NEW YORK
BEVERLY HILLS
NASHVILLE
LONDON
ROME
SYDNEY
MUNICH

WILLIAM MORRIS AGENCY, INC.

The
Agency
Of
The
Entertainment
World

NEW YORK—1350 Avenue Of The Americas, New York, N.Y. 10019 • (212) 586-5100, Telex 620165
BEVERLY HILLS—151 El Camino, Beverly Hills, Calif. 90212 • (213) 274-7451, (213) 272-4111,
Telex 673102
NASHVILLE—2325 Crestmoor Road, Nashville, Tenn. 37125 • (615) 385-0310, Telex 554472
LONDON—31/32 Soho Square, London W1V 5DG England • Phone 01-434-2191
Cable Address—"Willmorris London," Telex 851-27928
*ROME—Giosué Carducci 10-00187 Rome, Italy • Phone: 48-69-61
Telex 843-625614, Cable Address—"Willmorris Rome".
*MUNICH—Lamontstrasse 9, 8 Munich 80 • Telex "Alcap/Willmorris D"
*SYDNEY—50 Oxford Street, Paddington, N.S.W. Australia 202 • Phone: 61-02-360-3838

*Corresponding Offices

1989

INTERNATIONAL TELEVISION & VIDEO ALMANAC

34th Edition

Editor: JANE KLAIN

British Editor: WILLIAM PAY

Canadian Editor: PATRICIA THOMPSON

Quigley Publishing Company, Inc.

159 West 53rd Street, New York, N.Y. 10019

•

(212) 247-3100

Foreword

Recognizing the enormous growth of the video industry, this year the International Television and Video Almanac has extensively redesigned and expanded its coverage of and its data on the video market, while retaining the Almanac's easy-to-use, classic format. Additional international correspondents offer timely first-hand analysis of the television and video world market. Moreover, more than 400 new biographies have been added to the Almanac's near 5000 annually updated career profiles. I am proud to assume the editorship of this 34th edition of the Television and Video Almanac—the who, what, where and when of the Television and Video industries—and wish to thank the following friends who generously shared their expert knowledge, archival resources and loyal support: Alvin Marill, John Cocchi, Larry Cohn, David Bartholomew, Ernest Cunningham, Lloyd Ibert, Alan Barbour, Michael Schau, and Stephen Klain as well as Robert McDonald, Michelle Mart and Susan Gutterman for their tireless assistance. Most especially, I thank long-time Almanac editor Richard Gertner for his inestimable contributions and invaluable advice.

—JANE KLAIN

Ref
PN
1992.1
I57
34th ed.
1989

34th Edition
INTERNATIONAL
TELEVISION
& VIDEO
ALMANAC
For 1989
ISSN: 0539-0761
ISBN: 0-900610-41-7

PRINTED IN THE UNITED STATES OF AMERICA

Table of
Contents

A
Gulf+Western
Company ®

Paramount Pictures Corporation

ALPHABETICAL INDEX OF SUBJECTS

A

6A

7A

D

E

F

G

I

14A

T

15A

U

V

W

17A

X

Z

The Year in Review

1988 will long be remembered in the U.S. television industry as the Year of the Big Strike. Effects of the 22-week walkout by members of the Writers Guild of America are expected to reverberate for some time to come.

The major sticking point in reaching a settlement came from the writers' demands for a larger piece of the booming foreign market. The writers pointed to the fact that an hour-long drama once sold abroad for about $50,000 now goes for $300,000 and sometimes more. Members of the Alliance of Motion Picture & Television Producers countered by claiming that the foreign bonanza did not make up for the increasing losses producers have suffered in the domestic market (the demand for hour-long dramas in syndication by U.S. TV stations has slowed tremendously; game shows, costing much less to produce, are now much more popular).

What the writers settled for early in August was virtually what they had been offered in June: 1.2 per cent of a show's gross earnings overseas after the program has earned a certain amount of money for its producers. (The writers had sought 1.9 per cent.)

For the three major networks—ABC, CBS, and NBC—the strike was a hard blow, forcing a delay in the start of the fall season by a month to the end of October. Viewers, on the other hand, did not seem to notice, since the Summer Olympics played on NBC from September 15 to October 2 and prime time hours were filled with baseball on ABC and by the World Series on NBC (after October 15). CBS, unfortunately, had no "specials" to fill its prime time and could not start its new shows until late October.

Given this situation NBC was viewed by industry dopesters as certain to win the 1988–89 ratings race, just as it had in 1987–88, which would give it a third straight season at the top. NBC's margin of victory for 1987–88 had been the biggest for any network since the 1963–64 season when CBS was Number One. ABC was second for 1987–88, and CBS slipped to third for the first time in U.S. TV history.

Final averages, as tallied by the A.C. Nielsen Company, were a 16 rating (percentage of the nation's 88.6 million TV homes) and 26 share (percentage of sets in use) for NBC; a 13.7 rating/22 share for ABC; and a 13.5 rating/22 share for CBS. Ratings covered the period from September 21, 1987 to April 17, 1988.

NBC, which had never won a season before 1985–86, had the top four shows of the year: "The Cosby Show," "A Different World," "Cheers," and "Golden Girls." Number Five was ABC's "Growing Pains" followed by "Who's the Boss?" (ABC); "Night Court" (NBC); "60 Minutes" (CBS); "Murder, She Wrote" (CBS); and "The Wonder Years" (ABC).

For "60 Minutes" it was the 11th consecutive Top 10 finish, giving it the third-longest run for CBS behind "I Love Lucy" and "Gunsmoke" (13 seasons each).

The latest Nielsen ratings were based on its controversial new people meter methodology which had gone into effect at the start of the season in September. Detractors assert that the new method shows a loss in overall viewing that is at least twice the lost indicated from local tallies compiled all around the country. These latter results show a 3 per cent decline in viewership, compared with a 7 per cent loss when the national Nielsen results are applied.

Still Nielsen is now the only TV ratings company in the country. AGB Television Research, after a costly one-year attempt to set up an alternative service, suspended operations in August. CBS had been the only network subscriber to the system of AGB, which is owned by a British company called Mediamark Research, Inc. The U.S. experiment cost the company over $50 million.

That drop in overall viewing of the network shows is blamed by observers not so much on the WGA strike as on the continued growth of competition from cable and pay TV and home video cassettes. According to the Cabletelevision Advertising Bureau cable subscribers spend nearly as much time (33 per cent) watching cable programs as they do watching the three commercial networks (35 per cent). And in pay cable households, cable viewership outscores the three webs by 40 to 32 per cent. (For further recent statistics on the cable and home video industries, see those sections in this book).

The network created by Rupert Murdoch's Twentieth Century Fox in 1986 to compete with ABC, CBS and NBC—thus to form a "fourth network"—did not fare well in 1988. Projections showed that Fox Broadcasting Company, Inc. would probably lose $80 million for the year, and its future outlook was shaky.

Failure of the new project to catch on is blamed primarily on a soft market for television advertising. Fox had to depend a great deal on spillover from the big three webs of advertisers seeking national audiences who find that the ad time on the top-rated networks is sold out. When sales are weak, as is currently the case, overflow is small or non-existent.

On a more optimistic note the Turner Broadcasting System introduced a new cable entertainment network in October with nearly 10 million TV households signed up—well above an initial projection of seven million. The new network's programming will consist of movies drawn largely from the MGM library that TBS acquired in 1986.

This comes, however, after the failure of Home Box Office's Festival pay cable service introduced in June of 1987. The family-oriented program service had been able to attract subscribers at a rate of only 3.4 per cent from the 100 systems on which it was carried. (Less than 5 per cent is not considered viable.) Failure of Festival is attributed to lack of support from cable operators "who did not believe in it" or preferred to concentrate on promoting pay-per-view and basic cable rather than a service targeted for older viewers who usually shun pay TV or cable itself altogether. The service was discontinued at the end of 1988.

Finally, 1988 was the year in which the F.C.C. at last announced guidelines for high-definition TV which is expected to provide pictures twice as clear as those now available. Under the guidelines broadcasters must transmit high-definition signals at frequencies currently used in broadcasts, thus allowing viewers to continue to use their current sets. Only new sets will be able to provide a high-definition picture. The new standards are different from Japanese and European specifications for high-definition TV.

Statistics

Television and Station Operations

As of 1987, the FCC television station count is 1784: 511 UHF commercial; 544 VHF commercial; 218 UHF educational; 123 VHF educational; 282 UHF low-power; and 106 VHF low-power stations.

GROWTH OF COMMERCIAL TELEVISION STATIONS

	1960	1965	1970	1975	1980	1985	1988
Total	515	569	677	706	734	883	1055
VHF	440	481	501	514	516	520	544
UHF	75	88	176	192	218	363	511

VIEWING HABITS

TELEVISION USAGE

Number of TV homes	88,600,000
Number of color TV homes	85,000,000
Homes with two or more sets	53,500,000
Home with VCR	51,400,000

	1950	1970	1987
Avg. Hours per Home	4 hrs. 35 min.	5 hrs. 56 min.	7 hrs. 1 min.

COLOR TELEVISION

	1960	1975	1988
Homes	340,000	48,500,000	85,000,000
Per Cent of TV Homes	0.7	70.8	96

Source: A. C. Nielsen

TELEVISION USAGE

A BREAKDOWN OF TELEVISION VIEWERS

	Avg. Viewing Time Per TV Time Per Day (Hours and Minutes)
Total U.S.	7:48
By Household Income	
Under $15,000	7:59
$20,000 and over	7:45
$30,000 and over	7:39
$40,000 and over	7:42
By Age of Lady of House	
18–34	7:58
35–54	8:30
55 and over	7:42
By Household Size	
1 person	6:02
2 persons	7:02
3 persons	9:15
4 or more	9:37
By Education of Head of House	
Under 4 Yrs. H.S.	8:17
4 Yrs. H.S.	8:22
1+ Yrs. College	6:57
4+ Yrs. College	6:32
By Territory	
Northeast	7:58
East Central	8:35
West Central	7:21
South	7:52
Pacific	7:18
By County Size	
A	7:48
B	8:06
C & D	7:32

Source: A. C. Nielsen

TV EXPENDITURES

TOTAL ADVERTISING VOLUME (millions of dollars)

	1986	1987	% Change	% of Total
TELEVISION	$22,026	$22,941	+ 4.2	20.9
Newspapers	26,990	29,412	+ 9.0	26.8
Magazines	5,317	5,607	+ 5.5	5.1
Radio	6,949	7,206	+ 3.7	6.6
Cable	855	963	+12.6	0.9
Business Papers	2,382	2,458	+ 3.2	2.2
All Others	37,621	41,063	+ 9.1	37.5
Total Major Media	$102,140	$109,650	+ 7.4	100.0

Source: McCann-Erickson 5/88

NATIONAL ADVERTISING INVESTMENTS IN MAJOR MEDIA (millions of dollars)

	1986	1987	% Change	% of Total
TELEVISION	$15,512	$16,108	+ 3.8	53.4
Network	8,342	8,500	+ 1.9	28.2
Spot	6,570	6,846	+ 4.2	22.7
Nat'l Syndication	600	762	+27.0	2.5
Newspapers	3,376	3,494	+ 3.5	11.6
Magazines	5,317	5,607	+ 5.5	18.6
Radio (Network & Spot)	1,771	1,743	− 1.6	5.8
Cable	676	760	+12.5	2.5
Business Papers	2,382	2,458	+ 3.2	8.1
Total Major Media	$29,034	$30,170	+ 3.9	100.0

Source: McCann-Erickson 5/88

LOCAL ADVERTISING INVESTMENTS IN MAJOR MEDIA (millions of dollars)

	1986	1987	% Change	% of Total
TELEVISION	$ 6,514	$ 6,833	+ 4.9	17.9
Newspapers	23,614	25,918	+ 9.8	67.8
Retail	14,311	15,227	+ 6.4	39.8
Classified	9,303	10,691	+14.9	28.0
Radio	5,178	5,463	+ 5.5	14.3
Total Major Media	$35,306	$38,214	+ 8.2	100.0

Source: McCann-Erickson 5/88

LEADING LOCAL TV CATEGORIES

	add (000)			
	1984	1985	1986	1987
1. Restaurants & Drive-Ins	$577,598.6	$671,970.5	$744,800.0	$800,400.0
2. Auto and Truck Dealers*	257,027.5	311,211.7	339,000.0	371,400.0
3. Food Stores & Supermarkets	243,865.1	259,028.5	302,500.0	346,300.0
4. Furniture Stores	164,865.7	186,999.9	194,600.0	218,700.0
5. Banks, Savings & Loans	197,538.5	195,283.9	209,800.0	202,200.0
6. Movies				177,000.0
7. Department Stores	167,504.1	186,191.9	176,900.0	168,500.0
8. Radio Stations & Cable TV	128,577.5	134,482.4	147,000.0	152,500.0
9. Appliance Stores	85,586.4	121,883.1	141,600.0	143,800.0

Source: BAR   *Dealer Associations Not Included

LENGTH OF COMMERCIALS

Commercial Length	Non-Network				Commercial Length	Network			
	1984	1985	1986	1987		1984	1985	1986	1987
10 seconds	5.8%	5.5%	4.9%	5.3%	10 seconds	1.0%	1.3%	.05%	.02%
15 seconds	0.4	1.3	3.5	2.6	15 seconds	5.2	10.1	20.9	30.9
20 seconds	0.1	0.1	0.1	0.1	20 seconds	—	0.8	1.2	1.0
30 seconds	88.2	88.0	86.3	86.7	30 seconds	89.2	83.5	73.6	65.1
45 seconds	0.7	0.6	0.4	0.2	45 seconds	2.0	1.7	1.4	.09
60 seconds	2.8	2.7	2.9	2.9	60 seconds	2.1	2.2	1.8	1.5
90 sec. or more	2.0	1.8	1.9	2.1	90 sec. or more	0.5	0.4	0.6	0.4
	100%	100%	100%			100%	100%	100%	100%

Source: BAR

TELEVISION SET SALES (to dealers) 22,500,000 IN 1985

	Total	Color	Monochrome
1975	10,637,000	6,219,000	4,418,000
1980	18,532,000	11,803,000	6,729,000
1981	18,479,000	12,423,000	6,056,000
1982	16,406,000	11,484,000	4,922,000
1983	19,681,000	14,034,000	5,647,000
1984	22,384,000	17,190,000	5,194,000
1985	22,500,000	18,000,000	4,500,000
1986		18,134,000	3,434,000
1987		19,230,000	2,920,000

Source: EIA, Domestic & Imports

	Total Sales to Dealers in Units (Thousands)	Total Factory Sales in Dollars (Millions)	Average Value (Dollars per Unit)

COLOR TV RECEIVERS* (Excludes LCD and Projection Television)

	Total Sales to Dealers in Units (Thousands)	Total Factory Sales in Dollars (Millions)	Average Value (Dollars per Unit)
1985	16,971	5,555	327
1986	18,134	6,010	331
1987	19,230	6,250	325
1988 (est.)	19,300	6,310	327
1989 (est.)	19,400	6,365	328

Includes monitors for consumer use.

COLOR TV RECEIVERS WITH MTS (BUILT-IN STEREO CAPABILITY) (Included in Color TV Receivers Table)

	Total Sales to Dealers in Units (Thousands)	Total Factory Sales in Dollars (Millions)	Average Value (Dollars per Unit)
1985	1,500	900	600
1986	3,116	1,680	540
1987	4,349	2,218	510
1988 (est.)	5,300	2,600	490
1989 (est.)	6,200	3,010	485

STEREO-ADAPTABLE COLOR TV RECEIVERS (Included in Color TV Receivers Table)

	Total Sales to Dealers in Units (Thousands)	Total Factory Sales in Dollars (Millions)	Average Value (Dollars per Unit)
1985 (est.)	3,450	1,415	410
1986 (est.)	4,300	1,635	380
1987 (est.)	3,800	1,405	370
1988 (est.)	3,300	1,170	355
1989 (est.)	2,900	1,000	345

LCD COLOR TELEVISION (Excluded from Color TV Receivers Table)

	Total Sales to Dealers in Units (Thousands)	Total Factory Sales in Dollars (Millions)	Average Value (Dollars per Unit)
1985 (est.)	25	7	275
1986 (est.)	70	14	200
1987 (est.)	100	21	210
1988 (est.)	150	32	210
1989 (est.)	200	40	200

MONOCHROME TV RECEIVERS* (Excludes LCD Television)

	Total Sales to Dealers in Units (Thousands)	Total Factory Sales in Dollars (Millions)	Average Value (Dollars per Unit)
1985	3,504	289	82
1986	3,434	288	84
1987	2,920	242	83
1988 (est.)	2,800	210	75
1989 (est.)	2,700	205	75

Includes monitors (green, amber) for consumer use.

CABLE TV OPERATING SYSTEMS AND SUBSCRIBERS

	1960	1965	1970	1975	1980	1985
Operating Systems	640	1,325	2,490	3,366	4,048	6,600
Subscribers (millions)	0.7	1.3	4.5	9.8	15.5	37.3
% of TV Homes	1.4%	2.4%	7.6%	14.3%	20.5%	43.7%

Source: Television Digest

Emmy Award Winners

ACADEMY OF TELEVISION ARTS AND SCIENCES

**1987–88
TELEVISION ACADEMY AWARDS
Categories and Areas of Achievement
For the Emmy Award
FOR THE PERIOD
FROM July 1, 1987
THROUGH June 30, 1988**

OUTSTANDING COMEDY SERIES
The Wonder Years, Carol Black, Neal Marlens (executive producers); Jeff Silver (producer), ABC.

OUTSTANDING DRAMA SERIES
thirtysomething, Edward Zwick, Marshall Herskovitz (executive producers); Paul Haggis (supervising producer); Edward Zwick, Scott Winant (producers), ABC.

OUTSTANDING MINISERIES
The Murder of Mary Phagan, George Stevens Jr. (producer), NBC.

OUTSTANDING VARIETY, MUSIC OR COMEDY PROGRAM
Irving Berlin's 100th Birthday Celebration, Don Mischer (executive producer); Jan Cornell, David J. Goldberg (producers); Sara Lukinson (co-producer), CBS.

OUTSTANDING DRAMA/COMEDY SPECIAL: CLASSICAL PROGRAM/PERFORMING ARTS
Inherit the Wind, Peter Douglas (executive producer); Robert A. Papazian (producer), NBC.

OUTSTANDING CLASSICAL PROGRAM/PERFORMING ARTS
Nixon in China: Great Performances, Jac Venza (executive producer); David Horn (series producer); Michael Bronson (producer); John Walker (coordinating producer), PBS.

OUTSTANDING INFORMATIONAL SERIES
Buster Keaton: A Hard Act to Follow: American Masters, Kevin Brownlow, David Gill, producers; PBS; Nature, David Heeley, executive producer; Fred Kaufman, series producer; PBS.

OUTSTANDING INFORMATIONAL SPECIAL
Dear America: Letters Home From Vietnam, Bill Couturie, Thomas Bird (producers), HBO.

OUTSTANDING ANIMATED PROGRAM
A Claymation Christmas Celebration, Will Vinton (executive producer); David Altschul (producer); Will Vinton (director); Ralph Liddle (writer), CBS.

OUTSTANDING CHILDREN'S PROGRAM
The Secret Garden: Hallmark Hall of Fame, Norman Rosemont (executive producer); Steve Lanning (producer), CBS.

OUTSTANDING VARIETY/MUSIC EVENTS PROGRAMMING
The 60th Annual Academy Awards, Samuel Goldwyn Jr., producer; ABC.

OUTSTANDING LEAD ACTOR IN A COMEDY SERIES
Michael J. Fox, "Family Ties," NBC.

OUTSTANDING LEAD ACTOR IN A DRAMA SERIES
Richard Kiley, "A Year in the Life," NBC.

OUTSTANDING LEAD ACTOR IN A MINISERIES OR SPECIAL
Jason Robards, "Inherit the Wind," NBC.

OUTSTANDING LEAD ACTRESS IN A COMEDY SERIES
Bea Arthur, "The Golden Girls," NBC.

OUTSTANDING LEAD ACTRESS IN A DRAMA SERIES
Tyne Daly, "Cagney & Lacey," CBS.

OUTSTANDING LEAD ACTRESS IN A MINISERIES OR SPECIAL
Jessica Tandy, "Foxfire: Hallmark Hall of Fame," CBS.

OUTSTANDING SUPPORTING ACTOR IN A COMEDY SERIES
John Larroquette, "Night Court," NBC.

OUTSTANDING SUPPORTING ACTOR IN A DRAMA SERIES
Larry Drake, "L.A. Law," NBC.

OUTSTANDING SUPPORTING ACTOR IN A MINISERIES OR SPECIAL
John Shea, "Baby M," ABC.

OUTSTANDING SUPPORTING ACTRESS IN A COMEDY SERIES
Estelle Getty, "The Golden Girls," NBC.

OUTSTANDING SUPPORTING ACTRESS IN A DRAMA SERIES
Patricia Wettig, "thirtysomething," ABC.

OUTSTANDING SUPPORTING ACTRESS IN A MINISERIES OR SPECIAL
Jane Seymour, "Onassis: The Richest Man in the World," ABC.

OUTSTANDING GUEST PERFORMER IN A COMEDY SERIES
Beah Richards, "Frank's Place," CBS.

OUTSTANDING GUEST PERFORMER IN A DRAMA SERIES
Shirley Knight, "thirtysomething," ABC.

OUTSTANDING INDIVIDUAL PERFORMANCE IN A VARIETY OR MUSIC PROGRAM
Robin Williams, "ABC Presents A Royal Gala," ABC.

OUTSTANDING WRITING IN A COMEDY SERIES
Hugh Wilson, "Frank's Place: The Bridge," CBS.

OUTSTANDING WRITING IN A DRAMA SERIES
Paul Haggis, Marshall Herskovitz, "thirtysomething: Business As Usual, aka Michael's Father's Death," ABC.

OUTSTANDING WRITING IN A VARIETY OR MUSIC PROGRAM
Jackie Mason, "Jackie Mason on Broadway," HBO.

OUTSTANDING WRITING IN A MINISERIES OR A SPECIAL
William Hanley, "The Attic: The Hiding of Anne Frank: General Foods Golden Showcase," CBS.

OUTSTANDING DIRECTING IN A COMEDY SERIES
Gregory Hoblit, "Hooperman: Pilot," ABC.

OUTSTANDING DIRECTING IN A DRAMA SERIES
Mark Tinker, "St. Elsewhere: Weigh In, Way Out," NBC.

OUTSTANDING DIRECTING IN A VARIETY OR MUSIC PROGRAM
Patricia Birch, Humphrey Burton, "Celebrating Gershwin: Great Performances," PBS.

OUTSTANDING DIRECTING IN A MINISERIES OR A SPECIAL
Lamont Johnson, "Gore Vidal's Lincoln," NBC.

OUTSTANDING ACHIEVEMENT IN CHOREOGRAPHY
Alan Johnson, "Irving Berlin's 100th Birthday Celebration," CBS.

OUTSTANDING SOUND EDITING FOR A SERIES
William Wistrom, (supervising sound editor); Wilson Dyer, Mace Matiosian, James Wolvington (sound editors); Mace Matiosian (supervising ADR editor); Gerry Sackman (supervising music editor); "Star Trek: The Next Generation: 11001001," syndication.

OUTSTANDING SOUND EDITING FOR A MINISERIES OR A SPECIAL
Rich Harrison, (supervising sound editor); Tom Cornwell, Peter H. Harrison, Rich Harrison, Tom McMullen, Stan Siegel (sound editors); Tally Paulos (supervising ADR editor); Allan K. Rosen (supervising music editor); "The Murder of Mary Phagan, Part 2," NBC.

OUTSTANDING CINEMATOGRAPHY FOR A SERIES
Roy H. Wagner, ASC, "Beauty and the Beast: Pilot," CBS.

OUTSTANDING CINEMATOGRAPHY FOR A MINISERIES OR A SPECIAL
Woody Omens, ASC, "I Saw What You Did," CBS.

OUTSTANDING SOUND MIXING FOR A COMEDY SERIES OR A SPECIAL
Michael Ballin, M. Curtis Price, "Frank's Place: Food Fight," CBS.

OUTSTANDING SOUND MIXING FOR A VARIETY OR MUSIC SERIES OR A SPECIAL
Doug Rider, Carroll Pratt, David E. Fluhr, Dolly: Down in New Orleans, ABC.

OUTSTANDING SOUND MIXING FOR A DRAMA SERIES
Susan Chong, Thomas Huth, Tim Philben C.A.S., Sam Black, "Tour of Duty: Under Siege," CBS.

OUTSTANDING SOUND MIXING FOR A DRAMA MINISERIES OR A SPECIAL
Don MacDougall, Grover Helsley, Joe Citarella, Russell Williams, "Terrorist on Trial: The United States vs. Salim Ajami," CBS.

OUTSTANDING LIGHTING DIRECTION IN A COMEDY SERIES
Mark Buxbaum, "The Charmings: The Witches of Van Oaks," ABC.

OUTSTANDING LIGHTING DIRECTION FOR A VARIETY/ MUSIC OR DRAMA SERIES, MINISERIES OR SPECIAL
John Rock, "Julie Andrews: The Sound of Christmas," ABC.

OUTSTANDING EDITING FOR A SERIES (SINGLE CAMERA PRODUCTION)
Erwin Dumbrille, Christopher Nelson, "China Beach: Pilot," ABC; Marsh Hendry A.C.E., Robert Sounders, "Frank's Place: Food Fight," CBS; Elodie Keene, "L.A. Law: Full Marital Jacket," NBC.

OUTSTANDING EDITING FOR A MINISERIES OR A SPECIAL (SINGLE CAMERA PRODUCTION)
John A. Martinelli A.C.E., "The Murder of Mary Phagan: Part 2," NBC.

OUTSTANDING EDITING FOR A SERIES (MULTI-CAMERA PRODUCTION)
Andy Ackerman, "Cheers: The Big Kiss Off," NBC.

OUTSTANDING EDITING FOR A MINISERIES OR A SPECIAL (MULTI-CAMERA PRODUCTION)
Andy Zall, Mark West, Bob Jenkins, "Julie Andrews: The Sound of Christmas," ABC.

OUTSTANDING TECHNICAL DIRECTION/ELECTRONIC CAMERAWORK/VIDEO CONTROL FOR A SERIES
O. Tamburri (technical director); Jack Chisholm, Stephen A. Jones, Ritch Kenney, Ken Tamburri (camerapersons); Robert G. Kaufmann (senior video control); "The Golden Girls: Old Friends," NBC.

OUTSTANDING TECHNICAL DIRECTION/ELECTRONIC CAMERA/VIDEO CONTROL FOR A MINISERIES OR A SPECIAL
Mike Spencer, (technical director); David (Rocket) Barber, Bob Keys, Ron Sheldon, Gunther Degn (camerapersons); Mike Spencer (senior video control); "Julie Andrews: The Sound of Christmas," ABC.

OUTSTANDING ACHIEVEMENT IN MAKEUP FOR A SERIES
Werner Keppler, Michael Westmore, Gerald Quest, "Star Trek: The Next Generation: Conspiracy," syndication.

OUTSTANDING ACHIEVEMENT IN MAKEUP FOR A MINISERIES OR SPECIAL
Ronnie Specter (key makeup); Linda De Vetta, Pauline Heys (Farrah Fawcett's makeup); "Poor Little Rich Girl: The Barbara Hutton Story, Part 2," NBC.

OUTSTANDING ACHIEVEMENT IN HAIRSTYLING FOR A SERIES
Judy Crown, Monique De Sart, "Designing Women: I'll Be Seeing You," CBS.

OUTSTANDING ACHIEVEMENT IN HAIRSTYLING FOR A MINISERIES OR A SPECIAL
Claudia Thompson (key hairstylist); Aaron Quarles, Jan Archibald (Farrah Fawcett's hairstylists); Stephen Rose (key hairdresser); "Poor Little Rich Girl: The Barbara Hutton Story: Part 2," NBC.

OUTSTANDING COSTUME DESIGN FOR A SERIES
William Ware Theiss, "Star Trek: The Next Generation: The Big Goodbye," syndication.

OUTSTANDING COSTUME DESIGN FOR A MINISERIES OR A SPECIAL
Jane Robinson, "Poor Little Rich Girl: The Barbara Hutton Story: Part 2," NBC.

OUTSTANDING COSTUME DESIGN FOR A VARIETY OR MUSIC PROGRAM
Pete Menefee, Ret Turner, "Las Vegas—An All-Star 75th Anniversary Special," ABC.

OUTSTANDING ACHIEVEMENT IN COSTUMING FOR A SERIES
Paul Kaatz (women's costumer), "China Beach," Darryl Levine (men's costumer) "China Beach", ABC.

OUTSTANDING ACHIEVEMENT IN COSTUMING FOR MINISERIES OR SPECIAL:
Eddie Marks (costumer supervisor); Deborah Hopper, Radford Polinsky (costumers); "Shakedown on the Sunset Strip," CBS.

OUTSTANDING ART DIRECTION FOR A SERIES
John Mansbridge, (art director); Chuck Korian (set decorator), "Beauty and the Beast: Pilot," CBS.

OUTSTANDING ART DIRECTION FOR A VARIETY OR MUSIC PROGRAM
Charles Lisanby (production designer); "Barry Manilow: Big Fun on Swing Street," CBS.

OUTSTANDING ART DIRECTION FOR A MINISERIES OR SPECIAL
Jan Scott (production designer); Erica Rogalla (set decorator); "Foxfire: Hallmark Hall of Fame," CBS.

OUTSTANDING ACHIEVEMENT IN MUSIC COMPOSITION FOR A SERIES
Lee Holdridge,, "Beauty and the Beast: Pilot," CBS.

OUTSTANDING ACHIEVEMENT IN MUSIC COMPOSITION FOR A MINISERIES OR A SPECIAL
Laurence Rosenthal, "The Bourne Identity: Part 1," CBS.

OUTSTANDING ACHIEVEMENT IN MUSIC DIRECTION
Ian Fraser, Angela Morley (principal arrangers); "Julie Andrews . . . The Sound of Christmas," ABC.

OUTSTANDING ACHIEVEMENT IN MUSIC AND LYRICS
Larry Grossman (composer); Buz Kohan (lyricist); "Julie Andrews . . . The Sound of Christmas," ABC.

OUTSTANDING INDIVIDUAL ACHIEVEMENT— INFORMATIONAL PROGRAMMING—WRITING
Kevin Brownlow, David Gill, "Buster Keaton: A Hard Act to Follow, Part 1, American Masters," PBS; Bill Couturie, Richard Dewhurst, "Dear America: Letters Home From Vietnam," HBO.

INDIVIDUAL ACHIEVEMENT—INFORMATIONAL PROGRAMMING—DIRECTING
Kevin Brownlow, David Gill, "Buster Keaton: A Hard Act to Follow, Part 1, American Masters," PBS.

INDIVIDUAL ACHIEVEMENT—INFORMATIONAL PROGRAMMING—PERFORMING
Hal Holbrook, "Portrait of America: New York City," TBS.

INDIVIDUAL ACHIEVEMENT CLASSICAL MUSIC/DANCE PROGRAMMING—WRITING
David Gordon, "Dance in America: David Gordon's Made in U.S.A., Great Performances," PBS.

OUTSTANDING INDIVIDUAL ACHIEVEMENT—CLASSICAL MUSIC/DANCE PROGRAMMING—DIRECTING
Kirk Browning, "The Metropolitan Opera Presents: Turandot," PBS.

INDIVIDUAL ACHIEVEMENT—SPECIAL EVENTS PROGRAMMING—DIRECTING
Marty Pasetta, "The 60th Annual Academy Awards," ABC.

INDIVIDUAL ACHIEVEMENT—SPECIAL EVENTS PROGRAMMING—LIGHTING
Marc Palius (lighting director); Olin Younger (lighting consultant); "The 15th Annual American Music Awards," ABC.

INDIVIDUAL ACHIEVEMENT—SPECIAL EVENTS PROGRAMMING—PERFORMER
Billy Crystal, "The 30th Annual Grammy Awards," CBS.

INDIVIDUAL ACHIEVEMENT—SPECIAL EVENTS PROGRAMMING—ART DIRECTION
Charles Lisanby (production designer); Keaton Walker (art director); "The 60th Annual Academy Awards," ABC.

INDIVIDUAL ACHIEVEMENT—SPECIAL EVENTS— COSTUME DESIGN
Bob Mackie, Roy Aghayan, "The 60th Annual Academy Awards," ABC.

OUTSTANDING ACHIEVEMENT IN GRAPHICS AND TITLE SEQUENCE
Liz Friedman, "Strong Poison: A Dorothy L. Sayers Mystery," PBS.

OUTSTANDING SPECIAL VISUAL EFFECTS
Wil Vinton, Mark Gustafson, David Altshul, "Moonlighting: Come Back Little Shiksa," ABC.

OUTSTANDING ACHIEVEMENT IN ENGINEERING DEVELOPMENT
Optical Disc Corp. and the Sony Corp.

1987–88
TELEVISION ACADEMY AWARDS
Categories and Areas of Achievement
For the Emmy Award for Daytime Programs
FOR THE PERIOD
FROM March 6, 1987
THROUGH March 5, 1988

OUTSTANDING DRAMA SERIES
Santa Barbara, Jill Farren Phelps, Bridget Dobson (executive producers); Steven Kent (supervising producer); Leonard Friedlander, Julie Hanan, (producers), NBC.

OUTSTANDING GAME-AUDIENCE PARTICIPATION SHOW
The Price Is Right, Frank Wayne (executive producer); Phillip Wayne, Roger Dobkowitz (producers), CBS.

OUTSTANDING CHILDREN'S SERIES
Sesame Street, Dulcy Singer (executive producer); Lisa Simon (supervising producer); Arlene Sherman (coordinating producer), PBS.

OUTSTANDING CHILDREN'S SPECIAL
Never Say Goodbye (CBS Schoolbreak Special), Michael D. Little (executive producer); Susan Rohrer (producer); Craig S. Cummings (coproducer), CBS.

OUTSTANDING ANIMATED PROGRAM
Jim Henson's Muppet Babies, Margaret Ann Loesch, Lee Gunther, Jim Henson (executive producers); Bob Richardson (supervising producer); John Ahern, Bob Shellhorn (producers); Margaret Nichols (director); Sindy McKay, Larry Swerdlove (writers), CBS.

OUTSTANDING TALK/SERVICE SHOW
The Oprah Winfrey Show, Debra DiMaio (executive producer); Mary Kay Clinton, Dianne Atkinson Hudson, Ellen Sue Rakieten, Christine Tardio (producers), Syn.

OUTSTANDING LEAD ACTRESS, DRAMA SERIES
Helen Gallagher, "Ryan's Hope," ABC.

OUTSTANDING LEAD ACTOR, DRAMA SERIES
David Canary, "All My Children," ABC.

OUTSTANDING SUPPORTING ACTRESS, DRAMA SERIES
Ellen Wheeler, "All My Children," ABC.

OUTSTANDING SUPPORTING ACTOR, DRAMA SERIES
Justin Deas, "Santa Barbara," NBC.

OUTSTANDING INGENUE, DRAMA SERIES
Julianne Moore, "As the World Turns," CBS.

OUTSTANDING YOUNGER LEADING MAN IN A DRAMA SERIES
Billy Warlock, "Days of Our Lives," NBC.

OUTSTANDING GAME SHOW HOST
Bob Barker, "The Price Is Right," CBS.

OUTSTANDING TALK-SERVICE SHOW HOST
Phil Donahue, "Donahue," Syn.

OUTSTANDING DRAMA SERIES DIRECTING TEAM
Rudolph L. Vejar, Frank Pacelli, Heather Hill (directors); Randy Robbins, Betty Rothenberg (associate directors), "The Young And The Restless", CBS.

OUTSTANDING DRAMA SERIES WRITING TEAM
Agnes Nixon, Clarice Blackburn, Lorraine Broderick, Susan Kirshenbaum, Kathleen Klein, Karen L. Lewis, Victor Miller, Megan McTavish, Elizabeth Page, Peggy Sloane, Gillian Spencer, Elizabeth Wallace, Wisner Washam, Mary K. Wells, Jack Wood (writers), "All My Children," ABC.

OUTSTANDING GRAPHICS AND TITLE DESIGN
Wayne Fitzgerald, David Pfeil, "The Bold and the Beautiful," CBS.

OUTSTANDING ART DIRECTION/SET DECORATION/SCENIC DESIGN
Gary Panter (production designer); Wayne White, Ric Heitzman (co-production designers); Jeremy Railton (art director); James Higginson, Paul Reubens (set decorators), "Pee-wee's Playhouse," CBS.

OUTSTANDING ART DIRECTION/SET DECORATION/SCENIC DESIGN FOR A DRAMA SERIES
Sy Tomashoff, Jack Forrestel (art directors); Jay Garvin, Randy Gunderson (set decorators), "The Bold and the Beautiful," CBS.

OUTSTANDING CINEMATOGRAPHY
Tom Hurwitz (director of photography), ABC Afternoon Special ("Just a Regular Kid: An AIDS Story"), ABC.

OUTSTANDING WRITING IN A CHILDREN'S SERIES
Norman Stile (head writer); Christian Clark, Sara Compton, Judy Freudberg, Tony Geiss, Emily Kingsley, David Korr, Sonia Manzano, Jeff Moss, Cathi Rosenberg-Turow, Mark Saltzman, Nancy Sans, Luis Santeiro, Jocelyn Stevenson, Jon Stone, Belinda Ward, John Weidman (writers), "Sesame Street," PBS.

OUTSTANDING WRITING IN A CHILDREN'S SPECIAL
Victoria Hochberg, ABC Afterschool Special ("Just a Regular Kid: An AIDS Story"), ABC.

OUTSTANDING PROGRAM, WRITING AND DIRECTING—SPECIAL CLASS
(Directing) Dick Schneider, Macy's 61st Annual Thanksgiving Day Parade, NBC; Kirk Browning, "Un Ballo in Maschera," PBS.

OUTSTANDING MAKEUP
Ve Neill, "Pee-wee's Playhouse," CBS.

OUTSTANDING MAKEUP FOR A DRAMA SERIES
Carol Brown (head makeup artist); Keith Cary, Robert Sloan, Gail Hopkins, Lucia Bianca (makeup artists), "Days of Our Lives," NBC.

OUTSTANDING HAIRSTYLING
Bruce Geller (wig decorator); Victor Callegari (Mr. Pavarotti's wig); "Un Ballo in Maschera," PBS.

OUTSTANDING HAIRSTYLING FOR A DRAMA SERIES
Zora Sloan, Pauletta Lewis, "Days of Our Lives," NBC.

OUTSTANDING FILM SOUND MIXING
James Hodson (rerecording mixer), "ALF," NBC.

OUTSTANDING FILM SOUND EDITING
Bruce Elliot (supervising editor); William Koepnick (sound effects); Richard Gannon, Gregory K. Bowron, ADR; Stuart Goetz (music editor), "ALF," NBC.

OUTSTANDING FILM EDITING
John Craddock, CBS Schoolbreak Special ("What If I'm Gay?"), CBS.

OUTSTANDING VIDEOTAPE EDITING
John Ward Nielsen, "Pee-wee's Playhouse," ("Playhouse in Outer Space"), CBS.

OUTSTANDING VIDEOTAPE EDITING FOR A DRAMA SERIES
Marc Beruti, Dan Brumett, "The Young and the Restless," CBS.

OUTSTANDING COSTUME DESIGN
Lowell Detwiler, "Square One TV," PBS.

OUTSTANDING COSTUME DESIGN FOR A DRAMA SERIES
Lee Smith, "Days of Our Lives," NBC.

OUTSTANDING LIGHTING DIRECTION
Chenault Spence (lighting designer); Alan Adelman (lighting consultant); "Un Ballo in Maschera," PBS.

OUTSTANDING LIGHTING FOR A DRAMA SERIES
Howard Sharrott, "Loving," ABC.

OUTSTANDING MUSIC DIRECTION AND COMPOSITION
Bruce Hornsby, Peter Harris (music directors and composers), CBS Schoolbreak Special ("Soldier Boys"), CBS.

OUTSTANDING MUSIC DIRECTION AND COMPOSITION FOR A DRAMA SERIES
Liza Lachman (music director); Dominic Messinger (composer); Rick Rhodes (principal arranger), "Santa Barbara," NBC.

OUTSTANDING LIVE AND TAPE SOUND MIXING AND SOUND EFFECTS
Blake Norton, Tim Lester (production mixers); Dick Maitland (sound effects), "Sesame Street," PBS.

OUTSTANDING LIVE AND TAPE SOUND MIXING AND SOUND EFFECTS FOR A DRAMA SERIES
Scott A. Millan (preproduction and production mixer); Tommy Persson, (production mixer); Rafael O. Valentin, Donald D. Henderson (postproduction mixers); Maurice "Smokey" Westerfeld, Peter Romano (sound effects), "The Young and the Restless," CBS.

OUTSTANDING TECHNICAL DIRECTION/ELECTRONIC CAMERA/VIDEO CONTROL
Ray Angola (technical director); Joseph Arvizu, Cesar Cabreira, Keeth Lawrence, Martin Wagner (electronic camera); Allen Latter (video control), "The Price Is Right," CBS.

OUTSTANDING TECHNICAL DIRECTION/ELECTRONIC CAMERA/VIDEO CONTROL FOR A DRAMA SERIES
Chuck Guzzi (technical director); Ted Morales, Toby Brown, Gordon Sweeney, Mike Glenn, Pat Kenney (electronic camera); Roberto Bosio, Clive Bassett (video control), "The Bold and the Beautiful," CBS.

OUTSTANDING PERFORMER IN CHILDREN'S PROGRAMMING
Philip Bosco as "Gramps" in "Read Between the Lines," an ABC Afterschool Special, ABC.

OUTSTANDING DIRECTING IN CHILDREN'S PROGRAMMING
Jeff Brown, CBS Schoolbreak Special ("What If I'm Gay?"), CBS.

OUTSTANDING DIRECTING IN A GAME/AUDIENCE PARTICIPATION SHOW
Bruce Burmester, "$25,000 Pyramid," CBS.

OUTSTANDING DIRECTING IN A TALK/SERVICE SHOW
Russell Morash, "This Old House," PBS.

DIRECTORS GUILD OF AMERICA AWARDS 1948–49 TO 1987

(formerly Screen Directors Guild Awards)

1948–49: *Quarterly Awards* to FRED ZINNEMANN for The Search; HOWARD HAWKS for Red River; ANATOLE LITVAK for The Snake Pit; JOSEPH L. MANKIEWICZ for A Letter to Three Wives. *Annual Award* to JOSEPH L. MANKIEWICZ.

1949–50: *Quarterly Awards* to MARK ROBSON for The Champion; ALFRED L. WERKER for Lost Boundaries; ROBERT ROSSEN for All the King's Men; CAROL REED for The Third Man. *Annual Award* to ROBERT ROSSEN.

1950–1951: *Quarterly Awards* to BILLY WILDER for Sunset Boulevard; JOHN HUSTON for The Asphalt Jungle; JOSEPH L. MANKIEWICZ for All About Eve; VINCENTE MINNELLI for Father's Little Dividend. *Annual Award* to JOSEPH L. MANKIEWICZ for All About Eve.

1951: *May-July* to ALFRED HITCHCOCK for Strangers on a Train; *August–October* to GEORGE STEVENS for A Place in the Sun; *November–December* to VINCENTE MINNELLI for An American in Paris. *Annual Award* to GEORGE STEVENS for A Place in the Sun.

1952: *Quarterly Awards* to CHARLES CRICHTON for The Lavender Hill Mob; JOSEPH MANKIEWICZ for Five Fingers; FRED ZINNEMANN for High Noon; JOHN FORD for The Quiet Man. *Annual Award* to JOHN FORD.

1953: *Most Outstanding Directorial Achievement:* FRED ZINNEMANN for From Here to Eternity; *Outstanding Directorial Achievements:* CHARLES WALTERS for Lili; WILLIAM WYLER for Roman Holiday, GEORGE STEVENS for Shane, BILLY WILDER for Stalag 17. *Motion Picture Critic Award:* Bosley CROWTHER, New York Times.

1954: *Most Outstanding Directorial Achievement:* ELIA KAZAN for On The Waterfront; *Outstanding Directorial Achievement:* GEORGE SEATON for The Country Girl, ALFRED HITCHCOCK for Rear Window, BILLY WILDER for Sabrina, WILLIAM WELLMAN for The High and the Mighty; *Motion Picture Critic Award:* HAROLD V. COHEN, Pittsburgh *Post-Gazette.*

1955: *Most Outstanding Directorial Achievement:* DELBERT MANN for Marty; *Outstanding Directorial Achievement:* JOHN STURGES for Bad Day at Black Rock, JOHN FORD and MERVYN LEROY for Mister Roberts, ELIA KAZAN for East of Eden, JOSHUA LOGAN for Picnic. *Motion Picture Critic Award:* JOHN ROSENFIELD, Dallas *Morning Evening Star.*

1956: *Most Outstanding Directorial Achievement:* GEORGE STEVENS for Giant; *Outstanding Directorial Achievement:* MICHAEL ANDERSON for Around the World in 80 Days, WILLIAM WYLER for Friendly Persuasion, KING VIDOR for War and Peace, WALTER LANG for The King and I. *Motion Picture Critic Award:* FRANCIS J. CARMODY, Washington *News. D.W. Griffith Award:* KING VIDOR.

1957: *Outstanding Directorial Achievement:* DAVID LEAN for The Bridge On the River Kwai; JOSHUA LOGAN for Sayonara; SIDNEY LUMET for 12 Angry Men; MARK ROBSON for Peyton Place, and BILLY WILDER for Witness for the Prosecution. *Motion Picture Critic Award,* HOLLIS ALPERT and ARTHUR KNIGHT, critics for The Saturday Review.

1958: *Grand Award for Direction:* VINCENTE MINNELLI for Gigi; *D.W. Griffith Award for creative achievement in the film industry:* FRANK CAPRA; *Motion Picture Critic Award:* PHILIP K. SCHEUER, critic of the Los Angeles Times; *Special Award:* LOUELLA PARSONS; *Best Directed Non-English-Speaking Film:* RENE CLAIR for Gates of Paris (French); *Best Directed Television Film:* RICHARD BARE, for All Our Yesterdays, segment of the 77 Sunset Strip series.

1959: *Grand Award for Direction:* WILLIAM WYLER, Ben-Hur; *Most Outstanding Directorial Achievement:* Ben-Hur; *Motion Picture Critic Award:* JOHN E. FITZGERALD, entertainment editor of Our Sunday Visitor, a Sunday Supplement distributed by Catholic weeklies; *Guild's award for outstanding achievement in the television field:* THE UNTOUCHABLES (Part 1 and 2); *Director's Television Award:* PHIL KARLSON, The Untouchables.

1960: *Grand Award for Direction:* BILLY WILDER, The Apartment; *Motion Picture Critic Award:* PAUL BECKLEY, New York Herald Tribune; *Special Award of Honorary Membership:* Y. FRANK FREEMAN; *Television Director's Award:* GEORGE SCHAEFER, Macbeth; *Television Critic Award:* SHERWOOD KOHN, Louisville Times.

1961: *Directors Award:* ROBERT WISE, JEROME ROBBINS, West Side Story; *Critics Award:* John Beaufort of the Christian Science Monitor.

1962: *Director's Awards:* DAVID LEAN, Lawrence of Arabia; *Television Director's Award:* DAVID FRIEDKIN, The Price of Tomatoes, Dick Powell Show; *Television Critic's Award:* DONALD KIRKLEY, of The Baltimore Sun.

1963: *Film Director's Award:* TONY RICHARDSON, Tom Jones; *Outstanding Television Director's Award:* GEORGE SCHAEFER; *Motion Picture Critic's Award:* PAINE KNICKERBOCKER, San Francisco

Chronicle; *Television Critic's Award:* ROBERT LOUIS SHAYON, Saturday Review.

1964: *Film Director's Award:* GEORGE CUKOR, My Fair Lady; *Television Director's Award:* LAMONT JOHNSON; *Motion Picture Critic's Award:* JAMES MEADE, The San Diego Union.

1965: *Film Director's Award:* ROBERT WISE, The Sound of Music; *Critics Award:* SAM LESNER, Chicago Daily News; *D.W. Griffith Award:* WILLIAM WYLER.

1966: *Film Director's Award:* FRED ZINNEMANN, A Man for All Seasons; *Television Director's Award:* ALEX SEGAL.

1967: *Film Director's Award:* MIKE NICHOLS, The Graduate; *Television Director's Award:* GEORGE SCHAEFER.

1968: *Film Director's Award:* ANTHONY HARVEY, The Lion in Winter; *Television Director's Award:* GEORGE SCHAEFER; *D.W. Griffith Award:* ALFRED HITCHCOCK.

1969: *Film Director's Award:* JOHN SCHLESINGER, Midnight Cowboy; *Television Director's Award:* FIELDER COOK, Teacher, Teacher. *D. W. Griffith Award:* FRED ZINNEMANN.

1970: *Film Director's Award:* FRANKLIN SCHAFFNER, Patton; *Television Director's Award:* LAMONT JOHNSON, My Sweet Charlie; *D. W. Griffith Award:* None Presented.

1971: *Film Director's Award:* WILLIAM FRIEDKIN, The French Connection; *Television Director's Award:* (Special) BUZZ KULICK, Brian's Song.

1972: *Film Director's Award:* FRANCIS FORD COPPOLA, The Godfather: *Television Director's Award:* LAMONT JOHNSON, That Certain Summer.

1973: *Film Director's Award:* GEORGE ROY HILL, The Sting: *Television Director's Award:* JOSEPH SARGENT, The Marcus Nelson Murders.

1974: *Film Director's Award:* FRANCIS FORD COPPOLA, The Godfather, Part II: *Television Director's Award:* JOHN KORTY, The Autobiography of Miss Jane Pitman.

1975: *Film Director's Award:* MILOS FORMAN, One Flew Over the Cuckoo's Nest; *Television Director's Award:* SAM O'STEEN, Queen of the Stardust Ballroom.

1976: *Film Director's Award:* JOHN G. AVILDSEN, Rocky; *Television Awards—Specials:* DANIEL PETRIE, Eleanor and Franklin: *Comedy Series:* ALAN ALDA, Dear Sigmond episode of M∗A∗S∗H; *Dramatic Series:* GLENN JORDAN, Rites of Friendship; *Musical Variety:* TONY CHARMOLI, Shirley MacLaine's Gypsy in My Soul; *Documentary-News Special:* ARTHUR BLOOM, Democratic & Republican Conventions.

1977: *Film Director's Award:* WOODY ALLEN, Annie Hall; *Television Awards—Specials:* DANIEL PETRIE, Eleanor and Franklin—The White House Years; *Comedy Series:* PAUL BOGART, Edith's 50th Birthday episode of All in The Family; *Dramatic Series:* JOHN ERMAN, Show #2, Second Hour of Roots; *Musical Variety:* ART FISHER, Neil Diamond: Glad You're Here with Me Tonight; *News Specials/Sports:* RAY LOCKHART, A Day with President Carter; *Documentaries:* PERRY MILLER ADATO: Georgia O'Keeffe.

1978: *Film Director's Award:* MICHAEL CIMINO, The Deer Hunter; *Television Awards—Comedy Series:* PAUL BOGART, California, Here We Are, All in the Family; *Dramatic Series:* GENE REYNOLDS, Prisoner, Lou Grant; *Musical/Variety:* MERRILL BROCKWAY, Choreography by Balanchine, Part 3; *News Specials/Sports:* DON MISCHER, The Kennedy Center Honors; *Documentaries:* JOHN KORTY, Who Are the Debolts?; *Specials:* MARVIN CHOMSKY, Holocaust.

1979: *Film Director's Award:* ROBERT BENTON, Kramer Vs. Kramer; *Television Awards—Comedy Series:* CHARLES S. DUBIN, Period of Adjustment episode of M∗A∗S∗H; *Dramatic Series:* ROGER YOUNG, Cop segment of Lou Grant; *Musical/Variety:* TONY CHARMOLI, John Denver—The Muppets; *News Specials/Sports:* DON MISCHER, The Kennedy Center Honors; *Documentaries:* ALFRED R. KELMAN, The Magic Sense chapter of the Body Human; *Specials:* MICHAEL MANN, The Jericho Mile; *Commercials:* (directors judged by two or more examples of their work): ROBERT LIEBERMAN, Mary Ryan for McDonald's and Mary Lou for R.C. Cola.

1980: *Film Director's Award:* ROBERT REDFORD, Ordinary People; *Television Awards—Comedy Series:* NOAM PITLIK, Fog episode of Barney Miller; *Dramatic Series:* ROGER YOUNG, Lou episode of Lou Grant; *Musical/Variety:* DWIGHT HEMION, IBM Presents Baryshnikov on Broadway; *Actuality (recording live):* DON MISCHER, The Kennedy Center Honors; *Special:* JERRY LONDON, Shogun; *Documentaries:* (tie) PERRY MILLER ADATO, Picasso: A Painter's Diary; and ALFRED R. KELMAN, Body Beautiful segment of The Body Human.

1981: *Film Director's Award:* WARREN BEATTY, Reds; *Television Awards—Comedy Series:* ALAN ALDA, The Life You Save episode from M∗A∗S∗H; *Dramatic Series:* ROBERT BUTLER, Hill Street Station episode from Hill Street Blues; *Musical/Variety:* EMILE ARDOLINO, The Spellbound Child (Dance in America, PBS); *Actuality (recording live):* STAN HARRIS, Command Performance at Ford's Theatre—The Stars Meet the President; *Special:* HERBERT WISE, Skokie; *Documentary:* ROBERT GUENETTE, Great Movie Stunts: Raiders of the Lost Ark; *Commercials:* RICK LEVINE, First Love and Papa spots for Pepsi Cola and Summer Colt for Kodak.

1982: *Film Director's Award:* SIR RICHARD ATTENBOROUGH, Gandhi; *Television Awards—Comedy Series:* ALAN ALDA, Where There's a Will, There's a War, episode from M∗A∗S∗H; *Dramatic Series:*

Personal Foul, episode from Hill Street Blues; *Musical/Variety:* DON MISCHER, Shirley MacLaine, Illusions (CBS); *Dramatic Special:* MARVIN J. CHOMSKY, Inside the Third Reich (ABC Circle Film); *Documentary:* PERRY MILLER ADATO, Carl Sandburg—Echoes and Silences (American Playhouse); *Commercials:* JOE PYTKA, Baseball, Basketball and Future Gallup.

1983: *Film Director's Award:* JAMES BROOKS, Terms of Endearment; *Robert B. Aldrich Service Award (honorary):* ROBERT WISE; *Television Awards—Comedy Series:* JAMES BURROWS, Showdown Part II (episode of Cheers); *Dramatic Series:* JEFF BLECKNER, Life in the Minors (episode of Hill St. Blues); *Musical/Variety:* DON MISCHER, Motown 25: Yesterday, Today, Forever (NBC); *Dramatic Special:* EDWARD ZWICK, Special Bulletin (NBC); *Documentary:* HARRY MOSES, Willie Loman Comes to China; *Commercials:* (tie) BOB BROOKS, Hallmark Cards and STU HAGMANN, IBC Home Computers and LDS; *Daytime Drama:* SHARRON MILLER, The Woman Who Willed a Miracle (ABC).

1984: *Film Director's Award:* MILOS FORMAN, Amadeus; *D.W. Griffith Award for Life Achievement:* BILLY WILDER; *Televison Awards—Comedy Series:* JAY SANDRICH, The Bill Cosby Show (pilot); *Dramatic Series:* THOMAS CARTER, The Rise and Fall of Paul The Wall (episode of Hill Street Blues); *Musical Variety:* DON MISCHER and TWYLA THARP, Baryshnikov by Tharp with American Ballet Theatre (PBS); *Dramatic Special:* DANIEL PETRIE, The Dollmaker (ABC); *Documentary:* ALFRED R. KELMAN, The Journey Within (The Body Human) (CBS); *Sports:* SANDY GROSSMAN, Super Bowl XVIII (CBS); *Daytime Drama:* JOAN DARLING, Mom's on Strike (chapter of After School Special, ABC); *Commercials:* STU HAGMANN, spots for McDonald's, Latter Day Saints, IBM.

1985: *Film Director's Award:* STEVEN SPIELBERG, The Color Purple; *D.W. Griffith Award for Life Achievement:* JOSEPH L. MANKIEWICZ; *Robfert B. Aldrich Award (honorary):* George Sidney; *Television Awards—Comedy Series:* JAY SANDRICH, Golden Girls (pilot); *Dramatic Series:* WILL MacKENZIE, My Fair David (episode of Moonlighting); *Musical Variety:* DON MISCHER, Motown Returns to the Apollo; *Dramatic Special:* JOHN ERMAN, An Early Frost; *Documentary:* HARRY RASKY, Homage to Chagall: The Colors of Love; *Sports:* ANDY J. KINDLE and DAVID MICHAELS, Tour De France; *Daytime Drama:* CRAIG SANDY TUNG, The Day the Senior Class Got Married; *Commercials:* EDWARD BIANCHI, spots for National Institute of Drug Abuse, Diet Pepsi, American Express, Bounce.

1986: *Film Director's Award:* OLIVER STONE, Platoon; *D.W. Griffith Award for Life Achievement:* ELIA KAZAN; *Frank Capra Award (to an assistant director or unit production manager for outstanding service to the industry):* HENRY E. "BUD" BRILL; *Television Awards—Comedy Series:* WILL MacKENZIE, Atomic Shakespeare (episode of Moonlighting); *Dramatic Special:* LEE GRANT, Nobody's Child; *Documentary:* PERRY MILLER ADATO, Eugene O'Neill: A Glory of Ghosts; *Sports:* HARRY COYLE, Game 6 of the 1986 World Series; *Daytime Drama:* CATLIN ADAMS, Wanted: The Perfect Guy.

1987: *Film Director's Award:* BERNARDO BERTOLUCCI, The Last Emperor; *D.W. Griffith Award for Lifetime Achievement:* ROBERT E. WISE; Robert B. Aldrich Award (for work on behalf of the guild): SHELDON LEONARD; *Television Awards—Dramatic Special:* JUD TAYLOR, Foxfire. *Evening Series:* MARSHALL HERSKOVITZ, thirtysomething, pilot; *Comedy Series:* WILL MACKENZIE, My Name Is Alex (Family Ties); *Musical/Variety:* DWIGHT HEMION, Julie Andrews, Sound of Christmas; *Daytime Dramatic Show:* VICTORIA HOCHBERG, Just a Regular Kid: An AIDS Story (Afterschool Special); *Sports:* ROBERT A. FISHMAN, Syracuse-Indiana game (NCAA Basketball Championship); *Documentary:* ELENA MANNES, The Kingdom Divided (God and Politics); *Commercials:* RICK LEVINE, Pepsi Cola, Arnott's Biscuits and Dupont Commercials.

International Film Festivals and Markets

Listed alphabetically by country. Exact dates vary from year to year but months indicated are generally the same. Those marked with an asterisk are recognized by the International Federation of Film Producers Association, 33 Avenue Champs Elysées, 75008, Paris, France.

AUSTRALIA
*Adelaide (July)
*Sydney (June)
Melbourne (June)

AUSTRIA
*Vienna—Humor in Film (March)
Viennale (Vienna) (March)
Wels (Austrian) (October)

BELGIUM
Antwerp (March)
Brussels DIDACTA Audiovisual (June)
Brussels—Belgian Festival and Market (January)
Flanders (Ghent) (October)

BRAZIL
São Paolo (October)
Rio de Janeiro (November)

BULGARIA
Varna (June)

CANADA
Montreal World Film Festival (August)
Asian American International (Vancouver) (September)
Stratford (September)
Toronto (Festival of Festivals) (September)
Ottawa (Animation) (October)
Montreal (new cinema) (October)
Vancouver (October)

COLOMBIA
Cartagena Film Festival (June)

CUBA
Havana (December)

CZECHOSLOVAKIA
Prague Television Festival (June)
*Karlovy Vary (July)
Brno Film and TV Market (October)

EAST GERMANY
Leipzig (November)

ENGLAND
Birmingham (September)
London Multi-Media Market (October)
London Film Festival (November-December)

FINLAND
Tampere Film Festival (February)

FRANCE
Cannes MIDEM Music Market (January)
Rheims Sport Films (March-April)
Cannes MIP-TV Video Market (April)
Beaune Historical Films (May)
*Cannes Film Festival (May)
Grenoble Shorts (June-July)
Cannes VIDCOM (visual communications) (October)
Deauville (American Films) (September)
Riena (environmental) (September)
Noirmoutier (first films) (September)
Biarritz (Iberian, Latin American) (September)
Cherbourg (October)
Grenoble (Thrillers) (October)

GREECE
*Thessaloniki Film Festival (October)

HOLLAND
Dutch Film Days & Film Market (September)
Rotterdam Film International (February)
CineKid (Children's) (Amsterdam) (September)

HONG KONG
Hong Kong (March)

IRELAND
*Cork (September-October)

INDIA
New Delhi International Film Festival (January)

ITALY
Bergamo at San Remo (March)
MIFED (film and TV market) at Milan (April)
Trento (mountain films) (April-May)
Asolo (art and painting)
Alghero (June)

Fermo and Porto S. Giorgio (marine) (June)
*Trieste (science fiction) (July)
Taormina Festival of Nations (July)
Venice Film Festival (August)
Lucca (animation) (October-November)
Sorrento (Canadian) (September)
Rimini (new cinema) (September)
Prix Italia (TV) at Florence (September)
MIFED TV Market at Milan (October)
ORVIETO (folk art and artisans) (October)
Salerno (October)
Turin (youth films) (October)
Lucca (animation) (October-November)
Porretta Temer (November)
Festival dei Popoli at Florence (December)

MONTE CARLO
Monte Carlo TV Festival (February)

POLAND
*Cracow (shorts) (June)
Gdansk (September)
Katowice (scientific/technical) (November)

SCOTLAND
Edinburgh (August-September)

SPAIN
Fijon (children's) (June)
Cadiz (September)
*San Sebastian (September)
*Sitges (horror) (September-October)
Valencia (Mostra Cinema Mediterrani) (October)
*Valladolid (human values) (October)
*Barcelona (color) (October-November)
Barcelona (November)

SWITZERLAND
Montreux TV Festival (June)
Geneva Telecom (May)
*Locarno (August)
Montreux (new form) (August)
Les Diablerets (Alpine) (September)
*Nyon (shorts) (October)

TAIWAN
Taipei (Asian) (June)

UNITED STATES
Asian-American International Film Festival (touring)
*New York Animation Festival (January)
NATPE (Houston) (January)
Miami (February)
American Film Market (Los Angeles—March)
*Los Angeles International Film Exposition (Filmex) (March)
*San Francisco (March)
National Assn. of Broadcasters (Las Vegas) (April)
Philadelphia (May)
Aspen (independent) (September)
Intercom (industrial film/video, Chicago) (September)
*New York Film Festival (September-October)
American Independent Feature Film Market (New York) (October)
Denver (October)
San Diego (October)
Seattle International (May-June)
SMPTE (October, November)
Chicago (October)
Showeast (Atlantic City) (October)
International Film & TV (New York) (November)
Northwest Film & Video (Portland, OR) (November)
Hawaii (Honolulu) (December)

U.S.S.R.
*Tashkent (Afro-Asian) (May)
Teleforum (Moscow) (September)

VIRGIN ISLANDS
International Film Festival

WEST GERMANY
*Oberhausen (shorts) (April)
*Berlin (February)
Munich (Youth Prize—TV) (June)
Cologne Photokina (September-October)
Oberhausen Sports Festival (October)
Mannheim (October)
Hof (October)
Lubeck (Nordic films) (November)

YUGOSLAVIA
Belgrade Film Festival (February)
Belgrade (science and technology) (April)
*Zagreb (animation) (June)
Pula (national) (July)

Who's Who

In MOTION PICTURES and TELEVISION

A

AAMES, WILLIE: Actor. r.n. William Upton. b. California, July 15, 1960.
  PICTURES: Hog Wild, Scavenger Hunt, Zapped!, Cut and Run.
  TELEVISION: Series: We'll Get By, Courtship of Eddie's Father, The Odd Couple, Swiss Family Robinson, Wait Til Your Father Gets Home, Eight Is Enough, Charles in Charge. Movies: Eight is Enough Reunion.

AARON, PAUL: Director. Broadway shows include Salvation, Paris Is Out, '70 Girls '70, Love Me Love My Children, etc.
  PICTURES: A Different Story, A Force of One, Deadly Force, Maxie.
  TELEVISION: The Miracle Worker, Thin Ice, Maid in America, When She Says No, In Love and War, Save the Dog!

AARON, ROY H.: Executive. b. April 8, 1929. e. UCLA, BA; USC, LLB. Attorney in L.A. law firm of Pacht, Ross, Warne, Bernhard & Sears. Joined Plitt Companies in 1978 as snr. v.p. & gen. counsel. In 1980 named pres. & chief operating officer of Plitt Theatres, Inc. and related Plitt companies.

ABARBANEL, SAM X.: Producer, Writer, Publicist. b. Jersey City, NJ, March 27, 1914. e. Cornell U., U. of Illinois, B.S. 1935. Newspaperman Chicago before joining N.Y. exploitation dept. Republic, then to studio as ass't. publicity director. W.W.II in Europe with 103rd Div. After war independent publicist and producer. Co-prod. Argyle Secrets, 1948. Co-wrote orig. s.p., co-produced U.A.'s Prehistoric Women, 1950. Exec. Prod. U.A.'s Golden Mistress. In 1963 to Spain as associate prod. MGM's Gunfighters of Casa Grande, and Son of Gunfighter. Formed own co. in Spain, 1966. Produced Narco Men. Co-authored, prod. Last Day of War. Orig. & co-s.p. Avco's Summertime Killer, 1972.

ABELES, ARTHUR: Chairman, Filmarketeers, Ltd. b. 1914. Educated Duke U., Columbia U. 1939–41: general manager, West Indies, Warner. 1941. assistant general manager, Brazil, Universal. 1942–45: general manager, Uruguay, Warner. 1945–47: supervisor, Argentina, Chile, Uruguay, Paraguay, Warner. 1948–68: Managing director, Warner Bros. Pictures, Warner Theatres, Warner Bros. Production; Director Henderson Film Laboratories; Vice-pres., Warner Bros. Intl. in chg. of Europe, the Near East and North Africa. 1968–70; Managing director, Universal Pictures Ltd. 1970–77; Vice-president Universal International in charge of U.K., Continent and Middle East. 1970–77: Co-chairman, Cinema International Corporation. 1978: Co-chairman, A.M. Film Consultants Ltd. 1980: Chairman, Filmarketeers, Ltd.-Filmbond Group of Companies.

ABEND, SHELDON: Executive. b. New York, NY, June 13, 1929. Maritime Labor-Rel. Negotiator, 1954–56; chmn., Maritime Union, 1954–56; head, exec. dir. Authors' Research Co. rep. estates deceased authors, est. 1957. indep. literary negotiator, CC films, A.A.P., RKO General Inc., David O. Selznick, 1959–65; pres. American Play Co. Inc., Century Play Co. Inc., 1961–present; est. Million Dollar Movie Play Library, 1962; pres. Amer. Literary Consultants est. 1965; exec. v.p. Chantec Enterprises Inc. 1969–72. Marketing literary consultant for Damon Runyon Estate. Copyright analyst and literary rights negotiator, United Artists Corp. Founder and chrm., Guild for Author's Heirs, 1970–72, Literary negotiator and prod. consultant for Robert Fryer, 1974; Founder, Copyright Royalty Co. for Authors' Heirs, 1974; copyright consultant, Films, Inc. 1975; literary agent for Bway. play, Chicago, 1975. Owner of 53 classic RKO motion pictures for the non-theatrical markets, distributed by Films, Inc. Revived publishing of Damon Runyon stories in quality paperback in conjunction with Runyon-Winchell Cancer Fund. Published Cornell Woolrich mystery stories—all prod. by Alfred Hitchcock for TV & motion pictures, 1976. 1978, assoc. prod. of film, Why Would I Lie?; Originator of Million Dollar Movie

Book Theatre and Million Dollar Movie Sound Track Co., 1980; assoc. prod. of Broadway revival, Shanghai Gesture, 1981. Publ. 5 Cornell Woolrich books owned by S. Abend, 1982–83; Co-authored book, The Guardians; 1985, Romance of the Forties by Damon Runyon, 1986; 1985, founded American Concerts, Inc. and American Theatre Collections, Inc. Pres. of both. 1987, commenced pre-prod. work on Damon Runyon story, Madam La Gimp, as Bdwy. musical; published Into the Night by Cornell Woolrich. Packaged m.p. Bloodhounds of Broadway 1988; co-author s.p. Ultimate Demand.

ABRAHAM, F. MURRAY: Actor. b. Oct. 24, 1940. Attended U. of Texas, 1959–61; trained for stage at Herbert Berghof Studio with Uta Hagen. Stage debut in Los Angeles in The Wonderful Ice Cream Suit, 1965. New York debut in Fantasticks, 1966. Film debut in Serpico, 1974.
  THEATER: Antigone (NYSF, 1982), Uncle Vanya, The Golem (NYSF), Madwoman of Chaillot, Twelfth Night, Macbeth, A Midsummer's Night Dream.
  PICTURES: The Sunshine Boys, All the President's Men, They Might Be Giants, The Ritz, Madman, The Big Fix, Scarface, Amadeus. (AA-best actor), The Name of the Rose, The Favorite, Russicum, The Betrothed.
  TELEVISION: Love of Life, Kojak, Marco Polo, Sex and the Married Woman, How to Survive a Marriage, All in the Family, Dream West, etc.

ABRAHAMS, GARY: Executive. e. U. of Arizona, B.A. In 1968 joined Paramount TV as asst. to v.p.; 1974–75, asst. to prod., The Movies; 1971–78, assoc. dir., Los Angeles Intl. Film Exposition (Filmex); 1978, joined Marble Arch Productions as asst. to pres.; named dir. of corporate relations & merchandising, 1979; v.p., Cable Programming, Interscop Communications, 1982; assoc. dir., American Cinematheque, 1984–86; named pres., Great Entertainment Film Ventures, 1987.

ABRAHAMS, JIM: Producer, Writer, Director. b. Milwaukee, WI, May 10, 1944. e. U. of Wisconsin. Former private investigator. 1979, with friends David and Jerry Zukor, opened the Kentucky Fried Theatre in Madison, WI, a multimedia show specializing in live improvisational skits mixed with videotaped and film routines and sketches, with the threesome writing and appearing in them. Opened new theatre in Los Angeles in 1972 and developed large following. Trio wrote script for first film, The Kentucky Fried Movie, followed by Airplane! (1980) which they also wrote and jointly directed and served as executive producers.
  PICTURES: Top Secret! (co-dir., co-s.p.); Ruthless People (co-dir.), Big Business (dir.), The Naked Gun (co-s.p.), Cry Baby (exec. prod.).

ABRAHAMS, MORT: Producer. b. New York, NY. Dir. programming, prod., NTA, 1958–60; exec. prod. Cooga Mooga Prod. Inc., 1960–61. Producer: Target, The Corruptors 1961, Route 66, 1962–63; writer T.V. Shows, 1963–64; prod., Kraft Suspense Theatre, 1965; prod., Man from U.N.C.L.E., 1965–66; executive vice president, APJAC Prod. 1966. Assoc. prod. Doctor Dolittle, Planet of the Apes, Goodbye, Mr. Chips. Prod., The Chairman. Assoc. producer & writer, Beneath the Planet of the Apes; 1969, vice president in charge of production, Rastar Prods.: 1971–74 exec. prod. American Film Theatre & v.p. Ely Landau Org. in chg. West Coast prod. Exec. prod. on Luther, Homecoming, Man in the Glass Booth; exec. prod., The Greek Tycoon, Hopscotch, exec. prod.; exec. in chg. prod., The Chosen, Beatlemania; exec. prod., The Deadly Game; 1982, exec. prod. Separate Tables, Mr. Halpern and Mr. Johnson; prod., Arch of Triumph; exec. prod., The Holcraft Covenant; prod., Seven Hours to Judgement.

ABRAMS, DIANNE: Executive. Held posts with San Diego division Los Angeles Times; asst. acct. exec. with Hubbert Advertising; press and publicity dept. of KNBC. 1982, joined Warner Bros. as asst. to Robert G. Friedman, v.p. worldwide pub.; 1987, named WB dir. of natl. promotion.

ABULADZE, TENGIZ: Director, Writer. b. Soviet Georgia, Jan. 31, 1924. e. studied directing in Tbilisi then in Moscow at the Higher State Institute of Cinematography.
PICTURES: Documentaries: Dmitry Arakishvili; Our Palace; The Georgian State Dancing Company; An Open Air Museum; Features: Magdan's Donkey; Someone Else's Children; Me, Grandma, Iliko and Hillarion; Prayer, A Necklace for My Beloved, The Wishing Tree; Repentance, Hadji Murat.

ACKERMAN, BETTYE: Actress. b. Cottageville, SC, Feb. 28, 1928. e. Columbia U., 1948–52. Taught dancing 1950–54.
PLAYS INCLUDE: No Count Boy, 1954; Tartuffe, 1956; Sophocles' Antigone, and Oedipus at Colonus, 1956; The Merchant of Venice, 1971.
PICTURES INCLUDE: Face of Fire, 1959; Rascal.
TV: Alcoa Premiere, Alfred Hitchcock Presents, Perry Mason, Breaking Point, Dr. Maggie Graham on Ben Casey series for five yrs., Hope-Chrysler Theatre, Bonanza, FBI Story, Mannix, Ironsides, Medical Center, regular on Bracken's World, Colombo, Sixth Sense, Heat of Anger, Return to Peyton Place, (6 months 1972) Rookies, Barnaby Jones, Police Story, Gunsmoke, Harry O, Streets of San Francisco, S.W.A.T., Petrocelli, Wonder Woman, Police Woman, Chips, 240-Robert, The Waltons, Dynasty, Falcon Crest, Me and Mom, Trapper John M.D. TV Movies: Companions in Nightmare, A Day for Thanksgiving on Walton's Mountain, Confessions of a Married Man.
LP RECORDS: Salome & School for Scandal.

ACKERMAN, HARRY S.: Executive. b. Albany, NY, Nov. 17, 1912. e. Dartmouth Coll. m. actress Elinor Donahue. Began as writer, actor, producer. Joined Young & Rubicam adv. agcy. 1936; became v.p. of program operations, 1946. Exec. prod. CBS, 1948. Dir. of network programs—Hollywood, June, 1948; v.p. in charge network radio programs, 1950; v.p. chge. network TV programs CBS-TV, Hollywood, June, 1951; exec. dir. spec. progs. CBS network, 1956; formed independent company 1957; v.p. and exec. prod. Screen Gems Inc., 1958–1973; pres. Harry Ackerman Prods. nat'l pres., Academy TV Arts and Sciences, two terms; now pres., Harry Ackerman Prods.

ACKLAND, JOSS: Actor. b. London, England, Feb. 29, 1928. Member of Old Vic; toured U.S.S.R and U.S. with them. Spent time in Central Africa as a tea planter. Over 400 TV appearances.
PICTURES INCLUDE: Seven Days to Noon, Royal Flash, Crescendo, The House That Dripped Blood, Villain, England Made Me, The Black Windmill, Great Expectations, The Greek Tycoon, Someone Is Killing the Great Chefs of Europe, Saint Jack, The Apple, Rough Cut, Lady Jane, A Zed and Two Noughts, The Sicilian, White Mischief, To Kill a Priest, It Couldn't Happen Here.
TELEVISION: Queenie, Code Name: Kyril; Shadowlands; The Man Who Lived at the Ritz.

ADAM, KEN: Art director, Prod. Designer. b. Berlin, Germany, Feb. 5, 1921. e. St. Pauls Sch., London; London U., student of architecture. 6 years war service as RAF pilot. Ent. m.p. ind. as draughtsman 1947 (This Was a Woman). Art dir. The Devil's Pass, Soho Incident, Around the World in 80 Days, Trials of Oscar Wilde, Dr. No, Sodom and Gomorrah, Dr. Strangelove, Goldfinger, Thunderball, Ipcress File, You Only Live Twice, Funeral in Berlin, Chitty Chitty Bang Bang, Goodbye Mr. Chips, The Owl and the Pussycat, Diamonds Are Forever, Sleuth, The Last of Sheila, Barry Lyndon, (Acad. Award), Salon Kitty, 7% Solution, The Spy Who Loved Me, Moonraker, King David, Agnes of God, Pennies from Heaven, Crimes of the Heart, The Deceivers (prod. design), Dead-Bang.

ADAMS, BROOKE: Actress. b. New York, NY, Feb. 8, 1949. e. H.S. of Performing Arts; Inst. of American Ballet; Lee Strasberg. Made professional debut at age of six in Finian's Rainbow. Worked steadily in summer stock and TV until age 18. After hiatus resumed acting career.
THEATER: Split, Key Exchange, Linda Hur. Helps run small summer theater upstate NY.
PICTURES: The Lords of Flatbush, Car Wash, Shockwaves (Death Corps), Days of Heaven, Invasion of the Body Snatchers, Cuba, A Man, a Woman and a Bank, Utilities, The Dead Zone, Almost You, Key Exchange, Man on Fire.
TELEVISION: James Dean: Portrait of a Friend, The Last of the Belles, The Daughters of Joshua Cabe, Murder on Flight 502, The Bob Newhart Show, Police Woman, Lace, Special People, Lace II, The Lion of Africa; Paul Reiser: Out on a Whim. Series: O.K. Crackerby.

ADAMS, CATLIN: Actress. r.n. Barab. b. Los Angeles, CA, October 11, 1950. Began career as actress then studied directing at American Film Institute. Directorial debut: Wanted: The Perfect Guy (Emmy-winning ABC Afterschool Special). Also directed Little Shiny Shoes (short, written and prod. with Melanie Mayron).
THEATER: Safe House, Scandalous Memories, Dream of a Blacklisted Actor, The Candy Store.

PICTURES: As Actress: Katherine, Panic in Needle Park, The Jerk, The Jazz Singer. Director: Sticky Fingers (also co-s.p., co-prod.).
TELEVISION: How to Survive the 70's and Maybe Even Bump into a Little Happiness; She Loves Me, She Loves Me Not.

ADAMS, DON: Actor. b. New York, NY, April 13, 1926. Won Arthur Godfrey talent contest. Was nightclub impressionist before starting in TV.
PICTURE: The Nude Bomb.
TELEVISION: Bill Dana Show, Get Smart, The Partners, Hooray for Hollywood, Don Adams Screen Test, Three Times Daley, Inspector Gadget, Check It Out!

ADAMS, EDIE: Actress, Singer. b. Kingston, PA, April 16, 1931. e. Julliard Sch. of Music, Columbia Sch. of Drama.
STAGE: Wonderful Town, 1952–54; Lil Abner, 1956–57, Mame.
TELEVISION: The Chevy Show, 1958: Take a Good Look, 1960–61; Here's Edie, 1962–63; Movie: Ernie Kovacs' Between the Laughter, A Cry for Love, Fast Friends.
PICTURES INCLUDE: The Apartment, It's a Mad, Mad, Mad, Mad World, Call Me Bwana, Under the Yum, Yum Tree, Love With A Proper Stranger, Lover Come Back, The Best Man, Maid in Paris, The Honey Pot, Up in Smoke.

ADAMS, GERALD DRAYSON: Writer. b. Winnipeg, Manitoba. e. Oxford U. Export exec. 1925–30; literary agt. 1931–45. Member: Screen Writers' Guild.
PICTURES INCLUDE: (jt. orig. screen story) Magnificent Rogue, (jt. s.p.) Plunderers, (s.p.) Gallant Legion, (jt. s.p.) Big Steal; collab. story, Dead Reckoning; Orig. s.p. Battle of Apache Pass, Son of Ali Baba, Flaming Feather, Flame of Araby; collab. s.p. Lady from Texas, Steel Town, Untamed, Frontier; story, collab. s.p., Duel at Silver Creek; st., s.p., Princess of the Nile, Three Young Texans, Gambler from Natchez; st., Wings of the Hawk, Between Midnight and Dawn; st., adapt., Taza Son of Cochise; collab. s.p. story, Gambler from Natchez, Chief Crazy Horse, s.p. Golden Horde; adapt. s.p. Prince Who Was a Thief; orig. s.p., Sea Hornet; s.p., Three Bad Sisters; orig., s.p., Duel on the Mississippi; orig. Black Sleep, s.p., War Drums; story, collab. s.p., Gun Brothers; story, Affair in Reno; story, s.p., Frontier Rangers; story, s.p., Gold, Glory & Custer; orig. story, collab. s.p., Kissin Cousins. Orig. s.p. Harem Scarem.
TELEVISION: Maverick, G.E. Theatre, Northwest Passage, Broken Arrow, Cheyenne, 77 Sunset Strip.

ADAMS, JULIE: Actress. r.n. Betty May Adams. b. Waterloo, LA, Oct. 17, 1928. e. jr. coll., Little Rock, AK. Coll. dramatic; m.p. debut in Red Hot and Blue; Star of Tomorrow, 1953.
PICTURES INCLUDE: Bright Victory; as Betty Adams in: The Dalton Gang, Marshal of Heldorado, West of the Brazos; Hollywood Story, Finders Keepers, Bend of the River, Treasure of Lost Canyon, Horizons West, Lawless Breed, Mississippi Gambler, The Creature From the Black Lagoon, Private War of Major Benson, Man from the Alamo, Wings of the Hawk, Tickle Me, The Last Movie, MCQ, The Wild McCullochs, Killer Force, The Fifth Floor, Black Roses, Backtrack.
TELEVISION: Go Ask Alice, Capitol.

ADAMS, MASON: Actor. b. Feb. 26, 1919, NY, NY. ed. U. Wisconsin. B.A., 1940; M.A., 1941. Trained for stage at Neighborhood Playhouse. Began on radio in 1946, spending nearly two decades in title role of Pepper Young's Family. Broadway debut: Get Away Old Man (1943).
THEATER: Career Angel, Public Relations, Violet, Shadow of My Enemy, Inquest, The Sign in Sidney Brustein's Window, Tall Story, The Trail of the Catonsville Nine, Checking Out.
PICTURES: God Told Me To, Raggedy Ann and Andy, The Final Conflict.
TELEVISION: Series: Lou Grant (1977-1982), Morningstar/Eveningstar; Movies: The Deadliest Season, And Baby Makes Six, The Shining Season, Flamingo Road, The Revenge of the Stepford Wives, The Kid with the Broken Halo, Freedom to Speak, Solomon Northrup's Odyssey.

ADAMS, MAUD: Actress. r.n. Wikstrum. b. Lulea, Sweden, Feb. 12, 1945. Formerly a model. Film debut: The Christian Licorice Store.
PICTURES: U-Turn, Mahoney's Estate, The Man With the Golden Gun, Rollerball, Killer Force, The Merciless Man, Tattoo, Octopussy, Target Eagle, Grandpa and I.
TELEVISION: Laura—Shades of Summer, The Hostage Tower, Playing for Time, Chicago Story, Emerald Point, N.A.S., Nairobi Affair.

ADAMS, TONY: Producer. b. Dublin, Ireland, Feb. 15, 1953. Began career as asst. to dir. John Boorman and was associated with Burt Reynolds prior to joining Blake Edwards as a prod., 1973. Then Pres., Blake Edwards Entertainment; Pres., The Blake Edwards Company, 1988.
PICTURES: Assoc. Prod.: Return of the Pink Panther; The Pink Panther Strikes Again; Revenge of the Pink Panther;

"10"; S.O.B.; Victor-Victoria; Trail of the Pink Panther; The Man Who Loved Women. Prod.: Micki & Maude, That's Life, A Fine Mess, Blind Date, Sunset.
TELEVISION: Julie Andrews in Japan, Justin Case (prod.).

ADDISON, JOHN: Composer. b. West Chobham, Surrey, England, March 16, 1920. e. Wellington and Royal Coll. of Music. Entered m.p. ind. in 1948, Professor, Royal Coll. of Music.
PICTURES INCLUDE: (Music scores) Seven Days to Noon, The Man Between, The Maggie, Make Me An Offer, Privates Progress, Reach for the Sky, Lucky Jim, I Was Monty's Double, Carlton Brown of the Foreign Office, The Entertainer, The Honey Pot, Torn Curtain, A Fine Madness, I Was Happy Here, The Loved One, Guns at Batasi, The Uncle, Girl With Green Eyes, Tom Jones, The Loneliness of the Long Distance Runner, A Taste of Honey, The Charge of the Light Brigade, Smashing Time, Start the Revolution Without Me, Country Dance (in U.S., Brotherly Love), Forbush and the Penguins, Sleuth, Luther, Dead Cert, Ride a Wild Pony, Seven-Per-Cent Solution, Swashbuckler, Joseph Andrews, A Bridge Too Far, The Pilot, High Point, Strange Invaders, Grace Quigley, Code Name: Emerald, To Die For.
BALLETS INCLUDE: Carte Blanche (at Sadlers Wells and Edinburgh Festival).
PLAYS INCLUDE: The Entertainer, The Chairs, Luther, Midsummer Night's Dream, The Broken Heart, The Workhouse Donkey, Hamlet, Semi-Detached, The Seagull, Saint Joan of the Stockyards, Listen to the Mockingbird, Cranks (revue), Antony & Cleopatra, I Claudius, Twelfth Night, Bloomsbury, Antony and Cleopatra (LA Theatre Centre).
TELEVISION: Sambo and Snow Mountains, Detective, Hamlet, The Search for Ulysses, Way of the World, Back of Beyond, Black Beauty, The Bastard, Deadly Price of Paradise, Centennial, Pearl, Love's Savage Fury, Like Normal People, The French Atlantic Affair, Mistress of Paradise, Eleanor First Lady of The World, Charles and Diana: A Royal Love Story, Mail Order Bride, Ellis Island, Thirteen at Dinner, Dead Man's Folly, Mr. Boogedy, Something in Common, Firefighter, Amazing Stories, Bride of Boogedy, Strange Voices, Beryl Markham: A Shadow on the Sun (mini-series). Series: Nero Wolfe, Murder She Wrote.
STAGE MUSICALS: The Amazons, Popkiss.

ADELMAN, GARY: Executive. e. California State U., Long Beach State Coll. 1969, asst. dir. on feature, The Masterpiece; assoc. prod. on The Candy Snatchers. Produced first feature film, The Severed Arm, 1974. Assisted Winston Hock in development of 3-D process, 1975. 1976–82, pres. & COO of Monarch Prods. Post-prod. consultant for Jerry Gross Organization. 1983, founder and partial owner of New Image Releasing, Inc., new prod. & dist. co. Had post of secty./treas. 1987, named v.p., chg. prod., All-American Entertainment.

ADELMAN, JOSEPH A.: Executive. b. Winnipeg, Manitoba, Can., Dec. 27, 1933. e. New York U., B.A., 1954; Harvard Law Sch., J.D., 1957, graduated cum laude. Attorney, United Artists Corp., New York, 1958; named west coast counsel, Hollywood, 1964; named exec. assistant to the v.p. in charge of production 1968; named v.p., west coast business and legal affairs, 1972; appointed executive vice-president, Association of Motion Pictures and Television Producers, 1977; appointed v.p. in charge of business affairs, Paramount Pictures Corp., 1979; co-founder and exec. v.p. Kidpix, Inc. since 1984; founder and chief exec. officer of Kidpix Theaters Corp. since 1985; appointed senior v.p. for business/legal affairs, Color Systems Technology, Inc. 1986; names Pres. of CTS Entertainment, 1987. Admitted to New York, California and U.S. Supreme Court bars; member, Phi Beta Kappa; Alumni Achievement Award, NYU, 1982; American Bar Association; Los Angeles Copyright Society; Academy of Motion Picture Arts and Sciences; board of directors, AMPTP, 1969–1979; National Assn. of Television Programming Executives.; board of trustees, Theatre Authority, 1970–

ADELSON, GARY: Producer. b. 1954. e. U. of California at L.A. (B.A.). Son of Merv Adelson.
TELEVISION: Helter Skelter (prod. asst.); Sybil (assoc. prod.); Eight Is Enough (prod.); The Blue Knight (prod.); Too Good To Be True (exec. prod.) Our Family Business (exec. prod.); Cass Malloy (exec. prod.); John Steinbeck's The Winter of Our Discontent (exec. prod.); Lace (exec. prod.); Detective in the House (exec. prod.); Lace II (exec. prod.), Studio 5B (series, exec. prod.).
PICTURE: The Last Starfighter (prod.), The Boy Who Could Fly, In The Mood, Tap.

ADELSON, MERV: Producer. b. Los Angeles, CA, Oct. 23, 1929. e. U. of California at L.A. Bd. chmn., Lorimar Productions.
PICTURES INCLUDE: Twilight's Last Gleaming, The Choirboys, Who Is Killing the Great Chefs of Europe?, Avalanche Express, The Big Red One.
TELEVISION: The Waltons, Eight Is Enough, Dallas, Kaz, The Waverly Wonders, Knots Landing, Sybil, A Man Called Intrepid, The Blue Knight, Helter-Skelter.

ADJANI, ISABELLE: Actress. b. Germany, June 27, 1955.
PICTURES: The Slap, The Story of Adele H., The Tenant, Faustine, Barocco, The Driver, Nosferatu—The Vampire, The Bronte Sisters, Quartet, Next Year If All Goes Well, One Deadly Summer, Subway, Ishtar, Possession.

ADLER, ALLEN: Executive Producer. b. New York, NY, 1946. e. Princeton U., B.A.; Harvard Business Sch., M.B.A. Started with Standard & Poor's Inter-Capital; Then joined Alan Hirschfield at American Diversified Enterprises; next to Columbia Pictures 1973 as corporate officer. 1979, named sr. v.p., Columbia. 1981, teamed with Daniel Melnick in IndieProd Co.
PICTURE: Making Love.

ADRIAN, IRIS: Actress, r.n. Iris Adrian Hostetter. b. Los Angeles, CA, May 29, 1913. p. prof. Dancer, on stage N.Y. and abroad in Follies of 1931; m.p. debut in MGM two-reel color films.
PICTURES INCLUDE: Smart Woman, Out of the Storm, Paleface, Sky Dragon, There's a Girl in My Heart, Tough Assignment, Once a Thief, Always Leave Them Laughing, Stop That Cab, My Favorite Spy, Highway Magnet, Fast & The Furious, Crime Wave, Devil's Harbor, Carnival Rock, The Buccaneer, Blue Hawaii, The Errand Boy, Fate is the Hunter, That Darn Cat, The Odd Couple, The Love Bug, Freaky Friday.

AGAR, JOHN: Actor. b. Chicago, IL, Jan. 31, 1921. In service W.W.II. Film debut 1948: Fort Apache.
PICTURES INCLUDE: Adventure in Baltimore, I Married a Communist, Sands of Iwo Jima, She Wore a Yellow Ribbon, Breakthrough, Magic Carpet, Along the Great Divide, Woman of the North Country, Man of Conflict, Bait, Rocket Man, Shield for Murder, Golden Mistress, Revenge of the Creature, Hold Back Tomorrow, Tarantula, Star in the Dust, Joe Butterfly, St. Valentine's Day Massacre, Waco, Johnny Reno, Women of the Prehistoric Planet, Perfect Victims, Miracle Mile.

AGUTTER, JENNY: Actress. b. Taunton, England, 1952; e. Elmhurst Ballet Sch. m.p. debut East of Sudan, 1964. Emmy for best supporting actress, 1971; Variety Club of Grt. Britain Most Promising Artiste Award 1971; BAFTA best supporting actress award for Equus, 1976.
PICTURES: Ballerina, Gates of Paradise, Star!, I Start Counting, Walkabout, The Railway Children, War of Children, Logan's Run, The Eagle Has Landed, The Man in the Iron Mask, Equus, Dominique, Clayton & Catherine, The Riddle of the Sands, Sweet William, The Survivor, Amy, The American Werewolf, Secret Places, The Dark Tower.
PLAYS: School for Scandal, Rooted, Arms and the Man, The Ride Across Lake Constance, The Tempest, Spring Awakening, Hedda, Betrayal, 1982–83 Member, Royal Shakespeare Co.—King Lear, Arden of Taversham, The Body. Breaking the Silence, 1985. Shrew (Los Angeles), 1986.
TELEVISION: The Great Mr. Dickens, The Wild Duck, The Cherry Orchard, The Snow Goose, As Many as Are Here Present, A War of Children, The Man in the Iron Mask, A House in Regent Place, There's Love and Dove, Kiss Me and Die, A Legacy, The Waiting Room, Six Million Dollar Man, School Play, The Mayflower, Voyage of the Pilgrims, Beulah Land, Love's Labour's Lost, This Office Life, Magnum, The Two Ronnies, Silas Marner, The Twilight Zone, Murder She Wrote.

AIELLO, DANNY: Actor. b. June 20, 1933. On Broadway before entering films.
THEATER: Lampost Reunion, Wheelbarrow Closers, Knockout, The Floating Light Bulb, Hurlyburly, The House of Blue Leaves.
PICTURES: Blood Brothers, Fingers, Defiance, Hide in Plain Sight, Ft. Apache, the Bronx, Chu Chu and the Philly Flash, The Purple Rose of Cairo, Key Exchange, The Protector, Radio Days, Moonstruck, Man on Fire, The Pick-Up Artist, The January Man, Crack in the Mirror, Do The Right Thing, Russicum.
TELEVISION: Family of Strangers (Emmy, 1981), Lady Blue, Daddy, Alone in the Neon Jungle.

AIMEE, ANOUK: Actress. r.n. Françoise Dreyfus. b. April 27, 1934. Paris, France. Studied, Bauer-Therond dramatic school, Paris. Stage debut: 1946. La Maison Sous La Mer.
FILMS INCLUDE: Les Amants De Verone, The Golden Salamander, Le Rideau Cramoisi, Nuit D'Orage, La Bergere et Le Ramoneur (Cartoon), Mauvais Rencontres, Nina, Stresemann, Tous Peuvent Me Tuer, Pot Bouille, Modigliani of Montparnasse, Le Tete Contres Les Murs, Les Dragueurs, La Dolce Vita, Le Farceur, Lola, Les Amours de Paris L'Imprevu, 8½, Sodom and Gomorrah, La Fuga, A Man and a Woman, Un Soir, Un Train, The Appointment, The Model Shop, Justine, The Mandarins, Tragedy of a Ridiculous Man, Leap into the Void, A Man and A Woman: Twenty Years Later, The House of the Lord.

3

AKINS, CLAUDE: Actor. b. Nelson, GA, May 25, 1926. e. Northwestern U. Worked as salesman in Indiana before joining Barter Theatre for season. Came to New York; appeared in The Rose Tattoo. Spent several seasons with touring cos.
PICTURES INCLUDE: From Here to Eternity, The Caine Mutiny, Skyjacked, Flap, Devil's Brigade, Inherit the Wind, The Great Bank Robbery, Monster in the Closet, The Farm.
TELEVISION: Police Story, Cannon, McCloud, Marcus Welby, M.D., Mannix, The Streets of San Francisco, Movin' On, The Misadventures of Sheriff Lobo, The Rhinemann Exchange, Dream West, Mini-Series: Desperate Intruder, Celebrity, Movies: The Baron and the Kid, If It's Tuesday, It Still Must Be Belgium.

AKTER, MAHMOOD ALI KHAN: Producer, Distributor, Exhibitor: b. Hyderabad Deccan, India, April 12, 1926. Graduate of Arts. Formerly with Columbia Films of Pakistan Ltd., gen. mgr., Hussein & Co. controlling film dist. of United Artists Corp., Selznick Intl., London Films, Pathe Overseas. Participant foreign leaders prog. of Intl. Educational Exchange Service of U.S.A. State Dept.; mgr., Paramount Films of Pakistan, Ltd., 1959–64; mgr. dir., General Film Distributors, Lahore. Chm., Motion Picture Importer's Group, Lahore, Mgr. dir., Pak Boor Corp.

ALBECK, ANDY: Executive. Pres & chief exec. officer, United Artists Corp. b. U.S.S.R., Sept. 25, 1921. Industry career began in 1939 with Columbia Pictures Intl. Corp. 1947, Central Motion Picture Exchange. 1949, Eagle Lion Classics, Inc. Joined UA in 1951 in intl. dept., functioning in the area of operations. After filling a number of key posts, named asst. treas. in 1970. In 1972 became v.p. of UA and its subsidiary, UA Broadcasting, Inc. 1973, appt. pres. of UA Broadcasting and in 1976 named snr. v.p.—operations. Named UA Corp. pres. & chief exec. officer in 1978. Retired, 1981.

ALBERGHETTI, ANNA MARIA: Singer, Actress. b. Pesaro, Italy, May 15, 1936; d. Daniele Alberghetti, cellist. Concert debut in 1948 in Pesaro, then toured Italy, Scandinavia, Spain; Am. debut Carnegie Hall, 1950, sang with NY Philharmonic Society, Phila. Symphony, on television. Screen debut in The Medium, 1950; Broadway stage debut: Carnival, 1962. (Tony Award for best actress).
PICTURES: Here Comes the Groom, Stars Are Singing, Last Command, 10,000 Bedrooms, Cinderfella.
TELEVISION: Toast of the Town, Cavalcade of Stars, Arthur Murray Show, Bob Hope, Eddie Fisher, Red Skelton, Dinah Shore, Desilu Playhouse, G.E. Theatre, Chevy Show, Dupont Show, Voice of Firestone, Colgate Hour, Climax, Loretta Young, Ford Jubilee, Perry Como.

ALBERT, EDDIE: Actor. r.n. Eddie Albert Heimberger. b. Rock Island, IL, April 22, 1908. e. U. of Minnesota. Radio NBC.
BROADWAY: Brother Rat, Say Darling, The Music Man, Room Service, The Boys from Syracuse, Seven Year Itch, Our Town, No Hard Feelings, Reuben Reuben, Miss Liberty, You Can't Take It With You.
PICTURES INCLUDE: Brother Rat, Four Wives, Angel from Texas, Dispatch from Reuter's, Rendezvous With Annie, Perfect Marriage, Smash-Up, The Story of a Woman, Time Out of Mind, Hit Parade of 1947, Dude Goes West, You Gotta Stay Happy, Fuller Brush Girl, You're in the Navy Now, Carrie, Meet Me After the Show, Actors and Sin, Roman Holiday, Girl Rush, I'll Cry Tomorrow, Oklahoma Attack, Teahouse of the August Moon, Orders to Kill, Gun Runners, Roots of Heaven, The Young Doctors, The Longest Day, Captain Newman, The Heartbreak Kid, Miracle of the White Stallions, Seven Women, McQ, The Take, The Longest Yard, Escape to Witch Mountain, The Devil's Rain, Hustle, Birch Interval, Foolin' Around, Yesterday, The Concorde-Airport 79, The Border, Ladyfingers, How to Beat the High Cost of Living, Take This Job and Shove It, Yes, Giorgio, Bless 'em All, Dreamscape, Stitches, Head Office, Turnaround, Terminal Entry.
TELEVISION: Green Acres, Switch!, The Yeagers, Benjamin Franklin, The Borrowers, Killer Bees, Nutcracker, Anything Goes, Crash, The Word, Evening in Byzantium, Pirates Key, Living in Paradise, Oklahoma Dolls, The Plan, Peter and Paul, The Fall Guy, Goliath Awaits, Concord, Beyond Witch Mountain, Rooster, Love Boat, Rhode Island Demon Murder, Coalfire, In Like Flynn, Dress Gray, Mercy or Murder?, Highway to Heaven, Brenda Starr, War and Remembrances, Falcon Crest, Murder She Wrote.

ALBERT, EDWARD: Actor. b. Los Angeles, CA, Feb. 20, 1951. e. U. of California at L.A. Son of actor Eddie Albert and actress Margo. Was prod. asst. on Patton in Spain. Has appeared with father on radio and TV shows. Is photographer and has exhibited work in L.A.
PICTURES INCLUDE: Butterflies Are Free (debut), Forty Carats, Midway, The Domino Principle, The Greek Tycoon, When Time Ran Out, A Time To Die, Ellie, Getting Even, Distortions, The Rescue, The Underachievers, Fistfighter, The Rescue.
TELEVISION: Killer Bees, Yellow Rose, The Last Convertible, Falcon Crest, Beauty and the Beast, Daddy Can't Read.

ALBRIGHT, LOLA: Actress. b. Akron, OH, July 20, 1925. e. Studied piano 12 years. Switchboard operator and stenographer NBC; stenographer with WHAM and bit player; photographers' model. screen debut in The Pirate, 1948.
PICTURES INCLUDE: Easter Parade, Girl from Jones Beach, Tulsa, Champion, Good Humor Man, Bodyhold, When You're Smiling, Sierra Passage, Killer That Stalked New York, Arctic Flight, Silver Whip, Treasure of Ruby Hills, Magnificent Matador, Beauty on Parade, Tender Trap, A Cold Wind in August, Kid Galahad, Lord Love a Duck, Where Were You When the Lights Went Out?, The Impossible Years, The Money Jungle.
TELEVISION: Switch, The Eddie Capra Mysteries, Quincy, Airwolf.

ALCAINE, JOSE LUIS: Cinematographer. b. Tangier, Algeria, Dec. 26, 1938. e. Spanish Cinema Sch., Madrid. After graduation joined Madrid's Studio Moros doing commercials.
PICTURES INCLUDE: El Puente, El Sur, Taseo, Rustlers' Rhapsody, etc.

ALDA, ALAN: Actor, Writer-Director r.n. Alphonso D'Abruzzo b. New York, NY, Jan. 28, 1936. e. Fordham U., 1956 f. Robert Alda. Studied at Cleveland Playhouse on Ford Foundation Grant; performed with Second City, then on TV in That Was The Week That Was; Broadway credits include The Owl and The Pussycat, Purlie Victorious, Fair Game For Lovers (Theatre World Award), The Apple Tree (Tony Award nomination). Has won 5 Emmys, 2 Writer Guild Awards, 3 Directors Guild Awards, 5 Golden Globes, 7 People's Choice Awards, Humanitas Award for Writing.
PICTURES INCLUDE: Gone Are The Days, The Moonshine War, Jenny, The Mephisto Waltz, Paper Lion, To Kill a Clown, Same Time Next Year, California Suite, The Seduction of Joe Tynan (also s.p.), The Four Seasons (actor, dir., s.p.), Sweet Liberty (actor, dir., s.p.), A New Life (actor, dir., s.p.), Joint Venture.
TELEVISION: M*A*S*H (11 years), Isn't It Shocking?, Playmates, The Glass House, Kill Me If You Can, Free to Be You and Me, 6 Rms Riv Vu (actor, dir.), created series We'll Get By and The Four Seasons.

ALDREDGE, THEONI V.: Costume designer. b. Salonika, Greece, Aug. 22, 1932. m. actor Tom Aldredge. e. American School, Athens; Goodman Theatre School, Chicago, 1949–52. On Broadway (Timon of Athens, Two Gentlemen of Verona, A Chorus Line, Annie, 42nd Street, etc.) as well as theatrical films.
PICTURES INCLUDE: You're A Big Boy Now, No Way to Treat a Lady, Uptight, Last Summer, I Never Sang for My Father, Promise at Dawn, The Great Gatsby, Network, Semi-Tough, The Cheap Detective, The Fury, Eyes of Laura Mars, The Champ, The Rose, Rich and Famous, Middle Age Crazy, Annie, Ghostbusters, Racing With the Moon, Moonstruck.

ALEANDRO, NORMA: Actress. b. Argentina, 1941. Sister is actress Maria Vaner. As child, performed with parents in theater troupe they ran. Has performed in every theatrical genre and epoch, also directing in Argentina. Written published short stories (1986) and poems and has written screenplay for Argentinian film. Was in exile in Uruguay (18 months) and Spain 1976–82 because of the military junta in Argentina. Before exile had made 12 films; after return in 1982 starred in theatre and 7 films.
THEATER: U.S.: About Love and Other Stories (one-woman show), toured South America, then at La Mama and later off-Bdwy at Public Theater (1986); The Senorita of Tacna (written for her by Mario Varga-Llosa, 1987).
PICTURES: The Official Story (best actress award, Cannes Film Fest., 1986, shared with Cher); Gaby: A True Story (Acad. Award nom.); Cousins.

ALEXANDER, JANE: Actress. b. Boston, MA, Oct. 28, 1939. r.n. Jane Quigley. e. Sarah Lawrence Coll., U. of Edinburgh. Stage career includes appearances on Broadway, at Arena Stage, Washington, and Shakespeare Festival at Stamford, Conn.
THEATER: NY: The Great White Hope (Tony Award, 1969); Six Rms Riv Vu, Find Your Way Home, Hamlet, The Heiress, First Monday in October, Losing Time, Monday After the Miracle, Old Times, Night of the Iguana.
PICTURES: The Great White Hope, A Gunfight, The New Centurions, All the President's Men, The Betsy, Night Crossing, Testament, City Heat, Square Dance, Sweet Country, Matewan.
TELEVISION: Welcome Home, Johny Bristol, Miracle on 34th St., Death Be Not Proud, Eleanor and Franklin, Eleanor and Franklin: The White House Years, In the Custody of Strangers, Playing for Time (Emmy Award), When She Says No, Calamity Jane, Malice in Wonderland, Blood & Orchids, Open Admissions, A Friendship in Vienna.

ALEXANDER, RALPH: Executive. Began career with Universal Pictures in sales, 1949; various sls. jobs with 20th Century Fox and Lorimar. 1981–82, v.p., theatrical foreign sls., Filmway Pictures; 1982–84, v.p., sls, for Latin America & Southeast Asia, Embassy Pictures Intl. 1984, exec. v.p., multi-media foreign sls. for Robert Meyers Intl. Nov., 1985, joined Dino De Laurentiis Corp. as intl. sls. dir. in chg. all foreign sls. theatrical and ancillary rights except tv. 1986, promoted to v.p., intl. sls., DEG.

ALGAR, JAMES: Producer, Writer, Director. b. Modesto, CA, June 11, 1912. e. Stanford U., B.A., M.A. journalism. Entire career since 1934 with Walt Disney Prods. Animator: Snow White; Director: Fantasia, Bambi, Wind in the Willows, Ichabod & Mr. Toad.
 DOCUMENTARIES: war. health. True-Life Adventures: Seal Island, The Living Desert, Vanishing Prairie, The African Lion, Secrets of Life.
 FEATURE CREDITS: Ten Who Dared, The Incredible Journey, Gnome-Mobile, White Wilderness, Rascal, The Legend of Lobo, The Jungle Cat, Run, Cougar, Run.
 TELEVISION CREDITS: Producer: Run Light Buck, Run, The Not So Lonely Lighthouse Keeper, One Day on Beetle Rock, Wild Heart, Along the Oregon Trail, The Best Dog-goned Dog in the World, One Day at Teton Marsh, Solomon, the Sea Turtle, Manado the Wolverine, Wild Geese Calling, Two Against the Arctic, Bayou Ray, Secrets of the Pond, Boy Who Talked to Badgers, Big Sky Man. Wrote and co-produced Great Moments with Mr. Lincoln; New York World's Fair; Circarama, America the Beautiful, Circle Vision 1958 Brussels World's Fair, Disneyland, Hall of Presidents, Disney World, Florida.
 Shares in nine Oscars.

ALIN, MORRIS: Editor, Writer, Publicist, Lyricist. e. City Coll. of New York. Came into m.p. industry, auditor of Hunchback of Notre Dame, roadshow oper., 1924; asst. sls. prom. mgr. Universal, 1926–27; slsmn., Universal, 1927; assoc. editor, The Distributor–MGM publication, 1927; editor, 1928–33; writer, publicist, MGM Studio, 1933–34; writer, publicist, Hollywood, New York, 1935–38; rej. Universal. 1938, editor, Progress: (Univ. publication); Twice winner of award, International Competition on Industrial Journalism; Senior publicist and Progress editor, Universal, 1961–67; editor Enterprise Press, 1968; member, executive Enterprise Press 1973; American Guild of Authors and Composers, American Society of Composers, Authors and Publishers, National Academy of Popular Music, and Motion Picture Pioneers.

ALLAN, TED: b. Clifton, AZ. Comm. artist, actor SAG 1945, cameraman; photo training at Technicolor, Consolidated, MGM labs.; portrait photog., MGM, 20th-Century Fox, Selznick; created own film studio, 1952, prod. M.P. features, TV series, & pilots; Dir. of photog. 1956; 2 yr. contract Sinatra Enter.; 9 yrs. head CBS Cam. Dept. Hollywood; 3 yrs. 20th Cen. Fox, Pub-Stills & Featurettes for Von Ryan's Express, Fantastic Voyage, Sand Pebbles, Dr. Doolittle, The Detective, Lady in Cement, Tora, Tora, Tora. Featurettes for Universal: Seven Per Cent Solution, Hindenburg, Rollercoaster, Two Minute Warning, Gray Lady Down, The Promise, Dracula, Same Time Next Year.

ALLAND, WILLIAM: Producer. b. Delmar, DE, March 4, 1916. e. Baltimore. Acted in semi-professional groups; with Orson Welles' Mercury Theatre as actor, stage mgr.; asst. prod. Mercury Theatre radio series; actor, dialogue dir., Citizen Kane; act., Macbeth; U.S. Air Force, W.W.II; then radio writer; prod., Universal, 1952.
 PICTURES INCLUDE: The Raiders, Flesh and Fury, Stand At Apache River, It Came From Outer Space, Creature From The Black Lagoon, Johnny Dark, This Island Earth, Dawn At Socorro, Four Guns To The Border, Chief Crazy Horse, Revenge Of The Creature, Tarantula, Creature Walks Among Us, Gun for a Coward, Land Unknown, Deadly Mantis, Mole People, Raw Wind in Eden, The Lady Takes a Flyer, As Young As We Are; The Party Crashers, Colossus of New York, The Space Children; Look In Any Window, The Lively Set, The Rare Breed, The Lawless Breed.

ALLEN, COREY: Director, Actor. r.n. Alan Cohen. b. Cleveland, OH, June 29, 1934. e. UCLA, 1951–54; UCLA law sch. 1954–55. Actor turned dir. starred in Oscar-winning UCLA student film, appeared in 20 plays at Players Ring, Players Gallery and other L.A. theaters. Films as actor: Rebel Without a Cause (1955), Sweet Bird of Youth, Private Property, Party Girl, The Chapman Report; TV: Perry Mason, Alfred Hitchcock Presents. With partner John Herman Shaner, prod. Freeway Circuit Theatre. Led Actors Workshop with actor Guy Stockwell for 10 years.
 PICTURES: Pinocchio, Thunder and Lightning, Avalanche.
 TELEVISION: Director: This is the Life, Mannix, High Chaparral, Dr. Kildare, Streets of San Francisco, Ironside, Barnaby Jones, Police Woman, Rockford Files, Quincy, Dallas, Lou Grant, McClain's Law, Family Hovak, T.J. Hooker, Paper Chase: The Second Year, Hill Street Blues (Emmy), Sonny Spoons, Supercarrier, Pilots: Man Undercover, Stone, Capitol, Simon and Simon, Whiz Kids, Codename: Foxfire, Murder She Wrote, Dallas: The Next Generation. Movies: See the Man Run, Cry Rape!, Yesterday's Child, The Return of Frank Cannon, Man in the Santa Claus Suit, Brass, I-Man,

Destination America, Beverly Hills Cowgirl Blues, The Last Fling, Ann Jillian Story.

ALLEN, DAYTON: Performer. b. New York, NY, Sept. 24, 1919. e. Mt. Vernon H.S. Motion picture road shows, 1936–40; disc jockey, WINS, N.Y., 1940–41; writer, vaudeville comedy bits, 1941–45; then radio comic, puppeteer and voices; TV since 1948; film commercials; shows include Oaky Doky, Bonny Maid Varieties, Howdy Doody, Jack Barry's Winky Dink, Abe Lincoln in Illinois, The Circle of Chalk, The Steve Allen Show.

ALLEN, DEBBIE: Actress, choreographer. b. Houston, TX, Jan. 16, 1950. Sister of actress Phylicia Rashad. e. Howard U. Debut on television as one of the three women on NBC series 3 Girls 3 (1977).
 THEATER: Purlie, Raisin, West Side Story (revival), Sweet Charity (revival).
 PICTURES: Ragtime.
 TELEVISION: Roots—The Next Generation, Ben Vereen—His Roots; Fame (series; 3 Emmys as choreographer, 1982, 1983, 1 nom. as actress), Loretta Lynn in Big Apple Country, Texaco Star Theater—Opening Night, The Kids from Fame, Women of San Quentin, John Schneider's Christmas Holiday; A Tribute to Martin Luther King Jr.—A Celebration of Life, Celebrity, Motown Returns to the Apollo; A Different World (prod., dir.).

ALLEN, DEDE: Film editor. b. 1924. Once a messenger at Columbia Pictures, moved to editing dept., then to commercials and features.
 PICTURES INCLUDE: Odds Against Tomorrow (1959), America, America, Bonnie and Clyde, Rachel Rachel, Alice's Restaurant, Little Big Man, Serpico, Dog Day Afternoon, Slapshot, The Wiz, Reds (also exec. prod.), Harry and Son, Mike's Murder, The Breakfast Club, Off Beat, The Milagro Beanfield War (co-ed.).

ALLEN, HERB: Producer. b. San Francisco, CA, Dec. 24, 1913. e. U. of San Francisco, Pasadena Playhouse. Radio actor, anncr., Los Angeles, San Francisco; m.c.; packager. Meet the Champ, children's TV show; assoc. prod., Bob Crosby Show; prod., Johnny Carson show. CBS-TV.

ALLEN, IRWIN: Producer. b. New York, NY. e. Columbia U., City Coll. of New York, journalism & adv. ed. Hollywood; radio prod. dir., daily Hollywood program, 11 yrs.; radio & literary dir., own agency; then M.P. prod.
 PICTURES INCLUDE: Double Dynamite, Girl in Every Port (co-prod.); assoc., prod., Where Danger Lives; prod., Dangerous Mission, The Animal World; prod., co-writer, director, The Story of Mankind; prod., writer, director, Sea Around Us (Academy Award), prod., co-writer, The Big Circus; prod., co-writer, director, The Lost World, Voyage to the Bottom of the Sea, Five Weeks in a Balloon; prod., director action sequences, The Poseidon Adventure, The Towering Inferno. The Swarm (prod.-dir.); Beyond the Poseidon Adventure (prod.-dir.); When Time Ran Out (prod.).
 TELEVISION: Creator-prod., Voyage to the Bottom of the Sea, Lost in Space, Land of the Giant, The Time Tunnel, Adventures of the Queen, Swiss Family Robinson, Flood, Fire, The Return of Captain Nemo, Hanging by a Thread, Cave-In, Night the Bridge Fell Down, Memory of Eva Ryker. Producer: Code Red, Alice in Wonderland.

ALLEN, JAY PRESSON: Writer, Producer. b. Fort Worth, TX, March 3, 1922. Wrote play, Prime of Miss Jean Brodie, produced on Broadway and also for theatrical films and TV. Wrote Forty Carats for stage.
 PICTURES: Marnie, Prime of Miss Jean Brodie, Travels with My Aunt, Cabaret, Funny Lady, Just Tell Me What You Want, It's My Turn (also exec. prod.), Prince of the City (s.p. & exec. prod.), Deathtrap (exec. prod.), Lord of the Flies.
 TELEVISION: Family (creator), Clinic, Hothouse.

ALLEN, JOAN: Actress. b. Rochelle, IL, Aug. 20, 1956. Founding member of Steppenwolf Theatre Co., in Chicago where she performed in over 20 shows including A Lesson from Aloes, Three Sisters, The Miss Firecracker Contest, Cloud 9, Balm in Gilead, Fifth of July. Off Broadway in The Marriage of Bette and Boo, And a Nightingale Sang (Clarence Derwent, Drama Desk, Outer Critics' Circle and Theatre World Awards). Broadway debut: Burn This (1987, Tony Award).
 PICTURES: Compromising Positions (debut, 1985), Manhunter, Peggy Sue Got Married, Tucker: The Man and His Dream, In Country.
 TELEVISION: All My Sons.

ALLEN, KAREN: Actress. b. Carrollton, IL, Oct. 5, 1951. e. George Washington U., U. of Maryland. Auditioned for theatrical company in Washington, DC and won a role in Saint, touring with it for 7 months. Spent several years with Washington Theatre Laboratory Co. Moved to N.Y., acting in student films at New York U. and studying acting with Lee Strasberg at Theatre Institute. Major film debut in National Lampoon's Animal House in 1978.
 THEATER: Broadway debut: The Monday After the Miracle (Theatre World Award), Tennessee Williams: A Celebration

(Williamstown Theatre, MA), Extremities, The Glass Menagerie, (Williamstown), The Miracle Worker.
PICTURES: Manhattan, The Wanderers, Cruising, A Small Circle of Friends, Raiders of the Lost Ark, Shoot the Moon, Split Image, Strange Invaders, Until September, Starman, The End of the Line, Backfire, The Glass Menagerie, Animal Behavior, Scrooged.
TELEVISION: Circle of Children, Part II, East of Eden (1979), Alfred Hitchcock Presents (1986).

ALLEN, LEWIS: Director. b. Shropshire, England, Dec. 25, 1905. e. Tettenhall Coll., Staffs, Eng. Exec. in chg. of N.Y. & London prod. for Gilbert Miller; actor & stage dir. N.Y. & England; dir. (N.Y.) Laburnum Grove, Amazing Doctor Clitterhouse, Ladies & Gentlemen; (London) The Women, studied m.p. prod. at Paramount 2 yrs.; apptd. dir. with debut of The Uninvited 1943.
PICTURES INCLUDE: Appointment With Danger, Suddenly, Another Time Another Place, The Lorelei.

ALLEN, LEWIS M.: Producer. b. Berryville, VA, 1922.
PICTURES: The Connection, The Balcony, Fahrenheit 451, Fortune and Men's Eyes, Never Cry Wolf, Swimming to Cambodia, 1918, End of the Line (co-prod.), Dogfight (co-prod.), Miss Firecracker, Lord of the Flies (exec. prod.).

ALLEN, MEL: TV commentator b. Birmingham, AL, Feb. 14, 1913. e. U. of Alabama, A.B. 1932; U. Alabama Law Sch., LL.B. 1936. Started as sportscaster in Birmingham, while in law school; speech instructor in U. Ala. 1935–37; to N.Y. 1937, as staff announcer CBS to 1943; served in U.S. Army W.W.II in infantry until the war ended, then before discharge was transferred to work on NBC Army Hour; sportscasting throughout U.S., joined N.Y. Yankees, 1946, concurrently narrating many shorts incl. How to Make a Yankee, appearing on radio & video and in Babe Ruth Story; sports commentator Fox Movietonews; voted best sportscaster in Motion Picture Daily-Fame radio. TV polls; Monitor, NBC; NCAA TV College Football, NBC; World Series (1938–64), CBS-NBC; Rose Bowl (1951–62), NBC; Sports Broadcasters Hall Of Fame.

ALLEN, NANCY: Actress. b. New York, NY, June 24, 1950. e. H.S. Performing Arts, N.Y.
PICTURES: The Last Detail, Carrie, I Wanna Hold Your Hand, Home Movies, 1941, Dressed to Kill, Blow Out, Strange Invaders, The Buddy System, The Philadelphia Experiment, The Last Victim, Not for Publication, Terror in the Aisles, Robocop, Poltergeist III, Sweet Revenge, Out of the Dark, Limit Up.
TELEVISION: Movie: The Gladiator.

ALLEN, REX: Actor. b. Wilcox, AZ, Dec. 31, 1922. e. Wilcox H.S., 1939. Vaudeville & radio actor; WLS, Chicago, 5 yrs.; was rodeo star appearing in shows through U.S.
PICTURES INCLUDE: Arizona Cowboy, Hills of Oklahoma, Under Mexicali Stars, Thunder in God's Country, Rodeo King & the Senorita, I Dream of Jeannie, Last Musketeer, South Pacific Trail, Old Overland Trail, Down Laredo Way, Phantom Stallion, For the Love of Mike, Tomboy and the Champ; narr., Walt Disney.
TELEVISION: Perry Como Special; commercials, Wonderful World of Color (NBC) Frontier Doctor.
RECORDINGS: Crying in The Chapel, Don't Go Near the Indians, Warner Bros. Records. 1966 Radio Man of the Year; 1966 Cowboy Hall of Fame.

ALLEN, ROBERT: Actor. e. Dartmouth Coll. Began film career in 1926.
PICTURES INCLUDE: Love Me Forever, Party Wire, Winter Carnival, Crime and Punishment, Pride of the Marines, Black Room Mystery, Death Flies East, Air Hawks, Bob Allen Ranger Series, Craig's Wife, Awful Truth, Lady of Secrets, Keep Smiling, Meet the Girls, Everybody's Baby, The City, Winner Take All, Fire-Away, Pie In The Sky.
PLAYS INCLUDE: Blessed Event, Popsy, Kiss Them for Me, Show Boat, I Killed the Count, Auntie Mame, A Few Wild Oats, Time Out for Ginger.
TELEVISION: Kraft, Armstrong Theatre, Philco, The Web, Suspense, Ethel & Albert, Danger, Lux Playhouse, Pulitzer Prize Playhouse, Lamp Unto My Feet.

ALLEN, STEVE: Performer. b. New York, NY, Dec 26, 1921. m. actress Jayne Meadows. U.S. Army 1942; radio shows, Los Angeles; TV, N.Y., 1950; shows include: What's My Line, Steve Allen Show, Tonight, I've Got a Secret, Meeting of Minds, Laughback.
PICTURES INCLUDE: Down Memory Lane, Warning Shot, I'll Get By, Benny Goodman Story, College Confidential, Amazon Women on the Moon.
COMPOSER OR LYRICIST: This Could Be the Start of Something Big, Pretend You Don't See Her, South Rampart St. Parade, Picnic, Houseboat, On the Beach, Sleeping Beauty, Bell, Book and Candle, Gravy Waltz, Impossible, Score for Broadway musical Sophie, and TV musicals The Bachelor, and Alice in Wonderland.

AUTHOR: Fourteen For Tonight, Steve Allen's Bop Fables, The Funny Men, Wry On the Rocks, The Girls on the Tenth Floor, The Question Man, Mark It and Strike It, Not All of Your Laughter, Not All of Your Tears, Bigger Than a Breadbox, A Flash of Swallows, The Wake, Princess Snip-Snip and the Puppykittens, Curses, Schmock-Schmock!, Meeting of Minds, Ripoff, Meeting of Minds-Second Series, Rip-off, Explaining China, The Funny People, Talk Show Murders, Beloved Son: Story of the Jesus Cults, More Funny People, How To Make a Speech and How To Be Funny.

ALLEN, WOODY: Actor, Director, Writer. r.n. Allen Stewart Konigsberg. b. New York, NY, Dec. 1, 1935. Began writing comedy at age 17, contributing to various magazines and top TV comedy shows.
STAGE: Author of Play It Again, Sam; Don't Drink The Water.
PICTURES INCLUDE: What's New Pussycat? (story, screenplay, actor); Casino Royale (actor); What's Up Tiger Lily? (dubbed scr., act.); Take the Money and Run (co-story, co-scr., dir., act.); Bananas (scr., dir., act.); Everything You Always Wanted to Know About Sex* But Were Afraid to Ask (scr., dir., act.); Sleeper, (scr., dir., act.); Love and Death (s.p., act.); The Front (act.), Annie Hall (co. s.p., dir., act.); Interiors (s.p., dir.); Manhattan (co.-s.p., dir., act.); Stardust Memories (s.p., dir., act.); A Midsummer Night's Sex Comedy (s.p., dir.). Zelig (s.p., dir., act.), Broadway Danny Rose (s.p., dir., act.); The Purple Rose of Cairo (dir., s.p.); Hannah and Her Sisters (dir., s.p., actor); Radio Days (dir., s.p.), King Lear (actor only), September (dir., s.p.); New York Stories (co-dir., s.p.).

ALLEY, KIRSTIE: Actress. b. Wichita, KS, Jan. 12, 1955. m. actor Parker Stevenson. e. KS State U., U. KS.
PICTURES: One More Chance, Star Trek II—The Wrath of Khan; Blind Date; Champions; Runaways; Daddy's Home.
TELEVISION: Tow Heads; Highway Honeys; Masquerade (series, 1983–84), A Midsummers Night's Dream, A Bunny's Tale; North and South; Cheers (series).

ALLISON, FRAN: Performer. b. LaPorte City, IA. m. Archie Levington. e. Coe Coll., Cedar Rapids. Sch. teacher, Iowa; started radio career as songstress Iowa State U., 1934; starred in numerous programs, Chicago, 1937; Aunt Fanny of Breakfast Club; Fran of Kukla, Fran and Ollie on TV since 1947. Numerous commercials, daily TV variety show, 1958; Fac. mem., Careers Acad. Milwaukee.

ALLYSON, JUNE: Actress. r.n. Ella Geisman. b. Westchester, NY, Oct. 7, 1917. Started as chorus girl in school; m.p. debut in Best Foot Forward (1943). Voted one of ten best money-making stars in m.p. Herald-Fame poll, 1955.
BROADWAY INCLUDES: Best Foot Forward, 40 Carats, National Company, No No Nanette.
PICTURES INCLUDE: Girl Crazy, Thousands Cheer, Meet the People, Two Girls and a Sailor, Secret Heart, Reformer and Redhead, Right Cross, Too Young to Kiss, Girl in White, Battle Circus, Remains to be Seen, The Stratton Story, Little Women, Executive Suite, Glenn Miller Story, Woman's World, Strategic Air Command, The Strike, McConnell Story, You Can't Run Away From It, Opposite Sex, Interlude, My Man Godfrey, Stranger In My Arms, They Only Kill Their Masters, That's Entertainment!
TELEVISION: The June Allyson Show, Murder She Wrote, The Misfits of Science. Movie-of-the-Week: See the Man Run, Three on a Date, The Kid With the Broken Halo, 20th Century Follies.

ALMENDROS, NESTOR: Cinematographer. b. Barcelona, Spain, Oct. 30, 1930. e. Havana U. (Ph.D.). Worked with numerous directors in Europe—notably Eric Rohmer and François Truffaut—before coming to U.S. Decorated Chevalier, Order of Letters, France (1976). Author: A Man With a Camera (1980).
PICTURES INCLUDE: La Collectionneuse, My Night at Maud's, Clare's Knee, Love in the Afternoon, Perceval Le Gallois, The Wild Child, The Man Who Loved Women, The Story of Adele H., The Marquise of O, The Last Metro, Days of Heaven (Oscar, 1978), Goin' South, Madame Rosa, Kramer VS. Kramer, The Green Room, Love on the Run, The Valley, The Blue Lagoon, Still of the Night, Sophie's Choice, Improper Conduct (dir.), Heartburn, Places in the Heart, Nadine, Nobody Listened (co-prod., co-dir., co-s.p. with Jorge Ulla), New York Stories.

ALMOND, PAUL: Producer, Director, Writer. b. Montreal, Canada, April 26, 1931. e. McGill U., Balliol Coll., Oxford U. 1954–66 produced and directed over a hundred television dramas in Toronto, London, N.Y., and Hollywood; prod., dir., s.p., Isabel 1968, Act of the Heart; Etrog (dir.: best Canadian feature); Journey; Ups and Downs; Captive Hearts (dir.).

ALONSO, MARIA CONCHITA: Actress, Singer. b. Cuba, 1957. Family moved to Venezuela when she was five. 1971, Miss Teenager of the World. 1975, Miss Venezuela. Appeared in four feature films and 10 soap operas before coming to U.S. Recorded several albums as singer.

PICTURES: Moscow on the Hudson, Touch and Go, A Fine Mess, Extreme Prejudice, Colors, The Running Man, Vampire's Kiss.
TELEVISION: An American Cousin (RAI mini-series).

ALONZO, JOHN A: Cinematographer, Director. b. Dallas, TX, 1934.
PICTURES: Bloody Mama; Vanishing Point; Chinatown; Harold and Maude; Lady Sings the Blues; Sounder; Pete 'n' Tillie; Conrack; Farewell, My Lovely; The Fortune; I Will . . . I Will . . . For Now; Once Is Not Enough; The Bad News Bears; Black Sunday; Beyond Reason; Casey's Shadow; Close Encounters of the Third Kind; Which Way Is Up?; The Cheap Detective; Norma Rae; Tom Horn; Back Roads; Zorro, The Gay Blade; Blue Thunder; Cross Creek; Scarface; Out of Control; Runaway; Terror in the Aisles; Jo Jo Dancer, Your Life Is Calling; Nothing in Common; 50 Years of Action.
TELEVISION: Champions, A Love Story; Belle Star (also dir.); Blinded By the Light (also dir.); The Kid From Nowhere (also dir.).

ALTERMAN, JOSEPH GEORGE: Executive. b. New Haven, CT., Dec. 17, 1919. e. Wesleyan U., B.A., 1942; Inst. for Organization Management, Yale U. 1957–59. Exec. assist., SoundScriber Corp., 1945–48; district mgr., Industrial Luncheon Service, 1948–55; asst. secretary and admin. Secretary, Theatre Owners of America, 1955; Exec. dir. and vice pres., Natl. Assn. of Theatre Owners, 1966; Exec. v.p. COMPO., 1970. Retired May 1988.

ALTMAN, ROBERT: Director, Writer, Producer. b. Kansas City, MO, Feb. 20, 1925. e. U. of Missouri.
PICTURES: Debut: The James Dean Story, 1957 (co-prod.); The Delinquents (dir.), Countdown (dir.), That Cold Day in the Park, M*A*S*H; s.p. and dir., McCabe & Mrs. Miller, Brewster McCloud, Images, The Long Goodbye, Thieves Like Us, California Split, Nashville, Buffalo Bill and the Indians, The Late Show (prod.) Welcome to L.A. (prod.), Three Women (prod., dir., s.p.); A Wedding (prod., dir.); Remember My Name (prod.); Quintet (prod., dir.); A Perfect Couple (prod., dir.); Rich Kids (prod.); Health (prod., dir., s.p.), Popeye (dir.); Come Back to the Five & Dime, Jimmie Dean, Jimmie Dean (co-prod., dir.): Streamers (co-prod., dir.); Beyond Therapy (co-s.p., dir.); Aria (sequence), O.C. and Stiggs.
THEATER: Come Back to the Five & Dime, Jimmy Dean, Jimmy Dean (dir. on Broadway, 1982).
TELEVISION: Wrote, prod. and dir.: Roaring Twenties, Bonanza, Bus Stop, Combat, Kraft Theatre and pilots for The Gallant Men and The Long Hot Summer, Tanner '88 (dir., co-prod.) The Dumb Waiter, The Room, The Caine Mutiny Court-Martial (dir., co- prod.).

ALTON, JOHN: Cinematographer. b. Hungary, Oct. 5, 1901. Laboratory technician, MGM 1924; Paramount cameraman 1928; sent to Paris, France, chg. camera dept., 1931; installed studios for Lumiton & Sono Film (South America); writer, photographer & dir. many Spanish pictures; returned to U.S. 1937, cinematographer Hollywood; served in U.S. Signal Corps as Capt., W.W.II. Books include: Painting With Light, Photography and Lighting in General; received Sintonia Medal for best photography in Argentina, 1937. Academy Award best color photog. American in Paris ballet, 1951.
PICTURES INCLUDE: Witness to Murder, Big Combo, Catered Affair. Member: ASC, AMPAS.

ALVIN, JOHN: Actor. r.n. John Alvin Hoffstadt; b. Chicago, IL, Oct. 24, 1917. e. Pasadena (CA) Playhouse. On radio Chicago & Detroit; on N.Y. stage Leaning on Letty, Life of the Party. Screen debut 1944 in Destination Tokyo. Under contract four years to Warner Bros., featured in 25 films.
PICTURES INCLUDE: Objective Burma, Destination Tokyo, San Antonio, Beast With Five Fingers, Night and Day, Cheyenne, Missing Women, Two Guys from Texas, Bold Frontiersman, Train to Alcatraz, Shanghai Chest, Carrie, April In Paris, Roughly Speaking, The Very Thought of You, Shadow of a Woman, Three Strangers, Romance on the High Seas, Torpedo Alley, Irma La Douce, Legend of Lylah Claire, Mr. Tibbs, Marnie, Inside Daisy Clover, They Shoot Horses, Don't They?, Somewhere in Time.
TELEVISION: Meet Millie, Burns and Allen, Death Valley Days, Asphalt Jungle, Climax, Dragnet, Jack Benny Show, My Three Sons, The Texan, Adventures in Paradise, Rawhide, Rifleman, Omnibus, Wells Fargo, Alfred Hitchcock, Mannix, I Spy, Legend of Lizzie Borden, All in the Family, McDuff, Lineup, My Favorite Husband, Family Affair, The Incredible Hulk, The Lucy Show, Ironside, Nightstalker, MASH, Lou Grant Show, Hart to Hart, Yellow Rose, Dennis the Menace (2 Hour Pilot), Murder She Wrote, Monster Squad, House of Evil, Aftermash, General Hospital, Starsky & Hutch, Policewoman, Amazing Stories, Capitol, Passions (P.O.W.), The Quest, Vissions/KCET, Rachel, Sweet Rachel, Swallows Came Back (HBO Fall 1987).

AMATEAU, ROD: Director. b. New York, NY, Dec. 20, 1927. Staff writer, CBS radio; stage mgr., Lux Radio Theatre; U.S. Army, 1941; junior writer, 20th Century-Fox; then test dir., second

unit dir.; TV dir., numerous shows including Schlitz Playhouse of Stars, Four Star Playhouse, General Electric Theatre, Private Secretary, Dennis Day Show, Lassie, Ray Milland Show, Bob Cummings Show, dir. & prod. Burns & Allen Show, Dobie Gillis.
PICTURES INCLUDE: The Statue, Where Does It Hurt?, The Wilby Conspiracy, Drive-In, Lovelines, Sunset (story), Garbage Pail Kids (s.p., prod., dir.), One Is Hawaii (dir.).

AMECHE, DON: Actor. b. Kenosha, WI, 1908. e. Columbia Coll., U. of Wisconsin. In stock; on radio; m.p. debut 1936. In television from 1951; on Broadway in Silk Stockings, 1955; Holiday For Lovers, Goldilocks, 13 Daughters, Henry Sweet Henry.
PICTURES INCLUDE: Sins of Man, Ladies in Love, Ramona, You Can't Have Everything, Alexander's Ragtime Band, Swanee River, Four Sons, The Story of Alexander Graham Bell, Lillian Russel, That Night in Rio, Kiss the Boys Goodbye, Heaven Can Wait, So Goes My Love, That's My Man, Sleep My Love, Slightly French, A Fever in the Blood, Ring Around the World, Picture Mommy Dead, Suppose They Gave a War & Nobody Came, The Boatniks, Trading Places, Cocoon, Harry and the Hendersons, Coming to America, Things Change (best actor award Venice Film Fest., 1988); Cocoon II: The Return.
TELEVISION: International Showtime (host 1961–65), A Masterpiece of Murder, Pals, Mr. Smith, The Love Boat, Not in Front of the Kids (pilot), Detective in the House.

AMES, LEON: Actor. r.n. Leon Wycoff. b. Portland, IN, Jan. 20, 1903. Aviator; with Champlain Players, Lansford, PA, in stock and on stage; plays include: Tobacco Road, Male Animal, Land Is Bright; m.p. debut in Murders in the Rue Morgue, 1932; owner & vice-pres. Studio City Ford Co.
PICTURES INCLUDE: Meet Me in St. Louis, Thirty Seconds Over Tokyo, Yolanda and the Thief, Merton of the Movies, On an Island With You, Velvet Touch, Date With Judy, Battleground, Ambush, Big Hangover, Little Women, Dial 1119, Happy Years, Alias a Gentleman, Watch the Birdie, Cattle Drive, On Moonlight Bay, It's a Big Country, Angel Face, By the Light of the Silvery Moon, Let's Do It Again, Sabre Jet, Peyton Place, From the Terrace, Absent Minded Professor, Son of Flubber, Misadventures of Merlin Jones, The Monkey's Uncle, On a Clear Day You Can See Forever, Tora! Tora! Tora!, Testament, Peggy Sue Got Married.
TELEVISION: Life with Father, Father of the Bride, Mr. Ed, Bewitched, Frontier Judge, Maggie.

AMES, LOUIS B.: Executive. b. St. Louis, MO, Aug. 9, 1918. e. Washington U., St. Louis. m. Jetti Preminger. Began as music consultant and staff director of musical programs for NBC; music dir. 1948, WPIX; 1951 apptd. program mgr., WPIX; assoc. prod., Today, NBC TV, 1954; feature editor Home, 1957; Adm.-prod. NBC Opera, 1958; dir. cultural prog. N.Y. World's Fair, 1960–63; dir. RCA Pavillion, N.Y. World's Fair, 1963–65; 1966 dir., Nighttime, TV; 1969, dir. of programming N.W. Ayer & Sons, Inc. 1973 Mgr. Station Services, Television Information Office. NYC.

AMIS, SUZY: Actress. b. Oklahoma City, OK, 1962. m. actor Sam Robards. At 16 was introduced on the Merv Griffin Show by Eileen Ford whose modeling agency she worked for, as "The Face of the Eighties." After modeling and living in Europe, made film debut in Fandango (1985). Off-Broadway debut: Fresh Horses (Theatre World Award).
PICTURES: Fandango, The Big Town, Plain Clothes, Rocket Gibralter.

AMOS, JOHN: Actor. b. Newark, NJ, Dec. 27, 1941. e. Colorado State U, Long Beach City Coll. Worked as professional football player, social worker (heading the Vera Institute of Justice in NY), and advertising copywriter before writing television comedy material (for the Leslie Uggams Show) and performing as stand-up comedian in Greenwich Village. Has also dir. theatre with Bahamian Rep. Co. Starred in L.A. in Norman, Is That You? and Master Harold...And the Boys. Artistic dir. Keane-Brown Center Stage, NJ.
PICTURES: Vanishing Point (debut, 1971), The World's Greatest Athlete, Let's Do It Again, Touched By Love, The Beastmaster, Dance of the Dwarfs, American Flyers, Coming to America.
TELEVISION: Series: Mary Tyler Moore, The Funny Side, Maude, Good Times, Hunter, South by Southwest. Movies: The President's Plane is Missing, Willa, Roots (mini-series), Alcatraz—The Whole Shocking Story, Hang Tight, Willy Bill, Brother Tough, as well as guest appearances.

AMSTERDAM, MOREY: Producer, Writer, Composer, Musician, Actor. b. Chicago, IL, Dec. 14, 1914. e. U. of California, Berkeley. Boy soprano. Radio KPO, 1922; night club performer, Chicago, 1929; comedian, singer, musician. Rube Wolf Orchestra; comedian, Optimistic Doughnut Program, 1930; writer, vaudeville; comedian, writer, Al Pearce Gang, 1932; writer, MGM, 1937; co-writer, radio shows; m.p. Columbia, Universal; writer, performer, USO Shows, 1942–43; owner,

performer, the Playgoers-club; v.p. American International Pictures.
TELEVISION: Stop Me If You've Heard This One, Broadway Open House, Morey Amsterdam Silver Swan Show, Dick Van Dyke Show. Exec. Prod.-Star, Can You Top This. Movies: Side By Side.
PICTURES INCLUDE: Don't Worry . . . We'll Think of a Title, Machine Gun Kelly, Murder, Inc.
SONGS: Rum and Coca Cola, Why Oh Why Did I Ever Leave Wyoming, Yak A Puk, etc.

ANDERSON, DAPHNE: Actress. b. London, England, April 27, 1922. e. Kensington H.S. Stage debut in pantomime chorus, 1937; screen debut in Trottle True, 1948.
PICTURES INCLUDE: Cloudburst, Beggar's Opera, Hobson's Choice, A Kid for Two Farthings, The Prince and the Showgirl, No Time for Tears, Snowball, Stork Talk, Captain Clegg, The Launching, I Want What I Want.
TELEVISION: Silas Marner (serial), Gideon's Way (serial), Dr. Finlay's Casebook, Happy Family, The Imposter, The Harry Worth Show, The Whitehall Worrier, The Suede Jacket, Casanova, Haunted Series, Thirty Minute Theatre, Justice Is a Woman, Paul Temple, Today, 2 Cars.

ANDERSON, GERRY: Hon. F.B.K.S., Producer. b. London, England, 1929. Ent. ind. 1946. Chmn./man. dir. Gerry Anderson Productions, Ltd. Over 320 pictures produced for TV worldwide. 1981 Co-founded Anderson Burr Pictures. 1982 commenced production on Terrahawks in association with London Weekend Television; second series, Terrahawks, 1984; Space Police pilot for series in assoc. with TVS, 1985–6; Dick Spanner stop motion series for Channel Four 1987. Entered commercials as a dir.: "Shoes" for Royal Bank of Scotland, and campaign for Tennent's Pilsner.

ANDERSON, J. WAYNE: Executive. b. Clifton Forge, VA, Feb. 19, 1947. e. USA Signal School (1965–67); USN Service Schools (1967). USMC, 1965–69; opened 1st military 35mm m.p. theatre, DaNang, Vietnam, 1967–69; dist. mgr., R/C Theatres, 1971–75; v.p., 1976–83; pres. of opns., 1983–present.
MEMBER: Nat. Assn. of Theatre Owners technical advancement committee, 1981–present; Huntsman Condo bd. dir., 1979–83; pres., Huntsman 1982–83; Bd. of directors, NATO, 1987–present.

ANDERSON, DAME JUDITH: Actress. b. Adelaide, Australia, Feb. 10, 1898. Stage debut (Sydney) in Royal Divorce, 1915; on New York stage & in stock 1918; toured 1920; m.p. debut in Blood Money. 1933. Entertained U.S. Armed Forces overseas, W.W.II; received Donaldson Award 1948, New York Critics Award 1948, American Academy of Arts & Sciences Award for Best Speech 1948. N.Y. stage, 1952, In the Summer House, 1953.
PLAYS INCLUDE: Dear Brutus, Cobra, Dove, Strange Interlude, Old Maid, Mourning Becomes Electra, Macbeth, Medea.
PICTURES INCLUDE: King's Row, Rebecca, Forty Little Mothers, Free & Easy, All Through the Night, The Edge of Darkness, Jane Eyre, Laura, Spector of the Rose, Diary of a Chambermaid, Strange Love of Martha Ivers, Red House, And Then There Were None, Tycoon, Pursued, The Furies, Salome, Don't Bother to Knock, The Ten Commandments, Come of Age, Cinderfella, Cat on a Hot Tin Roof, Macbeth, A Man Called Horse, Inn of the Damned, Star Trek III.
TELEVISION: Series: Santa Barbara (1984), Episodes: Telephone Times, 1956. Specials: Macbeth (Hallmark, 1954 & 1960), The Cradle Song, Caesar and Cleopatra, The Moon & the Sixpence, Elizabeth the Queen, The Borrowers. Movies: The File of Devlin, The Chinese Prime Minister.

ANDERSON, KEVIN: Actor. b. Illinois, Jan. 13, 1960. e. Goodman School. Member of Chicago's Steppenwolf Theatre in which he starred in Orphans. Moved with the play when it transferred to New York (1985) and later starred in the London production, as well as the film version.
PICTURES: Risky Business, Pink Nights, A Walk on the Moon, Orphans, Miles from Home, In Country.

ANDERSON, LINDSAY: Director (cinema & theatre), Writer. b. Bangalore, India, 1923; e. Cheltenham Coll., Wadham Coll., Oxford (classical scholar). Ent. Ind. 1948 as writer-director in charge industrial film prod., also contributing editor independent film quarterly Sequence. Wrote Making a Film 1951; About John Ford (1981). Principal doc. films: O. Dreamland, Thursday's Children (collab. s.p. dir.) Guy Brenton: Hollywood Short Subject Award, 1954, Three Installations, Pleasure Garden, Wakefield Express, Every Day Except Christmas (Venice Grand Prix, 1957), March to Aldermaston. Founder mem. Free Cinema group. National Film Theatre 1956/9. Recent Doc.: The Singing Lesson (Documentary Studio, Warsaw). Artistic director, Royal Court Theatre 1969–70. Associate, 1970–76.
TELEVISION INCLUDES: Five episodes Robin Hood series, commercials, 1959–75. 1978 Dir. The Old Crowd. 1986

Free Cinema, Buston Keaton: A Hard Act to Follow (narrator); 1986–87: music videos for Carmel; 1988: movie masterclass My Darling Clementine, Sister Ruth.
PLAYS INCLUDE: The Long and the Short and the Tall, Billy Liar, The Fire Raisers, Serjeant Musgrave's Dance, The Cherry Orchard, Inadmissible Evidence (at Contemporary Theatre, Warsaw), In Celebration, The Contractor Home, The Changing Room, The Farm, Life Class, What the Butler Saw, The Sea Gull, The Bed Before Yesterday; The Kingfisher; Alice's Boys; Early Days; Hamlet; The Cherry Orchard; Playboy of the Western World; In Celebration (N.Y.); Hamlet (Washington, DC); Holiday.
PICTURES INCLUDE: This Sporting Life, 1963; The White Bus; If...; O Lucky Man!, In Celebration, 1975; Britannia Hospital; If You Were There; The Whales of August.

ANDERSON, LONI: Actress. b. St. Paul, MN, Aug. 5. 1946. m. actor Burt Reynolds. e. U. of Minnesota. Taught school before acting.
TELEVISION INCLUDES: Series: WKRP in Cincinnati, Three on a Date, Christmas in Opryland, Easy Street, My Mother's Secret Life, Stranded, Shaun Cassidy Special, Bob Hope specials, etc. Movies: The Jayne Mansfield Story, Sizzle, A Letter to Three Wives, Necessity, A Whisper Kills, Leave Her to Heaven.
PICTURES: Stroker Ace, All Dogs Go to Heaven (voice).

ANDERSON, MELISSA SUE: Actress. b. Berkeley, CA, Sept. 26, 1962. Took up acting at suggestion of a dancing teacher. Did series of commercials; guest role in episode of Brady Bunch; episode of Shaft. Gained fame as Mary Ingalls on Little House on the Prairie series.
PICTURE: Happy Birthday to Me.
TELEVISION: Very Good Friends, James at 15, The Loneliest Runner, The Survival of Dana, Which Mother is Mine? (Emmy Award, 1980), First Affair, An Innocent Love, Midnight Offerings; Series: Dark Mansions, The New Sea Hunt.

ANDERSON, MICHAEL: Director. b. London, England, 1920. e. France, Germany, Spain. Ent. m.p. industry as actor, 1936; asst. dir., unit manager on such films as In Which We Serve, Pygmalion, French Without Tears; Army service 1942–46; Co-dir., Private Angelo, 1949; since dir. Waterfront, Hell Is Sold Out, Night Was Our Friend, Will Any Gentleman?, The Dam Busters, 1984, Around the World in 80 Days, Yangtse Incident (Battle Hell), Chase a Crooked Shadow, Shake Hands with the Devil, The Wreck of the Mary Deare, All the Fine Young Cannibals, The Naked Edge, Flight From Ashiya, Monsieur Cognac, Operation Crossbow, The Quiller Memorandum, Shoes of the Fisherman, Pope Joan, Dr. Savage, Conduct Unbecoming, Logan's Run, Orca, Dominique, The Martian Chronicles, Bells, Apple and Pair, Separate Vacations, Vengeance, Millenium, The Goldsmith's Shop, The Long Walk Home.

ANDERSON, MICHAEL, JR.: Actor. b. London, England, 1943. Son of dir. Michael Anderson. Ent. films as child actor, 1954.
TELEVISION: Queen's Champion, Ivanhoe, The Monroes, The Martian Chronicles, Love Leads the Way.
PICTURES INCLUDE: Tiger Bay, The Moonraker, The Sundowners, Reach For Glory, In Search of the Castaways, Play It Cool, Greatest Story Ever Told, Dear Heart, Major Dundee, The Glory Days, The Sons of Katie Elder, Logan's Run.

ANDERSON, RICHARD: Actor. b. Long Branch, NJ, Aug. 8, 1926. U.S. Army, W.W.II. Began acting career in summer theatre in Santa Barbara and Laguna Playhouse where spotted by MGM executives who signed him to six-yr. contract. Appeared in 26 films for MGM before leaving studio.
PICTURES INCLUDE: 12 O'Clock High, The People Against O'Hara,, The Story of Three Loves, Escape from Fort Bravo, Forbidden Planet, The Long Hot Summer, Compulsion, Seconds, Paths of Glory, Tora! Tora! Tora!, Along Came a Spider, Macho Callahan, Doctors' Wives, Play It As It Lays, The Honkers, Stone, Redneck America.
TELEVISION: Bus Stop, Perry Mason, 12 O'Clock High (all regular), Ironside, The Big Valley, Mannix, My Friend Tony, The Mod Squad, Land of the Giants, The FBI, Gunsmoke. Series: The Six Million Dollar Man, The Bionic Woman, Movies: Kane & Abel, The Return of the Six Million Dollar Man and the Bionic Woman, Pearl, Perry Mason Returns, Hoover vs. the Kennedys, Stranger on My Land.

ANDERSON, RICHARD DEAN: Actor. b. Minneapolis, MN, Jan. 23, 1950. Planned to become professional hockey player, but broke both arms playing varsity hockey in high school. Became a street mime and jester in Elizabethan-style cabaret in L.A. Performed with his own rock band, Rick Dean and Dante.
PICTURES: Odd Jobs.
TELEVISION: General Hospital (1976–81); Series: Seven Brides for Seven Brothers; Emerald Point, N.A.S.; MacGyver.

ANDERSON, ROLAND: Art director. In 1933 collab. with Hans Dreier on This Day and Age, Par. Since then collaborated in art direction on many productions, including Lives of a Bengal Lancer, Hands Across the Table, Give Us This Night, Till We Meet Again, The Buccaneer, Union Pacific, North West Mounted Police, Love Thy Neighbor, The Crystal Ball, Story of Dr. Wassel, Road to Utopia, Let's Dance, Branded, Carried, Son of Paleface, Just For You, Here Come the Girls, White Christmas, Country Girl, We're No Angels, Court Jester.

ANDERSON, SYLVIA: Producer, Writer (Pinewood Studios). b. London, England. e. London U. Entered m.p. ind. 1960. First pub. novel, Love and Hisses. UK rep for Home Box Office of America.
TELEVISION: series created include: Thunderbirds, U.F.O.; Space 1999.

ANDERSON, WILLIAM H.: Producer; Member of Bd. of Dir. Walt Disney Productions. b. Utah, October 12, 1911. e. Compton Coll. Firestone Rubber Co.; Universal Credit Co.; Walt Disney Prods. 42 years.
PICTURES INCLUDE: Old Yeller, Swiss Family Robinson, Happiest Millionaire, The Computer Wore Tennis Shoes, Barefoot Executive, $1,000,000 Duck, Superdad, Strongest Man in the World, Apple Dumpling Gang, Treasure of Matecumbe, Shaggy D.A.
TELEVISION: Zorro Series 1958–59 (20 half-hour segments); 1959–60 (38 half-hour segments), Wonderful World of Disney: Zorro, Texas John Slaughter, Daniel Boone, The Swamp Fox, Pop Warner Football (1960–61), Johnny Shiloh, Mooncussers, 1962–63; Bristle Face, The Scarecrow of Romney Marsh (1963–64); The Legend of Young Dick Turpin (1965–66); Willie and the Yank (1966–67); A Boy Called Nuthin', The Young Loner (1967–68); The Wacky Zoo of Morgan City (1970–71); The Mystery of Dracula's Castle (1972–73); The Bull from the Sky, co-producer; 1975–76; Great Sleeping Bear Sled Dog Race, co-producer (1976–77).

ANDERSSON, BIBI: Actress. b. Stockholm, Sweden, Nov. 11, 1935. e. Royal Dramatic Theatre School.
PICTURES INCLUDE: (for director Ingmar Bergman) Smiles of a Summer Night, 1955; The Seventh Seal, Wild Strawberries, Brink of Life, The Magician, The Devil's Eye, Not to Mention All These Women, Persona; other films: My Sister, My Love Le Vio A Passion, Black Palm Trees, Story of a Woman, Duel at Diablo, The Kremlin Letter, The Passion of Anna, I Never Promised You a Rose Garden, Quintet, The Concorde: Airport '79, Enemy of the People, Babette's Feast.
TELEVISION: Wallenberg—A Hero's Story.

ANDES, KEITH: Actor. b. Ocean City, NJ, July 12, 1920. e. Temple U., Oxford. U. Radio work; on Broadway in Winged Victory, Kiss Me Kate, Maggie, Wildcat.
PICTURES INCLUDE: Farmer's Daughter, Clash By Night, Blackbeard the Pirate, Split Second, Life at Stake, Second Greatest Sex, Away All Boats, Pillars of the Sky, Back from Eternity, Damn Citizen, Surrender, Hells Bloody Devils, And Justice for All.
TELEVISION: This Man Dawson, Glynis.

ANDRESS, URSULA: Actress. b. Berne, Switzerland, 1936. m.p. Hollywood, 1955.
PICTURES INCLUDE: Dr. No, Four For Texas, Fun in Acapulco, Toys For Christmas, She, Tenth Victim, What's New Pussycat?, Chinese Adventures in China, Casino Royale, The Southern Star, Perfect Friday, The Red Sun, Scaramouche, Clash of the Titans.
TELEVISION: Peter the Great, Falcon Crest.

ANDREWS, ANTHONY: Actor. b. London, England, 1948.
PICTURES: Operation Daybreak, Under the Volcano, The Holcroft Covenant, The Second Victory, Hanna's War.
TELEVISION: A Beast With Two Backs, Romeo and Juliet, A War of Children, QB VII, Upstairs Downstairs, Danger UXB, Brideshead Revisited, Ivanhoe, The Scarlet Pimpernel, Sparkling Cyanide, A.D., Bluegrass, Suspicion, The Woman He Loved.

ANDREWS, DANA: Actor. b. Collins, MS., Jan. 1, 1909. e. Sam Houston Coll., Pasadena Community Playhouse. Accountant with Gulf Refining Co., 1930; chief accountant Tobins, Inc., 1931; acted with Pasadena Playhouse 3 yrs.; m.p. debut in The Westerner 1939; Vice Pres. Screen Actor's Guild, 1962–63, Pres. 1964–66.
PICTURES INCLUDE: The Best Years of Our Lives, Iron Curtain, My Foolish Heart, Forbidden Street Bway play, Two for the See-Saw, Laura, Edge of Doom, Where the Sidewalk Ends, Sealed Cargo, The Frogmen, I Want You, Assignment—Paris, Elephant Walk, Duel in the Jungle, Three Hours to Kill, Smoke Signal, Strange Lady in Town, While the City Sleeps, Comanche, Beyond a Reasonable Doubt, Spring Reunion, Night of the Demon, Zero Hour, Enchanted Island, The Fear Makers, The Crowded Sky, Madison Avenue, The Satan Bug, Crack in the World, In Harm's Way, Battle of the Bulge, Devil's Brigade, The Loved One, Innocent Bystander, The Last Tycoon, Airport, 1975, Born Again.
TELEVISION: Alas Babylon; G.E., The Playoff; Barbara Stanwyck; Dupont, Mutiny; 4 Star, Crazy Sunday; Checkmate, Alcoa, The Boy Who Wasn't Wanted; Twilight Zone, No Time Like The Past; Dick Powell, Last of the Big Spenders; Alcoa, The Town That Died, Bob Hope Chrysler, A Wind of Hurricane Force, One Small Step Forward (series), The Right Hand Man (Playhouse 90). Movies: Bright Promise, The Last Hurrah, Ike, Shadow in the Streets, The Failing of Raymond.
DINNER THEATRE: The Marriage-Go-Round; The Best of Friends, Angel Street, The Gang's All Here, Any Wednesday, A Man for All Seasons.

ANDREWS, HARRY: CBE, Actor. b. Tonbridge, Kent, England, Nov. 10, 1911. First stage appearance. Liverpool, 1933. London stage 1935, Worse Things Happen at Sea. To U.S., 1936, Hamlet. Army Service 1939–45. Screen debut 1952, The Red Beret.
PICTURES INCLUDE: The Black Knight, The Man Who Loved Redheads, A Hill in Korea, Alexander the Great, Moby Dick, Ice Cold in Alex, Devil's Disciple, Solomon and Sheba, In the Nick, Circle of Deception, Cleopatra, The Best of Enemies, Reach For Glory, The Inspector, Barabbas, 55 Days at Peking, The Snout, The System, The Hill, The Agony and the Ecstasy, The Sands of the Kalahari, The Deadly Affair, A Dandy in Aspic, The Charge of the Light Brigade, The Night They Raided Minsky's, The Seagull, A Nice Girl Like Me, Too Late the Hero, The Gaunt Woman, Country Dance (in U.S. Brotherly Love), Entertaining Mr. Sloane, Wuthering Heights, I Want What I Want, Nicholas and Alexandra, The Nightcomers, The Ruling Class, Man of La Mancha, Theatre of Blood, The Mackintosh Man, Man at the Top, The Skyriders, The Bluebird, The Passover Plot, The Prince and the Pauper, Equus, Superman, The Medusa Touch, The Big Sleep, Death on the Nile, SOS Titanic, Curse of King Tut's Tomb, Seven Dials Mystery, The Sound Machine, A Question of Guilt.
TELEVISION: Affair of Honour, Clayhanger, Two Gentle People, The Last Journey, Leo Tolstoy, A.J. Wentworth B.A., Lent, Dynasty, Return of Sherlock Holmes, Inside Story, All Passion Spent, Cause Celebre, To See Ourselves, Jack the Ripper.

ANDREWS, JULIE: Actress, Singer. r.n. Julia Wells. b. Walton-on-Thames. England. Oct 1, 1935. m. dir. Blake Edwards. debut, Eng. Starlight Roof Revue; pantomime of Cinderella. Film debut: Mary Poppins (1964; Academy Award).
PLAYS: The Boy Friend, My Fair Lady, Camelot.
PICTURES INCLUDE: The Americanization of Emily, The Sound of Music, Hawaii, Torn Curtain, Thoroughly Modern Millie, Star!, Darling Lili, The Tamarind Seed, "10," S.O.B, Victor/Victoria, The Man Who Loved Women, That's Life, Duet for One.
TELEVISION: High Tor, Julie and Carol at Carnegie Hall, The Andy Williams Show, The Julie Andrews Show, An Evening with Julie Andrews and Harry Belafonte, The World of Walt Disney, Julie and Carol at Lincoln Center, Julie Andrews Hour (ABC Television series 1972–73); Julie on Sesame Street, 1973; Julie Andrews' Christmas Special, 1973; Julie and Dick in Covent Garden, 1974; Julie Andrews and Jackie Gleason Together, 1974; Julie Andrews—My Favorite Things, 1975; Julie Andrews—The Sound of Christmas, 1987.
AUTHOR: Mandy, Last of the Really Great Whangdoodles, 1973.

ANDRIEUX, ROGER: Director, writer. b. France, Aug. 24, 1940. Began in French theatre, went to U. of California at L.A., took his M.F.A., made several short subjects as well as his first feature film in English.
PICTURES INCLUDE: Mr. Brown (s.p., dir.); Bonjour Amour (co-s.p., dir.); La Petite Sirene (s.p., dir., prod.), Envoyez les violons. (dir., s.p.).

ANGERS, AVRIL: Actress, Comedienne, Singer. b. Liverpool, England, April 18. Stage debut at age of 14; screen debut in 1947 in Lucky Mascot.
PICTURES INCLUDE: Miss Pilgrim's Progress, Don't Blame the Stork, Women Without Men, Green Man, Devils of Darkness, Be My Guest, Three Bites of the Apple, The Family Way, Two a Penny, The Best House in London, Staircase, There's a Girl in My Soup, Forbush and the Penguins, Gollocks (1973), Confessions of a Driving Instructor, Dangerous Davies.
TELEVISION: How Do You View, Friends and Neighbors, Dear Dotty, Holiday Town, Charlie Fainsbarn Show, Arthur Askey Show, All Aboard, The Gold Hunter, Bob Monkhouse Show, Before The Fringe, Hudd, Coronation Street, Dick Emery Show, Dad's Army, Bright Boffins, The More We Are Together, The Millionairess, Liver Birds, Looks Familiar, No Appointment Necessary, The Songwriters, All Creatures Great and Small, Coronation Concert, Minder, Smuggler, Just Liz, Give Up a Clue, Are You Being Served, Trelawney of the Wells, Cat's Eye, C.A.B., Rude Health.
PLAYS INCLUDE: The Mating Game; Musical, Cockie;

9

Murder at the Vicarage, Little Me, Norman, Is That You?, Blithe Spirit, Oklahoma!, Gigi, The Killing of Sister George, Cards on the Table, When We Are Married, Cinderella, Easy Virtue.

ANHALT, EDNA: Associate producer, Writer. b. New York, NY, April 10, 1914. e. Kathryn Gibbs Sch. 1932; U. doc. films; prod. mgr., Rockefeller Found. films. Academy Award, orig. story collab., Panic in the Streets.
PICTURES INCLUDE: (Orig. story, collab., assoc. prod., s.p.) Strange Voyage, Avalanche, Younger Brothers, Return of Frontiersman, Embraceable You, Sierra, The Sniper, My Six Convicts, Eight Iron Men, Member of the Wedding, Three Lives, The Big Kill, Not as a Stranger, Pride and the Passion, Girls, Girls, Girls, Decision at Delphi.
Member: Acad. of M.P. Arts & Sciences; S.W.G.

ANHALT, EDWARD: Writer. b. New York, NY. Academy Award. orig. story collab., Panic in the Streets.
PICTURES INCLUDE: The Young Savages, Becket (Acad. Award, s.p.), In Enemy Country, Boeing-Boeing, The Young Lions, Day of the Guns, Not As a Stranger, Madwoman of Chaillot, Member of the Wedding, Boston Strangler, Jeremiah Johnson, Q B VII (TV), Luther, Escape to Athena, Green Ice.

ANNAKIN, KENNETH: Director, Writer. b. Yorkshire, Eng., 1915. Graduated through Experimental Theatre and Documentary. Films incl: Across The Bridge, Swiss Family Robinson, Very Important Person, The Longest Day, The Fast Lady, The Informers, Those Magnificent Men in Their Flying Machines, Battle of the Bulge, The Long Duel, Monte Carlo or Bust, Call of the Wild, Paper Tiger, The Fifth Musketeer, Cheaper to Keep Her, The Pirate Movie, The New Adventures of Pippi Longstocking (dir., s.p., co-prod.).

ANNAUD, JEAN-JACQUES: Writer, Director. b. Draveil, France, Oct. 1, 1943. Began career as film director in French army, making educational pictures. Also directed 500 commercials.
PICTURES INCLUDE: Black and White in Color (Acad. Award, Best Foreign Film, 1977); Coup de Tete (dir. only); Quest for Fire (dir. only); The Name of the Rose (dir. only), The Bear (dir., co-s.p.).

ANN-MARGRET: Actress, singer. r.n. Ann-Margret Olsson. b. Valsjobyn, Sweden, April 28, 1941. m. Roger Smith, actor, dir., prod. e. grad., New Trier H.S., Winnetka, IL, attended Northwestern U. Radio shows, toured with band; worked with George Burns, Sahara, Las Vegas. TV debut, Jack Benny Show, April, 1961.
PICTURES INCLUDE: Pocketful of Miracles (debut, 1961), State Fair, Bye, Bye Birdie, Viva Las Vegas, Kitten With a Whip, Bus Riley's Back in Town, Once A Thief, The Cincinnati Kid, The Swinger, Stagecoach, Murderer's Row, The Pleasure Seekers, Made in Paris, The Tiger and the Pussycat, C. C. & Company, Carnal Knowledge, RPM, The Outside Man, The Train Robbers, Tommy, The Last Remake of Beau Geste, The Twist, Joseph Andrews, The Cheap Detective, Magic, The Villain, Middle Age Crazy, Lookin' to Get Out, I Ought To Be in Pictures, The Return of the Soldier, Twice in a Lifetime, 52 Pick-up, A Tiger's Tail, A New Life.
TELEVISION: Specials: Dames at Sea, When You're Smiling, Hollywood Movie Girls. Movies: Who Will Love My Children?, A Streetcar Named Desire, The Two Mrs. Grenvilles.

ANSARA, MICHAEL: Actor. b. Lowell, MA, April 15, 1922. e. Pasadena Playhouse. Served in U.S. Army; then summer stock, little theatre, road shows.
PICTURES INCLUDE: The Robe, Julius Caesar, Sign of the Pagan, Bengal Brigade, Soldiers Three, Only the Valiant, New Orleans Uncensored, Diane, Lone Ranger, Sol Madrid, Daring Game, The Bears and I, Mohammad, Messenger of God, The Manitou, Gas, Knights of the City.
TELEVISION: Broken Arrow, Law of the Plainsman, Westerner, Centennial, Guest: Simon and Simon, Gavilan, The Fantastic World of D.C. Collins, George Burns Comedy Week, Hunter, Hardcastle and McCormick, Buck Rogers in the 25th Century.

ANSPACH, SUSAN: Actress. b. New York, NY, Nov. 23, 1939. e. Catholic U., Washington, DC. After school returned to N.Y. and in 3 years had performed in 11 off-Broadway prods. Moved to Los Angeles and entered films.
PICTURES INCLUDE: Five Easy Pieces, The Landlord, Play It Again Sam, Blume in Love, The Big Fix, Running, The Devil and Max Devlin, Gas, Misunderstood, Blue Monkey.
TELEVISION: Yellow Rose, Space. Series: The Slap Maxwell Story.

ANSPAUGH, DAVID: Director. b. Decatur, IN, Sept. 24, 1946. e. Indiana U., 1965–70; U. of Southern CA, 1974–76. School teacher, Aspen, CO 1970–74. Awards for Hill Street Blues: Emmy 1982–83; DGA 1982, Golden Globes, 1981–82.
PICTURES: Hoosiers (dir.), Fresh Horses (dir.).
TELEVISION: Hill St. Blues (assoc. prod. 1980–81; prod.-dir. 1981–82; prod.-dir. 1983–84, dir. 1985); St. Elsewhere (dir.), Miami Vice (dir.).

ANTHONY, TONY: Actor, Producer, Writer. b. Clarksburg, WV, Oct. 16, 1939. e. Carnegie Mellon.
PICTURES INCLUDE: Force of Impulse, Pity Me Not, The Wounds of Hunger, A Stranger in Town, The Stranger Returns, A Stranger in Japan, Come Together, Blindman, Pete Pearl and the Pole, Let's Talk About Men, Get Mean, The Boy Who Owned a Melephant, Treasure of the Four Crowns, Comin' at Ya.

ANTON, SUSAN: Actress. b. Oak Glen, CA, Oct. 12, 1951. e. Bernardino Coll. Voted Miss California 1969. Worked in night clubs and did song recordings. (Country and western album: The First Time). Broadway debut: Hurlyburly (1985). Film debut, Golden Girl, 1979.
PICTURES: Spring Fever, Cannonball Run II.
TELEVISION: The Cliffhangers, Presenting Susan Anton, Susan Anton—and 10,000 GIs, The Boy Who Loved Trolls, Placido Domingo's Steppin' Out With the Ladies, How to Be a Man.

ANTONIO, LOU: Actor, Writer, Director. b. Oklahoma City, OK, Jan. 23, 1934. e. U. of OK.
THEATER: Actor: The Girls of Summer, The Good Soup; The Garden of Sweets; Andorra; The Lady of the Camellias; The Ballad of the Sad Cafe, Ready When You Are, C.B.
PICTURES: The Strange One; Splendor in the Grass; America, America; Hawaii; Cool Hand Luke; The Phynx; Mission Batangas (s.p.); Micki and Maude (exec. prod.).
TELEVISION: Actor: Snoop Sisters; Dog and Cat; Making It. Piece of Blue Sky; The Power and the Glory; Danny Thomas Hour; Partners in Crime; Sole Survivor; Where the Ladies Go; Director: Gentle Ben (and writer); Rich Man, Poor Man; Lannigan's Rabbi; The Young Rebels (and writer); Someone I Touched; The Girl in the Empty Grave; Something for Joey; The Critical List; Silent Victory—The Kitty O'Neil Story; Breaking Up Is Hard to Do; The Contender; We're Fighting Back; The Star Maker; Gage and Walker; The Steeler and the Pittsburgh Kid; Something So Right; A Good Sport; Threesome; Rearview Mirror, Face to Face.

ANTONIONI, MICHELANGELO: Director. b. Ferrara, Italy, Sept. 29, 1913. e. Bologna U. Film critic on local paper, then script writer and asst. director. First films as a director were documentaries, including: Gente del Po (1947) and N.U. First feature Love Story, 1950; since The Lady Without Camelias, Love in a City, I Vinti, The Friend, The City, L'Avventura, The Night, The Eclipse, The Red Desert, Blow-Up, Zabriskie Point, The Passenger.

ANTONOWSKY, MARVIN: Executive. b. New York, NY, Jan. 31, 1929. e. City Coll. of New York, B.A., M.B.A. Joined Kenyon and Eckhart in 1957 for which was media research dir.; named marketing v.p. With Norman, Craig, & Kummel as v.p., mktg. services. 1965, became v.p. in chg. of media research and spot buying at J. Walter Thompson. In 1969 joined ABC-TV as v.p. in chg. research. Left to become v.p. in chg. of programming at NBC-TV. 1976, sr. v.p., Universal-TV. 1979, joined Columbia Pictures as pres., mktg. & research. Rejoined MCA/Universal Pictures as pres, mktg., Nov. 1983.

ANTONY, SCOTT: Actor. b. Gosforth, Newcastle-upon-Tyne, England. e. Leeds U.; rec'd scholarship at Royal Acad. of Dramatic Art. Ken Russell found him there and gave him role in Savage Messiah, 1972. Has done much TV work in Britain.
PICTURES INCLUDE: Savage Messiah, The Mutations, Dead Cert.

APFEL, EDWIN R.: Executive. b. New York, NY, Jan. 2, 1934. e. Franklin and Marshall Coll., B.A., 1955. copywriter and account executive, Donahue and Coe, 1955–60; adv. publicity dept., Metro-Goldwyn-Mayer, 1960–62; dir. of adv. and creative services, MGM, Verve Records, 1962–63; dir. of adv., Embassy Pictures 1963–65; Advertising Writer, Consultant, 1965.

APPELBOOM, MAX: Producer. b. Amsterdam, Netherlands, March 7, 1924; e. art schools in Netherlands, Belgium and France. Started in the motion picture business in 1946 with J. Arthur Rank, then to RKO Radio Pictures. Worked from 1953–56 in Hollywood as writer, director and producer. Returned in 1956 to his home base, Amsterdam. Now heads Max Appelboom Productions, Inc. and Appletree Filmproductions Inc.
PICTURES INCLUDE: Floris, Monkey Business, Will o' the Wisp, Water For Waterland, The Bearboat, Gangrene, The Buggy Man and The New Adventures of Heidi.

APTED, MICHAEL: Director. b. Aylesbury, Eng., Feb. 10, 1941. e. Cambridge. Broke into show business at Granada TV in England in early 1960s as trainee, researcher, and finally director. By 1965 was producer-director for local programs and current affairs; then staff drama dir. for TV series, plays and serials. In late 1960s left Granada to freelance.
PICTURES INCLUDE: Triple Echo, Stardust, The Squeeze, Agatha, Coal Miner's Daughter, Continental Divide, Gorky

Park, Firstborn, Kipperbang, 7 Up, 28 Up, Critical Condition, Gorillas in the Mist.
TELEVISION: Poor Girl, High Kampf, Highway Robbery, Kisses at 50, The Collection (Intl. Emmy Award 28-Up (award winning documentary), Bring on the Night (doc. on Sting); Ptang Yang.

ARBEID, BEN: Producer. Films incl: The Barber of Stamford, Children of the Damned, Private Potter, The Jokers, Hoffman; The Hireling, (Grand Prix—Cannes), Murder Most Foul, Murder Ahoy, The Ace Murders, Assignment K, Before Winter Comes, Mahmud Bridge, The Water Babies, Eagles Wing, Enigma, 1986–87: retained by Turner Broadcasting System Inc. as exec. prod. for The Fourth Season.

ARCHER, ANNE: Actress. b. August 25, 1947. Daughter of actress Marjorie Lord and actor John Archer. Married Terry Jastrow, TV network sports producer-director and pres. Jack Nicklaus Prods.
THEATRE: Les Liaisons Dangereuses (Williamstown Fest., 1988).
PICTURES INCLUDE: The All-American Boy, Honkers, Cancel My Reservation, Trackdown, Lifeguard, Paradise Alley, Hero at Large, Raise the Titanic, Green Ice, Waltz Across Texas, The Naked Face, Too Scared to Scream, The Check Is in the Mail, Fatal Attraction.
TELEVISION: The Storefront Lawyers (1970), The Pirate (mini-series), The Blue Knight, Seventh Avenue, The Sky's No Limit, A Matter of Wife...and Death, The Dark Side of Innocence, A Different Affair, Falcon Crest, A Leap of Faith.

ARCHER, JOHN: Actor. r.n. Ralph Bowman, b. Osceola, NB, May 8, 1915. e. U. of Southern California. Won Jesse L. Lasky Gateway to Hollywood talent quest; m.p. debut in Flaming Frontiers 1938; on N.Y. stage also.
PICTURES INCLUDE: White Heat, After Nightfall, Destination Moon, Big Trees, Yank in Indo-China, Sound Off, Rodeo, Sea Tiger, The Stars Are Singing, Dragon's Gold, No Man's Woman, Emergency Hospital.

ARCHER, ROBERT V.: Executive. Joined Paramount Pictures in 1967 as adm. asst. to v.p. of facilities and TV prod. In 1975 named dir. of studio admin. 1977 promoted to dir. of studio operations and admin., responsible for prod. servicing and admin. depts. of studio.

ARCHERD, ARMY: Columnist, TV commentator. r.n. Armand Archerd, b. New York, NY, Jan. 13. e. U. of California at L.A., grad. '41, U.S. Naval Academy Post Graduate Sch., 1943. Started as usher at Criterion Theatre, N.Y., while in high school. After grad. U. of California at L.A., worked at Paramount studios before entering Navy, Lt., joined AP Hollywood bureau 1945, Herald-Express, Daily Variety as columnist, 1953. M.C. Hollywood premieres and Academy Awards. President, founder Hollywood Press Club, awards from Masquers, L.A. Press Club, Hollywood Foreign Press Club, and Newsman of the Year award from Publicists Guild, 1970; Movie Game. TV Series: People's Choice, co-host.

ARDANT, FANNY: Actress. b. France. Raised in Monte Carlo. Majored in political science in college. Served a 5-year apprenticeship in the French theater acting in Polyeucte, Esther, The Mayor of Santiago, Electra and Tete d'Or. After TV debut in Les Dames de la Côte, went on to star in films by Truffaut who became her mentor.
PICTURES: Les Chiens; Les uns et les Autres; The Woman Next Door; Life is a Novel; Confidentially Yours; Benevonata; Desire; Swann in Love; Love Unto Death; Les Enrages; L'Ete Prochain; Family Business; Melo; The Family, Three Sisters, Australia.

ARDEN, EVE: Actress. r.n. Eunice Quedens. b. Mill Valley, CA, 1912. Appeared with Alcazar stock co., Bandbox Repertory Theatre; Broadway debut in Ziegfeld Follies of 1936, also in Ziegfeld Follies of 1938, Autobiography: Three Phases of Eve, 1985.
PICTURES: Let's Face It, Night And Day, Cover Girl, Voice of the Turtle, Goodbye, My Fancy, We're Not Married, Our Miss Brooks, Anatomy of a Murder, Dark at the Top of the Stairs, Sergeant Deadhead, The Strongest Man in the World, Grease, Grease 2.
TELEVISION: Series: Our Miss Brooks, The Eve Arden Show, The Mothers-in-Law. Movies: A Very Special Person, The Dream Merchants, All My Darling Daughters, A Guide for the Married Woman, Faerie Tale Theatre (Cinderella).
STAGE: Mame, Hello Dolly, Butterflies Are Free.

ARDOLINO, EMILE: Producer, Director. Began career as dir. and prod. of Dance in America and Live From Lincoln Center series for Public TV 1975–81 before feature film debut as dir. Dirty Dancing (1988).
PICTURES: He Makes Me Feel Like Dancin' (prod., dir., Acad. and Emmy Award-winning doc., Peabody, Christopher, Cine Golden Eagle Awards, 1983), Dirty Dancing (dir.), Chances Are (dir.)
TELEVISION: Dance in America (prod., dir. 28 progs. include. Nuryev and the Joffrey Ballet in Tribute to Nijinsky,

Choreography By Balanchine IV-1979 Emmy, The Spellbound Child (DGA Award), Live From Lincoln Center (incld. New York City Ballet in Tribute to George Balanchine, Stravinsky and Balanchine: Genius Has a Birthday; The Saint of Bleeker Street), Baryshnikov at the White House, Mass by Leonard Bernstein, When Hell Freezes Over I'll Skate, Rumplestiltskin (Fairie Tale Theatre), Alice at the Palace, The Dance and The Railroad, A Midsummer Night's Dream, Good Morning Mr. Orwell, The Rise and Rise of Daniel Rocket (dir.).

ARKIN, ALAN: Actor, Director, b. New York, NY, March 26, 1934. e. Los Angeles City Coll., Los Angeles State Coll., Bennington (VT) Coll. Member folk singing group The Tarriers; off-Broadway, Second City, Man Out Loud, From the Second City; Broadway, Enter Laughing (Tony Award), Luv. Dir. Little Murders, White House Murders.
PICTURES INCLUDE: The Russians Are Coming, The Russians Are Coming, Wait Until Dark, The Heart Is a Lonely Hunter, Popi, Catch 22, Deadhead Miles, Last of the Red Hot Lovers, Freebie and the Bean, Rafferty and the Gold Dust Twins, Little Murders (also dir.), Hearts of the West, 7½ Per Cent Solution, The In-Laws (also exec. prod.), Simon, Chu Chu and the Philly Flash, The Return of Mr. Invisible, Joshua Then and Now, Bad Medicine, Big Trouble, Full Moon High.
TELEVISION: The Defection of Simas Kurdirka, The Other Side of Hell, A Deadly Business, Escape from Sobibor, The Visit (Trying Times, dir.).

ARKOFF, SAMUEL Z.: Producer, Motion Picture executive. Chairman & president of the Samuel Z. Arkoff Company (formed 1980) and Arkoff Int'l Pictures (formed 1981). b. Fort Dodge, IA, June 12, 1918. e. U. of Colorado, U. of Iowa, Loyola U. Law Sch. m. Hilda Rusoff. U.S.A.F. cryptographer W.W.II. Co-founder American Releasing, 1954, and American International Pictures, 1955. President and Chairman of the Board American International Pictures until 1979. Named with partner James H. Nicholson as Producers of the Year in 1963 by Allied States Association of Motion Picture Theatre Owners and in 1964 as Master Showmen of the Decade by the Theatre Owners of America. Also named Producers of the Year at the Show-A-Rama VIII, and in 1966 and 1967 voted among top ten producers in exhibitor ratings by the independent theatre owners. In Rome in 1970 honored by President of the Republic of Italy with decree naming him Commendatore of the Order of Merit. In 1971 he and Nicholson named Pioneers of the Year by the Foundation of the Motion Picture Pioneers, Inc. Since appointment in 1973, has served as International vice pres. of Variety Clubs International. Vice pres., Permanent Charities Committee. Appointed Member of the Board of Trustees of Loyola Marymount U., Los Angeles, in 1979. Honored by a retrospective on 25th anniversary of AIP at Museum of Modern Art, July–Sept., 1979.
PRODUCTION CREDITS: On more than 200 pictures including Amityville Horror, Dressed to Kill, How to Beat the High Cost of Living, The Earthling, Love at First Bite, Meteor, California Dreaming, Force Ten from Navarone, The House of Usher, Pit and the Pendulum, Tales of Terror, Master of The World, Premature Burial, Panic in the Year Zero, The Raven, Beach Party, Haunted Palace, Comedy of Terrors, Bikini Beach, Masque of the Red Death, Muscle Beach Party, Pajama Party Tomb of Ligeia, Wild Angels, Devil's Angels, The Trip, Three in the Attic, Wild in the Streets, The Oblong Box, Scream and Scream Again, Murders in the Rue Morgue, Cry of the Banshee, Bloody Mama, Wuthering Heights, Dr. Phibes, Frogs, Blacula, Dillinger, Heavy Traffic, Hennessy, Cooley High, Food of the Gods, Futureworld, Great Scout and Cathouse Thursday, Land that Time Forgot, People that Time Forgot, At the Earth's Core, Island of Dr. Moreau, and A Winning Season.

ARKUSH, ALLAN: Director. b. New York, NY, Apr. 30, 1948. e. Franklin & Marshall, New York U. Film Sch. With New World Pictures as film editor, trailer editor. Co-directed Hollywood Boulevard and Death Sport and was 2nd unit dir. of Grand Theft Auto before directing on own.
PICTURES: Rock 'n' Roll High School; Heartbeeps; Get Crazy; Caddyshack II.
TELEVISION: Fame, Summer, rock videos, St. Elsewhere; L.A. Law; Bronx Zoo; Moonlighting (Emmy nom., 1987).

ARLEDGE, ROONE: Executive. b. Forest Hills, NY, July 8, 1931. e. Columbia U. Entered industry with Dumont Network in 1952; joined U.S. Army, 1953, serving at Aberdeen Proving Ground in Maryland, where produced and directed radio programs. Joined NBC in 1954 where held various production positions. In 1960 went to ABC TV; 1964, named v.p. in chg. of ABC Sports. Created ABC's Wide World of Sports in April, 1961. Named pres. of ABC News in 1968; pres. of ABC News and Sports, 1977. Holds four George Foster Peabody Awards for sports reporting; 19 Emmy awards.

ARLING, ARTHUR E.: Cinematographer. b. Missouri, Sept. 2, 1906. e. N.Y. Inst. of Photography. Entered m.p. at Fox studio 1927 as asst. cameraman, 2nd cameraman 1931; operative cameraman on "Gone With the Wind" which won the

Academy Award for technicolor photography 1939. Lt. Comdr. U.S.N.R., W.W.II; received Academy Award as dir. of photography on "The Yearling" 1946. Member: Amer. Soc. of Cinematographers.
PICTURES INCLUDE: Homestretch, Captain from Castile, Mother Was A Freshman, You're My Everything, Wabash Avenue, My Blue Heaven, Call Me Mister, Belles on their Toes, The Glass Slipper, Three for the Show, Love Me or Leave Me, I'll Cry Tomorrow, Ransom, Great American Pastime, Tammy & the Bachelor, Pay the Devil, Story of Ruth, Pillow Talk, Lover Come Back, Notorious Landlady, Boys Night Out, My Six Loves.

ARMOUR, REGINALD: Foreign distributor, Producer. b. Chicago, IL, Nov. 28, 1905. e. Edinburgh, Scotland. Exec. RCA Victor Co. to 1933; estab. exch. India, Burma, Ceylon RKO Radio; Far East gen. mgr.; European gen. mgr. (Paris) 1937; exec. asst. to pres. RKO 1941; asst. gen. mgr. RKO studios 1942; British & European rep. Walt Disney Prod. 1942; financial field (N.Y.) 1943; exec. vice-pres. Richard Condon, Inc. 1944; with overseas br. OWI 1945; foreign rep. Columbia Internatl. Corp. (N.Y.) 1945–49; joined Republic Pictures Internatl. Corp. 1949; apptd. v.p., 1950; supvr., Europe & Near East for Republic 1952, exec. v.p. Republic Pictures International (Great Britain) and man. dir. Republic Prod. (Gt. Brit.) Ltd.; exec. v.p. Republic Pictures International Corp., 1955; pres., The Dorsey Corp., 1960; Vice Chmn., The Dorsey Corp., 1964; pres., SOS Photo-Cine-Optics, Inc., 1965; pres. FB/Ceco of Calif. Inc., 1967; pres. Instant Protection Systems, Inc., 1971. Exec. V.P. and Treas. The Quedo Corporation and International Producers Services, Inc. 1973; 1974, V.P. & Treas. Dyna-Soar, Inc.; 1977, exec. v.p. & treas., Two Feathers Prods.; 1981, pres., Armour Enterprises, Inc.; 1985, pres., Group Media Prods., Inc.

ARMSTRONG, BESS: Actress. b. Baltimore, MD, Dec. 11, 1953. m. producer John Fiedler. e. Brown U.
PICTURES INCLUDE: The Four Seasons, Jekyll and Hyde Together Again, High Road to China, Jaws 3-D, The House of God, Nothing in Common, Second Sight.
TELEVISION: On Our Own, Getting Married, How to Pick Up Girls, Walking Through the Fire, 11th Victim, Barefoot in the Park (HBO), This Girl for Hire, Lace, etc.

ARMSTRONG, GILLIAN: Director. b. Melbourne, Australia, 1950. e. Swinburne Coll. Among 1st class in dirs. course at National Aust. Film & TV School, Sydney. Worked as art dir. on a number of films. Did numerous shorts (Storytime, Old Man and Dog, One Hundred a Day, etc.) and documentaries (A Time and a Place, Tassie Wood, etc.) before turning to features.
PICTURES: My Brilliant Career; Starstruck; Mrs. Soffel; High Tide; Bingo, Bridesmaids and Braces (prod., dir.).

ARMSTRONG, GORDON: Executive. b. East Orange, NJ, Nov. 26, 1937. e. Arizona State U., graduate studies at New York U. Entered ind. as newspaper contact for MGM (1960–63); with Allan, Foster, Ingersoll and Weber 1963–70 as acct. exec.; joined 20th Century-Fox in 1970 as nat. pub. dir. In 1975 appt. dir. of adv.-pub.-promo. for Dino De Laurentiis Corp. In 1978, became vice pres., worldwide marketing for the company; 1980, named v.p., adv.-pub.-prom., Universal Pictures; 1984, named exec. v.p., mktg. MCA Recreation.

ARNALL, ELLIS GIBBS: Lawyer, executive. b. Newnan, GA, March 20, 1907; e. Mercer U., U. of the South, A.B. 1928, D.C.L. 1947; U. of Georgia LL.B. 1931; Atlanta Law Sch., LL.D. 1941; Piedmont Coll., LL.D 1943; Bryant Coll., LL.D. 1948. Georgia state representative from Coweta County, 1936–38; asst. Attorney-General (Ga.) 1938–42; Attorney-General (Ga.) 1942–43; Governor of Ga. 1943–47; pres. Dixie Life Insurance Co.; pres., Columbus National Life Insurance Co. senior mem. law firm Arnall, Golden & Gregory; pres. Georgia State Jr. Chamber of Commerce 1939; trustee U. of South; author of The Shore Dimly Seen 1946. What The People Want 1948; member U.S. Natl. Com. on UNESCO; member U.S. delegation to 4th annual conference UNESCO, Paris, France, 1949. Member: SIMPP (Pres. 1948); 1952 on leave as dir. Office of Price Stabilization, Washington; back to SIMPP, Sept. 1952; pres. Ind. Film Prod. Export Corp., 1953; member bd. of dir., exec. com., U.S. Nat'l Comm. for UNESCO, 1964–65, trustee, Mercer U. 1964–68; chair. bd. Coastal States Life Insurance Co., chair. bd. National Association of Life Companies. Member Academy Motion Picture Arts & Sciences; vice chm., Sun Life of America Group, Inc.

ARNAZ, JR., DESI: Actor, Singer, b. Jan. 19, 1953. Son of Lucille Ball and Desi Arnaz. Began appearing on I Love Lucy show on TV in infancy and on various Lucy shows since. Gained fame as rock singer and musician with the Dino, Desi and Billy group. Film debut in Red Sky at Morning in 1972.
PICTURES INCLUDE: Red Sky at Morning, Marco, Joyride, A Wedding, House of the Long Shadows.
TELEVISION: Flight to Holocaust, The Courage and the Passion, To Kill a Cop, How to Pick Up Girls, The Night the

Bridge Fell Down, She Lives, Voyage of the Yes, The Love Boat, Fantasy Island, Wacked Out, Automan, Paul Reiser: Out on a Whim.

ARNAZ, LUCIE: Actress. b. Los Angeles, CA, July 17, 1951. Daughter of Lucille Ball and Desi Arnaz. m. actor Laurence Luckinbill. Broadway show: They're Playing Our Song; National Touring Companies: Whose Life is It Anyway?, My One and Only, Social Security. Nightclubs: Lucie Arnaz—Latin Roots, Irving Berlin in Concert—In Sicily.
PICTURES: Billy Jack Goes to Washington, The Jazz Singer, Second Thoughts.
TELEVISION: Here's Lucy, The Black Dahlia, The Mating Season, The Washington Mistress, One More Try (pilot), The Lucie Arnaz Show, Who Gets the Friends?

ARNAUD, LEO: Composer, Arranger, Conductor. b. Lyons, France, July 24, 1904: e. Ormesson Music Acad., Ph.D. Faculty mem. & symph. cond., Ormesson Music Acad., 1922–27; mus. dir. & arr. in France & England, 1927–30; Fred Waring Orch., U.S., 1931–35; arr. vocal coach, comp., mus. dir., MGM, 1936–44; U.S. Armed Forces, 1945 dir. many orch. including; L.A. Concert Band, American Legion Band, Hollywood String Orch., Beverly Hills, Symph. Orch.; free-lance mus. dir., comp., arr. since 1945.
PICTURES INCLUDE: One Touch of Venus, Easter Parade, Date With Judy, Three Little Words, Lovely to Look At, Stars & Stripes Forever, Rose Marie, Seven Brides for Seven Brothers.

ARNELL, PETER: Producer. b. Bridgeport, CT. e. U. of Michigan, A.B. Pub. dir., prog., WJLS, Beckley, WV; m.c. & disc jockey, WPEN, Philadelphia; actor, announcer, N.Y.; creator of Rate Your Mate, Name's the Same; creator & prod. of Wheel of Fortune, Balance Your Budget, I'll Buy That, Take a Guess, What's in a Word? prod. Chance of Romance, Take a Good Look, Celebrity Talent Scouts, Face the Facts, Talent Scouts, Take My Word, Ernie Kovacs' Take a Good Look.

ARNESS, JAMES: Actor. b. Minneapolis, MN, May 26, 1923. e. Beloit Coll. Served in U.S. Army; worked in advertising, real estate; m.p. debut in The Farmer's Daughter (1947).
PICTURES INCLUDE: Battleground, Hell Gate, Man from Texas, People Against O'Hara, Iron Man, The Thing, Big Jim McLain, Horizon's West, Lone Hand, Island in the Sky, Veils of Bagdad, Hondo, Her Twelve Men, Them, Many Rivers to Cross, Flame of the Islands, Sea Chase.
TELEVISION: Gunsmoke (20 years), How the West Was Won, McLain's Law, The Alamo: 13 Days to Glory, Gunsmoke: Return to Dodge, Red River.

ARNOLD, DANNY: Writer, Actor. r.n. Arnold Rothman; b. New York, NY, Jan. 23, 1925. Appeared in summer stock, night clubs, vaudeville; entered m.p. ind. as sound effects ed., Columbia, 1944–46; then legit., night clubs, vaudeville, 1946–50. Appeared in m.p. Breakthrough, Inside the Walls of Folsom Prison, Sailor Beware, Jumping Jacks, Scared Stiff, Stars Are Singing,; featured on Martin and Lewis TV show 2 yrs., and wrote their Comedy Hours to 1953.
PICTURES INCLUDE: collab. s.p., story, The Caddy; collab., s.p., Desert Sands: story, s.p., Fort Yuma, story, s.p. Rebel in Town; s.p., Outside the Law.
TELEVISION: Writer: Tennessee Ernie Ford Show. Prod., writer, dir: The Real McCoys (1961–62), Bewitched (1963–64), The Wackiest Ship in the Army (1964–65), That Girl (1967–1969), My World and Welcome to It (1969–70), Barney Miller.

ARNOLD, EDDY: Singer. b. Henderson, TN, May 15, 1918. Radio performer, Nashville, TN; recording star since 1946; records include That's How Much I Love You, Anytime; star of Eddy Arnold Show, ABC-TV.

ARNOLD, JACK: Producer, Director. b. New Haven, CT, Oct. 14, 1912. e. Ohio State U., Amer. Acad. of Dramatic Arts. Actor on Broadway, Brit. m.p.; U.S. Air force, 1942–45; prod. 25 documentary films for State Dept., Army & private industry including With These Hands; dir., 1952. Producer, Universal 1956.
PICTURES INCLUDE: The Mouse That Roared, Bachelor in Paradise, Global Affair, The Incredible Shrinking Man, It Came from Outer Space, The Creature from the Black Lagoon, Girls in the Night, Revenge of the Creature, The Tattered Dress, Glass Web, Man in the Shadow, Man from Bitter Ridge; dir. story: Tarantula, Red Sundown, Decision at Durango, Outside the Law, Pay the Devil, No Name on the Bullet, The Lady Takes a Flyer, The Lively Set, High School Confidential. dir., Black Eye, Swiss Conspiracy (1975).

ARNOUL, FRANÇOISE: Actress. r.n. Françoise Gautsch. b. Algeria, June 3, 1931. Studied acting in Paris; m.p. debut in 1949.
PICTURES INCLUDE: Forbidden Fruit, Companions of the Night, Sheep Has Five Legs, The Bed, Inside a Girl's Dormitory, Tempest in the Flesh, Only the French Can (French CanCan), Last Exit Before Roissy, Night Patrol.

ARNOW, TED J.: Executive. b. Brooklyn, NY. e. St. Johns U., Washington and Lee U. Served as dir. of recreation for 262nd General Hospital in Panama. Veteran of over 50 yrs. in amusement industry. Is v.p. for adv., pub., & promo, for Loew's Theatres. Member: Motion Picture Pioneers, Variety Clubs, Will Rogers Hospital; former pres. of AMPA (Assoc. M.P. Advertisers).

ARQUETTE, ROSANNA: Actress. b. Aug. 10, 1960. Granddaughter of humorist Cliff Arquette (Charlie Weaver). Debut as teenage daughter on TV series Shirley (1979).
PICTURES: More American Graffiti, The World According to Garp, Off the Wall, S.O.B., Baby, It's You, The Aviator, Desperately Seeking Susan, After Hours, Silverado, Lies, 8 Million Ways To Die, Nobody's Fool, Amazon Women on the Moon, The Big Blue.
TELEVISION: The Dark Secret of Harvest Home; The Long Way Home; The Wall; The Executioner's Song; Johnny Belinda; One Cooks, the Other Doesn't; The Parade; Survival Guide; A Family Tree (PBS' Trying Times); Promised a Miracle.

ARTHUR, BEATRICE: Actress. r.n. Bernice Frankel. b. New York, NY, May 13, 1926. Franklin Inst. of Sciences & Art. Studied with Erwin Piscator at New School for Social Research; first stage role as Lysistrata; professional stage debut in Dog Beneath the Skin, 1947. Gas, Yerma, No Exit, Six Characters in Search of an Author. Stock appearances include Personal Appearance, Candlelight, Love or Money, The Voice of the Turtle.
THEATER: The Taming of the Shrew, (1948) The Owl and the Pussycat, The Threepenny Opera (1953 revival), The ShoeString Revue, What's the Rush?, Nature's Rush, Ulysses in Nighttown, Gay Divorcee, Fiddler on the Roof, Mame (Tony Award), The Floating Light Bulb, Night of the 100 Stars.
PICTURES INCLUDE: That Kind of Woman, Lovers and Other Strangers, Mame.
TELEVISION: Debut: Once Upon a Time (1951), Numerous guest appearances; Series: Maude; On the Air, Amanda's Place, Golden Girls, All Star Gala at Ford's Theater (host), Jay Leno's Family Comedy Hour, One More Time.

ARTHUR, EDWARD B.: Executive. b. New York, NY, Sept. 30, 1915. e. San Jose State Coll., Los Angeles Jr. Coll. Engaged in operation management, purchasing of films etc. in CA, NY, MO, IL; served in armored div. W.W.II, 1st Lt., at close of war Special Service unit (Germany) in chg. of distribution of films to service units; resumed his post as gen. mgr. Arthur Enterprises, Inc. which he had joined in 1935; named pres. St. Louis Amusement Co., 1946. Member: Variety Club.

ARTHUR, JEAN: Actress b. New York, NY, Oct. 17, 1908. On stage; minor roles. m.p. debut as lead in Warming Up, 1928.
PICTURES INCLUDE: Canary Murder Case, Mysterious Dr. Fu Manchu, Whirlpool, Mr. Deeds Goes to Town, You Can't Take It With You, Too Many Husbands, Talk of the Town, Lady Takes a Chance, Impatient Years, Foreign Affair, Shane.
N.Y. STAGE: Peter Pan, 1950.
TELEVISION: The Jean Arthur Show.

ARTHUR, KAREN: Director. b. Omaha, NB, Aug. 24, 1941. 1958–68: choreographer and musical comedy singer, dancer and actress. 1950–68: ballet dancer. 1968–75: actress, film, TV and theatre.
PICTURES: As director: Legacy (1975, International Film Critics Award, Best First Film, Josef Von Sternberg Award); The Mafu Cage, 1978; Lady Beware, 1986.
TELEVISION: Feature Films: Charleston; Return to Eden (mini-series, 1982); Victims for Victims (Christopher Award); A Bunny's Tale; The Rape of Richard Beck; Crossings (mini-series, 1986); Evil in Clear River, Cracked Up, A Bridge to Silence. Episodes: Rich Man, Poor Man; Emerald Point; Boone; Two Marriages; Hart to Hart; Remington Steele; Cagney & Lacey, (Emmy Award, best dir. dramatic episode, 1985).

ARTHUR, ROBERT: Actor. r.n. Robert Arthaud. b. Aberdeen, WA, June 18, 1925. e. U. of Washington (U.S. Navy training program). Won H.S. radio announcing contest; prof. announcer & disc jockey; m.p. debut in Roughly Speaking, 1945. Retired to run own insurance agency. Return to TV 1988: General Hospital, Highway to Heaven.
PICTURES INCLUDE: Nora Prentiss, Sweetheart of Sigma Chi, Devil on Wheels, Mother Wore Tights, 12 O'Clock High, September Affair, Air Cadet, Big Carnival, On the Loose, Belles on Their Toes, Just for You, The Ring, Young Bess, Take the High Ground, Return from the Sea, Top of the World, Desperados Are in Town, The System, Green Grass of Wyoming, Switchblade, Hellcats of the Navy, Young and Wild, Yellow Sky, Mother is a Freshman.

ARTZ, BOB: Theatre executive. b. Spokane, WA, Aug 21, 1946 e. B.T.A. Pasadena Playhouse College of Theatre Arts. Began in 1968 as doorman; then asst. mgr to mgr. with National General Theatre Corporation. Joined Plitt Theatres in 1978 as dist. mgr and ad/pub. director, West Coast. Joined General Cinema Theatre in 1986 as reg. marketing mgr; Western region.
MEMBER: Variety Club, Life Member: Pasadena Playhouse Alumni & Assoc.

ASH, RENE: Producer. b. Brussels, Belgium, March 14, 1939; e. U. of Omaha. Member of the Publicists Guild since 1968; Eastern Vice President of Pub Guild 1973–1981; Author of The Film Editor in Motion Pictures & Television; employed with I.A.T.S.E. 1968–1979, prior to which was assoc. editor, Greater Amusements; various articles published in foreign film magazines; editor-in-chief, Backstage; 1979–80; pres., Cinereal Pictures Nov., 1984–Oct, 1985; exec. v.p., Eagle Films Corp., since Nov., 1985, pres. Eagle/Zalon Ent. since Jan., 1987.

ASHBY, HAL: Director. b. Ogden, UT. e. Ogden High Sch. Began career as film editor. Worked with Norman Jewison on The Cincinnati Kid, The Russians Are Coming, The Russians Are Coming, In the Heat of the Night (AA) and also as assoc. prod on The Thomas Crown Affair and Gaily, Gaily, Directing debut, The Landlord, 1970.
PICTURES INCLUDE: Harold and Maude, The Last Detail, Shampoo, Bound for Glory, Coming Home, Second Hand Hearts, Being There, Lookin' to Get Out, Let's Spend the Night Together, The Slugger's Wife, 8 Million Ways to Die.
TELEVISION: Beverly Hills Buntz.

ASHCROFT, DAME PEGGY: Actress. b. Croyden, England, Dec. 22, 1907. e. Woodford Sch, Croyden, Central Sch. of Dramatic Art. On stage since 1926. London debut One Day More, 1927. Broadway debut High Tor (1937). Has had a long, extensive stage career in classics with Old Vic, Royal Shakespeare Co., National Theater, and Royal Court Theater. Film debut The Thirty-Nine Steps, 1933.
RECENT THEATER: John Gabriel Borkman, Happy Days, Tribute to the Old Lady, Old World, Watch on the Rhine, Family Voices, All's Well that Ends Well (1981).
PICTURES: The Nun's Story, The Wandering Jew, Rhodes of Africa, Quiet Wedding, Secret Ceremony, Three into Two Won't Go, Sunday Bloody Sunday, Joseph Andrews, A Passage to India (Acad. Award, supp. actress, 1984, L.A. Film Critics Award), Madame Sousatzka.
TELEVISION: The Shadow of Heroes, The Cherry Orchard, The Wars of Roses, Days in the Trees, Cream in My Coffee, Caught on a Train, The Jewel in the Crown.

ASHER, JANE: Actress. b. London, England, April 5, 1946. She has acted in many films and TV plays. Films: Greengage Summer, The Girl in the Headlines, Masque of the Red Death, Alfie, Deep End, Henry the Eighth and His Six Wives, Runners, Dream Child, Paris By Night.
TELEVISION: Brideshead Revisited, Voyage 'Round My Father, East Lynne, The Mistress, Wish Me Luck.

ASHLEY, ELIZABETH: Actress. b. Aug. 30, 1939. e. Studied ballet LA State U 1957–58; grad. Neighborhood Playhouse, 1961. Author: Postcards From the Road.
THEATER: Take Her She's Mine (1960 Tony Award), The Highest Tree, Barefoot in the Park, Legend, Cat on a Hot Tin Roof (B'way revival), Agnes of God.
PICTURES INCLUDE: The Carpetbaggers, Ship of Fools, The Third Day, The Marriage of a Young Stockbroker, Paperback Hero, Golden Needles, Rancho DeLuxe, 92 in the Shade, Great Scout and Cathouse Thursday, Coma, Windows, Captured, Paternity, Split Image, Dragnet, Vampire's Kiss, Grandpa and I.
TELEVISION: Stagecoach, Harpy, The Face of Fear, When Michael Calls, Second Chance, The Heist, Your Money or Your Wife, The Magician, One of My Wives is Missing, The War Between the Tates, Insight, Tom and Joann (pilot), A Fire in the Sky, Svengali, He's Fired, She's Hired; Warm Hearts Cold Feet, The Two Mrs. Grenvilles.

ASHLEY, JOHN: Actor, Producer. r.n. John Atchley. b. Kansas City, MO, Dec. 25, 1934. e. Oklahoma State U., B.A., 1956. Career started in Tulsa Little Theatre, 1956; screen debut, 1957, Dragstrip Girl; later: Motorcycle Gang, Suicide Battalion.
TV: Men of Annapolis, Sheriff of Cochise, Frontier Doctor; Matinee Theatre, Jefferson Drum, Something is Out There (co-exec. prod.), Prod: The A-Team, Werewolf.

ASHLEY, TED: Executive b. Brooklyn, NY, Aug. 3, 1922. e. City Coll. of New York. Sch. of Business Administration. 1937–39. With William Morris Agency, agent. 1939–46; formed Ted Ashley Associates, 1946; pres. Ashley Famous Agency, 1954; director and chairman of executive committee of Warner Communications Inc., 1967 to 1974; chairman of bd. and chief exec. officer, Warner Bros. 1969–75; chm. & co-CEO, 1977–80; 1981, sr. consultant, Warner Communications; 1982–84, vice chm. of bd., WC. Resigned 1988.

ASNER, EDWARD: Actor. b. Kansas City, KS, Nov. 15, 1929. e. U. of Chicago, where affiliated with campus acting group. Served two years with U.S. Army in France. Returned to Chicago to join Playwright's Theatre Club. Moved to N.Y.;

Broadway debut in Face of a Hero. Appeared off-Broadway (Ivanov, Threepenny Opera, Legend of Lovers, The Tempest, Venice Preserved), in stock, and with NY Shakespeare Festival (1960) and American Shakespeare Festival (1961). In 1961 moved to Hollywood to become active in films and TV. National pres. Screen Actors Guild (1981–85), With actress Timothy Blake founded Quince/Blake Productions. Winner of numerous humanitarian awards.

PICTURES: Kid Gallahad, The Slender Thread, The Satan Bug, The Venetian Affair, Eldorado, Peter Gunn, Change of Habit, Halls of Anger, They Call Me Mister Tibbs, Skin Game, Gus, Fort Apache—The Bronx, O'Hara's Wife, Daniel, Moon Over Parador (cameo).

TELEVISION: Series: Slattery's People, The Mary Tyler Moore Show (3 Emmy Awards), Lou Grant (2 Emmys), Off the Rack, The Bronx Zoo. Movies: The Doomsday Flight, Doug Selby, D.A., The House on Greenapple Road, The Old Man Who Cried Wolf, The Last Child, The Haunts of the Very Rich, Hey, I'm Alive, Twigs, Life and Assassination of the Kingfish, The Gathering, The Family Man, A Small Killing, A Case of Libel, Anatomy of an Illness, Vital Signs, Kate's Secret, The Christmas Star, Cracked. Mini-series: Rich Man, Poor Man (Emmy Award), Roots (Emmy Award), Tender Is the Night, A Friendship in Vienna.

ASSANTE, ARMAND: Actor. b. New York, NY, Oct. 4, 1949. e. American Acad. of Dramatic Arts. Appeared with regional theatre groups and off-Broadway. On Broadway in Boccaccio, Comedians, Romeo and Juliet, Kingdoms; Yankees 3, Detroit 0.

PICTURES: Lords of Flatbush, Paradise Alley, Prophesy, Little Darlings, Love and Money, Private Benjamin, I, the Jury, Unfaithfully Yours, Belizaire the Cajun, The Penitent, Animal Behavior.

TELEVISION: Human Feelings, Lady of the House, The Pirate, Sophia Loren—Her Own Story, Why Me?, Evergreen, A Deadly Business, Stranger in My Bed, Hands of a Stranger. Mini-Series: Napoleon and Josephine: A Love Story.

ASSEYEV, TAMARA: Producer. e. Marymont College; UCLA (MA, theatre arts). Began career as asst. to Roger Corman, working on 8 films with him. In 1967 started to produce films independently. Then co-produced films with Alex Rose, starting with Drive-In. In 1966 at 24, became youngest member of Producers Guild of Amer. Member: Costume Council, LA City Museum; founding member LA Museum of Contemporary Art.

PICTURES INCLUDE: The Wild Racers, Paddy, The Arousers, The History of Atlantic Records, Co-produced with Ms. Rose: Drive-In, I Wanna Hold Your Hand, Big Wednesday, Norma Rae.

TELEVISION: Movies: Penalty Phase, After the Promise, A Shadow on the Sun (also actress).

ASTIN, JOHN: Actor. b. Baltimore, MD, March 30, 1930. e. Washington and Jefferson Coll., Washington Drama Sch., Johns Hopkins U., grad. B.A., U. of Minnesota Graduate School. First prof. job., Off-Broadway, Threepenny Opera; Broadway debut, Major Barbara; dir., co-prod., A Sleep of Prisoners, Phoenix Theatre; during 1955–59, did voices in cartoons, commercials; TV Series: I'm Dickens . . . He's Fenster; The Addams Family, Harry Anderson's Sideshow (special).

STAGE: The Cave Dwellers, Ulysses in Nighttown, Tall Story.

PICTURES INCLUDE: West Side Story, That Touch of Mink, Candy, Viva, Max!, Bunny O'Hare, Get to Know Your Rabbit, Every Little Crook and Nanny, Freaky Friday, Teen Wolf Too, Return of the Killer Tomatoes, Nightlife.

ATHERTON, WILLIAM: Actor. b. New Haven, CT, June 30, 1947. While in high school became youngest member of Long Wharf Theatre Co. Given scholarship to Pasadena Playhouse; then switched to Carnegie Tech Sch. of Drama in 1965. Trained for stage with Aesthetic Realism Foundation, NY. In college years toured with USO prods in Europe and in stock and industrial shows. Came to N.Y. where first prof. job was in nat'l co. of Little Murders.

PICTURES INCLUDE: The New Centurions, Class of '44, The Sugarland Express, The Day of the Locust, The Hindenburg, Looking for Mr. Goodbar, Ghostbusters, Real Genius, No Mercy, Die Hard.

PLAYS: The House of Blue Leaves, The Basic Training of Pavlo Hummel, The Sign in Sidney Brustein's Window, Suggs, Rich and Famous, Passing Game, Happy New Year, The American Clock, Three Acts of Recognition, Caine Mutiny Court Martial.

TELEVISION: Centennial, Malibu, House of Mirth, The Equalizer.

ATKINS, CHRISTOPHER: Actor. b. Rye, NY, Feb. 21, 1961. e. Dennison U., Ohio. Early modelling jobs; theatrical film debut in The Blue Lagoon (1980).

PICTURES: The Pirate Movie, A Night in Heaven, Beaks, Mortuary Academy.

TELEVISION: Movie: Raid on Short Creek. Series: Dallas.

ATTENBOROUGH, DAVID: Broadcaster. b. London, England, May 8, 1926; e. Wyggeston Sch., Leicester; Clare Coll., Cambridge. Early career, editor in educational publishing house, ent. BBC-TC Sept. 1952. Prod. Zoo Quest series, Travellers Tales, Adventure and other prog., travel, Eastward with Attenborough, The Tribal Eye, Life on Earth, exploration natural History and anthropology. Controller BBC-2, 1965–68; Dir. of Prog. BBC-TV, 1969–72.

ATTENBOROUGH, SIR RICHARD: Actor, Producer, Director. b. Cambridge, England, Aug. 29, 1923. m. 1945 Sheila Beryl Grant Sim. e. Wyggeston Grammar Sch., Leicester. Leverhulme Scholarship to Royal Acad. of Dramatic Art, 1941 (Bancroft Medal). First stage appearance Ah, Wilderness, 1941. London debut in Awake and Sing, 1942. First film appearance in In Which We Serve, 1942. Appeared in The Little Foxes, Piccadilly Theatre, 1942; Brighton Rock, Garrick Theatre 1943. Joined R.A.F. 1943; seconded to R.A.F. Film Unit, 1944, and appeared in Journey Together; demobilized, 1946. Returned to stage, Jan. 1949, in The Way Back (Home of the Brave), To Dorothy, A Son, 1950; Sweet Madness, 1952; The Mousetrap, 1952–54; Double Image, 1956–1957; The Rape of the Belt, 1957–1958, 1959 formed Beaver Films with Bryan Forbes.

PICTURES INCLUDE: School for Secrets (Secret Flight), The Man Within (The Smugglers), Dancing with Crime, Brighton Rock (Young Scarface), London Belongs to Me (Dulcimer Street), The Guinea Pig, The Lost People, Boys in Brown, Morning Departure (Operation Disaster), Hell Is Sold Out, The Magic Box, Gift Horse (Glory at Sea), Father's Doing Fine, Eight O'Clock Walk, The Ship That Died of Shame, Private's Progress, The Baby and the Battleship, Brothers-in-Law, The Scamp, Dundirk, The Man Upstairs, Sea of Sand, Danger Within, I'm All Right Jack, Jetstorm, S.O.S. Pacific; The Angry Silence (also co-prod.); formed Allied Film Makers and appeared in their first film The League of Gentlemen; produced Whistle Down the Wind, appeared in Only Two Can Play, All Night Long, The Dock Brief (Trial & Error); produced The L-Shaped Room, appeared in The Great Escape, Seance on a Wet Afternoon (also prod.); appeared in The Third Secret, 1963; Guns at Batasi, 1964; The Flight of the Phoenix, 1965; The Bliss of Mrs. Blossom, Only When I Larf, 1968. Prod. and dir.: Oh! What a Lovely War, 1968. Appeared in The Last Grenade, A Severed Head, Loot, and made quest appearances in The Magic Christian and David Copperfield, 1969, 10 Rillington Place, 1970, Young Winston, 1972 appeared in Rosebud, Ten Little Indians, Brannigan. Conduct Unbecoming 1974, directed A Bridge Too Far, 1976. Appeared in The Chess Players, Magic, (dir.) The Human Factor, (actor) Gandhi (prod.-dir.); A Chorus Line (dir.), Cry Freedom (prod., dir.).

ATTERBURY, MALCOLM: Actor. b. Philadelphia, PA, Feb. 20, 1907, e. Hill Sch., PA. Radio editor, Phila. Ledger; prog. mgr., gen. mgr., performer, Phila. Ledger radio station, WHAT, 7 yrs.; concert, vaudeville, Schubert musicals, 7 yrs.; Tamarack Playhouse, 5 yrs.; owned, oper., Albany Playhouse, 6 yrs.; conducted thea. seminars, Skidmore, R.P.I., College of St. Rose.

TELEVISION: Hallmark Hall of Fame, Lux Video Thea., Playhouse 90, Studio One, G.E. Theatre, Cheyenne, Perry Mason, Gunsmoke, 77 Sunset Strip, Alfred Hitchcock Presents, Route 66, The Defenders, The Untouchables, Dr. Kildare, Profiles in Courage, Fugitive, FBI, Hazel, Bonanza, Voyage to the Bottom of the Sea, Judd.

PICTURES INCLUDE: Dragnet, Storm Center, Crime in the Streets, Reprisal, Crime of Passion, Toward the Unknown, No Time for Sergeants, Rio Bravo, North by Northwest, Wild River, From the Terrace, Summer and Smoke, Advise and Consent, The Birds, The Chase, Hawaii.

BROADWAY: One Flew Over the Cuckoo's Nest.

ATWATER, GLADYS: Writer. Has written many m.p. scripts; member of writing team with Robert Bren since 1939; v.p. Bremex, Inc., writings include: (collab. orig.) Man Who Found Himself; (collab. orig. story) Argentine Nights, First Yank into Tokyo, In Old California; (collab. s.p.) Criminal Lawyer, Crashing Hollywood, The Marriage Business, Crime Ring; (collab. story) El Paso, Tag for Murder, Blood on the Shrine, Legacy in Nylons, Aztec Dagger, Female Menagerie. Collab. story, s.p., Overland Pacific; collab. stor. Naked Alibi, Treasure of Pancho Villa; TV: Lone Wolf in Mexico, Stolen Train, Casey Jones series, Winds of the Four Seasons, collab. s.p.; collab. s.p. orig. story The Hawaiians.

AUBERJONOIS, RENE: Actor. b. New York, NY, June 1, 1940. e. attended Carnegie Mellon U.

THEATER: A Cry of Players, Dark of the Moon, Beyond the Fringe, Charley's Aunt, Coco (Tony Award), Tricks, The Ruling Class, Twelfth Night, The Good Doctor, The New York Idea, Break a Leg, Every Good Boy Deserves Favor; Richard III, The Misanthrope, Flea in Her Ear, Big River.

PICTURES INCLUDE: MASH, Brewster McCloud, McCabe and Mrs. Miller, Pete 'n Tillie, Images, My Best Friend Is a Vampire, Hindenberg, King Kong, Eyes of Laura Mars, Where the Buffalo Roam, 3:15, Walker, Police Academy 5: Assignment Miami Beach.

TELEVISION: Benson (series); Movies: The Birdmen, Dark Street at Harvest Home, More Wild Wild West, The Rhineman Exchange, Smokey Mountain Christmas, The Christmas Star, Fire, Longarm.

AUBREY, JAMES T., JR.: Executive. b. La Salle, IL, Dec. 14, 1918. e. Princeton U., 1941. m. Phyllis Thaxter, U.S. Air Force, 1941–45; salesman, Street and Smith, Condé Nast Pub., 1946–47; account exec., KNX, Los Angeles, 1948; account exec., KNXT, 1951; sales mgr., then gen. mgr., KNXT and CTPN, 1952. Man. network prog., Hollywood CBS-TV, 1956; V.P. programs and talent, ABC-TV 1957; v.p. CBS. 1958; exec. v.p. CBS-TV, 1959; pres. CBS-TV, 1959. In 1969–73 MGM pres.; now indep. prod.

PICTURES INCLUDE: Futureworld (prod.), The Hunger, Hostage (co-exec. prod.).

AUDRAN, STEPHANE: Actress. b. France, 1938. Ex-wife of French star Jean-Louis Trintignant; now married to director Claude Chabrol.

PICTURES INCLUDE: Les Cousins (debut under direction of Chabrol), The Champagne Murders, Les Biches, La Femme Infidele, The Beast Must Die, The Lady in the Car, Le Boucher, Without Apparent Motive, Dead Pigeon on Beethoven Street, The Discreet Charm of the Bourgeoisie, The Devil's Advocate, The Blackbird (American film debut), Silver Bears, Blood Relatives, Babette's Feast, Seasons of Pleasure, Faceless, Body-To-Body.

TELEVISION: Mistral's Daughter, The Blood of Others, The Sun Also Rises, Poor Little Rich Girl: The Barbara Hutton Story.

AUERBACH, NORBERT T.: President & Chief Executive Officer, United Artists Corp. b. Vienna, 1923. Educated in U.S. and served with U.S. Army Intelligence in Europe during W.W.II. Joined m.p. business in 1946 after graduation from U. of California at L.A. (business admin.). First asst. dir. at Service Studios in Calif. Moved to N.Y. to join domestic sales dept. of Film Classics. Left for position with Columbia Pictures in foreign dept. In 1950 assigned to Paris office, where remained for over decade, except for 18 mos. in Portugal as mgr. Returned to Paris in 1953 and filled number of exec. sls. positions for Columbia, ultimately rising to continental mgr. 1961, left Columbia to produce films in France. Resumed career in dist., this time at Paris office of United Artists, becoming continental mgr. In 1966 returned to production to make The Thief of Paris. 1967, joined Seven Arts Prods. heading theatrical and TV sls. operations in Paris. When Seven Arts acquired Warner Bros., he became continental sls. mgr. for Warners in Paris. 1968, set up European prod. and dist. oper. for CBS Cinema Center Films, operating from London. 1972, moved to L.A. as v.p., foreign mgr. for CCF. Returned to London in 1973 to be consultant in prod. and dist. Rejoined UA in 1977 as sls. mgr. for Europe and the Middle East. Named snr. v.p. & foreign mgr. in 1978. Named pres. & COO, Jan. 1981; pres., CEO, Feb. 1981. Co-pres., United Int'l Pictures, London, till 1982. In 1983 formed packaging and financing Co., Elikra, Inc. 1982, acting pres. and chief exec. officer of Almi Distribution Corp. Now Almi consultant.

AUMONT, JEAN PIERRE: Actor. b. Paris, France, 1909. e. Conservatoire of Drama. Roles French stage and films. U.S. pictures: Assignment in Brittany, Cross of Lorraine. In 1943 enlisted in Free French Army. Film debut, Jean de la Lune, 1932.

PICTURES INCLUDE: Assignment in Brittany, The Cross of Lorraine, Heartbeat, Siren of Atlantis, Affairs of a Rogue, Wicked City, Lili, Life Begins Tomorrow, Gay Adventure, Charge of the Lancers, Hilda Crane, Enemy General, The Devil at 4 O'Clock, Castle Keep, Cauldron of Blood, Cat and Mouse, Day for Night, The Happy Hooker, Mahogany, Catherine & Co., Blackout, Two Solitudes, Something Short of Paradise, Sweet Country.

STAGE: Tovarich, Incident at Vichy, Hostile Witness, Carnival, Camino Real, Murderous Angels, A Talent for Murder.

TELEVISION: Sins, Windmills of the Gods.

AURELIUS, GEORGE M.: Executive. b. Grasston, MN, Sept. 16, 1911. e. U. of Minnesota. Ent. m.p. ind. 1927 as usher Finkelstein & Ruben, St. Paul; asst. mgr. 1929–30; to Warner Theatres, New York 1931; man. Moss' Broadway; Minnesota Amusement Co. 1932–41; city mgr. Publix-Rickards-Nace. Paramount-Nace Theatres, Tucson, Ariz. 1941–46; v.p. ABC Theas. of Arizona, Inc. 1949–67; pres. ABC North Central Theatres, Inc., 1967–72; v.p., ABC Intermountain Theatres, Inc., v.p. ABC Theatres of California, Inc. 1972–1974; Mgmt. Consulting and ShoWest Convention & Trade Show since 1975, named exec. dir., 1979. Retired 1985.

AUSTIN, JOHN: Producer. b. Australia, 1923; Asst. Dir. of Entertainment for American Red Cross, 1942–45; assoc. West Coast rep. of Rodgers & Hammerstein, 1945–47; with Ministry of Info., Gov't of India, 1947–48; prod. TV films in Europe, 1949; shows include Intrigue, International Rendezvous, International Affair; prod. film Lasca. Since 1954, representative of leading foreign newspapers in Hollywood as correspondent for the entertainment industry. 1974–77, west coast editor, Screen International. 1977–81, international editor, The Hollywood Reporter. President: Inter-Global Film Consultants. Since 1982, vice president, editor in chief, Film News-International for VPA, Inc. Consultant to foreign producers on U.S. marketing and advertising techniques.

AUSTIN, RAY: Director, Writer, Producer. b. London, England, Dec. 5, 1932. Has written, produced and directed many TV series, specials and movies.

TELEVISION: Director of series: Avengers, The Champions, Department S, Randall & Hopkirk, Ugliest Girl in Town, Journey into the Unknown, Magnum P.I., Simon and Simon, House Calls, Kings Crossing, Fall Guy, Time Street, Spencer for Hire. Writer: Randall & Hopkirk, Department S. Producer-Director: The Perfumed Garden. Director: It's the Only Way to Go, Fun and Games, Space 1999, New Avengers, Hawaii Five-O, Sword of Justice, Webb, Barnaby Jones, Hardy Boys, Wonder Woman, Salvage, B.G. and the Bears, Hart to Hart, The Yeagers, Man Called Sloane, From Here to Eternity, Bad Cats, Westworld, Tales of the Gold Monkey (2-hr. pilot), The Return of the Man from U.N.C.L.E. Director-Writer: Black Beauty, Zany Adventures of Robin Hood, The Master, Hart to Hart (series); V, Air Wolf, Lime Street (pilot and episodes); Spenser for Hire (several episodes); Magnum P.I. (season premiere 2-hr. episode); Return of the Six Million Dollar Man (pilot); Our House (episodes).

PICTURES: Virgin Witches, House of the Living Dead.

AUTANT-LARA, CLAUDE: Director. Began career as scenic designer for French films in early 1920s; then asst. director; first solo venture experimental film, 1923; in Hollywood, 1930–32. dir. Parlor, Bedroom and Bath, Incomplete Athlete.

PICTURES INCLUDE: Devil in the Flesh, Seven Deadly Sins (seq.), Red Inn, Oh Amelia, Game of Love, Red and the Black.

AUTEN, H. WILLIAM: Executive. b. Cardiff, Wales, Mar. 7, 1921. e. Neville House, Eastbourne; U. Coll. Sch. of London. With sales dept., Warner Bros. (London) 1939; served as Major on Brit. Army Staff 1939–47, including custodianship of UFA, GMBH 1945–46; European & Near Eastern mgr. United Artists 1948; asst. foreign mgr. Eagle Lion Films, Inc. (N.Y.) 1948–49; founder & pres. Benagoss Productions, Inc. June, 1949, to produce and finance pictures; org. Ballentine Pict., 1951.

AUTEUIL, DANIEL: Actor. b. Algeria, Jan. 24, 1950.

PICTURES: L'Aggression/Sombres Vacanes; Attention Les Yeaux; La Nuit de Saint-Germain des Pres; Monsieuer Papa; L'Amour Viole; Les Heroes n'ont pas froid aux oreilles; A Nous Deux; Bete Mais Discipline; Les Sous-Doues; La Banquiere; Clara et les chic types Men Prefer Fat Girls; Pour 100 briques t'as plus rien maintentant; Que les gros salaires levent le doigt!!!; L'Indic; P'tit Con; The Beast; L'Arbalete; Palace; L'Amour en Douce, Jean la Florette; Manon of the Springs, Romauld and Juliette.

AUTRY, GENE: Actor. b. Tioga, TX, Sept. 29, 1907. Railroad telegrapher at Sapulpa, OK, 1925; became radio singer and recording artist (Columbia Records) 1928; screen debut 1934 at Mascot Pictures (later became Republic) as screen's first singing cowboy. Starred in 89 feature films and 91 half hour TV films. The Gene Autry Show, 1950–55. Formed Flying A Productions, produced Annie Oakley, The Range Rider, Buffalo Bill, Jr. and Adventures of Champion TV series. Wrote or co-wrote and recorded over two hundred songs, has 9 Gold Records, including all-time best seller, Rudolph the Red-Nosed Reindeer. Voted top money making Western star 1937–42, and in top Western stars 1936, 1946–54; first Western star to be in top ten money makers from 1938–42. Served in U.S.A.A.F. as flight officer, 1942–45; on USO tour overseas 3 mos.; immediately thereafter resumed radio career with former sponsor, the Wm. Wrigley Co., formed Gene Autry Productions, Inc., star of Madison Square Garden Rodeo first in 1940; composed & recorded song Here Comes Santa Claus; owner radio stations, California Angels baseball team and chairman of the board of Gene Autry Western Heritage Museum.

AVALON, FRANKIE: Entertainer. r.n. Francis Thomas Avalone. b. Philadelphia, PA, Sept 18, 1940. e. South Philadelphia H.S. Trumpet prodigy age 9 yrs. Recording contract, Chancellor Records, Inc., 1957; Gold Record, Venus 1959; Gold Album, Swingin' on a Rainbow, 1959; Night Clubs.

TELEVISION: Ed Sullivan, Perry Como, Pat Boone, Arthur Murray, Dick Clark Shows, Milton Berle, Golden Circle Spectacular; Dinah Shore Show, Steve Allen Show, Easy Does It (series, 1976), Happy Days.

PICTURES INCLUDE: Guns of the Timberland, The Alamo, Voyage to the Bottom of the Sea, Sail a Crooked Ship, Panic in the Year Zero, Bikini Beach, Beach Blanket Bingo,

Jet Set, I'll Take Sweden, Sgt. Deadhead, The Take, Grease, Back to the Beach.

AVEDON, DOE: Actress. b. Old Westbury, NY. Bookkeeper; then actress.
BROADWAY: Young and the Fair, My Name Is Aquilon.
PICTURES INCLUDE: High and the Mighty, Deep in My Heart, The Boss.
TELEVISION: Big Town.

AVERBACK, HY: Director. b. 1925. Theatrical director before turning to TV.
PICTURES: Chamber of Horrors; Where Were You When the Lights Went Out?, I Love You Alice B. Toklas, The Great Bank Robbery, Suppose They Gave a War & Nobody Came, Where the Boys Are—1984.
TELEVISION INCLUDE: The Brothers, The Real McCoys, Donna Reed Show, M*A*S*H, Friends, The New Maverick, Anna and the King, Needles and Pins, Movin' On, Look Out World, The Night Rider, A Guide for the Married Woman, The Girl, The Gold Watch, and Dynamite, She's in the Army Now; At Ease (also prod.), The Four Seasons.

AVILDSEN, JOHN G.: Director, Cinematographer, Editor. b. Chicago, IL. e. NYU. After service in Army made film with friend, Greenwich Village Story, then joined ad agency to write and produce film commercials. Entered m.p. industry as ass't cameraman on Below the Hill, followed with prod. mgr. job on Italian film made in U.S. Then made first theatrical short, Smiles. Asst. dir: Black Like Me; prod. mgr.: Mickey One, Una Moglie Americana; asst. dir.: Hurry Sundown. Produced, photographed & edited a short, Light, Sound, Diffuse. Returned to industry to make films for ad agencies before resuming theatrical career.
PICTURES INCLUDE: Turn on to Love (1st feature, dir., photo.), Out of It (asst. dir., dir. of photog.), Sweet Dreams (aka Okay, Bill; dir., photo., editor), Guess What We Learned in School Today? (dir., photo., editor), Joe (dir., photo.), Cry Uncle (dir., photo., editor), The Stoolie (dir. photog.), Save the Tiger (dir.), W. W. and the Dixie Dancekings (dir., editor), Foreplay (dir.), Rocky (dir.), Slow Dancing in the Big City (dir., editor, operator), The Formula (dir., editor), Neighbors (dir. supv. editor), Traveling Hopefully (documentary, dir.), A Night in Heaven (dir., editor, operator), The Karate Kid (dir., editor); Happy New Year (dir.); The Karate Kid: Part II (dir., editor); For Keeps (dir., editor), Lean On Me (dir.).
TELEVISION: From No House to Options House (2 On the Town).

AVNET, JON: Producer, Director. b. Nov. 17, 1947. e. U. of PA, Sarah Lawrence Coll. Began career as director of off-Bdwy. prods. Produced and directed low-budget film, Confusion's Circle, which brought a directing fellowship at American Film Institute. Joined Weintraub/Heller Prods. as assoc. prod., where met Steve Tisch, with whom formed Tisch/Avnet Prods.
PICTURES: Outlaw Blues (assoc. prod.), Coast to Coast (assoc. prod.), Risky Business, Deal of the Century (prod./exec. prod.), Less Than Zero (co-prod. The Avnet/Kerner Co. Prod.), Men Don't Leave.
TELEVISION: No Other Love, Homeward Bound, Prime Suspect, Something So Right, Silence of the Heart, Calendar Girl Murders, Call to Glory (pilot and series), The Burning Bed, In Love and War (Tisch/Avnet Prod., prod./exec. prod.); Between Two Women (The Jon Avnet Co./prod., dir., co-s.p.); Side By Side (The Avnet-Kerner Co., exec. prod.).

AXELROD, GEORGE: Playwright, writer, prod., dir. b. New York, NY, June 9, 1922. Stage mgr., actor, summer stock, 1940–41; radio writer, 1941–42; writer, novels: Beggar's Choice, Blackmailer; co-writer, night club musical: All About Love, 1951.
BROADWAY: The Seven Year Itch, Will Success Spoil Rock Hunter?, Visit to a Small Planet, Once More with Feeling, Goodbye Charlie.
PICTURES INCLUDE: Phfft, The Seven Year Itch, Bus Stop, Breakfast at Tiffany's, The Manchurian Candidate, Paris When It Sizzles, How to Murder Your Wife, Lord Love a Duck, The Secret Life of an American Wife (prod., s.p.), Candy Barr.

AXELROD, JONATHAN: Writer. b. New York, NY, July 9, 1948. Stepson of writer George Axelrod. Started as on-set "gofer" before writing screenplays.
PICTURES INCLUDE: The Dirty Movie, Every Little Crook and Nanny.

AYKROYD, DAN: Actor-Writer. b. Ottawa, Canada. July 1, 1952. m. actress Donna Dixon. Member of Toronto Co. of Second City Theater. Performed and recorded with John Belushi as the Blues Brothers. On TV in Coming Up Rosie (Canada), Saturday Night Live, 1975–79; as writer and performer.
PICTURES INCLUDE: Love at First Sight, Mr. Mike's Mondo Video, 1941, The Blues Brothers (and s.p.), Neighbors, Doctor Detroit, Trading Places, Twilight Zone—The Movie, Ghostbusters (and s.p.), Nothing Lasts Forever, Into the Night, Spies Like Us, Dragnet (also co-s.p.), The Couch Trip,

The Great Outdoors, Caddyshack II, My Stepmother is an Alien, The Von Metz Incident, Ghostbusters II.

AYRES, GERALD: Producer, Writer. e. Yale U. where had four plays produced. Became Broadway play doctor and then joined Columbia Pictures as freelance reader. Named story editor; exec. asst. to v.p. Mike Frankovich; then v.p. in chg. creative affairs in Hollywood. Left in 1970 to become independent. Formed Acrobat Films.
PICTURES INCLUDE: Cisco Pike, The Last Detail, Rich and Famous (s.p. only), Foxes (also s.p.).

AYRES, LEW: Actor. b. Minneapolis, MN, Dec. 28, 1908. Toured Mexico with own orchestra; played with Henry Halstead's Orchestra; screen debut in The Sophomore, The Kiss, 1929; served as medical corpsman & asst. chaplain W.W.II.
PICTURES INCLUDE: All Quiet on the Western Front, Common Clay, East is West, Doorway to Hell, Okay America, State Fair, Dr. Kildare series; (dir.) Hearts of Bondage, Dark Mirror, Unfaithful, Johnny Belinda, The Capture, New Mexico, No Escape, Donovan's Brain, The Carpetbaggers, Advise and Consent, Altars to the East (dir.-nar. star-prod.), Last Generation, 1971, Biscuit Eater, The Man, Battle for the Planet of the Apes, Battlestar Galactica.
TELEVISION: Hawaii Five-O (pilot), Earth II, She Waits, The Man, The Biscuit Eater, The Stranger, The Questor Tapes, Heatwaves, Frances Gary Powers, The End of the World, Salem's Lot, Of Mice and Men, Under Siege.

AZNAVOUR, CHARLES: Singer, Songwriter, Actor. b. Paris, France, May 22, 1924. r.n. Shahnour Varenagh Aznavourian. Studied dance and drama as a child and was performing at the age of 10. Encouraged by Edith Piaf, became one of France's leading performers by the mid-1950s and an international concert star by the 1970s. Has also composed music for film.
PICTURES: Adieu Cherie (1947), C'est arrive a 36 Chandelles, Les Dragueurs, Shoot the Piano Player; Le testament d'Orphee, Le Passage du Rhin, Un taxi pour Tobrouk, Horace 62, Tempo di Roma, Les Quatres Verites; Le Rat'd Amerique; Pourquoi Paris?; Paris in August; Candy; The Adventurers; And Then There Were None; The Twist; Sky Riders; Ciao, Les Mees; The Tin Drum; The Magic Mountain; the Hatter's Ghosts; What Makes David Run?; Edith and Marcel (lyrics); Long Live Life!

AZZATO, ANTHONY: Executive. b. New York, NY, Oct. 7, 1912. e. Fordham U., City Coll. of New York. Production supervisor, film editor, director, documentary and comm. films, 1938–48; Sound Masters, Inc.; U.S. Army Signal Corps, 1942–46; film editor, Paramount, 1932–42; asst'd director of film programs, WPIX, 1948; also film program consultant, KLAC, Los Angeles; dir. of station relations, National Telefilm Assoc., 1956; v.p., Swan & Mason Adv., 1961; v.p., Sales, Teledynamics Corp., v.p. Teledynamics Corp.

B

BABCOCK, DWIGHT V.: Writer. b. Ida Grove, IA, Feb. 19, 1909. e. Modesto Jr. Coll. Author short stories, novelist. First screenplay at Universal, 1943. 26 screen credits since at various studios. TV, freelance, includes 100 produced teleplays; co-author, Chautauqua.

BABENCO, HECTOR: Director. b. Buenos Aires, Argentina, Feb. 7, 1946. Early years spent in Mar del Plata. Left home at 17 and traveled throughout European capitals for 8 years working as a writer, house-painter, salesman, and, in Rome, as an extra at Cinecitta. Moved to Sao Paulo, Brazil where he made several short documentaries. First feature film, Rei Da Noite (1976).
PICTURES: Rei Da Noite, Lucio Flavio—Passageiro Da Agonia, Pixote (NY and LA Critics Awards, best foreign film), Kiss of the Spider Woman, Ironweed, Besame Mucho (prod. only).

BACALL, LAUREN: Actress. b. New York, NY, Sept. 16, 1924. e. American Acad. Dram. Arts. m. late Humphrey Bogart, actor. Fashion model; on stage, plays include: Johnny Two-by-Four, Franklin Street; m.p. debut in To Have and Have Not, 1944.
BROADWAY: Cactus Flower, Goodbye Charlie, Applause (Tony Award, best actress in musical), Woman of the Year, Sweet Bird of Youth (London).
PICTURES INCLUDE: Big Sleep, Confidential Agent, Dark Passage, Key Largo, Young Man with a Horn, Bright Leaf, How to Marry a Millionaire, Woman's World, Cobweb, Blood Alley, Written on the Wind, Designing Women, Flame over India, Shock Treatment, Gift of Love, Sex and the Single Girl, Harper, Murder on the Orient Express, The Shootist, Health, The Fan, Appointment with Death, Mr. North, The Tree of Hands.
TELEVISION: Petrified Forest, Applause, Perfect Gentlemen, Bacall on Bogart.

BACH, CATHERINE: Actress. b. Warren, Ohio, March 1, 1954.
PICTURES: The Midnight Man; Thunderbolt and Lightfoot;
Hustle; Cannonball Run II; Tunnels; Music City Blues.
TELEVISION: Series: The Dukes of Hazzard (1979–85);
The Dukes (cartoon, voice); guest on many specials; Movies:
Matt Helm; Strange New World, Murder in Peyton Place;
White Water Rebels.

BACHARACH, BURT: Composer-Conductor-Arranger. b. Kansas
City, MO, May 12, 1928. e. McGraw U., Mannes Sch. of
Music, Music Acad. of the West. Studied with composers
Darius Milhaud, Henry Cowell, and Bohuslav Martinu. Has
conducted for Marlene Dietrich, Vic Damone. As a performer
albums include: Burt Bacharach; Futures, Man! His Songs,
Books: The Bacharach-David Song Book (1978).
THEATER: Promises, Promises (Tony Award, best score,
1969).
PICTURES INCLUDE: The Man Who Shot Liberty Valance,
Wives and Lovers, Send Me No Flowers, A House is Not a
Home, What's Been Sleeping in My Bed?, What's New
Pussycat?, Casino Royale (Academy Award), The April Fools,
Promise Her Anything, Alfie (Oscar), Butch Cassidy and the
Sundance Kid (Academy Award, best song), Lost Horizon,
Arthur, Baby Boom.
TELEVISION: Burt Bacharach Special.

BACK, LEON B.: Exhibitor. b. Philadelphia, PA, Oct. 23, 1912. e.
Johns Hopkins U., B.E., 1932; U. of Baltimore, LL.B., 1933.
Entered m.p. ind. as mgr. for Rome Theatres, Baltimore,
Md., 1934; booker, ass't buyer, 1936; ass't to gen. mgr. 1939;
U.S. Navy 1944–46; v.p., gen. mgr., Rome Theatres, 1946;
Allied MPTO of Md. 1952–55; nat'l dir. Allied States, 1952–55;
nat'l secy. 1954; Pres. NATO of Maryland 1969–80; Pres.
USO Council, Greater Baltimore 1969–75; Chairman, board
of trustees, Employees Benefit Trust for Health & Welfare
Council of Central Maryland, 1970–79.

BACKE, JOHN DAVID: Executive. b. Akron, OH, July 5, 1932. e.
Miami U., B.S., 1954; Xavier U., M.B.A., 1961. Various
managerial positions in engineering, financing and marketing
functions, Gen. Electric Co., 1957–66; v.p., dir. mktg. Silver
Burdett Co., div. Gen. Learning Corp., 1969; pres., chief exec.
officer, 1969–73; pres. CBS Pub. Group, 1973–76; v.p., dir.,
CBS, Inc., 1973–76; pres., chief exec. officer, mem., fin.
comm., dir., 1976–80; now chm., Tomorrow Entertainment,
Inc., and chm., The Backe Group., Inc.
PICTURES: A Killing Affair.

BACKUS, JIM: Actor. b. Cleveland, OH, Feb 25, 1913. e. American
Acad. of Dram. Arts. Began in stock & vaudeville; radio
announcer; radio actor on Ilum on Stage in Hitch Your
Wagon; m.p. debut in Easy Living, Abner, Alan Young show &
own shows.
PICTURES INCLUDE: Half Angel, His Kind of Woman,
Bright Victory, Hollywood Story, Man with a Cloak, Iron Man,
Here Come the Nelsons, I'll See You in My Dreams,
Deadline, U.S.A., Androcles and the Lion, Don't Bother to
Knock, Pat and Mike, Above and Beyond, I Love Melvin,
Angel Face, Geraldine, Human Jundle, Francis in the Navy,
Rebel Without a Cause, Square Jungle, Meet Me in Las
Vegas, The Wonderful World of the Brothers Grimm, Critics
Choice, Six Loves, Boys' Night Out, The Horizontal Lieuten-
ant, Zoto!, Hello Down There, Pete's Dragon.
TELEVISION: I Married Joan, Gilligan's Island.
RECORDINGS: Delicious, Cave Man.
BOOKS: Rocks on the Roof, Back to Backus, What Are
You Doing After the Orgy?, Forgive Us Our Digressions (with
wife Henny).

BACON, KEVIN: Actor. b. Philadelphia, PA, July 8, 1958. Studied
at Manning U. Actor's Theatre. Apprentice at Circle-in-the-
Square in N.Y. Bdwy. debut in Slab Boys with Sean Penn.
Film debut in National Lampoon's Animal House, 1976.
THEATER: Off-Bdway debut: Getting Out, Album, Forty
Deuce, (Obie Award), Poor Little Lambs, Flux, Slab Boys,
Loot.
PICTURES: Friday the 13th, Hero at Large, Only When I
Laugh, Diner, Footloose, Quicksilver, Rites of Summer,
Planes, Trains & Automobiles, White Water Summer, Forty
Deuce, She's Having A Baby, End of the Line, Criminal Law,
The Big Picture, The Sixth Family.
TELEVISION: Movies: The Gift, Enormous Changes at the
Last Minute, The Demon Murder Case, Mr. Roberts, Lemon
Sky. Series: Search for Tommorrow, Guiding Light.

BADHAM, JOHN: Director. b. Eng. 1939, raised in Alabama. e.
Yale U., B.A.; Yale Drama School, M.F.A. Landed first job at
Universal Studio mailroom; later was Universal tour guide, a
casting dir. and assoc. prod. to William Sackheim. Made film
trailers and TV episodes. Twice nominated for Emmy Awards
for TV movies. First theatrical film: The Bingo Long Travelling
All-Stars and Motor Kings (1976).
PICTURES: Saturday Night Fever, Dracula, Whose Life Is
It Anyway?, Blue Thunder, War Games, Short Circuit, Stakeout (also exec. prod.), A Message From Salazar (co-exec.
prod.).

TELEVISION: The Law, Isn't It Shocking?, The Senator
Reflections of Murder, The Impatient Heart, The Gun.

BAER, JOHN G.: Executive, Engineer. b. New York, NY, May 8,
1934. e. U. of Tennessee, Chattanooga, B.S., physics, 1955.
Joined Bausch and Lomb, Inc. as optical and mechanical
engineer, 1957–67; director of research and development,
20th Century-Fox, New York 1967–72; sales/engineering,
Century Projector Corp., named pres. & chief exec. officer,
Jan. 1, 1975.
MEMBER: Optical Society of America; Society of American
Magicians; Intl. Brotherhood of Magicians; Magic Circle
(London); 25–30 Club (honorary). Fellow of SMPTE and dir.
Theatre Equip. Assn. Chm., PH-22 (motion picture) American
Natl. Standards Institute. U.S. delegate to Intl. Standards
Organization. Elected mayor West Windsor Township, NJ,
1977.

BAILEY, JOHN: Cinematographer. b. Missouri, August 10, 1942.
m. film editor Carol Littleton. e. U. of Santa Clara, Loyola U.,
U.S.C., U. of Vienna. Lecturer, American Film Institute, 1982
and 84.
PICTURES: Premonition (1972); End of August; Legacy;
Welcome to L.A.; The Mafu Cage; Boulevard Nights; Ameri-
can Gigolo; Ordinary People; Honky Tonk Freeway; Conti-
nental Divide; That Championship Season; Without a Trace; The Big Chill; Racing With the Moon; The
Pope of Greenwich Village; Mishima: A Life in Four Chapters:
Silverado; Crossroads; Brighton Beach Memoirs; Light of
Day; Swimming to Cambodia; Tough Guys Don't Dance;
Vibes; The Accidental Tourist.
TELEVISION: Battered; City in Fear.

BAILEY, JOSEPH W.: Attorney, Producer. b. Columbia City, IN,
Dec. 13, 1910. e. U. of Chicago, PHB, 1928–31, U. of Chicago
Law Sch., J.D., 1931–34. Practicing atty. at law, Chicago, Oct.
1934–June 1940; with Louis G. Cowan to Apr. 1942; U.S.
Navy 1942–46; v.p. & treas., Louis G. Cowan, 1946–49; mgr.,
radio-TV dept., Grey Adv. Agency, 1949; exec. prod., Robert
Montgomery Show & mgr., John Gibbs literary & talent
agency, 1950–57; prod. v.p. Ziv-United Artists, Inc. 1957–61.
Resigned June 1961 to become partner in firm, Bronstein,
Van Veen & Bailey; in practice of law specializing in allied
field of TV, motion pictures and the theatre.

BAILEY, PEARL: Entertainer. b. Newport News, VA, March 29,
1918. m. drummer Louis Bellson, Jr. e. Philadelphia and
Washington, DC. Career started when 15 years old, winner of
amateur stage contest; toured mining towns of Pennsylvania
as dancer; dancer and singer in vaudeville with Noble Sissle's
band; stage acting debut in St. Louis Woman (won Dona-
ldson Award, best newcomer of 1946); many night club
appearances and TV shows; screen debut 1947, Variety Girl.
PLAYS INCLUDE: Arms and the Girl, Bless You All, House
of Flowers, Hello Dolly.
PICTURES INCLUDE: Carmen Jones, Isn't It Romantic,
That Certain Feeling, St. Louis Blues, Porgy and Bess, All the
Fine Young Cannibals, The Landlord, Last Generation,
Norman, Is That You?, The Fox and the Hound (voice of Big
Mama).
TELEVISION: Trauma Center, Silver Spoons, An American
Portrait, Cindy Eller, The Pearl Bailey Show, Pearl Bailey and
Carol Channing on Broadway, One More Time, Member of
the Wedding (1982).

BAILEY, ROBIN: Actor. b. Hucknail (Nottingham), Eng., Oct. 5,
1919. e. Henry Mellish School, Nottingham.
STAGE: Barrets of Wimpole Street, Theatre Royal, Not-
tingham, 1938. Screen debut, School for Secrets, 1946.
PICTURES INCLUDE: Private Angelo, Portrait of Clare, His
Excellency, Gift Horse, Folly to Be Wise, Single Handed,
Sailor of the King, The Young Lovers, For Better, For Worse,
Catch Us If You Can, The Whisperers, Spy with a Cold Nose,
You Only Live Twice, The Eliminator, Blind Terror, Down by
the Riverside, Nightmare Rally, The Four Feathers, Jane and
the Lost City.
TELEVISION: Olive Latimer's Husband, Seven Deadly
Sins, The Power Game, Public Eye, Person to Person,
Troubleshooters, Armchair Theatre, Split Level, The New-
comers, Discharge of Trooper Lusby, Brett, Owen M.D.,
Solidarity, General Hospital, Murder Must Advertise, Vienna
1900, Justice, The Pallisers, The Couch, Way of the World,
Upstairs, Downstairs, Walk with Destiny, North and South, A
Legacy, The Velvet Glove, Crown Court, Took and Co., The
Good Companions, Cupid's Darts, Sorry, I'm a Stranger Here
Myself, Call My Bluff, Jane, Potter, Tales from a Long Room,
Sharing Time, Bleak House, Charters and Caldicott, Looks
Familiar, On Stage, Rumpole of the Bailey.

BAIO, SCOTT: Actor. b. New York, NY, Sept. 22, 1961. Started
career at 9 doing commercials and voice-overs.
PICTURES: Bugsy Malone, Skatetown USA, Foxes,
Zapped!
TELEVISION: Blansky's Beauties (series), Luke Was
There, Muggsy, Happy Days, Who's Watching the Kids?
(series), We're Moving (series), The Boy Who Drank Too

Much, Stoned, Joanie Loves Chachi, Charles in Charge (series), How to Be a Man. Movies: Senior Trip, Alice in Wonderland, The Truth about Alex.

BAKER, BLANCHE: Actress. r.n. Blanche Garfein. b. New York, NY, Dec. 20, 1956. Daughter of actress Carroll Baker and dir. Jack Garfein. e. Wellesley, Coll., studied acting with Uta Hagen. Acting debut, White Marriage, Yale Repertory Co. (1978), Regional Theater. Bdwy. debut in Lolita (1981).
PICTURES: The Seduction of Joe Tynan (debut, 1978), French Postcards, Raw Deal, Cold Feet, Sixteen Candles, Bum Rap.
TELEVISION: The Holocaust (Emmy Award, supp. actress, 1978), Mary and Joseph, The Day the Bubble Burst, Romeo and Juliet, The Awakening of Candra.

BAKER, CARROLL: Actress. b. Johnstown, PA, May 28, 1931. e. schools there and St. Petersburg (FL) Junior Coll. Career started as dancer in night clubs. Actors' Studio N.Y. Stage debut: Escapade. Then, All Summer Long; screen debut: Easy to Love, Autobiography: Baby Doll.
PICTURES INCLUDE: Giant, Baby Doll, But Not for Me, The Miracle, Bridge to the Sun, Something Wild, How the West Was Won, The Carpetbaggers, Station Six Sahara, Sylvia, Cheyenne Autumn, Mister Moses, Harlow, The Sweet Body of Deborah, Paranoia, Andy Warhol's Bad, Watcher in the Woods, Ironweed, Star 80, Native Son, The Secret Diary of Sigmund Freud.
TELEVISION: Hitler's S.S.: Portrait in Evil, On Fire.

BAKER, DON: Theatre Executive. b. St. Louis, MO, Dec. 16, 1931. e. St. Louis U. V.P., adv.-prom., Loews Theatres, N.Y. Member NATO, bd. dir. & nat'l chm. adv. comm., 1972–present; mem. bd. of dir., Will Rogers Memorial Fund, 1974; pub. chm., Variety Clubs Intl. in Western Hemisphere; Commissioner, NJ Film & TV Development Commission.

BAKER, GEORGE: Actor, Writer. b. Varna, Bulgaria, April 1, 1931. e. Lancing College, Sussex. Stage debut Deal Repertory Theatre, 1946. Film debut The Intruder, 1953.
PICTURES INCLUDE: Dam Busters, Ship That Died of Shame, Woman for Joe, Extra Day, Feminine Touch, A Hill in Korea, No Time for Tears, These Dangerous Years, Tread Softly Stranger, Lancelot and Guinevere, Curse of the Fly, Mister Ten Per Cent, Goodbye Mr. Chips, Justine, The Executioners, On Her Majesty's Secret Service, A Warm December, The Fire Fighters, The Spy Who Loved Me, Thirty-nine Steps, A Nightingale Sang in Berkeley Square, Hopscotch, North Sea Hijack.
TELEVISION: Fan Show, Ron Raudell's programme 1956, Guinea Pig, Death of a Salesman, The Last Troubadour, The Square Ring, Nick of the River, Mary Stuart, Probation Officers, Far Away Music, It Happened Like This, Boule de Suif, Maigret, Zero One, Rupert Henzau, Miss Memory, Any Other Business, The Navigators, Common Ground, Alice, The Queen and Jackson, The Big Man Coughed and Died, Up and Down, Call My Bluff, The Baron, St. Patrick, Love Life, Seven Deadly Virtues, The Prisoner, The Sex Games, Z Cars, Paul Temple, Candida, Fenn Street, Man Outside, The Persuaders, Main Chance, Ministry of Fear, Voyage in the Dark, Dial M for Murder, Zodiac, The Survivors, I, Claudius, Print Out, Goodbye, Darling, Chinese Detective, Triangle, Minder, Hart to Hart, Goodbye Mr. Chips, Woman of Substance. Writer: The Fatal Spring, Imaginary Friends, The Bird Fancier, Robin of Sherwood, Time after Time, If Tomorrow Comes, Coast to Coast, Dead Head, The Canterville Ghost, Room at the Bottom.
WRITER: The Fatal Spring, Imaginary Friends, Going for Broke, The Marches of Wales, The Hopkins, Just a Hunch.

BAKER, J. EDWIN: Executive. b. Detroit, MI, June 27, 1914. e. St. John's Coll. m. Marjorie R. Baker, actress. In 1935 produced Asylum of Horrors, stage show featuring the Frankenstein monster (in person), which played for over 40 years. Known professionally as Dr. Silkini. In 1960 organized Intl. Artists Pictures, of which he is pres., to produce films.
PICTURES INCLUDE: Phycoscope, Magic Land of Mother Goose, Santa Visits Mother Goose Land, Vampire's Coffin, Teenage Tramp, Aztec Mummy.

BAKER, JOE DON: Actor. b. Groesbeck, TX, Feb. 12, 1936. Began career on N.Y. stage, in Marathon 33 and Blues for Mr. Charlie. Film debut, Cool Hand Luke, 1967.
PICTURES INCLUDE: Guns of the Magnificent Seven, Adam at Six A.M., The Wild Rovers, Welcome Home, Soldier Boys, Junior Bonner, Walking Tall, Charley Varrick, The Outfit, Golden Needles, Mitchell, Framed, Wacko, The Natural, Fletch, Getting Even, The Living Daylights, The Killing Time, Leonard, Part 6, Criminal Law.
TELEVISION: The Abduction of Kari Swenson, Mongo's Back in Town, Power, To Kill a Cop, Eisheid (series).

BAKER, ROBERT H.: Management consultant. b. Springfield, OH, Oct. 14, 1943. e. Kent State U.A., 1965 (broadcasting); Michigan State U. M.A. 1966 (TV/radio management). Disc jockey, newsman, anchor at various Ohio and Mich. AM and

FM stations 1960–66. Storer Broadcasting Co.: local-regional acct. exec WSPD-TV, 1966–69; Storer TV Sales, national rep, 1969–72; WSPD-TV national sales mgr. 1972–74 and gen. sales mgr 1974–75. Owner-gen. mgr. WBIS-AM (Bristol, CT), 1975–76. Sales mgr WKDA-TV Pittsburgh 1976–79; Television Bureau of Advertising markting sales exec 1979– 81; v.p. local sales 1981–86; exec. v.p. operations 1986–88. President, Management Communications Consultants, Nashville, 1988–present. Mem.: National Speakers Assn. (and NY Metro chap.) 1988–present.

BAKER, ROBERT S.: Producer. b. London, 1916. Entered industry 1937 as assistant director. 1939–46: Army Film Unit. Produced 50 films including Crossplot, Sea of Sand.
TELEVISION: Produced: The Saint (1962–69), Gideon's Way. Directed: The Treasure of Monte Cristo, Hellfire Club, The Siege of Sidney Street, Jack the Ripper. Producer: The Persuaders, 1976–78: Return of the Saint. Devised: Return to Treasure Island. Executive Producer: The Saint in Manhattan.

BAKER, ROY: Producer, Director. b. London. e. Lycée Corneille, Rouen; City of London School. Ass't dir. with Gainsborough 1934–40; served in Army 1940–46.
PICTURES INCLUDE: Operation Disaster, Don't Bother to Knock, Inferno, One That Got Away, A Night to Remember, The Singer Not the Song, Flame in the Streets, Quartermass and the Pit, The Anniversary, Vampire Lovers, Dr. Jekyll and Mr. Hyde, Asylum (Paris Grand Prize), Seven Golden Vampires.
TELEVISION: The Human Jungle, The Saint, Gideon's Way, The Baron, The Avengers, The Champions, Department S., The Persuaders, Danger UXB, Minder.

BAKER, DR. WILLIAM F.: Executive. b. 1944. e. Case Western Reserve U., B.A., M.A., Ph.D. Began broadcasting career in Cleveland while still a student. Joined Scripps-Howard Broadcasting, 1971. Joined Group W as v.p. and general mgr., WJZ-TV, 1978; served as pres. and CEO, Group W Productions; pres. of Group W. Television, 1979; chmn., Group W Satellite Communications, 1981; 1983, carried Explorers Club flag to top of world, becoming one of few in history to visit both North and South Poles; April 1987, appointed pres. and CEO, WNET/Thirteen, N.Y. PBS station.

BAKSHI, RALPH: Animator-Writer-Director. b. New York, NY. Began career at Terrytoons at age 21. Created original "Deputy Dawg" and "Mighty Heroes."
PICTURES: Fritz the Cat, Heavy Traffic, Coonskin, Wizards, The Lord of the Rings, Hey, Good Lookin', American Pop, Fire and Ice.
TELEVISION: creator of Mighty Mouse: The New Adventures.

BALA, JOHN: Executive. e. Yale U., Harvard U., U. of California at L.A. Graduate Sch., management. After schooling joined Rand Corp. to work in public-policy research for 4 years; then to 20th Fox as mgr. of financial analysis in corporate development dept. 1982–83, dir. of finance research for Times-Mirror Videotex Services. Dec. 1983, joined 20th-Fox as v.p. of worldwide mkt. research.

BALABAN, A. J.: Theatre executive. b. Chicago, IL, April 18, 1889. In 1907 entered m.p. exhibition as operator of M.s. Nickelodeon Kedzie Theatre, Chicago; owned Movie Inn, restaurant with booths named for stars 1915; co-founder Balaban & Katz Corp. 1917; upon affiliation of B & K with Paramount named dir. of entertainment, then vice-pres.; abroad 9 yrs. returned to U.S. as circuit exhibitor 1935; gen. mgr. Roxy Theatre, N.Y., 1942; res. Jan 1, 1952, now consultant for 3 years; holds interest in Esquire, Carnegie theat., Chicago, with Harry and Elmer, brothers. Member: M.P. Pioneers, Jewish Theatrical Guild, French-American Club.

BALABAN, BOB: Actor. b. Chicago, IL, Aug. 16, 1945. Began working with Second City troupe while still in high school. Attended Colgate U. and New York U. while appearing on Broadway in Plaza Suite.
PICTURES: Catch 22, Midnight Cowboy, Girlfriends, Close Encounters of the Third Kind, Report to the Commissioner, Altered States, Prince of the City, Absence of Malice, Whose Life Is It Anyway?, 2010, End of the Line, Dead-Bang, Parents.
STAGE: You're a Good Man, Charlie Brown, The Inspector General, Who Wants to Be the Lone Ranger?, The Basic Training of Pavlo Hummel, The Children, The White House Murder Case, Some of My Best Friends, The Three Sisters.
TELEVISION: Amazing Stories.

BALABAN, ELMER: President, H. & E. Balaban Corp., Chicago, IL. e. U. of Pennsylvania, 1931. With Paramount Publix 1931; Balaban & Katz, 1933; then H. & E. Balaban Corp. Pres., Plains Television; interest in WTVO, Rockford, IL; interest in WHNB, Hartford, Conn. and numerous cable-TV systems.

BALDWIN, ALEC: Actor. b. Amityville, NY, April 3, 1958. e. George Washington U., NYU. Trained at Lee Strasberg

Theatre Inst. Started career in daytime TV on The Doctors while appearing on stage in A Midsummer Night's Dream. Moved to L.A. where cast in TV pilots, series and movies.
THEATER: Bdwy: The Wager, Summertree, A Life in the Theatre (Hartman), Study in Scarlet (Williamstown), Loot (Theatre World Award, 1986), Serious Money.
PICTURES: Forever Lulu (debut, 1986); She's Having a Baby; Beetle Juice, Married to the Mob, Working Girl, Talk Radio, Next of Kin.
TELEVISION: Knots Landing (series), Dress Gray (movie), The Alamo: 13 Days to Glory (movie).

BALIN, INA: Actress. b. Brooklyn, NY, Nov. 12, 1957. e. Forest Hills H.S.; parttime drama, psychology courses, New York U. Comm. model, salesgirl, receptionist. Prof. debut, Perry Como Show. Off-Bway, summer stock, Compulsion, Majority of One. N.Y. Stage. Film debut, The Black Orchid. TV and Broadway. Toured Europe 1961. Int'l Star of Tomorrow. Hollywood Foreign Press Golden Globe Award.
PICTURES INCLUDE: From the Terrace, Young Doctors, The Comancheros, The Greatest Story Ever Told, The Patsy, Charro!, The Projectionist.
TELEVISION: American Heritage, Stoney Burke, Adventures in Paradise, Kraft Theatre, The Lieutenant, Bonanza, The Loner, Voyage to the Bottom of the Sea, Run for Your Life, The Children of An Lac, The Hostage Flight.

BALL, LUCILLE: Actress. b. Jamestown, NY, Aug. 6, 1911. e. Chautauqua Inst. Music, John Murray Anderson Dram. School, p. Desiree Ball, concert pianist. Hattie Carnegie model, stage debut in Rio Rita; on Broadway in Hey Diddle, Diddle, Dream Girl, Wildcat; m.p. debut in Roman Scandals, 1933; entertained in Hollywood Canteen, W.W.II; Voted most promising star in Motion Picture Daily's TV poll, 1951; best performer, 1952; best comedy team, 1954; best comedienne 1952, 54–55, 57; pres. Desilu Prod., Inc.; exec. prod., The Lucy Show; pres. Lucille Ball Prods., 1967.
PICTURES INCLUDE: Roberta, Stage Door, Big Street, Du Barry Was a Lady, Easy to Wed, Ziegfeld Follies, Lured, Sorrowful Jones, Easy Living, Miss Grant Takes Richmond, Fuller Brush Girl, Fancy Pants, Magic Carpet, Long Long Trailer, Forever Darling, Facts of Life, Critics Choice, Yours, Mine and Ours, Mame.
TELEVISION: I Love Lucy, The Lucy Show, Here's Lucy, Movie: Stone Pillow.

BALLARD, CARROLL: Director. b. Los Angeles, Oct. 14, 1937. e. U. of California at L.A.
PICTURES: The Black Stallion; Never Cry Wolf; The Nutcracker.

BALLHAUS, MICHAEL: Cinematographer. b. Berlin, Germany, August 5, 1935.
PICTURES: Deine Zartlichkeiten; Two of Us; Whity; Beware of a Holy Whore; Tschetan; The Indian Boy; The Bitter Tears of Petra von Kant; Fox and his Friends; Mother Kusters Goes to Heaven; Summer Guests; Satan's Brew; I Only Want You To Love Me; Adolf and Marlene; Chinese Roulette; Bolweiser; Willie and the Chinese Cat; Women in New York; Despair; The Marriage of Maria Braun; Germany in Autumn; German Spring; The Uprising; Big and Little; Malou; Looping; Baby, It's You; Friends and Husbands; Dear Mr. Wonderful; Magic Mountain; Edith's Diary; Aus der Familie der Panzereschen; The Autograph; Heart Breakers; Old Enough, Reckless; After Hours; Under the Cherry Moon; The Color of Money; Sheer Madness; Baja Oklahoma; The House on Carroll Street, Broadcast News, The Last Temptation of Christ, Working Girl, Scoundrels.

BALSAM, MARTIN: Actor. b. New York, NY, Nov. 4, 1919. e. New School for Social Research. NY stage debut Ghost for Sale, 1941.
THEATER: Lamp at Midnight, The Wanhope Building, High Tor, A Sound of Hunting, Macbeth, Sundown Beach, The Closing Door, You Know I Can't Hear You When the Water's Running (Tony Award, 1967), Cold Storage (Obie Award).
PICTURES INCLUDE: On the Waterfront, (1954). Twelve Angry Men, Time Limit, Marjorie Morningstar, Al Capone, Middle of the Night, Psycho, Ada, Breakfast at Tiffany's, Cape Fear, Who's Been Sleeping in My Bed?, The Carpetbaggers, Youngblood Hawke, Seven Days in May, Harlow, The Bedford Incident, A Thousand Clowns (Academy Award), After the Fox, Hombre, 2001: A Space Odyssey, Trilogy, Catch 22, Little Big Man; Tora, Tora, Tora; The Anderson Tapes, The Stone Killer, Summer Wishes, Winter Dreams, The Taking of Pelham One Two Three, Murder on the Orient Express, Mitchell, All The President's Men, Two-Minute Warning, The Sentinel, Silver Bears, Cuba, The Goodbye People, St. Elmo's Fire, Death Wish, The Delta Force, Whatever It Takes, Private Investigations, Once Again.
TELEVISION: Actors Studio Theatre, US Steel Hour, Mr. Peepers, Alfred Hitchcock Presents, Arrest and Trial, Queenie, Archie Bunker's Place (series regular), Little Gloria, Happy at Last, Cold Storage, Space, Murder in Space, Raid on Entebbe, Grown Ups, Glitter, Kids Like These, The Child Saver.

BALTER, ALLAN: Executive. b. Detroit, MI, August 28, 1925. e. U. of Michigan, B.A. Asst. casting dept., 20th Century-Fox Film Corp. 1950–53; mgr., Encino theatre, 1953–54; asst. casting dept., MGM Studios, 1954–55; editor, Action mag., 20th Century-Fox house-organ 1955–56; trade planter, 20th Century-Fox publicity, 1956–57; unit publicist, Bryna Prods. (UA) 1957–58; unit publicist, 20th Century-Fox, 1958–62; dir. of pub., adv., Daystar Prods.

BANCROFT, ANNE: Actress. r.n. Anne Italiano; b. New York, NY, Sept. 17, 1931. m. director Mel Brooks. e. American Acad. of Dramatic Arts. Acting debut on TV, Studio One; many TV shows; film debut, Don't Bother to Knock.
PICTURES INCLUDE: Tonight We Sing, Treasure of the Golden Condor, Kid from Left Field, Demetrius and the Gladiators, Gorilla at Large, The Raid, Life in the Balance, New York Confidential, The Brass Ring, Naked Street, Last Frontier, Girl in the Black Stockings, Restless Breed, The Miracle Worker (Academy Award), The Pumpkin Eater, Slender Thread, The Graduate, Young Winston, The Prisoner of Second Avenue, The Hindenburg, The Turning Point, Fatso (also dir. & s.p.), The Elephant Man, To Be or Not to Be, Garbo Talks, Agnes of God, 'night Mother, 84 Charing Cross Road, Torch Song Trilogy, Bert Rigby You're a Fool.
PLAYS: Two For the Seasaw, The Miracle Worker, Mother Courage, The Devils, A Cry of Players, Golda.
TELEVISION: Mini-series: Jesus of Nazareth; Marco Polo; Specials: I'm Getting Married; Annie and the Hoods; Annie: The Woman and the Men in Her Life (dir., writer, star, Emmy Award, 1970).

BAND, ALBERT: Producer, Director. b. Paris, France, May 7, 1924. e. Lyceum Louis le Grand, won French-English Literature Prize 1938; entered film industry as cutter Pathe Lab.; prod. ass't to John Huston at MGM; first screen credit adaptation Red Badge of Courage novel; first direction, The Young Guns, Allied Artists; formed Maxim Productions, Inc., Sept. 1956; prod.-dir. Killer on the Wall for United Artists. 1958 prod.-dir. Face of Fire; 1962 dir. The Avenger; 1963 dir. Grand Canyon Massacre; 1965 prod.-dir. The Tramplers; 1966 prod. The Hellbenders. Recently formed Albert Band Intl. Prods., Inc.
PICTURES INCLUDE: The Young Guns, I Bury the Living, Face of Fire, A Minute to Pray, A Second to Die; Little Cigars, Dracula's Dog, She Came to the Valley, Metalstorm, The Destruction of Jared, Swordkill, Buy and Cell (exec. prod.), Troll, Terrorvision, Ghoulies II, Robojox.

BAND, CHARLES: Producer-Director. b. Los Angeles, CA, 1952. Son of Albert Band.
PICTURES: Crash; End of the World; Laserblast; Tourist Trap; The Alchemist; Parasite; MetalstormThe Destruction of Jared-Syn; Swordkill; Ghoulies; The Dungeonmaster; Future Cop; Re-Animator; I Eat Cannibals; Crawlspace; Troll; Elminators, Prison (exec. prod.), Deadly Weapon (exec. prod.), Ghoulies II (exec. prod.); Buy and Cell (exec. prod.), Catacombs (exec. prod.), Arena (exec. prod.), Pulse Pounders (prod.-dir.), Robojox (exec. prod.).

BANDY, MARY LEA: Director, Dept. of Film, Museum of Modern Art. b. Evanston, IL, June 16, 1943. e. Stanford U., B.A., 1965. Asst. editor, Harry Abrams and Museum of Modern Art. Administrator (1978–80) and since 1980 director, Dept. of Film, Museum of Modern Art. Editor of MOMA film publications includ.: Rediscovering French Film (1983). Member of Advisory Board, AFI's National Center for Preservation of Film and Video. Member of Film Advisory Comm., American Federation of Arts; Advisory Comm. on Film, Japan Society; member of Advisory Comm. NY State Motion Picture and Television Advisory Board. Co-president, National Alliance of Media Arts Center, 1986–87, 1987–88.

BANJERJEE, VICTOR: Actor. b. Calcutta, India. Was instrumental in forming the first Screen Extras Union in India, presently founding secretary. Won international recognition for A Passage to India (1985). Stage: Pirates of Penzance (at 5), An August Requiem (director, 1981), Desert Song, Godspell.
PICTURES: The Chess Players (debut). In India: Hullabaloo, Madhurban, Tanaya, Pratidan, Prarthana, Dui Prithvi, Kalyug, Arohan, Jaipur Junction (German), A Passage to India, The Home and the World, Hard to Be a God.
TELEVISION: Dadah Is Death.

BANNEN, IAN: Actor. b. Airdrie, Scotland, June 29, 1928. Early career Shakespeare Memorial Theatre (now RSC), Stratford-on-Avon. Film debut Battle Hell (1956).
STAGE: A View From the Bridge, The Iceman Cometh, Long Days Journey Into Night, Sergeant Musgrave's Dance. Royal Shakespeare Thea. Co. 1961–62. Toys in the Attic, Hamlet, As You Like It (with Vanessa Redgrave), Romeo and Juliet, Othello, The Knot, Devil's Disciple, The Iceman Cometh. Hedda Gabler. Translations (Drama Critics Award, 1981); Riverside Mermaid Theatres, 1983; Moon for the Misbegotten (London, Boston, Broadway).
PICTURES INCLUDE: Private's Progress, Rotten to the Core, Miracle in Soho, The Third Key, Behind the Mask, A Tale of Two Cities, The French Mistress, Carlton-Browne of

the F.O., Man in Cocked Hat, Macbeth, Station Six Sahara, Mister Moses, The Hill, Flight of the Phoenix, (nominated for AA), Sailor From Gibraltar, Penelope, Too Late the Hero, The Deserter, Jane Eyre, Fright, The Offence (BAFTA nomination), The Macintosh Man, Bite the Bullet, Watcher in the Woods, Eye of the Needle, Night Crossing, Gandhi, Gorky Park, Defense of the Realm, Lamb, Hope and Glory (BAFTA nomination), The Courier, On the Orient North, Circles in a Forest, The Match.
TELEVISION: Johnny Belinda, Jane Eyre, Terror From Within, Jesus of Nazareth, Tinker, Tailor, Soldier, Spy, Bookie, Dangerous Love.

BANNER, BOB: Producer, Director. b. Ennis, TX, Aug. 15, 1921. e. Southern Methodist U., B.A., 1939–43; Northwestern U., M.A., 1946–48. U.S. Naval Reserve 1943–46; faculty, Northwestern U., 1948–50; staff dir., NBC-TV in Chicago, 1949–50; dir., Garroway at Large, 1949–50; prod. & dir., Fred Waring Show, 1950–53; dir. Omnibus. Metropolitan Opera Prod., 1953; Nothing But the Best (prod. dir.), 1953; Omnibus, 1953–54; Dave Garroway Show, 1953–54; (prod. dir); Dinah Shore Show, 1954–57; exec. prod. Garry Moore Show; exec. prod. Candid Camera TV show; exec. prod., Carnegie Hall Salutes Jack Benny; exec. prod., Julie & Carol at Carnegie Hall; exec. prod., Carol & Co., 1963; Jimmy Dean Show, 1963–66; Calamity Jane, Once Upon A Mattress, 1964; The Entertainers, 1965; Carol × 2, 1966; Kraft Summer Music Hall, 1966, Carol & Co., Ice Follies, Carol Burnett Show, Peggy Fleming at Madison Square Garden, 1967; John Davidson at Notre Dame, Here's Peggy Fleming; Peggy Fleming at Sun Valley, The American West of John Ford; Love! Love! Love!—Hallmark Hall of Fame; To Europe with Love.
PICTURES INCLUDE: Mongo's Back in Town.
TELEVISION: Movies: Warning Shot, The Last Survivors, Journey From Darkness, My Sweet Charlie, Bud and Lou. Special: Peggy Fleming Visits the Soviet Union. Game Show: Almost Anything Goes. Specials: Perry Como's Lake Tahoe Holiday, Perry Como's Christmas In Mexico, Perry Como's Hawaiian Holiday, Perry Como's Spring In New Orleans. Daily Variety Series: Don Ho Show; Perry Como Las Vegas Style, Perry Como's Christmas in Austria, Jr. Almost Anything Goes, All-Star Anything Goes, Peggy Fleming and Holiday on Ice at Madison Square Garden; Julie Andrews, One Step Into Spring; Leapin' Lizards, It's Liberace; Perry Como's Easter By The Sea, Ford Motor Company's 75th Anniversary; Gift of Solid Gold; Specials starring Bob Hope, Julie Andrews, Andy Williams; Series: Solid Gold; Star Search; It's Showtime at the Apollo.

BAR, JACQUES JEAN LOUIS: Executive. Producer. b. Chateauroux, France, Sept. 12, 1921. e. Lycées Lakanal and Saint Louis, France. Formed Cinema-Theatre d'Avallon, 1944; Cite-Films S.A., 1947; Spira in assoc. with MGM, 1961; first Hollywood film, co-prod. Scratch A Thief, 1964; prod. 43 pictures in France, Spain, Italy, Switzerland, Japan and Brazil, 1948–64.
PICTURES INCLUDE: Where the Hot Wind Blows, Bridge to the Sun, Riffifi in Tokyo, A Very Private Affair, Swordsmen of Siena, Monkey in Winter, The Turfist, Any Number Can Win, The Day and the Hour, Joy House, Guns for San Sebastian.

BARBER, ARNOLD: Executive. b. London, England. Career in m.p. ind. started with RKO. Subsequently with AB-Pathe following war service until appointment with Warner-Pathe Dist. which led him through sales exec. positions until he headed company. Formed Sotia-Barber Distributors Ltd. in 1970. Now man. dir. Barber Intl. Films, Ltd.

BARBER, FRANCES: Actress. e. grad. studies in theatre, Cardiff U. Stage experience with fringe theaters including improvisational troupe Hull Truck Theatre Company, Glasgow Citizens and Tricycle Theatre (Killburn) before joining Royal Shakespeare Co. (Camille, Hamlet).
PICTURES: The Missionary, A Zed and Two Noughts, White City, Castaway, Prick Up Your Ears, Sammy and Rosie Get Laid, We Think the World of You.
TELEVISION: Jackie's Story; Home Sweet Home; Flame to the Phoenix; Reilly, Ace of Spies; Those Glory, Glory Days; Hard Feelings; Clem.

BARBERA, JOSEPH R.: Executive. b. New York, NY. e. New York U., American Institute of Banking. After schooling joined Irving Trust Co. in N.Y.; started submitting cartoon drawings to leading magazines selling one to Collier's. Left banking to seek career in cartooning. Joined Van Buren Associates as sketch artist, later going to work in animation dept. of MGM Studios. At MGM met William Hanna, who became his lifelong business associate. Made first animated short together in 1938, starting the famous Tom & Jerry series which they produced for 20 years. Left MGM in 1957 to form Hanna-Barbera Productions to make cartoons for TV. Series have included Yogi Bear, Huckleberry Hound, The Flintstones. Hanna-Barbera became a subsidiary of Taft Bdg. Co. in 1968 with both men operating studio under long-term agreements with Taft. Barbera was pres. until 1980. Company entered

theatrical production with Charlotte's Web in 1973. 1982: Heidi's Song.

BARBOUR, ALAN G.: Writer, Editor, Publisher. b. Oakland, CA, July 25, 1933. e. Rutgers U. m. Catherine Jean Callovini, actress, teacher, American Acad. of Dramatic Arts, American Mime Theatre. U.S. Army, worked as computer programmer. Formed Screen Facts Press in 1963, Screen Facts Magazine. Compiled, edited: The Serials of Republic, The Serials of Columbia, Great Serial Ads, The B Western, Serial Showcase, Hit the Saddle, The Wonderful World of B-Films, Days of Thrills and Adventure, Serial Quarterly, Serial Pictorial, Karloff—A Pictorial History, Errol Flynn—A Pictorial Biography, A Pictorial History of the Serial, A Thousand and One Delights, Cliffhanger, The Old-Time Radio Quiz Book. Direct Mktg. Div., RCA Records. Mgr., A & R, RCA Video Club.

BARBOUR, MALCOLM: Executive. b. London, England, May 3, 1934. e. Radley Coll., Oxford, England, Columbia Coll. At NBC was press info. asst., 1958–59; asst. magazine ed., 1959–62; assoc. mag. ed., 1962–64; sr. mag. ed., 1964–65; mgr. of magazine pub., National Broadcasting Co., 1965–67; pub. mgr., Buena Vista, 1967–68; Eastern story ed., Walt Disney Prod., 1968–69; dir. of adv. & pub. relations, Buena Vista, 1969.

BARDOT, BRIGITTE: Actress. b. Paris, France, Sept. 28, 1934. r.n. Camille Javal. e. Paris Conservatory. Model. Awarded French Legion of Honor, 1985. Active in the movement to preserve endangered animals. Auctioned her jewels and mementos from her film career, raising $500,000 to create an animal protection foundation, June 1987.
PICTURES INCLUDE: Le Trou Normand, Un Acte D'Amour, Helen of Troy, Le Fils De Caroline Cherie, Les Grandes Maneuvres, Doctor at Sea, En Effeuillant La Marguerite, The Bride Is Much Too Beautiful, Moonlight Jewelers, La Femme et Le Pantin, Will You Dance With Me, Manina, La Fille Sans Voiles, Si Versailles M'Etait Conte, Trahi, Futures Vedettes, La Lumiere D'En Face, Une Sacre Gamine, And God Created Woman, Le Parisienne, En Cas De Malheur, Love Is My Profession, Babette Goes to War, La Verite Contempt, A Very Private Affair, Two Weeks in September, Viva Maria, Shalako, Spirits of the Dead, Les Femmes, Les Novices, Boulevard du rhum, Les petroleuses, Don Juan, L'Historie tres bonne et tres joyeuse de Colinot troussechemise.

BARE, RICHARD L.: Producer, Director. b. Turlock, CA. Dir. for Warner: Smart Girls Don't Talk, Flaxy Martin, This Side of the Law, House across The Street, Return of Frontiersman; SDG Best Dir. TV award, 1959; author, The Film Director (Macmillan), 1971.
TELEVISION: 77 Sunset Strip, Maverick, 1956, So This is Hollywood (1955-NBC), The Islanders (1960), Dangerous Robin (1961), This Rebel Breed, Twilight Zone, Bus Stop (1962), Adventures in Paradise, The Virginian (1963), Kraft Theatre, Run For Your Life, Green Acres series (186 episodes-1969), Farraday and Son, 1974; Westwind (NBC) 1976.
PICTURES INCLUDE: Wrote, directed and produced: Wicked, Wicked, MGM, 1973; Story of Chang & Eng, City of Shame, Fox, Sudden Target.

BAREN, HARVEY M.: Executive. b. New York, NY, Nov. 25, 1931. e. State U. of New York. Served in U.S. Army, 1952–54; United Artists Corp., 1954–59 (contract dept., print dept., booker—N.Y. branch); asst. to general sls. mgr., Magna Pictures Corp., 1959–61; road show mgr., national sales coordinator, 20th Century-Fox, 1961–71; asst. general sales manager, Allied Artists Pictures, 1971–79; v.p., gen. sls. mgr., Nat'l. Screen Service, 1978–79; v.p., gen. sls. mgr., Cannon Pictures, 1979–80. 1980, pres. of Summit Feature Distributors; 1983, exec. V.P., dir., MGM/UA Classics; 1986, joined New Century/Vista as v.p., sls. admin.

BARENHOLTZ, BEN: Executive. b. Oct. 5, 1935. Whimsically describes ed. as Balcony U. Asst. manager: RKO Bushwick, Brooklyn, 1959–60. Manager: Village Theatre (Fillmore East), N.Y., 1966–68. Owner-operator: Elgin Cinema, 1968–72. President-owner: Libra Film Corp., 1982–84. Vice-president and partner: Circle Releasing, 1984–present.

BARI, LYNN: Actress. r.n. Marjorie Bitzer. b. Roanoke, VA, 1917. First Screen appearance as dancing girl in Dancing Lady (MGM). Became Fox contract player 1934.
PICTURES INCLUDES: Shock, Margie, Home Sweet Homicide, Nocturne, Amazing Mr. X, Kid from Cleveland, I'd Climb Highest Mountain, On the Loose, Sunny Side of the Street, Has Anybody Seen My Gal, I Dream of Jeanie, Francis Joins the WACs, AC Meet the Keystone Kops, Women of Pitcairn Island, Damn Citizen, Trauma.

BARISH, KEITH: Producer. b. Los Angeles, CA. Background in finance. 1984 formed partnership with Taft Broadcasting Co., Entertainment Div.
PICTURES: Endless Love (exec. prod.); Sophie's Choice (co-prod.); Kiss Me Goodbye (co-exec. prod.); Misunderstood (exec. prod.); 9½ Weeks (co-exec. prod.); Light of Day (co-prod.), The Running Man (co-exec. prod.), The Monster

Squad (co-exec. prod.), Ironweed (co-prod.), The Serpent and the Rainbow, Her Alibi, Hand-Carved Coffins.
TELEVISION: A Streetcar Named Desire (exec. prod.).

BARKER, ROBERT WILLIAM: TV host. b. Darrington, WA, Dec. 12. e. Springfield Central H.S., Drury Coll. News writer, announcer, disc jockey KTTS until 1949. News editor, staff announcer, Station WWPG; wife, Dorothy Jo. Emcee, Truth or Consequences, 1956. Pres. Bob Barker Prod., Inc., M.C. Miss USA Pageant, CBS-TV, since 1967, M.C. Miss Universe Pageant, CBS-TV since 1967, M.C. Rose Parade, since 1970. Prod.-M. C. Pillsbury Bakeoff, since 1970 CBS. Prod. Lucky Pair, syndicated, M.C. Price Is Right-CBS, 1972; Narrator, 500 Festival Parade, Indianapolis 1969–81.

BARKETT, STEVE: Actor, director, producer, film editor. b. Oklahoma City, OK, Jan. 1, 1950. Exhibited and scored over 52 feature length classic silent films prior to coming to Los Angeles in 1970. Executive in several nontheatrical releasing companies including Independent Film Associates. Est. Nautilus Film Co., 1978. Founded Capt. Nemo's Video (1985). Co-wrote and performed with Tricia Drake Schiotis, 42 episodes of Capt. Nemo's Video Review for radio (1987).
PICTURES INCLUDE: Actor: The Egyptians Are Coming, Corpsegrinders, Cruise Missile. Films as Actor, Director, Producer: The Movie People, Night Caller, The Aftermath. Actor-Director-Writer: Judgment Day. Actor-dir.-prod.-writer: The Journey Aftermath.

BARKIN, ELLEN: Actress. b. Bronx, NY, 1959. e. Hunter Coll.
PICTURES INCLUDE: Diner, Buckaroo Banzai, Harry and Son, Desert Bloom, The Big Easy, Siesta, Made in Heaven (unbilled), Sea of Love, Blood Money (aka Clinton and Nadine).
TELEVISION: Act of Vengeance, Parole, Terrible Joe Moran, Faerie Tale Theatre, Clinton and Nadine.

BARLOW, PHIL: Executive. Began career with National General Theatres in 1961 in Salt Lake City; later transferred to Los Angeles as Southern Calif. div. buyer. Worked as buyer for NGT and Syufy Theatres in San Francisco. Joined General Cinema Corp. in N.Y. as natl. coordinator of film. Served 10 years as v.p. with Edwards Theatre Circuit, being named sr. v.p. in January, 1985. Left to join Buena Vista Dist. Co. as v.p. & gen. sls. mgr. Promoted to senior v.p. & gen. sls. mgr., 1988.

BARNES, BILL: Producer, Manager. b. Wilson, NC, Jan 28, 1939. e. U. of North Carolina, Chapel Hill, B.A. Radio, TV, Motion Pictures. Casting dir. and story ed. for Otto Preminger 1962–1969; motion picture agent with IFA in 1970 and merged into Intl. Creative Management; joined Producer Circle Co., Jan. 1979 as v.p., creative affairs. Formed own personal mgt. co., 1983.

BARNETT, GABRIEL: Graduate U. of Southern California, 1925 with B.L.L., publisher of theatre programs and commercial film advertising. Established in 1938. Creator of the Barnett theatre clock. Now engaged in producing intermission music for motion picture theatres.

BARNHOLTZ, BARRY: Executive. b. St. Louis, MO, Oct. 12, 1945. e. California State U., Northridge; U. of Southern California; U. of California at L.A.; W.L.A.U. (studied law). Concert promotions in So. Calif. 1963–71; with Medallion TV as v.p. in chg. sls.; Barnholtz Organization, representing independent prod. cos. for feature films for cable; now sr. v.p. Vidmark, Inc.

BARON, MARK: Executive. Pub./mktg. career at Factors Etc., McFadden, Strauss & Irwin before joining Columbia Pictures as sr. exec. liaison to Coca-Cola Co., coordinating mktg. programs between parent co. and feature film div. Worked as dir. of pub./promo. on Annie and Gandhi. Left to go to Stone/Halinan Associates as exec. v.p., mktg./admin. 1985, formed own mktg./consulting firm specializing in independent film producers before joining Warner Bros. as v.p., pub., coordinating overall pub. & promo. efforts on specific WB film projects.

BARR, ANTHONY: Producer, Director, Actor. r.n. Morris Yaffe. b. St. Louis, MO, March 14, 1921. e. Washington U., B.S. 1942. Actor, asst. stage mgr., 1944–46; stage mgr., Katherine Dunham Dancers, 1946–47; teacher, actor, dir. in chg. Film Actors' Workshop, Professional Theatre Workshop, Hollywood; v.p. current prime time series, ABC-TV; v.p., current dramatic program production, CBS-TV; v.p., CBS Entertainment Prods.
BROADWAY: Jacobowsky and the Colonel, Winters' Tale, Embezzled Heaven.
PICTURES INCLUDE: (actor) People Against O'Hara, Border Incident, The Hollywood Story, The Mozart Story, (co-prod.) Dime with a Halo.
TELEVISION: (dir.) Art Linkletter's Houseparty, About Faces (ABC-TV), (assoc. dir.) Climax, Shower of Stars, (prod.) Climax, Summer Studio One, (assoc. prod. CBS-TV) Climax, Playhouse 90, Pursuit, G.E. Theatre, The Law and Mr. Jones, Four-Star.
BOOK: Acting for the Camera, 1982.

BARRAULT, MARIE-CHRISTINE: Actress. b. Paris, France, March 21, 1944.
PICTURES: My Night at Maud's; The Daydreamer; Lancelot of the Lake; The Aspern Papers; Les Intrus; La Famille Grossfeld; John Gluskstadt; Cousin Cousine; By the Tennis Courts; L'Etat Sauvage; Perceval; The Medusa Touch; Tout est a nous; Femme Entre Chien et Loup; Ma Cherie; Stardust Memories; Table for Five; Josephs Tochter; Eine Liebe in Deutschland; Les Mots Pour le Dire; Swann in Love; Grand Piano.

BARRETT, JAMES LEE: Screenwriter, Producer. b. Charlotte, NC, Nov. 19, 1929. e. Anderson Jr. Coll., Furman U., Pennsylvania State U., Art Students League. U.S. Marine Corps.
PICTURES INCLUDE: The D.I. (Marine Corps Combat Correspondents Award), The Greatest Story Ever Told, The Truth About Spring, Shenandoah, The Green Berets, Bandolero, The Undefeated, tick ... tick ... tick, The Cheyenne Social Club, Fools' Parade, Something Big, Smokey and the Bandit, Wild Horse Hank.
STAGE: Shenandoah (Tony Award, best musical book, 1974--75; Theatre Club annual award).
TELEVISION: The Awakening Land, Parts I and II (Certificate of Commendation, American Women in Radio and Television), Stubby Pringles' Christmas (Humanitas nomination), The Day Christ Died, Belle Starr, Angel City, Mayflower: The Pilgrim Experience, You Are the Jury, Big Bad John, The Defiant Ones, Stagecoach (Wrangler Award, National Cowboy Hall of Fame), Vengeance, Poker Alice, April Morning.
SERIES: Our House (creator).

BARRETT, RONA: News correspondent e. New York U. (communications major). Created the column, Rona Barrett's Young Hollywood, which led to featured column in 1960 in Motion Picture Magazine and a nationally syndicated column distributed to 125 newspapers by the North American Newspaper Alliance. Turned to TV; initial appearances, on ABC Owned Stations in 5 cities, providing two-minute reports for local newscasts. This resulted in a network morning program, co-hosted by Joanna Barnes, called Dateline Hollywood. In 1969 she created first daily syndicated TV news segment for Metromedia. 1975, became arts and entertainment editor for ABC's Good Morning America. 1980, joined NBC News. Then publisher and exec. editor, newsletter, The Rona Barrett Report. 1985, pres., Rona Barrett Enterprises, Inc., sr. corresp., Entertainment Tonight; Mutual Radio Network. 1988: creator of original novels for television, for NBC prods.

BARRIE, BARBARA: Actress. b. Chicago, IL, May 23, 1931. e. U. of TX, B.F.A., 1953. Trained for stage at Herbert Berghof Studio. NY stage debut, The Wooden Dish (1955). Film debut, Giant (1956).
THEATER: The Crucible; American Shakespeare Fest., Stratford, CT 1958–59; The Beaux Stratagem; The Taming of the Shrew; Conversations in the Dark; All's Well That Ends Well; Happily Never After; Horseman, Pass By; Company; The Selling of the President; The Prisoner of Second Avenue; The Killdeer; California Suite; Big and Little; Isn't It Romantic.
PICTURES: The Caretakers; One Potato, Two Potato (best actress, Cannes Film Fest, 1964); The Bell Jar; Breaking Away; Private Benjamin; Real Men; The Passage.
TELEVISION: Series: Diana (1973); Barney Miller (1975–76); Breaking Away; Tucker's Witch; Reggie; Double Trouble; Love of Life. Guest appearances: Ben Casey; The Fugitive; Dr. Kildare; Alfred Hitchcock Presents; The Defenders; Mary Tyler Moore Show; Lou Grant; Trapper John, M.D. Movies: To Be Young, Gifted and Black; 79 Park Avenue; Summer of My German Soldier; Roots, Part II; Tell Me My Name; To Race the Wind; Backstairs at the White House; Working; Barefoot in the Park; Two of a Kind; An American Romance, The Execution; Vital Signs.

BARRIE, GEORGE: Executive. b. Brooklyn, NY Feb. 9, 1918. e. New York U. Left school to embark on business career, beginning with soda fountain concessions in drugstores. Played in dance band and later became booker for bands. Turned to beauty products, forming co. Caryl Richards. In 1963 acquired Faberge, merging it with own firm. Entered leisure time field with records, books, films and TV.
PICTURES INCLUDE: A Touch of Class, Night Watch, Welcome to Arrow Beach, Book of Numbers, Hang-Up, Miracles Still Happen, Hugo the Hippo, Whiffs, Thieves.

BARRIE, MONA: Actress. b. London, England, Dec. 18, 1909. On stage Australia, England (Hay Fever, Bitter Sweet Autumn Crocus, others). From 1933 on screen.
PICTURES INCLUDE: Devil's Mask, Just Before Dawn, Secret of the Whistler, I Cover Big Town, Cass Timberlane, When a Girl's Beautiful, The First Time, Strange Fascination.

BARRON, ARTHUR RAY: Executive. b. Mt. Lake, MN, July 12, 1934. e. San Diego State U. 1956–60, B.S. Accounting. Certified public acc't, Calif., 1960. Coopers & Lybrand, 1960–63; Desilu Productions, Inc., 1963–67; v.p. finance and administration, Paramount Television, 1967–70 v.p. Finance, Paramount Pictures Corp., 1970; senior v.p. finance and administration, 1971; exec. v.p., finance & admin., 1974; exec. v.p. 1980; exec. v.p., Gulf & Western Industries, entertainment & communications group, 1983; promoted to pres., 1984–Feb., 1988. (retired).

BARRY, DONALD (Red): Actor, r.n. Donald Barry de Acosta; b. Houston, TX. e. Texas Sch. Mines. In 1936 in Night Waitress (RKO Radio), thereafter to 1939 in number of feature pictures, including The Woman I Love, Sinners in Paradise, The Crowd Roars. From 1939 in Westerns, attaining wide popularity as Republic Western star. Voted one of first ten Money-Making Western Stars in Motion Picture Herald-Fame Polls 1942, 1943, 1944.
PICTURES INCLUDE: Jesse James' Women, Untamed Heiress, Twinkle in God's Eye, I'll Cry Tomorrow, Seven Men From Now, Shalako, The Shakiest Gun in the West, Orca, The Swarm.

BARRY, GENE: Actor. r.n. Eugene Klass. b. New York, NY, June 14, 1921. e. New Utrecht H.S., Brooklyn. Appeared in little & summer theatre.
BROADWAY: Rosalinda, Catherine Was Great, Happy Is Larry, Bless You All, La Cage aux Folles, The Would-Be Gentleman.
PICTURES INCLUDE: Atomic City, Girls of Pleasure Island, War of the Worlds, Those Redheads from Seattle, Alaska Seas, Red Garters, Naked Alibi, Soldier of Fortune, Purple Mask, Houston Story, Back from Eternity, China Gato, 27th Day, Maroc 7.
TELEVISION: Bat Masterson, Burke's Law, The Name of the Game, The Adventurer. Movies: Prescription Murder, Aspen, A Cry for Love, Adventures of Nellie Bly.

BARRY, JOHN: Composer, arranger, conductor. b. York, England, 1933. Artist and prod., CBS Records.
PICTURES INCLUDE: Beat Girl, Never Let Go, The Amorous Prawn, From Russia With Love, Seance on a Wet Afternoon, Zulu, Goldfinger, The Ipcress File, The Knack, King Rat, Born Free, Thunderball, The Chase, The Wrong Box, The Quiller Memorandum, The Whisperers, Deadfall, Petulia, You Only Live Twice, The Lion in Winter, Midnight Cowboy, The Appointment, The Tamarind Seed, The Dove, The Day of the Locust, Robin and Marian, King Kong, The Deep, The Betsy, Moonraker, The Black Hole, Hanover Street, Starcrash, Game of Death, Raise the Titanic, Somewhere in Time, Inside Moves, Touched By Love, Body Heat, The Legend of the Lone Ranger, Hammett, High Road to China, Octopussy, The Golden Seal, Frances, Mike's Murder, Until September, The Cotton Club, A View to a Kill, Jagged Edge, Out of Africa, Howard the Duck, Peggy Sue Got Married, The Living Daylights, Hearts of Fire, Masquerade, A Killing Affair.
TELEVISION: Elizabeth Taylor in London, Sophia Loren in Rome.

BARRYMORE, DREW: Actress. b. Los Angeles, CA, Feb. 22, 1975. Daughter of John Barrymore, Jr. At 11 months was in first commercial.
PICTURES: Altered States, E.T.: The Extra Terrestrial, Firestarter, Irreconcilable Differences, Cat's Eye, See You in the Morning.
TELEVISION: Suddenly Love, Bogey, Babes in Toyland, Disneyland's 30th Anniversary, Night of 100 Stars II, Con Sawyer and Hucklemary Finn, The Screaming Woman, Conspiracy of Love.

BARRYMORE, JOHN BLYTH, JR.: Actor. b. Beverly Hills, CA, June 4, 1932. e. St. John's Military Acad., various public and private schools. p. late John Barrymore, Delores Costello (Mrs. John Vruwink). Debut in the Sundowners; many TV appearances.
PICTURES INCLUDE: High Lonesome, Big Night, Thunderbirds, While the City Sleeps, Shadow on the Window, War of the Zombies, Never Love a Stranger, The Night They Killed Rasputin, High School Confidential.

BART, PETER: Executive. e. Swarthmore Coll. and The London School of Economics. Served eight years as correspondent for The New York Times and wrote for such magazines as Harper's, The Atlantic, Saturday Review, etc. Joined Paramount Pictures in 1965. Named exec. ass't to Robert Evans, exec. in charge of world-wide production. Appointed v.p. prod. Resigned post in 1973 to develop and produce own films for Para. Appointed pres. Lorimar Films, 1978. Resigned, 1979, to be independent producer 1983, joined MGM as snr. v.p., prod., m.p. div. Resigned, 1985, to be indep. prod. Novels: Author-Thy Kingdom Come (1983); Destinies (1979).
PICTURES INCLUDE: Islands in the Stream, Fun with Dick and Jane (both co-prod.), Revenge of the Nerds (exec. prod.); Youngblood (co-prod.); Revenge of the Nerds II (co-prod.).

BARTEL, PAUL: Director, Writer, Actor. b. New York, NY, Aug. 6, 1938. e. U. of California at L.A., B.A.
PICTURES INCLUDE: Director: The Secret Cinema; Naughty Purse; Private Parts; Death Race 2000; Cannonball; Lust in the Dust. Actor: Piranha, Rock 'n' Roll High School;

Heart Like a Wheel, Into the Night, Amazon Women of the Moon, Baja Oklahoma, Mortuary Academy, Out of the Dark (exec. prod., actor). Actor-Writer-Director: Eating Raoul. Scenes From the Class Struggle in Beverly Hills. Director-Writer: Not for Publication.

BARTHOLOMEW, FREDDIE: Actor. b. London, England, March 28, 1924. Stage debut 1927; m.p. debut U.S. in David Copperfield, 1935.
PICTURES INCLUDE: Anna Karenina, Lloyds of London, Little Lord Fauntleroy, Devil Is a Sissy, Lord Jeff, Captains Courageous, Kidnapped, Swiss Family Robinson, Naval Academy, Yank at Eton, Junior Army, The Town Went Wild, St. Benny the Dip.

BARTKOWIAK, ANDRZEJ: Cinematographer. b. Lodz, Poland, 1950. Attended Polish Film School. Moved to US in 1972, gaining experience in TV commercials and low-budget features. Protege of Sidney Lumet, for whom did several pictures.
PICTURES: Deadly Hero, Prince of the City, Deathtrap, The Verdict, Daniel, Terms of Endearment, Garbo Talks, Prizzi's Honor, The Morning After, Nuts.

BARTLETT, HALL: Producer, Director, Writer. b. Kansas City, MO, Nov. 27, 1925. e. Yale U., B.A. 1942. U.S. Naval Reserve 1942–47; formed Hall Bartlett Productions, 1952; Author: The Rest of Our Lives.
PICTURES: prod. Navajo (winner of 27 nat'l awards & Festival of Brit. Award at Edinburgh); prod., s.p. Crazy-legs (winner of 9 nat'l awards, including Parents Mag. Gold Medal); prod., dir., s.p. Unchained (winner of Parents Mag. Gold Medal, Brotherhd. award of Nat'l Con. of Christians and Jews); prod., dir., s.p. Durango; prod. dir. s.p. Zero Hour, All the Young Men, Sol Madrid; photog., prod., Changes; prod. dir. Winner of the Sans Sebastian Festival, The Sandpit Generals, prod., dir., writer; winner of Grand Prize of VII International Film Festival of Moscow. Producer, director: Jonathan Livingston Seagull; Cleo Laine Special, Zubin Mehta Special; producer, director, The Children of Sanchez; prod., dir., s.p.: Comeback, Love Is Forever.

BARUCH, ANDRE: Announcer, Commentator. b. Paris, France. m. singer Bea Wain. e. Pratt Inst., Brooklyn; Columbia U.; Beaux Arts. Your Hit Parade (radio with Bea Wain). Commercials for L.A. Cellular, Belgian Waffles, Robinson's Western World Video, Lanvin Perfume. Fashion show commentator; sales conventions, M.C. Pres., Beand Products. (TV and radio.) Performed on over 7,000 radio and TV shows. Member, National Broadcasters Hall of Fame, Board of Pacific Pioneer Broadcasters.

BARUCH, RALPH M.: Executive. b. Paris, France, Aug. 5, 1923. e. The Sorbonne, Administrative aide, SESAC, Inc. 1944–48; account exec., DuMont Television Network, 1948–52; Eastern sales mgr., Consolidated Television Films, 1953–54; account exec., CBS Films, 1954; account supervisor, 1957; dir. international sales, 1959; v.p., CBS Enterprises, 1961–70; pres., Viacom Enterprises, 1971; pres., Viacom International, 1979; named chm. & chief exec. officer, Viacom International; pres., International Radio Television Society; chmn., Rewrite Committee (Communications Act), NCTA; former member of the board of directors and former chmn., Pay Cable Committee, NCTA; chm., NCTA Public Policy Planning Committee; gov. (New York), fellow of International Council of the National Academy of Television Arts Sciences.

BARWOOD, HAL: Writer, Producer, Director. e. U. of Southern California Sch. of Cinema. Has written scripts in collaboration with Matthew Robbins, Barwood branching out into producing with Corvette Summer in 1978 and directing with Warning Sign in 1985.
PICTURES INCLUDE: Screen plays, all with Robbins: The Sugarland Express, The Bingo Long Traveling All-Stars and Motor Kings, MacArthur, Corvette Summer (also prod.), Dragonslayer (also prod.), Warning Sign (also dir.).

BARYSHNIKOV, MIKHAIL: Dancer, Actor. b. Riga, Latvia, Jan. 27, 1948. Joined Kirov Ballet, Leningrad, 1969–74; defected to U.S. With American Ballet Theatre 1974–78; New York City Ballet Company 1978–79; named director of the American Ballet Theatre.
PICTURES: The Turning Point, That's Dancing!, White Nights, Dancers.
TELEVISION: Baryshnikov at the White House, Bob Hope on the Road to China, Baryshnikov on Broadway, AFI Salute to Fred Astaire, Baryshnikov in Hollywood, AFI Salute to Gene Kelly, David Gordon's Made in USA, All Star Gala at Ford's Theater.

BASCH, BUDDY: Print Media Syndicater, Publicist, Producer. b. South Orange, NJ, June 28, 1922. e. Columbia U. Began career as youngest radio editor in U.S. at 15, since written for national mags, syndicates, wire services, and newspapers. Edited and published "Top Hit Club News"-7 years old. Joined Donahue and Coe 1940 on m.p. accounts, U.S. Army in Europe 1942–45. 1945–67: own publicity and promotion office, working on m.p. company accounts and stars such as Burl Ives, Dinah Shore, Tony Martin, Danny Kaye, Peter Lorre, Tony Bennett, Gloria De Haven, McGuire Sisters, Rhonda Fleming, Sammy Davis, Jr., Anna Maria Alberghetti, Polly Bergen, Meyer Davis, The Beatles, Glenn Miller and Tommy Dorsey Orchestras. Produced many shows for radio, TV and stage in New York, Newark, Chicago, Hartford. Asst. to publisher, The Brooklyn Eagle 1962. 1966 formed Buddy Basch Feature Syndicate, covering assignments on show business, travel and general subjects for N.Y. Daily News, A.P., Travel/Holiday, Frontier Magazine, Kaleidoscope, True, United Features, Gannett Westchester-Rockland newspapers, Bergen (NJ) Record, Argosy, N.A.N.A., Womens' New Service, Today Magazine, Christian Science Monitor, New York Post, Inflight Magazine, Deseret News, California Canadian, Diversion. Member: Friars Club since 1959. Chairman, VIP Reception and Security for Friars luncheons and dinners. Served as Chairman of Elections (6 times). Member of Admission Comm. and House Committee. Contributing ed. Friars Epistle.

BASINGER, KIM: Actress. b. Athens, GA, Dec. 8, 1953. e. Neighborhood Playhouse. Began career as a Breck shampoo model (as her mother had been) then as a Ford model in New York. Pursued singing career under the nom-de-chant, Chelsea.
PICTURES: Hard Candy, Never Say Never Again, Mother Lode, The Man Who Loved Women, The Natural, 9½ Weeks, Fool for Love, No Mercy, Blind Date, Nadine, My Stepmother is an Alien.
TELEVISION: Series: Six Million Dollar Man (1977); Dog and Cat (1977). Movies: From Here to Eternity, Katie: Portrait of a Centerfold.

BASS, SAUL: Director, Producer. b. New York, NY, May 8, 1920. e. Arts Students League. Pres., Saul Bass/Herb Yager & Assoc. Has directed short films, m.p. titles/prologues/epilogues, TV show openings, TV commercials. Directorial feature debut in 1974 with Phase IV.
PICTURES INCLUDE: (shorts), The Searching Eye, From Here to There, Why Man Creates (Academy Award); Notes on the Popular Arts (AA nomination), The Solar Film (AA nomination), Bass on Titles, Quest; (titles) Carmen Jones, The Man With The Golden Arm, Anatomy of a Murder, Vertigo, Psycho, Around the World in 80 Days, West Side Story, That's Entertainment II.

BASSETT, LINDA: Actress. Extensive career in the English theatre.
THEATER: Began with Interplay Community Theatre Company. In 1977 joined Belgrade Theater-in-Education Company in Coventry as actress, writer, and director. 1982, joined Joint Stock Theatre Group for workshop production of Caryl Churchill's Fen (London and Public Theater, NY). Starred in Abel's Sister (London), The Cherry Orchard, Medea, Woyceck, The Bald Prima Donna and George Dandin with Leicester Haymarket Studio Season. Aunt Dan and Lemon (London and NY).
PICTURES: Debut as Gertrude Stein in Waiting for the Moon, Leave to Remain.

BATCHELOR, JOY: Director. b. Watford, England, May 12, 1914. e. grammar school & art school. Early career, illustrator & designer. Entered m.p. in 1935 & is connected with the production of over 500 cartoon films. Co-director, co-prod., collab. s.p., Animal Farm, first British full length color feature cartoon; dir. Dam the Delta, The Colombo Plan, The Commonwealth, Ruddigore, The Five, Wotdot, Contact, Ass and the Stick. Christmas Feast, Carry on Milkmaids.

BATEMAN, JASON: Actor. b. Rye, NY, Feb. 19, 1969. Brother of actress Justine Bateman. Son of prod.-theatrical mgr. Kent Bateman. Started career in commercials until cast in Little House on the Prairie at 12 (1981).
PICTURES: Teen Wolf Too (prod. by father).
TELEVISION: Series: Little House on the Prairie, Silver Spoons, It's Your Move, Valerie, Valerie's Family, The Hogan Family. Movies: The Fantastic World of D.C. Collins, The Thanksgiving Promise, Robert Kennedy and His Times, Can You Feel Me Dancing, The Bates Motel, Just a Little More Love (special).

BATEMAN, JUSTINE: Actress. b. Rye, NY, 1966. Sister of actor Jason Bateman. Daughter of prod.-theatrical mgr. Kent Bateman.
PICTURES: Satisfaction.
TELEVISION: Tales from the Dark Side, One to Grow On, It's Your Move, Glitter. Series: Family Ties. Movies: Right to Kill?, Family Ties Vacation, Can You Feel Me Dancing?. Specials: First the Egg, Whatta Year . . . 1986, Fame, Fortune and Romance.

BATES, ALAN: Actor. b. Allestree, Derbyshire, England, Feb. 17, 1934.
TV APPEARANCES: The Thug, A Memory of Two Mondays, The Jukebox, The Square Ring, The Wind and the Rain, Look Back in Anger, Three on a Gasring, Duel for Love, A Hero for Our Time, Plaintiff & Defendant, Two Sundays, The Collection, The Mayor of Casterbridge, The Trespasser, Very Like a Whale, Voyage Round My Father, An Englishman Abroad, Separate Tables, Dr. Fischer of Geneva, One for the Road, Pack of Lies.
STAGE: On London and New York stage. The Caretaker, Long Days Journey Into Night, Poor Richard, In Celebration, Hamlet, Butley (Tony Award), The Taming of the Shrew, Life Class, Otherwise Engaged, The Seagull, Stage Struck, A Patriot for Me, One for the Road, Victoria Station, Dance of Death, Yonadab, Melon.
PICTURES INCLUDE: The Entertainer, Whistle Down the Wind, A Kind of Loving, The Caretaker, Nothing But the Best, Zorba The Greek, Georgy Girl, King of Hearts, Three Sisters, Far from the Madding Crowd, The Fixer, Women in Love, Joe Egg, The Go Between, Impossible Object, Butley, In Celebration, Royal Flash, An Unmarried Woman, The Shout, Rose, Nijinsky, Quartet, The Return of the Soldier, The Wicked Lady, Duet for One, A Prayer for the Dying, We Think the World of You.

BATTY, PETER: Producer, Director, Writer. b. Sunderland, England, 1931. e. Bede Grammar Sch. and Queen's Coll., Oxford. Feature-writer both sides Atlantic 1954–58. Joined BBC TV 1958 dir. short films. Edited Tonight programme 1963–4. Exec. prod. ATV 1964–68. Awarded Grand Prix for doc. at 1965 Venice and Leipzig festivals. Official entries 1970 and 1971 San Francisco and Melbourne festivals. Nominated Intl. Emmy, 1986. Own company since 1968 prod. TV specials, series, commercials.
TV PRODUCTIONS INCLUDE: The Quiet Revolution, The Big Freeze, The Katanga Affair, Sons of the Navy Man, The Fall and Rise of the House of Krupp, The Road to Suez, The Suez Affair, Battle for the Desert, Vietnam Fly-In, The Plutocrats, The Aristocrats, Battle for Cassino, Battle for the Bulge, Birth of the Bomb, Search for the Super, Operation Barbarossa, Farouk: Last of the Pharaohs, Superspy, Spy Extraordinary, Sunderland's Pride and Passion, A Rothschild and His Red Gold, The World of Television, The Story of Wine, The Rise and Rise of Laura Ashley, The Gospel According to Saint Michael, Battle for Warsaw, Battle for Dien Bien Phu, Nuclear Nightmares. A Turn Up in A Million, Il Poverello, Swindle!, The Algerian War, Fonteyn and Nureyev: The Perfect Partnership, The Divided Union, Sons of the Navy Man. Contributed 6 episodes to Emmy-winning World at War series.

BAUER, HARALD P.: Executive. b. Berlin, Germany, March 16, 1928. e. M.A. Pol. Sci./Int. Law. Joined Associated Press 1950, foreign correspondent; 1970, appointed regional mgr. Joined United Press International 1971 as regional mgr. (Southwest U.S.); 1974, appointed gen. mgr. for Unicom Economic News Service; 1978 appointed gen. exec. for Europe; 1981, appointed v.p. for news and information services and corporate development; 1983, joined United International Pictures as pres., Pay-TV Group; 1985, v.p. & gen. mgr., United Media, New York.

BAUER, STEVEN: Actor. b. Cuba, Dec. 2, 1956. r.n. Steve Echervarria. Moved with family to Miami at age 3. e. Miami Dade Jr. Coll. where studied acting. Breakthrough came with selection for role in Que Pasa U.S.A.? for Public TV. Signed by Columbia TV and moved to California.
PICTURES: Scarface, Thief of Hearts, Running Scared, The Beast, Wildfire, Gleaming the Cube.
TELEVISION: Series: The Rockford Files, Doctors Private Lives, From Here to Eternity, Hill Street Blues, One Day at a Time. Movies: She's in the Army Now, Nichols and Dymes, An Innocent Love, Sword of Gideon.

BAUM, MARTIN: Executive. b. New York, NY, March 2, 1924. President, ABC Pictures; previously partner Baum & Newborn Theatrical Agency; head of West Coast office General Artists Corp., head of m.p. dept., Ashley Famous Agency; President of Martin Baum Agency; sr. exec. v.p. Creative Management Associations; president Optimus Productions, Inc., producing Bring Me the Head of Alfredo Garcia, The Wilby Conspiracy, and The Killer Elite. Partners with Michael Ovitz, Ron Meyer, Rowland Perkins, Bill Haber in Creative Artists Agency, Inc.

BAUMGARTEN, CRAIG: Executive. b. Aug. 27, 1949. Partner in independent prod. co., New America Cinema. Joined Paramount Pictures as prod. exec.; named v.p., prod. In 1980 went to Keith Barish Prods., of which was pres. three years. In 1983 appt. exec. v.p. & exec. asst. to the pres. & CEO, Columbia Pictures. Resigned 1985; joined Lorimar Motion Pictures as pres. Joined 20th Century Fox m.p. div. as exec. v.p. of production Oct. 1987.

BAUMSTONE, HAROLD: Executive. b. New York, NY, June 27, 1911. e. U. of North Carolina, B.A. 1932. Prod. & distrib. of short subjects; pres., Institutional Cinema Inc., National 16mm Film Exchange, representing Columbia Pictures,

Warner Bros., American International and ind. prod. Exclusive distributor for 16mm markets for foreign films.

BAXTER, BILLY: Executive. b. New York, NY, Feb. 8, 1926. e. Holy Cross, 1948. Mgr., Ambassador Brokerage Group, Albany, 1957–58; Bill Doll & Co., 1959–63; organ., prod., radio show, Earl Wilson Celebrity Column, 1962; prod. Broadway show, Mandingo, with Franchot Tone, 1962; dir. of promotion, spec. events, Rumrill Ad Agency, 1963–64; dir. of promotion, exploitation, Landau Co., 1964–65; dir. of adv. and pub., Rizzoli Co., 1965; resigned, Rizzoli, 1966. Consultant on special events to the Philip Morris Corp. and American Express. Coproducer on movies Love and Anarchy, Daughters-Daughters, Outrageous, One Man, Dawn of the Dead. Produced Diary of the Cannes Film Festival with Rex Reed, 1980.

BAXTER, KEITH: Actor. b. Monmouthshire, Wales, April 29, 1933. e. Wales, entered Royal Acad. of Dramatic Arts in 1951. 1952–55 in national service; returned to RADA. Did years of repertory work in Dublin, Croydon, Chichester, London's West End, and New York. Biggest stage hit in Sleuth, both London and N.Y.
PICTURES INCLUDE: The Barretts of Wimpole Street, Peeping Tom, Chimes at Midnight, With Love in Mind, Ash Wednesday, Berlin Blues.
TELEVISION: For Tea on Sunday, Hold My Hand Soldier, Saint Joan.

BAXTER, STANLEY: Actor. b. Glasgow, Scotland, 1928. e. Hillhead H.S., Glasgow. Principal comedian in Howard & Wyndham pantomimes. Summer revues. Televised regularly on BBC-TV, and also frequent broadcaster. M.P. debut 1955 in Geordie.
STAGE: The Amorous Prawn, On the Brighter Side, 1961, Chase Me Comrade, in Australia, 1965; Cinderella. 1966–68, What the Butler Saw; 1969; Phil The Fluter, 1969–70. Mother Goose Pantomime seasons 1970–74. Jack & The Beanstalk, 1975–78. Cinderella 1979–82; Mother Goose, 1982–85; Aladdin, 1985–87.
PICTURES INCLUDE: Very Important Person, Crooks Anonymous, The Fast Lady, Father Came Too Joey Boy.
TELEVISION: Baxter on (Series) 1964; The Confidence Course, The World of Stanley Baxter, Stanley Baxter Show, Stanley Baxter Show, Time for Baxter, The Stanley Baxter Big Picture Show, The Stanley Baxter Moving Picture Show, Part III, "Stanley Baxter's Christmas Box," Bing Crosby's Merrie Olde Christmas, Stanley Baxter's Greatest Hits, Baxter on Television, Stanley Baxter Series, The Stanley Baxter Hour, Children's Royal, Stanley Baxter's Christmas Hamper, Stanley Baxter's Picture Annual, 1986; Mr. Majeika (series, 1988).

BEAL, JOHN: Actor, r.n. J. Alexander Bliedung. b. Joplin, MO, Aug. 13, 1909. e. Wharton Sch., U. of Pennsylvania. On Broadway in Another Language, She Loves Me Not, Voice of the Turtle, Teahouse of the August Moon. Off Bdwy: Long Day's Journey into Night, Our Town. m.p. debut in Another Language, 1933; served in U.S.A.A.F., W.W.II.
PICTURES INCLUDE: Little Minister, Les Miserables, We Who Are About to Die, Man Who Found Himself, Arkansas Traveler, Cat and the Canary, Great Commandment, Doctors Don't Tell, Atlantic Convoy, Edge of Darkness; Stand By, All Networks, Key Witness, Madame X, Double Wedding, Beg, Borrow or Steal, Port of Seven Seas, Alimony, Song of Surrender, Chicago Deadline, My Six Convicts, Remains to Be Seen, The Vampire, The Sound and the Fury, That Night, Ten Who Dared, Amityville 3-D.

BEALS, JENNIFER: Actress. b. Chicago, IL, Dec. 19, 1963. Fashion model. Made film debut in small role in My Bodyguard, 1980.
PICTURES: Flashdance, The Bride, Vampire Kiss, Kid Gloves, Layover, Rider in the Dark, Split Decisions, The Lizard's Tale.
TELEVISION: The Picture of Dorian Grey, Cinderella (Faerie Tale Theatre).

BEAN, ORSON: Actor. b. Burlington, VT, July 22, 1928. r.n. Dallas Burrows. Performed in nightclubs as comic and on Broadway (School for Scandal, Will Success Spoil Rock Hunter?, Subways Are for Sleeping, Roar of the Grease Paint, the Smell of the Crowd, Ilya Darling.) Author: Me and the Orgone. Founder, administrator, dir. 15th St. School, NY.
PICTURES INCLUDE: How to Be Very, Very Popular (debut, 1955), Anatomy of a Murder, Lola, Skateboard, Forty Deuces.
TELEVISION: To Tell the Truth (reg. panelist).

BEATTY, NED: Actor. b. Lexington, KY, July 6, 1937. Worked at Barter Theatre in Virginia for seven years, appearing in over 70 plays. Broadway debut: The Great White Hope.
PICTURES INCLUDE: Deliverance (debut), The Thief Who Came to Dinner, Nashville, W.W. and the Dixie Dance Kings, All the President's Men, The Big Bus, Micky and Nickey, Silver Streak, Exorcist II: The Heretic, Network, The Great Georgia

Bank Hoax, Superman, Promises in the Dark, Hopscotch, The Incredible Shrinking Woman, Superman II, The Toy, Touched, Stroker Ace, Back to School, The Big Easy, The Fourth Protocol, Switching Channels, Rolling Vengeance, The Trouble With Spies, The Passage, The Unholy, Midnight Crossing, Smoke, Imagination.
TELEVISION: Pray TV, A Woman Called Golda, The Ballad of Gregorio Cortez, Kentucky Woman, The Last Days of Pompeii, Celebrity, Robert Kennedy and His Times, Murder She Wrote; Konrad (Wonderworks); Hostage Flight.

BEATTY, ROBERT: Actor. b. Hamilton, Ont., Canada, Oct. 19, 1909. e. U. of Toronto. London stage debut: Idiot's Delight, 1938. On screen first in Suspected Persons, 1942.
PICTURES INCLUDE: San Demetrio London, It Happened One Sunday, Appointment with Crime, Odd Man Out, Green Fingers, Against the Wind, Another Shore, Portrait from Life, Her Favorite Husband, Captain Horatio Hornblower, Calling Bulldog Drummond, Magic Box, Wings of Danger, The Gentle Gunman, The Oracle, The Net (Project M.7), Man on the Tightrope, Broken Horseshoe, The Square Ring, Albert RN (Break to Freedom), Loves of Three Women, Out of the Clouds, Portrait of Alison (Postmark for Danger),Tarzan and the Lost Safari, Something of Value, Time Lock, The Shakedown, The Amorous Prawn, Stanley Kubrick's 2001, Where Eagles Dare, Sitting Target, Pope Joan, The Pink Panther Strikes Again, Golden Rendezvous, Superman III, The Highlander, Superman IV, High Diamonds.
TELEVISION: Weekly guide, Saturday Night Out, Dial 999 (series), The Human Jungle (series), Court Martial (series), Time Lock, Man at the Top, The Venturers, Thriller, Jesus of Nazareth, Blake's Seven, Park Ranger, The Martian Chronicles, Walk with Destiny, Suez, The Rose, Medallion, Tales of the Unexpected, Murder of a Moderate Man, Minder on the Orient Express, Breakthrough at Reykjavik.

BEATTY, WARREN: Actor. b. Richmond, VA, March 30, 1938. Brother of Shirley MacLaine. e. Northwestern U. Small roles on television; Compulsion; winter stock, North Jersey Playhouse; Broadway debut, A Loss of Roses.
PICTURES INCLUDE: Splendor in the Grass, The Roman Spring of Mrs. Stone, All Fall Down, Lilith, Mickey One, Promise Her Anything, Kaleidoscope, Bonnie and Clyde (prod., actor), The Only Game in Town, McCabe and Mrs. Miller, Dollars, The Parallax View, Shampoo (prod., co-author, star), The Fortune, Heaven Can Wait (star, prod., co-dir, co-s.p.), Reds (star, prod., dir., co-s.p.), Ishtar (prod., star).
TELEVISION: The Many Loves of Dobie Gillis (series reg. 1959–60); Alcoa Presents, One Step Beyond, Wagon Train (1964).

BECK, ALEXANDER J.: Executive. b. Ung. Brod, Czechoslovakia, Nov. 5, 1926. e. Charles U., Prague, New York U. Owns 500 features and westerns for foreign distribution and library of 1400 shorts. Importer and exporter; Pres., chairman of bd. Alexander Beck Films, 1955; formed Albex Films and A.B. Enterprises, 1959; formed & pres., Beckman Film Corp., 1960; formed Alexander Beck Productions, 1964. Sept. '69 formed Screencom Int'l Corp., 1986, formed Beck Int'l Corp., 1987; formed Challenger Pictures Corp., 1988.

BECK, JACKSON: Actor-announcer-narrator. b. New York, NY. TV and radio commercials, children's records, comm. industrial films; Narrator.

BECK, JOHN: Actor. b. Chicago, IL. Jan. 28. Acted with midwestern theatre groups; had basic training in scores of TV series. Theatrical debut in Three in the Attic, 1968.
PICTURES INCLUDE: Three in the Attic, Mrs. Pollifax, Spy, Lawman, Pat Garrett and Billy the Kid, Sleeper, Deadly Honeymoon, Rollerball, Paperback Hero, The Big Bus, Audrey Rose, The Other Side of Midnight, Deadly Illusion, From Father to Son.
TELEVISION: Guest star roles on Bonanza, Mannix, Hawaii Five-0, Love American Style; The Silent Gun, Lancer, Gunsmoke. Movies: Attack on Terror, The FBI VS the Ku Klux Klan; Wheels, What Really Happened to the Class of '65; The Time Machine; Greatest Heroes of the Bible; Time Express, Mind over Murder, Gridlock, Partners in Crime, Peyton Place: The Next Generation.

BECK, MICHAEL: Actor. b. Memphis, TN, Feb. 4, 1949. e. Millsap Coll. on football scholarship (quarterback). Became active in college theatre. In 1971 attended Central Sch. of Speech and Drama, London; studied 3 years, following which toured England with repertory companies for 2 years. Returned to U.S.; cast as lead in independent film, Madman (shot in Israel in 1977).
PICTURES: Madman; Blackout; The Warriors; Xanadu; Battletruck; Megaforce; Warriors of the 21st Century; The Golden Seal; Triumphs of a Man Called Horse.
TELEVISION: Holocaust; Mayflower: the Pilgrim's Adventure; Alcatraz: The Whole Shocking Story; Fly Away Home; The Last Ninja; Celebrity; Chiller; The Streets; Rearview Mirror. Series: Houston Knights.

BECK, MYER P.: Sales, prod. rep. b. Meriden, CT. e. New York U. Sch. of Journalism. Newspaperman; publicist; publicity dir. United Artists; eastern mgr. Russell Birdwell Associates; formed own sls. prod. rep. office 1945, repr. Albert R. Broccoli; Jerome Hellman Productions, Stanley Kramer Pictures Corp.

BECKER, HAROLD: Director.
PICTURES INCLUDE: The Ragman's Daughter; The Onion Field; The Black Marble; Taps; Vision Quest, The Boost, Sea of Love.

BEDELIA, BONNIE: Actress. b. New York, NY, March 25, 1952. e. Hunter Coll.
THEATER: Enter Laughing (1963), The Playroom, My Sweet Charlie.
PICTURES: The Gypsy Moths, They Shoot Horses Don't They?, Lovers and Other Strangers, Between Friends, The Big Fix, Heart Like a Wheel, The Boy Who Could Fly, Death of an Angel, Violets Are Blue, Between Friends, The Strange Vengeance of Rosalie, Die Hard, The Prince of Pennsylvania.
TELEVISION: Hawkins on Murder, A Question of Love, Salem's Lot, Fighting Back, Alex: The Life of a Child, When the Time Comes, The New Land, No Means No, A Message to My Daughter, The Lady from Yesterday, Memorial Day.

BEERY, NOAH, JR.: Actor. b. New York, NY, Aug. 10, 1916. e. Urban and Harvard Mil. Acad. Son of Noah Beery, screen actor. Travelled with parents in stock company. Appeared as child in Mark of Zorro, 1920.
PICTURES INCLUDE: Father and Son, Road Back, Only Angels Have Wings, Doolins of Oklahoma, Davy Crockett, Indian Scout, Last Outpost, Savage Horde, Rocketship XM, Two Flags West, Tropic Zone, Cimarron Kid, Wagons West, Story of Will Rogers, Wings of the Hawk, War Arrow, The Yellow Tomahawk, Black Dakotas, White Feather, Jubal, Fastest Gun Alive, Journey to Shiloh, Heaven With A Gun, Walking Tall, The Spikes Gang, The Best Little Whorehouse in Texas.
TELEVISION: Yellow Rose.

BEGLEY, ED, JR.: Actor. b. Los Angeles, CA, Sept. 16, 1949. Son of late actor Ed Begley. Debut in a guest appearance on My Three Sons at 17.
PICTURES: Stay Hungry, Blue Collar, Citizens Band, The One and Only, Goin' South, Hardcore, Airport '79 The Concord, The In-Laws, Private Lessons, Buddy Buddy, Eating Raoul, An Officer and a Gentleman, Cat People, The Entity, Get Crazy, This Is Spinal Tap, Protocol, Streets of Fire, Transylvania 6-5000, The Accidental Tourist.
TELEVISION: Series: Room 222; Roll Out; St. Elsewhere (1982– 88). Movies and specials: Amateur Night at the Dixie Bar and Grill; A Shining Season; Riker; Rascals and Robbers—The Secret Adventures of Tom Sawyer and Huck Finn; Tales of the Apple Dumpling Gang; Voyagers; Not Just Another Affair; Still the Beaver; An Uncommon Love; Insight/ The Clearing House; Roman Holiday.

BEICH, ALBERT: Writer. b. Bloomington, IL, June 25, 1919. e. McGill U. Radio writer.
PICTURES INCLUDE: You Can't Beat the Law, Girls in Chains, Gangs of the Waterfront, Gay Blades, Bridge Goes Wild, Key to the City, Yellow Cab Man, The Milkman, Lieutenant Wore Skirts.

BEJTMAN, VINCENT: Executive. b. Poland. Started career producing entertainment films in native land. Came to U.S. during war. Named pres. of PIC Films, Inc., financed by Polish govt.-in-exile in London and the British Information Center. Company produced over 30 films depicting Polish participation in W.W.II. Formed Cine Classics Films, Inc. specializing in import of foreign films for U.S. market, including Rules of the Game, Zero De Conduit, etc. Produced documentaries (The Great Betrayal, Last Days of Warsaw.) Co-produced Naked Amazon. Now pres. of Vee Bee Productions, Inc. and involved in American-European co-production.

BELAFONTE, HARRY: Actor, Singer, Producer. b. New York, NY, March 1, 1927. Trained for stage at the Actors Studio, New Sch. for Social Research and American Negro Theatre. Professional debut; Royal Roost nightclub, N.Y., Village Vanguard, 1950. Broadway debut: John Murray Anderson's Almanac, 1953. Recording, concert artist.
THEATER: Juno and the Paycock, John Murray Anderson's Almanac. (Tony Award, supp. actor, 1953), Three for Tonight, A Night With Belafonte, To Be Young, Gifted and Black (prod.), Asinamali (co-prod.).
PICTURES INCLUDE: Bright Road, Carmen Jones, Island in the Sun, Odds Against Tomorrow, The World, The Flesh and the Devil, The Angel Levine, Buck and the Preacher, Uptown Saturday Night (prod., star), First Look, Beat Street (prod.).

BELFER, HAL B.: Executive producer, director, choreographer. b. Los Angeles, CA, Feb. 16. e. U. of Southern California (cinematography); U. of California (writing). Head of choreography dept. at 20th Century-Fox. Head of choreography dept.

at Universal Studios. Dir. of entertainment, in Las Vegas, Riviera and Flamingo Hotels. Prod., musical shows for Mexico City, Aruba, Puerto Rico, Montreal, Las Vegas. Dir., TV commercials and industrials. H.R. Pufnstuf TV series. Theatricals: Over 150 features. Producer-director-choreographer, Premore, Inc. Develop TV specials and sitcom, tape and film. Exec. prod., Once Upon a Tour and Dora's World, Rose on Broadway, Secret Sleuth, Inn by the Side of the Road, Imagine That! Special staging "Tony The Pony" Series and prod., segment of What a Way to Run a Railroad; TV specials. Talent development programs, Universal Studios, 20th Century-Fox. Personal management and show packager; 1982, exec. prod., Enchanted Inn (TV Special), Cameo Music Hall I, Stage mgr.: Promises, Promises, A Chorus Line (Sahara Hotel, Las Vegas).

BEL GEDDES, BARBARA: Actress. r.n. Barbara Geddes Lewis. b. New York, NY, Oct 31, 1922. p. Norman Bel Geddes, scenic designer. Stage debut in Out of the Frying Pan; toured USO camps in Junior Miss, 1941; screen debut in The Long Night, 1946; Star of Tomorrow, 1949. On TV in Dallas. Author-illustrator children's books: I Like to Be Me (1963), So Do I (1972). Also designer of greeting cards for George Caspari Co.
THEATER: The Moon Is Blue, Cat on a Hot Tin Roof, Mary, Mary, Everything in the Garden, Finishing Touches.
PICTURES INCLUDE: I Remember Mama, Blood on the Moon, Caught, Panic in Streets, Fourteen Hours, The Five Pennies, Five Branded Women, By Love Possessed, Summertree, The Todd Killings.
TELEVISION: Live TV in 1950s: Robert Montgomery Presents, Schlitz Playhouse of the Stars, etc., several classic Alfred Hitchcock Presents episodes including Lamb to the Slaughter; Our Town, Series: Dallas (1978–84; 1985–; Emmy, 1980).

BELL, TOM: Actor. b. Liverpool, England, 1932. Early career in repertory and on West End stage. First TV appearance in Promenade.
TELEVISION: No Trams to Lime Street, Love On the Dole, A Night Out, Cul de Sac, The Seekers, Long Distance Blue, The Virginian. Film debut 1960 in Payroll.
PICTURES INCLUDE: The Kitchen, H.M.S. Defiant, Prize of Arms, L-Shaped Room, Rebels Against the Light, Ballad in Blue, He Who Rides a Tiger, In Enemy Country, The Long Days Dying, Lock Up Your Daughters, Resurrection.

BELLAMY, EARL: Producer, Director. b. Minneapolis, MN, March 11, 1917. e. Los Angeles City Coll. Universal Studios. President, The Bellamy Productions Co.
PICTURES INCLUDE: Fluffy, Gun Point, Munsters Go Home, Side-winder, Speedtrap.
TELEVISION: Bachelor Father, Wells Fargo, Lone Ranger, Alcoa Premiere, Arrest and Trial, The Virginian, The Crusaders, Schlitz Playhouse, Heinz, Rawhide, The Donna Reed Show, Andy Griffith Show, Wagon Train, Laramie, Laredo, I Spy, Mod Squad, Medical Center.

BELLAMY, RALPH: Actor. b. Chicago, IL, June 17, 1905. Stock and repertory, 1922–30; pres. Actors Equity, 1952; council, Lambs, 1952; TV includes major live and film dramatic shows, voted many TV awards.
BROADWAY: Town Boy, Roadside, Tomorrow the World, State of the Union, Detective Story, Sunrise at Campobello.
PICTURES INCLUDE: Great Impersonation, Lady on a Train, Guest in the House, Delightfully Dangerous, Court Martial of Billy Mitchell, Sunrise at Campobello, The Professionals, Rosemary's Baby, Oh, God!, Trading Places, Disorderlies, Amazon Women on the Moon, Coming to America, The Good Mother.
TELEVISION: Space, The Winds of War, War and Remembrance.

BELLFORT, JOSEPH: b. New York, NY. e. New York U., Brooklyn Law Sch. Joined RKO Service Corp., Feb., 1930; trans. to RKO Radio Pictures, legal dept., May 1942; joined RKO Fgn. dept., Oct., 1944, handled Far Eastern division, Dec. 1946; then asst. to European gen. mgr.; gen. European mgr., 1949–1958; gen. sales mgr. National Screen Service, 1959; home office sup., Europe & Near East, 20th Century-Fox, 1963; home office intl. mgr., 20th Century-Fox, 1966. Ass't v.p. and foreign mgr. 20th Cent.-Fox, 1967; vice president 20th Century-Fox, Int. Corp. & Inter-America, Inc. 1968; named sr. v.p., 1975. Resigned from Fox, 1977, to become v.p., Motion Picture Export Assn. of America in New York. Retired 1983.

BELLOCCHIO, MARCO: Director, writer. b. Piacenza, Italy, Nov. 9, 1939. e. Milan (letters and philosophy); Centro Sperimentale di Cinematografia, Rome; School of Fine Arts, London 1959–63. Collaborated on Paola and Viva il primo maggio rosso.
PICTURES: Fists in the Pocket, China Is Near, Leap into the Void, In the Name of the Father, Strike the Monster on Page One (co-dir., co-s.p.), Vacations in Val Trebbia, The Eyes the Mouth, Henry IV, Sabbeth.

BELMONDO, JEAN-PAUL: Actor. b. Neuilly-sur-Seine, France, April 9, 1933. e. private drama school of Raymond Girard, and the Conservatoire d'Art Dramatique. Formed a theater group with Annie Girardot and Guy Bedos.
THEATRE INCLUDES: Jean Marais' production of Caesar and Cleopatra, Treasure Party. Oscar, 1958.
PICTURES INCLUDE: A Pied, A Cheval et En Voiture (By Foot, Horse and Car), Look Pretty and Shut Up, Drole de Dimanche, Les Tricheurs, Les Copains du Dimanche, Charlotte et Son Jules, A Double Tour, Breathless, Classe Tous Risques, Moderato Cantabile, La Francaise et l'Amour, Les Distractions, Mademoiselle Ange, La Novice, Two Women, La Viaccia, Une Femme Est une Femme, Leon Morin, Pretre, Les Amours Celebres, Un Singe en Hiver, Le Doulos, L'Aine des Ferchaux, La Mer A Boire, Banana Peel, That Man From Rio, Cent Mille Dollars au Soleil, Echappement Libre, La Chasse a l'Homme, Dieu a Choisi Paris, Weekend a Zuydcocte, Par Un Beau Matin d'Ete, Up to His Ears, Is Paris Burning?, The Thief of Paris, Tender Scoundrel, Pierrot le Fou, The Brain, Love Is a Funny Thing, Mississippi Mermaid, Borsalino, Inheritor, Stavisky, Fear Over the City.

BELSON, JERRY: Producer, Director, Writer. With Garry Marshall, writer of The Dick Van Dyke Show (Emmy), and prod. of The Odd Couple (Emmy). Together team wrote and prod. feature films: How Sweet It Is (1968) and The Grasshopper as well as co-authoring the Broadway play The Roast (1980).
PICTURES: Smile (s.p.); Fun With Dick and Jane (s.p.); The End (s.p.); Surrender (dir., s.p.); For Keeps (prod.).
TELEVISION: The Dick Van Dyke Show, The Odd Couple, The Tracey Ullmann Show (co-creator, co-exec. prod.).

BELUSHI, JAMES (Jim): Actor. b. Chicago, IL, June 15, 1954. e. DuPage Coll., Southern Illinois U. Brother, late John Belushi. Worked with Chicago's Second City Revue.
THEATER: Sexual Perversity in Chicago, Pirates of Penzance, True West.
PICTURES: Thief, Trading Places, The Man with One Red Shoe, Salvador, About Last Night, The Principal, Red Heat, Real Men, Homer and Eddie, King of the Mountain.
TELEVISION: Laverne and Shirley; Working Stiffs; Who's Watching the Kids?; The Joseph Jefferson Awards; The Best Legs in the 8th Grade; Saturday Night Live; Cinemax's Comedy Experiment's Birthday Boy (actor, prod., writer).

BENDHEIM, III, SAM: Executive. b. Richmond, VA, June 15, 1935. e. Washington & Lee U. Joined Neighborhood Theatre, Inc., 1958 as exec. trainee. Was dir. of adv. (1960–63); bd. member, ass't. treas. (1962); ass't to gen. mgr. (1963–67) v.p. (1967). Member: NATO of Virginia; former pres. & chm., NATO of Virginia; bd., pres. advisory council, exec. comm., NATO; bd., Foundation of Motion Picture Pioneers; pres. SKS Enterprises, Inc. & Bendheim Booking & Buying Service. Regional head film buyer, Cineplex Odeon Corp., Richmond, VA.

BENDICK, ROBERT: Indep. documentary prod., dir. b. New York, NY, Feb. 6, 1917. e. New York U., White School Photography. U.S Air Force, W.W.II. Documentary and still cameraman before joining CBS Television as cameraman and dir., 1940; rejoined CBS Television as dir. special events, 1946; promoted dir. news & special events; acting program dir. 1947; res. Oct. '51. Collab with Jeanne Bendick on Making the Movies, Electronics for Young People, Television Works Like This, Filming Works Like This, 1951; Prod. Peabody Award-winning U.N. show. The U.N. in Action; v.p., Cinerama Prod., co-prod. This Is Cinerama; co-dir., Cinerama Holiday; prod. Dave Garroway Show Today, prod., Wide Wide World 1955–56, NBC prod. dir. C.V. Whitney Pict., June, 1956; Merian C. Cooper Ent., 1957; prod. NBC, 1958. Prod.; Garroway Today Show, Bob Hope 25 Yrs. of Life Show, 1961; Bell Telephone Threshold Science Series, Merrily We Roll Along, US Steel Opening New York World's Fair, 1964. Prod. First Look Series 1965 (Ohio St. Award); prod. & dir. American Sportsman, ABC; prod., pilot, Great American Dream Machine (NET) (Emmy Award, 1971 and 1972); 1975, Co-exec. prod., Dick Cavett—Feeling Good. pres. Bendick Assoc. Inc.,; prod. of education audio-visual systems, Bd. of Governors, N.Y. Academy of TV Arts and Sciences. 1976, co-author with Jeanne Bendick, TV Reporting. Consultant, Warner Qube Cable Co.; 1978, produced/directed, Fight for Food (PBS). Program consultant to Times-Mirror Cable Co., L.A. Produced segment ABC 20/20. Member awards committee, National TV Acad. Arts & Science.

BENEDEK, LASLO: Director. b. Budapest, Hungary, March 5, 1907. e. U. of Vienna; Psycho-Analytic Clinic. Writer & photographer while in coll.; cameraman Budapest; first asst. cameraman several studios; cameraman UFA & Terra; film cutter; cutter & asst. prod. to Joe Pasternak; to Paris as cutter, then Engl dial. on Antonia; writer (England) 2 yrs.; montage dir. MGM 1937; writer (Mexico); assoc. prod. (Hollywood) on musicals; contract dir. MGM; Stanley Kramer Co., Col.; 1976–80, chairman of Graduate Film Program, New York U. 1983, visiting professor, Annenberg Sch. of Communication, U. of Pennsylvania, 1984, Film & TV Acad-

emy, Munich, Germany. Production advisor, S. Carolina ETV.
STAGE: Belial, Twelfth Night.
PICTURES INCLUDE: Kissing Bandit, Port of New York, Death of a Salesman, Storm Over Tibet, Wild One, Bengal Brigade; Sons, Mothers and a General, Affair in Havana, Moment of Danger, Recours en Grace, Namu, The Killer Whale, A Daring Game, The Night Visitor.
TELEVISION: 4 Star Playhouse, Dupont Theatre, Stage 7, Loretta Young Show, Telephone Time, Perry Mason, Naked City, Untouchables, Outer Limits, Alfred Hitchcock Hour.

BENEDICT, DIRK: Actor. r.n. Dirk Niewoehner. b. Helena, MT, March 1, 1945. e. Whitman Coll., Walla Walla, WA. Enrolled in John Fernald Academy of Dramatic Arts, Rochester, MI, after which had season with Seattle Repertory Theatre; also in summer stock at Ann Arbor, MI. Broadway debut, 1970, Abelard and Heloise. Film debut, Georgia, Georgia, 1972.
PICTURES INCLUDE: Sssssss, W, Battlestar Galactica, Scavenger Hunt, Ruckus, Underground Aces, Body Slam.
TELEVISION: Hawaii Five-O (one episode), Chopper One (series), Battlestar Galactica (series); The A Team (series), Scruples.

BENJAMIN, RICHARD: Actor. b. New York, NY, May 22, 1939. m. actress Paula Prentiss. e. Northwestern U.
THEATER: Central Park productions of The Taming of the Shrew, As You Like It; toured in Tchin Tchin, A Thousand Clowns, Barefoot in the Park, The Odd Couple. Broadway debut in Star Spangled Girl, 1966. Directed London productions of Barefoot in the Park, Packin' It In.
PICTURES INCLUDE: Goodbye, Columbus, Catch 22, Diary of a Mad Housewife, The Marriage of a Young Stockbroker, The Steagle, Portnoy's Complaint, The Last of Sheila, Westworld, The Sunshine Boys, Love at First Bite, Scavenger Hunt, The Last Married Couple in America, How to Beat the High Cost of Living, First Family, Director: My Favorite Year, Racing with the Moon, City Heat, The Money Pit, Little Nikita, My Stepmother Is an Alien.
TELEVISION: He and She, with Paula Prentiss, 1967.

BENNETT, ALAN: Author, Actor. b. Leeds, England, May 9, 1934. e. Oxford U. With Jonathan Miller, Dudley Moore and Peter Cook co-authored and starred in satirical revue Beyond the Fringe in London (1961) and on Bdwy (special Tony Award, 1963).
THEATER: Forty Years On (actor, author), Getting On, Habeas Corpus (also actor), Intensive Care (also appeared), Our Winnie, A Woman Of No Importance, Rolling Home, Marks, Say Something Happened, An Englishman Abroad.
PICTURES: A Private Function, Prick Up Your Ears.
TELEVISION: Famous Gossips, On the Margin (also actor), An Evening With, A Day Out, Sunset Across the Bay, A Little Outing, A Visit from Miss Prothero, Me—I'm Afraid of Virginia Wood, Doris and Doreen, The Old Crowd, Afternoon Off, An Office Story, All on the Sands, The Insurance Man.

BENNETT, BRUCE: Actor. r.n. Herman Brix. b. Tacoma, WA, 1909; e. U. of Washington.
PICTURES INCLUDE: My Son Is Guilty, Lone Wolf Keeps a Date, Atlantic Convoy, Sabotage, Underground Agent, More the Merrier, Sahara, Man I Love, Stolen Life, Nora Prentiss, Cheyenne, Treasure of Sierra Madre, Dark Passage, Smart Girls Don't Talk, Second Face, Great Missouri Raid, Last Outpost, Angels in the Outfield, Sudden Fear, Dream Wife, Dragonfly Squadron, Robbers Roost, Big Tipoff, Hidden Guns, Bottom of the Bottle, Strategic Air Command.

BENNETT, CHARLES: Writer, Director. b. Shoreham, England. British Army. Contract, Universal, 1937; wrote for British Ministry of Information, WWII; dir. s.p. over 50 TV shows, including Cavalcade of America, Schlitz Playhouse, The Christophers, Four Star.
PLAYS INCLUDE: Blackmail, The Last Hour, Sensation, The Danger Line, Page From a Diary, The Return, After Midnight.
PICTURES INCLUDE: Blackmail, The 39 Steps, Secret Agent, The Man Who Knew Too Much (orig.), Sabotage, The Girl Was Young, Balalaika, The Young in Heart, Foreign Correspondent, Reap the Wild Wind, Joan of Paris, They Dare Not Love, The Story of Dr. Wassell, Unconquered, Ivy, Sign of the Ram, Kind Lady, The Green Glove, Dangerous Assignment, Madness of the Heart (dir.), The Big Circus, The Lost World, Voyage to the Bottom of the Sea, Five Weeks in a Balloon.

BENNETT, HARVE: Producer. r.n. Harve Fischman. b. Chicago, IL, Aug. 17, 1930. e. U. of California at L.A. Quiz Kids radio show, 5 yrs.; newspaper columnist, drama critic; freelance writer; Assoc. prod., CBS-TV; free-lance TV writer; prod. of special events. CBS-TV; dir., Television film commercials; program exec., ABC, vice pres., programs west coast—ABC-TV; prod.-writer, Mod Squad. Creator-writer, The Young Rebels, Screen Gems; exec. prod., Six Million Dollar Man, Bionic Woman, Rich Man, Poor Man, Universal Studios; Pres., Bennett-Katleman. Productions at Columbia Studios, and exec. prod. on American Girls series, From Here to

Eternity, Salvage 1. Joined Paramount's Motion Picture Group, acting as exec. prod. & co-author of Star Trek II: The Wrath of Khan; prod. & author of Star Trek III: The Search for Spock. 1984, entered long-term deal with Para. Prod., co-writer: Star Trek IV: The Voyage Home.

BENNETT, HYWEL: Actor, Director. b. Garnant, South Wales. Early career National Youth Theatre where he played many leading Shakespearean roles followed by extensive work in British theatre. 1971–81: directed numerous stage productions. 1966: Film debut, The Family Way.
PICTURES: Twisted Nerve, The Virgin Soldiers, The Buttercup Chain, Loot, Percy, Endless Night, Alice in Wonderland, Murder Elite, War Zone.
TELEVISION: Where The Buffalo Roam, Malice Aforethought, Tinker Tailor Soldier Spy, series, Artemis 81, Myself A Mandarin, Frankie and Johnnie, Check Point Chiswick, Twilight Zone, The Idiot, The Traveller, Death of a Teddy Bear, Three's One, Pennies From Heaven, Shelley (series), The Critic, The Consultant, Absent Friends, The Secret Agent.

BENNETT, JILL: Actress. b. Penang, Federated Malay States, Dec. 24, 1931. Stage debut at Stratford-on-Avon, 1948; screen debut 1952 in Moulin Rouge.
PICTURES INCLUDE: Hell Below Zero, The Criminal, Extra-Day, Lust For Life, The Skull, The Nanny, Charge of Light Brigade, Inadmissible Evidence, I Want What I Want, Quilp, Full Circle, For Your Eyes Only, Britannia Hospital, Lady Jane, Hawks.
TELEVISION: The Heiress, Trilby, Jealousy, A Midsummer Night's Dream, The Three Sisters, Glimpse of the Sea, Return to the Sea, The Book Bag (Somerset Maugham Series), It's Only Us, The Parachute, Hotel in Amsterdam, Speaking of Murder, Intent to Murder, Jill and Jack, Almost A Vision, Hello Lola, The Old Crowd, Orient Express (French TV), The Aerodrome, Poor Little Rich Girls (series), Country, Paradise Postponed, Worlds Beyond.

BENNETT, JOAN: Actress. b. Palisades, NJ, Feb. 27, 1910. e. St. Margaret's Boarding School, Waterbury, CT; L'Ermitage, Versailles, France. Member of famous Bennett acting family; m. David Wilde, prod. On stage with father, Richard Bennett, in Jarnegan; m.p. debut in Bulldog Drummond, 1929 after small roles in The Valley of Decision, Power, The Divine Lady; vice-pres. & treas. Diana Prods. 1945. Author: The Bennett Playbill (1970, with Lois Kibbee).
PICTURES INCLUDE: Three Live Ghosts, Disraeli, The Mississippi Gambler, Puttin' on the Ritz, Crazy That Way, Moby Dick, Maybe It's Love, Scotland Yard, Doctors Wives, Hush Money, Many a Slip, She Wanted a Millionaire, Careless Lady, The Trial of Vivienne Ware, Week-ends Only, Wild Girl, Me and My Gal, Arizona to Broadway, Little Women, Pursuit of Happiness, Man Who Reclaimed His Head, Private Worlds, Mississippi, Two for Tonight, She Couldn't Take It, The Man Who Broke the Bank at Monte Carlo, Thirteen Hours By Air, Big Brown Eyes, Two in a Crowd, Wedding Present, Vogues of 1938, I Met My Love Again, The Texans, Artists and Models Abroad, Trade Winds, The Man in the Iron Mask, The Housekeeper's Daughter, Green Hill, The House Across The Bay, The Man I Married, The Son of Monte Cristo, Man Hunt, She Knew All the Answers, Wild Geese Chase, Confirm or Deny, Twin Beds, The Wife Takes a Flyer, Girl Trouble, Margin for Error, The Woman in the Window, Nob Hill, Scarlet Street, The Macomber Affair, The Woman on the Beach, Secret Beyond the Door, Hollow Triumph, Scar, Reckless Moment, For Heaven's Sake, Father of Bride, Father's Little Dividend, The Guy Who Came Back, Highway, Dragnet, We're No Angels, There's Always Tomorrow, Navy Wife, Desire in the Dust, House of Dark Shadows, Suspiria.
TELEVISION: Starred in Dark Shadows. Movies: Suddenly Love, A House Possessed, Divorce Wars.

BENSON, HUGH: Producer. b. New York, NY, Sept. 7, 1917. e. New York public schools. Six yrs. infantry, then Air Force. Exec. Prod., Screen Gems, 1966; prod., Cinema Center Films, 1969–71; prod., MGM, 1972; appointed exec. prod., MGM Television, 1972. 1975 indep. prod. On staff Col.-TV, 1975, pilots and long form.
PICTURES: Nightmare Honeymoon (prod.), Logan's Run (assoc. prod.), Billy Jack Goes to Washington (prod.).
TELEVISION: Producer: Contract On Cherry St., Child Stealers, Goldie and the Boxer, A Fire in the Sky, Confessions of a Lady Cop, The Dream Merchants, Goldie and the Boxer Go to Hollywood, Goliath Awaits, The Blue and the Gray, Hart to Hart, Master of Ballantrae (spvr. prod.); Anna Karenina, The Other Lover, I Dream of Jeannie 15 Yrs. Later, Miracle of the Heart: A Boy's Town Story, Crazy Like a Fox, In the Heat of the Night (pilot and series).

BENSON, LEON: Producer, Director. b. Cincinnati, OH, Nov. 9. e. New York U., U. of Cincinnati. Advertising Dept. Paramount, 1938, head of Trailer Dept., 1940. U.S. Army Air Corps, 1942–46, Major, First head of TV Dept. L.A. office of J. Walter Thompson Co., 1946–51. Head of Story Dept. Ziv TV, 1951; prod. and dir. West Point, 1955–56; Sea Hunt, 1956–60;

Ripcord, 1960–62. Prod.-Dir. Flipper TV series, 1963–64. Under contract, Universal, 1965–66, prod.-dir. episodes, Kraft Suspense Theatre, The Virginian, dir. episodes, Chrysler Theatre, Laredo. Prod. Tarzan TV series, 1966. Under contract, NBC Prods., 1967–70, as staff dir. Bonanza, High Chaparral. Prod. theatrical feature, Chosen Survivors, 1973. Also dir. Owen Marshall, Counsellor at Law, Mission Impossible, The Eleventh Hour, Ben Casey, Wild Wild West, Rat Patrol, The Lieutenant, Outer Limits, The Loner, Empire.

BENSON, ROBBY: Actor, Writer, Director. b. Dallas, TX, Jan. 21, 1956. m. actress Karla DeVito. Father, Jerry Segal, is writer, and mother, Ann Benson, veteran of Dallas stage and nat'l summer stock. (Currently head of nat'l promotions Merrill Lynch.). Appeared in commercials and summer stock at age five. First started on Bdwy at age 12 in Zelda. Also worked 6 mos. in Search for Tomorrow. Co-wrote One on One (1977) with father and starred in film. On Bdwy The Pirates of Penzance (1982). Dir. debut Crack in the Mirror (1988).
PICTURES: Jory, Jeremy, The Godfather—Part II, Ode to Billy Joe, Lucky Lady, One on One (co-s.p.), The End, Ice Castles, Walk Proud, Die Laughing (also prod., co-s.p.), Tribute, The Chosen, Running Brave, Harry and Son, Rent-A-Cop, Crack in the Mirror (dir., actor).
TELEVISION: Death Be Not Proud, Our Town, The Death of Richie, Remember When, Virginia Hill, All the Kind Strangers, Two of a Kind, California Girls, Alfred Hitchcock Presents (1985).
STAGE: Zelda, The Rothschilds, The Pirates of Penzance.

BENTON, ROBERT: Writer, Director. b. Waxahachie, TX, 1932. e. U. of Texas, B.A. Was art director and later consulting ed. at Esquire Magazine where he met David Newman, a writer-editor, and formed writing partnership. Together wrote a monthly column for Mademoiselle (10 years). Benton made directorial debut with Bad Company, 1972.
PICTURES INCLUDE: With Newman wrote: Bonnie and Clyde, There Was a Crooked Man, What's Up, Doc? Bad Company (also directed, solo s.p.), The Late Show (written and directed solo), Superman (with Mario Puzo and Tom Mankiewicz), Money's Tight. As dir.: Kramer vs. Kramer (5 Oscars) (dir. s.p.); Still of the Night (dir., s.p.); Places in Heart (dir., s.p.), Nadine (dir., s.p.), The House on Carroll Street (co-exec. prod.).
STAGE: It's a Bird . . It's a Plane . . . It's Superman (libretto), Oh! Calcutta (one sketch).

BERCUTT, MAX: Executive. b. Omaha, NB, Oct. 14, 1910. e. U. of Southern California, 1933. Pres., Paris-American Guide Services, Paris, France; publicist David O. Selznick Prod.; U.S. Navy officer, W.W.II; Warner Bros. field rep.; assistant to exec. vice-pres.; director of publicity, Warner Bros. Seven Arts Studio; resigned, September, 1969. Formed Max Bercutt Co., Jan. 1970.

BERENGER, TOM: Actor. b. Chicago, IL, May 31, 1950. e. U. of Missouri (drama). Acted in regional theatres and off-off-Broadway. Plays include The Rose Tattoo, Electra, Streetcar Named Desire, End as a Man (Circle Rep.). Film debut in the Beyond the Door (1975).
PICTURES: Sentinel, Looking for Mr. Goodbar, In Praise of Older Women, Butch and Sundance: The Early Days, The Dogs of War, The Big Chill, Eddie and the Cruisers, Fear City, Firstborn, Rustler's Rhapsody, Platoon, Someone to Watch Over Me, Shoot to Kill, Betrayed, Last Rites, Major League.
TELEVISION: One Life to Live (series), Johnny We Hardly Knew Ye, Flesh and Blood, If Tomorrow Comes.

BERENSON, MARISA: Actress. b. New York, NY Feb. 15, 1947. Granddaughter of haute couture fashion designer Scaparelli. Former model.
PICTURES: Death in Venice; Cabaret; Barry Lyndon; Killer Fish; S.O.B.; The Secret Diary of Sigmund Freud; La Tete Dans Le Sac; L'Arbalete.
TELEVISION: Tourist; Playing for Time.

BERESFORD, BRUCE: Director, Writer. b. Australia, 1949.
PICTURES INCLUDE: Director: The Adventures of Barry McKenzie, Barry McKenzie Holds His Own (also prod.), Don's Party, The Getting of Wisdom, Breaker Morant (also s.p.), The Club, Puberty Blues, Tender Mercies, King David, The Fringe Dwellers (also s.p.), Crimes of the Heart, Aria (sequence), Her Alibi.

BERG, DICK: Writer, Producer. b. New York, NY. e. Lehigh U. 1942; Harvard Business Sch. 1943. Prior to 1960 writer for TV shows Playhouse 90 Studio One, Robert Montgomery Presents, Kraft Television Playhouse. 1961–69 prod., writer for Universal Studios; exec. prod. The Chrysler Theatre, Alcoa Premiere, Checkmate. Created and wrote Staccato (series). 1971–85: prod., writer of over 50 TV movies via his Stonehenge Prods. TV films won 15 Emmies, 23 nominations. Twice elected pres. National Acad. of Television Arts and Sciences.
PICTURES: Prod.: Counterpoint, House of Cards, Banning Shoot (also s.p.), Fresh Horses.

TELEVISION: Prod. &/or writer: Mini-series: A Rumor of War, The Martian Chronicles, The World, Space, Wallenberg: A Hero's Story. Movies: Rape and Marriage: The Rideout Case, An Invasion of Privacy, Thief, Footsteps, Firehouse, American Geisha, Class of '63, Louis Armstrong, Chicago Style, Dolphin Bay.

BERG, JEFF: Executive. b. Los Angeles, CA, May 26, 1947. e. U of California, Berkeley, B.A., 1969. V.P., head lit. div., Creative Mgt. Associates, Los Angeles, 1969–75; v.p., m.p. dept., International Creative Associates, 1975–80; pres., 1980–. Dir., Joseph Intl. Industries.

BERGEN, CANDICE: Actress. b. Beverly Hills, CA, May 9, 1946. m. dir. Louis Malle. Daughter of ventriloquist Edgar Bergen. e. U. of Pennsylvania. Modeled during college; m.p. debut, The Group, 1965; freelance photo-journalist. Autobiography: Knock Wood (1984).
PICTURES INCLUDE: The Group, The Sand Pebbles, The Day the Fish Came Out, Live for Life, The Magus, The Adventurers, Getting Straight, Soldier Blue, Carnal Knowledge, The Hunting Party, T. R. Baskin, 11 Harrowhouse, Bite the Bullet, The Wind and the Lion, The Domino Principle, A Night Full of Rain, Oliver's Story, Starting Over, Rich and Famous, Gandhi, Stick.
TELEVISION: Hollywood Wives, Arthur the King, Murder: By Reason of Insanity, Mayflower Madam, Moving Day (Trying Times), Murphy Brown (series).

BERGEN, POLLY: Singer, Actress. b. Knoxville, TN, July 14, 1930. e. Compton Jr. Coll., CA. Prof. debut radio at 14; in light opera, summer stock; sang with orchestra and appeared in night clubs; Columbia recording star; pres. The Polly Bergen Co.; on stage, John Murray Anderson's Almanac, Champagne Complex, First Impressions.
PICTURES: At War With the Army, That's My Boy, The Stooge, Warpath, Arena, Escape from Ft. Bravo, Cape Fear, The Caretakers, Move Over Darling, Kisses for My President, Making Mr. Right.
TELEVISION: G.E. Theatre, Schlitz Playhouse, Playhouse 90, Studio One, Perry Como, Ed Sullivan Show, To Tell the Truth, Polly Bergen Show, Bob Hope Show, Bell Telephone, Wonderful World of Entertainment, Dinah Shore Show, Dean Martin Show, Andy Williams Show, Red Skelton Show, Mike Douglas Show. Movies: The Helen Morgan Story (Emmy Award, best actress, 1958), The Winds of War, War and Remembrance, Addicted to His Love.

BERGER, HELMUT: Actor. b. Salzburg, 1942. e. Feldkirk College and U. of Perugia. First film, small role in Luchino Visconti's The Witches (Le Streghe) in 1966.
PICTURES INCLUDE: The Young Tigers, The Damned, Do You Know What Stalin Did To Women?, The Garden of the Finzi-Continis, Dorian Gray, A Butterfly with Bloody Wings, The Greedy Ones, The Strange Love Affair, Ludwig, Ash Wednesday, Conversation Piece, The Romantic English-woman, Orders to Kill, Madame Kitty, Merry-Go-Round, Code Name: Emerald, The Glass Heaven, Faceless, The Be-trothed.

BERGER, RICHARD L.: Executive. b. Oct. 25, 1939. e. U. of California at L.A. In 1964 joined acct. dept., 20th Century-Fox; promoted to exec. position in Fox-TV. Was dir. of program-ming, then v.p. of programs. Appt. asst. v.p. prod. 20th-Fox. Left in 1975 to join CBS-TV as v.p. dramatic development. Returned to 20th-Fox in 1977 as v.p., domestic prod., 20th Century-Fox Pictures. Joined Warner Bros. Prods.; resigned 1984. Named sr. v.p., United Artists Corp., promoted to pres.

BERGERAC, JACQUES: Actor. b. Biarritz, France, May 26, 1927. Career includes Five Minutes With Jacques Bergerac on radio; in the theatre, on tour in Once More with Feeling; on most major network TV shows.
PICTURES INCLUDE: Twist of Fate, The Time is Now, Strange Intruder, Come Away With Me, Les Girls, Gigi, Man and His Past, Thunder in the Sun, Hypnotic Eye, A Sunday in Summer, Fear No More, Achilles, A Global Affair, Taffy and the Jungle Hunter, The Emergency Operation, Lady Chaplin, The Last Party, One Plus One.

BERGMAN, ALAN: Songwriter. b. New York, NY, Sept. 11, 1925. e. U. of North Carolina, U. of California at L.A. m. Marilyn Bergman with whom collaborates.
PICTURES INCLUDE: In the Heat of the Night, The Thomas Crown Affair, Happy Ending, Gaily, Gaily, Pieces of Dreams, Sometimes a Great Notion, The Way We Were, A Star Is Born, John and Mary, Life and Times of Judge Roy Bean, The One and Only, Same Time Next Year, And Justice for All, The Promise, A Change of Seasons, Yentl.
TELEVISION: Queen of the Stardust Ballroom, Hollow Image, Sybil, and themes for Maude, Good Times, Alice, Nancy Walker Show, etc.

BERGMAN, INGMAR: Writer, Director. b. Uppsala, Sweden, July 14, 1918. e. Stockholm U. Univershity play prods.; wrote & dir. Death of Punch, 1940; first theatrical success, dir., Macbeth, 1940; writer-director, Svensk Film-industri, 1942-present; first s.p, Frenzy, 1943; first directorial assignment, Crisis, 1946; chief prod., Civic Malmo, 1956–60. Directed Swedish prod. Hamlet for stage at Brooklyn Acad. of Music, 1988.
PICTURES INCLUDE: Kris, 1946 Det Regnar Pa Var Karlek, Skepp Till Indialand, Night is My Future, Port of Call, The Devil's Wanton, Three Strange Loves, Till Gladje, Summer Interlude (Illicit Interlude), High Tension, Bris (soap ads), Secrets of Women, Monika, The Naked Light, A Lesson in Love, Dreams, Smiles of a Summer Night, Sista Paret Ut, The Seventh Seal, Wild Strawberries, Brink of Life, The Magician, The Virgin Spring, The Devil's Eye, Through a Glass Darkly, Winter Light, The Silence, All These Women, Persona, Hour of the Wolf, Shame, The Passion of Anna, Cries and Whispers, Scenes from a Marriage, Face to Face, The Serpent's Egg, Autumn Sonata, Life of the Marionettes, Fanny and Alexander, After the Rehearsal.
AMERICAN TELEVISION: The Lie.

BERGMAN, MARILYN: Songwriter. b. New York, NY, Nov. 10, 1929. e. New York U. m. Alan Bergman with whom collabo-rates. See credits under his name.

BERLE, MILTON: Actor. r.n. Milton Berlinger; b. New York, NY, July 12, 1908. e. Professional Children's Sch., N.Y. In vaudeville; on N.Y. stage (Ziegfeld Follies 1936, Life Begins at 8:40, etc.): night clubs; concurrently on radio & screen. Author: Out of My Trunk (1945), Earthquake (1959), Milton Berle: An Auto-biography (1974).
TELEVISION: Star of own NBC show; Texaco Star Theatre, 1948–54, Kraft Music Hall TV Show, 1958–59, Jackpot Bowling, 1960–61, Doyle Against the House, Dick Powell Show, Chrysler TV special, 1962, The Milton Berle Show, 1966. Movies: Side By Side.
PICTURES INCLUDE: Tall, Dark and Handsome, Sun Valley Serenade, Over My Dead Body, Margin for Error, Always Leave Them Laughing, Let's Make Love, It's a Mad, Mad, Mad, Mad World, The Happening, Who's Minding the Mint, Where Angels Go . . . Trouble Follows, Can Hiero-nymus Merkin Ever Forget Mercy Humppe and Find True Happiness?, Lepke, Broadway Danny Rose.

BERLIN, IRVING: Composer. r.n. Israel Baline; b. Russia, May 11, 1888. To New York, 1893. As youth, singing waiter in N.Y.; early began writing songs. One of first successes, Alex-ander's Ragtime Band. Entered music pub.; member Water-son, Berlin & Snyder. W.W.I, sgt. inf. U.S. Army. Composer many indiv. and stage musical songs. In 1937 wrote songs for screen prod. Top Hat (RKO); in 1942 prod. stage musical This Is the Army for U.S. Army Fund; in 1943 assoc. with Warner Bros. in prod. film version. Member: Lambs, Friars (N.Y.); pres. Irving Berlin Music Corp., music pub.
PICTURES INCLUDE: Follow the Fleet, On the Avenue, Carefree, Alexander's Ragtime Band, Second Fiddle, Holiday Inn, Blue Skies, Easter Parade, Annie Get Your Gun, Call Me Madam, White Christmas, There's No Business Like Show Business.

BERLINGER, WARREN: Actor. b. Brooklyn, NY, Aug. 31, 1937. e. Columbia U.
STAGE: Annie Get Your Gun, The Happy Time, Bernar-dine, Take A Giant Step, Anniversary Waltz, Roomful of Roses, Blue Denim, Come Blow Your Horn, How To Succeed in Business Without Really Trying, (London) Who's Happy Now?, California Suite (1977–78 tour).
PICTURES INCLUDE: Teenage Rebel, Three Brave Men, Blue Denim, Because They're Young, Platinum High School, The Wackiest Ship in the Army, All Hand on Deck, Billie, Spinout, Thunder Alley, Lepke, The Four Deuces, I Will . . . I Will . . . for Now, Harry and Walter Go to New York, The Shaggy D.A., The Magician of Dublin, The Cannonball Run, The World According to Garp, Take Two, Outlaw Force.
TELEVISION: Secret Storm (serial), Alcoa, Goodyear, Armstrong, Matinee Theatre, Joey Bishop Show, The London Palladium, Kilroy, Billie, Bracken's World, The Funny Side, Touch of Grace, The Most Wanted Woman, The Other Woman, What Price Victory.

BERMAN, MONTY M.: Film and theatrical costumier. b. London, England, 1912. Personally costumed films and shows since 1931. Squad Leader RAF 1940–45; Bomber Command, M.B.E. Since war has costumed major films and shows and numerous TV prod.
PICTURES INCLUDE: Doctor Zhivago, Tom Jones, Long-est Day, My Fair Lady, Oliver, Cromwell, Patton, Fiddler on the Roof, A Bridge Too Far, Julia, The Slipper and the Rose, A Little Night Music, Star Wars, Superman, James Bond Films, The Four Musketeers, Mommie Dearest, Raiders of the Lost Ark, Chariots of Fire, Superman II and III, Gandhi, Yentl, The Dresser, Indiana Jones and The Temple of Doom, Cotton Club, Out of Africa, The Living Daylights.

BERMAN, PANDRO S.: Producer. b. Pittsburgh, PA, March 28, 1905. Son of late Harry M. Berman, gen. mgr. Universal, FBO. Asst. dir. film ed., FBO; film & title ed. Columbia Studios; chief film ed. RKO, later asst. to William Le Baron & David

Selznick; became prod. 1931 (RKO). A Champion of Champions Producers in Fame ratings. Joined MGM 1940.
PICTURES INCLUDE: What Price Hollywood, Symphony of Six Million, Bachelor Mother, The Gay Divorcee, Of Human Bondage, Morning Glory, Roberta, Alice Adams, Top Hat, Winterset, Stage Door, Vivacious Lady, Gunga Din, Hunchback of Notre Dame, Ziegfeld Girl, Honky Tonk, Seventh Cross, National Velvet, Dragon Seed, Portrait of Dorian Grey, Love Affair, Undercurrent, Sea of Grass, Three Musketeers, Madame Bovary, Father of the Bride, Father's Little Dividend, Prisoner of Zenda, Ivanhoe, All the Brothers Were Valiant, Knights of the Round Table, Long, Long Trailer, Blackboard Jungle, Bhowani Junction, Something of Value, Tea and Sympathy, Brothers Karamazov, Reluctant Debutante, Butterfield 8, Sweet Bird of Youth, The Prize, A Patch of Blue, Justine, Move.

BERMAN, STEVEN H: Executive. b. Middletown, OH, March 22, 1952. e. Ohio U., B.F.A. in playwriting, 1974; U. of Southern California, Annenberg Sch. of Communication studied management, 1977. m. Marcia Berman. Special research projects Paramount and ABC Television, 1977. Account exec., Gardner Advertising, 1978. Development exec., CBS Television, 1979–82. Director of comedy development, CBS Television, 1982–84. Five years at CBS in series development, comedy and drama. Vice pres., dramatic development, Columbia Pictures Television, 1984–85. Sr. vice pres., Creative Affairs, Columbia Pictures Television, 1985–87. Exec. vice pres., Columbia Television, division of Columbia/Embassy Television, 1987–present.

BERNARD, MARVIN A.: Executive. b. New York, NY, Oct. 1, 1934. e. New York U. Lab technician to v.p. in charge of sales, Rapid Film Technique, Inc., 1949–63; developed technological advances in film rejuvenation and preservation, responsible for public underwriting; 1964–69; real estate sales & investments in Bahamas, then with Tishman Realty (commercial leasing div.); v.p. and operating head of International FilmTreat 1970–1973; authored film damaged control chart, a critical analysis of film care and repair—1971; founded Filmlife Inc. with latest chemical/mechanical and technical advancement in field of film rejuvenation and preservation. 1973–75 bd. chmn, and chief operating officer of Filmlife Inc., motion picture film rejuvenation, storage and distribution company. Feb. 1975 elected President in addition to remaining bd. chairman. 1979 consultant to National Archives of U.S. on m.p. preservation. 1981 dev. m.p. rejuvenation and preservation for 8mm and S8mm. 1986 introduced this technology to private home movie use. 1987, active member of awards comm. for tech. achievements, National Acad. TV Arts & Sciences.

BERNHARD, HARVEY: Producer. b. Seattle, WA, March 5, 1924. e. Stanford U. In real estate 1947–50; started live lounge entertainment at the Last Frontier Hotel, Las Vegas, 1950. Partner with Sandy Howard, 1958–60; v.p. in chg. prod., David L. Wolper Prods., dividing time between TV and feature films, 1961–68; with MPC, v.p., chg. prod., 1968–70. Now pres. of Harvey Bernhard Ent., Inc.
PICTURES INCLUDE: The Mack (1973), The Omen, Damien—Omen II, The Final Conflict, The Beast Within, Ladyhawke (exec. prod.), Goonies (prod.), Lost Boys.

BERNSTEIN, ARMYAN: Director-Writer.
PICTURES INCLUDE: Thank God It's Friday (s.p.); One From the Heart (co-s.p.); Windy City (s.p., dir.); American Date (dir.), Satisfaction (co-exec. prod.), Cross My Heart (dir., co-s.p.).

BERNSTEIN, BOB: Executive. Began public relations career 1952 at DuMont TV Network, followed by 2 yrs. as press agent for Liberace. With Billboard Magazine as review editor 3 yrs. Joined Westinghouse Bdg. Co. as p.r. director 1959. In 1963 named p.r. director for Triangle Publications, serving in various capacities to 1971. Joined Viacom Intl. as director of information services. In 1975 formed own co., March Five Inc., p.r. and promotion firm.

BERNSTEIN, ELMER: Composer, Conductor. b. New York, NY, April 4, 1922. Scholarship, Juilliard. e. Walden Sch., New York U., U.S Army Air Force radio unit. After war 3 yrs. recitals, musical shows, United Nations radio dept; pres., Young Musicians Found.; 1st v.p. Academy of Motion Picture Arts & Sciences; co-chairman music branch. Music dir. Valley Symphony. Recording: United Artists. More than 90 major films. Pres. of Composers & Lyricists Guild of America.
PICTURES INCLUDE: The Ten Commandments, Man With the Golden Arm, The Great Escape, To Kill a Mockingbird (received ten Academy Award nominations and Oscar, 1967), The Carpetbaggers, The Magnificent Seven, Birdman of Alcatraz, Walk on the Wild Side, Hallelujah Trail, The Reward, Seven Women, Cast A Giant Shadow, Hawaii, Thoroughly Modern Millie, True Grit, Cahill, U.S. Marshall, McQ., Gold, The Trial of Billy Jack, Report to the Commissioner, From Noon Till Three, Sarah, The Shootist, Blood Brothers, The Great Santini, Meatballs, Saturn 3, Airplane!, Going Ape,

Stripes, An American Werewolf in London, Honky Tonk Freeway, The Chosen, Five Days One Summer, Airplane II: The Sequel, Spacehunter, Class, Trading Places, Bolero, Ghostbusters, Spies Like Us, Legal Eagles, Three Amigos, Amazing Grace and Chuck, Leonard Part 6, Da, Funny Farm.
TELEVISION: Specials: Hollywood: The Golden Years, The Race for Space; Parts I & II, D-Day, The Making of the President—1960 (won Emmy Award), Hollywood and the Stars, Voyage of the Brigantine Yankee, Crucification of Jesus, NBC Best Sellers Theme (1976). Series: Julia, Owen Marshall, Ellery Queen, Serpico, The Chisholms. Movies: Gulag, Guyana Tragedy.

BERNSTEIN, JACK B.: Producer. b. New York, NY, May 6, 1937. e. New York, B.A., sociology. U.S. Army-Europe, 1956–58; research bacteriologist, 1959–61. Entered industry in 1962 with S.I.B. Prods., Paramount, as gen. mgr.; 1964–66, v.p. gen. mgr. C.P.I. Prods, 1966–73 prod. mgr. asst. dir., free lance. 1973–1982, assoc. prod. exec. prod. at several studios. 1983–86, v.p. worldwide prod., Walt Disney Pictures; 1987, sr. v.p., worldwide prod., United Artists Pictures. Resigned 1988 to form indep. production firm. Member: DGA, Friars, Academy of MP Arts & Sciences; Academy of TV Arts & Sciences.
PICTURES: Assoc. Prod.: The Other Side of Midnight, The Fury, Butch Sundance, The Early Days, Six Pack, Unfaithfully Yours. Exec. Prod.: North Dallas Forty, Monsignore, The Beast Within.

BERNSTEIN, JAY: Producer, Personal manager. b. Oklahoma City, OK, June 7, 1937. e. Pomona Coll. 1963–76, pres. of Jay Bernstein Public Relations, representing over 600 clients. Formed Jay Bernstein Enterprises, acting as personal manager for Farrah Fawcett, Suzanne Somers, Kristy McNichol, Susan Hayward, Donald Sutherland, Bruce Boxleitner, Robert Conrad, Susan Saint James, Robert Blake, William Shatner, Linda Evans, Cicely Tyson, etc. Past pres., Bernstein-Thompson Entertainment Complex, entertainment and personal mgt. firm.
PICTURES: Exec. prod.: Sunburn, Nothing Personal.
TELEVISION: Exec. prod. Movies: The Return of Mike Hammer, Mickey Spillane's Margin for Murder; Wild, Wild, West, Revisited; More Wild, Wild West. Murder Me, Murder You, More Than Murder. Series: Bring 'Em Back Alive, Mike Hammer, Houston Knights (series).

BERNSTEIN, BARON SIDNEY, Baron cr 1969 (Life Peer) of Leigh; Sidney Lewis Bernstein LLd; Chairman; Granada Group PLC from 1934–79. Pres. since 1979. (Granada Television, Granada Theatres, Granada TV Rental, Granada Motorway Services, Novello & Co). b. 30 Jan. 1899. A founder, Film Society, 1924. Films Adviser, Min. of Inf. 1940–45; Liaison, British Embassy, Washington 1942; Chief, Film Section SHAEF 1943–45. Lecturer on Film and International Affairs, New York U. and Yale. Governor, Sevenoaks School. Member, Resources for Learning Committee, Nuffield Foundation, Member: Jerusalem Committee.

BERNSTEIN, WALTER: Director, Writer. b. New York, NY. Aug. 20, 1919. e. Dartmouth. Wrote for New Yorker Magazine; in W.W.II was roving correspondent for Yank Magazine. Returned to New Yorker after war. Wrote TV scripts; published book Keep Your Head Down (collection of articles).
PICTURES INCLUDE: Writer: The Molly McGuires, The Money Trap, Fail Safe, Paris Blues, Heller in Pink Tights, Semi-Tough, The Front, An Almost Perfect Affair, Yanks, Little Miss Marker (dir., debut), The House on Carroll Street (s.p.).

BERNSTEIN, WILLIAM: Executive. b. New York, NY, August 30, 1933. e. Yale Law Sch., LL.B., 1959; New York U., B.A., 1954. Exec. vice pres., Orion Pictures Corp. Asst. gen. counsel, then sr. v.p. United Artists 1959–78.

BERRI, CLAUDE: Actor, Director, Producer. b. Paris, July 1, 1934. r.n. Langmann. Began film career with short film Le Poulet (prod. and dir.; won Acad. Award, short subject, 1966).
PICTURES: The Two of Us (dir.); Marry Me, Marry Me (dir., actor); Le Pistonne (dir.); Le Cinema de Papa (prod.-dir.); Sex Shop (dir., s.p.); Male of the Century (dir., s.p., actor); The First Time (dir., s.p.); Tess (prod.); Inspecteur la Bavure (prod.); Je Vous Aime (prod., s.p.); Le Maitre d' Ecole (prod., dir., s.p.); A Quarter to Two Before Jesus Christ (prod.); L'Africain (prod.); Banzai (prod.); L'Homme Blesse (prod.); Garcon! Tchao Pantin (prod., s.p., dir.); Scemo Di Guerra; Jean la Florette; Manon of the Springs; The Bear (exec. prod.). The Door on the Left as You Leave the Elevator.

BERRY, JOHN: Director. b. New York, NY, 1917. Directed films in Hollywood mid and late '40s; went abroad during McCarthy era in U.S. where worked in French film industry. Later went to London to do stage work, acting as well as directing. Returned to U.S. to do stage work; returned to Hollywood to do TV.
PICTURES INCLUDE: Cross My Heart, From This Day Forward, Miss Susie Slagle's, Casbah, Tension, He Ran All the Way, Ça Va Barder, The Great Lover, Je Suis un

Sentimental, Tamango, On Que Mambo, Claudine, Maya, The Bad News Bears Go to Japan, Thieves, Il y a maldonne, 'Round Midnight (actor only), A Man in Love (actor only). TELEVISION: One Drink at a Time, Farewell Party, Mr. Broadway, Sister, Sister (also prod.); Angel on My Shoulder, Honeyboy.

BERRY, KEN: Actor. b. Moline, IL, Nov. 3.
PICTURES INCLUDE: Two for the Seesaw, Hello Down There, Herbie Rides Again, The Cat from Outer Space.
TELEVISION: The Reluctant Heroes, Wake Me When the War Is Over, Every Man Needs One (movie), Ken Berry Wow Show, Mayberry RFD, F. Troop, Mama's Family.

BERTINELLI, VALERIE: Actress. b. Wilmington, DE, April 23, 1960. Dramatic training at Tami Lynn Academy of Artists in California. Made early TV appearances in the series, Apple's Way, in commercials, and in public service announcements. Started own production company to acquire properties for self.
TELEVISION: Movies: Young Love, First Love; The Promise of Love, The Princess and the Cabbie, I Was a Mail Order Bride, The Seduction of Gina, Shattered Vows, Rockabye, Silent Witness, Ordinary Heroes. Specials: The Secret of Charles Dickens, The Magic of David Copperfield, etc., Pancho Barnes. Series: One Day at a Time. Mini-Series: I'll Take Manhattan.
PICTURE: Number One with a Bullet.

BERTOLUCCI, BERNARDO: Director, Writer, b. Parma, Italy, March 16, 1941. e. Rome U. Son of Attilio Bertolucci, poet and film critic. First worked in films at age of 20 as asst. dir. to Pier Paolo Pasolini on latter's first film, Accatone: in 1962 made debut film, The Grim Reaper, from script by Pasolini. 1962 published poetry book: In cerca del mistero. 1965–66: directed and wrote 3-part TV documentary: La vie del Petrolio for Ital. Oil co. in Iran. Collaborated on s.p. Ballata de un Milliardo, and Leone's Once Upon a Time in the West.
PICTURES INCLUDE: Before the Revolution, Partner, Love and Rage (one episode: Agony). The Spider's Strategem, The Conformist, Last Tango in Paris, 1900, Luna, Tragedy of a Ridiculous Man, The Last Emperor (Acad. Award, 1987).

BESMAN, MICHAEL: Executive. e. U. of California at L.A., B.A. in film studies. Gained first experience in m.p. industry as asst. to director Michael Wadleigh during post-production work on Wolfen. Served as asst. to prod. Aaron Russo in developing new projects, including Trading Places. 1983, joined Paramount Pictures as researcher for story dept. Named creative exec. with studio prod. dept. 1985, promoted to exec. dir., production, for Paramount M.P. Group.

BEST, BARBARA: Publicist. b. San Diego, CA, Dec. 2, 1921. e. U. of Southern California, AB, 1943. Pub., 20th Century-Fox, 1943–49; reporter, San Diego Journal, 1950 Stanley Kramer Co. 1950–53; own agency, Barbara Best & Associates, 1953–66; 1966 exec. v.p. Jay Bernstein Public rel.; Freeman and Best, 1967–74; Barbara Best Inc. publ. rel. 1975–85; Barbara Best Personal Management, current.

BEST, JAMES: Actor. b. Corydon, IN, July 26, 1926. Magazine model; on stage; in European roadshow cast of My Sister Eileen; served as M.P. with U.S.A.A.F., W.W.II; m.p. debut in Comanche Territory, 1949.
PICTURES INCLUDE: Winchester 73, Air Cadet, Cimarron Kid, Steel Town, Ma & Pa Kettle at the Fair, Francis Goes to West Point, Seminole, The President's Lady, City of Bad Men, Column South, Riders to the Stars, The Raid, Caine Mutiny, Return from the Sea, The Left-Handed Gun, They Rode West, Seven Angry Men, Come Next Spring, Baby, The Rack, Sounder, Ode to Billy Joe, The End, Hooper, Rolling Thunder.
RECENT TELEVISION: Hawkins, Savages, The Runaway, Barge, The Savage Bees, The Dukes of Hazzard (regular), Enos.

BETHUNE, ZINA: Actress, Dancer, Singer. b. New York, NY, 1950. Broadway: Most Happy Fella, National Tours: Sweet Charity, Carnival, Oklahoma!, Damn Yankees, Member of the Wedding, The Owl and The Pussycat, Nutcracker. New York City Ballet (Balanchine), Zina Bethune & Company Dance Theatre, Bethune Ballet Theatre Danse.
PICTURES: Sunrise At Campobello, Who's That Knocking at My Door.
TELEVISION: The Nurses, Lancer, Cains Hundred, Naked City, Route 66, Little Women, Santa Barbara, Judy Garland Show, Jackie Gleason Show, Gunsmoke, Dr. Kildare, Emergency, Planet of The Apes, Police Story, Chips, Hardy Boys, The Gymnast, Nutcracker: Money, Madness, Murder, Heart Dancing.

BETTGER, LYLE: Actor b. Philadelphia, PA, Feb. 13, 1915. e. Haverford School, Philadelphia, American Acad. of Dramatic Art, N.Y. m. Mary Rolfe, actress. Started in summer stock; in road cos. of Brother Rat, Man Who Came to Dinner.
STAGE: John Loves Mary, Love Life, Eve of St. Mark.

PICTURES INCLUDE: No Man of Her Own, Union Station, First Legion, Greatest Show on Earth, Sea Chase, Gunfight at OK Corral, Johnny Reno, Nevada Smith, Return of The Gunfighter, The Hawaiians, Carnival Story, The Seven Minutes.
TELEVISION: Court of Last Resort, Grand Jury, Hawaii 5-0, Police Story.

BETUEL, JONATHAN: Director.
PICTURES: My Science Project; Tripwire.

BEVILLE, HUGH M., JR.: Executive; b. April 18, 1908. e. Syracuse U., New York U. (MBA). To NBC 1930 statistician, chief statistician; Research mgr., dir., research; U.S. Army 1942–46; dir. of research and planning for NBC, v.p., planning and research, 1956; v.p., planning, 1964; consultant, 1968; professor Business Admin., Southampton Coll., 1968. Exec. dir., Broadcast Rating Council, 1971–82, author-consultant, contributing editor, TV/Radio Age, 1982–85. Author, Audience Ratings; Radio, Television, Cable, 1985, Elected member, Research Hall of Fame, 1986.

BEY, TURHAN: Actor. b. Vienna, Austria, March 30. Made U.S. m.p. debut in 1941.
PICTURES INCLUDE: Footsteps in the Dark, Burma Convoy, Bombay Clipper, Drums of the Congo, Destination Unknown, White Savage, Dragon Seed, Arabian Nights, Bowery to Broadway, Night in Paradise, Out of the Blue, Amazing Mr. X, Parole, Inc., Adventures of Casanova, Song of India, Prisoners of the Casbah, Stolen Identity.

BEYMER, RICHARD: Actor. r.n. George Richard Beymer, Jr., b. Avoca, IA, Feb. 21, 1939. e. N. Hollywood H.S., Actors Studio. Performer, KTLA, Sandy Dreams, Fantastic Studios, Inc., 1949, Playhouse 90.
PICTURES INCLUDE: Indiscretion of an American Wife, So Big, Johnny Tremaine, The Diary of Anne Frank, High Time, West Side Story, Bachelor Flat, Five Finger Exercise, Hemingway's Adventures of a Young Man, The Longest Day, The Stripper, Cross Country.

BIBAS, FRANK PERCY: Executive. b. New York, NY, 1917. e. Brown U., Columbia U. Capt., Army Air Corps, W.W.II. Entered m.p. ind. adv. dept., Donahue & Coe; later pub. dept. American Display, then to dist. dept., National Screen Service. In 1945 joined Casanave-Artlee Pictures Inc.; apptd. vice-pres. in charge of sales 1946 (dist. Selznick reissues in U.S.); vice-pres. Casanave Pictures, Inc. & Sixteen M.M. Pictures Inc., from 1949 mgr. m.p. dept., McCann-Erickson ad agency; joined Roland Reed TV Inc., v.p., prod., 1955. Prod-dir. with Hal Roach Studios, 1957. 1961 to present N.Y.C. partner, Bibas-Redford Inc. Production Co. 1962 won Academy Award for Project Hope, documentary. Member: S.M.P.T.E., Acad. of TV Arts and Sciences, Directors Guild of America.

BICK, JERRY: Producer. b. New York, NY, April 6, 1923. e. Columbia U., Sorbonne. Taught English at U. of Georgia and was radio sports announcer in Savannah, GA, before entering film industry in pub. dept. of MGM, N.Y. Opened own literary agency in Hollywood representing film, TV writers. Began career as producer in London; debut film, Michael Kohlhaas, 1969, made in Czechoslovakia. Oct. 1986–Jan. 1988, exec. v.p. worldwide prod., Heritage Entertainment.
PICTURES INCLUDE: The Long Goodbye, Thieves Like Us, Russian Roulette, Farewell My Lovely, The Big Sleep, Against All Odds (exec. prod.), Swing Shift.

BIEHN, MICHAEL: Actor. b. Nebraska, 1957. At 18 years moved to Los Angeles and studied acting. First professional job in 1977 in TV pilot for Logan's Run.
PICTURES INCLUDE: Coach, Hog Wild, The Fan, The Lords of Discipline, The Terminator, Aliens, The Boarder, The Seventh Sign, Rampage, In a Shallow Grave.
TELEVISION: Pilots for James at Fifteen and The Runaways; several movies-of-the-week, ABC Afternoon Specials. Series: Police Story, Family. Movies: China Rose, Deadly Intentions.

BIEN, WALTER H.: Producer. b. San Francisco, CA, April 16, 1923. e. U. of California at L.A., 1944. Entered m.p. ind. as film editor, MGM, 1943; Monogram, 1946; Eagle Lion, 1948; formed TV production company 1950, prod. live shows in L.A. area; Universal TV comm. dept., 1954; Warner Bros., to start comm. & ind. div., 1956; exec. prod. in chg. TV comm. ind. films div., prod. Bell System Science Series; pres., SIB Productions, Inc., SIB-Tower 12.

BILBY, KENNETH W.: Executive. b. Salt Lake City, UT, Oct. 7, 1918. e. Columbia U., U. of Arizona, B.A. With N.Y. Herald-Tribune, 47–50; author, New Star in the Near East, 1950; pub. rel. rep. to RCA Victor, Camden, NJ, 1950–54; exec. v.p. National Broadcasting Co., N.Y., 1954–60; V.p public affairs, RCA, 1960–62, exec. v.p. 1962–75; exec. v.p. corporate affairs, 1976–present.

BILIMORIA, N. M.: Distributor. b. Oct. 7, 1922, Partner in M. B. Bilimoria & Son, Bombay; dir. Dominion Films (P) Ltd.

Bombay; Modern Films Private Ltd., Bombay; Partner, Bilimoria & Lalji, Calcutta; Distributors Combine, Bombay; Bilimoria & Chhotubhai, Delhi; Moti Talkies, Delhi; Agent: Union Carbide India Ltd., Calcutta and Union Carbide International Co., N.Y.

BILL, TONY: Actor, Producer. b. San Diego, CA, Aug. 23, 1940. e. Notre Dame U. Began career in films in 1963 acting in Come Blow Your Horn. In 1971 founded Bill/Phillips Prods. with Julia and Michael Phillips. Left in 1973 to be independent.
PICTURES INCLUDE: Actor: You're a Big Boy Now, Castle Keep, Shampoo, Heartbeat, Less Than Zero. Co-producer: Deadhead Miles, Steelyard Blues, The Sting. Prod.: Hearts of the West, Harry and Walter Go to New York, Boulevard Nights (exec. prod.); Going in Style (co-prod.). Director: My Bodyguard, Six Weeks, Five Corners (also co-prod.).
TELEVISION: As actor: Washington Mistress, Running Out, Alfred Hitchcock Presents (Night Caller, 1985).

BILLITTERI, SALVATORE: Executive. b. Belleville, NJ, March 21, 1921. e. Fordham U. U.S. Air Force, 1943–45; ent. m.p. ind., doorman in N.Y. theatre, 1939; theatre mgr., 1947; film slsman, Casolaro Film Distributing Co., 1947–51; co-owner many foreign films; film editor, I.F.E., 1951; head of editing, prod. dept., Titra Sound Corp., 1956; head of east coast production, American International Pictures, 1961; dir. Post Prod., 1970; named v.p. 1974, sr. v.p. of Filmways Pictures, 1980; sr. v.p., post production, Orion Pictures Dist. Corp., 1982.

BILSON, BRUCE: Director. b. Brooklyn, NY, May 19, 1928. e. UCLA, BA, Theater Arts, 1950. m. actress Renne Jarrett. Father is prod. George Bilson, son is writer-dir. Danny Bilson. Asst. film ed. 1951–55; USAF photo unit 1952–53; asst. dir. 1955–65 including Andy Griffith Show, Route 66. Assoc. prod. The Baileys of Balboa. Dir. since 1965 of more than 300 TV shows. Emmy Award, Get Smart, DGA nom. The Odd Couple.
PICTURES: The North Avenue Irregulars, Chattanooga Choo Choo.
TELEVISION: Barney Miller, Get Smart, Hogan's Heroes, House Calls, Alice, Private Benjamin, Life With Lucy, Spenser: For Hire, Hotel, Dallas, Hawaii Five-O, The Fall Guy. Movies/pilots: The Dallas Cowboys Cheerleaders, BJ and the Bear, The Misadventures of Sheriff Lobo, Half Nelson, Finder of Lost Loves, The Girl Who Came Gift Wrapped, The Ghosts of Buxley Hall, The New Gidget, Barefoot in the Park, The Bad News Bears, The Odd Couple, Harper Valley PTA.

BINDER, STEVE: Producer, Director, Writer. b. Los Angeles, CA, Dec. 12. e. Univ. of Southern California. 1960–61 announcer in Austria and Germany with AFN, Europe. Prof. of Cinema, Univ. Southern CA. Mem.: DGA, Producers Guild of America, Writers Guild of America, NARAS, ATAS.
TELEVISION: Prod., Dir.: Steve Allen Show (1963–65, 1973); Elvis Presley Comeback Special; Barry Manilow Special (also writer, Emmy Award, 1977); Diana Ross in Central Park (dir., ACE Award), Diana Ross '81 (also writer); Ringling Bros & Barnum Bailey Circus (also writer), Pee-Wee's Playhouse (prod. only), Big Fun on Swing Street, Barry Manilow and over 200 major TV prods.
PICTURES: Give 'Em Hell, Harry! (dir.)

BINNS, EDWARD: Actor. b. Pennsylvania, 1916. Broadway debut in Command Decision, 1947. Has since appeared in TV, theatre, m.p. and commercial voice-overs.
PICTURES INCLUDE: Fail-Safe, Twelve Angry Men, Compulsion, Patton, The Americanization of Emily, Judgment at Nuremburg, Lovin' Molly, Night Moves, Oliver's Story, Before God, Private Tutor.
TELEVISION: Kraft Theatre, Studio One, Danger, Brenner (series), The Defenders, The Nurses, It Takes a Thief (series).
STAGE: Detective Story, Caligula, The Caine Mutiny Court Martial, A Touch of the Poet.

BIONDI, JR. FRANK J.: Executive. b. Jan. 9, 1945. e. Princeton U.; Harvard U., MBA (1968). Various investment banking positions 1968–74; asst. treas. Children's TV Workshop 1974–78; v.p. programming HBO 1978–82; pres. HBO 1983, then chm. & chief exec. off. 1984 joined Coca-Cola Co. as exec. v.p., entertainment business arm. Resigned 1987 to join Viacom International as pres. and CEO.

BIRCH, WILLIAM: Cinematographer. b. Chicago, IL, March 1, 1918. Asst., Movietonews, 1937–40; army signal corp, 1940–44; head of midwestern bureau, did camera, NBC News & Document.; established own service; estab. William Birch & Assoc. Inc.
Won two Emmys, cameraman of the yr., Nat. Headliners Award.

BIRMINGHAM, PAUL A.: Executive. b. Burbank, CA, Feb. 12, 1937. e. U. of California, U. of Southern California. Sr. v.p. studio operations and admin., Paramount Pictures.

BIRNEY, DAVID: Actor. b. Washington, DC, April 23, 1940. e. Dartmouth, U. of California at L.A. m. actress Meredith

Baxter Birney. Following college and the Army went to N.Y. where appeared in Lincoln Center prod. of Summertree. Appeared for two yrs. on TV daytime series, Love Is a Many Splendored Thing, doing other stage roles in same period.
THEATER: NY debut NY Shakespeare Fest; 3 seasons Lincoln Center Rep. Many NY and regional credits including: Amadeus, Benefactors, Man and Superman.
PICTURES INCLUDE: Caravan to Vaccares, Trial by Combat, Oh God, II, Goodbye, See You Monday, Prettykill, Nightfall.
TELEVISION: Series: St. Elsewhere, 6 Littles, Serpico, Bridget Loves Bernie (reg.). Mini-series: Seal Morning, Adam's Chronicles, Testimony of Two Men, Master of the Game, Valley of the Dolls, The Bible. Movies: The Deadly Game; OHMS; The 5 of Me; Mom, The Wolfman & Me; High Rise; The Champions; Bronc; The Long Journey Home (also co-exec. prod.), The Diaries of Adam and Eve (also prod.).

BIRNEY, MEREDITH BAXTER: Actress. b. Los Angeles, CA, June 21, 1947. On stage in Guys and Dolls; Butterflies Are Free; Vanities; Country Wife; Talley's Folly.
PICTURES: Ben, Bittersweet Love, All the President's Men.
TELEVISION: Series: The Interns, Bridget Loves Bernie, Family, Family Ties. Movies: The Night That Panicked America, The Stranger Who Looks Like Me, The Imposter, The Two Lives of Carol Leitner, Take Your Best Shot, The Rape of Richard Beck, Kate's Secret, The Long Journey Home (and co-exec. prod.), Winnie: My Life in the Institution. Mini-series: Beulah Land, Little Women, The Diaries of Adam and Eve (also prod.).

BIROC, JOSEPH F.: Cinematographer. b. New York, NY, Feb. 12, 1903. e. Emerson H.S., Union City, NJ.
PICTURES INCLUDE: Bwana Devil, Glass Wall, Tall Texan, Vice Squad, Donovan's Brain, Appointment in Honduras, Down Three Dark Streets, Lone Wolf, T-Men in Action, Man Behind the Badge, Dear Phoebe, Nightmare, Tension at Table Rock, Attack, Black Whip, Run of the Arrow, Ride Back, Garment Jungle, China Gate, Ice Palace, FBI Story, 13 Ghosts, Home Before Dark, Operation Eichmann, Devil at 4 O'clock, Gold of the Seven Saints, Reprieve, Opium Eaters, Hitler, Sail a Crooked Ship, Bye Bye Birdie, Toys in the Attic, Promises-Promises, Under the Yum-Yum Tree, Viva Las Vegas, Kitten With a Whip, Ride the Wild Surf, Renegade Posse, Gunfight at Commanche Pass, Hush . . . Hush, Sweet Charlotte, I Saw What You Did, Flight of the Phoenix, The Russians Are Coming, The Russians Are Coming, The Swinger, Warning Shot, Enter Laughing, Who Is Minding the Mint, Garden of Cucumbers, The Killing of Sister George, What Ever Happened to Aunt Alice?, Too Late the Hero, Mrs. Polifax Spy, Escape from the Planet of the Apes, The Organization, The Grissom Gang, Cahill, U.S. Marshall, The Longest Yard, The Towering Inferno, Hustle, The Duchess and the Dirtwater Fox, The Choirboys, Beyond the Poseidon Adventure, Airplane!, Hammet, All the Marbles, Airplane II: The Sequel.
TELEVISION: Four Star Theatre, Readers Digest, Superman, Richard Diamond, Alcoa Theatre, Grindl, Solo, Ghost Breakers, Take Her She's Mine, Heaven Help Us, Hardy Boys, Brian's Song, Gidget Gets Married, Ghost Story, Thursdays Game, Lonely Hearts, 555, Family Upside Down, S.S.T. Death Flight, Little Women, Scruples, The Gambler, A Death in California, A Winner Never Quits, Outrage.
TV PILOTS: Wonder Woman, Honky Tonk, The Moneychangers, Washington, D.C., Clone Master, Desperate Lives, Casablanca, Another Jerk, House Detective, Hell Town U.S.A., Flag, Time Out for Dad.

BISHOP, JULIE: Actress. b. Denver, CO, Aug. 30, 1917. e. Westlake, Kenwood, Schools for Girls. Former screen name Jacqueline Wells; m.p. debut 1941.
PICTURES INCLUDE: Nurse's Secret, International Squadron, Steel Against the Sky, Lady Gangster, Busses Roar, Cinderella Jones, Murder in the Music Hall, Idea Girl, Strange Conquest, Last of the Redmen, High Tide, Deputy Marshal, Threat, Sands of Iwo Jima, Westward the Women, Sabre Jet, High and the Mighty, Headline Hunters.

BISSET, JACQUELINE: Actress. b. Weybridge, England, September 13, 1944. e. French Lycée, London. After photographic modeling made film debut in The Knack, 1965.
PICTURES INCLUDE: Cul de Sac, Two For The Road, Casino Royale, The Sweet Ride, The Detective, Bullitt, The First Time, Airport, The Grasshopper, The Mephisto Waltz, Believe in Me, The Life & Times of Judge Roy Bean, Stand Up and Be Counted, The Thief Who Came to Dinner, Day for Night, Murder on the Orient Express, End of the Game, The Spiral Staircase, St. Ives, Sunday Woman, The Deep, The Greek Tycoon, Secrets, Who Is Killing the Great Chefs of Europe?, When Time Ran Out, Rich and Famous, Inchon, Class, Under the Volcano, High Season, Scenes From the Class Struggle in Beverly Hills, La Maison de Jade.
TELEVISION: Forbidden, Choices, Anna Karenina, Napoleon and Josephine: A Love Story.

BIXBY, BILL: Actor. b. San Francisco, CA, Jan. 22, 1934. e. U. of California, Berkeley. Worked in indust. films. Gen. Motors, Chrysler.
TELEVISION: Dobie Gillis, Danny Thomas Show, Joey Bishop Show, Andy Griffith Show, My Favorite Martian, The Courtship of Eddie's Father, The Incredible Hulk, Goodbye Beantown, International Airport, J.J. Starbuck, Agatha Christie's Murder Is Easy, The Incredible Hulk Returns (also exec. prod.).
STAGE: Fantasticks (nat'l company), Under the Yum Yum Tree.
PICTURES INCLUDE: Lonely Are the Brave, Irma La Douce, Under the Yum Yum Tree, Ride Beyond Vengeance, This Way Out Please.

BLACK, ALEXANDER F.: Publicist. b. New Rochelle, NY, Dec. 27, 1918. e. Brown U., BA, 1940. Joined Universal 1941. U.S. Navy 1942–45, Lt. Sr. Grade. Rejoined Universal 1946 serving in various capacities in Foreign Department, becoming Director of Foreign Publicity for Universal International Films, Inc. in 1967; 1974, named exec. in chg. intl. promotion for MCA-TV.

BLACK, KAREN: Actress. b. Park Ridge, IL, July 1, 1942. e. Northwestern U. Left school for New York to join the Hecscher House, where she appeared in several Shakespearean plays. In 1965 starred in Playroom, which ran only 1 month but won her a nom. as best actress of season by N.Y. Drama Critics. Made m.p. debut in 1966 in You're a Big Boy Now.
PICTURES INCLUDE: Hard Contact, Easy Rider, Five Easy Pieces, Drive, He Said, A Gunfight, Born To Win, Portnoy's Complaint, The Pyx, Rhinoceros, The Outfit, The Great Gatsby, Airport 1975, Law and Disorder, Day of the Locust, Nashville, Family Plot, Crime and Passion, Burnt Offerings, Capricorn One, Because He's My Friend, In Praise of Older Women, The Rip-off, Greed, Danny Travis, Chanel Solitaire, Come Back to the Five and Dime, Jimmie Dean, Jimmie Dean, Growing Pains, Martin's Day, Cut and Run, Invaders from Mars, It's Alive III, Hostage, After All These Years, The Invisible Kid, Eternal Evil, Homer and Eddie, Night Angel, Deadly Intent, Out of the Dark.
STAGE: Happily Never After, Keep It in the Family.
TELEVISION: Mr. Horn, Power, Trilogy of Terror, The Strange Possession of Mrs. Oliver, Full Circle Again (Canadian TV).

BLACK, NOEL: Director. b. June 30, 1940.
PICTURES: Skaterdater (short); Pretty Poison; Mirrors; A Man, a Woman, and a Bank; Private School; Mischief (s.p. only).
TELEVISION: I'm a Fool (1977); The Golden Honeymoon; The Electric Grandmother; The Other Victim; Prime Suspect; Cry of Innocence; Happy Endings; Quarterback Princess; Deadly Intentions (mini-series); Promises to Keep, A Time to Triumph, My Two Loves, The Doctors Wilde, Conspiracy of Love, The Town Bully, Meet the Munceys.

BLACK, STANLEY: Composer, conductor, musical director. Resident Conductor, BBC, 1944–52. Musical Director 105 feature films and Pathe Newsreel music: Music dir. Associated British Film Studios 1958–64. Guest Conductor, Royal Philharmonic Orchestra and London Symphony. Orchestra; many overseas conducting engagements including (1977) Boston Pops and Winnipeg Symphony. Associated Conductor Osaka Philharmonic Orchestra. Exclusive recording contract with Decca Record Co. since 1944.
PICTURES INCLUDE: Crossplot, The Long, The Short and The Tall, Rattle of a Simple Man, The Young Ones, Hell Is a City, Top Secret, Valentino.

BLACK, THEODORE R.: Attorney. b. New Jersey, Aug. 11, 1906. e. Harvard U., B.A., 1927, LL.B., 1930 (Sigma Alpha Mu fraternity). Formerly General Counsel, bd. member, Republic Pictures Corp. Member: Nat'l Panel of Arbitrators, American Arbit. Assn., Bd. N.Y. Ethical Culture Society.

BLACKMAN, HONOR: Actress. b. London, England. Stage debut. The Gleam 1946. Screen debut, Fame Is the Spur.
TELEVISION: African Patrol, The Witness, Four Just Men, Probation Officer series, Top Secret, Ghost Squad, Invisible Man, The Saint, The Avengers series.
PICTURES INCLUDE: Quartet, Daughter of Darkness, A Boy A Girl and a Bike, Diamond City, Conspirator, So Long at the Fair, Set a Murderer, Green Grow the Rushes, Come Die My Love, Rainbow Jacket, Outsiders, Delavine Affair, Three Musketeers, Breakaway, Homecoming, Suspended Alibi, Dangerous Drugs, A Night to Remember, The Square Peg, A Matter of Who, Present Laughter, The Recount, Serena, Jason & the Golden Fleece, Goldfinger, The Secret of My Success, Moment to Moment, Life at the Top, A Twist of Sand, Shalako, Struggle for Rome, Twinky, The Last Grenade, The Virgin and the Gypsy, Fright, Something Big, Out Damned Spot, Ragtime, Summer, Cat and the Canary.

BLADES, RUBEN: Actor, Composer, Singer, Writer. b. Panama City, Panama, July 16, 1948. e. U. of Panama (law and political science, 1974), Harvard U., L.L.M., 1985. Attorney, Banco Nacional de Panama, 1972–74. Legal advisor, Fania Records, Inc. 1975–78. Recorded award-winning albums (Buscando America, Escenas, Agua de Luna) for Elektra/Asylum Records. With his band Seis del Solar has toured U.S., Central America and Europe.
PICTURES: The Last Fight (debut, 1982), Crossover Dreams (also co-s.p.), When the Mountains Tremble, Beat Street, Critical Condition, The Milagro Beanfield War, Fatal Beauty, Waiting for Salazar.
TELEVISION: Sesame Street.

BLAIN, GERARD: Actor-Director. b. Oct. 23, 1930, Paris. Began his professional career in 1943 as an extra in Marcel Carne's The Children of Paradise. Appeared on stage in Marcel Pagnol's Topaze (1944). Military service in a parachute regiment. In 1955 Julien Duvivier gave him his first major role in Voici le Temps des Assassins (Murder a la Carte). By 1969 had appeared in more than 30 stage and film roles before becoming a director and co-author.
PICTURES: Les Mistons (1957), Le Beau Serge, Les Cousins. In Italy: The Hunchback of Rome, L'Ora di Roma, I Defini, Run with the Devil, Young Husbands. In Germany: The American Friend. As director and author or co-author: Les Amis, Le Pelican (also actor), Un Enfant dans la Foule, Un Second Souffle, Le Rebelle, Portrait sur Michel Tournier, Pierre et Djemila.

BLAINE, VIVIAN: Actress. r.n. Vivian S. Stapleton. b. Newark, NJ, Nov. 21, 1924. e. South Side H.S., Newark. Singer with various bands in New Jersey 1937–39, thereafter night clubs; 20th-Fox contract 1942. Personal appearance on Great Britain stage from 1947; created role of Adelaide in Guys and Dolls on Broadway, London and film. Hatful of Rain, Company, N.Y. stage.
Member: Academy of M.P. Arts & Sciences, AFTRA, Equity, S.A.G., A.G.V.A.
PICTURES INCLUDE: He Married His Boss, Thru Different Eyes, It Happened in Flatbush, Girl Trouble, Jitterbugs, Greenwich Village, Something for the Boys, Nob Hill, State Fair, Doll Face, Three Little Girls in Blue, If I'm Lucky, Skirts Ahoy, Public Pigeon No. 1, Guys and Dolls, The Dark, Parasite, I'm Going to Be Famous.
TELEVISION: Mary Hartman, Mary Hartman; A Year at the Top; The Cracker Factory; Fast Friends; Katie—Portrait of a Centerfold; Amanda's; Murder She Wrote.

BLAIR, BETSY: Actress. r.n. Betsy Boger. b. New York, NY, Dec. 11, 1923. m. director Karel Reisz.
BROADWAY: Beautiful People, Richard II, actress in little theatre groups.
PICTURES INCLUDE: Another Part of the Forest, Kind Lady, Othello, Marty, Halliday Brand, A Delicate Balance, Betrayed.
TELEVISION: Appearances on U.S. Steel Hour, Ford Theatre, Philco, Kraft, Suspicion (PBS).

BLAIR, JANET: Actress. b. Blair, PA, April 23, 1921. r.n. Martha Lafferty. With Hal Kemp's Orchestra; toured in South Pacific, 1950–52.
PICTURES INCLUDE: Three Girls About Town, Blondie Goes to College, Two Yanks in Trinidad, Burn Witch Burn, Broadway, My Sister Eileen, Something to Shout About, Once Upon a Time, Tars and Spars, Gallant Journey, Fabulous Dorseys, I Love Trouble, Black Arrow, Fuller Brush Man, Public Pigeon No. 1, Boys Night Out, The One and Only, Genuine, Original Family Band.

BLAIR, LARRY: Actor. r.n. Larry Bess. b. Newark, NJ, June 27, 1935; f. Herman Bess, N.Y.C. radio executive. e. public and private schools, Newark and Asbury Park, NJ Began in showbusiness, age 13 as D.J. and actor in N.Y.C.; 1954–55, production assistant, WABC-TV, N.Y.C.; 1955–62, associate director and director, WNEW-TV, N.Y.C.; 1962–71, D.J., newscaster with WFIL, Phila., WTIC, Hartford, WHN, WMCA, N.Y. 1971 to present, commercial spokesman, narrator and actor.

BLAIR, LINDA: Actress. b. St. Louis, MO, Jan. 22, 1959. Model and actress on TV commercials before going into films.
PICTURES: The Sporting Club, The Way We Live Now, The Exorcist, Airport '75, Sweet Hostage, Exorcist II: The Heretic, Hell Night, Chained Heat, Roller Boogie, Grotesque, SFX Retaliator, Silent Assassins, Night Patrol, Savage Streets, Savage Island, Night Force, Witchcraft.
TELEVISION: Born Innocent, Sarah T.—Portrait of a Teenage Alcoholic, Victory at Entebbe, Sweet Hostage, Stranger in Our House.

BLAIR, STEWART D.: Executive. b. Scotland, 1950. e. U. of Glasgow, M.A., economics and political science. Worked in London office of Chase Manhattan Bank, moving to NY to join its teaching staff lecturing on corp. finance, 1972 and becoming youngest v.p. at 27. Joined Tele-Communications

Inc. as dir. of finance and rose to v.p., finance, working directly for chm. John C. Malone, on acquisitions. When Tele-Communications acquired United Artists Communications Inc., named pres. and CEO of United Artists Communications, Inc.

BLAKE, AMANDA: Actress. r.n. Beverly Louise Neill; b. Buffalo, NY, Feb. 20, 1931. Telephone operator; in m.p. 1950.
PICTURES INCLUDE: Battleground, Stars in My Crown, Counterspy Meets Scotland Yard, Scarlet Angel, Cattle Town, Lili, Sabre Jet, Miss Robin Crusoe, About Mrs. Leslie, Adventures of Hajji Baba, A Star Is Born, Glass Slipper, High Society, B.O.R.N.
TELEVISION: Double Exposure; Schlitz Playhouse, General Electric Theater, Four Star Playhouse, Cavalcade of America, Lux Video Playhouse, My Favorite Husband, Professional Father, The Red Skelton Show, Climax, Gunsmoke (19 years). Movies: Betrayed; Gunsmoke—Return to Dodge.

BLAKE, DAVID M.: Producers' representative. b. Trincomalee, Ceylon, April 19, 1948. Ent. m.p. ind. 1968 British Lion Films, London. Lion Int'l. Films, O'Seas Division. Appointed 1970 U.S. representative. New York. British Lion Films, Shepperton Studios, Lion TV.

BLAKE, ROBERT: Actor. b. Nutley, NJ, Sept. 18, 1933. r.n. Michael Gubitosi. m. actress Sondra Kerry. Started as a child actor in Our Gang comedies as Bobby Blake, also Little Beaver in Red Ryder series. Later was Hollywood stunt man in Rumble on the Docks and The Tijuana Story. First acting job was in the Gallery Theater in Hatful of Rain.
PICTURES INCLUDE: As child in: Andy Hardy's Double Life, The Horn Blows at Midnight, Treasure of Sierra Madre, Revolt in the Big House, The Purple Gang. As adult: Town Without Pity, PT-109, The Greatest Story Ever Told, The Connection, This Property Is Condemned, In Cold Blood, Tell Them Willie Boy Is Here, Corky, Electra-Glide in Blue, Busting, Second Hand Hearts, Coast to Coast.
TELEVISION: Baretta (Emmy Award, 1975), Blood Feud, Joe Dancer, Hell Town (also s.p.), The Heart of a Champion—The Ray Mancini Story.

BLAKELY, SUSAN: Actress. b. Germany, Sept. 7, 1950, where father was stationed in Army. Studied at U. of Texas. m. writer Todd Merer. Became top magazine and TV commercial model in N.Y. Film debut in Savages, 1972.
PICTURES INCLUDE: The Lords of Flatbush, The Way We Were, The Towering Inferno, Report to the Commissioner, Shampoo, Capone, The Concorde—Airport '79, Over the Top.
TELEVISION: Rich Man, Poor Man. Movies: Secrets, The Heart of a Champion, International Airport, Blood & Orchids, The Annihilator, The Ted Kennedy Jr. Story, Will There Really Be A Morning?, April Morning, Fatal Confession: A Father Dowling Mystery, Broken Angel, Hiroshima Maiden.

BLANC, MEL: Man of 1000 voices. r.n. Melvin Jerome Blanc. b. San Francisco, CA, May 30, 1908. e. Lincoln H.S., Portland, OR, 1918–21. Musician, NBC Radio, San Francisco, 1928; orchestra conductor, Orpheum theatre, Portland, Ore., 1931; freelance, violin, tuba, bass player, 1925–30; voices on Warner Bros. Cartoons, Bugs Bunny, Porky Pig, Daffy Duck, etc. since 1937; running characters, Jack Benny Show, Radio & TV since 1940.
In radio: Point Sublime, 1942–44; Judy Canova Show, 1940–48; The Mel Blanc Show; Burns and Allen; Jack Carson Show; Abbott and Costello; Dagwood and Blondie; Al Pierce Show, 1938–50; Chairman of the Board, Blanc Communications Corp., 1960–88.
PICTURES: Who Framed Roger Rabbit (voice), Daffy Duck's Quackbusters (voice).
TELEVISION: The Bugs Bunny Show, The Porky Pig Show, Tweety 'n' Sylvester, Daffy-Speedy, The Munsters, Flintstones, Speed Buggy, Heathcliff, Jetsons, cartoon shows.

BLANCO, RICHARD M.: Executive. b. Brooklyn, NY. e. electrical engineering, Wentworth Institute. J.C., 1925–27; bus. admin., U. of California, 1939–40; U.S. Govt. Coll., 1942. Superv. Technicolor Corp., 1931–56; organ. and oper. Consumer Products, Kodachrome film process., Technicolor, 1956–62; dir. of MP Govt. and theatr. sales, N.Y. and Washington, DC, 1963–65; gen. mgr. of Technicolor Florida photo. operations at Kennedy Space Center., prod. document. and educ. films for NASA, 1965; VP of TV division, Technicolor Corp. of America; 1967 elected corporate v.p. Technicolor, Inc.; 1971 pres., Technicolor Graphic Services, Inc.; 1974, elected chm. of bd. of Technicolor Graphic Services; 1977, elected to board of directors of Technicolor Inc.

BLANE, RALPH: Composer. b. Broken Arrow, OK, July 26, 1914. e. Northwestern U. Started as singer, then vocal arranger for Broadway shows; appeared on NBC radio. Formed partnership with Hugh Martin, wrote Best Foot Forward; m.p. composer since 1939.
PICTURES INCLUDE: Best Foot Forward, Meet Me in St.

Louis, My Dream Is Yours, One Sunday Afternoon, My Blue Heaven, Friendly Island, Skirts Ahoy, French Line, Athena, Girl Rush, The Girl Most Likely, Who is Sylvia?, Ziegfeld Follies, Broadway Rhythm, Abbott and Costello in Hollywood, Easy to Wed.
TELEVISION: The Great Quillow. 1961; same in color for NBC, 1963.
BROADWAY: Three Wishes for Jamie, Tattered Tom, Something About Anne, Don't Flash Tonight.

BLANK, MYRON: Circuit executive. b. Des Moines, IA, Aug. 30, 1911. e. U. of Michigan. Son of A. H. Blank, circuit operator. On leaving coll. joined father in operatin Tri-States and Central States circuits. On leave 1943–46 in U.S. Navy, officer in charge visual educ. Now pres. Central States Theatre Corp.; pres. TOA, 1955; chmn. bd. TOA Inc. 1956–57; exec. chm. of NATO. Pres. of Greater Des Moines Comm.; treas. Iowa Methodist Medical Center; board, Iowa Des Moines Natl. Bank.; pres., Iowa Phoenix Corp., recipient of Brotherhood Award of National Conference of Christians & Jews; board, Simpson College; chm., Blank Park Zoo.

BLATT, DANIEL: Producer. Independent producer since 1978; prior posts: resident counsel, ABC Pictures; exec. v.p. Palomar Pictures; partner with Edgar J. Scherick. Blatt-Singer Prods. Now Daniel H. Blatt Prods.
PICTURES: I Never Promised You a Rose Garden; The American Success Company; The Howling; Independence Day; Cujo; Restless, The Boost.
TELEVISION INCLUDES: Co-prod. with Robert Singer: The Children Nobody Wanted, Sadat, V—The Final Battle, Raid on Entebbe, Sacred Vows, A Winner Never Quits, Sworn to Silence.

BLATTNER, ROBERT: Executive. b. Dover, DE, March 5, 1952. e. Harvard Coll., B.A., 1974; Harvard Business Sch., M.B.A., 1976. 1980–81, dir. sls., Columbia Pictures Home Entertainment; 1981–82, promoted to v.p. & gen. mgr.; 1982–83, v.p., gen. mgr., RCA/Columbia Pictures Home Video; named pres., 1983.

BLATTY, WILLIAM PETER: Writer, Producer. Novelist who wrote John Goldfarb, Please Come Home (filmed) and Twinkle, Twinkle, Killer Kane (prod., dir. also) before biggest success with The Exorcist, which became a 55-week best-selling book. He wrote s.p. and functioned as prod. on film version.
PICTURES INCLUDE: A Shot in the Dark (s.p.), What Did You Do in the War, Daddy? (s.p.), The Great Bank Robbery, Darling Lili (co. s.p.), The Exorcist (s.p., prod.), The Ninth Configuration (s.p., prod. dir.)

BLAU, MARTIN: Executive. b. New York, NY, June 6, 1924. e. Ohio U., 1948. Employed on newspapers in OH, TX, WV. Pub. dept., Columbia Pictures, 1951; asst. pub. mgr. 1959; pub. mgr., Columbia Internat'l, 1961; admin. asst. to v.p. of adv. & pub. Columbia Pictures, 1966. Dir. adv. and publicity, Columbia Pictures International, 1970; v.p., 1971; sr. v.p., 1985. Retired, 1988.

BLAUSTEIN, JULIAN: Producer. b. New York, NY, May 30, 1913. e. Harvard U., 1933. Ent. m.p. ind. as reader for Universal 1935; asst. story ed. 1935–36; story ed. 1936–38; in chg. story dept. Music Corp. of America 1938–39; story ed. Paramount 1939–41; Signal Corps Photo. Center 1941–46; edit. supervisor of Selznick 1946–48; to 20th-Fox as prod. 1949; apptd. exec. prod. 20th Cent.-Fox, 1951 to Dec. 1952.
PICTURES INCLUDE: Broken Arrow, Mister 880, Half Angel, Just One More Chance, Take Care of My Little Girl, Day the Earth Stood Still, Outcasts, Don't Bother to Knock, Desiree, The Racers, Storm Center, Cowboy, Bell, Book and Candle, The Wreck of the Mary Deare, Two Loves, The Four Horsemen of the Apocalypse, Khartoum.

BLAY, ANDRE: Executive. In 1979, sold Magnetic Video to 20th Century Fox, named pres., CEO, 20th Century Fox Home Video; 1981, formed The Blay Corporation; 1982, joined with Norman Lear and Jerry Perenchio, founders of Embassy Communications, as chairman and CEO of Embassy Home Entertainment; 1986, when Embassy sold to Nelson Group, left to form Palisades Entertainment Group with Elliott Kastner.
PICTURES: Exec. Prod.: Prince of Darkness, They Live, Homeboy, The Blob.

BLEAK, JANINE: Executive. e. U. of Southern California business school; degree in mktg. & finance. Nat'l media supr. with West Coast office of J. Walter Thompson. 1985, joined Warner Bros. as media mgr.

BLECKNER, JEFF: Director. b. Brooklyn, NY, Aug. 12, 1943. e. Amherst College, BA., 1965; Yale Sch. of Drama, MFA 1968. Taught drama at Yale, also participated in the theater co. 1965–68. 1968–75 theater dir. NY Shakespeare Fest. Public Theatre (2 Drama Desk Awards, 1 Tony nom. for Sticks and Bones); Basic Training of Pavlo Hummel (Obie Award, 1971), The Unseen Hand (Obie Award). Began TV career directing The Guiding Light, 1975.

TELEVISION: Hill Street Blues (Emmy Award, DGA Award, 1983), Concealed Enemies (Emmy Award, 1984), Daddy, I'm Their Momma Now, Do You Remember Love (Christopher, Humanitas, Peabody Awards), Fresno, Terrorist on Trial, Brotherly Love, My Father, My Son; Favorite Son.

BLEES, ROBERT: Writer, Producer. b. Lathrop, MO, June 9, 1922. e. Dartmouth, Phi Beta Kappa. Time and Life Magazines. Fiction: Cosmopolitan, etc. Exec. boards of Writers Guild, Producers Guild. Executive consultant, QM Prods.; BBC (England).
PICTURES INCLUDE: Magnificent Obsession, Autumn Leaves, The Glass Web, James Cain's Love's Lovely Counterfeit.
TELEVISION: Producer of Combat!, Bonanza, Bus Stop, Kraft Theater. Writer also of Alfred Hitchcock, Cannon, Barnaby Jones, Harry O, Columbo, co-creator, The New Gidget.

BLEIER, EDWARD: Executive. b. New York, NY, October 16, 1929. e. Syracuse U., 1951, City U. of New York, graduate courses. Reporter: Syracuse Herald Journal, Long Island Daily Press 1947–50. Sportscaster: WNEW, N.Y.; WSYR, Syracuse, 1947–50. American Broadcasting Company, 1952–57; 1959–68. Vice President in charge of Public Relations & Planning (Marketing, Advertising, Publicity), Broadcast Div.; Vice President in chg. of daytime Programming & Sales, ABC-TV Network; vice pres./gen. mgr. sales, ABC-TV Network; Account Executive, ABC-TV Network & WABC-TV. Vice Pres. Radio-Television-Film, Tex McCrary, Inc. 1958; Program Service Manager, DuMont Television Network, 1951; U.S. Army Psy. War School; Ex-chm., TV Committee, NASL; ex-Trustee, NATAS; founder-director & vice-chm., International TV Council (NATAS); past-pres., IRTS; ATAS; guest professor: several universities. Pres., pay-tv & network features and pres., animation, Warner Bros.

BLENDER, LEON PHILIP: Executive. b. Kansas City, MO, Feb. 15, 1920. e. Kansas State Coll., 1941. 20th Century-Fox Dist. Co., 1947–51; Kranz-Levin pictures, 1951–56. gen. sis. mgr. American International Film Dist. Corp., 1956–57; v.p. 1960; American Intl. Pictures, senior v.p., sales dist., later exec. v.p. sales and distribution; 1979, exec. v.p. sales & distribution, Film Ventures Intl.; 1983, exec. v.p., world-wide dist., Summa Vista Pictures.

BLOCH, ROBERT: Writer. b. Chicago, IL, April 5, 1917. Novelist short-story writer; 50 published books, incl. Psycho, Psycho II, The Night of the Ripper, etc.; wrote radio series, Stay Tuned for Terror, adapting own stories; national pres., Mystery Writers of Amer., 1970–71; entered films, 1960.
PICTURES INCLUDE: The Couch, Cabinet of Caligari, Straitjacket, The Night-Walker, The Psychopath, The Deadly Bees, (collab.) Torture Garden, The House that Dripped Blood, Asylum. (Films adapted from published work). Psycho, The Skull.
TELEVISION: Features: The Cat Creature, The Dead Don't Die. Approx. 70 credits on Hitchcock, Thriller, Star Trek, Tales from the Dark Side, Monsters.

BLOCK, WILLARD: Executive. b. New York, NY, March 18, 1930.; e. Columbia Coll., Columbia U. Law Sch., 1952. Counter-Intelligence Corps., U.S. Army, 1952–54, account exec., Plus Marketing, Inc. 1954–55; joined sales staff, NBC Television Network, 1955–57; sales staff, CBS Enterprises, Inc., 1957; international sales mgr, 1960; dir., international sales, 1965; v.p., 1967; v.p., Viacom Enterprises, 1971; pres., 1972; v.p. MCA-TV, 1973; v.p., gen. mgr., Taft, H-B International, Inc.; pres. Willard Block, Ltd.; 1979, named pres., Viacom Enterprises; 1982, pres. Viacom Worldwide Ltd.

BLOOM, CLAIRE: Actress. b. London, England, Feb. 15, 1931. e. Badminton Sch. (U.S.). Stage debut at Playhouse, Oxford, Sept., 1947; Old Vic seasons, etc.; screen debut in Limelight, 1951. Author: Limelight and After.
PICTURES INCLUDE: Innocents in Paris, The Man Between, Richard III, Alexander the Great, The Brothers Karamazov, Look Back in Anger, The Royal Game, The Wonderful World of the Brothers Grimm, The Chapman Report, The Haunting, Alta Infidelita, Il Maestro di Vigenuono, The Outrage, The Spy Who Came In From the Cold, Charley, The Illustrated Man, Three into Two Won't Go, A Severed Head, Red Sky at Morning, A Doll's House, Islands in the Stream, Clash of the Titans, Sammy and Rosie Get Laid.
TELEVISION: Misalliance, (Playhouse 90), Anna Karenina, Wuthering Heights, Ivanov, Wessex Tales, An Imaginative Woman, A Legacy, In Praise of Love, The Orestaia, Henry VIII, Brideshead Revisited, Hamlet, Cymbeline, King John, Ann and Debbie, Ellis Island, Separate Tables, Florence Nightingale, The Ghost Writer, Time and the Conways, Shadow Lands, Liberty, Promises to Keep, The Belle of Amherst, Hold the Dream, Anastasia, Queenie, Intimate Contact, Beryl Markham: A Shadow on the Sun, Oedipus the King, Dangerous Love.

BLOOM, VERNA: Actress. b. Lynn, MA, Aug. 7, 1939. e. Boston U. Studied drama at Uta Hagen-Herbert Berghof School. Performed with small theatre groups all over country; then started repertory theatre in Denver. Appeared on Broadway in Marat/Sade (played Charlotte Corday). Film debut, Medium Cool, 1969.
PICTURES INCLUDE: The Hired Hand, High Plains Drifter, Badge 373, National Lampoon's Animal House, After Hours, The Last Temptation of Christ.
TELEVISION: The Blue Knight, Contact on Cherry Street, Playing for Time, Rivlein—Bounty Hunter.

BLOOM, WILLIAM: Producer. b. New York, NY, Feb. 28, 1915. e. U. of Pennsylvania, B.A., 1935. Story dept., Columbia, N.Y., 1936; U.S. Army Signal Corps, 1941–45; asst. to Ender Bohem, Columbia, Hollywood; then prod. and asst. to B.B. Kahane, 1947–51; asst. to Julian Blaustein, Fox, 1951; prod., 1952.
PICTURES INCLUDE: Glory Brigade, Inferno, On the Threshold of Space.

BLOOMER STEPHEN J.: Exhibitor. b. Belleville, IL, Nov. 12, 1947. e. Northern Illinois U., B.S. in education, 1969. Elementary school band director, 1969–75; insurance sales, New York Life Insurance Co., 1975–77; asst. mgr., New York Life, 1977–1979; joined BAC Theatres Jan., 1979 as warehouse mgr.; Nov. 1979, named gen. mgr.

BLUM, HARRY N.: Executive. b. Cleveland, OH, Oct. 3, 1932. e. U. of Michigan, B.B.A., LL.B. Was attorney in Ohio, toy & hobby industry executive, management consultant, and venture capital and investment manager before entering industry. Now heads The Blum Group, entertainment financing, packaging, production and international marketing Co.
PICTURES INCLUDE: Executive Action (assoc. prod.); The Land That Time Forgot (assoc. prod.); At the Earth's Core (exec. prod.); Drive-In (assoc. prod.) Diamonds (exec. prod.); The Bluebird (assoc. prod.); Obsession (prod.); Skateboard (prod.); The Magician of Lublin (exec. prod.); Duran Duran—Arena (exec. prod.).

BLUM, MARK: Actor. b. Newark, NJ, May 14, 1950. Studied drama at U. of Minnesota and U. of Pennsylvania. Also studied acting with Andre Gregory, Aaron Frankel and Daniel Seltzer. Extensive Off-B'way work after debut in The Cherry Orchard (1976).
THEATER: Off-Broadway: The World of Sholem Aleichem, Brothers (New Brunswick, NJ), The Merchant (B'way), Say Goodnight, Gracie; Table Settings, Close Ties (Long Wharf), Key Exchange, Loving Reno, The Cherry Orchard (Long Wharf), Iago in Othello (Dallas), Messiah. At the Mark Taper Forum: An American Clock, Wild Oats, Moby Dick Rehearsed and An American Comedy, It's Only a Play (off-B'way), Little Footsteps, Cave Life.
PICTURES: Desperately Seeking Susan, Just Between Friends, Crocodile Dundee, Blind Date, The Presidio.
TELEVISION: Sweet Surrender, Miami Vice (guest).

BLUMENSTOCK, SID: Ad. exec. New York, NY. Publicity dir. Warner Bros. Atlantic City theatres 1934–38; joined 20th Fox adv. dept. 1938; asst. exploitation mgr. 1944–49; advertising mgr. Paramount 1949; asst. nat'l dir. adv. pub., exploit, 1951–58; MPH Coord. 1959 Academy telecast; v.p. Embassy Pictures, 1959; v.p. Chas. Schlaifer Agency, Hollywood, October, 1959–62; v.p. Safranski Prod., Inc.; adv. dir., Embassy Pictures, 1964–67; Walter Reade Org., 1967–70 Levitt-Pickman Film Corp., adv. dir., 1971–72.

BLUMOFE, ROBERT F.: Producer. b. New York, NY. e. Columbia Coll., AB, Columbia U. Sch. of Law, JD. v.p., West Coast oper., U.A., 1953–66; independent prod., pres. RFB Enterprises, Inc; American Film Institute, director, AFI-West, Sept. 1, 1977–81. Now indep. prod.

BLYTH, ANN: Actress. b. Mt. Kisco, NY, Aug. 16, 1928. e. New Wayburn's Dramatic Sch. On radio in childhood; with San Carlos Opera Co. 3 years; Broadway debut in Watch on the Rhine; on tour.
PICTURES INCLUDE: Chip Off the Old Block, Merry Monahans, Brute Force, Swell Guy, Mr. Peabody and the Mermaid, Woman's Vengeance, Mildred Pierce, Free for All, Top o' the Morning, Our Very Own, Great Caruso, Katie Did It, Thunder on the Hill, I'll Never Forget You, Golden Horde, One Minute to Zero, World in His Arms, Sally and Saint Anne, All the Brothers Were Valiant, Rose Marie, The Student Prince, King's Thief, Kismet, Buster Keaton Story, Jazz Age, Slander, The Helen Morgan Story.

BOCHCO, STEVEN: Producer, Writer. b. New York, NY 1945. m. actress Barbara Bosson. e. Carnegie Tech, MFA. Won MCA fellowship in college, joined U-TV as apprentice. His shows typically feature several interwoven plots and characters, deal with social issues, and shift from comedy to drama within an episode.
PICTURES: Silent Running (co-s.p.).
TELEVISION: Writer and story ed.: Name of the Game; Columbo; McMillan and Wife; Delvecchio (writer-prod.); Paris

(exec. prod.); Richie Brockelman (co-creator); Turnabout (writer); Invisible Man (writer); Vampire (writer); Hill St. Blues (creator, prod., writer; Emmy's 1981, 1982, 1983, 1984); Every Stray Dog and Kid (exec. prod.); Bay City Blues (exec. prod., writer, creator); L.A. Law, Hooperman.

BOCHNER, HART: Actor. b. Toronto, Ontario, Dec. 3, 1956. Son of actor Lloyd Bochner. e. U. of. San Diego. Film debut, Islands in the Stream, 1975.
PICTURES: Breaking Away, Terror Train, Rich and Famous, Supergirl, The Wild Life, Making Mr. Right, Die Hard, Apartment Zero.
TELEVISION: Haywire, The Sun Also Rises, Having It All, East of Eden.

BOCHNER, LLOYD: Actor. b. Canada, July 29, 1924.
PICTURES: Drums of Africa, The Night Walker, Sylvia, Tony Rome, Point Blank, The Detective, The Horse in the Gray Flannel Suit, Tiger by the Tail, Ulzana's Raid, The Man in the Glass Booth, Hot Touch, The Lonely Lady, Louisiana.
TELEVISION: A Fire in the Sky, Greatest Heroes of the Bible, The Golden Gate Murders, Dynasty, Mazes & Monsters, Fantasy Island; Masquerade; The A-Team; Hotel; Crazy Like a Fox; A Mouse, a Mystery & Me.

BODE, RALF: Cinematographer. b. Berlin, Germany. Attended Yale where was actor with drama school and acquired degree in directing. Received on-job training teaching combat photography and making films for Army at Ft. Monmouth. First professional job in films was gaffer on Harry, followed by long association with director John G. Avildsen, for whom served as gaffer and lighting designer on Guess What We Learned in School Today, Joe, and Cry Uncle. Later served as dir. of photography for Avildsen on Inaugural Ball and as East Coast dir. phot. for Rocky.
PICTURES INCLUDE: Saturday Night Fever, Slow Dancing in the Big City, Rich Kids, Coal Miner's Daughter, Dressed to Kill, Raggedy Man, A Little Sex, Gorky Park, First Born, Violets Are Blue, Critical Condition, The Big Town, Distant Thunder.
TELEVISION: PBS Theatre in America, working as lighting designer and dir. of photo. Also many TV commercials.

BOEHM, SIDNEY: Writer. b. Philadelphia, PA, April 4, 1908. e. Lehigh U. 1935-29. m. Ellen Kasputis. Reporter, N.Y. Journal-American & I.N.S., 1930-45.
PICTURES INCLUDE: Union Station, Big Heat, Atomic City, Six Bridges To Cross, The Raid, Rogue Cop, The Savage, Violent Saturday, Hell on Frisco Bay, Tall Men, Bottom of the Bottle, Revolt of Mamie Stover, Woman Obsessed, Seven Thieves, Sylvia, Rough Night in Jericho.

BOETTICHER, BUDD: Producer, Director, Writer. r.n. Oscar Boetticher, Jr. b. Chicago, IL, July 29, 1918. e. Ohio State U. Bull fighter; then technical dir., Blood and Sand, 1941; asst. dir., Hal Roach studios and Columbia 1941-44; became feature director at Columbia in 1944; dir. Eagle Lion, 1946; dir., Universal; independ. prod., 1954. Autobiography: When in Disgrace, 1989.
PICTURES INCLUDE: Behind Locked Doors, Assigned to Danger, Black Midnight, Killer Shark, Wolf Hunters, Bullfighter and the Lady, Cimarron Kid, Bronco Busters, Red Ball Express, Horizons West, City Beneath the Sea, Seminole, Man from the Alamo, Wings of the Hawk, East of Sumatra, Magnificent Matador, Killer Is Loose, Seven Men From Now, Decision at Sundown, The Tall T, Buchanan Rides Alone, Ride Lonesome Westbound, The Rise and Fall of Legs Diamond, Comanche Station, The Carlos Arruza Story. Original s.p.: Two Mules for Sister Sara, A Time For Dying, My Kingdom For...A Horse for Mister Barnum.

BOGARDE, DIRK: Actor. b. Hampstead, London, England, March 28, 1921. e. Allen Glens Coll., Glasgow & University Coll., London. Started theatrical career with Amersham Repertory Co., then London stage; in Army in W.W.II; screen debut in Esther Waters. Top ten British star, 1953-54, 1956-64; number one British money-making star 1955, 1957, 1958, 1959; Variety Club Award—Best Performance 1961-64. British Academy Award, Darling, 1966.
PICTURES INCLUDE: Quartet, Once a Jolly Swagman, Mr. Prohack, Blue Lamp, Five Angles on Murder, Gentle Gunman, So Long at the Fair, Blackmailed, Woman in Question, Hunted (Stranger in Between), Penny Princess, Desperate Moment, They Who Dare, The Sleeping Tiger, Doctor in the House, For Better or Worse, The Sea Shall Not Have Them, Simba, Doctor at Sea, Appointment in London, Cast a Dark Shadow, Doctor At Large, Spanish Gardener, Ill Met by Moonlight, Campbell's Kingdom, A Tale of Two Cities, The Wind Cannot Read, The Doctor's Dilemma, Libel, The Angel Wore Red, Song Without End, The Singer Not The Song, Victim, H.M.S. Defiant, The Password Is Courage, I Could Go on Singing, The Mind Benders, The Servant (British Academy Award, 1964), Hot Enough for June, Doctor Distress, The High Bright Sun, King and Country, Darling. ., Modesty Blaise, Accident, Our Mother's House, Sebastion, The Fixer, Justine, Oh What a Lovely War, The Damned, Death in

Venice, Le Serpent, The Night Porter, Permission to Kill, Providence, A Bridge Too Far, Despair.
TELEVISION: (U.S.) The Little Moon of Alban, Hallmark, 1964. Blythe Spirit, Hallmark, 1966, Upon This Rock, The Patricia Neal Story. (U.K.) May We Borrow Your Husband?, The Vision (U.K.).

BOGART, PAUL: Director. b. New York, NY, Nov. 21, 1919. Puppeteer-actor with Berkeley Marionettes 1946-48; TV stage mgr., assoc. dir. NBC 1950-52; numerous Emmy Awards, Christopher Awards.
FILMS INCLUDE: Marlowe, Halls of Anger, Skin Game, Class of '44, Mr. Ricco, Oh, God! You Devil, Torch Song Trilogy.
TELEVISION: U.S. Steel Hour, Kraft Theatre, Armstrong Circle Theatre, Goodyear Playhouse, Hallmark Hall of Fame 1953-60; The Defenders; All in the Family (1975-). Specials: Ages of Man, Mark Twain Tonight, The Final War of Ollie Winter, Dear Friends, Secrets, The House Without a Christmas Tree, Look Homeward Angel, The Country Girl, Double Solitaire, The War Widow, The Thanksgiving Treasure, Tell Me Where It Hurts, The Adams Chronicles, Nutcracker: Money, Madness and Murder, Natica Jackson.

BOGDANOVICH, PETER: Director, Producer, Writer, Actor. b. Kingston, NY, July 30, 1939. e. Collegiate Sch., Stella Adler Theatre Sch., N.Y. 1954-58. Stage debut, Amer. Shakespeare Festival, N.Y. Shakespeare Festival, others, 1955-58. Off-Bway: dir.-co. prod. The Big Knife, 1959, Camino Real, Ten Little Indians, Rocket to the Moon, 1961, dir.-prod. Once in a Lifetime, 1964. Film critic and feature writer, general publications (Esquire, New York Times, Village Voice, Cahiers du Cinema, Los Angeles Times), 1958-85, Monographs for Museum of Modern Art Film Library on Orson Welles, Alfred Hitchcock, Howard Hawks, 1961-63. Books: John Ford, Fritz Lang in America, 1969; Allan Dwan—The Last Pioneer, 1971; Pieces of Time, 1973, enlarged 1985; The Killing of the Unicorn: Dorothy Stratten 1960-1980, 1984. Owner: Crescent Moon Prods. Inc., LA, 1986-present.
PICTURES: Second-unit dir.-writer, The Wild Angels, 1966. Dir.-prod.-writer-actor, Targets, 1968. The Last Picture Show (dir., s.p.), Directed by John Ford (dir., s.p.), What's Up Doc? (dir., s.p.), Paper Moon (dir., prod.), Daisy Miller (dir., prod.), At Long Last Love (dir., prod., s.p.), Nickelodeon (dir., s.p.), Saint Jack (dir, s.p., actor), They All Laughed (dir., s.p.), Mask (dir), Illegally Yours (prod., dir.).
TELEVISION: CBS This Morning (weekly commentary) 1987-88.
AWARDS: N.Y. Film Critics' Award, best s.p., British Academy Award, best s.p. (The Last Picture Show) 1971; Writer's Guild of America Award, best s.p. (What's Up Doc?) 1972; Silver Shell, Mar del Plata, Spain (Paper Moon, 1973); Best Director, Brussels Festival (Daisy Miller) 1974; Pasinetti Award, Critics Prize, Venice Festival (Saint Jack) 1979.

BOHEM, ENDRE: Producer, Writer. b. Hungary. e. U. of Vienna. Exec. Asst. to E. Mannix, MGM and Harry Cohn, Columbia. Prod. shorts series: Passing Parade, Nostradamus, What do You Think, Crime Does Not Pay, Tell Tale Heart.
PICTURES INCLUDE: Night Has a 1000 Eyes, The Redhead and the Cowboy, Alias Nick Beal, Streets of Laredo, Postal Inspector, Wonder of Women, Thirst, House with a 1000 Candles, Two Wise Maids, Little Orphan Annie, Lord Jeff, Crime of the Century, Twin Stars, Bengazi.
TELEVISION: Revlon Mirror, Ford Theatre, Rawhide.

BOLAN, JAMES: Actor. b. Sunderland, England. Ent. ind. 1960.
PICTURES: The Kitchen, A Kind of Loving, Loneliness of the Long Distance Runner, HMS Defiant, Murder Most Foul, In Celebration.
TELEVISION: Likely Lads, When The Boat Comes In, Only When I Laugh, The Beiderdecke Affair, Father Matthews Daughter, Room at the Bottom, Andy Capp.

BOLOGNA, JOSEPH: Actor, Writer. b. Brooklyn, NY., Dec. 30, 1938. e. Brown U. m. actress-writer Renee Taylor. Service in Marine Corps and on discharge joined ad agency, becoming director-producer of TV commercials. Collaborated with wife on short film, 2, shown at 1966 N.Y. Film Festival. Together they wrote Lovers and Other Strangers, Broadway play, in which both also acted. Wrote s.p. for film version. Both wrote and starred in Made for Each Other, and created and wrote TV series, Calucci's Dept.
PICTURES INCLUDE: Lovers and Other Strangers (co.-s.p.), Made for Each Other (co.-s.p., star), Cops and Robbers (actor), Mixed Company (actor), The Big Bus (actor), Chapter Two (actor), My Favorite Year (actor), Blame It on Rio (actor), The Woman in Red (actor), Transylvania 6-5000 (actor), It Had to Be You (actor, co-dir., co-s.p.).
TELEVISION: Calucci's Dept. (co.-s.p.), Honor Thy Father (movie—actor), Copacabana, Acts of Love and Other Comedies, Paradise, Torn Between Two Lovers, Chapter Two, A Time To Triumph. Series: Rags to Riches; Mini-Series: Sins, Not Quite Human.

BOLT, ROBERT: Writer, b. Sale, England, 1924. Ent. m.p. ind. 1961.
PICTURES INCLUDE: Lawrence of Arabia, Dr. Zhivago, A Man For All Seasons (play and film), Ryan's Daughter, Dir. own s.p. Lady Caroline Lamb, The Bounty.

BONANNO, LOUIE: Actor. b. Somerville, MA, Dec. 17, 1961. e. Bentley Coll., Waltham, MA, BS-economics, finance; AS Accountancy, 1983. Moved to NY, 1983 to study at Amer. Acad. of Dramatic Arts. Toured U.S. 1985–86 as Dangermouse for MTV/Nickelodeon.
PICTURES INCLUDE: Sex Appeal (debut, 1986), Wimps, Student Affairs.
TELEVISION: Eisenhower & Lutz (series).

BOND, ANSON: Producer, Writer. b. Cleveland, OH, March 21, 1914. e. Yale Prep & pre-legal, Stuyvesant Sch., Warrenton, VA. p. Charles Anson Bond, founder, Bond Clothing Co. & Bond Stores, Inc. Washington corr., 30 Ohio newspapers, 1930–33; asst. to pres., C.W. Hord Co., N.Y. 1933–36; apprenticeship in m.p. prod. 1936–39; dir., prod., writer. U.S. armed forces, 1940–45; head pub. firm, Bond-Charteris, prod. radio program. The Saint; publ. Craig Rice Crime Digest & Movie Mystery Magazine.
PICTURES INCLUDE: The Judge, Not Wanted, Vicious Years, (co-prod.) Journey Into Light, Japanese War Bride, China Venture.

BOND, DEREK: Actor, Scriptwriter. b. Glasgow Scotland, Jan. 26, 1920. e. Haberdasher' Askes Sch., London. Stage debut in As Husbands Go, 1937; served in Grenadier Guards H.M. Forces 1939–46, awarded Military Cross; m.p. debut in Captive Heart, 1946; author of Unscheduled Stop, Two Young Samaritans, Ask Father Christmas, Packdrill, Double Strung, Order to Kill, The Riverdale Dam, Sentence Deferred, The Mavroletty Fund. Many TV appearances. Pres., British Actors Equity, 1984–86.
PICTURES INCLUDE: Nicholas Nickleby, Joanna Godden, Uncle Silas, Scott of the Antarctic, Marry Me, Poets Pub, Weaker Sex, Broken Journey, Christopher Columbus, Tony Draws a Horse, Quiet Woman, Hour of Thirteen, Distant Trumpet, Love's a Luxury, Trouble in Store, Svengali, High Terrace, Stormy Crossing, Rogues Yarn, Gideon's Day, The Hand, Saturday Night Out, Wonderful Life, Press For Time, When Eight Bells Toll, Intimate Reflections, Vanishing Army.

BONET, LISA: Actress. b. Los Angeles, CA, Nov. 16, 1967. First gained recognition on The Cosby Show as Denise Huxtable at the age of 15.
PICTURES INCLUDE: Angel Heart.
TELEVISION: Series: The Cosby Show, A Different World.

BONET, NAI: Actress, Producer. Worked in entertainment field since age of 13, including opera, films, TV, stage, night clubs and records.
PICTURES INCLUDE: Actress: The Soul Hustlers, The Seventh Veil, Fairy Tales, The Soul of Nigger Charlie, The Spy with the Cold Nose, John Goldfarb Please Come Home, etc. Wrote and starred in Nocturna and Hoodlums.
TELEVISION: Johnny Carson Show, Merv Griffin Show, Joe Franklin Show, Beverly Hillbillies, Tom Snyder Show.

BONO, SONNY: Singer, actor, director, writer. b. Detroit, MI, Feb. 16, 1935. r.n. Salvatore Bono. Started writing songs at age 16; entered record business with Specialty Records as apprentice prod. Became ass't. to Phil Spector, rock music prod. and did background singing. Has recorded albums with former wife Cher and made two feature films, and formed nightclub act with her. CBS comedy-variety series began as summer show in 1971 and made regular later that year.
PICTURES INCLUDE: Good Times, Chastity (prod., s.p.), Escape to Athena, Airplane II: The Sequel, Special Delivery, Troll, Hairspray, Under the Boardwalk.
TELEVISION: Sonny & Cher Comedy Hour, Sonny Comedy Revue.

BOOKE, SORRELL: Actor. b. Buffalo, NY, Jan. 4, 1930. e. Columbia U. Joined summer stock company in Charleston, WV, and later in Provincetown, MA. After stint with armed forces returned to New York and off-Broadway plays. Broadway debut in The Sleeping Prince, followed by appearances in over 100 plays.
PICTURES INCLUDE: Special Delivery, What's Up Doc?, Freaky Friday, The Other Side of Midnight.
TELEVISION: Series: Route 66, Soap, What's Happening!, The Dukes of Hazzard, Alice, Newhart.

BOOKMAN, ROBERT: Executive. b. Los Angeles, CA. e. U. of California, Yale Law Sch. Motion picture literary agent, IFA 1972–74, ICM 1974–79. 1979 joined ABC Motion Pictures as v.p., worldwide production; 1984, Columbia Pictures, exec. v.p., world-wide prod. 1986, Creative Artists Agency, Inc. as motion picture literary and directors' agent.

BOONE, JR., ASHLEY A.: Executive. b. 1939. e. Brandeis U. Started career at United Artists in adv./pub.; later with Cinema Center Films; adm. asst., Motown Records; assoc.

prod. for Sidney Poitier's E & R Productions. Joined 20th-Fox in 1972 in sls. dept.; advanced to sr. sls. & mktg. positions in feature film operation. In 1979 appt. pres. of 20th-Fox Distribution & Marketing. Joined Ladd Co., v.p. in chg. dist. & mktg., 1983; Pres., Columbia Pictures Mktg. & Dist. Group, 1984. Resigned 1985 but remained special mkt. consultant. 1986, joined Lorimar Pictures as pres., mktg. & dist.

BOONE, PAT: Singer. b. Jacksonville, FL, June 1, 1934. e. David Lipscomb Coll., North Texas State Coll., grad. magna cum laude, Columbia U. Winner of Ted Mack's TV show; joined Arthur Godfrey TV show, 1955. m.p. debut in Bernadine. Most promising new male star, Motion Picture Daily-Fame Poll 1957. One of top ten moneymaking stars, M.P. Herald-Fame Poll, 1957.
AUTHOR: Twixt Twelve and Twenty, Between You & Me and the Gatepost, The Real Christmas.
RECORDINGS: Ain't That a Shame, I Almost Lost My Mind, Friendly Persuasion, Love Letters in the Sand, April Love, Tutti Frutti.
PICTURES INCLUDE: Bernadine, April Love, Mardi Gras, Journey to the Center of the Earth, All Hands on Deck, State Fair, The Main Attraction, The Yellow Canary, The Horror of It All, The Perils of Pauline, The Cross and the Switchblade.

BOORMAN, JOHN: Producer, Director. b. London, Eng., Jan. 18, 1933. Wrote film criticism at age of 17 for British publications; served in National Service in Army; joined independent Television News as film editor; prod. documentaries for Southern Television; joined BBC, headed BBC Documentary Film Unit including documentary about D.W. Griffith.
PICTURES INCLUDE: Catch Us If You Can, Point Blank, Hell in the Pacific, Leo The Last (Directors Award, Cannes), Deliverance (prod., dir.), Zardoz (prod., dir., s.p.), Exorcist II: The Heretic, Excalibur (prod., dir., s.p.), The Emerald Forest (prod., dir.), Hope and Glory (prod., dir., s.p.).

BOOTH, MARGARET: Film editor. b. Los Angeles, CA, 1898. Awarded honorary Oscar, 1977.
PICTURES INCLUDE: Why Men Leave Home, Husbands and Lovers, Bridge of San Luis Rey, New Moon, Susan Lenox, Strange Interlude, Smilin' Through, Romeo and Juliet, Barretts of Wimpole Street, Mutiny on the Bounty, Camille, etc. Supervising editor on Owl and the Pussycat, The Way We Were, Funny Lady, Murder by Death, The Goodbye Girl, California Suite, The Cheap Detective (also assoc. prod.), Chapter Two (also assoc. prod.); The Toy (assoc. prod.). Editor: Annie. Exec. Prod.: The Slugger's Wife.

BOOTH, SHIRLEY: Actress. b. New York, NY, Aug. 20, 1907. Joined Poli Stock Co., Hartford, CT, at 12; Broadway debut in Hell's Bells, 1925; on radio in Duffy's Tavern; m.p. debut in Come Back Little Sheba (Academy Award, Best Actress, 1952).
PLAYS: After Such Pleasures, 3 Men on a Horse, Philadelphia Story, My Sister Eileen, Tomorrow the World, Goodbye My Fancy, Come Back Little Sheba (Tony Award, 1950), A Tree Grows in Brooklyn, Time of the Cuckoo (Tony Award, 1953), The Desk Set, Look to the Lillies, Miss Isobel, Juno, Colettes Second String, The Glass Menagerie.
PICTURES INCLUDE: Come Back Little Sheba, About Mrs. Leslie, Hot Spell, The Matchmaker.
TELEVISION: Perle Mesta Story, Hazel (series, 1961–68; Emmy Awards, 1962 & 1963), A Touch of Grace, The Glass Menagerie.

BOOTHE, POWERS: Actor. b. Snyder, TX, 1949. e. Southern Methodist U. On Broadway in Lone Star.
TELEVISION: Skag, A Cry for Love, Guyana Tragedy–The Story of Jim Jones (Emmy Award), Philip Marlowe (series), Into the Homeland.
PICTURES INCLUDE: Cruising, Southern Comfort, A Breed Apart, The Emerald Forest, Extreme Prejudice, Stalingrad.

BORGE, VICTOR: Comedian, Pianist. b. Copenhagen, Denmark, Jan. 3, 1909. Child prodigy at age 10. Later became humorous concert artist. Wrote and starred in musical plays and films in Denmark. Fled Nazis in 1941, came to America. Appeared on Bing Crosby radio show. Concert and Nightclub tours. TV variety shows. One-man Broadway show. Comedy in Music. 1953, three-year run. Second edition in 1964. World tour. One-man TV show.

BORGNINE, ERNEST: Actor. b. Hamden, CT, Jan. 24, 1918. e. Randall Sch. of Dramatic Art, Hartford, CT. Served in U.S. Navy; then little theatre work, stock companies; on Broadway in Harvey, Mrs. McThing; many TV appearances; m.p. debut in Whistle at Eaton Falls, 1951.
PICTURES INCLUDE: The Mob, China Corsair, From Here to Eternity, Demetruis & the Gladiators, Johnny Guitar, Vera Cruz, Bad Day at Black Rock, Marty (Acad. Award best actor 1955), Run for Cover, Violent Saturday, Last Command, Square Jungle, Catered Affair, Jubal, Best Things in Life are Free, Three Brave Men, Pay or Die, Go Naked in the World, Rabbit Trap, 10 Years a Counterspy, Summer of the Seven-

teenth Doll, Barabbas, Chuka, The Dirty Dozen, The Wild Bunch, The Adventurers, Suppose They Gave a War and Nobody Came?, A Bullet for Sandoval, Bunny O'Hare, Hannie Caulder, The Revengers, Legend of Lylah Clare, The Poseidon Adventure, The Emperor of the North, Law and Disorder, The Devil's Rain, Hustle, Shoot, The Greatest, Crossed Swords, Convoy, The Black Hole, When Time Ran Out, Escape from New York, Deadly Blessing, The Graduates of Malibu High, Codename: Wild Geese, Throwback, Skeleton Coast, Spike of Bensonhurst.
TELEVISION: Philco Playhouse, General Electric Theater, Wagon Train, Laramie, Zane Grey Theater, Alcoa Premiere, McHale's Navy, Blood Feud, Last Days of Pompeii, The Dirty Dozen: The Next Mission, The Dirty Dozen: The Deadly Mission, Treasure Island (Ital. TV), The Dirty Dozen: The Fatal Mission.

BORIS, ROBERT: Writer, Director. b. NY, NY, Oct. 12, 1945. Did many screenplays before also turning to direction with Oxford Blues, 1984.
PICTURES: Electra Glide in Blue; Some Kind of Hero; Doctor Detroit; Oxford Blues (also dir.), Steele Justice (dir.); Buy and Cell (dir.).
TELEVISION: Birds of Prey; Blood Feud, Deadly Encounter, Izzy and Moe.

BORODINSKY, SAMUEL: Executive. b. Brooklyn, NY, Oct. 25, 1941. e. Industrial Sch. of Arts & Photography. Expert in film care and rejuvenation. Now exec. v.p., Filmtreat International Corp. Previously with Modern Film Corp. (technician) and Comprehensive Filmtreat, Inc. & International Filmtreat (service manager).

BOSLEY, TOM: Actor. b. Chicago, IL, Oct. 1, 1927. e. DePaul U. Had roles on radio in Chicago and in stock productions before moving to New York. Appeared off-Broadway and on road before signed to play lead in Fiorello! for George Abbott on Broadway. First actor to win Tony, Drama Critics, ANTA and Newspaper Guild awards in one season for that role. Has since done many plays, movies and TV appearances.
PICTURES: Love with the Proper Stranger, The World of Henry Orient, Divorce, American Style, Yours, Mine and Ours, The Secret War of Harry Frigg, Mixed Company, Gus, Million Dollar Mystery.
TELEVISION: Alice in Wonderland (1953), Arsenic and Old Lace, Focus, Naked City, The Right Man, The Nurses, Route 66, The Perry Como Show, The Rebels. Series: Debbie Reynolds Show, Sandy Duncan Show, Wait Til Your Father Gets Home, Happy Days, Murder She Wrote. Movies: The Girl Who Came Gift Wrapped, Death Cruise, The Night the Martians Landed, Love Boat. Specials: The Drunkard, Profiles in Courage, Testimony of Two Men, The Bastard, Fatal Confession: A Father Dowling Mystery.

BOSTICK, ROBERT L.: b. Waynesboro, GA, Oct. 25, 1909. e. Georgia Inst. of Technology, M.E., eng., 1932. Started with National Theatre Supply, Atlanta, salesman, Memphis, 1933; br. mgr. 1937; br. mgr. Dallas, 1942; Vice Pres., Southern Division Mgr., 1952; retired 1968. Chief Barker Variety Club Tent 20, Memphis 1950–51. Since 1957, has served as International Rep., International Ambassador-at-Large, and International Vice Pres. for Variety Clubs International. Since 1968, owner & operator of theatres in Memphis and Charlotte areas.

BOSTWICK, BARRY: Actor. b. San Mateo, CA, Feb. 24, 1945. e. USIU Sch. of Performing Arts, San Diego, BFA in acting; NYU Grad. Sch. of the Arts. Made prof. stage debut while in coll. working with Walter Pidgeon in Take Her, She's Mine, Joined APA Phoenix Rep. Co. making his Bdwy debut in Cock-A-Doodle Dandy.
THEATER: Salvation, House of Leather, Soon, The Screens, Colette. Grease (created role of Danny Zuko, 1972), They Knew What They Wanted, The Robber Bridegroom (Tony Award), She Loves Me. L'Historie du Soldat.
PICTURES: The Rocky Horror Picture Show, Movie Movie, Megaforce.
TELEVISION: Series: Foul Play. Movies: Scruples, Moviola—The Silent Lovers, Summer Girl, An Uncommon Love, A Woman of Substance, You Can't Take It With You, Once Upon a Family, Red Flag, Working, Deceptions, Betrayed by Innocence, George Washington: The Forging of a Nation, I'll Take Manhattan, Body of Evidence, Addicted to His Love.

BOSUSTOW, NICK: Producer. b. Los Angeles, CA, March 28, 1940. e. Menlo Coll., CA, administration. MCA, International sales, 1963. Pres., Stephen Bosustow Productions, 1967; pres., ASIFA-West; Academy Award '70 best short, Is It Always Right to Be Right?; 1973 Academy Award nomination, The Legend of John Henry. The Incredible Book Escape, Misunderstood Monsters, A Tale of Four Wishes, Wrong Way Kid (TV specials). 1977, pres., Bosustow Entertainment, Inc.

BOSUSTOW, TED: Producer, Director, Editor. b. Hollywood, CA, Feb 18, 1938. e. U. of California at L.A. cinema in Westwood; La Sorbonne, Paris.

PICTURES INCLUDE: Beware of Thin Ice, Big Boys Don't Cry, Avati and the Mezzotint. Edited short, Is It Always Right to Be Right? (AA, 1971).
TELEVISION: About a Week (community affairs series; Emmy award).

BOSWALL, JEFFERY: Producer, Director, Writer. b. Brighton, England, 1931. e. Taunton House School, Montpelier College, Brighton. Started career as an ornithologist for the Royal Society for the Protection of Birds. Joined BBC in 1958 as radio producer, moving to TV 1964 making films in diverse locations (Ethiopia and Antarctica). Contributed to 50 films as wildlife cameraman. Co-founder of British Library of Wildlife Sounds. 1987: returned to RSPB, currently head of Film and Video Unit. Chairman BKSTS Int'l Wildlife Filmmakers' Symposium.
TELEVISION: 18 films in the Private Lives series of which 4 (about the Kingfisher, Cuckoo, Starling and Jackass Penguin) won int'l awards. Animal Olympians, Birds For All Seasons, Where the Parrots Speak Mandarin, Wildlife Safari to Ethiopia. Contributed to studio-based programs, behind the scenes and as presenter.
AUTHOR: Birds for All Seasons. Ed. Look and Private Lives. Contrib.: Times, Countryman, the Field, Wildlife and Countryside, BBC Wildlife, Scientific Film, Journal of the Society of Film and TV Arts, Image Technology. Has written for scientific journals and writes annual update for Encyclopedia Britannica on ornithology.

BOTTOMS, JOSEPH: Actor. b. Santa Barbara, CA, April 22, 1954. Brother of Sam and Timothy Bottoms. Did plays in jr. high school in Santa Barbara and then with community theatre. Made m.p. debut in The Dove, 1974.
PICTURES INCLUDE: Crime and Passion, King of the Mountain, Blind Date, Open House, Born to Race.
TELEVISION: Owen Marshall, Winesburg, Ohio, Side By Side: The True Story of the Osmond Family, I Married Wyatt Earp, The Sins of Dorian Gray, Celebrity, Time Bomb; Murder She Wrote; Braker, Island Sons.

BOTTOMS, SAM: Actor. b. Santa Barbara, CA, Oct. 17, 1955. Brother of Timothy, Joseph and Ben Bottoms.
PICTURES: The Last Picture Show, Class of '44, Zandy's Bride, The Outlaw Josey Wales, Apocalypse Now, Up from the Depths, Bronco Billy, In 'n Out, Hunter's Blood, Gardens of Stone, Loner, Stranded, Private Tutor.
TELEVISION: Savages, Greatest Heroes of the Bible, East of Eden, Desperate Lives, Island Sons, Half Nelson, Cage Without a Key.

BOTTOMS, TIMOTHY: Actor. b. Santa Barbara, CA, Aug. 30, 1951. Brother of Joseph and Sam Bottoms. Early interest in acting; was member of S.B. Madrigal Society, touring Europe in 1967. Sang and danced in West Side Story local prod.
PICTURES INCLUDE: Johnny Got His Gun (debut), The Last Picture Show, Love and Pain, The Paper Chase, The White Dawn, The Crazy World of Julius Vrooder, Seven Men at Daybreak, A Small Town in Texas, Rollercoaster, The Other Side of the Mountain: Part II, Hurricane, First Hello, Hambone and Hillie, Invaders from Mars, The Drifter, Mio in the Land of Faraway, Return From the River Kwai, A Case of Law.
TELEVISION: Look Homeward Angel; The Story of David, The Money Changers, Escape, A Shining Season, East of Eden, Island Sons.

BOUCHIER, CHILI: Actress. r.n. Dorothy Irene Boucher. b. Fulham, London, England, Sept. 12, 1909. m. Bluey Hill, Australian film director (d. 1986). British stage appearances include: Open Your Eyes, 1930; Lavender; Magnolia Street; Mother Goose; A Little Bit of Fluff; Rendezvous; Age of Consent; Tons of Money; The Mousetrap; Harvey; I Can't Imagine Tomorrow; Rookery Nook; French Dressing; Conduct Unbecoming; The Best of Dorothy Parker; Follies, 1985; A Little Night Music, 1987. Originally a model at Harrods, London. After her screen debut in 1927, she quickly became one of Britain's first international stars in motion pictures.
PICTURES INCLUDE: A Woman in Pawn, Shooting Stars, Maria Marten, Dawn, Chick, You Know What Sailors Are, Warned Off, The Silver King, City of Play, Downstream, Enter the Queen, Call of the Sea, Kissing Cup's Race, Brown Sugar, Carnival, The Blue Danube, Ebb Tide, The King's Cup, Summer Lightning, Purse Strings, It's a Cop, To Be a Lady, The Office Wife, Death Drives Through, Royal Cavalcade, The Mad Hatters, Honours Easy, Lucky Days, Get Off My Foot, Mr. Cohen Takes a Walk, The Ghost Goes West, Faithful, Where's Sally?, Southern Roses, Gypsy, Mayfair Melody, The Minstrel Boy, Change for a Sovereign, The Dark Stairway, Mr. Satan, The Singing Cop, The Return of Carol Deane, Everything Happens to Me, The Mind of Mr. Reeder, My Wife's Family, Facing the Music, Murder in Reverse, The Laughing Lady, Mrs. Fitzherbert, The Case of Charles Peace, Old Mother Riley's New Venture, The Wallet, The Counterfeit Plan, The Boy and the Bridge, Dead Lucky.
TELEVISION: Yesterday's Witness, Looks Familiar, Saturday Night at the Pictures, Catch a Fallen Star.

BOUDOURIS, A: Executive. b. Toledo, OH, Jan. 31, 1918. e. U. of Toledo, 1945–47, USN, radio-radar, 1941–45; carrier pilot. Service, installation, projection equip., 1934–36; Strong Electric, 1936–41; Pres., Theatre Equip. Co., 1945–65; Theatre Operating Co., since 1947; pres. Eprad, Inc., 1949, bd. chmn., 1980. Member (ex-chrm.) of NATO'S Technical Advisory Comm., Pres. NATO of Ohio, NATO representative on American National Standards Committee; now Vice Pres. NATO. Chairman, NATO Statistical Committee; Member, Projection Practices and Sound Comm. of SMPTE; NATO Representative International Standards Organization (Geneva), Member National Electrical Code Committee Panel #15. Recipient, SMPTE Fellowship Award, 1980.

BOULTING, ROY: Producer, Director. b. Bray, Buckinghamshire, England, Nov. 21, 1913. e. McGill U., Montreal. Capt., Brit. Army, W.W.II. Dir. Charter Film, Charter Film Prod. Ltd. London; dir. British Lion Films, Ltd., 1958.
PICTURES INCLUDE: Inquest, Trunk Crime, Pastor Hall, Thunder Rock, Desert Victory, Burma Victory, Fame is the Spur, Brighton Rock, Guinea Pig, Seven Days to Noon, Lucky Jim, High Treason, Singlehanded (Sailor of the King), Seagulls Over Sorrento (Crest of the Wave), Josephine and Men, Private's Progress, Run for the Sun, Brothers in Law, Happy Is the Bride, Carlton-Browne of the F.O., I'm All Right Jack, The Risk, The French Mistress, Heavens Above!, Rotten to The Core, The Family Way, Twisted Nerve, There's a Girl in My Soup, Soft Beds, Hard Battles, 1977, co-author with Leo Marks of play, Favourites, Danny Travis, The Last Word, 1979; Agatha Christie's The Moving Finger (BBC).

BOWER, DALLAS: Producer, Director. b. London, 1907. Ent. film prod. 1927; film ed., writer, dir., prod. with BBC-TV 1936. Prod. and dir. opening program of BBC Television service, 1936. Commissioned in Royal Corps of Signals, 1939; supvr. film prod., Ministry of Inf., Films Div., 1942; prod. official and commercial documentaries; author, Plan for Cinema, 1936.
PICTURES AND TELEVISION INCLUDE: Aida, Tristan & Isolde, Master Peter's Puppet Show, Cinderella, Julius Caesar, The Tempest, The Taming of the Shrew, The Silver Box, The Mock Emperor, The Emperor Jones, Rope, Path of Glory, Victory over Space, Henry V, Alice in Wonderland, The Second Mrs. Tanquery, Fire One, Doorway to Suspicion, Adventures of Sir Lancelot. In prep. for TV, The Ring, The Trojans.

BOWIE, DAVID: Singer, Actor. b. Brixton, South London, England, Jan. 8, 1947. r.n. David Robert Jones. Broadway debut: The Elephant Man (1980).
PICTURES: Ziggy Stardust and the Spiders from Mars (1973, U.S. release 1983), The Man Who Fell to Earth, Just a Gigolo, The Hunger, The Cat People, Merry Christmas, Mr. Lawrence, Into the Night, Absolute Beginners (act., music), Labyrinth (act., music), The Last Temptation of Christ, Imagine—John Lennon.
TELEVISION: Christmas With Bing Crosby; The Midnight Special, Glass Spider Tour.

BOWSER, EILEEN: Curator, Film Archivist, Historian. b. Ohio, Jan. 1, 1928. e. Marietta Coll., B.A., 1950; U. of North Carolina, M.A., history of art, 1953. Joined Dept. of Film, Museum of Modern Art, 1954. Curator, Dept. of Film since 1976. Organized major exhib. of the films of D.W. Griffith, Carl-Theodor Dreyer, Art of the Twenties, recent acquisitions and touring shows. On exec. comm. of Federation Internationale des Archives du Film since 1969, v.p. FIAF 1977–85; pres. FIAF Documentation Commission 1972–81. Film Archives Advisory Comm. since 1971. Assoc. of Univ. Seminars on Cinema and Interdisciplinary Interpretation. Publications: The Movies, David Wark Griffith, Biograph Bulletins 1908–1912, Film Notes, D.W. Griffith, Carl Dreyer, Motion Picture Film (in Conservation in the Library), A Handbook for Film Archives. Has written numerous articles on film history.

BOX, BETTY, OBE: Producer. b. Beckenham, Kent, England, 1920. Assisted Sydney Box in prod. 200 propaganda films in W.W.II. Assoc. prod. Upturned Glass.
PRODUCTIONS INCLUDE: Dear Murderer, When the Bough Breaks, Miranda, Blind Goddess, Huggett Family series. It's Not Cricket, Marry Me, Don't Ever Leave Me, So Long At the Fair, The Clouded Yellow, Appointment With Venus (Island Rescue). Venetian Bird (The Assassin), A Day to Remember, Doctor in the House, Mad About Men, Doctor at Sea, The Iron Petticoat, Checkpoint, Doctor at Large, Campbell's Kingdom, A Tale of Two Cities, The Wind Cannot Read, The 39 Steps, Upstairs and Downstairs, Conspiracy of Hearts, Doctor in Love, No Love for Johnnie, No, My Darling Daughter, A Pair of Briefs, The Wild and the Willing, Doctor in Distress, Hot Enough for June (Agent 8¾), The High Bright Sun, (McGuire Go Home), Doctor in Clover, Deadlier Than the Male, Nobody Runs Forever, The High Commissioner, Some Girls Do, Doctor in Trouble, Percy, The Love Ban, Percy's Progress.

BOXLEITNER, BRUCE: Actor. b. Elgin, IL, May 12, 1950. After high school enrolled in Chicago's Goodman Theatre, staging productions in the city and working with lighting and set design in addition to acting. Film debut in The Baltimore Bullet (1980).
TELEVISION: Series: How the West Was Won, The Macahans, Bring 'Em Back Alive, Scarecrow and Mrs. King. Movies: Happily Ever After, Kenny Rogers as The Gambler, Kiss Me, Kill Me, Fly Away Home, Kenny Rogers as The Gambler: The Adventure Continues, Passion Flower, Angel in Green, The Last Convertible, Bare Essence, East of Eden, Kenny Rogers as the Gambler: The Legend Continues, Red River, The Town Bully.
PICTURES: The Baltimore Bullet, Tron.

BOYARS, ALBERT: Executive. b. New York, NY, Aug. 11: e. New York U. U.S. Navy, 1941–45. David O. Alber Assoc., 1945–51: Greater N.Y. Fund, Robert S. Taplinger Assoc., Michael Myerberg Prod., 1951–54: pub. rel. dir., Transfilm-Caravel Inc., and parent co. Buckeye Corp., 1954–63: director spec. projects in adv-pub-exploit. M-G-M, 1963–64; dir. of adv. & pub. Trans-Lux Corp., 1964, v.p. of adv. and pub. rel., Trans-Lux Multimedia Corp., 1976. Under his marketing aegis are the attractions The New York Experience, (in Rockefeller Center), and The Seaport Experience (at South Street Seaport, NY.).

BOYER, PHIL: TV Executive. b. Portland, OR, Dec. 13, 1940. e. Sacramento State U. Began broadcasting career as 12-year-old in Portland, establishing nation's first youth radio facility—a 5-watt facility in the basement of his home. At 16 began working at KPDQ, Portland; two years later joined KPTV, Portland, as announcer. In 1960 joined KEZI-TV, Eugene, OR, heading prod. and prog. depts. In 1965 named staff prod.-dir. for KCRA, TV, Sacramento, CA, becoming prod. mgr. in 1967 and prog. mgr. in 1969. In 1972 joined KNBC-TV, Los Angeles, as prog. dir. In 1974 named v.p., programming, of ABC Owned Television Stations; 1977, v.p.-gen. mgr., WLS-TV, Chicago; 1979, v.p.-gen. mgr. of WABC-TV, New York 1981–.

BOYETT, ROBERT LEE: Producer. e. Duke U., B.A.; Col. U., M.A., marketing. Began career in media and mkt. research at Grey Advertising, Inc. Was program development consultant for PBS. In 1973 joined ABC as dir. of prime time series TV, East Coast. In 1975 named ABC TV v.p. & asst. to v.p. programs for West Coast. In 1977 joined Paramount Pictures in newly created position of v.p., exec. asst. to pres. & chief operating officer. 1979, joined Miller-Milkis—Boyett Productions to produce for Paramount Television.
TELEVISION: Exec. prod.: Laverne and Shirley, Happy Days, Bosom Buddies, Mork and Mindy, Valerie.

BOYLE, BARBARA D.: Executive. b. New York, NY, Aug. 11, 1935. e. U. of California, Berkeley, B.A., 1957; U. of California at L.A., J.D., 1960. Named to bar: California, 1961; New York, 1964; Supreme Court, 1964. Atty. in busn. affairs dept. & corp. asst. secty., American Intl. Pictures, Los Angeles, 1969–65; partner in law firm, Cohen & Boyle, L.A., 1967–74; exec. & gen. counsel, COO, New World Pictures, L.A., 1974–82. Sr. v.p. prod., Orion Pictures, L.A., 1982–85; exec. v.p., prod., RKO Pictures, L.A., 1986–present. Co-chmn. 1979–80, Entertainment Law Symposium Advisory Committee, U. of California at L.A. Law Sch.
MEMBER: Academy of Motion Picture Arts & Sciences, Women in Film (pres., 1977–78), Women Entertainment Lawyers Assn., California Bar Assn., N.Y. State Bar Assn., Beverly Hills Bar Assn., Hollywood Women's Political Committee, American Film Institute, Women's Director Workshop bd. mem., Independent Feature Project/West board member, Los Angeles; Women's Campaign Fund, board mem.

BOYLE, PETER: Actor. b. Philadelphia, PA, Oct. 18, 1933. e. LaSalle Coll. Was monk in Christian Bros. order before leaving in early 60s to come to N.Y. Acted in off-Broadway shows and joined The Second City in Chicago. Also did TV commercials.
PICTURES INCLUDE: Joe (debut), T.R. Baskin, The Candidate, Steelyard Blues, Slither, The Friends of Eddie Coyle, Kid Blue, Crazy Joe, Young Frankenstein, Swashbuckler, F.I.S.T., Brinks' Job, Hardcore, Beyond the Poseidon Adventure, Where the Buffalo Roam, In God We Trust, Outland, Hammett, Yellowbeard, Johnny Dangerously, Turk 182, Surrender, Walker, Red Heat, The Dream Team.
TELEVISION: Tail Gunner Joe, From Here to Eternity, Echoes in the Darkness.

BRABOURNE, LORD JOHN: Producer. b. London, England, Nov. 9, 1924.
PRODUCTIONS INCLUDE: Harry Black, Sink the Bismarck, H.M.S. Defiant, Othello, The Mikado, Up the Junction, Romeo and Juliet, Dance of Death, Tales of Beatrix Potter, Murder on the Orient Express, Death On The Nile, Stories from a Flying Trunk, The Mirror Crack'd, Evil Under the Sun, A Passage to India, Little Dorrit.

BRACCO, LORRAINE: Actress. b. Brooklyn, NY. m. actor Harvey Keitel. At 16 began modelling for Wilhelmina Agency appear-

ing in Mademoiselle, Seventeen, Teen magazine. Moved to Paris where modelling career continued and led to TV commercials. After making her film debut in Duo sur Canape became a disc jockey on Radio Luxembourg, Paris. 1983 produced a TV special on fashion and music. In Lincoln Center workshop performance of David Rabe's Goose and Tom Tom, 1986.
PICTURES: Carmorra, The Pick-up Artist, Someone to Watch Over Me, Talk Radio, Sing.

BRACKEN, EDDIE: Actor. b. New York, NY, Feb. 7, 1920. e. Prof. Children's Sch. for Actors, N.Y. m. Connie Nickerson, actress. Vaudeville & night club singer; stage debut in Lottery, 1930; m.p. debut in Life with Henry. 1940.
PLAYS: Lady Refuses, Iron Men, So Proudly We Hail, Brother Rat, What A Life, Too Many Girls, Seven Year Itch, Shinbone Alley, Teahouse of the August Moon, You Know I Can't Hear You When The Water's Running, The Odd Couple, Never Too Late, Sunshine Boys, Hotline to Heaven, Hello, Dolly, Damn Yankees, Sugar Babies, Show Boat.
PICTURES INCLUDE: Fleet's In, Happy Go Lucky, Sweater Girl, Star Spangled Rhythm, Young and Willing, Hail the Conquering Hero, Miracle of Morgan's Creek, Girl From Jones Beach, Summer Stock, Two Tickets to Broadway, About Face, We're Not Married, Slight Case of Larceny, National Lampoon's Vacation.
TELEVISION: Masquerade Party, Murder She Wrote, Blacke's Magic, Amazing Stories, Tales of the Dark Side.

BRADEN, WILLIAM: Executive, Producer. b. Alberta, Canada, 1939. e. Vancouver, B.C. Began career as stuntman in Hollywood, and has worked in all aspects of industry for 23 years. Worked for Elliott Kastner as prod. executive with offices at Paramount and with Jeffrey Bloom, of Feature Films, Inc., as prod. and v.p. in chg. of prod. before joining, Dunatai Corp., as head of film and t.v. prod., now indep. prod.
PICTURES: Pyramid (assoc. prod., prod. supv.), Russian Roulette (prod. exec.) 92 in the Shade (prod. exec.), Breakheart Pass (prod. exec.), Dogpound Shuffle (asst. dir., prod. supv.); Dublin Murders (supvr. re-edit); He Wants Her Back (prod.); Goldengirl (prod. exec.); Running Scared (prod.); Death Valley (asst. dir.); The Seduction (prod. exec.); Slapstick (prod. exec.).
TELEVISION: Requiem for a Planet (series, prod./creator); Nothing Great is Easy (special, exec. prod.); King of the Channel (special, exec. prod.); I Believe (special, prod.); If My People. . . (special, prod.), Jude (pilot, prod.) America: Life in the Family (dir./prod.) Also various Movies of the Week for networks.

BRADLEY, BILL: Performer, r.n. William M. Silbert. b. Detroit, MI, Jan. 1, 1921. e. U. of Detroit, Southern Methodist U. Disc jockey, m.c., many radio-TV shows, Detroit; panelist, Songs for Sale, 1952; emcee, Bill Silbert show, Let's Go Bowling, 1952–53; Bill Silbert Show. WMGM radio; announcer, Red Buttons Show; Philco Phonorama Time; m.c., National Radio Fan Club; Magazine of the Air, Mutual #1 disc jockey, Billboard Magazine, 1955; KLAC Hollywood, Bill Bradley Show; KTLA, Hollywood, m.c. Crime Story, Greet the People, Ad Lib, Hollywood Diary. Sales mgr., KLOS, Los Angeles.
PICTURES INCLUDE: Bundle of Joy, Thunderjets, The Alligator People, Young Jesse James, Lost Missile, Breakfast at Tiffany's, Return to Peyton Place, Looking for Love, Goonies.
TELEVISION: Bronco, 77 Sunset Strip, Hawaiian Eye, Sugarfoot, Combat, Adventures in Paradise, Police Station, Michael Shayne, Roaring 20's, The Outlaws, Breaking Point, The Fugitive, Bill Dana Show, My Living Doll, Joey Bishop Show, Ben Casey, Bing Crosby Show. Many commercials, Mannix, Wild Wild West, Name of the Game.

BRADLEY, ED: Newscaster. b. Philadelphia, Pa., June 22, 1941. e. Chayney State Coll, B.S. Worked up through the ranks as local radio reporter in Philadelphia 1963–67 and NY 1967–71. Joined CBS News as stringer in Paris bureau, 1971; then Saigon bureau. Named CBS news correspondent, 1973. Became CBS News White House corr. and anchor of CBS Sunday Night News, 1976–81; principal correspondent and anchor, CBS Reports, 1978–81; co-editor and reporter 60 Minutes since 1982.
TELEVISION: Special reports: What's Happened to Cambodia; The Boat People; The Boston Goes to China; Blacks in America—with all Deliberate Speed; Return of the CIA; Miami...The Trial That Sparked the Riot (Emmy); The Saudis; Too Little, Too Late (Emmy); Murder—Teenage Style (Emmy, 1981); In the Belly of the Beast (Emmy, 1982); Lena (Emmy, 1982).
AWARDS: Aside from numerous Emmys, has received Alfred I. duPont-Columbia University and Overseas Press Club Awards; George Foster Peabody and Ohio State Awards; and George Polk Award.

BRADY, FRANK L.: Theatre executive. b. Columbus, GA, Jan. 11, 1914. Former pres., Martin Theatres.

BRAEDEN, ERIC: Actor. b. Kiel, Germany. r.n. Hans Gudegast.
PICTURES: Colossus, The Forbin Project, The Law and Jake Wade, The Ultimate Thrill, Morituri, Escape from the Planet of the Apes, Lady Ice, A Hundred Rifles, Herbie Goes to Monte Carlo.
TELEVISION: The Young and the Restless (series).

BRAGA, SONIA: Actress. b. Maringa, Parana, Brazil, 1951. Began acting at 14 on live children's program on Brazilian TV, Gardin Encantado. Stage debut at 17 in Moliere's Jorge Dandin, then in Hair! Starred in many Brazilian soap operas including Gabriella, as well as a prod. of Sesame Street in Saõ Paulo.
PICTURES: The Main Road, A Moreninha, Captain Bandeira Vs. Dr. Moura Brasil, Mestica, The Indomitable Slave, The Couple, Dona Flor and Her Two aHusbands, Gabriella, I Love You, A Lady in the Bus, Kiss of the Spider Woman, The Milagro Beanfield War, Moon Over Parador.
TELEVISION: The Man Who Broke 1000 Chains, The Bill Cosby Show.

BRAND, NEVILLE: Actor. b. Kewanee, IL, Aug. 13, 1921. e. high sch., Kewanee. U.S. Army, 10 yrs to 1946; studied acting in N.Y.: film debut in D.O.A. (1949).
PICTURES INCLUDE: Halls of Montezuma, Only the Valiant, The Mob, Flame of Araby, Stalag 17, Charge at Feather River, Man Crazy, Gun Fury, Riot in Cell Block 11, Long Gun, Prince Valiant, Return from the Sea, Fury at Gunsight Pass, The Prodigal, Return of Jack Slade, Bobby Ware Is Missing, Mohawk, Raw Edge, The Adventures of Huckleberry Finn, The Desperadoes, Three Guns for Texas, Birdman of Alcatraz, That Darn Cat, Scalawag, Cahill, U.S. Marshall, The Deadly Trackers, Psychic Killer, Evils of the Night.
TELEVISION: The Untouchables, Arroyo, Laredo, Captains and the Kings, The Eddie Capra Mysteries, Harper Valley, The Seekers, The Quest, The Barbary Coast.

BRANDAUER, KLAUS MARIA: Actor. b. 1945. Was established in the German and Austrian theater before debut in Hungarian film Mephisto (1981; best actor award, Cannes Film Fest.).
PICTURES: Never Say Never Again, Colonel Redl, Out of Africa, The Lightship, Streets of Gold, The Death Ship, Burning Secret, Hanussen, Oskar Schindler—An Angel in Hell, Hitlerjunge Salomon.
TELEVISION: Quo Vadis?

BRANDO, JOCELYN: Actress. b. San Francisco, CA, Nov. 18, 1919. e. Lake Forest Coll. m.p. debut in The Big Heat; on Broadway in Mr. Roberts, Desire Under the Elms, Golden State.
PICTURES INCLUDE: China Venture, Ten Wanted Men, Mommie Dearest.
TELEVISION: Dark Night of the Scarecrow, A Question of Love, Starflight—The Plane that Couldn't Land.

BRANDO, MARLON: Actor. b. Omaha, NB, April 3, 1924. e. Shattuck Military Acad., Faribault, MN. Studied Dramatic Workshop, N.Y.; played stock Sayville, Long Island. Broadway debut: I Remember Mama, then Truckline Cafe, Candida, A Flag Is Born, A Streetcar Named Desire. One of top ten Money-Making Stars, M.P. Herald-Fame poll, 1954–55.
PICTURES INCLUDE: A Streetcar Named Desire, Viva Zapata, Julius Caesar, Wild One, On the Waterfront (Acad. Award, best actor, 1954), Guys and Dolls, Teahouse of the August Moon, Sayonara, The Young Lions, Mutiny on the Bounty, One-Eyed Jacks, The Ugly American, Bedtime Story, The Saboteur, Code Name, Morituri, The Fugitive Kind, The Chase, Appaloosa, The Countess From Hong Kong, Reflections in a Golden Eye, Night of the Following Day, Candy, Burn!, The Nightcomers, The Godfather (Acad. Award, best actor, 1972), Last Tango in Paris, The Missouri Breaks, Superman, The Formula, The White Russian Season, Jericho.
TELEVISION: Roots: The Next Generations (Emmy Award, best supporting actor).

BRANDT, JANET: Actress. b. New York, NY. Acting debut at 6 years old with Yiddish Theater. Over 100 stage appearances in New York where she studied with Martha Graham and with Michael Chekov. Lectured on Shakespeare at the Strasberg Institute in L.A.
PICTURES INCLUDE: A Cold Wind in August, Kotch, Mad Adventures of Rabbi Jacob, Sheila Levine, Semi-Tough, Dialogue Director: Battle of the Bulge, El Cid, Phaedre, View from the Bridge, King of Kings, etc.
TELEVISION: The Super, Odd Couple, Mannix, Lou Grant.

BRANDT, RICHARD PAUL: Executive. b. New York, NY, Dec. 6, 1927. e. Yale U., BS, Phi Beta Kappa. Chief exec. off. & chrf. Trans Lux Corp.; chm., Brandt Theatres; dir., Presidential Realty Corp., member President's Advisory Council, National Association of Theatre Owners; chrm. emeritus & trustee, American Film Institute; trustee: American Theatre Wing.

BRANDY, HOWARD: Executive. b. Brooklyn, NY, 1929. e. Emory U. Served with Marine Corps in Korean War. Worked as N.Y. press agent; in 1956 went with NBC. Was columnist for

Hollywood Reporter in Las Vegas then went back into publicity as asst. exec. for Rogers and Cowan. Started own business; clients included Frankie Avalon, Fabian, Monkees, Fifth Dimension, Johnny Cash, etc. Joined Commonwealth United in London working for co. 5 yrs. before it folded. Entered film prod.
PICTURES INCLUDE: Blood from the Mummy's Tomb, The Take.

BRASLOFF, STANLEY H.: Producer, director. b. Philadelphia, PA, July 23, 1930. In U.S. Army was entertainment dir., Heidelberg military post, 1948–50; prod., dir. & acted for various little theatre & summer stock groups, 1950–60; created, wrote, co-prod., dir. & starred in Time For Teens, TV show (Chicago); formed VCS Pictures Ltd., prod. & dir. Two Girls for a Madman, 1967; formed SHB Productions, Inc., prod. Nightmare at Ghost Beach, 1968; wrote, co-prod. & dir. Toys Are Not for Children, 1971.

BRAUDY, SUSAN: Executive. b. July 8, 1941. e. Bryn Mawr Coll. Taught writing at Brooklyn Coll., 1974. 1970–72, editor and writer at Newsweek; same post at Ms. Magazine, 1973–78. Worked in 1978 for producer Alberto Grimaldi. Has published numerous articles in New York Magazine, New Journal (Yale), The Atlantic, Village Voice, etc. In 1981 appt. Warner Bros. v.p., east coast production. 1981, novel, Who Killed Sal Mineo?, published.

BRAUER, LE ROY: Executive. b. Cincinnati, OH, Sept. 30, 1902. e. Columbia. U. Salesman, Cincinnati Standard Film Service, 1919. Universal, 1921–46, as salesman, branch mgr., Supvsr., China, Japan; br. mgr. New Orleans, other cities, then sales mgr., Europe, Middle East and India. Columbia Pictures, Intl. Corp. 1949–1951. Man. dir. Australia, 1951; chmn. bd., Exotic TV Film Distribs. Pty. Ltd.

BRAUNSTEIN, GEORGE GREGORY: Producer. b. New York, NY, May 23, 1947. e. Culver Military Acad., U. of California, B.A., biology, chemistry, 1970. U. of W.L.A. Law School J.D. 1987. Father is Jacques Braunstein (Screen Televideo Prods. At War with the Army, Young Lions, etc.). 1971, co-founder of The Crystal Jukebox—record productions, music management, music publishing co. Produced 12 hit albums for Decca Records of England and London Records, U.S.A. Entered m.p. production in 1975–76 producing Train Ride to Hollywood for Taylor-Laughlin Co., Pres. of Solar Survival Film Corp. 1981.
FILMS: Train Ride to Hollywood, Fade to Black, Surf II, And God Created Woman, Out Cold.

BRAVERMAN, CHARLES: Producer, Director. b. Los Angeles, CA, March 3, 1944. e. Los Angeles City Coll., U. of Southern California, B.A. m. Kendall Carly Browne, actress. Child actor, 1950–57. Two time Emmy winner.
TELEVISION: An American Time Capsule, The Smothers Brothers Racing Team Special, How to Stay Alive, David Hartman . . . Birth and Babies, Breathe a Sigh of Relief, The Television Newsman, Getting Married, The Making of a Live TV Show, Televisionland, Nixon: Checkers to Watergate, Braverman's Condensed Cream of Beatles, Two Cops, Peanuts to the Presidency; The Jimmy Carter Campaign; The Making of Beatlemania, Willie Nelson Plays Lake Tahoe, Tony Bennett Sings, What's Up, America?, The Big Laff Off, Engelbert at the MGM Grand, Oscar's First 50 Years, Frankie Valli Show, The Sixties, Showtime Looks at 1981, Roadshow, Kenny Rodger's America; St. Elsewhere; DTV (Disney Channel); Crazy Like a Fox; Dreams; The Richard Lewis Special; Prince of Bel Air, Brotherhood of Justice (both ABC movies); The Wizard; Heart of the City; Rags to Riches; The New Mike Hammer.
PICTURES: Dillinger, Soylent Green, Same Time Next Year (all montages, titles), Can't Stop the Music (titles), Hit and Run (prod./dir.).

BRAVERMAN, MILLICENT: Adv. agency president (Braverman-Mirisch Inc.) KFAC AM & FM, syndicated radio Los Angeles commentator on books, literary critic, publishing specialist. b. New York, NY. B-M. Inc. founded 1963 to date. General advertising, print and broadcast media nationally.

BRAY, PAUL JR.: e. Rensselaer Polytechnic Inst. Experienced airline transport pilot and instrument flight instructor. Writer and director specializing in motion picture scripts and productions on all phases aviation, engineering and electronic from theoretical to practical industrial personnel training, and for Armed Forces and Vocational-Technical school instruction.

BRAZZI, ROSSANO: Actor. b. Bologna, Italy, 1916. e. U. of Florence. Started career on Italian stage; has appeared in numerous Italian pictures.
PICTURES INCLUDE: (U.S.) Little Women, Three Coins in the Fountain, Barefoot Contessa, Summertime, South Pacific, Light in the Piazza, The Battle of Villa Fiorita, Rome Adventure, Dark Purpose, The Christmas That Almost Wasn't, The Bobo, Woman Times Seven, Krakatoa, East of Java, The Adventurers, Psychout for Murder, The Great Waltz, The Final Conflict, Fear City.

TELEVISION: (U.S.) June Allyson Show, Run For Your Life, The Name of the Game, Hawaii Five-O, Fantasy Island, Charlie's Angels, Hart to Hart, The Survivors, Honeymoon With a Stranger, The Far Pavillions, Christopher Columbus.

BREACHER, HAROLD: Executive. b. June 17, 1910. e. U. of California at L.A., B.A.; U. of Southern California, LL.B., J.D. Attorney at Law, 7 years. Bergerman-Breacher Motion Picture Agency, part owner. William Morris Agency, exec. agent; Famous Artists Agency, head Television Dept.; Ashley-Famous Agency, exec. packaging agent; United Artists Pictures Corp., head of sales & distribution United Kingdom, Europe, Middle East and Africa (TV); director, sales, U.K., Europe, Middle East & South Africa, Warner Bros. Television.

BRECHER, IRVING: Writer. b. New York, NY, Jan. 17, 1914. Yonkers Herald reporter; network programs writer for Milton Berle, Willie Howard, Al Jolson, etc., m.p. writer since 1937.
PICTURES INCLUDE: (collab. s.p.) Shadow of the Thin Man, Best Foot Forward, Meet Me in St. Louis; (collab. adapt.) Summer Holiday: (s.p.), Go West, At the Circus, Du Barry Was a Lady, Yolanda and the Thief, Life of Riley, Somebody Loves Me, Cry for Happy, Bye Bye Birdie, Sail a Crooked Ship.
TELEVISION: The People's Choice, The Life of Riley.

BREGMAN, MARTIN: Producer. Writer. b. New York, NY, May 18, 1931. m. actress Cornelia Sharpe. e. Indiana U., New York U. Began career as business and personal mgr. to Barbara Streisand, Faye Dunaway, Candice Bergen, Al Pacino, etc. Chairman NY Advisory Council for Motion Pictures, Radio and TV (co-founder, 1974).
PICTURES INCLUDE: Serpico, Dog Day Afternoon, The Next Man, The Seduction of Joe Tynan, Simon, The Four Seasons, Eddie Macon's Run, Venom, Scarface, Sweet Liberty, Real Men, A New Life, Sea of Love, Nesting.
TELEVISION: Prod.: S*H*E (movie), The Four Seasons (series).

BREN, ROBERT J.: Producer, writer. b. Guanajuato, Mexico. Film writing debut with Looking for Trouble, 1934; in U.S. Signal Corps, W.W.II, also coordinator Inter-American Affairs as m.p. program office head, N.Y. & Washington, DC. Formed Bremex, indep. picture co., 1963.
PICTURES INCLUDE: This Marriage Business, Crime Ring, Parents on Trail, American Empire, Underground Agent, Charter Pilot, In Old California, Gay Senorita, Five Little Peppers and How They Grew, prod. First Yank into Tokyo, assoc. prod. El Paso, Overland Pacific; Naked Alibi, Treasure of Pancho Villa, The Great Sioux Uprising, Siege at Red River, Without Orders, Maltrata (O.S., S.P., producer) for Bremex Corp., Mexico; Cajeme (O.S., S.P., producer) for Bremex, S.A., Mexico.
TELEVISION: Lone Wolf in Mexico, Stolen Train, Casey Jones series. collab. s.p., Winds of the Four Seasons; collab. s.p., orig. story, The Hawaiians, 1967. Wrote & collaborated on Blood On the Shrine, Legacy in Nylons, Aztec Dagger, Female Menagerie, Tag for Murder.

BRENNAN, EILEEN: Actress. b. Los Angeles, CA, Sept. 3, 1935. e. Georgetown U., American Acad. of Dramatic Arts, N.Y. Daughter of silent film actress Jean Manahan. Big break came with lead in off-Broadway musical, Little Mary Sunshine (Obie Award, 1960).
PICTURES INCLUDE: Divorce, American Style, The Last Picture Show, Scarecrow, The Sting, Daisy Miller, At Long Last Love, Hustle, Murder by Death, The Cheap Detective, Private Benjamin, Clue, Rented Lips, Sticky Fingers, The New Adventures of Pippi Longstocking, It Had to Be You.
STAGE: The Miracle Worker (tour), Hello, Dolly! (Broadway), and revivals of The King and I, Guys and Dolls, Camelot, Bells Are Ringing, etc. Did one-women revue, An Evening with Eileen Brennan.
TELEVISION: Series: Private Benjamin (Emmy Award), Off the Rack. Special: Working. Movies: The Blue Knight, Black Beauty, My Old Man, Playmates, When the Circus Comes to Town, Off Duty.

BRENNER, JOSEPH: Executive. b. Brooklyn, NY, Oct. 27, 1918. e. Brooklyn Coll. Started as usher, 1935, becoming mgr., Rogers Theatre, 1936; salesman, Eagle Lion Films, 1946; Screen Guild Prods., 1948; sales mgr., Ellis Films, 1949; formed Joseph Brenner Associates, 1953.

BRESSON, ROBERT: Writer, director. b. France, Sept. 25, 1907. PICTURES: Les Anges du Peche, Les Dames du Bois de Boulogne, Le Journal d'un Cure de Campagne, Pickpocket, The Trial of Joan of Arc, Au Hazard Balthasar, Mouchette, Une Femme Douce, Lancelot du Lac, Le Diable Probablement, De Weg Naar Bresson.

BREST, MARTIN: Director. b. Bronx, NY, 1951. e. New York U. Sch. of Film. Made award-winning short subject, Hot Dogs for Gauguin. Accepted into fellowship program at American Film Institute, making first feature, Hot Tomorrows, as AFI project.
PICTURES: Going in Style, Beverly Hills Cop, Midnight Run (prod., dir.).

BRETT, JEREMY: Actor. b. Berkwell Grange, Warwickshire, Eng., Nov. 3, 1933. r.n. Jeremy Huggins. e. Eton, Central Sch. of Speech and Drama. London stage debut, Troilus and Cressida (Old Vic, 1956); NY stage debut, Richard II (1956).
THEATER: Selected London shows: Meet Me by Moonlight, Variations on a Theme, Mr. Fox of Venice, Marigold, The Edwardians, Johnny the Priest, The Kitchen, A Month in the Country, Macrune's Guevara, A Voyage Round My Father, Traveller Without Luggage, Design for Living. U.S.: With Old Vic in Amphytrion 38, Richard II, Macbeth, Romeo and Juliet, Troilus and Cressida, The Deputy, Robert and Elizabeth (L.A.), Dracula (L.A.), Aren't We All?
PICTURES: War and Peace, My Fair Lady, The Medusa Touch.
TELEVISION: Romeo and Juliet (1957), Macbeth, Florence Nightingale, Deceptions, Jennie, Katherine Mansfield, The Merry Widow, Rebecca, The Adventures of Sherlock Holmes (1985–86), Picture of Dorian Gray, Dinner with Family, The School for Scandal, Hart to Hart.

BREWER, ROY M.: b. Cairo, NB, Aug. 9, 1909. Was projectionist 1925; chief projectionist, Capitol Theatre, Grand Island, NB 1927–39; pres. Nebraska State Fed. of Labor 1933; active in Nebraska labor movement in this period; NRA labor compliance officer for Nebraska 1934–35; campaigned for U.S. Senator George W. Norris in chg. campaign hdqts. 1936; re-elected pres. Nebraska State Federation of Labor 1937; covered legislature for Federation 1939, 1941, 1943; chief, plant & community facilities service War Prod. Bd. Washington 1943–45; apptd. specl. internl. rep. LATSE 1945; then made internl. rep. in Hollywood, rep. Richard F. Walsh, LATSE pres.; exec. ass't Steve Broidy, Allied Artists president, October, 1953; mgr. of br. oper., 1955; apptd. admin. sls. asst. to Edward Morey, vice-pres., Allied Artists, 1962; mgr. prod. dev., 1965. Member: Hollywood AFL Film Council, M.P. Ind. Council, M.P. Alliance, Pres, Perm Char. Committee 1965 Studio mgr. and prod. rep. for West Coast.

BRIALY, JEAN-CLAUDE: Actor. b. Aumale, Algeria, March 30, 1933. e. Strasbourg U. (philosophy) also attended drama classes at Strasbourg Conservatoire. Made several short films with Jacques Rivette and Jean-Luc Godard. Popular actor in films of French New Wave directors.
PICTURES: Elena et les Hommes; Elevator to the Scaffold (1958); Les Cousins; Le Beau Serge; The 400 Blows; Tire au Flane; La Chambre Ardente; A Woman is a Woman; The Devil and Ten Commandments; La Ronde; Un Homme de Trop; Lamiel; King of Hearts; Le Rouge et le Noir; The Bride Wore Black; Claire's Knee; A Murder is a Murder; The Phantom of Liberty; Catherine et Cie; The Accuser; L'Annee Sainte; Robert and Robert; Eglantine; Les Violets Clos; L'oiseau Rare; Un Amour De Pluie; Bobo Jacco; L'oeil Du Maitre; La Banquiere; La Nuit de Varennes; Cap Canaille; Le Demon Dan L'Isle; Edith and Marcel; Sarah; Stella; The Crime; Papy Fait de la Resistance; Pinot, Simple Flic.

BRIAN, DAVID: Actor. b. New York, NY, Aug. 5, 1914. e. City Coll. of New York. Doorman; chorus boy. Stage debut in New Moon.
STAGE: You Said It, Bittersweet, Princess Charming, Let 'Em Eat Cake, Crazy Quilt, Beat the Band, Candle in the Wind. By Jupiter and night club singer & dancer; in vaudeville; m.c. in South American night club; served as instructor in U.S. Coast Guard 1942–45; m.p. debut 1949, in Flamingo Road.
PICTURES INCLUDE: Intruder in the Dust, Beyond the Forest, Breakthrough, Damned Don't Cry, Inside Straight, Forth Worth, Inside Walls of Folsom Prison, This Woman is Dangerous, Springfield Rifle, Million Dollar Mermaid, Ambush at Tomahawk Gap, Perilous Journey, Dawn at Socorro, High and the Mighty, Timberjack, Fury at Gunsight Pass, The Rabbit Trap, The Seven Minutes.
TELEVISION: Mr. District Attorney, The Immortal.

BRICKMAN, MARSHALL: Writer, Director. b. Rio de Janeiro, Brazil. e. U. of Wisconsin. With folk group The Tarriers, The Journeymen before starting to write for TV. Writer: Candid Camera 1966, The Tonight Show 1966–70; prod. Dick Cavett Show 1970–72.
PICTURES: Writer (with Woody Allen): Sleeper; Annie Hall; Manhattan; Writer/director: Simon, Lovesick. Producer-Director-Writer: The Manhattan Project.

BRICKMAN, PAUL: Writer, Director. b. Highland Park, IL. e. Claremont Men's Coll., U. of Southern California. Worked as camera asst., then story analyst at Paramount, Columbia, and Universal. Debut script: Citizen's Band (1977; also called Hard To Handle). Debut as director with Risky Business (1983).
PICTURES: The Bad News Bears in Breaking Training (s.p.), Risky Business, (dir., s.p.), Deal of the Century (s.p.).

BRIDGES, BEAU: Actor. b. Hollywood, CA, Dec. 19, 1941. e. U. of California at L.A., U. of Hawaii. f. Lloyd Bridges. After several feature film bit parts and numerous TV credits, made screen feature debut in The Incident (1967).

PICTURES INCLUDE: For Love of Ivy, Gaily, Gaily, The Landlord, Adam's Woman, The Christian Licorice Store, Hammersmith Is Out, Child's Play, Your Three Minutes Are Up, Lovin' Molly, The Other Side of the Mountain, Dragonfly, Swashbuckler, Two Minute Warning, Greased Lightning, Norma Rae, The Runner Stumbles, The Fifth Musketeer, Honky Tonk Freeway, Night Crossing, Heart Like a Wheel, Love Child, The Hotel New Hampshire, The Killing Time, The Wild Pair (also dir.), The Iron Triangle, Seven Hours to Judgement (also dir.), One For Sorrow, Two for Joy.
TELEVISION: Ensign O'Toole, Sea Hunt, Ben Casey, Dr. Kildare, Mr. Novak, Combat, Eleventh Hour, Space, A Fighting Choice, Outrage, Cimarron Strip, The Kid from Nowhere, Dangerous Company, Witness for the Prosecution, Red Light Sting, Alice in Wonderland, Amazing Stories, The Thanksgiving Promise (also dir.).

BRIDGES, JAMES: Actor, Writer, Director. b. Paris, AK, Feb 3, 1936. e. Arkansas Teachers Coll; USC. Appeared as an actor in 50 TV shows and five feature films. Has written 16 plays and is published in New Theatre for Now, 18 hour Hitchcock Shows and one Great Adventure, Go Down Moses. Worked as writer on 14 features. As director, worked in New York, Edinburgh Festival, Mark Taper and Ahmanson in Los Angeles.
PICTURES INCLUDE: Limbo (s.p.), The Appaloosa (s.p.), Forbin Project (s.p.); The Baby Maker (s.p., dir.); The Paper Chase (s.p., dir.); September 30, 1955 (s.p., dir.); The China Syndrome (dir., co-s.p.); Urban Cowboy (co-s.p., dir.), Mike's Murder (dir., s.p.); Perfect (prod., dir., s.p.); Bright Lights, Big City (dir., co-s.p.).

BRIDGES, JEFF: Actor. b. Los Angeles, CA, Dec. 4, 1949. Made acting debut at eight in the TV series Sea Hunt starring his father, Lloyd Bridges. Studied acting at Herbert Berghof Studio, NY. Mil. service in Coast Guard reserves. Acad. Award nom.: The Last Picture Show (supp.); Thunderbolt and Lightfoot (supp.), Starman. Brother of actor, director Beau Bridges.
PICTURES: Halls of Anger (1969), The Yin and Yang of Mr. Go, The Last Picture Show, Bad Company, Fat City, The Iceman Cometh, The Last American Hero, Lolly-Madonna XXX, Thunderbolt and Lightfoot, Hearts of the West, Rancho Deluxe, King Kong, Stay Hungry, Somebody Killed Her Husband, The American Success Company, Winter Kills, Heaven's Gate, Kiss Me Goodbye, Cutter's Way (Cutter and Bone), Tron, Against All Odds, Starman, Jagged Edge, 8 Million Ways to Die, The Morning After, Nadine, Tucker, See You in the Morning.
TELEVISION: Silent Night, Lonely Night; In Search of America; Faerie Tale Theatre (Rapunzel).

BRIDGES, LLOYD: Actor. b. San Leandro, CA, January 15, 1913. Went into stock from college dramatics.
PICTURES INCLUDE: Miss Susie Slage's, Abilene Town, Canyon Passage, Ramrod, Trouble with Women, Hideout, Calamity Jane and Sam Bass, Trapped, Rocketship XM, Try and Get Me, Colt .45, Three Steps North, Whistle at Eaton Falls, Last of the Comanches, High Noon, Plymouth Adventure, Tall Texan, Kid from Left Field, City of Bad Men, Limping Man, Pride of the Blue Grass, Deadly Game, Apache Woman, Wichita, Wetbacks, The Rainmaker, Daring Game, The Goddess, The Happy Ending, The Fifth Musketeer, Airplane!, Airplane II, Weekend Warriors, The Wild Pair, Tucker: The Man and His Dream, Cousins.
TELEVISION: Early work on Bigelow Theatre (1950), Kraft Suspense Theatre. Series: Police Story, Sea Hunt (1957–61), The Lloyd Bridges Show (1962–63), The Loner, San Francisco International Airport, Joe Forrester (1975–76); Movies: Silent Night, Lonely Night; Roots, Disaster on the Coastliner, East of Eden. Movieola, The Blue and the Gray, George Washington, Dress Gray, North & South Book II, Paper Dolls, The Thanksgiving Promise.

BRIEN, LIGE: Executive, b. Pittsburgh, PA, March 23. e. U. of Pittsburgh, B.A. Asst. theatre mgr. 1937; theatre mgr. (PA); winner of many prizes for publicity, exploitation, grosses; winner of M.P. Herald Bronze Grand Award 1939, Silver Award 1944 & War Showmanship Award; press-book ed. PRC Pictures 1945, appt'd exploitation mgr., 1946; since exploit. mgr. Eagle Lion Classics; to U.A. as dir., spcl. events, April, 1951. Pres. AMPA, 153–54; asst. exploitation mgr., 20th Fox, 1960; nat'l dir. mdsg., Paramount Pictures, 1961–65; Expl. Dir., Seven Arts Pictures. (Warner Bros.). Then Warner Bros. exploitation liaison between Hollywood studio and New York offices, 1982, started new co., Golden Triangle Promotions.

BRIGHT, RICHARD: Actor. b. Brooklyn, NY, June 11. e. trained for stage with Frank Corsaro, John Lehne and Paul Mann.
THEATER: The Balcony (1959), The Beard, The Salvation of St. Joan, Gogol, The Basic Training of Pavlo Hummel, Richard III, Kid Twist, Short Eyes as well as regional theater.
PICTURES: Odds Against Tomorrow, Lion's Love, Panic in Needle Park, The Getaway, Pat Garrett and Billy the Kid, The Godfather, The Godfather II, Rancho Deluxe, Marathon Man,

Citizens Band, Looking For Mr. Goodbar, On the Yard, Hair, The Idolmaker, Vigilante, Once Upon a Time in America, Two of A Kind, Crackers, Crimewave, Cut and Run, Brighton Beach Memoirs, 52-Pick-up, Time Out.
TELEVISION: Lamp Unto My Feet, Armstrong Circle Theater, The Verdict Is Yours, Kraft Television Theatre, Studio One, Cagney and Lacey, Beacon Hill, Hill Street Blues, From These Roots. Movies: A Death of Innocence, The Connection, The Gun, Cops and Robin, Sizzle, There Must Be A Pony, Penalty Phase. Mini-series: From Here to Eternity, Skag.

BRIGHT, RICHARD S.: Executive. b. New Rochelle, NY, Feb. 28, 1936. e. Hotchkiss Sch., 1953–54; Wharton Sch. of Finance, U. of Pennsylvania, 1954–58. With U.S. Army Finance Corp., 1959–60. Was corporate exec. prior to founding in 1973 Persky-Bright Organization, private investment group to finance films. Now bd. chm., Persky-Bright Productions, Inc.; adjunct professor at Columbia U. Sch. of Fine Arts.
PICTURES INCLUDE: Last Detail, Golden Voyage of Sinbad, For Pete's Sake, California Split, The Man Who Would Be King, Funny Lady, The Front, and Equus. Financing/production services for: Hard Times, Taxi Driver, Missouri Breaks, Bound for Glory, Sinbad and the Eye of the Tiger, Hair, Still of the Night.
TELEVISION: The President's Mistress (co-producer).
STAGE: A History of the American Film (1978); Album (Off-Broadway, co-producer) 1980; Currently preparing with James Nederlander for Broadway, Dennis The Menace.

BRIGHTMAN, HOMER H.: Writer b. Port Townsend, WA. e. Washington State Nautical School-ship. Apprentice at 14, spent 10 years at sea as 2nd and 3rd officer; claims dept., Dollar Steamship Lines Shanghai, Hong Kong, Singapore: Academy Award for short Lend a Paw 1939; assoc. Walt Disney Prod. 13 years; created It's a Dog's Life, TV show; animated cartoon shorts for MGM, Walter Lantz, U.P.A.
PICTURES INCLUDE: Saludos Amigos, Three Caballeros, Make Mine Music, Fun and Fancy Free, Melody Time, Cinderella. Writer (collab.) TV shorts.

BRIMLEY, WILFORD: Actor. b. Salt Lake City, UT, Sept. 27, 1934. Formerly a blacksmith, ranch hand and racehorse trainer, begain in films as an extra and stuntman.
PICTURES: The Electric Horseman; Brubaker; The China Syndrome; Borderline; Death Valley; Absence of Malice; The Thing; Tender Mercies; Tough Enough; High Road to China; 10 to Midnight; Hotel New Hampshire; Harry and Son; The Natural; Country; Cocoon; Remo Williams: The Adventure Begins, End of the Line; Cocoon II: The Return.
TELEVISION: The Wild Wild West Revisited; Thompson's Last Run; Act of Vengeance; Joe Dancer; The Firm; Our House (series).

BRINKLEY, DAVID: TV news correspondent. b. Wilmington, NC, July 10, 1920. Started writing for hometown newspaper. e. U. of North Carolina, Vanderbilt U. Joined United Press before entering Army, W.W.II. After discharge in 1943 joined NBC News in Washington as White House corr. Co-chm. for many years with late Chet Huntley on NBC Nightly News. Then began David Brinkley's Journal. Moved to ABC to co-anchor nightly news, then to host This Week with David Brinkley.

BRISKIN, MORT: Producer, Writer. b. Oak Park, IL, 1919. e. U. of Southern California; attended Harvard and Northwestern law schools, being admitted to the bar at 20. Practiced law before entering m.p. industry in management with such stars as Mickey Rooney. Turned to production and also wrote screenplays for 16 of his 29 films. Created nine TV series and was prod. or exec. prod. of some 1,350 TV segments of which he wrote more than 300.
PICTURES INCLUDE: The River, The Magic Face, No Time for Flowers, The Second Woman, Quicksand, The Big Wheel, The Jackie Robinson Story, Ben, Willard, Walking Tall, Framed.
TELEVISION: Sheriff of Cochise, U.S. Marshal, The Texan, Grand Jury, The Walter Winchell File, Official Detective, Whirlybirds.

BRITTANY, MORGAN: Actress. b. Hollywood, CA, Dec. 5, 1951. r.n. Suzanne Cupito.
PICTURES: Marnie, The Birds, Gypsy, Gable and Lombard.
TELEVISION: Series: Dallas. Movies: Amazing Howard Hughes, Delta County U.S.A., Going Home Again, The Dream Merchants, Moviola, The Scarlett O'Hara War, The Wild Women of Chastity Gulch, LBJ: The Early Years, Perry Mason: The Case of the Scandalous Scoundrel.

BRITTON, TONY: Actor, b. Birmingham, England, 1924. e. Thornbury Grammar Sch., Glos. Early career as clerk and in repertory; TV debut, 1952, The Six Proud Walkers (serial), m.p. debut, 1955 in Loser Takes All.
PLAYS INCLUDE: The Guv'nor, Romeo and Juliet, The Scarlet Pimpernel, The Other Man, The Dashing White Sergeant, Importance of Being Earnest, An Ideal Husband,

School for Scandal, A Dream of Treason, That Lady, The Private Lives of Edward Whiteley, Affairs of State, The Night of The Ball, Gigi, The Seagull, Henry IV Part 1, Kill Two Birds, Cactus Flower, A Woman of No Importance, The Boston Story, Lady Frederick, My Fair Lady, Move Over Mrs. Markham, No No Nanette, Dame of Sark, The Chairman, Murder Among Friends, The Seven Year Itch, St. Joan, The Tempest, King Lear, A Man for All Seasons.
PICTURES INCLUDE: Birthday Present, Behind the Mask, Operation Amsterdam, The Heart of a Man, The Rough and the Smooth, The Risk, The Horsemasters, Stork Talk, The Break, There's a Girl in My Soup, Forbush and The Penguins, Sunday Bloody Sunday, Night Watch, The Day of the Jackal.
TELEVISION: Melissa series, Father Dear Father series, The Man Who Understood Women, Ooh La La, Call My Bluff, The Nearly Man. Robins Nest series, Friends and Brothers, Don't Wait Up series.

BROADNAX, DAVID: Producer, Writer, Actor. b. Columbus, GA, Dec. 16.
PICTURES: The Landlord (act.), Come Back Charleston Blue (act.), Sharpies (prod., co-s.p., act.), Zombie Island Massacre (prod., act., original story).
TELEVISION: As the World Turns, Another World, Edge of Night, Love Is a Many Splendored Thing, Search for Tomorrow, Saturday Night Live.

BROCCOLI, ALBERT: Producer. b. New York, NY, April 5, 1909. e. City Coll. of New York. Agriculturist in early years; entered m.p. ind. as asst. director, 20th Century-Fox, 1938. Worked with theatrical agent Charles Feldman 1948–51; producer, Warwick Films 1951–60.
PRODUCTIONS INCLUDE: Red Beret (Paratrooper), Hell Below Zero, Black Knight, Prize of Gold, Cockleshell Heroes, Safari, Zarak, April in Portugal, Pickup Alley, Fire Down Below, Arrivederci Roma, Interpol, How to Murder a Rich Uncle, Odongo, High Flight, No Time to Die, The Man Inside, Idle on Parade, Adamson of Africa, Bandit of Zhobe, Jazz Boat, In the Nick, Let's Get Married, The Trials of Oscar Wilde, Johnny Nobody, Carolina, Dr. No, Call Me Bwana, From Russia with Love, Goldfinger, Thunderball, You Only Live Twice, Chitty Chitty Bang Bang, On Her Majesty's Secret Service, Diamonds Are Forever, Live and Let Die, The Man with the Golden Gun, The Spy Who Loved Me, Moonraker, For Your Eyes Only, Octopussy, A View to a Kill, The Living Daylights, License Revoked.

BROCKMAN, JOHN J.: Executive. Vice pres. and gen. mgr. Microband Wireless Cable of New York, Inc. b. Sheboygan, WI, July 12, 1946. e. U. of Wisconsin, B.S., 1969; Bowling Green State U. M.S., 1971. Graduate asst., Bowling Green State U., 1969–70. 1972–75: system mgr. for Teltron Cable TV of The Milwaukee Journal Co. 1975–77: gen. mgr. for Lynchburg Cablevision and American Cablevision of Amer. Television & Communications Corp., Englewood, CO. 1977–78: gen. mgr. for Citizens Cable Communications, Inc., Ft. Wayne, IN. 1978–83: mid-east. and mid-central region mgr., Cox Cable Communications, Inc., Norfolk, VA and Ft. Wayne, IN. 1984–86: corp. v.p., corporate operating comm. member, pres. of operating cable co., Adams-Russell Co., Inc., Waltham, MA. 1986: consultant to Arthur D. Little, Inc., Cambridge, MA. 1974–75: co-chmn., technical comm., Wisc. Cable Communications Assns. 1975–76: advisor comm., Cable TV Curriculum, Indiana Vocational and Technical Coll. 1980: annual grad. school alumni lecturer, Today's Operating Communications Media, Bowling Green State U. 1981–82: founding comm. member and moderator for Great Lakes Cable Exposition. 1978–83: v.p. and dir., Illinois-Indiana Cable Assn.

BROCKMAN, MICHAEL: Executive. b. Brooklyn, NY, Nov. 19, 1938. e. Ithaca Coll. Became ABC v.p., daytime programming, ABC Entertainment, 1974; later v.p., tape prod. operations and admin. Left to become v.p., daytime programs, NBC Entertainment, 1977–1980. Became v.p. programs, Lorimar Prods. 1980–82; v.p. daytime and children's prog. CBS Entertainment, 1982–86. Added Late Night to title 1986.

BRODERICK, MATTHEW: Actor. b. New York, NY, Aug. 21, 1962. Son of late actor James Broderick and writer-dir. Patricia Broderick. Acted in a workshop prod. of Horton Foote's Valentine's Day with his father (1979). Theatrical film debut in Max Dugan Returns, 1983.
PICTURES: War Games, Ladyhawke, 1918, On Valentine's Day, Ferris Bueller's Day Off, Project X, Biloxi Blues, Torch Song Trilogy.
STAGE: Torch Song Trilogy, Brighton Beach Memoirs (Tony Award), Biloxi Blues.
TELEVISION: Master Harold . . . and the Boys.

BRODKIN, HERBERT: Producer. b. New York, NY, Nov. 9, 1912. e. U. of Mich., B.A.; Yale Drama Sch., M.F.A. (directing and design.) Army major, served as film dir. for Signal Corps, directing 40 films on military subjects, then transferred to Special Services to launch legit. play prog. for U.S.O. and Army, supervising prod. of 300 plays in 2 years. Worked in summer stock and rep. as designer and in Hollywood as scenery designer. Designed Bdwy plays and operas for City Center and Theater Guild. After Army, designed scenery at Buck's County Playhouse and Westport Country Playhouse, also prod. manager and director. Began as scenic designer for CBS. Charlie Wild, Private Detective, first TV show as prod. and designer. Has prod. nearly 600 shows for TV. 1960 formed Titus Productions, Inc., prod. and COO.

PICTURES INCLUDE: Sebastian, The People Next Door.

TELEVISION: Series: ABC Album (1951), The TV Hour, The Motorola TV Hour, Center Stage, The Elgin Hour, The Alcoa Hour, Goodyear Playhouse, Studio One, Playhouse 90 (21 shows, won 2 Emmys), Brenner, The Defenders (1961–65, 3 Emmys and other awards), The Nurses, Espionage, For the People, Coronet Blue, The Doctors and Nurses, Shane. Specials, pilots, movies: The Happeners (pilot), One Eyed Jacks are Wild (pilot), Dear Friends, The People Next Door (3 Emmys), Lights Out (pilot), Crawlspace, RX For The Defense, Pueblo (Golden Hugo Award, Chicago Film Fest.), Peabody Award and 5 Emmys), F. Scott Fitzgerald and the Last of the Belles (Silver Phoenix, Atlanta Film Fest.), The Missiles of October (Golden Hugo, Chicago Film Fest), Land of Hope, F. Scott Fitzgerald in Hollywood, The Four of Us, The Deadliest Season, Siege, Holocaust (mini-series, winner of 40 awards, including San Francisco Film Fest, Peabody and 8 Emmys), The Last Tenant, Hollow Image, Death Penalty, Dr. Franken, The Henderson Monster, F.D.R. The Last Year, King Crab, Skokie, My Body, My Child; Benny's Place, The Firm, Ghost Dancing, Sakharov (DACE Awards), Doubletake, Murrow, Welcome Home, Bobby; Johnny Bull, Night of Courage, Mandela, Stones For Ibarra.

BRODNEY, OSCAR: Writer, Producer. b. Boston, MA, 1905. e. Boston U., LL.B., 1927; Harvard, LL.M., 1928. Atty., MA Bar, 1928–35.

PICTURES INCLUDE: She Wrote the Book, If You Knew Susie, Are You With It?, For the Love of Mary, Mexican Hayride, Arctic Manhunt, Yes Sir, That's My Baby, Double Crossbones, Gal Who Took the West, South Sea Sinner, Comanche Territory, Harvey; story, Frenchie, Francis Goes to the Races, Little Egypt, Francis Covers the Big Town, Willie and Joe Back at the Front, Scarlet Angel, Francis Goes to West Point, Walking My Baby Back Home, Sign of the Pagan, Glenn Miller Story, Black Shield of Falworth, Captain Lightfoot, The Spoilers, Purple Mask, Lady Godiva, Day of Fury, Star in the Dust, Tammy and the Bachelor, When Hell Broke Loose, Bobkins, Tammy Tell Me True, The Right Approach, All Hands on Deck, Tammy and the Doctor, The Brass Bottle, I'd Rather Be Rich.

BRODSHAUG, MELVIN: Producer. b. Davenport, ND, May 22, 1900. e. North Dakota State U., B.S., 1923; Litt.D. 1958; U. of Chicago, M.A. 1927; Columbia U., Ph.D. 1931. Supt. of Schools, Arnegard, ND 1923–28; research assoc. Erpi Classroom Films 1930; apptd. dir. research Encyclopedia Britannica Films Inc., apptd. vice-pres. 1945, in chg. of product development; apptd. member bd. dir. 1951, Dean of Boston U. Sch. of Public Relations & Communications, 1954–62,dir., Boston U. film library, 1962–65. Prof. and consultant, Norfolk State Coll., VA, 1965–70; independent educational film producer 1970.

BRODSKY, JACK: Producer. b. Brooklyn, NY, July 3, 1932. e. George Washington H.S. Writer for N.Y. Times; joined 20th-Fox publicity in N.Y. in 1956. Left in 1961 to head national ad-pub for Filmways. Joined Rastar Productions to work on Funny Girl; later named v.p. in charge of prod. In 1976 named v.p. in chg. film prod. prom., Rogers & Cowan; 1978, Columbia Pictures v.p., adv., pub., promo.; 1979, named exec. v.p. of Michael Douglas' Big Stick Productions; 1983; joined 20th-Fox as exec. v.p., worldwide adv., pub., exploit. Resigned 1985 to resume career as producer.

PICTURES INCLUDE: Little Murders, Everything You Always Wanted To Know About Sex (exec. prod.), Summer Wishes, Winter Dreams, Jewel of the Nile, Dancers (co-exec. prod., actor).

AUTHOR: The Cleopatra Papers, with Nat Weiss.

BROKAW, NORMAN R.: Executive. b. New York, NY, April 21, 1927. Joined William Morris Agency as trainee, in 1943, junior agent, 1948; sr. agent, company exec. in m.p. and TV, 1951; 1974, v.p., William Morris Agency, World Wide all areas. 1981, named exec. v.p. & member of board, William Morris Agency, worldwide; 1986, named co-chm. of bd., WMA, worldwide. Member Academy of TV Arts & Sciences, Academy M.P. Arts & Sciences. Member bd. of dir. of Cedars-Sinai Medical Center, Los Angeles; pres., The Betty Ford Cancer Center. Clients include former President and Mrs. Gerald R. Ford.

BROKAW, TOM: TV Host, Anchorman. b. 1940, Yankton, S.D., Feb. 6. e. U. of South Dakota. Joined KMTV, NBC affiliate in Omaha, in 1962; 1965, joined WSB-TV, Atlanta. Worked in L.A. bureau of NBC News, anchored local news shows for KNBC, NBC station (1966–73). In 1973 named NBC News' White House correspondent; was anchor of NBC Saturday Night News. Named host of Today show in August, 1976. In

1982 co-anchor, NBC Nightly News; Conversation with Mikhail S. Gorbachev.

BROLIN, JAMES: Actor. b. Los Angeles, CA, July 18, 1940. e. UCLA. Debut in Bus Stop (TV series); named most promising actor of 1970 by Fame and Photoplay magazines.

PICTURES INCLUDE: Take Her She's Mine, Goodbye, Charlie, Von Ryan's Express, Morituri, Our Man Flint, The Boston Strangler, Skyjacked, Westworld, Gable and Lombard, The Car, Capricorn One, The Amityville Horror, The Gringos.

TELEVISION: The Monroes, Marcus Welby, M.D., (Emmy award), Short Walk to Daylight, Class of '63, Hotel, Beverly Hills Cowgirl Blues, Hold the Dream, Intimate Encounters, Deep Dark Secrets, Voice of the Heart.

BROMHEAD, DAVID M.: Executive. b. Teaneck, NJ, Jan. 7, 1960. e. Leighton Park Sch., Reading, England, 1973–78. Overseas sls. exec., Rank Film Dist., 1980; joined New World Pictures, 1984, dir. intl. dist.; named dir., TV dist., 1986.

BRON, ELEANOR: Actress. b. Stanmore, Middlesex, Eng., 1934. Started career in Establishment Club, London, and on American tour. Leading lady on British TV show Not So Much a Programme, More a Way of Life.

PICTURES INCLUDE: Help, Alfie, Two for the Road, Bedazzled, Women in Love, The Millstone, Little Dorrit.

THEATRE: The Doctor's Dilemma, Howard's End, The Prime of Miss Jean Brodie.

TELEVISION: (U.S.) The Day Christ Died; The Attic: The Hiding of Anne Frank.

BRONDFIELD, JEROME: b. Cleveland, OH, Dec. 9, 1913. e. Ohio State U., 1936. Reporter, ed. on Columbus Dispatch, Associated Press, story ed., script head, RKO Pathe, Oct., 1944; writer, dir. & supvr. of many doc. shorts incl. This Is America series; TV writer; short story writer; collab. s.p., Below the Sahara; s.p. Louisiana Territory; doc. film writer; Author, Woody Hayes, The 100-Yard War, Knute Rockne, The Man and the Legend.

BRONSON, CHARLES: Actor. b. Ehrenfeld, PA, Nov. 3, 1920. r.n. Charles Buchinsky. m. Jill Ireland, actress. Worked as a coal miner. Studied at Pasadena Playhouse. Starred on his own TV series Meet McGraw, Man With a Camera, Travels of Jamie McPheeters.

PICTURES INCLUDE: Red Skies of Montana, Pat and Mike, House of Wax, Drumbeat, Vera Cruz, Jubel, Lonely Are the Brave, Machine Gun Kelly, Never So Few, A Thunder of Drums, The Magnificent Seven, The Great Escape, The Sandpiper, The Battle of the Bulge, Pancho Villa, The Dirty Dozen, This Property Is Condemned, Once Upon a Time in the West, Goodbye, Friend, Rider in the Rain, You Can't Win Em All, Someone Behind the Door, Red Sun, Chato's Land, The Mechanic, The Valachi Papers, The Stone Killer, Mr. Majestyk, Death Wish, Breakout, Hard Times, Breakheart Pass, From Noon Till Three, St. Ives, The White Buffalo, Telefon, Borderline, Caboblanco, Death Hunt, Death Wish II, The Evil That Men Do, Death Wish 3, Murphy's Law, Assassination, Death Wish IV; Kinjite, Messenger of Death.

TELEVISION: Guest on Philco Playhouse (Adventure in Java); Medic, A Bell for Adano, Gunsmoke, Have Gun Will Travel, The FBI, The Fugitive, The Virginian. Movies: Act of Vengeance, Raid on Entebbe.

BRONSTON, SAMUEL: Producer. b. Bessarabia, Russia, March 26, 1908. e. Sorbonne, Paris. Film distributor, Paris; prod. exec. Columbia Studios, Hollywood; Martin Eden, City Without Men, Producer, Columbia Pictures; resigned to form Samuel Bronston Pict., Inc.; exec. prod. Jack London, A Walk in the Sun. color documentaries produced first time in Vatican; prod. John Paul Jones 1959; Received U.S. Navy Meritorious Pub. Serv. Citation; pres. Samuel Bronston Productions; 1960 prod. King of Kings, El Cid; 1962, 55 Days at Peking; 1963. The Fall of the Roman Empire; prod. Circus World, 1964, Condor Award, Society for Pan American Culture—for El Cid, 1962 (award shared with Stanford U.), The Hollywood Foreign Press Association Golden Globe for the achievement of his outstanding production of El Cid, 1962, Italian Order of Merit with Medal of Commendatore. Grand Cross of Merit by the Equestrian Order of the Knights of the Holy Sepulchre (the highest honor of the Catholic Church), the Encomienda of the Order of the Great Cross of Isabel la Catolica. President Samuel Bronston Studios, Madrid, Spain.

BROOK, PETER: Director. b. London, England, March 21, 1925. e. Magdalen Coll., Oxford. Gained fame as stage director before doing films. (Man and Superman, Marat/Sade, A Midsummer Night's Dream, etc.)

PICTURES INCLUDE: The Beggar's Opera, Moderato Cantabile, Lord of the Flies, Marat/Sade, Tell Me Lies, King Lear, Meetings with Remarkable Men, The Tragedy of Carmen, The Mahabharata.

BROOKE, PETER R.: Writer. b. Berlin, Germany, April 12, 1929. e. Germany, Switzerland, England. With Warner Bros., 1944–

46, mail room, pub. dept., then asst. casting dir.; contract writer, Robert Riskin Prod., Paramount; then free lance; radio writer many shows; TV writer for Teevee Prod., Celebrity Playhouse, Science Fiction Theatre; staff writer, Universal Pictures; left Universal to join Excelsior under new banner of Warbrook Inc. as writer-producer.
PICTURES INCLUDE: Basketball Fix, Sweet Violence orig., Outside the Law.
TELEVISION: Sea Hunt, 77 Sunset Strip, Sugar Foot, The Fugitive, Six Million Dollar Man.

BROOKS, ALBERT: Director, Writer, Actor. r.n. Einstein. b. Los Angeles, CA, July 22, 1947. e. Carnegie Tech. Son of late comedian Harry Einstein (Parkyakarkus); brother, Bob Einstein.
PICTURES: Taxi Driver (act. only); Real Life (dir., s.p., actor); Private Benjamin (act. only); Modern Romance (dir., s.p., actor); Twilight Zone—The Movie (act. only); Unfaithfully Yours (act. only); Lost in America; Broadcast News (actor).
TELEVISION: Gold-diggers of 1969 (actor); Saturday Night Live.

BROOKS, DICK: Executive. b. New York, NY, 1930. e. U. of Georgia. Reporter, Atlanta (GA) Journal; sports ed. Gainesville Times; correspondent, Pacific Stars & Stripes; entered m.p. business as staff writer, 20th Century-Fox pub. dept; nat'l pub. dir, Seven Arts Productions, Paramount pub. dir.; nat'l pub. dir. 20th Century-Fox; adv-pub. dir, Rastar Prods; Warner Bros. pub. dir; formed Dick Brooks Unlimited, Beverly Hills entertainment p.r. company 1980. Formed Bay Entertainment, prod. company, 1988.

BROOKS, JAMES L.: Director, Producer, Writer. b. North Bergen, NJ, May 9, 1940. e. NYU. Copyboy for CBS News, N.Y.; promoted to newswriter. 1965 moved to L.A. to work for David Wolper's documentary prod. co. 1969 conceived idea for series, Room 222; formed partnership with fellow writer Allan Burns. Together they created Mary Tyler Moore Show in 1970. 1977, established prod. co. on Paramount lot with other writers, producing and creating the series, The Associates and Taxi.
PICTURES: Modern Romance (actor only); Starting Over (s.p., co-prod.); Terms of Endearment (dir., prod., s.p.) (Academy Award, best film, dir., s.p., 1983); Broadcast News (dir., prod., s.p.); Big (co-prod.); Say Anything (exec. prod.).
TELEVISION: Thursday's Game (writer, prod., 1971); Rhoda (writer, prod.); The New Lorenzo Music Show, 1976 (writer); Lou Grant, 1977 (co-exec. prod.); Co-creator, and/or exec. prod: Taxi, Cindy, The Associates, Cheers, Tracey Ullman Show.

BROOKS, JOSEPH: Producer, Director, Writer, Composer, Conductor. Well-known for composing music for TV commercials before turning to producing, directing, writing and scoring theatrical feature, You Light Up My Life, in 1977. Winner of 21 Clio Awards (made by adv. industry); created music for 100 commercials. Has also composed for theatrical films.
PICTURES INCLUDE: Scores: The Garden of the Finzi-Continis, Marjoe, Jeremy, The Lords of Flatbush. Produced, directed, wrote, and composed, arranged and conducted music for You Light Up My Life. Produced, directed, wrote starred in and composed music for If Ever I See You Again.

BROOKS, MEL: Writer, Director, Actor. b. Brooklyn, NY, 1926. r.n. Kaminsky. m. actress Anne Bancroft. As child did impressions and was amateur drummer and pianist. First appearance as actor in Golden Boy in Red Bank, NJ. Was also director and social director in the Catskills. Became writer for Sid Caesar on TV's Broadway Review and Your Show of Shows, writing for latter for decade. Teamed with Carl Reiner for comedy record album, 2000 Year Old Man and The 2000 and 13 Year Old Man.
PICTURES INCLUDE: The Critic (short, s.p., narrator), The Producers, The Twelve Chairs, Blazing Saddles, Young Frankenstein, Silent Movie, High Anxiety (prod., dir., s.p.). History of the World—Part 1 (prod., dir., s.p., actor, composer), To Be or Not To Be (prod., actor), 84 Charing Cross Road (exec. prod.); Spaceballs (prod., dir. co-s.p., actor).
TELEVISION: Get Smart (writer), When Things Were Rotten (creator).
STAGE: Shinbone Alley, All-American (books for musicals).

BROOKS, RICHARD: Writer, Director. b. Philadelphia, PA, May 18, 1912. e. Temple U. Radio writer, narrator and commentator, NBC. Author of several short stories. Novels, Brick Fox Hole, Boiling Point, The Producer.
PICTURES INCLUDE: Swell Guy, Brute Force, To the Victor, Crossfire, Key Largo, Mystery Street, Storm Warning, Deadline U.S.A., Battle Circus, Take the High Ground, Flame and the Flesh, Last Time I Saw Paris, Blackboard Jungle, Last Hunt, Catered Affair, Something of Value, The Brothers Karamazov, Cat on a Hot Tin Roof, Elmer Gantry (Academy Award for s.p. 1961); Sweet Bird of Youth, writer, Lord Jim, The Professionals, In Cold Blood, The Happy Ending, Dollars, Bite the Bullet, Looking for Mr. Goodbar, Wrong Is Right (also prod.), Fever Pitch (also prod.), Saxo (actor only).

BROSNAN, PIERCE: Actor. b. Ireland, May 16, 1953. On stage in London (Wait Until Dark, The Red Devil Battery Sign, etc.)
PICTURES: The Mirror Crack'd, The Long Good Friday, Nomads, The Fourth Protocol, The Deceivers, Taffin.
TELEVISION: Remington Steele (series), Murphy's Stroke, The Manions of America, Nancy Astor, Noble House, Around the World in 80 Days.

BROUGH, WALTER: Writer. With Stage Society, LA. 5 years as v.p. Wrote musicals: Part of the Blues, John Henry, Superstitionist, Caprock County.
PICTURES: Gabriella; A New Life; No Place to Hide; Run Wild, Run Free; The Desperadoes; Funeral for an Assassin (also prod.); On a Dead Man's Chest (also prod.); Jed and Sonny (also prod.).
TELEVISION: Doctor Kildare; The Fugitive; Branded; Name of the Game; Mannix; Mission Impossible; The Magician; Man From Atlantis; Lucas; Police Story; Wildside; Heart of the City; Spencer for Hire; Law & Harry McGraw.

BROUGHTON, BRUCE: Composer. b. Los Angeles, CA , March 8, 1945. e. U. of Southern California, B.M., 1967. Music supvr., CBS-TV, 1967–77. Since then has been freelance composer for TV and films. Member: Academy of TV Arts & Sciences; Society of Composers & Lyricists, Academy of Motion Picture Arts & Sciences. Nominated 11 times for Emmy; won in 1981 for Buck Rogers, in 1983 for Dallas and in 1984 for Dallas and The First Olympics. Nominated in 1986 for Oscar for Silverado.
TELEVISION: Series: Hawaii Five-0, Gunsmoke, Quincy, How the West Was Won, Logan's Run, The Oregon Trail, Buck Rogers, Dallas. Movies: The Paradise Connection, Desperate Voyage, The Return of Frank Cannon, Desperate Lives, Killjoy, One Shoe Makes It Murder, The Master of Ballantrae, MADD, The Candy Lightner Story, Cowboy, A Thanksgiving Promise. Mini-Series: The Blue and the Gray, The First Olympics–Athens: 1896, George Washington II.
PICTURES: The Prodigal, The Ice Pirates, Silverado, Young Sherlock Holmes, Sweet Liberty, The Boy Who Could Fly, Square Dance, Harry and the Hendersons, Monster Squad, Big Shots, Cross My Heart, The Rescue, The Presidio.

BROUMAS, JOHN G.: Executive. b. Youngstown, OH, Oct. 12, 1917. e. Youngstown. Usher, Altoona Publix Theatres, 1933, usher to asst. mgr., Warner Thea. 1934–39; mgr. Grand 1939–40; mgr. Orpheum 1940–41. W.W.II active, Officer Chemical Corps, past commander 453rd Chem. Grp. (Reserve); Member Reserve Officers Assoc.; Gen. mgr. Pitts & Roth Theatres 1946–54; President, Broumas Theatres; bd. govnrs., Variety Club, Tent No. 11, 1959–73; Wash., first asst. chief barker, 1964 & 1971; chief barker, 1965–1966, 1972 V.P.T.O.A. 1965; V.P. NATO, 1969; past pres. & bd. chmn. Maryland Theatre Owners; bd. of directors of NATO of Va., Md., D.C.; pres., Broumas Theatre Service; bd. chmn., Showcase Theatres; mem. bd., Foundation of Religious Action (FRASCO). Mem. Nat'l Immigration Comm. Founder of John G. Broumas Scholarship for Drama at Youngstown State Univ.; past pres. & Board Chairman Maryland Theatre Owners; v.p. & bd. of dir.—Virginia Theatre Owners bd. of dir. NATO of D.C.; pres. B.C. Theatres; Sponsor of Andre G. Broumas Memorial Award—West Point; pres., McLean Theatre Corp.; member, Motion Picture Pioneers; sponsor, Broumas Scholastic and Athletic Scholarship for AHEPA Wash. D.C. area; director, McLean Bank McLean, Va.; honorary member, West Point Class 1954; Secretary-Treasurer, Tenley Circle Twin Theatre Corp.; President, Cinema Mgt. Corp; Director: Motion Picture Pioneers; Advisory Council: Will Rogers Memorial Hospital; Chief Barker: Washington, D.C. Variety Club, Tent #11, 1978–79 and bd. chmn., 1980; Life Patron, Variety Clubs Int'l, 1978; AHEPA Humanitarian Award, 1981; Dept. of Army, Patriotic Civilian Service Medal, 1982; WOMPI "good guy" award, 1974; Gold Medal for distinguished service to m.p. industry, 1978; bd. chm., Tantaloon Country Club, Oxon Hill, MD.; Chm. bd., McLean Bank.

BROWN, BLAIR: Actress. b. Washington, DC, 1948. e. National Theatre Sch. of Canada.
PICTURES: Paper Chase, The Choirboys, One-Trick Pony, Altered States, Continental Divide, Flash of Green. Stealing Home, Strapless.
TELEVISION: Mini-series: Captains and the Kings, James Michener's Space, Eleanor and Franklin, Arthur Hailey's Wheels, The Bad Seed, Kennedy, Hands of a Stranger; The Days and Nights of Molly Dodd (series).

BROWN, BRYAN: Actor. b. Australia, 1947. Began acting professionally in Sydney. Worked in repertory theatres in England with the National Theatre of Great Britain. Returned to Australia to work in films while continuing stage work with Theatre Australia. Theatrical film debut, Love Letters from Teralba Road, 1977.
PICTURES: The Irishman, Weekend of Shadows, Newsfront, Third Person Plural, Money Movers, Palm Beach, Cathy's Child, The Odd Angry Shot, Breaker Morant, Blood

Money, Stir, Winter of Our Dreams, Far East, F/X, Tai-Pan, The Good Wife, Cocktail, Gorillas in the Mist, Shall We Dance.

TELEVISION: Mini-series: Against the Wind, A Town Like Alice, The Thorn Birds.

BROWN, DAVID: Executive, Producer. b. New York, NY, July 28, 1916. e. Stanford U., A.B., 1936; Columbia U. Sch. of Journalism, M.S., 1937. Apprentice reporter, copy-editing, San Francisco News & Wall Street Journal, 1936; night ed. asst. drama critic, Fairchild Publications, N.Y., 1937–39; edit. dir. Milk Research Council, N.Y., 1939–40; assoc. ed., Street & Smith Publ., N.Y., 1940–43; assoc. ed., exec. ed., then ed.-in-chief, Liberty Mag., N.Y., 1943–49; edit. dir., nat'l education campaign, Amer. Medical Assn., 1949; assoc. ed., man. ed., Cosmopolitan Mag., N.Y., 1949–52; contrib. stories & articles to many nat'l mags.; man. ed., story dept., 20th-Fox, L.A., Jan., 1952; story ed. & head of scenario dept., May, 1953–56; appt'd. member of exec. staff of Darryl F. Zanuck, 1956; mem. of exec. staff, 20th-Fox studios, and exec. studio story editor, 1956–1960; Prod. 20th-Fox Studios, Sept. 1960–62; Editorial v.p. New American Library of World Literature, Inc., 1963–64; exec. story opers., 20th Century-Fox, 1964–67; vp. dir. of story operations, 1967; exec. vice-pres., creative operations and members, Board of Directors, 1969–71. Exec. v.p., member board of directors Warner Bros., 1971–1972; partner and director, The Zanuck/Brown Co., 1972–1988. Pres., Manhattan Project Ltd., 1988–; mbr., bd. of trustees, American Film Institute, 1972–80.

FILMS INCLUDE: The Sugarland Express, The Black Windmill, Sssssss, The Eiger Sanction, The Sting, MacArthur, Jaws, Jaws 2, Willie Dynamite, The Girl from Petrovka, The Island, Neighbors, The Verdict, Cocoon, Target, Cocoon II: The Return, Blue Lightning.

BROWN, GEORG SANFORD: Actor, Director. b. Havana, Cuba, June 24, 1943. m. actress Tyne Daly. Acted on stage with the New York Shakespeare Fest., NY, in the 1960s. Gained fame as one of the rookie cops in the 1970s TV series The Rookies before turning to TV directing.

THEATER: All's Well That Ends Well; Measure for Measure; Macbeth; Murderous Angels; Hamlet; Detective Story.

PICTURES: The Comedians; Dayton's Devils; Bullitt; Colossus; The Forbin Project; The Man; God Bless You, Uncle Sam.

TELEVISION: The Rookies (series); Barefoot in Athens; The Young Lawyers; Next Time, My Love; Dawn: Portrait of a Teenage Runaway; Roots; Roots: The Next Generations; The Night the City Screamed; Grambling's White Tiger (dir.); The Greatest American Hero (dir.); Cagney and Lacey (dir. Emmy, best dir., 1986); The Kid With the Broken Halo; In Defense of Kids; The Jesse Owens Story. Dir. of episodes: Charlie's Angels; Starsky and Hutch; Dynasty; Hill Street Blues.

BROWN, HAROLD: Executive. Pres., International Picture Show Co. since Dec., 1980. Previously pres., American International TV; v.p. & bd. mbr., American International Pictures (now Filmways).

BROWN, HENRY: Executive. b. New York, NY, Feb. 18, 1899. e. City Coll. of New York, 1920; Columbia U. 1923. Pres., Lakewood Amusement Corp.; pres., Atlas TV Corp.; pres. Capt. Zero Prods., Inc.

BROWN, HIMAN: M.P. Producer, Director, b. New York, NY, July 21, 1910. e. City Coll. of New York, St. Lawrence U. Radio & TV package prod. since 1927 include: Inner Sanctum, Thin Man, Bulldog Drummond, Dick Tracy, Terry and the Pirates, Joyce Jordan MD, Grand Central Station, CBS Radio Mystery Theatre, pres. Production Center, Inc.

PICTURES INCLUDE: That Night, Violators, The Stars Salute, The Price of Silence, The Road Ahead.

BROWN, HOWARD C.: Executive. b. Newport, NH, Aug. 15, 1901. e. Boston U. Assoc. with Technicolor Motion Picture Corp., Before org. Colorart Pictures, 1926. Merged with Synchrotone Pictures & Kennedy Pictures, 1929, forming Colorart Synchrotone Corp. In 1930 org. Brown-Nagel Productions. Since 1933 has produced numerous shorts. Sales mgr., Cinecolor, 1936–37; pres. Howard C. Brown Co. 1937–1938. Sales mgr., Trimble Laboratories, Inc. 1947; formed Howard C. Brown Productions 1948, to release for United Artists. Prod. Kangaroo Kid; prod. Mating Urge, inter-nations, documentary; 1969, Film Exporter.

BROWN, JIM: Actor. b. St. Simons Island, GA, Feb. 17, 1936. e. Manhasset H.S., Syracuse U. For nine years played football with Cleveland Browns; in 1964 won Hickock Belt as Professional Athlete of the year; founder, Black Economic Union.

PICTURES INCLUDE: Rio Conchos, The Dirty Dozen, Ice Station Zebra, The Split, Riot, Dark Of The Sun, 100 Rifles, Kenner, Tick . . . Tick . . . Tick, The Grasshopper, Slaughter, Slaughter's Big Rip-Off, I Escaped from Devil's Island, The Slams, Three the Hard Way, Take a Hard Ride, The Running Man.

BROWN, TOM: Actor. b. New York, NY, Jan. 6, 1913. e. N.Y. Prof. Children's Sch. Son of Harry Brown, actor-producer, and Marie Francis, actress. On radio, then dram. stage (Neighbors, Many a Slip, Pardon My Glove, etc.). Screen debut in A Lady Lies, 1929.

PICTURES INCLUDE: Buck Privates Come Home, Duke of Chicago, Operation Haylift, Fireman Save My Child.

TELEVISION: General Hospital.

BROWN, WILLIAM: Executive. b. Ayr, Scotland, June 24, 1929. e. Ayr Acad., U. of Edinburgh, where graduated Bachelor of Commerce, 1950. Served to Lieutenant, Royal Artillery, 1950–52. Sales mgr. for Scotland Television Ltd. in London, England, 1958 to 1961, sales director 1961 to 1963. Deputy mng. dir. of Scottish Television Ltd. at Glasgow 1963–66, mng. dir. in 1966. Deputy chm. and mng.-dir. of STV from 1974. Director, independent TV Publications, London, England, 1968. On board of directors for Scottish National Orchestra, 1973. Member of Independent TV Companies Association, and chairman of same 1978–80. Holds C.B.E. honor from British royalty.

BROWN, WILLIAM H., JR.: Director, concert mgr., Juilliard Sch. of Music, 1946; TV prod., Young and Rubicam, 1948; dir., Life with Father, Climax, CBS-TV, 1954, Studio One 1955; prod. Paramount Television, 1958; Exec. prod., Shirley Temple Show, NBC, 1960; TV prod., Norman, Craig and Kummel, 1962; Compton, 1963; Post-Keyes-Gardner, 1965; Freelance, 1967.

BROWN, WILLET HENRY: Executive. Assist. gen. mgr., Don Lee, Inc., 1932–33; exec. v.p. Don Lee Broadcasting System, Hollywood, 1938–48; pres. Don Lee Broadcasting System, 1949–58; consultant, R.K.O. General Inc.: pres. Don Lee, Inc. pres. Laurie Leasing Corp.: pres. Pacific States Invest. Corp.: pres. Hillcrest Motor Company: Operating: KXOA-AM & KXOA- FM, Sacramento, CA and KKSF-FM, San Francisco, CA. Pres., KGB INC, KGB-AM and KGB-FM, San Diego, Calif.: gen. partner, Brown Bdcstng. Co., operating KYNO FM & AM, Fresno, CA, and KKAT-FM, Salt Lake City, UT.

BROWNE, CORAL: Actress. b. Melbourne, Australia, July 23, 1913. Wife of actor Vincent Price. Theatre includes Mated, The Golden Gander, Death Asks a Verdict, The Man Who Came to Dinner, The Rehearsal, Lady Windermere's Fan, What the Butler Saw, The Waltz of the Toreadors, etc.

PICTURES: The Amateur Gentlemen, Pygmalion, The Prime Minister, Quartet, Madeleine, All at Sea, Rooney, The Ruling Class, The Killing of Sister George, The Drowning Pool, American Dreamer, Dreamchild.

TELEVISION: Eleanor: First Lady of the World, Time Express, An Englishman Abroad.

BROWNE, ROSCOE LEE: Actor, Director, Writer. b. Woodbury, NJ, 1925. e. Lincoln U., PA; postgraduate studies in comparative literature and French at Middlebury Coll., VT, Columbia U., N.Y. Taught French and lit. at Lincoln U. until 1952. National sales rep. for Schenley Import Corp. 1946–56; United States' international track star and a member of ten A.A.U. teams. Twice American champion in the 1000-yard indoor competition, twice all-American and, in 1951 in Paris, ran the fastest 800 meters in the world for that year. Professional acting debut, 1956, in Julius Caesar at the N.Y. Shakespeare Festival; published poet and short story writer. Trustee: Millay Colony Arts, NY; Los Angeles Free Public Theatre.

BROADWAY: The Ballad of the Sad Cafe, The Cool World, General Seeger, Tiger, Tiger Burning Bright!, The Old Glory; A Hand is on the Gate (dir., actor); My One and Only; Off-Broadway—The Connection, The Blacks, Aria da Capo, Benito Cereno (Obie Award).

PICTURES INCLUDE: The Comedians, Uptight, The Liberation of L. B. Jones, The Cowboys, World's Greatest Athlete, The Big Ripoff, Superfly T.N.T., Topaz, Uptown Saturday Night, Logan's Run, Twilight's Last Gleaming, The Fifth Door.

TELEVISION: Space, King, Dr. Scorpion.

BROWNING, KIRK: TV Director; b. New York, NY, March 28, 1921. e. Brooks School, Andover, MA, Avon Old Farms, Avon, CT., and Cornell U. 1940, reporter to News-Tribune in Waco, Texas; with American Field Service, 1942–45; adv. copywriter for Franklin Spier, 1945–48; became floor manager NBC-TV 1949; app't asst. dir. NBC-TV Opera Theatre in 1951 directing NBC Opera Theatre, TV Recital Hall, and Toscanini Simulcasts.

TELEVISION: Trial of Mary Lincoln; Jascha Heifetz Special; Harry and Lena; NBC Opera Theatre; Producers Showcase; Evening with Toscanini; Bell Telephone; The Flood; Beauty and the Beast; Lizzie Borden; World of Carl Sandburg; La Gioconda (Emmy, 1980); Big Blonde; Working; Ian McKellan Acting Shakespeare; Fifth of July; Alice in Wonderland; Live From the Met—Centennial.

BROWNLOW, KEVIN: Film historian, Writer, Director, Film Editor. b. Crowborough, Eng., June 2, 1938. e. University College

Sch. Film editor, World Wide Pictures, London, 1955–61; joint director, 1964; film editor, Samaritan Films, 1961–65; film editor, Woodfall Films, 1965–68. Director Thames Television 1980–present.
BOOKS: How It Happened Here (1968); The Parade's Gone By...; Adventures with D.W. Griffith (editor); The War, the West and the Wilderness (1979); Hollywood: The Pioneers (1980); Napoleon: Abel Gance's Classic Film.
PICTURES: It Happened Here (dir. with Andrew Mollo) 1966; Charge of the Light Brigade (editor); Winstanley; Napoleon (restoration and editor of 1927 film, released 1980).
TELEVISION: Hollywood (dir., s.p.); Unknown Chaplin (dir.), Movie: Charm of Dynamite (co-dir.).

BRUBAKER, JAMES D.: Producer. b. Hollywood, CA, March 30, 1937. e. Eagle Rock H.S. Transportation coordinator 15 years before becoming unit prod. mgr., 1978–84. Then assoc. prod., exec. prod. & prod.
PICTURES: Assoc. Prod.: True Confessions, Rocky III, Rhinestone. Exec. Prod.: The Right Stuff, Beer, Rocky IV, Cobra, Over the Top. Prod.: Rambo III.

BRUCE, BRENDA: Actress. b. Manchester, England, 1922. e. privately. London stage debut, 1066 And All That; On screen 1944; Millions Like Us; TV Best Actress Award 1962.
PICTURES INCLUDE: Night Boat to Dublin, I See a Dark Stranger, They Came to a City, Carnival, Piccadilly Incident, While the Sun Shines, When the Bough Breaks, My Brother's Keeper, Don't Ever Leave Me, The Final Test, Law and Disorder, Behind the Mask, Peeping Tom, Nightmare, The Uncle.
BROADWAY: Gently Does It (1953), This Year Next Year, Happy Days, Woman in a Dressing Gown, Victor Eh!, Merry Wives of Windsor, The Revenger's Tragedy, Little Murders, Winter's Tale, Pericles, Twelfth Night, Hamlet.
TELEVISION: Mary Britton series, Nearer to Heaven, Wrong Side of the Park, The Lodger, The Monkey and the Mohawk, Love Story, A Piece of Resistance, Give the Clown His Supper, Knock on Any Door, The Browning Version, Death of a Teddy Bear, Softly, Softly, The Girl, Happy, Family at War, Budgie.

BRUCKHEIMER, JERRY: Producer. b. Detroit, MI. e. U. of Arizona. Was adv. agency exec. in TV commercials before becoming producer of films. 1983, formed Don Simpson/Jerry Bruckheimer Prods. with Don Simpson and entered into deal with Paramount Pictures to produce.
PICTURES: Assoc. Prod.: Culpepper Cattle Company, Rafferty and the Gold Dust Twins. Producer: Farewell My Lovely, March or Die, Defiance, American Gigolo, Thief, Cat People (exec. prod.), Young Doctors in Love, Flashdance, Thief of Hearts, Beverly Hills Cop, Top Gun, Beverly Hills Cop II.

BRUNING, RICHARD R.: Executive. b. Kansas City, MO. e. Yale U., Harvard Business Sch. Asst. treas. Transamerica Corp., parent corp. of United Artists, from 1972. In 1979 named treas. of UA. 1980, named v.p. and treas. of UA Corp.

BRYAN, DORA: Actress. b. Southport, Lancashire, Eng., Feb. 7, 1924. e. Council Sch. Stage debut 1935. Screen debut The Fallen Idol, 1948.
PICTURES INCLUDE: No Room at the Inn, Once Upon a Dream, Blue Lamp, Cure for Love, Now Barabas, The Ringer, Women of Twilight, The Quiet Woman, The Intruder, You Know What Sailors Are, Mad About Men, See How They Run, Cockleshell Heroes, Child in the House, Green Man, Carry on Sergeant, Operation Bullshine, Desert Mice, The Night We Got the Bird, A Taste of Honey, Two a Penny, Apartment Zero.
TELEVISION: According to Dora (1968), Both Ends Meet.

BRYON, KATHLEEN: Actress. b. London, England, Jan. 11, 1922. e. London U., Old Vic. co. student, 1942. Screen debut in Young Mr. Pitt, 1943.
PICTURES INCLUDE: Silver Fleet, Black Narcissus, Matter of Life and Death, Small Back Room, Madness of the Heart, Reluctant Widow, Prelude to Fame, Scarlet Thread, Tom Brown's Schooldays, Four Days, Hell Is Sold Out, I'll Never Forget You, Gambler and the Lady, Young Bess, Night of the Silvery Moon, Profile, Secret Venture, Hand in Hand, Night of the Eagle, Hammerhead, Wolfshead, Private Road, Twins of Evil, Craze, Abdication, One of Our Dinosaurs Is Missing, The Elephant Man, From a Far Country.
TELEVISION: The Lonely World of Harry Braintree, All My Own Work, Emergency Ward 10, Probation Officer, Design for Murder, Sergeant Cork, Oxbridge 2000, The Navigators, The Worker; Hereward the Wake, Breaking Point, Vendetta, Play To Win, Who Is Sylvia, Portrait of a Lady, Cadfan, You're Wrecking My Marriage, Take Three Girls, The Confession of Mariona Evans, Paul Temple, The Worker, The Moonstone, The Challengers, The Golden Bowl, The Edwardians, The New Life, Menace, The Rivals of Sherlock Holmes, The Brontes, On Call, Edward VII, Sutherland's Law, Crown Court, Anne of Avonlea, Heidi, Notorious Woman, General Hospital, North & South, Angelo, Within these Walls, Jubilee,

Z Cars, Tales from the Supernatural, Secret Army, An Englishman's Castle, The Professionals, Forty Weeks, Emmerdale Farm, Blake Seven, The Minders, Together, Hedda Gabler, Nancy Astor, God Speed Co-operation, Take Three Women, Reilly.

BUCHHOLZ, HORST: Actor. b. Berlin, Germany, Dec. 4, 1933. e. high school. In radio and stage plays. Film debut Marianne (French), 1955.
PICTURES INCLUDE: Himmel Ohne Sterne (No Star in the Sky), Robinson Must Not Die, Mon Petit, The Confessions of Felix Krull, Tiger Bay, Fanny, One, Two, Three, Nine Hours to Rama, The Empty Canvas, The Great Waltz, Cervantes, Sahara, Code Name: Emerald, And the Violins Stopped Playing.
TELEVISION: Raid on Entebbe, Crossings.

BUCK, JULES: Producer. b. St. Louis, MO, July 30, 1917. Asst. to prod., The Killers; assoc. prod., Brute Force, Naked City, We Were Strangers; prod., Love Nest, Fixed Bayonets, Treasure of the Golden Condor, O.S.S., TV series; prod., The Day They Robbed the Bank of England, Great Catherine; formed Keep Films with Peter O'Toole. Co-prod., Under Milkwood. Prod., The Ruling Class. Exec. Prod., Man Friday. Prod., The Great Scout and Cathouse Thursday.
TELEVISION: (U.S.) Berlin Tunnel, The French Atlantic Affair, Raid on Entebbe, The Savage Bees.

BUCKLEY, BETTY: Actress. b. Fort Worth, TX, July 3, 1947. e. Texas Christian U., BA. Studied acting with Stella Adler. NY Stage debut: 1776 (1969); London debut: Promises Promises. Made film debut as the gym teacher in Carrie (1976) and starred as the mother in the Bdwy musical Carrie (1988).
THEATER: Johnny Pott; What's a Nice Country Like You Doing in a State Like This?; Pippin; I'm Getting My Act Together and Taking It on the Road; Cats (Tony Award, supp. actress, 1983); The Mystery of Edwin Drood; Carrie.
PICTURES: Carrie; Tender Mercies; Frantic.
TELEVISION: Series: Eight is Enough (1977–81); The Devil's Work; The Ordeal of Bill Carney; Bobby and Sarah; Salute to Lady Liberty; The Three Wishes of Billy Grier; Evergreen.

BUCKLEY, DONALD: Executive. b. New York, NY, June 28, 1955. e. C.W. Post Coll, NY, Sch. of Visual Arts. Ad. mgr., United Artists Theatres, 1975–78; acct. exec., Grey Advertising, 1978–80. Joined WB in 1980 as New York adv. mgr.; 1986, promoted to east. dir. of adv/promo. for WB.

BUCKNER, ROBERT H.: Producer. Writer. b. Crewe, VA, May 28, 1906. e. U. of Virginia., U. of Edinburgh, Scotland. Newspaper corresp. New York World. 1926–27 in England: instructor, Belgian Mil. Acad. 1927–28: with Alfred A. Knopf, Inc., Doubleday, Doran, N.Y., pub., 1928–33; corresp. in Russia, Scandinavia, 1933–35; contrib. fiction, Amer. & Brit. mags., 1926–36. Author & collab. many s.p. A Champion of Champion Producer in Fame ratings.
PICTURES INCLUDE: Gold Is Where You Find It, Jezebel, Dodge City, Virginia City, Knute Rockne, Santa Fe Trial, Dive Bomber, Yankee Doodle Dandy, Desert Song. In 1943 prod. Gentleman Jim, Mission to Moscow, Desert Song, The Gang's All Here, Cheyenne, Life with Father, prod. Rogue's Regiment. Sword in the Desert; Free For All, Deported, Bright Victory, The Man Behind the Gun, Safari.

BUJOLD, GENEVIEVE: Actress. b. Montreal, Canada, July 1, 1942. e. Montreal Conservatory of Drama. Worked in a Montreal cinema as an usherette; American TV debut: St. Joan.
STAGE: The Barber of Seville, A Midsummer Night's Dream, A House ... A Day.
PICTURES INCLUDE: La Guerre est Finie, La Fleur de L'Age, Entre La Mer et L'eau Douce, Final Assignment, King of Hearts, The Thief, Isabel, Anne of the Thousand Days, The Act of the Heart, The Journey, Earthquake, Swashbuckler, Alex and the Gypsy, Kamouraska, Obsession, Swashbuckler, Another Man, Another Chance, Coma, Murder by Decree, The Last Flight of Noah's Ark, Monsignore, Tightrope, Choose Me, Trouble in Mind, The Suspect, The Moderns, Dead Ringers, Mistress of Paradise, White Earth.
TELEVISION: Antony and Cleopatra, Mistress of Paradise.

BURGER, HENRY: Executive. b. Pittsburgh, PA, March 26, 1915. Asst. mgr. and mgr., various theatres in Pittsburgh and West Virginia; asst. ad. pub. mgr., Pittsburgh Zone Warner Bros. Theatres, 1942; ad., pub. mgr., 1948; district mgr., Stanley Warner Theatres, Erie district, 1951; district mgr., Pittsburgh City Theaters, zone ad. pub. mgr., 1953; Zone mgr., Stanley Warner Midwest-Zone Theatres, 1962; nat. adv. pub. dir., Stanley Warner Theatres, 1965; zone manager, 1967.

BURKE, ALFRED: Actor. b. London, England, 1918. Ent. films 1954.
PICTURES INCLUDE: The Angry Silence, Moment of Danger, The Man Inside, The Man Upstairs, No Time To Die, Law and Disorder, Yangtse Incident, Interpol, Bitter Victory.
TELEVISION: The Crucible, Mock Auction, Parole, No

Gun, No Guilt, The Big Knife, Parnell, The Strong Are Lonely, Home of the Brave, The Birthday Party, The Watching Eye, Public Eye series.

BURKE, PAUL: Actor. b. New Orleans, LA, July 21, 1926. e. prep schools, New Orleans, Pasadena Playhouse.
TELEVISION: Five Fingers, Harbor Master, Noah's Ark, Naked City, Playhouse 90, Studio One, Medic, Frontier, Men in Space, Man and the Challenge, Target, M-Squad, Black Saddle, Philip Marlowe, Martin Kane, Line Up, Dragnet, Man Without a Gun, Tightrope, Panic, Highway Patrol, Men of Annapolis, Flight, Naked City, 12 O'Clock High, Magnum P.I., Dynasty, Hotel, T.J. Hooker, The Seduction of Gina, Finder of Lost Loves, Murder She Wrote.
PICTURES INCLUDE: Once You Kiss a Stranger, Daddy's Gone A-Hunting, Valley of the Dolls.

BURKS, J. COOPER: Executive. b. Pilot Point, TX, April 26, 1919. e. Oklahoma City U., Oklahoma City Law Sch., American Inst. of Banking (special finance courses), U.S. Navy Schools at Wesleyan Coll., Middletown, CT, U. of North Carolina, Chapel Hill,, Virginia Polytechnic Inst., Blacksburg, Virginia Military. Commander USNR-Ret. W.W.II PT boats, North Atlantic then as Naval Aviator—latter part W.W.II and Korean War. Business experience: Prior to theatre business, was in banking & construction business. Formed present company March, 1970. Now president at chairman of the board of AATI (American Automated Theatres, Inc.) in Oklahoma City. Military Affairs Committee, Chamber of Commerce, Life Member-Navy League.

BURLINSON, JOHN J., JR.: Executive. b. New York, NY, Dec. 26, 1930. e. Collegiate Sch. NY, Fordham U. Dir. promotion and adv., Henry Regnery Co. (book publishers). 1960; sls. mgr. Regnery, 1962; N.Y. rep., U.S. Press Association, 1963; v.p., Quigley Publishing Co., N.Y., 1964. Ad Dir. Better Theatres Theatre vending; adv. mgr. Motion Picture Daily, 1966; National Screen Service Corp. 1970, dir. inter-corporate promotion. 1972; dir. of admin., National Theatre Supply; 1974, gen. mgr., NTS; 1977, v.p. & gen. mgr., EPRAD, Inc.; 1980, named pres., EPRAD; 1983, dir., mktg., sls., adv., Strong International. Elected exec. dir. & treasurer of TESMA in 1967. Co-director NATO/NAC/TESMA Trade Show; sec. & dir., M.P. Pioneers, 1970; hon. dir. TESMA, 1971; member SMPTE, Variety Club. 1972; Vice President Equipment Assoc.; 1974; bd. mem. TEA and Conference chm.; 1982: TEA secty.; Chm. annual N.Y. Variety Golf Tournament 1972–75; vice chairman, Motion Picture Div., Catholic Charities of N.Y., 1972–75. 1984–86, exec. dir., Variety Clubs Intl. 1986, consultant on medical treatment for third-world children.

BURNETT, CAROL: Actress, Comedienne, Singer; b. San Antonio, TX, April 26, 1933; Jody and Louise (Creighton) Burnett. e. Hollywood H.S., UCLA. children: Carrie Louise (actress), Judy Ann, Erin Kate Hamilton. Introduced comedy song, I Made a Fool of Myself over John Foster Dulles, 1957; regular performer Garry Moore TV show, 1959–62; appeared several CBS-TV spls., 1962–63. Recipient outstanding comedienne award Am. Guild Variety Artists, 5 times; 5 Emmy awards for outstanding variety performance, Acad. TV Arts and Scis. TV Guide award for outstanding female performer 1961, 62, 63; Peabody Award, 1963; Golden Globe award for outstanding comedienne of year, Fgn. Press Assn.; Woman of Year award Acad. TV Arts and Scis. Voted one of the world's 20 most admired women in 1977 Gallup Poll. First Annual National Television Critics Award for Outstanding Performance, 1977. Inducted Acad. of Television Arts and Sciences Hall of Fame, 1985.
THEATER: Once Upon a Mattress (debut, 1959); Fade Out-Fade In (1964). Regional: Plaza Suite (1970); I Do, I Do; Same Time, Next Year (1977).
PICTURES INCLUDE: Who's Been Sleeping in My Bed? (1963); Pete 'n Tillie, The Front Page, A Wedding (Best Actress, San Sebastian Film Fest.); Health; The Four Seasons; Chu Chu and the Philly Flash; Annie.
TELEVISION: The Garry Moore Show 1959–62; Julie & Carol at Carnegie Hall (1963); Carol & Company; Calamity Jane; Once Upon a Mattress; Carol + 2; The Carol Burnett Show (1966–77, now in syndication as Carol Burnett and Friends.); Julie & Carol at Lincoln Center; 6 Rms Riv Vu; Twigs; Sills & Burnett at the Met; Dolly & Carol in Nashville; The Grass Is Always Greener Over the Septic Tank; Friendly Fire; The Tenth Month; Life of the Party: The Story of Beatrice; Between Friends; The Laundromat; Burnett Discovers Domingo; Hostage.

BURNS, GEORGE: Actor. r.n. Nathan Birnbaum; b. New York, NY, Jan. 20, 1896. In vaudeville as singer in children's quartet, later as roller skater, then comedian; formed team Burns & (Gracie) Allen, 1925; m. partner 1926. Team many years on Keith and Orpheum vaudeville circuits, then on screen in Paramount short subjects, on radio in England; in 1930 began long career Amer. radio. Feature picture debut 1932 in The Big Broadcast.
PICTURES INCLUDE: International House, Love in Bloom, College Swing, Honolulu, Two Girls and A Sailor, The Sunshine Boys, Oh, God, Just You and Me, Kid, Oh, God! Book II, Oh, God! You Devil, 18 Again.
TELEVISION: Co-star Burns & Allen show, CBS-TV. Movies: Two of a Kind; Grandpa, Will You Run With Me?; Wendy and Me; Disney's Magic in the Magic Kingdom (host).

BURNS, RALPH: Composer, Musical conductor. b. Newton, MA, June 29, 1922.
PICTURES: Lenny, Cabaret (AA), Lucky Lady, New York, New York, Movie, Movie, All That Jazz (AA), Urban Cowboy, Jinxed, Annie, My Favorite Year, Star 80, Perfect, Kiss Me Goodbye; National Lampoon's Vacation; After the Promise.
TELEVISION: Baryshnikov on Broadway, Liza and Goldie Special (both Emmy awards), Ernie Kovacs—Between the Laughter.

BURR, RAYMOND: Actor. b. New Westminster, B.C., Canada, May 21, 1917. e. Stanford U., U. of California, Columbia U., U. of Chungking. Forestry svce.: appeared on stage in many countries in Night Must Fall, Mandarin, Crazy with the Heat, Duke in Darkness; dir., Pasadena Community Playhouse, 1943; on radio. Formed Royal Blue Ltd, TV prod. co. with business partner Robert Benevides, 1988.
PICTURES INCLUDE: Pitfall, Raw Deal, Key to the City, His Kind of Woman, Place in the Sun, New Mexico, Meet Danny Wilson, Mara Maru, Horizons West, Blue Gardenia, Fort Algiers, Casanova's Big Night, Gorilla at Large, Khyber Patrol, Rear Window, Passion, They Were So Young, You're Never Too Young, A Man Alone, Count Three and Pray, Please Murder Me, Godzilla King of the Monsters, Great Day in the Morning, Secret of Treasure Mountain, Cry in the Night, P.J., Airplane II: The Sequel.
TELEVISION: Perry Mason (series, 1957–66); Ironside (series, 1967–75); Kingston: Confidential, 79 Park Ave., Centennial, 1978. Movies: Perry Mason Returns; Perry Mason: The Case of the Murdered Madam; Perry Mason: The Avenging Ace; The Case of the Lady in the Lake; The Case of the Scandalous Scoundrel.

BURRILL, TIMOTHY: Producer, Executive. b. North Wales, 1931. e. Eton Coll., Sorbonne U. Paris. Grenadier Guards 2 yrs, then London Shipping Co. Ent. m.p. ind. as resident prod. mgr. Samaritan Films working on shorts, commercials, documentaries, 1954. Ass't. dir. on feature films: The Criminal, The Valiant Years (TV series), On The Fiddle, Reach for Glory, War Lover, Prod. mgr: The Cracksman, Night Must Fall, Lord Jim, Yellow Rolls Royce, The Heroes, Of Telemark, Resident producer with World Film Services. 1968–1969: Privilege, Oedipus the King, 1969–1970: A Severed Head, Three Sisters, 1970 produced two films on pop music for Anglo-EMI. 1971 assoc. prod. Macbeth. 1972 first production administrator National Film School in U.K. 1973 Prod. Alpha Beta. 1974 Post production administrator The Three Musketeers. 1974: Prod. TV Special The Canterville Ghost; 1975; assoc. prod, That Lucky Touch; 1976: UK Administrator, The Prince and the Pauper; 1977: North American Production controller, Superman 1; 1974–1983 Council Member of BAFTA: Co-produced Polanski's Tess; 1979–80 Managing Director Allied Stars (Breaking Glass, Chariots of Fire); 1981 co-produced NYSF Prod. Pirates of Penzance; 1979–80 V. Chmn. Film BAFTA; 1980–1983 Chmn. BAFTA: 1981 Gov. National Film School, Executive BFTPA Mbr. Cinematograph Films Council. 1982 Gov National Theatre; Prod.: Supergirl, The Fourth Protocol; 1987, chairman, Film Asset Developments.

BURROWS, JAMES: Director. b. Los Angeles, CA, Dec. 30, 1940. e. Oberlin, B.A.; Yale, M.F.A. Son of late Abe Burrows, composer, writer, director. Directed off-Bdwy. and theatrical film, Partners.
TELEVISION: Series: Mary Tyler Moore; Bob Newhart; Laverne and Shirley; Rhoda; Phyllis; Fay; Taxi; Lou Grant; Cheers; Dear John. Movies: More Than Friends; Like Father Like Daughter; Goodbye Doesn't Mean Forever; In the Lion's Den.

BURROWS, JOHN, H.: Producer. b. Brooklyn, NY, September 4, 1924. e. Yale U., New York U. Law with interruption for service. U.S. Navy, W.W.II, lieut., son of George D. Burrows, vice-president Allied Artists, started film career as salesman for AA later joining studio; asst. prod. Lindsley Parsons Productions.

BURROWS, ROBERTA: Executive. e. Brandeis U; Academia, Florence, Italy. Career includes freelance writing and post as dir. of pub. for Howard Stein Enterprises and with Rogers & Cowan and Billings Associates. Joined Warner Bros. as sr. publicist 1979; named dir. east coast publicity, 1986.

BURRUD, BILL: Executive. b. Los Angeles, CA, Jan. 12, 1925. e. U. of Southern California, B.S.; Harvard Business Sch. Ent. ind. as child actor; U.S. Navy, W.W. II; formed Bill Burrud Prods., 1954.
TELEVISION: Animal World, World of the Sea, Safari to Adventure, Challenging Sea, Secret World of Reptiles, Vanishing Africa, The Great American Wilderness, Predators of the Sea, Creatures of the Amazon, The Amazing Apes, The Amazing World, Animals Are the Funniest People.

BURSTYN, ELLEN: Actress. b. Detroit, MI, Dec. 7, 1932. r.n. Edna Rae Gilhooley. Majored in art; was fashion model in Texas when 18. Moved to Montreal as dancer; then N.Y. to do TV commercials (under the name of Ellen McRae), appearing for a year on the Jackie Gleason show (1956–57). In 1957 turned to dramatics and won lead in Bdwy show, Fair Game. Then went to Hollywood to do TV and films. Returned to N.Y. to study acting with Lee Strasberg; worked in TV serial, The Doctors. Co-artistic dir. of Actor's Studio. Pres. Actors Equity Assn. 1982–85. On 2 panels of Natl. Endowment of the Arts and Theatre Advisory Council (NY).
   THEATER: Same Time, Next Year (Tony Award, 1975); 84 Charing Cross Road.
   PICTURES INCLUDE: For Those Who Think Young, Goodbye, Charlie, Tropic of Cancer, Alex in Wonderland, The Last Picture Show, The King of Marvin Gardens, The Exorcist, Harry and Tonto, Alice Doesn't Live Here Anymore (Acad. Award), Providence, A Dream of Passion, Same Time Next Year, Resurrection, Silence of the North, The Ambassador, Twice in a Lifetime, Dear America: Letters Home From Vietnam (reader), Hanna's War.
   TELEVISION: Surviving, Act of Vengeance, Into Thin Air, Thursday's Game; The People vs. Jean Harris; Something in Common, Pack of Lies. Series: The Ellen Burstyn Show.

BURTON, BERNARD: Producer. Started as film ed.; prod. "Vagabond Lady" 1935.
   PICTURES INCLUDE: She Gets Her Man, Fighting Youth, Invisible Ray, Showboat, When Love is Young, One Hundred Men and a Girl, You're a Sweetheart, Midnight Intruder, Little Tough Guy, Three Smart Girls Grow Up, Spring Parade, Moonlight in Havana, Get Help to Love, Gentleman Joe Palooka, Fighting Mad, Smart Woman, Underworld Story, Cry Danger, The Highwayman, Triple Cross, Beast from 20,000 Fathoms.

BURTON, KATE: Actress. b. Geneva, Switzerland, Sept. 10, 1957. e. Yale Drama Sch. D. of late Richard Burton. m. director Michael Ritchie. Worked at Yale Repertory Theatre, Hartford, Stage Co., the Hartman, Williamstown, Berkshire Theatre festivals. Performed on Bdwy. and off-Bdwy and on TV. Theatrical film debut: Big Trouble in Little China, 1986.
   TELEVISION: Ellis Island, Evergreen, Alice in Wonderland, Uncle Tom's Cabin.
   STAGE: Present Laughter (debut, 1982, Theatre World Award), Alice in Wonderland, Winners, The Accrington Pals, Doonesbury, The Playboy of the Western World.

BURTON, LeVAR: Actor. b. Landstuhl, Germany, Feb. 16, 1957. e. U. of Southern California. Signed to play role of Kunta Kinte in TV series, Roots, while still in school. Has hosted Public TV children's shows, Bebop, and The Reading Rainbow.
   PICTURES: Looking for Mr. Goodbar, The Hunter.
   TELEVISION: Roots; Almos' A Man; Billy: Portrait of a Street Kid; Battered; Guyana: the Story of Jim Jones; The Ron LeFlore Story; Dummy; The Jesse Owens Story; A Special Friendship; Star Trek: The Next Generation; Roots Christmas.

BUSCH, H. DONALD: Exhibitor. b. Philadelphia, PA, Sept. 21, 1935. e. U. of Pennsylvania, physics, math, 1956; law school, 1959. 1960 to 1987 practiced law, anti-trust & entertainment. 1984, named pres., Budco Theatres, Inc. 1975–1987, pres., Busch, Grafman & Von Dreusche, P.C. 1987, pres. & CEO, AMC Philadelphia, Inc.
   MEMBER: Former posts: Suburban General Hospital (dir.); Rainbow Fund (dir.); NATO (dir.); Philadelphia All-Star Forum (dir.); Montgomery County Bar Assn. (dir.). Dir. & pres., Abington, PA school board (1974–77); dir., Sports Legends, Inc. (1972–84).

BUSCH, NIVEN: Writer. b. New York, NY, April 26, 1903. e. Princeton U. p. Briton Niven Busch, former v.p., Lewis J. Selznick Enterprises; Exec. prod., Samuel Goldwyn Productions. Assoc. ed. Time mag., 1923–31; assoc. ed. & contrib. New Yorker, 1927–31; numerous articles, many national magazines. Regents professor, U. of California, 1971–78. Special lectures on film. Regents professor, U. of California, Irvine, 1971–75. San Diego, 1974; Lecturer Berkeley, 1977. Lecturer, Princeton U., 1985, Ferris Teaching Fellow, Princeton U., 1986.
   AUTHOR: Books: Twenty One Americans, Carrington Incident, Duel in the Sun, They Dream of Home, Day of the Conquerors, The Furies, The Hate Merchant, The Actor, California Street, The San Franciscans, The Gentlemen from California, The Takeover, No Place for a Hero, Continent's Edge.
   PICTURES INCLUDE: The Crowd Roars, In Old Chicago, The Westerner, The Postman Always Rings Twice, Duel in the Sun, Till the End of Time, Pursued, Moss Rose; prod., The Capture, Distant Drums, Man from the Alamo, Moonlighter, Treasure of Pancho Villa, Moss Rose, He Was Her Man, The Angels Wash Their Face, Big Shakedown, Little Miss Pinkerton.

BUSEY, GARY: Actor, Musician. b. Goose Creek, TX, June 29, 1944. Played drums with the Rubber Band 1963–70. Also drummer with Leon Russell, Kris Kristofferson, Willie Nelson as Teddy Jack Eddy.
   PICTURES INCLUDE: Last American Hero, Lolly Madonna, Gumball Rally, Alex and the Gypsy, A Star Is Born, Straight Time, Big Wednesday, The Buddy Holly Story, Foolin' Around, Carny, Barbarosa, D.C. Cab, The Bear, Silver Bullet, Let's Get Harry, Eye of the Tiger, Lethal Weapon, Act of Piracy, Bulletproof.
   TELEVISION: Bloodsport, The Execution of Private Slovik, The Texas Wheelers (1974–75), A Dangerous Life (miniseries).

BUTTERFIELD, ELIZABETH: Production manager. b. London, England. e. London. Extensive theatrical experience as stage manager for The Old Vic Company (Michael Benthall, Tyrone Guthrie) and Donald Wolfit Company. Emigrated to Canada in 1957. Television experience includes: Quentin Durgens M.P. and Whiteoaks Of Jaina for C.B.C., Seaway, Ind.
   PICTURES INCLUDE: A Fan's Notes, (1971), Sunday in the Country, It Seemed Like a Good Idea at the Time, Find the Lady, Running, Middle Age Crazy, Torment.

BUTTOLPH, DAVID: Music director. b. New York, NY, Aug. 3, 1902.
   PICTURES INCLUDE: Phantom of Rue Morgue, Secret of the Incas, Bounty Hunter, Long John Silver, Jump into Hell, Target Zero, Lone Ranger, Steel Jungle, Santiago, Burning Hills, Cry in the Night.

BUTTONS, RED: Performer. r.n. Aaron Chwatt; b. New York, NY, Feb. 5, 1919. Singer at the age of 13; comic, Minsky's. U.S. Army, 1943; in Army and film version of Winged Victory.
   TELEVISION: Many TV appearances; star of Red Buttons Show CBS-TV, 1953; Best Comedian award 1953; NBC-TV, 1954; Alice in Wonderland, The Dream Merchants, Leave 'Em Laughing, Louis Armstrong—Chicago Style; Knots Landing (series); Reunion at Fairborough.
   PICTURES INCLUDE: Vickie, Wine, Women and Song, Barefoot Boy With Cheek, Hold It; Sayonara (Acad. Award, supp. actor, 1957), Imitation General, The Big Circus, Five Weeks in a Balloon, Harlow, They Shoot Horses Don't They, Who Killed Mary What's 'er name?, The Poseidon Adventure, Gable and Lombard, Viva, Knievel!, Movie Movie, When Time Ran Out, 18 Again.

BUTTS, R. DALE: Composer. b. Lamasco, KY, March 12, 1910. e. Louisville Conservatory of Music. Started in vaudeville at 16, later playing, arranging for dance bands; staff arranger, pianist, radio stations; to Republic Pictures, 1944.
   PICTURES INCLUDE: The Plunderers, Too Late for Tears, House by the River, Sea Hornet, The Outcast, Geraldine, Shanghai Story, Hell's Outpost, Santa Fe passage, Fighting Chance, No Man's Woman, Headline Hunter's, Lay That Rifle Down, Double Jeopardy, City of Shadows, Terror at Midnight, Stranger at My Door, Dakota Incident.

BUXBAUM, JAMES M.: Executive, Producer, Writer. b. Jamaica, NY, March 8. e. Harvard U., B.A., 1949; Columbia Law Sch., LL.B., 1955; spec. studies, The Hague Acad., Netherlands, 1953. Story ed. ZIV, Ivan Tors' Sea Hunt series, then assoc. prod., ZIV-CBS, Ivan Tors' Aquanauts series, story ed., 1957–60. Attorney, Wm. Morris Agency, 1962–63. Joined Ivan Tors Films, Inc. as v.p., prod. and wrote many episodes of Flipper series, 1964; exec. v.p. Ivan Tors Miami Studios, 1967–69; exec. v.p. Ivan Tors Films, Inc. 1968–69. Gen. mgr. Amer. Film Institute Center, Beverly Hills, 1969. Member: State Bar of CA, Amer. Bar Assoc. Exec. in charge of prod. for Island of the Lost.

BUZZI, RUTH: Actress. b. Wequetequock, CT, July 24, 1939. e. Pasadena Playhouse. Launched TV career on Garry Moore Show as comedy partner of Dom DeLuise. Created character Gladys Ormphby with Artie Johnson on TV's Laugh-In plus over 150 other characters.
   PICTURES INCLUDE: Nightfalls, The Being, The Trouble with Hello, Record City, Freaky Friday, The Apple Dumpling Gang Rides Again, The North Avenue Irregulars, The Villian, Surf Two, Skatetown USA, Chu Chu and the Philly Flash, The Bad Guys, Dixie Lanes, Nightfalls.
   TELEVISION: Lead on 7 TV series including: Rowan & Martin's Laugh-In; The Steve Allen Comedy Hour; The Donny & Marie Show and Carol Burnett's The Entertainers; semiregular on 12 other series including Flip, Tony Orlando & Dawn, That Girl, The Dean Martin Variety Hour; guest on 75 TV series and specials including Medical Center, Trapper John M.D., Love Boat. Eight cartoon voice-over series and over 150 on-camera commercials.
   STAGE: Sweet Charity (Broadway), 4 off-Broadway shows incld. A Man's Man, Little Mary Sunshine, 18 musical revues and Las Vegas club act.
   AWARDS: 4 Grammy nominations; Golden Globe winner, AGVA Variety Artist of the Year, 1977, Rhode Island Hall of Fame, Presidential commendation for outstanding artist in the field of entertainment, 1980.

BYGRAVES, MAX: Comedian, actor. b. London, England, October 16, 1922. e. St. Joseph's R.C. School, Rotherhithe. After RAF service, touring revues and London stage, M.P. debut 1949 in Skimpy in The Navy. TV debut in 1953, with own show. Received O.B.E., New Year's Honours 1983.
TELEVISION: Roamin' Holiday series.
PICTURES INCLUDE: Tom Brown's Schooldays, Charlie Moon, A Cry from the Streets, Boobikins, Spare the Rod. Autobiography, I Wanna Tell You A Story, pub. 1976.
NOVEL: The Milkman's on His Way, pub. 1977.

BYRD, CARUTH C.: Production executive. b. Dallas, TX, March 25, 1942. Multi-millionaire businessman, chm. of Caruth C. Byrd Enterprises, Inc., who entered entertainment industry forming Communications Network Inc. in 1972, producer of TV commercials. Was principal investor in film Santee (1972) and in 1973 formed Caruth C. Byrd Prods. to make theatrical features. 1983, chrm., Lone Star Pictures.
PICTURES INCLUDE: Allan and Murph the Surf, The Monkeys of Bandapur (both exec. prod.).

BYRD, JOHN: Writer, Director, Producer. Entered m.p. industry 1934 via scenario dept. Rock Studios, Elstree; visited Hollywood to study requirements of U.S. market, 1939; 1940–45 B.B.C. War Correspondent, 1945–46 Riverside Studios, 1947–8 British National Studios.
PICTURES INCLUDE: Murder in Reverse, World Owes Me a Living, Waltz Time. 1949 formed own org. prod. bus. TV films. Prod. films in South Africa, Uganda, Kenya, Portugal and Mexico. Filming Durgapur Steelworks project, India, 1961; Steel Strides Ahead, Concerning Colour, Design for Tall Building, Jungle to Steel Town, Steelworks in Action, 1962–4; Dryer Felt Loom, Bridging the Highways, 1965; Filming in Afghanistan, 1966; Filming in South Africa, 1967; Built from Top, 1968; Building with Steel and Plastics, 1969; The Desert Will Yield, 1970; Long Sea Outfall, One Steelworks, One Contract, Highweld Process. 1971: Go-Con Process, Mechanical Handling, 1972. Undersea Tunnel to Hong Kong. 1973: Contract 1306—Zambia, Bridge Across the Avon; 1974 filming for British Steel Corp.
OTHER PICTURES: Murder in Reverse, World Owes Me a Living, Waltz Time. 1974–5 Anchor Project for British Steel Corporation. 1976–77 Filming in Mexico AHMSA Steelworks project. 1977, More Steel for Mexico; 1978, Filming in South Africa; 1979–80, Filming in France & Spain; 1982, Filming Construction of Humber Bridge; 1983–84, New Zealand on steel development project. 1984, Better Coal for Kellingly; 1985, SCAW Metals Project; 1986, SAPPI Paper Mill Project; 1987, More Steel for New Zealand, documentary.

BYRNE, DAVID: Actor, Singer, Director. b. Scotland. Moved to Baltimore at 7. e. Rhode Island Sch. of Design studying photography, performance and video. Prod. and dir. music videos. Awarded MTV's Video Vanguard Award, 1985. Best known as the lead singer and chief songwriter of Talking Heads. Composed and performed original score for choreographer Twyla Tharp's The Catherine Wheel (Bdwy). Wrote music for Robert Wilson's The Knee Plays. Composed theme music and appeared in TV's Alive From Off Center.
PICTURES: Stop Making Sense (conceived and stars in concert film), True Stories (director, s.p., narrator), Married to the Mob (music).
TELEVISION: A Family Tree (Trying Times).

BYRNE, GABRIEL: Actor. b. Dublin, Ireland, 1950. e. University Coll., Ireland. Worked as archaeologist. Then became a Spanish teacher at girls' school. Participated in amateur theater before acting with Ireland's Focus Theatre, an experimental rep. co. and joining Dublin's Abbey Theatre Co. Cast in long-running TV series the Riordans. Also worked with National Theater in London.
PICTURES: Excalibur, Wagner, Hanna K, Defence of the Realm, Gothic, Lionheart, Siesta, Hello Again, A Soldier's Tale, The Courier.
TELEVISION: Series: The Riordan's, Branken, Movies: Mussolini, Christopher Columbus.

BYRNES, EDWARD: Actor. b. New York, NY, July 30, 1933. e. Harren H.S. Prof. debut, Joe E. Brown's Circus Show; appeared on stage in Tea and Sympathy.
PICTURES INCLUDE: Periscope, Marjorie Morningstar, Secret Invasion, Wicked, Wicked, Star Wars, Grease, Mankillers.
TELEVISION: Matinee Theatre, Crossroads, Jim Bowie, Wire Service, Navy Log, Oh Susanna!, 77 Sunset Strip, Throb, Rags to Riches, Troup Beverly Hills, Slaves: A True Story.

BYRON, WARD: TV Producer, Writer, Director. b. New York, NY, June 2, 1910. e. New York. Orchestra leader, 1929–32; radio prod., writer, 1932–39. Ent. TV as asst. to prog. dir. of ABC; writer & producer of Paul Whiteman Show & The Ameche-Langford Show; app'td exec. prod. of ABC-TV in 1950. Exec. prod., Canadian TV Young & Rubicam, 1955–57. Freelance writer prod., TV Specials & film series, v.p. gen. mgr. Trans-Nat'l Communications O'way Recording Studios;

1970, v.p. & sec. International Coproductions, motion picture distributors. Named pres. in 1979. Currently lecturing on early radio and TV.

BYRUM, JOHN: Writer, Director. b. Winnetka, IL, March 14, 1947. e. New York U. Film School. First job as "go-fer" on industrial films and cutting dailies for underground filmmakers. Went to England where wrote 1st s.p., Comeback. From 1970–73 was in N.Y. writing and re-writing scripts for low-budget films.
PICTURES INCLUDE: Mahogany (s.p.), Inserts (s.p., dir.) Harry and Walter Go to New York (story, s.p.), Heart Beat (s.p. dir.), Sphinx (s.p.), Scandalous (co.-s.p.), The Razor's Edge (co-s.p., dir.), The Whoopee Boys (dir.), The War at Home (dir., s.p.).
TELEVISION: Alfred Hitchcock Presents (1985).

C

CAAN, JAMES: Actor. b. Bronx, NY, March 26, 1940. e. Hofstra U. Studied with Sanford Meisner at the Neighborhood Playhouse. Appeared off-Broadway in La Ronde, 1961. Also on Broadway in Mandingo; Blood, Sweat and Stanley Poole.
PICTURES INCLUDE: Lady in a Cage, The Glory Guys, Red Line 7000, Eldorado, Games, Journey to Shiloh, Submarine X-1, Rain People, Rabbit, Run, The Godfather, Slither, Cinderella Liberty, Freebie and the Bean, T.R. Baskin, The Gambler, Godfather II, Funny Lady, Rollerball, The Killer Elite, Harry and Walter Go To New York, Silent Movie, A Bridge Too Far, Another Man, Another Chance, Comes a Horseman, Chapter Two, Hide in Plain Sight (also dir.), Thief, Kiss Me Goodbye, Gardens of Stone, Outer Heat.
TELEVISION: Much series work (Naked City, Route 66, Wagon Train, Ben Casey, Alfred Hitchcock Presents, etc.) 1962–69; Brian's Song (Emmy nom., 1971).

CACOYANNIS, MICHAEL: Producer, Director, Writer. b. Cyprus, June 11, 1922. Studied law in London, admitted to bar at age 21. Became a producer of BBC's wartime Greek programs while attending dramatic school. After acting on the stage in England, left in 1952 for Greece, where he made his first film, Windfall in Athens, with his own original script. While directing Greek classical plays, he continued making films.
PICTURES INCLUDE: Stella, The Girl in Black, A Matter of Dignity, Our Last Spring, The Wastrel, Electra, Zorba the Greek, The Day the Fish Came Out, The Trojan Women, Sweet Country.

CAESAR, IRVING: Author, Composer, Publisher. b. New York, NY, July 4, 1895. e. City Coll. of New York. Abroad with Henry Ford on Peace Ship, W.W.I; songwriter since then, several songs with George Gershwin, songwriter for stage, screen and radio, including Swanee, Tea for Two, Sometimes I'm Happy, I Want to Be Happy, Lady Play Your Mandolin, Songs of Safety, Songs of Friendship, Songs of Health and Pledge of Allegiance to the Flag.

CAESAR, SID: Performer. b. Yonkers, NY, Sept. 8, 1922. Musician. Joined Coast Guard in 1942. Appeared in Tars and Spars. Signed for Broadway Revue by Max Liebman, 1949. Star of Your Show of Shows on NBC-TV 1950–54; star of Caesar's Hour, 1954–1957; voted best comedian (tied) in M.P. Daily's TV poll, 1951. Best Comedian, Best Comedy Team (with Imogene Coca), 1953; 5 Emmy Awards 1957; Sylvania Award, 1958. Sid Caesar Invites You, 1958; Formed Shelbrick Corp., TV, 1959; TV series As Caesar Sees It, 1962; Bway Play: Little Me, 1962–64; The Sid Caesar Show, 1963–64. Author: Where Have I Been? (autobiography, 1982).
PICTURES INCLUDE: It's a Mad, Mad, Mad, Mad World, The Spirit is Willing, The Busy Body, Guide for the Married Man, Ten from Your Show of Shows, Airport 1975, Silent Movie, Fire Sale, Grease, The Cheap Detective, Grease II, History of the World—Part I, Over the Brooklyn Bridge, Cannonball Run III, The Emperor's New Clothes.
TELEVISION: Movies: Found Money, Love Is Never Silent, Alice in Wonderland, Freedom Fighter, Side By Side.

CAGE, NICOLAS: Actor. b. Long Beach, CA, Jan. 7, 1964. r.n. Nicholas Coppola. Nephew of Francis Ford Coppola. First starring role in Valley Girl (1983).
PICTURES: Rumble Fish, Racing with the Moon, The Cotton Club, Birdy, The Boy in Blue, Raising Arizona, Peggy Sue Got Married, Moonstruck, Vampire's Kiss.

CAHN, SAMMY: Lyricist, Producer. b. New York, NY, June 18, 1913. e. Seward Park H.S. Org. dance band with Saul Chaplin; collab. song writer for shows. m.p. 30 Acad. Award Nominations, Four Oscars for Three Coins in Fountain, All the Way, High Hopes, and Call Me Irresponsible! Only TV Emmy ever given a song, Love & Marriage from the TV award winning Our Town. 1972, inducted into Songwriters' Hall of Fame.
PLAYS INCLUDE: High Button Shoes, Skyscraper, Walking Happy many songs.

PICTURES INCLUDE: Anchors Aweigh, Three Coins in Fountain, Romance on High Seas, Some Came Running, Robin & Seven Hoods, The Tender Trap, Pocketful of Miracles, Thoroughly Modern Millie.

CAIN, SUGAR: Actress. r.n. Constance McCain. b. Jerome, AZ, March 13. e. U. of Washington, B.A., radio-drama; Colorado Woman's Coll., A.A., journalism; Columbia U., grad TV. MP. Reg. on radio serials. Hopalong Cassidy, Clyde Beatty Show, Night club act, Mexico; appeared TV, Hollywood & N.Y. Plays include: nat. tours, Pajama Tops, In One Bed, Idiots Delight, Streetcar Named Desire, The Rainmaker, Dead End, Druid Circle.
PICTURES INCLUDE: Breakstone Affair, Life with Edmer, I've Been Here Before, Monster from 20,000 Fathoms, Dalton Women, I Shot Billy the Kid, Hostile Country, Dalton Gang, Africa Screams; Sporting Club, Apple Man, Klute, Panic in Needle Park, The French Connection, Effect of Gamma Rays, Summer Wishes, Winter Dreams; Dir.-writer, m.p. short, Rama.

CAINE, MICHAEL: Actor. b. London, England, March 14, 1933. Asst. stage mgr. Westminster Rep. (Sussex, UK 1953); Lowestoft Rep. 1953–55. TV: 1957–63. Theater: Next Time I'll Sing For You (1963).
TELEVISION: The Compartment, The Playmates, Hobson's Choice, Funny Noises with Their Mouths, The Way with Reggie, Luck of the Draw, Hamlet, The Other Man, Jack the Ripper.
PICTURES INCLUDE: A Hill in Korea, How to Murder A Rich Uncle, Zulu, Ipcress File, Alfie, The Wrong Box, Gambit, Funeral in Berlin, Hurry Sundown, Billion Dollar Brain, Deadfall, The Magus, Play Dirty, Italian Job, The Battle of Britain, Too Late the Hero, Get Carter, Kidnapped, Zee and Company, Pulp, Sleuth, The Black Windmill, The Destructors, The Wilby Conspiracy, Peepers, The Romantic Englishwoman, The Man Who Would Be King, Harry and Walter Go to New York, The Eagle Has Landed, A Bridge Too Far, The Silver Bears, The Swarm, Ashanti, California Suite, Beyond the Poseidon Adventure, The Island, Dressed to Kill, The Hand, Victory, Deathtrap, The Jigsaw Man, Educating Rita, Beyond the Limit, Blame It on Rio, Water. The Holcroft Covenant, Hannah and Her Sisters, Sweet Liberty, Half Moon Street, Mona Lisa, The Whistle Blower, Surrender, The Fourth Protocol, Jaws—The Revenge, Without a Clue, Dirty Rotten Scoundrels.

CALHOUN, RORY: Actor. r.n. Francis Timothy Durgin. b. Los Angeles, CA, Aug. 8, 1923. e. Santa Cruz H.S. Worked as logger, miner, cowpuncher, for firefighter; m.p. debut in Something for the Boys, 1944.
PICTURES INCLUDE: Sunday Dinner for a Soldier, Nob Hill, Great John L, Red House, Adventure Island, That Hagen Girl, Sand, Massacre River, Ticket to Tomahawk, County Fair, I'd Climb the Highest Mountain, Rogue River, Meet Me After the Show, With a Song in My Heart, Way of a Gaucho, The Silver Whip, Powder River, How to Marry a Millionaire, River of No Return, Yellow Tomahawk, Bullet Is Waiting, Dawn at Socorro, Four Guns to the Border, The Looters, Ain't Misbehavin', Shotgun, Domino and Actor; actor, Treasure of Pancho Villa, The Spoilers, Red Sundown, Raw Edge, Flight to Hongkong, Utah Blaine, Big Caper, Adventures of Marco Polo, Colossus of Rhodes, Gun Hawk, Young and the Brave, Face in the Rain, Call Me Bwana, Black Spur, Lady of the Nile, Night of the Lepus, Won Ton Ton, Father Keno Story, Revenge of Bigfoot, Motel Hell, Angel, Rollerblade Warriors, Hell Comes to Frogtown.
TELEVISION: The Road Ahead, Day Is Done, Bet the Wild Queen, Zane Grey Theater, The Texan, U.S. Camera (series 1957–60); Killer Instinct, Lands End, The Blue and the Gray, Capitol.

CALLAN, MICHAEL: Actor, singer, dancer. b. Philadelphia, PA, 1935. Singer, dancer, Philadelphia night clubs; to New York in musicals, including The Boy Friend and West Side Story; dancer Copacabana; in short-run plays, Las Vegas: 5 month run starred in That Certain Girl. Guest starred on major dramatic TV shows and Occasional Wife (series, star).
PICTURES INCLUDE: debut, They Came to Cordura, The Flying Fontaines, Because They're Young, Pepe, Mysterious Island, Gidget Goes Hawaiian, 13 West Street, Bon Voyage, The Interns, The Victors, The "New" Interns, Cat Ballou, Frasier, The Sensuous Lion, Lepke, The Photographer, The Cat and The Canary (1977), Record City, The Donner Party, Freeway.
TELEVISION: Blind Ambition, Scruples.

CALLEY, JOHN: executive. b. New Jersey, 1930. Dir. of night time programming, dir. programming sales, NBC, 1951–57; prod. exec. and TV prod. Henry Jaffe Enterprises, 1957; v.p. in charge of Radio and Television, Ted Bates Advertising Agency, 1958; joined Filmways, Inc., 1960; exec. v.p. and prod. to 1969; exec. v.p. chg. world-wide prod. Warner Bros.; Pres., W.B. from Jan. 6, 1975; vice chm. bd., 1977. Now consultant.
PICTURES INCLUDE: Wheeler Dealer, The Americaniza-

tion of Emily, Topkapi, The Cincinnati Kid, Loved One, Don't Make Waves, Ice Station Zebra, Catch-22.

CALLOW, EVERETT C.: Publicist. b. Perth Amboy, NJ. e. St. John's Coll. On ed. staff N.Y. World; service staff chief Paramount Theas., N.Y., 1926; mgr. Keith & Albee Theas., Phila., 1928; mgr. Stanley Theatre, Phila., 1929–31; dist. theatre mgr. various dists. in NJ, PA & DE; apptd. dir. of adv. & publicity Warner Bros., Phila. zone, 1938; winner Quigley Silver Award, 1940; Lt. Col. U.S.M.C., 1943; returned to Warner post after war; 1950–51, internat'l dir. adv., pub., Cinerama, Feb., 1954. Member: American Legion Variety Post 713 (past commdr.); Military Order of Foreign Wars of U.S.; Adv. pub. dir., National Screen Service, 1965; VP in charge of adv. and pub. sales. TV, Foreign; pres. United Screen Arts, Inc. 1966; worldwide dist. and adv. and production. Presently consultant.

CALLOW, SIMON: Actor, Writer. b. London, June 13, 1949. e. Queens, U. of Belfast, The Drama Centre. Originated role of Mozart in London premiere of Amadeus. Author: Being an Actor; Charles Laughton: A Difficult Actor.
THEATER: London: Plumber's Progress; The Doctor's Dilemma; Soul of the White Ant; Blood Sports, The Resistible Rise of Arturo Ui; Amadeus (and Bdwy); Restoration; The Beastly Beatitudes of Balthazar B, Titus Andronicus (Bristol Old Vic), Faust.
PICTURES INCLUDE: Amadeus; A Room With a View; The Good Father; Maurice; Manifesto; For a Night of Love.
TELEVISION: Man of Destiny; La Ronde; All the World's a Stage; Wings of Song; The Dybbuk; Instant Enlightenment; Chance of a Lifetime (series), David Copperfield, Honour, Profit and Pleasure.

CALVET, CORINNE: Actress. r.n. Corinne Dibos. b. Paris, France, April 30, 1925. e. U. of Paris School of Fine Arts; Comedie Francaise. French stage and radio. Screen debut in France; La Part de L'Ombre, Nous Ne Sommes Pas Maries, Petrus. American screen debut: Rope of Sand.
PICTURES INCLUDE: When Willie Comes Marching Home, My Friend Irma Goes West, Quebec, On the Riviera, Peking Express, Thunder in the East, Sailor Beware, What Price Glory?, Powder River, Flight to Tangier, The Far Country, So This Is Paris, Mail Order Bride, Apache Uprising, Bluebeard's Ten Honeymoons, Adventures of a Young Man, Pound, Side Roads.

CAMERON, JAMES: Director, Writer. b. Kapuskasing, Ontario, Aug. 16, 1954. e. CA State U. (physics). Supported himself as truck driver while writing screen plays. First film work was with Roger Corman's New World Pictures as miniature set builder, process projection supervisor and art dir. on Battle of the Stars.
PICTURES: Pirhana II—The Spawning (dir., co-s.p.); The Terminator (dir.), Rambo: First Blood part II (co-s.p.); Aliens (dir.), Outer Heat (s.p.), The Abyss (dir., s.p.).

CAMERON, JOANNA: Actress, director. r.n. Patricia Cameron. b. Aspen, CO, Sept. 20. e. U. of California, Sorbonne, Pasadena Playhouse, 1968. Guinness Record: Most network programmed TV commercials. Prod., dir., documentary, Razor Sharp, 1981. Prod., dir.: El Camino Real (doc. 1987).
PICTURES INCLUDE: How To Commit Marriage (debut), P.S., I Love You, Pretty Maids All in a Row.
TELEVISION: Features: The All-American Beauty Contest, It Couldn't Happen to a Nicer Guy, High Risk. Other: The Survivors, Love American Style, Daniel Boone, Mission Impossible, The Partners, Search, Medical Center, Isis, Name of the Game, The Bold Ones, Marcus Welby, Petrocelli, Columbo, Switch, Bob Hope Special, Bob Hope 25th NBC Anniversary Special, Westwind, MacMillian, Spiderman, Swan Song, Johnny Carson, numerous commercials. Director: Various commercials, CBS Preview Special, closed circuit program host U.S.N., all TV equipped ships—actress and director, Razor Sharp (prod., div.), 1982.

CAMERON, KIRK: Actor. b. Canoga Park, CA, 1971. Started doing TV commercials at age 9. Appeared in TV movies, series episodes, and Two Marriages (short-lived series). Now in ABC series, Growing Pains.
PICTURES: Like Father, Like Son, Mismatch.
TELEVISION: Movie: Goliath Awaits.

CAMP, COLLEEN: Actress. b. San Francisco, 1953. Performing since age of three. Spent 2 years as a bird trainer before being noticed by an agent and cast on TV. TV debut on The Dean Martin Show; feature film debut, Battle for the Planet of the Apes (1973). Assoc. prod. on Martha Coolidge's film The City Girl.
PICTURES: Smile, Funny Lady, Apocalypse Now, They All Laughed, The Seduction, Smokey and the Bandit III, Valley Girl, The Joy of Sex, Police Academy II, D.A.R.Y.L., Clue, Doin' Time, Illegally Yours, Track 29, Walk Like a Man, Strike It Rich, Wicked Stepmother.
TELEVISION: Magnum P.I., Dukes of Hazzard, WKRP in Cincinnati, Dallas, Addicted to His Love.

CAMP, JOE: Producer-Director-Writer. b. St. Louis, MO, Apr. 20, 1939. e. U. of Mississippi, B.B.A. Acct. exec. McCan-Erickson Advt., Houston 1961–62; owner Joe Camp Real Estate 1962–64; acct. exec. Norsworthy-Mercer, Dallas 1964–69; dir. TV commercials; founder and pres. Mulberry Square Prods.
PICTURES: Benji, Hawmps, For the Love of Benji, The Double McGuffin, Oh Heavenly Dog, Benji the Hunted.
TELEVISION: The Phenomenon of Benji, Benji's Very Own Christmas Story, Benji at Work, Benji at Marineland.

CAMPAGNOLA, GINO: Executive. Joined Paramount Pictures in 1975; held various sales positions, including v.p., sls. admin. In 1980 named v.p., asst. gen. sls. mgr.; now sr. v.p.

CAMPANELLA, TOM: Executive. Joined Paramount Pictures 1968 as asst. business mgr.; later worked for corporate div. and Motion Picture Group. Named exec. dir., nat'l adv. 1979, made v.p., nat'l adv. 1982, appt. sr. v.p., adv., for M.P. Group. of Paramount, 1984.

CAMPBELL, GLEN: Actor, singer. b. Delight, AK, April 22, 1936. After forming local band became guitarist in Hollywood; records won two Grammy awards, 1967.
PICTURES INCLUDE: True Grit, Norwood.
TELEVISION: The Smothers Brothers Comedy Hour, The Glen Campbell Goodtime Hour, many specials.

CAMPBELL, MAE E.: Actress. b. St. Louis, MO, March 19. Studied with the Actors Studio and Lee Strasberg.
PICTURES INCLUDE: The Old Boyfriends; two industrial films for the Veterans Administration Hospital.

CAMPBELL, ROBERT MAURICE: Producer, Director. b. Detroit, MI, Feb. 16, 1922. e. Michigan Conservatory of Music, Detroit Inst. of Musical Arts, American Theatre Wing. Featured player. assoc. dir., Detroit stage prod.; numerous radio appearances; pub. relations, U.S. Coast Guard, W.W.II; since 1946 dir., off-Broadway show; dir.-prod., Springer Pictures, Inc.; TV show: All-Star News; exec., Visual Transcriptions, Inc.; prod. Jazz Dance (Robert J. Flaherty Award, Edinburgh Film Festival Merit Award); co-author, prod. designer, See No Evil.

CAMPBELL, WILLIAM: Actor. b. Newark, NJ. e. Feagin Sch. of Drama. Appeared in summer stock. Broadway plays; m.p. debut in The Breaking Point (1950).
PICTURES: People Against O'Hara, Holiday for Sinners, Battle Circus, Code Two, Big Leaguer, Escape from Fort Bravo, High and the Mighty, Man Without a Star, Cell 2455 Death Row, Battle Cry, Running Wild, Backlash, Pretty Maids All in a Row, Black Gunn.

CANALE, GIANNA MARIA: Actress. b. Reggio Calabria, Italy, Sept. 12. e. Florence. Debut in Mysterious Knight.
PICTURES INCLUDE: Kiss of a Dead Woman, Count Orgolino, Son of D'Artagnan, Go for Broke, Adventure in Algiers, Eternal Chain, Theodora Slave Empress, Madame DuBarry, The Whole Truth.

CANBY, VINCENT: Journalist, Critic. b. Chicago, IL, July 27, 1924. e. Dartmouth Coll. Navy officer during W.W.II. Worked on newspapers in Paris and Chicago. Joined Quigley Publications in 1951 in editorial posts on Motion Picture Herald. Reporter for Weekly Variety 1959–1965. Joined New York Times film news staff, 1965; named film critic, 1969. Author: Living Quarters (1975); End of the War (play, 1978); Unnatural Scenery (1979); After All (play, 1981); The Old Flag (1984).

CANDY, JOHN: Actor, writer. b. Toronto, Ont., Oct. 31, 1950. Began acting in 11th grade and continued while studying journalism at Centennial Community College, Toronto. First professional job as member of children's theatre group; performed in satirical review, Creeps. Had roles in several low-budget Canadian films before joining in 1972 Chicago's Second City Theatre for two years. Returned to Toronto to join Second City group there, which evolved into SCTV television series. Contributed as both performer and writer, earning two Emmy Awards (writing) when show picked up by NBC.
PICTURES: The Class of '44, Tunnelvision, The Clown Murders, Faceoff, 1941, Lost and Found, The Blues Brothers, Heavy Metal, Stripes, National Lampoon's Vacation, Strange Brew, Going Berserk, Splash, Brewster's Millions, Volunteers, Summer Rental, Armed and Dangerous, Three Amigos, The Little Shop of Horrors; Spaceballs; Planes, Trains & Automobiles, The Great Outdoors, Hot to Trot, Who's Harry Crum? (also exec. prod.).
TELEVISION: Movies: Drums Over Malta (also s.p.); Comic Relief.

CANFIELD, ALYCE: Writer. b. Los Angeles, CA. e. U. of California. Magazine writer; author Mervyn LeRoy book It Takes More Than Talent; in collab. with Howard Duff original story for Models, Inc.; story Journey Into Fire, Assignment for Murder; s.p. for latter in collab. with Jerry Jerome; creator, exec. prod. Ziv TV series, Underground, USA.

CANNELL, STEPHEN J.: Writer, Producer. b. Los Angeles, CA, Feb. 5, 1942. Heads own TV prod. co.
TELEVISION: The Rockford Files, The Jordan Chance, The Duke, Stone, 10 Speed and Brownshoe, Nightside, Midnight Offerings, The Greatest American Hero, The Quest, The A-Team, Hardcastle and McCormick, The Rousters, Riptide, Brothers-in-Law, Baa, Baa Black Sheep, Hunter, Wise Guy, Sonny Spoon, Sirens (co-exec. prod.).

CANNON, DYAN: Actress. r.n. Samille Diane Friesen. b. Tacoma, WA, Jan. 4, 1937. e. U. of Washington. Studied with Sanford Meisner. Modelled.
TELEVISION: Playhouse 90, Movies: Diane's Adventure, The Virginia Hill Story, Lady of the House, Master of the Game, Arthur the King, Jenny's War, Rock 'n' Roll Mom.
BROADWAY: The Fun Couple, Ninety-Day Mistress.
ROAD TOUR: How to Succeed in Business Without Really Trying.
PICTURES INCLUDE: Bob and Carol and Ted and Alice (Academy Award nomination), Doctors' Wives, The Anderson Tapes; The Love Machine; The Burglars, Such Good Friends, Shamus, The Last of Sheila, Child Under a Leaf, Heaven Can Wait, Revenge of the Pink Panther, Coast To Coast, Honeysuckle Rose, Deathtrap, Caddyshack II.

CANNON, JUDY: Actress. b. Santa Fe, NM, June 16, 1938. e. Santa Monica City Coll., 1957. Teenage Adrian model, 1954–56; toured as band singer, Orlo Wagner Orchestra, 1957; appeared in: The Little Hut, Girls of Summer, Made in Japan, Los Angeles Little Theatre, 1959–61; midwest musical comedy tour group, 1962; m.p. debut, Lullaby, 1963; Critics Choice, '63; A Comedy Tale of Fanny Hill, 1964.
TELEVISION: Smothers Bros. Comedy Hour, Man From U.N.C.L.E., Chrysler Theatre, Run for Your Life, The Road West, My Three Sons, Death Valley Days.
PICTURES INCLUDE: More, (1970).

CANNON, WILLIAM: Writer, Producer, Director. b. Toledo, OH, Feb. 11, 1937. e. Columbia Coll., B.A., 1959, M.B.A., 1962. Dir. Off-Broadway, Death of a Salesman, Pirates of Penzance, 1960. Wrote, prod., dir., Square Root of Zero, Locarno and San Francisco Film Festivals, 1963–65; Distrib., Doran Enterprises, Ltd.; author, Skidoo, (Par-Otto Preminger), 1968, Author, Novel, The Veteran (E.P. Dutton) 1974; Publisher, Highlife and Movie Digest, 1978; The Good Guys, 1987. Co-inventor: Cardz (TM), 1988.

CANOVA, DIANA: Actress. b. West Palm Beach, FL, June 1, 1952. Daughter of actress Judy Canova and musician Filberto Rivero. NY Theater: They're Playing Our Song (1981). People's Choice award, favorite female performer, 1981.
PICTURE: The First Nudie Musical.
TELEVISION: Ozzie's Girls (debut); Happy Days; Love Boat; Fantasy Island; Hotel; Chico and the Man; Barney Miller; Soap (series); I'm a Big Girl Now (series); Throb (series). Movies: Peking Encounter; Night Partners; With This Ring; Death of Ocean View Park.

CANTON, ARTHUR H.: Motion Picture Producer. b. New York, NY. e. New York U., Columbia U. Capt. USAF. Pres., Canton-Weiner Films, indep. foreign films importers, 1947; Van Gogh (Acad. Award, short, 1949); MGM Pictures, eastern div. publicity manager, executive liaison, advertising-publicity, Independent Productions; public relations executive, v.p.; pres., Blowitz, Thomas & Canton Inc., 1964; pres., Arthur H. Canton Co. Inc.; prod. exec., Warner Bros., 1968–70; advertising-publicity v.p., Columbia Pictures, 1971; executive v.p. of advertising and publicity, Billy Jack Productions, 1974–76. Co-founder of Blowitz & Canton Co. Inc., 1976, chairman of the board. Now pres. of Arthur H. Canton Co. Member Academy of Motion Picture Arts and Sciences, Film Information Council.

CANTON, MARK: Executive. b. New York, NY, June 19, 1949. e. U. of California at L.A., 1978. v.p., m.p. devlp., MGM; 1979, exec. v.p., JP Organization; 1980, v.p., Warner Bros.; named sr. v.p., 1983 and pres. w-w theatrical prod. div., 1985.

CAPRA, FRANK: Producer, Director. b. Palermo, Italy, May 18, 1897. e. Manual Arts H.S., California. Inst. of Technology, B.Sc., 1918. dir., The Strong Man, Long Pants, Platinum Blonde, American Madness, Bitter Tea of General Yen, Lady for a Day, Broadway Bill, It Happened One Night, 1934; Mr. Deeds Goes to Town, You Can't Take It With You, Lost Horizon, Mr. Smith Goes to Washington, Meet John Doe, Arsenic and Old Lace, It's a Wonderful Life, State of the Union, Riding High, Here Comes the Groom, A Hole in the Head, Pocketful of Miracles; prod., dir., Why We Fight Series, U.S. Army; pres. Academy of Motion Picture Arts and Sciences, 1935–39; pres., Directors Guild of America, 1938–40, 1959. 1964 Prod. & Dir. Rendezvous in Space. 1952–56, produced and directed four educational science films: Our Mr. Sun, Hemo The Magnificent, Strange Case of Cosmic Rays and Unchained Goddess.

51

CAPRA, FRANK, JR: Executive. Son of famed director Frank Capra. Served in various creative capacities on TV series (Zane Grey Theatre, Gunsmoke, The Rifleman, etc.). Associate producer on theatrical films (Planet of the Apes, Play It Again Sam, Marooned, etc.). Joined Avco Embassy Pictures in March, 1981, as v.p., worldwide production. In July, 1981, became pres. of A-E. Resigned May, 1982 to become indep. producer. Now with Pinehurst Industry Studios, NC.
PICTURES INCLUDE: Producer: Born Again, The Black Marble, An Eye for an Eye, Vice Squad, Firestarter, Marie. Exec. prod.: Death Before Dishonor.

CAPSHAW, KATE: Actress. b. Ft. Worth, TX, 1953; e. U. of Missouri. Taught school before moving to New York to try acting. Success came on TV before theatrical debut in A Little Sex, 1981.
PICTURES INCLUDE: Indiana Jones and the Temple of Doom, Best Defense, Dreamscape, Windy City, Power, SpaceCamp.
TELEVISION: The Quick and the Dead, The Edge of Night, Missing Children: A Mother's Story, Her Secret Life, Internal Affairs.

CAPUCINE: Actress. r.n. Germaine Lefebvre. b. Toulon, France, January 6, 1935. e. attended schools at Saumur, France, B.A. Photographer's model, Paris. Came to N.Y. to model. Signed contract, Famous Artists.
PICTURES INCLUDE: debut, Song Without End, North To Alaska, Walk On the Wild Side, The Lion, The 7th Dawn, What's New Pussycat?, The Honey Pot, Fraulein Doktor, Fellini's Satyricon, Red Sun, Arabian Adventure, Trail of the Pink Panther, Story of a Woman.
TELEVISION: Sins.

CAPUTO, GEORGE: Executive. b. Genoa, Italy, Oct. 24, 1916. e. Lycée de Nice, France, 1930; Sorbonne, Paris, 1934. Partner, gen. mgr., Caputo & Co., Colombia, S.A.; pres. Master Films Dist., Inc., 1950; pres. Fiesta Tele-Cinema, S.A.; pres. International Sound Studios Inc.; pres., Fall River Investments S.A.; acquired Latin America and South America rights in perpetuity to full RKO package feature films library, 1961.

CARA, IRENE: Singer, Actress. b. New York, NY, March 18, 1959. Off-Broadway shows include The Me Nobody Knows, Lotta, etc. On Broadway in Maggie Flynn, Ain't Misbehavin', Via Galactica, etc.
PICTURES INCLUDE: Aaron Loves Angela, Sparkle, Fame, D.C. Cab, City Heat, Certain Fury, Killing 'em Softly, Paradiso.
TELEVISION: Roots—The Next Generation, Guyana Tragedy, For Us the Living, Tribute to Martin Luther King, Jr., etc.

CARDIFF, JACK: Director-Cinematographer. b. Yarmouth, Eng., Sept. 18, 1914. Early career as child actor, later cinematographer on Stairway to Heaven, Black Narcissus, Red Shoes, Scott of the Antarctic, Black Rose, Under Capricorn, Pandora and the Flying Dutchman, African Queen, Magic Box, The Brave One, War and Peace, The Vikings, Avalanche Express, The Fifth Musketeer, A Man, a Woman and a Bank; The Awakening; started as dir. 1958.
PICTURES: as director: Intent to Kill, Beyond This Place, Scent of Mystery, Sons and Lovers, Fanny, My Geisha, The Lion, The Long Ships, Young Cassidy, The Liquidator, Dark of the Sun, The Girl on the Motorcycle, Penny Gold, The Mutations, Ride A Wild Pony, The Prince and The Pauper, Behind the Iron Mask, Death on the Nile, The Dogs of War and Ghost Story (Cinematographer), The Wicked Lady, Scandalous, Cat's Eye, Conan the Destroyer, Blue Velvet, Tai-Pan, Million Dollar Mystery.
TELEVISION: As cinematographer: The Far Pavillions, The Last Days of Pompeii.

CARDINALE, CLAUDIA: Actress. b. Italy, Apr. 15, 1939.
PICTURES INCLUDE: Persons Unknown, 1958; Upstairs and Downstairs, Il Bell' Antonio, Rocco and His Brothers, Cartouche, The Leopard, Eight and a Half, The Pink Panther, Circus World, Of A Thousand Delights, Blindfold, Last Command, The Professionals, Don't Make Waves, The Queens, The Red Tent, Conversation Piece, Escape to Athena, Immortal Bachelor, History, Torrents of Spring.
TELEVISION: Princess Daisy, Jesus of Nazareth.

CAREY, HARRY JR.: Actor. b. Saugus, CA, May 16, 1921. e. Newhall, CA, public school, Black Fox Military Acad., Hollywood. m. Marilyn Fix. Summer stock, Skowhegan, ME., with father; page boy, NBC, New York; U.S. Navy 1941–46; Screen debut: Pursued, then Red River, Moonrise.
PICTURES INCLUDE: Three Godfathers, She Wore a Yellow Ribbon, Wagonmaster, Rio Grande, Copper Canyon, Warpath, Wild Blue Yonder, Monkey Business, San Antone, Island in the Sky, Gentlemen Prefer Blondes, Beneath the 12-Mile Reef, Silver Lode, The Outcast, Long Gray Line, Mister Roberts, House of Bamboo, Great Locomotive Chase, The Undefeated Big Jake, Something Big, One More Train To Rob, The Long Riders, Endangered Species, Mask, The Whales of August, Cherry 2000.
TELEVISION: Black Beauty, The Shadow Riders, Wild Times, Once Upon a Texas Train.

CAREY, MACDONALD: Actor. b. Sioux City, IA, March 15, 1913. e. Phillips Exeter Acad., U. of Wisconsin, U. of Iowa. On stage (stock); in radio serials. On Broadway in Anniversary Waltz; m.p. debut in 1942.
PICTURES INCLUDE: Dr. Broadway, Take a Letter Darling, Wake Island, Suddenly It's Spring, Variety Girl, Dream Girl, Hazzard, Streets of Laredo, Song of Surrender, South Sea Sinner, Copper Canyon, Great Missouri Raid, Mystery Submarine, Excuse My Dust, Meet Me After the Show, Let's Make It Legal, Cave of the Outlaws, My Wife's Best Friend, Count the Hours, Outlaw Territory, Fire Over Africa, Stranger At My Door, Tammy and the Doctor, Broken Sabre, End of the World, American Gigolo, It's Alive III.
TELEVISION: Days of our Lives (since 1965), Roots, Miracle on 34th Street, The Rebels.

CAREY, PHIL: Actor. b. Hackensack, NJ, July 15, 1925. e. Mohawk U., U. of Miami. U.S. Marines; New England stock; m.p. debut in Operation Pacific.
PICTURES INCLUDE: Inside the Walls of Folsom Prison, This Woman Is Dangerous, Springfield Rifle, Calamity Jane, Gun Fury, The Nebraskan, Massacre Canyon, Outlaw Stallion, They Rode West, Pushover, The Long Gray Line, Wyoming Renegades, Mister Roberts, Count Three and Pray, Three Stripes in the Sun, The Time Traveler, Once You Kiss a Stranger, Three Guns for Texas, The Seven Minutes. TV: Laredo.

CARISCH, GEORGE: Exhibitor. b. Minneapolis, MN, Dec. 12, 1935. e. Hamline U., B.S.; U. of Minnesota, B.E.E. Chm., Carisch Theatres, Inc.

CARLIDGE, WILLIAM: Executive. b. Fenton, England, May 2, 1910. e. Grafton Boys' Sch. Entered m.p. ind. in 1930 as mgr. Ilford Hippodrome; circuit mgr. Union Cinemas, 1935; supervisor for Northern Ireland. Associated British Cinemas Ltd., 1947; first regional controller for Northern Region, personal asst. to man. dir. 1949; gen. man. Associated British Cinemas Ltd. 1951; dir. 1955; asst. man. dir. 1959; Board of Associated British Corp., 1964, now known as EMI Film and Theatre Corp.

CARLINO, LEWIS JOHN: Writer. b. New York, NY, Jan. 1, 1932. e. U. of Southern California. Early interest in theatre, specializing in writing 1-act plays. Winner of Obie award (off-Broadway play). Won Rockefeller Grant for Theatre, the Int'l. Playwriting Competition from British Drama League, Huntington Hartford Fellowship.
PICTURES INCLUDE: Seconds, The Brotherhood, The Fox (co-s.p.), The Mechanic, The Sailor Who Fell From The Sea, (s.p., dir.), I Never Promised You a Rose Garden (co. s.p.), The Great Santini (s.p., dir.), Resurrection (s.p.), Class (dir.), Haunted Summer (s.p.).
PLAYS: Cages, Telemachus Clay, The Exercise, Double Talk, Objective Case, Used Car for Sale, Junk Yard.
TELEVISION: Honor Thy Father, In Search of America, Where Have All the People Gone?

CARLISLE, ROBERT: Producer. b. Los Angeles, CA, Sept. 19, 1906. Cutter, Metro; Universal; John Stahl; Columbia; film ed. in chf. Columbia; prod. short subjects with Jerry Fairbanks including: Popular Science, Unusual Occupations, Speaking of Animals (two Academy of M.P. Arts & Sciences awards); prod. industrials for Dupont, Union Pacific RR; trophy at Italy's Cortina Sports Film Festival for ski film, 1957; prod. and dir. films on world affairs for Dept. of Defense; prod. Wondsel, Carlisle & Dunphy, Inc., 1963.

CARLTON, RICHARD: Executive. b. New York, NY, Feb. 9, 1919. e. Columbia U., Pace Inst. Columbia Pictures 1935–41; U.S. Army 1941–45; National Screen Serv. 1945–51; Sterling Television 1951–54; U.M. & M. TV Corp. 1955; v.p. in charge of sales, Trans-Lux Television Corp., 1956; exec. vice-pres., Television Affiliates Corp., 1961; exec. v.p. Trans-Lux Television Corp.; v.p. Entertainment Div. Trans-Lux Corp., 1966. Pres., Schnur Appel, TV, Inc. 1970; Deputy Director, American Film Institute, 1973. Pres., Carlton Communications Corporation, 1982; exec. dir., International Council, National Academy of Television Arts and Sciences, 1983.

CARMEN, JEAN: See Jean Carmen Dillow.

CARMICHAEL, IAN: Actor. b. Hull, England, June 18, 1920. e. Scarborough Coll., Bromsgrove Sch. Stage debut: R.U.R. 1939. Film debut: Bond Street, one of the top ten British money making stars M.P.H.—Fame Poll 1957, 1958.
TELEVISION: New Faces, Twice Upon a Time, Passing Show, Tell Her The Truth, Lady Luck, Give My Regards to Leicester Square, Jill Darling, Don't Look Now, Regency Room, Globe Revue, Off the Record, Here and Now, The Girl at the Next Table, Gilt and Gingerbread, The Importance of Being Earnest, Simon and Laura, 90 Years On, The World of Wooster, The Last of the Big Spenders, The Coward Revue, Odd Man In, Bachelor Father, Lord Peter Wimsey, Alma Mater, Comedy Tonight, Song by Song, Country Calendar, Down at the Hydro.
PICTURES INCLUDE: Trottie True, Mr. Prohack, Time

Gentlemen Please, Meet Mr. Lucifer, Betrayed, Colditz Story, Storm Over the Nile, Simon and Laura, Private's Progress, Brothers in Law, Lucky Jim, Happy Is the Bride, The Big Money, Right, Left and Center, I'm Alright Jack, School for Scoundrels, Light Up the Sky, Double Bunk, The Amorous Prawn, Hide and Seek, Heavens Above, Smashing Time, The Magnificent Seven, Deadly Sins, From Beyond the Grave, The Lady Vanishes.

CARNEY, ART: Performer. b. Mt. Vernon, NY, Nov. 4, 1918. Many radio shows. U.S. Army, 1944–45; performer, Jackie Gleason's Honeymooners.
TELEVISION: Studio One, Kraft, Omnibus, Chevy Show, Playhouse 90, Dupont Show of the Month—Harvey, Sid Caesar Show, Alfred Hitchcock Presents—Safety for the Witness, Art Carney Meets Peter and the Wolf, Playhouse 90—Fabulous Irishman, Charley's Aunt, Velvet Alley, Art Carney Meets the Sorcerer's Apprentice, The Sid Caesar-Art Carney Show, Our Town, Very Important People, Man in the Dog Suit, Call Me Back, Batman, Carol Burnett Show, Jonathan Winters Show, The Cavanaughs. Movies: The Night They Saved Christmas, A Doctor's Story, Terrible Joe Moran, Izzy and Moe, Faerie Tale Theater (The Emperor's New Clothes), Blue Yonder.
PICTURES INCLUDE: Harry and Tonto, W. W. and the Dixie Dancekings, Won Ton Ton, The Late Show, Take This Job and Shove It, Better Late Than Never, Firestarter, The Naked Face, Sunburn, Going in Style, Defiance, Roadie, Night Friend.
STAGE: The Rope Dancers, Take Her She's Mine, (Broadway), The Odd Couple (Broadway), Lovers (Broadway), The Prisoner of Second Avenue (Broadway).

CARNEY, FRED: Producer, Director. b. Brooklyn, NY, June 10, 1914. e. Mt. Vernon H.S., 1932. Actor on Broadway & summer stock; prod. mgr. for radio show, Truth or Consequences; asst. to prod.-dir of Kraft TV Theatre, 3 yrs.; dir, Kraft, Pond's Show; creator-prod., Medical Horizons; dir., Lux Video Theatre; prod. commercials at Cunningham & Walsh. Assoc. Prod. Everybody's Talking for ABC-TV. Ass't. Exec. Dir., Hollywood Chpt., Nat'l Acad. TV; Assoc. prod. 40th Acad. Award show, ABC-TV Arts & Sciences; currently acting in feature films and TV.

CARON, LESLIE: Dancer, Actress. b. Paris, France, July 1, 1931. e. Convent of Assumption, Paris; Nat'l Conservatory of Dance, Paris. 1947–50; Ballet de Paris 1954; joined Ballet des Champs Elysees. In 1950, signed MGM lead film role in An American in Paris.
THEATER: Orvet, Ondine, 13 Rue de l'Amour The Rehearsal, Women's Games, On Your Toes, One For the Tango.
PICTURES: Man with a Cloak, Glory Alley, Story of Three Loves, Lili, Glass Slipper, Daddy Long Legs, Gaby, Gigi, The Doctor's Dilemma, The Man Who Understood Women, The Subterraneans, Fanny, Guns of Darkness, The L Shaped Room, Father Goose, Promise Her Anything, A Very Special Favor, Is Paris Burning, Head of the Family, The Beginners, Madron, Chandler, Purple Night, Valentino, The Man Who Loved Women, Golden Girl, Contract.
TELEVISION: Master of the Game, Love Boat, Tales of the Unexpected, Carola, QB VII, Falcon Crest (series), The Man Who Lived at the Ritz.

CARPENTER, CARLETON: Actor. b. Bennington, VT, July 10, 1926 e. Bennington H.S., Northwestern U. (summer scholarship). Began career with magic act, clubs, camps, hospitals, New Eng.; then toured with carnival; first N.Y. stage appearance in Bright Boy. Appeared night clubs; radio; as model magazines, TV debut, Campus HoopLa show. Screen debut Lost Boundaries (also wrote song for film, I Wouldn't Mind). Member: SAG, AFTRA, AEA, ASCAP, Dramatists.
NY STAGE: Career Angel, Three To Make Ready, The Magic Touch, The Big People, Out of Dust, John Murray Anderson's Almanac, Hotel Paradiso, Boys in the Band, Dylan, Hello Dolly!
PICTURES INCLUDE: Summer Stock, Father of the Bride, Three Little Words, Two Weeks With Love, Whistle at Eaton Falls, Fearless Fagan, Sky Full of Moon, Vengeance Valley, Take the High Ground, Some of My Best Friends Are. . ., The Prowler, Simon, Byline.

CARPENTER, JOHN: Director, Writer. b. Carthage, NY, Jan. 16, 1948. e. U. of Southern California. At U.S.C. became involved in film short, Resurrection of Bronco Billy, which won Oscar as best live-action short of 1970. Also at U.S.C. began directing what ultimately became Dark Star, science fiction film that launched his career.
PICTURES: Assault on Precinct 13, Halloween (also music), Eyes of Laura Mars (s.p. only), The Fog (also music), Escape from New York (also music); The Thing (dir.); Christine (dir., music); Starman (dir.); The Philadelphia Experiment (exec. prod.); Big Trouble in Little China (dir., music); Prince of Darkness (dir., music, and as Martin Quatermass, music), They Live (dir., music).
TELEVISION: Elvis, Someone is Watching Me (also s.p.), Zuma Beach (s.p.).

CARPENTER, ROBERT L.: Executive. b. Memphis, TN, March 20, 1927. Joined Universal Pictures in 1949 as booker in Memphis exchange; promoted to salesman there in 1952 and branch mgr. in 1958. In 1963 named Los Angeles branch manager. In Dec. 1971 moved to New York to become asst. to general sales mgr. Named gen. sls. mgr. on April 16, 1972, replacing Henry H. Martin when latter became pres. of Universal. Left in 1982 to become consultant and producer's rep. 1984, joined Cannon Releasing Corp. as east. div. mgr.

CARR, ALLAN: Producer, Personal Manager. b. Highland Park, IL, 1939. e. Lake Forest College, Northwestern U. First venture in show business as one of creators of Playboy Penthouse TV series in Chicago which subsequently inspired the Playboy Clubs for Hugh Hefner. Asst. to Nicholas Ray on King of Kings shot in Madrid. Became talent scout, launching Marlo Thomas in West Coast premiere of Sunday in New York. As personal manager guided careers of Ann-Margret, Peter Sellers, Tony Curtis, Marvin Hamlisch, Paul Anka, Herb Alpert and Melina Mercouri. Special marketing of The Deer Hunter, Tommy, The Natural.
PICTURES: Producer: The First Time, C.C. and Company, Grease (co-prod. and adapt.), Can't Stop the Music (co-prod. co. s.p.), Grease 2 (co-prod.), Where the Boys Are, Cloak and Dagger, Survive.

CARR, ARNOLD: Publicist. b. Chicago, IL, Aug. 9, 1931. e. U. of Missouri. Began public relations handling tour with Dimitri Mitropoulos, U.S. State Dept.; Columbia Broadcasting System; pub. dir., KABC-TV; Screen Gems; pub. rel. dir., Hanna-Barbera Prod.; formed own firm, 1962; partnered with Richard Carter 1964; resumed business under own name, Arnold Carr Public Relations.

CARR, JOHN: Ex. Producer, Director, Writer. b. West Virginia, Jan. 19, 1930. Now pres. of Pan-American Pictures Corp.
PICTURES: Sanitarium, Gretta (dir.); The Dark Side of Love, The Rebel's Mistresses, The Runaways, The Talisman (s.p.).

CARR, MARTIN: Producer, Director, Writer. b. New York, NY, Jan 20, 1932. e. Williams Coll. Worked for all three networks.
TELEVISION: PBS Smithsonian World (exec. prod.). For CBS produced, wrote and directed CBS Reports: Hunger in America, The Search for Ulysses, Gauguin in Tahiti, Five Faces of Tokyo, Dublin Through Different Eyes. For NBC produced, wrote and directed NBC White Paper: Migrant, NBC White Paper: This Child Is Rated X. Also directed drama, dance, music, opera specials and daytime serial for CBS-TV. ABC Close-Up. The Culture Thieves. PRS Global Paper: Waging Peace, ABC News 20/20; NBC, The Human Animal.
AWARDS: Winner of 5 Emmys; 3 Peabody awards; 2 Du-Pont Col. Journalism awards; Robert F. Kennedy award; Sidney Hillman award; Writers Guild Award.

CARR, THOMAS: Director. b. Philadelphia, PA, July 4, 1907. On screen at 2½ yrs. for Lubin Co., Phil.; starred in Little Britches at 5 yrs.; actor on stage, radio & screen until 1937; then became dialogue clerk, Republic Studios, advancing to script; asst. assoc. prod; assoc. prod. 1944; dir. 1945. Retired 1970.
PICTURES: Include many westerns, Bobby Ware is Missing, Superman (serial), Dino, Three For Jamie Dawn.
TELEVISION: Superman; Rawhide; Trackdown; Wanted, Dead or Alive; Richard Diamond; 4 Star Theatre; Bonanza; Wild Bill Hickock; Laramie; Honey West; Stagecoach West; Shenandoah; Daniel Boone.

CARRADINE, DAVID: Actor. b. Hollywood, CA, Dec. 8, 1936. e. San Francisco State U. f. John Carradine. Began career in local repertory; first TV on Armstrong Circle Theatre and East Side, West Side; later TV includes Shane series and Kung Fu; N.Y. stage in The Deputy, Royal Hunt of The Sun.
PICTURES INCLUDE: Taggart, Bus Riley's Back in Town, Too Many Thieves, The Violent Ones, Heaven With a Gun, Young Billy Young, The Good Guys and the Bad Guys, Gallery of Horrors, The McMasters, Macho Callahan, A Gunfight, McCabe & Mrs. Miller, Boxcar Bertha, Death Race 2000, Bound for Glory, The Serpent's Egg, Gray Lady Down, Deathsport, Circle of Iron, The Long Riders, Cloud Dancer, The Winged Serpent, Safari 3000, Lone Wolf McQuade, Americana, Kain of Dark Planet, P.O.W. The Escape, Armed Response, Wheels of Terror, Warlords, Crime Zone, Night Children; Wizard of the Lost Age 2.
TELEVISION: Movies: Jealousy, The Bad Seed, Kung Fu: The Movie, Six Against the Rock. Mini-series: North & South; Book II, I Saw What You Did.

CARRADINE, JOHN: Actor. b. New York, NY, Feb. 5, 1908. On stage in Shakespearean roles. A Funny Thing Happened on the Way to the Forum. On screen from 1936.
PICTURES INCLUDE: Fallen Angel, House of Dracula, Captain Kidd, Face of Marble, House of Frankenstein, It's in the Bag, Private Affairs of Bel Ami, C-Man, Cassanova's Big Night, Thunder Pass, Johnny Guitar, The Egyptian, Stranger

on Horseback, Hidden Guns, Court Jester, Desert Sands, The Kentuckian, Dark Venture, Black Sheep, The Good Guys and the Bad Guys, Boxcar Bertha, Everything You Always Wanted to Know About Sex*, The Shootist, The Last Tycoon, The Sentinel, Zorro, The Gay Blade, House of the Long Shadows, Evils of the Night, Monster in the Closet, Demented Death, Farm Massacres, Evil Spawn.

CARRADINE, KEITH: Actor. b. San Mateo, CA, Aug. 8, 1950. e. Colorado State U. Son of actor John Carrradine, brother of David. Got first break in rock opera Hair. Screen debut in A Gunfight, 1971. Composer: I'm Easy (Nashville, Academy Award Best Song, 1975). Theater: Foxfire, 1982.
PICTURES INCLUDE: McCabe and Mrs. Miller, Idaho Transfer, Emperor of the North, Thieves Like Us, Nashville, Lumiere, Welcome to L.A., The Duellists, Pretty Baby, Old Boyfriends, An Almost Perfect Affair, The Long Riders, Southern Comfort, Maria's Lovers, Choose Me, Trouble in Mind, Backfire, The Moderns, The Investigation, Street of No Return, Cold Feet.
TELEVISION: A Rumor of War; Chiefs, Scorned and Swindled, A Winner Never Quits, Murder Ordained; His Eye is on the Sparrow; Stones for Ibarra; My Father, My Son.

CARRADINE, ROBERT: Actor. b. San Mateo, CA, March 24, 1954. Son of John Carradine; brother of Keith and David Carradine.
PICTURES: The Cowboys, Mean Streets, Aloha Bobby and Rose, Jackson County Jail, The Pom Pom Girls, Cannonball, Massacre at Central High, Joyride, Orca, Blackout, Coming Home, The Long Riders, The Big Red One, Heartaches, Wavelength, Just the Way You Are, Number One with a Bullet, Revenge of the Nerds, Revenge of the Nerds II, Buy and Cell, All's Fair.
TELEVISION: Movies: Footsteps, Rolling Man, Go Ask Alice, The Hatfields and the McCoys, The Survival of Dana, The Sun Also Rises, Monte Carlo, The Liberators, As Is, I Saw What You Did; Alfred Hitchcock Presents (1985); Disney's Totally Minnie.

CARRERA, BARBARA: Actress. Fashion model before film debut in The Master Gunfighter, 1976.
PICTURES: Embryo, The Island of Dr. Moreau, When Time Ran Out, Condorman, I the Jury, Lone Wolf McQuade, Never Say Never Again, Wild Geese II, The Underachievers, Loverboy, The Favorite, Wicked Stepmother.
TELEVISION: Centennial, Matt Houston, Masada, Emma: Queen of the South Seas.

CARRERAS, SIR JAMES K.C.V.O. M.B.E.: Chairman Hammer Film Productions Ltd. 1949–1980. President, Variety Clubs Int'l. 1961–63; 22 years: past chairman; vice chairman, Royal Naval Film Corporation; Friends of the Duke of Edinburgh's Award Scheme; Mem. of board, Services Kinema Corp. 12 years; president, London Federation of Boys' Clubs 5 years; trustee of the council, Cinema and Television Benevolent Fund. Chairman of the Cinema Veteran, 1982–83.

CARROLL, CARROLL: Writer, Producer, b. New York, NY, April 11, 1902. m.p. critic, feature writer, N.Y. Sunday World; free lance writer, nat'l mags: radio writer, J. Walter Thompson, N.Y. 1932–36; West Coast, 1936–46; v.p., writer, prod., Ward Wheelock Co., West Coast, 1946–53. CBS, NBC, JWT, East Coast 1957–67. Now based in Hollywood.
SHOWS INCLUDE: (radio) Bing Crosby, Al Jolson, Rudy Vallee, Eddie Cantor, Burns & Allen, Joe Penner, Kraft Music Hall, Edgar Bergen, Frank Sinatra, Bing Crosby, Corliss Archer, Double or Nothing. Club 15; (TV) head writer, Bob Crosby Show; CBS-TV creative staff, 1953–55; General Electric Hour; Young & Rubicam TV, 1955; NBC-TV creative staff, 1956–57; ed. dept., J. Walter Thompson Co., 1957–67. Writer, prod., Chase & Sanborn 100th Anniv. Radio Show with Edgar Bergen, 1964; C & S 101. Anniv. Show with Fred Allen, 1965; 1966 NBC 40th Anniv. Show. Free-lance writer and adv. consultant, 1967–77. Book Reviewer for Variety and Columnist, And Now a Word from. . . in Variety, 1967–84.
AUTHOR: None of Your Business or My Life with J. Walter Thompson, 1970. My Life With. . . 1978. Co-author with Henny Youngman: Take My Wife . . . Please! Editorial consultant Liberace. Editorial consultant Mike Douglas: My Story, Co-author with Ed McMahon, Here's Ed. Co-author with Bob Hope: I Never Left Home, So This is Peace. Author, Carroll's First Book of Proverbs, or Life Is a Fortune Cookie.

CARROLL, DIAHANN: Actress, singer. b. New York, NY, July 17, 1935. m. singer Vic Damone. On Broadway in House of Flowers, No Strings, Agnes of God. Film debut in Carmen Jones, 1954.
PICTURES: Porgy and Bess, Goodbye Again, Paris Blues, Hurry Sundown, The Split, Claudine.
TELEVISION: Series: Julia, Dynasty. Movies: I Know Why the Caged Bird Sings, Sister Sister; Roots, The Next Generation, many specials.

CARROLL, GORDON: Producer. b. Baltimore, MD, Feb. 2, 1928. e. Princeton U. Advtg. exec., Foote, Cone & Belding, 1954–

58; Ent. industry, Seven Arts Prods., 1958–61; v.p., Staff Prod., Jalem Prods., 1966–1969; Independent Producer to present.
PICTURES INCLUDE: How to Murder Your Wife, Luv, Cool Hand Luke, The April Fools, Pat Garrett and Billy the Kid, Alien, Blue Thunder, The Best of Times, Aliens, Red Heat.

CARROLL, PAT: Performer. b. Shreveport, LA, May 5, 1927. e. Immaculate Heart Coll., L.A, Catholic U., Washington, DC. Joined U.S. Army in capacity of civilian actress technician. Night club entertainer in N.Y., 1949.
TELEVISION: Red Buttons, George Gobel, Jimmy Durante and Mickey Rooney; Caesar's Hour, (Emmy, 1956), Broadway, Masquerade Party (panelist); Keep Talking (regular); You're in the Picture (reg.); Busting Loose; The Ted Knight Show (series); She's the Sheriff (series); Cinderella; Gertrude Stein.
STAGE: Catch a Star (debut, 1955); Gertrude Stein, Gertrude Stein (Drama Desk, Outer Critics Circle, Grammy Awards); The Last Resort; Dancing in the End Zone.
PICTURES: With Six You Get Eggroll, RTH Brother O'Toole.

CARSON, JEANNIE: Actress. b. Yorkshire, England. Amer. Citizen, 1966. In musicals Ace of Clubs, Love from Judy; Ent. motion pictures in 1954 in As Long as They're Happy; Alligator Named Daisy, Mad Little Island. 1979: founded Hyde Park Festival Theatre with husband William Biff McGuire. Has taught music and drama at U. of Washington.
THEATER: U.S.: The Sound of Music, Blood Red Roses, Finian's Rainbow (revival). Also extensive work with the Seattle Repertory Theatre as actress, and dir. with Seattle Bathhouse Theatre.
TELEVISION: Best Foot Forward, Little Women, Berkeley Square, The Rivals, Frank Sinatra Show, Series, Hey Jeannie and Jeannie Carson Show.

CARSON, JOHNNY: Comedian. b. Corning, IA, Oct. 23, 1925. e. U. of Nebraska. U.S. Navy service; with station KFAB, Lincoln, Neb.; WOW radio-TV, Omaha, 1948; announcer, KNXT, Los Angeles, 1950; then program, Carson's Cellar; quiz- master, Earn Your Vacation, 1954; writer for Red Skelton; star of Johnny Carson Show, CBS-TV; Who Do You Trust, ABC-TV; The Tonight Show Starring Johnny Carson, NBC-TV.

CARSTENSEN, VERN: Executive. b. Clinton, IA, May 24, 1914. e. U. of Iowa, 1933–38.
RADIO: announcer, 1936–38, WSUI, Iowa City, WOC, Davenport, WHBF, Rock Island, CBS, Chicago; prog. dir., sls. prom., KROS, Clinton, 1939–42; U.S. Army, 1942–46, Armed Forces Radio Network, No. Africa, orig. Mobile Radio Station, Italy, Armed Forces Radio Service Hdqtrs., Hollywood, OIC overseas liaison; prod. mgr., Mayfair Transcription Co., 1946–51; exec. asst., Alan Ladd Enterprises Inc., 1951–58; assoc. prod., exec. coord., Jaquar Prods., 1958–61; v.p., sec., Eagle Animation Corp.; sec.-treas., Juggernaut Prods. Inc., 1962–64; exec. v.p. Dale Robertson Assoc., 1963; exec. v.p., United Screen Arts Inc. 1964–66; exec. v.p Juggernaut, Inc. 1966–68, v.p. Entertainment Associates, Inc. 1968–70; v.p. Tommy Walker Productions 1970–73; pres. Center Features, Inc. 1973–1976; 1977–1978, exec. v.p., Justin & Assoc. Inc.; 1979–81, v.p. Great Rollerworks Corp.

CARTER, DIXIE: Actress. b. McLemoresville, TN, May 25, 1939. m. actor Hal Holbrook. e. U. of Tennessee, Knoxville, Rhodes Coll.; Memphis, Memphis State U. Off-Bdwy debut, A Winter's Tale with NY Shakespeare Fest (1963). London debut, Buried Inside Extra (1983). Lincoln Center musicals: The King & I, Carousel, The Merry Widow.
THEATER: Pal Joey (1976 revival), Jesse and the Bandit Queen, Fathers and Sons, Taken in Marriage, A Coupla White Chicks Sitting Around Talking, Buried Inside Extra, Sextet.
PICTURE: Going Berserk.
TELEVISION: The Edge of Night. Series: On Our Own, Filthy Rich, Out of the Blue, Different Strokes, Designing Women. Movies: The Killing of Randy Webster, OHMS.

CARTER, HELENA BONHAM: Actress. b. England, May 26, 1966. Great granddaughter of Liberal Prime Minister Lord Asquith. e. Westminster. Appeared on BBC in A Pattern of Roses; seen by director Trevor Nunn who cast her in Lady Jane, 1986, theatrical film debut.
PICTURES: Lady Jane, A Room with a View, Maurice, Francesco, The Mask, Getting It Right.
TELEVISION: Miami Vice. Movies: A Hazard of Hearts, The Vision (U.K.).

CARTER, JACK: Actor, r.n.: Jack Chakrin. b. New York, NY, June 24, 1923. e. Brooklyn Coll., Feagin Sch. of Dramatic Arts. Worked as comm. artist for adv. agencies. Debut Broadway in Call Me Mister, 1947; starred in TV Jack Carter Show. Seen on most major variety, dram. programs, incl. Ed Sullivan Show. Emmy nom. 1962 for Dr. Kildare seg. Played most major nightclubs. Broadway in Top Banana; Mr. Wonderful.

PICTURES INCLUDE: The Horizontal Lieutenant, Viva Las Vegas, The Extraordinary Seaman, The Resurrection of Zachary Wheeler, Red Nights.

CARTER, LYNDA: Actress. b. Phoenix, AZ, July 24. e. Arizona State U. Wrote songs and sang professionally in Arizona from age of 15; later toured for 4 yrs. with rock n' roll band. Won beauty contests in Ariz. and became Miss World-USA in 1973. Dramatic training with Stella Adler and Charles Conrad.
TELEVISION: The New Adventures of Wonder Woman; 5 variety specials; Movies: Baby Brokers; Last Song; Hotline; Rita Hayworth, Love Goddess; Stillwatch (also exec. prod.).

CARTER, MAURICE: Art director, Designer. b. London, England, 1913. Grad. of the Royal Society of Art Masters. Early career as interior decoration designer. Ent. m.p. ind. 1934/5 Islington Studios, became art dir. 1938. Involved in development back projection. Has art dir. or designed over eighty features include Man in Grey, Becket, The Battle of Britain, Anne of the Thousand Days, Innocent Bystanders, The Land that Time Forgot, At the Earth's Core, The People that Time Forgot, The Great Train Robbery. Specializes in period subject and special effect. Three times nominated for American Academy awards and twice for British Film Academy awards. Founder of Guild of Film Art Directors.

CARTER, NELL: Actress. b. Birmingham, AL, Sept. 13, 1948.
THEATER: Hair, Dude, Don't Bother Me, I Can't Cope, Jesus Christ Superstar, Ain't Misbehavin' (Tony Award), Ain't Misbehavin' (1988 revival).
TELEVISION: Baryshnikov on Broadway; The Big Show; Lobo; An NBC Family Christmas; Ain't Misbehavin' (Emmy Award); Gimme a Break (series); Christmas in Washington; Nell Carter, Never Too Old To Dream.
PICTURES: Hair; Quartet; Back Roads; Modern Problems.

CARTER, TRACY: Actress. r.n. Tracy Olsen. b. Los Angeles, CA, Feb. 16, 1940. e. Hollywood Sch. of Drama, 1957-58; Pasadena Playhouse, 1958-61. Pianist, 15 years, Los Angeles Conservatory.
TELEVISION: Have Gun Will Travel, Ripcord, 77 Sunset Strip, Fred McMurray Show, The Deputy, June Allyson Show, Michael Shayne, Betty Hutton Show, Divorce Court, Kraft Suspense Theatre, Bonanza, Beauty Fair.
PLAYS: Desperate Hours, Look Back in Anger, Puss n Boots, The Thousand Dollar Mule, Taming of the Shrew, Richard III.
PICTURES INCLUDE: The Couch, Boy on the Run, Terrified, Dust Is My Tomorrow, Sweet Hell, I'll Love You Forever, Johnny Reno, Waco, Red Tomahawk, Journey to the Center of Time.

CARTLIDGE, WILLIAM: Director, Producer. b. England. Ent. m.p. ind. 1959. Early career in stills dept., Elstree Studios. Later worked as an asst. dir. on The Young Ones, Summer Holiday, The Punch & Judy Man, The Naked Edge. As 1st asst. dir. pictures included Born Free, Alfie, You Only Live Twice, The Adventurers, Young Winston, Friends. As assoc. prod., Paul and Michelle, Seven Nights in Japan, The Spy Who Loved Me, Moonraker. Prod.: Educating Rita, Not Quite Paradise, Consuming Passion.

CARTWRIGHT, VERONICA: Actress. b. Bristol, Eng., 1949. Sister of actress Angela Cartwright. Began career as a child actress on TV series Daniel Boone, 1964-66.
PICTURES: Love and War; The Children's Hour; The Birds; One Man's Way; Spencer's Mountain, Inserts; Goin' South; Invasion of the Body Snatchers; Alien; Nightmares; The Right Stuff; My Man Adam; Flight of the Navigator, Wisdom; The Witches of Eastwick.
TELEVISION: Leave It to Beaver; Twilight Zone; Guyana Tragedy—the Story of Jim Jones; Joe Dancer; Prime Suspect; Robert Kennedy and His Times.

CARVER, STEVE: Director. b. Brooklyn, NY, April 5, 1945. e. U. of Buffalo; Washington U., MFA. Directing, writing fellow, Film Institute Center for Advanced Studies, 1970. (Writer, dir. films Patent and the Tell-Tale Heart). Teacher of filmmaking art and photo. Florissant Valley Col., MO 1966-68. News photographer, UPI. Instructor, film and photography, Metropolitan Ed. Council in the Arts; St. Louis Mayor's Council on the arts, Give a Damn (dir., prod.); asst. dir. Johnny Got His Gun; writer, editor with New World Pictures. Member: Sierra Club, National Rifle Assn.
PICTURES: Arena; Big Bad Mama; Capone; Drum, Fast Charlie, The Moonbeam Rider; Steel; An Eye for an Eye; Lone Wolf McQuade (also prod.); Oceans of Fire; Jocks (also co-s.p.); Bulletproof (also co-s.p.).

CASS, PEGGY: Actress. b. Boston, MA, May 21, 1924. On Broadway in Burlesque, Bernardine, Auntie Mame, Don't Drink the Water, Front Page, Last of the Red Hot Lovers, etc.
PICTURES: The Marrying Kind, Auntie Mame, Gidget Goes Hawaiian, The Age of Consent, Paddy, etc.
TELEVISION: The Hathaways, Garry Moore Show, To Tell the Truth, Women in Prison.

CASSAVETES, JOHN: Director, Actor. b. New York, NY, Dec. 9, 1929. e. Colgate Coll., New York Acad. of Dramatic Arts. m. Gena Rowlands. Actor in stock co.; asst. stage mgr. for Broadway play Fifth Season; many TV credits including Omnibus, Elgin Playhouse.
PICTURES INCLUDE: Taxi, Night Holds Terror, Crime in the Streets, Edge of the City, Fever Tree, Shadows (dir.), Too Late Blues (dir., s.p.), A Child Is Waiting (dir), Faces, Husbands (actor, s.p., dir.), Minnie & Moskowitz (s.p., dir.), Devil's Angels, The Dirty Dozen, Rosemary's Baby, Machine Gun McCann, Woman Under the Influence, (dir.), Mikey and Nicky, Killing of a Chinese Bookie (dir., s.p.); Two Minute Warning (actor); Opening Night, 1977 (s.p., dir.), The Fury (actor), Brass Target (actor), Gloria (s.p., dir., prod.), Whose Life Is It Anyway? (actor); Tempest (actor); Marvin and Tige (actor); Love Streams (dir., co. s.-p., actor); Big Trouble (dir.).

CASSEL, ALVIN I.: Executive. b. New York , NY, July 26. e. U. of Michigan, B.A., 1938. Capt. in U.S. Army European Theatre, 1941–45. Surveyed Central Africa for MGM, 1946–50, then assumed duties as asst. mgr. for MGM South Africa. Continued with MGM in West Indies, 1950–51 and Philippines, 1951–57. In 1957 joined Universal as mgr./supvr. for Southeast Asia; back to MGM in 1963 as supvr. S.E. Asia; 1967, with CBS Films as Far East supvr. In 1972 established Cassel Films to secure theatrical films for foreign distributors, principally in Far East, 1979, consultant for Toho-Towa co. of Japan and other Far East distributors.

CASSEL, JEAN-PIERRE: Actor. b. Paris, France, Oct. 27, 1932. Began as dancer, attracting attention of Gene Kelly in Left Bank nightspot, who gave him film work. Appeared in plays before becoming established as leading French screen star.
PICTURES INCLUDE: Games of Love, The Gay Deceiver, Five Day Lover, The Vanishing Corporal, The Male Companion, A Woman Passed By, Is Paris Burning?, Those Magnificent Men in Their Flying Machines, The Killing Game, Oh! What a Lovely War, The Bear and The Doll, The Rupture, The Boat on the Grass, Baxter!, The Discreet Charm of the Bourgeoisie, The Three Musketeers, Le Mouton Enrage, Murder on the Orient Express, Who Is Killing the Great Chefs of Europe?, Chouans!
TELEVISION: Casanova (U.S.).

CASSEL, SEYMOUR: Actor. b. Detroit, MI, Jan. 22, 1935. As a boy travelled with a troupe of burlesque performers including his mother. After high school appeared in summer stock in Michigan. Studied acting at American Theatre Wing and Actor's Studio. After joining a workshop taught by John Cassavetes, began a long creative association with the director-actor. Broadway: The World of Suzy Wong, The Disenchanted.
PICTURES: Murder Inc.; Too Late Blues; Shadows; Juke Box Racket; Coogan's Bluff; The Revolutionary; Faces; Minnie and Moskowitz; Black Oak Conspiracy; Death Game; The Killing of a Chinese Bookie; Scott Joplin; Opening Night; The Last Tycoon; Valentino; California Dreaming; Convoy; Ravagers; Sunburn; King of the Mountain; The Mountain Men; I'm Almost Not Crazy...John Cassavetes—The Man and His Work (doc.); Love Streams; Eye of the Tiger; Tin Men; Plain Clothes; Track 29; Wicked Stepmother.
TELEVISION: The Killers; Beverly Hills Madame; Blood Feud; Angel on My Shoulder; I Want to Live.

CASSIDY, DAVID: Actor. b. April 12, 1950. Son of Shirley Jones and late Jack Cassidy; brother of Shaun.
THEATER: Joseph and the Amazing Technicolor Dreamcoat (Bdwy. 1983).
TELEVISION: The Partridge Family, Man Undercover, The Night the City Screamed.

CASSIDY, JOANNA: Actress. b. Camden, NJ, Aug. 2, 1944. e. Syracuse U.
PICTURES: Bullitt, The Fools, The Laughing Policeman, The Outfit, Bank Shot, The Stepford Wives, Stay Hungry, Prime Time, The Late Show; Night Child, Stunts, The Glove, Our Winning Season, Night Games, Blade Runner, Club Paradise, The Fourth Protocol, Who Framed Roger Rabbit?, Under Fire, 1969.
TELEVISION: 240–Robert, Buffalo Bill, Reunion, The Children of Times Square, Pleasures, The Devlin Connection, Family Tree, Invitation to Hell; Codename: Foxfire; Hollywood Wives; A Father's Revenge; Nightmare at Bitter Creek.

CASSIDY, SHAUN: Actor, Singer, Composer. b. Los Angeles, CA, Sept. 27, 1958. One of 3 sons of Shirley Jones and late Jack Cassidy. e. Beverly Hills H.S. Began recording in 1976 and toured Europe and Australia, appearing on numerous TV shows. Has had several hit records.
TELEVISION: Hardy Boys Mysteries, Matlock. Movies: Once Upon a Texas Train, Roots Christmas. Numerous specials.
PICTURES: Born of Water (debut for Ameri. Film Inst.).

Cas-Cha

CASTELL, ANTONIO: Executive. b. Havana, Cuba, Dec. 9, 1911. e. U. of Havana. Publicity dir., Cuba, 1937; motion picture exhibitor, 1937–48; distributor, Cooperative Cinematografica; owner dir., Alex and Atlas Films, up to 1961; distributor, Spanish pictures for the Americas.

CASTELLANO, RICHARD S.: Actor, Producer. b. New York, NY, September 4, 1933. e. Commerce H.S., Columbia U. Before acting career was owner of construction company and employed as construction consultant.
  THEATRE: 1963: New Yiddish Theatre; 1965–66: starred off-Broadway in A View From The Bridge; 1966: on Broadway in The Investigation and That Summer That Fall; 1967: Stratford Shakespeare Company Festival; 1968: Mike Downstairs, Why I Went Crazy. Also on Broadway in Sheep on the Runway and Lovers and Other Strangers (Tony nomination).
  PICTURES: A Fine Madness, Lovers and Other Strangers (Academy nomination), Night of the Juggler, The Godfather.
  TELEVISION: NYPD, The Super, Incident on a Dark Street, Honor Thy Father, Joe and Sons, Gangster Chronicles.

CASTLE, NICK: Writer, Director. b. Los Angeles, CA, Sept. 21, 1947. e. Santa Monica Coll., U. of Southern California.
  PICTURES: Kiss Me, Kill Me; (dir. only); Skatedown USA (s.p. only); Tag: The Assassination Game; Escape from New York (s.p. only); The Last Starfighter (dir. only); The Boy Who Could Fly (dir. only), Tap.

CASTLE, WALTER H.: Cinematographer. b. Santa Ana, CA, May 19, 1905. Engaged continuously in photographic work for 27 years with Fox Films Corp. and 20th Century-Fox Film Corp., as director of photography; Walt Disney Prod., TV, Hardy Boys, American Dairy Story, Spin, Mickey Mouse Club, Our Friend the Atom, Saga of Andy Burnett; spec. effects for Trapeze.

CATES, GILBERT: Director, Producer. b. New York, NY, June 6, 1934. e. Syracuse U. Began TV career as guide at NBC studios in N.Y., working way up to prod. and dir. of game shows (Camouflage, Haggis Baggis, Mother's Day, etc.). Created Hootenanny and packaged and directed many TV specials.
  PICTURES INCLUDE: The Painting (short), Rings Around the World, I Never Sang for My Father, Summer Wishes, Winter Dreams (dir. only); One Summer Love, (prod.-dir.); The Promise, The Last Married Couple in America; Oh, God!—Book II; Backfire; One More Time.
  TELEVISION: International Showtime (1963–65 exec. prod.-dir.), Electric Showcase Specials (dir.-prod.), To All My Friends on Shore (dir.-prod.), The Affair (dir.), After the Fall (dir.-prod.), Johnny, We Hardly Knew Ye, (prod.-dir.), The Kid from Nowhere (prod.); Country Gold (dir.); Hobson's Choice (dir.); Burning Rage (dir.); Consenting Adult (dir.).
  STAGE: Director: Tricks of the Trade, Voices, The Price (Long Wharf Theatre). Producer: Solitaire/Double Solitaire, The Chinese and Mr. Fish, I Never Sang for My Father, You Know I Can't Hear You When the Water's Running.

CATES, JOSEPH: Producer, Director. b. 1924. e. New York U. Brother of Gilbert Cates. One of first producers of live TV with Look Upon a Star, 1947. Prod., Jackie Gleason Cavalcade of Stars, game shows, ($64,000 Question, $64,000 Challenge, Stop the Music, Haggis Baggis).
  THEATER: Prod. on B'way: What Makes Sammy Run?, Joe Egg, Spoon River Anthology, Gantry, Her First Roman.
  PICTURES: Who Killed Teddy Bear (dir.), The Fat Spy, Girl of the Night.
  TELEVISION: Series: International Showtime (Don Ameche Circuses). Prod.-dir. of spectaculars and special programs, 1955–1988; Johnny Cash, David Copperfield, Steve Martin; Emmy Awards as prod: Anne Bancroft: The Woman in the Life of Man, Jack Lemmon and Fred Astaire, S'marvelous, S'wonderful, S'Gershwin, Annual Ford Theater Salutes to the President, Country Music Awards Show, Miss Teen Age America, Junior Miss pageants. Movies: Prod.: The Quick and the Dead, The Last Days of Frank and Jessie James, The Cradle Will Fall, Special People.

CATES, PHOEBE: Actress. b. New York, NY, 1964. Daughter of TV producer Joseph Cates. Dance prodigy and fashion model before launching acting career in Paradise. Studied with Actors Circle theatre group. NY stage debut The Nest of the Wood Grouse (1984).
  PICTURES: Paradise, Fast Times at Ridgemont High, Private School, Gremlins, Bright Lights Big City; Shag; Date With an Angel, Hearts of Dixie.
  TELEVISION: Series: Mr. and Mrs. Dracula. Movies: Baby Sister, Lace, Lace II.

CATTRALL, KIM: Actress. b. Liverpool, Eng., Aug. 21, 1956. e. American Acad. of Dramatic Arts, N.Y. Started stage career in Canada's Off-Bdwy. in Vancouver and Toronto; later performed in L.A. in A View from the Bridge, Agnes of God, Three Sisters, etc. On Bdwy in Wild Honey. Theatrical film debut in Rosebud (1975).

PICTURES: The Other Side of the Mountain—Part II, Tribute, Ticket to Heaven, Porky's, Police Academy, Turk 182, City Limits, Hold-Up, Big Trouble in Little China, Just in Time, Mannequin, Masquerade, Midnight Crossing, Palais Royale, For Better or For Worse, The Return of the Musketeers.
  TELEVISION: The Bastard, The Night Rider, The Rebels, Scruples, The Gossip Columnist, Sins of the Past.

CAULFIELD, JOAN: Actress. b. Orange, NJ, June 1, 1922. e. Columbia U. Harry Conover model 1942–43; on stage 1943–44; screen debut in Miss Susie Slagle's, 1945.
  PICTURES INCLUDE: Dear Ruth, Variety Girl, Unsuspected, Sainted Sisters, Larceny, Pretty Girl, Lady Said No, Rains of Ranchipur, Buckskin.
  TELEVISION: Sally, My Favorite Husband, The Magician (series); Murder She Wrote.

CAULFIELD, MAXWELL: Actor. b. Glasgow, Scotland, Nov. 23, 1959. m. actress Juliet Mills. First worked as a dancer at a London nightclub. After coming to NY in 1978, ran the concession stand at the Truck and Warehouse Theatre. Won a Theatre World Award for Class Enemy.
  THEATER: Entertaining Mr. Sloane, Salonika.
  PICTURES: Grease 2, Electric Dreams, The Boys Next Door.
  TELEVISION: The Colbys (series); The Parade.

CAVANAUGH, ANDREW: Executive. Held positions with Norton Simon, Inc. and Equitable Life Insurance Co. before joining Paramount Pictures in 1984 as v.p., human resources. 1985, appt. sr. v.p., administration, mng. personnel depts. on both coasts. Also oversees corp. admin. function for Paramount.

CAVETT, DICK: Actor, Writer. b. Kearny, NE, Nov. 19, 1937. e. Yale U. Acted in TV dramas and Army training films. Was writer for Jack Paar, and his successors on the Tonight Show and had comedy writing assignments with Merv Griffin, Jerry Lewis, Johnny Carson. In 1967 wrote for self and appeared in night clubs. On TV starred in Where It's At (special on ABC Stage 67) and What's In (special). Began daytime series for ABC-TV in 1968, three-weekly series summer of 1969. The Dick Cavett Show.
  THEATRE: Otherwise Engaged, Into the Woods.
  Author: Cavett (with Christopher Porter) 1974.
  PICTURES: Beetlejuice, Before God, Private Tutor (cameo), Moon Over Parador (cameo).

CAZENOVE, CHRISTOPHER: Actor. b. Winchester, Eng., Dec. 17, 1945. m. Angharad Rees. e. Eton, Oxford U., trained at Bristol Old Vic Theatre School. West End theater includes Hamlet (1969); The Lionel Touch; My Darling Daisy; The Winslow Boy; Joking Apart; In Praise of Rattigan; The Life and Poetry of T.S. Eliot. Broadway debut: Goodbye Fidel (1980).
  PICTURES: There's a Girl in My Soup (1970); Royal Flash; East of Elephant Rock; The Girl in Blue Velvet; Zulu Dawn; Eye of the Needle; From a Far Country; Heat and Dust; Until September; Mata Hari; The Fantastist; Souvenir; Hold My Hand I'm Dying.
  TELEVISION: The Rivals of Sherlock Holmes (1971); The Regiment; Affairs of the Heart; Jennie: Lady Randolph Churchill; The Duchess of Duke Street; The Darkwater Hall Mystery; Ladykillers—A Smile Is Sometimes Worth a Million; The Red Signal; Lou Grant; The Letter; Jenny's War; Lace 2; Kane and Abel; Dynasty (series); Windmills of the Gods; Shades of Love; Dangerous Love; A Fine Romance.

CELENTINO, LUCIANO: Producer, Director, Writer. b. Naples, Italy, 1940. e. Rome, Paris, London. Ent. ind. 1959. Wrote, prod., dir. many plays incl: Infamita di Questa Terra, Black Destiny, Honour, Stranger's Heart, Youth's Sin, Wanda Lontano Amore. Stage musicals such as Songs...Dots...And Fantasies, Night Club's Appointment, Filumena, Serenada, Mamma. Since 1964 film critic of Il Meridionale Italiano. From 1962 co-writer and first asst. director to Luigi Capuano and Vittoria De Sica. 1972: formed own company, Anglo-Fortunato Films. Co-wrote, prod., dir. Blood Money. Dir. Bandito (in Italy). Wrote and dir. Toujours, Parole, Jackpot.

CELLAN-JONES, JAMES: Director. b. Swansea, Wales, July 13, 1931. e. St. John's Coll., Cambridge. Best known for his adaptations of classic novels for the BBC and PBS (shown on Masterpiece Theatre), he has been called "master of the mini-series."
  PICTURES: The Nelson Affair; Sleeps Six (also prod.).
  TELEVISION: The Scarlet and the Black; The Forsythe Saga; Portrait of a Lady; The Way We Live Now; Sold; The Roads to Freedom; Eyeless In Gaza; The Golden Bowl; Jennie; Caesar and Cleopatra; The Adams Chronicles; The Day Christ Died; The Ambassadors; Unity Mitford; The Comedy of Errors; Fortunes of War.

CHABROL, CLAUDE: Director. b. Paris, France, June 24, 1930. m. actress Stephane Audran. One of the first directors involved in the French New Wave.
  PICTURES INCLUDE: Le Beau Serge, The Cousins, Leda, Les Bonnes Femmes, Les Godelureaux, The Third Lover,

56

Seven Capital Sins, Ophelia, Landru, Le Tigre Aime la Chair Fraiche, Marie-Chantal Contre le Docteur Kah, Le Tigre Se Parfume a la Dunamite, Paris vu par . . . Chabrol, La Ligne de Demarcation, The Champagne Murders, The Route to Corinth, Les Biches, La Femme Infidele, This Man Must Die, Le Boucher, La Rapture, Ten Days' Wonder, Just Before Nightfall, Dr. Popaul, Les Noces Rouges, Nada, The Blood of Others (TV in U.S.), The Horse of Pride, Alouette, je te plumera; (The Lark)(actor only), Women's Affairs (dir. co.-s.p.).

CHAFFEY, DON: Director. b. Hastings, England, 1917. Trained as artist; secured work in art dept. of Gainsborough Studios in early 40s. Eventually moved to Gaumont British International where directed first film, a documentary on dog-fish.
PICTURES INCLUDE: Time Is My Enemy, The Girl in the Picture, The Flesh is Weak, A Question of Adultery, The Man Upstairs, Danger Within, Dentist in the Chair, Greyfriars Bobby, Nearly a Nasty Accident, A Matter of Who, The Prince and the Pauper, Jason and the Argonauts, A Jolly Bad Fellow, One Million Years B.C., The Viking Queen, A Twist of Sand, Creature the World Forgot, The Three Lives of Thomasina, The Horse Without a Head, Ride a Wild Pony.

CHAIKIN, WILLIAM E.: Executive. b. Cleveland, OH, April 7, 1919. e. Ohio State U., B.S., journalism, M.S., political science. Was newspaper reporter and columnist for paper in Ohio, Indiana and Florida before joining 20th-Fox pub. dept. in 1945. And in pub. depts. of Republic and Eagle Lion Films. Later pres., Chaikin-Perret, p.r. firm. Became v.p. and treas. of Standard Capital, investment banking firm, where financed and supervised prod. of over 60 films. In 1963 named pres. and bd. chm. of Charter Title Insurance Co. in Los Angeles. Is member of the Board of Mariners Savings and Loan. Is mem. of bd. of Mariners Financial Corp., financial holding co. diversified building firm. From 1968–74 was v.p. in chg. of West Coast operations of Avco Embassy Pictures Corp. and asst. to James R. Kerr, pres. of Avco Corp. In July, 1974, assumed presidency of Avco Embassy Pictures Corp. to 1980.

CHAKERES, MICHAEL H.: Executive b. Ohio. e. Wittenberg U. Pres. and chm. of bd. of Chakeres Theatres of Ohio and Kentucky. U.S. Army AF 1942–45. Bd. of Dir.: National NATO, NATO of Ohio, Will Rogers Hospital, Motion Picture Pioneers, Society National Bank, Wittenberg U., Mercy Medical Center. Member: Variety Club, Masons, Scottish Rite, I.O.O.F. Order of AHEPA, Ohio Heart Ass'n., Rotary Club, City of Hope.

CHAKIRIS, GEORGE: Actor. b. Norwood, OH, Sept. 16, 1934. Entered m.p. industry as a dancer in There's No Business Like Show Business; White Christmas and Brigadoon; academy award for West Side Story. Starred in the Young Girls of Rochefort, The Big Cube, Why Not Stay for Breakfast?
TELEVISION: Fantasy Island, Chips, Matt Houston, Scarecrow and Mrs. King, Hell Town, Dallas, Falcon Crest.

CHAMBERLAIN, RICHARD: Actor. b. Los Angeles, CA, March 31, 1935. Studied voice, LA Conservatory of Music 1958; acting with Jeff Corey. Founding mem. City of Angels, LA Theater Company. TV series: pilot: Paradise Kid. Became TV star in Dr. Kildare series, 1961–66. Film debut in 1962, A Thunder of Drums. Founded prod. co. Cham Enterprises.
THEATER: Breakfast at Tiffany's, Night of the Iguana, Fathers & Sons, Blithe Spirit.
PICTURES INCLUDE: Secret of Purple Reef; Twilight of Honor, Joy in the Morning, Petulia, The Madwoman of Chaillot, Julius Caesar, The Music Lovers, Lady Caroline Lamb, The Three Musketeers, The Towering Inferno, The Four Musketeers, The Slipper and the Rose, The Last Wave, The Swarm, Murder by Phone, King Solomon's Mines, Alan Quartermain and the Lost City of Gold.
TELEVISION: Hamlet, 1970. Portrait of a Lady (BBC); Movies: The Woman I Love; F. Scott Fitzgerald and the Last of the Belles, The Lady's Not For Burning; The Man in the Iron Mask; The Count of Monte Cristo, Cook and Perry: The Race to the Pole, Wallenberg: A Hero's Story, Casanova. Mini-Series: Centennial, Shogun, The Thorn Birds, Dream West, The Bourne Identity.

CHAMBERS, EVERETT: Producer, Writer, Director. b. Montrose, CA; Aug. 19, 1926. e. New School For Social Research, Dramatic Workshop, N.Y. Entered industry as actor; worked with Fred Coe as casting dir. and dir., NBC, 1952–57; prod., dir. Run Across the River. Author: Producing TV Movies.
PICTURES: The Kiss (1958, dir., nom. best short film, Acad. Awards), The Lollipop Cover (prod., writer, dir., best film and actor awards, Chicago Film Fest.).
TELEVISION: Producer: Series: Johnny Staccato (also writer), Target the Corrupters, The Dick Powell Theatre, The Lloyd Bridges Show (also writer); Peyton Place (4 years); Columbo (4 years), Future Cop, Lucan (also writer). Movies: Beverly Hills Madam, A Matter of Sex (exec. prod.) Partners in Crime, Airwolf (also writer), Timeslip (exec. prod., writer). (1985 Christopher Award, A.W.R.T. Award), Will There Really Be a Morning?, Berlin Tunnel 21 (sprv. prod.), Night Slaves

(also writer), Moon of the Wolf, Trouble Comes to Town, Great American Beauty Contest, Can Ellen Be Saved? (also writer), Jigsaw John, Street Killing, Nero Wolfe, Twin Detectives (also writer), The Girl Most Likely to. . ., Sacrifice the Queen. Co-Writer: Movies: The Perfect Town for Murder, Last Chance (pilot).

CHAMPION, JOHN C.: Director, Producer, Writer. b. Denver, CO, Oct. 13, 1923. e. Stanford U., Wittenberg Coll. p. Lee R. Champion, Supreme Court judge. Col. Entered m.p. in Fiesta; did some radio work; in stock at MGM briefly; co-pilot Western Air Lines, Inc., 1943; served in U.S. Army Air Force, air transport command pilot 1943–45; public relations officer AAF; writer & prod. for Allied Artists; v.p. prod. Commander Films Corp.: press. Champion Pictures, Inc.; prod., MGM, Warner, Para., Universal. Member: SAG, SWG, SIMPP, SPG; TV Academy, Prod. Member, MIRISCH-U.A.; prod. TV Laramie series; created McHales Navy; author, novel, The Hawks of Noon, 1965; National Cowboy, Hall of Fame Award, 1976.
PICTURES INCLUDE: Panhandle, Stampede, Hellgate, Dragonfly Squadron, Shotgun, Allied Artists; Zero Hour, Paramount; The Texican, Columbia; Attack on the Iron Coast, Submarine X-1, The Last Escape, Brother of the Wind, dir-prod-writer, Mustang Country, Universal.

CHAMPION, MARGE: Dancer, Actress. b. Los Angeles, CA, Sept. 2, 1923. e. Los Angeles public schools. p. Ernest Belcher, ballet master. In Blossom Time, Student Prince for Los Angeles Civic Opera; Dark of the Moon. Beggar's Holiday in N.Y. Made debut with former husband Gower Champion as dancing team, played many night clubs; m.p. Debut in Mr. Music; then signed by MGM; Fame Star of Tomorrow, 1952; on Broadway in 3 for Tonight, 1955; toured, invitation to A March 1962.
PICTURES INCLUDE: Show Boat, Lovely to Look At, Everything I Have Is Yours, Give a Girl a Break, Three for the Show, Jupiter's Darling, The Swimmer, The Party, The Cockeyed Cowboys of Calico County, Whose Life Is It Anyway? (choreographer).
TELEVISION: GE Theatre, Chevy Show, Telephone Hour, etc.

CHAN, DARLENE K.: Executive. e. U. of California at L.A. Worked as prod. asst. on various independent films, including pilot for Disney Channel. 1983, joined Paramount Pictures as creative executive. 1985, named exec. dir. of prod., Walt Disney Pictures.

CHANCELLOR, JOHN: TV Anchorman, News Reporter. b. Chicago, IL, 1927. e. U. of Illinois. Following military service joined Chicago Sun-Times (1948) and after two years moved to NBC News as Midwest corr. In 1948 assigned to Vienna bureau. Subsequently reported from London; was chief of Moscow bureau before appt. as host of Today program for one year (1961). Left NBC 1965–67 to become dir. of Voice of America. In recent yrs. anchorman for special coverage of moon landings, political conventions, inaugurations etc. Anchorman, NBC Nightly News, 1970–82. Now sr. commentator, NBC News, delivering news commentaries on NBC Nightly News.

CHANDLER, CHICK: Actor. b. Kingston, NY, 1905. m. stage actress Eugenie Frontai. On screen from 1934.
STAGE: Great Magoo, Best Man, Harvey, Our Town, Dinner at Eight, Star Dust, Show Boat, Maytime, Roberta, Firefly, Our Town.
MUSICAL COMEDY: Pajama Game, Damn Yankees, Pleasure Bound, Brigadoon.
PICTURES INCLUDE: Sing and Be Happy, Hotel for Women, Hollywood Cavalcade, Star for a Night, City Girl, Irish Eyes are Smiling, Speed to Burn, Blood Money, Big Shot, Alexander's Ragtime Band, Mother Wore Tights, Time Out for Romance, Swanee River, Bride Came C.O.D., Battle Cry, It's a Mad Mad Mad World, Lost Continent and over 100 more.
TELEVISION: Soldiers of Fortune, One Happy Family, major TV shows including Loretta Young, and Vincent Price.

CHANNING, CAROL: Actress. b. Seattle, WA, Jan. 31, 1923. e. Bennington Coll. Long career on Broadway and road; most notably in Gentlemen Prefer Blondes, Lend an Ear, and Hello Dolly! (Tony Award), Lorelei, Legends (on tour with Mary Martin).
PICTURES: First Traveling Saleslady, Thoroughly Modern Millie, Skidoo.
TELEVISION: Svengali and the Blonde, Three Men on a Horse, Crescendo; many guest appearances.

CHANNING, STOCKARD: Actress. r.n. Susan Stockard. b. New York, NY, Feb. 13, 1944. e. Radcliffe Coll., B.A., 1965. With Theater Co. of Boston, experimental drama company, 1967. Has performed in some 25 plays winning 2 Tony nominations and a Tony Award (best actress, 1985).
THEATER: Two Gentlemen of Verona, No Hard Feelings, Vanities (Mark Taper Forum, LA), The Rink, Joe Egg (Tony Award).

PICTURES INCLUDE: Comforts of Home (1970); The Fortune, The Big Bus, Sweet Revenge, Grease, The Cheap Detective, The Fish That Saved Pittsburgh, Without a Trace, Heartburn, The Men's Club, A Time of Destiny, Boys Life.
TELEVISION: Silent Victory: The Kitty O'Neil Story; The Girl Most Likely To; Stockard Channing Show (series, 1979–80), Not My Kid, The Room Upstairs, Echoes in the Darkness.

CHAPIN, DOUG: Producer. Began career as actor; then switched to film production, making debut with When a Stranger Calls, 1979.
PICTURES INCLUDE: Pandemonium, American Dreamer.
TELEVISION: Movies: Belle Starr, Missing Pieces, Second Sight.

CHAPIN, SLOCUM: Executive. b. Quincy, MA, May 12, 1913. e. Dartmouth Coll., 1936. With Broadcast Builders, Hanover, NH; sales prom., World Broadcasting System; sales exec., WOC, Davenport, IA; sales mgr., WKBN, Youngstown, OH; gen. mgr., WSTC, Stamford, CT; network sales staff, ABC, 1942–48; east. TV sales mgr., ABC, 1948–51; v.p. in charge of owned TV stations, ABC, 1951; sales vice pres., ABC-TV, 1954; V.P. client relations, 1957; v.p. sls., Western division 1959; v.p. sls. National division, 1963; v.p. exec. relations, 1964.

CHAPLIN, CHARLES S.: Executive. b. Toronto, Ont., Canada, June 24, 1911. Studied Law. Entered m.p. ind. 1930 as office boy with United Artists; then office mgr. booker, St. John, N.B., 1933; br. mgr. 1935; to Montreal in same capacity 1941; named Canadian gen. mgr., June 11, 1945; resigned January 1962. Vice-pres. Canadian sls. mag.: Seven Arts Prod., 1962; chief exec. off., v.p., dir. TV sls., Europe-Africa, Middle East-Socialist countries, 1968–70; v.p., WB-Seven Arts, 1970–72; exec. v.p. intl. film dist., NTA (Canada) Ltd., Toronto Intl. Film Studios, 1972–80; pres., Charles Chaplin Enterprises, specializing in theatrical and TV sls. and prod. Pres.: B'nai Brith-, Toronto Bd. of Trade, various charitable org., many trade assns., past pres. Canadian M.P. Dist. Assn., Chmn. m.p. section Com. Chest, chmn. publ. rel. comm. & past-chmn., M.P. Industry Council; Natl. Board Council Christians & Jews, U. of Haifa, etc.

CHAPLIN, GERALDINE: Actress. b. Santa Monica, CA, July 3, 1944. e. Royal Ballet School, London. Daughter of Charles Chaplin. Starred in over 20 European productions, including seven with Spain's leading filmmaker, Carlos Saura.
PICTURES INCLUDE: Doctor Zhivago, Stranger in the House, I Killed Rasputin, The Hawaiians, Zero Population Growth, Innocent Bystanders, The Three Musketeers, The Four Musketeers, Nashville, Buffalo Bill and the Indians, Welcome to L.A., Cria, Roseland, Remember My Name, A Wedding, The Mirror Crack'd, Voyage en Douce, Bolero, L'Amour Par Terre, The Moderns, White Mischief, The Return of the Musketeers, I Want to Go Home.
TELEVISION: The Corsican Brothers, My Cousin Rachel.

CHAPLIN, SAUL: Musical director, Producer. b. Brooklyn, NY, Feb. 19, 1912. e. New York U., 1929–34. Wrote vaudeville material, 1933–36; songwriter Vitaphone Corp.; other, 1934–40; Columbia, 1940–48; MGM, from 1948; songs include: Bei Mir Bist Du Schoen, Shoe Shine Boy, Anniversary Song.
PICTURES INCLUDE: Acad. Award, collab. best scoring of mus., American in Paris, 1951, 7 Brides for 7 Brothers, 1954; West Side Story, 1961; mus. dir., Lovely to Look At, Give A Girl a Break, Kiss Me Kate, Jupiter's Darling; mus. supve. Interrupted Melody, High Society; assoc. prod. Les Girls; music assoc. prod. Merry Andrew; assoc. prod. Can Can, West Side Story, The Sound of Music; prod. Star, 1968; assoc. prod., The Man of La Mancha, 1972; co-prod. That's Entertainment, Part Two.

CHAPMAN, MICHAEL: Cinematographer. b. New York, NY, Nov. 21, 1935. m. film editor—dir. Amy Jones. Early career in N.Y. area working on documentaries before becoming camera operator for cinematographer Gordon Willis on The Godfather, Klute, End of the Road, The Landlord. Also operated Jaws.
PICTURES: The Last Detail, White Dawn, Taxi Driver, The Front, The Next Man, Fingers, The Last Waltz, Invasion of the Body Snatchers, Hard Core, The Wanderers, Raging Bull, Dead Men Don't Wear Plaid, Personal Best, The Man With Two Brains, All the Right Moves (dir.); The Clan of the Cave Bear (dir.); Shoot to Kill.
TELEVISION: Death Be Not Proud; King, Gotham. Dir.: The Annihilator (pilot).

CHAPMAN, TEDWELL: Playwright, Journalist. b. Chicago, IL, April 12, 1917. e. De Paul U., Loyola U., Columnist, Hollywood Feature Syndicate, editor, Tailwagger Magazine, Hoja de Lunes (weekly, Malaga, Spain).
CREDITS: Abroad With Two Yanks (collab. orig. story & s.p.), The Fabulous Suzanne (collab. orig. s.p.), The Flanagan Boy (collab. s.p.), Drop In Anytime (orig. s.p.), Forever Is a Long Time (TV, orig. story & s.p.), The Crowded Bed (TV,

orig. s.p.), Twice Upon a Time (Stage), The Intriguing Stranger (Stage), Bedlam (Stage), The Shame of Cain (Stage, book & lyrics), South of Granada (Stage, book & lyrics).

CHARI, V.K.N.: Public relations counsel, Publicity advisor. b. Salem, 1913. Till 1956 publicity & pub. relations officer, Gemini Studios, Madras. Presently film publicity adviser to film studios and film producers. Editor: Advertiser's Vademecum, Indian Advertising Year Book, An Economic Guide to India, The Languages of India. Refer-india, etc. Hon. Genl. Secretary. The Indian Council of Public Affairs, Madras. Journalist & news correspondent, B44 First mainroad Sastrinagar, Madras 20.

CHARISSE, CYD: Dancer, Actress. r.n. Tula Ellice Finklea. b. Amarillo, TX, March 8, 1923. e. Hollywood Prof. Sch. m. Tony Martin, singer. Toured U.S. & Europe with Ballet Russe; screen debut in Something to Shout About, 1943. Elected Star of Tomorrow 1948.
PICTURES INCLUDE: Mission to Moscow, Three Wise Fools, Till the Clouds Roll By, On an Island with you, Words and Music, Kissing Bandit, Tension, East Side, West Side, Mark of the Renegade, Wild North, Singin' in the Rain, Sombrero, Band Wagon, Easy to Love, Brigadoon, Deep in My Heart, It's Always Fair Weather, Meet Me in Las Vegas, Silk Stockings, Black Tights, Two Weeks in Another Town, The Silencers, Maroc 7.
TELEVISION: Movie: Portrait of an Escort; many specials.

CHARLES, MARIA: Actress. b. London, England, Sept. 22, 1929. Trained at Royal Acad. of Dramatic Art. London Stage Debut 1946 in Pick Up Girl. Subseq.
STAGE (London): Women of Twilight, The Boy Friend, Divorce Me, Darling!, Enter A Free Man, They Don't Grow on Trees, Winnie the Pooh, Jack the Ripper, The Matchmaker, Measure for Measure, Annie (1979–80), Fiddler on the Roof, Steaming, Peer Gynt, The Lower Depths, When We Are Married.
PICTURES INCLUDE: Folly To Be Wise, The Deadly Affair, Eye of the Devil, Great Expectations, The Return of the Pink Panther, Cuba, Victor/Victoria.
TELEVISION: The Likes of 'Er, The Moon and the Yellow River, Down Our Street, Easter Passion, Nicholas Nickleby, The Voice of the Turtle, The Fourth Wall, The Good Old Days, Turn Out the Lights, Angel Pavement, The Ugliest Girl in Town, Other Peoples Houses, Rogues Gallery, The Prince and the Pauper, Crown Court, Bar Mitzvah Boy, Secret Army, Agony, Never the Twain, La Ronde, Shine of Harvey Moon, Sheppey.

CHARLESON, IAN: Actor. b. Edinburgh, Scotland, Aug. 11, 1949. e. Edinburgh U.; trained for stage at London Acad. of Music and Dramatic Art. On London stage: Cat on a Hot Tin Roof, 1988.
PICTURES: Jubilee, Chariots of Fire, Gandhi, Ascendancy, Greystoke, Opera.
TELEVISION: Rock Follies, Churchill's People, The Paradise Run, Antony and Cleopatra, Something's Got to Give, Master of the Game, A Month in the Country, The Devil's Lieutenant, Code Name: Kyril.

CHARTERIS, LESLIE: Writer, Producer. b. Singapore, 1907; e. Cambridge U. Novelist; creator The Saint, protagonist of mystery novels and series of pictures based on them prod. by RKO from 1938 and by Julian Lesser from 1952.

CHARTOFF, ROBERT: Producer. b. New York, NY., Aug. 26, 1933. e. Union College, A.B.; Columbia U., LL.B. Met Irwin Winkler through mutual client at William Morris Agency (N.M.) and established Chartoff-Winkler Prods. Currently pres., Chartoff Prods., Inc.
PICTURES INCLUDE: Double Trouble, Point Blank, The Split, They Shoot Horses Don't They?, The Strawberry Statement, Leo The Last, Believe in Me, The Gang That Couldn't Shoot Straight, The New Centurions, Up the Sandbox, The Mechanic, Busting, The Gambler, SPYs, Breakout, Nickelodeon, New York, New York, Valentino, Rocky, Comes a Horseman, Uncle Joe Shannon, Rocky II, Raging Bull, True Confessions, Rocky III, The Right Stuff, Rocky IV, Beer, The Return of the Musketeers.

CHASE, BRANDON: Producer, Director. President MPA Feature Films, Inc.; newscaster-news director NBC-TV 1952–57. Executive director Mardi Gras Productions, Inc. and member of Board of Directors. Now pres., Group I Films, Ltd., and V.I. Prods., Ltd.
PICTURES INCLUDE: The Dead One, The Sinner and the Slave Girl, Bourbon Street Shadows, Verdict Homicide, Face of Fire, Four for the Morgue, Mission To Hell, The Wanton, Harlow, Girl In Trouble, Threesome, Wild Cargo, Alice in Wonderland, The Models, The Four Of Us, Against All Odds, The Giant Spider Invasion, House of 1,000 Pleasures, The Rogue, Eyes of Dr. Chaney, Alligator, Crash!, Take All of Me, The Psychic, UFOs Are Real, The Actresses, The Sword and the Sorcerer.

TELEVISION: Wild Cargo (series prod.-dir.); This Strange and Wondrous World (prod.-dir.), Linda Evans: Secrets to Stay Young Forever.

CHASE, CHEVY: Actor. r.n. Cornelius Crane. b. New York, NY, Oct. 8, 1944. e. Bard Coll.; MIT, MA. Studied audio research at CCS Institute. Worked as artist for Mad Magazine 1969. Teamed with Kenny Shapiro and Lane Sarasohn while still in school to collaborate on material for underground TV, which ultimately became Off-Broadway show and later movie called Groove Tube. Co-wrote and starred in Saturday Night Live on TV, winning 2 Emmys for outstanding continuing or single performance by a supporting actor in variety and music and as writer for show. Wrote Paul Simon Special 1977, (Emmy Award). Feature film debut in Foul Play in 1978.
PICTURES: Oh, Heavenly Dog, Caddyshack, Seems Like Old Times, Under the Rainbow, Modern Problems, National Lampoon's Vacation, Deal of the Century, Fletch, National Lampoon's European Vacation, Spies Like Us, Follow That Bird, Three Amigos, The Couch Trip, Funny Farm, Caddyshack II, Fletch II.

CHASE, STANLEY: Producer. b. Brooklyn, NY, May 3. e. New York U., B.A.; Columbia U., postgraduate. m. actress/artist Dorothy Rice. Began career as assoc. prod. of TV show Star Time; story dept., CBS-TV; then produced plays Off-Broadway and on Broadway, winner Tony and Obie awards for Threepenny Opera. Joined ABC-TV as dir. in chg. programming; exec. consultant, Metromedia Producers Org.; prod. & exec. Alan Landsburg Productions. Formed Stanley Chase Productions, Inc. in 1975, which heads as pres.
PICTURES INCLUDE: The Hell with Heroes, Colossus: The Forbin Project; High-Ballin' (exec. prod.); Fish Hawk (exec. prod.); The Guardian (HBO).
TELEVISION: Inside Danny Baker (pilot); Al Capp special (prod., writer); Happily Ever After (pilot; prod., writer); Bob Hope Presents the Chrysler Theatre series; Jigsaw (pilot); Fear on Trial (Emmy nomination); Courage of Kavik (exec. prod.); An American Christmas Carol, Grace Kelly.
STAGE: Producer of following Bdwy. plays: Threepenny Opera, The Potting Shed, The Cave Dwellers, A Moon for the Misbegotten, European Tour: Free and Easy.

CHASMAN, DAVID: Executive. b. New York, NY, Sept. 28, 1925. e. Sch. of Industrial Art, 1940–43; Academie De La Grande-Chaumiere, 1949–50. Monroe Greenthal Co., Inc. 1950–53; Grey Advertising Agency, Inc., 1953–60. Freelance consultant to industry 1950–60; worked on pictures for UA, 20th-Fox, Columbia, Samuel Goldwyn, City Film; Adv. mgr. United Artists, 1960; exec. dir. adv., United Artists, 1962; exec. production, United Artists, London, 1964; v.p. in prod. United Artists, 1969; v.p. of west coast operations, U.A. 1970; Senior Vice President in charge of Production, U.A. 1972; President, Convivium Productions Inc., 1974. Joined Columbia 1977, named exec. v.p. worldwide theatrical prod. 1979. Joined MGM 1980; named exec. v.p.-worldwide theatrical prod.
PICTURES: Exec. prod.: Brighton Beach Memoirs, The Secret of My Success.

CHATELAIN, DIDIER: Production executive. b. Paris, France, Jan. 24. e. Paris and Polytechnic, London. Degree in Business Administration, Marketing & Advertising. Entered industry in 1970 joining Herman Cohen Productions in London and Hollywood, starting with the advertising & promotion of Crooks and Coronets, 1971; Trog, 1972, Today We Kill . . . Tomorrow We Die!, 1973; The Strangers Gundown, 1974. Assistant Producer, Craze, 1974. Now v.p., Cobra Media, Inc.

CHAUDHRI, AMIN QAMAR: Director, Cinematographer, Editor. b. Punjab, India, April 18, 1942. e. Hampstead Polytechnic, London, City U. of New York. Pres., Filmart Enterprises Ltd. & Filmart Int'l Ltd., Pres./CEO, Continental Film Group Ltd.
PICTURES INCLUDE: Director: Kashish, Sweet Vengeance, Khajuraho, Eternal, Urvasi, Konarak, Black Rodeo, The Land of Buddha, Producer: The Whitmore's Are Having Company, Producer/Director: Once Again, An Unremarkable Life, Tiger Warsaw (dir., co-prod.), Lydia.
CINEMATOGRAPHY: Right On, Sweet Vengeance, The Hopefuls, The Wicked Die Slow, The Love Statute, Who Says I Can't Ride a Rainbow, Black Rodeo, Medium Is the Message, Death of a Dunbar Girl, Kashish, Deadly Vengeance, Lydia.
TELEVISION: Reflections of India (prod.-dir.).

CHER: Singer, Actress. r.n. Cherilyn Sarkisian. b. El Centro, CA, May 20, 1946. Began singing as backup singer for Crystals and Ronettes then, with then husband Sonny Bono in 1965; first hit record I Got You Babe, sold 3 million. Made two films and then debuted nightclub musical-comedy act in 1969. CBS comedy-variety series started as summer show in 1971; became regular following December. NY stage debut: Come Back to the Five and Dime, Jimmy Dean, Jimmy Dean (1982).
PICTURES INCLUDE: Good Times, Chastity, Come Back to the Five and Dime, Jimmy Dean, Silkwood, Mask, The Witches of Eastwick, Suspect, Moonstruck (Acad. Award, 1987).

TELEVISION: Sonny & Cher Comedy Hour (1971–74), Cher; The Sonny and Cher Show (1976–77).

CHEREN, ROBERT M.: Executive. b. Winthrop, MA, June 12, 1947. e. Graham Coll., 1967. 1968, joined 20th Century Fox sales dept. in Boston; 1969, named branch mgr. 1975, transferred by Fox to Los Angeles as dist. mgr.; 1976, promoted to west. div. mgr. mgr. 1979, to Columbia Pictures as west. div. mgr.; 1981, joined Filmways (later Orion Pictures) as v.p. & gen. sls. mgr. 1984, named Orion exec. v.p., then pres., Orion Pictures Dist. Corp.
MEMBER: Academy of Motion Picture Arts & Sciences, Variety Club New York, Variety Club Tent 25 So. Calif.; Foundation of Motion Picture Pioneers.

CHERMAK, CY: Producer, Writer. b. Bayonne, NJ, Sept. 20, 1929. e. Brooklyn Coll., Ithaca Coll.
TELEVISION: Prod.: Ironsides, The Virginian, The New Doctors, Amy Prentiss, Night Stalkers, Barbary Coast, CHIPS. TV movie: Murder at the World Series.

CHERTOK, HARVEY: Executive. b. New York, NY, Oct. 29, 1932. e. New York U., grad. school, bus. admin. Merchandising mgr., National Telefilm Assocs., Jan. 1956–Aug. 1959; supv., adv., United Artists Associated, Aug. 1959–March 1961; dir., adv., sls. prom., publicity, Seven Arts Associated Corp., 1961–1968; prod., 7 Surprizes, 1964; 1968 TV v.p. advertising-publicity, Warner-7 Arts, co.-prod., The Great Charlie Chan (Golden Press) 1968; pres. The Children's Movie of the Month, Inc., 1969–71; marketing consultant, United Artists Television, 1972–73; v.p.-special-projects, The American Film Theatre, Inc. 1973–75; v.p. adv., sls. pro., pub. for Time-Life Television, 1975; named v.p., adv./promo, Time Life-tv, 1978–81. Formed Quartel Int'l. to dist. foreign TV rights.
PICTURES: The Impossible Spy (exec. prod.).

CHERTOK, JACK: Producer. b. Atlanta, GA, July 13, 1906. Began career as script clerk, MGM; later asst. cameraman, asst. dir., head of music dept., short subjects prod. (including Crime Does Not Pay, Robert Benchley, Pete Smith series.) Feature prod. MGM 1939–42 (The Penalty, Joe Smith, American, Kid Glove Killer, The Omaha Trail, Eyes in the Night, etc.). In July 1942, apptd. Hollywood prod. chief, Co-Ord. Inter-Amer. Affairs, serving concurrently with regular studio work. Left MGM 1942 and prod. for Warner Bros. to late 1944; pres.: Produced The Corn is Green and Northern Pursuit for Warner Bros. Pres. Jack Chertok TV, Inc.
TELEVISION: Prod.: My Favorite Martian, Lone Ranger, Sky King, Cavalcade, Private Secretary, My Living Doll.

CHESTER, HALE: Producer. b. Brooklyn, NY, March 6, 1921. On N.Y. stage; film debut in Crime School 1937, followed by Little Tough Guy series. Juvenile Court; personal appearance tour of U.S. and Canada 1941–44; entered m.p. production 1944, doing a series of musical shorts. Member: IMPPA. Joe Palooka series begin with Joe Palooka Champ, 1946, released via Monogram, Smart Woman; v.p. in chge. prod., Mutual Films Corp., 1951.
PICTURES INCLUDE: Joe Palooka in The Squared Circle, Underworld Story, The Highwayman, Triple Cross, Models, Beast from 20,000 Fathoms, Crashout, Bold and The Brave, The Weapon, The Haunted, School for Scoundrels, Two-Headed Spy, His and Hers, Hide and Seek, The Comedy Man, The Double Man, The Secret War of Harry Frigg.

CHETWYND, LIONEL: Executive, writer. b. London, England, 1940. Emigrated to Canada, 1948. e. economics, Sir George Williams U., Montreal, BA, economics; BCL-McGill U., Montreal. Graduate Work-Law—Trinity Coll. Oxford. Admitted to bar—Province of Quebec, 1968. C.B.C.—TV-Public Affairs and Talks, 1961–1965. CTV network 1965–67. Controller commercial TV and film rights, Expo '67. Freelance writer and consultant 1961–68. Joined Columbia Pictures Intern. New York July 1968, transferred to Columbia Pictures Corp. Ltd., London, Sept. 1968. Asst. man. dir. January 1969. Asst. man. dir. Columbia-Warner UK, 1971. Story and book for musical Maybe That's Your Problem, 1971–1973.
PICTURES: The Apprenticeship of Duddy Kravitz (s.p.), The Hanoi Hilton (dir., s.p.), Redline.
TELEVISION: The Guest Room (s.p.), Sadat, To Heal a Nation (writer, exec. prod.).

CHIKADA, TADASHI: Executive. b. Japan, Nov. 20, 1919. e. Tokyo Foreign Language U. 1940–6 with Showa Tsusho in Japan and China; 1947–50 Izumi Sangyo, transferring to Nihon Eiga Shizai (Japan Movie Equipment Co.) which later became Toshiba Photo Phone Co.; appt. director and gen. mgr. of Trade Div. in 1972, and in 1974 director in charge of trade.

CHILDS, RICHARD B. (REG): Executive. b. Oakland CA, March 14, 1937. e. Stanford U., 1964. President and Chief Operating Officer, Nelson Entertainment.

CHIN, ELIZABETH MAE: Executive. b. New York, NY, Nov. 2, 1938. e. George Washington H.S., 1956; City Coll. of New York, Business Administration, 1960. Internal Auditor 1960;

International trade and entrepreneur of international dairy franchise 1968. Entered motion picture industry in 1974 as agent for independent film distribution in theatrical and television. Presently, executive of Far East Enterprises, and Emcee World Associates, Inc. and Bergen Intl. Corp.

CHING, WILLIAM: Actor. b. St. Louis, MO, Oct. 2, 1913. e. Spring Hills Coll. Radio Singer; on Broadway in Allegro.
PICTURES INCLUDE: Pat and Mike, Never Wave at a WAC, Give a Girl a Break, Scared Stiff, The Moonlighter, Tall Man Riding, Magnificent Matador.
TELEVISION: featured actor, Our Miss Brooks.

CHINICH, JESSE: Executive. b. Hoboken, NJ, Dec. 17, 1921. e. New York U. Law School, LLB, 1938. Lawyer with Hovell, Clarkson and Klupt, 1938–41; Capt., Air Force Intelligence, Pacific Theatre, 1941–46; joined Paramount Theatres as film buyer, 1946–51; circuit supervisor, Rugoff & Becker, NYC, 1951–53; western div. sales mgr., Buena Vista Film Dist., Co., 1953–61; Ass't gen. sales mgr. co-ordinator Cinema V Dist.; ass't sales mgr., Allied Artists; sales executive, special projects, Warner Bros. Dist. Corp. Now Publisher of weekly newsletters.

CHINICH, MICHAEL: Producer. b. New York, NY. e. Boston U. Began career as casting agent in N.Y.; moved to L.A. to join MCA-Universal Pictures as executive in casting. Named head of feature film casting; then prod. v.p. Began association with director John Hughes at Universal, later joining him at Paramount.
PICTURES: Exec. Prod.: Pretty in Pink, Ferris Bueller's Day Off, Some Kind of Wonderful, Planes, Trains and Automobiles (co-exec. prod.).

CHOMSKY, MARVIN J.: Director. b. Bronx, NY, May 23, 1929. Started in theatre business at early age as art dir. with such TV credits as U.S. Steel Hour, Playhouse 90, Studio One, etc. Later worked with Herb Brodkin who advanced him to assoc. prod. with such TV shows as The Doctors and The Nurses. Brought to Hollywood in 1965 as assoc. prod. for Talent Associates, producing series of TV pilots.
PICTURES INCLUDE: Evel Knievel, Murph the Surf, Mackintosh and T.J., Tank.
TELEVISION: The Wild, Wild West, Gunsmoke, Star Trek, Then Came Bronson, and many Movies of the Week: Holocaust, Victory at Entebbe, Roots, Attica, The Narobi Affair, Life and Times of Robert Kennedy, Evita, Peter the Great, The Deliberate Stranger, Anastasia, Billionaire Boys Club (sprv. prod., dir.), Angel in Green (dir.).

CHONG, RAE DAWN: Actress. b. Vancouver, 1962. Daughter of director-comedian Tommy Chong. Debut at 12 in The Whiz Kid of Riverton (TV).
PICTURES: Quest for Fire, The Corsican Brothers, Beat Street, Fear City, American Flyer, Choose Me, Commando, The Color Purple, Soul Man, The Squeeze, The Principal, Beat Street, City Limits, Walking After Midnight, Loon, Far Out Man.
TELEVISION: Badge of the Assassin.

CHONG, TOMMY: Singer, Actor, Writer, Director. b. Edmonton, Alta., May 24, 1938. Was guitar player with various Canadian rhythm and blues combinations, teamed with Richard Marin (Cheech) in improvisational group. Has made comedy recordings.
PICTURES: Cheech and Chong's Up in Smoke, Cheech and Chong's Next Movie, Cheech and Chong's Nice Dreams, Things Are Tough All Over, It Came from Hollywood, Still Smokin', The Corsican Brothers (also s.p., dir.), After Hours, Far Out Man (also dir., s.p.).
TELEVISION: Trial and Error (co-exec. prod.).

CHOOLUCK, LEON: Producer, Director. b. New York, NY, March 19, 1920. e. City Coll. of New York, 1938. Production, distribution, editing with Consolidated Film Industries 1936–40; Army Pictorial Service as news photographer 1941–45; Indep. as ass. dir. and prod. mgr. 1946–56; prod. for Regal Films and Orbit Pro., 1957–58; dir. Highway Patrol, 1958. Various occupations on stage 1947–58; prod. mgr., assoc. prod., Daystar Prods., 1962–63; prod. supv., Encyclopedia Britannica Films, in Spain, 1964; prod. supv., U.S. Pictures, Battle of the Bulge; loc. mgr., Three F Prods., assoc. prod. I Spy, TV Series, 1965–67. Vice Pres. Fouad Said Cinemobile Systems, 1969–70.
PICTURES INCLUDE: Hell on Devil's Island, Plunder Road, Murder by Contract, City of Fear, The Fearmakers, Day of the Outlaw, Bramble Bush, Rise and Fall of Legs Diamond, Studs Lonigan, Three Blonds in His Life, El Cid, The Outer Limits, Midas Run, The Grissom Gang, Kotch, Payday; Three the Hard Way, Take a Hard Ride, Apocalypse Now, Loving Couples. Wonders of China for Disney Circlevision (supervisor).
TELEVISION: Prod. supvr. 1974–76; Specials: Strange Homecoming, Michener's Dynasty, Judge Horton and the Scottsboro Boys, Pearl, A Rumor of War, Murder in Texas.

CHOW, RAYMOND: Producer. b. Hong Kong. e. St. John's U., Shanghai. Worked as journalist for Hong Kong Standard; then joined the U.S. Information Agency, establishing its Chinese radio station which broadcast to the Chinese mainland. In late 1950s joined Shaw Brothers as head of their publicity operations. In next 12 years became right-hand man of Run Run Shaw and head of production. In 1971 formed The Golden Harvest Group to produce Chinese-language films in Hong Kong. Two kung-fu films featuring Bruce Lee put Harvest into int'l market. Started English-language films in 1977, beginning with The Amsterdam Kill and The Boys in Company C.
FILMS: Lassiter, Cannonball Run II.

CHRISTIAN, LINDA: Actress. r.n. Blanca Rosa Welter. b. Tampico, Mexico, Nov. 13, 1924. e. Mexico, Venezuela, Palestine, South Africa, Holland, Italy; attended medical school in Palestine. Worked for British Censorship Bureau in Palestine; asst. to plastic surgeon; screen debut in Holiday in Mexico (1946).
PICTURES INCLUDE: Green Dolphin Street, Tarzan and the Mermaids, The Happy Time, Battle Zone, Slave of Babylon, Athena, Thunderstorm, The VIPs.

CHRISTIANSEN, ROBERT W.: Producer. b. Porterville, CA. e. Bakersfield Coll. Spent 3 years in Marine Corps. Worked on Hollywood Reporter in circulation and advertising. Joined Cinema Center Films; prod. asst. on Monte Walsh and Hail Hero. Co-produced first feature in 1970, Adam at Six A.M., with Rick Rosenberg, with whom co-produced all credits listed.
PICTURES INCLUDE: Adam at Six A.M., Hide in Plain Sight.
TV: Features: Suddenly Single, The Glass House, Gargoyles, A Brand New Life, The Man Who Could Talk to Kids, The Autobiography of Miss Jane Pittman, I Love You . . . Goodbye, Queen of the Stardust Ballroom, Born Innocent, A Death in Canaan, Strangers, Robert Kennedy and His Times, Kids Don't Tell, As Summers Die, Gore Vidal's Lincoln, Red Earth, White Earth.

CHRISTIE, HOWARD J: Producer. b. San Francisco, CA, Sept. 16, 1912. e. U. of California, Berkeley. Entered m.p. ind. following graduation from coll. in 1934, as actor; asst. dir. 1936–40; assoc. prod., 1942–44, Deanna Durbin pictures. Member: Screen Directors Guild, Screen Producers Guild, Delta Tau Delta, vice pres., Reeve M.C.A. Inc., 1961.
PICTURES INCLUDE: Lady on a Train, Because of Him I'll Be Yours, Abbott & Costello Meet the Invisible Man, Golden Horde, Comin' Round the Mountain, Lost in Alaska, Against All Flags, Yankee Buccaneer, Seminole, Lone Hand, Abbott and Costello Go to Mars, Abbott and Costello Meet Dr. Jekyll and Mr. Hyde, Back to God's Country, Yankee Pasha, Abbott and Costello Meet Keystone Kops, Smoke Signal, The Looters, Purple Mask, Abbott and Costello Meet the Mummy, Price of Fear, Congi Crossing, Showdown at Abilene, Toy Tiger, Away All Boats, I've Lived Before, Wagon Train, The Raiders, Sword of Ali Baba, Senes, Laredo, Ride to Hangman's Tree, Journey to Shiloh, Nobody's Perfect, A Man Called Gannon.
TELEVISION: The Virginian.

CHRISTIE, JULIE: Actress. b. Chukua, Assam, India, July 14, 1941. e. year in France followed by drama school in England. TV debut in A for Andromeda. Birmingham Rep.; Royal Shakespeare Co.; East European and American tour, Starred (N.Y.) in Uncle Vanya.
PICTURES INCLUDE: Crooks Anonymous (1962); Fast Lady, Billy Liar, Young Cassidy, Darling (Academy Award, 1965); Dr. Zhivago, Farenheit 451, Far from the Madding Crowd, Petulia, In Search of Gregory, The Go-Between, McCabe and Mrs. Miller, Don't Look Now, Shampoo, The Demon Seed, Heaven Can Wait, Memories of a Survivor, The Return of the Soldier, Golddiggers, Heat and Dust, Power, Miss Mary.
TELEVISION: Debut: A is for Andromeda (UK series, 1962); Fathers and Sons (Italian TV); Dadah Is Death (Amer. TV debut, 1988).

CHRISTINE, VIRGINIA: Actress. b. Stanton, IA, March 5, 1920. e. U. of California at L.A. Has appeared in more than 400 motion pictures and television productions.
PICTURES INCLUDE: Mission to Moscow, Counter Attack, The Killers, Cover Up, The Men, Cyrano De Bergerac, Cobweb, High Noon, Not as a Stranger, Spirit of St. Louis, Three Brave Men, Judgment At Nuremberg, The Prize, Four For Texas, Edge of Darkness, The Mummy's Curse, Girls of the Big House, Murder is My Business, The Wife of Monte Cristo, Dragnet, Flaming Star, Cattle King, A Rage to Live, Guess Who's Coming to Dinner, Hail Hero, Daughter of the Mind.
TELEVISION: Dragnet, Abbot & Costello, Dangerous Assignment, Racket Squad, Superman, Schlitz Playhouse, Four Star Playhouse, The Whistler, Code 3, Ford Theatre, You Are There, Stage 7, Passport to Danger, Soldier of Fortune, Heinz

Show, Anthology, Four Star Playhouse, Cavalcade of America, Alfred Hitchcock Presents, Father Knows Best, Crusader, Kellogg, Front Row Center, The Twisted Road, Matinee, Private Secretary, Fort Laramie, Big Town, Science Fiction, Frontier Detective, Lone Ranger, Jim Bowie, Wire Service, Whirlybirds, Gunsmoke, Las Vegas Story, Trackdown, The Thin Man, San Francisco Beat, Stranger In Town, T Men, Casey Jones, Climax, Mickey Spillane, The Millionaire, Behind Closed Doors, Target, Peter Gunn, Zane Grey Theatre, Wyatt Earp, Secret Mission, The Donna Reed Show, Wanted Dead Or Alive, Buckskin, Loretta Young Show, Starperformance, Rescue 8, Steve Canyon, State Trooper, Twilight Zone, General Electric Theatre, How to Marry A Millionaire, Rifle Man, June Allyson Show, Rawhide, M Squad, Coronado 9, Man From Black Hawk, Grand Jury, Riverboat, 77 Sunset Strip, Happy, The Thriller, Lawless Years, The Untouchables, Death Valley Days, Verdict Is Yours, Deputy, Perry Mason, Wagon Train, Mr. Ed, Maverick, The Shirley Temple Show, Asphalt Jungle, Harrigan and Son, Tales of Wells Fargo, Bronco, Line of Duty, The New Breed, Going My Way, Stoney Burke, Bonanza, The Eleventh Hour, Ben Casey, The Virginian, The Fugitive, Day in Court, Hazel, Singing Nun, Billy the Kid, The Big Valley, The FBI, Laredo, A Man Called Shenandoah, Jericho, Judd for the Defense, The Invaders, Lancer, Nanny and the Professor.
STAGE: Hedda Gabler, Mary, Queen of Scots, Miss Julie, Desdemona.

CHRISTOPHER, DENNIS: Actor. b. Philadelphia, PA, Dec. 2, 1955. e. Temple U. NY stage debut, Yentl the Yeshiva Boy (1974). Other NY theater: Dr. Needle and the Infectious Laughter Epidemic, The Little Foxes, Brothers. Regional theater.
PICTURES: Blood and Lace (1971); Fellini's Roma; Salome; Three Women; September 30, 1955; A Wedding; California Dreaming; The Last Word; Breaking Away; Fade to Black; Chariots of Fire; Don't Cry, It's Only Thunder; The Falling; Flight of the Spruce Goose; Jake Speed; Friends.
TELEVISION: Cagney & Lacey; Moonlighting; Trapper John M.D.; Jack and the Beanstalk (Faerie Tale Theatre); Tales of the Unexpected; Berenice Bobs Her Hair.

CHRISTOPHER, JORDAN: Actor, Musician. b. Youngstown, OH. Oct. 23, 1941. e. Kent State U. Led rock 'n' roll group, The Wild Ones. Broadway debut, Black Comedy, 1967.
PICTURES INCLUDE: Return of the Seven, The Fat Spy, The Tree, Pigeons, Brainstorm, Star 80.

CHUNG, CONNIE: TV News Anchor. r.n. Constance Yu-Hwa Chung. b. Washington, D.C., Aug. 20, 1946. e. U. of Maryland, B.A. Entered field 1969 as reporter for WTTG-TV, Washington; 1971, named Washington corr., CBS; 1976, anchor KNXT, Los Angeles; 1983, anchor, NBC News at Sunrise; Summer Sunday USA; Summer Showcase.

CIANNELLI, LEWIS E.: Associate producer. b. New York, NY, Jan. 12, 1923. e. U. of California, 1941; Stanford U., AB, 1947; Meschini Institute, Rome, 1950. W.W.II 1942–46. Acct. exec. adv. firm 1947–48. Actor: TV and motion pictures, 1948–50. Exec. asst. Industrie Cinematografiche Sociali, 1950, Director of Foreign Sls. I.C.S. and on board of A.N.I.C.A. 1953. Production exec. Lux Film, Rome 1953. Head of Production Republic Pictures, Italy 1954–55; assoc. prod. The Best of the Post; assoc. prod., exec. asst. Ponti & Girosi, That Kind of Women; Heller in Pink Tights, assoc. prod. NBC-TV; Ford Startime, Chevy Special Mexico, Rivak The Barbarian, The Americans, Outlaws.
PLAYS: OK Nero!, Twin Trouble, The Bed.

CILENTO, DIANE: Actress. b. Queensland, Australia, April 2, 1934. e. Toowoomba. Went to New York and finished schooling and then American Acad. of Dramatic Art. First theatre job at 16; toured U.S. with Barter Co.; returned to London and joined Royal Acad. of Dramatic Art; several small parts and later repertory at Manchester's Library Theatre.
PICTURES INCLUDE: Angel Who Pawned Her Harp, Passing Stranger, Passage Home, Woman for Joe, Admirable Crichton, Truth About Women, Stop Me Before I Kill!, I Thank a Fool, Jet Storm, The Full Treatment, The Naked Edge, Tom Jones, Rattle of a Simple Man, The Agony and the Ecstacy, The Breaking Point, Once Upon A Tractor for UN, Hombre, The Boy Who Had Everything.
THEATRE: London stage: Tiger at the Gates, I Thank a Fool, The Third Secret, Tom Jones, The Rattle of a Simple Man, The Agony and the Ecstasy, Hombre, Once Upon a Tractor, Negatives, The Four Seasons, The Bonne Soup, Heartbreak House. (NY), the Big Knife, Orpheus, Altona, Castle in Sweden, Naked, Marys, I've Seen You Cut Lemons.
TELEVISION: La Belle France (series), Court Martial, Blackmail, Dial M for Murder, Rogues Gallery, Rain, Lysistrata, The Kiss of Blood, For the Term of His Natural Life.

CIMINO, MICHAEL: Writer-Director. b. 1943. e. Yale U. BFA, MA. Protege of Clint Eastwood, who signed him to do s.p. for Magnum Force and then to write and direct Thunderbolt and Lightfoot, in both of which Eastwood starred.

PICTURES: Silent Running (s.p.); The Deer Hunter (Academy Award, best dir., best film 1978.), Heaven's Gate, Year of the Dragon, The Sicilian (dir., prod.).

CIPES, ARIANNE ULMER: Executive. b. New York, NY, July 25; E. Royal Acad. of Dramatic Arts, London, U. of London. Daughter of film director Edgar G. Ulmer. Actress, then production and dubbing, Paris; CDC, Rome; Titra, New York; 1975–77, v.p., Best International Films (international film distributor), Los Angeles; 1977 co-founder and sr. v.p./sales & services of Producers Sales Organization, 1981, named exec. v.p., American Film Marketing Assn. 1982, founded AUC Films, consulting and international sales-producers rep.

CIPES, JAY H.: Executive. b. New York, NY, Dec. 14. e. Cornell U. 1960–66, independent producer-packager-distributor European features for U.S. TV sales; 1967, producer, 20th Century-Fox TV; 1970, producer, Four Star TV; 1971, marketing exec. Technicolor, Inc.; 1973, v.p., marketing, Technicolor, Inc.; 1979 sr. v.p., director worldwide marketing, Technicolor, Inc. Professional Film Division.

CLAGETT, MANNING (TIM): Executive. b. Washington, DC, Aug. 22, 1913. e. U. of Southern California; U. of California at L.A.; George Washington U. Correspondent for Washington Herald, Washington Times-Herald 1937–41; Washington Star, 1941–48. Joined U.S. Merchant Marine 1943–44; corr., Washington Post 1945–46; own news bureau 1946–48. Assoc. Director of information, Motion Picture Assoc. of America, Washington, 1948–1958; dir. pub. rel. MPAA, 1953; dir. State Leg. Service, MPAA, 1956; v.p., 1961; special consultant, 1970.

CLARK, BOB: Director. b. New Orleans, LA, Aug. 5, 1941. e. Hillsdale Coll.
PICTURES: The Emperor's New Clothes; Children Shouldn't Play with Dead Things (as Benjamin Clark); Dead of Night; Black Christmas; Breaking Point; Murder by Decree; Tribute; Porky's (also prod., s.p.); Porky's II—The Next Day (also prod., s.p.); A Christmas Story (also prod., s.p.); Rhinestone; Turk 182; The Von Metz Incident (dir., co.-s.p.).

CLARK, CANDY: Actress. b. Norman, OK, June 20, 1947. Was successful model in N.Y. before landing role in Fat City, 1972. Off-Broadway debut 1981: A Couple of White Chicks Sitting Around Talking.
PICTURES INCLUDE: Fat City, American Graffiti, The Man Who Fell To Earth, Citizens Band, The Big Sleep, When You Comin' Back, Red Ryder, More American Graffiti, National Lampoon Goes to the Movies, Blue Thunder, Amityville 3-D, Hambone and Hillie, Cat's Eye, At Close Range, The Blob.
TELEVISION: Amateur Night at the Dixie Bar and Grill, Johnny Belinda, Popeye Doyle, James Dean, Where the Ladies Go, Rodeo Girl.

CLARK, DANE: Actor. b. New York, NY, Feb. 18, 1915. e. Cornell U., Johns Hopkins U. In radio series 2 yrs.; on N.Y. stage (Of Mice and Men, Dead End, etc.).
PICTURES INCLUDE: Glass Key, Sunday Punch, Pride of the Yankees, Tennessee Johnson, Action in the North Atlantic, Destination Tokyo, Very Thought of You, Hollywood Canteen, God Is My Co-Pilot, Her Kind of Man, That Way With Women, Deep Valley, Embraceable You, Moonrise, Whiplash, Without Honor, Backfire, Barricade, Never Trust a Gambler, Fort Defiance, Highly Dangerous, Gambler and the Lady, Go Man Go, Blackout, Paid to Kill, Thunder Pass, Port of Hell, Toughest Man Alive.
TV: No Exit, The Closing Door, Wire Service, Bold Venture (series), The French Atlantic Affair, Police Story.

CLARK, DICK: Performer; Chairman, CEO, Dick Clark Prods., Inc. b. Mt. Vernon, NY, Nov. 30, 1929. e. Syracuse U. graduated 1951, summer announcer WRUN, Utica 1949, staff announcer WOLF, Syracuse 1950. After graduation 1951, took regular job with WOLF. Rejoined WRUN, Utica, then joined WKTV, Utica. Announcer WFIL Philadelphia 1952. Host of American Bandstand ABC-TV nationwide, the Dick Clark Beechnut Show, Dick Clark's World of Talent, The Object Is, Missing Links, Record Years, Years of Rock. Producer of TV shows, Where The Action Is, Swinging Country, Happening, Get It Together, Shebang, Record Years, Years of Rock. Author of Your Happiest Years, Random House...1959, Author of Rock, Roll & Remember, T.Y. Crowell, 1976 and To Goof or Not to Goof, Bernard Geis, 1963.... Dick Clark's Easyguide Guide to Good Grooming, Dodd, Mead 1986... The History of American Bandstand, Ballantine, 1986. Formed Dick Clark Productions 1956 (television and motion picture production). In-person concert division, marketing and communications division, cable TV programing department, compact disc label, home video and radio division. Host and Producer of two weekly radio programs: Countdown American and Rock Roll & Remember. Founder and principal owner of United Stations Radio Network. Host of the $25,000 Pyramid, $100,000 Pyramid.
PICTURES: Because They're Young, The Dark, The Young

Cla-Clo

Doctors, Psychout, The Savage Seven, Killers Three, Remo Williams: The Adventure Begins, Backtrack.
TELEVISION: Executive Producer: American Music Awards, Academy of Country Music Awards, Dick Clark's New Year's Rockin' Eve, Golden Globe Awards, Soap Opera Awards, Superstars and Their Moms; TV series: American Bandstand, TV's Bloopers & Practical Jokes, Puttin' on the Hits, Puttin' on the Kids, Dick Clark's Nitetime, Inside America, In Person From the Palace, Getting in Touch; TV movies: Elvis, Man in the Santa Claus Suit, Murder in Texas, Reaching for the Stars, The Demon Murder Case, The Woman Who Willed a Miracle, Birth of the Beatles, Copacabana; Promised a Miracle, The Town Bully, TV specials: Live Aid—An All-Star Concert for African Relief, Farm Aid III, TV Censored Bloopers, American Bandstand's 33⅓ Celebration, America Picks the #1 Songs, You Are the Jury, Thanks for Caring, Supermodel of the World. Winner of 5 Emmys. Took company public in January 1987 (NASDAQ: DCPI), serves as chm. & CEO.

CLARK, DUNCAN C.: Executive. b. July, 1952, Sutton, Surrey, England. Entered industry in 1972. Appointed director of publicity and advertising, CIC, January 1979, taking up similar post in 1981 for United Artists. On formation of U.I.P. in 1982, appointed director of publicity and advertising, and deputy managing director, July 1983. February 1987 appointed vice president of advertising and publicity, Columbia Pictures International (NY). In Aug. 1987, senior v.p. International Marketing for Columbia (Burbank). On formalization of Columbia Tri-Star Film Distributors, Inc., appointed senior v.p. for the newly-formed company (NY).

CLARK, GREYDON: Producer, Director, Writer. b. Niles, MI, Feb. 7, 1943. e. Western Michigan U., B.A., theatre arts, 1963. Heads own company, World Amusement Corp., Sherman Oaks, CA.
PICTURES: Writer: Satan's Sadists, Psychic Killer. Dir.-writer: Mothers, Fathers, and Lovers, Bad Bunch. Prod.-writer-dir.: Hi-Riders, Angel's Brigade, Without Warning, Joysticks (prod., dir), Uninvited (dir.).

CLARK, HILARY J.: Executive. e. U. of Southern California, B.A., 1976. Began industry career 1978 as ad-pub admin. in co-op adv. dept., Buena Vista Dist. Co. Promoted to mgr. of natl. field pub & promo. Acted as unit publicist on numerous films (Explorers, Sylvester, Swing Shift, Crossroads, etc.) before returning to BV 1986 as natl. pub. dir. for Walt Disney Pictures.

CLARK, JOHN L.: Executive. b. Owenton, KY, Sept. 13, 1907. e. U. of Tennessee. Talent scout, Brunswick Phono. Co.; mgr., WLW, Cincinnati; formed Transamerican Broad. & Tele. Corp. with Warner Bros.; prod. 50 TV films, 1941–44; created & prod. many radio & TV programs; pres. & sole owner, Transamerican.

CLARK, KENNETH: Journalist, Executive. b. Dekalb, IL, Aug. 1, 1899. e. U. of Illinois. Washington & foreign corresp. United Press, Internatl. News Service, Universal Service. Joined M.P. Prod. & Dist. Amer., 1936. Leave of absence 1942 to join U.S. Army; Maj., Lt. Col. and Col.; Returned to MPAA, Nov., 1945; v.p., 1953; exec. v.p., MPAA, 1962; v.p., MPEAA, 1953, Retired, 1984.

CLARK, PETULA: Actress, Vocalist. b. Ewell, Surrey, England, Nov. 15, 1932. On British stage in Sound of Music. Winner of two Grammy Awards, 1964, 1965.
PICTURES INCLUDE: The Huggets, Dance Hall, White Corridors, The Card, Made In Heaven, Gay Dog, Runaway Bus, That Man Opposite, Finian's Rainbow, Goodbye Mr. Chips.

CLARK, SUSAN: Actress. b. Canada, March 8, 1943. r.n. Nora Golding. Trained at Royal Acad. of Dramatic Art, London. Made m.p. debut in Banning, 1967.
PICTURES INCLUDE: Banning, Coogan's Bluff, Madigan, Colossus: The Forbin Project, Tell Them Willie Boy Is Here, Skullduggery, Skin Game, Valdez Is Coming, Showdown, The Midnight Man, Night Moves, Airport 1975, The Apple Dumpling Gang, The North Avenue Irregulars, Murder by Decree, City on Fire, Promises in the Dark, Porky's, Nobody's Perfekt. Producer: Jimmy B and Andre, Word of Honor.
TELEVISION: Webster (series); The Astronaut, Amelia Earhart, Babe, The Choice, Jimmy B and Andre, Maid in America (prod.).

CLAYBURGH, JILL: Actress. b. New York, NY, April 30, 1944. m. playwright David Rabe. e. Sarah Lawrence Coll. 1966. Former member of Charles Playhouse, Boston.
THEATER: The Nest (off-Broadway), The Rothschilds, Jumpers, Pippin, In the Boom Boom Room, Design For Living.
PICTURES INCLUDE: The Wedding Party, Portnoy's Complaint, The Thief Who Came to Dinner, Terminal Man, Gable and Lombard, Silver Streak, Semi-Tough, An Unmarried Woman, Starting Over, Luna, It's My Turn, First Monday in

October, I'm Dancing as Fast as I Can, Hannah K, Where Are The Children?, Shy People.
TELEVISION: Search For Tomorrow, Miles To Go, Hustling, Griffin and Phoenix, Who Gets the Friends?

CLAYTON, JACK: Producer, Director. b. 1921. Ent. m.p. 1935 as asst. dir. for London Films, Fox, Warner. Served H.M. Forces 1940–46; Naples is a Battlefield (dir., co-cine., s.p., 1944); prod. man. Ideal Husband; assoc. prod.: Queen of Spades, Flesh and Blood, Moulin Rouge, Beat the Devil, The Good Die Young, I Am a Camera.
PICTURES: Bespoke Overcoat (prod., dir. Oscar best short, 1956); Venice Festival prize-winning film; prod.: Sailors Beware, Dry Rot, Three Men in a Boat; dir.: Room at the Top, (BAFTA award best film 1958), The Innocents, The Pumpkin Eater; prod.-dir., Our Mother's House, dir.; The Great Gatsby; Something Wicked This Way Comes; The Lonely Passion of Judith Hearne.

CLEESE, JOHN: Actor. b. Weston-Super-Mare, England, Oct. 27, 1939. e. Clifton Coll., Cambridge U. Member Monty Python's Flying Circus.
PICTURES: Interlude, The Best House in London, The Rise and Rise of Michael Rimmer, And Now for Something Completely Different, The Love Ban, Monty Python and the Holy Grail, The Life of Brian (co-s.p.), The Great Muppet Caper, Time Bandits, Privates on Parade, Monty Python's The Meaning of Life, Yellowbeard, Silverado, Clockwise, The Secret Policeman's Third Ball, A Fish Called Wanda (co-exec. prod., co-s.p.), The Big Picture (cameo).
TELEVISION: Taming of the Shrew, Doctor in the House, Monty Python's Flying Circus, Fawlty Towers, etc.

CLEMENS, BRIAN: Writer, Producer, Director. b. Croydon, England, 1931. Early career in advertising then wrote BBC TV play. Later TV filmed series as writer, script editor and features. Script editor "Danger Man"; Won Edgar Allen Poe Award for Best TV Thriller of 1962 (Scene of the Crime for U.S. Steel Hour). Various plays for Armchair Theatre; ATV Drama 70; Love Story. Writer and Producer of The Avengers (two Emmy nominations for Best Production 1967 and 1968), Winner two Edgar Allen Poe Awards, Cinema Fantastique Award for best screenplay.
PICTURES INCLUDE: The Tell-Tale Heart, Station Six-Sahara, The Peking Medallion, And Soon The Darkness, The Major, When The Wind Blows, See No Evil, Dr. Jekyll and Sister Hyde, Golden Voyage of Sinbad, Watcher in the Woods, Stiff.
TELEVISION: Wrote and prod.: The New Avengers, The Professionals, Escapade (in U.S. for Quinn Martin).

CLIFFORD, GRAEME: Director.
PICTURES: Frances; Burke & Wills; Gleaming the Cube.
TELEVISION: The Boy Who Left Home; Little Red Riding Hood (Faerie Tale Theatre).

CLIFT, DENISON: Author, Director. b. May 2, 1893. e. Stanford U. Editor, Overland Monthly and other publications; publicity expert, San Francisco, 1917. Scenario writer and dir. for Fox, Paramount, MGM; dir. Honor Among Men, Ports of Call, This Freedom, A Bill of Divorcement, Paradise, The Mystery of the Mary Celeste, etc. Dir. for British International, Ideal Films, Gainsborough Pictures and Hammer Prod., London. Author of novels, Guns of Galt, Man About Town, The Mighty Thing, I Belong to You. Author of the New York plays, The Woman Disputed, Scotland Yard; and London plays, The Moon Is Red and Gentle Rain.

CLORE, LEON: Producer. Co-prod.: Conquest of Everest, Virgin Island, Every Day Except Christmas (Grand Prix Venice), Apaches, Executive Producer: Time Without Pity. Producer: Sunday by the Sea. (Grand Prix Venice), Bow Bells, We Are the Lambeth Boys (Grand Prix Tours), Dispute (British Film Academy Award), I Want to Go to School, All Neat in Black Stockings, Morgan—A Suitable Case For Treatment, The French Lieutenant's Woman.

CLORK, HARRY: Writer. r.n. Clarke; b. Galveston, TX. e. St. Paul's Academy, Garden City, NY. Was husband of late Nora Bayes, writer of her stage material; author several stage plays (Smiling Faces, The Milky Way, See My Lawyer) (collab., filmed in 1936 by Paramount); adapt. many plays for Shubert stage enterprises; radio writer. From 1935 writer many s.p. & adapt.
PICTURES INCLUDE: Thrill of Brazil, Mighty McGurk, Sainted Sisters, Painting the Clouds with Sunshine, Tea for Two, Ma and Pa Kettle at Waikiki, The Prisoner.
TELEVISION: Beulah, Life of Riley.

CLOSE, GLENN: Actress. b. Greenwich, CT., Mar. 19, 1947. e. Coll. of William and Mary. Began performing with a repertory group Fingernails, then toured country with folk-singing groups. Professional debut at Phoenix Theatre, New York, in season of plays including Love for Love, The Member of the Wedding, Rules of the Game. Also accomplished musical performer (lyric soprano).

THEATER: The Crucifer of Blood (1978), The Singular Life of Albert Nobbs (Obie Award), Rex, Barnum, The Real Thing (Tony Award, 1984), Benefactors, Wine Untouched, Uncommon Women and Others.
PICTURES: The World According to Garp (debut), The Big Chill, The Natural, The Stone Boy, Jagged Edge, Maxie, Fatal Attraction, Light Years (voice), Orders, Les Liaisons Dangereuses, The White Crow.
TELEVISION: Movies: The Orphan Train, Too Far To Go, Something About Amelia, Stones for Ibarra.

CLOVER, DAVID: Actor. b. November 10.
TELEVISION INCLUDES: Policewoman, Police Story, McLaren's Raiders; Kate McShane; One Day At A Time; Delphi Bureau; On The Rocks; The Dick Cavett Special.

CLUG, A. STEPHEN: Executive. b. New York, NY, Apr. 2, 1929. e. Colgate U., Columbia Law Sch. Was special agent, U.S. Army Counter Intelligence Corps, Far East Command, 1951–54. Started with industry as branch mgr., Paramount Films of Indonesia, 1954; mgr. dir., Paramount Films of India, Ltd., supervising India, Burma, Pakistan, Persian Gulf, 1955–57; Far East supvr. for special handling, The Ten Commandments, 1957–8; co-ordinator world-wide program theatrical re-releases, Paramount Intl., 1958–9; mgr., dir., Paramount Films of Brasil, 1959–65; v.p. & exec. prod., Gold Dolphin Prods., Inc., N.Y. 1965–69; gen. mgr. & supvr. Central America/Caribbean areas, MGM Intl. Inc., Panama, 1969–71; gen. mgr., MGM Puerto Rico/supvr. Caribbean area/MGM Cinemas, 1971–3; dir. sls. & asst. continental supvr. for Europe, UK, Middle East, MGM Intl., Inc. 1973–79; v.p./sls. mgr., MGM Intl., headquartered in Paris, 79–82; joined MPEAA as v.p. and regional rep. for Far East and Australia, headquartered in Singapore, 1982.

COBE, SANDY: Executive, Producer, Distributor. b. New York, NY, Nov. 30, 1928. e. Tulane U., B.A., fine arts. U.S. Army W.W.II & Korea, combat photographer; produced 11 features for Artmark Pictures, N.Y. General Studios, exec. v.p., distribution; First Cinema Releasing Corp., pres. Formed Sandy Cobe Productions, Inc., producer, packager, European features for U.S. theatrical & television. Pres., Intercontinental Releasing Corporation, domestic and foreign distribution of theatrical features.
MEMBER: Dir. of bd., American Film Marketing Assn., Dir. of bd., Scitech Corp. USA, 14 year mem., Academy of Television Arts and Sciences, 32nd degree Mason, Shriner, Variety Club Int'l. Special commendations from: Mayor of Los Angeles, California State Senate, City and County of L.A., California Assembly and Senate, and Governor of CA.
PICTURES: Terror on Tour (prod.), Access Code (exec. prod.), A.R.C.A. D.E. (prod.), Terminal Entry (exec. prod.).

COBE, SHARYON REIS: Executive. b. Honolulu, HI, e. U. of Hawaii, Loyola Marymount U. Dancer Fitzgerald, & Sample, N.Y. United Air Lines, N.Y.; v.p., story editor, Gotham Publishing N.Y.; v.p., distribution-foreign sales, World Wide Film Distributors, L.A.; exec. v.p., Intercontinental Releasing Corp., L.A.
MEMBER: Women in Show Business, Ladies of Variety (tent 25).
PICTURES: Terror on Tour (prod. co-ordinator), Home Sweet Home (prod. mgr.), To All a Good Night (assoc. prod.), Access Code (co-prod.), Terminal Entry (prod.).

COBLENZ, WALTER: Producer.
PICTURES: The Candidate; All the President's Men; The Onion Field; The Legend of the Lone Ranger; Strange Invaders; Sister Sister; 18 Again!; For Keeps.

COBURN, JAMES: Actor. b. Laurel, NB, Aug. 31, 1928. e. Los Angeles City Coll., where he studied drama. Served in U.S. Army. First acting role in coast production of Billy Budd. Later to New York, where he worked on TV commercials, then in teleplays on Studio One, GE Theatre, Robert Montgomery Presents. Summer stock in Detroit before returning to Hollywood. First film, 1959, was Ride Lonesome.
PICTURES INCLUDE: Foes of the Fugitive, The Magnificent Seven, Hell Is for Heroes, The Great Escape, Charade, The Americanization of Emily, The Loved One, Major Dundee, A High Wind in Jamaica, Our Man Flint, What Did You Do in the War, Daddy?, Dead Heat on a Merry-Go-Round, In Like Flint, Waterhole No. 3, Candy, Hard Contract, The Last of the Mobile Hot Shots, The Carey Treatment, The Honkers, Duck, You Sucker, The Last of Sheila, Harry in Your Pocket, A Reason to Live, A Reason to Die, The Internecine Project, Bite the Bullet, Hard Times, Sky Riders, The Last Hard Men, Midway, Cross of Iron, Firepower, The Big Bullet, Loving Couples, Looker, Martin's Day, Death of a Soldier, Walking After Midnight, Train to Heaven.
TELEVISION: Draw!, Sins of the Fathers, Malibu, The Dain Curse, Valley of the Dolls, Pinocchio (Faerie Tale Theater).

COCA, IMOGENE: Actress. b. Philadelphia, PA, Nov. 18, 1908. p. the late Joe Coca, orchestra leader, and Sadie Brady, retired vaudevillian. At 11, debut tap dancer in New York vaudeville; solo dancer Broadway musicals; as comedienne, in New Faces of 1934; with former husband, Bob Burton, in Straw Hat Revue in 1939, and others through 1942. New York night clubs, Cafe Society and Le Ruban Bleu, New York; Palmer House, Chicago; Park Plaza, St. Louis. 1949 to TV via Broadway Revue, evolved routines with Sid Caesar, Your Show of Shows, 1950–54. NBC-TV; Imogene Coca Show, 1954, 1955; Sid Caesar Invites You, 1958, Glinda.
PICTURES INCLUDE: Under the Yum Yum Tree, Rabbit Test, National Lampoon's Vacation, Nothing Lasts Forever, Buy and Cell.
TELEVISION INCLUDES: Glinda (series); Ruggles of Red Gap; Moonlighting. Movies: Alice in Wonderland, Return of the Beverly Hillbillies.

COCCHI, JOHN: Writer, Critic. b. Brooklyn, NY, June 19, 1939. e. Fort Hamilton H.S., 1957; Brooklyn College, A.A.S., 1961. U.S. Army, 1963–65. Puritan Film Labs, manager,1967–9. Independent-International Pictures, biographer-researcher, 1969. Boxoffice Magazine, critic, reporter, columnist, 1970–79. Co-author: The American Movies Reference Book (Prentice-Hall). Contributor: Screen Facts, Film Fan Monthly, Films in Review. Actor in: The Diabolical Dr. Ongo, Thick as Thieves, Captain Celluloid VS. the Film Pirates. Worked on dubbing: Dirtymouth, 1970. Author, The Westerns, a Movie Quiz Book. Contributor to various books on films. Author, Second Feature (A History of the B' Movie). Now free lance writer, researcher, agent. Recent credits: researcher for American Movie Classics (Rainbow Programming Service); contributor to books, 500 Best American Films, 500 Best British and Foreign-Language Films. Consultant to Killiam Shows, Prof. Richard Brown, Phototeque, Star Magazine.

COCHRAN, RON: Producer, Writer, Narrator. b. Saskatchewan, Canada, Sept. 20, 1912. e. Parsons Coll., U. of Florida. Newscaster for radio stations in Rock Island, IL, Des Moines, St. Louis; special agent, FBI 1942–45; then returned to radio as news dir., dir. of news WCOP Boston 1945–51; joined CBS-TV news staff, 1951, in Washington; newscaster, Late News Show; news roundups, CBS radio; moderator, Capitol Cloakroom, Where Do You Stand, Man of the Week; CBS news staff, N.Y., 1954; newscaster. The Late News; moderator, Youth Takes a Stand, One O'clock Report, CBS-TV; In Person, CBS-Radio; News, ABC-TV, 1962; Ron Cochran With the News 1967; Pres., Ron Cochran Enterprises Inc., producer and syndicator or radio and television.

COEN, ETHAN: Producer, Writer. b. St. Louis Park, MN, 1958. e. Princeton U. Co-wrote s.p. with brother, Joel, XYZ Murders (renamed Crime Wave).
PICTURES: Blood Simple (prod., co-s.p., co-edited under pseudonym Roderick James); Raising Arizona (prod., co-s.p.).

COEN, GUIDO: Producer and Executive Prod. series pictures for Fortress Films and Kenilworth Films.
PICTURES INCLUDE: One Jump Ahead, Golden Link, The Hornet's Nest, Behind the Headlines, Murder Reported, There's Always a Thursday, Date with Disaster, The End of the Line, The Man Without a Body, Woman Eater, Kill Her Gently, Naked Fury, Operation Cupid, Strictly Confidential, Dangerous Afternoon, Jungle Street, Strongroom, Penthouse, Baby Love, One Brief Summer, Burke and Hare, Au Pair Girls, Intimate Games, Twickenham Studios.

COEN, JOEL: Director, Writer. b. St. Louis Park, MN, 1955. e. Simon's Rock College, MA; studied film at NYU. Was asst. editor on the Evil Dead and worked with rock video crews. Co-wrote with brother, Ethan, s.p. for XYZ Murders (renamed Crime Wave.)
PICTURES: Blood Simple (dir., co-s.p., co-editor with brother, Ethan under pseudonym Roderick James), Raising Arizona (dir., co-s.p.).

COHEN, CHARLES: Executive. b. Brooklyn, NY, Sept. 15, 1912. e. Brooklyn Coll. Pub. dept., MGM, 1931; U-I, 1948–50; 20th-Fox, 1950; assoc. adv. mgr.; eastern asst. adv. & pub. mgr. Allied Artists, 1955; home off. pub. mgr. Warner Bros., 1957. Eastern adv. mgr. 1958; eastern adv., pub. mgr., 1960; Exec. ass't to adv. pub. director, 1960; expl. dir., Embassy Pictures, 1961; nat. adv. & pub. dir., Cinema V Dist., 1964; Adv. & Pub. Dir., Sigma III, 1968; adv., pub. mgr., The Cannon Group, 1970, v.p., adv.-pub. rel. 1971; Adv.-Pub. Dir., U.A. Eastern Theatres, 1973–77 (retired). Since 1978, has served as volunteer writer for Variety Clubs International magazine, the Barker, and in the creation of institutional fund-raising ad campaigns for V.C.I. Co-author with Morton Sunshine of This Is Variety, a brochure tracing the origins, development and accomplishments of Variety Clubs around the world.

COHEN, ELLIS A.: Producer, Writer. b. Baltimore, MD, Sept. 15, 1945. e. Baltimore Jr. Coll., A.A. Since 1983 pres., Hennessey Entertainment, Ltd. 1980, pres. Ellis A. Cohen Prods., 1978, Director of TV Network Boxing Events, Don King Productions, Inc., N.Y. 1978, Account Exec., Solters & Roskin P.R. L.A. 1977, Prod., Henry Jaffe Enterprises, Inc., 1974–76 dir., worldwide pub./adv., William Morris Agency, 1963, talent coordinator, Cerebral Palsy Telethon, WBAL-TV, Baltimore; 1964, p.r. asst. Campbell-Ewald Adv. Agency, L.A.; 1966, and mgr., Hochschild Kohn Dept. Stores, Baltimore; 1968–69, asst. dir., p.r. entertainment, talent booking for Club Venus Night Club, Baltimore; 1968, created-edited The Forum Oracle, national entertainment mag. 1969–72, dir., p.r., Jewish Community Center of Baltimore; 1970, leave of absence to work as corr. in Israel, Denmark & London; 1972, dir., p.r.& adv., The Camera Mart, New York; 1972–74 creator & editor-in-chief, TV/New York Magazine, nationwide TV mag.; Producer, New York Area Emmy Awards Telecast (1973 & 1974), WOR-TV (prod.), chm., exec. prod. of TV Academy Celebrity drop-in luncheon series; 1972, talent coordinator Bob Hope's Celebrity Flood Relief Telethon. Member: Writers Guild of America, Producers Guild of America, Friars Club, Amer. Newspaper Guild, Intl. Press Corp., Israeli Press Corp., National Academy of TV Arts & Sciences, Academy of Television Arts & Sciences, Screen Arts Guild. Mayor Beame's Committee in the Public Interest for N.Y.C.; executive producer, 1976 Democratic National Convention Gala.

TELEVISION: Aunt Mary (prod.-story by); New York Area Emmy Awards, 1973 (prod.) and 1974, (prod.). First Steps, Love Mary.

COHEN, HERMAN: Producer, Writer. b. Detroit, MI. Age 12, usher, Detroit, Dexter theatre; chief of service, Detroit, Fox theatre; mgr., booker, Dexter Theatres; military service; house mgr., Fox theatre; sales mgr. Columbia Pictures, Detroit; prod., Realart, Jack Broder Productions, Hollywood; formed own prod. Co., 1953; owner, Fox and Cinderella Theatres, Detroit; prod. pictures for Columbia and Warner Bros. Heads Cobra Media, Inc.

PICTURES INCLUDE: River Beat, Magnificent Roughnecks, The Brass Legend, Target Earth, Crime of Passion, Horrors of the Black Museum, I was a Teenage Werewolf, I Was a Teenage Frankenstein, Blood of Dracula, How to Make a Monster, Konga, Headless Ghost, Black Zoo, A Study in Terror, Berserk, Crooks and Coronets, TROG, Craze.

COHEN, IRWIN R.: Exhibition Executive. b. Baltimore, MD, Sept. 4, 1924. e. U. of Baltimore, (LLB) 1948, admitted to Maryland and U.S. Bar same year. Active limited practice. R/C Theatres outgrowth of family business started in 1932. One of founders of Key Federal Bank, chairman of board Loan Comm., director and member of exec. comm. Pres. NATO of Virginia 1976–78, chairman 1978–80. Director, member of exec. comm., and chairman of finance comm. National NATO. Member of Motion Picture Pioneers, and various other orgs.

COHEN, LARRY: Writer, Director. b. Chicago, IL, April 20, 1947. e. U. of Wisconsin.

PICTURES: Writer: Carrie, God Told Me To, The American Success Company, The Jury. Writer-Director: The Winger Serpent (also prod.), Special Effects, Perfect Strangers, Full Moon High (also prod.), It's Alive III, Deadly Illusion (co-dir., s.p.); Best Seller (s.p.); Maniac Cop (prod., s.p.).

COHEN, MILTON E.: Distributor. b. Chicago, IL. e. U. of Illinois. Entered motion picture industry as salesman. United Artists, Chicago, 1925–29; Columbia, Chicago, 1929–31; salesman, Detroit, 1931–38; sales mgr., RKO, Detroit, 1938; branch mgr., 1943; Eastern-Central dist. mgr., 1946; Eastern sales mgr., Eagle Lion Classics, 1948; genl. sales mgr., 1951; western & southern sales mgr., United Artist, 1951; Eastern & Southern sales mgr., 1952; supervisor, sales, Around The World In 80 Days, 1958; Eastern Canadian sales mgr., 1959; national dir., Roadshow Sales, 1961; retired. United Artists, 1969; exec. v.p. in charge of theatrical distrib. for Trans Globe Films, Inc., 1971.

COHEN, ROB: Producer, Director. b. Cornwall-on-the-Hudson, NY, March 12, 1949. e. Harvard U. BA. Formerly exec. v.p. in chg of m.p. and TV for Motown. Started as dir. of m.p. for TV at 20th Century-Fox. Joined Motown at age of 24 to produce films. Headed own production co. 1985, appt. pres., Keith Barish Prods.

PICTURES INCLUDE: Mahogany, Bingo Long and the Traveling All-Stars, Scott Joplin, Almost Summer, Thank God It's Friday, The Wiz, A Small Circle of Friends (dir.), Scandalous (dir., co- s.p.), The Razor's Edge (prod.), The Legend of Billie Jean (prod.), Light of Day (co-prod.), The Witches of Eastwick (co-exec. prod.), The Monster Squad (co-exec. prod.); Ironweed (co-exec. prod.); The Running Man (co-exec. prod.); The Serpent and the Rainbow, A Message From Salazar (co-exec. prod.).

TELEVISION: Miami Vice (dir.).

COHEN, ROBERT B.: Executive. e. George Washington U., B.A., Southern Texas Sch. of Law. 1980–84. Atty. for Greenberg, Glusker, Fields, Clamans and Machtinger (L.A.). Was asst. gen. counsel for Columbia Pictures. Joined Paramount 1985 as sr. atty. for M.P. Group. to oversee legal functions for assigned feature films; 1988 named v.p. in charge of legal affairs, Motion Picture Group of Paramount.

COHN, ROBERT: Producer. b. Avon, NJ, Sept. 6, 1920. e. U. of Michigan, B.A., 1941. p. Jack Cohn. Joined Columbia as asst. dir. In W.W.II, as Signal Corps film cutter. Air Corps Training Lab. unit mgr., combat aerial m.p. camera man with 13th A.A.F. Awarded: DFC, Air Medal & 3 clusters, Purple Heart. Assoc. prod. Lone Wolf In London, 1947; prod. Adventures in Silverado, 1948, all Col. Headed Robert Cohn prod. unit at Columbia, pres. International Cinema Guild. Columbia European prod.: exec. Columbia Studios. Hollywood: formed Robert Cohn Prod.

PICTURES INCLUDE: Black Eagle, Rusty Leads the Way, Palomino, Kazan, Killer That Stalked New York, The Barefoot Mailman, Mission Over Korea, The Interns, The New Interns, The Young Americans.

COLBERT, CLAUDETTE: Actress: r.n. Lily Chauchoin. b. Paris, Sept. 13, 1903. e. public schools, Paris, New York; Art Students League, N.Y. On N.Y. stage (debut, Wild Wescotts; following Marionette Man, We've Got to Have Money, Cat Came Back, Kiss in a Taxi, Ghost Train, The Barker, Dynamo, etc.). First screen role in Love O' Mike (silent); Academy Award best actress, 1934 (It Happened One Night); voted one of ten best Money Making Stars in Fame Poll, 1935, '36, '47.

PICTURES INCLUDE: Cleopatra, I Cover the Waterfront, No Time for Love, Practically Yours, Since You Went Away, So Proudly We Hail, Guest Wife, Tomorrow Is Forever, The Egg and I, Sleep My Love, Family Honeymoon, Bride for Sale, Three Came Home, The Secret Fury, Thunder on the Hill, Let's Make It Legal, Outpost in Malaya, Daughters of Destiny, Texas Lady, Parrish.

BROADWAY: Marriage Go Round, Irregular Verb to Love, The Kingfisher, Aren't We All?

TELEVISION: The Two Mrs. Grenvilles.

COLBY, RONALD: Producer, Director, Writer. b. New York, NY. e. Hofstra U., New York U. Began career as playwright at Cafe La Mama and Caffe Cino; performed in off-Bdwy shows; spent year as actor-writer in residence at Pittsburgh Playhouse. Served as dialogue coach and asst. to Francis Coppola; was v.p. of Zoetrope Studios. Directed several documentaries and short films.

PICTURES: Rain People (prod.), Hammett (prod.), Some Kind of Wonderful (exec. prod.), She's Having a Baby (exec. prod.).

COLE, GEORGE: Actor. b. London, Eng., Apr. 22, 1925. e. secondary sch. Surrey. Stage debut in White Horse Inn, 1939; m.p. debut in Cottage to Let, 1941.

PICTURES INCLUDE: Henry V, Quartet, My Brother's Keeper, Laughter in Paradise, Scrooge, Lady Godiva Rides Again, Who Goes There (Passionate Sentry), Morning Departure (Operation Disaster), Top Secret (Mr. Potts Goes to Moscow), Happy Family, Will Any Gentleman, Apes of the Rock, The Intruder, Happy Ever After (Tonight's the Night), Our Girl Friday (Adventures of Sadie), Belles of St. Trinian's, Prize of Gold, Where There's a Will, Constant Husband, Quentin Durward, The Weapon, It's a Wonderful Life, Green Man, Bridal Path, Too Many Crooks, Blue Murder at St. Trinians, Don't Panic Chaps, Dr. Syn, One Way Pendulum, Legend of Young Dick Turpin, The Great St. Trinian's Train Robbery, Cleopatra, The Green Shoes, Vampire Lovers, Fright, The Bluebird.

TELEVISION: Life of Bliss, A Man of Our Times, Don't Forget To Write, The Good Life, Minder.

COLE, SIDNEY: Producer, Director, Writer. b. London, England, 1908. e. Westminster City Sch., London U., B.Sc. Began at Stoll Studios 1930; then various feature and documentary studios. Dir. Roads Across Britain. Spanish ABC. Behind the Spanish Lines. Ed. Gaslight. Mr. Pimpernel Smith, San Demetrio, London, Nine Men, etc.; tech. adviser First of the Few; writer and assoc. prod. They Came to a City, Return of the Vikings; assoc. prod Dead of Night, Loves of Joanna Godden, Against the Wind, Scott of the Antarctic, The Magnet, Man in the White Suit, Train of Events (co-dir.); Operation Swallow (Eng. adapt.); The Angel Who Pawned Her Harp (writer-prod.); s.p., North Sea Bus. Assoc. prod. Escapade; prod. Sword of Sherwood Forest; prod. s.p. The Kitchen; prod. We Are The Engineers, One in Five.

TELEVISION: prod. Adventures of Robin Hood, The Buccaneers, Sword of Freedom, The Four Just Men, Danger Man (Secret Agent), Man in a Suitcase, Adventures of Black Beauty, Dick Turpin, Smuggler, Adventurer.

COLEMAN, DABNEY: Actor. b. Austin, TX, Jan. 3, 1932. e. VA Military Inst. 1949–51; U. Texas 1951–57; Neighborhood Playhouse School Theater 1958–60. A regular on the TV series, Mary Hartman, Mary Hartman.

PICTURES INCLUDE: This Property Is Condemned, The Slender Thread, The Scalphunters, The Other Side of the Mountain, The Black Streetfighter, Rolling Thunder, Viva Knievel, North Dallas Forty, Nothing Personal, How To Beat the High Cost of Living, Melvin and Howard, Nine to Five, On Golden Pond, Modern Problems, Young Doctors in Love, The Muppets Take Manhattan, Tootsie, WarGames, Cloak and Dagger, The Man with One Red Shoe, Dragnet, Hot to Trot.

TELEVISION: Movies: Apple Pie, When She Was Bad, Murrow, Guilty of Innocence, Sworn To Silence (Emmy Award), Plaza Suite, Baby M. Mini-Series: Fresno. Series: Forever Fernwood, Buffalo Bill, The Slap Maxwell Story.

COLEMAN, GARY: Actor. b. Zion, IL, Feb. 8, 1968. Gained fame as star of TV's Diff'rent Strokes.
TELEVISION: The Little Rascals, America 2-Night, Good Times, The Jeffersons, Diff'rent Strokes, Lucy Moves to NBC, The Big Show, etc. Movies: The Kid from Left Field, Scout's Honor, Playing with Fire, The Kid With the Broken Halo; The Kid with the 200 I.Q.
PICTURES: On the Right Track, Jimmy the Kid.

COLEMAN, NANCY: Actress. b. Everett, WA, Dec. 30, 1917. e. U. of Washington. In radio serials; on New York stage (with Gertrude Lawrence, in Theatre Guild productions). Desperate Hours, 1955; m.p. debut, 1941, American Theatre Guild Rep. Co. tour of Europe and So. America.
PICTURES INCLUDE: Kings Row, Dangerously They Live, Gay Sisters, Desperate Journey, Edge of Darkness, In Our Time, Devotion, Violence, Mourning Becomes Electra, That Man from Tangier, Slaves.
TELEVISION: Valiant Lady Producers Showcase, Adams Chronicles.

COLEMAN, THOMAS J.: Executive. b. Connecticut, Apr. 13, 1950. e. Boston U. Pres., Twalzo Music Corp., 1972–73; natl. sls. mgr., United Intl. Pictures, 1973–74; founded Atlantic Releasing Corp., 1974; Atlantic Television, Inc., 1981. All Atlantic corps. consolidated into Atlantic Entertainment Group, 1986. Co. has distributed over 100 films and produced 30 features and TV movies.
PICTURES: Producer or Exec. Prod.: Valley Girl, Alphabet City, Roadhouse, Night of the Comet, Starchaser, Teen Wolf, Extremities, The Men's Club, Modern Girls, Nutcracker, Teen Wolf Too (exec. prod.); Cop (exec. prod.); Patty Hearst (exec. prod.).

COLER, JOEL H.: Executive. b. Bronx, NY, 1931. e. Syracuse U., B.A., journalism. Worked as adv. asst. NBC; acct. exec. Grey advertising. Joined 20th Century-Fox 1964 as adv. coordinator Fox Intl.; 1967, named intl. adv./pub. mgr. 1974, named v.p. dir., intl. adv./pub.

COLLERAN, BILL: Producer-Director. b. April 16. Story department 20th Century-Fox 1945–46; Director Louis de Rochemont 1946–50; stage mgr. NBC 1951; Assoc. Dir. The Hit Parade 1952–53; Dir. The Hit Parade, various TV specs. 1954–56; Dir. Cinerama Windjammer 1956; TV Specs. Bing Crosby, Frank Sinatra, Debbie Reynolds 1957–60; various TV specs. 1960–65, Exec. Prod. Judy Garland Show, Dean Martin Show, 1965–66; Dir. Richard Burton's "Hamlet" film, Prod. "Popendipity" ABC-TV spec. various other TV specs. 1967–70; 1971–77 Various TV specials and series; 1978–83, prod., dir., writer for Hill-Eubanks Group and Little Joey, Inc.; 1984–86, dir. music video for Simba; developing film and TV projects for own production co.

COLLIN, REGINALD: Producer/Director. Trained at the Old Vic Theatre School as actor. Directed in repertory, also pantomimes and summer shows. Entered television 1958. Producer ITV's First Arts Programme Tempo. Producer of Callan, Mystery And Imagination, Special Branch, Napoleon And Love. 1975: Producer/director two Armchair Cinemas, also documentary on the Royal Shakespeare Theatre. 1976: Vice-Chairman of the British Academy of Film and Television Arts. Chairman of the Awards Committee. Director of BAFTA 1977–87. Fellow of the RTS.

COLLINS, JOAN: Actress. b. London, Eng., May 23, 1933. e. Francis Holland Sch., London. Made stage debut in A Doll's House, Arts Theatre 1946. Screen debut in I Believe in You, 1952. TV appearances include Dynasty series.
PICTURES INCLUDE: I Believe in You, Judgment Deferred, Decameron Nights, Cosh Boy, The Square Ring, Turn the Key Softly, Our Girl Friday (Adventures of Sadie), The Good Die Young, Land of the Pharaohs, Virgin Queen, Girl in the Red Velvet Swing, Opposite Sex, Sea Wife, Island in the Sun, Wayward Bus, Stopover Tokyo, The Bravados, Rally Round the Flag Boys, Seven Thieves, Esther and the King, Warning Shot, Can Hieronymus Merkin Ever Forget Mercy Humpe and Find True Happiness?, The Executioner, Tales from the Crypt, The Bawdy Adventures of Tom Jones, Empire of the Ants, The Big Sleep, Sunburn, The Stud, The Bitch.
TELEVISION: Movies: The Cartier Affair, The Making of a Male Model, Her Life as a Man, Paper Dolls, The Wild Women of Chastity Gulch, Hansel and Gretel (Faerie Tale Theater). Mini-Series: Sins, Monte Carlo (also exec. prod.).

COLLINS, PAT: Performer. r.n. Patricia Colinaka Allan. b. Detroit, MI, May 7, 1935. e. U. of Illinois, 1953. District mgr., Yardley Created Prods., Chicago; played in various nightclubs, Chicago, Miami, Las Vegas, etc. On CBS Morning News.
PICTURE: Experiment in Nightmares.
TELEVISION (1963–65): Steven Allen, Bill Dana Show, No

Time for Sergeants, Mike Douglas, Art Linkletter, Honey West.

COLLINS, STEPHEN: Actor. b. Des Moines, IA, Oct. 1, 1947. Appeared off-Bdwy. in several Joseph Papp productions before acquiring role on Bdwy. in The Ritz. Also on Bdwy. in Moonchildren, Anatol.
PICTURES: All the President's Men, Between the Lines, The Promise, Star Trek, Fedora, Loving Couples, Brewster's Millions, Jumpin' Jack Flash, Choke Canyon, The Big Picture.
TELEVISION: Tales of the Gold Monkey, Chiefs, Dark Mirror, Threesome, Hold the Dream, Inside the Third Reich, The Two Mrs. Grenvilles, Weekend War, Tattinger's (series).

COLT, MARSHALL: Actor. b. New Orleans, LA, Oct. 26. e. Tulane U. B.S. Physics. Did naval tour in Southeast Asia during Vietnam War. Acted in local stage productions in San Francisco (Hotel Universe, Who's Afraid of Virginia Woolf?, Zoo Story, etc.).
PICTURES: Bimbo (short), North Dallas Forty, Those Lips, Those Eyes, Jagged Edge.
TELEVISION: Series: Family, Paper Chase, Streets of San Francisco, Barnaby Jones, McClain's Law, Lottery! Movies: Colorado C-1, Sharon: Portrait of a Mistress, Once an Eagle, To Heal a Nation, Mercy or Murder, Justice Delayed.

COLTRANE, ROBBIE: Actor. b. Rutherglen, Scotland, 1950. Ent. ind. 1974. Early career at Traverse Theatre, Edinburgh. Work included John Byrn's Slab Boys Trilogy.
TELEVISION: Kick Up The Eighties, Alfresco, Laugh I Nearly Paid My Licence Fee, Comic Strip Presents Five Go Mad in Dorset, Beat Generation, Susie, Gino and Bullshitters, Tutti Frutti.
PICTURES: Subway Riders, Ghost Dance, Krull Caravaggio, Defence of the Realm, Chinese Boxes, Supergrass, Mona Lisa, Fruit Machine.

COLUMBUS, CHRIS: Director, Writer: b. Spangler, PA, 1959. Grew up in Ohio. Started making short super 8 films in high school, studied screenwriting at New York U. Film Sch., graduated 1980. Sold first s.p., Jocks, while at college. Wrote for and developed TV cartoon series, Galaxy High School.
PICTURES: wrote screenplay for: Reckless, Gremlins, The Goonies, Young Sherlock Holmes; worked on third Indiana Jones s.p., Little Nemo in Slumberland (animated film). Directing debut: Adventures in Babysitting (1987), Heartbreak Hotel (dir., s.p.).
TELEVISION: Amazing Stories, Twilight Zone, Alfred Hitchcock Presents.

COLVILLE, JOHN: Producer, Director. Started in theatre. Worked in all departments before becoming Film Editor on Features, Documentaries, and Television Series for both BBC/ITV. Extensive experience in Greece, Singapore, Spain, Switzerland—now establishing new Unit, Studios, and Producing films in Nigeria.

COMDEN, BETTY: Writer. b. Brooklyn, NY, May 3, 1919. e. New York U. Nightclub performer, 1939–44 in the Revuers; writer book, sketches & lyrics for many Bway. shows.
THEATER: all with Adolph Green: On the Town (1944); Billion Dollar Baby; Bonanza Bound!; Two on the Aisle (sketches and lyrics); Wonderful Town (Tony Award, 1953); Peter Pan; Bells Are Ringing; Say, Darling; A Party With Comden and Green; Do Re Mi; Subways Are For Sleeping; Fade Out-Fade In; Leonard Bernstein's Theatre Songs; Hallelujah, Baby (Tony Award, 1968); Applause (book), Tony Award; Lorelei (revision to book); By Bernstein (book and some lyrics); On the Twentieth Century (book and lyrics); A Doll's Life.
PICTURES INCLUDE: All with Adolph Green: Good News, On the Town, Barkleys of Broadway, Singin' in the Rain, Band Wagon, It's Always Fair Weather, What a Way to Go, Bells Are Ringing, Auntie Mame, Say Darling.

COMO, PERRY: Singer. b. Canonsburg, PA, May 18, 1912. e. Canonsburg local schools. p. Pietro and Lucille Travaglini Como. Barber at 15; joined Carlone Band, then Ted Weems in 1936; CBS sustaining show; played many night clubs, records for Victor. Screen debut, Something for the Boys (1944). Knight Commander and Lady Com. (Mrs. Como) of Equestrian Order of Holy Sepulchre of Jerusalem; personality of the yr., Variety Club, 1956.
PICTURES INCLUDE: Doll Face, If I'm Lucky, Words and Music.
TELEVISION: Perry Como show. NBC-TV. Best Male vocalist M.P. Daily, TV poll, 1955; radio poll, 1954. Best Male vocalist M.P. Daily, TV Poll, 1956: best TV performer M.P.D.—Fame poll 1957. Interfaith Award, 1953; Emmy, Peabody, Christopher Awards, 1955–56; Perry Como Kraft Music Hall, NBC-TV.

COMPTON, JOYCE: Actress. b. Lexington, KY. e. Tulsa U. Screen debut in Ankles Preferred.
PICTURES INCLUDE: The Awful Truth, Spring Madness, Sky Murder, Turnabout, A Southern Yankee, If I Had a Million, Christmas in Connecticut, Artists and Models Abroad,

Rustlers of Red Dog, The White Parade, Wild Party, Three Sisters, Grand Canyon, Jet Pilot, The Persuader, Girl in the Woods.

CONAWAY, JEFF: Actor. b. New York, NY, Oct. 5, 1950. Started in show business at the age of 10 when he appeared in Bdwy. production, All the Way Home. Later toured in Critics Choice before turning to fashion modeling. Toured with musical group, 3½, as lead singer and guitarist. Entered theatre arts program at New York U. Film debut at 19 in Jennifer on My Mind.
THEATER: Grease, The News.
PICTURES: The Eagle Has Landed, Pete's Dragon, I Never Promised You a Rose Garden, Grease, The Patriot, Elvira: Mistress of the Dark, Cover Girl.
TELEVISION: From Sea to Shining Sea (1974); Joe Forrester, The Mary Tyler Moore Show, Happy Days, Movin' On, Barnaby Jones, Kojak, Wizards and Warrior, Mickey Spillane's Mike Hammer, Taxi (regular), Benengers. Movies: Having Babies, Delta County, U.S.A., Breaking Up Is Hard to Do, For the Love of It; Nashville Grab, The Making of a Male Model, Bay Coven, The Dirty Dozen: The Fatal Mission.

CONDE, RITA: Actress. b. Cuba. r.n. Elizabeth Eleanor Conde Griffiths. Now American citizen. In numerous films and on TV in Hollywood and starred in Mexican film, El Ahijado de la Muerte.
PICTURES INCLUDE: Ride the Pink Horse, Two Roaming Champs, No Sad Songs for Me, Topaz, Change of Habit, Barquero, World's Greatest Lover, Love at First Bite, etc.
TELEVISION INCLUDES: I Love Lucy, Zorro, I Spy, Thriller, Night Gallery, Ironside, Chico and the Man, Days of Our Lives, Capitol.

CONDON, CHRIS J.: Producer, Director, Motion Equipment Designer. b. Chicago, IL, Dec. 7, 1922. e. Davidson Inst., U. of Southern California. U.S. Air Force 1943–46. Founded Century Precision Optics, 1948. Designed Athenar telephoto lenses, Century Super wide-angle lenses and Duplikins. Co-founded StereoVision International, Inc. 1969 specializing in films produced in new 3-D process.
FILMS PRODUCED: The Wild Ride, The Surfer, Girls, Airline, The New Dimensions, Member SMPTE. Lecturer and consultant on motion picture optics and 3-D motion picture technology.

CONLEY, DICK: Executive. r.n. Richard Glen. b. La Cygne, KS, Feb. 7, 1920. e. Lamar Union H.S., Lamar, CO. Atlas Theatre Corp., Denver, 1938–43; merchandising specialist, National General Corp., 1944–62; district mgr., Kansas City-St. Louis area, 1962–68; area superv. Kansas City-Omaha-Des Moines-St. Louis area; pres., Petite Amusement Corp., Kansas City.

CONN, ROBERT A.: Executive. b. Philadelphia, PA, Jan. 16, 1926. e. Lehigh U. 1944; U. of Pennsylvania, 1948. 1st Lt. Army Security Agency, 1944–46, 1951–52; furniture dist., Philadelphia, 1948–51; band & act. dept., MCA, 1952–53; dir. of adv. & prom. Official Films N.Y. 1954; head of Official Films Philadelphia sales office serving Pennsylvania, Baltimore, Washington, Cleveland and Detroit, 1956. Eastern Reg. Sls. Mgr. Flamingo Films, 1957; acct. exec. Dunnan and Jeffrey, Inc., June, 1961; v.p., Dunnan and Jeffrey, Jan. 1962; pres., adv. mgr., Suburban Knitwear Co., 1963; exec. v.p. Rogal Travel Service, 1964–68. 1968–78, pres. RAC Travel, Inc., Jenkintown, Pa. and pres. Royal Palm Travel, Inc. Palm Beach, Florida, 1978; Rosenbluth Travel Service, 1979; v.p., natl. retail mktg., E.F. Hutton & Co. (N.Y.), 1983.

CONNELY, PAUL V.: Executive. b. Boston, MA, June 11, 1923. e. Boston Coll., MA, 1951, B.S.B.A.; 1949; Fordham U., 1951–54; Asst. professor of Economics, Manhattan Coll., 1950–54; treas., America Corp. (formerly Chesapeake Industries), 1957–59; treas., dir., Pathe-America Dist. Co. Inc., Sutton Pictures Co.; vice-pres., dir., Pathe Labs., Inc.; pres., dir., Pathe-Deluxe of Canada, Ltd. 1959–65; pres. International Business Relations, 1965–67; v.p., treas., dir. Movielab, Inc., 1968; v.p.—finance, Tele-Tape Corp., 1970.

CONNER, CHARLES M.: Writer, Producer, Director. b. Covington, IN, April 19, 1925. e. U. of Wisconsin. Active in designing and creating pressbooks for theatrical m.p. producers and distributors, plus theatrical m.p. still photography, locations and studio sets. Now heads Charles M. Conner Film & Video Cassette Distribution & Marketing. Member: Writers Guild of America, West, both screen & TV branches. Winner, 1965–66 regional Emmy award, Guns Are for Killing.
CREDITS INCLUDE: Guns Are for Killing, Fulfillment, Something Worth Remembering, Albuquerque Lawman, The Protector, Bay of Pigs, Richest Man in the World, Tiger, Thru These Eyes, The Sound of Christmas Around the World, House of Sin, The Female Art of Man Hunting, Surfside Six, Far Out West, The Bunny Snatch, Listen, Girl Hunters, America's Greatness, Meet the Under World, Introduction, Christmas Tree, The Wounded Are Dangerous, Gorilla.

CONNERY, SEAN: Actor. b. Edinburgh, Scotland, Aug. 25, 1930. r.n. Thomas Connery. Worked as a lifeguard and a model before landing role in chorus of London prod. of South Pacific, 1953.
TELEVISION: Requiem for a Heavyweight, Anna Christie, Boy with the Meataxe, Women in Love, The Crucible, Riders to the Sea, Colombe, Adventure Story, Anna Karenina, Macbeth (Canadian TV).
PICTURES INCLUDE: No Road Back (1955), Time Lock, Hell Drivers, Action of the Tiger, Another Time, Another Place, Darby O'Gill and the Little People, Tarzan's Greatest Adventure, Frightened City, On the Fiddle, The Longest Day, Dr. No, From Russia With Love, Marnie, Woman of Straw, Goldfinger, The Hill, Thunderball, A Fine Madness, You Only Live Twice, Shalako, The Molly Maguires, The Red Tent, The Anderson Tapes, Diamonds Are Forever, The Offence, Zardoz, Ransom, Murder on the Orient Express. The Wind and The Lion, The Man Who Would Be King, Robin and Marian. The Next Man, A Bridge Too Far, The Great Train Robbery, Meteor, Cuba, Outland, Time Bandits, Wrong Is Right, Five Days One Summer, Never Say Never Again, Highlander, The Name of the Rose, The Untouchables (Academy Award, 1987), The Presidio, Indiana Jones and the Last Crusade.
Prod. dir., The Bowler and the Bonnet (film doc.), I've Seen You Cut Lemons (London stage). Director of Tantallon Films Ltd. (First production: Something Like the Truth).

CONNOR, KENNETH: Actor. b. London, England. Ent. m.p. industry 1949 in The Lady Killers.
TELEVISION: Ted Ray Show, Show Called Fred, Charlie Farnabarn's Show, Alfred Marks Time, As You Like It, Dickie Valentine Show, Black and White Minstrel, Anne Shelton, Hi Summer, series Don't Say a Word, Room at the Bottom, On the Houses, Frankie Howard Reveals All, Allo Allo, Hi de Hi, That's My Boy.
PICTURES INCLUDE: Carry on Sergeant, Carry on Nurse, Carry on Constable, Watch Your Stern, Carry on Regardless, Nearly a Nasty Accident, What a Carve Up, Call Me a Cab, Carry on Cleo, Captain Nemo, Carry On Up The Jungle, Carry On Matron, Carry On Abroad, Carry on England, Carry On Emanuelle.

CONNORS, CHUCK: Actor. r.n. Kevin Joseph Connors. b. Brooklyn, NY, April 10, 1921. e. Adelphi Acad., Seton Hall Coll., U.S. Army 3 yrs., then prof. baseball player with Brooklyn Dodgers, 1949; Chicago Cubs 1951. On stage in Chicago 1971–79 (My Three Angels, Mary, Mary.
PICTURES INCLUDE: Pat and Mike, Code Two, Trouble Along the Way, South Sea Women, Dragonfly Squadron, Naked Alibi, Human Jungle, Target Zero, Three Stripes in the Sun, Good Morning Miss Dove, Hold Back the Night, Hot Rod Girl, Tomahawk Trail, Walk the Dark Street, Designing Woman, Hired Gun, Lady Takes a Flier, Old Yeller, Death in Small Doses, The Big Country, Geronimo, Kill Them All and Come Back Alive, Move Over Darling, Ride Beyond Vengeance, Capt. Nemo and the Underwater City, Proud, Damned and Dead, Profane Comedy, The Deserter, Support Your Local Gunfighter, Pancho Villa, Embassy, The Mad Bomber, Soylent Green, 99 and 44/100% Dead, The Sea Wolf, The Tourist Trap, Virus, The Women of Jeremias, Day of the Assassin, Red Alert West, Mortuary, Balboa, Valley Girls, Target Eagle, Airplane II: The Sequel, Kelsey and Son, The Butterfly Revolution, Summer Camp Nightmare, Terror Squad, Mania, Hell's Hero, Trained to Kill, Mania.
TELEVISION: Series: The Rifleman (1958–63), Arrest and Trial, Branded (1964–65), Police Story (1972–75, pilot and episodes), Stone (1979), Werewolf (1987). Movies: Cowboy in Africa, Set the Town on Fire, The Profane Comedy, Birdman in Batham County, The Night They Took Miss Beautiful, Standing Tall, The Texans, Walking Tall, Great Mysteries of Hollywood, The Capture of Grizzly Adams, Celebrity Daredevils, Lone Star, The Yellow Rose, The American Cowboy, Steel Collar Man (pilot), Spenser for Hire (pilot), Once Upon a Texas Train. Guest: Six Million Dollar Man, Fantasy Island, Best of the West, Love Boat, Murder She Wrote.

CONNORS, MIKE: Actor. r.n. Krekor Ohanian. b. Fresno, CA, Aug. 15, 1925. e. U. of California at L.A. Film debut in Sudden Fear (1952).
PICTURES INCLUDE: Sky Commando, Day of Triumph, Flesh and Spur, Seed of Violence, Harlow, Good Neighbor Sam, Where Love Has Gone, Avalanche Express, Too Scared to Scream, Fistfighter.
TELEVISION: Tightrope, Mannix (Golden Globe award). Movies: Casino, High Midnight, Revenge for a Rape.

CONRAD, ROBERT: Actor, Singer. r.n. Conrad Robert Falk; b. Chicago, IL, March 1, 1935. e. public schools, Northwestern U. Prof. debut, nightclub singer. Formed Robert Conrad Production, 1966. Later, A Shane Productions.
TELEVISION: Lawman, Maverick, 77 Sunset Strip, Hawaiian Eye (series), Wild Wild West (series), Baa, Baa, Black Sheep (series), Centennial (mini-series), A Man Called Sloane (series). Movies: Wild Wild West Revisited, More Wild

Wild West, Breaking Up Is Hard To Do, Will: G. Gordon Liddy, Confessions of a Married Man, Hard Knox, Two Fathers' Justice, Assassin, Charley Hannah, The Fifth Missile, One Police Plaza, High Mountain Rangers (also dir., co-story).
PICTURES: Thundering Jets, Palm Springs Weekend, Young Dillinger, Murph the Surf, Sudden Death, The Women in Red, Wrong Is Right, Moving Violations, Uncommon Courage.

CONRAD, WILLIAM: Actor, Producer, Director. b. Louisville, KY, Sept. 27, 1920. e. Fullerton Coll. Announcer-writer-director for L.A. radio station KMPC before becoming WWII fighter pilot in 1943; returned to radio drama as original Matt Dillon of Gunsmoke Series; m.p. debut in The Killers, 1946; later acting credits include 30, Body and Soul, Sorry, Wrong Number, East Side, West Side, The Naked Jungle; TV credits include This Man Dawson, Klondike (produced and directed), 77 Sunset Strip (producer), True (directed 35 episodes); as m.p. producer for Warner Bros. credits include: Two on a Guillotine, Brainstorm, An American Dream, A Covenant with Death, First to Fight, The Cool Ones, The Assignment.
TELEVISION: Acting credits include The Brotherhood of the Bell; The D.A., Conspiracy to Kill; O'Hara, U.S. Treasury, Cannon (series), Vengeance: The Story of Tony Cimo, Jake and the Fatman (series).

CONROY, THOMAS: Executive. r.n. Coleman Thomas Conroy. b. Camden, NJ, Nov. 3, 1924. e. Yale U. Hd. prof. camera dept., Bell and Howell Inc., New York, 1951; hd. camera dept., Cinerama Inc., 1952–55; National Theatres Inc., 1955; hd. camera dept., Cinemiracle; v.p. prod., prod. supv., Cinerama, Inc. 1960. Developed Cinerama single-lens system; v.p., production, Shannon Prod., Inc., 1967.
PICTURES INCLUDE: This Is Cinerama, Cinerama Holiday, Seven Wonders of the World, Windjammer, The Wonderful World of the Brothers Grimm, How the West Was Won, The Best of Cinerama, The Golden Head.

CONTE, JOHN: Actor, Singer. b. Palmer, MA.. e. Lincoln H.S., Los Angeles. Actor, Pasadena Playhouse; radio anncr., m.c.; Armed Forces, W.W.II. Pres. KMIR-TV, Channel 36, Desert Empire Television Corp., Palm Springs.
THEATRE: On Broadway in Windy City, Allegro, Carousel, Arms and the Girl.
TELEVISION: John Conte's Little Show (1950–52); Max Liebman Spectaculars and dramatic shows, host and star of NBC Matinee Theatre; (1955–58). TV Hour of Stars; Mantovani Welcomes You.
PICTURES INCLUDE: Debut in Man With the Golden Arm, The Carpetbaggers.

CONTI, BILL: Composer. b. Providence, RI, April 13, 1943. Studied piano at age 7, forming first band at age 15. e. Louisiana State U., Juilliard School of Music. Toured Italy with jazz trio where scored first film, Candidate for a Killing. Returned to U.S. to be music supvr. on Blume in Love. for Paul Mazursky.
PICTURES: Harry and Tonto; Next Stop, Greenwich Village; Rocky, Handle with Care, F.I.S.T., Slow Dancing in the Big City, The Big Fix, Uncle Joe Shannon, An Unmarried Woman, The Seduction of Joe Tynan, The Formula, Neighbors, The Karate Kid, The Karate Kid II, Hurricane, Paradise Alley, Rocky II, Golden Girl, A Man, a Woman, and a Bank; Gloria, Private Benjamin, For Your Eyes Only, Victory, Rocky III, Carbon Copy, Split Image, Bad Boys, I, The Jury; That Championship Season; The Right Stuff (Acad. Award, best score), Unfaithfully Yours, The Bear, Mass Appeal, Gotcha, Nomad, Big Trouble, Beer, F/X, A Prayer for the Dying, Masters of the Universe, Baby Boom, For Keeps, A Night in the Life of Jimmy Reardon, Betrayed, Cohen and Tate.
TELEVISION: Kill Me If You Can, Stark, North and South, Napoleon and Josephine. Series themes: Cagney and Lacy, Dynasty, Falcon Crest, Kenya.

CONTI, TOM: Actor. b. Paisley, Scotland, Nov. 22, 1941. Trained at Royal Scottish Academy of Music, Glasgow. Did repertory work in Scotland before going to London, appearing with Paul Scofield on stage in Savages, 1973. Film debut in Galileo, 1975. On Bdwy. stage in Whose Life Is It Anyway?, 1980 (Tony Award). Dir: Last Licks (NY, 1979).
PICTURES: The Duellists, The Haunting of Julia (Full Circle), Blade on the Feather, Merry Christmas, Mr. Lawrence, Reuben, Reuben, American Dreamer, Miracles, Saving Grace, Beyond Therapy, Gospel According to Vic, Two Brothers Running, White Roses.
TELEVISION: Mother of Men (1959), The Glittering Prizes, Madame Bovery, Treats, The Norman Conquests, The Wall, Nazi Hunter, The Quick and the Dead, Roman Holiday, The Dumb Waiter, Faerie Tale Theater.

CONVERSE, FRANK: Actor. b. St. Louis, MO, May 22, 1938. e. Carnegie Tech. Early training on stage in New York. Active in repertory theatres. Two seasons with Amer. Shakespeare Fest.
PICTURES INCLUDE: Hurry Sundown, Hour of the Gun.

TELEVISION: Mod Squad, Medical Center, The Bold Ones, N.Y.P.D. (series) Coronet Blue (series), The Guest Room, Movin' On, The Widowing of Mrs. Holyrod. Movies: The Rowdyman, Shadow of a Gunman, Tattered Web, Dr. Cook's Garden, Anne of Green Gables—The Sequel; Alone in the Neon Jungle.
STAGE: The Seagull, Death of a Salesman, Night of the Iguana, A Man for All Seasons, The House of Blue Leaves, First One Asleep Whistle, Arturo Ui, A Streetcar Named Desire (1988 revival).

CONVY, BERT: Actor. b. St. Louis, MO, July 23, 1934. e. U. of California at L.A. Was professional baseball player before turning to acting. On Broadway in The Matchmaker, Billy Barnes Revue, Cabaret, Nine.
PICTURES: Gunman's Walk, Susan Slade, Act One, Semi-Tough, Jennifer, Hero at Large, The Cannonball Run.
TELEVISION: Dallas Cowboys Cheerleaders, Ebony, Ivory and Jade, Man in the Santa Claus Suit, Valley of the Dolls. Host on game show, Tattletales, Love Thy Neighbor.

CONWAY, GARY: Actor. r.n. Gareth Carmody. b. Boston, MA, 1939. e. U. of California at L.A. As college senior was chosen for title role in Teen-Age Frankenstein. After graduating served in military at Ford Ord, CA. In 1960 began contract with Warner Bros., doing bits for films and TV. Has also appeared on stage. Has given several one-man shows as painter.
PICTURES INCLUDE: Young Guns of Texas, Once Is Not Enough, The Farmer (also prod.), American Ninja (also s.p.), Over The Top (s.p.).
TELEVISION: Burke's Law, Land of the Giants (series).

CONWAY, KEVIN: Actor. b. New York, NY, May 29, 1942. Gained reputation on N.Y. stage, winning Obie and Drama Desk Awards for performance in When You Comin Back, Red Ryder? Also on and off Broadway in such plays as One Flew Over the Cuckoo's Nest, Of Mice and Men, Moonchildren, Life Class, Saved, The Elephant Man, Other Places, King John (NYSF). Dir.: Mecca, Short Eyes (revival), One Act Play Fest. (Lincoln Center), Milk Train Doesn't Stop Here Anymore (revival), The Elephant Man (tour).
PICTURES INCLUDE: Slaughterhouse Five, Shamus, Believe in Me, Portnoy's Complaint, F.I.S.T., Paradise Alley, The Fun House, Flashpoint, Homeboy, The Sun and the Moon (dir., prod.).
TELEVISION: Rage of Angels, Johnny We Hardly Knew You, The Deadliest Season, The Scarlet Letter, The Lathe of Heaven, Something About Amelia, Jesse, The Elephant Man.

CONWAY, TIM: Actor. b. Willoughby, OH, Dec. 15, 1933. e. Bowling Green State U. After 2 yrs. Army service joined KWY-TV in Cleveland as writer-director and occasional performer. Comedienne Rose Marie discovered him and arranged audition for the Steve Allen Show on which he became regular. In 1962 signed for McHale's Navy, series. Also has done night club appearances.
PICTURES INCLUDE: McHale's Navy, The World's Greatest Athlete, The Apple Dumpling Gang, Gus, The Shaggy D.A., Cannonball Run II, The Longshot (also s.p.), Cyclone.
TELEVISION: The Steve Allen Show, The Garry Moore Show, McHale's Navy, guest appearances on Hollywood Palace and shows starring Carol Burnett, Red Skelton, Danny Kaye, Dean Martin, Cher, Doris Day, The Tim Conway Show, The Longshot, Plaza Suite, many specials.

CONWAY, SHIRL: Actress. r.n., Shirl Conway Larson; b. Franklinville, NY, June 13, 1916. e. U. of Michigan, 1934–38. Singer, comedian, nightclubs.
PLAYS: Gentlemen Prefer Blondes, Plain and Fancy.
TELEVISION: The Doctors and The Nurses.

COOK, ELISHA, JR.: Actor. b. San Francisco, CA, Dec. 26, 1907. e. St. Albans, Chicago boarding school. Joined Frank Bacon in Lightnin' at the age of 14.
THEATRE: Appeared with Ethel Barrymore in Kingdom of God, in Henry, Behave, Many a Slip, Three Cornered Moon, in London in Coquette. Played in vaudeville and summer stock companies. Appeared in Chrysalis, then Ah, Wilderness, Theatre Guild success. Signed by Par. in 1936: Two in a Crowd.
PICTURES INCLUDE: Pigskin Parade, The Maltese Falcon, Up in Arms, Casanova Brown, Cinderella Jones, Dillinger, The Big Sleep, The Long Night, Don't Bother to Knock, I the Jury, Shane, Thunder Over the Plains, Drum Beat, Outlaw's Daughter, Timberjack, Indian Fighter, The Killing, Voodoo Island, Rosemary's Baby, Welcome to Hard Times, Blacula, The Great Northfield, Minnesota Raid, Emperor of the North, Electra-Glide in Blue, The Outfit, The Black Bird, The Champ, Carny, Hammett.
TELEVISION: Chicago Story, Terror at Alcatraz, Bring 'em Back Alive; It Came Upon a Midnight Clear; The Man Who Broke 1000 Chains.

COOK, FIELDER: Producer, Director. b. Atlanta, GA, Mar. 9, 1923. e. Washington & Lee U., B.A., 1947; U. of Birmingham, Eng., post grad., 1948. Doctor of Fine Arts (Hon) (1973) (W & L). USNR, 1944; 7th Amphibious Force, 1944–45, J. Walter Thompson Co., 1947–56.

TELEVISION FILMS/SPECIALS: Family Reunion; Gauguin, The Savage; John Updike's Too Far to Go; Maya Angelou's I Know Why the Caged Bird Sings; My Luke And I—The Lou Gehrig Love Story; Judge Horton & The Scottsboro Boys; Beacon Hill (series); Miles To Go Before I Sleep: This Is the West That Was; Miracle on 34th Street; The Homecoming (pilot, The Waltons); The Hands of Carmac Joyce; Sam Hill; Beauty and the Beast; Teacher, Teacher; The Rivalry; Valley Forge; The Price; Harvey; Goodbye, Raggedy-Ann (also exec.-prod.) Brigadoon (also prod.); Will There Ever Be a Morning?; Why Me?, Evergreen, A Special Friendship, Saul Bellow's Seize the Day.

PICTURES INCLUDE: Patterns, Home Is the Hero, A Big Hand for the Little Lady, How to Save a Marriage and Ruin Your Life, Prudence and the Pill, Eagle in a Cage, From the Mixed Up Files of Mrs. Basil E. Frankweiler.

PLAYS: A Cook For Mr. General, Maneuvers.

AWARDS: Various for (after 1956): Patterns, Project Immortality; Big Deal in Laredo; Teacher, Teacher; Ben Casey Pilot; The Price; Brigadoon; Judge Horton and the Scottsboro Boys; The Homecoming, Too Far to Go, Seize the Day.

COOK, KWENAM DAVID: Executive. b. Seoul, Korea, Mar. 16, 1922. e. Waseda U., Tokyo, Japan. ROK national assembly-man (Congress) 1959–61. Pres. Korean Gymnastic Assoc. 1967–70. Chairman: Century Co., Ltd., Seoul, producers, distributors, exhibitors, and importers of films. Honorary consul general for Peru.

COOK, RICHARD: Executive. Began career 1971 as Disneyland sls. rep.; promoted 1974 to mgr. of sls. Moved to studio in 1977 as mgr., pay TV and non-theatrical releases. 1980, named asst. domestic sls. mgr., for Buena Vista; 1981 promoted to v.p. & asst. gen. sls. mgr.; 1984, promoted to v.p. & gen. sls. mgr., B.V.; 1985, appt. sr. v.p., domestic distribution. 1988: appointed president Buena Vista Distribution.

COOKE, ALISTAIR: Journalist, Broadcaster. b. Eng., Nov. 20, 1908. e. Jesus Coll., Cambridge U.; Yale U.; Harvard U. Film crit. of BBC 1934–37. London corr. NBC 1936–37. BBC commentator in U.S. since 1937. Chief Amer. corr., Manchester Guardian, 1948–72; English narrator, The March of Time, 1938–39; v.o. narrator, Sorrowful Jones, 1948; narrator, Three Faces of Eve, 1957; narrator, Hitler, 1973; Peabody award winner for International reporting, 1952, 1973–83; author, Douglas Fairbanks, Garbo & The Night Watchmen. A Generation on Trial, One Man's America, Christmas Eve, The Vintage Mencken, etc.; m.c. Omnibus, TV show, 1952–61; m.c. prod. U.N.'s International Zone, Emmy Award, 1958; m.c., Masterpiece Theatre since 1971. Writer & narrator, America: A Personal History of The United States, TV series BBC, NBC, PBS, for which 5 Emmy Awards, 1973; Franklin Medal, Royal Society of Arts, 1973; Knighted, KBE, 1973.

BOOKS: America, 1973; Six Men, 1977; Talk About America, 1968; The Americans, 1979; Above London, 1980; Masterpieces, 1981; The Patient Has the Floor, 1986, America Observed, 1988.

COOLIDGE, MARTHA: Director, Writer, Producer. b. New Haven, CT, 1946. e. Rhode Island Sch. of Design, School of Visual Arts, and Columbia U., NYU Inst. of Film and TV grad. sch. m. producer Michael Backes. Started directing short films while in school. Worked on commercials and political doc. film crews. Has produced, directed and written several documentaries which have won festival awards, including Passing Quietly Through; David: Off and On (American Film Festival), Old Fashioned Woman (CINE Golden Eagle Award). 1968 wrote and prod. child children's TV show Magic Tom in Canada. Made student film Mondo Linoleum (co-star and dir.). First feature film Not a Pretty Picture (won Blue Ribbon Award, Amer. Film Fest.) Helped start assn. of Indep. Video and Filmmakers, Inc. As an AFI/Academy Intern worked with Robert Wise on his film Audrey Rose, 1976. Wrote orig. story that was filmed as the The Omega Connection. Directed short film Bimbo.

PICTURES: The City Girl, Valley Girl, National Lampoon's Joy of Sex, Glory Days, Real Genius, Plain Clothes, The Friendly.

TELEVISION: The Twilight Zone; Sledge Hammer (pilot); House and Home (pilot), Roughhouse.

COONEY, JOAN GANZ: Executive, Producer. b. Phoenix, AZ, Nov. 30, 1929. e. U. of Arizona. After working as a reporter in Phoenix, moved to NY in 1953 where she wrote soap-opera summaries at NBC. Then was publicist for U.S. Steel Hour. Became producer of live weekly political TV show Court of Reason (Emmy Award) and documentaries (Poverty, Anti-Poverty and the Poor) before founding Children's Television Workshop and Sesame Street in 1969. Currently exec. dir. CTW.

COOPER, BEN: Actor. b. Hartford, CT, Sept. 30, 1933. e. Columbia U. On stage in Life with Father, (1942); numerous radio, TV appearances (500 shows), first show May 1945.

PICTURES INCLUDE: Woman They Almost Lynched, A Perilous Journey, Sea of Lost Ships, Flight Nurse, Fortune Hunter, Johnny Guitar, Hell's Outpost, Eternal Sea, Last Command, Fighting Chance, Headline Hunters, Rose Tattoo, Rebel in Town, Chartroose Caboose, Red Tomahawk, The Fastest Gun Alive, One More Train to Rob, Support Your Local Gunfighter, Arizona Raiders, Gunfight at Comanche Creek, Outlaws Son.

COOPER, HAL: Director, Performer. b. New York, NY, Feb. 22, 1923. e. U. of Michigan. m. Marta Salcido; child actor in various radio prog. since 1932; featured Bob Emery's Rainbow House, Mutual, 1936–46; asst. dir. Dock St. Theatre, Charleston, SC, 1946–48.

TELEVISION: Your Sch. Reporter, TV Baby Sitter, The Magic Cottage as writer and producer; dir., Valiant Lady, Search for Tomorrow, Portia Faces Life; dir., assoc. prod. Kitty Foyle; prod. dir. Indictment; assoc. prod. dir. The Happy Time; prod. dir. For Better or Worse; dir., The Clear Horizon; Assoc., prod.., dir., Surprise Package; dir., Dick Van Dyke Show; prod., dir., The Art Linkletter Show, The Object Is. Dir.: Death Valley Days, I Dream of Jeannie, That Girl, I Spy, Hazel, Gidget, Gilligan's Island, NYPD, Mayberry, Courtship of Eddie's Father, My World and Welcome to It, The Odd Couple, Mary Tyler Moore, All in the Family. Exec. prod., dir. Maude, 1972–78; Phyl and Mikky, 1980; Love, Sidney, 1982–83; Gimme a Break, 1983–87.

COOPER, JACKIE: Actor, Director, Producer. b. Los Angeles, CA, Sept. 15, 1922. Began theatrical career at age of 3 as m.p. actor; was member of Our Gang comedies. First starring role in 1930 in Skippy. Worked at every major studio, always with star billing. At 20 enlisted in Navy. After three-yr. tour of duty went to N.Y. to work in live TV. Appeared on Broadway stage in Mr. Roberts and on natl. tour and in London. Directed as well as acted in live and filmed TV. Served as v.p. in chg. of TV prod., for Screen Gems, from 1964 to 1969, when resigned to return to acting, directing, producing.

PICTURES INCLUDE: Actor—Movietone Follies, Sunny Side Up, Skippy, Sooky, The Champ, When a Fellow Needs a Friend, Lumpy, Lost, The Bowery, Treasure Island, O'Shaughnessy's Boy, The Devil Is a Sissy, Gangster's Boy, Seventeen, Gallant Sons, Her First Beau, Syncopation, Stork Bites Man, Kilroy Was Here, Everything's Ducky, The Love Machine, Chosen Survivors, Superman, Superman II, Surrender. Director: Stand Up and Be Counted.

TELEVISION: People's Choice (directed 71 segments; also starred), Hennesey (dir. 91 segments; also starred) 1975 series: Mobile Two (star). Movies: The Last Detail; Perfect Gentlemen; Having Babies; Rainbow; White Mama (dir.); Leave 'Em Laughing (dir.); Rosie (also prod.); (dir.), Glitter; The Night They Saved Christmas (dir.), Izzy and Moe (dir.).

COOPER, SHELDON: Executive. e. Indiana U. Joined WGN Television, 1950 holding various positions in prod. including floor mgr., dir., prod.; 1961, named mgr. prod.; 1961 became exec. prod. for station; 1964, named asst. prog. mgr.; 1965, mgr. of dept.; 1966, v.p. prog. dev. with WGN Continental Productions Co.; elected to bd. of dir., Continental Broadcasting Co. and appointed station mgr., WGN TV, April 1974.; 1975, named v.p. and gen. mrg., WGN Continental Broadcasting.; 1977, dir., broadcasting; 1979, pres. and gen. mgr., WGN Television; 1982, chief exec. of newly formed Tribune Entertainment Co. and dir. of Tribune Co. Syndicate, Inc., 1982–present. One of founders of Operation Prime Time, consortium of independent stations. Awarded Emmys: 1960 as television's "man of the year behind the cameras" and 1964 for continuing excellence as writer, prod., executive, WGN TV. Chmn., Assoc. of Independent TV Stations, Inc. (INTV), 1980 and 1981; Naitonal v.p., Muscular Dystrophy Assoc.; 1980, on bd. National Assoc. of TV Prog. Executives (NATPE); first v.p., Chicago chap. Acad. of TV Arts and Sciences; v.p., trustee of national chap.

COOPERMAN, ALVIN: Producer. b. Brooklyn, NY. Started career with Lee & J. J. Shubert, 1939–51; color team, dev. color TV for FCC approval, 1953; prod. first color TV shows with mobile unit, 1954; developed & prod. first Wide Wide World, June 1955; mgr. program sls., NBC Network, 1955; exec. prod. Producers Showcase, Dodsworth, Rosalinda, 1956; prod. Jack and the Beanstalk, Festival of Music, 1957; dir. prog. NBC-TV, Apr. 1957; joined HJ Enterprises as prod. NBC-TV, The Shirley Temple Storybook, 1957; exec. prod. Screen Gems, 1958; prod. Du Pont Show, 1959; exec. prod. Roncom Prod. 1960; Prod., Untouchables, 1961–63; exec. dir., Shubert Thea. Ent. 1963; v.p., special programs, NBC, 1967–68; exec. v.p., Madison Square Garden Center, 1968–72; President, Madison Square Garden Center, Inc.; Chairman of the Board, Athena Communications Corporation. Pres., NY Television Academy, 1987–89.

TELEVISION: Producer: Romeo and Juliet, (Emmy nominee); Pele's Last Game; The Fourth King; Amahl and the

Night Visitors; Live from Studio 8H—A Tribute to Toscanini, (Emmy Award); Live from Studio 8H—An Evening with Jerome Robbins and the New York City Ballet, (Emmy Award); Live from Studio 8H—Caruso Remembered; Ain't Misbehavin', (Emmy nominee, NAACP Image Award, Best TV Show of the Year); Pope John Paul II; My Two Loves, Safe Passage; Family Album, U.S.A. (26 half hours).

COPPOLA, CARMINE: Composer. b. New York, NY, June 11, 1910. Father of director Francis Coppola and actress Talia Shire. Studied flute and composition at Juilliard and Manhattan School of Music. Orchestra musician and arranger at Radio City Music Hall in the 1930s. First flutist, Detroit Symphony. Conductor of orchestra of Broadway shows: Kismet; Once Upon a Mattress; 110 in the Shade, La Plume de ma Tante, Stop the World, I Want to Get Off; The Great Waltz. Played first flute with NBC Symphony Orchestra under Toscanini.
PICTURES: The Godfather; The Godfather, Part II (Academy Award); Apocalypse Now; The Black Stallion; Napoleon; Gardens of Stone, Blood Red, Tucker: The Man and His Dream (additional music).
TELEVISION: The People (TV).

COPPOLA, FRANCIS FORD: Writer, Producer, Director. b. Detroit, MI, April 7, 1939. e. Hofstra U, B.A., 1958; U. of California at L.A., 1958–68, M.A., cinema. While at UCLA he was hired as asst. to Roger Corman as dialogue dir., sound man and assoc. prod. 1969; est. American Zoetrope, a prod. center in San Francisco.
PICTURES INCLUDE: Dementia 13 (dir., s.p.); Is Paris Burning? (co-s.p.); You're a Big Boy Now (dir., s.p.); Reflections in a Golden Eye (s.p.); Finian's Rainbow (dir.); The Rain People (dir., s.p.); Patton (co-s.p., Acad. Award); THX 1138 (exec. prod.); The Godfather (dir., co-s.p., prod., Acad. Award, best picture and s.p.); American Graffiti (exec. prod.); The Conversation (prod., dir., s.p.); The Godfather Part II (co-s.p., dir.; Acad. Award, s.p., dir., picture); The Great Gatsby (s.p.); Apocalypse Now (prod., dir., co-s.p.); The Black Stallion (exec. prod.); One From the Heart (prod., dir., co-s.p.); Hammett (exec. prod.); The Outsiders (prod., dir., s.p.); The Escape Artist (prod.); The Black Stallion Returns (prod.); Rumble Fish (prod., dir., s.p.); Mishima (prod.); Peggy Sue Got Married (dir.); Gardens of Stone (dir.); Lionheart (exec. prod.), Tucker: The Man and His Dream (dir.); New York Stories (co-dir., s.p.).
TELEVISION: The People; Rip Van Winkle (Faerie Tale Theatre).

CORD, ALEX: Actor. r.n. Alexander Viespi. b. Floral Park, NY, May 3, 1933. Early career in rodeo; left to become actor. Studied at Shakespeare Academy (Stratford, Conn.) and Actor's Studio (N.Y.). Spent two yrs. in summer stock; in 1961 went on tour with Stratford Shakespeare Co. Made m.p. debut in Synanon, 1965. Author of novel Sandsong.
PICTURES INCLUDE: Stagecoach, The Scorpio Letters, The Prodigal Gun, The Brotherhood, Stiletto, The Dead Are Alive, Chosen Survivors, Sidewinder One, Grayeagle, Uninvited.
TELEVISION: Airwolf (series), Hunter's Man; Genesis II, Beggerman Thief, The Girl Who Saved America, The Dirty Dozen: The Fatal Mission.

CORDAY, BARBARA: Executive. b. New York, NY, Oct. 15, 1944. m. Barney Rosenzweig, TV producer. Began career as publicist in N.Y. and L.A. Turned to writing for TV; named v.p., ABC-TV, in chg. of comedy series development. 1982–84, headed own production co. in association with Columbia Pictures TV. June, 1984–1987; pres., Columbia Pictures TV.; Aug., 1988: appointed CBS Entertainment, exec. v.p. primetime programs. Member: Caucus of Writers, Producers & Directors; Hollywood Women's Coalition.
TELEVISION: Writer: American Dream (pilot); and co-creator, Cagney and Lacey (series), etc.

COREY, JEFF: Actor. b. New York, NY, Aug. 10, 1914. e. Feogin Sch. of Dram. Art. On stage in Leslie Howard prod. of Hamlet, 1936; Life and Death of an American, 1938. Screen debut 1940 in All That Money Can Buy, In the Matter of J. Robert Oppenheimer and Hamlet-Mark Taper Forum, L.A. King Lear, Beverly Music Center '73.
PICTURES INCLUDE: Syncopation, The Killers, Ramrod, Joan of Arc, Roughshod, Black Shadows, Bagdad, Outriders, The Devil and Daniel Webster, My Friend Flicka, Canyon City, Singing Guns, Seconds, In Cold Blood, Golden Bullet, Boston Strangler, True Grit, Butch Cassidy and The Sundance Kid, Beneath the Planet of the Apes, Getting Straight, Little Big Man, They Call Me Mister Tibbs, Clear and Present Danger, High Flying Lowe, Catlow, Something Evil, Premonition, Shine, Rooster, Oh, God!, Butch and Sundance: The Early Days, Up River, Conan the Destroyer, Secret Ingredient, Messenger of Death, The Judas Project, Messenger of Death.
TELEVISION: The Untouchables, The Beachcomber, The Balcony, Yellow Canary, Lady in a Cage, Outer Limits, Channing, The Doctors and the Nurses, Perry Mason, Gomer

Pyle, Wild, Wild West, Run for Your Life, Bonanza, Iron Horse, Judd for Defense, Garrisons Gorillas, Gunsmoke, Hawaii Five O, Star Trek, dir. The Psychiatrist, Night Gallery, Alias Smith and Jones, Sixth Sense, Hawkins, Owen Marshall, Police Story, Bob Newhart Show, Six Million Dollar Man, Doctors Hospital, Starsky and Hutch, Land of the Free (film), Kojak, McCloud, Captains Courageous (Bell Tel. Hr.), Bionic Woman, Barney Miller, One Day at a Time, The Pirate, Lou Grant, The Powers of Jonathan Starr, Cry for the Strangers, Today's FBI, Knots Landing, Archie Bunker's Place, Faerie Tale Theatre, Night Court, Helltown (series), Morning Star/Evening Star (series), New Love American Style, Starman, The A Team.

CORMAN, GENE: Producer. b. Detroit, MI, Sept. 24, 1927. e. Stanford U. Went to work for MCA as agent; left to produce his first feature film, Hot Car Girl. Partner with brother Roger in Corman Company and New World Distributors. Vice pres. 20th Century Fox Television.
PICTURES INCLUDE: Attack of the Giant Leaches, Not of This Earth, Blood and Steel, Valley of the Redwoods, Purple Reef, Beast from Haunted Cave, Cat Burglar, Tobruk, You Can't Win Em All, The Intruder, Von Richthofen and Brown, I Escaped from Devil's Island, Secret Invasion, Vigilante Force, F.I.S.T. (exec. prod.), The Big Red One.
TELEVISION: A Woman Called Golda (won Emmy and Christopher Awards as prod.).

CORMAN, ROGER WILLIAM: Executive, Director, Producer, Writer, Distributor. b. Detroit, MI, April 5, 1926. e. Stanford U. 1947; Oxford U., England 1950. U.S. Navy 1944; 20th Century-Fox, production department, 1948, story analyst 1948–49; Literary agent, 1951–52; story, s.p., assoc. prod. Highway Dragnet. Formed Roger Corman Prod. and Filmgroup. Produced over 200 feature films and directed over 60 of them. Formed production-releasing company, organization, New World Pictures, Inc., 1970. Formed production co., New Horizons, 1984; distribution co., Concorde, 1985.
PICTURES INCLUDE: Five Guns West (1953), House of Usher, Little Shop of Horrors, Pit and the Pendulum, The Intruder, Masque of the Red Death, Tomb of Ligeia, The Secret Invasion, The Wild Angels, The Trip, Bloody Mama, Von Richtofen and Brown, Gasss, St. Valentine's Day Massacre, Box Car Bertha, Big Bad Mama, Death Race 2000, Eat My Dust, Capone, Jackson County Jail, Fighting Mad, Thunder & Lightning, Grand Theft Auto, I Never Promised You A Rose Garden, Deathsport, Avalanche, Battle Beyond the Stars, St. Jack, Love Letters, Smokey Bites the Dust, Galaxy of Terror, Slumber Party Massacre Part II (prod.), Death Stalker, Barbarian Queen, Munchies, Stripped To Kill, Big Bad Mama II (prod.); Sweet Revenge (co-exec. prod.); The Drifter (exec. prod.); Daddy's Boys (prod.); Singles (exec. prod.).

CORNELL, JOHN: Producer, Director, Writer. b. Kalgoorlie, Western Australia, 1941. m. actress Delvene Delancy. Grew up Bunbury. e. studied pharmacy for two years in Perth. Won internship at Western Australian Newspapers at 19, becoming columnist then London editor at 26. As Melbourne prod. of TV show, A Current Affair, discovered bridge rigger Paul Hogan, putting him on show, becoming his manager and forming JP Productions with him in 1972. Prod. The Paul Hogan Show and making appearances as "Strop." Formed movie co. with Hogan, Rimfire Films.
PICTURES: Crocodile Dundee (prod., co-s.p.); Crocodile Dundee II (prod., dir., editor).

CORNFELD, STUART: Producer. b. Los Angeles, CA. e. U. of California, Berkeley. Entered America Film Institute's Center for Advanced Film Studies as producing fellow, 1975. Joined Brooksfilm as asst. to Mel Brooks on High Anxiety. Assoc. prod., History of the World Part I. Debut as producer, Fatso (1980).
PICTURES: The Elephant Man, National Lampoon's European Vacation (co-prod.), Girls Just Want to Have Fun, The Fly, Moving, The Fly II (exec. prod.).

CORNFIELD, HUBERT: Director-Writer-Producer. b. Istanbul, Turkey. e. U. of Pennsylvania. Actors' Studio, 1952–54. Story analyst Allied Artists 1954. Directed first picture 1955. Has lived in Paris since 1964.
PICTURES INCLUDE: Sudden Danger, Lure of the Swamp, Plunder Road, The Third Voice, Pressure Point, The Night of the Following Day.

CORRI, ADRIENNE: Actress. b. Glasgow, Scotland, Nov. 13, 1933. Ent. Royal Acad. of Dramatic Art at 13; parts in several stageplays including The Human Touch; m.p. debut in The River.
PICTURES INCLUDE: Quo Vadis, The Kidnappers, A Clockwork Orange, Lease of Life, Make Me An Offer, Feminine Touch, The Big Chance, Corridors of Blood, Doctor of Seven Dials, The Rough and the Smooth, Hellfire Club, The Tell-Tale Heart, Dynamite Jack, Doctor Zhivago, Epilogue to Capricorn, Rosebud. Numerous TV appearances.

CORT, BUD: Actor. r.n. Walter Edward Cox. b. New Rochelle, NY, March 29, 1950. e. New York U. School of the Arts. Stage debut in Wise Child, Bdwy. Theatrical film debut in M*A*S*H, 1970. Television debut in The Doctors.
PICTURES: Brewster McCloud, Harold and Maude, Why Shoot the Teacher?, The Secret Diary of Sigmund Freud, Invaders from Mars, Burnin' Love, Maria's Lovers, The Chocolate War, Out of the Dark.
TELEVISION: Brave New World, Bernice Bobs Her Hair, Faerie Tale Theatre, The Hitchhiker; Made for Each Other (HBO), The Bates Motel.

CORT, ROBERT W.: Executive. e. U. of Pennsylvania (Phi Beta Kappa). Moved into feature production after having worked primarily in marketing/advertising. Joined Columbia Pictures as v.p., 1976; elevated to v.p., adv./pub./promo. Named exec. v.p. of mktg. for 20th-Fox, 1980. Moved into feature production as senior v.p., 1981. In 1983 named exec. v.p., prod., 20th-Fox Prods. 1984, joined Interscope Communications as pres., entertainment division.
PICTURES: Co-prod.: Critical Condition, Outrageous Fortune, Revenge of the Nerds II, Three Men and a Baby, The Seventh Sign; Cocktail.

CORTESA, VALENTINA: Actress. b. Milan, Italy, Jan. 1, 1925. Started career at 15 in Rome. Screen debut: La Cens Delle Beffe, 1941; brought to Hollywood by 20th Century-Fox, following picture, A Yank in Rome; experience on dramatic stage in variety of roles inc. Shakespeare, O'Neill, Shaw.
PICTURES INCLUDE: Cagliostro, Glass Mountain, House on Telegraph Hill, Thieves' Highway, Les Miserables, Secret People, Barefoot Contessa, Shadow of the Eagle, Magic Fire, The Legend of Lylah Clare, Juliet of the Spirits, Day for Night, When Time Ran Out, The Adventures of Baron Munchausen.

CORTEZ, STANLEY: Dir. Photography. b. New York, NY. e. New York U. br. Ricardo Cortez, actor. Began working with portrait photographers (Steichen, Pirie MacDonald, Bachrach, etc.), N.Y. Entered film industry with Paramount Pictures; to Hollywood as camera asst. and later second cameraman, various studios; pioneer in use of montage; Signal Corps W.W.II, Yalta, Quebec, etc. Received Film Critics of Amer. award for work on Magnificent Ambersons. Under personal contract to David O. Selznick, Orson Welles, Walter Wanger, David Wolper. Contributor, Encyclopedia Britannica.
PICTURES INCLUDE: Man on the Eiffel Tower, Shark River (A.A. nominee), Since You Went Away (A.A. nominee), Bad Lands of Dakota, Magnificent Ambersons, Eagle Squadron, Powers Girl, Since You Went Away, Smash Up, Flesh and Fantasy, Captain Kidd, Secret Beyond the Door, Fort Defiance, Riders to the Stars, Black Tuesday, Night of the Hunter, Man from Del Rio, Three Faces of Eve, Top Secret Affair, Angry Red Planet, Dionosaurus, Back Street, Shock Corridor, Nightmare in the Sun, The Naked Kiss, Blue, The Bridge of Remagen, The Date, Another Man, Another Chance. Special sequences on Damien, Omen II, Day the World Ended, Le Bon Vivant.

CORWIN, BRUCE CONRAD: Exhibitor. b. June 11, 1940, Los Angeles, CA. e. Wesleyan U. Pres., Metropolitan Theatres Corp.; chmn., Will Rogers Hospital area ind. campaigns; pres., Variety Boys Club; Board of Trustees American Film Institute; Board of Trustees U.C.L.A. Foundation; pres., Variety Club Tent 25; Pres., L.A. Children's Museum.

CORWIN, NORMAN: Writer, Producer, Director. b. Boston, MA, May 3, 1910. Sports ed. Greenfield, Mass. Daily Recorder, 1926–29; radio ed., news commentator, Springfield Republican & Daily News, 1929–36; prog. dir., CBS, 1938. Bok Medal "for distinguished services to radio," 1942; Peabody Medal, 1942; awarded grant by Amer. Acad. of Arts & Letters, 1942; Page One Award, 1944; Distinguished Merit Award, Nat'l Conf. of Christians & Jews, 1945; Unity Award, Interracial Film & Radio Guild, 1945; Wendell Willkie One World Flight Award, 1946; Met. Opera Award for modern opera in collab. Bernard Rogers, 1946; first award, Res. Comm. of U.N., 1950; Radio & TV first award, Nat'l Conf. of Christians & Jews, 1951; Honor Medal of Freedom Foundation for TV show, Between Americans, 1951; ent., Radio Hall of Fame, 1962. Hon. doctorate Columbia Col. of Comms., 1967; Valentine Davies Award, WGA, 1972; P.E.N. Award, 1986; author of Thirteen by Corwin, More by Corwin, Untitled & Other Plays; The Plot to Overthrow Christmas, Dog in the Sky, Overkill and Megalove, Prayer for the 70s. Holes in a Stained Glass Window, Trivializing America; lectured at various colleges; taught courses U. of California at L.A., U.of Southern California, San Diego State U., regents lecturer, U.of California at Santa Barbara; Chairman, Creative Writing, U.S.C.-Isomata; U. of Alberta, U.S.C., Witswatersrand U., Rand Afrikaans U., So. Africa, Cantatas, The Golden Door, 55; Yes Speak Out Yes (commissioned by U.N., 1968). Faculty, U.S.C. Sch. of Journalism, 1980–. Industry Achievement Award, Broadcast Promotion Assn. 1984; Stasheff lecturer, Univ. Michigan, 1984; sect'y., M.P. Academy Foundation, 1985.
STAGE PLAYS: The Rivalry, The World of Carl Sandburg,

The Hyphen, Overkill and Megalove, Cervantes. Together Tonight: Jefferson, Hamilton and Burr.
PICTURES INCLUDE: Once Upon a Time, Blue Veil, The Grand Design, Scandal in Scourie, Lust for Life, The Story of Ruth.
TELEVISION: Inside the Movie Kingdom, The FDR series, The Plot to Overthrow Christmas, Norman Corwin Presents (for Westinghouse), The Court Martial of General Yamashita, Network at 50 (CBS). Wrote and hosted Academy Leaders (PBS).
Chmn. Doc. Award Com., Motion Picture Academy 1965–86; elected to bd. of governors, 1980. Chm., writers' exec. comm., M.P. Academy; co-chmn. scholarship com., m.p. Academy; member, Film Advisory Bd.; L.A. County Museum; Norman Corwin Presents series; member, bd. of trustees, Advisory Board, Filmex, member, board of directors, WGA. Secretary, Academy Foundation.

COSBY, BILL: Actor, Comedian. b. Philadelphia, PA, July 12, 1938. e. Temple U., U. of Mass., Ed.D. Served in United States Navy Medical Corps. Started as night club entertainer. Has appeared many times on TV variety shows, in numerous one-nighters across the country, and concert tours. Books: Fatherhood, Time Flies.
TELEVISION: Emmy Award 1966, 1967, 1968: Best Actor in Dramatic Series—I Spy; Emmy Award, 1969; The First Bill Cosby Special, I Spy, The Bill Cosby Special, The Second Bill Cosby Special, The Bill Cosby Show, Fat Albert, Fat Albert and the Cosby Kids, The Cosby Show; A Different World (exec. prod. only).
COMEDY ALBUMS: Bill Cosby Is A Very Funny Fellow . . . Right!; I Started Out As a Child; Why Is There Air?; Wonderfulness; Revenge; To Russell, My Brother, Whom I Slept With; 200 MPH; It's True, It's True; 8:15, 12:15.
SINGING ALBUMS: Silverthroat, Hooray for the Salvation Army Band. Grammy Award, 1964, 1965, 1966, 1967, 1969: Best Comedy Album.
RADIO: The Bill Cosby Radio Program.
PICTURES INCLUDE: Man and Boy, Uptown Saturday Night, Let's Do It Again, Mother, Jugs and Speed, A Piece of the Action, California Suite, The Devil and Max Devlin, Bill Cosby Himself, Leonard: Part VI (also co-prod., and story).

COSLOW, SAM: Producer, Songwriter. b. New York, NY, Dec. 27, 1905. Writer popular songs, many for screen prod. (Cocktails for Two, Just One More Chance, Sing You Sinners, etc.). In 1941 formed RCM Prod., Inc., with James Roosevelt. Apptd. Paramount prod. 1944. Academy Award (with Jerry Bresler), best two-reel short, 1943 (Heavenly Music). In 1945 joined Mary Pickford Prods. as prod.
PICTURES INCLUDE: Out of This World, Copacabana, Dreaming Out Loud.

COSELL, HOWARD: Sports Commentator. b. Winston-Salem, NC, 1920. Studied law and practiced. Broadcasting career began in 1953 when hired to host program on which N.Y. area Little Leaguers were introduced to baseball stars. In 1956 ABC hired him for ten five-minute sports shows on weekends. He dropped legal work to concentrate on sports reporting. Has had wide variety of roles in TV: commentator on ABC Monday Night Football, Monday Night Baseball, and various sports specials. Has hosted the Howard Cosell Sports Magazine for 4 yrs. and hosts 14 shows each week on American Contemporary Radio Network. Has guested on numerous prime-time TV shows.
PICTURES: Bananas, Sleeper, The World's Greatest Athlete.

COSMATOS, GEORGE P.: Director, Producer, Writer. b. Jan. 4, 1941. e. London U. Asst. dir., Exodus and Zorba the Greek.
PICTURES: Restless (co.-prod., s.p., dir.); Massacre in Rome (co-s.p., dir.); The Cassandra Crossing (co.-s.p., dir.); Escape to Athena (co-s.p., dir.); Of Unknown Origin (dir.); Rambo: First Blood Part II (dir.), Cobra (dir.), Leviathan (dir.).

COSTA-GAVRAS, CONSTANTIN: Director. b. Athens, Greece, 1933. French citizen. e. Studied at the Sorbonne; Hautes Etudes Cinematographique, (IDHEC). Worked as second, then first assistant to Marcel Ophuls, Rene Clair, and Rene Clement; dir. and wrote s.p. The Sleeping Car Murders. Second film Un Homme De Trop won prize at the Moscow Festival, 1966. Dir. and collab. s.p. Z (won Acad. Award, Best Foreign Lang. Film). L'Aveu (The Confession), State of Siege, Special Section, Claiz de Femme, Missing (also co-s.p.), Hannah K. (also co.-s.p.), Family Business (also s.p.), Betrayed.

COSTNER, KEVIN: Actor. b. Los Angeles, CA, Jan. 18, 1955. e. CA. State U, Fullerton. Acted with community theater gp. while at coll.
PICTURES: Shadows Run Black (debut, 1981), Sizzle Beach, U.S.A., Night Shift, Testament, Stacy's Knights, Table for Five, Silverado, Fandango, American Flyers, The Untouchables, No Way Out, Bull Durham, Shoeless Joe, Revenge.

COTTEN, JOSEPH: Actor. b. Petersburg, VA, 1905. m. actress Patricia Medina. In stock and on New York Stage, 1930–40, including Accent on Youth, Philadelphia Story; also Orson Welles' Federal Theatre's productions and Mercury Theatre of the Air. Autobiography: Vanity Will Get You Nowhere (1988).
STAGE: Sabrina Fair, Once More With Feeling, Prescription: Murder, Calculated Risk.
TELEVISION: narrator, Hollywood and the Stars; Alfred Hitchcock Presents; On Trial; Desilu Playhouse; Movies: Aspen; The Lindbergh Kidnapping Case; Cutter's Trail; Casino, The Screaming Woman.
PICTURES INCLUDE: Citizen Kane, Lydia, Magnificent Ambersons, Journey Into Fear, Shadow of a Doubt, Hers to Hold, Temptation, The Last Sunset, Two Flags West, September Affair, Walk Softly, Stranger, Half Angel, Peking Express, Man With a Cloak, The Untamed Frontier, The Steel Trap, Niagara, Blueprint for Murder, Special Delivery, Bottom of the Bottle, Killer Is Loose, Halliday Brand, From the Earth to the Moon, The Angel Wore Red, The Great Sioux Massacre, The Oscar, The Hellbenders, The Tramplers, The Money Trap, They Also Killed, The White Comanche, Petulia, The Grasshopper, The Abominable Dr. Phibes, Soylent Green, A Delicate Balance, Twilight's Last Gleaming, Airport '77, Caravans, Heaven's Gate.

COTY, HENRI ROLAND: Executive. b. Neuilly-sur-Seine, France, Feb. 13, 1922. e. Lycee Descartes, Tours, France. Baccalaureat, 1939–40, St. Jean DePassy. W.W.II Buchmaster Underground network; arrested 1942, deported to Dachau, Dora, Mauthausen, Bergen-Belsen concentration camps; liberated, 1945. Sales mgr., Coty Perfume Co., 1946–55; found own company, s.a. Coty & Co., promotion, publicity, public relations, printing, now TV program prod.

COULOURIS, GEORGE: Actor. b. Manchester, England, Oct. 1, 1903. Stage debut, 1926, Outward Bound. Began screen career in 1933.
PICTURES INCLUDE: Citizen Kane, Watch on the Rhine, Hotel Berlin, Doctor in the House, King of Kings, Arabesque, Papillon, Murder on the Orient Express, It's Not the Size that Counts, The Long Good Friday.

COURTENAY, TOM: Actor. b. Hull, England, Feb. 25, 1937. e. University Coll., London, Royal Acad. of Dramatic Art, 1960–61; Old Vic. Ent. TV 1961 in Private Potter and the Lads; I Heard the Owl Call My Name (U.S.).
STAGE: Billy Liar, Andorra, Hamlet, She Stoops to Conquer, Otherwise Engaged (N.Y. debut), The Dresser.
PICTURES INCLUDE: Loneliness of the Long Distance Runner, Private Potter, Billy Liar, King and Country, Operation Crossbow, King Rat, Dr. Zhivago, Night of the Generals, The Day the Fish Came Out, A Dandy in Aspic, Otley, One Day in the Life of Ivan Denisovich, The Dresser, Happy New Year, Leonard: Part VI.
TELEVISION: Series: The Lads; Ghosts; Private Potter; Movies: I Heard the Owl Call My Name, Jesus of Nazareth.

COURTLAND, JEROME: Actor-Producer-Director. b. Knoxville, TN, Dec. 27, 1926. Began career in 40s as actor, then turned to directing and producing.
PICTURES INCLUDE: Actor: Kiss and Tell, Man from Colorado, Battleground, The Barefoot Mailman, The Bamboo Prison, Tonka, Black Spurs. Director: Run, Cougar, Run, Diamond on Wheels. Producer: Escape to Witch Mountain, Ride a Wild Pony, Return from Witch Mountain, Pete's Dragon.
TELEVISION: Actor: The Saga of Andy Burnett, Tonka. Director: Hog Wild (also co-prod.), Harness Fever. Director: Knots Landing, Dynasty, Hotel, Love Boat, Fantasy Island.

COUSTEAU, JACQUES-YVES, CAPTAIN: Producer. b. St. Andre de Cubzac, Gironde, 1910. e. French Naval Acad. Trained as Navy flier, switched to Gunnery office and started diving experiments. 1943 with Emile Gagnan conceived and released Aqua-Lung, first regulated compressed air breathing device for deep sea diving. After WWII org. Experimental Diving Unit, performed oceanographic research. 1951 perfected first underwater camera equipment for TV. Founded environmental org. The Costeau Society 1974. Awarded Chevalier de la Legion d Honneur for work in Resistance. Member National Acad. of Sciences.
PICTURES: 20 short documentaries 1942–56; The Silent World (Acad. Award, 1957; Grand Prize Cannes, 1956); The Golden Fish (Acad. Award, short subject, 1959), World Without Sun (Acad. Award, 1965), Voyage to the Edge of the World.
TELEVISION: Nearly 70 TV films on his series: The World of Jacques-Yves Costeau; The Undersea World of Jacques Cousteau; (including 8 Emmy's) Oasis in Space; The Costeau Series; The Costeau Odyssey series; Amazon and Rediscovery of the World.

COUTARD, RAOUL: Cinematographer. b. Paris, France, 1924. Spent 4 years in Vietnam working for French Military Info. Service, later a civilian photographer for Time and Paris-Match. During WWII worked in photo labs. After war returned to France and formed prod. co. making documentaries. Joined Jean-Luc Godard as his cinematographer on Breathless (1960). His use of hand-held camera and natural light established him as a seminal cameraman of the French New Wave, working with Godard, Truffaut and later with Costa Gavras.
PICTURES: Breathless, Shoot the Piano Player, Lola, Jules and Jim, Bay of Angels, Les Carabiniers, Alphaville, The Soft Skin, Pierrot le Fou, La 317 eme Section, Weekend, Sailor From Gibralter, The Bride Wore Black, Z, The Confession, Le Crabe Tambour, Passion, First Name: Carmen, Dangerous Moves, Salt on the Skin, La Garce, Max My Love, Burning Beds.

COWAN, THEODORE: Executive. b. Letchworth, Eng. e. Parmiters Sch. Entered m.p. ind., J. Arthur Rank Productions, pub. div., asst. dir. pub. & adv., 1960. Formed own pr. & publ. Co., 1962.

COWAN, WARREN J.: Publicist. b. New York, NY, Mar. 13. e. Townsend Harris H.S., U of California at L.A., graduated 1941. Entered public relations, 1941, with Alan Gordon & Associates; three yrs. Air Force; joined Henry C. Rogers office in 1945; became partner, 1949, and changed name to Rogers & Cowan, Public Relations; Advisor, Rogers & Cowan, Inc., 1960; pres. Rogers & Cowan, Inc., 1964; named bd. chm., 1983. Active in various entertainment industry, civic and philanthropic organizations, including current post as national communications chm. for the United Way of America. On advisory board of the National Association of Film Commissioners; serves on the Second Decade Council of the American Film Institute. On bd. L.A. County High School for the Arts.

COX, ALEX: Director. b. Liverpool, Eng., Dec. 15, 1954. Studied law at Oxford U. where he dir. and acted in plays for school drama society. Studied film prod. Bristol U. Received Fulbright Scholarship to study at UCLA film school, 1981.
PICTURES: Repo Man, Sid and Nancy, Straight to Hell, Walker (dir., co-editor).

COX, RONNY: Actor. b. Cloudcroft, NM, Aug. 23, 1938. e. Eastern New Mexico U.
PICTURES: The Happiness Cage, Deliverance, Hugo the Hippo, Gray Lady Down, Harper Valley PTA, The Onion Field, Taps, Beverly Hills Cop, Vision Quest, Steel Justice, Beverly Hills Cop II, Robocop, One Man Force.
TELEVISION: Movies: Transplant, When Hell Was in Session, Fugitive Family, Alcatraz—The Whole Shocking Story, Two of a Kind, The Jesse Owens Story, The Abduction of Kari Swenson, Baby Girl Scott, The FBI Murders, Apple's Way (series); St. Elsewhere (series), Bloody Friday, Roughhouse.

COYOTE, PETER: Actor. r.n. Cohon. b. 1942. Studied with San Francisco Actors Workshop, Theatre includes The Minstrel Show (dir.), Olive Pits (also co-writer), The Red Snake, True West, The Abduction of Kari Swenson, Baby Girl Scott.
PICTURES: Die Laughing, Tell Me a Riddle, The Pursuit of D.B. Cooper, Southern Comfort, E.T.: The Extra Terrestrial, Endangered Species, Timerider, Cross Creek, Stranger's Kiss, Slayground, Heartbreakers, Jagged Edge, Outrageous Fortune, A Man in Love, Baja Oklahoma, Out (released on Video), Heart of Midnight.
TELEVISION: Movies: The People vs. Jean Harris, In the Child's Best Interest, Up and Coming, Golden Gate, Scorned and Swindled, Child's Cry, Time Flyer, Sworn to Silence, Echoes in the Darkness.

CRAIG, MICHAEL: Actor. b. India, 1929. At 16 joined Merchant Navy. 1949 returned to England and made stage debut in repertory. M.P. debut as crowd artist 1950.
PICTURES INCLUDE: Malta Story, The Love Lottery, Passage Home, The Black Tent, Yield to the Night, Eye-Witness, House of Secrets, High Tide At Noon, Sea of Sand, Sapphire, Upstairs and Downstairs, The Angry Silence, Cone of Silence, Doctor In Love, The Mysterious Island, Payroll, No My Darling Daughter, A Pair of Briefs; A Life for Ruth, The Iron Maiden, Captive City, Summer Flight, Of a Thousand Delights, Life at the Top, Modesty Blaise, Star, a Town Called Hell, Ride a Wild Pony, The Irishman, Turkey Shoot, The Timeless Land, Appointment with Death.

CRAIN, JEANNE: Actress. b. Barstow, CA, May 25, 1925. Model; crowned Miss Long Beach of 1941: Camera Girl of 1942.
PICTURES INCLUDE: Home in Indiana, In the Meantime Darling, Winged Victory, State Fair, Leave Her to Heaven, Margie, Centennial Summer, You Were Meant for Me, Apartment for Peggy, Letter to Three Wives, Pinky, Cheaper by the Dozen, Take Care of My Little Girl, People Will Talk, Model and the Marriage Broker, Belles on Their Toes, O. Henry's Full House, City of Bad Men, Dangerous Crossing, Vicki, Duel in the Jungle, Man Without a Star, Second Greatest Sex, Gentlemen Marry Brunettes, Fastest Gun Alive, Tattered Dress, The Joker, Guns of the Timberland, Skyjacked.

CRAMER, WM. DOUGLAS: Executive. b. Aug. 22, 1931. e. Northwestern U., Sorbonne, U. of Cincinnati, B.A.; Columbia U.M.F.A. m. Joyce Haber, columnist. Taught at Carnegie Inst. of Tech., 1954–55; Production asst. Radio City Music Hall 1950–51; MGM Script Dept. 1952; Manag. Dir. Cincinnati Summer Playhouse 1953–54. TV supvr. Procter and Gamble 1956–59; Broadcast supvr. Ogilvy, Benson and Mather, Adv. 1959–62; V-P Program Dev. ABC-TV 1962–66; V-P Program Dev. 20 Cent.-Fox TV 1966; Exec. v.p. in chg. of production, Paramount Television, 1968.
PLAYS: Love is a Smoke, Whose Baby Are You, Call of Duty.

CRAVEN, GEMMA: Actress. b. Dublin, Ireland, June 1, 1950. e. Loretto Coll. Studied acting at Bush Davies School. London stage debut, Fiddler on the Roof (1970). Considerable work in musical theater throughout England and Ireland.
THEATER: London: Audrey, Trelawny of the Wells, Dandy Dick, They're Playing Our Song, Song and Dance, Loot, A Chorus of Disapproval.
PICTURES: Kingdom of Gifts; Why Not Stay for Breakfast; The Slipper and the Rose; Wagner.
TELEVISION: Pennies From Heaven; Must Wear Tights; She Loves Me; Song by Song by Noel Coward; Song by Song by Alan Jay Lerner; East Lynne; Robin of Sherwood; Treasure Hunt; Gemma Girls and Gershwin.

CRAVEN, WESLEY: Director. b. Cleveland, OH, Aug. 2, 1949.
PICTURES: The Last House on the Left; The Hills Have Eyes; Deadly Blessing; Swamp Thing; The Hills Have Eyes Part II; A Nightmare on Elm Street; Deadly Friend, The Serpent and the Rainbow.
TELEVISION: Series: Twilight Zone (1985, 7 episodes: Word Play, A Little Peace and Quiet, Shatterday, Chameleon, Dealer's Choice, The Road Less Traveled, Pilgrim Soul.). Movies: A Stranger in Our House, Invitation to Hell, Chiller, Casebusters.

CRAWFORD, MICHAEL: O.B.E. Actor. b. Salisbury, England, Jan. 19, 1942. Early career as boy actor in children's films, as a boy soprano in Benjamin Britten's Let's Make an Opera and on radio. Later star of TV's Not So Much a Programme, More a Way of Life.
TELEVISION: Still Life, Destiny, Byron, Move After Checkmate, Three Barrelled Shotgun, Home Sweet Honeycomb, Some Mothers Do 'ave 'em, Chalk and Cheese, BBC Play for Today, Private View, Barnum.
PICTURES INCLUDE: Soap Box Derby (1950), Blow Your Own Trumpet, Two Left Feet, The War Lover, Two Living, One Dead, The Knack...And How to Get It, A Funny Thing Happened on the Way to the Forum, The Jokers, How I Won the War, Hello, Dolly!, The Games, Hello and Goodbye, The Adventures of Alice in Wonderland, Condorman.
STAGE: Come Blow Your Horn, Traveling Light, The Anniversary, White Lies and Black Comedy (N.Y.), No Sex Please We're British, Billy, Same Time Next Year, Flowers for Algernon, Barnum, The Phantom of the Opera (London-Laurence Olivier Award; and New York; Tony, Drama Desk and Outer Circle Critics Award, 1988).

CRENNA, RICHARD: Actor. b. Los Angeles, CA, Nov. 30, 1927. e. Belmont H.S., U. of Southern California.
RADIO: Boy Scout Jambouree, A Date With Judy, The Great Gildersleeve, Johnny Dollar, Our Miss Brooks.
TELEVISION: Our Miss Brooks, The Real McCoys, Slattery's People, All's Fair. Movies: Passions, A Case of Deadly Force, The Day the Bubble Burst, The Rape of Richard Beck, Doubletake, The Price of Passion, Police Story: The Freeway Killings, Plaza Suite, Kids Like These, On Wings of Eagles, Internal Affairs.
PICTURES INCLUDE: Pride of St. Louis, It Grows on Trees, Red Skies Over Montana, John Goldfarb, Please Come Home, Pendick Enterprises, The Sand Pebbles, Star, Marooned, The Deserter, Doctor's Wives, Red Sky at Morning, A Man Called Noon, Catlow, Dirty Money, Death Ship, First Blood, Table for Five, The Flamingo Kid, Rambo: First Blood Part II, Summer Rental, Rambo III, Leviathan.

CRICHTON, CHARLES: Director. b. Wallasey, Aug. 6, 1910. e. Oundle & Oxford. Collab. dir. Dead of Night.
PICTURES INCLUDE: Painted Boats, Hue and Cry, Against the Wind, Another Shore, Dance Hall, Lavender Hill Mob, Hufted (Stranger in Between), Titfield Thunderbolt, The Love Lottery, Divided Heart, Man in the Sky, Floods of Fear, Battle of the Sexes, The Third Secret, He Who Rides a Tiger, A Fish Called Wanda.
TELEVISION: The Wild Duck, Danger Man, The Avengers, Man in a Suitcase, The Strange Report, Shirley's World, Black Beauty, The Protectors, Space 1999, Return of the Saint, Dick Turpin 1 & 2 Series, Smuggler, Video Arts Shorts.

CRICHTON, MICHAEL: Writer-Director. b. Chicago, IL, Oct. 23, 1942. e. Entered Harvard Medical School in 1960's; while there completed first novel, Easy God, under pseudonym, John Lange. Has written 15 books under four different names, including A Case of Need (filmed as The Carey Treatment)

and The Andromeda Strain (first book to appear under his own name). Did post-graduate work at Salk Institute in La Jolla 1969–70. Also wrote novels Dealing and The Terminal Man, both filmed. Recipient Edgar award, Mystery Writers Amer. 1968, 1980. Name medical writer of year, Assn. of Amer. Med. Writers, 1970.
PICTURES INCLUDE: Westworld (s.p., dir.), Coma (s.p., dir.), The Great Train Robbery (s.p., dir.), Looker (s.p., dir.), Runaway (s.p., dir.), Smoke (dir.).
TELEVISION: Pursuit (Movie of Week), dir.; script by Robert Dozier based on Chrichton's book, Binary.

CRIST, JUDITH: Journalist, Critic. b. New York, NY, May 22, 1922. e. Hunter College, Columbia U. School of Journalism. Joined New York Herald Tribune, serving as reporter, arts editor, assoc. drama critic, film critic. Continued as film critic for New York World Journal Tribune, NBC-TV Today Show, New York Magazine, New York Post, Saturday Review, TV Guide, WWOR-TV. Now regular film critic for Coming Attractions. Teaches at Col. Grad. School of Journ.
AUTHOR: The Private Eye, The Cowboy and the Very Naked Girl; Judith Crist's TV Guide to the Movies; Take 22: Moviemakers on Moviemaking.

CRISTALDI, FRANCO: Producer. b. Turin, Italy, Oct. 3, 1924. Owner, prod. Vides Cinematografica; President of Italian Producer's Union.
PICTURES INCLUDE: White Nights, The Strawman, The Challenge, Big Deal On Madonna Street, Kapo, The Dauphins, Salvatore Giuliano, The Assassin, Divorce Italian Style, The Organizer, Bebo's Girl, Seduced and Abandoned, Time of Indifference, Sandra, A Rose for Every-One, China Is Near, A Quiet Couple, The Red Tent.
TELEVISION: Marco Polo.

CRITCHFIELD, EDWARD: Producer. B. Cleveland, OH, Jan. 9, 1919. e. Glenville H.S., 1937. Gen. insurance broker; real estate mortgage financing; motion picture financier, Delta Diamond Productions; then joined Bernfield Publications Inc., as vice-pres.; assoc. prod. Terrified.

CRON, JOHN B.: Executive. b. Mt. Vernon, NY, June 11, 1923. e. Princeton U.: Exec. v.p., Robert Lawrence Productions; managing dir., Screen Gems (Europe); sales dir., N.B.C. Film Division; v.p., sales dir. SIB Productions.

CRONENBERG, DAVID: Writer, Director. b. Toronto, Ont., May 15, 1943. e. U. of Toronto. In college produced two short movies on 16mm. 1971, to Europe on a Canadian Council grant where shot in 1975 his first commercial, Shivers.
PICTURES: They Came From Within, Rabid, Fast Company (both dir. only), The Brood, Scanners, Videodrome, The Dead Zone, Dead Ringers (dir., co-prod., co-s.p.).

CRONKITE, WALTER: Correspondent. b. St. Joseph, MO, Nov. 4, 1916. e. U. of Texas. Reporter: radio reporter; U.P. Correspondent. Joined CBS as Washington news correspondent, 1950; anchorman and mng. editor, CBS Evening News, 1962–81; special correspondent, CBS News, 1981–present. Many TV shows including You Are There, Twentieth Century, Eyewitness to History: CBS Reports: 21st Century, Walter Cronkite's Universe. Past nat'l pres. & mem. bd. Trustees, Acad. TV Arts & Sciences. Managing Editor of CBS Evening News since 1963; Special correspondent, Children of Apartheid.

CRONYN, HUME: Actor, Writer, Director. b. London, Ont., Canada, July 18, 1911. e. Ridley Coll., McGill U., Amer. Acad. of Dramatic Art; m. Jessica Tandy, actress. m.p. acting debut in Shadow of a Doubt.
STAGE: (Actor N.Y. plays) High Tor, Escape This Night, Three Men on a Horse, Boy Meets Girl, Three Sisters, Mr. Big, The Survivors; dir. plays Now I Lay Me Down to Sleep, Hilda Crane, Madam Will You Walk, The Fourposter, 1951–53; Madam Will You Walk; The Honeys, A Day by the Sea; The Man in the Dog Suit; Directed The Egghead, 1957; Directed and toured with his wife, Miss Tandy, in Triple Play; Big Fish, Little Fish (also in London); The Miser; The Three Sisters; Hamlet; The Physicists; Produced Slow Dance on The Killing Ground; Appeared at the White House; Hear America Speaking; Richard III; Revival The Miser; A Delicate Balance (1966 and tour, 1967); The Miser; Hadrian VII tour; Caine Mutiny Court Martial; Promenade All; Krapp's Last Tape, Happy Days, Act Without Words; Coward In Two Keys; Concert recital Many Faces Of Love; National tour, Noel Coward in Two Keys, Merchant of Venice and A Midsummer Night's Dream, at (Stratford Festival Theatre), Canada. Appeared in The Gin Game (Long Wharf Thea., New Haven, CT, Bdwy. 1977, co-prod. with Mike Nichols; also toured U.S., Toronto, London, U.S.S.R., 1978–79). Co-authored and acted in Foxfire at Stratford, Ont., 1980, Minneapolis, 1981 and N.Y., 1982–83, Traveler in the Dark (Amer. Repertory Theatre, Cambridge, MA), Foxfire (Ahmanson, LA 1985–86), The Petition (NY 1986).
TELEVISION: The Marriage, and other network dramatic shows, 1957. Co-authored The Dollmaker, Foxfire (and co-author), Day One.

PICTURES INCLUDE: Cross of Lorraine, Lifeboat, Seventh Cross, Main Street, After Dark, The Sailor Takes a Wife, A Letter for Evie, The Green Years, Brute Force, Bride Goes Wild, Postman Always Rings Twice, Top o' the Morning, People Will Talk, Crowded Paradise, Sunrise at Campobello, Cleopatra, Gaily, Gaily, The Arrangement, There Was a Crooked Man, Conrack, Parallax View, Honky Tonk Freeway, Rollover, Garp, Impulse, Brewster's Millions, Cocoon, Batteries Not Included, Cocoon II: The Return.

CROSBY, BOB: Band leader, Actor. r.n. George Robert C. b. Spokane, WA, Aug. 23, 1913. Brother of late singer-actor Bing Crosby. e. Gonzaga U. Began as singer; later featured vocalist Jimmie & Tommy Dorsey band. Org. own band (Bobcats); appeared with orch. on screen in Let's Make Music, 1940.
PICTURES INCLUDE: Sis Hopkins, Reveille with Beverly, Thousands Cheer, Presenting Lily Mars, See Here Private Hargrove; Meet Miss Bobby Socks, Kansas City Kitty, My Gal Loves Music, Pardon My Rhythm, Singing Sheriff, Two Tickets to Broadway.
TELEVISION: Bob Crosby Show.

CROSBY, CATHY LEE: Actress. b. Los Angeles, CA, Dec. 2. e. Grad. of U. of Southern California. Studied with Lee Strasberg. Theatrical film debut in The Laughing Policeman (1973), They Shoot Horses, Don't They? (wrote 1st theatrical adapt.).
PICTURES: Call Me by My Rightful Name, Trackdown, The Dark, Coach, Training Camp (writer), San Sebastian (writer).
TELEVISION: Movies: Wonder Woman, Keefer, Kingston Confidential, Mommy's Little Girl (writer), 5th & Philly (writer). Series: That's Incredible, Specials: A Special Evening in Egypt, Battle of the Network Stars, Circus of the Stars, Bob Hope Specials. Mini-series: World War III, Intimate Strangers, Roughnecks.

CROSBY, KATHRYN: Actress. r.n. Kathryn Grandstaff. b. Houston, TX, Nov. 25, 1933. e. U. of Texas, U. of California at L.A. m. Bing Crosby.
PICTURES: Forever Female, Rear Window, Living It Up, Arrowhead, Casanova's Big Night, Unchained, Cell 2455 Death Row, Tight Spot, Five Against the House, Reprisal, Guns of Fort Petticoat, Phoenix City Story, Wild Party, Mister Cory, Night the World Exploded, Brothers Rico, Operation Mad Ball, The Big Circus.
TELEVISION: Bob Hope Chrysler Theatre, Bing Crosby Christmas Specials, Suspense Theatre, Ben Casey, The Kathryn Crosby Show KPIX-TV, San Francisco.

CROSS, BEN: Actor. b. London, England, 1948. e. Royal Acad. of Dramatic Art. Stage work before films.
PICTURES: Chariots of Fire, The Assisi Underground. The Unholy, The Goldsmith's Shop, Paperhouse, The House of the Lord.
TELEVISION: The Far Pavilions, Coming Out of the Ice, Arthur Hailey's Strong Medicine, Steal the Sky, Pursuit.

CROSS, PERRY: Performer. b. Brooklyn, NY, Feb. 26. e. Rhode Island State Coll. At various clubs; to NBC, 1947. Guest relations staff, then TV production supervisor, coordinator, unit mgr.
TELEVISION: Ernie Kovacs Show, Henie Ice Spectacular, Ruggles of Red Gap, Tonight, Jack Paar Show, Today, TV network programs, night time.

CROUSE, LINDSAY: Actress. b. New York, NY, May 12, 1948. m. playwright-dir. David Mamet. Daughter of playwright Russel Crouse. e. Radcliffe. Began career as modern and jazz dancer; is also flutist and pianist. Has worked in films, theatre and TV.
THEATER: Was member of Circle Repertory Co. NY. The Shawl, The Cherry Orchard, Foursome, Present Laughter (Kennedy Center), Long Day's Journey Into Night, Hamlet (Circle Rep.), Twelfth Night (Circle Rep.), Reunion (Obie Award), Serenading Louie.
PICTURES INCLUDE: All the President's Men, Slap Shot, Between the Lines, The Verdict, Daniel, Iceman, Places in the Heart, House of Games, Communion: A True Story.
TELEVISION: Eleanor and Franklin, The Tenth Level, Lemon Sky.

CROWTHER, LESLIE: Actor, Comedian. b. Nottingham, England. Ent. TV ind. 1960. Early career incl: Hi Summer revue, Crackerjack, Black and White Minstrel Show. Stage: Let Sleeping Wives Lie, and Pantomine. 1971–72. Own TV series (LWT). 1978–82 Hi Summer series (LWT). Starred in Bud 'n Ches (stage). Since 1985 presented The Price is Right (Central TV).

CRUEA, EDMOND D.: Executive. b. Jersey City, NJ, June 3. Joined Grand National Pictures, L. A., 1935; Monogram Pictures, 1938–41, L.A. & Seattle; U.S. Army Signal Corp., 1942–46; Monogram Pictures, Seattle, 1946–48; branch mgr., 1948–49; branch mgr. and district mgr. Allied Artists, 1950–65 (Seattle, Portland, San Francisco, and Los Angeles); v.p.-gen. sls. mgr., Allied Artists 1965–71; dir. distribu-

tion, Abkco Films div. of Abkco Industries, Inc., 1971–73; pres. of Royal Dist. Corp., 1974; pres., Esco Film Corp., 1975; joined Film Ventures Intl. in 1976 as exec. v.p., succeeding to pres. and chief operating officer in August, 1976. Resigned Sept. 1977 to form Fil-Mark Inc. Co-founded New Image Releasing, Inc., 1982, as pres. & CEO 1985, v.p. theatrical, Cinetel Films; 1987 theatrical dist. consultant, Sony Pictures (NY) and Shining Armour Commun (London).

CRUISE, TOM: Actor. b. Syracuse, NY, 1962. m. actress Mimi Rogers. Acted in high school plays; secured role in dinner theatre version of Godspell. First film role in Endless Love (1981).
PICTURES: Taps, Losin' It, The Outsiders, Risky Business, All the Right Moves, Legend, Top Gun, The Color of Money, Cocktail, Rainman, Born on the 4th of July.
TELEVISION: Amazing Stories.

CRYER, JON: Actor. b. 1965. Son of actor David Cryer and songwriter-actress Gretchen Cryer. On Bdwy. stage in Brighton Beach Memoirs. Film debut: No Small Affair (1984).
PICTURES INCLUDE: Pretty in Pink, O.C. and Stiggs, Superman IV, Morgan Stewart, Hiding Out, Dudes.

CRYSTAL, BILLY: Actor. b. Long Island, NY, Mar. 14, 1947. e. Marshall U., New York U. Father, Jack, produced jazz concerts; family owned Commodore jazz record label. Worked with Alumni Theatre Group at Nassau Community College. Later teamed with two friends (billed as 3's Company) and toured coffee houses and colleges. Became stand-up comedian on own, appearing on TV.
PICTURES INCLUDE: Rabbit Test, Spinal Tap, Running Scared, The Princess Bride, Throw Mama From the Train, Memories of Me (actor, co-prod., co-s.p.), Boy Meets Girl.
TELEVISION: Tonight Show, Dinah, Mike Douglas Show, That Was the Year That Was, All in the Family, Love Boat, Soap, Saturday Night Live. Movies: Death Flight, Breaking Up Is Hard to Do.

CULBERG, PAUL S.: Executive. b. Chicago, IL, June 14, 1942. Began career in record industry, holding positions with Elektra Records & Wherehouse Record; 1977–80; v.p. sls. mktg., Cream Records.; 1980–82, dir. sls. mktg., Paramount Home Video; 1982, v.p. sls. mktg., Media Home Entertainment; 1984 to present, pres., New World Video.

CULLEN, BILL: Performer. b. Pittsburgh, Pa., Feb. 18, 1920; U. of Pittsburgh, B.A. Asst. disc jockey; announcer, KDKA, Pittsburgh; sportscaster; staff announcer. CBS radio, 1943; then m.c., panel member; shows include: m.c. Three on a Match, To Tell the Truth, Winning Streak, 25,000 Pyramid; Love Experts.

CULLEN, JAMES V.: Executive. b. San Francisco, CA, Dec. 29, 1938. e. City Coll. of San Francisco. Sales mgr., M.P.I. Toys, Los Angeles, 1963–65; entered film industry 1965 with 20th-Fox in S.F. exchange as ass't. field man; Named Southwest ad-pub. mgr. for Fox 1966 and Western Division ad-pub mgr. 1968. Appointed Fox director of exploitation 1971; then nat'l. dir. field adv. & pro.; Joined Sandy Howard Prods., v.p. creative affairs, 1974. Produced The Devils' Rain, 1975.

CULP, ROBERT: Actor, Writer, Director. b. Berkeley, CA, Aug. 16, 1930. e. Stockton, College of the Pacific, Washington U., San Francisco State; to N.Y. to study with Herbert Berghof. Starred in off B'way prod. He Who Gets Slapped. Best Actor of the Year in an off B'way Play; motion picture debut, 1962; P.T. 109; television guest appearances in Rawhide, Wagon Train, Bob Hope Presents the Chrysler Theatre; wrote and acted in Rifleman, Cain's Hundred, The Dick Powell Show.
PLAYS: The Prescott Proposals, He Who Gets Slapped, A Clearing in the Woods.
TELEVISION: Series: Trackdown, I Spy. Movies: The Calendar Girl Murders, Brothers-in-Law, The Blue Lightning, The Gladiator, Thou Shalt Not Kill, Her Life as a Man, No Man's Land, The Key to Rebecca, Flood, Combat High, A Cry for Help, What Price Victory.
PICTURES INCLUDE: PT 109, Sammy, The Way Out Seal, The Raiders, Sunday in New York, Rhino, The Hanged Man, Bob & Carol & Ted & Alice, The Grove, Hannie Caulder, Hickey and Boggs, Sky Riders, Great Scout and Cathouse, Thursday, Turk 182, Big Bad Mama II.

CUMMINGS, BOB: Actor, Director. b. Joplin, MO, June 9, 1910. Godson of Orville Wright. e. Drury Coll., Carnegie Inst. of Tech., American Acad. of Dramatic Arts: on dram. & musical stage, also radio. Has toured Dinner Theater Circuit since '73 and established new attendance records in 16 theaters playing Never Too Late, Marriage Go Round, No Hard Feelings, Harvey, Fun and Games.
TELEVISION: Bob Cummings Show; My Hero, Twelve Angry Men (Emmy, 1954). The Great American Beauty Contest.
PICTURES INCLUDE: Three Smart Girls Grow Up, Spring Parade, Saboteur, Heaven Only Knows, So Red the Rose, Kings Row, Flesh and Fantasy, Princess O'Rourke, You Came Along, Reign of Terror, The Accused, Free for All, Tell It

to the Judge, Paid in Full, Petty Girl, For Heaven's Sake, Barefoot Mailman, The Lost Moment, Free and Easy, First Time, Marry Me Again, Lucky Me, Dial M for Murder, How to Be Very Very Popular, My Geisha, Beach Party, The Carpetbaggers, What A Way to Go, Stage Coach, Promise Her Anything, Gidget Grows Up.

CUMMINGS, CONSTANCE: O.B.E. Actress. b. Seattle, WA, May 15, 1910. p. D.V. Halverstadt, attorney, and Kate Cummings, concert soprano; m. Benn Levy, English playwright. Was chorus girl in The Little Show and also appeared in June Moon. Broadway debut: Treasure Girl, 1928; London debut: Sour Grapes, 1934. Film debut: Movie Crazy 1932. Joined National Theatre Co. 1971.
THEATER: Recent work: A Long Day's Journey into Night (with Laurence Olivier), The Cherry Orchard, Wings (Tony, Obie Awards 1979), The Chalk Garden.
PICTURES INCLUDE: Behind the Mask, Washington Merry-Go-Round, Broadway; Through a Keyhole, Remember Last Night?, Channel Crossing, Glamour, Doomed Cargo, Busman's Honeymoon, This England, The Outsider, The Foreman Went to France, Somewhere in France, Blithe Spirit, Into the Blue, The Scream, John and Julie, The Intimate Stranger, Battle of the Sexes, A Boy 10 Feet Tall.
TELEVISION: Touch of the Sun, Clutterbuck, The Last Tycoon, Ruth, Late Summer, Long Day's Journey Into Night, Wings, Agatha Christie's Dead Man's Folly.

CUMMINGS, JACK: Producer. b. New Brunswick, Canada, Feb. 16, 1905. Started at MGM as office boy. Later worked as script boy, assistant director, director, producer of short subjects. Became producer of feature pictures. In 1934 produced The Winning Ticket.
PICTURES INCLUDE: Bathing Beauty, I Dood It, Broadway Melody, Girl from Rectors, Romance of Rosy Ridge, Neptune's Daughter, Two Weeks with Love, Three Little Words, Excuse My Dust, Texas Carnival, Lovely to Look At, Fiesta, Stratton Story, Sombrero, Give a Girl a Break, Kiss Me Kate, Seven Brides for Seven Brothers, Last Time I Saw Paris, Many Rivers to Cross, Interrupted Melody, Teahouse of the August Moon, Can Can, Bachelor Flat, Viva, Las Vegas.

CUMMINGS, SANDY: Executive. r.n. Sanford Cummings. b. Oct. 31, 1913. e. U. of Southern California. Child actor; Broadway. Summer stock, 1935; asst. prod., Paramount; assist. to Walter Wanger, 1936; started Hollywood office of Benton & Bowles, 1937; major, army, 1939—46; Head American Forces Network, Germany; prod. Columbia, 1946; ABC Coordinator, Walt Disney Studios, 1954; manager, TV Net Programs, Western Div. ABC, 1957; dir. TV Net Prog., 1958; V.P. & Dir. of pgms., Western Div., 1958—62; prod. specials, STV, 1964; prod., 20th Fox Television, 1965—66; NBC Broadcast Standards; 1969 mgr., live night-time and special programs, NBC.

CUMMINS, DWIGHT W.: Writer. b. San Francisco, CA, Feb. 20, 1901. e. U. of California at L.A., B.A. 1926. m. Dorothy Yost, writer. Tech. dir. & prod. asst. Film Booking Office studio, 1926—27. Began writing scripts 1927. Ed. & story asst. various major producers 1932—38. Instructor in Cinematog., U. of Southern California, 1938—42. Member Phi Gamma Delta.
PICTURES INCLUDE: Naughty but Nice, None but the Brave, The River, Thunderhead, Smoky, The Strawberry Roan, The Saginaw Trail.
TELEVISION: Gene Autry, Range Rider; TV writer for Roy Rogers, 1955—60; TV freelance.

CUMMINS, PEGGY: Actress. b. Prestatyn, North Wales. e. Alexandra Sch., Dublin, Gate Theatre, Dublin. Starred in Let's Pretend on London Stage 1938. Made Dr. O'Dowd WB, Eng., 1939. In 1942: Salute John Citizen; Welcome Mr. Washington; On London Stage in Junior Miss, Alice in Wonderland, Peter Pan. From 1946 Hollywood, starred in Late George Apley.
PICTURES INCLUDE: Moss Rose, Green Grass of Wyoming, Escape, That Dangerous Age, Gun Crazy, My Daughter Joy, Returned to Eng. 1950. Who Goes There (Passionate Sentry), Street Corner (Both Sides of the Law), Meet Mr. Lucifer, Always a Bride, Love Lottery, To Dorothy a Son, Cash on Delivery, March Hare, Carry on Admiral, Night of the Demon, Hell Drivers, The Captain's Table, Your Money or Your Wife, Dentist in the Chair, In the Doghouse.
TELEVISION: The Human Jungle, Looks Familiar.

CUNNINGHAM, SEAN S.: Producer, Director. b. New York, NY, 1941. e. Franklin & Marshall, B.A.; Stanford U., M.F.A. Worked briefly as actor, moving into stage-managing. Became producer of Mineola Theatre (Long Island, NY) and took several productions to Broadway. Formed Sean S. Cunningham Films, Ltd., 1971. Produced commercials, industrial film, documentaries, features.
PICTURES: Together (prod.-dir.), Last House on the Left (prod.); The Case of the Full Moon Murders (prod.); Here Come the Tigers (prod.-dir.); Kick (prod.-dir.); Friday the 13th (prod.-dir.); A Stranger Is Watching (prod.-dir.); Spring Break (prod.-dir.); The New Kids (prod., dir.); House (prod.); House

II (prod.), A Taste of Hemlock (dir.); House III, Deep 6 (prod., dir.).

CURTIN, JANE: Actress. b. Cambridge, MA, Sept. 6, 1947. e. Northeastern U. On stage in Proposition, Last of the Red Hot Lovers, Candida. Author, actress off-Bdwy musical revue Pretzel 1974—75.
PICTURES: Mr. Mike's Mondo Video, How to Beat the High Cost of Living, O.C. and Stiggs.
TELEVISION: Series: Saturday Night Live 1974—79; Kate & Allie. Movies: What Really Happened to the Class of '65, Divorce Wars—A Love Story, Candida, Suspicion.

CURTIS, DAN: Producer, Director. b. Bridgeport, CT, Aug. 12. e. U. of Bridgeport, Syracuse U., B.A. Was sales exec. for NBC and MCA before forming own company, Dan Curtis Productions, which he now heads. Producer/owner of CBS Golf Classic (1963—73).
PICTURES INCLUDE: House of Dark Shadows, Night of Dark Shadows (features for MGM, prod.-dir.), Burnt Offerings (prod., dir., co-s.p.).
TELEVISION: Producer: Dark Shadows (ABC serial, 1966—71). Movies: The Night Stalker, Frankenstein, The Picture of Dorian Gray. Producer-Director of movies: The Night Strangler, The Norliss Tapes, The Turn of the Screw, Dracula, The Scream of the Wolf, Purvis, The Winds of War; War and Remembrance. Director: The Last Ride of the Dalton Gang, The Long Days of Summer, I Think I'm Having a Baby, Mrs. R's Daughter.

CURTIS, JAMIE LEE: Actress. b. Los Angeles, CA, Nov. 22, 1958. m. actor, dir. Christopher Guest. Daughter of Janet Leigh and Tony Curtis.
PICTURES: Halloween, The Fog, Terror Train, Halloween II, Road Games, Prom Night, Love Letters, Grandview, USA, Perfect, Trading Places, 8 Million Ways to Die, Amazing Grace and Chuck, A Man in Love, Dominick and Eugene, A Fish Called Wanda, Blue Steel.
TELEVISION: Callahan (pilot), Tall Tales (Annie Oakley). Movies: As Summers Die, Death of a Centerfold, Money on the Side, She's in the Army Now, Operation Petticoat.

CURTIS, KEN: Actor. b. Lamar, CO, July 2, 1916. e. Colorado Coll. Success as songwriter for college prod. steered him to musical career in Hollywood. Sang with several groups, including Sons of the Pioneers, Tommy Dorsey Orchestra, Shep Fields band. In infantry and anti-aircraft unit in W.W.II. Signed by Columbia Pictures for series of westerns with "Big Boy" Williams in 1945.
PICTURES INCLUDE: The Searchers, The Alamo, The Quiet Man, Cheyenne Autumn, How the West Was Won, The Killer Shrews, The Giant Gila Monster, My Dog, Buddy.
TELEVISION: Ripcord, Perry Mason, Rawhide, Have Gun, Will Travel, Gunsmoke (joined later series as Festus Haggen in 1963), The Yellow Rose (series); Gunsmoke: Return to Dodge, Once Upon a Texas Train.

CURTIS, TONY: Actor. r.n. Bernard Schwartz. b. New York, NY, June 3, 1925. e. Seward Park H.S. In U.S. Navy, amateur dramatics, N.Y., started Empire Players Theatre, Newark, NJ, with Dramatic Workshop, Cherry Lane Theatre, Jr. Drama Workshop of Walt Whitman School; first prod. work with Stanley Woolf Players; m.p. debut in Criss-Cross; signed with U-I. Star of Tomorrow, 1953.
PICTURES INCLUDE: City Across the River, Johnny Stool Pigeon, Francis, Sierra, I Was a Shoplifter, Winchester 73, Kansas Raiders, Prince Who Was a Thief, Flesh and Fury, Son of Ali Baba, No Room for the Groom, Houdini, All American, Forbidden, Beachhead, Johnny Dark, Black Shield of Falworth, 6 Bridges to Cross, So This Is Paris, Purple Mask, Square Jungle, Rawhide Years, Trapeze, Mister Cory, Midnight Story, Sweet Smell of Success, Some Like It Hot, Spartacus, Operation Petticoat, Who Was That Lady?, The Rat Race, The Defiant Ones, Perfect Furlough, The Great Impostor, The Outsider, Taras Bulba, 40 Pounds of Trouble, Paris When It Sizzles, The List of Adrian Messenger, Captain Newman, M.D., Wild and Wonderful, Sex and the Single Girl, Goodbye, Charlie, The Great Race, Boeing-Boeing, Arrivederci, Baby!, Not with My Wife, You Don't!, Don't Make Waves, On My Way to the Crusades I Met a Girl Who—; The Boston Strangler; Those Daring Young Men in Their Jaunty Jalopies, Suppose They Gave a War and Nobody Came; You Can't Win 'Em All, Lepke, The Last Tycoon, The Manitou, Bad News Bears Go to Japan, The Mirror Crack'd, Insignificance, The Last of Philip Banter, Welcome to Germany, Midnight for Morticia.
TELEVISION: Series: The Persuaders, Vegas; Movies: The Second Girl on the Right, The Count of Monte Cristo, Moviola: The Scarlett O'Hara War, Harry's Back, Mafia Princess, Murder in Three Acts, Portrait of a Showgirl.

CUSACK, CYRIL: Actor. b. Durban, South Africa, Nov. 26, 1910. e. Newbridge, Co. Kildare; University Coll., Dublin, Eire. LL.D (Honoris Causa-National U. of Ireland); D. Litt (Hon. Causa-Dublin U.). Litt. D. (Hon. Causa-New U. of Ulster). Stage

debut: Candida, Abbey Theatre, 1932. Screen debut: Odd Man Out, 1945.
PICTURES INCLUDE: Esther Waters, Escape, The Blue Lagoon, Once a Jolly Swagman, All Over the Town, Small Back Room, The Elusive Pimpernel, Soldiers Three, Blue Veil, Secret of Convict Lake, Gone to Earth (Wild Heart), Saadia, Passage Home, Man in the Road, Man Who Never Was, March Hare, Jacqueline, Spanish Gardener, Ill Met by Moonlight, Rising of the Moon, Miracle in Soho, Shake Hands with the Devil, Floods of Fear, Gideon's Day, A Terrible Beauty, Johnny Nobody, The Waltz of the Toreadors, I Thank a Fool, 80,000 Suspects, Passport to Oblivion, The Spy Who Came In from The Cold, Fahrenheit 451, Taming of the Shrew, I Was Happy Here, Oedipus Rex, Galileo, King Lear, Country Dance, David Copperfield, Harold and Maude, Sacco and Vanzetti, La La Polizia Ringrazia, The Day of the Jackal, Juggernaut, Homecoming, Galileo, Tristan and Iseult, True Confessions, Little Dorrit, My Left Foot.
TELEVISION: The Dummy, The Moon and Sixpence, What Every Woman Knows, The Enchanted, The Power and The Glory, The Chairs, Don Juan in Hell, The Lotus Eater, Krapp's Last Tape, Murder in the Cathedral, Six Characters in Search of An Author, The Big Toe, Workhouse Ward, In the Train, Purgatory, The Moon in the Yellow River, Passage to India, Deirdre, The Tower, Dial M for Murder, St. Francis, The Physicists, Trial of Marshal Petain, In the Bosom of the Country, Uncle Vanya, A Time of Wolves and Tigers, Them, Clochemerle, The Golden Bowl, The Reunion, I Stand Well With All Parties, Catholics, Crystal & Fox, Jesus of Nazareth, The Plough and The Stars, You Never Can Tell, Accidental Death, Oedipus the King (Theban plays), The Hitchhiker, Menace Unseen, The Small Assassin, Glenroe.

CUSACK, JOAN: Actress. b. Evanston, IL, 1964. Sister of actor John Cusack; e. U. of Wisconsin, Madison. Studied acting at Piven Theatre Workshop, Evanston, IL. While in coll. joined The Ark, local improvisational comedy group. Joined Saturday Night Live as regular for 1985–86 season.
PICTURES: My Bodyguard (debut, 1980), Class, Sixteen Candles, Grandview U.S.A., Cutting Loose, Broadcast News, Stars and Bars, Married to the Mob, Say Anything, Working Girl, Heart of Midnight, Men Don't Leave.

CUSACK, JOHN: Actor. Brother of actress Joan Cusack. Member of Piven Theatre Workshop, IL. 10 years beginning when 8.
PICTURES: Class (debut, 1983); Sixteen Candles; Grandview, U.S.A.; The Sure Thing, Journey of Natty Gann, Better Off Dead, Stand By Me, One Crazy Summer, Hot Pursuit, Eight Men Out, Tapeheads, Say Anything, Dog Fight.

CUSHING, PETER: Actor. b. Kenley, Surrey, Eng., May 26, 1913. e. Purley Secondary Sch. Stage debut with Worthington Repertory Co.
TELEVISION: Asmodee, Anastasia, 1984, Gaslight, Home at Seven, Tovarich, Beau Brummell, Epitaph for a Spy, Pride and Prejudice, The Moment of Truth, Uncle Harry, Eden End, Rookery Nook, The Creature, The Browning Version, Winslow Boy, Peace With Terror, Julius Caesar (Cassius), Monica. Daily Mail TV award actor, 1953–54; Guild of TV award, 1955; News Chronicle T.V. Top Ten award, 1956, The Plan, Caves of Steel, Sherlock Holmes series, 1968, Morecambe & Wise Show, Wild-life Spectacular, The Zoo Gang, Orson Welles Great Mysteries, Space 1999, The New Avengers, The Great Houdini, A Land Looking West, A Tale of Two Cities (1981); The Vordal Blade, Tales of the Unexpected (1982); Helen and Teacher (1983).
PICTURES INCLUDE: Vigil in the Night, Moulin Rouge, Hamlet, Black Knight, End of the Affair, Alexander the Great, Magic Fire, Time Without Pity, Curse of Frankenstein, Abominable Snowman, Dracula, John Paul Jones, The Hound of the Baskervilles, Violent Playground, The Mummy, Suspect, The Flesh and the Friends, The Revenge of Frankenstein, Cone of Silence, Bride of Dracula, Sword of Sherwood Forest, The Naked Edge, Cash on Demand, The Devil's Agent, Captain Clegg, Fury at Smuggler's Bay, Hell-Fire Club, The Man Who Finally Died, The Evil of Frankenstein, The Gorgon, Dr. Terror's House of Horrors, She, The Skull, Dr. Who and Daleks, The Frighten Bed Island, Daleks Invade Earth, Frankenstein Created Woman, Torture Garden, Some May Live, The Night of the Big Heat, Corruption, Death's Head Moth, Frankenstein Must Be Destroyed, Doctors Wear Scarlet, The Vampire Lovers, Scream and Scream Again, House That Dripped Blood, I Monster, Twins of Evil, Tales from the Crypt, Dracula Today, Fear in the Night, Horror Express, The Creeping Flesh, Asylum, Nothing But the Night, Bride of Fengriffen, Frankenstein and the Monster from Hell, The Satanic Rites of Dracula, The Revenge of Dr. Death, From Beyond the Grave, The Beast Must Die, Dracula and the Legend of the Seven Golden Vampires, Shatter, Tender Dracula, The Ghoul, Logond of the Werewolf, The Devil's People, Death Corps, Trial by Combat, At The Earth's Core, Star Wars, Battleflag, The Uncanny, Hitler's Son, Touch of the Sun, Arabian Adventure, Black Jack, House of the Long Shadows, Sword of the Valiant, Top Secret!, Biggles.

DA COSTA, MORTON: Director, Actor. b. Philadelphia, PA, March 7, 1914. e. Temple U. Director of many Bdwy. musicals and plays, including Man and Superman, The Wild Duck, Plain and Fancy, No Time for Sergeants, Auntie Mame, The Music Man, Hot Spot, Maggie Flynn, The Women (revival).
PICTURES: Auntie Mame (dir., prod.), The Music Man, Island of Love.

DAFF, ALFRED EDWARD: Executive. b. Melbourne, Australia, Aug. 18, 1902. e. McDonald's Private Coll., Melbourne. Office boy Progressive Films, night asst. projectionist Moonee Ponds Theatre 6 mos., then in chg. of dispatch, adv. & accessory depts. Cooperative Films; joined Universal Mar., 1920 booker & suburban salesman 2 yrs., asst. mgr., then mgr. of Victoria & Tasmania; apptd. managing dir. of Japanese subsidiaries, 1935; Far Eastern supvr., 1938; also of Far and Middle East, 1940; to N.Y., 1942; apptd. foreign supvr. 1943; vice-pres. Universal Internatl Films, Inc., 1944; pres. same co., 1950; v.p. dir. world sales, Universal Pictures Co., since 1951. Named dir. Universal, May, 1952; exec. v.p., July, 1952; res. 1958; consultant motion pictures, TV.

DAFOE, WILLEM: Actor. b. Appleton, WI, July 22, 1955. Worked with experimental group Theatre X on the road before coming to New York. Built sets and debuted with the Wooster Group at the Performing Garage playing (literally) a chicken heart in Spalding Gray's Nayatt School. Current member of the Wooster Group. Film debut: The Loveless (1983, as a biker-poet).
PICTURES: The Hunger (1983); Streets of Fire; To Live and Die in L.A.; Platoon (nominated for an Oscar as best supporting actor), Off Limits, The Last Temptation of Christ, Mississippi Burning.

DAHL, ARLENE: Actress, Writer, Designer. b. Aug. 11, 1928, Minneapolis, MN. e. MN Business Coll.; U. of Minnesota, summers 1941–44; Minneapolis. Coll. of Music. m. Marc A. Rosen. Mother of actor Lorenzo Lamas. Acting career began at age 8, playing heroine of children's adventure serials on radio, Broadway stage debut in Mr. Strauss Goes to Boston, 1946; Appts: Internationally syndicated beauty columnist, Chgo. Tribune-N.Y. News Syndicate, 1951–71; Pres. Arlene Dahl Enterprises, (1951–75), Sleepwear Designer, A.N. Saab & Co., 1952–57; Nat. Beauty Advisor, Sears Roebuck & Co., 1970–75; v.p. Kenyon & Eckhart Advg. Co., pres., Women's World Div., Kenyon-Eckhart, 1967–72, Fashion Consultant, O.M.A. 1975–78, Int'l. Director of S.M.E.I., 1973–76, Designer, Vogue Patterns 1978–85. Pres., Dahlia Parfums Inc., 1975, pres., Dahlia Prods., 1978–81: pres. Dahlmark Prods. 1981–. Publs: Always Ask a Man, 1965 (6th ed.); Your Beautyscope (series of 12), 1969, Secrets of Hair Care, 1971, Your Beautyscope (series of 12) 1977–78. Profl. Assns. include: Screen Actors Guild, Actors Equity, Am. Fedn. of TV & Radio Artists, International Platform, Inc., Acad. of Motion Picture Arts and Sciences. Honrs. include: 8 Motion Picture Laurel Awards, 1948–63; Hds. of Fame Award, 1971, Woman of the Year, N.Y. Adv. Council, 1969. Mother of the Year, 1979; Coup de Chapeau, Deauville Film Fest 1983.
THEATER: Broadway starring roles include: Cyrano de Bergerac; Applause; other starring roles onstage in major US cities include: Questionable Ladies, The King and I, One Touch of Venus, I Married an Angel, Mame, Pal Joey, Bell Book and Candle, The Camel Bell, Life With Father, A Little Night Music, Lilliom, Marriage Go Round, Blythe Spirit.
PICTURES: My Wild Irish Rose (debut, 1947), The Bride Goes Wild, A Southern Yankee, Ambush, The Black Book, Three Little Words, Desert Legion, Here Come the Girls, Sangaree, The Diamond Queen, Bengal Brigade, Slightly Scarlet, Woman's World, Journey to the Center of the Earth, Kisses for My President, Jamaica Run, Caribbean, Gold, The Landraiders.
TELEVISION: Arlene Dahl's Beauty Spot, 1965; Hostess, Model of the Year Show, 1969, Arlene Dahl's Starscope, 1980, Arlene Dahl's Lovescopes, 1982, One Life to Live (1981–84), Night of One Hundred Stars, Happy Birthday, Hollywood, Who Killed Max Thorn?

DALE, JIM: Actor. b. Rothwell, Northants, England, Aug. 15, 1935. Debut as solo comedian at the Savoy, 1951. Joined National Theatre Co. in 1969 playing in Love's Labour's Lost, The Merchant of Venice, The National Health, etc. Toured Europe. U.S. theater: Mark Taper Forum: Comedians, Privates on Parade. NY Theater: Taming of the Shrew, Scapino, Barnum (Tony and Drama Desk Award), Joe Egg, Me and My Girl. Has written songs and music for films: Twinky, Shalako, Joseph Andrews, Georgy Girl.
PICTURES: Raising the Wind, Carry on Spying, Carry On Cleo, The Big Job, Carry On Cowboy, Carry on Screaming, Lock Up Your Daughters, The National Health, Digby, Joseph Andrews, Pete's Dragon, The Unidentified Flying Oddball, Scandalous.

DALEY, ROBERT: Producer. Began career in TV; later joined Clint Eastwood's Malpaso Co.
PICTURES INCLUDE: Dirty Harry, Magnum Force (both exec. prod.), Thunderbolt and Lightfoot (prod.), The Enforcer (prod.), The Gauntlet (prod.), Every Which Way But Loose (prod.), Escape from Alcatraz (exec. prod.), Any Which Way You Can (exec. prod.); Bronco Billy (exec. prod.); Stick (exec. prod.).
TELEVISION: The Untouchables, Ben Casey, The FBI, 12 O'Clock High, The Invaders, etc.

DALSIMER, SUSAN: Executive. Editor for E.P. Dutton before joining Lorimar Prods., as v.p. of east coast development. Left to become consultant for original programming at Home Box Office. 1987, named v.p., creative affairs, east coast, for Warner Bros.

DALTON, TIMOTHY: Actor. b. Colwyn Bay, Wales, March 21, 1946.
THEATER: Anthony and Cleopatra, The Taming of the Shrew, A Touch of the Poet.
PICTURES: The Lion in Winter, Cromwell, The Voyeur, Wuthering Heights, Mary Queen of Scots, Lady Caroline Lamb, Permission to Kill, Sextette, Agatha, Flash Gordon, Chanel Solitaire, The Doctor and the Devils, The Living Daylights, Brenda Starr, Hawks, License Revoked.
TELEVISION: Movies: Mistral's Daughter, Sins, The Master of Ballantrae, Florence Nightingale, The Flame is Love. Mini-Series: Jane Eyre, Centennial.

DALTREY, ROGER: Singer-Actor. b. London, England, March 1, 1944. Lead vocalist with The Who.
PICTURES: Woodstock, Tommy, Lisztomania, The Legacy, The Kids Are Alright, McVicar (also prod.), The Beggar's Opera.

DALY, JIM: Executive Director, Rank Organisation plc. b. 1938. Managing Director of Film and Television Services Division which includes: Pinewood Film Studios, Rank Film Laboratories, Rank Film Distributors, Rank Advertising Film, Rank Theatres, Rank Video Services. Appt. exec. dir., Rank Organ., 1982.

DALY, JOHN: Chm., Hemdale Group Ltd. b. London, England, 1937. After working in journalism joined Royal Navy. On leaving Service after three years, trained as underwriter with an Assurance Company. In 1966 became David Hemmings manager and in 1967 formed the Hemdale Company. Subsequently, in 1968, Hemdale obtained public status.
PICTURES INCLUDE: Images, Sunburn (co-prod., co-s.p.), High Risk, Going Ape, Deadly Force, Carbon Copy, Yellowbeard, Falcon and the Snowman, Terminator, Salvador, Rivers Edge, At Close Range, Hoosiers, Platoon, Best Seller, Shag (exec. prod.), Vampire's Kiss (exec. prod.), Miracle Mile (prod.), Criminal Law (co-exec. prod.), War Party (prod.), The Boost, Scenes From the Goldmine.

DALY, ROBERT A.: Executive. b. New York, NY, Dec. 8, 1936. e. Brooklyn Coll., Hunter Coll. Joined CBS-TV in 1955; dir. of program acct.; dir. of research and cost planning; dir. of business affairs. Later named v.p., business affairs, NY; exec. v.p. of network on April, 1976. Named president, CBS Entertainment, Oct. 1977. In Oct. 1979 became responsible for CBS Theatrical Films as well as the TV operation. In Nov. 1980, appointed co-chmn. and co-chief exec. officer of Warner Bros. Sole title holder since Jan., 1982.

DALY, TYNE: Actress. b. Madison, WI, Feb. 21, 1946. Daughter of late actor James Daly. Wife of Georg Stanford Brown. On stage in L.A. in Come Back Little Sheba (1987).
PICTURES: John and Mary, Angel Unchained, Play It As It Lays, The Entertainer, The Enforcer, Telefon, Speedtrap, Zoot Suit, The Aviator, Movers & Shakers.
TELEVISION: Series: Cagney and Lacey. Movies: Larry, Better Late Than Never, The Women's Room, A Matter of Life or Death, Your Place or Mine, Kids Like These.

DAMON, MARK: Executive. b. Chicago, IL, April 22, 1933. e. U. of California at L.A., B.A. Literature, M.A. Business Administration. Actor: 1958 under contract to 20th Century Fox, 1960 winner Golden Globe Award—Newcomer of the Year; early career includes The Fall of The House of Usher, The Longest Day; 1961 moved to Italy, stayed 16 years appearing in leading roles in 50 films; 1973 co-producer of The Arena with Roger Corman; 1974 head of foreign department for PAC, a leading film distributor in Italy; 1976 returned to the U.S.A. as exec. prod. of The Choirboys and in charge of its foreign distribution; 1977 founder and pres. of Producers Sales Organization, international distribution organization. 1987: formed Vision Int'l.
PICTURES: 1984: The Neverending Story (co-exec. prod.); High Spirits (exec. prod.).

DAMONE, VIC: Singer, Actor. r.n. Vito Farinola. b. Brooklyn, NY, June 12, 1928. m. actress-singer Diahann Carroll. e. Lafayette H.S., Brooklyn. Winner Arthur Godfrey talent show,

1945; then night clubs, radio, theatres, hotels. Film debut in Rich, Young and Pretty (1951); U.S. Army, 1951–53.
PICTURES INCLUDE: The Strip, Athena, Deep in My Heart, Hit the Deck, Kismet, Hell to Eternity.
TELEVISION: Vic Damone Show, 1958. Lively Ones, 1962.

DAMSKI, MEL: Director. b. New York, NY, July 21, 1946. e. Colgate U., AFI. Worked as reporter, journalism professor. USC Cinema instructor.
PICTURES: Yellowbeard, Mischief, Happy Together.
TELEVISION: M*A*S*H, Lou Grant, Long Journey Back, The Child Stealer, Word of Honor, The Legend of Walks Far Woman, American Dream, For Ladies Only, Making the Grade, An Invasion of Privacy, Badge of the Assassin, A Winner Never Quits, Attack on Fear, Hero in the Family, Murder by the Book, Hope Division, The Three Kings.

DANA, BILL: Actor, Writer. b. Quincy, MA, 1924. In night clubs and on TV.
PICTURES: The Right Stuff (actor), Busy Body (actor), The Nude Bomb (writer, actor).
TELEVISION: The Steve Allen Show (performer, head writer, 1961), The Bill Dana Jose Jimenez Show (star, writer), Ed Sullivan Show (performer), Spike Jones Show (prod., writer, performer), Milton Berle Show (prod., writer, performer), All in the Family (writer). Actor: Facts of Life, Too Close for Comfort, Golden Girls, Zorro and Son, Hollywood Palace, St. Elsewhere.

D'ANGELO, BEVERLY: Actress. b. Columbia, OH, 1954. Studied visual arts and was exchange student in Italy before working as cartoonist for Hanna-Barbera Studios in Hollywood. Toured Canada's coffeehouse circuit as singer and appeared with rock band called Elephant. Joined Charlotte Town Festival Company. Bdwy. debut in rock musical, Rockabye Hamlet. Film debut in The Sentinel (1977).
PICTURES: Annie Hall, First Love, Every Which Way But Loose, Hair, Coal Miner's Daughter, National Lampoon's Vacation, Finders Keepers, Paternity, National Lampoon's European Vacation, Big Trouble, Aria, Maid to Order, In the Mood, Trading Hearts, High Spirits.
TELEVISION: Captains and the Kings, A Streetcar Named Desire, Doubletake, Sleeping Beauty (Faerie Tale Theater), Slow Burn, Hands of a Stranger.

DANCE, CHARLES: b. Worcestershire, Eng., Oct. 10, 1946. e. Plymouth Coll. Art., Leicester Coll. of Art (graphic design degree). After first working as a West End theatre stagehand, made acting debut in 1970 in a touring company of It's a Two-Foot-Six-Inches-above-the Ground World. Worked in provincial repertory theaters. Joined the Royal Shakespeare Company 1975–80: Hamlet, Richard III, As You Like It. Lead in Henry V (1975, N.Y.), and Coriolanus (1979, Paris).
THEATER: revival of Irma La Douce (West End), Turning Over at London's Bush Theatre.
PICTURES: For Your Eyes Only, Plenty, The Golden Child, Good Morning, Babylon; White Mischief, The Hidden City, Pascali's Island.
TELEVISION: The Jewel in the Crown, Out On a Limb, BBC's The Secret Servant, Rainy Day Woman.

DANGERFIELD, RODNEY: Actor, Comedian. b. Babylon, NY, 1921. Performer in night clubs as Jack Roy 1941–51. Businessman 1951–63. Comedian 1963–present. Founder Dangerfields Nightclub 1969.
PICTURES: The Projectionist, Caddyshack, Easy Money (also co. s.p.), Back to School, Moving, The Scout.

DANIEL, SEAN: Executive. b. 1952. e. California Inst. of Arts film school. Was journalist for Village Voice before starting m.p. career as documentary filmmaker and asst. dir. for New World Pictures. In 1976 joined Universal Pictures as prod. exec.; 1979, named v.p. Now pres., production.

DANIELEWSKI, TAD: Director-Writer. b. Poland. Studied Royal Acad. of Dramatic Art, London; Ohio U.; State U. of Iowa. At Johns Hopkins Univ. won national award for research in prod. and dir. methods for TV. Produced and directed a series of dramatic shows on WAAM-TV in cooperation with NBC-TV, 1953–54.
PICTURES INCLUDE: Imperial Woman (co-writer), No Exit (dir.), The Guide (writer-dir.), Spain (writer-dir.), Copernicus (writer-dir. of English version).
TELEVISION: Omnibus, Wide Wide World, Eddie Fisher Show, Matinee Theatre, Robert Montgomery Presents, etc.
STAGE: Artistic director New York Repertory Theatre; directed Man with a Load of Mischief (London), A Desert Incident (Bdwy.), Brouhaha (off-Bdwy.).

DANIELS, HAROLD: Director, Producer, Writer. b. Buffalo, NY. e. Carnegie Tech. Drama Dept. B.A., U. of Pittsburgh, PHG.
STAGE: Director in Pittsburgh for Prof. Stage Guild Co., N.Y., Rhode Island and Boston Repertoire. Directed over 50 plays.
PICTURES INCLUDE: Joined MGM in 1940, directed shorts and won award from M.P. Council; joined David Selznick as director, 1943–45; produced, directed and wrote

Prince of Peace, won spec. award for dir., directed Woman from Tangier, Sword of Venus, Port Sinister, Roadblock, Daughter of the West Classics, Terror in the Haunted House, Date with Death, My World Dies Screaming, Bayou, Poor White Trash, Ten Girls Ago; directed, Night of the Beast, House of Black Death, Annabelle Lee, Moonfire. Pigmy, 1971.
TELEVISION: directed over 200 half-hour and hour films including My Hero, Readers Digest, Fury, Colt 45, Ellery Queen, Jim Backus Theatre, G.E. Theatre, etc. Wrote many original screenplays for both films and TV. The Phantom, On Guard, Death Valley Days, Hannibal Cobb.

DANIELS, JEFF: Actor. b. Georgia. 1955. e. Central Michigan U. Apprentice with Circle Repertory Theatre, New York.
THEATRE: Brontosaurus, Short-Changed Review, The Farm, Fifth of July, Johnny Got His Gun (Obie Award), Lemon Sky, The Three Sisters, The Golden Age.
PICTURES: Ragtime (debut), Terms of Endearment, The Purple Rose of Cairo, Marie, Something Wild, Heartburn, Radio Days, The House on Carroll Street, Sweet Hearts Dance, Checking Out, Love Hurts.
TELEVISION: Movies: A Rumor of War, Invasion of Privacy, Fifth of July, The Caine Mutiny Court Martial, The Visit (Trying Times). Series: Breaking Away (pilot), Hawaii 5-0.

DANIELS, PAUL: TV performer, magician. b. South Bank, England, 1938. Early career starring in British and overseas theatres. 1983, Magician Of The Year Award by Hollywood's Academy of Magical Arts. 1985, his TV special (BBC TV) awarded Golden Rose of Montreux trophy. Presenter of Every Second Counts and Paul Daniels Magic Show. Devised children's TV series, Wizbit and radio series Dealing With Daniels.

DANIELS, WILLIAM: Actor. b. Brooklyn, NY, Mar 31, 1927. m. actress Bonnie Bartlett. e. Northwestern U. Stage debut in Life with Father. Brought to national attention by role in A Thousand Clowns in original Bdwy. play and film version.
PICTURES: The Graduate, Marlowe, The Parallax View, Two for the Road, Black Sunday, Oh God, Sunburn, The Blue Lagoon, Blind Date.
TELEVISION: East Side/West Side; For the People; Tomoa, The Rockford Files; Rehearsal for a Murder; Drop Out Father; The Adams Chronicle, A Case of Rape, Blind Ambition, The Nancy Walker Show, Captain Nice, Knight Rider, St. Elsewhere (regular). Movie: The Little Match Girl.
STAGE: On a Clear Day You Can See Forever, 1776, Dear Me, The Sky Is Falling, A Little Night Music, etc.

DANNER, BLYTHE: Actress. b. Philadelphia, PA, Feb. 3, 1943. e. Bard Coll. m. writer-producer Bruce Paltrow. Appeared in repertory cos. in U.S. before Lincoln Center (N.Y.) productions of Cyrano de Bergerac, Summertree, and The Miser (Theatre World Award for last).
THEATER: Butterflies Are Free (Tony Award, 1971), Major Barbara, Twelfth Night, The Seagull, Ring Around The Moon, Betrayal, Blithe Spirit, A Streetcar Named Desire, Much Ado About Nothing.
PICTURES INCLUDE: 1776, To Kill a Clown, Lovin' Molly, Hearts of the West, Futureworld, The Great Santini, Man, Woman and Child, Brighton Beach Memoirs.
TELEVISION: Dr. Cook's Garden, To Confuse the Angel, George M, To Be Young, Gifted and Black, The Scarecrow, Adam's Rib (series), F. Scott Fitzgerald and The Last of the Belles; A Love Affair: Eleanor and Lou Gehrig, Too Far to Go: Eccentricities of a Nightingale, Inside the Third Reich, In Defense of Kids, Helen Keller: The Miracle Continues; Guilty Conscience. Series: Adam's Rib, Tattingers.

DANO, ROYAL: Actor. b. New York, NY, Nov. 16, 1922. On Broadway stage before entering films.
PICTURES: The Red Badge of Courage, Bend of the River, The Far Country, Moby Dick, Death of a Gunfighter, The Outlaw Josey Wales, In Search of the Historic Jesus, Take This Job and Shove It, Something Wicked This Way Comes, The Right Stuff, Red-Headed Stranger, Killer Klowns From Outer Space, Ghoulies II.
TELEVISION: Death Valley Days, Planet of the Apes, Heroes of the Bible, From Here to Eternity, Once Upon a Texas Train.

DANSON, HAROLD L.: Executive. b. New York, NY, Nov. 15, 1905. e. Brooklyn Polytechnic Institute, 1926. Feature ed., Brooklyn Eagle, 1927; press rep., Shubert Theatrical Co., asst. city ed., Newark Star-Eagle, 1928; dir. of adv. pub., RCA Photophone, 1929–30; asst. nat'l adv. mgr., RKO, 1930–32; exploit. mgr., studio adv. dir., asst. nat'l adv. dir., head of trailer prod., Paramount, 1932–44; account exec., 20th Century-Fox, 1944–46; nat. adv. dir., Eagle Lion, 1946–49; v.p., gen. sales mgr., Adler Communications Labs., 1951–54; dir. of adv. pub., TV National Screen Service Corp., 1955; acct. exec. ZIV TV Programs, 1956; Nat'l Telefilm Assoc. program sales, 1959; nat'l sales mgr., syndication Independent Television Corp., 1961–68; consultant 1969.

DANSON, TED: Actor. b. Dec. 29, 1947. e. Kent Sch., Stanford U., Carnegie-Mellon U. Studied at Actors Inst. with Dan Fauci. New York stage debut, The Real Inspector Hound, 1972. Film debut in The Onion Field, 1979. Television debut, The Doctors.
PICTURES: Body Heat, Creepshow, Little Treasure, A Fine Mess, Just Between Friends, Three Men and a Baby, Cousins, The Hard Way.
TELEVISION: Somerset, The Women's Room, The Good Witch at Laurel Canyon, Cowboy, Something about Amelia, Quarterback Princess, When the Bough Breaks, We Are the Children. Series: Cheers.

DANTE, JOE: Director. b. Morristown, NJ. Managing editor for Film Bulletin before going to Hollywood to work in advertising, creating campaigns for many films. Became protege of Roger Corman, co-directing Hollywood Boulevard. Edited Grand Theft Auto.
PICTURES: Piranha (dir., co-editor), Rock n' Roll High School (co-s.p. only), Grand Theft Auto (editor, only), The Howling (also co-editor), Twilight Zone—The Movie (segment), Gremlins, Explorers, Innerspace, Amazon Women on the Moon (co-dir.), The 'Burbs.

DANTON, RAY: Actor. b. New York, NY, Sept. 19, 1931. e. Horace Mann Sch., Carnegie Tech. m. Julie Adams. Radio actor on many programs; summer stock; London prod. of Mr. Roberts; U.S. Army, 1951–53; then TV actor numerous programs. Became dir. in 1976 with Psychic Killer (also co-s.p.).
PICTURES: Chief Crazy Horse, The Looters, The Spoilers, I'll Cry Tomorrow, Outside the Law, The Night Runner, Onionhead, Too Much Too Soon, Ice Palace, Legs Diamond, Tarawa Beachhead, Majority of One, The George Raft Story, Fever In The Blood, Portrait of a Mobster, The Chapman Report, The Longest Day, Sandokan, FBI Code 98, New York Calling Superdrago.
TELEVISION: Vietnam Story Home (dir.).

D'ANTONI, PHILIP: Producer. Director. b. New York, NY, Feb. 19, 1929. e. Fordham U., business administration. Joined CBS in mailroom, advanced into prod., sales development, prog. analysis, mkt. rsrch. Became indep. radio-TV repr. in 1954 for two years; then joined Mutual Broadcasting as sales manager; later, exec. v.p. Resigned in 1962 to form own prod. co. Made theatrical film debut with Bullitt as producer; directing debut with The Seven Ups. Heads Phil D'Antoni Prods.
PICTURES INCLUDE: Producer: Bullitt, The French Connection (Academy Award). Prod.-Dir.: The Seven Ups.
TELEVISION: Movin' On (series, 1969), Elizabeth Taylor in London, Sophia Loren in Rome, Melina Mercouri in Greece, Jack Jones Special, This Proud Land, and two movies: Mr. Inside/Mr. Outside, The Connection.

DANZ, FREDRIC A.: Executive. b. Seattle, WA, Feb. 28, 1918. Is chairman of Sterling Recreation Organization Co., Seattle; member, Foundation of M.P. Pioneers; v.p., Variety Club Intl.

DANZA, TONY: Actor. b. Brooklyn, NY, Apr. 21, 1951. e. U. of Dubuque. Professional boxer before tested for role in TV pilot (Fast Lane Blues) which he won. Back to New York and fighting until called to coast to appear as Tony Banta in Taxi series.
PICTURES: Hollywood Knights, Going Ape, Cannonball Run, Daddy's Little Girl.
TELEVISION: Series: Taxi, Who's the Boss. Movies: Doing Life, Single Bar, Single Women; Freedom Fighters (also co-exec. prod.).

DARBY, KIM: Actress. r.n. Derby Zerby. b. Hollywood, CA, July 8, 1948. e. Swanson's Ranch Sch., Van Nuys H.S. Studied at the Desilu Workshop in Hollywood. Professional debut on the Mr. Novak TV series.
TELEVISION: Eleventh Hour, Gunsmoke, Flesh and Blood (special); Enola Gay; Embassy; The People; Rich Man, Poor Man.
PICTURES INCLUDE: Bus Riley's Back in Town, True Grit, Generation, Norwood, The Strawberry Statement, The Grissom Gang, The One and Only, Better Off Dead, Teen Wolf Too.

DARK, JOHN: Producer. Films include, as associate: Light Up the Sky, Lost Innocence, The 7th Dawn, Casino Royale. Production exec., Paramount Pictures, exec. producer: Half a Sixpence, There's a Girl in My Soup. Produced: Wind of Change, Bachelor of Arts, Land That Time Forgot, At the Earth's Core, People That Time Forgot, Warlords of Atlantis, Arabian Adventure, Slayground.

DARLEY, DICK: Director, Producer network TV series and specials. Over 180 TV film shows; over 1,370 TV live/tape shows. Numerous pilots and commercials. Credits in U.S. and 27 foreign countries include drama, musical-variety, comedy, sports and documentary.

DARNBOROUGH, ANTONY: Producer, Director. b. London, Eng., ent. m.p. ind. 1944.
PICTURES INCLUDE: Seventh Veil, Years Between, Day-

break, Girl in a Million, Upturned Glass, When the Bough Breaks, Dear Murderer, The Calendar, My Brother's Keeper, The Girl in the Painting, Helter Skelter, Once Upon a Dream, Traveller's Joy, Boys in Brown, The Astonished Heart, So Long at the Fair, Quartet, Trio, Highly Dangerous, Encore, The Net (Project M. 7), Personal Affair, To Paris with Love, Baby and the Battleship.
TELEVISION: Also made many TV and documentary films for own co. and in assoc. with NSS.

DARREN, JAMES: Actor. b. Philadelphia, PA, June 8, 1936. Studied with Stella Adler group. Film debut: Rumble on the Docks (1956).
PICTURES INCLUDE: The Brothers Rico, Guns of Navarone, Gidget Goes Hawaiian, The Lively Set, 633 Squadron, Venus in Furs.
TELEVISION: T.J. Hooker, Fantasy Island, One Day at a Time.

DARRIEUX, DANIELLE: Actress. b. Bordeaux, France, May 1, 1917. e. Lycée LaTour, Conservatoire de Musique.
PICTURES INCLUDE: La Crise Est Finis, Mayerling, Club des Femmes, Abus de Confiance, Counsel for Romance, Mademoiselle Ma Mere, Katia, Orders from Tokyo, Oh Amelia, Rage of Paris, Rich Young and Pretty, 5 Fingers, La Ronde, Le Plaisir, Earrings of Madame De, Alexander the Great, Adorable Creatures, A Friend of the Family, Loss of Innocence, Scene of the Crime.
THEATRE: Coco, The Ambassador (Bdwy).

DARTIGUE, JOHN: Executive. b. Port-au-Prince, Haiti, Sept. 12, 1940. e. Brandeis U., B.A., 1961; Columbia U., M.A., 1965. United Artists: named director of worldwide pub. in 1975; appointed executive assistant to the senior vice president for advertising and publicity in 1977; named v.p. adv.-pub., 1978. Joined Warner Bros. in 1978 as project executive. Named sr. exec. asst. to the exec. v.p. of worldwide adv./pub., Jan., 1980, v.p., publicity July 1980.

DARTNALL, GARY: Executive. b. Whitchurch, Eng., May 9, 1937. e. Kings Coll., Taunton. Overseas Div., Associated British Pathe; Eur. rep., 1958–60; Middle & Far East rep., Lion International Films; Amer. rep., 1962; pres., Lion International Inc., 1963; Amer. rep., Alliance International Films Distributors, Ltd., and London Independent Producers, Ltd.; pres., Alliance International Films Corp. & Dartnall Films Ltd., 1966; managing dir., Overseas Division, Walter Reade Organization, 1969. pres., EMI Film Distributors, Inc., 1971; vice chairman, EMI Television Programs, Inc., 1976; pres., EMI Videograms, Inc., 1979; pres., VHD Programs, Inc. & VHD Disc Mfg. Co., 1980; chm. & chief exec. officer, Thorn EMI Films, Ltd., & Thorn EMI Video, 1983. Also pres. & CEO, Thorn EMI Films, Inc.; chm., Thorn EMI Cinemas; CEO, Thorn EMI Screen Entertainment Ltd. 1987: Acquired Southbrook Intl. Television and formed Palladium Inc., chairman and chief exec. officer.

da SILVA, RAUL: Creative consultant, Writer, Director, Producer, b. New York, NY, June 12, 1933. e. Adelphi U., B.A. 1958, elected to Academy of Distinction, Adelphi Alumni Assoc. 1978. Specializes in unusual conceptualization and plotting rework, stressing classic artistry and production values. Corporate AV dir., exec. prod. adv. agencies; indep. writer, producer, dir., univ. lecturer (business aspects of film prod. writing).
PUBLICATIONS: Making Money in Film & Video (Simon & Schuster, 1986); The World of Animation (Kodak, 1979); The Business of Filmmaking (Kodak, 1978); SOUND, Magnetic Recording for Motion Pictures (Kodak, 1977). Wrote articles for Millimeter, American Cinematographer, Back Stage and many other trades.
PICTURES: Fear No Evil (creative consultant).
TELEVISION: Nat Hurst, M.D. (dir., prod.), Standing Tall (script consultant). On home video cassette: The Rime of the Ancient Mariner.
AWARDS: 1984 Writer's Digest screenwriting award and numerous as dir.-prod. for films; six in 1975–76 for Coleridge and his masterpiece, The Ancient Mariner with Sir Michael Redgrave.

Da SILVA, RAY: Director and designer of animated films, Animator, Illustrator, Character designer. b. New York, NY, July 13, 1934. e. School of Visual Arts, N.Y., also instructor there. Specializes in animation direction, character design. Numerous national and international TV spots for the advertising industry.
PICTURES: Raggedy Ann & Andy; Heavy Metal.
TELEVISION: The Strangest Voyage, Noah's Animals, The Little Brown Burro, Ichabod Crane.

DASSIN, JULES: Director. b. Middletown, CT, Dec. 18, 1911. m. actress Melina Mercouri. Actor on dramatic stage several years; radio writer. Joined MGM, 1940, as dir. short subjects; later dir. features.
PICTURES INCLUDE: Canterville Ghost, Brute Force, Naked City, Thieves' Highway, Night and the City, Rififi, He

Who Must Die, The Law, Never on Sunday, Topkapi, Phaedra, 10:30 p.m. Summer, Promise at Dawn, Uptight, The Rehearsal, A Dream of Passion, Circle of Two.
PLAYS: Ilya, Darling, 1967.

DAVEE, LAWRENCE W.: Engineer. b. Foxcroft, ME, March 28, 1900. e. U. of Maine., B.S., elec. eng. Research eng. Bell Telephone Lab.; Fox Case Corp.; studio mgr. Fox Hearst Corp.; Bronx Studio. Elec. Research Prods., Inc.; Century Projector Corp., N.Y.; engineer & sales mgr.; pres. 1959. Member: 25–30 Club (Honorary). Lifemember, N.Y. State Projectionists.

DAVENPORT, NIGEL: Actor. b. Cambridge, England, May 23, 1928. e. Trinity Coll., Oxford. Began acting after stint in British military at 18 years. First 10 years of professional career in theatre. Majority of screen work in British films in 1960s and 70s.
PICTURES INCLUDE: Peeping Tom, A High Wind in Jamaica, A Man for All Seasons, Play Dirty, Virgin Soldiers, Royal Hunt of the Sun, No Blade of Grass, Villain Mary, Queen of Scots, Island of Dr. Moreau, Zulu Dawn, Nighthawks, Chariots of Fire, Greystoke, Without a Clue, Caravaggio.
TELEVISION: A Christmas Carol (1984), Dracula, The Picture of Dorian Gray, The Ordeal of Dr. Mudd, Masada.

DAVID, PIERRE: Producer. b. Montreal, Canada. e. U. of Montreal. Joined radio sta. CJMS 1966 as pub. relns. & spec. events dir. 1968, formed CJMS Prods., which became Mutual Prods., prod.-dist. co. which is part owner of Filmplan Intl. 1983, pres., Film Packages Intl.; 1985, exec. v.p. Larry Thompson Org. and pres. m.p. div.
PICTURES: The Brood; Hog Wild; Scanners; Dirty Tricks; Gas; Visiting Hours; Videodrome; Going Berserk; Of Unknown Origin; Covergirl; Breaking All the Rules; For Those I Loved, A Long Dark Night.

DAVID, SAUL: Producer. b. Springfield, MA., June 27, 1921. e. Classical H.S., Springfield; Rhode Island Sch. of Design. Started in radio, newspaper work and as editorial director for Bantam Books. Worked for Columbia Pictures, 1960–62; Warner Bros., 1962–63; 20th Century-Fox, 1963–67, and Universal, 1968–69; Executive story editor at MGM, 1972.
PICTURES INCLUDE: Produced Von Ryan's Express, Our Man Flint, Fantastic Voyage, In Like Flint, Skullduggery, Logan's Run, Ravagers (exec. prod.).

DAVIDSON, JOHN: Actor, Singer. b. Pittsburgh, PA, Dec. 13, 1941. e. Denison U. In numerous school stage prods. before coming to N.Y. in 1964 to co-star with Bert Lahr in Bdwy. show, Foxy. Signed as regular on The Entertainers with Carol Burnett.
PICTURES INCLUDE: The Happiest Millionaire, The One and Only Genuine Original Family Band, The Concorde—Airport '79, The Squeeze.
TELEVISION: The Fantasticks, USA, The FBI, The Interns, Owen Marshall, Kraft Summer Music Hall (own variety series), The Tonight Show, The Girl with Something Extra, The John Davidson Talk Show (1980), That's Incredible, Host of the New Hollywood Squares, Time Machine (game show), Incredible Sunday.

DAVIDSON, MARTIN: Director. b. New York, NY, Nov. 7, 1939. Acted in and directed off-Bdwy. plays, wrote material for Sid Caesar, worked as agent with N.Y. offices of Int'l. Famous Artists.
PICTURES: The Lords of Flatbush, Almost Summer, Hero at Large, Eddie and the Cruisers (also s.p.), Heartbreak Hotel.
TELEVISION: Series: Cold Steel and Neon, Family Honor, Call to Glory. Movies: Long Gone.

DAVIES, WILLIAM C.: Director. b. Auburn, NY, June 17, 1932. e. Auburn Community Coll., Sch. of Radio Technique. Radio & TV announcer & narrator, then cameraman & editor. Formed Virgo Productions, 1965.
PICTURES INCLUDE: Legend of Horror, Orgy of the Dead, The Seekers, Day the Adults Died, Pink Garter Gang, Night at the Feast, Laughter in Hell, The Crimson Cult, Submarine X-1.

DAVIS, ARTHUR: Executive. b. New York, NY, Dec. 28, 1927. e. New York U. Began as exhibitor in U.S.; founded Arthur Davis Organization in Tokyo, Japan, in 1963, representing European and American films for sales to Japanese TV and motion picture industry. 1979, released two documentaries, Brutes and Savages, The Art of Killing.

DAVIS, BETTE: Actress. b. Lowell, MA., April 5, 1908. e. Cushing Acad.; Mariarden Sch. of Dancing; John Murray Anderson Dram. Sch. Stage debut in Broadway (Rochester, NY); with Provincetown & Cape Players; on Broadway in: Broken Dishes, Solid South, Night of the Iguana, Sandburg; m.p. debut in Man Who Played God. 1932; won Academy Award twice: best actress 1935, in Dangerous and 1938, in Jezebel; voted one of the 10 best Money-Making Stars in Motion

Picture Herald-Fame Poll 1939, 40, 41, 44; founder & pres. Hollywood Canteen 1942; pres. AMPAS 1940. Received American Film Institute Life Achievement Award, 1977; 1979, Emmy for performance in Strangers; 1982, Film Advisory Board's Life Achievement Award; Amer. Acad. of Arts, 1983; Dept. of Defense Medal for Distinguished Public Service, 1983; Women in Films Crystal Award, 1983; Caesar Award French Cinema, Paris, 1986; Legion of Honor, French government, 1987; Kennedy Center Honors Award, 1987.
PICTURES INCLUDE: Of Human Bondage, Fog over Frisco, Sisters, Dark Victory, Juarez, Old Maid, Private Lives of Elizabeth and Essex, All This and Heaven Too, Letter, Now Voyager, Corn Is Green, Little Foxes, Deception, Winter Meeting, June Bride, Beyond the Forest, All About Eve, Payment on Demand, Another Man's Poison, Phone Call From a Stranger, The Star, Virgin Queen, Catered Affair, Storm Center, John Paul Jones, The Scapegoat, A Pocketful of Miracles, What Ever Happened to Baby Jane, Dead Ringer, Empty Canvas, Where Love Has Gone, Hush . . . Hush Sweet Charlotte, The Nanny, The Anniversary, Connecting Rooms, Bunny O'Hare, Madame Sin (TV in U.S.), Scientific Card Game, Burnt Offerings, Return from Witch Mountain, Death on the Nile, Watcher in the Woods, The Whales of August, Wicked Stepmother.
TELEVISION: The Disappearance of Aimee, Laugh-In, The Dark Secret of Harvest Home, Strangers: The Story of a Mother and Daughter, White Mama, Skyward, Family Reunion, A Piano for Mrs. Cimino, Little Gloria—Happy at Last, Right of Way, Hotel, Murder with Mirrors, As Summers Die.

DAVIS, BRAD: Actor. b. Florida, Nov. 6, 1949. Won music talent contest at 17; moved to Atlanta and acted in theatres before settling in New York, N.Y. stage debut in Crystal and Fox; did several off-Bdwy. plays including The Normal Heart in 1985. Appeared in TV soap opera, How to Survive a Marriage, for 10 months.
THEATER: The Elusive Angel, Entertaining Mr. Sloane, The Normal Heart.
PICTURES: Midnight Express, A Small Circle of Friends, Chariots of Fire, Querelle, Heart, Cold Steel.
TELEVISION: Walt Whitman, Sybil, Roots, A Rumor of War, The Greatest Man in the World, Chiefs, Robert Kennedy and His Times, Vengeance: The Story of Tony Cimo, Blood Ties, When the Time Comes, The Caine Mutiny Court Martial.

DAVIS, COLIN: Executive. Held executive positions in Canada in adv., bdcst., & p.r. with several companies, including Procter & Gamble, Young & Rubicam. Joined MCA TV Canada as v.p. & gen. mgr., 1977. Named dir. intl. sls., 1978. In 1986 appt. pres., MCA TV Int'l.

DAVIS, FRANK I.: Executive. b. Poolesville, MD, Feb. 18, 1919. e. U. of Maryland, A.B., 1941; Harvard Law School, LL.B., 1948. Law firm, Donovan, Leisure, Newton, Lombard and Irvine, 1948–50; v.p., gen. counsel, Vanguard Films, 1951; v.p., gen. counsel, Selznick Releasing Org., 1951–55; pres., The Selznick Company, 1953–55; v.p., Famous Artists Corp., 1956–62; v.p. George Stevens Productions Inc., 1962–65; exec. prod., The Greatest Story Ever Told; v.p. in charge of m.p. affairs, Seven Arts, 1966; exec. in chg. talent and exec. asst. to v.p. in chg. prod., MGM, 1967; dir. m.p. business affairs, MGM, 1970; v.p., business affairs, MGM, 1972; sr. v.p., motion picture business affairs, MGM/UA, 1983, exec. v.p., business affairs, MGM Pictures, 1986.

DAVIS, GEENA: Actress. b. Wareham, MA, 1959. m. actor Jeff Goldblum. e. Boston U. Acted with Mount Washington Repertory Theatre Co., NH. Model before debut in Tootsie, 1982.
PICTURES: Fletch, Transylvania 6-5000, The Fly, Beetlejuice, The Accidental Tourist, Earth Girls Are Easy.
TELEVISION: Series: Buffalo Bill, Sara.

DAVIS, GEORGE W.: Art director. b. Kokomo, IN, Apr. 17, 1914. e. U. of Southern California.
PICTURES INCLUDE: The Robe, The Diary of Anne Frank, Love Is A Many Splendored Thing, All About Eve, David and Bathsheba, Americanization of Emily, Unsinkable Molly Brown, Funny Face, Cimarron, Period of Adjustment, Mutiny on the Bounty, Twilight of Honor, How the West Was Won, Patch of Blue, The Wonderful World of the Brothers Grimm, Mr. Buddwing, The Shoes of the Fisherman, etc. Including 200 feature films and 2000 TV segments.

DAVIS, JORDAN P.: Executive. b. New York, NY, Oct. 29, 1933. e. Lehigh U., 1954; Columbia U. Law Sch., 1958. Attorney for five years. Director of Business Affairs, ABC TV Network, 1963–67. NBC TV Network 1967–69. Director of Talent and Program Admin. v.p. Warner Bros. Television, 1969–72. Executive, The Sy Fischer Company, 1972–73. Executive in charge of production, Four D. Productions, Inc.; The Mimus Corp., The Triseme Corporation, 1973–82. Pres., Jorlee Ltd., 1982–present.

DAVIS, JUDY: Actress. b. Australia. m. actor Colin Friels. Left convent school as teenager to become a singer in a rock band. Studied at West Australia Institute of Technology and National Institute of Dramatic Art. Worked with theatre companies in Adelaide and Sydney. Theatrical film debut in My Brilliant Career, 1979.
PICTURES: Hoodwink, Heatwave, Winter of Our Dreams, The Final Option, A Passage to India, Kangaroo, High Tide.
TELEVISION: A Woman Called Golda.

DAVIS, LUTHER.: Writer, Producer. b. New York, Aug. 29, 1921. Solo s.p., The Hucksters, B.F.'s Daughter, Black Hand, A Lion Is in the Streets, The Gift of Love, Holiday for Lovers, The Wonders of Aladdin; Across 110th St.; collab. book B'way musical Kismet (Tony Award), collab. s.p.; author, prod., Lady In A Cage; s.p. Across 110th St. Prod. and wrote book for Bdwy musical, Timbuktu!, 1978–79. Co-prod., Eden Court and Not About Heroes (off-Bdwy. plays, 1985 and 1986), Double Life of Harry Ptyffe.
TELEVISION: Wrote, prod., Kraft Suspense Theatre and many pilots for series (Run for Your Life, Combat, The Silent Force, Eastside, Westside, etc.). Wrote, prod. Arsenic and Old Lace (TV special). Prod.: The People Trap (TV special). Wrote teleplays for MOW's Daughter of the Mind, The Old Man Who Cried Wolf, Colombo.

DAVIS, MAC: Singer, Songwriter, Actor. b. Lubbock, TX, Jan 21, 1942. e. Emory U., Georgia State Coll. Employed as ditch digger, service station attendant, laborer, probation officer and record company salesman before gaining fame as entertainer-singer in 1969. Recording artist and composer of many popular songs.
PICTURES: North Dallas Forty, Cheaper to Keep Her, The Sting II.
TELEVISION: Brothers-In-Law, What Price Victory?

DAVIS, MARTIN S.: Executive. b. New York, NY, Feb. 5, 1927. e. City Coll. of New York, New York U. U.S. Army, 1943–46; joined Saml. Goldwyn Prod., Inc., 1944; Allied Artists, 1955; Paramount Pictures, 1958. Dir. adv., pub. expl. 1960; vice-pres., 1963; exec. v.p., 1966; exec. comm. & bd. of dir. Member of Bd., Gulf & Western, 1967. Exec. v.p. Gulf & Western, member exec. comm. 1983, elected G&W chm., CEO, & Chm. of exec. comm.

DAVIS, OSSIE: Actor, Writer, Director. b. Cogdell, GA, Dec. 18, 1917. e. Howard U., Washington, DC. m. actress Ruby Dee. Studied acting in N.Y. with Rose McLendon Players, leading to Broadway debut in 1946 in Jeb. For 11 years thereafter was one of best-known black actors on Broadway stage (Anna Lucasta, Jamaica, The Green Pastures, Wisteria Tree, A Raisin in the Sun, etc.) Wrote and starred in Purlie Victorious, repeating role for film version. Directed and appeared with Ms. Dee in her musical Take It From the Top. Co-hosted Ossie Davis and Ruby Dee Story Hour on radio (3 years). Published plays: Purlie Victorious, Langston, Escape to Freedom, Curtain Call, Mr. Aldredge, Sir. 1987: I'm Not Rapaport.
PICTURES INCLUDE: Actor: The Joe Louis Story, Fourteen Hours, Shock Treatment, No Way Out, The Cardinal, The Hill, Man Called Adam, The Scalphunters, Sam Whiskey, Let's Do It Again, Harry and Son, Avenging Angel, School Daze, The Right Thing, Her Alibi. Director: Cotton Comes to Harlem, Black Girl, Gordon's War, Countdown at Kusini (also star).
TELEVISION: Author: East Side/West Side, The Eleventh Hour. Acted in many top dramatic series. (Name of the Game, Night Gallery, Bonanza, etc.), Martin Luther King: The Dream and the Drum; Co-host and co-prod.: With Ossie and Ruby; Today is Ours (writer, dir.), Movies: All God's Children, Roots: The Next Generations, King, Teacher, Teacher.

DAVIS, PETER: Director. Filmmaker. b. Santa Monica, CA, Jan. 2, 1937. e. Harvard Coll., 1953–57. Parents were screenwriter Frank Davis, and novelist, screenwriter Tess Slesinger. Writer-interviewer, Sextant Prods., FDR Series, 1964–65. Host, The Comers, PBS 1964–65. Author: Hometown (1982), Where Is Nicaragua? (1987), articles for Esquire, NY Times Mag., The Nation, NY Woman, TV Guide.
PICTURES: Hearts and Minds (prod., dir.; Acad. Award, best documentary, 1975; Prix Sadoul, 1974).
TELEVISION: Writer-prod.: Hunger in America (assoc. prod., Writers Guild of America Award, 1968); The Heritage of Slavery; The Battle of East St. Louis, (Saturday Review Award, 1970; 2 Emmy nom.); The Selling of the Pentagon (Writers Guild, Emmy, Peabody, George Polk, Ohio State, Sat. Review Awards, 1971); 60 Minutes (segment prod.); Middletown (series, prod., Dupont Citation, Emmy noms. 1983); The Rise and Fall of the Borscht Belt.

DAVIS, ROGER H.: Attorney. b. Chicago, IL, June 19, 1923. e. U. of California, Berkeley, 1951, A.B., LL.B. Private law practice, partner, Loeb and Loeb, Los Angeles, 1951–61; atty., William Morris Agency, head of west coast legal, literary and M.P. depts., exec./admin., asst. sec. WMA, Inc., 1969–present, made v.p., 1974. exec. v.p. & bd. member, 1980.

DAVIS, SAMMI: Actress. b. Worcestershire, England. Convent-educated before taking drama course subsequently performed in stage productions with local drama society in Midlands, then Birmingham Rep. and Big Brum Theatre Co. Plays include The Home Front, The Apple Club, Nine Days, Databased, Choosey Susie. London stage debut: A Collier's Friday.
PICTURES: Mona Lisa, Lionheart, Hope and Glory, A Prayer for the Dying, Consuming Passions, The Lair of the White Worm, The Rainbow.
TELEVISION: Auf Wiedersehn Pet, The Day After The Fair.

DAVIS, SAMMY, JR.: Entertainer. b. New York, NY, Dec. 8, 1925. Father: Sammy Davis, Sr., entertainer. Professional debut at age 2, Gibson Theatre, in act with father and uncle, Will Mastin; singer, dancer, comedian, vocal and acting impressions; song writer; recording artist; starred in Mr. Wonderful, & Golden Boy on B'way; in many major TV shows.
PICTURES INCLUDE: Anna Lucasta, Porgy & Bess, Ocean's 11, Robin and the Seven Hoods, Salt and Pepper, A Man Called Adam, Sweet Charity, One More Time, The Cannonball Run, Cannonball Run II, Moon Over Parador, Tap.

DAVISON, BRUCE: Actor. b. Philadelphia, PA, 1946. e. Pennsylvania State U., New York U. debut, Lincoln Center Repertory.
THEATER: The Front Page (Long Wharf), Streamers (Westwood Playhouse, LA Critics Award), King Lear (Lincoln Center), The Elephant Man, Richard III (NY Shakespeare Fest.), The Glass Menagerie, The Caine Mutiny Court Martial (Ahmanson), The Normal Heart (Las Palmas Theatre), Downside (Long Wharf).
PICTURES INCLUDE: Last Summer, The Strawberry Statement, Willard, Been Down So Long It Looks Like Up To Me, The Jerusalem File, Ulzana's Raid, Mame, Mother, Jugs, and Speed, Short Eyes, Brass Target, French Quarter, High Risk, A Texas Legend, Lies, Crimes of Passion, Spies Like Us, The Ladies Club, Wheels of Terror, Misfit Brigade.
TELEVISION: Taming of the Shrew. Movies: Deadman's Curve, Summer of My German Soldier, Alfred Hitchcock Presents (1985), Mind Over Murder, The Gathering, Tomorrow's Child, Ghost Dancing, Poor Little Rich Girl: The Barbara Hutton Story; Amazing Stories, Hunter (series).

DAVISON, DALE: Executive. b. North Hollywood, CA, March 21, 1955. e. U.C.L.A., B.A., 1978. Entered the motion picture industry in 1973 working for Pacific Theatres. Employed with Great Western Theatres 1974–77 as manager, dir. of concessions, and asst. vice pres. Partner with Great Western Theatres, 1978–1984. Founder and CEO, CinemaCal Enterprises, Inc., 1985–present.

DAVISON, JON: Producer. b. Haddonfield, NJ, July 21, 1949. e. New York U. Film School. Taught film history there one summer and ran New York U. Cinema two years. 1972, joined New World Pictures as natl. dir. of publ./adv.; 1977, named in charge of prod.; 1980, became indep. prod.
PICTURES: Hollywood Boulevard, Grand Theft Auto, Piranha, Airplane!, White Dog, Twilight Zone—The Movie (episode), Top Secret! RoboCop.

DAWBER, PAM: Actress, Singer. b. Detroit, MI, Oct. 18, 1954. m. actor Mark Harmon. e. Farmington H.S., Oakland Community Coll. Travelled nationally to trade shows to introduce new auto model; also began working in commercials. In 1971 came to New York; hired as model, also doing commercials. First professional performance as singer in Sweet Adeleine at Goodspeed Opera House, East Haddam, CT. On TV in comedy special, Sister Terri. Played Mindy in Mork and Mindy.
STAGE: The Pirates of Penzance.
PICTURE: A Wedding (1978).
TELEVISION: Movies: Remembrance of Love, Through Naked Eyes, Last of the Great Survivors, American Geisha, This Wife For Hire. Series: My Sister Sam.

DAY, DORIS: Singer, Actress. r.n. Doris Kappelhoff. b. Cincinnati, OH, Apr. 3, 1924. e. dancing, singing. Toured as dancer; radio and band singer; screen debut in Romance on the High Seas, 1948. Voted one of Top Ten Money-Making Stars in Motion Picture Herald-Fame poll, 1951–52. Best female vocalist. M. P. Daily radio poll, 1952.
PICTURES INCLUDE: Young Man With a Horn, Tea for Two, Storm Warning, West Point Story, Lullaby of Broadway, On Moonlight Bay, I'll See You in My Dreams, Starlift, Winning Team, April in Paris, By the Light of the Silvery Moon, Calamity Jane, Lucky Me, Young at Heart, Love Me or Leave Me, Man Who Knew Too Much, Julie, Pajama Game, Teacher's Pet, Pillow Talk, Please Don't Eat the Daisies, Midnight Lace, Lover, Come Back, That Touch of Mink, Jumbo, Thrill of It All, Move Over, Darling, Do Not Disturb, Send Me No Flowers, Glass Bottom Boat, Caprice, The Ballad of Josie, Where Were You When the Lights Went Out, With Six You Get Eggrolls.
TELEVISION: The Doris Day Show (1968–73); Cable show: Doris Day and Friends (1985–86).

DAY, LARAINE: Actress. r.n. Laraine Johnson. b. Roosevelt, UT, Oct. 13, 1917. In school dramatics; with Players Guild, Long Beach, Calif.; toured in church prod. Conflict; Professionally on stage in Lost Horizon, The Women, Time of the Cuckoo, Angel Street; m.p. debut in Border G-Men 1938.
PICTURES INCLUDE: Story of Dr. Wassell, Those Endearing Young Charms, Locket, Tycoon, My Son, My Son, Foreign Correspondent, Woman on Pier 13, Without Honor, High and the Mighty, Mr. Lucky, Toy Tiger, Three for Jamie Dawn, The Third Voice, Yank on the Burma Road, The Bad Man, Fingers at the Window, Bride By Mistake, My Dear Secretary.
TELEVISION: Climax, Playhouse 90, Alfred Hitchcock, Wagon Train, Let Freedom Ring, Name of the Game, FBI, Sixth Sense, Medical Center, Murder on Flight #504 (movie), Fantasy Island, Love Boat, Lou Grant, Airwolf, Hotel, Murder She Wrote.

DAY, ROBERT: Director. b. England, Sept. 11, 1922. Started as cinematographer before turning to direction.
PICTURES: Director: The Green Man, Grip of the Stranger; First Man into Space; Corridors of Blood; Bobikins; Two-Way Stretch; The Rebel; Operation Snatch; Tarzan's Three Challenges; She; Tarzan and the Valley of Gold; Tarzan and the Green River; Logan's Run; The Man with Bogart's Face.
TELEVISION: Pilots include: Banion, Kodiak; Dan August; Sunshine, Switch, Kingston, Dallas. Movies include: Ritual of Evil; The House of Greenapple Road; In Broad Daylight; Having Babies; The Grass Is Always Greener over the Septic Tank; Peter and Paul; Running Out; Scruples; Cook and Peary—The Race to the Pole; Hollywood Wives; The Lady from Yesterday; Diary of a Perfect Murder; Celebration; Family.

DAY-LEWIS, DANIEL: Actor. b. London, England, 1958. Son of late C. Day-Lewis, poet laureate of Eng., and actress Jill Balcon. Grandson of late Sir Malcolm Balcon who prod. Hitchcock's Brit. films. e. Bristol Old Vic. Theatre School. First professional job at 12 as ruffian scratching cars with broken bottle in film, Sunday Bloody Sunday. Then acted with Bristol Old Vic and Royal Shakespeare Co. First gained fame as stage actor, appearing on West End in, among others, Another Country.
PICTURES: Gandhi, The Bounty, A Room With a View, My Beautiful Laundrette, The Unbearable Lightness of Being, Stars and Bars, Ever Smile New Jersey.
TELEVISION: How Many Miles to Babylon?, The Insurance Man.

DAYTON, LYMAN D.: Producer. b. Salt Lake City, UT. Aug. 17, 1941. e. Brigham Young U. m. Elizabeth Doty Dayton. After college worked in film lab at MGM, 1967–68; joined Screen Gems and General DeLuxe, 1968–69; became indep. prod. 1969. Heads Doty-Dayton Productions.
PICTURES INCLUDE: Where the Red Fern Grows, Seven Alone, Against A Crooked Sky, Pony Express Rider, Baker's Hawk, Young Rivals, Powder Keg.

DEAN, EDDIE: Actor. r.n. Edgar D. Glosup. b. Posey, TX. 1930–33 in radio throughout middle west; 1934 National Barn Dance, Station WLS; 1935 on CBS & NBC with same program. Featured male singer on TV KTLA Western Varieties 1944–55. Came to Hollywood in 1936; since then has starred in many westerns. Featured performer in western series for PRC in 1945. Voted one of the ten best money making Western Stars in Motion Picture Herald-Fame Poll 1936–47; recording artists, personal appearances, rodeos, fairs, etc.; 1966 V.P. Academy of Country & Western Music; 1967–68 on Bd. of Dir. of Academy of Western Music, Calif. Winner, Pioneer Award of Academy of Country Music, 1978. In 1983 named ACM v.p.; also v.p. in 1985. Recorded video cassette 1986, A Tribute to Eddie Dean.

DEAN, JIMMY: Performer. b. Plainview, TX, Aug. 10, 1928. Joined armed forces, 1946–49; first appeared in various clubs in Wash., 1949; then app. on Town and Country Jamboree; toured Caribbean and Europe with his troupe.
SONGS: Composer: Bummin' Around, Freight Train Blues, Glad Rags, Hello, Mr. Blues, I Found Out, Big Bad John, PT-109, Little Black Book, This Ole House.
TELEVISION: Sunday Night at the Palladium (London), The Jimmy Dean Show.

DEAN, MERRILL C.: Executive. b. May 24, 1941. e. U. of California at L.A., M.B.A., bus. admin. 1967–68, involved with Walt Disney Productions, 11 yrs. starting in m.p. distribution internationally with Buena Vista Intl., concentrating on Latin America. Later involved with worldwide publications and gen. mgr. of direct mktg. Was v.p. & gen. mgr. Walt Disney Records Music Division, four years. 1978–82, pres. of Televisa Intl. Distribution Corp., whose activities are principally involved with dist. of films to the Hispanic mkt. in U.S. & Puerto Rico. Now pres. InterFilm, Inc., Los Angeles, and Azimuth Communications Corp.

DEAN, MORTON: Television Newsman. b. Fall River, MA, Aug. 22, 1935. e. Emerson Coll. News dir., N.Y. Herald Tribune Net, 1957; corr. WBZ, 1960, corr. WCBS-TV, 1964; anchor, WCBW-TV News, 1967; corr., CBS News, 1967; anchor, CBS Sunday Night News, 1975; anchor, Sunday edition CBS Evening News, 1976; co-anchor, Independent Network News, 1985.

DEARDEN, JAMES: Writer, Director, b. London, England, 1949. Son of late British director Basil Dearden. e. New Coll., Oxford U. Entered film industry in 1967 as production runner. After editing commercials and documentaries, and working as asst. dir., wrote, prod. and dir. first short film, The Contraption (Silver Bear Award, 1978 Berlin Film Fest.), began dir. commercials and made short, Panic (Cert. of Merit, 1980 Chicago Film Fest.). 1979, made 45-min film Diversion, which became basis for Fatal Attraction (Gold Plaque, best short drama, 1980 Chicago Film Fest.).
PICTURES: Fatal Attraction (s.p.); Pascali's Island (dir., s.p.).
TELEVISION: The Cold Room (dir., s.p., Special Jury Prize, dir., 1985 Fest. Intl. d'Avoriaz du Film Fantastique).

De BELDER, GUIDO: Actor, Author, Screenwriter. b. Tienen, Belgium, Mar. 14, 1949.
PICTURES INCLUDE: Mirliton, Obsessie, Spielgelvan Het Geluk, Mireille Dans La Vie Des Autres, Exit Seven, Ten Years After, Chock, Slachtwee, Deterugtocht, Mama Dracula, Traverses Traversees, Une Femme en Fuite, The Afterman.
TELEVISION: De Machinist (serial in 3 parts), Portrait of Guido De Belder (documentary).

De BELSO, RICHARD: Executive. e. New York U., 1965. Began career in adv./research dept. at Benton & Bowles. Served as research dept. group head for Kenyon and Eckhart; group head for Gruden/Appell/Haley Research Co. (now known as A/H/F/ Marketing Research (N.Y.). Two years as assoc. dir. of mktg., research for Grey Advertising (N.Y.). Joined MCA/Universal in 1977 as assoc. dir., mktg. research. In 1980 named v.p. & dir. of mktg. research for Warner Bros.

De BROCA, PHILIPPE: Director. b. 1933. French director.
PICTURES INCLUDE: Les Jeux de l'Amour, L'Amant, de Cinq Jours, Cartouche, That Man from Rio, Un Monsieur de Compagnie, Tribulations, Chinoise en Chine, King of Hearts, Devil by the Tail, Give Her the Moon, Chere Louise, Le Magnifique, Dear Inspector (and s.p.), The Skirt Chaser, Someone's Stolen the Thigh of Jupiter, The African, Louisiana (TV in U.S.), The Gypsy, Chouans! (dir., co-s.p.).

De CAESAR, GABRIEL: Producer. b. New York, NY, Nov. 15, 1928. e. Los Angeles City College, 1952. Dir.-mgr. Little Theatre, L.A. Group, 3 yrs.; actor, 6 years; acting member Catholic Coll. Thea., Santa Monica Thea. Group, Pilgrimage Play Thea. Group, 3 yrs., producer: Three Wishes for Jamie, Bullfight; assoc. prod., asst. prod., Viscount Films, Inc. 1957–59; dir., N.A.B.E.T.; acted: Unexpected, TV series; producer, TV pilots, 1958; asst. prod., pictures; Tank Battalian, Speed Crazy; pres., exec. prod. Marqhis Productions, Inc., 1959; assoc. prod., Why Must I Die?

De CAMP, ROSEMARY: Actress. b. Prescott AZ, 1913.
TELEVISION: Robert Cummings Show, That Girl, Life of Riley (with Jackie Gleason); Death Valley Days; Partridge Family; Love American Style, Police Story, Rockford Files, Days of Our Lives, Misadventures of Sheriff Lobo, Love Boat, Blind Ambition, B.J. & the Bear.
PICTURES INCLUDE: Cheers for Miss Bishop, Hold Back the Dawn, Jungle Book, Yankee Doodle Dandy, Eyes in the Night, Pride of the Marines, Look for the Silver Lining, Story of Seabiscuit, Big Hangover, Scandal Sheet, On Moonlight Bay, Treasure of Los Canyon, By the Light of the Silvery Moon, Main Street to Broadway, So This Is Love, Many Rivers to Cross, Strategic Air Command, Saturday the 14th.

De CAPRIO, AL: Producer-director. e. Brooklyn Tech., New York U. Started as radio engineer, cameraman, tech. dir., prod. & dir. CBS; dir. Sgt. Bilko, Car 54 Where Are You?, Musical specials for ABC, CBS, NBC; v.p. exec. prod. dir., MPO Videotronics, Pres. World Wide Videotape.

De CARLO, YVONNE: Actress. b. Vancouver, B.C., Sept. 1, 1926. e. Vancouver School of Drama, Fanchon & Marco, Hollywood. Specialty dancing at Florentine Gardens, Earl Carroll's; m.p. debut in This Gun for Hire, 1942. One-woman club act and 7-person club act.
PICTURES INCLUDE: Harvard Here I Come, Youth on Parade, Road to Morocco, Story of Dr. Wassell, Salome, Where She Danced; Frontier Gal, Brute Force, Song of Scheherazade, Black Bart, Casbah, River Lady, Criss Cross, Gal Who Took the West, Calamity Jane and Sam Bass, Buccaneer's Girl, Tomahawk, Hotel Sahara, Silver City, Scarlet Angel, San Francisco Story, Hurricane Smith, Sombrero, Sea Devils, Fort Algiers, Border River, Captain's Paradise, Passion, Tonight's the Night, Shotgun, Magic Fire, Flame of the Islands, Ten Commandments, Raw Edge, Death of a Scoundrel, Band of Angels, Timbuktu, Law of the Lawless, Hostile Guns, The Power, McClintock, Play Dead, American Gothic, Cellar Dweller.
BROADWAY STAGE: Follies.
TELEVISION: The Munsters (series), The Mark of Zorro, A Masterpiece of Murder.

De CORDOVA, FREDERICK: Director. b. New York, NY, Oct. 27, 1910. e. Northwestern U., B.S. 1931. Gen. stage dir. Shubert enterprises, N.Y., 1938–41; same for Alfred Bloomingdale Prods., N.Y., and prod. Louisville (Ky.) Amphitheatre 1942–43; m.p. dir. Author: Johnny Come Lately, 1988.
PICTURES INCLUDE: (dial. dir.) San Antonio, Janie, Between Two Worlds; (dir.) Too Young to Know, Her Kind of Man, That Way with Women, Always Together, Wallflower, For the Love of Mary, Countess of Monte Cristo, Illegal Entry, Girl Who Took the West, Buccaneer's Girl, Peggy, Desert Hawk, Bedtime for Bonzo, Katie Did It, Little Egypt, Finders Keepers, Here Come the Nelsons, Yankee Buccaneer, Bonzo Goes to College, Column South.
TELEVISION: prod., dir. Burns and Allen, 1955–56; prod., December Bride, 1954–55; prod. and dir., Mr. Adams and Eve, prod. dir. December Bride; prod. dir. George Gobel Show; prod. dir., Jack Benny Program, 1960–63; dir., program planning, Screen Gems, 1964; prod. dir., Smothers Bros. Show, 1965–66; 1965 dir. I'll Take Sweden and Frankie & Johnny; 1966–70 dir. My Three Sons; 1971–present, prod., Tonight Show.

DeCUIR, JOHN: Art Director-Production Designer. b. San Francisco, CA. 1918. Universal 1938–49; Mark Hellinger Prods., 1946. 20th Fox 1949. Nominated for Acad. Award 11 times.
PICTURES INCLUDE: The Naked City, Snows of Kilimanjaro, My Cousin Rachel, Call Me Madam, Three Coins in the Fountain, There's No Business Like Show Business, Daddy Long Legs, The King and I (A.A., Art Dir.), Island in the Sun, South Pacific, The Big Fisherman, A Certain Smile, Cleopatra (A.,A.: Prod. Des.), The Agony and the Ecstasy, The Honey Pot, Zefferelli's Taming of The Shrew, Dr. Faustus, Hello, Dolly! (A.A.: Prod. Des.), On A Clear Day You Can See Forever, The Great White Hope, Once Is Not Enough, That's Entertainment, Too!, The Other Side of Midnight, Ziegfeld: The Man and His Women, Love and Bullets, Charlie, Raise the Titanic, (prod. design), Monsignor, Ghostbusters, (prod. design), Jo Jo Dancer, Legal Eagles.

DeCUIR, JR., JOHN F.: Art Director, Production Designer. b. Burbank, CA, Aug. 4, 1941. e. U. of Southern California, bachelor or architecture, 1965. Son of John F. De Cuir, Sr. 1966–68, U.S. Coast Guard (holds commission with rank of Lt. Commander, USCGR). 1968–72, project designer, Walt Disney World, Walt Disney Prods. 1972–74, dir. of design, Six Flags Corp. 1974–9, project designer, EPCOT, Walt Disney Prods. 1980–85, pres., John F. De Cuir, Jr. Design Consultants, Inc.
PICTURES: Illustrator: Cleopatra, The Honey Pot. Design Concepts: The Agony and the Ecstasy. Art Director: Raise the Titanic, (art dir.), Dead Men Don't Wear Plaid, Monsignor (also special effects consultant), Ghostbusters. (art dir.). Producer: The Building Puzzle. Production Designer: Fright Night.
TELEVISION: Art Director: Frank Sinatra Special—Old Blue Eyes Is Back, Annual Academy Awards Presentation 1971; Earth * Star Voyager (prod. designer).

DEE, RUBY: Actress. b. Cleveland, OH, Oct. 27, 1924. e. Hunter Coll. m. Ossie Davis. Stage appearances include Jeb, Raisin in the Sun, Purlie Victorious, Wedding Band, Checkmates.
PICTURES: Jackie Robinson Story, Take a Giant Step, St. Louis Blues, A Raisin in the Sun, Purlie Victorious, Buck and the Preacher, Do the Right Thing.
TELEVISION: The Atlanta Child Murders, Go Tell it on the Mountain, Windmills of the Gods, Gore Vidal's Lincoln.

DEE, SANDRA: Actress. b. Bayonne, NJ, April 23, 1942. Modeled, Harry Conover and Huntington Hartford Agencies, N.Y., 1954–56; signed long term exclusive contract, U-I, 1957.
PICTURES INCLUDE: Until They Sail, The Restless Years, Stranger in My Arms, The Reluctant Debutante, Gidget, The Wild and the Innocent, Imitation of Life, Summer Place, Portrait in Black, Romanoff and Juliet, Come September, Tammy Tell Me True, If a Man Answers, Tammy and the Doctor, Take Her, She's Mine, I'd Rather Be Rich, That Funny Feeling, Doctor You've Got to Be Kidding!, Rosie, The Dunwich Horror.

DEELEY, MICHAEL: Producer. b. London; England, 1932. Ent. m.p. ind. 1951 and TV, 1967, as ed. Air. Harlech Television Ltd. Film editor, 1951–58. MCA-TV 1958–61, later with Woodfall as prod. and assoc. prod. Proc. One Way Pendulum. Assoc. prod. The Knack, The White Bus, Ride of the Valkyrie, Prod. Robbery, The Italian Job. Executive prod. Long Days Dying, Where's Jack, Sleep Is Lovely, Murphy's War, Convoy, The Deer Hunter (AA), Blade Runner, A Gathering of Old Men (exec. prod.). Great Western Investments Ltd.; 1972; Great Western Festivals Ltd.; 1973, man. dir. British Lion Films Ltd. 1975, purchased BLF, Ltd. Appt. Jnt. man. dir. EMI Films Ltd.,

1977; pres., EMI Films, 1978, Member Film Industry Interim Action Committee, 1977–82; Deputy Chairman, British Screen Advisory Council, 1985. Appt. Chief Executive Officer, Consolidated Television Production & Distribution Inc., 1984.

De HAVILLAND, OLIVIA: Actress b. Tokyo, Japan, July 1, 1916. Sister of actress Joan Fontaine. e. California schools and Notre Dame Convent, Belmont. Acting debut, Max Reinhardt's stage prod., Midsummer Night's Dream; film debut in m.p. version, 1935; won Academy Award twice, best actress performance in To Each His Own, 1946, and The Heiress, 1949; N.Y. Film Critics award twice, 1948–49; Women's Natl. Press Club Award, 1949; Look award, best perf. 3 times, 1941-48-49. Autobiography: Every Frenchman Has One (1960).
PICTURES INCLUDE: Anthony Adverse, Gone With the Wind, Strawberry Blonde, Hold Back the Dawn, Princess O'Rourke, Dark Mirror, Snake Pit, My Cousin Rachel, Not as a Stranger, Ambassador's Daughter, Proud Rebel, Libel, Light in the Piazza, The Adventurers, Pope Joan, Airport '77, The Swarm.
STAGE: Romeo and Juliet, 1951; U.S. tour Candida, 1951–52, N.Y., 1952; A Gift of Time, Bdwy. 1962.
TELEVISION: Noon Wine (Stage 67). North & South Book II (mini-series), Anastasia, Agatha Christie's Murder is Easy, The Royal Romance of Charles and Diana, The Screaming Woman, The Woman He Loved.

DEIN, EDWARD: Director, Writer. b. Chicago, IL.
PICTURES INCLUDE: Dir., s.p. Shack Out on 101, Seven Guns to Sin, Curse of the Undead, Calypso Joe, I Trust My Wife, Hard Yellow, Come Die My Love (Spain), The Naked Sword (Mexico), Gaby (Brazil); story s.p. The Fighting Guardsman, Calling Dr. Death, The Gallant Blade, Leopard Man, All This and More, 13 French Street, Hang Me High; dir., prod., wrote, Capito, in Italy.
TELEVISION: Lawless Years, Hawaiian Eye, Bronco, Philip Marlowe, Not for Hire, Wild, Wild West series.

De LANE LEA, JACQUES: Executive. b. Nice, France, 1931. Early career as prod. shorts, second features; later prod. sup. features. Ent. m.p. ind. 1952, prod. own films. Became man. dir. De Lane Lea Ltd., after death his father 1964. Also dir. Delmore Film Productions Ltd., Mole-Richardson (England) Ltd., Humphries Holdings, Ltd., Int'l Library Service Ltd., CTS Ltd. Pres., dir. gen., SIS (1982), Paris. Director, Video-London Sound Studios, Ltd.

DELANNOY, JEAN: Director. b. Noisy-le-Sec, France, Jan. 12, 1908. e. Université de Paris, Lycée Montaigne, Lycée Louis le Grand, La Sorbonne; actor, 1927–29; film edit., 1929–37; dir., 1937–52.
PICTURES INCLUDE: Black Diamond, The Eternal Return, Symphonie Pastorale, The Chips Are Down, Souvenir, The Secret of Mayerling, Savage Triangle, Moment of Truth, Daughter of Destiny, The Bed, Action Man, La Peau de Torpedo, Pas folle la guêpe..

De LAURENTIIS, DINO: Producer. b. Torre Annunziata, Italy, Aug. 8, 1919. m. actress Silvana Mangano. Took part in Rome Experimental Film Center; dir., prod. Chairman of the Board and CEO, De Laurentiis Entertainment Group Inc.; founded in 1984 the DEG Film Studios in Wilmington, NC. Resigned 1988.
PICTURES INCLUDE: L'amore Canta, Il Bandito, La Figlia del Capitano, Riso Amaro, La Lupa, Anna, Ulysses, Mambo, La Strada, Gold of Naples, War and Peace, Nights of Cabiria, The Tempest, La Grande Guerra, Five Branded Women, Barabbas, The Bible, Operation Paradise, The Witches, The Stranger, Diabolik, Anzio, Barbarella, Waterloo, Valachi Papers, Stone Killers, Serpico, Death Wish, Casanova, Mandingo, Three Days of the Condor, Drum, Face to Face, Buffalo Bill and the Indians, King Kong, The Shootist, Orca, White Buffalo, Serpent's Egg, King of the Gypsies, The Brink's Job, Hurricane, Flash Gordon, Halloween II, Ragtime, Conan the Barbarian, Fighting Back, Amityville II: The Possession, Halloween III, The Dead Zone, Amityville 3-D, Firestarter, The Bounty, Conan the Destroyer, Stephen King's Cat's Eye, Red Sonja, Year of the Dragon, Marie, Silver Bullett, Raw Deal, Maximum Overdrive, Tai-Pan, Blue Velvet, the Bedroom Window, Crimes of the Heart, King Kong Lives, Million Dollar Mystery, Weeds.

De LAURENTIIS, RAFFAELLA: Executive. Daughter of Dino De Laurentiis. Independent producer.
PICTURES: Beyond the Reef, Conan the Barbarian, Conan the Destroyer, Dune, Tai-Pan.

De La VARRE, ANDRE, JR.: Producer-Director. b. Vienna, Austria, Oct. 26, 1934. Prod. Grand Tour travelogues; producer of promotion films for KLM, Swissair, tourist offices, recent productions: Bicentennial films for state of Virginia, city of Charleston, NY state; winner, Atlanta Film Festival, Sunset Travel Film Festival; Burton Holmes Travelogue subjects; V-P-R Educational Films; producer, director, lecturer, narrator.

DELERUE, GEORGES: Composer-Conductor. b. Roubaix, France, 1924. Studied with Busser and Milhaud at Paris Cons. Was conductor for RTF (Radio-TV Français).
PICTURES INCLUDE: Hiroshima Mon Amour (1958), Jeux de L'Amour, Shoot the Piano Player, Jules and Jim, The Soft Skin, The Pumpkin Eater, Viva Maria, A Man for All Seasons, King of Hearts, The 25th Hour, Interlude, Women in Love, The Conformist, The Horsemen, The Day of the Jackal, The Day of the Dolphin, The Slap, Julia, Tender Cop, Dear Inspector, Get Out Your Handkerchiefs, A Little Romance (Acad. Award, 1979), Love on the Run, Day for Night, True Confessions, The Woman Next Door, Rich and Famous, A Little Sex, Partners, Richard's Things, The Last Metro, Broken English, The Escape Artist, Man, Woman and Child, The Black Stallion Returns, Confidentially Yours, Exposed, One Deadly Summer, Silkwood, The Vultures, Mesmerized, Agnes of God, Family Council, Maxie, Salvador, Crimes of the Heart, The Pick-Up Artist, Platoon, The Lonely Passion of Judith Hearne, Paris By Night, The House on Carroll Street, Biloxi Blues, A Summer Story, Chouans!, Memories of Me, Heartbreak Hotel.
TELEVISION: Le Chandelier, Photo Souvenir, A Smile for the Crocodile, Our World (Emmy, 1968), Easter Island, The Nile, Borgia, Deadly Intentions, Aurora, Arch of Triumph, Amos, Silence of the Heart, Sword of Gideon, The Execution.

DELFONT, BERNARD LORD: President, First Leisure Corporation PLC. b. Tokmak, Russia, September 5, 1909. Brother of Lord Lew Grade. e. London, England. Dir. more than 30 companies incl. Delfont Productions. Ent. theatrical management 1941. Since presented over 250 shows in London; pantomimes in provinces and seaside shows; presented annual Royal Variety Performance. Controls Prince of Wales Theatre in London's West End. 1969: Chief Barker (Pres.) Variety Club of Great Britain; Companion of the Grand Order of Water Rats, President of Entertainment. Artistes' Benevolent Fund, member of Saints and Sinners organisation.

DELMAINE, BARRY: Writer, Director. b. London. Began motion picture career as extra. Later roles in comedies; then asst. dir. for Gloria Swanson prod. in England. From 1936–39 wrote sketches, lyrics London stage musicals; radio scripts. In 1939 apptd. chief scenarist Gaumont-British Instructional. In 1941 dir. films for Brit. Ministry of Information; 1942–43 scenarist, Brit. War Office mi. training films. In 1944 author & dir. Here We Come Gathering, J. Arthur Rank experimental film for child audiences. In 1946 joined Film Producers Guild, writer, dir.; 1949–50, dir. Concord Productions, Ltd., freelance writer films, radio, TV; s.p. Heir Conditioned; dir. ind. films, Concord Prod. Ltd., ass't dir. Advance Films; The Great Game, Les Parent Terrible (Eng. version), Is Your Honeymoon Really Necessary? Unit dir. Don't Blame the Stork; Unit dir., loc. mgr. Douglas Fairbanks Ltd.; prod. mgr. 1955; prod. mgr. Chase a Crooked Shadow, Ice Cold in Alex, Jetstream; prod. sup. The Night We Dropped a Clanger. Prod. Sup., Nothing Barred; prod. mgr., The Hellions; prod. The Golden Rabbit; prog. sup., Man of The World, Sentimental Agent, assoc. prod., Danger Man (secret agent) series. Assoc. prod., Man in the Suitcase series; Assoc. prod., Strange Report series; assoc. prod. Mr. Jerico feature. TV series: assoc. prod. The Firechasers; prod. Shirley's World; assoc. prod. The Adventurers. Assoc. prod., Three For All. Currently: Freelance Writer and Prod. Consultant.

DELON, ALAIN: Actor. b. Sceaux, France, Nov. 8, 1935. Discovered by Yves Allegret. Served in French Navy as a Marine. Worked as cafe waiter, heavy-load carrier.
PICTURES INCLUDE: When a Woman Gets Involved, Be Beautiful, and Keep Quiet, Plein Soleil and Quelle Joie de Vivre, Rocco and His Brothers, L'Eclipse, The Leopard, The Big Crab, The Black Tulip, The Felines, The Yellow Rolls Royce, The Killers of San Francisco, The Centurions, Is Paris Burning?, Texas, Here We Come, The Adventurers, Extraordinary Stories, Le Samourai, Diaboliquement Votre, The Motorcycle, Goodbye Friend, The Swimming Pool, Jeff, The Sicilian Clan, Borsalino, Red Sun, Assassination of Trotsky, Scorpio, Dirty Money, Mr. Klein, The Concorde-Airport '79, Swann in Love, Separate Rooms, Cop's Honor, The Passage, Let Sleeping Cops Lie.

Del ROSSI, PAUL R.: Executive. b. Winchester, MA, Oct. 19, 1942. e. Harvard Coll. 1964; Harvard Business Sch., 1967. Sr. v.p., The Boston Co., 1977–1980; sr. consultant, Arthur D. Little, Inc.; presently pres., General Cinema Theatres.

De LUISE, DOM: Comedian, Actor. b. Brooklyn, NY, Aug. 1, 1933. e. Tufts Coll. Spent two seasons with Cleveland Playhouse. Launched TV career on The Garry Moore Show with character, Dominick the Great, a bumbling magician.
PICTURES INCLUDE: Fail Safe, The Busybody, The Glass Bottom Boat, 12 Chairs, Who Is Harry Kellerman?, Every Little Crook and Nanny, The Adventures of Sherlock Holmes' Smarter Brother, Silent Movie, The World's Greatest Lover, The End, The Cheap Detective, The Last Married Couple in America, Fatso, Hot, Stuff (dir.); Wholly Moses, Smokey and the Bandit II, History of the World—Part I, The Cannonball

Run, The Best Little Whorehouse in Texas, Cannonball Run II, Johnny Dangerously, Haunted Honeymoon, My African Adventure, A Taxi Driver in New York, Going Bananas, The Von Metz Incident.
TELEVISION: The Entertainers, The Dean Martin Summer Show, Dom DeLuise Variety Show, The Barrum-Bump Show, The Dean Martin Show, The Tonight Show, Lotsa Luck. Movie: Happy (also exec. prod.).
STAGE: The Student Gypsy, Last of the Red Hot Lovers, Here's Love.

del VALLE, JOHN: Publicist. b. San Francisco, CA, Mar. 23, 1904. e. U. of California. Adv., edit. staff various newspapers including asst. drama ed. S.F. Call-Bulletin, L.A. Mirror; adv.-publicity dir. San Francisco Fox Theatre 1933–36; publicist, Paramount Studio, 1936–42; dir. pub., adv. Arnold Prod. 1946; Chaplin Studios, 1947; Nat Holt Prod., 1948–52; Editor, TV Family mag., N.Y., 1952–53; adv. pub. dir. Century Films, 1954; pub. rel. Academy M.P. Arts & Sciences, 1965; publicist, various U.A. indep. film prod., 1955–56; unit publicist, Para., 1956; TC-F 1957–62, Para., 1962–63; Universal 1964–65; Mirisch Corp.—UA Filming, Hawaii, 1965; pub. re. and editor, Atomics Int'l div. North American Rockwell, 1966–71; present, freelance writer.

DEMBY, EMANUEL H.: Producer, Writer. b. New York, NY, Dec. 12, 1919. e. City Coll. of New York, New School, Chung Ang U., Ph.D. Pioneered new programs for radio, 1936–47; story dept., Universal Pictures, 1937; writer, Gangbusters, Crime of the Week, Thrill of the Week (NBC, CBS); TV shows: What's Playing, 1950–52; Hollywood to Broadway, How To Be a Cowboy; The Shadow; prod., theatrical features, filmed commercials; pub. rel. consultant. Author: My Forty Year Fight for Korea; Indonesia; King of the Hill; Hot Tip on Wall St.; prod. Cavalcade of Music (TV); The World in Space (TV, theatrical); The Edge of Violence (stage); Man Into Space; Year III-Space Age (TV); The Communications Gap, The Creative Consumer, (P.R. films). Book: Who's Alienated, Youth or Society? Research Consultant, NBC TV News; consultant, Radio Advertising Bureau, Smash, Crash, Pow! (feature).

DEMME, JONATHAN: Director-Writer-Producer. b. Rockville Centre, NY, 1944. e. U. of Florida. First job in industry as usher; was film critic for college paper, The Florida Alligator and the Coral Gable Times. Did publicity work for United Artists, Avco Embassy; sold films for Pathe Contemporary Films; wrote for trade publication, Film Daily, 1966–68. Moved to England in 1969; served as musical co-ordinator on Irving Allen's EyeWitness in 1970. In 1972 co-produced and co-wrote first film, Angels, Hard As They Come.
PICTURES: Hot Box (prod., co-writer); Caged Heat (writer-dir.); Crazy Mama (writer-dir.); Fighting Mad (writer-dir.); Citizen's Band (also called Handle With Care, dir.), Last Embrace (dir.), Melvin and Howard (dir.), Swing Shift (dir.), Stop Making Sense (dir.), Something Wild (co-prod., dir.), Swimming to Cambodia (dir.), Married to the Mob (dir.).
TELEVISION: Who Am I This Time (dir.), (PBS); Accumation with Talking plus Water Motor (doc. on choreographer Trisha Brown); Survival Guides; numerous music videos (for UB40, Chrissie Hynde, Sun City Video of Artists United Against Apartheid); A Family Tree (Trying Times series, PBS); Haiti: Dreams of Democracy.
VIDEO: Suzanne Vega's Solitude Standing.

De MORNAY, REBECCA: Actress. b. California, 1961. Spent childhood in Europe, graduating from high school in Austria. Returned to America, enrolling at Lee Strasberg's Los Angeles Institute; apprenticed at Zoetrope Studios. Film debut: One From the Heart.
THEATER: Born Yesterday (Pasadena Playhouse).
PICTURES: Risky Business, Testament, The Slugger's Wife, Runaway Train, The Trip to Bountiful, Beauty and the Beast, And God Created Woman, Feds, The Return of the Musketeers.
TELEVISION: The Murders in the Rue Morgue.

DEMOSS, LYLE: Executive. b. Anthony, KS, Sept. 14, 1907. e. York Coll., U. of Nebraska Sch. of Music; 1925. KGBZ in York, Nebr.; 1928. KFAB in Lincoln, Nebr.; in 1932 became Prog. Mgr. of KFAB-KFOR; held same position for WOW from 1936 to 1946; asst. gen. mgr. Meredith WOW, 1946–59. Allen & Reynolds v.p. radio-TV dept. Omaha Advertising Club, Variety Club Canvasman, past pres. Omaha Ad. Club. Radio KLNG, 1965–67; freelance TV; Elected to Nebr. Broadcasters Hall of Fame—1972; KYNN-community relations director.

DEMPSEY, PATRICK: Actor. b. Lewiston, ME, 1966. In high school became State downhill skiing champion. Juggling, magic and puppetry led to performances before Elks clubs and community org. Cast by Maine Acting Co. in On Golden Pond. In 1983 acted in Torch Song Trilogy in San Francisco and toured in Brighton Beach Memoirs.
PICTURES: Heaven Help Us, Meatballs III, In the Mood, Can't Buy Me Love, In a Shallow Grave, Happy Together, Loverboy, Some Girls, Iron Will.

TELEVISION: A Fighting Choice (debut), Fast Times at Ridgemont High (series).

DEMY, JACQUES: Director, Writer. b. Pont-Chateau, France, 1931. After completing studies in art and film, worked as asst. to Paul Grimault and Georges Rouquier. Made shorts before dir. first feature Lola (1961).
PICTURES: Lola, Seven Capital Sins, Bay of Angels, The Umbrellas of Cherbourg (Golden Palm Award, Cannes, 1964), The Young Girls of Rochefort (also music), Model Shop, Donkey-Skin, The Pied Piper, The Slightly Pregnant Man, Lady Oscar, A Room in Town, Parkway, Three Seats for the 26th.

DENBAUM, DREW: Director, Screenwriter. b. New York, NY, Dec. 12, 1949. e. The Lawrenceville Sch., 1967; Yale U., 1971; New York U. Grad. Institute of Film & TV, 1973–75, assistant to visiting directors Frank Perry and Gilbert Cates. Represented by William Morris Agency.
PICTURES INCLUDE (Writer-Director): Nickel Mountain (based on novel by John Gardner); Lovesick (dramatic short); The Last Straw (dramatic short based on play by Charles Dizenzo).
AWARDS INCLUDE: First Prize, 20th Century Fox Screenwriting Competition (Caught In the Act); Silver Medal, Chicago Film Festival (Lovesick); Academy Award Finalist (Lovesick); Leo Jaffe Producer's Award (New York U. Grad. Inst. of Film & TV); Saybrook Fellows Prize (Yale Univ.); American Legion Award (1964). Lovesick and The Last Straw featured in Cineprobe Series, New York Museum of Modern Art.

DENCH, JUDI, O.B.E.: Actress. b. York, England, 1934. Studied for stage at Central Sch. of Speech and Drama. Theatre debut Old Vic, 1961. Recent Theatre: Cymbeline, Juno and the Paycock, A Kind of Alaska, Importance of Being Earnest, Pack of Lies, Mr. and Mrs. Nobody, Antony and Cleopatra.
TELEVISION: Major Barbara, Pink String and Sealing Wax, Talking to a Stranger, The Funambulists, Age of Kings, Jackanory, Hilda Lessways, Luther, Neighbours, Parade's End, Marching Song, On Approval, Days to Come, Emilie, The Comedy of Errors, Macbeth (both RSC productions), Langrishe Go Down, On Giant's Shoulders, Love in a Cold Climate, Village Wooing, A Fine Romance (series), The Cherry Orchard, Going Gently, Saigon, Year of the Cat, Ghosts, Behaving Badly.
PICTURES: He Who Rides a Tiger, Study in Terror, Four in the Morning, A Midsummer Night's Dream (RSC Production), The Third Secret, Dead Cert, Wetherby, A Room With a View, 84 Charing Cross Road, A Handful of Dust.

DENEAU, SIDNEY, G.: Sales executive. Head film buyer Fabian Theatres; U.S. Army 1942–46; gen. mgr. Schine Theatres 1947; v.p., gen. sales mgr., Selznick Releasing Orgn., 1949; 1956; v.p. asst. gen. sls. mgr., Para. Film Dist., 1958; exec. v.p., Rugoff Theatres, 1964. Resigned, September, 1969 to engage in own theatre consultant business.

DENEUVE, CATHERINE: Actress. r.n. Catherine Dorleac. b. Paris, France, Oct. 22, 1943. Sister was the late Françoise Dorleac.
PICTURES INCLUDE: Les Petits Chats (1956), Les Collegiennes, The Doors Slam, Vice and Virtue, Satan Leads the Dance, Umbrellas of Cherbourg, (received the French Film Academy's best actress award); Repulsion, Le Chant du Monde, La Vie de Chateau, Les Creatures, The Young Girls of Rochefort, Belle de Jour, Benjamin, Manon 70, Mayerling, La Chamade, April Fools, Mississippi Mermaid, Tristana, It Only Happens to Others, Dirty Money, Hustle, Lovers Like Us, Act of Agression, March or Die, La Grande Bourgeoise, The Last Metro, A Second Chance, Reporters, The Hunger, Fort Saganne, Scene of the Crime, FM—Frequency Murder.

DENHAM, MAURICE: Actor. b. Beckenham, Kent, England, Dec. 23, 1909. e. Tonbridge Sch. Started theatrical career with repertory com. 1934. Served in W.W.II and since demobilization played in numerous plays, films & radio shows.
PICTURES INCLUDE: Blanche Fury, London Belongs To Me, It's Not Cricket, Traveller's Joy, Landfall, Spider and the Fly, No Highway in the Sky, The Net, Time Bomb, Street Corner (Both Sides of the Law), Million Pound Note (Man With a Million), Eight O'Clock Walk, Purple Plain, Simon and Laura, 23 Paces to Baker Street, Checkpoint, Carrington V.C. (Court Martial), Doctor at Sea, Night of the Demon, Man With a Dog, Barnacle Bill, The Captain's Table, Our Man in Havana, Sink the Bismark, Two-Way Stretch, Greengage Summer, Invasion, Quartette, The Mark, HMS Defiant.
RECENT PICTURES: The Very Edge, Paranoiac, The Set Up, Penang, The King's Breakfast, Downfall, Hysteria, The Uncle, Operation Crossbow, Legend of Dick Turpin, The Alphabet Murders, The Night Callers, The Nanny, Those Magnificent Men in Their Flying Machines, Heroes of Telemark, After the Fox, The Torture Garden, The Long Duel, The Eliminator, Danger Route, Attack on the Iron Coast, The Best House in London, Negatives, The Midas Run, Some Girls Do, The Touch of Love, The Virgin and the Gypsy, Bloody Sunday, Countess Dracula, Nicholas and Alexandra, The Day

of the Jackal, Luther, Shout at the Devil, Julia, The Recluse, From a Far Country, Mr. Love, The Chain, Monsignor Quixote, Murder on the Orient Express, 84 Charing Cross Road.

TELEVISION: Uncle Harry, Day of the Monkey, Miss Mabel, Angel Pavement, The Paraguayan Harp, The Wild Bird, Soldier Soldier, Changing Values, Maigret, The Assassins, Saturday Spectacular, Vanishing Act, A Chance in Life, Virtue, Somerset Maugham, Three of a Kind, Sapper, Pig in the Middle, Their Obedient Servants, Long Past Glory, Devil in The Wind, Any Other Business, The Retired Colourman, Sherlock Holmes (series), Blackmail, Knock on Any Door, Danger Man, Dr. Finley's Casebook, How to Get Rid of Your Husband, Talking to a Stranger, A Slight Ache, From Chekhov with Love, Home Sweet Honeycomb, St. Joan, Julius Caesar, Golden Days, Marshall Petain, The Lotus Eaters, Fall of Eagles, Carnforth Practice, The Unofficial Rose, Omnibus, Balzac, Loves Labour Lost, Angels, Huggy Bear, The Portrait, The Crumbles Murder, A Chink In The Wall, Porridge, For God's Sake, Bosch, Marie Curie, Upchat Line, Secret Army, My Son, My Son, Edward and Mrs. Simpson, Gate of Eden, Potting Shed, Double Dealer, Minder, Agatha Christie Hour, Chinese Detective, The Old Men at the Zoo, The Hope and the Glory, Luther, Love Song, Mr. Palfrey, The Black Tower, Boon, Rumpole, All Passions Spent, Trial of Klaus Barbie, Miss Marple.

DE NIRO, ROBERT: Actor. b. New York, NY, Aug. 17, 1943. Studied acting with Stella Adler and Lee Strasberg.

THEATER: One Night Stand of a Noisy Passenger (off-Bdwy); Cuba and His Teddy Bear (Public Theater and Bdwy, 1986).

PICTURES INCLUDE: Greetings (1968); The Wedding Party, Jennifer on My Mind, Bloody Mama; Hi, Mom; Born to Win, The Gang That Couldn't Shoot Straight, Bang the Drum Slowly, Mean Streets, Godfather II (Academy Award, best supporting actor, 1974), Taxi Driver, 1900, The Last Tycoon, New York, New York, The Deer Hunter, Raging Bull (Academy Award, 1980), True Confessions, The King of Comedy, Once Upon a Time in America, Falling in Love, Brazil, The Mission, Angel Heart, The Untouchables, Midnight Run, Dear America: Letters Home From Vietnam (reader), Jacknife, Stanley and Iris, We're No Angels.

DENISON, MICHAEL: Actor. b. Doncaster, York, Eng., Nov. 1, 1915. e. Harrow, Magdalen Coll., Oxford and Webber Douglas Sch. m. Dulcie Gray, actress. Served overseas, Capt. Intelligence Corps, 1940–46. On stage first, 1938, Charlie's Aunt. Screen debut 1940, Tilly of Bloomsbury.

THEATRE: 50 London plays including Ever Since Paradise, Rain on the Just, Queen Elizabeth Slept Here, Fourposter, Dragon's Mouth, Bad Samaritan; Shakespeare Season Stratford-on-Avon; Edinburgh Festival. Meet Me By Moonlight, Let Them Eat Cake, Candida, Heartbreak House, My Fair Lady (Australia), Where Angels Fear to Tread, Hostile Witness, An Ideal Husband, On Approval, Happy Family, No. 10, Out of the Question, Trio, The Wild Duck, The Clandestine Marriage, The Dragon Variation, At the End of the Day, The Sack Race, Peter Pan, The Black Mikado, The First Mrs. Fraser, The Earl and the Pussycat, Robert and Elizabeth, The Cabinet Minister, Old Vic Season: Twelfth Night, Lady's Not for Burning, Ivanov, Bedroom Farce, The Kingfisher, Relatively Speaking, Coat of Varnish, Capt. Brassbound's Conversion, School for Scandal, Song at Twilight, See How They Run, The Tempest, Ring Round the Moon, The Apple Cart, Court in the Act, You Never Can Tell.

PICTURES INCLUDE: Hungry Hill, My Brother Jonathan, The Blind Goddess, The Glass Mountain, Landfall, The Franchise Affair, Angels One Five, Tall Headlines, Importance of Being Earnest, There Was a Young Lady, Contraband Spain, The Truth About Women, Faces in the Dark.

TELEVISION: Boyd QC Series, Funeral Games, Unexpectedly Vacant, Tale of Piccadilly, The Twelve Pound Look, The Provincial Lady, Subject: This Is Your Life, Bedroom Farce, Private Schultz, Blood Money, The Critic, Scorpion, Cold Warrior, Good Behavior.

DENNEHY, BRIAN: Actor. b. Bridgeport, CT, 1939. e. Columbia U. In Marine Corps five years, including Vietnam. After discharge in 1965 studied with acting coaches in N.Y., while working at part time jobs as a salesman, bartender, truck driver. Cast by Michael Ritchie in Semi-Tough, 1977.

THEATER: Streamers, Galileo (Goodman Theatre), The Cherry Orchard.

PICTURES INCLUDE: Looking for Mr. Goodbar, Foul Play, F.I.S.T., 10, Butch and Sundance: The Early Days, Little Miss Marker, Split Image, First Blood, Never Cry Wolf, Gorky Park, Finders Keepers, River Rat, Cocoon, Silverado, The Check Is in the Mail, F/X, Twice in a Lifetime, Legal Eagles, Best Seller, The Belly of an Architect, Return to Snowy River, Part II, Cocoon II: The Return, Miles From Home, Indigo.

TELEVISION: Films: It Happened at Lake Wood Manor (1977), Johnny We Hardly Knew Ye, Pearl, Real American Hero, A Death in Canaan, Ruby and Oswald, The Jericho Mile, Dummy, Silent Victory: The Kitty O'Neil Story, A Rumor

of War, The Seduction of Miss Leona, Skokie, Fly Away Home, I Take These Men, Off Sides, Blood Feud, The Last Place on Earth, Evergreen, Annie Oakley, Acceptable Risks, Private Sessions, The Lion of Africa, A Father's Revenge, Day One. Series: Big Shamus, Little Shamus, Star of the Family, Cagney and Lacey, Hunter, Tall Tales (Annie Oakley).

DENNIS, SANDY: Actress. b. Hastings, NB, April 27, 1937. m. Gerry Mulligan. Joined the Lincoln Community Theatre group. Made her professional acting debut in summer stock at London, NH. Studied with Herbert Berghof, N.Y. Understudy for N.Y. prod. Dark at the Top of the Stairs. Broadway debut in Burning Bright (1960).

THEATER: Face of A Hero; The Complaisant Lover; A Thousand Clowns (Tony Award, best sup. actress, 1963); Any Wednesday (Tony Award, 1964); Daphne in Cottage D; How the Other Half Loves; Let Me Hear You Smile; Absurd Person Singular; Same Time, Next Year; Come Back to the 5 & Dime, Jimmy Dean, Jimmy Dean; Buried Inside Extra.

PICTURES INCLUDE: Who's Afraid of Virginia Woolf? (Acad. Award, best supporting actress), Up the Down Staircase, Sweet November, The Fox, Thank You All Very Much, That Cold Day in the Park, The Out-of-Towners, Nasty Habits, The Four Seasons; 976-EVIL, Parents.

TELEVISION: The Execution, Perfect Gentlemen, Something Evil, Alfred Hitchcock Presents (1985).

DE NORMAND, GEORGE: Actor, Director. b. New York, NY, Sept. 22. Actor many westerns & TV series; dir., TV series, Man of Tomorrow. Member: SAG, SEG, NSTP.

DENVER, BOB: Actor. b. New Rochelle, NY, 1935.

PICTURES INCLUDE: Take Her She's Mine, For Those Who Think Young, Who's Minding the Mint? The Sweet Ride, Do You Know the One About the Travelling Saleslady?

TELEVISION: Dobie Gillis, Gilligan's Island, Dusty's Trail, The Castaways on Gilligan's Island; Bring Me the Head of Dobie Gillis.

DENVER, JOHN: Singer, Actor. r.n. Henry John Deutschendorf. b. Roswell, NM, Dec. 31, 1943. Records, concerts, nightclubs.

PICTURES: Oh, God!, America Censored.

TELEVISION INCLUDES: An Evening with John Denver (Emmy, 1975), Rocky Mountain Christmas, John Denver and the Muppets, Rocky Mountain Holiday, Salute to Lady Liberty, Jacques Costeau—The First 75 Years, Julie Andrews . . . The Sound of Christmas. Movie: The Christmas Gift, Foxfire, Higher Ground.

DE PALMA, BRIAN: Director. b. Newark, NJ, Sept. 11, 1940. e. Columbia U.,B.A.; Sarah Lawrence, M.A. While in college made series of shorts, including Wotan's Wake, winner of Rosenthal Foundation Award for best film made by American under 25. Also judged most popular film of Midwest Film Festival (1963); later shown at San Francisco Film Festival.

PICTURES INCLUDE: The Wedding Party, Murder a La Mod, Greetings, Hi Mom, Dionysus in '69, Get To Know Your Rabbit, Sisters, Phantom of the Paradise, Obsession, Carrie, The Fury, Home Movies (dir., s.p. and co-prod.), Dressed to Kill (also s.p.), Blow Out (also s.p.), Scarface, Body Double (prod., dir., s.p.), Wiseguys (dir.), The Untouchables (dir.), Casualties of War.

DEPARDIEU, GERARD: Actor. b. Chateauroux, France, Dec. 27, 1948. Studied acting at Theatre National Populaire in Paris. Made film debut at 16 in short by Roger Leenhardt (Le Beatnik et Le Minet). Acted in feature film by Agnes Varda (uncompleted).

PICTURES INCLUDE: Going Places, Stavisky, 1900, Vincent François, Paul and the Others; Maitresse, The Last Woman, Barocco, Le Camion, Get Out Your Handkerchiefs, Loulou, The Last Metro, Mon Oncle d'Amerique, The Woman Next Door, La Chevre, The Return of Martin Guerre, The Moon in the Gutter, Les Comperes, Fort Saganne, Police, One Woman or Two, Menage, Jean de Florette, Under Satan's Sun, Traffic Jam, Five Days in June, I Want to Go Home.

DEPEW, RICHARD H.: Executive. b. New York, NY, Jan. 16, 1925. e. Princeton U. U.S. Navy; American Broadcasting Co., 1947; television director, 1950; assistant, Eastern TV network program director, 1953; mgr. of TV network program oper., 1954–57; Cunningham & Walsh; Radio & TV acct. supv. & programming coordinator, 1961–65 v.p. & dir. of TV programming; 1965 Broadcast supr., Ogilvy and Mather; 1967, v.p. dir. TV programing Fuller & Smith & Ross. V.P. Media and Programming 1969, FSR.; 1973, Director of Corporate Underwriting Department WNET/13, Educational Broadcasting Corp. 1977 Management Supervisor, J. Walter Thompson, N.Y.; 1978, v.p., Account Director, 1980, Marsteller, Inc., mgt. supvr., v.p., corporate adv.; Doremus & Co., 1983; exec. v.p., Knox Minisk & Harwood, Stowe, VT.

DEREK, BO: Actress. r.n. Cathleen Collins. b. Torrance, CA., Nov. 20, 1956. Discovered by John Derek, actor turned filmmaker. Now married to him. Film debut in Orca (1977).

PICTURES INCLUDE: 10, Once Upon A Time, Change of

Seasons, Tarzan, the Ape Man (also prod.), Bolero (also prod.).

DEREK, JOHN: Actor, Producer, Director. b. Hollywood, CA, August 12, 1926. Acting debut in 1945 in I'll Be Seeing You; appeared in numerous films throughout 1950s. In 1963, Nightmare in the Sun (debut as prod., dir., cinematographer), followed by Once Before I Die, 1965.
PICTURES: Actor: Knock on Any Door, All the King's Men, Mask of the Avenger, Scandal Sheet, Mission Over Korea, The Adventures of Hajji Baba, Prince of Players, Run for Cover, The Leather Saint, The Ten Commandments, Omar Khayyam, Prisoner of the Volga, Exodus. Prod., dir., s.p., cinematography: A Boy . . . a Girl, Childish Things, Once Upon a Time, Tarzan, The Ape Man (dir., cinematography), Bolero (dir., s.p., cinematography).

DERN, BRUCE: Actor. b. Chicago, IL, June 4, 1936. e. U. of Pennsylvania. Studied acting with Gordon Phillips, member, Actor's Studio, 1959 after N.Y. debut in Shadow of a Gunman. Broadway: Sweet Bird of Youth, Orpheus Descending.
PICTURES: The Trip, The Wild Angels, Hush, Hush, Sweet Charlotte, Support Your Local Sheriff, Thumb-tripping, Drive, He Said; They Shoot Horses, Don't They?; The Cowboys, Silent Running, The King of Marvin Gardens, The Laughing Policeman, The Great Gatsby, Smile, Posse, Family Plot, Won Ton Ton, Black Sunday, Coming Home, The Driver, Middle Age Crazy, Tattoo, That Championship Season, On the Edge, The Big Town, World Gone Wild, 1969, The 'Burbs.
TELEVISION: Space, Toughlove, Roses Are for the Rich, Uncle Tom's Cabin.

DERN, LAURA: Actress. b. 1966. Daughter of actors Diane Ladd & Bruce Dern. Was an extra in several of her father's films and her mother's Alice Doesn't Live Here Anymore. Film debut at age 11 in Foxes (1980).
PICTURES: Teachers, Mask, Smooth Talk, Blue Velvet, Haunted Summer.
TELEVISION: Happy Endings, Three Wishes of Bill Greer.

De SANTIS, GIUSEPPE: Director. b. Italy, 1917. Film publicist; asst. dir.
PICTURES INCLUDE: Tragic Hunt, Bitter Rice, Under the Olive Tree, Rome 11 O'Clock, A Husband for Anna Zaccheo, Days of Love.

DE SANTIS, GREGORY JOSEPH: Producer, Writer, Director. b. Los Angeles, CA, July 12, 1947. e. U.S.C., Canaan Coll, Franklin Pierce Coll, Durham U., Hatfield Coll. 1970–74 owned commercial prod. co.: wrote, prod., dir. radio and TV commercials; 1972–74 owned marketing firm; 1974– present pres. of prod. placement co. that phased into prod. of TV documentary Volleyball: A Sport Come of Age. Cameo performance in Moon Rise (1947). Pres. & CEO The Beverly Hills Org. and Beverly Hills Productions Ltd.
PICTURES: Prod.: Diary of a Surfing Film, The Companion, Die Sister Die, Our Musical (also writer), Zioux (s.p. only), Car Trouble, Pass the Buck (also dir., s.p.), Beverly Hills (s.p.).
TELEVISION: California Day (co-prod.), The Bell (prod.).

De SCHAAP, PHILIP: Dutch correspondent, Quigley Publications, N.Y. b. Amsterdam, Holland, May 26, 1911. Entered m.p. ind. 1934 as publicity mgr., MGM br. office, Amsterdam; in 1936 corresp. for Quigley Publications. Also in 1937 exploitation mgr., RKO Radio Pictures, Amsterdam; to Paris 1938 as spec. publicity repr. in Paris and Brussels, RKO: in 1939 orig. own co. for exploitation and publicity; non-active 1940–45; on Oct. 1, 1945 estab. Phidesa Publiciteitsbureau voor de Filmbranche.

DESCHANEL, CALEB: Cinematographer, Director. b. Philadelphia, PA, Sept. 21, 1941. e. Johns Hopkins U., U. of Southern California Film Sch.
PICTURES: Cinematographer: More American Graffiti, Being There, The Black Stallion, The Right Stuff, Let's Spend the Night Together (co-cinematographer), The Natural, The Slugger's Wife, The Escape Artist (dir.); Crusoe (dir.).

De TITTA ARTHUR A.: Newsreel editor. b. North Bergen, NJ, July 9, 1904. Began work 1916 in employ newspaper in Union City, NJ; joined Fox Film Corp., N.Y. office & lab. staff; later became asst. & second cameraman, performing in that capacity numerous pictures Fox and other producers. (The Mountain Woman, When Knighthood Was in Flower, The Royale Girl, East Side, West Side, Untamed, etc.). In 1928 joined Movietonews, Inc.; Wash. (D.C.) supvr. to 1938; asst. Europ. supvr. to 1940; Pacific Coast supvr. to 1943. Commis. Lt. USNR, assigned to M.P. Sect., 1943; ret. 1944. Appt. news ed. Movietonews; west coast supervr., 1951–63; pub. rel., prod., documentaries; West Coast Bureau mgr. for foreign editions of Movietone News, now retired.

De TOTH, ANDRE: Writer-Director-Producer. b. Hungary. Dir.-writer European films, 1931–39; U.S. assoc. Alexander Korda prod., 1940; dir. Columbia, 1943; assoc. David Selznick, 1943; assoc. Hunt Stromberg-UA, 1944–45; staff dir., Enterprise 1946–47; dir., 20th-Fox, 1948–49; collab. story, The Gunfight-

er; dir., Columbia & Warner Bros., 1951; contract dir., Warner Bros., 1952; U.A. Columbia, W.B., 1953–55; Palladiums U.A., Denmark, 1956; Col. U.A. 1957; Columbia, 1960; assoc., Sam Spiegel, Horizon Pictures, Columbia, 1962; Harry Saltzman, Lowndes Prod., U.A. 1966–68; National General, 1969–70.
PICTURES INCLUDE: Passport to Suez, None Shall Escape, Since You Went Away, Pitfall, Springfield Rifle, Thunder Over the Plains, House of Wax, Bounty Hunter, Tanganyika, Indian Fighter, Monkey on My Back, Two Headed Spy, Man on a String, Morgan, The Pirate, The Mongols, Gold for the Caesars, Billion Dollar Brain, Play Dirty, El Condor, The Dangerous Game, Thane.

DEUTCH, HOWARD: Director. b. New York, NY. e. Ohio State U. Son of music publisher Murray Deutch. Spent almost 10 yrs. working in various film media, including music videos and film trailer advertising, before feature directorial debut with Pretty in Pink, 1986.
PICTURES: Some Kind of Wonderful, The Great Outdoors.

DEUTCHMAN, IRA J.: Executive. b. Cherry Point, NC, Mar. 24, 1953. e. Northwestern U., B.S., majoring in film. Began career with Cinema 5, Ltd. serving, 1975–79, as non-theatrical sls. mgr.; dir. theatrical adv./pub./dir. acquisitions. Joined United Artists Classics, 1981 as dir. of adv./pub. 1982, left to become one of the founding partners in Cinecom Intl. Films, where headed mktg./dist. div. from inception. Adjunct prof. Columbia U. film dept. Serves on board of Independent Feature Project-West and Collective for Living Cinema. On advisory bds. U.S. Film Festival and the Sundance Institute.
PICTURES: Miles From Home (co-exec. prod.).

DEUTSCH, ARMAND S.: Producer. b. Chicago, IL, Jan. 25, 1913. e. U. of Chicago, 1935, B.A. Producer, MGM.
PICTURES INCLUDE: Ambush, Right Cross, Magnificent Yankee, Three Guys Named Mike, Kind Lady, Girl in White, Carbine Williams, Girl who Had Everything, Green Fire, Slander.

DEUTSCH, DAVID: Producer, Writer. b. Birmingham, England, January 10, 1926. e. in Birmingham and Queen Mary Coll., London U. Ent. m.p. ind. apprentice at Gainsborough Pictures, Ltd.; 1949; asst. Sydney Box, 1954; J. Arthur Rank asst. to prod. 1955 Lost; assoc. prod. High Tide at Noon, The One That Got Away, Floods of Fear; prod. Blind Date; Anglo Amalgamated Film Dist. Ltd., as exec. in chrg. prod., 1960. Prod., Play It Cool, 1962, Nothing But the Best, Catch Us If You Can, Interlude, Lock Up Your Daughter, A Day in the Death of Joe Egg; Co-prod. The Day of the Jackal; s.p., The Blue Train, The Jacaranda Tree; Prod. Shakespeare Lives; prod. The Chain; prod. The Verger, Mr. Knowall and The Colonel's Lady.

DEUTSCH, HELEN: Writer. b. New York, NY. e. Barnard Coll., B.A. Author: The Provincetown. Wrote book of Broadway musical, Carnival, 1961.
PICTURES INCLUDE: Seventh Cross, National Velvet, King Solomon's Mines, Golden Earrings, Kim, Plymouth Adventure, Lili, The Glass Slipper, I'll Cry Tomorrow, Forever Darling.
TELEVISION: Jack and the Beanstalk, NBC Gen. Motors 50th Anniv. Show, 1957.

DEUTSCH, STEVEN: Producer. b. Los Angeles, CA, June 30, 1946. e. U. of California at L.A., B.A.; Loyola Law Sch. Son of late S. Sylvan Simon. Stepson of Armand Deutsch. Private law practice before joining Rastar 1976 as asst. to Ray Stark; 1977, sr. v.p., Rastar; entered independent prod. 1978.
PICTURES: Somewhere in Time; All the Right Moves, Russkies (co-exec. prod.), Daddy's Little Girl.

DEVANE, WILLIAM: Actor. b. New York, NY, Sept. 5, 1939. Appeared in some 15 productions with N.Y. Shakespeare Festival and off-Bdwy. shows before heading for California and films and TV.
PICTURES: Bad News Bears in Breaking Training, Rolling Thunder, Marathon Man, Butch and Sundance: The Early Years, Yanks, Honky Tonk Freeway, Testament.
TELEVISION: The Big Easy, Jane Doe, The Missiles of October, Fear on Trial, From Here to Eternity (series), Knots Landing, Timestalker, With Intent to Kill, Black Beauty.

De VITO, DANNY: Actor. b. Asbury Park, NJ, Nov. 17, 1944. m. actress Rhea Perlman. e. Oratory Prep Sch. Studied at American Acad. of Dramatic Arts. Wilfred Acad. of Hair and Beauty Culture. At 18 worked as hair dresser for 1 yr. at his sister's shop. On stage in Down the Morning Line, The Line of Least Existence, The Shrinking Bride, Call Me Charlie, Comedy of Errors, etc. Performance in One Flew Over the Cuckoo's Nest led to casting in the film version.
PICTURES: Goin' South, Lady Liberty, Scalawag, Hurry Up or I'll be 30, Terms of Endearment, Romancing the Stone, Johnny Dangerously, Head Office, Jewel of the Nile, Wiseguys, Ruthless People, Tin Men, Throw Mamma from the Train (also dir.), Twins, War of the Roses (dir., actor).
TELEVISION: Series: Taxi (also dir.); Mary (as dir.); The Rating Game (dir.); All the Kids Do It (Afterschool Special).

DEWHURST, COLLEEN: Actress. b. Montreal, Canada, June 3, 1926. e. Downer Coll., Milwaukee; Acad. of Dramatic Art; student of Harold Clurman and Joseph Anthony. Theater debut: The Royal Family (1946). Gained fame as stage actress.
THEATER: Desire Under the Elms, Tamberlain the Great, Camille, The Eagle Has Two Heads, The Country Wife, All The Way Home, Great Day in the Morning, Ballad of the Sad Cafe, Taming of the Shrew, Hello and Goodbye, Good Woman of Setzuan, More Stately Mansions, Children of Darkness, All Over, Moon For the Misbegotten, Mourning Becomes Elecktra, An Almost Perfect Person, The Queen and the Rebels, Dance of Death, You Can't Take It With You, Who's Afraid of Virginia Woolf? (revival), Ah! Wilderness, Long Day's Journey into Night.
PICTURES: The Nun's Story, A Fine Madness, McQ, The Cowboys, The Last Run, Annie Hall, Ice Castles, When a Stranger Calls, Tribute, The Dead Zone, The Boy Who Could Fly, Obsessed.
TELEVISION: The Price, The Crucible, The Hands of Cormac Joyce, Jacob and Joseph, Studs Lonigan, The Kitty O'Neill Story, And Baby Makes Six, The Blue and the Gray, The Glitter Dome, You Can't Take It With You, A.D., Between Two Women (Emmy Award), Johnny Bull, Sword of Gideon, Anne of Green Gables—the Sequel: Anne of Avonlea.

DE WITT, JOYCE: Actress. b. Wheeling, W V, April 23, 1949. e. Ball State U., B.A., theatre. Performed in summer stock musical comedies (Damn Yankees, Li'l Abner, etc.). Worked at Indianapolis dinner theatres, directing, staging and starring in musical revues.
TELEVISION: Baretta, The Tony Randall Show, Most Wanted, Risko, Three's Company, Finder of Lost Loves. Movie: With This Ring, Saturday's the Place.

DEY, SUSAN: Actress. b. Pekin, IL, Dec. 10, 1952. Signed as magazine teen model at age 15. Made professional TV debut at 17, appearing in The Partridge Family, 1970–74.
TELEVISION: Series: Barnaby Jones, Hawaii Five-0, Switch, Loves Me, Loves Me Not, L.A. Law. Movies: Cage Without a Key, Terror on the Beach, Mary Jane Harper Cried Last Night, Little Women, The Comeback Kid, The Gift of Life, Sunset Limousine, Echo Park, Angel in Green, A Place at the Table.
PICTURES: Skyjacked, First Love, Looker, Echo Park.

DE YOUNG, CLIFF: Actor. b. Inglewood, CA, Feb. 12, 1947. e. California State Coll., Illinois State U. On stage in Hair, Sticks and Bones.
PICTURES: Sunshine, Shock Treatment, Independence Day, The Hunger, Reckless, Protocol, Secret Admirer, F/X, Flight of the Navigator, In Dangerous Company, Bulldance.
TELEVISION: Sticks and Bones, Centennial, The Lindbergh Kidnapping Case, Scared Straight, Invasion of Privacy, This Girl for Hire, The Awakening of Candra, Master of the Game, Deadly Intentions, King, Sunshine, Senior Prom.

DEZEL, ALBERT: Exhibitor. b. Russia, May 21, 1900. e. Chicago Acad. of Fine Arts; also Art Inst., Crane Coll., Chicago. Art work, theatre publicity, exploitation & Middle West. Org. Albert Dezel Roadshows, exploitation films, 1926; in 1945 owner, operator, Film Classics Franchise, Detroit, Cleveland, Cincinnati; in 1946 acquired rights in same territory for Screen Guild Products; operator, operator, Avon Art Theatre, South Bend; Cinema, Hamilton Theatre, Indianapolis; Guild Theatres, Detroit.

DIAMANT, LINCOLN: Executive. b. New York, NY, Jan. 25, 1923. e. Columbia Coll., A.B. cum laude 1943. Cofounder, Columbia U. radio station. Advertising mgr., World Publ. Co.; writer-prod. CBS; prod.-dir., Blue Network (NBC); prom. dir., Book Find Club; creative dir., Ben Sackheim; group hd., McCann-Erickson; copy chief, DKG; Sr. TV prod., Ogilvy & Mather; TV prod. super., Grey Adv; founder, pres., Spots Alive, Inc., broadcast advertising consultants, 1969; author, The Broadcast Communications Dictionary, Anatomy of a Television Commercial, Television's Classic Commercials, contrib., to Effective Advertising, to Messages and Meaning; member, Broadcast Pioneers, Acad. TV Arts & Sciences; v.p. Broadcast Advertising Producer's Society of America. Adjunct faculty member, Pace Coll., Hofstra U. Fellow, Royal Society of Arts. President, Teatown Lake Reservation of Brooklyn Botanic Garden.

DIAMOND, BERNARD: Theatre Executive. b. Chicago, IL, Jan. 24, 1918. e. U. of Indiana, U. of Minnesota. Except for military service was with Schine Theatre chain from 1940 to 1963, working up from ass't. mg., booker, buyer, dir. of personnel to gen. mgr. Then joined Loews Theatres; last position, exec. v.p. Retired, 1985.

DIAMOND, NEIL: Singer, Songwriter. b. Brooklyn, NY, Jan. 24, 1941. Many concert tours.
PICTURES: Jonathan Livingston Seagull (music), Every

Which Way But Loose (music), The Last Waltz (actor), The Jazz Singer (actor, music).

DICKINSON, ANGIE: Actress. b. Kulm, ND, Sept. 30, 1931. e. parochial schools, Heart Coll., Glendale Coll., secretarial course. Beauty contest winner.
PICTURES INCLUDE: Sins of Rachel Cade, Rio Bravo, Bramble Bush, Ocean's 11, Jessica, Capt. Newman, M.D., The Killers, The Art of Love, The Chase, The Last Challenge, Point Blank, Sam Whiskey, Young Billy Young, Pretty Maids All in a Row, The Outside Man, Dressed to Kill, Charlie Chan and the Curse of the Dragon Queen, Death Hunt, Big Bad Mama II.
TELEVISION: Movies: One Shoe Makes It Murder, Jealousy, Hollywood Wives, A Touch of Scandal, Pearl, Stillwatch, Police Story, The Freeway Killings, Once Upon A Texas Train. Series: Police Woman.

DICKINSON, ROBERT: Actor, Engineer, Chemical-Electrical; Prof. Writer; Teacher, Drama; Producer. b. Newhall, WV. e. Va. Polytechnic Inst. & State U.; New York U.; U. of California at L.A.; Pasadena Playhouse; private drama schools, five. U.S. Army Signal Corps, W.W.II; U.S. chemical-aerospace firms: 10 yrs.; Approx. 819 total performances in 58 show biz shows, incl. nigh clubs & circus, across U.S. Chemical engr.-prof., gag writer; legit. Stage plays include: Murder in the Red Barn; Career; The Ponder Heart; & 25 Other plays. Motion pictures include: The Brain Eaters; Her Conversion. Elected member Int'l. Platform Ass'n; Assoc. Member: American Inst. of Chemical Engineers; AFTRA; SAG; AEA; DAV; Amer. Legion; Tau Beta Pi; Phi Lambda Upsilon; Phi Kappa Phi; First United Methodist Church; Boy Scouts.
TELEVISION: The Rank & File (Playhouse 90 series, CBS), 1952–59; Weather Channel 9, Pulaski, VA.

DIEHL, WALTER F.: Executive. International President, I.A.T.S.E. b. Revere, MA, April 13, 1907. e. Northeastern U., Boston Catholic Labor Guild Sch. Became projectionist in Boston in 1927 and member of Boston Moving Picture Machine Operators Local 182 in 1933. After several years of service on the executive board became business agent in 1946 and held that post until 1953, when he resigned to accept an appointment as an International Representative, handling assignments throughout New England until 1957, when was appointed assistant international president. In 1952 made a member of the Minimum Wage Commission for the amusement industry in the state of Massachusetts. Also served several years on the executive board of the Boston Central Labor Union and as Labor Representative on the Suffolk County March of Dimes. Elected IATSE pres. March, 1974., currently International Pres. emeritus, IATSE.

DIETRICH, MARLENE: Actress. r.n. Maria Magdalene von Losch. b. Berlin, Germany, Dec. 27, 1901. e. pvt. schs., Weimar; Musical Acad., Berlin. m. Rudolph Sieber; d. Maria Riva, actress. Stage training, Max Reinhardt's Sch. of Drama; debut in Viennese version of play, Broadway; then mus. com. Film debut Der Mensch am Wege (1923). With Army overseas (USO) 1942–45.
PICTURES INCLUDE: In Germany, Blue Angel; in Hollywood: Morocco, Dishonored, Blonde Venus, Shanghai Express, Scarlet Empress, Song of Songs, The Devil is a Woman, Desire, Angel, Garden of Allah, Knight Without Armour, Destry Rides Again, Seven Sinners, Flame of New Orleans, Manpower, The Lady is Willing, Pittsburgh, The Spoilers, Follow the Boys, Kismet, Golden Earrings, Martin Roumagnac (French), Foreign Affair, Stage Fright, No Highway in the Sky, Rancho Notorious, The Monte Carlo Story, Around the World in 80 Days, Witness for the Prosecution, Touch of Evil, Judgment at Nuremberg, Paris When it Sizzles, Just a Gigolo.

DIFFRING, ANTON: Actor. b. Koblenz, Germany, Oct. 20, 1918. Early career Academy of Drama, Berlin. Acted in Canada and U.S. before ent. m.p. ind. in Britain, 1951. Since 1970 in Rome, Munich, and Cannes.
PICTURES INCLUDE: I Am a Camera, Seven Thunders, House of Secrets, Albert RN, Circus of Horrors, The Man Who Could Cheat Death, A Question of Adultery, Lady of Vengeance, The Traitor, The Crooked Sky, The Sea Shall Not Have Them, The Colditz Story, The Black Tent, Enter Inspector Duval, Incident at Midnight. 1963/65 working in Germany, The Heroes of Telemark, The Blue Max, Fahrenheit 451, The Double Man, Counterpoint, Where Eagles Dare, Michael Kohlhaas, Horse Dealer, Uccidete Rommel, Piggies, Zeppelin, L'Iguana dalla lingua del Fuoco, Sutjeska, Corringa, Assassination of Little Sister, Dead Pigeon on Beethoven St., Der Stoff aus dem die Traume sind, The Day the Clown Cried, Das Schicksal ist der Jager, Tony Arzenta, The Beast Must Die, Shatter, Swiss Conspiracy, Vanessa, Operation Daybreak, Potato Fritz, Valentino, Les Indiens sont encore loin, L'Imprecateur, Waldrausch, Anna Ferroli, Das Einhorn, Return to Munich, Arsene Lupen, Escape to Victory,

Dil-Dix

Jer Schnüffler S.A.S. Malko, The Perfume of Old Memories, Operation Dead End, Faceless.
TELEVISION: The Last Hours, A Small Revoltion, Wedding Day, The One Who Came Back, The Man in Half Moon Street, The Queen and the Rebels, The Cold Light, The Magnificent Egoist, The One Who Got Away, Autumn Crocus, The Fourposter, Dear Charles, Cross of Iron, One Step Beyond, Ghost Squad, Dr. Korczak and His Children, Dixon of Dock Green, The Joel Brandt Story, Firebrand, Scobie in September, The Trouble Shooters, The Million Pound Note, Strange Report, Kommissar, A Place in the Sun, Die Krise, Assignment Vienna, Liebe 74, Yoster, Kiss Me and Die, Die Himmlischen Tochter, Car along the Pass, MM Le Mutant, Flambards, Plutoniumaler Alte. Der Gast (Durbridge), The Winds of War, Tanzschule Kaiser Les Voleurs Des Moutons Weltunter Gang, End of the World, The Masks of Death, The Gentle Art of Murder.

DILLER, BARRY: Executive. b. Feb. 2, 1942. Joined ABC in April, 1966, as asst. to v.p. in chg. programming. In March, 1968, made exec. asst. to v.p. in chg. programming and dir. of feature films. In May, 1969, named v.p., feature films and program development, east coast. In Feb., 1971, made v.p., Feature Films and Circle Entertainment, a unit of ABC Entertainment, responsible for selecting, producing and scheduling The Tuesday Movie of the Week, The Wednesday Movie of the Week, and Circle Film original features for airing on ABC-TV, as well as for acquisition and scheduling of theatrical features for telecasting on ABC Sunday Night Movie and ABC Monday Night Movie. On May 30, 1973, named v.p. in chg. of prime time TV for ABC Entertainment. In 1974 joined Paramount Pictures as bd. chm. and chief exec. officer. 1983, named pres. of Gulf & Western Entertainment and Communications Group, while retaining Paramount titles. Resigned from Paramount in 1984 to join 20th Century-Fox as bd. chm. and chief. exec. officer. Named chm. & CEO of Fox, Inc. (comprising 20th Fox Film Corp., Fox TV Stations & Fox Bdcstg. Co.), Oct., 1985. Named to bd., News Corp. Ltd., June, 1987.

DILLER, PHYLLIS: Comedienne. b. Lima, OH, July 17, 1917. e. Sherwood Music Sch., 1935–37; Bluffton Coll., OH, 1938–39.
PICTURES INCLUDE: Boy, Did I Get a Wrong Number! 1966; Mad Monster Party, Eight on the Lam, Did You Hear the One About the Traveling Saleslady, The Private Navy of Sergeant O'Farrell, The Adding Machine, Motel: The Great American Tradition, Yips, Dr. Hackenstein.
TELEVISION: Series: The Phyllis Diller Show, ABC 1966–67; The Beautiful Phyllis Diller Show, 1968. Guest spots on major shows here and abroad.
BOOKS: Phyllis Diller's Housekeeping Hints, 1968, Phyllis Diller's Marriage Manual, Phyllis Diller's The Complete Mother, The Joys of Aging and How to Avoid Them.
RECORDS: Verve and Columbia
THEATER: Hello, Dolly! (Bdwy), Nunsense (San Francisco)
CONCERTS: A dozen annual piano concerts with symphony orchestras.

DILLMAN, BRADFORD: Actor. b. San Francisco, CA, April 14, 1930. m. actress-model Suzy Parker. e. Yale U., 1951.
THEATER: The Scarecrow (1953), Third Person, Long Day's Journey into Night (premiere), The Fun Couple.
PICTURES INCLUDE: A Certain Smile, In Love and War, Compulsion, Crack in the Mirror, Circle of Deception, Sanctuary, Francis of Assisi, A Rage to Live, Sergeant Ryker, Bridge at Remagen, Jigsaw, Suppose They Gave a War and Nobody Came, Mastermind, Brother John, The Mephisto Waltz, Escape from the Planet of the Apes, The Way We Were, The Iceman Cometh, Chosen Survivors, 99 and44/100% Dead, Gold, Bug, A Black Ribbon for Deborah, One Away, The Enforcer, Amsterdam Kill, The Lincoln Conspiracy, The Swarm, Love and Bullets, Piranha, Guyana-Crime of the Century, Running Scared, Sudden Impact, Treasure of the Amazon, Man Outside.
TELEVISION: Movies: The Legend of Walks Far Woman, Covenant, Adventures of the Queen, Fear No Evil, Jennifer-A Woman's Story, The Memory of Eva Ryker, Revenge.

DILLON, KEVIN: Actor. b. Mamaroneck, NY, 1965. Younger brother of actor Matt Dillon. Stage work includes Dark at the Top of the Stairs, The Indian Wants the Bronx.
PICTURES: Heaven Help Us (debut, 1985); Platoon; Dear America: Letters Home from Vietnam; Remote Control; The Rescue; The Blob; War Party.

DILLON, MATT: Actor. b. New Rochelle, NY, Feb. 18, 1964. Casting director found him at age 14 in junior high school and put him in Over the Edge, 1978. Theater debut: Boys of Winter.
PICTURES: Little Darlings, My Bodyguard, Tex, The Outsiders, Rumble Fish, The Flamingo Kid, Target, Rebel, Native Son, The Big Town, Kansas, Bloodhounds of Broadway.

DILLON, MELINDA: Actress. b. Hope, AZ, Oct. 13, 1939. Launched career an Broadway in original company of Who's Afraid of Virginia Woolf? Screen debut with bit in The April Fools, 1969.
PICTURES INCLUDE: Bound for Glory, Slap Shot, Close Encounters of the Third Kind, F.I.S.T., Absence of Malice, A Christmas Story, Songwriter, Harry and the Hendersons, Boy's Life.
TELEVISION: Space, The Shadow Box, Fallen Angel, Right of Way, Transplant, Shattered Innocence.

DILLOW, JEAN CARMEN: Producer, Writer, Actress, Director. Began as baby star at age 5 on stage, screen. Last of the Wampas Baby Stars. Film work in England, Germany, Switzerland, Mexico, Italy. Play writing with George S. Kaufman; screenplay-writing with Andrew Solt. Wrote and produced with John Croydon, London producer. Wrote produced, directed and starred in TV feature The Pawn, filmed in Italy, Vienna. Stage: There Is No Other Prince but Aly (London), Stage Door, The Man Who Came to Dinner, What a Life. Completed scripts Spirit-Doll. The Resurrection, for Pinewood Studios, London. Starred in series of westerns for Republic, Monogram First National, Universal. Sang and danced in musicals and nightclubs. See Carmen Productions under Corporations. 1979, non-fiction books on phenomena: Do You Hear the Voices? and The Kidnapping of Aldo Moro. 1983 book Western Bullets are Blank, Mommy Angel; screenplay The Shoe of the Ghost, India-Rome locale; teleplays: Jikoku-ten, The Ghost of Palazzo Palladio, Give the Highest Award to Mommy Angel; The House in Athens. 1986, produced, directed and co-starred in film with Rossano Brazzi. Resides in Charleston, SC and Rome, co-starring and producing with son Guy.

DIMMOCK, PETER: C.V.O., O.B.E. Vice President-Managing Director, ABC Sports Worldwide Enterprises Ltd. & ABC Sports Intl., Inc., Director Screensport. b. Dec. 6, 1920. e. Dulwich Coll. & in France. R.A.F. pilot & staff officer during war. TV as prod. commentator BBC Outside Broadcasts Dept., 1946. Prod. more than 500 TV relays including telecast from Windsor Castle of King George VI's funeral, 1952. Coronation telecast Westminster Abbey; State Opening Parliament. Commentator, introduced BBC-TV weekly Sportsview, 1954–64. Head of BBC-TV Outside Broadcasts 1954–72. Head of BBC Enterprises 1973, v.p. ABC Cos., Inc., 1977. Fellow Royal TV Society.

DI PIETRA, ROSEMARY: Executive. Joined Paramount Pictures in 1976, rising through ranks to become director-corporate administration. 1985, promoted to exec. dir.-corporate administration.

DISHY, BOB: Actor. b. Brooklyn, NY.
THEATER: From A to Z, Second City, Flora the Red Menace, By Jupiter, Something Different, The Goodbye People, The Good Doctor, The Creation of the World and Other Business, An American Millionaire, Sly Fox, Murder at Howard Johnsons, Grown Ups, Cafe Crown.
PICTURES: Tiger Makes Out, Lovers and Other Strangers, The Big Bus, The Last Married Couple in America, First Family, Author! Author!, Brighton Beach Memoirs.
TELEVISION: The Cafeteria, The Comedy Zone, etc.

DISNEY, ROY E.: Producer, Director. Writer, Cameraman, Film editor. b. Los Angeles, CA, Jan. 10, 1930. e. Pomona Coll. CA. 1951 started as page, NBC-TV. Asst. film editor Dragnet TV series. 1952–78, Walt Disney Prods., Burbank, Calif., various capacities; vice chm. of the board, The Walt Disney Co.; bd. chm., Shamrock Holdings, Inc., bd. dir., Walt Disney.
PICTURES INCLUDE: Perri, Mysteries of the Deep, Pacific High.
TELEVISION: Walt Disney's Wonderful World of Color; The Hound That Thought He Was A Raccoon, Sancho, The Homing Steer, The Silver Fox and Sam Davenport, Wonders of the Water World, Legend of Two Gypsy Dogs, Adventure in Wildwood Heart. Also, The Postponed Wedding, (Zorro series), (Wonder World of Color); An Otter in the Family, My Family is a Menagerie, Legend of El Blanco, Pancho, The Fastest Paw in the West, The Owl That Didn't Give A Hoot, Varda the Peregrine Falcon, Cristobalito, The Calypso Colt, Three Without Fear, Hamade and the Pirates, Chango, Guardian of the Mayan Treasure, Nosey, the Sweetest Skunk in the World, Mustang!, Call It Courage, Ringo, the Refugee Raccoon, Shokee, the Everglades Panther, Deacon, the High-Noon Dog, Wise One, Whale's Tooth, Track of African Bongo, Dorsey, the Mail-Carrying Dog.

DIXON, BARBARA: Executive. b. Pasadena CA. e. U. of Southern California. Served as staff member of Senate Judiciary Committee and was deputy dir. of legislation for Sen. Birch Bayh, 1974–79. Left to become dir. of Office of Government & Public Affairs of Natl. Transportation Safety Board. Named v.p., Fratelli Group, p.r. firm in Washington; took leave of

87

Dix-Don

absence in 1984 to serve as deputy press secty. to Democratic V.P. candidate, Geraldine Ferraro. In 1985 joined Motion Picture Assn. of America as v.p. for public affairs.

DIXON, DONNA: Actress. b. Virginia, 1957. m. actor, writer Dan Aykroyd. e. Studied anthropology and medicine, Mary Washington U. Left to become a model, both on magazine covers and in TV commercials (Vitalis, Max Factor, Gillette). TV debut on comedy series Bosom Buddies.
PICTURES: Dr. Detroit; Twilight Zone—The Movie; Spies Like Us; The Couch Trip; It Had To Be You; Mr. Christmas Dinner.
TELEVISION: Series: Berengers.

DIXON, WHEELER: Educator, Writer, Filmmaker. b. New Brunswick, NJ, March 12, 1950. e. Rutgers U. In 1960s asst. writer for Time/Life publications; also writer for Interview magazine. 1976, directed TV commercials in NY. Two years with TVTV, Los Angeles, as post-prod. suprv.; produced programming for Theta Cable there. 1978, formed Deliniator Films, Inc., serving as exec. prod./dir. 1982, consultant to Vestron Industries, acquiring classic feature films. Since 1984 has directed film prod. program at Univ. of Nebraska, where holds rank of tenured assoc. prof. 1988, made chair, Film Studies prog.; received Rockefeller Foundation grant. Author: The 'B' Directors, 1985; The Cinematic Vision of F. Scott Fitzgerald, 1986; PRC: A History of Producer's Releasing Corp., 1986; books on Freddie Francis, Terence Fisher, Reginald Le Borg, 1989.

DMYTRYK, EDWARD: Director. b. Grand Forks, B.C., Canada, Sept. 4, 1908. Entered employ Paramount 1923, working after school. Film editor 1930–1939; dir. from 1939.
PICTURES INCLUDE: Murder My Sweet, Back to Bataan, Cornered Crossfire, So Well Remembered, Till the End of Time, Give Us This Day, Mutiny, The Sniper, Eight Iron Men, The Juggler, Caine Mutiny, Broken Lance, End of the Affair, Left Hand of God, Soldier of Fortune, The Young Lions, Where Love Has Gone, Mirage, Alvarez Kelly, Anzio, Bluebeard.

DODD, WILFRID E.: Executive. b. Hamburg, Germany, March 19, 1923. e. Institut Fisher, Montreux, Switzerland; Downside Coll., Bath, England; Royal Military Coll., Sandhurst, England. In the '50s formed the Canadian Investing Banking firm: Oswald Drinkwater & Graham Ltd., Vice Pres. and partner. Pres. Allied Artists International Corp., 1964. President of Allied Artists Productions, Inc., 1969. Formed Cinepix Inc., Canadian dist. firm, 1963.

DOLGEN, JONATHAN L.: Executive. e. Cornell U., New York U. Sch. of Law. Began career with Wall Street law firm, Fried, Frank, Harris, Shriver & Jacobson. In 1976 joined Columbia Pictures Industries as asst. gen. counsel and deputy gen. counsel. 1979, named sr. v.p. in chg. of worldwide business affairs; 1980, named exec. v.p. Joined Columbia m.p. div., 1981; named pres. of Columbia Pay-Cable & Home Entertainment Group. Also pres. Columbia Pictures domestic operations, overseeing Music Group. 1985, joined 20th-Fox in newly created position of sr. exec. v.p. for telecommunications.

DOLLINGER, IRVING: Exhibitor. Columbia Amusement Co. b. New York, NY, Sept. 20, 1905. e. U. of Pennsylvania. Stanley-Fabian mgr., 1926. Then with Warner Theatres in New Jersey. Owner and operator of theatre since 1929. Past pres. Allied Theat. Owners of N.J. Pres., Assoc. Theats. of N.J., booking org. 1938–44; v.p. & buyer, Independent Theatre Service Eastern regional v.p. Allied States Assoc., 1949–54; treas., Nat'l Allied, 1955–56; partner, Triangle Theatre Service, 1957; chief barker, N.Y. Tent 35, Variety Club, 1966.

DOMINGUEZ, MARINE: Filmmaker. b. El Paso, TX, Oct. 6, 1952. e. Western New Mexico U., 1970–72; Michigan State U., 1972–74; U. of San Francisco, B.P.A., 1980. Educational counselor and director for non-profit community service org., assisting Hispanic youth with admission into academic or technical progs. and univs. Taught photography and Spanish to adults in recreational prog. Since 1982 has developed Hearts on Fire, fictional film about the prod. of the 1954 labor film Salt of the Earth. Produces television progs. and industrial videos. President, Saldeterre Productions, Inc.

DONAHUE, PHIL: Television Personality. b. Cleveland, OH, Dec. 21, 1935. e. Notre Dame, BBA. m. actress Marlo Thomas. Began as announcer at KYW-TV & AM, Cleveland; news dir. WABJ, Adrian, MI, moved to WHIO-TV to do morning newscasts. Interviews with Jimmy Hoffa and Billy Sol Estes picked up nationally by CBS. Host of Conversation Piece, phone-in talk show. Debuted The Phil Donahue Show, daytime talk show in Dayton, Ohio, 1967. Syndicated 2 years later. Moved to Chicago, 1974. Host, Donahue, now in 165 outlets in U.S. In 1979 a mini-version of show became 3-times-a-week segment on NBC's Today Show. Winner of several Emmys.

DONAHUE, TROY: Actor. r.n. Merle Johnson, Jr. b. New York, NY, Jan. 17, 1937. e. Bayport H.S., N.Y. Military Acad. Directed, wrote, acted in school plays. Columbia U., Journalism. Summer stock, Bucks County Playhouse, Sayville Playhouse; contract, Warner Brothers, 1959.
PICTURES INCLUDE: Tarnished Angels (1957), Man Afraid, This Happy Feeling, The Perfect Furlough, Imitation of Life, A Summer Place, The Crowded Sky, Parrish, Susan Slade, Palm Springs Weekend, Rome Adventure, A Distant Trumpet, My Blood Runs Cold, Rocket to the Moon, Come Spy With Me, Sweet Savior, Godfather, Part II, Tin Man, Grandview, U.S.A., Low Blow, Cyclone, Deadly Prey, American Revenge, Back to the Beach, I Was a Teenage Sex Mutant, Sexpot.
TELEVISION: Series: Hawaiian Eye (1959–60), Surfside 6. Guest: Matt Houston, Malibu.

DONALDSON, ROGER: Director. b. Ballarat, Australia, Nov. 15, 1945. Emigrated to New Zealand at 19. Established still photography business; then began making documentaries. Directed Winners and Losers, a series of short dramas for NZ-TV. First theatrical feature, Sleeping Dogs.
PICTURES INCLUDE: Smash Palace (also s.p.), The Bounty, Marie, No Way Out, Cocktails.

DONEN, STANLEY: Producer, Director. b. Columbia, SC, April 13, 1924. e. local schools, high schools, U. of South Carolina.
PICTURES INCLUDE: Royal Wedding; Singin' in the Rain; It's Always Fair Weather, Deep in My Heart, Seven Brides for Seven Brothers, On the Town, Funny Face, Pajama Game, Kiss Them for Me, Indiscreet, Damn Yankees, Once More with Feeling, The Grass Is Greener, Charade, Arabesque, Two for the Road, Bedazzled, Staircase, The Little Prince, Lucky Lady, Movie, Movie, Saturn 3 (prod., dir.), Blame It on Rio (prod., dir.).

DONIGER, WALTER: Writer, Director, Producer. b. New York NY, 1917. e. Valley Forge Military Academy, Duke U., Harvard U. Graduate Business Sch. Entered m.p. business as writer later writer-prod-dir. Wrote documentaries in Army Air Forces M.P. Unit in W.W.II. WGA award nominee.
PICTURES INCLUDE: Rope of Sand; Desperate Search; Cease Fire, Safe At Home, House of Women, Duffy of San Quentin, Along the Great Divide, Tokyo Joe, Alaska Seas, Steel Cage, Steel Jungle, Hold Back the Night, Guns of Fort Petticoat, Unwed Mother, Jive Junction (dir., prod.).
TELEVISION: Movies of Week: Kentucky Woman, Mad Bull, The Outlaws. 50 different series including: Delvecchio, Mad Bull, Switch, Moving On, Baa, Baa, Blacksheep, McCloud, The Man and the City, Sarge, Owen Marshall, Peyton Place (200 episodes), Mr. Novak, The Greatest Show on Earth, Travels of Jaimie McPheeters, Outlaws, Hong Kong, Checkmate, Bat Masterson, The Web, Bold Venture, Tombstone Territory, Maverick, Rough Riders, Captain Grief, Lockup, Dick Powell, The Survivors, Bracken's World, Bold Ones, Kung Fu, Barnaby Jones, Marcus Welby, Lucas Tanner.

DONLAN, YOLANDE: Actress. b. Jersey City, NJ, June 2, 1920. e. Immaculate Heart Convent, Hollywood, CA. English stage debut in Born Yesterday at the Garrick Theatre (London) 1947; screen debut in Miss Pilgrim's Progress 1950. Autobiography: Shake the Stars Down, 1976.
PICTURES INCLUDE: To Dorothy a Son, The Body Said No, Traveller's Joy, Mr. Drake's Duck, Penny Princess, They Can't Hang Me, Expresso Bongo, Jigsaw, 80,000 Suspects, The Adventurers, Seven Nights in Japan.
TELEVISION: I Thought They Died Years Ago.

DONNELLY, DONAL: Actor. b. Bradford, Eng. July 6, 1931. Studied for theatre at the Dublin Gate Theatre. Broadway debut: Philadelphia, Here I Come (1966). Other NY theater includes: Joe Egg, Sleuth (NY and U.S. tour), The Elephant Man, The Faith-Healer, The Chalk Garden, My Astonishing Self, Big Maggie, Execution of Justice.
PICTURES: Rising of the Moon (1957); Gideon's Day; Shake Hands With the Devil; Young Cassidy; The Knack; Up Jumped a Swagman; The Mind of Mr. Soames; Waterloo; The Dead.
TELEVISION: Juno and the Paycock (BBC, 1958); Home Is the Hero, The Venetian Twins; The Plough and the Stars; Playboy of the Western World; Sergeant Musgrave's Dance; Yes-Honestly (series).

DONNELLY, RALPH E.: Executive. b. Lynbrook, NY, Jan. 20, 1932. e. Bellmore, NY public school; W. C. Mepham H.S., 1949. Worked for Variety (publication) as writer, 1950; Long Island Press as daily columnist, 1951; joined Associated Independent Theatres, 1953, as gen. mgr.; later film buyer; in 1973 left to become independent buyer and booker for Creative Films; film buyer and v.p., RKO/Stanley Warner Theatres, 1976–79; v.p. & gen. mgr. for Cinema 5 Ltd. circuit, N.Y., 1980–87; now exec. v.p. City Cinemas, N.Y.

DONNENFELD, BERNARD: Executive. b. New York, NY, Oct. 28, 1926. e. New York U., LL.B. Admitted to New York, California

Bar. Spvsr., corp. affrs., legal dept., Paramount Pictures Corp., New York, 1957–61; exec. asst., asst. secy. corp., Hollywood Studio, 1961–64; asst. to pres., asst. secy. corp., New York, 1964–65; assoc. hd. stud. activities, asst. secy. corp., Hollywood Studio, 1965, v.p. in charge of World Wide Production, Administration, Paramount, 1965–69. Pres. The Filmakers Group, 1970.

DONNER, CLIVE: Director. b. London, Eng., Jan 21, 1926. Ent. m.p. ind. 1942.
PICTURES INCLUDE: The Card, Meet Me Tonight, Genevieve, Million Pound Note, Purple Plain, I Am a Camera, The Secret Place, Heart of a Child, Marriage of Convenience, Some People, The Caretaker, Nothing But the Best, What's New Pussy Cat, Luv, Here We Go Round the Mulberry Bush, Alfred the Great, Vampira, Spectre, Rogue Male, Three Hostages, She Fell Among Thieves, The Thief of Baghdad, The Nude Bomb, Charlie Chan and the Curse of the Dragon Queen, Stealing Heaven.
TELEVISION: Danger Man, Sir Francis Drake, Mighty and Mystical, British Institutions, Tempo. Movies: Oliver Twist, The Scarlet Pimpernel, Arthur the King, To Catch a King, A Christmas Carol, Dead Man's Folly, Babes in Toyland.

DONNER, RICHARD: Director. b. New York, NY, 1939. Began career as actor off-Bdwy. Worked with director Martin Ritt on TV production of Maugham's Of Human Bondage. Moved to California 1958, directing commercials, industrial films and documentaries. First TV drama: Wanted: Dead or Alive (Steve McQueen series).
TELEVISION: Episodes of Have Gun Will Travel; Perry Mason; Cannon; Get Smart; The Fugitive; Kojak; Bronk; Lucas Tanner. Movies: Portrait of a Teen-Age Alcoholic; Senior Year; A Shadow in the Streets.
PICTURES: The Omen, Superman, The Final Conflict, The Toy (exec. prod.), Ladyhawke (prod.-dir.), Goonies (co-prod., dir.), Lethal Weapon (co-prod., dir.), Scrooged (dir., co-prod.).

DONOVAN, ARLENE: Producer. b. Kentucky. e. Stratford Coll., VA. Worked in publishing before entering industry as asst. to late dir. Robert Rosen on Cocoa Beach, uncompleted at his death. Worked as story editor, Columbia Pictures. 1969–82, literary head of m.p. dept. for ICM; involved in book publishing as well as stage and screen projects. Debut as film producer, Still of the Night, 1982.
PICTURES: Places in the Heart, Nadine, The House on Carroll Street (co-exec. prod.).

DONOVAN, HENRY B.: Executive, Producer. b. Boston, MA. Entered m.p. ind. for RKO Pathe Studios, property master, special effects dir., unit mgr., asst. dir., prod. mgr.; worked on over 310 pictures; Harry Sherman, Hopalong Cassidy features. 10 yrs., U.S. Army Signal Corps, as head of dept. of California studios prod. training m.p.; pres.: Telemount Pictures, Inc. Prod., dir., writer Cowboy G Men (TV series). Wrote novel, Corkscrewed, Live Television.
PICTURES INCLUDE: Hopalong Cassidy Features, Gone with the Wind, Becky Sharp, dir. Our Flag; Magic Lady (live-action TV show); Magic Lady (13 one-reel features), others. Prod. writer, Cowboy G Men (39 films).
TELEVISION: programming, financing, distribution. Global Scope; International TV; Dist., Financing, programming; sls. consultant, Internat'l TV & motion pictures. Cable TV & distribution & program development, collector of movie memorabilia; DBS TV programming & financing; production software. World-wide TV consultant.

DOOHAN, JAMES: Actor. b. Vancouver, B.C., Mar. 3, 1920. W.W.II capt. in Royal Canadian Artillery. 1946 won scholarship to Neighborhood Playhouse in N.Y. and taught there later. 1953, returned to Canada to live in Toronto, becoming engaged in acting career on radio, TV and in film. Then to Hollywood and chief fame as Chief Engineer Scott in TV series, Star Trek.
PICTURES: The Wheeler Dealer, The Satan Bug, Bus Riley's Back in Town, Fellowship;, Star Trek—The Motion Picture, Star Trek II: The Wrath of Khan, Star Trek III: The Search for Spock, Star Trek IV: The Voyage Home.
TELEVISION: Hazel, Bonanza, The Virginia, Gunsmoke, Peyton Place, The Fugitive, Marcus Welby MD, Ben Casey, Bewitched, Fantasy Island, etc.

DOOLEY, PAUL: Actor. b. Parkersburg, WV, Feb. 22, 1928. Began career on N.Y. stage in Threepenny Opera. Later member of Second City. Bdwy. credits include The Odd Couple, Adaptation/Next, The White House Murder Case, Hold Me, etc. Co-creator and writer for The Electric Company on PBS. Owns co. called All Over Creation, which produces original industrial films and shows and has created over 1,000 radio commercials.
PICTURES INCLUDE: What's So Bad About Feeling Good?, Slap Shot, Gravy Train, Death Wish, The Out-of-Towners, A Wedding, A Perfect Couple, Rich Kids, Breaking Away, Popeye, Paternity, Endangered Species, Kiss Me Goodbye, Health, Strange Brew, Going Berserk, 16 Candles, Little Shop of Horrors, O.C. and Stiggs, Big Trouble, Monster in the Closet.

TELEVISION: Faerie Tale Theater, The Firm, The Murder of Mary Phagan. Series: Coming of Age.

DORAN, LINDSAY: Executive. b. Los Angeles, CA. e. U. of California at Santa Cruz. Moved to London where was contributing author to The Oxford Companion to Film and the World Encyclopedia of Film. Returned to U.S. to write and produce documentaries and children's programs for Pennsylvania public affairs station WPSX-TV. Career in m.p. industry began in story dept. at Embassy Pictures which she joined in 1979; 1982 promoted to dir. of development; then v.p., creative affairs. 1985, joined Paramount Pictures as v.p., production, for M.P. Group. 1987, promoted to senior v.p., production.

DORFMAN, IRVIN S.: Executive. b. New York, NY, Sept. 3, 1924. e. Yale U., B.A., 1945. Following three years in U.S. Navy, joined Dorfman Associates, press rep. organ. handling film, and TV personalities. Handled pub. and promotion for more than 100 B'way shows and worked for 20th Cen.-Fox and U.A. Also produced off-B'way The Lion in Love. Top ranking amateur tennis star, 1950; pres., Surrogate Releasing and Dandrea Releasing.

DORTORT, DAVID: Executive Producer. b. New York, NY, Oct. 23, 1916. e. City Coll. of New York. Served U.S. Army, 1943–46. Novelist and short story writer, 1943–49. Also TV writer. Now pres. of Xanadu Prods., Aurora Enterprises, Inc., and Bonanza Ventures, Inc. & Pres. TV branch, WGA, West, 1954–55; TV-radio branch, 1955–57; v.p. PGA, 1967; pres. 1968. Chairman of The Caucus for Producers, Writers and Directors, 1973–75. Pres., PGA, 1980–81; campaign director, Permanent Charities Comm., 1980–81; chm., Interguild Council 1980–81.
AUTHOR: Novels include Burial of the Fruit and The Post of Honor.
PICTURES INCLUDE: The Lusty Men, Reprisal, The Big Land, Cry in the Night, Clash by Night, Going Bananas (exec. prod.).
TELEVISION: Creator and exec. prod., Bonanza; High Chaparral, The Chisholms. Producer: The Restless Gun, The Cowboys. Creator, story and exec. prod. Bonanza: The Next Generation.

DOUGHERTY, MARION: Executive. Gained fame as casting director. Acted as co-executive producer on Smile, 1975. In 1977 named v.p. in chg. talent for Paramount Pictures. In 1979 joined Warner Bros. v.p. in chg. talent to work with production dept. and producers and directors.
CASTING: A Little Romance (co-casting), Urban Cowboy (co-), Honky Tonk Freeway, Reds, Fire-Fox Honkytonk Man, The World According to Garp, Sudden Impact, The Man With Two Brains (co-), The Killing Fields (co-), Swing Shift, The Little Drummer Girl.

DOUGLAS, GORDON: Director. b. New York, NY, Dec. 15, 1907. Actor. Hal Roach stock company; writer; collab. Topper series, Housekeeper's Daughter; dir., 30 Our Gang shorts.
PICTURES INCLUDE: Saps at Sea, Broadway Limited, Devil with Hitler, First Yank into Tokyo, San Quentin, If You Knew Suzie, Black Arrow, Walk a Crooked Mile, Doolins of Oklahoma, Mr. Soft Touch, The Nevadan, Between Midnight and Dawn, Kiss Tomorrow Goodbye, Great Missouri Raid, Only the Valiant, I Was a Communist for the FBI, Come Fill the Cup, Mara Maru, Iron Mistress, She's Back on Broadway, So This Is Love, The Charge at Feather River, Them, Young at Heart, McConnell Story, Sincerely Yours, Santiago, The Big Land, Bombers B-52, Fort Dobbs, Yellowstone Kelly, Rachel Cade, Gold of 7 Saints, Follow That Dream, Call Me Bwana, Rio Conchos, Robin and the Seven Hoods, Sylvia, Harlow, Stagecoach, Way Way Out, In Like Flint, Chuka, Tony Rome, The Detective, Lady in Cement, Barquero, They Call Me Mr. Tibbs, Slaughter's Big Rip Off.
TELEVISION: Nevada Smith.

DOUGLAS, KIRK: Actor, Producer, Director. r.n. Issur Danielovitch (changed to Demsky). b. Amsterdam, NY, Dec. 9, 1918. m. Anne Buydens, pres. of Bryna Prod. Co. Father of Michael, Joel, Peter, Eric. e. St. Lawrence U, B.A. Stage debut in New York: Spring Again. U.S. Navy during W.W.II; resumed stage work. Did radio soap operas. Signed by Hal B. Wallis. Screen debut: The Strange Love of Martha Ivers. Autobiography: The Ragman's Son (1988).
AWARDS: Recipient of U.S. Presidential Medal of Freedom, 1981. Three Academy Award nominations: Champion, The Bad and the Beautiful, Lust for Life. N.Y. Critics Award, Best Actor for Lust for Life. Cecil B. DeMille Award–1968. Cited in Congressional Record three times: on discrimination (1977), on good will ambassador work (1964), testimony on abuse of elderly (1985). Received Jefferson Award in 1983 for public service by a private citizen. Made Goodwill Ambassador to U.S. State Dept. and U.S.I.A, 1963. 1979: Commander in the Order of Arts and Letters, Chevalier de la Legion d'Honneur, 1985. American Cinema Award, 1987. Golden Kamera Award (Germany 1988).
THEATER: Spring Again, Three Sisters, Kiss and Tell, Trio, The Wind is Ninetry, Star in the Window, Man Bites Dog, One

Flew Over the Cuckoo's Nest, The Boys of Autumn.
TELEVISION: Mousey, 1974; The Money Changers, Draw! (HBO), Victory at Entebbe, Holocaust 2000, Remembrance of Love, Amos, Queenie, Inherit the Wind.
PICTURES INCLUDE: Out of the Past, I Walk Alone, Mourning Becomes Electra, The Walls of Jericho, My Dear Secretary, Letter to Three Wives, Champion, Young Man with a Horn, The Glass Menagerie, The Big Carnival (a.k.a. Ace in the Hole), Along the Great Divide, Detective Story, The Big Trees, The Big Sky, Bad and the Beautiful, Story of Three Loves, The Juggler, Act of Love, Ulysses, Man Without a Star, 20,000 Leagues Under the Sea, The Racers, The Indian Fighter, Lust for Life, Top Secret Affair, Gunfight at the OK Corral, Paths of Glory, The Vikings, Last Train from Gun Hill, The Devil's Disciple, Strangers When We Meet, Spartacus, The Last Sunset, Town Without Pity, Lonely Are the Brave, Two Weeks in Another Town, The Hook, List of Adrian Messenger, For Love or Money, Seven Days in May, In Harm's Way, Cast a Giant Shadow, Is Paris Burning?, The Way West, The War Wagon, The Heroes of Telemark, A Lovely Way to Die, The Brotherhood, The Arrangement, There Was a Crooked Man, A Gunfight, The Light at the Edge of the World, Catch Me a Spy, Master Touch. Producer: The Indian Fighter, The Vikings, Spartacus, Lonely Are the Brave, List of Adrian Messenger, Seven Days in May, The Brotherhood, Summertree, (prod.) Scalawag; (prod., dir., act.) Once Is Not Enough, Posse (prod., dir., act.) The Chosen, The Fury, The Villain, Saturn III, Home Movies, The Final Countdown, The Man from Snowy River, Eddie Macon's Run, Tough Guys.

DOUGLAS, MICHAEL: Actor, Producer. b. New Brunswick, NJ, Sept 25, 1944. f. Kirk Douglas. e. Black Fox Military Acad., Choate, U. of California. Worked as asst. director on Lonely Are The Brave, Heroes of Telemark, Cast a Giant Shadow; after TV debut in The Experiment, appeared off-Broadway in City Scene, Pinkville; m.p. debut in Hail Hero (1969).
PICTURES: Adam at 6 A.M., Summertree, Napoleon and Samantha, Coma, China Syndrome (also prod.). Co-prod., One Flew over the Cuckoo's Nest; Running (actor). It's My Turn (actor). Star Chamber (actor). Romancing the Stone (prod., actor), Starman (exec. prod.); A Chorus Line (actor); Jewel of the Nile (prod., actor); Fatal Attraction; Wall Street (Acad. Award, 1987); Black Rain; The Tender (co-exec. prod.).
TELEVISION: The FBI, Medical Center, When Michael Calls, Streets of San Francisco (series).

DOUGLAS, MIKE: TV host, Commentator. r.n. Michael Delaney Dowd, Jr. b. Chicago, IL, 1925. Started career singing with bands in and around Chicago. In 1950 became featured singer with Kay Kyser's band, staying four years. In 1953 became host of WGN-TV's Hi Ladies in Chicago; also featured on WMAQ-TV, NBC, Chicago, as singer and host. Moved to Hollywood in late '50s, working as piano bar singer. In 1961 hired as host for new show on station KYW-TV in Cleveland, owned by Westinghouse Bdg. Co., featuring celebrity guests. This became the Mike Douglas Show which was later nationally syndicated and moved base of operations to Philadelphia, then Los Angeles. Ran 21 years til Mid-1982.

DOUGLAS, VALERIE: Executive. b. Hollywood, CA, Dec. 3. e. U. of California at L.A., journalism. Uncle was actor Elmo Lincoln (first Tarzan). 1945–46, publicist, Vic Shapiro Public Relations; 1946–49, sub-agent, Manning O'Conner Agency; 1949–51, TV coordinator, Bing Crosby Enterprises, Fireside Theatre Series; 1951–52, publicist, RKO Studios; 1952–59, personal mgr., Richard Burton; v.p. & dir. Denham Films, Ltd., London; 1959–61, pub. coordinator, Hecht-Lancaster-Hill; 1961–64, dir. of pub. relations, IPAR Productions, France; 1964–67, v.p., Illustra Films, West Coast branch; 1967–75, asst. dir. pub., United Artists Corp., West Coast; 1975–78, exec. v.p., Guttman & Pam Public Relations; 1978, formed Suvarie, Inc., m.p. representation, of which is pres.

DOURIF, BRAD: Actor. b. Huntington, WV, Mar. 18, 1950. Stage actor, three years with Circle Repertory Co., NY (When You Comin Back, Red Ryder?); before films and TV.
PICTURES INCLUDE: Split, W. W. and the Dixie Dancekings, One Flew Over the Cuckoo's Nest (Acad. Award nom., Golden Globe, British Oscar), Group Portrait with Lady, Eyes of Laura Mars, Wise Blood, Heaven's Gate, Ragtime, Dune, Impure Thoughts, Blue Velvet, Fatal Beauty, Sonny Boy, Child's Play, Mississippi Burning.
TELEVISION: Guest: Miami Vice, The Hitchhiker, Spencer for Hire, Tales of the Unexpected. Movies: Mound Builders, The Gardener's Son, Sgt. Matlovitch vs. the U.S. Air Force, Studs Lonigan, Guyana Tragedy—The Story of Jim Jones, I Desire: The Story of a Female Vampire, Vengeance: The Story of Tony Cimo, Rage of Angels: The Story Continues.

DOWN, LESLEY-ANNE: Actress. b. London, England, March 17, 1954. At age of 10 modeled for TV and film commercials, leading to roles in features. Stage debut at 14 in All the Right Noises.
PICTURES INCLUDE: Pope Joan, Scalawag, Brannigan, The Pink Panther Strikes Again, The Betsy, A Little Night

Music, The Great Train Robbery, Hanover Street, Sphinx, Rough Cut, Nomads, Scenes from the Goldmine.
TELEVISION: Series: Upstairs, Downstairs; Heartbreak House, North & South Book II. Movies: The One and Only Phyllis Dixey, The Last Days of Pompeii, Arch of Triumph, Indiscreet.
STAGE: Great Expectations, Hamlet, etc.

DOWNEY, ROBERT, JR.: Actor. b. New York, NY, April 4, 1965. Son of independent filmmaker Robert Downey. Made film debut in his father's Greaser's Palace (1972) and Up the Academy. Later appeared in father's film This is America The Movie, Not the Country (a.k.a. America). Was a cast regular on Saturday Night Live, 1985–86.
PICTURES: Baby, Its You; Back to School, Firstborn, Tuff Turf, Weird Science, To Live & Die in L.A., America, Less Than Zero; The Pick-Up Artist; Johnny B. Goode, Rented Lips, True Believer, 1969, Chances Are.
TELEVISION: Mussolini: The Untold Story.

DOWNS, HUGH: Broadcaster. b. Akron, OH, Feb. 14, 1921. e. Bluffton Coll., 1938. Wayne U., 1941. Col. U., N.Y., 1955; Supervisor of Science Programming, NBC's Science Dept. one yr.; science consultant for Westinghouse Labs., Ford Foundation, etc.; chm. of bd., Raylin Prods., Inc. Today, Chairman, U.S. Committee for UNICEF. Chm., National Space Institute.
TELEVISION: Hawkins Falls, Kukla, Fran & Ollie, Short Story Playhouse, American Inventory, Home, Sid Caesar Show, Tonight (Jack Paar Show), Concentration, Today. Host: ABC-TV 20/20 Program, Host: Over-Easy, PBS Network.
RADIO: NBC's Monitor.

DOYLE, KEVIN: Executive. b. Sydney, Australia, June 21, 1933. e. N. Sydney Tech. HS., Aust. Jr. exec., asst. adv. & pub. div., 20th Century-Fox, Aust., 1947–59; adv. & pub. dir., Columbia Pictures Aust., 1960–66; international ad/pub. mgr.; Columbia Pictures Int'l, N.Y. 1966; intl. pub./promo. mgr., 1980; 1987, Columbia Int'l. rep., Coca-Cola promotions/mktg. sub-committee; int'l pub./promo. mgr. Columbia Tri-Star Film Distributors Inc., 1988.

DRABINSKY, GARTH: Executive. b. Toronto, Canada, 1950. e. U. of Toronto, LL.D. Co-founder, Pan-Canadian Film Distributors; Chm, CEO and pres., Cineplex Odeon Corp., theatre circuit in Canada and U.S. Dir., CFMT-TV, Toronto. Former publisher, Canadian Film Digest.
PICTURES: Co-prods. with Joel B. Michaels: The Silent Partner, The Changeling; Tribute; The Amateur; Losin' It.

DRAGOTI, STAN: Director. b. New York, NY, Oct. 4, 1932. Worked in ad agency and did TV commercials (including I Love New York campaign). Theatrical director debut with Dirty Little Billy (1972).
PICTURES: Love at First Bite, Mr. Mom, The Man with One Red Shoe, Daddy's Little Girl.

DRAI, VICTOR: Producer. b. Casablanca, Morocco, July 25, 1947. e. Lycée de Port Lyautey, 1957–63. In real estate in Los Angeles 1976–82; clothing designer/mfg. in Paris, France, 1969–76. Began producing features in 1984, The Woman in Red.
PICTURES: The Man with One Red Shoe, The Bride.

DRAKE, CHARLES: Actor. r.n. Charles Ruppert; b. New York, NY, Oct. 2, 1914. e. Nicholas Coll., 1937. With Electric Boat Co., Groton, CT; adv. salesman; in little theatres; in m.p. as an actor.
PICTURES INCLUDE: I Wanted Wings, Man Who Came to Dinner, Now, Voyager, Air Force, Mr. Skefflington, Whistle Stop, Pretender, You Came Along, Tender Years, Bowie Knife, Comanche Territory, Air Cadet, Winchester '73, Harvey, Little Egypt, You Never Can Tell, Treasure of Lost Canyon, Red Ball Express, Bonzo Goes to College, Gunsmoke, Lone Hand, It Came from Outer Space, War Arrow, Glenn Miller Story, Tobor the Great, Four Guns to the Border, Female on the Beach, All That Heaven Allows, Price of Fear, The Arrangement.

DRAKLICH, NICK: Executive. b. Bakersfield, CA, Oct. 16, 1926. e. Fresno State Coll., Stanford U., Claremont Graduate Sch. Sr. v.p.—home entertainment for Republic Pictures Corp.

DRAZEN, LORI: Executive. Began career as asst. to dir. of adv. for Orion Pictures; gen. mgr., Seiniger Advertising; creative dept. mgr., Kenyon & Eckhardt. Joined Warner Bros. 1985 as dir., world-wide adv. & pub. services.

DREIFUSS, ARTHUR: Producer, Director, Writer. b. Frankfurt on Main, Germany, March 25, 1908. e. U. of Frankfurt on Main, Conservatory of Music, Columbia U. Choreographer, producer; many U. lectures; legit. producer: Allure, Baby Pompadour; producer many night club shows; associate producer Fanchon & Marco, Hollywood; dir. over 50 features and 53 TV shows for Columbia, RKO, Universal, Allied Artists, other majors; director Paul Muni debut Screen Gems-Ford Theatre, TV 1953; executive producer New Age Productions, 1970 to 1972; executive producer The Peter Hurkos Show, CBS;

writer Owl Hill; Dolls behind Walls, 1973, director, Wildlife in Crisis, Viacom TV series 1975. Assoc. prod. Chennault China Tiger (Genson Prods.), 1978; assoc. video editor Creative Editing, Inc., 1979; dir. literary dept, Georg Michaud Agency, 1979–86; dir., literary dept., Schoeman Agency. 1987; dir. literary dept. William Carroll Agency, 1988.
PICTURES: prod.-dir.: features Secret File and Assignment Abroad, 1956; dir.: The Last Blitzkrieg; Life Begins at Seventeen; Juke Box Rhythm; writer-dir.: Brendan Behan's The Quare Fellow; dir.: Riot on Sunset Strip; The Love-Ins; For Singles Only; The Young Runaways; A Time to Sing; assoc. prod.: Angel, Angel, Down We Go.

DREXLER, ELIAS J.: Executive. b. New York, NY, Dec. 24, 1911. e. Columbia U., Columbia Law Sch., LL.B., 1936. Special agent. Div. of Investigations, U.S. Dept. of Interior, 1937–40; dir., Preclusive operations, 1940–45; dir., Surplus Property Div., Foreign Economic Admin; exec., National Screen Service, 1945–56; general counsel and nat. sales mgr. AGFA-Gavaert; 1956–65; nat. sales mgr. and exclusive U.S. and Mexican dist. of motion picture products manufactured by Fuji Photo Film Co., Ltd., Tokyo, Japan, 1965–present.

DREYFUSS, RICHARD: Actor. b. Brooklyn, NY, Oct. 29, 1947. e. Beverly Hills H.S.; San Fernando Valley State Coll. 1965– 67. Prof. career began at Gallery Theatre (L.A.) in In Mama's House. Has also acted off-Bdwy. and on Bdwy.
PICTURES INCLUDE: Hello Down There, The Young Runaways, American Graffiti, The Apprenticeship of Duddy Kravitz, Jaws, Inserts, Close Encounters of the Third Kind, The Goodbye Girl (Acad. Award), The Big Fix (also co-prod.) The Competition, Whose Life Is It Anyway?, The Buddy System, Down and Out in Beverly Hills, Stand by Me, Tin Men, Stakeout, Nuts, Moon Over Parador.
TELEVISION: The Big Valley, Room 222, Judd for the Defense, Mod Squad, The Bold Ones, Funny, You Don't Look 200 (host, co-prod., co-writer).
STAGE: Journey to the Day, Incident at Vichy, People Need People, Enemy, Enemy, Line, Whose Little Boy Are You, But Seriously, Major Barbara, The Time of Your Life.

DROMGOOLE, PATRICK: Film director, Stage prod. Man. Dir. HTV Ltd., since April 1987. b. Iqueque, Chile, Aug. 30, 1930; e. Dulwich Coll., University Coll., Oxford. Joined BBC Radio as dir. 1954, later directing TV plays for BBC and ABC, incl. Armchair Theatre, Frontier, Dracula, Mystery Imagination. Joined HTV as West Country Programme Controller, 1968; dir. award-winning dramas; Thick as Thieves, Machinegunner. Developed Company's drama output and promoted policy of international pre-sales with such dramas as Jamaica Inn, Separate Tables, Catholics, Kidnapped, Robin of Sherwood, Arch of Triumph, Mr. Halpern and Mr. Johnson, Jenny's War, Codename Kyril, Wall of Tyranny, Strange Interlude, The Woman He Loved, Grand Larceny, Maigret. Made Fellow of RTS, 1978.
THEATER: Director: incl. first plays of Charles Wood, Joe Orton, David Halliwell, Colin Welland; Peter O'Toole in Man and Superman.
PICTURES: Two Vale South, Hidden Face, Dead Man's Chest, Anthony Purdy Esq., Point of Dissent, The Actors.

DRU, JOANNE: Actress. r.n. Joanne La Cock; b. Logan, WV, Jan. 31, 1923. Sister of Peter Marshall. John Robert Powers model: on stage as showgirl in Hold on to Your Hats; a Samba Siren at Ritz Carlton & Paramount; with theatrical group under Batami Schneider. Hollywood: m.p. debut in Abie's Irish Rose, 1946.
PICTURES INCLUDE: Red River, She Wore a Yellow Ribbon, All the King's Men, Wagonmaster, Vengeance Valley, 711 Ocean Drive, Mr. Belvedere Rings the Bell, Siege at Red River, Outlaw Territory, Southwest Passage, Three Ring Circus, Day of Triumph, Hell on Frisco Bay, Sincerely Yours, The Warriors, Thunder Bay, My Pal Gus, Pride of St. Louis, September Storm, Light in the Forest, Forbidden, Return of the Texan, Duffy of San Quentin, Supersnoopers.
TELEVISION: Guestward Ho (series).

DRURY, JAMES: Actor. New York, NY, 1934. e. New York U. Acting debut at age 8 in biblical play for children at Greenwich Settlement Playhouse. Performed on stage while youngster. Signed by MGM in 1955, working one day in each of seven movies that year, including Blackboard Jungle. Then got two-year contract at 20th-Fox. Gained fame as hero of TV series, The Virginian, which had nine-year run.
PICTURES INCLUDE: Love Me Tender, Bernardine.
TELEVISION: The Virginian (series), The Devil and Miss Sarah (movie of the week), Firehouse (series).

DRUXMAN, MICHAEL B.: Publicist, Producer. b. Seattle, WA, Feb. 23, 1941. e. U. of Washington. Exec. v.p., Seattle Civic Playhouse, 1962–63; founder, exec. dir., Actor's Theatre, Seattle; formed public relations firm, Michael B. Druxman and Associates.
CREDITS: Genesis (wrote, prod., dir.); produced and directed plays in the Los Angeles area—A Shot in the Dark, A Thousand Clowns.

DUBAND, WAYNE: Executive. Joined Warner Bros. 1969 as mgr. trainee in Australia. 1973, transferred to South Africa as mgr. dir.; 1977 gen. mgr. of CIC/Warner Bros. joint venture, also managing the CIC theatre operation there. 1980, named exec. asst. to Myron D. Karlin, pres. WB Intl., in Burbank. 1981, mgr. dir. of Warner/Columbia joint venture in France. 1985, appt. v.p. of sls. for WB Intl. division. 1987, appt. senior v.p. for Warner Bros. Intl. division.

DUBBINS, DON: Actor. b. Brooklyn, NY, June 28, 1929. Appeared in national company of Mr. Roberts, also Tea and Sympathy. Many television shows including Ed Sullivan show.
PICTURES INCLUDE: From Here to Eternity, Caine Mutiny, Tribute to a Bad Man, These Wilder Years, The D.I., Gunfight in Abilene, The Illustrated Man, The Prize.

DUBE, JACKSON E.: Executive. b. New York, NY. e. U of North Carolina. m. Pat Lavelle, actress. USAF 1942–45 Radar-Gunner, AAF, Italy. Writer: Television and programming 1947–48; reviews of recorded music. 1947–51, Consol Film Inds. Penthouse Prods. Dist: E. sales mgr. Atlas Tel. Corp, 1951–54; vp & gen. mgr., Craftsman Film Greatest Fights of the Century 1954; vp, Conquest Prods. CBS Net. Docus. 1954–57. TV and radio dir. Cote Fischer & Rogow Adv., 1957–59; exec vp, Bon Ami Film; dist: UA Feats. abroad 1959–63; prod's rep. Le Vien Prods—Finest Hours King's Story; E. sls. mgr. Desilu, 1964–67; exec vp, UCC Films; dist. RKO feature library abroad, 1969–70; pres. JED Prns. Corp Dist. London Films, Rank children's features, 1967–88. Consultant: New Century Ent., Windsor Pdns., Turner Program Services, 1985–88.

DUBENS, STANLEY: Writer, Producer. b. London, England, 1920. e. St. Paul's Sch. s. of Harry Dubens. Royal Corps Signals 1939–1945. From 1946, agent and theatrical productions. Ent. film production 1963. 1975 formed with Roger Moss, The Original Electric Picture Company, making commercials, doc., video, AV presentations.
THEATRE: prod. incl. Sweet and Low, And No Birds Sing, The Train for Venice, The Man Who Let It Rain, The Hands of Eurydice, I Want to See Mioussov, Sign Here Please.
PICTURES INCLUDE: Operation Snatch, Live Now Pay Later, The World Ten Times Over, Modesty Blaise, Marble Heroes, Matchgirls, Archie's Caper.

DUBS, ARTHUR R.: Executive, Producer, Director, Writer, President and Owner of Pacific International Enterprises, b. Medford, OR, Feb. 26, 1930. e. Southern Oregon State Coll. Founded Pacific International Enterprises, 1969.
PICTURES: Producer-Director: American Wilderness, Vanishing Wilderness, Wonder of It All. Exec. Prod.: Challenge to Be Free. Prod.: Adventures of the Wilderness Family, Wilderness Family Part 2 (also s.p.), Mountain Family Robinson (also s.p.), Across the Great Divide, Sacred Ground, Mystery Mansion, Dream Chasers (also co-dir.). Co-Prod.: Windwalker.

DUDELHEIM, HANS R.: Producer, Director, Editor. Began film career in Germany after W.W.II. Hired by U.S. Army Signal Corps as photographer, being sent to Far East Command. Came to New York, where joined ABC-TV as film editor. Beginning with hard news, moved to documentaries, editing many films. In 1981 established Cinema Arts Associates, Inc. as film society; 1966 expanded into indep. m.p. prod. co., of which he is pres.

DUDELSON, STANLEY E.: Executive. b. Cleveland, OH, July 12, 1924. Regnl. sales mgr., Hygo-Unity; natl. sales mgr. Screen Gems; producer's rep., Selma Ent., Italian Intl. Inter-Export Films of Rome, AIP; first vice pres., American Intl. Television, Inc. Joined New Line Dist. Corp., pres., New Line Intl. Releasing. Co- exec. prod. Nightmare on Elm Street. Left 1985 to be pres. & chief exec., Inter-pictures Releasing Corp.

DUFF, HOWARD: Actor. Bremerton, WA, Nov. 24, 1917. e. Repertory Playhouse, Seattle. With KOMO radio station 1935; served with U.S. Army 1941–5; entered m.p. 1947. Radio's original Sam Spade. Film debut: Brute Force (1947).
PICTURES INCLUDE: Brute Force, Naked City, All My Sons, Calamity Jane and Sam Bass, Illegal Entry, Johnny Stoolpigeon, Woman in Hiding, Shakedown, Lady From Texas, Models Inc., Spaceways, Roar of the Crowd, Jennifer, Tanganyika, Private Hell 36, Women's Prison, Yellow Mountain, Flame of the Islands, Broken Star, Sierra Stranger, Blackjack Ketchum Desperado, While the City Sleeps, Boy's Night Out, Syria Against Babylon, Panic in the City, The Late Show, A Wedding, Kramer vs. Kramer, Oh, God! Book II, Monster in the Closet, No Way Out.
TELEVISION: Series: Mr. Adams and Eve, Dante, Felony Squad; Flamingo Road; Knots Landing; Guest: Detective in the House. Hotel; Murder She Wrote; Movies: The D.A., The Heist, East of Eden, This Girl for Hire, Roses Are for the Rich.

DUFFY, JAMES E.: Executive. b. Decatur, IL, April 2, 1926. e. Beloit Coll. Radio announcer, then reporter; joined publicity dept., ABC in 1949; named director of adv. & promo., then account exec. for Central division of ABC Radio Network;

director of sales ABC Radio, 1957; central division account exec., ABC Television Network, 1955; natl. director of Sales, ABC Radio central division, 1960; vice president, ABC Radio Network, 1961; exec. v.p. & natl. director of sales, 1962; vice president in charge of sales, ABC Television Network, 1963; president, ABC Television Network, 1970–85; pres., communications, 1985–86; v.p. Capital Cities/ABC, Inc.; pres., communications, ABC Network & Bdgst. Divisions.

DUFFY, PATRICK: Actor. b. Townsend, MT, March 17, 1949. e. U. of Washington. Became actor-in-residence in state of Washington, where performed with various statefunded groups. Acted off-Bdwy. Taught mime and movement classes in summer camp in Seattle. Moved to L.A. and began TV acting career.
TELEVISION: The Last of Mrs. Lincoln; George Burns Comedy Week; Alice in Wonderland. Movies: The Stranger Who Looks Like Me, Hurricane, 14 Going on 30, Leave Her to Heaven. Series: Man from Atlantis (star), Switch (guest), Dallas (star).

DUIGAN, JOHN: Writer, Director. b. Australia. e. Melbourne U., philosophy, M.A. Taught for several years at Melbourne U. and Latrobe U. before entering films. Made experimental short, The Firm Man (1974).
PICTURES: The Trespassers, Mouth to Mouth, Dimboola (d., only), Winter of Our Dreams, Far East, The Year My Voice Broke (dir., s.p.).

DUKAKIS, OLYMPIA: Actress. b. Lowell, MA, June 20, 1931. m. actor Louis Zorich. e. Boston U., B.A., M.F.A. Was a founding member of The Charles Playhouse in Boston, establishing summer theatre 1957–60. Taught acting at NYU 1967–70 as instructor, 1974–83 as master teacher, and at Yale U. 1976. With husband conceived and guided artistic dev. of The Whole Theatre Co., Upper Monclair, NJ, since 1977, artistic dir. Has adapted plays for her co. and dir. theater there, at Williamstown Theatre Fest. and Delaware Summer Fest. Appeared in more than 100 plays on Bdwy, Off-Bdwy and in regional and summer theater.
THEATER: Who's Who in Hell, The Aspern Papers, Night of the Iguana, The Breaking Wall, Curse of the Starving Class, Snow Orchid, The Marriage of Bette and Boo (Obie Award), Social Security.
PICTURES: Lilith, Made for Each Other, Deathwish, Twice a Man, The Idolmaker, Rich Kids, The Wanderers, National Lampoon Goes to the Movies, Flanagan, Moonstruck (Acad. Award, supp. actress, 1987), Daddy's Home, Steel Magnolias.
TELEVISION: The Rehearsal, Sisters, Nicky's World, Search for Tomorrow; FDR—The Last Days, One of the Boys, King of America.

DUKE, PATTY: Actress. r.n. Anna Marie Duke. b. New York, NY, Dec. 14, 1946. e. Quintano Sch. for Young Professionals. Pres. Screen Actors Guild, 1985–88. Author: Surviving Sexual Assault; Call Me Anna.
THEATRE: The Miracle Worker, Isle of Children.
PICTURES: I'll Cry Tomorrow (debut 1955), Somebody Up There Likes Me, The Goddess, Happy Anniversary, The Miracle Worker (Acad. Award, best supp. actress, 1963), Valley of the Dolls, Billie, My Sweet Charlie, Me, Natalie, The Swarm.
TELEVISION: Series regular: Patty Duke Show (1963–66); It Takes Two (1982–83); Hail to the Chief (1985). Episodes: Armstrong Circle Theatre (1955), U.S. Steel Hour (1959), All's Fair (1982); Movies: The Prince and the Pauper, Wuthering Heights, Swiss Family Robinson, Meet Me in St. Louis, The Power and the Glory, My Sweet Charlie, The Miracle Worker (Emmy Award, 1979), Before and After, The Baby Sitter, The Women's Room, Something So Right, Perry Mason: The Avenging Ace, Fatal Dosage, See You in the Morning. Miniseries: Captains and the Kings; George Washington.

DUKES, DAVID: Actor. b. San Francisco, CA. On Bdwy. in Don Juan, The Visit, Holiday, School for Wives, Dracula, Travesties, Frankenstein, Bent, Amadeus, M. Butterfly.
PICTURES: The Wild Party, A Little Romance, The First Deadly Sin, Only When I Laugh, Without a Trace, The Men's Club, Catch the Heat, Date With an Angel, Deadly Intent, See You in the Morning, Rawhead Rex.
TELEVISION: Beacon Hill (series); 79 Park Avenue, Family, Some Kind of Miracle, The Triangle Factory Fire Scandal, Mayflower—the Pilgrim Adventure, Margaret Sanger–Portrait of a Rebel, George Washington, Sentimental Journey, Space, Kane and Abel, Strange Interlude, The Winds of War, War and Remembrance.

DULLEA, KEIR: Actor. b. Cleveland, OH, May 30, 1936. e. San Francisco State Coll., Sanford Meisner's Neighborhood Playhouse. Worked as ice cream vendor, carpenter with a construction co. Acted as resident juvenile at the Totem Pole Playhouse in PA. N.Y. theatre debut in the revue Sticks and Stones, 1956; appeared in stock co. prods. at the Berkshire Playhouse and Philadelphia's Hedgerow Theatre, 1959, off-Broadway debut in Season of Choice, 1969.

THEATER: Dr. Cooks Garden, Butterflies Are Free, Cat on a Hot Tin Roof, P.S. Your Cat is Dead.
TELEVISION: All Summer Long, Law and Order, Legend of the Golden Gun.
PICTURES INCLUDE: The Hoodlum Priest, David and Lisa (Best Actor Award, San Francisco Int'l Film Festival), Thin Red Line, Mail Order Bride, The Naked Hours, Madame X, Bunny Lake Is Missing, The Fox, 2001: A Space Odyssey, de Sade, Pope Joan, Paul and Michelle, The Paperback Hero, Silent Night, Evil Night, Leopard in the Snow, Brainwave, 2010, Devil in the Brain, Black Christmas, Welcome to Blood City, Full Circle.

DUNAWAY, FAYE: Actress. b. Bascom, FL, Jan. 14, 1941. e. Texas, Arkansas, Utah, Germany, U. of Florida. Awarded a Fulbright scholarship in theatre. Boston U. of Fine Applied Arts. Appeared on N.Y. stage in: A Man for All Seasons, After the Fall (with Lincoln Center Repertory Co., three years), Hogan's Goat.
PICTURES INCLUDE: The Happening, Bonnie and Clyde, Hurry Sundown, The Thomas Crown Affair, The Extraordinary Seaman, A Place for Lovers, The Arrangement, Puzzle of a Downfall Child, Little Big Man, Doc, Oklahoma Crude, The Three Musketeers, Chinatown, The Towering Inferno, The Four Musketeers, Three Days of the Condor, Network (Acad. Award, 1976), Voyage of the Damned, Eyes of Laura Mars, The Champ, The First Deadly Sin, Mommie Dearest, The Wicked Lady, Ordeal by Innocence, Supergirl, Barfly, Midnight Crossing, Burning Secret, Circe and Bravo, The Match.
TELEVISION: Portrait: The Woman I Love, The Disappearance of Aimee, Evita, Ellis Island, 13 at Dinner, Beverly Hills Madam, The Country Girl, Christopher Columbus, Casanova, The Raspberry Ripple.

DUNCAN, SANDY: Actress. b. Henderson, TX, Feb. 20, 1946. m. singer-dancer Don Correia. e. Len Morris Coll.
THEATER: The Music Man (NY debut, 1965); The Boyfriend, Ceremony of Innocence, Your Own Thing, Canterbury Tales, Peter Pan, My One and Only.
PICTURES INCLUDE: $1,000,000 Duck, Star Spangled Girl, The Cat from Outer Space.
TELEVISION: Funny Face (1971), The Sandy Duncan Show, Roots, Valerie's Family.

DUNING, GEORGE: Composer, Conductor, Arranger. b. Richmond, IN, Feb. 25, 1908. e. Cincinnati Conservatory of Music, U. of Cincinnati. Musical director; music scores for many m.p. including: Jolson Sings Again, Eddy Duchin Story, From Here to Eternity, Picnic, World of Susie Wong, Devil at 4 O'Clock, Toys in the Attic, Any Wednesday, The Man with Bogart's Face. TV: No Time for Sergeants, Wendy and Me, The Farmer's Daughter, Big Valley, The Long Hot Summer, The Second Hundred Years, Star Trek, Mannix, Then Came Bronson; music dir. Aaron Spelling Prods., 1970–71, Bobby Sherman Show, Movies of the Week. Bd. of Dir., ASCAP.

DUNLAP, RICHARD D.: Producer, Director. b. Pomona, CA, Jan. 30, 1923. e. Yale U., B.A., 1944; M.F.A., 1948. U.S. Navy 1943–46; Instructor, English dept., Yale U., 1947–48; Prod.-dir., Kraft TV Theatre, 3 years; Dir. Assoc. Prod., Omnibus, 3 seasons; Dir., 25 half-hr. Dramatic Film Shows. Frank Sinatra Specials, Prod.-Dir., 11 Academy Award Shows, 4 Emmy Award Shows. Artistic dir. Berkshire Theatre Festival.

DUNNE, DOMINICK: Producer. Began career as stage manager at NBC-TV; then produced shows for CBS Studio One. Later exec. prod. at 20th-Fox TV, v.p. at Four Star.
PICTURES INCLUDE: Boys in the Band (exec. prod.), The Panic in Needle Park, Play It as It Lays, Ash Wednesday.

DUNNE, GRIFFIN: Actor, Producer. b. New York, NY, June 8, 1955. Studied at Neighborhood Playhouse and with Uta Hagen. On Stage in Album, Marie and Bruce, Coming Attractions, Hotel Play, etc.
PICTURES: Actor: American Werewolf in London; Head Over Heels (also prod.); The Fan; Almost You; Johnny Dangerously; After Hours (also co-prod.), Who's That Girl, Amazon Women on the Moon, Big Blue, Me and Him. Producer: Baby It's You, Running on Empty.

DUNNE, IRENE: Actress. b. Louisville, KY, Dec. 20, 1904. e. Loretta Acad. in St. Louis, MO; Chicago Coll. of Music, D.M., 1945; N.Y. One child, Mary Frances. Screen debut Leathernecking 1930. Kennedy Center Honors (1986).
THEATRE: Stage prods. include Sweetheart Time, The City Chap, Show Boat.
PICTURES INCLUDE: Cimarron, Consolation Marriage, Back Street, Silver Cord, Ann Vickers, The Age of Innocence, Sweet Adeline, Roberta, The Magnificent Obsession, Showboat, The Awful Truth, Invitation to Happiness, My Favorite Wife, Penny Serenade, Lady in a Jam, A Guy Named Joe, The White Cliffs, Together Again, Over 21, Anna and the King of Siam, Life with Father, I Remember Mama, Never A Dull Moment, The Mudlark, It Grows on Trees, Love Affair, Theodora Goes Wild.
TELEVISION: Schlitz Playhouse (host).

DUNNE, PHILIP: Writer, Producer, Director. b. New York, NY, Feb. 11, 1908. p. Finley P. and Margaret Abbott Dunne. e. Harvard U. m. Amanda Duff.
PICTURES INCLUDE: How Green Was My Valley, Stanley and Livingstone, The Rains Came, Johnnie Apollo, Son of Fury, Suez, Lancer Spy, The Last of the Mohicans, The Count of Monte Cristo, The Late George Apley, Forever Amber, The Ghost and Mrs. Muir, Escape, Luck of the Irish, Pinky, David and Bathsheba, Anne of the Indies, Lydia Bailey, Way of a Gaucho, Demetrius and the Gladiators, The Egyptian, Prince of Players, View from Pompey's Head, Hilda Crane, Three Brave Men, Ten North Frederick, In Love and War, Blue Denim, Wild In The Country, Lisa, Blindfold, The Agony and the Ecstasy.
PUBLICATIONS: Mr. Dooley Remembers, Atlantic-Little Brown. Take Two (McGraw Hill, 1980).

DUNNING, JOHN: Film editor. b. Los Angeles, CA, May 5, 1916. e. U. of California at L.A., A.B., 1939. With MGM since 1935; U.S. Armed Forces, 1942–45. Post prod.supervisor, MGM, Inc.
PICTURES INCLUDE: Cass Timberlane, Homecoming, Julia Misbehaves, Battleground, Show Boat, Take the High Ground, Rhapsody, Last Time I Saw Paris, Tender Trap, Interrupted Melody, The Swan, Brothers Karamozov, Raintree County, Cimarron, Ben-Hur (Academy Award).

DUNNOCK, MILDRED: Actress. b. Baltimore, MD, Jan. 25, 1906. e. Goucher Co., Baltimore. Teacher, Brearly Sch., N.Y.; acted in summer stock.
THEATRE: B'way debut: Life Begins; since in Corn Is Green; Richard III, Vicki, Lute Song, Another Part of the Forest, Death of a Salesman, Cat on a Hot Tin Roof, The Chinese, Colette.
PICTURES INCLUDE: Corn Is Green, Kiss of Death, I Want You, Death of a Salesman, Viva Zapata, Girl in White, The Jazz Singer, Bad for Each Other, Hansel & Gretel (voice), Children of Fortune, Trouble with Harry, Love Me Tender, Baby Doll, The Nun's Story, Story on Page One, Farewell Eugene, Butterfield 8, Sweet Bird of Youth, Seven Women, Barefoot in the Park, Whatever Happened to Aunt Alice?, Dragonfly, The Pick-Up Artist.
TELEVISION: The Power and the Glory, Death of a Salesman.

DUPONT, ADLEY: Actress. r.n. Adley Stoltz. b. New York, NY, Aug. 7, 1946. e. Geller Sch. of Theatre, Film Industry Workshop, Desilu Sch.
PICTURES INCLUDE: Movie Star, The Golden Poodle.

DURNING, CHARLES: Actor. b. Highland Falls, NY, Feb. 28, 1933. Many stage credits on Broadway (That Championship Season, The Happiness Cage, etc.).
PICTURES INCLUDE: Harry and Walter Go to New York, Twilight's Last Gleaming, The Choirboys, Breakheart Pass, The Hindenburg, Enemy of the People, The Sting, Dog Day Afternoon, The Fury, The Greek Tycoon, Tilt, The Muppet Movie, North Dallas Forty, Starting Over, When a Stranger Calls, The Final Countdown, True Confessions, Sharky's Machine, Tootsie, The Best Little Whorehouse in Texas, To Be or Not to Be, Two of a Kind, Stick, Mass Appeal, The Man with One Red Shoe, Big Trouble, Stand Alone, Happy New Year, Tough Guys, Where the River Runs Black, The Rosary Murders, A Tiger's Tail, Cop, Far North, Ballerina.
TELEVISION: Captains and the Kings, The Rivalry, The Dancing Bear, The Cop and the Kid (1975 series), Queen of the Stardust Ballroom, Studs Lonigan, Working, Mr. Roberts, Side by Side (pilot), P.O.P. (pilot), Eye to Eye, Death of a Salesman, Kenny Rogers as The Gambler III—The Legend Continues, The Man Who Broke 1000 Chains, Case Closed.

DURSTON, DAVID E.: Writer, Director. b. Newcastle, PA, Sept. 10, 1925. e. Evanston Township H.S. Served as TV-radio director, Lynn Baker Adv. Agency, 1952–57; assoc. producer, Your Hit Parade, 1957–58. Acting credits include Winged Victory (B'way, film), Young Man's Fancy (B'way); Radio includes The Woolworth Hour (prod.), CBS Workshop (writer), Tournament of Roses Parade (exec. prod., 1954 & 55).
PICTURES INCLUDE: Felicia, Love Statue, Reflections, Blue Sextet (also edited), I Drink Your Blood, Stigma.
TELEVISION: as writer: Tales of Tomorrow, Navy Log, Hart to Hart, Ladies Man, The New Adventures of Flipper (story editor).

DURWOOD, RICHARD M.: Executive. b. Kansas City, MO, Aug. 18, 1929. e. Brown U., A.B. Pres. Crown Cinema Corp. Member: Motion Picture Assn. of Kansas City (pres.); United Motion Pictures Assn. (pres. 1972–73); Young NATO (chm., 1968–69); National NATO bd., Past Chief Barker, Tent #8; exec. comm., National NATO.

DURWOOD, STANLEY H.: Chairman of the Board, American Multi-Cinema, Inc. b. 1921; e. Harvard Coll., B.S. (football, wrestling). Air Force navigator 3 years; six children. Member: Harvard Club of Kansas City; Harvard Club of New York;

Chamber of Commerce (board of directors); Downtown, Inc. (board of directors), United Motion Picture Assoc. of America, Variety Club International. On board of United Missouri Bankshares.

DUSSAULT, NANCY: Actress. b. Pensacola, FL, Jun. 30, 1936. e. Northwestern U. On Bdwy. in Street Scene, The Mikado, The Cradle Will Rock, Do Re Mi, Sound of Music, Carousel, Fiorello, The Gershwin Years, etc.
PICTURE: The In-Laws.
TELEVISION: The Beggars Opera, Good Morning America (hostess), Too Close for Comfort.

DUTFIELD, RAY: Executive. Early career as chief accountant in Hawker Siddeley Group. Ent. m.p. ind. 1957, as exec. accountant with Rank Film Laboratories, gen. man., 1967; Appt. to board of dir., 1969; Appt. man. dir., 1970. Appt. man. dir., Rank Leisure Services, 1976 and vice-chm., Rank Film Laboratories. 1979 January appt. chmn. and chief executive officer, Technicolor Limited, Fellow Member of Inst. Chartered Accounts, SMPTE, BKSTS, Member Institute of Directors, Institute of Marketing.

DUVALL, ROBERT: Actor. b. San Diego, CA, Jan. 5, 1931. Studied at the Neighborhood Playhouse, NY.
THEATER: A View From the Bridge (Obie Award, 1965); Wait Until Dark; American Buffalo.
PICTURES INCLUDE: To Kill a Mockingbird, Captain Newman, M.D., The Chase, Countdown, The Detective, Bullitt, True Grit, The Rain People, M*A*S*H, The Revolutionary, THX-1138, Lawman, The Godfather, Tomorrow, The Great Northfield, Minn. Raid, Joe Kidd, Lady Ice, Badge 373, The Outfit, The Conversation, Godfather, Part II, Breakout, The Killer Elite, 7% Solution, Network, The Eagle Has Landed, The Greatest, The Betsy, True Confessions, The Pursuit of D.B. Cooper, Tender Mercies (Acad. Award, 1984; co-prod.); Apocalypse Now, The Great Santini, The Stone Boy, The Natural, The Lightship, Let's Get Harry, Hotel Colonial, Colors, Orders, The White Crow, Convicts, Roots in a Parched Ground. Writer-Director: Angelo, My Love.
TELEVISION: The Outer Limits; Guilty or Not Guilty; Movies: Fame is the Name of the Game, Ike; Lonesome Dove.

DUVALL, SHELLEY: Actress. b. Houston, TX, 1949.
PICTURES INCLUDE: Brewster McCloud, McCabe and Mrs. Miller, Thieves Like Us, Nashville, Three Women, Annie Hall, The Shining, Popeye, Time Bandits, Roxanne.
TELEVISION: Bernice Bobs Her Hair, Producer: Faerie Tale Theatre, Tall Tales and Legends.

DYER, TONY: Actor. b. Feb. 8, 1919. e. U. of Missouri, Alvine Sch. of Theatre. Acting debut: Cotton Blossom Showboat and Arthur Casey-Mary Hart Repertoire.
PICTURES INCLUDE: To Please A Lady, Children of An Loc, Apocalypse Now, Up from the Lower Depths, Bushido Blade.
TELEVISION: Shogun.

DYSART, RICHARD A.: Actor. On Bdwy. in The Quare Fellow, Our Town, Six Characters in Search of an Author, A Man for All Seasons, The Little Foxes, A Place without Doors, That Championship Season, etc.
PICTURES: Petulia; The Lost Man; The Sporting Club; The Hospital; The Terminal Man; The Crazy World of Julius Vrooder; The Day of the Locust; The Hindenberg; Prophecy; Meteor; Being There; An Enemy of the People; The Thing; The Falcon and the Snowman; Mask; Warning Signs; Pale Rider; Wall Street.
TELEVISION: Movies: The Autobiography of Miss Jane Pittman; Blood and Orchids; First You Cry; Bogie; The Ordeal of Dr. Mudd; Churchill and the Generals; People Vs. Jean Harris; A Bitter Harvest; The Last Days of General Patton; The Seal; Missing Children—A Mother's Story; Concealed Enemies; Malice in Wonderland, Day One. Series: L.A. Law. Special: Jay Leno's Family Comedy Hour; Moving Target.

E

EASTWOOD, CLINT: Actor, Producer, Director. b. San Francisco, CA, May 31, 1930; e. Oakland Technical H.S., Los Angeles City Coll. Worked as a lumberjack in Oregon before being drafted into the Army. Starred in TV series Rawhide, 1958–65. Formed Malpaso Productions, 1969.
PICTURES INCLUDE: Revenge of the Creature (debut, 1955), Francis in the Navy, Lady Godiva, Tarantula, Never Say Goodbye, The First Traveling Saleslady, Star in the Dust, Escapade in Japan, Ambush at Cimarron Pass, Lafayette Escadrille, A Fistful of Dollars, For a Few Dollars More, The Witches, The Good The Bad and The Ugly, Hang 'Em High, Coogan's Bluff, Where Eagles Dare, Paint Your Wagon, Kelly's Heroes, Two Mules For Sister Sara, Beguiled, Play Misty For Me (dir. and star); Dirty Harry, Joe Kidd, Breezy (dir.); High Plains Drifter, Magnum Force, Thunderbolt &

Lightfoot; The Eiger Sanction (also dir.), The Outlaw Josey Wales (also dir.), The Enforcer, The Gauntlet (dir., star), Every Which Way But Loose, Escape from Alcatraz, Bronco Billy (dir., star), Any Which Way You Can, Firefox (prod., dir., star), Honky Tonk Man (prod., dir., star), Sudden Impact (prod., dir., star), Tightrope, City Heat, Pale Rider (dir., star), Heartbreak Ridge (prod., dir., star); The Dead Pool (prod., star), Bird (dir. only).

EBERSON, DREW: Architect, Stamford, CT. b. Hamilton, OH, Feb. 29, 1904. e. Northwestern Military and Naval Acad., U. of Pennsylvania. Architect U.S. and England. WB production, Burbank. In 1931–38: Director, Coronet Pictures. Then theatre architect practicing throughout U.S. in 1942: Colonel, Corps of Engineers.

EBSEN, BUDDY: Actor. r.n. Christian Ebsen, Jr. b. Belleville, IL, April 2, 1908. e. U. of Florida, Rollins Coll. Won first Broadway role as dancer in Ziegfeld's Whoopee in 1928. Sister, Vilma, became dancing partner and they played nightclubs and did road tours. Went to Hollywood and appeared in many musicals as single. Later became dramatic actor and appeared on TV.
PICTURES INCLUDE: Broadway Melody of 1936, Captain January, Banjo on My Knee, Four Girls in White, My Lucky Star, Thunder in God's Country, Red Garters, Davy Crockett, Attack, Breakfast at Tiffany's, Mail Order Bride, The One and Only Original Family Band.
TELEVISION: Hawaii Five-O, Gunsmoke, The Beverly Hillbillies, Davy Crockett, Barnaby Jones, Stone Fox. Movies: Fire on the Mountain, The Bastard, Tom Sawyer.
STAGE: Take Her, She's Mine, Our Town.

EBY, GEORGE W.: Executive. b. Pittsburgh, PA, Jan. 2, 1914. e. Carnegie Tech., Pennsylvania State U., B.A. 1934. pres., Ice Capades, Inc., 1963–78, chm., Jan. 1, 1979; Int. Chief Barker Variety Clubs, 1958–60. Retired, 1983.

ECCLES, TED: Executive. Began career with Modern Film Effects developing special effects & title sequences for feature films. At Paramount Pictures for year as admin., west coast audio visual services. Joined Walt Disney Pictures 1985 as dir. of creative film svcs.

ECKERT, JOHN M.: Producer, Production Executive. b. Chatham, Ontario, Canada, 1948. e. Ryerson Polytechnical Inst., 1968–71 (film major). 12 features as unit prod. mgr. or asst. dir. (including Sudden Fury, Second Wind, Rituals, Find the Lady). Member: DGA, DGC.
PICTURES INCLUDE: Power Play (assoc. prod.), Running (co-prod.), Middle Age Crazy (co-prod.), Dead Zone (unit prod. mgr.), Cats Eye (exec. in charge of prod.), Silver Bullet (assoc. prod.), Home Is Where the Heart Is (prod.), Millenium (suprv. prod.).
TELEVISION: Terry Fox Story (assoc. prod.), Special People (prod., Christopher Award), Danger Bay (series supv. prod., 1985–87).

EDDINGTON, PAUL: Actor. b. London, England, 1927. Since 1944 extensive career on stage. Ent. TV ind. 1955. Numerous television plays and series incl: Quartet, Blithe Spirit, Outside Edge, Murder at the Vicarage, The Adventures of Robin Hood, Fall of Eagles, The Rivals of Sherlock Holmes, Danger Man, The Prisoner, The Avengers, Van der Valk, Frontier, Special Branch, The Good Life, Yes, Minister, Yes, Prime Minister.

EDELE, DURAND (BUD) J.: Executive. e. St. Louis U., Washington U. Reportorial staff, St. Louis Globe Democrat, 1934–35; booking dept., Paramount, 1935; booker & salesman, Warner Bros., 1936–41; branch & dist. mgr., Film Classics, 1946; branch mgr., United Artists, 1952–60; managed various divisions, United Artists, 1960–63; gen. sales mgr., v.p., Avco Embassy Pictures Corp., 1964, gen. sales mgr., Venture Dist. Inc., 1976; Consultant, RCMC 1976–78.

EDEN, BARBARA: Actress. b. Tucson, AZ, Aug. 23, 1934. e. San Francisco Conservatory of Music. Pres. Mi-Bar Productions. Dir. Security National Bank of Chicago.
PICTURES: Back from Eternity, Twelve Hours to Kill, Flaming Star, Voyage to the Bottom of the Sea, Five Weeks in a Balloon, The Wonderful World of the Brothers Grimm, The Brass Bottle, Seven Faces of Dr. Lao, Harper Valley PTA.
TELEVISION: Series: How to Marry a Millionaire, I Dream of Jeannie, etc. Movies: The Feminist and the Fuzz, Guess Who's Sleeping in My Bed, The Stranger Within, Let's Switch, How to Break Up a Happy Divorce, A Howling in the Woods, I Dream of Jeannie: 15 Years Later, The Stepford Children, Happily Ever After.

EDWARDS, ANTHONY: Actor. b. Santa Barbara, CA, July 19, 1963. Grandmother designed Walt Disney Studios in the 1930s and worked for Cecil B. De Mille as conceptual artist. Acted in 30 plays from age 12 to 17. At 16 worked professionally in TV commercials. 1980 attended Royal Acad. of Arts, London. and studied drama at USC. Film debut: Fast Times at Ridgemont High (1982).

PICTURES: Heart Like a Wheel, Revenge of the Nerds, The Sure Thing, Gotcha, Top Gun, Summer Heat, Mr. North, Miracle Mile, Hawks, How I Got Into College.
TELEVISION: Series: It Takes Two. Movies: The Bill Johnson Story, The Killing of Randy Webster.

EDWARDS, BLAKE: Writer, Director, Producer. r.n. William Blake McEdwards. b. Tulsa, OK, July 26, 1922. m. actress Julie Andrews. e. Beverly Hills H.S. Coast Guard during war. Film acting debut, Ten Gentlemen from West Point (1942).
RADIO: Johnny Dollar, Line-up; writer-creator: Richard Diamond.
TELEVISION: creator: Dante's Inferno, Peter Gunn, Mr. Lucky.
PICTURES INCLUDE: Writer: Panhandle, Stampede, Sound Off, Bring Your Smile Along, All Ashore, Cruisin' Down the River, Rainbow Round My Shoulder, He Laughed Last, Drive a Crooked Road, My Sister Eileen, Mr. Cory, This Happy Feeling, The Perfect Furlough, Operation Mad Ball, Notorious Landlady. Director: Operation Petticoat, High Time, Breakfast at Tiffany's, Experiment in Terror, Days of Wine and Roses, Soldier in the Rain, The Pink Panther, Shot in the Dark, The Great Race, What Did You Do in the War, Daddy, Gunn, Darling Lili, The Party, The Wild Rovers, Carey Treatment, The Tamarind Seed (dir. s.p.) The Return of the Pink Panther (prod., dir., co-s.p.), The Pink Panther Strikes Again (prod., dir., co-s.p.), Revenge of the Pink Panther (prod., dir., co-s.p.); "10" (co-prod., dir., s.p.). S.O.B. (co-prod., dir., Victor/Victoria (co-prod., dir., s.p.); Trail of the Pink Panther (co-prod., dir., co-s.p.); The Man Who Loved Women (prod., dir., co-s.p.); Micki and Maude (dir.); A Fine Mess (dir., s.p.); That's Life (dir., co-s.p.); Blind Date (dir.); Sunset (dir., s.p.); Skin Deep, Changes.
TELEVISION: Justin Case (exec. prod., dir., writer).

EDWARDS, DOUGLAS: News Correspondent. b. Ada, OK, July 14, 1917. Became radio reporter in Troy, AL, at 15 yrs. e. U. of Alabama, Emory U., U. of Georgia. News reporter for WAGF, Dothan, AL; ass't. news editor for Atlanta Journal and its station, WSB. Transferred to WXYZ, Detroit, returning to WSB as ass't. news editor 2 yrs. later. Joined CBS Radio News staff, 1942, appearing on Report to the Nation, and The World Today. Chief of CBS News Paris Bureau. First major newsman to make transition to TV, 1947. Anchorman on CBS Afternoon News and Douglas Edwards with the News for 15 years on CBS-TV. CBS Mid-Day News with Douglas Edwards. Retired from CBS, 1988.

EDWARDS, JAMES H.: Executive. President, Storey Theatres, Inc. b. Cedartown, GA, Aug. 14, 1927. e. Georgia State. U.S. Navy, 1948–50. With Ga. Theatre Co., 1950–1952; Storey Theatres, 1952–present. Formerly pres. & chm., NATO of Ga; formerly pres., Variety Club of Atlanta. Former dir. at large, Nat'l. NATO. Director, numerous theatre cos.

EDWARDS, RALPH: Producer, Emcee. b. Merino, CO, June 13, 1913. e. U. of California, Berkeley. Began career in radio in 1929 as writer-actor-producer-announcer at station KROW, Oakland. Later joined CBS & NBC Radio in New York as announcer. 1940, originated, produced and emceed Truth or Consequences for both radio & TV. Also has produced and hosted This Is Your Life, The Ralph Edwards Show, Name That Tune, Cross Wits, The People's Court, This Is Your Life (special edition, 1987).

EDWARDS, VINCE: Actor. b. New York, NY, July 9, 1928. e. Ohio State U., U. of Hawaii, American Acad. of Dramatic Arts. N.Y. stage. High Button Shoes.
TELEVISION APPEARANCES INCLUDE: Studio One, Philco, Kraft, Ben Casey (series), The Untouchables, General Electric Theatre, Hitchcock, The Deputy. Movies: Firehouse, The Rhinemann Exchange, The Dirty Dozen: The Deadly Mission, The Return of Ben Casey.
PICTURES INCLUDE: Sailor Beware, Hiawatha, Rogue Cop, Night Holds Terror, Serenade, The Killing, Hit and Run, The Scavengers, The Three Faces of Eve, City of Fear, Murder by Contract, The Victors, Devil's Brigade, The Desperados, Las Vegas, Los Angeles, The Seduction, Space Raiders, Deal of the Century, Cellar Dweller.

EGGAR, SAMANTHA: Actress. b. London, Eng., March 5, 1939.
PICTURES INCLUDE: The Wild and the Willing, Dr. Crippen, Doctor in Distress, Psyche 59, The Collector, Walk Don't Run, Return From the Ashes, Doctor Dolittle, Molly Maguires, The Lady in the Car, Walking Stick, The Grove, Light at the Edge of the World, 7% Solution, Demonoid, Why Shoot the Teacher, Blood City, The Uncanny, Curtains, Loner.
TELEVISION INCLUDES: Anna and the King (series), Man of Destiny, Double Indemnity, The Hope Diamond, Columbo, Baretta, The Hemingway Play, Love Story, Kojak, McMillan & Wife, Streets of San Francisco, Starsky and Hutch, Love Among Thieves, Hart to Hart, Murder She Wrote, Finder of Lost Loves, George Burns Comedy Week.

EHRLICH, ROSEANNE: Executive. e. Sarah Lawrence Coll., B.A., English literature. Entered m.p. industry as freelance reader for Warner Bros., Avco Embassy and Robert Stigwood Organization. 1977–80, East Coast story editor for Lorimar Productions. 1981, joined Paramount Pictures as dir. of literary affairs. 1985, promoted to v.p., production, East Coast for M.P. Group.

EICHHORN, LISA: Actress. b. Reading, PA, 1952. Went to England for literature studies at Oxford. Studied at Royal Acad. of Dramatic Art. Made film debut in Yanks (1979).
PICTURES: The Europeans, Why Would I Lie?, Cutter and Bone, Opposing Force.
TELEVISION: Murder in Three Acts.

EIKENBERRY, JILL: Actress. b. New Haven, CT, Jan. 21, 1947. e. Yale U. Drama Sch. m. Michael Tucker.
THEATER: Broadway: All Over Town, Saints, Uncommon Women and Others, Watch on the Rhine, Onward Victoria, Porch, Life Under Water.
PICTURES: Between the Lines, The End of the World in Our Usual Bed in a Night Full of Rain, An Unmarried Woman, Butch and Sundance: The Early Days, Orphan Train, Rich Kids, Hide in Plain Sight, Arthur, Grace Quigley, The Manhattan Project.
TELEVISION: The Deadliest Season, Orphan Train, Swan Song, Uncommon Women and Others, Sessions, Kane & Abel, Assault and Matrimony, Family Sins, Incident on the Tile Mill Road. Series: L.A. Law.

EILBACHER, LISA: Actress. b. May 5, Saudi Arabia. Moved to California at age 7; acted on TV as child.
PICTURES: An Officer and a Gentleman, Ten to Midnight, Beverly Hills Cop, Deadly Intent, Leviathan, Never Say Die.
TELEVISION: Series: Wagon Train, Laredo, My Three Sons, Gunsmoke, Combat, Ryan's Four. Movies: The War Between Men and Women, The Patty Hearst Story, Love for Rent, To Race the Wind, This House Possessed, Deadly Deception. Mini-Series: The Winds of War.

EISNER, MICHAEL D.: Executive. b. Mt. Kisco, NY, March 7, 1942. e. Denison U., B.A. Started career with programming dept. of CBS TV network. Joined ABC in 1966 as mgr. talent and specials. Dec., 1968 became dir. of program development—east coast. In March, 1971 named v.p., daytime programming, ABC-TV. In June, 1975 made v.p., program planning and development. In May, 1976 named sr. v.p., prime time production and development, ABC Entertainment. In Nov., 1976, left ABC to join Paramount Pictures as pres. & chief operating officer. 1984, joined Walt Disney Prods. as chm. & CEO.

EKBERG, ANITA: Actress. b. Malmö, Sweden, Sept. 29, 1931. Started career as a model.
PICTURES INCLUDE: Man in the Vault, Blood Alley, Artists and Models, War and Peace, Back from Eternity, Zarak, Pickup Alley, Sheba and the Gladiator, Sign of the Gladiator, La Dolce Vita, Boccaccio '70, The Alphabet Murder, The Cobra, Fellini's Clowns, Federico Fellini's Intervista.

EKLAND, BRITT: Actress. b. Stockholm, Sweden, Sept. 29, 1942.
TELEVISION: England: A Cold Peace. U.S.A.: Trials of O'Brien, McCloud, Six Million Dollar Man.
PICTURES INCLUDE: After the Fox, Double Man, Bobo, Night They Raided Minsky's, At Any Price, Stiletto, Cannibals, Tintomara, Percy, Carter, Night, Endless Night, Baxter, Asylum, Wicker Man, Ultimate Thrill, Man With Golden Gun, Royal Flash, Slavers, King Solomon's Treasure, Fraternity Vacation, Moon in Scorpio, Scandal.

ELAM, JACK: Actor. b. Miami, AZ, Nov. 13, 1916. e. Santa Monica Jr. Coll., Modesto Jr. Coll. Worked in Los Angeles as bookkeeper and theatre mgr.; served in Navy in W.W.II. Introduction to show business was as bookkeeper for Sam Goldwyn. Later worked as controller for other film producers. Given first acting job by producer George Templeton in 1948; has since appeared in over 100 films.
PICTURES: Rawhide, Kansas City Confidential, The Moonlighter, Vera Cruz, Moonfleet, Kiss Me Deadly, Gunfight at OK Corral, Baby Face Nelson, Edge of Eternity, The Comancheros, The Rare Breed, The Way West, Firecreek, Once Upon a Time in the West, Support Your Local Sheriff, Rio Lobo, Support Your Local Gunfighter, Dirty Dingus Magee, The Cannonball Run, Cannonball Run II.
TELEVISION: The Texas Wheelers, The Dakotas, Temple Huston, Gunsmoke. Series: The Texas Wheelers, Struck by Lightning, Easy Street. Movies: Black Beauty, Once Upon a Texas Train, Where the Hell's the Gold!!!?.

ELEFANTE, TOM: Executive. Began career as usher at Loews Riviera in Coral Gables, FL; progressed through ranks to asst. mgr., mgr. & Florida division mgr. 1972, joined Wormetco Theatres as gen. mgr. 1975, returned to Loews Theatres as southeast div. mgr.; 1979, named natl. dir. of concessions, moving to h.o. in New York. 1987, appt. sr. v.p. & gen. mgr., Loews. Served as pres. and chm. of NATO of Florida.

ELFAND, MARTIN: Executive. b. Los Angeles, CA, 1937. Was talent agent for ten years with top agencies; joined Artists

Entertainment Complex in 1972. First film project as producer: Kansas City Bomber, first venture of AEC, of which he was snr. v.p. In 1977 joined Warner Bros. as production chief. 1980.
PICTURES: Prod.: Clara's Heart, It's My Turn, An Officer and a Gentleman, King David.

ELG, TAINA: Actress, Dancer. b. Helsinki, Finland, March 9, 1931. e. Helsinki, Sadler's Wells Ballet. Toured with Marquis de Cuevas Ballet; m.p. debut in The Prodigal.
PICTURES INCLUDE: The Prodigal, Diane, Gaby, Les Girls, Watusi, Imitation General, The 39 Steps.

ELIAS, HAL: Executive. b. Brooklyn, NY, Dec. 23. Publicity dir., State Theatre, Denver; western exploitation mgr., MGM; adv. dept., pub. dept., MGM, Culver City studios; Head, MGM cartoon studio (Tom and Jerry); UPA Pictures, Inc., vice-pres. studio mgr.: Hollywood Museum; bd. dir., Academy of Motion Picture Arts & Sciences, 35 years; treasurer, AMPAS 1976–1979. Academy Oscar, 1979, for dedicated and distinguished service to AMPAS.

ELIZONDO, HECTOR: Actor. b. New York, NY, Dec. 22, 1936. m. actress Carolee Campbell. Studied with Ballet Arts Co. of Carnegie Hall and Actors Studio. Many stage credits in N.Y. and Boston.
STAGE: Island in Infinity, Madonna of the Orchard, Drums in the Night, The Prisoner of Second Avenue, Dance of Death, Steambath (Obie Award), The Great White Hope, Medal of Honor Rag, Sly Fox.
PICTURES INCLUDE: Pocket Money, Born to Win, Deadhead Miles, Stand Up and Be Counted, One Across, Two Down, The Taking of Pelham One Two Three, Report to the Commissioner, American Gigolo, The Flamingo Kid, Young Doctors in Love, Nothing in Common, Leviathan.
TELEVISION: Debut: The Wendie Barrie Show (1947), The Impatient Heart, Kojack, the Jackie Gleason Show, All in the Family. Series: Popi (1976); A.K.A. Pablo (also dir.), Freebie and the Bean; Foley Sq. Movies: Casablanca, Medal of Honor Rag, The Dain Curse, Courage, Honeyboy, Out of the Darkness, Death on a Day Pass, Natica Jackson, Addicted to His Love.

ELKINS, HILLARD: Producer. b. New York, NY, Oct. 18, 1929. e. New York U., B.A., 1951. Exec., William Morris Agy., 1949–51; exec. v.p., Gen. Artists Corp., 1952–53; pres., Hillard Elkins Mgmt., 1953–60; Elkins Prods. Intl. Corp., N.Y., 1960–71; Elkins Prods. Ltd., 1972–; Hillard Elkins Entertainment Corp., 1974–; Media Mix Prods., Inc., 1979–82.
Member: Academy of Motion Picture Arts & Sciences, Academy of TV Arts & Sciences, Dramatists Guild, League of New York Theatres, American Federation of TV & Radio Artists.
PICTURES: Alice's Restaurant; A New Leaf; Oh, Calcutta!; A Doll's House; Richard Pryor Live in Concert; Sellers on Sellers.
THEATRE: Come On Strong; Golden Boy; Oh, Calcutta!; The Rothschilds; A Doll's House; An Evening with Richard Nixon; Sizwe Banzi Is Dead, etc.
TELEVISION: The Importance of Being Earnest; The Deadly Game, Princess Daisy.

ELKINS, SAUL: Producer. b. New York, NY, June 22, 1907. e. City Coll. of New York, B.S., 1927. Radio writer, dir., prod. 1930–2; dir., prod. stock co. touring Latin America 1932–4; writer Fox Films, 20th Century-Fox; writer RKO, Columbia 1937–42; writer, dial-dir., dir. Warner Bros. 1943–7; prod. Warner Bros. since 1947. Member: AMPAS, Screen Writer's Guild. Exec. prod., Comprenetics, Inc. Dir., Pioneer Prods., 1982.
PICTURES INCLUDE: Younger Brothers, One Last Fling, Homicide, House Across the Street, Flaxy Martin, Barricade, Return of the Frontiersmen, This Side of the Law, Colt 45, Sugarfoot, Raton Pass, The Big Punch, Smart Girls Don't Talk, Embraceable You.

ELLIOTT, DENHOLM: C.B.E. Actor. b. London, Eng., May 31, 1922; e. Malvern Coll. Screen debut in Dear Mr. Proback, 1948; NY stage: Write Me A Murder, The Seagull, 1964.
PICTURES INCLUDE: The Sound Barrier, The Holly and the Ivy, The Ringer, The Cruel Sea, Heart of the Matter, They Who Dare, Man Who Loved Redheads, Lease of Life, Night My Number Came Up, Pacific Destiny, Scent of Mystery; Nothing But the Best, Station Six Sahara, King Rat, You Must Be Joking, The High Bright Sun, Alfie, Here We Go Round The Mulberry Bush, The Night They Raided Minskys, The Seagull, Too Late the Hero, The Rise and Rise of Michael Rimmer, A Doll's House, The Apprenticeship of Duddy Kravitz, Robin & Marian, To The Devil A Daughter, Russian Roulette, Voyage of the Damned, The Boys from Brazil, St. Jacques, Zulu Dawn, A Game for Vultures, Cuba, Illusions, Saint Jack, Bad Timing, Sunday Lovers, Marco Polo, Brimstone and Treacle, The Missionary, The Wicked Lady, Trading Places, The Razors Edge, A Private Function, A Room with a View, Defense of the Realm, Whoopee Boys, Maurice, September, Stealing Home, Return from the River Kwai, Indiana Jones and the Last Crusade.

TELEVISION: Bleak House, Marco Polo, Camille, Hotel du Lac, Mrs. Delafield Wants To Marry, A Child's Christmas in Wales, Noble House, Code Name: Kyril, The Bourne Identity.

ELLIOTT, LANG: Producer, Director. b. Los Angeles, CA, Oct. 18, 1949. Given first job in films by his uncle, the late actor William Elliott (known as Wild Bill Elliott). Worked as actor from early years; employed by, among others the McGowan Brothers. Turned to film production; co-founded distribution co., The International Picture Show Company, serving as exec. v.p. in chg. of financing, production & distribution. Under banner of TriStar Pictures, Inc. also finances productions. 1982, formed Lang Elliott Productions, Inc.
PICTURES: Produced Ride the Hot Wind, Where Time Began, The Farmer, The Billion Dollar Hobo, They Went That-a-Way & That-a-Way, The Prize Fighter. Produced and directed the Private Eyes.
TELEVISION: Experiment in Love (prod.), Boys Will Be Boys (writer).

ELLIOTT, RICHARD B.: Executive. b. San Francisco, CA, Oct. 20, 1952. e. Stanford U., M.B.A., 1983; U. of California, B.S., 1974. Worked for Price Waterhouse & Co. in Brussels, Belgium, as sr. tax acct., 1976–78; Touche Ross & Co. in Brussels, tax spvr., 1978–81; mgr. planning & special projects, Pay Cable and Home Entertainment Group of Columbia Pictures, 1983; dir. opns., Pay Cable & Home Entertainment Group, 1984; v.p., sls. planning, Marketing and Distribution Group, 1985.

ELLIOTT, SAM: Actor. b. Sacramento, CA, Aug. 9, 1944; m. actress Katharine Ross. e. U. of Oregon.
PICTURES: Debut as card player in Butch Cassidy and the Sundance Kid, The Games, Frogs, Molly and Lawless John, Lifeguard, The Legacy, Mask, Fatal Beauty, Shakedown, Road House.
TELEVISION: Movies: The Challenge, Assault on the Wayne, The Blue Knight, I Will Fight No More Forever, The Sacketts, Shadow Riders, A Death in California. The Blue Lightning, Houston: The Legend of Texas, The Quick and the Dead. Series: Mission: Impossible (1970–71), Once and Eagle, Aspen, The Yellow Rose.

ELLSWORTH, JAMES: Producer. b. Deltaville, VA, March 12, 1927. e. U. of California at L.A., 1949. Pro. baseball player.
TELEVISION SERIES: Champions of Sports.
PICTURES INCLUDE: Naked Fury, Marine, Life Story of Lt. General Lewis B. (Chesty) Fuller, Door to Door Maniac (Five Minutes to Live).

ELSON, NORMAN: Executive. b. New York, NY, July 5, 1907. e. U. of Maryland. Contact clerk for Columbia; accessory mgr. N.Y. Columbia Exchange; district mgr. film buyer & gen. mgr. Brandt Theatres; gen. mgr. Trans-Lux Theatre Circuit, then apptd. vice-pres. 1950. Guild Enterprises, Inc., circuit pres. operating 7 theatres in New York City.

ELWES, CARY: b. London, England, Oct. 26, 1962. e. Harrow. Studied for stage with Julie Bovasso at Sarah Lawrence, Bronxville, NY. Theatrical film debut, Another Country, 1984.
PICTURES: Oxford Blues, The Bride, Lady Jane, The Princess Bride.

ENDERS, ROBERT: Producer, Writer. Began in television, being responsible for 64 hrs. of live programming weekly for industry and govt. as pres. of Robert J. Enders, Inc. In 1961 turned to theatrical prod. and writing. 1973: formed Bowden Prods. with partner Glenda Jackson. Made countless award-winning documentaries for govt. and industry including Dept. of Defense, U.S. Air Force, Civil Defense, Ford Motor Co., etc.
PICTURES INCLUDE: A Thunder of Drums (prod.), The Maltese Bippy (prod.), How Do I Love Thee (prod.), Rowan and Martin at the Movies, Zig Zag (story), Voices (prod., s.p.), The Maids, (also s.p.), Hedda (prod.), Out of Season (exec. prod.), Conduct Unbecoming (s.p. and prod.), Nasty Habits (prod., s.p.), Stevie (prod., dir.), How to Score a Movie (dir., prod., s.p.), Seeing the Unseen (doc.), The Visit.
TELEVISION: The Best of the Post (prod. of series), Ben Franklin, High Noon (prod., special), Co-prod. of Acad. Award Show, 1968, The Princess and the Goblin (dir., writer, prod.), They Went That-Away (prod.), Strange Interlude (exec. prod., writer).

ENGEL, CHARLES F.: Executive. b. Los Angeles, CA, Aug. 30, 1937. e. Michigan State U., U. of California at L.A. Son of writer-producer Samuel G. Engel. Pgm. devel., ABC-TV, 1964–68; v.p. Univ.-TV, 1972; sr. v.p., 1977; exec. v.p., 1980; pres., MCA Pay-TV New Programming, 1981.

ENGELBERG, MORT: Producer. b. Memphis, TN. e. U. of Illinois, U. of Missouri. Taught journalism; worked as reporter for UPI, AP. Worked for US government, including USIA, Peace Corps., Office of Economic Opportunity; President's Task Force on War on Poverty. Left government service in 1967 to become film unit publicist, working on three films in Europe:

Dirty Dozen, Far From the Madding Crowd, The Comedians. Returned to U.S.; appt. pub. mgr. for United Artists. Sent to Hollywood as asst. to Herb Jaffe, UA head of west coast production, which post he assumed when Jaffe left. Left to join with independent producer, Ray Stark.
PICTURES: Smokey and the Bandit, Hot Stuff, The Villain, The Hunter, Smokey and the Bandit II, Smokey and the Bandit III, Nobody's Perfekt, The Heavenly Kid, The Big Easy, Maid to Order, Dudes, Three For the Road, Russkies, Pass the Ammo, Trading Hearts, Fright Night II, Rented Lips, Remote Control.

ENGLANDER, MORRIS: Executive. e. Wharton Sch., U. of Pennsylvania. With General Cinema Corp. circuit before joining RKO Century Warner Theatres 1984 as exec. v.p., develp.; later co-vice chm. of circuit. 1986, sr. real estate advisor, American Multi-Cinema. 1988: v.p. real estate Hoyts Cinema Corp.

ENGLUND, GEORGE H.: Producer, Director. b. Washington, DC, June 22, 1926. Producer, Paramount, Pennebaker Prods.; prod., MGM; prod.-dir., Universal.
PICTURES INCLUDE: The World the Flesh and the Devil, The Ugly American, Signpost to Murder, Snow Job.
TELEVISION: The Vegas Strip War (exec. prod., dir., s.p.), A Christmas to Remember, Dixie: Changing Habits; Terrorist on Trial: The United States vs. Salim Ajami (exec. prod.).

ENGLUND, KEN: Writer. b. Chicago, IL, May 6, 1914. e. Lane Tech., Chicago. Started career as magazine writer; then vaudeville routines, comedy radio shows. Bdwy revues and musicals. Twice elec. pres. screen branch Writers Guild of America, West, then pres. of WGAW. Member national council.
TELEVISION SHOWS INCLUDE: Jackie Gleason Show, Dear Phoebe, Ray Milland Show, Loretta Young Show, several spectaculars. Prod.-writer CBS-TV staff 1957; Sonja Henie Spect. London, 1958; 20th Fox and Warner Bros. TV Films, My Three Sons; sev. teleplays, Bewitched, 1965, That Girl!, Dr. Joyce Brothers (head writer for series).
PICTURES INCLUDE: Big Broadcast of 1938, Artists and Models Abroad, Good Girls Go to Paris, Slightly Honorable, Doctor Takes a Wife, No No Nanette, This Thing Called Love, There's That Woman Again, Nothing But the Truth, Springtime in the Rockies, Sweet Rosie O'Grady, Here Comes the Waves, Secret Life of Walter Mitty, Androcles and the Lion, Good Sam, A Millionaire for Christy, The Caddy, Never Wave at a WAC, Vagabond King, The Wicked Dreams of Paula Schultz, Surviving the Savage Sea.
AUTHOR: Tour D'Amour, Larks in a Casserole; Co-author (with George Marshall) The Ghost in Emily's Trunk.

EPSTEIN, JULIUS J: Screenwriter. b. New York, NY, Aug. 22, 1909. e. Pennsylvania State U. Worked as publicist before going to Hollywood where began writing. Had long collaboration with twin brother, Philip G. Epstein. Under contract with Warner Bros. over 17 years.
PICTURES INCLUDE: Casablanca (AA), Arsenic and Old Lace, The Man Who Came to Dinner, Four Daughters, Saturday's Children, Mr. Skeffington, My Foolish Heart, Pete n' Tillie, Reuben, Reuben (and co-prod.).

EPSTEIN, MEL: Producer. b. Dayton, OH, Mar. 25, 1910; e. Ohio State U. Adv. & edit. depts. on newspapers; entered m.p. ind. as player in 1931; then asst. dir., unit prod. mgr., second unit & shorts dir.; U.S. Army Signal Corps (1st Lt.); apptd Para. prod., 1946. Now retired.
PICTURES INCLUDE: Whispering Smith, Hazard, Copper Canyon, Dear Brat, Branded, The Savage, Alaska Seas, Secret of the Incas.
TELEVISION: Broken Arrow, Men into Space, The Islanders, Asphalt Jungle, Rawhide, Long Hot Summer, The Monroes, Custer, Lancer (pilot); unit mgr. Lancer (series), Medical Center (series).

ERDMAN, RICHARD: Actor, Director. b. Enid, OK, June 1, 1925. e. Hollywood H.S.
PICTURES INCLUDE: Janie, Objective Burma, Time of Your Life, Four Days Leave, The Men, Cry Danger, Jumping Jacks, Happy Time, The Stooge, Stalag 17, The Power and the Prize, Saddle the Wind, Namu, The Killer Whale. Director: Bleep, The Brothers O'Toole.
TELEVISION: Ray Bolger Show, Perry Mason, Police Story, Tab Hunter Show, Alice, Bionic Woman, One Day at a Time, Playhouse of Stars, Twilight Zone, The Lucy Show, Lou Grant. Director: The Dick Van Dyke Show, Mooch (special).

ERICSON, JOHN: Actor. b. Dusseldorf, Germany, Sept. 25, 1926. e. American Acad. of Dramatic Arts. Appeared in summer stock; m.p. debut, Teresa, 1951, then Stalag 17 on Broadway.
PICTURES INCLUDE: Rhapsody, Student Prince, Green Fire, Bad Day at Black Rock, Return of Jack Slade, Pretty Boy Floyd, Bedknobs and Broomsticks.
TELEVISION: Honey West.

Erl-Eva

ERLICHT, LEWIS H.: Executive. b. New York, NY. e. Long Island U. Began career with ABC in 1962 with Television Spot Sales. Promoted to mgr. of research for spot sales in 1965 became sls. mgr., gen. sls. mgr. of WABC-TV, New York, from 1969 to 1974. Named v.p., gen. mgr. of WLS-TV, Chicago, in 1975. Moved to ABC Entertainment in 1977; named v.p., gen. mgr., in 1978; v.p., asst. to pres. in 1979. In 1980 made snr. v.p. & asst. to pres.; 1981, sr. v.p., prime time. Promoted to pres. of ABC Entertainment in June, 1983.

ERMAN, JOHN: Director. b. Chicago, IL, Aug. 3, 1935. e. U. of California. Debut as TV director, Stoney Burke, 1962.
TELEVISION: Green Eyes, Alexander the Other Side of Dawn, Child of Glass, Just Me and You, My Old Man, Roots: The Next Generation, Family, Moviola, The Letter, Eleanor First Lady of the World, Who Will Love My Children?, The Atlanta Child Murders, A Streetcar Named Desire, An Early Frost (also prod.); The Two Mrs. Grenvilles (also spvr. prod.), When the Time Comes, The Attic: The Hiding of Anne Frank (sprv. prod.-dir.), David (also spvr. prod.).
PICTURES: Making It, Ace Eli and Rodger of the Skies.

ESBIN, JERRY: Executive. Joined Paramount Pictures in 1975 as mgr. of branch operations; later named v.p., asst. sls. mgr. In 1980 named v.p., gen. sls. mgr. 1981, snr. v.p., domestic sls. & mktg. 1981, joined United Artists as snr. v.p., mktg. & dist.; 1982, named pres., MGM/UA m.p. dist. & mktg. div; 1983, sr. v.p., domestic dist., Tri-Star Pictures; 1985, promoted to exec. v.p.

ESMOND, CARL: Actor. b. Vienna, Austria, June 14, 1906. e. U. of Vienna. On stage Vienna, Berlin, London, etc. (Shakespeare, Shaw, German modern classics). Originated part of Prince Albert in Victoria Regina (London). On screen in Brit. prod. including Blossom Time, Even Song, Invitation to the Waltz. To U.S. in 1938. Guest star on many live and filmed TV shows.
PICTURES INCLUDE: Dawn Patrol, First Comes Courage, Address Unknown, Margin for Error, Master Race, Ministry of Fear, Story of Dr. Wassell. The Catman of Paris, Smash-up, Story of a Woman, Slave Girl, Walk a Crooked Mile, The Navy Comes Through, Sundown, Lover Come Back, This Love of Ours, Without Love, Mystery Submarine, The World in His Arms, Agent for H.A.R.M., Morituri.

ESSENFELD, BARRY: Executive. b. Bronx, NY, Feb. 16, 1936. e. De Witt Clinton H.S., New York U. Acct., American Broadcasting Company, 1957–62; division controller, International Paper Co., 1962–67; group controller & division exec., New England Industries, 1968–70; Controller & asst. secty., Allied Artists Pictures Corp., 1970–73; named asst. treas. & dir. admin., Sept. 1973; gen. sls. mgr. 1979. Allied Artists Industries, v.p., finance, 1980–.

ESSERT, GARY: Executive. b. Oakland, CA, Oct. 15, 1938. e. U. of California at L.A. Entered entertainment field through m.p. exhibition; managed theatres in San Francisco and Los Angeles; has created advertising art campaigns for major studios and main titles for feature films. Technical consultant for professional motion picture presentation installations; coordinated and supervised design and planning of U.C.L.A. Motion Picture Center—Melnitz Hall (1964–67). Technical coordinator for the American Film Institute's Center for Advanced Film Studies (1968–70) designing and outfitting complete facilities. Co-owned and operated a multi-media dance/concert hall in Hollywood known as The Kaleidoscope. Produced The Movies, a two-part, four-hour compilation documentary on the history of American motion pictures, telecast 1975. Founder (1971) and CEO for 13 years of the Los Angeles International Film Exposition (Filmex). Founder (1983) and current artistic director of the American Cinematheque in Hollywood.

ESSEX, DAVID: Actor, Singer. b. Plaistow, London, Eng. July 23, 1947. e. Shipman Sch., Custom House. Started as a singer-drummer in East London band. 1967: Joined touring Repertory Co. in The Fantasticks, Oh, Kay, etc. 1970: West End debut in Ten Years Hard, 1972: Jesus Christ in Godspell, 1978: Che in Evita; 1981: Lord Byron in Childe Byron, 1983/4: Fletcher Christian in own musical Mutiny! on album and stage. Phonogram recording artist. Variety Club of Great Britain show business personality of 1978. Many gold & silver disc intl. awards.
TELEVISION: appearances include: Top of the Pops, Own Specials, BBC series. Appearances on TV: France, Japan, Germany, Spain, Denmark, Australia.
PICTURES INCLUDE: Assault, All Coppers Are. . ., That'll Be the Day, Stardust, Silver Dream Racer.
U.S. TV: Merv Griffin, Johnny Carson, Dinah Shore, American Bandstand, Midnight Special, Grammy Awards, Salute To The Beatles, Don Kirshner's Rock Concert, A.M. America, Phil Everly in Session, Paul Ryan Show.

ESSEX, HARRY J.: Writer. b. New York, NY, Nov. 29, 1915. e. St. John's U., Brooklyn, B.A. With Dept. Welfare. Wrote orig. story, Man Made Monster, for Universal. During W.W.II in U.S.

Army Signal Corps; scenarist, training films on combat methods, censorship.
PICTURES: Boston Blackie and the Law (orig. s.p.), Dangerous Business, Desperate Bodyguard, He Walked by Night, Dragnet, Killer That Stalked New York, Wyoming Mail, The Fat Man, Undercover Girl, Las Vegas Story, Models, Inc., Kansas City Confidential, The 49th Man, It Came From Outer Space; I the Jury (dir., s.p.); Creature from the Black Lagoon; collab. s.p., story, Southwest Passage; adapt., Devil's Canyon; Mad at the World (dir., s.p.); Teen-age Crime Wave (collab. s.p.); Raw Edge; Lonely Man (story, s.p.); collab.: Sons of Katie Elder, Man and Boy; s.p. & dir. Octman, s.p., dir., prod. The Cremators, The Amigos (story and s.p.). Collaboration with Oscar Saul; Chrysalis, in collaboration with Ray Bradbury.
TELEVISION: Untouchables, The Racers, Alcoa Hour, Westinghouse, Desilu; story consultant and head writer: Target, The Corruptors, The Dick Powell Show, Bewitched, I Dream of Jeannie, Kraft Suspense Theatre, Hostage Flight.
NOVELIST: I Put My Right Foot In (Little Brown); Man and Boy, (Dell), 1971, Marina (Playboy Press), 1981.
PLAYS: Something for Nothing, Stronger Than Brass, Neighborhood Affair, One for the Dame, Fatty, Twilight, When the Bough Breaks, Dark Passion, Casa D'Amor.

ESTEVEZ, EMILIO: Actor. b. 1963. Oldest son of actor Martin Sheen; brother of actor Charlie Sheen.
PICTURES: Tex, The Outsiders, Repo Man, The Breakfast Club, That Was Then This is Now, (also s.p.), St. Elmo's Fire, Wisdom (also s.p., dir.), Stakeout, Young Guns.
TELEVISION: In the Custody of Strangers (movie).

ESTRADA, ERIK: Actor. r.n. Enrique Estrada. b. New York, NY, Mar. 16, 1949. Began professional career in Mayor John Lindsay's Cultural Program, performing in public parks. Joined American Musical Dramatic Acad. for training. Feature film debut in The Cross and the Switchblade (1970).
PICTURES: The New Centurions, Airport '75, Midway, Trackdown, Where Is Parsifal?, Lightblast, The Repentant, House of the Assassin, The Lost Idol.
TELEVISION: Series: CHiPS, guest roles on Hawaii Five-0, Six Million Dollar Man, Police Woman, Kojak, Medical Center, Hunter, Alfred Hitchcock Presents (1988). Movies: Fire!, Honeyboy, Grandpa, Will You Run With Me?, The Dirty Dozen: The Fatal Mission.

ETKES, RAPHAEL: Executive. b. Paris, France, May 6, 1930. Joined MCA in 1961; named v.p. of Universal Pictures in 1973. Appt. v.p. of MCA, Inc. in 1978; named sr. v.p., Universal Pictures, 1979; 1980, named prs. chief exec. off., AIP; 1981, joined United Artists as snr. v.p.—Worldwide Prod; 1983–85, pres., production, Embassy Pictures. Resigned April 1985.

ETTINGER, EDWIN D.: Publicist. b. New York, NY, 1921. Entered m.p. ind. as office boy, MGM; pub. rel. and publ. for industrial, comm. clients, 1944–52; joined Ettinger Co., pub. rel., 1952; pub. rel. dir., Disneyland Inc., 1955; marketing dir., Disneyland, 1955–65; v.p., M.C.A. Enterprises, Inc., 1955.

ETTLINGER, JOHN A.: Producer, Director, Distributor. b. Chicago, IL, Oct. 14, 1924. e. Peddie Inst., Cheshire Acad. Signal Corps Photog. Center, 1942–45; with Paramount Theatres Corp., 1945–47; dir., KTLA, Paramount TV Prod., Inc., Los Angeles, 1948–50; radio-TV dir., Nat. C. Goldstone Agency, 1950–53; pres. Medallion TV Enterprises, Inc.; TV prod., View the Clue, Greenwich Village, High Road to Danger, Sur Demande, Star Route, Las Vegas Fights, Celebrity Billiards; Pres., KUDO-FM, Las Vegas.

EVANS, ANDREW C.: Executive. Joined Paramount Pictures 1977 as dir. of financial reporting. Named v.p., corporate controller, 1980; sr. v.p., 1984. Same year named exec. v.p., finance, for Motion Picture Group of co. 1985, promoted to sr. v.p., finance.

EVANS, BARRY: Actor, Director. b. Guildford, England, 1943. Trained Central School. Repertory: Barrow, Nottingham, Chester, Royal Court, Nat. Theatre, Hampstead Th. Club, Chips with Everything, London and B'way. Young Vic. Theatre Clwyd Mold.
TELEVISION: Redcap, Undermined, The Baron, The Class, Armchair Theatre, Love Story, Doctor at Large, Short Story, Crossroads, Mind Your Language, Dick Emery Show.
PICTURES INCLUDE: The White Bus, Here We Go 'Round the Mulberry Bush, Alfred the Great, Die Screaming, Marianne, The Adventures of a Taxi-Driver, Under the Doctor.

EVANS, GENE: Actor. b. Holbrook, AR, July 11, 1924. e. Colton H.S. Started career in summer stock, Penthouse Theatre, Altadena, CA. Screen debut: Under Colorado Skies, 1947.
PICTURES INCLUDE: Crisscross, Larceny, Berlin Express, Assigned to Danger, Mother Was a Freshman, Sugarfoot, Armored Car Robbery, Steel Helmet, I Was an American Spy, Force of Arms, Jet Pilot, Fixed Bayonets, Mutiny, Park Row, Thunderbirds, Donovan's Brain, Golden Blade, Hell and High Water, Long Wait, Cattle Queen of Montana, Wyoming Renegades, Crashout, Helen Morgan Story, Bravados, Sad

97

Sack, The Hangman, Operation Petticoat, Support Your Local Sheriff, War Wagon, Nevada Smith, Young and Wild, Ballad of Cable Hogue, There Was a Crooked Man, Support Your Local Gunfighter, Camper John, Walking Tall, People Toys, Pat Garrett and Billy the Kid, Magic of Lassie, Blame It on the Night.

TELEVISION: Matt Helm (series), Spencer's Pilots (series); Kate Bliss & Ticker Tape Kid, Fire, The Sacketts, Shadow Riders, Travis McGee, The Alamo: 13 Days to Glory, Once Upon a Texas Train.

EVANS, LINDA: Actress. b. Hartford, CT, Nov. 18, 1942. e. Hollywood H.S., L.A. TV commercials led to contract with MGM and film debut in Twilight of Honor, 1963.

PICTURES: The Klansman, Avalanche Express, Tom Horn.

TELEVISION: Series: The Big Valley, The Hunter, The Love Boat, Dynasty. Movies: Nowhere to Run, Standing Tall, Gambler II, The Alice Marble Story (also prod.). Mini-Series: Bare Essence, North & South Book II, The Last Frontier.

EVANS, MAURICE: Actor. b. Dorchester, Eng., June 3, 1901. On the stage since 1926.

THEATRE: London theatrical career included Justice, Loyalties, Diversion, Journey's End, The Man I Killed, The Queen Bee, The Swan, See Ourselves, The Heart Line and starred for one season at the Old Vic; to U.S. 1935 and appeared in Romeo and Juliet, St. Helena, Henry II, Hamlet (Entirety), Henry IV (Part I), Twelfth Night, Macbeth, 1942; after War returned to Broadway, 1945 and appeared in G.I., Hamlet, Man and Superman, The Devil's Disciple, The Wild Duck, Dial 'M' For Murder, The Apple Cart, Heartbreak House, Tenderloin, The Aspern Papers, Shakespeare Revisited, A Program for Two Players. Producer: Teahouse of the August Moon, No Time for Sergeants, N.Y. stage.

PICTURES INCLUDE: Kind Lady, Androcles and the Lion, Gilbert and Sullivan, Macbeth, Warlord, Planet of the Apes, Rosemary's Baby, The Body Stealers.

TELEVISION: Hamlet, Richard II, Macbeth, Devil's Disciple, Taming of the Shrew, Man and Superman, The Tempest, St. Joan, series of 7 plays for Hallmark, NBC; G.E. Theatre (Caesar and Cleopatra), Theatre Guild, Bewitched (series).

EVANS, RAY: Songwriter. b. Salamanca, NY, Feb. 4, 1915. e. Wharton Sch. of U. of Pennsylvania. Musician on cruise ships, radio writer spec. material. Hellzapoppin', Sons o' Fun.

SONGS INCLUDE: To Each His Own, Golden Earrings, Buttons and Bows (Academy Award, 1948), Mona Lisa (Academy Award, 1950), Whatever Will Be Will Be (Academy Award, 1956), A Thousand Violins, I'll Always Love You, Dreamsville, Love Song from Houseboat, Tammy, Silver Bells, Dear Heart, Angel, Never Let Me Go, Almost in Your Arms, As I Love You, In the Arms of Love, Wish Me a Rainbow.

PICTURES INCLUDE: Paleface, Sorrowful Jones, Fancy Pants, My Friend Irma, Capt. Carey U.S.A., Off Limits, Here Come the Girls, Red Garters, Man Who Knew Too Much, Stars Are Singing, Tammy, Houseboat, Blue Angel, A Private's Affair, All Hands on Deck, Dear Heart, The Third Day, What Did You Do in the War Daddy?, This Property Is Condemned.

BROADWAY MUSICAL: Oh Captain! Let It Ride!, Sugar Babies.

TELEVISION THEMES: Bonanza, Mr. Ed, Mr. Lucky, To Rome With Love.

EVANS, ROBERT: Producer. b. New York, NY, June 29, 1930. Made appearance on radio as actor at age 11; went on to appear in more than 300 radio programs on major networks. Also appeared on TV in its early days. At 20 joined brother, Charles, and Joseph Picone, as partner in women's clothing firm of Evan-Picone, Inc. In 1957 signed by Universal to play Irving Thalberg in The Man of a Thousand Faces after recommendation by Norma Shearer, Thalberg's widow. Signed as independent producer by 20th Century-Fox. In August, 1966, joined Paramount Pictures as head of prod., a post he held ten years. Resigned to become indep. prod. again; has exclusive contract with Paramount.

PICTURES INCLUDE: Actor: The Sun Also Rises, The Fiend Who Walked the West, The Best of Everything. Independent Producer: Chinatown, Marathon Man, Black Sunday, Players, Urban Cowboy, Popeye, The Cotton Club.

EVERETT, CHAD: Actor. r.n. Ray Canton. b. South Bend, IN, June 11, 1936. e. Wayne State U., Detroit. Signed by William T. Orr, head of TV prod. for Warner Bros. to 3-year contract. Appeared in many TV series as well as films. Next became contract player at MGM.

PICTURES INCLUDE: Claudelle Inglish, The Chapman Report, The Singing Nun, The Last Challenge, Made in Paris, Johnny Tiger, Return of the Gunfighter, The Impossible Years, Airplane II: The Sequel, Fever Pitch, Jigsaw.

TELEVISION: Hawaiian Eye, 77 Sunset Strip, Surfside Six, Lawman, Bronco, The Dakotas, The Lieutenant, Redigo, Route 66, Ironside, Medical Center, The Rousters.

EVERETT, RUPERT: Actor. b. Norfolk, England, 1959. e. Ampleforth Central School for Speech & Drama. Apprenticed with Glasgow's Citizen's Theatre. Originated role of Guy Bennett in Another Country on London stage in 1982 and made feature film debut in screen version in 1984.

PICTURES: Real Life, Dance with a Stranger, Duet for One, Chronicle of a Death Foretold, The Right Hand Man, Hearts of Fire, Haunted Summer, The Gold-Rimmed Glasses, Jigsaw.

TELEVISION: Arthur, the King, The Far Pavilions, Princess Daisy.

EVERSON, WILLIAM K.: Writer. b. Yeovil, Eng., April 8, 1929. Pub. dir., Renown Pictures Corp., Ltd., London, 1944; film critic; m.p. journalist; in armed forces, 1947–49; thea. mgr., pub. & booking consultant, Monseigneur News Theatres, London, 1949; pub. dir., Allied Artists Inc. Corp., 1951; prod.; writer Paul Killiam Dorg., 1956. Writer-editor-researcher on TV series Movie Museum and Silents Please, also on TV specials and theatrical features Hollywood the Golden Years, The Valentino Legend, The Love Goddesses and The Great Director.

AUTHOR: Several books on movie history, including The Western, The Bad Guys, The American Movie, The Films of Laurel & Hardy, The Art of W. C. Fields, Hal Roach. The Detective in Film, Classics of the Horror Film, Claudette Colbert.

Lecturer, archival consultant, American Film Institute representative. Film History instructor at New York U., The New School and Sch. of Visual Arts, all in New York. Also, Harvard U.

EWELL, TOM: Actor. r.n. Yewell Tompkins. b. Owensboro, KY, April 29, 1909. e. U. of Wisconsin. Active in coll. dramatics; salesman at Macy's. NY stage debut: They Shall Not Die, 1934; thereafter many unsuccessful plays. U.S. Navy 1942–46.

THEATRE: Returned to stage in John Loves Mary; Small Wonder; on road in Stage Door, Tobacco Road, Roberta, Key Largo; on Broadway in Seven-Year Itch, Tunnel of Love.

PICTURES INCLUDE: Adam's Rib, Mr. Music, A Life of Her Own, American Guerilla in the Philippines, Up Front, Finders Keepers, Lost in Alaska, Willie & Joe Back at the Front, Seven-Year Itch, Lieutenant Wore Skirts, Girl Can't Help It, Tender Is the Night, State Fair, Suppose They Gave A War and Nobody Came?, To Find a Man, They Only Kill Their Masters, The Great Gatsby, Easy Money.

TELEVISION: The Tom Ewell Show; Baretta (series); Promise Him Anything; The Return of Mod Squad; Terror at Alcatraz.

F

FABRAY, NANETTE: Actress. b. San Diego, CA, Oct. 27, 1920. e. Los Angeles City Coll. d. Raoul Fabares and Lillian (McGovern) Fabares. m. Ranald MacDougall 1957, deceased 1973. First prof. stage appearance at age of three in vaudeville as Baby Nan. Leading lady in Charlie Chan radio series. Member of the cast, radio, Showboat. 1938, won two-year scholarship to Max Reinhardt school in Hollywood, and starred in his CA productions of The Miracle, Six Characters in Search of an Author, and Servant With Two Masters.

PICTURES INCLUDE: Elizabeth and Essex, A Child is Born, The Happy Ending, Cockeyed Cowboys, The Bandwagon, That's Entertainment II, Magic Carpet, Amy, Personal Exemptions.

TELEVISION: Own TV Series, Yes, Yes Nanette 1961–62. Two years on Caesar's Hour. One Day at a Time (series); George M!; High Button Shoes; Alice Through the Looking Glass; many specials.

BROADWAY SHOWS: Meet the People, By Jupiter, Jackpot, May Dear Public, Let's Face It, Bloomer Girl, Arms and the Girl, High Button Shoes, Make a Wish, Love Life, Mr. President, No Hard Feelings, Yes-Yes-Yes Nanette! (one-woman show by Danny Daniels). .

AWARDS: Two Donaldson Awards for High Button Shoes and Love Life; Three Emmy Awards for Caesar's Hour as best comedienne, 1955, 1956, best supporting actress 1955; Woman of the Year, 1955, Radio and TV Editors of America; Hollywood Women's Press Club, 1960; Honorary Mayor of Pacific Palisades 1967–68; One of Ten Best Dressed Women in America, Fashion Academy Award, 1950. President's Distinguished Service Award, 1970; Eleanor Roosevelt Humanitarian Award; Public Service Award; Amer. Acad. of Otolaryngology, 1977; Woman of the Year, CA Museum, Science and Industry 1975; Award of Merit, Amer. Heart Assoc. 1975; Screen Actors Guild Humanitarian Award, 1986.

FABRIZI, ALDO: Actor. b. Rome, Italy, 1905. Stage actor to 1942.

PICTURES INCLUDE: Go Ahead, Passengers, Square of Rome, Open City, My Son, the Professor, To Live in Peace, Christmas at Camp 119, Emigrants, Welcome, Reverend, First Communion (Father's Dilemma), Flowers of St. Francis,

Mishappy Family, Thieves and Cops, Times Gone By, Lucky Five, Too Young for Love, Voice of Silence, Lucky Five, The Angel Wore Red, Three Bites of the Apple, Those Were the Days, We All Loved Each Other So Much.

FADIMAN, CLIFTON: Writer, Performer. b. Brooklyn, NY, May 15, 1904. e. Columbia U. Contributor to magazines since 1924. Asst. ed. Simon & Schuster, 1927–29, ed. 1929–35. Book ed. The New Yorker, 1933–43. Mc. on Information Please radio program 1938–48; TV, 1952; edit. com., Book of the Month Club, since 1944; Mc. This Is Show Business, TV; author, Party of One; Any Number Can Play; Enter Conversing; The Lifetime Reading Plan; editor, American Treasury, 50 years; m.c., Conversation, 1954; m.c., Quiz Kids, 1956; Metropolitan Opera Roving Reporter, 1955–60; m.c., Alumni Fun, 1964; bd. of editors, Encyclopaedia Britannica; Advisory Board, CRICKET: The Magazine for Children, Co-author, The Joys of Wine, 1975. Co-author, The Wine Buyers Guide, 1977; Co-author, Empty Pages: A Search for Writing Competence in School and Society, 1979; editor, World Treasury of Children's Literature, 1984–85; commentator, First Edition, 1983–84; editor, Little, Brown Book of Anecdotes, 1985; editor, The World of the Short Story, 1986.

FAIMAN, PETER: Director. b. Australia. Entered entertainment business through TV, involved early in production-direction of major variety series in Australia. Assoc. prod. of over 20 programs for The Paul Hogan Show and two Hogan specials filmed in England (1983). Developed Australia's most popular and longest-running national variety program, The Don Lane Show. Responsible for creative development of the TV Week Logie Awards on the Nine Network. For 4 years headed Special Projects Division of the Nine Network Australia. Resigned to establish own prod. co., Peter Faiman Prods. Pty Ltd. 1984. Made m.p. theatrical film debut as director of Crocodile Dundee.

FAIN, SAMMY: Composer. b. New York, NY, June 17, 1902. e. public and high schools. Self taught on piano. Commenced career in Tin Pan Alley as teenage staff pianist-composer for leading music publishers, then in vaudeville. Recording contract at Harmony Records (Columbia); featured solo performer on many New York radio stations. Joined ASCAP, 1926. Wrote first song hit, Let A Smile Be Your Umbrella. Lyrics by Irving Kahal, 1927.
 STAGE: Scores for Hellzapoppin', Son's of Fun, George White's Scandals, Ed Wynn's Boys & Girls Together, Flahooley, Christine & others.
 PICTURES INCLUDE: Scores & Songs—Big Pond, Young Man of Manhattan, Footlight Parade, Sweet Music, Harold Teen, New Faces of '37, Geo. White's Scandals, Call Me Mister, Alice in Wonderland, Peter Pan, Jazz Singer, Weekend at the Waldorf, Anchors Aweigh, Imitation of Life, Mardi Gras, Calamity Jane, April Love, Marjorie Morningstar, Certain Smile, Love Is a Many Splendored Thing, Tender Is the Night, Made in Paris, The Stepmother and many others.
 SONGS: Let a Smile Be Your Umbrella, Wedding Bells Are Breaking Up That Old Gang of Mine, When I Take My Sugar to Tea, You Brought a New Kind of Love to Me, Was That the Human Thing to Do, By A Waterfall, Are You Having Any Fun, I'm Late, I Can Dream Can't I, That Old Feeling, I'll Be Seeing You, Dear Hearts and Gentle People, April Love, A Certain Smile, A Very Precious Love, Tender Is the Night, Secret Love, Love Is a Many Splendored Thing, many others. Elected to Songwriters' Hall of Fame.
 CITATIONS: Oscar awards for Secret Love and Love is a Many Splendored Thing, plus eight Acad. Oscar nominations; International awards—Diploma Di Benemerenza most coveted honor by the Hall of Artists in Nice, France, and Augusto Messinesse Gold Award from Messina, Italy. Also two Laurel Awards.

FAIRBANKS, DOUGLAS, JR.: Actor, Producer, Business executive. b. New York, NY, Dec. 9, 1909. e. Pasadena (CA) Polytech. Sch.; Harvard Mil. Acad., Los Angeles; Bovee and Collegiate Sch., N.Y.; also Paris, London. son of late Douglas Fairbanks. Began as screen actor 1923 in Stephen Steps Out; thereafter in more than 75 pictures. Stage from 1927 in U.S., U.K. (Young Woodley, Saturday's Children, etc.); 1934 in Manchester, England (The Winding Journey), London (Moonlight in Silver), 1968–77 My Fair Lady, The Secretary Bird, Present Laughter (U.S.), The Pleasure of His Company (U.S., U.K., Ireland, Australia and Hong Kong), Out on a Limb, Sleuth (U.S.). Since sound in both British & U.S. prods.; formed own co. 1935, prod. & starring, The Amateur Gentleman, etc.; U.S. Navy, 1941; Silver Star Combat Legion of Merit; K.B.E., D.S.C., Legion of Honor, Croix de Guerre, etc. 1949. Entered TV film prod., 1952. Autobiography: The Salad Days (1988).
 PICTURES INCLUDE: (since sound) Dawn Patrol, Little Caesar, Outward Bound, Union Depot, Captured, Catherine the Great, Accused, The Prisoner of Zenda, Having Wonderful Time, Gunga Din, Morning Glory, Angels Over Broadway, The Corsican Brothers, The Exile, Sinbad the Sailor, That Lady in Ermine, Joy of Living, Fighting O'Flynn, State Secret;

prod.: Another Man's Poison, Chase Crooked Shadow, Ghost Story.
 TELEVISION: prod. Douglas Fairbanks Presents, The Rheingold Theatre; Movie: The Restless Heart.

FAIRBANKS, JERRY: Executive Producer. b. San Francisco, CA, Nov. 1, 1904. Cameraman, 1924–29; prod., shorts, Universal, 1929–34; prod., Popular Science, Unusual Occupations, Speaking of Animals Series, Para., 1935–49; Winner two Acad. Awards; set up film div., NBC, 1948; formed, NBC Newsreel, 1949; devel. Zoomar Lens and Multicam System; formed Jerry Fairbanks Prods., 1950.
 TELEVISION: Public Prosecutor (first film series for TV); other series: Silver Theatre, Front Page Detective, Jackson and Jill, Hollywood Theatre, Crusader Rabbit.
 PICTURES INCLUDE: The Last Wilderness, Down Liberty Road, With This Ring, Counterattack, Collision Course, Land of the Sea, Brink of Disaster, The Legend of Amaluk, North of the Yukon, Damage Report, The Boundless Seas.

FAIRCHILD, MORGAN: Actress. b. Dallas, TX, Feb. 3, 1950. e. Southern Methodist U.
 PICTURES: Bullet for Pretty Boy, The Seduction, Red-Headed Stranger, Campus Man, Sleeping Beauty, City Blue.
 TELEVISION: Search for Tomorrow, Murder in Music City, The Memory of Eva Ryker, Flamingo Road (series), Magnum P.I. (series), Honeyboy, Falcon Crest (series), The Dream Merchants, The Initiation of Sara, The Zany Adventures of Robin Hood, Time Bomb, North and South Book II, Paper Dolls, 79 Park Avenue, Deadly Illusion, Street of Dreams.

FAIRCHILD, WILLIAM: Director, Screenwriter, Playwright, Novelist. b. Cornwall, England, 1918. e. Royal Naval Coll., Dartmouth. Early career Royal Navy.
 PICTURES INCLUDE: Screenplays: Morning Departure, Outcast of the Islands, The Gift Horse, The Net, Newspaper Story, Malta Story, The Seekers, Passage Home, Value For Money, Star!, Embassy, Dir.: John and Julie, The Extra Day, The Horsemasters, The Silent Enemy.
 TELEVISION PLAYS INCLUDE: The Man with the Gun, No Man's Land, The Signal, Four Just Men, Some Other Love, Cunningham 5101, The Break, The Zoo Gang, Lady with a Past.
 STAGE: Sound of Murder, Breaking Point, Poor Horace, The Pay-Off, The Flight of the Bumble B.
 BOOKS: A Matter of Duty, The Swiss Arrangement, Astrology for Dogs, Astrology for Cats, Catsigns (U.S.), The Poppy Factory, No Man's Land (U.S.).

FALK, PETER: Actor. b. New York, NY, Sept. 16, 1927. e. Syracuse U.
 THEATRE: Off-Broadway: The Iceman Cometh, Comic Strip, Purple Dust, Bonds of Interest, The Lady's Not for Burning, Saint Joan, Diary of a Scoundrel. On Broadway: Saint Joan, The Passion of Josef D., The Prisoner of Second Avenue.
 TELEVISION: Studio One, Kraft Theatre, Alcoa Theatre, N.T.A. Play of the Week, Armstrong Circle Theatre, Omnibus, Robert Montgomery Presents, Brenner, Deadline, Kraft Mystery Theatre, Rendezvous, Sunday Showcase, The Untouchables, The Sacco—Vanzetti Story, Dick Powell Show (The Price of Tomatoes, Emmy Award, 1962), Danny Kaye Show, Edie Adams Show, Bob Hope Chrysler Hour, Columbo (series, 1971–77, Emmy Awards 1972, 1975, 1976).
 PICTURES INCLUDE: Wind Across the Everglades; The Bloody Brood; Pretty Boy Floyd; The Secret of the Purple Reef; Murder, Inc.; Pocketful of Miracles; The Pressure Point; The Balcony, Robin and the Seven Hoods; Mad, Mad, Mad World; Italiani Brava Gente; Penelope; Luv; Castle Keep; Anzio; Husbands; Machine Gun McCann; A Woman Under the Influence; Mikey and Nicky; Murder by Death; The Cheap Detective; Brinks' Job; The In-Laws; The Great Muppet Caper; All the Marbles; Big Trouble; Happy New Year; The Princess Bride; Vibes; Wings of Desire; Cookie.

FANTOZZI TONY: Theatrical Agent. b. New Britain, CT, May 1, 1933. William Morris Agency.

FARBER, BART: Executive. Joined United Artists Corp. in early 1960s when UA acquired ZIV TV Programs. Served as v.p. United Artists Television and United Artists Broadcasting. In 1971 named v.p. in charge of legal affairs of the cos. In January 1978, named snr. v.p., TV, video and special markets; indep. consultant, TV, Pay TV, home video. 1982, joined Cable Health Network as v.p., legal & business affairs; 1984, v.p., business & legal affairs, Lifetime Network; 1986, independent communications consultant.

FARENTINO, JAMES: b. Brooklyn, NY, Feb. 24, 1938. e. American Acad. of Dramatic Arts.
 THEATRE: Broadway: Night of the Iguana. A Streetcar Named Desire (revival, 1973).
 TELEVISION INCLUDES: Naked City, daytime soap operas, Laredo, Route 66, The Alfred Hitchcock Hour, Ben Casey, Twelve O'Clock High, Death of a Salesman, Sins,

Far-Fel

That Secret Sunday; Something So Right; The Cradle Will Fall; License to Kill; Blue Thunder; A Summer to Remember; Family Sins; The Red Spider; Who Gets the Friends?
PICTURES INCLUDE: The Pad (And How to Use It) (Golden Globe Award, 1966), The Ride of Hangman's Tree, Banning, Rosie!, The Story of a Woman, The Final Countdown, Dead and Buried, Her Alibi.

FARGO, JAMES: Director. b. Republic, WA, Aug. 14, 1938. e. U. of Washington (B.A.).
PICTURES INCLUDE: The Enforcer; Caravans; Every Which Way But Loose; Forced Vengeance; Born to Race; Voyage of the Rock Aliens; Riding the Edge.
TELEVISION: Tales of the Gold Monkey; Gus Brown and Midnight Brewster; The Last Electric Knight.

FARNSWORTH, RICHARD: Actor. b. Los Angeles, CA, Sept. 1, 1920. Active as stuntman for 40 years before turning to acting.
PICTURES: Comes a Horseman, Tom Horn, Resurrection, Ruckus, The Legend of the Lone Ranger, The Grey Fox, The Natural, Into the Night, Sylvester.
TELEVISION: Anne of Green Gables, Chase, Ghost Dancing, Wild Horses, Travis McGee.

FARR, FELICIA: Actress. b. Westchester, NY, Oct. 4, 1932. e. Pennsylvania State Coll. m. Jack Lemmon. Stage debut: Picnic (Players Ring Theatre).
PICTURES INCLUDE: Timetable, Jubal, Reprisal, First Texan, Last Wagon, 3:10 to Yuma, Hell Bent for Leather, Kiss Me Stupid, Kotch, Charley Varrick, That's Life!

FARR, JAMIE: Actor. r.n. Jameel Joseph Farah. b. Toledo, OH, July 1, 1934. e. Columbia Coll. Trained for stage at Pasadena Playhouse. Film debut in Blackboard Jungle, 1955. Nightclub comedy entertainer, 1975. Gained fame as Klinger in TV series, MASH.
PICTURES: Cannonball Run, Murder Can Hurt You, Return of the Rebels, Cannonball Run II, Scrooged, Run Till You Fall.
TELEVISION: Dear Phoebe, The Red Skelton Show, The Dick Van Dyke Show, The Danny Kaye Show, Chicago Teddy Bears, MASH (series reg.), After MASH (also dir. of both MASH series), The Love Boat, For Love or Money, The New Love American Style, Murder She Wrote.

FARRELL, CHARLES: Actor. b. Onset Bay, MA, Aug. 9, 1901. e. Boston U. Entered m.p. ind. in silent films. U.S. Navy, 1942–45; mayor of Palm Springs since 1947.
PICTURES INCLUDE: Seventh Heaven, Street Angel, Lucky Star, Sunny Side Up, Wild Girl, Big Shakedown, Moonlight Sonata, Just Around the Corner, Tailspin.
TELEVISION: My Little Margie; The Charles Farrell Show.

FARRELL, HENRY: Author of novels and screenplays
SCREENPLAYS INCLUDE: Whatever Happened to Baby Jane? Hush . . . Hush, Sweet Charlotte, and What's the Matter with Helen?
TELEVISION: How Awful About Allan, The House That Would Not Die.

FARREN, JACK: Producer, Writer. b. New York, NY. e. New York U., B.A. Theatre: prod., Take a Giant Step, Lorenzo 1967, Robert Anderson's You Know I Can't Hear You When the Water's Running; 1968, The Education of Hyman Kaplan.
PICTURES INCLUDE: Silent Night, Lonely Night; Fuzz.
TELEVISION: Goodson-Todman Productions; NBC, CBS.

FARROW, MIA: Actress. b. Los Angeles, CA, Feb. 9. 1945. d. of actress Maureen O'Sullivan and late dir. John Farrow. e. Marymount, Los Angeles, Cygnet House, London. Screen debut: Guns at Batasi (1964).
PICTURES INCLUDE: Guns at Batasi, A Dandy in Aspic, Rosemary's Baby, John and Mary, Secret Ceremony, See No Evil, The Public Eye, The Great Gatsby, Full Circle, A Wedding, Death on the Nile, Hurricane, A Midsummer Night's Sex Comedy, Zelig, Broadway Danny Rose, Supergirl, The Purple Rose of Cairo, Hannah and Her Sisters, Radio Days, September.
TELEVISION: Peyton Place (series), Johnny Belinda.
THEATRE: Debut: Importance of Being Earnest (Madison Ave. Playhouse, NY, 1963); Royal Shakespeare Co. (Twelfth Night, A Midsummer Night's Dream, Ivanov, Three Sisters, The Seagull, A Doll's House), Mary Rose (London). B'way debut: Romantic Comedy (1979).

FASS, M. MONROE: Theatre Broker. b. New York, NY, Feb. 26, 1901. e. City Coll. of New York, M.E., engineering. Firm: Fass & Wolper. Entered real estate business in 1925, making first deal with Marcus Loew for land on which Paradise Theatre, Bronx, NY, was built. Thereafter made theatre deals (sale or lease of land or building) in most major cities in the U.S. and in major shopping centers. Member: Real Estate Board of N.Y.: Natl. Institute of Real Estate Brokers, Natl. Assoc. of Real Estate Board; Amer. Society of Real Estate Appraisers, Natl. Assoc. of Theatre Owners.

FAWCETT, FARRAH: Actress. b. Corpus Christi, TX, Feb. 2, 1947. e. U. of Texas. Picked as one of the ten most beautiful girls while a freshman; went to Hollywood and signed by Screen Gems. Did films, TV shows, and made over 100 TV commercials. Off B'way debut: Extremities (1983).
PICTURES INCLUDE: Love Is a Funny Thing, Myra Breckinridge, Logan's Run, Somebody Killed Her Husband, Sunburn, Strictly Business, The Helper, Saturn III, Cannonball Run, Extremities, See You in the Morning, Candy Barr.
TELEVISION: Owen Marshall, Counselor at Law, The Six Million Dollar Man, Rockford Files, Charlie's Angels (regular). Movies: The Girl Who Came Gift-Wrapped, Murder on Flight 502, Murder in Texas, The Feminist and the Fuzz, The Burning Bed, Red Light Sting, Between Two Women, Nazi Hunter, Poor Little Rich Girl: The Barbara Hutton Story, Rock Mama.

FAY, PATRICK J.: Director, Producer. b. June 7. e. Carnegie Tech. Dumont TV Network, 10 years. Director of over 100 Army training films.
TELEVISION: Bishop Sheen, Broadway to Hollywood, Manhattan Spotlight, Life is Worth Living, Front Row Center, Ilona Massey Show, Alec Templeton Show, Maggi McNellis Show, Key to Missing Persons, Kids and Company; co-prod., dir., Confession; dir., TV film series, Confession; dir. IBM Industrials, IBM World Trade, Europe Industrial, The Big Picture.
AUTHOR: Melba, The Toast of Pithole, The Last Family Portrait in Oil, Coal Oil Johnny, French Kate, No Pardon in Heaven, An Ill Wind, Tighten Your G-String.
FILMS: Director for RCA, General Electric H.G. Peters Company, Bransby Films.

FEHR, RUDI: Executive. b. Berlin, Germany; m. Maris Wrixon actress. Started career with Tobis-Klangfilm, Berlin. Joined Warner Bros. editorial department, 1936. Became producer, 1952; promoted to executive, 1956; Post Production Exec. Warner Bros.; WB title changed to dir. of editorial & post-prod. operations. Now retired; is consultant to industry. Co-edited One From the Heart. Nominated for Oscar as co-editor of Prizzi's Honor.

FEINBERG, MILTON: Executive. b. Milwaukee, WI. e. U. of Minnesota, School of Bus. Admin. Salesman, 20th Century-Fox, Des Moines, 1942–44; branch mgr., National Screen Service, Des Moines, 1945–57; branch mgr., in Chicago, superv. Chicago, Milwaukee, Des Moines exchange territories, National Screen Service, 1958–65; gen. sales mgr., NSS, 1966; v.p. & gen. sls. mgr. 1967; May, 1974, sr. v.p., N.S.S.

FEINSTEIN, ALAN: Actor. b. New York, NY, Sept. 8.
TELEVISION: Series: Edge of Night, Love Of Life, Search for Tomorrow. Movies: The Other Side of Dawn, The Users, Visions, The Runaways, The Two Worlds of Jenny Logan, Masada, The Wedding, On Fire, Jigsaw John, Berrengers.
PICTURE: Looking for Mr. Goodbar.
STAGE: Malcolm, Zelda, A View from the Bridge, As Is, A Streetcar Named Desire.

FEITSHANS, BUZZ: Executive. Worked for 10 years at American-International as supvr. of prod., jobs including film editing and supervision of editing and dubbing. Bowed as producer on Dillinger (1973). In 1975 formed A-Team Productions with John Milius.
PICTURES: Big Wednesday (prod.), Hardcore (prod.), 1941 (prod.), Extreme Prejudice (exec. prod.). Conan the Barbarian, First Blood, Uncommon Valor, Rambo II, Red Dawn, Rambo III (prod.).

FELD, FRITZ: Actor. b. Berlin, Germany, Oct. 15, 1900. e. U. of Berlin; Max Reinhardt Sch. of Drama, Berlin. Actor, prod. asst. dir. for Reinhardt in Berlin 7 yrs.; on screen 1918 in The Golem, UFA. Since found variously assoc. U.S. m.p. prod., as writer, director, actor: has appeared in more than 410 pictures. 1971: nat'l bd. dir., Screen Actors Guild. 1968 chairman of the American National Theatre Comm., Southern California Chapter. 1976 chairman Hollywood Museum Project committee—Screen Actors Guild, 20th Century-Fox Film corp. staged A Tribute to Fritz Feld—60 Years in the Movies and the Los Angeles City named a theater in Brentwood the Fritz Feld Community Theatre. In April 1979, elected honorary Mayor of Brentwood by the Chamber of Commerce.
TELEVISION: Dangerous Assignment, Racket Squad, Mr. & Mrs. North, Jimmy Durante Show, Jack Paar, Thin Man, Chevy Show, Red Skelton, Milton Berle, Colonel Flack, Accused, Peter Gunn, General Electric Thea., Kraft Music Hall, Danny Thomas, Bachelor Father, Adventures in Paradise, Follow the Sun, The Donna Reed Show, Valentine Day, No Time for Sergeants, The Farmer's Daughter, The Bing Crosby Show, Batman, Lost in Space, The Man From U.N.C.L.E., Laredo, Please Don't Eat the Daisies, Girl From U.N.C.L.E., The Smothers Bros., The Wild, Wild, West, Bewitched, Donald O'Connor Show, The Beverly Hillbillies, Land of the Giants, Arnie, Love, American Style, The Merv

100

Griffin Show, The New Bill Cosby Show, The Julie Andrews Hour, Fire House, The Odd Couple, The Night Couple, The Night Stalker, Only with Married Men, The Mike Douglas Show, The Tonight Show, Tabitha, The Hardy Boys, Flying High, Over Easy, Hizzonner, General Hospital, Heidi, Supertrain, Love, Sidney, No Soap, Radio, Magnum P.I., Simon & Simon, Amazing Stories.
STAGE: The Miracle, Once More With Feeling, Would Be Gentleman, Midsummer Night's Dream, Arsenic and Old Lace, You Can't Take It With You.
PICTURES INCLUDE: Wives and Lovers, Promises, Promises, Who's Minding the Store?, Four for Texas, The Patsy, Harlow, Made in Paris, Three on a Couch, Way . . . Way Out, The Comic, Hello, Dolly!, The Computer Wore Tennis Shoes, The Phynx, Which Way to the Front? Herbie Rides Again, The Strongest Man in the World, Only With Married Men, Hoyt Axton's Country Western Rock 'Roll Show, The Sunshine Boys, Won Ton Ton, the Dog Who Saved Hollywood, Broadway Rose, Silent Movie, Pennsylvania Lynch, Freaky Friday, The World's Greatest Lover, Herbie Goes Bananas, History of the World, All the Marbles, The Last of the Great Survivors, A Fine Mess, Shell Game.

FELDMAN, COREY: Actor. b. Reseda, CA, July 16, 1971. Has been performing since the age of 4 in commercials, television and films.
PICTURES: The Fox and the Hound (voice); Friday the 13th—The Final Chapter; Friday the 13th—A New Beginning; The Goonies; Gremlins; Stand by Me; License to Drive; The 'Burbs.
TELEVISION: Series: The Bad News Bears (1979–80); Madame's Place.

FELDMAN, EDWARD S.: Producer. b. New York, NY, Sept. 5, 1929. e. Michigan State U. Trade press contact, newspaper and mag. contact, 20th Century Fox, 1950; dir. info. services, Dover Air Force Base. 1954–56; publicity coordinator, The World of Suzie Wong, Para., 1959; joined Embassy, dir. of publicity, 1969; vice pres. in chg., adv. & pub, Seven Arts Prods., 1962; v.p. exec. asst. to head prod. Warner-7 Arts Prods., 1967, pres., m.p. dept., Filmways, 1970; exec. prod., What's the Matter With Helen?, 1971, exec. prod. Fuzz, 1972, Save the Tiger, 1972; prod. The Other Side of the Mountain, 1974; prod. Two-Minute Warning, 1976; exec. prod. 21 Hours At Munich, 1976; prod., King, 1977. Formed Edward S. Feldman Co., 1978. Co-prod. The Last Married Couple in America; Six Pack (co. exec. prod.); Hot Dog. . .The Movie!; Witness, Explorers, The Golden Child, Wired.
TELEVISION: Exec. Prod.: Valentine, 300 Miles for Stephanie, Charles and Diana: A Royal Love Story, The Hitcher, Near Dark. Prod.: The Sender.

FELDMAN, PHIL: Producer. b. Boston, MA. Jan. 22, 1922. e. Harvard U., 1943; Georgetown U., 1946; Harvard Business Sch., 1947; Harvard Law Sch., 1949. First Lieutenant, U.S. Army, 1943–46. Owner, Wholesale and retail dry goods firm, 1946–49. Law practice, 1950–51. Legal counsel Famous Artists Corp. 1951–53. Assoc. Dir. of Business Affairs CBS, 1953; Dir. of Business Affairs CBS, 1954–57. V.P. Talent & Contract Properties CBS, 1957–60. Exec. v.p. Broadcast Management, 1960–62. Head Business Relations 20th-Century Fox, 1962. V.P. 7 Arts Assoc. Corp. 1962–66 Pres., Phil Feldman Prods., Inc., 1967. Pres., First Artists, 1969; 1980, joined Rastar Films as exec. v.p.
PICTURES INCLUDE: You're a Big Boy Now, The Wild Bunch, The Ballad of Cable Hogue, Blue Thunder (exec. p.).

FELL, NORMAN: Actor. b. Philadelphia, PA, March 24, 1924. e. Temple U. Studied acting with Stella Adler. Member, Actors Studio. Professional debut at Circle-in-the-Square Theatre in N.Y. in Bonds of Interest.
Summer Stock; appearances on TV; moved to Hollywood in 1958 to begin theatrical film career.
PICTURES INCLUDE: The Graduate, Pork Chop Hill, Oceans 11, Rat Race, Inherit the Wind, Bullitt, If It's Tuesday, This Must Be Belgium, Catch 22, The End.
TELEVISION: Over 150 live plays from New York and some 200 shows filmed in Hollywood. Series: Dan August, 87th Precinct, Joe and Mable, Tom Ewell Show, Needles and Pins, Three's Company, The Ropers, Matt Houston, Crazy Like a Fox, Simon and Simon. Mini-Series: Rich Man, Poor Man, Roots: The Next Generations. Movies: The Jessie Owens Story.

FELLINI, FEDERICO: Director. b. Rimini, Italy. Jan. 8, 1920. m. actress Giulietta Masina. e. U. Rome. Journalist 1937–39; writer of radio dramas 1939–42, also cartoonist, caricaturist; then m.p. writer, actor, s.p., dir.
PICTURES INCLUDE: Writer: Open City, Paisan, Ways of Love, Senza Pieta; director: Variety Lights, The White Sheik, I Vitelloni, The Matrimonial Agency (Love in the City), Il Bidone, The Wastrels, La Strada (Acad. Award, best foreign film, 1954); The Swindlers, La Dolce Vita, Boccaccio '70, "8½"(Acad. Award, foreign film), The Nights of Cabiria (Acad. Award, foreign film, 1957); Juliet of the Spirits, Spirits of the Dead, Fellini Satyricon, The Clowns, Fellini's Roma, Amar-

cord (Acad. Award, foreign film, 1975); Casanova, Orchestra Rehearsal, City of Women, And The Ship Sails On, Ginger and Fred, Federico Fellini's Intervista.

FELLMAN, DANIEL R.: Executive. b. Cleveland, OH, March 14, 1943. e. Rider Coll., B.S., 1964. Joined Paramount N.Y. 1964; later sales mgr. Washington DC, Dallas. Next branch mgr. Cleveland; then Chicago. In 1969 joined Loews Theatres as film buyer. In 1971 joined Cinema National Theatres, division of Carrols Development Corp., as v.p./chief film buyer. In 1973 named v.p./dir., Cinema National Theatres. 1977, pres., American Theatre Mgt. Joined Warner Bros. in 1978 as eastern sales mgr. 1979 named v.p. 1982, v.p., sls. mgr., WB. 1985, named v.p. & gen. sls. mgr.; senior v.p., gen sales mgr., 1987. President Variety Club Tent 35, 1977–78. 1986, board mem. and chm., Will Rogers Fund raising; member of board 1987 Will Rogers, bd. member and v.p. Motion Picture Pioneers; bd. member Streisand Center for Performing Arts.

FELLMAN, NAT D.: Executive. b. New York, NY, Feb. 19, 1910. Started as office boy, Warner Bros. Pictures, 1928; transferred to Warner Bros. Theatres, asst. to chief booker; handled pool, partnership operations; head buyer, booker for Ohio zone, 1941; asst. to chief film buyer in New York, 1943; apptd. chief film buyer, 1952; exec. asst. to v.p. and gen. mgr., Stanley Warner Theatres, 1962; acting gen. mgr., Stanley Warner Theatres, July, 1964; Stanley Warner Theatres, v.p. and gen. mgr., 1965; v.p., NGC Theatre Corp. and division mgr. Fox Eastern Theatres, 1968; v.p. National General Corp., and pres., National General Theatres, 1969; 1974, formed Exhibitor Relations Co., operations consultant; sold it and retired in 1982. Served as vice pres., Variety Clubs International and NATO, Chrm., presidents' advisory comm.

FENADY, ANDREW J.: Producer, Writer. b. Toledo, OH, Oct. 4, 1928. e. U. of Toledo, 1946–50. Radio-prod.-actor-writer.
PICTURES INCLUDE: Stakeout on Dope Street, The Young Captives, Ride Beyond Vengeance, Chisum, Terror in the Wax Museum, Arnold, The Man with Bogart's Face.
TELEVISION: The Rebel, Branded series, Hondo. Movies: The Woman Hunter, Voyage of the Yes, The Stranger, The Hanged Man, Sky Heist, Mayday 40,000 Ft., The Hostage Heart, Masterpiece of Murder, Who Is Julia?

FENNELLY, VINCENT M.: Producer. b. Brooklyn, July 6, 1920. e. Holy Cross, 1938–42. U.S. Navy, 1942–46; salesman, Monogram, Des Moines, 1947; entered prod. field, 1949; indep. prod. for Monogram, 1950; Ent. TV field, 1957; prod. Transwestern Films, Inc., Frontier Pictures, Silvermine Productions Co., Allied Artists; Malcolm Enterprises, Hilgarde Enter.
PICTURES INCLUDE: Kansas Territory, Wagons West, Fargo, Marksman, Star of Texas, Topeka, Texas Bad Man, Bitter Creek, The Desperado, Seven Angry Men, Dial Red O, Bobby Ware Is Missing, At Gunpoint, Crime in the Streets, Last of the Badmen.
TELEVISION: Four Star Films, Alcoa-Goodyear, Trackdown, Wanted Dead or Alive, David Niven Show, Richard Diamond, Stagecoach West, The Dick Powell Theatre, Target, The Corruptors, Rawhide; A Man Called Shenandoah.

FENNEMAN, GEORGE: M.C., Announcer. b. Peking, China, Nov. 10, 1919. e. San Francisco State U.
CREDITS INCLUDE: Groucho Marx Show, You Bet Your Life, M.C. Host: Surprise Package, Funny Funny Films, Talk About Pictures, On Campus, Donny & Marie, Spokesman for Home Savings of America/Savings of America.

FERRAZZA, CARL J.: Executive. b. Cleveland, OH, Aug. 29, 1920. e. Catholic U. of America, Washington, DC. Started career 1945: as asst. mgr. & mgr. for Loews Theatres. 1952, joined Cincinnati Theatre Co., first as mgr. for Keith's Theatre, Cincinnati, and after prom. dir. for circuit. 1963, field rep. for United Artists, covering midwest. 1968, UA prom. mgr., N.Y. 1975–83, dir. of field activities, MGM/UA; 1984, joined Orion Pictures Distributing Corp. as v.p. promotional and field activities.

FERRER, JOSE: Producer, Director, Actor. b. Santurce, Puerto Rico, Jan. 8, 1909. e. Princeton U. Director and actor, New York stage, prior to screen career.
THEATER: Let's Face It, Othello, Strange Fruit (prod., dir.), Stalag 17 (prod., dir.), Twentieth Century (1951), The Chase (prod., dir.), The Shrike (prod., dir., actor), Richard III, My Three Angels (dir.), The Dazzling Hour, The Girl Who Came to Supper, Man of La Mancha.
PICTURES INCLUDE: Joan of Arc, Whirlpool, Crisis, Cyrano de Bergerac, Anything Can Happen, Moulin Rouge, Miss Sadie Thompson, Caine Mutiny, Deep in My Heart, The Shrike, Cockleshell Heroes, Great Man, I Accuse, State Fair, Lawrence of Arabia, Stop Train 349 From Berlin, Enter Laughing, Voyage of the Damned, The Sentinel, The Swarm, Fedora, The Fifth Musketeer, The Big Brawl, A Midsummer Night's Sex Comedy, To Be or Not to Be, The Evil That Men Do, Dune.

TELEVISION: What Makes Sammy Run?, The Marcus-Nelson Murders, The Missing Are Deadly, The Art of Crime, Truman at Potsdam, The Rhinemann Exchange, Gideon's Trumpet, This Girl for Hire, Hitler's SS: Portrait in Evil, Samson and Delilah, Blood and Orchids, Newhart (series), Strange Interlude.

FERRER, MEL: Producer, Director, Actor. b. Elberon, NJ, Aug. 25, 1917. e. Princeton U. During coll. and early career spent summers at Cape Cod Playhouse, Dennis, MA; then writer in Mexico, authored juvenile book, Tito's Hats; later ed. Stephen Daye Press, VT. Left publishing upon reaching leading-man status at Dennis; first two Broadway appearances, dancing roles, You'll Never Know, Everywhere I Roam; others. Kind Lady, Cue For Passion; then to radio, serving apprenticeship in small towns; prod.-dir., NBC: dir. Land of the Free, The Hit Parade, and Hildegarde program. Entered m.p. ind., 1945, when signed by Columbia, dial. dir.: The Girl of the Limberlost; later, returned to Broadway, leading role, Strange Fruit; signed by David Selznick as producer-actor, on loan to John Ford as prod. asst. on The Fugitive; then to RKO for Vendetta. Acted in Lost Boundaries, Born to be Bad, Ondine on Bway., 1954.
PICTURES INCLUDE: The Secret Fury, The Brave Bulls, Rancho Notorious, Scaramouche, Lili, Knights of the Round Table, Saada, War and Peace, Paris Does Strange Things, The Vintage, The World, The Flesh, and the Devil, Blood and Roses, El Greco; prod. Wait Until Dark, "W."
TELEVISION: Falcon Crest (series). Movies: One Shoe Makes It Murder, Seduced, Outrages, Dream West, Peter the Great.

FETZER, JOHN E.: Executive. b. Decatur, IN, March 25, 1901. e. Purdue U., U. of Michigan, A.B., Andrews U. Hon LL.D., Western Michigan U. 1958. Chairman, owner Fetzer Broadcasting Co., Kalamazoo, MI; chmn., Detroit Baseball Club; pres., owner Fetzer Communications, Inc., Kalamazoo; chairman, dir., Cornhusker TV Corp.; Mem., former bd. dir., Amer. Nat'l Bank and Trust Co., former mem. Bd. of Trustees, Kalamazoo Coll. Radio research Europe, 1925; asst. dir., U.S. Censorship in charge of radio. 1944–46; served as war corr. in ETO, 1945; spl. assignment radio, TV, newspaper mission to Europe and Middle East, 1952. chmn., TV code review bd., NARTB, 1952–55. Pres., Pro Am Sports System, 1983; Member, bd., Domino's Pizza, 1983. Fellow, Royal Society of Arts, London; mem., Acad. of Polit. Science. Clubs: Park, Kalamazoo Country, Kalamazoo; Radio and Television Execs. Soc. (Assoc.); Broadcast Pioneers, N.Y.

FIEDLER, JOHN: Executive. Launched m.p. career with Technicolor as exec. in prod. svcs. in mktg. Joined Rastar as v.p., prod. devel. and asst. to Guy McElwaine, pres. & CEO. Joined Paramount as v.p. in prod.; then to Tri-Star Pictures in same post. Resigned to become exec. v.p., world-wide prod., at Columbia Pictures. 1987, left to become producer for Columbia.

FIELD, DAVID M.: Executive. b. Kansas City, MO. e. Princeton U. Worked as reporter on city desk at Hartford (CT) Courant. In 1968 with NBC News in N.Y. and Washington, DC. Entered film school at U. of Southern California (L.A.) after which joined Columbia Pictures as west coast story editor. In 1973 went to ABC-TV Network as mgr., movies of the week. 1975, moved to 20th-Fox as v.p., creative affairs. Joined United Artists in 1978; named snr. v.p.—west coast production. Left in 1980 to become 20th-Fox exec. v.p. in chg. of worldwide production 1983, resigned to enter independent production deal with 20th-Fox, Consultant, Tri-Star Pictures. Wrote and produced Amazing Grace and Chuck, 1987.

FIELD, SALLY: Actress. b. Pasadena, CA, Nov. 6, 1946. e. Actor's Studio 1973–75. Gained stardom as lead of TV series, Gidget, 1965, followed by The Flying Nun, 1967–68. Theatrical film debut in The Way West, 1967.
PICTURES INCLUDE: Stay Hungry, Smokey and the Bandit, Heroes, The End, Hooper, Norma Rae (Oscar), Beyond the Poseidon Adventure, Smokey and the Bandit II, Back Roads, Absence of Malice, Kiss Me Goodbye, Places in the heart (Oscar), Murphy's Romance (also exec. prod.), Surrender, Punchline, Steel Magnolias.
TELEVISION: Maybe I'll Come Home in the Spring, Marriage Year one, Home for the Holidays, Bridges, The Girl with Something Extra, Sybil (Emmy Award, 1977).

FIELD, SHIRLEY ANNE: Actress. b. London, 1938. Ent. films after repertory experience 1955. Under contract to Ealing-M.G.M. 1958.
THEATRE: The Lily White Boys, Kennedy's Children, Fire Wait Until Dark, The Life and Death of Marilyn Monroe, How the Other Half Loves.
PICTURES INCLUDE: Saturday Night and Sunday Morning, The Man in the Moon, War Lover, Lunch Hour, Kings of the Sun, Doctor in Clover, Alfie, Hell Is Empty, The Entertainer, The Damned, My Beautiful Laundrette.
TELEVISION: Risking It, Buccaneer.

FIELD, TED: Producer. e. U. of Chicago, Pomona Coll. Started career as one of owners of Field Enterprises of Chicago; transferred to west coast, concentrating on real estate. Founded Interscope Communications, diversified co., which develops and produces theatrical films, TV series and movies-of-the-week.
PICTURES: Revenge of the Nerds, Turk 182, Critical Condition, Outrageous Fortune, Three Men and a Baby, The Seventh Sign, Cocktail.
TELEVISION: The Father Clements Story (co-exec. prod.).

FIELD, VIRGINIA: Actress. r.n. Margaret Cynthia Field. b. London. e. England, Paris, Vienna. On N.Y. stage in Victoria Regina & others. On screen from 1934.
PICTURES INCLUDE: The Lady Is Willing, Little Lord Fauntleroy, Ladies in Love, Lloyds of London, Singapore Woman, Atlantic Convoy, The Crystal Ball, Christmas Eve, Repeat Performance, Ladies Man, Dial 1119, Weekend with Father, Veils of Bagdad.
THEATRE: The Doughgirls.

FIELDS, ALAN: Executive. Spent five years with Madison Square Garden before joining Paramount Pictures. Career there included various positions: v.p. for pay-TV and Home Video TV. Spent two years at studio lot in L.A. as part of network TV organization. 1981, named bd. director for Paramount Pictures (U.K.) in London, serving as liaison to United Intl. Pictures and Cinema Intl. Corp., serving on operating committees of both. 1985, appt. v.p., Entertainment & Communications Group of Gulf & Western Industries, Inc., parent co. of Paramount; C.O.O., exec. v.p. Madison Square Garden Corp.

FIELDS, FREDDIE: Executive. b. Ferndale, NY, July 12, 1923. Vice-pres., member of bd. of directors, MCA-TV, MCA Canada Ltd., MCA Corp.; mem., Pres. Club, Wash., D.C.; pres., Freddie Fields Associates Ltd.; 1960; Founder pres., chief exec. officer Creative Management Assoc. Ltd. Agency, Chicago, Las Vegas, Miami, Paris, Los Angeles, N.Y., London, Rome, 1961. Was exclusive agent of Henry Fonda, Phil Silvers, Judy Garland, Paul Newman, Peter Sellers, Barbra Streisand, Steve McQueen, Woody Allen, Robert Redford, Ryan O'Neal, Liza Minnelli and others. In 1975 sold interest in CMA (now International Creative Mgt.) but continued as consultant. Produced for Paramount Pictures. 1977: Looking for Mr. Goodbar. 1978: American Gigolo, Citizen's Band; 1981: Victory. In 1983 named pres. and COO, MGM Film Co. Resigned 1985 to become independent producer for MGM/UA. 1985: Fever Pitch. 1986: Poltergeist II, Crimes of the Heart, Millenium.

FINBERG, JACK GERALD: Writer technician. b. London, England. Asst. to exec. prod., story dept., British National Studios; Offic. shorthand writer, Royal Courts of Justice and Central Criminal court; hon. sec., Film Studios Club; personal asst. to Sam Spiegel; verbatim report, nuclear weapons, testing and disarmament conferences, UN; asst. prod., ABC TV; two feature writing credits; six major, 18 second feature film adaptations; Film/TV prod., Australia.

FINCH, JON: Actor. b. England, 1941. Came to acting via backstage activities, working for five years as company manager and director.
PICTURES: Vampire Lovers; Horror of Frankenstein; Sunday, Bloody Sunday; Macbeth; L'affaire Martine Desclos; Frenzy; Lady Caroline Lamb; The Final Programme; Diagnosis Murder; Une Femme Fidele; The Man of the Green Cross; Battleflag; El Mister; Death on the Nile; La Sabina; Gary Cooper Which Art in Heaven; Breaking Glass; Power Play; Doktor Faustus; Giro City; Plaza Real; Streets of Yesterday.
TELEVISION: (U.S.) The Martian Chronicles, Peter and Paul.

FINE, HARRY: Producer. e. St. Andrew's Coll. and Dublin U.
FILMS INCLUDE: Up The Junction, The Liquidator, The Penthouse, Long Days Dying, Vampire Lovers, Fright, Twins of Evil, Too Far to Go, Quadrophenia, McVicar, Journey to a Safe Place.
TELEVISION FILM SERIES: Sir Francis Drake, Man of The World, The Sentimental Agent.

FINESHRIBER, WILLIAM H., JR.: Executive. b. Davenport, IA, Nov. 4, 1909. e. Princeton U., B.A., 1931. Pub., CBS, 1931–34; mgr. Carnegie Hall, N.Y., 1934–37; script writer, dir., music comm., dir. of music dept., CBS, 1937–40; dir. of short wave programs, CBS, 1940–43; gen. mgr. CBS program dept. 1943–49; v.p. in charge of programs MBS, 1949–51; exec. v.p. & dir., MBS, 1951–53; v.p. & gen. mgr. of networks, NBC, 1953–54; v.p. in charge of Radio Network, NBC, 1955; v.p. Television Programs of America, 1956; director International operations, Screen Gems, 1957; v.p., Motion Picture Assoc. of America and Motion Picture Export Assoc. of America, 1960; bd. of dir., NARTB; exec. comm., bd. of dir., R.A.B.; v.p. Radio Pioneers.

FINKELMAN, KEN: Director.
PICTURES: Airplane II: The Sequel; Head Office.

FINKELSTEIN, HERMAN: Attorney. b. Torrington, CT, Jan. 9, 1903. e. Clark U., A.B.; Yale Law School, LL.B., member of CT, PA & NY, U.S. Sup. Ct. bar; honorary L.L.D., New England Coll. of Law. Director, ASCAP Nathan Burkan Memorial Competition; Mem.; American Law Institute; State Dept. Panel on intl. Copyright; U.S. National Commission for UNESCO 1957–62; Consultant to U.S. Delegation, Inter-Amer. Conf. of Copyright Exports, Wash., D.C., 1946; Mem. U.S. Delegation, Intergovernmental Conference on Universal Copyright Convention Geneva, 1952, Berne Convention-Stockholm Revision Conf. 1967, Paris Revision Conf. 1971, Communication Satellite Conf. 1973, past pres., Copyright Soc. U.S.A., past pres., Exec. Bureau, CISAC: past pres., SCRIBES.
AUTHOR: Numerous articles on copyright.

FINLAY, FRANK: Actor. b. Farnworth, Eng., Aug. 6, 1926. e. Studied acting at RADA. Appeared with Guildford Repertory Theatre Co. 1957. London stage debut: The Queen and the Welshman, 1957. Broadway debut, Epitaph for George Dillon, 1958. Extensive stage career, especially with the Royal Court, Chichester Fest., and National Theatre includes: Sergeant Musgrave's Dance; Chicken Soup with Barley; Roots; Platonov; Chips with Everything; Saint Joan; Hamlet; Othello (Iago to Olivier's Othello), Saturday, Sunday, Monday; Plunder; Watch It Come Down; Weapons of Happiness; Tribute to a Lady; Filumena, (and NY), Amadeus; Mutiny.
PICTURES: The Longest Day (1962); The Loneliness of the Long Distance Runner; Agent 8 3/4; Doctor in the Wilderness; Private Potter; The Comedy Man; Underworld Informers; A Study in Terror; Othello; The Jokers; The Shoes of the Fisherman; Inspector Clouseau; The Deadly Bees; Robbery; I'll Never Forget What's 'is Name; Twisted Nerve; Cromwell; The Molly Maguires; Assault; Gumshoe; Shaft in Africa; The Three Musketeers; The Four Musketeers; The Wild Geese; Murder by Decree; Enigma; The Ploughman's Lunch; 1919; Return of the Soldier; Lifeforce; The Return of the Musketeers.
TELEVISION: The Adventures of Don Quixote; The Thief of Baghad; Casanova; Julius Caesar; Les Miserables; This Happy Breed; The Lie; The Death of Adolph Hitler; Voltaire; The Merchant of Venice; 84 Charing Cross Road, Saturday, Sunday, Monday; Count Dracula; Aspects of Love; Sakharov; A Christmas Carol; Arch of Triumph.

FINNEY, ALBERT: Actor. b. Salford, England, May 9, 1936. Studied for stage at Royal Acad. Dramatic Art making his West End debut 1958 in The Party. Appeared at Stratford-on-Avon 1959 season playing title role in Coriolanus, etc. 1960; on West End stage in The Lily White Boys and Billy Liar; Luther; New York, 1963, Luther. National Theatre 1965; Much Ado About Nothing, Armstrong's Last Goodnight, Love for Love, Miss Julie, Black Comedy, A Flea in Her Ear; Broadway, Joe Egg; London Stage, Alpha Beta, Krapp's Last Tape, Cromwell, Chez Nous, Hamlet, Tamburlaine, Uncle Vanya, Present Laughter. National Theatre: The Country Wife, The Cherry Orchard, Macbeth, The Biko Inquest, Sergeant Mus-grave's Dance, (also dir.), Orphans.
PICTURES INCLUDE: The Entertainer, Saturday Night and Sunday Morning, Tom Jones, Night Must Fall, Two for the Road, Charlie Bubbles, (also dir.), Scrooge, Gumshoe, Alpha Beta, Murder on the Orient Express, Wolfen, Loophole, Looker, Shoot the Moon, Annie, The Dresser, Under the Volcano, Orphans, The Endless Game, Damnation Express.
TELEVISION: The Claverdon Road Job, The Miser, Pope John Paul II.

FINNEY, EDWARD: Producer. b. New York, NY, April 18, 1913. e. City Coll. of New York. Began as engineer, Western Electric. Then property man, Johnny Hines, C.C. Burr comedies. To MGM as press sheet ed.; sales promotion mgr., Pathe; asst. adv. dir. U.A; story ed. and adv. dir., Mon-Rep., prod. & adv. dir., Grand Natl.; then prod. Monogram, many westerns. In 1941 org. Edward Finney Prod. Discovered Tex Ritter and made his first 40 features. Prod. & dir. Silver Stallion, Code of the Redman, Queen of the Amazons, etc. Clubs: Masquers. ex. pres. Catholic Press Council, Board Member Permanent Charities, M.P. Acad. of Arts and Sciences Dramatic Guild; pres., Indep. M.P. Prod. Assn. Film chrm. Catholic Press Council.
PICTURES INCLUDE: Corregidor, Golden Stallion, Call of the Forest, Hi Diddle Diddle, Primitive Passion, Mormon Battalion, This Is Pippin (TV); Seven Wonders, Baron Munchausen, Enchanted Years, Buffalo Bill in Tomahawk Territory, Slash of the Knife, Gun Girls, Journey to Freedom, London After Dark, Dark Road, Halfway to Hell, The Pirate, Secret Tower, Barrels Away, Things That Make America Great, (TV); Spring Affair, Dragons Across Asia, The Mad-caps, The Happy Clown, The Great Dogtown Robbery.
TELEVISION: Pilots for Law and the People and the Circle Kids. Now preparing Small Crossing, Dog House Blues and The Italian.

FIRTH, PETER: Actor. b. Bradford, Yorkshire, Oct. 27, 1953. Selected to appear in local TV children's show where casting

director spotted him and got him role in series, The Flaxton Boys. Moved to London and worked in TV, first in children's show, later on dramas for BBC. Big break came in 1973 when signed for Equus at National Theatre, London, which role repeated for film.
PICTURES: Joseph Andrews, Aces High, Equus, When You Comin Back Red Ryder, Letter to Brezhnev, A State of Emergency, Born of Fire, The Tree of Hands, Prisoner of Rio.
STAGE: Equus, Romeo and Juliet, Spring Awakening.

FISCHOFF, RICHARD: Executive. 1977, joined Stanley Jaffe Productions as v.p. where he was assoc. prod. for Kramer vs Kramer and was involved in dev. and prod of Taps and Without a Trace; 1982, v.p. prod., Paramount where he supervised Jaffe-Lansing prods., Racing with the Moon, and Nate and Hays; 1984–86, pres., Carson Prods., assisted in dev. of The Big Chill; 1986–87, production pres., Jaffe-Lansing Prods., involved in prod. of Fatal Attraction and with dev. co.'s initial foray into TV; Nov. 1987, named senior v.p. prod., Tri-Star Pictures.
PICTURES: Kramer vs. Kramer (assoc. prod.); Desert Bloom (exec. prod.).
TELEVISION: Mistress.

FISHBURNE, LARRY: Actor. b. 1963. Made feature film debut at 12 as star of Cornbread, Earl and Me (1975).
PICTURES: Apocalypse Now, Willie and Phil, Death Wish II, Rumble Fish, The Cotton Club, The Band of the Hand, The Color Purple, Quicksilver, Gardens of Stone, School Daze.
TELEVISION: M*A*S*H, Trapper John, M.D., Spenser: For Hire, Pee-wee's Playhouse, Father Clements (movie). One Life to Live (series).

FISHER, AL: Executive. b. Brooklyn, NY. Entered m.p. industry as office boy, Fox Metropolitan Theatres; U.S. Army Provost Marshal General's Office, 1942–46; Universal Pictures, mgr., Park Avenue Theatre, N.Y. & Copley Plaza Theatre, Boston, 1946; Eagle Lion Film Co., mgr., Red Shoe's Bijou Theatre, N.Y., 1947; Stanley Kramer Prods., exploitation, Cyrano de Bergerac, 1951; press agent, 1951; prod., Bway show, Daphine, 1952; joined United Artists Corporation, 1952, named dir. of exploitation; now freelancing as producer's repr.

FISHER, CARRIE: b. Beverly Hills, CA, Oct. 21, 1956. e. London Central Sch. of Speech & Drama. Daughter of Debbie Rey-nolds and Eddie Fisher. On Broadway in the chorus of revival of Irene (1972) and Censored Scenes from King Kong.
PICTURES: Shampoo, Star Wars, Mr. Mike's Mondo Video, The Empire Strikes Back, The Blues Brothers, Under the Rainbow, Return of the Jedi, Garbo Talks, The Man with One Red Shoe, Hannah and Her Sisters, Appointment with Death, The Time Guardian, Amazon Women on the Moon, Loverboy, The 'Burbs, She's Back, Harry, This Is Sally.
TELEVISION: Laverne and Shirley (series); Come Back Little Sheba (1977), Leave Yesterday Behind, Classic Crea-tures: Return of the Jedi, Frankenstein, Tumblina (Faerie Tale Theater), Sunday Drive, George Burns Comedy Week, Paul Reiser: Out On a Whim.

FISHER, EDDIE: Singer. b. Philadelphia, PA, Aug. 10, 1928. Band, nightclub, hotel singer; discovered by Eddie Cantor, 1949; U.S. Army, 1951–53; many hit records include; Wish You Were Here, Lady of Spain; radio & TV shows, NBC.
PICTURES INCLUDE: Bundle of Joy, Butterfield 8, Nothing Lasts Forever.

FISHER, LUCY: Executive. b. Oct. 2, 1949. e. Harvard U., B.A. Story ed., Samuel Goldwyn Jr. Prods.; exec. story ed., MGM; exec. chg. creative affairs, MGM; v.p. creative affairs, 20th Century Fox; v.p. affairs, Fox. 1980, prod. v.p., Zoetrope Studios; 1981, v.p., sr. prod. exec., Warner Bros.; 1983, sr. v.p. prod., WB.

FISK, JACK: Director. b. Ipava, IL, Dec. 19, 1934. e. Cooper Union. m. Sissy Spacek. Career in films as designer turning to direction with Heart Beat (1980).
PICTURES: Director: Raggedy Man, Violets Are Blue.

FISZ, BENJAMIN: Producer. b. Warsaw, Poland, Nov. 4, 1922. Formed in assoc. Golden Era Films, 1954. Later Aqua Films Ltd., 1957 as ind. prod. for Rank Org. and formed S. Benjamin Fisz Prod. Ltd., 1963 formed Benton Film Prod. Ltd. in assoc. with Anthony Mann. 1967 Spitfire Prods. with Harry Saltzman. 1969 Benmar Prods. Incorporated into Scotia Investments Ltd. Formed Scotia Intl. under name group for dist. Dir., Scotia-Barber. 1970: Created studios complex, Spain Esterdios, Madrid. 1972: Formed Scotia Int. (Film Sales.) Jointly formed Scotia Deutschland and International Film Theatre Ltd. For Intl. Films Theatre Ltd. with Kenneth Rive. Formed Sintel Intl. Ltd. for worldwide dist., 1976. Formed London Leisure Centre and acquired Wembley Stadium Complex, 1983.
PICTURES INCLUDE: Capri, The Secret, Child in the House, Hell Drivers, Sea Fury, On the Fiddle, The Heroes of Telemark, The Battle of Britain, A Town Called Bastard, Aces High, A Nightingale Sang in Berkeley Square, Jigsaw Man.

Exec. in chg. prod.: Captain Apache, Bad Man's River, Pancho Villa, Royal Hunt of the Sun, Horror Express, Psychomania.

FITELSON, H. WILLIAM: Attorney, counsel to Fitelson, Lasky and Aslan, law firm, New York, specializing in the field of communications (publishing, motion pictures, theatre, television, radio); b. New York, NY, Jan. 21, 1905. e. Columbia U. (extension), New York Law School. Newspaper and editorial work, librarian and tutor New York Law School, Story Department Tiffany-Stahl Productions 1929, counsel Tiffany-Stahl Productions 1929–32, United States counsel to British and foreign motion picture and theatrical producers, counsel to The Theatre Guild and numerous members motion picture industry, theatre industry, newspaper and publishing, television and radio interests, managing director Theatre Guild Television and radio divisions, including U.S. Steel Hour. Non-legal consultant on communications projects to Allen & Co., and Columbia Pictures Industries.

FITZGERALD, GERALDINE: Actress. b. Dublin, Eire, Nov. 24, 1914. e. Dublin Art Sch. On stage Gate Theat., Dublin; then in number of Brit. screen prod. including Turn of the Tide, Mill on the Floss. On N.Y. stage in Heartbreak House. In U.S. screen prod. from 1939 Wuthering Heights. Founded Everyman Street Theatre with Brother Jonathan Ringkamp.
PICTURES: (U.S.) include Dark Victory, Till We Meet Again, Flight from Destiny, Gay Sisters, Ladies Courageous, Watch on the Rhine, Wilson, The Strange Affair of Uncle Harry, Three Strangers, Nobody Lives Forever, So Evil My Love, Obsessed, Ten North Frederick, The Pawnbroker, Rachel, Rachel, Believe in Me, The Last American Hero, Harry and Tonto, Echoes of a Summer, Arthur, Easy Money, Pope of Greenwich Village, Poltergeist II, Arthur 2: On the Rocks.
STAGE: Sons and Soldiers, Portrait in Black, The Doctor's Dilemma, King Lear, Hide and Seek, A Long Day's Journey Into Night, (1971), Ah, Wilderness, The Shadow Box, A Touch of the Poet, Songs of the Streets (one woman show), Mass Appeal (dir. only), The Lunch Girls (dir.).
TELEVISION: The Best of Everything, Dixie: Changing Habits, Kennedy, Street Songs, Do You Remember Love, Circle of Violence, Night of Courage.

FITZGERALD, PEGEEN: Commentator, executive. b. Norcatur, KS, Nov. 24, 1910. e. Coll. of St. Theresa, Winona, MN; Seton Hall U., LL.D. (hon). m. Ed Fitzgerald. Sales prom. adv. in retail field; magazine editor; originator (with husband) of husband and wife radio-TV conversation; radio-TV commentator, WOR, N.Y.; pres. Vivisection Investigation League; founder, Mercy Animal Clinic Special Fund, president Millennium Guild; co-author of Cast of Characters, author of Meatless Cooking pub. by Prentice-Hall.

FLAKS, STEPHEN: Executive. b. New York, NY, Jan. 1, 1941. e. City Coll. of New York, B.B.A. Early career as an investment banker & stock broker for various companies, including First Hanover, First Devonshire, 1962–69. Founded Flaks-Zaslow in 1969. Entered motion picture industry in 1974 in capacity of production financing. Established VideoVision, Inc., in 1978.

FLATTERY, THOMAS L.: Executive-Lawyer b. Detroit, MI, Nov. 14, 1922. e. U.S. Military Acad., West Point, B.S., 1944–47; U. of California at L.A., J.D., 1952–55; U. of Southern California, LL.M. 1955–65. Gen'l counsel and asst. sec'y, McCulloch Corp., CA, 1957–64; sec'y and corporate counsel, Technicolor, Inc., 1964–70; Vice President, Secretary & General Counsel, Amcord, Inc. (formerly American Cement Corporation) 1970–72; Vice President, Secretary & General Counsel, Schick Incorporated, 1972–75; counsel asst. secretary, C.F. Braun & Co., 1975–76; sr. vice pres., secretary & general counsel PCC Technical Industries, Inc. 1976–86; V.P. & gen counsel G & H Technology, Inc., 1986–87. General counsel and asst. secretary, 1988– present.

FLAXMAN, JOHN P.: Producer. b. New York, NY, March 3, 1934. e. Dartmouth U., B.A. 1956. 1st Lt. U.S. Army, 1956–58. Ent. m.p. industry in executive training program, Columbia Pictures Corp., 1958–63; exec. story consultant, Profiles in Courage, 1964–65; head of Eastern Literary Dept., Universal Pictures, 1965; writer's agent, William Morris Agency, 1966; partner with Harold Prince in Media Productions, Inc. 1967; pro. m.p. Something for Everyone. Founded Flaxman Film Corp., 1975 Prod. Jacob Two-Two Meets the Hooded Fang, 1976. President-Tricorn Productions 1977; pres. Filmworks Capital Corp., 1979–83; pres., Cine Communications, 1983–present. Producer Off-Broadway, Yours, Anne (1985).
TELEVISION: The Caine Mutiny Court-Martial (prod.).

FLEISCHER, RICHARD O.: Director. b. Brooklyn, NY, Dec. 8, 1916. e. Brown U., B.A.; Yale U., M.F.A. Stage dir.; joined RKO Pathe 1942.
PICTURES INCLUDE: Flicker Flashbacks (writer, prod.), This Is America (dir., writer), Design for Death (co-prod.), Child of Divorce, Banjo, So This Is New York, Bodyguard,

Follow Me Quietly, The Clay Pigeon, Narrow Margin, The Happy Time, Arena, 20,000 Leagues Under the Sea, Violent Saturday, Girl in the Red Velvet Swing, Bandido, Between Heaven and Hell, The Vikings, These Thousand Hills, Compulsion, Crack in the Mirror, The Big Gamble, Barabbas, Fantastic Voyage, Doctor Dolittle, Boston Strangler, Tora! Tora!, Ten Rillington Place, The Last Run, See No Evil, The New Centurions, Soylent Green, The Don Is Dead, The Spikes Gang, Mister Majestyk, Mandingo, The Incredible Sarah, Crossed Swords, Ashanti, The Jazz Singer, Tough Enough, Amityville 3-D, Conan the Destroyer, Red Sonja, Million Dollar Mystery.

FLEMING, JANET BLAIR: Executive. b. Ottawa, Canada, November 29, 1944. e. Carlton U., Ottawa, Canada, B.A. Secretary to Canada's Federal Minister of Transport 1967–72; 1973–77, asst. to Sandy Howard—business affairs; 1977, co-founder and v.p./sales & admin. of Producers Sales organization; 1981, named sr. v.p., admin.; 1982, sr. v.p., acquisitions; 1983, exec. v.p., Skouras Pictures; 1985 promoted to pres., intl. div.

FLEMING, RHONDA: Actress. r.n. Marilyn Lewis. b. Los Angeles, CA, Aug. 10, 1922. e. Beverly Hills H.S. p. Harold and Effie Graham Lewis, Screen debut: Spellbound (1945). L.A. Civic Light Opera in Kismet revival, 1976. Broadway debut in 1973: Revival of The Women.
PICTURES INCLUDE: Spiral Staircase, Adventure Island, Out of the Past; singing debut: A Connecticut Yankee in King Arthur's Court, The Last Outpost, Cry Danger, The Redhead and the Cowboy, The Great Lover, Crosswinds, Little Egypt, Hong Kong, Golden Hawk, Tropic Zone, Pony Express, Serpent of the Nile, Inferno, Those Redheads from Seattle, Jivaro, Yankee Pasha, Tennessee's Partner, While the City Sleeps, Killer Is Loose, Slightly Scarlet, Odongo, Queen of Babylon, Gunfight at the OK Corral, Buster Keaton Story, Gun Glory, Home Before Dark, Alias Jesse James, The Big Circus, The Crowded Sky, Instant Love, The American Wife, Won Ton Ton, The Dog Who Saved Hollywood, The Nude Bomb.
TELEVISION: Movie: The Last Hours Before Morning.

FLEMYNG, ROBERT: Actor. b. Liverpool, England, Jan. 3, 1912. e. Halleybury Coll. Stage debut: Rope, 1931. Screen debut; Head Over Heels, 1937.
PICTURES INCLUDE: Bond Street, The Guinea Pig, The Conspirators, The Blue Lamp, Blackmailed, The Magic Box, The Holly and the Ivy, Cast a Dark Shadow, Man Who Never Was, Funny Face, Let's Be Happy, Wisdom's Way, Blind Date, A Touch of Larceny, Radtus (Italian), The King's Breakfast, The Deadly Affair, The Spy with the Cold Nose, The Quiller Memorandum, Deathhead Avenger, Oh! What a Lovely War, Battle of Britain, Cause for Alarm, Young Winston, The Darwin Adventure, Travels with My Aunt, Golden Rendezvous, The Medusa Touch, The Four Feathers, The Thirty-Nine Steps, Paris By Night.
TELEVISION: appearances in England, U.S. inc.: Rainy Day, Playhouse 90, Wuthering Heights, Browning Version, After the Party, Boyd Q.C., They Made History, Somerset Maugham Show, Woman in White, The Datchet Diamonds, Probation Officer, Family Solicitor (series), Man of the World, Zero One, Compact, (serial), Day by the Sea, The Living Room, Hawks and Doves, Vanity Fair, The Inside Man, The Doctor's Dilemma, The Persuaders, Major Lavender, Public Eye, Florence Nightingale, Edward VIII, Spy Trap, The Venturers' Loyalties, The Avengers, Crown Court, Enemy at the Door, Rebecca, Edward and Mrs. Simpson, The Ladykiller, Professionals, Fame Is the Spur, Crown Court, Spider's Webb, Executive Suite, Small World.

FLETCHER, LOUISE: Actress. b. Birmingham, AL, 1934. e. North Carolina State U., B.S. Came to Hollywood at age 21; studied with Jeff Corey. Worked on TV shows (including Playhouse 90, Maverick). Gave up career to be housewife for 10 yrs.; returned to work in 1973.
PICTURES INCLUDE: Thieves Like Us, Russian Roulette, One Flew Over the Cuckoo's Nest (Acad. Award, 1975), Exorcist II: The Heretic, The Cheap Detective, Natural Enemies, The Lucky Star, Once Upon a Time in America, Brainstorm, Firestarter, Invaders from Mars, The Boy Who Could Fly, Flowers in the Attic, Two Moon Junction.
TELEVISION: Can Ellen Be Saved: A Summer to Remember, Second Serve, Thou Shalt Not Commit Adultery.

FLEXER, DAVID: Executive. b. Mt. Pleasant, TN, June 29, 1909. e. Wallace U. School, 1926; Vanderbilt U., 1930. m. Eleanor Handmacher, concert pianist. Was adv. rep. on national magazines, 1930–32; joined United Artists 1932–33 advertising exhib. 1933, head of Flexer Theatres, operating in Tenn. and Miss.; The Albany Corp.; Theatre Real Estate Corp.; v.p. Impossible pictures, Inc., producers of cartoons currently distrib. by Republic; constructed first drive-in theatres in Minneapolis, and St. Louis, 1947; pres., Flexer Theatres of Tenn., Inc., Flexer Theatres of Miss., Inc., The Albany Corp. Pres., Inflight Motion Pictures.

FLINN, JOHN C.: Publicist. b. Yonkers, NY, May 4, 1917. e. U. of California. p. late John C. Flinn, pioneer m.p. executive. In pub. dept. David O. Selznick, 1936–39; unit publicist, then head planner, Warner, 1936–46; joined Monogram as asst. to nat'l adv. & pub. head & pub. mgr. Aug. 5, 1946; apptd. nat'l dir. of pub. & adv. of Allied Artists Pictures Corp., March, 1951, appt'd studio dir. adv. & pub., Columbia, March, 1959; v.p., Jim Mahoney & Associates (pub. rel. firm) in 1971. Joined MGM West Coast publicity department as publicity coordinator, January, 1973; Rejoined Columbia Pictures in Feb., 1974 as studio pub. dir.; 1979, promoted to dir. industry relations. Joined MGM/UA pub. staff, 1988 to work on m.p. academy campaign for Moonstruck.

FLOREA, JOHN: Producer-Director. b. Alliance, OH, May 28, 1916. Served as photo journalist with Life magazine, 1940–50; assoc. editor Colliers magazine, 1950–53. Prod.-dir.
TELEVISION: Sea Hunt TV series, 1957–60; also dir. TV shows Bonanza, The Virginian, Honey West, Daktari, Gentle Ben, Cowboy in Africa. Prod.-dir. of film Islands of the Lost. With Ivon Tors Films. Nominated as one of the Top 10 directors in America by DGA for 1968 Mission Impossible episode. Dir. several Ironside episodes.
PICTURES INCLUDE: A Time to Every Purpose, The Astral Factor.

FLYNN, JOHN: Director-Writer. Began career as trainee script supvr. for dir. Robert Wise. Soon working as asst. dir. on MGM-TV shows. Made dir. debut with The Sergeant, 1969.
PICTURES INCLUDE: The Jerusalem File (dir.), The Outfit (s.p., dir.), Rolling Thunder (dir.), Defiance (dir.), Touched (dir.), Best Seller (dir.).

FOCH, NINA: Actress. b. Leyden, Holland, April 20, 1924; daughter of Consuelo Flowerton, actress, & Dirk Foch, symphony orch. conductor. Many stage, radio, television appearances. Prof., U. of Southern California, 1966–67; 1978–80, Adjunct professor, USC Cinema-TV grad. sch. 1986–; senior faculty, American Film Inst., 1974–77; Board of Governors, Hollywood Acad. of Television Arts & Sciences, 1976–77; Exec. Comm. Foreign Film Award, Acad. of Motion Picture Arts & Sciences, 1970–. Co-chmn., exec. comm. foreign language film award.
PICTURES INCLUDE: Nine Girls, Song to Remember, My Name is Julia Ross, An American in Paris, Scaramouche, Young Man in Hurry, Undercover Man, Sombrero, Fast Company, Executive Suite, Four Guns to the Border, Ten Commandments, Illegal, You're Never Too Young, Cry of the Werewolf, Escape in the Fog, I Love A Mystery, Johnny Allegro, Johnny O'Clock, Prison Ship, Return of the Vampire, Shadows In The Night, The Dark Past, The Guilt of Janet Ames, Three Brave Men, Spartacus, Cash McCall, Such Good Friends, Salty, Mahogany, Jennifer, Rich and Famous, Dixie Lanes.
TELEVISION: Trapper John, M.D.; Shadow Chasers.

FOGARTY, JACK V.: Executive, Producer, Writer. b. Los Angeles, CA. e. U. of California at L.A. Hd. travel dept., MGM, 1960–62; exec. prod. mgr., Cinerama, Inc., 1962–64; assoc. prod., The Best of Cinerama, 1963; est. own p.r. firm, 1965; pres., AstroScope, Inc., 1969–74. Partner, Sowards/Fogarty Prods.
TELEVISION: (writer) The Rookies, S.W.A.T., Charlie's Angels, Most Wanted, Barnaby Jones, A Man Called Sloane, Trapper John, T.J. Hooker, Crazy Like a Fox, The Equalizer, others. Story Editor, Charlie's Angels; exec. story consultant: Most Wanted, A Man Called Sloane, Sheriff Lobo, T.J. Hooker. Producer: T.J. Hooker. Co-prod.: Jessie.

FOGELSON, ANDREW: Executive. b. New Rochelle, NY, August 5, 1942. e. Union Coll., 1960–64. First entered m.p. industry in 1968 with Warner Bros., starting as copywriter and soon made exec. asst. to v.p. of adv.-pub. In 1973 appt. v.p., marketing services. Joined Columbia Pictures in Dec. 1973, as v.p. in chg. world-wide adv. In 1977 went to Warner Bros. as exec. v.p. in chg. worldwide adv.-pub. 1979 left to become pres. of Rastar Prods. Resigned 1981 to become indep. producer.
PICTURES: Wrong Is Right (exec. prod.), Blue Thunder (exec. prod.); Spring Break; Just One of the Guys.

FOLSEY, GEORGE: Cameraman. b. 1900. Began career in 1914. Joined Paramount's Astoria Studio, 1929; designed moveable camera. In 1933 moved to MGM. Amer. Society of Cinematographers Life Time Achievement Award, 1988.
PICTURES INCLUDE: Reunion in Vienna, Storm at Daybreak, Stage Mother, Going Hollywood, Men in White, Operator 13, Reckless, I Live My Life, The Great Ziegfeld, The Gorgeous Hussy, Hearts Divided, Meet Me in St. Louis, Mr. Imperium, Law and Lady, Lovely to Look At, Million Dollar Mermaid, All The Brothers Were Valiant, Executive Suite, Seven Brides for Seven Brothers, Deep in My Heart, The Cobweb, Fastest Gun Alive, House of Numbers, Imitation General, Cash McCall, Glass Houses, That's Entertainment.

FOLSEY, GEORGE, JR: Producer, Editor. b. Los Angeles, CA, Jan. 17, 1939. Son of cinematographer George Folsey Sr. e.

Pomona Coll., B.A., 1961.
PICTURES: Editor: Glass Houses (1973), Bone, Hammer, Black Caesar, Schlock, Trader Horn, Bucktown, J.D.'s Revenge, Norman...Is That You?, Tracks, The Chicken Chronicles, The Kentucky Fried Movie, Sourdough, National Lampoon's Animal House, Freedom Road, The Great Santini, The Blues Brothers. Producer: An American Werewolf in London, Twilight Zone—The Movie (assoc. Prod.); Trading Places (exec. prod.), Into the Night (co-prod.), Three Amigos, Coming to America (co-prod., co-editor).
VIDEO: Michael Jackson's Thriller (co-prod., editor).

FONDA, JANE: Actress. b. New York, NY, Dec. 21, 1937. e. Emma Willard Sch., Troy, NY. active in dramatics, Vassar. Father, late actor Henry Fonda. Husband Tom Hayden. Appeared with father summer stock production, The Country Girl, Omaha, NB. Studied painting, languages, Paris. Art Students League, N.Y. Appeared in The Male Animal, Dennis, MA. Modeled, appeared on covers, Esquire, Vogue, The Ladies Home Journal, Glamour, and McCall's, 1959.
PICTURES INCLUDE: Tall Story (debut), Walk on the Wild Side, The Chapman Report, Period of Adjustment, In the Cool of The Day, Sunday in New York, The Love Cage, La Ronde, Cat Ballou, The Chase, La Curee, Any Wednesday, The Game Is Over, Hurry Sundown, Barefoot in the Park, Barbarella, Spirits of the Dead, They Shoot Horses, Don't They? (Acad. Award nom.), Klute (Acad. Award, 1970), Steelyard Blues, F.T.A., A Doll's House, The Bluebird, Fun with Dick and Jane, Julia, Coming Home (Acad. Award, 1978), Comes a Horseman, California Suite, The China Syndrome, The Electric Horseman, Nine To Five, Roll-Over, On Golden Pond, Agnes of God, The Morning After, Union Street, Stanley and Iris.
STAGE: There Was A Little Girl, Invitation to a March, The Fun Couple, Strange Interlude.
TELEVISION: Lily—Sold Out, 9 to 5 (exec. prod.), Tell Them I'm a Mermaid, The Doll Maker (Emmy, 1984).

FONDA, PETER: Actor-Director. b. Feb. 23, 1940. Son of Henry Fonda. Brother of Jane Fonda.
PICTURES INCLUDE: Tammy and the Doctor, The Victors, Lilith, The Young Lovers, The Trip, The Wild Angels, Easy Rider (also writer, co-prod.), Idaho Transfer (dir.), The Last Movie, The Hired Hand (also dir.), Two People, Dirty Mary Crazy Larry, Open Season, Two People (also dir.), Race with the Devil, 92 In the Shade, Killer Force, Fighting Mad, Futureworld, Outlaw Blues, High Ballin!, Wanda Nevada (also dir.), Split Image, Smokey and the Bandit II, Certain Fury, Dance of the Dwarfs, Mercenary Fighters, Jungle Heat, Diajobu My Friend, Peppermint Frieden, Spasm.
TELEVISION: A Reason to Live, The Hostage Tower, A Time of Indifference, Sound, Certain Honorable Men.

FONTAINE, JOAN: Actress. b. Tokyo, Oct. 22, 1917. e. American School in Japan. Sister of Olivia de Haviland, actress. On B'way in Tea and Sympathy (1954); m.p. debut in Quality Street, 1937; won Academy Award best performance, 1941, for Suspicion. Acad. Award nom. for Rebecca and The Constant Nymph. Author: No Bed of Roses (1978).
PICTURES INCLUDE: The Women, Rebecca, The Man Who Found Himself, You Can't Beat Love, Music for Madame, Blond Cheat, Gunga Din, The Constant Nymph, Damsel in Distress, This Above All, Jane Eyre, Frenchman's Creek, Affairs of Susan, Emperor Waltz, Kiss the Blood Off My Hands, You Gotta Stay Happy, Letter from an Unknown Woman, Duke of West Point, Ivy, Born to Be Bad, Something to Live For, September Affair, Darling How Could You?, Ivanhoe, Decameron Nights, Flight to Tangier, The Bigamist, Casanova's Big Night, Island in the Sun, Until We Sail, A Certain Smile, Tender Is the Night, The Devil's Own, Bare Essence.
TELEVISION: Crossings, Dark Mansions, Cannon.

FOOTE, HORTON: Writer. b. Wharton, TX, March 14. Actor before becoming playwright. Plays include Out of My House, Only the Heart, Celebration, The Chase, Trip to Bountiful, Traveling Lady, etc.
PICTURES: To Kill a Mockingbird (Oscar, 1962); Tender Mercies (Oscar, 1983); 1918; The Trip to Bountiful, On Valentine's Day, Convicts, Roots on a Parched Ground.
TELEVISION: Trip to Bountiful, Young Lady of Property, Death of the Old Man, Flight, The Night of the Storm, Keeping On.

FORBES, BRYAN: Actor, Writer, Producer, Director. Former head of prod., man. dir., Associated British Prods. (EMI). b. Stratford (London), July 22, 1926. Stage debut, The Corn Is Green (London) 1942; screen debut, The Small Back Room, 1948.
PICTURES INCLUDE: All Over the Town, The Wooden Horse, Dear Mr. Prohack, Appointment in London, Sea Devils, Wheel of Fate, Million Pound Note (Man with a Million), An Inspector Calls, Colditz Story, Passage Home, Extra Day, It's Great to be Young, Satellite in the Sky, Quartermass 11, Cockleshell Heroes, Black Tent, House of Secrets, Baby and the Battleship, I Was Monty's Double, A Piece of Cake, Man

in the Moon, Whistle Down the Wind, League of Gentlemen, Only Two Can Play, The L-Shaped Room, Of Human Bondage, Station Six Sahara, Seance on a Wet Afternoon, King Rat, The Wrong Box, The Whisperers, Deadfall, The Madwoman of Chaillot, The Go-Between (executive producer), The Railway Children (exec. prod.) Tales of Beatrix Potter (exec. prod.) The Raging Moon (U.S. title, Long Ago Tomorrow), Goodbye Norma Jean and Other Things, The Stepford Wives (dir.), The Slipper and The Rose, International Velvet, Sunday Lovers, Jessie, Hopscotch (s.p.), Better Late Than Never (s.p./dir.) The Naked Face (s.p./dir.), Life of Henry Ford (s.p.).

TELEVISION: I Caught Acting Like the Measles (produced/directed), The Breadwinner, French Without Tears, Johnnie Was a Hero, The Gift, The Road, The Heiress. Theatre: Flarepath, Fighters Calling, Gathering Storm, September Tide, The Holly and the Ivy, Tobias and the Angel, A Touch of Fear, Three Way Switch, December Flower, First Among Equals, Sister Ruth.

PUBLICATIONS: Truth Lies Sleeping (short stories) 1951; Distant Laughter (novel) 1972; Notes For a Life (Autobiog.) 1973/4. The Slipper and the Rose (Book of Film) 1975/6. Ned's Girl, International Velvet 1978 (novel); Familiar Strangers (novel), 1979 (U.S. title, Stranger), That Despicable Race, 1980. the Rewrite Man 1983 (novel), The Endless Game (novel) 1986.

FORBES, DAVID: Executive. b. Omaha, NE, Nov. 9, 1945. e. U. of Nebraska. Began career with MGM in 1968 as field man in Detroit; later named asst. natl. field coordinator at studio. director, Metrovision, 1973. Director special projects for 20th-Fox, 1974; made natl. dir. marketing services, 1976. In 1977 left to join Rastar Prods. as marketing dir. Named v.p. & asst. to pres., Columbia Pictures, 1980; 1982, joined Almi Distributing Corp. as vice chm.

FORD, GLENN: Actor. r.n. Gwylin Ford; b. Quebec, Canada, May 1, 1916. On stage in western co. Children's Hour 1935; on Broadway in: Broom for a Bride, Soliloquy; served in U.S. Marine Corps 1942–45; m.p. debut in Heaven with a Barbed Wire Fence 1940.

PICTURES INCLUDE: Men Without Souls, Lady in Question, So Ends Our Night, Desperadoes, Stolen Life, Gilda, Framed, Mating of Millie, Return of October, Loves of Carmen, Mr. Soft Touch, Man from Colorado, Undercover Man, Lust for Gold, Doctor and the Girl, Flying Missile, The Redhead and the Cowboy, Follow the Sun, The Secret of Convict Lake, Green Glove, Young Man with Ideas, Affair in Trinidad, Man from the Alamo, Terror on a Train, Plunder of the Sun, Big Heat, Appointment in Honduras, Human Desire, The Americano, Violent Men, Blackboard Jungle, Interrupted Melody, Trial, Ransom, Fastest Gun Alive, Jubal, Teahouse of the August Moon, Don't Go Near the Water, Cowboy, The Sheepman, Imitation General, Torpedo Run, It Started with a Kiss, The Gazebo, Cimarron, Cry for Happy, The Four Horsemen of The Apocalypse, Experiment in Terror, Love Is a Ball, The Courtship of Eddie's Father, The Rounders, The Money Trap, Fate Is the Hunter, Dear Heart, The Last Challenge, Heaven with a Gun, Smith!, The Day of the Evil Gun, A Time for Killing, Midway, Superman, Happy Birthday to Me.

TELEVISION: Series: Cade's County; The Family Holvak; Movies: Once Upon an Eagle; Brotherhood of the Bell; Beggarman, Thief; Evening in Byzantium.

FORD, HARRISON: Actor. b. Chicago, IL, July 13, 1942. e. Ripon Coll. After acting in L.A. and films for 5 years, undertook carpentry work including building Sergio Mendes' recording studio. Returned to acting and won notice in American Graffiti.

PICTURES: Dead Heat on a Merry-Go-Round, Luv, Getting Straight, The Long Ride Home, Journey to Shiloh, Zabriskie Point, The Conversation, American Graffiti, Star Wars, Heroes, Force 10 from Navarone, Hanover Street, Apocalypse Now, The Frisco Kid, The Empire Strikes Back, Raiders of the Lost Ark, Blade Runner, Return of the Jedi, Indiana Jones and the Temple of Doom, Witness, The Mosquito Coast, Frantic, Working Girl, Indiana Jones and the Last Crusade.

TELEVISION: Dynasty, Trial of Lt. Calley, The Possessed.

FORD, TENNESSEE ERNIE: Singer. r.n. Ernest J. Ford. b. Bristol, TN, Feb. 13, 1919. Radio anncr., 1939–41; U.S. Air Force, 1942–45; radio anncr., San Bernardino, CA; hillbilly disc jockey, Pasadena; Capital Recording Star. Medal of Freedom recipient 1984.

TELEVISION: own TV shows, NBC; guest appearances on I Love Lucy, Red Skelton Show, Perry Como Show, George Gobel Show; own show, Tennessee Ernie Ford Show, ABC.

RECORDS INCLUDE: 16 Tons, many others.

FORD, TONY: Executive. b. New York, NY, August 6, 1925. e. St. Johns U. In U.S. Navy W.W.II; in life insurance business, 1946–48. Agent with MCA 1949–53. TV indep. prod., specials for Timex, Ringling Bros. Circus, Pontiac Victor Borge.

Re-entered agency business, General Artists Corp., v.p., TV dept. Headed own agency, Tony Ford Mgt., Inc., which was acquired by William Morris Agency. Headed creative services division WMA representing producers, directors, writers specializing in the packaging of TV series and specials, left Morris Agency Jan. 1, 1977 to re-open Tony Ford Productions; 1979, named v.p. Metromedia Producers Corp.; 1984, named exec. v.p. Gaylord Television Prods.

FOREMAN, JOHN: Producer. b. Idaho Falls, ID. Cofounder of CMA Agency. Resigned Jan., 1968, to form production co. with Paul Newman: Newman-Foreman Company.

PICTURES INCLUDE: Winning, Butch Cassidy and the Sundance Kid, WUSA (co-prod.), Puzzle of a Downfall Child, They Might Be Giants, Sometimes a Great Notion, Pocket Money, The Effect of Gamma Rays on Man-in-the-Moon Marigolds (exec. prod.), The Mackintosh Man, The Man Who Would Be King, Bobby Deerfield, The Great Train Robbery, The Ice Pirates, Prizzi's Honor.

FORMAN, SIR DENIS, O.B.E., M.A.: Executive. b. Moffat, Dumfriesshire, Scot., Oct. 13, 1917. e. Loretto Sch., Musselburgh, Pembroke Coll., Cambridge. Served in Argyll & Sutherland Highlanders, W.W.II. Entered film business May, 1946, production staff Central Office of Information, 1947; Chief Production Officer C.O.I. 1948; appointed dir. of the British Film Inst., 1949; joined Granada Television Ltd., 1955. Jnt. Mng. Dir., 1965 chm., British Film Inst., Bd. of Gov., 1971–73. Chmn. Granada T.V. 1975–1987. Chmn. Novello & Co. 1972. Fellow, British Acad. Film & TV Arts, 1976. Dep. chrm. Granada Group, 1986.

FORMAN, MILOS: Director. b. Czechoslovakia, Feb. 18, 1932. Trained as writer at Czech Film Sch. and as director at Laterna Magika. Won Int'l. attention with first film Black Peter, 1963. Emigrated to U.S. after collapse of Dubcek govt. in Czechoslovakia.

PICTURES INCLUDE: Peter and Pavla (Czech Film Critics Award, 1963; Grand Prix Locarno, 1964.). The Loves of a Blonde, Fireman's Ball, Taking Off, Visions of Eight (segment), One Flew Over the Cuckoo's Nest (Acad. Award, best dir. 1975), Hair, Ragtime, Amadeus (Acad. Award, best dir., 1984), Valmont (dir., co-s.p.), New Year's Day (actor only).

FORREST, FREDERIC: Actor. b. Dec. 23, 1936. Began career off-Broadway in Futz, Massachusetts Trust and Tom Paine, all with La Mama Troupe under direction of Tom O'Horgan. Moved to Hollywood in 1970. Film debut in When the Legends Die, 1972.

PICTURES INCLUDE: The Don Is Dead, The Conversation, The Gravy Train, Permission to Kill, The Missouri Breaks, It Lives Again, Apocalypse Now, The Rose, One from the Heart, Hammet, Valley Girl, The Stone Boy, Season of Dreams, Tucker.

TELEVISION: Movies: Best Kept Secrets, Calamity Jane, Right to Kill?, The Deliberate Stranger, Quo Vadis; Little Girl Lost; Saigon, Year of the Cat (U.K.); A Shadow on the Sun.

FORREST, STEVE: Actor. b. Huntsville, TX, Sept. 29, 1924. r.n. William Forrest Andrews. Brother of Dana Andrews. e. U. of California at L.A., 1950. Acted at La Jolla Playhouse; appeared on radio, TV; m.p. debut in Geisha Girl.

PICTURES INCLUDE: Bad and the Beautiful, Battle Circus, The Clown, Band Wagon, Dream Wife, So Big, Take the High Ground, Phantom of the Rue Morgue, Prisoner of War, Rogue Cop, Bedeviled, It Happened to Jane, Heller in Pink Tights, Five Branded Women, Flaming Star, The Second Time Around, Rascal, The Wild Country, The Late Liz, North Dallas Forty, Mommie Dearest, Sahara, Spies Like Us, Amazon Women on the Moon.

TELEVISION: Movies: The Hatfields and the McCoys, Wanted: The Sundance Women, The Last of the Mohicans, Testimony of Two Men, Maneaters are Loose, Hollywood Wives; Gunsmoke, Return to Dodge, Dallas. Series: The Baron, S.W.A.T., Hotel, Dallas.

FORSTATER, MARK: Producer. b. Philadelphia, PA, 1943. e. City Coll. of New York, Temple U. In 1967 moved to England; studied at U. of Manchester and London Intl. Film School. First job in industry with Anglia TV on program, Survival. Began producing in 1970 with British Film Institute. Set up Chippenham Films to make documentaries. Moved into features in 1974 with Monty Python and the Holy Grail.

PICTURES: The Odd Job, Marigolds in August, The Grass Is Singing, Xtro, Paint It Black, Wherever She Is, The Wolves of Willoughby Chase, Death of a Schoolboy, Streets of Yesterday, Wherever You Are (exec. prod.). Shorts: The Glitterball, Wish You Were Here.

TELEVISION: The Cold Room, Forbidden.

FORSTER, ROBERT: Actor. b. Rochester, NY, July 13, 1941. e. Heidelberg Coll., Alfred U., Rochester U., B.S.

THEATRE: Mrs. Dally, 1965. Summer tour, A Streetcar Named Desire, 1965.

PICTURES INCLUDE: Reflections in a Golden Eye, Medium Cool, Justine, Journey Through Rosebud, The Don is

Dead, The Black Hole, Alligator, Vigilante, Walking the Edge, Committed, Counterforce.
TELEVISION: Judd for the Defense, Banyon, Once a Hero.

FORSYTH, BILL: Director. b. Glasgow, Scotland, 1947. At 16 joined film co. For next 10 years made industrial films, then documentaries. Joined Glasgow Youth Theater.
PICTURES: That Sinking Feeling, Gregory's Girl, Local Hero, Comfort and Joy, Housekeeping, Breaking In, Rebecca's Daughters.
TELEVISION: Andrina.

FORSYTHE, JOHN: Actor. b. Penn's Grove, NJ, Jan. 29, 1918.
STAGE CREDITS: Mr. Roberts, All My Sons, Yellow Jack, Teahouse of the August Moon, and others.
TELEVISION: Started in 1947; appeared on Studio One, Kraft Theatre, Robert Montgomery Presents, and others. Series: Bachelor Father; To Rome with Love; Dynasty. Movie: The Mysterious Two, On Fire.
PICTURES INCLUDE: Captive City, It Happens Every Thursday, The Glass Web, Escape from Fort Bravo, Trouble with Harry, Ambassador's Daughter, Everything But the Truth, Kitten with a Whip, Madame X, In Cold Blood, The Happy Ending, Topaz, And Justice for All, Scrooge.

FORTE, FABIAN: Singer, Actor. b. Philadelphia, PA, Feb. 6, 1940. e. South Philadelphia H.S. At 14, discovered by Marcucci and DeAngelis, voice teacher. Chancellor Records; signed contract. Studied with Carlo Menotti.
RECORDS INCLUDE: Turn Me Loose, Tiger, I'm a Man, Hound Dog Man, The Fabulous Fabian (Gold album).
PICTURES INCLUDE: Hound Dog Man, High Time, North To Alaska, Love in a Goldfish Bowl, Mr. Hobbs Takes a Vacation, Ride the Wild Surf, Dear Brigette, Longest Day, 10 Little Indians, Fireball 500, Thunder Alley, Five Weeks in a Balloon, Devil's Eight, The Longest Day, A Bullet for Pretty Boy, Little Laura and Big John.

FOSSEY, BRIGITTE: Actress. b. Tourcoing, France, 1947. After a remarkable debut at the age of 5 in Rene Clement's Forbidden Games (1952) returned to school, studying philosophy and translating. Rediscovered by director Jean-Gabriel Albicocco and cast in Le Grand Meaulnes (1967).
PICTURES: Forbidden Games, The Happy Road, Le Grand Meaulnes, Adieu l'Ami, M Comme Matheiu, Making It, The Blue Country, The Man Who Loved Women, The Good and the Bad, The Swiss Affair, Quintet, Mais ou et donc Orincar, The Triple Death of the Third Character, A Bad Son, The Party, Chanel Solitaire, A Bite of Living, Imperativ, The Party-2, Enigma, Au nom de tous les Meins, Scarlet Fever, A Strange Passion, A Case of Irresponsibility, The Future of Emily, The False Confidences, New Cinema Paradise.

FOSTER, CHRISTINE: Executive. r.n. Mary Christine Foster Hunter. b. Los Angeles, CA, March 19, 1943. e. Immaculate Heart Coll, B.A. 1967. UCLA MJ, 1968. Teacher while member of Immaculate Heart Community, 1962–65. Teacher, Pacific U., Tokyo, 1968; dir., research and dev. Metromedia Producers Corp., 1968–71; dir., dev. and prod. services, The Wolper Org. 1971–76; manager, film progs. NBC Television Network 1976–77; v.p. movies for TV & mini-series, Columbia Pictures TV, 1977–81; v.p. series programs, Columbia Pictures TV 1981; v.p. prog. dev., Group W. Prods. 1981–87; v.p. television, The Agency, 1988. Member: exec. comm. Humanitas Awards, 1986– ; L.A. Roman Catholic Archdiocesan Communications Comm., 1986–; Immaculate Heart H.S. bd of trustees, 1981–; Women in Film, bd of dirs., 1977–78; Teacher UCLA Extension, 1987. University lecturer.

FOSTER, DAVID: Producer. b. New York, NY, Nov. 25, 1929. e. Dorsey H.S., U. of Southern California Sch. of Journalism. U.S. Army, 1952–54; entered public relations field in 1952 with Rogers, Cowan & Brenner; Jim Mahoney, 1956; Allen, Foster, Ingersoll & Weber, 1958; left field in 1968 to enter independent m.p. production. Partner in Turman-Foster Co.
PICTURES INCLUDE: Co-produced (with Mitchell Brower) McCabe and Mrs. Miller, The Getaway; co-produced (with Lawrence Turman), The Nickel Ride (exec. prod.), The Drowning Pool, The Legacy, Tribute (exec. prod.), Caveman, The Thing, Second Thoughts, Mass Appeal, The Mean Season (prod.), Short Circuit; Running Scared (co-prod.); Full Moon in Blue Water; Short Circuit II; Gleaming the Cube.
TELEVISION: Jesse.

FOSTER, JODIE: Actress. r.n. Alicia Christian Foster. b. Los Angeles, CA, Nov. 19, 1962. e. Yale U. Acting debut in Mayberry, R.F.D. TV series (1969). Followed with many TV appearances, from series to movies of the week.
PICTURES INCLUDE: Napoleon and Samantha (1972), Menace of the Mountain, One Little Indian, Tom Sawyer, Kansas City Bomber, Alice Doesn't Live Here Anymore, Taxi Driver, Echoes of a Summer, Bugsy Malone, Freaky Friday, The Little Girl Who Lives Down the Lane, Candleshoe, Foxes, Carny, The Hotel New Hampshire, Five Corners, Siesta, The Accused, Stealing Home, Backtrack.
TELEVISION: Series: The Courtship of Eddie's Father

(regular), My Three Sons (regular), Paper Moon (regular), The Secret Life of T.K. Dearing. Movies: Smile, Jenny, You're Dead, Rookie of the Year, The Blood of Others.

FOSTER, JULIA: Actress. b. Lewes, Sussex, England, 1944. First acted with the Brighton Repertory Company, then two years with the Worthing, Harrogate and Richmond companies. 1956, TV debut as Ann Carson in Emergency Ward 10.
PICTURES INCLUDE: Term of Trial, The Loneliness of the Long Distance Runner, The Small World of Sammy Lee, The System, The Bargee, One Way Pendulum, Alfie, Half A Sixpence.
TELEVISION: A Cosy Little Arrangement, The Planemakers, Love Story, Taxi, Consequences, They Throw It at You, Crime and Punishment, The Image.
STAGE: No. 1 tour of The Country Wife; 1969, What the Butler Saw.

FOSTER KEMP, CECIL R.: M.B.E. Associate Producer, Production Supervisor. b. Shanghai. e. Brighton Coll.
PICTURES INCLUDE: Paris Holiday, Interpol, Tarzan and the Lost Safari, Around the World in Eighty Days, Front Page Story, Appointment in London, South of Algiers, Under Capricorn, Scott of the Antarctic, Untamed, John Paul Jones, King of Kings, Offbeat, El Cid, Fifty Five Days at Peking, The Fall of the Roman Empire, William The Conqueror, Girl on the Motorcycle, Arthur! Arthur!, I Saw Him Die, Ferdinand and Isabella, Wild Violets.

FOSTER, MAURICE DAVID: Producer-Writer. e. St. Paul's. Ent. m.p. ind. 1943 as asst. to gen. man. and prod. sup. Easling Studios. From 1950–61, prod. sup. and dir. Film Finances, 1961–63, dir. and gen. man. MGM British Studios.
PICTURES INCLUDE: The Jokers, Assignment K, The Osterman Weekend.

FOSTER, MEG: Actress. b. May 10, 1948. e. N.Y. Neighborhood Playhouse.
PICTURES INCLUDE: Adam at 6 A.M., Promise Her Anything, A Different Story, Once in Paris, Carny, Ticket to Heaven, The Emerald Forest, The Wind, Blind Fury, They Live.
TELEVISION: Movies: The Death of Me Yet, Sunshine, Things In This Season, James Dean, Washington: Behind Closed Doors, Sunshine Christmas, Desperate Intruder, Desperate; Series guest: Here Comes the Brides, Mod Squad, Men at Law, Hawaii Five-O, Cagney and Lacey, Murder She Wrote, Miami Vice.

FOWLER, HARRY: Actor. b. Lambeth Walk, London, 1926. Stage debut, Nothing Up My Sleeve (London) 1950; Screen debut, 1941.
PICTURES INCLUDE: Demi-Paradise, Don't Take It to Heart, Champaigne Charlie, Painted Boats, Hue and Cry, Now Barabbas, The Dark Man, She Shall Have Murder, The Scarlet Thread, High Treason, The Last Page, I Believe in You, Pickwick Papers, Top of the Form, Angels One Five, Conflict of Wings (Fuss Over Feathers), A Day to Remember, Blue Peter, Home and Away, Booby Trap, Town on Trial, Lucky Jim, Birthday Present, Idle on Parade, Don't Panic Chaps, Heart of a Man, Crooks Anonymous, The Longest Day, Lawrence of Arabia, Flight from Singapore, The Golliwog, Ladies Who Do, Clash By Night, The Nanny, Life at the Top, Start the Revolution Without Me, The Prince and The Pauper, Fanny Hill.
TELEVISION: Stalingrad, I Remember the Battle, Gideon's Way, That's for Me, Our Man at St. Mark's, Dixon of Dock Green, Dr. Finlay's Case Book, I Was There, Cruffs Dog Show, The Londoners, Jackanory, Get This, Movie Quiz, Get This series, Going a Bundle, Ask a Silly Answer, London Scene, Flockton Flyer, Sun Trap, The Little World of Don Camillo, World's End, Minder, Dead Ernest, Morecambe Wise Show, Gossip, Entertainment Express, Fresh Fields, Supergram, A Roller Next Year, Harry's Kingdom, Body Contact.

FOWLEY, DOUGLAS: Actor. b. New York, NY, May 30, 1911. e. St. Francis Xavier's Mil. Acad., N.Y. In stock; operated dramatic sch. N.Y.; on screen in bit parts. From 1934 in regular roles. Has appeared in many pictures.
PICTURES INCLUDE: Battleground, Just This Once, This Woman Is Dangerous, Singin' in the Rain, Man Behind the Gun, Slight Case of Larceny, Naked Jungle, Casanova's Big Night, Lone Gun, High & Mighty, Three Ring Circus, Texas Lady, Broken Star, Girl Rush, Bandido, Nightmare in the Sun, The North Avenue Irregulars.
TELEVISION: The Moneychangers, Starsky and Hutch, Sunshine Christmas, Oregon Trail.

FOX, EDWARD: Actor. b. England, April 13, 1937. Comes from theatrical family; father was agent for leading London actors; brother of actor James Fox.
PICTURES INCLUDE: The Mind Benders, The Long Duel, Morgan, The Naked Runner, The Jokers, I'll Never Forget What's Its Name, The Battle of Britain, Oh! What a Lovely War, Skullduggery, The Breaking of Bumbo, The Day of The Jackal, A Doll's House, Galileo, The Squeeze, A Bridge Too Far, The Duellists, The Big Sleep, Force 10 from Navarone,

The Mirror Crack'd, Gandhi, The Dresser, The Bounty, Wild Geese II, Return From the River Kwai.
TELEVISION: Edward and Mrs. Simpson, A Hazard of Hearts; Anastasia: The Mystery of Anna; Shaka Zulu.

FOX, JAMES: Actor. b. London, England, May 19, 1939. Ent. films as child actor in 1950 as William Fox in The Magnet and The Miniver Story.
TELEVISION: The Door, Espionage, Love Is Old, Love Is New, Nancy Astor, Country, New World, Beryl Markham: A Shadow on the Sun, Farewell to the King, Sun Child.
PICTURES INCLUDE: The Loneliness of the Long-Distance Runner, Tamahine, The Servant, Those Magnificent Men in Their Flying Machines, King Rat, The Chase, Thoroughly Modern Millie, Arabella, Duffy, Loves of Isadora, Performance, Anna Pavlova, Runners, A Passage to India, Absolute Beginners, The Whistle Blower, Comrades, High Season, Finding Maubee.

FOX, MICHAEL J.: Actor. b. Edmonton, Canada, June 9, 1961. m. actress Tracey Pollan.
PICTURES INCLUDE: Midnight Madness, The Class of 1984, Back to the Future, Teen Wolf, Light of Day, The Secret of My Success, Bright Lights, Big City, Dear America: Letters Home From Vietnam (reader), Casualties of War.
TELEVISION: Palmerstown, U.S.A.; Trapper John, M.D.; Teachers Only; Time Travel: Fact, Fiction and Fantasy; Leo and Me; Letters from Frank; Family Ties (series, 2 Emmy Awards); High School USA, Poison Ivy.

FOX, RICHARD: Executive. Joined Warner Bros. Intl. as mgt. trainee in October 1975, working in Australia and Japan. 1977, named gen. mgr. of Columbia-Warner Dist., New Zealand. Served as gen. mgr. of WB in Tokyo, 1978–1981. Joined WB in L.A. as exec. asst. to Myron D. Karlin, pres. of WB Intl., 1981; appt. v.p., sls. 1982; 1983, promoted to exec. v.p. of intl. arm; 1985, named pres. of WB Intl., assuming post vacated by Karlin.

FOX, RICHARD A.: Executive. b. Buffalo, NY, Jan 5, 1929. e. U. of Buffalo, 1950. Chm., Fox Theatres Management Corp. Pres., Nat'l NATO 1984–86; chm., Nat'l NATO 1986–1988.

FOXWELL, IVAN: Producer. b. Feb. 22, 1914, London, Eng. Entered m.p. ind. 1933 as technician with British & Dominions Film Corp., subsequently with Paramount British & London Films; Assoc. with Curtis Bernhardt in Paris 1937 becoming producer & collaborating on story, s.p. of Carefour, Le Train pur Venise, Sarajevo, others. In W.W.II with BEF and AEF 1939–46. Returned to British films 1947 as producer, co-author screen adapt., No Room at the Inn; prod., collab. s.p., Guilt Is My Shadow; prod., Twenty-Four Hours of a Woman's Life; co-author s.p. and prod. The Intruder, The Colditz Story (TV series adapt. 1972), Manuela, A Touch of Larceny, Tiara Tahiti, The Quiller Memorandum; s.p. and prod. Decline and Fall. Director, Foxwell Film Prods. Ltd.

FOXWORTH, ROBERT: Actor. b. Houston, TX, Nov. 1, 1941. e. Mellon U. Began acting at age 10 at Houston Alley Theatre and stayed with stage part-time while completing formal education. Returned to theatre on full-time basis after graduation from Mellon. Made TV debut in Sadbird, 1969.
TELEVISION: The Storefront Lawyers (series), Mrs. Sundance, Hogan's Goat, Falcon Crest (series), The Return of the Desperado.
PICTURES: Treasure of Matecumbe (debut), The Astral Factor, Airport '77, Damien-Omen II, The Black Marble, Invisible Strangler.
STAGE: P.S., Your Cat Is Dead.

FOXX, REDD: Actor, Performer. r.n. John Elroy Sanford. b. St. Louis, MO, Dec. 9, 1922. Began career by running away from home to join a washboard band at age 13; Member of amateur music group Bon-Bons 1939–41. First nightclub appearances as a single, then with Slappy White 1947–51; 50 record albums in last 17 years.
TELEVISION: Sanford and Son (series); The Redd Foxx Comedy Hour 1977; Ghost of a Chance (movie).
PICTURE: Cotton Comes to Harlem; Norman, Is That You?

FRAKER, WILLIAM A.: Cinematographer-Director. b. Los Angeles, CA, 1923. Graduate, U. of Southern California Film Sch. Worked as operator with Conrad Hall; moved to TV before feature films.
PICTURES: Cinematographer: Games, The Fox, President's Analyst, Fade In, Rosemary's Baby, Bullitt, Paint Your Wagon, Dusty and Sweets McGee, Day of the Dolphin, Rancho Deluxe, The Killer Inside Me, Aloha, Bobby and Rose, Gator, Close Encounters of the Third Kind, Looking for Mr. Goodbar, Heaven Can Wait, Old Boyfriends, 1941, Divine Madness, The Legend of the Lone Ranger, Sharky's Machine, the Best Little Whorehouse in Texas, WarGames, Irreconcilable Differences, Murphy's Romance, Fever Pitch, Murphy's Romance, SpaceCamp, Burglar, Baby Boom, Life After Life. Director: Monte Walsh, Reflection of Fear, The Legend of the Lone Ranger.

TELEVISION: Stony Burke, Outer Limits, Ozzie and Harriet, Daktari.

FRANCIOSA, ANTHONY: Actor. b. New York, NY, Oct. 25, 1928. e. high school there. First stage part in YWCA play; joined Off-Broadway stage group; stock at Lake Tahoe, CA, Chicago and Boston.
THEATRE: N.Y. stage in End as a Man, The Wedding Breakfast, A Hatful of Rain.
PICTURES INCLUDE: A Face in the Crowd, This Could Be The Night, A Hatful of Rain, Wild Is The Wind, The Long Hot Summer, The Naked Maja, Career Story, On Page One, Go Naked in the World, Period of Adjustment, The Swinger, Fathom, A Man Called Gannon, The Sweet Ride, Rio Conchos, In Enemy Country, Across 110th Street, The Drowning Pool, Firepower, Death Wish II, Julie Darling, Ghost in the Noonday Sun, Death Is in Fashion.
TELEVISION: Valentine's Day, The Name of the Game, Search, Matt Helm, Stagecoach, Masquerade, The Love Boat, Finder of Lost Loves.

FRANCIS, ANNE: Actress b. Ossining, NY, Sept. 16, 1932. Child model; radio TV shows as child & adult; on B'way in Lady in the Dark.
PICTURES INCLUDE: Summer Holiday, So Young So Bad, Whistle at Eaton Falls, Lydia Bailey, Elopement, Dream Boat, Lion Is in the Streets, Rocket Man, Susan Slept Here, Rogue Cop, Bad Day at Black Rock, Battle Cry, Blackboard Jungle, Scarlet Coat, Forbidden Planet, The Rack, Great American Pastime, Don't Go Near the Water, Crowded Sky, Girl of the Night, Satan Bug, Brainstorm, Hook, Line, and Sinker, More Dead Than Alive, The Impasse, The Love God, Funny Girl, Born Again.
TELEVISION: Honey West (series), O'Malley; Riptide; Partners in Crime; Crazy Like a Fox; Jake and the Fatman; Twilight Zone; Dallas; Finder of Lost Loves. Movies: Rona Jaffe's Mazes and Monsters; Poor Little Rich Girl: The Barbara Hutton Story, Laguna Heat.

FRANCIS, ARLENE: Actress. r.n. Arlene Francis Kazanjian; b. Boston, MA, 1908. e. Convent of Mount St. Vincent Acad., Riverdale, NY, Finch Finishing Sch., Theatre Guild Sch., NY. m. Martin Gabel, late actor. Author: That Certain Something (1960); Arlene Francis—A Memoir (1978).
STAGE: The Women (1937), Horse Eats Hat (Mercury Theater), Danton's Death, All That Glitters, Doughgirls, The Overtons, Once More With Feeling, Tchin-Tchin, Beekman Place, Mrs. Dally, Dinner at Eight, Kind Sir, Lion in Winter, Pal Joey, Who Killed Santa Claus?, Gigi.
TELEVISION: Soldier Parade 1949–55; Regular panelist What's My Line; Home, Arlene Francis Show; Talent Patrol, etc.
RADIO: Arlene Francis Show, Emphasis, Monitor, Luncheon at Sardis.
PICTURES INCLUDE: Stage Door Canteen, All My Sons, One, Two, Three, The Thrill of It All, Blind Date.

FRANCIS, CONNIE: Singer. r.n. Constance Franconero. b. Newark, NJ, Dec. 12, 1938. Appeared, Star Time when 12 years old; won Arthur Godfrey's Talent Scout Show, 12 years old.
GOLD RECORDS: Who's Sorry Now, My Happiness. Numerous vocalist awards: All Major TV shows.
PICTURES INCLUDE: Where the Boys Are, Follow the Boys, Looking For Love.

FRANCIS, FREDDIE: Producer, Director, Cameraman. b. London, 1917. Joined Gaumont British Studios as apprentice to stills photographer; then clapper boy at B.I.P. Studios, Elstree; camera asst. at British Dominion. After W.W.II returned to Shepperton Studios to work for Korda and with Powell and Pressburger as cameraman.
PICTURES INCLUDE: Director: Paranoiac, Vengeance, Evil of Frankenstein, Nightmare, Hysteria, Dr. Terror's House of Horrors, The Skull, Traitor's Gate, The Psychopath, The Deadly Bees, They Came from Beyond Space, Torture Garden, Dracula Has Risen from the Grave, Girly, Trog, Tales from the Crypt, The Creeping Flesh, Tales That Witness Madness, The Ghoul, Legend of The Werewolf, The Doctor and the Devils. Cameraman: Moby Dick (second unit photo., special effects), Room at the Top, Saturday Night and Sunday Morning, Sons and Lovers (Oscar), The Innocents, The Elephant Man, The French Lieutenant's Woman, Dune, Code Name: Emerald, Clara's Heart, Her Alibi. Director-camera: Dark Tower.

FRANCIS, KEVIN: Producer, Executive. b. London, England, 1948. 1967–70, production mgr., assoc. producer. 1970–72, produced It's Life, Passport, Trouble with Canada. 1972 founder, Tyburn Productions Limited; 1973, produced Persecution; 1974, produced The Ghoul and Legend of the Werewolf; 1975, founder, Tyburn Productions Inc.; 1976, prod. Film Techniques Educ. Course for BFI. Since 1977 exec. prod., Master of the Shell, The Masks of Death, Courier, Murder Elite, The Abbot's Cry, etc.

FRANCISCUS, JAMES: Actor. b. Clayton, MO, Jan. 31, 1934. e. Taft Prep, Yale U.
PICTURES INCLUDE: Four Boys and a Gun, I Passed for White, The Outsiders, The Miracle of the White Stallions, Youngblood Hawke, The Valley of Gwangi, Marooned, Beneath the Planet of the Apes, The Cat O' Nine Tails, Hell Boats, The Amazing Dobermans, Puzzle, Good Guys Wear Black, The Greek Tycoon, Greed, Concorde, City on Fire, When Time Ran Out, Butterfly.
TELEVISION: Naked City, Mr. Novak, Longstreet (TV film feature). Movies: The 500 Pound Jerk, The Pirate, The Dream Makers, Jacqueline Bouvier Kennedy.

FRANK, EDMOND: Executive. b. New York, NY, Feb. 11, 1945. e. American U., B.A., Washington Coll. of Law, J.D. Admitted to Fla. Bar 1971. Vice-pres. and gen. counsel, World Film. pres., South Florida Entertainment Counsel Guild.

FRANKEL, DANIEL: Executive. b. New York, NY, Aug. 21, 1903. e. U. of Michigan, U. of Berlin, Germany. Gen. mgr., Films Erka, Paris, 1925–30. Ran Theatre des Champs Elysees, 1928–29. Produced two French pictures. Returned to New York and joined Pathe 1930; dir. foreign dept., later of all sales to 1941; resigned to engage in prod. unit org. Liaison to New York and Four Continents Films, 1945; with U.A. in Europe 1953–56; ret. U.S. & org., pres., Zenith Int'l Film Corp., 1956, distr., Lovers, 400 Blows, Hiroshima, Mon Amour, etc. Governor IFIDA.

FRANKENHEIMER, JOHN: Director. b. Malba, NY, Feb. 19, 1930. e. Williams Coll. Actor, dir., summer stock; radio-TV actor, dir., Washington, DC; then joined CBS network. Theater: The Midnight Sun (dir., 1959).
TELEVISION: Mama, You Are There, Danger, Climax, Studio One, Playhouse 90, Du Pont Show of the Month; Ford Startime, Sunday Showcase; The Comedian, For Whom the Bell Tolls, The Turn of the Screw, The Browning Version, The Rainmaker (1982).
PICTURES INCLUDE: The Young Stranger, The Young Savages, Birdman of Alcatraz, All Fall Down, The Manchurian Candidate, Seven Days in May, The Train, Seconds, Grand Prix, The Extraordinary Seaman, The Fixer, The Gypsy Moths, I Walk the Line, Horsemen, The Impossible Object, The Iceman Cometh, 99 and 44/100% Dead, French Connection II, Black Sunday, Prophecy, The Challenge, The Holcroft Covenant, 52 Pick-Up, Dead-Bang.

FRANKLIN, BONNIE: Actress. b. Santa Monica, CA, Jan. 6, 1944. e. U. of California at L.A. On Bdwy. in Dames at Sea, Your Own Thing, Applause.
TELEVISION: Series: One Day at a Time. Movies: Breaking Up Is Hard to Do, A Guide for the Married Woman, Portrait of a Rebel: Margaret Sanger, Your Place or Mine, Sister Margaret and Saturday Night Ladies, Shalom Sesame.

FRANKLIN, MICHAEL HAROLD: Executive. b. Los Angeles, CA, Dec. 25, 1923. e. U. of California, A.B., U. of Southern California, LL.B. Admitted to CA bar, 1951; pvt. practice in L.A. 1951–52; atty. CBS, 1952–54; atty. Paramount Pictures, 1954–58; exec. dir. Writers Guild Am. West, Inc. 1958–78; national exec. dir., Directors Guild of America 1978–. Mem. Am. Civil Liberties Union, Los Angeles Copyright Soc., Order of Coif.

FRANKLIN, PAMELA: Actress. b. Tokyo, Japan, Feb. 4, 1950. Attended Elmshurst Ballet Sch., Camberley, Surrey.
PICTURES INCLUDE: The Innocents, The Lion, Flipper's New Adventure, The Prime of Miss Jean Brodie, The Night of the Following Day, And Soon the Darkness, The Legend of Hell House, Food of the Gods.

FRANKLIN, RICHARD: Director. b. Melbourne, Australia, July 15, 1948.
PICTURES: The True Story of Eskimo Nell; Fantasm; Patrick (also co-prod.); The Blue Lagoon (co-prod. only); Road Games (also prod.); Psycho II; Cloak and Dagger; Into the Night (act. only).
TELEVISION: Beauty and the Beast (pilot), A Fine Romance.

FRANKLIN, ROBERT A.: Executive. b. New York, NY, April 15. e. U. of Miami, B.B.A., 1958; Columbia Pacific U., M.B.A., 1979; Ph.D., 1980 majoring in marketing. Before entering film industry worked with House of Seagram (1959–64); Canada Dry Corp. (1964–66); J. M. Mathes Adv. (1966–67). In 1967 joined 20th Century-Fox as dir. of mkt. planning. Formed RP Marketing Intl. (entertainment consulting firm) in 1976 and World Research Systems (computer software marketer). In 1981 joined MPAA; 1983, named v.p., administration and information services. In 1986, named v.p. worldwide market research. Chm., MPAA research comm.; member, AMA and ESOMAR.

FRANKLYN, ARTHUR R.: b. New York, NY, July 19, 1928. Child actor with Life With Father, Farewell Tour and Just Because. New York stage 1941–44. Featured skater, Ice Frolic Latin American tour, 1948–49; star and prod. ice revues at Havana

Coliseum, 1949–50; served with U.S. Marines, Korea 1950–51; prod. dir., Los Angeles Ice Palace, 1951–56; exploitation and special events, Fox West Coast Theatres, 1956–59; Lippert Theatres, 1960; purchased Amador Chain of Central California Theatres. Pres. U.S. Bowling Photographers, Inc.; 1960–65 Dist. Mgr. Theatre Amuse Co., Tarzana, CA.; Mgr. Florida State Theas., Dist. mgr. Arlo Enterprises.

FRANKOVICH, M. J.: Executive. b. Bisbee, AZ, Sept. 29, 1910. e. U. of California at L.A., B.A. Ent. Radio 1934 as producer, commentator; began writing screenplays for Universal, 1938; Republic Pictures, 1940–49 (except for period war service U.S. Army); to Europe 1949 to make Fugitive Lady, Lucky Nick Kane, Thief of Venice etc.; England 1952. prod., Decameron Nights, Malaga, Footsteps in the Fog, Joe Macbeth; apptd. man. dir. Columbia Pictures Corp. Ltd., in U.K. and Eire Aug. 1955; elected vice-pres., Columbia Pictures International Corp., Dec. 1955; head Col. Pictures Int. Prod., 1958; vice-pres., Col. Pics. Corp., 1959. Appt. Chmn., Columbia Pics. Corp. Ltd., 1959. Variety Club Crew Member; chief barker, Tent 36 Variety Club, 1957. dir., BLC Films; chmn., Screen Gems Ltd.; first v.p. chge. world prod., Columbia; resigned July, 1967 to return to independent production. Long Term Deal, 1969, rel. through Columbia. Won Jean Hersholt Humanitarian Award, 1984.
PICTURES INCLUDE: Bob & Carol & Ted & Alice, Marooned, Cactus Flower, The Looking Glass War, Doctors' Wives, There's A Girl in My Soup, The Love Machine, Dollars, Butterflies Are Free, Stand Up and Be Counted, 40 Carats, A Report to the Commissioner, From Noon Till Three, The Shootist.

FRANZ, ARTHUR: Actor. b. Perth Amboy, NJ, Feb. 29, 1920. e. Blue Ridge Coll., MD. U.S. Air Force. Radio, TV shows.
THEATRE: Streetcar Named Desire, Second Threshold.
PICTURES INCLUDE: Jungle Patrol, Roseanna McCoy, Red Light, Doctor and the Girl, Sands of Iwo Jima, Strictly Dishonorable, Submarine Command, Member of the Wedding, Flight Nurse, Bad for Each Other, Eddie Cantor Story, Caine Mutiny, Steel Cage, Battle Taxi, New Orleans Uncensored, Bobby Ware Is Missing, Atomic Submarine, The Human Factor, That Championship Season.

FRAWLEY, JAMES: Director. b. Houston, TX, 1937. Studied drama at Carnegie Tech. and Actors Studio, where later taught and ran the directors unit. Was charter member of comedy group, The Premise; has acted in plays on and off Bdwy. Won Emmy Award for Monkees series, where staged two musical numbers a week for two seasons.
PICTURES: Kid Blue, The Big Bus, The Muppet Movie, Fraternity Vacation.
TELEVISION: Columbo, Delancy Street, Capra, Cagney and Lacey, Assault and Matrimony.

FRAZER, AUSTIN: Prod. consultant. b. London, England. Early career, designer and writer. Fellow SIAD. Writer's Guild Award 1967, Dante's Inferno.

FRAZIER, CLIFF: Director, Actor. b. Detroit, MI, Aug. 27, 1934. e. Wayne State U., Harold Clurman. Exec. dir., The Community Film Workshop Council; was co-founder & artistic dir.: Stable Theatre, Detroit, 1960–63; Concept East Theatre, Detroit, 1962–64; co-produced and acted in Study in Color, 1964–65; assoc. dir., Theatre of Latin America, Inc., N.Y., 1968; dir. of drama, Mobilization for Youth, N.Y., 1966–68; East Coast dir. of rsch., Brooks Foundation, Santa Barbara, 1966–68.
TELEVISION ACTING INCLUDES: Today, Tell It Like It Is, NYPD. The Nurses, The Negro Experimental Theatre, Othello.
THEATRE: Stage repertories: Washington Theatre Club, Irish Hills Rep., Will-O-Way Playhouse.
Co-author, Discovery in Drama and book critic, Catholic Reporter, 1969.

FRAZIER, SHEILA E.: Actress. b. Bronx, NY, Nov. 13, 1948. e. Englewood, NJ. Was exec. sect'y. and high-fashion model. Steered to acting career by friend Richard Roundtree. Studied drama with N.Y. Negro Ensemble Co. and New Federal Theatre, N.Y.
PICTURES INCLUDE: Super Fly (debut), Superfly T.N.T., The Super Cops, California Suite, What Does It Take?, Three the Hard Way, The Hitter, I'm Gonna Git You Sucker.

FREARS, STEPHEN: Director. b. Leicester, Eng., 1941. e. Cambridge. Joined Royal Court Theatre, working with Lindsay Anderson on plays. Later asst. dir. on Morgan: A Suitable Case for Treatment; Charlie Bubbles, and Anderson's films: If . . . and O Lucky Man! Theatrical debut as director, Gumshoe (1971). Worked afterwards mostly in TV, directing and producing.
PICTURES: Gumshoe, Bloody Kids, The Hit, My Beautiful Laundrette, Prick Up Your Ears, Sammy and Rosie Get Laid, Les Liaisons Dangereuses.
TELEVISION: A Day Out (1971); England Their England; Match of the Day; Sunset Across the Bay; Three Men in a Boat; Daft as a Brush; Playthings; Early Struggles; Last

Summer; 18 Months to Balcomb Street; A Visit from Miss Protheroe; Abel's Will; Cold Harbour; series of six Alan Bennett plays; Long Distance Information; Going Gently; Loving Walter; Saigon, Year of the Cat; December Flower.

FREDERIC, MARC: Producer. b. New York, NY, Apr. 25, 1916. e. Washington & Lee U. Capt. U.S. Air Force. Prod., dist. Little Theatre, 1948, 104 episodes. First to make deal through AFTRA for kinescope release of live shows for dist. Tales of Tomorrow series. Org., Marc Frederic Prods., Inc.
PICTURES INCLUDE: Giant of the Unknown, She Demon, Missile to the Moon, Frankenstein's Daughter, Girl in Room 13, Career Girl, Festival Girl.

FREDERICKSON, H. GRAY, JR.: Producer. b. Oklahoma City, OK, July 31, 1937. e. U. of Lausanne, Switzerland, 1958–59; U. of Oklahoma. B.A., 1960. m. Victoria Schmidlapp. Worked one yr. with Panero, Weidlinger & Salvatori Engineering Co., Rome Italy. In 1979 named v.p. of feature films, Lorimar Films.
PICTURES INCLUDE: Candy, Inspector Sterling, Gospel 70, An Italian in America, The Man Who Wouldn't Die, The Good, the Bad and the Ugly, Intrigue in Suez, How to Learn to Love Women, God's Own Country, Wedding March, An American Wife, Natika, Echo in the Village, Little Fauss and Big Halsey, Making It, The Godfather, The Godfather, Part II, Hit (exec. prod.), Apocalypse Now (co.-prod.), One From the Heart, The Outsiders, UHF.
TELEVISION: Producer: The Return of Mickey Spillane's Mike Hammer, Houston Nights.

FREEDMAN, JERROLD: Director, Writer.
PICTURES: Kansas City Bomber, Borderline.
TELEVISION: Writer: A Cold Night's Death, Blood Sport, The Last Angry Man, Betrayal, Some Kind of Miracle, Legs. Director: The Streets of L.A., The Boy Who Drank Too Much, Victims, The Seduction of Gina, Best Kept Secrets, Seduced, Family Sins.

FREEMAN, AL, JR.: Actor. b. San Antonio, TX, March 21, 1934. e. LA City Coll.
THEATER: The Long Dream (1960), Kicks and Co., Tiger Tiger Burning Bright, Trumpets of the Lord, Blues for Mister Charlie, Conversation at Midnight, Look to the Lilies, Are You Now or Have You Ever Been?, The Poison Tree.
PICTURES: Torpedo Run, Dutchman, Finian's Rainbow, Castle Keep, The Lost Man, The Detective, A Fable (also dir.), Seven Hours to Judgement.
TELEVISION: My Sweet Charlie, Roots, King, One Life to Live (Emmy, 1979).

FREEMAN, EVERETT: Writer. b. New York, NY, 1912. Contrib. Sat. Eve. Post. From 1942 writer for screen.
PICTURES INCLUDE: George Washington Slept Here, Princess and the Pirate, It Happened on Fifth Ave., Secret Life of Walter Mitty, Too Young to Kiss, Lady Takes a Sailor, Jim Thorpe—All American, Pretty Baby, Million Dollar Mermaid, Destination Gobi, Kelly and Me, My Man Godfrey, Marjorie Morningstar, Sunday in New York, The Glass Bottom Boat, Where Were You When the Lights Went Out?, The Maltese Bippy, How Do I Love Thee.
TELEVISION: Prod. Bachelor Father series.

FREEMAN, JOEL: Producer. b. Newark, NJ, June 12, 1922. e. Upsala Coll. Began career at MGM studios in 1941. In Air Force Mot. Pic. Unit 1942–46. Became assist. dir. at RKO in 1946. In 1948 returned to MGM as asst. dir.; later assoc. prod. In 1956 entered indep. field as prod. supv. on various features and TV series. In 1960 to Warner Bros., assoc. producing Sunrise at Campobello, The Music Man and Act One. After such films as Camelot and Finian's Rainbow, became studio exec. at Warners. Presently senior v.p. prod., New Century Entertainment Corp.
PICTURES: Producer: The Heart Is a Lonely Hunter, Shaft, Trouble Man, Love at First Bite, Octagon, The Kindred.

FREEMAN, MORGAN: Actor. b. Memphis, TN, June 1, 1937. e. LA C Coll. Joined Air Force until 1959. Broadway debut in Hello Dolly! with Pearly Bailey. Took over lead role in Purlie. Became known nationally when he created Easy Reader on TV's The Electric Company (1971–76).
THEATER: The Mighty Gents (Drama Desk, Clarence Derwent Awards), Coriolanus (Obie Award), Mother Courage, Driving Miss Daisy (Obie Award), The Gospel at Colonus (Obie Award).
PICTURES: Who Says I Can't Ride a Rainbow! (1972), Brubaker, Eyewitness, Harry and Son, Teachers, Marie, That was then...This Is Now, Street Smart (NY, LA Film Critics Award, National Board of Review, supp. actor awards, 1987), Clean and Sober, Lean on Me.
TELEVISION: Clinton and Nadine.

FREEMAN, SIR N. BERNARD, C.B.E.: Executive. b. Sydney, Sept. 1, 1896. e. public schools, Xavier Coll.; Melbourne; established MGM throughout Australia, New Zealand, man. dir., chmn., retired 1967. European War, 1914–18.
Member: Admin. Comm. of Brit. Centre, 1944–46. Chairman: Anzac House Appeal 1945, Anzac House Trust 1946,

Miss Australia Quest, 1948–49. N.S.W. Comm. for World Refugee Year, 1960. Nat'l. Chmn., UNICEF, 1953; pres. Rotary Club of Sydney, 1960–61; Created C.B.E. (Civil) 1946; chmn., Motion Picture Distributors' Association of Australia, 1939–41, '63 Deputy Chairman, Council of International House, U. of Sydney.

FRELENG, FRIZ: Writer-Producer. b. Kansas City, MO, Aug. 21, 1906. Animator, Walt Disney Studio, 1928–29; Charles Mintz Studio, 1929–30, prod.-dir., Warner Bros., 1930–63. Formed partnership with David DePatie in 1963. Five Academy Awards, 3 Emmy Awards.
CARTOON FILMS INCLUDE: Bugs Bunny series, Daffy Duck, Sylvester, Yosemite Sam, Porky Pig, Tweetie Pie, Speedy Gonzales, Halloween Is Grinch Night, Pink Panther in Olympinks, Dr. Seuss' Pontoffel Pock. Recent compilations: The Looney, Looney Bugs Bunny Movie, Bugs Bunny's 3rd Movie: 1001 Rabbit Tales. Numerous series of television shows.

FRENKE, EUGENE: Producer. b. Russia, Jan. 1, 1907. m. Anna Sten.
PICTURES INCLUDE: Life Returns, Two Who Dared, Three Russians Girls, Let's Live a Little, Lady in Iron Mask, Miss Robin Crusoe, Heaven Knows, Mr. Allison, Barbarian and the Geisha, The Last Sunset, Royal Hunt of the Sun.

FRESCO, ROBERT M.: Writer. b. Burbank, CA, Oct. 18, 1928. e. Los Angeles City Coll. Newspaperman. Los Angeles, 1946–47; U.S. Army, 1948–49; staff writer, Hakim Prod., 1950–51; various screenplays, 1951–56.
PICTURES INCLUDE: Tarantula, They Came to Destroy the Earth, Monolith.
TELEVISION: Scripts for Science Fiction Theatre, Highway Patrol.

FRIED, MAX: Executive. b. New York City, 1910. e. James Madison H.S. Started with Warner Bros., 1927; 1940, buyer & booker for Century Theatres; 1950, exec. dir. & buyer, J.J. Theatres; 1957, buyer & booker for Seymour Florin Enterprises. Now pres. Maxi Cinema Enterprises; (consultant on m.p. industry); adv. & sls. rep. for Motion Picture Almanac and Television & Video Almanac; exec. dir., Motion Picture Bookers club. (also former pres.)
MEMBER: Variety Club Children's Charity; natl. chm., William Rogers Memorial Fund's Academy Award Sweepstakes' Drive; past. pres., cinema-radio-tv unit, B'nai B'rith.

FRIEDBERG, A. ALAN: Executive. b. New York, NY, Apr. 13, 1932. e. Columbia Coll., B.A.; Harvard Law School. President, Sack Theatres, Boston. NATO bd. mbr.

FRIEDKIN, JOHN: Executive. b. New York, NY, Dec. 9, 1926. Entered industry in New York as publicist for Columbia Pictures; spent eight years at Young & Rubicam adv. agency. Formed Sumner & Friedkin with Gabe Sumner as partner; left to join Rogers & Cowan, where named v.p. In 1967 resigned to join 20th-Fox, moving to California in 1972 when home offices were transferred. Appointed Fox v.p. worldwide publ. & promo. In 1979 joined Warner Bros. as v.p.—adv. pub. for intl. div.

FRIEDKIN, WILLIAM: Director. b. Chicago, IL, 1939. Joined WGN-TV, 1957, worked for National Education TV, did TV documentaries before feature films.
PICTURES INCLUDE: Good Times, The Night They Raided Minsky's, The Birthday Party, The Boys in the Band, The French Connection. (Academy Award, best picture, dir. 1971), The Exorcist (10 Acad. Award nominations), Sorcerer (prod.-dir.), Cruising (dir.-s.p.), Deal of the Century, To Live and Die in L.A. (dir., co-s.p.), Rampage (dir., s.p.).
TELEVISION: C.A.T. Squad (dir., exec. prod.).

FRIEDMAN, ARNOLD J.: Executive. b. New York, NY. Entered m.p. industry as exploiteer for Columbia Pictures Corp. 1957–60; advng dept. United Artists Corp. 1960–62; adv. mgr., Embassy Pictures Corp. and later director of adv., publi., prom. for Embassy Pictures Television, 1962–67; pres. Arnold Friedman's Company, 1967–70; dir. of ad./pub./promo for Metromedia Producers Corp., 1970–72; creative dir., ITC, 1973–74; vice pres. of theatrical TV & adv./pub./promo. for Cinema Shares International Television. Ltd., 1976–79; pres., Arcady Communications, 1980–present.

FRIEDMAN, DAVID F.: Executive. b. Birmingham, AL, Dec. 24, 1923. e. Cornell U. With U.S. Army Signal Corps, 1944–46. With Paramount Pictures as booker office manager 1946–50; circus press agent, 1950–51; Para. publ. agent, 1952–55; partner, Modern Film Distributors, 1956–60; partner, Sonney Amusement, 1960–64. Formed Entertainment Ventures, Inc. in 1965, of which he is pres. Produced a total of 59 features between 1958 and 1988.

FRIEDMAN, JOSEPH: Executive. b. New York, NY. e. City Coll. of New York, 1940–42, New York U., 1946–47. U.S. Navy 3 yrs. Asst. to nat'l. dir. field exploitation, Warner Bros. Pictures, 1946–58; nat'l. exploitation mgr., Paramount Pictures, 1958–60; exec. asst. to dir. of adv., publicity & exploitation, Para.,

1961; dir. adv. & pub., Paramount 1964; a v.p., Para., 1966; v.p. in charge of Marketing, 1968; v.p., adv., and p.r., Avco Embassy Pictures, 1969; v.p., p.r. American Film Theatre, 1973; v.p., adv. and p.r., ITC, motion picture div., 1976, pres., Joseph Friedman Marketing and Advertising, Inc., 1977. Exec. dir. New Jersey M.P. & T.V. Commission, 1978; v.p. worldwide adv./pub./promo., Edie & Ely Landau, Inc., 1980; exec. dir., New Jersey Motion Picture & Television Commission, 1981.

FRIEDMAN, MARTIN: Executive. b. New York, NY, Oct. 9. Warner 1928 sls. and contract dept.; booking sales, Cleveland 1939–42; U.S. Marine Corps, production until 1945 joined A.W. Schwalberg at Artists Producers, when company was dissolved in 1946 then joined Liberty Films as ass't. to E.K. (Ted) O'Shea. Liberty was taken over by Paramount Pictures; remained with Paramount in their sales division until 1957 at which time joined American Broadcasting-Paramount Theatres as their producers representative. Production was stopped, then Friedman assigned to the theatre division in 1960; v.p., gen. mgr., ABC Theas. of Penn. Inc., ABC Theas. of N.Y., Inc., New England Theas., Inc.; pres., Countrywide Theaters, 1970. In 1973 formed own corp., Martin Films, Inc., of which is pres. Co. buys and distributes indep. product.

FRIEDMAN, ROBERT L.: Executive. b. Bronx, NY, March 1, 1930. e. DeWitt Clinton H.S. Started as radio announcer and disc jockey with Armed Forces Radio Service in Europe and U.S. v.p., marketing, United Artists Corp.; pres. domestic distribution, Columbia Pictures. 1984, named pres., AMC Int'l., subsidiary of AMC Entertainment.
MEMBER: M.P. Associates Foundation, Phila., pres. 2 yrs.; Variety Club (on board) M.P. Pioneers; (on board) area chm. and N.Y. participation in Will Rogers Hospital Foundation, American Film Inst., Academy of M.P. Arts & Sciences.

FRIEDMAN, SEYMOUR MARK: Director. b. Detroit, MI, Aug. 17, 1917. e. Magdalene Coll., Cambridge, B.S. 1936; St. Mary's Hospital Medical Coll., London. Entered m.p. ind. as asst. film ed. 1937; 2nd asst. dir. 1938; 1st asst. dir. 1939, on budget pictures; entered U.S. Army 1942; returned to ind. 1946; dir. Columbia Pictures 1947. Vice president & executive production for Columbia Pictures Television, division of Columbia Pictures Industries, 1955.
MEMBER: Screen Directors Guild.
PICTURES INCLUDE: To the Ends of the Earth, Rusty's Birthday, Prison Warden, Her First Romance, Rookie Fireman, Son of Dr. Jekyll, Loan Shark, Flame of Calcutta, I'll Get You, Saint's Girl Friday, Khyber Patrol, African Manhunt, Secret of Treasure Mountain.

FRIEDMAN, STEPHEN: Writer, Producer. b. March 15, 1937. e. U. of Pennsylvania, Harvard Law School. Worked as lawyer for Columbia Pictures (1960–63) and Ashley-Famous Agency. 1963–67: Paramount Pictures. Formed and heads Kings Road Productions.
PICTURES INCLUDE: Producer: The Last Picture Show, Lovin' Molly (also s.p.), Slap Shot, Bloodbrothers, Fast Break, Hero at Large, Little Darlings, Eye of the Needle, All of Me, Creator, Enemy Mine.

FRIEND, PHILIP: Actor. b. Horsham, Sussex, England, Feb. 20, 1915. e. Bradfield Coll. m. Eileen Erskine, prof.
THEATRE: With musical comedy tour 1935; at Drury Lane Theatre 1936; Broadway debut in French Without Tears 1937; plays include: Pink Strings and Sealing Wax, First Gentlemen, Hide Out, 1969; Dictator's Slippers, The Ladder, 1970. Blindsight, Forgotten Factor, 1970.
Brit. m.p. debut in Midas Touch 1939; on Brit. radio; served in Brit. Army 3 yrs. W.W.II; made training m.p. for Brit. govt.
PICTURES INCLUDE: My Own True Love, In Which We Serve, Next of Kin, Great Day, Enchantment, Sword in the Desert, Buccaneer's Girl, The Highwayman, Thunder on the Hill, Desperate Moment, Background (Edge of Divorce), The Diamond, The Betrayal, Son of Robin Hood, Web of Suspicion, The Solitary Child, Stranglehold, The Fur Collar, Manutara.
TELEVISION: Rendezvous, Invisible Man series, The Third Man Series, Z Cars, Freewheelers, Short Story, Dial M for Murder, Moody & Peg, Suez.

FRIES, CHARLES W.: Executive. b. Cincinnati, OH, Sept. 30, 1928. e. Ohio State U., B.S. Exec.-prod., Ziv Television; v.p., prod., Screen Gems; v.p., prod., Columbia Pictures; exec. v.p., prod. and exec. prod., Metromedia Prod. Corp., 1970–74; pres., exec. prod., Alpine Prods. and Charles Fries Prods. 1974–83; chm. & pres., Fries Entertainment, 1984. Nat'l. treas., TV Academy; pres., Alliance TV Film Producers; exec. comm., MPPA. Chm., Caucus of Producers, Writers and Directors, board of governors and exec. comm. of Academy of TV Arts and Sciences. Bd. governors, secretary & chm., TV committee, American Film Institute.
PICTURES: Exec. Prod.: Flowers in the Attic; Troup Beverly Hills.
TELEVISION: Movies: Toughlove; The Right of the People; Intimate Strangers; Bitter Harvest; A Rumor of War; Blood

Vows: The Story of a Mafia Wife; The Alamo: 3 Days to Glory; Intimate Betrayal; Two Women; Drop Out Mother; LBJ: The White House Years; The Crucible; The Rose Kennedy Story; It's Howdy Doody Time: A 40 Year Celebration; Crash Course; Supercarrier.

FRISCH, LARRY: Producer, Director, Writer. b. Indianapolis, IN, Dec. 27, 1929. e. U. of Southern California, 1947–49; Columbia U, 1951–54. Prof. child actor, Radio 1944–47; writer/dir. with Caravel Films, N.Y., 1950; Assist. dir., Exodus, El Cid (Spain); Dir.; Writer, Tel Aviv Taxi, 1956 (Israel), Pillar of Fire 1962 (Israel), Casablan, 1963 (Greece).
TELEVISION: Dir., Story of a Teenage Drug Addict, Power of Pot Roast, Beyond Three Doors, Destination Vietnam, Bus to Sinai (NBC-TV), Biafra Eye-Witness (UPI-TV); Metromedia TV News, overseas correspondent 1969–71; prod., Miracle of Survival (TV special), An American Family In China, 1971.

FRONTIERE, DOMINIC: Executive, Composer. b. New Haven, CT, June 17, 1931. e. Yale School of Music. Studied composing, arranging and conducting; concert accordionist, World's Champion Accordionist, 1943; An Hour with Dominic Frontiere, WNHC-TV, New Haven, 3 years, 1947; exec. vice-pres., musical dir., Daystar Prods. Composer or arranger over 75 films.
PICTURES INCLUDE: Giant, Gentlemen Prefer Blondes, Let's Make Love, High Noon, Meet Me in Las Vegas, 10,000 Bedrooms, Hit the Deck; composer-conductor; Marriage-Go-Round, The Right Approach, One Foot in Hell, Hero's Island, Popi, Barquero, Chisum, A for Alpha, The Aviator.
TELEVISION: Composer-conductor: The New Breed, Stoney Burke, Bankamericard commercials (Venice Film Festival Award Best Use of Original Classical Music for filmed TV commercials), Outerlimits, Branded, Iron Horse, Rat Patrol, Flying Nun, The Invaders, Name of the Game, That Girl, Twelve O'Clock High, Zig Zag, The Young Rebel, The Immortal, Jean C. Killy, Fugitive, The Love War.

FROST, LINDA SMITH: Executive. Vice pres. marketing, Media Home Entertainment. b. Louisville, KY, March 13, 1956. e. Wellesley College. Dir. of marketing, South Coast Plaza. e. of marketing Rouse Company. dir. special events and marketing, Broadway Dept. Stores. V.P. marketing Media home Entertainment.

FRUCHTMAN, MILTON A.: Producer, Director. b. New York, NY, e. Columbia U. B.S.; Columbia U., M.S.
TELEVISION: High Adventure Series, Every Man's Dream, ABC, Verdict for Tomorrow, (Peabody Award, 1962), Assignment Southeast Asia, It Happened in Naples; Son of Sultan, The Secret of Michaelangelo, Every Man's Dream (Peabody), Dance Theatre of Harlem, Those Who Sing Together, worked for Columbia and independent producers in various production capacities, set up first worldwide TV network, Eichmann Trial, Capital Cities Broadcasting, The Makebelievers, Odyssey Prods.; received numerous Peabody, Emmy, and Gabriel awards, Gold Hugo Awards (Chicago Film and TV Festival), Martin Luther King Festival Award, DGA Award.

FRYE, WILLIAM: Producer. Was agency exec. before beginning prod. career as associate prod. of Four Star Playhouse in assoc. with late Dick Powell, David Niven and Charles Boyer. Later joined Revue Prods., which became Universal TV; he produced General Electric Theatre and other series. Has produced many Movie of the Week entries for ABC-TV.
PICTURES INCLUDE: The Trouble with Angels, Where Angels Go, Trouble Follows, Airport 1975, Airport 1977, Raise the Titanic, Apt Pupil.

FUCHS, LEO L.: Independent producer. b. Vienna, June 14, 1929. Moved to U.S., 1939. e. Vienna and New York. U.S. Army cameraman 1951–53; int'l. mag. photographer until entered motion pictures as producer with Universal in Hollywood in 1961.
PICTURES INCLUDE: Gambit, A Fine Pair; Jo (French version of The Gazebo), Sunday Lovers, Just the Way You Are.

FUCHS, MICHAEL: Executive. b. New York, NY, March 9, 1946. e. Union Coll., NYU Law School (J.D. degree). Show business lawyer before joining Home Box Office in 1976, developing original and sports programming. Named chairman and CEO of HBO in 1984 till present. HBO pres. & chief exec. officer.

FUEST, ROBERT: Director. b. London, 1927. Early career as painter, graphic designer. Ent. TV industry as designer with ABC-TV, 1958. 1962: directing doc., commercials. 1966: Wrote and dir. Just Like a Woman, 1967–68; dir. 7 episodes of The Avengers, 1969: wrote and directed 6 episodes of The Optimists.
PICTURES: And Soon the Darkness, Wuthering Heights, Doctor Phibes, Doctor Phibes Rides Again (also .p.); The Final Programme (also s.p., design), The Devil's Rain, The Geller Effect (s.p. only), The New Avengers, The Gold Bug, Revenge of the Stepford Wives, The Big Stuffed Dog, Mystery on Fire Island, Aphrodite, Worlds Beyond, Cat's Eyes.

FULLER, JACK DUBOSE: Exhibitor. b. Columbia, SC, March 7, 1921. e. U. of South Carolina, B. S. Palmetto Theatre Co. 1936–42; U.S. Navy, 1942–45; theatre mgr. Wilby-Kincey Service Corp., 1945–47; booker, 1947–51; partner Irvin-Fuller Theatres, operate 24 theatres NC & SC, since 1951; Pres., Theatre Owners of N.C. and S.C. 1957; dir. NATO since 1956.

FULLER, SAMUEL: Director, Writer, Producer. b. New York, NY, 1911. Copy boy, N.Y. Journal; reporter, rewrite man, N.Y. Graphic, N.Y Journal, San Diego Sun; journeyman reported many papers. Author of novel The Dark Page; many orig. s.p.; in U.S. Army, 16th Inf. 1st U.S. Inf. Div. 1942–45; s.p., dir., I Shot Jesse James, Baron of Arizona; prod., dir., also screen play author of The Steel Helmet; dir., Fixed Bayonets; s.p. dir., prod., Park Row; s.p., dir., Pickup On South Street; s.p., dir., Hell and High Water, House of Bamboo; prod. dir., s.p. Run of the Arrow, China Gate, Forty Guns, Verboten, The Crimson Kimono, Underworld U.S.A., Merril's Marauders, (collab. s.p., dir.), s.p., dir., prod. Shock Corridor, s.p. prod., dir., The Naked Kiss; s.p. dir., Dead Pigeon on Beethoven Street; s.p. dir., The Big Red One; co-s.p., dir., White Dog, Thieves After Dark, Return to Salem's Lot (actor only), Street of No Return (dir., s.p., actor), All Night Long (actor only).
AUTHOR: Novel, Crown of India. Novel; 144 Piccadilly Street; Dead Pigeon on Beethoven Street; The Rifle; The Big Red One, The Dark Page, La Grande Melee (Battle Royal), Pecos Bill and the Soho Kid.

FUNT, ALLEN: Producer, Performer. b. New York , NY, Sept. 16, 1914. Best known as producer and creator of Candid Camera series which originated on radio in 1947 as Candid Microphone which inspired theatrical film shorts. TV version began in 1948 as Candid Mike, changed in 1949 to Candid Camera which played off and on until 1960 when became regular series on CBS, lasting until 1967. Revived briefly in early '70s and again in mid '80s in new format; then syndicated as The New Candid Camera. Candid Camera Christmas Special, 1987. Funt produced and starred in film, What Do You Say to a Naked Lady?

FURIE, SIDNEY J.: Director, Writer, Producer. b. Toronto, Canada, Feb. 28, 1933. Ent. TV and films 1954. Canadian features include: Dangerous Age, A Cool Sound from Hell. Also dir. many Hudson Bay TV series. To England 1960. Films since include Dr. Blood's Coffin, During One Night, Brewster's Millions, The Young Ones, The Boys. 1961 appt. exec. dir. Galawor ldfilm Productions, Ltd.
PICTURES INCLUDE: The Leather Boys, Wonderful Life, The Incress File, The Appaloosa, The Naked Runner, The Lawyer, Little Fauss and Big Halsy, Lady Sings the Blues, Hit!, Sheila Levine, Gable and Lombard, The Boys in Company C, The Entity, Purple Hearts (prod., dir., s.p.), Iron Eagle, Iron Eagle II-Battle Beyond the Flag.

FURNESS, BETTY: Actress, TV Correspondent. b. New York, NY, Jan. 3, 1916. Stage and screen actress in the '40s; TV commercial spokeswoman for Westinghouse in '50s, leading consumer advocate in '70s. Host on both local TV and radio shows in New York (Dimension in a Woman's World, At Your Beck and Call, Ask Betty Furness, etc.). Named President Johnson's asst. for consumer affairs in 1967. 1970, chmn, exec. dir. of New York state's consumer protection board. Commissioner NY City dept. Consumer Affairs. Joined WNBC-TV in 1974 as consumer reporter and weekly contributor to Today Show. 1988: Betty's Attic.
PICTURES: Professional Sweetheart, Emergency Call, Lucky Devils, Beggars in Ermine, Keeper of the Bees, Magnificent Obsession, Swing Time, The President's Mystery, Mama Steps Out, North of Shanghai.

FURSE, RUSSELL L.: Executive. b. Humansville, MO, Jan. 27, 1908. e. Colorado Teachers Coll., Greely. Film. dir., prod. Warner Bros., Hal Roach: Prod. vice pres. Televisions Programs, Inc. Executive prod., ABC Television, Hollywood, Gen. mgr. network prog. dept., CBS Television: dir; prog. oper.; KEY T Santa Barbara. Gen. mgr. CHEK TV Victoria, B.C. Santa Barbara; exec. v.p. Santa Maria Telecasting Corp. Co-founder Academy of Television Arts & Sciences. Chmn. of board, Communications Foundation, pres. Tri-County Public Service Corporation, pres. KBBY-KBBQ Radio Oxnard, member Affiliated Producers Work Shop, Board of Directors Affiliates University of California Santa Barbara, Founder, Riviera Park Research & Communications Center; pres. & chief exec. off., California Video Communications.

FURST, AUSTIN O.: Executive. e. Lehigh U., B.S. in economics/marketing. Began career in marketing dept., Proctor and Gamble; 1972 joined Time Inc. as dir., new subscription sales for Time magazine; later joined Time Inc.'s new magazine dev. staff for People magazine; named circulation mgr., People magazine, 1974; 1975 named pres., Time Inc.'s Computer Television Inc., a pay-per-view hotel operation and was responsible for successful turnaround and sale of co.; 1976, vice pres., programming, Home Box Office; named

exec. v.p. HBO, 1979; appointed pres. and CEO, Time-Life Films, Inc., 1980; 1981 established Vestron after acquiring home video rights to Time/Life Video Library; chmn. and CEO, Vestron, Inc.

FURST, RENEE: Publicist. President, Renee Furst Advertising and Public Relations. b. New York, NY, Oct. 23. e. New School, Columbia U. m. Peter Furst, journalist. Adv. acct. exec. for Cinema 5 Theatres at Diener Hauser. 1974–87: has done p.r. on such films as Missing, Napoleon, The Gods Must Be Crazy, Fanny and Alexander, Cousin Cousine, Official Story, Barfly, Mephisto, Madame Rosa, Blood Simple, Breaker Morant. Worked on adv. and p.r. for Astor Pictures on classics such as La Dolce Vita, Last Year at Marienbad, Rocco and His Brothers.

G

GABOR, ZSA ZSA: Actress. r.n. Sari Gabor. b. Hungary, Feb. 6, 1918. e. Budapest, Lausanne, Switzerland. Stage debut in Europe. Author: Zsa Zsa's Complete Guide to Men (1969); How to Get a Man, How to Keep a Man and How to Get Rid of a Man (1971).
PICTURES INCLUDE: Lovely to Look At, We're Not Married, The Story of Three Loves, Lili, Moulin Rouge, Three Ring Circus, Death of a Scoundrel, Girl in the Kremlin, For the First Time, Boys' Night Out, Picture Mommy Dead, Jack of Diamonds, Won Ton Ton, the Dog Who Saved Hollywood.

GAFFNEY, ROBERT: Producer. Director. b. New York, NY, Oct. 8, 1931. e. Iona Coll., 1949–51. Staff, Louis de Rochemont; prod., Rooftops of New York, in assoc. with Robert Associates, prod. staff, Cinerama Holiday, Man on a String; camera technical consultant, Cinemiracle prod., Windjam-McCarty, 1960; prod. industrial films, Seneca Prods., Prod., Light Fantastic; prod., Troublemaker; assoc. prod., Harvey Middleman Fireman; dir., Frankenstein Meets the Space Monster.

GALANTE, M. CHRISTINA: Executive. b. Tucson, AZ, Aug. 30, 1942. e. U. of Arizona, New School for Social Research, N.Y. Started career as child model in 1948. Entered film career as stunt double in 1955 working in dozens of major films made in Arizona, 1962–66, feature vocalist with big bands for USO tours and major night clubs. 1967–70, spokeswoman and actress in TV commercials and feature films. 1970–74, television commercials producer. 1974–77, film coordinator for mayor's office, City of New York, coordinating and supervising all m.p. and television filming in City. 1977 named special consultant to California Motion Picture Council. 1980, named to Council by Governor Edmund G. Brown and elected its chairman. 1980, named to Los Angeles Film Commission by Mayor Tom Bradley, currently on executive board. 1981–82, special consultant for m.p. & TV development for city of Los Angeles. Currently creative services director, Rogers and Cowan (public relations).

GALE, BOB: Writer, Producer. b. St. Louis, MO, 1951. e. U. of Southern California School of Cinema. Joined with friend Robert Zemeckis to write screenplays, starting with episode for TV series, McCloud. Also co-wrote story for The Nightstalker series. Turned to feature films, co-writing with Zemeckis script for I Wanna Hold Your Hand, on which Gale also acted as associate producer.
PICTURES: 1941 (s.p.); Used Cars (prod., co-s.p.); Back to the Future (co.-prod., s.p.).

GALE, GEORGE: Executive. e. Sorbonne U., Paris, France. Feature editor, Budapest Ed., U.S. Army Pictorial Service. Feature and TV editor MGM, Hal Roach, Disney Studios; prod. and prod. exec. Ivan Tors; American National Enterprises, Inc. Producer and director. Supervised the production of over 30 features for television syndication and numerous theatrical and TV features. Member ACE and Academy of Motion Picture Arts and Sciences. Formed George Gale Productions, Inc. in 1976.

GALLIGAN, ZACK: Actor. b. New York, NY, 1963. e. Columbia U.
PICTURES: Gremlins, Nothing Lasts Forever, Waxwork.
TELEVISION: Crossings, Surviving, The Return of Hickey.

GALLOP, RICHARD C.: Executive. e. Harvard Law Sch. Now managing dir., Allen & Co., Inc. Previously, pres. & chief operating officer, Columbia Pictures Industries (appt. 1983); also chm. of m.p. div., Columbia Pictures. Previously exec. v.p-finance, law and admin. of Columbia (since 1982); also served as gen. counsel, 1981–83. Joined Columbia as sr. v.p. & gen. counsel, 1981. Began career in 1963 as associate of law firm, Milbank Tweed Hadley & McCloy, New York; named partner, 1970. 1979, partner of Washington, DC law firm, Caplin & Drysdale, specializing in corporate and financial matters. In that capacity served as outside corporate legal counsel to Columbia two yrs. Member: finance committee, Williams Coll.; board of trustees, Marymount Coll.

GAMBON, MICHAEL: Actor. b. Dublin, Ireland, 1940. Ent. Ind. 1966. Early experience in theatre. 1985–87 Acting at National Theatre and London's West End.
PICTURES: The Beast Must Die, Turtle Diary, Paris By Night.
TELEVISION: Uncle Vanya, Ghosts, Oscar Wilde, The Holy Experiment, Absurd Person Singular, The Singing Detective, (serial).

GANIS, SIDNEY M.: Publicist. b. New York, NY, Jan. 8, 1940. e. Brooklyn Coll. Staff writer, newspaper and wire service contact, 20th Century-Fox 1961–62; radio, TV contact and special projects, Columbia Pictures 1963–64. Joined Seven Arts Prod. 1965 as publicity mgr.; 1967, appt. prod. publicity mgr. Warner-7 Arts, Ass't prod., The Marquis a Crooked Man, 1969. Studio Publicity dir., Cinema Center Films, 1970. Director of Ad-Pub for Mame, Warner Bros., 1973; Director of Advertising, Warner Bros., 1974; named WB v.p., worldwide adv. & pub., 1977; 1979, snr. v.p., Lucasfilm, Ltd.; 1982 Emmy winner, exec. prod., best documentary, The Making of Raiders of the Lost Ark. 1986, joined Paramount Pictures as pres., worldwide mktg. 1986, elected to board of dir. University Art Museum, Berkeley, CA.

GANZ, BRUNO: Actor. b. Zurich, Switzerland, March 22, 1941.
THEATER: Was part of the Berlin Theater troupe, Schaubuhne. Hamlet (1967), Dans La Jungle Des Villes, Torquato Tasso, La Chevauchee Sur Le Lac de Constance, Peer Gynt, Hamlet (1984).
PICTURES: Der Sanfte Lauf (1967), Sommergaste (1975), The Marquise of O, Lumiere, The Wild Duck, The American Friend, The Lefthanded Woman, The Boys from Brazil, Black and White Like Day and Night, Knife in the Head, Nosferatu the Vampyre, Return of a Good Friend, 5% Risk, An Italian Woman, Polenta, La Provinciale, La Dame Aux Camelias, Der Erfinder, Etwas Wird Sichtbar, Circle of Deceit, Hande Hoch, Logik Der Gerfuhls, War and Peace, In the White City, System Ohne Schatten, Der Pendler, Wings of Desire, Bankomatt.
TELEVISION: Father and Son (Italian TV).

GARBO, GRETA: Actress. r.n. Greta Gustafson. b. Stockholm, Sept. 18, 1906. e. Stockholm. Stage career as a dancer in Sweden. Hollywood screen career started 1926 with Torrent. Voted one of the Ten Best Money-Making Stars in Motion Picture Herald-Fame Poll 1932. Spec. Academy Award, 1954.
PICTURES INCLUDE: Temptress, Flesh and the Devil, Love, Divine Woman, Mysterious Lady, Single Standard, Wild Orchids, Woman of Affairs, Kiss, Anna Christie, Susan Lennox, Her Fall and Rise, Romance, Mata Hari, Grand Hotel, Queen Christina, Anna Karenina, Camille, Conquest, Ninotchka, Two-Faced Woman.

GARCIA, ANDY: Actor. b. Havana, Cuba, 1956. e. Florida International U, Miami. Family moved to Miami Beach in 1961. Spent several years acting with regional theaters in Florida.
PICTURES: Blue Skies Again (debut, 1983), The Mean Season, 8 Million Ways to Die, The Untouchables, Stand and Deliver, American Roulette, The Sixth Family.
TELEVISION: Hill Street Blues, Brothers, Foley Square, Clinton and Nadine.

GARDENIA, VINCENT: Actor. r.n. Vincent Scognamiglio. b. Naples, Italy, Jan. 7, 1922. f. was actor and singer who brought Vincent to U.S. at age 2, formed theatrical co. in which Vincent took part. U.S. Army, W.W.II, and after landed first English-speaking role in summer stock prod. of Burlesque. Trained at Italian Theater, NY. Made off-Bdwy. debut in The Man with the Golden Arm; first Bdwy. role in The Visit, 1958, with the Lunts. Film debut: Murder, Inc. (1960).
PICTURES INCLUDE: Cop Haters, Cold Turkey, Little Murders, Hickey and Boggs, Bang the Drum Slowly, Luciano, The Manchu Eagle, Death Wish, The Front Page, Heaven Can Wait, Firepower, Home Movies, The Last Flight of Noah's Ark, Movers and Shakers, Little Shop of Horrors, Moonstruck, Freedom Fighter.
TELEVISION: All in the Family, (series) Breaking Away.
STAGE: Shoe Shine (1927 Brooklyn); The Man With the Golden Arm; The Visit; The Cold Wind and the Warm; Rashomon; The Power of Darkness; Only in America; Machinal, The Wall, Gallows Humor, Daughter of Silence; Endgame; Seidman and Son; Little Murders; Passing Through from Exotic Places, The Prisoner of Second Avenue (Tony Award, 1972); California Suite; God's Favorite; Sly Fox, Buried Inside Extra, Glengary Glen Ross; I'm Not Rappaport.

GARDINER, PETER R.: Executive. Independent still photographer and industrial film-maker before joining Paramount, 1973, in feature post-prod. 1979, joined Warner Bros. as asst. dir., corporate services. 1987, promoted to v.p., opns., WB corporate film-video services.

GARDNER, ARTHUR: Producer. b. Marinette, WI. Entered m.p.ind. as actor, in orig. cast All Quiet on the Western Front, 1929. Juvenile leads in: Waterfront, Heart of the North, Assassin of Youth, Religious Racketeer; production asst. dir. King Bros. 1941, then asst. prod. U.S. Air Force 1st Motion Picture Unit, 1943–45. Formed Levy-Gardner-Laven Prods. with Jules Levy, Arnold Laven, 1951.
PICTURES INCLUDE: (Asst. dir.) Paper Bullets, I Killed That Man, Rubber Racketeers, Klondike Fury, I Escaped From the Gestapo, Suspense; (Asst. prod.) Gangster, Dude Goes West, Badmen of Tombstone, Gun Crazy, Mutiny, Southside 1–1000; Prod.: Without Warning, Vice Squad, Down Three Dark Streets, Return of Dracula, The Flame Barrier, The Vampire, The Monster that Challenged the World, Geronimo, The Glory Guys, Clambake, Scalphunters, Sam Whiskey, Underground, McKenzie Break, The Honkers, Hunting Party, Kansas City Bomber, White Lightning, McQ, Brannigan, Gator, Safari 3000.
TELEVISION: Rifleman, Robert Taylor's Detectives, Law of the Plainsman, The Big Valley.
MEMBER: Producers Guild of America, Directors Guild of America, Screen Actors Guild, Actors Equity.

GARDNER, AVA: Actress. b. Smithfield, NC, Dec. 24, 1922. e. Atlantic Christian Coll.
PICTURES INCLUDE: We Were Dancing, Joe Smith, American, Lost Angel, Three Men in White, Maisie Goes to Reno, Whistle Stop, The Killers, The Hucksters, Singapore, One Touch of Venus, The Bribe, Great Sinner, East Side, West Side, Show Boat, Pandora and the Flying Dutchman, Lone Star, Snows of Kilimanjaro, Ride Vaquero, Mogambo, Knights of the Round Table, Barefoot Contessa, Bhowani Junction, Little Hut, The Naked Maja, On the Beach, The Fair Bride, 55 Days at Peking, Night of the Iguana, The Bible, Mayerling, Life and Times of Judge Roy Bean, The Devil's Widow, Earthquake, The Bluebird, Permission to Kill, The Cassandra Crossing, The Sentinel, City on Fire, Priest of Love.
TELEVISION: Harem, The Long Hot Summer, Falcon Crest (series).

GARFIELD, WARREN: Writer, Publicist. b. Nov. 18, 1936. e. U. of California at L.A., Loyola of Los Angeles Sch. of Law. Story analyst, assistant to dir., Hecht-Hill-Lancaster, 1948–58; casting dir. Assist., assist. film editor, Columbia Pictures, films, featurettes, trailers, TV spots, Paramount Pictures, 1966–68; creative film services, Walt Disney Productions, 1968–present. Member: Academy of Motion Picture, Arts & Sciences.
CREDITS: A Stranger in Town (wrote s.p.), Cat Ballou, Wild and Wonderful, Flight From Ashiya, Taras Bulba (as assist. to Harold Hecht); The High Chaparral (wrote, TV).

GARFINKLE, LOUIS: Writer, Director, Producer. b. Seattle, WA, February 11, 1928. e. U. of California, U. of Washington, U. of Southern California. Writer KOMO, Seattle, 1945; Executive Research, Inc., 1948; Writer, educ. doc. screenplays, Emerson Films, EBF. 1948–50; s.p. You Can Beat the A-Bomb (RKO), 1950; Writer-dir. training films, info. films, Signal Photo, 1950–53; Copy, Weinberg Adv., 1953; Head of Doc. Research in TV, U. of California, Berkeley, 1954–55; staff, Sheilah Graham Show, 1955; story and s.p. The Young Guns (AA), formed Maxim Prod. Inc. with Albert Band, 1956; story, s.p. and co-producer I Bury the Living (UA), 1957 (Killer on the Wall); s.p. and co-producer Face of Fire (AA), 1958; Writer, 712 teleplays for Day in Court, Morning Court, Accused for Selmur—ABC-TV, 1959–66; Co-writer-creator Direct Line pilot, Selmur, 1960; Story and t.p. June Allyson Show, Threat of Evil, 1960; s.p. in collab. The Hellbenders 1967; story and t.p. Death Valley Days, Crullers At Sundown, 1967; story, Death Valley Days, Captain Dick Mine, 1967; s.p. in collab. A Minute to Pray A Second to Die 1968; story, s.p. and co-producer The Love Doctors 1969; story, s.p. and director Beautiful People, 1970; s.p. (collab.) The Models, 1971; head writer, No. 3 Peanut Place (pilot), 1972; story & s.p. (collab.) The Doberman Gang, 1971; story & s.p. (collab.) Little Cigars 1973; The Deer Hunter 1978, (story collab.)

GARFUNKEL, ART: Actor, Singer, Composer. b. New York, NY, Oct. 13, 1942. e. Columbia U. Began singing at age 4. Long partnership with Paul Simon began in grade school at 13 in Queens, NY; first big success in 1965 with hit single, Sound of Silence. Partnership dissolved in 1970. Film debut in Catch 22 (1969). Winner of 4 Grammy Awards.
PICTURES: Carnal Knowledge, Bad Timing/A Sensual Obsession.

GARLAND, BEVERLY: Actress. b. Santa Cruz, CA, Oct. 17, 1930. e. Glendale Coll., 1945–47.
TELEVISION: starred, Decoy, Bing Crosby; Twilight Zone, Dr. Kildare, Medic, (Emmy Nomination, 1954); My Three Sons; Scarecrow and Mrs. King, Magnum P.I., Remington Steele. Movies: This Gun for Hire.
PICTURES INCLUDE: The Mad Room, Where the Red Fern Grows, Airport, 1975, Roller Boogie, It's My Turn.

GARNER, JAMES: Actor. b. Norman, OK, April 7, 1928. ie. high school there. Then joined Merchant Marine, U.S. Army ser. in Korean War. Prod. Paul Gregory suggested acting career. Studied drama at N.Y. Berghof School. Toured with road companies; Warner Bros. studio contract followed with screen debut in Toward the Unknown (1956).

PICTURES INCLUDE: Shoot-out at Medicine Bend, Darby's Rangers, Sayonara, Up Periscope, Cash McCall, The Children's Hour, The Great Escape. Thrill of It All, Move Over Darling, The Americanization of Emily, 36 Hours, The Art of Love, Mister Buddwing, Duel at Diablo, Grand Prix, Hour of the Gun, Support Your Local Sheriff, Marlowe, Support Your Local Gunfighter, Skin Game, They Only Kill Their Masters, One Little Indian, Hawaiian Cowboy, Health, The Fan, Victor/Victoria, Tank, Murphy's Romance, Sunset.
TELEVISION: Cheyenne, Maverick, Rockford Files. Movies: The Long Summer of George Adams, The Glitter Dome, Heartsounds, Promise (also exec. prod.), Obsessive Love. Mini-Series: Space.

GARR, TERI: Actress. b. Lakewood, OH, 1949. Began career as dancer, performing S.F. Ballet at 13. Later appeared with L.S. Ballet and in original road show co. of West Side Story. Did commercials; appeared in film written by a fellow acting student, Jack Nicholson, Head. Career boosted by appearance on TV as semi-regular on The Sonny and Cher Show.
PICTURES: The Conversation, Young Frankenstein, Won Ton Ton, The Dog Who Saved Hollywood, Oh, God!, Close Encounters of the Third Kind, Mr. Mike's Mondo Video, The Black Stallion, One from the Heart, The Sting II, Tootsie, The Black Stallion Returns, Mr. Mom, Firstborn, Lies, Miracles, After Hours, Full Moon in Blue Water, Out Cold.
TELEVISION: Series regular: The Ken Berry "Wow" Show, (1972), Burns and Schreiber Comedy Hour, Girl With Something Extra, The Sonny and Cher Comedy Hour, The Sonny Comedy Revue. Movies: Law and Order, Prime Suspect; The Tale of the Frog Prince (Faerie Tale Theatre); Winter of Our Discontent, To Catch a King, Intimate Strangers, Pack of Lies, Drive, She Said (Trying Times), Paul Reiser: Out on a Whim. Mini-Series: Fresno.

GARRETT, BETTY: Singer, Actress. b. St. Joseph, MO, May 23, 1919. e. scholarships; Annie Wright Seminary, Tacoma, WA, Neighborhood Playhouse, N.Y. Sang in night clubs, hotels, Broadway shows (1942–46); won Donaldson award for best musical comedy performance of 1964, Spoon River Anthology, Star of Tomorrow, 1949.
PICTURES INCLUDE: (Screen debut) The Big City, 1947, Words and Music, Take Me Out to the Ball Game, Neptune's Daughter, On the Town, My Sister Eileen, Shadow on the Window.
TELEVISION: Series: Laverne and Shirley, All in the Family, Murder She Wrote, Movies: All the Way Home.

GARRETT, LAWRENCE G. JR.: Executive. b. San Francisco, Nov. 5, 1942. e. U. of California; Thunderbird Graduate Sch. 1967, joined Columbia Pictures Intl., Panama, Mexico; 1969, Paramount Pictures, mgr., Venezuela; 1973, MCA-TV asst. mgr., Mexico; 1973–76, Shearson Hayden Stone Institutional investment; 1977, United Artists, Argentina, Austral-Asia mgr. dir.; 1980, Avco Embassy, sls. supvr. Latin American-Far East; 1981, head intl. sls., Shapiro Entertainment; 1982, head intl. sls., Goldfarb Distributors; 1983–86, dir./intl. sls. & acquisitions, Arista Films; 1987, v.p. intl. theatrical & video sls., ITC Entertainment.

GARRISON, PAUL: Writer, Producer, Director. Adv. photog, in N.Y., Hollywood; production of TV films since 1948; dir. first series of half hour TV pictures made, Cases of Eddie Drake; dir., writer for more than 100 TV film shows; in chge. of TV Workshop, Hollywood.

GARSON, GREER: Actress. b. County Down, Northern Ireland, 1912. e. London U., B.A. cum laude; Grenoble U. Screen debut 1939 in Goodbye, Mr. Chips. Academy Award best performance by actress, 1942 (Mrs. Miniver, MGM). Voted one of the ten best Money-Making Stars in Motion Picture Herald-Fame Poll 1942–46 inclusive. Photoplay Mag. Gold Medal 1944–45.
THEATRE: Stage debut Birmingham (England) Rep. theat. 1932 in Street Scene; London debut 1935 in Golden Arrow; continued London stage to 1938 (Vintage Wine, Mademoiselle, Accent on Youth, Page from a Diary, Old Music, etc.).
PICTURES INCLUDE: Pride and Prejudice, Blossoms in the Dust, When Ladies Meet, Mrs. Miniver, Random Harvest, Mme. Curie, Mrs. Parkington, Valley of Decision, Adventure, Desire Me, Julia Misbehaves, That Forsythe Woman, The Miniver Story, The Law and the Lady, Scandal at Scourie, Julius Caesar, Her Twelve Men, Strange Lady in Town, Sunrise at Campobello, The Singing Nun, The Happiest Millionaire.
TELEVISION: Crown Matrimonial, My Father Gave Me America, Little Women, Holiday Tribute to Radio City, Perry Como's Christmas in New Mexico, A Gift of Music (host).

GARTNER, MICHAEL G.: Executive. b. 1939. e. Carleton Coll., Northfield, MN; NYU Sch. of Law. Began newspaper career at 15 with The Des Moines Register in Iowa. Became the paper's editor, later pres., COO and editorial chmn. of the parent Des Moines Register and Tribune Co. Worked for 14 years at the Wall Street Journal in various positions. Served as editor of Gannett-owned Louisville Courier-Journal and Louisville Times, and owner of the Daily Tribune of Ames, IA. Appointed president of NBC News, August 1988.

GASSMAN, VITTORIO: Actor. b. Genoa, Italy, Sept. 1, 1922. e. Acad. of Dramatic Art, Rome. Stage actor, 1943; m.p. debut, 1946.
PICTURES INCLUDE: Daniele Cortis, Mysterious Rider, Bitter Rice, Lure of Sila, The Outlaws, Anna, Streets of Sorrow; to U.S., Cry of the Hunted, Sombrero, The Glass Wall, Rhapsody, Girls Marked Danger, Mambo, War and Peace, World's Most Beautiful Woman, Tempest, The Love Specialist, The Great War, Let's Talk About Women, Il Successo, The Tiger, Woman Times Seven, Ghosts—Italian Style, Scent of a Woman, Viva Italia!, A Wedding, Quintet, Immortal Bachelor, The Nude Bomb, Sharky's Machine, Tempest, I Picari, The Family, The Uncle, The House of the Lord, The Hateful Dead.

GATWARD, JAMES: Executive. b. London, England. Ent. Ind. 1957. Early career as freelance drama prod. dir. in Canada, USA, UK (with ITV & BBC). Prod. dir. various intern. co-productions in UK, Ceylond, Australia, Germany. Currently Chief Executive and Dep. Chmn. TVS Television Ltd., Chrm. Telso Communications Ltd., Dir. of ITN, Channel Four, Super Channel, Oracle Teletext.

GAVIN, JOHN: Actor. b. Los Angeles, CA, April 8, 1932. m. actress Constance Towers. e. St. John's Military Acad., Villanova Prep at Ojai, Stanford Univ., Naval service: air intelligence officer in Korean War. Broadway stage debut: Seesaw, 1973. 1961–73 public service experience as spec. advisor to Secretary Gen. of OAS, performed gp. task work for Dept. of State and Exec. Office of the President. Pres. Screen Actors Guild, 1971–73. Named U.S. Ambassador to Mexico, 1981–86. Joined UNIVISA Communications Gp. as pres. satellite communications. Consultant to Dept. of State and serves on many boards.
PICTURES INCLUDE: A Time to Love and a Time to Die, Imitation of Life, Spartacus, A Breath of Scandal, Romanoff and Juliet, Tammy, Tell Me True, Back Street, Thoroughly Modern Millie, Mad Woman of Chaillot, Psycho, Midnight Lace.

GAYLARD, JAMES W., III: Exhibitor b. Knoxville, TN, Sept. 18, 1943. e. Henderson H.S., Troy, AL., 1961; Troy State U., 1965, B.S. mathematics. Ent. industry, managed theatres, Troy Drive-In Theatres, Inc. 1966.

GAYLE, PETER: Producer, Writer, Actor. b. New York, NY. Attended American Acad. of Dramatic Arts, New York Sch. of Theatre Arts. Columbia Pictures Talent School.
TELEVISION: (Specials) Producer, writer, The World of Brigitte Bardot, The Goldie Hawn Special, The Rolling Stones in Concert, Hollywood: The Magic Kingdom, On Location With ABBA; Boy George Live from the London Paladium, John Belushi Remembered.
TELEVISION: (Series) The Young Rebels, The Protectors, Spindletop, The Legends of Rock and Roll.
PICTURES INCLUDE: Without Each Other (winner of Cannes Film Festival), The Gang; Never Too Young to Rock; Black Cobra; Shoot; The Boy Who Owned a Melephant (winner of the Venice Film Festival); Intercept; State Park; Cannabis Row; The Beatles: From the Beginning.

GAYNOR, MITZI: Actress. r.n. Francisca Mitzi Von Gerber. b. Chicago, IL, Sept. 4, 1931. e. Powers Professional H.S., Hollywood. Studied ballet since age four; was in L.A. Light Opera prod. Roberta.
OPERA: Fortune Teller, Song of Norway, Louisiana Purchase, Naughty Marietta, The Great Waltz.
PICTURES INCLUDE: My Blue Heaven, Take Care of My Little Girl, Golden Girl, The I Don't Care Girl, We're Not Married, Bloodhounds of Broadway, There's No Business Like Show Business, Anything Goes, Three Young Texans, Down Among the Sheltering Palms, Birds and the Bees, The Joker, Les Girls, South Pacific, Surprise Package, Happy Anniversary, For Love or Money.

GAZZARA, BEN: Actor. b. New York, NY, Aug. 28, 1930. e. Studied at CCNY 1947–48. Won scholarship to study with Erwin Piscator; joined Actor's Studio, where students improvised a play, End as a Man, which then was performed on Broadway with him in lead. Screen debut (1957) in film version of that play retitled The Strange One.
PICTURES INCLUDE: Anatomy of a Murder, Joy of Laughter, The Passionate Thief, The Young Doctors, Convicts Four, Conquered City, A Rage to Live, The Bridge at Remagen, Husbands, Capone, High Velocity, Killing of a Chinese Bookie, Voyage of the Damned, Bloodline, They All Laughed, Inchon, Tales of Ordinary Madness, Road House, Quicker Than the Eye.
TELEVISION: Arrest and Trial, Run for Your Life. Movies: A Question of Honor; An Early Frost, A Letter to Three Wives, Police Story: The Freeway Killings, Downpayment on Murder.
THEATER: Jezebel's Husband, End as a Man, Cat on a Hot Tin Roof, A Hatful of Rain, The Night Circus, Epitaph for

George Dillon, Two for the Seesaw, Strange Interlude, Traveler Without Luggage, Hughie, Who's Afraid of Virginia Woolf.

GEARY, ANTHONY: Actor. b. Coalville, UT, May 29, 1947. e. U. of Vermont. On screen in Johnny Got His Gun.
TELEVISION: Bright Promise, The Young and the Restless, Osmond Family Holiday Special, General Hospital, Intimate Agony, Sins of the Past, The Imposter, Kicks, Perry Mason: The Case of the Murdered Madam.
PICTURES INCLUDE: Private Investigations, Disorderlies, Penitentiary III, You Can't Hurry Love, Pass the Ammo, Dangerous Love, Singles, It Takes Two.

GEBHARDT, FRED: Producer, Writer, Exhibitor. b. Vienna, Austria, Mar. 16, 1925. e. Schotten Gymnasium, Vienna, U. of California at L.A., 1939. Usher Boyd Theatre, Bethlehem, PA; Mgr., Rivoli Thea. L.A., 1944; 18 yrs. mgr. many theatres. Fox West Coast, then Fine Arts Theatre. Writer, prod.: 12 To the Moon, The Phantom Planet; prod., Assignment Outer Space, Operation M; s.p., All But Glory, The Starmaker, Shed No Blood, Fortress in Heaven, Eternal Woman.
BOOKS: Mental Disarmament, All But Glory, Starmaker, Shed No Blood, The Last of the Templars.
Pres., Four Crown Prods., Inc.; recipient of Medal of Americanism, D.A.R., 1963; Honorary Lifetime Member, P.T.A., Young Man of The Year Award, 1956, 24 Showmanship Awards; Mem. Acad. M.P. Arts and Sciences, Ind. M.P. Prod. Assoc.

GEE, CHARLOTTE: Executive. Served for 6 years as adv.-pub. mgr. for Village Roadshow Corp., Warner Bros. Australian dist. Left to join Apogee (special effects co.) as v.p., mktg. 1986, joined WB as dir. project pub. 1987, named WB v.p., pub.

GEESON, JUDY: Actress. b. Arundel, Sussex, England, Sept. 10, 1948. e. Corona Stage Sch. Began professional career on British TV, 1960.
PICTURES INCLUDE: To Sir with Love, Circus of Blood, Here We Go Round the Mulberry Bush, Hammerhead, Three into Two Won't Go, Two Gentlemen Sharing, The Executioner, 10 Rillington Place, Brannigan, The Eagle Has Landed, Carry On England, It's Not the Size That Counts, Horror Planet, Dominique (made 1977).
TELEVISION: Dance of Death, Lady Windermere's Fan, Room with a View, The Skin Game, Star Maidens, Poldark, She, The Coronation, Murder She Wrote.
THEATRE: Othello, Titus Andronicus, Two Gentlemen of Verona, Section Nine, An Ideal Husband.

GEFFEN, DAVID: Executive. b. New York, NY, Feb. 21, 1943. Career began in 1964 in mail room of William Morris Agency. In 1968 left with co-worker Elliot Roberts to form Geffen-Roberts Management, clients eventually including Joni Mitchell, Crosby, Stills and Nash, Neil Young, Jackson Browne. Founded Asylum Records, later merging it with Elektra; roster including Joni Mitchell, Linda Ronstadt, Queen, Carly Simon, Bob Dylan, etc. In 1975 named vice chm. of Warner Bros. Pictures. Resigned 1978 to teach at Yale. Produced first film Personal Best, 1981. Theatrical productions include Dreamgirls, Cats, Little Shop of Horrors, Master Harold . . . and the Boys, Good, etc.
PICTURES INCLUDE: Prod.: Personal Best, Risky Business, Lost in America, Little Shop of Horrors.

GELBART, LARRY: Writer. b. Chicago, IL, Feb. 25, 1925. Began writing at 16; first break was writing material for Danny Thomas on Fanny Brice Show. Followed by Duffy's Tavern, shaping routines for Eddie Cantor, Bob Hope, Jack Paar. Was one of Sid Caesar's stable of comedy writers on Show of Shows.
THEATER: The Conquering Hero, A Funny Thing Happened on the Way to the Forum (with Burt Shevlove); Sly Fox.
PICTURES INCLUDE: The Notorious Landlady, The Wrong Box, Not With My Wife Don't, Oh, God!, Movie. Movie; Neighbors, Tootsie (co-s.p.), Blame It on Rio (exec. prod., co.-s.p.).
TELEVISION: M*A*S*H (Emmy, 1974, also co-prod.), United States, Karen.

GELFAN, GREG: Executive. Was entertainment atty. with two firms before joining Paramount Pictures in 1983 as dir. of business affairs. 1985, named v.p., business affairs, for M.P. Group of Paramount.

GELLER, BRIAN L.: Executive. b. New York, NY, Feb. 3, 1948. e. Queens Coll. Entered industry with Columbia Pictures as sls. trainee in 1966, leaving in 1968 to go with American Intl. Pictures as asst. branch mgr. In 1969 joined Cinemation Industries as eastern div. sls. mgr.; 1978, left to become gen. sls. mr. of NMD Film Distributing Co. 1982, named dir. of dist., Mature Pictures Corp. 1983, gen. sls. mgr., Export Pix. Now with Cinema Group as east. sls. mgr.
Member: Motion Picture Bookers Club of N.Y.; Variety Tent 35.

GENDECE, BRIAN K.: Producer, Executive. b. St. Louis, MO. e. Drury Coll., Springfield, MO. 1981–85, Director of Business Affairs, Weinstein/Skyfield Productions and Skyfield Management. 1986–87, dir. of business affairs,Cannon Films; 1987–88, dir. creative affairs, Cannon Films.
PICTURES INCLUDE: Runaway Train, Salsa, Rebel Yell.
STAGE: Jack Klugman as Lyndon.
VIDEO: Bad Habits, Shape Up with Arnold, Laura Branigan's Your Love.

GEORGE, GEORGE LOUIS: Director. b. Moscow, Russia, July 31, 1907. e. U. of Paris, law. Began as cutter, later asst. dir., French prods. Re-entered prod. 1939 as asst. dir. & prod. French version of The Four Hundred Million; in similar capacity numerous French versions of Hollywood prods. thereafter. In 1942 asst. prod. Our Russian Front. Became assoc. Natl. Film Board of Canada in prod. war information films; also dir. The Labor Front for World in Action series. In 1944 dir. University Town for Co-ord. Inter-Amer. Affairs; 1946–49 dir. 16 films for Signal Corps Photo. Center, Astoria, L.I., incl. Acad. Award winner Toward Independence. In 1949 dir. in TV, also Women of Tomorrow, WB. 1950, dir. in Israel for Palestine Films; dir., prod., TV & documentary films, 1950–55; exec. secr., Screen Directors International Guild, 1956–63; admin., SDIG Trust Fund, 1963–67; member, Natl. Bd., Directors Guild of America 1966–69; since 1966, member Eastern Directors Council, DGA; pres. Film & TV Book Club, Inc. 1967–69. Currently freelancing.

GEORGE, GEORGE W.: Writer, Producer. b. New York, NY, Feb. 8, 1920. e. Williams Coll. U.S. Navy, 1941–44; screenwriter since 1948. President, The Saga Group, Inc. N.Y. based, Industrial Video/film company.
PICTURES INCLUDE: Bodyguard, The Nevadan, Woman on Pier 13, Peggy Mystery Submarine, Red Mountain Experiment, Alcatraz, Fight Town, Smoke Signal, Desert Sands, Uranium Boom, Halliday Brand, Doc, The James Dean Story, The Two Little Bears.
PRODUCER STAGE: Dylan, Any Wednesday, Ben Franklin in Paris, The Great Indoors, Happily Never After, Night Watch, Via Galactica, Bedroom Farce.
PRODUCER PICTURES: A Matter of Innocence, Twisted Nerve, Hello-Goodbye, Night Watch, Rich Kids, My Dinner with Andre.
TELEVISION: Climax, Screen Gems, Loretta Young Show, The Rifleman, Peter Gunn, The Real McCoys, Adventures in Paradise, Hong Kong, Follow the Sun.

GEORGE, LOUIS: Executive. Pres. & chief executive officer, Arista Films, Inc. b. Karavas, Kyrenia, Cyprus, June 7, 1935. e. Kyrenia Business Acad., Cyprus (honored 1951). Emigrated to U.S. in 1952. After brief stint in Foreign Exchange Dept. of City National Bank, New York, served in U.S. Army, 1953–55. Entered industry in 1956 as theatre manager with Loew's Theatres in N.Y. metro area, managing Metropolitan, Triboro, New Rochelle, between 1958–66. In 1966 joined MGM as dir. of intl. theatre dept. In 1969 promoted to dir. of world-wide non-theatrical sales. From 1972 to 1974 served as regional dir. of MGM Far East operations. In 1974 left MGM to establish Arista Films, Inc., an indep. prod./dist. co.
PICTURES INCLUDE: Slaughterhouse Rock, Buying Time, Violent Zone.

GEORGE, SUSAN: Actress, Producer. b. Surrey, England, 1950. m. actor-prod. Simon MacCorkindale. e. Corona Acad. m.p. debut Million Dollar Brain, 1965.
PICTURES: The Sorcerers, Up the Junction, The Strange Affair, The Looking Glass War, All Neat in Black Stockings, Twinky, Spring and Port Wine, Eye Witness, Die Screaming Marianne, Fright, Straw Dogs, Sonny and I, Dr. Jekyll and Mr. Hyde, Dirty Mary Crazy Larry, Mandingo, Out of Season, A Small Town in Texas, Tiger Shark, Tomorrow Never Comes, Venom, A Texas Legend, House Where Evil Dwells, Jigsaw Man, The White Stallion, Stealing Heaven (exec. prod.), The Lifeguard, White Roses.
TELEVISION: Swallows and Amazons, Adam's Apple, Weaver's Green, Compensation Alice, The Right Attitude, Dracula, Lamb to the Slaughter, Royal Jelly, Masquerade, Czechmate, Hotel, Blacke's Magic, Jack the Ripper.

GERALD, HELEN: Actress. b. New York, NY, Aug. 13. e. U. of Southern California, 1948. Stage: Italian Teatro D'Arte, Les Miserables, The Civil Death, Feudalism.
PICTURES INCLUDE: The Gay Cavalier, The Trap, Tarzan and the Leopard Woman, Cigarette Girl, Meet Miss Bobby Socks, G.I. War Brides, Gentleman's Agreement, A Bell for Adano, Tomorrow Is Forever, Janie, Grand Prix, The Sandpiper, Make Mine Mink, Best of Everything.
TELEVISION: Robert Montgomery Presents, Frontiers of Faith, Valiant Lady, Kraft Theatre, Gangbusters, Adventures of The Falcon, Schlitz Playhouse of Stars, This Is the Answer, Man from U.N.C.L.E., Run for Your Life, Perry Mason.

GERARD, GIL: Actor. b. Little Rock, AK, Jan. 23, 1940. On stage in I Do! I Do!

PICTURES: Airport '77, Buck Rogers in the 25th Century.
TELEVISION: The Doctors, Killing Stone, Buck Rogers in the 25th Century, Sidekick. Movies: Washington Mistress, Not Just Another Affair, Hear No Evil, Johnny (pilot), For Love or Money, Stormin' Home, International Airport.

GERARD, LILLIAN: Publicist, Writer. Publicity, Rialto Theatre, 1936; publicity-adv. Filmarte Theatre, 1938, Gerard Associates, 1938–47; V.P. and managing dir. of Paris Theatre, 1948–62; publicity-adv. dir., Rugoff Theatres, 1962. Film consultant to Times Films, Lopert Films, Landau Co., 1964–65. Exec. secy. to the National Soc. of Film Critics, 1966–68. Adjunct Professor, Film, 1968–70, Columbia U., Sch. of the Arts, Special Projects Co-Ordinator, Museum of Modern Art, 1968–80. Contributor to American Film. Published by American Film Inst. Now associated with Philip Gerard in Gerard Associates.

GERARD, PHILIP R.: Executive. b. New York, NY, Aug. 23, 1913. e. City Coll. of New York, B.B.A. 1935; Columbia U.. Publicity dir. Mayer-Burstyn 1936–39; Gerard Associates, 1939–41; in public relations U.S. War Dept. 1942–44; with MGM 1944–48; with Universal Pictures since 1948; Eastern pub. mgr., 1950–59; Eastern ad. and pub. dir., Dec. 1959; N.Y. Production Exec., 1968–76. As of Jan. 1, 1977 formed Gerard Associates, film consultants on marketing, production and acquisitions. N.Y.C. Advisory Council of CSS/RSVP (Retired Seniors Volunteer Program); Community Service Society. Member: Visitor's Day Comm., New York Hospital.

GERBER, DAVID: Executive. b. Brooklyn, NY. e. U. of the Pacific. m actress Laraine Stephens. Joined Batten, Barton, Durstine and Osborn ad agency in N.Y. as TV supvr. Left to become senior v.p. of TV at General Artists Corp. In Jan., 1956, named v.p. in chg. sales at 20th-Fox TV where sold and packaged over 50 prime-time series and specials. Entered indep. prod. with The Ghost and Mrs. Muir, followed by Nanny and the Professor. In 1970 was exec. prod. of The Double Deckers, children's series made in England. In 1971 was exec. prod. of Cade's County (CBS). In 1972 he joined Columbia Pictures Television as an independent producer and in 1974 was named exec. v.p. worldwide production for CPT. In 1976 he returned to independent production and was exec. prod. of Police Story (Emmy, best dramatic series), Police Woman, The Lindbergh Kidnapping Case, Joe Forrester, The Quest and Gibbsville, To Kill a Cop, Power, Medical Story, Born Free, Beulah Land, The Night the City Screamed, Follow the North Star. 1985, joined MGM/UA TV broadcasting group in chg. world-wide prod. President, MGM/UA Television.

GERBER, MICHAEL H.: Executive. b. New York, NY, Feb. 6, 1944. e. St. Johns U., B.A., 1969; St. Johns U. School of Law, J.D., 1969. Atty. for Screen Gems, 1969–71; asst. secy. & asst. to gen. counsel, Columbia Pictures Industries, 1971–74; corporate counsel and secretary, Allied Artists Pictures, 1974, v.p. Corporate affairs, Allied Artists, 1978; v.p., business affairs, Viacom Intl.

GERE, RICHARD: Actor. b. Philadelphia, PA, Aug. 29, 1949. e. U. of Massachusetts. Started acting in college; later joined Provincetown Playhouse and Seattle Repertory Theatre. Composed music for productions of these groups. Appeared on Broadway in Grease, Soon, Habeas Corpus, Bent, A Midsummer Night's Dream (Lincoln Center); and in London in Taming of the Shrew with Young Vic. Off-B'way in Killer's Head.
PICTURES INCLUDE: Report to the Commissioner, Baby Blue Marine, Looking for Mr. Goodbar, Days of Heaven, Bloodbrothers, Yanks, American Gigolo, An Officer and a Gentleman, Breathless, Beyond the Limits, The Cotton Club, King David, Power, No Mercy, Miles From Home.
TELEVISION: Kojak, Strike Force (movie).

GERETY, T. MICHAEL: Executive. b. Rockville Center, NY, Oct. 30, 1942. U.S., Navy, 1961–64. Started industry career in Chicago with MGM as regional adv/pub. repr.; transferred to Atlanta in same capacity, 1966 and then to Dallas, 1967–70. Joined Durwood Theatres in Dallas in 1971 as div. operations mgr. In 1972 returned to MGM as south west div. dir. adv./pub. in Dallas. Moved to MGM Studios in 1973 as asst. natl. adv. coordinator. In 1974 joined American International as dir. of cooperative adv./exploit. In 1980 joined the Milton I. Moritz Co., film marketing firm, as v.p. In 1981, named v.p., Market Relay Systems, a mktg./communications co. 1982–83, pres., The Newslink Corp. (videotext news service). Joined Hanson & Schwam p.r., 1985. Member: Academy of MP. Arts & Sciences.

GERTZ, IRVING: Composer, Musical director. b. Providence, RI, May 19, 1915. e. Providence Coll. of Music, 1934–37. Assoc. with Providence Symph. Orch., comp. choral works for Catholic Choral Soc.; music dept., Columbia, 1939–41; U.S. Army, 1941–46; then comp. arranger, mus. dir. for many cos. incl. Columbia, U-I, NBC, 20th Century Fox.
PICTURES INCLUDE: Bandits of Corsica, Gun Belt, Long Wait, The Fiercest Heart, First Travelling Saleslady, Fluffy,

Nobody's Perfect, Marines, Let's Go! It Came from Outer Space, The Man from Bitter Ridge, Posse from Hell, The Creature Walks Among Us, The Incredible Shrinking Man, Hell Bent for Leather, Seven Ways from Sundown, Francis Joins the WACS, Raw Edge, East of Sumatra, A Day of Fury, To Hell and Back, Cult of the Cobra, Plunder Road, Top Gun, Tombstone Express, The Alligator People, Khyber Patrol, The Wizard of Baghdad.
Record album (Dot Records) Leaves of Grass; published works for mixed voices; Fluffy, feature, Universal. Marines, Let's Go! feature, 20th Century Fox Serenata for String Quartet, Divertimento for String Orchestra, Tableau for Orchestra.
TELEVISION: Orig. theme & scores: America, The Golden Voyage, Across the Seven Seas, The Legend of Jesse James, Daniel Boone, Voyage to the Bottom of the Sea, Peyton Place, Land of the Giants, Lancer, Medical Center, Boutade for Wood-Wind Quartet, Salute to All Nations, A Village Fair, Liberty! Liberte! (for symphony orchestra).

GETTY, J. RONALD: Producer. b. Berlin, Germany, Dec. 19, 1929. e. Zurich U., Heidelberg U., U. of Southern California. Prior to entering m.p. industry was oil executive, Tidewater Oil Co., mgn. dir. Veedol GmbH, 1955; Getty Oil, Hamburg, 1954–61; pres. & chm. of bd., Veedol Petroleum Int'l, Switzerland, 1961–69; dir., Huiles Veedol France, 1961–69. President & Chm. of bd., Getty Picture Corp.; pres. & chm., Getty Labs, Inc.; dir., Home Theatre Network.
PICTURES: Flare Up, Zeppelin, Shelia.

GETZ, DON: Executive. b. Chicago, IL. Early career in radio until 1952. 1952: Ent. dist. with GBD Int. Releasing handling US and foreign dist. for Mr. Hulot's Holiday, Jour de Fete, Diabolique, Holiday for Henrietta, Ali Baba. 1957: formed Getz-Buck Productions and prod. number of films in UK and France. 1961: formed Playpont Films Ltd., for prod. and dist. of TV and theatrical films in UK and Continent. 1963: formed Artxo Films with Artie Shaw to dist. imported films in the USA. 1964: joined Official Films Inc. as vice-pres. Int. 1968: consultant to Humphries Group. 1971: reactivated Playpont Films as sales agent for foreign producers handling The Great Catherine, Foxtrot, Caligula, One Away, Disappearance, The Illusionist, The Pointsman, Turkish Delight, The Lift, Chain Reaction, Year of the Quiet Sun, Shadow of Victory, Istanbul, Iris, Good Hope, One Month Later, Great Rock 'n Roll Swindle.

GIANNINI, GIANCARLO: Actor. b. Spezia, Italy, Aug. 1, 1942. Acquired degree in electronics but immediately after school enrolled at Acad. for Drama in Rome. Cast by Franco Zeffirelli as Romeo at age of 20. Subsequently appeared in a play also directed by Zeffirelli, Two Plus Two No Longer Make Four, written by Lina Wertmuller.
PICTURES INCLUDE: Love and Anarchy, The Seduction of Mimi, Swept Away by an Unusual Destiny in the Blue Sea of August, Seven Beauties . . . That's What They Call Him, How Funny Can Sex Be?, A Night Full of Rain, The Innocent, Buone Notizie (also prod.), Revenge, Travels with Anita, Lili Marleen, Lovers and Liars, La Vita e Bella, Picone Sent Me, Immortal Bachelor, American Dreamer, Fever Pitch, Saving Grace, I Picari, The Uncle, Snack Bar Budapest, Oh King.
TELEVISION: Sins.

GIBBS, MARLA: Actress. b. Chicago, IL, June 14, 1931. e. Cortez Peters Business School, Chicago. Worked as receptionist, switchboard operator, travel consultant (1963–74) before co-starring as Florence Johnston on the Jeffersons (1974–85). Formed Marla Gibbs Enterprises, Los Angeles, 1978. Member of CA State Assembly, 1980. Image Award NAACP, 1979–83.
TELEVISION: Series: The Jeffersons, Florence, 227.
Movies: You Can't Take It With You, Tell Me Where It Hurts, The Moneychanger, Nobody's Child.
PICTURES: Black Belt Jones, Sweet Jesus, Preacher Man.

GIBSON, HENRY: Actor. b. Germantown, PA, Sept. 21, 1935. e. Catholic U. of America. Appeared as child actor with stock companies, 1943–57; Bdwy. debut in My Mother, My Father and Me, 1962.
PICTURES: The Nutty Professor, Kiss Me Stupid, Charlotte's Web, The Long Goodbye (best supp. actor, Nat'l Soc. Film Critics, 1975), Nashville, The Last Remake of Beau Geste, Kentucky Fried Movie, The Incredible Shrinking Woman, The Blue Brothers, Tulips, Health, A Perfect Couple, Monster in the Closet, Brenda Starr, Inner Space, Switching Channels, The 'Burbs.
TELEVISION: Laugh-In co-star (1968–72). Movies: Every Girl Should Have One, Escape from Bogen County, The Night They Took Miss Beautiful, Evil Roy Slade, Amateur Night at the Dixie Bar & Grill, For the Love of It, Jailhouse Grab, Long Gone, Slow Burn.

GIBSON, MEL: Actor. b. New York, NY, 1957. Emigrated in 1968 to Australia with family. Attended Nat'l Inst. of Dramatic Art in Sydney; in 2nd yr. was cast in his first film, Summer City (1977). Graduated from NIDA, 1977. Joined South Australian

Theatre Co. in 1978, appearing in Oedipus, Henry IV, Cedoona. Also on TV in The Sullivans and The Oracle series.
PICTURES: Summer City, Mad Max, Tim, Attack Force Z, Gallipoli, The Road Warrior (Mad Max II), The Year of Living Dangerously, The Bounty, The River, Mrs. Soffel, Mad Max Beyond Thunderdome, Lethal Weapon, Tequila Sunrise.

GIELGUD, SIR JOHN: Actor. b. London, England, Apr. 14, 1904. e. Westminster Sch., Lady Benson's Sch. (dram.), London; Royal Acad. of Dramatic Art. Knighted, 1953.
THEATRE: Began stage career in Shakespearean roles; on London stage also in the Constant Nymph, The Good Companions, Dear Octopus, The Importance of Being Earnest, Dear Brutus, etc., various Shakespearean seasons, London & N.Y. 1988: The Best of Friends.
PICTURES INCLUDE: On screen 1932 in Brit. prod. Insult; later (Brit.) films The Good Companions, Secret Agent, The Prime Minister, Other films: Julius Caesar, Richard III. Around the World in 80 Days, Barretts of Wimpole Street, Becket, Tʰᵉ ˪oved One, Chimes at Midnight, St. Joan, Sebastian, The Assignment, Charge of the Light Brigade, The Shoes of the Fisherman, Oh, What a Lovely War, Eagle in a Cage, Lost Horizon, 11 Harrowhouse, Gold, Murder on the Orient Express, Providence, Portrait of the Artists as a Young Man, Joseph Andrews, Murder by Decree, The Human Factor, The Elephant Man, The Formula, Sphinx, Lion of the Desert, Arthur, Chariots of Fire, Priest of Love, Gandhi, The Wicked Lady, Scandalous, Wagner, Appointment with Death, Whistle Blower; Bluebeard, Bluebeard; Arthur 2 on the Rocks.
TELEVISION: A Day by the Sea, The Browning Version (U.S.), The Rehearsal, Great Acting, Ages of Man, Mayfly and the Frog, Cherry Orchard, Ivanov, From Chekhov With Love, St. Joan, Good King Charles' Golden Days, Conversation at Night, Hassan, Deliver Us from Evil, Heartbreak House, Brideshead Revisited, The Canterville Ghost; The Hunchback of Notre Dame; Inside the Third Reich; Marco Polo; The Scarlet and the Black; The Master of Ballantrae; The Far Pavillions; Camille; Romance on the Orient Express; Funny, You Don't Look 200, Oedipus the King, A Man For All Seasons.

GIL, DAVID: Producer. b. Tel Aviv, Israel, Jan. 24, 1930. e. U. of Jerusalem. m. Joan Andre. After commission in Israeli Army worked for Israeli Embassy, Paris, 1950–52; Israeli Film ind., 1953–55; prod. educational films, 1955–61; headed Gilart Productions, 1962–68; foreign sales dir., Commonwealth United, 1968; prod. Guess What We Learned in School Today, Joe, A Journey Through Rosebud, A Change in the Wind, Gas Pump Girls.

GILBERT, ARTHUR N.: Producer. b. Detroit, MI, Oct. 17, 1920. Lt., U.S.M.C., 1941–45. e. U. of Chicago, 1946. Special Agent, FBI, 1946–53; world sales dir., Gen. Motors, Cadillac Div., 1953–59; investments in mot. pictures and hotel chains, 1959–64; exec. prod., Mondo Hollywood, 1965; exec. prod. Jeannie-Wife Child, 1966; assoc. prod., The Golden Breed, 1967; commissioned rank of Colonel U.S.M.C., 1968.
PICTURES INCLUDE: The Glory Stompers, Fire Grass, Cycle Savages, Bigfoot, Incredible Transplant.

GILBERT, BRUCE: Producer. b. Los Angeles, CA, March 28, 1947. e. U. of California. Pursued film interests at Berkeley's Pacific Film Archive; in summer involved in production in film dept. of San Francisco State U. Founded progressive preschool in Bay Area. Became story editor in feature film division of Cine-Artists; involved in several projects, including Aloha, Bobby and Rose. Partnered with Jane Fonda and IPC Films, Inc. President, American Filmworks, 1980–
PICTURES INCLUDE: Coming Home (assoc. prod.); The China Syndrome (exec. prod.); Nine to Five (prod.); On Golden Pond (prod.); Rollover (prod.); The Morning After (prod.); Another World (dir.).
TELEVISION: Nine to Five (series-exec. prod.); The Dollmaker (movie-exec. prod.).

GILBERT, LEWIS: Producer, Writer, Director, Actor. b. London, England, Mar. 6, 1920. In RAF, W.W.II. Screen debut, 1932; asst. dir. (1930–39) with London Films, Assoc. British, Mayflower, RKO-Radio; from 1939–44 attached U.S. Air Corps Film Unit (asst. dir., Target for Today). In 1944 joined G.B.I. as writer and dir. In 1948, Gainsborough Pictures as writer, dir., 1949; Argyle Prod. 1950; under contract Nettlefold Films, Ltd. as dir.
PICTURES INCLUDE: Under One Roof, I Want to Get Married, Haunting Melody, Once a Sinner, Scarlet Thread, There Is Another Sun, Time Gentlemen Please, Emergency Call, Cosh Boy, Johnny on the Run, Albert R.N., The Good Die Young, The Sea Shall Not Have Them, Reach for the Sky, Cast a Dark Shadow, The Admirable Crichton, Carve Her Name with Pride, A Cry from the Street, Ferry to Hong Kong, Sink the Bismarck, Light Up the Sky, The Greengage Summer, H.M.S. Defiant, The Patriots, Spare the Rod, Alfie, The Seventh Dawn, You Only Live Twice, The Adventurers, Friends, Paul & Michelle, Operation Daybreak, Seven Nights in Japan, The Spy Who Loved Me. Dir: Moonraker, Educating Rita, Not Quite Paradise.

GILBERT, MELISSA: Actress. b. Los Angeles, May 8, 1964. Made debut at age of 3 in TV commercial. Comes from show business family: father, late comedian Paul Gilbert; mother, former dancer-actress Barbara Crane. NY Off-B'way debut A Shayna Madel (1987).
TELEVISION: Gunsmoke, Emergency, Tenafly, The Hanna-Barbera Happy Hour, Christmas Miracle in Caufield U.S.A., Love Boat, Little House on the Prairie (regular). Movies: Splendor in the Grass, Choices of the Heart, Choices, Penalty Phase, Family Secrets.
PICTURE: Sylvester (debut), Ice House.

GILER, DAVID: Producer, Writer, Director. b. New York, NY. Son of Bernie Giler, screen and TV writer. Began writing in teens; first work an episode for ABC series, The Gallant Men. Feature film career began as writer on Myra Breckenridge (1970).
PICTURES: Writer: The Parallax View, Fun with Dick and Jane, The Blackbird (also dir.), Southern Comfort (also prod.), Alien (prod. only), Rustlers' Rhapsody (prod. only).
TELEVISION: Writer: The Kraft Theatre, Burke's Law, The Man from U.N.C.L.E., The Girl from U.N.C.L.E.

GILFORD, JACK: Actor. r.n. Jacob Gellman. b. New York, NY, July 25, 1907. m. actress-producer Madeline Lee. Made first stage appearances in amateur night performances as stand-up comic at Cafe Society Downtown 1939, and Cafe Society Uptown, 1946. Wrote own material, specializing in imitations. Author 170 Years of Show Business, with wife and Zero and Kate Mostel, 1987: returned to cabaret act at the Ballroom, NY.
THEATER: (Selected NY credits): Frank Fay Vaudeville (debut, 1939); Meet the People, They Should Have Stood in Bed, Count Me In; Meet the People; Alive and Kicking; The Live Wire; Die Fledermaus (Met. Opera); The World of Sholom Aleichem; The Passion of Gross; Once Over Lightly (revue); The Diary of Anne Frank; Romanoff and Juliet; Drink to Me Only; Look After Lulu; Once Upon a Mattress; The Tenth Man; A Funny Thing Happened on the Way to the Forum; Cabaret; Three Men on a Horse; No, No Nanette; Sly Fox; The Supporting Cast; The World of Sholom Aleichem (1982); Of Thee I Sing; Let Them Eat Cake (Brooklyn Acad. of Music).
PICTURES: Hey, Rookie (debut, 1944); The Reckless Age; Main Street to Broadway; Mister Budwing; A Funny Thing Happened on the Way to the Forum; Enter Laughing; Who's Minding the Mint; The Incident; Harry and Walter Go to New York; Catch-22; They Might Be Giants; Save the Tiger; Cheaper to Keep Her; Wholly Moses; Cave Man; Cocoon; Arthur 2 On the Rocks; Cocoon II: The Return; The Island on Bird Street.
TELEVISION: The Arrow Show (1948); Paul Sand in Friends and Lovers; Apple Pie (1974–75); The Defenders; All in the Family; Rhoda; Soap; Taxi; Trapper John M.D. Specials: The World of Sholom Aleichem; Once Upon a Mattress; Of Thee I Sing; The Cowboy and the Tiger; the Very Special Jack Gilford Special; Anna to the Infinite Power; Twigs. Movies: Seventh Avenue; Hostage Flight; Goldie and the Bower Go to Hollywood.

GILLASPY, RICHARD M.: Producer, Director. b. St. Louis, MO, Dec. 10, 1927. Joined NBC in New York as exec. trainee, 1947; headed Marine Corps Radio, 1952–54; rejoined NBC-TV as stage mgr., became prod. dir.; won Emmy Award, 1960, for Nixon-Khrushchev debate; pres., Seven League Productions, 1961–63, owner, Radio Station WIII, Homestead, Fla., 1963–67; freelance prod. dir., 1967–70; v.p. of Ivan Tors Studios, N. Miami, 1970–72; pres. RMG Productions, 1972.

GILLIAM, TERRY: Writer, Director, Actor, Animator. b. Minneapolis, MN, Nov. 22, 1940. e. Occidental Coll. Freelance writer and illustrator for various magazines and ad agencies before moving to London. Member, Monty Python's Flying Circus (1969–76).
PICTURES: And Now for Something Completely Different (animator), Monty Python and the Holy Grail (co-dir.), Jabberwocky (dir.); Life of Brian (also s.p.), Time Bandits (prod., dir., co-s.p.), Monty Python's The Meaning of Life (s.p., act.), Brazil (s.p., dir.), The Adventures of Baron Munchausen (dir., co-s.p.).

GILLIAT, LESLIE: Producer. b. New Malden, England, 1917. e. Epsom Coll. Ent. m.p. ind. 1935.
PICTURES INCLUDE: Only Two Can Play, The Amorous Prawn, Joey Boy, The Great St. Trinians Train Robbery, A Dandy in Aspic, The Virgin Soldiers, The Buttercup Chain, Endless Night, Priest of Love (prod. supvr.), The Zany Adventures of Robin Hood (assoc. prod.).

GILLIN, DONALD T.: Executive. b. Council Bluffs, IA, June 17, 1914; e. U. of Minnesota., bus. adm., 1929–32. Sls., Warner Bros., 1932–39; W.W.II; home office sup., Warner Bros., 1946–48; sls. exec., Universal, 1948–50; v.p., gen. sls. mgr., mgr., Sol Lesser, 1950–59; establ., Donald T. Gillin Inc., producers' rep., 1960. Muchnic-Gillin Internat'l, Inc., 1961; Producers' Representatives, Inc., 1967.

GILLIS, ANNE: Actress. r.n. Alma Mable O'Connor. b. Little Rock, AK, Feb. 12, 1927. Screen debut 1936 in The Garden of Allah; thereafter in number child roles.
PICTURES INCLUDE: King of Hockey, Off to the Races, The Californian, The Adventures of Tom Sawyer, Peck's Bad Boy with the Circus, Little Orphan Annie, Edison the Man, All This and Heaven Too, Janie; A Wave, a Wac, a Marine; The Cheaters, Gay Blades, Big Town After Dark, 2001: A Space Odyssey.

GILMORE, WILLIAM S.: Producer. b. Los Angeles, CA, March 10, 1934. e. U. of California at Berkeley. Started career as film cutter before becoming asst. dir. and prod. mgr. at Universal Studios, where worked on 20 feature films. Headed prod. for Mirisch Co. in Europe; then formed Zanuck/Brown Co. as exec. in chg. prod. Produced several TV movies for EMI-TV. Sr. v.p./prod. of Filmways Pictures, supervising literary development, prod. and post-prod.
PICTURES: Swashbuckler (assoc. prod.), The Last Remake of Beau Geste, Rock n' Roll Hotel, Tough Enough, Deadly Blessing, Defiance, Against All Odds, Return of the Living Dead Part II, Midnight Run.
TELEVISION: Just You and Me, One in a Million—The Ron Leflore Story, The Legend of Walks Far Woman, S.O.S. Titanic, Another Woman's Child.

GILROY, FRANK: Writer, Director. b. New York, NY, Oct. 13, 1925. e. Dartmouth; postgrad. Yale School of Drama. TV writer: Playhouse 90, US Steel Hour, Omnibus, Kraft Theatre, Lux Video Theater, Studio One. Bdwy. playwright; won Pulitzer Prize & Tony for The Subject Was Roses, 1965. Other plays: Who'll Save the Plowboy?; The Only Game in Town; Present Tense; The Housekeeper; Last Licks. Novels: Private (with Ruth Gilroy); Little Ego; From Noon to 3.
PICTURES: The Fastest Gun Alive; The Subject Was Roses; The Gallant Hours; The Only Game in Town; Desperate Characters (also dir., prod.); From Noon Till Three (also dir.); Once in Paris (also dir.); The Gig (also dir.), The Luckiest Man in the World (also dir.).
TELEVISION: Dir.: Nero Wolfe, Turning Point of Jim Maloy.

GIMBEL, ROGER: Producer. b. March 11, 1925. e. Yale. Began television production career as copy and creative chief of RCA Victor TV, then became assoc. prod. of the Tonight Show for NBC. Subsequently named head of prog. dev. of NBC daytime programming; later became prod. of the 90-minute NBC Tonight Specials, including The Jack Paar Show and the Ernie Kovacs Show. Became prod. and co-packager of the Glen Campbell Goodtime Hour for CBS, 1969; vice pres. in charge of prod. for Tomorrow Entertainment, 1971. Formed his own production company, Roger Gimbel's Tomorrow Enterprises, Inc., 1975; prod. Minstrel Man. Became U.S. pres. of EMI-TV, 1976. Received special personal Emmy as exec. prod. of War of the Children, 1975. Produced 33 movies for TV under the EMI banner and won 18 Emmys. In January, 1984, EMI-TV became The Peregrine Producers Group, Inc., of which he was pres. & COO. 1987, spun off Roger Gimbel Prods. as an independent film co.
TELEVISION: The Autobiography of Miss Jane Pittman, Born Innocent, Birds of Prey, Brand New Life, Gargoyles, Glass House, In This House of Brede, I Heard the Owl Call My Name, I Love You, Good-Bye, Larry, Miles to Go, Queen of the Stardust Ballroom, Tell Me Where It Hurts, Things in Their Season, War of the Children (Emmy award, Outstanding Single Program, Drama or Comedy), Aurora, Rockabye, Blackout, Apology.

GINGOLD, DAN: Freelance Executive Producer, Producer, Director. Credits include all types live and film prod. Specialist in Special Events and Documentary. Awards include Emmy, Ohio State U., DuPont/Columbia U., Ed Murrow, Assoc. Press, San Francisco State, Cine Golden Eagle, NY Int'l. Film Fest. Asst prof., School of Journalism, U. of Southern California.

GINNA, ROBERT EMMETT, JR.: Producer, Writer. b. New York, NY, Dec. 3, 1925. e. U. of Rochester, Harvard U., M.A. In U.S. Navy, W.W.II. Journalist for Life, Scientific American, Horizon, 1950–55; 1958–61, contributor to many magazines. Staff writer, producer, director NBC-TV, 1955–58; v.p., Sextant, Inc., dir., Sextant Films Ltd., 1961–64; Founded Windward Productions, Inc., Windward Film Productions, Ltd., 1965. Active in publishing 1974–82; sr. ed. People; ed. in chief, Little Brown; asst. mging., Life. Resumed pres., Windward Prods., Inc., 1982; publishing consultant.
PICTURES: Young Cassidy (co-prod.); The Last Challenge (co-s.p.); Before Winter Comes (prod.); Brotherly Love (prod.).

GINSBERG, SIDNEY: Executive. b. New York, NY, Oct. 26, 1920. e. City Coll. of New York, 1938. Entered m.p. ind., as asst. mgr., Loew's Theatres; joined Trans-Lux 1943, as thea. mgr.; film booker; helped form Trans-Lux Distributing Corp., 1956; asst. to pres., Trans-Lux Dist. Corp.; asst. vice-pres., Trans-Lux Picture, Distributing and TV Corp., 1961, V.P. Trans-Lux Dist. Corp., 1967, V.P. in charge of worldwide sales, 1969.

Haven International Pictures, Inc., Haven Int'l 1970; IFIDA gov., 1970, v.p. sales, Scotia International Films, Inc., 1971; exec. v.p., Scotia American Prods; 1977, pres., Rob-Rich Films Inc.; 1979, exec. v.p., A Major Studio, Inc.; 1980, exec. v.p., The Health and Entertainment Corp. of America; 1982, sr. acct. rep., 3M-Photogard; 1984, pres., Rob-Rich Films.

GINSBURG, LEWIS S.: Distributor, Importer, Prod. b. New York, NY, May 16, 1914. e. City Coll. of New York, 1931–32. Columbia U., 1932–33. Ent. film industry, tabulating dept., United Artists, Sept. 1932; sls. contract dept. 1933; asst. to eastern district mgr., 1938; slsmn., New Haven exch., 1939. Army, 1943. Ret. to U.S., then formed first buying & booking service in Connecticut, 1945–55; in chg., New England Screen Guild Exchanges, 1955; TV film distr., 1955; Formed & org. International Film Assoc., Vid-EX Film Distr. Corp., 1961. Prod., TV half-hour series; vice-pres. in chg., dist., Desilu Film Dist. C., 1962; organized Carl Releasing Co., 1963; Walter Reade-Sterling Inc., 1964–65; formed L.G. Films Corp.; contract and playdate mgr., 20th Fox, 1965–68. Cinerama Releasing Corp. Adm. Ass't to sales mgr., 1968–69; 20th Cent.-Fox. Nat'l sales coordinator, 1969–present. 1970, 20th Century-Fox, Asst. to the Sales Mgr. 1971, Transnational Pictures Corp., v.p. in chg. of dist., pres., Stellar IV Film Corp., 1972.

GIRARDOT, ANNIE: Actress. b. France, Oct. 25, 1931. Studied nursing. Studied acting at the Paris Conservatory, made her acting debut with the Comedie Française. Has acted on the French stage and in reviews in the Latin Quarter.
PICTURES INCLUDE: Rocco and His Brothers, The Organizer, Les Galoises Bleues, Live For Life, Trois Chambres A Manhattan (Best Actress Award at the Venice Film Festival), Story of a Woman, Love Is a Funny Thing, The Slap, No Time for Breakfast, Traffic Jam, Five Days in June.

GISH, LILLIAN: Actress. b. Springfield, OH, Oct. 14, 1899. r.n. Lillian de Guiche. Sister of Dorothy Gish, actress. At 5 appeared in In Convict's Stripes, at Rising Sun, OH; following year danced in Sarah Bernhardt prod. in N.Y. In 1913 appeared with Mary Pickford in A Good Little Devil, N.Y. Began screen career 1912 with Biograph, beginning assn. with D. W. Griffith, dir., for whom she made 40 films including The Birth of a Nation, Intolerance, Hearts of the World, The Great Love, Broken Blossoms, Way Down East and Orphans of the Storm. One of the first women to dir. film (Remodeling Her Husband, 1920), and one of first actors to gain artistic control of projects (La Boheme, The Scarlet Letter). Continued in films: White Sister, Romola, The Wind, La Boheme, Scarlet Letter. From 1930 on N.Y. stage in number orig. prods. & classics Uncle Vanya, Camille, 9 Pine Street, Within the Gates, Hamlet, Star Wagon, Old Maid, Dear Octopus, Life With Father, Mr. Sycamore, The Marquise, Legend of Leonora, Crime and Punishment, Miss Mable, Curious Savage, A Passage to India, Too True to be Good; Romeo and Juliet, Stratford Shakespeare Theatre, 1965. 1969–71, One woman int'l. concert tour, Lillian Gish and the Movies. Received honorary Oscar, 1971. International touring with illustrated lecture on the art of film and TV, 1974. Lecture tour on Queen Elizabeth 2, 1975. Campaigned for film preservation and lobbied for D. W. Griffith commemorative stamp. Honoree Kennedy Center Honors, 1982; 1983, AFI Life Achievement Award, Commander of Arts & Letters from French govt.
PICTURES INCLUDE: One Romantic Night, His Double Life, Commandos Strike at Dawn, Duel in the Sun, Miss Susie Slagle's, Portrait of Jennie, Follow Me Boys!, Night of the Hunter, The Cobweb, The Unforgiven, Orders to Kill; Warning Shot, The Comedians, A Wedding (her 100th film), Hambone and Hillie, Sweet Liberty, The Whales of August.
PLAYS: Theatre Guild play The Trip to Bountiful, 1954; Chalk Garden, The Family Reunion; in Berlin, Ger., Portrait of a Madonna, Wreck of the 5:25, Uncle Vanya, 1973. All The Way Home, Anya, 1965; I Never Sang for My Father, A Musical Jubilee, (1976).
TELEVISION: I Mrs. Bibbs, Sound and the Fury, Ladies in Retirement, Detour, The Joyous Season, The Trip to Bountiful, Grandma Moses, The Quality of Mercy, The Corner Drugstore, Day Lincoln Was Shot, Mornings at Seven, The Grass Harp, Grandma T.N.T., Mr. Novak, Alfred Hitchcock Hour, Breaking Point, The Spiral Staircase, Arsenic and Old Lace, A Gift of Music, Kennedy Center Honors (1982), AFI Salute to Lillian Gish, The Silent Years (hostess). Movies: Twin Detectives; Thin Ice; Hobson's Choice.
AUTHOR: The Movies, Mr. Griffith and Me, (Prentice-Hall), 1969; Dorothy and Lillian Gish (Charles Scribner), October, 1973.

GITHENS, W. FRENCH: Executive. b. New York, NY, April 30, 1906. e. Columbia U. In 1928 secy. Amer. embassy Madrid. Entered m.p. ind. 1929 as member ed. staff Movietonews, editing program Embassy Newsreel theat., N.Y.; asst. ed. Pathe News 1933. On 1934 org. Newsreel Theats. (Embassy theat., Broadway, N.Y. & others), becoming pres. & dir. Org. Sound Masters 1937 to prod. industrial & educational films.

Lt. Comdr., U.S.N.R. Bureau Aeronautics W.W.II; com. U.S.N.R.; pres. National Educational Films, Inc.; on bd. of Viterama & Cinerama Corps. developers of 3-dimensional projection system, 1950. Mayor of Bernardsville, N.J., 2 terms; prod., Movietime Digest; prod., V.P. and dir. Steel Properties, N.Y.

GLASER, PAUL MICHAEL: Actor. b. Cambridge, MA, March 25, 1943. e. Tulane U., Boston U., M.A. Did five seasons in summer stock before starting career in New York, making stage debut in rock version of Hamlet in 1968. Appeared in numerous off-Bdwy. plays and got early TV training as regular in daytime series, Love of Life and Love Is a Many Splendored Thing.
PICTURES INCLUDE: Fiddler on the Roof, Butterflies Are Free. Director: Band of the Hand, The Running Man, Blue Lightning.
TELEVISION: Kojak, Toma, The Streets of San Francisco, The Rockford Files, The Sixth Sense, The Waltons. Movies: Trapped Beneath the Sea, The Great Houdini, Princess Daisy, Jealousy, Attack on Fear, Single Bars Single Women, Amazons (dir.). Series: Starsky and Hutch.

GLASER, SIDNEY: Exec. adv., Producer. b. New York, NY, July 12, 1912. e. City Coll. of New York, b. Eng., 1936; New York U., m. Eng., 1942. Office boy, adv. dept., Metro-Goldwyn-Mayer, 1929; prod. asst. 1934; prod. mgr., 1957; adv. prod. mgr., 1972; gen. adv. exec.

GLAZER, WILLIAM: Executive b. Cambridge, MA. e. State U. of New York, Entered m.p. ind. with Ralph Snider Theatres 1967–69; General Cinema Corp. 1969–71; Loews Theatres 1971–73; Joined Sack Theatres 1973 as Dist. mgr.; 1974 Exec. Asst. to Pres.; 1976 Gen. Mgr.; 1980 V.P. Gen. Mgr.; 1982 Exec. V.P. Member of SMPTE; NATO (Bd of Dir); Theatre Owners of New England (Bd of Dir); President Theatre Owners of New England 1982–1985.

GLAZIER, SIDNEY: Producer. b. Philadelphia, PA, May 29, 1918. Managed movie and legitimate theatres in Pennsylvania and Ohio. Air Force captain during W.W.II. Became v.p. of Washington Federal Savings and Loan Bank in Miami. Org. and became exec. dir. of Eleanor Roosevelt Cancer Foundation. Prod. network TV public service programs. First m.p. The Eleanor Roosevelt Story won Academy Award, 1966. Pres. of U-M Film Distributors, 1969.
PICTURES INCLUDE: The Producers, Take the Money and Run, The Gamblers, Quackser Fortune Has a Cousin in the Bronx, The 12 Chairs, Glen and Wanda, The Night Visitor, The Only Way.

GLEASON, LARRY: Executive. b. Boston, MA, Apr. 30, 1938. e. Boston Coll., M.A., 1960. Held various positions, western div., mgr., General Cinema Corp.; 1968–84; gen. mgr., Gulf States Theatres, New Orleans, 1984–85; pres., Mann Theatres, 1985; joined DeLaurentiis Entertainment Group as pres., mktg./dist., Dec., 1985.

GLENN, CHARLES OWEN: Executive. b. Binghamton, NY, March 27, 1938. e. Syracuse U., B.A., U. of Pennsylvania. Capt., U.S. Army, 1961–63. Asst. to dir. of adv., 20th Cent. Fox, 1966–67; asst. adv. mgr., Paramount, 1967–68; acct. spvsr. & exec., MGM record & m.p. div., 1968–69; nat'l adv. mgr., Paramount, 1969–70; nat'l. dir. of adv., Paramount, 1970–71; v.p. adv.-pub.-prom., 1971–73; v.p. marketing, 1974; v.p. prod. mktg., 1975; joined American Intl. Pictures as v.p. in chg. of adv./creative affairs, 1979. 1980, when Filmways took AIP over he was named their v.p. in chg. worldwide adv./pub./promo.; joined MCA/Universal in 1982 as exec. v.p., adv.-promo.; 1984, appt. Orion Pictures adv.-pub.-promo. exec. v.p.; 1987, appt. Orion mktg. exec. v.p.
MEMBER: Exec. comm. public relations branch, Academy of M.P. Arts & Sciences. Holder of NATO mktg. exec. of year (1983) award, Variety Club, Motion Picture Pioneers.

GLENN, SCOTT: Actor. b. Pittsburgh, PA, Jan. 26, 1942. e. William & Mary Coll. Worked as newspaper reporter before going to New York to study drama. Off-Bdwy. productions included Fortune in Men's Eyes, Long Day's Journey into Night. On Bdwy in Burn This. Member of Actors Studio. Film debut in The Baby Maker, 1970.
PICTURES: Nashville, Apocalypse Now, Urban Cowboy, Personal Best, The Challenge, The Right Stuff, The Keep, The River, Wild Geese II, Silverado, Verne Miller, Man on Fire, Off Limits, Two Telegrams, The Miss Firecracker Contest, Personal Choice.
TELEVISION: As Summers Die, Countdown to Looking Glass, Intrigue.

GLESS, SHARON: Actress. b. Los Angeles, CA, May 31, 1943.
TELEVISION: Movies: The Longest Night; All My Darling Daughters; My Darling Daughters' Anniversary; The Immigrants; The Scream of Eagles; The Last Convertible; Hardhat and Legs; The Kids Who Knew Too Much; Moviola; The Miracle of Kathy Miller; Palms; Hobson's Choice; The Sky's the Limit; Letting Go. Series: Turnabout, Faraday and Co.,

Switch, House Calls, Cagney and Lacey (2 Emmys). PICTURE: The Star Chamber.

GLICK, HYMAN J.: Executive. b. Russia, Dec. 15, 1904. e. New York U., B.C.S., 1926. C.P.A. (N.Y.); with public accounting firm, N.Y., 1923–29; own public accounting Business, 1929–32. Became assoc. m.p. ind. as member comptrollers' com., repr. Republic; 1932–36, tax & financial counsel Mascot Pictures Corp. Joined Republic 1936 as comptroller; apptd. asst. secy.-asst. treas. Jan., 1945. Retired, 1985.
Member: B'nai Brith Lodge 1325; State Soc. of Certified Public Accountants, Am. Inst. of Accountants. Resigned Republic, 1959; CPA (Calif.), member, Calif. Soc. of CPA; Own Accounting and Tax Practice.

GLICK, PHYLLIS: Executive. b. New York, NY. e. Queens Coll. of C.U.N.Y. Began career with Otto-Windsor Associates, as casting director; left to be independent. 1979, joined ABC-TV as mgr. of comedy series development; promoted 1980 to director, involved with all comedy series developed for network. 1985, joined Paramount Pictures as exec. dir., production, for M.P. Group.

GLICKMAN, JOEL: Producer. b. Los Angeles, CA, July 29, 1930. e. U. of California at L.A. (film dep't.). Was actor and director for L.A. little theatre groups and writer-director for industrial films. Early TV work on series, documentaries and commercials. Directed videotaping of off-Broadway shows. Was production assoc. on film, Wedding and Babies, 1958. Was assoc. prod. and prod. mgr. on films (Terror in the City, The Balcony, All the Way Home, For Love of Ivy, Hamlet (Richard Burton, assoc. director), Dion Brothers, Last Summer and TV (East Side, West Side, Mr. Broadway), N.Y.P.D., Love Song of Barney Kempinski, Among the Paths To Eden. Member, Motion Picture Academy & D.G.A. Has own co.: Selznick/Glickman Productions.
PICTURES INCLUDE: Brother John, Buck and the Preacher, Trial of the Catonsville Nine (exec. prod.).
TELEVISION: Night Terror, Angel on Horseback, Kennedy-Hoffa War (called Blood Feud for OPT), Hoover vs. the Kennedys (mini-series).

GLOBUS, YORAM: Producer. Has co-produced many films with Menahem Golan. Sr. exec. v.p., Cannon Group; Pres. and CEO Cannon Entertainment and Cannon Films.

GLOVER, DANNY: Actor. b. San Francisco, CA, 1947. e. San Francisco State U. Trained at Black Actors Workshop of American Conservatory Theatre. Appeared in many stage productions (Island, Macbeth, Sizwe Banzi Is Dead, etc.). On N.Y. stage in Suicide in B Flat, The Blood Knot, Master Harold...and the Boys (Theatre World Award).
PICTURES: Chu Chu and the Philly Flash, Iceman, Escape from Alcatraz, Witness, Places in the Heart, The Color Purple, Silverado, Lethal Weapon, Out (video); Bat-21.
TELEVISION: Hill Street Blues, Many Mansions, Chiefs, Face of Rage, Mandela, A Place at the Table, Lonesome Dove, A Raisin in the Sun.

GLOVER, JOHN: Actor. b. Salisbury, MD, Aug. 7, 1944. e. Towson State Coll., Baltimore. On regional theatre circuit; in plays off-Bdwy. (A Scent of Flowers, Subject to Fits, The House of Blue Leaves, The Selling of the President) with APA Phoenix Co. in Great God Brown (Drama Desk Award), The Visit, Don Juan, Chermin de Fer, Holiday. Other NY stage: The Importance of Being Earnest, Hamlet, Frankenstein, Whodunnit, Digby.
PICTURES: Julia, Annie Hall, She Killed Her Husband, Last Embrace, The American Success Company, Melvin and Howard, The Mountain Men, The Incredible Shrinking Woman, A Little Sex, The Evil That Men Do, White Nights, 52 Pick-Up, Masquerade, Moving Target, Hot Paint, A Killing Affair, The Chocolate War, Rocket Gilbraltar.
TELEVISION: A Rage of Angels, George Washington, Ernie Kovacs—Between the Laughter, An Early Frost, Apology (cable), Nutcracker: Money, Madness, and Murder, Paul Reiser: Out on a Whim, David.

GLYNN, CARLIN: Actress. b. Feb. 19, 1940. m. actor-writer Peter Masterson, mother of actress Mary Stuart Masterson. e. Sophie Newcomb College, 1957–58. Studied acting with Stella Adler, Wynn Handman and Lee Strasberg in NY. Debut, Gigi, Alley Theatre, Houston, TX 1959. NY stage debut Waltz of The Toreadors, 1960. On stage in The Best Little Whorehouse in Texas (Tony Award and Eleanora Duse Award), Winterplay, Alterations.
PICTURES: Three Days of the Condor, Continental Divide, Sixteen Candles.

GOATMAN, ALAN H.: Consultant. Entered m.p. industry 1934. Officer of the Venerable Order of St. John of Jerusalem. Fellow Society of Company and Commercial Accountants. Memb. Brit. Computer Soc. Fellow Brit. Inst. Management; member Inst. Data Processing; Management Dir. British Film & TV Producers Assoc.; Exec. mem., AGICOA, Geneva. Pres., AGICOA Services, S.A. Brussels, Freeman of the City of London.

God-Gol

GODARD, JEAN-LUC: Writer, Director. b. Paris, France, Dec. 3, 1930. e. Lycee Buffon, Paris. Journalist, film critic Cahiers du Cinema. Acted in and financed experimental film Quadrille by Jacques Rivette, 1951. 1954: dir. first short, Operation Beton. 1956, worked as film editor. 1957: worked in publicity dept. 20th Century Fox.
PICTURES: Breathless (feature debut, 1960), Le Petit Soldat, A Woman is a Woman, My Life to Live, Les Carabiniers, Contempt, Band of Outsiders, The Married Woman, Alphaville, Pierrot le Fou, Masculine-Feminine, Two or Three Things I Know About Her, La Chinoise, Weekend, Sympathy for the Devil, Le Gai Savoir, Tout a Bien (co-dir.), Numero Deux, Every Man For Himself, First Name Carmen, Hail Mary, Aria, King Lear, Keep Up Your Right (dir., edit, s.p., actor).

GODBOLD, GEOFF: Executive. b. London, England, 1935. Ent. ind. 1959. Specialized in supply of location requirements for film and TV prods. Formed Prop Workshops Ltd., co-promoted Television Recordings Ltd. Man. dir. Facilities (Screen & Television) Ltd. Dir. TV Recordings, Investments, Ltd.; Centrepoint Screen Prod. Ltd.; Tape Commercials, Ltd. Council Mem. Film and TV Contractors Assoc. Dir. Lancair Export Services Ltd.; 1968 Freelance production buyer, Screen Gems and Tigon. 1969. Feature Prod. Rep. Film Div. N.A.T.T.K.E. Man. Dir. Setpieces Ltd. Film & TV Prop. Hire. 1984: Carlton Communication. 1985: mng. dir., Set Pieces Ltd.
PICTURES INCLUDE: Dubious Patriot, Every Home Should Have One, Melody, Up Pompeii. Morocco location, Young Winston. The Asphyx, Our Miss Fred, Death of a Snow Queen, Man in the Iron Mask. TV: The Professionals.

GODDARD, PAULETTE: Actress. r.n. Marion Levy. b. Great Neck, NY, June 3, 1911. On N.Y. stage as a Ziegfeld girl at 14, then in Rio Rita; then member of Hal Roach Studios stock co. Became a Goldwyn girl in Hollywood. In 1936 opposite her then husband Charles Chaplin in Modern Times.
PICTURES INCLUDE: The Young in Heart, The Women, North West Mounted Police, The Great Dictator, Hold Back the Dawn, Reap the Wild Wind, Star Spangled Rhythm, I Love a Soldier, So Proudly We Hail, Standing Room Only, Duffy's Tavern, Kitty, The Diary of a Chambermaid, Unconquered, An Ideal Husband, Hazard, On Our Merry Way, Bride of Vengeance, Anna Lucasta, Babes in Bagdad, Vice Squad, Paris Model, Sins of Jezebel, Charge of the Lancers, Unholy Four, Time of Indifference.
TELEVISION: Female Instincts, The Snoop Sisters.

GODMILOW, JILL: Director, Producer, Editor.
PICTURES: Antonia: Portrait of a Woman (co-directed with Judy Collins) received Academy Award nomination and won Independent N.Y. Film Critics Award for Best Documentary, 1975; Nevelson In Process, Odyssey, (created with Susan Fanshel); The Popovich Brothers (co-dir., co-prod.); The Vigil (co-directed with Chiquita and Andre Gregory): At Nienadowka with Grotowsksi, Far from Poland; Waiting for the Moon.

GODUNOV, ALEXANDER: Dancer, Actor. b. Ujno-Sakalin, Soviet Union, Nov. 28, 1949. e. Riga Music Sch. 1958–67; trained for dance at Riga Choreography Sch. and for stage at Stella Adler Acting Sch. Dancer with Moiseyev's Ballet Co. 1958–66; principal dancer Bolshoi Dance Co. 1967–79; American Ballet Theatre, NY 1979–82.
PICTURES: Witness (debut, 1985), The Money Pit, Die Hard.
TELEVISION: Godunov: The World to Dance In (1983).

GODWIN, FRANK: Producer, Writer, Director.
PICTURES INCLUDE: Woman in a Dressing Gown, No Trees in the Street, Operation Bullshine, Don't Bother to Knock, The Small World of Sammy Lee, Danny the Dragon, Headline Hunters, Demons of the Mind, The Boy with Two Heads, The Firefighters, Sky Pirates, Sammy's Super T-Shirt, Electric Eskimo, The Boy Who Never Was, Break Out, Terry on the Fence.

GOEBEL, LAWRENCE A. JR.: Executive. b. Shreveport, LA, May 29, 1950. e. Marquette U., 1968–74; U. of Southern California. Cinema Dept. Graduate Sch. (1973–75). Began career as sports editor, Marquette Tribune, 1972; dir. of special events ticket sales—L.A. Sharks World Hockey Assn., 1973; freelance filmmaker, 1974–75. Now v.p., intl. & ancillary sls. for Film Ventures International.
MEMBER: American Film Marketing Assn's market advisory committee and fact book committee; 1986; Film Ventures' rep. for AFMA, 1983–86; film industry juror for L.A. Film Teacher's regional film festival, 1978–82.

GOLAN, MENAHEM: Producer, Director, Writer. b. Israel, 1929. e. NYU. Sr. exec. v.p., Cannon Group; chmn. of bd., Cannon Entertainment and Cannon Films.
PICTURES INCLUDE: Director/co-writer: Kasablan, Diamonds, Entebbe (Operation Thunderbolt), Teyve and His Seven Daughters, What's Good for the Goose? Lepke, The Magician of Lublin, The Goodsend, Happy Hooker Goes to Hollywood, Enter the Ninja. Producer-Writer-Director: The Threepenny Opera, Hanna's War. Producer-Director: The Uranium Conspiracy, Delta Force, Over the Brooklyn Bridge, Over the Top. Producer/Exec. prod.: Sallah, Runaway Train, Sallah, Fool For Love, Maria's Lovers, Cobra, Evil Angels, I Love You Rosa, Body and Soul, also: Deathwish II, The Last American Virgin, That Championship Season, House of Long Shadows, Revenge of the Ninja, Hercules, The Movie Tales (12 children's fairy tales films), The Wicked Lady, Cobra, Barfly (exec. prod.), Breakin', Missing in Action, Dancers (prod.), Surrender (exec. prod.), Death Wish 4: The Crackdown (exec. prod.), King Lear (prod.), Too Much (co-prod.), Powaqquatsi (exec. prod.), Mercenary Fighters (co-prod.), Doin' Time on Planet Earth (co- prod.), Manifesto (co-prod.), Kinjite (exec. prod.), Messenger of Death (exec. prod.), Alien From L.A. (prod.), Hero and the Terror (exec. prod.), Haunted Summer (exec. prod.), A Cry in the Darkness (exec. prod.).

GOLD, MELVIN: Executive. b. Chicago, IL, Sept. 3, 1909. In 1930 joined MGM, Chicago, as assistant office manager. To Reinheimer Circuit 1932 to operate theatres Hammond, IN; in 1940 organized own advertising agency, Sales, Inc., mgr.; mgr. Vogue Theatre, Hollywood, CA, 1943. Joined National Screen Service 1943 as editor Mister Showman; Feb., 1945 named director of advtsng. and publicity; assumed east coast film prod. and TV, Sept., 1948 to May, 1954. Formed Mel Gold Productions, Inc., June 1954.
Member Publicity Club of N.Y.; Associated Motion Picture Advertisers; founded National Television Film Council in 1948, elected Honorary Lifetime President, 1955. Partner Melmon Productions; Melvin L. Gold Enterprises, 1958; pres., Mesal Prods., Inc., 1961; wrote s.p., Not For Love, 1961; pres., Associated Motion Picture Advertisers, 1963–66; gen. sls. mgr., National Screen Service, 1963. Pres., Melvin L. Gold Enterprises, Inc. 1966. Pres. Manhattan Sound Studios 1967, v.p. in chg. m.p. div., National Showmanship Services, 1968; 1971, Pres. East Side Productions; Pres. Melvin L. Gold Enterprises. Motion picture consultant, Philip Morris, Inc., 1976–present. Operations director, Benson & Hedges 100, Film classics, 1976–79. Wrote s.p., The Sheriff Is a Lady, 1979.

GOLDBERG, BERNARD: Executive. b. Bronx, NY, Aug. 25, 1932. e. Queens Coll., B.A. Co-owner, Golden Theatre Mgt. Corp.; named vice pres. 1973.

GOLDBERG, FRED: Publicist. b. New York, NY, Aug. 26, 1921. e. Pace Coll., School of Marketing and Advertising. Expl., Paramount, 1946; asst. expl. mgr., trade paper contact, syndicate contact, N.Y. newspaper contact promotion mgr., 1946–52; ass't publ. mgr., RKO, 1952,; national publ. mgr.; IFE, 1953; v.p. Norton and Condon, pub., 1953; returned to IFE Sept., 1954, as nat'l pub. mgr.; head of N.Y. office, Arthur Jacobs, then Blowitz-Maskel, 1956; exec. asst. to dir. pub., adv., United Artists Corp., 1958; exec. dir. adv., pub., exploitation, United Artists Corp., 1961; named vice pres., 1962, senior vice president, 1972, Senior Vice President, Director of Marketing, 1977. Left in 1978 to be consultant with Piener, Hauser & Bates Agency. In 1979 joined Columbia Pictures as snr. v.p. in chg. adv./pub. Left in 1981 to form new company.

GOLDBERG, LEONARD: Executive. b. Brooklyn, NY, Nov. 24, 1934. e. Wharton Sch., U. of Pennsylvania. Began career in ABC-TV research dept.; moved to NBC-TV research div.; 1961 joined Batten, Barton, Durstine & Osborn ad agency in chg. of daytime TV shows and overall bdcst. coordinator. In 1963 rejoined ABC-TV as mgr. of program devel. In 1966 named VP in chg of network TV programming. Resigned in 1969 to join Screen Gems as VP in chg. of prod. Left for partnership with Aaron Spelling in Spelling/Goldberg Prods.; later produced TV and theatrical films under own banner, Mandy Prods. 1981: co-prod. All Night Long. 1983: War-Games. 1984: Space Camp; 1986, named pres., COO, 20th Century Fox.
TELEVISION: The Rookies (1972–76), Starsky and Hutch, Charlie's Angels, Family, Hart to Hart, T.J. Hooker, Paper Dolls, The Cavanaughs. Movies: Brian's Song, Letters From 3 Lovers, The Legend of Valentino, The Boy in the Plastic Bubble, This House is Possessed, Deadly Lessons, Something About Amelia, Alex: The Life of a Child.

GOLDBERG, WHOOPI: Actress. b. New York, NY, Nov. 13, 1949. Began performing at age 8 in N.Y. with children's program at Hudson Guild and Helen Rubenstein Children's Theatre. Moved to San Diego, CA, 1974, appearing in repertory theatre (Mother Courage, Getting Out, etc.). Joined Blake St. Hawkeyes Theatre in Berkeley, partnering with David Schein. Went solo to create The Spook Show, working in San Francisco and later touring U.S. & Europe. 1983 performance caught attention of Mike Nichols which led to Bdwy. show based on it and directed by him. Founding member of Comic Relief benefits. Theatrical film debut in The Color Purple (1985) (Image Award, NAACP, Golden Globe).
THEATER: small roles in B'way prods. of Pippin, Hair, Jesus Christ Superstar. 1988: toured in Living on the Edge of Chaos.

Gol-Gol

PICTURES: Jumpin' Jack Flash, Burglar, Fatal Beauty, The Telephone, Homer and Eddie, Clara's Heart, Beverly Hills Brats.
TELEVISION: Whoopi Goldberg on Broadway?, Carol, Carl, Whoopi and Robin, Moonlighting (Emmy nom., 1985), Funny, You Don't Look 200, Comedy Tonight (host).

GOLDBLUM, JEFF: Actor. b. Pittsburgh, PA, Oct. 22, 1952. m. actress Geena Davis. Studied at Sanford Meisner's Neighborhood Playhouse in New York. On Bdwy. in Two Gentleman of Verona, The Moony Shapiro Songbook.
PICTURES: Death Wish (debut), Nashville, Next Stop, Greenwich Village, Annie Hall, Between the Lines, Thank God, It's Friday, Invasion of the Body Snatchers, Threshold, The Big Chill, The Right Stuff, Buckaroo Banzai, Into the Night, Silverado, Transylvania 6-5000, The Fly, Beyond Therapy, Vibes, Earth Girls Are Easy, Camden Town Boy.
TELEVISION: Movies: The Legend of Sleepy Hollow, Rehearsal for Murder, Ernie Kovacs: Between the Laughter. Series: Tenspeed and Brownshoe.

GOLDEN, HERBERT L.: b. Philadelphia, PA, Feb. 12. e. Temple U., 1936, B.S. Reporter, rewrite man. asst. city ed., Philadelphia Record, 1933–38; joined Variety, 1938; on leave of absence, 1942–43, when asst. to John Hay Whitney and Francis Alstock, directors, M.P. Division, Coordinator of Inter-American Affairs (U.S.); commissioned in U.S. Navy, 1943, served on destroyer to 1946; then returned to Variety. M.p. ed. Consultant on motion pictures, Good Housekeeping magazine McGraw-Hill Publications, American Yearbook. Ent. Ind. Div. Bankers Trust Co., N.Y., 1952; named v.p. 1954–56; treas., Children's Asthma Research Institute, 1956; v.p. & mem. of bd. United Artists Corp., 1958; member of board, MPAA, 1959; pres., Lexington Int., Inc. investments, 1962; mem. bd., chmn. exec. com., Perfect Photo Inc., 1962; 1965 sect. & mem. bd. Century Broadcasting Group; chmn. G & G Thea. Corp.; pres. Diversifax Corp., 1966; consult. Pathe Lab, 1967; Mem. bd. Childhood Prod. Inc., 1967. Member bd. Music Makers Group, Inc., 1962. Mem. bd. Cinecom Corp., 1968; pres., Vere/Swiss Corp., 1977; mem. bd., Coral Reef Publications, Inc., 1977. Returned to Bankers Trust, 1979, to head its Media Group (service to film and TV industries).

GOLDEN, JEROME B.: Executive, Attorney. b. New York, NY, Nov. 26, 1917. e. St. Lawrence U., LL.B., 1942. Member legal dept., Paramount Pictures, Inc., 1942–50; United Paramount Theatres, Inc., 1950–53; American Broadcasting Companies, Inc., 1953; secy., ABC, 1958–86; vice-pres., ABC, 1959–86. Consultant.

GOLDENSON, LEONARD H.: Executive. b. Scottsdale, PA, December 7, 1905. e. Harvard Coll., B.A., Harvard Law School, LL.B. Practiced law, New York; counsel in reorg. Paramount theats. in New England, 1933–37; in 1937 apptd. asst. to vice-pres. Paramount in charge theat. operations; became head of theat. operations, 1938; elected pres. Paramount Theat. Service Corp., vice-pres. Paramount Pictures, Inc., 1938; dir. Paramount Pictures, 1942 (also pres. various Paramount theat. subsids., see Paramount circuits in Theatre Circuits section). Pres., chief exec. off. and director United Paramount Theatres, Inc., 1950, and of American Broadcasting-Paramount Theatres, Inc., 1953, result of merger of ABC and United Paramount Theatres, Inc.; name changed to American Broadcasting Companies, Inc. 1965; Chairman of the Board and Chief Executive Officer; of American Broadcasting Companies, Inc. since January 17, 1972; mem., board chm. of United Cerebral Palsy Assns.; trustee, John F. Kennedy Center for the Performing Arts; dir., Daughters of Jacob Geriatric Center; mem., International Radio and Television Society; Founder Member of Hollywood Museum; Trustee of Children's Cancer Research Foundation of the Children's Medical Center, Boston, Mass.; Director of Allied Stores Corporation; Trustee of Highway Users Federation for Safety and Mobility; Member of National Academy of Television Arts and Sciences; Member of Uptown Advisory Committee of Bankers Trust Company; Graduate Director of The Advertising Council, Inc.; Associate Trustee and Member of Advisory Council for the Performing Arts of University of Pennsylvania; Member of Broadcast Pioneers; Member of Inter Lochen Arts Academy-National Advisory Board; Member of Motion Picture Pioneers; Member of National Citizens' Advisory Committee on Vocational Rehabilitation; Member of United Negro College Fund-National Corporations Committee; Director of World Rehabilitation Fund, Inc.

GOLDFARB, HOWARD GERALD: Executive. b. New York, NY, Sept. 19, 1941. e. Wharton Sch. of Business. Exec. trainee, Columbia Pictures, 1962–64; mgr. dir., United Artists Corp., in Panama/Central America, 1964–69; v.p. & foreign mgr. Cannon Releasing Corp., 1970–72; pres., H.G. Entertainment Ltd. & Salt Water Releasing Co., Inc., 1972–75; dir. dist., C.I.C. (cassettes co.), 1976; v.p., dir. intl. opns., National Telefilm Associates, 1976–78; dir. intl. sls., Dino de Laurentiis Corp., 1978–79; pres., Goldfarb Distributors, 1979–1980, distributing films for independent producers worldwide. Now

represents Leisure Investment Co., Astral Films, National American, Hall Bartlett Films, Sewanee Prods., Western Pictures, Haruki Kadokawa Films, Highpoint Prods., Lawrence Schiller Prods., Market Prods.
PICTURES: Producer: The Unseen, Venus in 3-D, Mission Kills, Car Trouble, On the Fringe.

GOLDIN, BERNARD: Executive. Began career with Universal Pictures as branch mgr. in number of territories. Named Philadelphia mgr. for United Artists; 1977–81, Midwestern div. mgr. for Columbia Pictures. Returned to UA, 1981, as v.p. & asst. gen. sls. mgr.

GOLDING, DAVID: Executive. b. New York, NY, Oct. 20, 1915. e. U. of Wisconsin, B.A. Now operating public relations consultancy in London, David Golding and Associates Ltd. Formerly Universal advertising and publicity representative in UK. During war, mg. ed. Mediterranean edition, The Stars and Stripes. Also pub. dir. Samuel Goldwyn, 20th-Fox, Hecht-Hill-Lancaster, Otto Preminger.

GOLDMAN, BO: Writer.
PICTURES: One Flew Over the Cuckoo's Nest (Acad. Award, 1975), Murder on the Bridge, The Rose, Melvin and Howard, Shoot the Moon, Swing Shift.

GOLDMAN, EDMUND: Executive-Producer. b. Shanghai, China, Nov. 12, 1906. e. in Shanghai and San Francisco. Entered ind. as assst. mgr., for Universal in Shanghai, 1935–36; named mgr. Columbia Pictures' Philippine office, 1937. In 1951 named Far East. supvr. for Columbia, headquartering in Tokyo. From 1953 to present indep. m.p. dist., specializing in foreign marketing, representing indep. producers and distributors. Now v.p., Quixote Prods.
PICTURES: Surrender Hell (prod.), The Quick and the Dead (oxec. prod.).

GOLDMAN, JANE: Executive. e. Barnard Coll., New York U. School of Law. Represented Warner Bros. in special assignments while in general law practice; joined Warner Communications Inc. in N.Y. as full-time attorney, counselling dist. div. in copyright and anti-trust matters. 1985, named v.p., gen. counsel for WB Dist. Corp., at Warner Studio.

GOLDMAN, MARVIN: Executive. b. New York, NY. e. Fordham U., U. of Miami. Served in U.S. Navy in WWII, leaving with rank of Lt. commander. In 1947 went to Washington, D.C. to work for K-B Theatres; purchased the chain of five theatres. Circuit now operates 52 theatres in the DC, Maryland, Virginia area. (Partnership now includes son, Ronald.) Goldman also involved with son in indep. film prod. co., which has completed 6 features and planning more. Active in theatre organizations for many years; named pres. of National NATO in 1976. Former pres. of Metropolitan, Washington, DC area chapter of NATO and now bd. chmn. Past chief barker of Variety Club of Washington. Named exhibitor of year by IFIDA in 1966. With son operates European Classics, distributing imported films in U.S. & Canada.

GOLDMAN, MICHAEL F.: Executive. b. Manila, Philippines, Sept. 28, 1939. e. U. of California at L.A., B.S. in acct., 1962. C.P.A. certificate issued June, 1972. In 1962 incorporated Manson International, which was sold in 1986. Incorporated Quixote Prods., 1979. Also owner and sole proprietor Taurus Film co. of Hollywood, founded 1964. Co-founder and first chief financial officer of American Film Marketing Association, sponsor of First American Film Market in Los Angeles in 1981; v.p. of AFMA 1982 and 1983 and President AFMA 1984 and 1985. AFMA bd. mbr., 1981–87. Produced feature, Jessi's Girls in 1975.

GOLDMAN, SHEPARD: Writer, Producer. Pres., Scaramouche Productions. b. Brooklyn, NY; e. Hofstra U, NYU: Varied genres; novels and songs made into films.
PICTURES INCLUDE: An Unfinished Victory; Our Tender Hearts; Queens; Salsa (co-s.p.).
STAGE: The Last Salt of Summer.
TELEVISION: Chumbles Story Hour; Sensations.
AWARDS: Gold Medal–best adaptation, 15th Houston Int'l Film Festival; Gold Medal–best original comedy, 17th Houston Int'l Film Festival.

GOLDMAN, WILLIAM: Writer. b. Chicago, IL, 1931. e. Oberlin College, B.A., Columbia U., M.A. Novels include The Temple of Gold; Your Turn to Curtsy, My Turn to Bow; Soldier in the Rain (filmed); Boys and Girls Together; The Thing of It Is; No Way to Treat a Lady (filmed), Father's Day; The Season; The Princess Bride (filmed), Marathon Man (filmed), Magic (filmed), Tinsel, Control, The Silent Gondoliers, The Color of Light.
PICTURES INCLUDE: Harper, Butch Cassidy and the Sundance Kid (Acad. Award, screenplay), The Great Waldo Pepper, Marathon Man (based on own book), All the President's Men, A Bridge Too Far, Magic (based on own book), Heat (based on own book), The Princess Bride (s.p., based on his novel).

121

Gol-Goo

GOLDSMITH, JERRY: Composer. b. Los Angeles, CA, 1929. e. Los Angeles City Coll. Studied piano with Jacob Gimpel and music composition, harmony, theory with Mario Castelnuovo-Tedesco. Taught music; went with CBS radio first with own show (Romance) and then moved on to others (Suspense). Began scoring for TV, including Climax, Playhouse 90, Studio One, Gunsmoke, etc.
PICTURES INCLUDE: Black Patch (debut), Freud, Lilies of the Field, The Stripper, The Prize, Seven Days in May, In Harm's Way, Von Ryan's Express, A Patch of Blue, Our Man Flint, Stagecoach, The Blue Max, Seconds, Sand Pebbles, In Like Flint, Patton, Papillon, The Reincarnation of Peter Proud, The Cassandra Crossing, Islands in the Stream, MacArthur, Coma, Damien-Omen II, The Boys from Brazil, The Great Train Robbery, Alien, Players, Star Trek, The Final Conflict, Outland, Raggedy Man, Night Crossing, Poltergeist, The Challenge, Inchon, First Blood, Under Fire, The Lonely Guy, Gremlins, Psycho II, Twilight Zone, Explorers, Link, Supergirl, Runaway, Baby, Rambo: First Blood Part II, King Solomon's Mines, Legend, Poltergeist II, Hoosiers, Extreme Prejudice, Innerspace, Lionheart, Rent-a-Cop, Rambo III, Criminal Law, Outer Heat, Leviathan.

GOLDSMITH, MARTIN M.: Writer. b. New York, NY, Nov. 6, 1913. Bush pilot.
AUTHOR: Novels include: Double Jeopardy, Detour, Shadows at Noon, Miraculous Fish of Domingo Gonzales.
PICTURES INCLUDE: Detour, Blind Spot, Narrow Margin, Mission Over Korea, Overland Pacific, Hell's Island.

GOLDSTEIN, MILTON: Executive. b. New York, NY, Aug. 1, 1926. e. New York U., 1949. In exec. capac., Paramount; foreign sales coord., The Ten Commandments, Psycho; v.p. foreign sales, Samuel Bronston org.; asst. to Pres., Paramount Int'l., special prods., 1964; Foreign sales mgr., 1966; v.p., world wide sales, 1967, Cinerama; Sr. v.p. Cinema Center Films, 1969; pres., Cinema Center Films, 1971; v.p. Theatrical Mktg. & Sales, Metromedia Producers Corp., 1973; in March, 1974, formed Boasberg-Goldstein, Inc., consultants in prod. and dist. of m.p.; 1975, named exec. vice pres., Avco Embassy Pictures; 1978, named exec. v.p. & chief operating officer, Melvin Simon Prods. 1980, named pres.; 1985, pres. Milt Goldstein Enterprises, Inc.

GOLDSTONE, JAMES: Director. b. Los Angeles, CA. June 8, 1931. e. Dartmouth Coll., B.A., Bennington Coll., M.A. Film editor from 1950. Writer, story editor from 1957.
TELEVISION: From 1958, including pilots of Star Trek, Ironside, The Senator, etc., A Clear and Present Danger (Emmy nomination); Eric (Virgin Islands Int'l. Film Festival Gold Medal; Journey from Darkness (Christopher Award); Studs Lonigan (miniseries 1978), Kent State, (Emmy, best direction, special), Things in Their Season, Calamity Jane; The Sun Also Rises; Dreams of Gold; Earthstar Voyager.
PICTURES INCLUDE: Jigsaw, Man Called Gannon, Winning, Brother John, Red Sky at Morning, The Gang That Couldn't Shoot Straight, They Only Kill Their Masters, Swashbuckler, Rollercoaster, When Time Ran Out.

GOLDSTONE, RICHARD: Producer. b. New York, NY, July 14, 1912. e. U. of California at L.A., B.A., 1933. Capt., Army Air Forces, office of Motion Picture Services, W.W.II. Adv. exec. Entered m.p. ind. 1934 as writer, MGM; in 1935 asst. head short subjects dept.; in 1939 assoc. prod. short subjects; apptd. prod. mgr., MGM short subjects dept., co-holder 3 Academy Awards short subjects, 1942. Prod. The Set-Up, (Int'l Critics Grand Prix, Cannes, 1949), v.p. Dudley Pict. Corp.; v.p., Goldcoast Productions, Inc.
PICTURES INCLUDE: The Outriders, Yellow Cab Man, Dial 1119, Inside Straight, The Tall Target, Talk About a Stranger, Devil Makes Three, Terror on the Train, Tabor the Great, The Big Search, East of Kilimanjaro, South Seas Adventures; No Man Is an Island, Rage, The Sergeant, The Babymaker.
TELEVISION: Prod. Adventures in Paradise, Combat, Peyton Place, We Ask, Why Not? (doc.)

GOLDWURM, JEAN: Executive. b. Bucharest, Rumania, Feb. 21, 1893. e. U. of Vienna. pres. Times Film Corp. officer French Legion of Honor; commander Italian Order of Merit, Commander French Order of Arts and Letters.

GOLDWYN, SAMUEL, JR.: Producer, Director. b. Los Angeles, CA, Sept. 7, 1926. e. U. of Virginia. U.S. Army, 1944; following war writer, assoc. prod., J. Arthur Rank Org.; prod. Gathering Storm on London stage; returned to U.S., 1948; assoc. prod., Universal; recalled to Army service, 1951; prod., dir., Army documentary films including Alliance for Peace (Edinburgh Film Festival prize); prod. TV shows, Adventure series for CBS, 1952-53; prod. TV series, The Unexpected, 1954; pres., The Samuel Goldwyn Company.
PICTURES INCLUDE: Man With the Gun, The Sharkfighters, The Proud Rebel, The Adventures of Huckleberry Finn, The Young Lovers, Cotton Comes to Harlem, Come Back Charleston Blue, The Golden Seal.

TELEVISION: The Academy Awards, 1987; April Morning (co-exec. prod.); Acad. Awards, 1988 (prod.).

GOLIGER, NANCY: Executive. Began career in entertainment industry at Bill Gold Adv. & B.G. Charles. Joined Warner Bros. as natl. acct. mgr.; promoted to dir., creative adv. With Universal as dir. adv.; PolyGram Pictures, v.p., domestic & foreign adv./pub.; Seiniger Advertising, exec. v.p. & gen. mgr. 1985, joined Paramount Pictures as sr. v.p., prod./mktg. for M.P. Group.

GONZALEZ-GONZALEZ, PEDRO: Actor. b. Aguilares, TX, Dec. 21, 1926. Comedian in San Antonio Mexican theatres.
PICTURES INCLUDE: Wing of the Hawk, Ring of Fear, Ricochet Romance, High and the Mighty, Strange Lady in Town, Bengazi, I Died a Thousand Times, Bottom of the Bottle, Gun the Man Down, Wetbacks, The Love Bug, Hellfighters, Support Your Local Gunfighter.
TELEVISION: O'Henry Stories, Felix, the Fourth, Hostile Guns.

GOOD, CHARLES E.: Executive. b. 1922. Joined Buena Vista in 1957 in Chicago office; progressed from salesman to branch manager and then district manager. Later moved to Burbank as domestic sales manager in 1975; 1978, named v.p. & general sales manager; 1980, appointed pres., BV Distribution Co. Resigned presidency 1984; became BV consultant until retirement, April, 1987.

GOODMAN, DAVID Z.: Writer. e. Queens Coll., Yale School of Drama.
PICTURES: Straw Dogs, Lovers and Other Strangers, Farewell, My Lovely, Logan's Run, The Eyes of Laura Mars, Man, Woman and Child (co.-s.p.).

GOODMAN, GENE: Executive. Joined United Artists as salesman in 1954; promoted to branch mgr., Atlanta (1958–61). Served successively as branch mgr., New Orleans (1961–68); southern regional mgr. (1968–70); and southern div. mgr., (1970–78), New Orleans. Moved to N.Y. in 1978 to become asst. gen. sls. mgr. Promoted to v.p. & gen. sls. mgr. in 1980. Later in year named snr. v.p. for domestic sls.

GOODMAN, JOHN: Actor. b. St. Louis, MO, June 20, 1952. e. Southwest Missouri State U. Moved to NY in 1975 where he appeared off-off Broadway and in commercials. On Broadway in Big River.
PICTURES: Eddie Macon's Run (1983, debut), The Survivors, Revenge of the Nerds, C.H.U.D., Maria's Lovers, Sweet Dreams, The Big Easy, True Stories, Blind Date, Raisin' Arizona, Burglar, Punchline.
TELEVISION: Heart of Steel, The Face of Rape, The Mystery of Moro Castle, Chiefs (mini-series), Roseanne (series).

GOODMAN, JULIAN: Executive. b. Glasgow, KY, May 1, 1922. e. Western Kentucky U., B.A.; George Washington U., B.A. Office mgr., Comb. Prod. & Resources, 1943–45. History at NBC: news writer, WRC, NBC owned station in Washington, DC, 1945; Washington ed., News of the World, NBC Radio network; mgr. of news and special events, NBC-TV, 1951; dir. of news and public affairs, NBC News Div., 1959; v.p., NBC News, 1961; exec. v.p., 1965; sr. exec. v.p., Operations, Jan. 1, 1966; pres., NBC, April 1, 1966. Mem. bd. of dirs., NBC, 1966; chief executive officer, Jan. 1, 1970; elected director or RCA Corporation, Jan. 1, 1972; chmn., chief exec. off., NBC, April, 1, 1974; chmn., Jan. 5, 1977.

GOODMAN, MORT: Advertising, Public Relations Executive. b. Cleveland, OH, Oct. 17, 1910. e. Western Reserve U. With sports dept. Cleveland News 1928–29 joined pub. dept. Warner Bros. theatres (Ohio), 1930; transferred to Hollywood as pub. dir. for Pacific Coast zone, 1937; pub. dir. Republic Studios, 1946; res. 1952, apptd. v.p. Stodel Adv. Agcy., formed Mort Goodman Adv., 1953; formed Goodman Org., advertising agency, pub. rel., 1955. Currently pres., Goodman Nemoy and Partners, adv.-p.r. firm started 1977. In 1980 became adv. & p.r. consultant for m.p. industry.

GOODRICH, ROBERT EMMETT: Executive. b. Grand Rapids, MI, June 27, 1940. e. U. of Michigan, B.A., 1962; J.D., 1964; New York U. LL.M, 1966. Pres. & Secty., Goodrich Theaters, Inc. 1967–present, developed circuit from father's one theater to 40 screens at 7 locations in seven Mich. communities. Owns and operates AM/FM radio stations: Lansing & Muskegon, MI, Davenport, IA.
MEMBER: NATO; Will Rogers Inst. advisory comm; bd., Mich. Millers Mutual Insurance Co.; State of Mich. Bar Assn.

GOODSON, MARK: TV Producer; b. Sacramento, CA, Jan. 24, 1918; s. Abraham Ellis and Fannie (Gross) G.; U. of California, A.B., 1937. Announcer, newscaster, dir. Radio Sta. KFRC, San Francisco, 1938–41; radio announcer, dir., N.Y. 1941–43; producer—Appointment with Life, ABC, 1943; dir. Portia Faces Life, Young & Rubicam, adv. agy., 1944; radio dir. U.S. Treasury War Bond Drive, 1944–45; formed Goodson-Todman Prodns., 1946, originated radio shows Winner

Take All, 1946, Stop the Music, 1947, Hit the Jackpot, 1947–49. Creator of TV game programs What's My Line, It's News To Me, The Name's the Same, I've Got a Secret, Two for the Money, To Tell the Truth, The Price Is Right, Password, Match Game, Family Feud, and others; TV film series, The Web, The Rebel, Richard Boone Theater, Branded. 1st v.p. Capitol City Pub. Co.; v.p. New Eng. Newspapers, Inc.; dir. City Center Music and Drama, Board American Film Institute; trustee, Museum of Broadcasting. Recipient nat. television award Great Britain, 1951; Emmy award Acad. TV Arts and Scis., 1951, 52; Sylvania award. Pres. N.Y. Acad. TV Arts and Sci. 1957–58. Phi Beta Kappa.

GOODWIN, RICHARD: Producer. b. Bombay, India, Sept. 13, 1934. e. Rugby. Entered film world by chance: while waiting to go to Cambridge Univ. took temporary job as tea boy at studio which led to 20-year-long association with producer Lord Brabourne. First worked as asst. on Seven Thunders, of which Brabourne was assoc. prod. Named location manager for Brabourne's company, Mershal Productions; promoted to prod. mgr. Named assoc. prod. for Brabourne's British Home Entertainment Productions in 1960 (now defunct.)
PICTURES: Prod. Mgr.: The Sheriff of Fractured Jaw, Carve Her Name with Pride, The Grass Is Greener, Sink the Bismarck, HMS Defiant. Prod.: The Tales of Beatrix Potter. Co-Prod.: Murder on the Orient Express, Death on the Nile, The Mirror Crack'd, Evil Under the Sun, A Passage to India, Little Dorrit.

GOODWIN, RONALD: Composer, Arranger, Conductor. b. Plymouth, Eng., 1930. Early career: arranger for BBC dance orchestra; mus. dir. Parlophone Records; orchestra leader for radio, TV and records. Fut. m.p. ind., 1958. Many major film scores. Guest cond. R.P.O., B.S.O., Toronto Symph. Orch. New Zealand Symphony Orch., Sydney Symphony Orch. Scottish National Orch., BBC Scottish Symphony Orch., BBC Welsh Symphony Orch., BBC Radio Orch., BBC Concert Orch., London Philharmonic Orch., Gothenberg Symphony Orch., Norwegian Opera Orch. & Chorus, Halle Orchestra, Singapore Symphony Orch., Australian Pops Orch.
PICTURES INCLUDE: The Trials of Oscar Wilde, 633 Squadron, Those Magnificent Men in Their Flying Machines, The Trap, Where Eagles Dare, Monte Carlo or Bust, Battle of Britain, The Executioner, The Selfish Giant, Frenzy, Diamonds on Wheels, The Little Mermaid, The Happy Prince, One of Our Dinosaurs Is Missing, Escape From the Dark, Born to Run, Beauty and the Beast, Candleshoe, Force Ten from Navarone, Spaceman and King Arthur, Clash of Loyalties, Valhalla.

GORDON, ALEX: Producer. b. London, Eng., Sept. 8, 1922. e. Canford Coll., Dorset, 1939. Writer, m.p. fan magazines, 1939–41; British Army, 1942–45; pub. dir. Renown Pictures Corp., 1946–47; P.R. and pub. rep. for Gene Autry, 1948–53; v.p. and prod. Golden State Productions, 1954–58; prod. Alex Gordon Prods., 1958–66; producer Twentieth Century-Fox Television, 1967–76; film archivist/preservationist, 1976–84; v.p., Gene Autry's Flying A Pictures, 1985.
PICTURES INCLUDE: Lawless Rider, Bride of the Monster, Apache Woman, Day the World Ended, Oklahoma Woman, Girls in Prison, The She-Creature, Runaway Daughters, Shake Rattle and Rock, Flesh and the Spur, Voodoo Woman, Dragstrip Girl, Motorcycle Gang, Jet Attack, Submarine Seahawk, Atomic Submarine, The Underwater City, The Bounty Killer, Requiem for a Gunfighter.
TELEVISION: Movie of the Year, Golden Century, Great Moments in Motion Pictures.

GORDON, BERT I.: Producer, Director, Writer. b. Kenosha, WI; U. of Wisconsin.
PICTURES INCLUDE: Beginning of the End, The Amazing Colossal Man, The Fantastic Puppet People, The Cyclops, The Spider, Tormented, Boy and The Pirates, The Magic Sword, Village of the Giants, Picture Mommy Dead, How to Succeed With the Opposite Sex, Necromancy, Geronimo, The Mad Bomber, The Police Connection, The Food of the Gods, The Coming, The Big Bet.

GORDON, BRUCE: Executive. b. Sidney, Australia, Feb. 4, 1929. Began career in Australian entertainment industry 1952 with Tivoli Circuit, live theatre chain; acted as advance man, front-of-house mgr., adv. dir.; promoted to busn. mgr., 1958. Named Tivoli membr. bd. of management, 1960–62. Joined Desilu Studios in 1962, developing Far East territories; promoted 1968 when Paramount acquired Desilu to mng. dir. Para. Far East opns. Named to bd. of TV Corp., 1969, operator of Channel 9 TV stns. & co.'s theatres in Sydney, Melbourne. Dir. on bd. of Academy Investments, operator of Perth theatre chain; responsible for building Perth Entertainment Centre. Named pres., Paramount TV Intl. Services, Ltd., 1974, in New York office. Based in Bermuda since 1985.

GORDON, GALE: Actor. r.n. Charles T. Aldrich, Jr. b. New York, NY, Feb. 2, 1906. Stage debut in the Dancers; m.p. debut in The Pilgrimage Play, 1929.
PICTURES INCLUDE: Rally Round the Flag Boys, All in a

Night's Work, Don't Give Up the Ship, Visit to a Small Planet, All Hands on Deck, Speedway, The 'Burbs.
TELEVISION: Series: My Favorite Husband, Our Miss Brooks, The Brothers, Dennis The Menace, The Lucy Show, Here's Lucy.

GORDON, JACK: Executive. b. Brooklyn, NY, Mar. 13, 1929. e. U. of California at L.A. Father is Mack Gordon, songwriter. Started in industry as TV production asst. in 1949. Served in U.S. Infantry, Korea, 1951–52. Joined MGM in 1953; named dir. of non-theatrical div., 1956; v.p., MGM Intl., 1972. Appointed exec. v.p., MGM, Intl. 1979; sr. v.p., MGM/UA International Motion Pictures Distribution, 1981; pres., 1983.
Member: ASCAP, Motion Picture Pioneers, Academy of Motion Picture Arts & Sciences.

GORDON, LAWRENCE: Producer, Executive. b. Belzoni, MS, March 25, 1936. e. Tulane U. (business admin.). Assist. to prod. Aaron Spelling at Four Star Television, 1964. Writer and assoc. prod. on several Spelling shows. 1965, joined ABC-TV as head of west coast talent dev; 1966, TV and motion pictures exec. with Bob Banner Associates; 1968 joined AIP as v.p. in charge of project dev.; 1971 named v.p., Screen Gems (TV div. of Columbia Pictures) where he helped dev. Brian's Song and QB VII. Returned to AIP as v.p. worldwide prod. Formed Lawrence Gordon Prods. at Columbia Pictures; 1984–86, pres. and COO 20th Century Fox. Currently indep. prod. with projects in dev. at 20th Century Fox. Producer of musical Smile (Broadway).
PICTURES: Dillinger (1973), Hard Times, Rolling Thunder, The Driver, The End, Hooper, The Warriors, Xanadu, Paternity, Jekyll and Hyde, Together Again, 48 Hours, Streets of Fire, Brewster's Millions, Lucas, Jumpin' Jack Flash, Predator, The Couch Trip, The Wrong Guys, Die Hard, K-9, Shoeless Joe, Leviathan (exec. prod.), License to Drive.
TELEVISION: Matt Houston (creator and co-exec. prod.), Family Honor (co-creator and co-exec. prod.), Dog and Cat, The Renegades, Stunts Unlimited, The Missing Are Deadly, Lacey and the Mississippi Queen.

GORDON, MICHAEL: Director. b. Baltimore, MD, Sept. 6, 1909. e. Johns Hopkins U., B.A.; Yale, M.F.A. Stage experience as technician, stage mgr., actor, stage dir. (Stevedore, Home of the Brave, Anna Christie, One Bright Day). Member Group Theater 1935–40. m.p. debut: dial. dir. Columbia on over 20 films; dir. in 1942. Professor of Theater Arts, U. of California at L.A.
PICTURES INCLUDE: Boston Blackie Goes Hollywood, Underground Agent, One Dangerous Night, The Crime Doctor, The Web, Another Part of the Forest, An Act of Murder, The Lady Gambles, Woman in Hiding, Cyrano de Bergerac, I Can Get It for You Wholesale, The Secret of Convict Lake, Any Way the Wind Blows, Pillow Talk, Portrait in Black, Boy's Night Out, For Love or Money, Move Over Darling, Texas Across the River, A Very Special Favor, The Impossible Years, How Do I Love Thee?
OTHER PLAYS: Deadfall, The Lovers, Tender Trap, Male Animal, His & Hers, Champagne Complex, Home of the Brave, etc.

GORDON, RICHARD: Producer. b. London, Eng., Dec. 31, 1925. e. U. of London, 1943. Served in Brit. Royal Navy, 1944–46; ed. & writer on fan magazines & repr. independent American cos. 1946, with publicity dept. Assoc. Brit. Pathe 1947; org. export-import business for independent, British and American product; formed Gordon Films, Inc., 1949; formed Amalgamated prod., 1956; formed Grenadier Films, Ltd. 1971.
PICTURES INCLUDE: The Counterfeit Plan, The Haunted Strangler, Fiend Without a Face, The Secret Man, First Man into Space, Corridors of Blood, Devil Doll, Curse of Simba, The Projected Man, Naked Evil, Island of Terror; Tales of the Bizarre, Tower of Evil, Horror Hospital, The Cat and the Canary, Inseminoid.

GORDY, BERRY: Executive. b. Nov. 28, 1929. Was working on auto assembly line in Detroit when decided to launch record co., Motown. In 1961 wrote song, Shop Around; recording by Smokey Robinson made it his first million dollar record. Expanded into music publishing, personal mgt., recording studios, film and TV, also backing stage shows. Now bd. chm., Motown Industries.
PICTURES INCLUDE: Lady Sings the Blues (prod.), Mahogany (dir.), Almost Summer, The Last Dragon (exec. prod.).

GORING, MARIUS: Actor. b. Newport, Isle of Wight, 1912. e. Cambridge U., Universities of Frankfurt-on-Main, Munich, Vienna, Paris. Early career with Old Vic; stage debut 1927, Jean Sterling Rackinlay's Children's Matinees. 1940–46 served with H. M. Forces and Foreign Office.
PICTURES INCLUDE: Rembrandt, Dead Men Tell No Tales, Flying 55, Consider Your Verdict, Spy in Black, Pastor Hall, The Case of the Frightened Lady, The Big Blockade, The Night Raider, Lilli Marlene, Stairway to Heaven, Night Boat to Dublin, Take My Life, Red Shoes, Mr. Perrin and Mr. Traill, Odette, Pandora and the Flying Dutchman, Circle of Danger, Highly Dangerous, So Little Time, The Man Who

Watched Trains Go By, Rough Shoot, The Barefoot Contessa, Break in the Circle, Quentin Durward, Ill Met by Moonlight, The Moonraker, Family Doctor, Angry Hills, Whirlpool, Treasure of St. Teresa, Monty's Double, Beyond the Curtain, Desert Mice, The Inspector, Girl on a Motorcycle, Subterfuge.
TELEVISION: Numerous appearances, Sleeping Dog, Man in a Suitcase, Scarlet Pimpernel, The Expert.

GOROG, LASZLO: Writer. b. Hungary, Sept. 30, 1903. e. U. of Sciences, Budapest. Playwright, short story writer, asst. editor, Budapest, 1928–39.
PICTURES INCLUDE: Tales of Manhattan, The Affairs of Susan, She Wouldn't Say Yes, The Land Unknown, Mole People.
TELEVISION: 4 Star, Dupont, The Roaring Twenties, 77 Sunset Strip, Maverick, etc.

GORTNER, MARJOE: Actor, Producer. b. Long Beach, CA, Jan. 14, 1944. Was child evangelist, whose career as such was basis for documentary film, Marjoe (AA). Acted in films and TV; turned producer in 1978 for When You Comin' Back, Red Ryder.
PICTURES: Bobbie Joe and the Outlaw, The Food of the Gods, Viva Knievel, Sidewinder One, Earthquake, When You Comin' Back, Red Ryder, Mausoleum, Hellhole.
TELEVISION: Films: The Marcus-Nelson Murders, The Gun and the Pulpit, Pray for the Wildcats. Guest appearances on Police Story, Mayday: 40,000 Feet. Series: Falcon Crest.

GOSSET, LOUIS, JR.: Actor. b. Brooklyn, NY, May 27, 1936. e. New York U., B.S. On stage in Take a Giant Step, The Desk Set, Lost in the Stars, Raisin in the Sun, Golden Boy, The Blacks, Blood Knot, My Sweet Charley, Murderous Angels (L.A. Critics Award).
PICTURES: A Raisin in the Sun (debut, 1961), The Bushbaby, The Landlord, Skin Game, The Laughing Policeman, The White Dawn, River Niger, J.D.'s Revenge, Choirboys, The Deep, It Rained All Night the Day I Left, Private Benjamin, An Officer and a Gentleman (Oscar), Jaws 3-D, Finders Keepers, Enemy Mine, Iron Eagle, Firewalker, The Principal, Iron Eagle II: Battle Beyond the Flag, The Punisher.
TELEVISION: Movies: Campions in Nightmare, It's Good to Be Alive, Sidekicks, Delancey Street, The Crisis Within, Don't Look Back, Roots, Little Ladies of the Night, To Kill a Cop, The Critical List, Backstairs at the White House, This Man Stands Alone, Sadat, The Guardian, A Gathering of Old Men, The Father Clements Story, Roots Christmas. Series: The Power of Matthew Star, The Lazarus Syndrome, The Young Rebels, A Triple Play; Sam Found Out, Gideon Oliver (series).

GOTTESMAN, STUART: Executive. Started career in mailroom of Warner Bros., 1972; later named promo. asst. to southwestern regional fieldman; promoted to that post which held for 10 years. 1987, named WB dir. field activities.

GOTTLIEB, CARL: Writer, Director, Actor. b. March 18, 1938.
PICTURES: Writer: Jaws; Which Way Is Up?; Jaws II; The Jerk (also act.); Caveman (also dir.); Doctor Detroit; Jaws 3-D. Actor: The Committee, Into the Night, Amazon Women on the Moon (co-dir.).
TELEVISION: Writer: Smothers Bros. Show; The Odd Couple; Flip Wilson; Bob Newhart Show; The Super; Crisis at Sun Valley, The Deadly Triangle, Paul Reiser: Out on a Whim.

GOTTLIEB, STAN: Actor, Film Distributor. b. New York, NY, April 22, 1917. e. New York U., Columbia U. Has acted in films, theatrical, stage and TV since 1970. Gen. mgr. for Impact Films, Inc. 1966–72. Gen. Mgr., Mammoth Films (1973–76).
PICTURES INCLUDE: Actor: Putney Swope, You Gotta Walk It Like You Talk It, The Owl and the Pussycat, Pound, The Anderson Tapes, Cold Turkey, Slaughterhouse Five, Black Fantasy, Greaser's Place, Compliments to the World.
TELEVISION: Actor: Sticks & Bones, Hot I Baltimore, The Jeffersons.
STAGE: Steambath.

GOUGH, MICHAEL: Actor. b. Malaya, Nov. 23, 1917. e. Rose Hill Sch., in Kent, England, and at Durham School. Studied at Old Vic School in London; first stage appearance in 1936 at Old Vic Theatre. N.Y. stage debut 1937 in Love of Women. London debut in 1938 in The Zeal of Thy House. M.P. debut in 1948 in Blanche Fury; since in over 50 films.
PICTURES INCLUDE: Anna Karenina, The Man in the White Suit, Rob Roy, The Sword and the Rose, Richard III, Reach for the Sky, Horror of Dracula, The Horse's Mouth, Konga, Mr. Topaze, The Phantom of the Opera, The Skull, Women in Love, Julius Caesar, Trog, The Go-Between, Henry VIII and His Six Wives, Savage Messiah, The Legend of Hell House, The Boys from Brazil, The Dresser, Top Secret!, Caravaggio, Out of Africa, The Serpent and the Rainbow.
TELEVISION INCLUDES: Smiley's People, To the Lighthouse, The Citadel, Suez, Vincent the Dutchman, Heart Attack Hotel, Oxford Blues.

GOULD, ELLIOTT: Actor. b. Brooklyn, NY, August 29, 1938. Broadway debut in Rumple.
STAGE: Say Darling, Irma La Douce, I Can Get It for You Wholesale, On the Town (London), Fantasticks (tour), Drat the Cat, Little Murders, Luv (tour).
TELEVISION: Once Upon A Mattress, Come Blow Your Horn, Jack and the Jeanstalk (Faerie Tale Theater), George Burns Comedy Week, Paul Reiser: Out on a Whim. Movies: Vanishing Act, The Rules of Marriage, Conspiracy: The Trial of the Chicago 8. Series: E/R, Together We Stand.
PICTURES INCLUDE: The Night They Raided Minsky's, Bob & Carol & Ted & Alice, M*A*S*H, Getting Straight, Move, Little Murders, The Touch, I Love My Wife, The Long Goodbye, Busting, S*P*Y*S!, California Split, Who?, Nashville, (guest), Whiffs, I Will . . . I Will . . . For Now, Harry and Walter Go to New York, A Bridge Too Far, Capricorn One, Matilda, Escape to Athena, The Last Flight of Noah's Ark, The Devil and Max Devlin, Dirty Tricks, The Naked Face, The Silent Partner, Over the Brooklyn Bridge, Inside Out, The Muppet Movie, The Lady Vanishes, My First 40 Years, The Telephone, Lethal Obsession (Der Joker), Singles, The Big Picture, Dangerous Love, Story of a Woman, Cry Devil, The Wounded King.

GOULD, HAROLD: Actor. b. Schenectady, NY, Dec. 10, 1923. e. Cornell U., MA., Ph.D. Instructor of theatre and speech, 1953–56; asst. prof. drama and speech, 1956–60. Acted with Ashland, OR Shakespeare Fest. in 1950s and Mark Taper Forum (The Miser, Once in a Lifetime). Won Obie Award for Off-Bdwy debut in The Increased Difficulty of Concentration, 1969.
THEATER: The House of Blue Leaves, Fools, Grown Ups.
PICTURES: Two for the Seesaw, The Couch, Harper, Inside Daisy Clover, Marnie, An American Dream, The Arrangement, The Lawyer, Mrs. Pollifax: Spy, Where Does It Hurt?, The Sting, The Front Page, Love and Death, The Big Bus, Silent Movie, The One and Only, Seems Like Old Times, Playing for Keeps, Romero.
TELEVISION: Series: Rhoda, Soap. Movies: To Catch a Star, Feather and Father Gang, Park Place, Foot in the Door, Moviola, Washington Behind Closed Doors, Aunt Mary, Better Late Than Never, King Crab, Have I Got a Christmas for You, Man in the Santa Claus Suit, I Never Sang For My Father.

GOULD, JOSEPH: Executive. b. New York, NY, Jan. 30, 1915. e. New York U., B.A., 1935; Columbia U., Pulitzer School of Journalism, M.S., 1936. Adv. dept., United Artists, 1939–46; W.W.II service, 1944–46: Office Strategic Services (London), Office of Military Govt. for Germany (US); Berlin; Universal, 1947–48; asst. adv. mgr. 20th Century-Fox. 1949–52; adv. consultant, Joseph Burstyn. Louis De Rochemont Assoc., I.F.E. Releasing Corp. 1953–55; adv. mgr. United Artists, 1955–60; adv. mgr. Paramount Pictures, 1960–62; David Singer Associates, 1962–64; partner, Konheim Gould & Ackerman, 1968–74; principal, Joseph Gould Associates, 1974–77; creative services director, WIXT-TV, Syracuse, 1978–82; Joseph Gould Associates, Falls Church, VA, 1982–84; Center for Defense Information, Public Affairs, director, Washington, DC, 1984–.

GOULET, ROBERT: Singer, Actor. b. Lawrence, MA., Nov. 26, 1933. e. school, Edmonton; scholarship, Royal Conservatory of Music. Sang in choirs, appeared with numerous orchestras; disk jockey, CKUA, Edmonton; pub. rel., The Merrick Co.
STAGE: Camelot, The Happy Time, numerous tours.
TELEVISION: The Ed Sullivan Show, Garry Moore, The Enchanted Nutcracker, Omnibus, The Broadway of Lerner and Loewe, Rainbow of Stars, Judy Garland Show, Bob Hope Show, The Bell Telephone Hour; England: Granada—TV special, Jack Benny; Dean Martin; Andy Williams; Jack Paar; Red Skelton; Hollywood Palace; Patty Duke Show, Star of Robert Goulet Show, Blue Light (series), Brigadoon, Carousel, Kiss Me Kate, Fantasy Island, Matt Houston, Glitter.
PICTURES INCLUDE: Honeymoon Hotel, I'd Rather Be Rich, I Deal in Danger, Underground, Atlantic City, Beetlejuice.
RECORDS: Always You, Two of Us, Sincerely Yours, The Wonderful World of Love, Robert Goulet in Person, This Christmas I Spend With You, Manhattan Tower, Without You, My Love Forgive Me, Travelling On, Robert Goulet on Tour, Robert Goulet on Broadway, Robert Goulet on Broadway II, Camelot, Happy Time.

GOWDY, CURT: Sportscaster. b. Green River, WY, 1919. Basketball star at U. of Wyoming. All-Conference member; graduated U. of Wyoming. 1942. Officer in U.S. Air Force WWII, then became sportscaster. Voted Sportscaster of the Year, 1967, Nat'l Assn. of Sportswriters Broadcasters. Best Sportscaster, FAME, 1967. Did play-by-play telecasts for 16 World Series, 7 Super Bowls, 12 Rose Bowls, 8 Orange Bowls, 18 NCAA Final 4 college basketball championships. In 1970 was the first individual from the field of sports to receive the George Foster Peabody Award. Hosted the American Sportsman outdoor TV show on ABC for 20 years. (Received 8

Emmy Awards). Inducted into the Sportscasters Hall of Fame in 1981, the Fishing Hall of Fame in 1982, and the Baseball Hall of Fame in 1984.

GRADE, LORD LEW: Executive. r.n. Louis Winogradsky. b. Odessa, Dec. 25, 1906. Brother of Lord Bernard Delfont. Came to Eng. 1912. Was first a music hall dancer until 1934 when he became an agent. Joint managing dir. Lew and Leslie Grade Ltd. until 1955; deputy managing dir. Associated Television Ltd. 1958–; Chm. Stoll Theatre Corp., 1973–; Moss Empires 1973–; chmn, chief exec. Embassy Communications Int'l. 1982– Associated Communications Ltd. Chmn. & Chief exec., The Grade Co. Autobiography: Still Dancing (1988).

GRADE, MICHAEL: Executive. b. London, England, 1943. Entered industry 1966. Early career as newspaper columnist, became an executive at London Weekend Television then Embassy Television in Hollywood. Joined BBC Television, 1983 as controller of BBC 1 and director of Programmes (TV), 1986. Joined Channel 4 as chief executive, 1988.

GRADUS, BEN: Producer, Director, Writer. b. New York, NY. e. Brooklyn Coll. Is principal in Directors Group Motion Pictures, Inc. Positions held include v.p. Filmways, Inc.; prod.-dir. for Screen Gems. Specialist in educational and doc. films; also has done feature, children's comedy TV shows and series, Decision: The Conflicts of Harry S. Truman. Author, Directing the Television Commercial. Nominee for Emmy, Grammy.
CREDITS INCLUDE: Dawn over Ecuador, Gentlemen of the Jury, To Save Your Life, Lifewatch Six, Ford Around the World, Art Heritage, A Girl from Puerto Rico, Span of Life, Crowded Paradise.

GRAF, BILLY: Executive. b. 1945. Entered industry 1965. Was asst. dir.; unit/location mgr./production mgr. for American, British and European companies. Now line producer, production mgr., asst. director.
PICTURES INCLUDE: Alfie, A Man for All Seasons, Billion Dollar Brain, Scrooge, Run Wild Run Free, The Best House in London, Chitty Chitty Bang Bang, Galaxina, Khartoum, You Only Live Twice, Women in Love, Song of Norway, Prudence and the Pill, Hammerhead, Underground Aces, Purple Rain, Teen Wolf, Housesitter, The Spoiler.
TELEVISION: Secret Agent, The Saint, "Q" Branch, Private Eye Public Ear, The Avengers, Department "S," The Dave Cash Radio Show.

GRAF, WILLIAM N.: Executive. b. New York, NY, Oct. 11, 1912. Entered industry in 1934. 1937–42, exec. secty./asst. to Mark Hellinger at Warner Bros. & 20th-Fox. 1942–45, writer of armed forces training films. 1946–50, exec. secty./asst. to Harry Cohn, pres., Columbia Pictures; 1951, prod. asst. to Jack Fier, prod. head, Columbia. 1952–65, Amer. repr. for British productions, Columbia Pictures; 1965–66, exec. asst. to J. J. Frankovich, Columbia Pictures, London; 1965–66, v.p., Columbia Pictures Int'l., London; 1969–70, indep. prod., Cinema Center Films; 1980, v.p. in chg. of prod., Legion Films, Inc., Beverly Hills; 1984, pres., Billy Graf Prods.
PICTURES: (Producer): The Red Beret, A Man for All Seasons, Sinful Davey, The African Elephant.

GRAFF, RICHARD B.: Executive. b. Milwaukee, WI, Nov. 9, 1924. e. U. of Illinois. Served U.S. Air Force; Universal Pictures 1956 to 1964 in Chicago, Detroit, Chicago and New York home office as asst. to genl. sales manager; 1964 went to National General in Los Angeles. In 1967 became v.p. and general sales mgr. of National General Pictures and formed and operated company. 1968, exec. v.p. in charge of worldwide sales and marketing. 1968 v.p. of parent company; v.p. general sales mgr. AIP in 1971; 1975, pres. Cine Artists Pictures; pres. The Richard Graff Company Inc 1977; pres., domestic distribution, MGM/UA June 1983. Appointed group president, worldwide theatrical distribution, Weintraub Entertainment Group, 1987.

GRANET, BERT: Producer, Writer. b. New York, NY, July 10, 1910. e. Yale U. Sch. of Fine Arts (47 workshop). From 1936 author s.p. orig. & adapt. numerous pictures. Exec. prod.: Universal, 1967–69, CBS, Desilu Studios.
PICTURES INCLUDE: Quick Money, The Affairs of Annabel, Mr. Doodle Kicks Off, Laddie, A Girl a Guy and a Gob, My Favorite Wife, Bride by Mistake, Sing Your Way Home, Those Endearing Young Charms, The Locket, Do You Love Me?, The Marrying Kind, Berlin Express, The Torch, Scarface, Mob.
TELEVISION: Desilu (1957–61), Twilight Zone, The Untouchables (pilot), Scarface Mob; Loretta Young Show (1955–56), Walter Winchell File 1956–57, Lucille Ball-Desi Arnaz Show 1957–60, Westinghouse Desilu Playhouse, The Great Adventure.

GRANGER, FARLEY: Actor. b. San Jose, CA, July 1, 1925. e. Hollywood. School prior to m.p. career; screen debut in North Star 1943; in U.S. Armed Forces 1944–46. Joined Eva Le Gallienne's National Rep. Co. in the 1960s (The Sea Gull).

PICTURES INCLUDE: The Purple Heart, They Live by Night, Rope, Enchantment, Roseanna McCoy, Side Street, Our Very Own, Edge of Doom, Strangers on a Train, Behave Yourself, I Want You, O. Henry's Full House, Hans Christian Andersen, Story of Three Loves, Small Town Girl, Summer Hurricane, Brass Ring, Naked Street, Girl in the Red Velvet Swing, Arrow Smith, The Heiress, The Prisoner of Zenda, Senso, The Serpent, A Man Called Noon, Those Days in the Sun, The Chief of Homicide, The Painter and the Red Head, Call Me Trinity, The Syndicate, Arnold, A Crime for a Crime, The Imagemaker.
TELEVISION: Playhouse of Stars, U.S. Steel Hour, Producer's Showcase, Climax, Ford Theatre, Playhouse 90, 20th Century Fox Hour, Robert Montgomery Presents, Arthur Murray Dance Party, Wagon Train, Masquerade Party, Kojak, 6 Million Dollar Man, Ellery Queen, 9 Lives of Jenny Dolan, Widow, One Life to Live, As the World Turns.

GRANGER, STEWART: Actor. r.n. James Stewart. b. May 6, 1913. e. medicine; Webber-Douglas Sch. of Acting, London. In Brit. Army, W.W.II. On stage from 1935, Hull Repertory theat.; Birmingham Repertory; Malvern Festivals (1936–37); Old Vic Co. Film debut. A Southern Maid (1933). Voted one of Brit. top ten money-making stars in M.P. Herald-Fame Poll, 1943, 1944, 1945, 1946, 1947, 1949.
PICTURES INCLUDE: In Great Britain: So This Is London, Convoy, Secret Mission, Thursday's Child, Man in Grey, The Lamp Still Burns, Fanny by Gaslight, Love Story, Waterloo-Road, Madonna of the Seven Moons, Caesar and Cleopatra, Caravan, Magic Bow, Captain Boycott, Blanche Fury, Saraband for Dead Lovers, Woman Hater, Adam and Evalyn. In U.S.: King Solomon's Mines, Soldiers Three, Light Touch, Wild North, Scaramouche, Prisoner of Zenda, Salome, Young Bess, All the Brothers Were Valiant, Beau Brummell, Green Fire, Moonfleet, Footsteps in the Fog, Bhowani Junction, Last Hunt, The Little Hut, Gun Glory, The Whole Truth, Harry Black, North to Alaska, Sodom and Gomorrah, Swordsman of Siena, Last Patrol, The Secret Invasion, The Last Safari, The Trygon Factor, The Wild Geese, Hell Hunters.
TELEVISION: The Hound of the Baskervilles, Crossings, A Hazard of Hearts, Royal Romance of Charles and Diana.

GRANT, HUGH: Actor. b. London. e. New Coll., Oxford U. Acted with OUDS before landing role in Oxford Film Foundation's Privileged (1982) that began career. Acted at Nottingham Playhouse and formed revue group, The Jockeys of Norfolk.
PICTURES: Maurice (debut, 1987), The Lair of the White Worm, The Dawning.
TELEVISION: The Last Place on Earth (mini-series); The Demon Lover; The Detective; Handel: Honour, Profit and Pleasure; Ladies in Charge, Dangerous Love.

GRANT, LEE: Actress. r.n. Lyova Rosenthal. b. New York, NY, Oct. 31, 1931. m. producer Joseph Feury. At 4 was member of Metropolitan Opera Company; played princess in L'Orocolo. Member of the American Ballet at 11. e. Juilliard Sch. of Music, studied voice, violin and dance. At 18 with road co. Oklahoma as understudy. Acting debut: Joy to the World.
THEATRE: acted in a series of one-acters at ANTA with Henry Fonda. 1949, played shoplifter in The Detective Story (won Critics Circle Award); Lo and Behold, A Hole in the Head, Wedding Breakfast; road co. Two for the Seesaw, The Captains and the Kings; toured with Electra, Silk Stockings, St. Joan, Arms and the Man, The Maids (Obie Award), Prisoner of Second Avenue.
TELEVISION: Studio One, The Kraft Theatre, Slattery's People, The Fugitive, Ben Casey, The Nurses, The Defenders, East Side/West Side, Peyton Place (Emmy Award, Best Supporting Player, 1966), One Day at a Time, Fay (series), Bob Hope Show (Emmy nom.). Movies: The Love Song of Bernard Kempenski, BBC's The Respectful Prostitute, The Neon Ceiling (Emmy Award), The Spell, Thou Shalt Not Kill, Bare Essence, Plaza Suite, Will There Really Be A Morning?, Mussolini—The Untold Story (mini-series) Director: Nobody's Child, Shape of Things, When Women Kill, A Matter of Sex, Down and Out in America.
PICTURES INCLUDE: The Detective Story, Terror in the Streets, Affair of the Skin, The Balcony, Divorce American Style, Valley of the Dolls, In the Heat of the Night, Buona Sera, Mrs. Campbell, The Big Bounce, Marooned, The Landlord, There Was a Crooked Man, Plaza Suite, Portnoy's Complaint, Shampoo (Acad. Award, supp. actress, 1975), Voyage of the Damned, Airport '77, When You Comin' Back, Red Ryder, Charlie Chan and the Curse of the Dragon Queen, Teachers, The Big Town. Dir.: Tell Me a Riddle, Willmar Eight, Boy's Life.

GRASGREEN, MARTIN: Executive. b. New York, NY, July 1, 1925. Entered m.p. ind. Jan., 1944, Columbia Pictures h.o. in contract dept. Promoted to travelling auditor April, 1946. Appt. office mgr. Omaha branch Doc., 1948; salesman Omaha, Dec., 1950. Transferred to Indianapolis, 1952, as city salesman; transferred to Cleveland as sales mgr., 1953. Left Columbia in 1960 to become 20th-Fox branch mgr. in Cleveland. Transferred to Philadelphia in 1965 as branch mgr.; transferred to N.Y. in 1967 as Eastern dist. mgr. Resigned in 1970 to form Paragon Pictures, prod.-dist. co. In Jan., 1975, formed Lanira Corp., representing producers for U.S. sales and dist. of films in U.S. Retired.

GRASSHOFF, ALEX: Writer, Producer, Director. b. Boston, MA, Dec. 10, 1930. e. Tufts Coll., U. of Southern California. 3 Academy Award nominations for feature documentaries; 1974, Journey to the Outer Limits; 1966, Really Big Family; 1968, Young Americans won Oscar; Future Shock: 1973 Cannes Film Festival. T.V. Series (Dir.): The Rockford Files, Chips, Night Stalker, Toma, Barbary Coast, Movin' On, CHiPs. The Wave (Emmy), The Unforgiveable Secret, Counterattack—Crime in America, Sometimes I Don't Love My Mother, Backwards—The Riddle of Dyslexia.

GRAVES, PETER: Actor. b. London, Oct. 21, 1911. e. Harrow. With Knight, Frank & Rutley, then Lloyds prior to theat. career. First stage appearance 1934 in Charles B. Cochran's Streamline.
THEATRE: Novello musicals at Drury Lane; repertory at Windsor, Old Chelsea, The Merry Widow, The Sound of Music, Private Lives. Recent: The Reluctant Peer, The Last of Mrs. Cheyney, Dear Charles, An Ideal Husband (S. Africa), A Boston Story (tour), His, Hers, and Theirs, The Great Waltz, No Sex Please We're British.
PICTURES INCLUDE: Mrs. Fitzherbert, Spring in Park Lane, Maytime in Mayfair, Lady With a Lamp, Encore, Derby Day (Four Against Fate), Lilacs in the Spring (Let's Make Up), Admirable Crichton, Alfie, The Wrong Box, The Jokers, I'll Never Forget What's Is Name, How I Won the War, Assassination Bureau, The Adventurers, The Slipper and the Rose.
TELEVISION: Those Wonderful Snows, Chelsea at 9, One O'Clock Show, Lunch Box, 2 Cars, Dickie Henderson Show, Ivor Novello Series, East Lynne, Ninety Years On, The Sleeping Doe, The Frobisher Game, The Jazz Age series, Kate series, Crown Court, Softly, Softly, 10 from the 20s, Quiller, Duchess of Duke Street, Looks Familiar, Bulman, Shades of Darkness, God Knows Where's Port Talbot, Campaign, The Woman He Loved, Shadow on the Sun.

GRAVES, PETER: Actor. r.n. Peter Aurness. b. Minneapolis, MN, March 18, 1926. e. U. of Minnesota. Brother, James Arness. Played with bands, radio announcer, while at school; U.S. Air Force 2 yrs.; summer stock appearances; m.p. debut in Rogue River (1950).
PICTURES INCLUDE: Fort Defiance, Stalag 17, East of Sumatra, Beneath the 12-Mile Reef, The Raid, Black Tuesday, Wichita, Long Gray Line, Night of the Hunter, Naked Street, Fort Yuma, Court Martial of Billy Mitchell, The Ballad of Josie, Sergeant Ryker, The Five Man Army, Sidecar Racers, Airplane!, Airplane II: The Sequel.
TELEVISION: Series: Fury, 1955–58, Mission Impossible, 1967–73. Movies: Winds of War, If It's Tuesday, It Still Must Be Belgium. Host/narrator: Discover! The World of Science (1985–88); Biography (1987– 88).

GRAVES: RUPERT: Actor. Before film debut worked as a clown with the Delta travelling circus in England.
THEATER: Sufficient Carbohydrates, Amadeus.
PICTURES: A Room with a View, Maurice, A Handful of Dust.
TELEVISION: British: Vice Versa (1980–81); A Life of Puccini; Fortunes of War.

GRAY, COLEEN: Actress. r.n. Doris Jensen. b. Staplehurst, NB, Oct. 23, 1922. e. Hamline U., B.A. summa cum laude, 1943, Actor's Lab. m. Fritz Zeiser. Member: Nat'l Collegiate Players, Kappa Phi, a capella choir, little theatres, 1943–44; screen debut State Fair, 1945.
PICTURES INCLUDE: Kiss of Death, Nightmare Alley, Fury at Furnace Creek, Red River, Sleeping City, Riding High, Father Is a Bachelor, Models Inc., Kansas City Confidential, Sabre Jet, Arrow in the Dust, The Fake, The Vanquished, Las Vegas Shakedown, Twinkle in God's Eye, Tennessee's Partner, The Killing, Wild Dakotas, Death of a Scoundrel, Frontier Gambler, Black Whip, Star in the Dust, The Vampires, Hell's Five Hours, Copper Sky, Johnny Rocco, The Leech Woman, The Phantom Planet, Town Tamer, P.J., The Late Liz, Cry from the Mountain.
TELEVISION: Days of Our Lives, (1966–67). Family Affair, Ironside, Bonanza, Judd for the Defense, Name of the Game, Bright Promise, The FBI, The Bold Ones, World Premiere, Mannix, Sixth Sense, McCloud, The Best Place to Be, Tales from the Dark Side.

GRAY, DULCIE: C.B.E. Actress b. Malaya, Nov. 20, 1919. e. Webber Douglas Sch. London Stage debut 1939, Aberdeen, Hay Fever, Author: Love Affair (play), 18 detective novels, book of short stories. 8 radio plays; co-author with husband Michael Denison, An Actor and His World; Butterflies on My Mind, The Glanville Women, Anna Starr; Mirror Image.
STAGE: 40 West End plays including Little Foxes, Brighton Rock, Dear Ruth, Rain on the Just, Candida, An Ideal Husband, Where Angels Fear to Tread, Heartbreak House, On Approval, Happy Family, No. 10, Out of the Question, Village Wooing, Wild Duck, At The End of the Day, The Pay

Off, A Murder Has Been Announced, Bedroom Farce, A Coat of Varnish, School for Scandal, The Living Room.
PICTURES INCLUDE: Two Thousand Women, A Man About the House, Mine Own Executioner, My Brother Jonathan, The Glass Mountain, They Were Sisters Wanted for Murder, The Franchise Affair, Angels One Five, There Was a Young Lady, A Man Could Get Killed, The Trail of the Pink Panther, The Curse of the Pink Panther.
TELEVISION: Milestones, The Will, Crime Passionel, Art and Opportunity, Fish in the Family, The Governess, What the Public Wants, Lesson in Love, The Happy McBaines, Winter Cruise, The Letter, Tribute to Maugham, Virtue, Beautiful Forever, East Lynne, Unexpectedly Vacant, The Importance of Being Earnest, This Is Your Life, Crown Court, Making Faces, Read All About It, The Voysey Inheritance, Life After Death, The Pink Pearl, Britain in the Thirties, Rumpole (The Old Boy Net.), Cold Warrior, Hook, Line and Sinker, Howard's Way, 1985–88.

GRAY, GORDON: Broadcast Management Consultant. b. Albert Lea, MN, Nov. 16, 1905. e. U. of Missouri. Entered broadcasting ind. 1932, v.p., gen. mgr., WOR, WOR TV; pres. WKTV, Utica, N.Y., KAUZ, Wichita Falls, Tex. Founded Central N.Y. Cable, Utica, N.Y. Chm., Board of Governors, WFTV, Orlando, Fla. and management consultant, presently.

GRAY, SPALDING: Performance artist, Actor, Writer. b. Barrington, RI, 1941. Began career as actor in regional and off-Bdwy theater. In 1969 joined the Wooster Group, experimental performance group. Has written and performed autobiographical monologues (Sex and Death to the Age 14, Swimming to Cambodia) throughout U.S, Europe and Australia. Has taught theater workshops for adults and children and is recipient of Guggenheim fellowship. Artist in resident Mark Taper Forum, 1986–87.
PICTURES: Actor: The Killing Fields, Swimming to Cambodia, True Stories, Stars and Bars, Clara's Heart.
TELEVISION: Terrors of Pleasure (HBO Special).

GRAYSON, KATHRYN: Actress. r.n. Zelma Hedrick. b. Winston-Salem, NC, Feb. 9, 1923. e. St. Louis schools. Singer. Screen debut; Andy Hardy's Private Secretary, 1940. Achieved stardom in Anchors Aweigh, 1945.
PICTURES INCLUDE: The Vanishing Virginian, Rio Rita, Seven Sweethearts,Thousands Cheer; Ziegfeld Follies of 1946, Two Sisters from Boston, Showboat, That Midnight Kiss, Grounds for Marriage, The Toast of New Orleans, The Kissing Bandit, Lovely to Look At, Desert Song, So This Is Love, Kiss Me Kate, Vagabond King.
TELEVISION: GE Theatre, (Emmy nomination), 1960; Die Fledermaus, ABC, 1966; Murder, She Wrote.
STAGE: Debut in N.Y. and tour, Camelot, 1963; Rosalinda, Merry Widow, Kiss Me Kate, Showboat (N.Y. and U.S. tour).

GRAZER, BRIAN: Producer. b. Los Angeles, CA, July 12, 1953. e. U. of Southern California. Started as legal intern at Warner Bros.; later script reader (for Brut/Faberge) & talent agent. Joined Edgar J. Scherick-Daniel Blatt Co.; then with Ron Howard as partner.
PICTURES: Night Shift; Splash; Real Genius, Like Father, Like Son (co-prod.).
TELEVISION: Zuna Beach; Thou Shalt Not Commit Adultery, O'Hara (exec. prod.).

GREEN, ADOLPH: Writer, Actor. b. New York, NY, Dec. 2, 1915. m. actress-singer Phyllis Newman. Began career in the cabaret act The Revuers with partner Betty Comden and Judy Holliday (1944). Wrote book, sketches & lyrics for many Broadway shows including: On the Town, Billion Dollar Baby, Bonanza Bound! (also actor), Two on the Aisle, Wonderful Town, Peter Pan (Mary Martin); Say Darling; Bells are Ringing; Do Re Mi; Subways Are For Sleeping; Fade Out, Fade In; Halleuljah, Baby; Applause (Tony Award), Lorelei or Gentlemen Still Prefer Blondes (new lyrics), By Bernstein (book), On the Twentieth Century (Tony Award, best score 1978).
PICTURES INCLUDE: Good News, On the Town, Barkleys of Broadway, Take Me Out to the Ball Game, Singin' in the Rain, Bandwagon, It's Always Fair Weather, Auntie Mame; What a Way to Go, all in collab. with Betty Comden. As actor: Simon.

GREEN, GUY: Director. b. Somerset, Eng. 1913. Joined Film Advertising Co. as projectionist & camera asst. 1933; camera asst., Elstree Studios (BIP) 1935; started as camera operator on films including One of Our Aircraft Is Missing, In Which We Serve, This Happy Breed. 1944: Director of Photography; Dir of Allied Film Makers Ltd.
PICTURES INCLUDE: The Way Ahead, Great Expectations, Oliver Twist, Captain Horatio Hornblower, I Am A Camera, River Beat, Tears For Simon, House of Secrets, Sea of Sand, The Angry Silence, The Mark, Light In The Piazza, Diamond Head, A Patch of Blue, Pretty Polly, A Matter of Innocence, The Magus, A Walk in the Spring Rain, Luther, Once Is Not Enough, The Devil's Advocate, The Outlander.
TELEVISION: (U.S.) Incredible Journey of Dr. Meg Laurel;

Isabel's Choice; Jennifer: A Woman's Story; Arthur Hailey's Strong Medicine.

GREEN, JANET: Actress, Screen Writer. b. Hertfordshire, England, 1914. Early career as actress; Wrote first play, 1945; Ent. m.p. ind. 1947, wrote orig. s.p., The Clouded Yellow; further orig. s.p. incl. The Good Beginning, Lost Eye Witness, The Long Arm (in coll.), The Fever Tree, Sapphire, Cast a Dark Shadow, Midnight Lace, Gathering of Eagles, Ashenden, Victim, Life for Ruth, Christobel; Show Me A Murderer, Walk in the Shadow, Seven Women, The Golden Keel, It Happened in Havana, My Turn Now, Gutsy, The Sweetest Voice in the World (U.S.), The Fox Is Female, Little Individual.

GREEN, JOHN, (JOHNNY): Composer, Music Director, Conductor, Arranger, Pianist. b. New York, NY, Oct. 10, 1908. e. Horace Mann Sch., Harvard U., A.B., 1928. Entered m.p. industry as rehearsal pianist. Paramount Astoria, N.Y.; composer-conductor 1930–32. Conductor, Paramount-Publix Theatres, 1930–33. Name band leader, 1933–40. Made numerous shorts, appeared on many TC commercial radio programs. Composer of songs: Coquette, I'm Yours, Out of Nowhere, I Cover the Waterfront, Song of Raintree County, Body and Soul, Easy Come, Easy Go, I Wanna Be Loved etc.; also symphonic works performed by major orchestras U.S. and abroad; Symphony, Mine Eyes Have Seen, 1978 Joined MGM, composer-conductor, 1942–46; Univ. Internat'l. 1947; returned to MGM for Easter Parade (Acad. Award, scoring of musical); Warner 1948–49. Inspector General (Golden Globe Award 1949, best score of year). Apptd. gen. music dir. and exec-in-chg-of-music MGM 1949; produced shorts series MGM Concert Hall (Acad. Award, best one reel short 1953); Acad. Award, best scoring of musical, American in Paris 1951; composed score Raintree County (Acad. Nom. 1957); left MGM to freelance 1958. Prod. Desilu 1958–59. Comp. many original scores. V.p., Academy M.P. Arts and Sciences, 1953–55; chmn. Music Br. several terms: Acad. Life Member; prod. Acad.'s first Award Show TV, 1953. Acad. Award, best scoring of musical, West Side Story, 1961, nominated for Acad. Award, 14 times. Other films incl. High Society, Bye Bye Birdie, The Great Caruso, etc. Music dir. film, Oliver, won Acad. Award, 1968. Assoc. prod. They Shoot Horses, Don't They? (Acad. Award nomination, best music score). Pres. Screen Comp. Assoc., U.S.A. 1966–72; Member Bd of Governors Performing Arts Council L.A. Music Center, 1965–71; Chmn. bd. Emeritus, Young Musicians Foundation since 1965. Pres., Young Musicians Foundation 1973–77; Since 1949, guest conductor, many U.S. orchestras; 1983–31st. season Hollywood Bowl; co-chairman, music branch and v.p., Academy of Motion Picture Arts and Sciences, 1973–77; Music Branch Exec. Committee, 1980; 1981, ASCAP board; 1985, asst. secty.

GREEN, JOSEPH: Executive. b. Warsaw, Poland, Apr. 23, 1905. e. high school, prep school. Industry, legitimate theatre prod. Foreign film dist. Since 1933; headed Green Film Co., Warsaw, Poland; head of Sphinx Film Dist. Co., N.Y., until 1940. Co-owner, Art Theatre Circuit, N.Y., 1940–52; pres., Globe Dist. Co. of Foreign Films; formed President Films, Inc., 1954, now Globe Pictures, Inc. Beginning in 1979 a renaissance of Joseph Green's Yiddish film Classics produced in Poland in pre-W.W.II days, including Yiddle with He's Fiddle, Abriele der Mamen, Der Purinspieler, Mamele.

GREEN, MALCOLM C.: Theatre Executive. b. Boston, MA, Mar. 1, 1925. e. Harvard Coll. Began career as asst. mgr., Translux Theatre, Boston & Revere Theatre, Revere, MA. Treas., Interstate Theatres, 1959–64. Film Buyer, Interstate, 1959–72. Formed Theatre Management Services in 1972 with H. Rifkin and P. Lowe and Cinema Centers Corp. with Rifkin and Lowe families in 1973. Treas., Cinema Center, & pres., Theatre Mgmt. Services. Cinema Center grew to 116 theatres in 6 Northeast states, sold to Hoyts Cinemas Corp., 1986. Now senior v.p., Hoyts Cinemas Corp. Pres., NATO, 1986–88. Chmn Bd, 1988. Pres., Theatre Owners of New England, 1964–65; chmn bd., 1955–69; treas., 1970–84. Dir., Natl. Assoc. Theatre Owners. Chm., NATO of New York State. Chmn., Vision Foundation.

GREEN, MICHAEL L.: Executive-chm., Entertainment Film Distributors Ltd., chm., Entertainment in Video Ltd., chm., Michael Green Enterprises Ltd., mng. dir., Blackwater Film Productions Ltd.

GREEN, NATHANIEL CHARLES: Executive (retired). b. Spokane, WA. Feb. 16, 1903. e. Pleasant Prairie Sch. until 14 yrs. old. Ent. banking bus., Spokane & Eastern Trust Co., until 1921; came to CA, became associated Bank of America. Br. bank mgr., 26 yrs. of age, youngest in the U.S. at the time; became vice-pres., 1941; Jan. 1960 became v.p., and senior pub rel. officer between bank and m.p. and TV industry.

GREENE, CLARENCE: Producer, Writer. b. New York, NY, 1918. e. St. John's U., L.L.B. Author of play Need a Lawyer. Formed Greene-Rouse prods. with Russell Rouse; Acad. Oscar co-

orig. story Pillow Talk. Acad. award nom. co-orig. s.p. The Well. Two Writers Guild nominations. Writers Guild award outstanding teleplay, One Day in the Life of Ivan Denisovitch. PICTURES INCLUDE: Prod., collab. s.p. The Town Went Wild, D.O.A., The Well, The Thief, Wicked Woman, New York Confidential, A House Is Not a Home, The Oscar. Prod.: Unidentified Flying Objects, The Gun Runners, Fastest Gun Alive, Thunder in the Sun, The Caper of the Golden Bulls. collab. prod., writer TV series Tightrope, D.O.A. (story, 1988).

GREENE, DAVID: Director, Writer. b. Manchester, Eng., Feb. 22, 1921. Early career as actor. To U.S. with Shakespeare company early 1950's; remained to direct TV in Canada, New York and Hollywood. TELEVISION: The Defenders. Emmy Awds. The People Next Door, Rich Man, Poor Man, Roots, Friendly Fire, The Trial of Lee Harvey Oswald, Red Earth, White Earth; The Guardian, Fatal Vision, Guilty Conscience, Miles to Go, Circle of Violence, The Betty Ford Story, After the Promise; Inherit the Wind, Liberace. PICTURES INCLUDE: The Shuttered Room, Sebastian, The Strange Affair, I Start Counting, Madame Sin, Godspell, Count of Monte Cristo, Gray Lady Down, Hard Country (prod., dir.).

GREENE, ELLEN: Actress, Singer. b. Brooklyn, NY, Feb. 22. e. Ryder Coll. After coll. joined musical road show. Appeared in cabaret act at The Brothers & the Sisters Club and Reno Sweeney's, NY. Off-Bdwy debut, Rachel Lily Rosenbloom. Bdwy in the The Little Prince and The Aviator. With NY Shakespeare Fest. in In the Boom Boom Room, The Sorrows of Steven, The Threepenny Opera (Tony nom.). Film debut Next Stop, Greenwich Village (1976). Off Bdwy. co-starred in musical Little Shop of Horrors 1982, repeated role in film. PICTURES: Next Stop, Greenwich Village; I'm Dancing As Fast as I Can; Little Shop of Horrors; Me and Him; Talk Radio. TELEVISION: Rock Follies; Sister Ruth.

GREENFIELD, IRVING H.: b. Nov. 15, 1902. e. Brooklyn Law Sch. Formerly president, Cinema Lodge, B'nai B'rith. Former sec'y, attorney, Metro-Goldwyn-Mayer, Inc. and Key chairman M.P. Amusement Div. of U.J.A. Federation. Engaged in law practice: Greenfield, Lipsky, and Bress.

GREENFIELD, LEO: Executive, b. New York, NY, April 25, 1916. e. St. John's U, Coll. of Arts & Sciences. v.p., gen. sales mgr. Buena Vista, 1962; Columbia road show sales mgr. 1966; v.p.-gen. sales mgr., Cinerama Rel. Corp. 1966; pres.-gen. sales mgr., Warners, 1969; sr. v.p. worldwide distribution, MGM 1975; v.p. distribution & marketing, Marble Arch Productions, 1978; exec. v.p. Associated Film Distribution, 1979; pres., Greenlee Assoc., Inc., 1985; pres., distribution, F/M, 1986; pres., dist., Kings Road Entertainment, 1987.

GREENWALD, ROBERT: Director, Producer, Teacher. b. New York, NY, Aug. 8, 1945. e. Antioch Coll., New School for Social Research. Teaches film and theatre at New York U., New Lincoln, New School. Formed Robert Greenwald Prods. PICTURES: Xanadu (dir.), Sweethearts Dance (exec. prod., dir.). TELEVISION: Prod: The Desperate Miles, 21 Hours at Munich, Delta Country USA, Escape From Bogen County, Getting Married, Portrait of a Stripper, Miracle on Ice, The Texas Rangers, The First Time; Director: In the Custody of Strangers, Burning Bed; Katie: Portrait of a Centerfold. STAGE: A Sense of Humor, I Have a Dream, Me and Bessie.

GREENWOOD, JACK: Producer. b. 1919. PICTURES INCLUDE: Horrors of the Black Museum, Concrete Jungle, Invasion, Act of Murder, We Shall See, Face of A Stranger, Scotland Yard, The Scales of Justice 1967–68. TELEVISION: Edgar Wallace series, Avengers series, From a Bird's Eye View, TV series with Sheldon Leonard 1969. Prod. exec. with ATV Network (ITC) since 1970.

GREER, JANE: Actress. b. Washington, DC, Sept. 9, 1924. Orchestra singer; photograph as WAC on Life Magazine cover won screen debut in Pan-Americana 1945. PICTURES INCLUDE: They Won't Believe Me, Out of the Past, Station West, Big Steal, You're in the Navy Now, The Company She Keeps, You For Me, Prisoner of Zenda, Desperate Search, The Clown, Down Among the Sheltering Palms, Run for the Sun, Man of a Thousand Faces, Where Love Has Gone, Billie, The Outfit, Against All Odds, Just Between Friends.

GREGORY, JOHN R.: Executive, Producer, Writer. b. Brooklyn, NY, Nov. 19, 1918. e. Grover Cleveland H.S., 1935, New Inst. of M.P. & Telev., 1952; Sls., adv. dept. Fotoshop, Inc., N.Y., 1938–42; Spec. Serv., Photo. instructor, chief projectionist, supv., war dept. theatres, U.S. Army, 1942–46; sls. mgr., J. L. Galef & Son, N.Y.; 1948–49, gen. mgr., Camera Corner Co.; 1949–58, pres.; City Film Center, Inc., 1957; exec. v.p., Talent Guild of New York, 1958; pres., Teleview Prods., Inc., 1961;

127

Gri-Gro

executive producer, City Film Productions, 1970. Executive post-production supervisor, Jerry Liotta Films, 1977.
AUTHOR: many articles in nat'l publications dealing with m.p. practices and techniques; tech. editor, Better Movie-Making magazine, 1962; editor, pub., National Directory of Movie-Making Information, 1963; assoc. ed., Photographic Product News, 1964; contrib. editor, U.S. Camera. M.P. columnist, contributing ed. Travel and Camera magazine, 1969; Advisory panelist, Photo-methods (N.Y.), 1975. Consultant, Photographic Guidance Council, 1957, assoc. Society of M.P. & Television-Engineers, 1952.

GREIST, KIM: Actress. b. Stamford, CT, May 12, 1958. e. New Sch. for Social Research. Film debut C.H.U.D., 1984.
THEATER: Second Prize: Two Months in Leningrad, Twelfth Night (NY Shakespeare Fest.).
PICTURES: Brazil, Manhunter, Throw Momma from the Train, Punchline.
TELEVISION: Miami Vice, Tales From the Darkside.

GRESHLER, ABNER J.: Producer. b. New York, NY. e. Fordham U., St. John's U. Sch. of Law. Prior to entering m.p. ind., prod. shows for resort hotels; mgd., booked artists for vaudeville, hotels, cafes. Now pres., York Pictures Corp.; Abner J. Greshler Prod., Inc. Executive prod. At War with the Army, 1951; Hundred Hour Hunt, Yesterday and Today, 1953; Johnny and the Gaucho, 1955; prog. consultant, NBC; coord. of prog. development dept., NTA; pres., R.G. Prod., Ltd. Pres. Damond Artists Ltd.; dir. Yesterday and Today, The Fugitive, Odd Couple; v.p., Astron Prod Ltd.

GREY, JENNIFER: Actress. Daughter of actor Joel Grey.
PICTURES: The Cotton Club (debut, 1984), Reckless, Red Dawn, Ferris Bueller's Day Off, Dirty Dancing, Bloodhounds of Broadway, The Sixth Family.

GREY, JOEL: Actor, Singer. b. Cleveland, OH, April 11, 1932. Son of performer Mickey Katz; father of actress Jennifer Grey. e. Alexander Hamilton H.S., L.A. Acting debut at 9 years in On Borrowed Time at Cleveland Playhouse. Extensive nightclub appearances before returning to theatres and TV.
PICTURES INCLUDE: About Face, Calypso Heat Wave, Come September, Cabaret (Acad. Award, supp. actor, 1972), Man on a Swing, Buffalo Bill and the Indians, 7 Percent Solution, Remo Williams.
TELEVISION: Maverick, December Bride, Ironside, Night Gallery, Jack and the Beanstalk (special), The Burt Bacharach Show, The Tom Jones Show, The Englebert Humperdinck Show, George M! (special), The Carol Burnett Show, The Julie Andrews Hour, Queenie (mini-series).
STAGE: Come Blow Your Horn, Stop the World—I Want to Get Off, Half a Sixpence, Harry, Noon and Night, Littlest Revue, Cabaret (Tony Award), George M!, Goodtime Charley, The Grand Tour, Cabaret (1987, Bdwy revival).

GREY, VIRGINIA: Actress. b. Los Angeles, CA, March 22, 1923. Screen career started 1935 with She Gets Her Man.
PICTURES INCLUDE: Who Killed Doc Robbin, Bullfighter and the Lady, Highway 301, Slaughter Trail, Desert Pursuit, Perilous Journey, Forty-Niners, Target Earth, Eternal Sea, Last Command, Rose Tattoo, All That Heaven Allows, Tammy Tell Me True, Bachelor In Paradise, Back Street, Madame X, Rosie, Airport.

GRIEM, HELMUT: Actor. b. Hamburg, Germany, 1940; e. Hamburg U.
PICTURES: The Damned, The Mackenzie Break, Cabaret, Ludwig, Voyage of the Damned, Sergeant Steiner, Breakthrough, The Glass Cell, Berlin Alexanderplatz, La Passante, The Second Victory.
TELEVISION: Peter the Great.

GRIFFIN, MERV: Executive, Singer, M.C. b. San Mateo, CA, July 6, 1925. e. U. of San Francisco, Stanford U. w. Julann Wright. The Merv Griffin Show, KFRC-Radio, 1945–48; vocalist, Freddy Martin's orch., 1948–52; Contract Warner Bros., 1952–54. co-starred, So This Is Love, The Boy From Oklahoma; toured Niteclubs, 1954–55; Prod. Finian's Rainbow, City Center, N.Y., 1955; Vocalist, Morning Show, and Robt. Q. Lewis Show, 1956; M.C., Look Up and Live, Going Places, 1957, Merv. Griffin Show, 1958, Play Your Hunch, 1960; M.C., Keep Talking, 1960; Merv. Griffin Show, 1962; Word for Word, 1963; Merv. Griffin Show, Westinghouse Broadcasting, 1965–86; Secrets Women Never Share (exec. prod., host, 1987). Chairman, Merv Griffin Prods.

GRIFFITH, ANDY: Actor. b. Mount Airy, NC, June 1, 1926. e. U. of North Carolina. Began career as standup comedian, recording artist.
THEATRE: Broadway: No Time for Sergeants, Destry Rides Again.
TELEVISION: Series: The Andy Griffith Show, Andy of Mayberry, No Time for Sergeants, The Headmaster, Matlock. Movies: Go Ask Alice, Salvage I, Murder in Coweta County, The Demon Murder Case, Fatal Vision, Crime of Innocence, Diary of a Perfect Murder, Return to Mayberry, Under the Influence.

PICTURES INCLUDE: A Face in the Crowd, No Time for Sergeants, Onionhead, The Second Time Around, Angel in My Pocket, Hearts of the West, Rustler's Rhapsody.

GRIFFITH, MELANIE: Actress. b. New York, NY, Aug. 9, 1957. Daughter of actress Tippi Hedren. Moved to Los Angeles at 4. e. Catholic academies until Hollywood Prof. Sch., 1981. Studied acting with Stella Adler.
PICTURES: Night Moves, The Drowning Pool, Smile, Roar, One on One, Joyride, Underground Aces, Fear City, Body Double, Something Wild, Cherry 2000, The Milagro Beanfield War, Stormy Monday, Working Girl.
TELEVISION: Once an Eagle, Carter Country, Starmaker, Steel Cowboy, She's in the Army Now, Golden Gate, Alfred Hitchcock Presents.

GRILLO, BASIL F.: Executive. b. Angel's Camp, CA, Oct. 8, 1910. e. U. of California, Berkeley, A.B. Certified public accountant, exec. vice-pres., dir., Bing Crosby Ent., Inc., 1948–57; bus. mgr., Bing Crosby, 1945; co-organizer, dir., 3rd pres., & treas., Alliance of T.V. Film Producers, 1950–54; exec. prod., BCE, Inc., shows incl. Fireside Thea., Rebound, Royal Playhouse, The Chimps; dir., KCOP, Inc., 1957–60; dir. KFOX, Inc., 1958–62; pres., dir., Bing Crosby Prods., 1955–72; dir., Seven Leagues Ent., Inc., 1958; dir. Electrovision Prods., 1970, chief exec. off., Bing Crosby Enterprises.

GRIMALDI, ALBERTO: Producer. b. Naples, 1927. Studied law, serving as counsel to Italian film companies, before turning to production with Italian westerns starring Clint Eastwood and Lee Van Cleef. Is pres. of P.E.A. (Produzioni Europee Associate, S.A.S.).
PICTURES INCLUDE: For a Few Dollars More, The Good, the Bad and the Ugly, Three Steps in Delerium, Satyricon, Burn!, The Decameron, The Canterbury Tales, 1001 Nights, Salo, or the 100 Days of Sodom, Bawdy Tales, Man of La Mancha, Last Tango in Paris, Avanti, Fellini's Casanova, 1900, The True Story of General Custer.

GRIMES, GARY: Actor. b. San Francisco, CA, 1955. Family moved to L.A. when he was nine. Made film debut at 15 in Summer of '42, 1971. Voted Star of Tomorrow in QP poll, 1971.
PICTURES INCLUDE: The Culpepper Cattle Company, Cahill, United States Marshall, Class of '44, The Spikes Gang, Gus.

GRIMES, TAMMY: Actress. b. Lynn, MA, Jan. 30, 1934. Mother of actress Amanda Plummer. e. Stephens Coll. Member of staff Westport Playhouse, CT 1954.
THEATER: Look After Lulu (1959); Littlest Revue, Stratford (Ont.) Shakespeare Fest., Bus Stop, Cradle Will Rock, Unsinkable Molly Brown (Tony Award), High Spirits, Finian's Rainbow, Only Game in Town, Private Lives (Tony Award), California Suite, 42nd Street, Tartuffe, A Month in the Country, The Importance of Being Earnest, Mademoiselle Columbe, Tammy Grimes: A Concert in Words and Music.
PICTURES: Three Bites of an Apple, Play It as It Lays, Somebody Killed Her Husband, The Runner Stumbles, Can't Stop the Music, America, Mr. North, No Big Deal.
TELEVISION: Omnibus, Hollywood Sings, Hour of Great Mysteries, Four Poster, St. Elsewhere, Last Unicorn, The Tammy Grimes Show. Movies: The Other Man, The Horror at 37,000 Feet, The Borrowers, You Can't Go Home Again.

GRISSMER, JOHN: Executive. b. Houston, TX, Aug. 28, 1933. e. Xavier U., B.S., 1955; Catholic U., M.F.A., dramatic writing, 1959. Taught drama courses, directed student productions at U. of Connecticut & American U., Washington, DC. Produced and co-wrote House That Cried Murder, 1973; co-produced, wrote and directed Scalpel; directed Nightmare at Shadow Woods. Partner in P.J. Productions Co. & Producer's Marketing Group, Ltd.

GRIZZARD, GEORGE: Actor. b. Roanoke Rapids, NC, April 1, 1928. Debut on Broadway in The Desperate Hours. Has been member of APA repertory company and Tyrone Guthrie resident company in Minneapolis. Broadway plays include The Disenchanted, The Country Girl, The Royal Family, Who's Afraid of Virginia Woolf, You Know I Can't Hear You When the Water's Running, California Suite, Another Antigone.
PICTURES: From the Terrace, Advise and Consent, Warning Shot, Happy Birthday, Wanda June, Comes a Horseman, Firepower, Wrong Is Right, Bachelor Party.
TELEVISION: Robert Kennedy and His Times, Attica, The Shadey Hill Kidnapping, International Airport, The Deliberate Stranger, Embassy, The Adams Chronicles, Oldest Living Graduate, Perry Mason: The Case of the Scandalous Scoundrel, David.

GRODIN, CHARLES: Actor, Director. b. Pittsburgh, PA, April 21, 1935. e. U. of Miami. Studied acting with Uta Hagen and Lee Strasberg; began directing career in New York 1965 as asst. to Gene Saks. Has appeared in some 75 plays all over country. Has also written scripts produced plays.
THEATER: Tchin-Tchin (Bdwy debut, 1962); Absence of a

Cello; Same Time, Next Year; It's a Glorious Day . . . And All That (dir., co-author); Lovers and Other Strangers (dir.), Thieves (prod., dir.); Unexpected Guests (prod.,dir.).
PICTURES INCLUDE: Actor: Rosemary's Baby, Catch-22, The Heartbreak Kid, 11 Harrowhouse, Thieves, King Kong, Heaven Can Wait, Real Life, Sunburn, It's My Turn, Seems Like Old Times, The Incredible Shrinking Woman, Great Muppet Caper, The Lonely Guy, The Woman in Red, Movers and Shakers (also co-prod., s.p.), Last Resort, Ishtar, The Couch Trip, You Can't Hurry Love, Midnight Run.
TELEVISION: Candid Camera (writer, dir.); Simon and Garfunkel Special (writer, dir.); Acts of Love and Other Comedies (dir.); Paradise (prod., dir.); Fresno (actor); Grown Ups (actor).

GROSS, JERRY: Executive, Producer, Writer, Director. e. N.Y. pub. schools, night sch. Pres., Jerry Gross Productions, 1962; Pres., Cinemation Industries, Inc., 1964–75. Pres., Jerry Gross Org., 1979.
PICTURES INCLUDE: Girl on a Chain Gang, Teen Age Mother and Female Animal.

GROSS, KENNETH H.: Executive. e. New School for Social Research, U. of London. Conducted film seminars at New School and active in several indep. film projects. Published film criticism in various journals and magazines. Joined ABC Entertainment Oct. 1971. Named supvr. of feature films for ABC-TV. Appt. mgr. of feature films, Jan. 1974. Promoted in Nov, 1975 to program executive, ABC Entertainment Prime Time/West Coast. Moved to L.A. offices, Nov. 1975, promoted to exec. producer, movies for TV, ABC Ent. 1976; 1978, with literary agency F.C.A. as partner in Los Angeles; 1979 producer for Lorimar; then with Intl. Creative Mgt; 1982, formed own literary talent agency, The Literary Group; 1985, merged agency with Robinson-Weintraub & Assoc. to become Robinson-Weintraub-Gross & Assoc.

GROSS, MICHAEL: Actor. b. Chicago, IL, June 21, 1947. m. casting dir. Elza Bergeron. Brother of actress-comedienne Mary Gross. e. U. Illinois, B.A., Yale School of Drama, M.F.A. Broadway: Bent, The Philadelphia Story.
TELEVISION: Series: Family Ties, Movies: FDR: The Last Years, A Girl Named Sooner, Little Gloria Happy at Last, Cook and Peary—The Race to the Pole, Summer Fantasies, Bloody Friday, Right to Die, The FBI Murders.

GROSSBARD, ULU: Director. b. Antwerp, Belgium. Jan. 9, 1929. e. U. of Chicago, B.A. 1952. Trained at Yale Sch. of Drama 1952–53. Asst. dir. to Eliza Kazan Splendor in the Grass, 1961; asst. dir.: West Side Story, The Hustler, The Miracle Worker. Unit mgr.: The Pawnbroker.
THEATER: The Days and Nights of Beebee Fenstermaker, The Subject Was Roses, A View From the Bridge, The Investigation, That Summer—That Fall, The Price, American Buffalo, The Woods, The Wake of Jamie Foster.
PICTURES: The Subject Was Roses, Who Is Harry Kellerman?, Straight Time, True Confessions, Falling in Love.

GROSSBERG, JACK: Producer, Executive. b. Brooklyn, NY, June 5, 1927. Member: Academy of Motion Picture Arts & Sciences. New York Friars Club, Producers Guild of America, Directors Guild of America.
PICTURES: Requiem For A Heavyweight, Pretty Poison, The Producers, Don't Drink the Water, Take the Money and Run, Bananas, Everything You Always Wanted To Know About Sex, Sleeper, A Delicate Balance, Luther, Rhinoceros, Leadbelly, King Kong, The Betsy, Fast Break, A Stranger is Watching, Brainstorm, Strange Brew, Touch and Go, The Experts, Little Monsters.

GROSSMAN, ERNIE: Executive. b. New York, NY, Sept. 19, 1924. Still dept., pressbook edit., asst. field mgr., Warner Bros., 1940–58; Studio publicist, 1958–60; exploitation, promo. mgr. field dept., 1960–64; nat'l mgr., pub., exploit., promo.; 1964–67 exec. co-ord. adv., pub. & promo., Warner-7 Arts, 1967; WB nat'l supv. ad.-pub., 1970. exec. assist. to Richard Lederer, 1971–72; 1973 nat'l dir. of Pub. & Promotion, Warner Bros. Inc.; 1977, natl. dir. of adv.-pub.; 1980–85, natl. dir. promo. 1987, named south-west coast special events dir.

GRUEN, ROBERT: Executive. b. New York, NY, Apr. 2, 1913, e. Carnegie Mellon U., B.A. Stage designer, 1934–35; designer, 20th-Fox, 1936; prod. exec., National Screen Service Corp., 1936; head, Robert Gruen Associates, ind. design org.; 1940; nat. pres. Industrial Designers Inst., 1954–55; dir. and v.p., National Screen Service Corp. since 1951; senior v.p. 1975–78; dir., NSS Corp., Continental Lithograph and NSS, Ltd., 1978–85.

GRUENBERG, JERRY: Executive. b. Minneapolis, MN, June 7, 1927, e. U. of Minnesota. United Artists, Minneapolis, 1952; m.p. industry CEO Wisconsin Theatres 1952–67; v.p. Sigma III Corp. 1965–67. division mgr., 20th Century-Fox, 1967–71; senior v.p., general sales mgr., Allied Artists Pictures, 1971–79. Pres., Blossom Pictures, Inc. 1979–present. Member of Variety Club, Friars Club. Director of Will Rogers Memorial Fund.

GRUENBERG, LEONARD S.: Executive. b. Minneapolis, MN, Sept. 10, 1913, e. U. of Minnesota. Began as salesman Republic Pictures, Minneapolis, 1935; with RKO in same capacity, 1936; promoted to city sales mgr., St. Louis, 1937, then branch mgr., Salt Lake City, 1941; later that year apptd. Rocky Mt. Dist. Mgr. (hqts., Denver, CO); 1946 Metropolitan, div. mgr., v.p. NTA, v.p. Cinemiracle Prods.; Pres., Chmn. of bd., Sigma III Corp., 1962. Chmn. of bd., Filmways, 1967. Chmn. of bd. Gamma III Dist. Co. & Chmn of bd. and Pres. Great Owl Corp., 1976. Member variety Club, Sigma Alpha Mu Fraternity; Lieut. Civil Air Patrol, Lieut. Comdr., U.S.N.R.

GRUSIN, DAVID: Composer, Conductor, Performer. b. Littleton, CO, 1934. Directed music for the Andy Williams Show on TV for 7 yrs in the 1960s, where met Norman Lear and Bud Yorkin, producers of the series, who signed him to score their first feature film, Divorce, American Style (1967).
PICTURES INCLUDE: Winning, The Heart Is a Lonely Hunter, Tell Them Willie Boy Is Here, The Front, Murder by Death, The Yakuza, Three Days of the Condor, Bobby Deerfield, And Justice for All, The Champ, The Electric Horseman, My Bodyguard, Absence of Malice, On Golden Pond, Reds, Author! Author!, Tootsie, Scandalous, Racing with the Moon, The Pope of Greenwich Village, The Little Drummer Girl, Falling in Love, Goonies, The Milagro Beanfield War.
TELEVISION: Movies: Deadly Dream; Prescription: Murder; Scorpio Letters; Eric; The Family Rico; The Death Squad; themes to many series.

GUARDINO, HARRY: Actor. b. Brooklyn, NY, Dec. 23. 1925, e. Haaren H.S.
STAGE: B'way: End as a Man, A Hatful of Rain, Anyone Can Whistle, One More River, Natural Affection, The Rose Tattoo (revival), Seven Descents of Myrtle, Woman of the Year.
TELEVISION: Studio One, Playhouse 90, The Alcoa Theatre, Naked City, Dr. Kildare, The Untouchables, The Dick Powell Show, The Reporter (series), The New Perry Mason. Movies: Contract on Cherry Street, Police Story, Sophisticated Gentry, The Last Child, Evening in Byzantium.
PICTURES INCLUDE: Pork Chop Hill, The Five Pennies, Houseboat, The Pigeon That Took Rome, Treasure of San Grennaro, Madigan, Lovers and Other Strangers, Red Sky at Morning, Dirty Harry, They Only Kill Their Masters, St. Ives, The Enforcer, Rollercoaster, Matilda, Any Which Way You Can.

GUBER, PETER: Producer. b. 1939. e. Syracuse U., B.A.; U. at Florence (Italy), S.S.P.; New York U. Sch. of Law, J.D., L.L.M. Recruited by Columbia Pictures as exec. asst. in 1968 while pursuing M.B.A. at New York U. Graduate Sch. of Business Adm. With Col. seven yrs. in key prod. exec. capacities, serving last three as exec. v.p. in chg. of worldwide prod. Formed own company, Peter Guber's Filmworks, which in 1976 was merged with Casablanca Records to become Casablanca Record and Filmworks. He was chm of bd. of co. called PolyGram, and co.-mgr. dir.; May 1980 formed Boardwalk with Neil Bogart and Jon Peters, retaining connection with Polygram of which he was 50% owner; 1981 Boardwalk partnership dissolved; Jan. 1982 sold interest in Polygram. Formed Guber-Peters.
PICTURES INCLUDE: The Deep (first under own banner), Midnight Express (6 Golden Globes, 2 Oscars), An American Werewolf in London, Missing, Flashdance (exec. prod.), D.C. Cab (exec. prod.), Six Weeks (co-prod.), Visionquest (co-prod.), Clue (exec. prod.), The Color Purple (exec. prod.), The Witches of Eastwick (co-prod.), Innerspace (exec. prod.), Who's That Girl (co-exec. prod.); Gorillas in the Mist (co-exec. prod.); Caddyshack II (co- prod.), Batman (co-prod.).
TELEVISION: Mysteries of the Sea (doc.), Television and the Presidency (exec. prod.), Double Platinum (exec. prod.), Dreams (exec. prod.), The Toughest Man in the World (exec. prod.), Bay Coven (co-exec. prod.), Nightmare at Bitter Creek (co-exec. prod.)

GUEST, CHRISTOPHER: Actor, Writer, Composer. m. actress Jamie Leigh Curtis. b. New York, NY, Feb. 5, 1948. Wrote the musical score and acted in National Lampoon's Lemmings off-Bdwy. On Bdwy in Room Service, Moonchildren. Cast member Saturday Night Live 1984–85.
PICTURES: Actor: Girlfriends, The Last Word, The Long Riders, The Missing Link, The Fortune, Death Wish, The Hot Rock, Heartbeeps, This is Spinal Tap, Little Shop of Horrors, The Princess Bride, Beyond Therapy, The Big Picture (also dir.).
TELEVISION: The TV Show, The Chevy Chase Special (also writer); The Billion Dollar Bubble; Lily Tomlin (also writer, Emmy Award, 1976), A Nice Place to Visit (writer only), A Piano for Mrs. Cimino, The Million Dollar Infield, Haywire, Blind Ambition.

GUEST, LANCE: Actor. b. Saratoga, CA, July 21, 1960. e. U. of California at L.A.
PICTURES: I Ought To Be in Pictures, Halloween II, The

Gue-Gwy

Last Starfighter, Jaws—The Revenge, The Wizard of Loneliness.
TELEVISION: Lou Grant, St. Elsewhere. Movies: Between Two Loves, Why Us?, Please Don't Hit Me Mom, Confessions of a Married Man, One Too Many, My Father My Rival, The Roommate, Favorite Son.

GUEST, VAL: Writer, Director, Producer. b. London, England, 1911. e. England and America. Journalist with Hollywood Reporter, Zit's Los Angeles Examiner and Walter Winchell.
PICTURES INCLUDE: Murder at the Windmill, Miss Pilgrim's Progress, The Body Said No, Mr. Drake's Duck, Happy Go Lovely, Another Man's Poison, Penny Princess, The Runaway Bus, Life With the Lyons, Dance Little Lady, Men of Sherwood Forest, Lyons in Paris, Break in the Circle, It's A Great Life, Quatermass Experiment, They Can't Hang Me, The Weapon, The Abominable Snowman, Carry on Admiral, It's a Wonderful World, Camp on Blood Island, Up the Creek, Further Up the Creek, Life Is a Circus, Yesterday's Enemy, Expresso Bongo, Hell Is a City, Full Treatment, The Day the Earth Caught Fire, Jigsaw, 80,000 Suspects, The Beauty Jungle, Where the Spies Are, Casino Royale, Assignment K, When Dinosaurs Ruled the Earth, Tomorrow, The Persuaders, Au Pair Girls, The Adventures, Confessions of a Window Cleaner, Killer Force, Diamond Mercenaries.
TELEVISION: Space 1999, The Shillingbury Blowers, The Band Played On, Sherlock Holmes & Dr. Watson, Shillingbury Tales, Dangerous Davies, The Last Detective, The Boys in Blue, In Possession, Mark of the Devil, Child's Play, Scent of Fear.

GUILLAUME, ROBERT: Actor. b. St. Louis, MO, Nov. 30. e. St. Louis U., Washington U. Studied voice; acting career debut in Carousel. Has appeared in many Bdwy. plays and musicals including Fly Blackbird, Kwamina, Guys and Dolls.
TELEVISION: Dinah, Mel and Susan Together, Rich Little's Washington Follies, Jim Nabors, All in the Family, Sanford and Son, The Jeffersons, Marcus Welby, M.D., Soap, (series), Benson, (series), Purlie, North and South (mini-series), The Kid with the Broken Halo, The Kid with the 100 I.Q.; Perry Mason: The Case of the Scandalous Scoundrel, The Robert Guillaume Show.
PICTURES: Seems Like Old Times.

GUILLERMIN, JOHN: Director. b. London, England, Nov. 11, 1925. e. City of London Sch., Cambridge U. RAF pilot prior to entering film industry.
PICTURES INCLUDE: The Waltz of the Torreadors, Guns at Batasi, Rapture, The Blue Max, House of Cards, The Bridge of Remagen, El Condor, Skyjacked, Shaft in Africa, The Towering Inferno, King Kong, Death on the Nile, Mr. Patman, Sheena, King Kong Lives, The Favorite.
TELEVISION: The Tracker.

GUINNESS, SIR ALEC: Actor. b. London, Eng., April 2, 1914; e. Pembroke Lodge, Southbourne & Roborough Sch., Eastbourne. Created C.B.E. 1955; Knighted 1959. Stage debut: London, 1934. Theatre appearances in London, New York & Continent. Special AA, 1979, for services to film.
PICTURES INCLUDE: Great Expectations, Oliver Twist, Kind Hearts & Coronets, Run For Your Money, Last Holiday, The Mudlark, Lavender Hill Mob (Academy Nomination), The Man in the White Suit, The Card (The Promoter), Malta Story, Captain's Paradise, Father Brown (The Detective), To Paris with Love, The Prisoner, The Ladykillers, The Swan, The Bridge on the River Kwai (Academy Award 1957, best actor); The Horse's Mouth (Academy nomination for s.p.), The Scapegoat, Our Man in Havana, Tunes of Glory, A Majority of One, H.M.S. Defiant, Lawrence of Arabia, Dr. Zhivago, The Comedians, Cromwell, Scrooge, Brother Sun and Sister Moon, Hitler: The Last Ten Days, Murder by Death, Star Wars (Academy nomination), The Empire Strikes Back, Return of the Jedi, Lovesick, A Passage to India, Little Dorrit, A Handful of Dust.
TELEVISION: The Wicked Scheme of Jebel Deeks (National Academy nomination), Twelfth Night, Conversation at Night, Solo, E.E. Cummings, Little Gidding, The Gift of Friendship, Caesar and Cleopatra, Little Lord Fauntleroy, Tinker, Tailor, Soldier, Spy (7-part series), Smiley's People (mini-series), Edwin, Monsignor Quixote.

GULAGER, CLU: Actor. b. Holdenville, OK, Nov. 16, 1928. Father, John Gulager, cowboy entertainer. e. Baylor U. Starred at school in original play, A Different Drummer, where spotted by prod. of TV's Omnibus; invited to New York to recreate role on TV.
PICTURES INCLUDE: The Killers, The Last Picture Show, Winning, Company of Killers, McQ, The Other Side of Midnight, A Force of One, Touched by Love, The Initiation, Into the Night, Prime Risk, The Return of the Living Dead, Hunter's Blood, The Hidden, Tapeheads, Uninvited, I'm Gonna Git You Sucka.
TELEVISION: The Virginian, San Francisco International, Glass House, Ski Lift to Death, Space, Living Proof: The Hank Williams Jr. Story, Bridge Across Time, King, Once an Eagle, North and South II, Space.

GUMBEL, BRYANT: Announcer, News Show Host. b. Chicago, IL, Sept. 29, 1948. e. Bates Coll. Started as writer for Black Sports Magazine, NY, 1971; sportscaster, then sports dir., KNBC, Los Angeles. Sports host NBC Sports NY 1975–82. Now co-host on Today Show, New York (Emmy Awards, 1976, 1977).
TELEVISION: Super Bowl games, Games People Play, Different as Night and Day.

GUMPERT, JON: Executive. e. Cornell U. Law Sch. Sr. v.p., business affairs, MGM/UA Entertainment; pres., World Film Services, Inc., indep. prod. co. in N.Y. 1985, named v.p., business affairs, Warner Bros.

GUNN, MOSES: Actor. b. St. Louis, MO, Oct. 2, 1929. e. Tennessee State U. Taught speech and drama at Grambling Coll. Came to N.Y. and first cast in off-Bdwy. prod. of Genet's The Blacks. Later joined Negro Ensemble Company.
PICTURES INCLUDE: WUSA, The Great White Hope, The Wild Rovers, Shaft, Shaft's Big Score, Eagle in a Cake, Hot Rock, The Iceman Cometh, Amazing Grace, Rollerball, Aaron Loves Angela, Ragtime, Amityville II: The Possession, Firestarter, Heartbreak Ridge, Leonard Part 6, Dixie Lanes.
STAGE: In White America, Day of Absence, Song of the Lusitanian Bogey, Summer of the 17th Doll, Daddy Goodness, Harvest, Titus Andronicus, Measure for Measure, Romeo and Juliet, The Tempest, As You Like It, Macbeth, Othello, A Hand Is on the Gate, Sty of the Blind Pig, The Poison Tree, First Breeze of Summer, King John.
TELEVISION: Mr. Carter's Army, The Borgia Stick, Of Mice and Men, Haunts of the Very Rich, Hawaii Five-O, The FBI, Kung Fu; If You Give a Dance, You Gotta Pay the Band; The Cowboys, Roots, First Breeze of Summer.

GUNSBERG, SHELDON: Executive. b. Jersey City, NJ, Aug. 10, 1920. e. St. Peters Coll., New Jersey State Normal, New York U. With Night of Stars, Madison Sq. Garden, 1942; for. pub., 20th-Fox 1942; United Artists, 1945–47; Universal, roadshows. Rank product, asst. adv., pub. dir. 1947–54; v. pres., Walter Reade Theatres; exec. v.p. & dir., Walter Reade Org. 1962; Made chief operating officer, 1971; president, and Chief Executive Officer, 1973; chm. & CEO, 1984.

GUNZBURG, M.L.: President, Natural Vision Corporation. b. Denver, CO. e. U. of California at L.A., Columbia U. Newspaper man, columnist, Los Angeles Times, New York Times; radio writer, screen writer many m.p. cos.
Developed 3-D process, Natural Vision; contract Polaroid Corp. for 3-D, 1953.

GURIAN, PAUL R.: Executive. b. New Haven, CT, Oct. 18, 1946. e. Lake Forest Coll., U. of Vienna, New York U. Started producing films in 1971 with Cats and Dogs, a dramatic short which won prizes at Chicago Int. Film Fest and Edinburgh Fest. In 1977 formed Gurian Entertainment Corp., to acquire film properties for production.
PICTURES INCLUDE: The Garden Party (PBS program), Profile Ricardo Alegria (short), Bernice Bobs Her Hair (shown at 1977 N.Y. Film Festival); Cutter and Bone; Peggy Sue Got Married, The Seventh Sign (exec. prod.).

GUTTENBERG, STEVE: Actor. b. Brooklyn, NY, Aug. 24, 1958. e. Sch. of Performing Arts, N.Y. Off-Bdwy. in The Lion in Winter; studied under John Houseman at Julliard; classes with Lee Strasberg and Uta Hagen. Moved to West Coast in 1976; landed first TV role in movie, Something for Joey. Theatrical film debut in The Chicken Chronicles (1977).
PICTURES INCLUDE: The Boys from Brazil, Players, Can't Stop the Music, Diner, The Man Who Wasn't There, Police Academy, Police Academy 2, Cocoon, Bad Medicine, Police Academy 3, Short Circuit, The Bedroom Window, Police Academy 4: Citizens on Patrol, Three Men and a Baby, Surrender, Amazon Women on the Moon, High Spirits, Cocoon II: The Return.
TELEVISION: Series: Billy, No Soap, Radio, Police Story, Doc, etc. Movies: To Race the Wind, Miracle on Ice, The Day After, Gangs (co-prod.).

GWYNNE, FRED: Actor. b. New York, NY, July 10, 1926. e. Harvard U. Copywriter J. Walter Thompson 1955–60. On stage in Mrs. McThing, Irma La Douce, Twelfth Night, Texas Trilogy, The Lincoln Mask, Cat on a Hot Tin Roof, Winter's Tale, Arsenic and Old Lace.
PICTURES: On the Waterfront, Munster Go Home, Luna, Simon, So Fine, The Cotton Club, Off Beat, Water, The Boy Who Could Fly, Ironweed, Fatal Attraction, Waiting for Salazar.
TELEVISION: Series: Car 54, Where Are You? (1961–63); The Munsters (1964–66); Specials: Harvey, The Hasty Heart, Arsenic and Old Lace, The Lesson, Dames at Sea. Movies: Captains Courageous, Vanishing Act, The Christmas Star, Murder by the Book. Mini-Series: Kane & Abel.

130

H

HABEEB, TONY G.: Executive. b. San Francisco, CA, Oct. 26, 1927. e. San Francisco City Coll., 1945–47, U. of California, 1947–49, Lincoln U. Law Sch., LL.B, 1949–53. TV Editor, San Francisco Chronicle, 1949–54; Information Specialist, U.S. Army, 1954–56; managing editor; Torrance Press, 1956–57; CBS-TV Network Press information Division, 1957–61; ass't. dir. promo. and pub., Screen Gems, 1961–63; dir. promo. and pub., Screen Gems, 1963–67; world-wide dir. advertising, pub. and promo., Paramount Television; 1967–70. v.p., adv. and publicity, Metromedia Producers Corp. 1970–74. v.p. adv. and publicity, Irwin Allen Productions, 1974–81, pres., Publicist Guild of America; dir., adv., Warner Bros.-TV. 1987: senior v.p. publicity and promotion New Century/Vista Film Co. 1988: senior v.p. promotion and marketing Fries Entertainment.

HABER, JOYCE: Writer, syndicated Hollywood columnist. r.n. Mrs. Joyce Haber Cramer. b. New York, NY, Dec. 28, 1932. e. Brearley Sch., N.Y., class of 1948; Bryn Mawr Coll., 1949–50, cum laude list; Barnard Coll., B.A., 1953.
Researcher, Time magazine, 1953–63; Hollywood Reporter, L.A. Bureau Time, 1963–66; Columnist, Los Angeles Times, 1966–75; contributing editor, Los Angeles Magazine, 1977–80.
Published Caroline's Doll Book, illus. by R. Taylor, 1962. freelance writing: Esquire, Herald Tribune's New York Magazine, Harper's Bazaar, New York Magazine, Town and Country. Published The Users, a novel, 1976.

HACK, SHELLEY: Actress. b. CT, July 6. e. Smith Coll. Made modeling debut at 14 on cover of Glamour Magazine. Gained fame as Revlon's Charlie Girl on TV commercials.
PICTURES: Annie Hall, If Ever I See You Again, The King of Comedy, Troll, A Long Dark Night.
TELEVISION: Death Car, Charlie's Angels, Jack and Mike. Movies: Trackdown, Found Money, Single Bars Single Women.

HACKER, CHARLES R.: Executive. b. Milwaukee, WI, Oct. 8. e. U. of Wisconsin. Thea. mgr., Fox Wisc. Amuse. Corp., 1940; served in U.S.A.F., 1943–45; rejoined Fox Wisconsin Amusement Corp.; joined Standard Theatres Management Corp. 1947, on special assignments; apptd. district mgr. of Milwaukee & Waukesha theatres 1948; joined Radio City Music Hall Corp. as administrative asst. July, 1948; mgr. of oper., 1952; asst. to the pres., Feb. 1957; v.p., Radio City Music Hall Corp., 1964; appointed executive vice president and chief operating officer, February 1, 1973. Pres., Landmark Pictures, May, 1979. Elected treas. Will Rogers Memorial Fund, 1978. Award: Quigley Silver Grand Award for Showmanship, 1947. Member: U.S. Small Business Admin. Region 1, Hartford Advisory Council since 1983.

HACKETT, BUDDY: Actor, Comedian. b. Brooklyn, NY, Aug. 31, 1924. Prof. debut, borscht circuit.
TELEVISION: Stanley series, Bud and Lou (movie).
THEATRE: B'way, Call Mr. Mister, Lunatics and Lovers, I Had a Ball.
PICTURES INCLUDE: Walking My Baby Back Home, God's Little Acre, All Hands on Deck, The Music Man, The Wonderful World of Brothers Grimm, Everything's Ducky, It's a Mad, Mad, Mad, Mad World, Golden Head, Muscle Beach Party, The Love Bug.

HACKFORD, TAYLOR: Director. b. Dec. 3, 1944. e. USC, BA (international relations). Was Peace Corp. volunteer in Bolivia 1968–69. Began career with KCET in Los Angeles 1970–71. As prod.-dir. won Oscar for short, Teenage Father, 1978. Theatrical film debut as director with The Idolmaker (1980). Formed New Visions Inc. which merged with New Century Entertainment 1988 to become New Century/New Visions.
PICTURES: An Officer and a Gentleman, Against All Odds (also co.-prod.), White Nights (also co-prod.), La Bamba (co-prod. only), Chuck Berry: Hail! Hail! Rock 'n Roll (dir.); Everyone's All-American (dir., co-prod.), Rooftops (exec. prod.).

HACKMAN, GENE: Actor. b. San Bernardino, CA, Jan. 30, 1930. First major broadway role in Any Wednesday. Other stage productions include: Poor Richard, Children from their Games, A Rainy Day in Newark, The Natural Look. Formed own production co., Chelly Ltd.
TELEVISION: CBS Playhouse's My Father, My Mother, The F.B.I., The Invaders, The Iron Horse, etc.
PICTURES INCLUDE: Lilith, Bonnie and Clyde (Acad. Award nom. for Best Supporting Actor), First to Fight, Out by the Country Club, Hawaii, Riot, The Split, The Gypsy Moths, Downhill Racer, Marooned, I Never Sang for My Father, Doctor's Wives, Cisco Pike, The French Connection (Acad. Award best actor, 1971), Prime Cut, The Poseidon Adventure, Scarecrow, The Conversation, Zandy's Bride, Young Frankenstein, Night Moves, Bite the Bullet, French Connection II, Lucky Lady, The Domino Principle, A Bridge Too Far, March or Die, Superman, All Night Long, Superman II., Eureka,

Under Fire, Uncommon Valor, Misunderstood, Power, Target, Twice in a Lifetime, Hoosiers, No Way Out, Full Moon in Blue Water, Mississippi Burning, Bat-21, Split Decisions, The Von Metz Incident.

HADLOCK, CHANNING M.: Marketing. TV Executive. b. Mason City, IA. e. Duke U., U. of North Carolina. Newspaperman, Durham, NC Herald, war corr., Yank; NBC, Hollywood; television prod.-writer, Cunningham & Walsh Adv.; v.p. account supr. Chirug & Cairns Adv.; v.p. Marketing Innovations; dir. mktg. Paramount Pictures; mktg. svcs, Ogilvy & Mather; mktg, Time Life Books.

HAGERTY, JULIE: Actress. b. Cincinnati, OH. Studied drama for six years before leaving for New York. Made acting debut in her brother Michael's theatre group in Greenwich Village called the Production Company. Film debut in Airplane!, 1980.
THEATER: The Front Page (Lincoln Center).
PICTURES: A Midsummer Night's Sex Comedy, Airplane II: The Sequel, Lost in America, Bad Medicine, Beyond Therapy, Aria.
TELEVISION: The Visit (Trying Times).

HAGGAR, PAUL: Executive. Veteran of over 30 yrs. with Paramount Pictures, working way up from studio mail room to become apprentice editor in 1953; promoted to asst. editor 1955; music editor, 1957. In 1968 named head of post-prod. for all films made by Paramount. 1985, named sr. v.p., postprod. for Studio Group.

HAGGARD, PIERS: Director. b. Scotland, 1939. e. U. of Edinburgh. Son of actor Stephen Haggard; great grandnephew of author Rider Haggard. Began career in theatre in 1960 as asst. to artistic dir. at London's Royal Court. Named director at Glasgow Citizens' Theatre. 1963–65 worked with the National Theatre, where co-directed Hobson's Choice and The Dutch Courtesan. Has directed many plays and series for TV.
PICTURE: Venom, The Fiendish Plot of Dr. Fu Manchu, A Summer Story.
TELEVISION: Pennies from Heaven, Quatermass, A Triple Play: Sam Found Out.

HAGMAN, LARRY: Actor. b. Fort Worth, TX, Sept. 21, 1931. e. Bard Coll. Son of actress Mary Martin. First stage experience with Margo Jones Theatre in the Round in Dallas. Appeared in N.Y. in Taming of the Shrew; two years with London production of South Pacific. 1952–56 was in London with US Air Force where produced and directed show for servicemen. Returned to N.Y. for plays on and off Bdwy. (God and Kate Murphy, The Nervous Set, The Warm Peninsula, The Beauty Part). Starred in daytime serial, Edge of Night, for over 2 years.
PICTURES: Fail Safe, Ensign Pulver and the Captain, The Group, In Harm's Way, Beware!, The Blob, The Cavern, Stardust, 3 in the Cellar, Mother, Jugs and Speed, Harry and Tonto, The Eagle Has Landed, Superman, etc.
TELEVISION: Series: I Dream of Jeannie, The Good Life, Here We Go Again, Dallas. Movies: The President's Mistress, Last of the Good Guys, Battered, Deadly Encounter.

HAHN, HELENE: Executive. b. New York, NY. e. Loyola U. Instructor of entertainment law at Loyola. Attorney for ABC before joining Paramount in 1977 in studio legal dept. 1979, moved to business affairs; promoted to dir. 1980, v.p., 1981; sr. v.p., 1983. Left in 1985 to join Walt Disney Pictures as sr. v.p., business & legal affairs for m.p. division. 1987, promoted to exec. v.p., Walt Disney Studios.

HAIM, COREY: Actor. b. Toronto, Canada, 1972. Performed in TV commercials at 10; signed as regular on children's show, The Edison Twins. Theatrical m.p. debut, Firstborn (1984).
PICTURES: Secret Admirer, Silver Bullet, Lucas, Murphy's Romance, License to Drive, Dream a Little Dream, Watchers.
TELEVISION: A Time to Live; Roomies (series).

HAIMOVITZ, JULES: Executive. b. New York, NY, 1951. e. Brooklyn Coll., B.A., M.A., theoretical mathematics. Worked at ABC-TV in operations and audience research before joining Viacom International for 11 years finally as pres. of Viacom Networks Group with responsibility for Showtime/The Movie Channel, MTV and other pay TV networks. Sept. 1987, named pres. and COO, Aaron Spelling Productions, Inc.

HALAS, JOHN: Director. b. Budapest, Apr. 16, 1912. e. Hungary, Paris. Entered m.p. ind. 1928; prod. over 500 documentary, educational shorts & cartoons, including Masters of Animation (series 13 TV programs).
PICTURES INCLUDE: Animal Farm, The Owl and the Pussycat (3-D), History of the Cinema, Animal, Vegetable and Mineral, The Candlemaker; anim. seq., The First 99, The Energy Picture, Habatales, A Christmas Visitor, Hamilton Cartoon series, Automania 2000, Is There Intelligent Life on Earth, Midsummer Nightmare, Hoffnung Cartoon Series, Dodo, The Kid from Outer Space (series), Ruddigore, The Question, Children and Cars, Parkinson's Law, Tomfoolery

Show, Max and Moritz series, Ten for Survival, Autobahn, Dilemma, Players, Botticelli—A New Vision, Toulouse-Lautrec, Leonardo da Vinci.

HALE, ALAN: Actor. b. Los Angeles, CA, 1918. Son of late Alan Hale, actor.
PICTURES INCLUDE: Short Grass, The Gunfighter, West Point Story, At Sword's Point, Wait Till the Sun Shines Nellie, Big Trees, Lady in the Iron Mask, Springfield Rifle, Man Behind the Gun, Capt. John Smith and Pocahontas, Iron Glove, Silver Lode, Rogue Cop, Young at Heart, Many Rivers to Cross, Destroy, A Man Alone, Sea Chase, Indian Fighter, Killer Is Loose, Up Periscope, Advance to the Rear, Hang 'Em High, The True Story of Jesse James, Hambone and Hillie.
TELEVISION: The Lucy Show, Hazel, Wagon Train, Cheyenne, Maverick, Route 66, Jack Benny Show, Biff Baker, U.S.A. (series), Casey Jones (series), Gilligan's Island (series), The Law and Harry McGraw.

HALE, BARBARA: Actress. b. DeKalb, IL, April 18, 1922. Mother of actor William Katt. e. Chicago Acad. of Fine Arts. Beauty contest winner, Little Theatre actress. Screen debut, 1943: Higher and Higher. On TV in Perry Mason series.
PICTURES INCLUDE: Belle of the Yukon, Goin' to Town, Boy with Green Hair, Window, Jolson Sings Again, And Baby Makes Three, Emergency Wedding, Jackpot, Lorna Doone, First Time, Last of the Comanches, Seminole, Lone Hand, Lion Is in the Streets, Unchained, Far Horizons, Houston Story, Buckskin, Airport.
TELEVISION: Perry Mason Returns (1985) and other Perry Mason's: The Case of the Murdered Madam; The Avenging Ace, The Case of the Lady in the Lake, The Case of the Scandalous Scoundrel.

HALEY, JR., JACK: Executive. b. Los Angeles, CA, Oct. 25, 1933. e. Loyola U. Son of late film star. 1959–67 Wolper Prods., 1967–73. Sr. v.p. at Wolper before joining MGM. Named dir. of creative affairs. Produced, wrote and directed That's Entertainment! (1974). Left Nov., 1974, to join 20th Century-Fox as pres. of TV Div. and v.p., TV for 20th-Fox Film Corp. Winner of 2 Peabody Awards, best prod. at Int'l. TV Festival at Monte Carlo and 3 Silver Lion Awards at Venice Film Festival. Won Emmy for best dir. in music or variety shows for Movin' On with Nancy. Directed M.P. Academy Awards Show in 1970; prod. it in 1974 and 1979. Left Fox 1976 to be indep. prod. 1985: That's Dancing.
PICTURES: Norwood, The Love Machine, That's Entertainment, Better Late Than Never (prod.)
TELEVISION: The Incredible World of James Bond, The Legend of Marilyn Monroe, The Supremes, The Hidden World, Movin' with Nancy (Emmy, dir., 1968), With Love Sophia, Monte Carlo, Life Goes to War: Hollywood and the Homefront; Heroes of Rock n' Roll (exec. prod.), 51st Academy Awards (Emmy, 1979), Hollywood, the Golden Years (with David Wolper), Ripley's Believe It or Not, The Night They Saved Christmas.

HALL, ANTHONY MICHAEL: Actor. b. New York, NY, 1968.
PICTURES: Six Pack, National Lampoon's Vacation, Sixteen Candles, The Breakfast Club, Weird Science, Out of Bounds, Johnny Be Good.
TELEVISION: Rascals and Robbers: The Secret Adventures of Tom Sawyer and Huck Finn.

HALL, ARSENIO: Actor. Comedian. b. Cleveland, OH. e. Kent State U. Became interested in magic at 7, which later led to own local TV special, The Magic of Christmas. Switched from advertising career to stand-up comedy, 1979. Discovered at Chicago nightclub by singer Nancy Wilson.
PICTURES: Amazon Women on the Moon (debut, 1987), Coming to America.
TELEVISION: The 1/2 Hour Comedy Hour (1983, co-host), Thicke of the Night (regular), Solid Gold, The Late Show (host), The Arsenio Hall Show.

HALL, CONRAD: Cinematographer. b. Tahiti, 1926. Worked as camera operator with Robert Surtees, Ted McCord, Ernest Haller; moved to TV as director of photography before feature films.
PICTURES INCLUDE: Wild Seed, The Sabateur—Code Name Morituri, Harper, The Professionals, Rogue's Gallery, Incubus, Divorce, American Style, In Cold Blood, Cool Hand Luke, Hell in the Pacific, Butch Cassidy and the Sundance Kid, Tell Them Willie Boy Is Here, The Happy Ending, Fat City, Electra-Glide in Blue, The Day of the Locust, Smile, Marathon Man, Black Widow, Tequila Sunrise.
TELEVISION: It Happened One Christmas.

HALL, HUNTZ (HENRY): Actor. b. Boston, MA, 1920. In 1937 appeared in stage and screen production Dead End.
PICTURES INCLUDE: Crime School, Angels with Dirty Faces, They Made Me a Criminal, Hell's Kitchen, Muggs Rides Again, Live Wires, A Walk in the Sun, Jinx Money, Smuggler's Cove, Fighting Fools, Blues Busters, Bowery Battalion, Ghost Chasers, Crazy Over Horses, Let's Go Navy,

Here Come the Marines, Hold That Line, Feudin' Fools, No Holds Barred, Private Eyes, Paris Playboys, Bowery Boys Meet the Monsters, Clipped Wings, Jungle Gents, Bowery to Bagdad, High Society, Spy Chasers, Jail Busters, Dig That Uranium, Up in Smoke, Second Fiddle to a Steel Guitar, Gentle Giant, Cyclone.
TELEVISION: The Teddy Bears (series).

HALL, KEN G.: Producer, Director. b. Sydney, Australia, Feb. 22, 1901. Reporter. Joined pub. dept., Union Theats., Sydney; adv. mgr. 1920. In 1922 adv. mgr. FN (Asia) Ltd. Became adv. mgr. & pub. dir., State theat., Sydney, 1928; then asst. to managing dir., Union Theats. In 1931 gen. mgr. & dir., Cinesound Prods., Ltd.
PICTURES INCLUDE: (dir.) On Our Selection, Squatter's Daughter, Tall Timbers, Lovers and Luggers, Mr. Chedworth Steps Out, Vengeance of the Deep, Pacific Adventure.

HALMI, ROBERT: Producer: b. Budapest, Hungary, Jan 22, 1924. Originally writer-photographer under contract to Life Magazine.
PICTURES:: Documentaries for U.N. Features include: Hugo the Hippo; Visit to a Chief's Son; One and Only; Brady's Escape.
TELEVISION: Bold Journey (dir.-cin.); American Sportsman; The Oriental Sportsman; The Flying Doctor; The Outdoorsman; Julius Boros Series; Rexford; Who Needs Elephants; Calloway's Climb; Oberndorf Revisited; True Position; Wilson's Reward; Nurse; Buckley Sails; A Private Battle; My Old Man; Mr. Griffin and Me; When the Circus Came to Town; Best of Friends; Bush Doctor; Peking Encounter; Svengali; China Rose; Cook and Peary—The Race to the Pole; Terrible Joe Moran; Nairobi Affair; The Night They Saved Christmas.

HALPERN, NATHAN L.: Executive. b. Sioux City, IA, Oct. 22, 1914. e. U. of Southern California, B.A. 1936; Harvard Law Sch., L.L.B. 1939. With general counsel's office, U.S. Securities & Exchange commission, 1939–41; exec. asst. to dir., Civilian Supply, U.S. War Prod. Board, 1941–43; naval officer, Psychological Warfare Div., Supreme Headquarters, Allied Expeditionary Force, 1943–45; exec. asst. to dir., U.S. Information Service, Paris, 1945; asst. to pres., Columbia Broadcasting System, 1945–49; 1949–present; pres., TNT Communications, Inc.

HAMADY, RON: Producer. b. Flint, MI, June 16, 1947. e. U. of California, B.A. 1971, co-founder of The Crystal Jukebox, record productions, music management and music publishing co. Produced 12 hit albums for Decca Records of England and London Records, U.S. Entered m.p. industry in 1975–76, producing Train Ride to Hollywood for Taylor-Laughlin dist. Co.
PICTURES INCLUDE: Fade to Black, Surf II, And God Created Woman (1987), Out Cold.

HAMEL, VERONICA: Actress. b. Philadelphia, PA, Nov. 20, 1943. e. Temple U. Moved to NY and began a modelling career with Eileen Ford Agency. Off B'way debut: The Big Knife. Acted in dinner theater prods. Moved to L.A. 1975.
PICTURES: Cannonball, Beyond the Poseidon Adventure, When Time Ran Out, A New Life.
TELEVISION: Ski Lift, 79 Park Avenue, The Gathering, The Gathering II, Valley of the Dolls, Sessions, Kane and Abel. Series: Hill Street Blues (5 Emmys).

HAMILL, MARK: Actor. b. Oakland, CA, Sept. 25, 1952. Started in TV, including General Hospital (serial) and the Texas Wheelers (series). Film debut in Star Wars (1977). B'way debut: The Elephant Man. Then in The Nerd.
PICTURES INCLUDE: Star Wars, Corvette Summer, The Big Red One, The Empire Strikes Back, The Night the Lights Went Out in Georgia, Return of the Jedi, Slipstream.
TELEVISION: Eric Mallory: Circumstantial Evidence, Delancy Street; The Crisis Within; The City; Sarah T: Portrait of A Teenage Alcoholic; The F.B.I.; Owen Marshall; Room 222; The Partridge Family.

HAMILL, PETE: Journalist, Writer. b. Brooklyn, NY, June 24, 1935. Worked as ad designer, NBC page boy and sheet metal worker before joining staff of New York Post. In 1962 won Mike Berger Award of Columbia U. Graduate Sch. of Journalism for N.Y.'s worst slum. Received citation from Newspaper Reporters' Assn. for series on N.Y. Police Dept. Made s.p. writing debut with Doc, 1971.
PICTURES INCLUDE: Doc, Death at an Early Age, Badge 373, Report from Engine Co. 82.
TELEVISION: Laguna Heat, Adaptations of novels Flesh and Blood, The Gift.
BOOKS: A Killing for Christ (novel), Irrational Ravings (collection of N.Y. Post columns), The Seventeenth Christmas (novel), The Invisible City: A NY Sketchbook.

HAMILTON, GEORGE: Actor. b. Memphis, TN, Aug. 12, 1939. e. grammar, Hawthorne, CA; military sch., Gulfport, MS, N.Y. Hackley Prep Sch., FL, Palm Beach H.S. Won Best Actor Award for the state of Florida, high sch. contest.

TELEVISION: Rin Tin Tin, The Donna Reed Show, The Veil, Roots, Two Fathers' Justice, Monte Carlo, Poker Alice. Series: Spies.
PICTURES INCLUDE: Crime and Punishment, USA (debut), Home from the Hill, All The Fine Young Cannibals, Angel Baby, Where the Boys Are, By Love Possessed, A Thunder of Drums, Light in the Piazza, Two Weeks in Another Town, The Victors, Your Cheatin' Heart, Viva Maria, That Man George, Doctor, You've Got to Be Kidding!, The Long Ride Home, Jack of Diamonds, A Time for Killing, The Power, Evel Knievel, The Man Who Loved Cat Dancing, Once Is Not Enough, Love at First Bite (also exec. prod.), Zorro, the Gay Blade (also co-prod.)

HAMILTON, GUY: Director. b. Paris, Sept. 1922. Ent. m.p. industry 1939 as apprentice at Victorine Studio, Nice; Royal Navy, 1940–45, in England asst. dir., Fallen Idol, Third Man, Outcast of the Islands, African Queen.
PICTURES INCLUDE: The Ringer, The Intruder, An Inspector Calls, Colditz Story, Manuela, The Devil's Disciple, A Touch of Larceny, The Best of Enemies, The Party's Over, Man in the Middle, Goldfinger, Funeral in Berlin, Battle of Britain, Diamonds Are Forever, Live and Let Die, The Man with the Golden Gun, Force Ten from Navarone, The Mirror Crack'd, Evil Under the Sun, Remo Williams.

HAMLIN, HARRY: Actor. b. Pasadena, CA, Oct. 30, 1951. e. U. of California, Yale U., 1974 in theatre, psychology. Joined American Conservatory Theatre, San Francisco, for two years' study before joining as professional actor. Screen debut in Movie, Movie, 1979.
PICTURES: King of the Mountain, Clash of the Titans, Making Love, Blue Skies Again.
TELEVISION: Mini-series: Studs Lonigan, Master of the Game, Space, Laguna Heat, Favorite Son. Series: L.A. Law.
STAGE: Hamlet, Awake and Sing.

HAMLISCH, MARVIN: Composer. b. New York, NY, June 2, 1944. e. Juilliard. Accompanist and straight man on tour with Groucho Marx 1974–75; debut as concert pianist 1975 with Minn. Orch. Scores of Broadway shows: A Chorus Line (Tony Award); They're Playing Our Song, Smile.
PICTURES INCLUDE: The Swimmer (1968); Take the Money and Run; Bananas; Save the Tiger, Kotch; The Way We Were (Oscars for original score and song), The Sting (Oscar for adaptation), Same Time, Next Year; Ice Castles; Chapter Two; Seems Like Old Times; The Spy Who Loved Me, Starting Over, Ordinary People, The Fan, Sophies' Choice, I Ought to Be in Pictures, Romantic Comedy, D.A.R.Y.L., Three Men and a Baby, Little Nikita.
TELEVISION: Good Morning, America (theme); The Entertainer (also prod.); A Streetcar Named Desire; The Two Mrs. Grenvilles.

HAMMOND, PETER: Actor, Writer, Director. b. London, Eng., Nov. 15, 1923. e. Harrow Sch. of Art. Stage debut: Landslide, Westminster Theatre. Screen debut: Holiday Camp.
PICTURES INCLUDE: The Huggetts, Helter Skelter, Fools Rush In, The Reluctant Widow, Fly Away Peter, The Adventurers, Operation Disaster, Come Back, Peter, Little Lambs Eat Ivy, Its Never Too Late, The Unknown, Morning Departure, Confession, dir.: Spring and Port Wine.
TELEVISION: William Tell, Robin Hood, The Buccaneers series. 1959–61. writ., dir. TV plays. TV dir. credits: Avengers, 4 Armchair Theatres, Theatre 625, BBC classic serials Count of Monte Cristo, Three Musketeers, Hereward the Wake, Treasure Island, Lord Raingo, Cold Comfort Farm, The White Rabbit, Out of the Unknown, Follyfoot; Lukes Kingdom, Time to Think, Franklin's Farm, Sea Song, Shades of Greene, Our Mutual Friend, The House that Jack Built, The King of the Castle, The Black Knight, Kilvert's Diary, Turgenev's Liza, Wuthering Heights, Funnyman, Little World of Don Camillo, Rumpole of the Bailey, Bring on the Girls, Hallelujah Mary Plum, Aubrey Beardsley, The Happy Autumn Fields, The Combination, Tales of the Unexpected, The Glory Hole, The Hard Word, Shades of Darkness—The Maze, The Blue Dress.

HAMNER, EARL: Producer, Writer. b. Schuyler, VA, July 10, 1923. With WLW, Cincinnati, as radio writer-producer; joined NBC 1949 as writer; 1960, freelance.
PICTURES: Spencer's Mountain, You Can't Get There from Here, The Homecoming.
TELEVISION: The Waltons (creator, co-prod.); Joshua's World, Falcon Crest (exec. prod.); A Wedding on Walton's Mountain (exec. prod.); A Day of Thanks on Walton's Mountain (exec. prod. actor), The Gift of Love—A Christmas Story (exec. prod., s.p.).

HAMPSHIRE, SUSAN: Actress. b. London, Eng., May 12, 1941.
STAGE: Expresso Bongo, Follow That Girl, Fairy Tales of New York, Ginger Man, Past Imperfect, She Stoops to Conquer, On Approval, The Sleeping Prince, A Doll's House, Taming of the Shrew, Peter Pan, Romeo & Jeanette, As You Like It, Miss Julie, The Circle, Arms and the Man, Man and Superman, Tribades, An Audience Called Edward, The

Crucifer of Blood, Night and Day, The Revolt, House Guest, Blithe Spirit, Married Love.
TELEVISION: Andromeda, The Forsyte Saga, Vanity Fair, Katy, The First Churchills; An Ideal Husband, The Lady Is a Liar, The Improbable Mr. Clayville, musical version of Dr. Jekyll and Mr. Hyde, The Pallisers, Barchester Chronicles, Leaving, Leaving II, Going to Pot I, II, and III.
PICTURES INCLUDE: The Three Lives of Thomasina, Night Must Fall, Wonderful Life, Paris Au Mois d'Aout, The Fighting Prince of Donegal, The Trygon Factor, Monte Carlo or Bust, Rogan, David Copperfield, A Room in Paris, Living Free, Time for Loving, Malpertius, Baffled, Neither the Sea nor the Sand, Roses and Green Peppers, David the King, Bang.

HANCOCK, JOHN: Director. b. Kansas City, MO, Feb. 12, 1939. e. Harvard. Was musician and theatre director before turning to films. Dir. play A Man's a Man, NY 1962. Artistic dir. San Francisco Actors Workshop 1965–66. Nominated for AA for short, Sticky My Fingers, Fleet My Feet.
PICTURES INCLUDE: Let's Scare Jessica to Death, Bang the Drum Slowly, Baby Blue Marine, California Dreaming, Weeds (also co-s.p.), Steal the Sky.
TELEVISION: The Twilight Zone (1986).

HAND, BETHLYN J.: Executive. b. Alton, IL. e. U. of Texas. Entered motion picture industry in 1966 as administrative assistant to president of Motion Picture Association of America, Inc. In 1975 became associate director of Code for advertising of MPAA. In 1976 became director of Code for advertising; v.p.—west coast activities, board of directors, Los Angeles. S.P.C.A. 1981, appointed by Governor to Calif. Motion Picture Council 1983, elected vice chm., California Motion Picture Council.

HANDEL, LEO A.: Producer. b. Vienna. Dir. audience research, MGM, 1942–51; organized Meteor Prod., 1951; organized Leo A. Handel Prod., for TV films, 1953; author, Hollywood Looks at Its Audience, also TV plays; pres., Handel Film Corp; prod. TV series including Everyday Adventures, Magic of the Atom. Exec. prod. & v.p., Four Crown Prods., Inc., exec. prod., Phantom Planet, 1961; prod.-writer-dir., feature film, The Case of Patty Smith, 1961; Americana Series, 1963; book, A Dog Named Duke, 1965. TV specials, Age of the Atom, 1966; Sweden-Vikings Now Style, Benjamin Franklin, The Mexican American Heritage and Destiny, The American Indian, Police Dog (TV special), Art in America, 10 half-hour films, Stress-Distress (special), Computer and You, Thailand, The Philippines, Germ Wars, Measuring Things, Safety for Seniors, The Dropouts, 1986; Singapore—Crossroad of the Orient, Black American Odyssey.

HANKS, TOM: Actor. b. Oakland, CA, July 9, 1956. e. California State U. Began career with Great Lakes Shakespeare Festival, Cleveland (3 seasons).
PICTURES: He Knows You're Alone, Splash, Bachelor Party, The Man with One Red Show, Volunteers, The Money Pit, Nothing in Common, Every Time We Say Goodbye, Dragnet, Big, Punchline, The 'Burbs.
TELEVISION: The Love Boat, Bosom Buddies (series), Taxi, Happy Days, Family Ties. Movie: Rona Jaffe's Mazes and Monsters; Saturday Night Live (host).

HANNA, WILLIAM: Executive. b. Melrose, NM, July 14, 1911. e. Compton Coll. Studied engineering and journalism. Joined firm in CA as structural engineer; turned to cartooning with Leon Schlessinger's company in Hollywood. In 1937 hired by MGM as director and story man in cartoon dept. There met Joseph H. Barbera and created famous cartoon series Tom & Jerry, continuing to produce it from 1938 to 1957. Left MGM in 1957 to form Hanna-Barbera Productions to make cartoons for TV. Series have included Yogi Bear, Huckleberry Hound, The Flintstones. Hanna-Barbera became a subsidiary of Taft Broadcasting Co. in 1968 with both men operating studio under long-term agreements with Taft (which became Great American Broadcasting, 1987). Hanna is senior v.p. of Hanna-Barbera Productions. Company entered theatrical production with Loopy De Loop in 1960, Hey There It's Yogi Bear, Man Called Flintstone, Charlotte's Web, Heidi's Song.

HANNAH, DARYL: Actress. b. Chicago, IL, 1960. Niece of cinematographer Haskell Wexler. e. U. of California at L.A. Studied with Stella Adler.
PICTURES: The Fury (debut, 1978), Hard Country, Blade Runner, Summer Lovers, Splash, The Pope of Greenwich Village, Reckless, Clan of the Cave Bear, Legal Eagles, Roxanne, Wall Street, High Spirits, Steel Magnolias.
TELEVISION: Paper Dolls.

HANNEMANN, WALTER A.: Film editor. b. Atlanta, GA, May 2, 1914. e. U. of Southern California, 1935. Editorial training, RKO 1936–40; edit. supvr., Universal, 1941–42; consultant 1970–75 national educational media.
PICTURES INCLUDE: Interval, The Revengers, Dream of Kings, Guns of the Magnificent Seven, East of Java, Pay or Die, Al Capone, Hell's Five Hours, Armoured Command,

Han-Har

Only the Valiant, Time of Your Life, Kiss Tomorrow Goodbye, Blood on the Sun, Guest in the House, Texas Masquerade, Cannon for Cardoba, El Condor, Maurie, Lost in the Stars, Mad Mad Movie Making, Big Mo, Two Minute Warning, (Oscar nominee) The Peter Hill Puzzle, Smokey and the Bandit, Other Side of the Mountain—Part II, The Visitor, The Villain, Return of Maxwell Smart.
  TELEVISION: Death Valley Days, Reader's Digest, Rosemary Clooney Show, The New Breed, The Fugitive, Twelve O'Clock High, The Invaders, Hawaii Five-O, Streets of San Francisco, Cannon, Barnaby Jones, Caribe.

HANSEN, PETER: Actor. b. Oakland, CA, Dec. 5, 1921. e. Cranbrook Acad. of Arts, Bloomfield Hills, MI; U. of Michigan, 1940–41. p. Sydney and Lee Hansen. Studied acting at Pasadena Playhouse, CA, 1946, following war service as marine fighter pilot. Campagne, Arsenic and Old Lace, This Happy Breed; m.p. debut in Branded (1950).
  PICTURES INCLUDE: Molly, Something to Live For, When Worlds Collide, Passage West, Darling How Could You, The Savage, Violent Men, Proud and Profane, Harlow.
  TELEVISION: Matinee Theatre; New Dir. KCOP-TV: Day in Court; General Hospital (series, since 1965; Emmy supp., 1975).

HARBACH, WILLIAM O.: Producer. b. Yonkers, NY, Oct. 12, 1919, e. Brown U. p. Otto Harbach, lyricist, author. U.S. Coast Guard, 1940–45; actor, MGM, 1945–47; broadcast co-ordinator. NBC, 1947–49; stage mgr., 1949–50; dir., NBC, 1950–53; prod., Tonight, 1954; prod. Steve Allen Show, 1960–61 prod., dir., Bing Crosby shows; prod., Milton Berle Special, 1962; prod., Hollywood Palace Shows, 1963–69.; co-produced Julie Andrews Show, 1972–73. Emmy for Shirley MacLaine's Gypsy in My Soul, 1976; Bob Hope Special, 1981 and 1982.

HARBERT, TED: Executive. b. New York, NY, June 15, 1955. e. Boston U., B.S. magna cum laude, 1977, degree in bdcst. & film. Started career as producer in news dept. WHDH Radio in Boston, 1976. Joined ABC in 1977 as feature film coordinator for ABC Entertainment. Named spvr., feature film and late-night program planning, 1979. Named mktg. dir., program planning & scheduling, 1979. Named asst. to v.p. program planning-scheduling, 1981. V.P., program planning & scheduling, 1983. Promoted to newly created position of v.p., motion pictures, ABC Entertainment, 1986; given title v.p. motion pictures and scheduling, 1987; v.p. primetime ABC Entertainment, 1988.

HARDIMAN, JAMES W.: Publicist. b. Brighton, England 1926. Director advtg. & pub., Rank Organisation of Canada & Odeon Canada, 1947–56. Asst. dir. ad & pub, National Theatres, 1956–58. Dir. radio & TV promotion, Walt Disney, 1959–60. Dir. Screen Gems Hollywood, 1960–64. Dir. press infmtn, CBS TV Network, Hollywood, 1964–67. Studio dir. promtn. & pub, Screen Gems, Hollywood, 1967–70. VP Yuni public rels, Tokyo and v.p. and resident director, Sijohn o Enterprises, Japan, 1970–75. Dir. pub, (entertainment) Rogers & Cowan, Beverly Hills, 1975–77. President, Suhosky & Hardiman Public Rels, 1977 to date. 1968 named Hollywood Showman of the Year by the Publicists Guild.

HARE, DAVID: Director, Writer. b. Sussex, England, 1947. e. Lancing Coll., Jesus Coll., Cambridge. After leaving univ. in 1968 formed Portable Theatre Company, experimental touring group. Hired by Royal Court Theater as literary manager, 1969. 1970, first full-length play, Slag, prod. at Hampstead Theatre Club. Resident dramatist, Royal Court (1970–71), and Nottingham Playhouse (1973). West End debut, Knuckle.
  THEATER: Slag, Brassneck, Knuckle, Fanshen, Teeth 'n' Smiles, Plenty, A Map of the World.
  PICTURES: Plenty (writer); Wetherby (dir., s.p.); Paris by Night (dir., s.p.).
  TELEVISION: Licking Hitler (1979, dir., s.p.); Dreams of Leaving; Saigon: Year of the Cat.

HAREWOOD, DORIAN: Actor. b. Dayton, OH, Aug. 6. m. actress Ann McCurry. e. U. of Cincinnati.
  THEATER: Jesus Christ Superstar (road co.), Two Gentlemen of Verona, Miss Moffat, Streamers, Over Here, Don't Call Back, The Mighty Gents, Bloodshot Wine.
  PICTURES: Foster & Laurie, Gray Lady Down, Looker, Tank, Against All Odds, The Falcon and the Snowman, Full Metal Jacket.
  TELEVISION: Panic in Echo Park, Siege, Roots—The Next Generations, An American Christmas Carol, High Ice, Beulah Land (mini-series), Strike Force, The Ambush Murders; I, Desire; Trauma Center, The Jesse Owens Story, Dirty Work, Guilty of Innocence, Amerika, Hope Division, God Bless the Child.

HARGREAVES, JOHN: Executive. b. Australia. e. Australian National Inst. of Dramatic Art. Joined Gainsborough Pictures 1945. Transferred to Denham Studios 1946 and later Pinewood Studios. Joined Allied Film Makers 1960, then Salamander Film Productions as Bryan Forbes' financial controller and Asst. Prod. 1965. Joined EMI Film Prods. Ltd. as Asst.

Man. Dir. and prod. controller May 1969–May 1972. Produced Don Quixote (with Rudolf Nureyev, in Australia), 1973. Asst. Prod. The Slipper and The Rose 1975, Man. Dir; Cinderella Promotions Ltd, 1978: assoc. prod., International Velvet. Orion repr., 1979, The Awakening; post prod. exec., Fiendish Plot of Dr. Fu Manchu, 1980; Orion rep. for Excalibur, 1981; MGM rep., Year of Living Dangerously, Australia, 1982. 1983, U.K. production executive for Completion Bond Company, Inc.

HARMON, MARK: Actor. b. Burbank, CA, Sept. 2, 1951. Son of actress Elyse Knox and football star Tom Harmon. m. actress Pam Dawber.
  PICTURES: Beyond the Poseidon Adventure; Comes a Horseman; Summer School, The Presidio, Stealing Home, Worth Winning.
  TELEVISION: Series: Sam, Laverne & Shirley, Nancy Drew, Police Story, Adam-12, 240-Robert, St. Elsewhere (regular), Moonlighting. Movies: Eleanor and Franklin: The White House Years, Little Moe, Getting Married, The Deliberate Stranger, Prince of Bel Air.

HARMON, TOM: Performer. b. Rensselaer, IN, Sept. 28, 1919. e. U. of Michigan, B.S., 1941. m. Elyse Knox, actress. All American football player, 1939–40; 1940 Heisman Trophy Winner. U.S. Air Corps, 1941–46; sports dir., WJR, Detroit, 1941; KFI, Los Angeles, 1947; broadcaster, many football, baseball games; sports dir., Columbia Pacific Radio Network, 1948–61; Tom Harmon Sports Show (ABC) 1961–70; Golden West Broadcasters (Channel 5, Hollywood), 1970; 1974—Hughes Television Network—sports dir.; 1976—Editor-Publisher—Tom Harmon's Football Today. (weekly national football paper).

HARNELL, STEWART D.: Executive. b. New York, NY, Aug. 18, 1938. e. U. of Miami, U. of California at L.A., New School for Social Research. Entertainer with Youth on Parade in Coral Gables, FL, 1948–55, performing for handicapped children, Variety Club, etc. Singer, dancer, musician. Had own bands, Teen Aces & Rhythm Rascals, 1950–56; performed on Cactus Jim TV show and Wood & Ivory, 1953–54, WTVJ, Miami. Catskills, Sand Lake, NY, 1954–55. Joined National Screen Service as exec. trainee in 1960 in Chicago; worked as booker & salesman. Transferred to N.Y. home office, 1963; worked in special trailer production. Promoted to asst. gen. sls. mgr., 1964–66; New Orleans branch mgr., 1966–67; Atlanta division mgr., 1967–70. Formed own independent distribution co., 1970–Harnell Independent Productions. Resumed post as gen. sls. mgr. of NSS, New York, 1977–78; resigned to become pres. of Cinema Concepts Theatre Service, Atlanta, in 1978 to present. Pres. of Variety Club of Atlanta, Tent 21, 1972, 1976, 1979. In 1986 formed Cinema Concepts Communications, film-video animation studio in Atlanta. Chief barker Variety Club of Atlanta, Tent 21, 1988.

HARPER, JESSICA: Actress. b. Chicago, IL, 1949. e. Sarah Lawrence Coll. Understudied on Broadway for Hair for one year. Appeared in summer stock and off-Bdwy shows. Theatrical film debut in Phantom of the Paradise (1974).
  PICTURES: Inserts, Taking Off, Love and Death, Stardust Memories, Suspiria, Shock Treatment, Pennies from Heaven, My Favorite Year, The Imagemaker, Once Again, The Blue Iguana, Hunchback.
  TELEVISION: Series: Little Women. Mini-series: Aspen, Studs Lonigan.

HARPER, JOE: Theatre Executive. b. Dallas, TX, Aug. 11, 1941. e. El Centro Coll., Dallas; Georgia. State U. Was in public relations, N.Y., 1961–65 when joined Academy Theatres, Dallas. In 1968–69, with American Multi-Cinema, Dallas. In 1969 joined R. C. Cobb Theatre, Atlanta. Now v.p. in chg. booking, buying, Member: Democratic Executive Committee, Officer Ruritan International. Active in Scouting and Little League sports.

HARPER, TESS: Actress. b. Mammoth Springs, AR. e. Southwest Missouri State Coll., Springfield. Worked in Houston, then Dallas in children's theater, dinner theater, and commercials.
  PICTURES: Tender Mercies (debut, 1982); Amityville 3-D; Silkwood; Flashpoint; Crimes of the Heart (Acad. Award nom.); Ishtar; Criminal Law.
  TELEVISION: Chiefs (mini-series); Celebrity; Kentucky Woman; A Summer to Remember; Promises to Keep; Far North; Little Girl Lost.

HARPER, VALERIE: Actress. b. Aug. 22, 1940. Suffern, NY. e. Hunter Coll., New Sch. for Social Research. Started as dancer in stage shows at Radio City Music Hall. First professional acting in summer stock in Conn.; actress with Second City Chicago 1964–69; Appeared on Bdwy. in Take Me Along, Wildcat, Subways Are for Sleeping, Something Different, Story Theatre, Metamorphoses. Won 3 Emmys for best performance in supporting role in comedy for portrayal of Rhoda on The Mary Tyler Moore Show.

PICTURES INCLUDE: Freebie and the Bean, Chapter Two, The Last Married Couple in America, Blame It on Rio. TELEVISION: Series: The Mary Tyler Show, Rhoda, Valerie. Movie: The Execution, Fun and Games, The Shadow Box, The Day the Loving Stopped, Strange Voices, Drop Out Mother, The People Across the Lake.

HARPER, WILLIAM A.: Producer. b. Port Jervis, NY, Sept. 3, 1915. e. U. of Southern California, B.S., 1936. Founder member Delta Kappa Alpha fraternity (cinematography), U.S.C.; started in m.p. ind. in pub.; later asst. dir., prod. mgr., director; In W.W.II Major, USMC. Organized Marine Corps Photo Service, then in chg. Marine Corps Photo activities Pacific Ocean Areas. End of war organized Reliance Film Co., Inc., eng. in prod., dist., early TV prod. Recalled active duty for Korean War, headed USMC Photo Service. Co-prod. with Navy (Adm. John Ford) feat. documentary, This is Korea; govt. liaison with March of Time, Crusade in Pacific and with NBC U.S. Navy Victory at Sea; prod. dir., writer, Loucks & Norling Studios, 1952; free lance writer-director 1953–55; with Fred Feldkamp Prods. 1955–56; in Europe 1956–58. Assoc. prod. The Silken Affair (RKO) 1956; Producer, The Stranding in Holland 1957; prod. advisor The Last Blitzkreig (Col.), Europe, (1958); producer, The Stone, 1962; Managing Director, St. James Productions Ltd., (England) and Pres. American-European Entertainments, Inc. (Paris).

HARRINGTON, CURTIS: Director, Writer. b. Los Angeles, CA, Sept. 17, 1928. e. U. of Southern California, B.A. Exec. assts. to Jerry Wald, 1955–61 Associate Producer at 20th Cent. Fox.
PICTURES INCLUDE: Hound Dog Man, Return to Peyton Place, The Stripper, Night Tide, Queen of Blood, What's the Matter with Helen? Gingerbread House, The Killing Kind, Games, Who Slew Auntie Roo?.
TELEVISION: Series: Hotel, Dynasty, Tales of the Unexpected, Logan's Run, Twilight Zone (1986). Movies: The Cat Creature, The Dead Can't Die, How Awful About Alan, Killer Bees, Devil Dog.

HARRINGTON, PAT (JR.): Actor. b. New York, NY, Aug. 13, 1929. e. Fordham U. Served USAF as 1st Lt., 1952–54. Time salesman for NBC, 1954–58. Some 150 TV appearances on Jack Paar, Steve Allen and Danny Thomas TV shows, 1958–61; nightclub appearances, 1960–63. TV and films, 1963 to present. Television series include: Mr. Deeds Goes to Town, Owen Marshall, and One Day at a Time.
PICTURES INCLUDE: The Wheeler Dealers, Move Over Darling, Easy Come, Easy Go, The President's Analyst, 2000 Years Later, The Candidate.

HARRIS, BARBARA: Actress. b. Evanston, IL, July 25, 1935. e. Wright Junior Coll., Chicago; Goodman Sch. of the Theatre; U. of Chicago. Joined acting troup, The Compass. Founding member, Second City Players, 1960. Came to N.Y. where first role was in Oh, Dad, Poor Dad, Mamma's Hung You in the Closet and I'm Feeling So Sad, repeating in m.p.
THEATER: Mother Courage and Her Children, Dynamite Tonight, On a Clear Day You Can See Forever, The Apple Tree (Tony Award), Mahogany.
PICTURES INCLUDE: A Thousand Clowns, Plaza Suite, Who Is Harry Kellerman?, The War Between Men and Women, Mixed Company, Nashville, Freaky Friday, Family Plot, Movie Movie, The North Avenue Irregulars, The Seduction of Joe Tynan, Peggy Sue Got Married, Nice Girls Don't Explode.
TELEVISION: The Return of Ben Casey.

HARRIS, BURTT: Producer, Actor. Began career as actor; later worked with Elia Kazan as prod. asst. and asst. dir. on America America, Splendor in the Grass, and The Arrangement. Worked as second unit dir. and asst. dir. on many films as well as producer and actor.
PICTURES INCLUDE: Associate Producer: Little Murders, The Wiz, Cruising, Gilda Live. Executive Producer: The Verdict, Just Tell Me What You Want. Producer: Prince of the City, Daniel, Deathtrap, Garbo Talks, The Glass Menagerie. Co-Producer: D.A.R.Y.L. Actor: Splendor in the Grass, Fail Safe, The Taking of Pelham 1-2-3, The Wanderers, The Verdict, Daniel, Garbo Talks, D.A.R.Y.L., Running on Empty.

HARRIS, ED: Actor. b. Tenafly, NJ, Nov. 28, 1950. m. actress Amy Madigan. Played football 2 years at Columbia U. prior to enrolling in acting classes at OK State U. Summer stock. Grad. CA Institute of the Arts, 1975. Worked in West Coast Theater.
THEATER: Fool For Love (off-Bdwy debut), Precious Sons.
PICTURES: Coma, Borderline, Knightriders, Creepshow, The Right Stuff, Under Fire, Swing Shift, Places in the Heart, Alamo Bay, A Flash of Green, Sweet Dreams, Code Name: Emerald, The Suspect, Walker, To Kill a Priest, Jackknife, The Abyss.
TELEVISION: The Amazing Howard Hughes, The Seekers, The Aliens Are Coming, The Last Innocent Man.

HARRIS, EDWARD M.: Exhibitor. b. Holdenville, OK, Aug. 21, 1916. e. Tulsa U. Theatre mgr. in Neosho, MO, since 1933; now mgr., co-owner, Gardner Theatres there. Member: Kans.-Mo. Theatre Assn. (pres. 1954–56).

HARRIS, JAMES B.: Producer, Director, Writer. b. New York, NY, Aug. 3, 1928. e. Juilliard Sch. U.S. film export, 1947; Realart Pictures, 1948; formed Flamingo Films, 1949; formed Harris-Kubrick Productions, 1954. Producer of The Killing, Paths of Glory, Lolita; formed James B. Harris Prods., Inc., 1963; prod., dir., The Bedford Incident, 1965; produced, directed & wrote screenplay, Some Call It Loving, 1973; prod., Telefon, 1977; Fast-Walking, 1981 (prod., dir., s.p.); Cop (prod., dir., s.p.).

HARRIS, JULIE: Designer. b. London, England. e. Chelsea Arts Sch. Entered industry in 1945 designing for Gainsborough Studios. First film, Holiday Camp.
PICTURES INCLUDE: Greengage Summer, Naked Edge, The War Lover, Fast Lady, Chalk Garden, Psyche 59, A Hard Day's Night, Darling, Help, The Wrong Box, Casino Royale, Deadfall, Prudence and the Pill, Decline and Fall, Goodbye Mr. Chips, Sherlock Holmes, Follow Me!, Live and Let Die, Rollerball, Slipper and The Rose, Dracula.
TELEVISION: Laura (with Lee Radziwill), Candleshoe, The Sailor's Return, Lost and Found, The Kingfisher, Arch of Triumph, Sign of Four, Hound of the Baskervilles, A Hazard of Hearts.

HARRIS, JULIE: Actress. b. Grosse Pointe, MI, Dec. 2, 1925. e. Yale Drama Sch. m.p. debut in Member of the Wedding (1952).
THEATER: Sundown Beach, Playboy of the Western World, Macbeth, Young and the Fair, Magnolia Alley, Monserrat, Member of the Wedding, I Am a Camera, Colombe, The Lark; A Shot in the Dark; Marathon 33; Ready When You Are, C.B.; Break a Leg; Skyscraper; Voices; And Miss Reardon Drinks a Little; The Last of Mrs. Lincoln (Tony Award); In Praise of Love; The Belle of Amherst.
PICTURES INCLUDE: East of Eden, I Am a Camera, The Trouble with Women, The Haunting, Harper, Reflection in a Golden Eye, The Poacher's Daughter, You're a Big Boy Now, The Split, The People Next Door, The Hiding Place, The Moving Target, Voyage of the Damned, The Bell Jar, Gorillas in the Mist.
TELEVISION: Little Moon of Alban, Johnny Belinda, A Doll's House, Ethan Frome, The Good Fairy, The Lark, He Who Gets Slapped, The Heiress, Victoria Regina, Pygmalion, Anastasia, The Holy Terror, The Power and The Glory, The Woman He Loved, Leave Her to Heaven. Series: Thicker Than Water, Knot's Landing.

HARRIS, JULIUS: Actor.
PICTURES: Nothing But a Man, Live and Let Die, The Taking of Pelham 1-2-3, Looking for Mr. Goodbar, Hell Up In Harlem, Let's Do It Again, The Fox, Superfly, Islands in the Stream, Shaft's Big Score, Alambrista, First Family, My Chauffeur, A Gathering of Old Men, Berserk, The Enchanted.
THEATER: on B'way and in National tour of No Place To Be Somebody.
TELEVISION: To Kill a Cop; Blue and The Gray; Victory at Entebbe; Rich Man, Poor Man.

HARRIS, PHIL: Orchestra leader. b. Linton, IN, June 24, 1906. m. Alice Faye, actress. In 1933: with orchestra in Melody Cruise. In 1936: Vitaphone short prod. In 1937: Turn Off the Moon. In 1939: Man About Town. In 1940: Buck Benny Rides Again, Dreaming Out Loud.
PICTURES INCLUDE: I Love a Bandleader, Wabash Avenue, Wild Blue Yonder, Starlift, High and the Mighty, Anything Goes, Good-Bye My Lady, The Aristocrats (voice of Scat Cat). Co-starred with Alice Faye in weekly radio show; many TV appearances.

HARRIS, RICHARD: Actor. b. Limerick, Ireland, Oct. 1, 1930. Attended London Acad. of Music and Dramatic Arts. Prod.-dir. Winter Journey 1956. Prof. acting debut in Joan Littlewood's prod. of The Quare Fellow, Royal Stratford, 1956.
THEATER: London: A View from the Bridge; Man, Beast and Virtue; The Ginger Man. (U.S.): Camelot.
PICTURES INCLUDE: Alive and Kicking, Shake Hands With the Devil, The Wreck of the Mary Deare, A Terrible Beauty, The Long, The Short and The Tall, Guns of Navarone, Mutiny on the Bounty, This Sporting Life, The Red Desert (Italy), Major Dundee, The Heroes of Telemark, The Bible, Hawaii, Camelot, The Molly Maguires, A Man Called Horse, Cromwell, Bloomfield (actor & dir.), Man in the Wilderness, The Snow Goose, The Deadly Trackers, Gulliver, 99 and 44/100% Dead, Juggernaut, Echoes of a Summer, Robin and Marian, Return of the Man Called Horse, The Cassandra Crossing, Orca, Golden Rendezvous, The Wild Geese, The Ravagers, The Number, Game for Vultures, High Point, Your Ticket Is No Longer Valid, Martin's Day.
TELEVISION: Camelot.

135

HARRIS, ROBERT: Executive. Senior v.p., Universal TV, with responsibility of supervising Universal programming on CBS network. In 1981 named pres. of Universal TV. Pres. MCA, Television Group.

HARRIS, ROSEMARY: Actress. b. Ashby, Suffolk, Sept. 19, 1930. e. India and England. Early career, nursing; studied Royal Acad. of Dramatic Art, 1951–52. Screen debut in Beau Brummell (1954).
PLAYS INCLUDE: Climate of Eden (NY debut 1952), Seven Year Itch, Confidential Clerk (Paris Festival), and with Bristol Old Vic in The Crucible, Much Ado About Nothing, Merchant of Venice; also in The Tale of Two Cities, Dial M for Murder, etc. On stage, at Old Vic, 1955–56; U.S. tour, 1956–57; U.S. stage, 1958–63. Chichester Festivals 1962 and 63; Nat'l Theatre 1963–64; You Can't Take It With You, 1965; The Lion in Winter (Tony Award, 1966), 1967, APA Repertory Co., Heartbreak House, The Royal Family, A Pack of Lies, Hay Fever.
TELEVISION: Cradle of Willow (debut, 1951); Othello, The Prince and the Pauper, Twelfth Night; Wuthering Heights, Notorious Woman, (Emmy, 1976), Blithe Spirit, Holocaust, Profiles in Courage, To the Lighthouse, Strange Interlude, The Old Reliable.
PICTURES INCLUDE: Beau Brummell, The Shiralee, A Flea in Her Ear, Camelot, The Boys from Brazil, The Ploughman's Lunch, Crossing Delancey.

HARRISON, GEORGE: Singer, Composer, Producer. b. Liverpool, England, Feb. 25, 1943. Member, The Beatles. Winner of 2 Grammys on own in addition to Beatles' group awards.
PICTURES: As individual. Score: Let It Be. Exec. Prod.: Life of Brian; Time Bandits; Monty Python Live at the Hollywood Bowl; The Missionary; Privates on Parade; Scrubbers; Bullshot; A Private Function; Water; Mona Lisa; Shanghai Surprise, Withnail and I, Five Corners, Bellman and True, The Lonely Passion of Judith Hearne, Track 29, The Raggedy Rawney, How to Get Ahead in Advertising, Powwow Highway, Checking Out.

HARRISON, GREGORY: Actor. b. Avalon, Catalina Island, CA, May 31, 1950. Started acting in school plays; then joined Army. Studied at Estelle Harman Actors Workshop; later with Lee Strasberg and Stella Adler. Film debut in Jim, the World's Greatest (1976). Formed Catalian Productions with Franklin Levy.
THEATER: Picnic, The Hasty Heart, Journey's End.
PICTURES: Fraternity Row, Razorback, North Shore.
TELEVISION: Series: Logan's Run, M*A*S*H, Barnaby Jones, Trapper John. Movies: The Gathering, Enola Gay, Trilogy in Terror, The Best Place To Be, The Women's Room, For Ladies Only, The Fighter, Seduced, Oceans of Fire, Hot Paint (co-exec. prod., star), Red River (co-exec. prod., actor). Mini-series: Centennial, Fresno.

HARRISON, JOAN: Writer, producer. b. Guildford, Surrey, England, 1911. e. U. Sorbonne; Oxford U., B.A. Began screen career in England as asst. & writer with Alfred Hitchcock, dir. To U.S. 1939 to write s.p. Rebecca.
PICTURES INCLUDE: Foreign Correspondent, Suspicion, Saboteur, Phantom Lady (prod.); Dark Waters, The Strange Affair of Uncle Harry, Ride a Pink Horse, Circle of Danger, Eye Witness.
Prod. Alfred Hitchcock Presents, TV.

HARRISON, REX: Actor. b. Derry House, Huyton, Lancashire, Eng., Mar. 5, 1908. In the RAF W.W.II. Stage debut 1924 in Thirty Minutes in a Street, Liverpool Repertory Theatre, England; later on British tour (Charley's Aunt, Alibi, etc.) London debut 1930 in Getting George Married. NY debut Sweet Aloes (1936). Voted one of top ten British moneymaking stars in Motion Picture Herald-Fame Poll, 1945–46. Top ten world box office star, 1966.
THEATER: London, repertory, tour. New York stage: Anne of a Thousand Days (Tony Award, 1949), Henry VIII, 1948; Cocktail Party (London) 1950; Bell, Book and Candle, NY, 1951; Venus Observed, Love of 4 Colonels, (NY): Bell, Book and Candle, (London). My Fair Lady, 1956–57 (NY) (Tony Award), (1958–59, London); The Fighting Cock, 1959–60; Platonov (London), 1960; 1961, August for The People. Both Seasons at Royal Court Theatre (London). In Praise of Love (spec. Tony Award, 1969); Heartbreak House, Aren't We All?
PICTURES INCLUDE: Began screen career, 1929. Films include Men Are Not Gods, Storm in a Teacup, School for Husbands, Over the Moon, The Citadel, Ten Days in Paris, Sidewalks of London, Night Train, Major Barbara, Blithe Spirit. To Hollywood, 1946. I Live in Grosvenor Square, The Rake's Progress, Anna and the King of Siam, The Ghost and Mrs. Muir, Foxes of Harrow, Escape, Unfaithfully Yours, The Long Dark Hall, The Four Poster, King Richard & the Crusaders, Constant Husband, The Reluctant Debutante, Midnight Lace, Once a Thief, Cleopatra (Acad. Award nom.), My Fair Lady (Acad. Award, NY Film Critics Award, Golden Globe 1965), The Yellow Rolls-Royce, The Agony and the Ecstasy, The Honey Pot, Dr. Doolittle, A Flea in her Ear,

Staircase, The Prince and the Pauper, Crossed Swords, Ashanti, The Fifth Muskateer, A Time to Die.
TELEVISION: Anastasia, The Mystery of Anna.

HARROLD, KATHRYN: Actress. b. Tazewell, VA, 1950. e. Mills Coll. Studied acting at Neighborhood Playhouse in N.Y., also with Uta Hagen. Appeared in Off-Off-Bdwy. plays for year; then joined experimental theatre group, Section Ten, touring East, performing and teaching at Connecticut Coll. and New York U. Cast in TV daytime serial, The Doctors.
PICTURES: Nightwing (debut), The Hunter, Modern Romance, The Pursuit of D.B. Cooper, Yes, Gorgio, The Sender, Into the Night, Raw Deal.
TELEVISION: Movies: Son-Rise, a Miracle of Love, Vampire, Bogie, An Uncommon Love, Women in White, Man Against the Mob. Series: Starsky and Hutch, Bronx Zoo.

HARRYHAUSEN, RAY: Producer, Writer, Special Effects Expert. b. Los Angeles, CA. e. Los Angeles City Coll. While at coll. made 16mm animated film, Evolution, which got him job as model animator for George Pal's Puppetoons in early '40s. Served in U.S. Signal Corps; then made series of filmed fairy tales with animated puppets for schools and churches. In 1946 worked on Mighty Joe Young as ass't. to Willis O'Brien. Designed and created special visual effects for The Beast from 20,000 Fathoms; then began evolving own model animation system called Dynarama. In 1952 joined forces with prod. Charles H. Schneer, using new process for first time in It Came from Beneath the Sea. Subsequently made many films with Schneer in Dynarama.
PICTURES INCLUDE: Twenty Million Miles to Earth, The Three Worlds of Gulliver, Jason and the Argonauts, the First Men in the Moon, One Million Years B.C., The Valley of Gwangi, The Golden Voyage of Sinbad, Sinbad and the Eye of the Tiger, Clash of the Titans (co. prod., special effects).

HART, HARVEY: Director. b. Canada, Mar. 19, 1928. Began career on TV in native country then went to Hollywood.
PICTURES INCLUDE: Dark Intruder, Bus Riley's Back in Town, Sullivan's Empire, The Sweet Ride, Fortune and Men's Eyes, The Pyx, Aliens Are Coming, The High Country, Utilities.
TELEVISION: East of Eden, This Is Kate Bennett, Maserati and the Brain, Born Beautiful, Master of the Game (co-dir.), Reckless Disregard, Beverly Hills Madam, Stone Fox.

HARTFORD, K.: Executive. b. New York, NY, July 5, 1922. Graduate U. of Cincinnati, Los Angeles City Coll. Active in film financing, co-production, packaging. Executive of Hartford Industries, Latin American Development & Investment Co., Western International. Has offices in 8 countries.

HARTLEY, MARIETTE: Actress. b. New York, NY, June 21, 1940. Student Carnegie Tech. Inst. 1956–57; studied with Eva Le Gallienne. Appeared with Shakespeare Festival, Stratford 1957–60. Co-host Today Show, 1980. Returned to stage in King John (NYSF in Central Park).
PICTURES: Ride the High Country, Marooned, Skyjacked, Marnie, Improper Channels, O'Hara's Wife, 1969.
TELEVISION: Peyton Place, Stone, the Incredible Hulk, Second Time Around, The Hero, Good Night Beantown. Movies: Earth II, Sandcastles, Genesis II, Killer Who Wouldn't Die, Last Hurrah, Silence of the Heart, My Two Loves, Co-host on CBS Morning Show, 1987.

HARTMAN, DAVID: Actor. b. Pawtucket, RI, May 19, 1935. e. Duke U., 1956. Was 2nd Lt. in Air Force; entered American Acad. of Dramatic Arts, N.Y. Appeared in off-Bdwy. musicals and summer stock; toured with Belafonte singers. Bdwy. debut in Hello, Dolly!
PICTURES INCLUDE: The Ballad of Josie, Nobody's Perfekt, Ice Station Zebra, The Island at the Top of the World.
TELEVISION: World Premiere: I Love a Mystery. Series: The Virginian, The Bold Ones, Lucas Tanner, Berth and Babies (prod.). Host ABC's Good Morning, America, The Shooters (writer, exec. prod.; narrator), David Hartman—The Future Is Now (also exec. prod.; writer).

HARTZ, JIM: TV Newsman, Panelist. b. Feb. 3, 1940, Tulsa, OK. Pre-med student at U. of Tulsa, where worked in spare time as reporter for radio station KRMG. In 1963 left studies for career as newsman and joined KOTV in Tulsa. In 1964 moved to NBC News in New York, acting as reporter and anchorman. In 1974 became co-host of Today Show, joined Barbara Walters.

HARVEY, ANTHONY: Director. b. London, Eng., June 3, 1931. Royal Acad. of Dramatic Art. Two yrs. as actor. Ent. m.p. ind. 1949 with Crown Film Unit.
PICTURES INCLUDE: As actor or editor: Private's Progress, Brothers-in-Law, Man in the Cocked Hat, Carlton Brown of the F.O., I'm Alright Jack, The Angry Silence, The Millionairess, Lolita, The L-Shaped Room, Dr. Strangelove, Spy Who Came In From the Cold, The Whisperers, Director: Dutchman; The Lion in Winter, They Might Be Giants, Eagles' Wing, Players, The Abdication, Richard's Things, The Ultimate Solution of Grace Quigley.

TELEVISION: The Disappearance of Aimee, The Missiles of October, Svengali, The Patricia Neal Story, The Glass Menagerie.

HARWOOD, RONALD: Writer. b. Cape Town, South Africa, 1934. TELEVISION: The Barber of Stamford Hill, Private Potter, Take a Fellow Like Me, The Lads, Convalescence, Guests of Honor, The Guests. Adapted several of the Tales of the Unexpected, Mandela, Breakthrough at Roykjavik.
PICTURES INCLUDE: Barber of Stamford Hill, Private Potter (written with Casper Wrede), subsequently High Wind in Jamaica, Eye Witness, One Day in the Life of Ivan Denisovich, Operation Daybreak, The Dresser, The Doctor and the Devils.

HASSANEIN, RICHARD C.: Executive. b. New York, NY, Aug. 13, 1951; e. Staunton Military Acad., 1966–70; American U., 1970–74. Booker/real estate dept. opns., United Artists Theater Circuit, 1974–77; joined United Film Distribution Co., 1977; named pres. 1978. Resigned as pres. Feb. 1988. Currently pres. of Myriad Enterprises, NY.

HASSANEIN, SALAH M.: Executive. b. Suez, Egypt, May 31, 1921. e. British Sch., Alexandria, Egypt. Nat'l Bank of Egypt, Cairo, 1939–42. Asst. division mgr. Middle East, 20th-Fox, Cairo, Egypt, 1942–44: U.S. armed forces, 1944–47; usher, asst. mgr., Rivoli Theatre, N.Y., 1947–48. Film buyer, booker, oper. v.p. U.A. Eastern Theas., 1948–59; pres. 1960; exec. v.p. U.A. Communications, Inc. 1960; v.p. United Artists Cable News Corp.; pres. Todd-AO Corp., 1963. Exec. v.p., Todd-AO Corp., 1987. President, Warner Bros. International Theaters, 1988.
PICTURES: Exec. prod.: Knightriders; Creepshow; Hello Again; Love or Money.

HASSELHOFF, DAVID: Actor. b. Baltimore, MD, July 17, 1952. PICTURE: Starcrash, Witchcraft.
TELEVISION: The Young and the Restless, Knight Rider (series). Movies: Griffin and Phoenix, Semi Tough, After Hours—Getting to Know Us, The Cartier Affair, Bridge Across Time, Perry Mason: The Case of the Lady in the Lake.

HASTINGS, DON: Performer; b. Brooklyn, NY, Apr. 1, 1934. e. Professional Children's Sch. On B'way in Life With Father, I Remember Mama, Summer and Smoke, etc.; on various radio shows, Video Ranger on Capt. Video 1949–55; The Edge of Night, 1956–60; As the World Turns since 1960. Author of scripts for As the World Turns, The Guiding Light.

HATFIELD, BOBBY: Performer. b. Beaver Dam, WI, Aug. 10, 1940. e. Long Beach State Coll. Member, Righteous Bros. recording group.
TELEVISION: Shindig, The Danny Kaye Show, Ed Sullivan Show.
PICTURES INCLUDE: Beach Ball, Swingin' Summer.

HATFIELD, HURD: Actor. b. New York, NY, 1918. e. Morrisson prep, Horace Mann H.S., Riverdale Acad., Columbia U., Chekhov Drama Sch., Devonshire, Eng. On dramatic stage, Lower Depths, Twelfth Night, Cricket on the Hearth, King Lear, then screen debut Dragon Seed, The Picture of Dorian Gray, 1943–44.
PICTURES INCLUDE: The Unsuspected, Joan of Arc, Destination Murder, Tarzan and Slave Girl, Left-Handed Gun, Mickey One, Harlow, Von Richtofen and Brown, King David, Crimes of the Heart, Her Alibi.
N.Y. stage 1952, Venus Observed. TV appearances.

HATFIELD, TED: Executive. b. Wilton Junction, IA, Aug. 26, 1936. e. Hot Springs, AR. U.S. Army-NCO Academy, 1954. 1947–67 ABC Paramount Theatres, advanced from usher to district mgr. 1967–70 MGM asst. exploitation dir.; 1970–83, MGM national advertising coordinator; 1983–87, MGM/UA v.p., field operations. 1987–present, MGM/UA (v.p.) exhibitor relations.
MEMBER: Motion Picture Pioneers; Western LA Council, Boy Scout Commissioner, Culver City Chamber of Commerce, past v.p./presidents award; Jaycees, Past State v.p.; Advertising Federation, past state pres., Culver City Commissioner.

HAUER, RUTGER: Actor. b. Breukelen, Netherlands, Jan. 23, 1944. Stage actor in Amsterdam for six years. Motion picture debut in Turkish Delight, 1975.
PICTURES INCLUDE: The Wilby Conspiracy, Keetje Tippl'e, Max Havelaar, Soldier of Orange, Pastorale 1943, Femme Entre Chien et Loup, Mysteries, Nighthawks, Blade Runner, Chanel Solitaire, Eureka, The Osterman Weekend, A Breed Apart, Ladyhawke, Flesh and Blood, The Hitcher, Wanted: Dead or Alive; Bloodhounds of Broadway, Blind Fury, The Legend of the Holy Drinker, Salute of the Juggler, Ocean Point.
TELEVISION: Escape from Sobibor, Inside The Third Reich.

HAUSMAN, MICHAEL: Producer. Former stockbroker and still photographer. Entered film industry as assoc. prod. and prod.

mgr. on The Heartbreak Kid and Taking Off. Worked as head of prod. for Robert Stigwood on Saturday Night Fever.
PICTURES: I Never Promised You A Rose Garden; Alambrista!; Heartland; Rich Kids; One-Trick Pony; Ragtime (exec. prod.); The Ballad of Gregorio Cortez; Silkwood; Amadeus (exec. prod.); Places in the Heart (exec. prod.); Desert Bloom; Flight of the Spruce Goose; No Mercy; House of Games; Things Change; Valmont, Homicide.
TELEVISION: Lip Service (exec. prod.).

HAVOC, JUNE: Actress. r.n. Hovick. b. Seattle, WA, 1916. Sister of late Gypsy Rose Lee, actress. Made film bow when two in Hal Roach prod. Danced with Anna Pavlova troupe, then entered vaudeville in own act. Later, joined Municipal Opera Company, St. Louis, and appeared in Shubert shows. Musical comedy debut: Forbidden Melody (1936). To Hollywood, 1942.
PICTURES INCLUDE: Hello Frisco, Hello, No Time for Love, Sweet and Low Down, Brewster's Millions, Intrigue, Gentleman's Agreement; Red, Hot and Blue; Chicago Deadline, Once a Thief, Follow the Sun, Lady Possessed, Can't Stop the Music, The Accidental Tourist.
PLAYS: Pal Joey, Sadie Thompson, Mexican Hayride, Dunnigan's Daughter, Dream Girl, Affairs of State, The Skin of Our Teeth, A Midsummer Night's Dream (Stratford, CT. American Shakespeare Fest, 1958), Tour for U.S. Dept. of St., 1961; wrote Marathon 33. The Ryan Girl, The Infernal Machine, The Beaux Strategem, A Warm Peninsula, Dinner at Eight, Habeas Corpus. An unexpected evening with June Havoc (one woman show, London 1985), Toured England in The Gift, 1987.
TELEVISION: Anna Christie, The Bear, Cakes and Ale, Daisy Mayme, The Untouchables; co-owner, Willy, MacMillan & Wife, The Paper Chase, Murder She Wrote. Series: More Havoc (1964–65).

HAWN, GOLDIE: Actress. b. Washington, DC, November 21, 1945. Was a professional dancer (performed in Can-Can at the NY World's Fair, 1964), and made TV debut dancing on an Andy Griffith Special; TV acting debut Good Morning World followed by Laugh-In. Screen debut: Cactus Flower (1969).
PICTURES INCLUDE: There's A Girl In My Soup, Dollars, Butterflies Are Free, The Sugarland Express, The Girl from Petrovaka, Shampoo, The Duchess and the Dirtwater Fox, Foul Play, Private Benjamin (also prod.), Seems Like Old Times, Best Friends, Swing Shift, Protocol (also exec. prod.); Wildcats; Overboard.

HAWTHORNE, NIGEL: Actor. b. Coventry, England, 1929. Extensive career on stage. Ent. TV ind. 1953. Films, 1957.
TELEVISION: Mapp and Lucia, The Knowledge, The Miser, The Critic, Barchester Chronicles, Marie Curie, Edward and Mrs. Simpson, Yes, Minister, Yes, Prime Minister.
PICTURES: Gandhi, Firefox, The Chain.

HAYES, HELEN: Actress. r.n. Helen H. Brown. b. Washington, DC, Oct. 10, 1901. e. Sacred Heart Convent, Wash. Wife of the late writer, Charles MacArthur. Started film career in 1931. Dubbed "The First Lady of the American Stage."
PLAYS INCLUDE: What Every Woman Knows, Coquette, Petticoat Influence, The Good Fairy, Mary of Scotland, Victoria Regina, Harriet, Happy Birthday, Wisteria Trees, Mrs. McThing, Skin of Our Teeth, Glass Menagerie, The Show Off, Front Page (revivals).
PICTURES INCLUDE: Arrowsmith, The White Sister, Another Language, Night Flight, A Farewell to Arms, The Sin of Madelon Claudet (Academy Award 1931–32), My Son, John, Main Street to Broadway, Anastasia, Airport (AA, 1970), Herbie Rides Again, One of Our Dinosaurs Is Missing, Candleshoe.
TELEVISION: Twelve Pound Look, Mary of Scotland, Dear Brutus, Skin of Our Teeth, Christmas Tie, Drugstore on a Sunday Afternoon, Omnibus, A Caribbean Mystery, Murder with Mirrors.

HAYES, JOHN MICHAEL: Writer. b. Worcester, MA, May 11, 1919. e. U. of Massachusetts, 1941.
PICTURES INCLUDE: Red Ball Express, Thunder Bay, Torch Song, War Arrow, Rear Window, To Catch a Thief, Trouble with Harry, It's A Dog's Life, Man Who Knew Too Much, The Matchmaker, Peyton Place, But Not for Me, Butterfield 8, The Children's Hour, Where Love Has Gone, The Chalk Garden, Judith, Nevada Smith.

HAYES, PETER LIND: Actor: b. San Francisco, CA, June 25, 1915. m. Mary Healy. Was radio singer, actor, vaudeville, night clubs. Producer, Grace Hayes Lodge Review: on TV show with Mary Healy.
PICTURES INCLUDE: Million Dollar Legs, All Women Have Secrets, These Glamour Girls, Seventeen, Dancing on a Dime, Playmates, Seven Days Leave, 5000 Fingers of Dr. T, Once You Kiss a Stranger.

HAYNES, TIGER: Actor. b. St. Croix, V.I., Dec. 13, 1907. Organized singing group The Three Flames, whose hit record

Open the Door, Richard led to a vaudeville career, 39 weeks on radio and nightclub and TV dates.
THEATER: introduced in New Faces of 1956, Finian's Rainbow, Kiss Me Kate (City Center revival), 110 in the Shade, Fade Out-Fade In, Two Gentlemen of Verona, The Great White Hope (National Company), The Wiz (Tin Woodsman), A Broadway Musical, Comin' Uptown, My One and Only. Off-B'way: Bags, Louis, Taking My Turn.
PICTURES: Times Square, Moscow on the Hudson, All that Jazz, Trading Places, Ratboy, The Mosquito Coast, The Long Lost Friend, Enemy Territory, A Gathering of Old Men.

HAYS, ROBERT: Actor. b. Bethesda, MD, July 24, 1947. e. Grossmont Coll., San Diego State U. Left school to join Old Globe Theatre for five years.
PICTURES: Airplane, Take This Job and Shove It!, Some Summer Day, Airplane II: The Sequel, Utilities, Trenchcoat, Touched, Scandalous, Cat's Eye, For Better or Worse.
TELEVISION: Series: Love Boat, Harry O, Laverne and Shirley, Most Wanted, Wonder Woman, Angie, Starman. Movies: California Gold Rush, Murder by the Book. Miniseries: Will Rogers: Champion of the People, The Girl, The Gold Watch, and Everything.

HAZEN, JOSEPH H.: Attorney b. Kingston, NY, May 23, 1898. e. George Washington U. Law Sch. Formerly assoc. as member of firm, Thomas and Friedman. In 1939 member ind. com. in discussions with Commerce Dept. Member com. which negotiated consent decree. Member ind. Committee of Six, lawyers to study and reorganize ind. activities. Mem. War Activities Committee. In 1944 resigned as v.p. and dir., Warner Bros. to join Hal Wallis Prods. as pres., 1944–48; pres. Wallis-Hazen, Inc., Tillco. dissolved, June 1953; photoplay prod., Hal B. Wallis, Paramount Pictures Corp., since 1953. Dir. USO Camps, Inc., M.P.A.A.

HEADLY, GLENNE: Actress. b. New London, CT., March 13, 1955. m. actor John Malkovich. e. High Sch. of Performing Arts. Studied at HB Studios then American Coll. of Switzerland. In Chicago joined St. Nicholas New Works Ensemble. Won 3 Joseph Jefferson awards for work with Steppenwolf Ensemble in Say Goodnight Gracie, Miss Firecracker Contest, Balm in Gilead, Coyote Ugly, Loose Ends. Directed Canadian Gothic. Film debut: Fandango, 1985.
THEATER: Arms and the Man, Extremities, The Philanthropist.
PICTURES: Nadine, Making Mr. Right, Eleni, Purple Rose of Texas, Stars and Bars, Paperhouse, Scoundrels.

HEALY, JOHN T.: Executive. e. Brooklyn Coll. Taught economics and was associated with Lehigh Valley Industries and General Food Corp. before joining ABC, Inc. in 1970 as assoc. dir. of corp. planning. Named dir. of planning and develop. June, 1972. Elected v.p., planning and admin. of ABC Leisure Group, March, 1974; elected vice pres. of corporate planning, Feb., 1976.

HEARD, JOHN: Actor. b. Mar. 7, 1946. Married, actress Margot Kidder. Career began at Organic Theatre, starring in Chicago & N.Y. productions of Warp. Other stage roles include Streamers, G.R. Point, Othello, The Glass Menagerie.
PICTURES: Between the Lines, On the Yard, Head Over Heels, Heartbeat, Cutter and Bone, Cat People, Heaven Help Us, Lies, After Hours, The Trip to Bountiful, The Telephone, The Milagro Beanfield War, The Seventh Sign, Big, Betrayed, Beaches.
TELEVISION: The Scarlet Letter, Tender Is the Night, Out on a Limb, Necessity.

HEATHERTON, JOEY: Actress. b. Rockville Centre, NY, Sept. 14, 1944.
PICTURES: Twilight of Honor, Where Love Has Gone, My Blood Runs Cold, Bluebeard, The Happy Hooker Goes to Washington.

HECKART, EILEEN: Actress. b. Columbia, OH, Mar. 29, 1919. e. Ohio State U., American Theatre Wing. m. Jack Yankee.
THEATER: Voice of the Turtle, Brighten the Corner, They Knew What They Wanted, Hilda Crane, Picnic, The Bad Seed, A View From the Bridge, Family Affair, Pal Joey, Invitation to a March, Everybody Loves Opal, Dark at the Top of the Stairs, And Things That Go Bump in the Night, You Know I Can't Hear You When the Water's Running, Too True to Be Good, Barefoot in the Park, Butterflies Are Free, Veronica's Room, The Effect of Gamma Rays on Man in the Moon Marigolds.
PICTURES INCLUDE: Miracle in the Rain (debut), Somebody Up There Likes Me, Bus Stop, Hot Spell, Heller in Pink Tights, My Six Loves, Up the Down Staircase, No Way to Treat a Lady, Butterflies Are Free (Acad. Award), Zandy's Bride, The Hiding Place, Burnt Offerings, Heartbreak Ridge.
TELEVISION: Kraft, Suspense, Philco Playhouse, The Web, Mary Tyler Moore.
AWARDS: Daniel Blum and Outer Circle (Picnic), Foreign Press, and Donaldson, Oscar nom. and Film Daily Citation, (Bad Seed), TV Sylvania for the Haven, Variety Poll of N.Y.

and Drama Critics (Dark at The Top of the Stairs); Emmy, (Save Me a Place at Forest Lawn).

HECKERLING, AMY: Director. b. New York, NY, May 7, 1954. m. writer Neal Israel. e. Art & Design H.S., New York U., American Film Institute. Made shorts (Modern Times, High Finance, etc.) before turning to features.
PICTURES: Fast Times at Ridgemont High, Johnny Dangerously, Permanent Record, Daddy's Home.
TELEVISION: Twilight Zone (1986), Fast Times at Ridgemont High (series).

HEDLUND, DENNIS: Executive. b. Hedley, TX, Sept. 3, 1946. e. U. of Texas, Austin, B.A., business admin., 1968. Captain U.S. Marine Corps, 1966–70. 1970–74, newscaster and disc jockey, KGNC, Amarillo, TX; KOMA, Oklahoma City, OK; WTIX, New Orleans, LA; WFLA, Tampa, FL; 1974–77, national sales mgr., Ampex Corp., NY; 1977–80, vice pres., Allied Artists Video Corp., NY; 1980–present, founder and president, Kultur Video.

HEDWIG, GORDON W.: President, Nu-Art Films, Inc. b. Jersey City, NJ, April 27, 1913. e. Newtown H.S., Rensselaer Polytechnic Inst. p. William K. and Elsa Hedwig. Lt., Signal Corp. W.W.II. Part-time work film lab., 1927–33; salesman, 1933–35. Started 16 mm. distribution in 1935 as Nu-Art Film co., an individual enterprise and incorporated as Nu-Art Films, Inc., 1937. President NuArt Films, Inc., org. Telecast Films, Inc., org. in 1947 for TV film distribution. Sec. Theatre-on-films, Inc. Now active in all corporations, in TV & nontheatrical.

HEFFNER, RICHARD: Executive. b. Aug. 5, 1925. e. Columbia U. Instrumental in acquisition of Channel 13 (WNET) as New York's educational tv station; served as its first general manager. Previously had produced and moderated Man of the Year, The Open Mind, etc. for commercial TV. Served as dir. of public affairs programs for WNBC-TV in N.Y. Was also dir. of special projects for CBS TV Network and editorial consultant to CBS, Inc. Editorial Board. Was radio newsman for ABC. Exec. editor of From The Editor's Desk on WPIX-TV in New York. Taught history at U. of California at Berkeley, Sarah Lawrence Coll., Columbia U. and New School for Social Research, N.Y. Served as American specialist in communications for U.S. Dept. of State in Japan, Soviet Union, Germany, Yugoslavia, Israel, etc. Producer and moderator, The Open Mind on public TV stations in New York, Washington DC, Los Angeles, etc. Channel 11 (WPIX) in New York and is exec. editor of From The Editor's Desk. Is Univ. Prof. of Communications and Public Policy at Rutgers U. In July, 1974 appt. chmn. of classification and rating admin. rating board.

HEFFRON, RICHARD T.: Director. b. Chicago, Oct. 6, 1930.
PICTURES INCLUDE: Fillmore, Newman's Law, Trackdown, Futureworld, Outlaw Blues, I, the Jury.
TELEVISION: The Morning After, Dick Van Dyke Special, I Will Fight No More Forever, Toma (pilot), Rockford Files (pilot), North and South (mini-series). Movies: The California Kid, Young Joe Kennedy, A Rumor of War, A Whale for the Killing, The Mystic Warrior, V: The Final Battle, Anatomy of an Illness, Convicted: A Mother's Story, Guilty of Innocence, Samaritan, Napoleon and Josephine: A Love Story, Broken Angel.

HEIDER, FREDERICK: Producer. b. Milwaukee, WI, April 9, 1917. e. Notre Dame U., Goodman Theatre, Chicago. Actor in Globe Theatre, Orson Welles' Mercury Theatre.
TELEVISION & RADIO: Chesterfield Supper Club, Sammy Kaye's So You Want to Lead a Band, Frankie Carle Show, Jo Stafford Show, prod., writer, Paul Whiteman Goodyear Revue, Billy Daniels Show, Martha Wright Show, Earl Wrightson Show, Club Seven, Mindy Carson Show; prod., ABC, Ted Mack Family Hour, Dr. I.Q., Miss America Pageant, Bishop Sheen's Life Is Worth Living, Voice of Firestone, Music for a Summer Night. Music for a Spring Night, The Bell Telephone Hour. Publisher, Television Quarterly, National Academy of Television Arts and Sciences. Currently columnist, The Desert Sun, Palm Springs, CA.

HELD, DAVID: Executive. Entered industry as atty. in United Artists' legal dept. 1976, joined Paramount as sr. atty. in legal dept.; transferred to business affairs 1977; promoted to v.p., business affairs, 1979. Left for sabbatical 1983; re-entered industry with Samuel Goldwyn Co. as v.p., business affairs. 1984, returned to Paramount as sr. v.p. in chg. business affairs.

HELLER, FRANKLIN: Producer, Director. b. Dover, NJ. e. Carnegie Inst. of Technology, B.A., 1934. Actor, 1934–36; stage mgr., Sam Harris-Max Gordon Prods., 1936–44; exec. prod., USO shows N.Y., 1944–45; prod. & dir., Paramount, 1945–47; dir., summer stock, 1947–48; prod. & dir., CBS TV, 1949–54; exec., prod. and dir. Goodson-Todman Prods., 1954–69; exec. prod. Protocol Prods., 1969–72 Literary Representative 1972. Dirs. Guild of America, Nat'l bd. 1965–77; Treas. 1965–69; Sec. 1970–73; Chr. Publications 1966–76.

TELEVISION SHOWS: What's My Line?, Beat the Clock, The Front Page, The Web, Danger, To Tell the Truth, I've Got a Secret.

HELLER, LUKAS: Writer. b. Germany, 1930. Started as reader at Pinewood Studios, England; later working in various production capacities. Writing career began when Robert Aldrich assigned him to script for What Ever Happened to Baby Jane?, 1962. Long collaboration with Aldrich followed.
PICTURES: The Killing of Sister George, The Flight of the Phoenix, Too Late the Hero, The Dirty Dozen, Hush . . . Hush Sweet Charlotte, Monty Walsh, The Deadly Trackers, Damnation Alley, Blue City.
TELEVISION: Hitler's SS—Portrait in Evil.

HELLER, PAUL M.: Producer. b. New York, NY, Sept. 25, 1927. e. Hunter Coll., Drexel Inst. of Technology. President, Intrepid Productions. Studied engineering until entry into U.S. Army as member of security agency, special branch of signal corps. Left Army and went into fine arts and theatre. Worked as set designer (Westport, East Hampton, Palm Beach) and in fine TV and then on theatrical films. Involved with the NY Experience and South Street Venture. Debut as film producer, David and Lisa, 1963. From 1964 to 1969 was president of MPO Pictures Inc. Joined Warner Bros. as prod. exec., 1970. In 1972 founded Sequoia Pictures, Inc. with Fred Weintraub. Pres. of Paul Heller Prods. Inc. formed in 1978.
PICTURES INCLUDE: David and Lisa, The Eavesdropper, Secret Ceremony, Enter the Dragon, Truck Turner, Golden Needles, Dirty Knight's Work, Outlaw Blues, The Pack, The Promise, Pygmalion (cable), First Monday in October, Withnail and I.

HELLMAN, JEROME: Producer. b. New York, NY, Sept. 4, 1928. e. New York U. Joined ad dept. of New York Times then went to William Morris Agency as apprentice. Made asst. in TV dept. Worked as agent for Jaffe Agency. After hiatus in Europe joined Ashley-Steiner Agency (later IFA) where clients included Franklin Schaffner, Sidney Lumet, George Roy Hill, John Frankenheimer. Functioned as TV prod., including Kaiser Aluminum Hour. Left to form own agency, Ziegler, Hellman and Ross. Switched to feature prod. with The World of Henry Orient in 1964.
PICTURES INCLUDE: A Fine Madness, Midnight Cowboy (AA), The Day of the Locust, Coming Home, Promises in the Dark (also dir.), The Mosquito Coast.

HELMOND, KATHERINE: Actress. b. Galveston, TX, July 5, 1934. Initial stage work with Houston Playhouse and Margo Jones Theatre, Dallas. Joined APA Theatre, NY, and Trinity Square Rep. Co., RI, Hartford Stage, CT and Phoenix Rep. NY. In 1950s opened summer stock theatre in the Catskills. Taught acting at American Musical and Dramatic Acad., Brown U. and Carnegie-Mellon U. 1983, accepted into AFI's Directing Workshop for Women. Directed Bankrupt.
THEATER: The Great God Brown, House of Blue Leaves (Clarence Derwent, NY and LA Drama Critics Awards, 1972).
PICTURES: The Hindenberg; Baby Blue Marine; Family Plot; Time Bandits; Brazil; Shadey; Lady in White; The Lies of Muenchhausen.
TELEVISION: Series: Soap; Who's The Boss? (also dir); Benson (dir. only). Movies: The Autobiography of Miss Jane Pittman; The Legend of Lizzie Borden; Wanted: The Sundance Woman; Diary of a Teenage Hitchhiker; Honeymoon Hotel; Rosie: The Rosemary Clooney Story; World War III; Meeting of the Minds.

HEMINGWAY, MARGAUX: Actress. b. Portland, OR, Feb. 1955. Granddaughter of writer Ernest Hemingway. Model. Sister of Mariel Hemingway.
PICTURES: Lipstick, Killer Fish, A Fistful of Chopsticks, Over the Brooklyn Bridge, Porta Mi La Luna.

HEMINGWAY, MARIEL: Actress. b. Nov. 22, 1961. Granddaughter of writer Ernest Hemingway. Sister of Margaux Hemingway, model and actress.
PICTURES: Lipstick (debut, 1976), Manhattan, Personal Best, Star 80, The Mean Season, Creator, Sunset, The Suicide Club (also co-prod.)
TELEVISION: I Want to Keep My Baby, Amerika, Steal the Sky.

HEMMINGS, DAVID: Actor, Director. b. Guildford, England, 1938. Early career in opera. Ent. m.p. ind. 1956.
THEATER: Dylan Thomas in Adventures in the Skin Trade.
TELEVISION: Auto Stop, The Big Toe, Out of the Unknown, Beverly Hills Cowgirl Blues, In the Heat of the Night (dir.).
PICTURES INCLUDE: Some People, Two Left Feet, The System, The Eye of the Devil, Blow Up, Camelot, Charge of the Light Brigade, Only When I Larf, Barbarella, The Best House in London, Alfred the Great, The Walking Stick, Fragment of Fear, Unman Wittering and Zigo, Voices, Juggernaut, Crossed Swords. Running Scared (director), The 14, Quilp, Profundo Rosso, Islands in the Stream, The Squeeze, Murder by Decree, Man, Woman, and Child, Prisoners (also exec. prod.), The Rainbow.

HENDERSON, SKITCH: Music director. r.n. Lyle Henderson. b. Birmingham, England, Dec. 7, 1918. e. U. of California.
TELEVISION: Steve Allen Show, Tonight Show.

HENDRICKS, BILL L.: Owner/Director, Bill Hendricks Films; writer, prod. dir. of documentaries & shorts and TV commercials. b. Grand Prairie, TX, May 3. e. St. John's Coll. Formerly Warner Bros. Studio Publicity Director; special asst. to Jack Warner; and Director WB Cartoon Studios. Winner first Quigley Grand Award; mgr., Friendship Train & Merci Train. Author: Encyclopedia of Exploitation with Howard Waugh; Showmanship in Advertising with Montgomery Orr; writer, prod., A Force in Readiness, (Academy Award). The John Glenn Story (Oscar nomination), The FBI, Seapower, The Land We Love, A Free People, Top Story, A World of Pleasure, Red Nightmare, Star Spangled Revue, This is Eucom, An American Legend, Scenes to Remember, Freedom and You, Jobs, Wonderful World of Warner, Global Marine; Football Safety; An American Partnership, Free Enterprise, Today's Demand, Tomorrow's Challenge, That's Us in the USA, A Special Day. As ASCAP lyricist, songs include Wintersong; Vaya Con Dios, Amigo; March of the Americans; Paris Je T'aime; Hollywood!; Toys For Tots Parade; Merry Christmas!; Happy Song; On With the Show; Ho! To the West; Wait For Me. Colonel, USMCR (Ret); Founder Marine Corps Toys For Tots program.

HENKIN, HOWARD, H.: Executive writer, Producer, Director. b. New York, NY, Sept. 13, 1926. e. U. of Delaware, 1944. U.S. Army, 1944–46, U.S. dept., Newell Emmett Agency, 1947–48; gen. mgr., TelePrompter, 1950–54; eastern sales mgr., Shamus Culhane Prod. 1955–57; Academy Pictures 1957–58; pres. HFH Productions, 1958; pres., Henkin Prods. Inc. & Henkin-Faillace Prods. Inc., 1962–68; ch. of bd., Trio Prods., Inc., 1968–80; author of The Dot System.

HENNER, MARILU: Actress. b. Chicago, IL, Apr. 6, 1952. e. U. of Chicago. Studied singing and dancing, appearing in musicals in Chicago and on Broadway in Over Here and Pal Joey. Gained fame as Elaine in TV series, Taxi.
PICTURES: Between the Lines, Blood Brothers, Hammett, The Man Who Loved Women, Cannonball Run II, Johnny Dangerously, Perfect, Rustler's Rhapsody.
TELEVISION: Movies: Dream House, Stark, Love with a Perfect Stranger.

HENNING, LINDA KAY: Actress, Singer. b. Toluca Lake, CA, Sept. 16, 1944. e. San Fernando Valley State Coll.
STAGE: Gypsy, Applause, Damn Yankees, I Do, I Do, Pajama Game, Sugar, Wonderful Town, Fiddler on the Roof, Sound of Music, Vanities, Born Yesterday, Mary, Mary, Bus Stop, etc.
PICTURES INCLUDE: Bye Bye Birdie.
TELEVISION: Series: Petticoat Junction, Happy Days, Mork & Mindy, Double Trouble, Barnaby Jones, Love American Style, Adam 12. Pilots: Kudzu, The Circle, Family. Movies: The Dog Days of Arthur Kane, The Return of the Beverly Hillbillies, Gift of Terror.

HENNING, PAUL: TV Producer, Writer. b. Independence, MO, Sept. 16, 1911. e. Kansas City Sch. of Law, grad. 1932. Radio singer and disc jockey. Also acted, ran sound effects, sang, wrote scripts. To Chicago 1937–38, to write Fibber McGee and Molly. w. Don Quinn. To Hollywood as writer for Rudy Vallee, 1939. Wrote scripts for Burns and Allen 10 years, including transition radio to TV. In 1953 wrote, produced live and film shows for Dennis Day. Created, wrote, produced Bob Cummings Show, 1954–59. Wrote Beverly Hillbillies, 1962 to date. Created, prod. wrote Petticoat Junction. Exec. prod. Green Acres series. Wrote motion pictures, Lover Come Back, Bedtime Story.

HENREID, PAUL: Actor, Director. b. Trieste, Italy, 1908. e. Maria Theresianishe Acad. Inst. Graphic Arts, Vienna. Son of Carl Alphons Hernried Knight of Wasel-Waldingau. With book pub. taking night courses at Konservatorium, dramatic arts school in Vienna. In Max Reinhardt's Vienna Theat., then in many Austrian plays and films. London: on dramatic stage including Jersey Lily and Victoria Regina. Films: Goodbye Mr. Chips, An Englishman's Home, Nighttrain to Munich. Arrived in N.Y. 1940 for stage play Flight to the West. In Brit. film Night Train. In 1980 awarded Austrian Cross of Honor, 1st Class, for Science and Arts. 1980: Received The American Classic Screen Award from National Film Society. 1983: Texas Film Society Award for Artistic Achievement. 1984: Legend Silver Screen Award. 1988: Golden Star of Honor for meritorious deeds about the land Vienna.
PICTURES INCLUDE: Joan of Paris, Now Voyager, Casablanca, Of Human Bondage, Song of Love, In Our Time, Devotion, Deception, Between Two Worlds, The Spanish Main, Conspirators, Rope of Sand, Last of the Buccaneers, Pardon My French, So Young—So Bad, Stolen Face, Man in Hiding, Pirates of Tripoli; actor: For Men Only. Actor, dir., Acapulco; Actor, prod.: Hollow Triumph, Ten Thousand Bedrooms, etc. Actor; Holiday for Lovers, Never So Few, The Four Horsemen of The Apocalypse, The Great Spy Mission;

dir., Live Fast Die Young, Take Five From Five, Deadringer, Blues For Lovers. Actor: The Madwoman of Chaillot, Colors of Love, Exorcist II: The Heretic; dir., Bracken's World, dir., The Man and the City (dir.), 1972–73, Starred in Don Juan in Hell on major theatrical tour in the U.S. and Canada for 6 months.
TELEVISION: Dir. of TV films for Revue Productions, Warner, CBS, Screen Gems, Universal, 20th Century-Fox Studios, Film: Any Number Can Kill and many other films and series as actor and director.

HENRY, BUCK: Actor, Writer. b. New York, NY, 1930. r.n. Henry Zuckerman. e. Dartmouth Coll. Acted in Life with Father, tour, 1948; Fortress of Glass, Circle in the Square; Bernardine, Bdwy; 1952–54, U.S. Army; No Time for Sergeants, Nat'l. Co.; The Premise, improvis. theatre, off-Bwy; TV's The Steve Allen Show, writer, performer; That Was the Week That Was, writer, performer.
TELEVISION: Garry Moore Show; Steve Allen Show; Get Smart, co-creator with Mel Brooks, story editor; producer of Captain Nice series, Alfred Hitchcock Presents (1985, actor and s.p.), Falcon Crest (series).
PICTURES INCLUDE: The Troublemaker; The Graduate (s.p.), Catch 22 (s.p. & actor); Taking Off, Candy (s.p.), The Owl and the Pussycat (s.p.), What's Up, Doc?, The Day of the Dolphin (s.p.), The Man Who Fell to Earth, Heaven Can Wait (actor, co-dir., co-s.p.), Old Boyfriends, Gloria, First Family (s.p., dir., act.), Protocol (s.p.), Aria (actor), Dark Before Dawn.

HENRY, FRED: Producer. b. Los Angeles, CA, May 30. e. U. of Southern California, journalism and business administration. CBS-LA radio station KNX newscaster, writer; news, spec. events dir., KMPC-LA. Co-News commentator, CBS, Let's Talk Over the News; Served, U.S.N. Office of Naval Intelligence, Radio Relations Officer on Staff of Supreme Allied Commander, C-B-I Theatre, Admiral Lord Louis Mountbatten; officer, chg. short-wave broadcasting, AFRS, S.F.; 1945; appointed news, spec. events dir., KLAC, Don Fedderson; prg. dir. asst. gen. mgr., prg. dir. combined radio-tv operations, KLAC; res. KLAC, Jan. 1954, as vice-pres., exec. prod., Don Fedderson Prod.; supv. prod.: The Millionaire, Do You Trust Your Wife, Betty White Show, Date With Angels, Liberace, Life with Elizabeth, Who Do You Trust; My Three Sons, 1960; Family Affair, 1966; To Rome With Love, 1969; Henry Fonda Show, 1970.

HENRY, JUSTIN: Actor. b. Rye, NY, May 25, 1971. Debut at 8 in Kramer vs. Kramer, 1979.
PICTURES: Sixteen Candles, Martin's Day, Sweet Hearts Dance.
TELEVISION: Tiger Town.

HENSLEY, PAMELA: Actress. b. Los Angeles, CA, Oct. 3, 1950. Game show model on the New Treasure Hunt at age 18. Under contract to Universal Studios for seven years, appearing in TV series and movies.
PICTURES: Buck Rogers, Rollerball, Doc Savage, Double Exposure.
TELEVISION: Movies: Any Member Can Kill, Mrs. R., Kingston, Confidential. Series: Toma, Banacek, The Six Million Dollar Man, Switch, Marcus Welby, Buck Rogers, 240 Robert, Matt Houston.

HENSON, JIM: Producer, Director, Writer. b. Greenville, MS, Sept. 24, 1936. e. U. of Maryland. Early TV work with Washington station, appearing with puppets he built called The Muppets. Did commercials in Washington area, followed by bookings on Today, Tonight shows and Ed Sullivan Show. Followed with Sesame Street, The Muppet Show, Fraggle Rock, The Storyteller, and series of TV specials he produced and/or directed. Heads own production company, Jim Henson Productions. First theatrical feature: The Muppet Movie, 1979.
PICTURES: The Great Muppet Caper (dir.), The Dark Crystal, (co-prod.), co-dir.), The Muppets Take Manhattan, Labyrinth, The Witches (exec. prod.).

HENSON, LISA: Executive. e. Harvard U. Joined Warner Bros., 1983, as exec. asst. to head of prod. 1985, named dir. of creative affairs. 1985, promoted to v.p., prod.

HEPBURN, AUDREY: Actress. b. Brussels, May 4, 1929. Appeared on London stage; screen debut in Laughter in Paradise (1951); on B'way in Gigi, Ondine; named Star of Tomorrow, 1954.
PICTURES INCLUDE: One Wild Oat, Young Wives' Tales, Lavender Hill Mob, Secret People, Roman Holiday (Academy Award, best actress, 1953), Sabrina, War and Peace, Funny Face, Love in the Afternoon, Green Mansions, The Nun's Story, The Unforgiven, Breakfast at Tiffany's, Paris When It Sizzles, Charade, My Fair Lady, Two for the Road, Wait Until Dark, Robin and Marian, Bloodline, They All Laughed.
TELEVISION: Producers Showcase, Mayerling, 1957; Love Among Thieves, 1986.

HEPBURN, KATHARINE: Actress. b. Hartford, CT, Nov. 8, 1909. On stage in Death Takes a Holiday, Warrior's Husband, The Lake, The Philadelphia Story, (film version) 1940), As You

Like It, Millionairess. Film debut A Bill of Divorcement (1932); then Christopher Strong and won Academy Award same year for Morning Glory. Returned to stage in Merchant of Venice, Taming of the Shrew, Measure for Measure, Coco, A Matter of Gravity, West Side Waltz. Author: The Making of the African Queen, 1987.
PICTURES INCLUDE: A Bill of Divorcement, Christopher Strong, Morning Glory, Little Women, Spitfire, The Little Minister, Alice Adams, Sylvia Scarlett, Mary of Scotland, A Woman Rebels, Quality Street, Stage Door, Bringing Up Baby, Holiday, The Philadelphia Story, Woman of the Year, Keeper of the Flame, Dragon Seed, Without Love, Song of Love, State of the Union, Adam's Rib, Sea of Grass, African Queen, Pat and Mike, Summertime, Iron Petticoat, The Rainmaker, Desk Set, Suddenly Last Summer, Long Day's Journey Into Night, Guess Who's Coming to Dinner (Acad. Award), Lion in Winter (Acad. Award), The Madwoman of Chaillot, The Trojan Women, A Delicate Balance, Rooster Cogburn, Olly, Olly, Oxen Free, On Golden Pond (Acad. Award), Grace Quigley.
TELEVISION: The Glass Menagerie, Love Among the Ruins (Emmy Award), The Corn Is Green, Mrs. Delafield Wants To Marry, Laura Lansing Slept Here.

HEPPEL, ALAN: Executive. e. Harvard U., B.A., Yale U., Stanford Law Sch. With Haldeman and Peckerman as associate, practicing entertainment law. 1985, joined Paramount Pictures as atty. for M.P. Group. Member, California Bar Assn.

HERALD, PETER: Executive. e. U. of California at L.A., B.A. US Gov't. film officer in Germany 4 years. In charge of continental European prod. operation, Walt Disney Prods., 6 years. Supervisory prod. manager, Columbia Pictures, 3 years.
PICTURES INCLUDE: assoc. prod.: Almost Angels, Magnificent Rebel, Miracle of the White Stallions, Waltz King, Emil and the Detectives, The Young Loner; prod. supr.: There Was a Crooked Man, Soldier Blue; co-prod., Outrageous Fortune, Ballerina, National Lampoon's Class Reunion, Doctor Detroit, D. C. Cab; assoc. prod.; The Great Waltz, Assignment: Vienna, Crazy World of Julius Vrooder, Foul Play, Nightwing. Also: W. W. and the Dixie Dancekings, Mandingo, W. C. Fields and Me, Alex and the Gypsy, Silver Streak, Fire Sale, Star Wars.

HERB, THOMAS: Executive. Joined Warner Bros. Intl. 1981 as trainee; 1981–82 in Australia, also as trainee, before moving to Brazil as asst. gen. mgr., 1982–84. Returned to Burbank 1984 as asst. dir. of sls. 1985, named dir. of sls. for WBI.

HERDER, W. ED: Producer. b. New York, NY. U. of Miami, B.B.A. Pres. and chm. of bd., Worldfilm Corp. Financial investor in many m.p. and TV prods.
PICTURES INCLUDE: Without Each Other, Force of Impulse, Black Cobra, Shoot, Never Too Young to Rock, The Siberian Move, The Gang, Intercept, Scenes from a Murder.
TELEVISION: The World of Brigitte Bardot, The Goldie Hawn Special, The Rolling Stones in Concert, The Janis Joplin Special, The Young Rebels, Hollywood: The Magic Kingdom.

HERMAN, NORMAN: Producer, Director. b. Newark, NJ, Feb. 10, 1924. e. Rutgers U., New York U. Was accountant in California; in 1955 switched to film ind., joining American Int'l Pictures. Headed AIP prod. dept. 4 years, incl. prod., postprod., labor negotiations, supervising story dept., etc. Now pres. of Zide-Herman Co., Inc.
PICTURES INCLUDE: Prod. except as noted: Sierra Stranger, Tokyo After Dark (also dir.), Hot Rod Girl, Hot Rod Rumble, Crime Beneath Seas, Look in any Window, Mondy Teeno (also dir., co-s.p.), Glory Stompers, Three in the Attic, Bloody Mama, Pretty Boy Floyd, Dunwich, Three in the Cellar, Angel Unchained, Bunny O'Hare, Psych-Out, Killers Three, Frogs, Blacula, Legend of Hell House, Dirty Mary Crazy Larry.
TELEVISION: Writer: Robert Taylor Detectives, Iron Horse, Invaders, Adam 12, Lancer. Director-Producer: Hannibal Cobb, You Are the Judge.

HERMAN, PEE-WEE: Actor, Writer. r.n. Paul Rubenfeld. Professional name Paul Reubens. b. Sarasota, FL, July, 1952.
As Paul Reubens, appeared as Pinocchio on Faerie Tale Theatre. First performed with The Pee-wee Herman Show, a live show which gave 5 months of sold-out performances at the Roxy in L.A. and was later taped for HBO special. Guest appearances on Late Night With David Letterman, The Gong Show and The Dating Game before film debut in Pee-wee's Big Adventure.
PICTURES: Pee-wee's Big Adventure (also co-s.p.); Big Top Pee-Wee (also co-s.p., co-prod.).
TELEVISION: Pinocchio (as Paul Reubens, Faerie Tale Theatre), Pee-wee's Playhouse (creator, co-dir., co-writer; 6 Emmys).

HERMAN, PINKY: Journalist, Songwriter. b. New York, NY, Dec. 23, 1905. e. New York U. Song writer; member, ASCAP. Counsel member, S.P.A.; writer, M.P. News, 1930; 1934;

charter member, Songwriters Protective Assoc.; writer, M.P. Daily, 1935–43; columnist, Radio Daily, 1943–50; TV columnist for M.P. Daily. Retired, 1973. Councilman; The Lambs. Exec. prod., Lambs Club Productions (1960–69). Former TV editor, Quigley Publications.
SONGS INCLUDE: (collab.) Face the Sun, All Around the Town, Boom Ta Ra Ra, It Must Be LUV, Piano Teacher Song, Manhattan Merry Go Round, Lucky, I'm Still in Love With You, Havin' A Wonderful Time, Where Can You Be, Seven Days a Week, Texas Lullaby, Lighthouse in the Harbor, I'm Cuckoo Over Your, It's a Coincidence, If I Had a Million Dollars, Masquerade of Love, Mademoiselle Hortensia, Come Back to Me My Love, Someday When Shadows Fall, Myrtle the Turtle & Flip the Frog, Cowboy Isn't Speaking to His Horse, Gotta Horse That Loves to Rhumba, Girl on My Grandfather's Shaving Mug, Definition Song, Got a Gal in a Town Way Out West, Sing Something Irish, Little Sweetheart of the Mountains, Make a Million, Music Sets Me Free, She's the Daughter of the Sweetheart of Sigma Chi, Who Wants Love, Good-Lookin' It's Good Lookin' at You, Carib Gold, What Makes the Rainbow, Right Across de Ribber, Shadows in the Moonlight, Bible My Mother Left to Me, Poor Little Doll, Little Bit O'Rythm in the Best of Us, Lovely Lady, When a Girl's in Love, Never Leave A Lady When She Loves You, Without You, That's The Way to Live, It's Time to Sing, Acapulco (By The Sea).

HEROUX, CLAUDE: Producer. b. Montreal, Canada, Jan. 26, 1942. e. U. of Montreal. 1979, prod. v.p., Film Plan Intl., Montreal.
PICTURES INCLUDE: Valerie; L'Initiation; L'Amour Humain; Je t'aime; Echoes of a Summer; Jacques Brel Is Alive and Well and Living in Paris; Breaking Point; Born for Hell; Hog Wild; City of Fire; Dirty Tricks; Gas; Visiting Hours; Videodrome; The Funny Farm; Going Berserk; Of Unknown Origin; Covergirl.
TELEVISION: The Park is Mine, Popeye Doyle.

HERRMANN, EDWARD: Actor. b. Washington, DC, July 31, 1943. e. Bucknell U. Postgrad. Fulbright scholar, London Acad. Music and Dramatic Art 1968–69. Acted with Dallas Theater Center 4 years.
THEATER: Moonchildren, Mrs. Warren's Profession (Tony Award, supp. actor), Journey's End, The Beach House, The Philadelphia Story, Plenty, Tom and Viv, Julius Caesar, Not About Heroes.
PICTURES: The Paper Chase, The Day of the Dolphin, The Great Gatsby, The Great Waldo Pepper, The Betsy, The North Avenue Irregulars, Brass Target, Take Down, Harry's War, Reds, Death Valley, A Little Sex, Annie, Mrs. Soffel, The Purple Rose of Cairo, Overboard, Big Business.
TELEVISION: Beacon Hill, Eleanor and Franklin, Eleanor and Franklin: The White House Years, The Lou Gehrig Story, Portrait of a Stripper, Freedom Road, MASH, Valley Forge, Sorrows of Gin, The Private History of The Campaign That Failed, Murrow, Dear Liar, The Gift of Life, Concealed Enemies, The Return of Hickey.

HERSHEY, BARBARA: Actress. r.n. Barbara Herzstein. b. Los Angeles, CA, Feb. 5, 1948. e. Hollywood H.S. Briefly in the mid-1970s acted under the name Barbara Seagull. Screen debut in With Six You Get Eggroll.
PICTURES INCLUDE: Last Summer, Heaven With a Gun, The Liberation of Lord Byron Jones, The Baby Maker, The Pursuit of Happiness, Boxcar Bertha, Dealing, Angela—Love Comes Quietly, Vrooder's Hooch, Diamonds, The Last Hard Men, The Stunt Man, Choice of Weapons, Take This Job and Shove It, The Entity, The Right Stuff, The Natural, Hannah and Her Sisters, Hoosiers, Tin Men, Shy People, A World Apart (best actress award, Cannes, 1988), The Last Temptation of Christ, Beaches.
TELEVISION: Gidget, The Monroes (series), The Farmer's Daughter, Run for Your Life, The Invaders, Daniel Boone, CBS Playhouse, Chrysler Theatre, Kung Fu, Alfred Hitchcock Presents (1985). Movies: From Here to Eternity, My Wicked, Wicked Ways, Passion Flower, In the Glitter Palace, Just a Little Inconvenience, Sunshine Christmas, Angel on My Shoulder, A Man Called Intrepid.

HERSKOVITZ, ARTHUR M.: Executive. b. Mukden, China. Nov. 28, 1920. e. City Coll. of New York, 1939. Joined RKO, scenario dept., 1939. U.S. Army, 1942–46; appt. mgr., RKO Radio Pictures of Peru, 1955; RKO Pict. Peru, 1958; Warner Bros., Peru, 1958–64; MGM, Panama, 1965–67; MGM rep. in Japan, 1968; Far East supvr., 1970; Joined National General Pictures, 1973 as foreign sls. mgr. In 1974 appt. dir. of sls., JAD Films Int'l.; named v.p., 1977; pres., 1979.

HERZOG, WERNER: Producer, Director. r.n. Werner Stipetic. b. Sachrang, Germany, September 5, 1942. e. U. of Munich, Duquesne U., Pittsburgh. First st.p. 1957; 1961 worked nights in steel factory to raise money for films; 1966, worked for U.S. National Aeronautics and Space Admin.
PICTURES INCLUDE: Signs of Life, Even Dwarfs Started Small, Fata Morgana, The Land of Silence and Darkness; Aguirre—Wrath of God, The Great Ecstasy of the Sculptor Steiner,

Every Man for Himself and God Against All, Soufriere, Heart of Glass, Stroszek, Kaspar Hauser, Nosferatu, Woyzeck (also s.p.), Fitzcarraldo, Where the Green Ants Dream, Slave Coast (dir., s.p.).

HERTZ, WILLIAM: Executive. b. Wishek, ND, Dec. 5, 1923. e. U. of MN. Began theatre career in 1939; 1946 joined Fox West Coast Theatres; theatre mgr., booking dept.; 1965 appointed Los Angeles first-run district mgr.; promoted to Pacific Coast Division Mgr., National General Corp., 1967; v.p. Southern Pacific Div. Mgr., National General Theatres, Inc. 1971. Now with Mann Theatres as dir. of marketing, public relations, and labor relations.

HESSEMAN, HOWARD: Actor. b. Salem, OR, Feb. 27, 1940. Started with the San Francisco group, The Committee and worked as a disc jockey in San Francisco in the late 1960s.
PICTURES: Petulia, Billy Jack, Steelyard Blues, Shampoo, The Sunshine Boys, Jackson County Jail, The Big Bus, The Other Side of Midnight, Silent Movie, Honky Tonk Freeway, Private Lessons, Loose Shoes, Doctor Detroit, Spinal Tap, Police Academy 2—Their First Assignment, Heat, Amazon Women on the Moon.
TELEVISION: Series: Mary Hartman, Mary Hartman, Fernwood 2night, WKRP in Cincinnati, One Day at a Time, Head of the Class. Movies: Hustling, The Amazing Howard Hughes, The Ghost on Flight 401; The Great American Traffic Jam, Loretta Lynn—The Lady The Legend, Victims, One Shoe Makes It Murder, How To Be a Man, The Great Diamond Robbery.

HESSLER, GORDON: Producer, Director. b. Berlin, Germany, 1930. e. Reading U., England. Dir., vice pres., Fordel Films, Inc., 1950–58; dir., St. John's Story (Edinborough Film Festival), March of Medicine Series, Dr. Albert Lasker Award; story edit., Alfred Hitchcock Presents 1960–62; assoc. prod., dir., Alfred Hitchcock Hour, 1962; prod., Alfred Hitchcock Hour; prod., dir., Universal TV 1964–66.
PICTURES INCLUDE: The Woman Who Wouldn't Die, The Last Shot You Hear, The Oblong Box, Scream and Scream Again, Cry of the Banshee, Murders of the Rue Morgue, Sinbad's Golden Voyage, Medusa, Embassy, Puzzle, Pray for Death, Rage of Honour, The Misfit Brigade, The Girl on the Swing (also s.p.), Out on Bail.
TELEVISION: Alfred Hitchcock Presents, 1960–62; Alfred Hitchcock Hour, 1962–65; Run For Your Life, Convoy, Bob Hope Chrysler Show, 1964–66; ABC Suspense Movies of the Week, ABC Movies of the Week, 1973. Lucas Tanner, Night Stalker, Amy Prentiss, Switch; Kung Fu, Sara, Hawaii Five-O; Blue Knight; Wonder Woman, Master, Chips, Tales of the Unexpected.   Pilot: Tender Warriors.

HESTON, CHARLTON: Actor. b. Evanston, IL, Oct. 4, 1924. e. Northwestern U. Sch. of Speech. Radio, stage, TV experience. Following coll. served 8 yrs. 11th Air Force, Aleutians. After war, co-acted (leads) and dir. with wife, Thomas Wolfe Memorial Theatre, Asheville, NC in State of the Union, Glass Menagerie; member, Katharine Cornell's Co., during first year on Broadway; Anthony and Cleopatra, other Bway. plays, Leaf and Bough, Cockadoodle Doo; Studio One (TV): Macbeth, Taming of the Shrew, Of Human Bondage, Julius Caesar; 1988: The Caine Mutiny Court-Martial (director, in China).
RECENT THEATER: A Man for All Seasons, The Caine Mutiny.
PICTURES INCLUDE: Dark City, Greatest Show on Earth, The Savage, Ruby Gentry, President's Lady, Pony Express, Arrowhead, Bad for Each Other, Naked Jungle, Secret of the Incas, Far Horizons, Lucy Gallant, Private War of Major Benson, Ten Commandments, The Maverick, Ben Hur, Wreck of the Mary Deare, El Cid, The Pigeon That Took Rome, 55 Days at Peking, Major Dundee, The Agony and the Ecstasy, The War Lord, The Greatest Story Ever Told, Khartoum, The Battle Horns, Planet of the Apes, Beneath the Planet of the Apes, The Omega Man, Antony and Cleopatra (star & dir.), Skyjacked, Soylent Green, The Three Musketeers, Airport 1975, Earthquake, The Four Musketeers, The Last Hard Men, Midway, Two Minute Warning, The Prince and the Pauper (Crossed Swords); Gray Lady Down, The Awakening, Mother Lode (also dir.).
TELEVISION: Chiefs, The Nairobi Affair, The Colbys, The Proud Man, A Man For All Seasons (also dir.).

HETZEL, RALPH D.: Executive. b. Corvallis, OR, August 18, 1912. e. Pennsylvania State U., A.B., 1933; U. ef London, 1935–36. Private secy. to Gov. Pinchot of PA, 1933–35; did research & study, 1936–39; exec. secty. natl. hdqts., CIO, 1937–40; economic dir., 1938–40; in service, 1942–45. Consultant on labor, Natl. Selective Service hdqts., 1942; manpower consultant War Prod. Bd., 1942–43; dept. vice chmn., manpower requirements, W.P.B., 1943–45; acting vice-chmn., 1945; dir. Office of Labor Requirements, Civilian Prod. Admin., 1945–46; asst. to Secy. of Commerce, U.S. Dept. of Comm., 1946–48; asst. to secty. & dir. Office of Program Planning, 1948–51; asst. admin., Economic Stabilization Agency, 1951; exec. v.p. Motion Picture Association, MP Export Assn., 1951–71, Past president, International Federation of Film Producers Assns.; member of Board of Trustees, California Institute of the Arts and of Pennsylvania State U.; member of Film Advisory Committee of Museum of Modern Art, and of Advisory Council of Edward R. Murrow Center of Public Diplomacy at Tufts U. Dean, Coll. of Fine and Professional Arts, Professor of Art, Kent State U., 1971–76; provost and vice president, academic affairs, California Inst. of the Arts 1976–80; faculty member, 1976–.

HEYMAN, JOHN: Producer. b. England, 1933. e. Oxford U. Started with British TV, creating writing and producing entertainment and documentary programs; expanded into field of personal management, forming International Artists, largest independent p.r. agency in Europe. 1963, formed World Film Services, Ltd. to produce, package and finance films. 1973, formed Genesis Project, educational film co. whose first venture was to translate the Bible onto film.
PICTURES: Privilege, Boom!, Secret Ceremony, Twinky, Bloomfield, The Go-Between, Daniel, Beyond the Limit, The Dresser, A Passage to India (co-prod.), Martin's Day, Steaming, D.A.R.Y.L.

HEYWOOD, ANNE: Actress. b. England, 1931. m. late producer Raymond Stross.
PICTURES INCLUDE: Checkpoint, Doctor at Large, Dangerous Exile, The Depraved, Violent Playground, Floods of Fear, Heart of a Man, Upstairs and Downstairs, A Terrible Beauty, Carthage in Flames, Petticoat Pirates, Stork Talk, Over My Dead Body, The Very Edge, 90 Degrees in the Shade, The Fox, A Run on Gold, The Most Dangerous Man in the World, The Nun of Monza, I Want What I Want, and Presumed Dead.
TELEVISION: The Equalizer.

HICKMAN, DARRYL: Actor. b. Hollywood, CA, July 28, 1930. Started screen career 1938 with The Starmaker. Was with CBS as exec. prod., daytime programming. Returned to acting with Network in 1977.
PICTURES INCLUDE: Grapes of Wrath, Young People, Jackass Mail, Northwest Rangers, Keeper of the Flame, And Now Tomorrow, Salty O'Rourke, Captain Eddie, Kiss and Tell, Leave Her to Heaven, Black Gold, Happy Years, Submarine Command, Destination Gobi, Island in the Sky, Sea of Lost Ships, Southwest Passage, The Human Comedy, Men of Boys Town, Fighting Father Dunn, Tea and Sympathy, Network, Looker, Sharky's Machine.

HICKS, CATHERINE: Actress. b. Scottsdale, AZ, Aug. 6, 1951. e. Notre Dame. On Bdwy. in Tribute.
PICTURES: Death Valley, Better Late Than Never, Garbo Talks, The Razor's Edge, Fever Pitch, Star Trek IV: The Voyage Home; Peggy Sue Got Married, Like Father, Like Son; Souvenir, Secret Ingredient, Daddy's Little Girl.
TELEVISION: Ryan's Hope. Movies: The Bad News Bears, Marilyn—the Untold Story, Valley of the Dolls 1981, Tucker's Witch, Happy Endings, Laguna Heat, Childsplay.

HIFT, FRED: Executive. b. Vienna, Nov. 27, 1924. e. Vienna, London, Chicago. Early career reporter Chicago Sun and radio work with CBS News, New York. 1946 joined Boxoffice magazine; 1947 Quigley Publications; 1950 Variety. 1960 began career as publicist on Exodus. 1961 dir. pub., The Longest Day for Darryl Zanuck. 1962 joined Fox in Paris as ad-pub. dir. for Europe. 1964 became dir. European prod. pub. with headquarters London. Formed own pub., p.r. co., Fred Hift Associates, 1970. 1979, joined Columbia Pictures as dir. of eastern ad-pub operations in N.Y.; 1980, to United Artists as intl. adv./pub. v.p. Left to establish Fred Hift Associates, intl. mktg. consultant in New York. 1983, joined Almi Pictures as v.p., mktg. 1985, reactivated F.H.A.

HILL, ARTHUR: Actor. b. Saskatchewan, Canada, Aug. 1, 1922. e. U. of British Columbia. Moved to England in 1948, spending ten years in varied stage & screen pursuits; starred on Broadway in The Matchmaker, Home of the Brave, The Male Animal, Look Homeward Angel, All the Way Home, Who's Afraid of Virginia Woolf? (Tony Award), later in More Stately Mansions; film debut in Miss Pilgrim's Progress; other British work includes The Body Said No, Raising A Riot, The Deep Blue Sea.
PICTURES INCLUDE: The Young Doctors, The Ugly American, In the Cool of the Day, Moment to Moment, Harper, Petulia, Don't Let the Angels Fall, The Chairman, The Pursuit of Happiness, Rabbit Run, The Andromeda Strain, The Killer Elite, Future World, A Bridge Too Far, A Little Romance, The Champ, Dirty Tricks, Making Love, The Amateur, One Magic Christmas.
TELEVISION: Owen Marshall, Counselor-At-Law (series). Movies: Death Be Not Proud, Churchill and the Generals, The Guardian.

HILL, BENJAMIN (BENNY): TV performer. b. Southampton, England, Jan. 21, 1925. TV debut 1952; since many TV appearances including Showcase, Benny Hill Show; Midsummer Night's Dream, 1964; winner Daily Mail Award TV

personality of the year 1954; m.p. debut, Who Done It, 1955; Light Up the Sky, 1960; Those Magnificent Men in Their Flying Machines, 1965; Chitty Chitty Bang Bang.

HILL, DEBRA: Producer. b. Haddonfield, NJ. Started in film business with Adventure Films helping make documentaries in Africa, the Caribbean, etc. Career on feature films started with work as script supvr., asst. and 2nd unit dir. of 13 pictures. Producer's debut with Halloween, 1980, for which also co-wrote script with director John Carpenter.
PICTURES: The Fog (and co-s.p.), Escape from New York, Halloween II (and co-s.p.), Halloween III: Season of the Witch, The Dead Zone, Head Office, Adventures in Babysitting, Big Top Pee Wee (co-prod.), Heartbreak Hotel (co-prod.).

HILL, GEORGE ROY: Director. b. Minneapolis, MN, Dec. 20, 1921. e. Yale U., Trinity Coll., Dublin. Started as actor, Irish theatres and U.S. Shakespeare repertory company, also off-Broadway. Served as Marine pilot in W.W.II and Korean War. Wrote TV play, My Brother's Keeper, for Kraft Theatre, later rose to director with show. TV assignments included A Night to Remember, The Helen Morgan Story, Judgment at Nuremberg. Directed first Broadway play in 1957, Look Homeward Angel, followed by The Gang's All Here, Greenwillow. First film, Period of Adjustment, 1962.
PICTURES INCLUDE: Toys in the Attic, The World of Henry Orient, Hawaii, Thoroughly Modern Millie, Butch Cassidy and the Sundance Kid, Slaughterhouse Five, The Sting, The Great Waldo Pepper, Slap Shot, A Little Romance, The World According to Garp, The Little Drummer Girl, Funny Farm.

HILL, JAMES: Producer, Director, Writer. b. Yorkshire, England. Ent. ind. 1938. Early career as asst. dir. and asst. editor. Wrote and dir. many documentaries incl. Giuseppina (Oscar), The Home-Made Car, several children's features. Dir. The Kitchen, Born Free, The Dock Brief, Lunch Hour, Black Beauty, The Belstone Fox, A Study in Terror, Cuba Si (TV series), A Sunday in September, The Saint TV series, The Avengers, The Wild and the Free, Worzel Gummidge (TV series.) Prod. dir. The Young Visitors (Channel 4).

HILL, TERENCE: Actor. r.n. Mario Girotti. b. Venice, March, 1941. First attracted attention as actor in Visconti's The Leopard, 1963. Gained fame in European-made westerns. Formed Paloma Films.
PICTURES INCLUDE: God Forgives, I Don't, Boot Hill, Ace High, Barbagia, Anger of the Wind, They Call Me Trinity, Trinity Is Still My Name, My Name Is Nobody, Mr. Billion, March or Die; Don Camillo (dir., actor), Renegade Luke (also exec. prod.).

HILL, WALTER: Director, Writer, Producer. b. Long Beach, CA, Jan. 10, 1942. e. Michigan State U.
PICTURES INCLUDE: Writer: Hickey & Boggs, The Getaway, The Thief Who Came to Dinner, The Mackintosh Man, The Drowning Pool. Writer-Director: Hard Times, The Driver, The Warriors, The Long Riders, Southern Comfort, 48 Hrs., Streets of Fire, Alien (co-prod.), Brewster's Millions (dir.), Crossroads (dir.), Blue City (co-prod., co-s.p.), Extreme Prejudice (dir.), Aliens (co-prod, co.-s.p.), Red Heat (dir., co.-prod., co-s.p.).

HILLER, ARTHUR: Director. b. Edmonton, Alberta, Can., Nov. 22, 1923. e. U. of Alberta, U. of Toronto, U. of British Columbia.
TELEVISION: Matinee Theatre, Playhouse 90, Climax, Alfred Hitchcock Presents, Gunsmoke, Ben Casey, Rte. 66, Naked City, The Dick Powell Show.
PICTURES INCLUDE: The Careless Years, Americanization of Emily, Tobruk, The Tiger Makes Out, Popi, The Out-of-Towners, Love Story, Plaza Suite, The Hospital, Man of La Mancha, The Man in the Glass Booth, W. C. Fields and Me, Silver Streak, Nightwing, The In-Laws (also co-prod.), Author, Author; Making Love, Romantic Comedy, Lonely Guy (also prod.), Teachers, Outrageous Fortune, The Hard Way.

HILLER, DAME WENDY: D.B.E., 1975, O.B.E., 1971, Hon. LLD, Manchester, 1984. Actress. b. Bramhall, Cheshire, England, Aug. 15, 1912. e. Winceby House Sch., Bexhill. On stage 1930, Manchester Repertory Theatre, England; then on British tour. London debut 1935 in Love On the Dole; to N.Y., same role 1936. m.p. debut in Lancashire Luck, 1937.
PLAYS: First Gentleman, Cradle Song, Tess of the D'Urbervilles, Heiress, Ann Veronica, Waters of the Moon, Night of the Ball, Old Vic Theatre, Wings of the Dove, Sacred Flame, Battle of Shrivings, Crown Matrimonial, John Gabriel Borkman, Waters of the Moon (revival), Aspern Papers (revival), The Importance of Being Earnest.
PICTURES INCLUDE: Pygmalion, Major Barbara, I Know Where I'm Going, Outcast of the Islands, Single Handed (Sailor of the King), Something of Value, Uncle George, Separate Tables, Sons and Lovers, Toys in the Attic, Man For All Seasons, Murder on the Orient Express, Voyage of The Damned, The Elephant Man, Making Love, The Lonely Passion of Judith Hearne.

TELEVISION: The Curse of King Tut's Tomb, David Copperfield, Witness for the Prosecution, Anne of the Green Gables—The Sequel.

HILLMAN, WILLIAM BRYON: Writer, Director, Producer. b. Chicago, IL, Feb. 3. e. Oklahoma Military Acad., U. of California at L.A. Head of production at Intro-Media Productions; Fairchild Entertainment; Spectro Productions; Double Eagle Entertainment Corp; Excellent Films Inc.; Creative consultant for The Hit 'Em Corp. Presently head of SpectroMedia Entertainment.
PICTURES INCLUDE: Back on the Street (dir., s.p., co-prod.), Loner (dir., s.p., co-prod.), Fast & Furious (dir., s.p.), The Master (dir., s.p.), Lovelines (s.p.), Double Exposure (dir., s.p., co-prod.), The Passage (dir. s.p.), Campus (dir., s.p.), The Photographer (dir., prod., s.p.), The Man From Clover Grove (dir., s.p., co-prod.), Thetus (dir., s.p.), The Trail Ride (dir., s.p., co-prod.), Betta Betta (dir., s.p., prod.).
TELEVISION: Working Together (pilot s.p.), Disco-Theque Pilot (dir., s.p.), Everything Will Be Alright (s.p.), Money (dir., s.p.), RIPA (CBS movie, s.p.).
NOVELS: Silent Changes, The Combination, The Liar, Additives The Perfect Crime, Why Me, The Loner.

HILLERMAN, JOHN: Actor. b. Denison, TX, Dec. 20, 1932. e. U. of Texas. While in U.S. Air Force joined community theatre group and went to New York after completing military service. Studied at American Theatre Wing, leading to summer stock and off-Bdwy.
PICTURES: The Last Picture Show, What's Up Doc?, Paper Moon, At Long Last Love, Lawman, Blazing Saddles, The Day of the Locust, Chinatown, Up the Creek.
TELEVISION: Series: Ellery Queen, The Betty White Show, Magnum P.I. (Emmy Award). Movies: The Law, Kill Me If You Can, A Guide for the Married Woman, Betrayal, Marathon, Battles, Little Gloria . . . Happy at Last, Assault and Matrimony, Street of Dreams.

HINES, GREGORY: Actor-Dancer. b. NY, Feb. 14, 1946. Early career as junior member of family dancing act starting at age 2. Nightclub debut at 5 as Hines Kids with brother Maurice; B'way debut at 8 in The Girl in Pink Tights. Continued dancing with brother until 1973; film debut in Wolfen, 1981.
THEATER: The Last Mistral Show (close out of town), Eubie (Tony nom.), Comin' Uptown, Sophisticated Ladies.
PICTURES: History of the World—Part I, Deal of the Century, The Cotton Club, White Nights, Running Scared, Off Limits, Tap.

HINGLE, PAT: Actor. b. Miami, FL, July 19, 1924. e. U. of Texas, 1949. Studied at Herbert Berghof Studio, American Theatre Wing, Actor's Studio.
THEATRE: End as a Man (NY debut, 1953), The Rainmaker, Festival, Cat on a Hot Tin Roof, Girls of Summer, Dark at the Top of the Stairs, J.B., The Deadly Game, Macbeth and Troilus and Cresida (with American Shakespeare Festival, Stratford, CT.), Strange Interlude, Blues for Mr. Charlie, A Girl Could Get Lucky, The Glass Menagerie, The Odd Couple, Johnny No-Trump, The Price, Child's Play, The Selling of the President, That Championship Season, The Lady from the Sea, A Life, Thomas Edison: Reflections of a Genius (one man show).
RADIO: Voice of America.
PICTURES INCLUDE: On the Waterfront, The Strange One, No Down Payment, Splendor in the Grass, All the Way Home, The Ugly American, Sol Madrid, Hang 'em High, Jigsaw, Norwood, Bloody Mama, WUSA, Corporal Crocker, The Carey Treatment, One Little Indian, The Super Cops, The Gauntlet, When You Comin' Back, Red Ryder, Norma Rae, Sudden Impact, Running Brave, Going Berserk, The Falcon and the Snowman, Brewster's Millions, Baby Boom.
TELEVISION: Gunsmoke, MASH, Blue Skies, (series), Stone, Matlock, Twilight Zone, The Untouchables, Trapper John M.D., Murder She Wrote. Movies: The Lady from Yesterday, LBJ: The Early Years, If Tomorrow Comes, Elvis, The Last Angry Man, Sunshine Christmas, Of Mice and Men, Stranger on My Land, The Town Bully, War and Remembrance.

HINKLE, ROBERT: Actor, Producer, Director. b. Brownfield, TX, July 25, 1930. e. Brownfield H.S. Joined Rodeo Cowboys Association, 1950 and rodeoed professionally until 1953 when began acting career in Outlaw Treasure. Pres. Hinkle Pictures, Inc.
PICTURES INCLUDE: Giant, All the Fine Young Cannibals, Hud, The First Texan, Dakota Incident, Gun the Man Down, The Oklahoman, First Traveling Saleslady, No Place to Land, Under Fire, Speed Crazy, The Gunfight at Dodge City, Broken Land, Law in Silver City, Ole Rex (award for Family Entertainment), Born Hunter, Trauma, Something Can Be Done, Mr. Chat, Stuntman, Hud, Jumping Frog Jubilee, Mr. Chat-Mexico Safari, Trail Ride, Virginia City Cent., Texas Today, Texas Long Horns, Kentucky Thoroughbred Racing, Produced & Directed country music, Guns of a Stranger, Old Rex.
TELEVISION: Test Pilot, Dial 111, Juvenile Squad, X13 Vertijet, Cellist Extraordinary, Sunday Challenge.

HIRD, THORA: Actress. b. Morecambe, Lancashire, Eng., May 28, 1914. e. The Nelson Sch., Morecambe.
PICTURES INCLUDE: (Screen debut, 1940) The Black Sheep of Whitehall; Street Corner, Turn the Key Softly, Personal Affair, The Great Game, Storks Don't Talk, Shop Soiled, For Better or Worse; Love Match, One Good Turn, Quatermass Experiment, Simon and Laura, Lost, Sailor Beware, Home and Away, Good Companions, The Entertainer, A Kind of Loving, Term of Trial, Bitter Harvest, Rattle of a Simple Man, Some Will, Some Won't, The Nightcomers, Consuming Passions.
TELEVISION: The Winslow Boy, The Bachelor, What Happens to Love, The Witching Hour, So Many Children, The Queen Came By, Albert Hope, All Things Bright and Beautiful, Say Nothing, Meet the Wife, Who's a Good Boy Then? I AM! Dixon of Dock Green, Romeo and Juliet, The First Lady, Ours Is a Nice House, The Foxtrot, Seasons, She Stoops to Conquer, Villa Maroc, When We Are Married, In Loving Memory, Flesh and Blood, Your Songs of Praise Choice, Hallelujah, Happiness, That's the Main Thing, Intensive Care, In Loving Memory, Praise Be, Last of the Summer Wine, The Fall.

HIRSCH, JUDD: Actor. b. New York, NY, March 15, 1935. e. City Coll. of New York. Studied physics but turned to acting; first acting job in 1962 performing with stock co. in Colorado. Returned to N.Y. to work on stage and since has also done films and TV.
THEATER: Barefoot in the Park; Scuba Duba; Mystery Play; Hot L Baltimore; King of the United States; Knock, Knock; Chapter Two; Talley's Folly (Obie Award), I'm Not Rappaport (Tony Award).
PICTURES INCLUDE: King of the Gypsies, Serpico, Ordinary People, Without a Trace, The Goodbye People, Teachers, Running on Empty.
TELEVISION: Medical Story, Delvecchio, Taxi (series), Dear John (series),. Movies: Fear on Trial, Valentino, The Law, The Keegans, Brotherly Love, First Steps, The Last Resort, The Halloween That Almost Wasn't, The Great Escape: The Final Chapter.

HIRSCHFIELD, ALAN J.: Executive. b. Oklahoma City, OK; Oct. 10, 1935. e. U. of Oklahoma, B.A.; Harvard Business School, M.B.A. Film Corp. V.P., Allen & Co., 1959–66; Financial v.p. & dir. Warner/7 Arts, 1967–68; v.p. & dir., American Diversified Enterprises, 1969–73; pres. & chief exec. officer, Columbia Pictures Industries, 1973–78; consultant, Warner Communications, 1979, 1980–85, chm. and chief exec. officer, 20th Century-Fox. Current: Investments.
Vice Chairman and trustee: Cancer Research Institute. Director: American Film Institute. Stendig Corp., Jackson Hole Land Trust, Motown Records.

HIRSHAN, LEONARD: Theatrical Agent. b. New York, NY, Dec. 27, 1927. e. New York U. Joined William Morris Agency as agent trainee, New York, 1951. Agent legit theatre & TV dept. 1952–54. Sr. exec. agent M.P. dept., California office, 1955; sr. v.p., 1983; head of m.p. dept., west coast, 1986.

HIRT, AL: Musician. b. New Orleans, LA, Nov. 7, 1922. e. Cincinnati Conservatory of Music. Military service four years. Played with Tommy and Jimmy Dorsey bands, Ray McKinley and Horace Heidt; appeared, Dunes Hotel, Harrah's Club, Basin Street East, Cloisters, Palmer House, Eden Roc Hotel, Greek Theatre. European tour concerts. Inaugural Ball, President John F. Kennedy, Jan., 1961.
TELEVISION: Dinah Shore Show, Jack Paar Show, Ed Sullivan, NBC Special Home For the Holidays, Bell Telephone Hour Rainbow of Stars, Andy Williams Show, Tonight Show, Today Show, Perry Como Show, Lively Ones, Jerry Lewis Show.
PICTURES INCLUDE: World By Night, Rome Adventure.
RECORDINGS: RCA: The Greatest Horn in the World, Al—He's the King—Hirt, Horn-A-Plenty, Al Hirt at the Mardi Gras, Trumpet & Strings, Our Man in New Orleans, Honey in the Horn, Beauty and the Beard, Pop Goes the Trumpet, Boston Pops.

HITZIG, RUPERT: Producer. e. Harvard. At CBS as doc. writer-producer-director; later moved into dramas and comedy. Alan King's partner in King-Hitzig Prods.
TELEVISION: Much Ado About Nothing; The Wonderful World of Jonathan Winters; Playboy After Dark; How to Pick Up Girls; Return to Earth, Saturday Night Live, television series and numerous specials.
PICTURES: Electra Glide in Blue; Happy Birthday, Gemini; Cattle Annie and Little Britches; Jaws 3-D; Wolfen (also 2nd unit dir.); The Last Dragon, The Squeeze, Cry Devil (dir.).

HOBERMAN, DAVID: Executive. Started career as prod. exec. with TAT Communications for five years. 1982–85, worked as m.p. agent with Writers and Artists Agency and later at Ziegler Associates and ICM. 1985, named v.p. of prod. for Walt Disney Pictures based at studio. 1987, promoted to sr. v.p., prod. 1988, named president, production.

Hob-Hol

HOBIN, BILL: TV Producer, Director. r.n. Charles W. Hobin; b. Evanston, IL, Nov. 12, 1923. e. U. of Southern California. Prod. mgr., Coronet Instructional Films, Glenview, IL; dir., Garroway at Large, Wayne King Show from Chic., 1949–51; dir., Assignment Manhunt; Nothing But the Best; Les Paul and Mary Ford; Your Show of Shows, 1951–54; assoc. prod.-dir., Max Liebman Presents (Spectaculars), prod. dir. Fred Waring Show, Andy Williams Show, Pat Boone, Timex All-Star Jazz Show. dir. Your Hit Parade. Prod.-dir. The Golden Circle, 1959; The Bell Telephone Hour, 1959–60; The American Cowboy; Sing Along with Mitch, 1960–63; dir., Judy Garland Show; prod., dir., Victor Borge at Carnegie Hall; dir., m.p. Chrysler Show-Go-Round, N.Y. World's Fair. Dir.: Meredith Willson Special; Jack Jones on the Move Special; Red Skelton Hour, 1964–68; prod.; Red Skelton Hour, 1968–70; prod. and dir. The Bill Cosby Special I, 1968; prod., dir., The Tim Conway Comedy Hour; prod., dir. The CBS Newcomers series; dir. An Evening With My Three Sons special, prod., dir. Michel Legrand Special; prod., dir. Fred Astaire special; director, Maude; director, A Touch of Grace; prod.-dir.: Dinah, Won't You Please Come Home!; Bobby Goldsboro Show (syn); Your Hit Parade; prod.-dir. Flip Wilson Special, Dionne Warwick Special, Wayne Newton Special, all 1975; 1976— dir., Welcome (Back), Kotter, Prod.-dir., Monty Hall's Variety Special. dir., Bert Convy Show; dir., George Burns Special; McLean Stevenson Show; dir., Three's Company. Producer-director Bob Hope Specials, (1978–79); director Celebrity Challenge of the Sexes, 1979; director, Steve Allen Special; director, No Soap Radio, 1982.

HOBLEY, McDONALD: b. Port Stanley, Falkland Islands. e. South America; Brighton Coll. Early career in repertory cos., tours, etc.; entered TV in 1946 as TV announcer; won Nat'l TV Award for Personality of the Year, 1953–54; resigned from BBC, 1956; now freelance.
PICTURES INCLUDE: Checkpoint, The Entertainer.
TELEVISION: Holiday Town Parade, The Dave King Show, Tell the Truth, The Tommy Steele Show, Close-up.

HOCK, MORT: Executive. b. New York, NY, June 24, 1929. Blaine-Thompson Agency; A. E. Warner Bros., 1948; David Merrick B'way Prod., 1958; asst. adv. mgr., Paramount Pictures Corp., 1960; adv. mgr., United Artists Corp., 1962; dir. adv., United Artists Corp., July 1964; adv. dir., Para., 1965; v.p. advertising and public relations, Paramount Pict. Corp., 1968–71; v.p., marketing, Rastar Prods., 1971; exec. v.p., Charles Schlaifer & Co., 1974; sr. v.p. entertainment div., DDB Needham World-wide, 1983.

HODGE, PATRICIA: Actress. b. Lincolnshire, England, 1946.
PICTURES: The Elephant Man, Betrayal, Sunset, Falcon's Malteser.
TELEVISION: Behind Enemy Lines.

HOFFMAN, DUSTIN: b. Los Angeles, CA, Aug. 8, 1937. e. Los Angeles Conservatory of Music, Santa Monica Coll., Pasadena Playhouse, 1958. m. Lisa Hoffman. Worked as an attendant at a psychiatric institution, a demonstrator in Macy's toy dept., and a waiter. First stage role in Yes Is for a Very Young Man, at Sarah Lawrence Coll. Acted in summer stock, television and dir. at community theatre. Broadway and Off Broadway plays include: 1964, Harry, Noon and Night (American Place Theatre); 1966, Journey of the Fifth Horse (APT, won Obie Award); Eh? (won Vernon Rice & Theatre World Award); Jimmy Shine. Asst. Dir.: A View from the Bridge. Dir. (1974): All Over Town; 1984, Death of a Salesman (Drama Desk Award).
TELEVISION: Journey of the Fifth Horse, The Star Wagons, Death of a Salesman (Emmy Award).
PICTURES INCLUDE: The Tiger Makes Out (debut, 1967), Madigan's Millions, The Graduate (Acad. Award nom.); Midnight Cowboy (Acad. Award nom.); John and Mary, Little Big Man, Who Is Harry Kellerman?, Straw Dogs; Alfredo, Alfredo; Papillon, Lenny (Acad. Award nom), All the President's Men, Marathon Man, Straight Time, Agatha, Kramer vs. Kramer (Acad. Award), Tootsie, Ishtar, Rainman.

HOFFMAN, HERMAN: Writer, Director. b. Montgomery, AL. e. Baltimore City Coll. U.S. Navy.
FEATURE DIRECTING: The Bar Sinister, Great American Pastime, The Invisible Boy, The Battle of Gettysburg.
FEATURE WRITING: Attack on the Iron Coast, Guns of the Magnificent Seven, Escapeline, Reluctant Heroes (Movie-of-Week), The Icemen.
TV DIRECTING: Alcoa Premiere, Untouchables, Bonanza, Virginians, M-Squad, The Nurses, Room 222, Run Joe Run, Monster Squad, The Phantom Rebel.

HOFFMAN, JOSEPH: Writer. b. New York, NY, Feb. 20, 1909. e. UCLA. Newspaperman, screen writer, magazine writer. TV prod. Now TV and screen freelance writer.
PICTURES INCLUDE: China Sky, Don't Trust Your Husband, Gung-Ho, And Baby Makes Three, Weekend with Father, Duel at Silver Creek, At Sword's Point, Has Anybody Seen My Gal?, Against All Flags, No Room for the Groom, Lone Hand, Yankee Pasha, Rails into Laramie, Tall Man

Riding, Chicago Syndicate, Live a Little, How to Make Love and Like It, Sex and the Single Girl.
TELEVISION: Producer: Ford Theatre, Colt 45. Writer: Leave It to Beaver, My Three Sons, The Virginian, Love American Style, etc.

HOGAN, PAUL: Actor, Writer. b. Australia, 1942. Worked as rigger before gaining fame on Australian TV as host of nightly current affairs show (A Current Affair) and The Paul Hogan Show. Shows now syndicated in 26 countries. In U.S. gained attention with commercials for Australian Tourist Commission. 1985, starred in dramatic role on Australian TV in series, Anzacs. Made m.p. theatrical debut in Crocodile Dundee, 1986, Crocodile Dundee II (actor, exec. prod., co-s.p.).
TELEVISION: Anzacs: The War Down Under.

HOGARTH, JOHN M.: Executive. b. Hampstead, London, England, 1931. Man. Dir. Enterprise Pictures Ltd. 1977.

HOLBROOK, HAL: Actor. b. Cleveland, OH, Feb. 17, 1925. m. actress Dixie Carter. e. Denison U., 1948. Summer stock 1947–53. Gained fame as impersonator of Mark Twain on stage.
THEATER: Recent: Tartuffe, The Apple Tree, I Never Sang For My Father, Man of La Mancha, Does a Tiger Wear a Necktie?
PICTURES INCLUDE: The Group, Wild in the Streets, The People Next Door, The Great White Hope, They Only Kill Their Masters, Magnum Force, The Girl from Petrovka. All the President's Men, Midway, Julia, Capricorn One, Natural Enemies, The Fog, Creepshow, Star Chamber, Wall Street, The Unholy, Fletch II.
TELEVISION: The Whole World is Watching, A Clear and Present Danger, Travis Logan, Suddenly Single, Goodbye Raggedy Ann, That Certain Summer, The Pueblo, Sandburg's Lincoln (Emmy Award), Our Town, The Awakening Land, When Hell Was in Session, The Senator (Emmy), Mark Twain Tonight, Celebrity, George Washington, Underseige, Behind Enemy Lines, Dress Gray, North and South Book II, The Fortunate Pilgrim, Plaza Suite, Designing Women (series), Emma, Queen of the South Seas, Day One.

HOLDEN, GLORIA: Actress. b. London, Eng. Sept. 5, 1911. e. American Acad. of Dramatic Arts. Church soloist and singer, artists' & clothes model; mgr. Elizabeth Arden salon, Southampton, L.I.; stage and radio roles, lead in As Husbands Go, Theatre Guild road tour. Began screen career 1937.
PICTURES INCLUDE: Life of Emile Zola, The Girl of Limberlost, Dracula's Daughter, Test Pilot, Girls' School, Behind the Rising Sun, The Hucksters, Kiss for Corliss, Dream Wife, Music by Duchin.
TELEVISION: Lux Theatre, Hallmark Theatre.

HOLDRIDGE, LEE: Composer. b. Port-au-Prince, Haiti, March 3, 1944. e. Manhattan School of Music. Music arranger for Neil Diamond, 1969–73, with whom he collaborated on the score for Jonathan Livingston Seagull. Wrote score for Bdwy musical Into the Light (1986).
PICTURES: Winterhawk, Forever Young, Forever Free; Goin' Home; Mustang Country; The Other Side of the Mountain-Part 2; The Pack; Moment By Moment; Oliver's Story; French Postcards; Tilt; American Pop; The Beastmaster; Mr. Mom; Micki and Maude; Splash; Sylvester; 16 Days of Glory; Transylvania 6-5000; The Men's Club.
TELEVISION: Themes: McCloud; Hec Ramsey; Moonlighting; Beauty and the Beast. Movies: East of Eden; Fly Away Home; The Day the Loving Stopped; For Ladies Only; Skyward Christmas; The Sharks; Thou Shalt Not Kill; This is Kate Bennett; In Love With an Older Woman; Running Out; Thursday's Child; Wizards and Warriors; The Mississippi; Legs; I Want to Live; He's Fired, She's Hired; Letting Go; My Africa.

HOLLENDER, ALFRED L.: Advertising executive. b. Chicago, IL. e. U. of Illinois. Was associated with Radio Stations WIND-WJJD, Chicago as continuity ed., program dir. & asst. to pres.; entered military service in 1943; exec. v.p. & partner of Louis G. Cowan, Inc., exec. v.p. and dir. radio-TV dept., Grey Adv. Agency; pres., Grey Int'l.

HOLLIMAN, EARL: Actor. b. Tennass Swamp, Delhi, LA, Sept. 11, 1928. e. University of Southern Cal.
STAGE: Camino Real (Mark Taper Forum), A Streetcar Named Desire (Ahmanson).
PICTURES INCLUDE: Pony Soldier, Girls of Pleasure Island, Destination Gobi, East of Sumatra, Devil's Canyon, Tennessee Champ, Bridge at Toko-Ri, Broken Lance, Big Combo, I Died a Thousand Times, Forbidden Planet, Giant, Burning Hills, The Rainmaker, Gunfight at the OK Corral, Don't Go Near the Water, Hot Spell, The Trap, Last Train From Gun Hill, Visit to a Small Planet, Armored Command, Summer and Smoke, The Sons of Katie Elder, A Covenant with Death, The Power, Anzio, Smoke, Sharky's Machine.
TELEVISION: Series: Hotel de Paree (1959–60); Wide Country (1962–63); Police Woman (1974–78). Movies: Trapped, Where Ladies Go, I Love You, Goodbye; Cry Panic;

Country Gold, Tribes, Alexander: The Other Side of Down, The Solitary Man; The Thorn Birds; Gunsmoke: Return to Dodge.

HOLLOWAY, STERLING: Actor. b. Cedartown, GA, 1905. e. Georgia Military Acad., Atlanta, American Acad. of Dramatic Art. On screen from 1927.
THEATRE: N.Y. Plays include: Shepherd of the Hills, The Failures, Garrick Gaieties (4 editions), Donna Magana; vaude.; night clubs; radio; U.S. armed forces, 1943.
PICTURES INCLUDE: Casey at the Bat, Elmer the Great, Gold Diggers of 1933, Gift of Gab, Down to Their Last Yacht, Maid of Salem, Varsity Show, Remember the Night, Cheers for Miss Bishop, The Lady Is Willing, Twilight in Rio Grande, The Adventures of Huckleberry Finn, Walk in the Sun, Death Valley, Beautiful Blonde from Bashful Bend, Her Wonderful Lie, Alice in Wonderland, Life Begins at Forty, Live a Little, Love a Little, The Jungle Book (voice), The Aristocats (voice), Won Ton Ton, The Dog Who Saved Hollywood, Thunder and Lightning.
TELEVISION: The Life of Reilly, Willy, The Baileys of Balboa.

HOLM, CELESTE: Actress. b. New York, NY, Apr. 29, 1919. e. Univ. Sch. for Girls, Chicago, Francis W. Parker, Chicago, Lyceé Victor Durui (Paris), U. of Chicago, U. of California at L.A. e. Theodor Holm and Jean Parke Holm. m. actor Wesley Addy.
THEATRE: On Bdwy incl. Time of Your Life, Return of the Vagabond, Papa Is All, Oklahoma, Bloomer Girl, Affairs of State, Anna Christie, The King and I, Third Best Sport, Invitation to a March, A Month in the Country; Theatre-in-Concert for the U.S. State Department in 8 countries May–July 1966. Habeas Corpus (Bdwy), The Utter Glory of Morrissey Hall.
PICTURES INCLUDE: The Little Girls in Blue, Gentlemen's Agreement (Acad. Award, 1947), Come to the Stable, All About Eve, Snake Pit, Road House, Chicken Every Sunday, Everybody Does It, Champagne for Caesar, Tender Trap, High Society, Bachelor Flat, Doctor, You've Got To Be Kidding, Tom Sawyer, Bittersweet Love, Three Men and a Baby.
TELEVISION: A Clearing House in the Wood, Play of the Week, Cinderella, Backstairs at the White House, Midnight Lace, The Shady Hill Kidnapping, Trapper John, M.D., This Girl for Hire, Murder by the Book.
RADIO: People at the U.N.

HOLM, IAN: Actor. b. Ilford, Essex, England, Sept. 12, 1931. r.n. Ian Cuthbert. e. Royal Acad. of Dramatic Art. On British stage—Love Affair, Titus Andronicus, Henry IV, Ondine, Becket, The Homecoming, The Seat, etc.—before entering films.
PICTURES: The Bofors Gun, A Midsummer Night's Dream, The Fixer, A Severed Head, Nicholas and Alexandra, Mary Queen of Scots, Young Winston, The Homecoming, Juggernaut, Shout at the Devil, Alien, Chariots of Fire, Time Bandits, Return of the Soldier, Brazil, Dreamchild, Dance With a Stranger, Greystoke: The Legend of Tarzan, Langerhouse, Wetherby.
TELEVISION: Les Miserables, S.O.S. Titanic, Napoleon, We, the Accused, All Quiet on the Western Front, Holocaust, Man in the Iron Mask, Jesus of Nazareth.

HOMEIER, SKIP: Actor. r.n. George Vincent Homeier. b. Chicago, IL, Oct. 5, 1930. e. U. of California at L.A. Started in radio, 1936–43; on B'way stage, Tomorrow the World, 1943–44.
PICTURES INCLUDE: Tomorrow the World, Boy's Ranch, Mickey, Arthur Takes Over, The Big Cat, The Gunfighter, Halls of Montezuma, The Black Widow, Cry Vengeance, Dakota Incident, The Captives, No Road Back, Decision at Durango, Showdown.
TELEVISION: Playhouse 90, Alcoa Hour, Kraft Theatre, Studio 1, Armstrong Circle Theatre, Alfred Hitchcock, The Wild Wild West Revisited.

HONG, WILSON S.: Cinematographer. b. Butte, MT, Dec. 18, 1934. e. Montana State U., Brooks Inst. of Photography. 1965, Freelance photographer for national magazine and worldwide newspaper syndication; 1966, Photographic Director of U.S Forest Service Fire & Research Division; 1967, first cameraman on various documentaries, industrials, commercials, sports specials.
PICTURES INCLUDE: Bigfoot, Operation North Slope, John Wayne's No Substitute for Victory', The Hellcats, Dear Dead Delilah, Zodiac Killer, Velvet Vampire, Mrs. McGrudy, The Day the Adults Died, Sundown in Watts, Parallax View, 1776, Don't Go West, Drum, White Buffalo, MacArthur, An Enemy of the People, Sergeant Pepper's Lonely Hearts Club Band, Mulefeathers, Winter Kills, Mission to Glory, The Unfinished, They Only Kill Their Masters, The Fearless Five.
TELEVISION: Snowmobile Grand Prix, Indianapolis International Drag Races, The Great Outdoors (23 episodes), Thank you America (spec.), The Unser Story, Gun Hawks (pilot), Keep it Up (pilot), Where are they Now? (pilot), Hunting

and Fishing the North American Continent (spec.), The Blue Knight, A Dream for Christmas, The Toy Game, Moose (pilot), The Jerry Show, Apple's Way, The Moneychangers, Young Maverick, Rudi Gernreich/Future, Ours, Max Factor and Pepsi-Cola commercials, The Groovy Seven (pilot).

HOOKS, KEVIN: Actor. b. Philadelphia, PA, Sept. 19, 1958. Son of actor-director Robert Hooks.
PICTURES: Sounder; Aaron Loves Angela; A Hero Ain't Nothin' But a Sandwich; Take Down.
TELEVISION: Just an Old Sweet Song; The Greatest Thing That Almost Happened; Friendly Fire; Backstairs at the White House; White Shadow; Can You Hear the Laughter?—The Story of Freddie Prinze; For Members Only; Roots Christmas.

HOOKS, ROBERT: Actor, Director, Producer. b. Father of actor Kevin Hooks. b. Washington, D.C., April 18, 1937. Co-founder and exec. dir. Negro Ensemble Co. NY 1968–present. Founder DC Black Theatre, Washington, D.C. 1973–77. Co-star of TV series; NYPD, 1967–69.
THEATER: Tiger, Tiger Burning Bright (Bdwy. debut, 1962); Ballad for Bimshire; The Blacks; The Dutchman; Henry V; Happy Ending; Day of Absence; Where's Daddy?; Hallelujah, Baby?; Kongi's Harvest; A Soldier's Play (Mark Taper Forum, LA). Co-prod.: with Gerald S. Krone: Song of the Lusitanian Bogey, Daddy Goodness, Ceremonies in Dark Old Men, Day of Absence; The Sty of the Blind Pig; The River Niger; The First Breeze of Summer.
PICTURES: Hurry Sundown, The Last of the Mobile Hotshots; Trouble Man; Aaron Loves Angela; Airport '77; Fast-Walking; Star Trek III: The Search For Spock.
TELEVISION: Pilots: The Cliff Dweller; Two for the Money; Down Home. Movies: Carter's Army; Vanished; The Cable Car Murder; Crosscurrent; Trapped; Ceremonies in Dark Old Men; Just an Old Sweet Song; The Killer Who Wouldn't Die; The Courage and the Passion; To Kill A Cop; A Woman Called Moses; Hollow Image; Madame X; The Oklahoma City Dolls; The Sophisticated Gents; Cassie and Co.; Starflight—The Plane that Couldn't Land; Feel the Heat; Sister, Sister; The Execution.

HOOPER, TOBE: Director. b. Texas. Began film career making documentary and industrial films and commercials in Texas. Was asst. dir. of U. of Texas film program, continuing filmmaking while working with students. First feature film: Eggshells.
PICTURES: Eaten Alive, The Texas Chainsaw Massacre, Funhouse, Poltergeist, Lifeforce, Invaders from Mars, The Texas Chainsaw Massacre Part 2.
TELEVISION: Salem's Lot, Amazing Stories.

HOPE, BOB: Actor. b. Eltham, England, May 29, 1903. Started in vaude.; plays include: Roberta, Ziegfeld Follies, Red, Hot & Blue; director, They Got Me Covered, I Never Left Home, So This Is Peace. Voted one of ten best Money-Making Stars in M.P. Herald-Fame Poll, 1941–47, 49–53. On radio and TV. Emmy Governors Award, 1984.
PICTURES INCLUDE: Big Broadcast of 1938, College Swing, Give Me a Sailor, Thanks for the Memory, Never Say Die, Some Like It Hot, Cat and Canary, Road to Singapore, Ghost Breakers, Road to Zanzibar, Caught in the Draft, Louisiana Purchase, My Favorite Blonde, Road to Morocco, Nothing But the Truth, They Got Me Covered, Star Spangled Rhythm, Let's Face It, Road to Utopia, Princess and Pirate, Monsieur Beaucaire, My Favorite Brunette, Where There's Life, Road to Rio, Paleface, Sorrowful Jones, Great Lover, Fancy Pants, Lemon Drop Kid, My Favorite Spy, Son of Paleface, Road to Bali, Off Limits, Here Come the Girls, Casanova's Big Night, Seven Little Foys, That Certain Feeling, Iron Petticoat, Beau James, Paris Holiday, Alias Jesse James, Facts of Life, Bachelor in Paradise, Road to Hong Kong, Call Me Bwana, A Global Affair, I'll Take Sweden, Boy Did I Get a Wrong Number, Eight on the Lam, The Private Navy of Sgt. O'Farrell, How to Commit Marriage, Cancel My Reservation.

HOPE, HARRY: Producer, Director, Writer. b. May 26, 1926. e. U. of California at L.A., Etudes Universitaires Internationales, Ph.D. Entered m.p. industry as special effects man, Republic Studios, 1944; associate producer Star Productions; formed Blue Bird Film Co. Has since produced, directed and written 33 feature films, including Like the Gull, 1967, which won creative classical film award as Asian Film Festival. Founded Western International and directed First Leisure Corp. as exec. v.p. until 1972. From then until present, pres. of Harry Hope Production. Among recent film credits: Smokey and the Judge, Sunset Cove, Doomsday Machine, Death Dimension, Thunderfist, Tarzana, The Mad Butcher, Death Blow.

HOPKINS, ANTHONY: Actor. b. Port Talbot, South Wales, Dec. 31, 1937. Trained at Royal Acad. of Dramatic Art; Cardiff Coll. Drama. Joined National Theatre, gaining fame on stage in England, then TV and films.
THEATER: Julius Caesar (debut, 1964), Juno and the Paycock, A Flea in Her Ear, The Dance of Death, Three

Sisters, As You Like It, The Architect and the Emperor of Assyria, Equus (London and NY).
PICTURES INCLUDE: White Bus, Lion in Winter, Hamlet, The Looking Glass War, When Eight Bells Toll, Young Winston, The Girl from Petrovka, Juggernaut, A Doll's House, Audrey Rose, A Bridge Too Far, International Velvet, Magic, Change of Seasons, The Elephant Man, The Bounty, 84 Charing Cross Road, The Good Father, The Threepenny Opera.
TELEVISION: QB VII, War and Peace, The Lindbergh Kidnapping Case (Emmy Award, 1976), All Creatures Great and Small, The Bunker, Peter and Paul, A Married Man, Hollywood Wives, Guilty Conscience, Arch of Triumph, The Dawning, The Tenth Man.

HOPKINS, BO: Actor. b. Greenwood, SC, Feb. 2, 1942. Studied with Uta Hagen in N.Y. then went to CA with Desilu Playhouse training school in Hollywood. Parts in several prods. that group won him an agent, an audition with director Sam Peckinpah and his first role in latter's The Wild Bunch.
PICTURES INCLUDE: Monte Walsh, The Culpepper Cattle Co., The Moonshine War, White Lightning, The Getaway, The Man Who Loved Cat Dancing, American Graffiti, The Nickel Ride, The Day of the Locust, Posse, The Killer Elite, A Small Town in Texas, More American Graffiti, The Fifth Floor, Sweet Sixteen, Night Shadows, Trapper Country, The Bounty Hunter, The Stalker, Nightmare at Noon, The Tenth Man.
TELEVISION: Series: Doc Elliott, Aspen, The Rockford Files, Dynasty. Movies: A Smoky Mountain Christmas, Beggerman Thief, Down the Long Hills, Last Ride of the Dalton Gang, Casino.

HOPPER, DENNIS: Actor. b. Dodge City, KS, May 17, 1936. e. San Diego, CA, public schools. Author: Out of the Sixties (1988), book of his photographs.
TELEVISION: Medic, Loretta Young Show, Stark.
PICTURES INCLUDE: Jagged Edge, Rebel Without a Cause; I Died a Thousand Deaths, Giant, Story of Mankind, Gunfight at OK Corral, Night Tide, Key Witness, From Hell to Texas, Glory Stompers, The Trip, The Sons of Katie Elder, Hang 'Em High, Cool Hand Luke, True Grit, The American Dreamer, Kid Blue, The Sky is Falling, James Dean-The First American Teenager, Mad Dog Morgan, Tracks, Out of the Blue (actor, dir.), Easy Rider (dir., s.p., actor), The Last Movie, Hex, The American Friend, Apocalypse Now, King of the Mountain, Rumble Fish, The Osterman Weekend, The Texas Chainsaw Massacre Part 2, Blue Velvet, Hoosiers, Black Widow, River's Edge, Colors (dir. only), The Pick Up Artist, O.C. and Stiggs, Riders of the Storm, Backtrack (also dir.).

HOPPER, JERRY: Director. b. Guthrie, OK, July 29, 1907. Wrote radio scripts; asst. dir. & actor. Universal, MGM; casting office, Paramount; Combat/photog—U.S. Army, m.p. div.; asst. edit. dept. head, Paramount; dir., Paramount.
PICTURES INCLUDE: The Atomic City, Hurricane Smith, Pony Express, Alaska Seas, Secret of the Incas, Everything But the Truth, Something to Live For, Naked Alibi, Smoke Signal, Private War of Major Benson, One Desire, Square Jungle, Never Say Goodbye, Toy Tiger, Shark Fighters, Missouri Traveler, Blueprint for Robbery, Maharlica, Madron.
TELEVISION: pilots—Bachelor Father, Leave it to Beaver, Naked City, Wagon Train, Wichita Town. Many television productions, including The Fugitive, Addams Family, Gilligan's Island, Perry Mason, Get Smart, Voyage to the Bottom of the Sea, The Rifleman, Time Tunnel. Specials: Bob Hope shows, Nanette Fabray shows, over 300 series.

HORDERN, SIR MICHAEL: Actor. b. Berkhampstead, England, 1911. e. Brighton Col. Early career in business before stage appearance, 1937. M.P. debut The Girl in the News, 1939. TV debut 1946. 1939–45 Naval Service. Knighted 1983.
PICTURES INCLUDE: Passport to Pimlico, The Constant Husband, Alexander the Great, The Black Prince, Storm Over The Nile, Pacific Destiny, The Baby and the Battleship, The Spanish Gardener, No Time for Tears, Windom's Way, Monty's Double, Girls at Sea, Moment of Danger, Sink the Bismarck, Man in the Moon, El Cid, Cleopatra, V.I.P.s, Dr. Syn, The Yellow Rolls Royce, Ghengis Khan, The Spy Who Came in From the Cold, Khartoum, Cast a Giant Shadow, A Funny Thing Happened on the Way to the Forum, Taming of the Shrew, The Jokers, How I Won the War, I'll Never Forget What's 'is Name, Prudence and the Pill, The Bed-sitting Room, Where Eagles Dare, Anne of the Thousand Days, Futtocks End, Some Will, Some Won't, Up Pompeii, The Possession of Joel Delaney (U.S.), Pied Piper, Blood Will Have Blood, England Made Me, Girl Stroke Boy, Alice's Adventures in Wonderland, Theatre of Blood, The Mackintosh Man, Quilp, Barry Lyndon (narrator), The Slipper and the Rose, Joseph Andrews, The Medusa Touch, Wildcats of St. Trinians, Gandhi, Ivano, Oliver Twist, The Missionary, Yellowbeard, Robin Hood, Trouble at the Royal Rose, Lady Jane, Comrades, The Trouble With Spies.
TELEVISION: Doctor's Dilemma, The Great Adventure, The Witness, The Indifferent Shepherd, Dock Brief, Mr. Kettle

and Mrs. Moon, Guinea Pig, The Gathering Dusk, Farewell My City, Flowering Cherry, I Have Been Here Before, Without the Grail, The Outstation, The Square, Any Other Business, The Stone Dance, The Quails, A Waltz on the Water, August for the People, Land of My Dreams, Condemned to Acquittal, Nelson, The Browning Version, Whistle and I'll Come to You, The Man Who Murdered in Public, A Crack in the Ice, Sir Jocelyn the Minister Would Like a Word, Six Dates with Barker, Don Juan in Hell, Tartoffe, Tall Stories, The Magistrate, Edward VII, King Lear, Cakes and Ale, Chester Mystery Cycle, Paddington Bear (story teller), The Saints Go Marching In, Mrs. Bixby and the Colonel's Coat, Romeo and Juliet, The Tempest, All's Well That Ends Well, You're Alright: How Am I?, King Lear, Rod and Line, Cymbeline, Trelawney of the Wells, Paradise Postponed,The Secret Garden, Suspicion.

HORN, ALAN: Executive. b. New York, NY, Feb. 28, 1943. e. Union Coll., Harvard Business Sch. 1972, joined Tandem Prods., 1972; named v.p., business affairs, and of sister co., T.A.T. Communications, 1973; 1977, exec. v.p. & COO; pres., 1978. In 1983 named pres. Embassy Communications. 1986 joined 20th Century Fox as pres. COO. Left Fox Sept. 1986. Co-founded Castle Rock Entertainment 1987.

HORNE, LENA: Vocalist, Actress. b. Brooklyn, NY, June 30, 1917.
THEATRE: Blackbirds, Dance With Your Gods, Jamaica, Lena Horne: The Lady and Her Music (Tony Award).
Radio with Noble Sissle, Charlie Barnet, other bands. Floor shows at Cotton Club, Cafe Society, Little Troc, etc. Started screen career 1942.
PICTURES INCLUDE: Panama Hattie, Cabin in the Sky, Stormy Weather, I Dood It, Thousands Cheer, Broadway Rhythm, Swing Fever, Two Girls and a Sailor, Ziegfeld Follies, Till the Clouds Roll By, Words and Music, Meet Me in Las Vegas, Death of a Gunfighter, The Wiz.

HORNER, HARRY: Art director, Director. b. Holic, Czechoslovakia, July 24, 1910. e. U. of Vienna, Dept. of Architecture, 1928–33; Acad. of the Theatre, Vienna, 1930–32, Max Reinhardt's Seminary. Joined Max Reinhardt Thea. Co., Vienna and Salzburg Festivals; to U.S. as asst. to Reinhardt on pageant, The Eternal Road. Stage designer, N.Y. theatre 10 yrs. (Lady in the Dark, Family Portrait, others). First m.p. as prod. designer, 1938, Our Town (co-credit, Wm. Cameron Menzies). later Little Foxes, Stage Door Canteen. Army service, 1942–45; designed Winged Victory for Air Force. In 1949, won Acad. award black and white art dir., The Heiress. Other films designed: Born Yesterday, Separate Tables, They Shoot Horses; Acad. nomination, The Hustler; (Acad. award). Since 1959 prod., dir., TV series, The Royal Canadian Mounted Police; exec. prod., dir., Enterprise Films of Can., Anglo Ent. Films, London; co-prod., Fahrenheit 451, 1966, They Shoot Horses, Don't They? (Acad. nom.), Who Is Harry Kellerman?, Up the Sandbox.
FURTHER PICTURES INCLUDE: Born Yesterday, He Ran All the Way, Androcles and the Lion, Outrage. Films Directed: Beware My Lovely, Red Planet Mars, Vicki, New Faces, Life in the Balance, Step Down to Terror, Lonesome Gun, Wild Party Man From Del Rio, Winner of 2 acad. awards, 6 acad. nominations for Art Dir. 1975: The Black Bird, Harry and Walter Go to New York, Audrey Rose, The Driver, Moment by Moment, The Jazz Singer.
TELEVISION: Omnibus, Cavalcade, Reader's Digest, Author's Playhouse, Four Star Theatre, Gunsmoke, Revue Productions, Dupont Theatre.
OPERA: designer & director at San Francisco Opera, Metropolitan Opera, N.Y., Vancouver Festivals, Hollywood Bowl. Operas designed & directed: David, Joan at the Seake, Magic Flute. Amer. Premiere of New Opera, Midsummer Night's Dream. Designed Idiots Delight, Ahmanson Theatre, 1970, winner, L.A. Drama Critics Award, best stage design. Designed Time of the Cuckoo, Ahmanson Theatre 1974.

HORSLEY, LEE: Actor. b. Muleshow, TX, May 15, 1955. e. U. of No. Colorado. Appeared in stage productions locally of Oklahoma, Fiddler on the Roof, Lion in Winter, etc. Did stage work in New York. Starred in theatrical film, The Sword and the Sorcerer.
TELEVISION: Series: Nero Wolfe, Matt Houston. Movies: The Wild Women of Chastity Gulch, When Dreams Come True, Paradise.

HORTON, ROBERT: Actor. b. Los Angeles, CA, July 29, 1924. e. Miami U., U.of California at L.A. U.S. Coast Guard; many legit. plays; many radio & TV appearances; co-star, Wagon Train; screen debut in the Tanks Are Coming. Star of Broadway musical 110 in the Shade.
PICTURES INCLUDE: Return of the Texan, Pony Soldier, Apache War Smoke, Bright Road, The Story of Three Loves, Code Two, Arena, Prisoner of War, Men of the Fighting Lady, The Green Slime.
TELEVISION: Wagon Train, As the World Turns, Red River.

HORWITZ, SOL: Executive. b. Chicago, IL, April 2, 1920. e. U. of Chicago. U.S. Navy, 1942–45. Film booker and buyer for Balaban and Katz and Allied Theatres of Illinois, in Chicago before moving to New York where served in same capacity for Walter Reade Org., Cinema 5, Loews, Inc. In sls. divisions of EDP Films, Screenvision, and Castle Hill Prods. Now project administrator for Short Film Showcase and v.p. development, Angelika Films.

HOSKINS, BOB: Actor. b. England, Oct. 26, 1942. Porter and steeplejack before becoming actor at 25. Veteran of Royal Shakespeare Co. Appeared with Britain's National Theatre (Man Is Man, King Lear, Guys and Dolls, etc.)
PICTURES: Royal Flash, Zulu Dawn, The Wall, The Long Good Friday, Beyond the Limit, Lassiter, The Cotton Club, Brazil, Sweet Liberty, Mona Lisa, A Prayer for the Dying, The Lonely Passion of Judith Hearne, Who Framed Roger Rabbit?, The Secret Policeman's Third Ball (voice of the Secret Policeman), The Raggedy Rawney (dir., debut; actor and co-s.p.).
TELEVISION: Flickers, Pennies from Heaven, Othello.

HOUGH, JOHN: Director. b. London, Eng., Nov. 21, 1941. Worked in British film prod. in various capacities; impressed execs. at EMI-MGM Studios, Elstree, London, so was given chance to direct The Avengers series for TV. Began theatrical films with Sudden Terror for prod. Irving Allen, 1971.
PICTURES INCLUDE: Twins of Evil, Treasure Island, The Legend of Hell House, Dirty Mary Crazy Larry, Escape to Witch Mountain, Return to Witch Mountain, Brass Target, Watcher in the Woods, Biggles—Adventures in Time, Howling IV—The Original Nightmare.
TELEVISION: A Hazard of Hearts (dir., co-prod.), Dangerous Love (prod., dir.).

HOUSEMAN, JOHN: Producer, Director, Writer. r.n. J. Haussmann. b. Rumania, Sept. 22, 1902. e. Clifton Coll., Eng. Scholarship Trinity Coll, Cambridge. Instead 1920 moved to Argentina working on cattle ranch, then in bank. Returned Eng. 1923, worked in grain brokerage house. To U.S. 1925 continued in grain brokerage while writing; contrib. to magazines; adapt. plays from German, French. In 1932 prod. Four Saints in Three Acts; later dir. Valley Force, Panic, for Theatre Guild. Assoc. with Orson Welles in founding Mercury Theat., 1937; apptd. assoc. prof. English at Vassar same yr. Prod. Julius Caesar, Native Son for stage. Co-author Woodrow Wilson (prod. on stage as In Time to Come), bought by 20th Century-Fox. Wrote radio scripts for Helen Hayes. Exec. Selznick Prod., 1941–42. Chief of overseas Program bureau Office of War Information, 1942–43. In 1943–44 (joint s.p.) Jane Eyre; New York stage; dir. Lute Song, 1948; King Lear, 1950; Coriolanis, 1953. 1966 became producing director A.P.A. Repertory Co. (directing Pantagleize, Macbeth, etc.) Dir. The Country Girl, (1971), 1968 apptd. head of drama div., Juilliard School at Lincoln Center—also artistic dir., The Acting Co. until 1976.
PICTURES: Producer: Miss Susie Slagle's, The Unseen, Blue Dahlia, Letter from an Unknown Woman, They Live by Night, The Company She Keeps; prod. On Dangerous Ground, Holiday for Sinners, The Bad and The Beautiful, Julius Caesar, Executive Suite, Her Twelve Men, Moonfleet, The Cobweb, Lust For Life, All Fall Down, Two Weeks in Another Town, In the Cool of the Day. Actor: Seven Days in May, The Paper Chase (Acad. Award, 1973), Rollerball, Three Days of the Condor, St. Ives, The Cheap Detective, Old Boyfriends, The Fog, Wholly Moses, Ghost Story, Murder by Phone; Bright Lights, Big City.
TELEVISION: Paper Chase (series), Silver Spoons (series), The Displaced Person, Six Characters In Search of an Author, Captains and the Kings, Washington, Aspen, The Associates, Gideon's Trumpet, Christmas Without Snow, Marco Polo, The Winds of War, A.D., Noble House, Gore Vidal's Lincoln.
AUTHOR: Numerous magazine articles in Harper's, Vogue, Theatre Arts, Show, The Nation, New York Times. Memoirs: Run Through (1972), Front and Center (1979), Final Dress (1983), Entertainers and the Entertained (1986), Unfinished Business (1986).
AWARDS: Citation of Amer. Educational Theatre Assc., Outer Circle Critics Award, 1971; New Eng. Theatre Conference Annual Award; National Arts Club Medal of Honor. 1984: Conservator of the Arts, Amer. Conservatory Theatre; Algur Meadows Award for Excellece in the Arts, from So. Methodist U., Congressional Arts Caucus Award, Liberty Award of NY City (1986). 1986: John Houseman Theatre Center opened in NY.

HOWARD, CY: Producer, Director. b. Milwaukee, WI, Sept. 27, 1915. e. U. of Minnesota, U. of Wisconsin. Entered radio Station KTRH, Houston, TX as writer, prod., actor; served 1 yr. Army Air Corps; to WBBM, Chicago, as writer, prod., actor; 1942; to Jack Benny's radio writing staff; actor, Storm Operation (stage, 1943); to ABC as writer, comedian on What's New program; to NBC where orig. wrote Palmolive Party; radio writer for Milton Berle, Danny Thomas, Bert Lahr, Jerry Lewis; orig. My Friend Irma, tie with Luigi, radio and TV shows; to Hal B. Wallis Prod. as writer and assoc. prod. My Friend Irma; exec. prod., Desilu Studios, created and

produced Harrigan and Son, Westward Ho, Fair Exchange, My Friend Irma Goes West (films), That's My Boy; writer, Marriage on the Rocks; co-writer: Won Ton Ton, The Dog Who Saved Hollywood; director, Lovers and Other Strangers and Every Little Crook and Nanny.

HOWARD, CYRIL: C.B.E. Managing Director of Rank's Pinewood Studios, England. Formerly Secretary and general manager of the studios. Joined Rank Organisation 1941.

HOWARD, KEN: Actor. b. El Centro, CA, March 28, 1944. e. Yale Drama Sch. Left studies to do walk-on in Bdwy. musical, Promises, Promises. Starred as Thomas Jefferson in 1776 on Bdwy. (Theatre World Award) and in film version.
PICTURES: Tell Me That You Love Me, Junie Moon (debut), Such Good Friends, 1776, Second Thoughts.
TELEVISION: Series: Manhunter, Bonanza, Medical Center, Adam's Rib, The White Shadow, It's Not Easy. Movies: The Trial of George Armstrong Custer, He's Not Your Son, Rage of Angels: The Story Continues, Strange Interlude, The Man in the Brown Suit.
STAGE: Promises, Promises; Child's Play, Seesaw, 1600 Pennsylvania Avenue, The Norman Conquests, Equus.

HOWARD, ROBERT T.: Executive. b. Red Bank, NJ, June 18, 1927. e. U. of Virginia, Columbia U., N.Y. Began prof. career as NBC page, joining guest relations staff in N.Y., 1947. Moved up to NBC TV research dept., where worked in program testing and audience measurement. Became head of research for NBC Radio Spot Sales in 1953; 1955, promoted to acct. exec. in same dept. Joined TV Spot Sales in 1959 and named natl. sales mgr. of WNBC-TV, New York in 1963 named gen. mgr. of KNBC, Los Angeles. Elected v.p. of NBC a month later. Returned to N.Y and named pres. of NBC TV Network April 1, 1974. Elected to NBC bd. and named exec. v.p.; 1977, v.p. & gen. mgr. WNBC TV, New York; 1980, pres. & chm., Citicom Communications Co.

HOWARD, RON: Actor. b. Duncan, OK, March 1, 1954. e. U. of Southern California. Acting debut at age of two with parents, Rance and Jean Howard, in The Seven Year Itch at Baltimore's Hilltop Theatre. Two years later travelled to Vienna for his first film, The Journey. Many TV appearances over years. Is brother of Clint Howard, also actor from childhood.
PICTURES INCLUDE: Actor: Frontier Woman, The Journey, Wild Country, Five Minutes to Live, The Music Man, Courtship of Eddie's Father, A Village of the Giants, Happy Mother's Day . . . Love, George, American Graffiti, The Spikes Gang, The Shootist, More American Graffiti. Director: Grand Auto Theft (dir., debut, 1974), also co-s.p. and actor), Night Shift, Splash, Cocoon, Gung Ho (also exec. prod.), Willow, Vibes (co-exec. prod.), Clean and Sober (exec. prod.).
TELEVISION: Red Skelton Hour, Playhouse 90, Dennis, the Menace, Many Loves of Dobie Gillis, Five Fingers, Twilight Zone, Dinah Shore Show, Andy Griffith Show (regular), The Fugitive, Dr. Kildare, Big Valley, I Spy, Danny Kaye Show, Gomer Pyle, USMC, The Monroes, The FBI, Judd for the Defense, Daniel Boone, Lancer, Land of the Giants, Gentle Ben, Gunsmoke, Disney TV films (A Boy Called Nuthin', Smoke), Happy Days (regular), No Man's Land (co-exec. prod), Huckleberry Finn, Act of Love, Bitter Harvest. Director: Cotton Candy, Through the Magic Pyramid, Skyward.

HOWARD, SANDY: Producer. b. Aug. 1, 1927. e. Fla. So. Coll. Ent. m.p. ind. 1946.
PICTURES INCLUDE: Perils of the Deep, One Step to Hell, Jack of Diamonds, Tarzan and the Trappers, A Man Called Horse, Man in the Wilderness, Together Brothers, Neptune Factor, The Devil's Rain, Sky Riders, The Last Castle, Embryo, Magna I—Beyond the Barrier Reef, The Battle, Island of Dr. Moreau, Circle on Fire, Death Ship (exec. prod.), Avenging Angel, The Boys Next Door, Street Justice, Nightstick, Dark Tower (exec. prod.).
TELEVISION: Over 50 TV series.

HOWELL, C. THOMAS: Actor. b. Dec. 7, 1966. Former junior rodeo circuit champ.
PICTURES: E.T.: The Extra Terrestrial, The Outsiders, Tank, Grandview U.S.A., Red Dawn, Secret Admirer, The Hitcher, Soul Man, A Tiger's Tale, Far Out Man, Young Toscanini, The Return of the Musketeers.
TELEVISION: Series: Little People (only 4 yrs. old), Two Marriages, Into the Homeland.

HOWELLS, URSULA: Actress. b. Sept. 17, 1922. e. St. Paul's Sch., London. Stage debut, 1939, at Dundee Repertory with Bird in Hand followed by several plays inc. Springtime for Henry in N.Y., 1951; m.p. debut in Flesh and Blood, 1950; TV debut in Case of the Frightened Lady for BBC, 1948.
TELEVISION: Many appearances including The Small Back Room, A Woman Comes Home, For Services Rendered, Mine Own Executioner, The Cocktail Party.
PICTURES INCLUDE: The Oracle (Horse's Mouth), Track the Man Down, They Can't Hang Me, Keep It Clean, Long

Arm (Third Key), Death and The Sky Above, Mumsy, Nanny, Sonny, and Girly.

HOWERD, FRANKIE: Performer. b. York, Eng. March 6, 1921. e. Shooters Hill, London, Sch. Stage debut, Sheffield Empire, 1946. Film: Runaway Bus; BBC radio & TV appearances include Tons of Money, Frankie Howerd Show, Howerd Crowd.
PICTURES INCLUDE: Jumping for Joy, An Alligator Named Daisy, The Lady Killers, A Touch of the Sun, Further Up the Creek, Cool Mikado, Fast Lady, The Great St. Trinian's Train Robbery, Carry On Doctor, Up Pompeii, Up the Chastity Belt, Up the Front, The House in Nightmare Park, Sgt. Pepper's Lonely Hearts Club Band.
TELEVISION: BBC series. Comedy Playhouse, Frankie Howerd Show, Up The Convicts—Series (4) (Australia 1975), The Frankie Howerd Show—Series (13) (Canada 1976), Up Pompeii. TV-Video: HMS Pinafore, Trial by Jury.
STAGE: Old Vic Midsummer Night's Dream, A Funny Thing Happened on the Way to the Forum, Way Out in Piccadilly, Wind in the Sassafras Trees, Die Fledermaus.

HUDGINS, TORRENCE B.: Film Buyer. b. Merkel, TX. e. Southern Methodist U. Interstate Theatres, Inc. 1923–52; Trans-Texas Theatres, 1951–54, advertising; Cinema Art Theatres Inc., 1954–74, film buyer and advertising. 1974–78 Torrence Hudgins Buying and Booking Service.

HUDDLESTON, DAVID: Actor, Producer. b. Vinton, VA, Sept. 17, 1930. e. American Acad. of Dramatic Arts. On stage in A Man for All Seasons, Front Page, Everybody Loves Opal, Ten Little Indians, Silk Stockings, Fanny, Guys and Dolls, The Music Man, Desert Song, Mame. Broadway: The First; Death of a Salesman.
PICTURES: All the Way Home, A Lovely Way to Die, Slaves, Norwood, Rio Lobo, Fools Parade, Country Blue, Bad Company, Blazing Saddles, McQ, Capricorn I, World's Greatest Lover, Gorp, Smokey and the Bandit II, Santa Claus: The Movie; Frantic.
TELEVISION: Series: Hizzoner, Tenafly, Petrocelli. Movies: The Priest Killer, The Homecoming, Brian's Song, How the West Was Won, Winner Take All, Heatwave, The Oregon Trail, Sherlock Holmes in New York, Kate Bliss and the Ticker Tape Kid, Finnegan Begin Again, Family Reunion, Spot Marks the X, The Tracker.

HUDSON, HUGH: Producer, Director. b. England. e. Eton. Began career with ad agency in London; left for Paris to work as editor for small film co. Returned to London to form Cammell-Hudson Film Co., production house., turning out documentaries. 1970, joined with Ridley Scott to make TV commercials. 1975, formed Hudson Films to produce. Debut as director of theatrical features with Chariots of Fire, 1982.
PICTURES: Greystoke: The Legend of Tarzan, Lord of the Apes (prod./dir.), Revolution (dir.).

HUGGINS, ROY: Writer, Director. b. Litelle, WA, July 18, 1914. e. U. of California 1935–39; U. of California Graduate School, 1939–41. m. Adele Mara, actress. Spec. rep., U.S. Civil Service Comm., 1941–43; industrial eng., 1943–46; writer 3 novels and many stories for Sat. Eve. Post; pres., Public Arts, Inc., 1968. V.P., 20th Century-Fox TV, 1961.
PICTURES INCLUDE: I Love Trouble, Too Late for Tears, Lady Gambles; story, Fuller Brush Man, Good Humor Man; adap., Woman in Hiding; collab., s.p., Sealed Cargo; s.p., dir., Hangman's Knot; collab. s.p., Gun Fury, Three Hours to Kill; s.p., Pushover; prod. A Fever in the Blood.
TELEVISION: Prod. Warner Bros. Presents Cheyenne series, anthologies, 1955–56; Conflict (series); produced pilots of Colt .45, 77 Sunset Strip, Maverick, prod. Maverick, 1957–58; won Emmy Award 1958. Created, The Fugitive, 1962; v.p., MCA Revue, 1963; exec.-prod. Run for Your Life, 1965; exec. prod., The Outsiders, The Bold Ones, Alias Smith and Jones, Toma, 1968–74. ABC Movie of Week, Pretty Boy Floyd. 1974: Co-creator of The Rockford Files pilot and series for NBC; 1975: Co-creator of City of Angels for NBC; 1976: Captains and the Kings, (exec. prod.) 1977: Aspen (exec. prod.) 1978: Wheels, (exec. prod.), The Last Convertible.

HUGHES, BARNARD: Actor. b. Bedford Hills, NY, July 16, 1915. Winner of Emmy for role as Judge in Lou Grant series (1978) and Tony for Da (1978).
PICTURES INCLUDE: Midnight Cowboy, Oh, God!, Where's Poppa, The Hospital, Rage, Sisters, Cold Turkey, Pursuit of Happiness, Deadhead Miles, Tron, Best Friends, Maxie, Where Are the Children?, Da.
TELEVISION: Series: Doc, Mr. Merlin, The Cavanaughs. Movies: Guilty or Innocent, The Sam Sheppard Murder Case, See How She Runs, The Caryl Chessman Story, Tell Me My Name, Look Homeward, Angel, Father Brown: Detective, Nova, Homeward Bound, The Sky's No Limit, A Caribbean Mystery, Night of Courage, A Hobo's Christmas, Day One.

HUGHES, JOHN: Writer, Director, Producer. Editor of National Lampoon before writing film scripts of National Lampoon's Class Reunion (1982); National Lampoon's Vacation and Mr.

Mom (both in 1983). Co-wrote Nate and Hayes. Made directorial debut with Sixteen Candles in 1984 which also wrote. In 1985 entered into deal with Paramount Pictures to write, direct and produce films with his own production unit, The John Hughes Co.
PICTURES: The Breakfast Club (s.p., dir.); Weird Science (s.p., dir.); Pretty in Pink (s.p., dir., prod.); Planes, Trains & Automobiles (s.p., dir., prod.), She's Having a Baby (prod., dir., s.p.); The Great Outdoors (s.p., exec. prod.).

HUGHES, KATHLEEN: Actress. r.n. Betty von Gerkan; b. Hollywood, CA, Nov. 14, 1928. e. Los Angeles City Coll., U. of California at L.A. m. Stanley Rubin, producer, mother of 4, Michael played Baby Matthew on Peyton Place. Studied drama; under contract, 20th-Fox, 1948–51; starred in Seven Year Itch 1954, La Jolla Playhouse; signed by UI, 1952.
PICTURES INCLUDE: For Men Only, Sally and Saint Anne, Golden Blade, It Came From Outer Space, Thy Neighbor's Wife, Glass Web, Dawn at Socorro, Cult of the Cobra, Three Bad Sisters, Promise Her Anything, The President's Analyst, The Late Liz, The Take.
TELEVISION: Bob Cummings Show, Hitchcock, 77 Sunset Strip, G.E. Theatre, Bachelor Father, The Tall Man, Dante, Tightrope, Markham, I Dream of Jeannie, Peyton Place, Gomer Pyle, Kismet, Ghost and Mrs. Muir, Bracken's World, The Survivors, Julia, Here's Lucy, To Rome with Love, The Interns, The Man and the City, Mission Impossible, The Bold Ones, Lucas Tanner, Marcus Welby, Barnaby Jones, Medical Center, Babe (movie), Forbidden Love.

HUGHES, KEN: Writer, Director. b. Liverpool, Eng., 1922. Ent. ind. as sound engineer with BBC, 1940; Doc. films, Army training films. Novels: High Wray, The Long Echo. Scripts: The Matarese Circle, Tussy is Me, The Queen's Own, Rats.
PICTURES INCLUDE: Joe Macbeth, Confession, The Trials of Oscar Wilde, The Small World of Sammy Lee, Arrivederci Baby, Casino Royale, Chitty Chitty Bang Bang, Cromwell, Internecine Project, Sextette.
TELEVISION: Eddie (Emmy Award), Sammy (Brit. Acad. Award). Serials: Solo for Canary, Enemy of the State. Series: Lenin 1917 (The Fall of Eagles), The Haunting, The Voice, Oil Strike North, Colditz, Churchill.
AWARDS INCLUDE: Golden Globe, Emmy, British TV Acad. Award (Script Writer of Year), Avorias Festival Merit Award, British Writer's Guild Award, British Critics Award (best serial).

HUKE, BOB, B.S.C.: Cinematographer. Ent. m.p. ind. 1937, Asst. cameraman Pygmalion, French Without Tears, etc.; 1939–44 Royal Navy. 1945–9 camera operator Great Expectations, Uncle Silas, Seven Days to Noon and others. 1950–56 Brazil. Contract dir. of photo. for Cia Cinematographica Vera Cruz, 1957–59 dir. own company, Zenith, 1960. dir. photo, 3 Dinah Shore Shows, Spain, Paris, Copenhagen. NBC 1961. Dir. photo. Reach For Glory, The War Lover, The Very Edge, 1962; The Brain, 8 Danny Thomas Shows in Europe. 1963 Sandres of the River. 1964, Ballad in Blue, License to Share. TV & cinema commercials, 1955. 1966, 2nd Unit You Only Live Twice; 1968, 2nd Unit, Battle of Britain, 1969; dir. photo, The Virgin and the Gypsy. 1971; Under Milk Wood.

HULCE, THOMAS: Actor. b. White Water, WI, Dec. 6, 1953. e. NC School of the Arts. Understudied and then co-starred in Equus on Broadway. Directorial stage debut Sleep Around Town. Film debut September 30, 1955 (1977).
THEATER: Memory of Two Mondays; Julius Caesar; Candida; The Sea Gull; The Rise and Rise of Daniel Rocket.
PICTURES: National Lampoon's Animal House; Those Lips, Those Eyes; Amadeus; Echo Park; Dominick and Eugene; Shadowman.
TELEVISION: Emily, Emily; The Rise and Rise of Daniel Rocket.

HUNNICUT, GAYLE: Actress. b. Fort Worth, TX, February 6, 1943. e. U. of California at L.A., B.A., with honors, theater arts & English major. Early career, community theatres in Los Angeles. Ent. m.p. ind. 1967.
PICTURES INCLUDE: Eye of the Cat, Marlowe, Fragment of Fear, The Freelance, Voices, Running Scared, New Face in Hell, Scorpio, L'Homme Sans Visage, The Spiral Staircase, The Sell Out, Tony Siatta, Once in Paris, One Take Two, Fantomas, Return of the Man from U.N.C.L.E, Privilege, Sherlock Holmes, Target, Dream Lover, Turnaround, Hard to Be a God.
TELEVISION: Man and Boy, The Golden Bowl, The Ripening Seed, Fall of Eagles, The Switch, Humboldts Gift, The Life and Death of Dylan Thomas, Return of the Saint, Martian Chronicles, A Man Called Intrepid, Kiss Inc., Love Boat—The Mallory Quest, The Lady Killers, Philip Marlowe, The Quest, Fantasy Island, Taxi, Savage in the Orient, The First Olympics: Athens 1896, Dream West, Strong Medicine.
THEATER: The Ride Across Lake Constance, Twelfth Night, The Tempest, Dog Days, The Admirable Crichton, A Woman of No Importance, Hedda Gabler, Peter Pan, Macbeth, Uncle Vanya, The Philadelphia Story, Miss Firecracker

Contest, Exit The King, The Doctor's Dilemma, So Long on Lonely Street, The Big Knife.

HUNT, LINDA: Actress. b. Morristown, NJ, Apr. 2, 1945. e. Interlochen Arts Acad., MI, and Chicago's Goodman Theatre & Sch. of Drama.
PICTURES: Popeye, The Year of Living Dangerously (Acad. Award, supp. actress, 1985), Dune, The Bostonians, Silverado, Eleni, Waiting for the Moon.
THEATRE: Long Wharf Theatre, New Haven: (Hamlet, The Rose Tattoo, Ah, Wilderness); Mother Courage, End of the World (Tony nom.), A Metamorphosis in Miniature (Obie Award), Top Girls (Obie Award), Aunt Dan and Lemon, The Cherry Orchard.
TELEVISION: The Room Upstairs, The Room.

HUNT, MARSHA: Actress. b. Chicago, IL, Oct. 17, 1917. Screen debut 1935.
B'WAY PLAYS INCLUDE: Joy to the World, Devils Disciple, Legend of Sarah, Borned in Texas, Tunnel of Love, The Paisley Convertible.
PICTURES INCLUDE: Virginia Judge, College Holiday, Easy to Take, Blossoms in the Dust, Panama Hattie, Joe Smith American, These Glamour Girls, Winter Carnival, Irene, Pride and Prejudice, Flight Command, The Affairs of Martha, Kid Glove Killer, Seven Sweethearts, Cheers for Miss Bishop, Trial of Mary Dugan, Thousands Cheer, The Human Comedy, None Shall Escape, Lost Angel, Cry Havoc, Bride by Mistake, Music for Millions, Valley of Decision, A Letter for Evie, Smash-Up, Carnegie Hall, Raw Deal, Take One False Step, Actors and Sin, Happy Time, No Place To Hide, Bombers B-52, Blue Denim, Johnny Got His Gun.
TELEVISION: Philco, Studio One, Ford Theatre, Show of Shows, G.E. Theatre, Climax, Hitchcock, Peck's Bad Girl Series, The Defenders, Twilight Zone, Cains Hundred, Gunsmoke, The Breaking Point, Outer Limits, Profiles in Courage, Ben Casey, Accidental Family, Run For Your Life, My Three Sons, The Outsiders, Name of the Game, Univ.'s 120, Ironside, Marcus Welby, M.D., Police Story, The Young Lawyers, Harry-O, The Mississippi, Hot Pursuit, Shadow Chaser, Matlock, Murder She Wrote, Star Trek: The Next Generation.

HUNT, PETER: Director, Editor. b. London, England. March 11, 1928. e. Romford, England and Rome, Italy, London Sch. of Music. Actor English Rep. Entered film as camera asst. Documentary, later asst film editor documentary, then asst editor features. London Films then editor—credits incl. Hill in Korea, Admirable Crichton, Cry From the Streets, Greengage Summer (Loss of Innocence in U.S.), Ferry To Hong Kong, H.M.S. Defiant (Damn the Defiant in U.S.), Supervising editor/2nd Unit Director, Dr. No, Call Me Bwana, From Russia With Love, Goldfinger, Ipcress File, Thunderball, You Only Live Twice; associate producer, Chitty Chitty Bang Bang; director, On Her Majesty's Secret Service, Gullivers Travels (Live & Animation) Gold, Shout at the Devil, Death Hunt; Wild Geese II, Hyper Sapien, Assassination.
TELEVISION: Director: The Persuaders, Shirley's World, The Pencil, Smart Alec Kill (Philip Marlowe), The Beasts in the Streets, Last Days of Pompeii.

HUNT, PETER H.: Director. b. Pasadena, CA, Dec. 16, 1938. e. Hotchkiss, Yale U., Yale Drama School. m. actress Barbette Tweed. Director for Williamston Theatre since 1957. Lighting designer on Bdwy. (1963–69)
PICTURES INCLUDE: 1776; Give 'Em Hell, Harry; Bully; Adventures of Huckleberry Finn.
TELEVISION: Huckleberry Finn (mini-series), It Came Upon the Midnight Clear, The Parade, Life on the Mississippi, A Private History of a Campaign That Failed, A New Start, Skeezer, Mysterious Stranger. Pilots: Adam's Rib, Hello Mother Goodbye, Ivan the Terrible, Quark, Mixed Nuts, Flying High, Wilder and Wilder, Rendezvous Hotel, The Main Event, Nuts and Bolts, The Good Witch of Laurel Canyon, Masquerade, Stir Crazy, Charley Hannah, The Wizard of Elm Street, Travelling Man, My Africa.
CABLE: Sherlock Holmes, Bus Stop.
STAGE: 1776 (London & Bdwy.), Georgy (Bdwy.), Scratch (Bdwy.), Goodtime Charley (Bdwy.), Give 'Em Hell Harry, Magnificent Yankee (Kennedy Center). Tours: Bully, Three Penny Opera, Sherlock Holmes, Bus Stop.
AWARDS: Tony, Ace, Peabody (twice), N.Y. Drama Critics, London Drama Critics, Edgar Allan Poe, Christopher.

HUNT, WILLIE: Executive Producer. b. Van Nuys, CA, Oct. 1, 1941. e. Utah State U., B.A., 1963. m. writer Tim Considine. Started in industry as secretary at Warner Bros., 1965; named exec. secty. to Ted Ashley, WB, 1969; story analyst, WB, 1974; story editor, WB, 1975; named West Coast story editor for WB, 1978; joined MGM in 1979 as v.p., motion picture development. Moved to United Artists as v.p.-prod., 1982. In 1983 sr., v.p. of prod. at Rastar Prods.; 1984, indep. prod., Tri-Star Pictures; 1986, sr. v.p., Freddie Fields Prods. 1988: Loverboy (co-prod.)

HUNTER, HOLLY: Actress. b. Atlanta, GA. March 20, 1958. e. studied acting Carnegie Mellon. Appeared Off-Broadway in Battery (1981) and Weekend Near Madison. Appeared in four Beth Henley plays: The Miss Firecracker Contest (Off-B'way), as a replacement in Crimes of the Heart (B'way) The Wake of Jamey Foster (B'way) and Lucky Spot (Williamstown Theater Festival). Film debut: The Burning.
PICTURES: Swing Shift, The End of the Line, Raising Arizona, Broadcast News, End of the Line, Animal Behavior, Miss Firecracker Contest.
TELEVISION: A Gathering of Old Men.

HUNTER, KIM: Actress. r.n. Janet Cole; b. Detroit, MI, Nov. 12, 1922. e. public schools. d. Donald and Grace Mabel (Lind) Cole. Student acting with Carmine Lantaff Camine, 1938–40, Actors Studio; First stage appearance, 1939; played in stock, 1940–42; Broadway debut in A Streetcar Named Desire, 1947; frequent appearances summer stock and repertory theater, 1940–; appeared Am. Shakespeare Festival, Stratford, CT, 1961. Autobiography-cookbook: Loose in the Kitchen (1975).
STAGE: Two Blind Mice (tour), 1950; Darkness at Noon, 1951; The Chase; They Knew What They Wanted (tour); The Children's Hour (revival); The Tender Trap; Write Me a Murder; Weekend; The Penny Wars; And Miss Reardon Drinks a Little (tour); The Glass Menagerie (Atlanta), The Women; In Praise of Love (tour); The Lion in Winter (NJ); The Cherry Orchard; The Chalk Garden (PA); Elizabeth the Queen (Buffalo); Semmelweiss (Buffalo); The Belle of Amherst (NJ); The Little Foxes (MA); To Grandmother's House We Go, 1987; Another Part of the Forest (Seattle); When We Dead Awaken; Ghosts (Garden City and Tarrytown, NY), 1982; Territorial Rites; Death of a Salesman (Stratford, Ont.); Cat on a Hot Tin Roof; Life With Father (Coconut Grove, FL); Sabrina Fair (BTF, MA); Faulkner's Bicycle (Yale Repertory and Joyce Theatre, N.Y.); Antique Pink (U. of Michigan Theatre); The Belle of Amherst (NH); Painting Churches (Stamford, CT & E. Carolina U. Theatre, NC); A Delicate Balance (BTF, MA); Jokers (Goodspeed at Chester, CT); Remembrance (Boston, MA) 1987; Man and Superman (Roundabout, NY) 1987–88; The Gin Game (Lancaster, PA), 1988, A Murder of Crows.
PICTURES: Film debut in The Seventh Victim, 1943; Tender Comrade, 1943; When Strangers Marry (re-released as Betrayed); You Came Along; A Canterbury Tale; Stairway to Heaven; A Streetcar Named Desire; Anything Can Happen; Deadline: U.S.A.; Bermuda Affair; The Young Stranger; Money, Women and Guns; Lilith; Planet of the Apes; The Swimmer; Beneath the Planet of the Apes; Escape from the Planet of the Apes; Dark August; The Kindred.
TELEVISION: Made TV debut on Actors Studio Program, 1948; numerous TV appearances include: Requiem for a Heavyweight, 1956; The Comedian, 1961 (both on Playhouse 90); Give Us Barabbas; Love, American Style; Columbo; Cannon; Night Gallery; Mission Impossible; The Magician, 1972–73; Marcus Welby; Hec Ramsey; Griff; Police Story; Ironside; Medical Center; Bad Ronald; Born Innocent; Once an Eagle; Baretta; Gibbsville; Hunter; The Oregon Trail; Project: U.F.O.; Stubby Pringle's Christmas; Backstairs at the White House; Specter on the Bridge; Edge of Night; F.D.R.'s Last Year; Skokie; Scene of the Crime; Private Sessions; Three Sovereigns for Sarah; Hot Pursuit; Martin Luther King, Jr.: The Dream and the Drum; Drop-out Mother.
RECORDED: From Morning 'Til Night (and a Bag Full of Poems), RCA Victor, 1961; Come, Woo Me—Unified Audio Classic, 1964.
AWARDS: Recipient Donaldson Award for best supporting actress in A Streetcar Named Desire, 1948, also on Variety N.Y. Critics Poll, 1948, for film version, 1952; winner Acad. Award, LOOK award, Hollywood Fgn. Corrs. Golden Globe award; Emmy nominations for Baretta, 1977, Edge of Night, 1980; Carbonnell award for Big Mama in Cat on a Hot Tin Roof, So. Fla., 1984.

HUNTER, ROSS: Producer. r.n. Martin Fuss. b. Cleveland, OH, May 6, 1926. e. Western Reserve U., M.A. School teacher, 1938–43; actor, Columbia Pictures, 1944–46; returned to school teaching; stage prod. & dir.; m.p. dialogue dir.; assoc. prod. U-I, 1950–51; prod., U-I, 1951. Moved production Co. from Universal to Columbia, 1971. Moved to Paramount, 1974.
PICTURES INCLUDE: As actor: Louisiana Hayride, Ever Since Venus, Bandit of Sherwood Forest, Groom Wore Spurs. As producer: Take Me to Town, All I Desire, Tumbleweed, Taza Son of Cochise, Magnificent Obsession, Naked Alibi, Yellow Mountain, Captain Lightfoot, One Desire, The Spoilers, All That Heaven Allows, There's Always Tomorrow, Battle Hymn, Tammy and the Bachelor, Interlude, My Man Godfrey, The Wonderful Years, Stranger in My Arms, Imitation of Life, Pillow Talk, Portrait in Black, Midnight Lace, Back Street, Flower Drum Song, Tammy and the Doctor, The Thrill of It All, The Chalk Garden, I'd Rather Be Rich, The Art of Love, Madame X, The Pad, Thoroughly Modern Millie, Rosie, Airport, Lost Horizon.

TELEVISION: Lives of Jenny Dolan, The Moneychangers, The Best Place to Be, Sid and Nancy, A Family Upside Down, Suddenly Love.

HUNTER, TAB: Actor. b. New York, NY, July 11, 1931. U.S. Coast Guard; odd jobs. Discovered in 1948.
PICTURES INCLUDE: The Lawless, Island of Desire, Gun Belt, Steel Lady, Return to Treasure Island, Track of the Cat, Battle Cry, Sea Chase, Burning Hills, Girl He Left Behind, Lafayette Escadrille, Gunman's Walk, Damn Yankees, That Kind of Woman, Pleasure of His Company, The Golden Arrow, War Gods of the Deep, Ride the Wild Surf, Hostile Guns, Life and Times of Judge Roy Bean, Grease 2, Lust in the Dust (also prod.), Cameron's Closet, Grotesque, Out of the Dark.

HUNTER, TIM: Director.
PICTURES: Tex, Sylvester, Paint It Black.

HUNTLEY, RAYMOND: Actor. b. Birmingham, England, Apr. 23, 1904. On stage from 1922 repertory, tour; London debut in Back to Methuselah, 1924; N.Y. debut in Venetian Glass Nephew, 1931; m.p. debut 1934; many TV appearances.
PICTURES INCLUDE: Rembrandt, Knight Without Armour, Night Train to Munich, They Came to a City, Pimpernel Smith, Freedom Radio, Way Ahead, I See a Dark Stranger, School for Secrets, Broken Journey, So Evil My Love, Mr. Perrin and Mr. Traill, It's Hard to Be Good, Passport to Pimlico, Trio, I'll Never Forget You, The Last Page, Laxdale Hall, Meet Mr. Lucifer, Mr. Denning Drives North, Hobson's Choice, Orders Are Orders, Constant Husband, Geordie, The Prisoner, Doctor at Sea, Dam Busters, Teckman Mystery, Green Man, Brothers in Law, Room at the Top, Carlton-Browne of the F.O., Suspect, A French Mistress, Pure Hell of St. Trinians, Only Two Can Play, Waltz of the Toreadors, Crooks Anonymous, On the Beat, Carry On Nurse, The Great St. Trinian's Train Robbery, Hostile Witness, The Gaunt Woman, Arthur! Arthur!, Young Winston, That's Your Funeral, Symptoms.
TELEVISION: Lord Jeffrey, the Family Solicitor on Upstairs, Downstairs.

HUPPERT, ISABELLE: Actress. b. Paris, France, March 16, 1955. e. Conservatoire National d'Art Dramatique.
PICTURES: Faustine et le Bel Ete, Cesar and Rosalie, Going Places, Rosebud, The Rape of Innocence, The Lacemaker, Violette (Cannes, best actress award, 1977), The Bronte Sisters, Loulou, Heaven's Gate, The True Story of Camille, Wings of the Dove, Deep Water, The Trout, Cactus, Signed Charlotte, The Bedroom Window, The Possessed.

HURLOCK, ROGER W.: Pres. Hurlock Cine-World. b. Cambridge, MD, May 30, 1912. e. Baltimore City Coll. Ent. m.p. ind. as publicist, Hippodrome Theatre, Balt.; asst. mgr., Lessor-operator Imperial and Majestic Theatres, Balt., 1931–35; real estate, bldg., farming, Maryland and Alaska, 1936–58; elected bd. mem., Allied Artists, 1958; asst. to pres., 1961–63; chmn. budget comm., 1963; chmn. policy comm., 1964; c.p. exec. comm. member, 1964; v.p., chf. operating officer 1965; chmn. exec. comm., 1966; pres., 1967. pres., Hurlock Cine-World, 1969.

HURT, JOHN: Actor. b. Shirebrook, Derbyshire, Jan. 22, 1940. e. St. Martin's Sch. for Art, London. Debut in British film, The Wild and the Willing (1962).
PICTURES: A Man for All Seasons, Before Winter Comes, Sinful Davey, In Search of Gregory, 10 Rillington Place, Forbush and the Penguins, East of Elephant Rock, Disappearance, Spectre, Pied Piper of Hamelin, The Ghoul, Little Malcolm, The Shout, Midnight Express, Alien, Heaven's Gate, The Elephant Man, Partners, Night Crossing, The Osterman Weekend, Champions, The Hit, From the Hip, Aria, White Mischief, Jake Speed, Slaves of New York, Little Sweetheart, Scandal.
TELEVISION: Playboy of the Western World, A Tragedy of Two Ambitions, Green Julia, Nijinsky, Shades of Green, Ten from the Twenties, The Peddler, The Naked Civil Servant, I, Claudius, Crime and Punishment, The Storyteller (series host).
STAGE: The Dwarfs, Little Malcolm and His Struggle Against the Eunuchs, Man and Superman, Belcher's Luck, Ride a Cock Horse, The Caretaker, Romeo and Juliet, Ruffian on the Streets, The Dumb Waiter, Travesties, The Arrest, The Seagull.

HURT, MARY BETH: Actress. b. Marshalltown, IA, Sept. 26, 1948. m. writer-director Paul Schrader. e. New York U. Sch. of Arts. Stage debut in 1973 in N.Y. Shakespeare Festival prod., More Than You Deserve.
THEATER: As You Like It (Central Park), 2 seasons with Phoenix Theater, Love For Love, Tralawny of the Wells, Secret Service, Boy Meets Girl, Father's Day, Crimes of the Heart, The Misanthrope, The Nest of the Wood Grouse, The Day Room.
PICTURES: Interiors, Head Over Heels, Change of Seasons, The World According to Garp, D.A.R.Y.L., Compromising Positions, Slaves of New York, Parents.

TELEVISION: Secret Service (NET Theatre), Kojak, Baby Girl Scott (movie).

HURT, WILLIAM: Actor. b. Washington, DC, Mar. 20, 1950. Lived as child in South Pacific when father was dir. of Trust Territories for U.S. State Dept. e. Tufts as theology major, switched to drama in jr. year, Juilliard. Oregon Shakespearean Fest. Leading actor with New York's Circle Repertory Company since 1976, appearing in, among other plays, The Fifth of July, My Life, Ulysses in Traction, The Runner Stumbles, Hamlet, Childe Byron. Also appeared with the New York Shakespeare Festival—Henry V (1976) and Midsummer's Night's Dream (1982), and in Hurlyburly off-Bdwy and on Bdwy.
PICTURES: Altered States (debut), Eyewitness, Body Heat, The Big Chill, Gorky Park, Kiss of the Spider Woman (Academy Award), Children of a Lesser God, Broadcast News, A Time of Destiny, The Accidental Tourist.
TELEVISION: Verna: USO Girl, Best of Families, All The Way Home.

HUSSEIN, WARIS: Director. b. India, 1938.
TELEVISION INCLUDES: Sleeping Dog, Death of a Teddy Bear, Toggle, Spoiled, Days In the Trees, A Passage to India, Girls in Uniform, St. Joan, A Casual Affair, Divorce His, Divorce Hers, Shoulder to Shoulder, Georges Sand, Chips With Everything, The Glittering Prizes, Love Letters on Blue Paper, Sarah Bernhardt, Blind Love, Romance, Daphne Laureola, Waiting for Sheila, Armchair Thriller, Edward and Mrs. Simpson, Death Penalty, And Baby Makes Six, The Henderson Monster, Baby Comes Home, Callie and Son, Coming Out of the Ice, Little Gloria: Happy at Last, Princess Daisy, Winter of Our Discontent, Arch of Triumph, Copacabana, Surviving, When the Bough Breaks, Intimate Contact, Downpayment on Murder, Onassis: The Richest Man in the World.
PICTURES INCLUDE: A Touch of Love, Quackser Fortune, Melody, The Possession of Joel Delaney, Henry VIII and His Six Wives.

HUSTON, ANJELICA: Actress. b. CA, 1952. Daughter of John Huston. Granddaughter of actor Walter Huston. Raised in St. Clerans, Ireland.
PICTURES: Sinful Davey, A Walk with Love and Death, The Last Tycoon, The Postman Always Rings Twice, Swashbuckler, This is Spinal Tap, The Ice Pirates, Prizzi's Honor (Acad. Award, supp. actress, 1985), Gardens of Stone, Captain Eo, The Dead, Mr. North, A Handful of Dust, The Witches.
TELEVISION: The Cowboy and the Ballerina (movie), Faerie Tale Theatre, A Rose for Miss Emily, Lonesome Dove.

HUSTON, DANNY: Director. b. Rome, Italy, May 14, 1962. Youngest son of director-actor John Huston and actress Zoe Sallis. Brother of actress Anjelica and screenwriter Tony Huston. e. Overseas School, Rome; Intl branch of Milfield School in Exeter, London Film School. A constant visitor to his father's sets throughout the world, he began working on his father's films, beginning in Cuernavaca, Mexico as second-unit dir. on Under the Volcano. Directed TV doc. on Peru and on making of Santa Claus: The Movie; and TV features Bigfoot and Mr. Corbett's Ghost. Feature film debut, Mr. North (1988).

HUSTON, VIRGINIA: Actress. b. Omaha, NB, Apr. 24, 1925. Did radio and stage work while in school; acted at Omaha Community playhouse; started in m.p. with RKO 1945.
PICTURES INCLUDE: Nocturne, Out of the Past, Tarzan's Peril, The Highwayman, Racket, Flight to Mars, Night Stage to Galveston, Sudden Fear, Knock on Wood.

HUTTON, BETTY: Actress. b. Battle Creek, MI, Feb. 26, 1921. Made screen debut in 1942.
PICTURES INCLUDE: The Fleet's In, Star Spangled Rhythm, Happy Go Lucky, Miracle of Morgan's Creek, Incendiary Blonde, And the Angels Sing, Here Come the Waves, Duffys Tavern, The Stork Club, Perils of Pauline, Annie Get Your Gun, Let's Dance, The Greatest Show on Earth, Somebody Loves Me, Spring Reunion.
TV: Goldie (series).

HUTTON, BRIAN, G.: Director. b. New York, NY, 1935.
PICTURES INCLUDE: The Wild Seed, The Pad, Sol Madrid, Where Eagles Dare, Kelly's Heroes, X, Y, and Zee, Night Watch, The First Deadly Sin, High Road to China.
TELEVISION: Someone is Watching Me, Institute For Revenge.

HUTTON, LAUREN: Actress. r.n. Mary Hutton. b. Charleston, SC, Nov. 17, 1943. e. U. of South Florida, Sophie Newcombe Coll. As model featured on more covers than any other American.
PICTURES: Paper Lion (debut, 1968), Little Fauss and Big Halsey, The Gambler, Gator, Welcome to L.A., A Wedding, American Gigolo, Zorro, the Gay Blade, Paternity, Starflight One, Lassiter, Once Bitten, Malone, Bulldance.
TELEVISION: The Cradle Will Fall, The Rhinemann Exchange, Someone Is Watching Me, Scandal Sheet, Sins,

Monte Carlo, Timestalker, Perfect People, Falcon Crest (series).

HUTTON, ROBERT: Actor. r.n. R. Winne. b. Kingston, NY, June 11, 1920. e. Blair Acad., NJ. In summer stock prior to screen career, 1943.
PICTURES INCLUDE: Destination Tokyo, Janie, Roughly Speaking, Hollywood Canteen, Too Young to Know, Love and Learn, Always Together, Steel Helmet, New Mexico, Racket, Slaughter Trail, Casanova's Big Night, Cinderella; co-prod., dir., star, The Slime People; asso. prod., Now It Can Be Told. The Vulture, You Only Live Twice, They Came From Beyond Space, Torture Garden, Tales from the Crypt.

HUTTON, TIMOTHY: Actor. b. Malibu, CA, Aug. 16, 1960. Father, late actor Jim Hutton. m. actress Debra Winger. In high school plays; toured with father in Harvey during vacation. Film debut in Ordinary People, 1980.
TELEVISION: Movies: Zuma Beach, Best Place To Be, Baby Makes Six, Sultan and the Rock Star, Young Love, First Love, Friendly Fire.
PICTURES: Ordinary People (Acad. Award, supp. actor, 1980), Taps, Daniel, Iceman, The Falcon and The Snowman, Turk 182, Made in Heaven, A Time of Destiny, Everybody's All American, Showers.

HUYCK, WILLARD: Writer, Director. e. U. of Southern California. Went to work as reader for Larry Gordon, executive at American-International Pictures; named Gordon's asst., working on scene rewrites for AIP films. First screen credit on The Devil's Eight as co-writer with John Milius, also U.S.C. graduate. Left AIP to write original scripts, joining with Gloria Katz. Both signed by Francis Ford Coppola to write and direct films for his America Zoetrope but projects never materialized. Co-wrote American Graffiti with Katz (1973) and Lucky Lady (1975). Huyck made directorial debut in 1979 with French Postcards, co-written with Katz, who also produced.
PICTURES: Indiana Jones and the Temple of Doom (co.-s.p.); The Best Defense (co.-s.p.); Howard the Duck (dir., co.-s.p.).
TELEVISION: A Father's Homecoming (co-prod., co-s.p.).

HYAMS, JOSEPH: Advertising & Publicity Executive. b. New York, NY, Sept. 21, 1926. e. New York U. Ent. industry, 1947. Various publicity posts, 20th Century-Fox, Columbia Pictures, 1947–55; eastern pub. mgr., Figaro Prods., 1955–56; West Coast pub. mgr., Hecht-Hill-Lancaster, 1955–58; pub. adv. dir., Batjac Prods. 1959–60 national adv. & pub. dir., Warner Bros., Seven Arts, 1960. v.p., world-wide pub., Warner Bros., Inc., 1970–1987; appointed sr. v.p., special projects, Dec., 1987.

HYAMS, PETER: Director, Writer. b. New York, NY, July 26, 1943. e. Hunter Coll., Syracuse U. Joined CBS news staff N.Y. and made anchor man. Filmed documentary on Vietnam in 1966. Left CBS in 1970 and joined Paramount in Hollywood as writer. Hired by ABC to direct TV features.
PICTURES INCLUDE: Busting (s.p., dir.), Our Time (dir.), Peeper, Telefon (co-s.p.), Capricorn One (s.p., dir.), Hanover Street (dir., s.p.), The Hunter (co-s.p.), Outland (dir., s.p.), Star Chamber (s.p., dir.), 2010 (prod., dir., s.p.), Running Scared (exec. prod., dir.), The Monster Squad (co-exec. prod.), The Presidio (dir., cinematographer).
TELEVISION: The Rolling Man, Goodnight My Love (both s.p., dir.).

HYDE, JOHN W.: Executive. b. Jackson, MI. e. New York U., B.A. 1963. Joined ABC upon graduation from N.Y.U. 1963 hired by MCA-Universal as exec. assist. to then v.p. Ned Tanen becoming assoc. prod. on several MCA features. Also wrote, produced and directed musical shorts for MCA Records. 1969 joined Filmways, Inc. as v.p. and exec. asst. to then-pres. Richard R. St. Johns. 1972 formed own company, Acmelab, Ltd., multi-faceted special effects, commercial and post-production facility, which included Cinefex, Videoconversion and Acme Film Laboratories. 1976 Hyde sold Acmelab to produce The Ravagers for Columbia Pictures. During production of that film, Hyde rejoined Richard St. Johns as v.p. of the Morison Film Group, a Guinness co.; 1977 became v.p. in charge of production for all Morison films; 1981, named pres. of MFG.
TELEVISION: The Andy Williams Show, The Lloyd Thaxton Show.
PICTURES INCLUDE: Games, Midnight Patient, Skulduggery, The Ravagers, Death Hunt, Rituals, The Uncanny, Silent Flute (Circle of Iron), Matilda, The Wanders, Nightwing, The Mountain Men, The Final Countdown, A Change of Seasons, Dead and Buried, American Pop, Venom, Fire and Ice, UHF.

HYDE, TOMMY: Executive. r.n. Thomas L. b. Meridian, MS, June 29, 1916. e. Lakeland H.S., grad., 1935. Worked E.J. Sparks Theatres, 1932–41. Florida State Theatres, 1941–42. U.S. Navy, 1942–46. Florida State Theatres, 1946–47; city mgr. (Tallahassee). Talgar Theatres, 1947–58; v.p. and gen. mgr. Kent Theatres, 1958–86; vice-pres. Motion Picture Films,

Inc.; pres., NATO of Florida, 1961–62; chmn. bd. 1963–70; 1987–88, theatre consultant.

HYER, MARTHA: Actress. b. Fort Worth, TX, Aug. 10, 1924. e. Northwestern U., Pasadena Playhouse.
PICTURES INCLUDE: Thunder Mountain, Indian Summer, Roughshod, Velvet Touch, The Lawless, Outcast of Black Mesa, Salt Lake Raiders, Frisco Tornado, Abbott and Costello Go to Mars, Scarlet Spear, So Big, Sabrina, Kiss of Fire, Paris Follies of 1956, Francis in the Navy, Red Sundown, Showdown at Abilene, Kelly and Me, Battle Hymn, Mister Cory, My Man Godfrey, Paris Holiday, Once Upon a Horse, Houseboat, Some Came Running, Big Fisherman, Best of Everything, Ice Palace, Desire in the Dust, The Right Approach, The Last Time I Saw Archie, Girl Named Tamiko, Man from the Diner's Club, Wives and Lovers, Pyro, The Carpetbaggers, First Men in the Moon, Blood on the Arrow, Bikini Beach, Sons of Katie Elder, The Chase, Night of the Grizzly, Picture Mommy Dead, The Happening, Some May Live, House of a Thousand Dolls, Once You Kiss a Stranger, Crossplot.

HYSON, KEVIN: Executive. b. Duxford, U.K., Jan. 7, 1951. e. Kings' School, Ely, U.K. 1960–1969. Joined Universal Pictures Ltd., London, 1969 in print and technical dept. Joined Cinema International Corp. London, 1970; gen. mgr., Cinema International Corp., Dominican Republic, 1974–76; gen. mgr., Cinema International Corp., Panama and Central America, 1976–79; mng. dir., CIC/Warner, South Africa, 1979–81; v.p., YK Cinema International Corp., Japan, 1981–83. Joined Columbia Pictures International, 1983; v.p., Latin America and Pacific for Columbia Pictures Int'l, 1984; v.p., advertising and publicity, 1985; exec. v.p., theatrical distribution and marketing, Columbia Pictures Int'l, 1986. Joined Walt Disney Pictures as v.p. int'l marketing, 1988.

I

IANNUCCI, SALVATORE J.: Executive. b. Brooklyn, NY, Sept. 24, 1927. e. New York U., B.A.; 1949; Harvard Law School, J.D., 1952. 2 yrs. legal departments RCA and American Broadcasting Companies, Inc.; 14 yrs. with CBS Television Network: asst. dir. of bus. affairs, dir. of bus. affairs, v.p. of bus. affairs; 2 yrs. v.p. admin. National General Corp.; 2½ yrs. pres. of Capital Records; 4½ yrs. Corpor. vice pres. and dir. of Entertainment Div. of Playboy Enterprises, Inc.; 4 yrs. partner with Jones, Day, Reavis & Pogue in Los Angeles office, handling entertainment legal work; Pres., Filmways Entertainment, and sr. v.p., Filmways, Inc.; exec. v.p., Embassy Communications; COO, Aaron Spelling Prods.; now sr. partner Bushkin, Gaims, Gaines & Jonas.

IBBETSON, ARTHUR: Cinematographer. b. England, 1922.
PICTURES INCLUDE: The Horse's Mouth, Tunes of Glory, Whistle Down the Wind, Nine Hours to Rama, I Could Go on Singing, The Chalk Garden, A Countess from Hong Kong, Where Eagles Dare, Anne of the Thousand Days, A Doll's House, A Little Night Music, The Prisoner of Zenda, Hopscotch, Nothing Personal (co-cin.), The Bounty, Santa Claus: The Movie.
TELEVISION: Frankenstein: the True Story, Little Lord Fauntleroy (Emmy), Brief Encounter, Babes in Toyland, Witness for the Prosecution, Master of the Game.

IBERT, LLOYD: Executive. Began career as mgng. editor, Independent Film Journal. 1973, joined Paramount Pictures pub. dept.; named sr. publicist. 1985, appointed dir., natl. pub. for M.P. Group.

IDLE, ERIC: Actor, Writer. b. South Shields, Durham, Eng., March 29, 1943. e. Pembroke Coll., Cambridge, 1962–65. Member Monty Python's Flying Circus appearing on BBC, 1969– 74.
STAGE: Oh What a Lovely War, Monty Python Live at the Hollywood Bowl, 1970; Monty Python Live (NY, 1976). Author: Pass the Butler, 1982.
BOOKS: Hello Sailor, The Rutland Dirty Weekend Book, as well as co-author of Monty Python books: Monty Python's Big Red Book, The Brand New Monty Python Book, Monty Python and the Holy Grail, The Complete Works of Shakespeare and Monty Python.
PICTURES: And Now for Something Completely Different, Monty Python and the Holy Grail, Monty Python's Life of Brian, Yellowbeard, Monty Python Live at the Hollywood Bowl, Pirates of Penzance (s.p. only), The Secret Policeman's Other Ball, Monty Python's The Meaning of Life, National Lampoon's European Vacation, The Adventures of Baron Munchausen.
TELEVISION: The Frost Report, Do Not Adjust Your Set, Monty Python's Flying Circus, Faerie Tale Theater, Saturday Night Live.

IMAMURA, SHOHEI: Director, Producer. b. Tokyo, Japan, Sept. 15, 1926. e. Waseda U. Joined Shochiku Ofuna Studio 1951 asst. dir., transferred Nikkatsu in 1954 as asst. dir., director

Stolen Desire 1958 then 4 more films before refusing to work on any film distasteful to him; and wrote play later made into film directed by him in 1968; later turned to documentaries and from 1976 onward as independent; Ballad of Narayamá awarded Golden Palm Prize, Cannes Festival, 1983.
PICTURES: Stolen Carnal Desire, Big Brother, Hogs and Warships, Insect Woman, God's Profound Desire, Human Evaporation, Postwar Japan, Vengeance Is Mine, Swing Along.

IMI, TONY: Cinematographer. b. London, 1937. Ent. ind. 1959. Has worked primarily in England and Germany.
PICTURES: The Slipper and the Rose, International Velvet, Brass Target, Ffolkes, The Sea Wolves, Night Crossing, Nate and Hayes, Not Quite Jerusalem, Enemy Mine, Empire State, American Roulette, Buster, Options Wired.
TELEVISION: Queenie, The Return of Sherlock Holmes, Oceans of Fire, The Last Days of Frank and Jesse James, Reunion at Fairborough, A Christmas Carol, Sakharov, Princess Daisy, John Paul II, Little Gloria-Happy at Last, Inside the Third Reich, Dreams Don't Die, For Ladies Only, Nicholas Nickleby, A Tale of Two Cities.

IMMERMAN, WILLIAM J.: Producer. b. Dec. 29, 1937. Joined 20th Century-Fox in 1972 as v.p., business affairs. Promoted 1975 to senior vice pres., administration and worldwide business affairs of the Feature Film Division. Previously was with American International Pictures for 7 yrs. as v.p. business affairs & assoc. counsel. From 1963–65 was deputy dist. atty. for Los Angeles County. Was founder of and bd. chm. of Cinema Group, Inc. 1979–82. Presently president of Salem Prods. Inc. and counsel to law firm of Barash and Hill. Exec. prod., Highpoint, Southern Comfort, Hysterical, Primal Rage, Welcome to Spring Break, Mind Games, Take this Job and Shove It.

INGALLS, DON: Producer, Writer. b. Humboldt, NB. e. George Washington U. Columnist, Washington Post; producer-writer, ATV England and Australia; writer-producer, Have Gun Will Travel, CBS, also produced for TV: The Travels of Jamie McPheeters, The Virginian, Honey West, Serpico, Kingston: Confidential. Exec. story consultant The Sixth Sense; producer, Fantasy Island, T.J. Hooker.
WRITER: Gunsmoke, Have Gun Will Travel, The Bold Ones, Marcus Welby M.D., Mod Squad, Star Trek, Honey West, Bonanza, The Sixth Sense, Then Came Bronson, Police Story, World Premier Movie, Shamus, Flood, Capt. America, The Initiation of Sarah, Blood Sport, and others.
FEATURE FILMS: Airport-1975, Who's Got the Body?

INGELS, MARTY: Actor. Former Comedian, Executive. b. Brooklyn, NY, Mar. 9, 1936. m actress-singer Shirley Jones. U.S. Infantry 1954–58. Ent. show business representing Army, Name That Tune. Stage: Sketchbook revue, Las Vegas. Pres., Celebrity Brokerage, packaging celebrity events and endorsements. Active in community affairs and charity funding.
TELEVISION: Phil Silvers Show, Steve Allen, Jack Paar, Playboy Penthouse, Bell Telephone Hour, Manhunt, Ann Sothern Show, Peter Loves Mary, The Detectives, Joey Bishop Show, Hennessey, Dick Van Dyke Show, I'm Dickens ... He's Fenster (series), Burke's Law, Hollywood Palace, Family.
PICTURES INCLUDE: Ladies Man, Armored Command, Horizontal Lieutenant, Busy Body, Wild and Wonderful, Guide for a Married Woman, If It's Tuesday It Must be Belgium, For Singles Only.

INGSTER, BORIS: Writer, Director. b. 1913. In 1935; collaborated on adaptation, The Last Days of Pompeii, RKO. In 1936: Dancing Pirate, RKO. In 1937: collaborated on screen play Thin Ice, 20th-Fox. In 1938: Happy Landing.
PICTURES INCLUDE: Judge Steps Out, Southside 1–1000; Something for the Birds, Abdullah's Harem, California-story, Cloak & Dagger, The Amazing Mrs. Holliday.
TELEVISION: Wagon Train, The Alaskans, The Roaring 20's, Travels of Jaimie McPheeters, The Man From U.N.C.L.E.

INSDORF, ANNETTE: Film professor, critic, translator, and television host. b. Paris, France, July 27, 1950. e. 1963–68 studied voice at Juilliard Sch. of Music and performed as singer; Queens Coll. (summa cum laude), B.A. 1972; Yale U., M.A., 1973; Yale U., Ph.D., 1975. 1973: soloist in Leonard Bernstein's Mass (European premiere in Vienna and BBC/WNET TV). 1975–87: professor of film, Yale Univ. Author of François Truffaut (1979); Indelible Shadows: Film and the Holocaust. Since 1979: frequent contributor to NY Times (Arts and Leisure), Los Angeles Times, San Francisco Chronicle, Elle, and Premiere. Named Chevalier dans l'ordre des arts et lettres by French Ministry of Culture, 1986. Director of Undergraduate Film Studies, Columbia U., and professor in the Graduate Film Div. 1987: exec-prod. Shoeshine (short film written and dir. by Tom Abrams, nominated for Oscar). 1981–84: host for TeleFrance Cine-club (national cable TV prog. Host for Years of Darkness (PBS, 1983). Host for

Holocaust film series (WNYC, 1985). Moderator-translator since 1979 for seminars and directors Telluride Film Festival; trans. for Truffaut, AFI Retrospective (Wash. and L.A.) 1979; since 1979 trans. for Polish dirs. NY Film Fest.; since 1984 trans. Cannes Film Fest. Since 1981 coordinated and hosted lecture series at 92nd St. Y (NY) including Holocaust on Film, Critics on Criticism, Screenwriters on Screenwriting.

IRELAND, JILL: Actress. b. London, England, April 24, 1936. m. actor Charles Bronson. Began career in music halls of England at age of 12; went on to sing, dance and entertain at London's Palladium, in cabarets and a tour of the continent in ballet. Began acting in West End repertory; then signed to major film studio contract at 16 by J. Arthur Rank. Screen debut as ballet dancer in Oh, Rosalinda, first of 16 feature films for Rank. Author: Life Wish, Lifeline.
PICTURES INCLUDE: Three Men in a Boat, Hell Drivers, Robbery Under Arms, Carry On, Nurse, Raising the Wind, Twice Round the Daffodils, Villa Rides, Rider on the Rain, Cold Sweat, The Family, Someone Behind the Door, The Mechanic, The Valdez Horses, The Valachi Papers, Breakout, Hard Times, Breakheart Pass, From Noon Till Three, Death Wish II, Assassination, Caught.
TELEVISION: Shane (series), The Man from U.N.C.L.E., Ben Casey, Night Gallery, Daniel Boone, Mannix, Star Trek (series).

IRELAND, JOHN: Actor. b. Vancouver, B.C., Jan. 30, 1916. Prof. debut at Abbey Theatre, Dublin. To Hollywood, 1945 and has appeared in over 200 films.
THEATRE: On N.Y. stage: Macbeth, Moon Is Down, Native Son, Counter Attack, Robert W. Service (one-man show), Dublin Theatre Fest., Oxford Playhouse, The Pleasure of His Company (Toronto, 1985).
PICTURES INCLUDE: A Walk in the Sun, Wake Up and Dream, My Darling Clementine, Red River, The Gangsters, Roughshod, All The King's Men (Acad. Award nom.), Return of Jesse James, Vengeance Valley, Red Mountain, Basketball Fix, Bushwackers, Hurricane Smith, 49th Man, Combat Squad, Southwest Passage, Security Risk, Steel Cage, Outlaw Territory, Fast and Furious, Good Die Young, Queen Bee, Gunfight at OK Corral, Party Girl, Spartacus, The Ceremony, The Fall of the Roman Empire, Faces in the Dark, I Saw What You Did, Fort Utah, Once Upon a Time in the West, The Adventurers, The Dirty Heroes, Madam Kitty, Escape to the Sun, The Incubus, Messenger of Death, Farewell, My Lovely, Martin's Day.
TELEVISION: Crossbar (CBC), The Last Tycoon, The Cheaters (UK, series), Take Over, Marilyn: The Real Story, A Little Late Lamented, Cassie & Co., Bonanza: The Next Generation; Perry Mason: The Case of the Lady in the Lake.

IRETON, KIKUKO MONICA: Managing Editor. Movie/TV Marketing; Tokyo, Japan. b. May 22, 1929. e. Seijo Gaguen, Tokyo. Daughter of late Shoichiro Kobayashi, manager of Bank of Japan in New York (1937–41) and later director. Co-founder with husband (Glenn F. Ireton) of Far East Film News in 1953, renamed Movie Marketing in 1961, Movie/TV Marketing in 1966.

IRONS, JEREMY: Actor. b. Isle of Wight, 1948. m. actress Sinead Cusack. e. Sherborne Sch., Dorset. Stage career began at Marlowe Theatre, Canterbury, where he was student asst. stage manager. Accepted at Bristol Old Vic Theatre Sch. for two-yr. course; then joined Bristol Old Vic Co. In London played in Godspell, Much Ado About Nothing, The Caretaker, Taming of the Shrew, Wild Oats, Rear Column, An Audience Called Edouard, etc. N.Y. stage debut, The Real Thing (Tony Award, 1984).
PICTURES: Nijinsky, The French Lieutenant's Woman, Moonlighting, Betrayal, The Wild Duck, Swann in Love, The Mission, Dead Ringers.
TELEVISION: The Pallisers, Notorious Woman, Love for Lydia, Langrishe Go Down, Brideshead Revisited.

IRVIN, JOHN: Director. b. England, May 7, 1940. In cutting rooms at Rank Organisation before making first film—documentary Gala Day on grant from British Film Inst. Other documentaries before turning to features.
PICTURES: Dogs of War, Ghost Story, Champions, Turtle Diary, Raw Deal, Hamburger Hill, Next of Kin.
TELEVISION: Hard Times, Tinker Tailor Soldier Spy.

IRVINE, RICHARD H: Executive. b. 1942. e. U. of Southern California. Early career in marketing positions with Time-Life & Campbell Soup Co.; dir. of mktg., Disneyland; suprv. worldwide non-theatrical dist. for Walt Disney Prods. Pres. & CEO of Straight Arrow Publishing; v.p.-mktg. for Trans American Video, Inc. Served as exec. v.p. & COO of Talent Payments, Inc., Production Payments, Inc. & Central Casting Corp., all subsidiaries of IDC Services, Inc., of which he was also corp. sr. v.p.–west coast, 1976–78. In 1978 joined in formation of Aurora Pictures, of which is pres. & CEO.
PICTURES: Exec. Prod.: Why Would I Lie?, The Secret of NIMH, Eddie and the Cruisers, Heart Like a Wheel, East of the Sun, West of the Moon.

IRVING, AMY: Actress. b. Palo Alto, CA, Sept. 10, 1953. e. American Conservatory Theatre, London Acad. of Dramatic Art. Daughter of late Jules Irving and actress Priscilla Pointer. m. director-prod. Steven Spielberg.
THEATER: Heartbreak House, Road to Mecca.
PICTURES: Carrie, The Fury, Honeysuckle Rose, The Competition, Voices, Yentl, Micki and Maude, Rumpelstiltskin, Crossing Delancey.
TELEVISION: Movies: James Dean, Dynasty, Panache, Once an Eagle, Anastasia, The Mystery of Anna.

IRWIN, CHRISTOPHER: Producer, Executive. b. England 1948. e. U. of Sussex, Eng., B.A., social studies. From 1967 to 1969 worked as freelance producer-presenter for BBC Radio Brighton. Was with the Federal Trust (the institute concerned with European affairs) 1969 to 1975, during which time worked for the Secretariat of the North Atlantic Assembly. Joined the BBC's External Services as talks producer in 1975, moving in 1977 to the BBC's central Secretariat. From 1977 to 1978 was seconded to the International Institute for Strategic Studies. In 1978 went to Scotland as Secretary, BBC Scotland, and was closely associated with early stages of Radio Scotland. Member of BBC's Future Policy Group, the "think tank" of the Corporation. Appointed Head of Radio Scotland May 1980.

ISAACS, CHERYL BOONE: Executive. Entered m.p. industry 1977 as staff publicist for Columbia Pictures. Worked five years after that for Mel Simon Prods., named v.p. Left to become dir. of adv./pub. for The Ladd Co. 1984, named dir., pub. & promo., West Coast, for Paramount Pictures. Currently vice pres., publicity, Paramount Pictures since 1986.

ISAACS, PHIL: Executive. b. New York, NY, May 22, 1922. e. City Coll. of New York. In U.S. Navy, 1943–46. Joined Paramount Pictures in 1946 as bookers asst., N.Y. exch. Branch mgr. in Washington; then mgr. Rocky Mt. div. In 1966 was Eastern-Southern sls. mgr.; 1967 joined Cinema Center Films as v.p. domestic dist. In 1972 named v.p., marketing, for Tomorrow Entertainment; joined Avco-Embassy 1975 as v.p., gen. sls. mgr., named exec. v.p., 1977. 1978 joined General Cinema Corp. as v.p. 1980 v.p., gen. sls. mgr., Orion Pictures. 1983, formed Phil Isaacs Co.

ISRAEL, NEAL: Writer, Director.
PICTURES: Tunnelvision (exec. prod., s.p.); Cracking Up (s.p.); Americathon (dir., s.p.); Police Academy (s.p.); Bachelor Party (dir., s.p.); Moving Violations (dir., s.p.); Real Genius (s.p.); It's Alive III (s.p.); Buy and Cell (co-s.p.).
TELEVISION: Lola Falana Special (s.p.); Mac Davis Show; Ringo; Marie (prod.); Twilight Theatre (writer, prod.).

ITAMI, JUZO: Director, Actor. b. Kyoto, Japan, 1933. m. actress Nobuko Miyamoto. Son of Mansaku Itami, pioneering Japanese film director. After successful stint as commercial artist, became an actor as well as essayist (Listen, Women, a collection of his work). Directing debut The Funeral (1984).
PICTURES: Actor: 55 Days at Peking, Lord Jim, I Am a Cat, The Makioka Sisters, The Family Game. Director: The Funeral (1984 Japanese Acad. Awards), Tampopo, A Taxing Woman (8 Japanese Acad. Awards), A Taxing Woman's Return (dir., s.p.).

IVANEK, ZELJKO: Actor. b. Ljubljana, Yugoslavia, Aug. 15, 1957. Came to U.S. with family in 1960 and returned to homeland before settling in Palo Alto, CA, in 1967. Studied at Yale, majoring in theatre studies; graduated in 1978. Also graduate of London Acad. of Music and Dramatic Arts. Regular member of Williamstown Theatre Festival, appearing in Hay Fever, Charley's Aunt, Front Page. Bdwy. debut in The Survivor.
THEATER: Brighton Beach Memoirs, Loot, Master Harold . . . and the Boys (Yale Rep. premiere prod.). Off B'way: Cloud 9, A Map of the World, The Cherry Orchard.
PICTURES: Tex, The Sender, The Soldier, Mass Appeal, Rachel River.
TELEVISION: The Sun Also Rises, All My Sons, Echoes in the Darkness.

IVERS, IRVING N.: Executive. b. Montreal, Canada, Feb. 23, 1939. e. Sir George Williams U. Worked for 10 years in radio and TV in variety of executive capacities in station management before entering film business. Joined Columbia Pictures in 1973, serving as director of mktg. and dir. of adv. 1973–77; named Canadian sls. mgr. 1977–78; v.p. of adv./pub. 1978–80. In 1980 joined 20th Century-Fox as snr. v.p. of adv./pub./promo.; exec. v.p., worldwide adv., pub., promo. 1980–83; pres., worldwide mkt., MGM/UA/Entertainment Co., 1983–86. In 1986 to Warner Bros. as v.p., intl. adv./pub.

IVES, BURL: Ballad singer, Actor. b. Hunt Township, IL, June 14, 1909. e. Teacher's Coll., Charleston, IL. Professional football player, itinerant worker, radio singer, specializing ballads.
STAGE: On B'way in Cat on a Hot Tin Roof.
PICTURES INCLUDE: Smoky, Green Grass of Wyoming, Station West, So Dear to My Heart, Sierra, East of Eden, The Big Country (Acad. Award, supp., 1958), Cat on a Hot Tin

Roof, Day of the Outlaw, Our Man in Havana, Robin and the Seven Hoods, Just You and Me, Kid, Earthbound, Two Moon Junction.
TELEVISION: Rudolph the Red-Nosed Reindeer (narrator), Frosty the Snowman (narrator), Poor Little Rich Girl, Captains and the Kings, Roots, The Ewok Adventure.

IVEY, JUDITH: Actress. b. El Paso, TX, Sept. 4, 1951. e. Illinois State U. Acted with the Goodman Theatre, Chicago. Stage debut in The Sea in Chicago, 1974. Film debut in Harry and Son, 1984. Television debut in The Sandy Hill Kidnapping.
STAGE: Bedroom Farce, The Goodbye People, Oh, Cow-ard!, Design for Living, Piaf, The Rimers of Eldritch, Pastorale, Two Small Bodies, Steaming (Tony and Drama Desk Awards), Second Lady (off-B'way work she helped develop), Hurlyburly (Tony and Drama Desk Awards), Precious Sons, Blithe Spirit.
PICTURES: The Lonely Guy, The Woman in Red, Compromising Positions, Brighton Beach Memoirs, Hello Again, Sister, Sister, Miles from Home, Love Hurts.
TELEVISION: Dixie: Changing Habits, We Are the Children, The Long Hot Summer, Jesse and the Bandit Queen.

IVORY, JAMES: Director. b. Berkeley, CA, June 7, 1928. e. U. of Oregon, U. of Southern California. First film Venice: Theme and Variation (doc. made as thesis, 1957). American director who first gained his reputation making films in India (The Sword and the Flute, The Delphi Way). Formed Merchant-Ivory Productions with producer Ismail Merchant.
PICTURES: The Householder, Shakespeare Wallah, The Guru, Bombay Talkie, Savages, The Wild Party, Autobiography of a Princess, Roseland, Hullabaloo Over Georgie & Bonnie's Pictures, The Europeans (also prod.), The Five Forty Eight, Jane Austen in Manhattan, Quartet, Heat and Dust, The Bostonians, A Room with a View, Maurice (also co-s.p.), Slaves of New York.

J

JACKSON, ANNE: Actress. b. Allegheny, PA, Sept. 3, 1926. e. Neighborhood Playhouse, Actors Studio. Married to actor Eli Wallach. Stage debut in The Cherry Orchard, 1944. Film debut in So Young So Bad, 1950. Autobiography: Early Stages.
THEATER: Major Barbara, Middle of the Night, Typists and the Tiger, LUV, Twice Around the Park, Summer and Smoke, Nest of the Woodgrouse, Marco Polo Sings a Solo, The Mad Woman of Chaillot, Cafe Crown.
PICTURES: The Secret Life of an American Wife, Zig Zag, Lovers and Other Strangers, Dirty Dingus Magee, The Shining.
TELEVISION: Out on a Limb (movie); Everything's Relative (series), 84 Charing Cross Road, Golda, Private Battles, Baby M.

JACKSON, BRIAN: Actor, Film/Stage Producer. b. Bolton, England, 1931. Early career in photography then numerous stage performances incl. Old Vic, Royal Shakespeare. Ent. film/TV industry 1958. Formed Quintus Plays, 1965; formed Brian Jackson Productions 1966; formed Hampden Gurney Studios Ltd. 1970. Co-produced The Others 1967; presented The Button, 1969; co-produced the documentary film Village in Mayfair, 1970; 1971: Formed Brian Jackson Films Ltd.; produced Steaming, The Red Deer; 1972: produced The Story of Tutankhamen.
TELEVISION INCLUDES: Moon Fleet, Private Investigator, Life of Lord Lister, Z Cars, Vendetta, Sherlock Holmes, Mr. Rose, Hardy Heating International, Nearest & Dearest, The Persuaders, The Paradise Makers, The New Avengers, Smugglers Bay, The Tomorrow People, Secret Army, Last Visitor for Hugh Peters, Six Men of Dorset, Commercials: As the man from Delmonte.
PICTURES INCLUDE: Incident in Karandi, Carry On Sergeant, Gorgo, Jack the Ripper, Taste of Fear, Heroes of Telemark, Only the Lonely, The Deadly Females, The Revenge of the Pink Panther, Deceptions.
STAGE INCLUDES: Mame, Drury Lane, Fallen Angels, Seasons with Old Vic and Royal Shakespeare Co., In Praise of Love.

JACKSON, FREDA: Actress. B. Nottingham, Eng., Dec. 29, 1909. e. U. Coll., Nottingham. Stage debut 1933, Northampton Repertory Theatre; London debut 1936, Old Vic; screen debut in Canterbury Tale, 1942.
PICTURES INCLUDE: Henry V, Beware of Pity, Great Expectations, No Room at the Inn, Flesh and Blood, Women of Twilight, The Good Die Young, The Crowded Day, The Enchanted Doll, Bhowani Junction, Last Man to Hang, The Flesh Is Weak, Brides of Dracula, Greyfriar's Bobbie, Shadow of the Cat, Attempt to Kill, West Eleven, Monster of Terror, The Third Secret, Gwangi, Tom Jones, Clash of the Titans.
TELEVISION: Macadam and Eve, Sorry Wrong Number, Trial of Marie Lafarge, Release, Colombe, Maigret in Mont-

Jac-Jae

martre, Sergeant Musgrave's Dance, Dr. Finlay's Casebook, Sunset, Knock On Any Door, The Spies, Adam Adamant, Midland Profile, Owen Md., The Kilvert Diaries, She Fell Among Thieves, Randall and Hopkirk, The Old Curiosity Shop, Blake's Seven.

JACKSON, GLENDA: Actress. b. Birkenhead, England, May 9, 1936. State debut: Separate Tales (Worthing, Eng. 1957). Ent. m.p. ind. 1955.
THEATER: (Eng.): All Kinds of Men, Hammersmith, The Idiot, Alfie. Joined Royal Shakespeare Co in experimental Theatre of Cruelty season. Marat Sade (London, NY), Three Sisters, The Maids, Hedda Gabler, The White Devil, Rose, Strange Interlude (NY), Macbeth (NY).
PICTURES INCLUDE: Marat-Sade, Negatives, Women in Love (Acad. Award, 1970), The Music Lovers, Sunday, Bloody Sunday, Mary Queen of Scots, Triple Echo, The Nelson Affair, A Touch of Class (Acad. Award, 1973), The Maids, The Tempter, The Romantic Englishwoman, Hedda, Sarah, Nasty Habits, House Calls, Stevie, The Class of Miss McMichael, Lost and Found, Health, Hopscotch, Giro City, The Return of the Soldier, Turtle Diary, Beyond Therapy, Business as Usual, Salome's Last Dance, The Rainbow, The Visit.
TELEVISION: The Patricia Neal Story, Queen Elizabeth, Sakharov, Strange Interlude.

JACKSON, GORDON: Actor. b. Glasgow, Scotland, Dec. 19, 1923. e. Glasgow. On radio since 1939; screen debut in Foreman Went to France, 1940. Best known as Hudson on Upstairs, Downstairs.
PICTURES INCLUDE: Nine Men, San Demetrio, Millions Like Us, Pink String and Sealing Wax, Captive Heart, Against the Wind, Eureka Stockade, Whiskey Galore, Floodtide, Stop Press Girl, Bitter Springs, Happy Go Lovely, The Lady with the Lamp, Meet Mr. Lucifer, Malta Story, Castle in the Air, Quatermass Experiment, Pacific Destiny, Baby and the Battleship, Sailor Beware, Seven Waves Away (Abandon Ship), As Long as You're Happy, Hell Drivers, Rockets Galore, Bridal Path, Yesterday's Enemy, Blind Date, Cone of Silence, Tunes of Glory, Greyfriar's Bobbie, Mutiny on the Bounty, The Great Escape, The Long Ships, Those Magnificent Men in Their Flying Machines, The Great Spy Mission, The Ipcress File, Cast a Giant Shadow, Fighting Prince of Donegal, Night of the Generals, Triple Cross, The Eliminator, Prime of Miss Jean Brodie, Run Wild, Run Free, Hamlet, Scrooge, Kidnapped, Madame Sin, Russian Roulette, Spectre, Golden Rendezvous, Medusa Touch, Last Giraffe, Shooting Party, The Masks of Death, Whistle Blower, Gunpower.
TELEVISION: Numerous TV appearances incl: Upstairs, Downstairs, The Professionals, A Town Like Alice, Hart to Hart, My Brother Tom, Shaka Zulu, Noble House, Dangerous Love.

JACKSON, JOHN HENRY: Executive. b. New York, NY, April 27, 1916. e. Holy Cross Acad., 1930; Professional Children's Sch., 1934; Georgia Tech, 1936. Performed as vaudeville artist touring Europe, 1928–29; Fair dates and indoor circus, 1929–34; Billy Rosie's Jumbo, 1935; Texas Centennial, 1936; George Abbott's Too Many Girls, 1938. Joined Radio City Music Hall, 1943 with Glee Club; stage manager, 1944–51; director of stage operations, 1958; v.p., 1970; prod., 1971; pres., Tri-Marquee Productions, Ltd., 1979. Retired 1980. Produced p.r. events W.R. Grace Co. 1980–86.

JACKSON, KATE: Actress. b. Birmingham, AL, Oct. 29, 1949. e. U. of Mississippi, Birmingham Southern U. Did summer stock before going to N.Y. e. enter American Acad. of Dramatic Arts, appearing in Night Must Fall, Constant Wife, Little Moon of Alban, etc. Worked as model and became tour guide at NBC. First role on TV in Dark Shadows (series).
PICTURES INCLUDE: Thunder and Lightning, Dirty Tricks, Making Love, Loverboy.
TELEVISION: The Jimmy Stewart Show (pilot). Movies: Killer Bees, The Shrine of Lorna Love, The Jenny Storm Homicide, Listen to Your Heart, Topper, Thin Ice. Series: Charlie's Angels, Scarecrow and Mrs. King, Baby Boom.

JACKSON, MICHAEL: Singer, Composer. b. Aug. 29, 1958. Musical recording artist with family group known as Jackson 5: all brothers, Jackie, Tito, Marlon, Randy and Michael. Sister is singer Janet Jackson.
PICTURE: The Wiz, Moonwalker.
TELEVISION: Motown on Showtime: Michael Jackson.

JACOBI, DEREK: Actor. b. London, England, Oct. 22, 1938. e. Cambridge. On stage in Pericles, The Hollow Crown, Hobson's Choice, The Suicide, Breaking the Code (London, NY).
PICTURES INCLUDE: Day of the Jackal, Blue Blood, The Odessa File, The Medusa Touch, The Human Factor, Enigma, Little Dorrit, The Tenth Man.
TELEVISION: She Stoops to Conquer, Man of Straw, The Pallisers, I, Claudius, Philby, Burgess and MacLean, Hamlet. Movies: Othello, Three Sisters, Interlude, Charlotte, The Man Who Went Up in Smoke, The Hunchback of Notre Dame, Inside the Third Reich, The Secret Garden, The Tenth Man. Series: Minder, Tales of the Unexpected, Mr. Pye.

JACOBS, BARRY: Executive. b. London, England, 1924. Ent. m.p. ind. 1938. Served in RAF 1943–46. Circuit rep. Warner Bros. 1938–59. Overseas sales rep. independent producers 1960–62. Formed Eagle Films Ltd. dist. organization UK 1962. Entered prod. 1969. Exec. prod. The Wife Swappers, Groupie Girl, Bread, Naughty, The Love Box, Sex and The Other Woman, On the Game, Eskimo Nell. Formed Elephant Entertainment Ltd. & Elephant Video Ltd., 1986.

JACOBS, JOHN: Executive. b. New York, NY. e. Syracuse U.'s Newhouse Communications Sch. Full-service agency background, including 13 years with Grey Advertising agency, where handled Warner Bros. & Warner Home Video accts. Supvr. media on RCA, ABC-TV, Murdoch Publishing, Radio City Musical Hall, etc. Named v.p. & group media dir. for Grey. 1986, left to join Warner Bros. as v.p., media.

JACOBY, FRANK DAVID: Director, Producer. b. New York, NY, July 15, 1925. e. Hunter Coll., Brooklyn Coll. m. Doris Storm, producer/director educational films, actress. 1949–52: NBC network TV director; 1952–56: B.B.D.O., Blow Co., TV producer/director; 1956–58 Metropolitan Educational TV Association, Director of Production; 1958–65: United Nation, film producer/director; 1965 to present: President, Jacoby/Storm Productions, Inc., Westport, Conn., documentary, industrial, educational films and filmstrips. Clients include Xerox Corp., Random House, Publ., Lippincott Co., IBM, Heublein, G.E., and Pitney Bowes. Winner, Sherwood Award, Peabody Award. Member, Director's Guild of America; winner, Int'l TV & Film Festival, National Educational Film Festival, American Film Festival.

JACOBY, JOSEPH: Producer, Director, Writer. b. Brooklyn, NY, 1942. e. New York U. Sch. of Arts and Sciences, majoring in m.p. As undergraduate worked part-time as prod. asst. on daytime network TV shows and as puppeteer for Bunin Puppets. In 1963 joined Bill Baird Marionettes as full-time puppeteer, working also on Baird film commercials. Made feature m.p. debut as prod.-dir of Shame, Shame, 1968.
PICTURES INCLUDE: Hurry Up, or I'll Be 30, The Great Georgia Bank Hoax (co.-prod., dir., s.p.).

JACOBY, SCOTT: Actor. b. Chicago, IL, Nov. 19, 1956.
PICTURES: The Little Girl Who Lives Down the Lane, Midnight Auto Supply, Our Winning Season, To Die For.
TELEVISION: Movies: No Place to Run, That Certain Summer, (Emmy Award, supp. 1973), The Man Who Could Talk to Kids, Bad Ronald, Smash-Up on Interstate 5, 79 Park Avenue, No Other Love, The Diary of Anne Frank.

JACON, BERNARD: Executive. b. Louisiana. Manager, promotion, Small & Strausberg Theatres, New York; buyer & gen. mgr., Mantell Theatres N.Y., gen. mgr. & assoc., Rockaway Beach Theatres, Universal Pictures, home office & field, br. operations & sales. Mgr., sales & dist. (Continental Films in chg. of sales & dist., Lux Film Distributing Corp., N.Y., 1949–52; v.p. sales, dist. IFE Releasing, 1952–55; org. nat'l distrib. co., Jacon Film Distributors, Inc., as pres., 1956; nat'l consultant to independent distributors, producers & exhibitors, member of the Pioneers & Variety; 1979, formed Bernie Jacon, Inc., natl. co-ordinator for producers and distributors.

JACQUEMIN, ROBERT: Executive. Began career as media buyer; later in station representation as v.p. of regional sls. for Telerep, Inc. Entered syndication as pres. of Television Marketing Services, St. Louis. Joined Paramount Domestic Television and Video Programming as midwest div. mgr. in St. Louis; later sr. v.p., sls. in N.Y. 1981, named exec. v.p., sls. & mktg. 1985, joined Walt Disney Pictures as sr. v.p., domestic TV dist., a new syndication div. formed by the co.

JACQUES, ROBERT C.: Film editor. b. Cincinnati, OH, Feb. 24, 1919. e. U. of Michigan, U. of Southern California. Asst. film ed., RKO Radio 1939–42; film ed., Pathe News, 1942–44; chief film ed., NBC Television, 1944–48; prod. chief, Ziv TV film dept. 1944–58; free lance m.p. film ed., 1951–52; supervising film ed., prod. mgr., American Film Prod., 1952–53; prod. supvr., ed., Telenews and Screen Gems 1953; film ed., RKO Radio, 1953–55; supervising film ed., George Blake Enterprises, 1955–57; v.p. Peter Elgar Productions 1957–60; supv. film editor, Transfilm-Caravel Inc. 1960–62; v.p. in chg. of completion, Filmex, Inc., 1962. V.P. in charge of completion, Filmex Inc. 1962–69. Free lance film editor, May–Nov. 1969. V.P. of own co., Double Image Inc., film and videotape editorial service, Nov. 1969–1983. Freelance post-prod. consultant, 1983. Retired 1983.

JAECKEL, RICHARD HANLEY: Actor. b. Long Beach, NY, Oct. 10, 1926. e. Hollywood H.S., 1943. Performed odd jobs upon graduation, with plans toward entering Merchant Marine when of age; worked as delivery boy in mail room, 20th Century-Fox; Film debut Guadalcanal Diary (1943).
PICTURES INCLUDE: The Gunfighter, Sea Hornet, Hoodlum Empire, My Son John, Come Back Little Sheba, Big Leaguer, Sea of Lost Ships, Shanghai Story, Violent Men, Apache Ambush, Sands of Iwo Jima, Fragile Fox, 3:10 to

154

Yuma, The Gallant Hours, The Dirty Dozen, Sometimes a Great Notion, Ulzanas Raid, Pat Garrett and Billy the Kid, The Outfit, Chosen Survivors, The Drowning Pool, Part II—Walking Tall, Chisum, Twilights Last Gleaming, All the Marbles, Starman.
TELEVISION: U.S. Steel Hour, Elgin Hour, Goodyear Playhouse, Kraft, Producer's Showcase, The Petrified Forest. Movies: The Red Pony, Born Innocent, Firehouse, The Last Day Reward, Dirty Dozen: The Next Mission. Series: Spenser for Hire, Supercarrier.

JAFFE, HERB: Executive, Producer. b. New York, NY. e. Brooklyn Coll., Columbia U. Press agent; then talent agent, MCA personal appearance div.; sales exec., MCA-TV, Ltd., syndic. film div.; eastern sales mgr., Motion Pictures for Television; joined Official Films as v.p., sales mgr.; Herb Jaffe Assoc. 1957; sold Herb Jaffe Assoc. to Ashley-Steiner-Famous Artists, Inc.; v.p. in prod., United Artists, 1965; v.p. of West Coast Operations, 1966. 1970, v.p. charge of World-Wide prod, 1973 entered field of independent motion picture production. Now pres., TVO Productions, Inc.
PICTURES: The Wind and the Lion, Demon Seed, Who'll Stop the Rain, Time After Time, Those Lips, Those Eyes, Motel Hell, Jinxed, The Lords of Discipline, Little Treasure, Fright Night, The Gate, 3 for the Road, Maid to Order, Nightflyers, Pass the Ammo, Dudes, Fright Night—Part Two, Trading Hearts (co-prod.), Remote Control.

JAFFE, LEO: Executive. b. April 23, 1909. e. New York U. Started at Columbia, 1930; v.p., Columbia Pictures, January, 1954; 1st v.p., treas., member of board, 1956; v.p. & treas., 1958; exec. v.p., Columbia Pictures, 1962; Pres. Columbia Pictures, 1968; pres., Columbia Pictures Industries, Inc, 1970, president & chief executive officer, Columbia Pictures Industries, Inc., Chairman of board of directors to Aug., 1978. Currently chm. emeritus. Industry honors: Motion Picture Pioneer of the Year, 1972; Acad. of Motion Picture Arts and Sciences Jean Hersholt Humanitarian Award, 1979.

JAFFE, STANLEY R.: Producer. b. New Rochelle, NY, July, 1940. Graduate of U.of Pennsylvania Wharton Sch. of Finance. Joined Seven Arts Associates, 1962; named exec. ass't to president, 1964; later, head of East Coast TV programming. Produced Goodbye, Columbus, in 1968 for Paramount; then joined that company as exec. v.p., 1969. Produced A New Leaf, 1969. Named pres. of Paramount in 1970; resigned June 10, 1971 to form own prod. unit. First film: Bad Company (1972); Man on the Swing, Bad News Bears. Joined Columbia as exec. v.p. of global prod. in 1976, but resigned to be independent producer. 1979: Kramer vs. Kramer; 1981: Taps (co. prod.); 1983: Without a Trace (prod.-dir.). 1984: Racing with the Moon, Firstborn. 1987: Fatal Attraction (co-prod.), The Accused (co-prod.), Black Rain (co-prod.).

JAFFE, STEVEN-CHARLES: Producer. b. 1954. e. U. of Southern California, cinema. Worked on production in Holland and Switzerland; served as prod. asst. on The Wind and the Lion in Spain. Assoc. prod. on Demon Seed (written by brother Robert); served as location mgr. on Who'll Stop the Rain; assoc. prod. on Time After Time. Full producer on Those Lips, Those Eyes, Motel Hell (also co-s.p.).

JAFFE, WILLIAM B.: Attorney. b. New York, NY, Mar. 11, 1904. e. Union Coll., A.B., 1926; Columbia U. Law Sch., LL.B., 1929. m. Evelyn Annenberg. Assoc. Nathan Burkan 1929–35; gen. counsel Allied Artists; 1933–69 spcl. counsel to interests financing independent prod.; to leading personalities m.p. ind.; dir. MPPDA rep. Columbia; gen. counsel & dir. Allied Artists Internat'l 1933–69; chmn. Manning Plan, State of N.Y.; counsel, War Manpower Commission, N.Y. Region Spec. counsel to Revlon, Inc., in TV field; s.p. counsel Triangle Pub.; chmn., Art Advisory Committee Dartmouth College; trustee, Union Coll., Schenectady, N.Y. Vice Chr. & Bd. of Gov. Jewish Museum, N.Y.; benefactor, Metropolitan Museum of Art; patron, Museum of Modern Art; Group Chairm. United Hospital Fund 1964–69; Trustee, Phi Epsilon Pi Foundation. Recipient Phi Epsilon Pi Achievement Award, 1964; Doctor Humane Letters, Dartmouth Coll. 1964; Trustee Mt. Sinai Hospital, N.Y., N.Y. Eye & Ear Infirmary. Partner, law firm, Shea, Gallop, Climenko & Gould.

JAFFEY, HERBERT: Executive. b. Somerville, NJ. Cap't. U.S. Army, pressbook writer, 20th Century-Fox; theatre management, Loew's; field exploitation, United Artists, Ad. pub. dir. 20th Century-Fox Int and Inter-Amer. Corp.; dir., adv. & publicity, Rugoff Theatres; Independent Film Prod.; Paramount Foreign Advertising & Publicity Manager, screenplay writer.

JAGGER, DEAN: Actor. b. Lima, OH, Nov. 7, 1903. e. Wabash Coll., Crawfordsville, IN. On N.Y. stage, stock, vaudeville. Screen debut 1929 in Woman from Hell. Academy Award sup. role 1949 for 12 O'Clock High.
PICTURES INCLUDE: College Rhythm, Home on the Range, Car 99, Woman Trap, 13 Hours by Air, Woman in Distress, Escape by Night, Brigham Young, Western Union,

Valley of the Sun, I Escaped from the Gestapo, North Star, Alaska, When Strangers Marry, Pursued, Driftwood, Dark City, Rawhide, Warpath, Denver and Rio Grande, My Son John, It Grows on Trees, The Robe, Executive Suite, Private Hell 36, White Christmas, Bad Day at Black Rock, The Eternal Sea, On the Threshold of Space, It's a Dog's Life, Red Sundown, Great Man, Three Brave Men, The Nun's Story, Cash McCall, Elmer Gantry, Parrish, Jumbo, Stay Away Joe, Firecreek, Smith, The Kremlin Letter, Vanishing Point, Tiger by the Tail, Evil Town.
TELEVISION: Glass House, Mr. Novak (series), Brotherhood of the Bell, The Lie, Gideon's Trumpet, Haywire.

JAGGER, MICK: Singer, Composer, Actor. b. Dartford, Kent, England, July 26, 1943. Lead singer with Rolling Stones.
PICTURES: Performance, Ned Kelly, Gimme Shelter, Sympathy for the Devil, Ladies and Gentlemen, The Rolling Stones, The London Rock 'n' Roll Show, Let's Spend the Night Together.

JAGLOM, HENRY: Director, Writer, Editor. b. New York, NY, Jan. 26, 1943. Studied acting, writing and directing at U. of Pennsylvania and with Actors Studio. Did off-Bdwy. shows; went to West Coast where appeared in TV series (Gidget, The Flying Nun, etc.). Started shooting documentary film in Israel during Six Day War; turned it into 3-hr. silent film. Hired to edit Easy Rider by producer Bert Schneider. Acted in Drive, He Said and Last Movie. Directed first feature, A Safe Place, in 1971.
PICTURES: Tracks; Sitting Ducks; Can She Bake a Cherry Pie?; A Lovely Ride; Always; Someone to Love; New Years Day (dir., s.p.).

JALBERT, JOE JAY: Executive. e. U. of Washington. Was ski captain in school and began film career as technical director on Downhill Racer, 1969, also cinematographer and double for Robert Redford. 1970, produced Impressions of Utah, documentary, with Redford. Won Emmy for cinematography on TV's Peggy Fleming Special. In 1970 formed Jalbert Productions, Inc., to make feature films, TV sports, specials, commercials, etc. Co. has produced official films at Innsbruck Winter Olympics (1976), Lake Placid (1980), Sarajevo (1984).

JAMES, CLIFTON: Actor. b. Portland, OR, May 29, 1925. e. U. of Oregon. Studied at Actors Studio. Made numerous appearances on stage and TV, as well as theatrical films.
PICTURES INCLUDE: On The Waterfront, The New Centurions, Live and Let Die, The Last Detail, Bank Shot, Juggernaut, The Man with the Golden Gun, Rancho DeLuxe, The Untouchables, Eight Men Out.

JAMES, DENNIS: Performer. b. Jersey City, NJ, Aug. 24, 1917. e. St. Peter's Coll., Jersey City. TV personality for over 30 years. Formerly M.C., actor, sports commentator in Radio; award winning sports commentator for wrestling, 25 TV first to credit; currently pres., Dennis James Prod.
TELEVISION: Chance of a Lifetime, High Finance, First Impressions, What's My Line?, PDQ, Your All-American College Show; host New Price Is Right, Nightime; Host, Name That Tune, Daytime.

JAMES, POLLY: Writer. b. Ancon, Canal Zone. e. Smith Coll. Newspaper work, Panama; with trade mag., N.Y.; screenwriter since 1942.
PICTURES INCLUDE: Mrs. Parkington, The Raiders, Redhead from Wyoming, Quantrill's Raiders.
TELEVISION: Several shows.

JAMESON, JERRY: Director. b. Hollywood, CA. Started as editorial asset; then editor and supv. editor for Danny Thomas Prods. Turned to directing.
PICTURES: Dirt Gang, The Bat People, Brute Core, Airport '77, Raise the Titanic.
TELEVISION: Movies: Heatwave!, The Elevator, Hurricane, Terror on the 40th Floor, The Secret Night Caller, The Deadly Tower, The Lives of Jenny Dolan, The Call of the Wild, The Invasion of Johnson County, Superdome, A Fire in the Sky, High Noon—Part II, The Return of Will Kane, The Red Spider.

JANKOWSKI, GENE F.: Executive. b. Buffalo, NY, May 21, 1934. e. Canisius U., B.S., Michigan State U., M.A. in radio, TV and film. Joined CBS radio network sls, 1961 as acct. exec.; eastern sls. mgr., 1966; moved to CBS-TV as acct. exec. 1969; gen. sls. mgr. WCBS-TV, 1970; dir. sls, 1970; v.p. sls., CBS-TV Stations Divisions, 1973; v.p., finance & planning, 1974; v.p., controller, CBS Inc. 1976; v.p. adm., 1977; exec. v.p. CBS Broadcast Group, 1977; pres., CBS Broadcast/Group, 1977; 1988, appointed chairman CBS/Broadcast Group. Member: Pres., Intl. Council of National Acad. of Television Arts & Sciences; trustee Amer. Film Institute; trustee, Catholic U. of Amer.; director, Georgetown U.; bd. of gov. American Red Cross; member: National bd. dirs., Boys Hope; vice chmn., business comm. Metropolitan Museum of Art.
AWARDS: Received Distinguished Communications Medal from South Baptist Radio & Television Commission; honorary

Doctorate of Humanities, Michigan State U.; Humanitarian Award, National Conference of Christians and Jews.

JANNI, JOSEPH: Producer. b. Milan, Italy, May 21, 1916. e. Milan U., Rome Film Sch. Entered m.p. industry 1941. Assistant producer. Founded Vic Films Ltd.
PICTURES INCLUDE: Own productions: The Glass Mountain, White Corridors, Something Money Can't Buy, Romeo and Juliet (co-prod.), A Town Like Alice (prod.); The Captain's Table, Savage Innocents, A Kind of Loving, Billy Liar, Darling, Modesty Blaise, Far from the Madding Crowd, Poor Cow, In Search of Gregory, Sunday, Bloody Sunday, Made, Yanks (co-prod.).

JARMAN, CLAUDE, JR.: Actor. b. Nashville, TN, Sept. 27, 1934. e. MGM Sch. Film debut in The Yearling, 1946.
PICTURES INCLUDE: High Barbaree, Sun Comes Up, Intruder in the Dust, Roughshod, Outriders, Inside Straight, Rio Grande, Hangman's Knot, Fair Wind to Java, Great Locomotive Chase.
TELEVISION: Centennial.

JARMUSCH, JIM: Director, Writer, Composer, Actor. b. Akron, OH, 1953. e. attended Columbia U., went to Paris in senior year. New York U. Film Sch., studied with Nicholas Ray and became his teaching asst. Appeared as an actor in Red Italy and Fraulein Berlin. Composed scores for The State of Things and Reverse Angle. Directorial debut Permanent Vacation (1980). Wrote and directed New World using 30 minutes of leftover, unused film from another director. (Won International Critics Prize, Rotterdam Film Festival.) Expanded it into Stranger Than Paradise.
PICTURES: Stranger Than Paradise (Best Film Award, National Society of Film; Golden Leopard, Locarno Film Festival; Camera d'Or best new director, Cannes), Down by Law, All Night Long (actor only), Tuesday Night in Memphis.

JARRE, MAURICE: Composer. b. Lyon, France, 1924. Studied at Paris Cons. Was orchestra conductor for Jean Louis Barrault's theatre company four years. In 1951 joined Jean Vilar's nat'l theatre co., composing for plays by Shakespeare, Moliere, O'Neill, Eliot, and Victor Hugo. Started composing film scores in 1952.
PICTURES INCLUDE: Hotel des Invalides, La Tete contre les Murs, Eyes Without a Face, Crack in the Mirror, Sundays and Cybele, The Longest Day, Lawrence of Arabia (AA, 1962), The Collector, Is Paris Burning?, Weekend at Dunkirk, Dr. Zhivago (AA, 1965), Night of the Generals, The Professionals, Grand Prix, Five Card Stud, Isadora, The Damned, Ash Wednesday, The Life and Times of Judge Roy Bean, The Mackintosh Man, The Effect of Gamma Rays on Man-in-the-Moon Marigolds, Island at the Top of the World, Mandingo, Posse, Winter Kills, The Magician of Lublin, Resurrection, The American Success Company, The Black Marble, Taps, Firefox, Young Doctors in Love, Don't Cry, It's Only Thunder, The Year of Living Dangerously, Dreamscape, A Passage to India, Top Secret!, Witness, Mad Max Beyond Thunderdome, Solarbabies, The Mosquito Coast, Tai-Pan, No Way Out, Julia and Julia, Fatal Attraction, Gaby—A True Story, Moon Over Parador, Gorillas in the Mist, Wildfire, Distant Thunder.

JARRICO, PAUL: Writer, Producer. b. Los Angeles, CA, Jan. 12, 1915.
PICTURES INCLUDE: Salt of the Earth, Tom, Dick and Harry (Academy nomination), Thousands Cheer, The Search (Academy Award), The White Tower, Not Wanted, The Girl Most Likely, Messenger of Death (s.p.).
TELEVISION: Great Expectations, Enola Gay, Apology, Samson and Delilah, Shogun, Jesus of Nazareth, The Users, The Murder of Mary Phagan.

JARROTT, CHARLES: Director. b. London, England, June 16, 1927. Son of British businessman and former singer-dancer at Gaiety Theatre. Joined British Navy; wartime service in Far East. After military service turned to theatre as asst. stage mgr. with Arts Council touring co. In 1949 joined Nottingham Repertory Theatre as stage dir. and juvenile acting lead. In 1953 joined new company formed to tour Canada; was leading man and became resident leading actor for Ottawa Theatre. In 1955 moved to Toronto and made TV acting debut opposite Katharine Blake whom he later wed. In 1957 made directing debut in TV for Canadian Bdcstg. Co. Became CBC resident dir. Moved to London to direct for Armchair Theatre for ABC-TV. Then became freelance dir., doing stage work, films, TV.
PICTURES INCLUDE: Anne of the Thousand Days, Mary, Queen of Scots, Lost Horizon, The Dove, The Littlest Horse Thieves, The Other Side of Midnight, The Last Flight of Noah's Ark, Condorman, The Amateur, The Boy in Blue.
TELEVISION: The Hot Potato Boys, Roll On, Bloomin' Death, Girl in a Birdcage, The Picture of Dorian Gray, Rain, The Rose Affair, Roman Gesture, Silent Song, The Male of the Species, The Young Elizabeth, A Case of Libel, Dr. Jekyll and Mr. Hyde, A Married Man, Poor Little Rich Girl: The Barbara Hutton Story; The Woman He Loved.

STAGE: The Duel, Galileo, The Basement, Tea Party, The Dutchman, etc.

JASON, RICK: Actor. b. New York, NY, May 21, 1926. e. American Acad. of Dramatic Arts.
THEATRE: Broadway debut: Now I Lay Me Down To Sleep (Theatre World Award).
PICTURES INCLUDE: Sombrero, Saracen Blade, This Is My Love, Lieutenant Wore Skirts, Wayward Bus.
TELEVISION: The Case of the Dangerous Robin, Combat (series).

JAY, LESLIE: Executive. b. New York, NY, May 12. e. Fordham U., B.A., 1977. Entered industry in 1969 as publicist with Bob Perilla Associates. 1970, pub. asst. on Such Good Friends, 1976—present, with Penthouse Films Intl., Ltd., asst. to producers on Caligula; then world-wide project coordinator on Caligula. Director of pub. & promo. for Omni: The New Frontier for Omni Productions Intl., Ltd. Director of p.r. for Penthouse Int'l., Ltd; 1984, v.p. & dir. public relations, Penthouse.

JAYSTON, MICHAEL: Actor. b. Nottingham, England, Oct. 28, 1935. Member of Old Vic theatre Co. & Bristol Old Vic.
PICTURES INCLUDE: Cromwell, The Nelson Affair, Nicholas and Alexandra, A Midsummer Night's Dream, The Public Eye.
TELEVISION: She Fell Among Thieves, Tinker, Tailor, Soldier, Spy.

JEFFEE, SAUL: Executive. b. Elizabeth, NJ, March 30, 1918. Established Movielab, Inc., 1936, pres., bd. chmn., & chief exec. officer. Also chm. & CEO, Movielab Video, Inc.; chm. & pres. 619 West 54th St. Corp.; chm. & pres., MLH Realty Corp.; chm. & pres., Film Recoupment Corp.; Life Fellow, SMPTE, Treas.; Pres. & chm., Movielab Theatre Service; Pres. Assoc. of Cinema Labs, 1963; American Tech. Rep. & Deleg. in the U.S.-U.S.S.R. Cult. Exch. 1965; Trustee, UJA Federation of Jewish Philanthropies, Chmn. Enter. & Commu. Div., U.J.A., 1967–68; Life member, Motion Picture Pioneers, Friars, City Athletic Club; Author of Narcotics—An American Plan, chmn. Bd. of Trustees, Lorge School, 1968–81; Pres. & Chm., Movielab-Hollywood, Inc., vice chmn., Film Society of Lincoln Center, Patron, Lincoln Center for The Performing Arts, life member, chmn., Life Patron Program, Variety Clubs International, holder of 16 patents, Professional Motion Picture Equipment, Trustee, Federation of Jewish Philanthropies; Trustee, Will Rogers Memorial Fund; Mason (Shriner, 32 deg); Life Member, The Jewish Chautagui Society. Member, National Advisory Committee for the Handicapped Boy Scouts of Amer.; Advisory Board, Cinema Lodge No. 6000 B'nai B'rith. Academy of Motion Picture Arts & Sciences; Mayor of N.Y.C. Advisory Council on Motion Pictures. Member, Natl. Academy of TV Arts & Sciences, Film Acquisition Comm., U.S.I.A.; Member, Int'l. Radio & TV Society.

JEFFREYS, ANNE: Actress. b. Goldsboro, NC, Jan. 26, 1923. m. actor Robert Sterling. Named by Theatre Arts Magazine as "one of the 10 outstanding beauties of the stage." Trained for operatic career. Sang with NY's Municipal Opera Co. while supplementing income as a Powers model. Appeared as Tess Trueheart in Dick Tracy features.
PICTURES INCLUDE: I Married an Angel, Step Lively, Dillinger, Sing Your Way Home, Trail Street, Riffraff, Return of the Bad Men, Boys' Night Out.
THEATRE: On Bway. in Street Scene, Kiss Me Kate, Romance, Three Wishes for Jamie, Kismet.
TELEVISION: Series: Topper, Love That Jill, Bright Promise, Delphi Bureau, General Hospital, Finder of Lost Loves; appearances on Falcon Crest, Hotel, Murder She Wrote.
STOCK: Camelot, King & I, Kismet, Song of Norway, Bells Are Ringing, Marriage Go Round, No Sex Please, We're British, Take Me Along, Carousel, Anniversary Waltz, Do I Hear a Waltz, Ninotchka, Pal Joey, Name of the Game, Destry Rides Again, The Merry Widow, Bitter Sweet, Desert Song, High Button Shoes, Sound of Music.

JEFFRIES, LIONEL: Actor. b. Forest Hill, London, England, 1926. Ent. m.p. ind. 1952.
PICTURES INCLUDE: The Nun's Story, Two-Way Stretch, The Trials of Oscar Wilde, Fanny, The Notorious Landlady, The Wrong Arm of the Law, First Men in the Moon, Call Me Bwana, The Truth About Spring, You Must Be Joking, The Crimson Blade, Arrivederci Baby, Spy with the Cold Nose, Journey to the Moon, Camelot, Chitty Chitty Bang Bang, Eye Witness, The Prisoner of Zenda, Railway Children, (dir., s.p.), Gingerbread House, Baxter, (dir.), The Amazing Mr. Blunden, (dir., s.p.), The Water Babies.
TELEVISION: Father Charlie, Tom, Dick, and Harriet, Cream in My Coffee, Minder.

JENKINS, CHARLES: Animation producer. b. Yorkshire, England, 1941. Ent. m.p. ind. 1957. Joined T.V.C. as gen. ass't 1958. Animated and prod. various prods. Joined Dick Williams, pioneered use of Oxberry Camera for animation, 1966. Esta.

Trickfilm Ltd., prod. optical effects for Yellow Submarine, 1967.

JENKINS, DAN: Public Relations Executive. b. Montclair, NJ, Dec. 5, 1916. e. U. of Virginia. 1938. U.S. Army, 1940–45; major, infantry. P.R. officer, Hq. Eighth Army. Mng. ed., Motion Picture Magazine, 1946–48; editor, Tele-Views Magazine, 1949–50; TV editor, columnist, Hollywood Reporter, 1950–53; Hollywood bureau chief, TV Guide, 1953–63; v.p., exec. dir. TV dept., Rogers, Cowan & Brenner, Inc., 1963–71. Formed Dan Jenkins Public Relations, Inc. 1971. Joined Charles A. Pomerantz Public Relations, Ltd. as v.p., 1975, while retaining own firm. Sr. associate, Porter, Novelli, Assocs., 1981.Mem. bd. trustees, Natl. Academy of TV Arts & Sciences; bd. gov., Hollywood chapter, Natl. Academy of TV Arts & Sciences, 1967–71. Rejoined Rogers & Cowan, 1983, v.p., TV dept. Retired, 1988.

JENKINS, GEORGE: Art dir. b. Baltimore, MD, Nov. 19, 1911. e. U. of Pennsylvania. Hollywood-New York art dir. since 1946; TV pictures for Four Star Playhouse and revue productions; NBC-TV opera, Carmen; color dir., CBS-TV, 1954; NBC color spec. Annie Get Your Gun, 1957; TV music with Mary Martin, 1959. Professor, Motion Picture Design, U. of California at L.A., 1985–87.
STAGE: Mexican Hayride, I Remember Mama, Dark of the Moon, Lost in the Stars, Bell, Book and Candle, Bad Seed, Happiest Millionaire, Two for the Seesaw, Ice Capades. Jones Beach spec., Song of Norway, Paradise Island, Around the World in 80 Days, Mardi Gras, Miracle Worker, Critics Choice, A Thousand Clowns, Jennie, Generation, Wait Until Dark, Only Game in Town, Night Watch, Sly Fox.
PICTURES INCLUDE: Best Years of Our Lives, Secret Life of Walter Mitty, Miracle Worker, Mickey One, Up the Down Staircase, Wait Until Dark, Subject Was Roses, Klute, 1776, Paper Chase, Parallax View, Night Moves, Funny Lady, All the President's Men (Acad. Award), Comes a Horseman, China Syndrome, Starting Over, The Postman Always Rings Twice, Rollover, Sophie's Choice, Orphans, See You in the Morning.
TELEVISION: The Dollmaker.

JENNINGS, PETER. TV Newsman. b. Toronto, Canada, July 29, 1938. Son of Canadian broadcaster Charles Jennings. e. Carleton U.; Rider Coll. Worked as a bank teller and late night radio host in Canada. Started career as host of Club Thirteen, a Canadian American Bandstand-like dance prog., then as a newsman on CFJR (radio), Ottawa; then with CJOH-TV and CBS before becoming co-anchor of first national news program on Canadian commercial network, CTV. Joined ABC in 1964 as NY corr.; 1965, anchor, Peter Jennings with the News; 1968, natl. corr., ABC News; 1969, overseas assignments; 1975, Washington corr. and anchor for AM America; 1977, chief foreign corr.; 1978, foreign desk anchor; 1978, foreign desk anchor, World News Tonight; 1983, anchor, sr. editor, World News Tonight.

JENS, SALOME: Actress. b. Milwaukee, WI, May 8, 1935. e. Northwestern U. Member Actors Studio. On stage in The Disenchanted, Far Country, Night Life, Winter's Tale, Mary Stuart, Antony and Cleopatra, After the Fall, Moon For the Misbegotten, The Balcony.
PICTURES: Angel Baby, The Fool Killer, Seconds, Me, Natalie, Cloud Dancer, Harry's War, Just Between Friends.
TELEVISION: Movies: In the Glitter Palace, Sharon: Portrait of a Mistress, From Here to Eternity, The Golden Moment: An Olympic Love Story, A Killer in the Family, Playing with Fire, Uncommon Valor, Mary Hartman, Mary Hartman, Falcon Crest (series).

JEPHCOTT, SAMUEL C.: Executive. b. 1944, Southampton, England. e. Arts Educational Sch., London. Entered industry as child actor The Grove Family BBC TV, 1956. Eight years in advertising producing TV Commercials. Emigrated to Toronto, Canada in 1968. Exec. Secty., Directors Guild of Canada, 1969–72. Film production management, 1972–75. Joined Compass Film Sales Ltd., a division of Quadrant Film Ltd. 1975–77. Joined Nielsen-Ferns Intl. Ltd. in chg. of distribution and production, 1977–81. Mgr. distribution, CBC Enterprises, 1982–84. Currently president, Canadian Film & TV Assn., pres., Cyclops Communications Corp. Is director of the Canadian Association of Motion Picture Producers.
PICTURES INCLUDE: The Hard Part Begins (prod. manager); Sunday In The Country (2nd A.D.); Me (prod. manager); Lions For Breakfast (prod. manager), It Seemed Like a Good Idea at the Time, (2nd A.D.); Love at First Sight, (prod. accountant); Find the Lady (stills); The New Avengers, TV, (prod. manager); The Wars (prod. supvr.); (TV) The Last Frontier (TV prod.), Mako Films, 1985–87.

JERGENS, ADELE: Actress. b. Brooklyn, NY, Nov. 28, 1922. Began career in musical shows during summer vacation at 15; won contest, New York's World Fair, as model; appeared on New York stage; night clubs, U.S. and abroad.
PICTURES INCLUDE: Edge of Doom, Side Street, Abbott and Costello Meet the Invisible Man, Sugarfoot, Try and Get Me, Show Boat, Somebody Loves Me, Aaron Slick from

Punkin' Crick, Overland Pacific, Miami Story, Fireman Save My Child, Big Chase, Strange Lady in Town, The Cobweb, Girls in Prison, The Lonesome Trail.

JESSEL, IAN: Executive. b. London, England, 1939. e. Oxford. Joined Rank Organisation in 1962 as graduate trainee and became responsible for acquisition of indep. product. Formed Target International Pictures in 1968. In 1970 joined World Film Sales becoming man. dir. 1972. World Film Sales merged with ITC in 1974. Elected to board 1975. Appointed dir. Classic Cinemas and ITC Film Distributors (UK), 1979. Appt. man. dir. ITC Films Int., 1980. Joined CBS Theatrical Films, Sept. 1981, as vice-pres. int. distribution, now based in Los Angeles.

JEWISON, NORMAN P.: Producer, Director. b. Toronto, Canada, July 21, 1926. e. Malvern Collegiate Inst., Toronto, 1940–44; Victoria Coll., U. of Toronto, 1946–50, B.A. Awarded 1988 Acad. of Canadian Cinema and Television Special Achievement Award.
TELEVISION: Exec. prod. of 8 Judy Garland shows; prod.-dir., Judy Garland specials.
PICTURES INCLUDE: 40 Pounds of Trouble, The Thrill of It All, Send Me No Flowers, Art of Love, The Cincinnati Kid, The Russians Are Coming, The Russians Are Coming, Dir. In The Heat of the Night. Prod.-dir. Gaily, Gaily, Prod.: The Landlord, Fiddler on the Roof, Prod./dir.: Jesus Christ Superstar; Prod.: Billy Two Hats; Prod.-dir.: Rollerball. Prod.-dir.: F.I.S.T.; co-prod.-dir.: And Justice for All; co.-prod.-dir.: Best Friends; co-prod.: Iceman; co-prod., dir.: A Soldier's Story; co-prod., dir.: Agnes of God; co-prod., dir., Moonstruck; co-prod.: The January Man, dir., co.-prod.: In Country.

JHABVALA, RUTH PRAWER: Writer. b. Cologne, Germany, May 7, 1927. Emigrated with her family to England, 1939. e. Hendon County Sch., Queen Mary Coll., London U. (degree in English). m. architect C.S.H. Jhabvala, 1951 and moved to Delhi. Novels published in England: 1955–60: To Whom She Will, Esmond in India, The Nature of Passion, The Householder; 1962: Get Ready for Battle. 1975: Heat and Dust. Has written most of the screenplays for the films of Ismail Merchant and James Ivory.
PICTURES: The Householder (1963, wrote s.p. based on her novel), Shakespeare Wallah (with Ivory), The Guru (with Ivory), Bombay Talkie (with Ivory), Autobiography of a Princess, Roseland, Hullabaloo Over Georgie and Bonnie's Pictures, (TV), The Europeans, Jane Austen in Manhattan, Quartet, Heat and Dust (based on her own novel), A Room with a View; Madame Sousatzka (co.-s.p.).

JILLIAN, ANN: Actress. b. Cambridge, MA, Jan. 29, 1951. Began career at age 10 in Disney's Babes in Toyland; in film version of Gypsy at age 12. On stage in musical, Sugar Babies. Has own company: 9-J Productions, developing TV movies.
PICTURES: Gypsy, Mr. Mom.
TELEVISION: Series: Hazel, It's a Living, Jennifer Slept Here. Many appearances on series (Love Boat, Fantasy Island). Mini-series: Ellis Island. Movies: Mae West, Death Ride to Osaka, Killer in the Mirror, Convicted: A Mother's Story, Alice in Wonderland, Perry Mason: The Case of the Murdered Madam; The Ann Jillian Story.

JOELS, MERRILL E.: Performer. b. Hartford, CT. Began career, Hartford, 1930; organ. Mark Twain Masquers Thea.; radio, New York since 1945; TV since 1946; actor, announcer, narrator; over 500 TV shows; feature, Army, Navy and industrial films; narr., children's records, dir., AFTRA; member, The Players; Credits also Off-Broadway, Summer Stock, Daytime TV Drama. Announcer and Co-host WEVD Home Show 29 years. Announcer-engineer, WEVD.
AUTHOR: Acting Is a Business, How to Get into Show Business, Touring in Theatre of Peretz and Three by Chayefsky; Talking Books for Library of Congress.

JOFFE, CHARLES H.: Executive. b. Brooklyn, NY, July 16, 1929. e. Syracuse U. Joined with Jack Rollins to set up management-production org., clients including Woody Allen, Ted Bessell, Billy Crystal, David Letterman, Tom Poston, Robin Williams.
PICTURES INCLUDE: Produced: Don't Drink the Water, Take the Money and Run, Everything You Always Wanted to Know About Sex but Were Afraid To Ask, Love and Death, Annie Hall, House of God, Arthur. Exec. prod.: Play It Again Sam, Bananas, Sleeper, Arthur, Manhattan, Interiors, Stardust Memories, A Midsummer Nights' Sex Comedy, Zelig, Broadway Danny Rose, The Purple Rose of Cairo, Hannah and Her Sisters, Radio Days, September.
TELEVISION: Woody Allen specials. Star of the Family, Good Time Harry.

JOFFE, EDWARD: Producer, Director, Writer. Worked in m.p., theatre, commercial radio and as journalist before ent. TV ind. in Britain 1957 as writer/prod with ATV. Has prod. & dir. over 4000 progs. 1959–61 staff prod. Granada TV, 1962, dir., Traitor's Gate & Traveling Light for Robt Stigwood, prod. dir., numerous series for Grampian TV; 1967, dir. film The Price of a Record—Emmy finalist, Special Mention Salerno Film Fest shown in over 70 countries; 1967—8 films, Columbia's Folk & So Many Partings ITV entries in Golden Harp Fest.; 1968, prod. dir. Up At The Cross; prod. dir. ind. film, Will Ye No' Come Back Again; dir., This Is . . . Tom Jones; prod. dir., The Golden Shot; 1971, senior production lecturer, Thomson TV College; dir., films for U.S. for London Television Service; Evening Standard Commercials for Thames TV. Co. prod. dir.,ind. film Sound Scene, 1972–8, Contract prod. dir. Thames TV various series: Magpie, Today, Opportunity Knocks. The David Nixon Show, Seven Ages of Man, Problems, Finding Out; 1980; production consultant, CBC-tv, 1978–82, prod. dir. series Writers' Workshop, About Books; 1978, film, Places & Things (British Academy Award nom.) film, Who Do You Think You Are? (British Academy Award nom., ITV's Japan Prize entry, Special Jury Award San Francisco Intl. Film Fest), 1981, Film Images, (British Academy Award nom.); Gold Plaque Chicago Intl. Film Fest.); The Protectors (medal winner Intl. Film & TV Festival, N.Y.). 1982–86: Film Rainbow Coloured Disco Dancer. 1988: The Buzz. Various Series: Taste of China, Jobs Ltd. Spin-Offs.

JOFFE, ROLAND: Director. b. London, Eng., Nov. 17, 1945. e. Manchester U., England. Worked in British theatre; 1973 became youngest director at National Theatre. 1978, moved into directing TV as preparation for career in films making debut in 1984 with The Killing Fields.
   TELEVISION: Documentaries: Rope, Anne, No, Mama No. Plays: The Spongers, Tis Pity She's a Whore, United Kingdom (also co-wrote). Series: The Stars Look Down.
   PICTURES: The Killing Fields, The Mission.

JOHNS, GLYNIS: Actress. b. Durban, South Africa, Oct. 5, 1923. e. in England. Daughter of Mervyn Johns, actor, and Alys Steele, pianist. On London stage from 1935 (Buckie's Bears, The Children's Hour, A Kiss for Cinderella, Quiet Week-End; Gertie, N.Y. stage, 1952; Major Barbara, N.Y., 1956–57.) On screen 1936: South Riding. Voted one of top ten British Money-making stars in Motion Picture Herald-Pathe poll, 1951–54.
   STAGE: N.Y. 1964, Too Good to Be True, London, 1967: The King's Mare; 1970, Come as You Are. 1971–2 Tour of Britain, Canada and U.S. in The Marquise, A Little Night Music, NY 1973 (Tony Award); Cause Celebre (London, 1977); Harold and Maude (Canada, 1977); Hay Fever (U.K. tour, 1978); The Boy Friend (Toronto, 1984).
   PICTURES INCLUDE: Murder in Family, Prison Without Bars, Mr. Brigg's Family, 49th Parallel, Adventures of Tartu, Half-Way House, Perfect Strangers, This Man Is Mine, Frieda, An Ideal Husband, Miranda, Third Time, Lucky Mr. Proback, The Great Manhunt, Flesh and Blood, No Highway in the Sky, Appointment With Venus (Island Rescue), Encore, The Card (The Promoter), The Sword and the Rose, Rob Roy, Personal Affair, The Weak and the Wicked, The Seekers (Land of Fury), The Beachcomber, Mad About Men, Court Jester, Josephine and Men, Loser Takes All, Day They Gave Babies Away, Another Time Another Place, Shake Hands with the Devil, The Sundowners, The Spider's Web, The Chapman Report, Mary Poppins, Dear Brigette, Don't Just Stand There, Lock Up Your Daughters, Zelly and Me, Nuckie.
   TELEVISION: Series: Glynis, Coming of Age. Episodes of: Dr. Kildare, Roaring Twenties, Naked City, The Defenders, Danny Kaye Show. Also: Noel Coward's Star Quality, Mrs. Amworth, All You Need Is Love, Across a Crowded Room, Little Gloria, ... Happy at Last, Skagg.

JOHNSON, ARTE: Actor. b. Chicago, IL, Jan. 20, 1934. Gained fame on Rowan and Martin's Laugh-In.
   PICTURES: Miracle in the Rain, The Subterraneans, The Third Day, The President's Analyst, Love at First Bite, A Night at the Magic Castle, Tax Season.
   TELEVISION: Alice in Wonderland, Bud and Lou, Condominium.

JOHNSON, BEN: Actor. b. Pawhuska, OK, 1918, Stunt rider & performer in rodeos, touring country; did stunt work in War Party; m.p. debut in Mighty Joe Young.
   PICTURES INCLUDE: Three Godfathers, She Wore a Yellow Ribbon, Wagonmaster, Rio Grande, Wild Stallion, Fort Defiance, Shane, Rebel in Town, The Wild Bunch, The Undefeated, Chisum, The Last Picture Show, (Academy Award, best supporting actor, 1971), Junior Bonner, The Getaway, Dillinger, The Train Robbers, Kid Blue, The Sugarland Express, Bite The Bullet, Hustle, The Town That Dreaded Sundown, The Greatest, Grayeagle, The Swarm, The Hunter, Terror Train, Tex, Champions, Let's Get Harry, Dark Before Dawn, Cherry 2000.
   TELEVISION: Blood Sport, Dream West, Locusts, The Shadow Riders, Red Pony, The Sacketts, Wild Horses, Wild Times, Stranger on My Land.

JOHNSON, DON: Actor. b. Flatt Creek, MO, Dec. 15, 1950. Worked at ATC, San Francisco.
   PICTURES: The Magic Garden of Stanley Sweetheart (debut, 1970), The Harrad Experiment, A Boy and His Dog,

Zachariah, Return to Macon County, Soggy Bottom, USA, Cease Fire, Sweet Hearts Dance, Dead-Bang.
   TELEVISION: The Rebels, Miami Vice (series). Movies: From Here to Eternity—The War Years, Beulah Land, Revenge of the Stepford Wives, Amateur Night at the Dixie Bar and Grill, Elvis and the Beauty Queen, The Long Hot Summer.

JOHNSON, G. GRIFFITH: Executive. b. New York, NY, Aug. 15, 1912. e. Harvard U., 1934, A.M. 1936, Ph.D. 1938. U.S. Treasury Dept. 1936–39; Dept. of Comm., 1939–40; O.P.A. & predecessor agencies, 1940–46; consulting economist, 1946–47; dir., Econ. Stab. Div., Nat'l. Security Resources Bd., 1948–49; chief econ., U.S. Bur. of Budget, 1949–50; econ. advisor to Econ. Stab. Admin. 1950–52; Exec. v.p. MPEAA 1965, MPAA, 1971; Asst. Sec'y of State for Economic Affairs, 1962–65; v.p. MPAA, 1953–62; Author of several books & articles.

JOHNSON, J. BOND: Producer, Executive. b. Fort Worth, TX, June 18, 1926. e. Texas Wesleyan Coll., B.S., 1947; Texas Christian U., M.Ed., 1948; Southern Methodist U., B.D., 1952; U. of Southern California, Ph.D., 1967. Army Air Forces, W.W.II; public information officer, captain, U.S. Marine Corps. Korean War. Formerly member Marine Corps Reserve, Motion Picture Production Unit, Hollywood. Now Colonel, U.S. Army Reserve. Newspaper reporter, Fort Worth Star Telegram, 1942–48; pres., West Coast News Service, 1960; pres., exec. prod., Bonjo Prods., Inc., 1960, President, chief executive officer, Cine-Media International, 1975 managing partner, Capra-Johnson Productions, Ltd., 1978.
   PICTURES INCLUDE: Sands of Iwo Jima, Retreat Hell, Flying Leathernecks; photographed aerial portions, Jamboree 53, Norfleet, Devil at My Heels, Kingdom of the Spiders, Ordeal at Donner Pass, Place of the Dawn, Lies I Told Myself, Backstretch, Airs Above The Ground, The Jerusalem Concert, The Berkshire Terror, The Seventh Gate.
   TELEVISION: Creator, story consultant, tech. advisor, Whirlpool, 1962, one hour dramatic series for Screen Gems/CBS-TV, Executive Producer, Creator, On The Go (TV News-Sports series), 1977, Coasties (series), 1978, Desert Rangers (series) 1979. Producer, Fandango (series), 1981.

JOHNSON, LAMONT: Director, Producer, Actor. b. Stockton, CA, Sept. 30, 1922. e. U. of California at L.A.
   TELEVISION: The Defenders, Profiles in Courage, Twilight Zone, That Certain Summer, My Sweet Charlie, The Execution of Pvt. Slovik, Fear on Trial, Ernie Kovacs: Between the Laughter, Wallenberg: A Hero's Story (co-prod., dir.), Unnatural Causes, Gore Vidal's Lincoln.
   PLAYS: The Egg, Yes is For a Very Young Man; dir., two operas, L.A. Philharmonic, 1964; founder, dir., UCLA Professional Theatre Group.
   PICTURES INCLUDE: Covenant With Death, McKenzie Break, A Gunfight, The Groundstar Conspiracy, You'll Like My Mother, The Last American Hero, Lipstick, One on One, Somebody Killed Her Husband, Sunny Side, Foxes, Cattle Annie and Little Britches, Spacehunter.

JOHNSON, LAURIE: Music Composer, Director. b. 1927. Studied Royal Coll. of Music.
   STAGE: Lock Up Your Daughters, Pieces of Eight, The Four Musketeers.
   PICTURES INCLUDE: Good Companions, Moonraker, Girls at Sea, Operation Bullshine, Tiger Bay, I Aim at the Stars, Spare The Road, What a Whopper, Bitter Harvest, Seige of the Saxons, Dr. Strangelove, The First Men in the Moon, Beauty Jungle, East of Sudan, Hot Millions, And Soon the Darkness, Mister Jerico, Cause for Alarm, The Beltstone Fox, Hedda, It Lives Again, All Things Bright and Beautiful.

JOHNSON, RICHARD: Actor. b. Essex, England, July 30, 1927. Studied at Royal Acad. of Dramatic Art. First stage appearance Opera House, Manchester; then played in John Gielgud's repertory season, 1944. Served in Royal Navy 1945–48. Subsequent stage appearances incld. The Madwoman of Chaillot, The Lark. Visited Moscow with Peter Brook's production of Hamlet. Royal Shakespeare Thea.: Stratford, London, 1957–62. Royal Shakespeare Company 1972–73. National Theatre, 1976–77. Founded United British Artists, 1983. Produced Turtle Diary, Castaway, The Lonely Passion of Judith Hearne.
   PICTURES INCLUDE: The Haunting, 80,000 Suspects, Moll Flanders, Operation Crossbow, Khartoum, La Strega in Amore, Deadlier than the Male, The Rover, Danger Route, Twist of Sand, Oedipus the King, Trajan's Column, Lady Hamilton, Some Girls Do, Julius Caesar, The Deserters, The Beloved, Hennessy, Aces High, The Four Feathers, Turtle Diary.
   TELEVISION: (U.S.): The Flame is Love, Haywire, The Four Feathers, Portrait of a Rebel: Margaret Sanger.

JOHNSON, RUSSELL: Actor. b. Ashley, PA, 1924. e. Girard Coll, Actors Laboratory, L.A. W.W.II, Army Air Corps.
   PICTURES INCLUDE: A Town of the 80's, Stand at Apache Landing, A Distant Trumpet, Ma & Pa Kettle at Waikiki, Rogue

Cop, Loan Shark, Seminole, Tumbleweed, Blue Movies, It Came From Outer Space, Many Rivers to Cross, Law and Order, Black Tuesday, For Men Only, The Greatest Story Ever Told, MacArthur.
TELEVISION: Black Saddle (series), Mobile One (series), The Great Adventure (narrator), Jane Powell Show, Climax, You Are There, Rawhide, Twilight Zone, Gilligan's Island (series), Vanished, Harry Truman Biography, Truman vs. MacArthur.

JOHNSON, VAN: Actor. b. Newport, RI, Aug. 25, 1916. Began in vaudeville; then on N.Y. stage New Faces of 1937, Eight Men of Manhattan, Too Many Girls, Pal Joey. Film debut in Too Many Girls (1940). Voted one of the top ten Money Making Stars in Motion Picture Herald-Fame Poll 1945–46. Stage includes The Music Man (London), La Cage aux Folles (NY) and numerous tours.
PICTURES INCLUDE: Murder in Big House, War Against Mrs. Hadley, Dr. Gillespie's New Assistant, Pilot No. 5, Dr. Gillespie's Criminal Case, Guy Named Joe, Three Men in White, Two Girls and a Sailor, Thirty Seconds Over Tokyo, Ziegfeld Follies, Between Two Women, Thrill of Romance, Week-End at the Waldorf, Romance of Rosy Ridge, Bride Goes Wild, State of the Union, Command Decision, In the Good Old Summertime, Scene of the Crime, Battleground, Big Hangover, Three Guys Named Mike, Grounds for Marriage, Go For Broke, Too Young to Kiss, It's a Big Country, Invitation, When in Rome, Washington Story, Plymouth Adventure, Confidentially Connie, Remains to Be Seen, Easy to Love, Caine Mutiny, Siege at Red River, Men of the Fighting Lady, Brigadoon, Last Time I Saw Paris, End of the Affair, Bottom of the Bottle, Miracle in the Rain, 23 Paces to Baker Street, Slander, Kelly and Me, The Lost Blitzkreig, Beyond This Place, Subway in the Sky, Web of Evidence, Enemy General, Wives and Lovers, Where Angels Go . . . Trouble Follows, Eagles Over London, The Purple Rose of Cairo.
TELEVISION: Black Beauty; Pied Piper of Hamelin; Rich Man, Poor Man; Call Her Mom; Doomsday Flight; San Francisco International Superdome; Murder She Wrote.

JOHNSTON, MARGARET: Actress. e. Sydney U., Australia. London stage debut: Murder Without Crime. Screen debut: Rake's Progress, 1945.
TELEVISION: Always Juliet, Taming of the Shrew, Man with a Load of Mischief, Light of Heart, Autumn Crocus, Androcles and the Lion, Sulky Five, Windmill Near a Frontier, The Shrike, The Out of Towners, Looking for Garrow, The Typewriter, The Glass Menagerie, That's Where the Town's Going, The Vortex.
PICTURES INCLUDE: A Man about the House, Portrait of Clare, The Magic Box, Knave of Hearts, Touch and Go, Night of the Eagle, The Nose on My Face, Life at the Top, Schizo, Mr. Sebastian.
THEATRE: Ring of Truth, The Masterpiece, Lady Macbeth, Merchant of Venice, Measure for Measure, Othello.

JOHNSTONE, DAVID: b. Kilmarnock, Scotland, July 4, 1926. e. Ayr Acad. Journalist: Ayrshire Post; Glasgow Herald. Night News Editor, Scottish Daily Mail; Scottish Correspondent, News Chronicle. Joined Scottish Television May, 1958 as News Editor. Later producer, director. Originated daily magazine, Here and Now. Producer ITV World Cup (part) 1976. Head of News, Current Affairs, Documentaries and Sport. Assistant controller of programmes; controller (now director) of programmes, 1977.

JOLLEY, STAN: Producer, Director, Production Designer, Art Director. b. New York, NY, May 17, 1926. e. U. of Southern California, col. of architecture. Son of actor I. Stanford Jolley. In Navy in W.W.II. Has acted in capacities listed for many feature films and TV series. Nominated for AA, Witness.
PICTURES INCLUDE: Producer and Production Designer: Knife For the Ladies. Assoc. Producer and Prod. Designer, The Good Guys and the Bad Guys; assoc. prod. & prod. designer, Jessie; Director: Today's FBI, Macgyver; 2nd Unit director, Superman. Production Designer: The Good Mother, Witness, Taps, Caddyshack, Cattle Annie and Little Britches, Americathon (also second unit director), Swarm, Drum, Framed, Dion Brothers, Mixed Company, Walking Tall, Terror in the Wax Museum, Night of the Lepus (also second unit director), War Between Men and Women, Law Man, The Phynx. Art Director: Young Billy Young, Ride Beyond Vengeance, Broken Saber, The Restless Ones, Mail Order Bride, Toby Tyler, Nine Lives of Elfego Baca. Assoc. producer & prod. designer & 2nd unit director, Happily Ever After.
TELEVISION FEATURES: 2nd Unit Director and Production Designer: Swiss Family Robinson, Adventures of the Queen, Woman Hunter, Production Designer: Abduction of Carrie Swenson, Eagle One, No Man's Land, Last of the Great Survivors, Like Normal People, Howard Hughes, Flood, Voyage of the Yes, The Stranger, Punch & Jody, City Beneath the Sea, Women of San Quentin.
TELEVISION SERIES: Art Director: Walt Disney Presents, Pete and Gladys, Gunsmoke, Mr. Ed., Branded, Voyage to

the Bottom of the Sea, Land of the Giants, O'Hara, etc. Production Designer: Walking Tall, Today's F.B.I., For Love and Honor, Macgyver. Pilots: 8, including Get Smart.

JONES, AMY HOLDEN: Director, Writer. b. Philadelphia, PA, Sept. 17, 1953. m. cinematographer, Michael Chapman. e. Wellesley Coll., B.A., 1974; film and photography courses, Massachusetts Inst. of Technology. Winner, first place, Washington National Student Film Festival, 1973.
PICTURES: Editor: Hollywood Boulevard (debut, 1976), American Boy, Corvette Summer, Second Hand Hearts; Director: Slumber Party Massacre, Love Letters (dir., s.p.), Mystic Pizza (s.p. only), Maid to Order (dir., co-s.p.), It Had to Be Steve (co-s.p.).

JONES, CHUCK: Prod., Dir., Writer, Animator. b. Spokane, WA, Sept. 21, 1912. e. Chouinard Art Inst. Dir., Warner Bros. Animation until 1962 where he created and directed Roadrunner & Coyote, Pepe le Pew; created and helped create Bugs Bunny, Porky Pig, Daffy Duck etc. Created Snafu character, U.S. Armed Service. Co-prod., wrote, dir., Bugs Bunny Show, ABC-TV. Headed MGM Animation Dept. dir. How the Grinch Stole Christmas, Horton Hears a Who, The Dot and the Line, Pogo, The Phantom Tollbooth. Lecturer and teacher at many universities. Currently independent, Chuck Jones Enterprises, Producer, Director, Writer (for ABC-TV) The Cricket in Times Square; A Very Merry Cricket; Yankee Doodle Cricket and (for CBS-TV) Rudyard Kipling's Rikki-Tikki-Tavi; The White Seal; Mowgli's Brothers, Saint-Saens' The Carnival of the Animals, Ogden Nash lyrics, with Daffy Duck & Bugs Bunny; A Connecticut Rabbit in King Arthur's Court, based on Mark Twain's original story, with Bugs Bunny, Daffy Duck, Porky Pig, Elmer Fudd, etc., two specials featuring Raggedy Ann and Andy in The Great Santa Claus Caper and The Pumpkin Who Couldn't Smile; plus a feature compilation of past work: Chuck Jones' Bugs Bunny/Road Runner Movie. Most recently: Daffy Duck's Thanks-for-Giving Special and Bugs Bunny's Bustin' Out All Over.
AWARDS: Recipient Academy Award for best animated cartoons for Scenti-Mental Reasons, 1950, The Dot and The Line, 1965; best documentary short subject for So Much for So Little, 1950. Honored with retrospectives at Deauville Film Festival, 1978, British Film Inst., 1979. N.Y. Film Festival, 1982; Telluride Film Festival, 1976. N.Y. Museum of Modern Art, 1985, 25 gallery exhibition of cartoon art and unique art, 1983–84–85. Cartoon and other art displayed in gallery exhibitions throughout U.S., 1983–84. Honored at Cambridge Film Festival, 1985; received Great Director Award, U.S.A. Film Festival, 1986; received best animation award from National Society of Cartoonists, 1986, 1987 & 1988; appeared for Children's Hospital Telethon New Orleans, 1985–88; Children's Hospital Benefit St. Louis, 1985; Lecturer Emeritus, U. of California, San Diego, 1986; Children's book William the Backwards Skunk, 1986 by Crown Publ. Autobiography WW Norton Publishers, lifetime Achievement Awards from Zagreb Film Festival (1988), Chicago Film Festival (1987), Houston Film Fest. (1988).

JONES, CHUCK: Public Relations Executive. b. Detroit, MI, Dec. 6. e. Michigan State U., B.A., advertising. U.S. Marine Corps 1964–66. Staff writer, Pacific Stars & Stripes, Tokyo, Japan and DaNang, Vietnam. Contributing editor, Leatherneck Magazine, Naval Aviation News, Navy Times. Entered motion picture industry 1969. Critic/writer Motion Picture Daily, 1969. Publicist, Harold Rand & Co., Public Relations, 1970–71. Publicist, American International Pictures, 1971. Radio/TV, newspaper, magazine & syndicate contact, United Artists Corp., 1972–73. Established Chuck Jones Public Relations in 1973 and has been pres. since then. Had stint as eastern adv./pub. dir., Embassy Pictures, 1981–82.

JONES, CLARK R.: Producer, Director. b. Clearfield, PA, April 10, 1920. e. Northwestern U.
TELEVISION SHOWS INCLUDE: The Tony Awards, Peter Pan, Sleeping Beauty Ballet, Ford 50th Anniversary Show, Caesar's Hour, Your Hit Parade, Jack and the Beanstalk, Romeo & Juliet, Perry Como, Bell Telephone Hour, Carol Burnett series; Carol Channing and Pearl Bailey on Broadway, Tony Awards, 6 Rms Riv Vu, Twigs, CBS 50th Anniversary, Emmies, Miss U.S.A., Miss Universe.

JONES, DAVID: C.B.E. until retirement. Publicity Director, EMI Films Ltd. and also of EMI Cinemas. b. London, Eng., 1913. Entered industry through the CEA organ, Cinematograph Times; editorial assistant RKO-Radio, 1930–36; served in advertising and editorial sections, London Hollywood Reporter; rejoined RKO-Radio as exploiteer, appointed press representative, 1938; became director of publicity, 1942 until 1958, chairman, FIPC, 1951–52, 1955–62; president FIPC, 1952–54, 1960–63; Press Guy, Variety Club of Gt. Britain, 1949–50, 1953–63, Chief Barker, Variety Club, 1964, International Press Guy Variety Club of Great Britain, 1965–88.

JONES, DAVID: Director, Producer. b. Poole, Eng., Feb. 19, 1934. e. Christ's Coll., Cambridge U., B.A., 1954, M.A., 1957. Immigrated to U.S. in 1979. Artistic controller, then assoc. dir.,

Royal Shakespeare Co., 1964–75; artistic dir, RSC at Aldwych Theatre 1975–78; artistic dir, Brooklyn Acad. of Music Theatre Co., NY 1979–81; prof. Yale Sch. of Drama, 1981.
THEATER: Sweet Agonistes (debut, 1961); U.S.: Summerfolk, Loves Labour's Lost.
PICTURES: Betrayal, Jacknife.
TELEVISION: Prod.: Monitor 1958–64 (BBC series); Play of the Month (prod.); dir.: Shakespeare series, BBC 1982–83; prod. The Beaux' Stratagem, Langarishe Go Down; Ice Age.

JONES, DEAN: Actor. b. Morgan County, AL, Jan. 25, 1936. e. Asbury Coll., Wilmore, KY. Prof. debut as blues singer, New Orleans; U.S. Navy, 1953.
TELEVISION: Series: Ensign O'Toole, The Teddy Bears.
STAGE: There Was a Little Girl, Company, Into the Light.
PICTURES INCLUDE: Handle with Care, Never So Few, Under the Yum-Yum Tree, The New Interns, That Darn Cat, Two on a Guillotine, The Ugly Daschshund, Monkeys, Go Home, Blackbeard's Ghost, The Love Bug, The $1,000,000 Duck, Snowball Express, Mr. Super Invisible, The Shaggy D.A., Herbie Goes to Monte Carlo, Born Again.

JONES, GEMMA: Actress. b. London, Eng., Dec. 4, 1942. e. Royal Acad. of Dramatic Art.
THEATER: Baal; Alfie; The Cavern; The Pastime of M Robert; Portrait of a Queen; Next of Kin; The Marriage of Figaro; And A Nightingale; Breaking the Silence.
PICTURES: The Devils; Paperhouse; On the Black Hill.
TELEVISION: The Lie; The Way of the World; The Merchant of Venice; The Duchess of Duke Street (series).

JONES, GRACE: Singer, Actress. b. Spanishtown, Jamaica, May 19, 1952. e. Syracuse U. Modelled and appeared in several Italian pictures before career as singer.
PICTURES: Conan the Destroyer, A View to a Kill, Siesta.

JONES, GRIFFITH: Actor. b. London, England, 1910. e. University College, London; Royal Acad. of Dramatic Art (gold medal 1932). In H.M. Forces, W.W.II. Stage debut, London, 1930, in Carpet Slippers; N.Y. debut 1935 in Escape Me Never. Many stage successes. In many Brit. pictures from 1932.
PICTURES INCLUDE: Escape Me Never, The Faithful Heart, Catherine the Great, The Mill on the Floss, A Yank at Oxford, Four Just Men, Atlantic Ferry, This Was Paris, The Day Will Dawn, Uncensored, Henry V. Rake's Progress, Wicked Lady, They Made Me a Fugitive, Good Time Girl, Miranda, Look Before You Love, Once Upon a Dream, Honeymoon Deferred, Star of My Night, Scarlet Web, The Sea Shall Not Have Them, Face in the Night, Wanted on Voyage, The High Wall, Hidden Homicide, Strangler's Web, Decline and Fall.
PLAYS: The Moonraker, Quadrille, Alice Thro' the Looking Glass, Love Machine, Dead on Nine, The Entertainer, Expresso, The Sound of Murder, Treasure Island, Two Accounts Rendered, The Cavern, The Doctor's Dilemma, Jockey Club Stakes. 1973, Nottingham P'House, 1974 Crucible, Sheffield. Member of Royal Shakespeare Co. 1975–80, 1981–86.
TELEVISION: The Breaking Point, The Ware Case, When in Rome, A Moment in the Sun, Hell Hath No Fury, Margret, No Hiding Place, The Collection, By Invitation Only, A Woman of No Importance, Freedom in September, Blythe Spirit, Treasure Island, The Three Sisters, Emergency Ward, Vendetta, The Cabinet Papers, Man in a Suitcase, Boy Meets Girl, Troubleshooters, Strange Report, Avengers, Inside Man, A Matter of Principle, Doom Watch, Warm Feet, Warm Heart, Paul Temple, The Persuaders, The Lotus Eaters, The Black Arrow, Arrow, Spy Trap, Crown Court, Fallen Eagles, The Apple Cart, Comedy of Errors, Macbeth, The Three Sisters, Nicholas Nickleby.

JONES, HENRY: Actor. b. Philadelphia, PA, Aug. 1, 1912. e. St. Joseph's Coll. On stage in Hamlet, Henry IV, Time of Your Life, My Sister Eileen, The Solid Gold Cadillac, Bad Seed, Sunrise at Campobello (Tony Award, 1958), Advise and Consent.
PICTURES: The Girl Can't Help It, Will Success Spoil Rock Hunter?, Vertigo, Never Too Late, Support Your Local Sheriff, Rascal, Angel in My Pocket, Butch Cassidy and the Sundance Kid, Rabbit Run, Dirty Dingus Magee, Skin Game, Tom Sawyer, Pete 'n' Tillie, The Outfit, Nine to Five, Death Trap.
TELEVISION: Series: Phyllis, I Married Dora.

JONES, JAMES EARL: Actor. b. Arkabutla, MS, Jan. 17, 1931. e. U. of Michigan. Son of actor Robert Earl Jones. Awarded Hon. Doctor of Fine Arts (Yale, Princeton); Medal for Spoken Language (Amer. Acad. and Inst. of Arts and Letter; Hon. Doctor of Humane Letters (Columbia Coll. & U. of Mich.).
THEATER: The Cool World, Othello, Paul Robeson, Les Blancs, The Great White Hope (Tony Award, 1969), The Iceman Cometh, Of Mice and Men, A Lesson from Aloes, Master Harold . . . and the Boys, Fences (Tony Award, 1986).
PICTURES: Dr. Strangelove, The Comedians, The End of the Road, The Great White Hope, The Man, Claudine, The

Swashbuckler, The Bingo Long Travelling All-Stars and Motor Kings, The Greatest, The Last Remake of Beau Geste, A Piece of the Action, The Bushido Blade, Conan the Barbarian, Soul Man, Alan Quartermain and the Lost City of Gold, Gardens of Stone, My Little Girl, Matewan, Coming to America, Fugitives, Shoeless Joe, Convicts.
TELEVISION: Movies: The UFO Incident, Jesus of Nazareth, The Greatest Thing That Almost Happened, Roots: The Next Generations, Guyana Tragedy—The Story of Jim Jones, Golden Moment: An Olympic Love Story, Philby, Burgess and MacLean, The Atlanta Child Murders, The Vegas Strip War, King Lear, Soldier Boy, Mathnet.

JONES, JENNIFER: Actress. r.n. Phyllis Isley. b. Tulsa, OK, Mar. 21, 1919. e. Northwestern U., American Acad. of Dramatic Arts. Daughter of Phil R., Flora Mae (Suber) Isley, exhib. m. David O. Selznick, prod. Toured with parents stock company as child; in summer stock in East; little theat. East & West. Began screen career (as Phyllis Isley) in several Republic Westerns, first major role The Song of Bernadette (Acad. Award, 1943).
PICTURES INCLUDE: Since You Went Away, Love Letters, Duel in the Sun, Cluny Brown, Portrait of Jennie, We Were Strangers, Madame Bovary, Carrie, Wild Heart, Ruby Gentry, Indiscretion of an American Wife, Beat the Devil, Love Is a Many-Splendored Thing, Good Morning Miss Dove, Man in the Gray Flannel Suit, Barretts of Wimpole Street, Farewell to Arms, Tender Is the Night, The Idol, Angel, Down We Go, The Towering Inferno.

JONES, KATHY: Executive. Joined Paramount Pictures in 1977 as exec. dir., field mktg. Left to join Time-Life Films as v.p., domestic mktg., for m.p. div. Returned to Paramount 1981 as v.p., domestic pub. & promo. 1984, appt. sr. v.p., domestic pub. & promo. for Motion Picture Group, Paramount.

JONES, QUINCY: Composer, Arranger, Producer. b. Chicago, IL, March 14, 1935. Formerly in trumpet section of Lionel Hampton's band; played with Dizzy Gillespie, Count Basie and arranged for orchs. singers-Ray Anthony, Count Basie, Sarah Vaughn, Peggy Lee, Lesley Gore before scoring films.
PICTURES INCLUDE: In the Heat of the Night, In Cold Blood, (Acad. Award nom.), The Pawnbroker, Mirage, The Slender Thread, Made in Paris, Walk, Don't Run, Banning, The Deadly Affair, Enter Laughing, A Dandy in Aspic, The Counterfeit Killer, For Love of Ivy, The Split, Bob & Carol & Ted & Alice, The Lost Man, Cactus Flower, John and Mary, The Last of the Mobile Hotshots, The Out-of-Towners, They Call Me Mister Tibbs, Brother John, Dollars, The Anderson Tapes, The Hot Rock, The New Centurions, The Getaway, The Color Purple (also co-prod.), Stalingrad (exec. prod.).
TELEVISION: Roots (Emmy, 1977).

JONES, SAM J.: Actor. b. Chicago, IL, Aug. 12, 1954.
PICTURES: "10," Flash Gordon, My Chauffeur, Silent Assassins, White Fire, One Man Force.
TELEVISION: Stunts Unlimited, Code Red (series), No Man's Land, The Highwayman.

JONES, SHIRLEY: Actress. b. Smithton, PA, March 31, 1934. m. actor-prod. Marty Ingels.
THEATRE: Appeared with Pittsburgh Civic Light Opera in Lady in the Dark, Call Me Madam. Broadway: South Pacific, Me and Juliet, Maggie Flynn.
PICTURES INCLUDE: Oklahoma, Carousel, Bobbikins, Elmer Gantry (Acad. Award, supp., 1960), Pepe, A Ticklish Affair, The Secret of My Success, Fluffy, The Happy Ending, Beyond the Posiedon Adventure.
TELEVISION: Widow, Silent Night, Lonely Night, The Partridge Family (series), The Slap Maxwell Story (series).

JONES, TERRY: Writer, Actor. b. Wales, 1942. Worked with various rep. groups before joining BBC script dept. Member of Monty Python's Flying Circus.
PICTURES: And Now for Something Completely Different; Monty Python and the Holy Grail (and co-dir.); Monty Python's Life of Brian (also dir.); Monty Python's The Meaning of Life (dir, music), Labyrinth (s.p.).
TELEVISION: Late Night Lineup; The Late Show; A Series of Birds; Do Not Adjust Your Set; The Complete and Utter History of Britain; Monty Python's Flying Circus, Secrets.

JONES, TOMMY LEE: Actor. b. San Saba, TX, Sept. 15, 1946. Worked in oil fields; studied acting at Harvard, where earned a degree in English. Broadway debut in A Patriot for Me; appeared in Four in a Garden, Ulysses in Nighttown, Fortune and Men's Eyes. Film debut in Love Story, 1970.
PICTURES INCLUDE: Jackson County Jail, Rolling Thunder, The Betsy, Eyes of Laura Mars, Coal Miner's Daughter, Back Roads, Nate and Hayes, River Rat, Black Moon Rising, The Big Town.
TELEVISION: The Amazing Howard Hughes, The Executioner's Song, The Rainmaker, Cat on a Hot Tin Roof, Broken Vows, The Park is Mine; Yuri Nosenko: KGB; Gotham, Stranger on My Land; Lonesome Dove, April Morning.

JORDAN, GLENN: Producer, Director. b. San Antonio, TX, April 5, 1936. e. Harvard, B.A.; Yale Drama Sch. Directed plays off-Bdwy. and on tour.
PICTURES: Director: Only When I Laugh; The Buddy System; Mass Appeal.
TELEVISION: Writer: Hogan's Goat; Paradise Lost; Benjamin Franklin (Emmy); Family; In the Matter of Karen Ann Quinlan; Sunshine Christmas; Delta County; The Women's Room (also prod.); Lois Gibbs and the Love Canal; Heartsounds, Eccentricities of a Nightingale, Dress Grey, Promise, Echoes in the Darkness (prod., dir.), Jesse.

JORDAN, HENRIETTA: Executive. b. New York, NY, Feb. 26. Ent. m.p. ind. as ass't to exec. v.p., UPA Pictures, 1950; v.p. in charge of sales, Format Prods, Inc. v.p. and assoc. prod., 1962–71. Assoc. prod. Levitow-Hanson Films, Inc., 1972–74; Producer, Image West, Ltd., 1975–84; dir. sls., Cause & EFX, 1984–85; dir. sls., Modern Videofilm Graphics, 1986.

JORDAN, NEIL: Director, Writer. b. Sligo, Ireland, 1950. Entered industry when hired by John Boorman as script consultant on Excalibur. Also made doc. on making of that film.
PICTURES: Dir.-s.p.: Traveller (writer only), Angel, The Company of Wolves, Mona Lisa, High Spirits, The Courier (co-exec. prod. only).

JORDAN, RICHARD: Actor. b. New York, NY, July 19, 1938. e. Harvard.
PICTURES: The Yakuza, Rooster Cogburn, Old Boyfriends, Interiors, Raise the Titanic, A Flash of Green (also prod.), Dune, The Mean Season, The Men's Club, Solarbabies, Romero.
TELEVISION: Captains and the Kings, Les Miserables, The French Atlantic Affair, The Bunker, Washington Mistress, The Murder of Mary Phagan, The Equalizer (series).

JOSEPH, KENNETH: Executive. b. New York, NY, July 15, 1922. e. Syracuse U. Entered industry as announcer and program director of various N.Y. radio stations, including WNYC, 1946–53; exec. in various capacities of United Artists Television and predecessor companies, 1953–68; exec. v.p., syndication, Four Star Entertainment Corp., 1968–70; exec. v.p., world-wide syndication, Metromedia Producers Corp., 1970 to present.

JOSEPHSON, ERLAND: Actor, Director, Writer. b. Stockholm, Sweden, June 15, 1923. Acted in over 100 plays in Sweden. Joined Sweden's Royal Dramatic Theatre in 1956 replacing Ingmar Bergman as head of the theater, 1966–76. Closely associated with Bergman, with whom he staged plays in his late teens. Co-authored s.p. with The Pleasure Garden and Now About These Women. Also has pub. poetry, six novels, and scripts for stage, screen and radio. American stage debut: The Cherry Orchard, 1988.
PICTURES: It Rains on Our Love, To Joy, Brink of Life, The Magician; Hour of the Wolf; The Passion of Anna; Cries and Whispers; Scenes from a Marriage; Face to Face; Beyond Good and Evil; I'm Afraid; Autumn Sonata; To Forget Venice; One and One (also dir.); The Marmalade Revolution (also dir., s.p.); Montenegro; Sezona Mira u Parizu; Fanny and Alexander; Bella Donna; Nostalgia; House of the Yellow Carpet; After the Rehearsal; Angela's War; Behind the Shutters; A Case of Irresponsibility; Dirty Story; Amarosa; The Flying Devils; Garibaldi, The General; The Last Mazurka, The Sacrifice; Saving Grace; Unbearable Lightness of Being; Hanussen.

JOSEPHSON, MARVIN: Executive. b. New York, NY, June 5, 1935. e. Long Island U. Started with Liebling-Wood Agency as agent; later with Music Corp. of America, General Artists Corp., Agency for the Performing Arts.

JOSEPHSON, MARVIN: Executive. b. Atlantic City, NJ, March 6, 1927. e. Cornell U., B.A., 1949; L.L.B. May, 1952. Lawyer at CBS Television 1952–55; founded Broadcast Management Inc. which became Josephson International Inc. in 1955. Josephson International Inc. is the parent co. of International Creative Management, Inc. and ICM Artists Ltd.

JOSIAH, JR., WALTER J.: Executive. b. New York, NY. e. Fordham U., B.S.:SS, 1955–58: Harvard Law School, LL.B., 1962. U.S. Air Force, 1955–58, First Lt. and Pilot. Associate, Simpson Thacher & Bartlett, 1962–67. Legal staff, Paramount Pictures, 1967–69. Asst. resident counsel, 1969; chief resident counsel, 1970 and v.p. & chief resident counsel, 1971–82. ex.-v.p. & general counsel, Motion Picture Association of America, Inc., 1983.
Professional Associations: Chairman, Committee 307, Authors Rights, 1981–82, Patent, Trademark & Copyright Law Section of the American Bar Assn.; Association of the Bar of the City of New York (Committee on Copyright and Literary Property, 1976–79, 1982–85, chairman 1986–89): Copyright Society of the U.S.A.—Member of the Board of Trustees commencing June, 1981; vice president, from June 1988; member, Motion Picture Academy of Arts and Sciences; Copyright Office Advisory Committee, 1981–82; National Sculpture Society—advisor to the president; Advisory Board,

Publication: Communications and the Law; Member, President's Club Executive Committee and Annual Fund Council, Fordham U.

JOURDAN, LOUIS: Actor, b. Marseille, France, June 19, 1921. Stage actor prior to m.p.
PICTURES INCLUDE: Her First Affair, La Boheme, L'Arlesienne, La Belle, Adventure, Felicie Nanteuil, The Paradine Case, Letter from an Unkown Woman, Madame Bovary, Bird of Paradise, Anne of the Indies, The Happy Time, Three Coins in the Fountain, No Minor Voices, Decameron Nights, The Swan, Julie, Gigi, Streets of Montmartre, Story of the Count of Monte Cristo, VIP's, Made in Paris, A Flea in Her Ear, To Commit a Murder, Silver Bears, Octopussy, The Return of the Swamp Thing, Counterforce.
TELEVISION: The French Atlantic Affair, The Count of Monte Cristo, The Man in the Iron Mask, Beverly Hills Madam.

JOY, ROBERT: Actor. b. Montreal, Canada, Aug. 17, 1951. e. Newfoundland U. Rhodes Scholar. Acted in regional and off-Broadway theatre. Off-Bdwy debut The Diary of Anne Frank (1978). Has composed music for stage, radio and film. On board of Canadian Center for Advanced Film Studies.
THEATER: NY Shakespeare Fest. (Found a Peanut, Lenny and the Heartbreakers; The Death of von Richtofen); Life and Limb; Fables for Friends; Welcome to the Moon; What I Did Last Summer; Lydie Breeze; Romeo and Juliet (La Jolla Playhouse, Drama-Logue Award); Hay Fever (Bdwy debut); Big River (premiere); The Nerd.
PICTURES: Atlantic City, Ragtime, Threshold, Ticket to Heaven, Terminal Choice, Amityville 3-D, Desperately Seeking Susan, Joshua Then and Now, Adventure of Faustus Bidgood (also co-prod. music), Big Shots, The Suicide Club, She's Back!, Millenium.
TELEVISION: The Prodigious Hickey, The Return of Hickey, One Life to Live, The Equalizer, Moonlighting.

JUDD, EDWARD: Actor. b. Shanghai, 1934. e. Far East. Stage; The Long and the Short and the Tall, The Tinker. Numerous TV appearances.
PICTURES INCLUDE: The Day the Earth Caught Fire, Stolen Hours, The World Ten Times Over, Mystery Submarine, The Long Ships, First Men on the Moon, Strange Bedfellows, Invasion, Island of Terror, The Vengeance of Shee, Shakedown, The Kitchen Toto.

JULIA, RAUL: Actor. b. San Juan, PR, Mar. 9, 1940. e. U. of Puerto Rico; studied for theatre with Wynn Handman. New York stage debut in La Vida Es Sueño, 1964. Film debut in Panic in Needle Park, 1971.
THEATER: The Marriage Proposal (1966); Macduff in Macbeth (first assgn. with NY Shakespeare Fest., 1966); The Ox Cart; Titus Andronicus; No Exit; The Memorandum; Your Own Thing; The Cuban Thing (Bdwy debut); Paradise Gardens East; Conercio Was Here to Stay; City Way; The Castro Complex; Pinkville; Two Gentlemen of Verona; Hamlet (Delacorte Theater); As You Like It; King Lear; The Robber Bridegroom, Via Galactica; Where's Charley; Threepenny Opera (Lincoln Center); Dracula; The Taming of the Shrew; Betrayal; Othello; Nine; The Tempest; Design for Living; Arms and the Man.
PICTURES: The Organization Man, Been Down So Long It Looks Like Up to Me, Gumball Rally, The Eyes of Laura Mars, Strong Medicine, Tempest, The Escape Artist, One from the Heart, Kiss of the Spider Woman, The Morning After, La Gran Fiesta, The Penitent, Moon Over Parador, Trading Hearts, Tequila Sunrise, Tango Bar, Romero, The Threepenny Opera.
TELEVISION: Sesame Street (recurring role), King Lear, The National Health, McCloud, Love of Life, Aces Up. Movies: Death Scream, Florida Straits, Onassis: The Richest Man in the World.

JUNKIN, RAYMOND: Executive. b. New York, NY, Nov. 4, 1918. e. U. of Alabama, U. of Pennsylvania. Air Force, W.W.II. Eastern sls. mgr., Robert H. Clark Co., southwestern sls. mgr., then ass't to president; v.p., director of sales, Official Films, Inc., 1951–58; self-employed as a film and program consultant, 1959–60; pres. Program Sales Inc.; gen. sls. mgr., Programs For Television, Inc., since 1961; v.p. & gen. mgr., Screen Gems (Canada), Ltd.; v.p. Domestic Sales Mgr. Screen Gems Internat'l; 1967 gen. sls. mgr., Trans-Lux TV Corp., v.p. & gen. sls. mgr., 1968 to date. CTV Television Network Ltd.

JURADO, KATY: Actress. r.n. Maria Christina Jurado Garcia. b. Guadalajara, Mexico, 1927. Numerous Mexican films m.p. columnist for Mexican publications; American m.p. debut in Bullfighter and the Lady (1951).
PICTURES INCLUDE: High Noon, San Antone, Arrowhead, Broken Lance, The Racers, Trial, Trapeze, Man from Del Rio, The Badlanders, One Eyed Jacks, Barabbas, A Covenant with Death, Pat Garrett and Billy the Kid, Under the Volcano.
TELEVISION: Lady Blues.

161

JUROW, MARTIN: Producer. b. New York, NY. Dec. 14, 1911. e. William and Mary, Harvard Law Sch. Associated with MCA, William Morris, pres., Famous Artists; prod., G & E Productions; co-prod. with Richard Shepherd Jurow-Shepherd Productions.
PICTURES INCLUDE: The Hanging Tree, The Fugitive Kind, Love in a Goldfish Bowl, Breakfast at Tiffany's, The Great Race, Soldier in the Rain, Terms of Endearment, Sylvester, Pink Panther, Papa Was a Preacher.

JUSTIN, GEORGE: Executive. Major credits include producer on Middle of the Night and The Tiger Makes Out; assoc. prod. for Marathon Man and On the Waterfront; prod. exec. on The Goddess and Twelve Angry Men. V.p. & exec. prod. mgr. at Paramount Pictures; four years; left to join Columbia as prod. exec, where was assoc. prod. for The Deep and Prod. exec. on The Eyes of Laura Mars. In April, 1979 joined Orion Pictures; named exec. prod. mgr. Promoted to v.p./exec. prod. mgr. in April, 1980.
PICTURES: Rollover (exec. prod.); No Small Affair (exec. prod.)

K

KAEL, PAULINE: Critic. b. June 19, 1919, Sonoma County, CA. e. U. of California, Berkeley, 1936–40, majoring in philosophy. Managed two art theaters in CA for which she wrote program notes. Broadcast weekly about films on Pacifica network. Made experimental shorts. Has written on films for many magazines. Since 1968 movie critic for The New Yorker.
AUTHOR: I Lost It at the Movies, Kiss, Kiss, Bang, Bang, Going Steady, The Citizen Kane Book, Deeper into Movies, Reeling, When the Lights Go Down, 5001 Nights at the Movies, Taking It All In, State of the Art.
AWARDS: Guggenheim Fellow, 1964; George Polk Memorial Award for Criticism, 1970; The National Book Award, 1974, for Deeper into Movies; Front Page Award for best magazine column in 1974 from Newswomen's Club of N.Y and for distinguished journalism, 1983.

KAGAN, JEREMY PAUL: Director, Writer. b. Mt. Vernon, NY, Dec. 14, 1945. e. Harvard; NYU, MFA; student Amer. Film Inst. 1971. Film animator, 1968; multi-media show designer White House Conf. on Youth and Ed.
PICTURES: Heroes, The Big Fix, The Chosen, The Sting II, The Journey of Natty Gann, Russian Dressing, A Loving Gentleman, Hunchback.
TELEVISION: Columbo, The Bold Ones, Unwed Father, Judge Dee, My Dad Lives in a Downtown Hotel, Katherine (also s.p.), Scott Joplin, Courage, Conspiracy: The Trial of the Chicago 8.

KAHN, JUDITH: Executive. Background in mktg., including graphic design, adv./promo. Creative dir. at Intralink Film Graphic Design; art dir. for Seiniger & Associates. 1983, returned to New York as consultant to corporate clients, including cable, TV, and m.p. accts. 1985, joined Paramount Pictures as v.p., creative svcs. of M.P. Group.

KAHN, MADELINE: Actress, Singer. b. Boston, MA., Sept. 29. e. Hofstra U. Broadway bow in New Faces of '68. Featured in off-Broadway musical Promenade. Trained as opera singer and appeared in La Boheme, Showboat, Two by Two, Candide.
PICTURES INCLUDE: What's Up Doc? (debut), Paper Moon, From the Mixed-Up Files of Mrs. Basil E. Frankweiler, Blazing Saddles, At Long Last Love, Young Frankenstein, The Adventures of Sherlock Holmes' Smarter Brother, Won Ton Ton, High Anxiety, The Cheap Detective, Simon, Happy Birthday, Gemini, Wholly Moses, First Family, History of the World—Part I, Yellowbeard, City Heat, Clue.
THEATER: Two by Two, In the Boom Boom Room, On the Twentieth Century.
TELEVISION: Oh Madeline! (series), Mr. President (series); The Perfect Guy (afterschool special), Celebrating Gershwin: The Jazz Age.

KAHN, MILTON: Publicist. b. Brooklyn, NY, May 3, 1934. e. Syracuse U., Ohio U., B.S.J. 1957. Formed Milton Kahn Associates, Inc. in 1958.

KAHN, RICHARD: Executive. b. New Rochelle. NY, Aug. 29, 1929. e. Wharton Sch., U. of Pennsylvania, B.S., 1951; U.S. Navy, 3 yrs.; joined Buchanan & Co., 1954; ent. m.p. ind., pressbook writer, Columbia Pictures, 1955; exploitation mgr., 1958; natl. coord. adv. and pub., 1963; natl. dir. of adv., pub. and exploitation, 1968; v.p., 1969; 1974 v.p. in chg. of special marketing projects; 1975; moved to MGM as v.p. in chg. of worldwide advertising, publicity and exploitation; 1978, named sr. v.p. in chg. worldwide mktg. & pres., MGM Intl. 1980, elected bd. of governors, m.p. Academy of Arts & Sciences. 1982, named exec. v.p. of adv., pub., promo. for MGM/UA; 1983, formed the Richard Kahn Co., dist. & mktg. consultancy. Elected v.p., M.P. Academy of Arts & Sciences.

KALB, MARVIN: TV news reporter. e. City Coll. of New York; Harvard, M.A., 1953, Russian Language Sch., Middlebury Coll. Worked for U.S. State Dept., American Embassy, Moscow; CBS News, 1957; writer, reporter-researcher. Where We Stand: reporter-assignment editor; Moscow Bureau Chief, 1960–63; first dip. corres., Washington Bureau, 1963. Chief diplomatic corr. CBS News and NBC News, moderator Meet the Press; Teacher and lecturer; first dir. Joan Shorenstein Barone Center on the Press, Politics and Public Policy at John F. Kennedy Sch. of Govt. of Harvard U., since June, 1987. Host of PBS series, Candidates '88.
BOOKS: Eastern Exposure, Kissinger, Dragon in the Kremlin, Roots of Involvement, The U.S. in Asia, 1784–1971, Candidates '88 (with Hendrik Hertzberg).

KALISH, EDDIE: Executive. Reporter/reviewer, Variety, 1959–64; sr. publicist, Paramount Pictures, 1964–65; adv./pub./promo dir., Ken Greengras Personal Management, 1965–66; pub. dir., Harold Rand & Co., 1966–67; independent publicist overseas, 1967–75; rejoined Paramount Pictures in 1975 as dir. of intl. mktg.; later named v.p.; 1978, named v.p., worldwide pub. & promo. In 1979 appt. senior v.p., worldwide mktg. In 1980 joined United Artists as v.p.—domestic mktg.; sr. v.p., adv., pub., promo, for MGM/UA 1981–82; became sr. v.p., worldwide mkt., PSO, 1982–1986. Now pres., Kalish/Davidson Marketing.

KALSER, KONSTANTIN: Executive, b. Munich, Germany, Sept. 4, 1920. e. Switzerland, U. of California at L.A. Color photographer, newsreel cameraman, founded Marathon International Prods., Inc., pres., executive producer; Crashing the Water Barrier, 1956 (Acad. Award); Give and Take (Venice Award), The Carmakers, Chris Award. Director, The One for the Road, 1973 Gold Award, Intl. Film & Festival of N.Y. Director, We Did It! 1978 Gold Medal Intl. Film & TV Festival of N.Y.; Production Executive, The Unknown War 1978 Grand Award, Intl. Film & TV Festival of N.Y. 1984, For Years To Come! (dir., s.p.), winner of CINE Golden Eagle.

KAMBER, BERNARD M.: Executive. e. U. of Pennsylvania. New England exploitation rep. U.A. 1940; Army service 1941–43; dir. special events dept. U.A., 1943; asst. to Gradwell L. Sears, nat'l distrib. chmn. 6th War Loan Drive; dir. pub. 7th War Loan Drive, 1943–47; dir. pub. & prom. Eagle Lion Classics, 1951; org. Kamber Org., pub. rel. rep. for ind. prod. v.p. sales, adv. pub. Ivan Tors Prod. Greene-Rouse Prods.; June 1953; exec. asst. Hecht-Hill-Lancaster, chg. of N.Y. off., 1957; v.p. Hecht-Hill-Lancaster Companies, 1958; formed Cinex Distr. Corp., 1962; Pres. Cinex and Posfilm, Inc.; 1967 v.p. in chg. sls. Du Art Film Lab. Inc; 1975 joined Technicolor, Inc.

KAMEY, PAUL: Executive. b. New York, NY, Aug. 25, 1912. Worked on newspapers including NY Journal American. Ent. m.p. industry 1938; worked for MGM and 20th Century Fox; during war, writer, Office of War information; joined Universal, 1949; eastern pub. mgr., Universal Pictures. 1968, Freelance publicist.

KANANACK, ARTHUR: Executive. e. Cornell U., Cornell Law School. Started in industry in business affairs dept., ABC-TV, New York. Moved to London 1963 with Horizon Pictures; 1966 with Creative Management Associates (now ICM); returned to N.Y. 1968 to join UMC Pictures as exec v.p.; then business affairs dept. of 20th Century Fox. 1971–79, v.p., Warner Bros of business affairs intl., London. 1979–82, V.P., business affairs, WB-TV Distribution. 1982, joined ITC Productions as exec. v.p. 1985, named pres., ITC Entertainment. 1987, named president, Viacom Enterprises.

KANE, CAROL: Actress. b. Cleveland, OH, June 18, 1952. e. Professional Children's Sch., NY. Began professional acting career at age 14, touring in The Prime of Miss Jean Brodie. Other stage credits include, Arturo UI, The Enchanted, The Tempest, Macbeth, Tales of the Vienna Woods, Frankie and Johnny in the Claire de Lune.
PICTURES INCLUDE: Carnal Knowledge, Wedding in White, The Last Detail, Hester Street, Dog Day Afternoon, Harry and Walter Go to New York, Annie Hall, Valentino, The World's Greatest Lover, The Muppet Movie, The Mafu Cage, When a Stranger Calls, Over the Brooklyn Bridge, Racing with the Moon, The Secret Diary of Sigmund Freud, Transylvania 6-5000, Jumpin' Jack Flash, Ishtar, The Princess Bride, Sticky Fingers, License to Drive, The Lemon Sisters.
TELEVISION: Many Mansions, Taxi (Emmy Award), Faerie Tale Theatre, Paul Reiser: Out on a Whim; Drop-Out Mother.

KANE, JOHN: Publicity Manager. b. New York, NY. e. Rutgers, B.A.; NYU, M.A. Publicist, Solters & Roskin, 1976–80. Unit publicist: Fame, Tender Mercies, Prince of the City, 1980– 82. 1982–present, Home Box Office, unit publicist, manager.

KANE, STANLEY D.: Judge. b. Minneapolis, MN, Dec. 21, 1907. e. U. of Minnesota, B.A. (magna cum laude) 1930;, M.A., 1931; Minnesota Coll. of Law, LL.B., 1940. Instructor, U. of Minnesota, 1930–33. Exec. sec. Allied Theatre Owners of the Northwest, 1933–37; city attorney, Golden Valley, MN, 1940–

63; City Atty., Champlin, MN, 1955–60; on faculty, Minnesota Coll. of Law, 1940–44; trial attorney & trial examiner, National Labor Relations Board, Minneapolis, New Orleans, N.Y., 1943–46; special, gen. counsel, Puerto Rico Labor Relations Bd., 1946; exec. vice-pres. & gen. counsel, North Central Allied Independent Theatre Owners, 1946–63; recording sec. Allied States Assn., 1947 to 1956; Dist. Court Judge, Hennepin County, 1963; elected to 6-yr. term, 1964; re-elected, 1970; serving full-time as sr. judge since 1978.

KANEW, JEFF: Director.
PICTURES: Black Rodeo; Natural Enemies; Eddie Macon's Run; Revenge of the Nerds; Gotcha; Tough Guys, Troup Beverly Hills.
TELEVISION: Alfred Hitchcock Presents (1985).

KANIN, FAY: Writer. b. New York, NY. e. Elmira Coll., U. of Southern California. m. Michael Kanin, writer. Contrib. fiction to mags.; mem. and officer of WGA., AMPAS. also bd. mem. of latter. Co-chair, National Center for Film and Video Preservation; Bd. of trustees, Amer. Film Institute.
PICTURES INCLUDE: Blondie for Victory, Sunday Punch, My Pal Gus, Rhapsody, The Opposite Sex, Teacher's Pet, Swordsman of Siena, The Right Approach.
BROADWAY: Goodbye My Fancy, His and Hers, Rashomon, The Gay Life, Grind (1985).
TELEVISION: Heat of Anger, 1972; Tell Me Where It Hurts, 1974 (Emmy Award); Hustling, Friendly Fire (also co-prod., Emmy Award), Heartsounds.

KANIN, GARSON: Director, Writer. b. Rochester, NY, Nov. 24, 1912. e. American Acad. of Dramatic Arts. m. the late actress Ruth Gordon. Musician, actor, appearing in Spring Song, Little Ol' Boy, and others. Prod. assist. George Abbott on Three Men on a Horse, Brother Rat, Room Service; dir. Hitch Your Wagon, Too Many Heroes, Broadway plays; In June, 1937, Samuel Goldwyn's prod. staff, 1938, joined RKO, prod.-dir. contract. In 1942: prod. for U.S. Office of Emergency Management. Joined armed forces, W.W.II; co-prod. True Glory.
PICTURES INCLUDE: A Double Life, Adam's Rib, Born Yesterday, Marrying Kind, Pat and Mike, It Should Happen to You, Next Time I Marry, Man to Remember, Great Man Votes, Bachelor Mother, My Favorite Wife, They Knew What They Wanted, Tom, Dick and Harry, From This Day Forward, The Girl Can't Help It, The Rat Race, High Time, The Right Approach, Where It's At, Some Kind of a Nut, Woman of the Year, The More the Merrier.
THEATRE: Born Yesterday, The Smile of the World, The Rat Race, The Live Wire, A Gift of Time, Do Re Mi, Come on Strong, The Amazing Adele, The Good Soup, Dreyfus in Rehearsal. (writer and/or dir.) Dir.: The Rugged Path; Years Ago; How I Wonder; The Leading Lady; The Diary of Anne Frank; Into Thin Air; Small War on Murray Hill; Hole in the Head; Sunday in New York; Funny Girl; I Was Dancing; A Very Rich Woman; We Have Always Lived in a Castle; Idiot's Delight; Ho! Ho! Ho!, Happy Ending.
BOOKS: Remembering Mr. Maugham, Cast of Characters, Tracy and Hepburn; Hollywood; Blow Up a Storm; The Rat Race; A Thousand Summers; One Hell of an Actor; It Takes a Long Time to Become Young; Moviola, Smash, Together Again!, Cordelia.
TELEVISION: Hardhat and Legs (movie); Mr. Broadway (series, 1964).

KANIN, MICHAEL: Writer. b. Rochester, NY, Feb. 1, 1910. m. Fay Mitchell Kanin. Member SWG, officer; WGA, AMPAS. Commercial artist, musician, N.Y. prior to m.p. career; contrib. fiction mags.; s.p. Panama Lady, They Made Her a Spy, 1939.
PICTURES INCLUDE: Anne of Windy Poplars, Woman of the Year, Sunday Punch, The Cross of Lorraine, Centennial Summer Honeymoon, A Double Life, My Pal Gus, When I Grow Up (also dir.), Rhapsody, The Opposite Sex, Teacher's Pet, The Right Approach, The Swordsman of Siena, The Outrage, How to Commit Marriage.
BROADWAY: Goodbye My Fancy, Seidman and Son, His and Hers, Rashomon, The Gay Life.

KANTER, HAL: Writer, Director, Producer. b. Savannah, GA, Dec. 18, 1918. Writer, Danny Kaye Show, Amos 'n Andy, Bing Crosby Show, Jack Paar; Beulah; Ed Wynn TV Show, 1949; creator, writer, prod., stager, George Gobel Show; writer, Paramount, 1951–54; dir., RKO, 1956; Prod., dir., writer, Kraft Music Hall, 1958–59; exec. prod., TCF-TV; Valentine's Day; writer, prod. dir. Chrysler Theatre 1966–67. Creator W.D.P., Julia, NBC, 1968–71; creator W.D.P., Jimmy Stewart, 1971. W.P. Many TV specials. 1975–76 exec. prod. All In The Family. Sup. Prod. Chico & The Man, 1976–77; exec. prod., WB-TV, 1978; prod./writer, Lucille Ball Prod., 1979–80; dir./writer, ABC TV Movies, 1980; Walt Disney Prods., 1981; Savannah Prods., 1982–86. Writer, AFI Life Achievement Awards: Henry Fonda, Alfred Hitchcock; writer, 21 Annual Academy Awards; prod./writer, You Can't Take It With You (TV series, 1987–88).
PICTURES INCLUDE: My Favorite Spy, Off Limits, Road to Bali, Casanova's Big Night, About Mrs. Leslie, Money from Home, Artists and Models, Mardi Gras, Rose Tattoo, I

Married a Woman, Loving You, Once Upon a Horse, Blue Hawaii, Pocketful of Miracles, Bachelor in Paradise, Move Over, Darling, Dear Brigitte, etc.

KANTER, JAY: Executive. b. 1926. Entered industry with MCA, Inc., where was v.p. Left after more than 20 yrs. to become indep. prod., then pres. of First Artists Production Co., Ltd. In 1975 joined 20th-Fox as v.p. prod.; 1976, named sr. v.p., worldwide prod. Named v.p., The Ladd Co., 1979. Joined MGM/UA Entertainment Co. as pres., worldwide prod., Motion Picture Division, 1984. In 1985, named pres., worldwide prod., UA Corp.; now pres., production MGM Pictures Inc.

KANTOR, IGO: Producer, Film Editor. b. Vienna, Austria, Aug. 18, 1930. e. U. of California at L.A., A.A. 1950; B.S., 1952; M.S., 1954. Foreign corres., Portugal magazine, FLAMA, 1949–57; music supvr., Screen Gems, Columbia 1954–63; post-prod. supvr., film ed., features, TV; assoc. prod., 1963–64; prod., exec., International Entertainment Corp., 1965. pres., Synchrofilm, Inc., post-production co. and Duque Films, Inc., production co. 1968–74. 1975—present, produced and edited films. 1982, pres., Laurelwood Prods.
PICTURES INCLUDE: Bye Bye Birdie, Under the Yum Yum Tree, Gidget Goes to Rome, A House Is Not a Home, Pattern for Murder, Willy. Co.-prod., editor: Assault on Agathon; assoc., prod., editor, Dixie Dynamite; prod., editor, music supvr., Kingdom of the Spiders; assoc. prod., The Dark; prod. supvr., Good Luck Miss Wyckoff; prod., Hardly Working; Kill and Kill Again; Mutant, Shaker Run, Act of Piracy.
TELEVISION: From Hawaii with Love (1984); The Grand Tour; It's a Wonderful World (prod.-dir.); Nosotros Golden Eagle Awards (prod.), United We Stand (pre-Olympic special).

KAPLAN, BORIS: Executive. b. New York, NY, Sept. 23, 1897. e. City Coll. of New York. m. General mgr. of Selwyn Theatrical Enterprises, 1925–32. Prod. Plays for legitimate stage, Broadway; joined Paramount Pictures Corp., 1933; head of eastern casting and talent dept., Paramount 1936–62; independent casting dir.; m.p. consultant.

KAPLAN, GABRIEL: Actor, Comedian. b. Brooklyn, NY, March 31, 1945. After high school worked as bellboy at Lakewood, NJ hotel, spending free time studying comedians doing routines. Put together a comedy act, landing engagements in small clubs and coffee houses all over U.S. Made several appearances on Tonight Show, Merv Griffin Show, Mike Douglas Show, etc. Has played Las Vegas clubs.
TELEVISION: Welcome Back, Kotter (series), Gabriel Kaplan Presents the Future Stars, Love Boat, Lewis and Clark.
PICTURES INCLUDE: Fast Break, Tulips, Nobody's Perfect.

KAPLAN, JONATHAN: Director, Writer. b. Paris, Nov. 25, 1947. e. U. of Chicago, B.A.; New York U., M.F.A. Member of tech. staff Fillmore East, NY 1969–71. New World Pictures' Roger Corman post-grad. sch. of filmmaking, Hollywood, 1971–73. As actor on B'way in Dark at the Top of the Stairs, Happy Anniversary. In film: Rumplestiltskin.
PICTURES: Night Call Nurses; Student Teachers; The Slams; Truck Turner; White Line Fever (dir., co-s.p.); Mr. Billion; Over the Edge; The Accused (dir.), Heart Like a Wheel; Project X.
TELEVISION: The 11th Victim; The Hustler of Muscle Beach; The Gentleman Bandit; Girls of the White Orchid.

KAPLAN, MURRAY M.: Executive. In motion picture distribution since 1936. Distributor for Warner Bros., Paramount, Monogram, Eagle-Lion, United Artists, Allied Artists, Cinemation Industries. Became independent distributor in 1950, independent producer in 1966. Co-founder of PRO-International Films, 1975; 1978, formed M & M Films, to produce and distribute worldwide. Member: Motion Picture Pioneers of America.

KAPOOR, SHASHI: Actor. b. Calcutta, India, 1938. Son of late Prithviraj Kapoor, Indian film and stage actor. As child worked in Prithvi Theatre and in brother, Raj's films. Toured with father's co. at 18 and joined the Kendals' Shakespeareana Co. in India. Starred in over 200 Indian films as well as several Merchant-Ivory Prods.
PICTURES: Pretty Polly, Siddhartha, The Householder, Bombay Talkie, Shakespeare Wallah, Heat and Dust, USTAV (Festival of Love, also prod.), The New Delhi Times, Sammy and Rosie Get Laid, The Deceivers, Nomads.

KARDISH, LAURENCE: Curator, Dept. of Film, Museum of Modern Art. b. Ottawa, Ontario, Canada, Jan. 5, 1945. e. Carlton U. Ottawa, Canada, 1966, Honors B.A. in philosophy; Columbia U., Sch. of the Arts, 1968, M.F.A. in film, radio, and television. 1965–66: Canadian Film Inst., programmer for National Film Theatre, Ottawa; researched a history of Canadian filmmaking. 1965: founded first film society in Canada to exhibit Amer. avant-garde films (Carleton U. Cine Club); directed summer seminar on film, Carleton U., 1966. 1966–68: New American Cinema Group, Inc., NY, worked for

Kar-Kat

the Film-Makers' Distribution Center. 1968: joined Dept. of Film, MOMA; made curator 1984. Since 1968 involved with Cineprobe prog., since 1972 participated in selection of films for New Directors/New Films series; directed exhibitions of surveys of national cinemas (Senegal, Scandinavia, French-speaking Canada) and retrospectives of indep. Amer. film-makers (includ. Rudolph Burkhardt, Stan Brakhage, Shirley Clarke), The Lubitsch Touch, Columbia Pictures, Warner Bros., MGM, Universal, RKO, and directors. 1980: toured Europe with prog. of indep. Amer. films. Author of: Reel Plastic Magic (1972); as well as essays and monographs–Mark Rappaport and the Scenic Route; Senegal: 15 Years of an African Cinema; New Cinema from Iceland; Of Light and Texture: Andrew Noren and James Herbert; Michael Balcon and the Idea of a National Cinema; International Avant-Garde: Scattered Pieces; Berlin and Film. Directed feature film Slow Run (1968). On jury for Channel 13's Independent Focus series and on Board of Advisors, Collective for Living Cinema, NY. 1982–82: Board of Directors of National Alliance of Media Arts Centers; 1987–89: on Jerome Foundation panel. 1986 on Camera d'Or jury, Cannes Film Fest.

KARINA, ANNA: Actress. b. Copenhagen, Denmark, 1940. r.n. Hanna Karin Bayer. Had appeared in Danish shorts before going to Paris at 17 and working in commercials. Gained international renown in the 7 films she made with former husband Jean-Luc Godard.
PICTURES: Celo From Five to Seven, Three Fables of Love, My Life to Live, A Woman is a Woman, Sweet and Sour, Circle of Love, She'll Have to Go, Le Petit Soldat, Band of Outsiders, Pierrot le Fou, Alphaville, Made in U.S.A., The Stranger, La Religieuse, The Oldest Profession, The Magus, Before Winter Comes, Laughter in the Dark, Justine, Ren-devous a Bray, Willie and the Chinese Cat, Vivre Ensemble (also dir.), Story of a Mother, L'Ami de Vincent, Ave Maria.

KARLIN, FRED: Composer, Conductor. b. Chicago, IL, June 16, 1936. e. Amherst Coll., B.A. Composer and arranger for Benny Goodman and Harry James' Orchestras. Won Academy Award for Best Song for For All We Know (from Lovers and Other Strangers) and Emmy for original music in The Autobiography of Jane Pittman on TV. Adapted Huddie Ledbetter melodies for film Leadbelly.
PICTURES INCLUDE: Up the Down Staircase, Yours, Mine and Ours, The Sterile Cuckoo (including music for song, Come Saturday Morning), Westworld, Vasectomy: A Delicate Matter, Gravy Train, Mixed Company, Leadbelly, Loving Couples.
TELEVISION: More than 85 movies, including The Auto-biography of Miss Jane Pittman, Once Upon a Family, Marriage is Alive and Well, The Plutonium Incident, Baby Comes Home, Sophia Loren—Her Own Story, Fighting Back, Mom, The Wolfman, and Me; Broken Promise, Jacqueline Susann's Valley of the Dolls 1981, Inside the Third Reich, Hollywood—The Gift of Laughter, Not in Front of the Chil-dren, Missing Children—A Mother's Story, Deadly Encounter, The Gift of Love—A Christmas Story, Off the Rack, Robert Kennedy and His Times, Dadah is Death.

KARLIN, MYRON D.: Executive. b. Revere, MA, Sept. 21, 1918. e. U. of California at L.A. Joined m.p. business in 1946 as gen. mgr. for MGM in Ecuador. Two yrs. later assigned same spot for MGM in Venezuela. In 1952–53 was gen. sales mgr. for MGM in Germany, after which managing dir. in Argentina, returning to Germany as mgr. dir. in 1956. Named mgn. dir. for United Artists in Italy. 1960–68 was pres. of Brunswick Int'l., while also serving as advisor to World Health Organization and UNESCO. In 1969 was European mgr. for MGM and mgn. dir. in Italy. Joined Warner Bros. Int'l. in May, 1970 as v.p. of European dist. In March, 1972 appt. v.p. in chg. of int'l. operations for WB; 1977, appt. pres., WB Intl. & exec. v.p., Warner Bros., Inc; 1985, named exec. v.p., intl. affairs, WB, Inc. Now pres. & coo, Motion Picture Export Assn.

KARRAS, ALEX: b. Gary, IN, July 15, 1935. e. Univ. of Iowa. Former professional football player.
PICTURES: Blazing Saddles, Another Day at the Races, Jacob Two-Two Meets the Hooded Fang, When Time Ran Out, Nobody's Perfekt, Victor, Victoria.
TELEVISION: Movies: Hardcase, The 500-Pound Jerk, Babe, Mulligan's Stew, Mad Bull, Centennial. Series: Webster.

KASDAN, LAWRENCE: Writer, Director. b. West Virginia, Jan. 14, 1949. e. U. of Michigan. Clio award-winning advertising copywriter, Detroit and LA before becoming screen writer. Became director with Body Heat (1981).
PICTURES INCLUDE: The Empire Strikes Back (co-s.p.); Raiders of the Lost Ark (s.p.); Continental Divide (s.p.); Return of the Jedi (co-s.p.); Body Heat (dir., s.p.); The Big Chill (co-exec. prod., dir., co-s.p.); Silverado (prod., dir., co-s.p.), Cross My Heart (prod.), The Accidental Tourist (dir., co-prod., co-s.p.).

KASLOFF, STEVE: Executive. b. New York, NY, Nov. 13, 1952. e. Pratt Institute, 1974, cum laude. Writer/supvr., Young &

Rubicam, 1974–76; writer/sprv., Ally & Gargano, 1976; writer/supvr., Marsteller Inc., 1976–79; writer/creative supvr., Scali, McCabe, Sloves, 1979–82. hired as youngest v.p., Columbia Pictures, 1982; promoted to sr. v.p., creative dir., Columbia, 1983.
AWARDS: Winner of numerous Clio Awards when at ad agencies and over 100 other awards & medals for creative work (trailers, TV commercials, radio commercials, posters, etc.) on such films as Body Double, Tootsie, Karate Kid, Ghostbusters, Soldier's Story, Agnes of God, etc. Has directed stage production (Wait Until Dark), and commercials & special teaser trailers. Now working on screenplay.

KASSAR, MARIO: Executive, Producer.
At age of 18 formed own foreign distribution co. Kassar Films International, specializing in sale, dist. and exhibition of films in Asia and Europe. In 1976 became partners with Andrew Vajna who had own dist. co., forming Carolco. First prod. First Blood, followed by Rambo: First Blood Part II.
PICTURES: Exec. Prod.: Angel Heart, Extreme Prejudice, Rambo III, Red Head, Deep 6.

KASTNER, ELLIOTT: Producer. b. New York, NY, Jan. 7, 1933. e. U. of Miami, Columbia U. Was agent then v.p. with MCA, before becoming indep. prod., financing and personally producing 50 feature films in 25 yrs. Based in London.
PICTURES INCLUDE: Harper, Kaleidoscope, Sweet No-vember, Laughter in the Dark, Where Eagles Dare, When Eight Bells Toll, X, Y, Zee, The Nightcomers, Fear Is the Key, The Long Goodbye, Cops and Robbers, Jeremy, 11 Harrow-house, Rancho Deluxe, 92 in the Shade (exec. prod.); First Deadly Sin (co-exec. prod.); The Missouri Breaks (co-prod.); Equus (co-prod.), The Big Sleep (co-prod.); Ffolkes (prod.); Death Valley (prod.); Man, Woman, and Child (prod.); Garbo Talks (co-prod.); Oxford Blues (co-prod.); Angel Heart (co-prod.); The Big Picture (co-exec. prod.); Jack's Back (exec. prod.); The Blob; Likewise; White of the Eye; Zombie High; Never on Tuesday; Homeboy.

KATLEMAN, HARRIS L.: Executive. b. Omaha, NB, Aug. 19, 1928. e. U. of California at L.A., B.A. in admin., 1949. Joined MCA in 1949; in 1952 transferred to N.Y. as head of TV Packaging Dept. Left to join Goodson-Todman Prods. in 1955, where named v.p., 1956; exec. v.p., 1958; sr. exec. v.p., 1968. Was directly responsible for all film prod. in L.A., including such shows as The Rebel, Branded, The Richard Boone Show (Emmy nominations, Fame Award of Year), and Don Rickles Show, on which was exec. prod. Joined Metro-Goldwyn-Mayer in 1972 as v.p. of MGM-TV; promoted following year to pres., MGM-TV and sr. v.p. of MGM, Inc. Resigned as pres., MGM-TV September, 1977. Formed Bennett/Katleman Productions under contract to Columbia Pictures. Exec. prod.: From Here to Eternity, Salvage 1; 1980, named bd. chm. 20th-Fox Television.

KATSELAS, MILTON: Director. b. Pittsburgh, PA, Feb. 22, 1933. e. drama dept., Carnegie Inst. of Technology (now Carnegie Mellon U.). Has directed more than 30 stage prods., including in New York, The Rose Tattoo and Camino Real (both revivals), The Zoo Story, Butterflies Are Free, Private Lives.
PICTURES INCLUDE: Butterflies Are Free (debut), 40 Carats, Report to the Commissioner, When You Comin' Back, Red Ryder.
TELEVISION: The Rules of Marriage.

KATT, WILLIAM: Actor. b. Los Angeles, CA, 1955. Son of Barbara Hale and Bill Williams. e. Orange Coast Coll. Majored in music, playing piano and guitar. Acted with South Coast Repertory Theatre, later working in production at the Ahman-son and Mark Taper Theatres in L.A. Film debut in Carrie (1976).
PICTURES INCLUDE: Carrie, First Love, Big Wednesday, Butch and Sundance: The Early Days, Baby, House, White Ghost.
TELEVISION: The Greatest American Hero (series); Perry Mason Returns and 8 Perry Mason follow-ups (Murdered Madam; Avenging Ace; The Case of the Scandalous Scoun-drel; The Case of the Lady in the Lake); Lame Duck (series); The Rainmaker.

KATZ, GLORIA: Producer, Writer. e. U. of California at L.A. Film Sch. Joined Universal Pictures as editor, cutting educational films. Later joined forces with Willard Huyck, whom she had met at U.C.L.A. Pair signed by Francis Ford Coppola to write and direct for his newly created company, American Zoetrope. Projects didn't materialize but Katz and Huyck teamed to write script for America Graffiti for director George Lucas. Wrote Lucky Lady, 1975 together. Katz made debut as producer with French Postcards in 1979 which co-wrote with Huyck, who directed.
PICTURES: Indiana Jones and the Temple of Doom (co.-s.p.); The Best Defense (prod., co.-s.p.); Howard the Duck (prod., co.-s.p.).
TELEVISION: A Father's Homecoming (co-prod., co-s.p.).

KATZ, MARTY: Executive. b. Landsburg, West Germany, Sept. 2, 1947. e. U. of California at L.A., U. of Maryland. Served in Vietnam War as U.S. Army first lt.; awarded Bronze Star as combat pictorial unit director. 1971, dir. of film prod., ABC Circle Films; 1976, exec. v.p., prod., Quinn Martin Prods.; 1978–80, producer and consultant, Paramount Pictures' 1981–85, independent producer (Lost in America, Heart Like a Wheel). 1985, joined Walt Disney Prods. as senior v.p., motion picture & TV prod. Named exec. v.p. motion picture and TV production, 1988.

KATZ, NORMAN B.: Executive. b. Scranton, PA, Aug. 23, 1919. e. Columbia U. In U.S. Army 1941–46 as intelligence officer, airborne forces. Entered m.p. industry in 1947 with Discina Films, Paris, France, as prod. asst. Named exec. asst. to head of prod. in 1948. In 1950 named v.p. Discina Int'l. Films and in 1952 exec. v.p. In 1954 joined Associated Artists Prods. as foreign mgr.; named dir. of foreign operation in 1958. In 1959 became dir. of foreign operations for United Artists Associated. 1961 joined Seven Arts Associated Corp. of v.p. in chg. of foreign operations; named exec. v.p., Seven Arts Prods. In 1964. Named exec. v.p. Warner Bros.— Seven Arts Int'l. in 1967. In 1969 appt. exec. v.p. and chief exec. off. Warner Bros. International and bd. mem. of Warner Bros. Inc. In 1974 named snr. v.p. int'l. div. of American Film Theatre. Pres. of Cinema Arts Associated Corp. 1979, exec. v.p. and bd. member, American Communications Industries and pres., chief exec. off. of ACI subsidiary, American Cinema; 1983, pres., The NORKAT Co., Also, bd. chm., CEO, American Film Mktg. Assoc., 1985–87.

KATZENBERG, JEFFREY: Executive. b. 1950. Entered motion picture industry in 1975 as asst. to Paramount Pictures chmn. and CEO Barry Diller in NY. In 1977, became exec. dir. of mktg.; later same year moved to west coast as v.p. of programming for Paramount TV. Promoted to v.p., feature production for Paramount Pictures 1978; 2 years later assumed role of senior v.p. prod. of m.p. div.; 1982, pres of prod., m.p. and TV, Paramount Pictures. Left to join The Walt Disney Company, 1984; chairman of The Walt Disney Studios since 1984.

KATZKA, GABRIEL: Producer. b. New York, NY, Jan. 25, 1931. e. Kenyon Coll. Bdwy. prods. include Pal Joey, Hamlet, The Little Foxes, Anna Christie, The Comedians, etc.
PICTURES: Marlowe; Kelly's Heroes; Soldier Blue; The Parallax View; The Taking of Pelham 1-2-3; The Heartbreak Kid; Sleuth; A Bridge Too Far; Who'll Stop the Rain; Meteor; Butch and Sundance—The Early Days; The Beast Within; The Lords of Discipline; The Falcon and the Snowman.
TELEVISION: Kavik—The Wolf Dog; Isabel's Choice; Ellis Island.

KAUFMAN, HAL: Creative director, TV Writer, Producer. b. New York, NY, Dec. 16, 1924; e. U. of Texas, 1943–44; U. of Michigan, 1944–47. Started career as petroleum geologist, Western Geophysical Co., 1947–48; TV writer-prod-dir., KDYL-TV, Salt Lake City, 1948–49; prog. dir., WLAV-TV, Grand Rapids, 1949–51; prod. mgr., WOOD-TV, Grand Rapids, 1951–54; Radio-TV dir., Webber Advertising Agency, Grand Rapids, 1954–56; TV writer-prod., Leo Burnett Company, Chicago, 1957–58; TV writer-prod., Gordon Best Company, Chicago, 1958–59; senior writer, TV/Radio creative dept., Needham, Louis & Brorby, Inc., 1959; vice-pres., asst. copy dir., Needham, Louis & Brorby, Inc., 1962; dir., TV, Radio prod., Needham, Louis & Brorby, Inc., 1963; dir., broadcast design, production, Needham, Louis & Brorby, Inc., 1964; assoc. creat. dir., asst. Exec. v.p., Needham, Harper & Steers, Inc., 1965; Creat. dir. L.A., 1966; Sr. v.p. and Member Bd. of Dir., 1966. Aug. 1969, creative & marketing consultant in Beverly Hills. Aug., 1970; Exec. v.p., principle, Kaufman, Lansky Inc., Beverly Hills and San Diego; Member, Directors Guild of America, SAG, AFTRA. 1974; editor and publisher Z Magazine; program dir., Z Channel, Theta Cable TV. 1978 named snr. v.p./adv. & p.r. & asst. to pres. & bd. chmn., World Airways, Inc. 1982–v.p., Creative director, Admarketing, Inc., Los Angeles; 1985, mktg. & adv. consultant; copy dir., Teleflora, Inc.; 1981–pres. Hal Kaufman Inc., mktg. & adv. consultant.

KAUFMAN, J. L. (Les): Publicist. b. Chicago, IL, June 3: e. Morgan Park (IL) Military Acad. Police reporter, City News Bureau, Chicago. In 1926 adv. dept., Balaban & Katz Theats. In 1929 pub. Paramount Public Theats. To Columbia, 1933 asst. exploit, dir. In 1938 adv. & pub. dir., Fanchon & Marco Serv. Corp., St. Louis. Adv.-pub. dir., Republic Studios, 1944– 46; Nat'l. adv. pub. dir., International Pictures Corp. In 1947 named studio pub. dir., Universal-International; sales prom. counsel, Kaiser-Frazer Corp., 1950; v.p. in chge. West Coast, Ettinger Co., 1950; v.p. Grant Adv. Inc., Hollywood, Detroit, 1952–55; v.p., adv. dir., UPA Pictures, Inc., 1956; P.R. dir., Fedderson Productions & Lawrence Welk, 1957–83; My Three Sons, Hollywood Palladium, 1961, Family Affair, To Rome with Love. The Smith Family; pres., Hollywood Press Club, 1964–65, 1967–68. Bd. governors—NATVAS, Holly-

wood chapter. Director/promotion, Nederlander Companies, 1983.

KAUFMAN, LEONARD B.: Producer, Writer, Director. b. Newark, NJ, Aug. 31, 1927. e. New York U. In W.W.II served with Army Special Services writing and directing camp shows. Nat'l magazine writer, 1945–48; radio writer, including Errol Flynn Show, 1948–50; radio and TV writer, 1950–52. Headed own public relations firm: Kaufman, Schwartz, and Associates, 1952–64. Joined Ivan Tors Films as writer-prod., 1964. Films Corp., 1958.
PICTURES INCLUDE: Clarence, the Cross-eyed Lion, Birds Do It, Story.
TELEVISION: Daktari, Ivan Tors' Jambo, O'Hara, U.S. Treasury (pilot feature and series).

KAUFMAN, PHILIP: Writer, Director. b. Chicago, IL, Oct. 23, 1936. e. U. of Chicago, Harvard Law Sch. Was teacher in Europe before turning to film medium.
PICTURES INCLUDE: Goldstein, Fearless Frank, The Great Northfield, Minnesota Raid, The White Dawn, Invasion of the Body Snatchers, The Wanderers (dir., co-s.p.), The Right Stuff (dir., s.p.); The Unbearable Lightness of Being.

KAUFMAN, VICTOR: Executive. b. New York, NY, June 21, 1943. e. Queens Coll.; NYU Sch. of Law, J.D., 1967. Taught criminal law at UCLA before joining Wall St. law firm, Simpson Thacher & Bartlett. Joined Columbia Pictures as asst. general counsel, 1974. Named chief counsel, 1975; then made vice chmn. Columbia Pictures. Later exec. v.p. Columbia Pictures Industries and vice chmn. Columbia Pictures motion picture div. when conceived a new studio as a joint venture between Coca-Cola, Time Inc.'s Home Box Office and CBS, Inc. forming Tri-Star Pictures. Named chmn. and CEO Tri-Star, 1983. When Columbia Pictures and Tri-Star merged in late 1987, became pres. and CEO of new entity, Columbia Pictures Entertainment. In June 1988, dropped title of chmn. of Tri-Star.

KAUFMANN, CHRISTINE: Actress. b. Lansdorf, Graz, Austria, Jan. 11, 1945. e. school in Munich, Germany. Film debut as a dancer. Salto Mortale at 7 yrs of age.
PICTURES INCLUDE: Rosenrosli (Little Rosie), Schweigende Engel (Silent Angel), Maedchen in Uniform, Winter Vacation, The Last Days of Pompeii, Red Lips, Town Without Pity, Taras Bulba (first American-made film), Murder in the Rue Morgue, Bagdad Cafe.

KAVANAGH, DECLAN M.: Executive. b. Hollywood, CA, Oct. 29, 1956. e. California State U., B.A., acct. & mktg.; U. of Southern California, M.B.A. Co-producer of original Jane Fonda Workout, 1981; founded Video Associates (formerly Video Odyssey), 1981; co-producer home video, Everyday with Richard Simmons, 1982; organized first home video dist. deal with V.C.I. and Media Home Entertainment, 1983; founded Active Home Video, 1984; produced Bruce Jenner Winning Workout, 1984; sold Active Home Video, 1985. Now v.p. mktg. & sls., Video Associates, Inc.

KAVNER, JULIE: Actress. b. Los Angeles, Sept. 7, 1951. e. San Diego State U. Professional debut as Brenda Morgenstern on TV's Rhoda, 1974–78.
TELEVISION: Movies: The Girl Who Couldn't Lose (Afternoon Playbreak), No Other Love, The Revenge of the Stepford Wives, Katherine, A Fine Romance (pilot). Also on Lou Grant, Petrocelli, Taxi, The Tracey Ullman Show (series).
PICTURES: Bad Medicine, National Lampoon Goes to the Movies, Hannah and Her Sisters, Radio Days, Surrender.
STAGE: Particular Friendships (Off-B'way.), Two for the Seesaw (Burt Reynolds' dinner theater, FL), It Had to Be You (Canada).

KAY, GILBERT LEE: Director, Writer. b. Chicago, IL, June 28. e. Los Angeles City Coll. Was asst. dir. at various studios from 1942–53; started directing on own in 1954. Formed Pearly Gate Productions, London.
PICTURES INCLUDE: Three Bad Sisters, The Tower, Ocean's 11 (s.p.), Comeback, (s.p.), Take Five (s.p.), Fame! (s.p.), Anything for Money (s.p.), The Wrong Mrs. Wright, Now It Can Be Told (s.p.), It Happened in Lisbon (s.p.), The Secret Door, A Harvest of Evil (s.p., dir.), Sometimes I Love You (s.p.), White Comanche, Ragan, Devil May Care, Maybe September (s.p.), Recent screenplays: The Oedipus Vendetta, The Lotus Affair, Candle in the Wind, Royal Flush.
TELEVISION: Directed: Treasury Men in Action, Man Behind the Badge, Reader's Digest, Passport to Danger, Hollywood Profile, Highway Patrol, Arabian Nights, Telephone Time, Silent Service, The Grey Ghost, Man with a Camera, Adventures in Paradise, Shotgun Slade, Perry Mason, Follow the Sun, Frontier Circus. Wrote: The Uncivil Engineer, 8:46 to Southampton.
PLAYS: Directed: Two Faced Coin, Some Call It Love, French Without Tears, Burlesque, London by Night, The Man from Madrid, Paris, With Love. Wrote and Directed: West End, Please Omit Flowers, The Girl from Soho.

KAY, GORDON: Producer. b. Montreal, Canada, Sept. 6, 1916; e. Williams Coll., M.A. Asst. prod. Republic 1946, assoc. prod., 1947. apptd. secy.-treas.; exec. asst. to head of prod. at Republic, Feb., 1951; prod., Univ. 1955; pres. Gordon Kay & Assoc., 1958.
PICTURES INCLUDE: Wild Frontier, Bandits of Dark Canyon, Oklahoma Badlands, Bold Frontiersman, He Rides Tall, Fluffy, Taggart, Gunpoint, Beardless Warriors.

KAYAMA, YUZO: Actor. b. April 11, 1937. e. law school, Keio U. Debut Toho Studio 1959 in Man Against Man.
PICTURES INCLUDE: Westward Desperado, Man from the East, Blood in the Sea, Three Dolls series, Bull of Ginza, Tsubaki Sanjuro.

KAYLOR, ROBERT: Director.
PICTURES: Derby; Carny.

KAZAN, ELIA: Director. b. Constantinople, Turkey, Sept. 7, 1909. e. Williams Coll., Yale Dramatic Sch. With Group Theatre as apprentice & stage mgr.; on stage, 1934–41; plays include: Waiting for Lefty, Golden Boy, Gentle People, Five-Alarm, Lilliom; m.p. acting debut in City For Conquest, 1941; stage dir.; won Critics Award best direction of Skin of Our Teeth. All My Sons, Streetcar Named Desire, Death of a Salesman, Cat on a Hot Tin Roof; also dir.: One Touch of Venus, Harriet, Jocobowsky and the Colonel, Tea and Sympathy, Dark at the Top of the Stairs, J.B., Sweet Bird of Youth; co-dir., prod., Lincoln Center Repertory Theatre; dir., After The Fall, But For Whom Charlie; m.p. dir., 1944; Acad. Award best direction, 1947, for Gentleman's Agreement, 1954; for On the Waterfront. Author novels, The Arrangement, 1967, The Assassins, The Understudy, 1974; Acts of Love, The Anatolian, A Life (autobiography).
PICTURES INCLUDE: A Tree Grows in Brooklyn, Boomerang, Sea of Grass, Gentleman's Agreement, Panic in the Streets, Pinky, Streetcar Named Desire, Viva Zapata, Man on a Tightrope, On the Waterfront (Acad. Award, 1954), East of Eden, Baby Doll, Face in the Crowd, Wild River, Splendor in the Grass, America, America, The Arrangement, The Visitors, The Last Tycoon.

KAZAN, LAINIE: Singer, Actress. b. New York, NY, May 15, 1942. e. Hofstra U. On stage and performed in niteries.
PICTURES: Romance of a Horse Thief, Lady in Cement, Dayton's Devils, One from the Heart, My Favorite Year, Lust in the Dust, The Delta Force, Harry and the Hendersons, Beaches.
TELEVISION: A Cry for Love, Sunset Limousine, The Jerk Too, Obsessive Love, Family Business (pilot), The Lanie Kazan Show, Paper Chase, Karen Song, St. Elsewhere, Hotel, Johnny Carson Show, Dean Martin, Merv Griffin, Joan Rivers.

KAZANJIAN, HOWARD G.: Producer. b. Pasadena, CA, July 26, 1943. e. U. of Southern California Film Sch.; DGA Training Program.
PICTURES: Asst. Dir.: Camelot; Finian's Rainbow; The Wild Bunch; The Arrangement; The Front Page; The Hindenberg; Family Plot. Assoc. Prod.: Rollercoaster. Producer: More American Graffiti; Raiders of the Lost Ark; The Making of Raiders of the Lost Ark (exec. prod.); Return of the Jedi.

KAZURINSKY, TIM: Actor, Writer. b. Johnstown, PA. Worked as copywriter for Chicago ad agency. Took an acting class at Second City and quit job to become actor and head writer for Second City Comedy Troupe. Co-starred with John Candy in CTV/NBC's series Big City Comedy, 1980. Joined cast of Saturday Night Live as writer-actor 1981–84.
PICTURES: Actor: My Bodyguard, Somewhere in Time, Continental Divide, Neighbors, Police Academy II: Their First Assignment, Police Academy III: Back in Training, About Last Night (also co-s.p.), Police Academy IV, For Keeps (s.p. only), Road to Ruin (also s.p.), Hot to Trot.

KEACH, STACY: Actor, Director, Producer. b. Savannah, GA, June 2, 1942. Began professional acting career as Marcellus, Player King in Joseph Papp's 1964 production of Hamlet in Central Park. Performances since have won three Obie Awards, Vernon Rice Drama Desk Award for Macbird, Drama Desk Award, Tony Nomination for Indians.
PICTURES: The Heart Is a Lonely Hunter, End of the Road, The Traveling Executioner, Brewster McCloud, Doc, Judge Roy Bean, The New Centurions, Fat City, The Killer Inside Me, Conduct Unbecoming, Luther, Street People, The Squeeze, Gray Lady Down, The Ninth Configuration, Long-riders, (also exec. prod., co-s.p.), Road Games, Butterfly, Up in Smoke, Nice Dreams, That Championship Season.
TELEVISION: Caribe, The Blue and the Gray, Princess Daisy, Murder Me, Murder You, More Than Murder, Wait Until Dark, Mistral's Daughter, Mickey Spillane's Mike Hammer (series), Hemingway. Director: Incident at Vichy, Six Characters in Search of an Author.
STAGE: Long Day's Journey into Night, Macbird, Indians, Hamlet, Deathtrap, Hughie, Barnum, Cyrano de Bergerac, Peer Gynt, Henry IV Parts I & II, Idiot's Delight.

KEACH, SR., STACY: Executive. b. Chicago, IL, May 29, 1914. Father of actors, Stacy and James. e. Northwestern U., M.A. Was instructor in theatre arts at Northwestern and Armstrong College and dir. at Pasadena Playhouse before entering industry. For 4½ yrs. was under contract at Universal Pictures; 3 yrs. at RKO; had own productions on NBC, CBS. In 1946 began producing and directing industrial stage presentations for Union Oil Co. and from then on became full-time prod. of m.p. and stage industrial shows. In 1946 formed Stacy Keach Productions, of which he is pres. In addition to directing, producing and writing he occasionally appears as actor in films. Played Clarence Birds Eye on TV commercials as well as other commercials.

KEATON, DIANE: Actress. b. Santa Ana, CA, Jan. 5, 1946. e. Santa Ana Coll. Appeared in summer stock and studied at Neighborhood Playhouse in N.Y. Made prof. debut in Bdwy. prod. of Hair (1968); then co-starred with Woody Allen in Play It Again, Sam, repeating role for film version. Off-B'way: The Primary English Class. Author: photography books: Reservations (co-ed.), Still Life.
PICTURES INCLUDE: Lovers and Other Strangers, The Godfather, Play It Again, Sam, Sleeper, The Godfather, Part II, Love and Death, I Will . . . I Will . . . for Now, Harry and Walter Go to New York, Annie Hall (Acad. Award, 1977), Looking for Mr. Goodbar, Interiors, Manhattan, Reds, Shoot the Moon, The Little Drummer Girl, Mrs. Soffel, Crimes of the Heart, Radio Days, Baby Boom, The Good Mother, The Lemon Sisters.
DIRECTOR: What Does Dorrie Want? (short, 1982), Heaven.

KEATON, MICHAEL: Actor. b. Pittsburgh, PA, Sept. 9, 1951. Speech major, Kent State U. Taught school and became mem. of improvisational troup Jerry Vale. Started career as stand-up comic.
PICTURES: Night Shift, Mr. Mom, Johnny Dangerously, Touch and Go, Gung Ho, The Squeeze, Beetlejuice, Clean and Sober, The Dream Team, Batman.
TELEVISION: The Mary Tyler Moore Comedy Hour, Roosevelt and Truman, Working Stiffs, All's Fair, Report to Murphy.

KEEL, HOWARD: Actor. r.n. Harold Keel. b. Gillespie, IL, April 13, 1917. e. high school, Fallbrook, CA. m. Helen Anderson, dancer; d. Kaiye Liana. Stage and screen. Began career following George Walker scholarship award for singing, L.A.; appeared in plays, Pasadena Auditorium, concerts; won awards, Mississippi Valley and Chicago Musical Festivals. Stage debut: Carousel, 1945; principal role (Oklahoma). Screen debut, The Small Voice, London, 1948.
PICTURES INCLUDE: Annie Get Your Gun, Pagan Love Song, Three Guys Named Mike, Show Boat, Texas Carnival, Callaway Went Thataway, Lovely to Look At, Desperate Search, Ride Vaquero, Fast Company, Kiss Me Kate, Calamity Jane, Rose Marie, Seven Brides for Seven Brothers, Deep in My Heart, Jupiter's Darling, Kismet, Floods of Fear, Big Fisherman, Armored Command, Arizona Bushwackers.
PLAYS: Saratoga, No Strings, The Ambassador.
TELEVISION: Dallas (series).

KEESHAN, BOB: Performer. b. Lynbrook, NY, June 27, 1927. e. Fordham U. As network page boy became assistant to Howdy Doody's Bob Smith and originated role of Clarabelle the Clown; created children's programs Time for Fun, 1953; Tinker's Workshop, 1954; Captain Kangaroo, 1955–83; Mister Mayor, 1965.

KEITEL, HARVEY: Actor. b. Brooklyn, NY, 1941. m. actress Lorraine Baccro. Served in U.S. Marine Corps. Over 10 yrs. experience in summer stock repertory and little theatre after study at Actors Studio with Lee Strasberg and Frank Corsaro. Read for male lead in collegiate film prod. of Who's That Knocking at My Door?; Martin Scorsese, director, gave him the role. Has since become repertory member of Scorsese films.
THEATER: Death of a Salesman, Hurlyburly.
PICTURES INCLUDE: Who's That Knocking at My Door?, Street Scenes, Mean Streets, Alice Doesn't Live Here Anymore, Taxi Driver, Mother, Jugs and Speed, Buffalo Bill and the Indians, Welcome to L.A., The Duellists, Fingers, Blue Collar, Bad Timing, The Border, Exposed, Falling in Love, Off Beat, Wise Guys, The Men's Club, The Investigation, Blindside, The Pick-Up Artist, The January Man, Dear Gorbachev, The Last Temptation of Christ, In From the Cold.

KEITH, BRIAN: Actor. b. Bayonne, NJ, Nov. 14, 1921. p. Robert Keith, actor. U.S. Marines, 1942–45; worked in stock co., radio shows, comm. films for TV; on B'way in Mr. Roberts, Darkness at Noon; m.p. debut in Arrowhead (1953).
PICTURES INCLUDE: Jivaro, Alaska Seas, Bamboo Prison, Violent Men, Tight Spot, Five Against the House, Storm Center, Run of the Arrow, Nightfall, Sierra Baron, Those Calloways, The Raiders, The Young Philadelphians, Dino, A Tiger Walks, The Parent Trap, The Hallelujah Trail, Rare Breed, Nevada Smith, Reflections in a Golden Eye,

Krakatoa, East of Java, Gaily, Gaily, Suppose They Gave a War and Nobody Came, McKenzie Break, Scandalous John, Something Big, The Yakuza, The Wind and the Lion, Nickelodeon, Hooper, Meteor, Charlie Chan and the Curse of the Dragon Queen, Sharkey's Machine, Death Before Dishonor, Passage, Young Guns.
TELEVISION: Numerous dramas on Studio One, Suspense, Philco Playhouse. Series: Archer Family Affair, The Little People, The Westerner, Hardcastle and McCormick. Movies: Centennial, The Chisholms, 13 Days at the Alamo.

KEITH, DAVID: Actor. b. Knoxville, TN, May 8, 1954. e. U. of Tennessee, majored in drama. Appearance at Goodspeed Opera House in musical led to role in CBS sitcom pilot, Co-Ed Fever. Followed by first film role in The Rose (1979).
PICTURES: Actor: The Great Santini, Brubaker, Back Roads, Take This Job and Shove It, An Officer and a Gentleman, Independence Day, Lords of Discipline, Firestarter, White of the Eye, The Farm (dir.), The Curse (dir.), The Further Adventures of Tennessee Buck (dir., actor), Heartbreak Hotel.
TELEVISION: Are You in the House Alone?, Friendly Fire, Gulag, Golden Moment—An Olympic Story (mini-series), If Tomorrow Comes.

KEITH, PENELOPE: Actress. b. Sutton, Surrey, Eng., 1939. London stage debut, The Wars of the Roses (RSC, 1964). Extensive theater work including The Norman Conquests, Donkey's Years, The Apple Cart, Hobson's Choice, Captain Brassbound's Conversion, Hay Fever. Film debut, Think Dirty, 1970.
PICTURES: Take a Girl Like You, Penny Gold, Priest of Love.
TELEVISION: Series: Kate, The Good Life, To the Manor Born, Executive Stress; Movies: Private Lives, The Norman Conquests, Donkey's Years.

KELLER, MARTHE: Actress. b. Switzerland, 1946. e. Stanislavsky Sch. Munich. Joined a Heidelberg repertory group and Schiller Rep. in Berlin. Started acting in France and attracted attention of U.S. directors after appearing in Claude Lelouch's And Now My Love.
PICTURES INCLUDE: Funeral in Berlin, The Devil by the Tail, And Now My Love, Marathon Man, Black Sunday, Bobby Deerfield, Fedora, The Formula, The Amateur, Wagner, Femmes de Personne, Dark Eyes, Rouge Basier.

KELLERMAN, SALLY: Actress. b. Long Beach, CA, June 2, 1936. m. Jonathan Krane. e. Hollywood H.S. Studied acting in N.Y. at the Actors Studio and in Hollywood with Jeff Corey. Film debut Reform School Girls (1959).
TELEVISION: Mannix, It Takes a Thief, Chrysler Theatre, Centennial, Dempsey, Secret Weapons, September Gun, Faerie Tale Theatre, Dr. Paradise.
PICTURES INCLUDE: The Boston Strangler, The April Fools, M*A*S*H, Brewster McCloud, Last of the Red Hot Lovers, Lost Horizon, Slither, Rafferty and the Gold Dust Twins, The Big Bus, Welcome to L.A., A Little Romance, Foxes, Loving Couples, The Serial, Moving Violations, Back to School, That's Life!, Meatballs III, Three For the Road, Someone to Love, You Can't Hurry Love, Boris Natasha, Our Boy Badenov, Boardwalk, All's Fair.

KELLEY, DeFOREST: Actor. b. Atlanta, GA, Jan. 20, 1920.
PICTURES INCLUDE: Fear in the Night, Canon City, The Men, House of Bamboo, Man in the Gray Flannel Suit, Tension at Table Rock, Gunfight at the O.K. Corral, Raintree County, The Law and Jake Wade, Warlock, Where Love Has Gone, Marriage on the Rocks, Star Trek—The Motion Picture, Star Trek II—The Wrath of Khan, Star Trek III: The Search for Spock, Star Trek IV: The Voyage Home.
TELEVISION: Star Trek (series).

KELLEY PATRICK: Executive. Joined MCA in 1950 as agent; with them for 20 years; named v.p. in chg. of talent for Universal's theatrical and TV project in 1964. Left MCA in 1970 to form First Artists with star partners Barbra Streisand, Sidney Poitier, Paul Newman (later joined by Steve McQueen and Dustin Hoffman). Resigned 1975 as F.A. bd. chmn. to head Pan Arts Corp., prod. co. of which George Roy Hill is bd. chmn.
PICTURES INCLUDE: A Little Romance (exec. prod.), The Little Drummer Girl (exec. prod.), The World According to Garp (exec. prod.), Funny Farm (exec. prod.), Deadly Friend (exec. prod.).

KELLOGG, PHILIP M.: Executive. b. March 17, 1912, Provo, WA. e. U. of California at L.A. Special feature writer for Hearst papers and magazines, 1933–34; MGM story dept., production dept., Irving Thalberg unit, 1934–35; Warner Bros. Film editor, 1935–41; Berg-Allenberg Agency, 1941–50; U.S. Naval Reserve officer, 1941–46; William Morris Agency, 1950–present, co-head of m.p. dept., dir. WMA, Ltd., London.

KELLY, GABRIELLE: Producer. b. Ireland. e. U. of Sussex. Moved to U.S. in 1975, working at the New York Review of Books before going into independent film production. Has worked

with producers Jay Presson Allen, Burtt Harris and director Sidney Lumet, optioning, developing and producing projects. Co-producer of D.A.R.Y.L.

KELLY, GENE: Actor. b. Pittsburgh, PA, Aug. 23, 1912. e. Pennsylvania State U., U. of Pittsburgh. Bricklayer, concrete mixer, soda clerk, dance instructor before going on stage, in N.Y. prods. (Leave It to Me, One for the Money, The Time of Your Life, Pal Joey). On screen 1942 in For Me and My Gal; Special Academy Award for advancing dance films.
THEATER: Director: Flower Drum Song.
PICTURES INCLUDE: Pilot No. 5, Du Barry Was a Lady, As Thousands Cheer, The Cross of Lorraine, Christmas Holiday, Anchors Aweigh, Cover Girl, Ziegfeld Follies, The Pirate, Three Musketeers, Words and Music, Take Me Out to the Ball Game, Black Hand, On the Town, An American in Paris, Summer Stock, Singin' in the Rain, It's A Big Country, Devil Makes Three, Brigadoon, Crest of the Wave, Deep in My Heart, Invitation to the Dance, It's Always Fair Weather, The Happy Road, Les Girls, Gigot, A Guide for the Married Man, The Young Girls of Rochefort, Hello, Dolly!, The Cheyenne Social Club, 40 Carats, That's Entertainment, That's Entertainment, Part Two, Viva, Knievel!, Xanadu, That's Dancing.
TELEVISION: Jack and the Beanstalk, Going My Way (series), The Gene Kelly Show, many specials.

KELLY, JIM: Actor. b. Paris, KY. e. U. of Louisville. Studied karate at univ., winning trophies and int'l. middleweight championship. Opened school for karate in L.A. Did modelling and TV commercials. Was technical advisor for fight scenes on Melinda and played role in it.
PICTURES INCLUDE: Enter the Dragon (debut), Black Belt Jones, Three the Hard Way.

KELLY, NANCY: Actress. b. Lowell, MA, March 25, 1921. e. Immaculate Conception Acad., N.Y.; St. Lawrence Acad., L.I.; Bentley Sch. for Girls. In number of pictures as child, and on stage in Susan and God (N.Y. ed. 1937). Returned to screen in Submarine Patrol (1938).
PICTURES INCLUDE: Tailspin, Jesse James, Stanley and Livingstone, Tornado, Tailspin, Frontier Marshal, He Married His Wife, One Night in the Tropics, To the Shores of Tripoli, Tarzan's Desert Mystery, Women in Bondage, Gamblers Choice, Show Business, Double Exposure, Song of the Sarong, Woman Who Came Back, Murder in the Music Hall, Crowded Paradise, The Bad Seed.
STAGE: The Big Knife, Season in the Sun, 1950–51; Bad Seed, 1954–55 (Tony Award); The Gingerbread Lady (Nat'l tour); Remote Asylum.
TELEVISION: The Imposter (debut 1974); Medical Center.

KELSEY, LINDA: Actress. b. Minneapolis, MN, July 28, 1946. e. U. of Michigan, B.A.
TELEVISION: Lou Grant (series, 1977–82), The Picture of Dorian Gray, Something for Joey; Eleanor and Franklin, The Last of Mrs. Lincoln, A Perfect Match, Attack on Fear, His Mistress.

KEMENY, JOHN: Producer. b. Budapest, Hungary. Producer for National Film Board of Canada, 1957–69. Formed International Cinemedia Center, Ltd. in 1969 in Montreal, as partner.
PICTURES INCLUDE: The Apprenticeship of Duddy Kravitz, White Line Fever, Shadow of the Hawk, Ice Castles, Bay Boy, The Wraith, Quest for Fire (co-prod.), Nowhere to Hide (exec. prod.), Iron Eagle II—Battle Beyond the Flag.
TELEVISION: The Murderers Among Us: The Simon Wiesenthal Story (co-prod.).

KEMP, JEREMY: Actor. b. Chesterfield, England, Feb. 3, 1935. e. Abbotsholme Sch., Central Sch. of Speech and Drama. Service with Gordon Highlanders. Early career on stage incl. Old Vic Theatre Company, 1959–61. Recent theatre: Celebration, Incident at Vichy, Spoiled, The Caretaker. National Theatre, 1979–80.
TELEVISION: Z Cars, The Lovers of Florence, The Last Reunion, Colditz, Brassneck, Rhinemann Exchange, Lisa, Goodbye, Henry VIII, St. Joan, The Winter's Tale, Unity, The Contract, Winds of War, Sadat, King Lear, Sherlock Holmes, George Washington, Peter the Great, War and Remembrance, Slip-Up.
PICTURES INCLUDE: Cast a Giant Shadow, Operation Crossbow, The Blue Max, Assignment K, Twist of Sand, Strange Affair, Darling Lilli, The Games, The Saltzburg Connection, The Blockhouse, The Bellstone Fox, 7% Solution, A Bridge Too Far, East of Elephant Rock, Caravans, The Prisoner of Zenda, The Return of the Soldier, Top Secret!, Uncommon Valour, Why the Whales Came.

KEMP, MATTY: Producer, Director, Writer. b. Rockville Center, NY. e. St. Paul's Sch., Hemstead, NY. Entered as actor-writer 1926 Universal Pictures: variously employed by Mack Sennett, Fox, Paramount, RKO: prod. Authors' Guild show for radio and musical shorts. Served in U.S. Army 1942–45 in Signal Corps Pictorial, Information Education, and Training film branch. Prod. dir. for series of musical shorts Universal

1945; formed Cameo Productions (CA) 1946: formed Masque Productions with Gene Raymond 1948.
PICTURES INCLUDE: (prod., dir.) Linda Be Good, Million Dollar Weekend. (story) The French Line: (writer, prod., dir.) Pan American Showtime 13 half hour musical TV series. (prod., dir.) Meet the Family series (3) with Arthur Lake. (prod., dir.), Adventurous Hobby series (story, prod., dir.), The Birth of a Legend, documentary on Mary Pickford & Douglas Fairbanks. (Story, co-producer) America's Sweetheart, feature TV documentary. Managing dir., prod. executive, Mary Pickford Co.

KEMPER, VICTOR J.: Cinematographer. b. Newark, NJ, April 14, 1927. e. Seton Hall, B.S. Engineer Channel 13, Newark 1949–54; Tech. supervisor EUE Screen Gems NY 1954–56; v.p. engineering General TV Network. Pres. VJK Prods.
PICTURES: Husbands, The Magic Garden of Stanley Sweetheart, They Might Be Giants, Who is Harry Kellerman?, The Hospital, The Candidate, Last of the Red Hot Lovers, Shamus, The Friends of Eddie Coyle, Gordon's War, The Hideaways, The Gambler, The Reincarnation of Peter Proud, Dog Day Afternoon, Stay Hungry, The Last Tycoon, Mikey and Nicky, Slapshot, Audrey Rose, Oh God!, The One and Only, Coma, Eyes of Laura Mars, Magic, Night of the Juggler, And Justice for All, The Jerk, The Final Countdown, Xanadu, The Four Seasons, Chu Chu and the Philly Flash, Partner, Author! Author! National Lampoon's Vacation, Mr. Mom, The Lonely Guy, Cloak and Dagger, Secret Admirer, Pee Wee's Big Adventure, Clue, Bobo, Hot to Trot, Cohen and Tate, See No Evil, Hear Evil.

KEMP-WELCH, JOAN: Freelance, TV Director, Producer, Actress. b. Wimbleton, Eng., 1906. First appearance on stage 1927. Subsequently many stage parts and stage directorial assignments. First appeared in films 1938. Films included 60 Glorious Years, They Flew Alone, The Citadel, Busman's Honeymoon. Over 200 repertory and touring productions. West End theatre prods. include: Dead on Nine, Vicious Circle, Our Town, Desire Under the Elms. Since 1954 TV dir. Received TV Oscar for Light Entert., 1958. Desmond Davis Award for services to TV 1963. Silver Dove Monte Carlo Award, 1961 for Electra. The Lover, awarded Prix Italia 1963 (drama). Many other productions, incl. musicals, ballet, dramas, series, outside broadcasts. Dear Octopus, The Birthday Party, The Collection, View from the Bridge, Electra, 3 Sisters, A Midsummer Nights Dream, Dangerous Corner. Upstairs, Downstairs; prod. Armchair Theatre, 1973–74. 1974–75. French Without Tears, Wait Till Dark, The Price, Cranford Musical. 1976: The Other Side of the Swamp, TV. Romeo and Juliet. 1977 in S. Africa. Deep Blue Sea, The Kingfisher, The Monkey Walk in Vienna, The Circle 1978 Hay Fever. TV Hay Fever (London), It Happened in Harrods 1979. A Man and His Wife, You Can't Take It With You (South Africa), Home, Cause Celebre, Your Place or Mine, TV. The Piano 1980: Shades of Brown, Winter Journey, I Am Who I Am, TV Lady Killers. In S. Africa: The Elocution of Benjamin Franklin, Pitlochry. Gaslight & The Unvarnished Truth (S. Africa), Happy Birthday in Vienna, Murder at the Vicarage, Revival. Other Side of the Swamp, 1982 (Vienna). Dangerous Corner. Arsenic and Old Lace, The Killing of Sister George. 1983 (in Australia) On the Razzle, Romeo and Juliet. Tales from Chekhov (New York). Shades of Brown. 1984: On Golden Pond, The Voices; Sleuth (Vienna); An Inspector Calls in Cincinnati, USA; West Side Waltz, The Glass Menagerie (Frankfurt), 1986: The Amorous Prawn, Outside Edge; Catherine of Sienna; 1987: The Mousetrap; The Secret Garden. 1988: Blithe Spirit (Vienna), Death Trap (Frankfurt).

KENNEDY, ARTHUR: Actor. b. Worcester, MA, February 17, 1914. e. Carnegie Inst. of Technology. m. Mary Cheffey, prof. Has worked for George M. Cohan; Guthrie McClintic, Marc Connelly and others well known to theatregoers. Film debut: City for Conquest (1940).
PICTURES INCLUDE: They Died with Their Boots On, High Sierra, Strange Alibi, Knockout, Highway West, Air Force, Devotion, Boomerang, The Window, Champion, Chicago Deadline, The Glass Menagerie, Red Mountain, Bright Victory, Bend of the River, Rancho Notorious, Girl in White, Lusty Men, Man from Laramie, Trial, Naked Dawn, Desperate Hours, Crashout, Rawhide Years, Peyton Place, Some Came Running, Claudelle Inglish, Adventures of a Young Man, Barabbas, Lawrence of Arabia, Italiano Brava Gentle, Stay Away Joe, A Minute to Pray, a Second to Die, Hail Hero, Shark, My Old Man's Place, The Sentinel; One For Sorrow, Two For Joy.
TELEVISION: Many appearances between 1954–69. Movies: Murderer, Death of Innocence, Crawlspace, The President's Plane is Missing, Nakia.

KENNEDY, BURT: Director. b. Muskegon, MI, Sept. 3, 1922. Began as writer of TV and film scripts, and was writer, producer and director of Combat series and many TV and theatrical westerns.
PICTURES INCLUDE: Mail Order Bride (dir., prod., s.p.), The Rounders, The Money Trap, Return of the Seven, The War Wagon, Support Your Local Sheriff, Young Billy Young, The Devil's Backbone, Dirty Dingus Magee, Support Your Local Gunfighter, Hannie Caulder, The Train Robbers (also s.p.), The Trouble with Spies (prod., dir., s.p.).
TELEVISION: Movies: The Rhinemann Exchange, Wild Wild West Revisited, More Wild Wild West, Down the Long Hills, Sidekicks, Once Upon a Texas Train, Where the Hell's the Gold!!! (dir., prod., s.p.).

KENNEDY, GEORGE: Actor. b. New York, NY, Feb. 18, 1925. f. orchestra leader at N.Y. Proctor Theatre, m. dancer with Le Ballet Classique in vaudeville. At 2 acted in touring co. of Bringing Up Father. At 7, disc jockey with his own radio show for children. Joined W.W.II Army at 17, earned two Bronze Stars and combat and service ribbons. In Army 16 years, became Capt. and Armed Forces Radio and TV officer. 1957, opened first Army Information Office, N.Y. Served as technical advisor to Phil Silvers's Sergeant Bilko TV series. Began acting in 1959 when discharged from Army.
TELEVISION: Sugarfoot, Cheyenne, Blue Knight (series), Sarge (series). Movies: Jesse Owens Story, Liberty, Cry in the Wilderness, International Airport, Kenny Rogers as the Gambler III, The Gunfighters, Backstairs at the White House, What Price Victory.
PICTURES INCLUDE: Lonely Are the Brave, Strait Jacket, The Silent Witness, Island of the Blue Dolphins, The Man from the Diners Club, Little Shepherd of Kingdom Come, Mirage, See How They Run, McHale's Navy, Charade, In Harm's Way, The Sons of Katie Elder, Shenandoah, Hush . . . Hush Sweet Charlotte, The Dirty Dozen, Hurry Sundown, Cool Hand Luke (Acad. Award Best Supporting Actor), The Ballad of Josie, Jolly Pink Jungle, Bandolero!, The Boston Strangler, Guns of the Magnificent Seven, Gaily, Gaily, The Good Guys and the Bad Guys, Airport, . . . tick . . . tick . . . tick, Zig Zag, Dirty Dingus Magee, Fool's Parade, Lost Horizon, Cahill, Thunderbolt and Lightfoot, Airport 1975, Earthquake, The Human Factor, Airport '77, Death on the Nile, Brass Target, The Concorde—Airport 79, Death Ship, The Delta Force, Creepshow 2, Born to Race, Demon Warp, Counterforce, Nightmare at Noon, Private Roads, Uninvited, The Terror Within.

KENNEDY, KATHLEEN: Producer. e. San Diego State U. Early TV experience on KCST, San Diego, working as camera operator, video editor, floor director and news production coordinator. Produced talk show, You're On. Left to enter m.p. industry as prod. asst. on Steven Spielberg's 1941.
PICTURES: Raiders of the Lost Ark (prod. assoc.); Poltergeist (assoc. prod.); E.T.: The Extra-Terrestrial (co-prod.); Twilight Zone: The Movie (co-assoc. prod.), Indiana Jones and the Temple of Doom (assoc. prod.); Gremlins (exec. prod.); Goonies (exec. prod.); Back to the Future (exec. prod.); The Color Purple (co-prod.); Young Sherlock Holmes (co-prod.); An American Tail (co-exec. prod.); Innerspace (co-exec. prod.), Empire of the Sun (co-exec. prod.); Batteries Not Included (co-exec. prod.); Who Framed Roger Rabbit? (co-exec. prod.).
TELEVISION: Steven Spielberg's Amazing Stores, You're On (prod.).

KENNEY, H. WESLEY: Producer, Director, stage, TV, film. b. Dayton, OH, Jan. 3, 1926. grad. Carnegie Inst. of Technology. Six-time Emmy winner; 1974–75 dir., All in the Family; exec. prod. Days of Our Lives; 1979–81, dir., Ladies Man, Filthy Rich, 1981. Exec. prod. Young and Restless, 1981–86; now exec. prod., General Hospital.

KENT, JEAN: Actress. b. London, England, June 29, 1921. e. Marist Coll., Peekham, London; p. prof. Fields & Norrie. First stage appearance at 3 and at 10 played in parents' act; chorus girl at Windmill Theatre, London, 1935; 2 yrs. repertory; Screen debut: It's That Man Again, 1941.
PICTURES INCLUDE: Trottle True, Her Favorite Husband, The Reluctant Widow, The Woman in Question, The Browning Version, Big Frame, Before I Wake, Shadow of Fear, Prince and the Showgirl, Bon Jour Tristesse, Grip of the Strangler, Beyond This Place, Please Turn Over, Bluebeard's Ten Honeymoons, Shout at the Devil.
TELEVISION: A Call on the Widow, The Lovebird, The Morning Star, November Voyage, Love Her to Death, The Lion and the Mouse, The Web, Sir Francis Drake series, Yvette, Emergency Ward 10, County Policy, Coach 7, Smile on the Face of the Tiger, No Hiding Place, Kipling, This Man Craig, The Killers, Vanity Fair, A Night with Mrs. Da Tanka, United serial. The Family of Fred, After Dark, Thicker than Water series, The Young Doctors, Brother and Sister, Up Pompei, Steptoe and Son, Doctor at Large, Family at War, K is for Killing, Night School, Tycoon series, Crossroads (series), Lyttons Diary.

KENT, JOHN B.: Theatre executive, Attorney. b. Jacksonville, FL, Sept. 5, 1939. e. Yale U., U. of Florida, Law Sch., New York U. grad. sch. of law (L.L.M. in taxation, 1964). Partner in Kent, Ridge & Crawford, P.A.; Pres. & dir. of Kent Investments, Inc. (1977 to present); dir. and off. Kent Theatres, Inc. and affiliated corps (1961 to present); v.p. and gen. counsel, (1970 to present). Was pres. 1967–70 when resigned to devote full time to law practice. NATO dir. (1972) and Presidents' Advisory Cabinet, (1979 to present) v.p. NATO of Fla., 1968–72, dir; 1973 to present. Member of Rotary Club of Jacksonville, Fla. Bar Ass'n., American Bar Ass'n., American Judicature Society.

KENYON, CURTIS: Writer.
TV PLAYS: Cavalcade of America, Fireside Theatre, Schlitz Playhouse, U.S. Steel Hour, 20th Century-Fox Hour.
PICTURES INCLUDE: Woman Who Dared, Lloyds of London, Wake Up and Live, Love and Hisses, She Knew All the Answers, Twin Beds, Seven Days' Leave, Thanks for Everything, Princess and the Pirate, Bathing Beauty, Fabulous Dorseys, Tulsa, Two Flags West.

KERASOTES, GEORGE G.: Exhibitor. Springfield, IL. e. U. of Illinois, 1929–33; Lincoln Coll. of Law 1935–37. Past pres. Theatre Owners of Illinois. Past pres. Kerasotes Theatres, 1935–85. Past pres., Theatre Owners of America, 1959–60. Chmn. of board of TOA 1960–62; chmn. ACE Toll TV com.; bd. mem. NATO; treas.; bd. of dir., mem. exec. comm., chm. insurance comm. Chm., George Kerasotes Corp., GKC Theatres. Director St. Anthony's Hellenic Church—Hellenic Golf Classic. Director, Will Rogers Hospitals; Director, Pioneers.

KERKORIAN, KIRK: Executive. b. Fresno, CA, June 6, 1917. e. Los Angeles public schools. Served as capt., transport command, RAF, 1942–44. Commercial air line pilot from 1940; founder Los Angeles Air Service (later Trans Intl. Airlines Corp.), 1948; Intl. Leisure Corp., 1968; controlling stockholder, Western Airlines, 1970; chief exec. officer, MGM, Inc., 1973–74; chm. exec. com., vice-chm. bd., 1974–1978. Stepped down from exec. positions while retaining financial interest in MGM/UA.

KERR, DEBORAH: Actress. b. Helensburgh, Scotland, Sept. 30, 1921; e. Phyllis Smale Ballet Sch. m. Anthony Bartley. On stage 1939 in repertory. Began Brit. screen career 1940 in Major Barbara; voted "Star of Tomorrow" Motion Picture Herald-Fame Poll, 1942. Voted one of top ten British money-making stars in Motion Picture Herald-Fame Poll, 1947. B'way debut in Tea and Sympathy, 1953.
PICTURES INCLUDE: Major Barbara, Love on the Dole, Hatler's Castle, The Day Will Dawn, The Avengers, Perfect Strangers, Colonel Blimp, Black Narcissus, The Hucksters, If Winter Comes, Edward My Son, Please Believe Me, King Solomon's Mines, Quo Vadis, Thunder in the East, Prisoner of Zenda, Dream Wife, Julius Caesar, Young Bess, From Here to Eternity, End of the Affair, King and I, Proud and Profane, Tea and Sympathy, Heaven Knows Mr. Alison, Affair to Remember, Count Your Blessings, Beloved Infidel, Sundowners, The Grass Is Greener, The Innocents, The Naked Edge, The Chalk Garden, Night of the Iguana, Marriage On the Rocks, Casino Royale, Eye of the Devil, The Gypsy Moths, The Arrangement, The Assam Garden.
TELEVISION: A Woman of Substance, Reunion at Fairborough, Hold the Dream, Witness for the Prosecution.

KERR, FRASER: Actor. b. Glasgow, Scotland, 1931. Early career in repertory. Tours of Canada and America. Ent. TV 1956. Series incl. Emergency Ward 10, Dixon of Dock Green, Murder Bag. Many Shakespeare plays. Radio: BBC Drama Rep. Co., 39 Steps, The Ringer, The Bible, What Every Woman Knows.
STAGE & TELEVISION: Night Must Fall, Never a Cross Word, The Inside Man, On the Buses, Dr. Finlay's Casebook, Wicked Woman, Madeleine July, Doctor in the House, Counterstrike, Waggoner's Walk, Juno and the Paycock, Aquarius, Ev, Upstairs and Downstairs, Cover to Cover, Janine, Robert the Bruce, Caliph of Bagdad, Watch it, Sailor!, The Fosters, Weekend World, Doctor at Sea, Dads Army, Algernon Blackwood, Waiting for Sheila, Weekend Show, Mind Your Language, Yes, Minister, Dick Emery Show, Bottle Boys, The Hard Man.
PICTURES INCLUDE: What a Whopper, Carry on Regardless, Way of McEagle, Thomasina, Theatre of Death, Tom, Dick and Harriet, Granny Gets the Point, Nothing but the Night, The Lord of the Rings, Kidnapped, The Derelict, Bloomfield, Ace of Diamonds, Andy Robson, It's a Deal!, Howard's Way, One Step Beyond.
RECORD PRODUCER: Tales of Shakespeare Series, The Casket Letters of Mary Queen of Scots.

KERR, JOHN: Actor. b. New York, NY, Nov. 15, 1931. p. Geoffrey Kerr, actor, and June Walker, actress. e. Harvard U., B.A., Columbia U., M.A. Actor in summer stock, TV; on Broadway in Bernardine, Tea and Sympathy, All Summer Long.
PICTURES INCLUDE: The Cobweb, Gaby, Tea and Sympathy, The Vintage, South Pacific, Girl of the Night, Pit and the Pendulum, Seven Women from Hell.
TELEVISION: Peyton Place (series), Washington: Behind Closed Doors, Incident on a Dark Street.

KERSHNER, IRVIN: Director. b. Philadelphia, PA, April 29, 1923. e. Tyler Sch. of Fine Arts of Temple U., 1946; Art Center Sch., U. of Southern California. Designer, photography, adv., documentary, architectural; doc. film maker, U.S.I.S., Middle East, 1950–52; dir., cameraman, TV doc., Confidential File, 1953–55; dir.-prod.-writer, Ophite Prod.
PICTURES INCLUDE: Stakeout on Dope Street, Young Captives, Hoodlum Priest, The Luck of Ginger Coffey, A Fine Madness, The Flim Flam Man, Loving, Up the Sandbox, S*P*Y*s, Return of a Man Called Horse, Raid on Entebbe. (TV in U.S.), Eyes of Laura Mars, The Empire Strikes Back, Never Say Never Again, Wildfire (exec. prod.), Orders, The White Crow.
TELEVISION: The Rebel, Naked City, numerous pilots and other nat'l. shows.

KEYES, EVELYN: Actress. b. Port Arthur, TX, 1925. e. high school. Began career as a dancer in night clubs. Autobiography: Scarlett O'Hara's Younger Sister (1977).
PICTURES INCLUDE: The Buccaneer, Union Pacific, Gone with the Wind, A Thousand and One Nights, The Jolson Story, Mating of Millie, Johnny O'Clock, Enchantment, Mr. Soft Touch, The Prowler, The Killer That Stalked New York, Smuggler's Island, The Iron Man, One Big Affair, Shoot First, 99 River Street, Hell's Half Acre, Top of the World, Seven Year Itch, Around the World in 80 Days.
TELEVISION: Murder She Wrote.

KEYLOUN, MARK: Actor. b. Dec. 20, 1960. e. Georgetown U. Worked in New York theatre.
PICTURES: Those Lips, Those Eyes, Sudden Impact, Forty-Deuce, Mike's Murder.
TELEVISION: Evergreen, War Stories: The Mine.

KIDDER, MARGOT: Actress. b. Yellowknife, Canada, Oct. 17, 1948.
PICTURES INCLUDE: Gaily, Gaily, Quacker Fortune Has a Cousin in the Bronx, Sisters, The Great Waldo Pepper, Superman, Mr. Mike's Mondo Video, The Amityville Horror, Willy and Phil, Superman II, Some Kind of Hero, Little Treasure, Superman III, Keeping Track.
TELEVISION: Louisiana, The Glitter Dome, Bus Stop, Vanishing Act, Body of Evidence.

KIEL, RICHARD: Actor. b. Detroit, MI, Sept. 13, 1939.
PICTURES: The Human Duplicators, Skidoo, The Longest Yard, The Spy Who Loved Me, Force 10 from Navarone, They Went Thataway and Thataway, Flash and the Firecat, Moonraker, So Fine, Cannonball Run II, Pale Rider.

KILEY, RICHARD: Actor. b. Chicago, IL, Mar. 31, 1922. e. Loyola U. Started prof. career radio, Jack Armstrong, All American Boy.
STAGE: Streetcar Named Desire (touring co.), Misalliance, Kismet, Time Limit, Redhead (Tony Award), No Strings, Man of LaMancha, Her First Roman, The Incomparable Max, Voices, Absurd Person Singular.
PICTURES INCLUDE: The Mob, The Sniper, Eight Iron Men, Pick-Up on South Street, Blackboard Jungle, Phenix City Story, Spanish Affair, Pendulum, The Little Prince, Endless Love, Looking for Mr. Goodbar.
TELEVISION: The Thorn Birds, George Washington, The Bad Seed, A.D., Do You Remember Love, If Tomorrow Comes, A Year in the Life (series), One More Time.

KILLIAM, PAUL: Producer, Performer. b. Mass., Sept. 12, 1916. e. Harvard. News supervisor, WOR-Mutual; prod.-performer TV Hometown. Matinee in N.Y. units for CBS-TV Morning Show, NBC-TV Home Show; ind. prod. cartoons, shorts, comedies: prod. film series, Paul Killiam Show, Movie Museum, Silents Please.

KILMER, VAL: Actor. b. Los Angeles, CA, Dec. 31, 1959. e. Hollywood's Professional's Sch., Juilliard, NY. NY stage: Electra and Orestes. Co-wrote and starred in How It All Began (later presented at Public Theatre), Henry IV, Part One, and As You Like It (Gutherie, MN). Broadway debut, Slab Boys.
PICTURES: Top Secret! (debut, 1984), Real Genius, Top Gun, Willow.

KIMBLEY, DENNIS: Business Manager, Motion Picture, AV Television, Sales, Kodak Limited., in U.K. Early career in Kodak Testing Dept. responsible for quality control motion picture films. Joined Marketing Division 1966. Chairman BKSTS FILM 75 and FILM 79 Conference Committee. President BKSTS 1976–78. Governor, London International Film School, 1983.

KIMMINS, ANTHONY: Director, Writer. b. Harrow, Middlesex, England, Nov. 10, 1901; e. Royal Naval Coll., Dartmouth. Capt. in Royal Navy, W.W.II. Playwright (While Parents Sleep, Night Club Queen, Chase the Ace, Winter Sport, The Amorous Prawn.) Began screen career 1934 in How's Chances?; since author variously orig., s.p., collab., dial, many Brit. features (Talk of the Devil, Come On George, Laburnum Grove, etc.); in 1936 dir. & s.p. All at Sea; pictures dir. since include I See

Ice, It's in the Air, Trouble Brewing. In 1946 returned to m.p. to write, produce and direct.
PICTURES INCLUDE: Mine Own Executioner, Bonnie Prince Charlie, Flesh and Blood, Mr. Denning Drives North, Who Goes There (Passionate Sentry), Captain's Paradise, Smiley, Smiley Gets a Gun, The Amorous Prawn.

KING, ALAN: Actor, Producer. b. New York, NY, Dec. 26, 1927. Stars semi-annually at Sands Hotel, Las Vegas. Author, Anybody Who Owns His Own Home Deserves It, Help I'm a Prisoner in a Chinese Bakery.
TELEVISION: The Tonight Show, Kraft Music Hall, Comedy is King. Prod-star NBC-TV specials. Hosts and guest star, Tonight Show. Seventh Avenue (mini-series), On Location: An Evening with Alan King at Carnegie Hall.
STAGE: The Impossible Years, The Investigation, Dinner at Eight, The Lion in Winter, Something Different.
PICTURES INCLUDE: Bye Bye Braverman, Anderson Tapes, Just Tell Me What You Want, Author! Author! Producer: Happy Birthday, Gemini, Cattle Annie and Little Britches (co-prod.), Lovesick, Cat's Eye, Wolfen (exec. prod.), Memories of Me (actor, co-prod.).

KING, ANDREA: Actress, r.n. Georgette Barry; b. Paris, France, Feb. 7, 1915. e. Edgewood H.S., Greenwich, CT. m. N.H. Willis, attorney. Started career on N.Y. stage, following high school; in Growing Pains & Fly Away Home, Boy Meets Girl, Angel Street (Boston); Life with Father (Chicago); signed by Warner, 1943. Screen debut: The Very Thought of You.
PICTURES INCLUDE: My Wild Irish Rose, Ride the Pink Horse, Mr. Peabody and the Mermaid, Song of Surrender, Southside 1-10001, Dial 1119, Lemon Drop Kid, Mark of the Renegade, World in His Arms, Red Planet Mars, Daddy's Gone A-Hunting.
TELEVISION: Prescription Murder.

KING, HERMAN: Producer. b. Chicago, IL. Was engaged in vending machine business; mfr. Hollywood Talkitone Soundie Projectors; org. prod. co., King Bros. Prod. (with bros. Maurice and Franklin), 1941.
PICTURES INCLUDE: When Strangers Marry, Dillinger, Suspense, The Gangster, The Dude Goes West, Badman of Tombstone, Gun Crazy, Southside 1-1000, Drums in the Deep South, Mutiny, The Ring, Carnival Story, The Brave One, Gorgo, Captain Sinbad, Maya, Return of The Gunfighter, Heaven with a Gun.
TELEVISION: Maya series, King International Corp.

KING, PERRY: Actor. b. Alliance, OH, Apr. 30, 1948. e. Yale. Studied with John Houseman at Juilliard.
PICTURES INCLUDE: The Possession of Joel Delaney (debut), Slaughterhouse-Five, Big Truck, Poor Clare, The Lords of Flatbush, Mandingo, The Wild Party, Lipstick, Andy Warhol's Bad, The Choirboys, A Different Story, The Clairvoyant.
TELEVISION: Medical Center, Hawaii Five-O, Apple's Way, Cannon, I'll Take Manhattan, Riptide (series), The Last Convertible, Captain and the Kings, The Cracker Factory, Stranded, Perfect People, Shakedown on Sunset Strip.

KING, PETER: Executive. b. London, England, 1928. e. Marlborough Coll., Oxford U. Bd., Shipman & King Cinemas Ltd., 1956; borough councillor, 1959–61; chmn., London & Home counties branch, CEA, 1962–63; pres., CEA, 1964; dir. film ind. Defense Organization dir., Grade Org. 1966–68; man. dir. Shipman & King Cinemas Ltd., 1959–68. Ch. man. dir. Paramount Pictures (U.K.) Ltd. Britain, 1968–70. Man., dir., EMI Cinemas and Leisure Ltd., 1970–74. Chairman: King Publications Ltd.; Publisher: Screen International.

KING, STEPHEN: Writer. Best-selling novelist specializing in thrillers many of which have been adapted to film by others (Carrie, Salem's Lot, The Shining, The Dead Zone, Christine, Cujo, Firestarter, Cat's Eye). Stand By Me (The Body), The Running Man, Night Shift Collection (The Woman in the Room & The Boogey Man), Apt Pupil.
PICTURES INCLUDE: Creepshow (s.p., actor), Silver Bullet (s.p.), Maximum Overdrive (s.p., actor, dir.), Creepshow II (s.p., actor), Children of the Corn (s.p.).

KINGMAN, DONG: Fine Artist. b. Oakland, CA, Mar. 31, 1911. e. Hong Kong 1916–1920. 1928, mem. motion picture co., Hong Kong branch; 1935; began to exhibit as fine artist in San Francisco; promotional, advertising or main title artwork for following films: World of Suzie Wong, Flower Drum Song, 55 Days of Peking, Circus World, King Rat, The Desperados, The Sand Pebbles, Lost Horizon-1973. 1966–7, created 12 paintings for Universal Studio Tour for posters and promotion; 1968, cover painting for souvenir program for Ringling Bros.-Barnum and Bailey Circus; treasurer for Living Artist Production since 1954; Exec. V.P. 22nd-Century Films, Inc. since 1968, Prod. & dir. short, Hongkong Dong. Also short subject film Dong Kingman, filmed and directed by James Wong Howe.

KINGSLEY, BEN: Actor. b. Yorkshire, England, Dec. 31, 1943. Started career with Salford Players, amateur co. in Manches-

ter. Turned pro in 1966 and appeared on London stage at a Chichester Festival Theatre. 1967, joined Royal Shakespeare Co., where has been lead player in A Midsummer Night's Dream, Tempest, Measure for Measure, Merry Wives of Windsor, Volpone, Cherry Orchard, Hamlet, Othello, Judgement, Kean. (NY). Played Squeers in Nicholas Nickleby in 1980 in London. Film debut in Fear is the Key (1982).
PICTURES: Gandhi (Acad. Award, 1982), Betrayal, Turtle Diary, Harem, Slipstream, Testimony, Pascali's Island, Without a Clue, The Secret of the Sahara.
TELEVISION: Silas Marner, Kean, Oxbridge Blues, Camille, The Train, Sahara Secret, The Murderers Among Us: The Simon Wiesenthal Story.

KINGSLEY, DOROTHY: Writer. (Mrs. William W. Durney). b. New York, NY, Oct. 14, 1909. e. Detroit Arts and Crafts Acad. Radio writer for Bob Hope, 1938; Edgar Bergen, 1939–43.
PICTURES INCLUDE: Date With Judy, Neptune's Daughter, Two Weeks with Love, Angels in the Outfield, Texas Carnival, It's a Big Country, When in Rome, Small Town Girl, Dangerous When Wet, Kiss Me Kate, Seven Brides for Seven Brothers, Jupiter's Darling, Don't Go Near the Water, Pal Joey, Green Mansions, Can-Can, Pepe, Half a Sixpence, Valley of the Dolls.
TELEVISION: Created series, Bracken's World.

KINGSLEY, WALTER: Executive. b New York, NY, Oct. 20, 1923. e. Phillips Acad., Andover; Amherst Coll., B.A., 1947. Charter member Big Brothers of Los Angeles. WCOP, Boston, 1947–50; Ziv Television Programs, Inc., 1950–58; President, Independent Television Corp., 1958–62. Member bd. dir Big Brothers of Amer.; pres. Kingsley Co., 1962–66; exec. v.p. Wolper Prods. Metromedia Prods. Corp., 1966–72; faculty, Inter-Racial Council of Business Opportunity, N.Y.; 1972–82, pres., Kingsley Company, Commercial Real Estate; 1982–present, special consultant, American Film Inst.; Board Member: Big Brothers/Big Sisters of America; Big Brothers of Greater Los Angeles.

KINOSHITA, KEISUKE: Director. b. Japan, 1912. Entered Shochiku studio as film processor and progressed to director.
PICTURES INCLUDE: Twenty-four Eyes, Sun and Rose, Wild Chrysanthemum, A Japanese Tragedy, Times of Joy and Sorrow, Snow Flurry, Candle in the Wind, Carmen's Pure Love.

KINOY, ERNEST: Writer. Started career in radio writing sci. fic. programs (X Minus One, Dimension X). Wrote for nearly all early dramatic shows, including Studio One, Philco Playhouse, Playhouse 90.
PICTURES INCLUDE: Brother John, Buck and the Preacher, Leadbelly, White Water Summer (co-s.p.).
TELEVISION: The Defenders, Naked City, Dr. Kildare, Jacob and Joseph (special), David, the King (special), Roots I & II, Victory at Entebbe, Skokie, Murrow, The President's Plane is Missing, Stones for Ibarra, Gore Vidal's Lincoln, The Fatal Shore.

KINSKI, KLAUS: Actor. b. Poland, 1928. r.n. Nicolaus Nakszynski. Drafted into German army at 16; became British prisoner. After release began acting career in postwar German theatre. Since early 1950s has made nearly 170 films throughout Europe.
PICTURES INCLUDE: Cold Blooded Beast, Pleasure Girls, The Bloody Hands of the Law, Doctor Zhivago, For a Few Dollars More, Aguirre: The Wrath of God, Woyzeck, Nosferatu, the Vampyre, Love and Money (American debut), The Soldier, The Little Drummer Girl, Codename: Wild Geese, Cobra Verde, Paganini (dir., s.p., actor), Nosferatu in Venice.
TELEVISION: Beauty and the Beast (Faerie Tale Theatre), The Hitchhiker, Timestalkers.

KINSKI, NASTASSJA: Actress. b. Berlin, Germany, Jan. 24, 1960. Daughter of actor Klaus Kinski.
PICTURE: To the Devil a Daughter, Passion Flower Hotel, Stay as You Are, Tess, Cat People, Exposed, The Moon in the Gutter, Unfaithfully Yours, The Hotel New Hampshire, Maria's Lovers, Paris, Texas, Revolution, Silent Night, Showers.

KIRK, (BUSH), PHYLLIS: Actress. b. Syracuse, NY, Sept. 18, 1930. Perfume repr. model, Conover Agcy.; B'way play debut in My Name Is Aquilon; actress, summer stock; screen debut in Our Very Own; B'way production of Point of No Return. Worked as interviewer-host on all three major networks, Executive with ICPR and Stone Associates. Joined CBS News in Los Angeles, 1978; 1988 named v.p. media relations Stone/Hallinan Associates.
TELEVISION: The Thin Man.
PICTURES INCLUDE: A Life of Her Own, Two Weeks with Love, Mrs. O'Malley and Mr. Malone, Three Guys Named Mike, About Face, Iron Mistress, Thunder over the Plains, House of Wax, Crime Wave, River Beat, Canyon Crossroads, City After Midnight.

KIRKLAND, SALLY: Actress. b. NY, NY, Oct. 31, 1944. e. Actors Studio, studied acting with Uta Hagen and Lee Strasberg. Achieved notoriety in the 1960s for on-stage nudity (Sweet Eros, Futz), for work in experimental off-off Bdwy theater and as part of Andy Warhol's inner circle. Appeared as featured actress in over 25 films and countless avant-garde shows, before winning acclaim (and Acad. Award nom.) as the star of Anna (1987). 1983 founded Sally Kirkland Acting Workshop, a traveling transcendental meditation, yoga and theatrical seminar. Formed Artists Alliance Prods. with Mark and David Buntzman, 1988.
THEATER: The Love Nest, Futz, Tom Paine, Witness, One Night Stand of a Noisy Passenger, The Justice Box, Where Has Tommy Flowers Gone?, In the Boom Boom Room (L.A., Drama-Logue's best actress award, 1981), Largo Desolato.
PICTURES: Blue, Futz!, Coming Apart, The Sting, The Way We Were, Cinderella Liberty, Big Bad Mama, Bite the Bullet, A Star is Born, Pipe Dream, Private Benjamin, The Incredible Shrinking Woman, Human Highway, Love Letters, Fatal Games, Talking Walls, Anna, Melanie Rose, Crack in the Mirror, Paint It Black, Elizabeth From the Back County, Cold Feet.
TELEVISION: Willow B—Women in Prison, Georgia Peaches, Summer, Falcon Crest (series).

KIRKPATRICK, DAVID: Executive. e. California Inst. of Arts. Wrote screenplay, The Great Texas Dynamite Chase, produced by New World Pictures. Joined Paramount Pictures 1979 as analyst in story dept; left to head Sidney Beckerman's production co. at United Artists. Returned to Paramount 1982 as exec. dir. of production. 1984, promoted to v.p., prod., Paramount. 1985, named exec. v.p., prod. Named pres. mp. dev., Weintraub Entertainment Group, 1987.

KIRKWOOD, GENE: Producer. Company: Kanter-Kirkwood Entertainment.
PICTURES: Rocky ((Acad. Award, picture, 1976), New York, New York (assoc. prod.); Comes a Horseman; Uncle Joe Shannon; The Idolmaker; A Night in Heaven; Gorky Park; The Keep; The Pope of Greenwich Village; Legs Diamond; Ironweed, UHF (co-prod.).

KITT, EARTHA: Actress, Singer. b. Columbia, SC, Jan. 26, 1928. Professional career started as dancer in Katherine Dunham group; toured U.S., Mexico & Europe with group, then opened night club in Paris; in Orson Welles stage prod. of Faust for European tour; N.Y. night clubs; stage in U.S., New Faces of 1952; at Macambo Hollywood, 1953; author, Thursday's Child; A Tart Is not a Sweet; Alone with Me.
PICTURES: Accused, New Faces of 1952, The Mark of the Hawk, St. Louis Blues, Anna Lucasta; St. of Devil's Island, Synanon, Up the Chastity Belt, All By Myself (doc.); Dragonard.

KLAIN, JANE: Editor. b. New York, NY, Jan. 5. e. NYU, B.A., M.A. (film and theater). Reporter and film reviewer, Motion Picture Daily and Motion Picture Herald and asst. editor, Motion Picture Almanac and Television Almanac, Quigley Publishing Co.; asst. credit mgr., Seabury Press; assoc. ed., film and theater reviewer, Where Magazine, 1974–76; Video editor, Television & Video Almanac, 1986; assoc. editor, Motion Picture Almanac and Television and Video Almanac, 1987; editor, 1988. Also theater and film reviewer, Good Times, 1985–.

KLAIN, STEPHEN: Executive, Journalist. b. New York, NY, August 12. e. St. Julian's Sch., Portugal; Bedford Sch., Bedford, England; NYU (B.A., M.A.). Entered industry as reporter-reviewer, Motion Picture Daily & Motion Picture Herald, 1971; managing ed., M.P. & T.V. Almanacs, ed., Fame, 1973; Independent Film Journal, managing ed., 1973–76; joined Variety as reporter-reviewer, 1977; motion picture dept. editor, 1982–84; joined Tri-Star Pictures, March 1984, as asst. to exec. v.p. dist. & mktg; named v.p., intl. mktg., 1986; joined Columbia Tri-Star Film Distributors Inc. as v.p., intl. mktg., 1988.

KLEES, ROBERT E.: Executive. b. New York, NY, Feb. 21, 1927. e. Duke U., 1947–51; U. of California Graduate Sch. of Management, 1973–75. U.S. Navy, 1944–46; Union Carbide Corp., 1951–57; director of communications, Beckman Instruments, Inc., 1957–69; co-founder and v.p. mktg., International Biophysics Corp., 1969–73; sr. v.p., mktg., Deluxe Laboratories, Inc., 1975–83; Int'l. Exec. Service Corps & Senior Corps of Retired Executives, 1983–present. Member: Navy League of U.S., U.S. Naval Institute, Sons of American Revolution.

KLEIN, ALLEN: Producer. b. Dec. 18, 1931. Pres. ABKCO Films, a division of ABKCO Music & Records, Inc.
PICTURES INCLUDE: Force of Impulse, Pity Me Not, Mrs. Brown, You've Got A Lovely Daughter, Stranger in Town, The Stranger Returns, The Silent Stranger, Pete, Pearl & The Pole, The Grand Bouffe, Come Together, Let It Be, The Holy Mountain, El Topo, The Concert for Bangladesh, The Greek Tycoon, Personal Best, Blind Man, It Had to Be You, Sympathy for the Devil, Charlie Is My Darling.

KLEIN, HAROLD J.: Executive. b. New York, NY, e. U. of West Virginia, New York Law Sch. Reviewer, sales staff. Showman's Trade Review; booker, Brandt Theatres; booker, later vice-pres., gen. mgr., JJ Theatres, 1941–59; account executive, Exec. vice-pres., dir. of world-wide sales, ABC Films, Inc., N.Y., Pres., Klein Film Assn.; Exec. Vice President, Plitt Theatres, Inc. to Nov., 1985; now pres., H.J.K. Film Associates.

KLEIN, MALCOLM C.: Executive. b. Los Angeles, CA, Nov. 22, 1927. e. U. of California at L.A., grad., 1948; U. of Denver. Prod. dir. management, KLAC-TV (KCOP), L.A., 1948–52; acct. exec., KABC-TV, 1952–56; asst. gen. sales mgr., KABC-TV, 1956–59; exec. vice-pres. gen. mgr., NTA Broadcasting, N.Y., 1959; v.p., gen. mgr., RKO-General-KHJ-TV, 1960; joined National General Corp. 1968, vice-pres. Creative Services and Marketing. Pres. National General Television Productions, Inc., Pres. NGC Broadcasting Corp.; 1971, pres. Filmways TV Presentations; 1972, pres. Malcolm C. Klein & Assoc. mgmt. & mktg. consultants; 1973 gen'l. exec. Sterling Recreation Organization & Gen'l Mgr. Broadcast Division; pres., American Song Festival 1976; Exec. v.p. Telease Inc. & American Subscription Television; 1981, sr. v.p., mng. dir., STAR-TV (subscription TV); 1982, sr. v.p., InterAmerican Satellite TV Network. 1983: Pres. Malcolm C. Klein & Assoc., management consultant.

KLEIN, PAUL L.: Television Executive. b. Brooklyn, NY, Nov. 6, 1928. e. Brooklyn Coll. Veteran of U.S. Army Air Corps. Research analyst with Biow Co., ad agency, 1953–54; research manager for Doyle Dane Bernbach ad agency, 1955–60. Started with NBC in 1961 as supervisor, ratings, and rose to position of v.p., audience measurement in October, 1965. In August, 1970, left NBC to found Computer Television Inc., first independent pay-per-view TV co. in world. Time, Inc. bought his interest in CTI. Returned to NBC in March, 1976. as v.p., network mktg. & planning; then named v.p., programs. Appointed exec. v.p., programs, NBC-TV, November, 1977. Became independent 1978.

KLEINER, HARRY: Writer, Producer. b. Philadelphia, PA, 1916. e. Temple U., B.S.; Yale U., M.F.A.
PICTURES INCLUDE: Screenplay: Miss Sadie Thompson, Salome, Carmen Jones, Garment Jungle (also prod.), Fantastic Voyage, Bullitt (co-s.p.), Le Mans, Extreme Prejudice, Red Heat (co-s.p.).
TELEVISION: Writer: Rosenberg Trial.

KLEISER, RANDAL: Director, Producer. b. July 20, 1946. e. U. of Southern California.
PICTURES: Grease, Street People, The Blue Lagoon, Grandview, U.S.A., Summer Lovers, Flight of the Navigator, North Shore (exec. prod.), Big Top Pee Wee, Getting it Right (dir., co-prod.).
TELEVISION: Movies: All Together Now, Dawn: Portrait of a Teenage Runaway, The Boy in the Plastic Bubble, The Gathering. Series: Marcus Welby, M.D., The Rookies, Starsky and Hutch, Family.

KLINE, FRED W.: Publicist. b. Oakland, CA, May 17, 1918. e. U. of California, Berkeley. M.P. pub. rel. since 1934; pres. The Fred Kline Agency; pres. Kline Communications Corporation; Owner, Fred Kline Agency, Inc.; Kline Communications Corp.; Fred W. Kline Prod., Inc.; Capitol News Service, Sacramento; L.A. News Bureau; Capitol Radio News Service, Inc.; Commissioner, Motion Picture Council, State of California; Commissioner, Los Angeles County Fire Commission.

KLINE, KEVIN: Actor. b. St. Louis, MO, Oct. 24, 1947. e. Indiana U. Studied at Juilliard Theater Center (1968–72), and became founding member of John Houseman's The Acting Company, touring in classics, including The School for Scandal, She Stoops to Conquer, The Three Sisters, and modern works. Worked on Search For Tomorrow. Bdwy. debut in musical, The Robber Bridegroom (1977).
THEATER: Understudied Raul Julia in Lincoln Center's The Threepenny Opera, On the Twentieth Century (Tony Award), Loose Ends, The Pirates of Penzance (Tony Award), Richard III, Henry IV (Central Park), Arms and the Man, Hamlet, Much Ado About Nothing.
PICTURES: Sophie's Choice (debut, 1982), The Pirates of Penzance, The Big Chill, Silverado, Violets Are Blue, A Fish Called Wanda.
TELEVISION: Search For Tomorrow (1976–77), The Time of Your Life.

KLINGER, HENRY: Eastern story editor, 20th Century-Fox Film Corp. b. New York, NY, Mar. 15, 1908. e. City Coll. of New York, B.A.: New York U., B.B.A. Assoc. ed., Chatterbox, nat'l mag., 1931–33; pres. Booklovers' Guild, 1930–33; freelance story dept. work, RKO, Cosmopolitan & Fox Films, 1931–33; story dept., pub. contract, Fox, 1934; asst. story ed., 20th-Fox, 1936; acting story ed., 1941; assoc. story ed., 1942; story ed., 1956; exec. story ed., 1964; exec. aide, 1971–73. Lecturer, Author.

Kli-Koc

KLINGER, MICHAEL: Producer. President, Avton Films Int'l., Inc. b. Eng., Nov. 2, 1920.
PICTURES INCLUDE: Cul-de-Sac, Repulsion, Saturday Night Out, Study in Terror, The Penthouse, Baby Love, Something to Hide, Get Carter, Pulp, Rachel's Man, Tomorrow Never Comes, Gold, Shout at the Devil, Riding High. Exec. Prod. Confessions series, Blood Relatives, Death of a Soldier, The Assassinator, Retribution.

KLINGER, TONY: Producer/Writer. Chairman, Senior V.P., Avton Films International Inc. b. London, 1950. Ent. m.p. industry, 1966.
PICTURES INCLUDE: The Kids are Alright, Extremes, The Butterfly Ball, The Festival Gamer, Rock of Ages, Promo Man, The Assassinator (exec. prod.), Retribution (exec. prod.), Zombie Cop (prod.).

KLUGMAN, JACK: Actor. b. Philadelphia, PA, April 27, 1922. e. Carnegie Tech. m. Brett Somers. After several menial jobs appeared on Broadway in Saint Joan, Stevedore; later understudied in Mister Roberts, taking over the doctor role; recent stage work includes Gypsy, The Odd Couple (on tour and stock), I'm Not Rappaport.
PICTURES INCLUDE: Timetable, Twelve Angry Men, Cry Terror, The Scarface Mob, Days of Wine and Roses, I Could Go on Singing, The Yellow Canary, Act One, Hail Mafia, The Detective, The Split, Goodbye Columbus, Who Says I Can't Ride a Rainbow?, Two Minute Warning.
TELEVISION: The Defenders (Emmy Award for role in Blacklist segment), The FBI, Ben Casey, 90 Bristol Court, The Odd Couple (Emmy, 1971 and 1973), Quincy, M.E.; You, Again?, Around the World in 80 Days.

KNIGHT, ARTHUR: Critic, Educator. b. Philadelphia, PA, Sept. 3, 1916. e. City Coll. of New York, B.A., 1940. Asst. curator Museum of Modern Art Film Library, 1939–49; film consultant CBS-color television, Omnibus, Odyssey, Seven Lively Arts, etc; film courses at C.C.N.Y., New School for Social Research, Hunter Coll.; contributor to Encyclopedia Britannica, Collier's Encyclopedia, etc.; author: The Liveliest Art, The Hollywood Style; film critic, Hollywood Reporter; formerly Saturday Review; prof. U. of Southern California Sch. of Cinema/TV.

KNIGHT, DAVID: Actor. b. Niagara Falls, NY, Jan. 16, 1928. e. Whittier Coll. (CA). 1944–52 teacher Putney Sch., Vermont; 1952–53 student Royal Acad. of Dramatic Art.
LONDON STAGE: Trial of Mary Dugan, The Tenth Man, How to Succeed in Business Without Really Trying, Caine Mutiny Court Martial.
PICTURES INCLUDE: Young Lovers (Chance Meeting), Out of the Clouds, Lost, Eyewitness, Across the Bridge, V.I., The Story of David, Nightmare, Bedtime Story.
TELEVISION: Lincoln in Illinois, Berkeley Square, The Philadelphia Story, The Unquiet Spirit, A Question of Pride, Trial and Error.

KNIGHT, SHIRLEY: Actress. b. Goessell, KA, July 5, 1936. e. Lake Forest Coll., D.F.A., 1978.
PICTURES INCLUDE: Five Gates to Hell (debut), Ice Palace, The Dark at the Top of the Stairs, (Acad. Award nom.) The Couch, Sweet Bird of Youth (Acad. Award nom.), House of Women, Flight from Ashiya, The Group, Dutchman (Best Actress, Venice Film Fest.), Petulia, The Counterfeit Killer, The Rain People, Juggernaut, Beyond the Poseidon Adventure, Endless Love, The Sender, Prisoners.
TELEVISION: 21 Hours at Munich, Friendly Persuasion, Playing For Time, Return to Earth, Billionaire Boys Club.

KNOPF, DAVID A. Producer's Representative. b. Boston, MA, Feb. 9, 1942. e. U. of Wisconsin. m. Jane Gibbons. vice-pres., Knopf/Polier Representation. 1964 started in Universal Studios mailroom, moved up to publicity department. Began career in exhibition 1968 as film buyer, National General Theatres. Head film buyer for S. Cal. UA Theatres and General Cinema before joining Warner Bros. as sales exec. in Boston. Returned to Los Angeles as S. Cal. film buyer for Mann theatres. Started Knopf/Polier, 1979.

KNOTTS, DON: Actor. b. Morgantown, WV, July 21, 1924. e. U. of West Virginia, U. of Arizona. Drafted into U.S. Army where became part of show called Stars and Grapes, teamed with comedian Mickey Shaughnessy. After schooling resumed, was offered teaching fellowship but went to New York to try acting instead. Appeared on radio and TV, leading to role in No Time for Sergeants on Bdwy.; appeared in film version.
PICTURES: It's a Mad, Mad, Mad, Mad World, The Incredible Mr. Limpet, The Shakiest Gun in the West, The Apple Dumpling Gang, Herbie Goes to Monte Carlo, The Apple Dumpling Gang Rides Again, Cannonball Run II.
TELEVISION: Garry Moore Show, Steve Allen Show, Andy Griffith Show (played Barney Fife), The Don Knotts Show, Three's Company, Return to Mayberry.

KNOWLES, PATRIC: Actor. r.n. Reginald Lawrence Knowles; b. Horsforth, Yorkshire, England, Nov. 11, 1911. Joined Abby Repertory Theatre, 1930; Oxford Playhouse Repertory,

1932–33. Film debut (Ireland) in Irish Hearts, 1934; on London stage in By Appointment; U.S. m.p. debut in Charge of the Light Brigade, 1936; served in Canadian RAF & as civilian instructor USAF, W.W.II.
PICTURES INCLUDE: Honours Easy, Mister Hobo, Two's Company, Give Me Your Heart, It's Love I'm After, Expensive Husbands, Adventures of Robin Hood, How Green Was My Valley, Forever and a Day, Of Human Bondage, Bride Wore Boots, Ivy, Kitty, Monsieur Beaucaire, Dream Girl, Big Steal, Quebec, Three Came Home, Mutiny, Tarzan's Savage Fury, Jamaica Run, Flame of Calcutta, World Ransom, Khyber Patrol, No Man's Woman, Band of Angels, Auntie Mame, The Way West, In Enemy Country, The Devil's Brigade, Chisum, The Man, Terror in the Wax Museum, Arnold.

KNOX, ALEXANDER: Actor. b. Strathroy, Ont., Jan. 16, 1907. e. Western Ontario U. Author, novels: Bride of Quietness, Night of the White Bear, The Enemy I Kill, Raider's Moon, The Kidnapped Surgeon; plays, Old Master, The Closing Door, Red On White.
TELEVISION: Potsdam, Tinker Tailor Soldier Spy, Suez, Churchill And The Generals, Helen and Teacher, Empire, Darwin, Oppenheimer, The Last Place on Earth, Lovejoy.
STAGE: (N.Y.) Romeo and Juliet, The Three Sisters, Jupiter Laughs, Jason, The Closing Door; (London) King of Nowhere, Geneva, In Good King Charles' Golden Days, The Jealous God, Winter Journey, Henry VIII, Return to Tyassi, Burnt Flower Bed, When We Dead Awaken.
PICTURES INCLUDE: The Sea Wolf, This Above All, Commandos Strike at Dawn, None Shall Escape, Over 21, Wilson, Sign of the Ram, Judge Steps Out, Sister Kenny, I'd Climb the Highest Mountain, Saturday's Hero, Sleeping Tiger, Divided Heart, Crack in the Mirror, The Viking, The Night My Number Came Up, Reach for the Sky, High Tide at Noon, Davy, Operation Amsterdam, The Longest Day, Wreck of the Mary Deare, Man in the Middle, Woman of Straw, Mr. Moses, Accident, Villa Rides, Shalako, Skullduggery, Pupper on a Chain, Khartoum, Nicholas and Alexandra, Gorky Park, Joshua Then and Now.

KNOX, GORDON: Producer. b. Greenville, TX. e. U. of Missouri. In addition to making documentary films for several years has been employed by Warner Bros., and Walter Wanger Prods. Joined Princeton Film Center in 1940; Pres. SKS Prod. Inc., Santa Fe, NM Pres., PAC Productions, Inc., Princeton, NJ.

KOBAYASHI, MASAKI: Director. b. Japan, Feb. 4, 1916. e. Waseda U. Joined Shochiku 1941 as asst. Director. Army. Rejoined Shochiku 1946.
PICTURES INCLUDE: No Greater Love, Road to Eternity, A Soldier's Prayer, Black River, Room with Thick Walls, Somewhere Beneath Wide Sky, Fountainhead, I'll Buy You, The Human Condition, The Inheritance.

KOCH, HOWARD: Writer. b. New York, NY, Dec. 12, 1902. e. St. Stephen's Coll., 1922, B.A.; Columbia Law Sch., 1925. LL.B. Hon. degree Doctor of Human Letters, Bard Coll., 1972. Playwright (Give Us This Day, In Time to Come, Straitjacket). Began screen career collab. s.p. The Sea Hawk. Radio: wrote War of the Worlds play for Orson Welles' broadcast. book: The Panic Broadcast (Little, Brown & Co.); Academy Award best s.p. (Casablanca). As Time Goes By, Memoirs of a Writer in Hollywood, New York and Europe published by Harcourt, Brace and Jovanovich.
PICTURES INCLUDE: The Letter, Shining Victory, In This Our Life, Casablanca, Mission to Moscow, Letter From an Unknown Woman, The Thirteenth Letter, The War Lover, The Fox, Loss of Innocence, No Sad Songs for Me, Sergeant York, Three Strangers.

KOCH, HOWARD W.: Producer, Director. b. New York, NY, Apr. 11, 1916. Runner on Wall St. Began film career in Universal's contracts and playdate dept. in NY; asst. cutter, 20th-Fox; asst. dir., 20th-Fox, Eagle Lion, MGM; 2nd unit dir., freelance; In 1953, joined Aubrey Schenck Prod. forming Bel Air Prods., made films for U.A.; 1961–64, prod. Frank Sinatra Enterprises; v.p., chg. prod., Paramount Pictures Corp., 1964–66, Past pres. of the Academy of Motion Picture Arts and Sciences, 1977–79. On June 11, 1977, elected to the National Board of Directors Guild of America for two year term. 1980 honored by NATO as prod. of year. 1985 Silver Medallion Award of Honor, Motion Picture Television Fund. Produced eight Academy Award shows, 1972–1983. Has had a 24 year relationship with Paramount as exec., prod., and dir.
TELEVISION: Director, Miami Undercover, The Untouchables, Maverick, Cheyenne, Hawaiian Eye. Movies: The Pirate (prod.); Hollywood Wives (1985 mini-series), Crossings (1986 mini-series). Specials: Ol' Blue Eyes Is Back (prod.); Oscar's Best Actors (prod., dir.); Oscar's Best Movies (prod., dir.); Who Loves Ya Baby (prod.); On the Road with Bing (prod., dir.); The Stars Salute the Olympics (prod.).
PICTURES INCLUDE: Executive Producer: Come Blow Your Horn; Sergeant's Three; Manchurian Candidate; X-15; Robin and the Seven Hoods; None But The Brave; The President's Analyst; For Those Who Think Young; Dragonslayer. Producer: War Paint; Beachhead; Yellow Tomahawk;

Desert Sands; Fort Yuma; Quincannon; Frontier Scout; Ghost Town; Broken Star; Crimes Against Joe; Three Bad Sisters; Emergency Hospital; Rebel in Town; The Black Sheep; Pharaoh's Curse; Tomahawk Train; Revolt at Fort Laramie; War Drums; Voodoo Island; Hellbound; The Dalton Girls; The Odd Couple; On a Clear Day You Can See Forever; Plaza Suite; Star Spangled Girl; Last of the Red Hot Lovers; Jacqueline Susann's Once Is Not Enough; Some Kind of Hero; Airplane II: The Sequel; Collision Course. A Howard W. Koch Production: A New Leaf, Airplane!; Producer/Director: Badge 373. Director: Jungle Heat; Shield for Murder; Big House USA; Fort Bowie; Violent Road; Untamed Youth; Born Reckless; Frankenstein 1970; Andy Hardy Comes Home; The Last Mile; Girl in Black Stockings.

KOCH, HOWARD W., JR.: Producer. b. Los Angeles, CA, Dec. 14, 1945. Was asst. dir. and in other industry posts before turning to production. Pres. & chief exec. off., Rastar. 1987, set up own prod. co. at De Laurentiis Entertainment Group. Oct. 1987: named president of the De Laurentiis Entertainment Group, Resigned April 1988 to produce independently.
PICTURES: Heaven Can Wait, The Other Side of Midnight, The Frisco Kid (exec. prod.); Co-prod.: The Idolmaker, Gorky Park, Honky Tonk Freeway, The Keep, A Night in Heaven, The Pope of Greenwich Village, Rooftops.

KOCH, JOANNE: Executive Director, The Film Society of Lincoln Center. b. NY, NY, Oct. 7, 1929. e. Goddard College, B.A. political science, 1950. Dept. of Film, Museum of Modern Art, as circulation asst., film researcher, motion picture stills archivist, 1950. Early 1960s, technical dir., film dept. MOMA, supervised the implementation of MOMA's film preservation program. 1967, asst. to publisher of Grove Press, active in preparation of Grove's case in I Am Curious Yellow censorship trial. Joined film div., Grove, first in distribution then as tech. dir. and prod. coord. 1971 joined Film Society of Lincoln Center as prog. dir. of Movie-in-the-Parks. June, 1971 made admin. dir. Exec. dir. of NY Film Festival, Film Comment magazine, Movies-in-the-Park, Film-in-Education, New Directors/New Films and annual Film Society Gala.

KOENEKAMP, FRED J.: b. Los Angeles, CA, Nov. 11, 1922. Cinematographer. Member of American Society of Cinematographers.
PICTURES: Beyond the Valley of the Dolls, Billy Jack, Embryo, The Other Side of Midnight, The Champ, Amityville Horror, Love and Bullets, First Family, The Domino Principle, Towering Inferno (Acad. Award), The Hunter, When Time Ran Out, First Monday in October, Carbon Copy, Yes, Giorgio, Two of a Kind, Wrong is Right, Adventures of Buckaroo Banzai, Across the 8th Dimension, Mismatch.
TELEVISION: Nearly 30 TV movies including Disaster on the Coastline, Tales of the Gold Monkey, Money on the Side, Return of the Man from U.N.C.L.E., Summer Girl, Whiz Kids, Flight 90—Disaster on the Potomac, Obsessive Love, City Killer, Las Vegas Strip, A Touch of Scandal, Not My Kid.

KOENIG, WALTER: Actor, Writer, Director ,Producer. b. Chicago, IL, Sept. 14. e. Grinnell Coll. (IA), U. of California. Performed in summer stock; after college enrolled at Neighborhood Playhouse, N.Y.; first acting job in TV's Day in Court.
PICTURES: The Deadly Honeymoon, Star Trek—The Motion Picture, Star Trek II: The Wrath of Khan, Star Trek III: The Search for Spock.
TELEVISION: Actor: Colombo, Medical Center, Ironside, Mannix, Alfred Hitchcock Presents, Mr. Novak, Ben Casey, The Untouchables, Combat. Films: The Questor Tapes, Goodbye Raggedy Ann. Writer: Family, The Class of '65, The Powers of Matthew Starr.

KOHN, HOWARD E., II: Executive. b. McKeesport, PA. National dir. of adv., publicity, roadshow dept., United Artists; indep. prod., Hidden Fear, 1957; pres. Lioni-Warren-Kohn, Inc., 1958; national roadshow dir., Columbia Pictures, Porgy and Bess, 1959; World wide co-ordinator, national co-ordinator adv. & pub. for El Cid, June 1961; named world wide co-ordinator adv., pub. all Samuel Bronston Productions, April 1962; pres., Starpower Inc., 1968; exec. v.p., Avanti Films, 1970; v.p. Avariac Prods., 1971; Pres., Blossom Films, 1973. Elected member of ASCAP, 1975. Pres., Avanti Associates, 1976. Pres. Channel Television Prods., Inc., 1985.

KOHNER, PANCHO: Producer. b. Los Angeles, CA, Jan. 7, 1939. e. U. of Southern California, U. of Mexico, Sorbonne.
PICTURES: The Bridge in the Jungle (also dir-s.p.); The Lie; Mr. Sycamore; St. Ives; The White Buffalo; Love and Bullets; Why Would I Lie?; 10 to Midnight; The Evil That Men Do; Murphy's Law; Messenger of Death.

KOHNER, SUSAN: Actress. b. Los Angeles, CA. Nov. 11, 1936. m. designer John Weitz. Mother, Lupita Tovar, was one of Mexico's leading film actresses. Father was talent rep. Paul Kohner. e. U. of California, 1954–55. Currently does a weekly broadcast on In Touch Network for the Blind, and is play adviser to National Artists Management Co.
TELEVISION: Alcoa Hour, Schlitz Playhouse, Four Star

Theatre, Matinee Theatre, Climax, Suspicion, Playhouse 90, Route 66, Dick Powell Theatre.
STAGE: Love Me Little, He Who Gets Slapped, A Quiet Place, Rose Tatoo, Bus Stop, St. Joan, Sunday in New York, Take Her She's Mine, Pullman Car, Hiawatha, as well as summer stock.
PICTURES INCLUDE: To Hell and Back, The Last Wagon, Trooper Hook, Dino, Imitation of Life, The Big Fisherman, The Gene Krupa Story, All the Fine Young Cannibals, By Love Possessed, Freud.

KONCHALOVSKY, ANDREI: (also known as Mikhalov-Konchalovski) Director. b. Moscow, Soviet Union, 1937. Great grandfather: painter Sourikov; grandfather: painter Konchalovski; father is a writer; mother poet Natalia Konchalovskaia; brother is director Nikita Mikhalkov. e. as pianist Moscow Conservatoire, 1947–57; State Film Sch. (VGIK) under Mikhail Romm (1964). Worked as scriptwriter during 1960s especially with Andrei Tarkovsky. 1962: asst. to Tarkovsky on Ivan's Childhood. 1980: moved to US.
PICTURES INCLUDE: The Boy and the Pigeon (1961, short film, dir.); The Steamroller and the Violin (s.p.); Andrey Rublev (s.p.); The First Teacher (dir., s.p.); The Story of Asya Klyachina, Who Loved But Did Not Marry (dir., s.p.); A Nest of Gentlefolk (dir., s.p.); Tashkent City of Bread (s.p.); The Song of Manshuk (s.p.); Uncle Vanya (dir.); The End of Chieftain (s.p.); Romance for Lovers (dir.); Siberiade (Jury prize, Cannes, 1979); Split Cherry Tree (short for U.S., cable TV, 1982); Duet for One; Shy People (dir., story, co-s.p.), Homer and Eddie.

KONIGSBERG, FRANK: Executive. b. Kew Gardens, NY, March 10, 1933. e. Yale, Yale Law Sch. Worked as lawyer at CBS for six years; moved to NBC 1960–65 in legal dept. as dir. prog. and talent administration. Left to package TV special for Artists Agency Rep. (later AFA) in Los Angeles. being sr. v.p. of West Coast office seven years. Executive producer of many TV series, pilots, variety specials and made-for-TV movies. Formed own Konigsberg Company. Theatrical film debut as prod., Joy of Sex (1984).
TELEVISION: Movies (all exec. prod.): Pearl, Ellis Island, Bing Crosby: His Life and Legend, Dummy, Before and After, Guyana Tragedy, A Christmas Without Snow, The Pride of Jesse Hallam, Hard Case, Divorce Wars, Coming Out of the Ice, Onassis: The Richest Man in the World (co-exec. prod.), Where the Hell's the Gold!!!, Senior Prom. Series (all exec. prod.): It's Not Easy, Breaking Away, Dorothy.

KONTOS, SPERO L.: Thea. Equip. Dealer. b. Chicago, IL, Dec. 17, 1922. e. Illinois Inst. of Technology, B.S. B.M.. eng.; U. of California at L.A. Ent. Ind. as Chicago exhib., 1937; thea. mgmt. until 1942. U.S. Army, 1942–46; sis. eng., Abbott Theatre Equip. Co., 1946–48; sis. mgr., 1948–51; gen. mgr. 1951–54; sis. mgr. John P. Filbert Co. Inc., 1954–59; hd. Century 70/35 mm. projector program, 1959–60; Filbert Co., v.p. chg. sis. & eng., 1960–64; pres., 1964; pres. Theatre Equipment Dealers Assoc., 1965–67; bd. chm., TEDA, 1967–69; chief barker, L.A. Variety, 1971–72; pres., Megaron Corp., 1973, Academy of Motion Picture Arts & Sciences, 1975.

KOPELSON, ARNOLD: Producer, Packager, Financier, Distributor. b. New York, NY, Feb. 14, 1935. e. New York Law Sch., J.D., 1959; New York U., B.S. Has executive-produced, produced, packaged, developed or distributed over 100 films. Handled intl. dist. of Twice in a Lifetime. 1986, prod. Platoon. Chm., Film Packages Intl. Co-chm. Inter-Ocean Film Sales, Ltd.
PICTURES: Foolin' Around (prod.), The Legacy (exec. prod.), Lost and Found (exec. prod.), Night of the Juggler (exec. prod.), Platoon, Warlock (exec. prod.).

KORBAN, BERNARD: Executive. b. New York, NY, Nov. 28, 1923; e. RCA Inst. of Technology, New York U. U.S. Army 1942–46; 1951–58, Public Relations and Promotions for Davega Stores; 1959–62, exploitation fieldman for Universal Pictures; 1962–66, supvr. of fieldmen and exploitation activities; 1966–68, exec. in chrg. field activities; exec. assist. to v.p., adv. pub. and promotion; 1972 dir. of exploitation, National General Pictures; 1973, dir. of Marketing, promotion and worldwide distribution for Brut Prods; 1974, dir. of mkt., Avco Embassy Pictures, 1975, vice pres. of advertising/publicity/promotion, Cine Artists Pictures Corp.; advertising/publicity, United Artists Corp. West Coast ad. mgr.; then UA v.p., West Coast adv.; v.p. West Coast adv./promo., MGM/UA; 1983, v.p., gen. mgr., AC&R/DHB & BESS, San Diego.

KORMAN, HARVEY: Actor, Director. b. Chicago, IL, Feb. 15, 1927. e. Wright Junior Coll. Began dramatic studies at Chicago's Goodman Sch. of Drama at the Arts Inst. Acted in small roles in Broadway plays and did TV commercials until break came as comedian for Danny Kaye Show on TV. Staged comedy sketches for Steve Allen variety series in 1967. Became Carol Burnett's leading man on her show 1967 to 1978. Directed two episodes of The New Dick Van Dyke Show.
PICTURES INCLUDE: Actor: Three Bites of an Apple, Lord Love a Duck, Last of the Secret Agents, The April Fools, Blazing Saddles, Huckleberry Finn, High Anxiety, Ameri-

cathon, First Family, History of the World—Part I, Trail of the Pink Panther, Curse of the Pink Panther, The Longshot, Munchies.
TELEVISION: The Danny Kaye Show, Carol Burnett Show, Crash Course.

KORMAN, LEWIS J.: Executive. b. 1945. As a lawyer at Gelberg & Abrams, pioneered dev. of public limited partnerships, Delphi Partners, to help finance Columbia Pictures' and Tri-Star Pictures' films. 1985, became pres. of joint venture between Delphi Partners and Producers Sales Organization, PSO/Delphi. After co. dissolved, became consultant to Tri-Star involved in negotiations that led to acquisition of Loews Theatre Corp. in 1986. Joined Tri-Star, 1987, overseeing theater acquisitions. Named senior exec. v.p., Columbia Pictures Entertainment, Inc., 1987; appointed to additional post of chief operating officer and named dir., 1988.

KORTY, JOHN: Director, Producer, Writer, Cameraman, Animator. b. Lafayette, IN, June 22, 1936. e. Antioch Coll., B.A., 1959. President, Korty Films, Inc., Mill Valley, CA.
THEATRICAL FEATURES: Alex and the Gypsy; Oliver's Story; Twice Upon a Time.
TELEVISION FEATURES: The Autobiography of Miss Jane Pittman, (1974 Emmy, DGA Award); Farewell to Manzanar, 1976 (Humanitas, Christopher Awards); Forever (1977); A Christmas Without Snow (1980), A Deadly Business (1986); Resting Place (1986), Baby Girl Scott; Eye on the Sparrow. INDEPENDENT FEATURES: Crazy Quilt, (1964); Funnyman; Riverrun. DOCUMENTARIES: Who Are the De-Bolts?, (Oscar, Emmy, DGA Award); Can't It Be Anyone Else?; Stepping Out: The DeBolts Grow Up, The Ewok Adventure.
SHORT FILMS: The Language of Faces (AFSC, 1961); Imogen Cunningham, Photographer (AFI grant, 1970); The Music School. ANIMATION: Breaking the Habit, (Oscar nominee); Various children's films; Segments for Sesame Street and The Electric Company.

KORVIN, CHARLES: Actor. r.n. Geza Korvin Karpathi. b. Czechoslovakia, Nov. 21, 1907. e. U. of Paris, Sorbonne, 1933–36. Cameraman, dir., documentary films in Europe; to U.S. in 1937; Barter Theatre, 1940–42; on B'way, Dark Eyes, 1943; m.p. debut in Enter Arsene Lupin, 1945.
PICTURES INCLUDE: This Love of Ours, Temptation, Berlin Express, Killer That Stalked N.Y., Lydia Bailey, Tarzan's Savage Fury, Sangaree, Ship of Fools, The Man Who Had Power Over Women.

KOSCINA, SYLVA: Actress. b. Yugoslavia, Aug. 22, 1933. Grew up in Italy; as model placed under contract for films by Carlo Ponti.
PICTURES INCLUDE: The Railroad Man (debut), Juliet of the Spirits, Deadlier Than the Male, The Hornet's Nest, Casanova & Co., Sunday Lovers.

KOTCHEFF, WILLIAM THEODORE (Ted): Director. b. Toronto, Canada, 1931. Ent. TV ind. 1952. After five years with Canadian Broadcasting Corp. joined ABC-TV in London, 1957.
PLAYS INCLUDE: Of Mice and Men, Desperate Hours, The Human Voice, Edna the Inebriate Woman, Signalman's Apprentice, Lights Out, Rx for the Defence.
LONDON STAGE: Progress the Park, Play with a Tiger, Luv, Maggie May, The Au Pair Man, Have You Any Dirty Washing, Mother Dear?
PICTURES INCLUDE: Tiara Tahiti (debut, 1963), Life at the Top, Two Gentlemen Sharing, Outback, Billy Two Hats, The Apprenticeship of Duddy Kravitz, Fun with Dick and Jane, Who Is Killing The Great Chefs of Europe?, North Dallas Forty (also co-s.p.), First Blood, Split Image (also prod.), Uncommon Valor (also exec. prod.), Joshua Then and Now, Switching Channels, Winter People.

KOTTO, YAPHET: Actor. b. New York, NY, Nov. 15, 1937. Has many stage credits, including starring roles on Broadway in The Great White Hope, The Zulu and the Zayda. Off-Bdwy.: Blood Knot, Black Monday, In White America, A Good Place To Raise a Boy.
PICTURES INCLUDE: The Limit (star, prod.), Nothing But a Man, The Liberation of L. B. Jones, Live and Let Die, Across 110th Street, Truck Turner, Bone, Report to the Commissioner, Sharks' Treasure, Hey Good Lookin', Friday Foster, Night Chase, Drum, Monkey Hustle, Blue Collar, Alien, Brubaker, Fighting Back, Star Chamber, Eye of the Tiger, Prettykill, The Running Man, Midnight Run, Nightmare of the Devil (prod., dir., actor), Terminal Entry, Jigsaw.
TELEVISION: Movies: Raid on Entebbe, Rage, Playing With Fire, The Park Is Mine, Women of San Quentin, Badge of the Assassin, Harem, Desperado, Alfred Hitchcock Presents (1985), Perry Mason: The Case of the Scandalous Scoundrel.

KOVACS, LASZLO: Cinematographer. b. Hungary, May 14, 1933. Came to U.S. 1957; naturalized 1963. e. Acad. Drama and M.P. Arts, Budapest, MA 1956.

PICTURES INCLUDE: Hell's Angels on Wheels, The Savage Seven, Targets, Easy Rider, That Cold Day in the Park, Getting Straight, Alex in Wonderland, The Last Movie, Marriage of a Young Stockbroker, The King of Marvin Gardens, Pocket Money, What's Up, Doc?, Paper Moon, Huckleberry Finn, For Pete's Sake, Freebie and the Bean, Shampoo, At Long Last Love, Baby Blue Marine, Close Encounters of the Third Kind, Harry and Walter Go to New York, New York, New York, F.I.S.T., The Last Waltz, Paradise Alley, Butch and Sundance: The Early Days, The Runner Stumbles, Heart Beat, Inside Moves, The Legend of the Lone Ranger, Frances, The Toy, Crackers, Ghostbusters, Mask, Legal Eagles, Little Nikita, Say Anything.

KOZLOWSKI, LINDA: Actress. Began professional acting career soon after graduating from Juilliard Sch., N.Y., 1981. Stage debut in How It All Began at the Public Theatre. In regional theatre appeared in Requiem, Translations, Make and Break, as well as on Broadway and on tour with Dustin Hoffman in Death of a Salesman and the TV adaptation.
PICTURES INCLUDE: Crocodile Dundee, Crocodile Dundee II, Helena.
TELEVISION: Favorite Son.

KRABBE, JEROEN: Actor. b. Amsterdam, The Netherlands, Dec. 5, 1944. Trained for stage at De Toneelschool, Acad. of Dramatic Art, Amsterdam, 1965. Also studied at Acad. of Fine Arts, grad. 1981. Founded touring theater co. in the Netherlands and translated plays into Dutch. Also costume designer. As a painter, work has been widely exhibited. Author: The Economy Cookbook. Dir. debut, new stage adaptation of The Diary of Anne Frank, 1985 in Amsterdam.
PICTURES INCLUDE: Soldier of Orange (debut, 1979); A Flight of Rainbirds; Spetters; The Fourth Man; Turtle Diary; Jumpin' Jack Flash; No Mercy; The Living Daylights; Shadow of Victory; A World Apart; Crossing Delancey; Shadowman.
TELEVISION: Danton's Death (debut, 1966); William of Orange; World War Three. Movies: One for the Dance.

KRAMER, JEROME: Executive, Producer, Director. b. Los Angeles, CA, 1945. e. U. of Southern California Law Sch., 1971. Joined Braverman Productions, Inc. 1971; named exec. v.p. Co-producer with Charles Braverman of network specials (21 Years of A.I.P., Horror Hall of Fame), show titles (Rhoda, Cher) corporate and promotional films for Xerox, Petersen Publishing, etc. Producer and director of various television commercials (for Chevrolet, United Artists Records, Gulf Oil), educational films for United States Information Agency, special films and montages.

KRAMER, LARRY: Writer, Producer. b. Bridgeport, CT, 1935. e. Yale U., B.A. 1957. Ent. m.p. ind. 1958. Story edit. Columbia Pictures, N.Y. London 1960–65. Asst. to David Picker and Herb Jaffe, UA, 1965. Assoc. prod. and additional dialogue Here We Go Round the Mulberry Bush, 1968. Writ. prod. Women in Love, 1969. Lost Horizon, 1971 (s.p.). Novel: Faggots (1978). Theater: The Normal Heart. (NY Shakespeare Festival and throughout the world), Just Say No. Cofounder: Gay Men's Health Crisis, Inc. (community AIDS org.).

KRAMER, SIDNEY: Sales executive. b. New York, NY. e. New York Law Sch., LL.B., City Coll. of New York. Gen. sales mgr., RKO Pathe, June 1953; dir. and v.p. Cellofilm Corp. 1941–56; foreign sales mgr., RKO Radio, 1954–59; v.p. Cinemiracle Intl. 1960–61; v.p. T.P.E.A., 1960–61; foreign sls. mgr., Cinerama, Inc., 1962–65; Exec. Commonwealth Theatres, Puerto Rico, Inc., 1965–68; Exec. v.p. Cobian Jr. Enterprises Inc. 1968. M.P. consultant-exhibition, dist., foreign and Caribbean area, Oct., 1968–70. Pres. Coqui Internat'l. Inc.; 1970–80; vice. pres. of UAPR, Inc., Puerto Rico, U.A. Eastern Theatres, Inc. 1981–present, consultant in Florida, UA Theatres.

KRAMER, STANLEY E.: Executive producer, Director. b. New York, NY, Sept. 29, 1913; e. New York U., B.Sc., 1933. Entered m.p. ind. via back lot jobs; with MGM research dept.; film cutter 3 yrs.; behind m.p. ed.; m.p. & radio writer; served in U.S Signal Corps, 1st Lt.
PICTURES INCLUDE: Champion, Home of the Brave, The Men, Cyrano de Bergerac, Death of a Salesman, High Noon, My Six Convicts, The Sniper, The Four Poster, The Happy Time, Eight Iron Men, 5,000 Fingers of Dr. T, Wild One, The Juggler, Caine Mutiny, Not as a Stranger, Pride and the Passion; prod. dir., The Defiant Ones, On the Beach, Inherit the Wind, Judgment at Nuremberg; prod., dir., It's a Mad, Mad, Mad, Mad World, Invitation to a Gunfighter, prod., Ship of Fools, Prod. Dir. Guess Who's Coming to Dinner, The Secret of Santa Vittoria, R.P.M.*, Bless the Beasts and Children, Oklahoma Crude, The Domino Principle, The Runner Stumbles (prod., dir.).
TELEVISION: Guess Who's Coming to Dinner? (pilot).

KRANTZ, STEVE: Executive. b. New York, NY, May 20, 1923. e. Columbia U., B.A. Dir. progs., NBC, New York, 1953; dir. prog. dev., Screen Gems, N.Y., 1955; v.p., gen. mgr. Screen Gems,

Canada, 1958; dir. int. sls., 1960; formed Krantz Films, Inc. 1964.

TELEVISION': Steve Allen Show, Kate Smith Show, Hazel, Dennis the Menace, Winston Churchill—The Valiant Years, Telefilms, Marvel Super Heroes, Rocket Robin Hood, Animated Films. Mini-series: Princess Daisy, Sins, Mistral's Daughter, I'll Take Manhattan.

PICTURES INCLUDE: Fritz the Cat, Heavy Traffic (prod.), Cooley High, Ruby, Which Way Is Up?

KREIMAN, ROBERT T.: Executive. b. Kenosha, WI, Sept. 16, 1924. Served W.W.II Capt Army Corps of Engineers-ETO. e. Stanford U., 1943; U. of Wisconsin, 1942—1946-49. Dir., sales training, mgr., audio visual sales, Bell & Howell Co., 1949–58; V.P., Argus Cameras, Inc., 1958–61; V.P., gen. mgr., Commercial & Educ. Div., Technicolor 1961–69, v.p. gen. mgr., The Suburban Companies; 1969–71: pres. and chief exec. officer, Deluxe General, Inc. Pres. and Director of Movietonews, Inc. Bd. chm. Keith Cole Photograph, Inc. 1972–78. bd. chm., pres. and chief exec. officer, Pace International Corp., 1969 to present. past pres. of U.C.L.A. Executive Program Ass'n. Fellow SMPTE, Member M.P. Academy; TV Academy; assoc. mem., American Society of Cinematographers.

KRESS, HAROLD F.: Director, Film editor. b. Pittsburgh, PA, June 26, 1913. e. U. of California at L.A. Film ed., Command Decision, Madame Curie, Mrs. Miniver, The Yearling; crime shorts; 5-reel Army documentary short, Ward Care for Psychotic Patients. Member: Acad. of M.P. Arts and Sciences, Screen Directors Guild, Film Editors Guild.

PICTURES INCLUDE: Painted Hills, No Questions Asked, Apache War Smoke, Ride Vaquero, Saadia, Rose Marie, Valley of the Kings, The Cobweb, The Prodigal, I'll Cry Tomorrow, Teahouse of the August Moon, Silk Stockings, Until They Sail, Merry Andrew, Imitation General, The World, the Flesh and the Devil, Count Your Blessings, Home from the Hills, The Greatest Story Ever Told, Walk Don't Run, Alvarez Kelly, Academy Award for film editing on How the West Was Won.

FILM EDITOR: Poseidon Adventure, The Iceman Cometh, 99 and ⁴⁴/₁₀₀% Dead, The Towering Inferno.

KREUGER, KURT: Actor. b. St. Moritz, Switzerland, July 23, 1917. e. U. of Lausanne, U. of London. Came to U.S. 1937, partner in travel bureau; acted in Wharf Theat. group. Cape Cod, 1939; Broadway debut in Candle in the Wind with Helen Hayes, 1941.

PICTURES INCLUDE: Mademoiselle Fifi, Hotel Berlin, Paris Underground, Dark Corner, Unfaithfully Yours, Fear, The St. Valentine's Day Massacre, What Did You Do in the War Daddy?

KRIEGE, ALICE: Actress. b. Upington, South Africa, 1955. Moved to London at 22 and studied at School of Speech and Drama. Professional debut on British TV: The Happy Autumn Fields. In London prod. of Forever Yours, Maylou. West End debut, Arms and the Man, 1981. Two seasons with Royal Shakespeare Co. at Stratford and London (The Tempest, King Lear, The Taming of the Shrew, Cyrano de Bergerac.)

PICTURES: Chariots of Fire, Ghost Story, King David, Barfly, Baja Oklahoma, See You in the Morning, Haunted Summer.

TELEVISION: Wallenberg: A Hero's Story, Dream West, A Tale of Two Cities, Ellis Island, Second Serve.

KRIER, JOHN N.: Executive. b. Rock Island, IL. e. Augustana Coll. Joined A. H. Blank Theatres, Grad. Publix Theatres Manager Training Sch., 1930: managed theatres in Illinois, Iowa, Nebraska; joined Intermountain Theatres, Salt Lake City, 1937: appointed Purchasing Head, 1946: buyer-booker, 1952: v.p., gen. mgr., 1955: appt. v.p. gen mgr. ABC Theas., Arizona, 1968: appt. v.p. gen'l director Film Buying ABC Theatres of California & ABC Intermountain Theatres, Feb. 1972. Became consultant ABC Southern Theatres, 1974. Joined Exhibitors Relations Inc. as partner, 1978. Elected pres., 1982. Became owner, 1988.

KRIM, ARTHUR B.: Attorney. b. New York, NY, 1910. e. Columbia U., B.A., 1932. 1932 became member law firm Philips, Nizer, Benjamin, Krim & Ballon, N.Y. elected pres. United Artists Feb. 20, 1951; chairman of bd., 1969 to January 1978; Ch. of Board, Orion Pictures Company, March, 1978.

KRISEL, GARY: Executive. b. California. Senior vice-president, Network Television, Walt Disney Pictures.

KRISTOFFERSON, KRIS: Actor, Singer. b. Brownsville, TX, June 22, 1936. e. Pomona Coll., Oxford U. (Rhodes Scholar). Joined U.S. Army briefly and taught English literature at West Point. Started writing songs (country music) and hits have included Me and Bobby McGee, Why Me, Lord, Sunday Mornin' Comin' Down, etc. Film debut in Cisco Pike, 1971. Continues to make records, do concert tours and appear in films.

PICTURES: Cisco Pike, Pat Garrett and Billy the Kid, Blume in Love, Bring Me the Head of Alfredo Garcia, Alice

Doesn't Live Here Anymore, Vigilante Force, The Sailor Who Fell from Grace with the Sea, A Star Is Born, Semi-Tough, Convoy, Heaven's Gate, Roll-Over, Songwriter, Flashpoint, Trouble in Mind, Big Top Pee-wee, Millenium, Passage, Helena.

TELEVISION: Freedom Road, The Lost Honor of Kathryn Beck, Blood and Orchids, Stagecoach, The Last Days of Frank and Jesse James, Amerika, The Tracker.

KRONICK, WILLIAM: Writer, Director. b. Amsterdam, NY. e. Columbia Coll., A.B. U.S. Navy photography; wrote, dir. featurette, A Bowl of Cherries.

TV DOCS: Wrote, dir., prod.: The Ultimate Stuntman: a Tribute to Dar Robinson, To the Ends of the Earth, Mysteries of the Great Pyramid; George Plimpton Specials; National Geographic, Ripley's Believe It or Not, et. al. Wrote: Raiders of the Lost Ark: Great Movie Stunts. Prod.: In Search of . . . series.

FEATURE FILMS: Nights in White Satin (s.p.); Horowitz in Dublin (dir., s.p.); Flash Gordon and King Kong (2nd unit dir.); The 500 Pound Jerk (dir., TV movie).

KROST, BARRY: Producer. Partner with Doug Chapin and Mel Simon in The Movie Company, a film, TV, and theatrical production co. Also pres., BKM Management, involved in managing stars. Credits are as exec. prod.

PICTURES: When a Stranger Calls, Uforia, Pandemonium, American Dreamer.

TELEVISION: Movies: Second Sight, Missing Pieces, The Rules of Marriage, When the Circus Comes to Town, Belle Starr, Rearview Mirror.

KRUEGER, RONALD P.: Executive. b. St. Louis, MO, Oct. 19, 1940. e. Westminister Coll., 1961. Began working in theatres as a teenager. Assumed presidency Wehrenberg Theatres, 1962.

MEMBER: NATO and regional v.p.; American Film Inst.; Second Decade, advisory bd. mbr., Salvation Army; Motion Picture Pioneers; Demolay Legion of Honor.

KRUGER, HARDY: Actor. b. Berlin, Germany, April 12, 1928. Ent. m.p. ind. 1943; on stage since 1945.

PICTURES INCLUDE: The One That Got Away, Bachelor of Hearts. German version of The Moon Is Blue, The Rest Is Silence (German film of Hamlet), Blind Date (Britain). Has also starred in twenty-four German films. Filming in France and Germany. 1961–62: Films include: Taxi Pour Tobrouk (France), Hatari (Paramount, Hollywood), Les Dimanches de Ville d'Avray (France), Le Gros Coup (France), Les Pianos Mecaniques (France), Le Chant du Monde (France), Flight of the Phoenix (Hollywood), The Defector (U.S.), La Grande Sauterelle, Le Franciscain de Bourge (France), The Battle of the Neretva, The Red Tent, The Nun of Monza, The Secret of Santa Vittoria, Night Hair Child, Death of a Stranger (Israel), Le Solitaire (France), Barry Lyndon (England), Paper Tiger (England/Germany), Potato Fritz (Germany), A Bridge Too Far (England/U.S.), L'Autopsie d'un Monstre (France), The Wild Geese (England); Wrong Is Right (U.S.).

KRUGER, JEFFREY S.: Producer, Concert impresario, Record and music publisher, Film distribution executive. b. April 19, 1931, London, England. Chairman of the Kruger Organisation (Concert Promotions) Ltd., Bulldog Records, Ember Records, Kruger Leisure Organisation Ltd., Visual and Audio Leisure Co. Ltd. Produced feature films Rock You Sinners; Sweet Beat; The Amorous Sex. Distributor of Jack Nicolson's The Shooting, Love Child, Dial Rat For Terror, Starcrash; Kill the Shogun; Red Light In the Whitehouse; Enforcer from Death Row; A Whale of A Tale, Vengeance of the Barbarians, From Nashville with Music, Togetherness, Forbidden Love, Search for the Evil One, Gallery of Horrors, Grave of the Vampire, Tomb of the Undead, Sex and the Lonely Woman, House of Terror, Smoke in the Wind, Ten Fingers of Steel, Psychopath, Choppers, Deadwood 76, Good Time Outlaws, Ground Zero, Journey to the Centre of Time, and others. Produced (in association with B.B.C.-TV): 20 musical specials including six one-hour musicals starring Glen Campbell as well as shows starring Marvin Gaye, Jacksons, Charley Pride, George Burns, Charlie Rich, Anne Murray, Helen Reddy, Dionne Warwick, Blood Sweat and Tears, War, David Soul, Frankie Laine, Jerry Lee Lewis, others. Concert presentations include Glen Campbell, Helen Reddy, Anne Murray, George Burns, many more. Music publ. through Songs For Today. Own record production and distribution via Bulldog Records and Visual and Audio Leisure Co. Ltd. Director The Kruger Organisation (Concerts) Ltd. Songs For Today Ltd. Ember Enterprises Inc. Visual and Audio Leisure Co. Ltd. Hillbrow Productions Ltd. Recipient, certificate of merit from city of Beverly Hills & commendation from city of Los Angeles.

KUBRICK, STANLEY: Producer, Director, Writer. b. New York, NY, July 26, 1928. e. Taft H.S. Staff photog., Look magazine; writer, prod., dir., documentaries including Day of the Fight, Flying Padre; Received Luchino Visconti Award, Italy for contribution to cinema, 1988.

PICTURES: prod., dir., s.p., Fear and Desire, Killer's Kiss;

Kuh-Kwi

dir., s.p., The Killing; writer-dir., Paths of Glory; dir. Spartacus; prod. dir., Lolita; prod. dir., writer, Dr. Strangelove; prod. dir., writer, 2001; A Space Odyssey; A Clockwork Orange; Barry Lyndon; The Shining; Full Metal Jacket (dir., co-prod., co-s.p.).

KUHN, THOMAS G.: Executive. b. Chicago, IL, Nov. 10, 1935. e. Northwestern U., 1957; U. of Southern California, M.B.A., 1966. Singer on Roulette Records, 1958–59. KNBC-TV sales 1960–62; NBC business affairs, 1962–64; NBC mgr. live night time progs., 1965–67; dir. live night time progs., 1968–69. Warner Bros. TV, v.p. program dev. 1970; v.p. TV prod., 1971; exec. prod., Alice; exec. prod., The Awakening Land; exec. v.p. for Alan Landsburg Prods.; exec. prod., Torn Between Two Lovers; exec. prod., The Jayne Mansfield Story; Long Way Home. Staff, v.p., west coast, for RCA Selectavision Video Discs, 1980; division v.p., 1981. Pres., RCA Video Prods., 1984; pres., Lightyear Ent., 1987. Exec. prod.: Aria, The Return of the Swamp Thing.

KULIK, SEYMOUR (BUZZ): Producer, Director. b. New York, NY, 1923. Joined CBS-TV as prod.-dir., 1956; 1964: v.p. chg. West Coast Prods., Bob Banner Associates Inc., 1965; 1967 Prod-Dir. with Paramount Studios.
TELEVISION: Lux Video, Kraft; dir.: You Are There, Climax, Playhouse 90, Defenders, Dr. Kildare, Twilight Zone, Dick Powell Playhouse, Kentucky Jones (exec. prod.). Movies: Brian's Song, Women of Valor, Her Secret Life, Babe, Ziegfield: The Man and His Woman, Vanished, The Lindbergh Kidnapping Case, Her Secret Life, From Here to Eternity, Insight/Decision to Love; Kane and Abel, George Washington (supr. prod.-dir.), Rage of Angels, Too Young the Hero, Around the World in 80 Days.
PICTURES: Warning Shot, The Riot, Shamus, Villa Rides, The Hunter, Pursuit.

KUNO, MOTOJI: Sr. Managing Director. Tokyo Shibaure Electric Co., Ltd. (Toshiba), Tokyo, Japan. Graduated Law Dept., Tokyo Imperial U. Mar., 1923. Became Toshiba auditor June, 1941; dir. June, 1942; sr. managing dir. Nov., 1948, perm. auditor Apr. 1949; dir. Fem., 1950; exec. dir. May, 1952; sr. managing dir. May, 1958.

KUPPER, W. J.: Executive. b. New York, NY, Oct. 17, 1896. World Film Corp. 2 yrs.; h.o. 20th-Fox, Aug., 1919; asst. mgr. Dallas, 1920; br. mgr., Washington, Oct. 1921; later, br. mgr., Albany, Charlotte, Pittsburgh, Chicago; asst. gen. sales mgr., h.o., Jan., 1924; spcl. rep., 1928; west div. mgr., Aug., 1932; gen. sales mgr., U.S., Canada, 1942; mag. dir., 20th-Fox Films of Gt. Brit., 1947–54; v.p., gen. sales mgr. Chromart Colour Org., England; 1954. Member: M.P. Pioneers; Variety Club of Gt. Brit.

KURALT, CHARLES: TV News Correspondent. b. Wilmington, NC, Sept. 10, 1934. e. U. of North Carolina. Reporter-columnist for Charlotte News until joining CBS News as writer in 1957. Promoted to news assignment desk in 1958. Became first host of CBS News series, Eyewitness, in 1960. Named CBS News chief Latin American correspondent (based in Rio de Janeiro) in 1961 Appt. CBS News chief west coast correspondent in 1963; transferred to New York, 1964. Has worked on CBS Reports, CBS News Specials, and On the Road series for CBS Evening News. Now host of CBS News Sunday Morning. Author: To the Top of the World (1968), Dateline America (1979).

KUREISHI, HANIF: Writer. b. South London, Eng., Dec. 1956. e. King's Coll. (philosophy). At 18, first play presented at Royal Court Theatre where he ushered before becoming writer in residence. Early in career, wrote pornography as Antonia French. Stage and TV plays include: The Mother Country, Outskirts, Borderline and adaptations (Mother Courage). The Rainbow Sign, With Your Tongue Down My Throat (novella) and short stories have been pub. Anglo-Pakistani writer's first s.p. My Beautiful Laundrette earned Acad. Award nom., 1986, and began creative relationship with dir. Stephen Frears.
PICTURES: My Beautiful Laundrette, Sammy and Rosie Get Laid.

KURI, EMILE: Set decorator. b. Mexico City, Mex., June 11, 1907. e. Chaminade Coll., 1924–27. Interior decorator Be Hennesey Art Studio, 1929–32; then set decorator property dept. dir.
PICTURES INCLUDE: I'll Be Seeing You, Silver Queen, Spellbound, Duel in the Sun, Paradine Case, The Heiress (Academy Award, 1949), A Place in the Sun, Carrie, Shane, The Actress, Executive Suite, 20,000 Leagues Under the Sea (Academy Award, 1954); in charge of interior exterior decorations Disneyland. Several Golden Chair Awards (L.A. Furniture Mart). Mem.: Nat'l Acad. of TV Arts and Sciences, American Institute of Interior Designers, Bd. of Gov. Acad. of M.P. Arts and Sciences (1959–69). Honorary Sir Knights of Royal Rosarians, State of Oregon (1970), Decorating Consultant, Disney World, Fla.

KURI, JOHN A.: Producer, Writer. b. 1945. Son of set designer and Disneyland co-designer, Emile Kuri. At 16 worked at Disneyland in ride operations and construction maintenance

until joining set dressing crew at Disney Studios, 1969. 1971, became set decorator there. Exec. asst. to prod. Irwin Allen. Formed own co., 1976. Wrote and dir. doc. on city of Las Vegas.
PICTURES: Captive Hearts (prod., co-s.p. 2nd unit dir., co-lyrics.)
TELEVISION: The Red Pony (set decorator and art dir., Emmy nom., 1973), Through the Magic Pyramid (assoc. prod.), Skyward (prod., 2nd unit dir.), Skyward Christmas (prod., 2nd unit dir.), Airwolf (dir.); O'Hara (co-creator, series).

KURODA, TOYOJI: Executive. b. Tokyo. April 29, 1920. e. Waseda U. Joined Motion Picture Producers Association 1945; appointed inspectorate Board of Trade in export film division 1948. On occasion of founding of Association for Diffusion Japanese Films Abroad (UniJapan Film) became manager.

KUROSAWA, AKIRA: Director. b. Japan. March 23, 1910. Entered PCL Studio 1936 and made director 1943.
PICTURES INCLUDE: Sanshiro Sugata, The Most Beautiful, Those Who Tread on The Tiger's Tail, No Regrets for Our Youth, The Quiet Duel, Scandal, Stray Dog, Rashomon, The Seven Samurai, The Drunken Angel, The Lower Depths, The Idiot, Ikiru, I Live in Fear, The Hidden Fortress, Throne of Blood, Yojimbo, High and Low, Red Beard, The Bad Sleep Well, Sanjuro, Dersu Uzala, Kagemusha, Ran, Runaway Train (orig. s.p. only).

KURTIS, BILL: News Correspondent, Anchor. b. Pensacola, FL, Sept. 21, 1940. e. U. of Kansas, Washington U. Sch. of Law, Topeka. Member, American Bar Assn. Career in broadcast journalism began at WIBW Radio in Topeka. Joined CBS News as reporter-producer at Los Angeles bureau in 1970; named CBS news correspondent in 1971. Joined WBBM-TV, Chicago, in 1973 as co-anchor of news broadcasts. In 1982 returned to CBS News as correspondent and co-anchor of CBS Morning News. Left in 1985 to return to Chicago.

KURTZ, GARY: Producer, Director. b. Los Angeles, CA, July 27, 1940. e. U. of Southern California Cinema Sch. Began prof. career during college. Has worked as cameraman, soundman, editor, prod. supervisor and asst. dir. on documentaries and features. Worked on many low budget features for Roger Corman including: The Terror, Beach Ball, Track of the Vampire, Planet of Blood, The Shooting, Ride into the Whirlwind. Drafted into Marines. Spent 2 yrs. in Photo Field as cameraman, editor and still photo.
PICTURES INCLUDE: Two-Lane Blacktop (line prod.), Chandler (line prod.), American Graffiti (co.-prod.); Star Wars (prod.), The Empire Strikes Back (prod.); The Dark Crystal (prod., 2nd unit dir.), Return to Oz (exec. prod.), Slipstream (prod.).

KURTZ, SWOOSIE: Actress. b. Omaha, NB, Sept. 6, 1944. e. Studied at U. Southern Calif., Acad. of Music and Dramatic Art, Eng. Regional theatre 1966–70.
THEATER: Who's Afraid of Virginia Woolf? (with Mike Nichols and Elaine May), The Effect of Gamma Rays on Man-in-the Moon Marigolds, Enter a Free Man, Life Class, Children and the Middle Ages, Summer, Fifth of July (Tony Award), House of Blue Leaves (Tony and Obie Awards), Uncommon Women and Others.
PICTURES: Slap Shot, First Love, Oliver's Story, The World According to Garp, Against All Odds, Wildcats, True Stories, Vice Versa, Bright Lights, Big City, Baja Oklahoma, Les Liaisons Dangereuses.
TELEVISION: Uncommon Women, Marriage Is Alive and Well, Mating Season, Love Sidney, The Fifth of July, A Caribbean Mystery, Guilty Conscience, A Time to Live, House of Blue Leaves, The Visit (Trying Times).

KURYS, DIANE: Director. b. France. 1970 joined Jean-Louis Barrault's theatre group, acted for 8 years on stage, television and film. Adapted and translated staged plays. 1977, wrote screenplay for Diboio Menthe (Peppermint Soda) which she also directed and co-prod. Film won Prix Louis Deluc, Best Picture. Co-prod. Alexandre Arcady's Coup de Sirocco and Le Grand Pardon.
PICTURES: Cocktail Molotov (s.p., dir.); Entre Nous (s.p., dir.); A Man in Love (s.p., dir.).

KUTNER, MARTIN: Executive. Joined Paramount Pictures in 1971 as eastern div. mgr.; has held various positions in sls. dept. Named v.p., gen. sls. mgr.; in 1980 appt. senior v.p., domestic distribution; 1983, exec. v.p., distribution; 1984, exec. v.p., intl. mkt. & dist.

KWIT, NATHANIEL TROY, JR.: Executive. b. New York, NY, May 29, 1941. e. Cornell U., B.A.; New York U., M.B.A. 1964–68, American Broadcasting Co., Inc., exec. asst. to pres. of ABC Films. 1968–71, National Screen Service Corp., New York branch mgr., asst. genl. mkt. mgr. 1971, founder, CEO Audience Marketing, Inc., later acquired by Viacom International as operating subsidiary. 1974 named v.p. marketing services, Warner Bros., Inc. 1979, named v.p. in charge video and special markets division, United Artists Corp.; 1981, named sr. v.p. in chg. UA television, video, special market div. Following acquisition of UA Corp. by MGM in 1981 promoted to pres., dist. & mktg. for MGM/UA Entertainment Co. 1983, pres. & CEO, United Satellite Communications, direct broadcast TV co. formed with Prudential Insurance Co. backing.

KYO, MACHIKO: Actress. b. Osaka, Japan. e. Osaka. Dancer in Osaka and Tokyo music halls; entered films 1948 with Daiei Studio; has appeared in numerous Japanese films.
PICTURES INCLUDE: Rashomon, Gate of Hell, Golden Demon, Story of Shunkin, Tales of Genji, Street of Shame, Teahouse of the August Moon, Ugetsu.

L

LACHMAN, ED: Cinematographer. b. 1948. Son of a Morristown, NJ movie theater owner. e. Ohio U., BFA. Filmed documentaries Ornette: Made in America, Strippers, Huie's Sermon. Assisted Sven Nykvist on King of the Gypsies, Hurricane; Vittorio Storaro on Luna; Robby Muller on The American Friend and They All Laughed. Co-director of photography on Werner Herzog's La Soufriere and Stroszek and Wim Wenders' Lightning Over Water and A Tokyo Story.
PICTURES: Scalpel, Union City, Say Amen, Somebody, Little Wars, Split Cherry Tree, Strippers, The Little Sister, Insignificance (American sequences) Desperately Seeking Susan, True Stories, Making Mr. Right, Hail, Hail Rock and Roll, A Gathering of Old Men, Less Than Zero, Backtrack.

LADD, JR., ALAN: Executive. b. Los Angeles, CA, Oct. 22, 1937. Motion picture agent, Creative Management Associates, 1963−69. M.p. producer, 1969−73; produced 9 films in 4 yrs. Joined 20th Century-Fox in 1973 in chg. of creative affairs in feature div. Promoted to v.p., production, 1974. In 1975 named sr. v.p. for worldwide prod.; 1976, promoted to pres. of 20th Century-Fox Pictures. Resigned & formed The Ladd Co., 1979. In 1985 appt. pres. & COO, MGM/UA Entertainment Film Corp; appointed chairman of board, CEO Metro-Goldwyn-Mayer Pictures Inc., 1986; resigned Sept., 1988.
PICTURES: Prod.: Walking Stick, A Severed Head, Tam-Lin, Villian, Zee and Co., Exec. prod.: Fear is the Key.

LADD, CHERYL: Actress. r.n. Cheryl Stoppelmoor. b. Huron, S.D., July 2, 1951. Joined professional Music Shop Band while in elementary school; left with it on tour, ending up in Los Angeles. Cast as voice of Melody character in animated Josie and the Pussycats. Studied acting with Milton Katselas. Did TV commercials, small parts in TV, made film Jamaica Reef (unreleased).
TELEVISION: Series: Charlie's Angels. Guest star on Ben Vereen . . . His Roots, General Electric's All-Star Anniversary, John Denver and the Ladies, Police Woman, Happy Days, Switch, etc. Had 3 specials. Movies: When She Was Bad, Romance on the Orient Express, A Death in California, Crossings, Deadly Care, Grace Kelly Story, Bluegrass, Kentucky Woman.
PICTURE: Purple Hearts, Now and Forever, Millennium.

LADD, DAVID ALAN: Actor. b. Los Angeles, CA, Feb. 5, 1947. Son of late Alan Ladd. On stage in the Glass Menagerie and Alpha Beta.
PICTURES: The Lone Ranger, The Big Land, Raymie, Misty, R.P.M., Catlow, Deathline, Jamaica Reef, Day of the Locusts, Kansan, Wild Geese.
TELEVISION: Zane Gray Theatre, Wagon Train, Playhouse 90, Pursuit, Ben Casey, Gunsmoke, Love American Style, Kojak.

LADD, DIANE: Actress. b. Meridian, MS, Nov. 29, 1939. Mother of actress Laura Dern. e. St. Aloysius Acad.; trained for stage with Frank Corsaro in N.Y. Worked as model and as Copacabana nightclub dancer. At 18 in touring co. of Hatful of Rain. NY debut: Orpheus Descending. Film debut in Wild Angels, 1966.
THEATER: Carry Me Back to Morningside Heights, One Night Stands of a Noisy Passenger. The Wall, The Goddess, The Fantastiks, Women Speak, Texas Trilogy; Lu Ann Hampton Laverty.
PICTURES: Wild Angels, The Reivers, Macho Calahan, W.U.S.A., White Lightning, Alice Doesn't Live Here Anymore, Chinatown, Embryo, All Night Long, Something Wicked This Way Comes, Black Widow, Plain Clothes.
TELEVISION: Alice (series), Rose and Eddie, Addie and the King of Hearts, Willa, Black Beauty, The Secret Storm, Love Boat, Crime of Innocence, Celebration Family, Bluegrass.

LAFFERTY, PERRY: Executive. b. Davenport, IA, Oct. 3, 1920. e. Yale U. With CBS-TV as v.p., programs, Hollywood, 1965−76. Joined Filmways as exec. prod. In 1979 named sr. v.p., programs and talent, west coast, for NBC Entertainment. 1985, resigned. Now indep. producer.

LAFONT, BERNADETTE: Actress. b. Nimes, France, Oct. 28. Made her debut in 1957 in Truffaut's first film Les Mistons.

Has worked with such international directors as Chabrol, Szabo, Eustache.
PICTURES: Le Beau Serge, Leda, Male Hunt, Les Bonnes Femmes, The Thief of Paris, Such a Gorgeous Kid Like Me, The Mother and the Whore, Zig-Zag, Violette, Like a Turtle on Its Back, Il Ladrone (The Thief), Waiting for the Moon, The Seasons of Pleasure.

LAHTI, CHRISTINE: Actress. b. Birmingham, MI, April 4, 1950. m. dir., Thomas Schlamme. e. U. of Michigan. Trained for stage at Herbert Berghof Studios with Uta Hagen. TV commercials. As a mime, performed with Edinburgh Scotland's Travis Theatre. N.Y. stage debut in The Woods, 1978. Film debut in And Justice for All, 1980.
THEATER: The Zinger, Hooter (Playwrights Horizon), Loose Ends, Division St., The Woods, Scenes and Revelations, Present Laughter, The Lucky Spot, Summer and Smoke (LA).
PICTURES: Whose Life Is It, Anyway?, Swing Shift, Just Between Friends, Housekeeping, Stacking, Running on Empty.
TELEVISION: Love Lives On, Single Bars, Single Women, The Last Tenant, The Executioner's Song.

LAI, FRANCIS: Composer. b. France, April 26, 1933.
PICTURES INCLUDE: A Man and a Woman, Mayerling, House of Cards, Rider on the Rain, Love Story (Oscar), Le Petit Matin, Another Man, Another Chance, Wanted: Babysitter, Bilitis, The Good and the Bad, Widow's Nest, Cat and Mouse, The Body of My Enemy, Emmanuelle 2; The Forbidden Room, International Velvet, Oliver's Story (Oscar), Passion Flower Hotel, Robert and Robert, The Small Timers, By the Blood Brothers, Beyond the Reef, Bolero, A Second Chance, Edith and Marcel, My New Partner, Marie, A Man and a Woman: 20 Years Later, Bernadette.
TELEVISION: The Berlin Affair, The Sex Symbol, Sins.

LAMARR, HEDY: Actress. b. Vienna, 1915. At 15 starred in Ecstasy (awarded top Italian film-prize).
PICTURES INCLUDE: Algiers, I Take This Woman, Lady of the Tropics, Boom Town, Comrade X, Come Live with Me, Ziegfeld Girl; H. M. Pulham, Esq.; Tortilla Flat, Crossroads, White Cargo, Heavenly Body, Conspirators, Strange Woman, Samson and Delilah, A Lady Without a Passport, Dishonored Lady, Experiment Perilous, Let's Live a Little, Copper Canyon, My Favorite Spy, Story of Mankind, The Female Animal.

LAMAS, LORENZO: Actor. b. Los Angeles, CA, Jan. 20, 1958. e. Santa Monica City Coll. Son of the late Fernando Lamas and Arlene Dahl. Studied at Tony Barr's Film Actors Workshop (Burbank Studios).
PICTURES: Grease, Tilt, Take Down, Body Rock.
TELEVISION: Series: The Love Boat, Switch, Sword of Justice, California Fever, Secrets of Midland Heights, Falcon Crest. Movie: Detour.

LAMBERT, CHRISTOPHER: (also (CHRISTOPHE) Actor. b. New York , NY, 1958; reared in Geneva. Parents French. Studied at Natl Conservatory of Dramatic Art, Paris. Won role in small French film, Le Bar du Telephone.
PICTURES: La Dame de Coeur, Legitime Violence, Greystoke: The Legend of Tarzan, Lord of the Apes, Subway, Highlander, The Sicilian, Priceless Beauty, To Kill a Priest, After the Rain.

LAMBERT, VERITY: Producer. b. London, England. Ent. TV 1954, prod. Dr. Who, Adam Adamant Lives, Detective, Somerset Maugham (all BBC series). Since 1971: Shoulder to Shoulder (series), Budgie, Between The Wars. 1974: Appt. controller of Drama, Thames Television. 1979: Chief exec. Euston Films. 1983: Director of Production Thorn EMI Films Ltd. Relinquished her position as controller of Drama Thames Television and retaining pos. as chief exec., Euston Films. Became indep. prod. developing projects for BBC.
PICTURES: Exec. prod.: American Roulette, A Cry in the Darkness.

LAMOUR, DOROTHY: Actress. b. New Orleans, LA, Dec. 10, 1914. e. Spence's Business Sch. Miss New Orleans 1931; sang on radio programs; screen debut in Jungle Princess 1938.
PICTURES INCLUDE: Spawn of the North, St. Louis Blues, Man About Town, Disputed Passage, Johnny Apollo, Typhoon, Road to Singapore, Caught in the Draft, Star Spangled Rhythm, Road to Utopia, Practically Yours, Medal for Benny, Duffy's Tavern, My Favorite Brunette, Road to Rio, Wild Harvest, Miracle Can Happen, Lulu Belle, Girl from Manhattan, Lucky Stiff, Slightly French, Manhandled, The Greatest Show on Earth, Road to Bali, Road to Hong Kong, Donovan's Reef, The Phynx, Creepshow 2.
TELEVISION: Death at Love House (movie), Murder, She Wrote.

LANCASTER, BURT: Actor. b. New York, NY, Nov. 2, 1913. e. New York U. Was circus acrobat, in vaudeville; served in U.S. Army Special Service in Italy & N. Africa, W.W.II; NY stage debut: A Sound of Hunting (1945); screen debut in The

Killers, 1946. Formed Hecht-Lancaster Orgn. in partnership with Harold Hecht.
PICTURES INCLUDE: Desert Fury, I Walk Alone, Brute Force, Sorry Wrong Number, Kiss the Blood Off My Hands, Criss Cross, All My Sons, Rope of Sand, Mister 880, Flame and the Arrow, Vengeance Valley, Ten Tall Men, Jim Thorpe—All American, Crimson Pirate, Come Back Little Sheba, South Sea Woman, From Here to Eternity, His Majesty O'Keefe, Apache, Vera Cruz, The Kentuckian, Rose Tattoo, Trapeze, The Rainmaker, Gunfight at the OK Corral, Sweet Smell of Success, Separate Tables, The Devil's Disciple, Elmer Gantry (Acad. Award), The Young Savages, Birdman of Alcatraz, The Leopard, Seven Days in May, Hallelujah Trail, The Swimmer, The Gypsy Moths, Castlekeep, Airport, Valdez Is Coming, Lawman, Ulzana's Raid, Scorpio, Executive Action, The Midnight Man (prod. & dir. & star), Conversation Piece, Buffalo Bill and the Indians, The Cassandra Crossing, Twilight's Last Gleaming, The Island of Dr. Moreau, 1900, Go Tell the Spartans, Cattle Annie and Little Britches, Zulu Dawn, Atlantic City, Local Hero, The Osterman Weekend, Little Treasure, Tough Guys, The Suspect, Rocket Gibralter, The Goldsmith's Shop, Shoeless Joe.
TELEVISION: Moses, Victory at Entebbe, Marco Polo, Scandal Sheet, On Wings of Eagles, Barnum, Control, Legacy of the Hollywood Blacklist (narrator), Fathers and Sons (Ital. TV).

LANDAU, ELY A.: Executive. b. New York, NY, Jan. 20, 1920. Formed National Telefilm Associates, Inc., 1954; org. NTA Film Network, 1956; pres., chmn. of bd., National Telefilm Associates, Inc., 1957; resigned, 1961; formed Ely Landau Company, Inc., 1963; dist. The Servant, King and Country, Umbrellas of Cherbourg; prod. Long Day's Journey into Night, The Fool Killer, The Pawnbroker, A Face of War, The Madwoman of Chaillot. Prod. King—A Filmed Record—Montgomery to Memphis, 1968; organized, directed one-night simultaneous charity showing 633 theatres U.S., 1970; 1972 Formed American Film Theatre, and the Ely Landau Organization, Inc. 1972–74 produced Iceman Cometh, Rhinoceros, The Homecoming, A Delicate Balance, Luther, Lost in the Stars, Butley, Galileo, In Celebration, The Man in the Glass Booth. Also prod.: The Greek Tycoon; Hopscotch; The Chosen; Beatlemania—The Movie; The Deadly Game; Separate Tables; Mr. Halpern and Mr. Johnson; The Holcroft Covenant.
THEATER: Off-B'way: The Chosen (co-prod.) (1987).

LANDAU, MARTIN: Actor. b. New York, NY, June 20, 1931. e. Pratt Inst., Art Students League, Cartoon and staff artist on N.Y. Daily News; studied 3 yrs. at Actors Studio.
PICTURES INCLUDE: Pork Chop Hill, North by Northwest, Gazebo, Stagecoach to Dancer's Rock, Cleopatra, The Hallelujah Trail, The Greatest Story Ever Told, Decision at Midnight, Alien Attack, Nevada Smith, They Call Me Mister Tibbs, Operation Snafu, A Town Called Hell, Black Gunn, Welcome Home Johnny Bristol, Mission: Impossible vs. the Mob, Dark Shadows in an Empty Room, Meteor, The Savage Report, Death of Ocean View Park, Destination Moonbase Alpha, The Fall of the House of Usher, Without Warning, Trial By Terror, Cosmic Princess, Journey Through the Black Sun, Beauty and the Beast, The Last Word, The Return, Alone in the Dark, Access Code, Treasure Island, Run if You Can, W.A.R., Sweet Revenge, Cyclone, Real Bullets, Empire State, Delta Fever, Kung Fu: The Movie, Tucker: The Man and His Dream, Paint It Black.
TELEVISION: Series: Mission Impossible (1966–68), Space 1999. Numerous guest appearances.
STAGE: Middle of the Night, Uncle Vanya, Stalag 17, Wedding Breakfast, First Love, The Goat Song.

LANDAU, RICHARD H.: Writer. b. New York, NY, Feb. 21, 1914. e. U. of Arizona, Yale U. With Small-Landau agency handling writers and stories; shorts dept. writer MGM 1939; writer for RKO Radio since 1942; wrote documentaries and raining films for U.S. Army.
PICTURES INCLUDE: Gun in His Hand, Strange Confession, Challenge in the Night, Back to Bataan, Little Iodine, Christmas Eve, Crooked Way, Johnny One Eye, Roadblock, Lost Continent, F.B.I. Girl, Stolen Face, Bad Blonde, Spaceways, Sins of Jezebel, Blackout, Deadly Game, A Race for Life, Pearl of the South Pacific, Creeping Unknown.

LANDERS, HAL: Producer. b. Chicago, IL, June 26, 1928. Company: The Hal Landers Co.
PICTURES: Joy Ride; Damnation Alley; Gypsy Moths; Monte Walsh; The Hot Rock; Bank Shot; Death Wish; Death Wish II (exec. prod.).

LANDES, MICHAEL: Executive. b. Bronx, NY, Feb. 4, 1939. e. Fairleigh Dickinson, B.A., 1961; Rutgers, J.D., 1964; NYU, L.L.M., 1965. 20 years of corporate law and financing experience as partner in law firm of Hahn and Hessen. Co-chairman of The Almi Group (L.P.). Formed The Almi Group, 1978. Formed Almi Pictures, 1982. In July 1986, Almi sold its 97-screen RKO Warner Century Warner Theatre chain to Cineplex Odeon. Nov. 1986, Almi purchased Video Shack

chain. May 1987, RKO Warner Theatre Video acquired Salt Lake City-based Adventureland Video (franchise network). March 1988, RKO Warner Theatre Video purchased Super Video chain. May 1988, became chairman, Damon Creations, Inc. which merged with Enro Holding Corp. and Enro Shirt Co. into Damon Creations. Member: Young Presidents' Organization (YPO); exec. comm., Association for a Better New York; trustee, Citizens Budget Commission; trustee, Motion Picture Pioneers; member, Academy of Motion Picture Arts and Sciences.

LANDIS, JOHN: Director. b. Chicago, IL, Aug. 3, 1950.
PICTURES: Schlock (stuntman, dir., writer), Kentucky Fried Movie, National Lampoon's Animal House, The Blues Brothers (also co-s.p.), An American Werewolf in London (also s.p.), Trading Places, Twilight Zone—The Movie (prod., dir., s.p. also), Into the Night, Spies Like Us, Three Amigos (dir.), Amazon Women on the Moon (co-dir., co-exec. prod.), Coming to America (dir.).

LANDON, MICHAEL: Actor, Writer, Director. b. Forest Hills, NY, Oct. 31, 1936. e. U. of Southern California. Was athlete before signed by Warner Bros. to attend acting school. Roles in films and TV followed; big break came with Bonanza.
TELEVISION: Actor: Restless Gun, Bonanza, Little House on the Prairie; Highway To Heaven. Guest appearances on Variety Shows. Writer-Director: Love Came Laughing (Love Story series). Director: Roy Campanella Story. Producer: Little House on the Prairie, Highway to Heaven.

LANDRES, PAUL: Director. b. New York, NY, Aug. 21, 1912. e. U. of California at L.A. Started as asst. film editor at Universal 1931. Editor 1937 to 1949 of many feature films. Director of feature films and TV since 1949. Under directorial contract to Warner Bros. 1961–62. Director of 22 feature films for theatrical release.
PICTURES INCLUDE: Oregon Passage, A Modern Marriage, Mark of the Vampire, Navy Bound, The Curse of Dracula, Miracle of the Hills, 54 Washington Street and Son of a Gunfighter made in Spain for MGM release.
TELEVISION: 91 hour films and over 300 half hour shows including among many others, multiple episodes of Bonanza, Daktari, The Rifleman, 77 Sunset Strip, Maverick Hawaiian Eye, The Plainsman, Readers Digest, Topper, Wyatt Earp, Blondie, etc.

LANDSBURG, ALAN: Executive, Producer. b. New York, NY, May 10, 1933. e. New York U. Producer for NBC News Dept., 1951–59; producer-writer, CBS, 1959–60; exec. prod., Wolper Productions/Metromedia Producers Corp., 1961–70; chairman, The Alan Landsburg Company, 1970–present. Co-exec. prod.: Jaws 3-D, Porky's II: The Next Day.
TELEVISION: Biography, National Geographic Specials (exec. prod. 1965–70): The Undersea World of Jacques Costeau (exec. prod.); In Search of..., That's Incredible. Movies: Adam, Fear on Trial, Parent Trap II, Adam: His Song Continues, The George McKenna Story, Long Gone, Strange Voices, Bluegrass, A Place at the Table, Too Young the Hero (exec. prod.).

LANE, DIANE: Actress. b. New York, NY, Jan., 1965. Acted in stage classics (Medea, Electra, As You Like It) at La Mama Experimental Theatre Club, NY. Debut in A Little Romance, 1979.
PICTURES: Watcher in the Woods, Touched by Love, National Lampoon Goes to the Movies, Cattle Annie and Little Britches, Six Pack, Ladies and Gentlemen: The Fabulous Stains, Streets of Fire, The Outsiders, Rumble Fish, The Cotton Club, The Big Town, Lady Beware, Priceless Beauty, After the Rain.
STAGE: The Cherry Orchard, Agamemmon, Runaways.
TELEVISION: Child Bride of Short Creek, Summer, Miss All-American Beauty, Lonesome Dove.

LANG, CHARLES: Cinematographer. b. Bluff, UT, March 27, 1902. e. Lincoln H.S., Los Angeles; U. of Southern California. Entered m.p. ind. with Paramount Film Laboratory, then asst. cameraman; dir. of photography, Paramount, 1929–52; then freelance.
PICTURES INCLUDE: A Farewell to Arms (Academy Award for best photography, 1933); Ghost and Mrs. Muir, A Foreign Affair, September Affair, Ace in the Hole, Sudden Fear, Sabrina, Queen Bee, Man from Laramie, The Rainmaker, Some Like It Hot, The Magnificent Seven, Facts of Life, One-Eyed Jacks, Summer and Smoke, Charade, Father Goose, Wait Until Dark, Inside Daisy Clover, Hotel, Flim Flam Man, The Stalking Moon, Cactus Flower, Bob & Carol & Ted & Alice, The Love Machine, Doctors' Wives, Butterflies Are Free.

LANG, DAVID: Writer. b. New York, NY, Nov. 30, 1913. Was in Merchant Marine three years. Joined Charles Mintz Studio (Columbia) as cartoonist. Moved to MGM cartoon dept. 1938–40. Radio writer, Calling All Cars, KNX, Los Angeles, 1941. Contract writer at MGM, 1941–43. Yank on the Burma Road, Gambler's Choice, Hired Gun, North West Mounted

Lan-Lan

Police. For Par. Midnight Manhunt, People Are Funny, Caged Fury, One Exciting Night. For Warner Bros. Flaxy Martin, Smart Money. For Columbia, Chain of Circumstance, Ambush at Tomahawk, The Nebraskan, Black Horse Canyon for U.I. Also Screaming Eagles, Hellcats of the Navy, Buckskin Lady. For PRC, Queen of Burlesque.
TELEVISION: Cheyenne, 87th Precinct, Ford Theatre, Gallant Men, Westinghouse Theatre, Adventures in Paradise, Bonanza, Trackdown, Wanted Dead or Alive, Rifleman, Rawhide, Have Gun Will Travel. At least two hundred credits in above series. Novelist. Oedipus Burning. Publisher, Stein and Day.

LANG, JENNINGS: Executive. b. New York, NY, May 28, 1915. e. St. John's U. Law Sch. m. actress-singer Monica Lewis. Went into law practice in 1937 with Seligsburg and Lewis, m.p. law specialists. In 1938 went to Hollywood and became 2nd asst. dir. at Grand National Studios. Opened own office as actor's agent; first client, comedian Hugh Herbert. In 1940 joined Jaffe Agency; made partner and v.p. in 1942. Was pres. from 1948 to May, 1950, when resigned to join MCA. Worked in all phases of MCA operations; in 1952 made v.p. of MCA TV Ltd., and bd. mem. Involved with prod. and sales of TV prods. from inception of Revue (now Universal City Studios) in 1950. Organized Revue's New Projects Dept., creator and exec. in chg. of prog. dev. Involved with creation and sales of such series as Wagon Train, The Robert Cummings Show, Bachelor Father, Wells Fargo, Mike Hammer. Supvr. of Universal's World Premiere films. Made Executive Producer at MCA (Universal) for motion pictures.
PICTURES: exec. prod.: Winning, They Might Be Giants, Puzzle of a Downfall Child, Coogan's Bluff, The Beguiled, Act of the Heart, Tell Them Willie Boy Is Here, Play Misty for Me, Pete 'n Tillie, High Plains Drifter, Slaughterhouse Five, Charley Varrick, Breezy, The Great Waldo Pepper, Airport '75, Earthquake, Joe Kidd, The Great Northfield Minnesota Raid, The Eiger Sanction, Airport 1977, The Front Page, The Hindenburg. Producer: Swashbuckler, Roller Coaster, House Calls, Nunzio, Airport '79, The Concorde, Little Miss Marker, The Nude Bomb, The Sting II, Stick.

LANG, OTTO: Producer, Director, Four Academy Award nominations for Cinemascope Specials, Twentieth Century-Fox Film Corp. Saga of Western Man; ABC-TV Specials—The Legend of Cortez; Beethoven: Ordeal and Triumph.
TELEVISION: Man from U.N.C.L.E.; Daktari; Iron Horse; Cheyenne; Dick Powell Show; Zane Gray Theatre; Ann Sothern Show; Rifleman; Bat Masterson; Seahunt; The Deputy; Surfside 6; Hawaiian Eye. Prod. Twentieth Century Fox Hour. Dir. Man and the Challenge; Aquanauts; World of Giants. Dir. feature for Cinerama: Search for Paradise, Lancer, Felony Squad.
PICTURES: Prod., Call Northside 777; Five Fingers; White Witch Doctor. Specialist for foreign locations. Many segments for This World of Ours; Wide, Wide World. 1969. Assoc. prod: Tora! Tora! Tora!

LANGAN, GLENN: Actor. b. Denver, CO, July 8, 1917. e. Wheatridge H.S. Started career as asst. mgr. Elitch Gardens, Denver; traveled to N.Y., worked at odd jobs, until walk-on part in play, Swing Your Lady; signed by Hollywood after appearance in A Kiss for Cinderella, oppos. Luise Rainer.
PICTURES INCLUDE: Riding High, Four Jills in a Jeep, Something for the Boys, Margie, Homestretch, Forever Amber, Iroquois Trail, Treasure of Monte Cristo, Rapture, Hangman's Knot, One Girl's Confession, 99 River Street, Big Chase, Mutiny in Outer Space, Chisum.

LANGE, HOPE: Actress. r.n. Hope Elise Ross Lange; b. Redding Ridge, CT, Nov. 28, 1933. e. Reed Coll., Portland, OR; Barmore Jr. Coll., N.Y. Parents: John Lange, musician (Arr. music for stage shows, including Show Boat); Minnette Buddecke Lange, actress. Prof. stage debut at age 12 in The Patriots on Broadway; then in The Hot Corner. Film debut: Bus Stop (1956).
PICTURES INCLUDE: Jesse James, Peyton Place, The Young Lions, In Love and War, The Best of Everything, A Pocketful of Miracles, How the West Was Won, Love Is a Ball, Jigsaw, Death Wish, A Nightmare on Elm Street: Part 2, Blue Velvet.
TELEVISION: Series: The Ghost and Mrs. Muir, The New Dick Van Dyke Show. Movies: That Certain Summer, I Love You—Goodbye, Beulah Land, The Day Christ Died, Crowhaven Farm, A Family Tree (Trying Times).

LANGE, JESSICA: Actress. b. Cloquet, MN, Apr. 20, 1949. e. U. of Minnesota. Studied mime 2 years under Etienne Decroux in Paris. Dancer, Opera Comique, Paris; model with Wilhelmina agy, NY. Worked in experimental theatre in New York. Theatrical film debut in King Kong (1976).
PICTURES INCLUDE: All That Jazz, How to Beat the High Cost of Living, The Postman Always Rings Twice, Frances, Tootsie (Acad. Award, supp., 1982), Country (also co-prod.), Sweet Dreams, Crimes of the Heart, Far North, Everybody's All American, Men Don't Leave.
TELEVISION: Cat on a Hot Tin Roof.

LANGELLA, FRANK: Actor. b. Bayonne, NJ, Jan. 1, 1940. Studied acting at Syracuse U., later in regional repertory, summer stock, and on and off Bdwy. B'way debut: Seascape (1977, Tony Award). Film debut in The Twelve Chairs (1970).
THEATER: member Lincoln Ctr. Rep. co. 1963, Off B'way debut: The Immoralist (1963), Benito Cereno, The Old Glory (Obie Award), Good Day (Obie Award), The White Devil (Obie Award), Long Day's Journey Into Night, Yerma, The Devils, Dracula, A Cry of Players, Cyrano de Bergerac, other classics, The Tooth of the Crime, Ring Around the Moon, Passion, Design for Living, Sherlock's Last Case.
PICTURES: Diary of a Mad Housewife, The Deadly Trap, The Wrath of God, Dracula, Those Lips, Those Eyes, Sphinx, The Men's Club, And God Created Woman.
TELEVISION: Benito Cereno (1965), The Good Day, The Mark of Zorro, The Ambassador, The Sea Gull, The Amer. Woman: Portrait in Courage, Eccentricities of a Nightingale, Sherlock Holmes, Liberty.

LANGFORD, FRANCES: Singer, Actress. b. Lakeland, FL, April 4, 1913. e. Southern Coll. Stage experience in vaudeville, nightclubs, national radio programs. In 1935: collab. on lyrics and appeared in Every Night at Eight, Collegiate Broadway Melody of 1936, Palm Springs, Born to Dance, The Hit Parade, Hollywood Hotel, Dreaming Out Loud, Too Many Girls, The Hit Parade of 1941, All-American Coed, Swing It Soldier, Mississippi Gambler, Yankee Doodle Dandy, This Is the Army, Career Girl, The Girl Rush, Dixie Jamboree, Radio Stars on Parade, People Are Funny, Deputy Marshall, Purple Heart Diary, Glenn Miller Story; TV appearances with Don Ameche.

LANGNER, PHILIP: Producer. b. New York, NY, Aug. 24, 1926. e. Yale U. President of The Theatre Guild and Theatre Guild Films, Inc. Producer the Westport Country Playhouse 1947–53. Joined The Theatre Guild 1954. Produced 28 plays on Broadway at the Theatre Guild including the Matchmaker, Bells Are Ringing, The Tunnel of Love, Sunrise at Campobello, A Majority of One, The Unsinkable Molly Brown, A Passage to India, Seidman and Son, The Royal Hunt of the Sun, The Homecoming, Absurd Person Singular and Golda.
FILMS: Producer of The Pawnbroker, Slaves and Born to Win. Associate Prod., Judgment at Nuremberg, and A Child Is Waiting.

LANSBURY, ANGELA: Actress. b. London, England, Oct. 16, 1925. Sister of Bruce and Edgar Lansbury. e. South Hampstead Sch. for Girls, England; Acad. of Music, London; Feagin Dramatic Sch., N.Y. p. Moyna Macgill, actress; also rel. to Robert B. Mantell, actor, Rt. Hon. George Lansbury, gov't. official. Screen debut in Gaslight, 1943, which won Hollywood Foreign Correspondents' Assoc. award. Exercise and lifestyle video: Positive Moves.
PICTURES INCLUDE: National Velvet, Picture of Dorian Gray, Harvey Girls, Hoodlum Saint, Till the Clouds Roll By, Tenth Avenue Angel, If Winter Comes, State of the Union, Three Musketeers, Red Danube, Samson and Delilah, Kind Lady, Mutiny, Remains to Be Seen, Key, Man, Purple Mask, A Lawless Street, A Life at Stake, Court Jester, Please Murder Me, The Long Hot Summer, The Reluctant Debutante, The Summer of the 17th Doll, Season of Passion, Dark at the Top of the Stairs, A Breath of Scandal, All Fall Down, Hawaii, In the Cool of the Day, The Manchurian Candidate, The World of Henry Orient, Mr. Buddwing, Dear Heart, The Greatest Story Ever Told, Harlow, The Amorous Adventures of Moll Flanders, Something for Everyone, Bedknobs and Broomsticks, Death on the Nile, The Mirror Crack'd, The Pirates of Penzance.
BROADWAY: Hotel Paradiso (NY debut, 1957), A Taste of Honey, Anyone Can Whistle, Mame, Dear World, Gypsy, The King and I, Sweeney Todd, Mame (1983 revival).
TELEVISION: The Lady Vanishes, Sweeney Todd, Little Gloria...Happy at Last, Lace, The First Olympic Race, The Gift of Love; Rage of Angels: The Story Continues; Shootdown. Series: Murder She Wrote.

LANSBURY, BRUCE: Executive. b. London, England, Jan. 12, 1930. Brother of Angela and twin Edgar. e. U. of California at L.A. m. actress Moyna Macgill. Writer, prod. KABC-TV, Los Angeles, 1957–59; joined CBS-TV, 1959, was ass't. dir., program dev., Hollywood, director for daytime and nighttime programs, producer of Great Adventure series; and v.p., programs, New York; 1964–66, indep. prod., Broadway stage; 1966–69 producer, Wild Wild West, CBS series; 1969–72, prod. Mission: Impossible, Paramount Movies of Week; now v.p., creative affairs, Paramount TV.

LANSBURY, EDGAR: Producer, Designer. b. London, England, Jan. 12, 1930. e. U. of California at L.A. Brother of Angela and Bruce Lansbury. Started career as scenic designer and art director. 1955–60, art dir., CBS; 1962–63, exec. art dir. prod. for WNDT-TV, educational sta.; On Bdwy. produced such shows as The Subject Was Roses, Promenade, Waiting for Godot, Long Day's Journey into Night, Gypsy, The Night That Made America Famous, American Buffalo, etc.
PICTURES: Producer: The Subject Was Roses, Godspell,

Lan-Lat

The Wild Party, Squirm, Blue Sunshine, He Knows You're Alone, The Clairvoyant.
TELEVISION: The Defenders (art. dir.); Summer Girl (exec. prod.), etc.

LANSING, SHERRY: Executive. b. Chicago, IL, July 31, 1944. e. Northwestern U. Taught math, English and drama in L.A. city high schools, 1966–69. Acted in films (Loving, Rio Lobo) and numerous TV shows. Story editor for Wagner Intl. Prod. Co., 1972–74. Talent Associates, in chg. West Coast development (all projects), 1974–75. Appt. MGM story editor, 1975. In 1977 named MGM v.p. of creative affairs, Nov., 1977, appointed vice pres., production, at Columbia Pictures. January, 1980, appointed pres., Twentieth Century-Fox Productions. Resigned 1982 to form new production co. with Stanley R. Jaffee: Jaffee—Lansing Prods.
PICTURES: Co-prod.: Racing with the Moon, Firstborn, Fatal Attraction, The Accused, Black Rain.
TELEVISION: When the Time Comes (exec. prod.), Mistress.

LANTZ, WALTER: Animated cartoon producer. b. New Rochelle NY, April 27, 1900. Producer and creator of Woody Woodpecker, Andy Panda, Chilly Willy. Started with Gregory La Cava, 1916 with Katzenjammer Kids, Happy Hooligan and Krazy Kat. Joined J. R. Bray in 1922, producing Col. Heeza Liar, Dinky Doodle. Started with Universal Pictures in 1928. Produced first Technicolor cartoon for Paul Whiteman's King of Jazz. Produced Oswald Rabbit. Created Woody Woodpecker in 1941. Produced the first Woody Woodpecker TV show in 1957. Toured the Pacific War Zone on a handshake tour for the USO, with wife Gracie, the voice of Woody Woodpecker. Has been awarded the Golden Globe Award, the ASIFA Award, and in 1979 the Oscar for achievement in the field of animation. Now producing the Woody Woodpecker TV show. 1986, awarded a star on Hollywood Walk of Fame.

LARDNER, RING W., JR.: Writer. b. Chicago, IL, Aug. 19, 1915. p. Ring W. and Ellis A. e. Phillips Acad, Princeton U. Was reporter on New York Daily Mirror. Publ. writer, Selznick International. Shared orig. screenplay Academy Award with Michael Kanin for Woman of the Year, 1942. M*A*S*H (Acad. Award, s.p. based on material from another medium, 1970).
PICTURES INCLUDE: The Cross of Lorraine, Tomorrow the World, Forever Amber, Forbidden Street, Four Days Leave, Cloak and Dagger, The Cincinnati Kid, M*A*S*H, The Greatest.

LARKIN, JAMES J.: Executive. b. Brooklyn, NY, Nov. 2, 1925. e. Columbia U., 1947–52. U.S. Air Force, 1943–46; BOAC rep. to entertainment ind., 1948–60; pres., Transportation Counselors Inc., 1960–62; pres., Larkin Associates, Inc., 1962–65; exec. Radio N.Y. Worldwide, 1965–68, V.P. Grolier Educational Corp., 1968–69; V.P. Visual Informational Systems, 1969–73. Pres., Business Television Services, Inc., 1973; exec. prod., Madhouse Brigade, 1977–79; prod.-writer, All Those Beautiful Girls, 1979–80.

LARROQUETTE, JOHN: Actor. b. New Orleans, LA., Nov. 25, 1947. Disc jockey on FM radio during 1960's and early 70s. Acted on L.A. stage from 1973 (The Crucible, Enter Laughing, Endgame). Prof. debut, TV series Doctor's Hospital, 1976–78. Was narrator for film Texas Chainsaw Massacre.
PICTURES: Altered States; Heart Beat; Green Ice; Stripes; Cat People; Hysterical; Twilight Zone—the Movie; Choose Me; Meatballs, Part II; Star Trek III: The Search for Spock; Summer Rental; Blind Date; Second Sight.
TELEVISION: Series: Doctor's Hospital; Baa Baa Black Sheep; Night Court (Emmy, 1985 & 1986). Movie: Hot Paint.

LARSEN, KEITH: Actor. b. 1925. e. U. of Utah. Little theatre work.
TELEVISION: Series: The Hunter, Brave Eagle.
PICTURES INCLUDE: Green Glove, Son of Belle Star, Chief Crazy Horse, Desert Sands, Night Freight, Arrow in the Dust, Dial Red O, Security Risk, Wichita, Women of the Prehistoric Planet.

LARSON, BOB: Producer. e. U. of California at L.A. First job while in high school as prod. asst. on Sol Lesser's The Red House (1947). Worked way up after schooling thru film ranks; prod. mgr., Forty Pounds of Trouble, Freud, etc., for Universal Pictures. Joined Bryna Prods. as exec. in chg. prod. (Spartacus, The Vikings). Assoc. prod., asst. dir. for Clint Eastwood on Play Misty for Me. Rejoined Universal for decade; then went to David Wolper Prods. Became independent, producing TV pilot, Strange New World, at Warner Bros.; two films at Universal: Now partner with director Michael Apted, collaborating on Coal Miner's Daughter, Continental Divide, Bring on the Night, 28 Up, River Rat, Critical Condition.

LARSON, G. BENNETT: Executive. Joined KDYL, Salt Lake City as announcer, prog. mgr., 1926. Prod., dir., NBC, New York, 1929–34. Shows included Ed Wynn Texaco Show, Fleischmann House and Chase & Sanborn Hour. Radio exec. with Joseph Katz Co., Ruthrauff & Ryan, and Young & Rubicam, 1934–42. Gen. mgr. and part owner of WWDC,

Washington, 1942–45. Mgr. of WPEN, Phila., 1945–47. v.p. of TV, WCAU-TV 1947–50, App'd v.p. and gen. mgr., WPIX, New York, 1950; pres., Intermountain Broadcasting Corporation, KDYL AM-FM & TV, Salt Lake City, Utah, Exec. v.p. and gen. mgr. of Flower City Television Corporation, WOKR-TV, Rochester, New York, 1979–80, pres. Larson/Walker & Co., media brokers, Los Angeles; pres., G. Bennett Larson & Associates (broadcast consultants), 1981.

LASSALLY, WALTER: Cinematographer. b. Berlin, Germany, 1926. Family fled to Eng. during WWII where father prod. documentaries and shorts. Entered indust. as clapper-boy at Riverside Studios. During 1950s allied himself with Britain's Free Cinema filmmakers working for Lindsay Anderson, Gavin Lambert, Tony Richardson and Karel Reisz.
PICTURES: A Girl in Black (1956), Beat Girl, A Taste of Honey, Electra, The Loneliness of the Long Distance Runner, Tom Jones, Zorba the Greek (Acad. Award, 1965), Joanna, Savages, The Wild Party, Something for Everyone, Pleasantville, Shenanigans, Woman Across the Way, Hullabaloo Over George and Bonnie's Pictures, Something Short of Paradise, The Blood of Hussain, Angels of Iron, Memoirs of a Survivor, Too Far to Go, Heat and Dust, Private School, The Bostonians, Adventures of Huckleberry Finn, The Deceivers.
TELEVISION: Mrs. Delafield Wants to Marry, My Africa.

LASSER, LOUISE: Actress. b. New York, NY, April 11, 1941. e. Brandeis U., New School for Social Research. Appeared on stage before theatrical film debut in 1965 with What's New, Pussycat?
THEATER: I Can Get It For You Wholesale; The Third Ear; Henry, Sweet, Henry; Lime Green/Khaki Blue, The Chinese.
PICTURES: What's Up, Tiger Lily?, Take the Money and Run, Bananas, Everything You Always Wanted to Know About Sex, Such Good Friends, Slither, In God We Trust, Stardust Memories, Crimewave, Nightmare at Shadow Woods, Surrender, Sing.
TELEVISION: Masquerade, Mary Hartman, Mary Hartman (series); Movies: The Lie, Isn't It Shocking?, Just Me and You (also s.p.), For Ladies Only, Coffee, Tea or Me?.

LASZLO, ANDREW: Cinematographer. b. Hungary, Jan. 12, 1926.
PICTURES: One Potato, Two Potato, You're a Big Boy Now, The Night They Raided Minskys, Popi, Teacher, Teacher, The Out of Towners, Lovers and Other Strangers, The Owl and the Pussycat, Jennifer on Mind, To Find a Man, Class of 44, Countdown at Kussini, Thieves, Angela, Somebody Killed Her Husband, The Warriors, Shogun, The Funhouse, Southern Comfort, I, the Jury, First Blood, Love is Forever, Streets of Fire, Thief of Hearts, Remo Williams: The Adventure Begins, Poltergeist II, Innerspace.
TELEVISION: Documentaries: High Adventure with Lowell Thomas, The Twentieth Century. Series: The Phil Silvers Show, Joe and Mabel, Mama, Brenner, Naked City, The Nurses, Doctors and Nurses, Coronet Blue. Specials: New York, New York, The Beatles at Shea Stadium, Ed Sullivan specials. Movies and feature pilots: The Happeners, The Cliffdwellers, Daphne, Teacher, Teacher, Blue Water Gold, The Man Without a Country, The Unwanted, Spanner's Key, Thin Ice, Lover is Forever. Mini-series: Washington Behind Closed Doors, The Dain Curse, Top of the Hill, Shogun, and numerous commercials.

LATHROP, PHILIP: Cinematographer. b. Jan. 12, 1916.
PICTURES INCLUDE: Experiment in Terror, Lonely Are the Brave, Days of Wine and Roses, The Pink Panther, The Americanization of Emily, Thirty Six Hours, The Cincinnati Kid, The Russians Are Coming, Point Blank, Finian's Rainbow, The Gypsy Moths, The Illustrated Man, They Shoot Horses Don't They?, Airport '77, Earthquake, A Different Story, The Concorde—Airport '79, Little Miss Marker, Foolin' Around, Loving Couples, A Change of Seasons, All Night Long, Jekyll and Hyde Together Again, National Lampoon's Class Reunion, Deadly Friend.
TELEVISION: Captains Courageous, Celebrity, Malice in Wonderland, Picking Up the Pieces, Love on the Run, Christmas Show (Emmy Award, 1987), Little Girl Lost.

LATSIS, PETER C.: Publicist. b. Chicago, IL, Mar. 9, 1919. e. Wright Jr. Coll., Chicago. Newspaper reporter, Chicago Herald-American, 1942–45; Army, 1943; joined Fox West Coast Theatres, Los Angeles, in theatre operations 1945; adv.-pub. dept. 1946; asst. dir. adv.-pub. 1955; press rep. National Theatres, 1958; press relations dir., National General Corp., 1963; home office special field pub. repr., American International Pictures, 1973; Filmways Pictures, 1980–82; Recipient of Publicists Guild's Robert Yeager Award, 1983.

LATTANZI, MATT: Actor. m. actress-singer Olivia Newton-John.
PICTURES: Xanadu (1980), Rich and Famous, Grease 2, My Tutor, That's Life!, Blue Suede Shoes, Call Backs.

LATTUADA, ALBERTO: Director. b. Milan, Italy, 1914. Son of Felice Lattuada, musician, opera composer, and writer of scores of many of son's films. Studied architecture; founded the periodical Cominare. Later founded Italian Film Library, of

180

which he is still pres. Also, pres., Cinema D'Essay, First screen work as scriptwriter and asst. dir. of two films, 1940.
PICTURES INCLUDE: Mill on the Po, Anna, The Overcoat, La Lupa, Love in the City, White Sister, Flesh Will Surrender, Without Pity, The She Wolf, Tempest, The Unexpected, Mafioso, The Mandrake, Matchless, The Betrayal, The Steppe, Oh, Serafina, Stay as You Are.

LAUGHLIN, TOM: Actor, Producer, Director, Writer. b. Minneapolis, MN, 1938. e. U. of Indiana, U. of Minnesota where had athletic scholarships. m. actress Delores Taylor. Travelled around world, studying in Italy with Dr. Maria Montessori. Established, ran a Montessori school in Santa Monica for several yrs. Worked his way to Hollywood, where acted in bit parts until stardom came in Born Losers in 1967. Produced and starred in Billy Jack and The Trial of Billy Jack, also writing s.p. with wife under pseudonym Frank Christina. Heads own prod. co., Billy Jack Enterprises.
PICTURES INCLUDE: South Pacific, Tea and Sympathy, Gidget, Born Losers, The Trial of Billy Jack, The Master Gunfighter, Billy Jack Goes to Washington.

LAURENCE, DOUGLAS: Producer. b. Totowa, NJ, Dec. 16, 1922. U.S. Air Force. 1947–50; wrote, prod., dir., shows for NBC Radio. Exec. prod. talent buyer for Teleways Radio, TV Prod. 1958–59; ent. dir., Flamingo Hotel. Advisor to Brazilian govt. on building film industry.
PICTURES INCLUDE: Quick Before It Melts, Mister Buddwing, Doctor You've Got to Be Kidding, Speedway, Stay Away Joe, Live a Little Love a Little, The Outside Man, Rio Man.
STAGE: General Motors Motorama, L.A. Home Show, Calif., Wisc., Texas State Fairs, Ford Motor Auto Shows, Stay Eastern Univ. Dance Troupe, Jazz America.
TELEVISION: Strange Wills, John Charles Thomas Show, Sons of the Pioneers, All Star Hit Parade, John Gunther's High Road.

LAURENTS, ARTHUR: Writer, Director. b. New York, NY, July 14, 1918. e. Cornell U., B.A., 1937. First professional writing as radio script writer in 1939. In Army 1941–45.
STAGE PLAYS: Author: Home of the Brave, The Bird Cage, The Time of the Cuckoo, A Clearing in the Woods, Invitation to a March, West Side Story, Gypsy, Hallelujah, Baby!, The Enclave. Director: Invitation to a March, I Can Get It for You Wholesale, La Cage aux Folles (Tony Award). Author-Director: Anyone Can Whistle, Do I Hear a Waltz?
SCREENPLAYS: The Snake Pit, Rope, Caught, Anna Lucasta, Anastasia, Bonjour Tristese, The Way We Were (from his own novel), The Turning Point (also co-prod.).

LAURIE, PIPER: Actress. r.n. Rosetta Jacobs. b. Detroit, MI, Jan. 22, 1932. e. Los Angeles H.S. Acted in school plays, signed by U.I. in 1949; m.p. debut in Louisa (1950); Broadway, The Glass Menagerie (revival).
PICTURES INCLUDED: The Milkman, Francis Goes to the Races, Prince Who Was a Thief, Son of Ali Baba, Has Anybody Seen My Gal, No Room for the Groom, Mississippi Gambler, Golden Blade, Dangerous Mission, Johnny Dark, Dawn at Socorro, Smoke Signal, Ain't Misbehavin', Until They Sail, The Hustler, Carrie, Ruby, Return to Oz, Tim, Children of a Lesser God, Distortions, Appointment with Death, Tiger Warsaw, Dream a Little Dream.
TELEVISION: The Days of Wine and Roses, Rainbow, Thorn Birds, Love Mary, Tender Is the Night, Promise (Emmy Award).

LAUTER, ED: Actor. b. Long Beach, NY, Oct. 30, 1940.
PICTURES INCLUDE: The Last American Hero, Executive Action, Lolly Madonna, The Longest Yard, The French Connection II, Breakheart Pass, Family Plot, King Kong, Magic, Death Hunt, Timerider, Lassiter, Cujo, Finders Keepers, Death Wish 3, Youngblood, Raw Deal, Gleaming the Cube.
TELEVISION: Movies: Class of '63, The Migrants, The Godchild, Satan's Triangle, A Shadow in the Streets, Last Hours Before Morning, The Clone Master, The Jericho Mile, Undercover with the KKK, The Boy Who Drank Too Much, Guyana Tragedy—The Story of Jim Jones, Alcatraz—The Whole Shocking Story, The Last Days of Patton, The Thanksgiving Promise.

LAVEN, ARNOLD: Director, Producer. b. Feb. 23, 1922. Chicago, IL.
PICTURES INCLUDE: Without Warning, Vice Squad, Down Three Dark Streets, The Rack, Slaughter on Tenth Ave., Anna Lucasta, The Glory Guys, Rough Night in Jericho, Sam Whiskey.
TELEVISION: Part creator and director TV pilots: The Rifleman, Robert Taylor's Detectives, The Plainsmen. Many TV films.

LAVIN, LINDA: Actress. b. Portland, ME, Oct. 15, 1937. e. Coll. of William & Mary. First professional job in chorus of Camden County (N.J.) Music Circus. Worked in plays both off and on Broadway before turning to TV, where guest-starred on such series as Family, Rhoda, Phyllis and Harry O.
THEATER: Oh Kay! (Off-Bdwy debut, 1960); A Family

Affair, Revues: (Wet Paint, The Game Is Up); The Mad Show, member acting co., Eugene O'Neil Playwright's Unit, 1968; It's a Bird, It's a Plane...It's Superman, Something Different, Little Murders, Cop Out, The Last of the Red Hot Lovers, Story Theatre, Dynamite Tonight, Broadway Bound (Tony Award).
PICTURES: See You in the Morning, I Want to Go Home.
TELEVISION: Series: Barney Miller, Alice. TV movies: A Place to Call Home, Lena: My Hundred Children.

LAW, JOHN PHILLIP: Actor. b. Hollywood, CA, Sept. 7, 1937. e. U. of Hawaii. Trained at Repertory Theatre of Lincoln Center under Elia Kazan. Did numerous Italian films before discovery in U.S. Has made more than fifty films in more than 20 countries worldwide.
PICTURES INCLUDE: The Russians Are Coming, The Russians Are Coming, The Hawaiians, Barbarella, Von Richtofen and Brown, The Last Movie, The Sergeant, The Love Machine, The Golden Voyage of Sinbad, The Cassandra Crossing, Tarzan, the Ape Man, Night Train to Terror, American Commandos, Moon in Scorpio, A Case of Honor, Combat Force, Mutiny in Space.

LAW, LINDSAY: Producer. e. NYU School of the Arts. Producer of specials for Warner Bros. Television, head of drama for WNET/New York and prod. for Theatre in America before becoming exec. prod. of American Playhouse. Advisory Board of Independent Feature Project/West, U.S. Film Festival, AFI Television Comm.
PICTURES: On Valentine's Day; Smooth Talk; Native Son; In a Shallow Grave; One for Sorrow, Two for Joy (exec. prod.)
TELEVISION: Prod.: The Girls in Their Summer Dresses; The Time of Your Life; You Can't Take It With You; The Good Doctor; The Most Happy Fella; The Eccentricities of a Nightingale; Cyrano de Bergerac (assoc. prod.); Prod. for American Playhouse: Working; For Colored Girls Who Have Considered Suicide/When the Rainbow Is Enuf; Private Contentment; Concealed Enemies (exec. prod.); Land of Little Rain (exec. prod.).

LAWRANCE, JODY: Actress. r.n. Josephine Lawrence Goddard. b. Fort Worth, TX, Oct. 19, 1930. e. Beverly Hills H.S., Hollywood Professional Sch. Signed by Columbia; m.p. debut in Mask of Avenger (1951).
PICTURES INCLUDE: Family Secret, Son of Dr. Jekyll, Ten Tall Men, The Brigand, All Ashore, Capt. John Smith & Pocahontas, Scarlet Hour, Leather Saint, Stagecoach to Dancer's Rock.

LAWRENCE, BARBARA: Actress. b. Carnegie, OK, Feb. 24, 1930. e. U. of California at L.A. Mother Berenice Lawrence. Child model; successful screen try-out, 1944; screen debut in Billy Rose Diamond Horse Shoe (1945).
PICTURES INCLUDE: Margie, Captain from Castile, You Were Meant for Me, Give My Regards to Broadway, Street with No Name, Unfaithfully Yours, Letter to Three Wives, Mother Is a Freshman, Thieves Highway, Two Tickets to Broadway, Here Come the Nelsons, The Star, Arena, Paris Model, Her 12 Men, Oklahoma, Man with a Gun, Pay the Devil, Joe Dakota.

LAWRENCE, MARC: Actor. r.n. Max Goldsmith. b. New York, NY, Feb. 17, 1914. e. City Coll. of New York. On stage in Sour Mountain, Waiting for Lefty.
PICTURES INCLUDE: White Woman, Little Big Shot, Dr. Socrates, Road Gang, San Quentin, I Am the Law, While New York Sleeps, Dillinger, Flame of Barbary Coast, Club Havana, Don't Fence Me In, The Virginian, Life with Blondie, Yankee Fakir, Captain from Castile, I Walk Alone, Calamity Jane and Sam Bass, The Asphalt Jungle, Hurricane Island, My Favorite Spy, Girls Marked Danger, Helen of Troy, Custer of the West, Nightmare in the Sun, Krakatoa East of Java, Marathon Man, A Piece of the Action, Foul Play, Goin' Coconuts, Hot Stuff, Supersnooper, Dog and Cat, Night Train to Terror, The Big Easy.

LAWRENCE, STEVE: Actor. b. New York, NY, July 8, 1935. Singer in nightclubs and on TV.
PICTURES INCLUDE: Stand Up and Be Counted, The Blues Brothers, The Lonely Guy.
TELEVISION: Steve and Eydie Celebrate Irving Berlin, many specials: Police Story, Murder, She Wrote, Alice in Wonderland (mini-series).

LAWRENCE, VICKI: Actress. b. Inglewood, CA, March 26, 1949. Singer and recording artist appearing with Young Americans group for several years. Gained fame on The Carol Burnett Show as comedienne (1967–78). 1982: TV series, Mama's Family.
TELEVISION: Movie: Having Babies.

LAWSON, SARAH: Actress. b. London, Eng., Aug. 6, 1928. e. Heron's Ghyll Sch., Sussex. Stage debut in Everyman (Edinburgh Festival) 1947; screen debut in The Browning Version, 1953; TV debut in Face to Face, 1949.
PICTURES INCLUDE: Street Corner, You Know What Sailors Are, Blue Peter, It's Never Too Late, Links of Justice, Three Crooked Men, Man with a Dog, Night Without Pity, The

Lay-Leb

World Ten Times Over; The Stud, The Dawning (prod.).
TELEVISION: Face to Face, River Line, Whole Truth, Lady From the Sea, Mrs. Moonlight, Silver Card, An Ideal Husband, Love and Money, Rendezvous, Invisible Man, Saber Buccaneers, White Hunter, Flying Doctor, On the Night of the Murder, Haven in Sunset, The Odd Man, Zero 1 series, The Innocent Ceremony, Department S, The Marrying Kind, The Expert, The Persuaders, Trial, Starcast, The Midsummer of Colonel Blossum, Callen, Crimes of Passion, Full House, Father Brown, Within These Walls Series, The Standard, The Purple Twilight, The Professionals, Bergerac, Cuffy, Lovejoy.

LAYE, EVELYN: Actress, Singer. b. London, England, July 10, 1900. London stage debut 1918 The Beauty Spot. Subseq. in numerous musicals, dramas, London, including The Merry Widow, Madame Pompadour, Lilac Time, Blue Eyes, The New Moon, Paganini, Wedding in Paris, The Amorous Prawn, Strike a Light!, Let's All Go Down the Strand, Phil the Fluter, No Sex Please, We're British (1971–72). B'way stage debut, 1929, Bitter Sweet; m.p. debut 1927 silent production The Luck of the Navy.
PICTURES INCLUDE: One Heavenly Night, Waltz Time, Princess Charming, Evensong, The Night Is Young, Make Mine a Million, Theatre of Death, Within and Without, Say Hello to Yesterday.
TELEVISION: Stars and Garters, Not Just An Act; 1969: Late Night Line Up, The Golden Shot, The Simon Dee Show, The David Niven Show, This Is Your Life, Omnibus.
PUBLICATION: Boo to My Friends (Autobiography).

LAZARUS, PAUL N.: Executive. b. Brooklyn, NY, March 31, 1913. e. Cornell U., B.A., 1933. In U.S. Army, W.W.II. Entered m.p. ind. 1933 as gen. asst., press book dept., Warner Bros.; pres., AMPA, 1939–40. Joined Buchanan & Co., 1942 as m.p. account exec. To United Artists 1943 as dir. adv. & pub. Named asst. to pres., July 1948; joined Columbia exec. staff, New York, Aug. 1950; elected v.p. Columbia, Jan., 1954–62; exec. vice-pres. Samuel Bronston Prods., 1962–64; v.p., chg. Motion Pictures, Subscription Television Inc., 1964; exec. officer and partner, Landau Releasing Organization, 1964–65, exec. v.p., member bd. of dir., Nat'l Screen Serv. Corp., 1965–75. Lecturer and consultant, Film Studies Dept., U. of California at Santa Barbara. 1975 to present. Consultant to Kenya Film Corp., Nairobi, 1983. Director, Santa Barbara Intl. Film Festival, 1986–87. Chief of Staff, Santa Barbara Writers' Conference, 1976–.

LAZARUS, PAUL N. III: Motion Picture Executive. b. New York, NY, May 25, 1938. e. Williams Coll., BA.; Yale Law Sch, L.L.B. Third generation film exec. Began career with Palomar Pictures Int'l. as exec. v.p.; joined ABC Pictures Corp. as v.p. in chg. of creative affairs. Mng. dir., CRM Productions, maker of educational films; v.p. for motion pictures. Marble Arch Productions; 1983, v.p. in chg. of prod., Home Box Office.
PICTURES INCLUDE: Prod.: Extreme Close-Up, Westworld, Futureworld, Capricorn One, Hanover Street, Barbarosa.

LAZARUS, THEODORE R.: Executive. b. Brooklyn, NY, Aug. 5, 1919. e. Yale U., B.A., 1940. Adv. mgr., Eagle Lion Classics, 1951; adv., sales prom. mgr., WMGM, New York, 1951; then with Donahue and Coe adv. agency; secy., treas., George Blake Enterprises, TV film prod. firm, 1955; v.p. Gommi-TV, 1956; Charles Schlaifer and Co., Inc., 1957; adv. mgr., Paramount Pictures Corp., 1964; pres., Cinema Lodge, B'nai B'rith, 1968–71. Member, bd. of directors, NY chapter, Variety, The Children's Charity.

LEACHMAN, CLORIS: Actress. b. Des Moines, IA, June 30, 1930. e. Northwestern U. Broadway stage, television, motion pictures.
TELEVISION: Series: Lassie, Mary Tyler Moore Show (Emmy Award), Phyllis, The Facts of Life. Movies: A Brand New Life, The Migrants, Twigs, Ernie Kovacs: Between the Laughter, Deadly Intentions, Love Is Never Silent, Wedding Bell Blues.
PICTURES INCLUDE: Kiss Me Deadly, Butch Cassidy and the Sundance Kid, The Steagle, The Last Picture Show, (Acad. award, best supporting actress, 1971), W.U.S.A., Dillinger, Daisy Miller, Young Frankenstein, Crazy Mama, High Anxiety, The North Avenue Irregulars, Scavenger Hunt, Herbie Goes Bananas, History of the World—Part I, Shadow Play, Walk Like a Man, Hansel and Gretel.

LEACOCK, PHILIP: Producer, Director. b. London, England, Oct. 8, 1917. Moved from British film industry to American films and TV.
PICTURES: The Brave Don't Cry, Appointment in London, The Kidnappers, Escapade, The Spanish Gardener, High Tide at Noon, Innocent Sinners, The Rabbit Trap, Let No Man Write My Epitaph, Hand in Hand, Take a Giant Step, Reach for Glory, West Street, The War Lover, Tamahine, Adam's Woman.
TELEVISION: Movies: The Birdmen, When Michael Calls, The Daughters of Joshua Cabe, Baffled, The Great Man's Whiskers, Dying Room Only, Key West, Killer on Board, Wild

and Wooly, Three Sovereigns for Sarah. Series: Gunsmoke, Cimarron Strip, Hawaii 5-O.

LEAN, SIR DAVID: Director. b. Croydon, England, Mar. 25, 1908. e. Leighton Park. Entered m.p. ind. in 1919 as tea boy, later clapper boy, cutter, camera asst. Gaumont Pictures; asst. dir. & ed.; co-dir. 1942; dir. Knighted in 1984.
PICTURES INCLUDE: Pygmalion (editor), Invaders (editor) Major Barbara (editor, co.-dir.), One of Our Aircraft Is Missing (editor), In Which We Serve (co-dir.), This Happy Breed (and co-s.p.), Blithe Spirit, Brief Encounter, Great Expectations, The Passionate Friends, Oliver Twist, Escape Me Never (co-dir.), Madeleine, One Woman's Story. Breaking The Sound Barrier, Hobson's Choice, Summertime, The Bridge on the River Kwai (Academy Award 1957, best direction), Lawrence of Arabia (Academy Award), Dr. Zhivago, Ryan's Daughter, A Passage to India (also s.p. and editor).

LEAR, NORMAN: Producer, Director, Writer. b. New Haven, CT, July 27, 1922. e. Emerson Coll. In public relations 1945–49. Began in TV as co-writer of weekly one-hour variety show, The Ford Star Revue in 1950. Followed as writer for Dean Martin and Jerry Lewis on the Colgate Comedy Hour and for the Martha Raye and George Gobel TV shows. With partner, Bud Yorkin, created and produced such specials as Another Evening with Fred Astaire, Henry Fonda and the Family, An Evening with Carol Channing, and The Many Sides of Don Rickles. In 1965 their company, Tandem Productions, also produced the original Andy Williams Show. Moved into motion pictures in 1963, writing and producing Come Blow Your Horn. Formed Act III Communications, 1987.
PICTURES: Never Too Late (prod.), Divorce-American Style (prod., s.p.), The Night They Raided Minsky's (co.-prod., co-s.p.), Start the Revolution Without Me (exec.-prod.), Cold Turkey, (s.p., prod., dir.), The Princess Bride (exec. prod.), Breaking In (exec. prod.).
TELEVISION: Creator-dir.: TV Guide Award Show (1962), exec. prod. and creator or developer: Henry Fonda and the Family (1963), Andy Williams Specials, Robert Young and the Family, All in the Family, Maude, Good Times, Sanford and Son, The Jeffersons, Mary Hartman, Mary Hartman, One Day at a Time, All's Fair, A Year at the Top, All that Glitters, Fernwood 2 Night, The Baxters, Palmerstown, I Love Liberty, Heartsounds.

LEARNED, MICHAEL: Actress. b. Washington, DC, Apr. 9, 1939. Studied ballet and dramatics in school. Many stage credits include Under Milkwood, The Three Sisters, A God Slept Here, etc.; resident performances with Shakespeare festivals in Canada, Stratford, CT, and San Diego, CA. Gained fame on hit TV series, The Waltons, as the mother, Olivia. Theatrical film debut in 1980, Touched by Love.
TELEVISION: Gunsmoke, Police Story, Widow, Little Mo, A Christmas Without Snow, A Deadly Business, Mercy or Murder?, All My Sons, Picnic, Series: The Waltons (Emmy Award, 1973, 1974, 1976); Nurse (Emmy, 1982), Hothouse.

LEAUD, JEAN-PIERRE: Actor. b. Paris, France, 1944. Parents were screenwriter Pierre Leaud and actress Jacqueline Pierreux. At 14 chosen to play Antoine Doinel in Truffaut's The 400 Blows and subsequent autobiographical films Love at 20, Stolen Kisses, Bed and Board, Love on the Run. Also closely identified with major films by Jean-Luc Godard.
PICTURES: The 400 Blows, The Testament of Orpheus, Love at Twenty, Masculine-Feminine, Made in USA, Le Depart, La Chinoise, Weekend, Stolen Kisses, Le Gai Savoir, Pigsty, The Oldest Profession, Bed and Board, Last Tango in Paris, Day for Night, Lola's Lolos, Love on the Run, Rebelote, Detective, Just a Movie, Seen by...20 Years After, Treasure Island, The Grandeur and Decadence of a Small-Time Filmmaker, With All Hands, Time to Aim, Jane B, par Agnes V.; 36 Fillete, La Femme de Paille (The Straw Woman).

LE BORG, REGINALD: Director. b. Vienna, Austria, Dec. 11, 1902. e. U. of Vienna, B.A.; Sorbonne, Paris; Columbia U. Banker, playwright & stage dir., Europe; then staged musical and operatic sequences, Columbia, Paramount. To MGM as dir. short subjects. In 1941 joined Universal. Entered U.S. armed services, 1942; returned to Universal, 1944; Rec'd citation from OWL; freelance since 1946. Wrote Academy Award winning short Heavenly Music, 1945. directed two films in England, one in Mexico.
PICTURES INCLUDE: She's for Me, The Mummy's Ghost, Calling Dr. Death, Weird Woman, Dead Man's Eyes, Jungle Woman, Destiny, Honeymoon Ahead; San Diego, I Love You; (prod.), Philo Vance's Secret Mission; (dir.) Fighting Fools, Hold That Baby, The Squared Circle, Young Daniel Boone, Wyoming Mail, Triple Cross, G.I. Jane; Models, Inc., Bad Blonde, Great Jesse James Raid, Sins of Jezebel, Joe Palooka, Champ, Port Said, Fall Guy, Formed Cosmos Prod., prod., White Orchid (dir.), Black Sleep, Voodoo Island, War Drums, The Dalton Girls.
TELEVISION: for Sovereign, 4 Star Schlitz Playhouse, Wire Service, Navy Log, Maverick, Desilu Revue; Court of Last Resort, Warner Bros.; Screen Gems, MGM, Duo; recent features: The Flight That Disappeared, Deadly Duo, The

Diary of a Madman, The Eyes of Annie Jones, So Evil, My Sister.

LEDER, HERBERT JAY: Writer, Director, Producer, b. New York, NY, Aug. 15, 1922. e. B.A., Ph.D. Play Doctor on Broadway; Director TV dept., Benton and Bowles Adv. chg. all T.V. & Film production, 13 yrs.; Features: writer, Fiend Without a Face; writer-director co-prod., Pretty Boy Floyd; writer-director, co-producer, Nine Miles to Noon; writer, Aquarius Mission, Love Keeps No Score of Wrongs; writer, prod-dir., The Frozen Dead, It; Mia, writer-dir., Candyman, writer-director; writer, The Winners, The Way It Is, The Cool Crazies. Sponsored Films: Child Molester, Bank Robber, Shoplifter, Untouchables.

LEDERER, RICHARD: Executive. b. New York, NY, Sept. 22, 1916. e. U. of Virginia, B.S., 1938. Freelance writer, 1939–41; U.S. Army. Cryptanalyst, Signal Intell. Serv 1941–45; Adv. copywriter, Columbia Pictures, 1946–50; Adv. copywriter, Warner Bros., 1950–53; copy chief, Warner Bros., 1950–53; copy chief, Warner Bros., 1953–57; Asst. Nat'l Adv. mgr., Warner Bros. studios, 1957–59; Prod., theatrical, TV. Warner Bros. studios, 1959–60; Dir. of adv., publicity, Warner Bros. Pictures, 1960; v.p. Warner Bros. Pictures, 1963. V.P. production, Warner Bros. Studio, 1969–70; indep. prod. to May, 1971, when returned to WB as adv.-pub., v.p. Independent producer. 1980: Hollywood Knights. Joined Orion Pictures as v.p., adv. Resigned, 1984.

LEE, ANNA: Actress. M.B.E., 1983. r.n. Joan Boniface Winnifrith. b. Jan. 2, Kent, England. e. Central School of Speech Training and Dramatic Art, Royal Albert Hall. With London Repertory Theatre; toured in the Constant Nymph and Jane Eyre. In 1930s known as Britain's Glamour Girl. 1939 came to US to star in My Life With Caroline. Entertained troops with U.S.O. during WWII. 1950 moved to N.Y. to appear in live TV. PICTURES: British: The Camels Are Coming, Non Stop New York, King Solomon's Mines, You're in the Army Now, Passing of the Third Floor Back, Return to Yesterday, Young Man's Fancy, The Four Just Men. Hollywood: My Life With Caroline, Flying Tigers, How Green Was My Valley, This Earth is Mine, Flesh and Fantasy, Bedlam, Fort Apache, Horse Soldiers, Gideon of Scotland Yard, The Last Hurrah, Commandoes Strike at Dawn, Hangmen Also Die, Seven Women, The Sound of Music, In Like Flint. TELEVISION: Guest star on all major television shows from 1950 to 1977. Eleanor and Franklin, The Night Rider, The Beasts are Loose, Scruples, General Hospital (continuing role as Lila Quartermaine, 1978–present).

LEE, BONNI: Executive. Prod. exec. at MGM/UA, 1982; joined Warner Bros. as v.p.—creative affairs, 1984; v.p., production, 1986.

LEE, CHRISTOPHER: Actor. b. London, England, May 27, 1922. e. Wellington Coll. Served RAF 1940–46. Ent. m.p. ind. 1947. Over 40 TV films. PICTURES INCLUDE: Corridor of Mirrors, Hamlet, Moulin Rouge, Moby Dick, River Plate, Truth About Women, Tale of Two Cities, Curse of Frankenstein, Dracula, Man Who Could Cheat Death, The Mummy, Too Hot to Handle, Beat Girl, City of the Dead, Two Faces of Dr. Jekyll, The Terror of the Tongs, The Hands of Orlac, Taste of Fear, The Devil's Daffodil, Pirates of Blood River, Devil's Agent, Red Orchid, Valley of Fear, Katharsis, Faust '63, The Virgin of Nuremberg, The Whip and the Body, Carmilla, The Devil Ship Pirates, The Gorgon, The Sign of Satan, The House of Blood, The Dunwich Horror, Dr. Terror's House of Horrors, She, The Skull, The Mask of Fu Manchu, Dracula, Prince of Darkness, Rasputin, Theatre of Death, Circus of Fear, The Brides of Fu Manchu, Five Golden Dragons, Diabolica, Vengeance of Fu Manchu, Night of the Big Heat, The Pendulum, The Face of Eve, The Devil Rides Out, The Blood of Fu Manchu, The Crimson Altar, Dracula Has Risen from the Grave, The Oblong Box, De Sade 70, Scream and Scream Again, The Magic Christian, Julius Caesar, One More Time, Count Dracula, Bloody Judge, Taste the Blood of Dracula, Private Lives of Sherlock Holmes, El Umbragolo, Scars of Dracula, House That Dripped Blood, I Monster, Hannie Caulder, Dracula 72, Horror Express, Creeping Flesh, Death Line, Nothing but the Night, The Wicker Man, Poor Devil, Dark Places, Dracula Is Dead?, Eulalie Quitte les champs, The Three Musketeers, Earthbound, Man with the Golden Gun, The Four Musketeers, Killer Force, Diagnosis—Murder, Whispering Death, The Keeper, To the Devil a Daughter, Pere et Fils, Airport 77, Alien Encounter, The End of the World, Return from Witch Mountain, Caravans, The Silent Flute, The Passage, The Pirates, Jaguar Lives, Arabian Adventure, An Eye for an Eye, House of Long Shadows, Howling II, The Far Pavilions, The Return of Captain Invincible, Roadtrip, Dark Mission, Olympus Force, Murder Story, Mio In the Land of Faraway, The Girl, The Return of the Musketeers. TELEVISION: The Disputation, Metier du Seigneur, Captain America II, Charles and Diana: A Royal Love Story, Far Pavilions, The Pirate, Shaka Zulu, Goliath Await.

LEE, JOHN: Actor. b. Launceston, Tasmania, Australia, March 31, 1928. Early career on Australian stage and radio. Ent. m.p. ind. in England 1957. PICTURES INCLUDE: Dunkirk, Cat Girl, Silent Enemy, Flying Scot, Gypsy and The Gentleman, Under Ten Flags, The Liar, Seven Keys, The Secret Partner, Dr. Crippen, Stitch in Time, Go Kart Go, Space Flight. TELEVISION: Adventures of the Sea Hawk, International Detective, Rendezvous, Flying Doctor, Danger Man, Shadow Squad, Man and Superman, A Man Involved, Aren't We All, Probation Officer, Ladies of the Corridor, Golden Girl, After the Crash, The Net, Emergency Ward 10, Zero One, Sapper Series, Ca, Fancy, The Shifting Heart, Sergeant Cork, Dr. Who, The Materialists, The July Plot.

LEE, MICHELE: Actress. b. Los Angeles, CA, June 24, 1942. On Broadway in How to Succeed in Business Without Really Trying, Seesaw. PICTURES: How To Succeed in Business Without Really Trying, The Love Bug, The Comic. TELEVISION: Knots Landing (series), The Tim Conway Show. Movies: Bud and Lou, Dark Victory, Letter to Three Wives.

LEE, PEGGY: Singer, Actress. r.n. Norma Egstrom; b. Jamestown, ND, May 26, 1920. Began career as night club vocalist in Fargo & radio singer, WDAY, then with Sev Olsen, bandleader, Minneapolis, Will Osborne; Benny Goodman; collab. (with Dave Barbour) popular songs, Manana, It's a Good Day, What More Can a Woman Do? Leading feminine vocalist. TV & records; screen debut in Mr. Music (Bing Crosby) (1950); singer on Bing Crosby program, many TV specials. PICTURES INCLUDE: Jazz Singer, Pete Kelly's Blues, Lady and the Tramp (actress, song collab.).

LEE, SPIKE: Director, Writer, Actor. b. Atlanta, GA, 1957. r.n. Shelton Lee. Son of bass player, composer Bill Lee. e. Morehouse Coll (Mass communications), NYU Film Sch. Completed 2 student features and hour-long thesis: Joe Bed Stuy Barbershop: We Cut Heads which won student Acad. Award from Acad. M.P. Arts & Sciences. Wrote, prod., dir., co-starred in indep. feature, She's Gotta Have It, budgeted at $175,000, won L.A. Film Critics Award, best new dir., 1986. PICTURES: She's Gotta Have It (dir., prod., s.p., actor). School Daze (dir., prod., s.p., actor). Do the Right Thing (dir., s.p., actor).

LEEDS, MARTIN N.: Film-TV Executive. b. New York, NY, Apr. 6, 1916. e. New York U., B.S., 1936; J.D., 1938. Admitted N.Y. Bar, 1938, Calif. Bar, 1948; dir. indsl. relations Wabash Appliance Corp., 1943–44 indsl. bus. relations cons. Davis & Gilbert. 1944–45; dir. indsl. relations Flying Tiger Lines, 1947; dir. bus. affairs CBS. TV div., 1947–53; exec. v.p. Desilu Productions, Inc., 1953–60; v.p. Motion Picture Center Studios, Inc.: mem. Industry comm. War Manpower Comm., 1943; chmn. Com. to form Television Code of Ethics: U.S. Army 1941. Mem. Los Angeles Bar Assn., Century City Bar Assn.; exec. v.p. in chg. of West Coast oper. & member of bd. of dir. Talent Associates—Paramount Ltd., Hollywood, 1962; TV production consultant; exec. v.p., Electronovision Prods. Inc., 1964; TV prod. & MP prod. consultant, 1965. Pres., chief exec. officer member of bd., Beverly Hills Studios, Inc., 1969, senior v.p., American Film Theatre, 1973; 1975, motion picture and TV attorney & consultant.

LEENHOUTS, LEWIS GRANT: Executive. b. Los Angeles, CA. m. Edith Hargrave. 1934–38 variously stunt man, unit manager, cutter & asst. dir. Collab. orig. story No More Women, wrote orig. Heroes at Leisure. In 1939 wrote training films, U.S. Officer of Education; 1940–41 assoc. prod., writer, dir., Caravel Films Inc.; 1942–45 head of planning and production U.S. Navy Training Film & Motion Picture branch, Navy Dept.; 1946–47 gen. mgr. in charge of prod., National Educational Films, Inc. Later coordinator-producer, Industry Film Project, Motion Picture Assoc.; prod. California's Golden Beginning, Paramount assoc. chief and head of prod., International M.P. Div., U.S. Dept. of State, 1950–51; exec. v.p., Cinerama, Inc., 1952–53; planning and prod. head, Ford Foundation Fund for Adult Education, 1954, v.p., prod. head Cinerama, Inc., 1955–60. Ind. producer; prod. consultant Macbeth, Compass Prods. and Grand Prize Films, London; pres., Leehouts Prods., Inc., 1961; prod., 20th Century Fox, Movietone Digest, Children's Digest, 1963; Prod. Consultant, Cascade Pics. of Calif., 1964–65; 1967, dir. prod., Breakfast at the Capitol; prod., New Sounds in Africa; prod. head, Eddie Albert, Inc., 1971.

LEEWOOD, JACK: Producer. b. New York, NY. May 20, 1913. e. Upsala Coll., Newark U., New York U. 1926–31 with Gottes-man-Stern circuit as usher, asst. and relief mgr.; 1931–43 Stanley-Warner, mgr. of Ritz, Capitol and Hollywood theatres 1943–47. Joined Warner Bros. field forces in Denver-Salt Lake; Seattle-Portland, 1947–52. Dir. pub. & adv. Screen Guild Prod.; Lippert Productions; prod. exec. in chge. story dept.; 1953–56 Allied Artists; 1957–62 prod. 20th Cent. Fox;

Lef-Lei

1965–68 prod., Universal; 1976–78. Affiliated Theatre S.F. & HTN.; 1978–83. Hamner Prod.
PICTURES INCLUDE: Holiday Rhythm, Gunfire, Hi-Jacked, Roaring City, Danger Zone, Lost Continent, F.B.I. Girl, Pier 23, Train to Tombstone, I Shot Billy the Kid, Bandit Queen, Motor Patrol, Savage Drums, Three Desperate Men, Border Rangers, Western Pacific Agent, Thundering Jets, Lone Texan, Little Savage, Alligator, People, 13 Fighting Men, Young Jesse James, Swingin' Along, We'll Bury You, 20,000 Eyes, Thunder Island, The Plainsman, Longest 100 Miles, Escape to Mindanao, Dallas Cowboys Cheerleaders, When Hell Was in Session, Fugitive Family, Dallas Cowboys Cheerleaders II, Million Dollar Face, Portrait of a Showgirl, Margin For Murder, Anatomy of an Illness, Malibu.

LEFFERTS, GEORGE: Producer, Writer, Director. b. Paterson, NJ. Dir., numerous award-winning TV series, films, exec. prod.-Time-Life films 1977–78; prod./writer, Movie of the Week (NBC) 1977–78. Biog: Who's Who in America, Who's Who in the World. 1975 Emmy Award Benjamin Franklin Specials (CBS).
TELEVISION: 1969 Emmy Award, prod. Hallmark Hall of Fame Teacher Teacher, 1963 Emmy Award, wrote, prod., directed Purex Specials for Women. 1965 Producer's Guild Award, exec. prod. Breaking Point series. Other shows: The Bill Cosby Show, Studio One, Kraft Theatre, Chrysler Theatre, Sinatra Show, Lights Out, Alcoa, The Harness (Movie of the Week), The Bold Ones, Exec. prod., Bing Crosby Productions, prod., NBC 10 yrs, Independent.
PICTURES INCLUDE: The Stake, Mean Dog Blues, The Living End, The Boat, The Teenager.
BROADWAY: The Boat, 1968, Hey Everybody, 1970.

LEFKO, MORRIS E.: b. March 30, 1907. Entered m.p. ind. as poster clerk; booker, salesman, br. mgr., Indianapolis, RKO, June 1941; br. mgr., Pittsburgh, July 1944; East Central dist. mgr., July, 1948; appt. sales exec. of Ten Commandments Unit. Para. Film Dist. Corp., N.Y., 1956; v.p. in chg. sls., Michael Todd Co., 1958. Joined MGM, Inc., July 1960 sls. mgr., of road shows, Ben-Hur, King of Kings, Mutiny on the Bounty; vice pres., gen. sales mgr., MGM, 1963. Exec. consultant to Pres., Cinema 5 Ltd., Jan. 1970. v.p., Network Cinema Corp., 1972; American Film Theatre, Ely Landau Co., Nov., 1972; v.p., sls. mgr. Brut Prods., 1976.

LE GALLIENNE, EVA: Actress, Producer. b. London, England, Jan. 11, 1899. Stage career began in 1914. Founded Civic Repertory Theatre in 1926, starring in and directing such classics as Hedda Gabler, Romeo and Juliet, Alice in Wonderland, Camille, The Cherry Orchard. Also co-founder of American Repertory Theatre; 1946; toured with National Repertory Theatre. Won special Tony Award, 1964.
TELEVISION: Alice in Wonderland, The Corn Is Green, The Bridge of San Luis Rey, Mary Stuart, The Royal Family (Emmy award, 1977).
PICTURES: Prince of Players, The Devil's Disciple, Resurrection.

LEGRAND, MICHEL JEAN: Composer, Conductor. b. France, 1931. Son of well-known arranger, composer and pianist, Raymond Legrand. At 11 Michel, a child prodigy, entered Paris Cons. and graduated nine years later with top honors in composition and as solo pianist. In late fifties turned to composing for films and has composed, orchestrated and conducted scores of more than 50 films.
PICTURES INCLUDE: Lola, Eva, Vivre Sa Vie, La Baie des Anges, The Umbrellas of Cherbourg, Banda a Part, Un Femme Mariee, Les Demoiselles de Rochefort, Ice Station Zebra, The Thomas Crown Affair, Pieces of Dreams, The Happy Ending, Wuthering Heights, The Go-Between, Summer of '42, Picasso Summer, The Nelson Affair, Breezy, The Three Musketeers, Sheila Levine, Gable and Lombard, Ode to Billy Joe, The Savage, The Other Side of Midnight, The Fabulous Adventures of the Legendary Baron Munchausen, The Roads of the South, The Hunter, The Mountain Men, Atlantic City, Falling in Love Again, Melvin and Howard, Best Friends, A Love in Germany, Never Say Never Again, Yentl, Hell Train, Micki and Maude, Secret Places, Spirale, Parking, Switching Channels.
TELEVISION: Brian's Song, The Jesse Owens Story, A Woman Called Golda, As Summers Die, Crossings, Sins, Promises to Keep.

LEHMAN, ERNEST: Writer, Producer, Director. b. NY, NY, 1920. e. City Coll. of New York. Began career as financial editor and free-lance short story and novelette writer. Published first novel, The French Atlantic Affair followed by second, Farewell Performance, and first non-fiction book, Screening Sickness. First screenplays were Executive Suite, Sabrina, Sweet Smell of Success, based on own novelette. 1988: Acad. Awards show (co-writer).
PICTURES INCLUDE: The King and I, Somebody Up There Likes Me, North by Northwest, From the Terrace, West Side Story, The Prize, The Sound of Music. Became a prod.-wr. for first time with Who's Afraid of Virginia Woolf? Prod.-wr.

Hello Dolly; prod.-wr.-dir., Portnoy's Complaint; Family Plot (s.p.), Black Sunday (co.-s.p.).

LEHMAN, GLADYS: Writer, Scenarios identified with such Reginald Denny pictures as Out All Night, Clear the Deck, On Your Toes and Companionate Trouble; joined Columbia in 1929.
SCRIPTS INCLUDE: The Little Accident, A Lady Surrenders, The Cat Creeps, Many a Slip, Seed, Strictly Dishonorable, Back Street, Embarrassing Moments, Nice Women, Good Girls Go to Paris, Blondie, Two Girls and a Sailor, Thrill of a Romance, Her Highness and the Bellboy, This Time for Keeps, collab. s.p. Luxury Liner, Golden Girl.

LEIBMAN, RON: Actor. b. New York, NY, Oct. 11, 1937. m. actress Jessica Walter. e. Ohio Wesleyan U. Joined Actor's Studio in N.Y.; first professional appearance in summer theatre production of A View from the Bridge.
STAGE: The Premise, Dear Me, The Sky is Falling, We Bombed in New Haven, Cop Out, Room Service, I Oughta Be in Pictures.
PICTURES INCLUDE: Where's Poppa (debut), The Hot Rock, Slaughterhouse Five, Your Three Minutes Are Up, Super Cops, Law and Disorder, Won Ton Ton, Norma Rae, Up the Academy, Zorro, the Gay Blade, Romantic Comedy, Phar Lap, Rhinestone, Door to Door, Seven Hours to Judgement.
TELEVISION: Kaz (series). Movies: A Question of Guilt, Many Happy Returns, Christmas Eve, Rivkin—Bounty Hunter, Terrorist on Trial: The United States vs. Salim Ajami.

LEIBOWITZ, SAM: Executive. b. New York, NY, Feb. 12, 1913. Service mgr., Reel Photos, 1931–34; svg. mgr., Consolidated Film Ind., 1935; Apco Photo Co., Inc., treas., 1936–62; Apco-Apeda Photo Co., Inc., 1962–present, pres. & chief operating officer.

LEIDER, GERALD J.: Producer, Executive. b. Camden, NJ, May 28, 1931. e. Syracuse U., 1953; Bristol U., Eng., 1954, Fulbright Fellowship in drama. m. Susan Trustman. 1955 joined MCA, Inc., N.Y.; 1956–59 theatre producer in N.Y. London; Shinbone Alley, Garden District, and Sir John Gielgud's Ages of Man. 1960–61; director of special programs, CBS/TV; 1961–62, dir. of program sales, CBS-TV; 1962–69, vice pres., television operation, Ashley Famous Agency, Inc. Sept. 1969–Dec. 1974, pres. Warner Bros. Television, Burbank. Jan. 1975–Dec. 1976, exec. vice pres. foreign production Warner Bros. Pictures, Rome. Jan. 1977–1982, independent producer under Jerry Leider Productions; 1982–87, pres., ITC Prods., Inc. Named pres. and CEO, ITC Entertainment Group, 1987–present.
PICTURES: Wild Horse Hank, The Jazz Singer (1980), Trenchcoat.
TELEVISION: And I Alone Survived, Willa, The Hostage Tower, The Scarlet and the Black, Secrets of a Married Man, The Haunting Passion, Letting Go, A Time to Live, The Girl Who Spelled Freedom, Unnatural Causes, Poor Little Rich Girl.

LEIGH, JANET: Actress. r.n. Jeanette Helen Morrison; mother of actress Jamie Leigh Curtis. b. Merced, CA, July 6, 1927. e. Coll. of Pacific, music. Screen debut in Romance of Rosy Ridge, 1947.
PICTURES INCLUDE: If Winter Comes, Hills of Home, Words and Music, Act of Violence, Little Women, That Forsyte Woman, Red Danube, Doctor and the Girl, Holiday Affair, It's a Big Country, Two Tickets to Broadway, Strictly Dishonorable, Angels in the Outfield, Just This Once, Naked Spur, Confidentially Connie, Houdini, Walking My Baby Back Home, Prince Valiant, Living It Up, Black Shield of Falworth, Rogue Cop, My Sister Eileen, Pete Kelly's Blues, Safari, The Vikings, The Perfect Furlough, Psycho, The Manchurian Candidate, Bye, Bye, Birdie, Wives and Lovers, Kid Rodello, Grand Slam, Hello Down There, One Is a Lonely Number, Night of the Lepus, Boardwalk, The Fog.
TELEVISION: Honeymoon With a Stranger; Mirror, Mirror; Telethon; Murder at the World Series; Murder, She Wrote.

LEIGH, JENNIFER JASON: Actress. b. Los Angeles, CA, 1958. Daughter of the late Vic Morrow and TV writer Barbara Turner. Theatrical film debut in Wrong Is Right (1982). Won L.A. Valley Coll. best actress award for The Shadow Box on stage (1979).
PICTURES: Fast Times at Ridgemont High, Eyes of a Stranger, The Hitcher, Flesh and Blood, Sister, Sister; The Big Picture, Heart of Midnight, The Last Exit to Brooklyn.
TELEVISION: Movies: The Best Little Girl in the World, The Killing of Randy Webster, Angel City.

LEIGH, SUZANNA: Actress. b. England, 1945. Studied at the Arts Educational Sch. and Webber Douglas Sch. Film debut in Oscar Wilde (1961). 1964: TV series made in France, Three Stars. 1965–66: Under contract to Hal Wallis and Paramount, TV film series in West Indies, One On An Island. 1969: TV play, The Plastic People. 1970.
PICTURES INCLUDE: Bomb in High Street; To Love a

Vampire; Boeing Boeing; Paradise Hawaiian Style; The Deadly Bees; Deadlier Than the Male; The Lost Continent; Subterfuge; Beware My Brethren; Son of Dracula. TELEVISION: The Persuaders.

LEITCH, DONOVAN: Actor. Son of folksinger Donovan.
PICTURES: And God Created Women (1987), The In Crowd, The Blob.

LELOUCH, CLAUDE: Director, Cinematographer. b. Paris, France, Oct. 30, 1937. Began m.p. career with short subjects, 1956; French military service, motion picture department, 1957–60; formed Films 13, 1960; publicity Films and Scopitones, 1961–62.
PICTURES INCLUDE: Le Propre de L'homme (Man's Own), L'amour avec des Si (Love With Ifs), Une fille et des Fusils (Guns and a Girl), To Be a Crook, Un Homme et une Femme (A Man and A Woman), Vivre pour Vivre (Live for Life), Challenge in the Snow, Far From Vietnam, A Man I Like, Life, Love, and Death, Love Is a Funny Thing (dir., photog., s.p.); The Crook (dir., photog., s.p.), Simon the Swiss, Adventure Is Adventure (prod., dir., s.p.). Smic, Smac, Smoc, La Bonne Annee, And Now My Love, Seven Suspects For Murder, Another Man, Another Chance, Edith and Marcel (prod., s.p.); A Man and a Woman: 20 Years Later, Bandits.

LeMASTERS, KIM: Executive. e. U.C.L.A., B.A., 1971. Joined CBS in July, 1979 as director, dramatic program dev. Named vice pres., dramatic program dev., 1979; vice pres., comedy program dev., 1980; vice pres., program dev., Nov. 1981; and vice pres. program dev. and production, 1982. Left CBS to serve as vice pres., motion picture production for Walt Disney Productions 1984–85; returned to CBS, 1985 as vice pres., mini-series, CBS Entertainment; appointed vice pres., programs, 1986. Named president, CBS Entertainment, 1987.

LE MAT, PAUL: Actor. b. New Jersey. Studied with Milton Katselas, Herbert Berghof Studio, A.C.T., San Francisco, Mitchel Ryan-Actor's Studio.
PICTURES: American Graffiti, Citizen's Band, Melvin and Howard, Death Valley, Jimmy the Kid, Strange Invaders, The Hanoi Hilton, Private Investigations, More American Graffiti, P.K. and the Kid, Threats.
TELEVISION: Movies: Firehouse, The Night They Saved Christmas, The Burning Bed, Long Time Gone, Secret Witness. Mini-Series: On Wings of Eagles, Into the Homeland.

LEMLEIN, NEAL C.: Executive. e. Tulane U., New York U. Began career at Young & Rubicam in N.Y.; later joined Doyle Dane Bernbach, Inc., where named snr. acct. exec. assigned to 20th-Fox feature films account and CBS-TV Entertainment Division. In March, 1980, joined Universal Pictures as dir. of mktg.; 1986, v.p., mktg., 20th Century Fox.

LEMMON, JACK: Actor. b. Boston, MA. Feb. 8, 1925. e. Harvard U. Stage debut as a child; radio actor on soap operas; stock companies; U.S. Navy, W.W.II; many TV shows; B'way debut in Room Service 1953; other Broadway shows include: Face of a Hero (1960), Tribute (1978), Long Day's Journey into Night (1986). Other legitimate theatre appearances include: Idiot's Delight (1970, Los Angeles), Juno and the Paycock (1975, Los Angeles), Tribute (1979, Denver and Los Angeles), A Sense of Humor (Denver, L.A., S.F., 1983–84); Long Day's Journey into Night (Durham, NC, Washington, DC, London, Israel). m.p. debut in It Should Happen to You, 1953.
PICTURES INCLUDE: Three for the Show, Phfft, My Sister Eileen, Mr. Roberts (Acad. Award, supporting actor, 1955), You Can't Run Away from It, Fire Down Below, Operation Mad Ball, Bell Book and Candle, It Happened to Jane, Some Like It Hot, The Apartment, The Wackiest Ship in the Army, Notorious Landlady, Days of Wine and Roses, Irma La Douce, Under the Yum Yum Tree, Good Neighbor Sam, How to Murder Your Wife, The Great Race, The Fortune Cookie, Luv, The Odd Couple, The April Fools, The Out of Towners. Debut as director: Kotch, 1971, Save the Tiger (Acad. Award, Best Actor), Avanti, The Prisoner of Second Avenue, The Front Page, and the Gypsy, Airport '77, The China Syndrome (Cannes festival award for best actor, 1979), Tribute, Buddy, Buddy, Missing (Cannes award for best actor 1982), Mass Appeal, Macaroni, That's Life, Dad.
TELEVISION: Series: That Wonderful Guy (1949–50), Toni Twin Time (host), Ad Libbers, Heaven For Betsy (1952); Soap Operas: The Brighter Day, Road of Life; numerous dramatic shows (Goodyear Theatre, Alcoa Theatre etc.); Specials and Movies: The War Between Men and Women, 's Wonderful, 's Marvelous, 's Gershwin (TV Emmy Award 1972), The Entertainer, Long Day's Journey into Night, The Murder of Mary Phagan.

LEMONT, JOHN: Producer, Director, Screenwriter. e. Canada, U.S., England. Ent. m.p. ind. as actor and writer/technician. Early career working on features and documentaries. Service with Army Kinematograph Service as writ./dir. A.B.P. Director of Trans-Oceanic Telefilm Productions, Zodiac Productions Ltd., Venture Productions Ltd. V. Chmn. Writers Guild of Gt.

Britain. Awards: WGGB Laurel, Edgar Allen Poe, NY/USA Festival Gold Award.
PICTURES INCLUDE: Vacation Rhythm, The Patrol, The Green Buddha, Cross Channel, Missing Person, Harvest of the Seas, People's Playground, Port of London, Mirror and Markheim, And Women Shall Weep, The Shakedown, Konga, The Frightened City, Deep Waters, Horse Called Jester, Woman on the Stair.
TELEVISION: Fabian of the Yard, British Heritage, Frances Drake, Strange Study, Errol Flynn Theatre, Ivanhoe; prod., Sixpenny Corner, Dir. The Glorification of Al Toolum; dir, Witness in the Dark; TV Playhouse series.

LENZ, KAY: Actress. b. Los Angeles, CA, March 4, 1953.
PICTURES INCLUDE: American Graffiti, Breezy, White Line Fever, The Great Scout and Cathouse Thursday, Moving Violations, The Passage, Fast Walking, Stripped to Kill, House, Death Wish IV, Headhunter, Honor Betrayed.
TELEVISION: Movies: The Weekend Nun, Lisa, Bright and Dark, A Summer Without Boys, Unwed Father, The Underground Man, The FBI Story: The FBI Versus Alvin Karpis, Journey from Darkness, Rich Man, Poor Man, The Initiation of Sarah, The Seeding of Sarah Burns, Sanctuary of Fear, The Hustler of Muscle Beach, Midnight Caller.

LEON, SOL: Executive. b. New York, NY, July 2, 1913. e. New York U., City Coll. of New York, Brooklyn Law Sch., B.B.L., master of law. Sr. v.p., William Morris Agency, L.A.

LEONARD, SHELDON: Actor. r.n. Sheldon Leonard Bershad. b. New York, NY, Feb. 22, 1907. e. Syracuse U., B.A. Theatre mgr., Publix; N.Y. stage, 10 yrs.; sec., Directors Guild of America. 3 Emmy awards, Sylvania award, 4 TV Director of the Year nominations by D.G.A.
PICTURES INCLUDE: Another Thin Man, Tall, Dark and Handsome, Tortilla Flat, Rise and Shine, Lucky Jordan, Somewhere in the Night, Her Kind of Man, It's a Wonderful Life, The Gansters, If You Knew Susie, Sinbad the Sailor, My Dream Is Yours, Take One False Step, Iroquois Trail, Here Come the Nelsons, Young Man with Ideas, Stop You're Killing Me, Diamond Queen, Money from Home, Guys and Dolls; dir. Real McCoys, Pocketful of Miracles.
TELEVISION: dir. Make Room for Daddy, 1953–56: Damon Runyon, G.E. Theatre, Electric Theatre, Jewelers' Showcase, Jimmy Durante Show; prod.-dir. Danny Thomas Show; package & exec. prod., Andy Griffith Show, Dick Van Dyke Show; exec. prod., Gomer Pyle, U.S.M.C., I Spy, My World and Welcome To It. In 1975 starred in Big Eddie (series), 1977, exec. prod. and co-star in Top Secret.

LEONE, ALFRED: Producer, b. Nov. 30, 1926. In entertainment industry since 1958. Assistant producer for Braken Productions and Hallmark Productions. In 1968 formed Europa-America in Rome, Italy. 1974, formed Leone Intl. SPA in Rome. In 1978 opened offices in Beverly Hills. Produced and distributed over 35 films, among them: Vengeance, Four Times That Night, Baron Blood, Lisa And The Devil, House of Exorcism, Love by Appointment, Gold of the Amazon Women, The Snake.

LEONE, SERGIO: Director, Writer. b. Rome, Italy, 1921. Started career as asst. to dir. Robert Wise on Helen of Troy, followed by asst. to Fred Zinnemann on The Nun's Story, 1958. Served in same capacity for William Wyler on Ben Hur in 1959. Wrote screenplays for Italian films. Made debut as director in 1964 with A Fistful of Dollars (starring Clint Eastwood) under pseudonym Bob Robertson. Followed with several Italian "oaters" that gained him renown.
PICTURES: A Fistful of Dollars, For a Few Dollars More, The Good, the Bad and the Ugly, Once Upon a Time in the West, A Fistful of Dynamite, Duck, You Sucker! Once Upon a Time in America.

L'EPINE-SMITH, ERIC: Producer, Director, Writer. b. Thornton Heath, Eng. m. Brenda Cameron. Stage as actor, prod. playwright, formed own co. Aldwitch Films; joined Wieland's Agency; apptd. dir. of co.; casting dir. Warner Bros. 1st Natl.; assoc. prod. Edward Dryhurst Productions, then prod. Now artists' mgr., L'Epine-Smith, Ltd.
PICTURES INCLUDE: Down on the Farm, Pitchfork and Powder-Puff, Making a Man of Him, House of Silence, Five Pound Man, Coming of Age, While I Live, Noose, Romantic Age, Come Die My Love.

LERNER, JOSEPH: Producer, Director, Writer. m. Geraldine Lerner, film ed. radio stage mgr. & actor on Broadway; with RKO, Columbia and Republic as dir., dial. dir., writer, 2nd unit dir., test dir., dir-writer & head of special productions U.S. Army Signal Corps Photographic Center; writer of commercial and educational films 1946–47; vice-pres. in chg. of prod. Visual Arts Productions 1947; vice-pres. in chg. prod. Laurel Films 1949; prod.-dir., TV Gangbusters series, Grand Tour series; Girl on the Run, com. ind. films, Three Musketeers series TV, dir.-prod, 1961; Director, producer, writer, MPO Videotronics, Inc. 1967–73. President, The Place for Film Making, Inc.; pres., Astracor Associates Ltd. in production:

Les-Lev

The Ditch Digger's Daughter, The Little Hat, The Mapmakers, Trip the Light Fantastic. Also lecturer and instructor at New York U., Wm. Patterson Coll., Broward Community Coll. (FL), College at Boca Raton.
CREDITS INCLUDE: (writer-dir.) Fight Never Ends; (prod.-writer) Kings of the Olympics, Olympics Cavalcade; (prod.-dir.-writer) United Nations Case Book (for CBS-TV), C-Man; (prod.-dir.) Guilty Bystander, Mr. Universe, writer, director co-producer, The Dark of Day, Polish and/or rewrite. Many others in U.S. and abroad.

LESLIE, ALEEN: Writer. b. Pittsburgh, PA, Feb. 5, 1908. e. Ohio State U. Contributor to magazines; columnist Pittsburgh Press; orig. & wrote radio series A Date with Judy 1941–50. Bdwy play Slightly Married, 1943; wrote, prod. Date with Judy, TV series; author, The Scent of the Roses, The Windfall.
PICTURES INCLUDE: Doctor Takes a Wife, Affectionately Yours, Henry Aldrich Plays Cupid, Stork Pays Off, Henry Aldrich Gets Glamour, It Comes Up Love, Rosie the Riveter, Father Was a Fullback, Father Is a Bachelor.

LESLIE, JOAN: Actress. Star of Tomorrow, 1946. r.n. Joan Brodell; b. Detroit, MI, January 26, 1925. p. Agnes and John Brodell. e. St. Benedicts, Detroit; Our Lady of Lourdes, Toronto; St. Mary's Maternity Home, Immaculate Heart. H.S., L.A. Now on bd. of dir., St. Anne's Maternity Home, Damon Runyon Foundation.
PICTURES INCLUDE: The Sky's the Limit, This Is the Army, Yankee Doodle Dandy, Thank Your Lucky Stars, Rhapsody in Blue, Cinderella Jones, Hollywood Canteen, Where Do We Go From Here?, Too Young to Know, Repeat Performance, Northwest Stampede, Born To Be Bad, Skipper Surprised His Wife, Man in the Saddle, Hellgate, Flight Nurse, Jubilee Trail, Revolt of Mamie Stover.
TELEVISION: Ford Theatre, G.E. Theatre, Queen for a Day, Simon and Simon, Murder, She Wrote. Movies: Charley Hannah, The Keegans, Various commercials.

LESTER, MARK: Actor. b. Oxford, England, 1958. Ent. m.p. ind. 1963.
PICTURES INCLUDE: Allez France, Our Mother's House, 1967; Oliver, 1968; Run Wild, Run Free, 1969; The Boy Who Stole the Elephant, Eye Witness, SWALK (Melody), Black Beauty, Whoever Slew Auntie Roo?, Redneck, Crossed Swords.
TELEVISION: Special for Disney in Hollywood. 1970: American series for Krofft Television Productions, Scalawag, 1972; Graduation Trip, 1972; Danza Alla Porto Gli Olmi (Italian Entry Berlin '75), Seen Dimly Before Dawn '75.
STAGE: The Murder Game '76; The Prince and the Pauper '76.

LESTER, MARK LESLIE: Director. b. Cleveland, OH, Nov. 26, 1946. e. U. of California, Northridge, B.A.
PICTURES INCLUDE: Truck Stop Women; The Way He Was; Bobbi Jo and the Outlaw; Stunts; Roller Boogie; The Class of 1984; The Funhouse (exec. prod. only); Firestarter; Commando.
TELEVISION: Gold of the Amazon Women.

LESTER, RICHARD: Director, Composer. b. Philadelphia, PA, Jan. 19, 1932. Early career: dir. and mus. dir. TV, CBS, Phila., CBC-TV, Toronto. Ent. m.p. ind. 1957. TV: dir. TV Goon Shows. Composed (with Reg. Owen) Sea War Series. Films: composed and dir., Running, Jumping and Standing Still.
PICTURES INCLUDE: It's Trad, Dad, Mouse on the Moon, Hard Day's Night, The Knack, Help! A Funny Thing Happened on the Way to the Forum, How I Won the War, Petulia, The Bedsitting Room, The Three Musketeers, Juggernaut, The Four Musketeers, Royal Flash, Robin & Marian, The Ritz, Butch and Sundance: The Early Days, Superman (prod. only) Cuba, Superman II, Superman III, Finders Keepers (also exec. prod.), The Return of the Musketeers.

LESTZ, EARL: Executive. Affiliated for 18 years with Federal Department Stores, of which was sr. v.p. of operations for its Bullock's chain before joining Paramount Pictures in April, 1983, as sr. v.p. of studio operations. 1985, named pres., operations for Paramount Studio Group.

LETTER, LOUIS N.: Executive. b. New York, NY, August, 1937. e. Brooklyn Coll., business administration. v.p. and dir. of operations, Century Theatres, New Hyde Park, N.Y. Exec. v.p., RKO Century Warner Theatres, New York.

LETTERMAN, DAVID: Writer, Actor. b. Indianapolis, IN, Apr. 12, 1947. e. Ball State U. Began career as weatherman and talk show host on Indianapolis TV before going to Hollywood.
TELEVISION: Writer: Good Times, Paul Lynde Comedy Hour, John Denver Special, Bob Hope Special. Actor: Mary, Good Friends, Tonight Show (guest host from 1978), Late Night with David Letterman Show, An NBC Family Christmas.

LE VIEN, JACK: Producer, Director. b. New York, NY, 1918. Film ed., reporter, Pathe News; military service, 1941–46; news ed., gen. mgr., v.p., Pathe News; chmn, American Newsreel Assoc., 1956–59; dir. of prod., Hearst Metrotone News; prod. in assoc., ABC-TV, The Valiant Years; exec. prod., Black Fox; prod., The Finest Hours, A King's Story; chmn., exec. prod.,

Le Vien Films Ltd.; prod.; Other World of Winston Churchill, The Gathering Storm, Walk With Destiny, The Amazing Voyage of Daffodil and Daisy, The Queens Drum Horse, Where the Lotus Fell, Churchill and the Generals, The Glittering Crowd, A Question of Choice.

LEVIN, ALAN M.: Executive. b. New York, NY, 1943. e. Brooklyn Coll., Brooklyn Law Sch. In law practice before joining CBS News Business Affairs dept. in 1969 as asst. dir.; 1970, talent and program negotiator for network business affairs; 1971, assoc. dir. business affairs; 1974, dir. talent and program contracts; 1975, dir. talent and program negotiations; 1976, v.p., business affairs, CBS, New York; 1977, v.p. business affairs CBS Entertainment. April 1978, v.p. and asst. to pres.; then v.p., business affairs. In 1980 named to business affairs and admin.; 1982, exec. v.p.; 1984, head of CBS Productions.

LEVIN, IRVING H.: Executive. b. Chicago, IL., Sept. 8, 1921. e. grad., U. of Illinois. U.S. Air Force, 1943–45; entered m.p. ind. as partner of Kranz-Levin Pictures and Realart Pictures of Calif. Inc.; indep. exch. in 1948; formed Mutual Prod, 1952; pres., Filmakers Releasing Org., 1953; secy., Filmakers Prod., Inc., 1952; pres. AB-PT Pictures Corp., 1956; pres., exec. prod., Oakhurst Television Prod., Inc., Sindee Prod. Inc.; pres., exec. prod. Atlas Enterprises, Inc.; pres., prod. Atlantic Pictures, 1959; exec. vice-pres., mem. of bd. of dir., National General Corp. (formerly NTT) 1961 and Pres. National General Prod. Inc. 1966 & Pictures Corp. 1967. Pres. and chief operating officer, NGC. In 1975 formed Levin-Schulman Prods. 1983, pres., Royal Theatres, Hawaii.

LEVIN, ROBERT B.: Executive. b. Chicago, IL. e. U. of Illinois. Operated own adv. firm for five years. 1982, named sr. v.p., Needham Harper World Wide Advertising Agency, Chicago. 1985, joined Walt Disney Pictures as sr. v.p., mktg. 1988: Named pres. worldwide marketing, Walt Disney Pictures.

LEVINSON, BARRY: Director, Writer. b. Baltimore, MD, 1932. e. American U. Wrote and acted in tv comedy show in L.A., leading to work on network tv. Wrote and performed on The Carol Burnett Show. Worked on film scripts with Mel Brooks and co-wrote scripts with Valerie Curtin: And Justice for All, Inside Moves, Best Friends, Unfaithfully Yours.
PICTURES: Dir.: Diner, The Natural, Young Sherlock Holmes, Tin Men (also s.p.), Good Morning Vietnam, Rainman.
TELEVISION: Catholics (s.p.), Suspicion (prod., co-s.p.).

LEVINSON, NORM: Executive. b. New Haven, CT, March 17, 1925. Started theatre business as usher for Loew's Theatres, 1940. U.S. Army, 1943–46. Returned Loew's Theatres managerial positions New Haven and Hartford, CT. MGM press representative, Minneapolis, Jacksonville, Atlanta, Dallas. General Manager, Trans-Texas Theatres, Dallas. President, Academy Theatres, Inc., Dallas. Promoted Championship Boxing, Dallas and Johannesburg, South Africa. Executive Vice President, Cobb Theatres, Birmingham, Alabama; v.p., world-wide mktg., Artists Releasing Corp., Encino, CA.; head film buyer, Chakeres Theatres, Ohio & Kentucky.

LEVITT, RUBY REBECCA: Set decorator. b. Corinth, NY, Sept. 10, 1907. e. Pratt Inst., Brooklyn. Buyer, interior decorator, department stores; store mgr.; set decorator, Universal, since 1944.
PICTURES INCLUDE: Letter from an Unknown Woman, Magnificent Obsession, The Shrike, Six Bridges to Cross, Private War of Major Benson, This Earth Is Mine, Pillow Talk, 40 Pounds of Trouble, For the Love of Money, Sound of Music, Willie Boy, The Scavengers, Colossus, Change of Habit, Andromeda Strain, Vanished, Happy Birthday, Wanda June, The Other, Freebie and the Bean, The Manchu Eagle, Chinatown, Once Is Not Enough, Let's Do It Again, Harry and Walter Go to New York, A Star Is Born, New York-New York, Looking for Mr. Goodbar, The One the Only, Matilda, Promises in the Dark, The Jazz Singer.
TELEVISION: Mr. Ed, Addams Family, Double Life of Henry Phyffe, Movies of the Week, ABC, Banyon TV Series, Genesis II, Name of the Game, Love Story, Having Babies, Return Engagement.
Staff Decorator for television commercials, Filmways of California, Inc. Staff of Filmways of Calif., 1966. Universal Studios, 1968.

LEVY, BERNARD: Executive. b. Boca Raton, FL. e. Brooklyn Sch., L.L.B. Legal staff of Superintendent of Insurance of the state of New York in the rehabilitation and liquidation of guaranteed title and mortgage companies, 1934–36; private practice of law, 1936–46; legal staff, Paramount Pictures, Inc., 1946–50; legal staff, United Paramount Theatres, 1950–51; exec. asst. to Edward L. Hyman, vice-pres., American Broadcasting Companies, Inc., in chg. of theatre administration, north, 1951–62; apptd. exec. liaison officer for southern motion picture theatres, ABC, Inc., 1962–64; exec. liaison officer, m.p. theas., ABC, Inc., 1965–72; vice pres., ABC Theatre Division, 1973. Retired, 1976.

LEVY, BUD: Executive. b. Jackson Heights, NY, April 3, 1928. e. New York U. Exec. v.p. Trans-Lux Corp., N.Y. Member: Variety Clubs Int'l., M.P. Pioneers, bd. of Indep. Theatres Owners Ass'n.; dir., Trans-Lux Corp.; New York area chm., Will Rogers Memorial Fund; Member, President's Advisory Board-NATO; director: NATO, TOP, CATO. Elected pres., Trans-Lux Corp., 1980.

LEVY, DAVID: Executive. b. Philadelphia, PA, January 2. e. Wharton Sch., U. of Pennsylvania. As v.p. & assoc. dir., Young & Rubicam. Inc., 1938–59, acquisitions for clients include: Father Knows Best, Goodyear Playhouse, Life of Riley, Gunsmoke. Was v.p. in charge of network TV programs & talent, NBC, 1959–61. Acquisitions for network include: Bonanza, Dr. Kildare, Dick Powell Show, Saturday Night at the Movies, Bat Masterson, Klondike, Americans, Outlaws. Created: The Addams Family, Pruitts of Southampton, Savage. Developed: Double Life of Henry Phyffe, Name That Tune. Novels: The Chameleons, The Gods of Foxcroft, Network Jungle, as well as numerous TV plays and short stories.

LEVY, EUGENE: Actor, Writer. b. Hamilton, Canada, Dec. 17, 1946. e. McMaster U. Acted with coll. ensemble theater. Film debut in Ivan Reitman's Cannibal Girls, 1970, before joining Toronto's Second City troupe which eventually led to his work as writer-performer on Second City Television's various programs (Second City TV, SCTV Network 90, SCTV Network) 1977–83. Canadian theater: Godspell (1971), The Owl and the Pussycat, Love Times Four.
PICTURES: Cannibal Girls, Running, Strange Brew, Heavy Metal, Going Berserk, National Lampoon's Vacation, Splash, Armed and Dangerous, The Canadian Conspiracy, Club Paradise.

LEVY, HERMAN M.: Attorney. Hamden, CT. b. New Haven, CT, Sept. 27, 1904. e. Yale, B.A., 1927, Yale Law Sch., LL.B., 1929; Phi Beta Kappa, was in legal dept. RCA Photophone; newspaper reporter; admitted to Connecticut bar, 1929. In 1939 elected exec. secy. of MPTO of Connecticut. In 1943: Elected general counsel MPTOA. Elected gen. counsel, Theatre Owners of America, 1947–63. Pres., New Haven County Bar Assn., 1964; legislative agent, Conn. Assn. of Theatre Owners. Retired as legislative agent, 1981.
AUTHOR: More Sinned Against . . . Natl. Bd. of Review Magazine, 1941. Proving the Death of a Non-Resident Alien, Conn. Bar Journal, 1950; Need for a System of Arbitration M.P. Ind., Arbitration Journal, 1950; reprint of Industry Case Digest, 20th Century-Fox vs. Boehm in the Journal (Screen Producers Guild); Book Review of Antitrust in the Motion Picture Industry, by Michael Conant (Univ. of Calif. Law Review).

LEVY, JULES V.: Producer. b. Los Angeles, CA, Feb. 12, 1923. e. U. of Southern California. Property dept., W.B., 1941; First motion picture unit, Army Air Force, Culver City, CA.
PICTURES INCLUDE: The Vampire, Return of Dracula, Vice Squad, Without Warning, Down Three Dark Streets, Geronimo, Glory Guys, Clambake, Scalphunters, Sam Whiskey, Underground, McKenzie Break, The Hunting Party, The Honkers, McQ, Brannigan, White Lightning, Gator, Kansas City Bomber, Safari 3000.
TELEVISION: Rifleman, Robert Taylor's Detectives, Law of the Plainsman, The Big Valley.

LEVY, MICHAEL: Executive. b. Brooklyn, NY. e. Brown U. Started in industry in editorial dept. of trade-paper Variety; held posts in New York with ABC Motion Pictures and with Diener/ Hauser/Bates Advertising. Worked for Lawrence Gordon Productions as exec. asst. to Gordon and as story editor. Joined 20th Century Fox in January, 1985, as dir. of creative affairs for studio. 1986, named v.p., production, m.p. div., Fox; appointed senior v.p. production, 20th Century Fox, 1988.

LEVY, MIKE: Executive. b. England, 1910. Served RAF 1949–52. Joined Technicolor Ltd., 1953, diverse tech. assignments incl. technical control spvr. & plant supt. 1970, feature film sls. mgr. 1978, joined Rank Film Laboratories as int'l. sls. mgr. & adv. exec. 1981, sls. & mktg. controller. 1986, appt. mem. of board and sls. dir.

LEVY, NORMAN: Executive. b. Bronx, NY, Jan. 3, 1935. e. City Coll. of New York. In 1957 joined Universal Pictures, holding various sales positions; 1967, went to National General Pictures, ultimately being named v.p. and exec. asst. to pres.; 1974, Columbia Pictures, v.p., gen. sls. mgr. In 1975 named Columbia exec. v.p. in chg. of domestic sls.; 1977, exec. v.p., mktg; 1978. pres., Columbia Pictures Domestic Distribution. In 1980 joined 20th-Fox as pres. of Entertainment Group; 1981, vice-chm., 20th Century-Fox Film Corp. Resigned 1984 to become mktg./dist. consultant. 1986, joined New Century Productions as head of domestic production. Now head of New Century/Vista.

LEWELLEN, A. WAYNE: Executive. b. Feb. 16, 1944. e. U. of Texas. Joined Paramount Pictures 1973 as brch. mgr., Dallas-Oklahoma City territory; named South. dist. mgr.; 1978,

LEVY, BUD: Executive. b. Jackson Heights, NY, April 3, 1928. e.

South. div. mgr. July, 1984, named v.p., domestic dist., South. div.; 1985, appt. exec. v.p., gen. sls. mgr. (New York). 1986, named pres., domestic dist.

LEWINE, ROBERT F.: Executive. b. New York, NY, Apr. 16, 1913. e. Swarthmore Coll. Worked for restaurant chain, in real estate; U.S. Navy, 1942; creative staff, Cine-Television Studios, Inc.; v.p. in charge of oper., 1946; formed own co., 1947, for prod. of TV comm., industrial m.p.; also eastern rep., Dudley Films; radio-TV dir., Hirshon-Garfield, Inc., 1953; eastern prog. dir., ABC, 1953; dir., ABC-TV network prog. dept., 1954; v.p. in charge of programming and talent ABC-TV network, 1956; v.p., NBC, prog. dept. chg. nighttime programming, 1957; v.p. network programs, 1958; v.p. Figaro, Inc., 1958; v.p. programs, CBS Films, 1959; v.p. programs, Hollywood CBS Television Network, Apr., 1962; officer Acad. TV Arts & Sciences from 1954, Exec. comm., dir., Acad. TV Arts & Sciences. Pres., N.Y. Chapter 1959; nat'l. pres., 1961; nat'l. trustee, 1961–63; National pres., Academy TV Arts & Sciences, 1961–63; first vice pres., dir., Academy TV Arts & Sciences Foundation; pres., 1964; exec. v.p., Creative Management Associates Ltd.; v.p., Warner Bros., TV Pres. Nat'l Acad. of Television Arts and Sciences; trustee, Columbia College, L.A., Calif.; trustee, American Women in Radio and Television Foundation. 1977-NBC Television Network, exec. prod. dir.; chairman, PAW Society (Preservation of Animal Wildlife); Member International Advisory Council, Population Institute; Chairman of the Board, Riverside Broadcasting Company. Since 1978 guest lecturer at U. of California at L.A. and U. of Southern California.

LEWIS, ARTHUR: Producer, Director, Writer. b. New York, NY. e. U. of Southern California, Yale U. Began career as writer and assoc. prod. on the Jones Family TV series. Five years in U.S. Army; returned to screenwriting before producing Three Wishes for Jamie on Broadway and producing and directing Guys and Dolls in London's West End. In mid-60s produced plays with Bernard Delfont at Shaftesbury Theatre in London.
PICTURES: Producer: Loot, Baxter, The Killer Elite, Brass Target.
TELEVISION: Brenner, The Asphalt Jungle (prod. writer).

LEWIS, EDWARD: Producer. Began entertainment career as script writer, then co-produced The Admiral Was a Lady and teamed with Marion Parsonnet to bring the Faye Emerson Show to TV. Subsequently prod. first Schlitz Playhouse and China Smith series. Was v.p. of Kirk Douglas' indep. prod. co., where was assoc. prod. and writer-prod. Collaborated with John Frankenheimer on 8 films.
PICTURES INCLUDE: Lizzie (assoc. prod.), The Careless Years (prod., s.p.), Spartacus, The Last Sunset, Lonely Are the Brave, The List of Adrian Messenger, Seconds, Grand Prix, The Fixer (exec. prod.), The Gypsy Moths (exec.), I Walk the Line (exec.), The Horsemen, The Iceman Cometh (exec.), Rhinoceros, Lost in the Stars, Missing (co-prod.), Crackers, The River, Executive Action, Brothers (prod., s.p.).
TELEVISION: Islai: The Last of His Tribe (exec. prod.), The Thorn Birds (exec. prod.).

LEWIS, EMMANUEL: Actor. b. Brooklyn, NY, March 9, 1971. Began in TV commercials and has done TV and radio voice-overs. Singer and dancer and, following personal appearance tours in Japan, became recording star there. Theatrical debut in A Midsummer Night's Dream at N.Y. Shakespeare Festival (1982).
TELEVISION: Tonight Show, The Phil Donahue Show, Webster (series). Movie: Lost in London.

LEWIS, HAROLD G: Executive. b. New York, NY, Sept. 18, 1938. e. Union Coll., 1960, electrical engineer. Joined ATA Trading Corp. in 1960 and has been pres. since 1977. Producer of feature animation. Importer and exporter for theatrical and TV features, documentaries, series, classics, etc.

LEWIS, JERRY: Actor. r.n. Joseph Levitch. b. Newark, NJ, Mar. 16, 1926. e. Irvington H.S. Parents Danny and Rae Lewis, prof. entertainers. Debut at 5 at a NY Borscht Circuit hotel singing "Brother Can You Spare a Dime?" Worked as a drugstore lunch counter counterman, an usher at Loew's State in NY and a shipping clerk in a hat factory whle perfecting comedy routines. 1946 formed comedy-team with Dean Martin (singer, straight man) at 500 Club, Atlantic City, NJ; appeared Latin Casino, Phila., then other nightclubs, on NBC television; played many m.p. theatres; signed by Hal Wallis; team m.p. debut in My Friend Irma 1949. Partnership with Martin lasted for exactly 10 years, during which they made 16 films. 1959, signed contract between Paramount Pictures and Jerry Lewis Prods. for $10 million plus 60% of profits for 14 films over next 7 years. Partnership dissolved 1965. Voted Most Promising Male Star in Television in m.p. Daily's 2nd annual TV poll, 1950. Voted (as team) one of top ten money making stars in m.p. Herald-Fame poll, 1951, 1953–54–57. Number 1, 1952; best comedy team in m.p. Daily's 16th annual radio poll, 1951, 1952, 1953; 1956 formed Jerry Lewis Prods. Inc., functioning as prod., dir., writer & star. Full professor USC, taught grad. film dir. Book: The Total Filmmaker (1971) based on class-

room lectures. National Chairman Muscular Dystrophy Association 39 years and bd. member. Autobiography: Jerry Lewis In Person (1982).
PICTURES INCLUDE: My Friend Irma Goes West, At War with the Army, That's My Boy, The Caddy, Sailor Beware, Jumping Jacks, Scared Stiff, The Stooge, Money from Home, Living It Up, Three Ring Circus, You're Never Too Young, Artists and Models, Pardners, Hollywood or Bust, Delicate Delinquent, Sad Sack, Rock-A-Bye Baby, Geisha Boy, Don't Give Up the Ship, Visit to a Small Planet, Cinderfella, Bellboy, The Ladies Man, The Errand Boy, It's Only Money, The Nutty Professor, Who's Minding the Store?, The Patsy, The Disorderly Orderly, Boeing-Boeing, The Family Jewels, Three on a Couch, (dir. prod., star), Way . . . Way Out, The Big Mouth, (prod., s.p., star), Don't Lower the Bridge Raise the River, (prod., s.p., star), Hook Line and Sinker, Which Way to the Front?, (prod., dir., star), One More Time, (dir.), The Day the Clown Cried (star, dir., co.-s.p.), Hardly Working (star, dir., co-s.p.), King of Comedy, Smorgasbord (also dir.), To Catch a Cop, How Did You Get It?, Cookie.
TELEVISION: Fight for Life (movie).
RECORDS: Rock-A-Bye Your Baby.
AWARDS: AFL-CIO Murray-Green Award for Community Services, 1971; 1976 US Senate resolution of appreciation for fight against muscular dystrophy; NAPTE Award of the Year for humanitarian efforts, 1978; Amer. Institute for Public Service's Jefferson Award; Touchdown Club of Washington, D.C. Awarded Hubert H. Humphrey Humanitarian Award, 1980; Boston U Sch of Law's N. Neal Pike Prize for Service to the Handicapped, 1984; Inducted into French Legion of Honor and made Commander in the Order of Arts and Letters France, 1984; Dept. of Defense Medal for Distinguished Public Service, 1985; Doctor of Humane Letters, Mercy Coll., Westchester, NY, 1987.

LEWIS, JOSEPH H.: Director. b. New York, NY, Apr. 6, 1900. e. DeWitt Clinton H.S. Camera boy, MGM; then asst. film ed. in chge. film ed., Republic; dir. in chge. 2nd units; dir. Universal; U.S. Signal Corps., WW II; dir. RKO, Columbia, W.B.
PICTURES INCLUDE: My Name is Julia Ross, So Dark the Night, Jolson Story, The Swordsman, Return of October, Undercover Man, Gun Crazy, Lady Without Passport, Retreat Hell!, Desperate Search, Cry of the Hunted, Big Combo, A Lawless Street.
TELEVISION: Rifleman series, Barbara Stanwyck Show: The Big Valley.

LEWIS, MICHAEL J.: Composer. b. Wales, 1939. First film score 1968, The Mad Woman of Chaillot, won Ivor Novello Award for best film score. 1973: first Broadway musical, Cyrano, Grammy Nomination '74, Caesar and Cleopatra (T.V. '76); The Lion, the Witch, and the Wardrobe (Emmy, 1979).
PICTURES INCLUDE: The Man Who Haunted Himself, Julius Caesar. Upon This Rock, Unman, Wittering and Zigo, Running Scared, Baxter, Theatre of Blood, 11 Harrowhouse, 92 in the Shade, Russian Roulette, The Stick-Up, The Medusa Touch, The Legacy, The Passage, The Unseen, ffolkes, Sphinx, Yes, Giorgio, The Hound of the Baskervilles, On the Third Day, The Naked Face.

LEWIS, MONICA: Singer, Actress. b. Chicago, IL, May 5, 1925. e. Hunter Coll., N.Y. p. Leon Lewis, concert pianist, former medical dir. CBS; Jessica Lewis, child star with Nazimova; member Ben Greet's Shakespearean players, sang leading roles. Chicago Opera Co.; now vocal teacher. Started career as radio singer, own show, WMCA, N.Y.; on Beat the Band, 1946; co-star Chesterfield program; sang leading role, Girl Crazy, Ford Sunday Evening Hour, Own program, Monica Makes Music; co-star Revere Camera show. Among first ten female singers in country on recording polls. Vocalist: Stork Club, Astor Roof, Copacabana, Persian Room.
PICTURES INCLUDE: Inside Straight, Excuse My Dust, The Strip, Everything I Have Is Yours, Affair With a Stranger, Charlie Varrick, Earthquake, Roller Coaster, Airport '77, Nunzio, Concorde-Airport '79.

LIBERMAN, FRANK P.: Publicist. b. New York, NY, May 29, 1917. e. Cheshire Acad., CT, 1934; Lafayette Coll., Easton, PA, B.A. 1938. m. Patricia Harris, casting dir. Worked as copy boy, N.Y. Daily News, 1938–39. Began career as publicist at Warner Bros., home office as messenger, 1939, promoted to pressbooks dept., transferred to Warner's Chicago office as field exploitation man. U.S. Signal Corps, 1941, public relations officer, Army Pictorial Service, on temporary duty with War Dept., Bureau of Public Relations in Pentagon. Discharged as Capt., 1946. Rejoined Warner Bros. on coast 2 years, 1947, est. own public relations office, 1949. Owner, Frank Liberman and Associates, Inc.

LICCARDI, VINCENT G.: Executive. b. Brooklyn, NY. Started as messenger at Universal Pictures, asst. adv. mgr. on Around the World in 80 Days, asst. to exec. coord. of sales & Adv. on Spartacus; National Dir. of Adv. & Publ., Continental; Nat. Dir. Adv. & Publ., Braintree Prod., adv. pub. mgr. Allied Artists, ad. mgr. Paramount, National Dir. Adv.-Pub., UMC Pictures, Screenwriter, Playboy to Priest, The Rivals, The Rivals-Part

II, The Greatest Disaster of All Time, The Lady on the 9:40, All That Heaven Allows, All Mine to Love.

LIDER, EDWARD W.: Executive. b. New Bedford, MA, March 13, 1922. e. Dartmouth, Harvard Law Sch. Served as attorney-at-law, 1948–50. President & treasurer, Fall River Theatres Corp. & Nathan Yamins Enterprises, 1950 to present; member of bd., Theatre Owners of New England; past pres., Theatre Owners of New England; past member of bd. & past treas., Allied States Assoc. of M.P. Exhibitors; general manager of Sony & Eddy's Theatres in Boston: Exeter St., Academy, Harvard Square, Central Square, Allston C1nema-C2nema and Galeria Theatres.

LIEBER, PERRY W.: Publicist. b. Pleasant Prairie, WI, June 1, 1905. e. U. of Illinois. Was in adv. dept. of J. P. Seaburg Co., Chicago, IL. Pub. dept. RKO Radio Studio 1930; publ. dir. 1939; nat'l dir. pub., exploit. supv. N.Y. office, 1953–55. 20th Century-Fox pub. dept. 1956; in chg. studio adv. pub. dept., 20th Century Fox Studio, Aug. 1962. 1966 pub. dept. 20th Century-Fox. Mgr./P.R. Summa Corp. since 1970, Consultant, P.R., Summa Corp. since July, 1977.

LIEBERFARB, WARREN: Executive. e. Wharton Sch. of Commerce and Finance, U. of Pennsylvania, B.S., economics; U. of Michigan, M.B.A. Started career in industry at Paramount Pictures as dir. of mktg. and exec. asst. to Stanley Jaffe, then pres. Later joined 20th-Fox as v.p.—special market dist. (cable, pay-TV, non-theatrical). Joined Warner Bros. as v.p., exec. asst. to Ted Ashley, bd. chm.; later named v.p., intl. adv.-pub. In 1979 joined Lorimar as v.p., of Lorimar Productions, Inc., the parent company, based in New York, Promoted to snr. v.p. 1982, named v.p. mktg., Warner Home Video; named pres., 1985.

LIEBERMAN, ROBERT: Director.
PICTURE: Table for Five.
TELEVISION: Movies: Fighting Back—The Story of Rocky Blier; Will—G. Gordon Liddy.

LIEBERSON, SANFORD: Producer. b. Los Angeles, CA, 1936. 1979, named pres. of 20th-Fox Productions, which company he joined in 1977 as v.p.—European production. Previously an independent producer forming Goodtimes VPS, (Performance, Bugsy Malone, Jabberwocky, etc.). Prior to that exec. in chg. of European operations of Creative Management Associates. In 1980 named int'l. v.p. for Ladd Co., based in London. Supervising prod. chief, Goldcrest Film & TV (Outland, Blade Runner.) Returned to indep. prod. 1985. Prod.: Rita, Sue and Bob, Stars and Bars, Finding Maubee.

LIGHTMAN, M. A.: Exhibitor. b. Nashville, TN, Apr. 21, 1915. e. Southwestern U., Vanderbilt U., 1936, B.A. Bd. chmn. Malco Theatres, Inc., Memphis, Tenn.

LINDBLOM, GUNNEL: Actress, Director. b. Gothenburg, Sweden, 1931. Discovered by Ingmar Bergman while studying at drama school of Gothenburg Municipal Theatre (1950–53); she moved to Malmo, where he was director of the local Municipal Theatre. Under Bergman's direction she played in Easter, Peer Gynt, Faust, etc. between 1954–59. Later appeared in many Bergman films. Since 1968 has been on staff of Stockholm's Royal Dramatic Theatre, assisting Bergman and then beginning to direct on her own. Made film debut as director with Summer Paradise in 1977.
PICTURES INCLUDE: Actress: The Seventh Seal, Wild Strawberries, The Virgin Spring, Winter Light, The Silence, Rapture, Loving Couples. Director: Summer Paradise, Sally and Freedom, Summer Nights on Planet Earth.

LINDEN, HAL: Actor. b. Bronx, NY, March 20, 1931. e. City Coll. of New York. Began career as saxophone player and singer, playing with bands of Sammy Kaye, Bobby Sherwood, etc. Drafted and performed in revues for Special Services. After discharge enrolled at N.Y.'s American Theatre Wing; appeared on Bdwy. in Bells Are Ringing, replacing Sydney Chaplin.
THEATRE: On a Clear Day, Wildcat, Something More, Subways Are for Sleeping, Ilya Darling, The Apple Tree, Wildcat, The Education of HYMAN KAPLAN, Three Men on a Horse, Pajama Game, The Rothschilds (Tony Award), I'm Not Rappaport.
TELEVISION: Host on ABC series, Animals Animals Animals; Barney Miller (series), I Do! I Do!, The Best of Everything. Movies: Father Figure; My Wicked, Wicked Ways; The Other Woman; How to Break Up a Happy Divorce.
PICTURES: When You Comin' Back Red Ryder?, A New Life.

LINDFORS, VIVECA: Actress. b. Uppsala, Sweden, Dec. 29, 1920. e. Royal Dramatic Sch., Stockholm. Stage debut in Ann-Scofi Hedvig school prod. Screen debut in The Crazy Family, 1941; reached stardom in If I Should Marry the Minister. U.S. screen debut in Night Unto Night.
PICTURES INCLUDE: Adventures of Don Juan, Dark City, Flying Missile, Gypsy Fury, No Sad Songs For Me, Journey into Light, Four in a Jeep, The Raiders, No Time for Flowers,

Run for Cover, Captain Dreyfus, Coming Apart, Puzzle of a Downfall Child, The Way We Were, Welcome to L.A., Girl Friends, A Wedding, Voices, The Hand, Creepshow, The Sure Thing, Rachel River, Going Undercover, Misplaced.
TELEVISION: A Doctor's Story, Passions, The Three Wishes of Billy Grier; Playing for Time; Inside the Third Reich; Marilyn: The Untold Story; Secret Weapons; The Ann Jillian Story.

LINDNER, TERRELL M.: Executive. b. Dromana, Australia. Aug. 10, 1915. Entered m.p. ind. in pub. dep. Columbia Pictures, Melbourne, Australia, 1942. Columbia, mgr. Western Australia, Dec. 1946. gen. mgr. Columbia, New Zealand, 1948. United Artists home office rep. for India, Burma, Pakistan, Ceylon, 1952. apptd. United Artists dist. supvr. for Southeast Asia. hdqts. Bombay. Dec. 1953. Rank overseas. 1957. Opened West Indies offices. man. dir. Rank Filmes do Brasil, 1958. man. dir. Filmcenter Internacional Ltda., Brazil, (successors Rank) 1970.

LINDSAY, ROBERT: Actor. e. Royal Acad. of Dramatic Art. With Manchester's Royal Exchange Theatre Co. (Hamlet, The Cherry Orchard, The Lower Depths). Also in Godspell, The Three Musketeers, Me and My Girl, (London—Olivier Award, NY—Tony and Drama Desk Awards, 1987).
PICTURES: Loser Takes All; Bert Rigby, You're a Fool; Me and My Girl.
TELEVISION: Series: Citizen Smith, Give Us A Break (series), King Lear.

LINK, WILLIAM: Writer, Producer. With partner, late Richard Levinson, wrote and created numerous TV series and movies, specializing in detective-mystery genre.
TELEVISION: Series writer-creator: Mannix, Ellery Queen, Tenafly, Columbo (Emmy, 1972), Murder She Wrote (exec. prod.). Movies, writer: That Certain Summer, My Sweet Charlie (Emmy, 1970), The Execution of Private Slovik, The Gun, Stone, Crisis at Central High, Rehearsal For Murder, Take Your Best Shot, Prototype (also exec. prod.), The Guardian (also exec. prod.), Guilty Conscience (also exec. prod.).

LINKLETTER, ART: Emcee, Producer. b. Moose Jaw, Saskatchewan, Canada, July 17, 1912. e. San Diego State Coll. Radio prg. mgr., San Diego Exposition, 1935; radio pgm. mgr. S.F. World's Fair, 1937–39; freelance radio ann. and m.c. 1939–42; m.c. People are Funny since 1942. Starred Inside Beverly Hills, NBC-TV, 1955; exec. prod. host, NBC-TV spec. Salute to Baseball, 1956; host, Art Linkletter's Secret World of Kids, NBC-TV's Ford Startime, 1959; 1969 House Party series became the Linkletter Show.
Author of: The Secret World of Kids, 1959, Kids Say the Darndest Things, 1957, Linkletter Down Under, 1969, Yes, You Can, 1979; Old Age is Not For Sissies, 1988.

LINSON, ART: Producer, Director. b. Chicago, IL. e. U. of California at L.A. Was rock music manager before turning to film production. Debuted as director also with Where the Buffalo Roam.
PICTURES: Rafferty and the Gold Dust Twins, (co.-prod.), Wash, American Hot Wax (also co-s.p.), Melvin and Howard, The Wild Life (dir.), Singles, Fast Times at Ridgemont High (co-prod.), The Untouchables (prod. only) Scrooged (co-prod.), We're No Angels.

LIPPERT, ROBERT J., JR.: Producer, Director, Film editor. b. Alameda, CA, Feb. 28, 1928. e. St Mary's Coll., 1946; all conference football 1947. Film editor of 45 motion pictures. Produced and directed nine pictures for Lippert Pictures and 20th Century Fox. Present position is president, for Lippert Theatres headquartered in Pebble Beach, CA.

LIPSTONE, HOWARD H.: Executive, Producer. b. Chicago, IL, Apr. 28, 1928. e. U. of California at L.A., U. of Southern California. Ass't to gen. mgr. at KLTA, 1950–55; program dir. at KABC-TV, 1955–65; exec. ass't to pres. at Selmur Prods., ABC subsidiary, 1965–69. Ivan Tors Films & Studios as exec. v.p., 1969–70; pres.; pres., Alan Landsburg Prods., 1970–1985; The Landsburg Co., 1985 to present. Co-exec. prod.: The Outer Space Connection, The Bermuda Triangle, Mysteries, The White Lions, Jaws 3-D.
TELEVISION: exec. in charge of prod.: The Savage Bees, Ruby and Oswald, The Triangle Factory Fire Scandal, Strange Voices, A Place at the Table.

LIPTON, DAVID A.: Executive. b. Chicago, IL, Nov. 6, 1906. U.S. Army, W.W.II. Entered m.p. ind. 1921 as office boy, Balaban & Katz, Chicago; in 1922 joined pub. dept.; in 1929 transf. Detroit; in 1930 joined Famous Players Canadian Corp., org. pub. dept.; ret'd to Chicago office 1931; res. 1933 to become publ. dir. for Sally Rand. In 1937 joined CBS, N.Y. as press relations counsel. Named publ. dir. Universal N.Y., 1938; later to West Coast as studio publ. In 1941 to N.Y. as dir. adv. publ. & exploit., Columbia; returned to Universal as exec. coordinator of adv. & promotion, 1946; nat'l intl. adv. pub., Jan. 1949; elected v.p. in chge. adv. pub.; 1974, MCA Discovision, Inc., public relations director; 1979, consultant.

LISI, VIRNA: Actress. b. Ancona, Italy, Nov. 8, 1937.
PICTURES: How To Murder Your Wife, Casanova 70, Not with My Wife You Don't, Assault on a Queen, The Lady and the General, Arabella, Better a Widow, Ernesto.
TELEVISION: (U.S.) Christopher Columbus.

LISTER, MOIRA: Actress. b. Capetown, South Africa, b. Aug. 6, 1923. e. Holy Family Convent, Johannesburg. Stage debut at 6 yrs. of age in Vikings of Heligoland; screen debut in Shipbuilders, 1943. Numerous TV appearances.
PICTURES INCLUDE: Love Story, Wanted for Murder, Don Chicago, Uneasy Terms, So Evil My Love, Another Shore, Once a Jolly Swagman, Run for Your Money, Pool of London, White Corridors, Something Money Can't Buy, Cruel Sea, Grand National Night, Limping Man, Trouble in Store, John and Julie, Deep Blue Sea, Seven Waves Away, The Yellow Rolls Royce, Joey Boy, Double Man, Stranger in the House.

LITHGOW, JOHN: Actor. b. Rochester, NY, Oct. 19, 1945. Father was prod. of Shakespeare Fests. in midwest. e. Harvard. Fulbright fellowship to study at London Acad. of Music and Dramatic Art. Acted and directed in London with Royal Shakespeare Co. and Royal Court Theatre.
THEATER: The Changing Room (Tony Award, supp. 1973), My Fat Friend, The Comedians, A Memory of Two Mondays, Anna Christie, Once in a Lifetime, Requiem for a Heavyweight, The Front Page, M Butterfly.
PICTURES: Obsession, Rich Kids, Dealing, Blow Out, All That Jazz, The World According to Garp, Twilight Zone—The Movie, The Adventures of Buckaroo Banzai, Terms of Endearment, Footloose, 2010, Santa Claus: The Movie, The Manhattan Project, Harry and the Hendersons, Out Cold, Distant Thunder.
TELEVISION: Movies: The Day After, The Glitter Dome, Resting Place, Baby Girl Scott, Mesmerized.

LITTLE, CLEAVON: Actor. b. Chickasha, OK, June 1, 1939. e. San Diego Coll., B.A. 1965. Amer. Acad. of Dramatic Art, 1965–67.
THEATER: Macbeth, Scuba Duba, Hamlet, Jimmy Shine, Someone's Comin' Hungry, Purlie (Tony Award, 1970), All Over Town, The Poison Tree, I'm Not Rappaport.
PICTURES: What's So Bad About Feeling Good, Cotton Comes to Harlem, John and Mary, Vanishing Point, Blazing Saddles, FM, Greased Lightning, Scavenger Hunt, High Risk, Jimmy the Kid, Surf II, Toy Soldiers, Gig, Once Bitten, Fletch II.
TELEVISION: Series: The David Frost Revue (1971–73), Temperature's Rising. Movies: Don't Look Back, The Day the Earth Moved, Homecoming, Denmark Vesey's Rebellion, Now We're Cookin', Gore Vidal's Lincoln.

LITTLE, RICH: Actor. b. Ottawa, Canada, Nov. 26, 1938. Impersonator in night clubs. On screen in Dirty Tricks.
TELEVISION: Rich Little's Christmas Carol, Rich Little's Washington Follies, You Asked for It, Parade of Stars, The Christmas Raccoons, Rich Little and Friends in New Orleans, etc.

LITTMAN, LYNNE: Director, Producer. Wife of director Taylor Hackford. Researcher for Natl. Educational TV; exec. v.p., movies-for-TV, ABC, 1979–80.
PICTURES: In the Matter of Kenneth (doc.); Wanted-Operadoras (doc.); Till Death Do Us Part (doc.); Number Our Days (doc. short); Testament (co-prod., dir.).

LITTO, GEORGE: Executive. b. Philadelphia, PA, Dec. 9, 1930. e. Temple U. Joined William Morris Agency in New York and then became indep. literary agent. Opened own office in Hollywood, 1962. Packaged film and TV productions, including six films for Robert Altman. Hawaii Five-O for TV prior to entering indep. prod.; 1981–82, chm. bd. & CEO, Filmways; 1983–85 indep. prod. 20th Century Fox.
PICTURES INCLUDE: Thieves Like Us (exec. prod.), Drive-In (exec. prod.), Obsession (prod.), Over the Edge (prod.), Dressed To Kill (prod.). Blow Out (prod.), Kansas (prod.).
TELEVISION: Hawaii Five-O.

LITVINOFF, SI: Producer, Executive. b. New York, NY, April 5, 1929. e. Adelphi Coll., A.B.; New York U. Sch. of Law, LL.B. Theatrical lawyer, personal and business manager in New York until 1967 when left firm of Barovick, Konecky & Litvinoff to produce plays and films, June, 1987: senior v.p. for production and dev., Hawkeye Entertainment, Inc..
PICTURES: The Queen, All the Right Noises, Walkabout, A Clockwork Orange (exec. prod.), Glastonbury Fayre (exec. in chg. prod.); The Man Who Fell to Earth (exec. prod.)
STAGE: Leonard Bernstein's Theatre Songs, Cry of the Raindrop, Girl of the Golden West, Little Malcolm and His Struggle Against the Eunuchs, I and Albert (London).

LIVINGSTON, JAY: Composer, Lyricist. b. McDonald, PA, March 28, 1915; e. U. of Pennsylvania, 1937, U. of California at L.A., 1964–65. Army, W.W.II. Accompanist and arranger for various NBC singers and singing groups 1940–42, N.Y.; author music and special material for Olsen & Johnson, including various editions of Hellzapoppin', and Sons O'Fun: began

189

Liv-Lom

composing picture songs, 1944. Under contract to Paramount, 1945–55; then freelance. Composed songs for over 100 films. Writer of songs and special material for Bob Hope, 1965–present.

SONG HITS INCLUDE: G'bye Now, Stuff Like That There, To Each His Own, Golden Earrings, Silver Bells, Buttons and Bows (Acad. Award, 1949), Mona Lisa (Acad. Award, 1951), Que Sera Sera (Acad. Award, 1957), Tammy (Acad. nom.), Almost In Your Arms (Acad. nom.), Bonanza (TV Theme), Mister Ed (TV Theme), Dear Heart, (Acad. nom.), Wish Me a Rainbow, In the Arms of Love, Never Let Me Go, As I Love You, All the Time, Maybe September, Collab. music and lyrics for B'way show Oh Captain! 1958; Let It Ride, 1961. Two songs for Sugar Babies, 1980.

PICTURES INCLUDE: The Paleface, Fancy Pants, The Lemon-Drop Kid, Houseboat, Tammy and the Bachelor, The Man Who Knew Too Much, Dear Heart, Here Comes the Groom, My Friend Irma, The Night of the Grizzly, This Property Is Condemned, The Oscar, Never Too Late, Harlow, What Did You Do in the War Daddy?, Wait Until Dark, Red Garters, Sorrowful Jones.

LIVINGSTONE, PERCY: Pres. Society of Film Distributors, Cinema and Television Benevolent Fund. b. Leeds, England, 1913. e. City of Leeds Sch., Sch. of Accountancy. Entered m.p. industry Aug. 1931 in clerical capacity with old Fox Company. Joined sales force 3 years later; appointed Dublin Branch Manager, 1939; attached to Head Office, 1945 southern district mgr., 1948; assistant sales mgr., 1951; sales mgr., 1956; dir. of sales, 1957; bd. member; gen. sales mgr. Warner-Pathe Dist., 1959; man. dir. 20th Century-Fox, 1961; 20th Cent.-Fox Inter'l, N.Y., 1967; sr., v.p., 20th-Fox Intl. Corp., 1975; Chrm. 20th-Fox Film Co. Ltd. 1977; Chrm., 20th-Fox Productions Ltd.; pres., Society of Film Distributors; pres., Cinema & TV Benevolent Fund; chrm., All Industry Marketing.

LLOYD, CHRISTOPHER: Actor. b. Stamford, CT, Oct. 22, 1938. Studied at Neighborhood Playhouse, NY. Starred off-Bdwy. in Kaspar, winning Drama Desk and Obie Awards, 1973. Feature film debut in One Flew Over the Cuckoo's Nest, 1975.

PICTURES INCLUDE: Butch and Sundance: The Early Days, The Onion Field, The Black Marble, The Legend of the Lone Ranger, Mr. Mom, To Be or Not to Be, Star Trek III: The Search for Spock, Adventures of Buckaroo Banzai, Back to the Future, Clue, Who Framed Roger Rabbit?, Track 29, Walk Like a Man, Eight Men Out, The Dream Team.

TELEVISION: Taxi (series), Best of the West (series), The Dictator (series), Tales From Hollywood Hills: Pat Hobby—Teamed With Genius.

LLOYD, EUAN: Producer. b. Rugby, Warwick, England, Dec. 6, 1923. e. Rugby. Entered m.p. ind. in 1939 as theatre manager, then pub. dir.; dir. of Publ. Rank, 1946; joined Associated British-Pathe, Ltd. in same capacity; 1952 asst. to prod., Warwick Film Prod. Ltd. v.p. Highroad Productions, 1962–64. Rep. Europe Goldwyn's Porgy & Bess 1959.

PICTURES INCLUDE: April in Portugal, Heart of Variety, Invitation to Monte Carlo, The Secret Ways, Genghis Khan, Poppy Is Also a Flower, Murderer's Row, Shalako, Catlow, The Man Called Noon, Paper Tiger, The Wild Geese, The Sea Wolves, Who Dares Wins, Wild Geese II, The Final Option.

LLOYD, NORMAN: Producer. b. Jersey City, NJ, Nov. 8, 1914. e. New York U, 1932. Acted on Bdwy in: Noah, Liberty Jones, Everywhere I Roam, 1935–44; in various stock companies.

PICTURES INCLUDE: (actor) Spellbound, The Southerner, Green Years, Limelight. Prod. asst. on Arch of Triumph and The Red Pony, 1946. Assoc. prod. on The Alfred Hitchcock Show, 1957 (TV) and exec. prod. 1963. Also dir. of Up Above the World, Universal feature film; prod. of TV package deal, 2 hr. film.

STAGE: The Cocktail Party, The Lady's Not for Burning, Madame Will You Walk, The Golden Apple.

TELEVISION: Prod.-Dir.: The Alfred Hitchcock Hour, Actor: St. Elsewhere (series).

LOBELL, MICHAEL: Producer. b. New York, NY, May 7, 1941. e. Michigan State U.

PICTURES: Dreamer; Windows; So Fine; The Journey of Natty Gann, Chances Are.

LO BIANCO, TONY: Actor. b. New York, NY. Oct. 19, 1936. Performed on N.Y. stage as well as in films and TV. Former artistic dir. Triangle Theatre. Won Obie Award for performance in Yanks 3, Detroit 0, Top of the Seventh. Also acted on stage in The Office, The Rose Tattoo, The View From the Bridge, The Royal Hunt of the Sun.

PICTURES INCLUDE: Valentine, The French Connection, The Honeymoon Killers, The 7-Ups, McGee and the Lady, Separate Ways, F.I.S.T., Bloodbrothers, Blood Ties, City Heat, La Romana. Dir.: Too Scared to Scream.

TELEVISION: The Story of Joseph and Jacob, Hidden Faces, Legend of Black Hand, Lady Blue, Marco Polo,

Welcome Home Bobby, Blood Ties, Madigan; A Last Cry for Help; Mr. Inside, Mr. Outside; Marciano; Another Woman's Child; The Last Tenant; Goldenrod; Shadow in the Streets; Eugene O'Neill's A Glory of Ghosts, Police Story: The Freeway Killings, The Ann Jillian Story, Body of Evidence, Hizzoner (Emmy Award), Off Duty. Director: Police Story, Kaz, Cliffhangers.

LOCKE, SONDRA: Actress. b. Shelbyville, TN, May 28, 1947. Film debut in The Heart Is a Lonely Hunter, 1968.

PICTURES: Run, Shadow, Run; The Second Coming of Suzanne, Willard, A Reflection of Fear, The Outlaw—Josey Wales, The Gauntlet, Every Which Way But Loose, Bronco Billy, Any Which Way You Can, Sudden Impact. Debut as director: Ratboy, 1987 (also star).

TELEVISION: Rosie: The Rosemary Clooney Story; Friendships; Secrets and Lies; Amazing Stories.

LOCKHART, JUNE: Actress. b. New York, NY, June 25, 1925. p. Gene and Kathleen Lockhart. Bdwy debut For Love or Money, 1947. On TV in Lassie series.

PICTURES INCLUDE: A Christmas Carol (1938), All This and Heaven Too, Sergeant York, Miss Annie Rooney, Meet Me in St. Louis, Son of Lassie, White Cliffs of Dover, Keep Your Powder Dry, Bury Me Dead, T-Men, It's a Joke, Son, Time Limit, Troll, Rented Lips.

TELEVISION: Lost in Space, Petticoat Junction, General Hospital, Perfect People, A Whisper Kills.

LOCKWOOD, GARY: Actor. b. Van Nuys, CA, Feb. 21, 1937. Began in Hollywood as stuntman.

PICTURES INCLUDE: Tall Story, Splendor in the Grass, Wild in the Country, The Magic Sword, It Happened at the World's Fair, Firecreek, 2001: A Space Odyssey, They Came to Rob Las Vegas, Model Shop, The Body, R.P.M., Stand Up and Be Counted, The Wild Pair.

LOCKWOOD, ROGER: Executive. b. Middletown, CT, June 7, 1936. e. Ohio Wesleyan U. Sports writer for Akron Beacon Journal, 1960–62. On executive staff of Lockwood & Gordon Theatres; exec. v.p. SBC Theatres, 1969–73. In 1974 asst. to exec. v.p., General Cinema Corp. In 1975 formed Lockwood/Friedman Theatres, buying-booking and exhibition organization. Pres., Theatre Owners of New England, 1971–72; pres., Young NATO 1965–67; bd. of dir. NATO, 1962–1968. Board of dir. Tone, 1968–present; pres., Jimmy Fund, present; 1979–80, Variety Club of New England, pres. Director, Dana-Farber Cancer Institute, 1983–present.

LOGGIA, ROBERT: Actor. b. New York, NY, Jan. 3, 1930. e. U. of Missouri, B.A. Journalism, 1951. Studied with Stella Adler at Actors Studio. Broadway debut, The Man with the Golden Arm, 1955. Film debut, Somebody Up There Likes Me, 1956.

THEATER: Toys in the Attic, The Three Sisters, In the Boom Boom Room, Wedding Band.

PICTURES: The Greatest Story Ever Told, Cop Hater, Cattle King, The Garment Jungle, Che, First Love, Speed Trap, Revenge of the Pink Panther, The Sea Gypsies, The Ninth Configuration, An Officer and a Gentleman, S.O.B., Trail of the Pink Panther, Curse of the Pink Panther, Psycho II, Scarface, Jagged Edge, Prizzi's Honor, Armed and Dangerous, The Believers, That's Life, Over the Top, Big.

TELEVISION: Series: T.H.E. Cat, 1966–67; Emerald Point N.A.S. Play of the Week: Miss Julie; Movies: The Nine Lives of Elfego Baca (1958), No Other Love, Casino, A Woman Called Golda, A Touch of Scandal, Intrigue.

LOLLOBRIGIDA, GINA: Actress. b. Subiaco, Italy, July 14, 1927. e. Acad. of Fine Arts, Rome. Film debut (Italy) L'aguila nera, 1946.

PICTURES INCLUDE: Pagliacci, The City Defends Itself, The White Line, Fanfan the Tulip, Times Gone By, Beat the Devil, Crossed Swords, The Great Game, Beauties of the Night, Wayward Wife, Bread Love and Dreams, Bread Love and Jealousy, Young Caruso, World's Most Beautiful Woman, Trapeze, Hunchback of Notre Dame, Solomon and Sheba, Never So Few, Go Naked in the World, Come September, Imperial Venus, Woman of Straw, That Splendid November, Hotel Paradisio, Buona Sera, Mrs. Campbell, Bad Man's River, King, Queen, Knave, The Lonely Woman, Bambole, Plucked.

TELEVISION: Deceptions, Falcon Crest (series).

LOM, HERBERT: Actor. b. Prague, 1917. e. Prague U. Stage training London Embassy, Old Vic—Sadlers Wells and Westminster Schools. British film debut (Mein Kampf—My Crimes) (1941); on TV, The Human Jungle Series.

PICTURES INCLUDE: Tomorrow We Live, Secret Mission, Young Mr. Pitt, Dark Tower, Cage of Gold, Whispering Smith vs. Scotland Yard, Two on the Tiles, Mr. Denning Drives North, Hell Is Sold Out, Gaunt Stranger, Rough Shoot, The Net, The Love Lottery, Star of India, Beautiful Stranger, The Ladykillers, War and Peace Action, Fire Down Below, Hell's Drives, Chase a Crooked Shadow, Passport to Shame, Roots of Heaven, The Big Fisherman, North-West Frontier, I Aim at the Stars, Spartacus, Mysterious Island, Mr. Topaz, The

190

Frightened City, El Cid, Tiara Tahiti, The Phantom of the Opera, Horse Without a Head, A Shot in the Dark, Uncle Tom's Cabin, Return from the Ashes, Gambit, The Assignment, Three Faces of Eve, Villa Rides, Doppelganger, Mr. Jericho, Dorian, Mark of the Devil, Count Dracula, Murders in the Rue Morgue, Dark Places, Death in Persepolis, Return of the Pink Panther, The Pink Panther Strikes Again, Charleston, Revenge of the Pink Panther, The Man with Bogarts' Face, Hopscotch, The Acts of Peter and Paul, The Trail of the Pink Panther, The Curse of the Pink Panther, Memed, My Hawk, Dead Zone, King Solomon's Mines, Whoops Apocalypse, Coast of Skeletons, Master of Dragonard Hill, Going Bananas, Skeleton Coast.

LOMBARDO, GOFFREDO: Executive. b. Naples, Italy, May 13, 1920. President Titanus Films.
PICTURES INCLUDE: Rocco and His Brothers, Sodom and Gomorrah, The Leopard, Four Days of Naples.

LOMITA, SOLOMON: Executive. b. New York, NY, April 23, 1937. Entire industry career with United Artists Corp. as follows: adm., intl. dept., 1962; asst., intl. sales, same year. 1963, asst. intl. print mgr.; 1965, intl., print mgr. In 1973 appt. dir. of film services. 1981, v.p., film services. In 1985 named exec. v.p., post-prod., Orion Pictures.

LONDON, BARRY: Executive. Joined Paramount Pictures 1971 in L.A. branch office as booker; later salesman. 1973, sls. mgr., Kansas City-St. Louis; 1974, branch mgr. Transferred to San Francisco, first as branch mgr.; later as district mgr. 1977, eastern div. mgr. in Washington, DC, 1978-81, western div. mgr. In March, 1981, named v.p., gen. sls. mgr. June, 1983, advanced to sr. v.p., domestic distribution. 1984, named pres., domestic div., for Motion Picture Group of Paramount; 1985, named president, marketing and domestic distribution.

LONDON, JERRY: Director. b. Los Angeles, CA, Jan 21, 1937. Apprentice film editor, Desilu Prods., 1955; film ed., Daniel Boone, 1962; staged plays in local theater workshops; editor, assoc. prod., then dir. Hogan's Heroes. Formed Jerry London Prods., 1984.
PICTURES: Rent-a-Cop (feature debut, 1987).
TELEVISION: Series: Mary Tyler Moore Show, Love American Style, The Bob Newhart Show, Marcus Welby, M.D., Kojak, The Six Million Dollar Man, Police Story, Rockford Files. Mini-series: Wheels, Shogun (DGA, best dir., specials award), Chiefs (also sprv. prod.), Ellis Island (also sprv. prod.), If Tomorrow Comes, A Long Way From Home. Movies: Swan Song, Women in White, Evening in Byzantium, Father Figure, The Chicago Story, The Ordeal of Bill Carney (also prod.), The Gift of Life (also prod.), The Scarlet and the Black, Arthur Hailey's Hotel (also prod.), With Intent to Kill (exec. prod.), Manhunt For Claude Dallas, Family Sins, Macgruder and Loud (also prod.), Dadah Is Death.

LONDON, JULIE: Singer, Actress. r.n. Julie Peck. b. Santa Rosa, CA, Sept. 26, 1926. Launched as actress by agent Sue Carol (wife of Alan Ladd) who arranged screen test, followed by contract for 6 films. As singer has appeared in nightclubs and recorded.
PICTURES INCLUDE: The Red House, The Fat Man, The Great Man, Saddle the Wind, Man of the West, The Third Voice.
TELEVISION: Perry Como Show, Steve Allen Show, Ed Sullivan Show, Emergency (series).

LONDON, MILTON H.: Executive. b. Detroit, MI, Jan. 12, 1916. e. U. of Michigan, B.A., 1937. Wayne U. Law Sch., 1938. U.S. Army 1943-46. Invented Ticograph system of positive admissions control for theatres, 1950; pres. Theatre Control Corp., 1950-62; secy-treas. Co-op. Theas. of Michigan Inc., 1956-63; exec. comm., Council of M.P. Organizations, 1957-66; dir. M.P. Investors, 1960-67; exec. dir. Allied States Assoc. of M.P. Exhib., 1961-66; exec. dir. National Assoc. of Theatre Owners, 1966-69 pres., NATO of Michigan, 1954-74; Mich. State Fire Safety Bd., Chief Barker, Variety Club of Detroit, Tent No. 5. 1975-76; Life Patron and Lifeliner, Variety Clubs International; trustee, Variety Club Charity for Children; chm., Variety Club Myoelectric Center; dir., Motion Picture Pioneers; advisory comm., Will Rogers Inst.; trustee, Detroit Inst. for Children; pres., Metropolitan Adv. Co.; Intl. ambassador, Variety Clubs Int'l.

LONERGAN, ARTHUR: Art director. b. New York, NY, Jan. 23, 1906. e. Columbia U. Instructor in history of architecture, New York U.; architect with N.Y. Sch. of Decoration and Design. Joined MGM as illustrator in art dept., 1938; freelance art dir., 1945; pres. Soc. of M.P. Art Dir., 1952-54; Acad. Award nomination, art. dir., The Oscar. 1975—The Georges Melies Award for outstanding cinematic achievement for art direction in Science Fiction category. Design consultant on Disney Theme Park, Japan.
TELEVISION: Loretta Young Show, The Falcon, Mr. and Mrs. North, Topper, Life of Riley, Adventures of Hiram Holiday, Hitchcock Presents, GE Theatre, M. Squad, Restless Gun. etc.

PICTURES INCLUDE: Song in My Heart, Intrigue, Tender Years, Maneaters of Kumaon, Pitfall, Outpost in Morocco, Ride Vaquero, The Actress, It's Always Fair Weather, Tender Trap, Ransom, Forbidden Planet, On the Double, My Geisha, Who's Got the Action, Papa's Delicate Condition, A New Kind of Love, Who's Sleeping in My Bed, Robinson Caruso On Mars, Tickle Me, Red Line 7000, The Caper of the Golden Bull, Yours Mine and Ours, How Sweet It Is, Che, M*A*S*H, Plaza Suite.

LONG, ROBERT A.: Executive. b. McCune, KS, Oct. 31, 1931. e. U. of Kansas, 1957. Mng. partner, K.C., Arthur Andersen & Co., 1970-80; now exec. v.p., Commonwealth Theatres, Inc.
MEMBER: Past. pres., Civic Council of Greater Kansas City; past pres., Chamber of Commerce Greater Kansas City; Heart of America Council of Boy Scouts; United Way; bd. mbr., Rockhurst Coll., U. of Missouri at Kansas City, city trustees; Advisory Council, U. of Kansas, school of business & medicine; bd. trustees, Endowment Assoc. of U. of Kansas. Named Mr. Kansas City, 1981.

LONG, SHELLEY: Actress. b. Ft. Wayne, IN, Aug. 23, 1949. e. Northwestern U.
PICTURES: A Small Circle of Friends, Caveman, Night Shift, Losin' It, Irreconcilable Differences, The Money Pit, Outrageous Fortune, Hello Again, Troup Beverly Hills.
TELEVISION: Cheers (series), The Cracker Factory, Princess and the Cabbie, Promise of Love.

LONGSTREET, STEPHEN: Writer, Painter. b. New York, NY, April 18, 1907; e. Rutgers U.; Parsons Coll.; Rand Sch., London, B.A. Humorist, cartoonist (New Yorker, Collier's, etc.) 1930-37; ed. Free World Theat., radio plays; ed. film critic, Saturday Review of Literature, 1940, U.S. at War, Time 1942-43; writer for screen from 1942. On staff U. of California at L.A. Elected pres. Los Angeles Art Assoc. 1970. 1974: appointed Prof. English Dep., U. of Southern California. Modern Writing Course. Writers Guild, Comm. of Public Relations. Film and book critic for Readers' Syndicate since 1970. Professor performing arts dept. U. of Southern California since 1973, where in 1979, presented 12 great silent films, The Art & Entertainment of Silent Films in the cinema section of the college. Rutgers U., lecturer, 1986, on Griffith, Hawks, Hitchcock, Ford, Welles. L.A. Art Assoc. lecture series 1988 The Dreams That Swallowed the World: The Hollywood Scene 1940-88. Art show Movie Faces.
WRITINGS: Decade, The Golden Touch, The Gay Sisters, Last Man Around the World, Chico Goes to the Wars, Pedlocks, Lion at Morning, Promoters, Boy in the Model T, Sometimes I Wonder, Wind at My Back, The Young Men of Paris, The Wilder Shore, War Cries on Horseback, Yoshiwara, Geishas and Courtesans, Canvas Falcons, Men and Planes of World War I, We All Went to Paris. New publications in 1973: Chicago 1860-1919, (show business & society), Divorcing (a novel); The General (novel, 1974), All Star Cast, 1977; The Queen Bees (1979), Our Father's House (1985).
STAGE: High Button Shoes.
PICTURES INCLUDE: The Gay Sisters, Golden Touch, Stallion Road, Jolson Story, Silver River, Helen Morgan Story, First Traveling Saleslady, Untamed Youth, Duel in the Sun, Greatest Show on Earth, Streets of Montmarte, The Crime, Uncle Harry, Rider on a Dead Horse, The Imposter.
TELEVISION: Casey Jones (series), Clipper Ship, Agent of Scotland Yard, m.c. author of The Sea; m.c. Press & Clergy, 1960-63; Viewpoint; series Boy in the Model T, Young Man From Boston, 1967, Blue and the Grey. Appeared on Early Hollywood.

LONSDALE, PAMELA: Freelance Producer, Director. Devised and was first producer of Rainbow for Thames T.V. Other programs include: Ace of Wands, The Squad (also devised) Cranford, S.W.A.L.K., Marmalade Atkins, Spooky, Chocky and Mr. Stabs. Recently produced Exploits at West Poley, a film for the C.F.T.F. In 1975 won the British Academy Award for the best children's program.

LOOS, MARY: Writer. b. San Diego, CA, May 6, 1914. e. Stanford U., 1933. Actress m.p.; in public relations field N.Y. 1938; jewelry designer for Paul Flato; author of novel Return in the Vineyard, 1945. secy. Voyager Films, Inc., literary exec. M. J. Frankovich Prod. Novel: The Beggars Are Coming, Bantam Books, 1974, Belinda, 1976; The Barstow Legend, 1978; A Pride of Lovers, 1981.
PICTURES INCLUDE: Rose Marie, Maytime, Crusades, Cleopatra, Mr. Belvedere Goes to College, Mother Was a Freshman, Ticket to Tomahawk, When Willie Comes Marching Home, Father Was a Fullback, I'll Get By, Meet Me After the Show, Let's Do It Again, The French Line, Gentlemen Marry Brunettes, Over-Exposed, Woman's World.

LORD, JACK: Actor, Writer, Artist, Director, Producer. b. New York, NY, Dec. 30, 1930. e. New York U. (Chancellor Chase scholarship), B.S. Studied at Neighborhood Playhouse and Actors Studio. Artist, represented in various museums including Metropolitan Museum of Art, Museum of Modern Art,

Brooklyn Museum, in New York. Bibliotheque National, Paris; British Museum; Fogg Museum, Harvard U. St. Gaudens Plaque for Fine Arts; creator of Tramp Ship, McAdoo, Yankee Trader, The Hunter TV series. On Bway in Traveling Lady (Theatre World Award), Cat on a Hot Tin Roof. Fame Award, new male star, 1963, mem. of Directors Guild of America. Recent Awards: G. Washington Honor Medal from Freedom Foundation at Valley Forge, 1984; Veterans Administration, Administrator's Award, 1980; Salute to Hospitalized Veterans, Tripler Army Medical Center, 1985; East-West Center Distinguished Service Award, 1981.

PICTURES INCLUDE: The Court Martial of Billy Mitchell, Williamsburg Story, On a Dead Jockey, God's Little Acre, Man of the West, The Hangman, Walk Like a Dragon, Doctor No, Doomsday Flight, Ride to Hangman's Tree, Counterfeit Killer.

TELEVISION: Debut: Man Against Crime (series), Leads on all networks, including Omnibus Constitution series, Playhouse 90, Goodyear Playhouse, Studio One, U.S. Steel. Have Gun Will Travel (pilot), Untouchables, Naked City, Rawhide, Bonanza, The Americans, Route 66, Gunsmoke, Stagecoach West, Dr. Kildare, Greatest Show on Earth, Combat, Chrysler Theatre, 12 O'Clock High, The Loner, Laredo, The FBI, The Invaders, The Fugitive, The Virginian, Man from U.N.C.L.E., High Chaparral, Ironside, Star of Stoney Burke and Hawaii Five-O series. Director of Death with Father, How to Steal a Masterpiece; Honor Is an Unmarked Grave, The Bells Toll at Noon, Top of the World, Why Won't Linda Die, Who Says Cops Don't Cry episodes of Hawaii Five-O. Creator, director, and exec. Producer of M Station: Hawaii (2-hr special for TV), 1979. Pres., Lord and Lady Enterprises, Inc.

LORD, ROSEMARY: Actress, Writer. b. May 16, Taunton, Somerset, England. Now living in Hollywood.

PICTURES INCLUDE: Actress: The Whisperers, The Watchers, Touch of Class, Duchess and the Dirtwater Fox, Frances.

TELEVISION: Monty Python, Sherlock Holmes, Spyder's Web, Days of Our Lives.

LOREN, SOPHIA: Actress. b. Rome, Italy, Sept. 20, 1934. e. Naples. In films since 1950. m. producer Carlo Ponti.

PICTURES INCLUDE: Africa Beneath the Seas, Village of the Bells, Good People's Sunday, Neapolitan Carousel, Day in the District Court, Pilgrim of Love, Aida, Two Nights with Cleopatra, Our Times, Attila, Scourge of God, Too Bad She's Bad, Pride and the Passion, Gold of Naples, Boy on a Dolphin, Scandal in Lorrinto, Miller's Beautiful Wife, Desire Under the Elms, Houseboat, The Black Ordeal, That Kind of Woman, Heller With a Gun, Anatomy of Love, Breath of Scandal, Heller in Pink Tights, Bay of Naples, Two Women, El Cid, Boccaccio 70, Il Coltello nello Piaga, French, The Fall of the Roman Empire, The Great Spy Mission, Lady L, Marriage Italian Style, Judith, Arabesque, The Countess from Hong Kong, Happily Ever After, More than a Miracle, Ghosts—Italian Style, Sunflower, The Priest's Wife, Lady Liberty, White Sister, Man of La Mancha, The Voyage, The Verdict, The Cassandra Crossing, A Special Day, Angela, Brass Target, Firepower.

TELEVISION: Movies: Brief Encounter, Sophia Loren—Her Own Story; Softly, Softly, Rivals of Sherlock Holmes, Fantasy Island, Aurora, Courage, Mario Puzo's The Fortunate Pilgrim.

LOUIS, JEAN: Designer. b. Paris, France, Oct. 5, 1907. Head designer, Hattie Carnegie, 7 yrs., before accepting post as Chief Designer Columbia Pictures. Later Universal Studios. Free lance in m.p. & TV. Pres. Jean-Louis, Inc.

LOUISE, TINA: Actress. b. New York, NY, Feb. 11, 1934. e. Miami U., N.Y. Neighborhood Playhouse, Actors Studio, B'way.

STAGE: Two's Company, The Fifth Season, John Murray Anderson's Almanac, Li'l Abner, Fade Out, Fade In.

PICTURES INCLUDE: God's Little Acre, Day of the Outlaw, For Those Who Think Young, The Wrecking Crew, The Good Guys and the Bad Guys, How to Commit Marriage, The Happy Ending, The Stepford Wives, O.C. and the Stiggs, Dixie Lanes, The Pool.

TELEVISION: Gilligan's Island (series), Rituals (series), Mannix, Ironside, Kung Fu, Police Story, Kojak. Movies: Friendship, Secrets and Lies; Advice to the Lovelorn; The Day the Women Got Even, The Woman Who Cried Murder; SST Death Flight; Look What's Happened to Rosemary's Babies; Nightmare in Badham County.

LOWE, PHILIP L.: Executive. b. Brookline, MA, Apr. 17, 1917. e. Harvard. Army 1943–46. Checker, Lowe's 1937–39; treasurer, Theatre Candy Co., 1941–58; Pres.; ITT Sheraton Corp., 1969–70; Principal, Philip L. Lowe and Assoc.

LOWE, PHILIP M.: Executive. b. 1944. e. Deerfield Acad., Harvard Coll., cum laude in psychology, 1966; Columbia Business Sch., 1968. Work experience includes major marketing positions at General Foods, Gillette, Gray Advertising, and Estee Lauder Cosmetics before co-founding Cinema Centers Corp. and Theatre Management Services in Boston. Pres. of Lowe Group of Companies (cable television, broadcasting, hotels, real estate and management consulting). Past pres. and chm. of the bd; National Association of Concessionaires (NAC); past director, National Association of Theater Owners (NATO). Past professor of marketing, Bentley Coll., Waltham, MA.; Contributing Editor; The Movie Business Book, Prentice-Hall, Inc. 1983.

LOWE, ROB: Actor. b. Virginia, Mar. 17, 1964.

PICTURES: The Outsiders, Class, About Last Night . . ., The Hotel New Hampshire, Oxford Blues, St. Elmo's Fire, Youngblood, Square Dance, Illegally Yours, Masquerade.

TELEVISION: Schoolboy Father, A Matter of Time, Thursday's Child, A New Kind of Family (series).

LOWRY, DICK: Director. b. Bartlesville, OK. e. U. of Oklahoma. Commercial photographer before being accepted by AFI.

PICTURES: The Drought (short); Smokey and the Bandit—Part 3.

TELEVISION: Jayne Mansfield Story; Kenny Rogers as the Gambler; The Pigs V. the Freaks; Angel Dusted; Coward of the County; Few Days in Weasel Creek; Missing Children—A Motl 's Story; Living Proof; The Secret Adventures of Tom Sawyer and Huck Finn; Kenny Rogers as the Gambler—the Adventure Continues (also prod.); Wet Gold; The Toughest Man in the World; Murder with Mirrors, American Harvest, Kenny Rogers as The Gambler III (coexec. prod., dir.); Dream West (mini-series); Case Closed.

LOWRY, HUNT: Producer. b. Oklahoma City, OK, Aug. 21, 1954. e. Rollins Coll., & Wake Forest. Abandoned plans to study medicine to enter film-making industry; first job for New World Pictures where he met Jon Davison, with whom was later to co-produce. Next made TV commercials as prod. asst. and then producer. Left to go freelance as commercials producer 1980, appt. assoc. prod. to Davison on Airplane!

PICTURES: Humanoids from the Deep, Top Secret!, Get Crazy, Baja Oklahoma (exec. prod.), Wildfire (co-prod.).

TELEVISION: Rascals and Robbers: The Secret Adventures of Tom Sawyer and Huckleberry Finn.

LOY, MYRNA: Actress. r.n. Myrna Williams; b. Helena MT, Aug. 2, 1905. e. Westlake Sch. for Girls. Appeared in stage presentations, Grauman's Chinese theatre, then Hollywood. Film debut Pretty Ladies, 1925; thereafter in more than 100 pictures, variously starred, co-starred & featured. Voted one of the ten best Money-Making Stars in Motion Picture Herald-Fame Poll, 1937, 38.

STAGE: Marriage-Go-Round, There Must Be a Pony, Good Housekeeping, Barefoot in the Park, Dear Love, The Women, Don Juan in Hell, Relatively Speaking.

PICTURES INCLUDE: The Jazz Singer, The Desert Song, Last of the Duanes, Body and Soul, A Connecticut Yankee, Hush Money, Transatlantic, Arrowsmith, Vanity Fair, Love Me Tonight, The Mask of Fu Manchu, Animal Kingdom, Topaze, The Barbarian, The Prizefighter and the Lady, When Ladies Meet, Penthouse, Night Flight, Men in White, Manhattan Melodrama, The Thin Man, Evelyn Prentice, Wife Versus Secretary, The Great Ziegfeld, To Harry With Love, Libeled Lady, After the Thin Man, Test Pilot, The Rains Came, Another Thin Man, Third Finger, Left Hand; Shadow of the Thin Man, The Thin Man Goes Home, Best Years of Our Lives, The Bachelor and the Bobby Soxer, The Song of the Thin Man, Mr. Blandings Builds His Dream House, Red Pony, If This Be Sin, Cheaper by the Dozen, My Daughter Joy, Belles on Their Toes, Ambassador's Daughter, Lonely Hearts, From the Terrace, Midnight Lace, The April Fools, Airport 1975, The End, Just Tell Me What You Want.

TELEVISION: Meet Me in St. Louis, Minerva, George Gobel, Perry Como, Happy Birthday—June Allyson Show, Family Affair, The Virginians, Movies: Death Takes a Holiday (1970), Do Not Spindle or Mutilate, The Couple Takes a Wife, Ironside, The Elevator, It Happened at Lakewood Manor, Summer Solstice.

LUBCKE, HARRY R.: Registered Patent Agent. b. Alameda, CA, Aug. 25, 1905. e. U. of California, B.S., 1929. Holds numerous U.S. and foreign patents on television. In 1931: station W6XAO went on air on what is now television Channel No. 2 to become first station of kind in nation. New Mt. Lee studios built at cost of $250,000 in 1941, housing then largest TV stage 100x60x30 ft. Pioneered present television standard of 525 line (Aug., 1940). In 1942, television programs to promote war bonds sale. 1942–46 dir. war research for which certificates of commendation were received from Army & Navy.

MEMBER: Pres., Acad. TV Arts & Sciences, 1949. Dir. TV Don Lee Broadcasting System to Dec. 31, 1950; cons. TV engineer, 1951; registered patent agent, 1952. Life Fellow, 1951, IEEE, AAAS, SMPTE, 1967. Board of Governors, Patent Law Association of Los Angeles, 1974. Life Member National Academy of Television Arts & Sciences, member engineering Emmy Awards Committee. Member Blue Ribbon panel Emmy Awards Committee; 1978; Diamond Circle, of Pacific Pioneer Broadcasters, 1980; American Bar Assn., 1982.

LUBIN, ARTHUR: Director. b. Los Angeles, CA. Since 1935 has directed numerous pictures, including John Wayne's first four films at Universal: Hell on Ice, California Straight Ahead, Adventure's End, I Covered the War.
PICTURES INCLUDE: Buck Privates in the Navy, Hold That Ghost, Keep 'em Flying, Ride 'em Cowboy, Eagle Squadron, Phantom of the Opera, White Savage, Ali Baba and the Forty Thieves, Delightfully Dangerous, Francis, Queen for a Day, Francis Goes to the Races, Rhubarb, Francis Covers the Big Town, Francis Goes to West Point, It Grows on Trees, South Sea Woman, Star of India, Lady Godiva, Francis in the Navy, Footsteps in the Fog, First Traveling Saleslady, Escapade in Japan, The Thief of Baghdad, The Incredible Mr. Limpett, Rain for a Dusty Summer, Night in Paradise, The Spider Woman Strikes Back, New Orleans, Impact, Queen for a Day, Star of India, Hold On!
TELEVISION: Maverick (Henry Fonda episodes), 77 Sunset Strip, Bonanza, the entire Mister Ed series (prod.-dir.).

LUCAS, GEORGE: Producer, Director, Writer. b. Modesto, CA, 1944. e. U. of Southern California, cinema. Made short film called THX-1138 and won National Student Film Festival Grand Prize, 1967. Signed contract with WB. Ass't. to Francis Ford Coppola on The Rain People, during which Lucas made 2-hr. documentary on filming of that feature. Debut as director with THX-1138 for WB.
PICTURES INCLUDE: THX-1138 (dir., co-s.p.), American Graffiti (dir., co-s.p.), Star Wars (dir., s.p.); More American Graffiti (exec. prod.); The Empire Strikes Back (exec. prod.); Raiders of the Lost Ark (exec. prod.); Return of the Jedi (exec. prod., co-s.p.); Indiana Jones and the Temple of Doom (exec. prod.); Labyrinth (story; exec. prod.); Howard the Duck (exec. prod.); Willow (exec. prod., story); Tucker: The Man and His Dream (exec. prod.), The Land Before Time Began.
TELEVISION: The Ewok Adventure (exec. prod.).

LUCCHESI, GARY: Executive. b. San Francisco, CA, 1955. Entered industry as a trainee with the William Morris Agency, 1977. Joined Tri-Star, 1983, as vice pres. of production, became senior vice pres., 1985. Joined Paramount Pictures as exec. vice pres., April 1987; appointed head of motion picture production division, Dec. 1987.

LUCKINBILL, LAURENCE: Actor. b. Fort Smith, AZ, Nov. 21, 1934. m. actress Lucie Arnaz. e. U. of Arizona, Catholic U. of America. On Bdwy. in A Man for All Seasons, Arms and the Man, The Boys in the Band, Alpha Beta, The Shadow Box, etc.
PICTURES INCLUDE: The Boys in the Band, Such Good Friends, The Money, The Promise, Not for Publication, Cocktail, Messenger of Death.
TELEVISION: Movies: The Delphi Bureau, Death Sentence, Panic on the 5:22, Winner Take All, The Lindbergh Kidnapping Case, Ike, Lyndon Johnson (one-man show), Voices and Visions (narrator), To Heal a Nation.

LUDDY, TOM: e. U. of CA at Berkeley where he operated student film societies and rep. cinemas. Entered industry via Brandon Films. 1972, prog. dir. and curator of Pacific Film Archives. 1979, joined Zoetrope Studios as dir. of special projects where dev. and supervised revival of Gance's Napoleon and Our Hitler—A Film From Germany. Coordinated Koyaasnisqatsi, Every Man For Himself, Passion. A founder, Telluride Film Fest. Served on selection comm., NY and San Francisco Film Fest.
PICTURES: Mishima (co-prod.); Tough Guys Don't Dance (co-exec. prod.); Barfly (prod.)

LUDWIG, IRVING H.: Executive. b. Nov. 3. Rivoli Theatre, N.Y., mgr., theatre oper.; Rugoff and Becker, 1938–39; opened first modern art type theatre, Greenwich Village, 1940. With Walt Disney Prod. in charge of theatre oper. on Fantasia, 1940–41; buyer-booker, Rugoff and Becker, 1942–45; film sales admin., Walt Disney Prod. home office, 1945–53; v.p. and domestic sales mgr., Buena Vista Dist. Co., 1953; pres. gen. sales mgr., 1959–80.
MEMBER: Bd. of dir., Will Rogers Memorial Fund, Foundation of M.P. Pioneers; M.P. Bookers of NY; Academy of M.P. Arts & Sciences.

LUEDTKE, KURT: Writer. b. Grand Rapids, MI, Sept. 29, 1938. e. Brown U., B.A., 1961. Reporter Grand Rapids Press 1961–62. Miami Herald, 1963–65; Detroit Free Press (reporter, asst. photography dir., asst. mgr. ed., asst. exec. ed., exec. ed. 1965–78.).
PICTURES: Absence of Malice, Out of Africa (Acad. Award, 1985), Walls.

LUFKIN, DAN W.: Executive. Chairman of Exec. Comm., Columbia Pictures Industries (appt. July, 1978). Co-founder of Donaldson, Lufkin & Jenrette Securities Corp., investment banking and brokerage firm. Served as first commissioner of Dept. of Environmental Protection for state of Connecticut. Joined Columbia board in November, 1977.

LUKE, KEYE: Actor, Artist. b. Canton, China, 1904. e. Franklin H.S., Seattle. Formerly artist for Fox West Coast Theats. &

RKO Studios; also technical advisor on Chinese films. Screen debut as actor in Painted Veil, 1935.
STAGE: Flower Drum Song (3 yr).
PICTURES INCLUDE: Charlie Chan series, Oil for the Lamps of China, King of Burlesque, The Good Earth, International Settlement, Sued for Libel, Disputed Passage, Dragon Seed, Three Men in White, Between Two Women, First Yank in Tokyo, Tokyo Rose, Sleep My Love, Hell's Half Acre, World for Ransom, Bamboo Prison, Love Is a Many Splendored Thing, 80 Days Around the World, Their Greatest Glory, Battle Hell, Fair Winds to Java, Nobody's Perfect, Project X, The Chairman, The Hawaiians, Noon Sunday, Won Ton Ton, Amsterdam Kill, Just You and Me, Kid, They Call Me Bruce, Gremlins, A Fine Mess, Dead Heat, Finding Maubee.
TELEVISION: Gunsmoke, Danger, December Bride, Crusader, Wireservice, Crossroads, Soldiers of Fortune, My Little Margie, Annie Oakley, Ray Milland Show, Medic, Citizen Chang, Climax, Jerry Lewis, Trackdown, Perry Mason Show, The Littlest Hobo, This Is the Life, Smothers Bros., I Spy, FBI, Wackiest Ship in Army, Mickey Rooney Show, Johnny Quest, Kentucky Jones, Never Too Young, Bob Hope Chrysler Show, Family Affair, Big Valley, Dragnet, It Takes a Thief, Star-Trek, Adventures of Huck Finn, The Outsider, Scooby Doo, Paris 7000, Johnny Carson Show, Marcus Welby, M.D., Adam 12, Hawaii 5-O, Dinah Shore Show, The Lucy Show, Anna and the King of Siam, Kung Fu, Amazing Chan and Chan Clan, Follow The Sun, Target, The Corrupters, Fair Exchange, Cannon, Cat Creature, Love American Style, Judgment—Trial of Yamashita, Judge Dee, Khan, Harry O, M*A*S*H, Quincy, How the West Was Won, Meeting of Minds, Vegas, Battle of the Planets, The Yee Family, Might Man and Yukk, Rickety Racket, Tang Face, Charlie's Angels, Reach for the Sun, Fly Away Home, Brothers, Adventures of Goldie Gold, Spider Man, Unit Four, Remington Steele, Magnum P.I., Falcon Crest, Voyagers, The A-Team, Mike Hammer, Cocaine and Blue Eyes, Miami Vice, Street Hawk, Trapper John, Blade in Hong Kong, Mr. T, Night Court, Mac Gyver, T. J. Hooker, Crazy Like a Fox, Kung Fu, Golden Girls, Down to Earth, General Hospital, Sidekicks, Downtown, Friday the 13th, MacGyver, The Judge, 9 to 5, Beauty and the Beast.

LUKE, PETER: Playwright, Director. b. England, Aug. 12, 1919. Author of plays for TV: Small Fish Are Sweet, 1958; Pigs Ear with Flowers, 1960; Roll on Bloomin' Death, 1961; A Man on Her Back (with William Sansom), 1965; Devil a Monk Won't Be, 1966. wrote and directed films for BBC-TV: Anach 'Cuan (about the late Sean O Riada) 1967; Black Sound—Deep Song (about Federico Garcia Lorca) 1968; Author of Stage play, Hadrian VII, first produced at Birmingham rep in 1967 and has been staged around the world. Stage Play, Bloomsbury. Author of autobiography, Sisyphus & Reilly, publ., 1972, Prod. Phoenix Theatre 1974.

LUMET, SIDNEY: Director. b. Philadelphia, PA, June 15, 1924. e. Professional Children's Sch.; Columbia U. Child actor in plays: Dead End, George Washington Slept Here, My Heart's in the Highlands. U.S. Armed Forces, W.W.II, 1942–46; dir. summer stock, 1947–49; taught acting, H.S. of Prof. Arts. Assoc. dir. CBS, 1950, dir. 1951.
TELEVISION: Mama, Danger, You Are There, Omnibus, Best of Broadway, Alcoa, Goodyear Playhouse.
PICTURES INCLUDE: 12 Angry Men, Stage Struck, That Kind of Woman, The Fugitive Kind, A View From the Bridge, A Long Day's Journey into Night, Fail Safe, The Pawnbroker, The Hill, The Group, The Deadly Affair, Bye Bye Braverman, The Sea Gull, The Appointment, Last of the Mobile Hot-Shots, The Anderson Tapes, Child's Play, The Offence, Lovin' Molly, Serpico, Murder on the Orient Express, Dog Day Afternoon, Network, Equus, The Wiz, Just Tell Me What You Want (also co-prod.), Prince of the City (also co-s.p.), Deathtrap, The Verdict, Daniel (also co-exec. prod.), Garbo Talks, Power, The Morning After, Running on Empty.

LUNDGREN, DOLPH: Actor. b. Stockholm, Sweden, 1959. e. Washington State U., won Fulbright to Massachusetts Inst. of Technology, Royal Inst. of Technology, Stockholm, M.A. Was doorman at Limelight disco in NY while studying acting. Kick-boxing champion. Made workout video, Maximum Potential.
PICTURES: A View to a Kill, Rocky IV, Masters of the Universe, Red Scorpion, The Punisher.

LUPINO, IDA: Actress, Director. b. London, England, Feb. 4, 1918. e. Royal Acad. of Dramatic Art, London. Daughter of Stanley Lupino, English stage and screen comedian. Brit. m.p. debut in Her First Affair, 1932; in U.S. m.p. 1934; ent. independent prod., becoming one of the first major women director-screenwriters beginning with Not Wanted (also writer, prod.). Also maintained acting career at same time.
PICTURES INCLUDE: Money for Speed, High Finance, High Sierra, Ladies in Retirement, Moontide, The Hard Way, Devotion, Man I Love, Escape Me Never, Deep Valley, Road House, Lust for Gold, Not Wanted, Never Fear (dir.), Outrage (also dir., s.p.), Hard Fast & Beautiful (dir.), On Dangerous Ground, Beware My Lovely, The Hitch-Hiker (dir., s.p.), Jennifer, The Bigamist (dir.), Private Hell 36 (s.p.), Women's

Prison, Big Knife, While the City Sleeps, Trouble With Angels (dir.), Junior Bonner, The Devil's Rain, The Food of the Gods. TELEVISION: Mr. Adams and Eve (series), No. 5 Checked Out, The Trial of Mary Surrat, Honey West, Virginian, I Love a Mystery, Sam Benedict, Untouchables, G. E. Theater, Have Gun Will Travel, Thriller, Mr. Novak, Hong Kong, The Rogues, Chrysler Theatre, Kraft Theatre, Gilligan's Island, The Ghost and Mrs. Muir, The Bill Cosby Show, To Catch a Thief, Mod Squad, Family Affair.

LURASCHI, LUIGI G.: Exec. b. London, Jan 7, 1906. e. U. of Zurich. Long Island Studio, Paramount, 1929; home officer mgr. For. dept. hd, For. & dom. Censorship; Hollywood to 1960. Asst. Prod., Dino De Laurentiis Prod. 1960–65; asst. to pres. for prod. activities, Paramount, 1965. 1967 continental prod. exec. Paramount-Rome. Now v.p., intl.

LYDON, JAMES: Actor. b. Harrington Park, NJ, May 30, 1923; e. St. Johns Mil. Sch. On N.Y. stage in Prologue to Glory, Sing Out the News. On screen 1939, Back Door to Heaven.
PICTURES INCLUDE: Thoroughbreds, Naval Academy, Henry Aldrich series, Twice Blessed, Life With Father, Out of the Storm, Joan of Arc, Miss Mink of 1949, Tucson, Gasoline Alley, Island in the Sky, The Desperado, Battle Stations, My Blood Runs Cold (assoc. prod.), Brainstorm, An American Dream, A Covenant With Death, First to Fight, The Cool Ones, Chubasco, Countdown, Assignment to Kill, The Learning Tree, Scandalous John, Vigilante Force.
TELEVISION: Frontier Circus (assoc. prod.), Wagon Train, Alfred Hitchcock Hour, McHale's Navy, 77 Sunset Strip, Mr. Roberts. Series: So This Is Hollywood, The First Hundred Years, Love That Jill.

LYLES, A. C.: Producer. b. Jacksonville, FL. May 17, 1912. e. Andrew Jackson H.S. Paramount Publix's Florida Theatre, 1928; interviewed Hollywood celebrities, Jacksonville Journal, 1932; mail boy, Paramount Studios, Hollywood, 1937; publicity dept., 1938; hd. of adv., publ. dept., Pine-Thomas unit at Paramount, 1940; assoc. prod., The Mountain; prod., Short Cut to Hell; assoc. prod., Rawhide. President, A. C. Lyles Productions, Inc. (Paramount Pictures).
PICTURES INCLUDE: Raymie, The Young and the Brave, Law of the Lawless, Stage to Thunder Rock, Young Fury, Black Spurs, Hostile Guns, Arizona Bushwackers, Town Tamer, Apache Uprising, Johnny Reno, Waco, Red Tomahawk, Fort Utah, Buckskin, Rogue's Gallery, Night of the Lepus, The Last Day, Flight to Holocaust.
TELEVISION: A Christmas for Boomer, Here's Boomer (series), Dear Mr. President, Conversations With the Presidents.

LYNCH, DAVID: Director, Writer. b. Missoula, Montana, Jan. 20, 1946. e. Pennsylvania Acad. of Fine Arts, where received an independent filmmaker grant from America Film Institute. Made 16mm film, The Grandmother. Accepted by Center for Advanced Film Studies in Los Angeles, 1970. Wrote and directed Eraserhead (with partial AFI financing) which became cult movie. Co-wrote and directed The Elephant Man (1980). 1984: Dune. 1986: Blue Velvet (s.p., dir.), Zelly and Me (actor).

LYNCH, PAUL M.: Director. b. Nov. 6, 1946.
PICTURES: Hard Part Begins; Blood and Guts; Prom Night; Hummungus; Cross Country; Flying, Blindside.
TELEVISION: Series: Voyagers, Blacke's Magic, Murder She Wrote, Twilight Zone (1987), Moonlighting, Cameo By Night.

LYNCH, RICHARD: Actor. b. Feb. 12, 1942. Made Bdwy. debut in The Devils, both on and off Bdwy. Also in Live Like Pigs, The Orphan, The Basic Training of Pavlo Hummel, The Lady From the Sea, Arthuro-U, Lion in Winter. Film debut in Scarecrow (1973).
PICTURES: The Premonition, Steel, The Formula, The 7-Ups, The Sword and the Sorcerer, Invasion U.S.A., The Delta Fox, Savage Dawn, Cut and Run, Night Force, Little Nikita, Bad Dreams, Melanie Rose, Spirit.
TELEVISION: Vampire, Alcatraz—The Whole Shocking Story, The Last Ninja, Sizzle, Good Against Evil.

LYNDON, VICTOR: Producer, Writer. b. London. Ent. m.p. ind. as asst. dir., Gainsborough Pictures, 1946–56; prod. mgr., 26 feature pictures; since 1957 prod., assoc. prod., pictures for Columbia, United Artists, M-G-M, Paramount, British Lion. 1984: novel, Bermuda Blue.
PICTURES INCLUDE: as prod. mgr. The African Queen, Albert R.N., The Admirable Crichton, As assoc. prod., Dr. Strangelove, Darling, 2001 A Space Odyssey. As prod., Spare The Rod, Station Six—Sahara, The Optimists.

LYNE, ADRIAN: Director.
PICTURES: Foxes; Flashdance; 9½ Weeks; Fatal Attraction.

LYNLEY, CAROL: Actress. b. New York, NY, Feb. 13, 1942.
PICTURES: The Light in the Forest, Holiday for Lovers, Blue Denim, Return to Peyton Place, The Last Sunset, The

Stripper, The Cardinal, The Pleasure Seekers, Bunny Lake Is Missing, The Maltese Bippy, Norwood, The Poseidon Adventure, Harlow, The Cat and the Canary, The Shape of Things to Come, Dark Tower.
TELEVISION: Movies: Shadow on the Land, The Smugglers, The Immortal, Weekend of Terror, The Cable Car Murder, The Night Stalker, The Elevator, Death Stalk, Willow B, Women in Prison, Flood, Fantasy Island, Having Babies II, Cops and Robin, The Beasts Are on the Streets.

LYNN, ANN: Actress. b. London, England, 1934. Ent. films and TV, 1958.
PICTURES INCLUDE: Naked Fury, Piccadilly Third Stop, The Wind of Change, Strongroom, Flame in the Streets, Black Torment, Four in the Morning, Baby Love, Hitler—The Last Days.
TELEVISION: After the Show, All Summer Long, Trump Card, Man at the Top, The Expert, Hine, The Intruders, Too Far, King Lear, The Zoo Gang. Recent films incl: The Uncle, Morning Tide, Shot in the Dark, Estuary, Who Pays the Ferryman, The Professionals, Zeticula, Westway. The Perfect House, Minder, To the Sound of Guns, Crown Court, Just Good Friends, Starting Out, Paradise Park. TV film series: The Cheaters, The Other Side of the Underneath.

LYNN, JEFFREY: Actor. r.n. Ragnar Godfrey Lind. b. Auburn, MA, Feb. 16, 1909; e. Bates Coll. m.p. debut in 1938.
PICTURES INCLUDE: Four Daughters, Yes My Darling Daughter, Daughters Courageous, Espionage Agent, Roaring Twenties, Four Wives, Child Is Born, Fighting 69th, It all Came True, All This and Heaven, Too; My Love Came Back, Four Mothers, Million Dollar Baby, Law of the Tropics, Body Disappears, For the Love of Mary, Black Bart, Letter to Three Wives, Strange Bargain, Home Town Story, Up Front, Captain China, Lost Lagoon, Butterfield 8, Tony Rome.
BROADWAY: (Revival) Dinner at Eight.

LYON, EARLE: Producer, Executive. b. Waterloo, IA, April 9, 1923. e. U. of California at L.A. Entered m.p. industry 1947. Independent prod. 1954–55 and 1958–59; 20th Century-Fox prod., 1956–57; at Columbia, 1959–60; Universal, 1960–63; developed new TV projects with Bob Banner Assoc., 1963; v.p. and gen. mgr. United Pictures Corp.
PICTURES INCLUDE: Silent Raiders, The Lonesome Trail, The Silver Star, Stagecoach Fury, The Quiet Gun, The Rawhide Trail, The Rebel Set, The Destructors, Cyborg 2087, Dimension 5, Destination Inner Space, Haunting at Castle Montego, The Ten Billion Dollar Caper, Panic in the City. TV: Tales of Wells Fargo.

LYON, FRANCIS D. "PETE": Director. b. Bowbells, ND, July 29, 1905. e. Hollywood H.S., U. of California at L.A. WWII: writer, prod., OWI; assoc. with training, exploitation and information films. Maj. U.S. Army Signal Corps.
PICTURES INCLUDE: As film editor: Shape of Things to Come, Knight Without Armour, Rembrandt, Intermezzo, Adam Had Four Sons, The Great Profile, Four Sons, Daytime Wife, Body and Soul (Acad. Award), He Ran All the Way. As director: Crazylegs, The Bob Mathias Story (Christopher Award), Walt Disney's The Great Locomotive Chase, Cult of the Cobra, The Oklahoman, Gunsight Ridge, Bailout at 43,000, Escort West, parts of Cinerama South Seas Adventure, The Young and the Brave, Destination Inner Space, The Destructors, The Money Jungle, The Girl Who Knew Too Much. Producer: Tiger by the Tail.
TELEVISION: Laramie, Perry Mason, Zane Grey Theatre, Bus Stop, M. Squad, Wells Fargo, Kraft Suspense Theatre, Death Valley Days, Follow the Sun, etc.

LYON, SUE: Actress. b. Davenport, IA, July 10, 1946. e. Hollywood Prof. Sch.
PICTURES INCLUDE: Lolita, Seven Women, Night of the Iguana, The Flim Flam Man, Evel Knievel, Crash, End of the World, Astral Factor.

LYONS, RICHARD E.: Producer. b. Boston, MA; e. Titlon Jr. Coll., Dartmouth Coll. Eastern sls. dept., MGM Pictures, Field Photographic Br., U.S. Navy, 1941–46; eastern artist, repertoire exec., MGM Records, 1946–55; story ed., Edward Small Prod., 1955–56; assoc. story ed., Univ., 1956–57; staff prod., MGM Studios, 1960. Now lectures and holds film seminars at colleges.
PICTURES INCLUDE: Frontier Gun, The Sad Horse, The Miracle of the Hills, Ride The High Country, Mail Order Bride, The Rounders, The Plainsman, Winchester 73, Stranger on the Run, Something for a Lonely Man, Coogan's Bluff, Death of a Gunfighter, Dirty Dingus Magee.
TELEVISION: The Daughters of Joshua Cabe, The Jerico Mile, Shootout in A One Dog Town, The Daughters of Joshua Cabe Return; Welcome to Xanadu, Kate Bliss and the Ticker Tape Kid; Roughnecks, Metromedia Prod. I Married Wyatt Earp.

LYONS, STUART: Producer. b. Manchester, England, Dec. 27, 1928. e. Manchester U. Ent. m.p. ind. 1955. Asst. dir. TV series 1955–56. Casting dir. Associated British, 1956/60.

Freelance cast. dir., 1960/63. Joined 20th Century-Fox Productions as cast. dir., 1963. Appt. director 20th Century-Fox Productions Ltd., 1967, man. dir. 1968. 1971: left Fox on closure Europe prod. Joined Hemdale Group as head of production, May, 1972. Left Hemdale Aug. 1973 to resume indep. prod.

PICTURES INCLUDE: As casting director: Over thirty films including Those Magnificent Men in Their Flying Machines, Cleopatra, The Long Ships, Guns at Batasi, High Wind in Jamaica, Rapture, The Blue Max. As indep. producer: The Slipper and the Rose, Meetings with Remarkable Men, Danses Sacrees, Turnaround. As prod. consultant: Eleni.

M

MAC ARTHUR JAMES: Actor. b. Los Angeles, CA, Dec. 8, 1937. e. Harvard. p. Helen Hayes, Charles MacArthur. Stage debut, summer stock; The Corn Is Green, 1945; Life with Father, 1953.

PICTURES INCLUDE: The Young Stranger, The Light in the Forest, The Third Man on the Mountain, Kidnapped, Swiss Family Robinson, The Interns, Spencer's Mountain, The Love-Ins, Cry of Battle, Angry Breed.

TELEVISION: Strike a Blow, Hawaii Five-0 (series).

MACCHIO, RALPH: Actor. b. Long Island, NY, Nov. 4, 1962. Started with TV commercials; first theatrical film role in Up the Academy (1980). On Broadway in Cuba and His Teddy Bear, 1986.

TELEVISION: Eight is Enough (series, 1980–81); Movies: Journey to Survival, Dangerous Company, The Three Wishes of Billy Grier.

PICTURES INCLUDE: Up the Academy, The Karate Kid, Teachers, Crossroads, The Karate Kid: Part II, Distant Thunder.

MacCORKINDALE, SIMON: Actor, Producer. b. England, Feb. 2, 1952. m. actress Susan George. On stage in Dark Lady of the Sonnets, Pygmalion, French Without Tears, etc.

PICTURES: Death on the Nile, Riddle of the Sands, Quatermass Conclusion, Caboblanco, The Sword and the Sorcerer, Jaws 3-D, Sincerely Violet, Stealing Heaven (prod.), The Lifeguard (prod.), White Rose (prod.).

TELEVISION: I Claudius, Romeo and Juliet, Jesus of Nazareth, Manimal, Obsessive Love, Falcon Crest (series).

MAC DONALD, PHILIP: Writer. b. Scotland; e. St. Paul's Sch. London. Novelist, playwright. Began screen career 1933.

PICTURES INCLUDE: Sahara, Action in Arabia, The Body Snatcher, Strangers in the Night, Dangerous Intruder, Man Who Cheated Himself, Circle of Danger, Mask of the Avenger, Ring of Fear, Tobor the Great.

MAC GRAW, ALI: Actress. b. Pound Ridge, NY, Apr. 1, 1938. e. Wellesley Coll. Editorial asst. Harper's Bazaar Mag.; asst. to photographer Melvin Sokolsky. Was top fashion model.

PICTURES INCLUDE: Lovely Way to Die (debut, 1968). Goodbye Columbus, Love Story, The Getaway, Convoy Players, Just Tell Me What You Want.

TELEVISION: The Winds of War, China Rose, Falcon Crest (series).

MACKERRAS, SIR (ALAN) CHARLES (MACLAURIN): Kt 1979; CBE 1974; Chief Conductor, Sydney Symphony Orchestra, Australian Broadcasting Commission, from 1982–85; frequent Guest Conductor, Vienna State Opera, Geneva and Zurich Opera, Royal Opera House Covent Garden, English National Opera, San Francisco Opera; b. Nov. 17, 1925; s. of late Alan Patrick and Catherine Mackerras, Australia; m. 1947, Helena Judith (Née Wilkins); e. Sydney Grammar Sch. Principal oboist, Sydney Symphony Orchestra, 1943–46; staff conductor, Sadler's Wells Opera, 1949–53; principal conductor BBC Concert Orchestra, 1954–56; freelance conductor with most British and many continental orchestras; concert tours U.S.S.R., S. Africa, N. America, 1957–66; conductor, Hamburg State Opera, 1966–69; musical dir., Sadler's Wells Opera, later ENO, 1970–77; chief guest conductor, BBC SO, 1976–79; frequent radio and TV broadcasts; many commercial recordings, notably Handel series for DGG and Janáček operas for Decca; appearances at many internat. festivals and opera houses. Evening Standard Award for Opera, 1977; Janáček Medal, 1978; Gramophone Record of the Year Award, 1978, 1980 and 1983. Grammy Award for best opera recording 1981 The House of the Dead by Janáček. Prix Fondation Jacques Ibert and the Stereo Review's Records of the Year Award 1983 and 1985 for Cunning Little Vixen by Janáček. Publications: ballet arrangements of Pineapple Poll and of Lady and the Fool; articles in Opera Magazine, Music and Musicians and other musical jls. Musical dir., Welsh National Opera, from 1987.

MAC LAINE, SHIRLEY: Actress. b. Richmond, VA, April 24, 1934. Sister of actor-prod. Warren Beatty. e. Washington and Lee H.S., Arlington, VA. Dancer, singer; signed by Hal Wallis; film

debut in Trouble with Harry (1955). Producer of film documentary on China, The Other Half of The Sky. Star of video: Relaxing Within.

PICTURES INCLUDE: Artists and Models, Around the World in 80 Days, Hot Spell, The Matchmaker, The Sheepman, Some Came Running, Ask Any Girl, Career, Can-Can, The Apartment, All in a Night's Work, Two Loves, My Geisha, The Children's Hour, Two for the Seesaw, Irma La Duce, What A Way To Go, John Goldfarb Please Come Home, The Yellow Rolls Royce, Gambit, Woman Times Seven, The Bliss of Mrs. Blossom, Sweet Charity, Two Mules for Sister Sara, Desperate Characters, The Possession of Joel Delaney, The Turning Point, Being There, Loving Couples, Change of Seasons, Terms of Endearment (Acad. Award, 1983), Cannonball Run II, Madame Sousatzka, Steel Magnolias.

TELEVISION: Shirley's World, Specials. Mini-Series: Out on a Limb (also co-s.p.).

AUTHOR: Don't Fall off the Mountain, You Can Get There from Here, Out on a Limb, Dancing in the Light, It's All In the Playing. Editor: McGovern: The Man and His Beliefs (1972).

MACLEOD, GAVIN: Actor. b. Mt. Kisco, NY, Feb. 28, 1931. e. Ithaca Coll.

PICTURES: I Want to Live, Compulsion, Operation Petticoat, McHale's Navy, The Sand Pebbles, Deathwatch, The Party, Kelly's Heroes.

TELEVISION: Hogan's Heroes (series), Mary Tyler Moore Show, The Love Boat. Movies: The Intruders, Only with Married Men, Ransom for Alice, Murder Can Hurt You, Scruples, Student Exchange.

MAC MAHON, ALINE: Actress. b. McKeesport, PA, May 3, 1899. e. Erasmus Hall, Barnard Coll. stage experience; Once in a Lifetime, Candida, Yurma (Lincoln Center). Screen debut 1931 in Five Star Final.

PICTURES INCLUDE: The Mouthpiece, One Way Passage (1931), Life Begins, Once in a Lifetime, Gold Diggers of 1933, Heroes For Sale, World Changes, Babbitt, Side Streets, Kind Lady, I Live My Life, Ah Wilderness, When You're in Love, Back Door to Heaven, Out of the Fog, The Lady Is Willing, Dragon Seed, Guest in the House, Mighty McGurk, The Search, Roseanna McCoy, Flame and the Arrow, Eddie Cantor Story, Man From Laramie, Cimarron, I Could Go On Singing, All the Way Home.

MAC MURRAY, FRED: Actor. b. Kankakee, IL, Aug. 30, 1908. e. Carroll Coll., WI. Sang and played in orchestra to earn tuition. To Hollywood with band; extra roles on screen; to N.Y. with comedy stage band, then joined Three's a Crowd revue; vaudeville circuits, night clubs. Film debut, Girls Gone Wild (1929).

PICTURES INCLUDE: Friends of Mr. Sweeney, Grand Old Girl, Car 99, Gilded Lily, Alice Adams, Hands Across the Table, Bride Comes Home, Trail of the Lonesome Pine, 13 Hours By Air, The Princess Comes Across, The Texas Rangers, Maid of Salem, Champagne Waltz, Swing High, Swing Low; Exclusive, True Confession, Men with Wings, Coconut Grove, Sing You Sinners, Cafe Society, Invitation to Happiness, Honeymoon in Bali, Little Old New York, Remember the Night, Too Many Husbands, Rangers of Fortune, Virginia, One Night in Lisbon, New York Town, Dive Bomber, The Lady Is Willing, Take a Letter Darling, The Forest Rangers, Star Spangled Rhythm, Flight for Freedom, Above Suspicion, No Time For Love, Standing Room Only, Double Indemnity, Murder He Says, Practically Yours, Where Do We Go From Here?, Captain Eddie, Smoky, Pardon My Past, Suddenly It's Spring, Egg and I, Singapore, A Miracle Can Happen, Miracle of the Bells, Don't Trust Your Husband, Family Honeymoon, Father Was a Fullback, Borderline, Never a Dull Moment, Callaway Went Thataway, Millionaire for Christy, Fair Wind to Java, The Moonlighter, Caine Mutiny, Pushover, Woman's World, Far Horizons, There's Always Tomorrow, At Gunpoint, Rains of Ranchipur, Gun For a Coward, Quantez, Good Day for a Hanging, The Shaggy Dog, Face of a Fugitive, The Oregon Trail, The Apartment, The Absent Minded Professor, Bon Voyage, Son of Flubber, Kisses for My President, Follow Me Boys, The Happiest Millionaire, Charlie and the Angel, The Swarm.

TELEVISION: My Three Sons (1960–72), The Chadwick Family. Movie: Beyond the Bermuda Triangle.

MACNAUGHTON, ROBERT: Actor. b. New York, NY, Dec. 19, 1966. Entered entertainment industry in 1979. Member Circle Rep. Co., N.Y.

TELEVISION: Angel City, Big Bend Country, The Electric Grandmother, Hear My Cry.

PICTURES: E.T.: The Extra-Terrestrial, I Am the Cheese.

STAGE: Critic's Choice, A Thousand Clowns, Camelot, The Diviners, The Adventures of Huckleberry Finn, Henry V, Tobacco Road, Master Harold . . . and the Boys, Tomorrow's Monday, Talley and Son.

MacNICOL PETER: Actor. b. Dallas, TX, 1954. m. film prod. Marsue Cumming. e. U. of Minnesota. Screen debut, Dragonslayer, 1981.

THEATER: NY Shakespeare Fest. Public Theater: Found a Peanut, Rum and Coke, Twelfth Night, Richard II. Regional theatre includes Guthrie, Alaska Rep., Long Wharf, Dallas Theatre Center, Trinity Rep. (Providence, RI); Execution of Justice, Crimes of the Heart (B'way debut), The Nerd, Romeo and Juliet.
PICTURES: Sophie's Choice, Heat.
TELEVISION: Johnny Bull, Faerie Tale Theatre, Molly Dodd, Walt Whitman (narrator).

MAC RAE, JEAN: Actress. b. Montreal, Quebec, Mar. 24, 1930. Worked for National Film Bd. of Canada, Canadian Bdcst. Corp., and repertory theatre in Canada; U.S. studios, including MGM, 20th-Fox, Columbia, and Paramount; as TV studios at Desilu and 20th-Fox.

MADDEN, BILL: Executive. b. New York, NY, March 1, 1915. e. Boston U. Joined Metro-Goldwyn-Mayer as office boy, 1930; student salesman, 1938; asst. Eastern div. sales mgr., 1939; U.S. Navy, 1942–46; Philadelphia branch mgr., M.G.M., 1947–53; Philadelphia branch mgr., 1954–59; Midwest div. sales mgr., 1960–68; roadshow sales mgr., 1969; v.p., general sales mgr., 1969–74, M.G.M.; corp., v.p. & gen. sls. mgr., MGM, 1974; retired from MGM, 1975; 1976-present, exec. consultant to motion picture industry; lecturer and instructor at UCLA. Member: Academy M.P. Arts & Sciences, Motion Picture Associates, American Film Institute. Motion Picture Pioneers.

MADDEN, DAVID: Executive. e. Harvard U., 1976; U. of California at L.A., M.A., 1978. Joined 20th Century-Fox in Nov., 1978 as story analyst. Named story editor, 1980; exec. story editor, 1982. Appt. v.p., creative affairs for 20th-Fox Prods., 1983; v.p., prod., 20th Century-Fox Prods; 1980, v.p., production, Paramount Pictures.

MADIGAN, AMY: Actress. b. Chicago, IL, 1957. m. actor Ed Harris.
PICTURES: Love Child, Streets of Fire, Places in the Heart, Alamo Bay, Twice in a Lifetime, Nowhere To Hide, The Prince of Pennsylvania, Shoeless Joe.
TELEVISION: The Laundromat, The Day After, The Ambush Murders, Travis McGee, Victims, Crazy Times.

MADISON, GUY: Actor. r.n., Robert Moseley. b. Bakersfield, CA, Jan. 19, 1922. e. Bakersfield Jr. Coll. U.S. Navy; m.p. debut in Since You Went Away, 1944; Wild Bill Hickok radio and TV shows, Star of Tomorrow, 1954.
PICTURES INCLUDE: Till the End of Time, Honeymoon, Texas, Brooklyn and Heaven, Massacre River, Drums in the Deep South, Red Snow, Charge at Feather River, The Command, The Hard Man, Five Against the House, Beast of Hollow Mountain, Last Frontier, On the Threshold of Space, Hilda Crane, Bullwhip, Gunmen of The Rio Grande, Sandokan Fights Back, Sandokan Against the Leopard of Sarawak, Mystery of Thug Island, Shatterhand, Payment in Blood. 1960–75 starred in 45 foreign films; Pacific Connection, Cross Bow, River River.
TELEVISION: Red River.

MADONNA: Singer, Actress. r.n. Madonna Louise Veronica Cicone. b. Pontiac, MI, 1961. m. actor Sean Penn. e. U. of Michigan. Gained fame as rock & recording star before film debut in Desperately Seeking Susan, 1985. NY stage debut: Speed-the-Plow, 1988.
PICTURES: Shanghai Surprise, Who's That Girl?, Bloodhounds of Broadway.

MADSEN, VIRGINIA: Actress. b. Winnetka, IL, 1963. Mother is Emmy-winning Chicago filmmaker, brother is actor Michael Madsen. Studied with Chicago acting coach Ted Liss. Prof. debut, PBS, A Matter of Principle.
PICTURES: Class (debut, 1983), Dune, Electric Dreams, Creator, Fire With Fire, Modern Girl, Zombie High, Slam Dance, Mr. North, Hot to Trot, Heart of Dixie.
TELEVISION: The Hitchhiker. Movies: Mussolini: The Untold Story; The Hearst and Davies Affair, Long Gone, Gotham.

MAGNOLI, ALBERT: Director, Writer.
PICTURES: Jazz (dir. only); Purple Rain; American Anthem (dir. only).

MAGNUSON, ANN: Actress, Performance Artist. b. Charleston, WV, 1956. e. Denison Coll. Intern at Ensemble Studio Theatre when she came to NY in 1978. Ran Club 57, an East Village club, 1979. Has created various characters such as Sweet Pea, Raven and Lady Fresh in East Village clubs, downtown art spaces & on college campuses since 1980.
PICTURES: The Hunger, Desperately Seeking Susan, Making Mr. Right, A Night in the Life of Jimmy Reardon, Sleepwalk, Mondo New York.
TELEVISION: Night Flight (1986), Made for TV, Alive from Off Center.

MAHARIS, GEORGE: Actor. b. Sept. 1, 1928.
PICTURES: Exodus, Sylvia, Quick Before It Melts, The Satan Bug, Covenant with Death, The Happening, The Desperadoes, Sword and the Sorcerer, Last Day of the War, The Land Grabbers.
TELEVISION: Route 66 (series). Movies: Escape to Mindanao, The Monk, The Victim, Murder on Flight 502, Rich Man, Poor Man, Look What's Happened to Rosemary's Baby, SST-Death Flight, Return to Fantasy Island, Crash, A Small Rebellion.

MAHONEY, JOCK: Actor. r.n. Jacques O'Mahoney. b. Chicago, IL, Feb. 7, 1919. Stepfather of Sally Field. e. U. of Iowa. Fighter pilot instructor, U.S.M.C.; enter m.p. ind. as stuntman; then started in westerns; TV show, Range Rider, many appearances on Loretta Young Show. Personal appearances; 1974–present Gallant Charger Prods., advertising mgr.
PICTURES INCLUDE: Away All Boats, Day of Fury, Showdown at Abilene, Battle Hymn, I've Lived Before, Land Unknown, Joe Dakota, Money, Women and Guns, Moro Witch Doctor, Walls of Hell, Tarzan Goes to India, Tarzan's Three Challenges. Serials: Son of the Guardsman, Cody of Pony Express, Roar of Iron Horse; Speak of Brothers, Glory Stompers, Spirits of the Wild.
TELEVISION: Range Riders (series), Yancy Derringer (series), The Fall Guy, Simon and Simon.

MAHONEY, JOHN: Actor. b. Manchester, Eng. Mem. of Stratford Children's Theatre from age 10–13. Moved to U.S. at 19, taught Eng. at Western Illinois U. Then freelance ed. of medical manuscripts; assoc. ed., Quality Review Bulletin. At 35 quit medical book editing work to become an actor. Studied acting, Chicago's St. Nicholas Theatre. Prof. debut, The Water Engine, 1977. Joined Steppenwolf Theatre Co. (The Hothouse, Taking Steps, Death of a Salesman).
THEATER: Orphans (Theatre World Award), The House of Blue Leaves (Tony and Clarence Derwent Awards).
PICTURES: Mission Hill, Code of Silence, The Manhattan Project, Streets of Gold, Tin Men, Suspect, Moonstruck, Frantic, Eight Men Out, Betrayed, Say Anything, Love Hurts.
TELEVISION: Chicago Story. Movies: First Steps, Listen to Your Heart, Lady Blue, Dance of the Phoenix, The Killing Floor, Trapped in Silence, Favorite Son.

MAIBAUM, RICHARD: Writer, Producer. b. New York, NY, May 26, 1909. e. New York U., U. of Iowa, B.A., M.A., Phi Beta Kappa. Plays on Broadway: The Tree, Birthright, Sweet Mystery of Life, See My Lawyer (1939). Member, Shakespearean Repertory Theatre in New York as player, 1933, From 1935 to 1942 worked on screenplays in Hollywood: MGM (They Gave Him a Gun, Stablemates, etc.); Columbia (Amazing Mr. Williams); Paramount (I Wanted Wings); 20th-Fox (Ten Gentlemen from West Point). Army, 1942–46, dir. Combat Film Div., final rank Lt. Col. To Para. prod.-writer, 1946, wrote-produced O.S.S., Song of Surrender; collab. & prod. The Great Gatsby. Prod. Sainted Sisters, The Big Clock, Bride of Vengeance, Dear Wife, No Man of Her Own, Capt. Carey, U.S.A.; free lance, 1953; collab. s.p., Paratrooper; adapt., Hell Below Zero; writer of Teleplays; exec. prod. MGM-TV, 1958–60.
PICTURES INCLUDE: Ransom, Cockleshell Heroes, Bigger Than Life, Zarak, Tank Force, Killers of Kilimanjaro, The Day They Robbed the Bank of England, Battle at Bloody Beach, Dr. No, From Russia with Love, Goldfinger, Thunderball, Chitty, Chitty, Bang Bang, On Her Majesty's Secret Service, Diamonds Are Forever, The Man with the Golden Gun, The Spy Who Loved Me, For Your Eyes Only, Octopussy, A View to a Kill, The Living Daylights, License Revoked (co-s.p.).
TELEVISION: Jarrett (prod., s.p.), Combat, Wagon Train.

MAIN, DAVID: Writer, Producer. b. Essex, England, 1929. Extensive television experience in Britain producing and directing for A.T.V., Granada, A.B.C. and B.B.C. Emigrated to Canada in 1960. Directed Moment of Truth for N.B.C., and Quentin Durgens M.P. for C.B.C., Famous Jury Trials for 20th Century Fox. In 1977–78 directed King of Kensington, Le Club, A Gift to Last for CBC. President of Velvet Screen Plays Ltd. a subsidiary of Quadrant Films Ltd.
PICTURES INCLUDE: Sunday in the Country, 1973 (story & co-writer), and It Seemed Like a Good Idea at the Time (co-writer); Find the Lady (story, co-writer, co-producer); Double Negative (co-prod.); Nothing Personal (co-prod.).

MAJORS, LEE: Actor. b. Wyandotte, MI, April 23, 1940. Star athlete in high school; turned down offer from St. Louis Cardinals in final year at Eastern Kentucky State Coll. to pursue acting career. In L.A. got job as playground supervisor for park dept. while studying acting at MGM Studio.
PICTURES INCLUDE: Will Penny (debut), The Liberation of L. B. Jones.
TELEVISION: The Big Valley, The Man From Shiloh, The Six Million Dollar Man (series), The Fall Guy (series). Movies: The Ballad of Andy Crocker, Weekend of Terror, The Gary Francis Powers Story, The Cowboy and the Ballerina, A Rocky Mountain Christmas, The Return of the Six Million Dollar Man and the Bionic Woman, Danger Down Under (exec. prod., actor).

MAKEPEACE, CHRIS: Actor. b. Montreal, Canada, April 22, 1964. e. Jarvis Collegiate Institute. Trained for stage at Second City Workshop.
PICTURES: Meatballs (debut, 1979), My Bodyguard, The Last Chase, The Terry Fox Story, The Oasis, The Falcon and the Snowman, Hanauma Bay, Vamps, Aloha Summer.
TELEVISION: The Mysterious Stranger, Mazes and Monsters, The Undergrads. Series: Going Great (host, 1982–84), Why On Earth?

MALDEN, KARL: Actor. r.n. Mladen Sekulovich. b. Gary, IN, Mar. 22, 1914.
B'WAY PLAYS: Golden Boy, Key Largo, Flight to West, Missouri Legend, Uncle Harry, Counterattack, Truckline Cafe, All My Sons, Streetcar Named Desire, Desperate Hours, Desire Under the Elms.
PICTURES INCLUDE: Boomerang, The Gunfighter, Where the Sidewalk Ends, Hall of Montezuma, Streetcar Named Desire, (Acad. Award best supporting actor, 1951), The Sellout, Diplomatic Courier, Operation Secret, Ruby Gentry, I Confess, Take the High Ground, Phantom of the Rue Morgue, On the Waterfront, Bombers B-52, Desperate Hours, Fear Strikes Out, Egghead, The Hanging Tree, One Eyed Jacks, Parrish, Time Limit (dir.), Billion Dollar Brain, Hot Millions, Blue Hotel, Patton, Cat O'Nine Tails, Wild Rovers, Summertime Killer, Beyond the Poseidon Adventure, Meteor, The Sting II, Twilight Time, Billy Galvin, Nuts.
TELEVISION: Streets of San Francisco (series), Skag (series), Captains Courageous, Word of Honor, With Intent to Kill, Alice in Wonderland, Fatal Vision; My Father, My Son.

MALICK, TERENCE: Producer, Writer, Director. b. Texas, Nov. 30, 1943. e. Harvard. Attended Oxford on Rhodes scholarship. Worked for Newsweek, Life and The New Yorker; lectured for year in philosophy at M.I.T. Studied at American Film Inst. in Beverly Hills and made short funded by AFI.
PICTURES INCLUDE: Badlands (prod., dir., s.p.), Days of Heaven (s.p., dir.).

MALIN, AMIR JACOB: Executive. b. Tel-Aviv, Israel, Mar. 22, 1954. e. Brandeis U., 1972–76; Boston U. Sch. of Law, 1976–79. Staff atty., WGBH-TV, Boston, 1979–81; ABM Industries, chief exec. off., 1979; now chm., pres. & CEO, Cinecom Entertainment Group. Films acquired and distributed include Come Back to the Five and Dime, Jimmy Dean, Jimmy Dean; Metropolis; The Brother from Another Planet; Stop Making Sense; Coca-Cola Kid; A Room with a View; Swimming to Cambodia; Matewan; A Man in Love; Maurice, Miles From Home (exec. prod.).

MALKOVICH, JOHN: Actor, Producer, Director. b. Benton, IL, Dec. 9, 1953. m. actress Glenne Headley. e. Illinois State U. Founding member Steppenwolf Ensemble in Chicago with group of college friends 1976. Starred in Say Goodnight, Gracie and True West (Obie Award) which then was brought to New York. NY Stage work includes Death of a Salesman on Bdwy. and TV with Dustin Hoffman. Director: Balm in Gilead, Arms and the Man, The Caretaker. Actor: Burn This.
PICTURES: The Killing Fields (debut), Places in the Heart, Eleni, Making Mr. Right, The Glass Menagerie, Empire of the Sun, Miles From Home, Les Liaisons Dangereuses, The Accidental Tourist (co-exec. prod.).
TELEVISION: Death of a Salesman, Rocket to the Moon, American Dream, Word of Honor.

MALLE, LOUIS: Director. b. Thumeries, France, Oct. 30, 1932. m. actress Candice Bergen. e. Sorbonne (Pol. Science). Studied filmmaking at Institut des Hautes Etudes Cinematographiques 1951–53. Started in film industry as assistant to Robert Bresson. Began career somewhat ahead of most young French directors referred to as the Nouvelle Vague (New Wave). Became internationally known with Les Amants (The Lovers) in 1958. Has also acted in films.
PICTURES INCLUDE: The World of Silence (co-dir. with J. Y. Cousteau); A Man Escaped (asst. to Bresson); Elevator to the Gallows, The Lovers, Zazie in the Metro, A Very Private Affair, Vive Le Tour (doc.), The Fire Within, Bon Baisers de Bangkok (doc.), Viva Maria, The Thief of Paris, William Wilson, Spirits of the Dead, Calcutta (doc.), Phantom India (doc.), Murmur of the Heart, Humain, Trop Humain (doc.), Place de la Republique, Lacombe, Lucien, Black Moon, Pretty Baby, Atlantic City, My Dinner with Andre, Crackers, Alamo Bay (also prod.), Au Revoir Les Enfants (Goodbye, Children–winner of Golden Lion at Venice Film Festival, 1987).
TELEVISION: Documentaries: God's Country, And the Pursuit of Happiness.

MALLERS, ANTHONY: Theatre Owner. b. Portland, IN, Oct. 4, 1933. e. Indiana U., B.S., business admin. Entered industry in 1957. Now pres. of Mallers Theatres, headquartered in Muncie, Ind.

MALMUTH, BRUCE: Director. b. Brooklyn, NY, Feb. 4, 1937. e. City Coll. of New York, Brooklyn Coll. Grad. studies in film, Columbia U. and USC. Acted in and dir. college productions.

Moved to California and obtained job as page at NBC. In Army assigned to special services as director; reassigned to New York. Upon release began 10-year Clio-winning career as dir. of TV commercials. Debut as director of features with Nighthawks, 1981. Founder, Los Angeles Aspiring Actors and Directors Workshop.
PICTURES: Nighthawks, The Man Who Wasn't There, Where Are the Children?
TELEVISION: Baseballs or Switchblades? (prod., writer, dir., Emmy Award-winning doc.), A Boy's Dream.

MALONE, DOROTHY: Actress. b. Chicago, IL, Jan. 30, 1925. e. Southern Methodist U. Screen debut in The Big Sleep, 1946.
PICTURES INCLUDE: Young at Heart, Battle Cry, Pillars of the Sky, Written on the Wind (Acad. Award, best supporting actress, 1956), Man of a Thousand Faces, The Last Voyage, The Last Sunset, Beach Party, Abduction, Golden Rendezvous, Winter Kills.
TELEVISION: Dick Powell Theatre, Dr. Kildare, Bob Hope Show, Jack Benny Show, The Untouchables, The Greatest Show On Earth, Peyton Place (series), Peyton Place: The Next Generation (movie).

MAMET, DAVID: Writer. b. Chicago, IL, Nov. 30, 1947. e. Goddard Coll. Husband of actress Lindsay Crouse. Artist-in-residence, Goddard Coll. 1971–73. Artistic dir. St. Nicholas Theatre Co., Chicago, 1973–75. Co-founder Dinglefest Theatre; assoc. artistic dir., Goodman Theatre, Chicago. Plays include Lakefront, The Woods, American Buffalo, Sexual Perversity in Chicago, Duck Variations, The Long Canoe, Edmond, A Life in the Theatre, The Water Engine, Prairie du Chien, Glengarry Glen Ross (Pulitzer Prize 1984 + 4 Tony Awards), Speed-the-Plow.
PICTURES: The Postman Always Rings Twice, The Verdict, The Untouchables, House of Games (also dir.), Things Change (dir., co- s.p), We're No Angels, Homicide (dir.).
TELEVISION: L.A. Law, Lip Service (exec. prod.).

MANASSE, GEORGE: Producer. b. Florence, Italy, Jan. 1, 1938. e. U. of North Carolina. Producer, GSF Productions, Inc.; for Cannon was assoc. prod., Joe, Jump; prod. Who Killed Mary What's Her Name; for GSF was exec. prod., Journey Through Rosebud, Change in the Wind. Prod. mgr.: The Bell Jar, Neighbors, Porky's II, The Next Day. Prod.: He Knows You're Alone, Red Scorpion (co-prod.).

MANBY, C. R.: Executive. b. Battle Creek, MI, Feb. 24, 1920. e. Hillsdale Coll., MI, A.B., 1942; Harvard Grad. Sch. of Bus. Admin., 1953. v.p., RKO General Inc., 1955–58; pres. Show Corp. of Amer., 1958–75; pres., RKO Pictures, 1978–84; chm., 1985–86. Retired.

MANCIA, ADRIENNE: Curator, Dept. of Film, Museum of Modern Art. b. New York, NY. e. U. of Wisconsin. B.A.; Columbia U., M.A. Worked in film distribution industry in New York prior to joining Dept. of Film, Museum of Modern Art, 1964; responsible for film exhibition since 1965. In 1977, appointed curator. Restructured Museums' Auditorium Exhibition Prog., creating a balance between classic cinema and contemporary work. Initiated innovative programs such as Cineprobe and What's Happening? Served on numerous int'l film juries. Co-founder New Directors/New Films. Chevalier de l'ordre des arts et des lettres (Republic of France, 1985). Ufficiale dell Ordine al Meritor della Republica Italiana, 1988.

MANCINI, HENRY: Composer. b., Cleveland, OH, April 16, 1924. Arranged music for the Glenn Miller Story, The Benny Goodman Story, then began composing scores.
PICTURES INCLUDE: Touch of Evil, High Time, Breakfast at Tiffany's (AA, 1961), Bachelor in Paradise, Hatari, The Pink Panther, Charade, A Shot in the Dark, Dear Heart, What Did You Do in the War, Daddy?, Two for the Road, Visions of Eight, The Girl from Petrovka, The Great Waldo Pepper, W. C. Fields and Me, The Pink Panther Strikes Again, Silver Streak, Revenge of the Pink Panther, Who Is Killing the Great Chefs of Europe?, Prisoner of Zenda, Nightwing, "10," Little Miss Marker, Change of Seasons, Back Roads, S.O.B., Mommie Dearest, Victor, Victoria, Whose Little Girl Are You?, Trail of the Pink Panther, Curse of the Pink Panther, The Man Who Loved Women, Harry and Son, Life Force, Santa Claus: The Movie, That's Life!, Blind Date, The Glass Menagerie, Without a Clue.
TELEVISION: Peter Gunn, Mr. Lucky, Newhart (theme), The Moneychangers, The Shadow Box, Thorn Birds, Blue Knights, Best Place to Be, Justin Case.

MANCUSO, FRANK G.: Executive. b. Buffalo, NY, July 25, 1933. e. State U. of New York. Film buyer and operations supvr. for Basil Enterprises, theatre circuit, from 1958 to 1962. Joined Paramount as booker in Buffalo branch, 1962. Named sls. repr. for branch in 1964 and branch mgr. in 1967. In 1970 appt. v.p./gen. sls. mgr., Paramount Pictures Canada, Ltd., becoming pres. in 1972. In 1976 relocated with Paramount in U.S. as western div. mgr. in L.A. In Jan., 1977, appt. gen. sls. mgr. of N.Y., office; two months later promoted to v.p.—

domestic distribution; 1979, named exec. v.p., distribution & mktg. In 1983 made pres. of entire Paramount Motion Picture Division. 1984, appointed chm. and chief exec. officer, Paramount Pictures. Motion Picture Pioneers Man of the Year, 1987.
MEMBER OF BOARD: Acad. of M.P. Arts and Sciences, M.P. Association of America, Will Rogers Memorial Fund, Variety Clubs Intl., Sundance Institute, Amer. Film Institute, Motion Picture Pioneers.

MANCUSO, FRANK, JR.: Producer. b. Buffalo, NY, Oct. 9, 1958. Son of Frank G. Mancuso. e. Upsala Coll. Began with industry at age 14, booking short subjects in Canadian theatres. Worked in gross receipts dept. in Paramount corporate offices in New York and later with paralegal div. Initial prod. work as location asst. for Urban Cowboy in Houston, TX. Served as assoc. prod. of Friday the 13th Part II and prod. of Friday the 13th Part III in 3-D.
PICTURES: Off the Wall, The Man Who Wasn't There, April Fool's Day, Friday the 13th, Part IV: The Final Chapter; Friday the 13th, Part VII (exec. prod.); Back to the Beach; Permanent Record.
TELEVISION: Friday the 13th: The Series (exec. prod.).

MANDEL, LORING: Writer. Long career writing scripts for TV, dating back to 1955 when penned Shakedown Cruise.
PICTURES: A House His Own, Countdown, Promises in the Dark, The Little Drummer Girl, etc.
TELEVISION: Do Not Go Gentle Into that Good Night (Emmy, 1967), Breaking Up, Project Immorality (Sylvania Award, 1959), Trial of Chaplain Jensen.

MANDEL, ROBERT: Director.
PICTURES: Night at O'Rears; Independence Day; F/X; Touch and Go, Big Shots.

MANDELL, ABE: Executive. b. Oct. 4, 1922. e. U. of Cincinnati. Entered broadcasting as actor on Cincinnati radio station prior to W.W.II. Served U.S. Army in Southwest Pacific, 1942–45. Formed independent motion picture distribution company in the Far East. Company, which became the largest independent motion picture distributor in the Far East, also operated and owned motion picture theaters throughout the Phillipines and Indonesia, 1946–56; network-regional sales exec., Ziv Television, 1956–58; intl. foreign operations, Independent Television Corporation, 1958; v.p.-foreign oper., 1960; v.p.-sales and adm., 1961; exec. v.p., 1962; pres. 1965. In 1976 ITC changed its corporate name from Independent Television Corp. to ITC Entertainment, Inc. President to 1983 of ITC Entertainment.

MANES, FRITZ: Producer. TV ad exec. and stuntman before becoming exec. prod. on films for Clint Eastwood.
PICTURES: in various capacities: The Outlaw Josey Wales, The Enforcer. Assoc. prod.: The Gauntlet, Every Which Way But Loose, Escape From Alcatraz, Bronco Billy. Prod.: Any Which Way You Can (also 2nd asst. dir.), Firefox (exec. prod.), Honky Tonk Man (exec. prod.), Tightrope (prod.), Sudden Impact (exec. prod.), City Heat (prod.), Pale Rider (exec. prod.), Ratboy (exec. prod.), Heartbreak Ridge (exec. prod., prod. mgr.).

MANGANO, SILVANA: Actress. b. Rome, Italy. Apr. 23, 1930. m. prod. Dino De Laurentiis. e. Dance Acad. of Jia Ruskaja. Model to 1949; Named Miss Rome. Film debut in L'Elisir D'Amore (1946).
PICTURES INCLUDE: Bitter Rice, Lure of Sila, Musolino, The Brigand; Anna, Ulysses, Mambo, Gold of Naples, This Angry Age, Tempest, The Sea Wall, Five Branded Women, La Grande Guerra, Crimen, Una Vita Difficile, Il Giudizio Universale, Barabbas, Teorema, Le Streghe, Oedipus Rex, Medea, Death in Venice, Decameron, Ludwig, Conversation Piece, Dune, Dark Eyes.

MANKIEWICZ, DON M.: Writer. b. Berlin, Germany, Jan. 20, 1922. p. Herman J. Mankiewicz. e. Columbia, B.A., 1942; Columbia Law Sch. Served in U.S. Army, 1942–46; reporter, New Yorker magazine, 1946–48; author of novels See How They Run, Trial, It Only Hurts a Minute; magazine articles, short stories. President, Producers Guild of America (1987).
TELEVISION: Studio One, On Trial, One Step Beyond, Playhouse 90, Profiles in Courage. Exec. story consultant: Hart to Hart, Simon & Simon, Crazy Like a Fox, Adderly.
PICTURES INCLUDE: Trial, I Want to Live.
TV PILOTS: Ironside, Marcus Welby, M.D., Sarge; Lanigan's Rabbi (collab.); Rosetti and Ryan (collab.)

MANKIEWICZ, JOSEPH L.: Writer, Director. b. Wilkes-Barre, PA, Feb. 11, 1909. e. Columbia U. Asst. corr. in Berlin, Chicago Tribune; Ufa studio, translating subtitles into Eng. for release in Eng. & U.S.; returned to U.S. 1929 to join brother, Herman, on Paramount writing staff; MGM, 1933; Fox, 1943–51; dir., La Boheme, Metropolitan Opera House, 1953. Academy Awards: 1949, Letter to Three Wives, best s.p., dir.; 1950, All About Eve, best s.p., dir.
PICTURES INCLUDE: Skippy, Million Dollar Legs, If I Had

a Million, Alice in Wonderland, Fury, Gorgeous Hussy, Mannequin, Three Comrades, Shopworn Angel, Philadelphia Story, Woman of the Year, Keys of the Kingdom, Dragonwyck, Somewhere in the Night, No Way Out, Late George Apley, Ghost and Mrs. Muir, House of Strangers, Letter to Three Wives, All About Eve, People Will Talk, 5 Fingers, Julius Caesar, Barefoot Contessa, Guys and Dolls, Quiet American, Suddenly Last Summer, The Honey Pot, There Was a Crooked Man, Sleuth.

MANKIEWICZ, TOM: Writer. b. Los Angeles, CA, June 1, 1942. Specializes in adventure/suspense films.
PICTURES INCLUDE: The Sweet Ride (debut), Diamonds Are Forever, Live and Let Die, The Man with the Golden Gun, Mother, Jugs and Speed, The Cassandra Crossing, The Eagle Has Landed, Dragnet (also dir.).
TELEVISION: Hart to Hart (s.p., dir.).

MANKOWITZ, WOLF: Author, Playwright, Producer, Impresario. b. London, 1924. Journalist. Ent. m.p. in 1952. Musical play based his story Expresso Bongo. Musical play, Make Me An Offer; Belle; Pickwick; Passion Flower Hotel.
PICTURES INCLUDE: Make Me An Offer, Kid For Two Farthings, The Bespoke Overcoat, Trapeze, Expresso Bongo, The Millionairess, The Long and Short and Tall, The Day The Earth Caught Fire, Where the Spies Are, Assassination Bureau; Bloomfield: Black Beauty, Treasure Island: The Hireling.
TELEVISION: Make Me An Offer, The Baby, The Girl, Should Happen to a Dog, Conflict, The Killing Stones, A Cure for Tin Ear, The Model Marriage, ABC of Show Business, The Battersea Miracle, Dickens of London.

MANN, ABBY: Writer. b. Philadelphia, PA, 1927. e. New York U. First gained fame on TV writing for Robert Montgomery Theatre, Playhouse 90, Studio One, Alcoa, Goodyear Theatre. Acad. Award for film adaptation of own teleplay Judgment at Nuremberg into theatrical film.
PICTURES INCLUDE: Judgment at Nuremberg, A Child Is Waiting, The Condemned of Altona, Ship of Fools, The Detective, Report to the Commissioner, War and Love.
TELEVISION: Medical Center, Kojak (creator), The Marcus-Nelson Murders, The Atlanta Child Murders, King, War and Love, Skag, The Simon Wiesenthal Story: The Murderers Among Us (co-s.p., co-exec. prod.).

MANN, DANIEL: Director. b. New York, NY, Aug. 8, 1912. e. Erasmus Hall, Brooklyn; Professional Children's Sch. Started as musician in resort hotels; then in Canada, on road; U.S. Army, W.W.II; then received scholarship to Neighborhood Playhouse, N.Y.; dir. teaching, TV dir.
BROADWAY: Come Back Little Sheba, Rose Tattoo, Streetcar Named Desire (City Center prod.), Paint Your Wagon.
PICTURES INCLUDE: Come Back Little Sheba, About Mrs. Leslie, Rose Tattoo, I'll Cry Tomorrow, Teahouse of the August Moon, Hot Spell, Last Angry Man, Mountain Road, Butterfield 8, Ada, Judith; A Dream of Kings, Who's Got the Action?, Who's Been Sleeping in My Bed?, For Love of Ivy, Willard, The Revengers, Maurie, Interval, Lost in the Stars, Matilda.
TELEVISION: Playing for Time, The Day the Loving Stopped, The Man Who Broke 1000 Chains.

MANN, DELBERT: Director, Producer. b. Lawrence, KS, Jan. 30, 1920. e. Vanderbilt U., Yale U. U.S. Air Force, 1942–45; stage mgr., summer stock, dir. Columbia, S.C. Town Theatre, 1947–49; asst. dir., NBC-TV, 1949; dir., NBC-TV, 1949–55. Past pres. Directors Guild of America.
PROGRAMS: Philco-Goodyear TV Playhouse, Producer's Showcase, Omnibus, Playwrights '56, Playhouse 90, Ford Star Jubilee, Lights Out, Mary Kay and Johnny, The Little Show, Masterpiece Theatre, Ford Startime.
STAGE: A Quiet Place, Speaking of Murder, Zelda, opera: Wuthering Heights; New York City Center.
PICTURES INCLUDE: Marty (Academy Award, best director, 1955), Bachelor Party, Desire Under the Elms, Separate Tables, Middle of the Night, The Dark at the Top of the Stairs, The Outsider, Lover Come Back, That Touch of Mink, A Gathering of Eagles, Dear Heart, Quick Before It Melts, Mister Buddwing, Fitzwilly, The Pink Jungle, Kidnapped, Birch Interval, Night Crossing.
TELEVISION: Heidi, David Copperfield, Jane Eyre. The Man Without a Country, A Girl Named Sooner, Breaking Up, Tell Me My Name, Home to Stay, All Quiet on the Western Front, To Find My Son, All the Way Home, The Member of the Wedding, Bronte, The Gift of Love, Love Leads the Way, A Death in California, The Last Days of Patton, April Morning (co-prod., dir.).

MANN, MICHAEL: Producer, Director, Writer. b. Chicago, IL. e. U. of Wisconsin, London Film Sch. 1965–72, directed commercials and documentaries in England, including Insurrection for NBC in Paris during the 1968 riots. Directed short film, Jaunpuri, winner of Juris Prize at Cannes Film Festival. Returned to U.S. in 1972 to direct documentary, 18 Days

Down the Line. Wrote for prime-time TV (episodes of Starsky and Hutch, Police Story, Vegas).
PICTURES: Thief (exec. prod., s.p., dir.), The Keep (s.p. dir.), Manhunter.
TELEVISION: The Jericho Mile (s.p., dir.). (DGA, 1980 best director award). Miami Vice (exec. prod.), Crime Story (exec. prod.).

MANNE, S. ANTHONY: Executive. b. New York, NY, July 19, 1940. e. Wharton Sch., U. of Pennsylvania, B.S., economics. Joined Columbia Pictures 1963; international dept. 1964; asst. mgr., Brazil, 1968; mgr., Brazil, 1972–76. Joined JAD Films, 1976; United Artists, v.p., Latin American supervisor; 1980; Columbia Pictures Intl., v.p., continental mgr., 1981; appointed sr. v.p., sales manager, 1984; exec. v.p., Tri-Star Intl, 1987; appointed exec. v.p., foreign mgr. Columbia Tri-Star Film Distributors, 1988.

MANNIX, DAVID K.: Executive. b. Brooklyn, NY, 1952. e. Fordham U., B.S.; Pepperdine U., M.B.A. Joined Paramount Pictures in 1973 as supervisor, TV accounting; 1976, Mgr. financial analysis; 1978, asst. studio controller; 1979, director, production operations; 1981, executive director, studio operations; 1984, promoted to v.p. 1988, promoted to senior v.p. studio operations.

MANSON, ARTHUR: Executive. b. Brooklyn, NY, Feb. 21, 1928. e. City Coll. of New York, grad. Inst. Film Technique, 1945; editor, American Traveler, U.S. Army, 1946; Advance agent, co. mgr., Henry V, U.S., 1948–50; producer's publ. rep., Stanley Kramer Distributing Corp., Samuel Goldwyn Productions, Lopert Films, dir. of adv. and publ., MGM Pictures of Canada, Ltd., 1952–53; publ. and adv. rep., Cinerama Corp., 1953–58; worldwide ad-pub Cinerama (wide screen process) 1958–60; adv. mgr., Columbia Pictures, 1961–62; nat'l dir. of adv., publ., Dino De Laurentiis, 1962–64; exec. asst. to v.p. chg. adv. & pub., 20th Century-Fox, 1964–67; v.p. chg, adv. & pub. Cinerama. Inc., and Cinerama Releasing Corp.; 1967–74; exec. v.p., sales & marketing, BCP, service of Cox Broadcasting Corp., 1974–75; v.p. chg. worldwide adv.-pub. Warner Bros., 1976. In 1977 formed own company, Cinemax Mkt. & Dist. Corp. and is pres.

MANTEGNA, JOE: Actor. b. Chicago, IL, Nov. 13, 1947. e. Morton Jr. Coll., Goodman Sch. of Drama, 1967–69. Member: The Organic Theatre Company, Chicago (The Wonderful Ice Cream Suit, Cops, and 2 European tours with ensemble). Later mem. of Goodman Theater where he began long creative assoc. with playwright-dir. David Mamet (A Life in the Theatre, The Disappearance of the Jews). In national co. of Hair, Godspell, Lenny. Broadway debut: Working.
THEATER: Bleacher Bums (also conceived and co-author), Leonardo (L.A., co-author), Glengarry Glen Ross (Tony Award), Speed-the-Plow.
PICTURES: Towing, Second Thoughts, Compromising Positions, The Money Pit, Off Beat, Three Amigos, Critical Condition, House of Games, Weeds, Suspect, Things Change (Venice Film Fest., best actor award, 1988).
TELEVISION: Soap, The Comedy Zone, Open All Night, Bleacher Bums (Emmy).

MANULIS, MARTIN: Producer, Director. b. New York, NY, May 30, 1915. e. Columbia U., B.A. 1935. Head of prod. John C. Wilson, 1941–49; mgr. dir., Westport Country Playhouse, 1945–50; dir. B'way plays; staff prod. & dir. CBS-TV, 1951–58; head prod. 20th-Fox Television. Now pres. Martin Manulis Prods. Ltd. 1987, artistic dir., Ahmanson Theatre, L.A.
BROADWAY: (and on tour): Private Lives, Made in Heaven, The Philadelphia Story, Pride's Crossing, Laura, The Men We Marry, The Hasty Heart, The Show Off.
TELEVISION: Suspense, Studio One, Climax, Best of Broadway, Playhouse 90. Mini-Series: Chiefs, Space, The Day Christ Died.
PICTURES INCLUDE: Days of Wine and Roses, The Out-of-Towners, Luv, Duffy.

MARA, ADELE: Actress. r.n. Adelaida Delgado; b. Dearborn, MI, April 28, 1923. m. Roy Huggins. Singer, dancer with Xavier Cugat orchestra; TV: Wheels (1978).
PICTURES INCLUDE: Shut My Big Mouth, Blondie Goes to College, Alias Boston Blackie, You Were Never Lovelier, Riders of the Northwest Mounted, Magnificent Rogue, Passkey to Danger, Traffic in Crime, Exposed, The Trespasser, Blackmail, Campus Honeymoon, Sands of Iwo Jima, Sea Hornet, Count The Hours, Wake of the Red Witch, Back from Eternity, Curse of the Faceless Man, The Big Circus.

MARAIS, JEAN: Actor. b. Cherbourg, France, Dec. 11, 1913. e. Coll. St. Germain, Lycée Janson de Sailly, Lycée Condorcet. Painter; photog; stage actor; French Air Army; m.p. debut in Pavillon Brule.
PICTURES INCLUDE: Carmen, Eternal Return, Beauty and the Beast, Ruy Blas, Les Parents Terribles, Secret of Mayerling, Souvenir, Orpheus, Eagle with Two Heads, Inside a Girl's Dormitory, Royal Affairs in Versailles, Paris Does Strange Things, Le Capitan, Le Bossu, La Princesse de Cleves, Le Capitaine Fracasse, Honorable Stanilleu, Agent Secret, Patute, Fantomas, Le Gentleman de Cocody.

MARANS, MARDI: Executive. e. U. of California. Worked in L.A. office of Doyle Dane Bernbach ad agency. Joined Warner Bros. in March, 1975, as asst. to media director. In 1979 appt. v.p. and director of media for WB, responsible for planning and placement of all advertising for all films distributed by co. on world-wide basis. 1986, exec. v.p., worldwide mktg., Paramount Picture.

MARCH, DONALD: Production Executive. b. New York, NY, July 26, 1942. Held senior programming positions with ABC-TV network and Robert Stigwood Organization before joining CBS in 1977 as director, special projects, motion pictures for TV and mini-series. Later promoted to v.p., motion pictures for TV. Left CBS to serve as pres. of Filmways' theatrical division in early 1979; later that year rejoined CBS as v.p., theatrical films, with responsibility for selection, development and production of pictures for theatrical release. 1984, sr. v.p., HBO Premiere Films. Independent prod., 1987 with ITC.
TELEVISION: Billionaire Boys Club (exec. prod.), Clinton and Nadine (prod.), David.

MARCHAND, NANCY: Actress. b. Buffalo, NY, June 19, 1928. m. actor-dir. Paul Sparer. Stage debut The Late George Apley (In ME, 1946), Bdwy debut Taming of the Shrew (1951). Also in The Balcony (Obie Award, 1960), Playboy of the Western World, On the Town, The Duel, Parents' Day, Morning's at Seven, Awake and Sing. Film debut, Bachelor Party (1957).
PICTURES: The Rise and Rise of Michael Rimmer, Promise at Dawn, Goodbye Mr. Chips, Ladybug, Ladybug, Me, Natalie, Tell Me That You Love Me, Junie Moon, The Hospital, From the Hip.
TELEVISION: Little Women (1951), numerous live prods. Series: Lou Grant, Beacon Hill, Adams Chronicles, Love of Life, Search for Tomorrow. Movies: Some Kind of Miracle, Willa, The Golden Moment—An Olympic Love Story, Sparkling Cyanide. Mini-Series: North and South Book II.

MARCUS, LOUIS: Producer, Director, Writer. b. Cork, Ireland, 1936. e. National U. of Ireland, B.A., 1959. Based in Dublin since 1959, where has made nearly 30 theatrical documentary films. Produces and directs for Louis Marcus Documentary Film Production of Dublin and Louis Marcus Films Ltd. of London. In 1964 appt. by Irish govt. as bd. mem. of Dublin's Abbey Theatre. In 1972 appt. by govt. as mem. of Cultural Relations Comm. of Dept. of Foreign Affairs. Elected mem. of Academy of M.P. Arts & Sciences (short subject branch) 1974.
PICTURES INCLUDE: Fleadh Cheoil, Horse Laughs, Woes of Golf, Children at Work, Conquest of Light.
AUTHOR: The Irish Film Industry (1968).

MARENSTEIN, HAROLD: exec. b. New York, NY, e. City Coll. of New York, 1937. Shipping, picture checking service, Warner Bros., 1935–45; Booking, Loew's Inc., 1945–48; Booking, contracts, Selznick Rel. Org., 1948–51; contracts, Paramount, 1951–52; asst. sls. gr., International Rel. Org., 1952; asst. sls. mgr., Janus Films, 1961–64; sls. exec., Rizzoli Films, 1965; 1967, nat'l. sales dir., Continental Dist.; gen. sales mgr., Cinemation Industries, 1968. v.p.-sales, dir., Cinemation Industries, 1971; 1976, gen. sls. mgr., General National Films; 1980, gen. sls. mgr., Lima Productions. Now retired.

MARGOLIN, JANET: Actress. b. New York, NY, 1943. e. N.Y.H.S. of Performing Arts. Discovered by Frank Perry while rehearsing in Bdwy. show, Daughter of Silence, and hired by him for lead in David and Lisa (1963).
PICTURES: The Greatest Story Ever Told, Bus Riley's Back in Town, Morituri, Nevada Smith, Enter Laughing, Buona Sera, Mrs. Campbell, Take the Money and Run, Annie Hall, Last Embrace, Distant Thunder.
TELEVISION: Planet Earth, The Last Child, Lanigan's Rabbi, The Triangle Factory Fire Scandal, Plutonium Incident, Murder in Peyton Place.

MARGULIES, STAN: Producer. b. New York, NY, Dec. 14, 1920. e. De Witt Clinton H.S., New York U., B.S., June, 1940. Army Air Force, May, 1942; pub. rel. Air Force and the Infantry, wrote service magazines, newspapers including Yank; spec. feature writer & asst. Sunday editor, Salt Lake City Tribune; publicist, RKO Studios, Hollywood, March, 1947; continued publicity work at CBS-Radio, 20th Century-Fox, Walt Disney Productions. Bryna Films, 1955; became vice-pres., 1958; also served exec. prod., TV series, Tales of the Vikings; prod. aide. Spartacus. 1984, with ABC Circle Films. 1987, joined Telecom Entertainment, Inc.
PICTURES INCLUDE: 40 Pounds of Trouble, Those Magnificent Men in Their Flying Machines, Don't Just Stand There, The Pink Jungle, If It's Tuesday, This Must Be Belgium, I Love My Wife, Willy Wonka and the Chocolate Factory, One Is a Lonely Number, Visions of Eight.
TELEVISION: The Morning After, I Will Fight No More Forever, Collision Course, Roots, Roots: The Next Generation, Moviola, Murder Is Easy, The Thorn Birds, A Caribbean

Mystery, Sparkling Cyanide, A Killer in the Family, The Mystic Warrior, A Bunny's Tale, Out on a Limb, Broken Angel (exec. prod.).

MARILL, ALVIN H.: Executive Editor. b. Brockton, MA, Jan. 10, 1934. e. Boston U., 1955. Director music programming, writer/prod., WNAC, Boston 1961–65; director music prog., WRFM, NY 1966– 67; publicity writer, RCA Records 1967–72; senior writer/editor, RCA direct marketing 1972–80; partner, TLK Direct Marketing 1977–80; manager, A & R Administration, RCA Direct Marketing 1980–83; Television editor, Films in Review 1973–84; Author: Samuel Goldwyn Presents; Robert Mitchum on the Screen; The Films of Anthony Quinn; The Films of Sidney Poitier; Katharine Hepburn: A Pictorial Study; Boris Karloff—A Pictorial Biography; Errol Flynn—A Pictorial Biography; Movies Made for Television 1964—86. Co-author: The Cinema of Edward G. Robinson; The Films of Tyrone Power. Editor: Moe Howard & The 3 Stooges. Assoc. editor: Leonard Maltin's TV Movies; Writer/researcher: The Great Singers (record/tape collections). Jury member: 1983 Locarno Film Fest.

MARIN, RICHARD (CHEECH): Actor, Writer. b. Los Angeles, CA, July 13, 1946. e. California State U, B.S. Teamed with Tommy Chong in improvisational group, City Works (Vancouver). Has made comedy recordings with him, including Sleeping Beauty, Cheech and Chong Big Bama, Los Cochinos, The Wedding Album (Grammy Award).
PICTURES: Cheech and Chong's Up in Smoke, Cheech and Chong's Next Movie, Cheech and Chong's Nice Dreams, Things Are Tough All Over, It Came from Hollywood, Still Smokin', Cheech and Chong's The Corsican Brothers, After Hours, Born in East L.A. (also s.p., dir.), Fatal Beauty, Rude Awakening.

MARK, LAURENCE M.: Producer, Executive. b. New York, NY. e. Wesleyan U., B.A.; & New York U., M.A. Started career as trainee and publicist for United Artists; also asst. to producer on Lenny, Smile, etc. Joined Paramount Pictures as mktg./prod. liaison dir. and then exec. dir., pub. for m.p. division in New York. Named v.p., prod./mktg. at Paramount Studio; 1980, v.p., west coast mktg.; 1982 promoted to post as v.p., prod. 1984, joined 20th Century-Fox as exec. v.p., prod.; 1986, established Laurence Mark Productions at Fox.
PICTURES: Black Widow (exec. prod.); Cookie (prod.); Working Girl (exec. prod.); My Stepmother is an Alien (exec. prod.).

MARKHAM, MONTE: Actor. b. Manatee, FL, June 21, 1938. e. U. of Georgia. Military service in Coast Guard after which joined resident theatre co. at Stephens College, MO, where also taught acting. Joined ACT Theatre, San Francisco, for three years. Made TV debut in Mission: Impossible episode.
PICTURES INCLUDE: One Is a Lonely Number, Hour of the Gun, Guns of the Magnificent Seven, Midway, Airport '77, Ginger in the Morning, Jake Speed, Defense Play (also dir.).
TELEVISION: Series: The Second Hundred Years, Mr. Deeds Goes to Town, The New Perry Mason. Movies: Visions, The Astronaut, Death Takes a Holiday.
BROADWAY: Irene.

MARKLE, FLETCHER: Writer, Director, Producer. b. Canada, March 27, 1921. Writer, dir., prod. Canadian Broadcasting Co. & BBC, London, 1942–46; prod., dir. Studio One series, CBS, 1947–48; Ford Theatre, CBS, 1948–49; writer, ed. & narrator The Robot Bomb, prize-winning doc. short, 1941; first m.p. dir. Jigsaw, 1949; thereafter Night into Morning, The Man with a Cloak; prod. Studio One series, CBS, 1952–53; prod., dir., Life with Father, CBS-TV, 1953–55; Front Row Center, 1955. Contributing dir. and/or prod. to various TV film series: Mystery Theatre, Panic, No Warning, Colgate Theatre, Lux Playhouse, M Squad, Buckskin, Rendezvous, Tales of the Vikings, Thriller, Hong Kong, 1956–61. Dir. Father of the Bride, 1961; dir. m.p., The Incredible Journey, 1962; Telescope series, CBC-TV, 1963–72. Head of TV Drama, Canadian Broadcasting Corp. 1970–73, Exec. prod., CBC-TV features and writer in residence. University of Toronto, 1974–75.

MARKLE, PETER: Director.
PICTURES: The Personals; Hot Dog; Youngblood, Bat-21.

MARKOWITZ, ROBERT: Director. Mostly on TV before theatrical debut with Voices, 1979.
TELEVISION: Children of the Night, Phantom of the Opera, The Deadliest Season, Song of Myself, With All Deliberate Speed, The 34th Star, The Storyteller, Kojak: The Belarus File, My Mother's Secret Life, Pray TV, A Long Way Home, Alex: The Life of a Child, Adam: His Story Continues, Life or Death in the Emergency Room, The Wall.

MARKS, ALFRED: O.B.E. Actor-Comedian. b. London, 1921. TV, own series, Alfred Marks Time with wife, comedienne Paddie O'Neil.
PICTURES INCLUDE: Desert Mice, There Was a Crooked Man, Weekend with Lulu, The Frightened City, She'll Have to Go, Scream and Scream Again, Our Miss Fred, Valentino, Sleeps Six.

TELEVISION: Blanding's Castle, Hobson's Choice, Paris 1900, The Memorandum.

MARKS, ARTHUR: Producer, Director, Writer, Film Executive. b. Los Angeles, CA, Aug. 2, 1927. At 19 began work at MGM Studios as production messenger. Became asst. dir. in 1950, youngest dir. member of Directors Guild of Amer., 1957. President and board member of Arthur Prod., Inc. & Arm Service Co. Exec. head of prod., Henry Plitt Theatres. Exec. in chg. prod., Lionshead, Ltd.
PICTURES: Togetherness (prod., dir., s.p.), Class of '74 (dir., s.p.), Bonnie's Kids (dir., s.p.), Roommates (dir., s.p.), Detroit 9000 (prod., dir.), The Centerfold Girls (prod., dir.), A Woman For All Men (dir.), Wonder Woman (exec. prod.), The Candy Snatchers (exec. prod.), Bucktown (dir.), Friday Foster (prod., dir.), J.D.'s Revenge (prod.-dir.), Monkey Hustle (prod., dir.). Writer: Empress of the China Seas; Gold Stars; Mean Intentions; Hot Times.
TELEVISION: Prod. of Perry Mason series, 1961–66; dir. of over 100 Perry Mason episodes; writer-dir. of numerous TV shows including I Spy, Mannix, Starsky & Hutch, Dukes of Hazzard.

MARKS, RICHARD E.: Executive. e. U. of California at L.A.; UCLA Sch. of Law. 1978–82, v.p., legal & business affairs for Ziegler/Diskant Literary Agency. Appt. pres., Major Business Brokers. Joined Paramount Pictures 1984 as atty. for Network TV Div., as project atty. for Family Ties & Cheers. 1985, named sr. atty. for M.P. Group.

MARKSON, BEN: Writer. b. Creston, IA, Aug. 6. Army Capt., W.W.II. Reporter, feature writer columnist, playwright (Is My Face Red?). Joined Warners, 1932 as writer; since author orig. s.p. dial., adapt., collab., many pictures. Writes many TV plays.
PICTURES INCLUDE: Here Comes the Navy, Woman-Wise, Danger, Love at Work, Is My Face Red?, Brides Are Like That, Half-Naked Truth, Lady Killer, That I May Live, White Cockatoo, Goodbye Again, Great Mr. Nobody, The Beautiful Cheat, A Close Call for Boston Blackie, Prison Ship, The Falcon in San Francisco, Mr. District Attorney, It Happened on Fifth Ave., Edge of Eternity, With My Face to the Enemy.

MARLOWE, LOUIS J.: Producer, Director. r.n. L. J. Goetten. b. St. Cloud, MN, Jan. 4. e. Hollywood H.S., U. of Southern California. Prop man, asst. dir., unit mgr., dir. special effects, shorts, second units Warner Bros., freelance dir. comedy series; Director features both theatrical and TV programs.
PICTURES INCLUDE: On the Air, Always Tomorrow, Handing It Back, Tradition, One Above All, Just a Boy.

MARSH, JEAN: Actress, Writer. b. London, Eng., July 1, 1934. New York stage debut Much Ado About Nothing, 1959. As a child appeared in films: Tales of Hoffman, Where's Charley. Co-creator, co-author and starred as Rose, Upstairs, Downstairs.
THEATER: Broadway: Travesties, The Importance of Being Earnest, Too True to Be Good, My Fat Friend, Whose Life Is It Anyway?, Blithe Spirit.
PICTURES: Cleopatra, The Limbo Line, Frenzy, Dark Places, The Eagle Has Landed, The Changeling, Return to Oz, Willow, Danny the Champion of the World.
TELEVISION: Series: Upstairs, Downstairs (Emmy Award 1972, 1974, 1975), Nine to Five, The Grover Monster, A State Dinner with Queen Elizabeth II, Mad About the Boy: Noel Coward—A Celebration, Habeas Corpus, Uncle Vanya, Twelfth Night, Pygmalion, On the Rocks Theatre, The Corsican Brothers, Master of the Game.

MARSHALL, ALAN: Producer. b. London, Eng., Aug. 12, 1938. Co-founder Alan Parker Film Company, 1970. Formerly film editor. Received Michael Balcon Award, British Acad., Outstanding Contribution to Cinema, 1985.
PICTURES: Bugsy Malone, Midnight Express, Fame, Shoot the Moon, Pink Floyd: The Wall, Another Country (Cannes Film Fest, best artistic contribution award, 1984), Birdy (Special Jury Award, Cannes Film Fest., 1985), Angel Heart, Homeboy.
TELEVISION: No Hard Feelings, Our Cissy, Footsteps.

MARSHALL, E. G.: Actor. b. Minnesota, June 18, 1910. Acting debut with Oxford Players, 1933. Numerous TV appearances on all networks; film debut in House on 92nd St. (1945).
BROADWAY: Jason, Jacobowsky and the Colonel, Skin of Our Teeth, Iceman Cometh, Woman Bites Dog, The Survivors, The Gambler, The Crucible, The Little Foxes.
PICTURES INCLUDE: 13 Rue Madeleine, Call Northside 77, Caine Mutiny, Pushover, Bamboo Prison, Broken Lance, Silver Chalice, Left Hand of God, Scarlet Hour, 12 Angry Men, Bachelor Party, Town Without Pity, The Chase, Tora, Tora, Tora, The Bridge at Remagen, The Pursuit of Happiness, Interiors, Superman II, Creepshow, Power, My Chauffeur, La Gran Fiesta.
TELEVISION: The Defenders, The Bold Ones. Movies: The

Winter of Our Discontent, Under Siege, At Mother's Request, Emma, Queen of the South Seas.

MARSHALL, FRANK: Producer. Worked on first feature film in 1967 while still a student at UCLA. Protege of Peter Bogdanovich, working on his production crew and serving as assoc. prod. on Paper Moon, Daisy Miller, Nickelodeon, etc. Line producer on Orson Welles' The Other Side of the Wind (unreleased) and Martin Scorsese's The Last Waltz. Worked with Walter Hill on The Driver (assoc. prod.) and The Warriors (exec. prod.). Began collaboration with Steven Spielberg as prod. for Raiders of the Lost Ark.
PICTURES: Poltergeist (prod.); E.T.: The Extra-Terrestrial (prod. suprv.); Twilight Zone—The Movie (exec. prod.); Indiana Jones and the Temple of Doom (exec. prod.); Gremlins (exec. prod.); Goonies (exec. prod.); Back to the Future (exec. prod.); The Color Purple (co-prod.); Young Sherlock Holmes (co-prod.), An American Tail (co-exec. prod.); Innerspace (co-exec. prod.), The Money Pit (prod.), Empire of the Sun (co-exec prod.), Who Framed Roger Rabbit? (co-prod.); Indiana Jones III (exec. prod.).

MARSHALL, GARRY: Producer, Director, Writer. b. New York, NY, Nov. 13, 1934. Brother of Penny Marshall. e. Northwestern U. Copy boy and reporter for N.Y. Daily News while writing comedy material for Phil Foster, Joey Bishop. Was drummer in his own jazz band and successful stand-up comedian and playwright. Turned Neil Simon's play The Odd Couple into long running TV series (1970). Partner with Jerry Belson many years.
PICTURES: Writer-Producer: How Sweet It Is, The Grasshopper. Director: Young Doctors in Love (also exec. prod.), The Flamingo Kid (also s.p.), Overboard (dir. only), Beaches. Acted in Lost in America.
TELEVISION: Writer for Jack Paar Show, Joey Bishop Show, Danny Thomas Show, Lucy, Dick Van Dyke Show, I Spy, etc. Creator and exec. prod.: Happy Days, Laverne and Shirley, Mork and Mindy, Angie.

MARSHALL, LARRY: Comedian, Actor, Writer, Songwriter. b. Clarkston, Scotland. Trained Rutherglen repertory theatre. Own daily lunchtime television show for eight years. Appeared in many major television drama series; and light entertainment show; own evening shows; comedy and panel games. Since 1973 written, produced and starred in summer show, Jamie's Scottish Night Out running to 1987.

MARSHALL, PENNY: Actress. b. New York, NY, Oct. 15, 1942. Daughter of industrial filmmaker and Laverne and Shirley prod., Tony Marscharelli, and sister of prod.-dir. Garry Marshall. Dropped out of U. of New Mexico to teach dancing. Acted in summer stock and competed on The Original Amateur Hour before going to Hollywood to make TV debut in The Danny Thomas Hour (1967–68). Debut as theatrical director 1986: Jumpin' Jack Flash.
TELEVISION: Friends and Lovers (1974), Wives (pilot), The Bob Newhart Show, The Mary Tyler Moore Show, Chico and the Man, The Odd Couple (series), Laverne and Shirley (series). Movies: Let's Switch, Love Thy Neighbor, Challenge of a Lifetime, More Than Friends.
PICTURES: How Sweet It Is, The Savage Seven, The Grasshopper, 1941, Movers and Shakers, Jumping Jack Flash (dir.), Big (dir.).

MARSHALL, PETER: Actor, TV Show Host. r.n. Pierre La Cock. b. Clarksburg, WV, March 30. Brother of actress Joanne Dru. Began career as NBC page in N.Y. Did plays both on and off Bdwy., starring with Julie Harris in Skyscraper. Teamed with the late Tommy Noonan in comedy act for nightclubs, guesting on Ed Sullivan Show and other variety shows. In 1950 made Las Vegas stage debut and since has been headliner there and in Reno and Lake Tahoe. On London stage in H.M.S. Pinafore; Bye, Bye Birdie. In La Cage aux Folles (national company and B'way), 42nd St. (Atlantic City).
PICTURES INCLUDE: Ensign Pulver, The Cavern, Americathon, Annie.
TELEVISION: Two of the Most (local N.Y. show), The Hollywood Squares (host), many guest appearances.

MARSHALL, ZENA: Actress. b. Kenya, Africa, 1926. e. France, finishing school in Ascot, Eng. Made her stage debut in repertory. Many TV appearance U.S. and England including Bob Hope show, Harpers W.I., Ghost Squad.
PICTURES INCLUDE: Caesar and Cleopatra (debut, 1945), Good Time Girl, Miranda, Sleeping Car to Trieste, Marry Me, Dark Interval, Blind Man's Bluff, Love's a Luxury, Deadly Nightshade, My Wife's Family, Bermuda Affair, Let's Be Happy, Dr. No, The Guilty Party, Those Magnificent Men in Their Flying Machines, The Terrornauts.
TELEVISION: International Detective, Invisible Man, Dial 999, Danger Man, Sir Francis Drake, Man of the World, Human Jungle, Sentimental Agent, Court Martial.

MARTEL, GENE: Producer, director. b. New York, NY, June 19, 1916. e. City Coll. of New York , U. of Alabama, Sorbonne, Paris. Newspaperman, New York and Birmingham, AL;

dancer, actor, choreographer, director Broadway; prod. dir., many documentaries; films for State Department, others; dir. for Paramount Pictures. Joined Princess Pictures 1952 to make films in Europe; formed own company, Martel Productions Inc., 1954.
PICTURES INCLUDE: Check-mate, Double-barrelled Miracle, The Lie, Double Profile, Sergeant and the Spy, Black Forest, Eight Witnesses, Fire One, Phantom Caravan, Doorway to Suspicion, Diplomatic Passport, Immediate Disaster.

MARTENS, RALPH R.: Executive b. New York, NY. e. State U. of New York at Albany. USMC-USMCR 1962–present, 1970–73 Tampax Inc. 1973–79 Pannell Kerr Forster and Co., CPA's 1979–84, asst. treas. Motion Picture Association of America, MPEAA, AMPECA, AFRAM FILMS, 1984 Treas., MPAA, MPEAA, AMPECA and AFRAM.

MARTIN, DEAN: Actor. r.n. Dino Crocetti. b. Steubenville, OH, June 17, 1917. e. Steubenville H.S. Was amateur prizefighter; worked at odd jobs, mill hand, gasoline attendant, prior to acting career. Joined Jerry Lewis, comedian at 500 Club, Atlantic City, NJ, as straight man-singer, 1946; played many theatres, night clubs until 1956. Team film debut: My Friend Irma (1949). Voted (with Jerry Lewis) one of the top ten Money-Making Stars in Motion Picture Herald-Fame poll, 1951, 1953–55; Number One, 1952.
PICTURES INCLUDE: My Friend Irma Goes West, At War with the Army, That's My Boy, The Stooge, Sailor Beware, Jumping Jacks, The Caddy, Scared Stiff, Money from Home, Living It Up, Three Ring Circus, You're Never Too Young, Artists and Models, Pardners, Hollywood or Bust, 10,000 Bedrooms, The Young Lions, Some Came Running, Rio Bravo, Career, Who Was That Lady?, Bells Are Ringing, Ocean's 11, Ada, Sergeants 3, Who's Got the Action?, Toys in the Attic, Who's That Sleeping in My Bed, Robin and the Seven Hoods, Kiss Me Stupid, Sons of Katie Elder, Rough Night in Jericho, How to Save a Marriage, Airport, The Ambushers, The Wrecking Crew, Something Big, Showdown, Mr. Ricco, The Cannonball Run, Cannonball Run II.
TELEVISION: Club Oasis, Dean Martin Show. Golden Globe Award.

MARTIN, DEWEY: Actor. b. Katemcy, TX, Dec. 8, 1923. e. U. of Georgia. U.S. Navy, W.W.II; actor, little theatres & stock; film debut in Knock on Any Door (1949).
PICTURES INCLUDE: Kansas Raiders, The Thing, Big Sky, Tennessee Champ, Prisoner of War, Men of the Fighting Lady, Land of the Pharaohs, Desperate Hours, Proud and Profane, 10,000 Bedrooms.
TELEVISION: Daniel Boone (series), Doc Holliday (series), Wheeler and Murdoch.

MARTIN, EDWIN DENNIS: Executive. b. Columbus, GA, Jan. 30, 1920. e. U. of Georgia, B.S., 1940. Past pres., Martin Theatre Cos.; past pres. TOA, International. Retired.

MARTIN, MARY: Actress. b. Wetherford, TX, Dec. 1, 1914. e. Ward-Belmont Sch., Nashville, TN. Mother of actor Larry Hagman. m.p. debut in 1939. Received Special Tony Award, 1948. Autobiography: My Heart Belongs (1976).
STAGE: Lute Song, Leave It to Me, One Touch of Venus, South Pacific, Annie Get Your Gun, Kind Sir, Peter Pan (Tony Award, 1955), Jennie, Sound of Music (Tony Award, 1960), I Do I Do, Do You Turn Somersaults?, Legends (road tour with Carol Channing).
PICTURES INCLUDE: Great Victor Herbert (debut, 1939), Rhythm on the River, Love Thy Neighbor, Kiss the Boys Goodbye, New York Town, Birth of the Blues, Star Spangled Rhythm, True to Life, Happy Go Lucky, Night and Day, Main Street to Broadway.
TELEVISION: Ford anniversary show, Rodgers & Hammerstein Cavalcade show. Peter Pan (Emmy, 1955), Valentine, Together with Music (with Noel Coward), Over Easy (series host).

MARTIN, MILLICENT: Actress, Singer. b. Romford, Eng., June 8, 1934. Toured U.S. in The Boy Friend, 1954–57.
STAGE: Expresso Bongo, The Crooked Mile, Our Man Crichton, Tonight at 8, The Beggars Opera, Puss 'n Boots, The Card, Absurd Person Singular, Aladdin, Side by Side by Sondheim, King of Hearts, Move Over Mrs. Markham, Noises Off, Two Into One, Follies, 42nd Street (N.Y. & L.A.).
TELEVISION: International Detective Series, Millie, That Was the Week That Was, Harry Moorings; own series, Mainly Millicent, Kiss Me Kate; 1966 own series, Millicent TV; 1967: London Palladium Color Show, USA, Danny Kaye, Piccadilly London; From a Bird's Eye View (own series); Tom Jones show, Englebert Humperdinck show, Downtown with Michael Nouri, LA Law, Max Headroom, Network.
PICTURES INCLUDE: The Horsemaster, The Girl on the Boat, Nothing but the Best, Alfie, Stop the World I Want To Get Off.

MARTIN, PAMELA SUE: Actress. b. Westport, CT, Jan. 15, 1953. Did modelling and TV commercials before entering films.
PICTURES: To Find a Man, The Poseidon Adventure,

Buster and Billie, Our Time, The Lady in Red, Torchlight (also assoc. prod. & s.p.).
TELEVISION: Series: Nancy Drew Mysteries, Dynasty. Movies: The Gun and the Pulpit, The Girls from Huntington House, Angel on My Shoulder, Bay Coven.

MARTIN, STEVE: Actor. b. Waco, TX, 1945. m. actress Victoria Tennant. e. Long Beach Coll., U. of California at L.A. Writer for various TV comedy shows (Smothers Brothers, Sonny & Cher, etc.). Broadway debut Waiting For Godot, (with Robin Williams), 1988.
PICTURES: The Kids Are Alright, The Muppet Movie, The Jerk (also co-s.p.), Pennies from Heaven, Dead Men Don't Wear Plaid (also co.-s.p.), The Man with Two Brains (also co-s.p.), Lonely Guy, All of Me, Little Shop of Horrors, Three Amigos (also co-s.p. & exec. prod.); Roxanne (also exec. prod., s.p.); Planes, Trains & Automobiles, Dirty Rotten Scoundrels.
TELEVISION: Steve Martin—A Wild and Crazy Guy, Steve Allen Comedy Hours, Comedy Is Not Pretty, Saturday Night Live, Smothers Brothers Comedy Hour 20th Reunion.

MARTIN, TONY: Singer, Musician, Actor. b. Oakland, CA, Dec. 25, 1914. e. Alvin Morris. e. Oakland H.S., St. Mary's Coll. m. Cyd Charisse, actress-dancer. Sang, played saxophone & clarinet in high school band, engaged by nearby theatres for vaudeville; with Five Red Peppers, jazz group at 14 yrs.; two yrs. later with band, Palace Hotel, San Francisco; radio debut Walter Winchell program, 1932; joined Tom Gerund's band, World's Fair Chicago, 1933; played night clubs. First starring radio show, Tune Up Time (singer & emcee); on Burns and Allen program; own show for Texaco, Carnation Contented Hour.
RECORDINGS INCLUDE: Begin the Beguine, Intermezzo, The Last Time I Saw Paris, I'll See You in My Dreams, Domino, September Song, For Every Man There's a Woman.
PICTURES INCLUDE: Sing Baby Sing, Follow The Fleet, You Can't Have Everything, Ali Baba Goes To Town, Music in My Heart, Ziegfield Girl, The Big Store, Till The Clouds Roll By, Cabash, Two Tickets to Broadway, Here Come the Girls, Easy to Love, Deep in My Heart, Hit the Deck, Quincannon Frontier Scout, Let's Be Happy.

MARTON, ANDREW: Director. b. Budapest, Hungary, Jan. 26, 1904. Vita Film, Vienna, 1922; to Hollywood, with Ernst Lubitsch, 1923; started directing in Berlin, then in London, Wolf's Clothing, Secret of Stamboul, School for Husbands; in Hollywood, Little Bit of Heaven, Gentle Annie, Gallant Bess.
PICTURES INCLUDE: King Solomon's Mines, Wild North, Storm Over Tibet, Devil Makes Three, Gypsy Colt, Prisoner of War, Men of the Fighting Lady, Green Fire, Underwater Warrior, Cinerama Seven Wonders of the World, It Happened in Athens, The Longest Day, The Thin Red Line, Crack in the World, Clarence the Crosseyed Lion, Around the World Under the Sea, Birds Do It, Africa-Texas Style, Mohammed, Messenger of God.
TELEVISION: Man and the Challenge, Daktari, Cowboy in Africa, The Sea Hunt.

MARX, SAMUEL: Writer, Producer. b. New York, NY, Jan. 26, 1902.
PICTURES INCLUDE: Lassie Come Home, This Man's Navy, My Brother Talks to Horses, The Beginning or End, A Lady Without Passport, Grounds for Marriage, Kiss of Fire, Ain't Misbehavin', Waterloo, Rome, The Ravine.

MASEFIELD, JOSEPH R.: Executive, Producer, Director, Writer. b. New York, NY, June 20, 1933. e. American Acad. of Dramatic Arts, 1950. Writer-performer, club work (as Steve Parker). Later, actor in stock; formed EEF Film Productions, 1956; prod. A Story Like Two (short), A City Eats (doc.). In m.p. as unit mgr., asst. dir. and prod. Mgr. Later writer and film editor: Montage (Time-Life); Ages of Man (IBM); Festival of Two Worlds (Bell Telephone Hour) and special, The New Face of Israel. Asst. dir., prod. mgr., Mitgebracht Aus New York (German TV), The Devils Doubloon, (feature); Writer-director, Citizen Smith, feature documentary. Co-director and assoc. prod. Hear My Song, (Cavalier Films), 1969 producer The Spy. 1969, vice pres. in charge of prod. PCI, Inc. Public Relations director, The Max Steiner Music Society; pres., Joseph R. Masefield & Associates. In 1974, formed Majer Prods. with Steve Jerro.
PICTURES INCLUDE: A New Life, The Vanquished, Trio, Living Planet, The Burning Man.

MASINA, GIULIETTA: Actress. b. Giorgio di Piano, Italy, Feb. 22, 1921. m. director Federico Fellini. e. U. of Rome. Was a school teacher before acting on stage and on radio in Rome. Met Fellini when he asked her to audition for radio soap opera, 1942. Film debut: Rossallini's Paisan, 1946.
PICTURES: Without Pity, Variety Lights, The White Sheik, Behind Closed Shutters, The Greatest Love, La Strada, Forbidden Women, The Swindlers, Nights of Cabiria, Fortunella, Juliet of the Spirits, Non Stuzzicate la Zanazara, The Madwoman of Chaillot, Ginger and Fred.

MASLANSKY, PAUL: Producer, Director, Writer. b. New York, NY, Nov. 23, 1933. Studied filmmaking at Cinemateque Français where made a documentary (Letter from Paris) which won Cannes Festival award. Asst. dir. on Counterfeit Traitor; followed by prod. mgr. on several films in Europe, including The Running Man and Jason and the Argonauts. Wrote and produced Gothic horror films, including Castle of the Living Dead. Covered Israeli war in 1967 with CBS film group; spent year in Russia on The Red Tent, followed by The Blue Bird. Filmed Big Truck and Poor Claire in Israel; Miracles Still Happen in Brazil.
PICTURES: Damnation Alley (co-prod.), When You Comin' Back, Red Ryder (co-prod.), Hot Stuff, The Villain, Scavenger Hunt, Police Academy 2 (assoc. prod.), Circle of Iron (co-prod.), Love Child (prod.), Return to Oz, Police Academy 3, Police Academy 4, Police Academy 5: Assignment Miami Beach, For Better or Worse (exec. prod.), Police Academy 6 (co-prod.), The Lost (exec. prod.).
TELEVISION: The Gun and the Pulpit, King.

MASON, JOHN DUDLEY: Executive. b. Ashland, KY, Oct 29, 1949. e. Amherst Coll., B.A., cum laude, 1971; Claremont Graduate Sch. and University Center, M.A., 1973; Amos Tuck Sch. of Business Administration, Dartmouth Coll., M.B.A., 1978. Program officer, National Endowment for the Humanities, 1972–76; analyst (1978–79), asst. mgr. (1979–80), mgr. (1980) strategic planning, Consolidated Rail Corp.; Consultant, Frito-Lay, Division, PepsiCo (1980–82); mgr, corporate planning, The Dun & Bradstreet Corp. (1982–86); finance director, anti-piracy, Motion Picture Association of America, Inc. (1986–present). Chairman, Finance Comm. and mem., bd. of dir. Association de Gestion Int'l. Collective des Oeuvres Audiovisuelles (AGICOA) 1987–88. Director, Instituto Venezolano de Representacion Cinematografica (INVERECI), Caracas, Venezuela (1988–present). Director: Foundation for the Protection of Film & Video Works (FVWP), Taipei, Taiwan (1987–present).

MASON, KENNETH M.: Executive. b. Rochester, NY; Sept. 21, 1917. e. Washington and Jefferson Coll.; U. of Rochester, graduate work. Began career with Eastman Kodak Co. in Kodak Park cine processing dept. in 1935; transferred following year to film developing dept. at Kodak Research Laboratories. Returned to college in 1938 to complete studies and returned to Kodak year later to same dept. Later joined film planning dept., remaining there until entering military service in 1943. Returned to Kodak in 1946 as staff engineer in Kodak Office motion picture film dept. In 1950 appt. mgr. of Midwest Division, of M.P. Film Dept.; became gen. mgr., Midwest Division, m.p. products sales dept. in 1963; named sls. mgr. of New York City region in 1965; appt. regional sls. mgr., Pacific Southern Region, Hollywood, in 1970. On Jan. 1, 1974 appt. mgr., product programs and research, Motion Picture and Audiovisual Markets Division, Kodak Office. On March 18, 1974 named gen. mgr. of that division. Elected asst. v.p. of co. on March 28, 1974, v.p., Dec. 11, 1978. Retired Oct. 1, 1982. Former chm., Inter-Society Committee for the Enhancement of Theatrical Presentation.
MEMBER: Pres., Board of Trustees of Washington and Jefferson Coll.; past pres. of Society of Motion Picture & Television Engineers and honorary member; honorary fellow of British Kinematograph Sound & Television Society; mbr. of University Film Assn., Motion Picture Academy, American Society of Cinematographers, Variety Club. Board of Directors: Will Rogers Institute, Allied Film & Video, Univ. Film & Video Foundation.

MASON, MARSHA: Actress. b. St. Louis. April 3, 1942. e. Webster Coll. Came to N.Y. to continue dramatic studies and embark on theatre career. Member of American Conservatory Theatre, San Francisco.
THEATER: The Deer Park, Cactus Flower, The Indian Wants the Bronx, Happy Birthday, Wanda June, Private Lives, You Can't Take It With You, Cyrano de Bergerac, A Dolls House.
PICTURES INCLUDE: Blume in Love (debut), Cinderella Liberty, Audrey Rose, The Goodbye Girl, The Cheap Detective, Promises in the Dark, Chapter Two, Only When I Laugh, Max Dugan Returns, Heartbreak Ridge.
TELEVISION: Love of Life (series), Brewsie and Willie, Cyrano de Bergerac, Surviving, Trapped in Silence. Dir.: Little Miss Perfect.

MASON, PAMELA: Actress, Writer. b. Westgate. England. Mar. 10, 1918. Stage debut, 1936, The Luck of the Devil, London; also playwright (in collab. James Mason, Flying Blind, Made in Heaven), Author novels This Little Hand, A Lady Possessed, The Blinds Are Down, Ignoramus, Began Brit. screen career 1938, I Met a Murderer (orig. story & s.p.; cast); also in They Were Sisters, 1944. In 1946 (s.p. & cast) The Upturned Glass; (acted) Pandora and the Flying Dutchman; acted, collab. s.p. Lady Possessed, Syndicated TV, Pamela Mason Show, author Marriage Is the First Step Toward Divorce. syndicated TV The Weaker Sex?; author, The Female Pleasure Hunt; lectures at women's clubs countrywide.

MASSEN, OSA: Actress. b. Denmark, Copenhagen. Jan. 13, 1916.
PICTURES INCLUDE: Honeymoon in Bali, Honeymoon for Three, A Woman's Face, Accent on Love, You'll Never Get Rich, The Devil Pays Off, Ireland, Strange Journey, Night Unto Night, Deadline at Dawn, Gentleman Misbehaves, Rocketship XM.

MASSEY, ANNA: Actress. b. Sussex, England, Aug. 11, 1937. Daughter of Raymond Massey. Sister of Daniel Massey. On London stage in Spoiled, Doctor's Delimma, School for Scandal, etc.
PICTURES INCLUDE: Peeping Tom, Bunny Lake Is Missing, The Looking Glass War, David Copperfield, Frenzy, A Little Romance, Sweet William, Foreign Body, Mountains of the Moon.
TELEVISION: A Doll's House, Remember the Germans, Wicked Woman, The Corn Is Green, Sakharov, Hotel Du Lac, A Hazard of Hearts.

MASSEY, DANIEL: Actor. b. London, Eng., Oct. 10, 1933. e. Eaton and King's Colleges. Son of Raymond Massey. Brother of Anna Massey. Active on stage and TV. On Broadway in She Loves Me, Gigi.
PICTURES INCLUDE: Girls at Sea, Upstairs and Downstairs, The Queen's Guard, Go to Blazes, Moll Flanders, The Jokers, Star!, Fragment of Fear, Mary, Queen of Scots, Victory.
TELEVISION: Love with a Perfect Stranger, Intimate Contact.

MASSIE, PAUL: Actor. b. Ontario, Canada. July 7, 1932. Early career on Canadian stage. Attended Central Sch., London, 1952, later jnd. Scottish National Children's Theatre. Entered m.p. ind. 1954 in Orders to Kill.
PICTURES INCLUDE: High Tide at Noon, Sapphire, Libel, The Two Faces of Dr. Jekyll, The Rebel, The Pot Carriers, Raising the Wind.
STAGE: Cat On a Hot Tin Roof.
TELEVISION: The Mark of the Warrior, The Last of the Brave, Ring Around the Moon, Secret Mission and Her Romeo.

MASTERS, BEN: Actor. b. Corvallis, OR, May 6, 1947.
THEATER: The Cherry Orchard, Waltz of the Toreadors, Plenty, Captain Brassbound's Conversion, The Boys in the Band, Eden Court, What the Butler Saw, The White Whore and the Bit Player, Key Exchange.
PICTURES INCLUDE: Mandingo (1975), All That Jazz, Key Exchange, Dream Lover, Making Mr. Right.
TELEVISION: Barnaby Jones, Kojack. Movies: Celebrity, Class of '65, Riviera, The Shadow Box, Nightstalker, The Deliberate Stranger, Street of Dreams, Heart Beat.

MASTERSON, MARY STUART: Actress. b. New York, NY, 1967. Daughter of writer-director-actor Peter Masterson and actress Carlin Glynn. e. New York U. Made film debut at age 8 in The Stepford Wives (1975). Spent summer at Stage Door Manor in Catskills; two summers at Sundance Inst. Studied acting with Estelle Parsons. Off-B'way debut The Lucky Spot (Manhattan Theatre Club).
PICTURES INCLUDE: Heaven Help Us, At Close Range, Some Kind of Wonderful, Gardens of Stone, My Little Girl, Mr. North, Chances Are, Bloodhounds of Broadway, Parental Guidance.
TELEVISION: Love Lives On.

MASTERSON, PETER: Actor, Writer, Director. r.n. Carlos Bee Masterson, Jr. b. Houston, TX, June 1, 1934. m. actress Carlin Glynn. Father of actress Mary Stuart Masterson. e. Rice U., Houston, BA. 1957. NY stage debut, Call Me By My Rightful Name, 1961. Film debut Ambush Bay, 1965.
THEATER: Marathon '33, Blues for Mr. Charlie, The Trial of Lee Harvey Oswald, The Great White Hope, That Championship Season, The Poison Three, The Best Little Whorehouse in Texas (co-author, dir.), The Last of the Knucklemen (dir.).
PICTURES INCLUDE: Counterpoint, In the Heat of the Night, Tomorrow, The Exorcist, Man on a Swing, The Stepford Wives, The Best Little Whorehouse in Texas (s.p. only), The Trip to Bountiful (dir.), Full Moon in Blue Water (dir.), Palisades Park (dir.), Convicts (dir.).
TELEVISION: Camera Three, Pueblo; The Quinns; A Question of Guilt.

MASTORAKIS, NICO: Writer, Director, Producer. b. Athens, Greece, 1941. Writer of novels and screenplays, including Fire Below Zero, Keepers of the Secret, and The Ephesus Scrolls (co-author). Pres. Omega Entertainment Ltd. since Jan. 1978.
PICTURES: Writer/dir./prod.: The Time Traveller, Blind Date, Sky High, The Zero Boys, The Wind, Terminal Exposure, Nightmare at Noon, Glitch. Prod.: The Greek Tycoon, Red Tide, Grandmother's House, Darkroom, Bloodstone (exec. prod.), The Cold Room (prod.).

MASTRANTONIO, MARY ELIZABETH: Actress. b. Oak Park, IL, Nov. 17, 1958. m. e. U. of Illinois 1976–78. NY stage appearances, Copperfield (1981), Oh Brother, Amadeus, Sunday in

the Park With George (Playwright's Horizons), The Human Comedy, Henry V, Figaro, Measure For Measure, The Knife. Film debut: Scarface (1983).
PICTURES: The Color of Money, Slam Dance, The January Man, The Abyss.
TELEVISION: Mussolini: The Untold Story.

MASTROIANNI, MARCELLO: Actor. b. Fontana Liri, Italy, Sept. 28, 1924. e. U. of Rome theatrical company. Draftsman in Rome, 1940–43. WWII, drew military maps until captured by Nazis and escaped. Theatrical debut in Rome in Angelica, 1948. Film debut in I Mizrabili (1948). Formed indep. prod. co., Master Films, 1966.
PLAYS INCLUDE: Death of a Salesman, Streetcar Named Desire, Ciao Rudy.
PICTURES INCLUDE: Too Bad She's Bad, A Dog's Life, Three Girls from Rome, The Miller's Beautiful Wife, Fever to Live, The Ladykillers of Rome, Love a La Carte, Days of Love, White Nights, Big Deal on Madonna Street, Divorce Italian Style, La Notte, A Very Private Affair, Bell Antonio, Where the Hot Wind Blows, La Dolce Vita, The Organizer, 8½, Yesterday, Today and Tomorrow, Marriage Italian Style, Casanova '70, The 10th Victim, The Poppy Is Also a Flower, Shoot Loud, Louder . . . I Don't Understand, The Stranger, A Place for Lovers, Leo the Last, Diamonds for Breakfast, Sunflower, Jealousy Italian Style, The Priest's Wife, What?, The Grande Bouffe, Massacre in Rome, Down the Ancient Stairs, The Sunday Woman, A Special Day, Stay as You Are, Blood Feud, City of Women, Gabriella, La Nuit de Varennes, Macaroni, Ginger and Fred, Federico Fellini's Intervista, Dark Eyes, Miss Arizona, Traffic Jam, The Two Lives of Martia Pascal, Splendor.

MATALON, DAVID A.: Executive. Senior exec. v.p. and theatrical mgr. of Columbia Pictures International before joining Tri-Star Pictures in 1983 as exec. v.p. with responsibility for worldwide marketing and distribution. 1985, named Pres.

MATHESON, TIM: Actor. b. Los Angeles, CA, Dec. 31, 1947. e. California State U. Debut on TV at age 12 in My Three Sons. At 19 contract player for Universal regular on Bonanza. 1985, turned to direction: St. Elsewhere episode and music videos. Set up own productions co. at Burbank Studios 1985, acted off-Bdwy. in True West.
PICTURES: Divorce American Style, Yours, Mine and Ours, How to Commit Marriage, Magnum Force, Almost Summer, National Lampoon's Animal House, Dreamer, The Apple Dumpling Gang Rides Again, 1941, A Little Sex, To Be or Not To Be, Up the Creek, Impulse, Fletch, Blind Fury (also co-prod.).
TELEVISION: Movies: Owen Marshall, Counselor-at-Law, Lock, Stock and Barrel, Hitched, Remember When, The Last Day, The Runaway Barge, The Quest, Bus Stop, Classmates, Mary White, Obsessed with a Married Woman, Blind Justice, Warm Hearts Cold Feet, Bay Coven, Just in Time (co-exec. prod., actor).

MATHEWS, CAROLE: Actress. b. Montgomery, IL, Sept. 13. e. Aurora, IL H.S. Started as night club, radio entertainer; to Hollywood, 1944.
PICTURES INCLUDE: Massacre River, Great Gatsby, Special Agent, Meet Me at the Fair, Swamp Woman, Port of Hell, Shark River, Treasure of Ruby Hills, Requirement for a Redhead, Look In Any Window, Thirteen Men, Female Fiend, Tender Is the Night, End of the Road.
TELEVISION: Steel Hour, Kraft Theatre, Lux Video, Hitchcock Presents, Studio One, Californians, Texan, 77 Sunset Strip, Perry Mason, Four Star Theatre, M-Squad, Death Valley Days, Guestward Ho, Two Faces West, Johnny Midnight, Pete & Gladys, 87th Precinct, Ben Casey.

MATLACK, JACK D.: Theatre executive, Publicist. b. Manton, CA, Feb. 22, 1914. e. Chico (CA) State Teachers Coll. Entered m.p. ind. as doorman Criterion, Medford, OR; then mgr. dir.; joined J.J. Parker Theatres, Portland, OR, 1943; as exec. asst. to pres. and adv. dir. eight theatres; now pres. Jack Matlack Promotions. Portland OR, N.W.P.R. for studios; well known showman, winner 20 exploit. awards including Grand (Silver) Quigley Award, 1943; Quigley War Showmanship Award, 1942–44; numerous Quigley Pub. citations; cited by U.S. govt. for outstanding contrib. to W.W.II effort; active as civic worker; on bd. Portland, OR C. of C., Kiwanis, Portland City Planning Comm., Oregon Advertising Club; named First Citizen of Portland, 1944. Secretary/treasurer and co- founder, American Advertising Museum, Portland.

MATLIN, MARLEE: Actress. b. Morton Grove, IL, Aug. 24, 1965. Performed at Children's Theatre of the Deaf in Des Plaines at age 8, playing many leading roles. e. John Hershey H.S., Chicago, public school with special education program for deaf. e. William Rainey Harper Coll., majoring in criminal justice. As adult appeared in only one stage show. Theatrical film debut in Children of a Lesser God, 1986 (Acad. Award).
PICTURES: Children of a Lesser God, Walker, Fox.
TELEVISION: Bridge to Silence.

MATTHAU, WALTER: Actor. b. New York, NY, Oct. 1, 1920. Served in Air Force W.W.II. Studied journalism at Columbia U., then acted in summer stock. First Broadway role, 1948, in Anne of a Thousand Days.
THEATRE: Will Success Spoil Rock Hunter?, The Odd Couple.
PICTURES INCLUDE: A Face in the Crowd, The Kentuckian, Slaughter on Tenth Avenue, Indian Fighter, No Power on Earth, Middle of the Street, Onion Head, Voice in the Mirror, King Creole, Lonely Are the Brave, Strangers When We Meet, Who's Got the Action, The Gangster Story, Charade, Goodbye Charlie, Mirage, The Fortune Cookie, A Guide for the Married Man, The Odd Couple, Candy, Cactus Flower, Hello Dolly, A New Leaf, Plaza Suite, Pete n' Tillie, Charley Varrick, The Laughing Policeman, The Taking of Pelham One, Two, Three, The Front Page, The Sunshine Boys, The Bad News Bears, Casey's Shadow, House Calls, California Suite, Little Miss Marker (also exec. prod.), Hopscotch, First Monday in October, Buddy, Buddy, I Ought To Be in Pictures, The Survivors, Movers and Shakers, Pirates, The Couch Trip.
TELEVISION: Many appearances (1952–65); Awake and Sing, Inight, Muni.

MATURE, VICTOR: Actor. b. Louisville, KY, Jan. 29, 1916. TV retail store; trainee, Pasadena Theatre, Playbox Theatre; on B'way in Lady in the Dark; U.S. Coast Guard, W.W.II.
PICTURES INCLUDE: Housekeeper's Daughter, One Million B.C., Captain Caution, No No Nanette, I Wake Up Screaming, Shanghai Gesture, Song of the Islands, My Gal Sal, Footlight Serenade, Seven Days Leave, My Darling Clementine, Moss Rose, Kiss of Death, Cry of the City, Red Hot and Blue, Fury at Furnace Creek, Easy Living, Samson and Delilah, Wabash Avenue, Stella, Gambling House, Las Vegas Story, Androcles and the Lion, Million Dollar Mermaid, Something for the Birds, Glory Brigade, Affair with a Stranger, The Robe, Veils of Bagdad, Dangerous Mission, Betrayed, Demetrius & the Gladiators, The Egyptian, Chief Crazy Horse, Violent Saturday, Last Frontier, Safari, Zarak Pickup Alley, Tank Roce, The Bandit of Zhobe, Escort Wst., Big Circus, Timbuktu, Hannibal The Tartars, After the Fox, Every Little Crook and Nanny, Won Ton Ton, the Dog That Saved Hollywood, Firepower, The Screamer.
TELEVISION: Samson and Delilah.

MAUREY, NICOLE: Actress. b. France, 1925. Studied dancing; French films include Blondine, Pamela, Le Cavalier Noir; stage appearances in France; U.S. film debut in Little Boy Lost (1953).
PICTURES INCLUDE: Secret of the Incas, Bold and the Brave, House of the Seven Hawks, Day of the Triffids, The Very Edge, Gloria, Chanel Solitaire.

MAXWELL, RONALD F.: Writer, Director. b. Jan. 5, 1947. e. New York U. Coll. of Arts & Sciences; New York U. Sch. of the Arts, Inst. of Film & Television Graduate Sch., M.F.M., 1970. Producer-Director for PBS Theater-in-America.
PICTURES INCLUDE: The Guest, Little Darlings (dir.); The Night the Lights Went Out in Georgia (dir.); Kidco (dir.); The Killer Angels (prod., dir., co-s.p.).
TELEVISION: Sea Marks (prod., dir.); Verna: USO Girl (prod., dir.), Parent Trap II (dir.).

MAY, ELAINE: Actress, Screenwriter. b. Philadelphia, PA, April 21, 1932. Mother of actress Jeannie Berlin. Father was prod.-dir. Jack Berlin with whose travelling theater she acted with from age 6 to 10. Repertory theater in Chicago, 1954; comedy team with Mike Nichols, 1955. Appeared with improvisational theater group, The Compass, Chicago. Co-starred in An Evening with Mike Nichols and Elaine May.
PICTURES INCLUDE: Luv, Enter Laughing; A New Leaf (writer, dir., star); The Heartbreak Kid (dir.); Mikey and Nicky (dir., s.p.); Heaven Can Wait (co-s.p.); California Suite (actress); Ishtar (s.p., dir.), In the Spirit (actress).
TELEVISION: Jack Paar, Omnibus, Dinah Shore Show, Perry Como, Laugh Lines (panelist, 1959).

MAYEHOFF, EDDIE: Comedian. b. Baltimore, MD, July 7, 1914. e. Yale Sch. of Music. Adv. salesman, 1932; dance band leader, 6 yrs.; on radio with Norman Corwin; own show, Eddie Mayehoff on the Town; night clubs; B'way shows.
THEATRE: Let Freedom Sing, Early to Bed, Rhapsody, Billy Rose's Concert Varieties, Season in the Sun, Visit to a Small Planet.
TELEVISION: Adventures of Fenimore J. Mayehoff.
PICTURES INCLUDE: That's My Boy, The Stooge, Off Limits, Artists and Models, How to Murder Your Wife, Luv.

MAYER, BEN: Executive. b. Nov. 22, 1925. e. Manchester All Saints Sch. of Art, England; Royal Coll. of Art. President, Ben Mayer Design, Inc.

MAYER, GERALD: Producer, Director. b. Montreal, Canada; p. both deceased: Jerry G., mgr. MGM studio, and Rheba G Mayer (later Mrs. Hal Elias). e. Stanford U., journalism; corr. for San Francisco Examiner; pres. Sigma Delta Chi, prof.

journalism soc. Navy lieut. amphibious forces, W.W.II. Entered m.p. ind. in prod. dept. MGM studios; first dir. assignment Dial 1119 (1950).
PICTURES INCLUDE: Inside Straight, Sellout, Holiday for Sinners, Bright Road (Christopher Award for direction), The Marauders, African Drumbeat, and The Man Inside (Canadian).
TELEVISION: Canadian Broadcasting Corp. (prod./dir., TV drama), prod. The Swiss Family Robinson (British-Canadian, West German TV series). Director for U.S. TV: One Last Ride (mini-series), Airwolf, Night Heat, Lou Grant, Eight Is Enough, Quincy, Logan's Run, Mannix, Mission Impossible, Police Surgeon, Cimarron Strip, Peyton Place, Judd for the Defense, Bonanza, The Fugitive, Chrysler Thea., Ben Casey, Slattery's People, Profiles in Courage, The Defenders, Gunsmoke, etc.

MAYER, MICHAEL F.: Attorney, Executive. b. White Plains, NY, Sept. 8, 1917. e. Harvard Coll., B.S., 1939; Yale Law Sch., L.L.B., 1942. Armed Forces 1942–46, Air Medal (1945); vice-pres. Kingsley International Pictures Corp., 1954–62. Executive Director and General Counsel, Independent Film Importers and Distributors of America Inc. (IFIDA), 1959–67. Special Counsel, French Society of Authors, Composers and Publishers, 1961–72; British Performing Rights Society, 1962–67. Author: Foreign Films on American Screens (1966); Divorce and Annulment (1967); What You Should Know About Libel and Slander (1968); Rights of Privacy (1972); The Film Industries (1973)—revised edition published in 1978). Lectures on motion picture problems at New York U., Stanford U., U. of Pennsylvania, Dartmouth Coll., State U. of New York, Albany. Teacher of courses on Business Problems in Film, New School (1971–82). Secty. of Film Society of Lincoln Center, Inc. (1972–88).

MAYER, ROGER LAURANCE: Executive. b. New York, NY, Apr. 21, 1926. e. Yale U., 1948 graduate; Yale Law Sch., 1951 graduate. In 1952 was practicing attorney; joined Columbia Pictures that year as atty. and named corp. exec., 1957. Left in 1961 to join MGM Studio as asst. gen. mgr. Since with MGM as follows: v.p., operations, 1964; v.p., administration, 1975–84. Also exec. v.p., MGM Laboratories, 1974–83. Now pres., MGM Laboratories and sr. v.p., studio admin.
MEMBER: Los Angeles County Bar Assn., Los Angeles Copyright Society, Acad. of Motion Picture Arts & Sciences. Chm. & trustee for both Directors Guild Pension Plan and Producers Guild Pension Plan. Trustee, Motion Picture & TV Relief Fund and director, Permanent Charities.

MAYER, SEYMOUR R.: Executive. b. New York, NY, July 30, 1912. e. N.Y. schools. Div. mgr., Loew's in-town theatres, 1933; Armed Forces, W.W.II, as Major in charge of overseas m.p. service; with Loew's International: 1946, 1st v.p.; MGM Int'l.: 1963–69; pres., MGM Int'l.; worldwide sales, 1970; pres., MSD Int'l. worldwide sales.

MAYES, WENDELL: Writer. b. Hayti, MO, July 21, 1919. e. Johns Hopkins U., Columbia U. Military service in Pacific, W.W.II. Began career as actor legit theater, turned to writing for television. Gained television recognition before moving to Hollywood as motion picture writer.
PICTURES INCLUDE: Spirit of St. Louis, The Way to the Gold, Enemy Below, The Hunters, From Hell to Texas, The Hanging Tree, Anatomy of a Murder, Advise And Consent, In Harm's Way, Von Ryan's Express, Hotel, The Stalking Moon, The Poseidon Adventure, The Revengers, Bank Shot, Death Wish, Love and Bullets, Charlie, Go Tell the Spartans, Monsignor.

MAYO, VIRGINIA: Actress. r.n. Virginia Jones. b. St. Louis, MO, Nov. 30, 1920. e. St. Louis dramatic school. With Billy Rose's Diamond Horseshoe; then N.Y. stage, Banjo Eyes.
PICTURES INCLUDE: Kid from Brooklyn, Best Years of Our Lives, Secret Life of Walter Mitty, Out of the Blue, Smart Girls Don't Talk, The Girl from Jones Beach, Flaxy Martin, Colorado Territory, Always Leave Them Laughing, Flame and the Arrow, West Point Story, Along the Great Divide, Captain Horatio Hornblower, Painting the Clouds with Sunshine, Starlift, She's Working Her Way Through College, Iron Mistress, She's Back on Broadway, South Sea Woman, Devil's Canyon, King Richard & the Crusaders, Silver Chalice, Pearl of the South Pacific, Great Day in the Morning, Proud Ones, Congo Crossing, Big Land, Young Fury, Fort Utah, Castle of Evil, Won Ton Ton, The Dog Who Saved Hollywood, French Quarter.

MAYRON, MELANIE: Actress. b. Philadelphia, PA, Oct. 20, 1952. e. American Academy of Dramatic Arts, 1972. Debut Godspell (tour), NY stage debut: The Goodbye People, 1979. Gethsemane Springs, Mark Taper Forum, 1976. With Catlin Adams, co-prod., co-wrote short, Little Shiny Shoes.
PICTURES: Harry and Tonto (1974), The Great Smokey Roadblock, You Light Up My Life, Car Wash, Gable and Lombard, The Last of the Cowboys, Girl Friends (Best actress award, Locarno Film Festival) Heartbeeps, Missing, The Boss' Wife, Sticky Fingers (actress, co-s.p., co-prod. with Catlin Adams), Checking Out.

TELEVISION: Playing For Time, Will There Really Be a Morning?, Hustling, The Best Little Girl in the World, Lily Tomlin, Sold Out, Wallenberg: A Hero's Story, Rhoda, Thirty-something.

MAYSLES, ALBERT: Director, Cinematographer. b. Boston, MA, 1926. e. Boston U, M.A. Taught psychology there for 3 years. With late brother David (1933–87) pioneered in "direct cinema" documentary filmmaking, using hand-held cameras to capture slices of daily life, synchronous sound, no narration, and establishing rapport with the subject. Entered indust. photographing Primary with D.A. Pennebaker, Richard Leacock and John Drew, 1960. Formed Maysles Production Co., 1962, making commercials and corp. films.
    PICTURES: Showman (1962), Salesman, What's Happening! The Beatles in the U.S.A., Meet Marlon Brando, Gimme Shelter, Christo's Valley Curtain, Grey Gardens, Running Fence, Vladimir Horowitz: The Last Romantic, Ozawa, Islands, Horowitz Plays Mozart, The Umbrellas, Heart, Fellow Passengers.

MAZURKI, MIKE: Actor. b. Ukrainian descent; Tarnopal, Austria, Dec. 25, 1909. e. Manhattan Coll., N.Y., B.A., 1930. Toured United States and Canada as heavyweight wrestler. Screen debut 1941 in Shanghai Gesture.
    PICTURES INCLUDE: I Walk Alone, Unconquered, Nightmare Alley, Relentless, Neptune's Daughter, Come to the Stable, Rope of Sand, Samson and Delilah, Light Touch, Criminal Lawyer, Ten Tall Men, My Favorite Spy, The Egyptian, New Orleans Uncensored, New York Confidential, Blood Alley, Kismet, Davy Crockett, King of the Wild Frontier, Comanche, Around the World in 80 Days, It's a Mad, Mad, Mad, Mad World, Four for Texas, Cheyenne Autumn, 7 Women, Bullwhip Griffin, Challenge to Be Free, The Magic of Lassie, The Man with Bogart's Face, Doing Time.
    TELEVISION: Series: It's About Time, Chicago Teddy Bears.

MAZURSKY, PAUL: Producer, Director, Writer, Actor. b. Brooklyn, NY, April 25, 1930. e. Brooklyn Coll. Started acting in 1951 in the theatre (He Who Gets Slapped), the films (Film and Desire, 1951, Blackboard Jungle). Was nightclub comic 1954–1960 and directed plays. Began association with Larry Tucker by producing, directing, writing and performing in Second City, semi-improvisational revue. For four years they wrote the Danny Kaye TV show and created and wrote the Monkees series. First theatrical film I Love You, Alice B. Toklas, 1969, which he wrote with Tucker and both men acted as exec. prod.
    PICTURES INCLUDE: Bob and Carol and Ted and Alice, (dir., co-s.p.), Alex in Wonderland (dir., co-s.p., actor), Blume in Love (dir., s.p., prod., actor), Harry and Tonto (prod., dir., co-s.p.); Next Stop, Greenwich Village (prod., dir., s.p.); An Unmarried Woman (prod., dir., s.p.); A Man, a Woman and a Bank (actor); Willie and Phil (prod., dir., s.p.); Tempest (prod., dir., co-s.p.); Moscow on the Hudson (prod., dir., co-s.p.); Down and Out in Beverly Hills (prod., dir., co-s.p., actor), Moon Over Parador (dir., co-s.p., actor), Enemies, A Love Story (dir. prod.).

McBRIDE, JIM: Writer, Director. Began in underground film scene in New York. First film: David Holzman's Diary, 1967, which won grand prize at Mannheim and Pesaro Film Festivals.
    PICTURES INCLUDE: My Girlfriend's Wedding (actor, s.p., dir.), Glen and Randa (s.p., dir.), Pictures for Life's Other Side (dir.), Hot Times (dir., s.p.), Breathless (co.-s.p., dir.); The Big Easy (dir.), Great Balls of Fire (dir., s.p.).

McCALL, JOAN: Actress, Writer. b. Grahn, KY. e. Berea Coll. Starred on Broadway in Barefoot in the Park, The Star Spangled Girl, A Race of Hairy Men, and road companies of Barefoot in the Park, Star Spangled Girl, and Don't Drink the Water, Los Angeles company of Jimmy Shine.
    PICTURES INCLUDE: Grizzly, Act of Vengeance, The Devil Times Five. Screenwriter: The Predator, The Concision, Fly Away Home. 1980: Staff writer for The Days of Our Lives, Another World, As the World Turns, under the pen name Joan Pommer; 1982: Search for Tomorrow, 1984: Capitol, 1985: Santa Barbara.

McCALLUM, DAVID: Actor. b. Scotland, Sept. 19, 1933. Early career in rep. theatres and dir. plays for Army. Ent. m.p. Ind. 1953.
    PICTURES INCLUDE: The Secret Place, Hell Drivers, Robbery Under Arms, Violent Playground, A Night to Remember, The Long and the Short and the Tall, Billy Budd, Freud, The Great Escape, The Greatest Story Ever Told, To Trap a Spy, Three Bits of the Apple, Sol Madrid, Mosquito Squadron, Watcher in the Woods, The Wind.
    TELEVISION: The Man From U.N.C.L.E. (series), The Invisible Man (series); Teacher, Teacher; Hauser's Memory; Colditz (BBC series 1972–74); Frankenstein: The True Story; Behind Enemy Lines; Freedom Fighters; She Waits; The Man Who Lived at the Ritz.

McCALLUM, JOHN: Actor, Producer, Director. b. Brisbane, Australia, CBE. Mar. 14, 1918. e. Royal Acad. of Dramatic Art. Served in Australian Imperial Forces, W.W.II. Appeared in repertory with Old Vic & Stratford-on-Avon. On stage, 1937 in Judgment Day, Australian tour, 1955–56; on screen first 1944, Australia is Like This. Asst. man. dir. J. C. Williamson Theatres, Ltd., Australia, 1958; man. dir., 1960–66. Resigned chmn. Williamson-Powell Int. Films, 1965; chmn. Fauna Prod.; dir. Relatively Speaking on stage in Australia, 1968. Dir.; Plaza Suite, My Fair Lady, for Australian stage, 1969–70. Prod. TV Series, Skippy, Barrier Reef, Boney, Shannons Mob; London Stage 1973–74 Constant Wife. 1974 Comedy Theatre, Melbourne. 1976 Chichester Fest. 1976–77 The Circle. Exec. prod. Bailey's Bird, TV series. 1986, The Chalk Garden. 1987, The Kingfisher (tour, Far and Middle East), 1988, Hayfever, The Royal Baccarat Scandal Chichester Fest.
    PICTURES INCLUDE: A Son Is Born, Joe Goes Back, Root of All Evil, The Loves of Joanna Godden, It Always Rains on Sunday, Miranda, The Calendar, A Boy, a Girl and a Bike, Traveler's Joy, The Woman in Question, Valley of the Eagles, Lady Godiva Rides Again, Derby Day (Four Against Fate), Trent's Last Case, The Long Memory, Melba, Devil on Horseback, Trouble in the Glen, Smiley (in Australia), Safe Harbour, Nickel Queen (dir.); The Z Men (prod.); The Highest Honor (exec. prod.).

McCAMBRIDGE, MERCEDES: Actress. b. Joliet, IL, March 17, 1918. e. Mundelein Coll., Chicago, B.A. Did some radio work while in college; opposite Orson Welles two seasons, on Ford Theatre, other air shows; New York stage in: Hope for the Best, 1945; others: Place of Our Own, Twilight Bar, Woman Bites Dog, The Young and Fair; left latter play for Hollywood. Screen debut: All the King's Men (Academy Award for best supporting actress, 1950); own radio show, 1952. Member: National Inst. Alcohol Abuse and Alcoholism, Washington.
    PICTURES INCLUDE: Lightning Strikes Twice, Inside Straight, The Scarf, Johnny Guitar, Giant, A Farewell to Arms, Suddenly Last Summer, Cimarron, Angel Baby, Last Generation, Jigsaw, 99 Women, Thieves, The Concorde—Airport '79.
    AUTHOR: The Two of Us.
    TELEVISION: Numerous appearances, Who is the Black Dahlia?

McCARTHY, ANDREW: Actor. b. Westfield, NJ, 1962. e. New York U. Studied acting at Circle-in-the-Square; on Broadway in The Boys of Winter; Off Bdwy: Bodies, Rest and Motion; Life Under Water; Neptune's Hips, Mariens Hammer. Film debut, Class, 1984.
    PICTURES INCLUDE: Heaven Help Us, St. Elmo's Fire, Pretty in Pink, Manequin, Waiting for the Moon, Less Than Zero, Fresh Horse, Kansas.

McCARTHY, KEVIN: Actor. b. Seattle, WA, Feb. 15, 1914. Brother of author Mary McCarthy. e. U. of Minnesota. Acted in sch. plays, stock; B'way debut in Abe Lincoln in Illinois. In U.S. Army; On London stage in Death of a Salesman (1949–50). m.p. debut: Death of A Salesman.
    BROADWAY THEATER: Flight to West, Winged Victory, Truckline Cafe, Joan of Lorraine, Death of a Salesman, Anna Christie, Red Roses For Me, Love's Labour's Lost, Advise and Consent, The Day The Money Stopped, Two For the Seesaw, Cactus Flower, Alone Together, The Three Sisters, Happy Birthday Wanda June.
    PICTURES INCLUDE: Drive a Crooked Road, Gambler from Natchez, Stranger on Horseback, Annapolis Story, Nightmare, Invasion of the Body Snatchers, A Big Hand for the Little Lady, Hotel, Kansas City Bomber, Buffalo Bill and the Indians, Hero at Large, Those Lips, Those Eyes, Innerspace, Dark Tower, Hostage, Love or Money, Twilight Zone—The Movie, U.H.F.
    TELEVISION: Active on TV since 1949. Movies: The Making of a Male Model, Deadly Intentions, The Midnight Hour, A Masterpiece of Murder, Poor Little Rich Girl: The Barbara Hutton Story; The Long Journey Home; Once Upon a Texas Train; In the Heat of the Night, Channel 99. Series: The Colbys, e Survivors, Flamingo Road, Amanda's Second Start.

McCARTNEY PAUL: Singer, Musician. b. Liverpool, England, Feb. 25, 1942. As member of The Beatles co-starred in A Hard Day's Night, Help!, and Let It Be. Wrote songs for several films on own, including Live and Let Die (title), Oh Heavenly Dog. Formed group Wings for tours and recordings. Wrote script and music and acted in Give My Regards to Broad Street, cameo in Eat the Rich.

McCLANAHAN, RUE: Actress. b. Healdton, OK, Feb. 21, 1934. e. U. of Tulsa. On Bdwy. in Secret Life of Walter Mitty, Jimmy Shine, California Suite. Obie Award for Who's Happy Now (1970).
    PICTURES: They Might Be Giants.
    TELEVISION: Series: Maude, Topper, Mama's Family, Golden Girls (Emmy Award, 1987). Movies: Move Over Mrs. Markham; Rainbow; Mother and Me; The Great American Traffic Jam; Word of Honor; The Day the Bubble Burst, The Little Match Girl; Liberace; The Man in the Brown Suit.

McCLORY, SEAN: Actor. b. Dublin, Ireland, March 8, 1924. e. Jesuit Coll., U. of Galway. With Gaelic Theatre, Galway; Abbey Theatre. Dublin. Brought to U.S., in 1946 under contract to RKO Pictures. Prod. and dir. numerous plays, member of the Directors Guild of America and author of drama, Moment of Truth.
PLAYS INCLUDE: Shining Hour, Juno and the Paycock, Anna Christie, Escape to Autumn, King of Friday's Men, Lady's Not for Burning, Billy Budd, Dial M for Murder, The Winslow Boy, Shadow of a Gunman, Saint Joan.
PICTURES INCLUDE: Film debut: Dick Tracy vs. Cueball, Roughshod, Beyond Glory, Daughter of Rosie O'Grady, Storm Warning, Lorna Doone, What Price Glory, The Quiet Man, Diane, Island in the Sky, Ring of Fear, Them, Long Grey Line, Cheyenne Autumn, Plunder of the Sun Bay, Anne of the Indies, I Cover the Underworld, Botany Man in the Attic, Guns of Fort Petticoat, Kings Thief, Moonfleet, Bandolero, Day of the Wolves, Valley of the Dragons, Follow Me Boys, Rogues March, The Gnomobile, Well of the Saints, In Search of the Historical Jesus, Roller Boogie, My Chauffeur, The Dead.
TELEVISION: Matinee Theatre, Climax, Lost in Space, My Three Sons, Suspense, The Untouchables, Hitchcock, Thriller, Beverly Hillbillies, Bonanza, Gunsmoke, Mannix, Little House on the Prairie, Perry Mason, S.W.A.T., The New Daughters of Joshua Cabe, The Captains And the Kings, Once an Eagle, Fish, Columbo, How the West Was Won, Fantasy Island, Battlestar Galactica, Trapper John, Blue Knight. Falcon Crest, Simon and Simon, Murder She Wrote, Young Houdini. Co-starred in 3 series. The Californians, directing several episodes, and Kate McShane; Bring 'Em Back Alive, Guest in continuing role: General Hospital.

McCLURE, DOUG: Actor. b. Glendale, CA, May 11, 1935. e. U. of California at L.A.
PICTURES: Because They're Young, The Unforgiven, Shenandoah, Beau Geste, The King's Pirate, Nobody's Perfect, The Land That Time Forgot, At the Earth's Core, The House Where Evil Dwells, Warlords of Atlantis, Humanoids from the Deep, Cannonball Run II, 52 Pick-Up, Omega Syndrome, Nightside, Tapeheads, Prime Suspect, Dark Before Dawn.
TELEVISION: Movies: The Longest Hundred Miles, Terror in the Sky, The Birdmen, The Death of Me Yet, Playmates, The Judge and Jake Wyler, Shirts/Skins, Death Race, Satan's Triangle, Roots, SST-Death Flight, Search, Wild and Woolly, The Rebels, Checkmate, Men From Shiloh, Barbary Coast, Out of This World. Series: Overland Trail, The Virginian.

McCOWEN, ALEC: Actor. b. Tunbridge Wells, England, May 26, 1925. e. Royal Acad. of Dramatic Art. On stage in London in Ivanhoe, The Mask and the Face, Hadrian the Seventh, etc. On Bdwy. in Antony and Cleopatra, No Laughing Matter, After the Rain, The Assam Garden, etc.
PICTURES: The Cruel Sea, Time Without Pity, A Midsummer Night's Dream, The Loneliness of the Long Distance Runner, The Agony and the Ecstasy, The Devil's Own, The Hawaiians, Frenzy, Travels with My Aunt, Stevie, Hanover Street, Never Say Never Again, The Young Visitors, The Assam Garden, Personal Services, Cry Freedom.

McCREA, JOEL: Actor. b. Los Angeles, CA, Nov. 5, 1905. e. Pomona Coll. Husband of Frances Dee, actress. Stage experience: amateur dramatics and community plays taking male lead in The Patsy, Laff That Off and The Little Journey. In many pictures since 1932.
PICTURES INCLUDE: 1940, He Married His Wife, Primrose Path, Foreign Correspondent, Reaching for the Sun, Sullivan's Travels, The Great Man's Lady, The Palm Beach Story, The More the Merrier, Virginian, Ramrod, Four Faces West, South of St. Louis, Outriders, Colorado, Territory, Stars in My Crown, Saddle Tramp, Cattle Drive, San Francisco Story, Lone Hand, Shoot First, Border River, Black Horse Canyon, Stranger on Horseback, Wichita, First Texan, The Oklahoman, Trooper Hook, Fort Massacre, The Gunfight at Dodge City, Ride the High Country, Mustang Country, George Stevens: A Filmmaker's Journey.

McDOWALL, BETTY: Actress. b. Sydney, Australia. e. Mt. Bernard Convent, N. Sydney. Early career radio, stage in Australia; ent. BBC TV, 1952; since in West End plays, many TV and radio plays and films.
STAGE: Age of Consent, Ghost Train, The Kidders, The Dark Halo, Period of Adjustment, Rule of Three, Signpost to Murder, Hippolytus, The Winslow Boy, Woman in a Dressing Gown, As Long as It's Warm, Caprice—in a Pink Palazzo, Sweet Bird of Youth, There Was an Old Woman, What the Butler Saw, Two Dozen Red Roses, A Boston Story, The Man Most Likely To. . ., Sleeping Partner.
TELEVISION: Mid-Level and Glorification of Al Toolum, The Black Judge, Phone Call for Matthew Quade, Thunder on the Snowy, Shadow of Guilt, Traveling Lady, Torment, Biography, Notes for a Love Song, Esther's Altar, The Corridor People, The Beaten Beat, The Douglas Fairbanks, Ivanhoe, The Foreign Legion, Fabian of the Yard, Four Just Men, Flying Doctor, No Hiding Place, Z' Cars, Days of

Vengeance, Flower of Evil, Outbreak of Murder, Call Me Sam, The Prisoner, Public Eye, The Forgotten Door, All Out for Kangaroo Valley, Barry Humphries Scandals, Castle Haven, Albert and Victoria, Follyfoot, The Man Who Came to Dinner, Anne of Avoniea, Little Lord Fauntleroy, The Bass Player and the Blond (4 plays), The Gingerbread Lady. Series: Boyd Q.C.
PICTURES INCLUDE: First lead in England, Timelock, She Didn't Say No, Jack the Ripper, The Shiralee, Jackpot, Dead Lucky, Spare the Rod, Golliwog, Echo of Diana, First Men in the Moon, Ballad in Blue, The Liquidators, Willy Wagtails by Moonlight, The Omen.
RADIO: Anna Christie, The Little Foxes, Another Part of the Forest, The Archers.

McDOWELL, RODDY: Actor. b. London, England, Sept. 17, 1928. e. St. Joseph's, London. First appeared in Murder in the Family at age of 8. Later, You Will Remember, The Outsider, Just William, Hey, Hey, U.S.A., This England, all made in England. In 1940 signed by 20th Century-Fox. Star of Tomorrow, 1944.
PICTURES INCLUDE: Man Hunt, How Green Was My Valley, Confirm or Deny, Son of Fury, On the Sunny Side, The Pied Piper, My Friend Flicka, Lassie Come Home, White Cliffs of Dover, Macbeth, Act. assoc. prod., Rocky, Kidnapped, Big Timber, Tuna Clipper, Black Midnight, Killer Shark, Steel Fist, The Subterraneans, Midnight Lace, Cleopatra, The Longest Day, The Greatest Story Ever Told, Shock Treatment, That Darn Cat, The Loved Ones, The Third Day, Daisy Clover, Bullwhip Griffin, Lord Love A Duck, The Defector, It, The Cool Ones, Planet of the Apes, Hello, Down There, Midas Run, Escape from the Planet of the Apes, Conquest of the Planet of the Apes. Directorial Debut, The Devil's Widow, 1971. Actor: The Legend of Hellhouse, The Poseidon Adventure, Arnold, Funny Lady, The Cat from Outer Space, Scavenger Hunt, Charlie Chan and the Curse of the Dragon Queen, Evil Under the Sun, Class of 1984, Fright Night, Dead of Winter, Overboard (also exec. prod.), The Big Picture, Destroyer, Fright Night II, Cutting Class.
THEATRE: On B'way in Misalliance, Escapade, Doctor's Dilemma, No Time for Sergeants, Good as Gold, Compulsion, Handful of Fire, Look After Lulu, The Fighting Cock, 1959–60, Camelot, 1960–61, The Astrakhan Coat, 1966.
TELEVISION: Stratford Shakespeare Festival, 1955. Movies: This Girl for Hire, The Zany Adventures of Robin Hood, Hollywood Wives, Alice in Wonderland, Mae West, The Rhinemann Exchange, The Thief of Baghdad, Miracle on 34th Street, Around the World in 80 Days.

McDOWELL, MALCOLM: Actor. b. Leeds, England, June 13, 1943. Married actress Mary Steenburgen. Was spearholder for the Royal Shakespeare Co. in season of 1965–66 when turned to TV and then to films. NY stage: Look Back in Anger (also on video); In Celebration. Made debut in small role in Poor Cow, 1967.
PICTURES INCLUDE: If. . ., Figures in a Landscape, The Raging Moon, A Clockwork Orange, O Lucky Man!, Royal Flash, Aces High, Voyage of the Damned, Caligula, The Passage, Time after Time, Cat People, Britannia Hospital, Blue Thunder, Cross Creek, Get Crazy, The Caller, Sunset, Buy and Cell, The Big Picture, The Hateful Dead.
TELEVISION: Arthur the King, Gulag, Monte Carlo, Faerie Tale Theatre (Little Red Riding Hood).

McELWAINE, GUY: Executive. b. Culver City, CA, June 29, 1936. Started career in pub. dept. of MGM, 1955; 1959, joined m.p. div. of Rogers and Cowen. 1964, formed own public relations firm; then joined CMA. Left to become sr. exec. v.p. in chg. worldwide m.p. production, Warner Bros., 1975. In 1977 became sr. exec. v.p. in chg. worldwide m.p. activities and pres. of intl. film mktg. at Intl. Creative Management (ICM), formerly CMA. 1981, named pres. and chief exec. officer Rastar Films. Left in 1982 to become pres., Columbia Pictures; given additional title of chief exec. officer, 1983. In 1985 named chm. and on board of Columbia Pictures Industries. Resigned, 1986. Joined Weintraub Entertainment Group as exec. v.p. and chmn., m.p. div. 1987.

McEVEETY, BERNARD: Director. Comes from film family; father was pioneer as unit mgr. at New York's Edison Studios; brothers Vincent, also a dir., and Joseph, writer are at Disney Studios. Bernard's career began in 1953 at Paramount where was asst. dir. for 6 yrs. Earned full dir. responsibility on The Rebel, TV series.
PICTURES INCLUDE: Napoleon and Samantha, One Little Indian, The Bears and I.
TELEVISION: Numerous episodes on Bonanza, Gunsmoke, Combat and Cimarron Strip (also prod.), Centennial, Roughnecks, The Machans.

McEVEETY, VINCENT: Director. Joined Hal Roach Studios in 1954 as second asst. dir. Then to Republic for The Last Command. First Disney assignments: Davy Crockett shows and Mickey Mouse Club. Moved to Desilu as first asst. dir. on The Untouchables; made assoc. prod. with option to direct.

Did segments of many series, including 34 Gunsmoke episodes. First theatrical film: Firecreek, 1968.
PICTURES INCLUDE: $1,000,000 Duck, The Biscuit Eater, Charley and the Angel, Superdad, The Strongest Man in the World, Gus, Treasure of Matecumbe, Herbie Goes to Monte Carlo, Apple Dumpling Gang Rides Again, Herbie Goes Bananas.
TELEVISION: Blood Sport, Wonder Woman, High Flying Spy, Max Max, Gunsmoke: Return to Dodge.

McGAVIN, DARREN: Actor. b. San Joaquin Valley, CA, May 7, 1922. e. Coll. of the Pacific.
PLAYS INCLUDE: Death of a Salesman, My Three Angels, The Rainmaker, The Lovers, Dinner at Eight (revival).
PICTURES INCLUDE: Summertime, The Man with the Golden Arm, Court Martial of Billy Mitchell, Beau James, Delicate Delinquent, The Great Sioux Massacre, Bullet for a Badman, Mission Mars, Airport 77, A Christmas Story, The Natural, Turk 182, From the Hip, Dead Heat. Directorial debut: Happy Mother's Day . . . Love, George, 1973.
TELEVISION: Series: Mike Hammer, The Outsider, The Night Stalker. Movies: My Wicked Wicked Ways, The Rookies, Tribes, Something Evil, The Users, Inherit the Wind.

McGILLIS, KELLY: Actress. b. Newport Beach, CA, 1958. e. Juilliard.
PICTURES INCLUDE: Reuben, Reuben, Witness, Top Gun, Made in Heaven, Promised Land, The House on Carroll Street, The Accused, The Winter People, Lie Down With Lions.

McGOOHAN, PATRICK: Actor. b. New York, Mar. 19, 1928. Early career in repertory in Britain. London stage 1955 in Serious Charge; 1955 Orson Welles' Moby Dick. Ent. films 1955. On Broadway in Pack of Lies (1987).
PICTURES INCLUDE: Passage Home, High Tide at Noon, Hell Drivers, The Gypsy and the Gentleman, Nor the Moon by Night, Two Living, One Dead, All Night Long, The Quare Fellow, Thomasina, Dr. Syn, Ice Station Zebra, The Moonshine War, Brass Target, Scanners, Baby.
TELEVISION: Series: Danger Man; (also directed episodes); Secret Agent, The Prisoner. Movies: Jamaica Inn; Of Pure Blood, Man in the Iron Mask.

McGOVERN, ELIZABETH: Actress. b. Evanston, IL, July 18, 1961. Acted in high school in California; studied at American Conservatory Theatre, Julliard Sch. of Dramatic Art. Film debut in Ordinary People, 1980.
THEATER: To Be Young, Gifted and Black (1981, debut), My Sister in This House (Theatre World, Obie Awards), Painting Churches.
PICTURES: Ragtime, Lovesick, Racing with the Moon, Once Upon a Time in America, The Bedroom Window, Native Son, She's Having a Baby.

McGRATH, THOMAS J.: Producer. b. New York, NY. e. Washington Square Coll. of New York U., B.A., 1956; New York U. Sch. of Law, LL.B., 1960. Has practiced law in N.Y. from 1960 to date. Became indep. prod. with Deadly Hero in 1976; Author, Carryover Basis Under The 1976 Tax Reform Act, published in 1977.

McGREGOR, CHARLES: Executive. b. Jersey City, NJ, April 1, 1927. e. New York U. 1958–1969, co-founder, pres. and chief exec. officer, Banner Films, Inc. (World Wide TV Distribution), 1955–58, salesman and div. mgr., Flamingo Films (domestic TV Dist.). 1953–55; Professional mgr. ABC Music Publishing. 1951–53: Prod. and partner Telco Prods. and GM Productions (prods. of network and local shows). 1969–77: exec. v.p. in chg. of w-w dist., WB-TV; 1977: pres. WB-TV Distribution.

McGUIRE, DON: Writer, Director. b. Chicago, IL, Feb. 28, 1919. U.S. Army, 4 yrs.; press agent, Chicago and Hollywood; newsman, Hearst papers, Chicago; then actor, writer.
PICTURES INCLUDE: Double Deal, Dial 1119, Meet Danny Wilson, Willie and Joe in Back at the Front, Walking My Baby Back Home, Three Ring Circus, Bad Day at Black Rock, Artists and Models, Johnny Concho, Delicate Delinquent, Suppose They Gave a War and Nobody Came, Tootsie, Hear Me Good.
TELEVISION: Writer, dir., co-prod., Henessey (series); creator, series Not for Hire; creator, writer, prod. series, Don't Call Me Charlie, From Here to Eternity, Berlin Air Lift.
AUTHOR: Novels, The Day Television Died, 1600 Floogle Street, The Hell with Walter Cronkite.

McGUIRE, DOROTHY: Actress. b. Omaha, NB, June 14, 1919. e. Ladywood convent, Indianapolis; Pine Manor, Wellesley, MA.
STAGE: Our Town, My Dear Children, Swinging the Dream, Claudia, Legend of Lovers, Winesberg, Ohio, Night of the Iguana (1976), Cause Celebre; Another Part of the Forest; I Never Sang for My Father.
PICTURES INCLUDE: Claudia, A Tree Grows in Brooklyn, The Enchanted Cottage, Spiral Staircase, Claudia and David, Gentleman's Agreement, Mister 880, Callaway Went That-away, I Want You, Make Haste to Live, Invitation, 3 Coins in the Fountain, Trial, Friendly Persuasion, Old Yeller, The Swiss Family Robinson, This Earth Is Mine, Remarkable Mr.

Pennypacker, Dark at the Top of the Stairs, A Summer Place, Susan Slade, The Greatest Story Ever Told, Flight of the Doves.
TELEVISION: She Waits, Another Part of the Forest, The Runaways, The Philadelphia Story, Rich Man, Poor Man, Little Women, American Geisha, Ghost Dancing, The Incredible Journey of Dr. Meg Laurie, I Never Sang for My Father. Guest on: Love Boat, The Young & Restless, Highway to Heaven, Between Darkness and Dawn, Amos, Fantasy Island, St. Elsewhere.

McHUGH, JAMES: Agent, Manager. b. Boston, MA, Oct. 21, 1915. e. Holy Cross Coll. Joined MCA 1939. U.S. Army Signal Corps, 1944–46. MCA-British and European, 1945–50. Post grad. studies, Boston Coll. Formed James McHugh, Talent Agency 1953. Pres., Artists Mgr. Corp., pres., Turquoise Prod., Inc., v.p. Selective Activity.

McINTIRE, JOHN: Actor. b. Spokane, WA, June 27, 1907. e. local schools. m. Jeanette Nolan, actress. Radio announcer, actor teamed with wife.
PICTURES INCLUDE: Asphalt Jungle, Francis, Saddle Tramp, Winchester '73, Ambush, Scene of the Crime, You're in the Navy Now, Under the Gun, Raging Tide, Westward the Women, World in His Arms, Glory Alley, Sally & St. Anne, Horizons West, Lawless Breed, Mississippi Gambler, The President's Lady, Lion Is In the Street, War Arrow, Apache, Four Guns to the Border, Yellow Mountain, Far Country, Stranger on Horseback, Scarlet Coat, Phoenix City Story, Backlash, The Spoilers, The Kentuckian, World in My Corner, Away All Boats, The Tin Star, Who Was That Lady, Flaming Star, Two Rode Together, Summer and Smoke, Herbie Rides Again, Honkytonk Man, Cloak and Dagger.
TELEVISION: Series: Wagon Train, Naked City, The Virginian.

McKEE, LONETTE: Actress. b. Detroit, MI, 1954. Started career as singer at age of 14 on dance show, Swingin' Time. TV debut at 16 in The Wacky World of Jonathan Winters. Film debut in Sparkle, 1976. B'way debut as Mrs. Jackie Robinson in The First. On stage in revival of Showboat on Bdwy and off B'way in one woman show, Lady Day At Emerson's Bar and Grill.
PICTURES: Which Way Is Up?, Cuba, The Cotton Club, Brewster's Millions, 'Round Midnight, Gardens of Stone.
TELEVISION: Home Free (pilot), The Women of Brewster Place.

McKELLAR, KENNETH: Singer. b. Paisley, Scotland. singer, stage prods., radio & TV; appeared, concerts, Edinburgh International Festival; toured, Scots Concert groups; created role, Jamie in A Wish for Jamie, A Love for Jamie. Many BBC-TV and ITV appearances in V.K. Records regularly.

McKELLEN, IAN: Actor. b. Burnley, England, May 25, 1939. e. Cambridge. Many performances on London stage: A Scent of Flowers, Much Ado About Nothing, Trelawny of the Wells, A Lily in Little India, The Man of Destiny, Black Comedy, Dr. Faustus, King John, etc. On Bdwy. in The Promises, Amadeus (Tony, 1981), Ian McKellen Acting Shakespeare, Wild Honey (London and NY).
PICTURES: Alfred the Great, The Promise, A Touch of Love, Priest of Love, The Keep, Plenty.
TELEVISION: Hamlet, David Copperfield, The Scarlet Pimpernel, Hedda Gabler, Ian McKellen Acting Shakespeare, Every Good Boy Deserves Favor, Walter, Windmills of the Gods.

McKEON, DOUG: Actor. b. New Jersey, June 10, 1966. Theatre work includes Dandelion Wine and Truckload.
PICTURES: Uncle Joe Shannon, On Golden Pond, Night Crossing, Mischief.
TELEVISION: Edge of Night, Tell Me My Name, Centennial, Big Shamus Little Shamus, The Comeback Kid, An Innocent Love, Desperate Lives, At Mother's Request.

McKERN, LEO: Actor. r.n. Reginald McKern. b. Sydney, New South Wales, Australia, Mar. 16, 1920. On stage in She Stoops to Conquer, Hamlet, Merry Wives of Windsor, Cat on a Hot Tin Roof, A Man for All Seasons, etc.
PICTURES: All For Mary (1955), X the Unknown, Time Without Pity, The Mouse That Roared, Mr. Topaze, The Day the Earth Caught Fire, A Jolly Bad Fellow, King and Country, Moll Flanders, A Man for All Seasons, Ryan's Daughter, Help!, The Adventure of Sherlock Holmes' Smarter Brother, The Omen, Candleshoe, Damien: Omen II, The House on Garibaldi Street, The Last Tasmanian, The Blue Lagoon, The French Lieutenant's Woman, Voyage of Bounty's Child, Ladyhawke, The Chain, Traveling North.
TELEVISION: King Lear; Murder with Mirrors; House on Garibaldi Street; Reilly, Ace of Spies; Rumpole of the Bailey.

McLAGLEN, ANDREW V.: Dir. b. London, Eng., July 28, 1920. e. U. of Virginia, 1939–40. Prod. dept., Lockheed Aircraft Corp., 1940–44; asst. m.p. dir., 1944–54; dir., 1955–65; dir., CBS-TV, 1956–63.

PICTURES INCLUDE: Man in the Vault, Gun the Man Down, The Abductors, Freckles, The Little Shepherd of Kingdom Come, McLintock!, Shenandoah, The Rare Breed, Seven Men from Now, The Way West, The Ballad of Josie, Monkeys, Go Home, Devil's Brigade, Bandolero, The Undefeated, Fool's Parade, Something Big, One More Train to Rob, Cahill, U.S. Marshall, Mitchell, The Last Hard Men, The Wild Geese, ffolkes, The Sea Wolves, Sheena, Return from the River Kwai.

TELEVISION: Gunsmoke, Have Gun—Will Travel, Perry Mason, Rawhide, The Lineup, The Lieutenant, The Dirty Dozen: The Next Mission, On Wings of Eagles, The Blue and the Gray, The Shadow Riders, Travis McGee.

McLERIE, ALLYN ANN: Actress. b. Grand Mere, Quebec, Canada, Dec. 1, 1926. m. actor-singer George Gaynes. e. high school, N.Y. Dancer since 15 in many B'way shows.

SHOWS INCLUDE: One Touch of Venus, On the Town, Finian's Rainbow, Where's Charley, Miss Liberty, Time Limit, South Pacific (revival).

PICTURES INCLUDE: Words and Music (debut 1948), Where's Charley, Desert Song, Calamity Jane, Phantom of the Rue Morgue, Battle Cry, They Shoot Horses, Don't They?, The Cowboys, Jeremiah Johnson, The Magnificent Seven Ride, Cinderella Liberty, All the President's Men.

TELEVISION: Tony Randall Show (series) Punky Brewster (series), Days and Nights of Molly Dodd (series), The Thorn Birds, Oldest Living Graduate, The Entertainer, Beulah Land, Return Engagement.

McMAHON, ED: Performer. b. Detroit, MI, March 6, 1923. e. Boston Coll.; Catholic U. of America, B.A., 1949. U.S. Marines, 1942–53. First job on TV was as the clown on Big Top, 1950–51.

TELEVISION: Who Do You Trust?, Monitor, Fortune Phone, The Tonight Show Starring Johnny Carson (since 1962), Game show host: Missing Links, Concentration, Snap Judgment, Whodunnit (crime-quiz), Host: Kraft Music Hall (1968), NBC Adventure Theatre, Star Search, TV's Bloopers and Practical Jokes. Movies: Star Marker, The Great American Traffic Jam, The Kid From Left Field.

THEATRE: Stock Bdwy., Impossible Years.

PICTURES INCLUDE: The Incident, Fun with Dick and Jane, Butterfly.

McMAHON, JOHN J.: Executive. b. Chicago, IL, 1932. e. Northwestern U. Served with U.S. Army in Korea, beginning career on WGN-TV, Chicago; associated with ZIV-United Artists TV Productions during 1950s; joined ABC in 1958; v.p. & gen. mgr., WXYTZ-TV, Detroit, then KABC-TV, Los Angeles, 1968; v.p., ABC, 1968–72; joined NBC in 1972 as v.p., programs, west coast, NBC-TV; president, Hollywood Radio & Television Society; board member, Permanent Charities Committee. June, 1980, named pres. of Carson Prods. (Johnny Carson's prod. co.).

TELEVISION: If It's Tuesday, It Still Must Be Belgium (exec. prod.); My Father, My Son (exec. prod.).

McMARTIN, JOHN: Actor. Warsaw, IN, e. Columbia U. Off-Broadway debut: Little Mary Sunshine (1959).

THEATER: The Conquering Hero; Blood Sweat and Stanley Poole; Children from Their Games; A Rainy Day in Newark; Pleasures and Palaces (Detroit); Sweet Charity; Follies; The Great God Brown; Sondheim: A Musical Tribute; Forget-Me-Not-Lane (Mark Taper Forum); The Visit; Chemin de Fer, The Rules of the Game; A Little Family Business; Passion (Mark Taper); Solomon's Child.

PICTURES INCLUDE: What's So Bad About Feeling Good? (debut 1968); Sweet Charity; All The President's Men; Thieves; Brubaker; Pennies From Heaven; Legal Eagles; Dream Lover; Native Son.

TELEVISION: Mary Tyler Moore Show; Murrow; American Playhouse. Movies: Fear on Trial, Day One.

McMILLAN, KENNETH: Actor. b. Brooklyn, NY, July 2, 1932. e. H.S. of the Performing Arts; trained for theatre with Uta Hagen and Irene Dailey at HB Studios, NY. Stage debut in Sweet Bird of Youth, touring co., 1962.

PICTURES: Serpico, The Taking of Pelham 1, 2, 3, The Stepford Wives, Oliver's Story, Blood Brothers, Hide in Plain Sight, Little Miss Marker, Carny, Borderline, Eyewitness, Whose Life Is It Anyway?, True Confessions, Ragtime, Heartbeeps, The Killing Hour, Blue Skies Again, Head Over Heels, Reckless, Dune, Pope of Greenwich Village, Runaway Train, Armed and Dangerous, Malone, Fugitives.

TELEVISION: King, The Hustler of Muscle Beach, Breaking Up, Joe Dancer, Salem's Lot, Lou Grant, The Rockford Files, Kojak, Our Family Honor; Fran's Place; Murder She Wrote; Magnum, P.I.; In the Custody of Strangers; A Death in Canaan; Favorite Son. Series: Rhoda, Maggie Briggs, Love of Life.

McNALLY, STEPHEN: Actor r.n. Horace McNally. b. New York, NY, July 29, 1913. e. Fordham U., LL.B. In school dramatics; practiced law 2 yrs., N.Y.; stage, films, 1942.

PICTURES INCLUDE: Thirty Seconds Over Tokyo, Winchester 73, Wyoming Mail, No Way Out, Air Cadet, Apache Drums, Raging Tide, Lady Pays Off, Devil's Canyon, Make Haste to Live, A Bullet Is Waiting, Man from Bitter Ridge, Tribute to a Bad Man, Once You Kiss a Stranger, Black Gunn.

McNICHOL, KRISTY: Actress. b. Los Angeles, CA, Sept. 11, 1962. Made debut at age of 7 performing in commercials. Given regular role in Apple's Way; began appearing on such series as Love, American Style and The Bionic Woman. Attracted attention of Spelling-Goldberg Productions, who cast her as Buddy Lawrence in Family series 1976–80. (2 Emmy Awards, 1976–77); People's Choice Award 1980.

PICTURES: The End, Little Darlings, The Night the Lights Went Out in Georgia, Only When I Laugh, White Dog, The Pirate Movie, Just the Way You Are, Dream Lover, You Can't Hurry Love, Two Moon Junction.

TELEVISION: Movies: Like Mom, Like Me, Summer of My German Soldier, My Old Man, Love Mary, Women of Valor, Empty Nest (series).

McRANEY, GERALD: Actor. b. Collis, MI, Aug. 19, 1948. e. U. of Mississippi. Left school to become surveyor in oil fields after which joined acting company in New Orleans. Studied acting with Jeff Corey; landed guest role on TV series, Night Gallery.

TELEVISION: Series: The Incredible Hulk, The Rockford Files, The Dukes of Hazzard, Eight Is Enough, How the West Was Won, Hawaii Five-O, Barnaby Jones, Gunsmoke, Simon and Simon, Designing Women. Movies: Roots II, The Jordan Chance, Women in White, Trial of Chaplain Jenson, The Law, Love Story, The Haunting Passion, A Hobo's Christmas, Where the Hell's the Gold!!?, The People Across the Lake.

PICTURES: Night of Bloody Horror, Keep Off My Grass, The Neverending Story.

McSHANE, IAN: Actor. b. Blackburn, England, Sept. 29, 1942. e. Royal Acad. of Dramatic Art. Stage work includes The House of Fred Ginger, The Easter Man, The Glass Menagerie in England and The Promise on Bdwy. Los Angeles: Inadmissible Evidence, Betrayal.

PICTURES: The Wild and the Willing, The Pleasure Girls, The Battle of Britain, If It's Tuesday This Must Be Belgium, Pussycat Pussycat I Love You, Villain, The Last of Sheila, Ordeal by Innocence, Too Scared to Scream, Exposed, Ordeal By Innocence, Torchlight.

TELEVISION: Wuthering Heights, The Pirate, Disraeli, The Letter, Marco Polo, Bare Essence, Grace Kelly, Evergreen, A.D., The Murders in the Rue Morgue, Grand Larceny, War and Remembrance, Chain Letter.

MEANEY, DONALD V.: Executive. b. Newark, NJ. e. Rutgers U. Sch. of Journalism. Worked as reporter for Plainfield (NJ) Courier-News, Newark Evening News. Became news director of radio station WCTC in New Brunswick, NJ; later for WNJR, Newark. Joined NBC in 1952 as news writer; two years later became nat'l. TV news editor. Promoted to mgr., national news, 1960 and mrg., special news programs, 1961. Appt. dir. of news programs 1962 and gen. mgr., NBC News, 1965; v.p., news programming, NBC, 1967; v.p. news, Washington, 1974; mrg. dir., affiliate & intl. liaison, 1979; sr. mng. editor, intl. liaison, 1984; retired from NBC, 1985. Now on faculty of American U. Sch. of Communications.

MECHANIC, BILL: Executive. b. Detroit, MI. e. Michigan State U., B.A.; U. of Southern California, Ph.D. in film pending. Entered industry 1978 as dir. of programming for SelecTV; promoted to v.p., 1980. Joined Paramount 1982; 1984, to Disney as v.p., pay TV sls. 1985, named sr. v.p., video, of new Walt Disney video div.; 1987, named president, int'l theatrical distribution and worldwide video, Walt Disney.

MEDAK, PETER: Director. b. Budapest, Hungary. Entered industry in 1956 in London with AB-Pathe as trainee. Worked sound, editing and camera depts. Later was asst. dir., second unit dir. on various action pictures. In 1963 under contract to Universal Pictures, where started directing TV films. In 1967 under contract to Paramount Pictures.

PICTURES INCLUDE: Kaleidoscope (assoc. prod., 2nd unit dir.), Funeral in Berlin (2nd unit dir.), Fathom (assoc. prod.; 2nd unit dir.) Negatives (dir.), Day in the Death of Joe Egg (dir.), Ruling Class (dir.), Ghosts in the Noonday Sun (dir.), Odd Job, The Changeling, Zorro, the Gay Blade, Men's Club, Fatal Charm.

TELEVISION: Third Girl from the Left, The Babysitter, The Dark Secret of Black Bayou, Mistress of Paradise, Cry for the Stranger, Faerie Tale Theatre, Twilight Zone, Nabokov, Crime Story.

MEDAVOY, MIKE: Executive. b. Shanghai, China, Jan. 21, 1941. Lived in China until 1947 when family moved to Chile. Came to U.S. in 1957. e. U. of California at L.A., grad. 1963 with honors, history. Started working in mail room at Universal Studios and became a casting director, from which he went to work for Bill Robinson as an agent trainee. Two years later joined GAC and CMA where he was a v.p. in the motion picture department. In 1971 joined IFA as vice-president in charge of motion picture dept. Represented American and

foreign creative talents, among whom were Jane Fonda, Donald Sutherland, Michelangelo Antonioni, Jean-Louis Trintignant, Karel Reisz, Steven Spielberg, Robert Aldrich, George Cukor, John Milius, Terry Malick, Raquel Welch, Gene Wilder and Jeanne Moreau. While at IFA was involved in packaging The Sting, Young Frankenstein, Jaws and others, before joining United Artists Corp. in May, 1974, as senior v.p. in chg. of West Coast prod. In 1978 named exec. v.p., Orion Pictures Co. (In 1982 Orion team took over Filmways, Inc.) While production head received four Oscars for best picture: One Flew Over the Cuckoo's Nest, Rocky, Annie Hall, Amadeus, Platoon.
MEMBER: Filmex board; board of trustees, U.C.L.A. Foundation; advisory board, College for Intl. Strategic Affairs at U.C.L.A.; steering committee of Royce 270, U.C.L.A.; visiting committee, Boston Museum of Fine Arts; advisory board, Tel Aviv U.; board, Museum of Science & Industry; Co-Chmn.: Olympic Sports Federation, Music Center Unified Fund Campaign; board of governors, Sundance Inst.

MEDFORD, DON: Director. b. Detroit, MI, 1917. e. Purdue U., U. of North Carolina, B.A., Yale U., M.F.A. Actor, stage mgr., summer theatres; producer, B'way stage, Christopher Award.
TELEVISION: Kraft Theatre, General Electric Theatre, Alfred Hitchcock Presents, Climax, Twilight Zone, U.S. Steel Hour, Dick Powell, Eleventh Hour, Dr. Kildare, Fugitive, 12 O'clock High, The FBI, Man From U.N.C.L.E., Cimarron Strip, Baretta, Police Story, Kaz, Streets of San Francisco, Dynasty, Sizzle, Helltown.
FILMS: To Trap a Spy, Cosa Nostra, The Hunting Party, The Organization, The November Plan, Incident in San Francisco, The Coach.

MEDINA, PATRICIA: Actress. b. London, Eng. July 9, 1921. m. actor Joseph Cotten. In many British films.
PICTURES INCLUDE: Secret Journey, Hotel Reserve, Don't Take It to Heart, Waltz Time. U.S. screen debut: Secret Heart, 1946; others: Moss Rose, Foxes of Harrow, Sangaree, Drums of Tahiti, Phantom of the Rue Morgue, Black Knight, Pirates of Tripoli, Duel on the Mississippi, Uranium Boom, Stranger at My Door, The Killing of Sister George.

MEDMAN, EDWARD A: Executive. b. Philadelphia, PA, Nov. 11, 1937. e. U. of Pennsylvania Wharton Sch., 1955–58; U. of Pennsylvania Law Sch., 1958–61, J.D.S. General Counsel's staff, National Labor Relations Board, Washington, DC, 1962–66; Trial Attorney NLRB, New York 1966–69; joined law firm of Poletti, Freidin, Prashker, Feldman & Gartner, 1969; senior labor attorney, National Broadcasting Company 1970–72; joined The Burbank Studios, Dec. 1972, v.p., legal/business affairs.

MEDWIN, MICHAEL: Actor, Writer, Producer. b. England, 1925. e. Institut Fischer. Switzerland. Stage debut 1940; m.p. acting debut in Root of All Evil, 1946.
PICTURES INCLUDE: My Sister and I, Mrs. Christopher, Gay One, Children of Chance, Operation Diamond, Black Memory, Just William's Luck, Ideal Husband, Piccadilly Incident, Night Beat, Courtney's of Curzon Street, Call of the Blood, Anna Karenina, William Comes to Town, Woman Hater, Look Before You Love, Forbidden, For Them That Trespass, Queen of Spades, Trottie True, Boys in Brown, Trio, Long Dark Hall, Curtain Up, Street Corner (Both Sides of the Law), I Only Asked, Carry on Nurse, Wind Cannot Read, Heart of a Man, Crooks Anonymous, It's All Happening, Night Must Fall, I've Gotta Horse, 24 Hours To Kill. Prod: Charlie Bubbles, If. . ., Spring and Port Wine, O Lucky Man! Gumshoe, Law and Disorder, Memoirs of a Survivor, Falcon's Malteser.
TELEVISION: Granada's Army Game, Shoestring, The Love of Mike, Three Live Wires, Memorial Films Ltd.
THEATRE: Spring and Port Wine, Joe Egg, Forget-me-not Lane, Chez Nous, Alpha Beta, Another Country, Crystal Clear, Interpreters, Orpheus.

MEEKER, CHARLES R.: Producer. b. June 17. e. U. of Texas Sch. of Law. 1967–74, associated with Melveny & Myers, law firm specializing in entertainment industry. 1976, named active partner. Now pres., Feldman Meeker Co.; partnered with Edward S. Feldman.
PICTURES: Exec. Prod.: The Hitcher, Children of a Lesser God, Near Dark, Wired (co-prod.).

MELAMED, DAVID J.: Executive. b. N.Y., Dec. 11, 1911. e. New York U. Accountant, Columbia Pictures Corp., 1933–35; acct., RKO Radio Pictures, 1935–40; comptroller, Pathe Labs., Inc., 1941–43; U.S. Army, 1943–46; treas., Eagle Lion Films, 1947–51; exec. v.p., dir., Pathe Labs, Inc. 1952–58; dir. of adm., asst. to chmn. of bd., Nat'l General Corp., 1959–61; sr. exec. v.p., American International Pictures, 1961–80; v.p., SLM, Inc. 1981–84; presently director, Fries Entertainment.

MELCHIOR, IB: Director, Writer. b. Copenhagen, Denmark, Sept. 17, 1917. Son of late singer Lauritz Melchior. e. Coll., Stenhus, Denmark, 1936; U. of Copenhagen, 1937. Actor. stage mgr., English Players, 1937–38; co-dir. 1938; actor in 21 stage

prod. in Europe and U.S. on radio; set designer; stage man. dept., Radio City Music Hall, 1941–42; U.S. Military Intelligence, 1942–45; writer, dir., m.p. shorts for TV, 1947–48; TV actor, 1949–50; assoc. dir., CBS-TV, July, 1950; assoc. prod., G-L Enterprises, 1952–53; dir., Perry Como Show, 1951–54; dir. March of Medicine, 1955–56; writer, dir. of M.P. & TV films. 1957. Documentary writ. & dir. awarded Top Award by Nat'l. Comm. for Films for Safety, 1960. Golden Scroll Award, Acad. of Science Fiction, Best Writing, 1976; Hamlet Award, Shakespeare Society of America, excellence in playwriting, Hour of Vengeance, 1982.
PICTURES INCLUDE: When Hell Broke Loose, Live Fast Die Young, The Angry Red Planet, Reptilicus, Journey to the Seventh Planet, The Case of Patty Smith, Robinson Crusoe on Mars, The Time Travellers, Ambush Bay, Planet of the Vampires, Death Race 2000.
AUTHOR: Novel, Order of Battle, 1972; Sleeper Agent, 1975; The Haigerloch Project, 1977; The Watchdogs of Abaddon, 1979; The Marcus Device, 1980; The Tombstone Cipher, 1982; Eva, 1984; V–3, 1985; Code Name: Grand Guignol, 1987.

MELNICK, DANIEL: Executive. b. New York, NY, April 21, 1934. e. New York U. In 1954 was (youngest) staff prod. for CBS-TV; then exec. prod., East Side West Side and N.Y.P.D. Joined ABC-TV as v.p. in chg. of programming. Partner in Talent Associates. Joined MGM as v.p. in chg. of prod.; in 1974 named sr. v.p. & worldwide head of prod.; 1977 in charge of worldwide production, Columbia Pictures; named pres., 1978. Resigned to form independent production co., IndieProd. Company.
PICTURES INCLUDE: Straw Dogs (prod.), That's Entertainment! (exec. prod.); That's Entertainment, Two! (co-prod.); All That Jazz (exec. prod.); Altered States (exec. prod.); First Family (prod.), Making Love (co-prod.), Unfaithfully Yours (exec. prod.), Footloose (exec. prod.), Quicksilver (co-prod.); Roxanne (co-prod.), Punchline (co-prod.), Mountains of the Moon.
TELEVISION: Death of a Salesman (prod.), The Ages of Man (prod., Emmy Award, 1966); exec. prod. with David Susskind: East Side/West Side, N.Y.P.D., Get Smart.

MELNICK, SAUL: Executive. With a background in the video industry at CBS Video Enterprises, Pacifica Manufacturing Co. and Arista Records, joined MGM/UA Home Video in 1982 as national sales manager, rising to sales v.p. in 1983, and v.p. sales and marketing in 1984. Joined Tri-Star as pres. of home video unit, 1987; June 1988, appointed exec. v.p. Loews Theater Management.

MELNIKER, BENJAMIN: Motion Picture Producer, Attorney; b. Bayonne, NJ. e. Brooklyn Coll.; LL.B., Fordham Law Sch. Loew's Theatres usher, private law practice employed Legal Department Metro-Goldwyn-Mayer, vice president and general counsel, 1954–69, executive vice president, 1968–70, resigned from MGM December 1971; also member MGM bd. dir. and mem. MGM exec. com.; Adjunct associate professor, New York Law Sch., 1976–77; prod. & exec. prod. motion pictures, 1974–86; former motion picture chmn. Anti-Defamation League, B'nai B'rith; Mem. Am., N.Y. State bar assns., Bar Assn. City N.Y., Acad. of Motion Picture Arts and Scis.
PICTURES: Mitchell, Shoot, Winter Kills, Swamp Thing, Batman (exec. prod.).
TELEVISION: Three Sovereigns for Sarah, Television's Greatest Bets.

MENGERS, SUE: Talent Agent. b. Bronx, NY, Sept. 2, 1938. Started as receptionist, secretary with Music Corp. of America in New York. In 1963 became agent in small partnership. Two years later joined Creative Management Associates and sent to Hollywood. With Intl. Creative Mgt. (co. formed by merger of CMA and Marvin Josephson Associates). Clients have included Barbra Streisand, Gene Hackman, Ryan O'Neal, Tatum O'Neal, Ali MacGraw, Cybill Shepherd, Peter Bogdanovich, Sidney Lumet, Arthur Penn, Nick Nolte, Robin Williams, Roman Polanski, Michael Caine. 1988, appointed senior v.p. worldwide head of motion picture and m.p. literary division, William Morris Agency.

MENGES, CHRIS: Cinematographer, Director.
PICTURES: Cinematographer: If. . ., The Empire Strikes Back (second unit), Local Hero, Comfort and Joy, The Killing Fields (Acad. Award, 1984), Marie, The Mission (Acad. Award, 1986), Singing the Blues in Red, Shy People, High Season, A World Apart (dir. debut, 1988).
TELEVISION: World in Action, Opium Warlords, Opium Trail, East 103rd Street, etc.

MERCHANT, ISMAIL: Producer, Director. b. Bombay, India, 1936. e. St. Xavier's Coll., Bombay; New York U. Formed Merchant Ivory Prods., 1961 with James Ivory. First film, The Creation of Women (theatrical short, 1961, nom. for Acad. Award). Published cookbook, Ismail Merchant's Indian Cuisine; and book Hullabaloo in Old Jeypore (1989).
PICTURES: The Householder, Shakespeare Wallah, The Guru, Bombay Talkie, Savages, Autobiography of a Princess,

The Wild Party, Roseland, Hullabaloo Over Georgie and Bonnie's Pictures, The Europeans, Jane Austen in Manhattan, Quartet, Heat and Dust, The Bostonians, A Room With a View, Maurice, My Little Girl (exec. prod.), Slaves of New York (co-prod.), The Deceivers (prod.), The Perfect Murder (exec. prod.).
TELEVISION: Director: Mahatma and the Mad Boy, Courtesans of Bombay.

MERCHANT, LAWRENCE H., JR.: Producer. b. Cambridge, MA. e. Boston Latin Sch.; Hebron Acad., ME; Columbia U.; New York U. Pres., Educational Book Div., Prentice-Hall; pres., Pillsbury Productions; prod. exec., TV-Today, Home, Tonight, Milton Berle, Show of Shows, Hallmark Hall of Fame, Eye Witness, R. Montgomery Presents, Wide, Wide World, Walter Winchell; TV advisor, Gen. Dwight D. Eisenhower; prod. CBS films; pres., Kachina Productions.
PICTURES INCLUDE: Hands of Dr. Maniacal, Back Track, Present Tense of Love.

MERCOURI, MELINA: Actress. b. Athens, Oct. 18, 1925. m. dir.-prod. Jules Dassin. Schooling and training in Athens, fluent in French, German and English. Stage debut on Athens stage in avant-garde work; early stage career in Paris. Also made vocal recordings. Mem. of Greek Parliament for Port of Piraeus, 1977–present; Minister of Culture and Sciences for Greek Gov't. 1981–85; Minister of Culture, Youth and Sports, 1985–present.
PLAYS INCLUDE: Mourning Becomes Electra, La Nuit de Samaracande, Les Compagnons de la Marjolaine, Il Etait une Gare, Le Moulin de la Galette; to Greece 1954, in Stella. Also: A Streetcar Named Desire, Helen or the Joy of Living, The Queen of Clubs, The Seven Year Itch, Sweet Bird of Youth, Ilya Darling (Bdwy).
PICTURES INCLUDE: Stella, He Who Must Die, The Gypsy and the Gentleman, The Law, Never on Sunday, Phaedra, The Victors, Topkapi, 10:30 P.M. Summer, A Man Could Get Killed, Gaily, Gaily, Promise at Dawn, Earthquake, Once Is Not Enough, Nasty Habits, Maya and Brenda, A Dream of Passion.

MEREDITH, BURGESS: Actor. b. Cleveland, OH, Nov. 16, 1909. e. Amherst Coll., M.A. (hon.). m. Kaja Sundsten. Capt. U.S. Army Air Corps, W.W.II. On stage, 1929, Civic Repertory Co., N.Y.
STAGE PLAYS: Little Ol' Boy, She Loves Me Not, The Star Wagon, Winterset, High Tor, Remarkable Mr. Pennypacker, etc.
PICTURES INCLUDE: Began screen career 1936 in Winterset. Idiot's Delight, Of Mice and Men, Second Chorus, That Uncertain Feeling, Tom, Dick and Harry, Street of Chance, Miracles Can Happen, Story of G.I. Joe, Diary of a Chambermaid, Magnificent Doll, Mine Own Executioner, Man on the Eiffel Tower, Gay Adventure, Joe Butterfly, Advise and Consent, Hurry Sundown, Fortune Garden, Stay Away Joe, McKenna's Gold, Hard Contract, There Was a Crooked Man, The Clay Pigeon, Such Good Friends, Golden Needles, The Day of the Locust, 92 in the Shade, The Hindenburg, Burnt Offerings, Rocky, The Sentinel, The Manitou, Foul Play, Magic, The Great Georgia Bank Hoax, Golden Rendezvous, Rocky II, When Time Ran Out, Clash of the Titans, True Confessions, Rocky III, Santa Claus: The Movie, King Lear, Full Moon in Blue Water.
TELEVISION: Movies: The Last Hurrah, Johnny We Hardly Knew Ye, Tail Gunner Joe, Probe, Outrage!, Wet Gold.

MERRICK, DAVID: Producer. b. Hong Kong, Nov. 27, 1912. Famed Broadway stage impresario with long record of hits, including Fanny, The Matchmaker, Hello Dolly!, Look Back in Anger, The Entertainer, Jamaica, World of Suzie Wong, La Plume de Ma Tante, Destry Rides Again, Gypsy, Take Me Along, Irma La Douce, A Taste of Honey, Becket, Do Re Mi, Carnival, Sunday in New York, Oliver!, Marat/Sade, Rosencrantz and Guildenstern are Dead (Tony Award), 40 Carats, Promises, Promises, Play It Again Sam, Travesties, Very Good Eddie, I Do! I Do!, Private Lives, 42nd Street.
PICTURES: Child's Play (debut), The Great Gatsby, Semi-Tough, Rough Cut.

MERRILL, DINA: Actress. r.n. Nedinia Hutton; b. New York, NY, Dec. 9, 1928. e. George Washington U., 1940–41; American Acad. of Dramatic Arts. Fashion model, 1944–46. Acting debut: Here Today, Mrs. January and Mr. X, Newport (1944).
PLAYS INCLUDE: Regional theatre: My Sister Eileen, Major Barbara, Misalliance. Off-Broadway: Importance of Being Earnest, Smile of the Cardboard Man. Broadway: Angel Street, On Your Toes.
PICTURES INCLUDE: Desk Set (debut), Don't Give Up the Ship, Brass Ring, Catch Me If You Can, Operation Petticoat, The Sundowners, Butterfield 8, Running Wild, Twenty Plus Two, The Courtship of Eddie's Father, Young Savages, I'll Take Sweden, The Greatest, A Wedding, Just Tell Me What You Want, Do Me a Favor—Don't Vote For My Mom, Caddyshack II.
TELEVISION: debut, Kate Smith Show 1956; Four Star

Theatre, Playwrights '56, Climax!, Playhouse 90, Westinghouse Presents, The Investigators, Checkmate, The Rogues, Bob Hope Presents, To Tell the Truth, Hotel, Hawaii Five-O Hot Pursuit. Movies: Roots: The Next Generations, Seven in Darkness, The Letters, Family Flight, The Tenth Month, Sunshine Patriot.

MERRILL, GARY: Actor. b. Hartford, CT, Aug. 2, 1915. e. Loomis Prep. Sch., Bowdoin Coll., Trinity Coll. Stage career started in 1937, minor role, stage play, The Eternal Road; toured Brother Rat co.; then, Morning Star, See My Lawyer; on air in Young Dr. Malone, Helen Hayes Theatre, Theatre Guild, Gangbusters, Superman; army service 1941–45; upon disch. to stage in Born Yesterday, At War With the Army. Screen debut: Slattery's Hurricane (1949).
PICTURES INCLUDE: Twelve O'Clock High, Where the Sidewalk Ends, All About Eve, The Frogmen, Decision Before Dawn, Another Man's Poison, Phone Call From a Stranger, Girl in White, Night Without Sleep, Blueprint for Murder, Black Dakotas, Human Jungle, Pleasure of His Company, The Woman Who Wouldn't Die, Clambake, The Incident, The Last Challenge, The Power, Huckleberry Finn, Thieves.
TELEVISION: The Mask, Justice, Dr. Kildare.

MERSON, MARC: Producer. b. New York, NY, Sept. 9, 1931. e. Swarthmore Coll. Entered Navy in 1953; assigned as publicist to Admiral's Staff of Sixth Fleet Command in the Mediterranean. Upon discharge joined trade paper Show Business as feature editor. Joined CBS-TV as asst. to casting director. Left after 3 yrs. to work for Ely Landau as casting dir., packager and sometime producer of The Play of the Week on TV. Returned to CBS for 3-yr. stint doing specials and live programs. Left to organize Brownstone Productions as indep. prod. Now partner with Alan Alda in Helix Productions to package and produce TV shows.
PICTURES INCLUDE: The Heart Is a Lonely Hunter, People Soup (short), Leadbelly.
TELEVISION: Stage 67, Androcles and the Lion, Dummler and Son (pilot), The David Frost Revue (synd. series), We'll Get By.

MESMER, MARIE: Drama, Film reviewer. b. Newark, NJ, Feb. 14, 1920; e. Syracuse U., Brooklyn (NY) Inst. of Arts & Sciences. Radio adv. Crowell Pub. Co., 2 yrs.; danced with Ted Lewis and orchestra on tour; exhibiting artist in art galleries throughout U.S. for number years; currently drama reviewer Los Angeles (Calif.) Daily News, specializing in covering jazz music & personalities. Member: Los Angeles Press Club.

MESSICK, DON: Actor. b. Buffalo, NY, Sept. 7, 1926. e. Ramsay Streett, Sch. of Acting, Baltimore; American Theatre Wing, NY. Began performing as ventriloquist at age 13 in rural Maryland. Own radio show at 15 in Salisbury, MD (WBOC) for two years, writing and portraying all the characters in a one-man weekly comedy show. Worked in Hanna-Barbera cartoons since company began in 1958, voicing Ruff in their first series on NBC, 1959. Voiced Boo Boo Bear and Ranger Smith on Yogi Bear Show, Astro of The Jetsons. Voices: Scooby Doo and Scrappy Doo on Scooby Doo series; Papa Smurf and Azrael on Smurfs. Has done numerous national commercials.

MESTRES, RICARDO: Executive. b. New York, NY, 1958. e. Harvard U. Gained filmmaking experience during summers as prod. asst. on TV features. Joined Paramount Pictures as creative exec. 1981. Promoted to dir. of production, 1982 and to v.p., production in 1984. Named v.p. of prod., Walt Disney Pictures, 1985. Promoted to sr. v.p., prod.,1986. Named president, production, Touchstone Pictures, 1988.

METZGER, RADLEY: Producer, Director, Writer. b. 1930. Worked as asst. dir. also distributor of Swedish film I, A Woman before making own films.
PICTURES: Dark Odyssey (p.d., s.p.); Passionate Sunday, The Dirty Girls, The Alley Cats, Carmen, Baby (p.d.); Therese and Isabelle (p., d.); Camille 2000 (p.,d.); The Lickerish Quartet (p., d.); Score (p.d.); Little Mother (p., d.); Naked Came the Stranger (d.); The Image (d.), The Opening of Misty Beethoven; The Cat and the Canary; The Princess and the Call Girl.

METZLER, JIM: Actor. b. Oneonda, NY. e. Dartmouth Coll.
PICTURES: Four Friends, Tex, Hot to Trot.
TELEVISION: North and South, North and South Book II, On Wings of Eagles, Do You Remember Love, Princess Daisy, Christmas Star.

MEYER, BARRY M: Executive. With ABC-TV in legal and business affairs depts. before joining Warner Bros. TV in 1971 as dir. of business affairs. 1972, named v.p. of business affairs for Warner TV arm; promoted to exec. v.p. of div. 1978. 1984, named exec. v.p. of Warner Bros., Inc.

MEYER, NICHOLAS: Director. Writer. b. Dec. 24, 1945. e. U. of Iowa. Was unit publicist for Love Story, 1969. Story ed. Warner Bros. 1970–71. Author: The Seven-Per-Cent Solution,

Target Practice, The West End Horror, Confession of a Homing Pigeon.
PICTURES: The Seven-Per-Cent Solution (s.p.), Time After Time (s.p., dir.), Star Trek II: The Wrath of Khan (dir.), The Deceivers (dir.).
TELEVISION: Judge Dee (s.p.), The Night That Panicked America (s.p.); The Day After (dir.).

MEYER, RUSS: Producer, Director. b. Oakland, CA, March 21, 1922. In 1942 joined Army Signal Corps, learned m.p. photography and shot combat newsreels.
PICTURES INCLUDE: The Immoral Mr. Teas, Eve and the Handyman, Finders Keepers, Lovers Weepers, Goodmorning and Goodbye, Vixen, Beyond the Valley of the Dolls, The Seven Minutes, and Sweet Suzy, Beneath the Valley of the Dolls, The Breast of Russ Meyer, Ultra Vixens, Amazon Women on the Moon (actor).

MEYERS, ROBERT: Executive. b. Mount Vernon, NY, Oct. 3, 1934. e. New York U. Entered m.p. industry as exec. trainee in domestic div. of Columbia Pictures, 1956. Sales and adv. 1956–60; transferred to sales dep't. Columbia Pictures International, N.Y., posts there included supervisor of international roadshows and exec. ass't. to continental mgr. Joined National General Pictures as v.p.-foreign sales, 1969. Created JAD Films International Inc. in Feb. 1974 for independent selling and packaging of Motion Pictures around the world. September, 1977, joined Lorimar Productions Inc. as senior vice pres. of Lorimar Distribution International. Became pres. in April, 1978. Joined Filmways Pictures in 1980, named pres. & COO. Pres. of American Film Mktg. Assn.; 1982, formed new co., R.M. Films International.

MICHAELS, JOEL B.: Producer. b. Buffalo, NY, Oct. 24, 1938. Studied acting with Stella Adler. Many co-prods. with Garth Drabinsky, Cineplex Corp.
PICTURES: The Peace Killers; Your Three Minutes Are Up (prod. spvr.); Student Teachers (prod. spvr.); The Prisoners (asso. prod.); Lepke (asso. prod.); The Four Deuces (asso. prod.); Bittersweet Love; The Silent Partner; The Changeling; Tribute; The Amateur; Losin' It (exec. prod.); The Philadelphia Experiment.

MICHAELS, LORNE: Writer, Producer. b. Toronto, Canada, Nov. 17, 1944. r.n. Lorne Lipowitz. e. U. of Toronto, 1966. Rowan and Martin's Laugh-In (writer, 1968–69); CBC comedy specials (writer, prod., 1969–72); Lily Tomlin Specials (writer, prod., 1972–75, 2 Emmy Awards); Perry Como (writer, prod., 1974); Flip Wilson (writer, prod.); Saturday Night Live (creator, prod., writer 1975–80, 3 Emmys); Beach Boys (writer, prod.); Paul Simon (writer, prod., Emmy Award, 1978); The Rutles: All You Need Is Cash (writer, prod.); Steve Martin's Best Show Ever (prod.); Simon and Garfunkel: The Concert in Central Park (exec. prod.); The Coneheads (exec. prod.); The New Show (prod.); Emmy Awards, (prod., 1988); Coca-Cola Presents Live: The Hard Rock; On Location: The Kids in the Hall (exec. prod.); President, Broadway Video, since 1979.
PICTURES: Gilda Live (prod., writer); Nothing Lasts Forever (prod.); Bigshots in America; Three Amigos (prod.).

MICHAELS, RICHARD: Director. b. Brooklyn, NY, Feb. 15, 1936. e. Cornell U. Script supervisor 1955–64 and associate producer before starting directing career in 1968 with Bewitched (54 episodes), of which was also assoc. prod.
TELEVISION: Series: episodes of Love, American Style, Delvecchio, Ellery Queen, Room 222. Movies: Once an Eagle (mini-series), Charlie Cobb, Having Babies II, Leave Yesterday Behind, My Husband Is Missing, . . .And Your Name Is Jonah (winner, Christopher Award), Once Upon a Family, The Plutonium Incident, Scared Straight, Another Story (winner, Scott Newman Drug Abuse Prevention Award), Homeward Bound (winner, Banff Intl. TV Festival special & Christopher Award), Berlin Tunnel 21, The Children Nobody Wanted, One Cooks, The Other Doesn't, Sadat (mini-series), Jessie (pilot), Silence of the Heart, Heart of a Champion: The Ray Mancini Story, Rockabye, Kay O'Brien (pilot), I'll Take Manhattan (mini-series), Leg Work (pilot), Red River (movie), Indiscreet.
PICTURE: Blue Skies Again.

MICHEL, WERNER: Executive. b. March 5, 1910. e. U. of Berlin, U. of Paris, Ph.D. Radio writer, dir., co-author two Broadway revues, 1938, 1940; dir. French feature films; dir. Broadcast Div., Voice of America, 1942–46; prod., dir., CBS, 1946–48; asst. prog. dir., CBS, 1948–50; dir. of Kenyon and Eckhart TV dept., 1950–52; prod., DuMont TV network, 1952–55; dir., Electronicam TV-Film Prod., 1955–56; prod., Benton and Bowles; Procter and Gamble, 1956–57; v.p. & dir. TV-radio dept., Reach, McClinton Advertising, Inc., 1957–62; consultant, TV Programming & Comm'l-Prod., N. W. Ayer & Son, Inc.; v.p., dir., TV dept., SSCB Advertising, 1963, pgm. exec.; ABC-TV Hollywood, 1975; director, dramatic programs, 1976; sr. v.p., creative affairs, MGM-TV, 1977; exec. v.p., Wrather Entertainment Intl., 1979; sr. v.p., creative affairs, MGM-TV, 1980–82; COO, Guber-Peters TV, 1982–84; sr. v.p., corporate TV dept., Kenyon & Eckhart, & NY, 1984.

MICHELET, MICHEL: Composer. b. Kiev, Russia, June 27, 1899. Prof., Kiev & Vienna Conserv. Composed concert compositions, ballets, stage music; ent. m.p. industry, composed scores 105 films, in France, Italy and Germany; to U.S. 1941; author many concert compositions.
PICTURES INCLUDE: Voice in the Wind (AA nom.), Hairy Ape (AA nom.), Music for Millions, The Chase, Lured, Siren of Atlantis, Man on the Eiffel Tower, Once a Thief, Tarzan's Peril, Fort Algiers, Un Missionaire, Le Secret de Soeur Angele, Petersburger, Nachte, Challenge (Tribute to Modern Art). Also did scores for many U.S. Information Service documentaries; arr. of Russian music Anastasia; Afrodife (score); The January (orig. songs & arr. of Russian music). Member: French Soc. of Composers (SACEM).

MICHELL, KEITH: Actor. b. Adelaide, Australia, Dec. 1, 1926. Early career as art teacher, radio actor; toured Australia with Stratford Shakespearean Co. 1952–53; Stratford Memorial Theatre 1954–55, Old Vic Theatre 1956–57. Irma la Douce, Chichester, Art of Seduction, The First 400 Years, Robert & Elizabeth, Kain, The King's Mare, 1969: Man of La Mancha (London, N.Y.) 1970: Abelard & Heloise (London); 1971, (NY and LA), 1972, Hamlet, (London). Artistic Director, Chichester Festival Theatre. Toured Australia with Chichester Festival Co., London 1979: Crucifer of Blood, (London) 1980: On the Twentieth Century, (Melbourne Theatre Co.): Pete McGynty, (London): Captain Beaky Christmas Show. (Chichester): On the Rocks (Brisbane) 1982: The Tempest, (UK tour 1983): Amadeus (San Francisco). 1984–85: La Cage aux Folles (USA and Australia), Portraits, The Bacarat Scandal (Chicester, 1988).
TELEVISION: Pygmalion, Act of Violence, Mayerling Affair, Tiger at the Gates, Traveller Without Luggage, Guardian Angel, Wuthering Heights, The Bergonzi Hands, Ring Round The Moon, Spread of the Eagle, The Shifting Heart, Loyalties, Sister in Love, Hallmark Hall of Fame, series: Kain, The Ideal Husband, The Six Wives of Henry VIII (series). Keith Michell at various London theatres, Dear Love. Selections from Keith Michell in Concert at Chichester, Captain Beaky & his Band, Captain Beaky, Volume 2. 1983 TV Video: The Gondoliers, The Pirates of Penzance, Ruddigore, My Brother Tom (Australian and UK TV series, 1986), Capt. James Cook. (Aust. and UK TV series, 1987).
PICTURES INCLUDE: True as a Turtle, Dangerous Exile, Gypsy and the Gentleman, The Hellfire Club, All Night Long, Seven Seas to Calais, Prudence and the Pill, House of Cards, Henry VIII and his Six Wives, Moments, The Deceivers.

MIDLER, BETTE: Actress, Singer. b. Honolulu, HI, Dec. 1, 1945. e. U. of Hawaii. Appeared on Bdwy. in Fiddler on the Roof; Salvation, 1970; Tommy, Seattle Opera Co., 1971. Gained fame as singer-comic in nightclubs and cabarets. Has toured extensively with own stage shows: Divine Miss M, Clams on the Half-Shell. Author: The Saga of Baby Divine, 1983. Special Tony Award, 1973.
PICTURES: The Rose, Divine Madness, Jinxed, Down and Out in Beverly Hills, Ruthless People, Outrageous Fortune, Big Business, Beaches.
TELEVISION: Ol' Red Hair is Back (Emmy Award, 1978); Bette Midler's Mondo Beyondo.

MIFUNE, TOSHIRO: Actor. b. Tsingtao, China, April 1, 1920. e. Japanese schools. Served five years Japanese army. Joined Toho Studio 1946.
PICTURES INCLUDE: Snow Trail, Drunken Angel, Eagle of Pacific, Seven Samurai, I Live in Fear, Legend of Musashi, Throne of Blood, Riksha Man, Three Treasures, Last Gunfight, I Bombed Pearl Harbor, Rose in Mud, Rashomon, Yojimbo, Animus Trujano (Mexican), Kiska, Red Beard, High and Low, Judo Sag, The Lost World of Sinbad, Hell in the Pacific, Paper Tiger, Midway, Winter Kills, 1941, The Challenge, Inchon, The Bushido Blade, Princess from the Moon.
TELEVISION: (U.S.) Shogun.

MIGDEN, CHESTER L.: Executive. b. New York, NY, May 21, 1921; e. City Coll. of New York, B.A., 1941, Columbia U., LL.B, 1947. Member New York Bar. Attorney for National Labor Relations Board 1947–51. Currently exec. dir., Assn. of Talent Agents. Was exec of Screen Actors Guild 1952–81; nat'l. exec. secty., 1973–81.

MIKELL, GEORGE: Actor. b. Lithuania. In Australia 1950–56 acting with Old Vic Co. Ent. films 1955. TV 1957. To England 1957; since appeared in numerous film and TV prod.
TELEVISION: Counsel at Law, Six Eyes on a Stranger, The Mask of a Clown, Green Grows the Grass, Opportunity Taken, OSS Series, Espinage, The Danger Man, Strange Report, The Survivors, The Adventurer, Colditz, The Hanged Man, Quiller, Martin Hartwell, Flambards, Sweeney, The Secret Army, Sherlock Holmes, When the Boat Comes In, Brack Report, Bergerac, The Brief, Glass Babies (Australia), Hannay.
PICTURES INCLUDE: The Guns of Navarone, The Password Is Courage, The Great Escape, Deadline for Diamonds, Where The Spies Are, The Spy Who Came in From the Cold,

I Predoni Del Sahara, Sabina, The Double Man, Attack on the Iron Coast, Zeppelin, Young Winston, Scorpio, The Tamarind Seed, Sweeney Two, The Sea Wolves, Escape to Victory, Emerald, Kommissar Zufall (Germany).
STAGE: Five Finger Exercise, Altona, The Millionairess, Love from a Stranger, Portrait of a Queen, Farewell, Judas, Flare Path.

MIKHALKOV, NIKITA: Director, Writer. b. Moscow, Soviet Union, Oct. 21, 1945. His great grandfather was the painter Sourikov; his grandfather, painter Konchalovski; his father, Sergei Mikhalhov is a writer and chm. of USSR Writers Union. His mother is poet Natalia Konchalovskaia; brother is director Andrei Mikhalkov-Konchalovski. e. Theater School of Varkhtangok, and High School for Cinema. Directed first short film 1968: I'm Coming Home. Directed short film for graduation: A Quiet Day at the End of the War. Debut as actor in I'm Wandering Through Moscow (1964). Acted in more than 25 films including: The Call, A Nest of Noblemen, Song to Manchuk, The Red Tent, Siberiad.
PICTURES: Dir. and co-s.p.: At Home Among Strangers (1974), Ours Among Ours, The Slave of Love, Unfinished Work for Pianola (also actor), Five Evenings, Oblomov, Relatives (also actor), Without Witness, Dark Eyes, The Barber of Siberia.

MILES, CHRISTOPHER: Director. b. England, April 19, 1939. Brother of actress Sarah Miles.
PICTURES: Up Jumped a Swagman; The Virgin and the Gypsy; Time for Loving; The Maids; That Lucky Touch; Priest of Love (also prod.), Murder in Mesopotamia.

MILES, SARAH: Actress. b. Sept. 9, 1941. m. writer Robert Bolt. e. Royal Acad. of Dramatic Art. Film debut, Term of Trial (1963).
PICTURES INCLUDE: The Servant, The Ceremony, Six-Sided Triangle, Those Magnificent Men In Their Flying Machines, Blowup, Ryan's Daughter, Lady Caroline Lamb, The Man Who Loved Cat Dancing, The Sailor Who Fell from Grace with the Sea, The Big Sleep, Venom, Ordeal by Innocence, Steaming, Hope and Glory, White Mischief.
THEATRE: Vivat! Vivat Regina!
TELEVISION: James Michener's Dynasty; Great Expectations; Harem, Queenie.

MILES, VERA: Actress. b. Boise City, OK, Aug. 23, 1930. e. public schools, Pratt and Wichita, KS.
TELEVISION: Climax, Pepsi Cola Playhouse, Schlitz Playhouse, Ford Theatre. Movie: International Airport, Rough Necks, Baffled, McNaughton's Daughter, State Fair, Runaway, The Underground Man, The Strange and Deadly Occurrence, Smash-up on Interstate 5, Judge Horton and the Scottsboro Boys, Helen Keller—The Miracle Continues, Travis McGee.
PICTURES INCLUDE: For Men Only, Rose Bowl Story, Charge at Feather River, Pride of the Blue Grass, Wichita, The Searchers, 23 Paces to Baker Street, Autumn Leaves, Wrong Man, Beau James, Web of Evidence, FBI Story, Touch of Larceny, Five Branded Women, Psycho, The Spirit Is Willing, Gentle Giant, Sergeant Ryker, Kona Coast, It Takes All Kinds, Hellfighters, The Wild Country, One Little Indian, Psycho II, Brainwaves.

MILGRAM, HENRY: Theatre Executive. b. Philadelphia, PA, April 20, 1926. e. U. of Pennsylvania, Wharton Sch. In industry 41 years; now exec. v.p. Milgram Theatres. Variety Club Board member for past 20 years, past president and chairman of the board of Variety Club of Phila.; presently Variety Club Intl. v.p. Board member. Hahnemann University, trustee.

MILIUS, JOHN: Writer, Director. b. April 11, 1945. e. Los Angeles City Coll., U. of Southern California (cinema course). While at latter won National Student Film Festival Award. Started career as ass't. to Lawrence Gordon at AIP. Began writing screenplays, then became director with Dillinger (1973).
PICTURES INCLUDE: Devil's 8 (s.p.), Evil Knievel (s.p.), The Life and Times of Judge Roy Bean, Jeremiah Johnson (co-s.p.), Dillinger (s.p.-dir.), Magnum Force (co-s.p.), The Wind and the Lion (s.p., dir.), Big Wednesday (dir. co.-s.p.); Apocalypse Now (s.p.); Hardcore (exec. prod.), Used Cars (co-exec. prod.), 1941 (exec. prod., co.-s.p.); Conan the Barbarian (dir., co.-s.p.); Uncommon Valor (co-prod.), Red Dawn (dir., co-s.p.), Extreme Prejudice (story).

MILKIS, EDWARD: Producer. b. Los Angeles, CA, July 16, 1931. e. U. of Southern California. Began career as asst. editor, ABC-TV, 1952; Disney, 1954; MGM, 1957; editor, MGM, 1960–65; assoc. prod., Star Trek, 1966–69; exec. in chg. post-prod., Paramount, 1969–72; formed Miller-Milkis Prods., 1972; Miller-Milkis-Boyett, 1979. Now heads Edward K. Milkis Prods.
PICTURES: Silver Streak; Foul Play; The Best Little Whorehouse in Texas.
TELEVISION: Petrocelli; Bosom Buddies (exec. prod.); Happy Days; Laverne and Shirley; Feel the Heat.

MILLAR, STUART: Producer, Director. b. New York, NY, 1929. e. Stanford U.; Sorbonne, Paris. Ent. industry working for

Motion Picture Branch, State Dept., Germany. documentaries, Army Signal Corps, Long Island, Germany; journalist, International News Service, San Francisco; assoc. prod.-dir., The Desperate Hours; assoc. prod.-dir., Friendly Persuasion.
PICTURES INCLUDE: The Young Stranger; Stage Struck; Birdman of Alcatraz. I Could Go On Singing, The Young Doctors, Stolen Hours, The Best Man, Paper Lion, Little Big Man, When The Legends Die, Rooster Cogburn, Shoot the Moon (co-exec. prod.).
TELEVISION: Vital Signs.

MILLER, ANN: Actress. r.n. Lucille Ann Collier; b. Houston, TX, Apr. 12, 1923. e. Albert Sidney Johnson H.S., Houston; Lawler Prof. Sch., Hollywood. Studied dance as child; played West Coast vaudeville theatres. Screen debut: New Faces of 1937.
STAGE: George White's Scandals, 1940, Mame, 1969, Sugar Babies.
PICTURES INCLUDE: Life of the Party, Stage Door, New Faces of 1937, Radio City Revels, Having a Wonderful Time, Room Service, You Can't Take It with You, Too Many Girls, Time Out for Rhythm, Priorities on Parade, Reveille with Beverly, Jam Session, Eve Knew Her Apples, Thrill of Brazil, Easter Parade, The Kissing Bandit, On the Town, Watch the Birdie, Texas Carnival, Two Tickets to Broadway, Lovely To Look At, Small Town Girl, Kiss Me Kate, Deep in My Heart, Hit the Deck, Opposite Sex, Great American Pastime.

MILLER, ARTHUR: Writer. b. New York, NY, Oct. 17, 1915. e. U. of Michigan. Plays include All My Sons, Death of a Salesman, The Crucible, A View from the Bridge, After the Fall, Incident at Vichy, The Price, Up From Paradise, Situation Normal, The American Clock, Autobiography: Timebends (1987).
PICTURES: Film versions of plays: All My Sons, Death of a Salesman, The Crucible, A View From the Bridge, The Misfits (orig. s.p.).
TELEVISION: Death of a Salesman, Fame, After The Fall, Playing for Time.

MILLER, BARRY: Actor. b. Los Angeles, CA, Feb. 6, 1958. New York stage debut, My Mother, My Father and Me, 1980. Film debut, Saturday Night Fever, 1977.
THEATER: Forty Deuce, The Tempest, Biloxi Blues (Tony and Drama Desk Awards, 1985).
PICTURES: Voices, Fame, The Chosen, The Journey of Natty Gann, Peggy Sue Got Married, The Last Temptation of Christ.
TELEVISION: The Roommate, Joe and Sons, Szysznyk, The Bill Cosby Show.

MILLER, CHERYL: Actress. b. Sherman Oaks, CA, Feb. 4, 1943. e. U. of California at L.A., Los Angeles Conservatory of Music.
PICTURES INCLUDE: First film, Casanova Brown, age 19 days. Appeared in over 100 films as child, more recently in the Monkey's Uncle, Clarence the Cross-Eyed Lion, The Initiation, The Man from Clover Grove, Doctor Death.
TELEVISION: Perry Mason, Bachelor Father, Flipper and as co-star in Daktari, Donna Reed, Leave It to Beaver, Farmer's Daughter, Wonderful World of Color, Dobie Gillis, Bright Promise, Love American Style, Emergency, Cades County.

MILLER, DAVID: Director. b. Paterson, NJ, Nov. 28, 1909. U.S. Army, W.W.II. Film ed. 1930, Columbia; Walter Futter prods. In 1933 short subjects ed. MGM; then dir. short subjects. Dir. features 1941.
PICTURES INCLUDE: Billy the Kid, Sunday Punch, Flying Tigers, Love Happy, Top O the Morning, Our Very Own, Saturday's Hero, Sudden Fear, Twist of Fate, Diane, Opposite Sex, The Story of Esther Costello, Midnight Lace, Backstreet, Lonely Are the Brave, Captain Newman, MD, Hammerhead, Hail Hero, Executive Action, Bittersweet Love.
TELEVISION: Best Place to Be, Goldie and The Boxer, Love for Rent.

MILLER, DICK (RICHARD): Actor, Writer. b. New York, NY, Dec. 25, 1928. e. City Coll. of New York, Columbia U. Grad. NYU. Theater Sch. of Dramatic Arts. Commercial artist, psychologist (Bellevue Mental Hygiene Clinic, Queens General Hospital Psychiatric dept.) Served in U.S. Navy, W.W.II. Boxing champ, U.S. Navy. Semi-pro football. Broadway stage, radio disc jockey, The Dick Miller Show, WMCA, WOR-TV. Over 500 live shows. Did first live night talk show with Bobby Sherwood, Midnight Snack, CBS, 1950. Wrote, produced and directed radio and TV shows in NY in early 1950s. Wrote screenplays; T.N.T. Jackson, Which Way to the Front, Four Rode Out and others. Has appeared on all major TV series and Fame (3 years).
PICTURES INCLUDE: Has appeared in over 100 features, including: Not of This Earth, Thunder Over Hawaii, Rock All Night, Sorority Girl, The Terror, Bucket of Blood, Little Shop of Horrors, Targets, War of the Satellites, The Long Ride Home, St. Valentine's Day Massacre, Capone, Executive Action, White Line Fever, Cannonball, Mr. Billion, New York, New

York, Gremlins, Explorers, Inner Space, After Hours, Terminator, The 'Burbs.

MILLER, (DR.) GEORGE: Director. b. Chinchilla, Queensland, Australia, 1945. Practiced medicine in Sydney; quit to work on films with Byron Kennedy, who became longtime partner until his death in 1983. Early work: Violence in the Cinema Part One (short, dir., s.p.), Frieze—An Underground Film (doc., editor only), Devil in Evening Dress (doc., dir., s.p.). First worldwide success with Mad Max.
PICTURES: Mad Max (dir., s.p.), Chain Reaction (assoc. prod. only), The Road Warrior, Twilight Zone—The Movie (segment), Mad Max Beyond Thunderdome, The Witches of Eastwick.
TELEVISION: Five Mile Creek, The Cowra Breakout.

MILLER, GEORGE: Director. b. Australia.
PICTURES: In Search of Anna (asst. dir.), The Man from Snowy River, The Aviator, The Return of the Man from Snowy River.
TELEVISION: Cash and Company, Against the Wind, The Last Outlaw, The Dismissal, All the Rivers Run, Bodyline (also s.p.).

MILLER, JAMES R.: Executive. Began m.p. industry career in 1971 in legal dept. of United Artists (N.Y.). Left to go with Paramount Pictures in legal dept.; then moved to Columbia in 1977 as snr. counsel; later assoc. gen. counsel. In 1979 named Warner Bros. v.p.—studio business affairs; 1984, v.p. chg. world-wide business affairs; 1987, sr. v.p.

MILLER, JP: Writer. b. San Antonio, TX, Dec. 18, 1919. e. Rice U., 1937–41; Yale Drama Sch., 1946–47. U.S. Navy, Lieut., 1941–46; pub. poetry, short stories.
ORIGINAL DRAMAS INCLUDE: Philco TV Playhouse: Hide and Seek, Old Tasslefoot, The Rabbit Trap, The Pardon-me Boy; Playhouse 90, Days of Wine and Roses, CBS Playhouse, The People Next Door (Emmy Award, 1969), The Unwanted, The Lindbergh Kidnapping Case, Helter Skelter, Gauguin the Savage, The Preppie Killing.
PICTURES INCLUDE: The Rabbit Trap, (story, s.p.) Days of Wine and Roses (story s.p.) The Young Savages (co-author, s.p.) Behold A Pale Horse, (s.p.) The People Next Door (story, s.p.).
NOVELS: The Race for Home, Liv, The Skook.

MILLER, JASON: Writer, Actor. b. Scranton, PA, April 22, 1939. Entered regional playwriting contest during high school in Scranton, PA and since has moved back and forth between acting and writing. Wrote That Championship Season, winner of N.Y. Drama Critics Best Play award, 1972, Tony Award, 1973, and Pulitzer Prize for Drama.
PICTURES INCLUDE: The Exorcist (actor), That Championship Season (s.p.), The Nickel Ride (actor), A Home of our Own (actor), A Love Story (s.p.); Monsignor (actor), Light of Day (actor), The Ninth Configuration (actor).
TELEVISION: Actor: Deadly Care, Dain Curse, F. Scott Fitzgerald in Hollywood, Best Little Girl in the World, Vampire, A Home of Our Own, Henderson Monster, Marilyn: The Untold Story, Night Heat.

MILLER, MAX B.: Executive. Father, Max Otto Miller, producer silent features and shorts. e. Los Angeles Valley Coll., U. of California at L.A., Sherwood Oaks Coll. Writer of articles on cinema for American Cinematographer and other publications. Owns and manages Fotos Intl., entertainment photo agency with offices in 46 countries. Recipient of Golden Globe Award in 1976 for Youthquake, documentary feature. Also director of Films International (prod., Shoot Los Angeles) and pres. of MBM Prod., Inc. Active member of Hollywood Foreign Press Assn. (from 1974–82 bd member; twice chm.), Independent Feature Project, Acad. of TV Arts & Sciences, L.A. Int'l. Film Exhibition.

MILLER, ROBERT ELLIS: Director. b. New York, NY, July 18, 1932. Worked on Broadway and TV before feature film debut with Any Wednesday (1966).
PICTURES INCLUDE: Sweet November, The Heart Is a Lonely Hunter, The Buttercup Chain, Big Truck and Poor Claire, The Girl from Petrovka, The Baltimore Bullet, Reuben, Reuben, Hawks.
TELEVISION: The Voice of Charlie Pont, And James Was a Very Small Snail, The Other Lover, Madame X, Just an Old Sweet Song, Her Life as a Man, Ishi, Last of His Tribe; Intimate Strangers.

MILLER, RONALD W.: Producer. b. Los Angeles, CA, April 17, 1933. e. U. of Southern California. Football player with Los Angeles Rams. Two years U.S. Army. 1957 joined Walt Disney Productions as 2nd asst. dir. Old Yeller. Assoc. prod. TV series Walt Disney Presents; assoc. or co-prod. additional 37 episodes Disney TV. Exec. prod. Walt Disney's Wonderful World of Color. Assisted Walt Disney, Pageant Direct 1960 U.S. Olympics. By 1968, v.p., exec. prod. mem. bd. of dir. Walt Disney Productions. 1980, named pres. & chief operating off.;

1983, pres. & chief executive off., Disney Productions. Resigned in 1984.
PICTURES INCLUDE: Bon Voyage, Summer Magic, Son of Flubber, Moon Pilot, The Misadventures of Merlin Jones, A Tiger Walks, The Monkey's Uncle, That Darn Cat, Robin Crusoe, U.S.N., Monkey's Go Home, Prod. of: Never a Dull Moment, The Boatniks, The Wild Country, No Deposit, No Return, Treasure of Matecumbe, Freaky Friday, The Littlest Horse Thieves, Herbie Goes to Monte Carlo, Pete's Dragon, Candleshoe, Return from Witch Mountain, Cat from Outer Space, The North Avenue Irregulars, Herbie Goes Bananas, The Black Hole, Midnight Madness, Watcher in the Woods, The Last Flight of Noah's Ark. Exec. prod.: Condorman; The Devil and Max Devlin; Tex; Never Cry Wolf, Night Crossing, Tron.

MILLER, WINSTON: Writer. b. St. Louis, MO, June 22, 1910. e. Princeton U. In 1935 entered m.p. ind.
PICTURES INCLUDE: Good Morning, Judge, Song of Texas, Home in Indiana, One Body Too Many, They Made Me a Killer, Double Exposure, My Darling Clementine, Relentless, Station West, Last Outpost, Rocky Mountain, Hong Kong, Blazing Forest, Carson City, The Vanquished, Boy from Oklahoma, Jivaro, Bounty Hunter, Run for Cover, Far Horizons, Lucy Gallant, Tension at Table Rock, April Love, A Private's Affair, Hound Dog Man, Escapade In Japan, Mardi Gras.

MILLS, DONNA: Actress. b. Chicago, IL, Dec. 11, 1944. e. U. of Illinois. Left school to pursue career in theatre, beginning as dancer with stage companies around Chicago. Toured and landed in New York, breaking into TV as regular of soap opera, The Secret Storm. On Bdwy in Don't Drink the Water; theatrical film debut in The Incident.
TELEVISION: Series: Love Is a Many Splendored Thing, Lancer, Dan August, The Good Life, Knots Landing. Movies: Waikiki, Doctor's Private Lives, Superdome, The Hunted Lady, Woman on the Run, Fire!, The Bait. Mini-Series: Hanging by a Thread, Bare Essence, Intimate Encounters.
PICTURES: The Incident, Play Misty for Me, etc.

MILLS, HAYLEY: Actress. b. London, Eng., April 18, 1946. Daughter of actor John Mills. e. Elmhurst Boarding Sch., Surrey. m.p. debut Tiger Bay 1959; signed Disney contract 1960.
PICTURES INCLUDE: Pollyanna, The Parent Trap, Whistle Down the Wind, The Castaways, Summer Magic, The Chalk Garden, The Moonspinners, The Truth About Spring, Sky West and Crooked, Trouble with Angels, The Family Way, Pretty Polly, A Matter of Innocence, Twisted Nerve, Take a Girl Like You, Deadly Strangers, Silhouettes, What Changed Charley Farthing, The Diamond Hunters, That Darn Cat, Forbush and the Penguins, Endless Night, Appointment with Death.
TELEVISION: The Flame Trees of Thika, Parent Trap II, Amazing Stories, Illusion of Life, Good Morning Miss Bliss (series), Murder She Wrote.

MILLS, SIR JOHN: Actor, Producer. b. Suffolk, England, February 22, 1908, m. Mary Hayley Bell. Previously clerk. Film actor since 1933. One of top ten money-making Brit. stars in Motion Picture Herald-Fame Poll, 1945, 1947, 1949–50, 1954, 1956–58. Oscar for Ryan's Daughter. Recipient special award 1988, British Academy of Film and Television Arts.
PICTURES INCLUDE: We Dive at Dawn, The Young Mr. Pitt, In Which We Serve, This Happy Breed, Blue for Waterloo, Cottage To Let, Way to the Stars, Waterloo Road, Great Expectations, So Well Remembered, October Man, Scott of the Antarctic, Operation Disaster, Mr. Denning Drives North, Gentle Gunman, Long Memory, Hobson's Choice, End of the Affair, Colditz Story, Above Us the Waves, Escapade, It's Great to be Young, Around the World in 80 Days, War and Peace, Baby and the Battleship, Town on Trial, Monty's Double, Dunkirk, Summer of the 17th Doll, Tiger Bay, Swiss Family Robinson, Tunes of Glory, The Singer Not the Song, Flame In the Streets, Tiara Tahiti, The Valiant, The Chalk Garden, The Truth about Spring, The Great Spy Mission, King Rat, The Wrong Box, Sky West and Crooked (dir.), The Family Way, Cowboy in Africa, Chukka, A Black Veil For Lisa, Oh! What a Lovely War, Run Wild, Run Free, Ryan's Daughter, Adam's Woman, Dulcima, Oklahoma Crude, Young Winston, Lady Caroline, The Human Factor, Trial By Combat, Lamb, The Big Sleep, 39 Steps, Gandhi, Sahara, Who's That Girl.
STAGE: Good Companions, 1975; Great Expectations, 1976; Separate Tables, 1977; Goodbye, Mr. Chips, 1982; Little Lies, 1983; Little Lies (Toronto, 1984), The Petition, Pygmalion.
TELEVISION: Masks of Death, Murder with Mirrors, Woman of Substance, Hold the Dream, Edge of the Wind, When the Wind Blows, Around the World in 80 Days, Dangerous Love.

MILLS, JULIET: Actress. b. London, England, Nov. 21, 1941. Daughter of John Mills. Made stage debut at 14 in Alice Through the Looking Glass.

PICTURES: So Well Remembered, The History of Mr. Polly, No, My Darling Daughter, Twice Around the Daffodils, Nurse on Wheels, Carry on Jack, The Rare Breed, Wings of War, Oh, What a Lovely War!, The Challengers, Avanti!, Beyond the Door, The Second Power, The Last Melodrama. TELEVISION: Nanny and the Professor (series); Movies: Wings of Fire, The Challengers, Letters from Three Lovers, QB VII, Once an Eagle, Alexander: The Other Side of Dawn, The Cracker Factory, etc.

MILNER, JACK: Executive Producer. b. Jersey City, NJ, Nov. 2, 1910. e. Roosevelt H.S., L.A., CA. M.P. industry 1927. Worked many phases from laboratory-camera-editorial dept. to financing and co-producing feature pictures; formed Milner Bros. Productions with brother Dan Milner, 1955; prod. Phantom from 10,000 Leagues, From Hell It Came, Jail Break, etc.
TELEVISION: prod. My Dog Sheppy, From Here to Now, Come as You Are.

MILNER, MARTIN: Actor. b. Detroit, MI, Dec. 28, 1931. e. U. of Southern California. Debut in Life with Father, 1947; U.S. Army 1952–54, directed 20 training films.
PICTURES INCLUDE: Sands of Iwo Jima, The Halls of Montezuma, Operation Pacific, The Captive City, Battle Zone, Mr. Roberts, Pete Kelly's Blues, On the Threshold of Space, Gunfight at the O.K. Corral, Sweet Smell o' Success, Marjorie Morningstar, Too Much, Too Soon, Compulsion, 13 Ghosts, Valley of the Dolls.
TELEVISION: Series: The Stu Erwin Show (1954–55), The Life of Riley, Route 66 (1960–64), Adam-12 (1968–75), Swiss Family Robinson (1975–76). Movies: Black Beauty, The Last Convertible, Flood, Hurricane, The Seekers, Little Mo.

MILO, GEORGE: Set Decorator, r.n. George Milo Vescia. b. New York, NY, Dec. 19, 1909. e. high school, art schools. Landscape, seascape, still life painter, portrait sculptor; set decorator since 1937.
TELEVISION: Republic Studios, Revue Studios; Dangerous Assignment, Stories of the Century, Thriller, Alfred Hitchcock, Checkmate, General Electric.
PICTURES INCLUDE: Wake of the Red Witch, Fair Wind to Java, Borderline, Jubilee Trail, Make Haste to Live, Eternal Sea, Last Command, Come Next Spring, Psycho, Judgement at Nuremberg, The Last Cowboy, That Touch of Mink, The Birds.

MIMIEUX, YVETTE: Actress. b. Los Angeles, CA, Jan. 8, 1944. e. Vine Street Sch., Le Conte Jr. H.S., Los Angeles, Los Ninos Heroes de Chapultepec, Mexico City, Hollywood H.S., CA. Appeared with a theatrical group, Theatre Events; Sympn. Concert: Persephone, Oakland Orchestra, 1965, N.Y. Philharmonic, Lincoln Center, L.A. Philharmonic, Hollywood Bowl.
PICTURES INCLUDE: debut, Time Machine, Where the Boys Are, The Four Horsemen of the Apocalypse, Light in the Piazza, The Wonderful World of the Brothers Grimm, Diamond Head, Toys In the Attic, Joy In The Morning, Reward, Monkeys Go Home, Dark of the Sun, Caper of the Golden Bulls, Picasso Summer, Three in the Attic, Skyjacked, The Neptune Factor, Jackson County Jail, The Black Hole, Mystique.
TELEVISION: Tyger Tyger, 1964. 1970: series, Most Deadly Game, Berrengers. Movies: Death Takes A Holiday, Black Noon, Obsessive Love.
STAGE: I Am a Camera, 1963; Owl and the Pussycat, 1966.
CONCERTS: Persephone—Houston Symphony, London Royal Philharmonic.

MINER, STEVE: Director. b. Chicago, IL, June 18, 1951.
PICTURES: Friday the 13th Part 2 (also prod.); Friday the 13th Part 3; House, Warlock.
TELEVISION: The Wonder Years.

MINNELLI, LIZA: Actress, Singer. b. Mar. 12, 1946. p. Judy Garland & Vincente Minnelli. In concert with mother, London Palladium 1964. On B'way with Liza with a Z. In concert Carnegie Hall, 1979. After repertory work & off-broadway (Best Foot Forward, 1963), roles starred on Broadway in Flora, The Red Menace (Tony award), Chicago, The Act (Tony Award), The Rink. Also won Special Tony Award, 1974. Film debut as child with mother in In the Good Old Summertime (1949).
PICTURES INCLUDE: Charlie Bubbles, The Sterile Cuckoo, Tell Me That You Love Me, Junie Moon, Cabaret (Acad. Award, 1972), That's Entertainment!, Lucky Lady, Silent Movie, A Matter of Time, New York, New York, Arthur, Rent a Cop, Arthur 2 On The Rocks.
TELEVISION: Liza with a Z (Emmy Award). Liza at the Winter Garden, Liza and Goldie Together, Baryshnikov on Broadway, Faerie Tale Theater. Movie: A Time to Live, A Triple Play: Sam Found Out.

MINSKY, HOWARD G.: Writer, Producer, Sales and Distribution Exec. Paramount-Twentieth Century-Fox. Agency Exec. Wm.

Morris Pres. Cinema Consultants. Produced Love Story. 1970.

MIRISCH, DAVID: Executive. b. Gettysburg, PA, July 24, 1935. e. Ripon Coll. United Artists Corp., 1960–63; former exec. with Braverman-Mirisch adv. public rel. firm.

MIRISCH, MARVIN E.: Executive. b. New York, NY, March 19, 1918. e. City Coll. of New York, B.A., 1940. Print dept., contract dept., asst. booker, N.Y. exch.; head booker, Grand National Pictures, Inc., 1936–40; officer, gen. mgr. vending concession operation 800 theatres, Midwest, Theatres Candy Co., Inc., Milwaukee, Wisc., 1941–52; exec., corporate officer in chg., indep. producer negotiations, other management functions, Allied Artists Pictures, Inc., 1953–57; Chmn. of Bd., Chief Exec. Officer in chg. of all business affairs, admin. 7 financing, distr. liaison, The Mirisch Company, Inc., 1957 to present. Member of Board of Governors and former vice-president of Academy of Motion Pictures Arts & Sciences. Member Motion Pictures Pioneers. Past president of Academy of MPAS Foundation.
PICTURES: Exec. prod.: Dracula, Romantic Comedy.

MIRISCH, WALTER: Producer. b. New York, NY, Nov. 8, 1921. e. U. of Wisconsin, B.A., 1942; Harvard Grad. Sch. of Business Admin., 1943. In m.p. indust. with Skouras Theatres Corp., 1938–40; Oriental Theatre Corp., 1940–42. 1945 with Monogram, A.A.: apptd. exec. prod. Allied Artists, July, 1951; pres. and exec. head of prod. The Mirisch Company 1969; 1960–61; pres. Screen Prod. Guild; 1962, mem. bd. dir., MPAA; bd. Gvnrs., Academy of Motion Pictures Arts and Sciences, 1964; 1967, pres., Center Thea. Group of L.A.; bd. dir., Wisconsin Alum. Assn.; bd. of dir. Cedars-Sinai Medical Center, Bd. of Advisors, California State U.—Northridge, Board of Governors, Acad. of Motion Picture Arts & Sciences—1972. President, Permanent Charities Committee 1962–63; President, Acad. of Motion Picture Arts & Sciences—1973–77.
PICTURES INCLUDE: By Love Possessed, Two for the Seesaw, Toys in the Attic, Hawaii, Fitzwilly, In the Heat of the Night, They Call Me Mister Tibbs, The Organization, Mr. Majestyk, Midway, Gray Lady Down, Same Time, Next Year, Prisoner of Zenda, Dracula, Romantic Comedy.

MIRREN, HELEN: Actress. b. England, 1946. On stage in various Shakespearean roles as well as The Silver Tassle, Enemies, The Sea Gull, Faith Healer, etc.
PICTURES: Age of Consent, Savage Messiah, O! Lucky Man, Hamlet, Caligula, The Long Good Friday, The Fiendish Plot of Dr. Fu Manchu, Excalibur, Cal, 2010, White Nights, The Mosquito Coast, Pascali's Island, Why the Whales Came.
TELEVISION: Miss Julie, The Applecart, The Little Minister, A Midsummer Night's Dream, etc.

MISCHER, DON: Producer, Director. b. San Antonio, TX, March 5, 1941. e. U. of Texas, B.A. 1963, M.A. 1965. Prod.-dir. of specials starring Goldie Hawn, Shirley MacLaine, Barry Manilow, Cheryl Ladd, John Denver, Mikhail Baryshnikov. Directed The Kennedy Center Honors annually, Motown 25: Yesterday, Today, Forever (DGA & Emmy Award, 1982), The Great American Dream Machine; Donahue and Kids (Emmy, 1981), Ain't Misbehavin', Making Television Dance with Twyla Tharp, Shirley MacLaine...Illusions, An Evening with Robin Williams, Marlo Thomas Special; Goldie and Liza Together, Famous Lives, Happy Birthday Bob, Motown Returns to the Apollo (prod. also), AFI Salute to Gene Kelly. Founded Don Mischer Productions, 1978.

MR. T: Actor. r.n. Lawrence Tureaud. b. Chicago, IL, May 21, 1953. Professional bodyguard when hired by Sylvester Stallone in 1980 to play prizefighter in Rocky III.
TELEVISION: The A Team (series); T & T (series), The Toughest Man in the World (movie).
PICTURES: Rocky III, D.C. Cab.

MITCHELL, ANDREW: Producer. b. Giffnock, Scotland, 1925. e. Fettes Coll., Edinburgh. Early career, banking; Associated British Picture Corporation, Elstree Studios; gen. mgr., Elstree Distributors, 1961; dir., Kenwood Films Ltd., 1963; assoc. prod., Hand in Hand, The Young Ones, Summer Holiday, French Dressing, Wonderful Life. 1965; Prod.: Up Jumped a Swagman. Asst. to mgr. dir., Assoc. British Prods., Ltd. Prod. con. Associated British Productions Ltd. 1969–70: Film Finances, Mng. dir., Leslie Grade Film Ltd, 1973. Mng. Dir. Cannon, Elstree Studios. 1977 Prod. Are You Being Served?

MITCHELL, CAMERON: Actor. b. Dallastown, PA, Nov. 4, 1918. e. Theatre Sch., N.Y.; New York Theatre Guild, 1938–40. On stage with Lunt & Fontanne, Taming of the Shrew. Radio announcer, sportscaster before joining U.S. Army Air Forces 1942–44. Star of Tomorrow, 1954.
PICTURES INCLUDE: Mighty McGurk, High Barbaree, Cass Timberlane, Leather Gloves, The Sellout, Death of a Salesman, Japanese War Bride, Flight to Mars, Man in the Saddle, Outcasts of Poker Flat, Okinawa, Les Miserables,

Pony Soldier, Powder River, Man on a Tightrope, How to Marry a Millionaire, Hell & High Water, Gorilla at Large, Garden of Evil, Desiree, Strange Lady in Town, Love Me Or Leave Me, House of Bamboo, Tall Men, View from Pompey's Head, Carousel, Monkey on My Back, Face of Fire, Inside The Mafia, The Unstoppable Man, The Last of the Vikings, Three Came to Kill, Blood and Black Lace, Ride in the Whirlwind, Hombre, Island of the Doomed, Nightmare in Wax, Buck and the Preacher, Slaughter, The Midnight Man, The Klansman, Viva, Knievel!, The Swarm, Night Train to Terror, Low Blow, Night Force, Deadly Prey, Trapped, Rage to Kill, A Handful of Trouble, Terror in Beverly Hills.
TELEVISION: Series: High Chapparal, Swiss Family Robinson. Movies: Andersonville Trial, The Bastard, Black Beauty, How the West Was Won, Partners in Crime, Wild Times.

MITCHELL, GUY: Singer, Actor. b. Detroit, MI, Feb. 22, 1927 e. H.S., San Francisco. Studied singing; U.S. Navy, 1945–46; singer, radio stations; vocalist with Carmen Cavallaro orch.; sings with Columbia records; m.p. debut in Those Redheads from Seattle; also in: Red Garters.
TELEVISION: Guy Mitchell TV Show, Whispering Smith (series).

MITCHUM, JIM: Actor. b. Los Angeles, CA, May 8, 1941. m. actress Wendy Wagner. Son of Robert Mitchum. e. Univ. H.S., L.A. Went directly from school to Hollywood Professional Sch. On-job prof. training at Barter Theatre in Virginia.
PICTURES INCLUDE: Thunder Road (debut), The Last Time I Saw Archie, The Victors, Ambush Bay, Tramplers, In Harm's Way, Invisible Six, Moonrunners, Beat Generation, Ride the Wild Surf, Trackdown, Mercenary Fighters.

MITCHUM, ROBERT: Actor. b. Bridgeport, CT, Aug. 6, 1917. Odd jobs; to California; joined Long Beach Players Guild; appeared in Hopalong Cassidy series with William Boyd; in Westerns 8 yrs. RKO. Biography: It Sure Beats Working (1975, by Mike Tomkies).
PICTURES INCLUDE: Hoppy Serves a Writ (debut, 1943), The Leather Burners, Border Patrol, Follow the Band, Colt Comrades, The Human Comedy, We've Never Been Licked, Beyond the Last Frontier, Bar 20, Doughboys in Ireland, Corvette K-225, Aerial Gunner, The Lone Star Trail, False Colors, The Dancing Masters, Riders of the Deadline, Cry Havoc, Gung Ho, Johnny Doesn't Live Here Anymore, When Strangers Marry, The Girl Rush, Thirty Seconds Over Tokyo, Nevada, West of the Pecos; Gained recognition: Story of G.I. Joe, Undercurrent, Pursued Locket, Til' the End of Time, Desire Me, Crossfire, Out of the Past, Rachel and the Stranger, Blood on the Moon, Red Pony, Big Steal, His Kind of Woman, Where Danger Lives, Her Forbidden Past, Macao, Racket, One Minute to Zero, Lost Men, Angel Face, White Witch Doctor, Second Chance, She Couldn't Say No, River of No Return, Track of the Cat, Night of the Hunter, Not as a Stranger, Man with the Gun, Foreign Intrigue, Bandido, Heaven Knows Mr. Allison, Fire Down Below, Wonderful Country, Home from the Hill, Sundowners, The Last Time I Saw Archie, Cape Fear, The Longest Day, List of Adrian Messenger, Two for the Seesaw, Rampage, Mr. Moses, El Dorado, Anzio, Villa Rides, Five Card Stud, Secret Ceremony, Young Billy Young, Good Guys and the Bad Guys, Ryan's Daughter, Going Home, Wrath of God, Friends of Eddie Coyle, The Yakuza, Farewell My Lovely, Midway, The Last Tycoon, Amsterdam Kill, The Big Sleep, Matilda, That Championship Season, Maria's Lovers, The Ambassador, Mr. North.
TELEVISION: Mini Series: The Winds of War, North and South, War and Remembrance; Movies: A Killer in the Family, The Hearst and Davies Affair, Reunion at Fairborough, Promises to Keep, Thompson's Lost Run, Brotherhood of the Rose.

MOCIUK, YAR W.: Executive. b. Ukraine, Jan. 26, 1927. e. City Coll. of New York; World U.; Peoples U. of Americas, Puerto Rico. Expert in field of m.p. care and repair; holds U.S. patent for method and apparatus for treating m.p. film. Has also been film producer and director. Founder and pres. of CM Films Service, Inc. until 1973. Now chm. of bd. and pres. of Filmtreat International Corp. Member: M.P. & TV Engineers; Univ. Film Assn. Pres., Ukrainian Cinema Assn. of America.

MODINE, MATTHEW: Actor. Studied with Stella Adler.
PICTURES INCLUDE: Baby It's You, Private School, Streamers, Hotel New Hampshire, VisionQuest, Mrs. Soffel, Birdy, Full Metal Jacket, Orphans, Married to the Mob, The Match.
TELEVISION: Eugene O'Neill: Journey Into Greatness.

MOFFAT, DONALD: Actor. b. Plymouth, England, Dec. 26, 1930. Studied acting Royal Academy of Dramatic Art, 1952–54. London stage debut Macbeth, 1954. On stage with Old Vic before Broadway debut in Under Milkwood, 1957. Worked with APA-Phoenix Theatre Co. and as actor and dir. of numerous regional productions.
THEATER: The Bald Soprano; Jack; Ivanov; Much Ado About Nothing; The Tumbler; Duel of Angels; A Passage to

India; The Affair; The Taming of the Shrew; The Caretaker; Man and Superman; War and Peace; You Can't Take It With You; Rich You Are . . . If You Think You Are; School for Scandal; The Wild Duch; The Cherry Orchard; Cock-A-Doodle Dandy; Hamlet; Chemin de Fer; Father's Day; Painting Churches; Play Memory; Passion Play; The Iceman Cometh.
PICTURES: Pursuit of the Graf Spee (debut, 1957); Rachel, Rachel; The Trial of the Catonsville Nine; R.P.M.; Great Northfield Minnesota Raid; Showdown; Terminal Man; Earthquake; On the Nickel; Strangers; Health; Promises in the Dark; Popeye; License to Kill; The Land of No Return; The Thing; Monster in the Closet; The Right Stuff; Alamo Bay; The Best of Times; The Unbearable Lightness of Being; Far North.
TELEVISION: Guest: Camera Three (1958); You Can't Have Everything (U.S. Steel Hour); Murder, She Wrote; Dallas. Series: The New Land (1974); Logan's Run. Movies: Eleanor and Franklin; Sergeant Matlovich vs. the U.S. Air Force; Forget-Me-Not Lane; Tartuffe; Who Will Love My Children; Jacqueline Bouvier Kennedy; A Gift of Love.

MOGER, ART: Publicity executive. Author. b. Boston, MA, April 4. e. Boston U. Coll. of Journalism, B.S. Cartoonist & caricaturist, stage & screen attractions; feature writer. nat. mag.; script writer, guest appearances with Fred Allen, and many radio, TV shows (Mike Douglas Show, Merv Griffin); creator cartoon strip Seymour Shoze, dealing with m.p. and comic strip, Groucho, based on Groucho Marx: orig., About Faces, puzzle series; in 1937 syndicated cartoon series; pressbook cartoonist; handled personal appearances of celebrities. Pub. exec., Warner Bros. & other m.p. cos. Holds record for My Favorite Jokes in Parade Magazine (8 consecutive times). First honorary trustee of Nat'l. Broadcasters Hall of Fame; member Sigma Delta Chi, professional journalism society. Kentucky Colonel and Admiral. Pres., Advertising Enterprises, Boston; exec., Amuse-A-Menu Co.; dorArt Enterprises; pres. and originator Tub Thumpers of Amer. Charter member, Nat'l. Hall of Humor.
AUTHOR: You'll Dial Laughing, Pros and Cons, Some of My Best Friends Are People, The Complete Pun Book, Hello! My Real Name Is. . . , The Best Book of Puns.

MOGER, STANLEY H.: Executive. Pres., SFM Entertainment, Exec. Vice Pres., SFM Media Corp. b. Boston, MA, Nov. 13, 1936. e. Colby Coll., Waterville, ME, B.A., 1958. Announcer/TV personality/WVDA and WORL (Boston) 1953–54; WGHM (Skowhegan) 1955–56; WTWO-TV (Bangor) 1955; WMHB (Waterville) 1956–57; WTVL (Waterville) 1957–58; unit pub. dir., Jaguar Prods., 1958–59; US Army reserve, 1958–64, with calls to active duty in 1958–59 and 1961–62; account exec., NBC Films/California National Productions, Chicago; 1959–60, asst. sales manager, Midwest, RCA/NBC Medical Radio System; acct. exec. Hollingbery Co., Chicago, 1960–63; and New York 1963–66; account executive, Storer Television Sales, 1966–69; co-founded SFM, Sept. 29, 1969. In 1978, named pres., SFM Entertainment which was responsible for the revival of Walt Disney's Mickey Mouse Club, The Adventures of Rin-Tin-Tin; Mobil Showcase Network; SFM Holiday Network. Executive producer: Television-Annual 1978–79: Your New Day with Vidal Sassoon, The Origins Game; Believe You Can and You Can (from Disneyland), Walt Disney Presents Sport Goofy (series); The World of Tomorrow. March of Time . . . on the March (England), Sports Pros and Cons.
PROPERTIES INCLUDE: SFM Holiday Network, SFM Documentary Network, Car Care Central, Your New Day with Vidal Sassoon, March of Time series, Co-Packager Superstars; Adventures of the Wilderness Family; Across the Great Divide; Mysteries from Beyond Earth; To the Ends of the Earth; Challenge To Be Free; Wonder of It All; Great American Cowboy; Dayan; Sports Illustrated; General Foods Golden Showcase Network–Shock Trauma; 1983 official film of the America's Cup Challenge: Countdown to the Cup; Pinocchio in Outer Space; Rudyard Kipling's Jungle Book; The Heisman Trophy Annual Award Specials; Walt Disney World's Very Merry Xmas Parade; The Indomitable Teddy Roosevelt; Crusade in the Pacific; Rosepetal Place; Hugga-Bunch; Jayce and the Wheeled Warriors; Time Travel: Fact, Fiction and Fantasy; Zoobilee Zoo; Photon; Just the Facts (Dragnet special); Willie Nelson's Summer Picnic; Crusade in Europe; King Kong: The Living Legend; SFM Children's Theatre; Ghost Dance; Sea World's All-Star, Lonestar Celebration; George Stevens: A Filmmaker's Journey; Gorillas in the Mist Special; Tappin'; Care Bears (series); Crystal Light National Aerobics Championships (1986 & 87); U.S. Man of the Year Pageant; The Digital Discovery (series); The Infinite Voyage.

MOLINA, ALFRED: Actor. b. London, Eng. e. Guildhall Sch. of Music and Drama. Stand-up comic for street theatre group. Joined Royal Shakespeare Co., 1977 (Frozen Assets, The Steve Biko Inquest, Dingo, Bandits, Taming of the Shrew, Happy End), Also in Serious Money. Plays and Players' Most Promising New Actor Award for Accidental Death of an Anarchist.

Mol-Mon

PICTURES: Raiders of the Lost Ark, Meantime, Lady-hawke, Letter to Brezhnev, Prick up Your Ears, Manifesto.
TELEVISION: The Losers, Anyone for Dennis, Joni Jones, Number One, City Hospital, Russian Roulette.

MOLINARO, EDOUARD: Director. b. Bordeaux, France, May 13, 1928. Made amateur films at university and launched professional career via award-winning technical shorts. First feature film, Le Dos au Mur, 1957.
PICTURES INCLUDE: Girls for the Summer, A Ravishing Idiot, Gentle Art of Seduction, La Cage aux Folles (also Part II), Sunday Lovers, Just the Way You Are, The Door on the Left as You Leave the Elevator.

MOLL, ELICK: Writer. b. New York, NY, Mar. 20, 1907. e. U. of Illinois. U. of Chicago. Short story writer, novelist, playwright; Seidman and Son, Memoir of Spring, Night Without Sleep, Image of Tallie, Seidman and the Geisha, Perilous Spring of Morris Seidman; worked with Samuel Goldwyn, MGM, Fox, Columbia stories appear in magazines, texts on short story; won 2nd prize O. Henry Memorial Award Prize, Stories 1937.
PICTURES INCLUDE: You Were Meant for Me, Wake Up and Dream, House on Telegraph Hill, Night Without Sleep, Storm Center, Spring Reunion.
TELEVISION: Playhouse 90, Chrysler Theatre, others.
AWARDS: Academy of TV Arts & Sciences for best teleplay: Seidman & Son; TV Writers award for best script: The Fabulous Irishman.

MONASH, PAUL: Producer, Writer. b. New York, NY, June 14, 1917. e. U. of Wisconsin, Columbia U. Was in U.S. Army Signal Corps and Merchant Marine; newspaper reporter; high school teacher; and civilian employee of U.S. gov't. in Europe. Wrote two novels: How Brave We Live, The Ambassadors. Entered industry writing TV scripts on such shows as Playhouse 90, Studio One, Theatre Guild of the Air, Climax, etc. Authored two-part teleplay which launched The Untouchables. In 1958 won Emmy award for The Lonely Wizard, dramatization of life of German-born electrical inventor Charles Steinmetz. Made m.p. debut as exec. prod. of Butch Cassidy and the Sundance Kid, 1969.
PICTURES INCLUDE: Slaughterhouse-Five (prod.), The Friends of Eddie Coyle (prod., s.p.), The Front Page (prod.), Carrie (prod.), Big Trouble in Little China (prod.).
TELEVISION: Child Bride of Short Creek, The Day the Loving Stopped; Trial of Chaplain Jensen.

MONICELLI, MARIO: Director. b. Rome, Italy, May 15, 1915. Ent. m.p. industry in production; later co-authored, collab., comedies. Dir.: Big Deal on Madonna Street, The Great War, Tears of Joy, Boccaccio '70, The Organizer, Casanova, Girl With a Pistol, Amici Mie, Viva Italia!, Travels With Anita, Lovers and Liars (also, s.p.), Il Marchese de Grillo (also s.p.), Amici, Miei, Atto (All My Friends 2, also s.p.), Bertoldo, Bertoldino, E Cacasenna (also, s.p.), The Two Lives of Mattia Pascal, I Picari (dir., co-s.p.).

MONKHOUSE, BOB: TV-radio-cabaret Comedian, Comedy writer. b. Beckenham, Kent, June 1, 1928. e. Dulwich Coll. Debut 1948 while serving in RAF, own radio comedy series 1949–83 (winters), own TV series, BBC 1952–56, ITV 1956–83; BBC (ongoing). Several West End revues, Boys from Syracuse; Come Blow Your Horn; The Gulls; others. Films include: Carry On, Sergeant; Weekend with Lulu; Dentist in the Chair; She'll Have to Go; Bliss of Mrs. Blossom; others. Major cabaret attraction U.K., Australia, Hong Kong. British star of numerous TV series including: What's My Line?; Who Do You Trust?; Mad Movies; Quick on the Draw; Bob Monkhouse Comedy Hour; The Golden Shot (4 years); Celebrity Squares (4 yrs); I'm Bob, He's Dickie! (1978–81); Family Fortunes (1979–83); Bob Monkhouse Tonight (1983–ongoing). Regular dramatic guest spots ITV & BBC-TV, now under exclusive contract to BBC till 1986 for Tonight Show and new game shows.

MONKS, JOHN, JR.: Writer, Actor, Producer, Director. b. Brooklyn, NY. e. Virginia Military Inst., A.B. Actor, stock, B'way, radio, m.p. U.S. Marines, 1942; commissioned Major, 1945. Playwright Co-author Brother Rat.
PICTURES INCLUDE: Brother Rat, Co-author, Brother Rat and a Baby, Strike Up the Band, The House on 92nd Street, 13 Rue Madeleine, Wild Harvest, Dial 1119., The West Point Story, People Against O'Hara. Where's Charley. So This Is Love, Knock on Any Door, No Man Is an Island.
TELEVISION: Climax: The Gioconda Smile, A Box of Chocolates; 20th Century-Fox Hour: Miracle on 34th St.; Gen. Electric Theatre: Emily; CBS Special: High Tor; SWAT; Creator serial: Paradise Bay.

MONROE, CHAUNCEY: Actor, Writer, Prod., Dir., Stuntman, Singer. b. Gatlinburg, TN, July 7, 1950. e. Sonia Moore Studio of the Theater, NY; Amer. Stanislavski Inst., 1969–70; De Mille On Camera Workshop, CA 1983–85. Began artistic career at age 10 as professional portrait painter. First film role in A Walk in the Spring Rain. At 17 worked for Roy Acuff and formed own country five-piece group, The Highlanders.

Worked off-Bdwy., in film (as actor, singer, stuntman) and TV as well as MTV rock videos with Weird Al Yankovitch, Kim Carnes, etc. Formed Chauncey Monroe Productions, Extraordinaire, Ltd.
PICTURES INCLUDE: Batteries Not Included, Ten to Midnight, The Exterminator, Girls Just Wanna Have Fun, The Naked Cage, Smorgasbord, Star 80, Throwback.
TELEVISION: The Equalizer, Saturday Night Live, Search for Tomorrow, As the World Turns, Another World, Romance Theater, Divorce Court, General Hospital, Cagney and Lacey. Movies: The Day After, Copacabana.

MONTAGNE, EDWARD J.: Producer, Director. b. Brooklyn, NY. e. Loyola U., of Notre Dame. RKO Pathe, 1942; U.S. Army, 1942–46; prod. many cos. after army.
PICTURES INCLUDE: Tattooed Stranger, The Man with My Face, McHale's Navy, McHale's Navy Joins the Air Force, P.J.
TELEVISION: Man Against Crime, Cavalier Theatre, The Vaughn Monroe Show, The Hunter, I Spy, McHale's Navy; exec. prod. of film-CBS-N.Y., Phil Silvers Show. Prod. & head of programming, Wm. Esty Adv. Co., 1950; Program consultant, William Esty Co.; v.p. Universal TV prod. & dir.: 5 Don Knotts features; prod.: Andy Griffith, Angel in My Pocket, Ellery Queen, A Very Missing Person, Short Walk to Daylight, Hurricane, Terror on the 40th Floor, Francis Gary Powers, Million Dollar Ripoff, Crash of Flight 401, High Noon—Part 2, Harper Valley PTA.

MONTALBAN, RICARDO: Actor. b. Mexico City, Mex., Nov. 25, 1920. Appeared in Mexican pictures 1941–45; to U.S.
PICTURES INCLUDE: Fiesta, On an Island With You, Kissing Bandit, Neptune's Daughter, Battleground, Mystery Street, Right Cross, Two Weeks with Love, Across the Wide Missouri, Mark of Renegade, My Man and I, Sombrero, Border Incident, Latin Lovers, Saracen Blade, Life in The Balance, Sayonara, Hemingway's Adventures of a Young Man, The Reluctant Saint, Love Is a Ball, Sol Madrid, Blue, Sweet Charity, Conquest of the Planet of the Apes, The Train Robbers, Joe Panther, Won, Ton, Ton, the Dog Who Saved Hollywood, Star Trek II: The Wrath of Khan, Cannonball Run II, The Naked Gun.
TELEVISION: Series: Fantasy Island, The Colbys. Movies: The Pigeon, The Aquarian, Fireball Foreward, The Mark of Zorro, McNaughton's Daughter, Return to Fantasy Island.

MONTAND, YVES: Actor, Singer. r.n. Yvo Livi. b. Monsumano, Italy, Oct. 13, 1921. m. the late actress Simone Signoret. Worked as a truck loader, waiter in dockside bar, and barber. Performed in Marseilles as singer in clubs and music halls.
PICTURES INCLUDE: Etoile Sans Lumiere, Les Portes de La Nuit, L'Idole, Souvenir Perdus, Le Salaire de la Peur (Wages of Fear), Nostri Tempi, Mar, Napoleon, Les Heros Sont Fatigues, Marguerite de la Nuit, Uomini e Lupi, Les Sorcieres de Salem (The Crucible), La Lunga Strada, Un Denomme Squarcio, Le Pere et L'enfant, La Loi (Where the Hotwind Blows), Let's Make Love, Sanctuary, My Geisha, Goodbye Again, The Sleeping Car Murders, La Guerre est Finie, Is Paris Burning?, Grand Prix, Live for Life, Z, On a Clear Day You Can See Forever, The Vow, State of Siege, Jean de Florette, Manon of the Springs, Three Seats for the 26th.

MONTGOMERY, ELIZABETH: Actress. b. Los Angeles, CA, April 15, 1933. e. Amer. Acad. of Dramatic Arts. Daughter of the late Robert Montgomery. B'way debut: Late Love.
PICTURES: The Court Martial of Billy Mitchell, Johnny Cool, Who's Been Sleeping in My Bed?
TELEVISION: Series: Bewitched. Movies: The Victim, Mrs. Sundance, A Case of Rape, The Legend of Lizzie Borden, Dark Victory, A Killing Affair, The Awakening Land, Jennifer: A Woman's Story, Missing Pieces, Second Sight: A Love Story, Amos, Between Darkness and Dawn, Face to Face.

MONTGOMERY, GEORGE: Actor. r.n. George Montgomery Letz; b. Brady, MT, Aug. 29, 1916. e. U. of Montana. Armed Services, W.W.II.
PICTURES INCLUDE: Cisco Kid and the Lady (1939), Star Dust, Young People, Charter Pilot, Jennie, Cowboy and the Blonde, Accent on Love, Riders of the Purple Sage, Last of the Duanes, Cadet Girl, Roxie Hart, Ten Gentlemen from West Point, Orchestra Wives, China Girl, Brasher Doubloon, Three Little Girls in Blue, Lulu Belle, Belle Starr's Daughter, Girl From Manhattan, Sword of Monte Cristo, Texas Rangers, Indian Uprising, Cripple Creek, Pathfinder, Jack McCall Desperado, Fort Ti, Gun Belt, Battle of Rogue River, Lone Gun, Masterson of Kansas, Seminole Uprising, Robbers' Roost, Too Many Crooks, Stallion Trail, The Steel Claw, Watusi, Samar, Hallucination Generation, Hostile Guns, Ransom in Blood.

MONTY PYTHON: Group of six British comedians who performed on Monty Python's Flying Circus for BBC-TV during the '60s and '70s. They include Eric Chapman, John Cleese, Terry Gilliam, Eric Idle, Terry Jones, and Michael Palin.
PICTURES: And Now for Something Completely Different, Monty Python and the Holy Grail, The Life of Brian, Monty

Python at the Hollywood Bowl, Monty Python's The Meaning of Life.

MOONJEAN, HANK: Producer, Director. Began as asst. dir. at MGM. Later turned to producing.
PICTURES INCLUDE: Assoc. Prod.: The Great Gatsby, WUSA. Exec. Prod.: The Fortune, The End. Producer; Hooper, Smokey and the Bandit II, The Incredible Shrinking Woman, Paternity, Sharky's Machine, Stroker's Ace (prod.), Les Liaisons Dangereuses (co-prod.), Stealing Home (co-prod.).

MOORE, CONSTANCE: Actress. b. Sioux City, IA, Jan. 18, 1922. Sang on radio; Lockheed prog., 2 yrs; Jurgen's Show, 2 yrs. Screen debut 1938. TV shows, nightclubs. N.Y. Stage: The Boys from Syracuse, By Jupiter.
PICTURES INCLUDE: Prison Break, A Letter of Introduction, I Wanted Wings, Take A Letter Darling, Show Business, Delightfully Dangerous, Earl Carroll Sketchbook, In Old Sacramento, Hit Parade of 1947, Spree.

MOORE, DEMI: Actress. b. Roswell, NM, Nov. 11, 1962. r.n. Demi Guynes. m. actor Bruce Willis. Since age 16 worked as model. Appeared on TV series Kaz, Vegas. Off B'way debut: The Early Girl, 1987.
PICTURES INCLUDE: Choices (debut, 1981), Parasite, Young Doctors in Love, Blame It on Rio, No Small Affair, St. Elmo's Fire, One Crazy Summer, Wisdom, About Last Night, Wisdom, The Seventh Sign, Rapid Fire.
TELEVISION: General Hospital, Bedrooms.

MOORE, DICKIE: Actor. b. Los Angeles, CA, Sept. 12, 1925. m. actress Jane Powell. Began picture career when only 11 months old, appearing with John Barrymore in The Beloved Rogue. Appeared in numerous radio, television and stage prods. in NY and L.A. and over 100 films. Now in public relations.
PICTURES INCLUDE: Oliver Twist, Peter Ibbetson, Sergeant York, Heaven Can Wait, Dangerous Years, Out of the Past, Eight Iron Men, Member of the Wedding.

MOORE, DUDLEY: Actor, Writer, Musician. b. England, April 19, 1935. e. Oxford, graduating in 1958. Toured British Isles with jazz group before joining with three other Englishmen to put on revue, Beyond the Fringe, which was a hit in U.K. and N.Y. Appeared later with Peter Cook on Bdwy. in Good Evening. Composed film scores: 30 is a Dangerous Age, Cynthia; Inadmissible Evidence, The Staircase, Six Weeks.
PICTURES: Monte Carlo or Bust, The Wrong Box, 30 is a Dangerous Age, Cynthia; Alice in Wonderland, Those Daring Young Men in Their Jaunty Jalopies, The Bed Sitting Room, Bedazzled, The Hound of the Baskervilles, Foul Play, "10", Wholly Moses, Arthur, Six Weeks, Lovesick, Romantic Comedy, Unfaithfully Yours, The Best Defense, Micki and Maude, Santa Claus—The Movie; Like Father, Like Son; Arthur 2 On the Rocks (actor, exec. prod.), Sketch Life.

MOORE, ELLIS: Consultant. b. New York, NY, May 12, 1924. e. Washington and Lee U., 1941–43. Newspaperman in AK, TN, 1946–52. Joined NBC 1952; mgr. of bus. pub.; 1953; dir., press dept., 1954; dir., press & publicity, Dec. 22, 1959; vice-pres., 1961; pub. rel. dept., Standard Oil Co. (N.J.), 1963–66; v.p. press relations, ABC-TV Network, 1966–68; v.p. public relations ABC-TV Network, 1968–70; v.p. public relations, ABC, 1970, v.p. public relations, ABC, Inc., 1972; v.p. corporate relations, ABC, Inc., 1979; v.p. public affairs, ABC, Inc., 1982–85. P.R. consultant, 1985.

MOORE, GARRY: Performer. r.n. Thomas Garrison Morfit; b. Baltimore, MD, Jan. 31, 1915. Continuity writer, WBAL; announcer, sports commentator, KWK, St. Louis; comedian, writer, Club Matinee show, Chicago; Everything Goes, N.Y.; teamed with Jimmy Durante on radio to 1947; m.c., Take It or Leave It, Breakfast in Hollywood. Elected to TV Academy Hall of Fame.
TELEVISION: Star of Garry Moore Show, I've Got A Secret. Best TV daytime show: Fame Poll, 1958; To Tell The Truth.

MOORE, KIERON: Actor. b. Skibereen, Co. Cork, Eire, 1925. e. St. Mary's Coll., Dublin. Stage debut, 1945 in Desert Rats; appeared in Red Roses For Me. Film debut 1947 in A Man About the House.
PICTURES INCLUDE: Anna Karenina, Mine Own Executioner, Ten Tall Men, David and Bathsheba, Saints and Sinners, Naked Heart, Honeymoon Deferred, Man Trap (Man in Hiding), Conflict of Wings (Fuss Over Feathers), Green Scarf, Blue Peter, Satellite in the Sky, Three Sundays to Live, The Key, The Angry Hills, The Day They Robbed the Bank of England, League of Gentlemen, The Siege of Sidney Street, Faces of Evil, Lion of Sparta, Steel Bayonet, I Thank a Fool, Double Twist, The Day of the Triffids, The Thin Red Line, The Main Attraction, Crack in the World, Son of a Gunfighter, Never Love a Savage, Run Like a Thief, Custer of the West, Ryan International, The Dolmetch Story, Zoo Gang, The Progress of Peoples, The Parched Land.

MOORE, KINGMAN T.: Director. b. Macon, GA, Sept. 13, 1919. e. Wharton Sch. of Finance, U. of Pennsylvania, B.S.; member: Lambs Club, Phi Delta Theta. Actor, 1939–41; U.S. Army, 1941–46; asst. cutter, RKO Radio Pictures, 1946–47; production asst., 1947–48; CBS-TV, N.Y., 1948–49; NBC-TV, N.Y., Hollywood, 1949–52; dir. CBS shows include: Places Please, Backstage with Barry Wood, Kobbs Korner, Adventures in Jazz.
TELEVISION: Candid Camera, Lights Out, Your Show of Shows, Colgate Comedy Hour.

MOORE, MARY TYLER: Actress. b. Brooklyn. NY, Dec. 29, 1936. Began as professional dancer and got first break as teenager in commercials (notably the elf in Hotpoint appliance ads); then small roles in series Bachelor Father, Steve Canyon (1958) and finally as the switchboard oper. in Richard Diamond (though only her legs were seen). Broadway debut: Breakfast at Tiffany's, also Whose Life Is It, Anyway? (special Tony, 1980). Chairman of Bd., MTM Enterprises, Inc, which founded with then husband Grant Tinker.
TELEVISION: Bachelor Father, Steve Canyon, Richard Diamond, 77 Sunset Strip, Hawaiian Eye, Bachelor Father; Series: feature role on The Dick Van Dyke Show (1961–66, 2 Emmy awards); star, The Mary Tyler Moore Show (1970–77, 3 Emmys), The Mary Tyler Moore Hour (1979), Mary (1985–86). Movies: Love American Style, Run a Crooked Mile, Heartsounds, Finnegan Begin Again, First You Cry; Gore Vidal's Lincoln. Special: How to Survive the 70s.
PICTURES INCLUDE: X-15, Thoroughly Modern Millie, Don't Just Stand There, What's So Bad About Feeling Good, Change of Habit, Ordinary People, Six Weeks, Just Between Friends.

MOORE, ROGER: Actor, Director. b. London, England, Oct. 14, 1927. e. art school, London; Royal Acad. of Dramatic Art.
PLAYS: Mr. Roberts, I Capture the Castle, Little Hut, others.
BROADWAY: A Pin to See the Peepshow.
TELEVISION: Maverick, The Alaskans, Ivanhoe, The Saint, The Persuaders, Sherlock Holmes in New York.
PICTURES INCLUDE: Last Time I Saw Paris, Interrupted Melody, King's Thief, Diane, The Miracle, Gold of the Seven Saints, Rachel Cade, Rape of the Sabines, No Mans Land, Crossplot, The Man Who Haunted Himself, Live and Let Die, Gold, The Man with the Golden Gun, That Lucky Touch, Street People, Shout at the Devil, The Spy Who Loved Me, The Wild Geese, Escape To Athena, Moonraker, ffolkes, The Sea Wolves, Sunday Lovers, For Your Eyes Only, The Cannonball Run, Octopussy, The Curse of the Pink Panther, The Naked Face, A View to a Kill, The Magic Snowman (voice).

MOORE, TERRY: Actress. r.n. Helen Koford; b. Los Angeles, CA, Jan. 1, 1932. mother Luella Bickmore, actress. Photographer's model as a child; on radio; with Pasadena Playhouse 1940; in m.p. 1933. Star of Tomorrow: 1958. Formed Moore/Rivers Productions, 1988 with partner-manager Jerry Rivers.
PICTURES INCLUDE: Gaslight, Son of Lassie, Sweet and Low Down, Shadowed, Devil on Wheels, Return of October, Mighty Joe Young, He's a Cockeyed Wonder, Gambling House, Two of a Kind, Sunny Side of the Street, Man on a Tightrope, Beneath the 12-mile Reef, King of the Khyber Rifles, Daddy Long Legs, Shack Out on 101, Postmark for Danger, Come Back Little Sheba, Bernardine, Why Must I Die?, Platinum High School, A Private's Affair, Cast a Long Shadow, City of Fear, Black Spurs, Town Tamer, Waco, A Man Called Dagger, Death Dimension, Hellhole, Beverly Hills Brats.

MOORE, THOMAS W.: Executive. e. U. of Missouri. Naval aviator, USNR, 1940–45. Adv. dept., Star, Meridian, MS; v.p., adv. mgr., Forest Lawn Memorial Park; account exec., CBS-TV Film Sales, Los Angeles; gen. sales mgr., CBS-TV Film Sales, 1956; v.p. in chg. programming & talent, 1958; pres., ABC-TV Network, 1962; chmn. bd., Ticketron, 1968; pres., Tomorrow Entertainment, Inc. 1971; chm., 1981.

MOREAU, JEANNE: Actress. b. Paris, France, Jan. 23, 1928. e. Nat'l Conservatory of Dramatic Art. Stage debut with Comedie Française, acting there until 1952 when she joined the Theatre Nationale Populaire. Directorial debut: La Lumière (film), 1976.
PLAYS: A Month in the Country, La Machine Infernale, Pygmalion, Cat on a Hot Tin Roof.
PICTURES INCLUDE: She-wolves, Elevator to the Scaffold, The Lovers, Le Dialogue Des Carmelites, Les Liaisons Dangereuses, Moderato Cantabile, La Notte, Jules and Jim, A Woman Is a Woman, Eva, The Trial, Bay of Angels, The Victors, Le Feu Follet, Diary of a Chambermaid, The Yellow Rolls-Royce, The Train, Mata Hari, Viva Maria, Mademoiselle, Chimes at Midnight, Sailor From Gibraltar, The Bride Wore Black, The Immortal Story, Great Catherine, Monte Walsh, Alex in Wonderland, The Little Theatre of Jean Renoir, The Last Tycoon, French Provincial, La Lumière (actress, dir., s.p.), Mr. Klein, The Adolescent (dir., s.p. only), Plein Sud, Querelle, The Trout.

Mor-Mor

MORENO, FRANK: Executive. Distribution executive for First Artists and v.p. of dist. & world-wide mktg. for New World Pictures, before setting up own company, The Frank Moreno Co. In January, 1984, joined Almi Pictures as pres. & CEO. 1987, formed own dist. co., MC Releasing.

MORENO, RITA: Actress. r.n. Rosa Dolores Alvario. b. Humacao, Puerto Rico, Dec. 11, 1931. Spanish dancer since childhood; night club entertainer; m.p. debut in So Young, So Bad (1950). Has won Oscar, Tony and Grammy Awards.
 THEATER: debut Skydrift (1945), Sign in Sidney Brustein's Window, Gantry, Last of the Red Hot Lovers, The National Health (Long Wharf, CT), The Ritz (Tony Award, supp., 1975), Wally's Cafe.
 PICTURES INCLUDE: Pagan Love Song, Toast of New Orleans, Singin' in the Rain, The Ring, Cattle Town, Latin Lovers, Jivaro, Yellow Tomahawk, Garden of Evil, Untamed, Seven Cities of Gold, Lieutenant Wore Skirts, King and I, This Rebel Breed, Summer and Smoke, The Little Sister, Cry of Battle, West Side Story (Acad. Award, supporting actress, 1961), The Night of the Following Day, Marlowe, Popi, Carnal Knowledge, The Ritz, Happy Birthday, Gemini, The Four Seasons.
 TELEVISION: Nine to Five, Eva Peron, Anatomy of a Seduction, The Electric Company (series), The Muppet Show (Emmy, 1977), The Rockford Files (Emmy, 1978), Picture of a Showgirl, The Golden Land.

MORGAN, ANDRE: Producer. b. Morocco, 1953. e. U. of Kansas. Golden Harvest Films 1972–84, Producer. Exec. v.p., Golden Communications 1976–84. Formed Ruddy-Morgan Productions with Albert S. Ruddy, 1984.
 PICTURES INCLUDE: Enter the Dragon, The Amsterdam Kill, The Boys in Company C, Cannonball Run II, High Road to China, Lassiter, Farewell to the King.

MORGAN, DENNIS: Actor. r.n. Stanley Morner; b. Prentice, WI, Dec. 10, 1910. e. Carroll Coll. Started with State Lake Theat., Chicago. Toured midwest in Faust, sang in Empire Room of Palmer House, Chicago, appeared on NBC programs and sang lead in Xerxes. Screen debut, 1936. Star of Tomorrow (1941).
 PICTURES INCLUDE: Susy, The Fighting 69th, Three Cheers for the Irish, My Wild Irish Rose, Two Guys from Milwaukee, Two Guys from Texas, Cheyenne, Perfect Strangers, To the Victor, One Sunday Afternoon, Raton Pass, Pretty Baby, Painting the Clouds with Sunshine, This Woman Is Dangerous, Cattle Town, Gun That Won the West, Pearl of the South Pacific, Uranium Boom, Won Ton Ton, The Dog Who Saved Hollywood.
 TELEVISION: Beacon Street.

MORGAN, HARRY: Actor. r.n. Harry Bratsburg; b. Detroit, MI, Apr. 10, 1915. e. U. of Chicago. Screen debut 1942.
 TELEVISION: Series: December Bride, Pete and Gladys, M*A*S*H, Dragnet, After M*A*S*H, You Can't Take It With You, 14 Going on 30 (movie).
 PLAYS: Gentle People, My Heart's in the Highlands, Thunder Rock, Night Music, Night Before Christmas.
 PICTURES INCLUDE: To the Shores of Tripoli, Loves of Edgar Allen Poe, Orchestra Wives, Dragonwyck, Appointment with Danger, The Highwayman, When I Grow Up, The Well, Blue Veil, Bend of the River, Scandal Sheet, My Six Convicts, Boots Malone, High Noon, What Price Glory, Stop You're Killing Me, Arena, Torch Song, Glenn Miller Story, About Mrs. Leslie, Forty-Niners, Far Country, Not As a Stranger, Backlash, Strategic Air Command, Support Your Local Sheriff, Charlie and the Angels, Snowball Express, The Apple Dumpling Gang, The Greatest, The Shootist, Cat from Outer Space, The Apple Dumpling Gang Rides Again, Dragnet.

MORGAN, MICHELE: Actress. r.n. Simone Roussel; b. Paris, France, Feb. 29, 1920. e. Dieppe, dramatic school, Paris. Decided on acting career at 15 yrs., won role at 17 opposite Charles Boyer in Gribouille (later filmed as The Lady in Question, Hollywood). Made several pictures abroad; to U.S. 1940. First Amer. film Joan of Paris, 1942.
 PICTURES INCLUDE: Higher and Higher, Passage to Marseilles, The Chase, Symphonie Pastorale, Fallen Idol, Fabiola, 7 Deadly Sins, Moment of Truth, Daughters of Destiny, Naked Heart, Proud and the Beautiful, Grand Maneuver, Marguerite de la Nuit, The Mirror Has Two Faces, Landru, Oasis, Lost Command, Benjamin, Cat and Mouse, Seven Steps to Murder, Robert et Robert.

MORGAN, TERENCE: Actor. b. London, Eng., Dec. 8, 1921. e. Ewell Castle, Surrey, Royal Acad. of Dramatic Art. Stage debut: There Shall Be No Night, London 1943; m.p. debut: Hamlet, 1948.
 PICTURES INCLUDE: Capt. Horatio Hornblower, Encore, Mandy, It Started in Paradise, Steel Key, Street Corner, Turn the Key Softly, Always a Bride, Forbidden Cargo, Dance Little Lady, Femina, Svengali, They Can't Hang Me, March Hare, It's a Wonderful World, The Scamp, Tread Softly Stranger, The Shakedown, Picadilly Third Stop, The Curse of the

Mummy's Tomb, The Penthouse, Hide and Seek, The Lifetaker.
 TELEVISION: Crime Passionnel, Twelfth Night, The Bridesman's Danger, In Writing, Nothing to Declare, Perchance to Dream, More Than Robbery (serial), Now Barabbas, Women in Love, Sir Francis Drake (series of 26), Memoirs of a Chaise Lounge, No Place Like Earth, The Persuaders, King and Castle.

MORIARTY, MICHAEL: Actor. b. Detroit, MI, April 5, 1941. e. Dartmouth. Studied at London Acad. of Music and Dramatic Arts. Appeared with New York Shakespeare Festival, Charles Street Playhouse (Boston), Alley Theatre (Houston) and Tyrone Guthrie Theatre (Minneapolis). Broadway debut in The Trial of the Catonsville Nine.
 THEATER: Find Your Way Home (Tony Award, 1974), Richard III, Long Day's Journey Into Night, Henry V, G.R Point, Whose Life Is It Anyway (Kennedy Center), The Ballad of Dexter Creed, Uncle Vanya, Caine Mutiny Court Martial.
 PICTURES INCLUDE: Glory Boy (debut), Hickey and Boggs, Shoot It, Bang the Drum Slowly, The Last Detail, Report to the Commissioner, Who'll Stop the Rain, Shoot It Black, Shoot It Blue, Too Far To Go, The Winged Serpent, Pale Rider, The Stuff, Troll, The Hanoi Hilton, It's Alive III., Dark Tower.
 TELEVISION: The Glass Menagerie (Emmy Award), Girls of Summer, The Deadliest Season, Holocaust, Windmills of the Gods, Frank Nitti: The Enforcer.

MORIN, ROBERT B.: Executive. b. New York, NY, Nov. 24. e. Harvard Coll. Merch, Mgr., ad agency. AAP sls., 1955; AAP mgr. program sls., 1956; eastern sls. mgr., MGM-TV, 1957; sls. mgr., Lopert-UA, 1959; v.p., Allied Artists TV; formed Scandia Films, pres., 1965; joined RKO, 1966, in chg. foreign operations; 1968, pres. Lin Medallion Pict. Corp.; 1970–73, Talent Associates; 1973–76, exec. v.p., Heritage Eng.; 1976–78, v.p., MGM TV; 1978–80, pres. Lorimar Syndication; 1980, exec. v.p., 20th Century Fox; 1985, pres., New Century Telecommunications.

MORITA, NORIYUKI "PAT": Entertainer, Actor. b. CA, 1930. Began show business career as opening act in night clubs for such stars as Ella Fitzgerald, Johnny Mathis, Diana Ross and the Supremes, Glen Campbell, etc. Worked in saloons, coffee houses, and dinner theatres before becoming headliner in Las Vegas showrooms, Playboy Clubs, Carnegie Hall, etc. Guest on most TV talk and variety shows and regular on many series: M*A*S*H, Love Boat, Magnum, P.I., etc. Regular role on series, Happy Days.
 PICTURES: Thoroughly Modern Millie, Midway, Savannah Smiles, Jimmy the Kid, The Karate Kid, The Karate Kid: Part II, Captive Hearts, Collision Course.
 TELEVISION: The Vegas Strip War, Farewell to Manzanar, Amos, O'Hara (series).

MORITZ, MILTON I: Executive. b. Pittsburgh, PA, Apr. 27, 1933. e. Woodbury Coll., grad. 1955. Owned, operated theatres in L.A., 1953–55; U.S. Navy 1955–57; American International Pictures asst. gen. sls. mgr., 1957; nat'l. dir. of adv. and publ. 1958; v.p. and bd. mem. of American International Pictures, 1967; 1975, named Senior v.p.; in 1980 formed own co., The Milton I. Moritz Co., Inc., Inc., mktg. & dist. consultant. 1987, joined Pacific Theatres as v.p. in chg. of adv., p.r. & promotions. Pres. of Variety Club of Southern California Tent 25, 1975–76.

MORLEY, ROBERT: Actor, writer. b. Wiltshire, England, May 26, 1908. e. Royal Acad. of Dramatic Art, London. U.S. Air Force, 1943; prod., assoc. prod., Captain Gallant, Arsen, Chicot, Forbidden Cargo; TV Series: Captain Gallant; Scene of the Crime; TV Advisor, Telepictures of Morroco, Telerama, Ltd., Eng., 1954–59; helped org., Alliance of TV Film Producers; prod., Telerama, Inc., Georgetown Films, Inc., 1960; prod., dir., TV film series closeup, Telefilm, Inc. Presently president, Creative Assoc., Inc. and co-prod. with Helen Ainsworth; exec. prod. with Leon Fromkess, The Long Corridor.
 PLAYS: Brit. stage debut London 1929 in Treasure Island, also tour and repertory; N.Y. debut 1938 in Oscar Wilde; other appearances include Great Romancer, Pygmalion, 1948, Edward My Son, co-author, lead London and B'way stage; author several plays (Short Story, Goodness, How Sad, Staff Dance).
 PICTURES INCLUDE: Marie Antoinette, You Will Remember, Major Barbara, Big Blockade, This Was Paris, Foreman Went to France, Young Mr. Pitt, I Live in Grosvenor Square, Outcast of the Islands, African Queen, Edward My Son, Curtain Up, The Final Test, Melba, Gilbert and Sullivan, Beat the Devil, Beau Brummell, Rainbow Jacket, Good Die Young, Quentin Durward, Loser Takes All, Six Months Grace, Full Treatment, Hippo Dancing, Around the World in 80 Days, Sheriff of Fractured Jaw, The Journey, The Doctor's Dilemma, Battle of the Sexes, Libel, Oscar Wilde, Go To Blazes, The Young Ones, Nine Hours to Rama, Murder at the Gallop, Topkapi, Amanda, Take Her She's Mine, Genghis Khan, Hot Enough for June, The Alphabet Murders, Sinful Davey, Hot Millions, Some Girls Do, The Trygon Factor, Song of Norway,

The Blue Bird, Who Is Killing the Great Chefs of Europe?, Scavenger Hunt, The Human Factor, The Great Muppet Caper, The Wind, The Trouble With Spies, Little Dorrit.
TELEVISION: Call My Bluff (series), Charge!, Dangerous Love.

MORRICONE, ENNIO: Composer, Arranger. b. Rome, 1928. Studied with Goffredo Petrassi at the Acad. of Santa Cecilia in Rome.
PICTURES INCLUDE: A Fistful of Dollars, El Greco, Fists in the Pocket, Battle of Algiers, Matchless, Theorem, Once Upon a Time in the West, Investigation of a Citizen, Fraulein Doktor, Burn, The Bird with the Crystal Plumage, Cat O'Nine Tails, The Red Tent, Four Flies in Grey Velvet, The Decameron, The Black Belly of the Tarantula, Bluebeard, The Serpent, Blood in the Streets, Eye of the Cat, The Human Factor, Murder on the Bridge, Sunday Woman, The Inheritance, Partner, Orca, The Heretic, Exorcist II, 1900, La Cage aux Folles, Days of Heaven; Bloodline; Stay as You Are, The Humanoid, The Meadow, A Time to Die, Travels With Anita, When You Comin' Back Red Ryder?, Almost Human, La Cage aux Folles II, The Island, Tragedy of a Ridiculous Man; Windows; Butterfly, So Fine; White Dog, Copkiller, Nana, The Thing; Treasure of the Four Crowns, Sahara, Once Upon a Time in America, Thieves After Dark, The Cage, La Cage aux Folles III, The Forester's Sons, The Red Sonja, Repentier, The Mission, The Venetian Woman, The Untouchables, Quartiere (Neighborhood), Rampage, Frantic, A Time of Destiny.
TELEVISION: (U.S.): Marco Polo, Moses—The Lawgiver, Scarlet and the Black, C.A.T. Squad, The Endless Game.

MORRIS, HOWARD: Actor. b. New York, NY, Sept. 4, 1919. e. New York U. U.S. Army, 4 yrs.; dir, Who's Minding the Mint, Don't Drink the Water, End of the Line.
BROADWAY: Hamlet, Call Me Mister, John Loves Mary, Gentlemen Prefer Blondes.
TELEVISION: Your Show of Shows, Caesar's Hour.

MORRIS, JOHN: Composer. b. Elizabeth, NJ, Oct. 18, 1926. e. Juilliard; U. of Washington. Wrote music for the NY Shakespeare Fest. prods.: Richard III, As You Like It, Comedy of Errors, and American Shakespeare Fest. My Mother, My Father and Me, Camino Real, and Broadway musical, A Time for Singing.
PICTURES: The Producers, The Twelve Chairs, The Gambler, Blazing Saddles, The Bank Shot, Young Frankenstein, Sherlock Holmes' Smarter Brother, Silent Movie, The Last Remake of Beau Geste, The In-Laws, The World's Greatest Lover, In God We Trust, High Anxiety, The Elephant Man, History of the World, Part One, Yellowbeard, Table for Five, To Be or Not to Be, Johnny Dangerously, The First One In, The Woman in Red, Clue, The Doctor and the Devils, Haunted Honeymoon.
TELEVISION: Splendor in the Grass, The Electric Grandmother, The Scarlet Letter, The Adams Chronicles, Georgia O'Keefe, Doctor Franken, The Firm; The Tap Dance Kid (Emmy Award), The Desperate Hours, and musical specials: Anne Bancroft Specials, S'Lemmon, S'Gershwin, Wonderful, The Music of Harold Arlen, The Music of Cole Porter, The Canterville Ghost.

MORRIS, OSWALD: Cinematographer. b. London, Eng., 1915. Left school at 16 to work for two years as camera dept. helper at studios. Was lensman for cameraman Ronald Neame who gave Morris first job as cameraman; in 1949 when Neame directed The Golden Salamander he made Morris dir. of photography.
PICTURES INCLUDE: The Golden Salamander, The Card, The Man Who Never Was, Mister Moses, Moulin Rouge, Beat the Devil, Moby Dick, Heaven Knows, Mr. Allison, The Roots of Heaven, Reflections in a Golden Eye, The Mackintosh Man, Oliver!, Scrooge, The Pumpkin Eater, The Hill, The Spy Who Came in from the Cold, A Farewell to Arms, The Key, The Guns of Navarone, Lolita, Term of Trial, Fiddler on the Roof (Acad. Award), Sleuth, Goodbye, Mr. Chips; Lady Caroline Lamb; The Mackintosh Man; The Odessa File, The Man Who Would Be King, Seven Per Cent Solution, Just Tell Me What You Want; Equus, The Wiz; The Great Muppet Caper, The Dark Crystal.
TELEVISION: Dracula (1974).

MORRIS, RICHARD: Director, Writer. b. San Francisco, CA, May 14, 1924. e. Burlingame H.S., 1939–42; Chouinard Art Inst., 1946–47; Neighborhood Playhouse, 1947–48. U.S. Army special services, writing shows, Victory Bond; Universal-Int., talent dept., writing directing skits, writing music for acting class and Korean War entertainment troups; s.p. Take Me to Town, Finders Keepers.
AUTHOR, STAGE: The Unsinkable Molly Brown.
PICTURES INCLUDE: If a Man Answers, Thoroughly Modern Millie, Change of Habit.
TELEVISION: Wrote & dir. teleplays, Loretta Young Show, wrote & dir. The Pearl (Loretta Young Show), wrote teleplays,

Private Secretary, Ford Theatre, Kraft Television Theatre, dir., The Wild Swans (Shirley Temple Show-Christopher Award).

MORRIS, WILLIAM, JR.: Consultant, retired president, William Morris Agency, Inc. b. New York, NY, Oct. 22, 1899.

MORRISSEY, PAUL: Writer, Director. b. New York, NY, 1939. e. Fordham U. Service in Army. Was involved in indep. film prod. prior to joining Andy Warhol for whom he produced such films as Chelsea Girls, Four Stars, Bike Boy, Nude Restaurant, Lonesome Cowboys, Blue Movie, L'Amour, Women in Revolt.
PICTURES INCLUDE: Flesh, Trash, Heat, Flesh Fur, Frankenstein, Blood For Dracula, Forty Deuce, Madame Wang's, Mixed Blood, Throwback, Beethoven's Nephew (dir., co-s.p.), Spike of Bensonhurst (dir., s.p.).

MORRISON, HENRY T.: Executive. b. Mt. Pleasant, NY, Dec. 21, 1939. e. U. of Minnesota, B.A., 1963;, IMEDE, Switzerland, PED, 1971; Yale U. Divinity Sch., M.A., 1980. Episcopal priest 1983 to present. Positions in banking and marketing before entering m.p. industry 1972. 1976–85, independent financial consultant to industry. 1987, pres. & CEO, Mill City Entertainment, Minneapolis. 1987, pres. & CEO, Crocus Entertainment, Inc. MN. as well as Mill City Entertainment.
PICTURES: Dangerous Relations (assoc. prod.); Mitchell (assoc. prod.); The Devil's Men (exec. prod.) Author: Intercept, s.p., based on his own novel.

MORROW, JEFF: Actor. b. New York, NY, Jan. 13, 1917. e. Pratt Inst. Starred 2 years as radio's Dick Tracy, star of TV series Union Pacific, U.S. Steel, Wagon Train, etc.
BROADWAY: Cornell's Romeo and Juliet, St. Joan; Billy Budd. Starred in Lace On Her Petticoat, Three Wishes For Jamie. In Los Angeles Lincoln in Norman Corwin's Lincoln-Douglas Debates.
PICTURES INCLUDE: The Robe, Tanganyika, Sign of the Pagan, Captain Lightfoot, This Island Earth, Story of Ruth, Dino Risi's Giovane Normale (Italy) Hour of Decision (England).

MORSE, ROBERT: Actor. b. Newton, MA, May 18, 1931. Served U.S. Navy. Studied with American Theatre Wing, New York, where he had small role in film The Proud and the Profane, 1956. Following radio work, appeared on Broadway stage in The Matchmaker, 1956.
BROADWAY: Say, Darling, Take Me Along, How to Succeed in Business Without Really Trying (Tony Award, 1962), Sugar, So Long 174th Street.
PICTURES INCLUDE: The Matchmaker, Honeymoon Hotel, Quick Before It Melts, The Loved One, Oh Dad Poor Dad, How to Succeed in Business Without Really Trying, Guide for the Married Man, The Boatniks, Hunk, The Emperor's New Clothes.
TELEVISION: That's Life (series), The Stingiest Man in Town, Kennedy Center Tonight—Broadway to Washington, Masquerade, The Calendar Girl Murders.

MORTON, ARTHUR: Composer, Arranger. b. Duluth, MN, Aug. 8, 1908. e. U. of Minnesota, 1929. Composer for various film cos. including Universal, RKO, United Artists; with Columbia since 1948.
PICTURES INCLUDE: Night Life of the Gods, Princess O'Hara, Riding on Air, Fit for a King, Turnabout, Walking Hills, The Nevadan, Rogues of Sherwood Forest, Father is a Bachelor, Never Trust a Gambler, Harlem Globetrotters, Big Heat, Pushover, He Laughed Last.
ORCH. ARRANGEMENTS: Laura, Smokey, From Here to Eternity, Jolson Story, Salome, Phfft, No Sad Songs For Me, Born Yesterday, Long Gray Line, Man from Laramine, My Sister Eileen, Queen Bee, Picnic, Jubal, Autumn Leaves, Johnny Concho, Harder They Fall, 3:10 to Yuma, Full of Life, Garment Jungle, They Came to Cordura, Strangers When We Meet, Touch of Mink, Critics Choice, Diamond Head, Toys in the Attic, Man from the Diners' Club, Von Ryan's Express, The Saboteur, Code Name—Morituri, In Harm's Way, What a Way to Go, The New Interns, Rio Conchos, Dear Briggitte, Our Man Flint, Planet of the Apes, Film Flam Man, Justine, Patton, Tora Tora Tora, Mephisto Waltz, Ballad of Cable Hogue, Traveling Executioner, Escape From the Planet of the Apes, Cold Turkey, Wild Rovers, The Other, Ace Eli, One Little Indian, The Don is Dead, Papillon, Chinatown, Breakout, The Wind and the Lion, Logan's Run, The Omen, Islands in the Stream, Passover Plot, Twilight's Last Gleaming, Damnation Alley, MacArthur, Capricorn One, Coma, The Swarm, Omen II (Damien), Boys from Brazil, Magic, Superman, Alien, Players, Meteor, Star Trek, Inchon, Masada, The Final Conflict, Outland, Raggedy Man, Night Crossing, Poltergeist, The Secret of NIMH, First Blood, Psycho II, Twilight Zone, Under Fire, The Lonely Guy, Gremlins, Supergirl, Rambo: First Blood Part II, Explorers, King Solomon's Mines, Link, Poltergist II, Hoosiers, Lionheart, Extreme Prejudice, Innerspace, Rent a Cop, Rambo III.
TELEVISION: Black Saddle, Laramie, Bus Stop, Follow the Sun, My Three Sons, Peyton Place, Medical Center, Daniel Boone, Lancers, National Geographic, Say Goodbye, How to

Stay Alive, Hooray For Hollywood, The Waltons, Apple's Way, Medical Story.

MOSES, CHARLES ALEXANDER: Executive, Writer, Producer. b. Chicago, CA, March 1, 1923. e. Aeronautical U., Northwestern U., Englewood Eve. Jr. Coll., Antioch U. Pub. rel. dir., Goldblatt Bros. dept. store chain, Chicago; field adv-promo exec., United Artists, unit publicist for over 30 films, exec., Screen Gems; European adv-pub superv., Paris, United Artists; adv-pub dir., Bel Air Prod., V.P. adv-pub dir., Associates & Aldrich Co., adv-pub dir., Sinatra Enterprises, assoc. studio pub. dir., Universal Studios, adv-pub rep., Universal Studios from Paris for Europe, exec-in-chge New York domestic & foreign adv-pub dept., Universal, adv-pub superv., Orion Pictures Co. Own firm, Charles A. Moses Co., adv-marketing-pub. rel., acc'ts included United Artists, Columbia Picts., 20th Century-Fox, UA-TV, Brut Prod., Michael Klinger Ltd., ITT, Cinecom, Cinemation Industries, Hemdale Leisure Corp., Faberge, Stein & Day Publishers; Information, Inc., Automated Learning, Darrell Waters Ltd., Ebefilms, Phoenix Films, Valley Cable TV, Jensen Farley Picts., Taft Internat'l Picts, auto shows, TV shows, art galleries, events, guilds, Cinevent Prod., Dimitri Tiomkin, Dale Wasserman, American Internat'l Picts., Filmways. Orig. stories, Frankenstein 1970 (Allied Artists), Department Store (Brut Prod.); Prod., Radio Free Europe, Munich, Goldblatt radio, TV shows (WGN); Writer-prod-dir., documentaries, Carson Prod., Mason City; Screenplays, Abigail, The Callers; Musical book, Daddy. Past pres., The Publicists Guild of America (IATSE, Local 818).

MOSES, GILBERT: Director. b. Cleveland, OH, Aug. 20, 1942. Staff mem. Free Press, Jackson, MS 1963–64; editor, 1964; co-founder artistic dir. Free Southern Theatre; member Second City, Chicago, 1967. New York Stage director; m.p. debut Willie Dynamite (also score and lyrics) 1973; The Fish That Saved Pittsburgh, 1979.
STAGE: Ain't Supposed to Die a Natural Death, Slave Ship, The Taking of Miss Janie (Obie Award), 1600 Pennsylvania Avenue.
TELEVISION: Roots, A Fight for Jenny, The Greatest Thing That Almost Happened.

MOSLEY, ROGER E.: Actor. b. Los Angeles, CA. Planned career in broadcasting but turned to acting, first appearing in small roles in TV series: Night Gallery, Baretta, Kojak, Cannon, Switch, etc. Theatrical film debut in The New Centurions (1972).
PICTURES: Stay Hungry, The Greatest, Semi-Tough, Leadbelly.
TELEVISION: Series: Switch, Magnum P.I. Movies: I Know Why the Caged Bird Sings, The Jericho Mile, Attica, etc.

MOSS, ARNOLD: Actor, Director. b. New York, NY, Jan. 28, 1910. e. City Coll. of New York, B.A. (Phi Beta Kappa); Columbia U., M.A.; New York U., Ph.D.. Teacher, B'klyn Coll. 1932–39; visiting prof., U. of Connecticut, 1973; Pace U., 1975; Coll. of William and Mary, 1976; Purdue U., 1977. Neighborhood Playhouse Sch. of the Theatre, 1974–76; U. of Wyoming, 1985; Theatre, film opera & TV actor-director.
PICTURES INCLUDE: Temptation, Loves of Carmen, Reign of Terror, Border Incident, Kim, Mask of the Avenger, My Favorite Spy, Viva Zapata, Salome, Casanova's Big Night, Bengal Brigade, Hell's Island, Jump into Hell, The 27th Day, The Fool Killer, Caper of the Golden Bulls, Gambit.
TELEVISION: Star Trek, Bonanza, Alfred Hitchcock, Hallmark Hall of Fame, many others. Actor-writer, CBS Radio Mystery Theater (over 500 programs).

MOSS, CHARLES B., JR.: Theatre Executive, Producer. b. New York, NY, Aug. 29, 1944. e. U. of Pennsylvania, B.A., 1966; Boston U. Sch. of Law, LL.B., 1969. Was asst. prof. of law at Boston U., 1969–70. Entered ind. as v.p. of B.S. Moss Enterprises, 1970; now pres. Has produced three films: Let's Scare Jessica to Death, Stigma, Diary of the Dead.

MOSS, FRANK L.: Writer, Producer. b. New York, NY. e. Duke U., Columbia U. Reporter, drama & film critic, N.Y.; U.S. Army Air Force, 1942–46, Instructor, U. of California at L.A., 1985–86 on advanced screenplay writing. 1987–88 private tutoring on screenplay and TV writing.
PLAYS: author: Glamour Girl, Call To Arms, (collab), So Goes the Nation, (collab), Some People's Children, American Pastoral, City on a Hill.
PICTURES INCLUDE: The Unvanquished, Whiphand, Caribbean, Sangaree, Papago Wells, The Half Breed, Sweetheart of Sigma Chi. MILITARY: 22 Air Force Training Films; 17 documentaries.
TV PILOTS: Outer Limits, Grand Jury, The Texan.
TV SCRIPTS: Telephone Hour, Four Star Playhouse, Winston Churchill's Valiant Years, Route 66, Wagon Train, Laramie, Wild Wild West, The Texan, G.E. Theater, Wire Service, U.S. Marshall, M-Squad, Stoney Burke, Tales of the Texas Rangers, T.V. Readers' Digest, Sheriff of Cochise, Whirlybirds, Line-Up, Wyatt Earp, Rin Tin Tin, Walter Winchell File, Daniel Boone, Man Who Never Was, Felony Squad,

Richard Diamond, Lassie, Like the Rich People, Hired Mother, Shenandoah, Counterspy, White Hunter.
PROD-STORY ED: Screen Televideo, Sovereign Prod., Wire Service, T.V. Reader's Digest, Wyatt Earp.

MOSS, IRWIN: Executive. e. Syracuse U., Harvard Law Sch. Member NY State Bar. Began industry career as director of package negotiations for CBS-TV; 1970–80, exec. v.p. & natl. head of business affairs for I.C.M.; 1978–80, snr. v.p., NBC Entertainment; 1980, pres., Marble Arch TV. 1982, joined Paramount Pictures as snr. v.p. for motion picture div. 1984, exec. v.p., L. Taffner Ltd.

MOSTEL, JOSH: Actor. b. Dec. 21, 1946. Son of late Zero Mostel. m. producer Peggy Rajski. e. Brandeis U., B.A. 1970. Part of The Proposition, a Boston improvisational comedy group. Stage debut The Homecoming (Provincetown Playhouse, MA). Film debut Going Home, 1971.
STAGE: Unlikely Heroes, The Proposition, An American Millionaire, A Texas Trilogy, Gemini, Ferocious Kisses (dir.), Men in the Kitchen (Long Wharf, New Haven.), The Dog Play, The Boys Next Door, Love As We Know It (dir.).
PICTURES: Jesus Christ Superstar, Harry and Tonto, Sophie's Choice, Compromising Positions, Almost You, Star 80, Windy City, The Money Pit, Radio Days, Matewan, Wall Street.
TELEVISION: Seventh Avenue, Delta House, At Ease, The Boy Who Loved Trolls (PBS). Co-wrote Media Probes: The Language Show; Murphy's Law (series).

MOUND, FRED: Executive. b. St. Louis, MO, April 10, 1932. e. St. Louis U., Quincy Coll. 1946–52, assoc. with father, Charles Mound, at Park Theatre in Valley Park, Mo.; 1952–53, Universal Pictures (St. Louis); 1953, booker, UA, St. Louis; 1955 promoted to salesman in Kansas City; 1957, salesman, St. Louis; 1962, Indianapolis branch mgr. In 1967 named UA regional mgr., Dallas and in 1970 became S.W. Div. mgr; 1976–77, asst. gen. sls. mgr. for Southern, N.W. and S.W. Division operating out of Dallas. In June, 1977 appt. v.p., asst. gen. sls. mgr. of UA; Nov. 1978, appt. v.p. gen sls. mgr. for A.F.D. Pictures in Los Angeles; April, 1981, v.p. asst. gen. sls. mgr. for Universal Pictures; Jan., 1984, sr. v.p., gen. sls. mgr., Universal Pictures Distribution; named exec. v.p. Sept., 1988.

MOUNT, THOM: Executive. b. Durham, NC, May 26, 1948. e. Bard Coll.; CA Institute of the Arts, MFA. Started career with Roger Corman and as asst. to prod., Danny Selznick at MGM. Moved to Universal under prod. exec. Ned Tanen. At 26, named pres. and head of prod. at Universal. During 8-year tenure was responsible for dev. and prod. of more than 140 films (including Smokey and the Bandit, Animal House, Coal Miner's Daughter and Missing.) Also headed div. which created Broadway prods. (The Best Little Whorehouse in Texas, Nuts). 1985, founded The Mount Company, film, television, theatre and book publishing org.
PICTURES: Pirates (exec. prod.), Can't Buy Me Love, Frantic, Bull Durham (co-prod.); Stealing Home, Tequila Sunrise, Frankenstein, Singles.
TELEVISION: Son of the Morning, Star, Aquino (prod.).

MOYERS, BILL: TV Correspondent. b. Hugo, OK, June 5, 1934. e. U. of Texas; Southwestern Baptist Theological Sem. Asst. to Lyndon B. Johnson, 1959–60, 1961–63; assoc. dir., Peace Corps, 1961–63; spec. asst. to Pres. Johnson, 1963–67 and press secty. 1965–67. Editor and chief corr., CBS Reports. Bill Moyers Journal on PBS. Specials: Facing Evil.

MUDD, ROGER: Newscaster. b. Washington, DC, Feb. 9, 1928. e. Washington & Lee U., U. of North Carolina. Reporter for Richmond News-Leader, 1953; news. dir., WRNL, 1954; WTOP, Washington, 1956; joined CBS News 1961 as Congressional corr. 1977, Natl. Aff. corr.; 1978, corr., CBS Reports; 1980–87: NBC News as chief Washington corr.; chief political corr., co-anchor; 1987 joined The MacNeil/Lehrer News Hour as special correspondent; essayist, and chief congressional corr.

MUHL, EDWARD E.: Executive, Producer. b. Richmond, IN, Feb. 17, 1907. Gen. mgr., Universal 1948–53; v.p., chg. studio 1953–68. Bd. member, Cinema Group, Inc., 1984. Consultant, Alcor Prods., Dallas, 1985–87. Co-author, consultant, s.p., Soldier: The Other Side of Glory, 1987.

MUIR, E. ROGER: Producer. b. Canada, Dec. 16, 1918. e. U. of Minnesota. Partner Minn. Advertising Services Co.; Photographer, Great Northern Railway; motion picture producer Army Signal corps; NBC TV producer, Howdy Doody, exec. producer, Concentration. Now pres. Nicholson-Muir Prods, TV program packager, U.S. Sign-Off, Pay Cards, Canada Pay Cards, Headline Hunters, Definition, Celebrity Bowling, co-creator Newlywed Game, exec. prod. I Am Joe's Heart, I Am Joe's Lung, I Am Joe's Spine, I Am Joe's Stomach, The New Howdy Doody Show, Supermates, Second Honeymoon, Groaner, Generation Jury, Shopping Game, Guess What, I Am Joe's Kidney, I Am Joe's Liver, It's Howdy Doody Time: A 40 Year Celebration.

MULDAUR, DIANA: Actress. b. New York, NY, Aug. 19, 1938. e. Sweet Briar Coll. Began on New York stage the turned to films and TV, appearing on numerous major network shows.
PICTURES INCLUDE: The Swimmer, Number One, The Lawyer, One More Train to Rob, The Other, Chosen Survivors, Beyond Reason, McQ.
TELEVISION: Series: Born Free, Cannon, McCloud, The Survivors, Star Trek: The Next Generation. Movies: Murder in Three Acts, Black Beauty, Call to Danger, The Miracle Worker, A Year in the Life.

MULGREW, KATE: Actress. b. Dubuque, IA, April 29, 1955. e. New York U. Stage work includes stints with American Shakespeare Festival, O'Neill Festival and at Hartman Theatre, Stamford. Film debut: Lovespell (1978).
PICTURES: Jennifer, Tristan and Isolt, A Stranger Is Watching, Throw Momma from the Train.
TELEVISION: Ryan's Hope (1975–77), The Word, Jennifer, A Woman's Story, Mrs. Colombo, Kate Loves a Mystery, A Time for Miracles, The Manions of America, Mother Seaton, Roses Are for the Rich, Heat Beat, Roots Christmas.

MULHOLLAND, ROBERT E.: Executive. b. 1934. e. Northwestern U. Joined NBC News as newswriter in Chicago in 1962. In 1964 made midwestern field producer for Huntley-Brinkley Report. In 1964 moved to London as European producer for NBC News; 1967, named Washington producer of Huntley-Brinkley Report. Transferred to L.A. in 1967 to be director of news, west coast. Named exec. prod. of NBC Nightly News. In 1973 appt. v.p., NBC news.; 1974 exec. v.p. of NBC News. In 1977 appt. pres. of NBC Television Network; also elected to board of directors. Resigned, 1984.

MULL, MARTIN: Actor. b. Chicago, IL, Aug. 18, 1943. e. Rhode Island Sch. of Design. Started as humorist, making recordings for Warner Bros., Capricorn, ABC Records, etc. Theatrical m.p. debut, FM, 1978.
PICTURES: My Bodyguard, Serial, Take This Job and Shove It, Private School, Growing Pains, Flicks, Mr. Mom, Clue, O.C. and Stiggs, Home is Where the Hart Is, Rented Lips (actor, s.p., exec. prod.), Cutting Class.
TELEVISION: Mary Hartman Mary Hartman, Fernwood 2-Night, America 2-Night, Domestic Life, numerous talk shows, etc. Wrote produced and starred in The History of White People in America for HBO, Candid Camera Christmas Special (1987), Portrait of a White Marriage.

MULLER, PETER: Executive, Producer, Attorney. b. Teplitz-Sanov, Czechoslovakia, March 4, 1947. e. NYU, NYU Law Sch. Served as entertainment editor, Ambience and Women's Life magazines. Former CEO, Producers Releasing Corp., Pres. of PRC's entertainment div. Consultant to German TV show Am Laifen Band. Has worked with French and Eng. communication cos. Co-organizer: album and video of theater artists to fight world hunger, Broadway Feeds the World. Pres. and founder of The Muller Entertainment Group, Inc. Member: bd. of dirs. NYU Alumni Assoc., NYU's nominating comm.; American Bar Assoc.; ABA Forum on the Entertainment and Sports Industries; and ABA Forum on Patent, Trademark, Copyright Law; NY State Bar Assoc.; Volunteer Lawyers for the Arts.

MULLER, ROBBY: Cinematographer. b. Netherlands.
PICTURES: Saint Jack, Honeysuckle Rose, They All Laughed, Body Rock, Repo Man, Paris, Texas, The Longshot, To Live and Die in L.A., Down By Law, Tricheurs, Barfly.

MULLIGAN, RICHARD: Actor. b. New York, NY, Nov. 13, 1932. On stage in All the Way Home, Never Too Late, Thieves, etc.
PICTURES: The Mixed Up Files of Mrs. Basil E. Frankweiler, Irish Whiskey Rebellion, One Potato, Two Potato, The Group, the Big Bus, Little Big Man, Scavenger Hunt, S.O.B., Trail of the Pink Panther, Meatballs Part II, Teachers, Micki and Maude, Doin' Time, The Heavenly Kid, A Fine Mess, Quicksilver.
TELEVISION: Having Babies, Poker Alice, Series: The Hero, Diana, Soap (Emmy Award, 1980), Reggie, Empty Nest.

MULLIGAN, ROBERT: Director. b. Bronx, NY. Aug. 23, 1925. e. Fordham U., A.B. With CBS-TV, asst. supv. in radio oper.; prod. asst. on Supense, TV; then asst. dir. & dir.: TV Playhouse, NBC, Alcoa-Goodyear, Studio One, Playhouse 90, Hallmark Hall of Fame.
PICTURES INCLUDE: Fear Strikes Out (1957), The Rat Race, The Great Imposter, Come September, To Kill a Mockingbird, The Spiral Road, Love with the Proper Stranger, Baby the Rain Must Fall, Inside Daisy Clover, Up the Down Staircase, Pursuit of Happiness, Summer of '42, The Other, The Nickel Ride, Blood Brothers, Same Time Next Year, Kiss Me Goodbye (also prod.), Clara's Heart.

MURDOCH, RUPERT: Executive. b. Australia, March 11, 1931. Son of Sir Keith Murdoch, head of The Melbourne Herald and leading figure in Australian journalism. e. Oxford U., England. Spent two years on Fleet St. before returning home to take over family paper, The Adelaide News. Acquired more

Australian papers and in 1969 expanded to Britain, buying The News of the World. Moved to U.S. in 1973, buying San Antonio Express and News. Conglomerate in 1985 included New York Post, New York Magazine, The Star, The Times of London, The Boston Herald, The Chicago Sun-Times along with TV stations, book publishing companies, airline, oil and gas companies, etc. 1985, made deal to buy 20th Century-Fox Film Corp. from owner Martin Davis. Sold the NY Post, 1988 to conform with FCC regulations. Purchased Triangle Publications 1988 (including TV Guide).

MURPHY, BEN: Actor. b. Jonesboro, AR, March 6, 1942. e. U. of Illinois. Degree in drama from Pasadena Playhouse. Acted in campus productions and toured in summer stock. Film debut with small role in The Graduate, 1967.
PICTURES: The Thousand Plane Raid, Yours, Mine and Ours, Sidecar Racer.
TELEVISION: Series: The Name of the Game, Alias Smith and Jones, Griff, Gemini Man, The Chisholms, Lottery!, Berrengers, The Dirty Dozen. Movies: Wild Bill Hickock, Bridger, Heat Wave, Runaway, This Is the West That Was, Hospital Fire, The Cradle Will Fall. Mini-Series: The Winds of War.

MURPHY, EDDIE: b. Hempstead, NY, Apr. 3, 1961. Wrote and performed own comedy routines at youth centers and local bars at age 15. Worked on comedy club circuit; at 19 joined TV's Saturday Night Live. 1982, became writer for SNL as well as performer. Film debut, 48 Hrs., 1982.
PICTURES: 48 Hrs., Trading Places, The Best Defense, Beverly Hills Cop, The Golden Child, Beverly Hills Cop II, Eddie Murphy Raw, Coming to America (also story).

MURPHY, GEORGE: Actor, Former U.S. Senator. b. New Haven, CT, July 4, 1902. e. Yale U. Toolmaker for Ford Co., miner, real estate agent, nightclub dancer, actor. On stage from 1927 (Good News, Of Thee I Sing, Roberta, etc.). Screen debut 1934 in Kid Millions. Member: Screen Actors Guild (former pres.); Nat'l Com. WAC. Spcl. Academy Award (1951) "for interpreting m.p. ind. correctly to country at large," 1940; chmn., Hollywood Coordinating Com.; bd. mem., USO Inc.; v.p., Acad. of M.P. Arts & Sciences; div. of pub. rel., MGM, 1954–58; bd. mem. & past pres., Screen Actors Guild; bd. mem., M.P. Relief Fund. Joined Desilu Productions as v.p. in chg. public affairs, 1959; v.p., bd. of dir., Technicolor Corp. 1953, a year after last film, became chmn. Republican National Convention; Elected U.S. Senator, California, 1964–70. Autobiography: Say, Didn't You Used to Be George Murphy? (1970).
PICTURES INCLUDE: I'll Love You Always, You're a Sweetheart, London by Night, Broadway Melody of 1938, Risky Business, Two Girls on Broadway, A Girl, a Guy and a Gob, Tom, Dick and Harry, Ringside Maisie, Mayor of 44th Street, For Me and My Gal, Powers Girl, This Is the Army, Broadway Rhythm, Show Business, Step Lively, Having a Wonderful Crime, Up Goes Maisie, Arnelo Affair, Cynthia, Tenth Avenue Angel, Big City, Battleground, Border Incident, No Questions Asked, Talk About a Stranger, It's a Big Country, Walk East on Beacon, Jamboree (Boy Scout film), This Is the Army, Broadway Melody.

MURPHY, JOHN F.: Theatre Executive. b. Brooklyn, NY, Mar. 25, 1905. e. City Coll. of New York. Entire career with Loew's Theatres; started over 45 yrs. ago as asst. mgr. Hillside & Valencia Theatres, Jamaica, NY; apptd. gen. mgr. in chg. of out-of-town Theatres, 1942–54; v.p.; Loew's Theatres, Aug., 1954; dir., Loew's Theatres, Oct., 1956; exec. v.p., Loew's Theatre, 1959; ret. July 1963; continues on bd. as advisor and director emeritus.

MURPHY, MICHAEL: Actor. b. Los Angeles, CA, May 5, 1938. e. U. of Arizona. Taught English and Drama in L.A. city school system, 1962–64. N.Y. stage debut as director of Rat's Nest, 1978–79.
PICTURES: The Legend of Lylah Clare, The Arrangement, Brewster McCloud, MASH, McCabe and Mrs. Miller, What's Up Doc?, Nashville, An Unmarried Woman, The Front, Manhattan, The Year of Living Dangerously, Strange Behavior, Cloak and Dagger, Salvador.
TELEVISION: Saints and Sinners, Ben Casey, Dr. Kildare, Bonanza, Combat, Autobiography of Miss Jane Pittman, John Cheever's Oh Youth and Beauty, Two Marriages, Tanner '88: Dark Horse; The Caine Mutiny Court-Martial.

MURPHY, RICHARD: Writer. Director. b. Boston, MA, 1912. e. Williams Coll. Entered m.p. Ind. 1937 Capt. U.S. Army Sig. Corps. SWPA, 1942–45. Contract writer, 20th Century-Fox, 1945–54 Writer-Prod., 20th-Fox, 1964–72; pres. Cinecom World Ent. Ltd., 1974.
PICTURES INCLUDE: Boomerang, Deep Waters, Cry of the City, Panic in the Streets, You're in the Navy Now, Les Miserables, Desert Rats, Broken Lance, Three Strips in the Sun, Wackiest Ship in the Army, Compulsion, Last Angry Man.
TELEVISION: Our Man Higgins, creator, TV series, The Felony Squad, The Kidnapping of the President (s.p.).

MURRAY, BARBARA: Actress. b. London, England, Sept. 27, 1929. Stage debut in Variety, 1946; screen debut in Badger's Green, 1948. Various TV appearances.
PICTURES INCLUDE: Passport to Pimlico, Don't Ever Leave Me, Boys in Brown, Poets Pub, Tony Draws a Horse, Dark Man, Frightened Man, Mystery Junction, Another Man's Poison, Hot Ice, Street Corner (Both Sides of the Law), Meet Mr. Lucifer, Doctor at Large, Campbell's Kingdom, A Cry from the Streets, Girls in Arms.

MURRAY, BILL: Actor. b. Chicago, IL, Sept. 21, 1950. Was pre-med student; left to join brother, Brian Doyle-Murray, in Second City, the Chicago improvisational troupe. Appeared with brother on radio, National Lampoon Show, and in off-Bdwy. revue, of same name. Hired by ABC for Saturday Night Live; then by NBC.
PICTURES: Meatballs (debut), Mr. Mike's Mondo Video, Where the Buffalo Roam, Caddyshack, Stripes, Tootsie, Ghostbusters, The Razor's Edge (also co-s.p.), Nothing Lasts Forever, Little Shop of Horrors, Ghostbusters II.
TELEVISION: Series: Saturday Night Live (1977–80 also writer; Emmy-as writer 1977), Movies: All You Need Is Cash, Things We Did Last Summer. Specials: It's Not Easy Being Me—The Rodney Dangerfield Show, Second City—25 Years in Revue.

MURRAY, DON: Actor, Director, Writer. b. Hollywood, CA, July 31, 1929. Mother was a Ziegeld Girl, father was dance dir. for Fox Studio.
PLAYS: Insect Comedy, Rose Tattoo, The Skin of Our Teeth, The Hot Corner, Smith (a musical), The Norman Conquests; Same Time, Next Year.
PICTURES INCLUDE: Bus Stop, Bachelor Party, Hatful of Rain, The Hoodlum Priest (also prod., writer), Advise and Consent, Baby the Rain Must Fall, Sweet Love, Bitter, The Cross and the Switchblade (dir., s.p. only), Conquest of the Planet of the Apes, One Man's Way, The Plainsman, Escape from East Berlin, Shake Hands with the Devil, From Hell to Texas, Confessions of Tom Harris (also prod., s.p.), Call Me by My Rightful Name (also prod., co-s.p.), The Borgia Stick, Deadly Hero, Damien (dir., s.p. only), Endless Love, Radioactive Dreams, Peggy Sue Got Married, Scorpion, Made in Heaven, Ghosts Don't Do It.
TELEVISION: Series: The Outcasts, Knots Landing; Movies: The Sex Symbol, Rainbow, License to Kill, A Touch of Scandal, Something in Common, Stillwatch, The Stepford Children, The Borgia Stick, Return of the Rebels, Quarterback Princess, For I Have Loved Strangers, Hasty Heart, Billy Budd, Winterset, Alas Babylon, Mistress.

MURRAY, JAN: Performer. b. New York City, NY, 1917. Performed in nightclubs, vaudeville, B'way, radio, TV, films. Was m.c., Songs for Sale, and Sing It Again, CBS-TV; TV guest star many programs; on Dollar a Second; Jan Murray Time; Treasure Hunt.
PLAYS: A Funny Thing Happened on the Way to the Forum.
PICTURES INCLUDE: Who Killed Teddy Bear?

MUSANTE, TONY: Actor. b. Bridgeport, CT, June 30, 1936. e. Oberlin Coll. B.A. Directed local theatre, then appeared off-Broadway in regional theater and on Dupont Show of the Month (Ride With Terror).
THEATER: Bdwy: The Lady From Dubuque; P.S., Your Cat Is Dead; 27 Wagons Full of Cotton and Memory of Two Mondays; (Off-bdwy): Grand Magic; Cassatt; A Gun Play; Benito Cereno; L'Histoire du Soldat; Match-Play; The Zoo Story; The Pinter Plays (The Collection); Kiss Mama; The Balcony. Regional: The Big Knife, A Streetcar Named Desire, The Taming of the Shrew, APA Shakespeare Rep., others.
PICTURES INCLUDE: Once a Thief, The Incident, The Detective, The Mercenary, One Night at Dinner, The Bird with the Crystal Plumage, The Grissom Gang, The Last Run, Anonymous Venetian, The Trap, The Repenter, The Pisciotta Case, Goodbye and Amen, Break Up, Nocturne, The Pope of Greenwich Village.
TELEVISION: Chrysler Theatre, Alfred Hitchcock Hour, N.Y.P.D., The Fugitive, Trials of O'Brien, Police Story, Medical Story, Toma (series); Movies: Rearview Mirror, The Court Martial of Lt. William Calley, Desperate Miles, The Quality of Mercy, Nowhere to Hide, My Husband is Missing, The Story of Esther, High Ice. Mini-series: Nutcracker: Money, Madness & Murder; Breaking Up Is Hard To Do; the Legend of the Black Hand, Devil's Hill, Appointment in Trieste.

MUSTO, MICHAEL J.: Producer, Writer. b. New York, NY. e. S. Niagara U. Apprentice for J. J. Shubert. Comedy Workshop, N.Y. W-Co. Hellzapoppin, Wrote, Prod. Dir. Burlesque shows and stage revues. Prod. Industrial Films, Commercials, Operas, Fund Raising Shows. Prod. Films: The Glass House, Phenomena 7-7, Down Tin Pan Alley, Single Room Furnished, Educated Heart, Agnes, Spring Fancy, The Atheist, Man Who Cried Wolf, Several Robert Montgomery Presents, Hallmark Hall of Fame, TV Specials, The Bold Ones, Strange Is the Wind. Wrote: Due-Bill Marriage, Spring Fancy, Who's On First, Pratt's Fall, Charlie Daniels Band, Special Break,

Heads-Feed Cats, Seymour, Granada, Seppi and His Brothers, Amato and the Yenta, The Cliffdwellers, Other. Owner. Empire Films and Cinema City Studios, dinner theatres.

MUTSU, IAN YONOSUKE: Producer, Distributor. b. London, England, Jan. 14, 1907. e. U. of Birmingham, England. Journalist 1931–48. Daily Express, UPI, etc.; Japan repr. MGM-Hearst Metrotone News, U.S. Newsreel Pool, later Telenews, UPI-Movietone News, ITN London; 1952 pres. International Motion Picture Co. for news coverage, documentaries, custom films for worldwide clients; 1966 agent BBC TV sales, Modern Talking Picture Service NYC; 1973 founded Mutsu Inc. (Canada). Productions include numerous documentaries on Japan, Japanese background films for overseas clients.

MYERS, JULIAN F.: Public Relations. b. Detroit, MI, Feb. 22, 1918. e. Wayne U., 1935–37, U. of Southern California, 1937–39. Distribution, Loew's Detroit, 1941–42; asst. story editor, idea man, Columbia, 1942–46; publicist, 20th Century-Fox, 1948–62; public relations, Julian F. Myers, Inc., 1962; pres., Myers Studios, Inc., 1966; pres., New Horizons Broadcasting Corp., 1968–69; snr. publicist American Intl. Pictures, 1970–80. Executive Board Hollywood Press Club; member Variety Clubs; Academy of Motion Pictures Arts & Sciences; Board of Governors Film Industry Workshops, Inc. 1977, western vice-pres., The Publicists Guild; Recipient of Publicists Guild's Robert Yeager Award; 1979, re-elected western v.p., Publicists Guild. First male member Hollywood Women's Press Club. Co-founder HANDS (Hollywood Answering Needs of Disaster Survivors). Member, M.P. Pioneers. Winner, 1980 Publicists Guild Les Mason Award. Instructor in publicity, UCLA, 1979 to present. Filmways Pictures, pub. dept., 1980–81. Exec. v.p., worldwide m.p. and TV pub./mktg., Hanson & Schwam Public Relations 1981 to present.

MYERS, LAURENCE: Executive. Chairman, GTO Films & Video Intl. Handled Scum, The Wanderers, Breaking Glass and Caligula. Production credits incl. Never Too Young Too Rock, The Greek Tycoon (co-prod.), The Survivor (co-prod.), In the House of Death (exec. prod.), Bloodbath.

MYERS, PETER S.: Executive. b. Toronto, Ont., Canada, May 13, 1923. e. U. of Toronto. R.C.A.F. 1944–46. Toronto br. mgr., 20th Century-Fox, 1948; Canadian div. mgr., 1951; man. dir. Canada, 1959; gen. sales mgr. in chg. of dom. distribution, 1968; v.p., 1969; named snr. v.p.; domestic dist., 1979; snr. v.p., 20th-Fox Entertainment, 1980; pres., 20th-Fox Classics, 1983; pres., Hemdale Releasing Corp. and PSM Entertainment Inc., 1985.

MYERSON, BERNARD: Executive. b. New York, NY, March 25, 1918. Entered m.p. ind. with Fabian Theatres, 1938–63; last position as exec. v.p.; joined Loew's Theatres as v.p., 1963; exec. v.p. and board member, Loew's Corp.; pres. Loew's Theatres, 1971. Vice chm. & mem. of Executive Committee Corp., 1985. Chm. & pres., Loews Theatre Management Greater N.Y. Chapter, National Foundation of March of Dimes; Honorary chm. & bd. mem., Will Rogers Memorial Fund; Mem. exec. comm., bd., National Assn. Theatre Owners; bd. mem., Motion Picture Pioneers. Vice pres., Variety International; mem., finance comm.; Friars; Board of Directors Burke Rehabilitation Center; mem. N.Y.S. Governor's Council on M.P. & T.V. Development; mem. M.P. & T.V. Com. USIA.

N

NABORS, JIM: Actor. b. Sylacauga, AL, June 12, 1932. Developed a second career as a singer. Between 1966–72 had 12 albums on best selling charts.
PICTURES: The Best Little Whorehouse in Texas, Stroker Ace, Cannonball Run II, etc.
TELEVISION: Series: Andy Griffith Show, Gomer Pyle USMC, The Jim Nabors Show, etc. Movie: Return to Mayberry.

NADEL, ARTHUR: Producer, Director, Writer. b. New York, NY, April 25. Film editor for Paramount, 20th Century-Fox, Walt Disney, U.S. Air Force m.p. div., United Artists; superv. editor, McCann-Erickson; prod., dir., writer, Universal; v.p., Levy-Gardner-Laven. Currently exec. v.p. creative affairs, Filmation Studios, Co-chair, Documentary Comm. of Acad. of Motion Picture Arts and Sciences; Governor of Television Academy.
PICTURES INCLUDE: Clambake, Lola, Underground, No Trumpets, No Drum.
TELEVISION: The Rifleman, The Plainsman, Great Adventure, Arrest and Trial, Kraft Theatre, The Virginian, Big Valley, Daniel Boone, Cowboy in Africa, Bonanza, Delphi Bureau, Banyon, Streets of San Francisco; NBC Specials, Welcome Home (Emmy Winner); This Year in Jerusalem, Vortex in Oatmeal, The Chase; Crime Without Punishment (Emmy Award); Shazam, The Secrets of Isis, Bravestarr, He-Man; She-Ra, Bravo Bugzburg.

NADER, GEORGE: Actor. b. Pasadena, CA, Oct. 19, 1921. e. Occidental Coll., B.A.; Pasadena Playhouse. Served in U.S. Navy. Many TV appearances, film debut in Monsoon (1953). First novel, Chrome, (Putnam).
PICTURES INCLUDE: Carnival Story, Miss Robin Crusoe, Sins of Jezebel, Fours Guns to the Border, Six Bridges to Cross, Lady Godiva, Second Greatest Sex, Away All Boats, Congo Crossing, Unguarded Moment, Four Girls in Town, Man Afraid, Joe Butterfly, Nowhere to Go, The Secret Mark of D'Artagnan, The Great Space Adventure, Zigzag, The Human Afraid, House of a Thousand Dolls, Alarm on 83rd Street, Murder at Midnight, Count-Down for Manhattan, Dynamite in Green Silk, The Check and Icy Smile, The Murder Club From Bklyn, Death in a Red Jaguar, End Station of the Damned, Bullets on Broadway, Beyond Atlantis.
TELEVISION: Letter to Loretta, Fireside Theatre, Chevron Theatre, Ellery Queen, Man and the Challenge, Shannon.

NAIFY, MARSHALL: Executive. b. Sacramento, CA, March 23, 1920. e. U. of Southern California. U.S.A.F. Ch. exec. comm. & bd. chm., United Artists Communications, Inc.; pres., Magna Pictures Corp.

NAIFY, ROBERT: Executive. b. Sacramento, CA. e. Attended Stanford U. Worked for United California Theatres since 1946 in various capacities: theatre manager, purchasing agent, film buyer, general manager and president. 1963 became exec. vice president, United Artists Communications; and in 1971 became president and CEO until 1987. Currently president Todd-AO Corporation.

NAKAMURA, MOTOHIKO: Executive. b. Tokyo, Japan, Aug. 10, 1929. e. U. of California at Berkeley, U. of Pennsylvania, Tokyo U. Joined Fuji Film Co., Ltd. in Tokyo, 1953; assigned to Japan Camera Center, New York, 1956–67; North American rep. for Fuji Photo Film Co., Ltd., 1957–63; assistant export sales mgr., Fuji Photo Co., Ltd. in charge of international marketing of all products, 1964–71; exec. v.p., resident mgr., Fuji Photo Film Co. U.S.A., Inc.

NALLE, BILLY: Theatre concert organist, popular field, ASCAP Composer. b. Fort Myers, FL; graduate, The Juilliard Sch. Over 5000 major TV shows from New York; now artist-in-residence, Wichita Theatre Organ, Inc. Reader's Digest, Telarc & WTO Records Artist. Public Relations: Billy Nalle Music, Wichita.

NAMATH, JOE: Actor. b. Beaver Falls, PA, May 31, 1943. e. U. of Alabama. Former professional football star. Film debut in Norwood (1970).
PICTURES: C.C. & Co., The Last Rebel, Avalanche Express.
TELEVISION: The Waverly Wonders (series), Marriage Is Alive and Well, All American Pie, Kate and Allie.

NARDINO, GARY: Executive. b. Garfield, NJ, Aug. 26, 1935. e. Seton Hall U. Awarded honorary degree of Doctor of Laws. Entered industry in 1959 as agent, representing Lorimar Prods. and Talent Associates, among others. Named sr. v.p. of ICM's New York TV dept; then v.p. of William Morris Agency, heading N.Y. TV dept. Pres. of Paramount TV Production Division, 1977–83. Served as exec. prod. of Star Trek III: The Search for Spock. Now pres., of Gary Nardino Prods., Inc., formed 1983, to develop and produce theatrical features and TV programming.
PICTURES: Star Trek III (exec. prod.); Fire with Fire (prod.).
TELEVISION: Exec. prod.: Brothers, At Your Service, Joanna.

NARIZZANO, SILVIO: Producer, Director. b. Montreal, Canada, Feb. 8, 1927. e. U. of Bishop's, Lennoxville, Quebec, B.A. Was active as actor-director in Canadian theatre before going to England for TV and theatrical film work.
PICTURES INCLUDE: Director: Under Ten Flags (co-dir.), Die! Die! My Darling!, Georgy Girl, Blue, The Man Who Had Power Over Women, Loot, Redneck, The Sky Is Falling, Why Shoot the Teacher?, The Class of Miss MacMichael. Producer: Negatives, Fadeout, Redneck.
TELEVISION: Come Back Little Sheba, Staying On.

NASH, N. RICHARD: Writer. r.n. Nusbaum. b. Philadelphia, PA, June 8, 1913.
BROADWAY: author: Second Best Bed, The Young and Fair, See the Jaguar, The Rainmaker, Girls of Summer, Handful of Fire, Wildcat, 110 in the Shade, The Happy Time, Echoes, Wildfire, The Torch, Magic, The Bluebird of Happiness.
PICTURES INCLUDE: Nora Prentiss, The Vicious Years, The Rainmaker, Porgy and Bess, Sainted Sisters, Dear Wife, Welcome Stranger, Dragonfly.
TV: Many TV plays for Television Playhouse, U.S. Steel, General Electric.
NOVELS: Cry Macho; East Wind, Rain; The Last Magic; Aphrodite's Cave; Radiance; Behold the Man.

NATWICK, MILDRED: Actress. b. Baltimore, Md, June 19, 1908. e. Bryn Mawr Sch., Baltimore, Bennett Sch., Millbrook. Prof. stage debut in Carry Nation, 1932; London debut in Day I Forget.
PLAYS: Wind and the Rain, Distaff Side, End of Summer, Love from a Stranger, Candida, Missouri Legend, Stars in Your Eyes, Grass Harp, Blithe Spirit, (Barter Theatre award), Waltz of the Toreadors (nominated for Tony), The Firstborn, The Good Soup, Critic's Choice, Barefoot in the Park, Our Town, Landscape, 70, Girls 70, (nominated for Tony), Bedroom Farce.
PICTURES INCLUDE: Long Voyage Home, Enchanted Cottage, Yolanda and the Thief, Late George Apley, Woman's Vengeance, Three Godfathers, Kissing Bandit, She Wore a Yellow Ribbon, Cheaper by the Dozen, Quiet Man, Against All Flags, Trouble with Harry, Court Jester, Teenage Rebel, Tammy and the Bachelor, Barefoot in the Park (nominated for Oscar), If It's Tuesday This Must Be Belgium, Trilogy, The Maltese Bippy, Daisy Miller, At Long Last Love, Kiss Me Goodbye, Les Liaisons Dangereuses.
TELEVISION: Blithe Spirit (nominated for Emmy), House Without a Xmas Tree, Thanksgiving Treasure, Money to Burn, The Snoop Sisters (Emmy award), The Easter Promise, Little Women, McMillan and Wife, Hawaii Five-O, Love Boat, You Can't Take It With You, Alice—Made in America, Deadly Deception.

NAUGHTON, DAVID: Actor, Singer. b. Hartford, CT, Feb. 13, 1951. Brother of actor James Naughton. e. U. of Pennsylvania, B.A. Numerous TV commercials, including music for Dr. Pepper. On Bdwy. in Hamlet, Da, etc.
PICTURES: Midnight Madness; An American Werewolf in London; Separate Ways; Hog Dog—The Movie; Not for Publication, The Boy in Blue, Separate Vacations. Quite By Chance.
TELEVISION: Making It; I, Desire; At East; Getting Physical; My Sister Sam; Goddess of Love.

NAUGHTON, JAMES: Actor. b. Middletown, CT, Dec. 6, 1945. Brother of actor David Naughton. e. Brown U., A.B., 1967; Yale U., M.F.A., drama, 1970.
THEATER: I Love My Wife (Bdwy debut, 1977), Long Day's Journey Into Night (Theatre World, Drama Desk and New York Critics Circle Award, 1971), Whose Life Is It, Anyway?, Who's Afraid of Virginia Woolf? (Long Wharf), The Glass Menagerie (Long Wharf).
PICTURES: The Paper Chase (debut, 1972), Second Wind, A Stranger is Watching, Cat's Eye, The Glass Menagerie, The Good Mother.
TELEVISION: Look Homeward, Angel (1972); Series: Faraday and Company (1973–74); Planet of the Apes, Making the Grade; Trauma Center; Raising Miranda. Movies: F. Scott Fitzgerald and the Last of the Belles; The Last 36 Hours of Dr. Durant; The Bunker; My Body, My Child; Parole; The Last of the Great Survivors; Between Darkness and the Dawn; Sin of Innocence.

NEAL, PATRICIA: Actress. b. Packard, KY, Jan. 20, 1926. e. Northwestern U. Doctor's asst., cashier, hostess, model, jewelry store clerk. In summer stock; Broadway debut in Another Part of the Forest, 1947, (winning the Tony, Donaldson & Drama Critic Awards), also in Children's Hour. Autobiography: As I Am (with Richard DeNeut, 1988).
TELEVISION: The Bastard, The Homecoming, All Quiet on the Western Front (Emmy Award), Tail Gunner Joe, Love Leads the Way, Eric.
PICTURES INCLUDE: John Loves Mary (debut 1948), The Fountainhead, Hasty Heart, Bright Leaf, Three Secrets, Breaking Point, Raton Pass, Operation Pacific, Day the Earth Stood Still, Weekend With Father, Diplomatic Courier, Washington Story, Something for the Birds, Face in the Crowd, Hud (Academy Award, 1963), Psych 59, In Harms Way, The Subject Was Roses, The Night Digger, Baxter!, Happy Mother's Day . . . Love, George, The Passage, Ghost Story.

NEAME, RONALD: Cinematographer, Producer, Director. b. April 23, 1911. e. U. Coll. Sch., London. p. Elwin Neame, London photog., & Ivy Close, m.p. actress. Entered m.p. ind. 1928; asst. cameraman on first full-length Brit. sound Blackmail, dir. by Alfred Hitchcock, 1929; became chief cameraman & lighting expert, 1934; in 1945 joint assoc. prod., Noel Coward Prods.
PICTURES INCLUDE: Elizabeth of England, Invitation to the Waltz, Brief Ecstasy, It's in the Air, Gaunt Stranger, Four Just Men, Major Barbara, A Yank in the R.A.F. (Brit. flying sequence), One of Our Aircraft is Missing, In Which We Serve, This Happy Breed, Blithe Spirit, Brief Encounter, Great Expectations, Oliver Twist, Passionate Friends, Take My Life, Magic Box, Golden Salamander, The Card (The Promoter), Million Pound Note (Man With a Million), Man Who Never Was, Seventh Sin, Wisdom's Way, The Horse's Mouth, Tunes of Glory, Escape from Zahrain, I Could Go on Singing, The Chalk Garden, Mister Moses, Gambit, The Prime of Miss Jean Brodie, Scrooge, The Poseidon Adventure, The Odessa

Nee-Nel

File, Meteor, Hopscotch, First Monday in October, Foreign Body, The Magic Balloon.

NEEDHAM, HAL: Director, Writer. b. Memphis, TN, March 6, 1931. e. Student public schools. Served with Paratroopers U.S. Army 1951–54. Founder Stunts Unlimited, Los Angeles, 1956; stuntman Stunts Unltd. 1956–68; dir. and stunt coordinator second unit, 1968–86; dir., writer, 1976–present. Chmn. of bd., Camera Platforms International, Inc. 1986. Owner Budweiser Rocket Car (fastest car in the world). Member Screen Actors Guild, AFTRA.
PICTURES INCLUDE: Dir. and writer: Smokey and the Bandit (dir. debut), Hooper, The Villain, Smokey and the Bandit II, The Cannonball Run, Megaforce, Stroker Ace, Cannonball Run II, Rad, Body Slam.
TELEVISION: Hal Needham's Wild World of Stunts (syndicated series he wrote, directed and starred in): Directed Death Car on the Freeway (movie); Stunts Unlimited (pilot).

NEESON, LIAM: Actor. b. Ballymena, Northern Ireland. Was driving a fork lift truck for a brewery when he joined the Lyric Player's Theatre in Belfast. Made prof. debut in The Risen (1976) and stayed with rep. co. 2 years. Moved to Dublin as freelance actor before joining the Abbey Theatre. Stage includes The Informer (Dublin Theatre Fest.), Translations (National Theatre, London). Film debut: Excalibur (1981).
PICTURES: Krull, The Bounty, Lamb, The Innocent, Duet For One, The Mission, Prayer for the Dying, Suspect, Satisfaction, The Dead Pool, The Good Mother, Next of Kin.
TELEVISION: Merlin and the Sword, Across the Water (BBC), Ellis Island, A Woman of Substance, Sweet As You Are.

NEFF, HILDEGARDE: Actress, author. r.n. Hildegard Knef. b. Ulm, Germany, Dec. 28, 1925. e. Art Acad., Berlin. Film cartoonist for UFA, Berlin; on Berlin stage after war; appeared in German films: Murderers Are Among Us, Between Yesterday and Tomorrow, Film Without Title, The Sinner. On B'way in: Silk Stockings. U.S. m.p. debut in Decision Before Dawn. Author of best-selling autobiography, The Gift Horse, 1971.
PICTURES INCLUDE: Diplomatic Courier, Night Without Sleep, Snows of Kilimanjaro, Holiday for Henrietta, Man Between, Svengali, The Girl From Hamburg, Subway in the Sky, And So to Bed, Mozambique, The Lost Continent.

NEGULESCO, JEAN: Director. b. Craiova, Rumania , Feb. 29, 1900. e. Liceul Carol U., Rumania. Stage dir., artist, painter, Came to U.S. in 1927. Memoirs: Things I Did and Things I Think I Did (1983).
PICTURES INCLUDE: The Mask of Dimitrios, The Conspirators, Nobody Lives Forever, Three Strangers, Humoresque, Deep Valley, Johnny Belinda, Road House, Forbidden Street, Three Came Home, Under My Skin, Mudlark, Take Care of My Little Girl, The Full House, Phone Call From a Stranger, Lydia Bailey, Lure of the Wilderness, Titanic, Scandal at Scourie, How to Marry a Millionaire, The Rains of Ranchipur, Woman's World, Three Coins in the Fountain, Daddy Long Legs, Boy on a Dolphin, The Gift of Love, A Certain Smile, Count Your Blessings, The Best of Everything, Jessica, The Pleasure Seekers, Hello, Goodbye.

NEILL, SAM: Actor. b. New Zealand, 1948. e. U. of Canterbury. In repertory before joining N.Z. National Film Unit, acting and directing documentaries and shorts.
PICTURES: Landfall, Ashes, Sleeping Dogs, The Journalist, My Brilliant Career, Just Out of Reach, Attack Force Z, The Final Conflict, Possession, From a Far Country—Pope John Paul II, Enigma, The Country Girls, The Blood of Others, Robbery Under Arms, Plenty, A Cry in the Dark, Dead Calm.
TELEVISION: The Sullivans, Young Ramsay, Lucinda Brayford, Ivanhoe, Strong Medicine, Reilly Ace of Spies, Kane and Abel, Leap of Faith.

NELLIGAN, KATE: Actress. b. London, England, March 16, 1951. On stage in Barefoot in the Park, A Streetcar Named Desire, Playboy of the Western World, Private Lives, Plenty, Serious Money, Spoils of War.
PICTURES: The Romantic Englishwoman, Dracula, Mr. Patman, Eye of the Needle, Without a Trace, The Mystery of Henry Moore, Eleni.
TELEVISION: The Onedin Line, The Lady of the Camelias, Therese Raquin, Count of Monte Cristo, Victims, Kojak: The Price of Justice.

NELSON, BARRY: Actor. r.n. Robert Neilson. b. Oakland, CA, 1923. e. U. of California. London stage: No Time for Sergeants, 1957.
PICTURES INCLUDE: A Guy Named Joe, Winged Victory, Man with My Face, First Traveling Saleslady, Mary, Mary, The Borgia Stick, Airport, Pete 'n Tillie, The Shining.
BROADWAY: Light Up the Sky, Rat Race, Moon Is Blue, Mary, Mary, Cactus Flower, Everything in the Garden, Seascape, The Norman Conquests, The Act, 42nd Street.
TELEVISION: series: The Hunter, My Favorite Husband,

Washington: Behind Closed Doors, Climb an Angry Mountain, Seven In Darkness, Murder She Wrote.

NELSON, CRAIG T.: Actor. b. Spokane, WA, April 4, 1946. Began career as writer/performer on Lohman and Barkley Show in Los Angeles. Teamed with Barry Levinson as a comedy writer. Wrote for Tim Conway Show, Alan King TV special; guest appearances on talk shows and Mary Tyler Moore Show. Produced series of 52 half-hour films on American artists, American Still. Returned to L.A. in 1978 and acting career. Film debut in And Justice for All, 1979.
PICTURES: The Formula, Where the Buffalo Roam, Private Benjamin, Poltergeist, The Osterman Weekend, Silkwood, All the Right Moves, The Killing Fields, Poltergeist II, Red Riding Hood, Rachel River, Action Jackson, Me and Him, Troup Beverly Hills.
TELEVISION: Wonder Woman, Charlie's Angels, How the West Was Won, Diary of a Teenage Hitchhiker, Alex: The Life of a Child, The Ted Kennedy Jr. Story, Call to Glory, Coach (series), Murderers Among Us: The Simon Wiesenthal Story.

NELSON, DAVID: Actor. b. New York, NY, Oct. 24, 1936. e. Hollywood H.S., U. of Southern California. Son of Ozzie Nelson, Harriet Hilliard, brother of late Rick Nelson.
PICTURES INCLUDE: Here Comes the Nelsons, Peyton Place, The Remarkable Mr. Pennypacker, Day of the Outlaw, The Big Circus, "30," The Big Show, No Drums, No Bugles, The Wheel, The Sinners.
TELEVISION: Adventures of Ozzie and Harriet; dir.: Easy To Be Free (special), OK Crackerby series.

NELSON, GENE: Dancer, actor, director, choreographer. r.n. Gene Berg. b. Seattle, WA, March 24, 1920. e. Santa Monica, CA H.S. Began dancing and ice skating in school; joined Sonja Henie Hollywood Ice Revue, featured in It Happens on Ice, Center Theatre, NY; played in This Is the Army, W.W.II; after discharge. To Hollywood for I Wonder Who's Kissing Her Now; joined Hollywood group prod. stage musical, Lend an Ear; to Warner for Daughter of Rosie O'Grady (1950).
PICTURES INCLUDE: Apartment For Peggy, Gentlemen's Agreement, Tea for Two, Starlift, West Point Story, Lullaby of Broadway, Painting the Clouds With Sunshine, She's Working Her Way Through College, She's Back on Broadway, Three Sailors and a Girl, Crime Wave, So This Is Paris, Oklahoma, The Way Out, Atomic Man, 20,000 Eyes, The Purple Hills, Thunder Island. Director: The Hand of Death, Hootenany Hoot, The Cool Ones (also s.p.), Your Cheatin' Heart, Kissin' Cousins, Wake Me When the War Is Over, The Letters, Harum Scarum.
TELEVISION: Director: Mod Squad, I Dream of Jeannie, FBI, 12 O'Clock High, Hawaii Five-O, Farmer's Daughter, Donna Reed Show, Burke's Law, Felony Squad, Laredo, The Rifleman, The Wackiest Ship, Iron Horse, FBI, The Rookies, Quincy, Operation Petticoat. Movies: Wake Me When It's Over, The Letters.
BROADWAY: Follies, 1971; Music, Music, 1974, Good News.

NELSON, HARRIET: Singer, actress. r.n. Harriet Hilliard. b. Des Moines, IA, July 18, 1914, e. H.S., Kansas City. m. Ozzie Nelson. Appeared in dramatic & musical roles in shows; singer with Ozzie Nelson band; on radio shows: Believe It or Not, Seeing Stars, Red Skelton, Adventures of Ozzie & Harriet. Appeared in film: Here Come the Nelsons.
TELEVISION: Adventures of Ozzie and Harriet, (1952–66).
STAGE: Marriage-Go-Round; rec.: Ozzie and Harriet.
PLAYS: Impossible Years, State Fair.

NELSON, JUDD: Actor. b. Portland, ME, 1959. e. Haverford/Bryn Mawr Coll. Studied acting at Stella Adler Conservatory. Theatrical m.p. debut in Fandango, 1984.
PICTURES: Fandango, Making the Grade, The Breakfast Club, St. Elmo's Fire, Blue City, From the Hip, The Dark Backward.
TELEVISION: Moonlighting, Billionaire Boys Club.

NELSON, LORI: Actress. r.n. Dixie Kay Nelson; b. Santa Fe, NM, Aug. 15, 1933. e. H.S., L.A. Child actress; photographer's model; film debut in Ma and Pa Kettle at the Fair (1952).
PICTURES INCLUDE: Bend of the River, Francis Goes to West Point, All I Desire, All-American, Walking My Baby Back Home, Tumbleweed, Underwater, Destry, Revenge of the Creature, I Died a Thousand Times, Sincerely Yours, Mohawk, Day the World Ended, Pardners, Hot Rod Girl, Ma and Pa Kettle at Waikiki, Gambling Man, Untamed Youth.
TELEVISION: How to Marry a Millionaire (series), Wagon Train, Laramie, Bachelor Father, The Texan, Wanted Dead or Alive, Sam Spade, G.E. Theatre, Riverboat, Sugarfoot, The Young and the Restless, etc.

NELSON, WILLIE: Composer, Singer, Actor. b. Abbott, TX, April 30, 1933. Worked as salesman, announcer, host of country music shows on local Texas stations; bass player with Ray Price's band. Started writing songs in the 60s; performing in the 70s. Film debut in Electric Horseman, 1979.
PICTURES: Honeysuckle Rose, Thief, Barbarosa, Song-

224

writer, Red-Headed Stranger (also prod.), Baja Oklahoma, Walking After Midnight.
TELEVISION: Movies: The Last Days of Frank and Jesse James, Stagecoach, Coming Out of the Ice, Once Upon a Texas Train, Willie Nelson, Texas Style (star, prod.), Where the Hell's the Gold!!?

NETTER, DOUGLAS: Executive, Producer. b. Seattle, WA, May 23, 1921. e. Holy Cross, BS. After WW2 joined PRC (later merged with Eagle Lion) in sales dept.; 1947–55 gen. sales mgr. Altec; 1955–57, general manager Todd A.O.; 1958–60, Sam Goldwyn Productions; 1961–67, Formed own company representing producers; 1968–69, Jalem Productions; 1969–75, exec. vice president MGM; 1976, prod., Mr. Ricco. 1977, American co-prod., The Wild Geese.
TELEVISION: 1978, prod., Louis L'Amour's The Sacketts, (mini-series). 1979, exec. prod., The Buffalo Soldiers (pilot); prod., Wild Times, (mini-series); exec. prod. Roughnecks, (mini-series); exec. prod. Cherokee Trail (Walt Disney Productions and CBS). 1983–85, exec. prod., Five Mile Creek (Australian based TV series for Disney Channel); 1986, prod., Captain Power (pilot); exec. prod., Captain Power (syndicated series); exec. prod., Stealth F22 (film for Lockheed Aeronautical Systems).

NETTLETON, LOIS: Actress. b. Oak Park, IL. e. Studied at Goodman Theatre, Chicago and Actors Studio. Replaced Kim Hunter in Darkness at Noon on Broadway. Emmy Award: Performer Best Daytime Drama Spec., The American Woman: Portraits in Courage (1977). Also Emmy: Religious Program, Insight (1983).
PLAYS INCLUDE: Cat on a Hot Tin Roof, Silent Night, Lonely Night, God and Kate Murphy, The Wayward Stork, The Rainmaker, A Streetcar Named Desire.
PICTURES INCLUDE: Period of Adjustment, Come Fly with Me, Mail Order Bride, Valley of Mystery, Bamboo Saucer, The Good Guys and the Bad Guys, Dirty Dingus Magee, The Sidelong Glances of a Pigeon Kicker, The Honkers, Echoes of a Summer, Butterfly, Deadly Blessing, The Best Little Whorehouse in Texas.
TELEVISION: Brass, No Hiding Place, Medical Center, Barnaby Jones, Alfred Hitchcock, Series: Accidental Family (1967–68), All That Glitters. Movies: The Woman in White, The Light That Failed, Centennial, Any Second Now, Washington: Behind Closed Doors, Women in Chains, You Can't Take It With You (series).

NEWBERY, CHARLES BRUCE: Executive. b. Melbourne, Australia. e. All Saints Grammar Sch., Melbourne; Melbourne U. Entered m.p. ind. with Hoyt's Theatres, Ltd., Melbourne, 1929; publ. mgr., Fox Studios, Eng., 1934; controller, Fox Newsreel Theatres, 1935; managing dir., Fox Films, India, 1937; Supvr., India, China, Malaya, Fox Films, 1940; Film advisor, Government of India, 1941; estab. film studios & Newsreel for Government of India. suprv. Far East & Australia Republic, 1945; supvr. Middle, Near & Far East. Republic, 1947; supvr. Eng. & Europe, Republic, 1948; estab. Republic Productions Great Britain, 1952; v.p. bd. mem. dir. of sales, Republic, U.S.A., 1953; pres., Charles Newbery Assoc., Newbery-Warden Associates, London, 1960; mgr. dir., Santor Film Prods., Americon Prods, Inc., 1964; sen. v.p., bd. mem., administration, In-Flight Motion Pictures Inc., v.p., Intransit Motion Pictures, Inc., 1965. Senior v.p. Sales and Marketing 1967, President and Chief Operating Office, May 1973; vice chm. bd., Inflight, June, 1979; Dir. of Mktg., Life Services Co., of America June, 1979 chm. bd., Inflight and sls.—Europe, East and Africa, 1980. Bd. member/consultant to Inflight, 1985.
PICTURES INCLUDE: Deadlier Than the Male, Catch Me if You Can, Kiss Her Goodbye.

NEWBROOK, PETER: Producer, Director of photography. Entered m.p. ind. Warner Bros. Studios, Teddington. Chmn. Titan Int'l. Productions, Ltd. Esquire Records Ltd. & Esquire Music Co. Pres., British Society of Cinematographers.
PICTURES INCLUDE: After working on such pictures as The Sound Barrier, The Captain's Paradise, Hobson's Choice, Summer Madness, The Deep Blue Sea, Anastasia, The Bridge on the River Kwai; became dir. photog.: Lawrence of Arabia (2nd unit), 1961; In The Cool of the Day, That Kind of Girl, 1962; The Yellow Teddybears, Saturday Night Out, The Black Torment, Prod. and photog; Gonks Go Beat, prod. and photog; The Sandwich Man, Press For Time, Corruption, The Smashing Bird I Used to Know, Bloodsuckers, She'll Follow You Anywhere, Crucible of Terror, The Asphyx, The Wonderful World of Greece, Bosom Friends, Where's Your Sense of Humor?, Last of the Midnight Gardeners.
TELEVISION: Tales of the Unexpected, Coronation Street, Emerdale Farm.

NEWCOM, JAMES E.: Associate producer. b. Indianapolis, IN, Aug. 29, 1907. e. U. of California. Reader, MGM, 1926, then in stocks and bonds with E. F. Hutton; then actor and film editing dept., MGM, 1930; film ed. 1933; asst. prod., 1952. Now retired.

PICTURES INCLUDE: Gone With the Wind, Rebecca, Since You Went Away, Annie Get Your Gun, Trial, Somebody Up There Likes Me, Wings of Eagles, Until They Sail, Farewell to Arms, The Inn of the Sixth Happiness; Revue Television; Paramount Studios. Nine Hours to Rama, The Impossible Years, editor: Tora Tora Tora.

NEWELL, MIKE: Director. b. 1942.
PICTURES: The Awakening, Bad Blood, Dance With a Stranger, Sour Sweet.
TELEVISION: The Man in the Iron Mask, The Gift of Friendship, Blood Feud.

NEWGARD, ROBERT M.: Executive. b. Des Moines, IA, Jan. 14, 1925. e. U. of Notre Dame, 1948. Mirisch Bros., Theatres Candy Co., built and operated theas. in midwest, 1948–50; operated record dist. business 1949–53, Columbia and MGM records; prod. shows at KTTV Hollywood, 1952; Interstate Television Subsidiary Allied Artists, dist. and prod'n of TV films, 1953–56; midwestern and western sales mgr., Screen Gems, 1956–66; v.p. world syndication, Paramount Television, 1967–73; now v.p., intl. mkt., Film Services Corp.

NEWHART, BOB: Actor, Comedian. b. Chicago, IL, Sept. 5, 1929. e. Loyola U. In Army 2 yrs., then law school; left to become copywriter and accountant. Acted with theatrical stock co. in Oak Park; hired for TV man-in-street show in Chicago. Recorded comedy album for Warner Bros. Record Co., The Button Down Mind of Bob Newhart, which was big hit. Followed by two more successful albums. Did series of nightclub engagements and then acquired own TV variety series in 1961. Frequently appears in Las Vegas and headlines college concerts. Has guested on most major TV variety and comedy series.
PICTURES INCLUDE: Cool Millions, Catch 22, Cold Turkey, First Family.
TELEVISION: The Bob Newhart Show (series), Thursday's Game (movie), Newhart (series).

NEWLAND, JOHN: Director, Actor. b. Cincinnati, OH, Nov. 23, 1917. Began as a singer-dancer in vaudeville and on Bdwy; many TV appearances, especially as host of One Step Beyond. Actor, dir., Robert Montgomery Show, My Lover, My Son. Turned to full-time dir. and prod. in the 1960's.
PICTURES: Bulldog Drummond, That Night, The Violators, The Spy With My Face, Hush-a-Bye Murder.
TELEVISION: Producer: A Sensitive, Passionate Man; Overboard; Angel City; The Five of Me; Timestalker; The Next Step Beyond, The Suicide's Wife, Arch of Triumph (prod.).

NEWLEY, ANTHONY: Actor, Writer, Composer, Singer. b. Hackney, Eng., Sept. 24, 1931.
PICTURES INCLUDE: Cockleshell Heroes, Battle of the River Plate, Port Afrique, Fire Down Below, Good Companions, X the Unknown, High Flight, No Time to Die, The Man Inside, The Bandit, The Lady Is a Square, Idle on Parade, Killers of Kilimanjaro, Let's Get Married, Jazz Boat, In the Nick, The Small World of Sammy Lee, Dr. Dolittle; Can Hieronymus Merkin Ever Forget Mercy Humppee and Find True Happiness?, Sweet November, Quilp (star, music) Willie Wonka and the Chocolate Factory (score); Summer Tree (dir.).
TELEVISION: Sammy, Sunday Night Palladium, The Strange World of Gurney Slade (series), Saturday Spectaculars, The Johnny Darling Show, Hollywood Squares, Merv Griffin Show, The Tonight Show, Anthony Newley Special (London), Blade in Hong Kong (movie), Limited Partners.
PLAYS: West End stage; Stop The World—I Want to Get Off. N.Y. stage: Roar of the Greasepaint (wrote, composed with Leslie Bricusse), Good Old Bad Old Days, Chaplin.

NEWMAN, ALFRED S.: Executive. b. Brooklyn, NY, Nov. 16, 1940. e. New York U. Public relations work for Equitable Life Insurance, Trans World Airlines prior to joining Columbia Pictures in 1968 as writer in publicity dept.; named New York publicity mgr., 1970; national publicity mgr., 1972; joined MGM as East adv't-pub. dir., 1972; named director of adv't, pub. and promotion, 1974; named v.p., worldwide adv., pub., promo., 1976 v.p. pub./promo., MGM/UA, 1981. With 20th Century-Fox as v.p. adv./pub./promo. for TV & corporate, 1984–85; joined Rogers & Cowan as sr. v.p. & head of corporate entertainment, 1985; named exec. v.p., 1987; Oct. 1988 named pres. and CEO. Sterling Entertainment Co. and exec. v.p. worldwide marketing of parent co. MCEG.

NEWMAN, DAVID: Writer. b. New York, NY, Feb. 4, 1937. e. U. of Michigan, M.S., 1959. Was writer-editor at Esquire Magazine where he met Robert Benton, an art director, and formed writing partnership. All early credits co-written with Benton; later ones with Leslie Newman and others.
PICTURES INCLUDE: Bonnie and Clyde, There Was a Crooked Man, Floreana, What's Up, Doc?, Money's Tight, Bad Company, The Crazy American Girl, Superman (co-s.p.), Superman II (co-s.p.), Jinxed (co-s.p.), Superman III (co-s.p.), Sheena (co-s.p.), Still of the Night, Santa Claus—The Movie.

New-Nic

STAGE: It's a Bird ... It's a Plane ... It's Superman (libretto), Oh! Calcutta (one sketch).

NEWMAN, EDWIN: News Correspondent. b. New York, NY, 1919. Joined NBC News in 1952, based in N.Y. since 1961. Reports news on NBC-TV and often assigned to anchor instant specials. Has been substitute host on Today, appeared on Meet the Press and has reported NBC News documentaries. Host of interview series, Speaking Freely, on WNBC-TV, N.Y.; Television (PBS series, host).

NEWMAN, JOSEPH M.: Producer, Director, Writer. b. Logan, UT, Aug. 7, 1909. Started as office boy MGM, 1925; jobs in production dept. to 1931; asst. to George Hill, Ernst Lubitsch, etc., 1931–37; asstd. in organization of MGM British studios 1937; dir. short subjects 1938; dir. Crime Does Not Pay series 1938–42; Major in U.S. Army Signal Corps 1942–46; dir. 32 Army Pictorial Service Pictures. Member: AMPAS, SDG Masons.
PICTURES INCLUDE: Northwest Rangers, Abandoned, Jungle Patrol, Great Dan Pitch, 711 Ocean Drive, Lucky Nick Cain, Guy Who Came Back, Love Nest, Red Skies of Montana, Outcasts of Poker Flat, Pony Soldier, Dangerous Crossing, Human Jungle, Kiss of Fire, This Island Earth, Flight to Hong Kong, Fort Massacre, Big Circus, Tarzan The Ape Man, King of the Roaring Twenties, Twenty Plus Two, The George Raft Story, Thunder of Drums.

NEWMAN, LIONEL: Composer, Conductor. b. Los Angeles, CA, 1916. Began career at 16 as lead pianist with Earl Caroll's Vanities; wrote first song, Dust in Your Eyes, featured in Vanities. Joined brother, the late Alfred Newman, at 20th Century-Fox where Alfred was head of music dept.; succeeded him in 1970 when Alfred died. 1977, named v.p. of Fox; 1982, snr. v.p., 20th Century-Fox Feature Film and Television Divisions. Has composed or conducted for 250 films, earning 11 Academy Award nominations. Won Oscar, 1969, for Hello, Dolly. Retired from Fox, 1988. Named senior v.p. music, MGM/UA Communications Co., 1988.

NEWMAN, MARTIN H.: Executive. b. Brooklyn, NY, Nov. 16, 1913; e. New York U., 1934. Certified Public Accountant (N.Y.); Century Theatres, 1936–1974, exec. v.p. 1966–1974; National Association of Theatre Owners, 1975–1977; exec. dir., Will Rogers Memorial Fund, 1977–present.

NEWMAN, NANETTE: Actress, Writer. b. Northampton, Eng., 1934. m. to Bryan Forbes. Ent. films in 1946 and TV in 1951. Publications include God Bless Love, That Dog, Reflections, The Root Children, Amy Rainbow, Pigalev, Archie, Christmas Cookbook, Summer Cookbook, Small Beginnings.
TELEVISION: The Glorious Days, The Wedding Veil, Broken Honeymoon, At Home, Trial by Candlelight, Diary of Samuel Pepys, Faces in the Dark, Balzac (BBC), Fun Food Factory, TV series, Stay with Me Till Morning, Let There Be Love (series), West Country Tales, Jessie, Late Expectations.
FILMS INCLUDE: The Personal Affair, The League of Gentlemen, The Rebel, Twice Around the Daffodils, The L-Shaped Room, Wrong Arm of the Law, Of Human Bondage, Seance on a Wet Afternoon, The Wrong Box, The Whisperers, Deadfall, The Madwoman of Chaillot, The Raging Moon, (U.S. title: Long Ago Tomorrow), The Stepford Wives, It's A 2'2" Above the Ground World (The Love Ban), Man at the Top, International Velvet.

NEWMAN, PAUL: Actor, Director. b. Cleveland, OH, Jan. 26, 1925. m. actress Joanne Woodward. e. Kenyon Coll., Yale Sch. of Drama, The Actors Studio. Summer stock; on Broadway in Picnic, The Desperate Hours, Sweet Bird of Youth, Baby Want a Kiss. Formed First Artists Prod. Co. Ltd. 1969 with Sidney Poitier, Steve McQueen and Barbra Streisand.
TELEVISION: Philco, U.S. Steel, Playhouse 90. Dir.: The Shadow Box.
PICTURES INCLUDE: The Silver Chalice, The Rack, Somebody Up There Likes Me, Until They Sail, The Helen Morgan Story, The Long, Hot Summer, Cat on a Hot Tin Roof, The Left-Handed Gun, Rally Around the Flag Boys, The Young Philadelphians, Exodus, The Hustler, Paris Blues, Sweet Bird of Youth, Adventures of a Young Man, Hud, A New Kind of Love, The Prize, The Outrage, What a Way to Go, Lady L., Torn Curtain, Harper, Hombre, Cool Hand Luke, The Secret War of Harry Frigg, Winning, Butch Cassidy and the Sundance Kid. Dir. Rachel, Rachel. Sometimes A Great Notion (dir., actor), Pocket Money, Life & Times of Judge Roy Bean, The Effect of Gamma Rays (dir.), The Mackintosh Man, The Sting, The Towering Inferno, The Drowning Pool, Buffalo Bill and the Indians, Slap Shot, Quintet, When Time Ran Out, Fort Apache, The Bronx, Absence of Malice, The Verdict, Harry and Son (co-s.p., actor, dir., co-prod.), The Color of Money (Acad. Award), The Glass Menagerie (dir. only), Fat Man & Little Boy.

NEWMAN, SYDNEY.: O. C. (F.R.S.A.), Chief Creative Consultant for Canadian Film Development Corp. b. Toronto, Canada. Studied painting, drawing, commercial art at Central Techn. Sch. To Hollywood in 1938. Joined National Film Board of

Canada under John Grierson. Prod. over 300 shorts. Later became exec. prod. all Canadian government cinema films, 1947–52; Canadian Broadcasting Corp., 1952, as dir. outside broadcasts, features and documentaries. Later became drama sup. and prod. Canadian Television Theatre. Joined ABC-TV in England, 1958. as sup. of drama and producer of Armchair Theatre: Head of Drama Group, TV, BBC, 1963. Commissioned and prod. first TV plays by Arthur Hailey, Harold Pinter, Alun Owen, Angus Wilson, Peter Lake. Fellow Society of Film & TV Arts, 1968; Prod. Associated British Pictures. SFTA award 1968; Zeta award, Writers Guild, Gt. Btn., 1970. 1970: Special advisor, ch. dir., Broadcast Programmes branch, Canadian Radio & TV Commission, Ottawa. Aug., 1970: Appt. Canadian Govt. Film Commissioner and chm., National Film Board of Canada; Trustee, National Arts Centre, Ottawa; board member, Canadian Broadcasting Corporation, Canadian Film Development Corp., Canadian Picture Pioneers Special Award. Special Advisor on Film to the Secretary of State for Canada, 1975–77; pres., Sydney Newman Enterprises. 1981: Made Officer of the Order of Canada.

NEWMAN, WALTER BROWN: Writer. b. 1920.
PICTURES INCLUDE: Ace in the Hole (co-s.p.), Underwater, The Man with the Golden Arm (co-s.p.), The True Story of Jesse James, Crime and Punishment, USA, The Interns (co-s.p.), Cat Ballou (co-s.p.), Bloodbrothers, The Champ.

NEWTON-JOHN, OLIVIA: Actress, Singer. b. Sept. 26, 1948, Cambridge, Eng. m. actor Matt Lattanzi. Brought up in Melbourne, Australia, where won first talent contest at 15, with prize trip to England. Stayed there 2 yrs. performing as part of duo with Australian girl singer, Pat Carroll (Farrar), in cabarets and on TV. Started recording; several hit records. Became a regular guest on TV series, It's Cliff Richard. Gained world-wide prominence as singer, winning several Grammys and other music awards. 1983 opened Koala Blue, U.S. Clothing Stores featuring Australian style clothes and goods.
PICTURES: Grease, Xanadu, Two of a Kind.
TELEVISION: Olivia Newton-John—Let's Get Physical, Standing Room Only—Olivia Newton-John, Olivia Newton-John in Australia.

NEY, RICHARD: Actor, Writer, Producer, Financier. b. New York, NY, 1917. e. Columbia U., B.A. Acted in RCA TV demonstration, New York World's Fair; on stage in Life with Father. On screen 1942 in Mrs. Miniver. In armed services, W.W.II. Many TV shows. Financial advisor consultant, Richard Ney and Associates; financial advisor, lecturer; author, The Wall Street Jungle.
PICTURES INCLUDE: War Against Mrs. Hadley, Late George Apley, Ivy, Joan of Arc, The Fan, Secret of St. Ives, Lovable Cheat, Babes in Bagdad, Miss Italia, Sergeant and The Spy, The Premature Burial.

NIBLEY, SLOAN: Writer. b. Oregon; e. U. of Utah, U. of California at L.A. m. Linda Stirling, actress. Three yrs. U.S. Navy; employed as writer at major studios; contributor to mags.; wrote many western pictures incl.: Carson City, Springfield Rifle; prod., and writer many TV shows and live TV for Ralph Edwards.

NICHOLS, MIKE: Actor, Director. b. Berlin, Germany, Nov. 6, 1931. m. news correspondent Diane Sawyer. e. U. of Chicago. Compass Players, teamed with Elaine May; night clubs.
STAGE: Barefoot in the Park (Tony Award), The Knack, Luv (Tony Award), The Odd Couple, The Apple Tree, The Little Foxes, Plaza Suite (Tony Award), Uncle Vanya, The Prisoner of 2nd Avenue (Tony Award), Streamers, Comedians, The Gin Game, Drinks Before Dinner. Produced Annie, 1976. 1984: Directed The Real Thing (Tony award), Hurlyburly, Social Security.
PICTURES INCLUDE: Who's Afraid of Virginia Woolf, The Graduate (Acad. Award), Catch 22, Carnal Knowledge, The Day of the Dolphin, The Fortune, Gilda Live, Silkwood (also co-prod.), Heartburn, Biloxi Blues, Working Girl.
TELEVISION: Broadway, An Evening with Mike Nichols and Elaine May. Exec. prod.: Family, The Thorns.

NICHOLSON, JACK: Producer, Director, Actor, Writer. b. Neptune, NJ, April 22, 1936. Began career in cartoon department of MGM. Made acting debut in Hollywood stage production of Tea and Sympathy.
PICTURES INCLUDE: (Acting credits) The Shooting, Psych Out, Hell's Angels on Wheels, Little Shop of Horrors, The Raven, Ride the Whirlwind, Flight to Fury, Ensign Pulver, Too Young To Live, Studs Lonigan, Cry Baby Killer, Easy Rider, Five Easy Pieces, Carnal Knowledge, A Safe Place, (Writing credits) The Trip, Head, Flight to Fury, Ride the Whirlwind, Drive, He Said. (Producing credits) Ride the Whirlwind, The Shooting, Head, Drive, He Said. Directing debut with Drive, He Said, 1971. Acting: The Last Detail, 1973, Chinatown, Tommy, The Passenger, The Fortune, One Flew Over the Cuckoo's Nest (Acad. Award), The Missouri

Breaks, The Last Tycoon, Goin' South (also dir.), The Shining, The Postman Always Rings Twice, The Border, Reds, Terms of Endearment (Acad. Award, supp. actor), Prizzi's Honor, Heartburn, The Witches of Eastwick, Broadcast News, Ironweed, Batman.

NICKELL, PAUL: Director. e. Morehead, KY, State Teachers Coll., U. of North Carolina. English instructor, North Carolina State Coll.; then cameraman, asst. dir., dir. WPTZ, Philadelphia; dir. CBS-TV 1948.
TELEVISION: Studio One, Best of Broadway, Climax, Playhouse 90.

NICKSAY, DAVID: Executive. e. Mass., Hampshire Coll. Entered industry thru Directors Guild of America's training program, apprenticing on Rich Man Poor Man and rising to second asst. dir. on Oh, God. Producer of many TV projects and theatrical films with Edgar Scherick prod. co. 1986, joined Paramount Pictures as v.p., prod., for M.P. Group. Assoc. prod., prod. mgr.: I'm Dancing as Fast as I Can. Became senior v.p., prod. Paramount, M.P. Group, 1987.
PICTURES: Mrs. Soffel (prod.), Lucas (prod.).
TELEVISION: Call to Glory (pilot), Little Gloria Happy at Last, etc.

NICOL, ALEX: Actor, Director. b. Ossining, NY, Jan. 20, 1919; e. Fagin Sch. of Dramatic Arts, Actor's Studio. U.S. Cavalry.
THEATRE: Forward the Heart, Sundown Beach, Hamlet, Richard II, South Pacific, Mr. Roberts, Cat on a Hot Tin Roof.
PICTURES INCLUDE: Sleeping City, Target Unknown, Air Cadet, Raging Tide, Meet Danny Wilson, Red Ball Express, Because of You, Tomahawk, Redhead From Wyoming, Lone Hand, Law and Order, Champ for a Day, Black Glove, Heat Wave, About Mrs. Leslie, Dawn at Socorro, Strategic Air Command, Man from Laramie, Great Day in the Morning, Sincerely Yours, Five Branded Women, Via Margutta, Under 10 Flags, Gunfighters at Casa Grande, Sleeping Skull (dir.), Then There Were Three (dir.), The Brutal Land, Bloody Mama, Homer, The Gilded Cage, Point of Terror (dir.), Hells Black Night, Screaming Skull (dir.).

NIELSEN, LESLIE: Actor. b. Regina, Sask., Canada, Feb. 11, 1926. e. Victoria H.S., Edmonton. Disc jockey, announcer for Canadian radio station; studied at Neighborhood Playhouse; N.Y. radio actor summer stock.
TELEVISION APPEARANCES: Studio One, Kraft, Philco Playhouse, Robert Montgomery Presents, Pulitzer Prize Playhouse, Suspense, Danger, Justice, Man Behind the Badge, Death of a Salesman, The New Breed, Swamp Fox, Peyton Place, Ben Casey, Wild Wild West, The Virginian, The Loner, Blade in Hong Kong, Police Squad! (series), Fatal Confession: A Father Dowling Mystery.
PICTURES INCLUDE: Vagabond King, Forbidden Planet, Ransom!, Opposite Sex, Hot Summer Night, Tammy and the Bachelor, Night Train To Paris, Harlow, Dark Intruder, Beau Geste, Gunfight in Abilene, The Reluctant Astronaut, Counterpoint, Rosie, Dayton's Devils, How to Commit Marriage, Change of Mind, The Resurrection of Zachary Wheeler, The Poseidon Adventure, Viva, Knievel!, City on Fire, Airplane!, Wrong Is Right, Creepshow, The Patriot, Police Squad—The Movie, Wall Street, Nightstick, Nuts, The Naked Gun.

NILES, FRED A.: Executive. b. Milwaukee, WI, Sept. 12, 1918. e. U. of Wisconsin. Was radio news commentator and capt. of office of educ. and information of U.S. Army, W.W.II. Now heads own film studio, Fred A. Niles Communications Centers, Inc., Chicago.

NIMOY, LEONARD: Actor, director. b. Boston, MA, Mar. 26, 1931. Along with active career in films, TV and stage, has been writer and photographer. Author of three books on photography and poetry, as well as autobiography, I Am Not Spock. Has also been speaker on college lecture circuit.
PICTURES: Queen for a Day, Rhubarb, The Balcony, Catlow, Invasion of the Body Snatchers, Star Trek—The Movie, Star Trek II; The Wrath of Khan, Star Trek III: The Search for Spock (also dir.), Star Trek IV: The Voyage Home (also. dir.), Three Men and a Baby (dir. only), The Good Mother (dir. only), Star Trek V.
TELEVISION: Series: Star Trek, Mission: Impossible, In Search Of . . . (host); . Movie: The Sun Also Rises, Marco Polo, A Woman Called Golda, Baffled.
STAGE: Equus, Sherlock Holmes, Vincent (one-man show).

NIVEN, DAVID, JR.: Executive. b. London, England, Dec. 15, 1942. Joined William Morris Agency in Beverly Hills in 1963. Transferred same yr. to New York; in next five yrs. worked for agency's European offices in Rome, Madrid and London. In 1968 joined Columbia Pictures' U.K. office as a prod. exec.; 1972, named mng. dir. of Paramount Pictures in U.K. In 1976 became indep. prod., forming partnership with Jack Wiener.
PICTURES INCLUDE: The Eagle Has Landed, Escape to Athena, Monsignor, That's Dancing!

TELEVISION: The Night They Saved Christmas (exec. prod., s.p.).

NIX, WILLIAM PATTERSON: Executive. b. Philadelphia, PA, April 10, 1948. e. Georgetown U., A.B., 1970; Antioch Graduate Sch., M.A., 1971; Hofstra U. Sch. of Law, J.D., 1976; New York U. Sch. of Law, LL.M., 1979. Senior v.p. of both the Motion Picture Association of America and Motion Picture Export Assoc. of America. Chairman of MPAA committee on copyright and literary property matters, and worldwide director of film industry's anti-piracy programs. Member, Acad. of M.P. Arts & Sciences.

NIXON, AGNES: Writer, Producer. b. Nashville, TN, Dec. 10, 1927. e. Northwestern School of Speech, Catholic U. Landed 1st job writing radio serial dialogue three days after graduating from college. Became a freelance writer for TV dramatic series Studio One, Philco Playhouse, Robert Montgomery Presents, Somerset Maugham Theatre, Armstrong Circle Theatre, Hallmark Hall of Fame, My True Story, Cameo Theatre. Then wrote for daytime series Search For Tomorrow, As The World Turns, Guiding Light and Another World before creating her first soap opera. As creator-producer: One Life to Live, All My Children, Loving. Also evening mini-series The Manions of America. Credited with bringing social issues to daytime TV. Guest writer, the New York Times and TV Guide. Appeared on Good Morning America and other interview and news programs. Received National Acad. of Television Arts & Sciences' Trustee Award, 1981; Junior Diabetic Assn. Super Achiever Award, 1982; Communicator Award for American Women in Radio and Television, 1984.

NIXON, CYNTHIA: Actress. b. NY, NY, April 9, 1966. e. Barnard Coll. Started stage career at 12. Broadway: Hurlyburly, The Real Thing. Off-Broadway: Moonchildren, Romeo and Juliet.
PICTURES: Little Darlings (1980), Tatoo, Prince of the City, I Am the Cheese, Amadeus, The Manhattan Project.
TELEVISION: Tanner '88.

NIZER, LOUIS: Author, Attorney. b. London, Eng., Feb. 6, 1902. e. Columbia Coll., B.A., 1922; Columbia U. Law Sch., LL.B., 1924. Recipient of Columbia U. Curtis Oratorical Prize two times. Sr. partner of law firm, Phillips, Nizer, Benjamin, Krim & Ballon & special counsel to the Motion Picture Assn. of America. Writer of numerous books and articles in leading periodicals and newspapers; lecturer on legal subjects at many universities and bar associations. Also painter and writer of musical compositions.
BOOKS: Reflections without Mirrors, The Implosion Conspiracy, The Jury Returns, My Life in Court, What to Do With Germany, Thinking on Your Feet, Between You and Me, New Courts of Industry, Legal Essays. Excerpt from My Life in Court adapted to Bdwy. play, A Case of Libel, adapted for TV movie. Chapter of The Jury Returns adapted for TV movie.

NOBLE, PETER: Writer, Producer, Actor, TV personality. b. London, Eng., June 18; e. Hugh Myddelton Sch., Latymer Sch. Author several books on m.p. ind.; writer & conducts movie radio prog. for B.B.C. & Luxembourg (Film Time, Movie-Go-Round, Peter Noble's Picture Parade). Formed Peter Noble Productions, 1953; Acted in many pictures; Ed. Screen International since 1975. Editor Screen International Film & TV Yearbook since 1974. London Columnist; Hollywood Reporter etc. 1967–75.
PICTURES INCLUDE: Production assoc., Runaway Bus; asst. prod., To Dorothy a Son; co-prod., s.p. Fun at St. Fanny's; s.p.; Three Girls in Paris; assoc. prod., Lost; s.p., Captain Banner; prod., Strange Inheritance.
AUTHOR: Editor, British Film Year Book; author of biographies of Bette Davis, Erich Von Stroheim, Ivor Novello, Orson Welles. Author book, I Know That Face. Wrote screen plays, The King of Soho, Love in the Limelight, The Story of Ivor Novello, The Negro in Films.
TELEVISION: Find the Link, Other Screen, Film Fanfare, Movie Memories, Yakity Yak, Startime, Thank Your Lucky Stars, Juke Box, Jury, Simon Dee Show, Star Parade, Who's Whose, Movie Magazine, The Big Noise, The Name Game, Line Up, Tea Break, Today. Prod. consult. On The Braden Beat, The Frost Program, Dee Time. 1969–70 Prod. Cons. Simon Dee Show. Appeared on Anything You Can Do Looks Familiar, Password, Etc. 1971–1975. Wrote scripts and prod. consultant Movie Quiz (series). Appears frequently on Today TV series. 1976, Two's Company, Looks Familiar. Prod. con. Musical Time Machine BBC2 series, Talking about films on radio, including BBC Star Sound, Radio Luxembourg, Film Focus, Newsnight, Looks Familiar Nationwide, Hotel TV Network, 1981–3. Recent TV: The Time of Your Life, Channel 4 News, Nationwide. Numerous radio shows. TV series: Show Business, This Is Britain. TV appearances: Looks Familiar, Electric Picture Show, Gossip, Entertainment Tonight (USA). 1984–85: This Is Britain (TV cable series); Cannes Film Festival (Premiere TV Cable). 1986–87—The Colour Supplement (series); Good Afternoon New York (WOR weekly show U.S.); Loose Ends (BBC); The Golden Gong (TV film).

NOIRET, PHILIPPE: Actor. b. France, 1931. With Theatre National Populaire and worked as nightclub entertainer before film debut in Agnes Varda's short, La Pointe Court. Has played character roles in numerous international films.

PICTURES INCLUDE: Zazie dans le Metro, (1960), The Billionaire, Crime Does Not Pay, Therese Desqueyroux, None But the Lonely Spy, Death Where Is Thy Victory?, Les Copains, Lady L, La Vie de Chateau, Tender Scoundrel, The Night of the Generals, Woman Times Seven, The Assassination Bureau, Mr. Freedom, Justine, Topaz, Clemarbard, Give Her the Moon, A Room in Paris, Murphy's War, A Time for Loving, The Serpent, The Day of the Jackel, La Grande Bouffe, Let Joy Reign Supreme, The Old Gun, The Judge and the Assassin, A Woman at Her Window, Dear Inspector, Due Pezzi di Pane, Who Is Killing the Great Chefs of Europe?, Death Watch, Street of the Crane's Foot, A Week's Vacation, Heads or Tails, Three Brothers, Kill Birgitt Haas, Coup de Torchon, L'Etoile Du Nord, Amici, Miei, Atto 2, L'Africain, A Friend of Vincents, Le Grand Carnival, Fort Saganne, Les Ripoux, Souvenirs, Next Summer, The Gold-Rimmed Glasses, No Downing Allowed, My New Partner, 'Round Midnight, Let's Hope It's a Girl, The 4th Power, The Thrill of Genius, The Secret Wife, Twist Again in Moscow, The Family Chouans!, Young Toscanini, The Return of the Musketeers, Moments of Love, New Cinema Paradiso.

NOLTE, C. ELMER, JR.: Executive v.p. b. Baltimore, Md., Oct. 19, 1905. Managing dir., F. H. Durkee Enterprises, Baltimore. Pres., April 1955–56; treas., 1957–59; pres., 1952–66, 67–69. Now v.p. & gen. mgr.

NOLTE, NICK: Actor. b. Omaha, NB, Feb. 8, 1941. Attended 5 colleges in 4 yrs. on football scholarships, including Pasadena City Coll. and Phoenix City Coll. Joined Actors Inner Circle at Phoenix and appeared in several plays including Orpheus Descending, After the Fall, Requiem For a Nun. Did stock in Colorado. In 1968 joined Old Log Theatre in Minneapolis and after 3 yrs. left for New York, appearing at Cafe La Mama. Went to L.A. and did several TV series before big break in mini-series Rich Man, Poor Man as Tom Jordache.

PICTURES INCLUDE: Return to Macon County Line, The Deep, Who'll Stop the Rain, North Dallas Forty, Heart Beat, Cannery Row, 48 Hrs., Under Fire, Teachers, Grace Quigley, Down and Out in Beverly Hills, Extreme Prejudice, Weeds, Fugitives, Farewell to the King.

TELEVISION: Guest: Medical Center, Gunsmoke. Mini-series: Rich Man, Poor Man. Movies: Winter Kill, The California Kid, Death Sentence, Adams of Eagle Lek, The Treasure Chest Murder, The Runaways, Barge.

NORMAN, BARRY: Writer/presenter. b. London. Early career as show business editor London Daily Mail; humorous columnist The Guardian. Entered TV as writer, presenter FILM 72–81 and 83–88. 1982: presenter Omnibus. Writer/host: The Hollywood Greats and Talking Pictures. Radio work incl.: Going Places, The News Quiz, Breakaway, The Chip Shop. Books incl.: The Hollywood Greats, Movie Greats, Film Greats (all non-fiction). Seven novels incl.: A Series of Defeats, Have a Nice Day and Sticky Wicket.

NORRIS, CHARLES GLENN: Executive. b. Taylorsville, NC, Nov. 24, 1906; e. Nat'l U. Law Sch., Washington, DC. Asst. poster clerk, Fox Film Co., 1928; booker, Wash., D.C., 1934; ad-sales mgr., Aug., 1935; salesman, Phila., July, 1937; Baltimore, July, 1944; br. mgr., Wash., Jan. 1946; dist. mgr., July, 1946; br. mgr., Wash., Apr., 1948; Atlantic div. mgr., Wash., Jan., 1952; eastern sales mgr., April, 1954; central Canadian sales mgr., April, 1956; asst. gen. sales mgr., April, 1959; gen. sls. mgr., 1960–69; exec. capacity in distribution, 20th Century-Fox, The Glenoris Corp.

MEMBER: Variety Club, English Speaking Union, M.P. Pioneers.

NORRIS, CHUCK: Actor. r.n. Carlos Ray. b. Ryan, OK, 1939. Gained renown as karate expert. Film debut in The Wrecking Crew (1968).

PICTURES: Return of the Dragon, Breaker! Breaker!, Good Guys Wear Black, A Force of One, The Octagon, An Eye for an Eye, Slaughter in San Francisco, Silent Rage, Forced Vengeance, Lone Wolf McQuade, Missing in Action, Missing in Action 2, Code of Silence, Invasion U.S.A. (also s.p.), Delta Force, Firewalker, Braddock: Missing in Action III (also co-s.p.), Hero and the Terror, America's Red Army, Delta Force II.

TELEVISION: The Ultimate Stuntman: A Tribute to Dar Robinson (host).

NORTH, ALEX: Composer. b. Chester, PA, Dec. 4, 1910; e. Curtis Inst., 1928–29; Julliard Sch. of Music, 1932–34. Composer for ballet, radio, TV, theatre; U.S. Army, 1942–46; Guggenheim Fellowship, 1947–48; comp. 40 documentary films, 1937–50; comp. Revue for Clarinet & Orch. for Benny Goodman, 1947. Member ASCAP; Dramatists Guild.

PICTURES INCLUDE: Streetcar Named Desire, Death of a Salesman, Viva Zapata, Les Miserables, Pony Soldier, Member of the Wedding, Go Man Go, Desiree, Unchained, The Racers, Man with the Gun, Rose Tatoo, I'll Cry Tomorrow, Cleopatra (Composers and Lyricists Award, best film score, 1964), Shoes of the Fisherman (Golden Globe Award; best film score 1968), The Children's Hour, The Misfits, Cheyenne Autumn, Spartacus, The Rainmaker, The Agony and the Ecstacy, Who's Afraid of Virginia Woolf?, A Dream of Kings, Willard, Pocketmoney, Rebel Jesus, Once Upon a Scoundrel, Lost in the Stars, (musical director) Journey Into Fear, Shanks, Bite the Bullet, Somebody Killed Her Husband, Wise Blood, Carny, Dragonslayer, Under the Volcano, Prizzi's Honor, The Penitent, The Dead, Good Morning Vietnam. 15 Acad. Awards nominations.

TELEVISION: Rich Man, Poor Man; Death of a Salesman; The Word; Sister, Sister.

AWARDS: Honorary Oscar, 1986; ASCAP Golden Soundtrack Award, 1986; Society for Preservation of Film Music Award, 1986; American Society of Music Arrangers & Composers Golden Score Award, 1986.

NORTH, EDMUND H.: Writer. b. New York, NY, March 12, 1911. e. Stanford U. U.S. Army Signal Corps, five yrs., W.W.II, sep. as major.

PICTURES INCLUDE: One Night of Love, I Dream Too Much, Dishonored Lady, Flamingo Road, Young Man with a Horn, In a Lonely Place. collab. Only the Valiant; s.p. Day the Earth Stood Still, Outcasts of Poker Flat; collab. s.p., Destry, Far Horizons, Proud Ones; s.p. Cowboy; screen story and s.p., Sink the Bismarck!; collab. s.p., H.M.S. Defiant; collab. story and s.p. Patton; story and collab. s.p. Meteor.

TELEVISION: Fireball Foreward, Murderous Gang.

NORTH, SHEREE: Actress. r.n. Dawn Bethel. b. Los Angeles, CA, Jan. 17, 1933. e. Hollywood H.S. Amateur dancer with USO at 11; prof. debut at 13; many TV appearances; on Broadway in Hazel Flagg.

PICTURES INCLUDE: Excuse My Dust, Living It Up, How To Be Very Very Popular, Lieutenant Wore Skirts, Best Things in Life Are Free, Way to the Gold, Destination Inner Space, The Gypsy Moths, Charley Varick, The Outfit, Breakout, The Shootist, Telefon, Maniac Cop.

TELEVISION: Big Eddie, Bay City Blues, Archie Bunker's Place. Movies: The Seekers, Scorned and Swindled; Marilyn: The Untold Story; Legs; Vanished.

NOSSECK, NOEL: Producer, Director. Began as editor with David Wolper Prods; made documentaries; turned to features.

PICTURES: Best Friends; Las Vegas Lady; Dreamer; King of the Mountain.

TELEVISION: Return of the Rebels; The First Time; Night Partners; Summer Fantasies. Movies: Different Affair; Stark: A Mirror Image; Roman Holiday. Pilots: Aaron's Way; Half 'n Half.

NOURI, MICHAEL: Actor. b. Washington, DC, Dec. 9, 1945. e. Avon Old Farms, Rollins Coll., Emerson Coll. Studied for theatre with Larry Moss and Lee Strasberg. New York stage debut in Forty Carats, 1969. Film debut in Goodbye Columbus, 1969.

PICTURES: Flashdance, The Imagemaker, The Hidden, May the Best Man Win.

TELEVISION: Series: Beacon Hill, Downtown. Movies: The Gangster Chronicles, Contract on Cherry Street, Between Two Women, Rage of Angels: The Story Continues, Bay City Blues.

NOVAK, KIM: Actress. r.n. Marilyn Novak. b. Feb, 13, 1933. e. Wright Junior Coll., Los Angeles City Coll. Started as model, named World's Favorite Actress, Brussels World Fair; film debut in The French Line (1953).

PICTURES INCLUDE: Pushover, Phfft, Five Against the House, Picnic, Man with the Golden Arm, Eddy Duchin Story, Jeanne Eagles, Pal Joey, Middle of the Night, Bell, Book and Candle, Vertigo, Pepe, Strangers When We Meet, The Notorious Landlady, Boys' Night Out, Of Human Bondage, Kiss Me, Stupid, The Amorous Adventures of Moll Flanders, The Legend of Lylah Clare, The Great Bank Robbery, Tales That Witness Madness, The White Buffalo, The Mirror Crack'd.

TELEVISION: Falcon Crest (series), Alfred Hitchcock Presents (1985), Malibu, Santa's Triangle, Third Girl From the Left.

NOVELLO, DON: Writer, Comedian, Producer. b. Ashtabula, OH, Jan. 1, 1943. e. U. of Dayton, B.A., 1964. Best known as Father Guido Sarducci on Saturday Night Live. Was advertising copy writer before writing and performing on The Smothers Brothers Comedy Hour (1975). Writer for Van Dyke and Company, and writer-performer on Saturday Night Live 1978–80. Producer: SCTV Comedy Network (1982) and performer-writer on Broadway in Gilda Radner—Live From New York (1979) as well as filmed version (Gilda Live!). Author: The Laszlo Letters: The Amazing Real-Life Actual Correspondence of Laszlo Toth, American!

PICTURES: Tucker: The Man and His Dream.

NUREYEV, RUDOLF: Dancer, Actor. b. Russia, Mar. 17, 1938. e. Leningrad Ballet Sch. Joined Kirov Ballet Co. as soloist. Asked for and granted political asylum in 1961 in Paris while performing. Joined Marquis de Cuevas Ballet Co.
PICTURES: An Evening with the Royal Ballet, Swan Lake, Romeo and Juliet, The Sleeping Beauty, Don Quixote, Valentino, Exposed.
TELEVISION: Julie Andrews Invitation to the Dance with Rudolf Nureyev.

NYKVIST, SVEN: Cinematographer. b. Moheda, Sweden, Dec. 3, 1922. e. Stockholm Photog. Sch. Asst. cameraman 1941–44. Became internationally known through photographing most of Ingmar Bergman's pictures.
PICTURES INCLUDE: Sawdust and Tinsel, The Virgin Spring, Winter Light, Karin Mansdotter, The Silence, Loving Couples, Persona, Hour of the Wolf, Cries and Whispers (AA), The Dove, Black Moon, Scenes from a Marriage, The Magic Flute, Face to Face, One Day in the Life of Ivan Denisovich, The Tenant, The Serpents' Egg, Pretty Baby, Autumn Sonata, King of the Gypsies, Hurricane, Starting Over, Willie and Phil, From the Life of the Marionettes, The Postman Always Rings Twice, Cannery Row, Fanny and Alexander (Acad. Award), Swann in Love, The Tragedy of Carmen, After the Rehearsal, Agnes of God, Dream Lover, The Sacrifice, The Unbearable Lightness of Being, Katinka, New York Stories (co-cin.).
TELEVISION: Nobody's Child.

O

O'BRIAN, HUGH: Actor. r.n. Hugh J. Krampe. b. Rochester, NY, Apr. 19, 1930; U. of Cincinnati, UCLA. U.S. Marine Corps. Actor, stock cos.; actor with many m.p. cos.
PICTURES INCLUDE: Young Lovers, Never Fear, Vengeance Valley, Little Big Horn, On the Loose, The Cimarron Kid, Red Ball Express, Sally and Saint Anne, The Raiders, The Lawless Breed, Meet Me at the Fair, Seminole, Man from the Alamo, Back to God's Country, Saskatchewan, Fireman Save My Child, Drums Across the River, Broken Lance, There's No Business Like Show Business, White Feather, The Fiend Who Won the West, Twinkle in God's Eye, Brass Legend, Rope Law, Come Fly with Me, Love Has Many Faces, In Harm's Way, Ten Little Indians, Ambush Bay, Cowboy in Africa, Harpy, Killer Force, The Shootist, Game of Death, Doing Time on Planet Earth, Twins.
TELEVISION: Series: Wyatt Earp; Search, Probe; Specials: Dial M for Murder; A Punt, A Pass and A Prayer; It's a Man's World. Movies: Wild Women, Tomorrow is Now, Space in the Age of Aquarius, Murder on Flight 502, Fantasy Island, Cruise Into Terror.
THEATER: B'way Plays: Destry Rides Again, First Love, Guys and Dolls. National co. of Cactus Flower.
Pres. H.O.B. Inc. Bev. Hills, 1956. Founder, chm. and C.E.O.: Hugh O'Brian Youth Foundation; Nat'l Chmn., Cystic Fibrosis Research Foundation 1969–74; Co-founder and pres. Thalians 1956–57; Founder Hugh O'Brian Annual Acting Awards at U. of California at L.A.

O'BRIEN, LIAM: Writer. b. New York, NY, March, 1913. e. Fordham U., Manhattan Coll., A.B., 1935. Author B'way play Remarkable Mr. Pennypacker, 1953.
PICTURES INCLUDE: Chain Lightning, Redhead and the Cowboy, Of Men and Music, Diplomatic Courier, Here Comes the Groom, The Stars Are Singing, Young at Heart.

O'BRIEN, MARGARET: Actress. r.n. Angela Maxine O'Brien. Los Angeles, CA, Jan. 15, 1938. Screen debut at 4 in Babes on Broadway (1941). Acad. Award best child actress, 1944. Voted one of ten best money-making stars in Motion Picture Herald-Fame Poll 1945–46.
PICTURES INCLUDE: Journey for Margaret, Dr. Gillespie's Criminal Case, Lost Angel, Thousands Cheer, Madame Curie, Jane Eyre, The Canterville Ghost, Meet Me in St. Louis, Music for Millions, Our Vines Have Tender Grapes, Bad Bascomb, Three Wise Fools, Unfinished Dance, Tenth Avenue Angel, The Secret Garden, Big City, Little Women, Her First Romance, Glory, Heller in Pink Tights, Anabelle Lee, Diabolic Wedding, Amy.
TELEVISION: Guest: Marcus Welby (1972), Death in Space, Split Second to an Epitaph, Testimony of Two Men.

O'BRIEN, VIRGINIA: Actress. b. Los Angeles, CA, Apr. 18, 1919. Singer, comedienne with a distinctive dead-pan delivery. On stage in Meet the People. Screen debut 1940 in Hullabaloo; now retired.
PICTURES INCLUDE: The Big Store, Lady Be Good, Ringside Maisie, Ship Ahoy, Panama Hattie, DuBarry Was a Lady, Thousands Cheer, Meet the People, Two Girls and a Sailor, The Harvey Girls, Ziegfeld Follies, Till Clouds Roll By, The Showoff, Merton of the Movies.

O'CONNELL, JACK: Producer, Director, Writer, Lyricist. b. Boston, MA. After Germany in W.W.II got B.A. Princeton U., M.B.A.

Harvard U. Business Sch. After being creative group head in all media at D'Arcy and McCann-Erickson advertising and doing 500 TV commercials entered feature films working with Fellini on La Dolce Vita, then asst. director to Antonioni on L'Avventura, then writer-producer-director Greenwich Village Story, Revolution, Swedish Fly (a.k.a. Christa), Summer of Love. Features have been invited by critics to represent U.S. at Cannes, Locarno, Berlin and Venice Film Festivals.

O'CONNOR, CARROLL: Actor. b. New York, NY, Aug. 2, 1925. e. University Coll., Dublin; U. of Montana. Three years with Dublin's Gate Theatre, then N.Y. where stage credits include Ulysses in Nighttown, Playboy of the Western World, The Big Knife; m.p. debut in Fever in the Blood, 1960.
PICTURES INCLUDE: Lad Had a Dog, By Love Possessed, Lonely Are the Brave, Cleopatra, In Harm's Way, What Did You Do in the War, Daddy?, Hawaii, Not With My Wife You Don't, Warning Shot, Waterhole No. 3, The Devil's Brigade, For Love of Ivy, Kelley's Heroes, Doctors' Wives, Death of a Gunfighter, Law and Disorder.
TELEVISION: US Steel Hour, Armstrong Circle Theatre, Kraft Theatre, All in the Family (Emmy, Golden Globe awards), Of Thee I Sing, In the Heat of the Night (series). Movies: The Last Hurrah, The Sacco and Vanzetti Story, Brass, Convicted, The Father Clements Story.
AUTHOR: Ladies of Hanover Tower (play); Little Anjie Always, The Great Robinson (screenplays).

O'CONNOR, DONALD: Actor. Star of Tomorrow, 1943. b. Chicago, IL, Aug. 28, 1925. In vaudeville with family and Sons o' Fun (Syracuse, N.Y.) before screen debut 1938 in Sing You Sinners; in number other pictures 1938–39 (Sons of the Legion; Tom Sawyer, Detective, Beau Geste, On Your Toes, etc.); in vaudeville 1940–41, then resumed screen career with What's Cookin'?, 1942. Entered armed services, 1943.
PICTURES INCLUDE: Private Buckaroo, Give Out, Sisters, When Johnny Comes Marching Home, It Comes Up Love, Mr. Big, Top Man, Patrick the Great, Follow the Boys, The Merry Monahans, Bowery to Broadway, This Is the Life, Something in the Wind, Are You With It? Feudin', Fussin' and a-Fightin'. Yes Sir, That's My Baby, Francis series, Curtain Call at Cactus Creek, The Milkman, Double Crossbones, Singin' in the Rain, I Love Melvin, Call Me Madam, Walking My Baby Back Home, There's No Business Like Show Business, Anything Goes, Buster Keaton Story, Cry for Happy, That Funny Feeling, That's Entertainment, Ragtime, A Mouse, A Mystery and Me.
TELEVISION: Colgate Comedy Hour, 1953–54. Voted best TV performer, M.P. Daily poll, 1953, The Donald O'Connor Show.

O'CONNOR, PAT: Director. b. Ardmore, Ireland. After working in London at odd jobs (putting corks in wine bottles, paving roads), came to U.S. e. UCLA, B.A. Studied film and TV at Ryerson Institute in Toronto. 1970, trainee prod., dir. with Radio Telefis Eireann. 1970–78 prod. and dir. over 45 TV features and current affairs documentaries. (The Four Roads, The Shankhill, Kiltyclogher, One of Ourselves, Night in Ginitia). A Ballroom of Romance won British Acad. Award (1981).
PICTURES: Cal, (1984), A Month in the Country, Stars and Bars, The January Man.

OFFENHAUSER, WILLIAM H., JR.: Executive, Engineer; b. Brooklyn, NY, May 8, 1904. e. Columbia U. RCA, 1929–32; inventor MGM squeezetrack, 1929; contractor, Army Sig. Corps, 1933–34; sales eng., J. A. Maurer, Inc., 1936–39; mgr., Precisions Films Labs., N.Y., v.p., mem. of bd., J. A. Maurer, 1939–43; project eng., Johns Hopkins U., 1942–43; consultant, Sig. Corps. Photo Center, 1944–45; consultant, film in color TV, CBS, 1946–47, 1949–51; research project, Cornell U. Med. Coll., 1947–49, consultant, Telenews Prod., 1951–52; v.p., Andre Debrie of America, Inc., 1953; ind. consultant, films & TV, 1954. 1960–61, (Photo Staff) M.I.T. Lincoln Laboratory, Lexington, MA. Author, 16mm Sound Motion Pictures—A Manual; co-author, Microrecording-Industrial and Library Microfilming; ind. consultant, Films, TV, biological Acoustics and Biophysics; 1968, pres. Radio Club of America; 1969–73 Bd. Dir. Radio Club of America.

O'HANLON, GEORGE: Actor. b. Brooklyn, NY, Nov. 23, 1917. e. La Salle Acad.; Providence, RI. p. Sam Rice and Luly Beeson, prof., served in U.S. Air Corps, 1942–45. Appeared in stock, vaudeville and Broadway musicals. On screen first, 1941, New Wine.
PICTURES INCLUDE: The Hucksters, Headin' for Heaven, Triple Cross, Spirit of West Point, Are You with It? star in Joe McDoakes series: Park Row, Cattle Town, Tanks Are Coming, Lion and the Horse, Battle Stations, Million Dollar Duck, Bop Girl, The Rookie, Charley and the Angel, Rocky.
TELEVISION: Real George, Life of Riley, Desilu Playhouse, Pantomime Quiz, The Reporter, Nancy Drew.

O'HARA, GERRY: Director. b. Boston-Lincs., England 1924. e. St. Mary's Catholic Sch., Boston. Junior Reporter Boston Guard-

Oha-Oli

ian. Entered industry in 1942 with documentaries and propaganda subjects. Dir. debut 1963 That Kind of Girl.
PICTURES INCLUDE: Game for Three Lovers; Pleasure Girls (wrote & dir.); Maroc 7; Love in Amsterdam; All the Right Noises (orig. screenplay & dir.); Leopard in the Snow; The Bitch; Fanny Hill; Death on Safari (s.p.); Havoc in Chase County (s.p.).
TELEVISION: The Avengers; Man in a Suitcase, Journey into the Unknown, The Professionals (story editor, writer); Special Squad (story consultant); Cats Eyes (exec. story editor), Operation Julie (s.p., mini-series).

O'HARA, MAUREEN: Actress. r.n., Maureen FitzSimons. b. Dublin. Aug. 17, 1921. e. Abbey Sch. of Acting. Won numerous prizes for elocution. Under contract to Erich Pommer-Charles Laughton. Co-starred, Abbey & Repertory Theatre: U.S. film debut in Jamaica Inn (1939).
PICTURES INCLUDE: Hunchback of Notre Dame, A Bill of Divorcement, Dance, Girls, Dance, They Met in Argentina; How Green Was My Valley, To the Shores of Tripoli, Ten Gentlemen from West Point, The Black Swan, The Fallen Sparrow, Buffalo Bill, The Spanish Main, Do You Love Me?, Miracle on 34th Street, Foxes of Harrow, The Homestretch, Sitting Pretty, Woman's Secret, Forbidden Street, Sentimental Journey, Sinbad the Sailor, Father Was a Fullback, Comanche Territory, Tripoli, Bagdad, Rio Grande, At Sword's Point, Kangaroo, Flame of Araby, Quiet Man, Against All Flags, Redhead from Wyoming, War Arrow, Fire over Africa, Magnificent Matador, Lady Godiva, Long Gray Line, Everything But the Truth, Wings of Eagles, The Deadly Companions, Our Man in Havana, Mr. Hobbs Takes a Vacation, McLintock, Spencer's Mountain, The Parent Trap, The Rare Breed, The Battle of Villa Fiorita, How Do I Love Thee, Big Jake.
TELEVISION: The Red Pony, Mrs. Miniver, Scarlet Pimpernel, Spellbound, High Button Shoes, Who's Afraid of Mother Goose.

O'HERLIHY, DAN: Actor. b. Wexford, Ireland, May 1, 1919. e. National U. of Ireland (Bachelor of Architecture). Actor with Abbey Theatre, Dublin Gate, Longford Prod.; announcer on Radio Eireann; on Broadway in The Ivy Green. Extensive TV from 1952. Nom. Acad. Award, Best Actor, 1954.
PICTURES INCLUDE: Odd Man Out, Macbeth, At Swords Point, Adventures of Robinson Crusoe, Black Shield of Falworth, Cabinet of Dr. Caligari, Imitation of Life, Virgin Queen, Fail-Safe, Home Before Dark, Waterloo, Last Starfighter, 100 Rifles, The Tamarind Seed, MacArthur, Robocop, The Dead.
TELEVISION: Series: A Man Called Sloane, The Whiz Kids.

OHLMEYER, DONALD W. JR.: Executive, Producer, Director. b. New Orleans, LA, Feb. 3, 1945. e. U. of Notre Dame, B.A. (Communications), 1967. Producer and director at both ABC and NBC. Formed Ohlmeyer Communications Company, 1982 (diversified prod. and dist. of entertainment and sports prog.). Assoc. dir., ABC Sports, NY 1967–70; director, ABC Sports, 1971–72 (dir. 1972 Olympic Games); prod.: ABC Sports, NY 1972–77 (prod. and dir. 1976 Winter and Summer Olympics; prod. ABC's Monday Night Football, 1972–76); exec. prod.: NBC Sports, NY 1977–82 (exec. prod., 1980 Olympics, The World Series, The Super Bowl). Chairman and CEO, Ohlmeyer Communications Co., LA, 1982–present. Recipient of 11 Emmy Awards, Humanitas Prize, Award for Excellence, National Film Board. Member, Directors Guild of America.

OHMART, CAROL: Actress. b. Salt Lake City, UT, June 3, 1928. e. Lewis and Clark H.S., Spokane, WA. Newspaper writer, model, radio actress.
TELEVISION: Versatile Varieties, Studio One, Philco Playhouse, Colgate Comedy Hour.
THEATRE: On Broadway in Kismet.
PICTURES INCLUDE: The Scarlet Hour (debut, 1955); Wild Party, House On Haunted Hill, Born Reckless, Scavengers, Wild Youth, One Man's Way, Caxambu, The Spectre of Edgar Allen Poe.

O'HORGAN, TOM: Director. e. DePaul U. At age 12 wrote opera, Doom on the Earth. Is also musician, singer, actor. Responsible for developing many revolutionary off-off Bdwy. artistic innovations in such productions as The Maids, Tom Paine, Futz.
PICTURES INCLUDE: Futz, Rhinoceros.
STAGE: Broadway: Hair, Lenny, Jesus Christ, Superstar, Inner City, Dude.

OHTANI, HIROSHI: Executive. b. Tokyo, Nov. 2, 1910. e. Kobe Commercial C. 1935; entered Shochiku Co., Ltd., 1936; exec. dir. 1937; man. dir. 1944; dir. Taisho-kan Theatre Co., Ltd. 1948; dir. Chuei Co., Ltd. 1953; man. dir. 1953; aud. Schochiku Co., 1954; pres. 1960–62; pres., Chugai motion picture chain. 1962.

O'KEEFE, MICHAEL: Actor. b. Larchmont, NY, 1955. e. New York U. On Bdwy. stage in Streamers, Mass Appeal and Fifth of July.
PICTURES: Gray Lady Down, The Great Santini, Caddyshack, Split Image, Nate and Hayes, Finders Keepers, The Slugger's Wife, Ironweed.
TELEVISION: Friendly Persuasion, Panache, A Rumor of War, The Dark Secret of Harvest Home, Unholy Matrimony, Bridge to Silence.

OKON, TED: Producer, Director. b. New Kensington, PA, Oct. 27, 1929. e. U. of Pittsburgh, B.A., 1949. Started career as radio announcer, disk jockey; John Harris Enterprises, theatres and Ice Capades, 1 year; prod. dir., WDTV-TV, Pittsburgh, formed Togo Productions prod. live and film TV shows: Reach, Yates and Matoon. TV-radio dir. 1956; TV-radio pro. dir. Reach McClinton & Co., 1957. sr. v.p. pro. TV comm. Benton and Bowles Adv. 1958–63; Exec. TV prog. dir. art., Ogilvy, Benson & Mather Adv. 1963–65; v.p. prog. dir. Van Praag Prod.; Exec. prod. Girl Game, TV show, 1966; Pres. Rough & Ready, 1966–69; Pres. prod-dir. Tape 16, Teletronics 1969–70; Pres. 1970's Productions; Exec. prod. Women's Clubhouse, TV show, Pres., exec. prod., Pennysaver Productions, Inc., TV programming syndication. Exec. prod. The Pennysaver Place, Dance Party '76, $50,000 Crossword, Sho-Biz-Quizz, Polka Party, Salsa Time, Northstage Theatre Restaurant.

OLDMAN, GARY: Actor. b. New Cross, South London, Eng., March 21, 1958. Won scholarship to Rose Bruford Drama College, (B.A. Theatre Arts) after studying with Greenwich Young People's Theatre. Acted with Theatre Royal, York and joined touring theatre co. Then in 1980 appeared with Glasgow Citizens Theatre in Massacre at Paris, Chinchilla, Desperado Corner, A Waste of Time (also touring Europe and South America). London stage: Minnesota Moon, Summit Conference, Rat in the Skull, Women Beware Women, The War Plays, Real Dreams, The Desert Air, Serious Money (Royal Shakespeare Co.). The People Wedding (won Time Out's Fringe Award, best newcomer 1985–86; British Theatre Assc. Drama Mag. Award, Best Actor 1985).
PICTURES: Sid and Nancy, Prick Up Your Ears, Track 29, Criminal Law, We Think The World of You, Chattahoochee.
TELEVISION: Remembrance; Meantime; Morgan's Boy; Honest, Decent and True; Rat in the Skull.

OLEMBERT, THEODORA: Producer, Writer. Doctor of Law Criminology of Paris U. Entered films through documentaries on child delinquency. Worked during the war as assistant to Prof. René Cassin on Franco/British cultural relations including films. Afterwards joined Jean Benoit-Lévy, chief of the United Nations Film Section. Formed Triangle Films Ltd. for international coproductions; associated with l'Editon Française Cinématographique (Paris).
PRODUCED: Leonardo da Vinci, G. B. Shaw, Chopin, Teiva, The Sixth Day of Creation, Salvador Dali, Is Venice Sinking?, Edith Piaf and Corsica. Co-produced: Midnight Episode, Van Gogh, Molière, Mont St. Michel and Chinese Theatre. Preparing further films for international releases.

OLIVIER, LORD. (Sir Laurence Olivier): Actor, Director. b. Dorking, England, May 22, 1907. m. actress Joan Plowright. On stage, London, N.Y. since 1925. Stage includes, Caesar and Cleopatra, Antony and Cleopatra, London, 1951, N.Y. 1952; Venus Observed, London 1950; Sleeping Prince, London, 1953; Shakespeare Season, Stratford-upon-Avon, 1955; The Entertainer, London, N.Y., 1957–58; Titus Andronicus European Tour 1957; Coriolanus Stratford-upon-Avon, 1959. Rhinoceros, London, 1960; Becket, N.Y., 1960 & Tour 1961. dir., Chichester festival Theatre; 1962. dir., The Chances, The Broken Heart; Uncle Vanya, dir., acted, 1965; Othello, 1964. dir., National Theatre, 1962; Hamlet, Uncle Vanya. Recruiting Officer 1963–64. Othello Master Builder 1963–65; dir., The Crucible, 1965; Moscow, Berlin, Othello And Love For Love 1965; dir. Juno and the Paycock, 1965–66. Tour of Canada with National Thea. Co. in Love for Love, Dance of Death, Flea in Her Ear, 1967, Home and Beauty, 1969, Shylock in The Merchant of Venice, 1970; Long Day's Journey Into Night, 1972–74; Dir. Amphitryon 38, 1971; Saturday, Sunday, Monday, 1973; The Party, 1973; Eden End, 1974. Honorary Academy Awards, 1948, 1978.
PICTURES INCLUDE: As You Like It, Fire Over England, Divorce of Lady X, Wuthering Heights, Rebecca, Pride and Prejudice, That Hamilton Woman, Demi Paradise, Henry V (dir. & cast), Hamlet (prod., dir. & cast), Acad. Award, Best Actor, 1948, Carrie, Beggar's Opera, Richard III (prod. dir. & cast), Prince & the Showgirl, Devil's Disciple, Spartacus, The Entertainer, Term of Trial, Bunny Lake Is Missing, Othello, Khartoum, Shoes of the Fisherman, Oh! What a Lovely War, Battle of Britain, Dance of Death, David Copperfield, Three Sisters, Sleuth, Nicholas and Alexandra, Lady Caroline Lamb, 7% Solution, Marathon Man, A Bridge Too Far, The Betsy, The Boys from Brazil, A Little Romance, Dracula, Clash of the Titans, Inchon, The Jazz Singer, Wagner, The Bounty, The Jigsaw Man, Wild Geese II.
TELEVISION: John Gabriel Borkman, London. The Moon

and Sixpence, (Emmy, 1960); The Power and the Glory, N.Y., Uncle Vanya, Long Day's Journey Into Night, (Emmy, 1973), Merchant of Venice, World at War, Love Among the Ruins (Emmy, 1975), Jesus of Nazareth. Prod. and acted in The Collection, Cat on a Hot Tin Roof. Prod. and dir. Hindle Wakes. Prod. and acted in Come Back Little Sheba, Daphne Laureola. Prod. and acted in Saturday Sunday Monday, Brideshead Revisited (Emmy, supp., 1982), and King Lear (Emmy, 1984); Actor: The Last Days of Pompeii, Peter the Great.

OLMI, ERMANNO: Director. b. Bergamo, Italy, July 24, 1931. e. Accademia d'Arte Drammatica, Milan. Worked as a clerk for an electric company Edisonvolta 1949–52, until 1952 when he began directing theatrical and cinematic activities sponsored by co. 1952–61, directed or supervised over 40 short 16mm and 35mm documentary films. 1959 first feature film, semi-doc. Time Stood Still. With other friends and Tullio Kezich formed prod. co. 22 December S.P.A., 1961.
  PICTURES: The Sound of Trumpets, The Fiances, A Man Named John, One Fine Day, The Scavengers, (TV), During the Summer, The Circumstance, The Tree of the Wood Clogs (Palm d'or, Cannes, 1978), Camminacammina.

OLMOS, EDWARD JAMES: Actor. b. East Los Angeles, CA, February 24, 1947. e. East Los Angeles Coll., CA State U. Started as rock singer with group Eddie James and the Pacific Ocean. By the early 1970s acted in small roles on Kojak and Hawaii Five-O. 1978 starred in Luis Valdez's musical drama Zoot Suit at Mark Taper Forum, on Broadway and in subsequent film. Formed YOY Productions with director Robert Young.
  PICTURES: El Alambrista, Virus, Wolfen, Zoot Suit, Blade Runner, The Ballad of Gregorio Cortez, Saving Grace, Stand and Deliver.
  TELEVISION: Evening in Byzantium, 300 Miles for Stephanie, Seguin, Y.E.S. Inc., Miami Vice (series, Emmy, supporting actor, 1985).

O'LOUGHLIN, GERALD STUART: Actor. b. New York, NY, Dec. 23, 1921. e. Blair Acad., Lafayette Coll., U. of Rochester, Neighborhood Playhouse. U.S. Marine, W.W.II.
  THEATRE: Broadway: Streetcar, Shadow of a Gunman, Dark at the Top of the Stairs, A Touch of the Poet, Cook for Mr. General, One Flew over the Cuckoo's Nest, Calculated Risk. Off Broadway: Who'll Save the Plowboy (Obie Award), Harry, Noon and Night.
  PICTURES INCLUDE: Lovers and Lollypops, Cop Hater, Hatful of Rain, Ensign Pulver, A Fine Madness, In Cold Blood, The Valachi Papers, Desperate Characters, The Organization, Twilight's Last Gleaming, Frances, Quicksilver, Crimes of Passion.
  TELEVISION: The Defenders, Ben Casey, Dr. Kildare, 12 O'Clock High, For the People, Going My Way, Naked City, Alcoa Premiere, Child's Cry. Movies: Blind Ambition, The Blue and the Gray, Roots: The Next Generations; Woman in White, Something for Joey, Wilson's Reward, A Matter of Death & Life; Quincy; Too Close For Comfort, Riptide, Murder She Wrote, Voyage to Heaven, Perry Mason (Notorious Nun), Series: Mod Squad, The Rookies, Our House.

OLSON, DALE C: Executive. b. Fargo, ND, Feb. 20, 1934. e. Portland State Coll., OR. Owner, Dale C. Olson & Associates; formerly sn. v.p. & pres., m.p. div., Rogers & Cowan public relations. Journalist on Oregonian newspaper, West Coast editor, Boxoffice Magazine, 1958–1960; critic and reporter, Daily Variety, 1960–1966; director of publicity, Mirisch Corporation, 1966–1968; Rogers & Cowan, 1968–1985. Past pres., Hollywood Press Club, awarded Bob Yaeger and Les Mason award by Publicists Guild; v.p. Diamond Circle, City of Hope; delegate for U.S. to Manila International Film Festival.

OLSON, NANCY: Actress. b. Milwaukee, WI, July 14, 1928. e. U. of Wisconsin, U. of California at L.A. No prof. experience prior to films.
  PICTURES INCLUDE: Union Station, Canadian Pacific, Sunset Boulevard, Mr. Music, Submarine Command, Force of Arms, So Big, Boy from Oklahoma, Battle Cry, Pollyanna, The Absent-Minded Professor, Smith!, Airport 1975, Making Love.
  TELEVISION: Paper Dolls.

O'NEAL, FREDERICK: Actor, Director, Lecturer. b. Brooksville, MS, Aug. 27, 1905. e. public schools, Brooksville, St. Louis, MO, New Theatre Sch., American Theatre Wing. Acted primarily on stage. Pres. of Associated Actors and Artists of America. Named to Black Filmmakers Hall of Fame, 1975.
  PICTURES INCLUDE: Pinky, No Way Out, Something of Value, Anna Lucasta, Take a Giant Step.
  TELEVISION: Car 54, Where Are You? (series, 1961–62).

O'NEAL, PATRICK: Actor. b. Ocala, FL, Sept. 26, 1927. e. U. of Florida; Neighborhood Playhouse. In stock cos. before N.Y. TV, 1951. Has appeared in over 300 television shows (live and film).
  PICTURES INCLUDE: The Mad Magician, The Black

Shield of Falworth, From the Terrace, A Matter of Morals, The Cardinal, In Harm's Way, King Rat, Chamber of Horrors, A Fine Madness, Alvarez Kelly, Matchless, The Assignment, Where Were You When the Lights Went Out?, The Secret Life of an American Wife, Castle Keep, Stiletto, Corky, The Way We Were, The Stepford Wives, The Kremlin Letter, King Rat, Like Father, Like Son.
  TELEVISION: The Moneychangers, The Last Hurrah, Perry Mason Returns, To Kill a Cop. Series: Dick and the Duchess, Emerald Point NAS, Diagnosis: Unknown, Kaz, War Chronicles (mini-series).

O'NEAL, RON: Actor. b. Utica, NY, Sept. 1, 1937. e. Ohio State U. Spent 8 yrs. at Karamu House in Cleveland (inter-racial theatre) from 1957 to 1966, taking part in 40 plays. 1967–68 spent in N.Y. teaching acting in Harlem. Appeared in all-black revue 1968, The Best of Broadway, then in summer stock. Acted off-Broadway in American Pastorale and The Mummer's Play. 1970 joined Joseph Papp's Public Theatre. Big break came with No Place To Be Somebody, which won him top acting honors: the Obie, the Clarence Derwent, the Drama Desk and the Theatre World Awards.
  PICTURES INCLUDE: Move, The Organization, Super Fly, Super Fly TNT, The Master Gunfighter, Brothers, A Force of One, When a Stranger Calls, The Final Countdown, St. Helens, Red Dawn, Mercenary Fighters, Trained to Kill, Hero and the Terror.
  TELEVISION: Movies: North and South, As Summers Die, Brave New World, Freedom Road, Sophisticated Gents, Playing with Fire, The Equalizer (series), A Triple Play; Sam Found Out.
  STAGE: Tiny Alice, The Dream of Monkey Mountain.

O'NEAL, RYAN: Actor. r.n. Patrick Ryan O'Neal. b. Los Angeles, CA, April 20, 1941. Began as stand-in, then stunt man, then actor in Tales of the Vikings series, in Germany, 1959; freelanced in Hollywood; Screen Gems Pilots, Donny Dru, Our Man Higgins, and co-starred in series made from Empire; co-star, Peyton Place.
  PICTURES INCLUDE: The Big Bounce, The Games, Love Story, Wild Rovers, What's Up Doc, Paper Moon, The Thief Who Came to Dinner, Barry Lyndon, Nickelodeon, A Bridge Too Far, The Driver, Oliver's Story, Green Ice, Partners, So Fine, Irreconcilable Differences, Fever Pitch, Tough Guys Don't Dance, Chances Are.
  TELEVISION: Movie: Love, Hate, Love.

O'NEAL, TATUM: Actress. b. Los Angeles, CA, Nov. 5, 1963. Daughter of Ryan O'Neal and Joanna Moore. Won Acad. Award, 1973 for debut performance in Paper Moon.
  PICTURES INCLUDE: Paper Moon, The Bad News Bears, Nickelodeon, International Velvet, Little Darlings, Circle of Two, Prisoners, Certain Fury.

O'NEIL, THOMAS F.: Executive. b. Kansas City, MO, Apr. 18, 1915. e. Holy Cross Coll., 1933–37. Employed by General Tire and Rubber Co., 1937–41; U.S. Coast Guard, 1941–46; v.p., dir., Yankee Network, Boston, 1948–51; pres. chmn. of bd. RKO General, Inc., since 1952. Arranged purchase RKO Radio by General Teleradio, Inc. from Howard Hughes, July, 1955; chairman of the Board, RKO General, Inc., dir., General Tire & Rubber Co.

O'NEILL, JENNIFER: Actress. b. Rio de Janeiro, Brazil, Feb. 20, 1949. Model before entering films. Spokeswoman: CoverGirl cosmetics. Pres., Point of View Productions and Management.
  PICTURES: Rio Lobo (debut, 1970), Summer of '42, Such Good Friends, The Carey Treatment, Glass Houses, Lady Ice, The Reincarnation of Peter Proud, Whiffs, Caravans, Innocent, A Force of One, The Psychic, Scanners, Cloud Dancer, Steel, Committed.
  TELEVISION: Series: Bare Essence, Cover Up; Movies: Love's Savage Fury, Chase, The Red Spider, The Other Victim; Mini-series: A.D.

ONTKEAN, MICHAEL: Actor. b. Canada, Jan. 24, 1950. e. U. of New Hampshire. Son of Leonard and Muriel Cooper Ontkean, actors. Theater: Public Theatre, NY, Williamstown Theatre Fest., Mark Taper Lab, The Kitchen, Soho.
  PICTURES: The Peace Killers, Pick Up on 101, Necromancy, Hot Summer Weekend, Slap Shot, Voices, Willie and Phil, Making Love, Just the Way You Are, Street Justice, Maid to Order, Clara's Heart, The Allnighter, Bye Bye Blues.
  TELEVISION: The Rookies (series). Movies: The Blood of Others, Kids Don't Tell, The Right of the People, Man From the South, Summer.

OPATOSHU, DAVID: Actor. b. New York, NY, Jan. 30, 1918. e. Morris H.S. U.S. Army, 1942–46; played character roles, The Group Theatre at 21; appeared on Broadway.
  THEATRE: Me and Molly, Once More With Feeling, Silk Stockings, The Reclining Figure, The Wall, Bravo Giovanni, Does a Tiger Wear a Neck-Tie?
  PICTURES INCLUDE: Cimmarron, Naked City, The Brothers Karamazov, Exodus, Act of Mercy, Best of Enemies,

Enter Laughing, Romance of a Horse Thief, The Fixer, Public Enemy No. 1, The Light Ahead, Forty Days of Musa Dagh. TELEVISION: Movies: Conspiracy of Terror, Masada, Raid on Entebbe, Under Siege, Francis Gary Powers, The Smugglers.

OPHULS, MARCEL: Director, Writer. b. Frankfurt-am-Main, Germany, Nov. 1, 1927. r.n. Marcel Oppenheimer. Son of German director Max Ophuls. e. Occidental Coll., U. of California, Berkeley, Sorbonne (philosophy). Family moved to France, 1932, then to Hollywood, 1941. Military service with Occupation forces in Japan, 1946; performed with theater unit, Tokyo. 1951 began working in French film industry as 3rd asst. dir., using name Marcel Wall. 1956–59, radio and TV story ed., West Germany. Later worked for French TV as reporter and dir. news mag. features. 1968 doc. dir. for German TV. 1975–78 staff prod. CBS News, then ABC News.
PICTURES AND DOCUMENTARIES: Asst. dir.: Moulin Rouge (1953); Act of Love; Marianne de ma jeunesse, Lola Montes (dir. by father); Director and writer: Matisse; Love at 20; Banana Peel, (co-s.p.); Fire at Will (co-s.p.); Munich, or Peace in Our Time (TV); The Sorrow and the Pity (for TV, Navy Blues and Three Sons O'Guns, The Mortal Storm, The Big Street, Unholy Partners, Wicked, Wicked (exec. prod.).

OPOTOWSKY, STAN: Executive. e. Tulane U. Served in U.S. Marine Corps as combat corr. and later joined United Press, working in New Orleans, Denver, and New York. Published own weekly newspaper in Mississippi before returning to N.Y. to join New York Post as mgr. editor and traveling natl. corr. Is also cinematographer and film editor. Joined ABC News as TV assignment editor; named asst. assignment mgr. In 1974 named dir. of operations for ABC News TV Documentaries. In 1975 named dir. of TV News Coverage, ABC News.
AUTHOR: TV: The Big Picture, The Longs of Louisiana, The Kennedy Government, Men Behind Bars.

OPPENHEIMER, GEORGE: Writer. b. New York, NY, Feb. 7, 1900; e. Williams Coll., 1916–20; Harvard, 1921. Alfred A. Knopf, publishers, 1921–25; co-founder, Viking Press, 1925–33; W.W.II, 1942–45; playwright; short stories; radio.
PICTURES INCLUDE: Rendezvous, We Went to College, Libeled Lady, Day at the Races, Married Before Breakfast, Adventures of Don Juan, Anything Can Happen, Tonight We Sing, Decameron Nights.
TELEVISION: 30 Topper episodes.

OPPENHEIMER, JESS: Producer, Director, Writer. b. San Francisco, CA, Nov. 11, 1913. e. Stanford U. Radio, Packard Hour, Fred Astaire, 1937–39; head writer, Screen Guild Program, 1939–40; Writer: Rudy Vallee, John Barrymore Show, 1939–41; head writer, prod., dir., Baby Snooks, 1943–48; writer, prod., dir., Lucille Ball, My Favorite Husband, 1948–51.
TELEVISION: Creator, head writer, prod., I Love Lucy, The Glynis Johns Show. Prod., Get Smart, Gen. Motors 50th Anniversary Program, Danny Kaye Special, Emmy Show. Creator, prod., The Debbie Reynolds Show. Prod., writer: Ford Startime Special, Bob Hope Chrysler Hours (also dir.); creator, prod.-dir., Angel series. Writer, All in the Family.

ORBACH, JERRY: Actor. b. Bronx, NY, Oct. 20, 1935. e. U. of Illinois, Northwestern U. Trained for stage with Herbert Berghof and Lee Strasberg. N.Y. stage debut in Threepenny Opera, 1955.
THEATER: The Fantasticks (original cast, 1960); Carnival; The Cradle Will Rock; Guys and Dolls; Scuba Duba; Promises, Promises; 6 Rms Riv Vu, Chicago, 42nd Street.
PICTURES: Please Come Home, The Gang That Couldn't Shoot Straight, A Fan's Notes, Sentinel, Prince of the City, Brewster's Millions, F/X, The Imagemaker, Dirty Dancing, Someone to Watch Over Me, The Last Exit to Brooklyn.
TELEVISION: Shari Lewis Show, Jack Paar, Bob Hope Presents, Love American Style, Out on a Limb, Dream West, Love Among Thieves, Murder She Wrote, The Law and Harry McGraw (series).

OREAR, RICHARD: Executive. b. Kansas City, MO, June 11, 1911. e. Findlay Engineering Coll. Exhibitor since 1931 in various capacities. 1947, named to board of Commonwealth Theatres; 1955, exec. v.p.; 1959, bd. chmn.

ORKIN, AD: Executive. b. Jackson, MS, Dec. 7, 1922. e. U. of Mississippi. With Trans World Airlines as flt. eng. 1945–50. Previously co-owner of Orkin Amusements in Jackson. Now owner, Pike Triple Cinema in Troy area. Operates Orkin Badge Co. & Orkin Equipment Co.

O'ROURKE, JOHN J.: Executive. b. New York, NY, July 3, 1922. e. City Coll. of New York, 1950. Entered the industry 1939 Music Hall/New York. 20th Century Fox Film Corp. 1941–59, asst. to dir. of exploitation, MGM, 1960–62; asst. exploitation mgr. Astor Pictures 1962–63; exploitation mgr. 1963–67; National dir. of exploitation Avco Embassy Pictures, 1967; national coordinator roadshows, United Artists, 1968; asst. roadshow

mgr. Universal Pictures. 1969 joined Cinemation Industries as dir. advertising, publicity and exploitation. 1974, v.p., Harry K. McWilliams Assoc. Advertising, 1977, vice pres., Benjamin Philip Associates, Inc., Advertising.

ORR, WILLIAM T.: Executive. b. New York, NY, Sept. 27, 1917. e. Coburn Sch., Rumsey Hall, Philips Exeter Acad. Impersonator, Meet the People, revue. Contract, Warner Bros. Joined U.S. Air Force, 1942. Assigned production duties. Air Force's first motion picture unit, 1945. Joined Warner Bros. staff, 1946. Entertained, various night clubs and acting on Broadway stage, New York. Returned to Warner Bros., 1947 as exec. talent dept. and shortly named asst. to Steve Trilling, exec. asst. to Mr. Warner. Chg., studio's TV opers., 1955 as exec. prod. vice-pres., Warner Bros. Pictures, Inc., Nov. 29, 1957–62; vice-pres. in chg. of prod. both features and television, March 1961 to March 1962; vice pres. in chg. of television production, 1962–63; prod., Sex and the Single Girl; asst. to pres., exec. prod., TV div., J. L. Warner, 1963–65; formed Wm. T. Orr Co., 1966, for prods. of M.P.s and TV films.
PICTURES INCLUDE: My Love Came Back, Thieves Fall Out, Navy Blues and Three Sons O'Guns, The Mortal Storm, The Big Street, Unholy Partners, Wicked, Wicked (exec. prod.).

OSBORNE, JOHN: Dramatist. b. London, England, Dec. 12, 1929.
AUTHOR: Plays include 1956: Look Back in Anger. 1957: Epitaph for George Dillon. 1958: The Entertainer. 1959: The World of Paul Slickey. 1961: Luther. 1963: Plays for England. 1964: Inadmissible Evidence, A Patriot for Me, A Bond Honoured, Time Present, The Hotel in Amsterdam, West of Suez, Hedda Gabler (adaptn.).
PICTURES: Films of his plays include Look Back in Anger, The Entertainer. Film scripts: Tom Jones (Oscar, 1964), The Charge of the Light Brigade, Moll Flanders, Tomorrow Never Comes.
TELEVISION: The Right Prospectus, Very Like A Whale, A Subject of Scandal and Concern, The Gift of Friendship; Jack and Jill; You're Not Watching Me, Mummy; Try a Little Tenderness.

O'SHEA, MILO: Actor. b. Ireland, 1926. Member of Dublin Gate Theatre Co., before screen career. On Bdwy. in Staircase, Dear World, The Comedians, A Touch of the Poet, Mass Appeal, Corpse!
PICTURES: Carry on Cabby, Never Put it in Writing, Ulysses, Romeo and Juliet, Barbarella, The Adding Machine, The Angel Levine, Paddy, Sacco and Vanzetti, Loot, Digby, The Biggest Dog in the World, Arabian Adventure, The Verdict, The Purple Rose of Cairo, etc.
TELEVISION: Two by Forsyth, Ellis Island (series); QB VII, A Times for Miracles, Broken Vows, Angel in Green.

OSHIMA, NAGISA: Director, Writer. b. Kyoto, Japan, March 31, 1932. e. U. of Kyoto (law), 1954. Joined Shochiku Ofuna Studios in 1954 as asst. dir.; 1956 wrote film criticism and became editor-in-chief of film revue Eiga hihyo; 1959 promoted to director. 1962– 65 worked exclusively in TV; 1962–64 made documentaries in Korea and Vietnam; 1975 formed Oshima Productions. 1976, his book of Realm of the Senses seized by police. With editor, prosecuted for obscenity, acquitted. President of Directors Guild of Japan, 1980–present.
PICTURES: A Town of Love and Hope (1959); Cruel Story of Youth, The Sun's Burial; Night and Fog in Japan; The Catch, The Rebel; A Child's First Adventure; The Pleasures of the Flesh; Violence at Noon; Ban on Ninja; Death By Hanging; He Died After the War; The Ceremony; Dear Summer Sister; In the Realm of the Senses; Phantom Love; Empire of Passion; Merry Christmas, Mr. Lawrence; Max Mon Amour; Cruel Story of Youth.

OSMOND, DONNY: Singer, TV Host. b. Ogden, UT, Dec. 9, 1957. Seventh of 9 children, he was fifth member of family to become professional singer. (Four brothers, Alan, Wayne, Merrill and Jay, are original and present members of Osmond Bros., who originally sang barbershop quartet.) Made debut at 4 on Andy Williams Show. Has had 12 gold albums. Was co-host of Donny & Marie on TV with sister.
PICTURES: Goin' Cocoanuts (with Marie).
TELEVISION: Wild Women of Chastity Gulch.

OSMOND, MARIE: Singer, TV Host. b. Ogden, UT, Oct. 13, 1959. Began career at age of 7 while touring with her brothers. Her first album, Paper Roses, became a gold one. Appeared as co-host with brother Donny on TV's Donny & Marie.
TELEVISION: Gift of Love, I Married Wyatt Earp, Side By Side.

O'STEEN, SAM: Editor, Director. b. Nov. 6, 1923. Entered m.p. industry 1956 as asst. to editor George Tomassini on The Wrong Man. Became full editor in 1963 on Youngblood Hawke. Directorial debut with TV film A Brand New Life, 1972.
PICTURES: Editor: Kisses for My President; Robin and the 7 Hoods; Youngblood Hawke; Marriage on the Rocks; None

But the Brave; Who's Afraid of Virginia Woolf?; Cool Hand Luke; The Graduate; Rosemary's Baby; The Sterile Cuckoo (supr. ed.); Catch-22; Carnal Knowledge; Portnoy's Complaint; Day of the Dolphin; Chinatown; Straight Time; Sparkle (dir); Hurricane; Amityville II: The Possession, Silkwood; Heartburn; Nadine; Biloxi Blues; Frantic.
TELEVISION: Director: A Brand New Life; I Love You, Goodbye; Queen of the Stardust Ballroom (DGA Award); High Risk; Look What's Happened to Rosemary's Baby; The Best Little Girl in the World; Kids Don't Talk.

O'SULLIVAN, KEVIN P.: Executive. b. New York, NY, April 13, 1928. e. Queens Coll., Flushing, NY. Associated with television 40 yrs., initially as a talent; later as businessman. Entered entertainment world after winning first prize in Arthur Godfrey Talent Scouts competition in 1948. 1950–55 professional singer, actor on TV, in theatre, night clubs. 1955–57 on radio-TV promotion staff, Ronson Corp. 1958–61 salesman, Television Programs of America. 1961–67 director of program services, Harrington, Righter and Parsons. In 1967 joined ABC Films, domestic sales div. as v.p. & gen. sales mgr. In Jan., 1969 named v.p., gen. mgr., ABC Films, Inc.; in April same yr. named pres. In July 1970 made pres., ABC Int'l. TV, while retaining position as pres., ABC Films. In April, 1973 became pres., chief operating officer, Worldvision Enterprises, Inc., co. formed to succeed ABC Films when FCC stopped networks for TV program dist. Elected chm. & chief exec. officer Worldvision, 1982. Named president, Great American Broadcasting Group, 1987. Resigned, 1988.

O'SULLIVAN, MAUREEN: Actress. b. Boyle, Eire, May 17, 1911; mother of actress Mia Farrow. e. convents in Dublin, London; finishing sch., Paris. Film debut: Song O' My Heart (1930). On many TV shows.
PICTURES INCLUDE: A Connecticut Yankee, The Big Shot, MGM Tarzan series, Tugboat Annie, The Barretts of Wimpole Street, The Thin Man, David Copperfield, Anna Karenina, Cardinal Richelieu, The Voice of Bugle Ann, The Devil Doll, A Day at the Races, Big Clock, Bonzo Goes to College, Pride and Prejudice, All I Desire, Mission Over Korea, Duffy of San Quentin, Steel Cage, The Tall T, Never Too Late, Hannah and Her Sisters, Peggy Sue Got Married, Stranded.
STAGE: Never Too Late, The Front Page, 1971; No Sex Please, We're British, 1973, Mornings at Seven.
TELEVISION: The Crooked Hearts, The Great Houdinis.

OSWALD, GERD: Director. b. Berlin, Germany, June 9, 1919. Father Richard Oswald, Austrian prod. dir., founder of UFA. Child actor, Vienna 1938; asst. dir., Monogram, Republic, Goldwyn, Paramount; 1949–53, 20th-Fox, prod. mgr., 2nd unit dir., test dir. 1954, 20th-Fox, assoc., prod., Man on a Tightrope, Nightpeople. Prod. Oasis, 1955–58, dir., U.A., A Kiss Before Dying (San Sebastian Film Festival nominee); Brass Legend; Crime of Passion; Fury at Showdown; Valerie; Paris Holiday. 1959–67, dir., Columbia, Screaming Mimi. Prod.-dir., screenplay Germ., prod. The Day the Rains Came; J. Arthur Rank: Brainwashed, Bombay (Venice Film Festival nominee), dir., The Longest Day (St. Mere-Eglise Seq.). Prod. Dir. Italo-French, Co-prod., The Scarlet Eye; dir., Agent from H.A.R.M. 1970. Story prod.-dir. 80 Steps to Jonah, outstanding merit award by motion picture council; 1971 prod.-dir., Bunny O'Hare; 1976, dir. European co-prod.; To The Bitter End.
TELEVISION: Ford Theatre, G.E. Hour, Playhouse 90, Perry Mason, Rawhide, Black Saddle, The Virginian, Outer Limits (Soldier episode won HUGO award at world Sci-Fi convention), Fugitive, Blue Light, Felony Squad, Michner's Adventure in Paradise, Star Trek, Shane, Daniel Boone, Gentle Ben, Bonanza, It Takes A Thief, James Garner's Nichols; 1985–86: several episodes of new Twilight Zone.

O'TOOLE, ANNETTE: Actress. b. Houston, TX, April 1, 1953. e. U. of California at L.A.
PICTURES: Smile, One on One, King of the Gypsies, Foolin' Around, Cat People, 48 HRS, Superman III, Cross My Heart.
TELEVISION: Copacabana, Broken Vows, Strong Medicine, The Entertainer, The War Between the Tates, Stand By Your Man, Love For Rent, Vanities, The Kennedys of Massachusetts.

O'TOOLE, PETER: Actor. b. Ireland, Aug. 2, 1932. Studied at Royal Acad. of Dramatic Art. Early career with Bristol Old Vic. London Stage in The Long, the Short and the Tall. 1960, with the Stratford-on-Avon Company. Ent. films 1959 in Kidnapped. Partner with Jules Buck, Keep Films, Ltd.
PICTURES INCLUDE: The Savage Innocents, The Day They Robbed the Bank of England, Lawrence of Arabia, Becket, Lord Jim, What's New Pussycat, How to Steal a Million, The Night of the Generals, The Bible, Great Catherine, The Lion in Winter, Goodbye Mr. Chips, Brotherly Love, Murphy's War, Under Milk Wood, The Ruling Class, Man of La Mancha, Rosebud, Man Friday, Foxtrot, Caligula, The Stunt Man, My Favorite Year, Supergirl, Creator, Club Paradise, The Last Emperor, High Spirits, Helena.

TELEVISION: Movies: Svengali, Kim, Pygmalion; Strumpet City (serial), Masada (mini-series).

O'TOOLE, STANLEY: Producer. Earliest experience with production costs; worked on Cleopatra, Singer, Not the Song, No Love for Johnny, Victim, etc. In 1966 named chief cost acct. for Paramount in U.K.; 1967, promoted to prod. exec. Worked on Downhill Racer, Running Scared, etc. Produced The Last of Sheila in 1972; 1974–75 was in Prague working on Operation Daybreak. Produced The Seven-Per-Cent Solution. Formed own Martinat Co. and produced The Squeeze, The Boys from Brazil, Nijinsky, Sphinx, Outland, Enemy Mine, Lionheart, The Last Emperor.

OTWELL, RONNIE RAY: Theatre Executive. b. Carrollton, GA, Aug. 13, 1929. e. Georgia Inst. of Technology. Entered industry as mgr., Bremen Theatre (GA), 1950; dir. pub., adv., Martin Theatres, Columbus (GA), 1950–63; v.p., dir. Martin Theatres of Ga., Inc., 1963, Martin Theatres of Ala., Inc., 1963; dir. Martin Theatres of Columbus, 1963; sr. v.p., Martin Theatres Companies, 1971. Member: NATO, GA, NATO, Columbus C of C; Columbus Mus. Arts & Crafts; Assn. U.S. Army.

OWEN, ALUN: Writer. b. Liverpool, Eng., 1925.
STAGE: A Little Winter Love, Maggie May, Progress to the Park, The Rough and Ready Lot, There'll Be Some Changes Made, Norma (Mixed Doubles), Shelter, Fashion of Your Time, The Ladies, Lucia.
TELEVISION: The Ruffian, No Trams to Lime Street, After the Funeral, Lena O' My Lena (for ITV's Armchair Theatre); The Rose Affair (two awards, 1961), Ways of Love, You Can't Win 'Em All, A Hard Knock, Dare to be a Daniel, The Stag, The Strain, A Local Boy, Ruth, Funny, Pal, Giants and Ogres, The Piano Player, The Web Flight, Buttons, Lucky, Left. Ronnie Barker and Forget-me-not series, Lady of the Lake, The Look, Passing Through, The Runner, Sea Link, Kisch-Kisch, Colleagues, Francis.
PICTURES INCLUDE: The Criminal, A Hard Day's Night, Minding the Shop, Park People, You'll Be the Death of Me, McNeil, Cornelius, Emlyn.

OWEN, BILL: Actor. r.n. Bill Rowbotham. b. Acton, Eng., Mar. 14, 1915. Screen debut in Way to the Stars (1945). Numerous TV appearances.
PICTURES INCLUDE: School for Secrets, Daybreak, Dancing With Crime, Easy Money, When the Bough Breaks, My Brother's Keeper, Martha, Parlor Trick, The Roundabout, Trottie True, Once a Jolly Swagman, A Day to Remember, You See What I Mean, Square Ring, Rainbow Jacket, Ship That Died of Shame, Not so Dusty, Davy, Carve Her Name with Pride, Carry on Sergeant, Carry on Nurse, Night Apart, Cabby!, Secret of Blood Island, Georgy Girl, Headline Hunters, O Lucky Man!, Kadoyng, In Celebration, When The Screaming Stopped, Comeback, Laughter House.
TELEVISION: Last of the Summer Wine (1974–78 series).

OWENSBY, EARL: Producer, Actor. b. North Carolina, 1935. Set up his own studio in Shelby, NC. Built new studio in Gaffney, SC, 1985.
PICTURES: Challenge, Dark Sunday, Buckstone County Prison, Frank Challenge—Manhunter, Death Driver, Wolfman, Seabo, Day of Judgment, Living Legend, Lady Grey, Rottweiler, Last Game, Hyperspace, Hit the Road Running, Rutherford County Line.

OXENBERG, CATHERINE: Actress. b. NY, NY, Sept. 21, 1961. Daughter of the exiled Princess Elizabeth of Yugoslavia, raised among intl. jet set with Richard Burton acting as her tutor. Modeled before making TV debut in The Royal Romance of Charles and Diana (1983).
PICTURES: The Lair of the White Worm, The Return of the Musketeers.
TELEVISION: Dynasty (series), Roman Holiday.

OZ, FRANK: Puppeteer, Director. b. Herford, Eng., May 25, 1944. r.n. Frank Oznowicz. Gained fame as various characters on Sesame Street and the Muppet Show (Fozzie Bear, Miss Piggy, Animal, The Swedish Chef) 1976–81, winning Emmy Awards 1974, 1976, 1978. Feature film directorial debut The Dark Crystal. Vice president Wenson Associates.
PICTURES: The Blues Brothers; The Empire Strikes Back; The Muppet Movie; The Great Muppet Caper (also prod.); American Werewolf in London; The Dark Crystal (also dir.); Return of the Jedi; The Muppets Take Manhattan (also dir. and s.p.); Little Shop of Horrors (dir.); Scoundrels (dir.).
TELEVISION: Sesame Street, The Muppet Show, Big Bird in China; various variety shows.

P

PAAR, JACK: Actor. b. Canton, OH, May 1, 1918. Radio announcer in Cleveland, Buffalo; served in U.S. Armed Forces,

W.W.II; entertained in Pacific zone with 28th Special Service Div. On radio with own show; m.p. debut in Variety Time, 1948. CBS-TV; Jack Paar Show, NBC-TV. First host of The Tonight Show, various specials, Jack Paar is Alive and Well (prod., 1987), He Kids You Not.
PICTURES INCLUDE: Walk Softly Stranger, Footlight Varieties, Love Nest, Down Among the Sheltering Palms.

PACINO, AL: Actor. b. New York, NY, Apr. 25, 1940. Gained attention as stage actor initially at Charles Playhouse, Boston (Why Is a Crooked Letter, The Peace Creeps).
STAGE: The Indian Wants the Bronx (Obie award), Does a Tiger Wear A Necktie? (Tony Award), The Local Stigmatic, Camino Real, The Connection, Hello Out There, Tiger at the Gates, The Basic Training of Pavlo Hummel (Tony Award), American Buffalo, Julius Caesar.
PICTURES INCLUDE: Panic in Needle Park (debut), The Godfather, Scarecrow, Serpico, The Godfather II, Dog Day Afternoon, Bobby Deerfield, And Justice for All, Cruising, Author! Author!, Scarface, Revolution, Sea of Love.

PAGE, ANTHONY: Director. b. Bangalore, India, Sept. 21, 1935. e. Oxford. Stage work includes Inadmissible Evidence, Waiting for Godot, A Patriot for Me, Look Back in Anger, Uncle Vanya, Cowardice, etc.
PICTURES: Inadmissible Evidence, Alpha Beta, I Never Promised You a Rose Garden, Absolution, The Lady Vanishes.
TELEVISION: Pueblo, The Missiles of October, The Parachute, FDR—The Last Year, The Patricia Neal Story, Bill, Johnny Belinda, Grace Kelly, Bill—On His Own, Forbidden, Monte Carlo, Pack of Lies.

PAGE, PATTI: Performer, recording artist. r.n. Clara Ann Fowler. b. Claremore, OK, 1927. e. U. of Tulsa. Staff performer, radio stat. KTUL, Tulsa; Top recording star of the 1950s and 60s (The Tennessee Waltz, How Much is That Doggie in the Window, etc.). Appeared on CBS radio show; star Patti Page Show, TV film series, The Big Record; author, Once Upon a Dream.
PICTURES INCLUDE: Elmer Gantry, Dondi, Boys Night Out.

PAGET, DEBRA: Actress. r.n. Debralee Griffin. b. Denver, CO, Aug. 19, 1933; e. drama & dancing privately. Stage debut in Marry Wives of Windsor, 1946; in Jeanne D'Arc little theatre prod.; m.p.; debut in Cry of the City, 1948.
PICTURES INCLUDE: House of Strangers, Broken Arrow, Fourteen Hours, Bird of Paradise, Anne of the Indies, Belles on Their Toes, Les Miserables, Stars & Stripes Forever, Prince Valiant, Demetrius & the Gladiators, Princess of the Nile, Gambler from Natchez, White Feather, Seven Angry Men, Last Hunt, Ten Commandments, Tales of Terror, The Haunted Palace.

PAGETT, NICOLA: Actress. b. Cairo, Egypt, June 15, 1945. r.n. Nicola Scott. e. Royal Acad. of Dramatic Art. Appeared with Citizen's Rep. Theatre, Glasgow.
THEATER: Cornelia (debut, 1964, Worthing, U.K.); A Boston Story (London debut, 1968); A Midsummer Night's Dream; Widowers' Houses; The Misanthrope; A Voyage 'Round My Father; The Ride Across Lake Constance; Ghosts; The Seagull; Hamlet; The Marriage of Figaro; A Family and a Fortune; Gaslight; Yahoo; Old Times (L.A.).
PICTURES: Anne of the Thousand Days (1969); There's a Girl in My Soup; Operation Daybreak; Oliver's Story; Privates on Parade.
TELEVISION: Series: Upstairs, Downstairs (Elizabeth Bellamy); Movies: Frankenstein: The True Story; The Sweeney; Aren't We All; A Woman of Substance (mini-series); Anna Karenina.

PAIGE, JANIS: Actress (Star of Tomorrow, 1947). r.n. Donna Mae Jaden. b. Tacoma, WA, Sept. 16, 1923. Sang with Tacoma Opera Co. m.p. debut, 1944, Hollywood Canteen, N.Y. stage in 1951, and TV in 1956.
STAGE: Pajama Game, Remains to Be Seen, Alone Together.
PICTURES INCLUDE: Of Human Bondage, Two Gals and a Guy, Fugitive Lady, The Time the Place and the Girl, Two Guys from Milwaukee, Her Kind of Man, Cheyenne, Love and Learn, Wallflower, Winter Meeting, One Sunday Afternoon, Romance on High Seas, House Across the Street, Younger Brothers, Mr. Universe, Remains to be Seen, Please Don't Eat the Daisies, The Caretakers, Welcome to Hard Times.
TELEVISION: It's Always Jan (series), Roberta (1958 and 1969), Columbo, Banacek, Flamingo Road, St. Elsewhere, Baby Makes Five (series), Lanigan's Rabbi (series).

PAINE, CHARLES F.: Executive. b. Cushing, TX, Dec. 23, 1920. e. Stephen F. Austin U. Pres. Tercar Theatre Company; pres., NATO of Texas, 1972–73. NATO board member, 1973 to present; Motion Picture Pioneers member; Variety Club of Texas member.

PAKULA, ALAN J.: Producer, Director. b. New York, NY, April 7, 1928. e. Yale U., B.A., 1948. Prod. apprentice, MGM, 1950;

prod. asst., Para. 1951; prod. Para., 1955. Own prod. co., Pakula-Mulligan Prod. Stage prod. and m.p. dir. prod. 1988 received Eastman Award for Continued Excellence in M.P.
STAGE: Comes a Day, Laurette, There Must Be a Pony.
PICTURES INCLUDE: Fear Strikes Out, To Kill a Mockingbird, Love with the Proper Stranger, Baby the Rain Must Fall, Inside Daisy Clover, Up the Down Staircase, The Stalking Moon, The Sterile Cuckoo, Klute (dir., co-prod.), Love and Pain and the Whole Damned Thing, The Parallax View, All the President's Men (dir.), Comes a Horseman, Starting Over (co.-prod., dir.). Roll-over (dir.); Sophie's Choice (s.p., dir., prod.); Dream Lover (co-prod.-dir.), Orphans (prod., dir.), See You in the Morning (s.p., prod., dir.).
AWARDS: N.Y. Film Critics for best director, All the President's Men (1976); London Film Critics for best director, Klute (1971).

PALANCE, JACK: Actor. b. Lattimer, PA, Feb. 18, 1920. e. U. of North Carolina. Professional fighter; U.S. Air Corps. Broadway stage. Film debut: Panic in the Streets (1950).
STAGE: The Big Two, Temporary Island, The Vigil, Streetcar Named Desire, Darkness at Head.
PICTURES INCLUDE: Halls of Montezuma, Shane, Sudden Fear, Flight to Tangier, Man in the Attic, Sign of the Pagan, Silver Chalice, Kiss of Fire, Big Knife, I Died a Thousand Times, Attack!, Lonely Man, House of Numbers, Ten Seconds to Hell, Warriors Five, Barabbas, Contempt, Torture Garden, Kill a Dragon, They Came to Rob Las Vegas, The Desperadoes, Che, The Mercenary, Justine, Legion of the Damned, A Bullet for Rommel, The McMasters, Monte Walsh, Companeros, The Horsemen, The Professionals, Oklahoma Crude, Craze, The Four Deuces, The Diamond Mercenaries, Hawk the Slayer, Gor, Bagdad Cafe, Young Guns.
TELEVISION: Requiem for a Heavyweight, Dr. Jekyll and Mr. Hyde, Dracula, Bronk (series), Ripley's Believe It or Not (series host).

PALEY, WILLIAM S.: Executive. b. Chicago, IL, Sept. 28, 1901. e. U. of Pennsylvania. Took over operation Columbia Broadcasting System (now CBS, Inc.) as pres. 1928; chairman of the board from January, 1946 to April 1983, when named founder-chm.; built network to leading position and est. innovations in broadcasting. During war on leave to supervise OWI radio in Mediterranean area. Chief of radio of Psychological Warfare Division, SHAEF, 1944–45; Dep. Chief Info. Control Div. of U.S.G.C.C. 1945; Colonel, A.U.S. Deputy Chief Psychological Warfare Division, SHAEF, 1945; pres. & dir., William S. Paley Foundation, Inc.; partner, Whitcom Investment Co.; co-chm., Intl. Herald Tribune; pres. & dir., Greenpark Foundation, Inc. Founder and Chairman of the Board of Trustees of the Museum of Broadcasting; trustee, emeritus, Columbia U.; trustee and chairman, emeritus, Museum of Modern Art. Trustee, North Shore University Hospital 1949–73, Co-Chairman of the Board, 1954–73. Decorations include the Legion of Merit, Medal for Merit. Legion of Honor, Croix de Guerre with Palm. Chairman of President's Materials Policy Comm., 1951–52, which issued report, Resources for Freedom.

PALIN, MICHAEL: Actor, Writer. b. Sheffield, Yorkshire, England, May 5, 1943. e. Oxford. Member of Monty Python's Flying Circus. On stage with troupe both in London and on Bdwy.
PICTURES: And Now for Something Completely Different, Monty Python and the Holy Grail, Jabberwocky, Life of Brian, Time Bandits, The Missionary (also co-prod., s.p.), Monty Python's The Meaning of Life (also music), A Private Function, Brazil, A Fish Called Wanda.
TELEVISION: Do Not Adjust Your Set, The Frost Report, Marty Feldman Comedy Machine, How To Irritate People, Pythons in Deutschland, Secrets, Ripping Yarns, etc.

PALMER, BETSY: Actress. b. East Chicago, IN, Nov. 1, 1926. e. DePaul U. Studied at Neighborhood Playhouse, HB Studio with Uta Hagen. On Broadway in The Grand Prize, Affair of Honor, Cactus Flower, Roar Like a Dove, Eccentricities of a Nightingale, Same Time Next Year and many regional prods.
PICTURES: The Long Gray Line, Queen Bee, The Other Life of Lynn Stuart, The Tin Star, The Last Angry Man, Mister Roberts, Friday the 13th, Friday the 13th, Part II.
TELEVISION: All major live shows such as Studio One, U.S. Steel Hour, Kraft Theatre. Panelist, I've Got a Secret (11 years), No. 96 (series), Candid Camera (host), Wifeline (host), As the World Turns. Movies: Isabel's Choice, Windmills of the Gods.

PALMER, GREGG: Actor. r.n. Palmer Lee. b. San Francisco, CA, Jan. 25, 1927; e. U. of Utah. U.S. Air Force, 1945–46; radio announcer, disc jockey; then to Hollywood; many TV appearances.
PICTURES INCLUDE: Cimarron Kid, Battle at Apache Pass, Son of Ali Baba, Red Ball Express, Francis Goes to West Point, Sally and St. Anne, The Raiders, Back at the Front, Redhead From Wyoming, Column South, Veils of Bagdad, Golden Blade, The All American, Taza Son of Cochise, Magnificent Obsession, Playgirl, To Hell and Back,

Creature Walks Among Us, Hilda Crane, Zombies of Mora Tau, Revolt of Fort Laramie, Rebel Set, Thundering Jets, Forty Pounds of Trouble, Night Hunt, The Undefeated, Chisum, Rio Lobo, Big Jake, Providenza (Italy), Ci Risiamo Vero Providenza (Italy, Spain). The Shootist, The Man with Bogart's Face.

TELEVISION: Movies: Go West Young Girl, Hostage Heart, True Grit, Beggarman, Thief; The Blue and the Gray (miniseries).

PALMER, PATRICK: Producer. b. Los Angeles, CA, Dec. 28. Began career with 10-year apprenticeship at Mirisch Company, involved in making of West Side Story, Seven Days in May, The Fortune Cookie, etc. 1966, associated with Norman Jewison, serving as assoc. prod. on The Landlord, Fiddler on the Roof, Jesus Christ Superstar, Rollerball, etc. 1972, prod. with Jewison Billy Two Hats; exec. prod. on The Dogs of War.

PICTURES: Co-prod.: Best Friends, Iceman, A Soldier's Story, Agnes of God, Children of a Lesser God, Moonstruck.

PALTROW, BRUCE: Director, Producer, Writer. b. New York, NY, Nov. 26, 1943. e. Tulane U., B.F.A. m. actress Blythe Danner. Produced stage plays.

PICTURE: A Little Sex (co-prod., dir.).

TELEVISION: Shirts and Skins; You're Gonna Love It Here; Big City Boys; The White Shadow (creat. dir.); St. Elsewhere (exec. prod.-dir.), Tattinger's (co-exec. prod.).

PAM, JERRY: Publicist. b. London, England, Oct. 17, 1926. e. Cambridge, London U. Reporter, Paris, London; freelance writing, Australia; 1950–53. To U.S. in 1953, on Hollywood Reporter, drama ed. Beverly Hills Citizen, 1953–54; publicist, Moulin Rouge, MGM studios; drama ed., Valley Times 1959–61; partner, Pam and Joseph pub. rel. counsellors; est. Jerry Pam & Associates, pub. rel., April 1965; formed Guttman & Pam, Ltd., 1971. Exec. prod., Highpoint, 1979. Prod., On the Film Scene (weekly series on Z Channel).

PAMPANINI, SILVANA: Actress. b. Rome, Italy, Sept. 25, 1925. e. Academy of St. Cecilia. Studied singing, several concert appearances. Elected Miss Italia of 1946–47; m.p. debut in Secret of Don Giovanni.

PICTURES INCLUDE: Second Ark, Twin Trouble, O.K. Nero, City Stands Trial, A Husband for Anna, Songs of Half a Century, Songs Songs Songs, Matrimony, Enchanting Enemy, A Day in District Court, Loves of Half a Century, Slave of Sin, Orient Express, Merry Squadron, Princess of the Canary Islands, Mademoiselle Gobette, Don Juan's Night of Love, Roman Tales.

PAN, HERMES: Dance director. b. 1905. In 1935, handled Roberta, RKO stage ensembles. In 1938 won Academy Awards for dance direction Damsel in Distress.

PICTURES INCLUDE: Top Hat, Old Man Rhythm, In Person, I Dream Too Much, Follow the Fleet, Swing Time, Shall We Dance, Radio City Revels, Let's Dance, Three Little Words, Excuse My Dust, Texas Carnival, Lovely to Look At, Sombrero, Kiss Me Kate, Student Prince, Hit the Deck, Jupiter's Darling, Meet Me in Las Vegas, Porgy and Bess, Can-Can, Flower Drum Song, Cleopatra, My Fair Lady, Finian's Rainbow, Darling Lili, The Lost Horizon.

TELEVISION: An Evening with Fred Astaire (Emmy Award, choreography), Astaire Time, Sounds of America, Star-times Academy Awards of Songs, Remember How Great, Frances Langford Show.

PANAMA, CHARLES A. (CHUCK): Publicist. b. Chicago, IL, Feb. 2, 1925. e. Northwestern U., Beloit Coll., U. of California at L.A. Publicist, Los Angeles Jr. Chamber of Commerce; So. Calif. sports ed., Los Angeles bureau, INS; publicist, 20th Century-Fox Studios; adv.-pub. dir., Arcola Pics.; opened L.A. office, John Springer Associates; v.p. Jerry Pam & Assoc.; Account exec., Rogers, Cowan & Brenner, Inc.; dir. m.p. div., Jim Mahoney & Assoc.; v.p. Guttman & Pam, Ltd.; asst. pub. dir., 20th-Fox TV.

PANAMA, NORMAN: Writer, Producer, Director. b. Chicago, IL, April 21, 1914. Screen career: wrote, co-prod. & dir., with Melvin Frank, Li'l Abner, Facts of Life, The Road to Hong Kong, Mr. Blandings Builds His Dream House.

PICTURES INCLUDE: My Favorite Blonde, Happy Go Lucky, Star-Spangled Rhythm, Thank Your Lucky Stars, And the Angels Sing, Road to Utopia, Duffy's Tavern, Our Hearts Were Growing Up, Monsieur Beaucaire, It Had to Be You, Return of October, The Reformer and the Redhead, Strictly Dishonorable, Callaway Went Thataway, Above and Beyond, Knock on Wood, White Christmas, Court Jester, Not With My Wife You Don't, How to Commit Marriage, Coffee, Tea, or Me. Wrote and directed: I Will, I Will...For Now. Directed, Barnaby and Me; Wrote Fade In—Fade Out, The Stewardesses, Li'l Abner, for NBC-TV. Wrote: Co-authored The Glass Bed (novel), and two plays: A Talent for Murder & The Bats of Portobello. 1983: Mrs. Katz and Katz (TV pilot); 1984: Judgment Day (s.p.). 1985: 3 s.p.'s: Cheek to Cheek, The Marathon, Too Much Johnson. 1986: Checkmate!, Donovan.

PANTAGES, CLAYTON G.: Executive. b. Hartford, CT, March 6, 1927. e. Trinity Coll. Served various executive posts for 11 years with 20th Century-Fox; gen. sales mgr. Magna Pictures; Pres., International Coproductions, Inc., S.P. Films, Pantheon Entertainment Ltd., Clayton's Classics.

PAPAS, IRENE: Actress. b. near Corinth, Greece, 1926. Entered dramatic school at 12. At 16 sang and danced in variety shows. Film debut in 1951 Greek film, Lost Angels; 1958 Greek Popular theatre in Athens.

STAGE: The Idiot, Journey's End, The Merchant of Venice, Inherit the Wind, That Summer, That Fall, Iphigenia in Aulis.

PICTURES INCLUDE: Dead City, The Unfaithful, Attila the Hun, Theodora, Whirlpool, Tribute to a Bad Man, The Guns of Navarone, Antigone (Best Actress Award, Salonika Film Festival), Electra (Best Actress Award, Salonika Film Festival), Zorba the Greek, The Brotherhood, Anne of a Thousand Days, Z, A Dream of Kings, A Ciascuno il Suo, The Odyssey, The Trojan Women, Moses, Mohammed: Messenger of God, Lion of the Desert, Into the Night, The Assisi Underground, Sweet Country, High Season.

TELEVISION: Moses the Lawgiver.

PARE, MICHAEL: Actor. b. Brooklyn, NY, 1959. Debut as singer-actor in Eddie and the Cruisers (1983).

PICTURES: The Philadelphia Experiment, Under Cover (Aust.), Streets of Fire, The Women's Club, World Gone Wild.

TELEVISION: Series: The Greatest American Hero (1981–83), Houston Knights. Movies: Crazy Times.

PARISH, JAMES ROBERT: Film historian/marketing exec. b. Cambridge, MA e. U. of PA (BBA, Phi Beta Kappa); U. of PA Law School (LLB). Member of NY Bar. Founder Entertainment Copyright Research Co., Inc. 1968–69, film reporter, Motion Picture Daily, weekly Variety. 1969–70, entertainment publicist, Harold Rand & co (NY). Currently marketing consultant in direct marketing industry, contributor to arts sections of major national newspapers and entertainment trade papers, series editor of show business books and author of over 70 books on the entertainment industry including: The Great Combat Pictures; Black Action Pictures From Hollywood; The Great Detective Pictures; The Great Western Pictures II: The Great Gangster Pictures II: The Great Spy Pictures II; Actors TV Credits; The Best of MGM; The Forties Gals; The Great American Movies Book; Hollywood Happiness; The Funsters; Hollywood on Hollywood; The Hollywood Beauties; Elvis!; The Great Science Fiction Pictures; The Child Stars; The Jeannette MacDonald Story; Great Movie Heroes; Liza!; The RKO Gals; Vincent Price Unmasked; The George Raft File; and The Emmy Awards.

PARK, ROBERT H.: Executive. b. Atlanta, GA, May 11, 1916. e. U. of Texas. Attorney for Jefferson Amusement Co.; now bd. chm., Tercar Theatre Company.

PARKER, ALAN: Director, Writer. b. Islington, London, England, Feb. 14, 1944. Worked way up in advertising industry from mail room to top writer and director of TV commercials.

PICTURES: Melody (s.p., 1968); No Hard Feelings (dir., s.p.); Our Cissy (dir., s.p.); Footsteps (dir., s.p.); Bugsy Malone (dir., s.p.; 5 British Academy Awards, 1975); Midnight Express (2 Acad. Awards); Fame (2 Acad. Awards), Shoot the Moon, Pink Floyd—The Wall, Birdy, Angel Heart, Mississippi Burning.

TELEVISION: The Evacuees.

PARKER, ELEANOR: Actress. b. Cedarville, OH, June 26, 1922. In Cleveland play group; in summer stock Martha's Vineyard; at Pasadena Community Playhouse.

PICTURES INCLUDE: They Died With Their Boots On, Buses Roar, Mission to Moscow, Between Two Worlds, Very Thought of You, Crime By Night, Last Ride, Never Say Goodbye, Pride of the Marines, Of Human Bondage, Escape Me Never, Woman in White, Voice of the Turtle, Chain Lightning, Caged, Three Secrets, Valentino, Millionaire for Christy, Detective Story, Scaramouche, Above and Beyond, Escape from Fort Bravo, Naked Jungle, Valley of the Kings, Many Rivers to Cross, Interrupted Melody, Man with the Golden Arm, King and Four Queens, Lizzie, Seventh Sin, Home from the Hill, Return to Peyton Place, Madison Avenue, The Oscar, An American Dream, Warning Shot, The Eye of the Cat, The Sound of Music, Sunburn.

TELEVISION: Bracken's World, Vanished, Guess Who's Coming to Dinner (pilot), Murder She Wrote, Fantasy Island.

PARKER, FESS: Actor. b. Fort Worth, TX, Aug. 16, 1925. e. U. of Southern California. U.S. Navy, 1943–46; national co., Mr. Roberts, 1951; m.p. debut, Untamed Frontier, 1952.

PICTURES INCLUDE: No Room for the Groom, Springfield Rifle, Thunder Over the Plains, Island in the Sky, Kid from Left Field, Take Me to Town, Them, Battle Cry, Davy Crockett, King of the Wild Frontier, Davy Crockett and the River Pirates, Great Locomotive Chase, Westward Ho the Wagons, Old Yeller, The Light in the Forest, The Hangman, The Jayhawkers, Hell Is for Heroes, Smoky.

TELEVISION: Davy Crockett (series), Mr. Smith Goes to

Par-Pas

Washington (series), Daniel Boone (series), Jonathan Winters, Walt Disney presents, Ed Sullivan, Phyllis Diller, Joey Bishop, Dean Martin, Red Skelton, Glen Campbell.

PARKER, JAMESON: Actor. b. Baltimore, MD, Nov. 18, 1947. e. Beloit Coll. Professional stage debut in Washington Theatre Club production, Caligula. Acted with Arena Stage in DC; worked in dinner theatres and summer stock. Moved to N.Y., working in TV commercials and touring in play, Equus. Feature film debut in The Bell Jar (1979).
PICTURES: A Small Circle of Friends, White Dog, American Justice, Prince of Darkness, Crystal Eye.
TELEVISION: Series: Somerset, One Life to Live, Simon and Simon. Movies: Women at West Point, Anatomy of a Seduction, A Caribbean Mystery, Who Is Julia?

PARKER, SUZY: Actress. r.n. Cecelia Parker. b. San Antonio, TX, Oct. 28, 1933. m. actor Bradford Dillman. e. schools in NY, FL. Began career at 17 as fashion model; became known as highest paid fashion model and cover girl in U.S.; went to Paris under contract to fashion magazine; film debut as model in Funny Face (1957); signed by 20th-Fox prod. chief Buddy Adler for part opposite Cary Grant in Kiss Them for Me.
PICTURES INCLUDE: Ten North Frederick, The Best of Everything, Circle of Deception, The Interns.

PARKINS, BARBARA: Actress. b. Vancouver, Canada, May 22, 1943.
PICTURES: Valley of the Dolls, The Kremlin Letter, Puppet on a Chain, The Mephisto Waltz, Bear Island.
TELEVISION: Peyton Place (series). Movies: A Taste of Evil, Snatched, Law of the Land, Captains and the Kings, Young Joe, the Forgotten Kennedy, Testimony of Two Men, Ziegfield: The Man and His Women, The Critical List, To Catch a King, Calendar Girl Murders, Peyton Place: The Next Generation, The Manions of America, Jennie: Lady Randolph Churchill.

PARKS, BERT: Announcer, M.C. b. Atlanta, GA, Dec. 30, 1914. Announcer, then chief announcer in Atlanta radio station; announcer, network, N.Y., for Eddie Cantor; m.c. for Xavier Cugat's show; U.S. Army, W.W.II; radio shows include Break the Bank, Stop the Music, Double or Nothing. Announcer Miss America Pageant, 1956–79.
TELEVISION: Break the Bank, Stop the Music.

PARKS, GORDON: Director, Writer, Photographer, Composer, Poet, Photojournalist. b. Fort Scott, KS, Nov. 30, 1912. From the age of 15 worked as piano player, bus boy, dining car waiter and prof. basketball player in MN before taking up photog. in late 1930s. Awarded 1st Julius Rosenwald Fellowship in photog. 1942. Worked with Roy Stryker at Farm Security Admin., WWII Office of War Info. correspondent. Photo-journalist, Life Mag., 1949–68, editorial dir.: Essence Magazine 1970–73 (and founder). Film debut 1961 with doc. Flavio (dir. and writer), followed by Diary of a Harlem Family (doc.) (Emmy Award). Winner of numerous awards including NAACP's Spingarn Medal and Governor's Medal of Honor. Recipient of 19 honorary degrees in lit., fine arts, humane letters.
AUTHOR: The Learning Tree; A Choice of Weapons; A Poet and His Camera; Whispers of Intimate Things; In Love; Born Black, Moments Without Proper Names, Flavio, To Smile in Autumn, Shannon.
PICTURES INCLUDE: The Learning Tree, Shaft, Shaft's Big Score, Super Cops, Leadbelly.
TELEVISION: The Odyssey of Solomon Northrup.

PARKS, MICHAEL: Actor. b. 1938. Made m.p. debut in Wild Seed, 1964.
PICTURES INCLUDE: Bus Riley's Back in Town, The Bible, The Idol, The Happening, The Last Hard Men, Sidewinder One. ffolkes, Hard Country, Savannah Smiles, King of the City, The Return of Josey Wales, Spiker, Arizona Heat, Welcome to Spring Break, Prime Suspect.
TELEVISION: Along Came Bronson (series), numerous TV movies: Can Ellen Be Saved?, Savage Bees, Chase, Dangerous Affection.

PARRISH, ROBERT R.: Director, Producer. b. Columbus, GA, Jan. 4, 1916. Actor before joining RKO in 1933, first as assistant director, then film editor. With various companies since, including 20th Century-Fox, Universal, Columbia, United Artists, J. Arthur Rank, etc. Won Academy Award, best film editing, Body and Soul, 1947. U.S. Navy 1941–45; won documentary Academy Award, 1942 and 1943 for Battle of Midway and December 7th. Formed own independent production company, Trimark Productions, Inc., 1955. Autobiography: Growing Up in Hollywood, 1976.
PICTURES INCLUDE: City Lights, All Quiet on the Western Front, The Divine Lady, A Double Life, Caught, No Minor Vices, All the King's Men, Cry Danger (dir.), The Mob, San Francisco Story, Assignment–Paris, My Pal Gus, Shoot First, The Purple Plain, Lucy Gallant, Fire Down Below, Saddle the Wind, The Wonderful Country, In the French Style, Up From

the Beach, Casino Royale, The Bobo, Duffy, A Town Called Bastard, The Marseilles Contract, Flashman, Mississippi Blues (doc., co-dir. with Bertrand Tavernier).

PARSONS, ESTELLE: Actress. b. Marblehead, MA, Jan. 20, 1927. e. Connecticut Coll. for Women, Bachelor's degree in political science. Attended Boston U. Law Sch. Helped harvest crops in England with the Women's Land Army. Was active in politics; worked for the Committee for the Nation's Health in Wash. and the Republican Finance Committee in Boston. Was elected to public office in Marblehead, Mass. Joined NBC-TV's Today Show as prod. asst.; then writer, feature producer and commentator. Appeared in two Julius Monk revues, Jerry Herman's Nightcap and the Threepenny Opera. Has appeared with the Lincoln Center Repertory Theatre, Mahagonny.
STAGE: Happy Hunting; Whoop Up; Beg, Borrow or Steal; Mrs. Dally Has a Lover (Theater World Award), Next Time I'll Sing to You (Obie Award), In the Summer House (Obie Award), Ready When You Are, C.B. Malcolm, The Seven Descents of Myrtle, And Miss Reardon Drinks a Little, The Norman Conquests, Ladies of the Alamo, Miss Margarida's Way, Pirates of Penzance.
PICTURES INCLUDE: Ladybug, Ladybug, Bonnie and Clyde (Acad. Award, supporting actress, 1967), Rachel, Rachel, Don't Drink the Water, Strangers, Watermelon Man, I Never Sang For My Father, I Walk the Line, Two People, For Pete's Sake.
TELEVISION: Backstairs at the White House, The Front Page, All in the Family, The Gun and the Pulpit.

PARSONS, LINDSLEY: Executive Vice Pres., Film Finances, Inc. Pres., Completion Service Co., Hollywood. Toronto. b. Tacoma, WA, Sept. 12, 1915. e. U. of California at L.A. On ed. staff City News Service, L.A.: Alhambra Post-Advocate; Calexico Chronicle; Santa Rosa Press Democrat; Humboldt Times; San Marino News (ed. & pub.). Joined Monogram 1931 as pub. dir. in 1933 author s.p. Sagebrush Trails; then wrote orig. s.p. Westerns for Monogram, Republic, Grand Nat'l. In 1939 assoc. prod. Tough Kid; from 1940 prod. numerous westerns; prod. Wayne Morris & James Oliver Curwood series for Allied Artists; prod. Motion Pictures Int'l, 1956–72. Exec. v.p., dir., Film Finances, Inc.
PICTURES INCLUDE: Rocky Rhythm Inn, Casa Manana, Big Timber, Call of the Klondike, Sierra Passage, Yukon, Manhunt, Yellow Fin, Northwest Territory, Desert Pursuit, Torpedo Alley, Jack Slade, Loophole, Cry Vengeance, Finger Man, Return of Jack Slade, Come On, The Intruder, Cruel Tower, Dragon Wells Massacre, Portland Expose, Oregon Passage, Wolf Larsen, Crash Boat, The Purple Gang, Mara of the Wilderness, Good Times, The Big Cube.
TELEVISION: Gray Ghost (series); Files of Jeffrey Jones, The Whistler.

PARTON, DOLLY: Singer, Composer, Actress. b. Sevierville, TN, Jan. 19, 1946. Gained fame as country music singer, composer and radio and TV personality. Many awards for recordings.
PICTURES: Nine to Five, The Best Little Whorehouse in Texas, Rhinestone (also music), Steel Magnolias.
TELEVISION: Porter Wagoner Show, Cass Walker program, Bill Anderson Show, Wilbur Bros. Show. Movies: A Smoky Mountain Christmas. 1987: Dolly (series); A Tennessee Mountain Thanksgiving.

PARTRIDGE, DEREK: TV talk and magazine show host, Interviewer, Newscaster, Presenter, Narrator, Writer. b. London, England, 1935. Ent. journalism on the Daily Express. Ent. industry 1959 as documentary scriptwriter with Film Producers' Guild. 1976–78: Rhodesian TV: Chief news anchor, live magazine programme Frankly Partridge, quizmaster The Kwhizz Kids. 1979 (Miami): newscaster, daily What's Happening South Florida, and Focus (WKAT/ABC). 1980 (New York): To the Point, and Special Edition. 1981–82: TV (Los Angeles): Newscaster/writer/interviewer for Financial News Network. 1982: The Romance of Words. 1981–83: The Guinness Book of Records Specials (announcer). 1983: Video Aktuell (Hollywood celebrities for German TV). 1983–88: Financial Inquiry (anchor/interviewer). 1984: Election Coverage '84. 1985: The Story of a News Story (Emmy winner), Travel Time. 1986: Information Power (Emmy winner). 1986–88: Music programmes host (Gulf Air, Saudia, Royal Jordanian). Interviewer: TV's Bloopers & Practical Jokes. 1987: Health Line '87; American Life Styles; Star du Siècle (French TV); Sexuality—Today's Decisions. 1988: Law in America; World Access TV; Over 50. Corporate videos for: Bank of America, Transamerica, Hilton Hotels, Coca Cola, Mercedes Benz, Armand Hammer, Getty Oil, American Red Cross, Lincoln Mercury.

PASETTA, MARTY: Producer-Director. b. June 16, 1932. e. U. Santa Clara.
TELEVISION: A Gift of Song; Salute to Israel; Gene Kelly Special; Elvis in Hawaii; Oscar, Emmy and Grammy Award Shows; A Country Christmas (1979); Debbie Boone—The Same Old Brand New Me; The Monte Carlo Show (exec.

236

prod.); A Country Christmas, 1980; AFI Salute to Fred Astaire (dir.); Texaco Star Theatre—Opening Night; AFI Salute to John Huston (dir.); I Love TV Test (exec. prod., dir.); A Concert of the World (dir.); Live—and in Person; John Schneider's Christmas Holiday; Burnett Discovers Domingo; 56th Oscar Show; AFI Salute to Lillian Gish; Disneyland's 30th Anniversary Celebration.

PASSER, IVAN: Director, Writer. b. Prague, Czechoslovakia, July 10, 1933. e. Film Faculty of Acad. of Musical Arts, Prague. 1961, asst. dir. to Milos Forman on Audition which led to scripting for Forman. 1969, moved to U.S., worked in NY as longshoreman while studying Eng. U.S. dir. debut: Born to Win, 1971.
PICTURES INCLUDE: Writer: Loves of a Blonde, Fireman's Ball. Director: A Boring Afternoon (1965), Intimate Lighting, Born to Win, Law and Disorder, Crime and Passion, The Silver Bears, Cutter and Bone, Creator, Haunted Summer.
TELEVISION: (U.S.) Faerie Tale Theatre.

PASTER, GARY M.: Executive. b. St. Louis, MO, July 4, 1943. e. U. of Missouri, B.A.; U. of California at L.A., U. of Southern California Graduate Sch. of Business. 1970, joined The Burbank Studios as asst. to the pres. and as treas. 1976 v.p.—administration and chairman of the exec. committee. September, 1977 pres. Board of Directors/Trustees: Permanent Charities Committee of Entertainment Industry, St. Joseph Medical Center Foundation. American Women in Radio & TV, William H. Parker L.A. Police Foundation. Member: Academy of Motion Picture Arts and Sciences, Los Angeles Film Development Council, Hollywood Radio and T.V. Society, Academy of Television Arts and Sciences. Advisory bd., Kaufman Astoria Studios, N.Y.

PASTERNAK, JOE: Producer. b. Szilagysomlyo, Hungary, Sept. 19, 1901. 2nd asst. dir. Paramount 1923; asst. dir. Universal (Hollywood), 1926, then prod. mgr. Berlin; made pictures in Vienna and Budapest, returned to Hollywood 1937; assoc. prod. then prod. A Champion of Champion producers in Fame ratings. Autobiography: Easy the Hard Way, 1956.
PICTURES INCLUDE: Zwei Menschen, Unter Falscher Flagge, Grosse Schensucht, Unsichtbare Front, Fraulein Paprika, Gruss Und Gruss, Veronika, Scandal in Budapest, Csibi, Spring Parade, Katherine, Three Smart Girls, 100 Men and a Girl, Mad About Music, That Certain Age, Three Smart Girls Grow Up, Destry Rides Again, It's a Date, Nice Girl, It Started With Eve, Presenting Lily Mars, Thousands Cheer, Two Girls and a Sailor, Music for Millions, Thrill of a Romance, Anchors Aweigh, Her Highness and the Bellboy, Two Sisters from Boston, Holiday in Mexico, No Leave No Love, This Time for Keeps, Three Daring Daughters, On an Island With You, Date With Judy, In the Good Old Summertime, Big City, Unfinished Dance, Nancy Goes to Rio, Summer Stock, That Midnight Kiss, Toast of New Orleans, The Great Caruso, Rich, Young and Pretty, The Strip, Merry Widow, Skirts Ahoy!, Because You're Mine, Small Town Girl, Latin Lovers, Easy to Love, Flame and the Flesh, Student Prince, Athena, Hit the Deck, Love Me or Leave Me, Meet Me in Las Vegas, Opposite Sex, 10,000 Bedrooms, This Could Be the Night, Where the Boys Are, Jumbo, A Ticklish Affair, Girl Happy, Penelope, The Sweet Ride.

PATERSON, NEIL: Novelist, Screenwriter. b. Scotland, Dec. 15, 1916. e. Edinburgh U. War Service Lt. R.N.V.R. Early career as novelist. Awarded Atlantic Award in Literature, 1946. Dir. Grampian TV 1960–86. Member Chmn. of Production; dir., consultant: films of Scotland 1954–78. Gov., British Film Institute 1958–60. Gov., National Film School 1970–80. Gov., Pitlochry Fest. Theatre, 1966–76. Chm., Literature Comm. Scottish Arts Council 1967–76. Member Arts Council Gt. Britain 1974–76.
NOVELS: The China Run, Behold Thy Daughter, And Delilah, Man on the Tight Rope.
PICTURES INCLUDE: Man on a Tight Rope, The Little Kidnappers, Woman for Joe, High Tide at Noon, The Shiralee, Innocent Sinners, Room at the Top (s.p. Acad. Award, 1960), The Spiral Road, The Golden Fool, The Forty Days of Musa Dagh, Keeper of My Heart.

PATINKIN, MANDY: Actor. b. Chicago, IL, Nov. 20, 1947. e. U. of Kansas, Juilliard Sch. (Drama Div.) (1972–74). In regional theatre before coming to New York where played with Shakespeare Festival, Public Theater (Trelawny of the Wells, Hamlet, Rebel Women).
THEATER: Savages, Shadow Box (Bdwy debut), Evita (Tony Award), Henry IV, Part I (Central Park), Sunday in the Park With George (Tony Award), The Knifte, Follies in Concert.
PICTURES: The Big Fix, French Postcards, The Last Embrace, Night of the Juggler, Ragtime, Daniel, Yentl, Maxie, The Princess Bride, The House on Carroll Street, Alien Nation.
TELEVISION: That Thing on ABC, That 2nd Thing on ABC, Charleston (movie), Taxi, Sparrow, Streets of Gold, Midnight Special.

PATRICK, C.L.: Theatre Executive. b. Honaker, VA., Dec. 6, 1918. Former pres. of Fuqua Industries which owned Martin Theatres and Gulf States Theatres. Prior to this was pres. and chairman of Martin Theatres. Presently chairman of board Carmike Cinemas, Inc. Member NATO exec. com.; v.p. Variety International; director, Will Rogers Institute; Motion Picture Pioneer of 1976; Recipient of the Sherrill Corwin Award, 1984.

PATRICK, MICHAEL W.: Executive. b. Columbus, GA, May 17, 1950. e. Columbus Coll, B.S., 1972. Pres., Carmike Cinemas.
MEMBER: v.p., NATO; pres., Ga. Theatre Owners Assn.; exec. comm., Will Rogers Institute; Variety Intl.; Motion Picture Pioneers.

PATTON, WILL: Actor. b. Charleston, SC. e. NC School of the Arts, 1975.
THEATER: Tourists and Refugees #2 (La Mama E.T.C., Obie Award, Best Actor), Fool For Love (1982 Obie Award, Best Actor), Goose and Tomtom (Public Theatre), A Lie of the Mind.
PICTURES: Silkwood, After Hours, Desperately Seeking Susan, A Gathering of Old Men, Belizaire (the Cajun), No Way Out, Stars and Bars, Wildfire, The Lizard's Tale.
TELEVISION: Kent State, Ryan's Hope, Search For Tomorrow.

PAUL, M. B.: Cameraman, Director. r.n. Morrison Bloomfield Paul. b. Montreal, Canada. Sept. 30, 1909. e. De Paul U. Newsreel, publicity picture service; partner, Seymour Studios, 1930–33; film test biz. own studio. Hollywood, 1933–35; prod. adv. films, asst. in N.Y. E.W. Hammons, 1945–47; Acad. Award, one-piece color translucent background system, 1950. Dir. of photography, optical effects, Daystar, United Artists, Outer Limits, 1963; designed, patented, Scenoramic process, 1965. Camera, Paradise Road. Features, Film project supervision A/V consult. Sceno 360 surround system development. Mem. AMPAS, Friars, SMPTE.

PAUL, STEVEN: Director, Actor. b. New York, NY, May 16, 1958.
THEATER: Actor: Happy Birthday Wanda June, Burning.
PICTURES: Melissa; Falling in Love Again (prod., dir., s.p., actor); Slapstick; Emanon (exec. prod., actor).
TELEVISION: Actor: A Visiting Angel, Whatever Happened to Dobie Gillis?

PAULEY, JANE: TV host and journalist. b. Indianapolis, IN, Oct. 31, 1950. m. Doonesbury creator Garry Trudeau. e. Indiana U. Involved in Indiana state politics before joining WISH-TV, Indianapolis, as reporter. Co-anchored midday news reports and anchored weekend news reports. Co-anchor of nightly news at WMAQ-TV, NBC station in Chicago. Joined Today show in October, 1976, as featured regular, prior to which had made guest appearances on that program. Now co-host Today Show.

PAVAN, MARISA: Actress, r.n. Marisa Pierangeli. b. Cagliari, Sardinia, Italy, June 19, 1932. m. actor Jean Pierre Aumont. e. Torquato Tasso Coll. Twin sister of late Pier Angeli, actress. Came to U.S. 1950; m.p. debut in What Price Glory (1952).
PICTURES INCLUDE: Down Three Dark Streets, Drum Beat, Rose Tattoo, Diane, Man in the Gray Flannel Suit, John Paul Jones, Solomon and Sheba, Midnight Story.

PAVLIK, JOHN M.: Executive. b. Melrose, IA, Dec. 3, 1939. e. U. of Minnesota, B.A., 1963. Reporter, Racine (WI) Journal-Times, San Bernardino (CA) Sun-Telegram, 1963–66; Writer, News Bureau, Pacific Telephone, Los Angeles, 1966–68; asst. dir. of public relations, Association of Motion Picture and Television Producers, 1968–72; dir. of public relations, 1972–78; v.p., 1978–79; exec. administrator, Academy of Motion Picture Arts and Sciences, 1979–82; exec. dir., M.P. & TV Fund, 1982–88; member, board of dir., Permanent Charities Comm. of the Entertainment Industries, 1979–84; member, bd. of dir., Hollywood Chamber of Commerce, 1979–85; v.p., Los Angeles Film Dev. Committee, 1977– 78, member, exec. council, 1974–85; special consultant, California Motion Picture Council, 1974–79.

PAVLOW, MURIEL: Actress. b. June 27, 1924. e. England, France, Switzerland. Stage debut in Dear Octopus, 1938; screen debut in Quiet Wedding (1941).
PICTURES INCLUDE: Night Boat to Dublin, Shop at Sly Corner, It Started in Paradise, The Net (Project M7), Malta Story, Conflict of Wings (Fuss Over Feathers), Doctor in the House, Simon and Laura, Reach for the Sky, Eye Witness, Tiger in the Smoke, Doctor at Large, Rooney, Whirlpool, Meet Miss Marple.

PAY, WILLIAM: UK Manager Quigley Publishing Co., Inc. b. London, England. Joined London office Quigley Publications. Served in RAF, 1941–46; rejoined Quigley; dir. Burnup Service Ltd., 1951; London news ed., Quigley Pub., 1955. Dir., Quigley Pub. Ltd., 1961; appt. mgr. dir., 1963; mgr. dir., Burnup Company. Appt. Sec. British Kinematograph Sound & TV Society. Conference Co-ordinator biennial Intern. Film & TV Technology Conferences in U.K., 1975–87.

PAYNE, JOHN: Actor. b. Roanoke, VA, 1912. e. Mercersburg Acad., PA; Roanoke Coll. of Virginia; Columbia. On radio programs. Stage debut, 1973, Good News.
PICTURES INCLUDE: Dodsworth, Wings of the Navy, Indianapolis Speedway, Kid Nightingale, Stardust, Maryland, Great Profile, Tin Pan Alley, King of the Lumberjacks, Tear Gas Squad, Great American Broadcast, Sun Valley Serenade, Week-End in Havana, Remember the Day, To the Shores of Tripoli, Hello Frisco Hello, The Dolly Sisters, Sentimental Journey, Razor's Edge, Wake Up and Dream, Miracle on 34th Street, Larceny, Saxon Charm, El Paso, Crooked Way, Captain China, Eagle and Hawk, Passage West, Crosswinds, Blazing Forest, Caribbean, The Vanquished, Kansas City, Confidential, Raiders of the 7 Seas, 99 River Street, Rails into Laramie, Silver Lode, Hell's Island, Santa Fe Passage, Road to Denver, Tennessee's Partner, Hell's Island, Slightly Scarlet, Rebel in Town, The Boss, Bail Out at 43,000, Hidden Fear, The Gift of the Nile.
TELEVISION: The Restless Gun (series), Call of the West (series), The Philadelphia Story.

PAYNE, NORMAN: Artists' and writers' manager. b. London, England. Ent. entertainment ind., 1939. Early career music, then formed talent agency, J.P. Productions, 1945. Later bought by MCA, 1951. Became dir. MCA and head of light ent. for theatres and TV throughout Europe. On MCA terminating reformed agency. TV offices also in Germany, Australia.

PAYNTER, ROBERT: Cinematographer. b. London, England. e. Mercer Sch. First job in industry at 15 years as camera trainee with Government Film Dept.
PICTURES: Hannibal Brooks (debut, 1969), The Nightcomers, The Mechanic, Firepower, Superman, Superman II, Trading Places, An American Werewolf in London, The Final Conflict (co-cine.), Superman III, Why the Whales Came.

PAYS, AMANDA: Actress. b. Berkshire, England, 1959. Began as a model. Studied French, art and pottery at Hammersmith Polytechnic. Acting debut: Cold Room (HBO).
PICTURES: The Kindred, Oxford Blues, Off Limits, Leviathan.
TELEVISION: A.D. (mini-series), Max Headroom (series), The Pretenders.

PAYSON, MARTIN D.: Executive. Practiced law privately before joining Warner Communications, Inc. as v.p. 1970. Later named exec. v.p.–gen. counsel. 1987, appt. to 3-member office of pres., WCI.

PEAKER, E. J.: Actress, Singer, Dancer. Edra Jeanne Peaker. b. Tulsa, OK, Feb. 22. e. U. of New Mexico, U. of Vienna, Austria. Stage debut Bye, Bye Birdie; film debut Hello, Dolly (1969). Films include All American Boy, Private Roads, The Four Deuces, Graduation Day, Fire in the Night.
TELEVISION: That's Life series, The Flying Nun, That Girl, Movie of the Week, Love American Style, Odd Couple, Police Woman, Rockford Files, Get Christie Love.

PEARCE, RICHARD: Director, Cinematographer. b. San Diego, CA. e. Yale U., degree in Eng. lit., 1965. New School for Social Research, M.A., political economics. Worked with Don Pennebaker on documentaries and with a Seattle-based owner of TV stations in the Pacific Northwest. Photographed Emile de Antonio's America Is Hard to See. In 1970 went to Chile where he dir., photographed and edited Campamento, an award-winning documentary.
PICTURES: As photographer: Woodstock; Marjoe; Interviews With My Lai Veterans; Hearts and Minds.
PICTURES: As director: Heartland; Threshold; Country; No Mercy.
TELEVISION: The Gardener's Son; Siege; No Other Love; Sessions.

PECK, GREGORY: Actor, Producer. b. La Jolla, CA, April 5, 1916. e. U. of California; Neighborhood Playhouse Sch. of Dramatics. On dramatic stage (The Doctor's Dilemma, The Male Animal, Once in a Lifetime, The Play's the Thing, You Can't Take It With You, Sons and Soldiers, etc.); on screen 1944 in Days of Glory. Voted one of ten best Money-Making Stars Motion Picture Herald-Fame Poll, 1947, 1952. Co-prod. and starred in Big Country, for his company, Anthony Productions; prod. the Trial of the Catonsville Nine, The Dove (St. George Productions). Autobiography: An Actor's Life, 1978.
PICTURES INCLUDE: Keys of the Kingdom, Valley of Decision, Spellbound, Yearling, Duel in the Sun, Macomber Affair, Gentleman's Agreement, Paradine Case, Yellow Sky, 12 O'Clock High, Great Sinner, The Gunfighter, Only the Valiant, David and Bathsheba, Captain Horatio Hornblower, World in His Arms, Snows of Kilimanjaro, Roman Holiday, Night People, Man With a Million, Purple Plains, Man in the Gray Flannel Suit, Moby Dick, Designing Woman, The Bravados, Pork Chop Hill, On the Beach, Beloved Infidel, Guns of Navarone, Cape Fear, To Kill a Mockingbird (Acad. Award, 1963), Captain Newman, M.D., Behold a Pale Horse, Mirage, Arabesque, MacKenna's Gold, Stalking Moon, The

Chairman, Marooned, I Walk the Line, Shootout, Billy Two Hats, The Omen, MacArthur, The Boys from Brazil, The Sea Wolves, Amazing Grace and Chuck, The Old Gringo.
TELEVISION: The Blue and the Gray, The Scarlet and the Black.

PEERCE, LARRY: Director. b. Bronx, NY. Son of late singer Jan Peerce.
PICTURES INCLUDE: One Potato, Two Potato, The Incident, Goodbye Columbus, The Sporting Club, The Big TNT Show, A Separate Peace, Ash Wednesday, The Other Side of the Mountain, Two Minute Warning, The Other Side of the Mountain—Part II, The Bell Jar, Why Would I Lie?, Love Child, Hard to Hold, Wired.
TELEVISION: A Stranger Who Looks Like Me, Love Lives On, I Take These Men, The Fifth Missile, Prison for Children, Queenie, Elvis and Me.

PELLATT, JOHN: Production Executive. Abandoned school for theatre at age of 14. Became stage manager before serving in H.M. forces. Then became assistant director for Warner Bros., MGM, London Films, etc. Since 1955 worked as prod. manager/assoc. producer with British Lion, Columbia, Paramount, United Artists, Ivan Tors, American International. Also while assistant gen. prod. mgr. 20th Century Fox, associated with Inn of Sixth Happiness, Roots of Heaven, The Blue Angel, Sons and Lovers, Sink the Bismarck.
PICTURES INCLUDE: Noose, The Wooden Horse, Silent Dust, Lavender Hill Mob, Man in the White Suit, Ivanhoe, Innocents in Paris, Mogambo, Knights of the Round Table, A Kid for Two Farthings, Oh Rosalinda, The Twelve Days of Christmas, The Captain's Paradise, Zarak Khan, The Green Man, St. Trinians, Only Two Can Play, They're a Weird Mob, Age of Consent, Count Five and Die, Help, The Revolutionary, Wuthering Heights, Elephant Country, Who Slew Auntie Roo, Tower of Evil, The Diamond Mercenaries (Killer Force in U.S.), One Away. (South & S.W. Africa).
TELEVISION: Series for Incorporated Television Espionage. Worked in Europe, Middle and Far East, India, East and North Africa, Congo, Bahamas, Australia, Hollywood, Southern Africa, The Zoo Gang TV series, Born Free TV series (Kenya).

PENN, ARTHUR: Director. b. Philadelphia, PA, Sept. 27, 1922. e. Black Mountain Coll., Asheville, NC; U. of Perugia, U. of Florence in Italy. Began as TV dir. in 1953, twice winner of Sylvania Award. Dir. stage plays Two for the Seesaw, Miracle Worker (Tony Award), Toys in the Attic, All the Way Home, Golden Boy, Wait Until Dark, Sly Fox, Monday After the Miracle, Hunting Cockroaches. Entered m.p. as dir. of Left-Handed Gun in 1958.
PICTURES INCLUDE: The Miracle Worker, Mickey One, The Chase, Bonnie and Clyde, Alice's Restaurant, Little Big Man, Visions of Eight (co-dir.), Night Moves, The Missouri Breaks, Four Friends (also co-prod.), Target, Penn and Teller Get Killed (prod., dir.).
TELEVISION: North Beach and Rawhide.

PENN, CHRISTOPHER: Actor. Brother of actor Sean Penn.
PICTURES: Rumble Fish, All the Right Moves, Footloose, The Wild Life, Pale Rider, Return from the River Kwai.

PENN, SEAN: Actor. b. Burbank, CA, Aug. 17, 1960. Son of actor-director Leo Penn, actress Eileen Ryan. m. actress-singer Madonna. e. Santa Monica H.S. Served as apprentice for two years at Group Repertory Theatre, L.A. Acted in Earthworms, Heartland, The Girl on the Via Flaminia, etc. First prof appearance as guest star on TV's Barnaby Jones. On Bdwy. in Heartland, then Slab Boys.
PICTURES: Taps (debut), Fast Times at Ridgemont High, Bad Boys, Crackers, Racing with the Moon, The Falcon and the Snowman, At Close Range, Shanghai Surprise, Colors, Judgment in Berlin, Casualties of War.
TELEVISION: Movies: Concrete Cowboys, Hellinger's Law, The Killing of Randy Webster. Series: Barnaby Jones.

PENNEBAKER, D.A.: Director. b. Evanston, IL, 1926. r.n. Donn Alan Pennebaker. e. Yale U. Studied engineering, then set up own electronics firm. Worked in advertising before writing and directing experimental films. 1959 joined Richard Leacock and others in equipment-sharing film co-op, Filmakers. 1963 set up own co. Uses cinema verite approach, often shooting in 16mm and blowing up to 35mm.
PICTURES: Opening in Moscow (1959); Primary (co-dir.); Balloon (co-dir.); David; Jane; Mr. Pearson; Don't Look Back; Monterey Pop; Beyond the Law (co-photo, only); One P.M.; Sweet Toronto; Maidstone (co-photo only); From the Pole to the Equator (ed. only).

PEPPARD, GEORGE: Actor. b. Detroit, MI, Oct. 1, 1928. e. Dearborn H.S., Carnegie Tech., B.F.A., fine arts. U.S. Marine Corps. Legit. stage debut, Pittsburgh Playhouse, 1949. Worked as mason, construction laborer, fencing instructor, Braddock, PA. Discovered by Sam Spiegel to appear in The Strange One (debut, 1957).
STAGE: Girls of Summer, The Pleasure of His Company.

PICTURES INCLUDE: Pork Chop Hill, Home from the Hill, The Subterraneans, Breakfast At Tiffany's, How the West Was Won, The Victors, The Carpetbaggers, The Third Day, Operation Crossbow, The Blue Max, Tobruk, Rough Night in Jericho, P.J., House of Cards, What's So Bad About Feeling Good, Pendulum, Cannon for Cordoba, The Executioner, One More Train to Rob, The Groundstar Conspiracy, Newman's Law, Damnation Alley, Five Days From Home (also prod., dir.), Your Ticket Is No Longer Valid, Battle Beyond the Stars, Race to the Yankee Zephyr.
TELEVISION: Little Moon of Alban, Suspicion, U.S. Steel Hour, Alfred Hitchcock Presents, Matinee Theatre, Alcoa-Goodyear Playhouse, Studio One, Hallmark Hall of Fame, Banacek (series), The Bravos, Doctors Hospital, Story of Dr. Sam Sheppard, Crisis in Mid-Air, Torn Between Two Lovers, The A Team (series), Man Against the Mob.

PEPPERCORN, CARL: Executive. b. New York, NY. e. New York U. Ent. film ind. FBO (forerunner of RKO), held var. sls. positions, home office and branches. Lt. Comm. US Navy, WW II; pres. Military Bank of Naples, sales mgr. N.Y. branch RKO; asst. to Eastern sales mgr., RKO; gen'l sales mgr.,. RKO Canada; pres. Dairy-maid Chocolate Co., Toronto; v.p. Fairweather Dept. Stores, Canada; chmn. bd. Andako Mining Co., Canada; v.p. & gen'l sales mgr. Continental Dist. Inc.; v.p. & gen'l sales mgr. Embassy Pictures, Inc.; exec. v.p. and gen'l sales mgr. Cinema V Inc, pres. & sls. mgr., U.M. Film Distributors and Peppercorn-Wormser Film Distributors; Diversified Film Representatives, Inc., Peppercorn Enterprises.

PERAKOS, SPERIE P.: Executive. b. New Britain, CT, Nov. 12, 1915. e. Cheshire Acad., Yale U., Harvard Law Sch. Student mgr., Stanley-Warner thtrs., 1939–40; Perakos thtrs., 1940–41; Fellow, Pierson Coll., Yale, 1946–present; Yale Alumni Bd., 1949 to present; Yale Alumni Film Bd. 1952 to present; member Alumni Council for Yale Drama Sch.; past pres. Yale Club of New Britain, Conn.; dir. of Films & Filmings Seminars, Pierson Coll., Yale; prod. Antigone, 1962; pres. Norma Film Prod., Inc., 1962 to present. Past pres. now chm. Yale's Peabody Museum Associates and member of the University Council of the Peabody Museum. Pres., Perakos Theatres, Conn. Theatre Circuit, Inc.

PERENCHIO, ANDREW J.: Executive. b. Fresno, CA, Dec. 20, 1930. e. U. of California. Vice pres., Music Corp. of America, 1958–62; General Artists Corp., 1962–64; pres., owner, Chartwell Artists, Ltd., theatrical agency, Los Angeles, 1964; pres. & CEO, Tandem Productions, Inc., and TAT Communications Co., 1973–83, then became principal with Norman Lear in Embassy Communications. Held post of pres. & CEO of Embassy Pictures.

PERKINS, ANTHONY: Actor. b. New York, NY, Apr. 14, 1932. Son of late actor Osgood Perkins. e. Columbia U., Rollins Coll. Broadway stage in Tea and Sympathy. Wrote s.p. Last of Sheila, 1973.
TELEVISION: Kraft Theatre, Studio One, U.S. Steel Hour, Armstrong Theatre. Movies: How Awful About Allen, Les Miserables, Sins of Dorian Gray, First You Cry, Napoleon and Josephine: A Love Story.
PICTURES INCLUDE: The Actress, Friendly Persuasion, The Lonely Man, Fear Strikes Out, The Tin Star, This Bitter Earth, Desire Under the Elms, The Matchmaker, Green Mansions, On the Beach, Tall Story, Psycho, Goodbye Again, Phaedra, Five Miles to Midnight, The Trial, Two Are Guilty, The Fool Killer, The Adorable Idiot, Is Paris Burning, The Champagne Murders, Pretty Poison, Catch 22, Someone Behind the Door, Ten Days' Wonder, WUSA, The Life and Times of Judge Roy Bean, Play It As It Lays, Lovin' Molly, Murder on the Orient Express, Mahogany, Remember My Name, Winter Kills, The Black Hole, ffolkes, Double Negative, Twice a Woman, Psycho II, Crimes of Passion, Psycho III (also dir.), Shadow of Death, Mr. Christmas Dinner (dir.), Edge of Sanity.
STAGE: Look Homeward Angel, Greenwillow, Steambath (also dir.), Equus, Romantic Comedy.

PERKINS, ELIZABETH: Actress. b. Queens, NY, 1961. After high school moved to Chicago to study at Goodman School of Drama. Two months after moving to NY in 1984, landed a role in the national touring co. of Brighton Beach Memoirs, later performing part on Broadway. Acted with Playwright's Horizon, NY Ensemble Theater and Shakespeare in the Park.
PICTURES: About Last Night...(1987), From the Hip, Big, Sweethearts Dance.

PERKINS, JOHN HENRY ROWLAND II: Executive. b. July 10, 1934, Los Angeles, CA. e. U. of Southern California, U. of California at L.A. Joined William Morris Agency, 1959; exec. in TV dept. In January, 1975, co-founded Creative Artists Agency, of which is senior partner and first pres. Member Hollywood Radio & TV Society since 1964, and Academy of TV Arts & Sciences since 1962. Mem. bd. of dir. of HRTS and bd. of gov. Acad. of TV Arts and Sciences.

PERKINS, MILLIE: Actress. b. 1939.
PICTURES: The Diary of Anne Frank, Wild in the Country, Wild in the Streets, Lady Cocoa, Table for Five, At Close Range, Jake Speed, Slam Dance, Wall Street, Two Moon Junction.
TELEVISION: A.D., The Thanksgiving Promise, Penalty Phase, Anatomy of an Illness, Shattered Vows, License to Kill, Strange Voices, Broken Angel.

PERLMAN, RHEA: Actress. b. Brooklyn, NY, March 31. e. Hunter Coll. m. Danny DeVito.
TELEVISION: Movies: Mary Jane Harper Cried Last Night; I Want to Keep My Baby; Intimate Strangers; Drop-Out Father; Having Babies II, Dangerous Affection. Special: Funny, You Don't Look 200. Series: Cheers.
PICTURES: Love Child, My Little Pony.

PERLMUTTER, DAVID M.: Producer. b. Toronto, Canada, 1934. e. U. of Toronto. Pres., Quadrant Films Ltd.
PICTURES INCLUDE: The Neptune Factor, 1972; Sunday in the Country; It Seemed Like a Good Idea at the Time; Love at First Sight, Find the Lady; Blood and Guts, The Third Walker, Two Solitudes; Fast Company; Double Negative, Nothing Personal; Misdeal, Love.

PERMUT, DAVID A.: Producer. b. New York, NY, Mar. 23, 1954. e. U. of California, 1972. 1974, pres., Diversified Artists Intl.; 1975, pres., Theatre Television Corp.; 1979, formed Permut Presentations, Inc., of which is pres. Production deals with Columbia Pictures (1979), Lorimar Productions (1981), Universal (1985), and United Artists (1986).
PICTURES: Give 'Em Hell Harry (prod.); Fighting Back (exec. prod.); Love Leads the Way (exec. prod.); Blind Date (prod.); Richard Pryor—Live in Concert (exec. prod.); Dragnet (prod.).
TELEVISION: Mistress (sprv. prod.)

PERREAU, GIGI: Actress. r.n. Ghislaine Perreau; b. Los Angeles, CA, Feb. 6, 1941. sister of Janine Perreau & Richard Miles. Prof. m.p. debut in Madame Curie 1943; many stage and TV guest appearances.
PICTURES INCLUDE: Dark Waters, Abigail, Dear Heart, Family Honeymoon, Roseanna McCoy, High Barbaree, Song of Love, Green Dolphin Street, Two Girls and a Sailor, Shadow on the Wall, My Foolish Heart, For Heaven's Sake, Never a Dull Moment, Reunion in Reno, Lady Pays Off, Weekend with Father, Has Anybody Seen My Gal, Bonzo Goes to College, There's Always Tomorrow, Man in the Gray Flannel Suit, Dance With Me Henry, Tammy Tell Me True, Journey to the Center of Time, Hell on Wheels.

PERRINE, VALERIE: Actress. b. Phoenix, AZ, Sept. 3 1943. e. U. of Arizona. Was showgirl in Las Vegas before discovered by agent Robert Walker who got her contract with Universal Pictures. Film debut in Slaughterhouse Five (1972).
PICTURES INCLUDE: The Last American Hero, Lenny (N.Y. Film Critics Award, best supporting actress), W. C. Fields and Me, Mr. Billion, Superman, The Electric Horseman, Can't Stop the Music, Superman II, The Border, Water.
TELEVISION: When Your Lover Leaves, Malibu, The Couple Takes a Wife, Ziegfeld: The Man and His Women, Faerie Tale Theatre. Series: Leo and Liz in Beverly Hills.

PERRY, ANTHONY: Producer. b. London, England, 1929. Ent. m.p. ind. 1948 with Two Cities story dept. asst. story ed., Rank Prods. Wrote orig. story and prod. asst. Simba. Prod., The Secret Place in 1957. Created and prod. TV series, Interpol Calling, 1959; founded Eyeline Films, prod. many Brit. prize-winning commercials. Sold Eyeline Films, 1963; wrote, dir. Emma, 1964–65, res. prod. Keep Films/Embassy Prods., London, 1966–67; prod. Dare I Weep, Dare I Mourn, for ABC-TV, and Fernandel TV series. Admin. Yellow Submarine, joined Trickfilm as man. dir. Chmn. Film & TV Copyrights, Ltd.
PICTURES INCLUDE: The Impersonator, Girl on Approval, The Party's Over.

PERRY, EARL: Circuit Executive. b. Aug. 11, 1921. e. Tulane U. Spent 4 yrs. as Air Force officer in World War II. Worked for Twentieth Century Fox for four years; then entered exhibition in 1951 as vice pres. and gen. mgr. of Pittman Theatres; in 1966, formed Ogden-Perry Theatres, and as pres., operates theatres in Louisiana, Mississippi, Tennessee, and Florida. Past President of NATO of Louisiana; Past Chief Barker of Variety Club Tent 45.

PERRY, FRANK: Director, Producer, Writer. b. 1930. Served as apprentice, Westport, CT Country Playhouse; spent nine years in stock as stage mgr., prod. mgr., and managing director. U.S. Army, 1952–54; director-observer, Actors Studio, 1955; Theatre Guild, 1956–60; s.p. (with Eleanor Perry): Somersault, David and Lisa, and others.
PICTURES INCLUDE: The Swimmer, Ladybug, Ladybug, David and Lisa, Last Summer, Trilogy, Diary of a Mad Housewife, Doc, Play It As It Lays, The Man on the Swing, Rancho Deluxe, Mommie Dearest (also co-s.p.), Monsignor, Hello Again (prod., dir.).

TELEVISION: Truman Capote's A Christmas Memory, Thanksgiving Visitors, JFK—A One Man Show, Skag (premiere), Dummy.

PERRY, SIMON: Producer, Writer. b. England. Ent. ind. 1974. Early career in stage and television production. Prod. minibudget feature Knots; prod. dir. Eclipse. Served on bureau staff of Variety. Ran the National Film Development Fund for two years. In 1982 set up Umbrella Films to produce Another Time, Another Place, Loose Connections, Hotel Du Paradis, Nanon, White Mischief.

PERSCHY, MARIA: Actress. b. Eisenstadt, Austria, Sept. 23, 1940. e. Max Rheinhardt Seminar, Vienna. Widow of John Melson, writer. Started in 1958 with German film (Nasser Asphalt) and has appeared in over 50 European and U.S. features. Has also appeared on European TV. Recipient of Laurel Award in 1963.
PICTURES INCLUDE: Man's Favorite Sport, Squadron 633, Ride the High Wind, Murders in the Rue Morgue, Last Day of the War, The Desperate Ones, The Tall Woman, Witch Without a Broom, etc.
TELEVISION: General Hospital, Hawaii Five-O.

PERSKY, LESTER: Executive. b. New York, NY, July 6, 1927. e. Brooklyn Coll. Officer in U.S. Merchant Marine, 1946–48. Founder and pres. of own adv. agency, 1951–1964. Theatrical stage producer, 1966–69. Produced Fortune and Men's Eyes for MGM in 1971. In 1973 creative director and co-owner Persky Bright Org. (owner-financier of numerous motion pictures for private investment group). Films include Last Detail, Golden Voyage of Sinbad, For Pete's Sake, California Split, The Man Who Would Be King, The Front, Shampoo. Also Hard Times, Taxi Driver, Missouri Breaks, Funny Lady, Gator, Bound for Glory, Sinbad and the Eye of the Tiger. Lester Persky Productions, Inc.
PICTURES: Produced Equus, Hair, Yanks, Handcarved Coffins.
TELEVISION: Poor Little Rich Girl (mini-series)

PERSOFF, NEHEMIAH: Actor. b. Jerusalem, Israel, Aug. 2, 1919. e. Hebrew Technical Inst., 1934–37. Actors Studio electrician, 1937–39; signal maint., N.Y. subway, 1939–41. L.A. Critics Award 1971 for Sholem-Sholem Alecheim, and The Dybbuk.
STAGE: Sundown Beach, Galileo, Richard III, King Lear, Peter Pan, Peer Gynt, Tiger At the Gates, Colombe, Flahooly, Montserrat, Only in America. Tour: Fiddler on the Roof, Man of La Mancha.
PICTURES INCLUDE: Al Capone, Some Like It Hot, The Harder They Fall, The Badlanders, The Wrong Man, In Search of the Real Jesus, Men in War, This Angry Age, The Big Show, The Commancheros, Fate Is the Hunter, The Greatest Story Ever Told, The Wild Party, The Power, Mrs. Pollifax—Spy, Red Sky at Morning, Psychic Killer, Voyage of the Damned, Yentl, The Last Temptation of Christ, Testament, Twins.
TELEVISION: Philco-Goodyear Show, Kraft, Producers Showcase, Danger, You Are There, Untouchables, Route 66, Naked City, Wagon Train, Rawhide, Gunsmoke, Thriller, Hitchcock Thriller, Bus Stop, Five Fingers, Mr. Lucky, The Wild, Wild West, I Spy, Columbo, Barney Miller, Sadat, Adderly, The French Atlantic Affair, The Big Knife.

PERTWEE, JON: TV Performer. b. London, England, July 7, 1919. e. Sherborne, Royal Acad. of Dramatic Art. Early career, Arts League Traveling Theatre, 5 yrs. repertory; regularly on radio, TV, music hall, cabaret and circus.
PICTURES INCLUDE: Murder At the Windmill, Miss Pilgrim's Progress, Will Any Gentleman?, Gay Dog, It's A Wonderful Life, Mr. Drake's Duck, A Yank in Ermine, Ugly Duckling, Just Joe, Not a Hope in Hell, Nearly a Nasty Accident, Ladies Who Do, Carry on Cleo, I've Gotta Horse, Carry On Cowboy, Carry On Screaming, A Funny Thing Happened On the Way To The Forum, Up in the Air, The Hod, March of the Desert, One of our Dinosaurs Is Missing, The House that Dripped Blood, The Island of Young Tigers, The Boys in Blue.
TELEVISION: Own series, Sunday Night, London Palladium Compere Variety Show, Doctor Who series, Who Dunnit, Worzel Gummidge.
RADIO: Navy Lark.
STAGE: See You Inside, A Funny Thing Happened On The Way To The Forum, There's A Girl In My Soup, Oh Clarence, My Dear Gilbert, The Bedwinner, Don't Just Lie There, Say Something, Irene, Touch It Light.

PERTWEE, MICHAEL: Writer. b. April 24, 1916. e. Sherborne Sch., France. Early career, journalist; ent. m.p. ind. 1937. Coauthor, co-presentation many BBC plays and serials; many appearances panel games.
PICTURES INCLUDE: Laughter in Paradise, On Monday Next, Top Secret, Happy Ever After, Now and Forever, Against the Wind, Interrupted Journey, The Naked Truth, Too Many Crooks, Bottoms Up, Make Mine Mink, It Started in Naples, In the Doghouse, Mouse on the Moon, Ladies Who Do, Finders Keepers, Strange Bedfellows, A Funny Thing

Happened on the Way to the Forum, Salt and Pepper, One More Time, Don't Just Lie There Say Something, Digby the Biggest Dog in the World.
TELEVISION: Rainy Day, Strictly Personal, Grove Family, Man in a Moon, The Frightened Man, Yakity Yak (ATV 1956), The Old Campaigner, Terry Thomas series, B and B series, Never a Cross Word, Six of Rix, Men of Affairs.
STAGE: The Four Musketeers, Drury Lane, She's Done It Again, Don't Just Lie There Say Something, Birds of Paradise, A Bit Between the Teeth, Six of One, Ace In A Hole, Find the Lady, Do Not Disturb, Look No Hans!, Holiday Swap.

PESCOW, DONNA: Actress. b. Brooklyn, NY, March 24, 1954. e. American Acad. of Dramatic Arts. Started career on summer tour in Ah Wilderness in 1975. Did bit in ABC daytime series, One Life to Live. Film debut in Saturday Night Fever (1977).
PICTURES: Saturday Night Fever, Jake Speed.
TELEVISION: Advice to the Lovelorn, The Day the Bubble Burst, Policewoman Centerfold, Obsessed with a Married Woman, Angie (series), Out of this World (series).

PETERS, BERNADETTE: Actress. r.n. Bernadette Lazzara. b. New York, NY, Feb. 28, 1948. e. Quintano Sch. for Young Professionals, NY. Professional debut at age 5 on TV's Horn & Hardart Children's Hour, followed by Juvenile Jury and Name That Tune. Stage debut with N.Y. City Center production of The Most Happy Fella (1959). Screen debut, Ace Eli and Rodger of the Skies (1973).
THEATER: Gypsy (1961), This is Google, Riverwind, The Penny Friend, Curly McDimple, Johnny No-Trump, George M!, Dames at Sea, La Strada, W.C., On the Town (1971 revival), Tartuffe, Mack and Mabel, Sally and Marsha, Sunday in the Park With George, Song and Dance (Tony Award), Into the Woods.
PICTURES INCLUDE: Ace Eli and Roger of the Skies, The Longest Yard, W.C. Fields & Me, Vigilante Force, Silent Movie, The Jerk, Tulips, Pennies from Heaven, Heartbeeps, Annie, Slaves of New York, Pink Cadillac.
TELEVISION: All's Fair (series, 1976–77), The Martian Chronicles, They Said it with Music, The Starmakers, Lonely Man, House of Numbers, Ten Seconds to Hell, Warriors Five, Party at Annapolis, Rich, Thin and Beautiful (host), Faerie Tale Theatre, David, many specials.

PETERS, BROCK: Actor. b. Harlem, NY, July 2, 1927. e. U. of Chicago. Had numerous featured roles on and off Bdwy. in road and stock cos., nightclubs, TV. Toured with DePaul Infantry Chorus 3 seasons. Made m.p. debut, Carmen Jones (1955).
THEATER: King of the Dark Chamber, Othello, The Great White Hope, Lost in the Stars.
PICTURES INCLUDE: Carmen Jones, Porgy and Bess, To Kill a Mockingbird, Heavens Above, The L-Shaped Room, The Pawnbroker, Major Dundee, P.J., The Daring Game, The Incident, The McMasters, Black Girl, Soylent Green, Slaughter II, Lost in the Stars, Million Dollar Dixie Deliverance, Framed, Two-Minute Warning, Huckleberry Finn, Star Trek IV: The Voyage Home.
TELEVISION: The Young and the Restless, It Takes a Thief, Mannix, Mod Squad, SST—Death Flight, Broken Angels, To Heal a Nation.

PETERS, JON: Producer. b. Van Nuys, CA, 1947. Started hairstyling business; built it into multimillion-dollar firm before turning film producer. Formed Jon Peters Organization. 1980, joined with Peter Guber and Neil Bogart to form The Boardwalk Co. (dissolved 1981). Later Guber-Peters-Barris Company.
PICTURES INCLUDE: A Star Is Born, The Eyes of Laura Mars, The Main Event, Die Laughing, Caddyshack, An American Werewolf in London (co-exec. prod.), Missing (co-exec. prod.), Flashdance (co- exec. prod.), Six Weeks, D.C. Cab, Visionquest, Clue (exec. prod.), The Color Purple (exec. prod.), The Witches of Eastwick (co-prod.), Innerspace (exec. prod.), Who's That Girl (co-exec. prod.), Gorillas in the Mist (exec. prod.), Caddyshack II (prod.), Batman (co-prod.).
TELEVISION: Bay Coven (co-exec. prod.), Nightmare at Bitter Creek (co-exec. prod.).

PETERSEN, WILLIAM: Actor. b. Chicago, IL, 1953. Active in Chicago theatre; helped to found Ix, an ensemble acting group now called the Remains Theatre. Acted in Moby Dick, In the Belly of the Beast, A Streetcar Named Desire, etc. 1986, formed company with actor John Malkovich called High Horse Prods.
PICTURES: To Live and Die in L.A., Manhunter, Amazing Grace and Chuck.
TELEVISION: Long Gone (HBO movie), The Kennedys of Massachusetts.

PETERSEN, WOLFGANG: Director. b. Emden, Germany, Mar. 14, 1941. Career as asst. state director at Ernst Deutsch Theatre in Hamburg before starting to direct for television and later theatrical films.
PICTURES INCLUDE: Black and White Like Day, The

Consequence, Das Boot (The Boat), The NeverEnding Story, Enemy Mine.
TELEVISION: Scenes of the Crime (series).

PETERSON, S. DEAN: Executive. b. Toronto, Canada, December 18, 1923. e. Victoria Coll., U. of Toronto. W.W.II service RCNVR; 1946 TV newsreel cameraman NBC; founded own production company in 1947; incorporated Dordean Realty Limited to acquire new studios 1959; formed Peterson Production Limited in 1957 to make TV commercials and sponsored theatrical shorts; has international awards as producer, director, director of photography; formed Studio City Limited in 1965 to produce television series and features acquiring an additional studio complex and backlot in Kleinberg, Ontario; 1972 formed SDP Communications Ltd. to package M.P. and TV; 1970 incorporated Intermedia Financial Services Limited to provide specialized financing and consultation to companies in M.P. and TV industries.
Past-President Canadian Film and Television Association, mbr. Variety Club, Tent 28; Canadian Society of Cinematographers; Directors Guild of America, Directors Guild of Canada, SMPTE.

PETERSON, PAUL: Actor. b. Glendale, CA, Sept. 23, 1945. e. Valley Coll. Original Disney Mouseketeer (TV). In the late 1960's turned to writing—beginning with a Marcus Welby script followed by paperback novels in 1970's. Also book about Disney empire, Walt, Mickey and Me, 1977.
PICTURES INCLUDE: Houseboat, This Could Be the Night.
TELEVISION: The Donna Reed Show (series), Playhouse 90, Lux Video Theatre, GE Theatre, The Virginian, Ford Theatre, Valentine's Day, Shindig.

PETERSON, RICHARD W.: Executive. b. Denver, CO, June 15, 1949. e. Col. Sch. of Broadcasting, Harper Coll. Joined Kennedy Theatres, Chicago, 1966. In 1968 went with Great States Theatres (now Plitt Theatres), Chicago. Was city mgr. of Crocker and Grove Theatres, Elgin, IL. In 1973 joined American Automated Theatres, Oklahoma City, as dir. of adv., pub. Promoted to dir. of U.S. theatre operations. Worked for American International Pictures, Dallas, TX. Then moved to Dal Art Film Exchange and B & B Theatres as general mgr.; 1987 took over 7 screens from McLendon and formed own co., Peterson Theatres, Inc.

PETRIE, DANIEL: Director. b. Glace Bay, Nova Scotia, Nov. 26, 1920. e. St. Francis Xavier U., Nova Scotia; Columbia U., MA, 1945; postgrad. Northwestern U. Broadway actor 1945–46. TV director from 1950.
PICTURES INCLUDE: The Bramble Bush, A Raisin in the Sun; Lifeguard, Buster and Billie; Spy With A Cold Nose; The Idol; Stolen Hours; The Betsy, Resurrection, Fort Apache, The Bronx, Six Pack, The Bay Boy, Square Dance, Rocket Gibralter; Cocoon II: The Return.
THEATRE: Shadow of My Enemy; Who'll Save The Plowboy?; Mornin' Sun; Monopoly, The Cherry Orchard, Volpone, A Lesson from Aloes.
TV FILMS: Eleanor and Franklin (Emmy, 1976), Sybil, Eleanor and Franklin: The White House Years (Emmy, 1977), Silent Night, Lonely Night, Harry Truman, Plain Speaking, The Dollmaker, The Execution of Raymond Graham, Half a Lifetime.

PETROU, DAVID MICHAEL: Writer, Producer, Public Relations Executive. b. Washington, DC, Nov. 3, 1949. e. U. of Maryland, B.A.; Georgetown U., M.A. Publicity assoc., Psychiatric Institutes of America, Washington, DC, 1971; assoc. dir. of publicity & film liaison, Random House, 1974; guest lecturer, screen writing & film production, The American University Consortium, Washington, DC, spring, 1980; Woodrow Wilson Fellowship, 1971. Entered industry in 1975. Joined Salkind Organization in chg. of literary projects. Worked in numerous production capacities on Crossed Swords, Superman, Superman II. 1977, exec. in chg. of literary development, Salkind. Wrote Crossed Swords (1978) and The Making of Superman. Co-authored screenplay, Shoot to Kill. 1978–79, promotional development on Time after Time for Warner Bros.; 1980–83, dir., special projects Joseph Kennedy Foundation. Organized U.S. premiere of Superman II and The Empire Strikes Back; 1983–84, sr. editor for entertainment, Regardie's Magazine; 1984, organized Washington, DC premiere of Indiana Jones and the Temple of Doom; 1984–86, sr. exec., p.r. div., Abramson Associates; 1986–present, sr. v.p., Eisner, Held & Petrou, Inc., p.r. agency.

PEVERALL, JOHN: Producer. b. Islington, England. Started in entertainment industry in 1945 in mail room of J. Arthur Rank Prods. Promoted to asst. dir. Time out for military service in Royal Air Force Air-Sea Rescue Unit. Resumed career as asst. dir. and unit prod. mgr. on several films produced in Britain and throughout Europe. In 1969 became associated with newly-formed Cinema Center Films as prod. exec. in London. When firm suspended activities became freelance as asst. dir.
PICTURES INCLUDE: Conduct Unbecoming and The Man

Who Fell to Earth (both assoc. prod.), The Deer Hunter (prod.).

PEVNEY, JOSEPH: Director, Actor. b. New York, NY, 1920. e. New York U. m. the late Mitzi Green, child star, actress, nightclub entertainer. Began career in vaudeville at 13 as jr. mem. song & dance team; later stage in Home of the Brave. US Army ETO W.W.II. Actor turned director.
STAGE: Counsellor at Law, Key Largo, Native Son; (dir.) Swan Song, Let Freedom Sing.
PICTURES INCLUDE: (acting) Nocturne, Outside The Wall, Body & Soul; Counsellor at Law (dir.), Key Largo, Native Son. Director: The Strange Door, Shakedown, Air Cadet, Lady from Texas, Meet Danny Wilson, Iron Man, Flesh and Fury, Just Across the Street, Because of You, Desert Legion, It Happens Every Thursday, Back to God's Country, Yankee Pasha, Playgirl, Three Ring Circus, Six Bridges to Cross, Foxfire, Female on the Beach, Away All Boats, Congo Crossing, Tammy and the Bachelor, The Midnight Man, Man of a Thousand Faces, Twilight for the Gods, Torpedo Run, Cash McCall, The Plunderers (also prod.), Crowded Sky, Portrait of a Mobster, Night of the Grizzly.
TELEVISION: Trapper John M.D., Contract for Life: The S.A.D.D. Story. Movies: Who is the Black Dahlia, My Darling Daughter's Anniversary, Mysterious Island of Beautiful Women.

PEYSER, JOHN: Producer, Director. b. New York, NY, Aug. 10, 1916. e. Colgate U., 1938. In TV ind. since 1939, with Psychological Warfare Div., ETO., W.W.II; pres. Peypac productions, Madrid.
TELEVISION: Director: Hawaii Five-O, Mannix, Movin On, Swiss Family Robinson, Bronk, Combat, Untouchables, Rat Patrol, Honeymoon with a Stranger.
PICTURES: Spain, The Open Door; Kashmiri Run; Four Rode Out; Massacre Harbor.

PFEIFFER, MICHELLE: Actress. b. Santa Ana, CA, 1957.
PICTURES: Charlie Chan and The Curse of the Dragon (1980), Falling in Love Again, Hollywood Nights, Grease II, Scarface, Into the Night, Ladyhawke, Sweet Liberty, The Witches of Eastwick, Married to the Mob, Tequilla Sunrise, Les Liaisons Dangereuses.
TELEVISION: Delta House (series), B.A.D. Cats (series), Callie and Son, The Children Nobody Wanted, Splendor in the Grass, One Too Many, Natica Jackson.

PHILLIPS, D. JOHN: Motion Picture Theatre Consultant. b. New York, NY. Advertising and publicity mgr. Borden Co. Produce Sales Div., 1933–36; adv. & pub. mgr., Paul R. Dillon Co., Inc., 1936–41. Became field exploitation rep., United Artists Corp., 1941–42; Short Subjects & Paramount News adv. & pub. mgr. Paramount Pictures, 1942–47; exec. dir. Metropolitan Motion Pictures Theatres Assn., 1947–79, New York.

PHILLIPS, JULIA: Producer. b. Brooklyn, NY, April 7, 1944. e. Mt. Holyoke Coll. Production asst. at McCall's Magazine; later became textbook copywriter for Macmillan; story editor, Paramount; creative exec., First Artists Prods., NY. In 1970 with former husband, Michael and actor Tony Bill formed Bill/Phillips Productions to develop film projects.
PICTURES INCLUDE: Steelyard Blues, The Sting, Taxi Driver, The Big Bus, Close Encounters of the Third Kind, The Beat (co-prod.).

PHILLIPS, LESLIE: Actor, Producer. b. London, England, April 20, 1924. Early career as child actor. Ent. m.p. ind. 1935.
PICTURES INCLUDE: High Flight, Les Girls, Smallest Show on Earth, Carry on Nurse, King Ferdinand of Naples, This Other Eden, The Navy Lark, Doctor in Love, Please Turn Over, Watch Your Stern, No Kidding, Week-End With Lulu, VIP, Carry on Constable, Raising the Wind, In the Doghouse, Crooks Anonymous, Fast Lady, Father Came Too, Doctor in Clover, You Must Be Joking, Maroc 7, Some Will Some Won't, Doctor in Trouble, The Magnificent 7 & Deadly Sins, Not Now Darling, Don't Just Lie There, Spanish Fly, Not Now Comrade, Out of Africa, Empire of the Sun, Mountains of the Moon.
TELEVISION: Our Man at St. Marks, Impasse, The Gong Game, Time and Motion Man, Reluctant Debutante, A Very Fine Line, The Suit, The Culture Vultures (series), Edward Woodward Show, Casanova 74 (series), Redundant—or the Wife's Revenge. TV film: You'll Never See Me Again, Mr. Palfrey of Westminister, Monte Carlo.

PHILLIPS, LOU DIAMOND: Actor. b. Philippines, 1962. m. asst. dir of La Bamba, Julie Cypher. Raised in Arlington, TX. e. U. of Texas, Arlington (drama). Studied film technique with Adam Roarke, becoming asst. dir./instructor with the Film Actor's Lab, 1983–86. Regional theater includes: A Hatful of Rain, Whose Life Is It, Anyway?, P.S. Your Cat Is Dead, The Lady's Not for Burning, Doctor Faustus, Hamlet.
PICTURES: Angel Alley, Interface, Trespasses (also co-s.p.), Harley, La Bamba, Stand and Deliver, Young Guns, Lakota, Waiting for Salazar.
TELEVISION: Dallas, Miami Vice. Movie: Time Bomb.

241

PHILLIPS, MICHAEL: Producer b. Brooklyn, NY, Nov. 10, 1916. Mgr. & prof. pugilist (featherweight), 1930–36. Ent. m.p. ind. as secy to Ray Milland, 1937; apptd asst. dir., U.S. Army Special Service Div., 1942–45; script ed. & prod. activities, Eddie Bracken Radio Prod. until 1949 (orig. & s.p.) Double Cross; formed own prod. co. Demyrtha Prod., Inc. 1950.

PHILLIPS, MICHAEL: Producer. b. Brooklyn, NY, June 29, 1943. e. Dartmouth Coll., B.A., 1965. NYU, Law Sch. J.D., 1968. Securities analyst, NY 1968–70. Indep. m.p. prod. 1971. In 1970 formed prod. co. with former wife, Julia, and actor Tony Bill.
PICTURES INCLUDE: Steelyard Blues, The Sting, Taxi Driver, The Big Bus, Close Encounters of the Third Kind, Heartbeeps, Cannery Row, The Flamingo Kid, The Tender.

PHOENIX, RIVER: Actor. b. Madras, Oregon, August 23, 1971. Sisters Rainbow, Liberty and Summer and brother Leaf are also actors. Spent childhood traveling to South and Central America with parents who were then independent Christian missionaries. Returned to States at 7. First TV appearance, singing and playing guitar on Fantasy TV. Began acting career at 10 in Seven Brides for Seven Brothers on TV. Also plays guitar and records own original songs.
PICTURES: Explorers (debut, 1985), Stand By Me, Mosquito Coast, A Night in the Life of Jimmy Reardon, Little Nikita, Running on Empty.
TELEVISION: Hotel, It's Your Move, Family Ties. Movies: Celebrity, Robert Kennedy and His Times, Surviving: A Family in Crisis.

PIALAT, MAURICE: Director. b. Cunlhat, Puy de Dome, France, 1925. Worked as a painter and sometime actor before turning to film in 1952. Made a number of short films including L'Amour Existe (1960) which won an award at the Venice film festival. Worked in television before feature debut in 1967. Television: Janine (1961), Maitre Galip (1962), La Maison des Bois (1971).
PICTURES: L'Enfance Nue (1967, awarded Prix Jean Vigo); Nous Ne Vieillirons pas Ensemble (1972), La Gueule Ouverte (1974); Passe Ton Bac D'Abord (1979); Loulou (1979); A Nos Amours (1983, Prix Louis Delluc); Police (1985); Under Satan's Sun (1987, winner Golden Palm, Cannes Festival).

PICCOLI, MICHEL: Actor. b. Paris, France, Dec. 27, 1925. r.n. Jacques Piccoli. Since his film debut in The Sorcerer in 1945 has had impressive career on the French stage and in films working for major French dirs. Renoir, Bunuel, Melville, Resnais, Clouzot, Godard as well as Hitchcock. Until 1957 was mgr. of Theatre Babylone in Paris. Formed prod. co. Films 66. Produced: Themroc (1972); La Faille; Les Enfants Gates.
PICTURES: The Sorcerer, Le Point du Jour; French Can Can; The Witches of Salem; Le Bal des Espiona; Gina; Le Doulos; Contempt; Diary of a Chambermaid; Lady L; La Guerre Est Finie; The Young Girls of Rochefort; Un Homme de Trop; Belle de Jour; La Chamade; Dillinger Is Dead; L'Invasion; The Milky Way; Topaz; The Things of Life; Ten Days' Wonder; The Discreet Charm of the Bourgeoisie; Themroc; Wedding in Blood; La Grande Bouffe; The Last Woman; Leonor; 7 Deaths by Prescription; The Weak Spot; F For Fairbanks; Mado; Todo Modo; Rene the Cane; Spoiled Children; Strauberg Is Here; The Fire's Share; Little Girl in Blue Velvet; The Savage State; The Sugar; The Bit Between the Teeth; La Divorcement; Leap into the Void; The Price for Survival; Atlantic City; The Prodigal Daughter; Beyond the Door; The Eyes, The Mouth; Passion; A Room in Town; Will the High Salaried Workers Please Raise Their Hands!!!; The General of the Dead Army; La Passante; The Prize of Peril; Adieu, Bonaparte; Dangerous Moves; Danger in the House; Long Live Life!; Success Is the Best Revenge; The Sailor 512; Departure, Return; Mon beau-frere a tue ma soeur; The Nonentity; The Prude; Bad Blood; Undiscovered Country; Blanc de Chine.

PICERNI, PAUL: Actor. b. New York, NY, Dec. 1, 1922. e. Loyola U., Los Angeles. U.S. Air Force 1943–46; head of drama dept. Mt. St. Mary's Coll., 1949–50. TV credits include Untouchables (co-star).
TELEVISION: Philco Playhouse, Climax, Lux, Loretta Young Show, Desilu, Kojak, Mannix, Police Story, Lucy Special, Quincy, Alice, Trapper John, Vegas, Fall Guy, Capitol, Hardcastle and McCormick, Matt Houston, Simon and Simon.
PICTURES INCLUDE: Breakthrough, I Was a Communist for the FBI, Mara Maru, Desert Song, She's Back on Broadway, House of Wax, Shanghai Story, To Hell and Back, Miracle in the Rain, Bobby Ware Is Missing, Omar Khayyam, Brothers Rico, Young Philadelphians, The Young Marrieds, The Scalphunters, Airport, Kotch, Beyond the Posiedon Adventure, Dirty Dozen III.

PICKER, ARNOLD M.: Executive. b. New York, NY, Sept. 19, 1913. p. Celia and David V. Picker. e. City Coll. of New York, U. of London. Joined Columbia's foreign dept. in June, 1935.

Asst. to foreign mgr.; then vice-pres. 1945, Columbia International Corp.; v.p. charge foreign dist., Oct., 1951; exec. v.p. UA, and in charge all distribution, June 1961; chmn. exec. com., 1967. Retired.

PICKER, DAVID V.: Executive. b. New York, NY, May 14, 1931. e. Dartmouth Coll., B.A., 1953. Father Eugene Picker, exec. Loew's Theatres. Ent. industry in 1956 as adv. pub. & exploitation liaison with sls. dept., United Artists Corp.; exec. v.p. U.A. Records; asst. to Max Youngstein, v.p.; v.p. U.A.; first v.p. UA; pres. 1969 Resigned 1973 to form own production co. In 1976 joined Paramount Pictures as pres. of m.p. prod.; Lorimar Productions; independent; 1987, pres. & COO, Columbia Pictures. Resigned.
PICTURES INCLUDE: Juggernaut, Lenny, Smile, Royal Flash, Won Ton Ton, The One and Only, Oliver's Story, Bloodline (co-prod.), The Jerk (co-prod.), Dead Men Don't Wear Plaid (co-prod.), The Man with Two Brains, Beat Street (co-prod.).

PICKER, EUGENE D.: Executive b. New York, NY, Nov. 17, 1903. p. David V. and Celia C. Picker. e. New York U. and Sch. of Business. Started with father in Bronx theatres; joined Loew's Inc., 1920; in charge circuit operations, New York area, 1945; v.p. Loew's Theatres, Sept. 1954; member bd. of dir., 1956, exec. v.p. Sept. 1958; pres. Loew's Theatres, March 1959. Res. 1961 as pres. Loew's Theatres; joined U.A. as v.p., July 1961. Joined Trans-Lux Corp. as exec. v.p., Jan. 1967; pres. & chief oper. Officer of Entertainment Division of Trans-Lux Corp. to 1984 then confirmed as member bd. of directors; Exec. consultant motion picture industry Jan. 1, 1974 and Pres. E.D.P. Films Inc. as of June 1974 to 1982; pres. NATO, 1969–71, ch. bd., 1971–72, Bd. dir., Will Rogers Hospital, bd. ch. At present member board of directors, Trans Lux Corp. and Foundation of Motion Picture Pioneers and Broadway Association.

PICKMAN, JEROME: Executive. b. New York, NY, Aug. 24, 1916. e. St. John's U.; Brooklyn Law Sch. of St. Lawrence U., LL.B. Reporter N.Y. newspapers, 1930–40; U.S. Army World War II; Ad-pub exec. 20th-Fox, 1945–46; Eagle-Lion Films, 1947; Paramount Pictures, 1949; v.p., dir., adv. & pub., Paramount, 1951; v.p. domestic gen. sls. mgr., Paramount 1960–62; senior sls. exec. Columbia Pictures 1963–67; pres. Continental Motion Picture Div. of Walter Reade Org., 1967–70; pres., Levitt-Pickman Film Corp., 1971; snr. v.p., domestic distribution, Lorimar Productions, 1979–81; pres., Pickman Film Corp., Cineworld Enterprises Corp., 1982; pres. Scotti Bros. Pictures Distribution, 1986.

PIERCE, FREDERICK S.: Executive. b. New York, NY, April 8, 1933. e. Bernard Baruch Sch. of B.A., City Coll. of New York. Served with U.S. Combat Engineers in Korean War. Associated with Benj. Harrow & Son, CAP, before joining ABC in 1956. Served as analyst in TV research dep.; prom. to supvr. of audience measurements, 1957, named mgr. next year. In 1961 made dir. of research; 1962 dir. of research, sales devel. Named dir. of sales planning, sales devel. April, 1962; elec. v.p., Feb. 1964 and made nat. dir. of sales for TV. In 1968 named v.p., planning; March. 1970 named asst. to pres. In July 1972, named v.p. in chg. ABC TV planning and devel. and asst. to pres. ABC TV, March, 1973. Named sr. v.p., ABC TV, Jan., 1974. Elected pres., ABC Television Division, October, 1974. Pres. & chief operating off., ABC, Inc., 1983.

PIERSON, FRANK: Producer, Director, Writer. b. Chappaqua, NY, May 12, 1925. e. Harvard U. Was correspondent for Time magazine before entering show business as story editor of TV series, Have Gun, Will Travel. Later served as both producer and director for show. Developed a number of properties for Screen Gems before writing theatrical screenplays.
PICTURES INCLUDE: Cat Ballou (co-s.p.), Cool Hand Luke (s.p.), The Anderson Tapes (s.p.), The Looking Glass War, (s.p., dir.), Dog Day Afternoon (s.p., Acad. Award, 1975), A Star Is Born (dir., s.p.), King of the Gypsies (dir., s.p.), In Country (s.p.).
TELEVISION: Nicholas (series, prod.), Haywire (s.p.), The Neon Ceiling, Alfred Hitchcock Presents (1985).

PIGOTT-SMITH, TIM: Actor. b. England, 1946. Acted with Bristol Old Vic, Royal Shakespeare Co. On stage in As You Like It, Major Barbara, School for Scandal, Sherlock Holmes, The Benefactors, Entertaining Strangers.
PICTURES: Man in the Fog, Escape to Victory, Sweet William, Richard's Things, Clash of the Titans, Joseph Andrews, State of Emergency.
TELEVISION: The Lost Boys, Henry IV, Day Christ Died, Hunchback of Notre Dame, Fame Is the Spur, Glittering Prizes, The Jewel in the Crown, Dead Man's Folly, The Case of Sherlock Holmes.

PIKE, JOHN S.: Executive. Joined Paramount Pictures as v.p., video programming; promoted to sr. v.p., video prog. 1984, named sr. v.p., current network programming; 1985, promoted to exec. v.p., Paramount Network TV. 1986, appt. pres., Paramount Network TV Division.

PILCHER, TONY: Producer. b. Boston, England, 1936. e. Shrewsbury Sch. Ent. m.p. industry 1960 with Anglo-Scottish Pictures. Became prod. exec. 1961, German rep. and exec. 1963. Joined AB-Pathe as German rep., TV and Advertising Films division 1964. TV prod., Heumann Ogilvy & Mather, Frankfurt, 1966; prod. Chambers and Partners; Guild TV; Wace Film, Signal Films, Rayant TV, Filmshop, Europartners 1967 to date.

PILE, SUSAN: Executive. First west coast editor of Interview magazine before entering entertainment industry as media buyer and acct. exec. on m.p. accts for Diener/Hauser/Bates. After 6 years left to become partner in Proper Exposure, specialized mktg. firm in m.p. field. Natl.mag. contact, Universal Pictures; unit publicist for Universal & Warner Bros. 1980, joined Paramount as dir., west coast adv. & pub. 1981, named v.p., west coast pub. & promo; 1985, sr. v.p., west coast publ, promo. & adv. Resigned 1988.

PINCHOT, BRONSON: Actor. b. New York, NY, May 20, 1959. e. Yale U.
PICTURES: Risky Business (debut, 1983), Beverly Hills Cop, The Flamingo Kid, Hot Resort, After Hours, Second Sight.
TELEVISION: Series: Sara (1985), Perfect Strangers.

PINK, SIDNEY: Producer, Director, Writer. b. Pittsburgh, PA, Mar. 6, 1916. e. U. of Pittsburgh, B.S., 1934–37; U. of Southern California, law, 1940–41. Projectionist, mgr., booker, Warner Bros., PA, Fox West Coast, United Artists Theatres, Calif. Prod. budget mgr., Something to Sing About and Lost Horizon.
PICTURES INCLUDE: Bwana Devil, Angry Red Planet, Green-Eyed Elephant, Reptilicus, Journey to The Seventh Planet, Operation Camel, Valley of the Swords, Madigan's Millions.

PINSKER, ALLEN: Executive. b. New York, NY, Jan. 23, 1930. e. New York U. Mgr., Hempstead Theatre, 1950. In 1954 joined Island Theatre Circuit as booker-buyer; named head buyer 1958. In 1968 joined United Artists Eastern Theatres as film buyer; head buyer, 1969, v.p., 1970. Named v.p. United Artists Theatre Circuit, 1972. In 1973 named UAET exec. v.p., member bd., 1974. Appt. pres. & COO, UA Communications, Inc., theatre division 1987. March, 1987, named pres. and CEO, United Artists Theatre Circuit, Inc. and exec. v.p., United Artists Communications, Inc.; 1988, became member, bd. dir. United Artists Comm. Inc.

PINTER, HAROLD: Writer, Director, Actor. b. London, England, Oct. 10, 1930. Began career as actor then turned to writing and direction. Plays include The Dumb Waiter, Slight Ache, The Room, The Birthday Party, The Caretaker, The Home-coming, The Collection, Landscape, Silence, Old Times, No Man's Land, The Hot House, Betrayal.
PICTURES: The Caretaker, The Servant, The Pumpkin Eater, The Quiller Memorandum, Accident, The Go-Between, The Last Tycoon, The French Lieutenant's Woman, Betrayal, Turtle Diary, Reunion.
TELEVISION: A Night Out, Night School, The Lover, Tea Party, The Basement.

PIROSH, ROBERT: Writer, Director, Producer. b. Baltimore, MD, April 1, 1910. S.p. credits include A Day at the Races, I Married a Witch, Rings on Her Fingers, Up in Arms, Battleground (solo orig. s.p. Academy Award winner), Hell Is for Heroes, A Gathering of Eagles, What's So Bad About Feeling Good, S.p.-dir. credits include Go for Broke, Washington Story, Valley of the Kings, The Girl Rush, Spring Reunion.
TELEVISION: (Wrote, prod. pilots) Laramie, Combat. (Writer) Hawaii Five-0, Ellery Queen, Mannix, Bonanza, Ironside, The Waltons, Barnaby Jones, The Bold Ones, etc.

PISANO, A. ROBERT: Executive. e. San Jose State U.; U. of California, Berkeley. Member, State Bar of CA, Board of Directors, American Corp. Counsel Assn., American Bar Assoc., L.A. County Bar Assoc. Joined O'Melveny & Myers as associate 1969; made partner 1976. 1979–82 headed its Paris office. Returned to L.A. office to handle Paramount Pictures' litigation 1983–84. In 1985 joined Paramount as exec. v.p. & gen. counsel.

PISCOPO, JOE: Actor, Comedian. b. Passaic, NJ, June 17, 1951. Stage appearances in regional and dinner theaters in South and Northeast. Worked as stand-up comic at the Improvisa-tion and the Comic Strip clubs, NY 1976–80. Author: The Piscopo Tapes. Television debut as regular on Saturday Night Live, 1980–84.
PICTURES: American Tickler or the Winner of 10 Academy Awards (1976); Johnny Dangerously, Wise Guys.
TELEVISION: Saturday Night Live; Comic Relief (1986).

PISIER, MARIE-FRANCE: Actress. b. Indochina, 1944. First discovered by François Truffaut who cast her in Love at

Twenty (1976). When film completed returned to school for degree in political science. Continued to work in films.
PICTURES: French Provincial, Trans-Europe Express, Stolen Kisses, Celine et Julie Vont en Bateau, Cousin Cousine, Souvenirs d'en France, Barocco, The Other Side of Midnight, Serail, Love on the Run, Les Apprentis Sourciers, The Bronte Sisters, French Postcards, La Banquiere, Chanel Solitaire, Der Zauberberg (The Magic Mountain), Ace of Aces, Hot Touch, The Prize of Peril, Der Stille Ocean, L'Ami de Vincent, The Abyss.
TELEVISION: (U.S.) French Atlantic Affair, Scruples.

PLACE, MARY KAY: Actress, Songwriter. b. Tulsa, OK, Septem-ber, 1947. e. U. of Tulsa. Worked in production jobs also as Tim Conway's asst. for his TV show and as sect. for Norman Lear on Maude before starting to write for TV series (Mary Tyler Moore Show, Phyllis, Maude, M*A*S*H, etc.). Also involved in acting, appearing in episodes of All in the Family and Mary Tyler Moore Show and as Loretta Haggers on series, Mary Hartman, Mary Hartman (Emmy, best comedy actress).
PICTURES: Bound For Glory (debut, 1976), More Ameri-can Graffiti, New York, New York, Starting Over, Private Benjamin, Modern Problems, Waltz Across Texas, The Big Chill, Smooth Talk, A New Life.
TELEVISION: Fernwood 2-Night, Saturday Night Live, The Tonight Show, John Denver Special. Movies: The Girl Who Spelled Freedom, Act of Love, For Love or Money. Specials: Martin Mull's History of White People in America I & II, Portrait of a White Marriage, 4 specials on religion, white crime, stress and politics.

PLATT, MILT: Executive. b. New York, NY. e. City Coll. of New York, RCA Inst., Ohio State U. U.S. Army 1942–46; div. mgr., RKO Radio Pictures until 1957; gen. sls. mgr. Continental Dist., 1957–65; vice-pres. & gen. sls. mgr. Sherpix, 1965; v.p. & gen. sls. mgr., Comet Film Distributors, Inc., 1965; v.p. & sls. mgr., Times Film Corp., 1968. Pres. Eagle Amusement Co., 1970. Appointed member of the Appeals Board of the MPA rating system, 1971; pres. of Pisces Group, Ltd., 1972; v.p. & gen. sls. mgr., International Co-productions, Inc., 1974. pres., Milton Platt Co., 1975. Member governing committee, IFIDA

PLEASENCE, DONALD: Actor. b. Worksop, England, Oct. 5, 1919. Repertory, first London appearance in Twelfth Night. RAF, WW II. Since London stage, N.Y. stage, ent. m.p, ind. 1953.
STAGE: Vicious Circle, Saint's Day, Hobson's Choice, The Rules of the Game, The Lark, Ebb Tide, The Caretaker, Poor Bitos, The Man in the Glass Booth, Wise Child (N.Y.); voted actor of the year, 1958.
PICTURES INCLUDE: Manuela, The Man in the Sky, Heart of a Child, Tale of Two Cities, Battle of the Sexes, The Shakedown, The Horsemasters, Spare the Rod, No Love for Johnnie, The Caretaker, The Great Escape, The Greatest Story Ever Told, Hallelujah Trail, Fantastic Voyage, Cul-de-Sac, You Only Live Twice, Matchless, 13, Will Penny, Arthur! Arthur, THX 1138, Soldier Blue, Outback, Jerusalem File, Pied Piper, Innocent Bystanders, Death Line, Wedding in White, The Rainbow Boys, The Black Windmill, Journey Into Fear, Escape to Witch Mountain, Hearts of the West, The Devil Within Her, The Last Tycoon, Passover Plot, Trial by Combat, The Eagle Has Landed, Goldenrod, Oh God!, Fear, the Uncanny, Telefon, Escape from New York, Halloween, Halloween II, Terror in the Aisles, Warrior Queen, Prince of Darkness, Hanna's War, The Commander, Halloween IV, Off Balance, Paganini Horror, Metropolitan Animals, Nosferatu in Venice, Death on Safari.
TELEVISION: Fate and Mr. Browne, Small Fish Are Sweet, The Silk Purse, A House of His Own, The Traitor, The Millionairess, The Cupboard Machinal, The Hatchet Man, The Bandstand, Ambrose, Thou Good and Faithful Servant, Call Me Daddy, Taste, The Fox Trot, Omnibus, Julius Caesar, Occupations, The Joke, The Cafeteria, Kindle Wakes, Master of the Game, Arch of Triumph, The Great Escape: The Final Chapter, Scoop, Punishment Without Crime, The Room.

PLESHETTE, EUGENE: Executive. b. Brooklyn, NY, Jan. 7. e. City Coll. of New York, LaSalle U., Paramount Pict. Acting Sch. Stage actor; assoc. prod. and dir. three off-Broadway plays; treas. and house mgr. N.Y. Paramount; v.p. Reid-Singer Music; exec. mgr. Brooklyn Paramount thea., 1945; mgn. dir. 1953; v.p. in chg. of ABC Merchandising Inc., AB-PT, Inc. and American Broadcasting Co., 1962; exec. v.p., MSG-ABC Prods., Inc. 1965; exec. v.p. Don Reid TV Prod.; 1975, President, Pleshette Associates.

PLESHETTE, SUZANNE: Actress. b. New York, NY, Jan. 31, 1937. e. Performing Arts H.S., Finch Coll., Syracuse U. Broadway debut, Compulsion; m.p. debut Geisha Boy (1958).
STAGE: The Cold Wind and the Warm, The Golden Fleecing, The Miracle Worker, Compulsion, Two for the Seesaw, Special Occasions.
PICTURES INCLUDE: Rome Adventure, The Birds, 40 Pounds of Trouble, Wall of Noise, A Rage to Live, Youngblood Hawke, A Distant Trumpet, The Ugly Dachshund, Bullwhip

 # Ple-Pol

Griffin, Fate is the Hunter, Mr. Buddwing, Nevada Smith, Blackbeard's Ghost, The Power, If It's Tuesday This Must Be Belgium, Suppose They Gave a War and Nobody Came, Support Your Local Gunfighter, The Shaggy D.A., Oh, God! Book II.
TELEVISION: Series: The Bob Newhart Show (1972–78); Suzanne Pleshette Is Maggie Briggs (1984–85); Bridges to Cross. Movies: Flesh and Blood; For Love or Money; Fantasies; If Things Were Different; Help-Wanted-Male; Dixie Changing Habits; Starmaker; One Cooks, The Other Doesn't; Legend of Valentino; Kojak The Belarus File; A Stranger Waits; Alone in the Neon Jungle.

PLESKOW, ERIC: Executive. b., Vienna, Austria, April 24, 1924. Served as film officer, U.S. War dept., 1946–48; entered industry in 1948 as asst. mgr., Motion Picture Export Association, Germany; 1950–51, continental rep. for Sol Lesser Prods.; joined United Artists in 1951 as Far East Sales Mgr.; named mgr., S. Africa, 1952; mgr., Germany, 1953–58; exec. asst. to continental mgr., 1958–59; asst. continental mgr., 1959–60; continental mgr., 1960–62; v.p. in charge of foreign distribution, 1962; exec. v.p. & chief operating off., Jan. 1, 1973; pres. & chief exec. off., Oct. 1, 1973. Resigned in 1978 to become pres. and chief exec. officer of Orion Pictures Co.; 1982, became pres. & chief exec. off., Orion Pictures Corp.

PLITT, HENRY G.: Executive. b. New York, NY, Nov. 26, 1918. e. Syracuse U., St. Lawrence U. Law Sch. War service, 6 yrs.; Paramount Pictures International Corp.; United Detroit Theatres; asst. gen. mgr., North Ohio Theatres Corp.; div. mgr., then v.p., Paramount Gulf Theatres, New Orleans; pres. gen. mgr. Paramount Gulf Theatres; pres., ABC Films, 1959–65; Pres. ABC Great States Inc., Great States Theas. 1966; v.p. Prairie Farmer publications, 1971, v.p., ABC Theatre Holdings, Inc.; 1974, purchased Northern Theatre Circuit from American Broadcasting Company, consisting of 127 theatres, naming these theatres Plitt Theatres, Inc., of which he is bd. chmn. 1978, purchased rest of ABC theatres from American Broadcasting Company consisting of 272 screens, and renamed them Plitt Theatres. Sold circuit interest in 1985. Presently bd. chm., Showscan Film Corp.

PLOWRIGHT, JOAN: C.B.E. Actress. b. Scunthrope, Brigg, Lincolnshire, Eng., Oct. 28, 1929. m. Lord Laurence Olivier. Trained for stage at Laban Art of Movement Studio, 1949–50; Old Vic Theatre Sch. 1950–52; with Michel St. Denis, Glen Byam Shaw and George Devine. London stage debut The Duenna, 1954. Broadway debut The Entertainer, 1958. Won Tony Award in 1961 for A Taste of Honey. With Bristol Old Vic Rep., Royal Court, National Theatre in numerous classics and contemporary plays.
RECENT THEATER: Saturday, Sunday, Monday; The Seagull; The Bed Before Yesterday; Filumena; Enjoy; Who's Afraid of Virginia Woolf; Cavell; The Cherry Orchard; The Way of the World; Mrs. Warren's Profession.
PICTURES: Moby Dick (1956), Time Without Pity, The Entertainer, Three Sisters, Equus, Richard Wagner, Brimstone and Treacle, Britannica Hospital, The Dressmaker, Drowning By Numbers, The Divider.
TELEVISION: Odd Man In, Secret Agent, School for Scandal, The Diary of Anne Frank, Twelfth Night, Merchant of Venice, Daphne Laureola, Saturday, Sunday, Monday.

PLUMMER, AMANDA: Actress. b. New York, NY, March 23, 1957. e. Middlebury Coll. Daughter of Christopher Plummer and Tammy Grimes.
THEATER: You Never Can Tell, A Taste of Honey, Agnes of God (Tony Award, featured actress, 1982), The Glass Menagerie, Pygmalion, The Milk Train Doesn't Stop Here Anymore.
PICTURES: Cattle Annie and Little Britches, Daniel, The World According to Garp, The Hotel New Hampshire, Static, The Courtship, Made in Heaven.
TELEVISION: The Unforgivable Secret, The Dollmaker, Riders to the Sea, The Courtship, Gryphon.

PLUMMER, CHRISTOPHER: Actor. b. Toronto, Canada, Dec. 13, 1927. Stage career started with English repertory group visiting Canada; toured U.S. in Nina, 1953; Bway debut in The Constant Wife, 1954; on road and in N.Y. with The Dark is Light Enough; American Shakespeare Festival at Stratford, CT, in Julius Caesar and The Tempest; Shakespeare Festival at Stratford, Ont., in Henry V, Twelfth Night, and Hamlet; on Bway in The Lark and Cyrano (musical, Tony Award, 1974), Othello, Macbeth.
TELEVISION: Oedipus Rex, Omnibus, After the Fall, The Moneychangers, Desperate Voyage, The Shadow Box, When the Circus Came to Town, Dial M for Murder, Little Gloria— Happy at Last, The Scarlet and the Black, The Thorn Birds, The Velveteen Rabbit, Crossings, A Hazard of Hearts.
PICTURES INCLUDE: Across the Everglades, Stage Struck, Inside Daisy Clover, The Sound of Music, Triple Cross, The Battle of Britain, The Royal Hunt of the Sun, Lock Up Your Daughters, The Pyx, The Return of the Pink Panther, Conduct Unbecoming, The Man Who Would Be King,

International Velvet, The Silent Partner, Murder by Decree, Hanover Street, Somewhere in Time, Eyewitness, The Amateur, Dreamscape, Ordeal by Innocence, Lily in Love, The Boy in Blue, Dragnet, The Boss' Wife, Souvenir, Light Years (voice), Stage Fright, Nosferatu in Venice.

PODELL, ALBERT N.: Executive. b. New York, NY, Feb. 25, 1937. e. Cornell U., U. of Chicago. Articles editor, Playboy magazine, 1959–61; dir. of photog., Argosy magazine, 1961–64; account exec. on 20th Century-Fox at Diener, Hauser, Greenthal, 1966–68; national advertising dir., Cinema Center Films, 1969; account supervisor on Columbia Pictures at Charles Schlaifer; creator & dir. of Annual Motion Picture Advertising Awards sponsored by Cinema Lodge, B'nai B'rith.

PODESTA, ROSSANA: Actress. b. Tripoli, June 20, 1934. Discovered in Italy by French director Leonide Moguy, who starred her in Tomorrow Is Another Day. For 15 years appeared only in films by her husband, Marco Cicario; now divorced.
PICTURES INCLUDE: Cops and Robbers, La Red, Ulysses, Helen of Troy, Santiago, The Golden Arrow, Il Prete Sposato, Seven Golden Men, Pano, Burro e Marmelate, The Quiet Countrywoman, Sunday Lovers, Stasi, Hercules; Secrets, Secrets.

PODHORZER, MUNIO: Executive. b. Berlin, Germany, Sept. 18. e. Jahn-Realgymnasium, U. of Berlin Medical Sch. U.S. Army, 1943–47; pres. United Film Enterprises, Inc.; formerly secy.-treas. 86th St. Casino Theatre, N.Y.; former v.p. Atlantic Pictures Corp.; former pres. Casino Films, Inc.; former pres. Film Development Corp.; former rep. Export-Union of the German Film Ind.; former U.S. rep. Franco-London Film, Paris; former pres., Venus Productions Corp.; former U.S. rep. Atlas Int'l Film GmbH, Munich; former U.S. rep. Bavaria Atelier Gesellschaft U.S. past rep. Israfilm Ltd., Tel-Aviv; past rep. Tigon British Film Prod., London; past rep. Elias Querejeta, P.C., Madrid; past rep. Equiluz Films, Madrid, past rep. Airport Cine, Hawaii, Les Films Du Capricorne; Profilmes, Spain; Ligno, Spain; Films D'Alma, France; Intra Films, Italy. Member: Variety Club, Cinema Lodge, B'nai B'rith, Past Board of Governors IFIDA; past pres. CID Agents Assoc. Former gen. foreign sales mgr., theatrical division of National Telefilm Associates. Presently representing Atlas Film + AV, Germany; Barcino Films, S.A., Spain; Eagle Films Ltd., United Kingdom; Les Films Jacques Leitienne, France; Nero Films Classics U.S.A.; Schongerfilm Germany; Profilmes, S.A., Spain; KFM Films, Inc. U.S.A.; Compagnie France Film, Canada; Cia. Iberoamerican de TV, S.A. Spain; V.I.P. Ltd., Israel. Co-chm., entertainment div., United Jewish Appeal, Federation of Jewish Philanthropies, 1981–83.

PODHORZER, NATHAN: Executive. b. Brody, Poland, Nov. 27, 1919. e. City Coll. of New York, Rutgers U., U. of Southern California. U.S. Army, 1942–46; documentary film prod., Israel, 1946–57; vice pres., secy., United Film Enterprises, Inc.

POE, STEPHEN: Executive. Began career as lawyer with Rutan & Tucker; continues active entertainment law practice, recently being indep. counsel for United Artists Pictures. 1976, joined 20th Century-Fox as prod. counsel; later v.p., business affairs. Turned to producing in 1982, first in association with Frank Mancuso Jr. Productions. 1987, joined CBS/Fox Video as sr. v.p. of acquisitions and programming.

POITIER, SIDNEY: Actor. b. Miami, FL, Feb. 24, 1924. m. actress Joanna Shimkus. e. Miami, FL. Appeared on stage with Amer. Negro Theatre in Days of Our Youth. Formed First Artists Prod. Co. Ltd., 1969, with Paul Newman and Barbra Streisand. Autobiography: This Life (1980).
STAGE: Strivers Road, You Can't Take It With You, Anna Lucasta (Bdwy debut, 1948), Lysistrata, Freight, A Raisin in the Sun.
PICTURES INCLUDE: No Way Out (debut 1950), Cry the Beloved Country, Red Ball Express, Go Man Go, Blackboard Jungle, Good-Bye My Lady, Edge of the City, Something of Value, Porgy and Bess, All the Young Men, Devil at Four O'Clock, A Raisin in the Sun, The Long Ships, Lilies of the Field (Acad. Award, 1963), Slender Thread, A Patch of Blue, Duel at Diablo, To Sir With Love, In the Heat of the Night, Guess Who's Coming to Dinner, The Lost Man, They Call Me Mister Tibbs, Brother John, For Love of Ivy, Buck and the Preacher (also dir.), A Warm December (dir., star), Uptown Saturday Night (dir., star), The Wilby Conspiracy, Let's Do It Again (dir., star), A Piece of the Action (dir., star), Stir Crazy (dir.), Hanky Panky (dir.), Fast Forward (dir.), Shoot To Kill, Little Nikita.

POLANSKI, ROMAN: Director, Writer. b. Paris, France, Aug. 18, 1933. Lived in Poland from age of three. Early career, art school in Cracow; five years State Film College at Lodz. As actor in Amadeus (and dir., Warsaw), Metamorphosis (Paris, 1988). Autobiography: Roman (1984).
PICTURES: Wrote and dir. shorts: Two Men in a Wardrobe, Le Gros et Le Maigre, Mammals. Features: Knife in the Water (Poland), Repulsion, Cul-De-Sac, The Vampire Killers. Direc-

tor: Rosemary's Baby, Macbeth, What?, Chinatown. Director-writer: The Tenant (also actor), Tess, Pirates, Frantic.

POLIER, DAN A.: Executive. b. Atlanta, GA. e. Georgia Military Acad., U. of Illinois. Sports columnist, Charlotte (N.C.) News; sports editor, army wkly, Yank; entered m.p. industry adv. dept. 20th Century-Fox; head of booking dept. Fox West Coast Theatres; v.p. and director of film buying NTT Amusement Corp.; v.p. and co-director theatre operations, National General Corp. (formerly NTT); named v.p. in chg. of production, National General Productions, Inc., 1967. Joined Radnitz/Mattel Productions in 1972 as v.p. in chg. of distribution for Sounder; v.p. Mann Theatres Corp. of Calif., 1973. Rejoined Radnitz/Mattel Productions, 1975, as vice pres. in charge of marketing. Now pres., Knopf/Polier Representation.

POLL, MARTIN H.: Producer. b. New York, NY. e. Wharton Sch., U. of Pennsylvania. Pres. Gold Medal Studios; prod. Love Is a Ball, Sylvia, The Lion in Winter, The Appointment, The Magic Cⁿⁿⁿⁿ of Stanley Sweetheart, The Man Who Loved Cat Dancing, Night Watch, Love and Death (exec. prod.); The Sailor who Fell From Grace with the Sea, Somebody Killed Her Husband, The Dain Curse, Nighthawks, Arthur the King, Gimme an F, Haunted Summer.

POLLACK, SYDNEY: Director, Producer. b. South Bend, IN, July 1, 1934. m. Claire Griswold. e. Neighborhood Playhouse. Assistant to Sanford Meisner at Neighborhood Playhouse. Appeared as actor on Bdwy in A Stone for Danny Fisher, The Dark is Light Enough. As TV actor: Playhouse 90 segments, Shotgun Slade, 15 Ben Caseys, A Cardinal Act of Mercy (won 5 Emmy nominations), The Game on Bob Hope-Chrysler Theatre (won Emmy for direction), Two is the Number. Dir. debut in 1960. Dir. play at U. of California at L.A., P.S. 193. Prepared the American version of The Leopard.
  PICTURES INCLUDE: The Slender Thread (dir.), This Property is Condemned, The Scalphunters, Castle Keep, They Shoot Horses, Don't They?, Jeremiah Johnson, The Way We Were, The Yakuza, Three Days of the Condor, Bobby Deerfield, The Electric Horseman, Honeysuckle Rose (exec. prod. only), Absence of Malice (also prod.); Tootsie (also prod. and actor); Songwriter (prod. only); Out of Africa (also prod.), Bright Lights, Big City (prod. only), Scrooged (exec. prod.), The Comeback Kid (prod. only).

POLLEXFEN, JACK: Producer, Director, Writer. b. San Diego, CA, June 10, 1918. e. Los Angeles City Coll. Newspaperman, magazine writer, playwright: prod. for RKO, United Artists, Columbia, Allied Artists.
  PICTURES INCLUDE: Son of Sinbad, At Swords Point, Secret of Convict Lake, Desert Hawk, Lady in the Iron Mask, Dragon's Gold, Problem Girls, Captive Women, Captain Kidd and the Slave Girl, Neanderthal Man, Captain John Smith and Pocahontas, Return to Treasure Island, Sword of Venus, 1000 Years from Now, Daughter of Dr. Jekyll, Monstrosity, Son of Dr. Jekyll, Mr. Big, Man from Planet X.

POLLOCK, DALE: Executive. b. Cleveland, OH, 1950. e. Brandeis U., B.A. anthropology, San Jose State U, M.A. mass communication. Began journalistic career in Santa Cruz in early '70s, serving as reporter and film critic for Daily Variety from 1977 to 1980. Then joined Los Angeles Times as film writer, winning paper's Award for Sustained Excellence in 1984. In 1985 left to take post with The Geffen Film Co. as executive in chg. creative development. Joined A&M Films as v.p. in chg. prod., Jan. 1986. Author: Skywalking (about George Lucas). Co-exec. prod.: Finding Maubee.

POLLOCK, THOMAS: Executive. b. 1943. In 1971, after 3 years as business mgr. for American Film Institute's film marketing wing, formed law firm Pollock Bloom, and Dekom with young filmmakers such as George Lucas and Matthew Robbins as clients. Served as chmn. Filmex, 1973–81. 1986, named chmn. MCA's Universal motion picture group, also v.p., MCA, Inc.

POLONSKY, ABRAHAM: Director, Writer. b. New York, NY, Dec. 5, 1910. e. City Coll. of New York, B.A.; Columbia Law Sch. Taught at City Coll. 1932 until war. Wrote s.p. Golden Earrings, I Can Get it For You Wholesale. Wrote novels; The Enemy Sea, The Discoverers, The World Above, The Season of Fear, Zenia's Way. Wrote orig. story and s.p. Body and Soul; collab. s.p. and directed Force of Evil. Blacklisted from 1951–66; Odds Against Tomorrow (s.p.). Coll. s.p. Madigan 1968; dir. and s.p. Tell Them Willie Boy is Here, 1970; dir. Romance of a Horse Thief, 1971; Avalanche Express (s.p.); Monsignor, (s.p.) 1982.

PONTECORVO, GILLO: Director. b. Pisa, Italy, 1919. Younger brother of Prof. Bruno Pontecorvo, Harwell scientist who defected in 1950. Worked as asst. dir., directed documentary shorts before feature debut in 1957.
  PICTURES: Die Windrose Giovanna; La Grande Strada Azzurra; Kapo; The Battle of Algiers; Queimada!; (Burn); Ogro.

PONTI, CARLO: Producer. b. Milan, Italy, Dec. 11, 1913. m. actress Sophia Loren. e. U. of Milan, 1934. Prod. first picture in Milan, Little Old World; prod. Lux Film Rome; prod. first of a series of famous Toto pictures, Toto Househunting.
  PICTURES INCLUDE: A Dog's Life, The Knight Has Arrived, Musolino, The Outlaw, Romanticism, Sensuality, The White Slave, Europe 1951, Toto in Color, The Three Corsairs, Ulysses, The Woman of the River, An American of Rome, Attila, War and Peace, The Last Lover, The Black Orchid, That Kind of Woman, Marriage Italian Style, The Great Spy Mission, Happily Ever After, The Girl and the General, Sunflower, Best House in London, Lady Liberty, White Sister, What?, Andy Warhol's Frankenstein, The Passenger, The Cassandra Crossing, A Special Day.
  TELEVISION: Mario Puzo's The Fortunate Pilgrim (exec. prod.).

POOLE, FRANK S.: Executive. b. London, England, 1913. e. Dulwich Coll., 1925–31. Ent. m.p. ind. 1931. Early career with Pathe Pictures, Twickenham Film Distributors, until joining 20th Century Fox as London branch office supervisor 1939. War service 1940–46. Rejoined Fox 1946–53; appt. Leed Branch mgr. 1954–59; supv. 1959–61; asst. sls. mgr., 1961 until joined Rank Film Distrib. as asst. sls. mgr. 1962. Appt. sls. mgr. July 1965, and to board as dir. of sls. Aug. 1965. Appt. gen. mgr. 1968; jnt. mng. dir. 1969; appt. mng. dir. July 1970; appt. dir. Rank Overseas Film Dist. Ltd., 1972; appt. co-chmn Fox-Rank Distributors Ltd., Dec. 1972; appt. vice-chairman Rank Film Distributors Ltd. 1977. 1975, elected to Committee of Cinema & TV Veterans. Oct., 1978, retired from Rank Organisation. Appt. chmn., Appeal Tribunal for the Film Industry. Appt. chm., Grebelands Mgt. Committee & to exec. council of CTBF, 1979, assoc. Geoff Reeve & Associates. 1980, chm. & mng. dir., Omandry Intl. Ltd.

PORTER, DON: Actor. b. Miami, OK, Sept. 24, 1912. e. Oregon Inst. of Tech. Wide theatre work; then m.p, roles. U.S. Army, 3 yrs.
  TELEVISION: Co-star, Private Secretary, Ann Sothern Show, Gidget, Bionic Woman, Hawaii Five-O, Switch, Love Boat, Three's Company, The President's Mistress, The Murder That Wouldn't Die, The Last Song, Dallas; Old Money.
  STAGE: The Best Man, Any Wednesday, Generation, Plaza Suite, The Price, How To Succeed in Business Without Really Trying, Harvey.
  PICTURES INCLUDE: The Racket, The Savage, 711 Ocean Drive, Because You're Mine, Our Miss Brooks, Bachelor in Paradise, Youngblood Hawke, The Candidate, 40 Carats, Mame, White Line Fever.

POST, TED: Producer, Director. b. Brooklyn, NY, March 31, 1918. Dir. many stage plays; dir. CBS-TV Repertoire Thea.; Producer-dir., NBC-TV Coney Island of the Mind.
  TELEVISION: Studio One, Ford Theatre, Playhouse of Stars, Fred Astaire Show, Gunsmoke, Rawhide, Twilight Zone, Wagon Train, Combat, Peyton Place, Alcoa, Defenders, Route 66, Baretta, and Columbo. Movies: Dr. Cook's Garden, Girls in One Office, Cagney & Lacey, Night Slaves, Five Desperate Women, Stagecoach, Yuma, The Bravos, Do Not Fold, Spindle or Mutilate.
  MINI-SERIES: Rich Man, Poor Man II (episode 3).
  PICTURES INCLUDE: The Peachmaker (1956), The Legend of Tom Dooley, Magnum Force, Hang 'em High, Beneath The Planet of the Apes, The Harrad Experiment, Good Guys Wear Black, Whiffs, Go Tell the Spartans, Nightkill.

POSTER, STEVEN: Cinematographer. e. L.A. Art Center Coll. Started as commercial cinematographer before moving into feature films.
  PICTURES: Blood Beach, Dead and Buried, Spring Break, Strange Brew, Testament, The New Kids, The Heavenly Kid, Blue City, The Boy Who Could Fly, Aloha Summer.

POSTON, TOM: Actor. b. Columbus, OH, Oct. 17, 1927. Winner of Emmy for supporting work on Steve Allen Show (1959).
  PICTURES: The City That Never Sleeps; Zotz; The Old Dark House; Cold Turkey; The Happy Hooker; Rabbit Test; Up the Academy; Carbon Copy.
  TELEVISION: Movies: On the Rocks; We've Got Each Other; The Girl; The Gold Watch and Everything; Save the Dog! Series: Mork and Mindy, Fame, Newhart. Game Show: To Tell the Truth.

POTTER, DENNIS: Writer. b. Forest of Dean, Gloucester, Eng., May 17, 1935. e. New Coll., Oxford U.
  THEATER: Vote, Vote, Vote for Nigel Barton (1968); Son of Man; Only Make Believe; Brimstone and Treacle; Sufficient Carbohydrate.
  PICTURES: Pennies From Heaven; Gorky Park; Dreamchild; Track 29.
  TELEVISION: Series: Casanova; Mini-series: Pennies From Heaven; Blue Remembered Hills; Blade on the Feather, Rain on the Roof; Cream in My Coffee; Traitor; Paper Roses; The Singing Detective. PLAYS: The Confidence Courses; Stand Up Nigel Barton; Vote, Vote, Vote for Nigel Barton; Almost Cinderella; Son of Man; Lay Down Your Arms; Follow

Pot-Pre

the Yellow Brick Road; Only Make Believe; Joe's Ark; Schmoedipus; Late Call; Double Dare; Where Adam Stood; Brimstone and Treacle.
NOVELS: The Glittering Coffin; The Changing Forest; Hide and Seek.

POTTLE, HARRY: Production designer. b. London, England, 1925. e. Ealing Coll. of Arts. Fleet Air Arm, 1944–47. Ent. m.p. ind. 1947. Designed Blind Date, 1960. Human Jungle, Avengers (TV series). Art Director, You Only Live Twice, Chitty Chitty Bang Bang, The Adventurers. Production Designer, 39 Steps, Murder by Degree, Bear Island, Matarese Circle, Desert King.

POTTS, ANNIE: Actress. b. Nashville, TN, Oct. 28. e. Stephens Coll., MO. Began acting career in summer stock; on road in Charley's Aunt. Theatrical mp. debut, Corvette Summer (1978).
PICTURES: King of the Gypsies, Heartaches, Stick, Crimes of Passion, Ghostbusters, Pretty in Pink, Jumpin' Jack Flash, Pass the Ammo, Who's Harry Crumb?
TELEVISION: Movies: Flatbed Annie and Sweetie Pie, Cowboy, It Came Upon a Midnight Clear. Series: Goodtime Girls, Designing Women.

POUND, LESLIE: Executive. Entered industry in 1943 as reporter on British trade paper, Screen International. Following military service in India and Singapore returned to work for that publication until 1952 when joined Paramount pub. office in London on the The Greatest Show on Earth. Named dir. of adv./pub. in U.K. for Paramount. 1958, retained Para. position when Cinema Intl. Corp. was formed. 1977, joined Lew Grade in ITC Entertainment as worldwide dir. of pub./adv. 1982, intl. pub. chief for Embassy Pictures in Los Angeles. 1982, named Paramount Pictures v.p., intl. mktg. for motion picture div., N.Y. Now relocated in L.A. with mktg. div.

POWELL, CHARLES, M.: Executive. b. New York, NY, Feb. 17, 1934. e. New York U., B.S., journalism. Columbia Pictures national publicity mgr., national exploitation mgr., 1959–69. Paramount Pictures, national publicity coordinator, 1963–64. WNBC-Radio/TV, advertising/promotion mgr. 1965. Director adv., pub. for M. J. Frankovich 1969–71. Joined MGM as dir. adv. pub.-expl. in 1972; named div. v.p. & corp. v.p., 1974; Columbia Pictures, v.p. advertising/publicity/exploitation 1975. Universal Pictures, sr. v.p., 1976–80. Powell & Young, m.p. consultants; exec. v.p. & dir., Color Systems Technology, Inc. Board of Governors, Acad. of Motion Picture Arts & Sciences, since 1973. Member: Nat'l Acad. of Television Arts and Sciences. Founder & pres., Synagogue for the Performing Arts, L.A and Shofar Synagogue.

POWELL, JANE: Actress. r.n. Suzanne Burce. b. Portland, OR, Apr. 1, 1929. m. pub. relations exec. Dick Moore. Had own radio program over KOIN, Portland; singer on natl. networks; m.p. debut in Song of the Open Road, 1944. Star of Tomorrow, 1948. Autobiography: The Girl Next Door . . . and How She Grew (1988).
PICTURES INCLUDE: Holiday in Mexico, Three Daring Daughters, Luxury Liner, Date With Judy, Nancy Goes to Rio, Two Weeks With Love, Royal Wedding, Rich Young and Pretty, Small Town Girl, Three Sailors and a Girl, Seven Brides for Seven Brothers, Athena, Deep in My Heart, Hit the Deck, Girl Most Likely, The Enchanted Island.
STAGE: Irene (Broadway, 1974).
TELEVISION: Ruggles of Red Gap, Give My Regards to Broadway, Meet Me in St. Louis, Jane Powell Show.

POWELL, MICHAEL: Producer, Director, Writer. b. Canterbury, Kent, England, Sept. 30, 1905. Collaborated for many years with the late Emeric Pressburger in making films.
PICTURES INCLUDE: Writer only: Caste, Park Lane, The Star Reporter, Hotel Splendide, The Fire Raisers, Night of the Party, Lazybones, The Phantom Light, The Man Behind the Mask, etc. Writer-Producer-Director: The Edge of the World, The Spy in Black, The Thief of Baghdad, 49th Parallel, One of Our Aircraft is Missing, The Life and Death of Colonel Blimp, A Canterbury Tale, I Know Where I'm Going, A Matter of Life and Death, Black Narcissus, The Red Shoes, The Small Back Room, Gone to Earth, The Elusive Pimpernel, The Tales of Hoffman, Ill Met by Moonlight, Peeping Tom, Honeymoon, The Queen's Guards, They're a Weird Mob, Sebastian (prod. only), Age of Consent, The Boy Turned Yellow, Return to the Edge of the World.

POWERS, MALA: Actress. r.n. Mary Ellen Powers. b. San Francisco, CA, Dec. 29, 1921. p. George and Dell Powers, latter, dramatic coach. e. Max Reinhardt Dramatic Sch., Hollywood, CA, U. of California at L.A. Pasadena Playhouse in For Keeps, 1946; Distant Isle; Actor's Lab, Hollywood; did considerable radio work. Writer, narrator Children's Story, Tell-Story and Dial A Story (1979). Author: Follow the Year (1984).
PICTURES INCLUDE: Outrage, Edge of Doom, Cyrano de Bergerac, Rose of Cimarron, City Beneath the Sea, City That Never Sleeps, Geraldine, Yellow Mountain, Rage at Dawn,

Bengazi, Tammy and the Bachelor, Storm Rider, Flight of the Lost Balloon, Daddy's Gone-A-Hunting, Temple of the Ravens, Six Tickets to Hell.

POWERS, C. F. (MIKE) JR: Executive. b. San Francisco, CA, March 6, 1923. e. Park Coll., MO, Columbia U., N.Y., graduated U. of Oregon. Entered film business with P.R.C. in Portland, OR, 1947. Became Eagle Lion branch mgr. in Portland, 1950, and then United Artists. Moved to Seattle, WA as branch mgr. of 20th Century Fox, 1960. Was then western division mgr. for 20th Century Fox until 1967, then western division mgr. for Cinerama till 1973. Became exec. v.p., head film buyer for Robert L. Lippert Theatres, Transcontinental Theatres and Affiliated Theatres until 1978. Became western division mgr. for Filmways Pictures. President of Catholic Entertainment Guild of Northern Calif.; past Chief Barker of Variety Club Tent 32, San Francisco.

POWERS, STEFANIE: Actress. r.n. Stefania Federkiewicz. b. Hollywood, CA, Nov. 2, 1942. Theatrical m.p. debut in Among the Thorns, 1961. TV debut in The Girl from U.N.C.L.E. series.
PICTURES INCLUDE: Tammy Tell Me True, Experiment in Terror, The Inters, If a Man Answers, McClintock, Palm Springs Weekend, Fanatic, Die Die My Darling, Stagecoach, Love Has Many Faces, Warning Shot, Herbie Rides Again, Crescendo, Escape to Athena, Invisible Stranger (a.k.a. The Astral Factor).
TELEVISION: Feather and Father (series), Washington: Behind Closed Doors (mini-series), Hart to Hart (series). Movies: Family Secrets (also prod.), A Death in Canaan, Mistral's Daughter, Hollywood Wives, Deceptions, At Mother's Request, Beryl Markham: A Shadow on the Sun (also co-prod.).

PRATLEY, GERALD: Commentator, b. and e. London, Eng. Joined Canadian Broadcasting Corp., 1946; writer, narrator and producer of The Movie Scene and Music from the Films; asst. member British Film Academy, dir. Canadian Film Institute 1953; chairman Toronto and District Film Council 1956; co-dir. & founder A.G.E. Film Society, Toronto; contributor to U.S. and European film journals; film consult., Canadian Centennial Comm. Chmn., Canadian Film Awards; director, Stratford Film Festival; director, Ontario Film Institute, Toronto. Prof. of film, York U., U. of Toronto. Seneca Coll., McMaster U. Author: Cinema of John Frankenheimer; Otto Preminger; David Lean; John Huston, Torn Sprockets. Mem., classification board, Ontario Theatre branch. 1984, Mem. Advisory boards film depts., Humber College, Ryerson Polytechnical Institute; Mem. TV Ontario Adult Programming Order of Canada, 1984, Can. Picture Pioneers Assn. Cultural Executives, St. George's Society, Arts and Letters Club.

PRENTISS, PAULA: Actress. r.n. Paula Ragusa. b. San Antonio, TX, March 4, 1939. m. actor-director Richard Benjamin. e. Northwestern U., Bachelor degree in drama, 1959. On TV in He & She; on stage in As You Like It, Arf?
PICTURES INCLUDE: Where the Boys Are, The Honeymoon Machine, Bachelor in Paradise, Man's Favorite Sport, Catch 22, Move, The World of Henry Orient, In Harms Way, What's New Pussycat?, Scraping Bottom, Last of the Red Hot Lovers, The Parallax View, The Stepford Wives, The Black Marble, Buddy, Buddy, Saturday the 14th.

PRESLE, MICHELINE: Actress. r.n. Micheline Chassagne. b. Paris, France, Aug. 22, 1922. e. Raymond Rouleau Dram. Sch. m.p. debut in Je Chante; on stage in Colinette. Am. Stram Gram, Spectacle des Allies; to U.S., 1945.
PICTURES INCLUDE: Jeunes Filles en Detresse, L'Histoire de Rire, La Nuit Fantastique, Felicie Nanteuil, Seul Amour, Faibalas, Boule de Suif, Jeux Sont Faix, Diable au Corps, Under My Skin, American Guerilla in the Philippines, Adventures of Captain Fabian, Sins of Pompeii, House of Ricordi, Archipelago of Love, Thieves After Dark, Le Chien, At the Top of the Stairs, Fine Weather, But Storms Due Towards Evening, Confidences, Alouette, je te plumerai.
TELEVISION: The Blood of Others.

PRESSMAN, EDWARD R.: Producer. b. New York, NY. e. Fieldston Sch.; grad., Stanford U.; studied at London Sch. of Economics. Began career with film short, Girl, in collaboration with director Paul Williams in London. They formed Pressman-Williams Enterprises.
PICTURES INCLUDE: Out of It, The Revolutionary, Dealing: or the Berkeley to Boston Forty Brick, Lost Bag Blues, Sisters, Badlands (exec. prod.), Phantom of the Paradise; Paradise Alley (exec. prod.); Old Boyfriends (prod.); Heartbeat (co-exec. prod.); The Hand (prod.); Conan the Barbarian (exec. prod.); Das Boot (prod.); The Pirates of Penzance (exec. prod.); Crimewave (exec. prod.); Plenty (prod.); Half Moon Street (exec. prod.); True Stories (exec. prod.); Good Morning Babylon; Masters of the Universe (exec. prod.); Walker (exec. prod.); Wall Street (prod.); Cherry 2000 (co-prod.); Paris By Night (exec. prod.); Talk Radio (co-prod.); Martians Go Home (prod.); Blue Steel (co-prod.).

246

PRESSMAN, LAWRENCE: Actor. b. Cynthiana, KY, July 10, 1939. e. Kentucky Northwestern U. On Bdwy. in Man in the Glass Booth, Play It Again, Sam, etc.
PICTURES: Man in the Glass Booth, The Crazy World of Julius Vrooder, Hellstrom Chronicle, Shaft, Making It, Walk Proud, Nine to Five, Some Kind of Hero, The Hanoi Hilton.
TELEVISION: Movies; Cannon, The Snoop Sisters, The Marcus-Nelson Murder, Winter Kill, The First 36 Hours of Dr. Durant, Rich Man, Poor Man, Man from Atlantis, Mulligan's Stew (series), The Trial of Lee Harvey Oswald, The Gathering, Like Mom, Like Me, Blind Ambition, Little Girl Lost.

PRESSMAN, MICHAEL: Producer, Director. b. New York, NY, July 1, 1950. e. California Inst. of Arts. Comes from show business family; was actor in college.
PICTURES INCLUDE: The Great Texas Dynamite Chase, The Bad News Bears Breaking Training, Boulevard Nights (dir.), Those Lips Those Eyes (dir., co-prod.), Some Kind of Hero (dir.), Doctor Detroit (dir.).
TELEVISION: Director: Like Mom, Like Me, The Imposter, The Christmas Gift, Final Jeopardy, Private Sessions, Secret Passions, And the Children Shall Lead, Sirens, Haunted by Her Past, To Heal a Nation.

PREUSTER, CHRISTOPHER W.: Executive. b. Newark, NJ, Apr. 16, 1942. e. St. Peters Coll., Jersey City, 1960–64. Pub. acct. to many film cos. (UA, Fox, Universal), while with Peat Marwick Mitchell, 1964–67; joined Walter Reade Organization, 1968; named pres. 1984.

PREVIN, ANDRE: Composer, Conductor. b. Berlin, Germany, Apr. 6, 1929. Composed and conducted over 50 m.p. scores. Music director, Pittsburgh Symphony Orchestra, & conductor emeritus of London Symphony Orchestra. Music Director, Royal Philharmonic Orch., from 1985. Guest conductor of most major symphony orchestras in U.S. and Europe.
PICTURES INCLUDE: Three Little Words, Cause for Alarm, It's Always Fair Weather, Bad Day at Black Rock, Invitation to the Dance, Catered Affair, Designing Woman, Silk Stockings, Gigi (Academy Award), Porgy and Bess (Academy Award), Subterraneans, Bells are Ringing, Pepe, Elmer Gantry, Four Horsemen of the Apocalypse, One Two Three, Two for the Seesaw, Long Day's Journey Into Night, Irma LaDouce (Academy Award), My Fair Lady (Academy Award), Goodbye Charlie, Inside Daisy Clover, Fortune Cookie, Thoroughly Modern Millie, Valley of the Dolls, Paint Your Wagon, The Music Lover, Jesus Christ Superstar.

PRICE, FRANK: Executive. b. Decatur, IL, May 17, 1930. e. Michigan State U. following naval service. Joined CBS in N.Y. in 1951 as story editor and writer. Moved to Hollywood in 1953, serving as story editor first at Columbia and then NBC (Matinee Theatre). In 1958 joined Universal as an assoc. prod. and writer. In 1961 named exec. prod. of The Virginian TV series. Appt. exec. prod. of Ironside; later did It Takes a Thief and several World Premiere movies. In 1964 named v.p. of Universal TV; 1971, sr. v.p.; 1974, pres. Also v.p., MCA, Inc. In 1978 left to join Columbia as pres. of new company unit, Columbia Pictures Productions. In 1979 named chm. & CEO of Columbia Pictures. In 1984 joined Universal: named chm., motion picture group, pres. of Universal Pictures, and v.p. of MCA. In 1987 formed Price Entertainment Inc. as chm. & CEO to produce movies and create TV shows for dist. through Columbia Pictures Entertainment.

PRICE, ROGER: Performer. b. Charleston, WV, Mar. 6, 1920. e. U. of Michigan, American Acad. of Art, Max Reinhardt Dramatic Workshop. Appeared at many night clubs, many TV guest appearances; writing credits include the Don Knotts Show, Governor & J.J., Bob Hope, The Partners, The Bluffers. V.P. of Price, Stern, Sloan Publishers.
TELEVISION: Toast of the Town, Arthur Godfrey's Friends, Garry Moore Show, This Is Show Business, Jack Paar, Get Smart, Johnny Carson. creator of The Kallikaks (NBC); The Waltons, McMillan and Wife, Mike Douglas, Murder She Wrote, Ghost Chasers, Mama's Family, Superior Court.
PICTURES: Mame, Day of the Locust, The Strongest Man in the World, Mixed Company, At Long Last Love, Pete's Dragon, The Devil and Max Devlin, Love on the Run.

PRICE, VINCENT: Actor. b. St. Louis, MO, May 27, 1911. m. actress Coral Browne. e. Yale U., U. of London, Nuremberg U. Autobiography: I Know What I Like (1959).
PICTURES INCLUDE: The Song of Bernadette, Buffalo Bill, The Eve of St. Mark, Wilson, The Keys of the Kingdom, Laura, A Royal Scandal, Leave Her to Heaven, Dragonwyck, Shock, Long Night, Moss Rose, Three Musketeers, Rogues Regiment, The Web, The Bribe, Baron of Arizona, Champagne for Caesar, Bagdad, His Kind of Woman, Adventures of Captain Fabian, Las Vegas Story, House of Wax, Dangerous Mission, Mad Magician, Son of Sinbad, Serenade, While the City Sleeps, Mysterious House of Usher, Return of the Fly, The Bat, The Tingler, House on Haunted Hill, House of Usher, Pit and Pendulum, Tales of Terror, The Mask of the Red Death, War Gods of the Deep, Dr. Gold Foot and the Sex Machine, The House of 1,000 Dolls, More Dead Than Alive,

The Oblong Box, Scream and Scream Again, Dr. Phibes, Dr. Phibes Rise Again!, Theatre of Blood, Madman, Scavenger Hunt, House of the Long Shadows, The Whales of August, Dead Heat, Backtrack, The Offspring.
TELEVISION: What's a Nice Girl Like You. . ., Batman, Time Express (series), Mystery! (host), many dramatic roles in 1950s and 60s as well as hosting E.S.P. and The Chevy Mystery Show and panelist on Pantomime Quiz (1950–52).

PRIES, RALPH W.: Executive. b. Atlanta, GA, August 31, 1919. Graduated Georgia Inst. of Technology. V.P., MEDIQ, Inc.; pres. MEDIQ/PRN Life Support Services, Inc.; past pres., Odgen Food Service Corp.; exec. comm. and bd., Firstrust Savings Bank and chm. of audit comm.; Boards of St. Christopher's Hospital for Children, Moss Rehabilitation Hospital, United Hospital Corp., Philadelphia Heart Instit. Former intl pres., Variety Clubs Intl.; previously on bd. of Hahnemann U. and Hosp., chm. of bd. Likoff Cardiovascular Instit., pres. Main Line Reform Temple, Wynnewood, PA.

PRIMUS, BARRY: Actor. b. New York, NY, Feb. 16, 1938. e. Bennington Coll., City Coll. of NY.
THEATER: The King and the Duke (debut, 1953); The Nervous Set; Henry IV, Parts I and II; Creating the World; Teibele and the Demon.
PICTURES: The Brotherhood (1969); Been Down So Long It Looks Like Up to Me; New York, New York; Avalanche; Autopsy; Night Games; The Rose; Heartland; Absence of Malice; The River; Down and Out in Beverly Hills; Jake Speed; Space Camp; The Stranger.
TELEVISION: Series: The Defenders; Cagney and Lacey. Movies: Washington Behind Closed Doors; Heart of Steel; Brotherly Love.

PRINCE: Singer, Actor. r.n. Rogers Nelson. b. Minneapolis, MN, 1960. Famous as rock star and recording artist before film debut in Purple Rain (1984).
PICTURES: Purple Rain, Under the Cherry Moon, Sign O' the Times (dir., actor, songs).

PRINCE, HAROLD: Director, Producer. b. New York, NY, Jan. 30, 1928. e. U. of Pennsylvania. Worked as stage mgr. for George Abbott on three shows, later co-produced, produced and/or directed the following: The Pajama Game (Tony Award), Damn Yankees (Tony Award), New Girl In Town, West Side Story, A Swim in the Sea, Fiorello! (Tony/Pulitzer), Tenderloin, Take Her, She's Mine, A Funny Thing Happened on the Way to the Forum (Tony Award), She Loves Me, The Matchmaker (revival), Fiddler On The Roof, Poor Bitos, Baker Street, Flora, The Red Menace, Superman, Cabaret (Tony Award), Zorba, Company, Follies, The Great God Brown, The Visit, Love for Love (the last three all revivals), A Little Night Music (Tony Award), Candide (Tony Award), Pacific Overtures, Side by Side by Sondheim, Some of My Best Friends, On the Twentieth Century, Evita (London, 1978, Bdwy. 1979, LA, Australia & Chicago, 1980; Vienna & Mexico City, 1981), Sweeney Todd (Bdwy., Tony Award 1979; London, 1980), Merrily We Roll Along, A Doll's Life, Play Memory, End of the World, Diamonds, Grind, Roza, Cabaret (revival), Phantom of the Opera (London, 1986; NY, 1988) (Tony Award), and also directed the operas Ashmadei, Silverlake, Sweeney Todd and Candide for N.Y. City Opera, Girl of Golden West for Chicago Lyric Opera Co. and San Francisco Opera; Willie Stark for Houston Grand Opera; Madame Butterfly for Chicago Lyric Opera and Turandot for Vienna State Opera.
MOVIES: Co-producer: The Pajama Game (1957), Damn Yankees. Director: Something for Everyone, A Little Night Music.
AUTHOR: Contradictions, Notes on Twenty-Six Years in the Theatre (Dodd, Mead & Co., New York, 1974).

PRINCE, WILLIAM: Actor. b. Nichols, NY, Jan. 26, 1913. With Maurice Evans, actor, 2 yrs., radio announcer. On N.Y. stage, Ah, Wilderness; m.p. debut in 1943. Many TV credits.
STAGE: Guest in the House, Across the Board on Tomorrow Morning, The Eve of St. Mark, John Loves Mary, As You Like It, I Am a Camera, Forward the Heart, Affair of Honor, Third Best Sport, The Highest Tree, Venus at Large, Strange Interlude, The Ballad of the Sad Cafe, Mercy Street.
PICTURES INCLUDE: Destination Tokyo, Cinderella Jones, The Very Thought of You, Roughly Speaking, Objective Burma, Pillow to Post, Lust for Gold, Cyrano de Bergerac, Secret of Treasure Mountain, Macabre, Sacco and Vanzetti, The Heartbreak Kid, The Stepford Wives, Family Plot, Network, The Gauntlet, Rollercoaster, The Cat from Outer Space, The Promise, Bronco Billy, Love & Money, Kiss Me Goodbye, Movers and Shakers, Fever Pitch, Spies Like Us, Nuts, Vice Versa.

PRINCIPAL, VICTORIA: Actress. b. Fukuoka, Japan, Jan 3, 1950. Went to New York to become model; studied acting privately with Jean Scott at Royal Acad. of Dramatic Art in London before moving to Hollywood. Film debut in The Life and Times of Judge Roy Bean (1972).
PICTURES INCLUDE: The Naked Ape, Earthquake, I Will, I Will . . . for Now, Vigilante Force.

TELEVISION: Fantasy Island (pilot), Love Story, Love, American Style, Greatest Heroes of the Bible, Dallas (series). Movies: The Night They Stole Miss Beautiful, The Pleasure Palace, Last Hours Before Morning, Not Just Another Affair, Mistress.

PRINE, ANDREW: Actor. b. Jennings, FL, Feb. 14, 1936. e. U. of Miami. On stage in Look Homeward, Angel, A Distant Bell.
PICTURES: The Miracle Worker, Advance to the Rear, Company of Cowards, Bandolero!, The Devil's Brigade, This Savage Land, Generation, Chisum, Riding Tall, One Little Indian, The Centerfold Girls, Grizzly, The Town That Dreaded Sundown, Winds of Autumn, High Flying Lowe, The Evil, Amityville: The Possession, Playing with Fire, Eliminators.
TELEVISION: Series: The Wide Country, The Road West, W.E.B., Boone. Movies: Split Second to an Epitaph, Along Came a Spider, Night Slaves, Wonder Woman, Law of the Land, First Gunner Joe, Last of the Mohicans, A Small Killing, Mind over Murder, M-Station Hawaii, Christmas Miracle in Caulfield, Young Abe Lincoln, U.S.A., Donner Pass: The Road to Survival, V: The Final Battle (mini-series).

PROSKY, ROBERT, Actor. b. Philadelphia, PA. Won TV amateur talent search contest, leading to scholarship with American Theatre Wing. 23-year veteran with Washington's Arena stage. Taught acting and appeared in over 150 plays including Death of a Salesman, Galileo, The Caucasian Chalk Circle, You Can't Take it With You. Broadway prods. include Moonchildren, A View from the Bridge, Pale Horse, Pale Rider, Arms and the Man, Glengarry Glen Ross, A Walk in the Woods.
PICTURES INCLUDE: Thief, Hanky Panky, Monsignor, The Lords of Discipline, Christine, The Keep, The Natural, Outrageous Fortune, Broadcast News, Big Shots, The Great Outdoors, Things Change.
TELEVISION: World War III, The Ordeal of Bill Carny, Lou Grant, The Adams Chronicles, Old Dogs, Hill Street Blues (series), Into Thin Air, The Murder of Mary Phagan.

PROVINE, DOROTHY: Actress. b. Deadwood, SD, Jan. 20, 1937. e. U. of Washington.
TELEVISION: The Alaskans, The Roaring 20's.
PICTURES INCLUDE: The Bonnie Parker Story, It's A Mad, Mad, Mad World, Good Neighbor Sam, The Great Race, That Darn Cat, Who's Minding the Mint?, Never a Dull Moment.

PRYCE, JONATHAN: Actor. b. North Wales, 1947. e. Royal Acad. of Dramatic Art. On stage in Comedians, Taming of the Shrew, Antony and Cleopatra, Comedians, Hamlet, Macbeth, The Seagull, Uncle Vanya, Accidental Death of an Anarchist.
PICTURES: Voyage of the Damned, Breaking Glass, Loophole, Praying Mantis, The Ploughman's Lunch, Something Wicked This Way Comes, Brazil, Doctor and the Devils, Haunted Honeymoon, Man on Fire, Jumping Jack Flash, Consuming Passions, The Adventures of Baron Munchausen.
TELEVISION: Comedians, Playthings, Partisans, For Tea on Sunday, Timon of Athens, Murder Is Easy, Daft as a Brush, Martin Luther, Heretic; The Caretaker, Glad Day.

PRYOR, RICHARD: Actor. b. Peoria, IL, Dec. 1, 1940. At age 7 played drums with professionals. Appearances on TV (Johnny Carson, Merv Griffin, Ed Sullivan) established him as standup comic. Wrote TV scripts for Lily Tomlin and Flip Wilson; co-author of film, Blazing Saddles. Several albums are best-selling hits.
PICTURES INCLUDE: Actor: Lady Sings the Blues, Bingo Long and the Travelin' All Stars, Silver Streak, Greased Lightning, Which Way Is Up?, Blue Collar, The Wiz, California Suite, Wholly Moses, In God We Trust, Stir Crazy, Bustin' Loose (star, co-prod.), Live on Sunset Strip (prod.), Some Kind of Hero, Richard Pryor: Here and Now (dir., s.p.), The Toy (also s.p., dir.), Brewster's Millions, Jo Jo Dancer Your Life Is Calling (also prod.-dir.-s.p.), Critical Condition; Moving, See No Evil, Hear No Evil.

PRYOR, THOMAS M.: Journalist. b. New York, NY, May 22, 1912. Joined NY Times, 1929; m.p. dept. 1931 as reporter, editor, asst. film critic; Hollywood bureau chief, corres., NY Times, 1951–59; editor, Daily Variety, 1959–88; 1988— Consultant to Variety & Daily Variety.

PTAK, JOHN: Agent. b. San Diego, CA. Graduated U. of California at L.A. film department, 1968. Theatre mgr. and booker for Walter Reade Organization and Laemmle Theatres, 1966–1969. Admin. exec. at American Film Institute's Center for Advanced Studies, 1969–1971. Agent at the International Famous Agency (ICM), 1971–1975. Vice Pres., William Morris Agency, 1976 to present, representing motion picture and television talent. Responsible for the initial representation of such films as Jaws, The Sting, Taxi Driver, Close Encounters of the Third Kind, Coal Miner's Daughter, Airplane, National Lampoon's Vacation. Consultant for the National Endowment of the Arts.

PURCELL, PATRICK B.: Executive. b. Dublin, Ireland, Mar. 16, 1943. e. Fordham U., M.B.A., 1973. In pub. & acct., England, 1969–69; acct., Associated Hosp. Service, N.Y., 1968–70;

joined Paramount Pictures, 1970; v.p., fin., 1980–83; exec. v.p. fin. & admin. 1983–.

PURDOM, EDMUND: Actor. b. Welwyn Garden City, England, Dec. 19, 1924. e. St. Ignatius Coll., London. Played leads, character roles for Northampton Rep. Co., Kettering Rep., two seasons at Stratford-On-Avon; London stage in Way Things Go, Malade Imaginaire, Romeo and Juliet, played in Caesar and Cleopatra, Antony and Cleopatra, London and N.Y.; TV and radio appearances N.Y., London.
PICTURES INCLUDE: Titanic, Julius Caesar, Student Prince, The Egyptian, Athena, The Prodigal, King's Thief, Moment of Danger, Rasputin, The Comedy Man, The Beauty Jungle, Don't Open Till Christmas (also dir.), After the Fall of New York.
TELEVISION: Winds of War, Scarlet and the Black, Sophia Loren: Her Own Story.

PURL, LINDA: Actress. b. Greenwich, CT, Sept. 2, 1955. Moved to Japan at age 2. Appeared in Japanese theatre, TV. Back to US in 1971.
PICTURES: Jory; W.C. Fields & Me; Crazy Mama; Leo and Loree; The High Country; Visiting Hours; Vipers.
TELEVISION: Series: Beacon Hill, Young Pioneers, Happy Days, The Secret Storm, Matlock. Movies: Eleanor and Franklin; Little Ladies of the Night; Testimony of Two Men; A Last Cry for Help; Women at West Point; A Very Special Love; Like Normal People; The Flame is Love; The Night the City Screamed; The Adventures of Nellie Bly; The Last Days of Pompeii, The Manions of America, Sisterhood, Addicted to His Love.

PUTTNAM, DAVID, CBE D. Lih.: Producer. b. London, England 1941. e. Michenden Sch. In advertising before joining VPS/Goodtimes Prod. Co. Dir. of Britain's National Film Finance Corp. Also served on Cinema Films Council and governing council of the British Acad. of Film & Television Arts. Governor of National Film Sch. 1986, appt. Chm. & CEO, Columbia Pictures. Resigned 1987. Received Eastman 2nd Century Award, 1988. Sept., 1988 formed a joint venture for his Enigma Productions Ltd. with Warner Bros., Fujisankei Comm. Gp. of Japan, British Satellite Broadcasting & Country Nat West to prod. 6 films.
PICTURES INCLUDE: Melody, The Pier Piper, That'll Be The Day, Stardust, Mahler, Buggy Malone, The Duellists, Midnight Express; Foxes (co-prod.), Chariots of Fire, Local Hero, Cal, The Killing Fields, The Mission, Defence of the Realm. Co-produced documentaries: Swastika, James Dean—The First American Teenager, Double-Headed Eagle, Brother, Can You Spare a Dime?
TELEVISION INCLUDES: P'Tang Yang Kipperbang, Experience Preferred, Secrets, Those Glory Glory Days, Sharma and Beyond, Winter Flight.

PYKE, REX: Film-Television Producer, Director. Recent productions include Akenfield, Landscape, Eric Clapton's Rolling Hotel, Van Morrison in Ireland and Woodstock in Europe 1979.

Q

QUAID, DENNIS: Actor. b. Houston, TX Apr. 9, 1954. Brother of Randy Quaid. e. U. of Houston. Appeared in Houston stage productions before leaving for Hollywood. Movie debut: September 30, 1955 (1978). On N.Y. stage with his brother in True West, 1984. Performs with rock band The Electrics and wrote songs for films The Night the Lights Went Out in Georgia, Tough Enough, The Big Easy.
PICTURES INCLUDE: Crazy Mama, Our Winning Season, Seniors, Breaking Away, I Never Promised You a Rose Garden, Gorp, The Long Riders, All Night Long, Caveman, The Night the Lights Went Out in Georgia (also wrote songs), Tough Enough, Jaws 3-D, The Right Stuff, Dreamscape, Enemy Mine, The Big Easy (also composed and sang song), Innerspace, Suspect, D.O.A., Everyone's All- American, Great Balls of Fire, Lie Down With Lions.
TELEVISION: Bill: On His Own, Johnny Belinda, Amateur Night at the Dixie Bar and Grill.

QUAID, RANDY: Actor. b. 1950. Discovered by Peter Bogdanovich while still jr. at Drama Dept. at U. of Houston and cast in his The Last Picture Show, 1971. Off-B'way debut: True West (1983).
PICTURES INCLUDE: What's Up, Doc?, Paper Moon, Lolly-Madonna XXX, The Last Detail, The Apprenticeship of Duddy Kravitz, Breakout, The Missouri Breaks, Bound for Glory, The Choirboys, Midnight Express, Foxes, The Long Riders, Heartbeeps, The Wild Life, The Slugger's Wife, Fool for Love, The Wraith, Sweet Country, Moving, No Man's Land, Bloodhounds of Broadway, Out Cold, Caddyshack II, Parents.
TELEVISION: Niagra, Raid on Coffeyville, To Race The Wind, Mad Messiah, Of Mice and Men, Inside the Third Reich, Cowboy, A Streetcar Named Desire, LBJ: The Early Years, Evil in Clear River.

QUAYLE, ANTHONY: Actor, stage producer. b. Lancashire, England, Sept. 7, 1913. Early career acting with Old Vic Co., Elsinore and on tour Continent, North Africa. Army service, 1939–45; joined Stratford Memorial Theatre as director & actor 1948; many plays and acted Shakespearean roles; m.p. debut 1955, Oh Rosalinda; many TV credits in U.S. & England; Moses, David & Saul, Q.B. VII (Emmy).
PICTURES INCLUDE: Battle of the River Plate, The Wrong Man, No Time for Tears, Woman in a Dressing Gown, The Man Who Would Not Talk, Ice Cold in Alex, Serious Charge, Tarzan's Greatest Adventure, Guns of Navarone, H.M.S. Defiant, Lawrence of Arabia, The Fall of the Roman Empire, East of Sudan, Operation Crossbow, MacKenna's Gold, Before Winter Comes, Anne of a Thousand Days, Everything You Always Wanted to Know About Sex*, Bequest to the Nation, Tamarind Seed, The Eagle Has Landed, Murder by Decree, Dial M for Murder, Key to Rebecca, Quoth the Raven, Oedipus at Colonus, Silent Night, The Legend of the Holy Drinker, Buster.
RECENT TV: Ice Age, Henry IV, Masada, The Manions of America, The Last Bottle in the World, Testament of John, Lace, Last Days of Pompeii, The Bourne Identity, Oedipus at Colonus (Theban Plays).

QUIGLEY, MARTIN, JR.: Educator, Writer. b. Chicago, IL, Nov. 24, 1917. e. A.B. Georgetown U.; M.A., Ed. D, Columbia U. M.P. Herald, Oct. 1939; spcl. ed. rep., M.P. Herald & M.P. Daily, May, 1941; wartime work in U.S., England, Eire & Italy, Dec. 1941–Oct. 1945; assoc. ed., Quigley Pub., Oct. 1945; ed. M.P. Herald, July, 1949; also edit. dir. of all Quigley Pub., 1956; pres. Quigley Pub. Co., 1964; author, Great Gaels, 1944, Roman Notes, 1946, Magic Shadows—the Story of the Origin of Motion Pictures, 1948. Editor, New Screen Techniques, 1953; m.p. tech. section, Encyclopaedia Brit., 1956; co-author, Catholic Action in Practice, 1963. Co-author: Films in America, 1929–69, 1970. Pres., QWS, Inc., educational consultants, 1975–81. Adjunct professor of higher education, Baruch College Univ. City of New York 1977–. Village of Larchmont, N.Y., trustee, 1977–79; mayor, 1980–84. Board of managers, American Bible Society, 1984–; Religious Education Ass'n., treasurer, 1975–80 & Chairperson, 1981–84; Laymen's Nat'l. Bible Association, chm. education committee, 1983–; Will Rogers Institute, chm. Health education committee, 1980–.

QUIGLEY, WILLIAM J.: Executive. b. New York, NY, July 6, 1951. e. Wesleyan U., B.A.; Columbia U., M.S., 1983. From 1973 to 1974 was advt. circulation mgr. for Quigley Publishing Co. Taught school in Kenya in 1974; returned to U.S. to join Grey Advt. as media planner. In 1975 joined Walter Reade Organization as asst. film buyer; promoted to head film buyer in 1977. Named v.p., 1982. In 1986 joined Vestron, Inc. as sr. v.p. to establish Vestron Pictures. Named pres., Vestron Pictures, 1987.
PICTURES: Exec. prod.: Steel Dawn, The Dead, Salome's Last Dance, The Unholy, Waxwork, Burning Secret, The Lair of the White Worm, Paint It Black, The Rainbow.

QUILLAN, EDDIE: Actor. b. Philadelphia, PA, March 31, 1907. p. Sarah Owen and Joseph Quillan, professionals; stage training playing in the Quillan act with his family. In 1926 discovered by Mack Sennett who signed him to long-term contract. Made 18 2-reel comedies. Then signed by Cecil B. De Mille for The Godless Girl. Starred in many pictures at Pathe and RKO-Pathe (incl.: Show Folks, Geraldine, Noisy Neighbors).
PICTURES INCLUDE: The Sophomore, Night Work, Big Money, A Little Bit of Everything, The Big Shot, Dark Mountain, This Is the Life, Moonlight and Cactus, Song of the Sarong, A Guy Could Change, Sensation Hunters, Sideshow, Mutiny on the Bounty (Screen Actors Guild Award), Grapes of Wrath, Broadway to Hollywood, Hollywood Party, London By Night, Big City, Kid Glove Killer, Brigadoon, Did You Hear the One About the Traveling Saleslady?, Angel in My Pocket, How to Frame a Figg.
TELEVISION: Series: Valentine's Day, Julia, Little House on the Prairie, Hell Town, Highway to Hell.

QUINE, RICHARD: Actor. b. Detroit, MI, Nov. 12, 1920. In U.S. Coast Guard during W.W.II; in vaudeville 6 yrs.; also on radio in 1938. N.Y. stage debut in Very Warm for May, then in My Sister Eileen. First appearance on screen in The World Changes, 1932; variously acted, prod. & dir. many films.
PICTURES INCLUDE: Babes on Broadway, Tish, My Sister Eileen, For Me and My Gal, Dr. Gillespie's New Assistant, Stand By for Action, We've Never Been Licked, Rookie Fireman, Sunny Side of the Street, Purple Heart Diary, Rainbow Round My Shoulder, Sound Off, All Ashore, Cruisin' Down the River, Pushover, So This is Paris, Solid Gold Cadillac, Full of Life, Mad Ball, Drive a Crooked Road, Bell Book and Candle, It Happened to Jane, Strangers When We Meet, The World of Suzie Wong, Notorious Landlady, Paris When It Sizzles, Sex and the Single Girl, How to Murder Your Wife, Synanon. Oh Dad Poor Dad Mama's Hung You In The

Closet and I'm Feeling So Sad, Hotel (dir.), A Talent for Loving (dir.), "W" (dir.), Prisoner of Zenda (dir.).
TELEVISION: The Jean Arthur Show (exec. prod.).

QUINLAN, KATHLEEN: Actress. b. Pasadena, CA, Nov. 19, 1954. Played small role in film, One Is a Lonely Number, while in high school. Also did bit in American Graffiti. Major role debut in Lifeguard (1976).
PICTURES: Airport '77, I Never Promised You a Rose Garden, The Promise, The Runner Stumbles, Sunday Lovers, Hanky Panky, Independence Day, Twilight Zone— The Movie, Wild Thing, Sunset, Man Outside, Clara's Heart.
TELEVISION: Movies: When She Says No, Blackout, Can Ellen Be Saved: Children of the Night, Dreams Lost, Dreams Found.

QUINN, AIDAN: Actor. b. Chicago, IL, March 8, 1959. Moved back to Belfast with family while in high sch. Returned to Chicago at 19, worked as a tar roofer. Chicago stage: The Man in 605 (debut), Scheherazade, The Irish Hebrew Lesson.
THEATER: Off-Bdwy debut: Fool for Love, A Lie of the Mind, A Streetcar Named Desire.
PICTURES: Reckless, Desperately Seeking Susan, The Mission, Stakeout, Crusoe.
TELEVISION: All My Sons, An Early Frost, etc.

QUINN, ANTHONY: Actor. b. Mexico, Apr. 21, 1915. Began on screen, 1936. Acad. Award, best supp. actor, Viva Zapata, 1952, and Lust for Life, 1956.
PICTURES INCLUDE: Guadalcanal Diary, Buffalo Bill, Irish Eyes Are Smiling, China Sky, Back to Bataan, Where Do We Go From Here?, Black Gold, Tycoon, The Brave Bulls, Mask of the Avenger, The Brigand, World in His Arms, Against All Flags, Ride Vaquero, City Beneath the Sea, Seminole, Blowing Wild, East of Sumatra, Long Wait, Magnificent Matador, Ulysses, Naked Street, Seven Cities of Gold, La Strada, Attila the Hun, Lust for Life, Wild Party, Man from Del Rio, Ride Back, Hunchback of Notre Dame, The River's Edge, Hot Spell, Black Orchid, Last Train From Gun Hill, Warlock, Heller With a Gun, Heller in Pink Tights, Savage Innocents, The Guns of Navarone, Barabbas, Requiem for a Heavyweight, Behold a Pale Horse, Zorba the Greek, High Wind in Jamaica, The Visit, Guns for San Sebastian, The Secret of Santa Vittoria, A Dream of Kings, Flap, A Walk in the Spring Rain, R.P.M.*, Across 110th Street, Deaf Smith and Johnny Ears, The Don Is Dead, Mohammad, Messenger of God, The Greek Tycoon, Caravans, The Passage, Lion of the Desert, High Roll, Valentina, The Salamander, Treasure Island, A Man of Passion, Stradivarius, Grandpa and I.
TELEVISION: Much dramatic work in the early 1950s. Series: The City. Movies: Jesus of Nazareth, Treasure Island (Italian TV), Onassis: The Richest Man in the World.

QUINN, STANLEY J., JR.: Producer, Director. b. Brooklyn, NY, Mar. 18, 1915; e. Princeton U., 1932–36. Radio writer for Edgar Bergen show; mgr., J. Walter Thompson radio dept. in Australia, 1941–43; war corresp., 1943–45; radio prod. J. Walter Thompson, 1946; prod., dir., Kraft TV Theatre, NBC, 1947–53; ABC, Oct. 1953; vice pres., J. Walter Thompson, June 1954; exec. prod. Lux Video Theatre, 1954; pres. Quinn, McKenney Prod.; v.p. head radio, TV dept., D.C.S.S.; prod., Grey Adv. for Revlon commercials. Dir. of Admin. MGM-TV Studios 1963–64; dir. Radio-TV Center U. of Conn. 1965–76. Commercial dir. Kraft Foods, 1964–72; Director, Radio/TV Div., CIMT, Univ. Conn., 1976–80. Freelance TV dir., 1980.

R

RABE, DAVID WILLIAM: Writer. b. Dubuque, IA, March 10, 1940. m. actress Jill Clayburgh. e. Loras Coll.
PICTURES: I'm Dancing As Fast As I Can (exec. prod., s.p.); Streamers (s.p.).
PLAYS: The Basic Training of Pavlo Hummel (Obie Award, 1971); Sticks and Bones (Tony Award, 1971); The Orphan; In the Boom Boom Room; Streamers; Hurlyburly.
TELEVISION: Sticks and Bones.

RABINOVITZ, JASON: Executive. b. Boston, MA, e. Harvard Coll., B.A. where elected to Phi Beta Kappa. Following W.W.II service as military intelligence captain with paratroops, took M.B.A. at Harvard Business Sch., 1948. Started in industry in 1949 as asst. to secty.-treas., United Paramount Theatres. Asst. controller, ABC, 1953; adm. v.p., ABC-TV, 1956; joined MGM as asst. treas., 1957; named MGM-TV gen. mgr., director of business & financial affairs, 1958; treas. & chief financial officer, MGM, Inc., 1963; advanced to financial v.p. & chief financial officer, 1967. In 1971 named exec. v.p., Encyclopedia Brittanica Education Corp.; sr. v.p., American Film Theatre, 1974–75. Rejoined MGM as v.p./exec. asst. to the pres., 1976. Elected v.p. finance, 1979; promoted to sr. v.p., finance & corporate admin., MGM Film Co. & UA Prods. Resigned, 1984. Now film & TV consultant and independent producer.

RACKMIL, MILTON R.: Executive. b. New York, NY. e. New York U. Certified Public Accountant prior to assoc. with Brunswick Record Co. 1929; co-founder Decca Records, 1934; pres. Decca Records, 1949; pres. and member of board of dir. Universal Pictures, 1952, after Decca bought controlling stock interest in Universal; pres. emeritus, Universal, 1973.

RADIN, PAUL: Producer. b. New York, NY, Sept. 15, 1913. e. New York U. After college went in adv. Became v.p. in chg. of m.p. div. of Buchanan & Co. During the war posted in Middle East as film chief for Office of War Information for that area. On return to U.S. assigned by Buchanan to ad campaign for Howard Hughes' The Outlaw. Turned to talent mgr., joining the Sam Jaffe Agency. Then joined Ashley-Famous Agency. Became exec. prod. for Yul Brynner's indep. prod. co. based in Switzerland, with whom made such films as The Journey, Once More with Feeling, Surprise Package.
PICTURES INCLUDE: Born Free, Living Free, Phase IV, The Blue Bird.
TELEVISION: The Incredible Journey of Dr. Meg Laurel; The Ordeal of Dr. Mudd; Crime of Innocence; Series: Born Free; The Wizard.

RADNER, GILDA: Actress, Writer. b. Detroit, MI, June 28, 1946. m. actor-dir. Gene Wilder. e. U. of Michigan. Began career as part of Toronto's Second City improvisational group. Moved to NY when John Belushi invited her to work with him on National Lampoon Radio Hour as writer and performer. Soon after joined TV's Saturday Night Live. Appeared in Bdwy. in one-woman show, Gilda Radner—Live from New York, which was filmed for theatrical movie.
PICTURES: First Family, Gilda Live, Hanky Panky, It Came from Hollywood, The Woman in Red, Movers and Shakers, Haunted Honeymoon.

RADNITZ, ROBERT B.: Producer. b. Great Neck, NY, Aug. 9, 1924. e. U. of Virginia. Taught 2 years at U. of Virginia, then became reader for Harold Clurman; wrote several RKO This Is America scripts, then to Broadway where co-prod., The Frogs of Spring; prod. The Young and the Beautiful; to Hollywood working at United Artists, then as story consultant for 20th Century-Fox; prod. A Dog of Flanders (1960—first feature), first U.S. film to win Golden Lion Award at Venice Film Festival. Board of Directors, Producer Guild of America: v.p., last 3 years; first producer with retrospective at Museum of Modern Art. First producer honored by joint resolution of both houses of Congress, 1973. Sounder received four Academy Award nominations: best picture, best actor, best actress, best screenplay. Pres. Robert B. Radnitz Productions, Ltd. Vice pres., Producers Guild, 1982, 1984.
PICTURES INCLUDE: Misty, Island of the Blue Dolphins, And Now Miguel, My Side of the Mountain, The Little Ark, Sounder, Where the Lilies Bloom, Birch Interval, Sounder II, A Hero Ain't Nothin' But a Sandwich, Cross Creek (4 AA nominations).
TELEVISION: Mary White (Emmy for teleplay-nominated for best film) Christopher Award for TV special.

RAFELSON, BOB: Producer, Director, Writer. b. New York, NY, 1935. After Army Service did program promotion for a radio station; then hired by David Susskind to read scripts. Became script supervisor of Play of the Week for Susskind and Ely Landau; wrote 34 adaptations for the series. Joined Screen Gems in California, developing program idea for Jackie Cooper, then head of TV prod. arm of Columbia. Later formed BBS Productions with Bert Schneider and Steve Blauner; their first film, Head (1968).
PICTURES INCLUDE: Head (co-s.p); Five Easy Pieces (co-prod., dir.), The King of Marvin Gardens (prod.-dir.), Stay Hungry (co-prod., co-s.p., dir.), The Postman Always Rings Twice (co. prod.-dir.), Black Widow (dir.), Mountains of the Moon (dir., co-s.p.).

RAFFERTY, FRANCES: Actress. b. Sioux City, IA, June 26, 1922; e. U. of California, premedical student U. of California at L.A. TV shows, December Bride (series), Pete and Gladys (series).
PICTURES INCLUDE: Seven Sweethearts, Private Miss Jones, Girl Crazy, War Against Mrs. Hadley, Thousands Cheer, Dragon Seed, Honest Thief, Mrs. Parkington, Barbary Coast Gent, Hidden Eye, Abbott and Costello in Hollywood, Adventures of Don Coyote, Money Madness, Lady at Midnight, Old Fashioned Girl, Rodeo, Shanghai Story.

RAFFIN, DEBORAH: Actress. b. Los Angeles, CA, March 13, 1953. m. producer Michael Viner. Mother is actress Trudy Marshall. e. Valley Coll. Was active fashion model before turning to acting when discovered by Ted Witzer. Made m.p. debut in 40 Carats (1973). Publisher Dove Books On Tape. Head of Dove Films, prod. co.
PICTURES INCLUDE: The Dove, Once Is Not Enough, The Sentinel, Touched by Love, Death Wish 3.
TELEVISION: A Nightmare in Badham County, Willa, Haywire, Threesome, Sparkling Cyanide, James Clavell's Noble House, Windmills of the Gods (also co-prod.).

RAGLAND, ROBERT OLIVER: Composer. b. Chicago, IL, July 3, 1931. e. Northwestern U., American Conservatory of Music, Vienna Acad. of Music. Professional pianist at Chicago nightclubs. In U.S. Navy; on discharge joined Dorsey Bros. Orchestra as arranger. On sls. staff at NBC-TV, Chicago. 1970, moved to Hollywood to become composer for movies; has scored 43 feature films plus many TV movies and series segments. Has also written some 15 original songs.
PICTURES: The Touch of Melissa, The Yin and Yang of Mr. Go, The Thing with Two Heads, Project: Kill, Abby, Seven Alone, The Eyes of Dr. Chaney, Return to Macon County, The Daring Dobermans, Shark's Treasure, Grizzly, Pony Express Rider, Mansion of the Doomed, Mountain Family Robinson, Only Once in a Lifetime, Jaguar Lives, The Glove, Lovely But Deadly, "Q", The Day of the Assassin, A Time To Die, The Winged Serpent, Trial by Terror, The Guardian, Ten to Midnight, Dirty Rebel, Hysterical, Brainwaves, Where's Willie?, The Supernaturals, Nightstick, Messenger of Death.
TELEVISION: Photoplay's Stars of Tomorrow, Wonder Woman, Barnaby Jones, Streets of San Francisco, High Ice, The Girl on the Edge of Town, The Guardian, etc.

RAILSBACK, STEVE: Actor. b. Dallas, TX. Studied with Lee Strasberg. On stage in Orpheus Descending, This Property Is Condemned, Cherry Orchard, Skin of Our Teeth, etc.
PICTURES: The Visitors, Angela, The Stunt Man, Turkey Shoot, The Golden Seal, Deadly Games, Torchlight, Lifeforce, Distortions, Blue Monkey, The Wind, Deadly Intent, Nukie, Scenes From the Goldmine.
TELEVISION: Helter Skelter, From Here to Eternity.

RAKOFF, ALVIN: Producer, Director. b. Toronto, Canada, 1927. e. U. of Toronto. Early career as journalist. Dir. in French & U.S. T.V. England, Canada. Emmy Award Winner, 1968 for Call Me Daddy. Emmy Award, 1982 for A Voyage Around My Father.
STAGE: Hamlet.
PICTURES INCLUDE: On Friday at 11, The Comedy Man, Crossplot, Hoffman, Say Hello to Yesterday, City of Fire, Death Ship, Dirty Tricks.
TELEVISION: The Caine Mutiny Court Martial, Requiem for a Heavyweight, Our Town, The Velvet Alley, A Town Was Turned to Dust, Jokers Justice, Call Me Back, Day Before Atlanta, Heart to Heart, The Seekers, Sweet War Man, The Move after Checkmate, The Stars in My Eyes, Call Me Daddy, Summer & Smoke, Don Quixote, Shadow of a Gunman, The Impeachment of Andrew Johnson, Cheap in August, In Praise of Love, Nicest Man in the World, Dame of Sark, The Kitchen, Romeo and Juliet, Voyage Round My Father, Mr. Halpern and Mr. Johnson, The First Olympics—Athens 1896, Paradise Postponed.

RAKSIN, DAVID: Composer. b. Philadelphia, PA, Aug. 4, 1912. e. U. of Pennsylvania, studied music with Isadore Freed and Arnold Schoenberg. Composer of music for films, ballet, dramatic and musical comedy, stage, radio and TV, symphony orchestra and chamber ensembles. Arranger of music of Chaplin film, Modern Times; pres. Composers and Lyricists Guild of America, 1962–70; film cartoons include Madeline and The Unicorn in the Garden (UPA), professor of Music and Urban Semester, U. of Southern California, and faculty, U. of California at L.A. Sch. of Music. Coolidge Commission from the Library of Congress: Oedipus Meneitai (Oedipus Remembers) for bass/baritone, 6-part chorus and chamber orchestra premiered there under dir. of composer, Oct. 30, 1986.
PICTURES INCLUDE: Laura, Secret Life of Walter Mitty, Smoky, Force of Evil, Across the Wide Missouri, Carrie, Bad and the Beautiful, Apache, Suddenly, Big Combo, Jubal, Hilda Crane, Separate Tables, Al Capone, Night Tide, Too-Late Blues, Best of the Bolshoi (music for visual interludes), Two Weeks in Another Town, The Redeemer, Invitation to a Gunfighter, Sylvia, A Big Hand for the Little Lady, Will Penny, Glass Houses, What's the Matter with Helen?
TELEVISION: Wagon Train, Five Fingers, Journey, Life With Father, Tender is the Night, Father of the Bride, Ben Casey, Breaking Point, Prayer of the Ages, Report from America, Medical Center, The Olympics (CBC), The Day After.

RALSTON, RUDY: Producer. b. Prague, Czechoslovakia, Jan. 30, 1918. e. grad. eng., Realka U. Came to U.S. & joined Consolidated Lab.; exec. Republic Prod.; prod. Republic, 1950.
PICTURES INCLUDE: No Man's Woman, Double Jeopardy, Terror at Midnight, Hell's Crossroads, The Lawless Eighties, Last Stagecoach West, Man Who Died Twice.

RAMIS, HAROLD: Writer, Director, Actor. b. Chicago, IL, Nov. 21, 1944. e. Washington U., St. Louis. Assoc. ed. Playboy Mag. 1968–70; writer, Second City, Chicago 1970–73; National Lampoon Radio Show, Lampoon show 1974–75. Head writer and actor SCTV, 1977–78; prod., head writer Rodney Dangerfield Show 1982.
PICTURES: Writer, actor: National Lampoon's Animal House; Meatballs; Caddyshack (also dir.); Stripes; Ghostbusters. Director: National Lampoon's Vacation (also dir.); Club

Paradise; Baby Boom; Caddyshack II (co-s.p. only); Stealing Home; How to Get into College.

RAMPLING, CHARLOTTE: Actress. b. Sturmer, England, Feb. 5, 1946. e. Jeanne D'Arc Academie pour Jeune Filles, Versailles; St. Hilda's, Bushey, England. Ent. m.p. ind. 1966. TV credits include: Six More for BBC, The Superlative Seven—Avenger series, Mystery of Cader Iscom, The Fantasists, What's in it for Henry, Zinotchka, Sherlock Holmes, Infidelities.
PICTURES INCLUDE: The Knack, Rotten to the Core, Georgy Girl, The Long Duel, Sequestro di Persona, The Damned, Three, Ski Bum, Corky, Tis Pity She's a Whore, The Six Wives of Henry VIII, Asylum, The Night Porter, Giordano Bruno, Zardoz, Caravan to Vaccares, Yuppi Dui La Chair De L'orchidee, Farewell My Lovely, Foxtrot, Orca, The Mauve Taxi, Stardust Memories, The Verdicta, Viva La Vie, Angel Heart, Mascara, D.O.A., Max My Love, He Died with His Eyes Open, Paris By Night, The Riddle, Ocean Point.

RAMSAY, PATRICK: b. Bristol, Eng., 1926. e. Marlborough Coll., Jesus Coll., Cambridge, M.A., History. Served with Royal Naval Volunteer Reserve (Fleet Air Arm) 1944–46. Joined British Broadcasting Corporation 1949 as a report writer in monitoring service. Became assistant, appointments dept., 1953 and three years later re-joined BBC External Services as senior administrative assistant. In charge of news administration, radio and television 1958 to 1963, helping develop the U.K. regional television news network for BBC. 1963, appointed planning manager (projected arrangements), television. 1966 assistant controller, programme services, television, then assistant controller, program planning, television, from December 1969. Controller, programme services, television, April 1972. Appointed controller, BBC-Scotland, May 1979.

RAND, HAROLD: Executive. b. New York, NY, Aug. 25, 1928. e. Long Island U., B.S., 1948–50; City Coll. of New York, 1945–46. U.S. Army 1946–48; ent. m.p. ind. 1950, pub. dept. 20th-Fox; variety of posts incl. writer, trade press, newspaper contacts; joined Walt Disney's Buena Vista pub. mgr., 1957; pub. mgr. Paramount Pictures, 1959; formed own pub. rel. firm, 1961; dir. of pub. Embassy Picture Corp. 1962; dir. of world pub. 20th Century Fox 1962; resigned 1963; dir. of adv. & pub., Landau Co., 1963; dir. world pub., Embassy Pictures, 1964; est. Harold Rand & Co., Inc., 1966, pred. of p.r. & mktg. firm. Appt. mktg., dir., Kaufman Astoria Studios, 1984; elected v.p., 1985.

RANDALL, STEPHEN F.: Executive. Held marketing posts with United Vintners and Clorox. Joined Columbia Pictures in 1978 as director of research; named v.p. in 1980 and senior v.p. in 1982. 1983, joined Tri-Star Pictures as snr. v.p. of marketing; promoted to exec. v.p.

RANDALL, TONY: Actor. r.n. Leonard Rosenberg. b. Tulsa, OK, Feb. 26, 1920. e. Northwestern U. Prof. N.Y. debut as actor in Circle of Chalk; then in Candida and others; U.S. Army 1942–46; radio actor on many shows.
STAGE: Corn is Green, Antony & Cleopatra, Caesar & Cleopatra, Inherit the Wind, Oh Men Oh Women, Oh Captain, The Sea Gull, The Master Builder.
PICTURES INCLUDE: Oh Men Oh Women, Will Success Spoil Rock Hunter, No Down Payment, The Mating Game, Pillow Talk, Adventures of Huckleberry Finn, Let's Make Love, Lover Come Back, Boys' Night Out, 7 Faces of Dr. Lao, Send Me No Flowers, Fluffy, The Alphabet Murders, Bang! You're Dead, Hello Down There, Everything You Always Wanted to Know About Sex*, Foolin' Around, Scavenger Hunt, The King of Comedy, That's Adequate, It Had to Be You.
TELEVISION: One Man's Family, TV Playhouse, Mr. Peepers, Max Liebman Spectaculars, Sid Caesar, Dinah Shore, Playhouse 90, Odd Couple, The Tony Randall Show, Love Sidney (series), Walt Disney World Celebrity Circus. Movies: Sunday Drive, Hitler's SS; Off Sides; Kate Bliss and Ticker Tape Kid; Save the Dog!; The Man in the Brown Suit.

RANSOHOFF, MARTIN: Executive. b. New Orleans, LA, 1927. e. grad., Colgate U. Adv., Young & Rubicam, 1948–49; slsmn, writer, dir., Gravel Films, 1951; formed own co., Filmways, 1952; industrial films, commercials; formed Filmways TV Prods., Filmways, Inc., Filmways of Calif. chmn., bd. Filmways, Inc., resigned from Filmways in 1972 and formed own independent motion picture and television production company.
TELEVISION: Mister Ed, The Beverly Hillbillies, Petticoat Junction, Green Acres, The Addams Family.
PICTURES INCLUDE: The Americanization of Emily, The Sandpiper, Boys Night Out, The Loved One, The Wheeler Dealers, The Cincinnati Kid, See No Evil, Ten Rillington Place, King Lear, Topkapi, Fuzz, Castle Keep, Ice Station Zebra, Catch 22, Save The Tiger, The White Dawn, Silver Streak (exec. prod.), Nightwing, The Wanderers, Change of Seasons, American Pop, Hanky Panky, Class, The Jagged Edge, The Big Town (prod.), Switching Channels (prod.), Smoke (prod.), Passage.

RAPF, MATTHEW: Producer, Writer. b. New York, NY, Oct. 22, 1920. e. Dartmouth Coll., B.A., 1942; p. Harry Rapf, producer. U.S. Navy, W.W.II as Lt. (j.g.).
PICTURES INCLUDE: Adventures of Gallant Bess s.p., co-prod., assoc. prod., story, The Sellout; prod., Desperate Search, Big Leaguer, Half a Hero.
TELEVISION: Loretta Young Show, Frontier, Great Gildersleeve, The Web, Jefferson Drum, Man From Blackhawk, Two Faces West, Ben Casey, Slattery's People, Iron Horse, Young Lawyers, Hardcase, Terror In the Sky, Shadow On the Land, Marcus-Nelson Murders, Kojak, Switch, Doctor's Hospital, Eischied, Oklahoma City Rolls, Gangster Chronicles.

RAPHAEL, FREDERIC: Writer. b. Chicago, IL, Aug. 14, 1931. e. Charterhouse, St. John's Coll., Cambridge. First novel pub., 1956, subsequently, The Earlsdon Way, The Limits of Love, A Wild Surmise, The Graduate Wife, The Trouble With England, Lindmann, Orchestra and Beginners. 1970: Like Men Betrayed. 1971: Who Were You With Last Night? 1972: April, June and November. 1973: Richard's Things. 1975: California Time. 1976: The Glittering Prizes. 1979: Sleeps Six & Other Stories. 1980: Oxbridge Blues & Other Stories; 1985: Heaven & Earth; 1986: Think of England; 1988: After the War. Biographies: Somerset Maugham and His World; Byron; Translations: Poems of Catullus (with Kenneth McLeish); The Oresteia. Essays: Bookmarks, Cracks in the Ice. Ent. m.p. ind., 1956. Several plays for ATV, 1960–62.
PICTURES: Nothing But the Best (1964); Darling (Acad. Award, orig. s.p., 1965); Two for the Road, Far from the Madding Crowd; A Severed Head; Daisy Miller, The King's Whore.
TELEVISION: The Glittering Prizes (Royal TV Society Writer Award 1978), Rogue Male; School Play, Something's Wrong; Best of Friends; Richard's Things, Oxbridge Blues (ACE Award, best s.p.); After the War.
PLAYS: From the Greek (1979), An Early Life.

RAPHEL, DAVID: Executive. b. Boulogne-s/Seine, France, Jan. 9, 1925. e. university in France. Entered m.p. ind. as asst. to sales mgr. in France, 20th-Fox, 1950–51; asst. mgr. in Italy, 1951–54; mgr. in Holland, 1954–57; asst. to European mgr. in Paris, 1957–59; European mgr. for TV activities in Paris, 1959–61; Continental mgr. in Paris, 1961–64, transferred to N.Y. as vice-pres. in chge. of international sales, 1964; named pres., 20th Century-Fox International, 1973. In Feb., 1975, also appointed senior vice-pres., worldwide marketing, feature film division, for 20th-Fox, headquartered in Los Angeles. In November, 1976, joined ICM, appointed director general of ICM (Europe) headquartered in Paris. In 1979 elected pres. ICM with headquarters in Los Angeles. 1980, formed Cambridge Film Group Ltd.

RAPPER, IRVING: Director. b. London, Eng., 1900. e. New York U., B.A. Assoc. Gilbert Miller in stage prod. dir. Animal Kingdom, The Firebird, Five Star Final, The Late Christopher Bean.
PICTURES INCLUDE: Shining Victory, One Foot in Heaven, The Gay Sisters, The Adventures of Mark Twain, Rhapsody in Blue, The Corn Is Green, Deception; Now, Voyager; Voice of the Turtle, Anna Lucasta, The Glass Menagerie, Another Man's Poison, Forever Female, Bad For Each Other, The Brave One, Marjorie Morningstar, The Miracle, Joseph and His Brethren, Pontius Pilate, The Christine Jorgensen Story, Born Again, Justus.

RAPPOPORT, GERALD J.: Executive, Film Producer. b. New York, NY, 1925. e. New York U. U.S. Marine Corps. 1955–1958—pres., Major Artists Representatives Corp.; 1958–1960—director of Coast Sound Services, Hollywood; 1957 to present, pres., Sewan Music Publishers. 1960 to present, Pres. of International Film Exchange Ltd., N.Y., a subsidiary of Today Home Entertainment 1988.

RATHER, DAN: News Correspondent, Anchor. b. Wharton, TX, Oct., 1931. e. Sam Houston State Coll., BA journalism. Instructor there for 1 year. Worked for UPI and Houston Chronicle. Joined radio staff KTRH, Houston. Joined CBS News in 1962 as chief of southwest bureau in Dallas. Transferred to overseas burs. (including chief of London Bureau 1965–66), then Vietnam before returning as White House corr. 1966. White House Correspondent, 1964 to 1974. Covered top news events, from Democratic and Republican national conventions to President Nixon's trip to Europe (1970) and to Peking and Moscow (1972). Anchored CBS Reports, 1974–75. Presently co-editor of 60 minutes (since 1975) and anchors Dan Rather Reporting on CBS Radio Network (since 1977). Winner of numerous awards, including 5 Emmys. Now anchorman on CBS-TV Evening News.

RAUCHER, HERMAN: Writer. b. Apr. 13, 1928. e. New York U. Author of novels—Summer of '42 and Ode to Billy Joe—adapted to films by him.
PICTURES INCLUDE: Sweet November, Hieronymus Merkin, Watermelon Man, Summer of '42, Class of '44, Ode to Billy Joe, The Other Side of Midnight.

Rav-Red

TELEVISION: Studio One, Alcoa Hour, Goodyear Playhouse, Matinee Theatre, Remember When? (movie).

RAVELO, ROBERT F.: Executive. b. Santiago de Cuba, Oriente, Cuba, Aug. 30, 1947. Emigrated to U.S., 1961. e. U. of Connecticut, B.A. 1966–69, band leader and Latin percussionist. 1969–74, Winchester Intl. Marketing Dept. 1976–77, U.S. Air Force; capt., 1977–81. Entered industry in 1981 as prod. asst. to Robert Towne during filming of Personal Best. Now v.p./sls., v.p. production and operating officer, Arista Films, Inc.

RAVETCH, IRVING: Director, Scenarist, Producer. b. 1915. m. Harriet Frank.
PICTURES INCLUDE: The Long Hot Summer, The Sound and the Fury, Home from the Hill, The Dark at the Top of the Stairs, Hud, Hombre, The Reivers (also prod.), Conrack (co s.p.), Norma Rae (co.-s.p.), Murphy's Romance (co-s.p.).

RAY, ALDO: Actor. r.n. Aldo DaRe. b. Pen Argyl, PA, Sept. 25, 1926. e. U. of California. U.S. Navy, June, 1944–May, 1946: constable. Crockett, Calif., Nov. 1950–Sept. 1951: m.p. debut in Saturday's Hero (1950). Star of Tomorrow, 1954. Stage debut: Stalag 17 (La Jolla Playhouse 1983). Member: SAG, AFTRA. American Legion.
PICTURES INCLUDE: The Marrying Kind, Pat and Mike, Let's Do It Again, Miss Sadie Thompson, Battle Cry, We're No Angels, Three Stripes in the Sun, Nightfall, Men in War, God's Little Acre, Four Desperate Men, Day They Robbed the Bank of England, Sylvia, What Did You Do in the War Daddy?, To Kill A Dragon, Dead Heat on a Merry-Go-Round, Welcome to Hard Times, The Power, My True Story, The Green Berets, The Violent Ones, Angel Unchained, And Hope To Die, Psychic Killer, Seven Alone, Evils of the Night, The Sicilian, Terminal Force.
TELEVISION: Desilu Playhouse, K.O. Kitty, The Virginian, Bonanza, Women in White, Promise Him Anything, Deadlock.

RAY, SATYAJIT: Director, Writer, Composer. b. India, May 2, 1921. Gained international acclaim for his Apu Trilogy in the '50s.
PICTURES: Pather Panchali, The Unvanquished, The Music Room, The World of Apu, The Goddess, Kanchenjunga, The Adventures of Goopy and Bagha, The Adversary, Company Limited, Distant Thunder, The Middle Man, The Chess Player, The Elephant God, The Kingdom of Diamonds, The Home and the World, etc.

RAYBURN, GENE: Performer. b. Christopher, IL, Dec. 22, 1917. e. Knox Coll., Galesburg, IL. NBC guide; with many radio stations in Baltimore, Philadelphia, N.Y.; U.S. Army Air Force, 1942–45, Rayburn and Finch, show, WNEW, N.Y., 1945–52; Gene Rayburn Show, NBC radio; TV shows: Many appearances as host-humorist on game shows, variety shows, drama shows. Summer stock: leads in comedies.
BROADWAY: Bye Bye Birdie, Come Blow Your Horn.
TELEVISION: Helluva Town, The Match Game, Love Boat, Fantasy Island, Tonight Show.

RAYE, MARTHA: Actress. b. Butte, MT, Aug. 27, 1916. p. Reed and Hooper, professionals. On stage: sang and did comedy with Paul Ash's orchestra; was in Earl Carroll's Sketch Book; Lew Brown's Calling All Stars. Appeared in night clubs.
PICTURES INCLUDE: Rhythm on the Range, The Big Broadcast of 1937, Hideway Girl, College Holiday, Par, Waikiki Wedding, Mountain Music, Artists and Models, Double or Nothing, Par. Pin Up Girl, Four Jills and a Jeep, Monsieur Verdoux, Pufnstuf, The Concorde—Airport '79.
TELEVISION: All Star Revue, Martha Raye Show, Alice, Gossip Columnist, Alice in Wonderland, Murder She Wrote.

RAYMOND, GENE: Actor r. n. Raymond Guion. b. New York, NY, Aug. 13, 1908. Air Force Reserve, W.W.II. Formed ind. prod. co., Masque Prod., 1949. Song composer. Vice-pres. Arthritis Found.; Past pres. Motion Pic. and TV Fund; Pres. LA Chapt., Air Force Assn.; trustee, Falcon Found; trustee SGA; Bd., Acad. TV Arts and Sciences; Awarded Lion of Merit, USAF; Humanitarian Award, AF Assn.; Better World Award, VFW.
STAGE: Why Not?, The Potters, Cradle Snatchers, Take My Advice, Say When, Mirrors, Jones, Young Sinners, Broadway starred Shadow of My Enemy, 1957, National Co., The Best Man 1960, Write Me A Murder, Kiss Me Kate, Candida, Madly in Love.
PICTURES INCLUDE: Personal Maid, Ladies of the Big House, The Night of June 13th, Forgotten Commandments, If I Had A Million, Red Dust, Ex-Lady, Sadie McKee, Brief Moment, I am Suzanne, Flying Down to Rio, The Woman in Red, The House on 56th Street, Seven Keys to Baldpate, The Bride Walks Out, Hooray for Love, Zoo in Budapest, Behold My Wife, Mr. and Mrs. Smith, Smilin' Thru, The Locket, Sofia, Walking On Air, Coming Out Party, Life of the Party, She's Got Everything, Ann Carver's Profession, Transient Lady, The Best Man, I'd Rather Be Rich.
TELEVISION: Star-host, TV Fireside Theatre and TV Reader's Digest; Lux Video Theatre, Robert Montgomery Presents, Climax, Playhouse 90, Kraft Theatre, Red Skelton,

U.S. Steel Hour, The Man From U.N.C.L.E.; Matinee Theatre (actor, dir.), Girl from Uncle, Laredo, Ironsides, Julia, Judd For the Defense.

RAYMOND, PAULA: Actress. r.n. Paula Ramona Wright, b. San Francisco, CA. e. San Francisco Jr. Coll. 1942. Started career in little theatre groups, San Francisco; leading roles Ah! Wilderness, Peter Pan, other plays; model, Meade-Maddick Agency; TV appearance 1949.
PICTURES INCLUDE: Devil's Doorway, Inside Straight, Duchess of Idaho, Crisis, Grounds For Marriage, Tall Target, Texas Carnival, The Sellout, Bandits of Corsica, City That Never Sleeps, Beast from 20,000 Fathoms, King Richard & the Crusaders, Human Jungle, Gun That Won the West, The Flight That Disappeared, 5 Bloody Graves, Blood of Dracula's Castle.

RAYNOR, LYNN S.: Producer, Production Executive. b. 1940. Produced West Coast premiere of The Balcony by Genet, The Crawling Arnold Review by Feiffer. Joined Television Enterprises, 1965; Commonwealth United, 1968 as business affairs exec. later production supervisor. 1972 opened London branch of the Vidtronics Co. 1974, formed Paragon Entertainment. 1976, producer, PBS. 1977, producer, James Flocker Enterprises. 1979, exec. in charge of production, Lawrance Schiller Productions. 1981, producer, Polygram Pictures; 1984, producer, Newland-Raynor Prods.; 1985, Columbia Pictures TV.
TELEVISION: Waiting for Godot; Camp Wilderness (synd. series); Marilyn, The Untold Story (movie); The Execution; The Pete Gray Story.
PICTURES: Ghosts That Still Walk, Alien Encounters, Fanny Hill, Dangerously.

REAGAN, RONALD: Actor, Politician. b. Tampico, IL, Feb. 6, 1911. e. high school, Eureka Coll. m. Nancy Davis. Lifeguard. Wrote weekly sports column for a Des Moines, IA newspaper; broadcast sporting events. Signed as actor by Warner Bros. in 1937. In W.W.II. 1942–45, capt., USAAF. Actor until 1966 on TV as well. Program supvr., General Electric Theatre, Death Valley Days. Gov., California, 1967–74. Businessman and rancher. Elected Pres. of U.S., 1980. Re-elected, 1984.
PICTURES INCLUDE: Love Is On the Air, Submarine D-1, Sergeant Murphy, Swing Your Lady, Accidents Will Happen, Cowboy from Brooklyn, Boy Meets Girl, Girls on Probation, Going Places, Dark Victory, Naughty but Nice, Hell's Kitchen, Kings Row, Juke Girl, Desperate Journey, This is the Army, The Killers, That Hagen Girl, Night Unto Night, Voice of the Turtle, John Loves Mary, Girl from Jones Beach, Hasty Heart, Louisa, Last Outpost, Bedtime for Bonzo, Storm Warning, Hong Kong, She's Working Her Way Through College, Winning Team, Tropic Zone, Law & Order, Prisoner of War, Cattle Queen of Montana, Tennessee's Partner, Hellcats of the Navy, The Killers.

REARDON, BARRY: Executive. Began industry career with Paramount Pictures; named v.p.; left to join General Cinema Theatres Corp. as snr. v.p. Now with Warner Bros. as pres. of domestic distribution co.

REASON, REX: Actor. b. Berlin, Germany, Nov. 30, 1928. e. Hoover H.S., Glendale, CA. Worked at various jobs; studied dramatics at Pasadena Playhouse.
PICTURES INCLUDE: Storm Over Tibet, Salome, Mission Over Korea, Taza Son of Cochise, This Island Earth, Smoke Signal, Lady Godiva, Kiss of Fire, Creature Walks Among Us, Raw Edge, Miracle of The Hills, The Rawhide Trail.

REASONER, HARRY: News correspondent. b. Dakota, IA. Apr. 17, 1923. e. Stanford U., U. of Minnesota. Beg. journalism career, reporter, Minneapolis Times 1941–43; U.S. Army, W.W.II. Ret. to Times, drama critic 1946–48. Author, book, Tell Me About Women, 1946; newswriter, radio station WCCO. CBS affiliate. Minn., 1950–51; writer U.S. Information Agency Manila, 1951–54; news-dir., KEYD-TV (now KMSP-TV). Minn., 1954; Joined CBS News, N.Y., 1956; ABC News 1970–78. Rejoined CBS 1978; co-editor, 60 Minutes.

REDDY, HELEN: Singer. b. Australia, Oct. 25, 1942. Parents were producer-writer-actor Max Reddy and actress Stella Lamond. e. in Australia. Began career at age four as singer and had appeared in hundreds of stage and radio roles with parents by age of 15. Came to New York in 1966, subsequently played nightclubs, appeared on TV. First single hit record: I Don't Know How To Love Him (Capitol). Grammy Award, 1973, as best female singer of year for I Am Woman. Other Gold singles: Delta Dawn, Leave Me Alone, Angle Baby. Gold Albums: Love Song for Jeffrey, Free & Easy, No Way to Treat a Lady, I Don't Know How To Love Him, Music, Music. Platinum albums: I Am Woman, Long Hard Climb, Helen Reddy's Greatest Hits. Most Played Artist by the music operators of America: American Music Award 1974; Los Angeles Times Woman of the Year (1975); No. 1 Female Vocalist in 1975 and 1976; Record World, Cash Box and Billboard; one of the Most Exciting Women in the World because of her strong convictions, beauty and intelligence—

International Bachelor's Society, 1976. Heads prod. co. Helen Reddy, Inc..
PICTURES: Airport 1975 (debut), Pete's Dragon.
TELEVISION: David Frost Show, Flip Wilson Show, Mike Douglas Show, etc. The Helen Reddy Show (Summer, 1973), Permanent host of Midnight Special. Appearances on Tonight Show, Mac Davis Show. Hosted Merv Griffin Show, Sesame St.; Live in Australia (host, 1988); Tonight Show, Muppet Show.

REDFORD, ROBERT: Actor. b. Santa Monica, CA, Aug. 18, 1937. U. of Colorado, left to travel in Europe, 1957. Attended Pratt Inst. and American Acad. of Dramatic Arts. m. Lola Van Wangemen.
BROADWAY: Walk-on in Tall Story, also in The Highest Tree, Sunday in New York, Barefoot in the Park.
PICTURES INCLUDE: Warhunt, 1961; Situation Hopeless, But Not Serious, Inside Daisy Clover; The Chase, This Property Is Condemned, Barefoot in the Park, Tell Them Willie Boy is Here, Butch Cassidy and the Sundance Kid, Downhill Racer, The Crow Killer, The Hot Rock, The Candidate, Jeremiah Johnson, The Way We Were, The Sting, The Great Gatsby, The Great Waldo Pepper, Three Days of the Condor, All The President's Men, A Bridge Too Far, The Electric Horseman, Brubaker, The Natural, Out of Africa, Legal Eagles. Director: Ordinary People (AA), The Milagro Beanfield War (dir., co-prod.), Promised Land (co-exec. prod.).
TELEVISION: The Iceman Cometh; In the Presence of Mine Enemies, Playhouse 90.

REDGRAVE, CORIN: Actor. b. London, England, July 16, 1939. e. Cambridge. Son of the late Sir Michael Redgrave. Brother of Vanessa and Lynn Redgrave. On stage with England Stage Co., plays including A Midsummer Night's Dream, Chips with Everything, Lady Windermere's Fan, Julius Caesar, Comedy of Errors, etc.
PICTURES: A Man for All Seasons, The Deadly Affair, Charge of the Light Brigade, The Magus, Oh What a Lovely War, When Eight Bells Toll, Serail, Excalibur, Eureka, etc.

REDGRAVE, LYNN: Actress. b. London, England, Mar. 8, 1943. Sister of Vanessa and Corin Redgrave. Youngest child of late Sir Michael Redgrave and Rachel Kempson. m. dir., actor, manager John Clark. Ent. m.p. and TV, 1962. Broadway debut Black Comedy.
THEATER: NY: My Fat Friend (1974), Mrs. Warren's Profession, Knock Knock, Misalliance, St. Joan, Twelfth Night (Amer. Shakespeare Fest), Sister Mary Ignatius Explains It All for You, Aren't We All?, Sweet Sue.
PICTURES INCLUDE: Tom Jones, Girl With Green Eyes, Georgy Girl, The Deadly Affair, Smashing Time, The Virgin Soldiers, The Last of the Mobile Hot-Shots, Viva la Muerta Tua, Every Little Crook and Nanny, Everything You Always Wanted to Know About Sex*, Don't Turn the Other Cheek, The National Health, The Happy Hooker, The Big Bus, Sunday Lovers, Home Front, Morgan Stewart's Coming Home, Midnight For Morticia, Death of a Son, Getting It Right.
TELEVISION: Pretty Polly, Ain't Afraid to Dance, The End of the Tunnel, I Am Osango, What's Wrong with Humpty Dumpty, Egg On the Face of the Tiger, Blank Pages, A Midsummer Night's Dream, Pygmalion, Turn of the Screw, William, Vienna 1900, Daft as a Brush, Not For Women Only, Co-host U.S. talkshow and A.M. America. Movies: Seduction of Miss Leona, Gauguin, Beggerman Thief, Centennial, Rehearsal for Murder, The Bad Seed, My Two Loves. Series: House Calls, Teachers Only, The Muppet Show, Walking on Air, Candid Camera Christmas Special, Woman Alone, The Old Reliable.

REDGRAVE, VANESSA: O.B.E. Actress. b. London, England, Jan. 30, 1937. Sister of Lynn and Corin Redgrave. Early career with Royal Shakespeare Company. Ent. m.p. 1958 in Behind the Mask.
TELEVISION: A Farewell to Arms, Katherine Mansfield, Playing for Time (Emmy Award), My Body, My Child, Three Sovereigns for Sarah, Peter the Great, Second Serve, A Man For All Seasons.
STAGE: Daniel Deronda, Cato Street, The Threepenny Opera, Twelfth Night, As You Like It, Taming of the Shrew, Cymbeline, The Sea Gull, The Prime of Miss Jean Brodie, Antony & Cleopatra, Design for Living, Macbeth, Lady from the Sea, The Aspern Papers, Ghosts, Anthony and Cleopatra, Taming of the Shrew, Tomorrow Was War, A Touch of the Poet.
PICTURES INCLUDE: Morgan, A Suitable Case for Treatment, A Man for All Seasons, Blow-up, Red and Blue, 1967 to Hollywood for Camelot, Charge of the Light Brigade, Isadora, Oh! What a Lovely War, The Seagull, A Quiet Place in the Country, Drop Out, Trojan Women, The Devils, La Vacanza, Mary Queen of Scots, Murder on the Orient-Express, Out of Season, Seven-per-cent Solution, Julia (Acad. Award, supp. actress), Agatha, Yanks, Bear Island, Wagner, The Bostonians, Steaming, Wetherby, Prick Up Your Ears, Consuming Passions.

REDSTONE, EDWARD S.: Exhib. b. Boston, MA, May 8, 1928. e. Colgate U., B.A., 1949; Harvard Grad. Sch. of Bus. Admin., M.B.A., 1952. v.p., treas., Northeast Drive-In Theatre Corp.; v.p., Theatre Owners of New England, 1962; chmn., advis. coms., mem. bd. dirs., TOA; gen. conven. chmn., joint convention TOA & NAC, 1962; pres. National Assn. of Concessionaires, 1963; chief barker. Variety Club of New England, 1963; pres., Theatre Owners of New England; gen. chmn., 35th annual reg. convention.

REDSTONE, SUMNER MURRAY: Theatre Executive, Lawyer; b. Boston, MA, May 27, 1923; s. Michael and Belle (Ostrovsky) R. e. Harvard, B.A., 1944, LLB., 1947. Served to 1st Lt. AUS, 1943–45. Admitted to MA Bar 1947; U.S. Ct. Appeals 1st Circuit 1948, 8th Circuit 1957, 9th Circuit 1948; D.C. 1951; U.S. Supreme Ct. 1952; law sec. U.S. Ct. Appeals for 9th Circuit 1947–48; instr. U. San Francisco Law Sch. and Labor Management Sch., 1947; special asst. to U.S. Atty. General, 1948–51; partner firm Ford, Bergson, Adams, Borkland & Redstone, Washington, D.C. 1951–54; exec. v.p. Northeast Drive-In Theatre Corp., 1954–68; pres. Northeast Theatre Corp.; asst. pres., Theatre Owners America 1960–63, pres. 1964–65; bd. chm., National Association of Theatre Owners 1965–66; dir. ACE Prodns., Inc.; mem. Presidential Advisory Committee John F. Kennedy Center for the Performing Arts; chmn. Jimmy Fund, Boston 1960; met. div. Combined Jewish Philanthropies 1963; sponsor Boston Museum of Science; Trustee Children's Cancer Research Foundation; Art Lending Library; bd. dirs. Boston Arts Festival; v.p., exec. committee Will Rogers Memorial Fund; bd. overseers Dana Farber Cancer Institute; mem. corp. New England Medical Center; Motion Picture Pioneers; bd. mem. John F. Kennedy Library Foundation; 1984–85, 1985–86 State Crusade Chairman American Cancer Society; Board of Overseers Boston Museum of Fine Arts; Professor, Boston U. Law Sch. 1982–83, 1985–86; Chairman, Viacom International.
AWARDS: Decorated Army Commendation medal. Named one of ten outstanding young men Greater Boston Chamber of Commerce 1958; William J. German Human Relations Award Entertainment and Communications Division American Jewish Committee, 1977; 1985 recipient, Boston U. Law Sch. Silver Shingle Award for Distinguished Public Service; Communicator of the Year B'nai B'rith Communications, Cinema Lodge 1980.

REED, OLIVER: Actor. b. Wimbledon, England, Feb. 13, 1938. Nephew of late British dir. Sir Carol Reed. Dropped out of school in teens and worked as a bouncer, a boxer, and a taxi driver before debut in The Rebel (1960).
PICTURES INCLUDE: The Rebel, His and Hers, Beat Girl, The Angry Silence, League of Gentlemen, Two Faces of Dr. Jekyll, Sword of Sherwood Forest, Bulldog Breed, Paranoic, No Love for Johnnie, Curse of the Werewolf, Pirates of Blood River, Curse of Captain Clegg, The Damned, The Party's Over, Scarlet Blade, Assassination Bureau, Shuttered Room, The System, Brigand of Kandahar, The Trap, I'll Never Forget What's His Name, Hannibal Brooks, The Jokers, Oliver, The Girl Getters, Women in Love, Take a Girl Like You, The Lady in the Car, Hunting Party, The Devils, Zero Population Growth, Sitting Target, Triple Echo, Fury Rides the Wind, Dirty Weekend, Revolver, Blue Blood, Three Musketeers, Death in Persepolis, Tommy, The Four Musketeers, Ten Little Indians, Royal Flash, Sell Out, Burnt Offerings, The Great Scout and Cathouse Thursday, The Prince and the Pauper, Assault on Paradise, Tomorrow Never Comes, The Big Sleep, The Class of Miss MacMichael, The Broad, Lion in the Desert, Dr. Heckle and Mr. Hype, Condorman, Venom, The Great Question, Deathbite, The Sting II, Masquerade, Second Chance, Two of a Kind, Captive, Castaway, Dragonard; The Return of the Three Musketeers; Hold My Hand, I'm Dying; Fire With Fire; Rage to Kill; Skeleton Coast, Damnation Express.
TELEVISION: Dangerous Love.

REED, PAMELA: Actress. b. Tacoma, WA, 1953. Ran day-care center and worked with Head Start children before studying drama at U. of Washington. Worked on Trans-Alaska pipeline. Off-Broadway showcases. Television debut: series regular The Andros Targets, 1977. Off-Broadway debut: Curse of the Starving Class (1978).
THEATER: All's Well That Ends Well (Central Park), Getting Out, Fools, The November People (Broadway debut), Fen, Standing on My Knees, Elektra.
PICTURES: The Long Riders (1980), Melvin and Howard, Eyewitness, Young Doctors in Love, The Right Stuff, The Goodbye People, The Best of Times, Clan of the Cave Bear, Rachel River.
TELEVISION: Inmates—A Love Story; Until She Talks; I Want To Live; Heart of Steel; Scandal Sheet; Tanner '88; Hemingway.

REES, ROGER: Actor. b. Aberystwyth, Wales, May 5, 1944. e. Camberwell Sch. of Art, Slade Sch. of Fine Art. Stage debut Hindle Wakes (Wimbledon, U.K., 1964). With Royal Shake-

Ree-Rei

speare Co. from 1967. Starred in the title role The Adventures of Nicholas Nickleby (London and NY, 1980–81, Tony Award). Assoc. dir. Bristol Old Vic Theatre Co., 1966–present. Playwright with Eric Elice of Double-Double and Elephant Manse.
PICTURES: Star 80 (debut, 1983).
TELEVISION: Movies: A Christmas Carol, Place of Peace, Under Western Eyes, Bouquet of Barbed Wire, Saigon, Imaginary Friends, The Adventures of Nicolas Nickleby, The Comedy of Errors, Macbeth, The Voysey Inheritance, The Ebony Tower.

REEVE, CHRISTOPHER: Actor. b. New York, NY, Sept. 25, 1952. e. Cornell U., B.A.; graduate work at Julliard. National tour with Irregular Verb to Love, co-starring with Celeste Holm. Went to England, visiting repertory theatres; hired for backstage work by Old Vic. Returned to U.S.; played role on daytime TV series, Love of Life. On Bdwy. with Katharine Hepburn in A Matter of Gravity. Theater: Fifth of July, Summer and Smoke (L.A., 1988). Theatrical film debut, Gray Lady Down, 1978.
PICTURES: Superman, Somewhere in Time, Superman II, Deathtrap, Monsignore, Superman III, The Bostonians, The Aviator, Street Smart, Superman IV, Switching Channels.
TELEVISION: Love of Life, Faerie Tale Theatre, Enemies, The American Revolution, The Great Escape: The Final Chapter.

REEVES, STEVE: Actor. b. Glasgow, MT, Jan. 21, 1926. Delivered newspapers. Mr. Pacific, Mr. America, Mr. World, Mr. Universe; ent. theatrical field, Kismet. Appeared The Vamp, Wish You Were Here.
PICTURES INCLUDE: Athena, Goliath and the Barbarians, Sword of Siracusa, Judos, David and Goliath, Hercules, Giant of Marathon, Last Days of Pompeii, Hercules Unchained, White Warrior, Morgan the Pirate, The Thief of Baghdad, The Trojan Horse, The Private Prince, A Long Ride From Hell.

REHME, ROBERT G.: Executive. b. Cincinnati, OH, May 5, 1935. e. U. of Cincinnati. 1953, mgr., RKO Theatres, Inc., Cincinnati; 1961, adv. mgr., Cincinnati Theatre Co.; 1966, dir. of field adv., United Artists Pictures; 1969, named dir. of pub. and field adv./promotion, Paramount Pictures; 1972, pres., BR Theatres and v.p., April Fools Films, gen. mgr. Tri-State Theatre Service; 1976, v.p. & gen. sls. mgr., New World Pictures; Feb. 1978, joined Avco Embassy Pictures as snr. v.p. & chief operating officer; Dec. 1978, named exec. v.p.; 1979, named pres., Avco Embassy Pictures, Inc,. 1981, joined Universal Pictures as pres. of distribution & marketing; 1982, named pres. of Universal Pictures; 1983, joined New World Pictures as co-chm. & chief exec. officer.

REID, BERYL: Actress. b. Hereford, England, June 17, 1920. Career in radio before London stage debut in revue, After the Show, 1951. Also on stage in The Killing of Sister George, Spring Awakening, Campiello, Born in the Gardens, etc.
PICTURES: The Belles of St. Trinian's, The Extra Day, Inspector Clouseau, The Assassination Bureau, The Killing of Sister George, The Beast in the Cellar, Father Dear Father, No Sex Please We're British, Joseph Andrews, Carry on Emmanuelle, The Doctor and the Devils.
TELEVISION: Nellie McClung, Crossbar, Robbers, Rooftops and Witches, Death of a Salesman, Christmas Eve.

REID, KATE: Actress. b. London, England, Nov. 4, 1930. Performed in stock in Canada and Bermuda. Joined Stratford Shakespeare Festival in Canada to play many roles. On Bdwy. in Dylan, Cat on a Hot Tin Roof, Bosoms and Neglect, Death of a Salesman, etc.
PICTURES: This Property Is Condemned, The Side Glances of a Pigeon Kicker, Andromeda Strain, A Delicate Balance, Equus, Highpoint, Death Ship, Double Negative, Plague, Circle of Two, Atlantic City, The Blood of Others, Heaven Help Us, Fire with Fire, Sweet Hearts Dance, Bye Bye Blues.

REILLY, CHARLES E., JR.: Communications Executive. b. Philadelphia, PA, Nov. 14, 1928. e. St. Joseph's Coll. Network liaison, TV Guide Magazine; asst. to the v.p. & dir., corporate relations, Young & Rubicam, 1964–66; executive dir., National Catholic Office for Radio, 1966–71; Secretary, Communications Foundation (CCF) 1968–77; exec. v.p., Patrick Carr Associates 1971–73; corp. exec. Communispond Inc. of J. Walter Thompson Co., 1973–76; v.p., Speech Dynamics subsidiary, Ogilvy & Mather International, 1976–77; pres. & founder, In-Person Communications Inc. 1977–present. Also chm., Executive Communications Group.

REILLY, CHARLES NELSON: Actor, Director. b. New York, NY, Jan. 13, 1931. e. U. of CT. On Broadway mostly in comedy roles before turning to TV and films. Recently directed stage plays.
THEATER: As actor: Bye Bye Birdie (debut); How to Succeed in Business, Hello Dolly!; Skyscraper; God's Favorite. Acted in 22 off-Bdwy plays. Founded musical comedy dept. HB Studios. Conceived and dir.: The Belle of Amherst,

Paul Robeson, The Nerd (dir.). Resident dir.: Burt Reynolds' Jupiter Theatre.
PICTURES INCLUDE: A Face in the Crowd, Two Tickets to Paris, The Tiger Makes Out, Cannonball Run II, All Dogs Go to Heaven (voice).
TELEVISION: Guest host Tonight Show, Ghost and Mrs. Muir, Dean Martin Show, The Three Kings, game shows (host), Sweet Hearts.

REINAUER, RICHARD: Executive. b. Chicago, IL, April 28, 1926. e. U. of Illinois, grad. 1952. Prod., dir., freelance, 1952–59; bus. mgr., asst. prod., Showcase Theatre Evanston, 1952; prod., dir., NBC, Chicago, 1953–55; film dir., Kling Studios, 1956; asst. dir., Foote Cone & Belding, 1956–59; dir., radio, TV & m.p., American Medical Assoc., 1959–64; pres., Communications Counselors, 1963–64; exec. dir., TV Arts & Sciences Foundation, 1964; pres., Acad. of TV Arts & Sciences, Chicago Chapter, 1970–72. assoc. prod. & asst. dir. Wild Kingdom & asst. to pres., Don Meier Prods., 1965–present. Member–Illinois Nature Preserve Commission.

REINBERG, DEBORAH: Executive. Attorney in entertainment field for Manatt, Phelps, Rothenberg and Phillips before joining Elektra/Asylum Records as v.p., business affairs. July, 1984, joined Warner Bros. Inc. as dir. of music, business & legal affairs. 1985, promoted to newly created position of v.p., business affairs, music.

REINER, CARL: Performer, Director, Writer. b. New York, NY, March 20, 1923. Comedian on Bdwy., Call Me Mr., Inside U.S.A., Alive and Kicking; m.p. The Russians are Coming; on TV in Your Show of Shows, first Bob Hope Show, Caesar's Hour; Sid Caesar Invites You, 1958; prod.-writer, The Dick Van Dyke Show, CBS (Emmy Award-writing Comedy) 1961–62. Prod., The New Dick Van Dyke Show 1973; Heaven Help Us, 1975–76.
PICTURES INCLUDE: The Gazebo, writ. orig. s.p., The Thrill of It All, dir. co-author & co-prod. The Comic; Generation. A Performer: It's a Mad, Mad, Mad, Mad World; Happy Anniversary, Gidget Goes Hawaiian, The End. Co-author & dir: Enter Laughing; Dir: Where's Poppa, Oh, God!, The One and Only, The Jerk, Dead Men Don't Wear Plaid (s.p. & actor), The Man with Two Brains (co-s.p.-dir.), All of Me (dir.), Summer Rental (dir.), Bert Rigby, You're a Fool (dir., s.p.).
RECORDINGS: Carl Reiner and Mel Brooks, The 2000 Year Old Man, The 2001 Year Old Man, 2013 Year Old Man.
AUTHOR: Broadway plays: Enter Laughing, Something Different.

REINER, ROB: Actor, Writer, Director. b. New York, NY, March 6, 1945. Son of actor/writer/director Carl Reiner. Worked as actor with regional theatres and improvisational comedy troupes. Wrote for the Smothers Brothers Comedy Hour. Breakthrough as actor came in 1971 when signed by Norman Lear for All in the Family on TV, playing Mike Stivic (Meathead). Directorial debut with This Is Spinal Tap, 1984.
PICTURES: Enter Laughing (actor only), This is Spinal Tap (co-s.p., dir., act.); The Sure Thing (dir.), Stand By Me (dir.), The Princess Bride (dir.), Throw Momma from the Train (act. only), Harry, This is Sally (dir.).

REINHARDT, GOTTFRIED: Producer, Writer. b. Berlin, Germany, 1911. p. Max Reinhardt, noted theatrical prod.; Else Reinhardt, actress; brother, Wolfgang Reinhardt, prod. e. Berlin. Began career at 19 as asst. to prod. Ernst Lubitsch, father's friend, with m.p. Design For Living; asst. to Walter Wanger; later to Bernard H. Hyman (Saratoga; San Francisco). Wrote orig. story, I Live My Life, The Great Waltz; collab. Bridal Suite; book for NY musicals, Rosalinda, Helen of Troy. U.S. Army service, Signal Corps. 1942–46.
PICTURES INCLUDE: Comrade X, Rage in Heaven, Two-Faced Woman, (co-prod.) Homecoming, Command Decision, The Great Sinner, The Red Badge of Courage, Invitation, Young Man with Ideas, (dir. 2 seq.) Story of Three Loves, Betrayed, Town Without Pity (prod.); Situation Hopeless, But Not Serious (prod.), Hitler: The Last Ten Days (prod., co. s.p.).

REINHOLD, JUDGE: Actor. b. Wilmington, DE, 1956. e. Mary Washington Coll., North Carolina Sch. of Arts. Acted in regional theatres including Burt Reynolds dinner theater in FL. before signed to TV contract at Paramount. Theatrical film debut in Running Scared, 1979.
PICTURES: Stripes, Thursday the Twelfth, Fast Times at Ridgemont High, Lords of Discipline, Gremlins, Beverly Hills Cop, Roadhouse, Head Office, Off Beat, Ruthless People, Beverly Hills Cop II, Vice Versa, A Soldier's Tale.
TELEVISION: Wonder Woman, Magnum P.I., The Survival of Dana, Brothers and Sisters, A Step Too Slow, The Willmar Eight, Booker, Promised a Miracle.

REISENBACH, SANFORD E.: Executive. e. New York U. Associated with Grey Advertising for 20 years; exec. v.p. and pres. of Grey's leisure/entertainment division in N.Y. In August, 1979, joined Warner Bros. as exec. v.p. in chg. of worldwide adv. & pub.; named pres., worldwide adv. & pub., 1985.

REISNER, ALLEN: Director. b. New York, NY.
PICTURES: The Day They Gave Babies Away; St. Louis Blues, All Mine to Give.
TELEVISION: : Movies: The Captain and the Kings; Mary Jane Harper Cried Last Night, Your Money or Your Wife; To Die in Paris; The Cliff; Skag; They're Playing Our Song; The Gentleman From Seventh Avenue; Escape of Pierre Mendes-France; Deliverance of Sister Cecelia; The Sound of Silence.
TV FILM SERIES: Murder She Wrote, Twilight Zone, Hardcastle & McCormick, Airwolf, The Mississippi, Hawaii Five-O, Blacke's Magic, Law and Harry McGraw.
LIVE TV SERIES: Playhouse 90, Studio One, Climax, United States Steel Hour, Suspense, Danger, etc.

REISNER, DEAN: Writer. Began career as director: Bill and Coo, 1947. Has collaborated on following screenplays, among others: Coogan's Bluff, Dirty Harry, Play Misty for Me.

REISS, JEFFREY C.: Executive. b. Brooklyn, NY, April 14, 1942. e. Washington U., St. Louis, B.A., 1963. Consultant at New York U. and Manhattanville Coll. and instructor at Brooklyn Coll. before entering industry. Agt. in literary dept. for General Artists Corp., 1966. Supervised development in N.Y. of Tandem Prods. for Norman Lear, 1968. Produced off-Bdwy. plays 1968–70. Dir. of progm. devel. for Cartridge TV, Inc. (mfg. of video-players-recorders) 1970–73. Joined ABC Entertainment as director of network feature films, 1973–75. Founder and pres., Showtime Entertainment (pay TV), 1976–80. Co-founder, pres., & CEO, Cable Health Network, 1981–83. In March, 1983, named vice chm. & CEO, Cable Health Network. Chm. & CEO, Reiss Media Enterprises, 1984; founder & CEO, Request Television (pay-per-view svc.), 1985.

REISS, STUART A.: Set decorator. b. Chicago, IL, July 15, 1921. e. L.A. High Sch., 1939. Property man, 20th-Fox, 1939–42; U.S. Army Air Corps, 1942–45; set decorator, 20th-Fox since 1945; 6 Acad. nom.; 2 Acad. Awards, Diary of Anne Frank, Fantastic Voyage.
PICTURES INCLUDE: Titanic, How to Marry a Millionaire, Hell and High Water, There's No Business Like Show Business, Soldier of Fortune, Seven Year Itch, Man in the Grey Flannel Suit, Teen Age Rebel, What a Way to Go, Doctor Doolittle, Fantastic Voyage, Oh God!, Swarm, Beyond the Poseidon Adventure, Carbon Copy, All the Marbles, The Man Who Loved Women, Micki and Maude, A Fine Mess.

REISZ, KAREL: Director. b. Czechoslovakia, 1926. e. Britain. Wrt. Technique of Film Editing for British Film Academy. Worked with British Film Institute and National Film Library, 1954; co. dir. (with Tony Richardson) Momma Don't Allow, 1957; prod. Every Day Except Christmas, 1958; dir. We Are the Lambeth Boys, 1959–60; dir. Saturday Night & Sunday Morning, 1962; prod. This Sporting Life, 1963; dir. Night Must Fall, 1966; dir. Morgan, 1966; dir. Isadora; The Gambler, Dir. On the Road. (BBC-TV). Dir. Rag Soldiers (U.S. Title: Who'll Stop the Rain) (1978), The French Lieutenant's Woman, 1981 (also co-prod.), Sweet Dreams, 1985.

REITMAN, IVAN: Producer, Director. b. Czechoslovakia, Oct. 26, 1946. e. McMaster U. Moved to Canada, 1951.
THEATER: The Magic Show (co-prod.); Merlin (dir., prod.).
PICTURES: Foxy Lady, Cannibal Girls, Shivers, Death Weekend, Blackout, Animal House (prod.); Meatballs (prod.-dir.); Stripes (prod.-dir.); Heavy Metal (prod.); Spacehunter (exec. prod.); Ghostbusters (prod.-dir.); Legal Eagles (prod.-dir.), Big Shots (exec. prod.), Casual Sex? (exec. prod.); Twins (prod., dir.).
TELEVISION: The Delta House.

RELPH, MICHAEL: Producer, Director, Writer, Designer. b. England, 1915. 1942 art dir. Ealing Studios then assoc. prod. to Michael Balcon on The Captive Heart, Frieda, Kind Hearts and Coronets, Saraband (also designed; nominated Oscar). 1948 appt. producer and formed prod/dir. partnership Basil Dearden (until 1972). 1971–76 Governor Brit. Film Institute. Chairman B.F.I. Prod. Board. Chairman Film Prod. Assoc. of G.B., member Films Council.
PICTURES INCLUDE: (For Ealing) The Blue Lamp (Brit. Film Academy: Best Brit. Film 1950), I Believe in You, The Gentle Gunman, The Square Ring, The Rainbow Jacket, Out of the Clouds, The Ship That Died of Shame, Davy (for Brit. Lion), The Smallest Show on Earth. (for Rank) Violent Playground, Rockets Galore (Island Fling U.S.), Sapphire (Brit. Film Academy: Best Brit. Film 1959), 1960 Founder Dir. Allied Film Makers: Prod. The League of Gentlemen, Man in the moon (co-author s.p.), Victim, Life For Ruth (Walk in the Shadow U.S.). Also produced: Secret Partner, All Night Long, The Mind Benders, A Place To Go (author s.p.), Woman of Straw (co-author s.p.), Masquerade (co-author s.p.), The Assassination Bureau (prod., s.p., designer), The Man Who Haunted Himself (prod., co-author s.p.). 1978, exec. in chg. prod., Kendon Films, Ltd. exec. prod., Scum, 1982, co-prod., An Unsuitable Job for a Woman. 1984, exec. prod.: Treasure Houses of Britain; TV series, prod., Heavenly Pursuits, 1985–86; Gospel According to Vic (U.S.).

RELYEA, ROBERT E.: Producer. b. Santa Monica, CA, May 3, 1930. e. U. of California at L.A., B.S., 1952. In Army 1953–55. Entered industry in 1955. Started production of films in 1968 with Bullitt.
PICTURES INCLUDE: Bullitt, The Reivers, Day of the Dolphin.

REMBUSCH, TRUEMAN T.: Exhibitor. b. Shelbyville, IN, July 27, 1909. f. Frank J. Rembusch, pioneer exhibitor. e. U. of Notre Dame Sch. of Commerce, 1928. m. Mary Agnes Finneran. Ent. m.p. ind., 1928, servicing sound equip., father's circuit; became mgr., 1932; elect. bd. of dir., Allied Theatre Owners of Ind., 1936–45, pres. 1945–51, 1952–53; dir. chmn. Allied TV Committee, 1945–50; pres. Allied States Assn., 1950–51; 1952, named by Allied as one of triumvirate heading COMPO; elected chmn. Joint Com. on Toll TV, 1954; Nov. 1953 named by Gov. of Indiana as dir. State Fair Board. Currently pres. Syndicate Thea., Inc., Franklin, Ind. member, In Notre Dame Club of Indianapolis (Man of Yr., 1950); BPOE, 4th Degree K of C, Meridian Hills Country Club, Marco Island Country Club. American Radio Relay League (amateur & commerce, licenses); OX5 Aviation Pioneers; awarded patent, recording 7 counting device, 1951; dir. Theatre Owners of Indiana; dir. to NATO; dir. NATO member ad hoc comm; 1972 chair., NATO Statistical Committee; presently ch., trade practice comm.; 1976–NITE Award service to Independent Exhibition.

REMICK, LEE: Actress. b. Boston, MA, Dec. 14, 1935. e. Miss Hewitt's Sch., Barnard Coll. Started in summer stock; on tour in Jenny Kissed Me, The Seven Year Itch, Paint Your Wagon; first N.Y. stage appearance, Be Your Age; major TV shows incl. Studio 1, Playhouse 90, Armstrong Circle Theatre; m.p. debut in A Face in the Crowd (1956). 1988: became a full partner in (James) Garner/(Peter) Duchow Prods., forming Garner/Duchow/Remick Prods., Inc.
THEATER: Anyone Can Whistle, Wait Until Dark, Follies in Concert.
PICTURES INCLUDE: The Long Hot Summer, Anatomy of a Murder, Wild River, Sanctuary, Experiment in Terror, The Days of Wine and Roses, The Wheeler Dealers, Baby the Rain Must Fall, Hallelujah Trail, Hard Contract, A Severed Head, Sometimes A Great Notion, A Delicate Balance, Hennessy, The Omen, Telefon, The Medusa Touch, The Europeans, The Competition, Tribute.
TELEVISION: The Tempest, And No One Could Save Her, The Blue Knight, Queen's Bench VII, Jennie: Lady Churchill, Eleanor Roosevelt: In Her Words; A Girl Named Sooner, Hustling, Breaking, Wheels, Torn Between Two Lovers, Ike: The War Years, Haywire, The Women's Room, The Letter, A Good Sport, The Gift of Love, Mistral's Daughter, Rearview Mirror, Toughlove, Of Pure Blood, Nutcracker: Money, Madness and Murder, Jesse, A Bridge to Silence.

REMSEN, BERT: Actor. b. Glen Cove, NY, Feb. 25, 1925. e. Ithaca Coll.
PICTURES: Pork Chop Hill, Kid Galahad, Moon Pilot, Brewster McCloud, Thieves Like us, Baby Blue Marine, McCabe and Mrs. Miller, Sweet Hostage, Nashville, The Awakening Land, California Split, Tarantulas, A Wedding, Buffalo Bill and the Indians, The Rose, Uncle Joe Shannon, Carny, Borderline, Second Hand Hearts, Joni, Inside Moves, Looking to Get Out, Sting II, Code of Silence, Stand Alone, Eye of the Tiger, South of Reno, Independence Day, Remote Control.
TELEVISION: Who Is Julia?, The Awakening Land, Burning Rage, Crazy Times, Hobson's Choice, If Tomorrow Comes, Space, Love For Rent, Dallas (series), It's a Living, Mothers Against Drunk Driving, Little Ladies of the Night, Matlock, Jake and the Fatman, Memorial Day.

RESNAIS, ALAIN: Director. b. Cannes, France, June 3, 1922. Began career as asst. dir. to Nicole Vedres on compilation of film for Paris 1900. During '50s worked as asst. editor and editor; experimented with making his own 16mm films. Did series of shorts on various painters, culminating with documentary on Van Gogh, 1948, which he co-directed with Robert Hessens, with whom he later filmed Guernica. Co-directed The Statues Also Die, with Chris Marker.
PICTURES INCLUDE: Night and Fog, Hiroshima, Mon Amour, Last Year at Marienbad, Muriel, La Guerre Est Finie, Je t'Aime, Je t'Aime, Stavisky, Providence, Mon Oncle d'Amerique, Melo, I Want to Go Home.

RESNICK, JOEL H.: Executive. b. New York, NY. e. U. of Pennsylvania, B.A., 1958; New York Law Sch. 1961, admitted to N.Y. State Bar. In 1962 received Masters of Law degree in taxation. 1961–66 served as associate with New York law firm, Phillips, Nizer, Benjamin, Krim & Ballon. Was in-house counsel to United Artists Corp. 1967, joined UA as spec. asst. to the snr. v.p. & gen. mgr. 1970, moved to American Multi-Cinema, Inc., Kansas City, as asst. to pres. 1972, named v.p. in chg. development; 1976, promoted to v.p. in chg. film development. 1977, named exec. v.p. 1983, elected exec. v.p. & dir., AMC Entertainment. 1984, appt. to office of pres. as chm. & CEO, film mktg. 1986, resigned to join Orion Pictures Distribution Corp. as chm. Has served as co-chairman NATO

Ret-Ric

trade practices comm. since 1979. In 1982 elected pres., NATO; 1984, became chm. NATO bd.

RETCHIN, NORMAN: Writer, Producer. b. Chicago, IL, May 6, 1919. e. U. of Pennsylvania, 1940. U.S. Air Force, 1943–45; J. Walter Thompson adv. agency, 1946–51; story ed. & assoc. prod. Screen Televideo Co., 1951–55; story ed. Clover Prod. 1955; stage, orig. bk. and lyrics, The Genius Farm; TV, orig. prod., The Untouchables.
PICTURES INCLUDE: Uranium Boom, (collab.) Leather Saint, Ride Out for Revenge, Mission Mars, Into Thin Air, (orig. story).

RETTIG, TOMMY: Actor. b. Jackson Heights, NY, Dec. 10, 1941; on stage in Annie Get Your Gun. TV series: Lassie (1954–58).
PICTURES INCLUDE: Panic in the Streets, Two Weeks with Love, For Heaven's Sake, The Strip, Elopement, Gobs and Gals, Paula, Lady Wants Mink, 5000 Fingers of Dr. T., So Big, River of No Return, The Raid, The Egyptian, The Cobweb, Jackpot, The Last Wagon, At Gunpoint.
TELEVISION: Studio One, Wagon Train, Mr. Novak, Matinee Theater, Lawman, U.S. Steel Hour, Burns and Allen Show, Peter Gunn, Death Valley Days, Allan Young Show, many others.

REVERE, ANNE: Actress. b. New York, NY, June 25, 1907. e. Wellesley Coll., B.A. m. Samuel Rosen, director. On stage, Stuart Walker Stock Co., 1928–29, Double Door, 1933–34. Children's Hour, 1934–37, org. & dir. Surry Theat., Maine, N.Y., 1936–39; Acad. Award best supporting role, National Velvet, 1945.
PICTURES INCLUDE: Double Door, Howards of Virginia, Men of Boys Town, Remember the Day, Star Spangled Rhythm, Song of Bernadette, National Velvet (Acad. Award, supp., 1945), Keys of the Kingdom, Sunday Dinner for a Soldier, Dragonwyck, Forever Amber, Body and Soul, Gentleman's Agreement, Place in the Sun, Great Missouri Raid, Tell Me That You Love Me Junie Moon, Birch Interval.
TELEVISION: Two for the Money, Search for Tomorrow, Sesame Street.

REVILL, CLIVE: Actor. r.n. Selsby. b. Wellington, New Zealand, Apr. 18, 1930. e. Rongotai Coll., Victoria U. Film debut 1965.
STAGE: Irma La Douce, The Mikado, Oliver, Marat/Sade, Jew of Malta, Sherry, Chichester Season, The Incomparable Max (N.Y.), Sherlock Holmes (N.Y.), Lolita (N.Y.), Pirates of Penzance (L.A.).
PICTURES INCLUDE: Bunny Lake Is Missing, Once Upon a Tractor, Modesty Blaise, A Fine Madness, Kaleidoscope, The Double Man, Fathom, Italian Secret Service, Nobody Runs Forever, Shoes of the Fisherman, Assassination Bureau, The Private Life of Sherlock Holmes, The Buttercup Chain, A Severed Head, Boulevard de Rhum, Avanti!, Flight to the Sun, The Legend of Hell House, The Little Prince, The Black Windmill, Ghost in the Noonday Sun, One of Our Dinosaurs Is Missing, Galileo, Matilda, Zorro, The Gay Blade, Rumpelstiltskin, The Emperor's New Clothes.
TELEVISION: Chicken Soup with Barley, Volpone, Bam, Pow, Zapp. Candida, Platonov, A Bit of Vision, Mill Hill, The Piano Player, Hopcroft in Europe, A Sprig of Broome, Ben Franklin in Paris, Pinocchio, The Great Houdini, Show Business Hall of Fame, Feather and Father, Winner Take All, The New Avengers, Licking Hitler, Columbo, Centennial, A Man Called Sloane, Nobody's Perfect, Marya, Moviola, Diary of Anne Frank, Mikado, The Sorcerer, Wizards & Warriors, George Washington, Murder She Wrote, Faerie Tale Theatre.

REY, FERNANDO: Actor. r.n. Fernando Casado Arambillet. b. La Coruña, Spain, Sept. 20, 1917. e. Madrid Sch. of Architecture. Dubbed dialogue of foreign films into Spanish before beginning acting career. Has made over 150 films since 1939. Made Knight of Arts and Letters, Cannes, 1986.
PICTURES INCLUDE: Tierra Sedienta, Don Quixote, The Mad Queen, Don Juan, Welcome Mr. Marshall, Viridiana, Chimes at Midnight, The Return of the Seven, The Phantom of Liberty, Tristana, The Adventurers, The French Connection, The Discreet Charm of the Bourgeoisie, Seven Beauties, French Connection II, That Obscure Object of Desire, Voyage of the Damned, The Assignment, Quintet, Monsignor, The Stranger, The Hit, Rustler's Rhapsody, Padre Nuestro, Saving Grace, The Enchanted Forest, Traffic Jam, Pasodoble, El Tunel, Hard to Be a God, Moon Over Parador.
TELEVISION: A.D., Black Arrow, Jesus of Nazareth, Captain James Cook (Aust. TV).

REYNOLDS, BURT: Actor, Director. b. Waycross, GA, Feb. 11, 1936. Former Florida State U. football star. m. actress Loni Anderson. Won fame as actor on TV in series: Riverboat, Gunsmoke, Hawk and Dan August. Founded the Burt Reynolds Dinner Theater in Jupiter, FL, 1979.
PICTURES INCLUDE: Armored Command, Angel Baby, Operation CIA, Navajo Joe, Impasse, Shark, Sam Whiskey, 100 Rifles, Fade-In, Skullduggery, Everything You Wanted To Know About Sex, Fuzz, Deliverance, Shamus, White Lightning, The Man Who Loved Cat Dancing, The Longest Yard, W.W. & The Dixie Dancekings, At Long Last Love, Hustle,

Lucky Lady, Gator (dir.-star), Silent Movie, Nickelodeon, Smokey & The Bandit, Semi-Tough, The End (dir-star), Hooper, Starting Over, Rough Cut, Smokey & The Bandit II, Cannonball Run, Paternity, Sharky's Machine (dir.-star), The Best Little Whorehouse in Texas, Best Friends, Stroker Ace, The Man Who Loved Women, Cannonball Run II, Stick (also dir.), City Heat, Heat, Malone, Rent a Cop, Switching Channels, Smoke, All Dogs Go to Heaven (voice), Breaking In.
TELEVISION: Dir.: Alfred Hitchcock Presents (1985).

REYNOLDS, DEBBIE: Actress. r.n. Mary Frances Reynolds. b. El Paso, TX, April 1, 1932. Mother of actress Carrie Fisher. e. Burbank & John Burroughs H.S., Burbank, CA. With Burbank Youth Symphony during h.s.; beauty contest winner (Miss Burbank) 1948, signed by Warner Bros.; on stage in Personal Appearances, Blis-Hayden Theater, Star of Tomorrow, 1952. Autobiography: Debbie: My Life (1988).
PICTURES INCLUDE: The Daughter of Rosie O'Grady, Three Little Words, Two Weeks With Love, Mr. Imperium, Singing in the Rain, Skirts Ahoy, I Love Melvin, Give a Girl a Break, Affair of Dobie Gillis, Susan Slept Here, Athena, Hit the Deck, Tender Trap, Catered Affair, Bundle of Joy, Tammy and the Bachelor, The Mating Game, Say One for Me, It Started with a Kiss, The Gazebo, The Rat Race, Pleasure of His Company, Second Time Around, How the West Was Won, Goodbye Charlie, The Unsinkable Molly Brown, The Singing Nun, Divorce, American Style, What's The Matter with Helen?, That's Entertainment!
TELEVISION: The Debbie Reynolds Show, Aloha Paradise (series), Sadie and Son, Jack Paar Is Alive and Well.
STAGE: !rene.

REYNOLDS, MARJORIE: Actress. b. Buhl, ID, Aug. 12, 1921. On screen as child 1923 & later (Scaramouche, Svengali, Revelation, etc.).
PICTURES INCLUDE: Murder in Greenwich Village (1937), College Humor, Holiday Inn, Star-Spangled Rhythm, Dixie, Ministry of Fear, Up in Mabel's Room, Three Is a Family, Duffy's Tavern, Bring on the Girls, Meet Me on Broadway, Heaven Only Knows, Bad Men of Tombstone, Great Jewel Robber, Rookie Fireman, Home Town Story, No Holds Barred, Models, Inc., Silent Witness.
TELEVISION: The Life of Riley (series).

REYNOLDS, SHELDON: Writer, Producer, Director. b. Philadelphia, PA, 1923. e. New York U. Radio-TV writer; programs include My Silent Partner, Robert Q. Lewis Show, We the People, Danger; writer, prod., dir. Foreign Intrigue film; TV: prod. dir. s.p. collab. story, Foreign Intrigue.

REYNOLDS, STUART: Producer. b. Chicago, IL, March 22, 1907. e. Chicago law schools. Adv. exec., Lord and Thomas, BBDO. General Mills; sales exec. Don Lee-Mutual; formed Stuart Reynolds Prod., TV films. Now motion picture & TV program consultant.
TELEVISION: General Electric Theatre, Cavalcade of America, Your Jeweler's Showcase, Wild Bill Hickok. Producer and worldwide distributor of educational/training films; Eye of the Beholder.

RICH, DAVID LOWELL: Director. b. New York, NY, Aug. 31, 1920. Started career on live television in New York: Studio One, Playhouse, etc. 1950, left for Hollywood to work on TV series: Naked City, Route 66, etc.
PICTURES: Senior Prom, Hey Boy, Hey Girl, Have Rocket Will Travel, Madame X, The Plainsman, Rosie, A Lovely Way to Die, Eye of the Cat, Concorde—Airport '79, Chu Chu and the Philly Flash.
TELEVISION: Movies include See How They Run, Marcus Welby, M.D., The Mask of Sheba, The Sheriff, All My Darling Daughters, The Judge and Jake Wyler, Brock's Last Case, Crime Club, Satan's School for Girls, Sex Symbol, The Daughters of Joshua Cabe Return, You Lie So Deep My Love, Ransom for Alice, Telethon, Little Women, The Hearst and Davies Affair, His Mistress, Scandal Sheet, Infidelity.

RICH, JOHN: Producer, Director. b. Rockaway Beach, NY, July 6, 1925. e. U. of Michigan, B.A., Phi Beta Kappa, 1948; M.A. 1949; Sesquicentennial Award, 1967. bd. of dir., Screen Dir. Guild of America, 1954–1960; v.p. 1958–1960 Founder-Trustee, Producers-Directors Pension Plan, chmn. of bd. 1965, 1968, 1970; treasurer, Directors Guild of America, 1966–67; v.p. 1967–72.
TELEVISION: Academy Awards, The Dick Van Dyke Show, 1963; All in the Family, 1972 (director); All in the Family, 1973 (producer); Directors Guild Award, Most Outstanding Directorial Achievement, 1971. Christopher award: Henry Fonda as Clarence Darrow, 1975. NAACP Imog. Award, 1974; Golden Globe Awards, All in the Family, 1972–73, Mr. Sunshine, MacGyver, Second Start (dir., co-exec. prod.).
PICTURES INCLUDE: Boeing-Boeing; The New Interns; Wives and Lovers; Roustabout; Easy Come, Easy Go.

RICH, LEE: Producer. b. Cleveland, OH, Dec. 10, 1926. e. Ohio U. Adv. exec.; resigned as sr. v.p., Benton & Bowles, to become

256

producer for Mirisch-Rich TV, 1965 (Rat Patrol; Hey, Landlord). Resigned 1967 to join Leo Burnett Agency. Left to form Lorimar Productions in 1969 and served as pres. until 1986 when left to join MGM/UA Communications as chm. & CEO. Resigned 1988; signed 3-year deal with Warner Bros. setting up Lee Rich Prods. there.
PICTURES: Executive Producer: The Man, Who Is Killing the Great Chefs of Europe?, Marriage Is Alive and Well, The Big Red One.
TELEVISION INCLUDES: Executive Producer: Helter Skelter, The Waltons (Emmy Award), Sybil, Eric, Green Eyes, The Blue Knight, The Long Journey Back, Kaz, Eight is Enough, Dallas, Some Kind of Miracle, Mr. Horn, Studs Lonigan, A Man Called Intrepid, Big Shamus, Little Shamus, Young Love, First Love, Mary and Joseph—A Story of Faith, Knots Landing, Skag, Flamingo Road, Reward, Willow B—Women in Prison, Joshua's World, A Perfect Match, Secret of Midland Heights.
AWARDS: Honorary doctorate in communications, Ohio U., 1982; Distinguished Citizenship Award, Southwestern U. Sch. of Law, 1983; named Man of Year by Beverly Hills Lodge of B'nai B'rith, 1983. Has won 3 George Foster Peabody Awards, 4 Humanitas Awards, 2 Christopher Medals. Twice named Television Showman of the Year by Pub. Guild of Amer.

RICHARD, CLIFF: Singer, Actor. b. India, Oct. 14, 1940. Ent. show business 1958 in TV series Oh Boy. Other TV includes Sunday Night at the London Palladium, several Cliff Richard Shows; film debut in Serious Charge, 1959; star, play Aladdin, London Palladium Theatre, 1964–65. Top British Singer, 1960–71. Stageplays: Five Finger Exercise (1970), The Potting Shed (1971). Twice rep. U.K. in Eurovision Song Contest. 3 BBC TV series plus doc. series. 32 silver discs, 12 gold discs for single record releases. Has made three videos. Starred in Time, rock musical, London 1986–87.
PICTURES INCLUDE: Expresso Bongo, The Young Ones, Summer Holiday, Wonderful Life, Voted top box-office Star of Grt. Britain, 1962–63, 1963–64. Finder's Keepers, Two a Penny, Take Me High.

RICHARDS, BEAH: Actress. b. Vicksburg, MS. e. Dillard U. On Bdwy. in The Miracle Worker, A Raisin in the Sun, etc.
PICTURES: Take a Giant Step, The Miracle Worker, Guess Who's Coming to Dinner, In the Heat of the Night, Hurry Sundown, Great White Hope, Mahogany, Homer and Eddie.
TELEVISION: Movies: Footsteps, Outrage, A Dream for Christmas, Just an Old Sweet Song, Ring of Passion, Roots II—The Second Generation, A Christmas Without Snow.

RICHARDS, DICK: Producer, Director, Writer. b. New York, NY, 1936. In U.S. Army as photo-journalist; worked for Life, Look, Time, Esquire, etc. as photographer. Won over 100 int'l. awards, for commercials and photographic art work.
PICTURES: The Culpepper Cattle Co. (prod., dir., s.p.), Rafferty and the Gold Dust Twins (dir.), March or Die (dir.), Tootsie (co-prod.); Death Valley (dir.); Man, Woman and Child (dir.), Heat (dir.).

RICHARDSON, JOELY: Actress. Daughter of actress Vanessa Redgrave and director Tony Richardson, sister of actress Natasha Richardson. e. Lycee Français, St. Paul's Girl's School, London; Royal Acad. of Dramatic Art. Film debut with mother in Wetherby (1985).

RICHARDSON, MIRANDA: Actress. b. Lancashire, England, 1958. Studied acting at the drama program at Bristol. 1979, began acting on stage. Appeared in Moving, at the Queen's Theatre and continued in All My Sons, Who's Afraid of Virginia Woolf, The Life of Einstein in provincial theatres. Also A Lie of the Mind (London), The Changling.
PICTURES: Dance with a Stranger (debut, 1985), The Innocent, Empire of the Sun.
TELEVISION: The Hard Word, Sorrel and Son, A Woman of Substance, Underworld, Death of the Heart, The Black Adder (series).

RICHARDSON, NATASHA: Actress. Daughter of actress Vanessa Redgrave and director Tony Richardson. e. Central Sch. of Speech and Drama. Appeared at the Leeds Playhouse in On the Razzle, Top Girls, Charley's Aunt. Performed A Midsummer Night's Dream and Hamlet with the Young Vic. In 1985 starred with mother in The Seagull (London), also in the musical High Society.
PICTURES: Gothic, A Month in the Country, Patty Hearst, Dangerous Woman.
TELEVISION: In a Secret State, The Copper Beeches (epis. of Sherlock Holmes), Ghosts, The Barringtons.

RICHARDSON, TONY: Director. b. Shipley, Yorks., Eng., June 5, 1928. Father of actresses Natasha and Joely Richardson. e. Wadham Coll., Oxford, where he dir. number prod. for O.U.D.S. Began career with BBC TV and directed such plays as Othello and The Gambler. In 1955 joined English Stage Co. as assoc. artistic dir. Started with Look Back in Anger, Member of the Wedding, 1958 at Shakespeare Memorial

Theatre. 1960, N.Y. co-dir., A Taste of Honey. Recent stage work, dir., Seagull and St. Joan of the Stockyards, Threepenny Opera, I Claudius. Ent. m.p. ind. 1955 as co-dir. of short Mama Don't Allow. Through his Woodfall Films, dir. and produced the best of Britain's "Angry Young Man" films beginning with John Osborne's Look Back in Anger.
PICTURES INCLUDE: Look Back in Anger (1958, prod., dir.), The Entertainer (prod., dir.), Saturday Night and Sunday Morning (prod. only), Sanctuary, A Taste of Honey, Loneliness of the Long Distance Runner, Tom Jones (Acad. Award, 1963), The Loved One, Mademoiselle, The Sailor from Gibralter, Red and Blue, Charge of the Light Brigade, Laughter in the Dark, Hamlet, Ned Kelly, A Delicate Balance, Dead Cert, Joseph Andrews, The Border, The Hotel New Hampshire (also s.p.).
TELEVISION: Penalty Phase, A Death in Canaan, Beryl Markham: A Shadow on the Sun.

RICHE, ALAN: Executive. e. U. of Arizona. Began career as music agent with GAC, later moving into its TV dept. Joined CMA 1969 as m.p. & literary agent. With Guber-Peters Co. as v.p., creative affairs. 1987, named sr. v.p. of prod. for De Laurentiis Entertainment Group. Resigned Dec. 1987.

RICHMAN, (PETER) MARK: Actor. b. Philadelphia, PA, April 16, 1927. Stage credits incl. End as a Man, Masquerade, The Zoo Story, Detective Story, Rose Tattoo.
PICTURES INCLUDE: Friendly Persuasion, Dark Intruder, Agent for H.A.R.M., For Singles Only.
TELEVISION: Cain's Hundred (series); Dempsey, Blind Ambition, City Killer, House on Greenapple Road.

RICHMOND, TED: Producer. b. Norfolk, VA, June 10, 1912. e. Massachusetts Inst. of Technology. Ent. m.p. ind. as publicity dir., RKO Theats.; later mgr. Albany dist. Pub. dir. Fabian circuit, N.Y.; Paramount upper N.Y. state theats.; Grand Nat'l Pictures. Author Grand Nat'l series Trigger Pal, Six Gun Rhythm. Formed T. H. Richmond Prods., Inc., 1941. Formed Copa Prod. with Tyrone Power, 1954. Reactivated Copa Prod. Ltd., England, 1960.
PICTURES INCLUDE: Hit the Hay, The Milkman, Kansas Raiders, Shakedown, Smuggler's Island, Strange Door, Cimarron Kid, Bronco Buster, Has Anybody Seen My Gal, No Room for the Groom, Weekend with Father, The Mississippi Gambler, Desert Legion, Column South, Bonzo Goes to College, Forbidden, Walking My Baby Back Home, Francis Joins the Wacs, Bengal Brigade, Count Three and Pray, Nightfall, Abandon Ship, Solomon and Sheba, Charlemagne. Formed Ted Richmond Prod. Inc. for MGM release, 1959. Bachelor in Paradise, Advance to the Rear; Pancho Villa; Return of the 7; Red Sun; Producer, Papillon, The Fifth Musketeer.

RICHTER, W. D.: Writer. b. Connecticut. e. U. of Southern California Film Sch.
PICTURES: Slither, Peeper, Nickelodeon, Invasion of the Body Snatchers, Dracula, Brubaker, All Night Long, Adventures of Buckeroo Banzai (prod.-dir.).

RICKERT, JOHN F.: Executive. b. Kansas City, MO, Oct. 29, 1924. e. U. of Southern California. Joined Universal Pictures in 1951; left in 1957 to start independent productions From 1960 to 1968 handled indep. roadshow distribution (4-walling). In 1959 formed CineWorld Corporation, natl. dist. co., of which he is pres. In 1975–76 did tax shelter financing for 13 films. Currently involved in distribution, production packaging and intl. co-production as pres. of Coproducers Corp.

RIEGERT, PETER: Actor. b. New York, NY, Apr. 11, 1947. e. U. of Buffalo. Brief stints as teacher, social worker before turned actor, off-off Bdwy. Debuted on Bdwy. in Dance with Me. First film in short, A Director Talks About His Film.
PICTURES: National Lampoon's Animal House, Americathon, Head Over Heels, National Lampoon Goes to the Movies, The City Girl, Local Hero, Anne and Joey, The Big Carnival, The Stranger, Crossing Delancey.
TELEVISION: Concealed Enemies, Ellis Island, News at Eleven.

RIFKIN, HARMON "BUD": Theatre Executive. b. Springfield, MA, Apr. 1, 1942. e. Clark U., A.B., 1964; Boston Coll. Graduate Sch. of Business Admin., M.B.A., 1967. Worked for Rifkin Theatres while student; upon graduation continued in film and equipment purchasing and financial management for the circuit. 1972, co-founded Cinema Centers Copr. & Theatre Management Services; currently pres. and C.E.O. of Hoyts Cinema Corp. with responsibility for new theatre development and general operations.
MEMBER: Exec. Comm. and v.p. of Natl. Assoc. of Theatre Owners. Past program chm., v.p., pres. & chm. of Theatre Owners of New England.

RIFKIN, JULIAN: Exhibitor. b. Boston, MA, May 26, 1915. e. Massachusetts Inst. of Technology. Member bd. of dir. Allied States Assoc.of M.P. Exhibitors, and Theatre Owners of America. Pres. Theatre Owners of New England 1961–63. Chairman bd. Theatre Owners of New England. 1964–65.

Rig-Roa

Past pres. Allied Artists Corp. of New England. Pres., 1968–69, chmn. of bd. Nat'l Assoc. of Theatre Owners, 1970. Pres. Rifkin Theatres. Pres. Cinema Centers Corp. Chm. NATO Code and Rating Comm., 1968–79. Received Sherrill C. Corwin Memorial Award, 1985. Senior consultant, Hoyts Cinema Corp.

RIGG, DIANA: C.B.E. (1987). Actress. b. Doncaster, England. July 20, 1938. Formerly with the Royal Shakespeare Co. at Aldwych Theatre, 1962–64. Ent. TV in The Avengers series, 1965. Ent. films 1967. Recent London stage: Follies.
  PICTURES INCLUDE: The Assassination Bureau, On Her Majesty's Secret Service, Julius Caesar, The Hospital, Theatre of Blood, The Great Muppet Caper, A Little Night Music, Evil Under the Sun.
  TELEVISION: Diana (series), In This House of Brede; Witness for the Prosecution; King Lear; Bleak House; A Hazard of Hearts.

RINGWALD, MOLLY: Actress. b. Sacramento, CA, 1968. Daughter of jazz musician Bob Ringwald; began performing at age 4 with his Great Pacific Jazz Band. Professional debut at 5 in stage play, The Glass Harp. Appeared in TV's New Mickey Mouse Club, a West Coast stage production of Annie and in TV series, The Facts of Life, before theatrical film debut in Tempest (1982).
  PICTURES: Spacehunter: Adventures in the Forbidden Zone, Sixteen Candles, The Breakfast Club, Pretty in Pink, The Pick-Up Artist, For Keeps, King Lear, Fresh Horses, Loser Take All, Me and My Girl.
  TELEVISION: Movies: Packin It In, P.K. and the Kid, Surviving.

RISI, DINO: Director. b. Italy, 1916. Studied medicine but left for film job as assistant on Mario Soldati's Giacomo L'Idealista. Interned in Switzerland in W.W.II. Returned home to make documentaries and short films before directing Vacanze col Gangster in 1952.
  PICTURES INCLUDE: Sign of Venus, Poveri ma Bellis, Ill Sorpasso, Scent of a Woman, Sunday Lovers, Ghost of Love, Good King Dagobert (also s.p.), Madam at War (also s.p.).

RISSIEN, EDWARD L.: Executive. b. Des Moines, IA. e. Grinnell Coll., Stanford U., B.A., 1949. Army Air Force, W.W.II. Bdwy. stage, mgr., 1950–53; v.p., Mark Stevens. Prods., 1954–56; prod., v.p., Four Star, 1958–60; prog. exec., ABC-TV, 1960–62; v.p., Bing Crosby Prods., 1963–66; v.p., Filmways TV Prods.; assoc. producer, Columbia, 1968–69; indep. producer, 1970; prod., WB, 1971; exec. v.p., Playboy Prods., 1972–80; consultant & indep. prod., 1981–82; sr. consultant, cable, Playboy Prods., 1982–85; pres., Playboy Programs, 1985–present. Board of dirs.: Heritage Entertainment, Inc. 1985– present.
  PICTURES INCLUDE: Snow Job (prod., WB); Castle Keep (prod. exec.); The Crazy World of Julius Vrooder (prod.); Saint Jack (exec. prod.).
  TELEVISION: Movies: Exec. prod.: Minstrel Man; A Whale for the Killing; Ocean View Park; Big Bob Johnson; The Great Niagara; Third Girl from the Left; Summer Without Boys.

RISSNER, DANTON: Executive. b. New York, NY, March 27, 1940. Began as agent with Ashley Famous (later Int. Famous), 1967–69. In 1969 joined Warner Bros. as v.p., chg. European prod.; 1970, moved to United Artists as v.p., chg. European prod. 1973, named v.p. in chg. East Coast & European prod. for UA; 1975, v.p. in chg. of world-wide prod. Resigned 1978; 1981, exec. v.p., 20th Century-Fox. 1984, joined UA as sr. v.p., motion pictures.
  PICTURES: Prod.: Up the Academy, Backfire, A Summer Story.

RITCHIE, MICHAEL: Director. b. Waukesha, WI, Nov. 28, 1938. e. Harvard U. where he directed first production of Arthur Kopit's play, Oh Dad, Poor Dad, Mama's Hung You in the Closet and I'm Feeling So Sad. Professional career began as ass't. to Robert Saudek on Ford Foundation's Omnibus TV series. Later became assoc. prod. and then dir. on Saudek's Profiles in Courage series. Then had dir. assignments on top series (Man from U.N.C.L.E., Dr. Kildare, The Big Valley, Felony Squad).
  PICTURES INCLUDE: Downhill Racer, Prime Cut, The Candidate, Smile (also prod.), The Bad News Bears, Semi-Tough, An Almost Perfect Affair, The Island, Bette Midler's Divine Madness (also prod.), The Survivors, Fletch, Wildcats, The Golden Child, The Couch Trip, Fletch II.
  TELEVISION: Man from U.N.C.L.E., Dr. Kildare, The Big Valley, Felony Squad, Run for Your Life, The Outsider (pilot), The Sound of Anger.

RITT, MARTIN: Director. b. New York, NY, Mar. 2, 1920. e. Elon Coll., Burlington, KY. Started as actor with the Group Theatre in Golden Boy and Winged Victory. N.Y. stage; studied acting under Elia Kazan; dir. stage; Mr. Peebles and Mr. Hooker, The Man, Set My People Free, A View from the Bridge, N.Y.; acted in 150 and dir. 100 TV dramas.
  TELEVISION: Danger.

PICTURES INCLUDE: Edge of the City (dir. debut, 1956), No Down Payment, The Long Hot Summer, The Black Orchid, The Sound and the Fury, Adventures of a Young Man, Hud (also co-prod.), The Outrage, Spy Who Came in from the Cold, Hombre, The Brotherhood, The Molly Maguires, The Great White Hope, Sounder, Pete 'n' Tillie, Conrack, The Front, Casey's Shadow, Norma Rae, Back Roads, Cross Creek, Murphy's Romance, Stanley & Iris. Acted: End of the Game, The Slugger's Wife, Nuts.

RITTER, JOHN: Actor. b. Hollywood, CA, Sept. 17, 1948. Father was late Tex Ritter, country-western star. m. actress Nancy Morgan. Attended Hollywood H.S. Interest in acting began at U. of Southern California in 1968. Appeared with college cast at Edinburgh Festival; later with Eva Marie Saint in Desire Under the Elms. Gained fame as star of TV series, Three's Company.
  PICTURES: Americathon, Hero at Large, Wholly Moses, They All Laughed, Real Men, Changes.
  TELEVISION: Movies: Leave Yesterday Behind, In Love with an Older Woman, Love Thy Neighbor, Letting Go, Unnatural Causes, The Last Fling, Prison for Children. Series: Three's a Crowd, Hooperman, Have Faith (exec. prod.).

RIVE, KENNETH: Executive. b. London, England, July 26, 1919. Early career as actor, radio compere, theatrical agent. Served in Intell. Corps. during W.W.II. After demob. theatre sup. and gen. man. cinema co. promoted dir. 1947. Started in continental exhibition forming Gala Film Distrib. Ltd., 1950. Now dir., Cannon Group (UK) Ltd.; Cannon Film Distributors (UK) Ltd.; Gala Film Distributors Ltd.
  PICTURES INCLUDE: During One Night, The Boys, Devil Doll, Curse of Simba.

RIVERA, CHITA: Actress, Dancer. b. Washington, DC, Jan. 23, 1933. r.n. Concita del Rivero. m. dancer-director Anthony Mordente. Trained for stage at American School of Ballet.
  THEATER: Call Me Madam (1952); Guys and Dolls; Can Can; Shoestring Revue; Seventh Heaven; Mr. Wonderful; Shinebone Alley; West Side Story; Bye Bye, Birdie; Bajour; Sondheim: A Musical Tribute; Chicago; Hey Look Me Over; Merlin; The Rink (Tony Award).
  PICTURES: Sweet Charity (1969).
  TELEVISION: The New Dick Van Dyke Show; Kennedy Center Tonight—Broadway to Washington!; Pippin; Toller Cranston's Strawberry Ice; TV Academy Hall of Fame, 1985.

RIVERA, GERALDO: TV Reporter. b. New York, NY, July 4, 1943. e. U. of Arizona, Brooklyn Law Sch., 1969, Columbia Sch. of Journalism. Started legal career then switched to journalism, making several TV documentaries on such subjects as institutions for retarded, drug addiction, migrant workers, etc. Joined WABC-TV, New York, in 1970. Winner 3 national and local Emmys, George Peabody Award, 2 Robert F. Kennedy Awards.
  TELEVISION: Geraldo Rivera: Good Night America; Good Morning America (contributor); 20/20. Specials: The Mystery of Al Capone's Vault, American Vice: The Doping of a Nation; Innocence Lost: The Erosion of American Childhood; Sons of Scarface: The New Mafia; Murder: Live From Death Row, The Investigators (prods.).

RIVERS, JOAN: Actress, Writer, Director. r.n. Joan Molinsky. b. New York, NY, June 8, 1933. e. Barnard Coll. (Phi Beta Kappa). Formerly fashion coordinator Bond clothing stores. Most of career on TV and in nightclubs; with Second City 1961–62; TV debut: Johnny Carson Show, 1965; nat'l syndicated columnist, Chicago Tribune 1973–76, 1983–86 regular substitute guest host for Johnny Carson. 1986, hosted own TV talk show on Fox Network, The Late Show. Hadassah Woman of the Year, 1983; Jimmy Award for Best Comedian 1981; Chair. National Cystic Fibrosis Foundation. Author: Having a Baby Can Be a Scream (1974); Can We Talk? (1983); The Life and Hard Times of Heidi Abramowitz (1984).
  PICTURES: The Swimmer (act.); Rabbit Test (act., dir., s.p.); Uncle Sam (act.); The Muppets Take Manhattan (act.).

RIVKIN, ALLEN: Writer, Producer. b. Hayward, WI, Nov. 20, 1903. Newspaperman, novelist, playwright. Authored 85 s.p. including Farmer's Daughter, Battle Circus, Prisoner of War, Joe Smith American, Eternal Sea, Big Operator.
  TELEVISION: Prod. Troubleshooters series, 1960 entertainment director: Democratic Nat'l Convention; author (with Laura Kerr) Hello, Hollywood; past pres. scr. br. and currently dir. pub. rel., consultant WGAW. Recipient of Morgan Cox and Valentine Davies Awards.

ROACH, HAL, JR.: President, owner Hal Roach Studios. Unit mgr. 20th Century-Fox, 1944–45; gen. mgr., Rainbow Prod., 1945–46. Member of Acad. of M.P. Arts & Sciences, M.P. Producers Assoc., Pres. Alliance of TV Film Producers; treas. & bd. member and former pres. of Acad. of TV Arts & Sciences; pres. Rabco Corp., Hal Roach Prod., chmn. exec. officer, dir., F. I. Jacobs, Detroit; past chmn. bd., Mutual Broadcasting

System, bd. member, Vitapix Corp.; gen. exec., TV Prod., Seven Arts Associated.
PICTURES INCLUDE: Block Heads, A Chump at Oxford, One Million B.C., Road Show, All American Co-ed, Calaboose, Prairie Chickens, Army training films, Physical Education & Military Training, Military Justice of Court Martials, Fighting Man series.
TELEVISION: Stu Erwin Show, Racket Squad, Public Defender, My Little Margie, Passport to Danger, Screen Directors Playhouse, Stories of John Nesbitt, Code 3, Charlie Farrell Show, Gale Storm Show, Blondie, Forest Ranger.

ROBARDS, JASON, JR.: Actor. b. Chicago, IL, July 26, 1922. Served in Navy during W.W.II. Studied acting at Acad. of Dramatic Arts. Began with Children's World Theatre (1947), radio parts, asst. stage mgr. on Stalag 17. First major break 1953 in play American Gothic. To Hollywood, 1958. Film debut: The Journey (1958).
THEATER: The Iceman Cometh, Long Day's Journey into Night, The Disenchanted, Toys in the Attic, Big Fish, Little Fish, A Thousand Clowns, After the Fall (Tony Award, 1959), But for Whom Charlie, Hughie, The Devils, We Bombed in New Haven, The Country Girl, A Moon for the Misbegotten, Long Day's Journey Into Night (Brooklyn Acad. of Music, 1975, Bdwy. 1988), A Touch of the Poet, O'Neill and Carlotta, You Can't Take It With You.
PICTURES INCLUDE: The Journey, By Love Possessed, Long Day's Journey Into Night, Tender Is the Night, Act One, A Thousand Clowns, Any Wednesday, Divorce: American Style, The St. Valentine's Day Massacre, The Night They Raided Minsky's, Hour of the Gun, The Loves of Isadora, Once Upon a Time in the West, Ballad of Cable Hogue, Fools, Johnny Got His Gun, Murders in the Rue Morgue, Pat Garrett and Billy the Kid, All the President's Men (Acad. Award, supp., 1977), Julia, Comes a Horseman, Hurricane, Raise the Titanic!, Caboblanco, Melvin and Howard, Something Wicked This Way Comes, Max Dugan Returns, Square Dance, Bright Lights, Big City; The Good Mother, Dream a Little Dream, Reunion.
TELEVISION: The Iceman Cometh, The Doll's House, For Whom the Bell Tolls, You Can't Take It With You, Hughie, Washington: Behind Closed Doors, The Day After, The Atlanta Child Murders, FDR: The Last Days, Sakharov, Johnny Bull, The Long Hot Summer, Laguna Heat, Norman Rockwell's Breaking Ties, Inherit the Wind.

ROBBINS, MATTHEW: Writer, Director. e. U. of Southern California Sch. of Cinema. Writes scripts in collaboration with Hal Barwood, Robbins branching out into directing also with Corvette Summer in 1978.
PICTURES INCLUDE: Scripts, all with Barwood: The Sugarland Express, The Bingo Long Traveling All-Stars and Motor Kings, Corvette Summer (also dir.); Dragonslayer (also dir.).

ROBBINS, RICHARD: Composer. Studied piano and composition at New England Conservatory. Received Frank Hunting Beebe Fellowship to Austria where he studied musicology. Later became head of Mannes College of Music Preparatory School, N.Y. Has worked closely with James Ivory and Ismail Merchant.
PICTURES: The Europeans (supr. score), Jane Austen in Manhattan, Quartet, Heat and Dust, A Room with a View, Maurice.

ROBBINS, TIM: Actor. b. West Covina, CA, Oct. 16, 1958. Son of Greenwich Village folksinger, worked as actor while in high school. e. NYU. Transferred to UCLA theatre prog. Studied French with actor George Bigot of the Theatre du Soleil. 1981 co-founder The Actors Gang, in L.A.
PICTURES: Fraternity Vacation (1984), No Small Affair, The Sure Thing, Wendell, Toy Soldiers, Top Gun, Howard the Duck, Five Corners, Bull Durham, Tapeheads, Miss Firecracker.
TELEVISION: St. Elsewhere, Hill St. Blues.

ROBERT, PATRICIA HARRISON: Executive. b. Atlanta, GA, March 31, 1939. e. Manhattanville Coll. of the Sacred Heart, Ecole Française (Paris), U. of Virginia Graduate Sch. Dir. of pub. & pub. relations, Gerald Rafshoon Advertising, 1965–69; drama critic, Atlanta Magazine, 1965–68; drama critic, feature writer, The Atlanta Constitution, 1968–69; asst. to publicity director, The Walter Reade Organization, 1969–70; director of publicity—public relations, Radio City Music Hall, 1970. Became Director of Advertising—Public Relations, July, 1973; appt. v.p., 1976. Named east coast pub. dir., Universal Pictures, 1983. In 1984 appt. v.p., pub., Orion Pictures Dist. Corp.

ROBERTS, CURTIS: Producer. b. Dover, England. e. Cambridge U. Child actor. England, Germany; numerous pictures for Rank Org.; prod. England, on Broadway in Gertie, Island Visit; co-prod. on Broadway, Horses in Midstream, Golden Apple, Tonight or Never; tour and N.Y. The Journey, B'way. Now pres., CGC Films, Munich.
TELEVISION: Rendezvous, Deadly Species, Top Secret,

The Ilona Massey Show, When In Rome, Ethan Frome, Black Chiffon.
PICTURES INCLUDE: An Actress in Love, La Die, Hypocrite, Jet Over the Atlantic, The Vixen, Farewell Party, Polly's Return, Rain Before Seven, Halloween, Malaga, My Dear Children, Bus Stop, Eve Arden Show, Norma, The Lion's Consort, 1988.
BOOKS: History of Summer Theatre; The History of Vaudeville; Other Side of the Coin, 1969; History of Music (Popular) 1900–70, 1970; History of English Music Halls, 1972; Latta, 1972; Then There Were Some, 1979; I Live to Love, 1985; Gabor the Merrier, 1988.
TOURS: Blithe Spirit, Showboat, Kiss Me Kate, Generation, The Camel Bell, Farewell Party, Twentieth Century, Great Sebastians, Goodbye Charlie, Time of the Cuckoo, Under Papa's Picture, Everybody's Gal, Divorce Me Darling, Gingerbread Lady, September Song, 1975; Same Time Next Year, Funny Girl, Pal Joey, South Pacific, It Girl; Fanny, Breaking Up the Act (pre-Bdwy.), 1987, 1988.

ROBERTS, ERIC: Actor. b. Biloxi, MS, April 18, 1956. Father founded Actors and Writers Workshop in Atlanta, 1963. Began appearing in stage prods. at age 5. Studied in London at Royal Acad. of Dramatic Art, 1973–74. Returned to U.S. to study at American Acad. of Dramatic Arts. Stage debut in Rebel Women.
THEATER: Mass Appeal, The Glass Menagerie (Hartford Stage Co.), A Streetcar Named Desire, (Princeton's McCarter Theater), Alms for the Middle Class (Long Wharf), Burn This (Broadway).
PICTURES: King of the Gypsies (debut, 1978), Raggedy Man, Star 80, The Pope of Greenwich Village, The Coca Cola Kid, Runaway Train, Nobody's Fool, Rude Awakening.
TELEVISION: Paul's Case, Miss Lonelyhearts, To Heal a Nation.

ROBERTS, MARGUERITE: Writer. b. Clarks, NB. m. John Sanford, novelist.
PICTURES INCLUDE: Honky Tonk, Dragon Seed, Ziegfeld Girl, Sea of Grass, If Winter Comes, Ambush, Escape, Soldiers Three, Diamond Head, Love Has Many Faces, Five Card Stud, Norwood, Shootout, Red Sky at Morning, True Grit.

ROBERTS, PERNELL: Actor. b. Waycross, GA, May 18, 1930. e. U. of Maryland. Left college to begin working with summer stock companies, joining Arena Stage in Washington, DC in 1950. In 1952 began appearing off-Bdwy. (where he won a Drama Desk Award for Macbeth, 1957); made Bdwy. debut in 1958 in Tonight in Samarkand. Film debut in Desire Under the Elms, 1958.
PICTURES: The Sheepman, Ride Lonesome, The Magic of Lassie.
TELEVISION: Series: Bonanza (1959–65), Vegas, Trapper John M.D. (1979–86). Movies: High Noon Part II: The Return of Will Kane, Desperado, Around the World in 80 Days.

ROBERTS, STEPHEN: Executive. b. 1939. Started career at Columbia Pictures Industries in 1958; 1967, moved to intl. sls. div. of 20th Century-Fox. Named pres. of two Fox units: intl. theatres div. and licensing corp. In 1977 appt. pres. of Fox telecommunications div. and in 1979 chm. of Fox Video (formerly Magnetic Video). In 1982 named pres. of new CBS-Fox Co., video cassette and disc firm.

ROBERTS, TONY: Actor. b. New York, NY, Oct. 22, 1939. e. Northwestern U. On Bdwy. in Play It Again Sam, Promises Promises, Barefoot in the Park, Absurd Person Singular, Sugar, Doubles, NY City Opera: Brigadoon, South Pacific.
PICTURES: Million Dollar Duck, The Star Spangled Girl, Play It Again Sam, Serpico, The Taking of Pelham One Two Three, Lovers Like Us, Annie Hall, Just Tell Me What You Want, Stardust Memories, A Midsummer Night's Sex Comedy, Amityville 3-D, Key Exchange, Hannah and Her Sisters, Radio Days, 18 Again.
TELEVISION: The Lindbergh Kidnapping Case, Girls in the Office, If Things Were Different, The Way They Were, A Question of Honor, A Different Affair, The Thorns (series).

ROBERTS, WILLIAM: Writer, Producer. b. Los Angeles, CA. e. U. of Southern California.
PICTURES INCLUDE: The Mating Game, The Magnificent Seven, Wonderful World of the Brothers Grimm, Come Fly With Me, The Devil's Brigade, The Bridge At Remagen, One More Train to Rob, Red Sun, The Last American Hero, Posse, Ten to Midnight.
TELEVISION: created Donna Reed Show.

ROBERTSON, CLIFF: Actor. b. La Jolla, CA, Sept. 9, 1925.
STAGE: Mr. Roberts, Late Love, The Lady and the Tiger, The Wisteria Tree, Orpheus Descending.
PICTURES INCLUDE: Picnic, Autumn Leaves, Battle of the Coral Sea, As the Sea Rages, Underworld, USA, The Big Show, Gidget, All in a Night's Work, The Interns, PT 109, The Best Man, 633 Squadron, Masquerade, The Honey Pot, The Devil's Brigade, Charly, (Academy Award, Best Actor, 1969),

Too Late the Hero, The Great Northfield, Minnesota Raid, J. W. Coop (director, actor); Man On a Swing, Three Days of the Condor, Midway, Shoot, Dominique, Fraternity Row, Class, Brainstorm, Star 80, Shaker Run, Malone.
TELEVISION: Philco-Goodyear, Studio One, Robert Montgomery Presents; Man Without a Country; Washington: Behind Closed Doors; Dreams of Gold, Falcon Crest (series).

ROBERTSON, DALE: Executive, Actor, Producer (Star of Tomorrow, 1951). r.n. Dayle; b. Oklahoma City, OK, July 14, 1923. e. Oklahoma Military Coll. Prof. prizefighter; U.S. Army Sept. 1942–June 1945; Film debut in Fighting Man of the Plains (1949).
PICTURES INCLUDE: Caribou Trail, Two Flags West, Call Me Mister, Take Care of My Little Girl, Golden Girl, Lydia Bailey, Return of the Texan, Outcasts of Poker Flat, O. Henry's Full House, Farmer Takes a Wife, Gambler from Natchez, Sitting Bull, Son of Sinbad, Day of Fury, Law of the Lawless, Blood on the Arrow, The Walking Major, The Coast of Skeleton, The One-Eyed Soldier, The Last Ride of the Daltons, Dakota Incident, View from the Terrace, Fast and Sexy, Hell's Canyon.
TELEVISION: Series: Wells Fargo, The Iron Horse, Death Valley Days, J.J. Starbuck. Movies: Melvin Purvis, Kansas City Massacre.

ROBIN, DANY: Actress. b. Paris, France, 1927. Dancer since child. Played at the opera; acted on stage in Paris, then m.p.
PICTURES INCLUDE: Thirst of Men, Naughty Martine (L'Eventail); American Language debut in Act of Love, 1954. Holiday for Henrietta, Topaz, The Best House in London.

RODDAM, FRANC: Director. b. 1946, England. Studied at London Film Sch. Spent two years as adv. copywriter/prod. with Ogilvy, Benson, Mather before joining BBC as documentary filmmaker. Feature film debut, Quadrophenia.
PICTURES: The Lords of Discipline, Rain Forest, The Bride, Aria, War Party (co-exec. prod., dir.).
TELEVISION: The Family, Mini, Dummy, Aufwiedersehen Pet.

RODDENBERRY, GENE: Producer, Writer. b. El Paso, TX, Aug, 19, 1921. e. L.A. City Coll.; U. Miami; Columbia U.; U. Southern CA. Was airline pilot and L.A. Police Department sergeant. Freelance TV and m.p. writer 1953–62; Prod. TV and m.p. 1962– present.
PICTURES: Pretty Maids All in a Row (prod., s.p.). Star Trek—The Motion Picture.
TELEVISION: Star Trek (creator-prod.), Questor, The Lieutenant, Genesis 2; Star Trek: The Next Generation (exec. prod. and co- writer).

ROEG, NICOLAS: Director, Cameraman. b. London, England. Aug. 15, 1928. m. actress Theresa Russell. Entered film industry through cutting rooms of MGM's British Studios, dubbing French films into English. Moved into prod. as clapper boy and part of photographer Freddie Young's crew. Next became camera operator (Trials of Oscar Wilde, The Sundowners). Had first experience as cameraman on TV series (Police Dog and Ghost Squad). Feature film debut as cameraman on Doctor Crippen. Debut as director on Performance; co-directed with Donald Cammell. First solo dir. film, Walkabout.
PICTURES INCLUDE: Cameraman: The System, Every Day's a Holiday, The Caretaker, Nothing But the Best, A Funny Thing Happened on the Way to the Forum, Masque of Red Death, Fahrenheit 451, Far from the Madding Crowd, Petulia. Director-Cameraman: Performance (co.-dir.), Walkabout, Don't Look Now, The Man Who Fell To Earth, Bad Timing, Eureka. Director: Insignificance, Castaway, Aria, Track 29, The Witches.

ROEVES, MAURICE: Actor, Director, Writer. b. Sunderland, England. Ent. industry, 1964. Played Macduff to Alec Guinness's Macbeth, London stage. Early films: Ulysses, Oh! What a Lovely War, Young Winston, The Eagle Has Landed, Who Dares Wins. Dir. many stage plays.
TELEVISION: In USA and UK incl.: Scobie (series), The Gambler, Allergy, Magnum P.I., Remington Steele, Escape to Victoria, Inside the Third Reich, Journal of Bridgitte Hitler, Tutti Fruitti, Unreported Incident, Bookie, North & South Part II.

ROGERS, CHARLES (BUDDY): Actor. b. Olathe, KS, Aug. 13, 1904. m. Mary Pickford. p. Maude & Bert Henry Rogers. e. U. of Kansas, and was trained for screen in Paramount Picture Sch. Appeared in Fascinating Youth and others. In armed services W.W.II. In 1945 named v.p. & treas. Comet Prods., Inc. Assoc. prod. Sleep My Love, 1950, pres. PRB, Inc., prod. radio, video shows.
PICTURES INCLUDE: Wings, My Best Girl, Get Your Man, Abie's Irish Rose, The Lawyer's Secret, Road to Reno, Working Girls, This Reckless Age, Best of Enemies. Fox: Take a Chance, Dance Band, Old Man Rhythm, One In a Million, Let's Make a Night of It, This Way Please, Golden Hoofs, Mexican Spitfire's Baby, Sing for Your Supper, Mexi-

can Spitfire at Sea, Mexican Spitfire Sees a Ghost, Don't Trust Your Husband.

ROGERS, FRED: Television Host, Producer. b. Latrobe, PA, 1928. e. Rollins Coll., B.A., music composition. In 1951 served as asst. prod. of NBC-TV's The Voice of Firestone and NBC-TV Opera Theatre. Later promoted to network floor dir., supervising Your Lucky Strike Hit Parade, Kate Smith Hour, etc. In Nov., 1953, joined WQED-TV in Pittsburgh, educational TV station, to handle programming. In 1954 started Children's Corner series, writing, producing and performing; it ran 7 years. In 1963 was ordained minister of Presbyterian Church, dedicated to working with children and families through TV. Same year introduced character of Mister Rogers on Canadian Bdctg. Corp. of 15-min. daily program. Ran for one year—was similar in content to present half-hour program, Mister Rogers' Neighborhood. In 1964 programs were incorporated into larger, half-hour format on ABC affiliate in Pittsburgh. In 1966, 100 programs acquired by Eastern Educational Network, broadcast in Pittsburgh, and seen for first time in other cities. Program now carried over 300 PBS stations.
AWARDS: George Foster Peabody, NET Special, Saturday Review TV, General Federation of Women's Club, Ralph Lowell, Gabriel, many honorary doctoral degrees from universities. Emmy, 1980, Outstanding Individual Achievement in Children's Programming; Abe Lincoln Distinguished Communications Recognition Award. Odyssey Award, 1981; Ohio State Award, 1983; Christopher Award, ACT Awards, 1984; Emmy, 1985. Friends of Children Award, 1986: Special Recognition Award—National Directors of Special Ed., 1986: Parents Choice Award, 1985, 1986: Distinguished Service Award—Spina Bifida Assoc.—1985. Action for Children's Television Hall of Fame Award, 1988; Ollie Award, 1987; Commissioners Award for PA Public TV, 1988; Parents Choice Award, 1987.

ROGERS, GINGER: Actress. r.n. Virginia Katherine McMath. b. Independence, MO, July 16, 1911. On stage in vaudeville, m.p. theat. presentations & musical comedy (Girl Crazy). Film debut 1930. Voted among ten best Money-Making Stars in M.P. Herald-Fame Poll 1935, '37. In numerous pictures including Young Man of Manhattan, Gold Diggers of 1933, and others.
PICTURES INCLUDE: 42nd Street, Flying Down to Rio, The Gay Divorcee, Top Hat, Swing Time, The Story of Irene & Vernon Castle, Having Wonderful Time, Bachelor Mother, Tom Dick & Harry, Vivacious Lady, Stage Door, Primrose Path, Kitty Foyle (Acad. Award, 1940), Roxie Hart, The Major & the Minor, Once Upon a Honeymoon, Lady in the Dark, Tender Comrade, I'll be Seeing You, Week-End at the Waldorf, Heartbeat, Magnificent Doll, It Had to Be You, Barkeleys of Broadway, Perfect Strangers, Groom Wore Spurs, Storm Warning, We're Not Married, Dream Boat, Monkey Business, Forever Female, Black Widow, Twist of Fate, Tight Spot, First Traveling Saleslady, Oh! Men, Oh! Women, Teenage Rebel, Harlow, The Confession.
TELEVISION: Perry Como Show, Pontiac, Pat Boone, Dinah Shore, Bob Hope, Ed Sullivan, Hollywood Palace, Chrysler, Steve Allen, Jack Benny, Cinderella.

ROGERS, HENRY C.: Publicist. b. Irvington, NJ, April 19, 1914. e. U. of Pennsylvania, 1934. Formed Rogers & Cowan, 1949, with Warren Cowan; 1969, bd. chm., Rogers & Cowan, Inc.

ROGERS, KENNY: Singer, Actor, Songwriter. b. Crockett, TX, Aug. 21, 1938. Country and western singer. Member Bobby Doyle Trio, Christy Minstrels, 1966–67; The First Edition 1967–76. On screen in Six Pack (1982).
TELEVISION: Series: Rollin. Many specials and movies: Kenny Rogers as The Gambler, Coward of the County, The Gambler—The Adventure Continues, Wild Horses; Kenny Rogers as The Gambler—The Legend Continues.

ROGERS, LAWRENCE H., II: Executive. b. Trenton, NJ, Sept. 6, 1921. e. Princeton U. 1942, U.S. Army, 1942–1946; WSAZ, Huntington, WV. Radio & TV, V.P. & gen. mgr., 1949–55; WSAZ, Inc., President, 1955–59; Taft Broadcasting Co., v.p., 1959–63; Taft Broadcasting Co., President, 1963–76. Vice Chairman, Hanna-Barbera Productions, L.A., CA, and Cinemobile Systems, Hollywood. Director: Cine Artists International, Hollywood; Cincinnati Financial Corp.; Inter-Ocean Insurance Co., Cinti.; Cardinal Fund, Ohio; Federal Reserve Bank of Cleveland, Cincinnati Branch; Theater Development Fund, New York; Greater Cincinnati Foundation; Rockford Coll., Rockford, IL.

ROGERS, MIMI: Actress. b. Coral Gables, FL, Jan. 27. m. actor Tom Cruise. Made film debut in Blue Skies Again.
PICTURES: Blue Skies Again, Gung Ho, Street Smart, Someone to Watch Over Me, Finding Maubee, Hider in the House.
TELEVISION: Series: The Rousters, Paper Dolls. Episodes: Magnum, P.I., Hart to Hart, Quincy, M.E., Hill Street Blues. Movies: Divorce Wars, Hear No Evil, You Ruined My Life.

ROGERS, PETER: Executive. b. Rochester, Eng., Feb. 20, 1916. e. Kings Sch., Rochester. Journalist in theatre and BBC; joined G. W. H. Productions 1941 as script writer; with Gainsborough Studios; asst. scenario ed. to Muriel Box; assoc. prod.; personal asst. to Sydney Box 1949.
PICTURES INCLUDE: Dear Murderer, Holiday Camp, When the Bough Breaks, Here Come the Huggetts, Huggetts Abroad, Vote for Huggett, It's Not Cricket, Marry Me, Don't Ever Leave Me, Appointment with Venus (Island Rescue), The Clouded Yellow, The Dog and the Diamonds (Children's Film Found), Up to His Neck, You Know What Sailors Are, Cash on Delivery, To Dorothy A Son, Gay Dog, Circus Friends, Passionate Stranger, After the Ball, Time Lock, My Friend Charles, Chain of Events, Carry on Sergeant, Flying Scott, Cat Girl, Solitary Child, Carry On Teacher, Carry On Nurse, Carry On Constable, Please Turn Over, Watch Your Stern, The Tommy Steele Story, The Duke Wore Jeans, No Kidding, Carry On Regardless, Raising the Wind, Twice Around the Daffodils, Carry on Cruising, The Iron Maiden, Nurse on Wheels, Carry on Cabby, This Is My Street, Carry On Jack, Carry on Spying, Carry on Cleo, The Big Job, Carry on Cowboy, Carry on Screaming, Don't Lose Your Head, Follow that Camel, Carry on Doctor, Carry on Up the Khyber, Carry on Camping, Carry on Assault, Carry on Henry, Quest, Revenge, Carry on At Your Convenience, All Coppers Are. . ., Carry on Matron, Carry on Abroad, Bless This House, Carry on Girls, Carry on Dick, Carry on Behind, Carry on England, The Best of Carry On, Carry on Emmanuelle.
TELEVISION: Ivanhoe series, Carry on Laughing, Carry on Laughing (2), What a Carry on (2).

ROGERS, RODDY: Producer. b. Philadelphia, PA. e. St. George's Sch. R.I.; U. of Pennsylvania. Asst. acct. exec., Gray & Rogers Adv. Agency, Phila., 1946–48; stage mgr. and lighting coordinator at WFIL-TV, 1948; operations correlator, 1949; prod., dir., 1950; exec. prod. for WFIL-TV, 1951, prod. dir. Paul Whiteman TV Teen Club for ABC and Youth on the March, both on ABC-TV; dir. TV prod., WFIL-TV, 1953, mgr. radio, TV prod., Ward Wheelock Co., New York, 1954; prog. prod., radio-TV account supervisor N. W. Ayer & Son, 1955, N.Y.; chge. network sup. Ayer, N.Y. 1958; v.p., mgr. home office Ayer, 1959, pres. Agency Services Co.; pres. E. H. Rogers & Co., 1969.

ROGERS, ROY: Actor. r.n. Leonard Slye. b. Cincinnati, OH Nov. 5, 1911. Radio singer; many m.p. from 1937. Voted No. 1 Money-Making Western Star in M.P. Herald-Fame, 1943–54 inclusive; also voted one of ten best money-making stars in 1945, '46. Acting & prod. TV films, 1952 with wife, Dale Evans; one-hour spectaculars, Chevy Show, 1959–60; contracted for several TV specials and for nationwide appearances with Roy Rogers touring show in Canada & U.S., 1962; state fairs, rodeos since 1962; TV series. Happy Trails with Roy and Dale (cable). Star of 86 feature films and 104 TV episodes.
PICTURES INCLUDE: Under Western Stars, The Old Barn Dance, Billy the Kid Returns, Come On Rangers, Rough Riders, Round-Up, Frontier, Pony Express, Southward Ho!, In Old Caliente, Wall Street Cowboy, Heart of the Golden West, Sunset Serenade, Son of Paleface.

ROGERS, WAYNE: Actor. b. Birmingham, AL, April 7, 1933. e. Princeton U.
PICTURES: Odds Against Tomorrow, The Glory Guys, Chamber of Horrors, Cool Hand Luke, WUSA, Pocket Money, Once in Paris, Hot Touch, The Gig, The Killing Time.
TELEVISION: Series: Edge of Night, Housecalls, Stagecoach West, M*A*S*H, City of the Angels, High Risk (host). Movies: It Happened One Christmas, Making Babies II, The Top of the Hill, Chiefs, He's Fired She's Hired, The Lady from Yesterday, American Harvest, Drop-Out Mother, One Terrific Guy, Bluegrass.

ROGERS, WILL, JR.: Actor. b. New York, NY, Oct. 20, 1912. p. late Will Rogers, actor. e. Stanford U., 1935. Publisher, ed., Beverly Hills Citizen; for. corresp.; elected congressman from CA; U.S. Army, W.W.II; m.p. debut in Story of Will Rogers, since in Eddie Cantor Story, Boy From Oklahoma.

ROHM, MARIA: Actress, Assoc. prod. b. Vienna, Austria, 1949. Early career with Burgtheater in Vienna. Ent. TV 1963, Films 1966. Films incl: Million Eyes of Sumuru, Five Golden Dragons, House of a Thousand Dolls, 99 Women, Blood of Fu Manchu, Justine, Venus in Furs, Eugenie, Black Beauty, Treasure Island, Call of the Wild, The Assassin Is Not Alone, Ten Little Indians, End of Innocence. Flight to Hell, TV Series, Quatermain. Assoc. prod.: White Stallion; Black Arrow; Buried Alive.

ROHMER, ERIC: Director. Writer. r.n. Jean Maurice Scherer. b. Nancy, France, April 4, 1920. Professor of literature. Film critic for La Gazette du Cinema and its successor Cahiers du Cinema which he edited, 1957–63. With Claude Chabrol wrote book on Alfred Hitchcock, established film critic, 1957. 1959 directorial debut, Le Signe du Lion. In 1962 began a series of 6 Moral Tales; from 1980 with The Aviator's Wife

began another series of 7 films called Comedies and Proverbs. Staged Catherine de Heilbronn in Nanterre, 1979.
PICTURES: Short films: Presentation ou Charlotte et Son Steak (1951); Veronique et Son Cancre; Nadja a Paris; Place de L'etoile; Une Etudiante d'aujourd'hui; Fermiere a Montfaucon; Feature films: Le Signe du Lion; La Boulangere de Monceau; La Carriere Suzanne; My Night at Maude's; La Collectionneuse; Claire's Knee; Chloe in the Afternoon; The Marquise of O; Perceval; The Aviator's Wife; Le Beau Mariage; Pauline at the Beach; Full Moon in Paris; La Rayon Vert; Boyfriends and Girlfriends; Four Adventures of Reinette and Mirabelle.
TELEVISION: Carl Dreyer; Le Celluloid et le Marbre; Ville Nouvelle; Catherine de Heilbronn; between 1964–69 directed series of documentaries for French TV: Les Cabinets et Physique du XVIII siecle, Les Metamorphoses du Paysage Industriel; Perceval; Don Quichotte; Edgar Poe; Pascal; Louis Lumiere, etc.

ROIZMAN, OWEN: Cinematographer. b. Brooklyn, NY, Sept. 22, 1936.
PICTURES INCLUDE: The French Connection, The Gang That Couldn't Shoot Straight, Play It Again, Sam, The Heartbreak Kid, The Exorcist, The Taking of Pelham 1-2-3, The Stepford Wives, Independence, Three Days of the Condor, The Return of the Man Called Horse, Network, Straight Time, Sgt. Pepper's Lonely Hearts Club Band, The Electric Horseman, The Black Marble, True Confessions, Absence of Malice, Taps, Tootsie, Vision Quest.

ROLAND, GILBERT: Actor. r.n. Luis Alonso. b. Juarez, Mexico, Dec. 11, 1905. p. Father Francisco Alonso, a bullfighter in Spain. e. private schools in Mexico.
PICTURES INCLUDE: Captain Kidd, Pirates of Monterey, Dude Goes West, Malaya, We Were Strangers, Crisis, The Furies, The Torch, Bullfighter and Lady, Mark of Renegade, Ten Tall Men, My Six Convicts, Glory Alley, Miracle of Fatima, Apache War Smoke, Bad & the Beautiful, Thunder Bay, Diamond Queen, Beneath the 12-Mile Reef, French Line, Underwater, The Racers, That Lady, Treasure of Pancho Villa, Guns of the Timberland, The Wild Innocents, Eyes of Father Thomasino, The Big Circus, Samar, Cheyenne Autumn, The Reward, High Chaparral, Christian Licorice Store, Islands in the Stream, Caboblanco, Barbarosa.
TELEVISION: Bonanza, Alfred Hitchcock Presents, The FBI, Gunsmoke, The Fugitive, etc.

ROLLE, ESTHER: Actress. b. Pompano Beach, FL, Nov. 8. e. New School for Social Research. One of original members of Negro Ensemble Co. in N.Y. Has appeared both off and on Bdwy (in The Blacks, Amen Corner, Blues for Mister Charlie, Don't Play Us Cheap) and in several TV series.
PICTURES: To Kill a Mockingbird, Nothing But a Man, The Learning Tree, Cleopatra Jones, P.K. and the Kid, Finding Maubee.
TELEVISION: Guest roles in N.Y.P.D., Like It Is, The Winners. Regular on series: Maude, Good Times. Movies: I Know Why the Caged Bird Sings, Summer of My German Soldier (Emmy Award), A Raisin in the Sun.

ROLLINS, HOWARD E., JR.: Actor. b. Baltimore, MD, 1951. e. Towson State Coll. On stage in Traps, Streamers, The Mighty Gents, Medal of Honor Rag, G.R. Point.
PICTURES: Ragtime, The House of God, A Soldier's Story, Dear America: Letters Home From Vietnam (reader).
TELEVISION: The Edge of Night, King, Roots—The Next Generation, Member of the Wedding, My Old Man, A Doctor's Story, He's Fired She's Hired, In the Heat of the Night (series).

ROLLINS, JACK: Executive. Joined in partnership with Charles H. Joffe (see bio) to set up management-production org. Involved in production of many Woody Allen films with Joffe.
TELEVISION: Dick Cavett Show (exec. prod.).

ROMAN, LAWRENCE: Writer. b. Jersey City, NJ, May 30, 1921. e. U. of California at L.A., 1943. Wrote play, Buying Out, prod. in Buffalo, N.Y.; wrote play Crystal, Crystal Chandelier, prod. in Stockbridge, Mass. Broadway plays: If! If! If!, Alone Together.
PICTURES INCLUDE: (collab.) Drums Across the River, Vice Squad, (collab.) Naked Alibi, (collab.) One Desire, Man From Bitter Ridge, (s.p.) Kiss Before Dying, The Sharkfighters, (s.p.) Slaughter on Tenth Avenue, The Swinger, Author B'way play & collab. s.p. Under the Yum Yum Tree, Author B'way play P.S. I Love You. s.p. Paper Lion, collab. Red Sun, orig. s.p. A Warm December; McQ, (orig. s.p.) The Mayflower Number; (orig. s.p.) Abracadabra (orig. s.p.), Skeletons (orig. s.p.); Lovers Three (orig. s.p.). Omar Bradley (TV special movie), Anatomy of an Illness (TV movie) based on Norman Cousin's book; Badge of the Assassin (TV movie based on Robert Tanenbaum's book); Three Wishes for Jamie (TV movie).

ROMAN, RUTH: Actress. b. Boston, MA, Dec. 23, 1924. p. professionals. e. Girls H.S., Boston; Bishop Lee Dramatic Sch. Started career with little theatre groups: New Eng.

Rom-Ros

Repertory Co., Elizabeth Peabody Players. Screen debut in Universal serial, Queen of the Jungle, then minor roles; author stories, The Whip Son, The House of Seven Gables.
PICTURES INCLUDE: Good Sam, Belle Starr's Daughter, Whip Son, House of Seven Gables, The Window, Champion, Barricade, Beyond the Forest, Always Leave Them Laughing, Colt .45, Three Secrets, Dallas, Strangers on a Train, Tomorrow is Another Day, Invitation, Starlift, Mara Maru, Young Man With Ideas, Blowing Wild, Far Country, Shanghai Story, Tanganyika, Down Three Dark Streets, Joe Macbeth, Bottom of the Bottle, Great Day in the Morning, Rebel in Town, Bitter Victory, Look in Any Window, Miracle of the Cowards (Spanish prod.), Love Has Many Faces, The Killing Kind, Dead of Night, The Baby, Day of the Animals, Echoes.
TELEVISION: Naked City, Route 66, The Defenders, Breaking Point, Eleventh Hour, Producers Showcase, Dr. Kildare, The Long Hot Summer, Go Ask Alice (movie), Murder She Wrote.

ROMERO, CESAR: Actor. b. New York, NY, Feb. 15, 1907. e. Collegiate Sch., Riverdale Country Sch. In U.S. Coast Guard, W.W.II. In 1927 on N.Y. stage. Film debut: the Thin Man (1934).
PICTURES INCLUDE: British Agent, Show Them No Mercy, Metropolitan, Cardinal Richeleu, Love Before Breakfast, Wee Willie Winkie, Happy Landing, My Lucky Star, The Return of the Cisco Kid, The Little Princess, The Gay Caballero, Wintertime, Coney Island, Captain from Castile, Beautiful Blonde from Bashful Bend, Deep Waters, That Lady in Ermine, Diamond Jim Brady, Clive of India, Weekend in Havana, Springtime in the Rockies, Tales of Manhattan, Tall, Dark and Handsome, Once a Thief, The Jungle, Lost Continent, FBI Girl, Frontier Marshall, Happy Go Lovely, Scotland Yard Inspector, Prisoners of the Casbah, Shadow Man, The Americano, Vera Cruz, The Racers, Around the World in Eighty Days, Leather Saint, Ocean's 11, The Computer Wore Tennis Shoes, Madigan's Millions, Now You See Him, Now You Don't, The Spectre of Edgar Allan Poe, The Strongest Man in the World, Carioca Tiger, The Story of Father Kino, Lust in the Dust, Mortuary Academy, Street Law.
TELEVISION: Falcon Crest (series), Passport to Danger.

ROMERO, GEORGE A.: Director. b. 1939.
PICTURES INCLUDE: Night of the Living Dead, The Crazies; Hungry Wives; Dawn of the Dead; Knightriders (also s.p.); Creepshow; Day of the Dead, Monkey Shines (dir., s.p.).
TELEVISION: Tales from the Dark Side (exec. prod., s.p.)

ROONEY, ANDY: Writer, Director, Actor. b. Albany, NY, Jan. 14, 1920. e. Colgate U. Started career as writer for Arthur Godfrey then for Garry Moore, Sam Levenson, Victor Borge, etc. Produced, directed and performed in documentaries, including Black History—Lost, Strayed or Stolen, An Essay on War, In Praise of New York City, Mr. Rooney Goes to Work, etc. Regularly appears on 60 Minutes (CBS).

ROONEY, MICKEY: Actor. r.n. Joe Yule, Jr.; b. Brooklyn, NY, Sept. 23, 1920; son of Joe Yule & Nell Carter, vaudeville performers. U.S. Army, W.W.II. In vaudeville during early infancy with parents and others before m.p. debut and after; from age of 5 to 12 created screen version of Fontaine Fox newspaper comic character Mickey McGuire in series of short subjects of that title, also appeared in number of features (Not to be Trusted, Orchids and Ermine, The King, etc.). Adopting name of Mickey Rooney, ret. to vaudeville; resumed screen career 1932. Special Academy Award 1940 for Andy Hardy characterization; voted among first ten Money-Making Stars in M.P. Herald-Fame Poll. 1938–43. Broadway: Sugar Babies 1979. Autobiography: I.E. (1965). Honorary Academy Award, 1983.
PICTURES INCLUDE: As child: Information Kid, Fast Companions, My Pal the King, Beast of the City, The Big Cage, The Bowery, Broadway to Hollywood, The Big Chance, Manhattan Melodrama, A Midsummer Night's Dream, Reckless, Riff Raff, Little Lord Fauntleroy, Captains Courageous.
LATER FILMS: A Family Affair, Love Finds Andy Hardy, Babes in Arms, Strike Up the Band, Men of Boy's Town, Babes on Broadway, The Human Comedy, Girl Crazy, National Velvet, Words and Music, The Strip, Sound Off, Off Limits, All Ashore, Slight Case of Larceny, Drive a Crooked Road, Bridges at Toko-Ri, Atomic Kid, Twinkle in God's Eye, Bold and the Brave, Magnificent Roughnecks, The Last Mile, Big Operation, Private Lives of Adam and Eve, Platinum High School, King of the Roaring 20's, Breakfast at Tiffany's, It's a Mad, Mad, Mad, Mad World, Everything's Ducky. The Secret Invasion, The Extraordinary Seaman, The Comic, The Cock-eyed Cowboys of Calico County, Skidoo, Pulp, Richard, B.J. Presents, That's Entertainment!, The Domino Principle, Pete's Dragon, The Black Stallion, Arabian Adventure.
TELEVISION: Playhouse 90, Pinocchio, Eddie, Somebody's Waiting, The Dick Powell Theater, Hey Mickey (series), Bill, Bill: On His Own, Bluegrass, Golden Girls.

ROONEY, PAT: Performer stage, nightclubs, pictures. Producer. e. Denver U., Santa Monica Coll., U. of California at L.A., Marquette U. Entertainer vaudeville, theatres, stage, TV and pictures. Captain U.S. Army Air Corps. during Korean War.

Entertained troops Far East Commands. Producer, 1960, C.B.S. Films Inc., producing TV pilots and series. 1962, formed Pat Rooney Prods. with Del E. Webb, hotel and construction exec. 1963–68, producer for Jerry Buss Prods. %Paramount Pictures, Hollywood, making feature films.
MAJOR PICTURES INCLUDE: Dime with a Halo, Danger Pass, Caged, Law of the Lawless, Requiem for a Gunfighter, Bounty Killer, Young Once, Hells Angels, Fools, Christmas Couple, Black Eye, Jan and Dean, Deadman's Curve.

ROOS, FRED: Producer. b. Santa Monica, CA, May 23, 1934. e. UCLA, B.A. Directed documentary films for Armed Forces Radio and Television Network. Worked briefly as agent for MCA and story editor for Robert Lippert Productions. Worked as casting dir. in 1960s and served as casting dir. on The Godfather, beginning longtime association with filmmakers Francis Coppola and George Lucas.
PICTURES: The Conversation; The Godfather Part II; Apocalypse Now; The Black Stallion; The Escape Artist (exec. prod.); The Black Stallion Returns; Hammett; One From the Heart; The Outsiders; Rumble Fish; The Cotton Club; One Magic Christmas; Seven Minutes in Heaven; Peggy Sue Got Married (special consultant); Barfly; Gardens of Stone (co-exec. prod.); Tucker: The Man and His Dream.

ROOT, WELLS: Writer. b. Buffalo, NY, March 21, 1900. e. Yale U. Drama ed., NY World; dramatic and film critic, Time mag.; fiction, articles, various magazines; many TV dramas, various programs.
PICTURES INCLUDE: I Cover the Waterfront, Tiger Shark, Bird of Paradise, Prisoner of Zenda, Magnificent Obsession, Texas Across the River.

ROSE, ALEX: Producer. r.n. Alexandra Rose. b. 1946. e. U. of WI, BS. Started in m.p. distribution with Medford Films. Later became asst. sls. mgr. for New World Pictures.
PICTURES INCLUDE: (co-prod. with Tamara Asseyev), Drive-In, I Wanna Hold Your Hand, Big Wednesday, Norma Rae, Nothing in Common (co-prod. with Garry Marshall), Overboard (with Garry Marshall).
TELEVISION: Nothing in Common (co-exec. prod. with Garry Marshall), Pilots: Norma Rae, Just Us Kids.

ROSE, DAVID: Composer, Conductor. b. London, England, June 15, 1910. To U.S. 1914. Studied music, Chicago Coll. of Music. Pianist with Chicago orchestras; staff arranger for several radio stations; mus. dir., West Coast network; while in U.S. Army, comp. dir. of Winged Victory; songs include Holiday for Strings, Our Waltz.
PICTURES INCLUDE: Texas Carnival, Rich Young & Pretty, The Clown, Bright Road, Jupiter's Darling, Port Afrique.
TELEVISION: Musical dir., Red Skelton Show; composer-conductor, Bonanza. Little House on the Prairie, Highway to Heaven, Emmy, Fred Astaire special.

ROSE, JACK: Writer. b. Warsaw, Poland, Nov. 4, 1911. e. Ohio U. 1934, B.A. m. Audrey Mary Rose, writer, prod. Paramount Pictures, L.A.
PICTURES INCLUDE: Ladies Man, Sorrowful Jones, The Great Lover, It's A Great Feeling, Pale Face, My Favorite Brunette, Road to Rio, Daughter of Rosie O'Grady, Always Leave Them Laughing, On Moonlight Bay, Riding High, I'll See You in My Dreams, Room for One More, April in Paris, Trouble Along the Way, Living it Up, Seven Little Foys, Houseboat, Five Pennies, Beau James, It Started in Naples, Double Trouble, Papa's Delicate Condition, Who's Got the Action?, Who's Been Sleeping in My Bed?, A Touch of Class, The Duchess and the Dirtwater Fox, Lost and Found, The Great Muppet Caper.
TELEVISION: Academy Awards (1988, writer).

ROSE, REGINALD: Writer. b. New York, NY, Dec. 10, 1921. e. City Coll. of New York. Worked as clerk, publicist, Warner Bros.; adv. acct. exec., copy chief; U.S. Air Force, W.W.II; first TV play, Bus to Nowhere, 1951; since then numerous TV plays, Studio One, Playhouse 90. Creator of The Defenders, other programs.
PICTURES INCLUDE: Crime in the Streets, 12 Angry Men, Dino, Man of the West, The Man in the Net, Baxter, Somebody Killed Her Husband, The Wild Geese, The Sea Wolves, Whose Life Is It Anyway?, Wild Geese II, The Final Option.
TELEVISION: Dear Friends, Thunder on Sycamore Street, Tragedy in a Temporary Town, My Two Loves, The Rules of Marriage, Studs Lonigan, Escape from Sobibor.

ROSE, STEPHEN: Executive. Entered m.p. industry in 1964 with Columbia Pictures; named adv. dir. In 1970 joined Cinema V Distributing, Inc. as dir. of adv.; left in 1971 to take post at Cinemation Industries, where was named v.p. and bd. member. In 1975 joined Paramount Pictures as dir. of adv.; promoted to v.p./adv. In 1979 formed Barrich Prods. with Gordon Weaver. In Feb., 1982, rejoined Paramount as v.p., mktg; 1983, named v.p. of mktg. for Paramount; sr. v.p., mktg., 1983. Resigned in 1984 to form Barrich Marketing with Gordon Weaver.

262

ROSEN, ROBERT L.: Producer. b. New York, NY, Oct. 7, 1935. e. Lehigh U., B.S.C.
PICTURES: The French Connection II; Black Sunday; Prophecy; Going Ape; The Challenge; Courage (also dir.); Porky's Revenge, World Gone Wild.
TELEVISION: Puff the Magic Dragon; The Little Rascals' Christmas Special; The World of Strawberry Shortcake; Puff the Magic Dragon in the Land of Living Lies; Thanksgiving in the Land of Oz; etc.

ROSENBERG, FRANK P.: Producer, Writer. b. New York, NY, Nov. 22, 1913. e. Columbia U., New York U. Joined Columbia 1929; writer m.p. & radio; exploit, mgr., 1941; apptd. national dir. adv., publicity, exploitation, Columbia Pictures Feb. 1944. Pub. dir. M.P. Victory Loan, 1945; dir. pub. Columbia Pictures Studios, Hollywood, Jan. 1946. Resigned 1947 to enter production. Co-prod. Man Eater of Kumaon. Collab. adapt., assoc. prod. Where the Sidewalk Ends.
PICTURES INCLUDE: Secret of Convict Lake, Return of the Texan, The Farmer Takes a Wife, King of the Khyber Rifles, Illegal, Miracle in the Rain, Girl He Left Behind, One-Eyed Jacks, Critic's Choice, Madigan, exec. prod., The Steagle, prod. The Reincarnation of Peter Proud; sole adaptation, Gray Lady Down.
TELEVISION: Exec. prod. and prod. for Schlitz Playhouse programs during 1957–58; prod., The Troubleshooters; exec. prod., Arrest and Trial, 1963–64; exec. prod. Kraft Suspense Theatre, 1964–65; v.p. MCA Universal 1964; pres., Cutlass Prods., Inc.

ROSENBERG, GRANT E.: Executive. Started career in research dept., NBC; 1977, joined Paramount in research and later in development; 1984, v.p., dramatic develp.; then sr. v.p., develp., for TV group, Paramount. 1985, named sr. v.p., network TV for Walt Disney Pictures.

ROSENBERG, MARK: Executive. b. 1948. e. U. of Wisconsin. Started career in magazine publishing field in New York. Adv. exec. with Seiniger & Associates; agent in m.p. dept. of IFA (later became ICM). With literary agency of Adams, Ray, Rosenberg. In 1978 joined Warner Bros., as v.p., prod.; in 1980 promoted to snr. v.p. of prod.; 1983, pres., W B theatrical production division. 1986, partner with Sydney Pollack in Mirage Prods.
PICTURES: Bright Lights, Big City (co-prod.).

ROSENBERG, RICHARD K.: Executive. b. Paterson, NJ, Apr. 4, 1942. e. Indiana U. 1966–77 corp. & entertainment atty. for many major corps. & celebrities. 1974, produced Alice, Sweet Alice, debut film of Brooke Shields. Formed RKR Entertainment Group in 1977, with its subsidiaries, RKR Releasing, Inc., RKR Artists & RKR Prods.
PICTURES: Alice Sweet Alice, Hell's Angels Forever, Search for the Mother Lode, The Wild Duck.
PUBLICATIONS: Entertainment Industry Contracts, 1986.

ROSENBERG, RICK: Producer. b. Los Angeles, CA. e. Los Angeles City Coll., U. of California at L.A. Started career in mail room of Columbia Pictures, then asst. to prod. Jerry Bresler on Major Dundee and Love Has Many Faces. Asst. to Col. v.p., Arthur Kramer. Was assoc. prod. on The Reivers and in 1970 produced first feature, Adam at Six A.M., with Bob Christiansen, with whom co-produced all credits listed below.
PICTURES INCLUDE: Adam at Six A.M., Hide in Plain Sight.
TELEVISION: Features: Suddenly Single, The Glass House, A Brand New Life, The Man Who Could Talk to Kids, The Autobiography of Miss Jane Pittman, I Love You . . . Goodbye, Queen of the Stardust Ballroom, Born Innocent, A Death in Canaan, Strangers, Robert Kennedy and His Times, Kids Don't Tell, As Summers Die; Gore Vidal's Lincoln; Red Earth, White Earth.

ROSENBERG, STUART: Director, Producer. b. New York, NY, 1927. e. New York U. Emmy Award, 1962.
PICTURES INCLUDE: Murder, Inc., Cool Hand Luke, The April Fools, WUSA, Pocket Money, The Laughing Policeman, The Drowning Pool, Voyage Of The Damned, The Amityville Horror, Love and Bullets, Brubaker, The Pope of Greenwich Village.
PICTURES: Numerous episodes of such series as The Untouchables, Naked City, The Defenders, Espionage, Chrysler Theatre, Twilight Zone, Alfred Hitchcock Theater.

ROSENFELT, FRANK E.: Executive. b. Peabody, MA, Nov. 15, 1921. e. Cornell U., B.S.; Cornell Law Sch., L.L.B. Served as atty. for RKO Radio Pictures, before joining MGM in 1955 as member of legal dept. Appt. secty. in 1966. Named v.p., gen. counsel in 1969 and pres. in 1973. In 1974 also named chief exec. officer. Bd. chm. & chief exec. officer, MGM to 1981; now vice chm., MGM/UA Communications Co. Member: Bd. of Governors, Academy of M.P. Arts & Sciences for 9 years.

ROSENFIELD, JONAS, JR.: Marketing Consultant. b. Dallas, TX, June 15, 1915. e. U. of Miami, A.B. In U.S. Navy, W.W.II.

Warner Bros. advertising copy department, adv. mgr. Walt Disney, Adv. copywriter Donahue & Coe. Advertising copy chief 20th Century-Fox. Pres. N.Y. Screen Publicists Guild. In July 1942, ex-officio member industry's War Activities Committee. In 1945 apptd. asst. adv. mgr., 20th Cent.-Fox; adv. mgr., 1949–51; dir. of pub. rel. for Italian Films Export 1952; v.p. chg. adv. prom., pub. IFE Releasing Corp., 1953–55; exec. asst. to Paul Lazarus; v.p., of Columbia Pictures, 1955; exec. in chg., avd., pub. expl., Columbia, 1958; v.p. in chg. adv. pub. expl. Columbia, 1960; elected v.p., Columbia Int'l Pictures Corp., 1962; elected gen. exec. officer, Columbia Pictures, 1962; vice president, worldwide advertising, publicity and promotion, Twentieth Century-Fox, 1963–77; film mktg. consultant, 1977–78; lecturer in mktg., U. of Southern California, 1978–79; v.p. in chg. of worldwide mktg., Melvin Simon Productions, 1979. In 1980 named snr. v.p.; 1981, joined Filmways Pictures as exec. v.p., worldwide adv./pub., promo. 1982, film mkt. consultant, lecturer adjunct, U.S.C. Sch. of Cinema & TV; 1983, exec. dir., American Film Mktg. Assn.; 1985 to present, pres. AFMA.

ROSENMAN, HOWARD: Producer. b. Brooklyn, NY. Asst. to Sir Michael Benthall on Bdwy. show; prod., Benton & Bowles Agency; ABC-TV; RSO Prods. Now independent prod., Howard Rosenman Prods.
PICTURES: Sparkle; The Main Event; Resurrection, The War at Home.
TELEVISION: Virginia Hill; The Bees.

ROSENMAN, LEONARD: Composer. b. New York, NY, Sept. 7, 1924. Winner of two Oscars: Barry Lyndon, Bound for Glory; and two Emmys: Sybil, Friendly Fire.
PICTURES INCLUDE: East of Eden, Cobweb, Rebel Without a Cause, Edge of the City, The Savage Eye, The Chapman Report, Fantastic Voyage, Hellfighters, Beneath the Planet of the Apes, Barry Lyndon, Birch Interval, Race With the Devil, Bound For Glory, A Man Called Horse, The Car, September 30, 1955, The Enemy of the People, The Lord of the Rings, Promises in the Dark, Prophecy, Hide in Plain Sight, The Jazz Singer, Making Love, Miss Lonely Hearts, Cross Creek, Heart of the Stag, Star Trek IV: The Voyage Home, Circles in a Forest.
TELEVISION: Sylvia, Friendly Fire, City in Fear, Murder in Texas, Vanished, The Wall, Miss Lonelyhearts, Celebrity, The Return of Marcus Welby MD, Heartsounds, First Steps, Promised a Miracle.

ROSENSTEIN, GERTRUDE: Director. b. New York, NY. e. Barnard Coll., B.A., Neighborhood Playhouse. exec. asst. to George Ballanchine & Lincoln Kirstein, N.Y.C. Ballet. Assoc. with Gian Carlo Menotti, Festival of Two Worlds, Spoleto, Italy.
TELEVISION: Assoc. dir., NBC Opera, Emmy Awards, news programs, election coverages, Kennedy Memorial Mass; dir., Concentration. TV staff dir., NBC. Now freelance director.

ROSENTHAL, BUD: Executive. b. Brooklyn, NY, Mar. 21, 1934. e. Brooklyn Coll., B.A., 1954, New York U. U.S. Army, 1954–56; college correspondent, N.Y. Times; ent. m.p. ind. as associate editor, Independent Film Journal, 1957. Joined Columbia Pictures publicity dept. as trade paper contact and news writer, 1959, newspaper and syndicate contact 1960; appointed national publicity mgr., Columbia Pictures Corp., 1962–67; asst. prod. Something For Everyone; pub. dir., Anderson Tapes, Such Good Friends; story ed. and casting dir., Sigma Prods., 1972–75; associate, producer, Broadway play, Full Circle, 1973, assoc. prod., Rosebud, 1974; dir. intl. press relations, The Bluebird, 1975; Warner Bros. project coordinator, Superman, 1977–79; Superman II, 1980–81; Superman III, 1982–83; Columbia Pictures intl. mktg. coordinator, Ghostbusters, 1984–85; Tri-Star intl. mktg. coordinator, Labyrinth, 1986–87.

ROSENTHAL, RICK: Director. b. New York, NY, June 15, 1949. Launched career as filmmaker-in-residence with New Hampshire TV Network. Moved to Los Angeles to study at American Film Institute where filmed Moonface, 1973. Theatrical feature debut: Halloween II, 1981.
PICTURES: Bad Boys, American Dreamer, Russkies, Distant Thunder.
TELEVISION: Fire on the Mountain, Code of Vengeance, Secrets of Midland Heights.

ROSENTHAL, ROBERT M.: Producer. b. New York, NY, Dec. 28, 1936. e. Lawrence Acad., MA, 1952–56. U. of Pennsylvania Wharton Sch., 1956–60. Pictorial Officer, Prod.-dir. for U.S. Army Signal Corp., 1960–62; Chief, U.S. Army Production Facilities, France, 1961–62. Production mgr., Gurney Productions Inc., 1963; comptroller, Jalor Productions Inc., 1964; pres. Rosenthal Productions Inc., 1964; prod. Lieut. Wolf, I Wonder Why, Been Down So Long It Looks Like Up To Me. Producer/atty.-at-law, Southwestern U. Sch. of Law, 1973–76. Pres., Bel Air Broadcasting Corp., 1984.

ROSI, FRANCESCO: Director. b. Naples, Italy, 1922. Apprenticed as asst. to Visconti and Antonioni; directed first feature La Sfida (The Challenge) in 1958.
PICTURES INCLUDE: Salvatore Giuiliano, Hands Over the City, More Than a Miracle, Just Another War, Lucky Luciano, The Mattei Affair, Eboli, Three Brothers, Chronicle of a Death Foretold.

ROSS, DIANA: Singer, Actress. b. Detroit, MI, Mar. 26, 1944. Formed musical group at age 14 with two friends, Mary Wilson and Florence Ballard. In 1960 they auditioned for Berry Gordy, head of Motown Record Corp. and were hired to sing backgrounds on records for Motown acts. After completing high school, the trio was named the Supremes and went on tour with Motor Town Revue. Over period of 10 yrs. Supremes had 15 consecutive hit records and once had five consecutive records in no. one spot on charts. In 1969 Diana Ross went on her own, appearing on TV and in nightclubs.
PICTURES INCLUDE: Lady Sings the Blues (debut, 1973), Mahogany, The Wiz.
TELEVISION: Diana! (special; also exec. prod. & writer), Motown 25: Yesterday, Today, Forever; Motown Returns to the Apollo.

ROSS, FRANK: Producer, Writer. b. Boston, MA, Aug. 12, 1904. e. Exeter, Princeton U. President, Frank Ross Inc. In 1939, asst. prod. Of Mice and Men, UA, Road. In 1941, producer, The Devil and Miss Jones, RKO. Co-author of story and s.p. The More the Merrier. Spec. Acad. Award (1945) for prod. The House I Live In, short subject on tolerance.
PICTURES INCLUDE: The Lady Takes a Chance, Flame and the Arrow, The Lady Says No, The Robe, Demetrius and the Gladiators, Rain of Ranchipur, Kings Go Forth, Mr. Moses, Maurie (prod.), Where It's At.

ROSS, HERBERT: Director. b. New York, NY, May 13. Resident choreographer A.B.T., choreographer on Broadway for I Can Get It For You Wholesale, Tovarich, Anyone Can Whistle, Do I Hear a Waltz, On a Clear Day You Can See Forever, The Apple Tree. Broadway Director: Chapter Two. I Ought To Be in Pictures. Ent. m.p. ind. as choreographer/musical sequences dir.
PICTURES INCLUDE: As Director/Choreographer: Funny Girl. As director: Goodbye Mr. Chips, The Owl and the Pussycat, Play It Again, Sam, The Last Of Sheila (produced and directed), Funny Lady, The Sunshine Boys, The Seven-Per-Cent Solution (produced and directed), The Turning Point (produced and directed), The Goodbye Girl, California Suite, Nijinsky, Pennies from Heaven (prod.-dir.), I Ought To Be in Pictures (prod.-dir.), Max Dugan Returns (prod.-dir.), Footloose, Protocol, The Secret of My Success (prod.-dir.), Dancers (dir.), Steel Magnolias (dir.), Burn This (dir.).
TELEVISION: Bell Telephone Hour, Fred Astaire Special, Follies in Concert.

ROSS, KATHARINE: Actress. b. Los Angeles, CA, Jan. 29, 1943. m. actor Sam Elliott. e. Santa Rosa Coll. Joined the San Francisco Workshop, appeared in The Devil's Disciple, The Balcony, 1962, poetry festival. TV debut, 1962 in Sam Benedict segment.
TELEVISION: Doctors at Work, World Premiere, The Longest Hundred Miles, Ben Casey, The Bob Hope-Chrysler Theatre, The Virginian, Wagon Train, Kraft Mystery Theatre, the Lieutenant, The Road West, Secrets of a Mother and Daughter. Series: The Colbys.
PICTURES INCLUDE: Shenandoah, Mister Buddwing, The Singing Nun, Games, The Graduate (nom. for Acad. Award, Best Actress; voted Most Promising Female Newcomer, Golden Globe Award), Hellfighters, Butch Cassidy and the Sundance Kid, Tell Them Willie Boy is Here, They Only Kill Their Masters, The Stepford Wives, Voyage of the Damned, The Betsy, The Swarm, The Legacy, The Final Countdown, Wrong Is Right, Red-Headed Stranger.

ROSS, KENNETH: Writer. b. London, Sept. 16, 1941.
TELEVISION: The Roundelay, ATV Network, 1963. The Messenger, CBC Network, 1966.
THEATRE: The Raft, London, 1964. Under The Skin, Glasgow, 1968. Mr. Kilt & The Great I Am, London, 1970.
PICTURES INCLUDE: Entered industry 1970. Screenplays: Brother Sun, Sister Moon, Slag, The Reckless Years (also orig. story). Abelard & Heloise, The Day of the Jackal (nominated for Writers' Guild, SFTA, and Golden Globe Awards), The Devil's Lieutenant, The Odessa File (nominated for Writers' Guild Award), Quest, (orig. story, s.p.), Black Sunday (Edgar Allen Poe Award, Mystery Writers of America, 1977).

ROSELLINI, ISABELLA: Actress. b. Rome, Italy, June 18, 1952. Daughter of Ingrid Bergman and Roberto Rossellini. Came to America 1972. Worked as translator for Italian News Bureau. Model for Vogue, Harper's Bazaar, Italian Elle.
PICTURES: A Matter of Time (debut 1976 with her mother), The Meadow, White Nights, Blue Velvet, Tough Guys Don't Dance, Siesta, Zelly and Me, Cousins.

ROSSO, LEWIS, T.: Executive. b. Hoboken, NJ, Feb. 3, 1911. Ent. m.p. ind. 1930; prod. & mgt. for Consolidated Film Ind., 1930–44; Republic Prod., 1944–50; prod. mgr. Republic, 1950–55; asst. sec'y and asst. treas. Republic Pictures Corp., 1959; exec. asst. to exec. prod. mgr., 20th Century-Fox Films, 1960; plant mgr., Samuel Goldwyn Studios, 1961–71; exec. admin. asst. plant mgr., The Burbank Studios, 1972–86.

ROSSOVICH, RICK: Actor. b. CA, August 28, 1957. e. Sacramento State (art history). Studied acting with coach Vincent Chase. After a succession of appearances of episodic TV, made film debut in Lords of Discipline.
PICTURES: Losin It, Streets of Fire, The Terminator, Warning Signs, Top Gun, Roxanne, Paint It Black, Witching Hour, Spellbinder, Secret Ingredient.
TELEVISION: MacGruder and Loud (series). Movie: 14 Going On 30.

ROTH, BOBBY: Director.-Writer-Producer.
PICTURES: The Boss' Son; Circle of Power; Independence Day; Baja Oklahoma (dir., co-s.p.); Heartbreakers.
TELEVISION: Episodes of Miami Vice, The Insiders, Crime Story. Movies: Tonight's the Night, The Man Who Fell to Earth.

ROTH, PAUL A.: Executive. b. Asheville, NC, March 28, 1930. e. U. of North Carolina, A.B. political science, 1948–51; George Washington U. Law Sch., 1951–52. U.S. Army 1952–55. Dist. Mgr. Valley Enterprises, Inc. 1955–56. Vice Pres. Roth Enterprises, Inc. 1956–65. Pres. Roth Enterprises, Inc. 1965–present. President NATO of Virginia 1971–73. Chairman of Board NATO of Virginia, 1973–75. Member National NATO Board, 1971–present. Executive Committee NATO of Metro-D.C. 1970–present. Variety Club Tent 11 Board Member 1959–65. President National NATO, 1973–75; chairman National NATO board of directors 1975–77. Member Foundation Motion Picture Pioneers, 1973–present. Member & advisory committee, Will Rogers Hospital, 1973–present. Trustee American Film Institute, 1973–75. President, Valley Lanes, Inc., 1975–present. Director, Riggs Bank of Maryland, 1984–present. Director, Metro Mortgage Acceptance Corp., 1984–87. Vice-pres., CAPA, Ltd., 1976–present. Pres., Thrasher's Ocean Fries, Inc. 1987–present. Pres. Carolina Cinema Corp., 1980–present.

ROTH, RICHARD A.: Producer. b. Beverly Hills, CA, 1943. e. Stanford U. Law Sch. Worked for L.A. law firm before beginning film career as lawyer and literary agent for Ziegler-Ross Agency. In 1970 left to develop s.p. Summer of '42 with Herman Raucher.
PICTURES INCLUDE: Summer of '42, Our Time, The Adventures of Sherlock Holmes' Smarter Brother, Julia, Outland, In Country (co-prod.).

ROTHKIRCH, Dr. EDWARD v.: Producer. b. July 30, 1919. e. Friedrich Wilhelm U., Berlin; Rockhurst Coll., Midwestern Coll. Prod. asst., research, Pan American Prod.; 1941; research Pacific Films, 1942; U.S. Air Force, 1942–44; asst. prod., Pan American Productions 1945; analyst, Cambridge Prod., 1947; assoc. prod., Pentagon Films 1949; assoc. prod., Reelestic Pictures, 1950; assoc. prod. Cambridge-Meran Prod. Co., 1951; assoc. prod., Cambridge Prod., 1954; also v.-p. Continental Prod. Services; assoc. exec. prod. Trinity Hill Productions, produced Pan-American Highway 1954, The Keepers TV series, 1953–58, Famous Women of the Bible, 1955–58; To the Stars TV series, 1954–58; also sec.-treas. Crusader Records and v.p. Orbit Records. Member of many professional societies, director International Association of Independent Producers, presently Executive Producer—Galaxie Productions, and Encore Records also Executive Editor, Intercontinental Media Services, Ltd.

ROTHMAN, FRANK: Executive. b. Los Angeles, CA, Dec. 24, 1926. e. U. of Southern California, LL.B., 1951. Mem. Calif. Bar. Dept. city atty., Los Angeles, 1951–55; law firm, Wyman, Bautzer, Rothman, Kuchel & Silbert, Los Angeles 1955–82; chmn. bd., MGM/UA Entertainment Co., 1982–86. Now partner in law firm.

ROTUNNO, GIUSEPPE: Cinematographer. b. Italy. Gained fame as leading cinematographer of Italian films working with Federico Fellini. Also worked for Lina Wertmuller and Luchino Visconti. Later worked in Hollywood.
PICTURES: Scandal in Sorrento, White Nights, Anna of Brooklyn, The Naked Maja, The Angel Wore Red, On the Beach, Rocco and His Brothers, The Best of Enemies, The Leopard, Yesterday, Today and Tomorrow, Anzio, The Secret of Santa Vittoria, Fellini's Roma, Casanova, Amarcord, Satyricon, Sunflower, Carnal Knowledge, Man of La Mancha, The Stranger, The Organizer, Juliet of the Spirits, Fellini's Roma, Amarcord, Casanova, Orchestra Rehearsal, City of Women, Love and Anarchy, All Screwed Up, The Bible, End of the World in Our Usual Bed in a Night Full of Rain, All That Jazz, City of Women, Popeye, Five Days One Summer, Rollover, And the Ship Sails On, American Dreamer, Desire, Nothing Left to Do But Cry, The Assisi Underground, The Red Sonja,

Julia and Julia, Rent-a-Cop, Haunted Summer, The Adventures of Baron Munchausen.
TELEVISION: The Scarlet and the Black.

ROUNDTREE, RICHARD: Actor. b. New Rochelle, NY, July 9, 1942. e. Southern Illinois U. Former model, Ebony Magazine Fashion Fair; joined workshop of Negro Ensemble Company, appeared in Kongi's Harvest, Man, Better Man, Mau Mau Room; played lead role in Philadelphia road company of The Great White Hope before film debut.
PICTURES INCLUDE: Shaft, Shaft's Big Score, Shaft in Africa, Charley One-Eye, Earthquake, Man Friday, Diamonds, Escape to Athena, An Eye for an Eye, The Winged Serpent, Inchon, City Heat, Opposing Force, Maniac Cop, Homer and Eddie, Angel III: The Final Chapter, The Party Line, Cry Devil, Getting Even, American Cops.
TELEVISION: Shaft (series, 1973), Firehouse (movie), Roots, A.D., The Fifth Missile, Outlaws.

ROURKE, MICKEY: Actor. b. Schenectady, NY, 1950. Moved to Miami as a boy. Fought as an amateur boxer 4 years in Miami. Studied acting with Sandra Seacat while working as a nightclub bouncer, a sidewalk pretzel vendor and other odd jobs. Moved to LA, 1978. Debut: TV movie City in Fear (1978).
PICTURES: Fade to Black, 1941, Heaven's Gate, Body Heat, Diner, Eureka, Rumblefish, The Pope of Greenwich Village, 9½ Weeks, Year of the Dragon, Angel Heart, Barfly, Prayer for the Dying, Homeboy (and orig. story), Francesco.
TELEVISION: Rape and Marriage, The Rideout Case, Act of Love.

ROWAN, DANIELLE: Executive. Began career with Paramount Pictures 1980; asst. to pres. & gen. s.s. mgr. Canadian operations. 1984, transferred to N.Y. as asst. to sr. v.p., dist. 1985, appt. exec. administrator dist./mktg.

ROWE, ROY: Owner-operator, Rowe Amusement Co., Burgaw, NC. b. Burgaw, May 29, 1905. e. U. of North Carolina. Eng. instructor, private bus. coll., 1926–29; Publix Sch. for Mgrs., N.Y., 1930–31; mgr. theatres, Spartanburg, SC; Greensboro & Raleigh, NC; mgr., Warner Theatre, Pittsburgh, PA, 1931–34; city mgr. for Warner Theatres, Washington, PA, 1934–35; opened own theatres in NC 1935; member NC Senate, 1937, 1941, 1945, 1949, 1957, 1965; House of Rep., 1943; Major, Civil Air Patrol, W.W.II; pres. Carolina Aero Club, 1943–44; chmn. NC Aeornautics Comm., 1941–49; dir. Theatre Owners No. & So. Car. 1943–45; pres., Theatre Owners of S.C. & N.C. 1944–45; pres., Assn. of Governing Boards of State Universities, 1964. Owned and operated motel, Carolina Beach, NC, 1965–67., Rowe Insurance Agency, 1967–69. Mem. Exec. Bd., U. of N.C. Trustees, 1969. Principal Clerk, NC Senate 1969–75. Retired. Now watercolor artist and world traveller.

ROWLAND, ROY: Director. b. New York, NY, Dec. 31. e. U. of Southern California, law. Script clerk; asst. dir.; asst. to late W. S. Van Dyke on Tarzan pictures; dir. of shorts, "How to" Benchley series; Crime Does Not Pay series. Pete Smith Specialties.
PICTURES INCLUDE: Think First, Stranger in Town, Lost Angel, Our Vines Have Tender Grapes, Tenth Avenue Angel, Night patrol, Ski Soldier, Boys' Ranch, Romance of Rosy Ridge, Killer McCoy, Scene of the Crime, Outriders, Excuse My Dust, Two Weeks With Love, Bugles in Afternoon, 5000 Fingers of Dr. T. Affair with a Stranger, The Moonlighter, Witness to Murder, Rogue Cop, Many Rivers to Cross, Hit the Deck, Meet Me in Las Vegas, Slander, Somewhere I'll Find Him, Gun Glory, The Seven Hills of Rome, The Girl Hunters, Gunfighters of Casa Grande, They Called Him Gringo, Tiger of the Seven Seas, Thunder Over the Indian Ocean.

ROWLANDS, GENA: Actress. b. Cambria, WI, June 19, 1936. e. U. of Wisconsin. Came to New York to attend American Acad. of Dramatic Arts, where met and married John Cassavetes. Made Bdwy. debut as understudy and then succeeded to role of the Girl in The Seven Year Itch. Launched as star with part in The Middle of the Night, which she played 18 mos. Film debut in The High Cost of Living, 1958.
PICTURES INCLUDE: Lonely Are the Brave, The Spiral Road, A Child Is Waiting, Tony Rome, Faces, Minnie and Moskowitz, A Woman Under the Influence, Two Minute Warning, The Brink's Job, Gloria, Tempest, Love Streams, Light of Day, Another Woman.
TELEVISION: The Philco TV Playhouse, Studio One, Alfred Hitchcock Presents, Dr. Kildare, Bonanza, The Kraft Mystery Theatre, Columbo. Movies: Question of Love, Strangers: The Story of a Mother & Daughter, An Early Frost, The Betty Ford Story.

ROWLEY, JOHN H.: Executive. b. San Angelo, TX, Oct. 6, 1917. e. U. of Texas, 1935–39. Consultant, United Artists Theatre Circuit, Inc. Southwest Div.; past president, NATO of Texas; past Int'l Chief barker, Variety Clubs Int'l; past pres., TOA; pres., Variety Foundation of Texas.

ROZSA, MIKLOS: Composer. b. April 18, 1907, Budapest, Hungary. e. Leipzig Conservatory. Wrote great number of symphonic and chamber music works. Composed music for many m.p. In 1936, Knight Without Armor, Acad. Award best music scoring for drama or comedy (Spellbound) 1945; best music scoring for drama or comedy (Double Life) 1947; Ben-Hur, 1959. Pres., Screen Composers Assn. 1956. Cesar of French Academy for Providence, 1978.
PICTURES INCLUDE: Jungle Book, Thief of Bagdad, Double Idemnity, The Killers, Madame Bovary, The Lost Weekend, Spellbound, Asphalt Jungle, Quo Vadis, Ivanhoe, Julius Caesar, Story of Three Loves, Plymouth Adventure, Young Bess, Knights of the Round Table, A Time to Love and a Time to Die, The World the Flesh and the Devil, Ben Hur, Lust for Life, Something of Value, King of Kings, El Cid, Sodom and Gomorrah, The VIP's, The Power, The Green Berets, The Private Life of Sherlock Holmes, Sinbad's Golden Voyage, Providence, Secret Files of J. Edgar Hoover, Fedora, Last Embrace, Time After Time, Eye of the Needle, Dead Men Don't Wear Plaid.

RUBIN, JOSEPH: Director. b. Briarcliff, NY, 1951. e. U. of Michigan, majoring in theater and film; Brandeis U., B.A. Interest in film began in high sch. Bought a Super-8 camera and filmed his first movie, a teenage love story. First feature, The Sister-in-Law, a low budget feature which he wrote and dir. in 1975.
PICTURES: The Sister-in-Law (also s.p.), The Pom-Pom Girls (also s.p.), Joy Ride (also co-s.p.), Our Winning Season, Dreamscape, The Stepfather, True Believer.
TELEVISION: Breaking Away (pilot).

RUBIN, STANLEY: Producer, Writer. b. New York, NY, Oct. 8, 1917; ed. U. of California at L.A., 1933–37. Phi Beta Kappa. Writer—radio, magazines, pictures, 1937–41; U.S. Army Air Force, 1942–45; writer, prod., owner, Your Show Time, Story Theatre TV series; producer, RKO, 20th-Fox, U.I., MGM, Paramount, Pastar.
PICTURES INCLUDE: The Narrow Margin, My Pal Gus, Destination Gobi, River of No Return, Destry, Francis in the Navy, Behind the High Wall, Rawhide Years, The Girl Most Likely, Promise Her Anything, The President's Analyst.
TELEVISION: G.E. Theatre, Ghost and Mrs. Muir, Bracken's World, The Man and the City, Executive Suite. Movies: Babe (co-prod.), And Your Name is Jonah, Don't Look Back: The Story of Satchel Page, Escape From Iran: The Canadian Caper (exec. prod.).

RUBINSTEIN, JOHN: Actor, Composer. b. Los Angeles, CA, December 8, 1946. Son of concert pianist Arthur Rubinstein and dancer-writer Aniela Rubinstein. e. UCLA.
THEATER: Pippin (NY debut, 1972); Picture (Mark Taper, LA); Children of a Lesser God (Tony Award, Drama Desk, L.A. Drama Critics Awards, 1980); Fools; The Caine Mutiny Court-Martial.
PICTURES: Journey to Shiloh (debut, 1966); Zachariah; In Search of Historic Jesus; The Trouble With Girls; Getting Straight; The Wild Pack; The Car; The Boys From Brazil; Daniel; Someone to Watch Over Me.
TELEVISION: The Virginian (1966); Ironside; Dragnet; Room 222; The Psychiatrist; The Mary Tyler Moore Show; Cannon; The Mod Squad, Nichols; Hawaii Five-O; Barnaby Jones; Policewoman; Barbary Coast; The Rookies; The Streets of San Francisco; Harry O; Vegas; The Class of '65; Movin' On; Stop the Presses; Wonder Woman; Lou Grant; Fantasy Island; The Quest; Quincy; Trapper John M.D. Movies: The Marriage Proposal; God Bless the Children; A Howling in the Woods; Something Evil; All Together Now; The Gift of the Maji; Roots: The Next Generations; Just Make Me an Offer; The French Atlantic Affair; Corey: For the People; Happily Ever After; Moviola; Skokie; The Mr. and Ms. Mysteries; Killjoy; Freedom to Speak; Someone's Killing the High Fashion Models; I Take These Men; M.A.D.D.: Mothers Against Drunk Driving.
SCORES: FILMS: Paddy; Jeremiah Johnson; The Candidate; Kid Blue; The Killer Inside Me. TELEVISION: All Together Now; Emily, Emily; Stalk the Wild Child; Champions: A Love Story; To Race the Wind; The Ordeal of Patty Hearst; Amber Waves; Johnny Belinda; Secrets of a Mother and Daughter; Choices of the Heart; The Dollmaker; Family; The Fitzpatricks; The Mackenzies of Paradise Cove; The New Land: For Heaven's Sake; The Lazarus Syndrome.

RUBINSTEIN, RICHARD P.: Producer, Executive. b. New York, NY, June 15, 1947. e. American U. B.S. 1969; Columbia U. MBA 1971, Chairman and pres. Laurel Entertainment, Inc. TV: executive-producer, Tales From the Darkside (series) (shared credit); executive producer, Monsters (series).
PICTURES INCLUDE: Martin (1977); Dawn Of The Dead; Knightriders; Creepshow; Day Of The Dead; Creepshow 2; Pet Sematary (1988).

RUDDY, ALBERT S.: Producer. b. Montreal, Canada, March 28, 1934. e. U. of Southern California, B.S. in design, Sch. of Architecture, 1956.
PICTURES INCLUDE: The Wild Seed (Pennebaker); prod.,

Rud-Rut

Little Fauss & Big Halsey; Making It; prod. The Godfather, 1974; The Longest Yard, Coonskin; Matilda; The Cannonball Run; Megaforce; Lassiter, Cannonball Run II, Farewell to the King, Paramedics.

RUDIN, SCOTT: Executive. b. New York, NY, July 14, 1958. Began career as prod. asst. on Bdwy. for producers Kermit Bloomgarden, Robert Whitehead; then casting director. 1984, became producer for 20th Century Fox; named exec. v.p. prodn.; 1986, appt. pres. prodn., 20th-Fox. Resigned 1987.
TELEVISION: Little Gloria...Happy at Last (exec. prod.).

RUDOLPH, ALAN: Director, Writer. b. Los Angeles, CA, Dec., 1943. Son of Oscar Rudolph, TV director of '50s and '60s. Made his screen debut in The Rocket Man (1954, dir. by his father). Began in industry doing odd jobs in Hollywood studios. In 1969 accepted for assistant director's training program sponsored by the Director's Guild. Worked with Robert Altman on California Split and The Long Goodbye (asst. dir.) and co-writer on Buffalo Bill and the Indians.
PICTURES: Welcome to L.A. (debut as dir.), Remember My Name, Roadie, Endangered Species, Return Engagement, Songwriter, Choose Me, Trouble in Mind, Made in Heaven, The Moderns (dir., co-s.p.).

RUGOLO, PETE: Composer, Arranger. b. Sicily, Italy, Dec. 25, 1915. To U.S., 1919. e. San Francisco State Coll., Mills Coll., Oakland. Armed Forces, 1942–46; pianist, arr. for many orch. including Stan Kenton; m.p. and TV.
PICTURES INCLUDE: The Strip, Skirts Ahoy, Glory Alley, Latin Lovers, Easy to Love, Jack the Ripper.
TELEVISION: Richard Diamond, The Thin Man, Thriller, more than 25 movies.

RULE, ELTON H.: Executive. b. Stockton, CA, 1917. e. Sacramento Coll. With Amer. Bdg. Cos., Inc., since 1952; gen. sls. mgr., KABC-TV, 1953–60; gen. mgr., 1961–68; pres., ABC TV Network 1968–70; group v.p. Am. Bdg. Cos. Inc., 1969–72; pres., ABC div. 1970–72; pres., chief operating officer, mem. exec. comm., Amer. Bdg. Cos., 1972–83; vice chm., Amer. Bdg. Cos., Inc. & member exec. comm., 1983–84. Formed Rule/Starger Productions with Martin Starger.

RULE, JANICE: Actress. b. Cincinnati, OH, Aug. 15, 1931. e. Wheaton & Glenbard H.S., Glen Ellyn, IL. Dancer 4 yrs. in Chicago & New York nightclubs; stage experience in It's Great To Be Alive, as understudy of Bambi Lynn; in chorus of Miss Liberty; Broadway stage debut Picnic, 1953. Screen debut, Goodbye My Fancy (1951).
PICTURES INCLUDE: Starlift, Holiday for Sinners, Rogue's March, Woman's Devotion, Gun for a Coward, Subterraneans, Invitation to a Gunfighter, The Chase, Welcome to Hard Times, The Ambushers, Kid Blue, 3 Women, Missing, The Swimmer, Rainy Day Friends.

RUSH, BARBARA: Actress. b. Denver, CO, Jan. 4, 1930. e. U. of California. First stage appearance at age of ten, Loberto Theatre, Santa Barbara, CA, in fantasy, Golden Ball; won acting award in coll. for characterization of Birdie (The Little Foxes); scholarship, Pasadena Playhouse Theatre Arts Coll.
PICTURES INCLUDE: The First Legion, Quebec, Molly, When Worlds Collide, Flaming Feather, Prince of Pirates, It Came From Outer Space, Taza Son of Cochise, Magnificent Obsession, Black Shield of Falworth, Captain Lightfoot, Kiss of Fire, World in My Corner, Bigger Than Life, Oh Men! Oh Women!, Harry Black and the Tiger, The Young Philadelphians, Bramble Bush, Strangers When We Meet, Come Blow Your Horn, Robin and the Seven Hoods, Hombre, Airport, The Man, Superdad, Can't Stop the Music, Summer Lovers.
TELEVISION: Flamingo Road, The Seekers, Suddenly Single, Eyes of Charles, Sand.

RUSH, HERMAN: Executive. b. Philadelphia, PA, June 20, 1929. e. Temple U., Headed Flamingo Telefilms, Inc. 1957–60; 1960–71, pres., television div. of Creative Mgt. Assoc. Pres., Herman Rush Assoc. Inc., 1971–77. In 1977–78 chmn bd., Rush-Flaherty Agency, Inc. In 1970 headed Marble Arch TV. In 1980 named pres., Columbia TV; 1984, named pres. of newly formed Columbia Pictures TV Group. In 1986, named chm. of newly formed Coca-Cola Telecommunications, Inc. In 1988, chairman, Rush Entertainment Group.

RUSH, RICHARD: Director, Producer, Writer. b. New York, NY, 1930. Wrote, dir. prod., Too Soon To Love (U.I.), 1960; Of Love and Desire (Fox), 1963; dir. A Man Called Dagger (MGM) 1965; dir. Fickle Finger of Fate, 1966; dir. Thunder Alley, 1966; dir. Hell's Angels on Wheels, 1967; dir. wrote Psych-Out, 1967; dir. Savage Seven, 1968; dir., prod. Getting Straight (Columbia), 1970, dir. prod. Freebie and the Bean (Warner Bros.) 1974; dir., prod. wrote, The Stunt Man (Fox), 1980 (AA nominations for best dir., s.p.).

RUSSELL, CHARLES W.: Producer. b. New York, NY, Mar. 31, 1918. Actor, m.p. & radio.

PICTURES INCLUDE: The Purple Heart, The Late George Apley.
TELEVISION: CBS-TV prod., You Are There, Danger.

RUSSELL, CHUCK: Director. Asst. dir. and line prod. on many low-budget films for Roger Corman and Sunn Classics, including Death Race 2000.
PICTURES: Dreamscape (co-s.p., line prod.); Back to School (prod.); Nightmare on Elm Street III (dir., co-s.p.); The Blob (dir., co-s.p.).

RUSSELL, JANE: Actress. b. Bemidji, MN, June 21, 1921. e. Max Reinhardt's Theatrical Workshop & Mme. Ouspenskaya. Photographer's model; m.p. debut in Outlaw, 1943.
PICTURES INCLUDE: Young Widow, Paleface, Montana Belle, His Kind of Woman, Double Dynamite, Macao, Son of Paleface, Las Vegas Story, Gentlemen Prefer Blondes, French Line, Underwater, Gentlemen Marry Brunettes, Foxfire, Tall Men, Hot Blood, Revolt of Mamie Stover, Fuzzy Pink Nightgown, Darker Than Amber, Born Losers, Fate Is The Hunter, Waco.
TELEVISION: Yellow Rose (series).

RUSSELL, JOHN: Actor. b. Los Angeles, CA, Jan. 3, 1921. e. U. of California. Served in U.S. Marine Corps. 1942–44, as 2nd Lt. m.p. debut in Frame-Up.
PICTURES INCLUDE: Story of Molly X, Gal Who Took the West, Slattery's Hurricane, Yellow Sky, Sitting Pretty, Forever Amber, Somewhere in the Night, Within These Walls, Don Juan Quilligan, Bell for Adano, Barefoot Mailman, Man in the Saddle, Hoodlum Empire, Oklahoma Annie, Fair Wind to Java, Sun Shines Bright, Jubilee Trail, Hell's Outpost, Last Command, Rio Bravo, Yellowstone Kelly, Fort ·Utah, Honky Tonk Man, Pale Rider, Under the Gun.
TELEVISION: Lawman (series), Alias Smith and Jones, Soldiers of Fortune.

RUSSELL, KEN: Director. b. Southampton, England, 1927. e. Walthamstow Art Sch. Early career as dancer, actor, stills photographer, TV documentary film-maker. Ent. TV ind. 1959. Made 33 documentaries for BBC-TV. Also made numerous pop videos.
PICTURES INCLUDE: Prokofiev, Elgar, Bartok, The Debussy films, Isadora Duncan, Song of Summer—Delius, Dance of the Seven Veils, French Dressing, Billion Dollar Brain, Women in Love, The Music Lovers, The Devils, The Boy Friend, Savage Messiah, Mahler, Tommy, Lisztomania, Valentino, Altered States, Crimes of Passion, Gothic, Aria (sequence), Salome's Last Dance (dir., s.p., actor), The Lair of the White Worm (prod., dir., s.p.), The Rainbow (co-prod., dir., co-s.p.).

RUSSELL, KURT: Actor. b. Springfield, MA, March 17, 1951. Son of former baseball player turned actor Bing Russell (deputy sheriff on Bonanza). At 12 got lead in The Travels of Jamie McPheeters (1963–64). Starred as child in many Disney shows and films. Professional baseball player 1971–73. Host, Kurt Russell Celebrity Shoot Out, 4-day hunting tournament.
PICTURES: The Absent-Minded Professor, Follow Me Boys, The Horse in the Grey Flannel Suit, Charley and the Angel, Superdad, Used Cars, Escape from New York, The Fox and the Hound (voice only), The Thing, Silkwood, Swing Shift, The Mean Season, The Best of Times, Big Trouble in Little China, Overboard, Tequila Sunrise, The Winter People.
TELEVISION: Series: Travels of Jamie McPheeters, The New Land, The Quest. Movies: The Deadly Tower, Elvis, Amber Waves, Search for the Gods.

RUSSELL, ROBERT: Performer. b. Passaic, NJ. Baritone, Philadelphia Grand Opera Co.; then radio work as quiz master, m.c., singer, gagwriter, composer, writer spec. material; m.c., writer, composer, dir. eleven Miss America pageants; staged, wrote, dir. five Miss Universe pageants.
TELEVISION: Birthday Party, Bonny Maid Show, It's in the Bag, Toast of the Town, Live Like a Millionaire; now m.c. Stand Up and Be Counted, CBS-TV; pres. Pageant Productions, Inc.

RUSSELL, THERESA: Actress. r.n. Theresa Paup. b. San Diego, CA, 1957. m. dir.-cinematographer Nicolas Roeg. e. Burbank H.S. Began modeling career at 12. Studied at Actors' Studio in Hollywood. Professional film debut in The Last Tycoon, 1977.
PICTURES: Straight Time, Bad Timing/A Sensual Obsession, Eureka, The Razor's Edge, Insignificance, Black Widow, Aria, Track 29, Smoke.
TELEVISION: Blind Ambition (mini-series).

RUTHERFORD, ANN: Actress. b. Toronto, Canada, 1924. Trained by mother (cousin of Richard Mansfield); with parents in stock as child; later on Los Angeles radio programs. Screen debut, 1935.
PICTURES INCLUDE: Gone With the Wind, Laramie Trail, Happy Land, Bermuda Mystery, Two O'Clock Courage, Bedside Manner, The Madonna's Secret, Murder in the Music Hall, Secret Life of Walter Mitty, Operation Haylift, Adventures of Don Juan, They Only Kill Their Masters.

RYAN, ARTHUR N.: Executive. Joined Paramount in N.Y. in 1967 as asst. treas; later made dir. of admin. and business affairs, exec. asst. to Robert Evans and asst. scty. In 1970 appt. v.p.-prod. adm. In 1975 named senior v.p. handling all prod. operations for Paramount's m.p. and t.v. divisions, including supvr. of physical prod., business affairs, studio operations and coordination with co.'s creative personnel and film-makers. Named asst. to the Chairman and Chief Executive Officer 1976; Chairman and President Magicam, Inc.; Chairman Fortune General Corp.; Chairman Paramount Communications; co-chm. of scholarship comm. of Academy of Motion Picture Arts and Sciences; trustee of Univ. Film Study Center in Boston. Joined Technicolor in August 1976 as pres., chief operating officer and director; vice chm., 1983–85; chm. & CEO, 1985 to date. Chairman Technicolor Audio-Visual Systems International, Inc.; director Technicolor S.P.A.; director Technicolor, Film International; and chairman of executive committee, Technicolor Graphics Services, Inc.; director, Technicolor, Inc.; chairman, Technicolor Fotografica, S.A.; Chairman Technicolor Film International Service Company, Inc.; director and Deputy Chairman Technicolor Limited; chm. & dir., The Vidtronics Company, Inc.; chm. & CEO, Compact Video, Inc., 1984 to date; dir, Four Star Int'l., 1983 to date; dir., MacAndrews & Forbes, Inc. 1985 to date; Permanent charities committee of the Entertainment Industry; Hollywood Canteen Foundations. Vice-Chm. & Dir., Calif. Inst. of Arts. Trustee: Motion Picture & Television Fund. In 1985 named chm., Technicolor.

RYAN, MEG: Actress. b. Fairfield, CT, 1963. e. NYU. Supported herself while studying journalism by making commercials. Prof. debut on As the World Turns, 1983–85.
PICTURES: Rich and Famous (debut, 1981), Amityville 3-D, Top Gun, Armed and Dangerous, Innerspace, D.O.A., Promised Land, The Presidio, Harry, This is Sally.
TELEVISION: Wild Side (series).

RYAN, MITCHELL: Actor. b. Louisville, KY, Jan. 11, 1928. Entered acting following service in Navy during Korean War. Was New York stage actor working off-Bdwy. for Ted Mann and Joseph Papp; on Bdwy. in Wait Until Dark. Member of Arena Stage group in Washington.
PICTURES INCLUDE: Monte Walsh, The Hunting Party, My Old Man's Place, High Plains Drifter, The Friends of Eddie Coyle, Electra Glide in Blue, Magnum Force, Labyrinth.
TELEVISION: Series: Chase, Executive Suite, Having Babies, The Chisholms, Dark Shadows, High Performance, King Crossings; Movies: Angel City, The Five of Me, Death of a Centerfold—The Dorothy Stratten Story; Uncommon Valor; Medea, Kenny Rogers as the Gambler—The Adventure Continues, Robert Kennedy & His Times, Fatal Vision.

RYDELL, MARK: Producer, Director, Actor. b. March 23, 1934. e. Juilliard Sch. of Music. Studied acting with Sanford Meisner of N.Y. Neighborhood Playhouse. Became member of Actors Studio. Was leading actor for six years on daytime CBS serial, As The World Turns. Made Broadway debut in Seagulls over Sorrento and film bow in Crime in the Streets. Went to Hollywood as TV director (Ben Casey, I Spy, Gunsmoke, etc.). Theatrical feature debut: The Fox (1968). Partner with Sydney Pollack in Sanford Prods., film, TV prod. co.
PICTURES INCLUDE: Director: The Fox, The Receivers, The Cowboys, Cinderella Liberty (also prod.), Harry and Walter Go To New York, The Rose, On Golden Pond, The River, The Comeback Kid (prod., dir.). Actor: The Long Goodbye, Punchline.

S

SACKHEIM, WILLIAM B.: Producer, Writer. b. Gloversville, NY, Oct. 31, 1919. e. U. of California at L.A. Sr. v.p., Rastar Films. Joined Universal TV 1981 as creative consultant.
PICTURES: Smart Girls Don't Talk, One Last Fling, A Yank in Korea, Paula, Reunion in Reno, The Human Jungle, Border River, Chicago Syndicate, Art of Love, The In-Laws (co-prod.), The Competition, First Blood (co-s.p.), The Survivors (prod.), No Small Affair (prod.), The Hard Way (prod.).
TELEVISION: Jordan Oliver (series, exec. prod.).

SACKS, SAMUEL: Attorney, Agent. b. New York, NY, March 29, 1908. e. City Coll. of New York, St. Lawrence U. Law Sch., LL.B., 1930. Admitted Calif. Bar, 1943; priv. prac., law, N.Y. 1931–42; attorney, William Morris Agency, Inc., Sept. 1942; head of west coast TV business affairs, 1948–75. bd. of dir., Alliance of Television Film Producers, 1956–60. L.A. Copyright Society Treasurer, Beverly Hills Bar Assn., Los Angeles Bar Assn., American Bar Assn.; Academy of TV Arts & Sciences; Hollywood Radio & TV Society. Pres. Adat Shalom Synagogue, 1967–69, chmn. of bd., 1969–71; pres., American Field Service West L.A. Chapter 1970–72, United Synagogue of America (Pacific Southwest region), v.p., 1974–88. Counsel, entertainment field, Simon & Sheridan, 1975–88, Los

Angeles Citizens' Olympic Committee. Arbitrator for Screen Actors Guild, Assn. of Talent Agents and American Arbitration Assn. Chm. Task Force Project Caring; board of dir., Jewish Family Service of L.A.; exec. comm., Congregational Cabinet University of Judaism, 1975 to date.

SAFER, MORLEY: News Correspondent. b. Toronto, Ont., 1931. e. U. of Western Ontario. Started as corresp. and prod. with Canadian Broadcasting Corp. Joined CBS News as head of Saigon Bureau, 1965. Chief of CBS London bureau 1967–70. Joined 60 minutes as co-editor in Dec., 1970.

SAFFLE, M. W. "BUD": Executive. b. Spokane, WA, June 29, 1923. e. U. of Washington. In service 1943–46. Started in m.p. business as booker, 1948. Entire career with Saffle Theatre Service as buyer-booker; named pres. in 1970. Also pres. of Grays Harbor Theatres, Inc., operating theatres in Aberdeen, WA. Also operates d.i. in Centralia, WA. On bd. of NATO of WA for 15 yrs; pres. of same for 2 terms and secty.-treas. 6 yrs. Elected to National NATO bd. in 1972. Founder of Variety Tent 46, serving as chief barker three times.

SAFIR, SIDNEY: Executive. b. Vienna, Austria, Feb. 2, 1923. e. London U. Ent. m.p. ind. 1940, Shipman & King Cinemas; RKO Radio Picture, 1941; salesman, British Lion, 1943; European sls. mgr., Lion Int'l, 1958; gen. sls. mgr. Lion Int'l, 1960; president, Lion Int'l Inc., 1965; man. dir. Lion Int'l Ltd. 1969; dir., British Lions Film Ltd., 1972. Formed Safir Films Ltd. with his son Lawrence, 1977.

SAGANSKY, JEFF: Executive. b. 1953. Joined CBS 1976 in bdcst. finance; 1977, NBC, assoc. in pgm. development.; 1977, mgr. film pgms.; 1978, dir. dramatic dev.; 1978, v.p., dev. David Gerber Co.; 1981, returned to NBC as series dev. v.p.; 1983, snr. v.p. series programming; 1985, joined Tri-Star Pictures as pres. of production.

SAINT, EVA MARIE: Actress. b. Newark, NJ, July 4, 1924. e. Bowling Green State U., Ohio. Radio, TV actress; on Broadway in Trip to Bountiful; m.p. debut in On the Waterfront (Acad. Award, best supporting actress, 1954).
PICTURES INCLUDE: That Certain Feeling, Raintree County, Hatful of Rain, North by Northwest, Exodus, All Fall Down, Grand Prix, The Stalking Moon, Loving, Cancel My Reservation, Nothing in Common.
TELEVISION: How the West Was Won (series), Fatal Vision, The Last Days of Patton, A Year in the Life, Norman Rockwell's Breaking Ties, Series: One Man's Family, Moonlighting.

ST. JACQUES, RAYMOND: Actor, Director. r.n. James Johnson. b. 1930. e. student, Yale U. Began career as actor, asst. dir. and fencing dir. for American Shakespeare Festival, Stratford, CT. Made prof. acting debut in off-Bdwy. play, High Name Today. Made m.p. debut, Black Like Me, 1964.
STAGE: The Blacks, Night Life, The Cool World, Seventh Heaven.
PICTURES INCLUDE: The Pawnbroker, The Comedians, Mr. Moses, Madigan, Mister Buddwing, The Green Berets, Uptight, If He Hollers Let Him Go, Change of Mind, Cotton Comes to Harlem, Cool Breeze, Come Back Charleston Blue, Book of Numbers (also dir. debut), Lost in the Stars, Eyes of Laura Mars, The Evil That Men Do, The Wild Pair, They Live.
TELEVISION: Dark Mansions, Roots, Sophisticated Gents, Search for the Gods. Series: Superior Court.

SAINT JAMES, SUSAN: Actress. b. Los Angeles, CA, Aug. 14, 1946. r.n. Susan Miller. e. Connecticut Coll. for Women. Was model for six years; then signed to contract by Universal Pictures.
TELEVISION: Series: The Name of the Game, McMillan & Wife, Kate and Allie. Movies: SOS Titanic, I Take These Men, Fame is the Name of the Game, Sex and the Single Parent, Night Cries.
PICTURES INCLUDE: What's So Bad About Feeling Good?, Jigsaw, P.J., Where Angels Go . . . Trouble Follows, Magic Carpet, Outlaw Blues, Love at First Bite, How to Beat the High Cost of Living, Carbon Copy.

ST. JOHN, JILL: Actress. r.n. Jill Oppenheim. b. Los Angeles, CA, Aug. 19, 1940. On radio series One Man's family. Television debut, A Christmas Carol, 1948. Theatrical film debut, Summer Love, 1957.
PICTURES: The Remarkable Mr. Pennypacker, Holiday for Lovers, The Roman Spring of Mrs. Stone, Tender Is the Night, Come Blow Your Horn, Who's Been Sleeping in My Bed?, Honeymoon Hotel, The Oscar, Banning, Tony Rome, Diamonds Are Forever.
TELEVISION: Fame Is the Name of the Game, Dupont Theatre, Fireside Theatre, Emerald Point NAS (series), Hart to Hart, Brenda Starr, Spy Killer, Telethon, Rooster.

ST. JOHNS, RICHARD R.: Executive Producer. b. Los Angeles, CA, Jan. 20, 1929. Son of journalist Adela Rogers St. Johns. e. Stanford U., B.A., 1953; Stanford Law Sch., J.D., 1954. Joined law firm O'Melveny & Meyers 1954, specializing in

entertainment law. 1963 became partner in law firm. 1968 became senior v.p., Filmways, Inc., becoming president and chief operating office in 1969. 1972, formed Richard R. St. Johns and Associates, independent management and packaging firm. Formed Guinness Film Group in 1975, branching out into full-scale motion picture production.
PICTURES: (exec. prod.): The Uncanny, Death Hunt, Matilda, The Silent Flute (Circle of Iron), Nightwing, The Wanderers, The Mountain Men, The Final Countdown, A Change of Seasons, Dead & Buried, Death Hunt, American Pop and Venom, Fire and Ice.

SAKS, GENE: Director, Actor. b. New York, NY, Nov. 8, 1921. e. Cornell U. Attended dramatic workshop, New School for Social Research. Active in off-Broadway in 1948–49, forming cooperative theatre group at Cherry Lane Theatre. Joined Actor's Studio, followed by touring and stock. Also appeared in live TV dramas (Philco Playhouse, Producer's Showcase). Directed many Broadway plays before turning to film direction with Barefoot in the Park (1967).
BROADWAY: Director: Enter Laughing, Nobody Loves an Albatross, Generation, Half a Sixpence, Mame, A Mother's Kisses, Sheep on the Runway, How the Other Half Loves, Same Time Next Year, California Suite, I Love My Wife, Brighton Beach Memoirs, Biloxi Blues, The Odd Couple (1985), Broadway Bound. Actor: Middle of the Night, Howie, The Tenth Man, A Shot in the Dark, A Thousand Clowns.
PICTURES INCLUDE: Director: Barefoot in the Park, The Odd Couple, Last of the Red Hot Lovers, Mame, Cactus Flower. Actor: A Thousand Clowns, Prisoner of Second Avenue, The One and Only, Lovesick, The Goodbye People, Brighton Beach Memoirs.

SALANT, RICHARD S.: Executive. b. New York, NY, Apr. 14, 1914. e. Harvard Coll. A.B., 1931–35; Harvard Law Sch., 1935–38. Atty. Gen.'s Com. on Admin. Procedure, 1939–41; Office of Solicitor Gen., U.S. Dept. of Justice, 1941–43; U.S. Naval Res., 1943–46; assoc., Roseman, Goldmark, Colin & Kaye, 1946–48; then partner, 1948–51; pres. CBS news div., 1961–64; v.p. special asst. to pres. CBS, Inc., 1951–61, 1964–66; pres., CBS news div., 1966; mem. bd. of dir., CBS, Inc. 1964–69; vice chm., NBC bd., 1979–81; sr. adviser, 1981–83; pres. CEO, National News Council, 1983–84. Retired.

SALE, RICHARD: Writer, Director. b. New York, NY, Dec. 17, 1911. e. Washington & Lee, 1934. m. Irma Foster, designer. Author novels, over 400 published stories; honor roll Best Short Stories, 1935; ent. m.p. ind. with Paramount, 1944; member: WGAW, DGA: Acad. of M.P. Arts & Sciences, Authors League of Amer., BMI: pres. Voyager Films, Inc.; v.p. Libra Productions, Inc.
PICTURES INCLUDE: Strange Cargo, Rendezvous with Annie, Spoilers of the North, Campus Honeymoon, Lady at Midnight, Calendar Girl, Inside Story, Dude Goes West, Mother Is a Freshman, Father Was a Fullback, When Willie Comes Marching Home, Mr. Belvedere goes to College, Ticket to Tomahawk, I'll Get By, Driftwood, Meet Me After the Show, Half Angel, Let's Make It Legal, Girl Next Door, My Wife's Best Friend, Let's Do It Again, Torpedo Run, French Line, Suddenly, Women's World, Gentlemen Marry Brunettes, Abandon Ship, The Oscar, The White Buffalo, Assassination.

SALETRI, FRANK R.: Producer, Director, Writer. b. Chicago, IL, Jan. 20, 1928. Is criminal trial lawyer, member of Calif. bar. Heads FRSCO Prods., Ltd., m.p. prod.
PICTURES INCLUDE: Black Frankenstein—Blackenstein (s.p., prod.); Black the Ripper (s.p., dir.); The Return of the Ghost of the Son of the Bride of the House of Frankenstein, 1984 (s.p., dir.), The Skid Row Slasher, s.p., dir; The Secret of the Maltese Falcon, s.p. dir; Annually prod., s.p. & dir. for The Academy of Science Fiction, Horror and Fantasy Films. Annually prod., s.p. & dir. for The Annual Count Dracula Society Ann Radcliffe' Awards. (Both are documentaries).

SALKIND, ALEXANDER: Producer. b. Danzig/Gdansk, of Russian extraction. Grew up in Berlin where father, Miguel, produced films. Went to Cuba with father to assist him in film production. First solo venture a Buster Keaton comedy, 1945. Returned to Europe where made many pictures in Spain, Italy, France and Hungary.
PICTURES INCLUDE: The Three Musketeers, The Four Musketeers, The Prince and the Pauper, Superman, Supergirl, Santa Claus.

SALKIND, ILYA: Producer. b. Mexico City, 1948. e. U. of London. Grew up in many countries as father, Alexander, produced films. First film job as production runner on The Life of Cervantes for father. Was assoc. prod. on Light at the Edge of the World.
PICTURES: The Three Musketeers, The Four Musketeers, Superman, Superman II (exec. prod.); Supergirl (exec. prod.); Superman III (exec. prod.).

SALKOW, SIDNEY: Director, Writer. b. New York, NY, June 16, 1911. e. City Coll. of New York, B.A.; Harvard Law Sch. Stage dir. & prod. asst. number N.Y. dram. prods. (Dir. Bloodstream,

Black Tower, etc.) and mgr. summer theatre. From 1933 variously dialogue dir., assoc. dir., writer & dir. numerous pictures Paramount, Universal, Republic, Columbia, etc.; dir. number of pictures in Lone Wolf series (for Columbia), Tillie the Toiler, Flight Lieutenant, etc. In armed service, W.W.II.
PICTURES INCLUDE: Millie's Daughter, Bulldog Drummond at Bay, Admiral Was a Lady, Fugitive Lady, Golden Hawk, Scarlet Angel, Pathfinder, Prince of Pirates, Jack McCall Desperado, Raiders of the 7 Seas, Sitting Bull, Robbers' Roost, Shadow of the Eagle, Las Vegas Shakedown, Toughest Man Alive, Chicago Confidential, Iron Sheriff, Great Sioux Massacre, Martin Eden.
TELEVISION: Created, prod. dir., This is Alice series for Desilu, Lassie, Fury, Wells Fargo series. Headed prod. for FF Prod. in Rome, 1967–71.

SALMI, ALBERT: Actor. b. Coney Island, NY, 1928. After serving in W.W.II, studied 1948–54 with Dramatic Workshop, American Theatre Wing, Actors Studio. Appeared in many off-Bdwy. plays and live TV prods. Big hit on Bdwy. in Bus Stop. Other plays include The Rainmaker and The Brothers Karamazov. Has appeared in over 20 feature films and over 200 TV shows.
PICTURES INCLUDE: The Lawman, Something Big, The Deserter, The Crazy World of Jules Vrooder, Empire of the Ants, Dragonslayer, Love Child, Hard to Hold.
TELEVISION: Gunsmoke, Barnaby Jones, etc. Movies: Dress Gray, Fatal Vision, Best Kept Secrets, Once an Eagle, 79 Park Avenue, Night Games.

SALTER, HANS J.: Composer, Conductor. b. Vienna, Jan. 14, 1896. e. U. Acad. of Music, Vienna, Austria. Mus. dir.: Volksopera, Vienna; State Oper. Berlin; Metropole Theatre, Berlin; comp., cond., UFA, Berlin, 1929–33; European br., Universal, 1934–36; to U.S., Univ. 1938–47, 1950–52, wrote over 150 scores.
PICTURES INCLUDE: It Started With Eve, His Butler's Sister, Scarlet Street, Magnificent Doll, The Spoilers, Frenchie, Flesh and Fury, Golden Horde, The Sign of the Ram, Frightened City, Ghost of Frankenstein, Black Friday, House of Frankenstein, The Wolfman, Hold That Ghost, The Invisible Man Returns, the Mummy's Hand, Man-Eater of Kumaon, This Island Earth, Tomahawk, The Battle of Apache Pass, Please Believe Me, Apache Drums, Untamed Frontier, Lover Come Back, Thunder on the Hill, Bend of the River, Against All Flags, Black Shield of Falworth, Sign of the Pagan, Far Horizons, Man Without a Star, Wichita, Autumn Leaves, Red Sundown, Hold Back the Night, Rawhide Years, The Oklahoman, Three Brave Men, Pay the Devil, Law of the Trigger, Female Animal, Raw Wind in Eden, The Wild and the Innocent, Bat Masterson Story, Man in the Net, Come September, Follow That Dream, If a Man Answers, Bedtime Story, The Warlord, Beau Geste, Return of the Gunfighter.
TELEVISION: Wichita Town, Laramie, The Law and Mr. Jones, The Virginian, Wagon Train, Lost in Space, Maya.

SALTZMAN, HARRY: Producer. Lowndes Productions, Ltd. b. October, 1915. St. John, N.B., Canada. Ent. film ind. 1945. Chm. bd., H.M. Tenment, Ltd., London.
PICTURES INCLUDE: The Iron Petticoat, Look Back in Anger, The Entertainer, Saturday Night, Sunday Morning, Ipcress File, Funeral in Berlin, Billion Dollar Brain, Battle of Britain, Nijinsky (exec. prod.). Also co-producer of 10 James Bond films.

SALZBURG, JOSEPH S.: Producer, Editor. b. New York, NY, July 27, 1917. Film librarian, then rose to v.p. in chge. of prod., Pictorial Films, 1935–42; civilian chief film ed. U.S. Army Signal Corps Photo Center, 1942–44; U.S. Army Air Forces, 1944–46; prod. mgr., Pictorial Films, 1944–50; prod. mgr. Associated Artists Prod., then M.P. for TV, 1950–51; org. m.p prod. & edit. service for theatrical, non-theatrical & TV films 1951–56; prod. mgr., dir. of films oper., official Films. Oct. 1956–59; prod. sup. tech. dir. Lynn Romero Prod. features and TV; assoc. prod. Lynn Romero Prod. TV series, Counterthrust 1959–60; v.p., sec'y, B.L. Coleman Assoc., Inc. & Newspix, Inc. 1961; pres. National Production Assoc., Inc. 1960–1962, chief of production, UPI Newsfilm, 1963–66. Prod./account exec. Fred A. Niles Comm. Center, 1966. Appt. v.p., F.A. Niles Communications Centers Inc., N.Y., 1969. In 1979 appointed in addition exec. producer & gen. mgr., F. A. Niles Communication centers Inc., N.Y. studio.

SAMPSON, LEONARD E.: Exhibitor. b. New York, NY, Oct., 1918. e. City Coll. of New York, B.B.A., 1939. Entered m.p. industry as stagehand helper and usher; Skouras Park Plaza, Bronx 1932–36; asst. mgr. Gramercy Park, 1937–38; mgr., 5th Avenue Playhouse, 1939–41; mgr., Ascot Bronx, 1941–42. In Army 1942–46. On return entered into partnership with cousin Robert C. Spodick in Lincoln, a New Haven art house. Organized Nutmeg Theatres, operating 6 art and conventional theatres in CT, associated with Norman Bialek in Westport and Norwalk. Sold Nutmeg in 1968 to Robert Smerling. Retains partnership with Spodick in New Haven's York Sq., Lincoln, and Crown. Built Groton, CT, Cinemas I & II in 1970 and Norwich, CT, Cinema I & II, 1976 and acquired Village Cinemas I & II, Mystic, in association with Spodick and William Rosen. Acquired Westerly Cinema I & II, 1982.

SAMUELS, ABRAM: Executive. b. Allentown, PA, Sept. 15, 1920. e. Lehigh U. U.S. Army 1942–46; pres. Automatic Devices Co. 1946–76; named bd. chmn. in 1976.

SAMUELSON, DAVID W., F.R.P.S., F.B.K.S., B.S.C.: Executive. b. London, England, July 6, 1924. Son of early producer G. B. Samuelson. Joined ind. 1941 with British Movietone News. Later film cameraman, 1947. Left Movietone 1960 to join family company, Samuelson Film Service Ltd. Dir., Samuelson Group Plc, 1958–84. Past president British Kinematograph Sound & TV Soc., Chm, British Board of Film Classification past chm., London Intl. Film Sch. Author of Motion Picture Camera and Lighting Equipment, Motion Picture Camera Techniques, Motion Picture Camera Data, Samuelson Manual of Cinematography, and Cinematographers Computer Program. Currently consultant on technology film making, author, lecturer. Won Acad. Award for Engineering, 1980.

SAMUELSON, PETER GEORGE WYLIE: Producer. b. London, England, October 16, 1951. e. Cambridge U., M.A., English literature. Early career as interpreter and production assistant. 1979–84, exec. v.p., Interscope Communications, Inc. Pres., Starlight Foundation. Director, Friends of British Academy 1986–88, pres., Film Associates, Inc. chm., Samuelson Group, Inc. (USA).
PICTURES: Production Manager: Speed Merchants. (1973), High Velocity. One by One. 1976, Return of the Pink Panther, Sante Fe 1836. A Man, A Woman and a Bank (prod.); Revenge of the Nerds (prod.); Turk 182 (exec. prod.).

SAMUELSON, SYDNEY, C.B.E., B.S.C., Hon. F.B.K.S., Executive. b. London, England, Dec. 7, 1925. Early career as cinema projectionist, 1939–42; Gaumont British News, 1942–43; Royal Air Force, 1943–47; asst. cameraman, cameraman, director/cameraman until 1960; founded Samuelson Film Service, 1955; now chmn. Samuelson Group plc; Trustee and chmn. board of management, British Acad. of Film and Television Arts (chmn. of Council 1973–76). Trustee and member of Exec. Council (Pres. 1983–86) Cinema and Television Benevolent Fund. Member of Executive, Cinema & Television Veterans (pres. 1980–81); assoc. member, American Society of Cinematographers. Hon. Tech. Adviser, Royal Naval Film Corp. Hon. member, Guild of British Camera Technicians (1986); Member, British Society of Cinematographers. (governor, 1969–79; 1st vice pres., 1976–77).

SANDA, DOMINIQUE: Actress. b. Paris, France, March 11, 1951. r.n. Dominique Varaigne. e. Saint Vincent de Paul, Paris. Was a popular model for women's magazines when cast by Robert Bresson as the tragic heroine in his Dostoyevsky adaptation Un Femme Douce (1968).
PICTURES: Un Femme Douce; First Love, The Conformist; The Garden of the Finzi-Continis; La Notte Dei Fiori; Sans Mobile Apparent; Impossible Object; The Mackintosh Man; Steppenwolf; Conversation Piece; 1900; L'Eredita Ferramonti; Damnation Alley; Beyond Good and Evil; The Song of Roland; Utopia; The Navire Night; Travels on the Sly; Caboblanco; A Room in Town; Dust of the Empire; The Way to Bresson; The Sailor 512; With All Hands.

SANDERS, TERRY BARRETT: Producer, Director, Writer. b. New York, NY, Dec. 20, 1931. e. U. of California at L.A., 1951; Co-prod., photographed, A Time Out of War, 1954. Academy award best two-reel subject, and won first prize Venice Film Festival, etc.; co-wrote The Day Lincoln Was Shot, CBS-TV; s.p. The Naked and the Dead; prod. Crime and Punishment—USA., prod. War Hunt; prod. and dir. Portrait of Zubin Mehta for U.S.I.A. Assoc. dean, Film Sch., California Inst. of the Arts. Assoc. professor, UCLA.
TELEVISION: Prod. dir.: Hollywood and the Stars, The Legend of Marilyn Monroe, National Geographic Society specials, The Kids from Fame, Film Bios Kennedy Center Honors; Slow Fires; exec. v.p., American Film Foundation.

SANDRICH, JAY: Director. b. Los Angeles, CA, Feb. 24, 1932. e. U. of California at L.A.
PICTURES: Seems Like Old Times.
TELEVISION: The Lily Tomlin Show (DGA Award, 1975). Movies: The Crooked Hearts, What Are Best Friends For? Series: Mary Tyler Moore Show (1970–77; Emmy Awards 1971 & 1973); Soap (1977–78); Phyllis (pilot); Tony Randall Show (pilot); Bob Newhart Show (pilot); Benson (pilot); Golden Girls (pilot), Empty Nest (pilot), The Cosby Show (1985–87; Emmy Award 1985, 1986; DGA Award 1985), Dick Van Dyke Show (pilot), The Johnsons Are Home.

SANDS, JULIEN: Actor. b. Yorkshire, Eng. 1958. e. Central School of Speech and Drama, London. Professional debut: opposite Anthony Hopkins in British TV series A Married Man (1981).
PICTURES: The Killing Fields, Oxford Blues, After Darkness, Romance on the Orient Express, The Doctors and the

Devils, A Room with a View, Gothic, Siesta, Vibes, Wherever You Are, Warlock, Tennessee Waltz.
TELEVISION: The Room.

SANDS, TOMMY: Singer. b. Chicago, IL. e. Schools there and Greenwood, LA. Father, Benny Sands, concert pianist. Started career as guitar player, singer when 6, at KWKH station, Shreveport. One of pioneers of rock music. First manager was Col. Tom Parker. Acting debut: Kraft TV show The Singin' Idol; recording contract won him million record sales of Teen Age Crush.
PICTURES INCLUDE: Sing Boy Sing, Mardi Gras, Love in a Goldfish Bowl, Babes in Toyland, The Longest Day, Ensign Pulver, None But the Brave.

SANFORD, CHARLES: Musical Director. b. New York, NY, June 17, 1905. Has been conducting since age of 15; asst. cond. N.Y. Hippodrome; district musical supervisor, RKO; conducted various shows, assoc. cond. to Alexander Smallens, Porgy and Bess.
TELEVISION: Musical dir., Admiral Broadway Review, 1948; Your Show of Shows, 1950–54; Bob Hope, 1950–51; Elgin American Show, 1950; Beatrice Lillie Show, 1950–51; Max Liebman Presents, 1954–56; Producer's Showcase, 1957–58; Jerry Lewis, Patrice Munsel Shows; 1959–60 Max Liebman Specials, Phil Silvers, Sid Caesar Specials.

SANFORD, ISABEL: Actress. b. New York, NY, Aug. 29, 1917. e. Textile H.S., Evander Childs H.S. Began acting in elementary school and continued through high school. Joined American Negro Theatre in the 1930's (then The Star Players) which disbanded in W.W.II. Latter associated with YWCA project and off-Bdwy. plays. Bdwy. debut in The Amen Corner.
PICTURES: Guess Who's Coming to Dinner, Pendulum, Stand Up and Be Counted, The New Centurions, Love at First Bite.
TELEVISION: Series: The Carol Burnett Show, All in the Family, The Jeffersons, etc. Movie: The Great Man's Whiskers.

SANGSTER, JIMMY: Producer, Director, Screenwriter. b. England, Dec. 2, 1927. Ent. m.p. ind. 1943. Prod. man. for Break in the Circle, Men of Sherwood Forest, X the Unknown.
PICTURES INCLUDE: Man on the Beach, The Curse of Frankenstein, The Trollenberg Terror, The Georkel, The Blood of the Vampire, Dracula, Intent to Kill, The Revenge of Frankenstein, Jack the Ripper, The Mummy, The Brides of Dracula, The Man Who Could Cheat Death, The Siege of Sydney Street, The Criminal, The Hell Fire Club, See No Exit, 1960 prod. and scripted Taste of Fear for Hammer Films 1961. Prod. The Savage Guns; prod. s.p. Maniac, Nightmare, Devil Ship Pirates; prod. Hysteria, s.p., The Giants, Paranoiac; s.p. Brainstorm; prod., s.p. The Nanny, s.p. Deadlier Than the Male, The Bridge of Newgate Jail; s.p. Java Weed, s.p. The Anniversary, prod. s.p. Doubled in Diamonds, Hide and Seek, Foreign Exchange, Private I (prod.), s.p. The Killing Game, The Claw, Touchfeather, wrote, prod. dir. The Horror of Frankenstein; dir. Lust for a Vampire; co-wrote s.p. Gingerbread House, Murder by Month Club, A Taste of Evil, The Goldfish Bowl, s.p. prod., dir. Fear in the Night. Screenplay: The Fairytale Man, s.p. The Monstrous Defect, s.p. The Legacy, s.p., Phobia.
TELEVISION: Writing credits include: Motive for Murder, The Assassins, I Can Destroy the Sun; exec. story consultant Screen Gems-NBC short story series, McCloud, Banacek, Cannon, Ironside, etc. 1977–78; prod. Young Dan'l Boone; wrote & produced pilot for CBS: Ebony Ivory and Jade; wrote pilot: Adventure; wrote pilot for Murder in Music City; The Concrete Cowboys; Once Upon a Spy (movie), No Place To Hide; writer/prod./dir., Ripley's Believe It or Not.

SANSOM, LESTER A.: Executive. b. Salt Lake City, UT. e. U. of Utah. Radio singer under name of Jack Allen, 1930; ent. m.p. ind. in editorial dept., Fox Film Corp., Dec. 1931; served in U.S. Navy as head of film library, Washington, DC, 1942–45; head of edit. dept. & post-prod., Allied Artists, since 1953; assoc. prod. Skabenga; prod., co-writer, Battle Flame; assoc. prod. Hell to Eternity, exec. prod. The Thin Red Line, prod. Crack in the World; prod. Bikini Paradise, Battle of the Bulge, Custer of the West, Co-prod., Krakatoa—East of Java; exec. prod. 12 + 1.

SAPERSTEIN, HENRY G.: Executive. b. Chicago, IL, June 2, 1918. e. U. of Chicago. Theatre owner, Chicago, 1943–45; pres. Television Personalities, Inc., 1955–67 Mister Magoo, Dick Tracy, TV shows, 1960–62; 1960–67 Glen Films, Inc.; prod., All-Star Golf, 1958–62; prod. Championship Bowling, 1958–60; prod. Ding Dong School, 1959–60; pres. owner, UPA Pictures, Inc. Prod.: Mr. Magoo, Dick Tracy cartoon series, Mr. Magoo's Christmas Carol, T.N.T. Show, Turnon, Tune In Drop Out. Pres. Screen Entertainment Co., Benedict Pictures Corp., United Prod. of America; pres. H. G. Saperstein & Associates. Producer: The Vaudeville Thing; Tchaikovsky Competition, Gerald McBoing Boing Show
PICTURES: Producer: Gay Purr-ee, What's Up Tiger Lily,

T-A-M-I, Swan Lake, Hell in the Pacific, War of the Gargantuas, Invasion of the Astro Monsters.

SAPHIER, PETER: Executive. b. Los Angeles, CA, Aug. 5, 1940. e. Antioch Coll. Son of late James L. Saphier. Programmer, subscription TV, Santa Monica, CA 1964; prod. v.p., Universal, 1972–81; prod., Martin Bregman Prods.; sr. v.p., m.p. activities, Taft Entertainment Co., since 1984.
PICTURES: Scarface (co-prod.); Eddie Macon's Run (exec. prod.)
TELEVISION: The Four Seasons.

SARA, MIA: Actress. b. Brooklyn, NY, 1968. Started doing TV commercials; landed role in soap opera, All My Children. Theatrical m.p. debut, Legend (1986).
PICTURES: Ferris Bueller's Day Off, The Long Lost Friend, Apprentice to Murder, Imagination.
TELEVISION: Queenie.

SARAFIAN, RICHARD C.: Director. b. New York, NY. April 28, 1925. Studied medicine and law before entering film industry with director Robert Altman doing industrial documentaries. Made documentaries before starting TV career.
TELEVISION: Gunsmoke, Bonanza, Guns of Will Sonnet, I Spy Wild, Wild West; Maverick, Twilight Zone, Gangster Chronicles. Movies: Shadow on the Land, Disaster on the Coastline, Splendor in the Grass; A Killing Affair; Liberty; Golden Moment—An Olympic Love Story. As Actor: Foley Square (series).
PICTURES: Andy (debut, 1965), Run Wild, Run Free, Ballad of a Badman, Fragment of Fear, Man in the Wilderness, Vanishing Point, Lolly Madonna (XXX), The Man Who Loved Cat Dancing, The Next Man (also prod.), Sunburn, The Bear, Songwriter (actor only), Street Justice.

SARANDON, CHRIS: Actor. b. Beckley, WV, July 24, 1942. e. U. of West Virginia.
PICTURES: Dog Day Afternoon, Lipstick, The Sentinel, Cuba, The Osterman Weekend, Protocol, Fright Night, Collision Course, The Princess Bride, Childs Play, Forced March.
TELEVISION: You Can't Go Home Again, The Day Christ Died, A Tale of Two Cities, This Child Is Mine, Liberty, Mayflower Madam.

SARANDON, SUSAN: Actress. b. New York, NY, Oct. 4, 1946. e. Catholic U. Came to New York to pursue acting, first signing with Ford Model Agency. Made film debut in Joe (1970). Also appeared on TV in A World Apart series. Co-produced film, The Last of the Cowboys.
THEATER: A Coupla White Chicks Sitting Around Talking, Extremities.
PICTURES INCLUDE: Lovin' Molly, The Front, The Great Waldo Pepper, The Rocky Horror Show, Dragonfly, Crash, The Great Smokey Roadblock, Walk Away Madden, The Other Side of Midnight, Pretty Baby, King of the Gypsies, Loving Couples, Atlantic City, Tempest, The Hunger, In Our Hands, The Buddy System, Compromising Positions, The Witches of Eastwick, Bull Durham, The January Man, Sweet Heart's Dance, Married to the Mob, A Dry White Season.
TELEVISION: Search For Tomorrow, Calucci's Dept., Who Am I This Time?, A.D., Mussolini and I, Women of Valor, He'll See You Now, F. Scott Fitzgerald & the Last of the Belles, Oxbridge Blues.

SARGENT, ALVIN: Writer. Began career as writer for TV, then turned to theatrical films.
PICTURES INCLUDE: The Stalking Moon, Gambit, The Sterile Cuckoo, I Walk the Line, The Effect of Gamma Rays on Man-in-the-Moon Marigolds, Love and Pain (and the whole damn thing), Julia (Acad. Award, 1977), Bobby Deerfield, Straight Time, The Electric Horseman, Ordinary People (Acad. Award, 1980), Nuts (co-s.p.); Dominick and Eugene (co-s.p.).
TELEVISION: Footsteps, The Impatient Heart.

SARGENT, DICK: Actor. b. Carmel, CA, 1933. Veteran of over 140 TV shows, 17 feature films and four TV series.
PICTURES: Captain Newman, M.D., Operation Petticoat, Mardi Gras, Bernadine, Hardcore, Body Count.
TELEVISION: Bewitched.

SARGENT, JOSEPH: Director. r.n. Giuseppe Danielle Sargente. b. Jersey City, NJ, July 25, 1925.
PICTURES INCLUDE: The Hell With Heroes, The Forbin Project, White Lightning, The Taking of Pelham One Two Three, MacArthur, Goldengirl, Coast to Coast, Nightmares, Jaws... The Revenge (also prod.).
TELEVISION: One Spy Too Many, The Spy in the Green Hat, The Sunshine Patriot, The Immortal, The Man, Tribes, The Marcus-Nelson Murders (Emmy award for tv movie that was pilot for Kojak series), The Night That Panicked America, Sunshine, Friendly Persuasion, Amber Waves, Hustling, Terrible Joe Moran, Choices of the Heart (also prod.), Space, Love Is Never Silent, Passion Flower, Of Pure Blood, There Must Be a Pony, The Karen Carpenter Story.

SARLUI, ED: Executive. b. Amsterdam, The Netherlands, Nov. 10, 1925. Owner, Peruvian Films, S.A.; pres., Radio Films of Peru, S.A.; pres. Bryant Films Educatoriana, S.A.; partner, United Producers de Colombia Ltd.; pres. Royal Film N.V.; pres., United Producers de Centroamerica, S.A.; pres. United Producers de Mexico, S.A.; pres., United Producers Int'l, Inc., Continental Motion Pictures, Inc. 1988, formed Cinema Corp. of America with Moshe Diamant and Elliott Kastner.
PICTURES: Full Moon in Blue Water (co-exec. prod.), High Spirits (co-exec. prod.).

SARNOFF, ROBERT W.: Executive. b. New York, NY, July 2, 1918. e. Harvard U., B.A., 1939; Columbia Law Sch. 1940. In office of Coordinator of Info., Wash., DC, Aug. 1941; the U.S. Navy, Mar. 1942; asst. to publisher, Gardner Cowles, Jr., 1945; mem. of staff Look Mag., 1946, with NBC, 1948–65; pres., Dec. 1955–58; chmn. bd., 1958; bd. of dir. RCA, 1957; chmn bd. chief exec. officer, NBC, 1958–65; pres. RCA, 1966; Chief Exec. Officer, 1968; bd. chmn., 1970–75. Mem., TV Pioneers, 1957; pres., 1952–53; International Radio & TV Society, Broadcasters Committee for Radio Free Europe. Am Home Products, Inc., dir., of Business Committee for the Arts.

SARNOFF, THOMAS W.: Executive. b. New York, NY, Feb. 23, 1927. e. Phillips Acad., Andover, MA, 1939–43; Princeton U., 1943–45, Stanford U. grad. 1948, B.S. in E.E.; Grad Sch. of Bus. Admin. 1948–49. Sgt., U.S. Army Signal Corps, 1945–46; prod. & sales, ABC-TV, Hollywood, 1949–50; prod. dept. MGM, 1951–52; asst. to dir. of finance and oper., NBC, 1952–54; dir. of prod. and bus. affairs, 1954–57; vice pres., prod. and bus. affairs, 1957–60; v.p. adm. west coast, 1960–62; v.p. west coast, 1962; exec. v.p. 1965–77; bd. of dir., NBC prods 1961–77; bd of dir Hope Enterprises 1960–75; dir. NABCAT, Inc. 1967–75; dir. Valley County Cable TV, Inc. 1969–75; Pres. NBC Entertainment Corp. 1972–77; Pres. Sarnoff International Enterprises, Inc. 1977–81; pres., Sarnoff Entertainment Corp., 1981–; exec. v.p., Venturetainment Corp., 1980. Past pres. Research Foundation at St. Joseph Hospital of Burbank; past pres. Permanent Charities of the Entertainment Ind.; past ch. bd. of trustees, National Acad. of TV Arts and Sciences.

SARRAZIN, MICHAEL: Actor. r.n. Jacques Michel Andre Sarrazin. b. Quebec, Canada, May 22, 1940. Began acting at 17 on CBC TV; signed by Universal, 1965, appearing on several TV shows.
PICTURES INCLUDE: Gunfight in Abilene (debut), The Flim-Flam Man, The Sweet Ride, Journey to Shiloh, A Man Called Gannon, Eye of the Cat, In Search of Gregory, They Shoot Horses, Don't They?, The Pursuit of Happiness, Sometimes a Great Notion, Believe in Me, Harry in Your Pocket, For Pete's Sake, The Reincarnation of Peter Proud, Scaramouche, The Gumball Rally, Caravans, The Seduction, Fighting Back, Joshua Then and Now, Captive Hearts, Mascara, Keeping Track.
TELEVISION: Chrysler Theatre, The Virginian, World Premiere. Movies: Beulah Land, Frankenstein: The True Story.

SASSOWER, HARVEY L.: Advertising director. b. New York, NY, July 28, 1945. e. City Coll. of New York, B.A., advertising 1968 asst. to adv. mg., United Artists, 1969, asst. to adv. dir., 20th Century-Fox, 1969, appointed adv. mgr. of ABC Pictures Corp., dir. of adv., ABC Pictures, 1970; pres., Universal Spectrum, Inc. (design & adv. studio). Art director; author.

SAUL, OSCAR: Writer. b. Brooklyn, NY. e. Brooklyn Coll. Co-author play, Medicine Show; m.p. ed., U.S. Public Health Svce; numerous radio and TV plays.
PICTURES INCLUDE: collab. s.p., Once Upon a Time, Strange Affair; collab. story, Road House, Lady Gambles; s.p., Woman in Hiding, Secret of Convict Lake; adapt., Streetcar Named Desire; collab. sp. p., Thunder on the Hill, Affair in Trinidad; prod., Let's Do It Again; collab. s.p. Helen Morgan Story; s.p. Joker Is Wild; collab. story Naked Maja; collab. s.p. Second Time Around, Major Dundee; s.p. The Silencers; collab. s.p. Man and Boy, The Amigos. Novel: The Dark Side of Love (NBC movie). 1984, adapted A Streetcar Named Desire (ABC-TV).

SAVAGE, DAVID: Executive Producer, Advertising Executive, b. New York, NY, March 17, 1929. e. Rochester Inst. of Technology. In research development & testing div., Eastman Kodak Co., 2 yrs.; adv. mgr. asst. nat'l sales mgr., Official Films; org., film dept. mgr. WCBS-TV; dir. of film procurement, CBS; mgr. of film procurement, NBC; mgr. planning, merchandising, Recorded Tape Dept., RCA Records; promo. mgr., special products mktg. RCA Records Div.; v.p., opera., Wunderman, Rilotto, & Kline, 1970; pres., Response Industries, Inc., (adv. agency), 1973 which became affiliate of McCann Erickson, and was sr. v.p. of McCann Erickson in addition to continuing as pres. of R.I. Pres., Mattel Direct Marketing, 1982.

SAVAGE, JOHN: Actor. b. Long Island, NY, Aug. 25, 1949. Studied at American Acad. of Dramatic Arts. In Manhattan organized Children's Theatre Group which performed in public housing.

Has appeared in many plays both on and off Bdwy. Won Drama Circle Award for performance in One Flew Over the Cuckoo's Nest in Chicago and Los Angeles.
PICTURES: Bad Company, Steelyard Blues, All the Kind Strangers, The Deer Hunter, Hair, The Onion Field, Cattle Annie and Little Britches, Inside Moves, The Amateur, Brady's Escape, Maria's Lovers, Beauty and the Beast, Hotel Colonial, The Beat, Catacombs, War Shepherds.
STAGE: Fiddler on the Roof, Ari, Siamese Connections, The Hostage, American Buffalo.
TELEVISION: Gibbsville (series). Movies: Eric, Coming Out of the Ice, Silent Witness, The Nairobi Affair, Desperate, Date Rape (Afterschool Special).

SAVALAS, TELLY: Actor. r.n. Aristotle Savalas. b. Garden City, NY, Jan. 21, 1924. e. Columbia U., B.S. Joined Information Services of State Dept.; made exec. dir. Then named sr. dir. of news, special events for ABC, where created Your Voice of America series. Acting career began with debut in Bring Home a Baby on Armstrong Circle Theatre TV.
PICTURES INCLUDE: Birdman of Alcatraz, Young Savages, Cape Fear, Man from the Diner's Club, Battle of the Bulge, Greatest Story Ever Told, Beau Geste, Dirty Dozen, Buona Sera, Mrs. Campbell, Crooks and Coronets, Kelly's Heroes, On Her Majesty's Secret Service, Killer Force, Lisa and the Devil, Capricorn One, Escape to Athena, Beyond the Poseidon Adventure, Cannonball Run II, The Secret of the Sahara, Faceless.
TELEVISION: Series: Kojak. Movies: Mongo's Back in Town, Visions, The Marcus-Nelson Murders, The Dirty Dozen: The Deadly Mission, Alice in Wonderland, The Cartier Affair, Return to the Titanic (host), The Dirty Dozen: The Fatal Mission.

SAWELSON, MEL: Executive b. Los Angeles, CA, Sept. 5, 1929. e. U. of Southern California, 1947–48; U. of California at L.A. 1948–49. Entered M.P. industry in 1947; mgr., Acme Film Laboratories, Inc., 1952; pres. Sports-TV; 1957–59; produced, Olympic Films, International Olympic Organization, 1956; produced, Big 10 Hilites, PCC Hilites, All American Game of the Week, 1957–59; 1st m.p. lab. exec. to install videotape, 1959; created Acme-chroma process of transferring color videotape to film; pres., Acme Film & Videotape Labs., 1967–71; v.p. Consolidated Film Industries, 1971, exec. v.p. 1972; pres., Glen Glenn Sound Co., 1972.

SAWYER, DIANE: News Correspondent, Anchor. b. Glasgow, KY, Dec. 22, 1945. m. director Mike Nichols. e. Wellesley Coll. Studied law before deciding on career in TV. Worked for Nixon Administration in press office from 1970–74; assisted Nixon in writing memoirs, 1975–78. Joined CBS News as reporter in Washington bureau in 1978; named correspondent in 1980. Served as CBS State Dept. correspondent 1980–81. Joined Charles Kuralt as co-anchor of the weekday editions of CBS Morning News in 1981. From 1984 correspondent on 60 Minutes.

SAXON, JOHN: Actor. r.n. Carmine Orrico. b. Brooklyn, NY, Aug. 5, 1935. Model; m.p. debut: Running Wild. On TV in Scarecrow and Mrs. King, Falcon Crest (series).
PICTURES INCLUDE: The Unguarded Moment, Rock Pretty Baby, Summer Love, The Restless Years, The Reluctant Debutante, Cry Tough, Portrait in Black, The Unforgiven, The Plunderers, Posse from Hell, War Hunt, Nightmare, Evil Eye, For Singles Only, Joe Kidd, Enter The Dragon, Black Christmas, Strange Shadows in an Empty Room, The Electric Horseman, Wrong Is Right, The Big Score, Nightmare on Elm Street, Fever Pitch, Welcome to Spring Break, Death House (also dir.), Tunnels, My Mom's a Werewolf, Aftershock.
TELEVISION: Movies: 79 Park Avenue, Can Ellen Be Saved?, Golden Gate, The Immigrants, Once an Eagle, Raid on Entebbe.

SAYLES, JOHN: Writer, Director, Editor. b. Schnectady, NY, Sept. 28, 1950. e. Williams U. Wrote two novels: Pride of the Bimbos, 1975 and Union Dues, 1978; also The Anarchist's Convention, collection of short stories. First screenplay: Alligator, then Piranha (1978). Wrote and directed plays off-Bdwy (Turnbuckle).
PICTURES: Battle Beyond the Stars (s.p.), Lady in Red (s.p.), Return of the Secaucus Seven (s.p., dir., actor, editor), Alligator (s.p.), The Howling (co-s.p.), The Challenge (co-s.p.), Lianna (s.p., dir., editor), Baby, It's You (s.p., dir.), The Brother from Another Planet (s.p., dir., editor, actor), The Clan of the Cave Bear (s.p.), Wild Thing (s.p.), Matewan (dir., s.p. actor), Eight Men Out (dir., s.p., actor), Breakin' In (s.p. only).
TELEVISION: A Perfect Match, Unnatural Causes (actor, s.p.).

SCACCHI, GRETA: Actress. b. Milan, Italy. e. England and Australia.
PICTURES: Heat and Dust, Defense of the Realm, The Coca Cola Kid, A Man in Love, Good Morning, Babylon,

White Mischief, Paura e Amore (Three Sisters), Woman in the Moon, Schoolmates.
TELEVISION: Camille.

SCARDINO, DON: Actor. b. Canada. On Bdwy. in Godspell, King of Hearts, Johnny No Trump, As You Like It, etc.
PICTURES: The People Next Door, Homer, Squirm, Cruising, He Knows You're Alone.

SCARWID, DIANA: Actress. b. Savannah, GA. Went to N.Y. after high school to attend American Acad. of Dramatic Arts, Pace U. Member of National Shakespeare Conservatory (Woodstock, NY) and worked in regional theatres before moving to Hollywood 1976. Motion picture debut in Pretty Baby, 1978.
PICTURES: Inside Moves, Honeysuckle Rose, Mommie Dearest, Rumble Fish, Strange Invaders, Silkwood, The Ladies Club, Heat, Brenda Starr.
TELEVISION: Gibbsville (series), Studs Lonigan (miniseries), and films: The Guyana Tragedy, Kingston Confidential, The Glitter Palace, Battered, Desperate Lives, Thou Shalt Not Kill, A Bunny's Tale, After the Promise.

SCHAEFER, CARL: Publicist, b. Cleveland, OH, Sept. 2. e. U. of California at L.A. Contr. to mag., including Vanity Fair, Hollywood Citizen-News, 1931–35; Warner Bros., 1935.; Huesped de Honor, Mexico, 1943; OSS W.W.II, 1944–45; Int'l Comt. AMPS, chmn. 1966–67; Italian Order of Merit, 1957; Chevalier de l'ordre de la Couronne, Belgium, 1963. Pres., Foreign Trade Assn. of Southern Calif., 1954; chmn. of bd., 1955; British-American C. of C., Dir., 1962; Chevalier French Legion d'Honneur, 1955; Comm. Hollywood Museum; dir., International Relations, Warner Bros. Seven Arts Int'l Corp., 1960; formed own firm, Carl Schaefer Enterprises, 1971. Dir. pub. rel., British-American Chamber of Commerce, 1971; dir. pub. rel. Iota International Pictures, 1971; dir. pub. rel. Lyric Films International, 1971; bureau chief (Hollywood) Movie/TV Marketing, 1971; managing dir., International Festival Advisory Council, 1971; dir. pub. rel. & adv. Francis Lederer Enterprises (Inc. American National Academy of Performing Arts, and Canoga Mission Gallery) 1974; West Coast rep. Angelika Films of N.Y. 1974, Hwd. rep Korwitz/Geiger Products. 1975–; Hwd. corresp. Movie News, S'pore, & Femina, Hong Kong, 1974–; member Westn. Publications Assn. 1975–; field rep. Birch Records 1975; Hollywood rep Antena Magazine, Buenos Aires; dir pub rel Style Magazine. Coordinator Hollywood Reporter Annual Key Art Awards; coordinator Hollywood Reporter Annual Marketing Concept Awards; executive committee & historian ShoWest; Mem: National Panel of Consumer Arbitrators, 1985; Hollywood Corr., Gold Coast Times of Australia, 1986–87.

SCHAEFER, GEORGE: Producer, Director. b. Wallingford, CT, Dec. 16, 1920. e. Lafayette Coll., Yale Drama Sch. Bdwy. shows include The Linden Tree; Man and Superman; The Corn Is Green; The Heiress; Idiot's Delight; The Male Animal. Tovarich; Teahouse of the August Moon; Write Me a Murder; 1986, joined UCLA as chairman, Theatre, Film, TV.
PICTURES: Once Upon a Scoundrel; Generation; Doctors' Wives; Pendulum; Macbeth; An Enemy of the People.
TELEVISION: Hamlet; One Touch of Venus; The Corn Is Green; The Good Fairy; Born Yesterday; The Little Foxes; Little Moon of Alban; Harvey; Macbeth; The Magnificent Yankee; Kiss Me Kate; Pygmalion; F. Scott Fitzgerald; Blind Ambition; First You Cry; The People Vs. Jean Harris; A Piano for Mrs. Cimino; The Deadly Game; Children in the Crossfire; Right of Way; Stone Pillow; Mrs. Delafield Wants to Marry; Laura Lansing Slept Here.

SCHAFER, MARTIN: Executive. e. U. of California at L.A. Attorney-at-law. Served as producer on Modern Romance & The Awakening before joining Embassy Pictures as prod. exec. 1983; promoted to pres., prod. 1985, named exec. v.p., prod., for 20th Century Fox.
PICTURES: Co-prod.: The Mountain Men; The Awakening; Modern Romance.

SCHAFER, NATALIE: Actress. b. New York, NY, Nov. 5. e. Merrill Sch., Hamilton Inst.
BROADWAY: Lady in the Dark, Susan and God, The Doughgirls.
PICTURES INCLUDE: Marriage Is a Private Affair, Molly and Me, Dishonored Lady, The Time of Your Life, The Snake Pit, Caught, Anastasia, Oh Men! Oh Women!, Susan Slade, 40 Carats, The Day of the Locust, Beverly Hills Brats.
TELEVISION: I Love Lucy, Route 66, 77 Sunset Strip, Thriller, The Beverly Hillbillies, Gilligan's Island (series).

SCHAFFEL, ROBERT: Producer. b. Washington, DC, March 2, 1944. Partner with Jon Voight in Voight-Schaffel Prods. Now heads Robert Schaffel Prods.
PICTURES: Gordon's War; Sunnyside; Lookin' to Get Out; Table for Five, Distant Thunder, Jacknife (co-prod.).

SCHAFFNER, FRANKLIN: Director. b. Tokyo, Japan, May 30, 1920. e. Franklin & Marshall Coll. U.S. Navy, W.W.II. President, Directors Guild of Amer., 1987–
TELEVISION: Person to Person, Studio One. Kaiser-

Aluminum Hour, Playhouse 90, Kaiser Aluminum Hour (also prod.) DuPont Show of the Week (also prod.), Twelve Angry Men (Emmy, 1954), Caine Mutiny Court Martial (Emmy, 1955), The Defenders (Emmy, 1962).
PICTURES INCLUDE: The Stripper, (1962), The Best Man, War Lord, The Double Man, Planet of the Apes, Patton (Acad. Award, 1970), Nicholas and Alexandra, Papillon, Islands in the Stream, The Boys from Brazil, The Sphinx, Yes, Giorgio, Lionheart, Passage.

SCHATZBERG, JERRY: Director. b. New York, NY. Early career in photography as asst. to Bill Helburn.
PICTURES INCLUDE: Puzzle of a Downfall Child, Panic in Needle Park, Scarecrow, Sweet Revenge (prod.-dir.), The Seduction of Joe Tynan, Honeysuckle Rose, Misunderstood, No Small Affair, Street Smart, Reunion.
TELEVISION: Clinton and Nadine.

SCHEIDER, ROY: Actor. b. Orange, NJ, Nov. 10, 1932. e. Franklin and Marshall Coll. where he won the Theresa Helburn Acting Award twice. First professional acting in N.Y. Shakespeare Festival 1961 prod. of Romeo and Juliet. Became member of Lincoln Center Repertory Co. and acted with Boston Arts Festival, American Shakespeare Festival, Arena Stage (Wash., DC) and American Repertory Co.
PICTURES INCLUDE: Loving, Paper Lion, Stiletto, Star!, Puzzle of a Downfall Child, Klute, The French Connection, The Outside Man, The Seven Ups, The Inheritor, Sheila Levine, Jaws, Marathon Man, Sorcerer, Jaws II, Last Embrace, All That Jazz, Still of the Night, Blue Thunder, 2010, 52 Pick-up, The Men's Club, La Ciurma, Palisades Park, Mismatch, Cohen and Tate.
TELEVISION: Hallmark Hall of Fame, Studio One, N.Y.P.D., Assignment Munich, Jacobo Timerman, Tiger Town, Portrait of the Soviet Union (host).
STAGE: Richard III, Stephen D, Sergeant Musgrave's Dance, The Alchemist, Betrayal.

SCHELL, MARIA: Actress. b. Vienna, 1926. Sister of Maximillian Schell. Made debut at 12 in Swiss film, The Gravel Pit. Subsequently appeared in many British and American films.
PICTURES: Angel with a Trumpet, The Heart of the Matter, So Little Time, The Magic Box, The Brothers Karamazov, The Hanging Tree, Cimarron, The Odessa File, Voyage of the Damned, The Twist, Superman, 1919.
TELEVISION: (U.S.): Christmas Lilies of the Field; Inside the Third Reich; Martian Chronicles; Samson and Delilah.

SCHELL, MAXIMILIAN: Actor. b. Vienna, Dec. 8, 1930.
TELEVISION: Shows include: Playhouse 90, Judgment at Nuremberg, The Fifth Column, The Diary of Anne Frank, Turn The Key Deftly, Phantom of the Opera, Heidi, Peter the Great (mini-series).
PICTURES INCLUDE: Children, Mother and the General, The Young Lions, Judgment at Nuremberg (Acad. Award), Five Finger Exercise, The Condemned of Altona, Return from the Ashes, The Deadly Affair, Counterpoint, The Desperate Ones, The Castle, Krakatoa East of Java, The Odessa File, First Love (dir., starred); The Man in the Glass Booth (actor), End of the Game (dir., co-prod.), St. Ives, A Bridge Too Far, Cross of Iron, Julia, Players, The Black Hole, The Chosen, The Assisi Underground, Marlene (dir.).

SCHENCK, AUBREY: Producer. b. Brooklyn, NY, Aug. 26, 1908. e. Cornell U., New York U. With law firm of O'Brien, Driscoll & Raftery; buyer & attorney for Natl. Theatres, 1936; prod. for 20th Century-Fox 1945; exec. prod. Eagle Lion 1946; contract prod. Universal Internatl. 1948; Aubrey Schenck Productions, Inc.
PICTURES INCLUDE: Shock, Johnny Comes Flying Home, Strange Triangle, Repeat Performance, T-Men, Mickey, It's a Joke Son, Trapped, Port of New York, Wyoming Man, Undercover Girl, Fat Man, Target Unknown; formed own co. to prod. War Paint, Beachhead. Also: Yellow Tomahawk, Shield for Murder, Big House, U.S.A., Crime Against Joe, Emergency Hospital, Ghost Town, Broken Star, Rebels in Town, Pharaoh's Curse, Three Bad Sisters, Fort Yuma, Desert Sands, Quincannon, Frontier Scout, Black Sleep, Hot Cars, War Drums, Voodoo Island, Revolt at Fort Laramie, Tomahawk Trail, Untamed Youth, Girl in Black Stockings, Bop Girl Goes Calypso, Up Periscope, Violent Road, Reckless, Frankenstein 1970, Wild Harvest, Robinson Crusoe On Mars, Don't Worry, Ambush Bay, Kill a Dragon, Impasse, More Dead Than Alive, Barquero, Daughters of Satan.
TELEVISION: Miami Undercover, series.

SCHEPISI, FRED: Producer, Director, Writer. b. Melbourne, Australia, Dec. 26, 1939. Assessed student films at Melbourne's Swinburne Inst. of Tech., worked on gov. sponsored experimental Film Fund, Made TV Commercials. Founded The Film House prod. co.
PICTURES: The Priest (dir.), The Devil's Playground (dir., prod., s.p.), The Chant of Jimmie Blacksmith (dir., prod., s.p.), Barbarosa (dir.), Iceman (dir.), Plenty (dir.), Roxanne (dir.), A Cry in the Dark (dir., co-s.p.).

SCHERICK, EDGAR J: Executive Producer. e. Harvard U.; elected to Phi Beta Kappa. Introduced Wide World of Sports on TV through his co., Sports Programs, Inc. Was v.p. in chg. of network programming at ABC-TV. Pres. of Palomar Pictures Int'l. Now independent producer.
PICTURES INCLUDE: For Love of Ivy, The Birthday Party, Take the Money and Run, They Shoot Horses, Don't They?, The Killing of Sister George, Sleuth, The Heartbreak Kid, Law and Disorder, The Stepford Wives, I Never Promised You a Rose Garden, The American Success Company, I'm Dancing As Fast As I Can, Shoot the Moon, White Dog, Reckless, Mrs. Soffel.
TELEVISION: The Man Who Wanted to Live Forever (1970); The Silence; Circle of Children; Raid on Entebbe; Panic in Echo Park; Zuma Beach; An American Christmas Carol; The Seduction of Miss Leona; Revenge of the Stepford Wives; Hitler's SS; The High Price of Passion; The Stepford Children; Unholy Matrimony; Little Gloria...Happy at Last; On Wings of Eagles; Hands of a Stranger; Home Fires; He Makes Me Feel Like Dancin' (Emmy and Acad. Awards, 1983); Stranger on My Land (exec. prod.); And the Band Played On; The Kennedys of Massachusetts; Satin's Touch (exec. prod.).

SCHIAVONE, JAMES: Executive. b. Niagara Falls, NY, Nov. 14, 1917. e. U. of Michigan. Started career as newspaperman; general manager WWJ-AM-FM-TV, Detroit, 1952–68; pres.-gen. mgr., KSAT-TV, San Antonio, TX, 1969–present.

SCHICK, ELLIOT: Executive. b. Brooklyn, NY, Dec. 24, 1924. e. Brooklyn Coll., B.A.; New School for Social Research, drama workshop, directing 1945–46. Author of book for Ballet Theatre, Manfred; book, The Administration of the Economic and Social Council. 1942–48, prod. & dir. radio shows for WNYC, N.Y., composed and arranged music for radio and stage production; 1946–48; dialogue director, Republic Studios; 1948–50, prod. & dir. TV shows and commercials, Nova Productions; 1950–51, editor, United Nations Film Div.; 1951–53, editor, Candid Camera; 1953–55, asst. studio mgr., American Natl. Studios; 1955–56, prod. & dir. live and video tape shows for KCET; 1969, asst. dir., Tora, Tora, Tora; 1969–72, prod. mgr. for features: 3 in the Attic, Up in the Cellar, Bunny O'Hare, Halls, The Brothers Keeper & Boggs, Kansas City Bomber, White Lightning; 1973–77 spvr. prod. for AIP on Sugar Hill, Return to Macon County, Cooley High, Futureworld, Island of Dr. Moreau in 1977. Joined EMI Films, Inc. as v.p. prod.; 1978, exec.-in-chg.-prod., Deer Hunter; 1980, produced The Earthling; 1981, prod., Private Benjamin (TV series); supvr. prod., Pippin (TV); Blue Skies Again (exec.-in-chg.-prod.); Fools Die (prod.); Fast Eddie (prod.); Marie (exec. prod.); Cherry-2000 (co-prod.), Masters of the Universe (co-prod.). Farewell to the King (exec. in charge of prod.).

SCHIFRIN, LALO: Composer, b. Buenos Aires, Argentina, June 21, 1932. Father was conductor of Teatro Colon in B.A. for 30 years. Schifrin studied with Juan Carlos Paz in Arg. and later Paris Cons. Arranger for Xavier Cugat. Returned to homeland and wrote for stage, modern dance, TV. Became interested in jazz and joined Dizzie Gillespie's band in 1962 as pianist and composer. Settled in L.A. Pres. Young Musicians Fed. Music; dir. and conductor, Paris Philharmonic 1987.
PICTURES INCLUDE: The Cincinnati Kid, The Liquidator, Cool Hand Luke, The President's Analyst, The Fox, Kelly's Heroes, Hell's Chronicles, Dirty Harry, Magnum Force, Man on a Swing, The Four Musketeers, Voyage of the Damned, The Eagle Has Landed, Telefon, Nunzio, The Manitou, Boulevard Nights, The Concord—Airport '79, Love and Bullets, Serial, The Big Brawl, Brubaker, Escape to Athena, The Amityville Horror, The Nude Bomb, The Competition, When Time Ran Out, Caveman, Buddy, Buddy, The Seduction, A Stranger Is Watching, Amityville II: The Possession, The Sting II, The Osterman Weekend, Sudden Impact, The Mean Season, The New Kids, Doctor Detroit, Tank, The Silence at Bethany, Little Sweetheart, Berlin Blues (music and songs).
TELEVISION: Mission Impossible (theme), Hollywood Wives, A.D., Private Sessions, Foster and Laurie, Starsky and Hutch, Earth Star Voyager, Princess Daisy, Falcon's Gold, Kung Fu: The Movie.

SCHILLER, FRED: Playwright, Screen & TV writer. Awarded: New York Literary Prize, for McCall magazine story Ten Men and a Prayer. Member of Dramatists' Guild. Member of Smithsonian Institution, Member of Societé Des Auteurs et Compositeurs Dramatiques. Member of Los Angeles World Affairs Council. Formerly chief corres. European Newspaper Feature Services. Honored by the U. of Wyoming for literary achievements with a special Fred Schiller Collection for their library.
PICTURES FOR: MGM, Columbia, RKO, Republic and Henri Sokal Films, Paris.
TELEVISION: Wrote some 53 TV plays for all major networks. Adapted G.B. Shaw play, The Inca of Jerusalem, presented by NBC as special. Wrote TV special: Demandez

Vicky! for Paris and Finder BitteMelden! for Austrian TV. STAGE: Come On Up (U.S.), Anything Can Happen (London), Demandez Vicky (Paris), Finder Please Return (Athens, Madrid), Finder Bitte Melden (Berlin, Baden-Baden, and Vienna). Peter Sellars production at Kennedy Center, Come on Up; a Mae West revival.

SCHILLER, LAWRENCE J.: Producer, Director. b. New York, NY, Dec. 28, 1936. Photojournalist with Life Magazine & Saturday Evening Post, 1958–70; collaborated on numerous books including three by Norman Mailer: The Executioner's Song, Marilyn, and The Faith of Graffiti; Muhammad Ali with Wilfrid Sheed; Minamata with Eugene Smith.
PICTURES: The Man Who Skied Down Everest (editorial concept & direction); Lady Sings the Blues, Butch Cassidy & the Sundance Kid (conceived and executed special still montages & titles); The American Dreamer (prod./dir.).
TELEVISION: Hey, I'm Alive (prod./dir.); Producer: The Trial of Lee Harvey Oswald, The Winds of Kitty Hawk, Marilyn, The Untold Story, An Act of Love, Child Bride of Short Creek. 1983: The Executioner's Song (prod. & dir.), Peter the Great.

SCHINE, G. DAVID: Executive. b. Gloversville, NY, Sept. 11, 1927. e. Harvard U., Pres., gen. mgr. Schine Hotels 1950–63. Film exhibitor until 1966 in New York, Ohio, Kentucky, Maryland, Delaware, and West Virginia. Exec. prod. of French Connection, 1971. Writer, prod., dir. of That's Action!, 1977. Chief Exec. officer of Schine Productions (production) and Epic Productions (distribution), Visual Sciences, Inc., High Resolution Sciences, Inc., and Studio Television Services, Inc.

SCHLAIFER, CHARLES: Executive. President, Charles Schlaifer and Company, Inc., advertising agency with offices in New York and Los Angeles. b. Omaha, NB. Reporter Daily News, World-Herald, (Omaha). In 1930 apptd. adv. mgr. Paramount theatres, Omaha; then of Publix theats., Omaha; then of Tri-State circuit, Neb., Iowa; 1936–42 managing dir. United Artists Theats., San Francisco; advisor, nat'l adv., United Artists prod. In 1942 apptd. adv. mgr. 20th Cent.-Fox; named asst. dir. of adv., publicity, & exploitation, 1944; apptd. v.p. & dir. of advertising, pub., exploitation and radio, 1945. Resigned 20th-Fox post, Feb. 1, 1949, to establish own adv. agency. Pres., Charles Schlaifer & Co., Inc. Chmn. advertising advisory council, MPAA; instructor at New School for Social Research, N.Y., on m.p.; revised m.p. adv. code; permanent chmn. first MPAA pub rel. com. Member; Nat'l Advisory Mental Health Council to U.S. Surgeon General; Founder and vice-chmn. bd. of gov., Nat'l Assn. of Mental Health. Lecturer, writer on adv. & mental health bd. of gov., Menninger Foundation; founder, co-chmn., Nat'l Mental Health Comm., secy., treas., Joint Comm. on Mental Illness & Health; expert witness Congress, govt. hearings creating National Institute of Mental Health in U.S. Public Health Service. Elected Hon. Fellow of the Amer. Psychiatric Assn., 1959; V. chmn., trustee in chg., Mental Health and Mental Retardation Facilities, NY State, 1964; secy., treas., Joint Commission Mental Health for Children; vice chmn. bd. Foundation for Child Mental Welfare, 1963. Mem. bd. trustees Research Found. 1966. Mem.: White House Conference on the Handicapped, 1952–65; elected honorary fellow, Post Graduate Psychiatric Institute, 1968. Hon. Doctor of Letters, John F. Kennedy Coll., Wahoo, Neb., 1969; Chmn. N.Y. State Health and Mental Hygiene Facilities Improvement Corp., 1970; Hon. Fellow—American Ortho Psychiatric Assoc., 1970; Hon. Fellow British Royal Society of Health. Wisdom Award Hon. Wisdom Mag., 1969; social conscience award Karen Horney Clinic, 1972. Chmn, NY State Facilities Dev. Corp., 1973–; Advisory Council to the National Institute of Mental Health to the Surgeon General of the U.S. 1976–.

SCHLANG, JOSEPH: Executive. b. New York, NY, Feb. 24, 1911, e. New York U. Owner and leader in N.Y. real estate, and exec. dir. of many enterprises. Pres. of International Opera Co. & Opera Presentations, Inc. Has produced two weekly radio programs: Opera Stars of Tomorrow and 100 & More Ways to Improve N.Y.C. since April, 1973. Opera Presentations, Inc., a non-profit corp. distributes and exhibits opera, ballet and art films throughout America and the school system. Over 100 cultural films owned by Schlang are supplied to Opera Presentations free to use.

SCHLATTER, GEORGE: Producer, Director, Writer. b. Birmingham, AL, Dec. 31, 1932. m. former actress Jolene Brand. e. Pepperdine U. on football scholarship. First industry job was agent in band and act dept., MCA. Then gen. mgr. and show producer Ciro's nightclub where he met Dick Martin and Dan Rowan.
TELEVISION: Laugh-In (2 Emmys, 1968); Shirley MacLaine Specials; Great American Laugh-Off; Just for Laughs; Laugh-In Specials; Goldie Hawn Special; Goldie and Liza Together; Speak Up, America!; Real Kids; The Best of Times; Look at Us (exec. prod.); Real People (exec. prod.); Shape of Things (exec. prod. and writer); Magic or Miracle (exec. prod., writer); Salute to Lady Liberty (exec. prod.); S.O.S.—Secrets of Surviving (exec. prod., writer); The American Comedy

Awards; George Schlatter's Comedy Club; George Schlatter's Funny People.

SCHLESINGER, JOHN: Director, Producer. b. London, England, Feb. 16,d 1926. e. Oxford U., BBC dir. 1958–60: Wrote and dir. Terminus for British Transport Films (Golden Lion, best doc., Venice); The Class. Some episodes The Valiant Years series.
PICTURES INCLUDE: 1961: A Kind of Loving (Golden Bear, Berlin); Billy Liar; Darling (New York Film Critics Award); Far From the Madding Crowd. Midnight Cowboy (Best dir. and film, S.F.T.A. and Oscars' 1968); Sunday, Bloody Sunday (Best dir. and film, S.F.T.A.), Visions of Eight (sequence), The Day of the Locust, Marathon Man, Yanks, Honky Tonk Freeway, The Falcon and the Snowman (also co-prod.), The Believers (also co-prod.), Madame Sousatzka (dir., co-s.p.).
TELEVISION: Separate Tables, An Englishman Abroad (BAFTA award).
OPERA: Les Contes d'Hoffmann (Royal Opera House 1981); SWET award; Der Rosenkavalier (Royal Opera House 1984).
THEATRE: No Why (RSC), 1964; Timon of Athens (RSC); Days in the Trees (RSC); I And Albert (Piccadilly Theatre); Heartbreak House (NT); Julius Caesar (NT); True West (NT).

SCHLONDORFF, VOLKER: Director. b. Wiesbaden, Germany, March 31, 1939. Studied in France, acquiring interest in political science in Paris. Studied at French Intl. Film Sch. (IDHEC) before becoming asst. to Jean-Pierre Melville, Alain Resnais, and Louis Malle Debut film, Der Junge Torless (Young Torless), 1965.
PICTURES: A Degree of Murder; Michael Kohlhass; Baal; The Sudden Fortune of the Poor People of Kombach; Die Moral der Rugh Halbfass; A Free Woman; The Lost Honor of Katharine Blum; Le Coup de Grace; Valeska Gert; The Tin Drum; Circle of Deceit; Swann in Love.
TELEVISION: Death of a Salesman; A Gathering of Old Men.

SCHLOSSBERG, JULIAN: Producer, Distributor, Director, Radio TV Host. b. New York, NY, Jan. 26, 1942. e. N.Y. Joined ABC-TV network 1964 as asst. acct. rep.; named act. rep. 1965; 1966, joined Walter Reade Organization as asst. v.p. chg. of TV; 1969, moved to WRO Theatre Div.; 1970, joined faculty of School of Visual Arts; 1971 named v.p. of WRO Theatres; 1976, joined Paramount Pictures as v.p. in charge of feature film acquisition. Since 1978 pres. & owner of Castle Hill Productions; 1974, prod. & moderated An Evening with Joseph E. Levine at Town Hall, N.Y.; 1974 to 1980, host of radio show Movie Talk on WMCA (N.Y.), WMEX (Boston), WICE (Providence); 1982–83 host of syndicated TV show, Julian Schlossbergs' Movie Talk; producers' rep. for Elia Kazan, Dustin Hoffman, Elaine May, George C. Scott.
PICTURES INCLUDE: In the Spirit, Going Hollywood: The War Years, Hollywood Uncensored, Hollywood Ghost Stories, No Nukes.
THEATRE: It Had To Be You, An Evening with Nichols and May, Rainbow Room, N.Y., 1983.
TELEVISION: Steve Allen's Golden Age of Comedy; All the Best, Steve Allen.

SCHLOSSER, HERBERT S.: Executive. b. Atlantic City, NJ. e. Princeton U., Yale Law Sch. Joined law firm of Phillips, Nizer, Benjamin, Krim & Ballon, 1954; attorney, California National Productions (subsidiary of National Broadcasting Company) 1957; v.p. & gen. mgr., 1960; director, talent & program administration, NBC television network, 1961; v.p., talent & program admin., 1962; v.p. programs, west coast, 1966–72; exec. v.p., NBC-TV, 1972; president, NBC Television Network, 1973, pres. & chief operating officer, NBC, April 1, 1974–76; Pres. & chief executive officer, 1977–78; exec. V.P. RCA 1978–85; sr. advisor, broadcasting & entertainment, Wertheim, Schroder & Co., 1986.

SCHLUSSELBERG, MARTIN: Film Executive. b. Sept. 1936. e. Yeshiva U. Booking clerk. UA. 1956; head booker, Citation Films, 1958; head booker, Desilu Dist., Co., 1961; head booker, and asst. to gen. sls. mgr., Medallion Pictures Corp., 1963; World Ent. Corp., 1966, Sales Mgr.; Crystal Pictures, 1978, sls. mgr., v.p.

SCHMIDT, WOLF: Producer, Distributor. b. Freiburg/Br., Germany, June 30, 1937. Came to U.S. 1962 as freelance journalist. Started producing in 1969, distributing independently since 1972. Now heads Kodiak Films.
PICTURES INCLUDE: Ski Fever (prod.), Stamping Ground (co-prod.), Young Hannah (exec. prod.), Things Fall Apart (prod.),The Passover Plot (prod.), Run For the Roses (co-prod.). Ghost Fever (exec. prod.); Defense Play (prod.); Riding the Edge (prod.).

SCHMOELLER, DAVID: Writer, Director. b. Louisville, KY, Dec. 8, 1947. e. Universidad de Las Americas, 1967–69; studied film and theater under Luis Bunuel and Alejandro Jodorowsky, U. of Texas, B.A., M.A., 1969–74. Wrote and directed 7 short films while studying at U. of Texas; won 27 intl. awards. In

Hollywood spent 6 months working as intern to Peter Hyams on film, Capricorn One. Now heads own co., The Schmoeller Corp.
PICTURES: Tourist Trap (debut as dir.); The Seduction (Dir., s.p.); Crawlspace (dir., s.p.). As writer only: The Day Time Ended, The Peeper, Last Chance Romance, Thrill Palace, Warriors of the Wind (Eng. adaptation), Ghost Town (s.p.), Catacombs (dir.).
TELEVISION: James at 15 (s.p.); Kid Flicks (cable; s.p., prod.).
NOVEL: The Seduction.

SCHNEER, CHARLES H.: Producer, Director. b. Norfolk, VA, May 5, 1920. e. Columbia Coll. pres., Morningside Prods. Inc. & Pictures Corp.; 1956. Founded Andor Films 1974.
PICTURES INCLUDE: Prod. The 3 Worlds of Gulliver, The 7th Voyage of Sinbad, I Aim the Stars, Face of a Fugitive, Good Day for a Hanging, Battle of the Coral Sea, Tarawa Beachhead, Mysterious Island, Jason and the Argonauts, First Men In The Moon, Half A Sixpence, Land Raiders, Valley of Gwangi, The Executioner, The Golden Voyage of Sinbad, Sinbad & The Eye of the Tiger, Clash of the Titans.

SCHNEIDER, DICK: Producer, Director. b. Cazadero, CA, Mar. 7. e. Coll. of the Pacific. U.S. Navy, W.W.II. Winner of 3 Emmys.
TELEVISION: Dough Re Mi, NBC-TV, Wide Wide World, NBC-TV, Colgate Comedy Hours, Beatrice Lilly & Jackie Gleason Comedy Hours, Henry Morgan Show, Kate Smith Show, Big Story, Treasury Men in Action, Doorway to Danger, Today Show, Home, Tonight Show, General Mills Circus; dir. coverage of political conventions; dir. NBC-TV coverage, Princess Margaret's wedding and Paris summit conference; dir. Eleanor Roosevelt Specials, 1959–60; Something Special 61, At This Very Moment, Inauguration, Gemini, Emmys, 1962, 1963, 1964; Papal Mass for all networks at Yankee Stadium, 1965–66; 1966–67 Tonight Show, Orange Bowl, Macy's Parade; Jr. Miss Pageant; 1967–70 College Queen, Emmy Award. Prod.; Macy's Parade, 1968–69 Orange Bowl Parade, 1968–69; Prod.-dir., NBC Expt. in TV, New Communication; prod., Big Sur; prod.-dir., Jr. Miss Pageant, 1968–69; dir. Dream House, ABC; dir. Who, What or Where, NBC; produced in 1970: Macy's Parade, Junior Miss, Orange Bowl Parade. 1971–79 Macy's Parade, Stars and Stripes; in 1972: Post Parade, Stars and Stripes 1973–75; Rose Parade 1974–81; Salute to Sir Lew; Jeopardy; NBC Star Salute, 1980; Emmy winner, 1980; Rose Parade, 1981-84; Star Salute, 1981; UCP Telethons, 1981-86. Macy's Parade, 1980–87; Diabetes Telethon, 1983; NBC Affiliate Convention, 1980–85; 1986, People's Choice, Jeopardy. 1984–87. Four-time Emmy winner.

SCHNEIDER, JOHN: Actor. b. Mount Kisco, NY, Apr. 8, 1954. Active in drama club in high school in Atlanta. Got job as fashion model and played guitar and sang own compositions in various Atlanta clubs. Active in local community theatre. Summer stock in New Hampshire.
PICTURES INCLUDE: Smokey and the Bandit, Million Dollar Dixie Deliverance, Eddie Macon's Run, Cocaine Wars.
TELEVISION: Dukes of Hazzard; John Schneider—Back Home. Movies: Dream House, Happy Endings, Stagecoach, Christmas Comes to Willow Creek.

SCHNEIDER, JOHN, A.: Executive. b. Chicago, IL, Dec. 4, 1926. e. U. of Notre Dame, B.S. U.S.N.R., 1943–47. Exec. assignments with CBS-TV, in Chicago and New York 1950–58; VP, gen. mgr. WCAU-TV, Philadelphia 1958–64; WCBS-TV, New York 1964–65; pres. CBS-TV Network 1965–66; pres. CBS/Broadcast Group 1966–69, 1971–77; exec. VP CBS Inc. 1969–71, TV and MP consultant 1977–79; consultant WCI, 1979; pres., CEO Warner Amex Satellite Entertainment Corp., 1980.

SCHNEIER, FREDERICK: Executive. b. New York, NY, May 31, 1927; e. New York U., 1951, bus. admin.; New York U. Grad. Sch., M.B.A., 1953. Dir. sls. planning, Mutual Broadcasting System, 1947–53; media research dir., RKO Teleradio, 1953–55; RKO Teleradio Advisory Comm., 1955–56; exec. staff RKO Teleradio & dir., marketing services, 1956–58; exec. vice-pres., Showcorporation, 1958–71; v.p. TV programming, RKO General, 1972–1973; v.p.; Hemdale Leisure Corporation, 1973–79; Viacom Enterprises v.p., feature films, 1979; sr. v.p., program acquisitions & motion pictures, 1980–83; snr. v.p., acquisitions, Showtime/The Movie Channel, 1983–85; sr. v.p. program acquisitions, program enterprises, 1985–87; now exec. v.p., programming.

SCHNUR, JEROME: Producer, Director. b. New York, NY, July 30, 1923. e. Carnegie Tech. Film prod. & dir. many indep. cos., 1939–43; prod., dir., training films, U.S. Air Force 1943–46; indep. film prod., Hollywood, 1946–50: on bd. of dir., Alson Prod., Inc. & Burwood Pictures Corp.; prod., dir., CBS-TV, N.Y., 1950–51; prod., dir., Goodson-Todson Prod., 1951–56; pres., Holiday Prod., indep. TV prod., 1956; Metropole Prod., indep. film prod., 1956; exec. prod. chg. creative prog. Frank Cooper Assoc., 1958; pres., Jerome Schnur Prods., Inc. Packager and Producer TV and Film.

TELEVISION: It's News to Me, Two for the Money, The Name's the Same, What's My Line, Beat the Clock, Robert Q. Lewis Show, Judge for Yourself, Holiday film series, Fred Allen Show, Dotto, Make the Connection, Scene of the Crime, Who Pays, Shari Lewis Show, Bell Telephone Hour, U.S. Steel Spec., Private Eye—Private Eye, exec. prod., United Fund Simulcast This Is My Town; writer; dir., Mark of Cain, Chronicle, Science Special, Tomorrow Was Yesterday; dir., L'Enfance du Christ; exec. prod., Supermarket Sweep; dir., Michelangelo's Pauline Chapel. CBS News spec.; dir. Jeptha's Daughter. St. Joan. TV ballet specials. Exec. Prod. Everybody's Talking; dir. Missions of San Antonio; Light in the Wilderness, and David Wept; Exec. Prod. Politithon 1970— PBS. Exec. Prod. & Dir., Threatened Paradise A Time To Live 1972; Director, Questions of Abraham Special Cantata; American Ballet Theatre Special; Luther 1973. Exec. prod., Musical Chairs, Strategy, others, 1974; Director, Joffrey ballet, PBS special; dir. Jerusalem Symphony, CBS spec.; 1977; dir. Song of Songs, CBS spec., 1978, Director, All Star-Jazz Show, CBS Special 1976. Recipient 1970–71 Peabody Award, 1970–71 Saturday Review Award, 1972 Emmy Citation; 1975 Ohio State Award.

SCHOENFELD, JOE: Executive. b. New York, NY, June 2, 1907. e. New York schools. Reporter, Hearst newspapers, 1924–32; reporter & editor, Variety, 1932–43 William Morris Agency, 1944–50; editor, Daily Variety, 1950–59; M.P. agency exec., William Morris, 1959–74. Retired.

SCHOENFELD, LESTER: Executive. b. Brooklyn, NY, Dec. 6, 1916. e. City Coll. of New York, 1934–38. Asst. mgr., Randforce Amusement, 1936–38; mgr., Rugoff & Becker circuit, 1938–47; mgr., Golden & Ambassador Theatres, 1948; print & sales dept., Film Classics, 1948–50; chg. of Theatrical, non-theatrical & TV dist., Brit. Info. Serv.; est. Lester A. Schoenfeld Films, 1958; Schoenfeld Films Distributing Corp., 1960.

SCHONFELD, NORMAN J.: Theater Executive. b. Newark, NJ, June 25, 1934. e. U. of Pennsylvania, B.A., 1955. Captain, U.S.A.F., 1957, sls. rep. Bache & Co. 1963, v.p. Tiger Films, Inc., 1966 founder and president, Wood Theater Group.

SCHORR, DANIEL: Television News Correspondent. b. New York, NY, Aug. 31, 1916. e. City Coll. of New York. Started with various news services and newspapers. Joined CBS in 1953 on special assignment; 1955, reopened CBS bureau in Moscow; 1958–60, roving assignment; 1960–1966, chief German Bureau; 1966–76, chief of Washington Bureau; 1979, Public Radio and TV; 1980, correspondent for Cable News Network.

SCHRADER, PAUL: Writer, Director. b. Grand Rapids, MI, July 22, 1946. m. actress Mary Beth Hurt. e. Columbia U., U. of California at L.A., M.A., cinema. Served as film critic for L.A. Free Press and Cinema 1970–72.
PICTURES INCLUDE: The Yakuza, Taxi Driver, Rolling Thunder, Blue Collar (co-s.p., dir.). Hardcore (s.p., dir.), Old Boyfriends (co-s.p. and exec. prod.), American Gigolo (s.p., dir.), Raging Bull (co-s.p.), Cat People (dir.), Mishima (co-s.p., dir.), Light of Day (dir., s.p.); The Mosquito Coast (s.p.), The Last Temptation of Christ (s.p.), Patty Hearst (dir.).

SCHRODER, RICKY: Actor. b. Staten Island, NY, April 3, 1970. Started modelling while only four months; did many TV commercials before theatrical film debut in The Champ, 1979, at age nine.
PICTURES: The Last Flight of Noah's Ark, The Earthling, Apt Pupil.
TELEVISION: Silver Spoon (series). Movies: Little Lord Fauntleroy, Two Kinds of Love, A Reason to Live, Too Young the Hero, Terror on Highway 91.

SCHROEDER, BARBET: Producer-Director. b. Teheran, Iran, April 26, 1941. e. Sorbonne (philosophy degree). Worked as a jazz tour operator in Europe, a photo-journalist in India and critic for Cahiers du Cinema and L'Air de Paris, 1958–63. 1963: asst. to Jean-Luc Godard on Les Carabiniers. 1964: formed own prod. co. Les Films du Losange. Prod. and acted in Rohmer's La Boulangere de Monceau.
PICTURES AS PRODUCER: La Carriere de Suzanne (short); Mediterrannee; Paris Vu Par; The Collector; My Night at Maud's; Claire's Knee; Chloe in the Afternoon; Out One (co-prod.); The Mother and the Whore (co-prod.); Celine and Julie Go Boating; Flocons D'Or; The Marquise of O; Roulette Chinoise (co-prod.); The American Friend (co-prod.); Le Passe-Montagne; The Rites of Death; Perceval Le Gallois; Le Navire Night; Le Pont du Nord; Mauvaise Conduite.
PICTURES AS DIRECTOR: More (1969); Sing-Song (documentary); La Vallee; General Idi Amin Dada (doc.); Maitresse; Koko, The Talking Gorilla (doc.); Charles Bukowski (50 4-min. videos, 1982–84); Tricheurs; Barfly.

SCHULBERG, BUDD WILSON: Writer. b. New York, NY, Mar. 27, 1914. son of B. P. Schulberg, prod. e. Dartmouth Coll. Publicist, Paramount Pictures, 1931; writer for screen from

1932; addit. dial., A Star Is Born, Nothing Sacred; collab. s.p., Little Orphan Annie; orig. & collab. s.p., Winter Carnival. Weekend for Three; collab. orig., City Without Men; adap. Government Girl. Armed services W.W.II. Author, 3 best-selling novels including The Disenchanted. Harder They Fall; story, s.p. On the Waterfront (Acad. Award & Writers Guild Award, 1954), Face in the Crowd, Wind Across the Everglades. Recent books: Everything That Moves (novel), Moving Pictures: Memories of a Hollywood Prince; play and TV production of What Makes Sammy Run? Teleplay: A Question of Honor, A Table at Ciro's, and documentary, Joe Louis: For All Time (1985—Cine Golden Eagle). Non-fiction books; Writers in America, Swan Watch; Loser and Still Champion: Muhammad Ali.

SCHULTZ, MICHAEL: Director, Producer. b. Milwaukee, WI, Nov. 10, 1938. e. U. of Wisconsin, Marquette U. Theatre includes Kongi's Harvest; Does a Tiger Wear a Necktie?; Every Night When the Sun Goes Down; etc.
PICTURES: Director: Cooley High; Car Wash; Greased Lightning; Which Way Is Up?; Sgt. Pepper's Lonely Hearts Club Band; Scavenger Hunt; Carbon Copy; Bustin' Loose; The Last Dragon; Krush Groove, Disorderlies (prod., dir.).
TELEVISION: To Be Young, Gifted and Black; Ceremonies in Dark Old Men; Benny's Place; For Us The Living; The Jerk, Too; Fade Out—The Erosion of Black Images in the Media (documentary), Rock 'n' Roll Mom.

SCHULMAN, JOHN A.: Executive. b. Yale U.; law degree from Boalt Hall, U. of California, Berkeley, 1972. Founding partner in Beverly Hills law firm, Weissmann, Wolff, Bergman, Coleman & Schulman in 1981 after nine years with firm of Kaplan, Livingston, Goodwin, Berkowitz & Selvin. Joined Warner Bros. 1984 as v.p. & gen. counsel, reporting to Barry Meyer, exec. v.p.

SCHUMACHER, JOEL: Writer, Director. b. New York, NY, 1939. Art dir. & costume designer before turning to writing scripts.
PICTURES: Writer: Car Wash, Sparkle, The Wiz. Director: The Incredible Shrinking Woman; D.C. Cab (also s.p.); St. Elmo's Fire (also s.p.), The Lost Boys, Cousins.
TELEVISION: Writer, Director: Virginia Hill; Amateur Night at the Dixie Bar & Grill; Music video Devil Inside for rock group INXS (dir.).

SCHUMAN, EDWARD L.: Executive. b. Lisbon, CT, Sept. 3, 1916. e. Wayne U., 1932–34; U. of Michigan, 1934–37. Mathematician, 1937–51, assistant actuary, Detroit City Employees Pension Fund. Pres., Studio Theatre Corp, Detroit, 1951 to 1975; pres., Studio 8 Theatre Corp., Detroit, 1953 to 1975; secy.-treas., Studio New Center Theatre Corp. of Detroit, 1975; v.p. and gen. mgr. Art Theatre Guild, 1954–60; v.p. Rugoff Theatres, N.Y., 1960–63. V.P. and bd. member, Walter Reade Organization 1963–75; executive vice president & partner, Quartet Films 1980–86. Associate producer Broadway plays, Same Time Next Year, The Comedians, Anna Christie, and Asinamali. Assoc. prod. of First Monday in October. Co-prod., Torch Song Trilogy in London.

SCHWAB, SHELLY: Executive. Station mgr., WAGA-TV, Atlanta; various sls. & mgr. posts with CBS. Joined MCA, 1978, becoming exec. v.p., MCA-TV. 1986, appt. pres., MCA TV Enterprises.

SCHWARTZ, BERNARD: Producer. Brought to Hollywood by the late Howard Hughes to watch his film interests; Schwartz teamed with wily. Greg Bautzer to package movie deals for clients. Re-cut number of Buster Keaton's silent movies into documentary anthologies (The Golden Age of Comedy, When Comedy Was King, etc.). Subsequently made TV series, One Step Beyond, followed by The Wackiest Ship in the Army, Miss Teen International specials, etc. Named pres. Joseph M. Schenck Enterprises, for which made Journey to the Center of the Earth, Eye of the Cat, A Cold Wind in August, I Passed for White, The Shattered Room, Trackdown. Presently partnered with Alan Silverman of Essaness Theatres.
PICTURES: Coal Miner's Daughter (prod.), Road Games (exec. prod.) Psycho II (exec. prod.), St. Elmo's Fire (co-exec. prod.).
TELEVISION: Elvis and Me (co-exec. prod.).

SCHWARTZ, LESLIE R.: Exhibitor. b. New York, NY, June 7, 1915; e. Lehigh U., 1937. Entered m.p. ind. with Century Theatres Construction Co., 1937–39; film buyer, Century Theatres, 1940–42; personnel exec. 1942–43; U.S. Army service, 1943–45; with Andrews, Inc., Century Theat. concessions, 1945–48; apptd. gen. theatre mgr. 1948; pres., 1955. Member: Pi Lambda Phi; North Shore Country Club; pres., Metropolitan Motion Picture Assn., 1960–62; pres., 1955–present.

SCHWARY, RONALD L.: Producer. b. Oregon, May 23, 1944. e. U. of Southern California.
PICTURES: California Suite (assoc. prod.); Casey's Shadow (asst. dir.); Ordinary People; Absence of Malice; A Soldier's Story; Batteries Not Included.
TELEVISION: Tour of Duty.

SCHWARZENEGGER, ARNOLD: Actor. b. Graz, Austria, July 30, 1947. m. NBC reporter Maria Shriver. e. U. Wisconsin, B.A. Was Mr. Universe.
PICTURES: Stay Hungry, Pumping Iron, The Villain, Conan the Barbarian, Conan the Destroyer, Terminator, Red Sonja, Commando, Raw Deal, Predator, Running Man, Red Heat, Twins, Sgt. Rock.
TELEVISION: The Jayne Mansfield Story.

SCHYGULLA, HANNA: Actress. b. Kattowitz, Germany, Dec. 25, 1943. Worked with Rainer Werner Fassbinder in Munich's Action Theater; a founder of the "anti-theatre" group.
PICTURES INCLUDE: Love Is Colder Than Death, Gods of the Plague, Rio Das Mortes, Beware of a Holy Whore, The Merchant of Four Seasons, The Bitter Tears of Petra Von Kant, House by the Sea, Jail Bait, Effi Briest, The Marriage of Maria Braun, Berlin Alexanderplatz, Lili Marleen, The Night of Varennes, Passion, A Labor of Love, A Love in Germany, The Future Is a Woman, Forever, Lulu; Miss Arizona.
TELEVISION: (U.S.): Peter the Great, Barnum, Casanova.

SCOFIELD, PAUL: Actor. b. Hurstpierpoint, England, Jan. 21, 1922. Gained greatest fame on London stage in much Shakespeare and modern plays, including Staircase and Desire Under the Elms, I'm Not Rappaport.
PICTURES INCLUDE: That Lady, Carve Her Name with Pride, The Train, A Man for All Seasons (Oscar, 1966), King Lear, Scorpio, A Delicate Balance, 1919, Why the Whales Came.
TELEVISION: (U.S.): Anna Karenina, The Attic: The Hiding of Anne Frank.

SCOLA, ETTORE: Director. b. Treviso, Italy, May 10, 1931. e. U. of Rome. Began career 1947 as journalist; 1950, wrote for radio shows. Began career as script writer 1954; debut as director, 1964. Has directed or co-directed 20 films, all of which he also scripted or co-wrote. Also has written 50 other scripts, mostly comedies, for other directors.
PICTURES: Let's Talk about Women, Economical Crisis, One Sketch, The Archdevil, Will Your Heroes Find Their Friends Who Disappeared so Mysteriously in Africa?, Inspector Pepe, Pizza Triangle, Excuse Me My Name Is Rocco Papaleo, The Greatest Evening of My Life, We All Loved Each Other so Much, Down and Dirty, Signore e Signori Buonanotte, A Special Day, Viva Italia, Chi Si Dice a Roma, The Terrace, Passion of Love, The Night of Varennes, Le Bal, Macaroni, The Family (also co-s.p.), Le Capitain Fracassa, Splendor.

SCORSESE, MARTIN: Writer, Director, Editor. b. New York, NY, Nov. 17, 1942. Began career while film arts student at New York U., doing shorts What's A Nice Girl Like You Doing in a Place Like This? (dir., s.p.), It's Not Just You, Murray and The Big Shave.
PICTURES INCLUDE: Editor and asst. dir.: Woodstock, Medicine Ball Caravan, Elvis. Director: Who's That Knocking at My Door? (and assoc. prod.), Boxcar Bertha, Mean Streets (also co-s.p.), Alice Doesn't Live Here Anymore, Taxi Driver, New York, New York, The Last Waltz (also actor), Raging Bull, King of Comedy, After Hours, The Color of Money, The Last Temptation of Christ, The Grifters, New York Stories, Lost Under Cover.
TELEVISION: Amazing Stories.

SCOTT, GEORGE C.: Actor, Director. b. Wise, VA, Oct. 18, 1927. Served 4 years Marine Corps. e. U. of Missouri, appeared in varsity productions, summer stock, Shakespeare.
THEATRE: Off-Broadway in Richard III, As You Like It, Children of Darkness, Merchant of Venice, Desire Under the Elms, Antony and Cleopatra; Broadway in Comes a Day, The Andersonville Trial, The Wall, The Little Foxes, Plaza Suite, Uncle Vanya, director All God's Chillun Got Wings, Death of a Salesman (dir., actor), Sly Fox, Present Laughter.
PICTURES INCLUDE: The Hanging Tree (debut, 1959), Anatomy of a Murder, The Hustler, List of Adrian Messenger, Dr. Strangelove, The Bible, Flim-Flam Man, Patton (Acad. Award), They Might Be Giants, The Last Run, Hospital, The New Centurions, Oklahoma Crude, The Day of the Dolphin, The Hindenburg, Islands in the Stream, Crossed Swords, Movie Movie, Hardcore, The Changeling, The Formula, Taps, Firestarter.
Director-Actor, Rage; Director-Producer-Actor, The Savage Is Loose.
TELEVISION: Major TV playhouses including DuPont Show of the Month, Playhouse 90, Hallmark Hall of Fame, Kraft Theatre, Omnibus, Armstrong Theatre, Play of the Week, NBC Sunday Showcase, Dow Hour of Great Mysteries, Esso Theatre; East Side, West Side (series); The Crucible, Jane Eyre, The Price, Fear on Trial, Beauty and the Beast; The Andersonville Trial (dir.), A Christmas Carol, China Rose, Choices, The Last Days of Patton, The Murders in the Rue Morgue, Pals, The Ryan White Story. Mini-Series: Mussolini—The Untold Story, Mr. President (series).

SCOTT, GORDON: Actor. r.n. Gordon M. Werschkul. b. Portland, OR, Aug. 3, 1927. e. U. of Oregon. U.S. Army, 1944–47; then

Sco-Seg

worked as fireman, cowboy, life guard; signed by Sol Lesser Prod. for role of Tarzan; debut in Tarzan's Hidden Jungle (1955); since in: Tarzan and the Lost Safari, Tarzan's Greatest Adventure, The Tramplers.

SCOTT, GORDON L. T.: Producer. b. Edinburgh, Scotland, January 3, 1920. e. George Watson's Boys Coll. Served H.M. Forces 1939–46. Ent. m.p. ind. 1946 as 3rd asst. dir. with Ealing Studios. 1948: 1st asst. dir. on Passport to Pimlico, Train of Events; joined Associated British 1949 and worked on The Dancing Years, The Franchise Affair, Laughter in Paradise, Angels One Five, Isn't Life Wonderful, Will Any Gentleman, Rob Roy; 1953 prod. man. The Weak and the Wicked, It's Great To Be Young, The Dam Busters; 1956 appt. production exec. asst.; prod. Look Back in Anger, Sands of the Desert, Petticoat Pirates, The Pot Carriers, The Punch & Judy Man, Crooks in Cloisters, Forbush and the Penguins, Voices, The Maids, Snow Children, Out of Season, Hedda, The Abbess. Left Associated British 1969. Currently free-lance. Recent Prods: Spectre Hanover Street, Friend or Foe, Tightrope to Terror, Lace, Haunters of the Deep, Out of the Darkness.
TELEVISION: (Prod): International Detective Series, The Avengers, Pathfinders, The Maids, Snow Children, A Man Called Intrepid, Undying Love, The Eye of the Yemanja.

SCOTT, J.C.: Executive. e. U. of California at L.A. Worked as prod. asst. on The Waltons and prod. coordinator for America at the Movies; two years at Intl. Creative Mgt. She joined Edward S. Feldman Co. at 20th-Fox as dir. of creative affairs; then v.p. of creative affairs for Marvin Worth Prods. Left to join Walt Disney Pictures 1983 as exec. asst. to Richard Berger, pres. 1984, promoted to v.p., m.p. prod. Assoc. prod.: The Sender.

SCOTT, MARTHA: Actress. b. Jamesport, September 22, 1916. e. U. of Michigan. In little theatres over U.S.; summer stock N.Y.; on radio with Orson Welles; Broadway debut Our Town (1938), film debut in Our Town, 1940 (Oscar nom.). Theater producer since 1968 with Henry Fonda and Alfred De Liagre at Kennedy Center and on Bdwy (Time of Your Life, First Monday in October).
PICTURES INCLUDE: Cheers for Miss Bishop, They Dare Not Love, One Foot in Heaven, In Old Oklahoma; Hi Diddle Diddle; So Well Remembered, When I Grow Up, Desperate Hours, Ben Hur, Ten Commandments, Airport 1975, Turning Point, Doin' Time on Planet Earth.
PLAYS INCLUDE: Soldier's Wife, Voice of the Turtle, The Number, Male Animal, Remarkable Mr. Pennypacker, Forty-Second Cousin.
TELEVISION: Beulah Land, Adam, Father Figure, Charleston, The Word, Murder She Wrote, Hotel.

SCOTT, MORTON W.: Executive. b. San Francisco, CA, Jan. 17. e. Stanford U. Pres., Studio City Television Productions, Inc.

SCOTT, RIDLEY: Director. Producer. b. South Shields, Northumberland, Eng., 1939. Brother of director Tony Scott. e. Royal College of Art, London. Joined newly formed Film Sch. First film: Boy on Bicycle. Won design scholarship in NY. Returned to London and joined BBC as set designer (Z-Cars, The Informers series). Directed almost 3,000 commercials in 18 years.
PICTURES: The Duellists, Alien, Blade Runner, Legend, Someone to Watch Over Me (also exec. prod.), Black Rain.

SCOTT, TONY: Director. Began career in TV commercials, being partnered with his brother Ridley in prod. co. Winner of numerous Clios, Gold & Silver Lions, and other awards. Entered m.p. industry 1972, directing half-hr. film, One of the Missing, for British Film Inst. and Loving Memory, 1-hr. feature for Albert Finney.
PICTURES: The Hunger, Top Gun, Beverly Hills Cop II, Revenge.

SCOTT, WALTER M.: Set decorator. b. Cleveland, OH, Nov. 7, 1906. e. U. of Southern California, 1929; Chouinard Sch. of Art. Interior decorator, Fred B. Martin Co., 1929–30, asst. mgr., United Studios, 1930–31; joined Fox Film Corp., 1931; asst. set decorator, 1932; set decorator 1933; set decorator, 20th Century-Fox, 1935; supervising set decorator, 1952–72. Now consultant decorator for Fox.
PICTURES INCLUDE: Twenty-one Academy nominations—6 Oscars for Robe, King and I, Diary of Anne Frank, Cleopatra, Fantastic Voyage, Hello, Dolly. On Board of Governors of the Academy of Motion Picture Arts and Sciences 1968–76, 1980–81, 1981–85.

SCULLY, JOE: Talent Executive, Casting Director, Producer. b. Kearney, NJ, March 1, 1926. e. Goodman Memorial Theatre of the Art Inst. of Chicago, 1946. m. Penelope Gillette. Daughter, Samantha. Acted until 1951. CBS-TV, N.Y. Casting Dir., Danger You Are There, Omnibus, The Web, 1951–56. 1956–60, CBS-TV, Associate Prod., Studio One, Dupont Show of the Month, Playhouse 90. 1962–64, CBS Stations Div. KNXT, Producer, Repertoire Workshop. 1965–70 Casting Dir. 20th Century-Fox Films. 1970–74 Independent Casting

Director. 1974–75 Universal TV, Casting Dir. 1975, NBC-TV Manager, Casting & Talent. 1978, Re-established Joe Scully-Casting, independent service to the industry. 1983, casting director, Walt Disney Pictures.
PICTURES INCLUDE: Hello Dolly, In Like Flint, Valley of the Dolls, Planet of the Apes, The Flim-Flam Man, Sounder, Lady Sings the Blues, Play It as It Lays, The Stone Killer, Parallax View, Lifeguard, Man in the Glass Booth, Middle Age Crazy, Death Wish II.
TELEVISION: Peyton Place, Room 222, Pilots: Julia, The Ghost & Mrs. Muir. 1970, Joe Scully Casting, Indep., The Bill Cosby Show, 1971: TV Feature, Thief, Missiles of October, Earth II; Series, Search, Bonanza, Nichols, Snoop Sisters, Columbo, Switch, McMillan & Wife, Tales of the Unexpected, Gone are the Days (Disney Channel, 1983).

SEALEY, PETER S.: Executive. b. Aug. 26, 1940. e. U. of Florida, B.S., economics; Yale U. Graduate Sch., master of industrial admin. Joined Coca-Cola Co.. 1969; named v.p., mgr. of mktg. planning dept., 1976–79. 1979–82, v.p. & mktg. dir. of The Wine Spectrum, Coca-Cola subsidiary. 1982, elected v.p. of Coca-Cola and named mgr. of corporate mktg. operations. 1986, named exec. v.p., Columbia Pictures Industries: then pres. of mktg. & dist., Columbia Pictures. 1987, named pres. & COO, Coca-Cola Telecommunications.

SECOMBE, SIR HARRY, C.B.E.: Singer, Comedian, Actor. b. Swansea, Wales, Sept. 8, 1921. m.p. debut, Penny Points to Paradise, 1951; awarded, C.B.E., 1963. 1963–64: London stage starring in Pickwick. 1965: same role New York stage. 1967–68, The Four Musketeers; 1975, The Plumber's Progress.
PICTURES INCLUDE: Forces Sweetheart, Down Among the Z Men, Trilby, Davy, Jet Storm, Oliver, The Bed Sitting Room, Song of Norway, Rhubarb, Doctor in Trouble, The Magnificent Seven Deadly Sins, Sunstruck.
TELEVISION: Numerous appearances, incl. own series: Secombe and Friends, The Harry Secombe Show, Secombe with Music. Also special version, Pickwick. Presenter of Tyne Tees TV's Highway since 1983. Author of Twice Brightly, Goon for Lunch, Katy and the Nurgla, Welsh Fargo, Goon Abroad, The Harry Secombe Diet Book, Harry Secombe's Highway, The Highway Companion.

SEAGROVE, JENNY: Actress. b. Kuala Lumpur. Stage debut 1979. Early TV: The Brack Report, The Woman in White, Diana. Recent stage: Jane Eyre.
PICTURES INCLUDE: Local Hero, Savage Islands, A Shocking Accident, Tattoo, The Sign of Four, Appointment With Death, A Chorus of Disapproval.
TELEVISION: A Woman of Substance, Hold The Dream, In Like Flynn, Killer, Lucy Walker.

SEGAL, GEORGE: Actor. b. New York, NY, Feb. 13, 1934. m. Linda Rogoff. e. Columbia U., B.A., 1955. Worked as janitor, ticket-taker, soft-drink salesman, usher and under-study at N.Y.'s Circle in the Square theatre. Acting debut: Downtown Theatre's revival of Don Juan.
THEATER: 1956 revival: The Iceman Cometh, N.Y. Shakespeare Festival's Antony and Cleopatra, Leave It to Jane, The Premise (satiric improvisational revue), Rattle of a Simple Man, The Knack, Requiem for a Heavyweight.
Formed a nightclub singing act with Patricia Scott. Record album of ragtime songs and banjo music: The Yama, Yama Man. Dir. debut: Bucks County Playhouse prod. Scuba Duba.
TELEVISION: Death of a Salesman, Of Mice and Men, The Desperate Hours, The Cold Room, The Zany Adventures of Robin Hood, Not My Kid, Many Happy Returns, Take Five (series), Murphy's Law (series), Four Minute Mile.
PICTURES INCLUDE: The Young Doctors (1961), The Longest Day, Act One, The New Interns, Invitation to A Gunfighter, Ship of Fools, King Rat, The Lost Command, Who's Afraid of Virginia Woolf? (Acad. Award nom.), The Quiller Memorandum, The St. Valentine's Day Massacre, Bye Bye Braverman, No Way to Treat a Lady, The Southern Star, The Bridge at Remagen, The Girl Who Couldn't Say No, Loving, The Owl and the Pussycat, Where's Poppa?, Born to Win, Hot Rock, A Touch of Class, Blume in Love, The Terminal Man, California Split, The Black Bird, Russian Roulette, The Duchess and the Dirtwater Fox, Fun with Dick and Jane, Rollercoaster, Who Is Killing the Great Chefs of Europe?, Lost and Found, The Last Married Couple in America, Carbon Copy, Stick, All's Fair, Daddy's Home.

SEGAL, MAURICE: Publicist. b. New York, NY, July 22, 1921. e. City Coll. of New York, 1937–41. Entered m.p. ind., adv. dept., 20th Fox, 1941–42; U.S. Army 1942–46; feature writer, pub. dept., 20th Fox, April, 1946; asst. to dir., adv., pub., Century Circuit, 1947; press book dept., Paramount, 1949; trade press rep. 1950; trade press rep. RKO Radio, Nov. 1952; res. to join Richard Condon-Kay Norton, publicists, May, 1953; adv., pub. dept., U-I. Sept. 1954; asst. pub. mgr., United Artists Apr. 1957. Hollywood pub.-exploit., coordinator, 1958; exec. in chg. of M.P. press dept., Universal City Studios, 1966; West Coast adv.-pub. dir., National Gen. Pictures, 1971; Pres., Maurice E. Segal Co., 1974; dir., West Coast operations, Charles Schlai-

276

fer & Co., 1976; v.p., Max Youngstein Enterprises, 1979; exec. v.p., Taft Intl. Pictures, 1980; pres. Maurice E. Segal Co., 1982.

SEIDELMAN, ARTHUR ALLAN: Director, Producer, Writer. b. New York, NY, October 11. e. Whittier Coll., B.A.; UCLA, M.A. Former staff member, Repertory Theatre of Lincoln Center and Phoenix Theatre, NY.
  THEATER: The Beautiful People (dir., prod., L.A., 1960); The Awakening (dir., prod.); Director: Hamp, Ceremony of Innocence, The Justice Box, Billy, Vieux Carre, The World of My America, Awake and Sing; The Four Seasons, Inherit the Wind, as well as numerous regional prods. and national tours.
  PICTURES: Children of Rage (1978, dir., s.p.); Echoes, The Caller.
  TELEVISION: Ceremony of Innocence; Family; Magnum, P.I.; Murder She Wrote; Trapper John M.D.; Paper Chase; Knots Landing; Bay City Blues. Movies: Which Mother is Mine? A Special Gift; Schoolboy Father; A Matter of Time; I Think I'm Having a Baby; Sin of Innocence; Kate's Secret, Poker Alice; The People Across the Lake.

SEIDELMAN, SUSAN: Director. b. near Philadelphia, PA, Dec.11, 1952. e. Drexel Univ. B.A. Worked at a UHF television station in Phila., NYU film school M.F.A. Debut: 28-min. student film And You Act Like One Too. Then dir. Deficit (short, funded by AFI), and Yours Truly, Andrea G. Stern.
  PICTURES INCLUDE: Smithereens (dir., prod., co-s.p.; 1st Amer. indep. feature accepted into competition at Cannes Film Fest., 1982); Desperately Seeking Susan; Making Mr. Right, Cookie.

SELBY, DAVID: Actor. b. Morganstown, WV. Feb. 5, 1941. e. U. of West Virginia. Acted in outdoor dramas in home state and did regional theatre elsewhere. Was ass't. instructor in lit. at Southern Illinois U.
  PICTURES INCLUDE: Up the Sandbox, Super Cops, Lady in Blue, Night of Dark Shadows, Rich Kids, Rich and Famous.
  TELEVISION: Series: Dark Shadows, Flamingo Road, Falcon Crest. Movies: Washington: Behind Closed Doors, Telethon, Family, King of the Olympics: The Lives and Loves of Avery Brundage.

SELF, WILLIAM: Producer. b. Dayton, OH, June 21, 1921. e. U. of Chicago, 1943. Prod.-dir., Schlitz Playhouse of Stars, 1952–56; prod., The Frank Sinatra Show, 1957; exec. prod., CBS-TV, The Twilight Zone, Hotel De Paree. 1960–61 exec. prod., 20th Century-Fox TV. Hong Kong, Adventures in Paradise, Bus Stop, Follow the Sun, Margie; v.p. in chg. of prod., 20th Century-Fox TV, 1962; exec. v.p., 1964. Pres., FOX TV 1969; v.p. 20th Century Fox Film Corp., 1969; pres. of William Self Productions, Inc., partner, FrankovicCPSelf Productions; 1975; vice-pres., programs, Hollywood CBS Television Network, 1976; 1977, v.p. motion pictures for television and miniseries, CBS Television Network; 1982, pres., CBS Theatrical Films. In 1985, pres., William Self Prods. in association with CBS Prods.

SELIG, ROBERT WILLIAM: Exhibitor. b. Cripple Creek, CO. e. U. of Denver, 1932, B.A.; doctorate, 1959. Consultant, Pacific Theatres. Lifetime Trustee, U. of Denver. Member Kappa Sigma, Omicron Delta Kappa, Beta Gamma Sigma; Nat'l Methodist Church Foundation; Pres., Theatre Association of California; board of directors Los Angeles Chamber of Commerce; chm., ShoWest Conventions.

SELLECK, TOM: Actor. b. Detroit, MI, Jan. 29, 1945. e. U. of Southern California.
  PICTURES: Myra Breckenridge, Seven Minutes, Daughters of Satan, Midway, The Washington Affair, Coma, High Road to China, Lassiter, Runaway, Three Men and a Baby, Her Alibi.
  TELEVISION: Series: Bracken's World, The Young and the Restless, The Rockford Files, Magnum, P.I. (Emmy, 1984), Movies: Countdown at the Superbowl, The Sackets (miniseries), Gypsy Warriors, Boston and Kilbride, The Concrete Cowboys, Divorce Wars—A Love Story, Returning Home.

SELLERS, ARLENE: Producer. b. Sept. 7, 1921. e. U. of CA at Berkeley, BA, LLB, JD. In partnership as attorneys in L.A. for 20 years with Alex Winitsky before they turned to financing and later production of films.
  PICTURES INCLUDE: (co-prod. with Winitsky) End of the Game, The Seven-Per-Cent Solution, Cross of Iron, Night Calls, Silver Bears, Cuba, Blue Skies Again, Scandalous, Swing Shift, Bad Medicine.

SELTZER, ROGER: Executive. b. Chicago, IL, Oct. 7, 1937. e. Indiana U., B.S., 1958; Harvard Graduate Sch. of Business, M.B.A., 1961. Joined ASI Market Research as v.p., 1964; named exec. v.p. 1974. Now v.p., market research, Universal Pictures.

SELTZER, WALTER: Executive. b. Philadelphia, PA, Nov. 7, 1914. e. U. of Pennsylvania. Publicity mgr. for Warner Bros. Theatres, Philadelphia; Fox West Coast Theatres; to Hollywood with MGM 1936–39; Columbia, 1940–41. Enlisted U.S.

Marine Corp., 1941–44. Pub. dir., Hal Wallis, 1945–54; v.p. in chg. adv & pub., Hecht-Lancaster Orgn., Feb., 1954–55; assoc. prod., The Boss; partner, Glass-Seltzer, pub. rel. firm; v.p. & exec. prod, Pennebaker Production. 1982, v.p., M.P. & TV Fund. Pres., WSP Inc.
  PICTURES INCLUDE: One-Eyed Jacks, Shake Hands With the Devil, Paris Blues, The Naked Edge, Man in the Middle, Wild Seed, War Lord, Beau Geste, Will Penny, Number One, Darker Than Amber, The Omega Man, Sky-jacked, Soylent Green, The Cay, The Last Hard Men.

SEMEL, TERRY: Executive. b. New York, NY, Feb. 24, 1943. e. City Coll. of New York, M.B.A., 1967. Was with C.P.A. accounting firm, 1965–66. Entered ind. with Warner Bros. in 1966 as br. mgr., New York, Cleveland, Los Angeles. Domestic sls. mgr. for CBS—Cinema Center Films, 1971–73. In 1973 joined Buena Vista as v.p., gen. sls. mgr. In 1975 went to Warner Bros. as v.p., gen. sls. mgr. In 1978 named exec. v.p. and chief operating officer. Now pres., WB.

SEMPLE, LORENZO, JR.: Writer.
  PICTURES: Pretty Poison, Marriage of a Young Stockbroker, The Drowning Pool, Three Days of the Condor, King Kong, Hurricane (and exec. prod.), Flash Gordon, Never Say Never Again, Sheena (co-s.p.).
  TELEVISION: Rearview Mirror.

SEN, BACHOO: Producer, Distributor. Entered industry 1950 in India and 1958 in U.K. Director of English Film Co. Ltd., English Film Co. (Exports) Ltd. and English Film Co. (Productions) Ltd. Among 38 features produced: Her Private Hell, Loving Feeling, Love Is a Splendid Illusion, Tenderness, Adam and Nicole, The Intruders. In U.S., Nightmare Weekend. Chairman of Senemedici Inc. and All American Leisure Group Inc.

SENDREY, ALBERT: Music Composer, Arranger, Conductor. b. Chicago, IL, 1921. e. Trinity Coll. Music, London, U. of Southern California, Paris, & Leipzig Conservatories. Winner, Chi. Symphony Orch. prize for First Symphony, 1941; 1948, Reichhold Award Detroit Symph. Orch. for 2nd Symphony. Ohio Sesquicentenn. Award for Overture, Johnny Appleseed, 1953; French libretto: One Act Opera: The Telltale Stones, 1964; arr., Mary Martin at Radio City Music Hall, 1965. Compose, arr., orch. for many plays, films and TV.
  MEMBER: M.P. Academy, ASCAP, CLGA, ASMA, TV Academy.
  BROADWAY: orch., arr.: Peter Pan, Ziegfeld Follies, New Faces, At the Grand, Pink Jungle, The Great Waltz, Turn to the Right.
  PICTURES INCLUDE: Orch: The Yearling, Three Musketeers, Father's Little Dividend, Duchess of Idaho, Royal Wedding, Easy to Love, Great Caruso, American in Paris, Brigadoon, Athena, Finian's Rainbow, Guys and Dolls, Meet Me in Las Vegas, Opposite Sex, High Society, Raintree County, Let's Be Happy, Ride the High Country, Hallelujah Trail, The Hook, The Comancheros, Nevada Smith, The Oscar, Thoroughly Modern Millie, Hello Down There, Private Navy of Sgt. O'Farrell, Hard Times.
  TELEVISION: comp. music: Laramie, Wagon Train, Ben Casey, Wolper Documentaries, Americans Abroad, J. F. Kennedy Anthology; Young Man from Boston, High Chaparral, (collab. with Harry Sukman), Bonanza (with D. Rose), The Monroes, Ken Murray's Hollywood, SWAT (collab. B. de Vorzon), Hard Times, (collab.), Napoleon and Josephine (orch.).

SENECA, JOE: Actor. Has been acting since 1973. In the 1950's was part of a satirical singing group, The Three Riffs performing at a New York club, Le Ruban Bleu. In the 1950s and '60s wrote songs. 1970–73 was a writer for Sesame Street.
  THEATER: The Little Foxes (starring Elizabeth Taylor), Of Mice and Men (starring James Earl Jones), Sizwe Banzi Is Dead (Pittsburgh), Ma Rainey's Black Bottom (Yale Repertory and B'way).
  PICTURES: Kramer vs. Kramer, The Verdict, Silverado, The Evil Men Do, Crossroads, School Daze, The Blob.
  TELEVISION: The Wilma Rudolph Story, Terrible Joe Moran, Solomon Northrup's Odyssey, The House of Dies Drear, Dorothy and Son (Amazing Stories), A Gathering of Old Men.

SERNAS, JACQUES: Actor, Producer. b. Lithuania, July 30, 1925. Became naturalized French citizen, studying medicine in Paris. Was amateur boxer when heard Jean Gabin needed an acting boxer for The Mirror, in which he made professional debut as actor. Has appeared in over 80 films, made in recent years primarily in Italy, now his home.
  PICTURES INCLUDE: Lost Youth, The Golden Salamander, Helen of Troy, Jump into Hell, The First Night, La Dolce Vita, 55 Days in Peking, F.B.I.: Operation Baalbeck (also prod.), Operation Gold in the Balearic Islands (also prod.), Super Fly TNT.
  TELEVISION: The School of the Painters of Paris (prod.

only), The 18th Century Seen Through Its Famous Painters (prod. only), The Red Triangle (Ital. series).

SERPE, RALPH B.: Producer. b. Portland, ME, Dec. 23, 1914. e. Columbia U. Ind. thea. agent, 1936. U.S. Army, Spec. Services, 1942. v.p., Scalera Films, 1946; v.p., Italian Films Export, 1948; U.S. rep., assoc. prod., exec. asst., Dino De Laurentiis, 1952.
PICTURES INCLUDE: War and Peace, Ulysses, The Tempest, Under Ten Flags, Yovanka, Barabbas, The Bible, Drum, The Brinks' Job.

SEVAREID, ERIC: News commentator. b. Velva, ND, Nov. 26, 1912. e. U. of Minnesota, Paris. Started career as reporter: Minneapolis Journal, Paris Herald Tribune, United Press; joined CBS news staff in Paris at outbreak of W.W.II; with CBS radio, TV since; nat. corres; retired 1977.
BOOKS: author: Not So Wild a Dream, In One Ear, Small Sounds in the Night, This is Eric Sevareid.

SEVERINO, JOHN C.: Executive. b. New Haven, CT. e. U. of Connecticut. Joined ABC in 1965 as acct. exec. for WABC-TV; later served in various positions for ABC-TV Spot Sales in N.Y. and Chicago. In 1968 named sls. mgr., WLS-TV, Chicago; promoted to gen. sls. mgr., WXYZ-TV, Detroit, 1969. Returned to Chicago station in 1974 as v.p., gen. mgr. In 1974 named v.p., gen. mgr. of KABC-TV, Los Angeles. In 1981 named pres. of ABC Television.

SEWALL, BARBARA JEAN: Public Relations. b. Holly, CO, Jan. 6. e. Los Angeles City Coll., U. of California at L.A. Pub. dir. & adv. mgr., Saks Fifth Ave., Beverly Hills; owner-publicity agency representing actors and independent production cos. Hollywood Athletic Club; RKO, Samuel Goldwyn Prods., Inc., MGM, Edward Small Prod., Warner Bros., 20th Century-Fox, Lowell Thomas, Cinerama, Wrather Television, VideoTravel.

SEYMOUR, ANNE: Actress. b. New York, NY, Sept. 11, 1909. On many radio programs, including Story of Mary Marlin, Grand Hotel, etc.
PICTURES: All the King's Men, The Whistle at Eaton Falls, Man on Fire, Pollyanna, Desire Under the Elms, Gift of Love, Home from the Hill, Misty, Good Neighbor Sam, Mirage, How To Succeed in Business without Really Trying, Fitzwilly, Stay Away, Joe, Hearts of the West, Big Top Pee-Wee.
TELEVISION: Empire, General Hospital. Movies: I Never Said Goodbye, The Last Survivors, James at 15, Studs Lonigan, The Miracle Worker, Angel on My Shoulder, etc.

SEYMOUR, DAN: Actor. b. Chicago, IL, Feb. 22, 1915. Performer burlesque, nightclubs. Stage, screen and TV actor.
PLAYS: Rain, Amphitryon 38, Room Service, and others.
PICTURES INCLUDE: Casablanca, To Have and Have Not, Confidential Agent, Intrigue, Key Largo, Johnny Belinda, Rancho Notorious, Maru Maru, Glory Alley, Face to Face, The System, Second Chance, Big Heat, Human Desire, Moonfleet, Buster Keaton Story, Sad Sack, Watusi, Return of the Fly, Leader of the Pack, The Mummy, The Way We Were, Soft Touch, Escape from Witch Mountain, Rainbow Island.
TELEVISION: Casablanca, Restless Gun, Perry Mason, Untouchables, Holiday Inn, This Gun for Hire, 77 Sunset Strip, Hawaiian Eye, Get Smart, My Mother The Car, Batman, U.N.C.L.E., Beverly Hillbillies, Voyage to the Bottom of the Sea, My Favorite Martian, Don't Eat the Daisies, The Bob Hope Show, Kojak, The Chase, Barbary Coast, Fantasy Island.

SEYMOUR, JANE: Actress. r.n. Joyce Frankenberg. b. Hillingdon, England, Feb. 15, 1951. Dancer with London Festival Ballet at 13. Theatrical film debut, Live and Let Die, 1973. On Bdwy. in Amadeus (1980).
PICTURES: Oh! What a Lovely War (debut, 1968), The Only Way, Young Winston, Live and Let Die, Sinbad and the Eye of the Tiger, Battlestar Galactica, Oh, Heavenly Dog, Somewhere in Time, Lassiter, The Tunnel, Keys to Freedom.
TELEVISION: Movies: Frankenstein: The True Story, Captains and the Kings, Benny and Barney: Las Vegas Undercover, Seventh Avenue, Killer on Board, The Four Feathers, The Awakening Land, Love's Dark Ride, Dallas Cowboys Cheerleaders, Our Mutual Friend, East of Eden, The Haunting Passion, Dark Mirror, The Sun Also Rises, Obsessed with a Married Woman, Crossings, War and Remembrance, The Woman He Loved, Onassis: The Richest Man in the World, Jack the Ripper.

SEYRIG, DELPHINE: Actress. b. Beirut, Lebanon, 1932. Formal dramatic training in Paris; later at Actors Studio, N.Y.
PICTURES: Pull My Daisy, Last Year in Marienbad, Muriel, La Musica, Accident, Mr. Freedom, Stolen Kisses, Daughters of Darkness, Peau d'Ane, The Discreet Charm of the Bourgeoisie, The Day of the Jackal, The Black Windmill, Aloise, Doll's House, Dear Michael, Le Dernier Cri, India Song, Faces of Love, Le Chemin Perdu, I Sent a Letter to My Love, Le Petit Pommier, Freak Orlando, Le Grain de Sable, Dorian Gray, Sur le Boulevard de la Presse a Scandale, The Golden Eighties, Letters Home, Johanne d'Arc of Mongolia.

SHABER, DAVID: Screenwriter. b. Cleveland, OH. e. Western Reserve U., Yale U., Taught at Allegheny Coll. in speech and drama dept. Contributor to Cosmopolitan, Life, Esquire; had several short stories in O'Henry prize collections. Also wrote dramas (Shake Hands with the Clown, The Youngest Shall Ask, etc.). First screenplay was Such Good Friends for Otto Preminger.
PICTURES INCLUDE: The Last Embrace, The Warriors, Those Lips, Those Eyes, Night Hawks, Rollover.

SHAGAN, STEVE: Writer. b. New York, NY. Oct. 25, 1927. Apprenticed in little theatres, film lab chores, stagehand jobs. Wrote, produced and directed film short, One Every Second; moved to Hollywood in 1959. Was IATSE man, working as grip, stagehand, electrician to support film writing. Was freelance advertising man and publicist; produced Tarzan TV show. In 1968 began writing and producing two-hour films for TV.
PICTURES INCLUDE: Save the Tiger (prod., s.p.-AA nomination—WGA award, best original s.p.), Hustle (s.p.), Voyage of the Damned (co.-s.p.-AA nomination), The Formula (s.p., prod.), Nightwing (co-s.p.), The Sicilian (s.p.).
TELEVISION: Writer-producer: River of Mystery, Spanish Portrait, Sole Survivor, A Step Out of Line, House on Garibaldi Street (s.p.).
BOOKS: Save the Tiger, City of Angels, The Formula, The Circle, The Discovery, Vendetta.

SHALIT, GENE: b. New York, NY, 1932. e. U. of Illinois. Started as freelance writer; joined NBC Radio Network, working on Monitor. Has been book and film critic, sports and general columnist. In January, 1973 replaced Joe Garagiola as featured regular on NBC Today Show.

SHANLEY, JOHN PATRICK: Writer. b. New York, NY, 1950. e. NYU.
THEATER: Danny and the Deep Blue Sea; Savage in Limbo; Dreamer Examines His Pillow; Italian-American Reconciliation.
PICTURES: Five Corners; Moonstruck; The January Man; I Am Angry (short, 1987, dir., s.p.).

SHAPIRO, IRVIN: Executive. Formerly newspaperman; m.p. reviewer; director of national publicity campaigns. Publicity, RKO; active in ind. dist. & in export & import. Now pres., Films Around the World, Inc.; Filmworld Export Corp. which represents leading film producers and distributors throughout the world.

SHAPIRO, JACOB: Executive. b. Harbin, China, Aug. 26, 1928. e. Gakushuin U. (Peers' Sch.), Tokyo, Japan, B.A. Pol. Sci. Joined Columbia Pictures Intl., N.Y., 1961; Japan sales manager, 1961–65; Puerto Rico gen. mgr., 1965–68; appointed Japan and South Korea gen. mgr., Columbia, 1968; from 1970 became Columbia supv. for Philippines as well as gen. mgr. Japan and South Korea until Feb. 1981; from 1981 v.p. Far East and Australia, Twentieth Century Fox, Los Angeles.

SHAPIRO, KEN: Producer, Director, Writer, Actor. b. New Jersey, 1943. e. Bard Coll. Was child actor on TV and teacher in Brooklyn before opening "world's first video theatre" in East Village of Manhattan: Channel One, 90 mins. of TV lampoons and original material shown on TV monitors to live audience. Took 16 mm material on college dates with success, culminating in feature film: The Groove Tube, 1974.
PICTURE: Modern Problems (co-s.p., dir.).

SHAPIRO, ROBERT W.: Producer. b. Brooklyn, NY, March 1, 1938. e. U. of Southern CA. Joined William Morris Agency, Inc., 1958. dir. and head of motion picture dept., William Morris Agency (UK) Ltd., 1969; man. dir., 1970. 1974 vice president, head int'l. m.p. dept., William Morris, Inc. In March, 1977 joined Warner Bros. as exec. v.p. in chg. of worldwide production. 1981, named WB pres., theatrical production div. Resigned 1983 to produce films.
PICTURES: Pee-Wee's Big Adventure (prod.); Empire of the Sun (exec. prod.); Arthur 2 On the Rocks (prod.).

SHARAFF, IRENE: Costume Designer. b. 1910. Long career on stage and in films. Winner of Tony, two Donaldson Awards, five Academy Awards and 16 Oscar nominations. Has worked on more than 30 motion pictures.
PICTURES INCLUDE: Meet Me in St. Louis, Hello, Dolly, Guys and Dolls, Call Me Madam, Yolanda and the Thief, Brigadoon, Porgy and Bess, Flower Drum Song, The Best Years of Our Lives, The Taming of the Shrew, A Star is Born (1954), Mommie Dearest. Oscar winners include An American in Paris, The King and I, West Side Story, Cleopatra, Who's Afraid of Virginia Woolf?.

SHARE, MICHAEL: Executive. Began career with Paramount Pictures 1974 as booker in Indianapolis. 1975–76 appt. salesman; 1976–77 sls. mgr. in Philadelphia; 1977, Cincinnati branch mgr.; 1980, Chicago branch mgr. 1985, promoted to v.p., eastern div.

SHARIF, OMAR: Actor. r.n. Michel Shahoub. b. Alexandria, Egypt, April 10, 1932. e. Victoria Coll., Cairo.; pres. of College Dramatic Society. m. Faten Hamama. Starred in 21 Egyptian and two French films prior to Lawrence of Arabia.
PICTURES INCLUDE: Ciel d' enfer (1953, debut), The Blazing Sun, Goha, Lawrence of Arabia, Ghengis Khan, The Fall of the Roman Empire, The Yellow Rolls-Royce, Behold a Pale Horse, Doctor Zhivago, Night of the Generals, More Than a Miracle, McKenna's Gold, Che!, Funny Girl, The Appointment, Mayerling, The Horsemen, The Burglars, The Tamarind Seed, The Mysterious Island of Captain Nemo, Juggernaut, Funny Lady, Crime and Passion, The Baltimore Bullet, Green Ice, The Possessed, Paradise Calling, The Blue Pyramids, Keys to Freedom.
TELEVISION: The Far Pavilions, Pleasure Palace, Peter the Great, Harem, Anastasia, The Mysteries of the Pyramids Live (host).

SHARKEY, RAY: Actor. b. Red Hook, Brooklyn, NY, 1952. Began on TV, guesting in Kojak, Police Story, Barney Miller, etc. Also performed on stage in Los Angeles. Theatrical movie debut in Hot Tomorrows in 1976.
PICTURES: Trackdown, Stunts, Paradise Alley, Who'll Stop the Rain?, Heartbeat, Willie and Phil, The Idolmaker, Love and Money, Some Kind of Hero, No Mercy, Wise Guys, Private Investigations, Act of Piracy, Wired, Scenes From the Class Struggle in Beverly Hills.
TELEVISION: Behind Enemy Lines, Wiseguy (series).

SHARP, ALAN: Writer. b. Glasgow, Scotland. Writes western screenplays.
PICTURES INCLUDE: The Hired Hand, Ulzana's Raid, Billy Two Hats, Night Moves, The Osterman Weekend, Little Treasure (also dir.), Freeway.
TELEVISION: Coming Out of the Ice.

SHARP, DON: Writer, director. b. Hobart, Tasmania, Australia, 1922. Early career as actor in Australia. Ent. m.p. ind. in England with Group Three as screenwriter, 1951. Began directing 1955 with doc. children's films, 2nd unit work and filmed TV series.
PICTURES INCLUDE: Kiss of the Vampire, It's All Happening, Devil Ship Pirates, Witchcraft, Those Magnificent Men in Their Flying Machines (2nd unit), Curse of the Fly, The Face of Fu Manchu, Rasputin—The Mad Monk, Our Man in Marrakesh, The Brides of Fu Manchu, Rocket to the Moon, Taste of Excitement, The Violent Enemy, Puppet on a Chain, Psychomania, Dark Places, Callan, Hennessy, The Four Feathers, The 39 Steps, Bear Island.
TELEVISION: Ghost Squad, The Champions, The Avengers, House of Horror, Q.E.D., A Woman of Substance, Tusitala, Hold the Dream.

SHATNER, WILLIAM: Actor. b. Montreal, Quebec, Mar. 22, 1931. e. McGill U. Toured Canada in various stock, repertory companies. Bdwy. debut, Tamburlaine the Great, 1956.
PICTURES INCLUDE: The Brothers Karamazov, Judgment at Nuremberg, The Explosive Generation, The Intruder, The Outrage, Big Hot Mama, Dead of Night, The Devil's Rain, Kingdom of the Spiders, Star Trek—The Motion Picture, The Kidnapping of the President, Star Trek II: The Wrath of Khan, Airplane II: The Sequel, Star Trek III: The Search for Spock, Star Trek IV: The Voyage Home, Star Trek V (also dir., orig. story).
TELEVISION: Star Trek (series), The Statesman, The Bastard, Disaster on the Coastline, The Baby Sitter, Andersonville, T.J. Hooker (series), Secrets of a Married Man, North Beach and Rawhide, Top Flight (host), Broken Angel, Voice of the Planet (mini-series).

SHAVELSON, MELVILLE: Writer, Director. b. Brooklyn, NY, April 1, 1917. e. Cornell U., 1937, A.B. Radio writer: We The People, Bicycle Party, 1937, Bob Hope Show, 1938–43. Screen writer; apptd. prod., Warner Bros. 1951. Conceived for TV: Make Room for Daddy, My World and Welcome To It. Author: book, How To Make a Jewish Movie. Lualda, The Great Houdinis, The Eleventh Commandment, Ike. Pres., Writers Guild of America, West, 1969–71, 1979–81, 1985–87; Pres., Writers Guild Foundation 1978–88.
PICTURES INCLUDE: Princess & the Pirate, Wonder Man, Kid From Brooklyn, Sorrowful Jones, It's a Great Feeling, Daughter of Rosie O'Grady, Always Leave Them Laughing, Where There's Life, On Moonlight Bay, I'll See You in My Dreams, Room For One More, April in Paris, Trouble Along the Way, Living It Up, Seven Little Foys, Beau James, Houseboat, It Started in Naples, The Five Pennies, On the Double, The Pigeon That Took Rome, A New Kind of Love, Cast a Giant Shadow, Yours Mine and Ours, The War Between Men and Women, Mixed Company.
TV FEATURES: The Legend of Valentino, The Great Houdinis, Ike, The Other Woman, Deceptions; Academy Awards, 1988 (writer).

SHAVER, HELEN: Actress. b. St. Thomas, Ontario, Canada, Feb. 24, 1951. e. Banff Sch. of Fine Arts, Alberta. Worked on stage

and screen in Canada before coming to Los Angeles 1978. Theatrical film debut Starship Invasions, 1977.
PICTURES: Christina; High-Ballin'; The Amityville Horror; In Praise of Older Women; Who Has Seen the Wind; Gas; The Osterman Weekend; Harry Tracy; Best Defense; Desert Hearts; The Color of Money; The Believers; Bethune: The Making of a Hero, Walking After Midnight, The Tree of Hands.
TELEVISION: Series: United States, Jessica Novak. Movies: Many Happy Returns, The Park is Mine, Countdown To Looking Glass, Between Two Brothers, Lovey: Circle of Children II, Ray Bradbury Theater III, No Blame.

SHAWN, WALLACE: Playwright, Actor. b. New York, NY, Nov. 12, 1943. Son of former New Yorker editor William Shawn. e. Harvard; Oxford U. Taught English in India on a Fulbright scholarship.
PLAYS: Our Late Night (1975, Obie Award); The Mandrake (translation); A Thought in Three Parts; Marie and Bruce; The Hotel Play; The Music Teacher; Ode to Napoleon Bonaparte; Aunt Dan and Lemon.
THEATER: Actor: The Mandrake (1977); The Master and Margerita; Chinchilla; The First Time; Ode to Napoleon Bonaparte.
PICTURES: All That Jazz (1979); Manhattan; Starting Over; Atlantic City; The First Time; Simon; A Little Sex; My Dinner With Andre (also s.p.); Deal of the Century; Lovesick; Strange Invaders; Saigon—Year of the Cat; Crackers; The Bostonians; Heaven Help Us; The Hotel New Hampshire; Micki and Maude; Head Office; The Bedroom Window; Prick Up Your Ears; Nice Girls Don't Explode; The Princess Bride; The Moderns; Scenes From the Class Struggle in Beverly Hills.

SHAYE, ROBERT: Executive. b. Detroit, MI, Mar. 4, 1939. e. U. of Michigan, B.B.A.; Columbia U. Law. At 15 wrote, prod. dir. training film for father's supermarket staff. Later won first prize in Society of Cinematologists' Rosenthal Competition (best m.p. by American dir. under 25). Wrote, prod., dir., edited short films, trailers and TV commercials, including award-winning shorts, Image and On Fighting Witches (prod., dir.). Founded New Line Cinema 1967. Pres. & CEO, New Line Cinema.
PICTURES: Prod./exec. prod.: Stunts, XTRO, Alone in the Dark, The First Time, Polyester, Critters, Quiet Cool, My Demon Lover, A Nightmare on Elm Street (parts 1,2,3,4), The Hidden, Jack in the Box, Stranded, Critters 2, Hairspray.

SHAYNE, ROBERT: Actor. b. Yonkers, NY. On N.Y. stage, on screen 1943 in Shine on Harvest Moon.
PLAYS: Claudia, Night of January 16th, Both Your Houses, Yellow Jack, Whiteoaks, Without Love, etc.—70 in all
PICTURES INCLUDE: Mr. Skeffington, Christmas in Connecticut, Welcome Stranger, Neanderthal Man, North by Northwest, The Arrangement, Tora Tora Tora, Barefoot Executive, Million Dollar Duck—96 in all.
TELEVISION: Marcus Welby, M.D., Doris Day Show, S.W.A.T., Emergency, Superman Series—350 segments in all.

SHEA, JOHN: Actor. b. Conway, NH, April 14, 1949. Raised in MA. e. Bates Coll., ME; Yale Drama School (1970), graduated as a director, 1973. Worked as asst. dir. Chelsea Westside Theater; taught part-time at Pratt Inst.
THEATER: Yentl (debut 1975, Off-Bdwy and Bdwy), Sorrows of Stephen, The Master and Margerita, Romeo and Juliet (Circle in the Sq.); With Manhattan Theatre Club: American Days (Drama Desk Award), The Dining Room (Obie Award); End of the World; The Normal Heart (London, 1987).
PICTURES: It's My Turn (debut, but scenes cut), Hussy, Missing, Windy City, Honeymoon, A New Life, Unsettled Land, Stealing Home.
TELEVISION: The Nativity, The Last Convertible, Kennedy, Hitler's SS: Portrait in Evil, Family Reunion, Coast to Coast (BBC), A Case of Deadly Force, The Impossible Spy, Baby M.

SHEAFF, DONALD J.: Executive. b. Oct. 23, 1925. e. U.of California at L.A., 1948; Pierce Coll., 1957. Served 4 yrs. during W.W.II in Navy Air Corps in South Pacific. 1946, joined Technicolor Motion Picture Div. in supervisory capacity; 1957, lab. supervisor, Lookout Mountain Air Force Station, handling Top Secret film for Air Force and Atomic Energy Commission. Est. and org. the installation of Vandenberg Air Force Base Lab. facilities, which Technicolor designed. 1961 joined Panacolor Corp., 1963; joined Pacific Title and Art Studio in charge of color control for special effects and titles. Returned to Technicolor Corp. 1966, app't. Plant Mgr. of Television Div., Oct. 1966, V.P. & Gen. Mgr. of the Television Div., July, 1973 appt v.p. & gen. mgr., Motion Picture Division; 1976; mgr., special visual effects, Universal City Studios. Member: SMPTE, Nat'l Academy of Television Arts & Sciences. Has conducted scientific seminars for SMPTE.

SHEARER, HARRY: Writer, Actor. b. Los Angeles, CA, 1944. e. UCLA (pol. science); grad. work in urban gov., Harvard. At 7 appeared on The Jack Benny Show. Worked as freelance

journalist for Newsweek, L.A. Times and publ. articles in New West, L.A. Magazine and Film Comment. Also taught Eng. and social studies in high school and worked in CA State Legislature in Sacramento. Founding mem. The Credibility Gap, co-wrote, co-prod. and performed on comedy group's albums (A Great Gift Idea, The Bronze Age of Radio). Co-wrote, co-prod. Albert Brooks' album A Star is Bought. Host of Le Show, L.A. radio prog. Joined Saturday Night Live (1979–80).
PICTURES: Actor: Abbott and Costello Go to Mars (debut, 1953); Cracking Up; Real Life (also co-s.p.); Animalympics; The Fish That Saved Pittsburgh, Serial; One-Trick Pony; The Right Stuff; This is Spinal Tap (also co-s.p.); Plain Clothes.
TELEVISION: Fernwood 2-Night (creative consultant). Specials: Likely Stories; It's Just TV; Paul Shaffer: Viva Shaf Vegas; Comedy Hour.

SHEEDY, ALLY: Actress. b. New York, NY, June 13, 1962. e. U. of Southern California. Daughter of literary agent Charlotte Sheedy. At age 12 wrote children's book, She Was Nice to Mice; later pieces in The New York Times, The Village Voice, Ms. Began acting in TV commercials at 15. Film debut in Bad Boys, 1983.
PICTURES: WarGames, Oxford Blues, The Breakfast Club, St. Elmo's Fire, Twice in a Lifetime, Blue City, Short Circuit, Maid to Order, Heart of Dixie, Rapid Fire.
TELEVISION: Episodes of Hill Street Blues. Movies: Homeroom, Splendor in the Grass, Best Little Girl in the World, Day the Loving Stopped, The Violation of Sarah McDavid, We Are the Children.

SHEELER, MARK: Actor. r.n. Morris Sheeler. b. New York, NY, April 24, 1923. e. U. of California at L.A. Disc jockey 1942–48. Air Corp. Photog. during war. Voices, animated cartoons, commercials. M.p. debut in Born Yesterday.
PLAYS: Hillbarn Thea., Calif.: Harvey, The Happy Time, Time of Your Life, Amphitryon 38, Send Me No Flowers, The Gazebo, 3 Men on a Horse, etc.
PICTURES INCLUDE: The High and the Mighty, Blood Alley, It Came From Beneath the Sea, Apache Warrior, Tank Battalion, P.O.W., Book of Israel, Why Must I Die?, Irma La Douce, The Raven, Elmer Gantry, How the West Was Won, Mary Poppins, Unsinkable Molly Brown, Sound of Music, After the Fox, See the Man Run, Capricorn I, Damien, Omen II, The Hand, Blue Thunder.
TELEVISION: Hitchcock Presents, Kraft Thea., Day in Court, Defenders, East Side, West Side, Dr. Kildare, The Fugitive, Mr. Ed, Jack Benny Show, Life of Riley, Man from Uncle, Doctors & the Nurses, The Invaders, Batman, Here's Lucy, Dennis the Menace, Andy Griffith, Marcus Welby, Banachek, Moses the Lawgiver, All My Children, Kojak, Charlie's Angels, Police Woman, The Tonight Show, Mash, Fantasy Island, Photo Clinic (PBS), The C.C. Connection, Nero Wolfe, House Calls, China Smith, Highway Patrol, Three's Company, Ike: The War Years, Cagney and Lacey, Barnaby Jones, Mike Hammer, Trapper John, The D.A.'s Man, Mark of Zorro, Peoples Court.

SHEEN, CHARLIE: Actor. b. Los Angeles, 1966. Son of Martin Sheen. Brother of actor Emilio Estevez. Made debut as extra in TV movie, The Execution of Private Slovik (starring father) and as extra in Apocalypse Now (also starring father).
PICTURES: Grizzly II—The Predator, The Red Dawn, Lucas, Platoon, Ferris Buehler's Day Off, The Wraith, Three for the Road, Wall Street, No Man's Land, Never on a Tuesday, Eight Men Out, Johnny Utah, Young Guns, Beverly Hills Brats, Backtrack, Major League.
TELEVISION: Movies: Silence of the Heart, The Boys Next Door.

SHEEN, MARTIN: Actor. r.n. Ramon Estevez. b. Dayton, OH, Aug. 3, 1940. Father of actors Emilio Estevez and Charlie Sheen.
THEATER: The Connection (debut, 1959 with the Living Theater), Women of Trachis, Many Loves, In the Jungle of Cities, Never Live Over a Pretzel Factory, The Subject Was Roses, The Wicked Crooks, Hamlet, Romeo and Juliet, Hello Goodbye, The Happiness Cage, Death of a Salesman (with George C. Scott), Julius Caesar.
PICTURES INCLUDE: The Subject Was Roses, The Incident, Catch 22, No Drums No Bugles, Rage, Pickup on 101, Badlands, The Cassandra Crossing, The Little Girl Who Lives Down the Lane, Apocalypse Now, The Final Countdown, Gandhi, That Championship Season, Enigma, Man, Woman and Child, The Dead Zone, Firestarter, The Believers, A State of Emergency, Wall Street, Siesta, Walkway After Midnight, Personal Choice, Da (co-exec. prod., actor), Judgement in Berlin (exec. prod., actor), Beverly Hills Brats.
TELEVISION: As the World Turns. Movies: Then Came Bronson, Mongo's Back in Town, Welcome Home, Johnny Bristol, That Certain Summer, Letters for Three Lovers, Pursuit, Catholics, Message to My Daughter, The Execution of Private Slovik, The California Kid, The Missiles of October, The Story of Pretty Boy Floyd, Sweet Hostage, The Guardian, The Last Survivors, Blind Ambition, The Long Road Home, (Emmy, 1981), In the Custody of Strangers, Choices of

the Heart, Kennedy (mini-series), The Atlanta Child Murders, Consenting Adult, Shattered Spirits, News at Eleven, Out of the Darkness, Samaritan, Conspiracy: The Trial of the Chicago 8.

SHEFFER, CRAIG: Actor. b. York, PA. e. East Stroudsberg Coll., PA. Started career in tv commercials; in soap opera, One Life to Live. On off-Bdwy. stage in Fresh Horses and on and off-Bdwy. in Torch Song Trilogy.
PICTURES: That Was Then . . . This Is Now, Fire with Fire, Voyage of the Rock Aliens, Split Decisions.

SHEFFIELD, JOHN: Actor. b. Pasadena, CA, April 11, 1931. e. U. of California at L.A. Stage debut at 7 in On Borrowed Time. Created screen role of Tarzan's son; in Tarzan pictures since.
PICTURES INCLUDE: Babes in Arms, Lucky Cisco Kid, Little Orvie, Bomba series, Million Dollar Baby, Knute Rockne, The Golden Idol, Lord of the Jungle, The Black Sheep, Roughly Speaking, Cisco Kid.
TELEVISION: series: Bantu the Zebra Boy.

SHEFTER, BERT: Composer, Conductor. b. Russia, May 15, 1904. e. Carnegie Inst. of Technology, Curtis Inst., Damrosch Inst. Member of piano team, Gould & Shefter, on radio & in theatres; org. own band; concert pianist; comp., cond. for many films and TV.
PICTURES INCLUDE: compose, conduct: Tall Texan, No Escape, Great Jesse James Raid, Sins of Jezebel, The Big Circus, The Fly, Lost World, Jack the Giant Killer, Monkey on My Back, Cattle King, Curse of the Fly, Last Man on Earth, Voyage to the Bottom of the Sea, The Bubble, Dog of Flanders.
TELEVISION: Written shows for Sunset Strip, Surfside, Hawaiian Eye, Maverick, Sugarfoot, Lawman, Bourbon St., Roaring 20's.

SHEINBERG, SIDNEY JAY: Executive. b. Corpus Christi, TX, Jan. 14, 1935. e. Columbia Coll., A.B. 1955; LL.B., 1958. Admitted to Calif. bar, 1958; assoc. in law U. of California Sch. of Law, Los Angeles, 1958–59; Joined MCA, Inc, 1959. Pres., TV div., 1971–74; exec. v.p., parent co., 1969–73. Named MCA pres. & chief oper. off., 1973.

SHELDON, DAVID: Director, Writer, Producer. b. New York, NY. e. Yale U. Sch. of Drama, M.F.A.; Principia Coll., B.A.; Actors Studio, directors unit. Directed N.Y. & L.A. companies of The Star Spangled Girl, Alley Oop, Jimmy Shine, etc. From 1972–74 was exec. in chg. of development at American Intl. Pictures (now Orion Pictures) supervising various production & post-production aspects of such films as Dillinger, Sisters, Macon County Line, Reincarnation of Peter Proud, Slaughter, Dr. Phibes, Boxcar Bertha, Heavy Traffic. Mng. dir., The Gateway Playhouse in N.Y. where produced & directed over 50 plays and musicals.
PICTURES INCLUDE: Producer-Writer, Sheba, Baby, Grizzly, The Evil, Project: Kill. Producer: Just Before Dawn, Abby, Day of the Animals, The Manitou. Director: Bring Her Back Alive, Timelapse, Lovely But Deadly. Writer: The Predator.

SHELDON, JAMES: Director. r.n. Schleifer. b. New York, NY, Nov. 12. e. U. of North Carolina. Page boy, NBC; announcer-writer-dir., NBC Internat'l Div.; staff dir., ABC radio; staff prod. dir., Young & Rubicam; free lance prod. dir. of many programs live tape and film, N.Y. and Hollywood.
TELEVISION: prod., dir.: Mr. Peepers, Armstrong Circle Theatre, Robert Montgomery Presents, Schlitz Playhouse, West Point, Zane Grey Theatre, The Millionaire, Desilu Playhouse, Perry Mason, Twilight Zone, Route 66, Naked City, The Virginian, Alfred Hitchcock Presents, Fugitive, Espionage, Defenders, Nurses, Bing Crosby Show, Family Affair, Wonderful World of Disney, Man From UNCLE, Felony Squad, That Girl, Ironside, My World and Welcome To It, To Rome With Love, Owen Marshall, Room 222, Gidget Grows Up (ABC Movie), Apple's Way, Love American Style, McMillan and Wife, Sanford and Son, Ellery Queen, Rich Man, Poor Man II, Family, MASH, Switch, Loveboat, With This Ring (ABC Movie), Sheriff Lobo, Gossip Columnist (movie), Knots Landing, The Waltons, 240-Robert, Nurse, Dukes of Hazard, Topaz F.B.I., McLain's Law, 7 Brides for 7 Brothers, Lottery, Partners in Crime, Jessie, Santa Barbara, Half Nelson, Stir Crazy, The Equalizer, Sledge Hammer.

SHELDON, SIDNEY: Writer, Producer, Novelist. b. Chicago, IL, Feb. 11, 1917. e. Northwestern U. Novels made into films include Other Side of Midnight, Bloodline, Naked Face. Awards: Oscar, Writers Guild, Tony, Edgar.
PICTURES INCLUDE: Bachelor and the Bobbysoxer, (Acad. Award, 1947), Easter Parade, Annie Get Your Gun, Dream Wife, Jumbo, Pardners, The Buster Keaton Story (s.p., prod., dir.), You're Never Too Young, Birds and the Bees, Three Guys Named Mike, Remains To Be Seen, Gambling Daughters, Dangerous Lady.
TELEVISION: Created Patty Duke Show; Created and produced I Dream of Jeannie, Nancy and created Hart to Hart. Novels made into mini-series: Rage of Angels, Master of the Game, Windmills of the Gods, If Tomorrow Comes.

NOVELS: The Naked Face, The Other Side of Midnight, A Stranger in the Mirror, Bloodline, Rage of Angels, Master of the Game, If Tomorrow Comes.
THEATER: Redhead (Tony Award, 1959).

SHENSON, WALTER: Producer. b. San Francisco, CA. e. Stanford U., Calif.; Ent. m.p. ind. 1941; studio exec., writing, prod., prom. shorts, trailers, Columbia; sup. publ., expl., London, Columbia European production, 1955.
PICTURES INCLUDE: prod.: The Mouse That Roared, A Matter of Who, The Mouse on the Moon, A Hard Day's Night, Help!, 30 is a Dangerous Age, Cynthia, Don't Raise the Bridge Lower the River, A Talent for Loving, Welcome to the Club (prod.-dir.), The Chicken Chronicles, Reuben, Reuben; Echo Park.

SHEPARD, SAM: Writer, Actor. r.n. Samuel Shepard Rogers. b. Fort Sheridan, IL, Nov. 5, 1943. Grew up in California, Montana and South Dakota. Lived near San Francisco, where, in addition to writing, ran a drama workshop at the U. of California at Davis. Recipient of Brandeis U. Creative Arts Citation, 1976, and American Acad. of Arts and Letters Award, 1975.
PLAYS INCLUDE: Cowboys and Rock Garden (double bill), Chicago, Icarus' Mother, and Red Cross (triple bill—1966 Obie Award), La Turista (1967 Obie), Forensic and the Navigators, Melodrama Play, Tooth of Crime (1973 Obie), Back Dog Beast Bait, Operation Sidewinder, 4-H Club, The Unseen Hand, Mad Dog Blues, Shaved Splits, Rock Garden, Curse of the Starving Class (1978 Obie), Buried Child, A Lie of the Mind.
PICTURES: Actor: Days of Heaven, Resurrection, Raggedy Man, Frances, The Right Stuff, Country, Fool for Love, Crimes of the Heart, Baby Boom; Far North (dir., s.p. only), Steel Magnolias, Hot Spot.
SCREENPLAYS: Paris, Texas, Fool for Love.

SHEPHERD, CYBILL: Actress, Singer. b. Memphis, TN, Feb. 18, 1950. e. Hunter Coll., New York U., U. of Southern California. Was fashion model before acting debut in 1971. Debut record album, Cybill Does It . . . To Cole Porter, 1974.
PICTURES INCLUDE: The Last Picture Show (debut), The Heartbreak Kid, Daisy Miller, At Long Last Love, Taxi Driver, Special Delivery, Silver Bears, Chances Are.
TELEVISION: Yellow Rose, Secrets of a Married Man, A Guide for the Married Woman, Seduced, The Lady Vanishes, The Long Hot Summer, Moonlighting (series).

SHEPHERD, RICHARD: Producer. b. Kansas City, MO, June 4, 1927. e. Stanford U. In U.S. Naval Reserve, 1944–45. Entered ent. field as exec. with MCA, 1948, functioning in radio, TV, and m.p. fields until 1956, with time out for U.S. Army, 1950–52. In 1956 became head of talent for Columbia Pictures. In 1962 joined CMA talent agency on its founding, becoming exec. v.p. in chg. of m.p. div. Left to join Warner Bros. in Aug., 1972, as exec. v.p. for prod. Resigned Oct. 1, 1974 to become indep. prod. In 1976 named MGM sr. vp. & worldwide head of theatrical prod.
PICTURES INCLUDE: Twelve Angry Men, The Hanging Tree, The Fugitive Kind, Breakfast at Tiffany's (prod.), Alex and the Gypsy, Robin and Marian, Volunteers, The Hunger.

SHER, LOUIS K.: Executive. b. Columbus, OH, Feb. 25, 1914. e. Ohio State U., 1933. Exec., Stone's Grills Co., 1934–37; owned & operated, Sher Vending Co., 1937–43. U.S. Army, 1943–46. V.p., Sons Bars & Grills, 1947–54; org. & pres. Art Theatre Guild, 1954; opened art theatres for first time in many cities, org. opera film series, film classic series and similar motion picture activities in many cities. Org., Film Festival at Antioch Coll., 1960; pioneer in fighting obscenity laws in Ohio; operates 10 theatres in midwest and western states. Co-producer of the musical broadway production Shenandoah and American Dance Machine. Produced film, Deathmask.

SHERAK, THOMAS: Executive. b. Brooklyn, NY June 22, 1945. e. New York Community Coll., mktg. degree. 1967–69; US Army, Specialist E5 Sgt.; 1970, began career in m.p. industry, Paramount Pictures sls. dept.; 1974, R/C Theatres, booking dept.; 1977, joined General Cinema Theatres as district film buyer; 1978, promoted to v.p., films; 1982, promoted to v.p. head film buyer; 1983, joined 20th Century Fox as pres., domestic dist. & mktg.; 1985, pres., domestic dist.

SHERMAN, GEORGE: Director. b. New York, NY, 1908. 1985: Formed Ronsher Productions with Cleo Ronson for feature and TV productions.
PICTURES INCLUDE: The Bandit of Sherwood Forest, Red Canyon, Yes Sir That's My Baby, Sword in the Desert, Comanche Territory, Sleeping City, Spy Hunt, Tomahawk, Target Unknown, Golden Horde, Steel Town, Raging Tide, Against All Flags, Battle at Apache Pass, The Lone Hand, Veils of Bagdad, War Arrow, Border River, Johnny Dark, Dawn at Socorro, Chief Crazy Horse, Count Three and Pray, Treasure of Pancho Villa, Comanche, Reprisal, Flying Fontaines, Enemy General. Formed Shergari Corp. with F. H.

Ricketson, Jr., and Ted R. Gamble made For the Love of Mike; dir.: Panic Button, Wounds of Hunger, Jacquin Murieta, Smokey, Big Jake. In 1976 wrote, produced, and directed Artie-Charley and Friend, indep. feature.
TELEVISION: Prod. and/or dir. for 20th Century-Fox, and NBC, CBS. 1978, prod., Little Mo (movie).

SHERMAN, RICHARD M.: Composer, Lyricist. b. New York, NY, June 12, 1928. e. Bard Coll., B.A., 1949. Info. & Educ. Br., U.S. Army, 1953–55. Songwriter, composer, Walt Disney Prods.
SONGS: Things I Might Have Been, Tall Paul, Christmas in New Orleans, Mad Passionate Love, Midnight Oil, You're Sixteen, Pineapple Princess, Let's Get Together, Maggie's Theme, Chim Chim Cheree, Comedy Album: Smash Flops.
PICTURES INCLUDE: Nightmare, The Cruel Tower, Absent Minded Professor, The Parent Trap, Big Red, The Castaways, Moon Pilot, Bon Voyage, Legend of Lobo, Summer Magic, Miracle of the White Stallions, The Sword in the Stone, Merlin Jones, Mary Poppins, Those Calloways, The Monkey's Uncle, That Darn Cat, Symposium of Popular Songs, Winnie the Pooh, Bedknobs & Broomsticks, Tom Sawyer (s.p. and score.), Huckleberry Finn.
TELEVISION: Wonderful World of Color, Bell Telephone Hour.

SHERMAN, ROBERT B.: Composer, Lyricist, b. New York, NY, Dec. 19, 1925. e. Bard Coll., B.A., 1949. U.S. Army, W.W.II, 1943–45. Songwriter, 1952–60; pres., Music World Corp., 1958; songwriter, composer, Walt Disney, 1960–65.
SONGS: Things I Might Have Been, Tall Paul, Young & In Love, Midnight Oil, Pineapple Princess, You're 16, Let's Get Together, Maggie's Theme, Chim Chim Cheree.
PICTURES INCLUDE: Absent Minded Professor, The Parent Trap, Big Red, The Castaways, Moon Pilot, Bon Voyage, Legend of Lobo, Miracle of the White Stallions, Summer Magic, The Sword in the Stone, Merlin Jones, Mary Poppins, Those Calloways, The Monkey's Uncle, That Darn Cat, Winnie the Pooh, Symposium of Popular Songs, Bedknobs & Broomsticks, Tom Sawyer (s.p. and score.), Huckleberry Finn.
TELEVISION: Wonderful World of Color, Bell Telephone.

SHERMAN, ROBERT M.: Executive. Entered ind. as agent for MCA; later joined Arthur P. Jacobs pub. rel. firm. Became acc't. exec. when Jacobs merged with Rogers & Cowan. In 1964 joined CMA; 1967 made v.p. in m.p. div., serving both in London and Hollywood. In 1972 formed own prod. co., Layton Prods., with first film, Scarecrow for WB. In 1973 prod. Night Moves, also for WB. In 1974 named v.p., prod., for 20th-Fox. Returned to independent prod.: The Missouri Breaks, Convoy, Oh God! You Devil, Deadly Friend.

SHERMAN, SAMUEL M.: Producer, Director, Writer. b. New York, NY. e. City Coll. of New York, B.A. Entered m.p. ind. as writer, cameraman, film ed., neg. & sound cutter; nat'l mag. ed., Westerns Magazine 1959; pres., Signature Films; prod., dir., TV pilot, The Three Mesquiteers, 1960; prod., Pulse Pounding Perils, 1961; helped create, ed., dir., Screen Thrills Illustrated; exec. prod., Screen Thrills; v.p., Golden Age Films, 1962; prod., Joe Franklin's Silent Screen, 1963; N.Y. rep., Victor Adamson Productions; owns world rights; The Scarlet Letter; 1965; N.Y. rep., Tal prods., Hlywd.; adv. & pub. Hemisphere Pictures; ed., autobiog., Joe Bonomo; prod., writer, Chaplin's Art of Comedy, The Strongman; prod., Hollywood's Greatest Stuntman; story adapt., Fiend With the Electronic Brain. 1967, prod. Spanish version Chaplin Su Arte y Su Comedia; tech. consul., Hal Roach Studios, NBC, Music from the Land; 1968, N.Y. rep. East West Pict. of Hollywood. 1968, N.Y. rep., Al Adamson Prods. of Hollywood; post-prod'n consultant: The Fakers, Creatures of the Prehistoric Planet; sales U.K. of U.S. product; promo. consultant, Love Is a Woman, Blood Fiend; Brides of Blood, The Ghastly Ones. 1969, post prod'n and promo. consultant, Blood Demon, Mad Doctor of Blood Island. Ed.-in-chief, bk., The Strongman. Prod'n consultant, Satan's Sadists, The Blood Seekers. Pres., Independent-International Pictures Corp., assoc. prod. Horror of the Blood Monsters, Blood of Ghastly Horror; Producer-Writer Brain of Blood; prod. supervisor Dracula vs. Frankenstein; Exec. prod. Angels, Wild Women; pres., Producers Commercial Productions Inc.; producer-writer, The Naughty Stewardesses; producer, Girls For Rent; producer TV special, Wild Wild World of Comedy; executive producer, The Dynamite Brothers; producer-writer, Blazing Stewardesses; production consultant, In Search of Dracula; executive producer, Cinderella 2000; producer & orig. story, Team-Mates; Chairman of Creditors' Committee, Allied Artists Television Corp.; president, Independent-International Entertainment, TV div. Independent-International Pictures Corp. Pres., Technovision Inc.; pres., Super Video, Inc.; dir-s.p., Raiders of the Living Dead.

SHERMAN, VINCENT: Director. b. Vienna, GA, July 16, 1906. e. Oglethorpe U. B.A. Writer, actor, dialogue dir., prod. dir.
PICTURES INCLUDE: Dir: Return of Doctor X, Saturday's Children, Man Who Talked Too Much, Underground, Flight

from Destiny, The Hard Way, All Through the Night, Old Acquaintances, In Our Time, Mr. Skeffington, Pillow to Post, Janie Gets Married, Nora Prentiss, The Unfaithful, Adventures of Don Juan, Somewhere in the City, Hasty Heart, Damned Don't Cry, Harriet Craig, Goodbye, My Fancy, Lone Star, Assignment—Paris; prod. dir.: Affair in Trinidad, The Young Philadelphians, The Naked Earth, Second Time Around, Ice Palace, Fever in the Blood.
TELEVISION: 25 episodes of Medical Center; Westside Medical; Baretta; Waltons; Doctors Hospital; Movies: The Last Hurrah; Women at West Point; The Yeagers (pilot), Bogey, The Dream Merchants, Trouble in High Timber Country, High Hopes—The Capra Years.

SHERRIN, NED: Producer, Director, Writer. b. Low Ham, Somerset, England, Feb. 18, 1931. Early career writing plays and musical plays. Prod., dir., ATV Birmingham, 1955–57; prod., Midlands Affairs, Paper Talk, etc. Joined BBC-TV 1957 and produced many TV talk programmes. Novels: (with Caryl Brahms) Cindy-Ella or I Gotta Shoe (also prod. as stage play), Rappell 1910, Benbow Was His Name.
TELEVISION: England: prod.: Ask Me Another, Henry Hall Show, Laugh Line, Parasol. Assoc. prod.: Tonight series. Little Beggars, 1962; prod., creator: That Was The Week That Was, 1962–63; prod., dir.: Benbow Was His Name (co-author), 1964; Take a Sapphire (co-author), The Long Garden Party, The Long Cocktail Party. ABC of Britain revue. Prod., dir.: thrice-weekly series Not So Much a Programme, More a Way of Life, 1964–65. Appearances inc. Your Witness, Quiz of The Week, Terra Firma, Who Said That, The Rather Reassuring Programme, Song by Song.
PICTURES INCLUDE: prod.: The Virgin Soldiers (with Leslie Gilliat), Every Home Should Have One, Up Pompeii, Girl Stroke Boy (co-author with Caryl Brahms), Up the Chastity Belt, Rentadick, The Garnet Saga, Up the Front, The National Health, The Cobblers of Umbridge (dir. with Ian Wilson).

SHERWOOD, MADELINE: Actress. b. Montreal, Canada, Nov. 13, 1922. e. Yale Drama Sch. Trained with Montreal Rep. and Actors Studio. Has dir. prods. at Actors Studio and regional theaters.
THEATER: The Crucible, Sweet Bird of Youth, Invitation to a March, The Garden of Sweets, Camelot, Hey You, Light Man!, Brecht on Brecht, Night of the Iguana, Arturo Ui, Do I Hear a Waltz?, Inadmissible Evidence, All Over, Older People, Getting Out, The Suicide.
PICTURES: Baby Doll, Cat on a Hot Tin Roof, Sweet Bird of Youth, Parrish, The 91st Day, Hurry Sundown, Pendulum, Until She Talks, Mr. Preble Gets Rid of His Wife, The Changeling, Resurrection, Wicked, Wicked, Teachers.
TELEVISION: The Flying Nun (series), Rich Man, Poor Man, Nobody's Child.

SHIELDS, BROOKE: Actress. b. New York, NY, May 31, 1965. e. Princeton U. Discovered at age 11 months by photographer Francesco Scavullo to pose in Ivory Snow ads. Later became Breck girl in commercials; appeared in Richard Avedon's Colgate ads for 3 yrs.
PICTURES INCLUDE: Alice Sweet Alice (Communion), Pretty Baby, Tilt, King of the Gypsies, Wanda Nevada, Just You and Me, Kid, The Blue Lagoon, Endless Love, Sahara, Brenda Starr.
TELEVISION: The Prince of Central Park, After the Fall, Wet Gold, The Great Diamond Robbery and numerous specials.

SHIELDS, WILLIAM A.: Executive. b. New York, NY, 1946. e. El Camino Coll., California State Coll. Entered the motion picture industry in 1966 when he went to work for Pacific Theatres. Other industry affiliations included: MGM sales department, Los Angeles and Denver, 1970; New World Pictures, Western Division manager, 1972; branch manager, 20th Century-Fox, Washington, 1973; New York district manager, 20th Century-Fox, 1973–75. Joined Mann Theatres Corporation of California as head booker in 1975. Gen. sls. mgr., Far West Films, 1977–79; joined Avco Embassy as Western div. mgr., promoted to asst. gen. sls. mgr., 1980; promoted to v.p.-gen. sls. mgr., January, 1981. In 1983 joined New World Pictures as exec. v.p., world-wide mktg. & acquisitions. Promoted to pres., w-w sls. & mktg., 1985.

SHIFF, RICHARD: Executive. Joined Warner Bros. as sales analyst, 1977. In 1979 named dist. coordinator; 1980, asst. dir. sls. admin. 1982, promoted to post, dir. sls. admin. 1987, v.p., theatrical sls. opns.

SHIKATA, MASAO: Executive. b. Kyoto, Japan, Apr. 22, 1918. e. Naniwa Commercial Coll. Chm., Sansha Electric Manufacturing Co. Ltd., Tokyo and Osaka, makers of power semiconductors & applied electronic equipment; pres. Japan Motion Picture Equipment Manufacturers & Suppliers Assoc.; v.p., Japan Machinery Design Center; v.p., Japan Optical Industry Assoc.; director, Federation of Japanese Film Industries Inc.

SHIMA, KOJI: Director. b. Japan. Entered m.p. ind. as actor, 1930; then asst. dir., director. Dir., Daiei M. P. Co. (now defunct). Presently indep. director.
PICTURES INCLUDE: Golden Demon, Phantom Horse.

SHINBACH, BRUCE D.: Executive. b. South Bend, IN, June, 1939. e. U. of Colorado, B.A., 1963; New York Inst. of Finance; Northwestern U., M.A., 1965. Stockbroker for Harris, Upham & Co., 1964, shopping center developer, Dixie Associates, 1966 to present. Pres., Monarch Theatres.

SHIRE, DAVID: Composer. b. Buffalo, NY, July 3, 1937. e. Yale U., 1959, B.A. Composer of theater scores: The Sap of Life, Starting Here, Starting Now; Baby.
PICTURES INCLUDE: Farewell My Lovely, The Conversation, All the President's Men, Saturday Night Fever, Old Boyfriends, Norma Rae, The Hindenberg, The Taking of Pelham 1-2-3, Only When I Laugh, Paternity, The World According to Garp, Max Dugan Returns, 2010, Return to Oz, Short Circuit, 'night, Mother, Vice Versa, Monkey Shines.
TELEVISION: The Defection of Simas Kurdirka, Raid on Entebbe, Do You Remember Love, Echoes in the Darkness, God Bless the Child, Promise, Alice, Mayflower Madam, Hothouse (series).

SHIRE, TALIA: Actress. b. New York, NY, April 25, 1946. Raised on road by her father, arranger-conductor Carmine Coppola, who toured with Broadway musicals. After 2 yrs. at Yale Sch. of Drama she moved to L.A. where appeared in many theatrical productions. Sister of Francis Ford Coppola.
PICTURES INCLUDE: The Dunwich Horror, Gas-s-s, The Christian Licorice Store, The Outside Man, The Godfather, The Godfather, Part II, Rocky, Old Boyfriends, Rocky II, Windows, Rocky III, Rocky IV, RAD, Never Say Never Again (prod.), Lionheart (co-prod.).
TELEVISION: Rich Man, Poor Man, Kill Me If You Can, Foster and Laurie; Daddy I Don't Like It Like This.

SHIVAS, MARK: Producer, Director. TV credits incl: Presenter of Cinema. The Six Wives of Henry VIII, Casanova, The Edwardians, The Evacuees, The Glittering Prizes, Abide With Me, Rogue Male, 84 Charing Cross Road, The Three Hostages, She Fell Among Thieves, Professional Foul, Telford's Change, On Giant's Shoulders, & The Price, What If it's Raining?, The Story Teller. Now head of drama, BBC TV.
PICTURES: Producer; Richards' Things, Moonlighting, A Private Function. Exec. Prod.: Bad Blood; The Witches (prod.).

SHONFELD, PHIL: Executive. Began career in sls. dist. at Universal Pictures. Later asst. to western sls. mgr. for National General and western dist. mgr. for Buena Vista. Joined Warners in November, 1976 as asst. to v.p. & gen. sls. mgr. In 1979 promoted to v.p.—sls. admin., continuing to head playdate and contract depts. while becoming involved in all aspects of sls. dept.

SHORE, DINAH: Singer. r.n. Frances Rose Shore. b. Winchester, TN, Mar. 1, 1917. e. Vanderbilt U., B.A., 1939. Became singer WNEW, N.Y., 1938; joined NBC as sustaining singer, 1938; started contract RCA-Victor, 1940; star Chamber Music Soc. of Lower Basin St. program, 1940; joined Eddie Cantor radio pgm., 1941; star own radio program, General Foods, 1943; entertained troops European Theatre of operations, 1944; radio program, Procter & Gamble. Star TV show, Chevrolet, 1951–61; Dinah Shore Specials, 1964–65. 1969: Dinah Shore Special, Like Hep. 1970–71: Dinah's Place (Emmy, 1973, 1974), Dinah! (Emmy, 1976), Death Car on the Freeway.
PICTURES: Thank Your Lucky Stars, Up in Arms, Belle of the Yukon, Follow the Boys, Make Mine Music, Till the Clouds Roll By, Fun and Fancy Free, Aaron Slick from Punkin Crick.
AWARDS: Awarded New Star of Radio Motion Picture Daily Poll and World Telegram-Scripps-Howard Poll, 1940; Best Popular Female Vocalist M.P. Daily Fame's Annual Poll Radio and TV 1941–61; Michael Award Best Female Vocalist, Radio and TV, 1950, 51, 52; Billboard Award; Favorite Female Vocalist in radio, 1949; Billboard Award Favorite Female Vocalist in records, 1947; Gallup Poll One of Most Admired Women in the World, 1958–61; 6 Emmy Awards 1954 to 59. Recording of songs by Decca; Los Angeles Times Woman of the Year Award, 1957; TV-Radio Mirror mag. award, best female singer, radio, 1952, 53, 56, 57, 58; TV-Radio Mirror mag. award, TV's Best Musical Variety Show, 1956, 58, 59; Peabody TV Award, 1957; Fame's Critics' Poll, Best Female Vocalist, 1958, 63; Hollywood Foreign Press Assn's Golden Globe Award, 1959; Radio-TV Daily, Female Vocalist of the Year, 1949, 56.

SHORE, HOWARD: Composer, Musician. Began career as musical director for Saturday Night Live.
PICTURES: Scanners, Videodrome, The Brood, The Fly, After Hours, Heaven, Belizaire, The Cajun, Nadine, Moving, Big, Dead Ringers.

SHORE, SIG: Producer. b. New York, NY. Served as navigator in Air Force, W.W.II. First job in films in pub. dept. at Warner

Bros. Formed own ad agency on West Coast; then turned to TV production with The Errol Flynn Theatre. Engaged by David O. Selznick Films to dist. its films to TV outlets. Entered theatrical distribution, importing Hiroshima, Mon Amour, The 400 Blows, etc. In mid-50s became involved in cultural exchange program of US State Dept., importing and distributing Soviet films. Returned to TV production, turning out over 250 shows, including The Outdoor World for Shell Oil. Headed co. for Ivan Tors which made Flipper, Daktari, Gentle Ben series. In 1970 formed Plaza Pictures for theatrical dist.
PICTURES INCLUDE: Super Fly, Super Fly TNT, That's The Way of the World, Sudden Death. (s.p.-dir.).

SHORT, MARTIN: Actor, Comedian. b. Canada, 1951. e. McMaster U. Trained as social worker but instead performed on stage in Godspell as well as in revues and cabarets in Toronto, 1973–78 including a stint as a member of the Toronto unit of the Second City comedy troupe (1977–78). Best know for comic characters he created such as nerdy Ed Grimley and lounge lizard Jackie Rogers Jr. as well as impersonations of Katharine Hepburn and Jerry Lewis on Saturday Night Live (1985–86).
PICTURES: Three Amigos (debut, 1986); Innerspace; Cross My Heart; Fugitives; The Big Picture.
TELEVISION: Series: The Associates (1979); I'm a Big Girl Now; SCTV Network 90; Saturday Night Live; The Completely Mental Misadventures of Ed Grimley (cartoon series). Movies: All's Well That Ends Well; Really Weird Tales.

SHOWALTER, MAX: Actor, composer. s.n. Casey Adams. b. Caldwell, KS, June 2, 1917. e. Caldwell H.S.; Pasadena Playhouse. Composed background music for films: Vicki, Return of Jack Slade, Bdwy. Harrington 'n Hart (composer).
BROADWAY: Knights of Song, Very Warm for May, My Sister Eileen, Showboat, John Loves Mary, Make Mine Manhattan, Lend an Ear, Hello Dolly!, The Grass Harp.
PICTURES INCLUDE: Always Leave Them Laughing, With a Song in My Heart, What Price Glory, My Wife's Best Friend, Niagara, Destination Gobi, Dangerous Crossing, Vicki, Night People, Naked Alibi, Never Say Goodbye, Bus Stop, Down Three Dark Streets, Designing Woman, Female Animal, Voice In the Mirror, The Naked and the Dead, It Happened to Jane, Elmer Gantry, Return to Peyton Place, Summer and Smoke, Music Man, Smog, Bon Voyage, My Six Loves, Lord Love a Duck, The Anderson Tapes, Move Over Darling, Sex and the Single Girl, Fate Is the Hunter, How to Murder Your Wife, The Moonshine War, Racing with the Moon, 10, Sixteen Candles.

SHUE, ELISABETH: Actress. b. 1964.
PICTURES: The Karate Kid, Adventures in Babysitting, Link, Cocktail.
TELEVISION: Call to Glory.

SHULER, LAUREN: Producer. b. Cleveland, OH, June 23, 1949. Began filmmaking career as camera-woman in TV production, 1972; prod. TV movie: Amateur Night at the Dixie Bar and Grill for NBC.
PICTURES: Mr. Mom, Ladyhawke, St. Elmo's Fire, Pretty in Pink.

SHULL, RICHARD: Actor. b. Evanston, IL, Feb. 24, 1929. e. State U. of Iowa. U.S. Army, 1953. N.Y. stage debut in Minnie's Boys, 1970. Film debut in The Anderson Tapes, 1971.
PICTURES: B.S. I Love You, Such Good Friends, Slither, Hail to the Chief, The Black Bird, Cockfighter, Hearts of the West, The Fortune, Dreamer, Wholly Moses, Heartbeeps, Spring Break, Lovesick, Unfaithfully Yours, Splash, etc.
TELEVISION: Holmes & Yoyo, Rockford Files, Good Times, Love American Style, Hart to Hart, Lou Grant, etc.

SHURPIN, SOL: Executive. b. New York, NY, Feb. 22, 1914. e. Pace Inst., 1936. Law stenog., 1932–33; Joe Hornstein, Inc., 1933–41; National Theatre Supply, 1941–48; purchased interest in Raytone Screen Corp., became v.p., 1948; pres., Raytone, 1952; pres., Technikote Corp., which succeeded Raytone Screen, 1956–present; sole owner, Technikote Corp., 1962.

SHUTT, BUFFY: Executive. Joined Paramount 1973 as member of N.Y. pub. staff; 1975, natl. mag. contact. 1978, named dir. of pub.; later exec. dir. of pub. Promoted 1980 to v.p., pub. & promo. Resigned to join Time-Life Films; returned to Paramount in 1981 as v.p. & asst. to pres. of Motion Picture Group. 1984, appt. exec. v.p.-mktg. for M.P. Group, Paramount. 1986, resigned.

SIDARIS, ANDY: Producer, Director, Writer. b. Chicago, IL, Feb. 20, 1932. e. Southern Methodist U., B.A., radio-TV. Began television career in 1950 in Dallas, TX as a director at station WFAA-TV; now pres., The Sidaris Company. Won 8 Emmy Awards.
PICTURES INCLUDE: Dir., Stacey, The Racing Scene, M*A*S*H football sequences, Seven (prod.-dir.), Malibu Express (prod., dir., s.p.), Hard Ticket to Hawaii (dir., s.p.), Picasso Trigger (dir., s.p.), Savage Beach (dir., s.p.).

TELEVISION: Dir., The Racers/Mario Andretti/Joe Leonard/Al Unser, ABC's Championship Auto Racing, ABC's NCAA Game of the Week, 1968 Summer Olympics (Mexico City), 1972 Summer Olympics, 1976 Summer Olympics (Montreal), 1984 Summer Olympics (L.A.), 1964 Winter Olympics (Innsbruck), 1968 Winter Olympics (Grenoble), 1976 Winter Olympics (Innsbruck), 1980 Winter Olympics (Lake Placid), 1988 Winter Olympics (Calgary), Wide World of Sports, The Racers/Craig and Lee Breedlove, dir.: The Burt Reynolds Late Show, dir., Kojak episode, Nancy Drew, Dukes of Hazzard.

SIDNEY, GEORGE: Director, Producer. b. New York, NY, 1916. Son of L. K. Sidney, veteran showman and v.p. MGM, and Hazel Mooney, actress. From 1932 at MGM as test, second unit and short subjects dir. Several Academy Awards for shorts, Our Gang Comedies, Pete Smith etc. In 1941 made feature dir., MGM. Pres., Director's Guild of America, 16 yrs; spec. presidential assignment to Atomic Energy Commission and U.S. Air Force; 1961–66, Pres., Hanna-Barbera Productions; Doctorate of Science Hanneman Medical University and Hospital. Mem. ASCAP. Pres., Directors, Inc., since 1969; v.p., Directors Foundation; v.p., R.W. Griffith Foundation; life mem., ACTT (England) and DGA.
PICTURES INCLUDE: dir., prod.: Free and Easy, Pacific Rendezvous, Pilot No. 5, Thousands Cheer, Bathing Beauty, Anchors Aweigh, Harvey Girls, Cass Timberlane, Three Musketeers, Red Danube, Key to the City, Annie Get Your Gun, Holiday in Mexico, Show Boat, Scaramouche, Young Bess, Kiss Me Kate, Jupiter's Darling, Eddie Duchin Story, Jeanne Eagels, Pal Joey, Who Was That Lady, Pepe, Bye Bye Birdie, A Ticklish Affair, Viva Las Vegas, Who Has Seen the Wind?, U.N. special; The Swinger, Half a Sixpence.

SIDNEY, SYLVIA: Actress. b. New York, NY, Aug. 8, 1910. r.n. Sophia Kosow. e. Theatre Guild Sch. On stage, then screen debut in Through Different Eyes (1929).
PLAYS: Nice Women, Crossroads, Bad Girl, The Gentle People, etc.
PICTURES INCLUDE: City Streets, Five Minutes from the Station, Ladies of the Big House, Confessions of a Co-Ed, An American Tragedy, Street Scene, The Miracle Man, Merrily We Go to Hell, Madame Butterfly, Pick-Up, Jennie Gerhardt, Good Dame, Thirty Day Princess, Behold My Wife, Accent on Youth, Mary Burns—Fugitive, Trail of the Lonesome Pine, Fury, A Woman Alone, You Only Live Once, Dead End, You and Me, One Third of a Nation, The Wagons Roll at Night, Blood on the Sun, Mr. Ace, Searching Wind, Love from a Stranger, Les Miserables, Violent Saturday, Behind the High Wall, Summer Wishes, Winter Dreams, I Never Promised You a Rose Garden, Damien-Omen II, Hammett, Beetlejuice.
TELEVISION: Movies: Do Not Fold, Spindle or Mutilate, Death at Love House, Raid on Entebbe, The Gossip Columnist, FDR—The Last Year, The Shadow Box, A Small Killing, Come Along With Me, Having It All, Finnegan Begin Again, An Early Frost, Pals.

SIEGEL, DON: Director. b. Chicago, IL, Oct. 26, 1912. e. Jesus Coll., Cambridge U., England. Has appeared with the Royal Acad. of Dramatic Art, London, and Contemporary Theatre Group, Hollywood. Joined Warner Bros. as asst. film librarian, 1934; became asst. cutter and head of insert dept. Organized montage dept.; wrote and dir. all montages. Directed many TV shows 1953–66.
PICTURES INCLUDE: dir.: Star in the Night and Hitler Lives (two Academy Awards for distinctive achievement for shorts, 1945). dir.: The Verdict, Night Unto Night, Big Steal, Duel at Silver Creek, No Time For Flowers, Count the Hours, China Venture, Riot in Cell Block 11, Private Hell 36, Annapolis Story, Invasion of the Body Snatchers, Madigan, Coogan's Bluff, Two Mules for Sister Sara, The Beguiled, Dirty Harry; Play Misty for Me, (actor only), Charley Varrick, Black Windmill, The Shootist, Telefon, Escape from Alcatraz (also prod.), Rough Cut, Jinxed.
TELEVISION: Movies: The Killers, The Hanged Man, Stranger on the Run.

SIEGEL, SIMON B.: Financial vice-president, treas., American Broadcasting Paramount Theatres & mem. bd. of dir. Started career in ind. 1929, comptroller's staff Paramount Pictures, Inc.; asst. to comptroller of the company's theatre div., 1941; comptroller, 1949; joined United Paramount Theatres, 1950; in 1953 named treasurer when ABC & UPT were merged; named financial v.p. and treas., 1957; exec. vice-pres., ABC-Paramount Theatres.

SIKKING, JAMES B.: Actor. b. Los Angeles, CA, March 5, 1934. e. U. of California at L.A., B.A. Theatre includes Waltz of the Toreadors, Plaza Suite, Damn Yankees, The Big Knife.
PICTURES: The Magnificent Seven; Von Ryan's Express; The New Centurions; The Electric Horseman; Capricorn One; Outland; The Star Chamber; Up the Creek; Star Trek III—The Search for Spock; Morons from Outer Space.
TELEVISION: Series: Turnabout; General Hospital; Hill Street Blues. Movies: The Jesse Owens Story; First Steps;

Sil-Sim

The Golden Land; Ollie Hoopnoodles Haven of Bliss; Bay Coven; Leave Her to Heaven; Brotherhood of the Rose (miniseries).

SILBERT, STEPHEN D.: Executive. b. Los Angeles, CA, Sept. 4, 1942. e. Claremont McKenna Coll., CA, B.A., Masters in Business Economics; Boalt Hall Sch. of Law, U. of California, Berkeley, J.D. Member: American Bar Assoc., State Bar of CA. Senior partner, Wyman, Bautzer, Kuchel and Silbert; Sept. 1985–Oct. 1986, chairman of exec. committee of board of directors, MGM/UA Communications Co., and employed by Kirk Kerkorian; Oct. 1986–July 1988, president and COO, MGM/UA Communications; July 1988, became chairman of board and CEO, MGM/UA Communications Co. Resigned as of Jan 1989. Joined Tracinda Corp.

SILLIPHANT, STIRLING: Executive, Writer. b. Detroit, MI, Jan. 16, 1918. e. U. of Southern California, B.A., 1938. On pub. staff, Walt Disney Productions, Burbank 1938–41; 1941–42, exploit. & pub., Hal Horne Org. for 20th Century-Fox in New York & other key cities, 1942–43, asst. to Spyros P. Skouras. U.S. Navy, W.W.II. Since 1946, 20th-Fox; in chge. special events and promotions, June 1949; apptd. Eastern pub. mgr. Aug, 13, 1951.
PICTURES: Prod., Joe Louis Story; co-prod., collab. s.p., 5 Against the House; screenwriter, producer, Naked City, Route 66, The Slender Thread, In the Heat of the Night; s.p., Marlowe; collab., s.p., The Liberation of L. B. Jones; s.p., A Walk in the Spring Rain; p., Shaft, Shaft in Africa, (s.p.). The New Centurions (s.p.), The Poseidon Adventure, (s.p.). The Towering Inferno (s.p.), The Killer Elite (co.-s.p.), The Enforcer (co.-s.p.), Telefon (co-s.p.), The Swarm, Circle of Iron (co-s.p.), When Time Ran Out, Over the Top (co-s.p.).
TELEVISION: Series: The Naked City, Route 66, Space, Golden Gate, Fly Away Home, (prod., s.p.), Mussolini—The Untold Story; Pearl, (exec. prod., writer), Salem's Lot (exec. prod.), Welcome to Paradise (exec. prod., s.p.), Travis McGee, The Three Kings (prod., s.p.).

SILVA, HENRY: Actor. b. Puerto Rico, 1928.
PICTURES: Viva Zapata, Crowded Paradise, A Hatful of Rain, The Bravados, Green Mansions, Cinderfella, Ocean's Eleven, The Manchurian Candidate, Johnny Cool, The Return of Mr. Moto, The Reward, The Plainsman, The Hills Ran Red, Buck Rogers in the 25th Century, Thirst, Virus, Alligator, Sharkey's Machine, Wrong Is Right, Cannonball Run II, Lust in the Dust, Code of Silence, Alan Quartermain and the Lost City of Gold, Above the Law, Bulletproof, Fists of Steel, Trained to Kill.
TELEVISION: Contract on Cherry Street, Happy (series), Black Noon.

SILVER, JOAN MICKLIN: Writer, Director. b. Omaha, NB, May 24, 1935. m. producer Raphael Silver. e. Sarah Lawrence Coll. Began career as writer for educational films. Original s.p., Limbo, purchased by Universal Pictures. In 1972 Learning Corp. of Am. commissioned her to write and direct a 30-min. documentary, The Immigrant Experience. Also wrote and directed two children's films for same co. First feature was Hester Street, which she wrote and directed.
THEATER: Director: Album, Maybe I'm Doing It Wrong.
PICTURES INCLUDE: Hester Street (s.p., dir.); Bernice Bobs Her Hair (short, s.p.-dir., later shown on TV), Between the Lines (dir.); On the Yard (prod.), Head Over Heels (s.p., dir.; retitled Chilly Scenes of Winter), Crossing Delancey (dir.), Loverboy.
TELEVISION: Finnegan Begin Again (dir.), The Nightingale, Faerie Tale Theatre (s.p.).

SILVER, JOEL: Producer. e. New York U. Made first film, a short called Ten Pin Alley; moved to Los Angeles with job as asst. to Lawrence Gordon. Named pres., Lawrence Gordon Prods.; developed with Gordon and produced and marketed Hooper, The End, The Driver, The Warriors. At Universal Pictures as prod. v.p.; supervising Smokey and the Bandit II, Xanadu.
PICTURES: Co-Producer: 48 Hrs., Streets of Fire, Brewster's Millions. Producer: Weird Science, Commando, Jumpin' Jack Flash, Lethal Weapon, The Predator, Action Jackson, Road House, License to Drive, Die Hard.

SILVER, LEON J.: Executive. b. Boston, MA, March 25, 1918. e. U. of Southern California, 1935–39. Independent prod. of short subjects, 1939; story analyst, Paramount, 1940, film writer, U.S. Army Pictorial Service, 1941–45; freelance writer, 1946; film writer. prod., U.S. Public Health Service, 1946–51, asst. chief, foreign film prod., U.S. Dept. of State, 1951–54; acting chief, domestic film prod., U.S. Information Agency, 1955. Division Chief, Worldwide Documentary Film & Television Product, U.S. Information Agency, Apr. 6, 1968, 1978 to 1980, sr. advisor IV, film production. Resigned, 1980. Now TV network writer-producer-novelist.

SILVER, MILTON: Advertising executive. b. New York, NY. U.S. Army W.W.I. Co-ed. Who's Who on Screen and Little Movie Mirror books; co-author Broadway stage production, The Mystery Ship; dir. adv., exploit., Universal Pictures, trailer ed,

adv. manager, National Screen Service; exec. asst. to dir. adv. pub. Republic Pictures; to Souvaine Selective Pictures as adv., pub. dir., 1951; adv. pub. dept. United Artists 1953. Freelance writer since 1960.

SILVER, RAPHAEL D.: Producer. b. Cleveland, OH, 1930. e. Harvard Coll. and Harvard Graduate Sch. of Business Adm. Is pres. of Midwestern Land Devel. Corp. and Hodgson Houses, Inc. In 1973 formed Midwest Film Productions to produce Hester Street, written and directed by his wife, Joan Micklin Silver. Also distributed film independently. Also produced Between the Lines, directed by wife. Directed On the Yard and a Walk on the Moon, Crossing Delancey (exec. prod.).

SILVER, RON: Actor. b. New York, NY, July 2, 1946. e. U. of Buffalo, St. John's U., Taiwan, M.A. Trained for stage at Herbert Berghof Studios and Actors Studio. N.Y. stage debut in Kasper and Public Insult, 1971. Film debut in Semi-Tough, 1977. TV debut in Rhoda, 1976.
THEATER: El Grande de Coca Cola, Lotta, More Than You Deserve, Angel City (Mark Taper, LA), regional theater, Hurlyburly, Social Security, Hunting Cockroaches, Speed-the-Plow.
PICTURES: Tunnelvision, Welcome to L.A., Silent Rage, Best Friends, The Entity, Lovesick, Silkwood, Garbo Talks, Goodbye People, Eat and Run, Oh God! You Devil, Blue Steel.
TELEVISION: Hill Street Blues, Stockard Channing Show (series), Mac Davis Show, Bakers Dozen, Dear Detective. Movies: Betrayal, Word of Honor, A Father's Revenge, Drive, He Said (Trying Times), Billionaire Boys Club.

SILVERMAN, FRED: b. New York, NY, Sept., 1937. e. Syracuse U., Ohio State U., master's in TV and theatre arts. Joined WGN-TV, indep. sta. in Chicago. Came to N.Y. for exec. post at WPIX-TV, where stayed only six weeks CBS-TV hired him as dir. of daytime programs. Named v.p.—programs June, 1970. In May, 1975 left CBS to become pres., ABC Entertainment. In June, 1978, named pres. and chief exec. officer of NBC. Now Pres., Fred Silverman Company, Los Angeles.
TELEVISION: Prod./exec. prod.: Series: Perry Mason Movies, We Got It Made, Matlock, In the Heat of the Night, Jake and the Fatman, Father Dowling Mysteries, Braddock.

SILVERMAN, JIM: Executive. b. Des Moines, IA, June 26, 1950. e. U. of Hawaii, B.A., 1972; Taiwan National U., foreign language study, 1973. Exec. v.p. & co-founder, Commtron Corp., division of Bergen Brunswig Corp., 1975–83; pres. & founder, Continental Video, Inc., division of Cinema Group, Inc.

SILVERMAN, RON: Producer. Writer. b. Los Angeles, CA, June 13, 1933. e. U. of California at L.A., 1951–53; U. of Arizona, 1953–55. Reporter reviewer, Daily Variety, 1957–61; asst. to prod.-dir. Mark Robson, Red Lion Films, 20th Century-Fox, 1961–62; assoc. prod., Daystar Productions, 1961; v.p., 1964; assoc. prod. Crackerby TV series, 1965. Prod. exec., Warner Bros. TV, 1966; prod. & exec. Ted Mann Prods., 1967.
PICTURES INCLUDE: Buster and Billie (prod.), 1974, Lifeguard, Brubaker (prod.), Krull (prod.), Shoot to Kill (co-prod.).
TELEVISION: Wild Wild West (writer), 1967.

SILVERMAN, SYD: Executive. b. New York, NY, Jan 23, 1932. Grandson of Sime Silverman, founder of Variety in 1905. e. The Manlius Sch., 1946–50; Princeton U., 1950–54. Lt., U.S. Army, 1954–56. Publisher, Daily Variety and Weekly Variety.

SILVERSTEIN, ELLIOT: Director. b. Boston, MA, Aug. 3, 1927. e. Boston Coll., Yale U. Started career on television.
PICTURES: Cat Ballou, The Happening, A Man Called Horse, Deadly Honeymoon, The Car.
TELEVISION: Belle Sommers, Betrayed by Innocence, Night of Courage, Fight for Life.

SILVERSTEIN, MAURICE: Executive. b. Syracuse, NY, March 1, 1912. Booker, salesman, MGM domestic dep't; International Dep't, MGM; supervisor Southeast Asia Hdqts. Singapore, MGM, 1938–42; OWI chief, film distribution for Europe, hdqts. London, during W.W.II; asst. sales supervisor, Far East, MGM; regional director, Latin America, 1947; liaison exec. to handle independent productions MGM, 1956; vice-pres. MGM International, 1957; first vice-pres., 1958; pres., MGM International, 1963; vice-pres., parent company, Metro-Goldwyn-Mayer Inc. 1970; Silverstein Int'l Corp., pres.

SILVESTER, VICTOR, O.B.E.: Musical director. b. Wembley, England. e. St. John's Leatherhead, John Lyons, Harrow. Exclusive BBC contract; with his orchestra, records exclusively for Pye Records.

SIMMONS, ANTHONY: Director. Writer. b. London, England. e. Grad. from the LSE with LL.B. Practiced briefly as a barrister before entering the industry as writer/director of documentaries, then commercials and feature films. Awards: Grand Prix (shorts), Venice, Grand Prix, Locarno; 2 Int. Emmys.

284

PICTURES: Sunday By the Sea, Bow Bells, Four in the Morning, The Optimists, Black Joy, Little Sweetheart.
TELEVISION: On Giant's Shoulders, Supergran and the Magic Ray, Day After the Fair.

SIMMONS, JEAN: Actress. b. London, England, Jan. 31, 1929. e. Aida Foster Sch., London. Screen debut 1944, at 14 in Give Us the Moon. Voted one of top ten British money-making stars in M.P. Herald-Fame Poll, 1950–51. London stage: A Little Night Music.
PICTURES INCLUDE: Mr. Emmanuel, Meet Sexton Blake, Kiss the Boys Goodbye, Sports Day, Caesar and Cleopatra, Way to the Stars, Great Expectations, Hungry Hill, Black Narcissus, The Women In the Hall, Blue Lagoon, Hamlet, (Venice Film Fest., Best Actress), Adam and Evelyne, Trio, So Long as the Fair, Cage of Gold, The Clouded Yellow, Androcles and the Lion (U.S. film debut), Angel Face, Young Bess, Affair with a Stranger, The Actress, The Robe, She Couldn't Say No, A Bullet Is Waiting, The Egyptian, Desiree, Footsteps in the Fog, Guys and Dolls, Hilda Crane, This Could Be the Night, Until They Sail, The Big Country, Home Before Dark, This Earth Is Mine, Spartacus, The Grass Is Greener, All the Way Home, Elmer Gantry, Divorce American Style, Rough Night in Jericho, The Happy Ending (Acad. Award nom.), Say Hello to Yesterday, Dominique, Going Undercover, The Dawning.
TELEVISION: Beggarman Thief, The Easter Promise, The Dain Curse, The Home Front, Golden Gate, Jacqueline Susann's, Valley of the Dolls 1981, A Small Killing, The Thorn Birds (Emmy award, supp., 1983), North & South Book II, Inherit the Wind.

SIMMONS, JOHN: Producer, Director, Writer, Creative consultant. e. St. Clement Danes, U. of London, the Temple. Assoc. with many adv. doc. feature & TV films. Numerous International Festival awards, incl. Oscar nomin.; creative dir., Cinevista Ltd.; wrote, The Blue Bird, Loganberry Fair (lyrics, etc.), devised adv. campaigns, The Guns of Navarone, Summer Holiday; creative dir., John Simmons Creative Consultants Ltd. Join The Tea Set, Shell, Ovaltine, Waddington, Tide, Terylene, Marks & Spencer, Schweppes, Crown, Cleveland, Gold Camera Award (1st Place) for The Bosch Equation, U.S. Int. Ind. Film Festival, 1974. 1st Prize San Francisco Fest. 1975. Dev. & Dir. Cinema Ad. Awards, 1976. Corr. to Fin. Times, Variety, Campaign etc. Gold Camera Award 1977 for Stop Her, Silver Award, New York Fest. Consultant, Rank Advertising Awards (cinema) and commercial radio. Best radio commercial Award 1977. Award, Cannes 1978, A Clear Edge.

SIMMONS, MATTY: Producer. b. Oct. 3. Bd. chm., National Lampoon, Inc. Prod., National Lampoon Radio Hour; National Lampoon Lemmings; National Lampoon Show.
PICTURES: National Lampoon's Animal House; National Lampoon's Vacation; National Lampoon Goes to the Movies; National Lampoon's Class Reunion; National Lampoon's European Vacation.
TELEVISION: National Lampoon's Disco Beavers, National Lampoon's Class of '86 (exec. prod.), Delta House.

SIMMS, FRANK: Announcer. b. Tulsa, OK, June 8, 1921. e. U. of Tulsa, 1946. Radio announcer, U.S. Air Force, W.W.II; announcer, KVOO, Tulsa, to N.Y., 1953.
TELEVISION: I Love Lucy, My Little Margie, Public Defender, Garry Moore Show.

SIMON, MELVIN: Executive. b. New York, NY, Oct. 21, 1926. e. City Coll.of New York, B.B.A., 1949; graduate work at Indiana U. Law Sch. Owns and operates, in partnership with two brothers, over 90 shopping centers in U.S. In 1978 formed Melvin Simon Productions, privately owned corp., to finance films. Dissolved Co. in 1983.
PICTURES: Exec. Prod.: Dominique, When a Stranger Calls, The Runner Stumbles, Scavenger Hunt, Cloud Dancer, The Stunt Man, My Bodyguard, Zorro—the Gay Blade, Chu Chu and the Philly Flash, Porky's, Porky's II—The Next Day, Uforia, Wolf Lake, Porky's Revenge.
MEMBER: Friars Club; N.Y. div.; 1978, v.p., In-tl. Council of Shopping Centers; 1978, commerce and industry chm. of muscular dystrophy; mem. bd., Indiana Repertory Theatre 1978, corporate sponsor: Indianapolis 500 Festival, Indianapolis Museum of Arts, Indianapolis Children's Museum; Indianapolis Zoological Society.

SIMON, NEIL: Playwright. b. Bronx, NY, July 4, 1927. e. NYU, U.S. Army Air Force, 1945–46. Wrote comedy for radio with brother, Danny, also TV scripts for Sid Caesar, Red Buttons, Jackie Gleason, Phil Silvers, Garry Moore.
PLAYS INCLUDE: Come Blow Your Horn, Little Me, Barefoot in the Park, The Odd Couple, Sweet Charity, The Star Spangled Girl, Plaza Suite, Promises, Promises, The Last of the Red Hot Lovers, The Gingerbread Lady, The Prisoner of Second Avenue, The Sunshine Boys, The Good Doctor, God's Favorite, California Suite, Chapter Two, They're Playing Our Song, I Ought to Be in Pictures, Fools, Brighton Beach Memoirs, Biloxi Blues, The Odd Couple (female),

Broadway Bound, Rumors. Adapted several of own plays to screen and wrote original s.p.s, The Out-of-Towners, and The Slugger's Wife.
PICTURES: After the Fox, Barefoot in the Park, The Out-of-Towners, The Heartbreak Kid, The Prisoner of Second Avenue, The Sunshine Boys, Murder by Death, The Goodbye Girl, The Cheap Detective, California Suite, Seems Like Old Times, Only When I Laugh (also co-prod.), Chapter Two, I Ought to Be in Pictures (also co-prod.), Max Dugan Returns (also co-prod.), The Lonely Guy (adaptation), The Slugger's Wife, Brighton Beach Memoirs, Biloxi Blues.
TELEVISION: The Trouble With People, Plaza Suite.
AWARDS: Emmy Award: Sid Caesar Show (1957), The Phil Silvers Show (1959). Tony Award: The Odd Couple (1965), Biloxi Blues (1985). Writers Guild Screen Award: The Odd Couple (1969), The Out-of-Towners (1971).

SIMON, PAUL: Singer, Composer, Actor. b. Newark, NJ, Nov. 8, 1942. Teamed with Art Garfunkel, writing and performing own songs; they parted in 1970 to go separate ways. Reunited for concert in New York, 1982, which was televised on HBO.
PICTURES: The Graduate (songs), Annie Hall (actor), One Trick Pony (s.p., act., comp.)
TELEVISION: The Paul Simon Special (Emmy), Home Box Office Presents Paul Simon, The Graceland Concert.

SIMONE, SIMONE: Actress. b. April 23, 1914. Marseilles, France. Played in many films in Europe, among them Les Beaux Jours, and Lac aux Dames. On stage in Toi C'est Moi, and others.
PICTURES INCLUDE: Girl's Dormitory, Ladies in Love, Seventh Heaven, Love and Kisses, Josette, Johnny Doesn't Live Here Any More, Silent Bell, Temptation, Harbor, Lost Women, La Ronde, Pit of Loneliness, Le Plaisir, Double Destin, The Extra Day.

SIMPSON, DON: Producer. b. Anchorage, AL, Oct. 29, 1945. e. U. of Oregon, Phi Beta Kappa, 1967. Began career in industry as acct. exec. with Jack Woodel Agency, San Francisco, where supervised mktg. of Warner Bros. films. Recruited by WB in 1971 as mktg. exec. specializing in youth market; oversaw Woodstock, Clockwork Orange, Billy Jack, etc. Co-writer on low-budget films, Aloha, Bobby and Rose (Columbia) and Cannonball (New World). Joined Paramount as prod. exec. 1975; promoted 1977 to v.p., prod. Named sr. v.p. of prod., 1980; pres. of world-wide prod., 1981. Formed Don Simpson/Jerry Bruckheimer Prods. 1983, entering into exclusive deal with Paramount to develop and produce for m.p. and TV divisions.
PICTURES: Flashdance, Thief of Hearts, Beverly Hills Cop, Top Gun, Beverly Hills Cop II.

SIMPSON, GARRY: Producer, Director, Writer. e. Stanford U. Major shows with NBC-TV: Jimmy Durante Show, Armstrong Circle Theatre, Ed Wynn Show, Philco TV Playhouse, Ballet Theatre. Awards: Academy of TV Arts & Sci., Sylvania. Documentary film writer-producer awards: International Film & TV Festival, Chicago Film Festival, Broadcast Media Awards. Currently, independent prod.-dir.

SIMPSON, O.J.: Actor. b. San Francisco, CA, July 9, 1947. r.n. Orenthal James Simpson. e. U. of Southern California. Was star collegiate and professional football player.
PICTURES: The Towering Inferno, The Klansman, Killer Force, Cassandra Crossing, Capricorn One, Firepower, Hambone & Hillie, The Naked Gun.
TELEVISION: Movies: Roots, A Killing Affair, Goldie and the Boxer (also exec. p.), Detour to Terror (exec. p.), The Golden Moment—An Olympic Love Story, Student Exchange.

SIMS, JOAN: Actress. b. London, England, 1930.
PICTURES INCLUDE: Dry Rot, Off the Record, No Time for Tears, Just My Luck, The Naked Truth, The Captain's Table, Passport to Shame, Emergency Ward 10, Most of the Carry On' films, Doctor in Love, Watch Your Stern, Twice Round the Daffodils, The Iron Maiden, Nurse on Wheels, Doctor in Clover, Doctor in Trouble, The Garnett Saga, Not Now Darling, Don't Just Lie There Say Something, Love Among the Ruins, One of Our Dinosaurs Is Missing, Till Death Us Do Part, The Way of the World, Deceptions.
TELEVISION: Born and Bred, Worzel Gummidge, Ladykillers, Crown Court, Cockles, Fairly Secret Army, Tickle on the Tum, Miss Marple: A Murder Is Announced, Hay Fever, In Loving Memory, Drummonds, Farrington of the F.O., Dr. Who.

SINATRA, FRANK: Actor, Singer. b. Hoboken, NJ, Dec. 12, 1915. Sportswriter; then singer on radio various N.Y. stations; joined Harry James orchestra, later Tommy Dorsey. On screen as a band vocalist in Las Vegas Nights, Ship Ahoy, Reveille with Beverly. Spec. Academy Award 1945 for acting in The House I Live In, short subject on tolerance.
PICTURES INCLUDE: Higher and Higher, (acting debut, 1943), Step Lively, Anchors Aweigh, Words and Music, It Happened in Brooklyn, Till the Clouds Roll By, Miracle of the Bells, Kissing Bandit, Take Me Out to the Ball Game, On the

Town, Double Dynamite, Meet Danny Wilson, From Here to Eternity (Acad. Award. best supporting actor, 1953), Suddenly, Young at Heart, Not as a Stranger, Guys and Dolls, Tender Trap, Man With the Golden Arm, Johnny Concho, High Society, Around The World in 80 Days, Pride and the Passion, The Joker is Wild, Pal Joey, Kings Go Forth, Some Came Running, A Hole in the Head, Never So Few, Ocean's 11, Devil at Four O'Clock, Sergeants 3, The Manchurian Candidate, Come Blow Your Horn, The List of Adrian Messenger, 4 for Texas, Robin and the Seven Hoods, None But the Brave (dir.), Von Ryan's Express, Marriage on the Rocks, Cast a Giant Shadow, Assault on a Queen, The Naked Runner, Tony Rome, The Detective, Lady in Cement, Dirty Dingus Magee, That's Entertainment!, The First Deadly Sin, (also exec. prod.), Who Framed Roger Rabbit? (voice).
TELEVISION: The Frank Sinatra Show, numerous specials, etc. Won both an Emmy and a Peabody Award. Hersholt Humanitarian Award, 1971. 1977: Contract on Cherry Street (movie), Sinatra: Concert For the Americas, Magnum P.I.

SINCLAIR, ANDREW: Director, Writer. b. 1935. Early career as novelist and historian, playwright. Published over 20 books in U.K., U.S. Entered m.p. ind. 1968.
PICTURES INCLUDE: s.p.: Before Winter Comes, Adventures in the Skin Trade, The Voyage of the Beagle, You?; dir., writer: The Breaking of Bumbo, 1970; dir., writer: Under Milk Wood, 1971; prod. Malachi's Cove, 1973; Tuxedo Warrior, 1982; Writ. The Representative, The Scarlet Letter; Martin Eden.

SINCLAIR, MADGE: Actress. b. Kingston, Jamaica, April 28, 1938. e. Shortwood Women's College. Worked in Jamaica as a teacher and in the insurance business before moving to New York. Chairwoman, Madge Walters Sinclair Inc., women's wear manufacturer and distributor. Awards: NAACP Image Award, 1981 and 1983, best actress in dramatic series, Trapper John M.D.; Drama-Logue Critics Award, 1986, Boseman & Lena; Mother of the Year Award, 1984. Member: bd. of dir., Museum of African American Art, Gwen Bolden Foundation.
THEATER: Kumaliza (NYSF, debut, 1969); Iphigenia (NYSF, NY and with Young Vic, London); Mod Donna, Ti-Jean and His Brothers; Blood; Division Street (Mark Taper Forum); Boesman & Lena (LA Theatre Center); Tartuffe (L.A. Theatre Center); Trinity.
PICTURES INCLUDE: Conrack (debut, 1974); Cornbread, Earl & Me; Leadbelly; I Will, I Will...For Now; Convoy; Uncle Joe Shannon; Star Trek IV; Coming to America.
TELEVISION: Series: Grandpa Goes to Washington (1978–79); Trapper John M.D. (1980–86); O'Hara. Guest: Madigan, Medical Center, The Waltons; Joe Forester; Doctor's Hospital; Executive Suite; Medical Story; Serpico; The White Shadow; All in the Family; Mini-Series: Roots. Movies: I Love, You, Goodbye; One in a Million: The Ron LeFlore Story; The Autobiography of Miss Jane Pittman; I Know Why the Caged Bird Sings; High Ice; Jimmy B and Andre; Guyana Tragedy: The Story of Jim Jones; Victims; Look Away: The Emancipation of Mary Todd Lincoln, Divided We Stand.

SINDEN, DONALD: Actor. b. Plymouth, England, Oct. 9, 1923. Stage debut 1942 in fit-up shows; also with Shakespeare Memorial Theatre, then Old Vic. London stage includes London Assurance (also NY), Habeas Corpus, Shut Your Eyes and Think of England, Present Laughter, Two into One. TV debut 1948; screen debut in 1953, Cruel Sea.
PICTURES INCLUDE: The Cruel Sea, Mogambo, A Day to Remember, You Know What Sailors Are, Doctor in the House, The Beachcomber, Mad About Men, An Alligator Named Daisy, Black Tent, Eyewitness, Tiger in the Smoke, Doctor at Large, Rockets Galore, The Captain's Table, Operation Bullshine, Your Money or Your Wife, The Siege of Sydney Street, Twice Around the Daffodils, Mix Me a Person, Decline and Fall, The Island at the Top of the World, That Lucky Touch.
TELEVISION: Bullet in the Ballet, Road to Rome, Dinner With the Family, Odd Man In, Love from Italy, The Frog, The Glove, The Mystery of Edwin Drood, The Happy Ones, The Comedy of Errors, The Wars of the Roses, The Red House, Blackmail, A Bachelor Gray, Our Man at St. Marks (3 series), The Wind in the Tall Paper Chimney, A Woman Above Reproach, Call My Bluff, Relatively Speaking, Father Dear Father, The 19th Hole, Seven Days in the Life of Andrew Pelham (serial), The Assyrian Rejuvenator, The Organization (serial), The Confederacy of Wives, Tell It to the Chancellor, The Rivals, Two's Company (4 series), All's Well That Ends Well, Never the Twain (7 series).

SINGER, LORI: Actress. b. Corpus Christi, TX, Nov. 6, 1962. Sister of actor Marc Singer and daughter of symphony conductor Jacques Singer. Concert cellist while in teens. Won starring role in TV series Fame (1981). Motion picture debut in Footloose (1984).
PICTURES: The Falcon and The Snowman, The Man with

One Red Shoe, Trouble in Mind, Summer Heat, Made in U.S.A., Warlock.
TELEVISION: Born Beautiful.

SINGER, MARC: Actor. b. Vancouver, B.C., Canada, Jan. 29. Brother of actress Lori Singer. Son of symphony conductor Jacques Singer. Trained in summer stock and regional theatre.
PICTURES: Go Tell the Spartans, If You Could See What I Hear, The Beastmaster, Born to Race.
TELEVISION: Roots II, 79 Park Avenue, Journey from Darkness, The Contender, For Ladies Only, Her Life as a Man, "V" (movie and series), Dallas.

SINGER, ROBERT: Producer. b. Nyack, NY. e. New York U., B.S.
PICTURES: Independence Day; Cujo; The Howling; Restless.
TELEVISION: Lacy and the Mississippi Queen; Dog and Cat series; Night Stalker; 7 Wide World of Entertainment specials; The Children Nobody Wanted; Three Eyes; Sadat; V-The Final Battle (exec. prod.); V (series-exec. prod.).

SINGLETON, PENNY: Actress. r.n. Dorothy McNulty. b. Philadelphia, PA, September 15, 1908. e. Columbia U. First Broadway success came as top comedienne in Good News., exec. pres. AGVA.
PICTURES INCLUDE: 28 films in Blondie series; Go West Young Lady, Footlight Glamor, Young Widow, The Best Man.
TELEVISION: The Jetsons (voice).

SIODMAK, CURT: Director. b. 1902. e. U. of Zurich. Engineer, newspaper reporter, writer in Berlin; novelist, including F.P.1 Does Not Answer, adapt. 1932 for Ufa. Originals and screenplays in France and England including France (Le Bal), Transatlantic Tunnel, GB.
PICTURES INCLUDE: In U.S. originals and screenplays, many pictures including Her Jungle Love, Aloma of the South Sea, Par.; Invisible Woman; basis: Son of Dracula; s.p.: The Mantrap; (orig.) House of Frankenstein; collab. orig. s.p.: Shady Lady; s.p.: Beast with Five Fingers; collab. s.p., story: Berlin Express; collab. s.p.: Tarzan's Magic Fountain, Four Days Leave; dir.: Bridge of the Gorilla; collab. s.p., dir.: The Magnetic Monster; s.p.: Riders to the Stars; story, s.p.: Creature with the Atom Brain; story: Earth vs. the Flying Saucers.

SIPES, DONALD: b. 1928. Executive. Attorney. Worked for talent agencies early in career; also for NBC and CBS networks as business affairs official. Joined MCA Inc. in 1975, becoming pres. of its Universal TV unit in 1978 and corporate v.p. in June, 1981. In November, 1981, named MGM Film Co. pres. and chief operating officer. 1983, named UA Corp. Chm & CEO. In 1984, pres., Lorimar Dist. Group.

SKELTON, RED: Actor, Comedian. r.n. Richard Skelton. b. Vincennes, IN, July 18, 1913. Joined medicine show at 10; later in show boat stock, minstrel shows, vaudeville, burlesque, circus. Screen debut 1939 in Having Wonderful Time. On radio from 1936. Red Skelton Show, TV, since 1950. Composer of music, writer of short stories and painter.
PICTURES INCLUDE: Flight Command, Lady Be Good, The People vs. Dr. Kildare, Whistling in the Dark, Whistling in Dixie, Ship Ahoy, Maisie Gets Her Man, Panama Hattie, Du Barry Was a Lady, Thousands Cheer, I Dood It, Whistling in Brooklyn, Bathing Beauty, Ziegfeld Follies, Fuller Brush Man, Southern Yankee, Neptune's Daughter, Yellow Cab Man, Three Little Words, Watch the Birdie, Excuse My Dust, Texas Carnival, Lovely to Look At, The Clown, Half a Hero, Great Diamond Robbery, Public Pigeon No. 1, Those Magnificent Men in Their Flying Machines.

SKERRITT, TOM: Actor. b. Detroit, MI, Aug. 25, 1933. e. Wayne State U., UCLA. Appeared in Italian movies 1972–76.
PICTURES: War Hunt, M*A*S*H, Fuzz, Big Bad Mama, Harold and Maude, The Devil's Rain, The Turning Point, Ice Castles, Up in Smoke, Alien, Savage Harvest, Silence of the North, Fighting Back, A Dangerous Summer, The Dead Zone, Top Gun, Opposing Forces, Space Camp, Wisdom, Maid to Order, The Big Town, Poltergeist III, Steel Magnolias, Hunchback.
TELEVISION: Ryan's Four, (series), The Calendar Girl Murders, The Last Day, A Touch of Scandal, Miles to Go, Parent Trap II, Poker Alice, Moving Target, Nightmare at Bitter Creek.

SKILES, MARLIN: Composer. b. Harrisburg, PA, Dec. 17, 1906; e. Froehlich Sch. of Music, Harrisburg. Pianist for several dance orch.; mus. dir., pianist, arr. for Paul Whiteman, Irving Aaronson, others; to Hollywood, 1932; comp., arr. for radio & many m.p.
PICTURES INCLUDE: com., arr.: Over 21, Jolson Story, Gilda, Tonight and Every Night, Dead Reckoning, Callaway Went Thataway, Rose Bowl Story, Battle Zone, The Maze, Fighter Attack, Pride of the Blue Grass, Arrow in the Dust, Dial Red O, Annapolis Story, many Bowery Boys features, Sudden Danger, Fort Massacre, The Hypnotic Eye, The Strangler, The Resurrection of Zachary Wheeler.

SKIRBALL, WILLIAM N.: Exhibitor. b. Homestead, PA. Began career with Metro in Des Moines & Chicago; states rights distrib., Cleveland; assoc. with brother, Jack H. Skirball (of Skirball-Manning prod. team), educational films br. mgr.; also brother of Joseph Skirball, first nat'l franchise owner, Pittsburgh. Currently partner Skirball Bros. circuit (10 theatres, Ohio), hdqts., Cleveland, OH.

SKOLIMOWSKI, JERZY: Director. b. Poland, 1938.
PICTURES: Identification Marks—None, Walkover, The Barrier, The Departure, Hands Up, Dialogue, The Adventures of Gerard, Deep End, King Queen Knave, The Shout (also co-s.p.), Circle of Deceit (act.), Moonlighting (also s.p., prod.); Success Is the Best Revenge, The Lightship, White Nights (actor), Big Shots (actor), Torrents of Spring (dir.), Showers.

SLATER, DAPHNE: Actress. b. Bayswater, London, England, March 3, 1928. e. Haberdashers' Askes Sch.; Royal Acad. of Dramatic Art. Stage debut: The Rising Generation, 1945; several plays including King Lear; m.p. debut in Courtneys of Curzon Street, 1947; TV debut for BBC in I Want to Be an Actor, 1946.
TELEVISION: Emma, Shout Aloud Salvation, All the Year Round, They Fly by Twilight, Pride and Prejudice, The Affair at Assino, Beau Brummell, Jane Eyre, Precious Bane, The Dark Is Light Enough, Mary Rose, Julius Caesar, Berkeley Square, Less Than Kind, The Burning Glass, Persuasion, The Winslow Boy, She Stoops to Conquer, Nothing to Pay, The Father, The Bald Prima Donna, The Big Breaker, The Cocktail Party, Photo Finish, The Seagull, Love Story, Emergency Ward 10, Jackanory, The First Freedom, Man of Our Times, The Jazz Age, Callan, The Piano Tuner, Happy Ever After, The Pretenders, Virtue, Elizabeth R, The Staff Room, Footprints in the Sand.

SLATER, HELEN: Actress. b. New York, NY, Dec. 19, 1963. Off-Bdwy: Responsible Parties, Almost Romance.
PICTURES: Supergirl, The Legend of Billie Jean, Ruthless People, The Secret of My Success, Sticky Fingers, Happy Together.

SLATZER, ROBERT FRANKLIN: Writer, Director, Producer, Author; b. Marion, OH, April 4, 1927. e. Ohio State U., U. of California at L.A., 1947. Radio news commentator sportscaster, wrote radio serials; adv. dir., Brush-Moore Newspapers; feature writer, Scripps-Howard Newspapers; adv. exec., The Columbus Dispatch; syndicated columnist, New York Journal-American; wrote several guest columns for Walter Winchell and Dorothy Kilgallen; author of several western short stories and novels; wrote, directed, produced many industrial films, documentaries, sports specials and commercials; 1949–51, writer for Grand National Studios Productions, Monogram Pictures, Republic Studios, Eagle-Lion Films; 1951, publicist, Hope Enterprises; Pub. Dir., Paramount Pictures; 1952, personal manager to Marilyn Monroe, Ken Maynard, James Craig, Gail Russell and other stars; 1953, story editor and assoc. prod., Joe Palooka Productions; 1953–54, staff writer Universal Studios, RKO Radio Pictures, MGM, Columbia and Paramount Studios; 1958, formed Robert F. Slatzer Productions; 1960, exec. in chg. of prod., Jaguar Pictures Corp.; 1963–65, president Slatzer Oil & Gas Company; 1966–67, board director, United Mining & Milling Corp.; 1967–70, wrote and directed several feature films; 1970–74, exec., Columbia Pictures Corp.; 1974, resumed producing and financing features and television films; 1976, honored as "Fellow", Mark Twain Inst.
PICTURES INCLUDE: White Gold, The Obsessed, Mike and the Heiress, Under Texas Skies, They Came To Kill, Trail of the Mounties, Jungle Goddess, Montana Desperado, Pride of the Blue, Green Grass of Wyoming, The Naked Jungle, Warpaint, Broken Lance, Elephant Walk, South of Death Valley, The Big Gusher, Arctic Flight, The Hellcats, Bigfoot, John Wayne's No Substitute for Victory', Joniko—Eskimo Boy, Operation North Slope, Don't Go West, Mulefeathers, The Unfinished, Single Room Furnished, Viva Zapata, Inchon.
TELEVISION: The Great Outdoors, Adventures of White Arrow, Let's Go Boating, The Joe Palooka Story, Amos & Andy, I Am the Law, Files of Jeffrey Jones, Fireside Theatre, The Unser Story, Year of Opportunity (Award winning spec.), The Big Ones, Ken Maynard's West, Where are They Now?, The Groovy Seven, The Untouchables, The Detectives, Wild Wild West, Wagon Train, Playhouse 90, Highway Patrol, David Frost Special, Today Show, ABC News, 20/20.
AUTHOR: (novels) Desert Empire, Rose of the Range, Rio, Rawhide Range, The Cowboy and the Heiress, Daphne, Campaign Girl, Scarlet, The Dance Studio Hucksters, Born to be Wild, Single Room Furnished, The West is Still Wild, Gusher, The Young Wildcats; (biographies) The Life and Curious Death of Marilyn Monroe, The Life and Legend of Ken Maynard, Who Killed Thelma Todd?, The Duke of Thieves, Bing Crosby—The Hollow Man, Duke: The Life and Times of John Wayne.

SLAVIN, GEORGE: Writer. b. Newark, NJ, May 2, 1916; e. Bucknell U., drama, Yale U.

PICTURES INCLUDE: story, collab. s.p., Intrigue; collab. story, Woman on Pier 18; collab. s.p., The Nevadan, Mystery Submarine; collab. story & s.p. Peggy, Red Mountain, City of Bad Men; collab. story, Weekend with Father, Thunder Bay, Rocket Man; collab. story, collab. s.p., Smoke Signal, Uranium Boom; collab. s.p., Desert Sands, The Halliday Brand, Son of Robin Hood.

SLOCOMBE, DOUGLAS: Cinematographer. b. England, Feb. 10, 1913. Former journalist.
PICTURES: Dead of Night, The Captive Heart, Hue and Cry, The Loves of Joanna Godden, It Always Rains on Sunday, Saraband for Dead Lovers, Kind Hearts and Coronets, Cage of Gold, The Lavender Hill Mob, Mandy, The Man in the White Suit, The Titfield Thunderbolt, Man in the Sky, Ludwig II, Lease on Life, The Smallest Show on Earth, Tread Softly, Stranger, Circus of Horrors, The Young Ones, The Mark, The L-Shaped Room, Freud, The Servant, Guns at Batashi, A High Wind in Jamaica, The Blue Max, Promise Her Anything, The Vampire Killers, Fathom, Robbery, Boom, The Lion in Winter, The Italian Job, The Music Lovers, Murphy's War, The Buttercup Chain, Travels With My Aunt, Jesus Christ Superstar, The Great Gatsby, Rollerball, Hedda, The Sailor Who Fell From Grace With the Sea, Nasty Habits, Julia, Close Encounters of the Third Kind, Caravans, Lost and Found, Nijinsky, Raiders of the Lost Ark, Never Say Never Again, The Pirates of Penzance, Water, Indiana Jones and the Temple of Doom, Indiana Jones and the Last Crusade.
TELEVISION: Love Among the Ruins, The Corn Is Green, etc.

SLOTE, A. R.: Bureau Chief in Pakistan for Quigley Publications. b. Bagasra, India, June 9, 1935. e. Pakistan National H.S., Muslim Sch. and Art. Coll., Karachi. Booker, Columbia Pictures Int. Corp. Asst. mgr., Plaza Cinema, Paradise Theatres, Ltd. Editor: Filmlife, 1959–64; Karachi correspondent for Weekly Chitrali, Pakistan Daily Observer, Dhaka, 1966–70. Editor, publisher: Pakistan Filmdom, 1966; Sind Film Directory, 1981; Platinum Jubilee Film Directory, 1987. Film Page Incharge, The Star Daily of Karachi since 1971.

SMAKWITZ, CHARLES A.: e. Syracuse U. Named by Warner Bros. as dist. mgr. Albany, Troy and Utica, and named as zone mgr. Warner Bros., New York State Theatres. Made zone mgr. of Stanley Warner Theatres for the state of New Jersey and New York state theatres added to NJ Zone and made headquarters in Newark, NJ in 1955, transferred to New York home office as national director of public relations, publicity, advertising for Stanley Warner Corp. nation-wide. In the various areas was Mayor's Rehabilitation and Urban Development Com. of Albany, State Albany Chairman War Activities Committee, National Public Dir. Red Cross Fund Organized Albany V.C. Tent #9 and served as Chief Barker 3 years, 1949–1952, elected National Representative V.C. of America. Member NY State Program and Planning Committee, Pres. Heart Assn. of Albany County, NJ State Chairman Nat. Conf. of Christian and Jews 1955–62. Organized and Pres. of Syr. U. of Greater N.Y. Served as v.p. of V.C. of N.Y. Assistant to Spyros R. Skoveas 1969–71, served as International-Ambassador at large of V.C. International Consultant exhibition, production, promotion, real estate and public relations.

SMIGHT, JACK: Director. b. Minneapolis, MN, March 9, 1926. e. U. of MN, BA. Began as disc jockey then became TV dir. of One Man's Family (1953).
PICTURES INCLUDE: I'd Rather Be Rich, The Third Day, Harper, Kaleidoscope, The Secret War of Harry Frigg, No Way to Treat a Lady, Strategy of Terror, The Illustrated Man, The Travelling Executioner, Rabbit Run, Airport 1975, Midway, Damnation Alley, Fast Break, Loving Couples, Number One with a Bullet.
TELEVISION: Banacek, Columbo, Madigan. Movies: Eddie (Emmy, 1959), Roll of Thunder, Hear My Cry, Frankenstein—The True Story, Double Indemnity, Remembrance of Love, Linda, The Longest Night, The Screaming Woman.

SMITH, ALEXIS: Actress. b. Penticton, Can., June 8, 1921. m. actor Craig Stevens. e. Los Angeles City Coll. In summer stock British Columbia; star in coll. prod., Night of January 16th.
PICTURES INCLUDE: Smiling Ghost, Dive Bomber, Steel Against the Sky, Gentlemen Jim, Thank Your Luck Stars, Constant Nymph, Conflict, Adventures of Mark Twain, Rhapsody in Blue, Horn Blows at Midnight (Star of Tomorrow, 1943), One More Tomorrow, Night and Day, Of Human Bondage, Stallion Road, Two Mrs. Carrolls, Woman in White, Decision of Christopher Blake, Whiplash, South of St. Louis, Any Number Can Play, One Last Fling, Undercover Girl, Wyoming Hall, Montana, Here Comes the Groom, Cave of the Outlaws, Turning Point, Split Second, Sleeping Tiger, Eternal Sea, The Young Philadelphians, Once Is Not Enough, The Little Girl Who Lives Down the Lane, Casey's Shadow, Tough Guys.
BROADWAY: Follies (Tony Award), 1971, The Women, 1973, Summer Brave, 1975; Platinum, 1978.

TELEVISION: Movies: A Death in California, Dress Gray. Series: Hothouse.

SMITH, CHARLES MARTIN: Actor. b. Oct. 30, 1953. e. California State U. Father is animation artist Frank Smith.
PICTURES INCLUDE: Actor: The Culpepper Cattle Company, Fuzz, The Spikes Gang, American Graffiti, More American Graffiti, The Buddy Holly Story, Never Cry Wolf, Starman, The Untouchables, Trick or Treat (dir.), The Experts, Boris & Natasha in Our Boy Badenov.
TELEVISION: Series: The Brady Bunch, Monte Nash. Movies: Cotton Candy, Go Ask Alice, Law of the Land.

SMITH, CONSTANCE: Actress. r.n. Constance Smyth. b. Limerick, Ire., 1929. e. St. Louis Convent. Began career as model for Noel Mayne; winner of beauty contest Screen Magazine. Freelance actress, studios in Eng., prior to Hollywood m.p. debut in The Mudlark (1950).
PICTURES INCLUDE: Brighton Rock, Now Barrabas, Trottie True, Murder at the Window, Blackmail, The Perfect Woman, Room to Let, The 13th Letter, I'll Never Forget You, Red Skies of Montana, Treasure of the Golden Condor, Tiger By The Tail, Lure of the Wilderness, Taxi, Man in the Attic, Big Tipoff.

SMITH, HOWARD K.: News commentator. b. Ferriday, LA, May 12, 1914. e. Tulane U., 1936; Heidelberg U., Germany; Oxford U., Rhodes scholarship. United Press, London, 1939; United Press Bureau, Copenhagen; United Press, Berlin, 1940; joined CBS News, Berlin corr., 1941. Reported on occupied Europe from Switzerland to 1944; covered Nuremberg trials, 1946; ret. to U.S., moderator, commentator or reporter, CBS Reports, Face the Nation, Eyewitness to History, The Great Challenge, numerous news specials. Sunday night news analysis. CBS News Washington corr., 1957; chief corr. & mgr., Washington Bureau, 1961; joined, ABC News, Jan. 1962. News and comment, ABC news. Anchorman and commentator, ABC Evening News. Author: Last Train from Berlin, 1942, The State of Europe, 1949. Washington, D.C.—The Story of Our Nation's Capital, 1967.

SMITH, HY: Executive. b. New York, NY, June 3, 1934. e. Baruch Sch., City Coll. of New York, B.B.A. Joined Paramount Pictures 1967, foreign ad.-pub coordinator; 1969-joined United Artists as foreign ad.-pub mgr., named int'l. ad.-pub dir., 1970; named v.p.; intl. adv.-pub. 1976: Appointed vice pres. worldwide Advertising, publicity and promotion, July 1978; 1981, named first v.p., adv./pub./promo; 1982, joined Rastar Films as v.p., intl. project director for Annie. 1983, joined United Intl. Pictures as sr. v.p., adv/pub, based in London. 1984, named sr. v.p., mktg.

SMITH, JACLYN: Actress. b. Houston, TX, Oct. 26, 1947. Started acting while in high school and studied drama and psychology at Trinity U. in San Antonio. Appeared in many commercials as model.
PICTURES INCLUDE: Bootleggers, The Adventures, Deja Vu.
TELEVISION: McCloud, Get Christy Love, The Rookies, World of Disney, Switch, Charlie's Angels (series). Movies: The Night They Saved Christmas, Sentimental Journey, Florence Nightingale, George Washington, Rage of Angels: The Story Continues, Windmills of the Gods, The Bourne Identity.

SMITH, JACQUELINE: Executive. b. Philadelphia, PA, May 24, 1933. e. Antioch Coll., 1954. m. William Dale Smith, novelist (pseudonym David Anthony). Actress, Bermudiana Theatre in Bermuda, The Antioch Theatre, OH and several little theatres in Washington, DC; with the Stanford U. Players. Did research and writing for RCA, worked as a nursery school teacher and directed Little Theatre groups in the West Coast area. 1957: wrote and produced over 100 weekly children's programs at KPIX, San Francisco. Promotion director at WPIX-TV, N.Y. Worked with CBS TV Network for over 5 yrs. as general prog. exec. and exec. prod. of CBS West Coast daytime programs. Currently director of special projects at Warner Bros. Television Dept. and executive producer of Warner Bros. Animation Division.

SMITH, JOSEPH P.: Executive. b. Brooklyn, NY. e. Columbia U. Started career Wall Street; joined RKO Radio Pictures, served in sales and managerial posts; exec. vice-pres., Lippert Productions, Hollywood; vice pres., Telepictures, Inc., formed and pres., Cinema-Vue Corp.; pres., Pathe Pictures, Inc., Pathe News, Inc.

SMITH, MAGGIE: C.B.E. Actress. b. Ilford, England, Dec. 28, 1934. Early career Oxford Playhouse. With the Old Vic 1959–60. Also with Stratford Ontario Shakespeare Fest. 1976–78, & 1980. Received C.B.E. 1970. Numerous TV appearances Britain, America.
THEATER: Twelfth Night (debut, 1952), New Faces of 1956 (NY debut, as comedienne, 1956), Share My Lettuce, The Stepmother, Rhinoceros, The Rehearsal, The Private Ear, The Public Eye, Mary, Mary, The Recruiting Officer, Othello, The Master Builder, Hay Fever, Much Ado About Nothing,

Black Comedy, Miss Julie, Hedda Gabler, Private Lives (London & NY), Peter Pan, As You Like It, Macbeth, Night and Day, Virginia.
PICTURES INCLUDE: Nowhere to Go, The Pumpkin Eater, The V.I.P.s, Young Cassidy, Othello, The Honey Pot, Hot Millions, The Prime of Miss Jean Brodie (Acad. Award, Best Actress), Oh What a Lovely War, Love and Pain, Travels with my Aunt, Murder by Death, Death on the Nile, California Suite (Acad. Award), Clash of the Titans, Quartet, Evil Under the Sun, Better Late Than Never, The Missionary, A Private Function, Lily in Love, A Room with a View, The Lonely Passion of Judith Hearne.
TELEVISION: Much Ado About Nothing, Man and Superman, On Approval, Home and Beauty.

SMITH, MAURICE: Producer, Director, Writer. b. London, England, May 12, 1939. e. St. Ignatius Coll. Prior to entering m.p. industry, worked in bank in England, on newspaper in Canada, pool hustler, general contractor in Los Angeles, CA.
PICTURES INCLUDE: The Glory Stompers, Scream Free, Cycle Savages, Hard Trail, Diamond Stud, Love Swedish Style, November Children, How Come Nobody's On Our Side, Joys of Jezebel, Screwball Hotel, Grotesque (exec. prod.).

SMITH, ROGER: Actor, Producer. b. South Gate, CA, Dec. 18, 1932. m. actress-performer Ann Margret. e. U. of Arizona. Started career at age 7, one of the Meglin Kiddies, appearing at the Mayan Theater, Wilshire, Ebell.
PICTURES INCLUDE: No Time to Be Young, Crash Landing, Operation Madball, Man of a Thousand Faces, Never Steal Anything Small, Auntie Mame, Rogues Gallery.
TELEVISION: The Horace Heidt Show, Ted Mack Original Amateur Hour, 77 Sunset Strip (series), writer, ABC-TV, sings, composes, American folk songs. Producer: Ann-Margret Olsson; Ann-Margret Smith; Ann-Margret-Rhinestone Cowgirl.

SMITH, WILLIAM: Actor. b. Columbia, MO, May 24, 1932. e. Syracuse, U., BA; UCLA, MA.
PICTURES INCLUDE: Darker Than Amber, C.C. and Company, The Losers, Run, Angel, Run, Blood and Guts, Seven, Fast Company, No Knife, Twilight's Last Gleaming, The Frisco Kid, Any Which Way You Can, Red Dawn, Moon in Scorpio, Maniac Cop, Emperor of the Bronx, Nam, B.O.R.N., Hell Comes to Frogtown, Terror in Beverly Hills.
TELEVISION: Rich Man, Poor Man, Hawaii 5-0, The Jerk Too, The Rebels, Wild Times, Death Among Friends, Wildside.

SMOLEN, DONALD E.: Executive. b. New York, NY, Aug. 10, 1923. e. New York U., 1947; Pratt Inst., 1947, Ecole Des Beaux Arts, 1949. Art dept. Fox, 1940–41; art dept. Kayton Spiero Advtg., 1942; illustrator designer, Gilbert Miller Studios 1946–49; free lance illustrator, designer, 1951–65 servicing such accounts as UA, Fox, Warner Bros., TWA, Ford Motors; dir. of adv., UA. Resigned 1974 to form own co., Donald E. Smolen and Associates, consultant for m.p. adv.; 1975 merged to form Smolen, Smith and Connolly, advertising and marketing consultants to m.p. industry. Created ad campaigns for All the Presidents' Men, Fiddler on the Roof, Rocky, Superman, Star Wars. 1987, joined newly formed distribution arm, Kings Road Entertainment.

SNAPER, WILBUR: Exhibitor. b. Perth Amboy, NJ, Oct. 30, 1911. e. Yale U. 1933, N.J. Law, 1935. Pres. Snaper Theatres, New York, nat'l pres. Allied States Assn.; partner 1957. Member: Yale Club, Variety Club, N.Y. Bridge Club; pres. Triangle Theatres; pres., AIT Theatres, N.J.; pres. Triangle Theatres.

SNELL, PETER R. E.: Producer. b. 1941. Since in 1967: Prod.: Winters Tale, Some May Live, A Month in the Country, Carnaby 68; Subterfuge; Julius Caesar; Goodbye Gemini; Anthony and Cleopatra; The Wicker Man. Appt. head of prod. and man. dir. British Lion 1973. Joined Robert Stigwood group 1975. Hennessy. Returned to indep. prod., 1978; Bear Island. Motherlod. Appt. chief exec., Britannic Film & Television Ltd. 1985, purchased British Lion Film Prods., Ltd. from Thorn/EMI 1986–87. 1988: Chairman and chief executive British Lion. Produced Lady Jane, Turtle Diary, A Prayer for the Dying.

SNODGRESS, CARRIE: Actress. b. Chicago, IL, Oct 27, 1945. e. Northern Illinois U. and M.A. degree from the Goodman Theatre. Plays include All Way Home, Oh What a Lovely War, Caesar and Cleopatra and Tartuffe (Sarah Siddons Award, 1966), The Price, Vanities, The Curse of the Starving Class.
PICTURES INCLUDE: Rabbit, Run, Diary of a Mad Housewife, The Fury, A Night in The Attic, Murphy's Law, Pale Rider, Blueberry Hill, The Chill Factor, Blue Suede Shoes.
TELEVISION: World Premier (Silent Night, Lonely Night, The Whole World Is Watching), The Outsider, The Virginian, Judd for the Defense, Medical Center, Marcus Welby, M.D., The Dark Side, First Sight.

SNYDER, TOM: Newscaster, Show host. b. Milwaukee, WI, May 12, 1936. e. Marquette U. First job in news dept. of WRIT,

Milwaukee. Subsequently with WSAV-TV, Savannah; WAII-TV, Atlanta; KTLA-TV, Los Angeles; and KYW-TV, Philadelphia, before moving to KNBC in Los Angeles in 1970 as anchorman for weeknight newscast. Named host of NBC-TV's Tomorrow program in Oct., 1973, and moved to N.Y. in Dec., 1974, at which time began as anchorman of one-hour segment of NewsCenter 4. In Aug., 1975, inaugurated the Monday-thru-Friday editions of NBC News Update, one-minute prime time news spot. Host for Tomorrow talk show, Tom Snyder Show (ABC Radio).

SNYDER, WILLIAM L.: Producer, Executive. b. Baltimore, MD, Feb. 14, 1920. e. The Johns Hopkins U., B.A., 1940. Lt. Comnder., U.S. Navy W.W.II, 1941–45. Established Rembrandt Films, N.Y., 1948 as importer and dist. of foreign films. Co-prod. White Mane (UA, dom.), winner Cannes Fest. Grand Prize, seven other int'l awards, 1945. Prod. 13 Tom & Jerry Cartoons (MGM) and more than 100 Miss Nightingale, She, Little Lord Fauntleroy, The Secret Army (2 series). Popeye and Krazy Kat cartoons for U.S. TV plus number cartoons (Para.), 1956. Won Academy Award for cartoon Munro (Para.), 1961. Rec'd Academy nominations for Self Defense for Cowards (1962), The Game (1963), How to Avoid Friendship (1964) and Nudnik (1965). Prod. cartoon feature Alice in Paris (Childhood Prodns.), 1966. Prod. I a Woman II, 1968 (Chevron Picts.), and The Daughter (Chevron Picts.), 1970.

SOADY, WILLIAM C.: Executive. b. Oct. 7, 1943. Career with Universal Pictures started in 1970 when named Toronto branch mgr.; promoted to v.p. & gen. sls. mgr. of Universal Film (Canada) in 1971. Promoted to v.p. & gen. sls. mgr., Universal Pictures, 1981, in New York, relocating to L.A. in 1981. In 1983 named pres. of Universal Pictures Distribution, new dist. div. of Universal; resigned Sept., 1988.

SOAMES, RICHARD: Executive. b. London, England, 1936. Joined Film Finances Ltd. 1972; Appt. director Film Finances Ltd., 1977; Appt. man. dir. 1979. Appt. pres. Film Finances Canada Ltd. 1982: Appt. pres., Film Finances Inc.

SOBLE, RON: Actor. b. Chicago, IL, March 28, 1932. e. U. of Michigan. Served U.S. Army, 11th Airborne, in Japan. Studied acting in New York and was member of Jose Quintero's Circle in the Square Players. Acted in such plays as Romeo and Juliet, Murder in the Cathedral, The Petrified Forest; prod. assoc. on TV series Suspense and Danger, and appeared in 56 series. Co-star in The Monroes TV show.
PICTURES INCLUDE: Navajo Run, Al Capone, The Cincinnati Kid, Joe Kidd.

SOHMER, STEVE: Executive. b. 1942. 1977–82, v.p., adv./promo. CBS-TV. 1982, joined NBC as v.p. of adv./creative svcs. Promoted to exec. v.p., 1984. In 1985 joined Columbia Pictures as pres. & chief oper. officer. Resigned 1987. Heads Steve Sohmer Inc., creative boutique & advertising agency. Author of novel Favorite Son.
PICTURES: Leonard Part 6 (exec. prod. for Bill Cosby).

SOKOLOW, DIANE: Executive. b. New York, NY. e. Temple U. m. Mel Sokolow. 1975, v.p., East Coast operations, for Lorimar; with Warner Bros. 1977–81; served as v.p. of East Coast production. Left to form The Sokolow Co. with husband, Mel, to produce films. 1982, returned to WB as v.p., East Coast prod. 1984, joined Motown Prods. as exec. v.p.; Producer, MGM-UA 1986–present.
TELEVISION: The Preppie Killing (exec. prod.).

SOLDATI, MARIO: Director. b. Turin, Italy, 1906. e. Superior Institute of the History of Art, Rome. Lecturer, Columbia U.; author of America First Love, other books; m.p. dir. since 1939.
PICTURES INCLUDE: O.K. Nero, Wayward Wife, Stranger's Hand, Don Juan's Night of Love, Woman of the River.

SOLO, ROBERT H.: Producer. b. Waterbury, CT, Dec. 4, 1932. e. U. of Connecticut, BA. Early career as agent with Ashley-Famous; later production as exec. asst. to Jack Warner and Walter MacEwen at Warner Bros. In London prod. & prod. Scrooge for Cinema Center Films, 1970; co-prod. The Devils, 1971, 1971, named WB v.p., foreign production 1974, named exec. v.p., prod. at Burbank Studio. Now indep. prod.
PICTURES: Invasion of the Body Snatchers, The Awakening; I, The Jury; Bad Boys; Colors (prod.); Above the Law (exec. prod.).

SOLOMON, MICHAEL JAY: Executive. b. Jan. 20, 1938. e. Emerson, Boston; New York U. Evening Sch. of Commerce while working at first job with United Artists in 1956. Became student booker. Hired by Seymour Florin as booker for one year; returned to UA in int'l dept. January, 1960 went to Panama as asst. to mgr. of Central America. Transferred to Bogota after one yr.; made mgr. of UA in Peru and Bolivia. In 1964 joined MCA Latin American div., reorganizing office in Mexico and later opening office in Brazil. Made v.p., 1968, of MCA-TV. Supervised Latin American and Caribbean div.,

1973 made head of feature film sales to tv stations internationally while still supervising MCA business in Latin America. Resigned 1977 to form Michael Jay Solomon Films International, Inc. & Solomon International TV Newsletter. In 1978 formed Telepictures Corporation to distribute films worldwide and enter production. Was chm. & CEO. In 1986 merged with Lorimar to form Lorimar—Telepictures. Is member of 4-man office of the pres. Co. is a leading supplier of tv programs world-wide, produces films, has video co. & ad agency; bought MGM studios.
MEMBER: Vice-pres., N.Y. World TV Festival; bd. of dir., Intl. Council of NATAS; chm., Intl. Comm. of NATPE; bd., AFMA; bd., U.S. Magazine.

SOLOMON, T. G.: Executive. b. Jan. 5, 1920. e. Louisiana State U., 1941. Chairman of Board to Gulf States Theatres, New Orleans, LA, operating theatres in Louisiana, Mississippi, and Texarkana; Past chm. and past pres. of the National Association of Theatre Owners. Past chief barker, Variety Tent 45; past pres., Mississippi Theatre Owners; past pres., Texas Theatre Owners; chm., Louisiana Film Commission; past pres., Louisiana Theatres Assn.

SOLT, ANDREW: Writer. b. Budapest, Hungary, June 7, 1916; e. St. Stephen's Coll.
PICTURES INCLUDE: They All Kissed the Bride, Without Reservations, Joan of Arc, Little Women, Jolson Story, In a Lonely Place, Thunder on the Hill, Lovely to Look At; orig. s.p. For the First Time (orig., s.p.), Imagine (dir., co-prod., co-s.p.).
TELEVISION: Hitchcock Presents, Ford Theatre, Douglas Fairbanks Presents, Wire Service, General Electric Theatre, BBC and Stuttgart TV, Remembering Marilyn (exec. prod., dir.).
STAGE: 1973, Geld In Der Tasche, produced by Theatre am Kurfurstendamm, West Berlin.

SOLTZ, CHARLENE E.: Executive. b. New London, CT. Director of press relations and public affairs for Motion Picture Association of America, Inc.

SOMERS, SUZANNE: Actress. r.n. Suzanne Mahoney. b. San Bruno, CA, Oct. 16, 1946. e. Lone Mountain, San Francisco Coll. for Women. Pursued modeling career; worked as regular on Mantrap, syndicated talk show. Did summer stock and theatrical films. Wrote books: Touch Me Again, Some People Live More Than Others. Biggest TV success in Three's Company series (1977–81).
PICTURES: Bullitt, Daddy's Gone A-Hunting, Fools, Magnum Force, American Graffiti, Yesterday's Hero, Nothing Personal.
TELEVISION: One Day at a Time, Lotsa Luck, The Rockford Files, Starsky & Hutch, The Rich Little Show, Battle of the Network Stars, Us Against the World, Love Boat, Three's Company (series), She's the Sheriff (series). Movies: Happily Ever After, It Happened at Lakewood Manor, Zuma Beach, Ants, Hollywood Wives, Disney's Totally Minnie.

SOMMER, ELKE: Actress. r.n. Elke Schletz. b. Germany, Nov. 5, 1940. To Britain 1956. Ent. films in Germany, 1958, and since made films in Germany and Italy incl. Friend of the Jaguar, Traveling Luxury, Heaven and Cupid, Ship of the Dead. 1960: made debut in British films.
PICTURES INCLUDE: Don't Bother to Knock, The Victors, The Prize, Love the Italian Way, A Shot in the Dark, The Art of Love, The Oscar, Boy, Did I Get a Wrong Number, The Venetian Affair, Deadlier than the Male, Frontier Hellcat. Under contract to ABPC; The Corrupt Ones, The Wicked Dreams of Paula Schultz, They Came to Rob Las Vegas, The Wrecking Crew, Baron Blood, Zeppelin, Percy, Ten Little Indians, Lisa and the Devil, The Prisoner of Zenda, The Net, The Double McGuffin, Exit Sunset Blvd., The Man in Pyjamas, The Astral Factor, Lily in Love.
TELEVISION: Jenny's War, Peter the Great, Anastasia: The Mystery of Anya, Inside the Third Reich.

SOMMER, JOSEF: Actor. b. Greifswald, Germany, June 26, 1934. e. Carnegie-Mellon U. Studied at American Shakespeare Festival in Stratford, CT, 1962–64. US Army, 1958–60. NY stage debut in Othello, 1970. Film debut in Dirty Harry, 1971.
PICTURES: The Front, Close Encounters of the Third Kind, Oliver's Story, Hide in Plain Sight, Reds, Independence Day, Absence of Malice, Hanky Panky, Still of the Night, Rollover, Sophie's Choice (narrator), Silkwood, Iceman, D.A.R.Y.L., Witness, Target, The Rosary Murders, Chances Are.
TELEVISION: Morning Becomes Electra, The Scarlet Letter, Saigon, Sparkling Cyanide, The Betty Ford Story, A Special Friendship, Hothouse (series).

SONDHEIM, STEPHEN: Composer, Writer. b. New York, NY, March 22, 1930. e. Williams Coll. Writer for Topper TV series, 1953. Wrote incidental music for The Girls of Summer (1956). Winner of 4 Grammy Awards: Cast Albums 1970, 1973, 1980 and song of the year 1975.
THEATER: Lyrics only: West Side Story, Gypsy, Do I Hear a Waltz?. Music and lyrics: A Funny Thing Happened on the Way to the Forum, Anyone Can Whistle, Company (Tony

Award, 1971), Follies (Tony, 1972), A Little Night Music (Tony, 1973), The Frogs (Yale Repertory), Candide (new lyrics for revival), Pacific Overtures, Sweeney Todd, (Tony, 1979), Merrily We Roll Along, Sunday in the Park with George (Pulitzer Prize, 1985), Into the Woods. Anthologies of his songs: Side By Side By Sondheim; Marry Me a Little.
PICTURES: The Last of Sheila (s.p.), Stavisky (score), A Little Night Music (score).

SORIANO, DALE: Publicist, b. Brooklyn, NY. Ent. m.p. Ind. as a reelboy in projection room, later usher, sign painter, manager, film booker stagehand (NBC-CBS-ABC). Orchestra leader, director of info. for various N.Y. depts., licenses, real estate, law, public events and firearms control board. Publicist for Americana festivals, various veteran organizations. V.F.W., A.L., D.A.V., C.W.V. and Army & Navy Union and many philanthropic organizations. W.W.II served with 1st Marine Div. U.S.M.C. in S.W. Pacific thea. of opera. 1960–68 v.p. Publicists Association, I.A.T.S.E. conducted many TV and vet columns for the Brooklyn Eagle and independent newspapers. Show*Biz column 1st for the Brooklyn Daily Bulletin. Also stage, records, movies, radio and TV Editor. Pres. of Lighthouse Productions and pres. of Flatlands Chamber of Commerce; pres. National Council of Civic Assn. Member of Motion Picture Pioneers, National Publicists Association, American Newspaper Guild.

SORVINO, PAUL: Actor. b. New York, NY, 1939. Acted on Bdwy.; broke into films with Where's Poppa in 1970.
THEATER: Bajour, An American Millionaire, The Mating Dance, King Lear.
PICTURES: Day of the Dolphin, Made for Each Other, The Gambler, A Touch of Class, Oh, God, Bloodbrothers, Slow Dancing in the Big City, The Brink's Job, Lost and Found, Cruising, I, The Jury, That Championship Season, Off the Wall, Turk 182, The Stuff, Vasectomy.
TELEVISION: Seventh Avenue, Tell Me Where It Hurts, Chiefs, Surviving, With Intent to Kill, The Oldest Rookie (series).

SOTHERN, ANN: Actress. r.n. Harriet Lake. b. Valley City, ND, Jan. 22, 1919. e. Washington U. p. Annette Yde-Lake, opera singer. On stage, in m.p. since 1934.
PICTURES INCLUDE: Let's Fall in Love, Melody in Spring, Three Hearts for Julia, Swing Shift Maisie, Cry Havoc, Thousands Cheer, Maisie series, April Showers, Letter to Three Wives, Judge Steps Out, Words and Music, Nancy Goes to Rio, Blue Gardenia, Lady in a Cage, Sylvia, Chubasco, The Killing Kind, Golden Needles, Crazy Mama, The Manitou, The Little Dragons, The Whales of August (Acad. Award. nom).
TELEVISION: Private Secretary (series), Ann Sothern Show (series), My Mother The Car (voice of the car), Captain and the Kings, Letter to Three Wives.

SOUL, DAVID: Actor. r.n. David Solberg. b. Chicago, IL, Aug. 28, 1943. Attended several colleges but gave up studies to pursue a career in music. Made 25 singing appearances on The Merv Griffin Show where was spotted and given screen test. Signed contract with Screen Gems and given starring role in ABC-TV series, Here Come the Brides. Later Starsky and Hutch.
PICTURES INCLUDE: Johnny Got His Gun, Magnum Force, Dog Pound Shuffle, Appointment with Death, Hanoi Hilton, The Secret of the Sahara.
TELEVISION: Guest Star: The Streets of San Francisco, Cannon, Medical Center, The Rookies, Ironside, Star Trek, McMillan and Wife, Dan August, Circle of Fear, Owen Marshall, Counselor at Law. Movies: A Country Christmas, Swan Song (also prod.), Homeward Bound, Rage, The Manions of America, World War III, Through Naked Eyes, The Disappearance of Flight 412, Intertect, Movin' On, Little Ladies of the Night, The Fifth Missile, Harry's Hong Kong, The FBI Murders, Around the World in 80 Days. Series: Here Come the Brides, Starsky and Hutch, Casablanca, Yellow Rose, Bloody Friday.

SPACEK, SISSY: Actress. r.n. Mary Elizabeth. b. Quitman, TX, Dec. 25, 1949. m. director Jack Fisk. Cousin of actor Rip Torn. Was photographic model; attended acting classes in New York under Lee Strasberg.
PICTURES INCLUDE: Prime Cut (debut), Ginger in the Morning, Badlands, Carrie, Welcome to L.A., 3 Women, Heart Beat, Coal Miner's Daughter (Acad. Award, 1980), Raggedy Man, Missing, The River, Marie, Violets Are Blue, 'night, Mother, Crimes of the Heart.
TELEVISION: The Girls of Huntington House, The Migrants, Katherine (all TV movies), two episodes of The Waltons.

SPACEY, KEVIN: Actor. b. South Orange, NJ, 1960, raised in southern CA. e. L.A. Valley Coll., appearing in stage productions as well as stand-up comedy clubs, before attending Juilliard Sch. of Drama. Has appeared in numerous regional and repertory productions including the Kennedy Center

(The Seagull), American National Theatre and Seattle Rep. Theatre, and with New York Shakespeare Fest.
THEATER: Henry IV Part I, The Robbers, Barbarians, Ghosts, Hurlyburly, Long Day's Journey into Night (with Jack Lemmon).
PICTURES: Heartburn (debut); Rocket Gibralter.
TELEVISION: Long Day's Journey into Night, The Murder of Mary Phagan, Wiseguy (series).

SPADER, JAMES: Actor. b. Boston suburbs, MA, 1961. e. Phillips Academy. Studied acting at Michael Chekhov Studio.
PICTURES: Endless Love (debut, 1981); The New Kids; Tuff Turf; Pretty in Pink; Mannequin; Wall Street; Less Than Zero; Baby Boom; Jack's Back.
TELEVISION: The Family Tree (1983).

SPANO, VINCENT: Actor. b. New York, NY, Oct. 18, 1962. Film debut in The Double McGuffin, 1978. Stage debut at 14 in The Shadow Box (Long Wharf and Bdwy).
THEATER: Balm in Gilead.
PICTURES: Over the Edge, Rumblefish, The Black Stallion Returns, Baby It's You, Alphabet City, Maria's Lovers, Creator, Good Morning Babylon, And God Created Woman, Venetian Red.
TELEVISION: Search for Tomorrow, The Gentleman Bandit, Senior Trip, Blood Ties.

SPEARS, JR., HAROLD T.: Executive. b. Atlanta, GA, June 21, 1929. e. U. of Georgia, 1951. With Floyd Theatres, Lakeland, FL, since 1953; now pres.

SPECKTOR, FREDERICK: Executive. b. Los Angeles, CA, April 24, 1933. e. U. of Southern California, U. of California at L.A. M.P. agent, Ashley Famous Agency, 1962–64; Artists Agency Corp., 1964–68; exec. M.P. dept., William Morris Agency, 1968–78; exec. Creative Artists Agency, 1978–present.

SPELLING, AARON: Executive. b. Dallas, TX, Apr. 22, 1928. Was actor/writer before becoming producer at Four Star in 1957. In 1967, formed Thomas/Spelling Productions to produce several series and movies, including Mod Squad. In 1969, formed his own company, Aaron Spelling Productions, and then in 1972, partnered with Leonard Goldberg to produce The Rookies, Charlie's Angels, Fantasy Island, Starsky and Hutch, Hart to Hart, T.J. Hooker, and under own company banner, Love Boat, Vega$, Dynasty, Matt Houston, Hotel, The Colbys, Life with Lucy, Angels '88, HeartBeat and over 103 movies for television.
PICTURES: Mr. Mom (exec. prod.), Surrender, Three O'Clock High (exec. prod.), Satisfaction (co-prod.), Cross My Heart (co-exec. prod.).
TELEVISION: Recent: The Three Kings (exec. prod.), Nightingales (exec. prod.).

SPENGLER, PIERRE: Producer. b. Paris, France, 1947. Went on stage at 15; returned to language studies at Alliance Française. Entered film industry as production runner and office boy. Teamed for first time with friend Ilya Salkind on The Light at the Edge of the World, produced by Alexander Salkind.
PICTURES INCLUDE: Bluebeard, The Three Musketeers, The Four Musketeers, Crossed Swords, Superman, Superman II, Superman III, Santa Claus, The Return of the Musketeers.

SPENSER, JEREMY: Actor. b. Ceylon, 1937; e. Downshill Sch., Farnham, England. Ent. films 1947 in Anna Karenina.
PICTURES INCLUDE: It's Great To Be Young, The Prince and the Showgirl, Wonderful Things, Ferry to Hong Kong, Roman Spring of Mrs. Stone, Vengeance, King and Country, He Who Rides a Tiger.

SPEWACK, BELLA: Writer. b. Hungary, 1899. e. Washington Irving H.S., 1917. m. late Samuel Spewack, 1922; writer. Reporter N.Y. Call, N.Y. Mail, N.Y. World, N.Y. Evening World; feature writer, N.Y. Herald Tribune, N.Y. Times; nat'l pub. dir. Camp Fire Girls, then Girl Scouts; reporter under byline Bella Cohen for N.Y. World, and other newspapers 1922–26; author plays with husband include: Solitaire Man, Poppa, War Song, Clear All Wires, Spring Song, Boy Meets Girl, Leave It to Me, Kiss Me Kate, (Tony Award, 1949), My Three Angels, Festival. Member: Dramatists Guild; SWG; pres., N.Y. Girls Scholarship Fund.
PICTURES INCLUDE: Clear All Wires, Boy Meets Girl, Cat and the Fiddle, Rendezvous, The Nuisance, Three Loves of Nancy, My Favorite Wife, When Ladies Meet, Weekend at the Waldorf, Move Over Darling, We're No Angels (based on play My Three Angels).
TELEVISION: Mr Broadway, Kiss Me Kate, My Three Angels, The Enchanted Nutcracker, Kiss Me Kate, BBC.

SPHEERIS, PENELOPE: Director. b. 1945. e. U. of California at L.A. Film Sch.
PICTURES: Real Life (prod. only); The Decline of Western Civilization (documentary); Suburbia; The Boys Next Door; Hollywood Vice Squad, Dudes, The Decline of Western Civilization—Part II: The Metal Years.
TELEVISION: Saturday Night Live (prod. only).

SPIEGEL, LARRY: Producer, Writer, Director. b. Brooklyn, NY. e. Ohio U. With CBS-TV 1960–66; Benton & Bowles, 1966–67; Wells, Rich, Green, 1967–71; BBDO, 1972–73.. Now heads Appledown Films, Inc.
PICTURES INCLUDE: Hail (s.p.); Book of Numbers (s.p.); Death Game (prod.); Stunts (prod.); Spree (direc./s.p.); Phobia (prod.); Remo Williams: The Adventure Begins (prod.); Dove Against Death (prod.).
TELEVISION: Alexander (s.p., prod.); Incredible Indelible Magical Physical Mystery Trip (s.p.); Bear That Slept Through Christmas (s.p.); Never Fool With A Gypsy Ikon (s.p.); Mystery Trip Through Little Red's Head (s.p.); Planet of The Apes (animated) (s.p.); Jan Stephenson Golf Video (prod.); Remo Williams (pilot ABC; prod.).

SPIEGEL, TED: Publicist. b. New York, NY. e. New York U., B.S. 1948. Joined Columbia Pictures 1948 in adv. copy, exploitation, pub. depts.; foreign public rel., Columbia International 1956. Spec. adv., pub. rep., Kingsley Int'l Pictures, 1960; spec. asst. to pres. Kingsley Int'l Pictures, 1962; mgr. dir., theatre operations, The Landau Co., 1963; pub. exec., Embassy Pics. Corp., 1964; dir. pub., Avco Embassy Pictures, 1968. In 1976 joined A. Stirling Gold as dir. adv./pub. relations. In 1978 named acct. exec. for Solters & Roskin.

SPIELBERG, STEVEN: b. Cincinnati, OH, Dec. 18, 1947. m actress Amy Irving. e. California State Coll. Made home movies as child; completed first film with story and actors at 12 yrs. old in Phoenix. At 13 won film contest for 40-min. war movie, Escape to Nowhere. At 16 made 140-min. film, Firelight. At CSC made five films. First professional work, Amblin', 20 min. short which led to signing contract with Universal Pictures.
TELEVISION: Duel, Savage, Night Gallery, Something Evil, Steven Spielberg's Amazing Stories.
PICTURES INCLUDE: The Sugarland Express; Jaws; Close Encounters of The Third Kind; I Wanna Hold Your Hand (exec. prod.); 1941; Used Cars (exec. prod.); Raiders of the Lost Ark; Poltergeist (prod.-s.p.); E.T.: The Extra-Terrestrial (dir.); Twilight Zone—The Movie (prod.—dir.); Indiana Jones and the Temple of Doom (dir.); Gremlins (exec. prod.); Goonies (exec. prod.); Back to the Future (exec. prod.); The Color Purple (co-prod.-dir.); Young Sherlock Holmes (co-prod.); An American Tail (co-exec. prod.); Innerspace (exec. prod.), Empire of the Sun (dir., prod.), Batteries Not Included (co-exec. prod.), Who Framed Roger Rabbit? (co-exec. prod.), Indiana Jones and the Last Chance (dir.), The Land Before Time Began (co-exec. prod.).

SPIER, WILLIAM: Producer, Director, Novelist, Radio-TV Writer. Network exec., producer; prod. radio shows including March of Time, Columbia Work Shop, Adventures of Sam Spade, Philip Morris Playhouse, Suspense; co-dir. film, Lady Possessed.
TELEVISION: The Clock, 1951; Fred Waring, Omnibus, 1952–53; Medallion Theatre, Willy, 1954–55; Perry Mason, 1956; scripts for Omnibus, The Clock, 20th Century-Fox Hour, The Lineup, Reader's Digest, Passing Parade, Alfred Hitchcock, Steve Canyon, Peter Gunn, Desilu, Playhouse 90, The Untouchables, 77 Sunset Strip, Bourbon Street, Dragnet, Richard Diamond, CIC, The Islanders, Thin Man, etc. Winner of Peabody Award, Look Magazine, Mystery Writers of America, Writers' Guild Award, best hour script of 1961.

SPIKINGS, BARRY: Executive. b. Boston, England, Nov. 23, 1939. Ent. m.p. ind. 1973. Jnt. Mang. Dir. British Lion Films Ltd., 1975. Co-prod. Conduct Unbecoming, Man Who Fell to Earth, 1976. Appt. jnt. man. dir. EMI Films Ltd., 1977. Prod. The Deer Hunter, Convoy. 1979, appt. chm. & chief exec., EMI Film & Theatre Corp.; chm. & chief exec, EMI Films, Ltd., chm. EMI Cinemas, Ltd.; chm., Elstree Studios, Ltd. Chm. EMI-TV Programs, Inc., 1980; appt. chm. chief exec., EMI Films Group, Jan. 1982; June, 1985 Barry Spikings Productions Inc. (U.S.A.); June, 1985 became director Galactic Films Inc. (with Lord Anthony Rufus Issacs); Oct., 1986, acquired Embassy Home Entertainment from Coca Cola Co., renamed Nelson Entertainment Inc., appointed pres. and chief operating officer.

SPIRA, STEVEN S.: Executive. e. City Coll. of New York; Benjamin Cardozo Sch. of Law. Associated 10 years with N.Y. law firm, Monasch, Chazen & Stream. 1984, joined 20th Century Fox as sr. counsel; 1985, to Warner Bros. Now WB v.p., studio business affairs.

SPIRES, JOHN B.: Executive. b. New York, NY. e. New York U. Assistant manager Tribune Theatre, N.Y., 1934–36; Paramount Pictures lab., 1936–42; Capt. U.S. Army, 1942–46; Major U.S. Reserves, 1946–48; foreign rep., RKO, Europe, 1946; asst. foreign mgr., United World Films, 1947–48; in charge 16mm foreign oper., Universal 1949; asst. to European gen. mgr., Universal International, 1950; European gen. mgr., Continental Europe, Near East, Universal International, 1955; gen. mgr., foreign film sales, MCA-TV, 1958; dir., TV sis., 1964; named v.p. of MGM-TV, 1973; snr. v.p., MGM-TV, UK, Europe,

MGM-TV, 1961; dir., Int'l TV sis., MGM-TV, 1978. Founded Phoenix Intl. TV Associates, 1980; pres., Phoenix Intl.

SPITZ, HENRY: Producer. b. Paterson, NJ, Mar. 4, 1905. e. N.Y.M.A. Gen. mgr., Quackenbush Dept. Stores; on bd. Preakness Hill Country Club & Barnet Memorial Hosp.; e. Marshall-Matherson dept. store, 1930–34; ent. m.p. ind. as prod. & bus. mgr., Cameo Pictures, 1935; assoc. prod., Cameo-Imperial Pictures, 1936; asst. prod. mgr. & asst. dir. Conn Prod.; asst., prod. mgr. Universal through 1949. With Walter Wanger Prods. then indep. prod. Retired 1972.
PICTURES INCLUDE: I Demand Payment, High Hat, Here's Flash Casey, Headleys at Home, Hawaiian Nights, Private Affairs; assoc. prod. Two Dollar Bettor, Sudden Fear, Comanche, Beast of Hollow Mountain, The Big Doodle, Night in Havana, Jade Idol, For the Love of Mike, Geronimo, Love and Desire, A Thousand Clowns, The Group, Scalphunters, Charly, Lovers and Other Strangers, Jenny, Saber Jet, Interval.

SPITZ, JAMES R.: Executive. Began career in industry 1962 with Warner Bros., working way thru sls. dept. and holding various positions such as booker and office mgr. in New York, San Francisco, Salt Lake City, Seattle and Kansas City. Appt. branch mgr. of WB Seattle-Portland branch; then L.A. branch mgr. at United Artists 1972–77, joined U.A. L.A. branch mgr. and then western div. mgr. Joined Avco Embassy as asst. gen. sls. mgr., 1979. In 1980 left to go to Columbia Pictures as v.p. & gen. sls. mgr. In 1981 promoted to pres. of Columbia Pictures' domestic distribution.

SPIVAK, LAWRENCE E.: TV-radio Producer. b. New York, NY, 1900. e. Harvard U. LL.D. (hon.) Wilberforce U.; Litt. D. (hon.) Suffolk U. L.H.D. (hon.) Tampa U. Began as bus. mgr., Antiques Mag., 1921–30; asst. to the pub., Hunting and Fishing, Nat. Sportsman mags., 1930–33; bus. mgr., American Mercury, 1934–39; pub., 1939–44; editor, pub., 1944–50; founder, pub. until 1954, Ellery Queen's Mystery Mag., The Mag. of Fantasy and Science Fiction, Mercury Mystery Books, Bookseller Mysteries, Jonathan Press Books; originator, producer, panel member, TV program, Meet the Press. Recipient two Peabody Awards. Winner of Emmy Award for outstanding achievement in Coverage of Special Events and Honor Award from U. of Missouri for Distinguished Service in Journalism.

SPODICK, ROBERT C.: Exhibitor. b. New York, NY, Dec. 3, 1919. e. City Coll. of New York, 1940; ent. m.p. ind. as errand boy Skouras Park Plaza, Bronx 1932–33; reel boy, asst. mgr., Loew's Theatres; mgr., Little Carnegie and other art theatres; exploitation man, United Artists. Acquired Lincoln, New Haven art house in 1945 in partnership with cousin Leonard E. Sampson; developed Nutmeg Theatre circuit, which was sold in 1968 to Robert Smerling. Beginning in 1970, built Groton, CT., Cinemas I and II; Norwich Cinemas I and II, Village Cinemas I, II and III, Rosen, and Westerley Triple Cinemas in RI as Gemini Cinema Circuit in partnership with Sampson and William Rosen. Gemini sold to Interstate Theatres, 1986. With Sampson presently operates York Square Triple Cinemas in New Haven. Pres., Allied of CT, 1962–64; Pres. NATO of Conn. 1968–73. Past chm. exec. comm., CT Ass'n of Theatre Owners, and active member.

SPOTTISWOODE, ROGER: Director. b. England. Film editor of TV commercials and documentaries before turning to direction.
PICTURES: Editor: Straw Dogs, The Getaway, Pat Garrett and Billy the Kid, Hard Times, The Gambler, Who'll Stop the Rain? (assoc. prod.), Baby (exec. prod.). Director: Terror Train; The Pursuit of D.B. Cooper; Under Fire; The Best of Times, Shoot to Kill.
TELEVISION: The Renegades, The Last Innocent Man.

SPRADLIN, G.D.: Actor. b. Oklahoma. Started career as lawyer and active in local politics before turning to acting. Joined Oklahoma Repertory Theatre in 1964. Film debut in Will Penny (1968).
PICTURES INCLUDE: Monte Walsh, Tora! Tora! Tora!, The Hunting Party, The Godfather, Part II, North Dallas Forty, MacArthur, Wrong Is Right, The Formula, Apocalypse Now, The Lords of Discipline.
TELEVISION: Space, Nutcracker: Money, Madness, and Murder, Robert Kennedy and His Times, Resting Place, Dream West, Jayne Mansfield Story.

SPRINGER, PAUL D.: Executive. e. Brooklyn Law Sch. Served as assoc. for N.Y. law firm, Johnson and Tannebaum. Later with legal dept. of Columbia Pictures. 1970, joined Paramount Pictures N.Y. legal dept. 1985, promoted to sr. v.p., chief resident counsel, 1987, promoted to senior v.p., asst. general counsel responsible for all legal functions for Paramount's distribution and marketing depts. Mem., N.Y. Bar.

SPRINGFIELD, RICK: Actor, Singer, Songwriter. b. Australia, Aug. 23, 1949.
PICTURES: Battlestar Galactica, Hard to Hold (act., addl. music).

TELEVISION: General Hospital, An Evening at the Improv, Countdown '81.

SPRINGSTEEN, R. G.: Director. b. Tacoma, WA, Sept. 8, 1904. e. U. of Washington. With Universal Studios 1930; asst. dir. Fox; asst. dir. & dir. Republic.
PICTURES INCLUDE: Out of the Storm, Hellfire, Red Menace, Singing Guns, Honeychile, Toughest Man in Arizona, Gobs & Gals, Perilous Journey, Geraldine, I Cover the Underworld, Cross Channel, When Gangland Strikes, Come Next Spring, Track the Man Down, Secret Venture, Double Jeopardy, Johnny Reno, Red Tomahawk.

STACK, ROBERT: Actor. b. Los Angeles, CA, Jan. 13, 1919. e. U. of Southern California. In U.S. Armed Forces (Navy), W.W.II. Studied acting at Henry Duffy School of Theatre 6 mo. then signed a contract with Universal. National skeet champion at age 16. Autobiography: Straight Shooting.
PICTURES INCLUDE: First Love, When the Daltons Rode, Mortal Storm, Little Bit of Heaven, Nice Girl, Badlands of Dakota, To Be or Not To Be, Eagle Squadron, Men of Texas, Fighter Squadron, Date With Judy, Miss Tatlock's Millions, Mr. Music, Bullfighter and the Lady, My Outlaw Brother, Bwana Devil, War Paint, Conquest of Cochise, Sabre Jet, Iron Glove, High & the Mighty, House of Bamboo, Good Morning Miss Dove, Great Day in the Morning, Written on the Wind, John Paul Jones, Last Voyage, Killers of Kilimanjaro, The Caretakers, The Corrupt Ones, Story of a Woman, 1941, Airplane!, Uncommon Valor, Big Trouble, Plain Clothes, Caddyshack II.
TELEVISION: The Untouchables (series), Name of the Game (series), Most Wanted (series), Strike Force, Playhouse 90 (Panic Button), They Knew What They Wanted, George Washington, Hollywood Wives, Midas Valley (series), Unsolved Mysteries (host/narrator), Korea: The Forgotten War (host).

STAHL, AL: Executive. Syndicated newspaper cartoonist; asst. animator, Max Fleischer, gag ed. Terrytoons; U.S. Signal Corps; opened own studios, 1946; prod. first animated TV cartoon show; pres., Animated Prod.; prod. live and animated commercials; member of bd. NTFC.

STALLONE, SYLVESTER: Actor, Writer, Director. b. New York, NY, July 6, 1946. After high school taught at American Coll. of Switzerland instructing children of career diplomats, young royalty, etc. Returned to U.S. in 1967 and graduated from U. of Miami, 1969. Came to New York to seek acting career, taking part-time jobs, including usher for Walter Reade Theatres. Then turned to writing, selling several TV scripts. Back to acting in Woody Allen's Bananas and with lead role in The Lords of Flatbush (1974).
PICTURES INCLUDE: Capone, Death Race 2000, Rocky (also s.p.), F.I.S.T. (actor, co.-s.p.), Paradise Alley (actor, s.p., dir.). Rocky II (actor, s.p., dir.), Nighthawks, Victory, Rocky III (s.p.-dir.-actor); First Blood (co-s.p.-actor), Staying Alive (prod., dir., co-s.p.); Rhinestone (actor, co-s.p.); Rambo: First Blood Part II (actor, co-s.p.); Rocky IV (s.p.-dir.-actor); Cobra (s.p.-actor); Over the Top (actor, co-s.p.), Rambo III (co-s.p., actor).

STAMP, TERENCE: Actor. b. London, England, July 23, 1939. Stage experience including Alfie on Broadway. Recent stage: Dracula, The Lady from the Sea, Airborne Symphony.
PICTURES INCLUDE: Billy Budd (debut 1962, Acad. Award nom.), Term of Trial, The Collector (best actor award, Cannes, 1965), Modesty Blaise, Far from the Madding Crowd, Poor Cow, Blue, Tales of Mystery, Teorama, The Mind of Mr. Soames, A Season in Hell, Hu-Man, The Divine Creature, Strip-Tease, Superman, Meetings with Remarkable Men, The Thief of Baghdad, Together, Superman II, Death in the Vatican, The Hit, Link, Legal Eagles, The Sicilian, Wall Street, Outer Heat, Young Guns, Alien Nation.

STANDER, LIONEL: Actor. b. New York, NY, Jan. 11, 1908. e. coll. N.Y. stage, 1952. On TV in Hart to Hart.
PICTURES INCLUDE: Scoundrel, Page Miss Glory, Gay Deception, Music Goes 'Round, Mr. Deeds Goes to Town, A Star Is Born, Meet Nero Wolfe, Guadalcanal Diary, Big Show-Off, Specter of the Rose, In Old Sacramento, Kid from Brooklyn, Gentleman Joe Palooka, Pal Joey, Mad Wednesday, Call Northside 777, Unfaithfully Yours, Trouble Makers, Two Gals and a Guy, St. Benny the Dip, Cul de Sac, A Dandy in Aspic, The Gang That Couldn't Shoot Straight, Pulp, The Black Bird, The Cassandra Crossing, New York, New York, Matilda, 1941, Cookie, The Wicked Stepmother.

STANFILL, DENNIS C: Executive. b. Centerville, TN, April 1, 1927. e. Lawrenceburg H.S.; U.S. Naval Acad., B.S., 1949; Oxford U. (Rhodes scholar), M.A., 1953; U. of South Carolina, L.H.D. (hon.). Corporate finance specialist, Lehman Brothers 1959–65; v.p. finance, Times Mirror Company, Los Angeles, 1965–69; exec. v.p. finance, 20th Century-Fox Film Corp., 1969–71, pres., 1971, chmn. bd./chief exec. officer, 1971–81; pres., Stanfill, Doig & Co., venture capital firm, 1981–.

STANG, ARNOLD: Performer, b. Chelsea, MA, Sept. 28, 1927. Radio, 1935–50; on B'way, in five plays and in m.p. and short subjects; guest appearances on TV shows. Much voice-over cartoon work.
TELEVISION: Captain Video, Milton Berle, Danny Thomas, Perry Como, Ed Sullivan, Red Skelton, Frank Sinatra, Wagon Train, Top Cat, Jack Benny, Johnny Carson, December Bride, Playhouse 90, Batman, Bonanza, Bob Hope, Danny Kaye, Broadside, Jackie Gleason, Emergency, Feeling Good, Chico & the Man, Super Jaws & Catfish, Busting Loose, Flying High, Robert Klein Specials, Tales from the Dark Side.
PICTURES INCLUDE: Man with the Golden Arm, The Wonderful World of the Brothers Grimm, It's a Mad, Mad, Mad, Mad World, Pinocchio in Outer Space, Dondi, Alakazam the Great, Hello Down There, Skidoo, Walt Disney's Aristocats, Seven Days Leave, My Sister Eileen, Let's Go Steady, Raggedy Ann & Andy, Gang That Couldn't Shoot Straight, We Go Pogo, That's Life, Hercules in New York, They Got Me Covered.

STANLEY, KIM: Actress. r.n. Patricia Reid. b. Tularosa, NM, Feb. 11, 1925. e. U. of New Mexico. Began stage acting in college and later in stock. Worked as model in NY while training with Elia Kazan and Lee Strasberg at Actors Studio. In late 1960s and 1970s taught drama, Coll. of Santa Fe, NM.
THEATER: The Dog, Beneath the Skin (NY debut, 1948), Him, Yes Is For a Very Young Man, Montserrat, The House of Bernarda Alba, The Chase, Picnic (NY Drama Critics Award, 1953), The Traveling Lady, The Great Dreamer, Bus Stop, A Clearing in the Woods, A Touch of the Poet, A Far Country, Natural Affection, The Three Sisters.
PICTURES: The Goddess, Seance on a Wet Afternoon (Acad. Award nom.), Frances, The Right Stuff.
TELEVISION: Clash by Night, The Travelling Lady, A Cardinal Mercy (Emmy, 1963), The Three Sisters, Cat on a Hot Tin Roof.

STANLEY, PHYLLIS: Actress. b. London, England, Oct. 30. e. Beauclair Sch., London. On London stage in 1932–35.
STAGE: The Miracle, Words & Music, The Town Talks, Oh! You Letty, Happy Returns, Lights Up.
PICTURES INCLUDE: Side Street Angel (m.p. debut), St. Martin's Lane, Jeannie, One Exciting Night, Next of Kin, The Case of Lady Brooke, Lovely to Look At, Take Me To Town, Her 12 Men, Strange Lady in Town, Black Sleep, Seventh Veil.
TELEVISION: Fireside Theatre, Ford Theatre, Four Star Playhouse (Schlitz Playhouse, Lux Video Theatre, Matinee Theatre).

STANTON, HARRY DEAN: Actor. b. Kentucky, July 14, 1926. Acting debut at Pasadena Playhouse. Theatrical film debut in Tomahawk Trail, 1957.
PICTURES INCLUDE: The Proud Rebel, Pork Chop Hill, A Dog's Best Friend, Cool Hand Luke, Kelly's Heroes, Two-Lane Blacktop, Pat Garrett and Billy the Kid, Dillinger, Zandy's Bride, The Godfather Part II, Rancho Deluxe, Farewell, My Lovely, The Missouri Breaks, 92 in The Shade, Renaldo and Clara, Straight Time, The Rose, Wise Blood, Alien, Death Watch, The Black Marble, Private Benjamin, Escape from New York, One From the Heart, Young Doctors in Love, Tough Enough, Christine, Repo Man, Paris Texas, Uforia, Red Dawn, One Magic Christmas, Pretty in Pink, Fool for Love, The Bear, The Care Bears Movie, Slam Dance, Stars and Bars, Mr. North, The Last Temptation of Christ, Dream a Little Dream.
TELEVISION: I Want to Live, Flatbed Annie & Sweetiepie: Lady Truckers.

STANWYCK, BARBARA: Actress. r.n. Ruby Stevens; b. Brooklyn, NY, July 16, 1907. Film debut, Locked Door, 1929.
PICTURES INCLUDE: Ladies of Leisure, Night Nurse, So Big, Bitter Tea of General Yen, Brief Moment, Woman in Red, Annie Oakley, Plough and the Stars, Stella Dallas, Mad Miss Manton, Union Pacific, Golden Boy, Meet John Doe, Two Mrs. Carrolls, B.F.'s Daughter, Sorry, Wrong Number, Lady Gambles, East Side, West Side, Thelma Jordan, The Furies, No Man of Her Own, To Please a Lady, Man With a Cloak, Clash by Night, Jeopardy, All I Desire, Titanic, Blowing Wild, The Moonlighter, Executive Suite, Witness to Murder, Violent Men, Double Indemnity, Ball of Fire, Cattle Queen of Montana, Escape to Burma, There's Always Tomorrow, Maverick Queen, These Wilder Years, Crime of Passion, Trooper Hook, Forty Guns, Walk on the Wild Side, Roustabout, The Night Walker.
TELEVISION: Guest: Jack Benny, Ford, Zane Grey, Alcoa-Goodyear; The Big Valley (series, 1965–69), The Thorn Birds (Emmy award), The Colbys (series).

STAPLETON, JEAN: Actress. r.n. Jeanne Murray. b. New York, NY, Jan. 19, 1923. m. dir., prod. William Putch. e. Wadleigh H.S. Summer stock in NH, ME, MA, and PA. Broadway debut in In the Summer House (1953). President, Advisory bd., Women's Research Instit. (Wash., D.C.); bd.: Eleanor Roosevelt Val-kill, Hyde Park; bd.: Wonder Woman Foundation.
THEATER: Damn Yankees, Bells Are Ringing, Juno, Rhinoceros, Funny Girl, Arsenic and Old Lace and extensive

work at her husband's Totem Pole Playhouse, Fayettesville, PA.

PICTURES: Damn Yankees, Bells Are Ringing, Something Wild, Up the Down Staircase, Cold Turkey, Klute, The Buddy System.

TELEVISION: All in the Family. Movies: Eleanor: First Lady of the World, A Matter of Sex, Dead Man's Folly.

STAPLETON, MAUREEN: Actress. b. Troy, NY, June 21, 1925. Worked as a model and waitress while studying acting with Herbert Berghof in N.Y. in 1944 and became member of Actors Studio. Broadway debut, 1946, in The Playboy of the Western World. Became a star in 1951 in The Rose Tattoo. Film debut 1959 in Lonelyhearts.

THEATER: Anthony and Cleopatra, Detective Story, Bird Cage, The Rose Tattoo (Tony Award, 1951), The Emperor's Clothes, The Crucible, Richard III, The Seagull, 27 Wagons Full of Cotton, Orpheus Descending, The Cold Wind and the Warm, Toys in the Attic, The Glass Menagerie (1965 & 1975), Plaza Suite, Norman Is That You?, Gingerbread Lady (Tony Award, 1970), The Country Girl, Secret Affairs of Mildred Wild, The Gin Game, The Little Foxes.

PICTURES INCLUDE: The Fugitive Kind, A View from the Bridge, Bye Bye Birdie, Airport, Plaza Suite, Interiors, The Runner Stumbles, On the Right Track, Reds (Acad. Award, supp. 1981), Johnny Dangerously, Cocoon, The Money Pit, Made in Heaven, Heartburn, Sweet Lorraine, Nuts, Cocoon II—The Return.

TELEVISION: Series: What Happened? (panelist, 1952); Movies: For Whom the Bell Tolls, Among the Paths to Eden (Emmy, 1968), Tell Me Where It Hurts, Queen of the Stardust Ballroom, Cat on a Hot Tin Roof, The Gathering, The Gathering Part II, Letters From Frank, The Electric Grandmother, Little Gloria—Happy at Last, Family Secrets, Sentimental Journey, Private Sessions.

STARGER, MARTIN: Executive. b. New York, NY, May 8, 1932. e. City Coll. of New York. Served in U.S. Army Signal Corp., where prod. training films. Joined BBDO, starting in TV prod. dept.; later made v.p. & assoc. dir. of TV. Joined ABC in April 1966, as v.p. of programs, ABC-TV, East Coast. In March, 1968, prom. to v.p. and natl prog. dir; in 1969 named v.p. in chg. progr. Named pres., ABC Entertainment, July 17, 1972. In June, 1975 formed Marstar Productions Inc., M.P. & TV production company of which he is pres. In March 1978 formed Marble Arch Productions, of which he is pres. In 1984 produced Mask. Formed Rule/Starger Co. with Elton Rule, 1988.

PICTURES: Exec. prod.: Nashville, The Domino Principle, The Muppet Movie, Raise the Titanic, Saturn 3, The Great Muppet Caper, Hard Country, The Legend of the Lone Ranger, Sophie's Choice, Barbarosa.

TELEVISION: Escape from Sobibor, Earth Star Voyager.

STARK, RAY: Producer. e. Rutgers U. Began career after W.W.II as agent handling radio scripts, and later literary works for such writers as Costain, Marquand and Hecht. Joined Famous Artists Agency, where he represented such personalities as Marilyn Monroe, Kirk Douglas and Richard Burton; in 1957, resigned exec. position to form Seven Arts Prods. with Eliot Hyman, serving as exec. v.p. and head of production until July, 1966, when he left to take on personal production projects, including Reflections in a Golden Eye and Funny Girl.

PICTURES: The Sunshine Boys, Robin and Marian, Murder by Death, Casey's Shadow, The Cheap Detective, California Suite, The Electric Horseman, Chapter Two, Seems Like Old Times, Annie, The Slugger's Wife, Brighton Beach Memoirs, Biloxi Blues, Steel Magnolias.

STARK, WILBUR: Producer, Director. b. New York, NY, Aug. 10, 1922. e. Columbia U. Started career as actor, Brooklyn Academy Players; slsm. & producer radio station WMCA-NY, 1942–46; for 18 yrs. producer-director of theatrical feature films and over 1500 live dramas and over 300 TV movies, including 81 for CBS as producer (directing over 30).

PICTURES: The Thing (exec. prod.); The Cat People, (exec. consultant); My Lover, My Son (prod., story); Vampire Circus (prod., story); The Love Box (prod., dir. s.p.); A Policeman's Lot (prod., dir); All I Want Is You, and You. . . (prod.); The Petrified Prince (prod., dir.).

TELEVISION: Producer: Newsstand Theatre, Rocky King, Detective; Modern Romances with Martha Scott; True Story, Col. Humphrey Flack, My Father Is a Detective.

STARR, EVE: Columnist. b. Chicago, IL, May 1. e. Columbia U., Miami U., Julliard Sch. of Music. Radio-TV playwright, feature writer, actress. Hollywood foreign correspondent; m.p. writer, newspapers, mags.; m.p. columnist, Hollywood Citizen-News; Daily syndicated TV column, Inside TV—General Features Synd.; feature column, Tell It To Eve, International Newspapers; Traveling With Eve, Nat'l Syndicated Travel Column.

STARR, RINGO: O.B.E. Singer, Musician, Songwriter. r.n. Richard Starkey. b. Liverpool, England, July 7, 1949. Member of The Beatles. (Films: A Hard Day's Night, Help).

PICTURES ALONE: Actor: The Last Waltz, Sextette, The Kids Are Alright, Caveman, Give My Regards to Broad Street, Walking After Midnight.

TELEVISION: Actor: Princess Daisy, D.C. Beach Party—A Celebration.

STEEL, ANTHONY: Actor. b. London, Eng., May 21, 1920. e. private schools, south Ireland, Cambridge. Film debut in Saraband for Dead Lovers.

PICTURES INCLUDE: Portrait from Life, Christopher Columbus, Helter Skelter, Poet's Pub, The Blue Lamp, The Wooden Horse, Laughter in Paradise, The Mudlark, Where No Vultures Fly (Ivory Hunter), Another Man's Poison, Emergency Call, Something Money Can't Buy, The Planter's Wife (Outpost in Malaya), Malta Story, Master of Ballantrae, Albert, R.N. (Break to Freedom), West of Zanzibar, Sea Shall Not Have Them, Passage Home, Storm Over the Nile, Black Tent, Checkpoint, Valerie, A Question of Adultery, Harry Black, Honeymoon, The Switch, The Mirror Crack'd.

STEEL, DAWN: Executive. m. producer Charles Roven. Former sportswriter. Marketing exec. with Penthouse Magazine. Joined Paramount Pictures 1978 as dir. of merchandising and licensing; promoted 1979 to v.p.; named v.p., production 1980; promoted to sr. v.p. 1983, named pres., prod. 1985 with involvement and responsibility for Footloose, Top Gun, Star Trek IV, Beverly Hills Cop II, The Untouchables, Fatal Attraction. Joined Columbia Pictures 1987 as president, Columbia Pictures.

STEELE, TOMMY: Performer. r.n. Tommy Hicks. b. London, Dec. 17, 1936. Early career Merchant Navy. First TV and film appearances, 1956. Composed and sang title song for The Shiralee. Recent Stage Musical: Singin' in the Rain, London Palladium, 1983.

PICTURES INCLUDE: Kill Me Tomorrow, The Tommy Steele Story, The Duke Wore Jeans, Tommy the Toreador, Light Up the Sky, It's All Happening, The Happiest Millionaire, Half A Sixpence, Finian's Rainbow, Where's Jack?

TELEVISION: Tommy Steele Spectaculars, Richard Whittington Esquire (Rediffusion), Ed Sullivan Show, Gene Kelly Show, Perry Como Show, Twelfth Night, The Tommy Steele Hour, Tommy Steele in Search of Charlie Chaplin, Tommy Steele And A Show, Quincy's Quest.

STEENBURGEN, MARY: Actress. b. Newport, AZ, 1953. Studied at Neighborhood Playhouse. Married to actor Malcolm MacDowall.

PICTURES INCLUDE: Goin' South, Time after Time, Melvin and Howard (Acad. Award), Ragtime, A Midsummer Night's Sex Comedy, Cross Creek, One Magic Christmas, Dead of Winter, The Whales of August, End of the Line (also exec. prod.), Miss Firecracker Contest.

TELEVISION: Tender Is the Night, Faerie Tale Theatre, The Attic: The Hiding of Anne Frank.

STEIGER, ROD: Actor. b. Westhampton, NY, Apr. 14, 1925. e. Westside H.S., Newark, NJ. Served in U.S. Navy, then employed in Civil Service; studied acting at N.Y. Theatre Wing Dramatic Workshop Actors' Studio; numerous TV plays; on Broadway in ANTA prod. of Night Music; m.p. debut in Teresa (1951).

PICTURES INCLUDE: On the Waterfront, The Big Knife, Oklahoma!, Court Martial of Billy Mitchell, Jubal, The Harder They Fall, Back from Eternity, Run of the Arrow, Unholy Wife, Al Capone, Seven Thieves, The Mark, Reprieve, 13 West Street, Hands Upon the City, The Time of Indifference, The Pawnbroker, In the Heat of the Night (Acad. Award), The Girl and the General, No Way to Treat a Lady, And There Came a Man, The Illustrated Man, Three Into Two Won't Go, Duck, You Sucker, Happy Birthday, Wanda June, Waterloo, The Lolly-Madonna War, Lucky Luciano, Hennessy, W. C. Fields and Me, F.I.S.T., The Amityville Horror, Lion of the Desert, Cattle Annie and Little Britches, The Chosen, The Naked Face, The Kindred, The January Man, Tennessee Waltz, White Roses.

TELEVISION: Many appearances in 1950s including Marty; Race to the Pole, Hollywood Wives, Jesus of Nazareth, Sword of Gideon, Desperado: Avalanche at Devil's Ridge.

STEINBERG, DAVID: Actor, Writer, Director. b. Winnipeg, Canada, Aug. 9, 1942. e. U. of Chicago; Hebrew Theological Coll. Member Second City troupe; comedian at comedy clubs: Mr. Kelly's Hungry i, Bitter End. Starred in London and Bdwy. stage prods. Bdwy. includes Little Murders; Carry Me Back to Morningside Heights.

PICTURES: Actor: The End, Something Short of Paradise, Willow. Director: Paternity, Going Berserk (also co.-s.p.).

TELEVISION: Music Scene (writer, co-host); Tonight Show (guest host); David Steinberg Summer Show; Second City: 25 Years in Revue. Director: Newhart episodes, The Popcorn Kid, Golden Girls, One Big Family, Faerie Tale Theatre, Richard Belzer Special, Baby on Board, and many commercials.

Ste-Ste

STEINBERG, HERB: b. New York, NY, July 3, 1921. e. City Coll. of New York, 1937–41. Capt. U.S. Army, 1942–46; pub. PRC, 1946, Eagle Lion, 1946–49, Paramount 1949; pub. mgr. 1951; expl. mgr., 1954; studio adv. & pub. dir., 1958; exec. chg. of spec. proj., press dept., Universal City Studio, 1963; v.p., Universal Studio Tours, 1971; 1974 v.p., MCA Recreation Services. Appt. to California Tourism Commission, 1984; consultant, MCA, Inc., 1987; bd. trustees, Motion Picture & TV Fund, 1987; Communications dir. Alliance of Motion Picture & Television Producers.

STEINMAN, MONTE: Executive. Joined Paramount Pictures 1980 as sr. financial analyst. Series of promotions followed, culminating in appt. as dir. of financial planning of Gulf + Western's Entertainment and Communications Group, in February, 1984. In 1985, named exec. dir., financial planning.

STELOFF, ARTHUR "SKIP": Executive. b. New York, NY, Aug. 10, 1925. Son of Ike Steloff, "Saratoga Ike," professional gambler. Nephew of Gotham Book Mart owner Frances Steloff. e. U.S. Naval Acad. Served in the Navy. Sold television and radio spot time for WWDC in Washington, D.C. 1951–52. Sold ZIV film library for Matty Fox 1952–56; Sales mgr. C&C TV 1956–58. Founded Heritage Entertainment Inc. 1966 originally as a radio syndication business, then as indep. film prod. and dist. company. Chairman and CEO of Heritage.
PICTURES: Without Warning (co-exec. prod.); Mr. North.

STEMBLER, JOHN H.: Executive. b. Miami, FL, Feb. 18, 1913. e. U. of Florida Law Sch., 1937. Asst. U.S. att., South. dist. of Fla., 1941; U.S. Air Force, 1941–45; pres. Georgia Theatre Co., 1957; named chm., 1983; NATO member exec. comm. and past pres.; Major Gen. USAF (Ret); past bd. chm., National Bank of Georgia.

STEMBLER, WILLIAM J.: Executive. b. Atlanta, GA, Nov. 29, 1946. e. Westminister Sch., 1964; U. of Florida, 1968; U. of Georgia Law Sch., 1971. 1st. lt. U.S. Army, 1971; capt., U.S. Army Reserve; resigned 1976. Enforcement atty., SEC, Atlanta office, 1972–73; joined Georgia Theatre Co., 1973; pres. 1983–86; joined United Artists Communications, Inc., 1986, as v.p.
MEMBER: bd. of dir., Merchant Bank of Atlanta; bd. of dir., & v.p., NATO, 1983–present; mbr., NATO OF GA & past-pres., 1983–85.

STERLING, JAN: Actress. r.n. Jane Sterling Adriance. b. April 3, 1923. e. private tutors; Fay Compton Sch. of Dramatic Art, London. N.Y. stage debut: Bachelor Born.
STAGE: Panama Hattie, Present Laughter, John Loves Mary, Two Blind Mice, Front Page, Over 21, Born Yesterday, The November People.
PICTURES INCLUDE: Johnny Belinda (debut), Appointment with Danger, Mating Season, Union Station, Skipper Surprised His Wife, Big Carnival, Caged, Rhubarb, Flesh and Fury, Sky Full of Moon, Pony Express, The Vanquished, Split Second, Alaska Seas, High & the Mighty, Return From the Sea, Human Jungle, Women's Prison, Female on the Beach, Man with the Gun, 1984, The Harder They Fall, Love in a Goldfish Bowl, The Incident, The Minx.
TELEVISION: Series: You're in the Picture, (panelist, 1961), Made in America, The Guiding Light (1969–70), Movies: Backstairs at the White House; Dangerous Company; My Kidnapper, My Love.

STERLING, ROBERT: Actor. r.n. William Sterling Hart. b. Newcastle, PA, Nov. 13, 1917. e. U. of Pittsburgh. m. Anne Jeffreys, actress. Father of actress Tisha Sterling. Fountain pen salesman, day laborer, clerk, industrial branch credit mgr., clothing salesman on West Coast; served as pilot-instructor U.S. Army Corps. 3 yrs.
PICTURES INCLUDE: Blondie Meets the Boss, Only Angels Have Wings, Manhattan Heartbeat, Yesterday's Heroes, Gay Caballero, Penalty, I'll Wait for You, Get-Away, Ringside Maisie, Two-Faced Woman, Dr. Kildare's Victory, Johnny Eager, This Time for Keeps, Somewhere I'll Find You, Secret Heart, Roughshod, Bunco Squad, Sundowners, Show Boat, Column South.
TELEVISION: Series: Topper, Love That Jill, Ichabod and Me. Movie: Beggarman, Thief.

STERN, ALFRED E. F.: Public relations executive. b. Boston, MA, Aug. 4. e. Boston U. Reporter, editor, Lowell Sun, Quincy Patriot-Ledger, Dartmouth News; publicist, RKO Radio Pictures, 1946–54; publicity dir., 1955; West Coast publicity dir., NTA, 1958; own public relations org., Alfred E. F. Stern Co., Inc., 1960.

STERN, DANIEL: Actor. b. Bethesda, MD, Aug. 28, 1957.
PICTURES: Breaking Away, It's My Turn, One-Trick Pony, Stardust Memories, Diner, I'm Dancing As Fast As I Can, Blue Thunder, Get Crazy, The Boss' Wife, Hannah and Her Sisters, D.O.A., The Milagro Beanfield War, Leviathan, Crazy Horse.
TELEVISION: Samson and Delilah, Weekend War. Series: Hometown.

STERN, EDDIE: Film buyer. b. New York, NY, Jan. 13, 1917. e. Columbia Sch. of Journalism. Head film buyer and booker, specializing in art theatres, for Rugoff and Becker, N.Y.; Captain, USAF; joined Wometco Ent. in 1952 as asst. to film buyer; v.p. motion picture theatre film buying and booking, Wometco Enterprises, Inc. Retired from Wometco 1985. Now handling film buying and booking for Theatres of Nassau, Ltd.

STERN, EZRA E.: Attorney. b. New York, NY, Mar. 2, 1908. e. Southwestern U. 1930, LL.B. pres., Wilshire Bar Assn. Former legal counsel for So. Calif. Theatre Owners Association. Member: Calif. State Bar; member, Int'l Variety Clubs; former chief barker, Variety Club So. Calif. Tent 25; pres., Variety Int'l Boys' Club; board of dir., Los Angeles Metropolitan Recreation & Youth Services Council; bd. of trustees, Welfare Planning Council, Los Angeles Region; former mem. Los Angeles Area Council, Boys' Club of America; pres., Variety International Boys' Club 1976–77 and 1979–80. Member bd. dir., Will Rogers Institute, M.P. Pioneers. 1984, honored by Variety Boys and Girls Club as founder of youth recreational facility.

STERN, STEWART: Writer. b. New York, NY, Mar. 22, 1922. e. Ethical Culture Sch., 1927–40; U. of Iowa, 1940–43. Rifle Squad Leader, S/Sgt. 106th Inf. Div., 1943–45; actor, asst. stage mgr., The French Touch, B'way, 1945–46; dialogue dir. Eagle-Lion Studios, 1946–48. 1948 to date: screenwriter.
TELEVISION: (Plays) Crip, And Crown Thy Good, Thunder of Silence, Heart of Darkness, A Christmas to Remember, Sybil (Emmy, 1977).
PICTURES INCLUDE: Teresa, Benjy (orig. s.p.) Rebel Without a Cause, The Rack, The James Dean Story, The Outsider, The Ugly American, Rachel, Rachel, The Last Movie, Summer Wishes—Winter Dreams (orig. s.p.).

STEUER, ROBERT B.: Executive. b. New Orleans, LA, Nov. 18, 1937. e. U. of Illinois, & 1955–57; Tulane U., 1957–59, B.B.A. Booker-Southern D.I. circuit, New Orleans, 1959; assoc., prod., Poor White Trash; 1960; v.p. Cinema Dist. America, 1961; co-prod., Flesh Eaters, Common Law Wife, 1963; Flack Black Pussy Cat, 1966; partner, gen. mgr., radio station WTVF, Mobile, 1963; dir. special projects, American Intl. Pictures, 1967; so. div. sls. mgr., AIP, 1971; v.p. asst. gen. sls. mgr., AIP, 1974; partner, United Producers Organization, producing Screamers, 1977; v.p., sls., Ely Landau Org., 1979; v.p., gen. sls. mgr., Film Ventures Intl., 1981; exec. v.p. world-wide mktg., 1983; pres., FVI, 1986-to date. 1987, senior v.p. world-wide mktg. Film Ventures Intl; 1987–88 exec. prod. Operation: Take No Prisoners, Tunnels, Most Dangerous Women Alive, Mad Crush.

STEVENS, ANDREW: Actor. b. Memphis, TN, June 10, 1955. Son of actress Stella Stevens. e. Antioch U., L.A., B.A. (psychology). Studied acting with Strasberg, David Craig, Vincent Chase, and Pat Randall. Began balancing work between film, TV and stage. Owner, exec. prod. King Cod Prods., LA. Producer Catalina Production Group Ltd.
PICTURES INCLUDE: Shampoo, Day of the Animals, Ten to Midnight, Massacre at Central High, Las Vegas Lady, Vigilante Force, The Boys in Company C, The Fury, Death Hunt, The Seduction, Scared Stiff, Tusks, Fine Gold, The Attendant, The Ranch, A Man of Passion, The Little Mermaid, The Terror Within.
TELEVISION: Adam-12, Apple's Way, The Quest, Police Story, Shazan, Once an Eagle (mini-series), Oregon Trail, Code Red (series), Dallas (series), Forbidden Love, Miracle on Ice, Journey's End, Women at Westpoint. Movies: S Secrets, The Last Survivors, The Werewolf of Woodstock, The Bastard (mini-series), The Rebels (mini-series), Beggarman Thief (mini-series), Topper, Emerald Point NAS, Hollywood Wives.

STEVENS, CONNIE: Actress. r.n. Concerta Ann Ingolie. b. Brooklyn, NY, August 8, 1938. e. Sacred Heart Acad., Hollywood Professional Sch. Began career as winner of several talent contests in Hollywood; rep. debut, Hollywood Repertory Theatre's prod. Finian's Rainbow; recordings include: Kookie, Kookie, Lend Me Your Comb, 16 Reasons, What Did You Make Me Cry For, From Me to You, They're Jealous of Me, A Girl Never Knows, Tapeheads, Back to the Beach.
PICTURES INCLUDE: Eighteen and Anxious, Young and Dangerous, Drag Strip Riot, Rock-a-Bye Baby, Parish, Susan Slade, Palm Springs Weekend, Cruise A-Go-Go, The Grissom Gang, Last Generation, Grease 2.
TELEVISION: Call Her Mom, Scruples, Playmates, The Sex Symbol, Bring Me the Head of Dobie Gillis, Starting from Scratch (series).

STEVENS, CRAIG: Actor. r.n. Gail Shekles. b. Liberty, MO, July 8, 1918. m. actress Alexis Smith. e. U. of Kansas. Played in coll. dramatics. On screen 1941 in Affectionately Yours.
PICTURES INCLUDE: Since You Went Away, The Doughgirls, Roughly Speaking, Too Young to Know, Humoresque, The Man I Love, That Way With Women, Night Unto Night, Love and Learn, Lady Takes a Sailor, Phone Call from a

294

Stranger, French Line, Where the Sidewalk Ends, Duel on the Mississippi, The Name's Buchanan, Gunn, Limbo Line, The Snoop Sisters, "S.O.B."
TELEVISION: Lux Video Theatre, Four Star Playhouse, Loretta Young Show, Schlitz Playhouse, Dinah Shore, Ernie Ford Shows, Chevy Show, Summer on Ice, The Millionaire, The Bold Ones; Series: Peter Gunn (1958–61), Man of the World (ATV England); Mr. Broadway, Name of the Game, The Invisible Man, Rich Man, Poor Man (mini-series); Dallas; Movies: The Killer Bees; The Love Boat; The Cabot Connection; The Home Front; Supercarrier.
STAGE: Here's Love, King of Hearts, Plain and Fancy, Critics Choice, Mary Mary; Nat. Co. Cactus Flower.

STEVENS, GEORGE, JR.: Director, Writer, Producer. b. Los Angeles, CA, Apr. 3, 1932. Son of late director George Stevens. e. Occidental Coll., 1949–53, B.A. 1st Lieut. U.S. Air Force; TV dir., Alfred Hitchcock Presents, Peter Gunn, 1957–61; prod. asst. Giant Productions, 1953–54; prod. asst. Mark VII, Ltd., 1956–57; assoc. prod., dir., The Diary of Anne Frank, 1957–59; assoc. prod., dir., The Greatest Story Ever Told, 1959–62; dir. M.P. Service, U.S. Information Agency 1962–67; chmn., U.S. deleg. to Film Festivals at Cannes (1962, 1964), Venice (1962, 1963), Moscow (1963); prod. John F. Kennedy; Years of Lightning, Day of Drums. Founding director, American Film Institute, 1967–79; co-chm., American Film Institute, 1979 to present. Producer, America at the Movies (1976). George Stevens: A Filmmaker's Journey (dir.,writer, prod.) 1984.
TELEVISION: The American Film Institute's Salute to James Cagney (Emmy Award) 1975; American Film Institute's Salutes (producer/writer, 1973–88); The Stars Salute America's Greatest Movies, (executive producer, 1977); The Kennedy Center Honors, (producer/writer, 1978–87) (Emmy Award 1983, 1985); America Entertains Vice Premier Deng, (producer/writer, 1978). Christmas in Washington, (Exec. prod./s.p., 1982–87); The Murder of Mary Phagan (co-writer, prod., 1988).

STEVENS, K. T.: Actress, r.n. Gloria Wood. b. Hollywood, CA, 1919. e. U. of Southern California. Daughter of late director Sam Wood.
STAGE: You Can't Take It With You, The Man Who Came to Dinner, My Sister Eileen, Nine Girls, St. Joan, The Voice of the Turtle, The Tender Trap.
PICTURES INCLUDE: (debut) Peck's Bad Boy, The Great Man's Lady, Nine Girls, Address Unknown, Kitty Foyle, Harriet Craig, Vice Squad, Tumbleweed, Missile to the Moon, Bob and Ted and Carol and Alice, Pets, They're Playing With Fire.

STEVENS, LEE: President, Chief Executive Officer, William Morris Agency, Inc. b. March 10, 1930, New York, NY. e. New York U. Sch. of Commerce, B.S., 1951; New York U. Law Sch., J.D., 1957. Member of NY bar. With William Morris Agency 35 years.

STEVENS, LESLIE: Executive, Writer, Producer, Director. b. Washington, DC, Feb. 3, 1924. e. Westminister Sch., London, Yale Drama Sch., American Theatre Wing, N.Y. Sold first play, The Mechanical Rat at 15; wrote six plays for summer stock groups, 1941–42; U.S. Air Force, 1943; pres., exec. prod. Daystar Prods.; writer, producer, director, film TV and features.
STAGE: Bullfight (off B'way) 1953–54; wrote, Broadway: Champagne Complex; The Lovers; The Marriage-Go-Round; The Pink Jungle, Joy Joy.
TELEVISION: For Playhouse 90: Invitation to a Gunfighter, Charley's Aunt, Rumors of Evening, The Violent Heart, Portrait of a Murderer, The Second Man; Kraft TV Theatre, Duel; Four Star Playhouse, Award, Producers Showcase, Bloomer Girl; created, prod., dir. Stoney Burke, (series), 1962, created, prod., dir. Outer Limits, pilot It Takes a Thief; exec. prod. series; prod.-writer pilot McCloud; exec. prod. series; exec. prod. Men From Shiloh series; exec. prod., writer-dir., Name of the Game, (Leslie Stevens Productions), prod.-writer, pilot of Search, exec. prod., series creator, series Movie of Today, Paperback Playhouse, Earthside Missile Base. Exec. prod., Invisible Man, 1975. Supervising prod. Gemini Man, (1976 pilot and series), Battlestar Galactica (co-prod., pilot), Buck Rogers (co-s.p., 1979), The Highwayman (sprv. prod.).
PICTURES INCLUDE: author, The Left-Handed Gun 1958; co-prod.-wrote-dir. Private Property; wrote, The Marriage-Go-Round; wrote-prod.-dir. Hero's Island; Battlestar Galactica (co-prod.), Buck Rogers (writer, prod.), Three Kinds of Heat (dir., prod., s.p.).

STEVENS, MARK: Actor. r.n. Richard Stevens. b. Cleveland, OH, Dec. 13, 1922. e. privately; Beaux Arts and Sir George Williams Sch. of Fine Arts, Montreal. Had varied career before appearing on stage and radio in Canada; later joined station WAKB in Akron; then prod. mgr., WJW, Akron. Screen debut in Objective Burma. Formed Mark Stevens Prod., Mark Stevens Television Prod., 1955.
PICTURES INCLUDE: God Is My Co-Pilot, Pride of the

Marines, From This Day Forward, The Dark Corner, I Wonder Who's Kissing Her Now, Between Midnight and Dawn, Katie Did It, Little Egypt, Reunion in Reno, Mutiny, Big Frame, Torpedo Alley, Jack Slade, Cry Vengeance, Timetable, September Storm, Fate Is the Hunter, Frozen Alive, Sunscorched.
TELEVISION: Series: Martin Kane; Big Town (prod., starred, script), Murder She Wrote.

STEVENS, STELLA: Actress. b. Hot Coffee, MS, Oct. 1, 1938. e. Attended Memphis State U. Modeled in Memphis when she was discovered by talent scouts. Was briefly a term contract actress at 20th Century-Fox, later under exclusive contract to Paramount, then Columbia.
PICTURES INCLUDE: Say One For Me, The Blue Angel, Li'l Abner, Too Late Blues, Man Trap, The Courtship of Eddie's Father, The Nutty Professor, Advance to the Rear, Synanon, The Secret of My Success, The Silencers, The Ballad of Cable Hogue, Stand Up & Be Counted, Slaughter, The Poseidon Adventure, Arnold, Las Vegas Lady, Cleo Jones and the Casino of Gold, Nickelodeon, The Manitou, Wacko, Chained Heat, The Longshot, Monster in the Closet.
TELEVISION: Series: Ben Casey, Flamingo Road. Movies: Honky Tonk, Murder in Peyton Place, Day the Earth Moved, Amazons, Children of Divorce, Climb an Angry Mountain, French Atlantic Affair, Twirl, No Man's Land, Man Against the Mob, Fatal Confession: A Father Dowling Mystery.

STEVENSON, PARKER: Actor. b. Philadelphia, PA, June 4, 1953. e. Princeton U. Began professional acting career by starring in film, A Separate Peace, while high school senior, having attracted attention through work on TV commercials.
PICTURES INCLUDE: A Separate Peace (debut), Our Time, Lifeguard, Stroker Ace, Stitches.
TELEVISION: The Streets of San Francisco, Gunsmoke, Hardy Boys Mysteries, Falcon Crest, Probe. Mini-Series: North & South Book II. Movie: Shooting Stars, This House Possessed, That Secret Sunday.

STEWART, DOUGLAS DAY: Writer, Director.
PICTURES: Writer: The Blue Lagoon; An Officer and a Gentleman; Thief of Hearts (also dir.); Mismatched (also dir.).
TELEVISION: Boy in the Plastic Bubble, The Man Who Could Talk to Kids, Murder or Mercy.

STEWART, ELAINE: Actress. b. Montclair, NJ, May 31, 1929. b. Montclair, NJ, May 31, 1929. Usherette, cashier, m.p. theatre, Montclair; model, Conover Agcy., 1948; many TV shows; screen debut in Sailor Beware (1951); Star of Tomorrow, 1954.
PICTURES INCLUDE: Sky Full of Moon, The Bad and the Beautiful, Desperate Search, Code Two, Slight Case of Larceny, Young Bess, Take the High Ground, Brigadoon, Adventures of Hajji Baba, Tattered Dress, Rise and Fall of Legs Diamond, Most Dangerous Man Alive.

STEWART, JAMES: Actor. b. Indiana, PA, May 20, 1908. e. Mercersburg Acad.; Princeton U. With Falmouth Stock Co., Cape Cod; on N.Y. stage in Goodbye Again; stage mgr. for Camille with Jane Cowl (Boston). In films since 1935; joined U.S. Air Force 1942, commissioned Col. 1944. Retired as Brig. Gen. Voted one of top ten money-making stars, M.P. Herald-Fame poll, 1950, 52, 54, 57; No. 1 Money-Making Star, 1955. 1968, Screen Actors Guild Award. Mem.: Bd. of Trustees, Princeton U. Trustee, Claremont Coll.; exec. bd. of Los Angeles Council of Boy Scouts of America; bd. of dirs., Project Hope. Honorary Academy Award, 1984.
STAGE: Spring in Autumn, All Good Americans, Yellow Jack, Journey at Night, Harvey.
PICTURES INCLUDE: Murder Man, Rose Marie, Wife vs. Secretary, Next Time We Love, Small Town Girl, Speed, Gorgeous Hussy, Born to Dance, After the Thin Man, Seventh Heaven, You Can't Take It With You, The Last Gangster, Navy Blue and Gold, Of Human Hearts, Vivacious Lady, Shopworn Angel, Made For Each Other, Ice Follies of 1939, Mr. Smith Goes to Washington, It's A Wonderful World, Destry Rides Again, Shop Around the Corner, Mortal Storm, No Time For Comedy, The Philadelphia Story (Acad. Award, 1940), Come Live With Me, Pot O'Gold, Ziegfeld Girl, It's a Wonderful Life, Magic Town, Call Northside 777, On Our Merry Way, Rope, You Gotta Stay Happy, Stratton Story, Malaya, Winchester '73, Broken Arrow, Harvey, Jackpot, No Highway in the Sky, Greatest Show on Earth, Carbine Williams, Bend of the River, Naked Spur, Thunder Bay, Glenn Miller Story, Far Country, Rear Window, Strategic Air Command, Man From Laramie, Man Who Knew Too Much, Spirit of St. Louis, Night Passage, Vertigo, Bell Book and Candle, Anatomy of a Murder, FBI Story, The Mountain Road, Two Rode Together, Man Who Shot Liberty Valance, Mr. Hobbs Takes a Vacation, How the West Was Won, Take Her, She's Mine, Cheyenne Autumn, Dear Brigitte, Shenandoah, The Rare Breed, Flight of the Phoenix, Firecreek, Bandolero, Cheyenne Social Club, Fool's Parade, That's Entertainment, The Shootist, Airport '77, The Magic of Lassie, The Big Sleep.
TELEVISION: Series: The Jimmy Stewart Show (1971–72), Hawkins, 1973–74; Movies: Hawkins on Murder, Right of Way, 1984.

STEWART, JAMES L.: Executive. e. U. of Southern California, B.A. in cinema-TV and M.B.A. in finance. Worked for two years in sales for CBS Radio Network—West Coast. Spent four years with MGM in promotion and marketing. With Walt Disney Prods. for 12 years, functioning in marketing, management and administrative activities; named v.p.-corp. relations & admin. asst. to pres. In 1978 joined in formation of Aurora Pictures, of which is exec. v.p., secty., & COO.
PICTURES: Exec. Prod.: Why Would I Lie?, The Secret of NIMH, Eddie and the Cruisers, Heart Like a Wheel, East of the Sun, West of the Moon, Maxie.

STEWART, KEN: Executive. First affiliated with Universal as asst. to head of trailers dept. Joined Paramount in 1981 as member of West Coast pub. dep.; later administrator, audio visual services. 1984, appt. exec. dir. of creative services (New York).

STEWART, MARILYN: Public Relations Executive. b. New York, NY. e. Hunter Coll. Entered ind. as scty. in 1960 to Si Seadler, MGM dir. of adv. Promoted in 1963 to asst. to Seadler. Left in 1964 to become prom.-pub. for Verve/Folkways Records; duties also included ar and talent scouting. In 1966 joined 20th-Fox as mag. pub. coordinator. In 1969 went to Para. Pictures as mag. pub. coordinator. Following year named worldwide director of pub. for Para., including creation of overall mkt. concepts, becoming 1st woman to be appointed to that position at major co. Campaigns included Love Story and The Godfather. In 1972 opened own consulting office specializing in m.p. marketing and p.r. Headquarters in N.Y.; repr. in L.A. Has represented American Film Theatre, The Lords of Flatbush, Bang the Drum Slowly, The Kids Are Alright, Autumn Sonata, The Tin Drum, L.A. Film Exposition, Michael Moriarty, Fred Schepisi, Lucasfilm, etc.

STIGWOOD, ROBERT: Executive. b. Adelaide, Australia, 1934. e. Sacred Heart Coll. Began career as copywriter for Aust. ad agency; at 21 left home for England. Series of first jobs led to his opening a London theatrical agency. Began casting commercials for TV; produced records for clients. Became first independent record producer in Great Britain. In mid '60s joined forces with Brian Epstein, manager of Beatles, to become co-mgr. of NEMS Enterprises. At Epstein's death formed own company, launching careers of such artists as Bee Gees, Cream, etc. Moved into theatre production in London: Hair, Jesus Christ Superstar, Pippin, Oh Calcutta!, Evita. Entered film production with Jesus Christ Superstar. Formed RSO Records in 1973.
PICTURES INCLUDE: Jesus Christ Superstar, Tommy, Saturday Night Fever, Grease, Sgt. Pepper's Lonely Hearts Club Band, Moment by Moment, Times Square (co.-prod.), The Fan, Gallipoli, Grease 2, Staying Alive.

STING: Musician, Actor. r.n. Gordon Matthew Sumner. b. Newcastle-Upon-Tyne, England, Oct. 2, 1951. e. Warwick U. A schoolteacher before helping from rock group, The Police as songwriter, singer and bass player.
PICTURES: Quadrophenia, Radio On, The Great Rock 'n' Roll Swindle, Brimstone and Treacle, The Bride, Dune, Plenty, Bring on the Night, Julia and Julia, Stormy Monday, The Adventures of Baron Munchausen, The Passion.

STOCKWELL, DEAN: Actor. b. Hollywood, CA, Mar. 5, 1935. p. Harry and Betty Veronica Stockwell. e. Long Island public schools and Martin Milmore, Boston. On stage in Theatre Guild prod. Innocent Voyage. Appeared on radio in Death Valley Days and Dr. Christian. Named in 1949 M.P. Herald-Fame Stars of Tomorrow poll; 1976 retired to Santa Monica as a licensed real estate broker but soon returned to acting.
PICTURES INCLUDE: Anchors Aweigh (debut), The Valley of Decision, Abbott and Costello in Hollywood, The Green Years, Home Sweet Homicide, The Mighty McGurk, The Arnelo Affair, The Romance of Rosy Ridge, Song of the Thin Man, Gentleman's Agreement, Deep Waters, Down to Sea in Ships, Boy with Green Hair, The Secret Garden, Happy Years, Kim, Stars in My Crown, Cattle Drive, Compulsion, Sons and Lovers, Long Day's Journey Into Night, Psych-out, The Dunwich Horror, Ecstasy, The Last Movie, The Loners, Another Day at the Races, Werewolf of Washington, Won Ton Ton The Dog Who Saved Hollywood, Win, Place, or Steal, Tracks, Wrong Is Right, To Kill a Stranger, Paris, Texas, Dune, To Live and Die in L.A., Blue Velvet, Beverly Hills Cop II, Gardens of Stone, The Time Guardian, The Blue Iguana, Tucker: The Man and His Dream, Buying Time, Married to the Mob, Palais Royale, Backtrack.
TELEVISION: Miami Vice, Hart to Hart, Simon and Simon, The A-Team, Movies: The Failing of Raymond, The Gambler III: The Legend Continues.

STODDARD, BRANDON: Executive. b. Canaan, NY, March 31, 1937. e. Yale U., Columbia Law Sch. Was program ass't. at Batton, Barton, Durstine and Osborn before joining Grey Advertising, where was successively, program operations supvr., dir. daytime programming, v.p. in chg. of TV, radio programming. Joined ABC in 1970; named v.p. daytime programs for ABC Entertainment, 1972; v.p. children's pro-

grams, 1973. Named v.p., motion pictures for TV, 1974. In 1976 named v.p., dramatic programs and motion pictures for television. In June, 1979, named pres., ABC Motion Pictures. In 1985 appt. pres., ABC Entertainment.

STOLBER, DEAN: Executive. b. Philadelphia, PA, Sept. 2, 1944. e. Harvard, A.B., 1966; New York U. Sch. of Law, J.D., 1969. Acted on Broadway and in TV before starting career in law and business affairs in films. 1979, sr. v.p., business affairs, for United Artists Corp.; 1981 named exec. v.p.; 1982, sr. v.p., MGM/UA Entertainment Co.

STOLNITZ, ART: Executive. b. Rochester, NY, March 13, 1928. e. U. of Tennessee, LL.B., 1952. U.S. Navy Air Force. Legal dept., William Morris Agency, 1953, dir. business affairs, ZIV 1959; dir. new program development, ZIV-United Artists, 1960; literary agent, MCA, 1961; dir. business affairs, Selmur Productions, Selmur Pictures, 1963; v.p. ABC Pictures, 1969; v.p. Metromedia Producers Corporation, 1970, executive v.p. Metromedia Producers Corporation; 1975 exec. v.p. and prod. Charles Fries Prods. 1976, prod. Edgar J. Scherick Productions; 1976–77 prod., Grizzly Adams (TV); 1977; v.p. business affairs, Warner Bros.-TV; 1980, snr. v.p., business affairs.

STOLOFF, VICTOR: Producer, Writer, Director, Editor. b. March 17, 1913. e. French Law U. Ac. Fines Arts. Prod. dir. writer of award winning documentaries (Warner Bros. release); Prod. dir. writer first U.S. film made in Italy, When in Rome; First U.S. film made in Egypt; Collaborator William Dieterle films; Contract; writer, dir. to Sidney Buchman, Columbia, s.p. Volcano, The Sinner, Shark Reef. Journey Around the World. Prod. Writ. Of Love and Desire; producer-director, Intimacy, producer-director: The Washington Affair.
TELEVISION: Ford Theatre, Lloyd Bridges series, National Velvet, High Adventure, with Lowell Thomas, Prod. on location 22, Hawaii Five-O, The 300 Year Weekend, Why? Director (orig. s.p.) Created Woman of Iran, first of TV series.

STOLTZ, ERIC: Actor. b. American Samoa, 1961. Family moved to California when he was 8. Spent 2 years at U. of Southern California in theatre arts; left to study with Stella Adler and later William Traylor and Peggy Feury. Motion picture debut in Fast Times at Ridgemont High, 1982. Stage work with an American rep. co. in Scotland in Tobacco Road, You're a Good Man Charlie Brown, Working. Broadway debut Our Town (1988).
PICTURES: Lucky 13, Next of Kin, The Wild Life, Code Name: Emerald, Mask, Some Kind of Wonderful, Lionheart, Sister Sister, Haunted Summer, For a Night of Love, Manifesto, The Fly 2: The Insect Awakens, Torrents of Spring.
TELEVISION: Many series appearances. Movies: A Killer in the Family, Paper Dolls, Thursday's Child, The Violation of Sara McDavid, The Seekers, Things Are Looking Up.

STONE, ANDREW L.: Producer, Director. b. California, July 16, 1902. e. U. of California. Ent. ind. 1918 at Universal San Francisco exch.; later author, prod., dir. series of pictures for Paramount; prod., dir. for Sono-Art; 1932–36. org. and oper. Race Night company; prod., dir., The Girl Said No, 1936; Stolen Heaven, Say It in French, The Great Victory Herbert, Magician Music, 1940. Dir. Stormy Weather; formed Andrew Stone Prods., 1943.
PICTURES INCLUDE: The Great Victor Herbert, Stormy Weather, Hi Diddle Diddle, Sensations of 1945, Bedside Manner, Bachelor's Daughter, Fun on a Weekend, Highway 301, Confidence Girl, Steel Trap, Blueprint for Murder, Night Holds Terror, Julie, Cry Terror, The Decks Ran Red, The Last Voyage, Ring of Fire, Password is Courage, Never Put It in Writing, Secret of My Success, Song of Norway, The Great Waltz.

STONE, BURTON J.: Executive. b. Feb. 16, 1928; e. Florida Southern Coll. Was film ed., Hollywood Film Co. 1951–53; serv. mgr., sales mgr. and gen. mgr., Consolidated Film Inds., 1953–61; nat'l sales mgr., Movielab, 1961–63; pres., Allservice Film Laboratories, 1963–; v.p. Technicolor, Inc., 1963–70. Pres., Precision Film Labs., 1972–78. Pres., Deluxe Laboratories, Inc., a wholly-owned subsidiary of 20th Century Fox, 1978–present.
MEMBER: Board of directors, Will Rogers Foundation and Motion Picture Pioneers; member Acad. of Motion Picture Arts & Sciences, American Society of Cinematographers; awarded fellowship in Society of Motion Picture & Television Engineers; pres., Association of Cinema & Video Laboratories; awarded fellowship in British Kinematograph, Sound & Television Society.

STONE, DEE WALLACE: Actress. r.n. Deanna Bowers. b. Kansas City, MO, Dec. 14. m. actor Christopher Stone. e. U. of Kansas, theater and education. Taught high school English. Came to NY to audition for Hal Prince and spent 2 years working in commercials and industrial shows. First break in Police Story episode.
PICTURES: The Hills Have Eyes; 10; The Howling; E.T. the Extra-Terrestrial; Jimmy the Kid; Cujo; King of the City;

Critters; Secret Admirer; Shadow Play; The White Dragon; Stranger on My Land.
TELEVISION: Chips, Together We Stand (series). Movies: A Whale for the Killing, The Five of Me, Wait Till Your Mother Gets Home, Happy, I Take These Men, The Sky's the Limit, Terror in the Sky, The Christmas Visitor.

STONE, EZRA C.: Actor, Dir., Writer, Prod., Teacher, Lecturer, Farmer. b. New Bedford, MA, Dec. 2, 1917. e. American Acad. of Dramatic Arts, N.Y., 1934–35. Actor: National Junior Theatre, 1931; Broadway: Parade, Ah Wilderness, Oh Evening Star, Three Men on a Horse, Room Service, Brother Rat; created Henry Aldrich, What a Life, The Alchemist, She Stoops to Conquer; prod. asst. to George Abbott, 1935–40; created Henry Aldrich on radio's Aldrich Family, 1938; starred, Those Were the Days, This is the Army, USAAF, 1941–45; directed on Broadway: See My Lawyer, 1939, Reunion in New York, 1940.
STAGE: This Is the Army, 1942; January Thaw; At War with the Army; To Tell You the Truth; Me and Molly; Wake Up Darling; Make a Million; The Man That Corrupted Hadleyburg; The Pink Elephant; Dear Ruth; Come Blow Your Horn; God Bless Our Bank, Fallen Angels; Finishing Touches, 1978; Dracula—The Vampire King, 1978; Sweet Land (exec. prod., dir.); Centennial Celebration of Founding Newtown, PA (actor).
PICTURES INCLUDE: (docum.) Did 300 documentary films for IBM. Also American Heart Assn., Chapman Coll., University of Judaism, Jewish Theological Seminary; dir. live action sequences for The Daydreamer; The Forty Million (producer, director, co-narrator).
TELEVISION: Aldrich Family, Danny Thomas, Ed Wynn, Ezio Pinza, Martha Raye, Fred Allen, Herb Shriner, Life With Father, Sid Caesar, Joan Davis, dir. Joe and Mabel, prod., dir. Bachelor Father, Angel, The Hathaways, spec. Affairs of Antol, Shari Lewis, Bob Hope, My Living Doll, Munsters, Karen, Tammy, O.K. Crackerby, Please Don't Eat the Daisies; dir., writer Woody Allen pilot, Loredo, Pistols & Petticoats, Petticoat Junction, Phyllis Diller Show, Lost in Space, Tammy Grimes show, Julia, Flying Nun, Debbie Reynolds, The Jimmy Stewart Show, Lassie, Sandy Duncan Show, Tribute to the Lunts, Love American Style, Bob Newhart, Space Academy, Munster's Revenge, Quincy, ABC Circle Playhouse Project UFO, actor, (PBS Paul Muni, biography film). Has over 25 intl. film awards; Grand Prize, Barcelona Int'l Film Festival.
AUTHOR: Coming Major, 1945, co-author: Deems Taylor; Liberte, Puccini Opera, 1951; contributor to: Variety, Magazine Digest, N.Y. Post; Equity Magazine, etc. Teacher: American Acad. Dramatic Arts, assoc. dir., American Theatre Wing; American College Theatre Festival, Princeton, Yale, U. of California at L.A.: pres./dir., David Library of Amer. Revolution.

STONE, MARIANNE: Actress. b. London, England. Studied Royal Acad. of Dramatic Art, West End debut in The Kingmaker, 1946.
TELEVISION: Maigret, Bootsie and Snudge, Jimmy Edwards Show, Wayne and Schuster Show, Roy Hudd Show, Harry Worth Show, Steptoe and Son, Informer, Love Story, Father Dear Father, Bless This House, The Man Outside, Crown Court, Public Eye, Miss Nightingale, She, Little Lord Fauntleroy, The Secret Army (2 series), Shillingbury Tale, The Bright Side (series), Tickets for the Titanic (series), The Balance of Nature, Always, Hammer House of Mystery & Suspense.
PICTURES INCLUDE: Brighton Rock, Seven Days to Noon, The Clouded Yellow, Wrong Arm of the Law, Heavens Above, Stolen Hours, Nothing But the Best, Curse of the Mummy's Tomb, Hysteria, The Beauty Jungle, A Hard Day's Night, Rattle of a Simple Man, Echo of Diana, Act of Murder, Catch Us If You Can, You Must Be Joking, The Countess from Hong Kong, The Wrong Box, To Sir With Love; The Bliss of Mrs. Blossom, Here We Go Round the Mulberry Bush, Carry on Doctor, The Twisted Nerve, The Best House in London, Oh! What a Lovely War; The Raging Moon, There's a Girl in My Soup, All the Right Noises, Assault, Carry On at Your Convenience, All Coppers Are . . ., Carry on Girls, Penny Gold, The Vault of Horror, Percy's Progress, Confessions of a Window Cleaner, Carry on Dick, That Lucky Touch, Sarah, Carry on Behind, Confessions From a Holiday Camp, The Chiffy Kids, What's Up Superdoc?; The Class of Miss McMichael, The Human Factor, Dangerous Davies, Funny Money, Terry on the Fence, Carry on Laughing.

STONE, OLIVER: Director, Writer. b. New York, NY, Sept. 15, 1946. e. Yale U., NYU, B.F.A., 1971. U.S. Infantry 1967–68 in Vietnam.
PICTURES: Seizure (dir., s.p.), Midnight Express (s.p.— AA), The Hand (dir., s.p.), Conan the Barbarian (s.p.), Scarface (s.p.); Year of the Dragon (s.p.), Salvador (dir., co-s.p.), Platoon (dir., s.p.); Wall Street (dir., co-s.p.), Talk Radio (dir., co-s.p.), Born on the Fourth of July (dir., s.p.), Blue Steel (co-prod.).

STONE, PETER: Writer. b. Los Angeles, CA, Feb. 27, 1930. Won Oscar in 1964 for Father Goose; Emmy for segment of The Defenders.
THEATER: Kean, Skyscraper, 1776, Two By Two, Sugar, Full Circle, Woman of the Year, My One and Only.
PICTURES INCLUDE: Charade, Arabesque, Mirage, Secret War of Harry Frigg, Sweet Charity, Skin Game, The Taking of Pelham One Two Three, 1776 (adapted own stage musical book to screen), Silver Bears, Who Is Killing the Great Chefs of Europe?, Why Would I Lie?, Nesting.
TELEVISION: Androcles and the Lion, Adam's Rib (series), Ivan the Terrible.

STONEMAN, JAMES M.: Executive. b. Jan. 16, 1927. Pres., Interstate Theatres Corp., Boston. 1985, pres., Theatre Owners of New England. NATO bd.; Variety Club of New England & South Florida.

STORARO, VITTORIO: Cinematographer. b. Rome, Italy, 1940. Trained at Rome's Centro Sperimentale and began filming short films. His work as Bernardo Bertolucci's regular cameraman has won him an international reputation and award-winning work in Europe and America.
PICTURES: Giovinezza, Giovinezza (Youthful, Youthful, 1970); The Spider's Stratagem; The Conformist; 'Tis a Pity She's a Whore; Last Tango in Paris; Giordano Bruno; 1900; La Luna; Apocalypse Now (Academy Award); Submission; Agatha; Reds (Acad. Award); One From the Heart; Wagner; Peter the Great; Ladyhawke; The Last Emperor (Acad. Award); Tucker: The Man and His Dream; Zoe (Coppola's segment of New York Stories).

STOREY, FREDERICK: Executive. b. Columbus, GA, Nov. 12, 1909. e. Georgia Tech. Adv. staff Atlanta Journal, 1933–38; adv. staff C. P. Clark Adv. Agcy., 1938; partner 1940; U.S. Navy, 1941–46; staff Georgia Theatre Co., 1946; v.p. 1947–52. Founded Storey Theatres Inc., Atlanta, GA; 1952, now bd. chm. (formerly pres.) of Georgia State Theatres; dir. numerous theatre cos.; v.p. dir., Motion Picture Theatre Owners of Georgia, Dist. Alumnus award, Georgia Tech, 1979.

STORKE, WILLIAM F.: Producer. b. Rochester, NY. e. U. of California. In Navy in W.W.II. First position with NBC Hollywood guest relations staff, 1948. Moved to continuity acceptance dept. as comm. editor. Prom. to asst. mgr, comm. supvr. before joining NBC West Coast sales dept., 1953. Transferred to N.Y. as progr. acct. exec., 1955; named administrator, participating prog. sales, Nov., 1957. Named dir., participating program sales, 1959. Named dir., program adm., NBC-TV, Jan., 1964; in Feb. elected v.p., program adm. In 1967 named v.p., programs, East Coast; Nov. 1, 1968, appt. v.p., special programs, NBC-TV Network; 1979, pres., Claridge Group, Ltd.; exec. v.p. Entertainment Partners, Inc., N.Y., 1982–.
TELEVISION: Producer: Oliver Twist, 1982, To Catch A King, A Christmas Carol; The Last Days of Patton; A Special Friendship, The Ted Kennedy Jr. Story, Buck James (series, exec. prod.).

STORM, GALE: Actress. r.n. Josephine Cottle. b. Bloomington, TX, April 5, 1922. Won a "Gateway to Hollywood" talent contest while still in high school, in 1939. Made several minor films in the 1940s including several Roy Rogers westerns, before becoming popular comedienne on TV with My Little Margie (1952–55). Also launched successful recording career. Autobiography: I Ain't Down Yet (1981).
PICTURES INCLUDE: Tom Brown's Schooldays (debut, 1939), Foreign Agent, Nearly Eighteen, The Right to Live, Sunbonnet Sue, It Happened on Fifth Avenue, Abandoned, Between Midnight and Dawn, Underworld Story, Curtain Call at Cactus Creek, Al Jennings of Oklahoma, Texas Rangers, Woman of the North Country.
TELEVISION: Series: My Little Margie, Oh Susanna, radio show.

STOSSEL, JOHN: News Correspondent. b. 1947. e. Princeton U. Started as producer-reporter with KGW-TV in Portland, OR. Joined WCBS-TV in New York as investigative reporter and consumer editor, winning 15 local Emmy Awards. In June, 1981 joined ABC-TV, appearing on Good Morning America and 20/20 as consumer editor. Also provides twice-weekly consumer reports on ABC Radio Information Network. Author: Shopping Smart (1982).

STOVER, WENDY: Executive. Joined Orion Pictures (then Filmways Pictures) 1977 as asst. in legal dept. Named dir. of admin., heading insurance and personnel depts. 1985, named v.p., admin. 1987, sr. v.p. in chg. admin. Also holds title of v.p., branch admin. for Orion Pictures Distribution Corp.

STRADLING, HARRY, JR.: Cinematographer. b. New York, NY, Jan. 7, 1925. Son of Harry Stradling, renowned cinematographer.
PICTURES: Welcome to Hard Times, Support Your Local Sheriff, The Mad Room, Something Big, Fools Parade, The Way We Were, Bite the Bullet, Airport 77, Midway, The Big

Bus, Born Again, Convoy, Go Tell the Spartans, Prophecy, Carney, S.O.B., Buddy, Buddy, The Pursuit of D.B. Cooper, Micki and Maude, Blind Date, Caddyshack II.
TELEVISION: George Washington (mini-series).

STRAIGHT, BEATRICE: Actress. b. Old Westbury, NY, Aug. 2, 1918. Trained in classics; won Tony award early in career for best actress in Arthur Miller's The Crucible. Many films and TV programs.
THEATER: King Lear, Twelfth Night, The Possessed, Land of Fame, Eastward in Eden, The Heiress (Bdwy. & on tour), The Crucible, Phedra, Everything in the Garden, Ghosts, All My Sons, and regional theater (Streetcar Named Desire, A Lion in Winter, Old Times).
PICTURES: Phone Call from a Stranger, Patterns, The Nun's Story, Garden Party, Network (Acad. Award, supp. actress), Bloodline, The Promise, The Formula, Endless Love, Poltergeist, Two of a Kind, Power.
TELEVISION: Beacon Hill (series), The Dain Curse, The Borrowers, Murder on Board, King's Crossing (series), The Princess and the Pea (Faerie Tale Theatre), Morning Star/Evening Star, Jack and Mike (series), Robert Kennedy and His Times, Under Siege.

STRASBERG, SUSAN: Actress. b. New York, NY, May 22, 1938.; e. N.Y. Parents: late Lee Strasberg, stage dir. & dir. of Actors Studio, and Paula Miller, actress. Made stage debut in off-Bdwy. production of Maya; on TV in series, The Marriage, The Duchess and the Smugs, Catch a Falling Star; starred on Bway. in The Diary of Anne Frank.
PICTURES INCLUDE: Picnic, Stage Struck, Scream of Fear, Adventures of a Young Man, The Trip, Psych-Out, The Name of the Game Is Kill, Rollercoaster, The Manitou, In Praise of Older Women, The Delta Force, Prime Suspect, The Runnun Kind.
TELEVISION: Beggarman, Thief; The Immigrants; Toma; Frankenstein; Rona Jaffe's Mazes and Monsters; Murder She Wrote.

STRASSBERG, STEPHEN: Publicist. b. New York, NY. e. City Coll. of New York, B.S.S. Joined Loew's Inc., 1940; served in U.S. Army, WW II; publicist with Republic Pictures, 1946–49; asst. nat'l adv. dir., Film Classics, 1949–50; pub. dir., Eagle Lion Classics, 1950; publicist Lopert Films, Inc., 1951; dir. of adv., pub., Imperial Films, 1953; pub. dir., WABC, WABC-TV, N.Y., 1955; asst. dir., Press Information; ABC, 1957; dir. press info. ABC-TV Network, 1958; dir., News Information, ABC-TV Network, 1975.

STRATTON, JOHN: Actor. b. Clitheroe, England, 1925; e. Royal Grammar Sch., Clitheroe. Early career in repertory; m.p. and TV debut 1948.
TELEVISION: The First Mrs. Fraser, The Confidential Clerk, Adams Apple, You Know What People Are (series), Death of a Salesman, Quatermass In The Pit, The Wind and the Rain, The Secret Kingdom, Kipps, The Dobson Fund, The Problem of Mary Winshaw, A Perfect Woman, Climate of Fear, Thank You and Goodnight, What's In It for Walter, A Free Weekend, Workshop Limits, 24 Hour Call, 2 Cars, The Odd Man, It's Dark Outside, For the West, Man in Room 17, Julie's Gone, The Trouble Shooters, Turn out the Lights, Mr. Rose, The Black Doctor, Sir Arthur Conan Doyle, The Newcomers, Tickle Time, Letters from the Dead, Z Car, Wanted Single Gentleman, Softly Softly, Fall of the Goat, City '68, Artist in Crime, The First Lady, Print and Be Damned, The Expert, Resurrection (serial), Sherlock Holmes, Measure of Malice, The Elusive Pimpernel (serial), The Pallisers, Fall of the Eagles, Clayhanger, Trinity Tales, Witch of Pendle, When We Are Married, Just William, Backs to the Land, Forget Me Not, A Superstition, The Professionals, Mill on the Floss, The Good Companions, Great Expectations, The Forgotten Story, The Tales of Beatrix Potter, My Cousin Rachel, Dr. Who: Juliet Brajo.
PICTURES INCLUDE: Small Back Room, Seven Days to Noon, Appointment With Venus (Island Rescue), Happy Family, Cruel Sea, Long Arm, Man In the Sky, Seven Waves Away (Abandon Ship), The Challenge, Strangler's Web.

STRAUSS, PETER: Actor. b. Croton-on-Hudson, NY., Feb. 20, 1947. e. Northwestern U. Spotted at N.U. by talent agent and sent to Hollywood. Film debut in Hail Hero, 1969. Has acted at Mark Taper Theatre in Dance Next Door, The Dirty Man.
PICTURES INCLUDE: Hail, Hero!, Soldier Blue, The Trail of the Catonsville Nine, The Last Tycoon, Spacehunter.
TELEVISION: Man Without a Country, Attack on Terror, The FBI Story; Young Joe: The Forgotten Kennedy, The Jericho Mile (Emmy Award), Angel on My Shoulder; Heart of Steel, Under Siege. Mini-Series: Rich Man, Poor Man, Masada, Kane & Abel, A Whale for the Killing, Tender Is The Night, Penalty Phase, The Proud Men, Brotherhood of the Rose.

STRAUSS, PETER E.: Executive. b. Oct. 7, 1940. e. Oberlin Coll., London Sch. of Economics, Columbia U. Sch. of Law, L.L.B., 1965. Vice pres., University Dormitory Development Co., 1965–68; v.p., Allart Cinema 16, 1968–69; v.p. Production,

Allied Artists Pictures Corp., 1970; June 14, 1974 elected exec. v.p. Joined Rastar Films; left to become independent.

STREEP, MERYL: Actress. r.n. Mary Louise Streep. b. Bernardsville, NJ, April 22, 1949. e. Vassar. Acted for a season with traveling theater co. in VT. Awarded scholarship to Yale Drama School, 1972, where she was cast in 12–15 roles a year. NY stage debut: Trelawny of the Wells (1975) with New York Shakespeare Fest.
THEATER: Off-Broadway: 27 Wagons Full of Cotton, A Memory of Two Mondays, Secret Service, Henry V, (New York Shakespeare Fest.), Measure for Measure (NYSF), The Cherry Orchard, Happy End (Broadway debut, 1977), Taming of the Shrew (NYSF), Alice in Concert.
PICTURES: Julia, Manhattan, The Deer Hunter, The Seduction of Joe Tynan, Kramer vs. Kramer (Acad. Award, best supporting actress, 1979), The French Lieutenant's Woman, Still of the Night, Sophie's Choice (Acad. Award, 1982), Silkwood, Falling in Love, Plenty, Out of Africa, Heartburn, Ironweed, A Cry in the Dark, The Barber of Siberia.
TELEVISION: Holocaust, The Deadliest Season.

STREISAND, BARBRA: Singer, Actress. b. New York, April 24, 1942. e. Erasmus H.S., Brooklyn. Appeared in New York night clubs. NY stage debut: Another Evening with Harry Stoones (1961). On Broadway in I Can Get It For You Wholesale, Funny Girl.
PICTURES INCLUDE: Funny Girl (debut, Acad. Award, 1968), Hello Dolly, On A Clear Day You Can See Forever, The Owl and the Pussycat, What's Up Doc?, Up the Sandbox, The Way We Were, For Pete's Sake, Funny Lady, A Star Is Born, (star, prod.), The Main Event (star, co-prod.), All Night Long, Yentl (prod., dir., co.s.p., star), Nuts (actress, prod., music).
TELEVISION: My Name is Barbra, Color Me Barbra, Bell of 14th Street, A Happening in Central Park, Barbra Streisand: One Voice.

STRICKLYN, RAY: Actor. b. Houston, TX, October 8, 1930. e. U. of Houston.
PLAYS INCLUDE: Broadway debut in Moss Hart's The Climate of Eden. Tour: Stalag 17, Confessions of a Nightingale. Off-B'way: The Grass Harp. Los Angeles: Confessions of a Nightingale, Vieux Carre, Compulsion and The Caretaker, Naomi.
FILMS INCLUDE: The Proud and the Profane, Crime In the Streets, Somebody Up There Likes Me, The Catered Affair, The Last Wagon, Return of Dracula, 10 North Frederick, The Remarkable Mr. Pennypacker, The Big Fisherman, Young Jesse James, The Plunderers, The Lost World, Track of Thunder, Arizona Raiders, Dogpound Shuffle.
AWARDS: Broadway Theatre World Award; two Hollywood Foreign Press Golden Globe nominations (10 North Frederick and The Plunderers); Best Actor Awards 1984 & 86 for Vieux Carre and Confessions of a Nightingale (LA Drama Critics, L.A. Weekly Award, Drama-Logue, Robby Award, AGLA Media Award, Oscar Wilde Award).

STRINGER, HOWARD: Executive. e. Oxford U., B.A., M.A., modern history/international relations. Received Army Commendation Medal for meritorious achievement for service in Vietnam (1965–67). Joined CBS, 1965, at WCBS-TV, NY, rising from assoc. prod., prod. to exec. prod. of documentary broadcasts. Served as prod., dir. and writer of CBS Reports: The Palestinians (Overseas Press Club of America, Writers Guild Awards, 1974); The Rockefellers (Emmy Award, 1973). Won 8 Emmy Awards as exec. prod., prod., writer or dir: CBS Reports: The Boston Goes to China; CBS Reports: The Defense of the United States; CBS Evening News with Dan Rather: The Beirut Bombing; The Countdown Against Cancer; The Black Family. Exec. prod., CBS Reports; exec. prod., CBS Evening News with Dan Rather, 1981–84. Appointed exec. vice pres., CBS News Division, 1984; pres., CBS News, 1986; pres., CBS/Broadcast Group, 1988.

STRITCH, ELAINE: Actress. b. Detroit, MI, Feb. 2, 1926. Major career on stage. Bdwy debut 1946 in Loco.
THEATER: Made in Heaven, Angel in the Wings, Call Me Madam, Pal Joey, On Your Toes, Bus Stop, Goldilocks, Sail Away, Who's Afraid of Virginia Woolf?, Wonderful Town, Company.
PICTURES: The Scarlet Hour (debut, 1955), Three Violent People, A Farewell to Arms, The Perfect Furlough, Who Killed Teddy Bear?, Sidelong Glances of a Pigeon Kicker, The Spiral Staircase, Providence, September, Cocoon II—The Return.
TELEVISION: Series: Growing Pains (1949), Pantomine Quiz (regular, 1953–55, 1958), My Sister Eileen, The Trials of O'Brien, Two's Company, The Ellen Burstyn Show. Specials: Kennedy Center Tonight, Follies in Concert.

STROCK, HERBERT L.: Producer, Writer, Director, Film editor. b. Boston, MA, Jan. 13, 1918. e. U. of Southern California, A.B., M.A. in cinema. Prof. of cinema, U. of Southern California, 1941. Started career, publicity leg man, Jimmy Fidler, Hollywood columnist; editorial dept., MGM, 1941–47; pres., IMP-

PRO, Inc., 1955–59; assoc. prod.-supv. film ed., U.A.; dir., AIP; dir., Phoenix Films. Pres., Herbert L. Strock Prods.
PICTURES INCLUDE: Storm Over Tibet, Magnetic Monster, Riders to the Stars, The Glass Wall. Director: Gog, Battle Taxi, Donovan's Brain, Rider on a Dead Horse, Devil's Messenger, Brother on the Run, One Hour of Hell, Witches Brew, Blood of Dracula, I Was a Teenage Frankenstein, The Crawling Hand; Soul Brothers Die Hard, Monstroids. Writer-film editor, Hurray for Betty Boop (cartoon). Sound Effects editor on Katy Caterpillar (cartoon feature). Director: Witches' Brew. Editor: Night Screams. Past-prod. spvr.: King Kung Fu. Co-director: Deadly Presence.
TELEVISION: Highway Patrol, Harbor Command, Men of Annapolis, I Led Three Lives, The Veil, Dragnet, 77 Sunset Strip, Maverick, Cheyenne, Bronco, Sugarfoot, Colt 45, Science Fiction Thea., Seahunt, Cimarron Archer, Bonanza, Hallmark Hall of Fame, The Small Miracle, Hans Brinker, The Inventing of America (specials); What Will We Say to a Hungry World (5 hr. Telethon); They Search for Survival (special), Flipper (series). Documentaries: Atlantis, Legends, UFO Journals, UFO Syndrome, Legend of the Lochness Monster, China-Mao to Now, El-Papa—Journey to Tibet. Editor: Peace Corps' Partnership in Health. L.A. Dept. of Water & Power: Water You Can Trust; Olympic Comm. Your Olympic Legacy—AAF.

STRODE, WOODY: Actor. r.n. Woodrow Strode. b. 1914. Before W.W.II at U. of California at L.A. With Kenny Washington was one of first black players to integrate collegiate football. For 9 years after W.W.II was a professional wrestler. Worked for John Ford, Cecil B. DeMille, Henry Hathaway.
PICTURES: The Lion Hunters, (debut, 1951), The Gambler From Natchez, The Ten Commandments, Tarzan's Fight for Life, Pork Chop Hill, The Last Voyage, Sergeant Rutldge, Spartacus, The Sins of Rachel Cade, Two Rode Together, The Man Who Shot Liberty Valance, Genghis Khan, 7 Women, The Professionals, Shalako, Che!, The Revengers, The Gatling Gun, Winterhawk, Loaded Guns, The Black Stallion Returns, Vigilante, The Cotton Club.
TELEVISION: Breakout, Key West, A Gathering of Old Men.

STROLLER, LOUIS A.: Executive Producer. b. Brooklyn, NY, April 3, 1942. e. Nicholas Coll. of Business Administration, BBA, 1963. Entered film business in 1963 doing a variety of jobs in local NY studios, then TV commercials and unit manager on The Producers. Moved to L.A. in 1970s. First asst. dir. Charley, Take the Money and Run, Lovers and Other Strangers, They Might Be Giants, Man on a Swing, 92 in the Shade. Prod. manager on Mortadella, Sisters, Sweet Revenge, The Eyes of Laura Mars, Telefon. Assoc. prod.: Badlands, Carrie. In 1978 met prod. Martin Bregman beginning an assoc. with The Seduction of Joe Tynan (prod. manager).
PICTURES: Exec. prod. or prod.: Simon, The Four Seasons, Venom, Eddie Macon's Run, Scarface, Sweet Liberty, Real Men, A New Life, Sea of Love.
TELEVISION: Half a Lifetime (exec. prod.).

STRONG, JOHN: Producer, Director, Writer, Actor. b. New York, NY, Dec. 3. e. U. of Miami, Cornell U., B.S., architectural engineering. Began acting in small role in film Duel in the Sun; on B'way in Annie Get Your Gun and understudy for James Dean in Immoralist. Appeared in many radio and TV serials, regular on Captain Video and the Video Ranger, later under contract as actor to Universal and Warner Bros. Member, Writers Guild America West, Directors Guild of America, Producers Guild of America, Dramatists Guild.
PICTURES INCLUDE: Perilous Journey (exec. prod., writer), Eddie & the Cruisers (superv. prod.), Heart Like a Wheel (superv. prod.), For Your Eyes Only (writer), The Earthling (prod.), The Mountain Men (actor, prod.), Savage Streets (prod.).
TELEVISION: The John Strong Show (host, exec. prod.), The Nurse (special, writer), McCloud (prod., writer), The Thrill of the Fall (prod.), Search (prod., writer, 2nd unit dir.), Outer Limits (exec. chge. prod.), Name of the Game (exec. chge. prod.), I Spy (writer), Love American Style (writer), All in the Family (writer), Changes (prod., dir., writer), Charlie's Angels (writer), Hawaii Five O' (writer).

STROUD, DON: Actor. b. Honolulu, Hawaii, 1937.
PICTURES: Madigan, Games, What's So Bad About Feeling Good?, Coogan's Bluff, Bloody Mama, Explosion, Von Richtofen and Brown, Angel Unchained, Hat Full of Rain, Murf the Surf, Sudden Death, Slaughter, Tick Tick, Tick, Joe Kidd, Scalaway, The Killer Inside Me, The Choirboys, The House by the Lake, The Buddy Holly Story, The Amityville Horror, The Night the Lights Went Out in Georgia, Search and Destroy, Striking Back, Sweet Sixteen, Armed and Dangerous, Two to Tango, License Revoked.
TELEVISION: Mike Hammer (series).

STRUTHERS, SALLY: Actress. b. Portland, OR, July 28, 1948.
PICTURES INCLUDE: The Phynx, Charlotte, Five Easy Pieces, The Getaway.

TELEVISION: Summer Bros. Smothers Show, Tim Conway Comedy Hour, All in the Family (series), Gloria (series), 9 to 5 (series). Films: The Great Houdinis, Aloha Means Goodbye, Hey, I'm Alive, Intimate Strangers, And Your Name is Jonah, A Gun in the House.

STULBERG, GORDON: Executive. b. Toronto, Canada, Dec. 17, 1923. e. U. of Toronto, B.A., Cornell Law Sch., LL.B. Was assoc. & member, Pacht, Ross, Warne & Bernhard; ent. m.p. ind. as exec. asst. to v.p., Columbia Pictures Corp., 1956–60; v.p. & chief studio admin. off., 1960–67; pres. of Cinema Center Films (div. of CBS) 1967–71; pres. 20th Century-Fox, Sept. 1971–75; 1980, named pres. & chief operating officer, PolyGram Pictures. Member of NY, Calif. bars, Chairman, American Interactive Media (Polygram subsidiary).

STURGES, JOHN ELIOT: Director. b. Oak Park, IL, Jan. 3, 1910. e. Marin Jr. Coll. asst. in blueprint dept., RKO-Radio Pictures, 1932; art dept; asst. film ed.; prod. asst., David O. Selznick; film ed.; Captain, Air Corps, W.W.II; directed, edited, 45 documentaries, training films.
PICTURES INCLUDE: The Man Who Dared, Shadowed, Alias Mr. Twilight, For the Love of Rusty, Keeper of the Bees, Best Man Wins, Sign of the Ram, The Walking Hills, The Capture, Mystery Street, Right Cross, The Magnificent Yankee, Kind Lady, The People vs. O'Hara, The Girl in White, Jeopardy, Fast Company, Escape from Fort Bravo, Bad Day at Black Rock, Gunfight at the O.K. Corral, The Old Man and the Sea, Last Train from Gun Hill, Never So Few, The Magnificent Seven, By Love Possessed, Sergeants Three, A Girl Named Tamiko, The Great Escape, The Satan Bug, Hallelujah Trail, Hour of the Gun, Ice Station Zebra, Marooned, Joe Kidd, McQ, The Eagle Has Landed.

STURGIS, NORMAN: Director, Actor, Writer. b. Dallas, TX, 1922. Prod., Your Navy Sings, Evanston; TV dir. Space X, Theaterama, Plays Anthology, The Viewers, TV commercials, educational films and newsfilms.
TELEVISION: The Web, Gunsmoke, Twilight Zone, Alcoa Goodyear Theatre, Bat Masterson, The Untouchables.
PICTURES INCLUDE: Solid Gold Cadillac, Bernardine, Mardi Gras, Compulsion.

STYNE, JULE: Composer, Producer. r.n. Jules Stein. b. London, Eng., Dec. 31, 1905. To U.S. as a child; guest piano soloist with Chicago Symph. Orch. at 8; played with many dance bands; gen. mus. dir. Granada & Marbro Theat., Chicago; vocal coach, arranger, conductor & comp. for several m.p. studios; entertainment consult.
SONGS: I've Heard That Song Before, It's Magic, I'll Walk Alone, It's Been a Long, Long Time; Let It Snow, 3 Coins in the Fountain (Acad. Award in collab. Sammy Cahn, 1954), People.
STAGE: High Button Shoes, Gentlemen Prefer Blondes, Two on the Aisle, Hazel Flagg, Gypsy, Sugar, Peter Pan, Bells Are Ringing, Funny Girl, Hallelujah Baby (Tony Award), Bar Mitzvah Boy.
PICTURES INCLUDE: Kid from Brooklyn, It Happened in Brooklyn, Romance on the High Seas, It's a Great Feeling, West Point Story, Meet Me After the Show, Living It Up, My Sister Eileen.

SUBOTSKY, MILTON: Writer, Producer. b. New York, NY, Sept. 27, 1921. Early career studying engineering. Wrote, dir. and edited doc. & educational films. Ent. m.p. ind. 1938. Wrote and prod. live TV programs 1941. Wrote & prod. TV film series Junior Science 1954. Wrote & co.prod. Rock, Rock, Rock; Jamboree, The Last Mile, in U.S. In England: City of the Dead, It's Trad Dad, Just for Fun, Dr. Terror's House of Horrors, Dr. Who and The Daleks, Daleks' Invasion Earth 2150 A.D., The Skull, The Psychopath, The Deadly Bees, The Terrornauts, They Came From Beyond Space, Torture Garden, Danger Route, The Birthday Party, Thank You All Very Much (Brit. title: A Touch of Love), Scream and Scream Again, The Mind of Mr. Soames, The House That Dripped Blood, I Monster, What Became of Jack and Jill, Tales From the Crypt, Asylum, Vault of Horror, And Now the Screaming Starts, Madhouse, From Beyond the Grave, The Beast Must Die, The Land That Time Forgot, At The Earth's Core, The Uncanny, Dominique, The Martian Chronicles, The Monster Club, Cat's Eye, Maximum Overdrive. TV series: Classic Fairy Tales.

SUCHER, HENRY: Writer. b. New York, NY, Sept. 3, 1900. e. New York U. With A.E.F., W.W.I. M. Pearl Krex, Reporter, N.Y. Globe, then mag. ed. (Nugents, Garment Weekly, The Brooklynite); publicity adv. copywriter; contrib. light satirical verses and humorous bits to the Sat. Eve. Post, Colliers, The New Yorker and other nat'l mags. Began screen career 1941 with collab. orig. s.p. The Miracle Kid. In 1942 wrote Soundies for Roosevelt-Coslow-Mills Corp. Wrote serials, Jack Holt, G. Man, and others for Larry Darmoor at Columbia Studios. Contract writer, Eagle-Lion Studios.
PICTURES INCLUDE: Captive Wild Woman, The Mummy's Tomb, Mug Town, The Mummy's Ghost (adapt. & collab. orig.), The Frozen Ghost, Jungle Woman, Your Fate Is In Your

Hands, Lines of Destiny; short subjects released by RKO; now v.p. Edward Finney Prod., v.p. Boots and Saddles Pictures, Inc.

SUGAR, JOSEPH M.: Executive. b. New York, NY, June 4, 1916. e. NYU. Started with Republic Pictures 1938; after service, U.S. Army Air Force, went to Eagle Lion which was taken over by United Artists; 1953, U.A., N.Y., metropolitan district manager; 1959, Magna Pictures Corp., v.p. sls.; 1962, 20th Century-Fox, v.p. domestic distribution; 1967, Warner-7 Arts, exec. v.p.; 1968, pres., Cinerama Rel. Corp.; 1974, formed Joe Sugar, Inc.; 1976, joined A.I.P. as exec. v.p. worldwide sls. & pres., A.I.P. Distribution Co.—A.I.P. later became Filmways; 1983, Embassy Pictures, exec. v.p. distribution; 1986, Joe Sugar, Inc. when Embassy sold to Coca Cola. Member Cinema Lodge, B'nai B'rith; A.F.I.; Motion Picture Pioneers.

SUGARMAN, BURT: Producer. b. Beverly Hills, CA, Jan. 4. e. U. of Southern California. Chm. & CEO, Giant Group, Ltd., diversified co. traded on NYSE. Heads Barris Industries Inc.
PICTURES: Kiss Me Goodbye, Extremities, Children of a Lesser God, Crimes of the Heart.
TELEVISION: Midnight Special, Switched on Symphony, The Mancini Generation, Johnny Mann's Stand Up and Cheer, etc.

SUHOSKY, BOB: Publicist. b. Philadelphia, PA, Nov. 23, 1928. Marine Corps 1946–57; 20th Century Fox Television, publicist, 1959, publicity director, 1964–70; pres. Bob Suhosky Assoc., public relations, 1971–77. Chairman, Suhosky & Hardiman Public Relations, 1977 to date. Wrote s.p. for Lone Star Girls (theatrical film) and Code R (TV).

SULLIVAN, BARRY: Actor. r.n. Patrick Barry. b. New York, NY, Aug. 29, 1912. e. New York U., Temple U. Usher in theat.; buyer for dept. stores; N.Y. stage: The Man Who Came to Dinner, Brother Rat, Idiot's Delight, The Land is Bright, Caine Mutiny Court Martial, etc.
PICTURES INCLUDE: Woman of the Town, Lady in the Dark, Rainbow Island, Two Years Before the Mast, And Now Tomorrow, Duffy's Tavern, Three Guys Named Mike, Cause for Alarm, Grounds for Marriage, Life of Her Own, Nancy Goes to Rio, Inside Straight, Payment on Demand, Mr. Imperium, No Questions Asked, Unknown Man, Skirts Ahoy, Bad & the Beautiful, Jeopardy, Cry of the Hunted, China Venture, Loophole, Her 12 Men, Miami Story, Playgirl, Queen Bee, Texas Lady, Maverick Queen, Strategic Air Command, Purple Gang, Seven Ways from Sundown, Light in the Piazza, War Lords of Outer Space, Stage to Thunder Rock, Buckskin, Tell Them Willie Boy Is Here, Earthquake, The Human Factor, Oh, God!, Caravans.
TELEVISION: Series: Man Called X (1955–56); Harbourmaster, The Tall Man, The Immortal (series), Road West (series), Once an Eagle, Poor Man—Book II, Johnny Belinda, Night Gallery, Yuma.

SULLIVAN, J. CHRISTOPHER: Actor. b. Greenville, TX, Sept. 15, 1932. e. Prairie View A & M U.; Sorbonne (Paris); U. of Texas., Ph.D. Stage debut in The Sign in Sidney Brustein's Window. Also appeared in Hatful of Rain, Anna Lucasta, Ceremonies in Dark Old Men, Dark of the Moon, Take a Giant Step, Therese. First black to teach at any predominantly white university in the south as an instructor of speech and communications at U. of Texas, Austin, 1964. Winner NAACP Image Award 1986; best theatre actor, Anna Lucasta.
PICTURES INCLUDE: Night Call Nurses, The Venetian Affair, The Lost Man, Body Heat, Black Starlet, The Black Gestapo, The Happy Ending, D.C. Cab, Critters II, Arthur 2 On the Rocks.
TELEVISION: The White Shadow, Jeffersons, Good Times, One Day at a Time, General Hospital, Serpico, Starsky & Hutch, Death Flight, McClain's Law, Growing Pains, Hill Street Blues, Elvis and Me, Roots Christmas.

SULLIVAN, REV. PATRICK J., S.J., S.T.D.: Provost, Graduate Center at Tarrytown, Fordham U. b. New York, NY, March 25, 1920. e. Regis H.S.: Georgetown U., A.B., 1943; Woodstock Coll., M.A., 1944; Fordham U., 1945–47; S.T.L. Weston Coll., 1947–51; S.T.D. Gregorian U. (Rome), 1952–54. Prof. of Theology, Woodstock Coll., 1954–57; Consultor, Pontifical Commission for Social Communications.

SUNSHINE, MORTON: Honorary Executive Vice President, Variety Clubs Intl. special consultant; International executive director, Variety Clubs International, 1975–86. b. Brooklyn, NY, Sept. 20, 1915. B.S. in S.S., 1935; LL.B., 1938; J.S.D., 1939. Admitted to N.Y. Bar 1939. Federal Bar 1941. Practicing attorney, 1941–44; Federal investigator with U.S.C.S.C. 1944–45; business mgr., Independent Theatre Owners Assn. 1945–46; exec. dir. since 1946; member COMPO tax & legis. com., 1950; sp. rep. Org. of M.P. Ind. of City of N.Y., 1952–55; exec. coord. Tony Awards Amer. Theatre Wing, 1958–60, Sophie Tucker Golden Jubilee; ind. trib. to Jimmy Durante; Al Jolson; Will Rogers; A. Montague; Herman Robbins; S. H. Fabian; Rodgers-Hammerstein; Eric Johnston; Diamond Jubilee, Stagehands, 1962. Danny Thomas; indus. pub. rel.

consultant; (William Morris Agency, Movielab, etc.) exec. coord. IFIDA Int'l Film Awards Dinners; pres. cabinet, Nat'l Assn. of Theatre Owners, exec. dir., Variety Club of N.Y.; consultant to American Film Institute, 1973–75; executive director, Motion Picture Pioneers, 1970–75; Editor-Publisher, Independent Film Journal, 1947–75.

SUNSHINE ROBERT HOWARD: Publisher. b. Brooklyn, NY, Jan. 17, 1946. e. U. of Rhode Island; Brooklyn Law School, 1971. Admitted to NY State Bar, 1971. President of Pubsun Corp., owner of The Film Journal. Publisher of The Film Journal. Exec. dir., Theatre Equipment Association, 1979–present; exec. dir., Variety, The Children's Charity of New York, 1975–present; secretary and exec. dir. Foundation of the Motion Picture Pioneers, 1975–present; exec. dir., The National Association of Theatre Owners of New York State, 1985–present; Producer of Variety Telethon, 1985–present; coordinator and producer, Show East convention.

SURTEES, BRUCE: Cinematographer. Son of cinematographer Robert L. Surtees.
PICTURES INCLUDE: The Beguiled, Play Misty for Me, Dirty Harry, The Great Northfield Minnesota Raid, High Plains Drifter, Blume in Love, Joe Kidd, Lenny (A.A. nomination), Leadbelly, Night Moves, The Outlaw Josey Wales, The Shootist, Three Warriors, Sparkle, Dreamer, Big Wednesday, Escape from Alcatraz, Ladies and Gentlemen, the Fabulous Stains, White Dog, Firefox, Inchon, Honkytonk Man, Bad Boys, Risky Business, Sudden Impact, Tightrope, Beverly Hills Cop, Pale Rider, Psycho III, Out of Bounds, Ratboy, License to Drive.

SUSCHITZKY, PETER: Cinematographer. Spent long time in Latin America as documentary cinematographer. Later made commercials in France, England, and U.S. First feature It Happened Here, 1962.
PICTURES INCLUDE: Lisztomania, Leo the Last, Privilege, Charlie Bubbles, That'll Be the Day, The Rocky Horror Picture Show, Valentino, The Empire Strikes Back, Krull, Falling in Love, In Extremis, Dead Ringers.

SUTHERLAND, DONALD: Actor. b. St. John, New Brunswick, Canada, July 17, 1934. Father of actor Kiefer Sutherland. e. U. of Toronto. At 14 became a radio announcer and disc jockey. Worked in a mine in Finland. Theatre includes: The Male Animal (debut), The Tempest (Hart House Theatre, U. of Toronto), Two years at London Acad. of Music and Dramatic Art. Spent a year and a half with the Perth Repertory Theatre in Scotland, the repertory at Nottingham, Chesterfield, Bromley and Sheffield. London stage debut: August for the People.
STAGE: On a Clear Day You Can See Canterbury, The Shewing Up of Blanco Posnet, The Spoon River Anthology, Lolita.
PICTURES INCLUDE: The World Ten Times Over, The Castle of the Living Dead, Dr. Terror's House of Horrors, Fanatic, The Bedford Incident, Promise Her Anything, The Dirty Dozen, Billion Dollar Brain, Oedipus the King, Interlude, Joanna, The Split, Start the Revolution Without Me, The Act of the Heart, M*A*S*H*, Kelly's Heroes, Little Murders, Alex in Wonderland, Klute, Johnny Got His Gun, F.T.A., Steelyard Blues, Lady Ice, Alien Thunder, Don't Look Now, S*P*Y*S*, The Day of the Locust, Murder on the Bridge, Casanova, The Eagle Has Landed, 1900, The Disappearance, Blood Relatives, Kentucky Fried Movie, National Lampoon's Animal House, Invasion of the Body Snatchers, Murder by Decree, The Great Train Robbery, Bear Island, A Man, A Woman and a Bank, Nothing Personal, Ordinary People, Gas, Eye of the Needle, Max Dugan Returns, Threshold, Crackers, Ordeal by Innocence, Heaven Help Us, Revolution, The Rosary Murders, Bethune: The Making of a Hero, The Trouble With Spies, Apprentice to Murder, A Dry White Season.
TELEVISION: (British) Gore Vidal's Marching to the Sea, Albee's The Death of Bessie Smith, Hamlet at Elsinore, The Saint, The Avengers, Gideon's Way, The Champions, The Winter of Our Discontent.

SUTHERLAND, KIEFER: Actor. b. London, England, 1967. Son of actor Donald Sutherland and actress Shirley Douglas. Moved to Toronto at 10. m. actress Camelia (Kath) Sutherland. Debut with L.A. Odyssey Theater at 9 in Throne of Straw. Worked in local Toronto theater workshops. Film debut The Bay Boy (1984) for which he won Canadian equivalent of Acad. Award. TV debut: Trapped in Silence, 1986.
PICTURES: The Bay Boy; At Close Range; Crazy Moon; Stand By Me; The Lost Boys; The Killing Time; Bright Lights, Big City; 1969; Promised Land; Young Guns; Lakota.
TELEVISION: Trapped in Silence.

SUTTON, JAMES T.: Executive. b. California, Sept. 13. e. Columbia U. Film inspector, U.S. government; overseas m.p. service, WW II; co-owner, gen. mgr., Hal Davis Studios; hd. TV commercial div., Allan Sandler Films; Academy Art Pictures; pres., chmn. of bd., exec. prod., Royal Russian Studios, Inc., western hemisphere div.; pres. exec. prod. Gold Lion Prods., Inc.; pres. exec. prod. James T. Sutton-John L.

Carpenter Prods.; pres., exec. dir., Airax Corp.; pres. of Skyax (div. of Airax).

SUZMAN, JANET: Actress. b. Johannesburg, South Africa, Feb. 9, 1939. m. director Trevor Nunn. e. Kingsmead Coll., U. of Witwaterstrand. Joined the Royal Shakespeare Co. in 1962. London stage debut in The Comedy of Errors.
PICTURES: A Day in the Death of Joe Egg, Nicholas and Alexandra, The Black Windmill, Nijinsky, Priest of Love, The Draughtsman's Contract, And the Ship Sails On, A Dry White Season.
TELEVISION: The Three Sisters, Hedda Gabler, The House on Garibaldi Street, The Zany Adventures of Robin Hood, Macbeth, Mountbatten—Last Viceroy of India (series), The Singing Detective (series), Clayhanger(series), The Miser.

SVENSON, BO: Actor. b. Goteborg, Sweden, Feb. 13, 1941. e. U. of Meiji, 1960–63; UCLA, 1970–74. U.S. Marine Corps 1959–65. Immigrated to U.S., 1958. Was professional race car driver and professional hockey player. Third degree black belt in Judo. Far East heavyweight div. champion, 1961.
PICTURES: Maurie (1973), The Great Waldo Pepper; Part 2: Walking Tall; The Breaking Point; Special Delivery; Final Chapter—Walking Tall; Our Man in Mecca; Son of the Sheik; Snow Beast; Gold of the Amazon; North Dallas Forty; Virus; Thunder Warrior; Deadly Impact; Wizards of the Lost Kingdom; The Manhunt; The Delta Force; Choke Canyon; Heartbreak Ridge, War Bus 2.
TELEVISION: Series: Here Come the Brides (1968–70); Walking Tall.

SWAIM, BOB: Director, Writer. b. Evanston, IL, 1944. American director who has often worked in France. Began career making shorts: Le Journal de M Bonnafous, Self Portrait of a Pornographer, Vive les Jacques.
PICTURES: La Nuit de Saint-Germain-des-Pres (1977); La Balance; Half Moon Street; Masquerade.

SWALLOW, NORMAN: Producer. b. Manchester, Eng., Feb. 17, 1921. e. Manchester Grammar Sch., Keble Coll., Oxford U. British Army 1941–46; BBC as writer-prod. of docum., 1946; wrote 3 docum. films, 1948; TV as docum. prod., 1950; prods. include American Looks at Britain, with Howard K. Smith for CBS, Wilfred Pickles at Home series; orig. Speaking Personally series with appearance of people like Bertrand Russell; co-prod. TV coverage of Britain's general election, 1951; ed. prod. BBC monthly prog. Special Inquiry, 1952–56; World is Ours, 1954–56; study tour Middle East, India, Pakistan, Ceylon, 1956–57; writer, prod. Line of Defense, I Was a Stranger; asst. head films for BBC, 1957; writer-prod., On Target, 1959; apptd. chief asst. (doc. & gen.), BBC-TV, 1960; asst. editor, Panorama, BBC-TV, 1961. Joined Denis Mitchell films, May 1963; writer, prod., Pomp and Pageantry, The Right to Health, A Wedding on Saturday, 1964; The End of a Street, 1964; exec. prod., Report from Britain, 1964; writer, prod., Youth, British, Football; co-prod. This England. prod. A Railwayman for Me, 1966; co-prod. Ten Days That Shook the World, 1967. Co-prod. The Long Bridge, 1968. prod., dir., The Three Happiest Years; exec. prod. Omnibus series, 1968–70. Writer, prod., dir. To Leningrad With Love; exec. prod. Omnibus Series, 1968–72. Writer, co-prod. Eisenstein, 1970. BBC-TV Head of Arts Features 1972–74. Prod.-dir. series A Lasting Joy 1972. Exec. prod. Granada TV since 1974 of The Christians, This England, Clouds of Glory. Winner Desmond Davis Award (UK) 1977. Exec. prod. A Conductor At Work, A Pianist At Work, 1981. Prod., A Lot of Happiness (1982 Emmy Award). Freelance producer/director since 1985. The Last Day for BBC-TV, 1986.

SWAYZE, JOHN CAMERON: Reporter, Commercial spokesman. b. Wichita, KS, Apr. 4, 1906. e. U. of Kansas; Anderson-Milton Dramatic Sch. Reporter and ed., Kansas City, MO Journal-Post; news dept. KMBC, Kansas City; head of news, NBC western network, Hollywood; NBC radio news reports, N.Y.; covered political conv. TV 1948–52; began News Caravan on NBC in 1949–56; panel mem. Who Said That, 1949–51; Watch the World on NBC-TV, 1948–50; Sightseeing With The Swayzes (with family) NBC-TV, 1953; news program, ABC, 1957. Host: Circle Theatre, NBC, and panel member, To Tell the Truth, CBS. Voted best news commentator, M.P. Daily TV Poll, 1951–55.
MEMBER: Lambs Club; National Press Club, Washington, Greenwich, Conn., CC.

SWAYZE, PATRICK: Actor, Dancer. b. Houston, TX. Aug. 18, 1954. Son of Patsy Swayze choreographer (Urban Cowboy). Began as dancer appearing in Disney on Parade on tour as Prince Charming. Songwriter and singer with 6 bands. Studied dance at Harkness and Joffrey Ballet Schs. On Bdwy. in Goodtime Charley, Grease.
PICTURES: Skatetown USA, The Outsiders, Uncommon Valor, Red Dawn, Grandview USA (also choreographer), Youngblood, Dirty Dancing (co-wrote song and sings She's Like the Wind), Steel Dawn, Road House, Tiger Warsaw, Next of Kin.

TELEVISION: North and South: Books I and II, The New Season, Pigs vs. Freaks, The Comeback Kid, The Return of the Rebels, The Renegades.

SWERLING, JO: Writer. b. Russia, Apr. 8, 1897. Newspaper & mag. writer; author vaude. sketches; co-author plays, The Kibitzer, Guys and Dolls (Tony Award, 1951).
PICTURES INCLUDE: s.p., The Kibitzer, Guys and Dolls (co-author, orig. play); Platinum Blonde, Washington Merry-Go-Round, Dirigible, Man's Castle; collab. s.p., Whole Town's Talking; s.p., No Greater Glory, Pennies from Heaven, Double Wedding, Made for Each Other; collab. s.p., The Westerner; s.p., Confirm or Deny, Blood and Sand; collab. s.p., Pride of the Yankees; story, Lady Takes a Chance; s.p., Crash Dive, Lifeboat, Leave Her to Heaven, Thunder in the East.
TELEVISION: collab. The Lord Don't Play Favorites, NBC.

SWERLING, JO, JR.: Executive, Producer. b. Los Angeles, CA, June 18, 1931. e. UCLA, 1948–51; California Maritime Acad., 1951–54. Son of writer Jo Swerling. Active duty US Navy 1954–56. Joined Revue Prods./Universal Television, 1957–81, as prod. ccordinator, assoc. prod., producer, assoc. exec. prod., exec. prod., writer, director, actor; currently senior v.p. and supervising prod., The Cannell Studios.
TELEVISION: Series: Kraft Suspense Theater (prod.), Run for Your Life (prod., writer, Emmy, nom.), The Rockford Files (prod., writer), Cool Million (prod.), Alias Smith & Jones (assoc. exec. prod.), Baretta (prod., Emmy nom.), City of Angels (exec. prod.), Toma (exec. prod.), Jigsaw (prod.). The Bold Ones (prod., writer), Lawyers (prod., writer). Mini-series: Captains and the Kings (prod., Emmy nom.), Aspen (prod.), The Last Convertible (exec. prod.). Movies: Producer: This is the West That Was, The Whole World is Watching, The Invasion of Johnson County, The Outsider, Do You Take This Stranger, Burn the Town Down, The Three-Thousand Mile Chase, How to Steal an Airplane. Supervising prod. Stephen J. Cannell Productions: The Greatest American Hero, Quest, The A-Team, Hardcastle & McCormick, Riptide, The Last Precinct, Hunter, Stingray, Wiseguy, 20 Jump Street, J.J. Starbuck, Sonny Spoon, The Rousters.

SWIFT, DAVID: Producer, Director, Writer. b. Minneapolis, MN, 1919. Served with 8th Air Force in England, W.W.II. Entered m.p. ind. in Walt Disney animation dept. After service, comedy writer for radio. Later, starting in 1949, TV drama writer for Philco Playhouse, Studio One, Kraft Theatre, Omnibus. Created Mr. Peepers, Jamie. Writer-dir. Playhouse 90, Rifleman, Wagon Train, Climax, others. First feature film Pollyana (writer-dir.)
PICTURES INCLUDE: The Parent Trap, The Interns, Love Is a Ball, Under the Yum Yum Tree; pr.-dir.-writer, Good Neighbor Sam, How to Succeed in Business Without Really Trying, Candleshoe, Foolin' Around (co-s.p.).

SWIFT, LELA: Director.
TELEVISION: Studio One, Suspense, The Web, Justice, DuPont Show of the Week, Purex Specials For Women, (Emmy Award) Dark Shadows, Norman Corwin Presents, ABC Late Night 90 min. Specials, ABC Daytime 90 min. Play Break. Won three Emmy awards for best director of day-time serial: Ryan's Hope (1977, 1979, 1980). Monitor award for best director of a daytime serial: Ryan's Hope, 1985.

SWINK, ROBERT E.: Film editor, Director. b. Rocky Ford, CO, June 3, 1918. Joined editorial dept., RKO Radio, 1936; apptd. film ed., 1941. In U.S. Army Signal Corps, 1944–45; supv. editor, Fox studio. Edited numerous productions.
PICTURES INCLUDE: Detective Story, Carrie, Roman Holiday, Desperate House, Friendly Persuasion, The Big Country, The Diary of Anne Frank, The Young Doctors, The Children's Hour, The Best Man, The Collector, How To Steal A Million, Flim Flam Man, Funny Girl, The Liberation of L. B. Jones, The Cowboys, Skyjacked, Lady Ice, Papillion, Three the Hard Way, Rooster Cogburn, Midway, Islands in the Stream, Gray Lady Down, The Boys From Brazil, The In-Laws, Going in Style, The Sphinx.

SWISS, FERN: Executive. Executive director-financial planning for Motion Picture Group of Paramount Pictures. Joined co. in 1979 as financial analyst and advance to controller-TV in 1983. Named to present post, 1984.

SWIT, LORETTA: Actress. b. Passaic, NJ, Nov. 4, 1937. Stage debut in Any Wednesday. Toured in Mame for year. Arrived in Hollywood in 1969 and began TV career. Theatrical film debut in Stand Up and Be Counted, 1972.
PICTURES: Freebie and the Bean, Race with the Devil, S.O.B., Beer.
TELEVISION: M*A*S*H, (Emmy Awards, 1980, 1982), Gunsmoke, Mannix, Hawaii Five-O, Mission: Impossible, The Doctors, Cade's County. Films: Hostage Heart, Shirts/Skin, Coffeeville, Valentine, Mirrors, Mirror, Friendships, Secrets and Lies, Cagney & Lacey, (pilot as Cagney), Games Mother Never Taught You, The Walls Came Tumbling Down, First Affair, The Execution, Dreams of Gold, 14 Going on 30.

Swo-Tan

SWOPE, HERBERT BAYARD, JR.: Director, Producer, Commentator. b. New York, NY. e. Horace Mann Sch., Princeton U. U.S. Navy, 1941–46; rejoined CBS-TV as remote unit dir., 1946 directing many "firsts" in sportscasting; winner, Variety Show Management Award for sports coverage & citation by Amer. TV Society, 1948; joined NBC as dir., 1949; prod. dir., 1951; Lights Out, The Clock, The Black Robe, dir., Robt. Montgomery Presents; winner, Sylvania, 1952. TV Award Outstanding Achievement in Directorial Technique; became executive producer, NBC-TV in charge of Wide, Wide, World; directed Arsenic & Old Lace on Best of Broadway, CBS-TV, 1955; dir. Climax, CBS-TV, Film prod., 20th Century-Fox, Hilda Crane, Three Brave Men, True Story of Jesse James, The Bravados, The Fiend who Walked the West; 1960–62; exec. prod. 20th-Fox TV; Many Loves of Dobie Gillis, Five Fingers; dir. co-prod. on Broadway, Step On A Crack, Fragile Fox, Fair Game for Lovers. 1970–72 exec. at N.Y. Off-Track Betting Corp. 1973–74; vice-president, Walter Reade Organization, Inc.; 1975–76 producer-host, This Was TV, Growth of a Giant; 1976 to present commentator, Swope's Scope, (radio—WPBR-AM)); Critic (TV); Critic's Views; Herbert Swope Interviews (WPTV, Palm Beach).

SYKES, ERIC, O.B.E.: Scriptwriter, Comedian. b. Oldham, England, 1924. Early career actor; ent. TV industry, 1948; wrote first three series, BBC's Educating Archie and radio, TV comedy series for Frankie Howerd, Max Bygraves, Harry Secombe. BBC panel show member. Longterm contract ATV, 1956; own BBC series, 1958–78, Sykes Versus TV, The Frankie Howard Show; Sykes and a Big, Big Show, 1971, 1978 19th Year BBC-TV series. Toured extensively in Big Bad Mouse. 1977 Summer Show Sykes. 1978 Tour of Sykes to Rhodesia, Australia, Canada, The Plank, Rhubarb. Toured one man show, 1982. Time and Time Again, 1983; Run for Your Wife (London, Canada).
PICTURES INCLUDE: Watch Your Stern, Invasion Quartet, Village of Daughters, Kill or Cure, Heavens Above, The Bargee, One Way Pendulum, Those Magnificent Men and Their Flying Machines, Rotten to the Core, The Liquidator, Spy With The Cold Nose. Dir. s.p. The Plank, Shalako, The Monte Carlo Rally, Theatre of Blood.
TELEVISION: Varying specials, remade The Plank, If You Go Down to the Woods Today, It's Your Move, Mr. H is Late, Rhubarb.

SYLBERT, ANTHEA: Executive. b. New York, NY, Oct. 6, 1939. e. Barnard Coll., B.A.; Parsons Sch. of Design, M.A. Early career in costume design with range of Bdwy. (The Real Thing), off-Bdwy. and m.p. credits (Rosemary's Baby, F.I.S.T., Shampoo, The Fortune, A New Leaf, The Heartbreak Kid. Two A.A. nominations for creative costume designs for Julia and Chinatown. Joined Warner Bros. in October, 1977, as v.p., special projects, acting as liaison between creative executives, production dept., and creative talent producing films for company. In October, 1978, named v.p., production (projects included One Trick Pony, Personal Best, etc.). In March, 1980 appointed v.p.—production, for United Artists, working on Stab, Jinx, etc. For Warner Bros.: Swing Shift, Protocol, Wildcats.

SYMS, SYLVIA: Actress. b. London, Dec. 3, 1934. e. Convent and Grammar Sch. Film debut, 1955, My Teenage Daughter.
PICTURES INCLUDE: No Time For Tears, Birthday Present, Woman In A Dressing Gown, Ice Cold in Alex, The Devil's Disciple, Moonraker, Bachelor of Hearts, No Trees in the Street, Ferry to Hong Kong, Expresso Bongo, Conspiracy of Hearts, The World of Suzie Wong, Flame in the Streets, Victim, Quare Fellow, Punch & Judy Man, The World Ten Times Over, East of Sudan, The Eliminator, Operation Crossbow, The Big Job, Hostile Witness, The Marauders, The White Cold, Danger Route, Run Wild, Run Free, The Desperados, The Tamarind Seed, Give Us This Day, There Goes the Bride.
TELEVISION: The Human Jungle (series), Something to Declare, The Saint (series), The Baron (series), Bat Out of Hell, Department in Terror, Friends and Romans, Strange Report, Half-hour Story, The Root of All Evil, The Bridesmaid, Clutterbuck, Movie Quiz, My Good Woman, Looks Familiar, Love and Marriage, The Truth About Verity, I'm Bob, He's Dickie, Blankety Blank, The Story of Nancy Astor, Give Us a Clue, Sykes, Crown Court, A Murder Is Announced, Murder at Lynch Cross.

SZABO, ISTVAN: Director. b. Budapest, Hungary, Feb. 18, 1938. e. Academy of Theatre and Film Art, Budapest, 1961. Debut Koncert (short, diploma film) 1961.
PICTURES: Variations on a Theme (short), You (short), The Age of Daydreaming, Father, Piety (short), Love Film Budapest, Why I Love It (series of shorts), 25 Fireman's Street, Premiere, Budapest Tales, City Map (short), Confidence (Silver Bear, Berlin Festival), The Green Bird, Mephisto (Best screenplay, Cannes Festival; Hungarian Film Critics Award; Academy Award, Best Foreign Film, 1982), Colonel Redl, Hanussen (dir., co-s.p.), Opera Europa.

SZWARC, JEANNOT: Director. b. Paris, France, Nov. 21, 1939.
PICTURES: Extreme Close-Up; Bug; Jaws II; Somewhere in Time; Enigma; Santa Claus—The Movie; Supergirl.
TELEVISION: Ironside; To Catch a Thief; Kojak; Columbo; Night Gallery; Crime Club; True Life Stories; Twilight Zone (1986). Movies: Night Terror, You'll Never See Me Again, The Small Miracle, Murders in the Rue Morgue.

T

TAFFNER DONALD L.: Executive. b. New York, NY. e. St. Johns U. William Morris Agency, 1950–59; Paramount Pictures. 1959–63; D. L. Taffner Ltd., 1963-present.
TELEVISION: Prod.: Three's Company, Too Close For Comfort.

TAKEI, GEORGE: Actor. b. Los Angeles, CA, April 20. e. U. of California, U. of California at L.A. Professional debut in Playhouse 90 production while training at Desilu Workshop in Hollywood. Gained fame as Sulu in Star Trek TV series. Co-author of novel, Mirror Friend, Mirror Foe.
PICTURES INCLUDE: Ice Palace, A Majority of One, Hell to Eternity, An American Dream, Walk, Don't Run, The Green Berets, Star Trek—The Motion Picture, Star Trek II: The Wrath of Khan, Star Trek III: The Search for Spock, Star Trek IV: The Voyage Home, Star Trek V.
TELEVISION: Perry Mason, Alcoa Premiere, Mr. Novak, The Wackiest Ship in the Army, I Spy, Magnum PI, Trapper John M.D., etc.

TALBOT, LYLE: Actor. r.n. Lysle Hollywood. b. Pittsburgh, PA, Feb. 8, 1904. In Army Air Corps, W.W.II. First screen appearance in Vitaphone short; then in Love Is A Racket, 1932.
PICTURES INCLUDE: Up in Arms, Sensations of 1945, One Body Too Many, Dixie Jamboree, Gambler's Choice, Strange Impersonation, Vicious Circle, Mutineers, Sky Dragon, The Jackpot, Sea Tiger, Down Among the Sheltering Palms, Star of Texas, Capt. Kidd & the Slave Girl, Tobor the Great, Steel Cage, There's No Business Like Show Business, Jail Busters, Sudden Danger.
TELEVISION: Newhart (1987).
MEMBER: Masonic Lodge (Shriner), Lambs, Masquers, American Legion.

TAMBLYN, RUSS: Actor b. Los Angeles, CA, Dec. 30, 1935. e. No. Hollywood H.S. West Coast radio shows; on stage with little theatre group; song-and-dance act in Los Angeles clubs, veterans hospitals.
PICTURES INCLUDE: Boy with Green Hair, Reign of Terror, Samson and Delilah, Deadly Is the Female, Kid from Cleveland, Captain Carey, U.S.A., Father of the Bride, As Young As You Feel, Father's Little Dividend, Winning Team, Retreat Hell, Take the High Ground, Seven Brides for Seven Brothers, Many Rivers to Cross, Hit the Deck, Last Hunt, Fastest Gun Alive, Young Guns, Don't Go Near the Water, Peyton Place, High School Confidential, Tom Thumb, Cimarron, West Side Story, Wonderful World of the Brothers Grimm, The Haunting, Long Ships, Son of Gunfighter, The Last Movie, Aftershock, Commando Squad, Cyclone, Necromancer, B.O.R.N.

TANDY, JESSICA: Actress. b. London, Eng., June 7, 1909. wife of Hume Cronyn. On London, N.Y. stage, 1928–42.
THEATRE: N.Y. stage. A Streetcar Named Desire, Hilda Crane, The Four Poster, Coward In Two Keys; The Way of the World, Eve and A Midsummer Night's Dream at Stratford Festival 1976, Canada; limited tours of Many Faces of Love 1974–76 and for CBC, Canada 1977; performed in The Gin Game, Long Wharf Thea., New Haven, Conn. June 1977; Long Day's Journey Into Night, Theatre London, London, Canada 1977. Appeared in The Gin Game, Pulitzer Prize winning play at The Golden Thea. N.Y. 1977–78, and toured with it in U.S., Toronto, London and U.S.S.R., 1979 and Long Day's Journey Into Night, Foxfire;/Stratford Festival 1980, Rose Cort, N.Y. 1981; Foxfire, Guthrie Theatre, Minneapolis 1981 and N.Y., 1982–83; The Glass Menagerie, N.Y., 1983.
PICTURES INCLUDE: The Seventh Cross, Dragonwyck, The Green Years, Forever Amber, A Woman's Vengeance, September Affair, The Desert Fox, A Light In The Forest, Adventures of a Young Man, Butley, The Birds, Honky Tonk Freeway, Still of the Night, The World According to Garp, Best Friends, The Bostonians, Cocoon, Batteries Not Included, The House on Carroll Street, Cocoon II—The Return.
TELEVISION: The Marriage (summer comedy series with Hume Cronyn, 1954), The Fourposter, Moon and the Sixpence, Foxfire.

TANEN, NED: Executive. b. Los Angeles, CA, 1931. e. U. of California at L.A., law degree. Joined MCA, Inc. 1954; Appd. v.p. in 1968. Brought Uni Records, since absorbed by MCA Records, to best-seller status with such artists as Neil Diamond, Elton John, Olivia Newton-John. First became active in theatrical film prod. in 1972. In 1975 began overseeing feature prod. for Universal. In 1976 named pres.

of Universal Theatrical Motion Pictures, established as div. of Universal City Studios to encompass all theatrical film prod. activities. Left in 1982 to become independent producer. 1985, joined Paramount Pictures as pres. of Motion Picture Group.

TANKERSLEY, ROBERT K.: Executive. b. Decatur, IL, July 31, 1927. In U.S. Navy, 1945–46; Marine Corps, 1949–55. With Natl. Theatre Supply as salesman in Denver 13 yrs. 1959–87, pres. Western Service & Supply, Denver, theatre equip. co.; 1960–87, mgr., Tankersley Enterprises theatre equip. Also is CEO of Theatre Operators, Inc., Bozeman, Mont. Member: Theatre Equipment Assn. (past pres.), National NATO Presidents Advisory Council; Rocky Mt. Motion Picture Assn. (past pres.), SMPTE, Motion Picture Pioneers, past chief barker, Variety Club Tent #37. Colorado, Wyoming NATO (past pres.) chm.-elect Exhibitors West.

TANNER, WINSTON R.: Exhibitor. b. Appomattox, VA, Feb. 10, 1905. e. U. of Richmond. Entered m.p. ind., 1939 as asst. to owner, mgr. Free State Victoria Theatres, Kenbridge, Va.; dir. partner Kendig-Tanner Theatres, 1942; bought partner's interest in 1957; operator Tanner Theatres 7 houses, in Va.; operates Winston R. Tanner booking-buying service.

TAPLIN, JONATHAN: Producer. b. Cleveland, OH, July 18, 1947. e. Princeton U.
PICTURES: Mean Streets, The Last Waltz, Carny (exec. prod.), Grandview U.S.A. (co-exec. prod.), Under Fire, Baby, My Science Project.
TELEVISION: Six episodes of Shelly Duvall's Faerie Tale Theatre.

TAPS, JONIE: Producer. Executive. Columbia Studio.
PICTURES INCLUDE: Jolson Story, Down to Earth, Thrill of Brazil. Produced: When You're Smiling, Sunny Side of Street, Sound Off, Rainbow Round My Shoulder, All Ashore, Cruisin' Down the River, Drive a Crooked Road, Three for the Show, Bring Your Smile Along, He Laughed Last, Shadow on the Window.
MEMBER: Friars Club, Hillcrest Country Club.

TARADASH, DANIEL: Writer, Director. b. Louisville, KY, Jan. 29, 1913. e. Harvard Coll., B.A., 1933; Harvard Law Sch., LL.B., 1936. Passed NY Bar, 1937; won nationwide playwriting contest, 1938; U.S. Army W.W.II. Pres. Screen Writers Branch, WGA, 1955–56; v.p., Writers Guild of America, West 1956–59; mem. Writers Guild Council, 1954–65; mem., bd. of govrns. M.P. Acad. Arts & Sciences, 1964–74, and v.p. 1968–70; chmn., trustee, Producers-Writers Guild Pension plan 1960–73. Mem. Bd. of Trustees of American Film Institute 1967–69. WGA's Valentine Davies Award, 1971. Pres., Academy M.P. Arts & Sciences, 1970–73, member of Board of Trustees, Entertainment Hall of Fame Foundation. Member, Public Media General Programs panel for the National Foundation for the Arts, Pres. Writers Guild of America, West, 1977–79. Nat'l. chm., Writers Guild of America, 1979–81. WGA's Morgan Cox Award, 1988.
PICTURES INCLUDE: collab. s.p. Golden Boy, A Little Bit of Heaven, Knock on Any Door; s.p., Rancho Notorious, Don't Bother to Knock, From Here to Eternity (Acad. Award 1953); Desiree; collab. story, s.p. and dir., Storm Center; s.p., Picnic, Bell Book and Candle. The Saboteur Code Name—Morituri; col. s.p. Hawaii; collab. s.p. Castle Keep, s.p. Doctors' Wives; Collab. s.p. The Other Side of Midnight.

TARNOFF, JOHN B.: Producer. b. New York, NY, Mar. 3, 1952. e. U. of California at L.A., motion pictures & TV, 1973–74; Amherst Coll., B.A., 1969–73. Named field exec. with Taylor-Laughlin Distribution (company arm of Billy Jack Enterprises) 1974; left in 1975 to be literary agent with Bart/Levy, Inc.; later with Michael Levy & Associates, Paul Kohner/Michael Levy Agency; Headed TV dept., Kohner/Levy, 1979. Joined MGM as production exec., 1979; v.p., development, 1979–80; sr. v.p. production & devel., 1981–82; exec. v.p., Kings Road Prods., 1983–84; v.p., prod., Orion Pictures Corp., 1985; exec. prod., Out of Bounds, Columbia Pictures, 1986; v.p., prod., De Laurentiis Entertainment Group, 1987. Head of production, DeLaurentiis Entertainment, Australia, 1987–.

TARTIKOFF, BRANDON: Executive. b. New York, NY, Jan. 13, 1949. e. Yale U. Started TV career in 1971 in promo. dept. of ABC affiliates in New Haven, CT Joined promo. staff at ABC affiliate in Chicago. In 1976 went to New York, with ABC-TV as mgr., dramatic development; moved to NBC Entertainment in Sept., 1977, as dir., comedy programs. In 1978 appt. v.p., programs, West Coast, NBC Entertainment; 1980, named pres. of that division. Pres. NBC Entertainment since 1980. Also heads own prod. co., NBC Productions.
PICTURES: Square Dance, Satisfaction.

TASCO, RAI: Actor, Announcer. r.n. Ridgeway Tasco. b. Boston, MA, Aug. 12, 1917. e. Boston English High. 1935. U.S. Army, 1935–45. Grad., Cambridge Sch. of Radio & TV, New York, 1950. Appeared in most TV and radio dramatic shows, and stage plays, New York and Hollywood; Broadway stage & films; dramatic instructor.

TATUM, DONN B.: Executive. b. Los Angeles, CA, January 9, 1913. e. Stanford U., Oxford U. Director, retired chm. & chief exec., Walt Disney Co. 1943, lawyer, RCA, NBC, and ABC. 1949, v.p., counsel, Dir. of Don Lee Companies. Gen. Mgr., KABC, dir. of Television, Western Division ABC. 1956, prod. business mgr. for Walt Disney Productions; exec. v.p. Disneyland, v.p. TV sales; v.p. and adm. asst. to pres. and exec. comm.; exec. v.p.; president; chmn; now Member of Bd. of Dir.; a director of Greyhound Corp; director and chm. John Tracy Clinic; dir. & v.p. Community Building Funds of So. Calif.; trustee of Calif. Institute of the Arts, the Salk Institute, the St. John's Hospital Foundation; overseer, Huntington Library.

TAVERNIER, BERTRAND: Director, Writer. b. Lyon, France, April 25, 1941. After 2 yrs. of law study, quit to become film critic for Cahiers du Cinema and Cinema 60. Asst. to dir. Jean-Pierre Melville on Leon Morin, Priest (1961), also worked as film publicist. Wrote film scripts and a book on the Western and a history of American cinema. Partner for 6 yrs. with Pierre Rissient in film promotion company, during which time he studied all aspects of film-making. 1963: directed episode of Les Baisers. Debut picture: The Watchmaker of St. Paul (aka The Clockmaker) in 1974.
PICTURES INCLUDE: Let Joy Reign Supreme (dir., co-writer), The Judge and the Assassin, Spoiled Children, Deathwatch, A Week's Vacation, Clean Slate, Mississippi Blues (co-dir. with Robert Parusa), A Sunday in the Country, 'Round Midnight, Beatrice, Season of Fear.
TELEVISION: Phillippe Soupault.

TAVIANI, PAOLO and VITTORIO: Directors, Writers. b. San Miniato, Pisa, Italy, (Paolo: Nov. 8, 1931; Vittorio: Sept. 20, 1929); e. Univ. of Pisa (Paolo: liberal arts; Vittorio: law). The two brothers always work in collaboration from script preparation through shooting and editing. 1950: With Valentino Orsini ran cine-club at Pisa. 1954: In collab. with Caesare Zavattini directed short about Nazi massacre at San Miniato. 1954–59: with Orsini made series of short documentaries (Curatorne e Montanara; Carlo Pisacane; Ville della Brianza; Lavatori della pietra; Pitori in cita; I Pazzi della domenica; Moravia, Cabunara). Worked as assistant to Rosellini, Luciano Emmer and Raymond Pellegrini. 1960: collaborated on an episode of Italy Is Not a Poor Country.
FEATURE FILMS (all by both): A Man to Burn (1962); Matrimonial Outlaws (1964); The Subversives (1967); Under the Sign of Scorpio (1967) Saint Michael Had a Rooster (1971); Allonsanfan (1974); Padre Padrone (1977—winner of Best Film and International Critics Prize, Cannes Festival); The Meadow (1979); The Night of the Shooting Stars (1981—Best Director Award, National Society of Film Critics and Special Jury Prize, Cannes); Kaos (1985); Good Morning, Babylon (1987).

TAYLOR, ANTHONY: Producer. b. Los Angeles, CA, Feb. 5, 1931. e. U. of Southern California. U.S.A.F. 1954–56; mem. Chicago Board of Trade, 1962–65; columnist, L.A. Herald Examiner, 1964–65; also mem. N.Y. Mercantile Exchange, Chicago Mercantile Exchange; partner Commodity Futures Co., Westwood, CA; 1966, produced feature Incubus; 1966, award for motion picture excellence, San Francisco Int'l Film Festival; 1967, award Incubus, Cork Int'l Film Festival, Ireland; 1968: prod. feature, Possession.

TAYLOR, DELORES: Actress, Writer. b. Winner, SD. e. U. of South Dakota, studying commercial art. m. Tom Laughlin. First TV experience was heading art dept. at RCA wholesale center in Milwaukee. Made feature film debut as actress in Billy Jack in 1971. Wrote s.p. with husband for that and the sequel, The Trial of Billy Jack, under pseudonym Teresa Christina.
PICTURES INCLUDE: Billy Jack, The Trial of Billy Jack.

TAYLOR, DON: Actor, Director. b. Freeport, PA, Dec. 13, 1920. e. Pennsylvania State U. Appeared in Army Air Corps' Winged Victory; on stage & screen; author short stories, screenplays, one-act plays, TV shows, both half-hour and hour.
PICTURES INCLUDE: Actor: Girl Crazy, Naked City, For the Love of Mary, Battleground, Father of the Bride, Father's Little Dividend, Submarine Command, Flying Leathernecks, Blue Veil, Japanese War Bride, Stalag 17, The Girls of Pleasure Island, Destination Gobi, Johnny Dark, I'll Cry Tomorrow, Bold and the Brave. Director: Jack of Diamonds, Five Man Army, Escape from The Planet of the Apes, Tom Sawyer, Echoes Of A Summer, The Great Scout and Cathouse Thursday, The Island of Dr. Moreau, Damien-Omen II, The Final Countdown.
TELEVISION: Director: He's Not Your Son, Circle of Children, Broken Promise, Red Flag, Drop Out Father, September Gun, My Wicked Wicked Ways, Secret Weapons, Going for the Gold, Classified Cove, Ghost of a Chance.

TAYLOR, ELIZABETH: Actress. b. London, Eng., Feb. 27, 1932. e. Bryon House, London. When 3 years old danced before Princess Elizabeth, Margaret Rose. Came to U.S. on outbreak W.W.II. Film debut: There's One Born Every Minute (1942). Author: Elizabeth Takes Off (1988).

303

PICTURES INCLUDE: Lassie Come Home, Jane Eyre, National Velvet, Life with Father, Cynthia, Courage of Lassie, Little Women, White Cliffs of Dover, Date With Judy, Conspirator, Big Hangover, Father of the Bride, Father's Little Dividend, Love Is Better Than Ever, A Place in the Sun, Ivanhoe, The Girl Who Had Everything, Rhapsody, Elephant Walk, Beau Brummell, Last Time I Saw Paris, Giant, Raintree Country, Suddenly, Last Summer, Butterfield 8, Cleopatra, The V.I.P.'s, The Night of the Iguana, Who's Afraid of Virginia Woolf, The Taming of the Shrew, The Sandpiper, Doctor Faustus, The Comedians, Reflections In A Golden Eye, Boom!, Secret Ceremony, The Only Game in Town, X, Y, and Zee, Hammersmith Is Out, Night Watch, Ash Wednesday, That's Entertainment!, The Driver's Seat, The Blue Bird, A Little Night Music, The Mirror Crack'd, Young Toscanini.

TELEVISION: Elizabeth Taylor in London (1963), Here's Lucy (1970 with Richard Burton), General Hospital (1981), All My Children (1983). Movies: Divorce His, Divorce Hers, Victory at Entebbe, Repeat Performance, Between Friends, Malice in Wonderland, There Must Be a Pony, Poker Alice, North and South.

TAYLOR, MICHAEL: Executive. b. New York, NY, March 28. Joined United Artists in 1973 as trainee. Named asst. to v.p. in chg. of production, 1975. Appointed exec. in chg. of production in London, where worked in acquisition and production of properties, working on such pictures as The Spy Who Loved Me, Valentino, The Pink Panther Strikes Again, etc. Left U.A. to form Taylor/Wigutow Productions in 1977. Produced Last Embrace, The Pursuit of D. B. Cooper. In 1982 joined Orion Pictures as exec. asst. to pres; made corporate v.p., 1984.

TAYLOR, RENEE: Actress, Writer. b. March 19, 1945. Wife of actor Joseph Bologna, with whom she collaborates in writing. Their Bdwy. plays include Lovers and Other Strangers.
PICTURES: Actress: The Last of the Red Hot Lovers, The Errand Boys, The Detective, The Producers, A New Leaf, Lovers and Other Strangers (also s.p.), Made for Each Other (also s.p.), Lovesick, It Had to Be You (also co-dir., co-s.p.).
TELEVISION: Writer: Acts of Love and Other Comedies (Emmy), Paradise, Calucci's Department, The American Dream Machine, etc.

TAYLOR, ROD: Actor. b. Sydney, Australia, Jan. 11, 1930. e. Fine Arts Coll. Started out as artist then turned to acting on stage. After co-starring in film Long John Silver, to Hollywood in 1954. First film The Virgin Queen, followed by Giant, Separate Tables and Step Down to Terror. Also made a number of TV appearances. Formed own company, Rodler, Inc., for TV-film production.
PICTURES INCLUDE: Giant, Separate Tables, Step Down to Terror, Ask Any Girl, The V.I.P.'s, The Birds, Sunday in New York, Young Cassidy, The Time Machine, Seven Seas to Calais, A Gathering of Eagles, 36 Hours, Do Not Disturb, The Glass Bottom Boat, Hotel, Chuka, Dark of the Sun, High Commissioner, The Hell with Heroes, Zabriskie Point, The Train Robbers, Trader Horn, The Deadly Trackers, A Time To Die, On the Run.
TELEVISION: Cry of the Innocent, Jacqueline Bouvier Kennedy, Masquerade. Series: Hong Kong (1960–63), Bearcats, The Oregon Trail, Outlaws, Falcon Crest.

TAYLOR, RONNIE: Director of Photography. b. London, England, 1924. Ent. m.p. ind. 1941 at Gainsborough Studios.
PICTURES: Tommy, The Silent Flute, The Reef, Circle of Iron, Savage Harvest, Gandhi, High Road to China, The Hound of the Baskervilles, The Champions, Master of the Game (UK shoot), A Chorus Line, Foreign Body, Cry Freedom, Opera (Italy), The Experts, Sea of Love.

TAYLOR, RUSSELL JOHN: Writer, Critic. b. Dover, England, June 19, 1935. e. Cambridge U., B.A., 1956. Editor: Times Educational Supplement, London, 1959–60; film critic, The Times, London, 1962–73; art critic, 1978–; editor, Films and Filming, 1983–; prof., division of Cinema, USC, 1972–78. Member: London Film and TV Press Guild, London Critics Circle, NY Society of Cinematologists.
BOOKS: Joseph L. Mankiewicz: An Index; The Angry Theatre; Anatomy of a Television Play; Cinema Eye, Cinema Ear; Shakespeare: A Celebration (cont.); New English Dramatists 8 (ed. & intr.); The Hollywood Musical; The Second Wave: Hollywood Dramatists for the 70s; Masterworks of the British Cinema; Directors and Directions: Peter Shaffer; Hitch; Cukor's Hollywood; Impressionism; Strangers in Paradise; Ingrid Bergman; Alec Guinness: A Celebration; Vivien Leigh; Hollywood 1940s; Portraits of the British Cinema.

TAYLOR-YOUNG, LEIGH: Actress. b. Washington, DC, Jan. 25, 1945. e. Northwestern U.
PICTURES: I Love You, Alive B. Toklas, The Big Bounce, The Adventurers, The Buttercup Chain, The Horseman, The Gang That Couldn't Shoot Straight, Soylent Green, Can't Stop the Music, Looker, Secret Admirer, Jagged Edge, For Better or For Worse.

TELEVISION: Peyton Place (series), Marathon, Napoleon and Josephine: A Love Story, Who Gets the Friends.

TEAGUE, LEWIS: Director. b. 1941. e. New York U.
PICTURES: Dirty O'Neil (co-dir.); Lady in Red (also editor); Alligator; Fighting Back; Cujo; Cat's Eye; Jewel of the Nile.
TELEVISION: Alfred Hitchcock Presents; Daredevils.

TEITELBAUM, PEDRO: Executive. b. Porto Alegre, Rio Grande Do Sul, Brazil, Nov. 21, 1922. e. Colegio Uniao, Brazil, 1942, C.P.A.; Univ. of Porto Alegre, Brazil, 1945, economics & business admin. 1939; Columbia Pictures; 1943, Warner Brothers; 1958, Latin-American supervisor for Republic Pictures; 1957, producer, distributor, exhibitor in Brazil; 1968, area supervisor for United Artists; 1973, v.p. intl. sales; 1975, v.p. international sales & distribution; 1976, senior v.p. and foreign manager. In Jan., 1977, joined CIC as senior exec. v.p. Named pres., July, 1977.

TELLER, IRA Executive. b. New York, NY, July 3, 1940. e. City Coll. of New York & 1957–61; New York U. Graduate Sch. of Arts, 1961–62. Publicist, Pressbook Dept., 20th Century Fox., 1961–62; asst. to adv. mgr., Embassy Pictures Corp., 1962–63; asst. adv. mgr., Columbia Pictures Corp., 1963; adv. mgr., Columbia Pictures Corp., 1964, 1964–65; asst. to chmn. of bd., Diener, Hauser, Greenthal Agy., 1966; adv. mgr., 20th Century-Fox, 1966–67; 1967, adv. dir. 20th Cent.-Fox.; Dir. of Adv., Nat'l General Pictures Corp., 1969; eastern dir., adv.-pub., 1972; National Director, Adv-Pub., 1973; Bryanston Distributors, Inc. v.p. adv.-pub., 1974; Cine Artists Pictures Corp. v.p. adv-pub., 1975; Lorimar Productions, v.p., adv.-marketing, 1976–77. 1977-present, pres. Ira Teller and Company, Inc.

TEMPLE, SHIRLEY JANE: Actress, Diplomat. b. Santa Monica, CA, April 23, 1928. In 1932 screen debut, Red Haired Alibi. In 1933 To the Last Man; then leading figure in Baby Burlesque series Educational shorts until Stand Up and Cheer, 1934, which resulted in career as child and teen star. Voted one of ten best Money-Making Stars in Motion Picture Herald-Fame Poll, 1934–39. As an adult, turned her attention to government and international issues. Republican candidate for U.S. House of Representatives, 1967. Rep. to 24th General Assembly of U.N. (1969–70). Special asst. to chmn., President's Council on the Environment (1970–72). U.S. Ambassador to Ghana (1974–76). Chief of Protocol, White House (1976–77); member of U.S. delegation on African Refugee problems, Geneva, 1981. Autobiography: Child Star (1988).
PICTURES INCLUDE: Baby Takes a Bow, Bright Eyes, Now I'll Tell, Change of Heart, Little Miss Marker, Now and Forever, The Little Colonel, Our Little Girl, Curly Top, The Littlest Rebel, Captain January, Poor Little Rich Girl, Dimples, Stowaway, Wee Willie Winkle, Heidi, Rebecca of Sunnybrook Farm, Little Miss Broadway, Just Around the Corner, Little Princess, Susannah of the Mounties, The Blue Bird, Young People, Kathleen, Miss Annie Rooney. Since You Went Away, I'll Be Seeing You, Kiss and Tell, That Hagen Girl, Honeymoon, Fort Apache, Bachelor and the Bobby-Soxer, Mr. Belvedere Goes to College, Adventure in Baltimore, Story of Seabiscuit, Kiss for Corliss.
TELEVISION: Hostess, fairy tale series: Shirley Temple's Storybook; The Shirley Temple Show.

TENNANT, VICTORIA: Actress. b. London, England, Sept. 30, 1953. m. actor, writer Steve Martin. e. Central Sch. of Speech & Drama. Daughter of ballerina Irene Baronova and talent agent Cecil Tennant.
PICTURES: The Ragman's Daughter, The Speckled Band, The Killing, Strangers Kiss, Horror Planet, (Inseminoid), All of Me, Flowers in the Attic, Best Seller.
TELEVISION: Winds of War, Dempsey, Chiefs, War and Remembrance, Claire Booth Luce, Voice of the Heart.

TENNANT, WILLIAM: Executive. Partner in literary agency of Ziegler, Ross and Tennant. Turned to m.p. production with Cleopatra Jones for Warner Bros., following with writing and producing of sequel, Cleopatra and the Casino of Gold. In 1975 joined Columbia Pictures as v.p.-prod. headquartering at Burbank Studios. Named pres., Casablanca Filmworks; now pres., PolyGram Pictures m.p. division.
PICTURES INCLUDE: As exec. prod.: The Hollywood Knights, King of the Mountain, The Pursuit of D.B. Cooper (co-exec. prod.).

TERRY, SIR JOHN: Film Consultant. b. London, England, 1913. e. Mill Hill Sch. Early career as solicitor. Entered m.p. ind. Film Producers Guild 1946–47; then legal dept. Rank Organisation until 1949; joined National Film Finance Corporation; its chief solicitor 1949–57; sec., 1956–57; man. dir., 1958–78.

TESICH, STEVE: Writer. b. Yugoslavia, 1941. e. Indiana U., Columbia U. Came to U.S. at age 14. While doing graduate work in Russian literature at Columbia left to begin writing. Taken up by American Place Theatre which did his play, The Carpenters, in 1970 and then six others. Wrote screenplays; first produced was Breaking Away, 1979; then Four Friends; Eyewitness; The World According to Garp; Eleni.

TESLER, BRIAN: CBE. Chairman, Managing Director, London Weekend Television Ltd. b. London, England, 1929. e. Chiswick Country School and Exeter College, Oxford. Ent. TV ind. as trainee prod., BBC. 1952–56 Prod. Light Entertainment, BBC TV. 1957–59 Prod. Light Entertainment, ATV. 1960–63 joined ABC Television as head of features and light ent. then programme controller and director of programmes. 1968 appt. dir. of programmes, Thames Television. appt. dep. chief executive LWT. 1976 appt. man. dir. LWT. 1976. Appt. mem. Working Party on Future of British Film Industry. 1977 appt. governor, National Film and Television School. 1979 appt. dir. ITN. 1980 Appt. chairman, ITCA Council (until 1982). 1980–85 dir. Channel 4. Mem. board of management, Services Kinema Corporation. Dir. Oracle Teletext Ltd. 1981 appt. chrm. ITCA Cable and Satellite Television Working Party and subsequently chrm. Super Channel Steering Group. Dir. LWT International. 1982 appt. dep. chairman and man. dir. LWT becoming chairman and man. dir. 1984. 1986 appt. chrm. ITV Super Channel, governor BFI, chrm. The Music Channel (trading as Super Channel) and Network Programme Committee. 1986 awarded CBE.

TETZLAFF, TED: Director. b. Los Angeles, CA, June 3, 1903. Joined camera dept. Fox Studios, became first cameraman; dir., 1940; served in U.S. Air Corps as a Major, W.W.II.
PICTURES INCLUDE: cameraman: Enchanted Cottage, Notorious; dir.: World Premiere, Riffraff, Fighting Father Dunne, Window, Johnny Allegro, Dangerous Profession, Gambling House, White Tower, Under the Gun, Treasure of Lost Canyon, Terror on a Train, Son of Sinbad.

TEWKESBURY, JOAN: Writer, Director. e. U. of Southern California. Student American Sch. Dance 1947–54. Directed and choreographed Little Theatre prods. in L.A. area; taught in theatre arts depts. of two universities: U. of Southern California, Immaculate Heart. Became script supvr. for Robert Altman on McCabe & Mrs. Miller. Off-Bdwy: Cowboy Jack Street (writer, dir.). Teacher in film dept. UCLA.
PICTURES INCLUDE: Thieves Like Us (co.-s.p.), Nashville, (s.p.), Old Boyfriends (dir.), American Desire (s.p.), Hampstead Center (doc. of Anna Freud, writer, dir.), Angel's Dance Card (dir., s.p.), A Night in Heaven (s.p.), The Accused.
TELEVISION: The Acorn People (dir., s.p.), The Tenth Month (dir., s.p.), Alfred Hitchcock Presents (dir., s.p., 1986), Elysian Fields (pilot, writer, dir., prod.).

THACHER, RUSSELL: Producer, Writer. b. Hackensack, NJ, May 29. e. Bucknell U., New York U. Author of novels: The Captain, The Tender Age, A Break in the Clouds. Editor Omnibook Magazine, 1946–58; Book of the Month Club, 1958–63. Exec. story editor, MGM, 1963–69. Exec. prod., MGM, 1969–72. Dir., creative affairs, Samuel Goldwyn Co., 1983–84.
PICTURES INCLUDE: Travels with My Aunt (assoc. prod.), Soylent Green, The Cay, Last Hard Men, The Golden Seal (assoc. prod.), Once Bitten (assoc. prod.).

THALHIMER, JR., MORTON G.: Former Theatre Executive. b. Richmond, VA, June 27, 1924. e. Dartmouth Coll., 1948, B.A.; U. of Virginia, 1959. Naval aviator in W.W.II. Joined Century Theatres as trainee 1948; Jamestown Amusement, 1949–50. Past pres. Neighborhood Theatre, Inc. 1967–86. Charter member of Theatre Owners of America; continuing member and v.p. of NATO, served on finance comm. and Trade Practice comm. bd. member and past president of NATO of VA, 1973–75. Mem. Variety Club Int'l., Tent 11; patron life member, Variety Club of Israel, Tent 51.

THAXTER, PHYLLIS: Actress. b. Portland, ME, Nov. 20, 1921. e. St. Genevieve Sch., Montreal. Screen debut in Thirty Seconds Over Tokyo (1944).
PICTURES INCLUDE: Weekend at the Waldorf, Bewitched, Tenth Avenue Angel, Sign of the Ram, Blood on the Moon, The Breaking Point, Fort Worth, Jim Thorpe—All American, Come Fill the Cup, She's Working Her Way Through College, Operation Secret, Springfield Rifle, Women's Prison, The World of Henry Orient, Superman.
TELEVISION: Wagon Train, Alfred Hitchcock, Twilight Zone, Purex Specials For Women, Playhouse 90, The Fugitive, Defenders, The Longest Night, Three Sovereigns for Sarah, etc.

THEODORAKIS, MIKIS: Composer. b. Greece, 1925.
PICTURES: Eva, Night Ambush, Shadow of the Cat, Phaedra, Five Miles to Midnight, Zorba the Greek, The Day the Fish Came Out, The Trojan Women, State of Siege, Serpico, Iphigenia.

THINNES, ROY: Actor. b. Chicago, IL, April 6, 1938.
PICTURES: Journey to the Far Side of the Sun, Charlie One-Eye, Airport 75, The Hindenburg, Rush Week.
TELEVISION: Series: The Long Hot Summer, The Invaders, The Psychiatrist, Falcon Crest. Movies: The Other Man, God Bless the Children, Black Noon, The Horror at 37,000 Feet, The Norliss Tales, Satan's School for Girls, Death Race, The Manhunter, Secrets, Code Name: Diamond

Head, From Here to Eternity, Scruples, Sizzle, The Return of the Mod Squad, etc.

THOMAS, BILL: Fashion designer. b. Chicago, IL, Oct. 13, 1921. e. U. of South Carolina, A.B., 1941; Art Center, Los Angeles, 1941. Started career as designer on assignment to USO shows; Theatre Royale, Brisbane, Australia; from duty with U.S.A.F., 1941–46. Asst. to Irene, Irene Inc., 1948; asst. costume designer MGM Studios 1947–48; U-I Studios 1949–59; currently freelance.
PICTURES INCLUDE: High Time, Beloved Infidel, By Love Possessed, Babes in Toyland.

THOMAS, DANNY: Actor. r.n. Amos Jacobs. b. Deerfield, MI, Jan. 6, 1914. Father of actress Marlo Thomas. Began career in teens as a "candy butcher" in burlesque theater. Night club entertainer; on radio and TV, films. Formed prod. partnership with Sheldon Leonard and later Aaron Spelling (co. prod.): Andy Griffith Show, Dick Van Dyke Show, Gomer Pyle, U.S.M.C. and The Mod Squad). Endowed St. Jude's Children's Hospital, Memphis, TN.
TELEVISION: Own TV show, Make Room for Daddy (retitled The Danny Thomas Show) 1953–64; NBC-TV specials 1964–66, Danny Thomas Show, 1967–68; Specials 1967 & 1970. Make Room for Grandaddy (series) 1970–71; The Practice, 1976–77. Movie: Side By Side.
PICTURES INCLUDE: Unfinished Dance, Big City, Call Me Mister, I'll See You in My Dreams, The Jazz Singer.

THOMAS, DOUGLAS: Executive. b. London, England, 1954. Managing director Rank Screen Advertising. President: Cinema Advertising Association. Member of Council Advertising Association, Advertising Standards Board of Finance, British Code of Advertising Practice Committee, Screen Advertising World Association.

THOMAS, GERALD: Producer, Director. b. Hull, England, 1920. Entered m.p. industry 1946.
PICTURES INCLUDE: Tony Draws a Horse, Appointment With Venus, Venetian Bird, Sword and the Rose, A Day to Remember, Mad About Men, Doctor in the House, Above Us the Waves, A Novel Affair, After the Ball, Timelock, Vicious Circle, Chain of Events, Solitary Child, The Duke Wore Jeans, Carry on Sergeant, Carry on Nurse, Carry on Teacher, Please Turn Over, Carry on Constable, Watch Your Stern, No Kidding, Carry on Regardless, Raising The Wind, Twice Around the Daffodils, Carry on Cruising, The Iron Maiden, Nurse on Wheels, Call Me a Cab, Carry on Jack, Carry on Spying, Carry on Cleo, The Big Job, Carry On Cowboy, Carry on Screaming, Don't Lose Your Head, Follow That Camel, Carry on Doctor, Carry On Up The Khyber, Carry on Up the Jungle, Carry on Loving, Carry on Camping; Carry on Again, Doctor, Carry on, Henry, Carry on at Your Convenience, Carry on Matron, Carry on Abroad, Bless This House, Carry On Girls, Carry on Dick, Carry on Behind, Carry on England, That's Carry On, Carry on Emmanuelle, The Second Victory.
TELEVISION: Prod. and dir. Rob Roy, serial. Prod. on Christmas for Thames TV. Prod., Carry on Laughing for ATV. Dir. Best of Carry On. Prod. Odd Man Out, series for Thames TV. Dir., Carry on Laughing, Just for Laughs, Comedy Tonight (Canada), What a Carry On.

THOMAS, HARRY E.: Exhibitor. b. Monroe, LA, May 22, 1920. e. Louisiana State U., 1938–41. Psychological Branch of Army Air Force, 1942–46. Past pres., secy., and treas. of NATO of MS. Dir. of Design & Const. & Sec. Gulf State Theatres Inc. Retired 1978.

THOMAS, MARLO: Actress. b. Detroit, MI, Nov. 21, 1938. Father is Danny Thomas. m. Phil Donahue. Sister of TV producer Tony Thomas. e. U. of Southern California. Started career with small TV roles, summer stock. Appeared in London stage prod. of Barefoot in the Park. Debut in own TV series, That Girl, 1966. Most Promising Newcomer Awards from both Fame and Photoplay. Conceived book, record and TV special Free to Be You and Me (Emmy, 1974).
THEATER: Thieves, Social Security.
PICTURES INCLUDE: Jenny, Thieves, In the Spirit.
TELEVISION: Movies: The Lost Honor of Kathryn Beck (also exec. prod.), Consenting Adult, Nobody's Child.

THOMAS, PHILIP MICHAEL: Actor. b. Columbus, OH, May 26, 1949. e. Oakwood Coll.
PICTURE: Black Fist.
TELEVISION: Miami Vice (series); This Man Stands Alone, Valentine, Toma, A Fight for Jenny (movie), Disney's Totally Minnie.

THOMAS, RALPH: Director. b. Hull, Yorkshire, England, Aug. 10, 1915. e. Tellisford Coll., Clifton and University Coll., London. Journalist in early career, entered m.p. ind. 1932 as film ed.; service with 9th Lancers, 1939–45; then film director.
PICTURES INCLUDE: prod.: The Clouded Yellow; Dir: Appointment with Venus (Island Rescue), Day to Remember, Travellers' Joy, Venetian Bird, Once Upon a Dream, Doctor in the House, Mad about Men, Above Us the Waves, Doctor At Sea, Iron Petticoat, Checkpoint, Doctor at Large, Campbell's

Kingdom, A Tale of Two Cities, The Wind Cannot Read, The 39 Steps, Upstairs and Downstairs, Conspiracy of Hearts, Doctors in Love, No Love for Johnnie, No, My Darling Daughter, A Pair of Briefs, The Wild & the Willing, Doctor in Distress, Hot Enough for June, The High Bright Sun, Agent 008½, Doctor in Clover, Deadlier Than the Male, Nobody Runs Forever, Some Girls Do, Doctor in Trouble, Percy, Quest, The Love Ban, Percy's Progress, A Nightingale Sang in Berkeley Square, Pop Pirates.

THOMAS, RICHARD: Actor. b. New York, NY, June 13, 1951. e. Columbia U. Made TV debut at age 7 and featured in several series.
PICTURES INCLUDE: Last Summer, Red Sky at Morning, The Todd Killings, Cactus in the Snow, You'll Like My Mother, September 30th, 1955.
TELEVISION: Medical Center, Marcus Welby, M.D., The F.B.I., The Waltons (series). Movies: The Fifth of July, The Master of Ballantrae, All Quiet on the Western Front, Hobson's Choice, Final Jeopardy, Sister Ruth, Go Toward the Light.

THOMAS, ROBERT G. ("BOB"): Producer, Director. b. Glen Ridge, NJ, July 21, 1943. e. U. of Bridgeport, Fairleigh Dickinson U. Produced educational radio programs, 1962, WPKN-FM. Asst. stage manager at Meadowbrook Dinner Theatre, 1963. In March, 1964 began career as TV camera-man for New York stations. Worked both full-time and freelance for major TV and video tape studios. In January, 1968, started Bob Thomas Productions and began producing business/sales films and TV commercials. Has 8 awards from natl. film festivals; nominated for 5 Emmys for TV series called The Jersey Side he produced for WOR-TV.
PICTURES: Shorts: Valley Forge with Bob Hope, New Jersey—200 Years. Road-Eo '77.
TELEVISION: The Jersey Side (talk/entertainment), Jersey People (weekly talk/entertainment program); $10,000 Touch-down (game show). Sir Reginald and the 3rd Dimension (Children's Show) 3-D Television—for local TV station promo-tion The First Annual Comedy Awards (TV Special).

THOMAS, ROBERT J. ("BOB"): Columnist, Associated Press, Hollywood. b. San Diego, CA, Jan. 26, 1922. p. George H. Thomas, publicist. e. U. of California at L.A. Joined Associ-ated Press staff, Los Angeles, 1943; corr. Fresno, 1944; Hollywood since 1944. Writer mag. articles; appearances, radio; orig. story Big Mike.
BOOKS: author: The Art of Animation, King Cohn, Thalberg, Selznick, Winchell, Secret Boss of California; The Heart of Hollywood; Howard, The Amazing Mr. Hughes; Weekend '33; Marlon, Portrait of the Rebel as an Artist; Walt Disney, An American Original; Bud and Lou, The Abbott and Costello Story; The Road to Hollywood (with Bob Hope); The One and Only Bing, Joan Crawford; Golden Boy: The Secret Life of William Holden; Astaire: The Man, The Dancer; I Got Rhythm, The Ethel Merman Story; Liberace.

THOMOPOULOS, ANTHONY D.: Executive. b. Mt. Vernon, NY, Feb. 7, 1938. e. Georgetown U. Began career in broadcasting at NBC, 1959, starting as mailroom clerk and moving to radio division in prod. & admin. Shortly named to post in Interna-tional Division Sales, involved with programming for stations and in developing TV systems for other nations. Joined Four Star Entertainment Corp. as dir. of foreign sales, 1964; named v.p., 1965; exec. v.p., 1969. In 1970 joined RCA SelectaVision Div. as dir. of programming. In 1971 joined Tomorrow Enter-tainment as v.p. In 1973 joined ABC as v.p., prime-time programs in N.Y.; 1974, named v.p., prime-time TV creative operations, ABC Entertainment. In 1975 named v.p. of special programs, ABC Entertainment; 1976 made v.p., ABC-TV, assisting pres. Frederick S. Pierce in supervising all activities of the division. In Feb., 1978 named pres. of ABC Entertain-ment. In June 1983 promoted to be pres., ABC Broadcast Group in chg. all TV & radio operations. 1986, pres. & COO, United Artists Corp. Resigned Sept., 1988.

THOMPSON, J. LEE: Writer, Director, Producer. b. England, 1914. On Brit. stage; writer of stage plays including: Murder Without Crime, Cousin Simon, Curious Dr. Robson (collab.) Thou-sands of Summers, Human Touch. Writer and m.p. director.
PICTURES INCLUDE: The Middle Watch (s.p.), For Them That Trespass (s.p.), Murder Without Crime (dir., s.p.), The Yellow Balloon, Weak and the Wicked. Director: As Long as They're Happy, For Better or Worse, An Alligator Named Daisy, Yield To The Night, The Good Companions (co-prod., dir.), Woman In The Dressing Gown, Ice Cold in Alex, No Trees in the Street, Tiger Bay, I Aim at the Stars, The Guns of Navarone, Taras Bulba, Cape Fear, Kings of the Sun, What A Way to Go, John Goldfarb, Please Come Home, Return From the Ashes, Eye of the Devil, MacKenna's Gold, Battle for the Planet of the Apes, Before Winter Comes, The Chairman, Country Dance, Conquest of the Planet of the Apes, Huck-leberry Finn, The Reincarnation of Peter Proud, St. Ives, The White Buffalo, The Greek Tycoon, The Passage, Caboblanco, Happy Birthday To Me, The Ambassador, 10 to Midnight, The

Evil That Men Do, King Solomon's Mines, Murphy's Law, Firewalker, Death Wish IV, Messenger of Death, Kinjite.
TELEVISION: A Great American Tragedy, The Blue Knight, Widow.

THOMPSON, JACK: Actor. r.n. John Payne. b. Sydney, Australia, Aug. 31, 1940. e. Queensland U. Joined drama workshop at school; first part was in TV soap opera as continuing character.
PICTURES INCLUDE: Outback, Wake in Fright, Libido, Petersen, A Sunday Too Far Away; Caddie, Mad Dog Coll, The Chant of Jimmie Blacksmith, Breaker Morant (Australian award), The Earthling, The Club, The Man From Snowy River, Bad Blood, Merry Christmas, Mr. Lawrence, Flesh and Blood.
TELEVISION: The Last Frontier, A Woman Called Golda, Waterfront, The Letter, Beryl Markham: A Shadow on the Sun.

THOMPSON, LEA: Actress. b. Rochester, MN, 1962. Danced professionally since age of 14; won scholarship to Penn. Ballet Co., American Ballet Theatre, San Francisco Ballet. Gave up that career for acting. Motion picture debut in Jaws 3-D (1983).
PICTURES: All the Right Moves, Red Dawn, The Wild Life, Back to the Future, Space Camp, Howard the Duck, Some Kind of Wonderful, The Wizard of Loneliness, Casual Sex?, Going Undercover.

THOMPSON, MARSHALL: Actor. r.n. James Marshall Thompson; b. Peoria, IL, Nov. 27, 1926. e. Occidental Coll., L.A. In school dramatics; studied for clergy; wrote play Faith, prod. by Westwood Players; in Westwood Players as actor; m.p. debut in Reckless Age, 1944.
PICTURES INCLUDE: They Were Expendable, Gallant Bess, Valley of Decision, Homecoming, B.F.'s Daughter, Words and Music, Command Decision, Roseanna McCoy, Battleground, Dial 1119, Devil's Doorway, Mystery Street, Tall Target, Basketball Fix, My Six Convicts, Rose Bowl Story, The Caddy, Battle Taxi, Port of Hell, Cult of the Cobra, Crashout, To Hell and Back, Clarence, The Cross-eyed Lion, Around the World Under the Sea, The Turning Point, White Dog.
TELEVISION: Series: The World of Giants, Angel, Daktari, Mini-series: Centennial.

THOMPSON, SADA: Actress. b. Des Moines, IA, Sept. 27, 1929. e. Carnegie Inst. of Technology, Pittsburgh. First N.Y. stage appearance in Under Milkwood with Dylan Thomas. Bdwy. career has produced many awards topped by The Effects of Gamma Rays, for which she won Obie, Drama Desk, Variety Poll. Recent theater: Real Estate.
PICTURES: Desperate Characters.
TELEVISION: Sandburg's Lincoln, The Entertainer, Marco Polo, My Two Loves, Our Town, Princess Daisy, Fatal Confession: A Father Dowling Mystery, Home Fires Burning. Series: Family (Emmy Award, 1978).

THORPE, RICHARD: Director. b. Hutchinson, KS, Feb. 24, 1896. m. Belva Kay, prof. In vaudeville, stock & musical comedy, 1915–18. Now retired.
PICTURES INCLUDE: cast, Torchy Comedies, Three O'Clock in the Morning, Burn 'Em Up Barnes, Flame of Desire; dir. since 1933. dir., Night Must Fall, Ivanhoe, Double Wedding, Crowd Roars, Earl of Chicago, Huckleberry Finn, White Cargo, Two Girls and a Sailor, Sun Comes Up, Big Jack, Challenge to Lassie, Malaya, Black Hand, Three Little Words, Vengeance Valley, The Great Caruso, Unknown Man, It's a Big Country, Carbine Williams, Prisoner of Zenda, The Girl Who Had Everything, All the Brothers Were Valiant, Knights of the Round Table, Student Prince, Athena, Quentin Durward, The Prodigal, The Tartars, Honeymoon Machine, Horizontal Lieutenant, Follow The Boys, The Truth About Spring, That Funny Feeling, Scorpio Letters, Last Challenge.

THULIN, INGRID: Actress, Director. b. Solleftea, Sweden, Jan. 27, 1929. m. Harry Schein, founder and head of Sweden's Film Inst. Made acting debut at 15 at the Municipal Theatre in Norrkoping. Studied at Stockholm's Royal Dramatic Theatre. Worked with Malmo repertory. Appeared on Swedish stage in Gigi, Peer Gynt, Two for the Seesaw, Twelfth Night, Miss Julie. Has directed plays in Stockholm. N.Y. stage debut, 1967: Of Love Remembered.
PICTURES INCLUDE: For Ingmar Bergman: Wild Straw-berries, Brink of Life (Best Actress Award, Cannes Film Festival), The Magician, Winter Light, The Silence, The Hour of the Wolf, The Ritual, Night Games, The Bathers, Adelaide, La Guerre Est Finie, The Four Horsemen of the Apocalypse, Return From Ashes, The Damned, Cries and Whispers, Moses, The Cassandra Crossing, Madame Kitty, After the Rehearsal. Dir. short film: Devotion.

THUNA, LEONORA: Writer, Producer. b. May 3, 1929. e. Hunter Coll., A.B., 1951. Is produced playwright, author of The Natural Look, Broadway, 1967; Show Me Where the Good Times Are, 1970; Let Me Hear You Smile, 1973; Fugue, 1987; and other plays and musicals off-Bdwy. and on tour.

Tie-Tok

TELEVISION: Family Secrets (movie; s.p., co-prod.); The Natural Look (s.p., prod., pilot); I Know Why the Caged Bird Sings (s.p.); Madam (movie). Wrote episodes of Family, Lou Grant, and In the Beginning and worked on Starting Fresh (prod.); Grandpa Goes to Washington (co-exec. prod.); Angie (exec. prod.); The Goodtime Girls (co-creator & supvr. prod.). Also writer for Broadway variety special for Entertainment Channel.
PICTURE: How to Beat the High Cost of Living (story).

TIERNEY, GENE: Actress. b. Brooklyn, NY, Nov. 20, 1920. e. St. Margaret's Sch., Brilmont, Switzerland; Miss Farmer's Sch., Farmington, CT. Autobiography: Self Portrait (1979).
PICTURES INCLUDE: Return of Frank James, Hudson's Bay, Tobacco Road, Belle Starr, Sundown, Shanghai Gesture, Son of Fury, Heaven Can Wait, Laura, Bell for Adano, Leave Her to Heaven, Dragonwyck, Razor's Edge, Ghost and Mrs. Muir, Iron Curtain, That Wonderful Urge, Whirlpool, Where the Sidewalk Ends, Night and the City, Mating Season, On the Riviera, Secret of Convict Lake, Way of a Gaucho, Close To My Heart, Plymouth Adventure, Never Let Me Go, Personal Affair, The Egyptian, Black Widow, Left Hand of God, Advise & Consent.
TELEVISION: The F.B.I., Daughter of the Mind, Scruples.

TIERNEY, LAWRENCE: Actor. b. Brooklyn, NY, Mar. 15, 1919. Brother of actor Scott Brady. e. Manhattan Coll. Track athlete (natl. championship Cross Country team, N.Y. Athletic Club). On stage as actor. Screen debut 1943 in The Ghost Ship.
PICTURES INCLUDE: Youth Runs Wild, Dillinger, Mama Loves Papa, Badman's Territory, Step By Step, San Quentin, Devil Thumbs a Ride, Born to Kill, Bodyguard, Kill or Be Killed, Best of the Bad Men, Shakedown, Greatest Show on Earth, Hoodlum, Bushwackers, Steel Cage, A Child Is Waiting, Custer of the West, Such Good Friends, Midnight, Prizzi's Honor.
TELEVISION: Terrible Joe Moran, Hill Street Blues.

TIFFIN, PAMELA: Actress. r.n. Pamela Wonso. b. Oklahoma City, OK, Oct. 13, 1942. e. Hunter Coll. Started modeling as a teenager. Film debut in Summer and Smoke (1961).
PICTURES INCLUDE: One Two Three, State Fair, Come Fly with Me, For Those Who Think Young, The Pleasure Seekers, The Hallelujah Trail, Harper, Paranoia, Kiss the Other Sheik, Viva Max, Deaf Smith and Johnny Ears, Evil Fingers.
PLAY: Dinner at Eight.

TILLY, MEG: Actress. b. California, 1960. Raised in Victoria, B.C., where began acting and dancing in community theatrical prods. while in high school. To New York at 16; appeared on TV in Hill Street Blues. Film debut was a few lines in Fame.
PICTURES INCLUDE: Tex (debut), Psycho II, One Dark Night, The Big Chill, Rest in Peace, Impulse, Agnes of God, Off Beat, Masquerade, Valmont, The Girl in the Swing.
Television: The Trouble With Grandpa.

TINKER, GRANT A.: Executive. b. Stamford, CT., Jan. 11, 1926. e. Dartmouth Coll., 1947. Joined NBC radio prog. dept. 1949. In 1954 with McCann-Erickson ad agency, TV dept. In 1958, Benton & Bowles Ad Agency, TV dept. From 1961–66 with NBC, v.p., programs, West Coast; v.p. in chg. of programming, N.Y., 1966–67. Joined Universal Television as v.p., 1968–69; 20th-Fox, v.p., 1969–70. Became pres. MTM Enterprises, Inc. 1970. Named NBC bd. chm. & CEO, 1981. Formed indep. prod. co. G.T.G. Entertainment, 1988.

TISCH, LAURENCE A.: Executive. b. Brooklyn, NY, March 5, 1923. e. New York U., 1941; U. of Pennsylvania Wharton Sch., 1942; Harvard Law Sch., 1946. Pres. Tisch Hotels, Inc., 1950–59; pres. Americana Hotel, Inc., Miami Beach, 1956–59; Chmn. of bd. and chief executive officer of Loews Corp since 1960. Also chmn. of bd. of CNA Financial Corp since 1947. Chief executive officer and chmn. of board, CBS since 1986.

TISCH, PRESTON ROBERT: Executive. b. Brooklyn, NY, April 29, 1926. e. Bucknell U., Lewisberg, PA, 1943–44; U. of Michigan, B.A., 1948. Pres. Loew's Corporation. Postmaster General of the U.S. 1986–1988. March, 1988 returned to Loews Corp. as president and co-chief executive. Elected member of bd. CBS Inc. Sept., 1988.

TISCH, STEVE: Producer. b. Lakewood, NJ, 1949. e. Tufts U. Son of Preston Tisch. Worked during school breaks for John Avildsen and Fred Weintraub. Signed upon graduation as exec. asst. to Peter Guber, then prod. head at Columbia Pictures. Entered producer ranks with Outlaw Blues, 1977, collaborating with Jon Avnet with whom formed Tisch/Avnet Prods. Alliance with Phoenix Entertainment 1988.
PICTURES: Coast to Coast, Risky Business, Deal of the Century, Soul Man, Big Business, Hot to Trot.
TELEVISION: Homeward Bound, No Other Love, Prime Suspect, Something So Right, The Burning Bed (exec. prod.), Call to Glory (series), Silence of the Heart, In Love and War (sole prod.), Evil in Clear River, Dirty Dancing.

TOBACK, JAMES: Writer, Producer, Director. b. New York, NY, 1944. e. Harvard U. Taught literature at City Coll. of New York; contributed articles and criticism to Harper's, Esquire, Commentary, etc. Wrote book Jim, on actor-athlete Jim Brown (1971). First screenplay, The Gambler, filmed in 1974.
PICTURES: Fingers (s.p., dir.); Love and Money (s.p., dir., prod.), Exposed (dir., prod., s.p.), The Pick-Up Artist (dir., s.p.).

TODD, ANN: Actress. b. Hartford, England, 1909. e. Central Sch. of Speech Training & Dramatic Art. Wrote, prod. and dir. travel documentaries in the 1960s. Autobiography: The Eighth Veil, 1980.
BRITISH STAGE PLAYS INCLUDE: Service, When Ladies Meet, Man in Half-Moon Street, Peter Pan, Brit., Lottie Dundass. Ret. to theatre Feb., 1951 in stage version, Seventh Veil, So Evil My Love; Old Vic. Theatre, 1954–55: Doctor's Dilemma, Four Winds, Duel of Angels, One Woman's Story.
PICTURES INCLUDE: Keepers of Youth (debut, 1931), These Charming People, The Ghost Train, The Water Gypsies, The Return of Bulldog Drummund, Things to Come, Squeaker, Action for Slander, South Riding, Poison Pen, Danny Boy, Ships With Wings, Perfect Strangers, The Seventh Veil, Perfect Strangers, Gaiety George, Daybreak, So Evil My Love, Hollywood debut in Paradine Case. Passionate Friends, Madeleine, The Sound Barrier, Green Scarf, Time Without Pity, Taste of Fear, Son of Captain Blood, Ninety Degrees in The Shade, The Fiend, The Human Factor.
TELEVISION: Many appearances and TV films, New York, Hollywood, The Paradine Case, So Evil My Love. London incl.: Camille, The Vortex, The Door, Snows of Kilimanjaro, TV film, Hollywood. 1964: Prod., travelogue in Nepal, Love Story, Makes own Diary Documentaries and appears in them. Films for cinema and TV incl. Thunder in Heaven, Thunder of Gods, Thunder of Kings. Persian Fairy Tale. Free in the Sun, Thunder of Silence. Recent TV appearances, The Last Target, Maelstrom series, The McGuffon.

TODD, RICHARD: Actor. b. Dublin, Eire, June 11, 1919. e. Shrewsbury. In repertory, 1937; founder-member, Dundee Repertory Theatre, 1939; distinguished war service, 1939–46; Dundee Repertory, 1946–48; screen debut, 1948; For Them That Trespass, 1948. Founder-Director Triumph Theatre Productions.
PICTURES INCLUDE: The Hasty Heart, Lightning Strikes Twice (U.S.), Robin Hood, The Venetian Bird, Sword and the Rose, Rob Roy, A Man Called Peter (U.S.), Virgin Queen (U.S.), The Bed, Dam Busters, D-Day the Sixth of June (U.S.), Marie Antoinette, Yangtse Incident, Chase a Crooked Shadow, The Naked Earth, Danger Within, The Long the Short and the Tall, The Hellions, Never Let Go, The Longest Day, The Boys, The Very Edge, exec. prod., star own prod. Don't Bother to Knock, Operation Crossbow, Coast of Skeletons, Asylum, The Big Sleep, House of the Long Shadows.
STAGE: 1966–67, An Ideal Husband; Dear Octopus. Cofounder, Triumph Theatre Prods., Ltd. plays since 1970: Roar Like a Dove, Grass Is Greener, The Marquise (U.S.), Sleuth, 1972–73 (England and Australia). Murder by Numbers, The Hollow Crown (with RSC), Equus. On Approval, Quadrille, This Happy Breed, The Business of Murder, 1981–86 (London).

TODMAN, HOWARD: Executive. b. New York, NY, Nov. 24, 1920. e. Hamilton Coll., 1941. Dir. business affairs, Goodson-Todman Productions; treas., Goodson-Todman Associates, inc.; v.p. & treas., Goodson-Todman Enterprises, Inc.; Treasurer, Peak Prods., Inc.; Treas. Goodson-Todman Bcstg. Inc.; v.p. Price Productions, Inc.; v.p. Celebrity Productions, Inc.; chm., N.Y. Cancer Crusade, radio & TV.

TOGNAZZI, UGO: Actor. b. Cremona, Italy, March 23, 1922. Graduate of law. Started entertainment career in 1945 as comic in music hall revues. Film career began in 1950 with Les Cadets de Gascogne. Has produced four films and a detective series for TV. Also acted on stage.
PICTURES INCLUDE: His Women (also dir.), The Fascist, Queen Bee (aka The Conjugal Bed), The Magnificent Cuckold, An American Wife, Question of Honor, Barbarella, Property Is No Longer a Theft, Blowout, Duck in Orange Sauce, Goodnight Ladies and Gentlemen, Bishop's Bedroom, Viva Italia!, La Cage aux Folles, La Cage II, Sunday Lovers, Tragedy of a Ridiculous Man, Amici, Miei, Atto 2, Claretta and Ben, La Cage aux Folles 3: The Wedding, Ultimo Momento, Traffic Jam, Torrents of Spring.

TOKOFSKY, JERRY H.: Executive. b. New York, NY, Apr. 14, 1936. e. New York U., B.S., journalism, 1956; New York Law, 1959. Entered William Morris Agency while at NYU 1953, working in night club dept. to live TV. Moved to Beverly Hills office, 1959. Entered m.p. div. WMA, 1960. Joined Columbia Pictures, as prod. v.p., 1963–70. Now producer & exec. v.p., Zupnik Enterprises, Inc. Joined Paramount Pictures 1970 as prod. v.p. To MGM as prod. v.p., 1971.
PICTURES: Producer: Where's Poppa, Born to Win, Paternity, Dreamscape, Fear City, Wildfire.

TOM, C. Y.: Cinematographer, Distributor. b. Toy Shan, Kwangtung, China, Nov. 6, 1907. Graduated N.Y. Inst. of Photography, 1926. Photographed newsreels for The Great Wall Film Co. of Shanghai; in New York, 1926–29; in charge of production, Shanghai, 1929–32. Studied production techniques in Hollywood. Toured Europe, managing Chinese vaudeville, 1934–35. Studio mgr. and dir. photography for Chi Ming Motion Picture Co., 1935–41. President, Chinamerica Film Exchange and Chinamerica Film Studio, Hong Kong and Shanghai. Distributor, Monogram, Film Classics and Telenews, Hong Kong, Macao and China; asst. man. dir., Capitol Theatre, Hong Kong, 1948–59.

TOMBRAGEL, MAURICE: Writer.
PICTURES INCLUDE: Legion of Lost Flyers, Horror Island, Mutiny in the Arctic, Two Senoritas from Chicago, Lone Wolf in Mexico, Return of the Whistler, Prince of Thieves, The Creeper, Highway 13, Thunder in the Pines, Sky Liner, Arson Inc., Motor Patrol, Fort Bowie, Moon Pilot, s.p. Monkeys Go Home; v.p. Running Wild, Golden Circle Prods., 1973.
TELEVISION: Wild Bill Hickock, Stories of the Century, Annie Oakley, Soldiers of Fortune, Western Marshal, Wyatt Earp, Frontier Doctor, Texas Rangers, Sergeant Preston, Adventures of Jim Bowie, Bat Masterson, Walt Disney's Elfego Baca, John Slaughter TV series, Life of Johann Strauss, Escapade in Florence, Bristle Face. Gallegher series, The Tenderfoot series. For Disney, The Treasure of San Marco (2 parts), The Gentle Ben Series.

TOMLIN, LILY: Actress. r.n. Mary Jean Tomlin. b. Detroit, MI, Sept. 1, 1939. Wayne State U. (studied pre-med). Started inventing characters for comedy sketches in college, used them in cafe and night club dates. 1966 went to NY performing skits on coffee-house circuit and landing job on The Garry Moore Show. In December, 1969, first appeared on Laugh-In, TV series, gaining national attention.
THEATER: Appearing Nightly (Special Tony Award, 1977), The Search for Signs of Intelligent Life in the Universe (1986, on Bdwy and on tour).
TELEVISION: Laugh-In, The Lily Tomlin Show (Emmys as writer and star, 1974), The Paul Simon Special (Emmy, as writer 1978), Lily—Sold Out (also exec. prod., 2 Emmys as prod. and star, 1981), The Muppets Go to the Movies, Lily for President? Live—and in Person, Funny, You Don't Look 200.
PICTURES INCLUDE: Nashville, (debut, 1975; NY Film Critics Award, supp. actress; Acad Award nom.), The Late Show, Moment by Moment, Nine to Five, The Incredible Shrinking Woman, All of Me, Lily Tomlin (doc. behind the scenes of The Search for Intelligent Life); Big Business.
RECORDS: This Is a Recording, And That's The Truth, Appearing Nightly (Grammy Award, 1971).

TOOMEY, REGIS: Actor. b. Pittsburgh, PA, Aug. 13, 1902. e. U. of Pittsburgh; Carnegie Inst. of Technology (drama). On N.Y. & London stage 5 yrs; film debut in Alibi, 1929.
PICTURES INCLUDE: Spellbound, Big Sleep, Her Sister's Secret, Guilty, High Tide, Magic Town, Bishop's Wife, Boy With Green Hair, Mighty Joe Young, Come to the Stable, Cry Danger, Tall Target, People Against O'Hara, Show Boat, My Six Convicts, Battle at Apache Pass, Just For You, My Pal Gus, Never Wave at a Wac, It Happens Every Thursday, High and the Mighty, Top Gun, Guys and Dolls, Great Day in the Morning, 3 for Jamie Down, Dakota Incident, Warlock, Guns of the Timberland, The Day of the Gun, The Last Sundown, Journey to the Bottom of the Sea, Man's Favorite Sport, Peter Gunn, Change of Habit, Run Shadow Run, The Carey Treatment.
TELEVISION: Four Star Theatre, December Bride, Hey Mulligan, Dodsworth, Richard Diamond (series), Shannon (series), Burke's Law (series), Petticoat Junction (series).

TOPOL: Actor. b. Israel, Sept. 9, 1935. r.n. Chaim Topol. On Bdwy. in Fiddler on the Roof repeating role on screen.
PICTURES: Cast a Giant Shadow, Sallah, Before Winter Comes, Fiddler on the Roof, Follow Me, Galileo, Flash Gordon, For Your Eyes Only.
TELEVISION: House on Garibaldi Street, The Winds of War, Queenie.

TORME, MEL: Singer, Actor. b. Chicago, IL, Sept. 13, 1925. Singing debut at age of 4; won radio audition 1933; on radio; composed song Lament to Love; with Chico Marx's orchestra as drummer, arranger & vocalist 1942; served in U.S. Army, W.W.II; m.p. debut in Higher and Higher; 1943; org. vocal group Meltones; many recordings; in night clubs.
PICTURES INCLUDE: Pardon My Rhythm, Good News, Let's Go Steady, Janie Gets Married, Junior Miss, Night and Day, Good News, Words and Music, Duchess of Idaho, The Big Operator, Girls Town, Walk Like a Dragon, The Patsy, A Man Called Adam, The Land of No Return, Daffy Duck's Quackbusters (voice).

TORN, RIP: Actor. r.n. Elmore Torn, Jr. b. Temple, TX, Feb. 6, 1931. e. Texas A & M U., U. of Texas. Served in army. Signed as understudy for lead in Cat on a Hot Tin Roof on Broadway.

THEATER: Orpheus Descending, Sweet Bird of Youth, Daughter of Silence, Macbeth, Desire Under the Elms, Strange Interlude, Blues For Mr. Charlie, The Kitchen, The Deer Park (Obie Award), The Beard, The Cuban Thing, Dream of a Blacklisted Actor, The Dance of Death.
PICTURES INCLUDE: Baby Doll, A Face in the Crowd, Time Limit, Pork Chop Hill, King of Kings, Hero's Island, Sweet Bird of Youth, Critics Choice, The Cincinnati Kid, One Spy Too Many, You're a Big Boy Now, Beach Red, Sol Madrid, Beyond the Law, Coming Apart, Tropic of Cancer, Payday, Crazy Joe, Birch Interval, Maidstone, The Man Who Fell to Earth, Nasty Habits, Coma, The Seduction of Joe Tynan, One Trick Pony, First Family, Heartland, The Beastmaster, Jinxed, Airplane II: The Sequel, Cross Creek, Misunderstood, Songwriter, Flashpoint, City Heat, Summer Rental, Beer, Extreme Prejudice, Nadine, The Telephone (dir.), Cold Feet.
TELEVISION: Betrayal, The President's Plane is Missing, The FBI vs. the Ku Klux Klan, Song of Myself, The Execution, When She Says No, The Atlanta Child Murders, J. Edgar Hoover, Sophia Loren—Her Story, Rape and Marriage—The Rideout Case, Blind Ambition, Montserrat, Laguna Heat, Steel Cowboy, Cat on a Hot Tin Roof, The King of Love, April Morning.

TOTTER, AUDREY: Actress. b. Joliet, IL, Dec. 20, 1923. In many stage plays. On radio 1939–44; film debut in Main Street, 1944.
PLAYS INCLUDE: Copperhead, Stage Door, Late Christopher Bean, My Sister Eileen.
PICTURES INCLUDE: Her Highness and the Bellboy, Dangerous Partners, Sailor Takes a Wife, Cockeyed Miracle, Lady in the Lake, High Wall, Beginning or the End, Unsuspected, Alias Nick Beal, Saxon Charm, Any Number Can Play, Tension, Set-Up, Under the Gun, Blue Veil, Sellout, F.B.I. Girl, Assignment-Paris, My Pal Gus, Woman They Almost Lynched, Cruisin' Down the River, Man in the Dark, Mission Over Korea, Champ for a Day, Massacre Canyon, Women's Prison, A Bullet for Joey, Vanishing American, The Carpetbaggers, Chubasco, The Apple Dumpling Gang Rides Again.
TELEVISION: Series: Cimarron City, Our Man Higgins, Medical Center (series 1972–76); Movies: The Great Cash Giveaway, City Killer, Murder, She Wrote.

TOWERS, CONSTANCE: Actress. b. Whitefish, MT, May 20, 1933. m. John Gavin, actor and former U.S. Ambassador to Mexico. e. Juilliard Sch. of Music. Stage work on Broadway and tour.
THEATER: King and I (1977–79 opp. Yul Brynner).
PICTURES: Horse Soldiers, Sergeant Rutledge, Fate Is the Hunter, Shock Corridor, Naked Kiss, The Spy, Sylvester, Fast Forward.
TELEVISION: Series: Love Is a Many Splendored Thing, VTV, Capitol. Mini-Series: On Wings of Eagles, Home Show, The Loner, Murder, She Wrote, STN, Hour Mag.

TOWERS, HARRY ALAN: Executive, Producer. b. London, England, 1920. Prod. and wrote: 1963: Sanders of the River; 1964: Code Seven Victim Five.
PICTURES INCLUDE: City of Fear, Mozambique, Coast of Skeletons, Sandy the Seal, 24 Hours to Kill, The Face of Fu Manchu, Ten Little Indians, Marrakesh, Circus of Fear, The Brides of Fu Manchu, Sumuru, Five Golden Dragons, The Vengeance of Fu Manchu, Jules Verne's Rocket to the Moon, House of a Thousand Dolls, The Face of Eve, Blood of Fu Manchu, 99 Women, Girl From Rio, Marquis de Sade's Justine, Castle of Fu Manchu, Venus in Furs, Philosophy in the Boudoir, Eugenie, Dorian Gray, Count Dracula, The Bloody Judge, Black Beauty, Night Hair Child, The Call of the Wild, Treasure Island, White Fang, Death in Persepolis, Ten Little Indians, End of Innocence, Black Cobra, Black Velvet-White Silk, Night of The High Tide, King Solomon's Treasure, Shape of Things to Come, Klondike Fever, Fanny Hill, Frank and I, Black Venus, Christmas, Black Arrow, Pompeii, Love Circles, Lightning—White Stallion, Gor, Outlaw of Gor, Dragonard, Skeleton Coast, Master of Dragonard Hill, Nam, Fire With Fire, Jekyll and Hyde, River of Death, Death on Safari, Cobra Strike, The Howling IV—The Original Nightmare, Skeleton Coast, Edge of Sanity.

TOWNE, ROBERT: Writer, Director, Producer. b. 1936. Was member of Warren Beatty's production staff on Bonnie and Clyde and contributed to that screenplay.
PICTURES INCLUDE: Villa Rides, The Tomb of Ligeia, The Last Detail, Chinatown, Shampoo (co-s.p.), The Yazuka (co.-s.p.), Personal Best (s.p., prod., dir.), Greystoke: The Legend of Tarzan, The Pick-Up Artist (actor), Tequilla Sunrise (dir., s.p.).

TOWNSEND, CLAIRE: b. New York, NY, Feb. 20, 1952. e. Princeton U. Joined 20th Century-Fox in 1976; named west coast story editor & v.p. creative affairs. Left in 1978 to go to United Artists, where named v.p. of production, responsible for managing the acquisition, development and production of feature films. Now independent producer.

TOWNSEND, LEO: Writer. b. Faribault, MN, May 11, 1908. e. U. of Minnesota. Formerly radio and feature story magazine writer. In 1942 collab. s.p., It Started With Eve, collab. orig. s.p. Seven Sweethearts.
PICTURES INCLUDE: The Amazing Mrs. Halliday, Can't Help Singing, Chip Off the Old Block, Night and Day, Southside E-1000, One Big Affair, Dangerous Crossing, Siege at Red River, A Life in the Balance, White Feather, Running Wild, Fraulein, The Black Hand, Shadow On the Window, Flight to Hong Kong, That Way With Women, Seven Sweethearts, I'd Rather Be Rich, Bikini Beach, Beach Blanket Bingo, How to Stuff a Wild Bikini, Fireball 500.
TELEVISION: Jane Wyman Theatre, Wagon Train, Maverick, 77 Sunset Strip, Hawaiian Eye, Dinah Shore Chevy Show, Shirley Temple Show, Perry Mason, Bourbon Street Beat, Beulah, Bachelor Father, Surfside Six, Destry, Patty Duke Show, Gidget, Man From U.N.C.L.E., My Three Sons, The Munsters, Batman, Andy Griffith Show, Bewitched.

TOWNSEND, ROBERT: Producer, Director, Writer, Actor. b. Chicago, IL, Feb. 6, 1957. e. attended Illinois State U. and Hunter Coll. Planned baseball career before turning to acting. Veteran of experimental Black Actors Guild and Second City. Film debut: Cooley High (1974). TV commercials; stand-up comedy at NY Improvisation; taped Evening at the Improv.
PICTURES: Actor: Willie and Phil, A Soldier's Story, Streets of Fire, American Flyers, Odd Jobs, Ratboy. Producer-Director-Actor-Writer: Hollywood Shuffle ($100,000 budget), Eddie Murphy Raw (dir.), Finding Maubee (actor).
TELEVISION: Another Page (PBS series), Robert Townsend and His Partners in Crime; Take No Prisoners: Robert Townsend and His Partners in Crime II (HBO).

TRAMBUKIS, WILLIAM J.: Executive. b. July 26, 1926. Began career as usher with Loew's in Providence, RI, 1941. Served 1943–46 with Navy Seabees. Recipient of Quigley Awards. Managed/supervised Loew's Theatres in several New England cities, Harrisburg, PA, Syracuse, Rochester, Buffalo, NY, Washington, DC, Richmond, Norfolk, VA, Toronto, Canada, Atlanta, GA. Appt. Loew's NortheEastern Division mgr. 1964, Loew's gen. mgr. 1975: v.p. in 1976; sr. v.p., 1985. Retired, 1987.

TRAVANTI, DANIEL J.: Actor. b. Kenosha, WI, March 7, 1940. e. U. of Wisconsin, Yale Sch. of Drama. Woodrow Wilson fellow, 1961. On stage in Twigs, Othello, I Never Sang for My Father.
PICTURE: St. Ives, Midnight Crossing, Millenium.
TELEVISION: Hill Street Blues (series), A Case of Libel, Adam, Aurora, Murrow, Adam: His Song Continues, I Never Sang for My Father.

TRAVERS, BILL: Actor, Producer, Director. b. Newcastle-on-Tyne, England. Jan. 3, 1922. Actor in repertory co.; London stage in Cage Me a Peacock, Damask Cheek, Square Ring, I Captured the Castle; A Cook for Mr. General (Broadway); Royal Shakespeare Theatre Co., 1962. Abraham Cochrane, Peter Pan.
PICTURES INCLUDE: Square Ring, Romeo and Juliet, Geordie, Footsteps in the Fog, Bhowani Junction, Barretts of Wimpole Street, Smallest Show on Earth, Seventh Sin, Passionate Summer, Bridal Path, Gorgo, The Green Helmet, Two Living—One Dead, Born Free, Duel at Diablo, A Midsummer Night's Dream, Ring of Bright Water, Boulevard du Rhum, The Belstone Fox.
TELEVISION: A Cook for the General (Kraft), Episode, A Giant Is Born (U.S.), Espionage, Rawhide, CBS Voice of America (Rome), Lorna Doone, The Admirable Crichton. Producer/Director/Writer: The Lions Are Free, An Elephant Called Slowly, The Lion at Worlds End, Christian the Lion, Wild Dogs of Africa, Baboons of Gombe, The Hyena Story, Deathtrap, Lions of the Serengeti, River of Sand, Bloody Ivory, Sexual Encounters of the Floral Kind.

TRAVIS, J. MARK: Executive. b. Los Angeles, CA, , March 7, 1953. e. Yale. U. 1971, v.p., Sackheim Agency; 1973, pres., Entertainment 4; 1975, chm., CEO, Theatre Television Corp.; 1977, pres., Special Event Entertainment; 1979, Columbia Pictures—Travis Productions; 1980, Lorimar Productions—Travis; 1983, pres. & CEO, Movie Music Co., Inc.
PICTURES: Give em Hell Harry (prod.); Stop the World I Want to Get Off (prod.), Richard Pryor Live in Concert (prod.); Fighting Back (exec. prod.).

TRAVOLTA, JOHN: Actor. b. Englewood, NJ, Feb. 18, 1954. Quit school at 16 to pursue theatre career; first stage role in Who Will Save the Plowboy? Did off-Bdwy prod. of Rain; next to Broadway in Grease. Toured with latter for 10 months. Also in Over Here on Bdwy. with Andrew Sisters for 10 months.
PICTURES INCLUDE: Carrie, Saturday Night Fever, Grease, Moment by Moment, Urban Cowboy, Blow Out, Staying Alive, Two of a Kind, Perfect, The Experts, The Tender, Daddy's Home.
TELEVISION: Emergency, Owen Marshall, The Rookies, Medical Center, Welcome Back, Kotter (series), Movie: The Boy in the Plastic Bubble.

TREMAYNE, LES: Actor. b. London, England, Apr. 16, 1913. e. Northwestern U., Chicago Art Inst., Columbia U., U. of California at L.A. First professional appearance in British mp., 1916, with mother; stock, litte theatres, vaudeville, 1925–40; entered radio field, 1931; numerous shows on all networks.
SHOWS INCLUDE: Woman in My House (with wife, Alice Reinheart), Errand of Mercy, Your Are There, One Man's Family, Heartbeat Theatre, The First Nighter (lead 7 yrs.); on Broadway in Heads or Tails, Detective Story.
TELEVISION: Lux Video Theatre, 20th Century-Fox Hour, Navy Log, One Man's Family, Meet Mille, The Millionaire, The Whistler, Truth or Consequences, NBC Matinee, The Girl, O'Henry series, Rin Tin Tin, Bachelor Father, The Texan, Adventures of Ellery Queen, Court of Last Resort, Rifleman, State Trooper, Rescue 8, June Allyson-Dupont Show, Wagon Train, M Squad, Hitchcock Presents, Mr. Ed., Perry Mason.
PICTURES INCLUDE: The Racket, Blue Veil, Francis Goes to West Point, It Grows on Trees, I Love Melvin, Under the Red Sea, Dream Wife, War of the Worlds, Susan Slept Here, Lieutenant Wore Skirts, Unguarded Moment, Everything But the Truth, Monolith Monsters, Perfect Furlough, North by Northwest, Say One for Me, The Gallant Hours, The Angry Red Planet, The Story of Ruth, The Fortune Cookie.
Blue ribbon award for best perf. of the month for A Man Called Peter; dir. Hollywood Repertory Theatre, 1957; pres. Hollywood Actors' Council, 1951–58; chmn. Actors Div. workshop com. Acad. TV Arts & Sciences; Member of The Workshop Comm. of the Hollywood M.P. & TV Museum Commission.

TREVOR, CLAIRE: Actress. b. New York, NY, 1909. e. American Acad. of Dramatic Arts; Columbia U. On Broadway in Party's Over, Whistling in the Dark, Big Two.
PICTURES INCLUDE: Life in the Raw, Last Trail, Mad Game, Jimmy and Sally, Stagecoach, Allegheny Uprising, Dark Command, Murder, My Sweet, Johnny Angel, Crack-Up, Bachelor's Daughters, Born to Kill, Raw Deal, Valley of the Giants, Babe Ruth, Velvet Touch, Key Largo (Acad. Award), Lucky Stiff, Best of the Bad Men, Border Line, Hoodlum, Empire, Hard, Fast and Beautiful, My Man and I, Stop, You're Killing Me, Stranger Wore a Gun, High and the Mighty, Man Without a Star, Luch Gallant, The Mountain, Marjorie Morningstar, Two Weeks in Another Town, The Stripper, How to Murder Your Wife, Capetown Affair, Kiss Me Goodbye.
TELEVISION: Dodsworth (Emmy Award). Ladies in Retirement, Alfred Hitchcock Presents, The Untouchables, Love Boat, Murder, She Wrote.

TREXLER, CHARLES B.: Exhibitor. b. Wadesboro, NC, Feb. 8, 1916. From 1937 to Nov. 1948 was practicing CPA except for 2 yrs. in U.S. Army in W.W.II. Joined Stewart & Everett Theatres in 1948 as controller. In March, 1953 named gen. mgr.; Jan. 1, 1954, exec. v.p.; treas.; May, 1962 named pres.; Feb. 1, 1983, named bd. chm. Former bd. chm., NATO of North and South Carolina; v.p. & bd. mbr., National NATO.

TRIKONIS, GUS: Director. b. New York, NY. Started career in chorus of West Side Story on Bdwy. Turned to direction, making low-budget weekenders (films shot in 12 days only on weekends).
PICTURES: Moonshine County Express, The Evil Touched by Love, Take This Job and Shove It.
TELEVISION: Dark Side of Terror, Dressed To Kill, The Last Convertible (final three hours), Dempsey, Elvis and the Beauty Queen, Flamingo Road, Malice in Wonderland, Twilight Zone (1986).

TRINTIGNANT, JEAN-LOUIS: Actor. b. Aix-en-Provence, France, Dec. 11, 1930. m. Nadine Marquand, director. Theatre debut: 1951, To Each According to His Hunger. Then Mary Stuart, Macbeth (at the Comedie de Saint-Etienne). 1955 screen debut.
PICTURES INCLUDE: Si Tous Les Gars du Monde, La Loi des Rues, And God Created Woman, Club de Femmes, Les Liaisons Dangereuses, L'Ete Violent, Austerlitz, La Millieme Fenetre, Plein Feux sur L'Assasin, Coeur Battant, L'Atlantide, The Game of Truth, Horace 62, Les Sept Peches Capitaux (7 Capital Sins), Le Combat dans L'Ile, The Easy Life, Il Successo, Nutty, Naughty Chateau, Les Pas Perdus, La Bonne Occase, Mata-Hari, Meurtre a L'Italienne, La Longue Marche, Le 17eme Ciel, Un Jour a Paris, Is Paris Burning?, The Sleeping Car Murders, A Man and a Woman, Enigma, Safari Diamants, Trans-Europ-Express, Mon Amour, Mon Amour, Un Homme a Abattre, La Morte Ha Fatto L'Uovo, Les Biches, Grand Silence, Z, Ma Nuit Chez Maud (My Night at Maud's), The Conformist, The Crook, Without Apparent Motive, The Outside Man, The French Conspiracy, Simon the Swiss, Agression, Les Violons du Bal, The Sunday Woman, Under Fire, La Nuit de Varennes, Long Live Life!, Next Summer, Departure, Return, The Man With the Silver Eyes, Femme Je Personne, Confidentially Yours, A Man and a Woman: 20 Years Later, La Vallee Fantome; Rendezvous, Bunker Palace Hotel.

TROELL, JAN: Writer, Director, Cinematographer. b. Sweden, July 23, 1931. Was teacher before entering industry. In early 60s

photographed Bo Widerberg's first film, The Pram. Became apprentice in TV; made m.p. debut as director in 1965 with Stay in the Marshland.
PICTURES INCLUDE: Here Is Your Life, Eeny, Meeny, Miny, Mo, The Emigrants, The New Land, Zandy's Bride, Hurricane, The Fairytale Country (dir., editor).

TROSPER, GUY: Writer. b. Lander, WY. Started as reader, Samuel Goldwyn; then story ed.; screen writer since 1941.
PICTURES INCLUDE: Stratton Story (co-s.p.); Devil's Doorway, Inside Straight; Pride of St. Louis (story); Many Rivers to Cross (co-s.p.); The Americano, Girl He Left Behind, Jailhouse Rock, Darby's Rangers, One-Eyed Jacks (co-s.p.); Birdman of Alcatraz; The Spy Who Came in From the Cold (co-s.p.).

TRUMBULL, DOUGLAS: Cinematographer, Director, Writer. Chm., Showscan Film Corp. President, Berkshire Motion Picture.
PICTURES: Did special effects for Silent Running; 2001: A Space Odyssey; The Andromeda Strain; Close Encounters of the Third Kind; Blade Runner, Star Trek: The Motion Picture. Produced and directed Brainstorm and directed Silent Running.

TRYON, THOMAS: Actor. b. Hartford, CT, Jan. 14, 1926. e. Yale U. Served in U.S. Navy, W.W.II, studied at Art Students League; with Cape Playhouse, Dennis, MA, as set painter, asst. stage mgr., actor; prod. asst., CBS; then TV actor.
PLAYS INCLUDE: Wish You Were Here, Cyrano de Bergerac, Richard III.
PICTURES INCLUDE: m.p. debut in Scarlet Hour; since in Screaming Eagles, Three Violent People, Moon Pilot, Marines Let's Go, The Cardinal, The Glory Guys, The Other (exec. prod., s.p.), The Horsemen, Johnny Got His Gun (also prod.), Fedora (orig. story).
TELEVISION: Texas John Slaughter (series).
AUTHOR: The Other, Harvest Home, Lady, Crowned Heads.

TSUKASA, YOKO: Actress. b. Tottori, Japan, Aug. 20, 1934. e. Kyoritsu Coll. joined Toho Studio 1954 after period as magazine cover girl.
PICTURES INCLUDE: Don't Die My Darling, Blue Beast, Eternity of Love, End of Summer, Three Treasures, Yojimbo (The Bodyguard), Women of Design.

TUCKER, MELVILLE: Executive. b. New York, NY, Mar. 4, 1916. e. Princeton U. Asst. purchasing agent Consolidated Laboratories, N.Y., 1934–36; sound effects & picture ed., Republic Productions, Inc. 1936–8; then asst. production mgr. & first asst. dir., 1938–42; served in U.S. Army 1942–46; asst. prod. Republic 1946; assoc. producer, 1947–52; prod., Universal 1952–54; prod. exec. v.p., Universal, 1955–70; production exec. U-I, 1954–71; prod.-Verdon Prods., 1971–present.
PICTURES INCLUDE: The Missourians, Thunder in God's Country, Rodeo King and the Senorita, Utah Wagon Train. U-I prod., 1953: Drums Across the River, Black Shield of Falworth; prod. A Warm December, Uptown Saturday Night, Let's Do It Again, A Piece of the Action, exec. prod.: Stir Crazy, Hanky Panky, Fast Forward.

TUCKER, MICHAEL: Actor. b. Baltimore, MD, Feb. 6, 1944. m. actress Jill Eikenberry. e. Carnegie Tech. Drama Sch. Worked in regional theater (Washington's Arena Stage) and with the New York Shakespeare Festival in Trelawney of the Wells, Comedy of Errors, Measure for Measure, The Merry Wives of Windsor.
THEATER: Also includes Moonchildren, Modigliani, The Rivals, Mother Courage, Waiting for Godot, Oh, What a Lovely War, I'm Not Rappaport (American Place Theatre).
PICTURES: A Night Full of Rain (1977), The Eyes of Laura Mars, An Unmarried Woman, Diner, The Goodbye People, The Purple Rose of Cairo, Radio Days, Tin Men, Checking Out.
TELEVISION: Hill Street Blues. Series: L.A. Law. Movies: Concealed Enemies, Vampire, Assault and Matrimony, Day One.

TUCKERMAN, DAVID R.: Executive. b. Perth Amboy, NJ, Nov. 9, 1946. e. Monmouth Coll., Florida U., 1967–70; B.S.B.A. Entered industry at A.I.T. Theatres, 1967; gen. mgr., Music Makers Theatres, 1973; v.p., Leigh Group, MMT, head film buyer, 1976; sr. v.p., MMT, 1980; Loews Film Buyer, 1986.
MEMBER: SMPTE, Variety Intl., MPBC, AFI.

TUGGLE, RICHARD: Director, Writer. Wrote screenplays before directorial debut with Tightrope, 1984, which he also wrote. Previous work includes s.p. for Escape from Alcatraz.

TULIPAN, IRA H.: Publicist. b. New York, NY. e. New York U., B.S., 1934. Entered m.p. ind. as theatre mgr., Boston, 1934; pub. dept. Warner Bros. home office, 1935–40; joined 20th Century-Fox 1942; U.S. Army service 1943–46; returned to Fox upon disch., feature writer, press book ed.; trade paper contact; newspaper contact; pub. mgr. 1955; asst. dir. adv. pub. expl. Columbia Pictures. 1960; exec. adm. asst. to adv.,

publ., v.p., Columbia, 1963; dir. overseas prod. pub., 1966. Returned to U.S. in 1978 as eastern pub.-coordinator; 1984, pub. consultant, Universal Pictures.

TUNBERG, KARL: Writer. b. Spokane, WA, 1908. From 1937 collab. many Hollywood s.p.
PICTURES INCLUDE: You Can't Have Everything, My Lucky Star, Hold That Co-Ed, Down Argentine Way, Yank in the RAF, (collab. s.p.) My Gal Sal, Orchestra Wives, Tall, Dark and Handsome (s.p. & story); Weekend in Havana (s.p. & story), I Was an Adventuress (s.p.), Lucky Jordan, (collab. s.p.) Dixie, Standing Room Only, Bring on the Girls; (prod. & collab. s.p.) Kitty; (prod.) You Gotta Stay Happy; (collab. s.p.) Love That Brute, Night Into Morning, Law and the Lady, Because You're Mine, Scandal at Scourie, Valley of the Kings; s.p. Beau Brummell, Scarlet Coat, Seventh Sin, Ben Hur, s.p. Count Your Blessings; s.p. Libel, Taras Bulba; s.p., I Thank A Fool; s.p. The Seventh Dawn, Harlow (story); col. s.p., Where Were You When the Lights Went Out?

TUNE, TOMMY: Actor, Director, Dancer. b. Wichita Falls, TX, Feb. 28, 1939. Began professional career dancing in choruses of Bdwy. shows (Baker Street, A Joyful Noise, How Now Dow Jones, etc.). Signed by 20th-Fox and cast in Hello, Dolly! (1969).
PICTURE: The Boy Friend.
STAGE: Performer: Seesaw, My One and Only. Director: The Club, Cloud 9, The Best Little Whorehouse in Texas, Nine. Choreographer: A Day in Hollywood/A Night in the Ukraine.
TELEVISION: Dean Martin Presents the Golddiggers.

TURMAN, LAWRENCE: Producer. b. Los Angeles, CA, Nov. 28, 1926. e. U. of California at L.A. In textile business 5 years, then joined Kurt Frings Agency; left in 1960 to form Millar-Turman Prods.
PICTURES INCLUDE: (prod.) The Young Doctors, I Could Go on Singing, The Best Man. Formed own prod. co., Lawrence Turman, Inc., to make The Flim-Flam Man, The Graduate, Pretty Poison, The Drowning Pool, First Love, Heroes, Walk Proud, Caveman (co-prod.), The Thing, Second Thoughts (co-prod., dir., s.p.), Mass Appeal (co-prod.), The Mean Season (co-prod.), Short Circuit (co-prod.), Running Scared (co-prod.), Full Moon in Blue Water, Short Circuit 2 (co-prod.), Gleaming the Cube (co-prod.).
TELEVISION: Co-prod. with David Foster: The Gift of Love, The Morning After, News at Eleven, Between Two Brothers, She Lives, Unwed Father.

TURNER, CLIFFORD: Producer. b. Leeds, England, 1913. Ent. m.p. industry as cutting room asst. Gaumont British. Edited number early British pictures, before going to Hollywood in 1935. Subsequently edited for Warners, Columbia, Universal, Fox. Returned to England 1948 to edit The Small Back Room. Dir. and exec. producer since 1950 in Hollywood and New York. Formed Boulevard Film Productions Ltd., Screen Biographies International Inc., Television Enterprises Inc. Four Against the Bank of England. 1972: Utrillo, Rose of Cimarron, Mystery of the General Grant; La Cicatrice, The Valadon Story, Streets of Montmartre, The Murderess, Le Nain Rouge.

TURNER, FREDERICK: Executive. b. London, England. Ent. m.p. ind. 1946. Early career with Eagle-Lion before transferring to Rank Overseas Film Distributors, then Rank Film Distributors. Became financial controller and appt. managing director 1981. Currently responsible for Film Investments and Distribution, UK and Overseas, covering all media.

TURNER, KATHLEEN: Actress. b. Springfield, MO, June 19, 1954. e. U. of Maryland. Starred in NBC soap opera, The Doctors; on Bdwy. stage in Gemini. Starred in Camille (Long Wharf, CT, 1987). Film debut in Body Heat, 1981.
PICTURES: The Man With Two Brains, Romancing the Stone, Crimes of Passion, A Breed Apart, Prizzi's Honor, Jewel of the Nile, Peggy Sue Got Married, Switching Channels, Julia and Julia, Who Framed Roger Rabbit (voice), The Accidental Tourist, Dear America: Letters Home From Vietnam (reader).

TURNER, LANA: Actress. b. Wallace, ID, Feb. 8, 1921. Parents, Virgil Turner and Mildred Cowan.
PICTURES INCLUDE: They Won't Forget, Great Garrick, Adventures of Marco Polo, Love Finds Andy Hardy; Rich Man, Poor Girl; Dramatic School, Calling Dr. Kildare, These Glamour Girls, Dancing Coed. Two Girls on Broadway, We Who Are Young, Ziegfeld Girl, Dr. Jekyll and Mr. Hyde, Johnny Eager, Slightly Dangerous, Marriage Is a Private Affair, Keep Your Powder Dry, Week-End at the Waldorf, Postman Always Rings Twice, Green Dolphin Street, Cass Timberlane, Homecoming, Three Musketeers, Life of Her Own, Mr. Imperium, The Merry Widow, Bad & the Beautiful, Latin Lovers, Flame & the Flesh, Betrayed, The Prodigal, Sea Chase, Rains of Ranchipur, Diane, Lady and the Flyer, Imitation of Life, Portrait in Black, By Love Possessed, Bachelor in Paradise, Who's Got the Action?, Love Has Many

Faces, Madame X, The Big Cube, Persecution, Bittersweet Love.
TELEVISION: The Survivors (series), Love Boat, Falcon Crest.

TURNER, ROBERT EDWARD (TED): Executive. b. Cincinnati, OH., Nov. 19, 1938. e. Brown U. Began career in Savannah in family's outdoor adv. business, selling space on billboards. Bought co. in 1963 and in 1970 entered broadcasting with purchase of a failing TV station in Atlanta which he turned into WTBS, a "superstation" which in 1985 reached 80% of U.S. homes equipped with cable. 1980, established CNN a 24-hr. cable news service. Purchased MGM. Co-owner two professional sports teams in Atlanta: Braves (baseball) and Hawks (basketball). Started Turner Network Television 1988.

TURNER, TINA: Singer, Actress. r.n. Annie Mae Bullock. b. Brownsville, TX, Nov. 26, 1939. Previously married to Ike Turner and appeared with him on road in Ike and Tina Turner Revue. Many hit records.
PICTURES: Gimme Shelter, Soul to Soul, Tommy, Sound of the City, Mad Max Beyond Thunderdrome.
TELEVISION: Tina—Live From Rio.

TUSHINGHAM, RITA: Actress. b. Liverpool, England, March 14, 1940. m. director Ousama Rawi. Student at Liverpool Playhouse. M.p. debut 1961 in A Taste of Honey (1961).
THEATER: The Giveaway, Lorna and Ted, Mistress of Novices, The Undiscovered Country, Mysteries.
PICTURES INCLUDE: The Leather Boys, A Place to Go, Girl With The Green Eyes, The Knack, Dr. Zhivago, The Trap, Smashing Time, Diamonds for Breakfast, The Guru, The Bedsitting Room, Straight on 'til Morning, Situation, Instant Coffee, The Human Factor, Rachel's Man, The Slum Boy, The Black Journal, Bread, Butter and Jam, Mysteries, Felix Krull, Lady Killers, The Spaghetti Thing, Seeing Red, The Housekeeper, Resurrection.
TELEVISION: (U.S.) Green Eyes.

TUTIN, DOROTHY: Actress. b. London, Eng., Apr. 8, 1930. e. St. Catherine's Sch. Bramley, Guildford (Surrey). Stage debut in The Thistle & the Rose, 1949.
PLAYS INCLUDE: Much Ado About Nothing, The Living Room, I Am a Camera, The Lark, Wild Duck, Juliet, Ophelia, Viola, Portia, Cressida, Rosalind, The Devils, Once More With Feeling, The Cherry Orchard, Victoria Regina-Portrait of a Queen, Old Times, Peter Pan, What Every Woman Knows, Month in the Country, Macbeth, Antony and Cleopatra, Undiscovered Country, Reflections, After the Lions, Ballerina, A Kind of Alaska, Are You Sitting Comfortably?, Chalk Garden, Brighton Beach Memoirs.
PICTURES INCLUDE: Screen debut in The Importance of Being Earnest. Also: The Beggar's Opera, A Tale of Two Cities, Cromwell, Savage Messiah, The Shooting Party, Murder with Mirrors.
TELEVISION: Living Room, Victoria Regina, Invitation to a Voyage, Antigone, Colombe, Carrington V.C., The Hollow Crown, Scent of Fear, From Chekhov With Love, Anne Boleyn in The Six Wives of Henry VIII, Flotsam and Jetsam, Mother & Son, South Riding, Willow Cabins, Ghosts, Sister Dora, The Double Dealer, The Combination, La Ronde, Tales of the Unexpected, 10 Downing Street, Life After Death, King Lear, Landscape, The Father, The Demon Lover, Robin Hood.

TWAINE, MICHAEL: Actor, Director. b. New York, NY, Nov. 1, 1939. e. Ohio State U. Served U.S. Army. While studying with Lee Strasberg, worked as private detective, school teacher. Made stage debut City Center, 1956, in Mr. Roberts. Became village coffee house and club comedian 1968 to 1972.
PICTURES INCLUDE: Marriage Italian Style (voice only); American Soap, Blood Bath, Up! the Girls, F.I.S.T., Cheap Shots.
TELEVISION: The Silent Drum, Starsky & Hutch, Wonder Woman, Streets of San Francisco, Soap, Lou Grant, Diff'rent Strokes, Nurse, Stalk the Wild Child, The Courage and the Passion, Eischied.

TWIGGY: Recording Artist. r.n. Leslie Hornby. b. London, England, Sept. 19, 1949. m. actor Michael Witney. At 17 regarded as world's leading high fashion model. Made m.p. debut in The Boy Friend, 1971. Starred in many London West End Shows, including Cinderella and Captain Beaky Presents. Star of Broadway and touring stage productions of Funny Face. 1983: on Broadway in musical, My One and Only.
TELEVISION: Hosted and starred in major American & British music shows including Twiggy (U.K.), Twiggy and Friends (U.K.), and Juke Box (U.S.), Pygmalion (England), Sun Child (Eng.).
PICTURES INCLUDE: W, There Goes the Bride, The Blues Brothers, The Doctor and the Devils, Club Paradise, Madame Sousatzka.

TWYMAN, ALAN P.: Executive. b. Dayton, OH, May 30, 1934. e. U. of Cincinnati. Twyman Films, Inc. sales 1958, vice pres.-pres., 1975. NAVA board of directors, 1964–69; pres. 1970,

chm. of bd., 1972. In 1983 left to form own co., Alan Twyman Presents.

TYRRELL, SUSAN: Actress. b. San Francisco, CA, 1946. Made first prof. appearance with Art Carney in summer theatre tour prod. of Time Out for Ginger. Worked in off-Bdwy. prods. and as waitress in coffee house before attracting attention in Lincoln Center Repertory Co. prods. of A Cry of Players, The Time of Your Life, Camino Real.
PICTURES INCLUDE: The Steagle, Shoot Out, Fat City, Catch My Soul, The Killer Inside Me, Islands in the Stream, Andy Warhol's Bad, I Never Promised You A Rose Garden, Another Man, Another Chance, September 30, 1955, Forbidden Zone, Subway Riders, Tales of Ordinary Madness, Loose Shoes, Fast-Walking, Liar's Moon, Fire and Ice, Night Warning, Angel, The Killers, Avenging Angel, Flesh and Blood, Tapeheads, The Underachievers, Big Top Pee-Wee.
TELEVISION: If Tomorrow Comes, The Christmas Star, Poker Alice, Jealousy, Midnight Lace, Lady of the House, Windmills of the Gods, Open All Night (series).

TYSON, CICELY: Actress. b. New York, NY, Dec. 19, 1933. e. New York U. Studied at Actor's Studio. Former secretary and model. Co-founder, Dance Theatre of Harlem.
THEATER: The Blacks, Moon on a Rainbow Shawl, Tiger Tiger Burning Bright, The Corn Is Green.
PICTURES INCLUDE: Twelve Angry Men, Odds Against Tomorrow, Last Angry Man, A Man Called Adam, The Comedians, The Heart Is a Lonely Hunter, Sounder, The Blue Bird, The River Niger, A Hero Ain't Nothin, But a Sandwich, The Concorde—Airport '79.
TELEVISION: East Side, West Side (series), The Autobiography of Miss Jane Pittman (Emmy Award), Roots, A Woman Called Moses, King, Just An Old Sweet Song, The Marva Collins Story, Benny's Place, Wilma, Playing with Fire, Acceptable Risks, Samaritan, The Women of Brewster Place.

U

UGGAMS, LESLIE: Singer. b. New York, NY, May 25, 1943. e. Professional Children's Sch., grad., 1960. Juilliard. Beg. singing career age 5. TV debut as Ethel Waters' niece on Beulah. Also on Johnny Olsen's TV kids at age 7, Your Show of Shows as singer, 1953; Records for Columbia Records. Wrote The Leslie Uggams Beauty Book (1962).
STAGE: Hallelujah Baby (Tony Award, 1968), Her First Roman, Blues in the Night, Jerry's Girls.
PICTURES: Skyjacked.
RADIO: Peter Lind Hayes-Mary Healy Show, Milton Berle, Arthur Godfrey, Star Time.
TELEVISION: Beulah (1949), Kids and Company, Milton Berle Show, Name That Tune, Jack Paar Show, Garry Moore, Sing Along With Mitch, The Leslie Uggams Show (1969). Movies: Roots, Sizzle, Backstairs at the White House (miniseries), The Book of Lists (co-host). Fantasy (Emmy, 1983, host), I Love Men, Placido Domingo Steppin' Out With the Ladies.

ULLMAN, TRACEY: Actress, Comedian, Singer. b. Hackbridge, England. Attended the Italia Conti School for 4 years. Soon after appeared on British TV and onstage in Grease and The Rocky Horror Picture Show. Also performed in improvisational play Four in a Million (1981) at the Royal Court Theatre, London (London Theatre Critics Award). Recorded goldselling album You Broke My Heart in Seventeen Places. Film debut, Plenty (1985). U.S. TV debut, The Tracey Ullman Show (debuted April, 1987).

ULLMANN, LIV: Actress. b. Japan of Norwegian parents, Dec. 16, 1939. Accompanied parents to Canada when W.W.II began and later returned to Norway. Was catapulted to fame in a succession of Swedish films directed by Ingmar Bergman. Author: Changing, 1977. Choices.
THEATER: (U.S.) A Doll's House, Anna Christie, I Remember Mama (musical), Ghosts.
PICTURES INCLUDE: The Wayward Girl (debut, 1959), Swedish: Persona (debut), Hour of the Wolf, Shame, The Passion of Anna, The Emigrants, Face to Face, Cries and Whispers; Scenes From a Marriage, The Serpent's Egg, Autumn Sonata, American: The Devil's Imposter (formerly Pope Joan), Lost Horizon, 40 Carats, The New Land, Zandy's Bride, The Abdication, Leonor, Richard's Things, A Bridge Too Far, The Wild Duck, Bay Boy, The Night Visitor, Gaby—A True Story. Italian: Moscow Adieu (Donatello Award, Best Actress, 1987); A Time of Indifference, La Amiga.
TELEVISION: Lady From the Sea, Jacobo Timerman: Prisoner Without a Name, Cell Without a Number.

UNGER, ANTHONY B.: Executive, Producer. b. New York, NY, Oct. 19, 1940. e. Duke U., U. of Southern California. Prod. ass't Third Man, TV series, 1961. v.p. Unger Productions, Inc., 1964; v.p. Landau-Unger Co., Inc., 1965; v.p. Commonwealth United Entertainment in London, 1968; pres., Unger Prods. Inc., 1978–present.

PICTURES INCLUDE: 1966: assoc. prod., The Desperate Ones. 1968: assoc. prod., The Madwoman of Chaillot. 1969: exec. prod., The Battle of Neretva, The Magic Christian, Julius Caesar. 1970: exec. prod., The Devil's Widow. exec. prod., Don't Look Now; prod., The Unseen; prod., Silent Rage.

UNGER, KURT: Producer. b. Berlin, Jan. 10, 1922. Entered ind. in 1939 in chg. m.p. entertainment British troops in Middle East. Subsequently distributor for United Artists Corp. in Israel and Italy.
PICTURES INCLUDE: Judith, Best House in London, Puppet on a Chain, Pope Joan (The Devil's Imposter).

UNGER, STEPHEN A.: Executive. b. New York, NY, May 31, 1946. e. NYU, Grad. Film and Television Instit. Started as independent prod. and dist. of theatrical and TV films. In June, 1978, joined Universal Pictures Intl. Sales as foreign sls. mgr. Named v.p. Universal Theatrical Motion Pictures in 1979, responsible for licensing theatrical or TV features not handled by U.I.P. in territories outside U.S. & Canada and world-wide acquisitions. In 1980 joined CBS Theatrical Films as int'l. v.p., sls.; 1982–present, pres., Unger Int'l. Distributors, Inc.

URICH, ROBERT: Actor. b. Toronto, OH, Dec. 19, 1947. e. Florida State U., B.A., radio and TV communications; Michigan State U., M.A. Communications Mgmt. Appeared in university plays. Was sales account executive at WGN Radio, Chicago, before turning to stage acting (Ivanhoe Theatre, Chicago).
TELEVISION: The FBI, Gunsmoke, Kung Fu, Marcus Welby, MD, S.W.A.T., Bob & Carol & Ted & Alice, Soap, Tabitha, The Love Boat, Vega$, Spenser For Hire; Movies: Fighting Back, Bunco, When She Was Bad, Princess Daisy, Invitation to Hell, Mistral's Daughter, His Mistress, Scandal Sheet, Young Again, Spenser for Hire, Amerika, April Morning, The Comeback.
PICTURES: Magnum Force, Endangered Species, The Ice Pirates, Turk 182.

URMAN, MARK: Executive. b. New York, NY, Nov. 24, 1952. e. Union Coll., 1973; NYU, cinema, 1973–74. m. story analyst Deborah Davis. 1973, apprentice publicist, Universal Pictures; 1973–82, United Artists international dept. as assoc. publicist, senior publicist and ultimately asst. to v.p. worldwide ad-pub.; 1982–84, director of publicity and marketing, Triumph Films (Columbia/Gaumont); 1985–86, exec. dir. East Coast pub., Columbia Pictures; 1986–present, v.p. East Coast pub., Columbia Pictures. Member: Motion Picture Assoc. Ratings Appeal Board; advisory committee, U.S. Film Festival.

URQUHART, ROBERT: Actor, Writer. b. Scotland, October 16, 1922. e. George Heriots, Edinburgh. Served in Merchant Navy 1938–45; stage debut, Park Theatre, Glasgow; screen debut: You're Only Young Twice, 1951.
PICTURES INCLUDE: Isn't Life Wonderful, The House Of The Arrow, Knights of the Round Table, Happy Ever After (Tonight's the Night), Golden Ivory, The Dark Avenger, You Can't Escape, Yangtse Incident, Curse of Frankenstein, Dunkirk, The Trouble with Eve, Danger Tomorrow, Foxhole in Cairo, Murder in Mind, The Bulldog Greed, 55 Days At Peking, The Break, Murder at the Gallup, The Syndicate, The Limbo Line, The Looking Glass War, Brotherly Love (Country Dance), Playing Away, Restless Natives, Sharma and Beyond, P'Tang Bang Clipper Bang, Kitchen Toto.
TELEVISION: Tamer Tamed, Infinite Shoeblack, Morning Departure, The Human Touch, The Iron Harp, Sleeping Clergyman, The Naked Lady, For Services Rendered, The Bright One, Jango, Murder Swamp, She Died Young, Plane Makers series, Reporter, Inheritors series; 1976 series: Mr. Goodall, The Nearly Man, The Button Man, Happy Returns, Endless-Aimless, Bleak House, The Queens Arms, Shostakovich.
AUTHOR: (Wrote TV) House of Lies, End of the Tether, Landfall, The Touch of a Dead Hand.

USLAN, MICHAEL E.: Producer, Writer. b. Bayonne, NJ, 1951. e. Indiana U., A.B., M.S., J.D. Wrote 12 books, including Dick Clark's 1st 25 Years of Rock 'n' Roll; 1976–80 atty. with United Artists; Produced with Benjamin Melniker: First National Trivia Quiz (prod., writer); Dinosaurs (series, exec. prod., creator, writer); Three Sovereigns for Sarah (exec. prod.); Television's Greatest Bits (prod., creator, writer).
PICTURES: Swamp Thing, The Return of the Swamp Thing, Batman (exec. prod.).

USTINOV, PETER: Actor, Writer, Director. b. London, Eng., Apr. 16, 1921. e. Westminster Sch. In Brit. Army, W.W.II. On Brit. stage from 1937. Screen debut 1941 in Brit. picture Mein Kampf, My Crimes, Commander, Order of British Empire 1975. Awards: 2 Acad. Awards, supp. actor; Golden Globe; 3 Emmy Awards; 1 Grammy; NY Critics Award and Donaldson, best foreign play (The Love of Four Colonels); British Critics Award (Romanoff and Juliet).
THEATER: Romanoff and Juliet, N.Y., London; and 17 other plays. Dir., acted, Photo Finish; wrote, Life In My Hands,

The Unknown Soldier and His Wife, Half Way Up The Tree, King Lear, Beethoven's Tenth, etc.
PICTURES INCLUDE: The Goose Steps Out, One of Our Aircraft Is Missing, Let the People Sing, The Way Ahead, The True Glory, The Way Ahead (collab. s.p.); School for Secrets (wrote, dir. & co-prod.), Vice Versa; Private Angelo (adapt., dir., co-prod.), Odette, Quo Vadis, Hotel Sahara, The Egyptian, Beau Brummell, We're No Angels, Lola Montez, The Spies, An Angel Flew over Brooklyn, The Sundowners, Spartacus; prod., scripted, acted, Romanoff and Juliet; dir., prod./scpt., acted, Billy Budd, Topkapi, John Goldfarb Please Come Home; prod. dir., Lady L., Blackbeard's Ghost, The Comedians, Hot Millions, Viva Max. Dir. and acted, Hammersmith Is Out. Actor: Big Truck, Poor Clare, Logan's Run, Treasure of Matecumbe, One of Our Dinosaurs Is Missing, Le Taxi Mauve, The Last Remake of Beau Geste, Doppio Delitto, Death on the Nile, Charlie Chan and the Curse of the Dragon Queen, The Great Muppet Caper, Evil Under the Sun; Memed My Hawk (dir., prod., actor); Appointment with Death; Murder in Mesopotamia.
RECENT TV: The Well Tempered Bach, 13 at Dinner, Deadman's Folly, Peter Ustinov's Russia, World Challenge, Murder in Three Acts, The Secret Identity of Jack the Ripper (host), Around the World in 80 Days.

V

VACCARO, BRENDA: Actress. b. Brooklyn, NY, Nov. 18, 1939. e. Thomas Jefferson H.S., Dallas; studied two yrs. at Neighborhood Playhouse in N.Y. Was waitress and model before landing first Bdwy. role in Everybody Loves Opal. Toured in Tunnel of Love and returned to N.Y. for role in The Affair.
THEATER: The Affair, Children From Their Games, Cactus Flower (Tony Award, supp. actress, 1965), The Natural Look, How Now Dow Jones, The Goodbye People, Father's Day.
PICTURES INCLUDE: (debut) Midnight Cowboy, I Love My Wife, Summertree, Going Home, Once Is Not Enough, Airport '77, House by the Lake, Capricorn One, The First Deadly Sin, Zorro, the Gay Blade, Supergirl, Water, Cookie, Heart of Midnight, Death on Safari.
TELEVISION: The F.B.I., The Name of the Game, The Helen Reddy Show, The Shape of Things (special, Emmy, supp. actress, 1974). Series: Sara, Dear Detective, Paper Dolls. Movies: Sunshine, Deception, Julius and Ethel Rosenberg, Guyana Tragedy, Star Maker, Honor Thy Father, A Long Way Home, The Pride of Jesse Hallam.

VADIM, ROGER: Director, Writer. b. Paris, Jan. 26, 1928. r.n. Roger Vadim Plemiannikow.
PICTURES INCLUDE (s.p.): Futures Vedettes (s.p.). Writer-Director: And God Created Woman, Heaven Fell That Night, Les Liaisons Dangereuses, Warrior's Rest, Vice and Virtue, La Ronde, The Game is Over. Director: Barbarella, Pretty Maids All in a Row, Don Juan, Night Games, A Faithful Woman, Hot Touch, And God Created Woman (1988).
TELEVISION: Beauty and the Beast (Faerie Tale Theatre).

VAJNA, ANDREW: Executive. b. Budapest, Hungary, Aug. 1, 1944. e. U. of California at L.A. Exhibitor and dist. of feature films since 1970. Formed Carolco Service, Inc. (foreign sls. org.), 1977. Pres., American Film Mkt. Assn., 1983.
PICTURES: Exec. Prod.: The Silent Partner, The Changeling, Suzanne, The Amateur, Your Ticket Is No Longer Valid, Carbon Copy, First Blood, First Blood Part II, Angel Heart, Deep 6 (exec. prod.), Rambo III (co-exec. prod.), Red Heat (co-exec. prod.).

VALE, EUGENE: Writer. b. April 11, 1916. e. Zurich, Switzerland. m. Evelyn Wahl. Story and s.p., The Second Face, The Shattered Dream, 1954 SWG award nom., best written telefilm; The Dark Wave. 1957, m.p. academy award nominations.
PICTURES: A Global Affair, Francis of Assisi, The Bridge of San Luis Rey.
TELEVISION: Four Star Playhouse, Fireside Theatre, 20th Century Fox Hour, Schlitz Playhouse, Hollywood Opening Night, NBC, Crusader, Lux Video Theatre, Danger, CBS, Chevron Theatre, Douglas Fairbanks, Pepsi Cola Playhouse, Waterfront, Christophers, Cavalcade of America, Hallmark Hall of Fame.
AUTHOR: Technique of Screenplay Writing.

VALENTI, JACK J.: Executive. b. Sept. 5, 1921. e. U. of Houston, B.A., 1946; Harvard U., M.B.A., bus. admin., 1948. Air force pilot in European theatre, W.W.II; adv. and pub. rel. exec. in Houston; special asst. and advisor to Pres. Lyndon B. Johnson, 1963–66, elected pres., Motion Picture Association of America, MPEA and AMPTP, since June, 1966.

VALENTINE, KAREN: Actress. b. Sebastopol, CA, May 25, 1947.
PICTURES: Forever Young, Forever Free, Hot Lead and Cold Feet, The North Avenue Irregulars.
TELEVISION:Series: Room 222 (Emmy), Karen, My Friend Tony, Hollywood Squares, Laugh-In, The Bold Ones, Sonny

and Cher, Mike Hammer, Murder, She Wrote. Movies: Gidget Grows Up, The Daughters of Joshua Cabe, Coffee, Tea or Me?, The Girl Who Came Gift-Wrapped, The Love Boat, Having Babies, Murder at the World Series, Return to Fantasy Island, Go West, Young Girl, American 2100, Only the Pretty Girls Die, Muggable Mary, He's Fired, She's Hired; A Fighting Choice, Jane Doe, Skeezer, Money on the Side, Perfect People.

VALLI, ALIDA: Actress. r.n. Alida von Altenburger. b. Pola, Italy, May 31, 1921. e. M.P. Acad., Rome (dramatics); m. Oscar de Mejo, pianist-composer. In Italian m.p.; won Venice Film Festival Award in Piccolo Mondo Antico (Little Old World).
PICTURES INCLUDE: Vita Ricomincia, Giovanna; to U.S. 1947; U.S. m.p. debut in Paradine Case, 1947, Miracle of the Bells, The Third Man, Walk Softly Stranger, White Tower, Lovers of Toledo, Stranger's Hand, The Castilian, Ophelia, Spider's Stratagem, The Cassandra Crossing, Suspiria, 1900, Luna, Le Jupon Rouge, A Notre Regrettable epoux.

VALLONE, RAF: Actor. b. Turin, Italy, Feb. 17, 1916. e. U. of Turin. Newspaper writer; m.p. debut in Bitter Rice (1948).
PICTURES INCLUDE: Under the Olive Tree, Anna, Path of Hope, White Line, Rome 11 O'Clock, Strange Deception, Anita Garibaldi, Daughters of Destiny, Teresa Raquin, Riviera, The Secret Invasion. Two Women, El Cid, A View From the Bridge, Phaedra, Kiss The Girls and Make Them Die, The Desperate Ones, The Cardinal, The Italian Job, The Kremlin Letter, Summertime Killer, Rosebud, The Human Factor, The Other Side of Midnight, The Greek Tycoon, Lion of the Desert.
TELEVISION: Fame (Hallmark Hall of Fame), Honor Thy Father, Catholics, The Scarlet and the Black, Christopher Columbus, Goya.

VAN ARK, JOAN: Actress. b. New York, NY, June 16, 1943. e. Yale U. Starred in touring company, then on Broadway and in London in Barefoot in the Park. Television work includes Saturday morning cartoon voice work on series (Tarzan and the Super Seven, Heathcliff and the Dingbat, Spider Woman). Also appeared on Broadway with the APA-Phoenix Rep. Co. in the 1970s. As a runner has competed in 12 marathons.
THEATER: School for Wives (Theatre World Award), Cyrano de Bergerac, Ring Around the Moon, Chemin de Fer, As You Like It (L.A. Drama Critics Award).
PICTURES: The Frogs.
TELEVISION: The F.B.I., The Girl with Something Extra, Quark. Co-host: Miss USA and Miss Universe Pageants, Battle of the Network Stars. Series: Temperatures Rising, We've Got Each Other, Dallas, Knots Landing. Movies: A Testimony of Two Men, The Last Dinosaur, Big Rose, The Bionic Boy, The Judge and Jake Wyler, Red Flag—The Ultimate Game, Glitter, Shakedown on Sunset Strip.

VANCE, LEIGH: Scriptwriter, Producer. b. Harrogate, England, March 18, 1922. e. Shrewsbury Coll. Early career: reporter, critic. Ent. TV 1951, then films, many TV scripts; 1961, won Edgar Allan Poe Award, 1969 brought to Hollywood by Paramount.
PICTURES INCLUDE: The Flesh Is Weak, Heart of a Child, Picadilly Third Stop, Women Shall Weep, The Shakedown, Eyes of Youth, The Frightened City, It's All Happening Dr. Crippen, Outcast, Walk Like A Man, Cross Plot, Tall Cool Girl, The Black Windmill.
TELEVISION: Mannix, Mission Impossible, many pilots and movies-of-the-week. The Avengers, The Saint, Cannon (exec. story consultant, 1973), Caribe (exec. story consultant), Bronk (prod.), Baretta (exec. prod.), Switch (exec. prod.), The Phoenix (prod.), Hart to Hart (prod.).

VAN CLEEF, LEE: Actor. b. Somerville, NJ, Jan. 9, 1925. e. Somerville H.S., 1942. Joined U.S. Navy, 1942; asst. mgr. in summer camp, public accountant; then joined little theatre group.
PICTURES INCLUDE: High Noon, Beast from 20,000 Fathoms, Vice Squad, The Nebraskan, Gypsy Colt, Arrow in the Dust, Yellow Tomahawk, Dawn at Socorro, Princess of the Nile, Ten Wanted Men, The Conqueror, Big Combo, Treasure of Ruby Hills, I Cover the Underworld, Road To Denver, Posse from Hell, The Man Who Shot Liberty Valance, A Man Alone, Vanishing American, Tribute to a Bad Man, For a Few Dollars More, The Good, the Bad and the Ugly, The Big Gundown, Death Rides a Horse, Day of Anger, Barquero, El Condor, The Magnificent Seven Ride, Return of Sabata, Escape from New York, Amred Response, Codename: Wild Geese, The Commander.

VAN DEVERE, TRISH: Actress. b. Englewood Cliffs, NJ, March 9, 1945. e. Ohio Wesleyan U. Wife of actor George Scott. On Bdwy. in Sly Fox, Tricks of the Trade, etc.
PICTURES: Where's Poppa?, The Last Run, One Is a Lonely Number, The Day of the Dolphin, The Savage Is Loose, Fifty-Two Pickup, Movie, Movie, The Changeling, The Hearse, Findings, Messenger of Death.
TELEVISION: Mayflower—The Pilgrim's Adventure, All God's Children, Haunted.

VAN DOREN, MAMIE: Actress. r.n. Joan Lucille Olander. b. Rowena, SD, Feb. 6, 1933. e. Los Angeles H.S. Secy. law firm, L.A.; prof. debut as singer with Ted Fio Rita orch.
THEATRE: Appeared in many stock plays incl.: Once in a Lifetime, Boy Meets Girl, Come Back Little Sheba.
PICTURES INCLUDE: (m.p. debut) Forbidden; All American, Yankee Pasha, Francis Joins the Wacs, Ain't Misbehavin, Second Greatest Sex, Running Wild, Star in the Dust, Untamed Youth, Girl in Black Stockings, Teachers Pet, The Navy Vs. the Night Monsters.

VAN DYKE, DICK: Actor. b. West Plains, MO, Dec., 18, 1925. U.S.A.F., W.W.II. After discharged from service, opened advertising agency, Danville, IL; folded next year. Teamed with friend in nightclub act called Eric and Van, The Merry Mutes, and for 6 yrs. toured country doing a routine in which they pantomimed and lip-synched to records. 1953 hosted local TV show in Atlanta, then New Orleans. 1956 to NY as host of prime time cartoon show. Emmy Awards: Best actor in a series (1964, 1965); Best actor in a comedy series (1966); Star, best comedy-variety series (Van Dyke and Company, 1977), Best performer in children's prog. (The Wrong Way Kid, 1984).
THEATRE: The Girls Against the Boys, Bye Bye Birdie (Tony Award, 1961), The Music Man (revival).
PICTURES INCLUDE: Bye Bye Birdie, Mary Poppins, What a Way to Go, The Art of Love, Lieutenant Robinson Crusoe, Divorce American Style, What's New Fitzwilly?, Chitty Chitty Bang Bang, Some Kind of Nut, The Comic, Cold Turkey, The Runner Stumbles.
TELEVISION: The Merry Mute Show, The Music Shop, The Dick Van Dyke Show (series), CBS Cartoon Theater (host), The Chevy Showroom, The New Dick Van Dyke Show (series), The Carol Burnett Show, The Van Dyke Show (series, 1988–89). Movies: The Morning After, Drop-Out Father, Found Money, Ghost of a Chance.

VAN FLEET, JO: Actress. b. Oakland, CA, 1922. e. Coll. of the Pacific. Neighborhood Playhouse.
THEATRE: On Broadway in Winter's Tale, Whole World Over, Closing Door, King Lear, Flight into Egypt, Camino Real, Trip to Bountiful (Tony Award); Look Homeward Angel (Critics Award); The Glass Menagerie; The Alligators, Oh Dad, Poor Dad, Mama's Hung You in the Closet and I'm Feeling So Sad.
PICTURES INCLUDE: East of Eden (Academy Award, best supporting actress, 1955); I'll Cry Tomorrow (Look Award), Rose Tattoo, This Angry Age, King and Four Queens, Gunfight at the OK Corral; Wild River, Cool Hand Luke, I Love You, Alice B. Toklas, Gang Who Couldn't Shoot Straight, The Tenant.
TELEVISION: Cinderella, Bonanza, Mod Squad, Power, Paradise Lost, Seize the Day.

VANGELIS: Composer, Conductor. Full name: Vangelis Papathanassiou. b. Greece. Formed band Formynx in Greece; then Aphrodite's Child in Paris.
PICTURES: Chariots of Fire (Oscar), Missing, Blade Runner, The Bounty, Wonders of Life, Wild and Beautiful.

VAN HEUSEN, JIMMY: Composer. r.n. Edward Chester Babcock. b. Syracuse, NY, Jan. 26, 1913. e. Syracuse U. Pianist with publishing houses; songs for many m.p. Academy Award for Swinging on a Star, High Hopes, All the Way, Call Me Irresponsible.
PICTURES INCLUDE: Road to Rio, Emperor Waltz, Connecticut Yankee, Mr. Music, Riding High, Road to Bali, Bells of St. Mary's. Little Boy Lost. Emmy for Love and Marriage; Songwriters Hall of Fame. Many scores for Bing Crosby pictures, including Going My Way.

VANOCUR, SANDER: News Commentator. b. Cleveland, OH, Jan. 8, 1928. e. Northwestern U. Began career as journalist in London; City staff, NY Times 1955–57. Joined NBC in 1957, hosting First Tuesday series. Resigned in 1971 to be correspondent of the National Public Affairs Center for PBC. In 1977 joined ABC News as v.p., special reporting units 1977–80. Chief overview corr. ABC news, 1980–81; senior corr. 1981–present. Author: Business World.

VAN PALLANDT, NINA: Actress. b. Copenhagen, Denmark, July 15, 1932. e. U. of Southern California. Returned to Denmark where married Baron Frederik Van Pallandt with whom she had appeared as folk singer throughout Europe. Made 3 films with him; went on world tour together. Now divorced. Has appeared in New York as singer.
PICTURES: The Long Goodbye, A Wedding, Assault on Agathon, Quintet, American Gigolo, Cloud Dancer, Cutter and Bone, Asi Como Habian Sido, Time Out, O.C. and Stiggs.
TELEVISION: The Sam Shepherd Murder Case.

VAN PATTEN, DICK: b. New York, NY, Dec. 9, 1928. Began career as child actor with Bdwy. debut at 7 yrs., playing son of Melvyn Douglas in Tapestry in Gray. Has worked since in stage, radio, TV, films.

PICTURES INCLUDE: Making It, Joe Kidd, Soylent Green, Dirty Little Billy, Westworld, Gus, Treasure of Matecumbe, High Anxiety, The New Adventures of Pippi Longstocking.
TELEVISION: Guest Roles: Arnie, The Rookies, Cannon, Banyon, The Little People, The Streets of San Francisco, When Things Were Rotten. Series: I Remember Mama, The Partners, The New Dick Van Dyke Show, Eight Is Enough, Eight is Enough. Movies and specials: Jay Leno's Family Comedy Hour, A Mouse, A Mystery and Me, 14 Going On 30.
STAGE: The Lady Who Came to Stay, O Mistress Mine, On Borrowed Time, Ah, Wilderness, Watch on the Rhine, The Skin of Our Teeth, Kiss and Tell, Mister Roberts, I Was Dancing.

VAN PATTEN, JOYCE: Actress. b. New York, NY, March 9, 1936.
PICTURES: The Goddess, I Love You Alice B. Toklas, Mame, Something Big, Thumb Tripping, Mikey and Nicky, The Falcon and the Snowman, St. Elmo's Fire, Blind Date, Trust Me, Monkey Shines.
TELEVISION: Series: The Danny Kaye Show, The Good Guys, Mary Tyler Moore Variety Hour. Many specials and movies: Shadow of Fear, The Martian Chronicles, Eleanor First Lady of the World, Bus Stop, In Defense of Kids, Malice in Wonderland, Under the Influence, Sirens.

VAN PEEBLES, MELVIN: Director, Writer, Composer. b. 1932. Father of actor Mario Van Peebles. Was navigator-bombardier in Air Force, drove cable car in San Francisco.
AUTHOR: A Bear for the F.B.I., Don't Play Me Cheap (play) won 1st prize, Belgian Festival; and photoessay book on cable cars. Albums of his own music: Brer Soul, Ain't Supposed to Die a Natural Death. Composed music for Watermelon Man.
PICTURES INCLUDE: The Story of a Three-Day Pass, Watermelon Man, Sweet Sweetback's Baadasssss Song.
MEMBER: French Director's Guild; one of first black directors to be member of Directors Guild of America.
STAGE: Ain't Supposed to Die a Natural Death, Don't Play Us Cheap.
TELEVISION: The Sophisticated Gents (actor, s.p.), Just an Old Sweet Song (s.p.), Taking Care of Terrific. Series: Sonny Spoons.

VAN PRAAG, WILLIAM: Executive, Producer, Director, Writer, Editor. Advertising Consultant. b. New York, NY, Sept. 13, 1924. e. CREI, Columbia U. U.S. Army, 1942. Paramount, 1945; Brandt Bros. Prods., 1946; NBC, 1947; v.p. Television Features, 1948. Devlpd. vidicon system in m.p. prod., 1949. Started, pres., Van Praag Prod. Inc. 1951. Formed Ernst-Van Praag, Inc. 1971, a communications and marketing counseling firm (N.Y., Brussels, Tokyo). Pres., International Film, TV and A-V Producers Ass'n, 1969, Creator of Van-O-Vision. Winner of commercial, short subject and feature theatrical awards. Author of Color Your Picture, Primer of Creative Editing, and Van Praag's Magic Eye. Past pres., Film Producer's Ass'n, mem. DGA, SAG, 771 IATSE, National Academy of TV Arts and Sciences, International Radio and TV Executive Society and Soc. of MP and TV Engineers.

VAN RIKFOORD, HAROLD C.: Producer. b. New York, NY, Jan. 1, 1935. e. Bryant H.S., grad., 1952; New York U. Errand boy, stage mgr., N.Y., 1954–57. Co-prod. two Broadway plays. Prod., The Long Ride Home, Rome, 1957; prod., short subject films; prod., Moment of Crisis, 1959; prod., television pilot films; exec. prod., Jonathan Shields Prod.

VAN THAL, DENNIS: Executive. b. London, June 4, 1909. e. University Coll. Early career musical dir.; war service, Royal Navy; entered m.p. industry 1946; casting dir. Pinewood Studios; dir., Myron Selznick Ltd.; joined dir. Alexander Korda as prod. exec., 1953; apptd. dir., Big Ben Films, 1955; joined Ealing Films, 1956; prod. assoc. Anastasia; assoc. prod. The Admirable Crichton, Barnacle Bill, The Scapegoat; mgr. dir. London Management, Ltd.

VARDA, AGNES: Photographer, Director, Writer. b. France, 1928. Started as still photographer for The Theatre National Populaire de Jean Vilar. Became a photo-journalist. In 1954 wrote and directed first film, La Pointe Courte. Afterwards made both documentaries and features.
PICTURES INCLUDE: Cleo from 5 to 7, Le Bonheur, Les Creatures, Lion's Love, One Sings, The Other Doesn't, Kung Fu Master! (prod., dir., s.p.); Jane B. par Agnes V. (dir., editor, s.p., actress).

VARSI, DIANE: Actress. b. San Francisco, CA, 1938.
PICTURES: Peyton Place, Ten North Frederick, From Hell to Texas, Compulsion, Sweet Love, Bitter, Wild in the Streets, Killers Three, Bloody Mama, Johnny Got His Gun, I Never Promised You a Rose Garden.
TELEVISION: The People (movie).

VAUGHN, ROBERT: Actor. b. New York, NY, Nov. 22, 1932. e. L.A. State coll., B.S. and M.A. Theatre Arts 1956; USC, Ph.D. Communications, 1970. Gained fame as Napoleon Solo in The Man From U.N.C.L.E. TV series. Author: Only Victims, 1972.

PICTURES: Hell's Crossroads, No Time to Be Young, Unwed Mother, Good Day for a Hanging, The Young Philadelphians, The City Jungle (Acad. Award nom.), The Magnificent Seven, The Big Show, The Caretakers, To Trap a Spy, The Spy With My Face, One Spy too Many, The Venetian Affair, How to Steal the World, Bullitt, The Bridge at Remagen, The Mind of Mr. Soames, If It's Tuesday, This Must Be Belgium, Julius Caesar, The Statue, The Clay Pigeon, One of Our Spies Is Missing (TV, Great Britain), The Spy In the Green Hat (TV, Great Britain), The Towering Inferno, Starship Invasions, S.O.B., Superman III, The Delta Force, Black Moon Rising, Rampage, Fire With Fire, Skeleton Coast, B.U.D.
TELEVISION: Washington: Behind Closed Doors, The Blue and the Gray, Evergreen, International Airport, Murrow, Prince of Bel Air, Desperado, Full Circle Again, Ray Bradbury Theater III.

VEITCH, JOHN: Executive. b. New York, NY, June 22, 1925. Started production career as asst. director and moved through ranks as prod. mgr., assoc. prod., prod., second unit dir., and exec. prod. mgr. Appointed Columbia Pictures exec. asst. prod. mgr., 1961; became exec. prod. mgr., 1963. Named v.p. & exec. prod. mgr., 1966; promoted in 1977 to exec. v.p. & exec. prod. mgr. of world-wide productions. In 1979 named pres. of Columbia Pictures Productions. Resigned 1983 to be consultant and independent producer exclusively for Columbia.
PICTURES: Fast Forward, Suspect (exec. prod.).

VELAZCO, ROBERT E.: r.n. Emil Velazco, Jr. b. Dallas, TX, Jan 1, 1924. e. Columbia U., business administration, 1942–43. Started in film business with father, Emil Velazco, Inc. Following yrs. worked for Emil Velazco, Inc., NTA, Ross Gaffney, Inc. During this time worked on over 8,500 productions from 5 sec. to feature films. In charge of Velazco, Inc., Kansas City, MO, 1947–49. Owner and pres., Musifex Co., Inc., 1958. Opened Musifex Inc. Arlington, VA, 1972. Two films scored by Velazco nominated for Academy Award, 1978 and 1980. In 1983 expanded into video tape music editing and video mixing.

VELDE, JAMES R.: Executive. b. Bloomington, IL, Nov. 1, 1913. e. Illinois Wesleyan U. Entered m.p. ind. as night shipper Paramount ex. Detroit, 1934; then city salesman, office mgr. until joining Army, 1943, rejoining same ex. upon dischge., 1946; to Paramount, Washington as Baltimore city salesman, same yr.; br. mgr. Selznick Rel. Org. Pittsburgh, 1948; salesman Eagle-Lion Classics, Pittsburgh, 1949; br. mgr. ELC, Des Moines, 1949; br. mgr., ELC, Detroit, 1950; west coast dist. mgr., United Artists, April, 1951; Western div. mgr. UA, 1952; gen. sales mgr., 1956; v.p., 1958; dir., UA, 1968; sr. v.p., 1972. Retired, 1977.

VENORA, DIANE: Actress. b. Hartford, CT, 1952. Member of Juilliard's Acting Company and the Ensemble Studio Theatre. Theater includes A Midsummer Night's Dream, the title role in Hamlet (New York Shakespeare Festival), Uncle Vanya (at La Mama), Penguin Toquet, Tomorrow's Monday (Circle Rep).
PICTURES: All That Jazz, The Critical List, Wolfen, Terminal Choice, The Cotton Club, F/X, Bird.
TELEVISION: Mini-series: A.D. Movie: Cook and Peary: The Race to the Pole.

VERDON, GWEN: Actress, Dancer, Choreographer. b. Culver City, CA, Jan. 13, 1925. Married to late dir.-choreographer Bob Fosse. Studied dancing with her mother, E. Belcher, Carmelita Marrachi, and Jack Cole.
THEATER: Bonanza Bound! (1947), Magdalena (asst. choreographer to Jack Cole), Alive and Kicking (1950), Can-Can (Donaldson Award and Tony Awards), Damn Yankees (Tony Award), New Girl in Town (Tony Award), Redhead (Tony Award), Sweet Charity, Children! Children!, Milliken's Breakfast Show (Waldorf Astoria, 1973), Damn Yankees (revival Westbury, Long Island, 1974), Chicago, Dancin' (asst. choreographer, prod. supervisor road co.), Sing Happy (tribute to Kander and Ebb, 1978), Parade of Stars Playing the Palace (Actors' Fund benefit, 1983), Night of 100 Stars II (1985).
PICTURES: On the Riviera (debut, 1951), David and Bathsheba, Meet Me After the Show, The Merry Widow, The I Don't Care Girl, Farmer Takes a Wife, Damn Yankees, Cocoon, The Cotton Club, Nadine, Cocoon II: The Return.
TELEVISION: M*A*S*H, Fame, All My Children, Magnum P.I., The Equalizer, All is Forgiven, Legs, The Jerk Too.

VEREEN, BEN: Singer, Dancer, Actor. b. Miami, FL, Oct. 10, 1946. e. High School of Performing Arts. On stage in Hair, Sweet Charity, Jesus Christ Superstar, Pippin (Tony), Grind.
PICTURES: Gasss, Funny Lady, All That Jazz, The Zoo Gang, Buy and Cell.
TELEVISION: Movies: Louis Armstrong—Chicago Style, Roots, Ellis Island, Jesse Owens Story, A.D., Ten Speed and Brown Shoe (series), J.J. Starbuck (series). Specials: Ben Vereen—His Roots, Uptown—A Tribute to the Apollo Theatre, Ellis Island, A. D.

VERHOEVEN, PAUL: Director. b. The Netherlands, 1940. e. U. of Leiden, Ph.D., (mathematics and physics) where he began making films.
PICTURES: Soldier of Orange (debut, 1979), Spetters, The Fourth Man, Robocop.

VERNON, ANNE: Actress. r.n. Edith Antoinette Alexandrine Vignaud. b. Paris, Jan. 7, 1924. e. Ecole des Beaux Arts, Paris. Worked for French designer; screen debut in French films; toured with French theatre group; first starring role, Le Mannequin Assassine 1948. Wrote French cookbooks. Was subject of 1980 French TV film detailing her paintings, Les Peintres Enchanteurs.
PICTURES INCLUDE: Edouar et Caroline, Terror on a Train, Ainsi Finit La Nuit, A Warning to Wantons, Patto Col Diavolo, A Tale of Five Cities, Shakedown, Song of Paris, The Umbrellas of Cherbourg, General Della Rovere, La Rue L'Estrapade, Love Lottery.

VERNON, JOHN: Actor. b. Canada, 1936. e. Banff Sch. of Fine Arts, Royal Acad. of Dramatic Art.
PICTURES: Point Blank, Justine, Topaz, One More Train to Rob, Dirty Harry, Charlie Varrick, The Black Windmill, Fear Is the Key, Cat and Mouse, Brannigan, The Outlaw Josey Wales, Angela, A Special Day, National Lampoon's Animal House, Fantastica, Crunch, Herbie Goes Bananas, Chained Heat, Curtains, Savage Streets, Doin' Time, Ernest Goes to Camp, Blue Monkey, Nightstick, Deadly Stranger, Dixie Lanes, Killer Klowns From Outer Space, Imogit Yu Sucka, Office Party, Blood of Others, Curtains.
TELEVISION: Movies: Trial Run, Escape, Cool Million, Hunter, The Questor Tapes, Mousey, The Virginia Hill Story, The Imposter, Swiss Family Robinson, The Barbary Coast, Matt Helm, Mary Jane Harper Cried Last Night, The Sacketts, The Blue and the Gray, Rat Tales.

VERONA, STEPHEN: Director. b. Illinois, Sept. 11,1940. e. Sch. of Visual Arts. Directed some 300 commercials before turning to feature films in 1972, which he wrote as well.
PICTURES: The Rehearsal (short), Pipe Dreams, Board-walk (and co-s.p.), Talking Walls (dir., s.p.).
TELEVISION: Class of 1966 (prod. designer, ani. dir.); Diff'rent Strokes; The Music People; Double Exposure; Flatbush Avenue; Sesame Street; Take a Giant Step.

VETTER, RICHARD: Executive. b. San Diego, CA, Feb. 24, 1928. e. Pepperdine Coll., B.A., 1950; San Diego State Coll., M.A., 1953; U. of California at L.A., Ph.D., 1959. U.S. Navy: aerial phot., 1946–48, reserve instr., San Diego County Schools, 1951–54; asst. prof., audio-vis. commun., U.C.L.A., 1960–63. Inventor, co-dev., Dimension 150 Widescreen Process. 1957–63: formed D-150 Inc., 1963; exec. v.p. mem.: SMPTE, Technical & Scientific Awards Committee, AMPAS.

VICTOR, JAMES: Actor. r.n. Lincoln Rafael Peralta Diaz. b. Santiago, Dominican Republic, July 27, 1939. e. Haaren H.S., N.Y. Studied at Actors Studio West. On stage in Bullfight, Ceremony for an Assassinated Blackman, Latina, The Man in the Glass Booth, The M.C. (1985 Drama-Logue Critics, and Cesar best actor awards), I Gave You a Calendar (1983 Drama-Logue Critics Award), I Don't Have To Show You No Stinking Badges (1986 Drama-Logue Critics Award).
PICTURES: Fuzz, Rolling Thunder, Boulevard Nights, Defiance, Losin' It, Borderline; Stand and Deliver.
TELEVISION: Series: Viva Valdez, Condo, I Married Dora. Many appearances on specials. Movies: Robert Kennedy and His Times, Twin Detectives, The Hound of Hell, Remington Steel; The Streets of L.A.; I, Desire; Second Serve.
AWARDS: Cleo, 1975, for Mug Shot; L.A. Drama-Logue Critics Award, 1980, for Latina; Golden Eagle Award, 1981, for consistent outstanding performances in motion pictures.

VIETHEER, GEORGE C.: Executive. b. New York, NY, Feb. 27, 1910. e. Norwich U., B.S., 1932; Syracuse U., M.S., 1933. U.S. Army officer, 1933–37; chief service bureau, later Wash. rep. Panama Canal & R.R. Co., 1937–41; deputy dir., personnel, Office of Emergency Mgt., 1941–43; U.S. Army, 1943–46; mem., Nat'l Comm. on Manpower Shortages, 1946; deputy dir., personnel, U.S. Dept. of Commerce, 1946–50; U.S. rep. to U.N. Public Admin. Conf., 1950; deputy asst. admin. Econ. Stab. Agency, 1951; mgr., Washington office, MPAA, 1952; subsequently v.p., MPEAA and also v.p. American Motion Picture Export Co. (Africa) and v.p., Afram Films, Inc. Author: various pubs., articles on bus. mgt. Retired since 1977.

VILLECHAIZE, HERVE: Actor. b. Paris, France, April 23, 1943. Sought career as artist, studying in Paris and then coming to New York to the Art Students League. Studied acting with Julie Bovasso. First film, The Guitar, shot in Spain. On Broadway in Elizabeth the First and Gloria and Esperenze. Also performed mime in N.Y. City Opera productions.
PICTURES: Hollywood Blvd. No. 2, Hot Tomorrow, The Man with the Golden Gun, Crazy Joe, The Gang That Couldn't Shoot Straight, Seizure, The One and Only, Forbidden Zone, Two Moon Junction.
TELEVISION: Fantasy Island (series).

VINCENT, JAN-MICHAEL: Actor. b. Denver, CO, July 15, 1944. e. Ventura City (CA) Coll. as art major. Joined National Guard. Discovered by agent Dick Clayton. Hired by Robert Conrad to appear in his film, Los Bandidos, made in Mexico. Signed to 6-mo. contract by Universal, for which made Journey to Shiloh. Then did pilot TV movie for 20th-Fox based on Hardy Boys series of book. Originally called self Michael Vincent; changed after The Undefeated.
PICTURES INCLUDE: Los Bandidos, Journey to Shiloh, The Undefeated, Going Home, The Mechanic, The World's Greatest Athlete, Buster and Billie, Bite the Bullet, White Line Fever, Baby Blue Marine, Vigilante Force, Shadow of the Hawk, Damnation Alley, Big Wednesday, Hooper, Defiance, Hard Country, The Last Plane Out, Born in East L.A., Hit List, Deadly Embrace.
TELEVISION: Lassie, Bonanza, The Banana Splits Adventure Hour, The Survivors (series), Airwolf (series). Movies: Tribes, The Catcher, Sandcastle, Six Against the Rock.

VINCENT, JR., FRANCIS T: Executive. b. Waterbury, CT, May 29, 1938. e. Williams Coll. B.A., 1960; Yale Law Sch. LL.B., 1963. Bar, CT 1963; NY, 1964; D.C. 1969. 1969–78, partner in law firm of Caplin & Drysdale, specializing in corporate banking and securities matters. 1978, assoc. dir. of, Division of Corporation Finance of Securities & Exchange Commission. Trustee of Williams Coll. & The Hotchkiss Sch. Exec. v.p. of the Coca-Cola Company and pres. & CEO of its entertainment business sector. Also chm. & CEO of Columbia Pictures Industries, Inc.; appt. pres. CEO, 1978. Member of board of dir. of The Coca-Cola Bottling Co. of New York. 1987–June 1988. Rejoined law firm of Caplin & Drysdale, Washington, D.C., 1988.

VINCENT, KATHARINE: Actress. r.n. Ella Vincenti. b. St. Louis, MO, May 28, 1918. e. Two years of high school, left in 1937 to go on the stage. m. the late Pandeno Descanto, producer.
THEATRE: Broadway shows include: Love or Bust, 1938; Could She Tell?, 1939; Banners of 1939; Czarina Smith, 1940. Numerous roadshow tours.
PICTURES INCLUDE: Peptipa's Waltz, 1942 (debut), Error in Her Ways, Stars and Stripes on Tour, 1943, Skin Deep, 1944, The Hungry, Voodoo Village, Welcome to Genoa, 1950, Unknown Betrayal, 1956, The Hooker, 1962 (Descanto films).
TELEVISION: The Untouchables, Moses, The Lawgiver, Dolce Far Niente (mini-series TVF Roma).

VINER, MICHAEL: Producer, Writer. b. 1945. m. actress Deborah Raffin. e. Harvard U., Georgetown U. Served as aide to Robert Kennedy; was legman for political columnist Jack Anderson. Settled in Hollywood, where worked for prod. Aaron Rosenberg, first as prod. asst. on three Frank Sinatra films; then asst. prod. on Joaquin Murieta. In music industry was record producer, manager, executive, eventually heading own division, at MGM. Debut as writer-producer in 1976 with TV special, Special of the Stars. Theatrical film debut as prod.-co-writer of Touched by Love, 1980. Television: Windmills of the Gods (exec. prod.).

VITALE, JOSEPH A.: Actor. b. New York, NY, Sept. 6, 1901. In 1924, on dramatic stage (Hold on to Your Hats, Page Miss Glory, All Editions, I'd Rather Be Right, Common Ground). Screen debut, 1943.
PICTURES INCLUDE: None But the Lonely Heart, Lady Luck, Road to Rio, Where There's Life, Connecticut Yankee, Illegal Entry, Red Hot and Blue, Paleface, Fancy Pants, My Friend Irma Goes West, Stop You're Killing Me, Stranger Wore a Gun, Square Jungle, Rumble On the Docks, Apache Rifles.
TELEVISION: Climax, Lineup, Bengal Lancers, Wagon Train, Schlitz Playhouse, Cimmaron City, Telephone Time, Wyatt Earp, Rawhide, Red Skelton, The Thin Man, M Squad, Dawson, Ben Casey, Empire, Hazel, Mr. Ed, To Rome With Love, Fisherman's Wharf (pilot).

VITTI, MONICA: Actress. r.n. Monica Luisa Ceciarelli. b. Italy, 1933.
PICTURES: L'Avventura, La Notte, L'Eclipse, Dragees du Poivre, The Nutty, Naughty Chateau, The Red Desert, Modesty Blaise, The Chastity Belt, Girl with a Pistol, The Pacifist, Duck in Orange Sauce, An Almost Perfect Affair, The Mystery of Oberwald, The Flirt.

VOGEL, JESSE: Writer, Composer. b. New York, NY, Oct. 24, 1925. e. City Coll. of New York, B.S.Sc., 1947; Paris Conservatory of Music, 1949. Dir., Vogel Films, Paris, post-production services, English and Foreign versions. Screen-plays: Carmen, Baby; Therese and Isabelle. Produced: Who's Harriet? My Pleasure Is My Business.

VOIGHT, JON: Actor. b. Yonkers, NY. Dec. 29, 1938. e. Arch-bishop Stepinac H.S., White Plains, NY; Catholic U., B.F.A., 1960; studied acting at the Neighborhood Playhouse and in private classes with Stanford Meisner, four yrs. Off-Broadway in: A View From the Bridge (revival), 1964. Won the Theatre World Award for Broadway prod. That Summer, That Fall. Played Romeo, San Diego Shakespeare Festival.

315

TELEVISION: Public Broadcast Lab.'s The Dwarf, also Gunsmoke, Cimarron Strip.

PICTURES INCLUDE: Hour of the Gun, Fearless Frank, Midnight Cowboy (Acad. Award nom., Best Actor), Out of It, Catch 22, The Revolutionary, All American Boy, Deliverance, Conrack, The Odessa File, End of the Game, Coming Home, The Champ, Lookin' To Get Out (also co-s.p.), Table for Five, Runaway Train, Desert Bloom.

VOLONTE, GIAN MARIA: Actor. b. Milan, April 9, 1933. e. Rome's National Acad. of Dramatic Art, 1957 graduate. Entered on professional theatrical career, playing Shakespeare and Racine, along with modern works, Sacco and Vanzetti and The Deputy. On TV in Chekov's Uncle Vanya and Dostoyevsky's The Idiot. First major film roles in Un Uomo da Bruciare, 1961 and Il Terrorista, 1963. Called self John Welles in credits for spaghetti westerns.

PICTURES INCLUDE: For a Fistful of Dollars, For a Few Dollars More, Investigation of a Citizen Above Suspicion, The Working Class Goes to Heaven, Wind from the East, Sacco and Vanzetti, L'Attenat, Slap the Monster on Page One, Just Another War, The Mattei Affair, Lucky Luciano, Eboli, The Death of Mario Ricci, Chronicle of a Death Foretold.

VON SYDOW, MAX: Actor. b. Lund, Sweden, April 10, 1929. m. Keratin Olin, actress, 1951. Theatrical debut in a Cathedral Sch. of Lund prod. of The Nobel Prize. Served in the Swedish Quartermaster Corps two yrs. Studied at Royal Dramatic Theatre Sch. in Stockholm. Tour in municipal theatres. Has appeared on stage in Stockholm, London, Paris and Helsinki in Faust, The Legend and The Misanthrope. 1954 won Sweden's Royal Foundation Cultural Award.

PICTURES INCLUDE: Wild Strawberries, Brink of Life, The Magician, The Seventh Seal, The Virgin Spring, Through a Glass Darkly, Winter Light, Hawaii, The Greatest Story Ever Told, The Reward, Hour of the Wolf, Shame, The Kremlin Letter, The Passion of Anna, The Immigrants, Night Visitor, The Emigrants, The New Land, Three Days of The Condor, Voyage of the Damned, Exorcist II: The Heretic, March or Die, Flash Gordon, Victory, Conan The Barbarian, Never Say Never Again, Dreamscape, Dune, Code Name: Emerald, Hannah and Her Sisters, Duet for One, The Second Victory, Pelle the Conqueror, Katinka (dir.).

TELEVISION: Samson and Delilah, Christopher Columbus, Kojak: The Belarus File, Brotherhood of the Rose.

VONDERHAAR, RAYMOND T.: Executive. b. Rugby, N.D., Nov. 1, 1919. e. St. Cloud State. Spent entire career in exhibition. Pres., Allied Theatre Assn., 1963–64; pre., NATO North Central States, 1965–76; National NATO bd., 1965–84; also memb. exec. comm. 1965–84; NATO No. Central, chm., 1976–84.

VON ZERNECK, FRANK: Producer. b. New York, NY, Nov. 3, 1940. e. Hofstra Coll., 1962. Has produced plays in New York, Los Angeles, and on national tour and 45 films and miniseries. Founded (with Robert Greenwald) Moonlight Prods. Devised Portrait film genre for TV movies: Portrait of a Stripper, Portrait of a Mistress, Portrait of a Centerfold, etc.

TELEVISION: 21 Hours at Munich, Dress Gray, Miracle on Ice, Combat High, Queenie, In the Custody of Strangers, The First Time, Baby Sister, Policewoman Centerfold, Obsessive Love, Invitation to Hell, Romance on the Orient Express, Hostage Flight, The Tall Men, The Proud Men (exec. prod.), Man Against the Mob (co-exec. prod.), To Heal a Nation (exec. prod.).

Past chm. of California Theatre Council; former officer of League of Resident theatres; active member of League of New York Theatres & Producers; bd. of gov., Producers Guild of America, the Caucus for Producers, Writers, and Directors, Museum of Broadcasting.

VORHAUS, BERNARD: Director. b. 1898. In 1933, wrote and directed Money for Speed (UA-British). Recently has lectured on film.

PICTURES INCLUDE: 1934, The Ghost Camera, Crime on the Hill, Night Club Queen, Broken Melody, Blind Justice, Ten Minutes Alibi, Street Song, Last Journey, Twickenham, Dark World. Associate producer Broken Blossoms; director, Dusty Ermine, Twickenham; Cotton Queen, Rock Studios, Bury Me Dead, Winter Wonderland, The Spiritualist, So Young, So Bad, Pardon My French.

W

WADLEIGH, MICHAEL: Director. b. Akron, OH, Sept. 24, 1941. e. Ohio State U., B.S., B.A., M.A., Columbia Medical Sch. Directed Woodstock (1970), Wolfen (dir., co-s.p.), Out of Order, The Village at the End of the Universe (dir., s.p.).

WAGGONER, LYLE: Actor, b. Kansas City, KS, April 13, 1935. e. Washington U., St. Louis, Was salesman before becoming actor with road co. prod. of Li'l Abner. Formed own sales-

promo co. to finance trip to CA for acting career in 1965. Did commercials, then signed by 20th-Fox for new-talent school.

TELEVISION: The Carol Burnett Show (series), It's Your Bet (host), The New Adventures of Wonder Woman (series).

PICTURES INCLUDE: Love Me Deadly, Journey to the Center of Time, Catalina Caper, Surf II.

WAGNER, JANE: Writer, Director. b. Morristown, TN, Feb. 2, 1935. Bdwy. work includes Appearing Nitely and The Search for Signs of Intelligent Life in the Universe—both starring Lily Tomlin.

PICTURES INCLUDE: Moment by Moment (s.p., dir.); The Incredible Shrinking Woman (exec. prod., s.p.).

TELEVISION: Lily, Lily Tomlin, People, Lily—Sold Out, Lily for President?

WAGNER, LINDSAY: Actress. b. Los Angeles, CA, June 22, 1949. Appeared in school plays in Portland, OR; studied singing and worked professionally with rock group. In 1968 went to L.A. and decided to make acting her career. Signed to Universal contract in 1971.

PICTURES INCLUDE: Two People, Paper Chase, Second Wind, Nighthawks, Martin's Day.

TELEVISION: The F.B.I., Owen Marshall, Counselor at Law, Night Gallery, The Bold Ones, Marcus Welby, M.D., The Rockford Files, The Six Million Dollar Man, The Bionic Woman (series, Emmy, 1977), Jessie (series); Movies: Two Kinds of Love, Passions, Child's Cry, Convicted, This Child Is Mine, Young Again, Stranger in My Bed, The Return of the Six Million Dollar Man and the Bionic Woman, Scruples, Student Exchange, The Incredible Journey of Dr. Meg Laurel, Callie and Son, I Want to Live, Evil in Clear River, The Taking of Flight 847, Nightmare at Bitter Creek, Voice of the Heart.

WAGNER, RAYMOND JAMES: Producer. b. College Point, NY, Nov. 3, 1925. e. Middlebury Coll., Williams Coll. Joined Young & Rubicam, Inc., as radio-TV commercial head in Hollywood, 1950–59. Head of pilot development, Universal Studios, 1960–65. Produced Petulia for Warner Bros. (1967) and was exec. prod. of Loving for Columbia, 1969. V.p. of production (features) for MGM, 1972–79. Presently independent producer for 20th Century-Fox. 1985, Code of Silence (prod.), Rent-a-Cop (prod.).

WAGNER, ROBERT: Actor. b. Detroit, MI, Feb. 10, 1930. e. Saint Monica's H.S. Film debut in Halls of Montezuma (1950).

PICTURES INCLUDE: The Frogmen, Let's Make It Legal, With A Song In My Heart, What Price Glory, Stars and Stripes Forever, The Silver Whip, Titanic, (Star of Tomorrow, 1953). Beneath the 12-Mile Reef, Prince Valiant, Broken Lance, White Feather, Kiss Before Dying, The Mountain, True Story of Jesse James, Stopover Tokyo, The Hunters, In Love and War, Say One for Me, Between Heaven and Hell, All the Fine Young Cannibals, Sail a Crooked Ship, The Longest Day, The War Lover, The Condemned of Altona, Harper, Banning, The Biggest Bundle of Them All, Don't Just Stand There, Winning, The Towering Inferno, Midway, The Concorde—Airport '79, Curse of the Pink Panther, I Am the Cheese.

TELEVISION: Series: It Takes A Thief, Switch, Hart to Hart. Movies: Pearl, Cat on a Hot Tin Roof, To Catch a King, There Must Be a Pony, Love Among Thieves, Windmills of the Gods, Indiscreet.

WAHL, KEN: Actor. b. Chicago, IL, Feb. 14, 1960. No acting experience when cast in The Wanderers in 1978.

PICTURES INCLUDE: Fort Apache, The Bronx, Race for the Yankee Zephyr, Running Scared, Jinxed, The Soldier, Purple Hearts.

TELEVISION: The Dirty Dozen: The Next Mission, Double Dare, The Gladiator. Series: Wiseguy.

WAITE, RALPH: Actor. b. White Plains, NY, June 22, 1929. e. Bucknell U., Yale U. Social worker, publicity director, assistant editor and minister before turning to acting. Appeared in many Bdwy. plays, including Hogan's Goat, The Watering Place, Trial of Lee Harvey Oswald, etc., and off-Bdwy. and regional theatres. Biggest success on TV in The Waltons. Is founder of the Los Angeles Actors Theatre. Wrote, produced, directed and acted in theatrical film, On the Nickel.

PICTURES INCLUDE: Five Easy Pieces, Lawman, The Grissom Gang, Dime Box, The Sporting Club.

TELEVISION: Series: The Waltons, The Mississippi. Movies: Red Alert, The Secret Life of John Chapman, Ohms, Angel City, A Good Start, Crime of Innocence; Red Earth, White Earth. Mini-series: Roots.

WAITE, RIC: Cinematographer. Photographed more than 40 movies-of-the-week for TV, 1979–83. First theatrical film, The Other Side of the Mountain, 1975.

PICTURES INCLUDE: Defiance, On the Nickel, The Long Riders, The Border, Tex, 48 Hrs., Class, Uncommon Valor, Footloose, Red Dawn, Volunteers, Summer Rental, Brewster's Millions, Cobra, Adventures in Babysitting, The Great Outdoors.

TELEVISION: Captains and the Kings (Emmy, 1977), Tail Gunner Joe, Huey P. Long, Revenge of the Stepford Wives, Baby Comes Homes.

WAITS, TOM: Singer, Composer, Actor. Recorded numerous albums and received Acad. Award nom. for his song score of One from the Heart. Composed songs for On the Nickel, Streetwise, Paradise Alley, Wolfen. Has also starred in Chicago's Steppenwolf Theatre Co.'s Frank's Wild Years for which he co-wrote the music.
PICTURES: As actor: Paradise Alley (1978), Poetry in Motion, Wolfen, The Outsiders, Rumble Fish, The Cotton Club, Down by Law (also music), Ironweed, Big Time (also co-s.p., performer), Cold Feet.

WAJDA, ANDRZEJ: Director, Writer. b. Suwalki, Poland, March 6, 1927. e. Fine Arts Academy, Krakow, Poland, 1945–48; High School of Cinematography, Lodz, Poland, 1950–52. 1940–43, worked as asst. in restoration of church paintings. 1942, joined Polish gov. in exile's A.K. (Home Army Resistance) against German occupation. 1950–52, directed shorts (While You Sleep; The Bad Boy, The Pottery of Ilzecka) as part of film school degree; 1954, asst. dir. to Aleksander Ford on 5 Boys from Barska Street. Work flourished under easing of political restraints in Poland during late 1950s. 1981, concentrated on theatrical projects in Poland and film prods. with non-Polish studios. 1983, gov. dissolved his Studio X film prod. group. 1984, gov. demanded Wajda's resignation as head of filmmakers' assoc. in order to continue org.'s existence.
PICTURES: Dir.-Writer: A Generation (debut, 1957); I Walk to the Sun; Kanal; Ashes and Diamonds; Lotna; Innocent Sorcerers; Samson; Lady Macbeth of Mtsensk; Warszawa (episode of Love at 20); Ashes; Gates to Paradise; Everything for Sale; Landscape After the Battle; The Wedding; Promised Land; The Shadow Line; Man of Marble; Without Anesthetic; Invitation to the Inside; The Orchestra Conductor; The Girls from Wilko; Man of Iron (Golden Palm Award, Cannes, 1981); Danton; A Love in Germany; The Possessed, Land of Promise.
TELEVISION: Poly-Poly; The Birch Wood; Pilate and the Others; The Dead Class; November Night.

WALD, MALVIN: Writer, Producer. b. New York, NY, Aug. 8. e. Brooklyn Coll., B.A., J.D. Woodland U. Coll. of Law; graduate work Columbia U., New York U., U. of Southern California. Newspaper reporter and editor, publicist, social worker, radio actor. Screenplays and original stories for Columbia, 20th-Fox, UA, MGM, WB; U.S. Air Force; tech. sgt., wrote 30 documentary films for film unit. Exec. prod., 20th Century Fox TV Documentary Unit, 1963–64 writer-prod. U.S.I.A., 1964–65; writer-prod., Ivan Tors Films, 1965–69; prof., U. of Southern California Sch. of Cinema, Television, 1983–85 bd. of dir.; Writer's Guild of America; 1986–88, Trustee, Writers Guild Foundation; Acad. of Motion Picture Arts and Sciences, co-author of book, Three Major Screenplays. Contributor to books, American Screenwriters, Close-Ups. Published s.p., Naked City. Consultant, Natl. Endowment for Humanities and Corp. for Public Broadcasting. Visiting professor, Southern Illinois Univ. Pre-selection judge, Focus writing awards. Media & prod. consultant, Apache Mountain Spirit (PBS); actor-playwright, Group Repertory Theatre, ANTA-West. Co-author, L.A. Press Club 40th Anniversary Show, 1987. Dramatists Guild.
PICTURES INCLUDE: The Naked City (Acad. Award nomination, best story); Behind Locked Doors, The Dark Past, Ten Gentlemen from West Point, The Powers Girl, Two in a Taxi, Undercover Man, Outrage, On the Loose; (assoc. producer and sec.-treas., Filmakers Pictures, Inc.); Battle Taxi, Man on Fire, Al Capone, Venus in Furs. In Search of Historic Jesus. Legend of Sleepy Hollow. Shorts: An Answer, Employees Only (Academy Award nomin., best sht. doc.), Boy Who Owned a Melephant (Venice Children's Film Festival gold medal), Unarmed in Africa, The Policeman, James Weldon Johnson, Me an Alcoholic?. Problem Solving, Managerial Control.
TELEVISION: Many credits including Playhouse 90, Marilyn Monroe, Hollywood: The Golden Years, The Rafer Johnson Story, D-Day, Project: Man in Space, Tales of Hans Christian Andersen, John F. Kennedy, Biography of A Rookie, Alcoa-Goodyear Hour, Climax, Shirley Temple Storybook, Life of Riley, Peter Gunn, Perry Mason, Dobie Gillis, Combat, Moonport (U.S.I.A.; prod., writer), Daktari, (associate prod.) Primus, California Tomorrow, prod. Mod Squad, Untamed World, Around the World of Mike Todd, The Billie Jean King Show, Life and Times of Grizzly Adams, Mark Twain's America, Greatest Heroes of the Bible, Littlest Hobo. Rich Little's You Asked For It, Hugh Hefner's Bunny Memories.

WALD, RICHARD C.: Executive. b. New York, NY, 1931. e. Columbia Coll., Clare Coll. (Cambridge). Joined the New York Herald Tribune in 1951 as Columbia Coll. correspondent; religion editor, political reporter; foreign correspondent (London, Bonn), 1959–63; associate editor, 1963–65; managing editor from 1965 until paper ceased publication in 1966; Sunday editor, World Journal Tribune, 1966; managing editor, Washington Post, 1967; vice president, Whitney Communications Corp., 1967–68; joined National Broadcasting Company

as vice president, NBC News, 1968; exec. v.p., 1972; president, NBC News, 1973; sr. v.p., ABC News, 1978.

WALDMAN, WALTER: Publicist. b. New York, NY. e. City Coll. of New York, Columbia U. Newspaper reporter; magazine writer; radio-television-film critic; radio news writer, Current Events, Triangle Publications; The Bronx Home News; Grolier Society; Netherlands Information Bureau, station WLIB; freelance New York Times and New York Herald Tribune; writer, press book dept., 20th Century-Fox; copy writer, advertising dept., Republic Pictures; writer, Variety, Box Office Magazine; publicity writer, copy chief, publicity dept., Paramount Pictures; publicity copy chief, contact, MGM/United Artists Entertainment Co.

WALKEN, CHRISTOPHER: Actor. b. Astoria, NY, Mar. 31, 1943. Began career in off-Bdwy. musical, Best Foot Forward, starring Liza Minnelli. Continued in musicals until cast in original Bdwy. production of The Lion in Winter, winning Clarence Derwent Award for performance as King Philip. Switched to dramatic roles, winning Obie Award for title role in Kid Champion and Theater World Award for performance in N.Y. City Center revival of Rose Tattoo. 1984 Bdwy. appearance, Hurlyburly, N.Y.
PICTURES INCLUDE: The Anderson Tapes (debut), Next Stop, Greenwich Village, Roseland, Santa Fe–1936, The Sentinel, Annie Hall, The Deer Hunter, Heaven's Gate, The Dogs of War, Pennies from Heaven, Brainstorm, The War Zone, A View to a Kill, At Close Range, Biloxi Blues, Deadline, The Milagro Beanfield War, Puss n' Boots, Slaves of New York, Homeboy, Communion, Atuk, In From the Cold.

WALKER, CLINT: Actor. b. Hartford, IL, May 30, 1927. e. schools there. Joined Merchant Marine 1944, worked as sheet metal worker, carpenter, other jobs in Alton, IL; set out with wife and infant daughter for oil fields in TX; decided to try acting. Got screen test at Paramount Studios for Cecil B. De Mille; later landed contract to star in Cheyenne TV films at Warner.
PICTURES INCLUDE: Fort Dobbs, Yellowstone Kelly, None But the Brave, Pancho Villa, Maya, Night of the Grizzly, Gold of the Seven Saints, Send Me No Flowers, The Dirty Dozen, The Great Bank Robbery, Sam Whisky, More Dead Than Alive, The Legend of Grizzly Adams.
TELEVISION: Cheyenne (series), Hardcase, Killdozer, Bounty Man, Centennial, Scream of the Wolf, Yuma.

WALKER, E. CARDON: Executive. b. Rexburg, ID, Jan. 9, 1916. e. U. of California at L.A., B.A. 1938. Four years officer, U.S. Navy, Started with Walt Disney Productions 1938; camera, story, unit director short subjects, budget control. Headed, 1950, adv. & pub. 1956, v.p. in chg. of adv. & sales. 1960 member bd. of dir. & exec. comm. 1965 v.p., mkt. 1967 exec. v.p. operations 1968, exec. v.p. and chief operating officer; pres., 1971; Nov. 1976 pres. and chief executive officer; June, 1980, named bd. chm. & chief executive officer; May, 1983, became chm. of exec. committee, which position he retained until Sept. 1984. Remains a board member.

WALKER, KATHRYN: Actress. b. Philadelphia, PA, Jan. 9. m. singer-songwriter James Taylor. e. Wells Coll., Harvard. Studied acting at London Acad. of Music and Dramatic Art on Fulbright Fellowship. Stage roles include part in Private Lives with Elizabeth Taylor and Richard Burton, and Wild Honey with Ian McKellen.
PICTURES: Rich Kids, Slap Shot, Neighbors, D.A.R.Y.L., Dangerous Game.
TELEVISION: Series: Beacon Hill; Movies: Family Reunion, FDR: The Final Years, Special Bulletin, O Youth and Beauty, The Adams Chronicles (Emmy, 1978), The Murder of Mary Phagan.

WALKER, NANCY: Actress, Director. r.n. Anna Swoyer Barto. b. Philadelphia, PA, May 10, 1922. m. singer, vocal teacher David Craig. e. Bentley Sch., and Professional Children's Sch. As child toured Europe with her parents, The Barto and Mann vaudeville team. Pursued career as serious vocalist until George Abbott steered her toward comedy when she auditioned for Broadway prod., Best Foot Forward at 19 in 1941. Directed film, Can't Stop the Music, 1980.
STAGE: On the Town, Barefoot, Boy with Cheek, Look, Ma, I'm Dancin', Along Fifth Avenue Revue, A Month of Sundays, Phoenix '55 Revue, Fallen Angels, Copper and Brass, Pal Joey, Wonderful Town, Girls Against the Boys, Lucky Me, Do Re Mi, The Cherry Orchard, The Cocktail Party (both with APA Phoenix), A Funny Thing Happened on the Way to the Forum (Ahmanson, L.A.), Sondheim: A Musical Tribute.
PICTURES INCLUDE: Best Foot Forward, Girl Crazy, Broadway Rhythm, Meet the People, Stand Up and Be Counted, The World's Greatest Athlete, Forty Carats, Won Ton Ton, Murder by Death.
TELEVISION: Nearly every major TV show, plus series: Family Affair, McMillan & Wife, Rhoda, The Nancy Walker Show, Blansky's Beauties.

WALLACE, IRVING: Writer. b. Chicago, IL, March 19, 1916. e. Williams Inst., Berkeley, CA, 1935–36. For. correspondent in

Japan & China, Liberty Mag., 1940; U.S. Army doing m.p. & photog.; covered France, Germany, Spain for Sat. Evening Post, Collier's, Reader's Digest, 1946, 1947, 1949, 1953.
AUTHOR: The Fabulous Originals, 1955; The Square Pegs; The Sins of Philip Fleming; The Fabulous Showman; The Chapman Report; The Twenty-Seventh Wife; The Prize; The Three Sirens; The Man; The Sunday Gentleman; The Plot; The Writing of One Novel; The Seven Minutes; The Nympho and Other Maniacs; The Word; The Fan Club; The People's Almanac; The R Document; The Book of Lists; The Tow; The Pigeon Project; The Second Lady; The Almighty, Significa; The Miracle; The Seventh Secret; The Celestial Bed; The Golden Room; The Guest of Honor.
PICTURES INCLUDE: story, collab. s.p., West Point Story; s.p., Meet Me at the Fair; collab. s.p. Desert Legion, Gun Fury; collab. story and s.p., Split Second; s.p., The Burning Hills, Bombers B-52; novel (basis for film), The Chapman Report, The Prize, The Seven Minutes, The Man; The Word.

WALLACE, JEAN: Actress. b. Chicago, IL, Oct. 12, 1930. As teenager signed by Paramount as contract player and studied at Actors Laboratory (method school) in Hollywood. Later, switched to 20th Century-Fox. In 1951 went to Argentina to star in first film, Native Son. Board of Directors Permanent Charities Committee and (Womens Auxiliary), Antans (The Womens Auxiliary of the American National Theater and Academy); hospitality chm., Beverly Hills P.T.A. Member, So. Calif. Motion Picture Council and recipient of its Bronze Halo Award of Special Merit. Mbr., L.A.D.I.E.S; bd. of dir. of Screen Smart Set.
PICTURES INCLUDE: Storm Fear, The Big Combo, The Man on the Eiffel Tower, The Devil's Hairpin, Maracaibo, The Sword of Lancelot, Beach Red, No Blade of Grass.

WALLACE, MIKE: TV Commentator, Interviewer. b. Brookline, MA, May 9, 1918. e. U. of Michigan, 1939. Night Beat, WABD, N.Y., 1956; The Mike Wallace Interview, ABC, 1956–58; Newspaper col.; Mike Wallace Asks, N.Y. Post, 1957–58; News Beat, WNTA-TV, 1959–61; The Mike Wallace Interview, WNTA-TV, 1959–61; Biography, 1962; correspondent, CBS News, 1963, CBS Radio; Personal Closeup, Mike Wallace at Large; Co-editor, 60 Minutes, CBS News.

WALLACH, ELI: Actor. b. Brooklyn, NY, Dec. 7, 1915. e. U. of Texas. Capt. in Medical Admin. Corps during W.W.II. After college acting, appeared in summer stock. Made Broadway debut in Skydrift, 1945, followed by Antony & Cleopatra, The Rose Tattoo, Major Barbara, Rhinoceros, Luv, Twice Around the Park, Cafe Crown. Charter member, Actors Studio in 1947.
PICTURES INCLUDE: Baby Doll (debut, 1957), The Magnificent Seven, Seven Thieves, The Misfits, The Victors, Hemingway's Adventures of A Young Man, How the West Was Won, Act One, Genghis Khan, The Moonspinners, Lord Jim, How to Steal a Million, The Good, the Bad and the Ugly, The Tiger Makes Out, Band of Gold, How to Save a Marriage and Ruin Your Life, A Lovely Way to Die, Ace High, The Brain, Zigzag, The People Next Door, Romance of a Horse Thief, Cinderella Liberty, Crazy Joe, Movie Movie, The Hunter, Sam's Son, Tough Guys, Nuts.
TELEVISION: Studio One, Philco Playhouse, Playhouse 90, A Poppy Is Also a Flower (Emmy Award). Movies: Anatomy of an Illness, Murder: By Reason of Insanity, Something in Common, Executioner's Song, Christopher Columbus, Embassy, The Impossible Spy.

WALLACH, GEORGE: Producer, Writer, Director. b. New York, NY, Sept. 25, 1918. e. New York U. Actor in theatre & radio 1938–45; U.S. Navy 1942–45; supvr. radio-TV Div. of Amer. Thea. Wing 1946–48; dir., WNEW, 1947–48; prod./div., Wendy Barrie Show, 1948–49; prod.-dir. for WNBC-WNBT, 1950; Dir., news, spec. events WNBT-WNBC, 1951–52; prod. mgr., NBC Film Div. since 1953; CBS-TV; formed George Wallach Prod., 1956; prod. dir. It Happened in Havana, appt. TV officer, U.S.I.A., 1957. Film-TV officer American Embassy, Bonn, Germany, 1961. Film-TV officer American Embassy; Tehran, Iran, 1965–66; m.p. Prod. Officer, JUSPAO, American Embassy, Saigon, 1966; prod.-dir-wr., Greece Today, 1967–68. Exec. prod.-dir., George Wallach Productions, spec. doc., travel, and industrial films, chairman, Film-TV Dept., N.Y. Institute of Photography, 1968–75; Prof. film-TV-radio, Brooklyn Coll., 1975–80; presently international film consultant, China and Soviet Union.
PICTURES INCLUDE: NBC-producer: Inner Sanctum, The Falcon, His Honor Homer Bell, Watch the World; assoc. prod., prod. mgr. Bwana Devil; dir., Wanted, CBS-TV series.

WALSH, M. EMMET: Actor. b. 1935.
PICTURES INCLUDE: Midnight Cowboy, Stiletto, Alice's Restaurant, End of the Road, The Traveling Executioner, Little Big Man, Cold Turkey, Loving, The Jerk, Straight Time, Back Roads, Reds, Fast-Walking, The Escape Artist, Blade Runner, Silkwood, Blood Simple, The Pope of Greenwich Village, Missing in Action, The Best of Times, Wildcats, Critters, Raisin' Arizona, Red Scorpion, No Man's Land, The Milagro Bean-

field War, Sunset, Finding Maubee, War Party, Clean and Sober.
TELEVISION: Series: The Sandy Duncan Show (1972), Dear Detective. Movies: East of Eden, High Noon Part II, Hellinger's Law, Night Partners, You Are the Jury, The Deliberate Stranger, Resting Place, Broken Vows, Murder Ordained.

WALSH, RICHARD F.: President Emeritus International Alliance Theatrical Stage Employees and M.P. Machine Operators. b. Brooklyn, NY, 1900. In 1917 became apprentice stage electrician; 1920 full member Local 4, Brooklyn stagehand union IATSE & MPMO. Stage electrician various theatres. In 1924 elected pres. Local 4. 1926 business agent: 1934 int'l vice-pres. IATSE & MPMO; Nov., 1941 named pres. by exec. board; elected pres. by convention June, 1942; re-elected International pres. by convention thereafter; v.p., AFL-CIO, 1956; ch. of bd., Will Rogers Hospital; pres., Union Label Dept, retired as IATSE president in 1974.

WALSTON, RAY: Actor, Director. b. New Orleans, LA, Nov. 2, 1918. Dir. of Bdwy. musical, Damn Yankees, 1974.
TELEVISION: You Are There, Producers Showcase, There Shall Be No Night, Studio One, Playhouse 90, My Favorite Martian (series), Oh Madeline (series), Fast Times at Ridgemont High (series), Crash Course, Amos, Red River, Grandpa and I.
PICTURES INCLUDE: South Pacific, Damn Yankees, Kiss Them For Me, Say One for Me, The Tall Story, The Apartment, Portrait In Black, Convicts Four, Wives and Lovers, Who's Minding the Store, Kiss Me Stupid, Caprice, Paint Your Wagon, The Sting, Popeye, Fast Times at Ridgemont High, Johnny Dangerously, RAD, From the Hip, O.C. and the Stiggs, A Man of Passion, Blood Relations.

WALTER, JESSICA: Actress. b. Brooklyn, NY, Jan. 31, 1940. m. actor Ron Leibman. e. H.S. of the Performing Arts. Studied at Bucks County Playhouse and Neighborhood Playhouse. Many TV performances plus lead in series, For the People. Broadway debut in Advise and Consent, 1961. Also, Photo Finish (Clarence Derwent Award), Night Life, A Severed Head.
PICTURES INCLUDE: Lilith, The Group, Grand Prix, Bye Bye Braverman, Number One, Play Misty For Me, Going Ape, The Flamingo Kid, Tapeheads.
TELEVISION: Love of Life, Ironside, Amy Prentiss (Emmy, 1975), All That Glitters, Wheels, Bare Essence, Secret of Three Hungry Wives, She's Dressed to Kill, Scruples, The Execution, Aaron's Way.

WALTERS, BARBARA: TV Personality. b. Boston, MA, Sept. 25, 1931. m. Merv Adelson, executive. e. Sarah Lawrence Coll. Began working in TV right after graduation. Joined The Today Show in 1961 as writer, making occasional on-camera appearances. In 1963 became full-time on camera. In April, 1974, named permanent co-host. Also hosted own synd. prog., Not for Women Only. In 1976 joined ABC-TV Evening News; 20/20.

WALTERS, JULIE: Actress. b. Birmingham, England, 1950. Trained for 2 years to be a nurse before studying drama at Manchester Polytechnic, followed by year at Granada's Stables Theatre. Joined Everyman Theatre, Liverpool. Also toured Dockland pubs with songs, dance and imitations.
THEATER: Breezeblock Park, Funny Perculiar, The Glad Hand, Talent (written by Victoria Wood, with whom she began comedy partnership), Good Fun, Educating Rita (1980), Macbeth, Having a Ball.
PICTURES: Educating Rita, She'll Be Wearing Pink Pyjamas, Car Trouble, Personal Services, Prick Up Your Ears, Buster, The Threepenny Opera.
TELEVISION: Unfair Exchanges, Talent, Nearly a Happy Ending, Family Man, Happy Since I Met You, The Secret Diaries of Adrian Mole (series); Wood and Walters (series); Me—I'm Afraid of Virginia Woolf, Say Something Happened, Intensive Care, The Boys from the Black Stuff, Monologues, Victoria Wood as Seen on TV (series), The Birthday Party.

WALTON, FREDERICK R.: Director.
PICTURES: When a Stranger Calls; April Fool's Day.
TELEVISION: I Saw What You Did.

WANAMAKER, SAM: Actor, Stage producer, Film director. b. Chicago, IL, June 14, 1919. e. Drake U. On Broadway stage as actor, producer, presenter.
THEATER: London West End stage: Winter Journey, The Big Knife, The Threepenny Opera, The Rainmaker; 1956, acting, producing London and Liverpool stage; 1959–60, acting at Stratford-on-Avon; 1961–62, acting on New York stage in The Far Country; prod. dir. Children From Their Games, (N.Y.); Rhinoceros (Washington, D.C.). Opera prods.: King Priam, Forza Del Destino; A Case of Libel (dir.), Founder and exec. dir.: Globe Playhouse Trust. Dir. Sydney Opera House Opening, Bankside Festival (prod.), U.S. tour, Shakespeare's Globe, Aida, San Francisco Opera.

PICTURES: My Girl Tisa, Give Us This Day, Mr. Denning Drives North, The Secret, The Criminal, Taras Bulba, Man in the Middle, Those Magnificent Men in Their Flying Machines, The Spy Who Came in from the Cold, The Warning Shot, The Day the Fish Came Out, Voyage of the Damned; The Executioner (dir.), The Eliminator, The Chinese Visitor; Cat-low; Sinbad and the Eye of the Tiger; Private Benjamin, The Competition, The Aviator, Irreconcilable Differences, Raw Deal, Superman IV, Baby Boom, Judgement in Berlin, Secret Ingredient.
TELEVISION: The Big Wheel, The White Death, A Young Lady of Property (dir.), The Defenders, Oedipus Rex, Russian Self Impressions. Man of World (series), Espionage, Outer Limits. Dir. several episodes The Defenders series, Arturo Ui, War and Peace, The Ferret, Heartsounds, The Berrengers, The Ghost Writer, Sadie and Son, Deceptions, The Law, Baby Boom (series).

WANG, WAYNE: Director. b. Hong Kong, 1949. e. came to U.S. to study photography at College of Arts and Crafts, Oakland, CA. With a Master's Degree in film and television, returned to Hong Kong. Worked on TV comedy series. First dir. work, as asst. dir. for Chinese sequences of Golden Needle. First film A Man, A Woman and a Killer (award-winning short). Won grant from AFI and National Endowment of the Arts which was used to finance Chan is Missing (1982) which cost $22,000.
PICTURES: Chan is Missing (dir., s.p., editor, prod.), Dim Sum: A Little Big of Heart, Slam Dance, Eat a Bowl of Tea.

WARBURTON, JOHN: Actor. b. Liverpool, Eng., e. Oxford U. With British Army, W.W.I; then on stage Liverpool Repertory Theatre. To U.S. 1920.
STAGE: Journey's End, Bird In the Hand, Dishonorable Lady.
PICTURES INCLUDE: on screen 1933 in Cavalcade. Also: Chi Ci, Becky Sharp, Sisters, Saratoga Trunk, The White Cliffs, Marriage Is a Private Affair, Confidential Agent, Living in a Big Way, City Beneath the Sea, East of Sumatra, Royal African Rifles.

WARD, BURT: Actor, Executive. b. Los Angeles, CA, July 6, 1945. Pres. of Pinnacle Associates, Inc. and the World of Earlybird, a publicly traded holding co. and a children's social value education program, respectively.
TELEVISION: Batman (co-starred as Robin 1966–68).

WARD, DAVID S.: Writer, Director. b. Providence, RI, Oct. 24, 1945. e. U. of Southern California where attended film school. First script was Steelyard Blues produced at Warner Bros. in 1972 by producers Michael and Julia Phillips.
PICTURES: The Sting (Acad. Award, best orig. s.p.); Cannery Row (s.p., dir.); The Sting II (s.p.), The Milagro Beanfield War (co-s.p.), Major League.

WARD, FRED: Actor. b. San Diego, CA, 1943. Studied at Berghof Studio. On stage In The Glass Menagerie, One Flew over the Cuckoo's Nest.
PICTURES: No Available Witness, Tilt, Escape from Al-catraz, Southern Comfort, Timerider, The Right Stuff, Silk-wood, Uncommon Valor, Swing Shift, Uforia, Secret Admirer, Remo Williams: The Adventure Begins, Saigon, Train of Dreams, Off Limits, Big Business, The Prince of Pennsylva-nia, Backtrack, Miami Blues.
TELEVISION: Florida Straits, Belle Starr.

WARD, RACHEL: Actress. b. London, 1957. m. actor Bryan Brown. Top model before becoming actress. Studied acting with Stella Adler and Robert Modica; numerous commercials on TV.
PICTURES: Night School, Three Blind Mice, Sharky's Machine, Dead Men Don't Wear Plaid, Against All Odds, The Final Terror, The Good Wife, Hotel Colonial, How to Get Ahead in Advertising.
TELEVISION: The Thorn Birds, Fortress.

WARD, SARAH E.: Executive. b. Warrenton, VA, April 5, 1920. 1949–1962, office clerical positions with RKO, 20th Century-Fox, Todd AO Corp; v.p. sales mgr. for Europix Consolidated Corp., 1968; v.p.—sec'y for Europix International Ltd., 1971.

WARD, SIMON: Actor. b. Beckenham, England, Oct. 19, 1941. Ent. ind. 1964.
PICTURES: If, Frankenstein Must Be Destroyed, I Start Counting, Young Winston, Hitler—The Last Ten Days, The Three Musketeers, The Four Musketeers, Children of Rage, Deadly Strangers. All Creatures Great & Small, Aces High, The Battle Flag, Holocaust 2000, Zulu Dawn, Supergirl.
TELEVISION: Spoiled, Chips with Everything, The Corsi-can Brothers, Dracula, The Last Giraffe, Around the World in 80 Days.

WARDEN, JACK: Actor. b. Newark, NJ, Sept. 18, 1920. With Margo Jones theatre in Dallas.
TELEVISION: Philco Goodyear Producer's Showcase, Kraft. Movies: Raid on Entebbe, Robert Kennedy and His

Times, Hobson's Choice, A. D., Crazy Like a Fox (series), Hoover vs. The Kennedys, The Three Kings.
THEATRE: View from the Bridge, Very Special Baby.
PICTURES INCLUDE: From Here to Eternity, 12 Angry Men, Edge of the City, Bachelor Party, Escape from Zahrain, The Thin Red Line, Summertree, Who Is Harry Kellerman?, The Sporting Club, Welcome to the Club, Billy Two Hats, The Apprenticeship of Duddy Kravitz, Shampoo, All the Presi-dent's Men, Heaven Can Wait, Death on the Nile, And Justice for All, Being There, The Great Muppet Caper, Carbon Copy, So Fine, The Verdict, Crackers, The Aviator, September, The Presidio.

WARNER, DAVID: Actor. b. Manchester, England, July 29, 1941. e. Royal Acad. of Dramatic Art. Made London stage debut in Tony Richardson's version of A Midsummer Night's Dream (1962). Four seasons with Royal Shakespeare Co. Theater includes Afore Night Come, The Tempest, The Wars of the Roses, The Government Inspector, Twelfth Night, I, Claudius.
PICTURES INCLUDE: Tom Jones, Morgan, Work Is a Four Letter Word, The Bofors Gun, The Fixer, The Seagull, Michael Kohlhaas, The Ballard of Cable Hogue, Perfect Friday, Straw Dogs, A Doll's House, Tales from the Crypt, Providence, Cross of Iron, The Omen, Silver Bears. The 39 steps (remake), The Concorde—Airport '79, Time After Time, The Island, Time Bandits, Tron, The Man With Two Brains, The Company of Wolves, Hansel and Gretel, Hanna's War, Mr. North, My Best Friend is a Vampire, Waxwork, Silent Night, Office Party, Pulse Pounders, Keys to Freedom.
TELEVISION: Desperado, A Christmas Carol, Hitler's SS—Portrait in Evil, Holocaust, Marco Polo, Masada (Emmy, supp., 1981), SOS Titanic, Love's Labour's Lost.

WARNER, JACK JR.: Producer. b. San Francisco, CA, Mar. 27, 1916. p. Jack L. Warner, and Mrs. Albert S. Rogell. e. Beverly Hills H.S.; U. of Southern California, B.A. Entered Warner New York office studying distrib. and exhib. for 1½ years. Transferred to prod. dept. at West Coast studios, then to short subject dept. as assoc. prod. As reserve officer called to active duty in 1942 and served as combat photo unit officer in 164th Signal Photo Co. for one year. Transf. to Signal Corps Photographic Center, Astoria, NY, where participated in prod. Army Signal Corps training films. Was asst. to chief of training films prod. In 1944 assigned to Hq. First U.S. Army Group to assist in planning combat photography for invasion of Europe. Until cessation of hostilities was asst. chief Photo Branch Office of Chief Signal Officer in 12th Army Group and on fall of Germany was on staff of General Eisenhower in Frankfurt as asst. and acting photo officer, Office of the Chief Signal Officer, Theatre Service Forces European Theatre (TSFET). Released from active duty April 20, 1945. Commis-sioned Lt. Col. Signal Corps Reserve. In 1947 with Warner Bros. Pictures Distrib. Corp., making survey of exhib. and distrib. as related to prod.; liaison between Warner and Assoc. Brit. Pictures on The Hasty Heart, 1948–49; org. Jack M. Warner Prod., Inc., 1949; first film, The Man Who Cheated Himself, distrib. by 20th Cent.-Fox; prod. dept., Warner Bros., 1951; prod. exec. Warners 1953. In charge of TV film prod. for Warners 1955; exec. in charge of television comm. and ind. film dept., Warner Bros. 1956; v.p., Warner Bros. Pictures, Inc., Jan. 1958; Warner association terminated Jan. 1959. Reactivated independent motion picture company Jack M. Warner Prod. Future activities production of feature television and industrial films; pres., Jack Warner Prods., Inc., prod. theatrical films, 1961; prod., dir., Brushfire; Commissioned Colonel, Signal Corps. U.S. Army Reserve, 1962; 1977–78: Producer, TV series & films for theatrical and TV, Jack Warner Pdns; writer, 1979–81. Author: Bijou Dream (novel, 1982).1983-87: writer, projected TV series and theatrical films. Completing novel and screenplay.

WARNER, MALCOLM-JAMAL: Actor. b. Jersey City, NJ, Aug. 18, 1970. Raised in Los Angeles. Was 13 years old when signed to play Bill Cosby's son on The Cosby Show.
THEATER: Three Ways Home (off-Bdwy debut, 1988).
TELEVISION: The Cosby Show (series, since 1984); Movie: The Father Clements Story.

WARREN, CHARLES MARQUIS: Director, Producer, Writer. b. Baltimore, MD, Dec. 16, 1917. e. McDonogh Sch. (MD), Baltimore City Coll. Commander U.S. Navy, W.W.II; then to Hollywood. Writer for screen, magazines; author of books.
BOOKS INCLUDE: Only the Valiant, Valley of the Shadow, Wilderness, Deadhead, History of American Dental Surgery.
PICTURES INCLUDE: Only the Valiant, Beyond Glory, Redhead and the Cowboy, Streets of Laredo, Springfield Rifle, Day of the Evil Gun, Little Big Horn, Hellgate, Pony Express, Arrowhead, Flight to Tangier, 7 Angry Men, Trooper Hook, Tension at Table Rock, Cattle Empire, Charro!, Down to the Sea, Time of the Furies, Copper Sky, Ride a Violent Mile, Blood Arrow, The Unknown Terror, The Hunter, The Final Day, The Head of the Serpent.
TELEVISION: Creator of Gunsmoke, Rawhide, Gunslinger, and the Virginian, series as well as prod.-dir.-writer. Exec. prod. on Iron Horse series.

WARREN, GENE: Executive. b. Denver, CO, Aug. 12, 1916. Pres. of Excelsior Prods., production co. specializing in special effects and animation. Has headed 2 other cos. of similar nature over past 20 years, functioning at various times as prod., dir., studio prod. head and writer. Producer-director of following shorts: The Tool Box, Suzy Snowflake, Santa and the Three Dwarfs, Land of the Midnight Sun and these documentaries/training films: Mariner I, Mariner III, Apollo, U.S. Navy titles.
Special effects on theatrical features including. Black Sunday, McNamara's Band, Satan's School for Girls, My Name Is John, The Power, 7 Faces of Dr. Lao, Wonderful World of the Brothers Grimm, The Time Machine, Tom Thumb, etc. TV series include The Man from Atlantis, Land of the Lost, Star Trek, Outer Limits, Twilight Zone, Mission Impossible, etc.

WARREN, JENNIFER: Actress, Producer. b. New York, NY, Aug. 12, 1941. e. U. of Wisconsin, Madison, B.A. Grad work at Wesleyan U. Studied acting with Uta Hagen at HB Studios. As part of AFI Women's Directing Workshop, directed Point of Departure, short film which received Cine Golden Eagle Award at Aspen Film Festival. Formed Tiger Rose Productions, independent film-TV prod. co., 1988.
THEATER: Scuba Duba (off-Bdwy. debut, 1987); 6 RMS RIV VU; Harvey; P.S., Your Cat Is Dead; Saint Joan; Volpone; Henry V (Guthrie Theatre).
PICTURES: Night Moves (debut, 1975); Slapshot; Another Man, Another Chance; Ice Castles; Fatal Beauty.
TELEVISION: Kojak (1975) Series: The Smothers Brothers Comedy Hour (1967–69); Paper Dolls. Movies: Shark Kill; Steel Cowboy; First, You Cry; Champions: A Love Story; Angel City; Freedom; The Choice; The Intruder Within; Confessions of a Married Man; Celebrity; Amazons, Gambler.

WARREN, LESLEY ANN: Actress. b. New York, NY, Aug. 16, 1946. Studied acting under Lee Strasberg. Big break came in Rodgers and Hammerstein's Cinderella on TV, where seen by Disney scout. Broadway debut in 110 in the Shade (1963). Film debut in The Happiest Millionaire (1967).
PICTURES: Race to the Yankee Zephyr, Victor/Victoria (Acad. Award nom.), A Night in Heaven, Songwriter, Choose Me, Clue, Burglar, Blood on the Moon, Cop, Worth Winning.
TELEVISION: Series: Mission: Impossible (1970–71), Miniseries: Beulah Land, Pearl, 79 Park Avenue, Evergreen. Movies: Seven in Darkness, Assignment Munich, Portrait of a Stripper, Betrayal, A Fight for Jenny, Apology, Baja Oklahoma.

WARRICK, RUTH: Actress. b. St. Joseph, MO, June 29, 1916. Film debut in 1941: Citizen Kane.
PICTURES: Obliging Young Lady, The Corsican Brothers, Journey Into Fear, Forever and a Day, Perilous Holiday, Father of the Bride, The Iron Major, Secret Command, Mr. Winkle Goes to War, Guest in the House, China Sky, Song of the South, Driftwood, Daisy Kenyon, Arch of Triumph, The Great Dan Patch, Make Believe Ballroom, Three Husbands, Let's Dance, One Too Many, Roogie's Bump, The Great Bank Robbery, The Returning.
TELEVISION: Studio One, Robert Montgomery Presents, Lux Star Playhouse, Sometimes I Don't Love My Mother, Peyton Place—The Next Generation. Series: Peyton Place, All My Children.

WASHBURN, DERIC: Writer. b. Buffalo, NY. e. Harvard U., English lit. Has written number of plays, including The Love Nest and Ginger Anne.
PICTURES: Silent Running (co-s.p.), The Deer Hunter, The Border.

WASHINGTON, DENZEL: Actor. b. Mt. Vernon, NY, Dec. 28, 1954. e. Fordham U., B.A., journalism. Studied acting with American Conservatory Theatre, San Francisco.
THEATER: When the Chickens Come Home to Roost (Audelco Award); Coriolanus; Spell #7; The Mighty Gents; Ceremonies in Dark Old Men; A Soldier's Play; Checkmates.
PICTURES: Carbon Copy (1981); A Soldier's Story; Power; Cry Freedom; For Queen and Country; Finding Maubee.
TELEVISION: Movies: Wilma; Flesh and Blood; License to Kill. Series: St. Elsewhere (1982–88).

WASSERMAN, DALE: Writer, Producer. b. Rhinelander, WI, Nov. 2, 1917. Stage: lighting designer, dir., prod.; dir. for attractions, S. Hurok; began writing, 1954. Founding member & trustee of O'Neill Theatre Centre; Artistic Director Midwest Playwrights Laboratory; member, Acad. M.P. Arts & Sciences; awards include Emmy, Tony, Critics Circle (Broadway), Outer Circle; Writers Guild, etc.
TELEVISION: The Fog, The Citadel, The Power and the Glory, Engineer of Death, The Lincoln Murder Case, I Don Quixote, Elisha and the Long Knives, and others.
PLAYS: Livin' the Life, 998, One Flew Over the Cuckoo's Nest, The Pencil of God, Man of La Mancha, Play With Fire, Shakespeare and the Indians, Mountain High.

PICTURES INCLUDE: Cleopatra, The Vikings, The Sea and the Shadow, Quick, Before It Melts, Mister Buddwing, A Walk with Love and Death, Man of La Mancha.

WASSERMAN, LEW: Executive. b. Cleveland, OH, March 15, 1913. National dir. advertising and publ. Music Corporation of Amer. 1936–38; v.p. 1938–39; v.p. motion picture div. 1940; Chairman of the bd., Chief Executive Officer, MCA, Inc., Universal City, CA. Received Jean Hersholt Humanitarian Award, 1973.

WASSON, CRAIG: Actor. b. Eugene, OR, March 15, 1954. On stage in Godspell, All God's Chillun Got Wings, Death of a Salesman, The Glass Menagerie. Also musician.
PICTURES: The Boys in Company C (also music), Go Tell the Spartans, The Outsider, Carny, Schizoid, Night at O'Rears, Ghost Story, Second Thoughts, Four Friends, Body Double, The Men's Club, Bum Rap.
TELEVISION: Phyllis, Baa Baa Black Sheep, Serpico, Movies: Skag, Why Me?, Thornwell, The Silence, Mrs. R's Daughter.

WATANABE, GEDDE: Actor. b. Ogden, UT, June 26. Trained for stage at American Conservatory Theatre, San Francisco. Has appeared with N.Y. Shakespeare Festival Shakespeare in the Park series and with Pan Asian Repertory Theatre, N.Y.
THEATER: Pacific Overtures (debut, as Tree Boy, Bdwy. and on tour, 1976); Oedipus the King; Bullet Headed Birds; Poor Little Lambs.
PICTURES: Sixteen Candles (debut, 1984); Volunteers; Gung Ho; Vamp.
TELEVISION: Gung Ho (series).

WATERHOUSE, KEITH: Writer. b. Leeds, England, Feb. 6, 1929. Early career as journalist, novelist. Author of There is a Happy Land, Billy Liar, Jubb, The Bucket Shop. Ent. m.p. ind. 1960.
PICTURES INCLUDE: s.p. (with Willis Hall), Whistle Down The Wind, A Kind of Loving, Billy Liar, Man in the Middle, Pretty Polly, Lock Up Your Daughters, The Valiant, West Eleven.
TELEVISION: (series): Inside George Webley, Queenie's Castle, Budgie, Billy Liar, There is a Happy Land, Charters and Caldicott.

WATERS, JOHN: Director, Writer. b. Baltimore, MD, 1946. Renowned for elevating bad taste to outrageous high comedy. First short film Hag in a Black Leather Jacket (1964) shot in Baltimore, as are most of his films. Other shorts include Roman Candles, and Eat Your Makeup. Feature debut, Mondo Trasho.
PICTURES: Multiple Maniacs (dir., prod., editor, sound; film marked the debut of Waters' star Divine), Pink Flamingos, Desperate Living, Female Trouble, Polyester (filmed in "Odor-ama" complete with scratch and sniff cards), Hairspray (dir., s.p., co-prod.; actor), Cry Baby (dir., s.p.).

WATERSTON, SAM: Actor. b. Cambridge, MA, Nov. 15, 1940. e. Yale U. Spent jr. year at Sorbonne in Paris as part of the Amer. Actors' Workshop run by American dir. John Berry. Broadway debut in Oh Dad, Poor Dad...(1963). Film debut, The Plastic Dome of Norma Jean (1965). TV debut Pound (Camera Three). Has worked in New York Shakespeare Festival prods. since As You Like It (1963).
THEATER: N.Y. Shakespeare Festival: As You Like It, Ergo, Henry IV (Part I & II), Cymbeline, Hamlet, Much Ado About Nothing, The Tempest. Off Bdwy: The Knack, La Turista, Waiting for Godot, The Three Sisters. Broadway: The Paisley Convertible, Halfway Up the Tree, Indian, Hay Fever, The Trial of Cantonsville Nine, A Meeting by the River, Much Ado About Nothing (Drama Desk and Obie Awards), A Doll's House, Lunch Hour, Benefactors, A Walk in the Woods.
PICTURES: Fitzwilly, Three, Generation, Mahoney's Estate, Who Killed Mary What's 'er Name?, Savages, The Great Gatsby, Journey Into Fear, Rancho Deluxe, Dandy, Capricorn One, Eagle's Wing, Sweet William, Coup de Foudre, Interiors, Hopscotch, Heaven's Gate, The Killing Fields, Warning Sign, Hannah and Her Sisters, Just Between Friends, A Certain Desire, The Devil's Paradise, September.
TELEVISION: The Good Lieutenant, Much Ado About Nothing, The Glass Menagerie, Reflections of a Murder, Friendly Fire, Oppenheimer, O.E.D., In Defense of Kids, Games Mother Never Taught You, Dempsey, Finnegan Begin Again, Love Lives On, Steven Spielberg's Amazing Stories, The Fifth Missile, The Room Upstairs, Terrorist on Trial: The United States vs. Salim Ajami, Gore Vidal's Lincoln.

WATKIN, DAVID: Director of Photography. b. Margate, Eng., March 23, 1925. Entered British documentary industry in Jan., 1948. With British Transport Films as asst. cameraman, 1950–55; as cameraman, 1955–61. Feature film debut The Knack beginning long creative relationship with director Richard Lester.
PICTURES: The Knack (1964); Help!; Marat/Sade; How I Won the War; Charge of the Light Brigade; Catch 22; The

Devils; The Boyfriend; The Homecoming; A Delicate Balance; The Three Musketeers; The Four Musketeers; Jesus of Nazareth; Mahogany; To the Devil, a Daughter; Robin and Marian; Joseph Andrews; Cuba; Hanover Street; The Summer; Endless Love; Chariots of Fire; Return to Oz; Yentl; The Hotel New Hampshire; White Nights; Out of Africa (Acad. Award, 1985); Moonstruck; Sky Bandits; The Good Mother.

WATKINS, GRATH: Actor. b. London, Aug. 8, 1922. e. University Coll. Sch. Served in Royal Air Force 1944–45. Entered films in 1945 with role in The Captive Heart.
PICTURES INCLUDE: Bedelia, Gaiety George, A Matter of Life and Death, The Hanging Judge, Goodbye Mr. Chips, Cromwell, The Rise and Fall of Michael Rimmer, Virgin Witch, Fright, Naughty, Twins of Evil, Mary, Queen of Scots, Steptoe and Son, Henry VIII, Cinderella, The Omen.
TELEVISION: People in Conflict (Canada).

WATTLES, JOSHUA S.: Executive. Now sr. atty. for Paramount Pictures, working with Richard Zimbert, sr. v.p. & gen. counsel. Prior to joining para. legal dept. in 1981 was atty. in office of gen. counsel at ASCAP. Member N.Y. and Calif. Bars.

WAX, MO.: Publisher and editor of Film Bulletin. b. Philadelphia, PA. e. Villanova U. Also pres., Audienscope, Inc., Entertainment research organization.

WAX, MORTON DENNIS: Public Relations Executive. b. New York, NY, March 13, 1932. e. Brooklyn Coll., 1952. President of Morton Dennis Wax & Assoc., Inc., public relations and marketing firm servicing intl. creative marketplace, established 1956. Contributing writer to Box Office Magazine, intl. editorial consultant, Film Journal. Recent articles: Creativity (Advertising Age), Rolling Stone's Marketing Through Music, Words & Music, Campaign Magazine, Songwriters Guild of America National Edition. As sect. of VPA, conceptualized intl. Monitor Award, an annual event, currently under auspices of ITS. Public relations counsel to London Intl. Advertising Awards. Member: The Public Relations Society of America, National Acad. of Television Arts & Sciences, National Acad. of Recording Arts & Sciences, Publishers Publicity Assoc., Motion Picture Bookers Club, Friars Club, English Speaking Union.

WAYLAND, LEN: Actor. b. California, Dec. 28. e. Junior Coll., Modesto, CA. Wrote, prod. weekly radio series 1939–41, KPAS, KTRB, Calif. Service, radar navigator, 1941–45; en. theatre, Tobacco Road, 1946; 1973, formed Len Wayland Prods. for production of theatrical pictures and TV series. In 1976–77: produced/directed. Don't Let It Bother You. 1978, pro./dir., You're not there yet, for own company.
THEATRE: Played summer and winter stock 1947–49. B'way, Streetcar Named Desire, 1949, and tour; toured as lead, Heaven Can Wait; My Name Is Legion; toured, Love of Four Colonels, Stalag 17, 1954, A Time to Live (serial), First Love, 1955; Armstrong Circle Theatre, Justice, Sgt. Bilko, Kraft Theatre; Dr. Weaver, From These Roots. Off Broadway prod., USA, 1960; on Broadway, A Man For All Seasons, 1962.
TELEVISION: Profiles in Courage, Dr. Kildare, Gunsmoke, Slattery's People, Ben Casey, A Noise in the World, Love Is a Many Splendored Thing; Dragnet, Outsider; Ironside, Name of the Game, The Bold Ones, Daniel Boone, The Virginian, Project U.F.O., Sam (series), The Blue and the Gray.

WAYNE, DAVID: Actor, r.n. Wayne McKeekan; b. Traverse City, MI, Jan. 30, 1916. e. Western Michigan U., 1936; in marionette shows, 1937.
THEATRE: Finian's Rainbow (Tony Award, 1947), Mister Roberts, Teahouse of the August Moon (Tony Award, 1954).
PICTURES INCLUDE: Portrait of Jennie, Adam's Rib, Reformer and the Redhead, My Blue Heaven, Stella, M, Up Front, As Young As You Feel, With a Song in My Heart, Wait 'Til the Sun Shines, Nellie; Down Among the Sheltering Palms, The I Don't Care Girl, We're Not Married, O. Henry's Full House, Tonight We Sing, How to Marry a Millionaire, Hell and High Water, Tender Trap, The Three Faces of Eve, The Last Angry Man, The Big Gamble, The Andromeda Strain, The African Elephant (narrator), Huckleberry Finn, The Front Page, The Apple Dumpling Gang, Lassie: A New Beginning, House Calls, Finders Keepers.
TELEVISION: Series: Norby (1955), The Adventures of Ellery Queen, Dallas, House Calls. Specials: The Ruggles of Red Gap, The Devil and Daniel Webster, Escape Clause (Twilight Zone), Movies: The FBI vs. Alvin Karpis, Benjamin Franklin, Statesman, Once an Eagle, Gift of Love, Black Beauty, Loose Change, American Christmas Carol.

WAYNE, JOEL: Executive. Began career with Grey Advertising; in 17 years won many awards (60 Clios, 25 N.Y. Art Director Club Awards, etc.). Was exec. v.p. & creative dir. of agency when left in 1979 to join Warner Bros. as v.p., creative adv. 1987, named senior v.p., worldwide creative adv.

WAYNE, MICHAEL A.: Executive. r.n. Michael A. Morrison. b. Los Angeles, CA, Nov. 23, 1934. Son of late actor John Wayne. e.

Loyola H.S.; Loyola U., B.B.A. Asst. dir., various companies, 1955–56; asst. dir., Revue Prods., 1956–57; pres. Batjac Prods, and Romina Prods., 1961; asst. to producer: China Doll, 1957; Escort West; The Alamo; prod., McClintock; co-prod., Cast Giant Shadow; prod. The Green Berets; exec. prod. Chisum; prod. Big Jake; prod. The Train Robbers; prod. Cahill, U.S. Marshall, exec. prod. McQ, Brannigan.

WAYNE, PATRICK: Actor. b. July 15, 1939. Son of late actor John Wayne. Made film debut at age 11 in Rio Grande with father.
PICTURES INCLUDE: The Searchers, The Alamo, The Comancheros, McClintock, The Bears and I, Big Jake, Sinbad and the Eye of the Tiger, The People Time Forgot, Rustler's Rhapsody, Young Guns, Her Alibi.
TELEVISION: Last Hurrah, Sole Survivor, Yesterday's Child, Frank's Place.

WEAKLAND, KEVIN L.: Producer, Entertainer. b. Philadelphia, PA, Aug. 14, 1963. e. Holy Family Coll. 1977–82, entertainment consultant and actor; 1982–present, entertainment producer and financier as well as entertainer (singer-actor). Company: KLW International, Inc.
MEMBER: Association of Independent Video and Filmmakers; National Academy of Video Arts & Sciences; Mid-Atlantic Arts Consortium; National Music Publishers Assn.; New Jersey Associations of Media Artists.

WEAVER, DENNIS: Actor, Director. b. Joplin, MO, June 4, 1925. e. U. of Oklahoma, B.A., fine arts, 1948.
TELEVISION: Series: Chester, in Gunsmoke, 1955–64; title role, Kentucky Jones, 1964–65; Gentle Ben, 1967–69; McCloud, 1970–76; Stone (1979–80); Emerald Point NAS (1983–84); Buck James (1987–88). Movies: The Forgotten Man, Duel, The Rolling Man, The Great Man's Whiskers, Terror on the Beach, Intimate Strangers, Pearl, Centennial; Amber Waves, Dr. Mudd, Cocaine: One Man's Seduction, Go for the Gold. Bluffing It.
PICTURES INCLUDE: Duel at Diablo, Way Way Out, Gentle Giant, A Man Called Sledge, What's the Matter with Helen?, The Gallant Hours, Mission, Batangas.

WEAVER, FRITZ: Actor. b. Pittsburgh, PA, Jan. 19, 1926. e. U. of Chicago. On stage in Chalk Garden, Miss Lonelyhearts, All American, Shot in the Dark, Baker Street, Child's Play (Tony), The Price, etc.
PICTURES: Fail Safe (debut, 1964), The Maltese Bippy, A Walk in the Spring Rain, Demon Seed, Marathon Man, Black Sunday, The Day of the Dolphin, The Guns of August, The Big Fix, Creepshow, Power.
TELEVISION: Movies: The Borgia Stick, Berlin Affair, Heat of Anger, The Snoop Sisters, Hunter, The Legend of Lizzie Borden, Captains Courageous, Holocaust, The Hearst and Davies Affair, A Death in California, I'll Take Manhattan. Mini-Series: Dream West.

WEAVER, SIGOURNEY: Actress. r.n. Susan Weaver. b. New York, NY, Oct. 8, 1949. e. Stanford U., Yale U. Daughter of Sylvester "Pat" Weaver, former NBC pres. Mother, actress Elizabeth Inglis (one-time contract player for Warner Bros.). After college formed working partnership with fellow student Christopher Durang for off-Bdwy. improvisational productions. First professional appearance on stage in 1974 in The Constant Wife with Ingrid Bergman.
THEATER: Off-Bdwy: Titanic, Das Lusitania Songspiel; Gemini (by Yale class mate Albert Innaurato), Marco Polo Sings a Solo, Beyond Therapy, Hurlyburly (Broadway).
PICTURES: Alien (debut, 1979), Eyewitness, The Year of Living Dangerously, Deal of the Century, Ghostbusters, One Woman or Two, Aliens, Half Moon Street, Gorillas in the Mist, Working Girl.
TELEVISION: The Best of Families, Somerset, The Sorrows of Gin.

WEAVER, SYLVESTER L., JR.: Executive. b. Los Angeles, CA, Dec. 21, 1908. e. Dartmouth Coll. CBS, Don Lee Network, 1932–35; Young & Rubicam adv. agency, 1935–38; adv. mgr., American Tobacco Co., 1938–47; v.p. Young & Rubicam, 1947–49; joined NBC as v.p., chg. TV, 1949; appt'd v.p. chg. NBC Radio & TV networks, 1952; vice-chmn. bd., NBC, Jan. 1953; pres., NBC, Dec. 1953; bd. chmn., Dec. 1955; As head of NBC during TV's formative years, Weaver is credited as the father of TV talk/service program, founding both Tonight and Today shows, also innovated the rotating multi-star anthology series, the Wide Wide World series and concept of TV "special." Own firm, 430 Park Avenue., N.Y., 1956; chmn. of bd. McCann-Erickson Corp. (Intl.), 1959; pres., Subscription TV. Inc. Comm. Consultant in Los Angeles, CA and President, Weaver Productions, Inc. On magazine series Television: Inside and Out (1981–82).
AWARDS: Emmy Trustees' and Governor's Award (1967) and Governor's Award (1983).

WEBB, CHLOE: Actress. b. New York, NY. e. Boston Conservatory of Music and Drama. On stage with Boston Shakespeare Co., Goodman Theatre in Chicago and Mark Taper Forum, L.A. In Forbidden Broadway (Off-Bdwy. and L.A.) impersonat-

ing Angela Lansbury, Mary Martin and Carol Channing.
PICTURES: Sid and Nancy (debut, 1986); The Belly of an Architect.
TELEVISION: Remington Steele; China Beach (series); Movie: Who Am I This Time?

WEBB, ROBERT D.: Director. b. 1903.
PICTURES INCLUDE: assoc. prod., Lure of the Wilderness; dir., Glory Brigade, Proud Ones. Prod., dir.: Threshold of Space, Seven Cities of Gold, Beneath the 12 Mile Reef, White Feather, The Jackals, Capetown Affair, Love Me Tender, The Way to the Gold, Seven Women From Hell, The Agony and the Ecstasy (2nd unit), Capetown Affair, The Hawaiians.

WEBBER, ROBERT.: Actor. b. Santa Ana, CA, Oct. 14, 1924. e. Belmont H.S., Van Nuys H.S., Compton Jr. Coll. U.S.M.C., 1943–45. Summer stock. Co-starred, Wonderful Town, American Pavilion, Brussels World Fair, 1958.
THEATRE: Two Blind Mice, Goodbye My Fancy, Royal Family, No Time for Sergeants, Orpheus Descending, Fair Game, A Loss of Roses, Period of Adjustment.
PICTURES INCLUDE: Highway 301, Twelve Angry Men, The Stripper, The Sandpiper, The Third Day, Harper, The Silencers, The Hired Killer, Dead Heat on a Merry-Go-Round, Don't Make Waves, The Dirty Dozen, The Big Bounce, The Great White Hope, The French Mistress, $(Dollars), Every Man Is My Enemy, Bring Me the Head of Alfredo Garcia, Midway, Casey's Shadow, The Choirboys, The Revenge of the Pink Panther, 10, Private Benjamin, S.O.B., Sunday Lovers, Wrong Is Right, Who Dares Wins, Wild Geese II, Nuts.
TELEVISION: Over 400 shows from 1947 through 1988. Recent: Something is Out There.

WEBSTER, R.A.: Executive. b. Montreal, Canada, 1933. e. Bishop's Univ. (BA), Univ. of New Brunswick (BCL) and Univ. of London (LLM). Early career as barrister and solicitor. Ent. m.p. ind. 1961 as asst. company secretary, Associated British Picture Corp. 1966: booking director, Associated British Cinemas; 1974: managing director, Associated British Cinemas; 1979: chairman/managing director Thorn EMI Cinemas; 1981: director of product acquisition, Thorn EMI Screen Entertainment; 1986: president, theatre div., Cinema International Corp. BV (CIC).

WEDGEWORTH, ANN: Actress. b. Abilene, TX, Jan. 21, 1935. e. U. of Texas. On stage in Thieves, Blues for Mr. Charlie, Chapter Two, etc.
PICTURES: Handle with Care, Thieves, Bang the Drum Slowly, Scarecrow, Law and Disorder, Dragon Fly, The Birch Interval, No Small Affair, Sweet Dreams, The Men's Club, Made in Heaven, Far North.
TELEVISION: The Edge of Night, Another World, Somerset, All That Glitters, Three's Company, Filthy Rich, Right to Kill?, A Stranger Waits.

WEILER, GERALD E.: Producer. b. Mannheim, Germany, May 8, 1928. e. Harvard, 1946–48; Columbia, B.S., 1949–51; New York U. Grad. Sch., 1951–53. Writer, WHN, N.Y. writer, sports ed., news ed., Telenews Prod., Inc., 1948–52; asst. to prod., Richard de Rochemont, Vavin, Inc., 1952; U.S. Army, 1953–55; v.p., Vavin Inc. 1955–73; President, Weiler Communications Inc. 1973.

WEILL, CLAUDIA: Director. b. New York, NY 1947. e. Radcliffe, B.A., 1969. Teacher of acting, Cornish Institute, 1983; guest lecturer on film directing, NYU and Columbia U. Winner of Donatello Award, best director, 1979; Mademoiselle Woman of the Year, 1974; AFI Independent Filmmakers Grant, 1973. Worked as prod. asst. on doc. Revolution.
THEATER: An Evening for Merlin Finch (debut, 1975, Williamstown); Stillife; Found a Peanut; The Longest Walk.
PICTURES: Doc. shorts: This Is the Home of Mrs. Levant Grahame; Roaches' Serenade. Director: The Other Half of the Sky—A China Memoir; Girlfriends; It's My Turn.
TELEVISION: The 51st State; Sesame Street; Joyce at 34; The Great Love Experiment; thirtysomething (series).

WEINBLATT, MIKE: Television Executive. b. Perth Amboy, NJ, June 10, 1929. e. Syracuse U. Served in Army as counterintelligence agent, mostly in Japan (1952–53). Joined NBC in 1957; has headed two major TV network functions—talent/program admin. & sls. Joined network business affairs dept. in 1958 as mgr., business affairs, facilities operations; rose to post of director, pricing & financial services before moving to sales in November, 1962, as mgr., participating program sales. Named v.p., eastern sales, NBC-TV, 1968. Named v.p., talent & program admin., October, 1968; promoted to v.p. sales, February, 1973. January, 1975 named snr. v.p., sales; later became exec. v.p. Appointed exec. v.p. & gen. mgr. of NBC TV network in August, 1977. 1983, joined Showtime/Movie Channel as pres. & chief oper. off. 1984, pres., Multi Media Entertainment.

WEINSTEIN, HENRY T.: Executive Producer. b. New York, NY, July 12, 1924. e. City Coll. of New York, Carnegie Inst. of

Technology. Dir. of: the Brattle Theatre, Theatre in the Round, Houston, Texas. Prod. for The Theatre Guild, N.Y. Producer, 20th Century-Fox, M.G.M. Executive in charge of production, American Film Theatre, Skyfield Productions. Currently, v.p., creative affairs, Cannon Films.
PICTURES INCLUDE: Tender is the Night, Joy in the Morning, Cervantes, Madwoman of Chaillot, The Battle of Neretva, Magic Christian, A Delicate Balance, The Homecoming, The Iceman Cometh, Lost in the Stars, Butley, Luther, Rhinoceros, Galileo, The Man in the Glass Booth, In Celebration, Runaway Train, 52 Pick-Up.
TELEVISION: Play of the Week series, prod.

WEINSTEIN, PAULA: Independent Producer. b. Nov. 19, 1945. e. Columbia U. Daughter of late prod. Hannah Weinstein. Partnered with Gareth Wigan in WW Productions at Warner Brothers. Started as theatrical agent with William Morris and International Creative Management. With Warner Brothers, 1976–78 as production v.p.; left to go to 20th Century-Fox in same capacity. Named Fox snr. v.p., worldwide production. In 1980 appointed v.p., production, the Ladd Company. 1981, joined United Artists as pres., motion picture div. In 1983, began own production company at Columbia Pictures, also serving as a consultant for Columbia. 1987, joined MGM as exec. consultant. Prod.: A Dry White Season.

WEINTRAUB, FRED: Executive, Producer. b. Bronx, NY, April 27, 1928. e. U. of Pennsylvania Wharton Sch. of Business. Owner of The Bitter End Coffeehouse to 1971. Personal management, Campus Coffee House Entertainment Circuit; TV Production Hootenanny, Popendipity; syndicated TV show host: From The Bitter End; motion picture production; v.p., creative services, Warner Bros. 1969, executive in charge of Woodstock; producer motion pictures, Weintraub-Heller Productions, 1974.
PICTURES: Enter The Dragon, Rage, Black Belt Jones, Truck Turner, Golden Needles, Animal Stars, Hot Potato, The Ultimate Warrior, Dirty Knights Work, Those Cuckoo Crazy Animals, Crash, Outlaw Blues, The Pack, The Promise, Tom Horn, Battle Creek Brawl, Force Five, High Road to China, Out of Control, Gymkata, Princess Academy.
TELEVISION: My Father, My Son (prod.).

WEINTRAUB, JERRY: Producer. b. New York, NY, Sept. 26, 1937. Sole owner and chm. of Management Three, representing entertainment personalities, including John Denver, John Davidson, Frank Sinatra, Neil Diamond, etc. Also involved with Intercontinental Broadcasting Systems, Inc. (cable programming) and Jerry Weintraub/Armand Hammer Prods. (production co.). 1985, named United Artists Corp. chm. Resigned, 1986. 1987: formed Weintraub Entertainment Group.
PICTURES: Nashville, Oh, God!, Cruising, All Night Long, Diner, The Karate Kid.

WEINTRAUB, SY: Executive. b. New York, NY, 1923. e. U. of Missouri, B.A., journalism, 1947; graduate of American Theater Wing. Started career in 1949 forming with associates a TV syndication co., Flamingo Films, Inc., which merged with Associated Artists to form Motion Pictures for Television, Inc., largest syndicator at that time. He originated Superman and Grand Ol' Opry series for TV. In 1958 bought Sol Lesser Prods., owners of film rights for Tarzan, and began producing and distributing Tarzan films through Banner Productions, Inc. Also formerly chmn. of bd. of Panavision, Inc.; bd. mem. and pres. of National General Television Corp., and pres. of KMGM-TV in Minneapolis. In 1978 named chm. of Columbia Pictures Industries' new Film Entertainment Group, also joining Office of the Chief Executive of CPI.

WEIR, PETER: Director, Writer. b. Sydney, Australia, Aug. 8, 1944. Briefly worked selling real estate, traveled to Eng. 1965. Entered Australian TV industry as stagehand while prod. amateur revues.
PICTURES: First prof. credit: director-writer of Michael, an episode of the feature, Three To Go (1970). Writer-Director: The Cars That Ate Paris, The Last Wave, The Plumber. Director only: Picnic at Hanging Rock, Gallipoli, The Year of Living Dangerously, Witness, The Mosquito Coast, Dead Poet's Society.

WEIS, DON: Writer, Director, Producer. b. Milwaukee, WI, May 13, 1922. e. U. of Southern California.
PICTURES INCLUDE: (dial. dir.) Body and Soul, The Red Pony, Champion, Home of the Brave, The Men; (dir.) Letter From a Soldier, sequence in It's a Big Country, Bannerline, Just This Once, You for Me, I Love Melvin, Remains To Be Seen, A Slight Case of Larceny, Half a Hero, Affairs of Dobie Gillis, Adventures of Haiji Baba, Ride the High Iron, Catch Me If You Can, Gene Krupa Story, Critic's Choice, Looking for Love, The King's Pirate, Repo.
TELEVISION: Dear Phoebe. Best TV director, 1956, 1958. Screen Dir. Guild, The Longest Hundred Miles, It Takes a Thief, Ironside, M*A*S*H., Happy Days, Planet of the Apes, Bronk, Petrocelli, The Magician, Mannix, Night Stalker, Barbary Coast, Courtship of Eddie's Father, Starsky & Hutch,

Hawaii Five-O, Chips, Charlie's Angels, Love Boat, Fantasy Island.

WEIS, JACK: Producer, Director, Writer, Cinematographer, Film Editor. b. Tampa, FL, October 1, 1932. e. U. of Notre Dame, B.S.; U. of Chicago, M.S. Was in U.S. Air Force six yrs. Founded Associated Productions/Associated Advertising Productions, Inc. in New Orleans in Aug., 1967, and has been involved in over 120 films and approx. 1,500 commercials. Produced, directed and wrote original s.p.s. for several HEW youth rehabilitation pictures. Member: Cinematography Local 666, Chicago IATSE; Film Editor Local 780, IATSE, Chicago; Directors Guild of America; Writers Guild of America.
PICTURES INCLUDE: Quadroon (dir.), Storyville (prod., dir., s.p.), Damballa (prod., dir., s.p.); creature from Hony Island Swamp (prod.-dir., s.p.); Lehia (prod., dir., camera), You Never Gave Me Roses, (s.p., prod., dir.); The Perfect Circle (TV-s.p., prod., dir.); Crypt of Dark Secrets (prod., dir., s.p.); Mardi Gras Massacre, prod., dir., s.p., editor).

WEISBERG, BRENDA: Writer. b. Rowne, Poland. Magazine writer, social service, public health, drama instructor. Married to the late Morris Meckler.
PICTURES INCLUDE: s.p., China Sky; s.p., When a Girl's Beautiful, Burning Cross, Port Said, Rusty series, Girl's School; collab. s.p., Isle of Samoa; collab. orig., Reunion in Reno, Alias Mr. Twilight, King of the Wild Horses, Little Tough Guy, s.p. Shadowed. Collaborator, Scarlet Claw, Ding Dong Williams, Babes On Swing Street, Weird Woman, The Mummy's Ghost, The Mad Ghoul, Keep 'Em Slugging, Mug Town, Tough As They Come, Mob Town, There's One Born Every Minute, Hit the Road, Sing Another Chorus, You're Not So Tough.
TELEVISION: Fireside Theatre, Philco Theatre, Matinee Theatre.
AUTHOR: U (short stories), Woman's Home Companion, Collier's. American Mercury (Mencken's) Plain Talk, Forum, Papa Was a Farmer (book).

WEISS, STEVEN ALAN: Executive. b. Glendale, CA, Oct. 19, 1944. e. Los Angeles City Coll., A.A., 1964; U. of Southern California, B.S., 1966; Northwestern U., B.S., 1967; LaSalle Extension U., J.D., 1970. U.S. Navy-San Diego, Great Lakes, Vallejo & Treasure Island, 1966–67; shipyard liaison officer, Pearl Harbor Naval Shipyard, U.S. Navy, 1970; gen. mgr., Adrian Weiss Prods., 1970–74; organized Weiss Global Enterprises with Adrian Weiss 1974 for production, acquisition & distribution of films. Purchased with Tom J. Corradine and Adrian Weiss from the Benedict E. Bogeaus Estate nine features, 1974. Secty./treas. of Film Investment Corp. & Weiss Global Enterprises. (Cos. own, control or have dist. rights to over 300 features, many TV series, documentaries, etc.)
MEMBER: Natl. Assn. of TV Program Executive Intl.; National Cable TV Assn.; American Film Institute.

WEISSMAN, MURRAY: Executive. b. New York, NY, Dec. 23. e. U. of Southern California. Promotion mgr., TV Guide, 1952; asst. publicity director, KABC-TV, 1953–60; asst. dir. of press info., CBS, 1960–66; mgr., TV press dept., Universal Studio, 1966–68; executive in charge of m.p. press dept., Universal Studios & asst. secy., Universal Pictures, 1968–76; marketing exec., Columbia Pictures, 1976–77; vice pres. of advertising & publicity, Lorimar Productions, 1977; vice pres., ICPR Public Relations Company, 1978–81; now principal, Murray Weissman & Associates.

WEISSMAN, SEYMOUR J.: Executive, Producer, Director. Weissman Franz Productions. b. Brooklyn, NY, May 28, 1931. e. Kenyon Coll., Eng. Lit., A.B., 1953; U. of Southern California, cinema, 1955. Unity Films, 1954; Henry Strauss & Co., 1954; Dir. of motion pictures, White Sands Proving Grounds, N.M., 1954–55; M.P.O., 1955; Coleman Prod., 1956; prod. dir., Dynamic Films, Inc., 1958–59; prod., dir., Viston Assoc., 1959–64; dir., VPI Prods., 1966.

WEITMAN, ROBERT M.: Executive. b. New York, NY, August 18, 1905. e. Cornell U. Attended Paramount Managers' Training Sch. Assigned to Rialto Theatre, assistant manager, in 1926. Promoted to manager, Brooklyn Paramount. City manager of New York Paramount Public Theatres. Appointed managing director of New York Paramount Theatre in 1935. Managing dir. of N.Y. and Brooklyn Paramount Theatres. Vice-pres. United Paramount Theatres, supervising southern and Philadelphia houses; v.p. American Broadcasting-Paramount Theatres, Inc. in chge. of programming and talent; v.p. in charge of program development, CBS TV, 1956; v.p. chge. prod. MGM-TV 1960; v.p. in chg. prod., MGM, Inc., 1962; member MGM bd. directors; resigned MGM, July, 1967; v.p. in charge of studio production, Columbia, July, 1967. Dec., 1969 formed own prod. company.

WEITZLER, LINDA: Executive. Began career in entertainment industry at ABC-TV, where worked 11 yrs. Joined Columbia Pictures 1981 as v.p. talent relations, working with publicity and promotion depts.; 1984, moved to Universal Pictures in

similar capacity. 1987, appt. corporate p.r. dir. for corporate special projects.

WEITZNER, DAVID: Executive. b. New York, NY, Nov. 13, 1938. e. Michigan State U. Entered industry in 1960 as member Columbia Pictures adv. dep't; later with Donahue and Coe as ass't exec. and Loew's Theatres adv. dep't; later with Embassy Pictures, adv. mgr.; dir. of adv. and exploitation for Palomar Pictures Corp.; v.p. in charge of adv., pub., and exploitation for ABC Pictures Corp.; v.p., entertainment/ leisure div., Grey Advertising; v.p., worldwide adv., 20th Century Fox; exec. v.p. adv./pub./promo., Universal Pictures; exec. v.p., mktg. & dist., Embassy Pictures; 1985, joined 20th Century-Fox Films as pres. of mktg. 1987, pres., mktg., Weintraub Entertainment Group.

WELCH, RAQUEL: Actress. r.n. Raquel Tejada. b. Chicago, IL, Sept. 5, 1940. Mother of actress Tahnee Welch. e. La Jolla H.S. Fashion and photographic modeling. Co-hostess, Hollywood Palace. Broadway debut, Woman of the Year, 1981.
PICTURES INCLUDE: Roustabout; A House Is Not a Home; Swinging Summer; Fantastic Voyage; Shoot Louder . . . I Don't Understand; One Million Years B.C.; Fathom; Bedazzled; The Biggest Bundle of Them All; The Queens; Bandolero; Lady in Cement; 100 Rifles; Flare Up; The Magic Christian; Myra Breckinridge; Hannie Caulder; Kansas City Bomber; Fuzz; The Last of Sheila, The Three Musketeers; The Four Musketeers; The Wild Party; Mother, Jugs and Speed; Crossed Swords; L'Animal.
TELEVISION: From Raquel With Love (also writer), Legend of Walks Far Woman; Right to Die; Scandal in a Small Town.

WELD, TUESDAY: Actress. r.n. Susan Weld. b. New York, NY, Aug. 27, 1943. m. violinist Pinchas Zuckerman. e. Hollywood Professional Sch. Began modeling at 4 yrs. Film debut, Rock, Rock, Rock (1956).
PICTURES INCLUDE: Rally Round The Flag, Boys! The Five Pennies, The Private Lives of Adam and Eve, Return to Peyton Place, Wild in the Country, Bachelor Flat, Lord Love a Duck, Pretty Poison, I Walk the Line, A Safe Place, Play It As It Lays, Looking for Mr. Goodbar, Who'll Stop the Rain, Thief, Author! Author!, Once Upon a Time in America; Heartbreak Hotel.
TELEVISION: The Many Loves of Dobie Gillis (series, 1959–60). Movies: Mother and Daughter: The Loving War, Winter of Our Discontent, F. Scott Fitzgerald in Hollywood, Madame X, Seduced and Abandoned, Something in Common, Circle of Violence, The Rainmaker.

WELK, LAWRENCE: Orchestra leader. b. Strasburg, ND, March 11, 1903. Played accordion community dances, church socials, etc. Started own group. Biggest Little Band in America. Played hotels, ballrooms, music became known as Champagne Music. Signed Aragon Ballroom, Pacific Ocean Park, CA, 1951, with weekly television show. Champagne Music Makers, ABC-TV, July 2, 1955; The Lawrence Welk Show, ABC; signed lifetime contract, Hollywood Palladium, July 1961. Recording: Calcutta, 1961; syndicated network show started 1971.

WELLER, PETER: Actor. b. Stevens Point, WI, June 24, 1947. Acting since 10 years old. e. North Texas State U. Studied at American Acad. of Dramatic Arts with Uta Hagen. Member, Actor's Studio.
PICTURES: Butch and Sundance: The Early Years, Just Tell Me What You Want, Shoot the Moon, Of Unknown Origin, Vera, Buckeroo Banzai, Firstborn, Robocop, Shakedown, Leviathan, A Killing Affair, The Tunnel.
TELEVISION: Lou Grant, Exit 10. Movies: Two Kinds of Love, Kentucky Woman, The Silence, Apology.
STAGE: Sticks and Bones (moved up from understudy, Bdwy. debut), Summer Brave, Macbeth, The Wool-Gatherers, Rebel Women, Streamers, The Woods, Serenading Louie.

WELLS, FRANK G.: Executive. b. California, March 4, 1932. e. Pomona Coll., 1949–53; Oxford U., 1953–55; Rhodes Scholarship Jurisprudence. U.S. Army, Infantry first lieutenant, 1955–57; Stanford Law Sch. 1957–59. Joined Gang, Tyre & Brown (entertainment industry law firm) 1959; partner, 1962–69; mem., State Bar of Calif., American Bar Assoc., Los Angeles County Bar Assoc., vice chm., Warner Bros. Inc.; 1985, pres. & COO, Walt Disney Prods., Inc.

WENDERS, WIM: Director. b. Dusseldorf, Germany, August 14, 1945. Studied film 1967–70 at Filmhochschule in Munich. Worked as film critic 1968–70 for Filmkritik and Die Suddeutsche Zeitung. In 1967 made first short films (Schauplatze) and three others before first feature, Summer in the City, in 1970.
PICTURES INCLUDE: Die Angst Des Tormanns Beim Elfmeter, The Scarlet Letter, Aus Der Familie Der Panzerechsen, Falsche Bewegung, Alice in the Cities, The Goalie's Anxiety at the Penalty Kick, Kings of the Road, The American Friend, Lightning Over Water, Hammett, The State of Things, Paris, Texas, Tokyo-Ga, Wings of Desire, All Night Long (as actor), Till the End of the World.

WENDKOS, PAUL: Director. b. Philadelphia, PA, Sept. 20, 1922.
PICTURES: The Burglar; Tarawa Beachhead; Gidget; Face of a Fugitive; Because They're Young; Angel Baby; Gidget Goes to Rome; Miles to Terror; Guns of the Magnificent Seven; Cannon for Cordova; The Mephisto Waltz; Special Delivery.
TELEVISION INCLUDES: Hawkins: Murder in the Slave Trade; Fear No Evil; The Brotherhood of the Bell; A Death of Innocence; The Underground Man; The Woman I Love; The Legend of Lizzie Borden; Honor Thy Father; The Death of Ritchie; 79 Park Avenue; Ordeal of Doctor Mudd; The Five of Me; The Search for Patty Hearst; A Woman Called Moses; A Cry for Love; Cocaine; One Man's Poison; Celebrity; Intimate Agony; Scorned and Swindled; The Execution; Picking Up the Pieces; Hometown; LBJ: The Early Years; The Bad Seed; Six Against the Rock; Rage of Angels: The Story Continues; Right to Die; The Taking of Flight 847.

WERNER, PETER: Producer, Director. b. New York, NY, Jan. 17, 1947. e. Dartmouth Coll.
PICTURES: In the Region of Ice, Don't Cry It's Only Thunder, No Man's Land.
TELEVISION: Producer: Battered, Barnburning, Learning in Focus. Director: Aunt Mary, Hard Knox, I Married a Centerfold, Women in Song, Sins of the Father.

WERTHEIMER, THOMAS: Executive. Exec. v.p., MCA, Inc.; director and officer of subsidiaries. Member exec. committee.

WERTMULLER, LINA: Writer, Director. b. Rome, Aug. 14, 1928. After graduating high school enrolled in drama school. Began working in theatre in 1951; spent decade doing everything from puppetry to stage managing to writing and directing for radio and TV. Began film career as asst. to Fellini on 8½ in 1962. Following year wrote and directed first film, The Lizards. Had big TV success with series called Gian Burasca and then returned to theatre for a time. 1988, named Special Commissioner of Centro Sperimentale di Cinematografia.
PICTURES: This Time, Let's Talk About Men, The Seduction of Mimi, Love and Anarchy, All Screwed Up, Swept Away, Seven Beauties, A Night Full of Rain, A Joke of Destiny, Sotto Sotto, Summer Night.

WEST, ADAM: Actor. b. 1938. r.n. William West Anderson.
PICTURES: The Young Philadelphians; Geronimo; Soldier in the Rain; Robinson Crusoe on Mars; Mara of the Wilderness; Alexander the Great; Batman; The Girl Who Knew Too Much; Marriage of a Young Stockbroker; The Specialist; Hell River; Hooper; One Dark Night; Doin' Time on Planet Earth, Return Fire: Jungle Wolf II, Mad About You.
TELEVISION: Series: The Detectives; Batman; The Last Precinct; Movies: For the Love of It; I Take These Men; Nevada Smith; Poor Devil.

WEST, TIMOTHY: Actor. b. Yorkshire, England, Oct. 20, 1934. Ent. ind. 1960. Began acting 1956 after two years as recording engineer. Worked in regional repertory, London's West End and for Royal Shakespeare Company. Dec., 1979 appointed artistic controller of Old Vic. Has directed extensively in the theatre.
PICTURES: Twisted Nerve, The Looking Glass War, Nicholas and Alexandra, The Day of the Jackal, Hedda, Joseph Andrews, The Devil's Advocate, Agatha, The Thirty Nine Steps, Rough Cut, Oliver Twist, Cry Freedom, Consuming Passions.
TELEVISION: Edward VII, Hard Times, Crime and Punishment, Henry VIII, Churchill and the Generals, Brass, The Monocled Mutineer, The Good Doctor, Bodkin Adams, What the Butler Saw, Harry's Kingdom, The Train, When We Are Married, Breakthrough at Reykjavik, Strife, A Shadow on the Sun.

WESTCOTT, HELEN: Actress. r.n. Myrthas Helen Hickman. b. Hollywood, CA, 1929. e. Los Angeles Jr. Coll., 1946. In play The Drunkard, at 7, for 9 yrs.; many radio shows.
PICTURES INCLUDE: A Midsummer Night's Dream (as child), Adventures of Don Juan, Girl from Jones Beach, Mr. Belvedere Goes to College, Whirlpool, Dancing in the Dark, The Gunfighter, Three Came Home, Secret of Convict Lake, Phone Call from a Stranger, Return of Texan, With a Song in My Heart, Loan Shark, Abbott and Costello Meet Dr. J. & Mr. H., Charge at Feather River, Hot Blood, The Last Hurrah, I Love My Wife.

WESTON, JACK: Actor. b. Cleveland, OH, Aug. 21, 1915. Began career in 1934 in children's division of Cleveland Playhouse. In Army in W.W.II. Success came in Broadway hit, Season in the Sun. Was frequent performer in top TV shows during 1950s. Film debut in Stage Struck in 1958.
PICTURES INCLUDE: Stage Struck, Please Don't Eat the Daisies, All in a Night's Work, The Honeymoon Machine, It's Only Money, Palm Springs Weekend, The Incredible Mr. Limpet, Mirage, The Cincinnati Kid, Wait Until Dark, The Thomas Crown Affair, The April Fools, Cactus Flower, A New Leaf, Fuzz, Marco, Gator, The Ritz, Cuba, The Four Seasons, The Longshot, RAD, Ishtar, Dirty Dancing, Short Circuit 2.

TELEVISION: Studio One, Philco Theatre, Kraft Playhouse, Rod Browning of the Rocket Rangers. Movies: If Tomorrow Comes, 79 Park Avenue, Deliver Us From Evil, I Love a Mystery.

WESTON, JAY: Producer. b. New York, NY, March 9, 1929. e. New York U. Operated own pub. agency before moving into film prod. In 1965 launched Weston Production; sold orig. s.p., The War Horses, to Embassy Pictures; acquired and marketed other properties. Became prod. story exec. for Palomar-ABC Pictures in 1967.
PICTURES INCLUDE: For Love of Ivy (co-prod.), Lady Sings the Blues (co-prod.), W.C. Fields and Me, Chu Chu and the Philly Flash, Night of the Juggler, Buddy, Buddy.
STAGE: Does a Tiger Wear a Necktie (co-prod.).
TELEVISION: Laguna Heat (exec. prod.).

WESTON, ROBERT R.: Executive. b. New York, NY. e. Peekskill Military Acad., Fordham U. Publicity dir., WFUV-FM, 3 yrs.; copy writer, Columbia Pictures, asst. accnt. exec., Donahue & Coe, asst. adv. mgr., United Artists adv. dir., Embassy Pictures, v.p., asst. to exec. v.p.; v.p. asst. to pres., resigned to become independent film producer, 1971. Presently pres., Harold Robbins Int'l., film prod. co. Prod.: The Betsy, The Lonely Lady.

WEXLER, HASKELL: Cinematographer, Director. b. Chicago, 1926. Photographed educational and industrial films before features. Documentaries as cin. include: The Living City, The Savage Eye, T. for Tumbleweed, Stakeout on Dope Street, Brazil—A Report on Torture, Interviews With Mai Lai Veterans, Interview—Chile's President Allende, Introduction to the Enemy.
PICTURES INCLUDE: Studs Lonigan, Five Bold Women, The Hoodlum Priest, Angel Baby, A Face In the Rain, America, America, The Best Man, The Bus (also dir. prod.), The Loved One (also co-prod.), Who's Afraid of Virginia Woolf (Acad. Award, 1966), In the Heat of the Night, The Thomas Crown Affair, Medium Cool (also co-prod., dir., s.p.), Trial of Catonsville Nine, American Graffiti, One Flew Over the Cuckoo's Nest, Bound for Glory (Acad. Award, 1976), Days of Heaven (addit. photog.), Richard Pryor: Live on the Sunset Strip, No Nukes (also co-dir.), Second Hand Hearts, Lookin' to Get Out, Coming Home, The Man Who Loved Women, Matewan, Colors, Latino (dir., writer only), Fugitives.
TELEVISION: The Kid From Nowhere.

WHEATON, WIL: Actor. b. California. Began acting in commercials at age 7.
PICTURES: The Buddy System (debut, 1984); Hambone and Hillie; The Last Starfighter; The Farm; Stand by Me; The Curse.
TELEVISION: A Long Way Home (debut); The Shooting. Pilots: Long Time Gone, 13 Thirteenth Avenue; The Man Who Fell to Earth. Movies: The Defiant Ones. Series: Star Trek II: The Next Generation.

WHEELER, LYLE: Art director. b. Woburn, MA, Feb. 12, 1905. e. U. of Southern California. Mag. illustrator, industrial designer before entering m.p. ind. as art dir. of Garden of Allah. In 1944 apptd. supervising art dir. 20th Century-Fox. Academy Award, in collab. art-direction black & white for Anna and the King of Siam; Gone With the Wind, color art dir., collab., The Robe, 1953. Love Is a Many-Splendored Thing, Daddy Longlegs, The Diary of Anne Frank (Acad. Award, 1959), Journey to the Center of the Earth, The Cardinal.
TELEVISION: Perfect Gentlemen, Flight to Holocaust.

WHITAKER, FOREST: Actor. Stage credits include Swan, Romeo and Juliet, Hamlet, The Greeks, Ring Around the Moon, Craig's Wife, Whose Life Is It Anyway?, Beggar's Opera, Jesus Christ Superstar.
PICTURES: Tag, Fast Times at Ridgemont High, Vision Quest, The Color of Money, Platoon, Stakeout, Good Morning Vietnam, Bird.
TELEVISION: Hands of a Stranger, North and South, Parts I & II, The Grand Baby; Guest: Amazing Stories, Hill Street Blues.

WHITE, BETTY: Actress. b. Oak Park, IL, Jan. 17, 1924. Wife of late Allen Ludden. Began on radio in Blondie, The Great Gildersleeve, This Is Your F.B.I. Moved onto TV with live local show, L.A.
TELEVISION: Panelist: Make the Connection (1955), Match Game P.M., Liar's Club, Life with Elisabeth (Emmy), The Betty White Show (1954–58), A Date With the Angels (1957–58), Tonight Show, Mary Tyler Moore Show (Emmy 1975, 1976), The Pet Set, Macy's Thanksgiving Parade (hostess for 10 yrs.), The Betty White Show, The Best Place To Be, The Gossip Columnist, The Carol Burnett Show, Just Men (host, Emmy, 1983), Mama's Family, Golden Girls (Emmy, 1986).

WHITE, JESSE: Actor. b. Buffalo, NY, Jan. 13, 1919. e. Akron, OH H.S. Did odd jobs, then salesman; radio, vaudeville, burlesque, nightclubs and little theatre work; Broadway stage debut in Moon is Down, 1942; other shows include Harvey, Born Yesterday, etc. Has appeared on numerous radio and

TV shows, regular on Danny Thomas, Ann Southern Shows.
PICTURES INCLUDE: Harvey, Death of a Salesman, Callaway Went Thataway, Million Dollar Mermaid, Witness to Murder, Forever Female, Not as a Stranger, Bad Seed, Back from Eternity, Designing Woman, Marjorie Morningstar, Legs Diamond, Fever in the Blood, Sail a Crooked Ship, It's Only Money, The Yellow Canary, It's a Mad, Mad, Mad, Mad World, Looking For Love, A House Is Not a Home, Bless the Beasts and Children, The Cat from Outer Space.

WHITE, LAWRENCE R.: Executive. b. 1926. e. Syracuse U. Began career as producer-director for the Dumont Television Network in 1948. Dir. of programming, Benton & Bowles, Inc., 1951; joined CBS TV network as v.p., daytime programming, 1959; dir. of program development, CBS, 1963; joined NBC television network in 1965 as v.p., daytime programs; v.p. programs, east coast, 1969; v.p. programs, NBC-TV, 1972; ind. prod. affiliated with CPT, 1975. Resigned 1980 to become independent producer.
TELEVISION: Exec. prod.: Goliath Awaits, The Blue and the Gray, The Master of Ballantrae, The First Olympics—Athens 1896.

WHITE, LEONARD: Producer, Director, Actor. b. Sussex, Eng. TV dir., prod., CBS-TV (Canada), T.W.W. Ltd. T.T. TV & ABC-TV; Jupiter Thea., Inc.; Crest Theatre; Royal Alexandra Thea.; Toronto Thea., 1953–57. England, Playhouse, Oxford, Perth Repertory Thea., Hornchurch, Guilford Repertory Thea. Belgrade Thea., Coventry. Actor: U.S.A. debut in A Sleep of Prisoners, 1951–52; London West End. In the White Devil, He Who Gets Slapped, Macbeth, Still She Wished for Company, Point of Departure.
PICTURES INCLUDE: The Dark Man, The Large Rope, River Beat, Hunted, Martin Luther, Passage Home, Breakout, Circumstantial Evidence, At the Stroke of Nine, etc.
TELEVISION: All networks, G. Britain and CBC (Canada). Prod., ABC-TV, 1960–68. Series: Inside Story, Armchair Mystery Thea., Police Surgeon, The Avengers, Out of This World, Armchair Theatre. Prod., 1968–69; prod., Thames Television, 1969–70. Drama consultant CBC-TV Toronto. 350 drama productions for ITV (UK) Network.

WHITE, PAUL: Executive, Producer, Director. b. New York, NY. e. Columbia U. N.Y. Times Wide World Pictures; managing ed., Nation-Wide News Service; ed./publisher of Key Magazine; home office exec. Paramount Pictures. Author, alone & in collab., books including I Find Treason. Served in U.S. Marine Corps as officer-in-chg. combat photography in the Pacific W.W.II, prod. & dir. wire recording from foxholes of first sound ever made of actual warfare sounds under battle fire in the Marshalls. Joined David O. Selznick as gen. mgr. European operations 1946; formed own co., Paul White Productions, Inc. 1948; pres., PSI-TV 1953. Joined Subscription TV 1958 as v.p. in chg. pgmg; pioneer Cablevision and Pay-TV; pres. MCI; created 11 audio-visual inventions; 1973 Paul White Enterprises (consultants). Clients: RCA; Impresario S. Hurok; Radix Intl. Corp.; Motivational Systems, Inc.; Liberty Mint. The Education Guild; Hi-Tech Industries, Inc.; Creative Holographics, U.K.; 1929 co-founder & chm., Holoptics Network Intl. (N.Y./London) viz. Dimensional Imaging: Holography; Linear Optics; 3-D Film System (co-inventor) pat pend anticounterfeit ID labeling system with visible 3-D or animated tickets, labels, etc., invisibly encoded inside label, which portable mini computer can decode & display essential readout info re product, i.e. video cassettes, hi-tech equipment, records, toys, wearing apparel. 1984 co-founder, bd. chm. & CEO Holoptic 3D Systems, Inc. Optical inventions: The Holoptic Converters (enable standard 2D slide and m.p. 35mm cameras and projectors to shoot and show full color 3D images with polaroid glasses). The Holoptiscope (4 photographic dimension projector for slide and m.p. without need for viewer accessories). Currently dev. 3D TV syst.
PICTURES INCLUDE: Battle of the Marshalls, Saipan, Tinian, To the Shores of Iwo Jima, Song of Siam, Pearl of the Orient, Land of Fair Dinkum, Unusual Sports, Flying Doctor.
TELEVISION: Series Created and/or supervised incl.: Playhouse of Stars, China Smith, Play of The Week, Orient Express, prod. & dir. The Keys to Peace (Pope Paul's U.S. Visit); exec. prod. The Bolshoi Ballet; Bicentennial project; OP Sail 1976, The Tall Ships; Creative & technical svcs. for 3-D TV & multi-graphic applications.

WHITE, ROY B.: Executive, Exhibitor. b. Cincinnati, OH, July 30, 1926. e. U. of Cincinnati. Flight engineer, U.S. Air Force during W.W.II; worked in sales department of 20th Century-Fox, 1949–52; began in exhibition, 1952; past pres., Mid-States Theatres; pres., R. M. White Management, Inc.; past president, National Association of Theatre Owners, past Chairman of the Board, National Association of Theatre Owners: Board of Trustees—American Film Inst.; Board of Directors NATO of Ohio, v.p., Motion Picture Pioneers Foundation; Will Rogers Hospital, Nat'l. Endowment for Arts.

WHITELAW, BILLIE: Actress. b. Coventry, England, June 6, 1932. Acted on radio and television since childhood. Winner of the TV Actress of the Year and 1972, Guild Award, Best Actress,

1960. British Academy Award 1969; U.S. National Society of Film Critics Award for Best Supporting Actress, 1968. Evening News, Best Film Actress, 1977; Best Actress Sony Radio Radio Award 1987.
STAGE: 3 years with National Theatre of Great Britain. Revue: England, My England. Stage plays include: Progress to the Park, A Touch of the Poet, Othello, Trelawney of the Wells, After Haggerty, Not I, Alphabetical Order, Footfalls, Molly, The Greeks, Happy Days, Passion Play, Rockaby (also in N.Y. and Adelaide Festival), Tales from Hollywood, Who's Afraid of Virginia Woolf?
PICTURES INCLUDE: No Love for Johnnie, Mr. Topaze, Hell Is a City, Payroll, Charlies Bubbles, The Adding Machine, Twisted Nerve, Start the Revolution Without Me, Leo the Last, Eagle in a Cage, Gumshoe, Frenzy, Nightwatch, The Omen, The Water Babies, A Tale of Two Cities, An Unsuitable Job for a Woman, Slayground, Shadey, The Chain, Maurice, The Tangier Arrangement, Murder Elite, The Dressmaker, Joyriders.
TELEVISION: Over 100 leading roles incl. No Trains to Lime Street, Lady of the Camelias, Resurrection, The Pity of it All, You and Me, A World of Time, Dr. Jekyll and Mr. Hyde, Poet Game, Sextet (8 plays for BBC), Wessex Tales, The Fifty Pound Note, Supernatural (2 plays), Three plays by Samuel Beckett, Eustace and Hilda, The Oresteia of Aeschylus, The Haunted Man, Private Schultz, Jamaica Inn, Rockaby, Camille, Imaginary Friends, The Secret Garden, The Picnic.

WHITEMORE, HUGH: Writer. b. England, 1936. Studied acting at Royal Acad. of Dramatic Art. Has since written for television, film, theatre.
THEATER: Stevie, Pack of Lies, Breaking the Code, The Best of Friends.
PICTURES: All Neat in Black Stockings, All Creatures Great and Small, Stevie, The Return of the Soldier, 84 Charing Cross Road, Pack of Lies.
TELEVISION: Cider With Rosie (Writers' Guild Award 1971), Elizabeth R (Emmy Award 1971), Country Matters (Writers' Guild Award 1972), Dummy (RAT—Prix Italia 1979), Rebecca, All For Love, A Dedicated Man, Down at the Hydro, A Bit of Singing and Dancing, Concealed Enemies (Emmy, Neil Simon Awards 1984).

WHITFIELD, RICHARD ALLEN: Producer, Executive. b. Goldsboro, NC, 1946. e. U. of North Carolina. Adv. writer-producer for American Brands, Pepsicola, 1970–73; TV-film producer, industrial-educational, 1973–77; v.p., adv., Independents International Films, Inc., distributor, 1978; v.p.-producer, Rick Friedberg & Associates, 1979; pres. Golden Image Motion Picture Corp., feature production, 1980.
PICTURES INCLUDE: K-GOD (exec. prod.), Used Cars (video segments prod.), Bones of Peking (prod.).

WHITMAN, STUART: Actor. b. San Francisco, CA., Feb. 1, 1928. Army Corp. of Engineers (1945–1948), at Fort Lewis, WA; while in army, competed as light heavyweight boxer. Studied drama under G.I. Bill at Ben Bard Drama Sch. and L.A. City Coll. Performed in Heaven Can Wait and became member of Michael Chekhov Stage Society and Arthur Kennedy Group. Entered films in early 1950s. TV debut on 26 episodes Highway Patrol.
PICTURES INCLUDE: When Worlds Collide, The Day The Earth Stood Still, Rhapsody, Seven Men From Now, War Drums, Johnny Trouble, Darby's Rangers, Ten North Frederick, The Decks Ran Red, China Doll, The Sound and the Fury, These Thousand Hills, Hound Dog Man, The Story of Ruth, Murder, Inc., Francis of Assisi, The Fiercest Heart, The Mark (Acad. Award nom.), The Comancheros, Convicts 4, The Longest Day, The Day and the Hour (Fr./It.), Shock Treatment; Rio Conchos, Those Magnificent Men In Their Flying Machines, The Sands of the Kalahari, Signpost to Murder, An American Dream, The Last Escape; The Invincible Six; The Only Way Out Is Dead, Captain Apache (US/Sp.), The Man Who Wanted to Live Forever, Night Of The Lepus, Hostages; The Man Who Died Twice; Welcome To Arrow Beach/Tender Flesh, Call Him Mr. Shatter; Ransom; Crazy Mama, Las Vegas Lady; Tony Saitta/Tough Tony (It.), Strange Shadows In An Empty Room; Ruby; The White Buffalo; Death Trap/Eaten Alive; The Thoroughbreds; Maniac; Oil (It. as Red Adair), La Murjer de la Tierra Caliente (Sp./It.); Run For The Roses, Delta Fox; Guyana-Crime Of The Century (as Rev. Jim Jones, Mex.), Key West Crossing, Jamaican Gold, Treasure Of The Amazon.
TELEVISION: Cimarron Strip (series 1967–68), The Crowd Pleaser (Alcoa-Goodyear), Highway Patrol, Dr. Christian, Hangman's Noose (Zane Grey), The Last Convertible, Stillwatch, Condominium, Once Upon a Texas Train, Hemingway.

WHITMORE, JAMES: Actor. r.n. James Allen Whitmore, Jr. b. White Plains, NY, Oct. 1, 1921. e. Yale U. In Yale Drama Sch. players; co-founder Yale radio station, 1942; U.S. Marine Corps, W.W.II; in USO, in American Wing Theatre school, in stock. Broadway debut in Command Decision, 1947; m.p. debut in Undercover Man (1949). Star of Tomorrow.

PICTURES INCLUDE: Battleground, Asphalt Jungle, Next Voice You Hear, Mrs. O'Malley and Mr. Malone, Outriders, Please Believe Me, Across the Wide Missouri, It's a Big Country, Because You're Mine, Above and Beyond, Girl Who Had Everything, All the Brothers Were Valiant, Kiss Me Kate, The Command, Them, Battle Cry, McConell Story, Last Frontier, Oklahoma, Face of Fire, Eddie Duchin Story, Who Was That Lady?, Black Like Me, Chuka, Water Hole No. 3, Nobody's Perfect, Planet of the Apes, Madigan, The Split, Guns of the Magnificent Seven, Chato's Land, Where the Red Fern Grows, Give 'em Hell, Harry, The Serpent's Egg, The First Deadly Sin, Nuts.
TELEVISION: The Law and Mr. Jones (series), Temperature's Rising (series), Celebrity, All My Sons, The Word, I Will Fight No More Forever, Rage, The Challenge, Mark I Love You, Sister Ruth.

WHITTEL, JAMES: Executive. b. Clatterbridge, England, 1943. Ent. ind. 1962 holding various management positions with Odeon Cinemas. 1969: operations executive. 1972: operations executive Rank Motorway Service Areas. 1981: managing director: Rank Tuschinski, Netherlands. 1983: operations director Pizzerland Restaurants, UK. 1986 appointed managing director, Odeon Cinemas UK.

WIARD, WILLIAM O.: Director.
PICTURE: Tom Horn.
TELEVISION: Scott Free; The Girl, The Gold Watch and Everything; Ski Lift to Death; This House Is Possessed; Fantasies; Help Wanted: Male; Deadly Lessons; Kicks.

WICKES, MARY: Actress. r.n. Mary Wickenhauser. b. St. Louis, MO, June 13, 1916. e. Washington U., Doctor of Arts (hon.), 1969.
THEATRE: (B'way) The Man Who Came to Dinner, Town House, Stage Door, Danton's Death. Dramatic & musical comedy stock includes: St. Louis Municipal Opera, Starlight Theatre, Houston Music Theatre.
PICTURES INCLUDE: The Man Who Came to Dinner, Now, Voyager, White Christmas, The Music Man, The Trouble With Angels, Where Angels Go Trouble Follows, Napoleon and Samantha, Snowball Express, Touched by Love.
TELEVISION: The Halls of Ivy, The Danny Thomas Show, Dennis the Menace, Bonino, Alfred Hitchcock Presents, Studio One, Playhouse 90, Fatal Confession: A Father Dowling Mystery.

WIDMARK, RICHARD: Actor. b. Sunrise, MN, Dec. 26, 1914. e. Lake Forest U. Instructor, 1938. On radio, then stage, films.
PICTURES INCLUDE: Kiss of Death, Cry of the City, Road House, Street With No Name, Yellow Sky, Down to the Sea in Ships, Slattery's Hurricane, Night and the City, Panic in the Streets, No Way Out, Halls of Montezuma, The Frogmen, Red Skies of Montana, Don't Bother to Knock, O. Henry's Full House, My Pal Gus, Destination Gobi, Pickup on South Street, Take the High Ground, Hell & High Water, Broken Lance, Prize of Gold, The Cobweb, Backlash, Last Wagon, Saint Joan, Warlock, Kingdom of Man, The Long Ships, Run for the Sun, The Alamo, Judgment at Nuremberg, How the West Was Won, The Way West, Madigan, Death of a Gunfighter, When The Legends Die, Murder on the Orient Express, Twilight's Last Gleaming, The Domino Principle, Rollercoaster, Coma, The Swarm, Hanky Panky, The Final Option, Against All Odds.
TELEVISION: Madigan (series). Movies: Vanished (miniseries), The Last Day, Benjamin Franklin, A Whale For the Killing, All God's Children, Blackout, A Gathering of Old Men, Once Upon a Texas Train.

WIDOM, DIANE: Executive. Held marketing positions with Warner Bros., in New York, London, Burbank, for 10 years prior to joining 20th Century Fox in 1980 as West Coast pub. dir. 1982, named dir. of natl. mag. pub. & special photography. Promoted to natl. pub. dir. 1985, named v.p., pub., Fox m.p. div.

WIENER, JACK: Executive. b. Paris, France, June 8, 1926. Pub. rep., MGM, New Orleans, Jacksonville, FL, 1952–56; joined Columbia Pictures Int. Corp., 1956, continental publicity mgr., Columbia, Paris; v.p., Columbia Pics. Int'l. 1966; continental prod. exec., 1968; v.p. Columbia Pictures Corp., 1970. In 1972 became indep. prod., making Vampira, The Eagle Has Landed, Escape to Athena, Green Ice, F/X.

WIESEN, BERNARD: Producer, Director, Writer, Executive. b. New York, NY, Oct. 6, 1922. e. City Coll. of New York, B.B.A.; Pasadena Playhouse Coll. of Theatre, master of theatre arts; dramatic workshop of New School.
PICTURES INCLUDE: Producer-Director: Fear No More. Asst. Director on films, including The King and I, The Left Hand of God, The Rains of Ranchipur, To Catch a Thief, The Trouble with Harry.
TELEVISION: Director: How to Marry A Millionaire, Valentine's Day. Assoc. Producer: Valentine's Day, Three on an Island, Cap'n Ahab, Sally and Sam. Assoc. Prod.: Daniel Boone. Producer/Director: Julia, Co-Producer-Director: The

Jimmy Stewart Show. Prod. Exec.: Executive Suite (pilot). Exec. Paramount TV, director of current programming. Writer: Love 4 Love.
STAGE: First Monday in October (Bdwy.)—co. prod.

WIEST, DIANNE: Actress. b. Kansas City, MO, March 28, 1948. e. U. of Maryland. Studied ballet but abandoned it for theatre. Did regional theatre work (Yale Repertory, Arena Stage) and performed with N.Y. Shakespeare Festival. Film debut in I'm Dancing As Fast As I Can, 1982.
THEATER: Toured with Amer. Shakespeare Co.; Arena Stage (Heartbreak House, Our Town, The Dybbuk, Inherit the Wind). Public Theater (Ashes, Agamennon, Leave it to Beaver is Dead), Frankenstein (Bdwy), Othello, Beyond Therapy, Not About Heroes (dir., Williamstown Fest.)
PICTURES: It's My Turn; Independence Day; Footloose; Falling in Love; The Purple Rose of Cairo; Hannah and Her Sisters (Acad. Award); Radio Days; Lost Boys; September; Bright Lights, Big City; Cookie.
TELEVISION: Zalman or the Madness of God, Out of Our Father's House, The Wall, The Face of Rage.

WIGAN, GARETH: Executive. b. London, England, Dec. 2, 1931. e. Oxford. Agent, MCA London; 1957; John Redway & Associates, 1960; co-founder, agent Gregson & Wigan Ltd., 1961; co-founder, agent London Intl., 1968; independent prod., 1970; v.p., creative affairs, 20th Century Fox, 1975; v.p., prod., Fox, 1976; v.p., The Ladd Co., 1979–83. Company W.W. Prods.
PICTURES: Unman Wittering & Zigo; Running Scared; etc.

WIHTOL, ARN S.: Executive. Exec. v.p., international sales, Pacific International Enterprises. b. Millville, NJ, Sept. 4, 1944. e. San Jose State.
PICTURES: Production Executive and Co-Writer: Mystery Mansion. Casting and Controller: Dream Chasers. Producer's Assistant: Sacred Ground.

WILBY, JAMES: Actor. b. Rangoon, Burma, 1958. Lived a nomadic childhood moving from Burma to Ceylon, then Jamaica and finally England. e. Durham U. Trained at Royal Acad. of Dramatic Art where he played Shakespearean roles and landed a part in Oxford Film Foundation's Privileged (1982). West End stage debut Another Country. Also acted in regional theatre. 1988: The Common Pursuit.
PICTURES: Dreamchild (1985); A Room with a View (walk-on); Maurice; A Handful of Dust; A Summer Story.
TELEVISION: Sherlock Holmes; The Crooked Man; Dutch Girls.

WILCOX, CLAIRE: Actress. b. Toronto, Canada, 1955. Photographer's model, 3 yrs. of age; appeared on numerous national magazine covers; TV commercials; signed contract, Curtis Enterprises.
PICTURES INCLUDE: 40 Pounds of Trouble, Wives and Lovers.
TELEVISION: Harris Versus the World.

WILDE, ARTHUR L.: Publicist. b. San Francisco, CA, May 27, 1918. S.F. Daily News; Matson Lines; pub. dept., Warner Bros., 1936; dir. exploitation, CBS; pub. dir., Hal Wallis Prod.; pub. dept., Paramount; pub., Hecht-Hill-Lancaster; v.p., Arthur Jacobs, public rel.; Blowitz-Maskell Publicity Agency; pub. dir., C. V. Whitney Pictures; gen. v.p., 1958; owner, pub.-ad. agency, The Arthur L. Wilde Co., 1961–65; freelance publicist, 1965–66; pub. rel. consultant, Marineland of Florida, 1965; unit publicity dir., United Artists, National General, Paramount, 1966–69; free lance publicity, 1971; unit publicist, MGM, Paramount, United Artists, 1972–74; staff position; Features Publicity at Paramount Pictures, 1973. Freelance unit publicist again in 1976 at Universal, Paramount and Lorimar Productions. 1978–79, Columbia Pictures & Universal Studios; 1980, Marble Arch. Prods. & Northstar Intl. Pictures; 1981, studio pub. mgr., 20th Century-Fox; recently staff unit publicist for 20th-Fox; 1984–87, free lance unit publicist for feature films.

WILDE, CORNEL: Actor, Producer, Director, Author. b. New York, NY, Oct. 13, 1918; e. Columbia U.; City Coll. of New York; Art Sch., Budapest; Columbia Medical Sch.; studied drama with Strasberg, Bulgakov, Chekov. First screen role, 1941, High Sierra.
STAGE: Moon Over Mulberry Street, Love is Not So Simple, Daughters of Altreus, Having a Wonderful Time, Romeo & Juliet.
PICTURES INCLUDE: Wintertime, A Song to Remember, The Perfect Snob, A Thousand and One Nights, Leave Her to Heaven, Bandit of Sherwood Forest, Centennial Summer, Forever Amber, The Homestretch, It Had to be You, Walls of Jericho, Roadhouse, Four Days Leave, Two Flags West, Greatest Show on Earth, At Sword's Point, Saadia, Passion, Woman's World, Big Combo, Scarlet Coat, Hot Blood, Star of India, Beyond Mombasa, Omar Khayyam, Edge of Eternity, Constantine the Great; act., prod., dir.: Storm Fear, Maracaibo; act., prod., dir. cowriter: The Devil's Hairpin, The Sword of Lancelot; act., prod., dir.: The Naked Prey; act.,

prod., dir., co-author s.p.: Beach Red; prod., dir., co-author s.p.: No Blade of Grass; prod., dir., act., screenplay: Sharks' Treasure; actor: The Fifth Musketeer.
TELEVISION: Gargoyles (movie); Murder, She Wrote.

WILDER, BILLY: Producer, Director, Writer. r.n. Samuel Wilder. b. Austria, June 22, 1906. Newspaperman active Vienna, Berlin; then author screen story People on Sunday (debut, 1930) followed by 10 other German films. s.p.: Emil and the Detectives (in Museum of Modern Art), UFA. French films, wrote, dir., Mauvaise Graine, and wrote Adorable. To Hollywood 1934, Head Film Section, Psych. Warfare Div., U.S. Army, 1945, Am. Zone, Germany. American Film Institute Life Achievement Award 1987. Irving Thalberg Memorial Award 1988.
PICTURES: As co-writer: Music in the Air, Lottery Lover, Bluebeard's Eighth Wife, Midnight, Ninotchka, What a Life, Arise My Love, Ball of Fire, Hold Back the Dawn.
PICTURES: As director & co-writer: The Major and the Minor, Five Graves to Cairo, Double Indemnity, The Lost Weekend (Acad. Award, best dir., best co-s.p., 1945), The Emperor Waltz, A Foreign Affair, Sunset Boulevard (Acad. Award, best story and s.p., 1950); (collab. s.p., dir., prod) The Big Carnival (a.k.a. Ace in the Hole), Stalag 17, Sabrina, The Seven Year Itch, The Spirit of St. Louis, Love in the Afternoon, Witness for the Prosecution, Some Like It Hot, The Apartment (Academy Award for best direction, best story, and s.p., best picture, 1960); One, Two, Three, Irma La Douce; (co-prod.) Kiss Me, Stupid, The Fortune Cookie, The Private Life of Sherlock Holmes, Avanti, The Front Page, Fedora, Buddy, Buddy.

WILDER, GENE: Actor. r.n. Jerry Silberman. b. Milwaukee, WI, June 11, 1935. m. actress Gilda Radner. e. U. of Iowa. Joined Bristol Old Vic company in England, became champion fencer; in New York, worked as chauffeur, fencing instructor, etc. before N.Y. off-Broadway debut in Roots.
BROADWAY: The Complaisant Lover, Mother Courage, Luv.
PICTURES INCLUDE: Bonnie and Clyde, The Producers, Start the Revolution Without Me, Quackser Fortune Has a Cousin in the Bronx, Willy Wonka and the Chocolate Factory, Everything You Always Wanted to Know About Sex*, Blazing Saddles, Rhinoceros, Young Frankenstein, The Little Prince, Adventures of Sherlock Holmes Smarter Brother (s.p., dir., star), Silver Streak, The World's Greatest Lover (s.p., dir., star), The Frisco Kid, Stir Crazy, Sunday Lovers, (dir., s.p., act.), Hanky Panky, The Woman in Red (dir., s.p., act.), Haunted Honeymoon (dir., s.p., act.), See No Evil, Hear No Evil (also co-s.p.).
TELEVISION: The Trouble With People, Marlo Thomas Special (1973), Thursday's Game (movie).

WILDER, W. LEE: Producer, director. Brother of Billy Wilder. b. Austria. e. U. of Vienna. Awards: First prize 1950 Venice Film Festival musical documentary category.
PICTURES INCLUDE: The Vicious Circle, Shadows of Fire, The Pretender, Once A Thief, Three Steps North, Phantom from Space, Killers from Space, Snow Creature, Big Bluff, Manfish, Man Without a Body, Fright, Spy in the Sky, Bluebeard's Ten Honeymoons.

WILK, TED: Theatrical agent. b. Minneapolis, MN, Jan. 5, 1908. e. U. of Michigan, 1926–30. Publix Theatres, Duluth, MN, 1930; Warner Bros., Minneapolis, 1932–33; Film Daily, Hollywood, 1934–40; U.S. Army, 1941–46; Lou Irwin agency 1946–61; Ted Wilk Agency, since 1961.

WILLIAMS, BERT: Executive, Actor. b. Newark, NJ, April 12, 1922. e. U. of Southern California. Navy, 1942–45. Summer Stock, 1940–41; world's best diving champion, 1945–48; star diver, Larry Crosby, Buster Crabbe, Johnny Weismuller, Dutch Smith Shows, 1945–48; writer, asst. prod., Martin Mooney Prods., PRC, Goldwyn Studios; pres., Bert Prods., Bert Williams Motion Picture Producers and Distributors, Inc. Member, M.P. Academy of Fine Arts & TV Academy of Arts & Science.
THEATRE: roadshow plays include: Cat on a Hot Tin Roof, Hamlet, Run From The Hunter, Sugar and Spice, Hope Is a Thing Called Feathers, 69 Below, Tribute.
PICTURES INCLUDE: Actor, Angel Baby; prod., dir., actor, The Nest of the Cuckoo Birds; actor, Around the World Under the Sea; s.p. auth. Deathwatch 28; dir., Twenty Eight Watched, prod. dir. Adventure To Treasure Reef. s.p. Knife Fighters. orig. story & s.p.; Actor: Black Freedom; A Crime of Sex; The Masters. Crazy Joe, Serpico, Lady Ice, The Klansman, Report to the Commissioner, Tracks, All the President's Men, From Noon Till Three, While Buffalo, Helter Skelter, Shark Bait (writer), The Big Bus, Wanda Nevada, Cuba Crossing, Sunnyside, Cuba, The Last Resort, The All Night Treasure Hunt. Tom Horn, Kill Castro, Midnight Madness, The All-American Hustler, 10 to Midnight, Police Academy 2, One More Werewolf Picture, Murphy's Law, Cobra, Assassinations, Penitentiary III, Messenger of Death.
TELEVISION: Flipper, Sea Hunt, prod., Speargun, Gentle Ben, The Law (pilot) and Police Story (actor). Recent actor:

Get Christy Love, General Hospital, Columbo, Brenner for the People (actor), Mayday 40,000 Feet, Jigsaw John (Blue Knight episode), Police Woman, Chips, Mobil One, Street Killing, East of Eden, Rose for Emily, Brett Maverick, Today's F.B.I., The Judge. Produced, directed & wrote pilot, Fifth St. Gym. Appeared on Mike Douglas Show, Johnny Carson Show, Tales on Dark Side, The Last Car, This Is the Life, Deadly Intentions, Tales on the Dark Side, The Last Car, Divorce Court, Man Who Broke 1000 Chains.

WILLIAMS, BILL: Actor. r.n. William Katt. b. Brooklyn, NY, 1916. m. actress Barbara Hale. Father of actor William Katt. e. Pratt Inst., Brooklyn. In U.S. Army, W.W.II. Began as professional swimmer; later with Municipal Opera House, St. Louis; then on vaudeville tour, U.S. & England. Screen debut 1944 in Murder in the Blue Room.
PICTURES INCLUDE: Thirty Seconds Over Tokyo, Those Endearing Young Charms, Blue Blood, Great Missouri Raid, Operation Haylift, Cariboo Trail, Havana Rose, Rose of Cimarron, Son of Paleface, Bronco Buster, Pace That Thrills, Torpedo Alley, Racing Blood, Outlaw's Daughter, Apache Ambush, Hell's Horizon, Wiretapper, Broken Star, Dog's Best Friend, Buckskin, Tickle Me, Scandalous John.
TELEVISION: Series: Kit Carson (1952–54), Assignment Underwater.

WILLIAMS, BILLY DEE: Actor. b. New York, NY, April 6, 1937. e. National Acad. of Fine Arts and Design. Studied acting with Paul Mann and Sidney Poitier at actor's workshop in Harlem. Was child actor in the Firebrand of Florence with Lotte Lenya; Broadway adult debut in The Cool World in 1961.
STAGE: A Taste of Honey, Hallelujah, Baby, I Have a Dream, Fences.
PICTURES INCLUDE: The Last Angry Man (debut), The Out-of-Towners, The Final Comedown, Lady Sings the Blues, Hit! Mahogany, The Bingo Long Travelling All-Stars, The Empire Strikes Back, Nighthawks, Return of the Jedi, Marvin and Tige, Fear City, Number One with a Bullet, Deadly Illusion.
TELEVISION: Brian's Song, The Glass House, Christmas Lilies of the Field, Oceans of Fire, Chiefs, The Right of the People, Courage, Stranded, The Return of the Desperado, Scott Joplin, King of Ragtime and appearances on series: The F.B.I., The Interns, Mission Impossible, Mod Squad, Dynasty.

WILLIAMS, CARA: Comedienne. r.n. Bernice Kamiat. b. Brooklyn, NY, 1925. e. Hollywood Professional Sch. Ent. ind., 20th Century Fox, child actress.
PICTURES INCLUDE: Boomerang, Something For the Boys, Meet Me In Las Vegas, Never Steal Anything Small, The Defiant Ones, The Man from the Diners' Club, Doctors' Wives.
TELEVISION: Pete and Gladys, Alfred Hitchcock Presents, Desilu Playhouse, The Jackie Gleason Show, Henry Fonda Special, The Cara Williams Show.

WILLIAMS, CARL W.: Executive. b. Decatur, IL, March 9, 1927. e. Illinois State Normal U., B.S., 1949; U. of California at L.A., M.A., 1950. dir. adv. photo., Clark Equipment Co., 1951–54; film dir., WKAR-TV, E. Lansing, MI, 1954–56; Prod., dir., Capital Films, E. Lansing, MI, 1957; pdtr., A-V Laboratory, U.C.L.A., 1957–63; co-dev. Dimension 150 Widescreen process, 1957; formed D-150 Inc., 1963; Filbert Co., 1970, v.p., 1977; v.p., Cinema Equipment Sales of Calif., Inc., 1986. MAMPAS, SMPTE, AFI.

WILLIAMS, CINDY: Actress. b. Van Nuys, CA., Aug. 22, 1947. e. Los Angeles City Coll. Appeared in high school and college plays; first prof. role in Roger Corman's film Gas. Made TV debut in Room 222 and had continuing role.
PICTURES INCLUDE: Beware the Blob, Drive, He Said, The Christian Licorice Store, Travels with My Aunt, American Graffiti, The Conversation, Mr. Ricco, The First Nudie Musical, More American Graffiti, Uforia, Hunchback, Rude Awakening.
TELEVISION: Episodes of The Funny Side, The Neighbors, Barefoot in the Park, My World and Welcome to It, Love, American Style, Nanny and the Professor, The Bobby Sherman Show—Getting Together; Laverne and Shirley (series). Movies: The Migrants, Helped Wanted: Kids, Save the Dog, Tricks of the Trade.

WILLIAMS, DIAHN: Actress. b. Gainesville, FL, June 30. e. U. of Miami, B.A., psychology, speech; also attended U. of Florida, U. of California at L.A. m. Thomas J. McGrath, prod. & atty. Started as fashion model in New York, France, Germany. Top woman exec. as assoc. dir. of pub. rel. at Chesebrough-Ponds, 1971–72.
PICTURES INCLUDE: Chair de Poule, Another Nice Mess, Deadly Hero.
TELEVISION: Harry's Girls (series, 1963–64), Somerset (series, 1973–74) and guest-starred in many TV shows, including I Spy, Get Smart, Tarzan, Here Comes the Brides, Andy Griffith Show, G.E. Theatre, etc.

WILLIAMS, ELMO: Film editor. b. Oklahoma City, OK, Apr. 30, 1913. Film editor 1933–39, with British & Dominion Studio, England. Since then with RKO-Radio as film editor for numerous major productions; mgr., dir., 20th Century Fox Prod. Ltd. v.p., worldwide production, 20th Century-Fox Film 1971. President Ibex Films. Exec. v.p., Gaylord Prods., 1979; promoted to pres., worldwide prods.
PICTURES: Academy Award, best film ed. (collab.) High Noon, 1952; dir. film ed., Tall Texan; prod. dir., ed., The Cowboy; ed., 20,000 Leagues Under the Sea; dir. Apache Kid; second unit dir., film ed. The Vikings; dir. 2nd Unit DFZ prod., The Big Gamble; The Longest Day (assoc. prod.), Tora! Tora! Tora! (prod.), Sidewinder One (ed.), Caravans (ed.), Exec. prod.: Those Magnificent Men in Their Flying Machines, The Blue Max, Zorba The Greek, Man, Woman and Child (prod.).
TELEVISION: co-prod. dir., Tales of the Vikings.

WILLIAMS, ESTHER: Actress. b. Los Angeles, CA, Aug. 8, 1923. e. U. of Southern California. Swimmer San Francisco World's Fair Aquacade; professional model. On screen 1942 in Andy Hardy Steps Out. Voted one of Top Ten Money-Making Stars in M.P. Herald-Fame poll, 1950.
PICTURES INCLUDE: A Guy Named Joe, Bathing Beauty, Thrill of a Romance, This Time for Keeps, Ziegfeld Follies, Hoodlum Saint, Easy to Wed, Fiesta, On an Island With You, Take Me Out to the Ball Game, Neptune's Daughter, Pagan Love Song, Duchess of Idaho, Texas Carnival, Skirts Ahoy!, Million Dollars Mermaid, Dangerous When Wet, Easy to Love, Jupiter's Darling, Unguarded Moment, the Big Show, The Magic Fountain (s.p.).

WILLIAMS, JOBETH: Actress. b. Houston, TX, 1953. m. director John Pasquin. e. Brown U. One of Glamour Magazine's top 10 college girls, 1969–70. With repertory companies in Rhode Island, Philadelphia, Boston, Washington, DC, etc. Spent over two years in New York-based daytime serials, Somerset and The Guiding Light. Film debut in Kramer Vs. Kramer, 1979.
THEATER: Ladyhouse Blues (1979), A Coupla White Chicks Sitting Around Talking, Gardenia.
PICTURES INCLUDE: Stir Crazy, The Dogs of War, Poltergeist, Endangered Species, The Big Chill, American Dreamer, Teachers, Desert Bloom, Poltergeist II, Memories of Me, Passage.
TELEVISION: Fun and Games, Feasting with Panthers, Jabberwocky, The Day After, Adam, Kids Don't Tell, Adam: His Song Continues, Murder Ordained, Baby M.

WILLIAMS, JOHN: Composer. b. New York, NY, Feb. 8, 1932. e. U. of California at L.A., Juilliard Sch. Worked as session musician in '50s; began career as film composer in late '50s. Considerable experience as musical director and conductor as well as composer. Since 1977 conductor of Boston Pops.
PICTURES INCLUDE: I Passed for White, Because They're Young, The Secret Ways, Bachelor Flat, Diamond Head, Gidget Goes to Rome, The Killers, None But the Brave, John Goldfarb Please Come Home, The Rare Breed, How To Steal A Million, The Plainsman, Not with My Wife You Don't, Penelope, A Guide for the Married Man, Fitzwilly, Valley of the Dolls, Daddy's Gone A-Hunting, Good-bye Mr. Chips (mus. supvr. & dir.), The Reivers, Fiddler on the Roof (musc. dir.) The Cowboys, Images, Pete 'n' Tillie, The Poseidon Adventure, Tom Sawyer (musc. supvr.), The Long Goodbye, The Man Who Loved Cat Dancing, The Paper Chase, Cinderella Liberty, Conrack, The Sugarland Express, Earthquake, The Towering Inferno, The Eiger Sanction, Jaws, Star Wars, Close Encounters of the Third Kind, The Fury, Jaws II, Meteor, Quintet, Dracula, 1941, Close Encounters of the. Third Kind (special edition), The Empire Strikes Back, Heartbeeps, Raiders of the Lost Ark; E.T.: The Extra-Terrestrial, Return of the Jedi, Monsignor, Indiana Jones and the Temple of Doom, The River, Space Camp, The Witches of Eastwick.
TELEVISION: Once Upon a Savage Night, Jane Eyre (Emmy Award), Sergeant Ryker, Heidi (Emmy Award), The Ewok Adventure, NBC News Theme, Amazing Stories.

WILLIAMS, OSCAR: Writer, Producer, Director. e. San Francisco State U., getting degree in film, TV. Was director's intern on The Great White Hope (directed by Martin Ritt) through the American Film Inst.
PICTURES INCLUDE: The Final Comedown (s.p., prod. dir.); Black Belt Jones (s.p., assoc. prod.) Five on the Black Hand Side (dir.), Truck Turner (s.p.), Hot Potato (s.p., dir.).

WILLIAMS, PAUL: Actor, Composer. b. Omaha, NB. Sept. 19, 1940. Began career at studios as set painter and stunt parachutist. Bit and character parts in commercials followed. Seen briefly in The Chase and The Loved One. Became song writer, collaborating briefly with Biff Rose and later with Roger Nichols, with whom wrote several best-sellers, including We've Only Just Begun, Rainy Days and Mondays, Just an Old-Fashioned Love Song, Evergreen (Acad. Award with Barbra Streisand, 1976).

PICTURES INCLUDE: As actor: Watermelon Man, Planet of the Apes, The Cheap Detective, Smokey and the Bandit (& II), The End, Stone Cold Dead, The Muppet Movie (and score), The Chill Factor. Scores: Cinderella Liberty, Phantom of the Paradise (also actor), Bugsy Malone, A Star Is Born (songs), Grease (title song), Agatha, One on One.
TELEVISION: Rooster, Night They Saved Christmas, Wild, Wild West Revisited, Flight to Holocaust.

WILLIAMS, PAUL: Director. First gained attention as director of film short, Girl, which won Golden Eagle award. Made in collaboration with producer Edward R. Pressman, with whom he formed Pressman-Williams Enterprises.
PICTURES INCLUDE: Out of It, The Revolutionary, Dealing: or the Berkeley to Boston Forty Brick, Lost Bag Blues, Nunzio.

WILLIAMS, RICHARD: Producer, Painter, Film animator. b. March, 1933, Toronto, Canada. Entered industry in 1955. Founded Richard Williams Animation Ltd. in 1962, having entered films by producing The Little Island (1st Prize, Venice Film Festival) in 1955. His company produces TV commercials, entertainment shorts and animated films. Also designed animated feature titles for such films as What's New Pussycat?, A Funny Thing Happened On The Way To The Forum, Casino Royale, etc. (20 feature titles in 6 years). 1969: Animated sequences: Charge of the Light Brigade (Woodfall). 1971: A Christmas Carol, animated TV special for ABC-TV. His company makes TV commercials for England, America, France and Germany. His films have won awards at Festivals at Venice, Edinburgh, Mannheim, Montreal, Trieste, Melbourne, West Germany, New York, Locarno, Vancouver, Philadelphia, Zagreb, Hollywood, Cork, Los Angeles. 1973: Won Academy Award, best cartoon.

WILLIAMS, ROBIN: Actor, Comedian. b. Chicago, IL, July 21, 1952. e. Claremont Men's Coll. (CA), Coll. of Marin (CA) studying acting at latter. Continued studies at Juilliard with John Houseman in New York augmenting income as a street mime. As San Francisco club performer appeared at Holy City Zoo, Intersection, the Great American Music Hall and The Boardinghouse. In Los Angeles performed as stand-up comedian at Comedy Store, Improvisation, and The Ice House. First TV appearance on Laugh In, followed by The Great American Laugh Off. Guest on Happy Days as extraterrestrial named Mork from Ork.
TELEVISION: Series: The Richard Pryor Show (1977), Laugh-In (revival 1977–78), Mork and Mindy. Guest: America Tonight, Ninety Minutes Live, The Alan Hamel Show, E.T. & Friends, Faerie Tale Theatre, Seize the Day.
PICTURES: The Last Laugh, Popeye, The World According to Garp, The Survivors, Moscow on the Hudson, The Best of Times, Club Paradise, Good Morning Vietnam, Dear America: Letters Home From Vietnam (reader), The Adventures of Baron Munchausen, Dead Poet's Society.

WILLIAMS, ROGER: Pianist, Concert, film, TV Personality. b. Omaha, NB, Oct. 1, 1926. e. Drake U., Idaho State Coll. Hon. Ph.D. Midland and Wagner Colls. Served U.S. Navy W.W.II. Appeared as guest artist in number of films. Public debut on TV's Arthur Godfrey Talent Scouts and Chance of a Lifetime. Other TV appearances include Ed Sullivan, Hollywood Palace, Kraft Summer Series, Celanese Special. Tours in addition to U.S. and Australia. Concert Halls—Japan, Mexico, Union of South Africa. Recorded 75 Albums, Kapp (now MCA) Records, with sales over 15 million albums.

WILLIAMS, TREAT: Actor. r.n. Richard Williams. b. Rowayton, CT, 1952. e. Franklin and Marshall Coll. Landed role on Bdwy. in musical, Over There! also played leading role in Grease on Bdwy. Film debut in The Ritz (1975).
THEATER: Bus Stop (Equity Library Theatre), Once in a Lifetime, The Pirates of Penzance, Some Men Need Help.
PICTURES: Deadly Hero, The Eagle Has Landed, Hair, 1941, Why Would I Lie?, The Pursuit of D. B. Cooper, Prince of the City, Once Upon a Time in America, Flashpoint, Smooth Talk, The Men's Club, Dead Heat, Sweet Lies, Heart of Dixie, Night of the Sharks, Russicum.
TELEVISION: Movies: Dempsey, A Streetcar Named Desire, J. Edgar Hoover, Echoes in the Darkness.

WILLIAMS-JONES, MICHAEL: Executive. b. England, June 3, 1947. Joined United Artists as trainee, 1967; territorial manager, South Africa, 1969; territorial manager, Brazil, 1971; territorial manager, England, 1976; appt. v.p., continental European manager, 1978; sr. v.p. foreign manager, 1979; In 1982 joined United Intl. Pictures as sr. v.p. intl. sls., based in London. 1984, named pres. UIP motion picture group; 1986, named pres. & CEO.

WILLIAMSON, FRED: Actor, Director, Writer. b. Gary, IN, March 5, 1937. e. Northwestern U. Spent 10 yrs. playing pro football before turning to acting.
PICTURES INCLUDE: M*A*S*H, Tell Me That You Love Me, Junie Moon, The Legend of Nigger Charley, Hammer, Black Caesar, The Soul of Nigger Charley, Hell Up in Harlem,

That Man Bolt, Crazy Joe, Three Tough Guys, Black Eye, Three the Hard Way, Boss Nigger, Darktown, Bucktown, No Way Back (also prod., dir. s.p.), Take a Hard Ride, Adios Amigo, Death Journey (also prod., dir.), Joshua, Blind Rage, Fist of Fear Touch of Death, 1990: The Bronx Warriors; One Down Two to Go (also prod. dir.), Vigilante, Warriors of the Wasteland, Deadly Impact, The Big Score (dir., actor); The Last Fight (dir., actor); Foxtrap (prod., dir., actor); Warrior of the Lost World, Deadly Intent; Delta Force; Commando; Taxi Killer (prod.), Hell's Heroes.
TELEVISION: Julia (series), Police Story, Monday Night Football, Half Nelson.

WILLIAMSON, NICOL: Actor. b. England, Sept. 14, 1938. Has played many classical roles with Royal Shakespeare Co., including Macbeth, Malvolio, and Coriolanus. Starred on Broadway in Inadmissible Evidence; musical debut in Rex.
PICTURES INCLUDE: Six Sided Triangle, Inadmissible Evidence, The Bofors Gun, Laughter in the Dark, The Reckoning, Hamlet, The Jerusalem File, The Seven-Per-Cent Solution, The Goodbye Girl (cameo), The Cheap Detective, The Human Factor, Excalibur, Venom, I'm Dancing As Fast As I Can, Return to Oz, Black Widow, Apt Pupil.
TELEVISION: Passion Flower, Lord Mountbatten, The Word, Macbeth, Christopher Columbus.

WILLIAMSON, PATRICK: Executive. b. England, Oct. 1929. Joined Columbia Pictures London office 1944—career spanned advertising & publicity responsibilities until 1967 when apptd. managing director Columbia Great Britain in 1971. Also man. dir. on formation of Columbia-Warner. Promoted to executive position in Columbia's home office, New York, April, 1973 and president of international operations since Feb. 1974. Vice pres., Coca-Cola Export Corp., April, 1983; exec. v.p. Columbia Pictures Industries, 1985; director, CPI, 1985; exec. v.p., Coca-Cola Entertainment Business Sector, 1987; promoted to special asst. to pres. & CEO of Coca-Cola Entertainment Business Sector, July, 1987. Serves on boards of Tri-Star-Pictures, RCA/Columbia Home Video, RCA/Columbia Int'l. Video. 1987: named president Triumph Releasing Corp., a unit of Columbia Pictures Entertainment.

WILLIS, BRUCE: Actor. b. Germany, March 19, 1955. Moved to New Jersey when he was 2. After graduating high school, worked at DuPont plant in neighboring town. First entertainment work was as harmonica player in band called Loose Goose. Formed Night Owl Promotions and attended Montclair State Coll., NJ where he acted in Cat on a Hot Tin Roof. N.Y. stage debut: Heaven and Earth. Member of Barbara Contardi's First Amendment Comedy Theatre; supplemented acting work by doing Levi's 501 jeans commercials and as bartender in a N.Y. nightclub, Kamikaze.
THEATER: Fool for Love.
PICTURES: Blind Date, Die Hard, In Country.
TELEVISION: Hart to Hart, Miami Vice, Moonlighting (series).

WILLIS, GORDON: Cinematographer. Acted two summers in stock at Gloucester, MA, where also did stage settings and scenery. Photographer in Air Force; then cameraman, making documentaries. In TV did commercials and documentaries.
PICTURES INCLUDE: End of the Road, Loving, The Landlord, The People Next Door, Little Murders, Bad Company, Klute, Up the Sandbox, The Paper Chase, The Godfather, The Parallax View, The Godfather, Part II, The Downing Pool, All the President's Men, September 30, 1955, Annie Hall, Comes a Horseman, Interiors, Manhattan, Stardust Memories, Pennies from Heaven, A Midsummer Night's Sex Comedy, Perfect, Zelig, Broadway Danny Rose, The Purple Rose of Cairo, The Money Pit, The Pick-Up Artist, Bright Lights, Big City. Director: Windows (1980; debut).
TELEVISION: The Lost Honor of Kathryn Beck.

WILLIS, (LORD) TED: Screenwriter, Dramatist. b. England, Jan. 13, 1918.
PICTURES INCLUDE: The Blue Lamp (orig. treatment), Good-Time, Trouble in Store, One Good Turn, Top of the Form, Up to His Neck, Woman in a Dressing Gown, The Young and the Guilty, Great to Be Young, No Trees in the Street, The Horsemasters, Flame in the Streets, Bitter Harvest, The Naked Sun, Mrs. Harris M.P., Spy on Ice, Mrs. Hams Goes to New York, Mrs. Harris Goes to Moscow, Mrs. Harris Goes to Monte Carlo.
TELEVISION: Dixon of Dock Green, Big City, Look in Any Window, Strictly for the Sparrows, Scent of Fear, Inside Story, Hot Summer Night, Sergeant Cork, The Four Seasons of Rosie Carr, The Sullivan Brothers, Knock On Any Door, Virgin of the Secret Service, Crime of Passion, Black Beauty, Hunter's Walk, Valley of the Kings, A Place for Animals, The Campbells in Canada, Racecourse, Minna, Anna and Luzieci.

WILSON, ELIZABETH: Actress. b. Grand Rapids, MI, April 4, 1925. On Bdwy. in Picnic (debut, 1953), The Desk Set, The Tunnel of Love, Little Murders, Dark of the Moon, Sticks and Bones (Tony), Uncle Vanya, Morning's at Seven, Ah! Wilderness.
PICTURES: The Goddess, Little Murders, Day of the Dolphin, Man on the Swing, The Happy Hooker, The Prisoner of Second Avenue, Nine to Five, The Incredible Shrinking Woman, Grace Quigley, Where Are the Children?, The Believers.
TELEVISION: Doc (series), Million Dollar Infield, Miles to Go Before I Sleep, Sanctuary of Fear, Morning's at Seven, Nutcracker: Money, Madness and Murder, Conspiracy of Love.

WILSON, FLIP: Performer. r.n. Clerow Wilson. b. Newark, NJ, Dec. 8, 1933. Left school at 16 to join Air Force; played clubs in FL & Bahamas until 1965 when guest appearance on NBC began; The Flip Wilson Show debuted 1970–71 season, (won Emmy, 1971), Charlie and Company (1985–86 season).
PICTURE: Uptown Saturday Night, Skatetown USA, The Fish That Saved Pittsburgh.

WILSON, HUGH: Producer, Director, Writer. b. Miami, FL, Aug. 21, 1943. Gained fame for creating, writing, producing and directing TV series, WKRP in Cincinnati, and Frank's Place. Feature film dir. debut with Police Academy (1984).
PICTURES: Stroker Ace (co-s.p.), Police Academy (dir. and co-s.p.), Rustler's Rhapsody (s.p./dir.), Burglar (co.s.p.-dir.).

WILSON, RICHARD: Producer, Director. b. McKeesport, PA, Dec. 25, 1915. e. Denver U. Actor, announcer, Denver radio stations; radio actor, N.Y.; actor, asst. stage mgr., stage mgr., prod. asst. with Mercury Theatre, 1937–38; mgr., prod., summer theatres, 1939–40; assoc. with all Orson Welles films & radio shows to 1951; U.S. Air Force, 1942–45; assoc., prod., then prod., U-I.
PICTURES INCLUDE: assoc. prod., Lady from Shanghai, Macbeth, Ma and Pa Kettle on Vacation, Ma and Pa Kettle Go to Waikiki, Redhead from Wyoming; prod., Ma and Pa Kettle at Home, Golden Blade, Man with a Gun, Kettles in the Ozarks; dir. The Big Boodle; co-writer, dir. Man with a Gun; co-writer, dir., Raw Wind in Eden; dir., Al Capone; collab. s.p., dir. Invitation to a Gunfighter, Three in the Attic (prod.-dir.).

WILSON, SCOTT: Actor. b. Atlanta, GA, 1942. Was college athlete on basketball scholarship when injured and had to leave school. Moved to L.A. and enrolled in local acting class. Made film debut, In Cold Blood, 1968.
PICTURES INCLUDE: The Grissom Gang, The Gypsy Moths, Castle Keep, In the Heat of the Night, The New Centurions, Lolly-Madonna XXX, The Great Gatsby, The Passover Plot, The Ninth Configuration, The Right Stuff, The Aviator, On the Line, A Year of the Quiet Sun, Blue City, Malone.
TELEVISION: The Tracker.

WINCER, SIMON: Director. b. Australia. Directed over 200 hours of dramatic programs for Australian TV, including Cash and Company, Tandarra, Ryan, Against the Wind, The Sullivans, etc. Exec. prod. of The Man from Snowy River, then the top-grossing theatrical film in Australia.
PICTURES: Snapshot, Harlequin, Phar Lap, D.A.R.Y.L., The Lighthorsemen (dir., co.-prod.).
TELEVISION: The Last Frontier, Bluegrass.

WINCHELL, PAUL: Performer. b. New York, NY, 1924. e. Sch. of Industrial Arts. At 13 won first prize Major Bowes Radio Amateur Hour; signed by Ted Weems; created Jerry Mahoney when 17; Host of The Bigelow Show (1948–49), ventriloquist & star own Paul Winchell-Jerry Mahoney show (1950–54). Ringmaster Circus Time and panelist on Keep Talking. In The Treasure Chest (TV movie, 1975). Provides voices for numerous films (The Aristocats, Winnie the Pooh, The Fox and the Hound) and Saturday morning cartoons (Dastardly and Muttley, Goober and the Ghost Chasers). Made news in 1975 as inventor of an artificial heart.

WINDSOR, MARIE: Actress. r.n. Emily Marie Bertelsen. b. Maryvale, UT, Dec. 11, 1922. Winner of beauty contests, including Miss Utah. Worked as telephone girl, dancing teacher. Trained for acting by Maria Ouspenskaya. Won Look Mag. Award, best supporting actress, 1957.
PICTURES INCLUDE: Song of the Thin Man, Force of Evil, Dakota Lil, Little Big Horn, The Narrow Margin, The Eddie Cantor Story, The Bounty Hunter, Swamp Woman, The Killing, The Story of Mankind, Critics Choice, Mail Order Bride, Chamber of Horrors, Support Your Local Gunfighter, One More Train To Rob, Cahill, U.S. Marshall, The Outfit, Hearts of the West, Freaky Friday, Lovely But Deadly.
TELEVISION: Salem's Lot, J.O.E. and the Colonel, Manhunter, Wild Women.

WINELAND, FRED L.: Theatre Executive. b. Washington, DC, 1926. e. Southeastern U., 1957. Pres., Wineland Theatres, circuit which owns and operates two Maryland drive-ins, three Maryland indoor multi-cinemas and two Virginia multi-cinemas.

WINFIELD, PAUL: Actor. b. Los Angeles, CA, May 22, 1940. e. U. of California at L.A. Inducted in Black Filmmakers Hall of Fame.
THEATER: Regional work at Dallas Theatre Center (A Lesson From Aloes), Goodman Theatre (Enemy of the People), Stanford Repertory Theatre and Inner City Cultural Center, L.A.; At Lincoln Center in The Latent Heterosexual, and Richard III. Broadway: Checkmates.
PICTURES: The Lost Man, RPM, Brother John, Sounder, Gordon's War, Conrack, Hustle, Damnation Alley, The Greatest, A Hero Ain't Nothin' But a Sandwich, Twilight's Last Gleaming, Carbon Copy, Star Trek II—The Wrath of Khan, White Dog, On the Run, Mike's Murder, The Terminator, Blue City, Death Before Dishonor, Big Shots, The Serpent and the Rainbow.
TELEVISION: King, Backstairs at the White House, Angel City, Key Tortuga, The Sophisticated Gents, Dreams Don't Die, Sister Sister, The Blue and the Gray, For Us the Living, Go Tell It on the Mountain, Under Siege, The Roy Campanella Story, Women of Brewster Place, Roots II, The Charmings (series).

WINFREY, OPRAH: TV Talk Show Hostess, Actress. b. Kosciusko, MS, 1954. e. Tennessee State U. Started as TV news reporter-anchor in Nashville. Moved to Baltimore in same capacity, later having very successful morning talk show. Left Chicago to host own show which became top-rated in only a month; expanded to national syndication in 1986. Formed own production co., Harpo, Inc. in 1986 which assumed ownership and prod. of The Oprah Winfrey Show in 1988. Named Broadcaster of the Year by Intl. Radio and TV Soc., 1988. Theatrical film debut in The Color Purple (1985), Throw Momma From the Train (cameo).
TELEVISION: Movie: The Women of Brewster Place (actress, co-exec. prod.).

WINGER, DEBRA: Actress. b. Cleveland, OH, May 17, 1955. m. Timothy Hutton, actor. e. California State U. Began career in TV series Wonder Woman; also featured in TV film, Special Olympics. Feature film debut: Slumber Party, 1976.
PICTURES: Thank God, It's Friday, French Postcards, Urban Cowboy, Cannery Row, An Officer and a Gentleman, Mike's Murder, Terms of Endearment, Legal Eagles, Made in Heaven, Black Widow, Sundown, Betrayed.

WINITSKY, ALEX: Producer. b. New York, NY, Dec. 27, 1924. e. NYU, BS, LLB, JD. In partnership as attorneys in L.A. for 20 years with Arlene Sellers before they turned to financing and later production of films.
PICTURES INCLUDE: (co-prod. with Sellers) End of the Game, The Seven-Per-Cent Solution, Cross of Iron, Night Calls, Silver Bears, The Lady Vanishes, Breakthrough, Cuba, Blue Skies Again, Irreconcilable Differences, Scandalous, Swing Shift, Bad Medicine.
TELEVISION: Ford—The Man and the Machine.

WINKLER, HENRY: Actor. b. New York, NY, Oct. 30, 1945. e. Emerson Coll., Yale Sch. of Drama, MA. Appeared with Yale Repertory Co.; returned to N.Y. to work in radio. Did 30 TV commercials before starring in The Great American Dream Machine and Masquerade on TV.
PICTURES INCLUDE: The Lords of Flatbush (debut), Crazy Joe, Heroes, The One and Only, Night Shift, Memories of Me (dir.).
TELEVISION: The Mary Tyler Moore Show, The Bob Newhart Show, The Paul Sand Show, Rhoda, Happy Days (series), Laverne & Shirley. Specials: Henry Winkler Meets William Shakespeare, America Salutes Richard Rodgers, An American Christmas Carol. Movie: Katherine. Director: A Smoky Mountain Christmas, All the Kids Do It (actor and dir. and Emmy as exec. prod., 1985). Exec. prod.: Ryan's Four (series), Who Are The DeBolts—and Where Did They Get 19 Kids?, Scandal Sheet, When Your Loves Leaves, Starflight, Second Start.

WINKLER, IRWIN: Producer. b. New York, NY, May 28, 1931. e. New York U. Started in mailroom at William Morris Agency 1955–62. With I. Robert Chartoff formed production co., Chartoff-Winkler Prods. All films co-produced with Chartoff until Revolution (1985). Then solo producer-Irwin Winkler, Winkler Films.
PICTURES INCLUDE: Double Trouble, Point Blank, The Split, They Shoot Horses, Don't They?, The Strawberry Statement, Leo the Last, Believe in Me, The Gang That Couldn't Shoot Straight, The New Centurions, Up the Sandbox, The Mechanic, Busting, S*P*Y*S, The Gambler, Breakout, Rocky, Nickelodeon, New York, New York, Valentino, Comes a Horseman, Uncle Joe Shannon, Rocky II, Raging Bull, True Confessions, Rocky III, Author! Author!; The Right Stuff, Rocky IV, Revolution, 'Round Midnight, Betrayed.

WINNER, MICHAEL: Producer, Director, Writer. b. London, Eng., Oct. 30, 1935. e. Cambridge U. Ent. m.p. ind. as columnist, dir., Drummer Films.
TELEVISION: White Hunter series, Dick and the Duchess series.

PICTURES INCLUDE: orig. s.p., Man With A Gun; prod. dir., writ., Shoot to Kill, Swiss Holiday, Climb Up the Wall, Out of the Shadow, Some Like it Cool, Girls, Girls, Girls, It's Magic, Behave Yourself; Haunted England, Play It Cool, The Cool Mikado; dir., West 11; co-prod., dir., The System; co-author, dir. You Must Be Joking; co-prod. author. dir. The Jokers; prod. dir. I'll Never Forget What's 'Is Name; prod. dir., Hannibal Brooks, The Nightcomers, Chato's Land; dir. The Mechanic, Scorpio, The Stone Killer, Death Wish, (prod. dir.), Won Ton Ton, The Dog That Saved Hollywood (prod., dir.), The Sentinel (prod., dir.), The Big Sleep; Firepower; Death Wish II; The Wicked Lady (also co-s.p.); Scream for Help (prod., dir.); Death Wish 3 (prod., dir.); Appointment with Death (prod., dir., s.p.), A Chorus of Disapproval (prod., dir., s.p.).

WINNINGHAM, MARE: Actress. b. CA, May 6, 1959. TV debut at age 16 as a singer on The Gong Show.
PICTURES: One-Trick Pony (1980); Threshold; St. Elmo's Fire; Nobody's Fool; Miracle Mile.
TELEVISION: Off the Minnesota Strip; Operation Runaway; Amber Waves (Emmy Award, 1980); The Women's Room; Special Olympics; The Thorn Birds; Helen Keller—The Miracle Continues; Studs Lonigan (mini-series); Eye on the Sparrow; God Bless This Child.

WINTERS, DEBORAH: Actress. b. Los Angeles, CA. e. Professional Children's Sch., New York; began studying acting with Stella Adler at age 13 and Lee Strasberg at 16. Acting debut at age 9 in TV commercials. Casting dir.: Breakdancers for Mars.
PICTURES: Me, Natalie, Hail Hero!, The People Next Door, Kotch, Class of '44, Blue Sunshine, The Lamp, The Outing.
TELEVISION: Six Characters in Search of an Author, The People Next Door, The Winds of War, Crisis in Sun Valley, Gemini Man. Movies: Tarantulas: The Deadly Cargo, Little Girl Lost.

WINTERS, DAVID: Choreographer, Actor, Director. b. London, April 5, 1939. Acted in both Broadway and m.p. version of West Side Story (as A-rab). Directed and acted in number of TV shows. Choreography credits include films Viva Las Vegas, Billie, Send Me No Flowers, Tickle Me, Pajama Party, Girl Happy, The Swinger, Made in Paris, Easy Come, Easy Go, The Island of Doctor Moreau, Roller Boogie, A Star is Born, Blame It on the Night. Was choreographer for TV series Hullabaloo, Shindig, Donny and Marie Osmond, The Big Show, and Steve Allen Show, and several TV specials starring Joey Heatherton, Nancy Sinatra, Diana Ross.
THEATER: Of Love Remembered (Bdwy, dir.), Pajama Tops (prod.).
PICTURES INCLUDE: Racquet (dir., prod.), Welcome to My Nightmare (dir.), The Last Horror Film (prod., dir.), Fanatic (dir., prod.), Rage to Kill (dir., prod.), Mission Kill (dir.), Thrasin' (dir.).
TELEVISION: The Monkees (series, dir.), Where the Girls Are (dir.), Prod.: Leslie Uggams Special, The Spring Thing, Old Faithful, Go, Saga of Sonora, Hot Stuff, Story Theatre, Lucy in London; Exec. Prod.: Barbara McNair Show, Once Upon a Wheel (series), The Darin Invasion, The Lou Rawls Show, Bobby Sherman Special, Sonny and Cher Nitty Gritty Hour, 5th Dimension: Traveling Sunshine Show, Rolling on the River, Timex All-Star Swing Festival. Director-Producer: Ann-Margret From Hollywood With Love, Ann-Margret Show, The London Bridge Special, Racquel, Dr. Jekyll and Mr. Hyde, Diana Ross Show (world tour).

WINTERS, JERRY: Producer, Director. b. Waterbury, CT, Aug. 18, 1917. e. Antioch Coll., B.A., 1940. Photog., 1940–42; U.S. Air Force, 1942–46; photog., Hollywood, 1946–47; prod. assoc. Tonight on Broadway, CBS-TV, 1949; assoc. prod., College Bowl, ABC-TV, 1950–51; in charge N.Y. film prod., Television Varieties, Inc., 1951–54; Production head Eldorado Int'l Pictures Corp., 1964–67; vice president, Edutornics Corp., 1968; pres. Giralda Pros., 1971.
PICTURES INCLUDE: prod., Renoir; prod.-dir., Herman Melville's Moby Dick, Speak to Me Child; prod; English version, The Loves of Liszt.

WINTERS, JONATHAN: Performer. b. Dayton, OH, Nov. 11, 1925. e. Kenyon Coll.; Dayton Art Inst., B.F.A. Disc jockey, Dayton and Columbus stations; night club comedian. Performed at Blue Angel, NY and on Bdwy. in John Murray Anderson's Almanac. Author: Mouse Breath, Conformity and Other Social Ills.
TELEVISION: And Here's the Show, Columbus—TV, NBC Comedy Hour, Jonathan Winters Show, Masquerade Party (panelist), 'Tis the Season to Be Smurphy (voice), Hot Dog, The Wacky World of Jonathan Winters, Mork and Mindy.
PICTURES INCLUDE: It's A Mad, Mad, Mad World; Oh, Dad, Poor Dad; The Loved One, The Russians Are Coming, the Russians Are Coming, Penelope, On the Lam, Viva Max, The Fish That Saved Pittsburgh, The Longshot, Midnight Oil, Moon Over Parador.

WINTERS, ROLAND: Actor. b. Boston, MA, Nov. 22, 1905. Appeared on stage and in stock, 1923–33; numerous radio programs, 1933–47. On screen in 13 Rue Madeleine, Return of October. Starred as Charlie Chan in pictures for Monogram.
  PICTURES INCLUDE: West Point Story, Follow the Sun, Inside Straight, She's Working Her Way Through College, Jet Pilot, So Big, Loving.

WINTERS, SHELLEY: Actress. r.n. Shirley Schrift. b. St. Louis, MO, Aug. 18, 1922. e. Wayne U. Clerked in 5 & 10 cent store; in vaudeville; on dramatic stage (Conquest, Night Before Christmas, Meet the People, Rosalinda, etc.). Screen debut, Nine Girls (1943). Sailor's Holiday. N.Y. stage; A Hatful of Rain, Girls of Summer, Minnie's Boys.
  PICTURES INCLUDE: Knickerbocker Holiday, Cover Girl, Double Life, Cry of the City, Larceny, Take one False Step, Johnny Stool Pigeon, Great Gatsby, South Sea Sinner, Winchester '73, Place in the Sun, Untamed Frontier, My Man and I, Tennessee Champ, Executive Suite, Saskatchewan, Playgirl, Mambo, Night of the Hunter, I Am a Camera, Big Knife, Treasure of Pancho Villa, I Died a Thousand Times, Cash on Delivery, Diary of Anne Frank (Acad. Award, supp., 1959), Young Savages, Lolita, Chapman Report, A House Is Not a Home, A Patch of Blue (Acad. Award, supp., 1965), Alfie, Enter Laughing, The Scalphunters, Wild in the Streets, Buena Sera Mrs. Campbell, The Mad Room, Bloody Mama, What's the Matter with Helen?, The Poseidon Adventure, Cleopatra Jones, Something to Hide, Blume in Love, Diamonds, Next Stop Greenwich Village, The Tenant, Pete's Dragon, City on Fire, "S.O.B.", Over the Brooklyn Bridge, Ellie, Witchfire (also assoc. prod.), Deja Vu, The Delta Force., The Order of Things.
  TELEVISION: Two is the Number (Enemy, 1964), Big Rose, Alice in Wonderland, French Atlantic Affair, Death of Innocence, Adventures of Nick Carter, Elvis.

WINTMAN, MELVIN R.: Theatre Executive. b. Chelsea, MA. e. U. of Massachusetts, Northeastern U., J.D. Major, infantry, AUS, W.W.II. Attorney. Now consultant & dir., General Cinema Corp.; formerly exec. v.p., GCC and pres., GCC Theatres, Inc., Boston. Dir. Will Rogers Memorial Fund. Former pres. Theatre Owners of New England (1969–70); past dir. NATO (1969–70); treas., Nat'l Assoc. of Concessionaires (1960).

WISBERG, AUBREY: Writer, Producer, Director. b. London, Eng., Oct. 20, 1909. e. Columbia U. Newspaper writer, radio, TV dramatist U.S. Eng., Australia, radio diffusionist, Paris, France. Author novels Bushman at Large, Patrol Boat 999, This Is the Life; plays Virtue, Inc., Whiphand.
  PICTURES INCLUDE: s.p., prod. The Man From Planet X, Captive Women, Sword of Venus, The Neanderthal Man, Capt. John Smith & Pocahontas, Problem Girls, Dragon's Gold, Capt. Kidd & the Slave Girl, Return to Treasure Island, Murder is My Beat, The Women of Pitcairn Island, Port Sinister, Submarine Raider, Counter Espionage, Escape in the Fog, U-Boat Prisoner, Power of the Whistler, Adventures of Rusty, After Midnight, The Wreck of the Hesperus, The Big Fix, Betrayal from the East. The Falcon's Adventure, Son of Sinbad, At Swords Point, Hit Parade, They Came to Blow Up America, Bombers Moon, Rendezvous 24, The Lady in the Iron Mask, The Steel Lady, Treasure of Monte Cristo, Road to the Big House, The Burning Cross, St. Montana Mike, Casanova's Big Night, So Dark the Night, The Desert Hawk, s.p. Just Before Dawn, Out of the Depths, Target Minus Forty, Mission Mars, Ride the Wild Wind, Hercules in N.Y., Evil in the Blood.

WISDOM, NORMAN: Actor, Singer, Comedian. Musical and legit. b. London, Eng., Feb. 4. Many London West End stage shows including royal command performances. New York Broadway shows include Walking Happy and Not Now Darling. Two Broadway awards. Films include Trouble in Store, One Good Turn, Man of the Moment, Up in the World, Just My Luck, The Square Peg, There Was a Crooked Man, The Bulldog Breed, The Girl on the Boat, On the Beat, A Stitch in Time, The Early Bird, Press for Time, The Sandwich Man, What's Good for the Goose, and others mostly for the Rank Organisation and United Artists. In US: The Night They Raided Minsky's. TV musical: Androcles and the Lion.

WISE, ROBERT: Director, Producer. b. Winchester, IN, Sept. 10, 1914. e. Franklin Coll., Franklin, IN. No prior bus. experience. Ent. m.p. ind. in cutting dept. RKO, 1933; sound cutter, asst. ed.; film ed., 1938; dir., 1943; to 20th Century-Fox, 1949; ass'n. Mirisch Co. independent prod. 1959; assn. MGM independent prod., 1962; assn. 20th Century Fox Independent Prod. 1963. Partner, Filmakers Group, The Tripar Group.
  PICTURES INCLUDE: The Body Snatchers, Blood on the Moon, The Set Up, Day the Earth Stood Still, Captive City, So Big, Executive Suite, Helen of Troy, Tribute to a Bad Man, Somebody Up There Likes Me, Until They Sail, Run Silent Run Deep, I Want to Live, Odds Against Tomorrow, West Side Story, Two For the Seesaw, The Haunting, The Sound of Music, The Sand Pebbles, Star!, The Andromeda Strain, Two

People, The Hindenburg, Audrey Rose, Star Trek, Wisdom (exec. prod. only), Rooftops (dir.).

WISEMAN, FREDERICK: Documentary filmmaker. b. Boston, MA, Jan. 1, 1930. e. Williams College, B.A., 1951; Yale Law Sch., L.L.B., 1954. Member: MA Bar. Private law practice, Paris, 1956–57. Lecturer-in-Law, Boston U. Law Sch., 1959–61; Russell Sage Fndn. Fellowship, Harvard U., 1961–62; research assoc., Brandeis U., dept. of sociology, 1966–69; visiting lecturer at numerous universities. Author: Psychiatry and Law: Use and Abuse of Psychiatry in a Murder Case (American Journal of Psychiatry, Oct. 1961). Co-author: Implementation (section of report of President's Comm. on Law Enforcement and Administration of Justice).
  The award-winning producer, director, editor makes non-judgemental documentaries that record the detailed daily lives of various institutions (a mental institution, the Army, a meat-packing plant, the police), and are distributed through his Zipporah Films.
  PICTURES: Titicut Follies (1967); High School; Law and Order; Hospital; Basic Training; Essene; Juvenile Court; Primate; Welfare; Meat; Canal Zone; Sinai Field Mission; Manoeuvre; Model; Seraphia's Diary; The Store; Racetrack; Deaf, Blind, Multi-Handicapped; Adjustment and Work; Missile.

WISEMAN, JOSEPH: Actor. b. Montreal, Canada, May 15, 1918. Began acting in the thirties, including Bdwy. stage, radio, m.p. and later TV.
  PICTURES INCLUDE: Viva Zapata, Les Miserables, The Silver Chalice, The Garment Jungle, Dr. No, Bye Bye Braverman, The Night They Raided Minsky's, The Valachi Papers, The Apprenticeship of Duddy Kravitz, The Betsy.
  STAGE: King Lear, Golden Boy, The Diary of Anne Frank, Uncle Vanya, The Last Analysis, Enemies, Masada, QB VII, Rage of Angels.
  TELEVISION: Seize the Day.

WITHERS, GOOGIE: Actress. b. Karachi, India, Mar. 12, 1917. Trained as a dancer under Italia Conti, Helena Lehmiski & Buddy Bradley; stage debut Victoria Palace in Windmill Man, 1929. Best Actress Award, Deep Blue Sea, 1954. Began screen career at 18. TV also. Theatrical tours Australia, Sun Award, Best Actress, 1974. Awarded officer of the Order of Australia (A.O.) 1980.
  PICTURES INCLUDE: Traveler's Joy, Night and the City, White Corridors, Derby Day, Devil on Horseback, Safe Harbor, Nickel Queen.
  STAGE: (Britain) Winter Journey, Deep Blue Sea, Hamlet, Much Ado About Nothing. (Australia) Plaza Suite, Relatively Speaking, Beckman Place, Woman in a Dressing Gown, The Constant Wife, First Four Hundred Years, Roar Like a Dove, The Cherry Orchard, An Ideal Husband. (London) Getting Married, Exit the King. (New York) The Complaisant Lover, Chichester Festival Theatre and Haymarket, London, in The Circle, The Kingfisher, Importance of Being Earnest, The Cherry Orchard, Dandy Dick, The Kingfisher (Australia and Middle East), Time and the Conways (Chichester); School for Scandal (London), Stardust (UK tour). 1986: The Chalk Garden, Hay Fever, Ring Round the Moon.
  TELEVISION: Series, Within These Walls, Time After Time, Movies: Hotel Du Lac, Northanger Abbey.

WITHERS, JANE: Actress. b. Atlanta, GA, April 12, 1927. By 1934 attracted attention as child player on screen, after radio appearance in Los Angeles and experimental pictures parts, in 1934 in Fox production Bright Eyes, Ginger; thereafter to 1942 featured or starred in numerous 20th-Fox prod. Voted Money-Making Star M.P. Herald-Fame Poll, 1937, 1938. Starred as Josephine the Plumber in Comet commercials.
  PICTURES INCLUDE: North Star, Johnny Doughboy, My Best Gal, Faces in the Fog, Dangerous Partners, Affairs of Geraldine, Danger Street, Giant, The Right Approach, Captain Newman, M.D.

WIZAN, JOE: Executive. b. Los Angeles, CA, Jan. 7, 1935. e. UCLA. Started in industry as agent for William Morris Agency. Left to form London Intl. Artists, Ltd. in association with Richard Gregson, Alan Ladd, Jr. and Mike Gruskoff. When firm dissolved joined Creative Management Associates as v.p. in chg. of creative services. In 1969 formed own indep. prod. co. 1981, named pres., CBS Theatrical Film Div. 1982, returned to 20th Century-Fox as independent producer. 1983, named pres., 20th-Fox Prods.; Resigned in 1984.
  PICTURES: Jeremiah Johnson, Junior Bonner, Prime Cut, The Last American Hero, Audrey Rose, Voices, And Justice for All, Best Friends, Unfaithfully Yours, Two of a Kind, Tough Guys, Witching Hour, Split Decisions, Spellbinder (prod.).

WIZEMAN, JR., DONALD G.: Executive. b. Fort Smith, AK, Nov. 17, 1944. e. Old Dominion U. Formed Wizeman & Associates, Ltd. Advertising Agency and Artus Specialty Company in 1967; is pres. of both. In 1971 formed Filmakers, Ltd. which also heads.
  PICTURES INCLUDE: Moonchild (exec. prod.), Come Out of the Bathroom Hannibal Fry (exec. prod.).

WOLF, EMANUEL, L.: Executive b. Brooklyn, NY, Mar. 27, 1927. e. Syracuse U., B.A., 1950; Maxwell Sch., Syracuse U., M.A. 1952; Maxwell Scholar in Public Admin.-Economics; Chi Eta Sigma (Econ. Hon.). 1952–55. Management consultant, exec. office of Secretary of Navy & Dept. of Interior, Wash., DC, 1956. National dir. of Program & Admin. of a Veterans Org. 1957–61. Pres. E. L. Wolf Associates, Washington, DC, 1961–Jan. 1965. Treasurer, Kalvex, Inc. Dec. 1962. Director Kalvex, Inc. March 1963. Dir. Allied Artists Pictures Corp., Jan. 1965. Pres. Kalvex, Inc. April 1966–present, pres. & chmn. of the Bd. Kalvex, Inc.; Chmn. of the Bd. Vitabath, Inc.; Chmn. of the Bd. Lexington Instruments; pres. & chairman of the bd. Pharmaceutical Savings Plan, Inc. Syracuse U. Corporate Advisory Board, American Committee for the Weizmann Institute of Science (Bd. of Directors). Pres. & chm. of bd., Allied Artists Pictures Corp: January, 1976: pres., bd. chm. & chief executive officer of Allied Artists Industries Inc., created by Merger of Allied Artists Pictures Corp., Kalvex Inc. and PSP, Inc. 1985, formed independent prod. co., Mended Dreams, Inc.

WOLF, HERBERT: Producer. b. New York, NY, July 11, 1917. e. New York U., 1937. Radio & TV prod. Wolf Presentations, Inc. TELEVISION: (N.Y.) Masquerade Party, Break the Bank, Hold That Note, Keep Talking, Window Shopping.

WOLF, THOMAS HOWARD: TV news exec. b. New York, NY, April 22, 1916. e. Princeton U., B.A., magna cum laude, 1937. Time & Life Mag. 1937–39; 1937–39 NEA (Scripps-Howard) 1940–46; European mgr., NEA, 1942–46. War correspondent, ETO, MTO) NBC radio correspondent, Paris, 1944–45; co-owner, pres., Information Prod., Inc. founded 1951; co-owner, chairman. Butterfield & Wolf, Inc. founded 1955; prod. CBS series. Tomorrow, 1960; exec. prod., CBS daily live Calendar Show, 1961–62; senior prod., ABC News Report, 1963; exec. prod., ABC Scope, 1964–66. v.p. dir. of TV Documentaries, 1966; v.p., dir. of TV Public Affairs, 1974; dir. TV Cultural Affairs, 1976.

WOLFSON, RICHARD: Executive. b. New York, NY, Jan. 7, 1923. e. Harvard Coll., Yale Law Sch., 1945–47, law sect'y to Justice Wiley Rutledge, U.S. Supreme Court. Law instructor at New York U. Law Sch.; later received Guggenheim Fellowship; 1952, joined Wometco Ent. as counsel and asst. to pres.; named v.p. and dir. in 1959 and senior v.p. in 1962; named exec. v.p. and general counsel in 1973; named chm., exec. comm., 1976; co-author of Jurisdiction of the Supreme Court of the United States and author of articles in various legal publications. Retired from Wometco 1982; counsel, Valdes-Fanli, Cobb & Petrey, Miami, FL.

WOLPER, DAVID L.: Producer. b. New York, NY, Jan. 11, 1928. m. Gloria Diane Hill. e. Drake U., U. of Southern California. Treas., Flamingo Films, 1948; merged with Associated Artist to form M.P. for TV, Inc., acting as v.p. in chge of West Coast oper., 1950; v.p. reactivated Flamingo Films, 1954; also pres. Harris-Wolper Pictures, Inc.; pres. Wolper Prod. 1958; pres. Dawn Prod.; v.p. Bd. Dir. Metromedia, 1965; pres. Wolper Pictures Ltd. 1967; ch. of bd. Wolper Prod., Inc., 1967; pres. Wolper Pictures, 1968; pres. Wolper Productions, 1970; pres. & ch. of bd. of dir. The Wolper Organization, Inc., 1971; consultant to Warner Bros. & Warner Communications. Pres., David L. Wolper Prods., Inc. 1977. Received Jean Hersholt Humanitarian Award, 1985.
TV & M.P.: The Race For Space, 1958; Story of . . . series, 1962–63; Biography series, 1962–63; Hollywood and the Stars series, 1963–64; The Making of the President, 1960, 1964, 1968; Men in Crisis series, 1964; Four Days in November feature, 1965; National Geographic Society Specials, 1965–68, 1971–75; The March of Time series, 1965–66; The Rise and Fall of the Third Reich, 1967–68; The Undersea World of Jacques Cousteau, 1967–68; If It's Tuesday, This Must Be Belgium feature, 1968; Plimpton specials, 1970–72; Say Goodbye, 1971; Willy Wonka and the Chocolate Factory feature, 1971; Appointment With Destiny series, 1971–73; Visions of Eight feature, 1973; American Heritage specials, 1973–74; Primal Man specials, 1973–75; Get Christie Love series, 1974; Judgment specials, 1974; Birds Do It, Bees Do It feature, 1974; Chico and the Man series, 1974–; Smithsonian Specials, 1974–; Sandburg's Lincoln, 1974–76; Welcome Back, Kotter series, 1975–; I Will Fight No More, Forever, 1975; Collision Course, Victory at Entebbe, 1976; Roots, 1977; Roots: The Next Generation, 1978; Moviola, 1980; Agatha Christie: Murder Is Easy, 1981; The Man Who Saw Tomorrow (exec. prod.); Casablanca, 1982; The Thorn Birds, 1983; Opening & Closing Ceremonies, Olympic Games, 1984; North and South Book I, 1985; North and South, Book II, 1986; Liberty Weekend, 1986; Napoleon and Josephine, 1987, What Price Victory, Kunta Kinta's Gift: Roots Christmas, Imagine: John Lennon.

WOODARD, ALFRE: Actress. b. Tulsa, OK, 1953. e. Boston U., B.A. Soon after graduation landed role in Washington, D.C. theater in Horatio, and Saved.
THEATER INCLUDES: A Christmas Carol; Bugs, Guns; Leander Stillwell; For Colored Girls Who Have Considered Suicide/When the Rainbow Is Enuf; A Map of the World.
PICTURES: Health; Remember My Name; Cross Creek (Acad. Award nom.); Go Tell It on the Mountain; Extremities; Miss Firecracker Contest, A State of Independence.
TELEVISION: Palmerstown, USA; The Class of '65; Ambush Murders; Sophisticated Gents; Freedom Road; For Colored Girls Who Have Considered Suicide/When the Rainbow Is Enuf; Trial of the Moke; Tucker's Witch (series); The Killing Ground; Sweet Revenge; Hill Street Blues (Emmy, supporting actress, 1984); Sara (series); Unnatural Causes; The Killing Floor; Mandela; The Child Saver.

WOODS, DONALD: Actor. b. 1906.
PICTURES INCLUDE: Sweet Adeline (1933), Watch on the Rhine, Roughly Speaking, 13 Ghosts, Kissin' Cousins, Moment to Moment, A Time to Sing.
STAGE: Two for the Seesaw, L.A., 1961; Rosmersholm, N.Y., 1962; One by One, N.Y., 1964; Soldier, You Can't Take It With You, Chicago, 1969; Twelfth Night, Assassination 1865; Chicago, 1969–71.
TELEVISION: G.E. Theatre, Wagon Train, Thrillers, Sunset Strip, Ben Casey, Laramie, The Rebel, The Law and Mr. Jones, The Roaring 20's, Wild Wild West, Bonanza. Series: Craig Kennedy Criminologist (1953), Tammy.

WOODS, JAMES: Actor. b. Vernal UT, Apr. 18, 1947. e. Massachusetts Inst. of Technology (appeared in 36 plays at M.I.T., Harvard and Theatre Co. of Boston). Left college to pursue acting career in New York; appeared on Broadway. in Borstal Boy, Conduct Unbecoming, Saved (off-Bdwy.). Also in Trial of the Catonsville Nine, Moonchildren (Theatre World Award), Green Julia (off-Bdwy.), Finishing Touches, etc. Feature film debut in The Visitors (1971).
PICTURES: The Way We Were, Alex and the Gypsy, Distance, Night Moves, The Choirboys, The Onion Field, The Black Marble, Eyewitness, Captured, Fast Walking, Videodrome, Split Image, Against All Odds, Once Upon a Time in America, Cat's Eye, Joshua Then and Now, Salvador (Independent Film Project Spirit Award), Best Seller, Cop (also co-prod.), The Boost, True Believer, Parental Guidance.
TELEVISION: Movies: All the Way Home, The Great American Tragedy, And the Name is Jonah, The Disappearance of Aimee, Raid on Entebbe, Billion Dollar Bubble, Badge of the Assassin. Mini-series: Holocaust. Movies: Promise (Emmy, Golden Globe, Golden Apple Awards), In Love and War.

WOODWARD, EDWARD, O.B.E.: Actor, Singer. b. Croydon, England, June 1, 1930. e. Royal Acad. of Dramatic Art. 11 LPs. 2 Gold Discs. Television Actor of the Year, 1969–70; also Sun Award, Best Actor, 1970, 71, 72.
THEATRE: 16 West End plays and musicals, including The Art of Living, The Little Doctor, A Rattle of a Simple Man, The High Bid, The Male of the Species. On Bdwy in musical High Spirits, 1962. Latest: On Approval, Richard III, The Assassin.
TELEVISION: Sword of Honour, Callan series. Over 300 TV plays latest: Bassplayer and Blonde, Saturday, Sunday, Monday, 1990 series, Nice Work, Rod of Iron, The Trial of Lady Chatterly, Wet Job—Callan Special, Churchill: The Wilderness Years, Blunt Instrument, Killer Contract, Uncle Tom's Cabin, The Equalizer (series), Codename: Kyril (movie), Hunted, The Man in the Brown Suit.
PICTURES INCLUDE: Becket, File on the Golden Goose, Murders in the Rue Morgue, Julius Caesar, The Listener, Young Winston, Sitting Target, Hunted, Wicker Man, Callan, Stand Up Virgin Soldiers, Breaker Morant, The Appointment, Who Dares Wins, Forever Love, Merlin and the Sword, Champions, A Christmas Carol, King David.

WOODWARD, JOANNE: Actress. b. Thomasville, GA, Feb. 27, 1930. e. Louisiana State U. Studied at Neighborhood Playhouse Dramatic Sch. and the Actors Studio. m. Paul Newman. Appeared in many TV dramatic shows; on B'way in Picnic; m.p. debut in Count Three and Pray (1953).
THEATER: The Lovers, Baby Want a Kiss, The Glass Menagerie (Williamstown, The Long Wharf).
PICTURES INCLUDE: Kiss Before Dying, Three Faces of Eve (Acad. Award 1957, best actress); Long Hot Summer, No Down Payment, Rally Round the Flag Boys, The Sound and the Fury, From the Terrace, Fugitive Kind, Paris Blues, The Stripper, A New Kind of Love, Signpost to Murder, A Big Hand for the Little Lady, A Fine Madness, Rachel, Rachel (Acad. Award nom.); Winning, WUSA, They Might Be Giants, The Effect of Gamma Rays on Man-in-the-Moon Marigolds, Summer Wishes, Winter Dreams, The Drowning Pool, The End, Harry and Son, The Glass Menagerie.
TELEVISION: Movies: The Shadow Box, Crisis at Central High, Family (Thanksgiving special, dir.), Sybil, See How She Runs (Emmy, 1978), Passions, Do You Remember Love.

WOOLF, SIR JOHN: Producer. Chairman Romulus Films, Ltd. Chm., British and American Film Holdings, Plc. b. England, 1913. With brother James Woolf founded Romulus Films, 1949.
PICTURES INCLUDE: Pandora and the Flying Dutchman, African Queen, Moulin Rouge, Beat the Devil, Carrington

V.C., I am a Camera, Sailor Beware, Three Men in a Boat, The Story of Esther Costello, Room at the Top, The L-Shaped Room, Life At The Top, Oliver! (Oscar for best film 1969), The Day of the Jackal, No Sex Please We're British, The Odessa File.

WOOLRIDGE, SUSAN: Actress. b. London, England. Ent. ind. 1971.
THEATER incl.: Macbeth, School for Scandal, Merchant of Venice, The Cherry Orchard, Look Back in Anger.
PICTURES: The Shout, Butley, Loyalties, Hope and Glory, How to Get Ahead in Advertising, Bye Bye Blues.
TELEVISION: The Naked Civil Servant, John McNab, The Racing Game, The Jewel in the Crown, The Last Place on Earth, Hay Fever, Time and the Conways, Dead Man's Folly, The Devil's Disciple, The Dark Room, Pastoralcare, The Small Assassin.

WOPAT, TOM: Actor. b. Lodi, WI, Sept. 9, 1951. e. U. of Wisconsin.
Left school to travel for two years with rock group as lead singer and guitarist. Spent two summers at Barn Theater in MI. Came to New York; off-Bdwy. in A Bistro Car on the CNR. On Bdwy. in hit musical, I Love My Wife.
TELEVISION: The Dukes of Hazzard (series), Blue Skies (series). Movies: Christmas Comes to Willow Creek, Burning Rage.

WORKMAN, CHUCK: Director, Writer, Producer. b. Philadelphia, PA., June 5. e. Rutgers U., B.A.; Cornell U. Pres., International Documentary Assoc.; Member: Directors Guild of America Special Projects Comm., DGA Directors Council, 1987; Board member: Santa Monica Arts Foundation. Lecturer, U. of Southern California. Pres. Calliope Films, Inc. Winner Clio Award, 1969, 1970.
PLAYS INCLUDE: Bruno's Ghost (1981, writer, dir.), Diplomacy (writer, dir.), The Man Who Wore White Shoes (writer); Bloomers (writer).
PICTURES: Monday's Child (1967, editor); Traitors of San Angel (editor); The Money (dir., s.p.); Protocol (dir., media sequences); Stoogemania (dir., co-s.p.); Precious Images (Acad. Award, Best Live Action Short, 1986; Gold Hugo Award, Cannes Film Fest., N.Y. Film Fest.); Words (Best Short, Houston Fest., N.Y. Film Fest., 1988).
DOCUMENTARIES: Writer, Producer, Director: The Making of the Deep; The Director and the Image (CINE Golden Eagle Award, 1980); The Game; The Best Show in Town (CINE Golden Eagle); And the Winner Is. . .

WORTH, IRENE: Actress. b. Nebraska, June 23, 1916. e. UCLA.
Formerly a teacher. Bdwy. debut in The Two Mrs. Carrolls, after which went to London where made her home. Appeared with Old Vic and Royal Shakespeare Co.; returned to U.S. to appear on Bdwy. in the Cocktail Party.
THEATER: Hotel Paradiso, Mary Stuart, The Potting Shed, Toys in the Attic, Tiny Alice (Tony Award, 1965), Sweet Bird of Youth (Tony Award, 1976), Cherry Orchard; Old Times, Happy Days.
PICTURES: Orders to Kill (British AA, best actress), The Scapegoat, King Lear, Nicholas and Alexander, Rich Kids, Eyewitness, Deathtrap, Fast Forward.
TELEVISION:: The Lady from the Sea, The Duchess of Malfi, The Way of the World, Prince Orestes, Forbidden, The Big Knife.

WORTH, MARVIN: Producer, Writer. b. Brooklyn, NY. Jazz promoter and manager before starting to write special material for Alan King, Buddy Hackett, Joey Bishop, Lenny Bruce.
PICTURES: Writer: Boys Night Out, Three on a Couch, Promise Her Anything. Producer: Where's Poppa?, Malcolm X, Lenny, Fire Sale, The Rose, Up the Academy, Soup for One, Unfaithfully Yours, Rhinestone, Falling in Love, Less Than Zero (co-prod.), Patty Hearst (prod.), Running Mates.
THEATER: Lenny (prod.).
TELEVISION: Steve Allen Show, Jackie Gleason, Chevy Shows, Milton Berle Show, Colgate Comedy Hour, Martha Raye Show, Judy Garland Show, Get Smart.

WOWCHUK, HARRY N.: Actor, Writer, Photographer, Producer, Executive. b. Philadelphia, PA. Oct. 16, 1948. e. Santa Monica City Coll., U. of California at L.A., theater arts, 1970. Started film career as actor, stunt-driver-photographer. T.V. and commercial credits include: Warner Bros.; Columbia Records; R.C.A.; Playboy Magazine: TV Guide; Seal Test; Camel Cigarettes; Miller High Life; American Motors; Camera V; AW Rootbeer; Harold Robbins Productions. Former exec. v.p. International Cinema, in charge of prod. and distribution; V.P. J. Newport Film Productions; pres., United West Productions.
PICTURES INCLUDE: The Lost Dutchman, Las Vegas Lady, This Is A Hijack, Tidal Wave, Tunnel Vision, Incredible 2-Headed Transplant, Jud, Bad Charleston Charlie, Some Call It Loving, Summer School Teachers, Five Minutes of Freedom, Pushing Up Daisies, Money-Marbles-Chalk, The Models, Love Swedish Style, Up-Down-Up, Sunday's Child, Soul Brothers, Freedom Riders, Perilous Journey, Claws of Death, Georgia Peaches.

WOWCHUK, NICHOLAS: Executive, Producer, Writer, Editor, Financier. b. Philadelphia, PA. e. St. Basil's Coll., U. of California at L.A. Founder-publisher: All-American Athlete Magazine; Sports and Health Digest; The Spectator. Former sports writer: Phila. Evening Public Ledger; Phila. Daily Record; Phila. Inquirer. Founder & board chairman: Mutual Realty Investment Co.; Mutual Mortgage Co., Beverly Hills, CA. President: Mutual General Films, Bev. Hills, CA; Abbey Theatrical Films, N.Y.; Mutual Film Distribution Co.; Mutual Recording & Broadcasting Enterprises.
PICTURES INCLUDE: Exec. Prod.: Perilous Journey; Incredible 2-Headed Transplant; Pushing Up Daisies; Money-Marbles-Chalk; Five Minutes of Freedom; The Campaign; Claws of Death. Prod.: Scorpion's Web; Pursuit; Brave Men; Sea of Despair; The Hetman; Cossacks In Battle; The Straight White Line; Tilt, Rooster, To Live . . . You Gotta Win.

WRAY, FAY: Actress. b. Alberta, Canada, Sept. 10, 1907. m. Robert Riskin, writer. On stage in Pilgrimage Play, Hollywood, 1923; m.p. debut in Gasoline Love; thereafter in many m.p. for Paramount to 1930; then in films for various Hollywood and Brit. prod.
PICTURES INCLUDE: Streets of Sin, The Wedding March, The Four Feathers, The Texan, Dirigible, Doctor X, The Most Dangerous Game, The Vampire Bat, The Mystery of the Wax Museum, King Kong, The Bowery, Madame Spy, The Affairs of Cellini, The Clairvoyant, They Met in a Taxi, Murder in Greenwich Village, The Jury's Secret, Adam Had Four Sons, Small Town Girl, Treasure of the Golden Condor, Queen Bee, Rock Pretty Baby, Tammy, Out of Time, The Cobweb, Summer Love.
TELEVISION: Pride of the Family (series), Gideon's Trumpet (movie).

WRIGHT, ROBERT C.: Executive. President and Chief Exec. Off., NBC Bdcst. Co., as of September 1986. 1969, joined General Electric; lawyer in plastics div. Later moved into product & sls. management in that div. 1980, moved to Cox Cable as pres. Returned to GE 1983 heading small appliances div.; moved to GE Financial Services & GE Credit Corp. as pres., which posts he held when named head of NBC following purchase of NBC's parent RCA by GE.

WRIGHT, TERESA: Actress. b. New York, NY, Oct. 27, 1918. Ent. m.p. 1941, The Little Foxes, Goldwyn-RKO.
PICTURES INCLUDE: Pride of the Yankees, Mrs. Miniver (Acad. Award, supporting actress), Shadow of a Doubt, Casanova Brown, Best Years of Our Lives, Trouble with Women, Pursued, Imperfect Lady, Enchantment, The Capture, The Men, Something to Live For, California Conquest, Steel Trap, Count the Hours, The Actress, Track of the Cat, Hail Hero, The Happy Ending, Roseland, Somewhere in Time, The Good Mother.
STAGE: Tours: Mary, Mary, Tchin-Tchin, The Effect of Gamma Rays on Man-in-the-Moon Marigolds, Noel Coward in Two Keys, The Master Builder. Regional Theatre: Long Day's, Journey into Night, You Can't Take It With You, All The Way Home, Wings. New York: Life with Father, Dark at the Top of the Stairs, Mary, Mary, I Never Sang for My Father, Death of a Salesman, Ah, Wilderness!, Morning's at Seven (Broadway and London).
TELEVISION: The Margaret Bourke-White Story, The Miracle Worker, The Golden Honeymoon, Bill-on His Own, The Fig Tree.

WRIGHT, TONY: Actor. b. London, Dec. 10, 1925. Stage debut in repertory, South Africa; screen debut; Flanagan Boy, 1951.
PICTURES INCLUDE: A Toi De Jouer Callaghan, Plus De Whiskey, Pour Callaghan (France), Jumping for Joy, Jacqueline, Tiger in the Smoke, Seven Thunders, Broth of a Boy, Faces in the Dark, In the Wake of a Stranger, Journey to Nowhere, The Liquidator.
TELEVISION: Compact, Marriage Lines, No Hiding Place, The Saint, Mystery Theatre, Curtains for Sheila, Crossroads, Make Me A Widow, Wednesday's Train, Onedin Line, 6 Saints, Persuaders, The Jensen Code, Follow Me, Kidnapped.

WYATT, JANE: Actress. b. New York, NY, Aug. 10, 1913. e. Miss Chapin's Sch., Barnard Coll. m. Edgar B. Ward. Joined Apprentice Sch., Berkshire Playhouse, Stockbridge, Mass. Understudied in Tradewinds and The Vinegar Tree. Appeared in Give Me Yesterday and the Tadpole. In 1933 succeeded Margaret Sullavan in Dinner at Eight. New York stage, The Autumn Garden, 1951; other plays, The Bishop Misbehaves, Conquest, Eveninsong, The Mad Hopes.
PICTURES INCLUDE: Great Expectations, (1934), One More River, The Luckiest Girl in the World, Lost Horizon, Kisses for Breakfast, The Navy Comes Through, The Kansan, The Iron Road, None But the Lonely Heart, Boomerang, Gentlemen's Agreement, No Minor Vices, Bad Boy, Canadian Pacific, Pitfall, Task Force, Our Very Own, My Blue Heaven, Man Who Cheated Himself, Criminal Lawyer, Never Too Late, Treasure of Matecumbe.
TELEVISION: Father Knows Best (1954–59, winner 3 Emmy Awards), Bob Hope Chrysler Theater, The Virginian,

Wagon Train, U.S. Steel Hour, Bell Telephone Hour, Hostess moderator, Confidential For Women, My Father My Mother. Guest star—Star Trek, Barefoot in the Park (pilot), The Ghost and Mrs. Muir, Here Come the Brides, Love American Style, Katherine, Tom Sawyer; Father Knows Best Reunion, A Love Affair, Amelia Earhart, Superdome, Fantasy Island, Love Boat, The Nativity, The Millionaire, Missing Children—A Mother's Story.

WYMAN, JANE: Actress. r.n. Sarah Jane Fulks. b. St. Joseph, MO, Jan. 4, 1914. In 1936: My Man Godfrey, U; Cain and Mabel, Smart Blonde, Warner. From 1937 in many Hollywood pictures. Voted one of top ten money-making stars in M.P. Herald-Fame poll, 1954.
PICTURES INCLUDE: Larceny, Inc., My Favorite Spy, Footlight Serenade, Princess O'Rourke, Doughgirls, Make Your Own Bed, Crime by Night, Lost Weekend, One More Tomorrow, Night and Day, The Yearling, Cheyenne, Magic Town; Johnny Belinda (Acad. award, best actress, 1948), Three Guys Named Mike, Here Comes the Groom, Blue Veil, Just for You, Story of Will Rogers, Let's Do It Again, So Big, Magnificent Obsession, Lucy Gallant, All That Heaven Allows, Miracle in the Rain, Pollyanna, Holiday for Lovers, Bon Voyage, How to Commit Marriage.
TELEVISION: Series: Jane Wyman Theater (1956–60), Fireside Theatre, Amanda Fallon, Falcon Crest. Movies: The Failing of Raymond, The Incredible Journey of Dr. Meg Laurel.

WYMAN, THOMAS H.: Executive. b. 1931. Joined CBS, Inc. in 1980 as pres. & chief exec. Now chm. Prior career as chief exec. of Green Giant Co.; became v. chm. to 1988, of Pillsbury Co. when it acquired Green Giant in 1979.

WYMORE, PATRICE: Actress. b. Miltonvale, KS, Dec. 17, 1926. p. James A. Wymore, oper. exhib. film delivery service throughout Kans.; ret. Widow of actor Errol Flynn. Began career as child performer, tent shows, county fairs, vaudeville; later, toured night clubs in middle west, own song & dance act; modelled, Chicago understudy Betty Bruce, Up in Central Park, played role Hollywood Bowl; then, N.Y. stage, Hold It! All For Love; radio & TV roles.
PICTURES INCLUDE: Screen debut: Tea for Two, 1950, then Rocky Mountain, I'll See You in My Dreams, Star-Lift, Big Trees, Man Behind the Gun, She's Working Her Way Through College, She's Back on Broadway, Chamber of Horrors.

WYNN, TRACY KEENAN: Writer. b. Hollywood, CA, Feb. 28, 1945. Fourth generation in show business; son of actor Keenan Wynn; grandson of Ed Wynn; great-grandson of Frank Keenan Wynn, Irish Shakespearean actor who made Bdwy. debut in 1880.
PICTURES INCLUDE: The Longest Yard, The Drowning Pool (co-s.p.), The Deep (co. s.p.).
TELEVISION: The Glass House, Tribes, The Autobiography of Miss Jane Pittman, Quest, Bloody Friday.

WYNTER, DANA: Actress. b. London, England. June 8, 1930. e. Rhodes U. On stage in London; TV appearances include Robert Montgomery Show, Suspense, Studio One, U.S. Steel Hour.
PICTURES INCLUDE: Invasion of the Body Snatchers, View from Pompey's Head, D-Day, The Sixth of June, Something of Value, Fraulein, Shake Hands with the Devil, In Love and War, Sink the Bismarck, The List of Adrian Messenger, If He Hollers, Let Him Go, Airport.
TELEVISION: Playhouse 90, Dick Powell Show, Wagon Train, Virginian, Burkes Law, Bob Hope Presents, Alfred Hitchcock, Twelve O'Clock High, The Rogues, Ben Casey, FBI Story, My Three Sons, Wild Wild West, The Man Who Never Was, The Royal Romance of Charles and Diana.

Y

YABLANS, FRANK: Executive. B. Brooklyn, NY, Aug. 27, 1935. Ent. m.p. ind. as Warner Bros. booker, 1957. Warner Bros. salesman in N.Y., Boston, Milwaukee, Chicago, 1957–59. Milwaukee br. mgr. Buena Vista, 1959–66. Midwest sales mgr., Sigma III, 1966. Eastern sales mgr., 1967, sales v.p. 1968. V.P. general sales mgr., Paramount Pic. Corp., 1969; v.p.-dist., April 1970; sr. v.p.-mkt., Oct., 1970; exec. v.p., April 1971; named pres. May, 1971. In Jan., 1975, became an independent producer, his company called, Frank Yablans Presentations Inc. 1983, MGM/UA Entertainment Co. as bd. chm. & chief oper. off. Held titles of bd. chm. & chief exec. off. with both MGM and UA Corp when resigned, 1985. Same year teamed with PSO Delphi to form Northstar Entertainment Co.; 1986, non-exclusive deal with Empire Entertainment; 1988, non-exclusive 3-year deal with Columbia Pictures.
PICTURES: Silver Streak (exec. prod.), The Other Side of Midnight (prod.), The Fury (prod.), North Dallas Forty (prod.-co-s.p.), Mommie Dearest (prod.-co-s.p.); Monsignor (co.-prod), Star Chamber, Kidco, Buy and Cell (prod.).

YABLANS, IRWIN: Executive. b. Brooklyn, NY, June 25, 1934. Began career in industry at WB in 1956 after two-yr. stint in Germany with U.S. Army. Held m.p. sales posts in Washington, DC, Albany, Detroit, Milwaukee and Portland. In 1962 joined Paramount as L.A. mgr. In 1964 made western sales mgr. In 1972 entered production as assoc. prod. on Howard W. Koch's Badge 373. First prod. on own: The Education of Sonny Carson (1974). Pres. of Compass Int'l. Pictures. Exec. v.p., low budget films, Lorimar Productions. Resigned June, 1984. In 1985 named chm., Orion Pictures Distributing Corp. 1988: named chm. and CEO of newly formed Epic Pictures.
PICTURES: Exec. prod.: Halloween (also story), Fade To Black (story), Seduction (prod.), Halloween II, Halloween III, The Season of the Witch, Parasite, Tank, Hell Night, Prison Arena.

YATES, PETER: Producer, Director. b. Ewshoot, Eng., July 24, 1929. e. Royal Acad. of Dramatic Art. Ent. m.p. ind. as studio manager and dubbing asst. with De Lane Lea. Asst. dir.: The Entertainer, The Guns of Navarone, A Taste of Honey, The Roman Spring of Mrs. Stone. Stage: dir. The American Dream, The Death of Bessie Smith, Passing Game, Interpreters.
TELEVISION: Danger Man (Secret Agent), The Saint (series).
PICTURES INCLUDE: Summer Holiday, One Way Pendulum, Robbery, Bullitt, John and Mary, Murphy's War, The Hot Rock, The Friends of Eddie Coyle, For Pete's Sake, Mother, Jugs and Speed, The Deep, Breaking Away (dir., prod.), Eyewitness (dir., prod.), Krull, The Dresser (dir., prod.), Eleni, Suspect, The House on Carroll Street (prod., dir.).

YELLEN, LINDA: Producer, Director, Writer. b. New York, NY, July 13, 1949. e. Barnard Coll., B.A.; 1969; Columbia U., M.F.A., 1972; Ph.D., 1974. Also lecturer Barnard Coll., Yale U., asst. professor, City U. of New York. Member, executive council, Directors Guild of America.
PICTURES: Looking Up (prod., dir., 1978); Prospera; Come Out, Come Out.
TELEVISION: Mayflower: The Pilgrims' Adventure (prod.); Playing for Time (prod., Emmy, Peabody, Christopher Awards, 1980); Hardhat and Legs (prod.); The Royal Romance of Charles and Diana (exec. prod., co-s.p.); Prisoner Without a Name, Cell Without a Number (prod., dir., co-s.p.; Peabody, Writers Guild Awards, 1985), Liberace (exec. prod.).

YORDAN, PHILIP: Writer. b. Chicago, IL, 1913. e. U. of Illinois, B.A., Kent Coll. of Law, LL.D. Author, producer, playwright (Anna Lucasta). Began screen writing 1942 with collab. s.p. Syncopation.
PICTURES INCLUDE: Unknown Guest, Johnny Doesn't Live Here, When Strangers Marry, Dillinger (Acad. Award nom.), Whistle Stop, The Chase, Suspense; play & s.p. Anna Lucasta, House of Strangers; s.p. Edge of Doom; collab. s.p. Detective Story, (Acad. Award nom.) Mary Maru, s.p., Houdini, Blowing Wild; collab. s.p., Man Crazy, Naked Jungle; s.p., Johnny Guitar; story, Broken Lance (Acad. Award, 1954); adapt. Conquest of Space; collab. s.p. Man from Laramie, Last Frontier; prod. s.p. Harder They Fall, Men In War, No Down Payment, God's Little Acre; s.p. Bravados, Time Machine, The Day of the Outlaw, Studs Lonigan, King of Kings; collab., El Cid, 55 Days at Peking, Fall of the Roman Empire; prod., Crack in the World, Battle of the Bulge, Royal Hunt of the Sun, Brigham, Cataclysm, Night Train to Terror, Satan's Warriors, Cry Wilderness, Bloody Wednesday (prod., s.p.), The Unholy (co-s.p.).

YORK, DICK: Actor. r.n. Richard Allen York. b. Fort Wayne, IN, Sept. 4, 1928. e. De Paul U. Drama Sch. Appeared on radio shows; then films; on Broadway in Tea and Sympathy, Bus Stop; TV appearances.
TELEVISION: Omnibus, Robert Montgomery Show, Mr. D.A., The Web, Wagon Train, Alfred Hitchcock, Twilight Zone, Route 66, Series: Going My Way, Bewitched.
PICTURES INCLUDE: Inherit the Wind, Cowboy, They Came to Cordura, My Sister Eileen, Three Stripes in the Sun.

YORK, MICHAEL: Actor. b. Fulmer, England, March 27, 1942. Early career with Oxford U. Dramatic Society and National Youth Theatre; later Dundee Repertory, National Theatre.
THEATER: Any Just Cause, Hamlet, Outcry (Broadway), Ring Round the Moon (Los Angeles), Bent, Cyrano de Bergerac, The Little Prince.
PICTURES INCLUDE: The Taming of the Shrew, Accident, Red and Blue, Smashing Time, Romeo and Juliet, The Strange Affair, The Guru, Alfred the Great, Justine, Something for Everyone, Zeppelin, La Poudre D'Escampette, Cabaret, England Made Me, Lost Horizon, The Three Musketeers, Murder on the Orient Express, The Four Musketeers, Conduct Unbecoming, Logan's Run, Seven Nights in Japan, The Last Remake of Beau Geste, The Island of Dr. Moreau, Fedora, The Riddle of the Sands, The White Lions, Final Assignment, Success Is the Best Revenge, Dawn, Lethal Obsession (The Joker), The Return of the Musketeers, Off Balance, The Secret of the Sahara, City Blue, About That Strange Girl..., Killing Blue.

TELEVISION: The Forsyte Saga, Rebel in the Grave, Great Expectations, Jesus of Nazareth, True Patriot, Much Ado About Nothing, A Man Called Intrepid, The Phantom of the Opera, The Master of Ballantrae, Space, For Those I Loved, The Far Country, Dark Mansions, Sword of Gideon, Dynasty (series), Faerie Tale Theatre.

YORK, SUSANNAH: Actress. b. London, England, Jan. 9, 1941. Ent. TV 1959. Appearances include: The Crucible, The Rebel and the Soldier, The First Gentleman, The Richest Man in the World. Ent. films in 1960. Wrote two books: In Search of Unicorns and Lark's Castle.
THEATER: A Cheap Bunch of Flowers, Wings of the Dove, Singular Life of Albert Nobbs, Man and Superman, Mrs. Warren's Profession, Peter Pan, The Maids, Private Lives, The Importance of Being Earnest, Hedda Gabler (New York), Agnes of God, The Human Voice. Produced The Big One, a variety show for peace, 1984. Penthesilea, Fatal Attraction, The Apple Cart, Private Treason.
PICTURES INCLUDE: Tunes of Glory, There Was a Crooked Man, Greengage Summer, Freud, Tom Jones, While the Tiger Sleeps, The Seventh Dawn, Scene Nun—Take One, Sands of Kalahari, Scruggs, Kaleidoscope, A Man for All Seasons, Sebastian, The Killing of Sister George, Oh What a Lovely War, The Battle of Britain, Lock Up Your Daughters, They Shoot Horses Don't They? (Acad. Award nom.), Brotherly Love, Zee & Co., Happy Birthday Wanda June, Images, The Maids, Gold, Conduct Unbecoming, Heaven Save Us From Our Friends, Sky Riders, The Silent Partner, Superman, The Shout, Superman II, Falling in Love Again, Alice Loophole, The Awakening, Mio My Mio, Christmas Card, Prettykill, Bluebeard Bluebeard, A Summer Story, American Roulette, Falcon's Malteser, Just Ask For Diamond.
TELEVISION: Slaughter of St. Teresa's Day, Kiss On A Grass Green Pillow, Fallen Angels, Prince Regent, Second Chance, Betjeman's Briton, We'll Meet Again, Jane Eyre, A Christmas Carol, Star Quality, Macho, Dangerous Love.

YORKIN, BUD: Producer, Director. r.n. Alan "Bud" Yorkin. b. Washington, PA, Feb. 22, 1926. e. Carnegie Tech., Columbia U. U.S. Navy, 1942–45; Began career in TV in NBC's engineering dept. Moved into prod., first as stage mgr., then assoc. dir. of Colgate Comedy Hour (Martin and Lewis) and dir. of Dinah Shore Show. Formed Tandem Productions with Norman Lear; 1974 formed own production co.
TELEVISION: Song at Twilight, Martin & Lewis Show, Abbott and Costello Show, Ritz Bros. Show, Spike Jones Show; writer, prod. dir., Tony Martin Show, 1954–55; dir., George Gobel Show, 1954–55; prod. dir., The Ernie Ford Show 1956–57; An Evening with Fred Astaire (1958, 3 Emmys), Another Evening with Fred Astaire (1959); owner. co-prod. All In The Family; Sanford and Son; Maude; Good Times; What's Happening!!; Carter Country.
PICTURES: Come Blow Your Horn (dir., co-prod., adapt.), Dir. Never Too Late; Divorce American Style; Inspector Clouseau; prod.-dir. Start the Revolution Without Me; Thief Who Came to Dinner, The Night They Raided Minsky's (exec. prod.); Cold Turkey, (exec. prod.), Blade Runner (exec. prod.), Deal of the Century, (prod.), Twice in a Lifetime (dir., prod.), Arthur 2 on the Rocks (dir., co-prod.), Love Hurts (dir., co-prod.).

YOSHISAKA, KIYOJI: Executive. b. Shanghai, China 1908. e. Thomas Hambury Coll., Shanghai. Ent. ind. 1930 RCA Victor of China, 1932 Victor Talking Machine, 1938 Manchuria Talking Machine, 1940 Victor of Japan. Left Photophone Div. of Victor in 1950 for Tokyo Theatre Supply 1950–58; 1959–63 Rhythm Friend Corp.; exec. dir.s Nichior 1964–66; became consultant Nihon Eiga Shizai 1966 and after name changed to Toshiba Photo Phone became mgr. trade. div. 1969 then dir. and gen. mgr. of trade div. in 1970. Retired.

YOUNG, ALAN: Actor. r.n. Angus Young; b. North Shield, Northumberland, England, Nov. 19, 1919. Cartoonist, acted first as monologuist at 13 years in Canada; radio comedian 10 yrs. in Canada and U.S.; served in Canadian Navy as sub-lt. 1942–44; wrote, dir. and acted in comedy broadcasts; TV: Alan Young Show (2 Emmy Awards), Mister Ed.
PICTURES INCLUDE: Margie (debut, 1946), Chicken Every Sunday, Mr. Belvedere Goes to College, Aaron Slick from Punkin Crick, Androcles and the Lion, Gentlemen Marry Brunettes, Tom Thumb, Time Machine, The Cat from Outer Space.
TELEVISION: The Alan Young Show, Mr. Ed (series), Coming of Age (series).

YOUNG, BUDDY: Executive. b. New York, NY, June 15, 1935. e. City Coll. of New York. UA publicity dept. 1952; asst. pub. mgr., UA 1963; pub. dir. Fox, Oct. 1965; west coast coordinator of adv. and publicity UA. In 1975 joined Columbia Pictures as worldwide dir. of adv.-pub.-exp. In 1976 named MGM adv.-pub. co-ordinator. Joined Universal Pictures in 1976 as dir. of pub. & promo. promoted to v.p., of advertising, publicity and promotion; 1980, partner in m.p. consulting firm, Powell & Young; 1983, pres. & dir., Color Systems Technology, Inc.

YOUNG, BURT: Actor, Writer. b. New York, NY, April 30, 1940. Worked at variety of jobs (boxer, trucker, etc.) before turning to acting and joining Actor's Studio. Appeared in off-Bdwy. plays which led to Hollywood career.
PICTURES INCLUDE: Cinderella Liberty, The Gambler, The Killer Elite, Chinatown, Rocky, The Choirboys, Convoy, Uncle Joe Shannon (actor, s.p.), All the Marbles, Rocky III, Lookin' To Get Out, Amityville II: The Possession, Over the Brooklyn Bridge, Once Upon a Time in America, The Pope of Greenwich Village, Rocky IV, Back to School, Beverly Hills Brats, The Last Exit to Brooklyn.
TELEVISION: M*A*S*H, Baretta. Movies: A Summer to Remember, Serpico, Hustling, Daddy I Don't Like It Like This (also s.p.), The Great Niagara, This Deadly Game, Murder Can Hurt You.

YOUNG, CARROLL: Writer. b. Cincinnati, OH. e. St. Xavier Coll. Publicist for Pathe Studios, Fox West Coast Theatres, RKO Studios, MGM, 1930–35; story ed. Sol Lesser Prod., Ernst Lubitsch Prod., 1936–40; asst. to exec. prod., RKO, 1941; U.S. Army Air Force, 1942–44.
PICTURES INCLUDE: story, collab. s.p. Tarzan Triumphs; story, Tarzan's Desert Mystery; story, s.p. Tarzan and Leopard Woman, Tarzan and Mermaids; s.p. many in Jungle Jim series, Hidden City, The Jungle; story, Lost Continent; collab. s.p. Tarzan and the She-Devil; story s.p. Cannibal Attack; collab. story & s.p. Apache Warrior; collab. s.p. She-Devil, The Deerslayer; collab. s.p. Machete.

YOUNG, IRWIN: Executive. b. New York, NY. e. Perkiomen Sch., Lehigh U., B.S., 1950. Pres., Du Art Film Laboratories, Inc.

YOUNG, LORETTA: Actress. r.n. Gretchen Young; b. Salt Lake City, UT, Jan. 6, 1913. e. Ramona Convent, Alhambra, CA, Immaculate Heart Coll. Hollywood. After small part in Naughty But Nice, lead in Laugh Clown, Laugh. Played in almost 100 films. Acad. Award, best actress (Farmer's Daughter) 1947; NBC-TV Loretta Young Show, 1953–61; CBS-TV New Loretta Young Show 1962; won Emmy Awards, 1954–56–59. Has won innumerable other awards. Returned to TV, 1986; in movie: Christmas Eve (1986).

YOUNG, ROBERT: Actor. b. Chicago, IL, Feb. 22, 1907. Star numerous pictures before and after sound; from 1932 in many productions, various Hollywood producers.
PICTURES INCLUDE: The Sin of Madelon Claudet (debut, 1931), Strange Interlude, The Kid From Spain, Hell Below, Tugboat Annie, Lazy River, The House of Rothchild, Spitfire, Whom the God's Destroy, Remember Last Night?, West Point of the Air, It's Love Again, Secret Agent, Stowaway, The Emperor's Candlesticks, I Met Him in Paris, The Bride Wore Red, Josette, Frou, Frou, Three Comrades, Rich Man, Poor Girl, Honolulu, Miracles For Sale, Maisie, Northwest Passage, The Mortal Storm, Florian, Western Union, The Trial of Mary Dugan, Lady Be Good, H.M. Pulham, Esq., Joe Smith American, Cairo, Journey for Margaret, Claudia, Sweet Rosie O'Grady, The Canterville Ghost, Secrets in the Dark, Claudia and David, Lady Luck, They Won't Believe Me, Crossfire, Sitting Pretty, Adventures in Baltimore, And Baby Makes Three, Bride for Sale, Second Woman, That Forsyte Woman, Goodbye My Fancy, Half-Breed, Secret of the Incas.
TELEVISION: Father Knows Best (series), Window on Main Street, Marcus Welby, M.D. (series); Movies: Mercy or Murder, Conspiracy of Love, Little Women.

YOUNG, ROBERT M.: Director. b. New York, NY, Nov. 22, 1924. e. Harvard.
PICTURES: Nothing But a Man; Short Eyes; Rich Kids; One-Trick Pony; The Ballad of Gregorio Cortez; Alambrista!, Extremities, Dominick and Eugene, The Triumph.
TELEVISION: Sit-In; Angola—Journey to a War; The Inferno (a.k.a. Cortile Cascino, documentary; also prod., s.p. editor); Anatomy of a Hospital; Eskimo; Fight for Life (Emmy).

YOUNG, SEAN: Actress. b. Louisville, KY, Nov. 20, 1959. e. Interlochen Arts Acad., MI, studied dance. After graduating, moved to N.Y., worked as receptionist, model for 6 months and signed with ICM. Shortly after signed for film debut in Jane Austen in Manhattan (1980).
PICTURES: Jane Austen in Manhattan, Stripes, Blade Runner, Young Doctors in Love, Dune, Baby, The Secret of the Lost Legend, No Way Out, Wall Street, The Boost, Cousins, Batman.
TELEVISION: Under the Biltmore Clock, Tender Is the Night.

YOUNG, TERENCE: Director, Writer. b. Shanghai, China, June 20, 1915. e. Cambridge U. Served with Guards Armoured Div., W.W.II; ent. m.p. ind. 1936 at BIP Studios. Screenwriter turned director.
PICTURES INCLUDE: Writer: On the Night of the Fire, On Approval, Dangerous Moonlight, Theirs is the Glory; Director: Corridor of Mirrors, One Night With You, Woman Hater, They Were Not Divided, The Valley of the Eagles, Red Beret (Paratrooper), That Lady, Safari, Storm Over the Nile, Action

of the Tiger, Serious Charge, Black Tights, Dr. No. From Russia With Love, Moll Flanders, Thunderball, Triple Cross, The Rover, Wait Until Dark, Mayerling, The Christmas Tree, The Red Sun, Grand Slam, The Valachi Papers, War Goddess, The Klansman, Jackpot, Bloodline, Inchon, The Jigsaw Man, Takeover.

YOUNGSTEIN, MAX E.: Executive. b. March 21, 1913. e. Fordham U. Member New York Bar. Motion picture consultant and independent producer. Member, Producers Guild. Pres., Max E. Youngstein Enterprises. 1940–41, dir. adv. & pub., 20th Century Fox; later dir. studio special svcs.; asst. to pres. 1942–44, US Army Signal Corps. 1945, v.p. & gen. mgr., Stanley Kramer Prods. 1946–48, dir. adv. & pub., Eagle Lion Films; v.p. chg. adv. & pub. & prod. liaison. 1949–50, dir. adv. & pub., Paramount; mem. exec. comm. & v.p. & dir. dist. co. 1951–62, gen. v.p., partner, bd. mem., dir. adv. & pub., United Artists Corp. Formed UA Music Co. Pres., UA Records. 1977, consultant to Bart-Palevsky Prods. Advisor, Golden Harvest Films. Consultant, Rico-Lion. 1979, Consultant, Shamrock Prods., Rank Film Distributors, Taft Bdcst. Co., Encore Prods., Bobrun Prods., Selkirk Films. 1980, named chm. & CEO, Taft Int'l. Pictures. 1984, Consultant, Orion, 20th Century-Fox. 1985–86, pres., Great American Pictures. Consultant, H&M Trust, Color Systems Technology, Mickey Rooney Film Prods., Peachtree Prods.
PICTURES INCLUDE: Young Billy Young, Best of Cinerama, Man in the Middle, Fail Safe, The Money Trap, The Dangerous Days of Kiowa Jones, Welcome to Hard Times.

YULIN, HARRIS: Actor. On Bdwy. in Watch on the Rhine, A Lesson from Aloes, etc.
PICTURES: Doc, The Midnight Man, Night Moves, Steel, Scarface, The Believers, Candy Mountain, Fatal Beauty, Bad Dreams, Judgement in Berlin.
TELEVISION: The Thirteenth Day—The Story of Esther, When Every Day Was the Fourth of July, Last Ride of the Dalton Gang, Robert Kennedy and His Times.

Z

ZADORA, PIA: Singer, Actress. b. New York, NY, 1954. e. H.S. of Professional Arts. m. Meshulam Riklis. On stage in Henry Sweet Henry. Singer in nightclubs, concerts, records, and has appeared on numerous talk and variety TV shows.
PICTURES: Butterfly, Fakeout, The Lonely Lady, Voyage of the Rock Aliens, Hairspray.
TELEVISION: Pajama Tops (cable).

ZAENTZ, SAUL: Producer. b. Passaic, NJ.
PICTURES: One Flew Over the Cuckoo's Nest (Acad. Award), Three Warriors, The Lord of the Rings, Amadeus, The Unbearable Lightness of Being.

ZAMPA, LUIGI: Director. b. Rome, Italy, 1905. Playwright, studied at Experimental Film Center, Rome, 1935–1938; script writer, Neo-realist director.
PICTURES INCLUDE: American on Vacation, To Live in Peace, Difficult Years, Angelina, The White Line, City on Trial, Two Gentlemen in a Carriage, His Last 12 Hours, We Women, Woman of Rome, Art of Getting Along, A Flower in His Mouth, Tigers in Lipstick, Portrait of a Lovely, Lucky Woman (TV, 1985).

ZAMPI, GIULIO: Associate producer. b. London, Eng., Sept. 29, 1923. p. Mario Zampi. e. Rome U. Ed. to Marcel Varnel, then to Mario Zampi; dir. of Anglofilm Ltd. Transocean Films Ltd.
PICTURES INCLUDE: Phantom Shot, Fatal Night, Shadow of the Past, Come Dance with Me, Third Time Lucky, Laughter in Paradise, Top Secret, I Have Chosen Love, Happy Ever After (Tonight's the Night), Now and Forever, The Naked Truth, Too Many Crooks, Bottoms Up, Five Golden Hours.

ZANUCK, RICHARD DARRYL: Executive. b. Los Angeles, CA, Dec 13, 1934. e. Stanford U. 1952–56. f. Darryl Zanuck. Story dept., 20th Century Fox. 1954; N.Y. prod. dept., 1955; asst. to prod., Island in the Sun, 1957; The Sun Also Rises, 1956; v.p. Darryl F. Zanuck Prod. 1958; prod. Compulsion, 1959, DFZ Prod., 20th Century Fox; prod., Sanctuary, 1961; prod., The Chapman Report, 1962; asst. to prod., The Longest Day, 1962; president's prod. rep., 20th Century Fox Studio, 1963; v.p. charge prod., 20th Fox; pres., 20th Fox TV exec. v.p. chge. prod., 20th Fox, 1967. 1968: Chmn. of Bd., Television div., 20th Century Fox. 1969: Pres., 20th Century Fox Film Corp. Joined Warner Bros., March 1971, as sr. exec. v.p.; Resigned July, 1972 to form Zanuck-Brown Production Company, Universal Pictures. Joined 20th Century-Fox, 1980–83. To Warner Bros., 1983. To MGM Entertainment, 1986.
PICTURES: Sssssss, The Sugarland Express; Willie Dynamite; The Sting; The Black Windmill, The Girl from Petrovka; The Eiger Sanction; Jaws; MacArthur; Jaws 2; The Island; Neighbors; The Verdict; Cocoon; Target; Cocoon II—The Return.
TELEVISION: Barringtons.

ZANUSSI, KRZYSZTOF: b. Warsaw, Poland, 1939. e. Warsaw University, (physics); attended lectures on cinema at Polish Academy of Science's Institute of Arts. Made first film for Warsaw U. Amateur Film Club before enrolling as grad. student in philosophy at Cracow U., 1959. Grad. Lodz State College of Film, 1966. Made several short films before feature debut with the Structure of Crystals, 1969. Head of one of 3 gov.-supported film units in Poland. Was active in Solidarity. Has since maintained ties with Polish film indust. while making films abroad.
PICTURES: Shorts: The Way to the Skies, Proba Cisnienia; The Death of a Provincial; Industry; Computers; Face to Face; Zaliczenie; Mountains at Dusk; The Role; Behind the Wall; Hypothesis. Features: The Structure of Crystals; Family Life; Illumination; The Catamount Killing; A Woman's Decision; Penderecki, Lutoslawski, Baird; Camouflage; Anatomy Lesson; House of Women (TV); Spiral; Ways in the Night; My Cracow; The Constant Factor; Contract; From a Far Country—Pope John Paul II; Temptation; Imperative; The Unapproachable (TV); Vatican Capitale; Bluebeard; The Year of the Quiet Sun; The Power of Evil; Wherever You Are (dir., s.p.); The Young Magician (co-prod. only).

ZEFFIRELLI, FRANCO: Director. b. Italy, Feb. 12, 1923. Was stage director before entering film industry. Set designer 1949–52 for Visconti plays (A Streetcar Named Desire, The Three Sisters). Director of operas.
PICTURES INCLUDE: The Taming of the Shrew, Romeo and Juliet, Brother Sun, Sister Moon, The Champ, Endless Love, La Traviata, Otello, Young Toscanini.
TELEVISION: Jesus of Nazareth.

ZELNICK, STRAUSS: Executive. b. Boston, MA, June 26, 1957. e. Wesleyan U. B.A., 1979 (Summa Cum Laude); Harvard Grad. School of Business Administration, M.B.A.; 1983; Harvard Law School, J.D., 1983 (Cum Laude). 1983–86, vice president, international television sales, Columbia Pictures International Corp. President & chief operating officer, Vestron, Inc.

ZEMECKIS, ROBERT: Director, Writer. b. Chicago, IL, 1952. e. U. of Southern California Sch. of Cinema. At U.S.C. wrote, produced, directed a 14-minute film, A Field of Honor, which won special jury award at Second Annual Student Film Awards sponsored by M.P. Academy of Arts & Sciences, plus 15 international honors. Has film editing background, having worked as cutter on TV commercials in Illinois. Also cut films at NBC News, Chicago, as summer job. After schooling went to Universal to observe on set of TV series, McCloud. Wrote script for that series in collaboration with Bob Gale. Turned to feature films, directing I Wanna Hold Your Hand and co-writing s.p. with Gale and co-writing 1941 with him.
PICTURES: Used Cars, Romancing the Stone, Back to the Future, Who Framed Roger Rabbit?

ZENS, WILL: Producer, Director. b. Milwaukee, WI, June 26, 1920. e. Marquette U., U. of Southern California, B.A., M.A. Wrote, produced and directed many TV shows. Formed Riviera Productions in 1960 to produce theatrical motion pictures.
TELEVISION: Punch & Trudy, Your Police, Aqua Lung Adventures.
PICTURES INCLUDE: Capture That Capsule, The Starfighters, To the Shores of Hell, Road to Nashville, Hell on Wheels, From Nashville with Music, Yankee Station, Help Me . . . I'm Possessed!, Hot Summer in Barefoot County, The Fix.

ZETTERLING, MAI: Actress, Director. b. Sweden, May 24, 1925. e. Ordtuery Sch., Theater Sch. First m.p.: Sweden, Frenzy. Has made numerous stage and screen appearances since in Sweden. British screen debut, Frieda. Since 1969 directing plays & films in Sweden. Won Golden Lion at Venice in 1964 for The War Game.
PICTURES INCLUDE: Bad Lord Byron, Quartet, Portrait from Life, Romantic Age, Blackmailed, Hell is Sold Out, Desperate Moment, Knock on Wood, Dance Little Lady, Prize of Gold, Seven Waves Away (Abandon Ship), The Truth About Women, Jetstorm, Faces in the Dark, Piccadilly Third Stop, Offbeat, Only Two Can Play, The Main Attraction. 1965–66 wrote, dir. Loving Couples, Night Games. 1968: Dr. Glas, The Girls, The Rain Hat, We Have Many Names, The Witches.
TELEVISION: Idiot's Delight, Mayerling, Doll's House, Dance of Death, etc. dir. doc. for BBC and in Sweden. Wrote and dir. Scrubbers, Amorosa.

ZIDE, LARRY M: Executive. b. Flushing, NY, Oct. 16, 1954. 3rd generation in mp. industry. Started 1972 with American Intl. Pictures in sls. & adv.; 1973, named branch sls. mgr., Memphis. 1975, joined Dimension Pictures as print controller; 1978, formed Zica Films Co. serving m.p. industry. 1985, Zica merged with Filmtreat Intl. Corp; named pres., newly formed Filmtreat West Corp.

ZIDE, MICHAEL (MICKEY): Executive. b. Detroit, MI, May 31, 1932. Joined m.p. industry with American Intl. Pictures as

print controller; 1962, promoted to asst. gen. sls. mgr. Named
v.p., special projects, 1970; 1972, joined Academy Pictures as
v.p. of prod. Later went with Zica Film Co.; 1985, named exec.
v.p., Filmtreat West Corp.

ZIEFF, HOWARD: Director. b. Los Angeles, CA, 1943. Started as
artist and photographer, working as newsreel photographer
for L.A. TV station. Went to N.Y. to do still photography;
became top photo artist in advertising. Turned to film
direction with Slither in 1972.
PICTURES INCLUDE: Slither, Hearts of the West, House
Calls, The Main Event, Private Benjamin, Unfaithfully Yours,
The Dream Team.

ZIFKIN, WALTER: Executive. b. July 16, 1936. New York, NY. e. U.
of California at L.A., A.B., 1958; U. of Southern California,
LL.B., 1961. CBS legal dept., 1961–63; William Morris Agency
1963–present; exec. vice-pres.

ZIMBALIST, EFREM, JR.: Actor. b. New York, NY, Nov. 30, 1923.
Son of violinist Efrem Zimbalist and opera singer Alma Gluck.
Father of actress Stephanie Zimbalist. e. Fay Sch., South-
boro, MA; St. Paul's, Concord, NH; Yale. Studied drama,
Neighborhood Playhouse. N.Y. Stage debut, The Rugged
Path. Shows with American Repertory Theatre; Henry VIII,
Androcles and the Lion, What Every Woman Knows, Yellow
Jack, Appeared, Hedda Gabler. Co-prod., The Medium, The
Telephone, The Consul, (Critics Award, Pulitzer Prize).
Screen debut, House of Strangers (1949). Gave up acting
after death of his wife and served as asst. to father, Curtis
Inst. of Music for 4 years. Returned to acting, stock co.,
Hammonton, NJ, 1954.
TELEVISION: Philco, Goodyear Playhouse, U.S. Steel Hour.
Series: Maverick, 77 Sunset Strip, The FBI. Movies: The
Black Dahlia, Terror Out of the Sky, Scruples, The Gathering
II, A Family Upside Down, Best Place to Be, A Family of
Winners, Insight/Checkmate, Beyond Witch Mountain, Family
in Blue, Baby Sister, Shooting Stars, You Are the Jury (host).
PICTURES INCLUDE: Bomber B-52, Band of Angels, The
Deep Six, Violent Road, Girl on the Run, Too Much Too Soon,
Home Before Dark, The Crowded Sky, A Fever in the Blood,
By Love Possessed, Chapman Report, The Reward, Harlow
(electronovision), Airport 1975.

ZIMBERT, RICHARD: Executive. Member, California bar. Has
been with Paramount Pictures in executive capacities since
1975. In 1985 named exec. v.p. of co.

ZINNEMANN, FRED: Director. b. Vienna, Austria, Apr. 29, 1907.
e. Vienna U., law. Studied violin as a boy; after law, studied
photographic technique, lighting & mechanics (Paris); asst.
cameraman 1 yr. Paris; came to U.S. 1929; extra in m.p. All
Quiet on the Western Front, 1930; asst. to Berthold Viertel,
script clerk & asst. to Robert Flaherty, 1931; dir. Mexican
documentary The Wave; short subjects dir., MGM, winning
Academy Award for That Mothers Might Live, 1938; feature
dir. 1941; winner of first Screen Directors' Award 1948 with
The Search. 4 N.Y. Film Critics Awards; 2 Director's Guild
Annual Awards; 4 Acad. Awards. Other awards: U.S. Con-
gressional Life Achievement Award (1987), Gold Medal City
of Vienna, Donatello Award (Italy), Order of Arts & Letters
(France), Golden Thistle Award (Edinburgh, Scotland), etc.
PICTURES INCLUDE: The Seventh Cross, The Search,
The Men, Teresa, High Noon (N.Y. Film Critics Award), Benjy,
short for L.A. Orthopedic Hosp. (Acad. Award, best doc.
short, 1951); Member of the Wedding; From Here to Eternity
(Acad. Award, best dir., 1953, N.Y. Film Critics Award,
Directors' Guild Award), Oklahoma, Hatful of Rain, Nun's
Story (N.Y. Film Critics Award), Sundowners, Behold a Pale
Horse, A Man for All Seasons (Oscars, best picture &
direction, Directors' Guild Award) Day of the Jackal, Julia,
Five Days One Summer.

ZINNEMANN, TIM: Producer. b. Los Angeles, CA. e. Columbia U.
Son of dir. Fred Zinnemann. Began career industry as film
editor; then asst. dir. on 20 films. Production mgr. for 5
projects; assoc. prod. on The Cowboys and Smile. Produced
Straight Time for Warners with Stanley Beck.
PICTURES: A Small Circle of Friends, The Long Riders,
Tex, Impulse, Fandango, Crossroads, The Running Man.
TELEVISION: The Jericho Mile (ABC).

ZITO, JOSEPH: Director. b. New York, NY, May 14, 1946. e. City
Coll. of New York.
PICTURES: Abduction, The Prowler, Friday the 13th: The
Final Chapter, Missing in Action, Invasion U.S.A., Red
Scorpion.

ZOUARY, MAURICE H.: Executive. b. Brooklyn, NY, July 17, 1921.
e. Sch. of Industrial Design & Art, 1937. Trans-Lux Theatres,
1941; U.S. Armed Forces, 1943; production, acct. exec. ad
agencies; Bud Gamble Prod., 1948; TV dept., Edward S.
Kellogg Agency, L.A.; formed Zouary TV-Film Prod., 1950;
prod. supvr. Films for Industry, 1950–52; TV prod., Grey Adv.
Agency, 1952–54; prod, new commercials div., Guild Films,
1955–56; prod. Dore Prod., 1956–57; reactivated Zouary TV
Film Prod., 1957; formed Filmvideo Releasing Corp. film

stock shot library, 1957. Prod.: Freedom (feature film); Prod.
Kiddie Camera (TV series); Prod.: The Vaudevillains (TV
special); Prod.: Dr. DeForest. In 1975 formed TV National
Releasing Corp., supplier of TV programming. Wrote and
produced two cassettes for Movietronics: Buster Keaton &
The First Sound of Movies—The Case for Dr. Lee DeForest.

ZSIGMOND, VILMOS: Cinematographer. b. Czeged, Hungary,
June 16, 1930. e. National Film Sch. Began career photo-
graphing Hungarian Revolution of 1956. Later escaped from
Hungary with friend Laszlo Kovacs, also a cinematographer.
Winner of several int'l and domestic awards as dir. of TV
commercials through own co., Cinematic Directions (formed
1985).
PICTURES: The Time Travelers (1964), The Sadist, The
Name of the Game is Kill, Futz, Picasso Summer, The
Monitors, Red Sky at Morning, McCabe and Mrs. Miller, The
Hired Hand, The Ski Bum, Images, Deliverance, Scarecrow,
The Long Goodbye, Cinderella Liberty, Sugarland Express,
The Girl From Petrovka, Obsession, Close Encounters of the
Third Kind (Acad. Award, 1977), Winter Kills, The Deer
Hunter, The Rose, The Last Waltz, Heaven's Gate, Blow Out,
Jinxed, Table for Five, No Small Affair, The River, Real
Genius, The Witches of Eastwick, Adventure at Eagle Island.
TELEVISION: Flesh and Blood.

ZUCKER, DAVID: Producer, Director, Writer. b. Milwaukee, WI,
Oct. 16, 1947. e. U. of Wisconsin, majoring in film. With
brother, Jerry, and friend Jim Abrahams founded the Kentucky Fried Theatre in Madison in 1979 and wrote script for
film of that name released in 1977. Trio followed this with
Airplane, 1980, which they wrote and jointly directed while
serving as executive producers.
PICTURES: Top Secret (co-dir., co-s.p., co-prod.); Ruthless
People (co-dir.), Naked Gun (dir., co-s.p.).

ZUCKER, JERRY: Producer, Director. Writer. b. Milwaukee, WI,
Mar. 11, 1950. e. U. of Wisconsin, majoring in film. With
brother, David, and friend Jim Abrahams founded the Kentucky Fried Theatre in Madison in 1979 and wrote script for
film of that name released in 1977. Trio followed this with
Airplane! in 1980 which they wrote and jointly directed and
served as executive producers.
PICTURES: Rock 'n' Roll High School (2nd unit dir.), Top
Secret (co-dir., co-s.p.); Ruthless People (co-dir.), Naked Gun
(co-s.p.).

ZUGSMITH, ALBERT: Producer, Director, Writer. b. Atlantic City,
NJ, April 24, 1910. e. U. of Virginia. Pres. Intercontinental
Broadcasting Corp.; ed. publ. Atlantic City Daily World; v.p.
Smith Davis Corp.; Chmn of bd., Continental Telecasting
Corp., Television Corp. of America; assoc. ed. American
Press; pres. World Printing Co.; exec. CBS; pres. American
Pictures Corp.; pres. Famous Players Int'l Corp.
PICTURES INCLUDE: Written on the Wind, Man in the
Shadow, Red Sundown, Star in the Dust, Tarnished Angels,
The Incredible Shrinking Man, The Girl in the Kremlin, The
Square Jungle, Female on the Beach, Touch of Evil, Captive
Women, Sword of Venus, Port Sinister, Invasion U.S.A., Top
Banana, Paris Model, Slaughter on Tenth Avenue, The
Female Animal, High School Confidential, Night of the
Quarter Moon, Beat Generation, The Big Operator, Girls
Town, Violated!, Platinum High School, Private Lives of Adam
and Eve, Dondi, College Confidential, Confessions of an
Opium Eater, The Great Space Adventure, On Her Bed of
Roses, Fanny Hill, The Rapist! author, Private Lives of Adam
and Eve, The Beat Generation, How to Break Into the
Movies, The Chinese Room, Street Girl, The President's Girl
Friend, The Phantom Gunslinger, Sappho, Darling, Menage a
Trois, Two Roses and a Goldenrod, The Friendly Neighbors,
Why Me, God?, Tom Jones Rides Again, etc.

ZWICK, EDWARD: Writer, Producer, Director. b. Chicago, IL,
Oct. 8, 1952. e. Harvard U., B.A., 1974; American Film Inst.
Center for Advanced Film Studies, M.F.A., 1976. Editor and
feature writer, The New Republic and Rolling Stone maga-
zines, 1972–74. Author: Literature and Liberalism (1975).
Formed Bedford Falls Production Co. with Special Bulletin
collaborator Marshall Herskovitz.
PICTURE: About Last Night (dir., debut, 1986).
TELEVISION: Family (writer, then story editor, dir., prod.,
Humanitas Prize Award, 1980); Paper Dolls (dir.); Hang It All
(dir.); Special Bulletin (writer, prod., dir.; Directors Guild,
Writers Guild Awards, 2 Emmys, Humanitas Prize Award,
1983); thirtysomething (exec. prod. with Marshall Herskovitz).

ZWICK, JOEL: Director. b. Brooklyn, NY, Jan. 11, 1942. e.
Brooklyn Coll., B.A., M.A.
THEATER: Dance with Me.
PICTURE: Second Sight.
TELEVISION: Laverne and Shirley; Mork and Mindy; Angie
(pilot); It's a Living; Bosom Buddies (pilot); Struck by
Lightning (pilot); America 2100; Goodtime Girls; Hot W.A.C.S.
(and exec. prod.); Little Darlings; Joanie Loves Chachi; Star
of the Family (pilot); The New Odd Couple (and supv. prod.);
Webster; Brothers (supv. prod.).

Services

Film Distributors in Key Cities

ATLANTA

Alliance International, 161 Spring St., N.W. 30303; (404) 524-7579.
Atlantic Releasing Corp., 220 Northlake Pkwy., Suite 288, Tucker, GA 30084; (404) 491-7766
Bradley Films, 1876 De Foor Ave., N.W., 30318; (404) 352-3316. Gordon Bradley.
Buena Vista Distribution Co., 1190 W. Druid Hill Dr., P.O.B. 10517, 30329; (404) 634-6525.
Chappell Releasing Co., 2814 New Spring Rd. 30339; (404) 432-3361. Wayne Chappell, pres.
Clark Film, Inc., 2200 Northlake Pkwy., Tucker, GA 30084; (404) 491-7766. Lewis Owens.
Clark Film Releasing Co., 161 Spring St., NW, 30303; (404) 524-6588.
Columbia Pictures, 3100 Breckinridge Blvd., #135, Duluth, GA 30136; (404) 564-8521. Terry Tharpe, mgr.
Craddock Films, Inc., Atlanta Film Bldg., 161 Spring St., N.W.; Suite 417; (404) 523-5653.
General Film Distributing, 3950 Peachtree Rd., N.E. 30319; (404) 261-5363. C. L. Autry.
Harnell Independent Productions, 6065 Roswell Rd., 30328; (404) 256-3464. Walter Powell, gen. sls. mgr.
MGM/UA Distribution Co., 2600 Century Parkway, N.E., 30345; (404) 325-3470. Larry Terrell, mgr.
New World Pictures, 3301 Buckeye Rd., 30341; (404) 458-0975. Walter Powell.
Orion Pictures Distribution Corp., 2970 Clairmont, #240; (404) 325-7155. Glenn Simonds.
Paramount Film Distributing Corp., 2600 Century Parkway, 30345; (404) 325-7674. M. V. McAfee.
R.S. Films, Inc., 1455 Tullie Circle, N.W., 30329; (404) 325-0690.
Toddy Pictures Co., Box 150, 30301; (404) 355-9654. Ted Toddy, pres.
Transvue Pictures Corp., 161 Spring St., N.W.; (404) 523-6566.
Twentieth Century-Fox Film Corp., 2635 Century Parkway, N.E., 30345; (404) 321-1178. Larry Jameson.
Universal Film Exchange, 6060 McDonough Dr., Norcross GA 30093; (404) 448-8032. Curtis Fainn, Mgr.
Warner Bros., 2200 Century Pkwy., 30345; (404) 325-0301. Barry Nelson.

BOSTON

Association Films, 410 Great Road, Littleton, MA 01460; (617) 486-3518.
Buena Vista Distribution Co., 990 Washington St., Dedham, MA, 02026; (617) 461-0870. John Molson, Mgr.
Columbia Pictures Corp., 20 Park Plaza, 02116. (617) 426-8980; Gasper Urban, mgr.
Ellis Gordon Films, 46 Church St., 02116; (617) 542-5550. Ellis Gordon, mgr.
Lockwood & Friedman Film Corp., 20 Pickering St., Needham, MA 02192; (617) 449-7777.
MGM/UA Distribution Co., 100 Grandview Rd., Braintree, MA, 02184; (617) 849-0131.
New England Film Distributing, 31 St. James Ave., 02116; (617) 482-9025.
Orion Pictures Distribution Corp., 31 St. James Ave., 02116; (617) 542-0677. Beth Weiner, mgr.
Paramount Film Distributing Corp., 31 St. James Ave., 02116; (617) 426-1070. Joe Rathgeb.
Jud Parker Films, 46 Church St., 02116; (617) 542-0744.
20th Century Fox Film Corp., 545 Boylston St., Suite 1101, 02116; (617) 267-4800. Carl Bertolino.
Universal Film Exchanges, Inc., 44 Winchester St., 02116; (617) 426-8760. Joan Corrado.
Warner Bros. Pictures Dist. Corp., 45 Braintree Hill, Office P/C 301, 02184; (617) 848-2550. Andrew Silverman.

CHARLOTTE

Atlantic Releasing Corp., 230 S. Tyron St., 28202; (704) 376-5549
Buena Vista Dist. Co. Inc., 230 S. Tryon St., 28202; (704) 373-0724. Jack Kirby.
Carolina Booking Service, 230 S. Tryon St., 28202; (704) 377-9341.
Carolina Film Service Inc., 5012 Hovis Rd.; (704) 394-3129. E. J. Poole (ship); Marg. Miller (off.)

Charlotte Booking Service, N.W. Bank Bldg., 28230; (704) 376-5569. J. R. McClure.
Cinema Film Distributing, 222 S. Church, 28201; (704) 332-8539. Ron Witherspoon.
Clark Film Inc., 230 S. Tryon St., 28202; (704) 376-5569. Bob McClure, branch mgr.
Columbia Pictures Corp., 201 S. College St., 28244; (704) 375-0705. Ed. McLaughlin.
Dominant Pictures Corp., 1400 Charlotte Plaza, 28244; (704) 375-0705. Harry Kerr, mgr.
Galaxy Films, 222 S. Church St., 28202; (704) 372-6747. W. R. James, mgr.
Howco Exchange, 301 S. McDowell, 28204; (704) 834-8510. J. Francis White.
International Amusement Corp., 222 S. Church St., 28202; (704) 332-4163.
JACO Productions, 222 S. Church St., 28202; (704) 375-2519. K. Rogers, Charlie Mincey, branch mgrs.
Premier Pictures, 221 S. Church St., 28202; (704) 332-5101. Jerry Helms.
Pyramid Films, 221 S. Church St., 28202; (704) 333-2894.
Queens City Advertising & Amusement, Inc., 221 S. Church St., 28202; (704) 375-4419. Hugh M. Sykes, Jr.
Variety Films, Inc., 221 S. Church St., 28202; (704) 374-1611. Bob McClure, mgr.

CHICAGO

Apache Films, 32 W. Randolph, 60601; (312) 782-5620. Harry Goodman.
Atlantic Releasing Corp., 9575 W. Higgins Rd., Suite 602, Rosemont, IL 60018; (312) 692-2300
Azteca Films, Inc., 1233 S. Wabash Ave., 60605; (312) 922-6186. Edward G. Edwards, br. mgr.
Buena Vista Distribution Co. Inc. 8550 W. Bryn Mawr Ave., 60631; (312) 693-8580.
Don Buhrmester & Assoc., Inc., 203 N. Wabash Ave., 60601; (312) 782-0988. Don Buhrmester.
Clark Service, Inc., 2265 W. St. Paul Ave.; (312) 342-3140. Jack Bailey.
Columbia Pictures Corp., O'Hare Atrium Office Center, 2800 N. River Rd., Des Plaines, IL 60018; (312) 699-8168. Gene Gibbons.
Dudelson Film Distributing, 1325 S. Wabash Ave. 60605; (312) 922-3546. Moe Dudelson.
Empire Pictures, 999 E. Touhy Ave., Des Plaines, IL 60018; (312) 699-1055. Neil W. Wise.
Gilbreth Film Co., 32 W. Randolph St., 60601; (312) 726-6220. Jack Gilbreth.
J.M.G. Film Co., 32 W. Randolph St., 60601; (312) 346-6916. Virgil Jones.
Kaplan-Continental Pictures, 203 N. Wabash Ave., 60601; (312) 782-8413. Sam Kaplan.
William Lange & Associates, 32 W. Randolph St., 60601; (312) 332-1734. Bill Lange.
Orion Pictures Distribution Corp., 75 E. Wacker Dr., 60601; (312) 332-4755. David Sikich.
Paramount Film Distributing Co., 111 East Wacker Dr., 60601; (312) 380-4560. Clark Woods.
Select Film Co., 32 W. Randolph St., 60601; (312) 236-1233. Sam Seplowin.
Teitel Film Corp., 333 S. Michigan, 60601; (312) 346-2566. Chas Teitel, bd. chmn.
Topar Films, Inc. 345 Fullerton Parkway, 60614; (312) 348-0210. John McLaurin.
Twentieth Century Fox Film Corp., 1100 Woodfield Rd., Schaumburg, IL, 60173; (312) 843-3640. Robert Kaplowitz.
United Film Distribution Co., Suite 420, 625 Plainfield Rd., Willowbrook, IL 60521; (312) 789-1444. Sharon McAndrews, mgr.
Universal Film Exchanges, 425 N. Michigan Ave., 60611; (312) 822-0513. William Gehring, mgr.
Warner Bros. Dist. Corp., 1111 East Touhy Ave., Des Plaines, IL 60018; (312) 296-5070. Seymour Hite, div. mgr.

CINCINNATI

Buena Vista Distribution Co., Inc., 636 Northland Rd., 45240; (513) 742-0900. Norma Wethington, mgr.
J.M.G. Film Co., 636 Northland Blvd., 45240; (513) 851-9933. Jay Goldberg, mgr.

MGM/UA Distribution Co., 35 E. 7th St., 45202; (513) 241-1546. Frank Morris, br. mgr.
MYCO Films, 617 Vine St., 45202; (513) 579-8090. Jo Harrison.
Regency Film Distributing, 617 Vine St., 45202; (513) 621-2955. William Blum.
C. J. Ruff Film Distributing Co., 1601 Harrison Ave., 45214; (513) 921-8200.
Edward Salzberg, Inc., 35 E. Seventh St., 45202; (513) 241-3671.

CLEVELAND

Academy Film Service, Inc. 2108 Payne Ave., 44114; (216) 696-0661. Blair Mooney, pres. M. M. Blaettner, mgr.
Cine-Pix, 2108 Payne Ave., 44114; (216) 781-0622. Jack Kaufman.
Columbia Pictures Corp., 3 Commerce Park Square, 23200 Chagrin Blvd., 44122; (216) 292-3610. David Spero.
Imperial Pictures, 2108 Payne Ave., 44114; (216) 621-9376.
Selected Pictures Corp., 29001 Cedar Rd., Lyndhurst, OH 44124; (216) 461-9770. Jay Schultz, pres.
States Film Service, Inc., Warner Bldg., 2336 Payne Ave.; (216) 771-3723. Harry Lyman, mgr.

DALLAS

American National Enterprises, 11422 Harry Hines Blvd., 75231; (214) 243-5171. A. H. Watts.
Atlantic Releasing Corp., 700 S. Story Rd., Suite 1021, Irving, TX 75060; (214) 259-3636
Buena Vista Distribution, 10300 N. Central Expressway, 75206; (214) 363-9494.
Columbia Pictures, 12770 Merit Dr., 75251; (214) 770-4220. Kenneth Newbert, mgr.
Crump Distributors, Inc. 6545 Lange Circle, 75214; (214) 826-6331. Jim Crump.
Dal Art Film Exchange, 8235 Douglas St. 75225; (214) 987-2161. Fred Beiersdorf, pres.
Dimension General Eric Distributing, 10830 N. Central Expressway, 72531; (214) 692-7744. Eric Deneve, Don Scruggs.
Empire Pictures, 10300 N. Central Expressway Bldg., 75231; (214) 739-6966. Dale Smith.
Film Booking Service, 500 S. Ervay, Suite 603, 75201; (214) 744-3165. Bennie Lunch.
G&M Film Distributors, 500 S. Ervay St., 75201; (214) 748-7093. Frank Meyers, Jake Guiles.
Jaco Productions, 500 S. Ervay St., 75201; (214) 748-6145. Bill Hill.
MGM/UA Distribution Co., Suite 438, 6060 N. Central Expressway, 75206; (214) 692-0777. Don Evans, mgr.
Major Film Distributors, 1907 Elm St., 75201; (214) 744-4069. Jack Durrell.
Orbit Films, 4411 N. Central Expressway, 75205; (214) 522-7780. Al Weiner.
Orion Pictures Distribution Corp., 7557 Rambler Rd., 75231; (214) 363-7800. Kenneth Durbin, mgr.
R.S. Films, Inc., 6060 N. Central Expressway, 75206; (214) 368-8083.
Sack Amusement Enterprises, 1710 Jackson St., 75201; (214) 742-9445.
Southern Enterprises, 2344 Farrington St., 75207; (214) 634-2690. Carl Sims, gen. mgr.
Starline Pictures, 3220 Lemmon West, 75204; (214) 522-8300. James Prichard.
Topar Films, Inc., 1 No. Park East; (214) 691-7660. M. Parker, J. Kauffman.
Twentieth Century Fox Film Corp., 12222 Merit Dr., 75251; (214) 392-0101. Woodrow Townsend.
United Film Distribution Co., 1900 S. Central Expressway, 75215; (214) 421-1900. Sara Murray, mgr.
Universal Film Exchanges, Inc., 7502 Greenville Ave., 75231; (214) 360-0022. Mark Gaines, br. mgr.
Variety Film Distributors, 4308 N. Central Expressway, 75206; (214) 827-7800. Mark Gaines.
Warner Bros. Distributing Corp., 8144 Walnut Hill Lane 920, 75231; (214) 691-6101. Jackie Stanley.

DENVER

Buena Vista Dist. Co., Inc., 3650 S. Yosemite, 80237; (303) 779-6160. Andrew Hersh, mgr.
Crest Films, 1860 Lincoln St., 80203; (303) 623-1221. Jack Felix, branch mgr.
J&B Independent Films, 1860 Lincoln, 80203; (303) 255-0495.
McGee Film Distributing, 655 S. Alton Way; (303) 343-3413.
Mountain States Film Dist., 2145 Broadway; (303) 623-1377. David Inget.
Paramount Pictures Corp., 158 Fillmore St., 80206; (303) 399-7582. Mike Morrison.

DETROIT

D&R Distributors, 13131 Fenkell Ave., 48227; (313) 491-2180. Al Dezel, George Rossman.
Gail Film Distributors, 16300 W. 9 Mile Rd., Southfield, MI 48075; (313) 557-5024. Arthur Weisberg, pres.
J.M.G. Films, 2330 Greenfield Rd., Oak Park, 48237; (313) 968-0500.
Levin Film Distributors, 29501 Greenfield Rd., Southfield, MI, 48072; (313) 559-1101. Nate Levin.
Orion Pictures Distribution Corp., 24700 Northwestern Hwy., Southfield, MI 48075; (313) 358-0733. Linda Victel, mgr.
R. Distributors, 13131 Fenkell, 48227; (313) 491-2180.
Regency Film Distributing, 24655 Southfield Rd., Southfield, 48075; (313) 354-3245. Herb Gillis.
C. J. Ruff Films, 23300 Greenfield Rd., Oak Park, 48237; (313) 968-7770. Dennis Glenn.

HONOLULU, HI

Hawaii Nichibel Film Co. Inc., 728 9th Ave., 96816; (808) 737-3455.
Pacific Motion Picture Co. Ltd., 1190 Nuuanu Ave., 96817; (808) 538-1035.

HOUSTON, TX

Conner, Charles M. Productions, 4713 Braeburn Dr., Bellaire, TX; (713) 668-9900.

JACKSONVILLE, FL

Atlantic Releasing Corp., 905 North St., 32211; (904) 721-2112
Clark Film Releasing, 905 North St., 32211; (904) 721-2122. Harry Clark, pres. Belton Clark, gen. mgr.
South Eastern Entertainment, 10348 Atlantic Circle, 32216; (904) 356-7216. Robert Capps.
United Film Distribution Co., 9333 Atlantic Blvd., 32211; (904) 725-4077. Richard Settoon, mgr.

KANSAS CITY, MO

Atlantic Releasing Corp., 3859 W. 95 St., Overland, KS 66206; (913) 381-2058
Buena Vista Distribution Co., 4220 Johnson Dr., Shawnee Mission, KS 66205; (913) 362-9500. Doug Finlay, mgr.
Marcus Film Distributing, 3773 W. 95th St., Overland Park, KS, 66206; (913) 381-6222. Ben Marcus, pres.
Mercury Film Co., 3865 W. 95th St., KS, Overland Park, 66206; (913) 383-3880. Bev. Miller.
Midwest Films, 3879 W. 95th St., Shawnee Mission, KS 66206; (913) 381-2058. Gene Irwin.
Orion Pictures Distribution Corp., 3101 Broadway, 64111; (816) 932-6500. Jack Klug, mgr.
Thomas/Shipp Film Distributing, 207 Westport Rd., 64111; (816) 561-0202. Howard Thomas, John Shipp.
United National Distributors, 1703 Wyandotte, 64108; (816) 474-5330. Gene Irwin.

LOS ANGELES

Amerikana Film Co., 6255 W. Sunset Blvd., L.A. 90046; (213) 464-3131.
Atlantic Releasing Corp., 8255 Sunset Blvd., Suite 104, L.A. 90046; (213) 650-2500.
Azteca Films, Inc., 555 N. La Brea Ave., 90036; (213) 938-2413.
BFA Educational Media, 2211 Michigan Ave., Santa Monica, 90212; (213) 829-2901.
Seymour Borde Associates, 1800 N. Highland Ave., Hollywood, CA 90028; (213) 461-3936.
Buena Vista Dist. Co. Inc., 3800 W. Alameda Ave., Burbank, 91505; (818) 569-7300.
Carlyle Films Ltd., 6430 Sunset Blvd., 90028; (213) 466-0864.
Cavalcade Pictures, Inc., 8950 Venice Blvd., 90034; (213) 836-2048.
Columbia Pictures, Corp., Columbia Plaza South, Burbank, CA 91505; (818) 954-3084. Richard Sands.
Cori Films International, 2049 Central Park E., #1200, 90067; (213) 557-0173.
Counselor Films, 8816 Sunset Blvd, L.A.; 90069; (213) 659-5720.
Crest Film Distributors, 116 No. Robertson Blvd., 90052; (213) 652-8844. J. Persell.
Crown International Pictures, 8701 Wilshire Blvd., B.H. 90211; (213) 657-6700.
Empire Pictures, 1551 N. La Brea Ave., 90028; (213) 850-6110. Jim Rogers.

341

Favorite Films of California, Inc., 292 La Cienega Blvd., B.H.; (213) 657-6700.
Film Investment Corp. 333 S. Beverly Dr., B.H., 90211; (213) 553-5806.
Hollywood International Film Corp. of America, 1044 S. Hill St., L.A. 90015; (213) 749-2067.
International Film Enterprises, Inc., 721 N. La Brea Ave., 90038; (213) 655-2534.
MGM/UA Distribution Co., 11111 Santa Monica Blvd., 90025; (213) 444-1600. Robert Wood, mgr.
Manson International, 9145 Sunset Blvd., 90069; (213) 273-8640. Michael F. Goldman, pres.
National Telefilm Associates, Inc., 12636 Beatrice St., 90066; (213) 306-4040.
Orion Pictures Distribution Corp., 11500 W. Olympic Blvd., 90064; (213) 473-5073. Bob Wood, mgr.
Paramount Film Dist. Corp. 9440 Santa Monica Blvd., Beverly Hills, 90210; (213) 550-8600. Walter Lange.
Services Marketing & Distribution Co., P.O. Box 85, Ross, CA 94957.
Summit Film Distributors, 116 N. Robertson Blvd., 90048; (213) 652-7702.
Toho Co., Ltd., 2049 Century Park E., 90067; (213) 277-1081.
Topar Films, Inc., 18321 Ventura Blvd., Tarzana, CA 91356; (213) 881-9115.
Tower Film Co., 8400 W. Sunset Blvd., L.A. 90069; (213) 654-4414.
Twentieth Century Fox Film Corp., 15250 Ventura Blvd., Sherman Oaks, CA 91403; (818) 995-7975. Donna Wolfe.
United Film Distributing Co., 6380 Wilshire Blvd., Suite 1111, 90048; (213) 655-5044. Steven Naify, mgr.
Universal Film Exchange, 8901 Beverly Blvd., 90048; (213) 550-7461. Jack Finn, mgr.
Warner Bros. Pictures Distribution Corp., 15821 Ventura Blvd., #685, Encino, 91436; (818) 784-7494. Shirley Becker.

MEMPHIS

Blue Ribbon Pictures, 942 Normandy Ave., 38137; (901) 683-3949.
Clark/Pabst Films, Inc., 1188 Perkins Rd. S. 38117; (901) 683-8182.
Dimension General, 138 Huling St., 38102; (901) 278-4442. Jeff Williams.
Don Kay Enterprises, 138 Huling St., 38102; (901) 527-4023. Fordyce Kaiser, branch mgr.
Starline Pictures, 100 N. Main Bldg., 38103; (901) 527-9424. Bailey Prichard, owner.
Tab Films, 2999 Overton Crossing, 38127; (901) 353-4100. Charles Arendall.

MILWAUKEE

Independent Film Distributor, 6421 Milwaukee Ave.; 771-9470. Fern Anderson, mgr.
Mescop Distributing, 9235 W. Capitol Dr., 53222; (414) 466-1700. Fred Florence, pres.

NEW ORLEANS

Atlantic Releasing Corp., 5515 Pepsi St., Jefferson, LA 701213; (504) 733-3555
Blue Ribbon Pictures, Inc., International Trade Mart, Suite 1400, 2 Canal St., 70130; 522-8788-89. George Pabst, owner.
Clark/Pabst Film, Inc., P.O. Box 7865, Metairie, LA, 70010; (504) 733-3555.
I.F.I. Films, 4117 Heaslip Ave., Metairie, LA 70011; (501) 837-6106.
Jaco Productions, 822 Perdido, 70112; (504) 524-4218. Ken Rodgers.
Southern Film Distributing, 143 N. Rampart St., 70112; (504) 837-5200.

NEW YORK

Atlantic Releasing Corp., 475 Park Ave. S., 32nd floor, 10016; (212) 689-2026
Bedford Entertainment, 51 E. 42 St., 10017; (212) 697-6188.
Buena Vista Distribution Co., 500 Park Ave., 10022; (212) 593-8900.
Cinevista Releasing, 347 W. 39 St., 10018; (212) 947-4373.
Columbia Pictures, 1700 Broadway, 10019; (212) 765-5860. Joseph Curtin.
Films, Inc., 440 Park Ave. S., 10016; (212) 889-7910.
First Run Features, 153 Waverly Place, 10011; (212) 243-0600.
Grange Communications, 45 W. 60 St., 10023; (212) 582-4261.
Gray City, Inc., 853 Broadway, 10001; (212) 473-3600.
Independent International Pictures Corp., 223 State Hwy. #18, East Brunswick, NJ 08816; (201) 249-8982.

Italtoons Corp., 32 W. 40 St., 10018; (212) 730-0280.
ITM Releasing Corp., 321 W. 44 St., 10036; (212) 582-6946.
Marvin Films, Inc., 1560 Broadway, 10019; (212) 575-7753.
Miramax Films, 211 W. 56 St., 10019; (212) 247-4264.
Orion Pictures Distribution Corp., 9 W. 57 St., 10019; (212) 980-1117. Redmond Gautier.
Paramount Film Distributing Corp., 1 Gulf & Western Plaza, 10023; (212) 333-7000. Pam Pritzler.
Promovision International Films, Ltd., 347 W. 39 St., 10018; (212) 947-4373.
Third World Newsreel, 335 W. 38 St., 10018; (212) 947-9277.
Times Film Corp., 157 W. 57 St., 10019; (212) 757-6980.
Twentieth Century Fox Film Corp., 40 W. 57 St. 10019; (212) 977-5500. Ronald Polon, mgr.
United Film Dist. Co., 11 Middleneck Rd., Great Neck, NY 11021; (212) 895-7100. R. Hassanein.
Universal Film Exchange, 445 Park Ave., 10022; (212) 759-7500. Gary Rocco, mgr.
Warner Bros. Distributing Corporation, 75 Rockefeller Plaza, 10019; (212) 484-6230. Charles Barcellona.

PHILADELPHIA

Alan Pictures, 900 Kings Highway N., Cherry Hill, NJ 08034; (215) 561-0800. Alan Strulson, pres.
Buena Vista Distribution, One Cherry Hill, Cherry Hill, NJ 08002; (609) 779-8804.
Capital Film Exchange, 309 N. 13th St. 19107; (215) 567-2698.
Columbia Pictures Corp., 1700 Market St., 19103; (215) 568-3889. Joe Saladino.
Magill Films, 1612 Market St., 19103; (215) 563-7428. Mort Magill.
M.Y. Film Co., 1518 Walnut St., 19102; (215) 732- 6543. Emanuel Youngerman, pres.
Orion Pictures Distribution Corp., 1530 Chestnut St., 19103; (215) 568-6684. Richard Bonanno, mgr.
United Film Distribution Co., 2201 Route 38, Suite 230, Cherry Hill, NJ 08002; (215) 563-5827. Ed Potash, mgr.
Warner Bros. Pictures Dist. Corp., 1800 J.F. Kennedy Blvd., 19103. (215) 557-7030. William Waynberg.

SAN FRANCISCO

Buena Vista Dist. Co., Inc., 901 Market St., 94103; (415) 957-9876.
Cardinal Films, 1255 Post St., 94102; (415) 776-2626. R. Stafford.
Orion Pictures Distribution Corp., 90 New Montgomery St., 94105; (415) 995-2200. Robert Coley, mgr.
Pacific Film Enterprises, 1 Hallidie Plaza, 94102; (415) 479-8223. Paul Williams.
Paramount Film Distributing Inc., 1700 Montgomery St., 94111; (415) 433-8660. Larry St. John
Ted Reisch Enterprises, 1325 Laurel St., San Carlos, 94070; (415) 593-7060.
United Film Distributors Corp., 172 Golden Gate Ave., 94102; (415) 928-3200. Steven Naify, mgr.
Warner Bros. Pictures Distributing Corp., 150—4th St., 91403; (415) 543-8015. Mike Timko.

SEATTLE

Buena Vista Dist. Co. Inc., 975 John St., 98109; (206) 624-0186.
MGM/UA Distribution Co., 225-108th Ave., N.E. Bellevue, WA 98004. S. Amato, mgr.
Paramount Film Distributing Corp., 975 John St., 98109; (206) 747-1176. Joe Vigil.
Parnell Film Distributors Inc., 4223 Northeast 103 Place, WA 98125; (206) 527-8804.

WASHINGTON, DC

Association-Sterling Films, 1701 N. Fort Meyer Dr., Arlington, VA; 525-4475. C. Edgar Bryant, sales mgr.
Empire Pictures, 501 Church St., Vienna, VA 22180; (703) 255-0655. John Nau.
Key Theatre Ent., 1325½ Wisconsin Ave., N.W., 20007; (202) 965-4401. David Levy.
Orion Pictures Distribution Corp., 5205 Leesburg Pike, Falls Church, VA 22041; George Shepard, mgr.
Twentieth Century Fox Film Corp., 1156 15th St., N.W. 20005; (202) 223-6320. Francis X Gormley.
Warner Bros. Dist. Corp., 1700 Rockville Pike, Rockville, MD 20852; (301) 230-1324. Daniel Chinich.

Film Processing, Raw Stock, Preservation, Storage

Film Labs, Processing

ATLANTA

CINEFILM LABORATORY, 2156 Faulkner Rd., 30324; (404) 633-1448.
SOUTHERN FILM LAB INC., 2050-H Chamblee Tucker Rd., Chamblee, GA 30341; (404) 458-0026.

BOSTON

CINE SERVICE LABORATORIES, INC., 1380 Soldiers Field Rd., Brighton, 02135; (617) 254-7882.
COLORTEK, 330 Newbury St., 02115; (617) 267-6503.
D-4 FILM STUDIOS, INC., P.O. Box 187, Needham Heights, MA 02194; (617) 235-1119.
FILM SERVICE LAB, 93 Harvey St., Cambridge, MA 02140; (617) 542-8501.
MASTER COLOR SERVICE, 44 Piedmont St., 02116; (617) 426-3592.
SPORTS FILM LAB, 361 W. Broadway, South Boston 02127; (617) 268-8388.

CHICAGO

ALLIED FILM & VIDEO SERVICES, 1322 W. Belmont Ave., 60657; (312) 348-0373.
ASTRO COLOR LAB, 61 W. Erie, 60610; (312) 280-5500.
CINEMA VIDEO PROCESSORS, 211 E. Grand Ave., 60611; (312) 527-4050.
EDITEL, INC., 301 E. Erie, 60611; (312) 440-2360.
FILMACK, 1327 S. Wabash, 60605; (312) 427-3395.
SPECTRUM MOTION PICTURE LAB, 399 Gundersen, Carol Stream, IL 60187; (312) 665-4242; (800) 345-6522.

CINCINNATI

MARATHON MOVIE LABORATORY, 2436 Vine St., 45219; (513) 621-5313.

COLUMBIA, SC

SOUTHEASTERN FILM COMPANY, 3604 Main St., 29203; (803) 252-3753.

COLUMBUS, OH

JOHN R. BENNETT, 2553 Cleveland Ave., 43211; (614) 267-7007.

DALLAS

ALLIED FILM LABORATORY & VIDEO SERVICES, 4 Dallas Communications Complex, #115, Irving 75039; (214) 869-0100.
SOUTHWEST FILM LABORATORY, INC., 3024 Fort Worth Ave., 75211; (214) 331-8347.

DAYTON, OH

VALDHERE INC., 3060 Valleywood Dr., Dayton, 45429; (513) 293-2191.

DETROIT

ALLIED FILM & VIDEO SERVICES, 7375 Woodward Ave., 48202; (313) 871-2222.
FILM CRAFT LAB., INC., 66 Sibley, 48201; (313) 962-2611.
MULTI-MEDIA INC., 7154 E. Nevada St., 48234; (313) 366- 5200.
PRODUCERS COLOR SERVICE, 2921 E. Grand Blvd., 48202; (313) 874-1112.
WILLIAMS SERVICE, 601 W. Fort, 48226; (313) 962-9070.

HOLLYWOOD-LOS ANGELES

ALPHA CINE LABORATORY INC., 5724 W. Third St., Suite 311, Los Angeles, 90038; (213) 934-7793.

ASHLAND FILM LAB., 747 N. Seward St., Hollywood 90038; (213) 462-3231.
AUDIO VISUAL HEADQUARTERS CORP., 361 N. Oak, Inglewood 90302; (213) 419-4040.
CINEMA RESEARCH CORP., 6860 Lexington Ave., Los Angeles, 90038; (213) 460-4111.
CINESERVICE, INC., 6518½ Santa Monica Blvd., Los Angeles, 90038; (213) 463-3178.
CONRAD FILM DUPLICATING COMPANY, 6750 Santa Monica Blvd., Hollywood, 90038; (213) 463-5614.
CONSOLIDATED FILM INDUSTRIES, 959 N. Seward St., Hollywood, 90038; (213) 960-7444.
CREST NATIONAL FILM & VIDEO LABS, 1141 N. Seward St., Hollywood, 90038; (213) 466-0624; 462-6696.
DELUXE GENERAL INC., 1377 N. Serrano Ave., Hollywood, 90027; (213) 462-6171; (800) 233-5893.
EASTMAN KODAK LABORATORY 1017 N. Las Palmas Ave., Los Angeles, 90038; (213) 465-7152; (800) 621-1234.
FILM TECHNOLOGY CO. INC., 6900 Santa Monica Blvd., Los Angeles, 90038; (213) 464-3456
FILMSERVICE & VIDEO LABS, INC., 6327 Santa Monica Blvd., Hollywood, 90038; (213) 464-5141.
FLORA COLOR, 3767 Overland Ave. #109, Los Angeles, 90034; (213) 559-4369.
FOTO-KEM FOTO-TRONICS, 2800 W. Olive Ave., Burbank, 91505; (818) 846-3101.
FOTORAMA, 1507 N. Cahuenga Blvd., Los Angeles, 90028; (213) 469-1578.
GETTY FILM LAB, 7641 Densmore Ave., Van Nuys, CA 91406; (818) 997-7801.
HOLLYWOOD FILM ENTERPRISES, INC., 6060 Sunset Blvd., Hollywood, 90028; (213) 464-2181.
IMAGE TRANSFORM LABORATORY, 3611 N. San Fernando Rd., Burbank, 91505; (818) 841-3812.
MGM/UA ENTERTAINMENT CO. LABS., INC. 10202 W. Washington Blvd., Culver City, 90230; (213) 558-5858.
METROCOLOR LAB, (div. of Lorimar Telepictures), 10202 W. Washington Blvd., Culver City, 90232-3783; (213) 202-2000.
MORCRAFT FILMS, 837 N. Cahuenga Blvd., Los Angeles, 90038; (213) 464-2009.
MOVIELAB-HOLLYWOOD, INC., 6823 Santa Monica Blvd., Los Angeles, 90038; (213) 469-2211.
MULTI-LAB, 1633 Maria St., Burbank, 91504; (213) 415- 9970.
NEWELL COLOR LAB, 221 W. Westmoreland Ave., Los Angeles, 90004; (213) 380-2980.
NEWSFILM LABORATORY, INC., 516 N. Larchmont Bl., Hollywood, 90004; (213) 462-6814.
PACIFIC TITLE & ART STUDIO, 6350 Santa Monica Blvd., Los Angeles, 90038; (213) 464-0121.
PEERLESS FILM PROCESSING CORP., 730 Salem, Glendale, 91203; (818) 242-2181.
RANK FILM—TECHNICAL SERVICES, P.O. Box 1166, Malibu, 90265; (213) 461-8483.
REVERSALS UNLIMITED ENTERPRISES, 6750 Santa Monica Blvd., Los Angeles, 90038. (213) 463-5654.
SINA'S CUSTOM LAB, 3136 Wilshire Blvd., Los Angeles, 90010; (213) 381-5161.
TECHNICOLOR INC., (Professional Film Division), 4050 Lankershim Bl., North Hollywood, 91608; (818) 769-8500.
UNITED COLOR LAB. INC., 835 N. Seward, Hollywood, 90038; (213) 461-9921.
UNIVERSAL FACILITIES RENTAL DIVISION, 100 Universal City Plaza, Universal City, 91608; (818) 777-3000.
YALE LABS, 1509 N. Gordon St., Los Angeles, 90028; (213) 464-6181.

HOUSTON

THE PHOTOGRAPHIC LABORATORIES, 1926 W. Gray, 77019; (713) 527-9300.

INDIANAPOLIS, IN

FILMCRAFT COLOR LABORATORIES, 5216 Keystone, 46220; (317) 251- 9568.

MEMPHIS, TN

MOTION PICTURE LABORATORIES, INC., 781 S. Main St. 38101; (901) 774-4944; (800) 238-2636.

MIAMI, FL

CAPITAL FILM LABORATORIES, INC., 1998 N.E. 150 St., 33161; (305) 949-4252.
CONTINENTAL FILM LABS, INC., 1998 Northeast 150 St., N. Miami, 33181; (305) 949-4252; (800) 327-8396.

MILWAUKEE, WI

CENTRAL FILM LABORATORY & PHOTO SUPPLY, 1003 North Third St., 53203; (414) 272-0606.

NEW ORLEANS

PAN AMERICAN FILMS, 822 N. Rampart St., 70116; (504) 522-5364.

NEW YORK CITY

A-ONE FILM LABS. CORP., 333 W. 39 St., 10018; (212) 239-9530.
ACCURATE FILM LABS, 45 W. 45 St., 10036; (212) 730-0555.
BEBELL LABS, 420 E. 55 St., 10022; (212) 486-6577.
CINELAB CORP., 475 Tenth Ave., 10018; (212) 244-7400.
DELUXE GENERAL INC., 630 Ninth Ave., 10036; (212) 489-8800.
DU-ART FILM LABORATORIES, 245 W. 55 St., 10019; (212) 757-4580.
GUFFANTI FILM LABORATORIES INC., 630 Ninth Ave., 10036; (212) 265-5530.
HBO STUDIO PRODS., 120A E. 23 St., 10010; (212) 512-7800.
HUEMARK FILMS INC., 277 E. 44 St., 10017; (212) 986-5066.
J & D LABS INC., 12 W. 21 St., 10010; (212) 691-5613.
JAN FILM LAB, INC., 302 W. 37 St., 10018; (212) 279-5438.
KIN-O-LUX, INC., 17 W. 45 St., 10036; (212) 869-5595.
LAB-LINK, INC., 115 W. 45 St., 10036; (212) 302-7373.
LAB POWER, 630 Ninth Ave., #910, 10036-3770; (212) 977-8980.
KEN LIEBERMAN LABORATORIES INC., 118 W. 22 St., 10011; (212) 633-0500.
MAGNO SOUND & VIDEO, 729 Seventh Ave., 10019; (212) 302- 2505.
MAGNO VISUALS, 115 W. 45 St., 10036; (212) 575-5162; 575- 5159.
MOVIELAB INC., 619 W. 54 St., 10019; (212) 586-0360.
PRECISION FILM & VIDEO LABS, 630 Ninth Ave., 10036; (212) 489-8800.
RAPID FILM TECHNIQUE, INC., 37-02 27th St., Long Island City, 11101; (212) 786-4600.
STUDIO FILM LABS INC., 321 W. 44 St #512, 10036; (212) 582-5578.
STUDIO WEST LTD., 321 W. 44 St., #504, 10036; (212) 489-1190.
TVC LABS, INC., 311 W. 43 St., 10036; (212) 397-8600.
TECHNICOLOR INC., 321 W. 44 St., 10036; (212) 582-7310.
VAN CHROMES CORP., 311 W. 43 St., 14th floor, 10036; (212) 582-0505.

OMAHA

CORNHUSKER FILM PROCESSING LAB, 1817 Vinton St., 68108; (402) 341-4290.

PHILADELPHIA

NEWS REEL LABORATORY, 1725 N. 24th St., Philadelphia 19121; (215) 763-3400.

PITTSBURGH

WRS MOTION PICTURE LAB., 210 Semple St., 15213; (412) 687-3700.

PORTLAND OR

TEKNIFILM INC., 909 N.W. 19th, 97209; (503) 224-3835.

SALT LAKE CITY, UT

ALPHA CINE LAB. INC., 450 S. 900 St., #205, 84102; (801) 363-9465.

SAN FRANCISCO

DINER/ALLIED FILM & VIDEO, 620 Third St., 94107; (415) 777-1700.

HIGHLAND LABS., 840 Battery St., 94111; (415) 981-5010.
INTERFORMAT, 1000 Brannan St., 94103; (415) 626-1100.
LUCASFILM LTD., P.O. Box 2009, San Rafael, CA 94912; (415) 662-1800.
MONACO LABORATORIES, INC., 234 Ninth St., 94103; (415) 864-5350.

SEATTLE, WA

ALPHA CINE LABORATORY, 1001 Lenora St., 98121; (206) 682-8230; (800) 426-7070.
FORDE MOTION PICTURE LABORATORY, 306 Fairview Ave. N., 98109; (206) 682-2510; (800) 682-2510.

SPRINGFIELD, MA

PENFIELD PRODUCTIONS LTD., 35 Springfield St., Agawarm 01001; (413) 786-4454.

TAMPA, FL

BEACON FILM LABORATORY, 3705 N. Nebraska Ave.; (813) 932-9636.

Film Preservation

ACCUTREAT FILMS, INC., 630 Ninth Ave., #1101, New York, NY 10036; (212) 247-3415.
AFD/PHOTOGRAD FILM COATING LAB, 1015 N. Cahuenga Blvd., Hollywood, CA 90038; (213) 469-8141.
BARTCO CO., 924 N. Formosa, Hollywood, CA 90046; (213) 851- 5411.
BONDED SERVICES, 487 Edward H. Ross Dr., Elmwood Park, NJ 07407; (201) 794-6550.
BONDED SERVICES, 5260 Vineland Ave., N. Hollywood, CA 91601; (818) 761-4058.
THE DURAFILM CO., 137 No. La Brea Ave., Hollywood, CA 90036; (213) 936-1156. Madelon Cohen, pres.
FILMLIFE INCORPORATED, Filmlife Bldg., 141 Moonachie Road, Moonachie, NJ 07074; (201) 440-8500. Marvin A. Bernard, bd. chm. & pres.
FILMTREAT INTERNATIONAL CORP., 42-24 Orchard St., Long Island City, NY 11101; (212) 784-4040. Y. W. Mociuk, pres. (See display ad on P. 345.)
FILMTREAT WEST CORP., 5537 Satsuma Ave., North Hollywood, CA 91601; (818) 506-3276. Larry M. Zide, pres.
HOLLYWOOD VAULTS, 742 N. Seward St., Los Angeles, CA 90038; (213) 461-6464.
PEERLESS FILM PROCESSING CORPORATION, 42-24 Orchard St., Long Island City, NY 11101; (212) 784-4040. Y. M. Mociuk, pres.
PERMAFILM INT'L CORP., 280 High St., Milford, CT. 06460; (203) 877-7746.
RESEARCH TECHNOLOGY, INC., 4700 Chase Ave., Lincolnwood, IL 60646; (312) 677-3000.

Photo Reproduction Labs

APCO-APEDA/RIK SHAW, 525 W. 52 St., New York, NY 10019; (212) 586-5755.
BEBELL INC., 420 E. 55 St., New York, NY 10019; (212) 486-6578. 16mm. 35mm. reversal processing, black & white and color release prints. Slides and slide films, camera masters, dupes. Giant size color prints, plus transparencies.
FRANKLIN PHOTOS, INC., 370 W. 35 St., New York, NY 10001; (212) 279-1950.

Film Storage Vaults

ATLANTA

BENTON FILM FORWARDING CO., 168 Baker St., N.W.; (404) 577-2821. William B. Langston, mgr.

FORT LEE, NJ

BONDED FILM STORAGE, 550 Main St., Fort Lee, NJ 07024; (212) 557-6732.
BONDED SERVICES, 2050 Center Ave., 07024; (201) 592-7868; (212) 695-2034 (NY).
FORT LEE FILM STORAGE & SERVICE, 504 Jane St., 07024; (201) 944-1030.

**THE LEADER IN MOTION PICTURE FILM CARE
AND REJUVENATION FOR OVER A HALF CENTURY**

CONTACT:

SAM BORODINSKY   JERRY MOCIUK

Filmtreat International Corporation
42-24 Orchard Street, Long Island City, N.Y. 11101
Tel. (718) 784-4040

CONTACT:
LARRY ZIDE

Filmtreat West Corporation
5537 Satsuma Avenue, North Hollywood, CA 91601
Tel. (818) 506-3276

BONDED SERVICES, 2050 Center Ave., 07024; (201) 592-7868; (212) 695-2034 (NY).

FORT LEE FILM STORAGE & SERVICE, 504 Jane St., 07024; (201) 944-1030.

HOLLYWOOD-LOS ANGELES

(Hollywood studios have their own storage vaults)

AMERICAN ARCHIVES, INC., 11120 Weddington St., North Hollywood, 91601; (818) 506-STOR; (818) 506-6688.

ARCHIVES FOR ADVANCED MEDIA, 838 N. Seward St., Los Angeles, 90038; (213) 466-2454.

BEKINS RECORDS MANAGEMENT, 1025 N. Highland Ave., Hollywood, 90038; (213) 466-9271.

BELL & HOWELL RECORDS MANAGEMENT, 510 Sixth St., Los Angeles, 90014; (213) 466-9271.

BONDED SERVICES, 5260 Vineland Ave., North Hollywood, 91601; (818) 761-4058.

CONSOLIDATED FILM INDUSTRIES, 959 N. Seward St., Hollywood CA 90038; (213) 462-3161. (Stores only film which Consolidated Laboratory is handling.)

RAY HACKIE FILM SERVICE, 1613½ W. 20th St., Los Angeles, 90007; (213) 734-5418; (213) 737-6062.

HOLLYWOOD FILM CO., 5446 Carlton Way, Hollywood, 90027; (213) 462-1971.

HOLLYWOOD VAULTS, INC., 742 N. Seward St., Hollywood 90038; (213) 461-6464.

INTERNATIONAL CINE SERVICES, INC., 733 Salem St., Glendale, 91203; (818) 242-3839.

TYLIE JONES/WEST, 10718 Riverside Dr., North Hollywood, 91602; (818) 980-7300.

PACIFIC TITLE ARCHIVES, 4800 W. San Vicente Blvd., Los Angeles, 90019; (213) 938-3711; 561 Mateo St., Los Angeles, 90013; (213) 617-8650; 6350 Santa Monica Blvd., Los Angeles, 90038; (213) 464-0121.

PRODUCERS FILM CENTER, 948 N. Sycamore Ave., Hollywood, 90038; (213) 851-1122.

TAPE-FILM INDUSTRIES (TFI), 941 N. Highland Ave., Hollywood 90038; (213) 461-3361.

THEATRE TRANSIT, INC., 8401 E. Slauson Ave., Pico Rivera, 90660; (213) 949-6659.

THE VAULT WORKS, 4306 Coldwater Canyon Ave., North Hollywood 91605; (818) 764-0685.

NEW YORK CITY

ANI LIVE FILM SERVICE, INC., 45 W. 45 St., 10036; (212) 819-0700.

BEKINS ARCHIVAL SERVICES, INC., 609 W. 51 St., 10019; (212) 489-7890.

BELL & HOWELL RECORDS MGT., 609 W. 51 St., 10019; (212) 489-7890; 225 Varick St.; New York, NY 10014; (212) 645-0868.

BONDED SERVICES, 535 W. 46 St.; 10036; (212) 582-7540.

PAT FILM SERVICES, INC., 630 Ninth Ave., 10036; (212) 247-0900.

RAPID FILM TECHNIQUE, INC., 37-02 27th St., Long Island City, 11101; (212) 786-4600.

TAPE-FILM INDUSTRIES, 619 W. 54 St., 10019; (212) 708-0500.

Raw Stock Manufacturers

AGFA CORPORATION, MOTION PICTURE PRODUCTS DIVISION. (Manufacturer, distributor 35mm 16mm color, black, white raw stock. Executive offices: 100 Challenger Rd., Ridgefield Park, NJ 07660; (201) 440-2500 or (212) 563-5500.
BRANCHES:
San Francisco, 94080; 601 Gateway Blvd., Ste. 500, South San Francisco, Ca; (415) 589-0700.
Los Angeles, 90067: 1801 Century Park East, Suite 110; (213) 552-9622.

EASTMAN KODAK CO., 343 State St., Rochester, NY; Tel.: (716) 325-2000. 1901 W. 22nd St., Oakbrook, IL 60521; Tel.: (312) 654-5300. 6700 Santa Monica Blvd., Hollywood, CA, 90038; Tel.: (213) 464-6131. 1133 Ave. of the Americas, New York, NY 10036; Tel.: (212) 930-7538.

FUJI PHOTO FILM U.S.A., INC., (distributor of Fuji Professional Motion Picture Film) 350 Fifth Ave., New York, NY; 736-3335. Northeast Region Sales & Dist. Ctr., 4200 Central Blvd., Carlstadt, NJ 07072; (201) 935-6022; Corp. headquarters: 555 Taxter Rd., Elmsford, NY 10523; (914) 789-8100.

GAF CORP., Binghamton, NY 13902; (607) 777-4421.

GEVAERT COMPANY OF AMERICA, INC., (see Agfa Corporation).

ILFORD, INC., 70 W. Century Rd., Paramus, NJ 07562; (201) 265-6000.

3M COMPANY (MINNESOTA MINING & MANUFACTURING CO.), Photographic Products Division, manufacturer and distributor of Ferrania 3M motion picture films; 2501 Hudson Rd., St. Paul, MN 55101, (612) 733-0020; 845 Third Ave., New York, NY, (212) LT-1-1416; 3130 Damon Way, Burbank, CA 91505; (818) 843-5935.

RESEARCH TECHNOLOGY, INC., 4700 Chase Ave., Lincolnwood, IL 60646; (312) 677-3000.

Stock-Shot Film Libraries

HOLLYWOOD-LOS ANGELES

ACADEMY OF MOTION PICTURE ARTS & SCIENCES LIBRARY, 8949 Wilshire Blvd., Beverly Hills, CA 90211; (213) 278-4313.

AFTER IMAGE INC., 3807 Wilshire Blvd., Suite 250, Los Angeles, 90010; (213) 480-1105.

AMERICAN FILM INSTITUTE LIBRARY, 2021 N. Western Ave., Los Angeles, 90027; (213) 856-7600; 856-7655.

TOM ANDERSON FILMWORKS, 6362 Hollywood Blvd., Suite 308, Los Angeles, 90028; (213) 464-0386.

BISON ARCHIVES, Raleigh Studios, 650 N. Bronson Ave., Suite 146, Hollywood, 90004; (213) 275-3624.

BUDGET FILMS, 4590 Santa Monica Blvd., Los Angeles, 90029; (213) 660- 0187.

CAMEO FILM LIBRARY, 10620 Burbank Blvd., North Hollywood, 91601; (818) 980-8700.

CINEMAPHILE AMALGAMATED PICTURES, P.O. Box 8054, Universal City, 91608; (213) 939-9042.

DICK CLARK MEDIA ARCHIVES, INC., 3003 W. Olive Ave., Burbank, CA 91505; (818) 841-3003.

THE CLIP JOINT FOR FILM, 5304 Agnes Ave., North Hollywood, CA 91607; (818) 761-0545; 761-3228.

COLLECTORS BOOK STORE, 1708 N. Vine St., Hollywood, CA 90028; (213) 467-3296.

THE WALT DISNEY CO., 500 S. Buena Vista St., Burbank, 91521; (818) 840-1000.

LARRY DORN ASSOCS., 5550 Wilshire Blvd., #303, Los Angeles, 90036; (213) 935-6266.

DREAMLIGHT IMAGES, INC., 932 N. La Brea Ave., Suite C, Hollywood, 90038; (213) 850-1996.

ENERGY PRODUCTIONS, 2690 Beachwood Dr., Los Angeles, 90068; (213) 457-8081.

FILM BANK, 3306 W. Burbank Blvd., Burbank, 91505; (818) 841-9176.

FILM SEARCH, 1449 S. Rexford Dr., #7, Los Angeles, 90035; (213) 277-5880.

JAMES FOSHER COLLECTION OF ARCHIVAL FOOTAGE, 6363 Sunset Blvd., Suite 714, Hollywood, 90028; (213) 461-0178.

G-FORCE INTERNATIONAL ENTERTAINMENT CORP., 279 S. Beverly Dr., Suite 1038, Beverly Hills, 90212; (213) 271-0700.

SHERMAN GRINBERG FILM LIBRARIES, INC., 1040 N. McCadden Pl., Hollywood, CA 90038; (213) 464-7491.

H.B. HALICKI PRODS., 17902 S. Vermont Ave., P.O. Box 2123, Gardena 90248; (213) 770-1744; 327-1744.

HERITAGE ENTERTAINMENT INC., 11500 W. Olympic Blvd., Suite 300, Los Angeles, 90064; (213) 477-8100.

HOLLYWOOD FILM ARCHIVE, 8344 Melrose Ave., #22, Hollywood, 90069; (213) 933-3345.

HOLLYWOOD NEWSREEL SYNDICATE INC., 1622 N. Gower St., Hollywood, 90028; (213) 469-7307.

INTERVIDEO, 733 N. Victory Blvd., Burbank 91502; (818) 843- 3633; 843-6884; 569-4000.

PALISADES WILDLIFE LIBRARY, 1205 S. Ogden Dr., L.A., 90019; (213) 931-6186.

PHOTO-CHUTING ENTERPRISES, 12619 S. Manor Dr., Hawthorne, 90250; (213) 678-0163.

PRODUCERS LIBRARY SERVICE, 7325 Santa Monica Blvd., Hollywood 90046; (213) 851-2201; 851-2202; 1051 N. Cole Ave., Hollywood, 90038; (213) 465-0572.

RON SAWADE CINEMATOGRAPHY, 3724 Berry Dr., Studio City, 91604; (818) 769-1747.

THE STOCK HOUSE, 6922 Hollywood Blvd., Suite 621, Los Angeles, 90028; (213) 461-0061.

UNITED AIRLINES, (stock footage), 626 Wilshire Blvd., Los Angeles, 90017; (213) 482-2000.

UNIVERSAL CITY STUDIOS, 100 Universal City Plaza, Universal City, 91608; (818) 777-1000.

VIDEO TAPE LIBRARY LTD., 1509 N. Crescent Heights, Blvd. #2, Los Angeles, 90046; (213) 656-4330.

WARNER RESEARCH COLLECTION, 110 N. Glenoaks Blvd., Burbank 91503; (818) 847-9743.

WORLDWIDE ENTERTAINMENT CORP., 5912 Ramirez Canyon, Malibu, 90265; (213) 457-8081.

MIDWEST

WHITE JANSSEN, INC., 604 Davis St., Evanston, IL 60201; (312) 328-2221.

MILL VALLEY, CA

STOCK SEARCH, 44 Ralston Ave., Mill Valley, 94941; (415) 381-6972. (National database for stock footage and photos. Serves as clearing house to locate footage, but does not supply footage.)

NEW YORK CITY

AMERICAN MUSEUM OF NATURAL HISTORY FILM ARCHIVES, Central Park West at 79 St., 10024; (212) 769-5419.

ARCHIVE FILM PRODUCTIONS, INC., 530 W. 25 St., 10001; (212) 620-3955.

BROADCAST NEWS SERVICE, Pier 62, W. 23 St., 10011, (212) 466-0234.

COE FILM ASSOCIATES, INC., 65 E. 96 St., 10128; (212) 831-5355.

FILM SEARCH, 232 Madison Ave., 10016, (212) 532-0600.

SHERMAN GRINBERG FILM LIBRARIES, INC., 630 Ninth Ave., NY 10036; (212) 765-5170.

HALCYON DAYS PRODUCTIONS, 102 E. 30 St., 10016; (212) 686-8744.

HEARST METROTONE NEWS, 235 E. 45 St. 10017; (212) 682-7690.

IMAGEWAYS, INC. 440 W. 47 St., 10036; (212) 265-1287.

KILLIAM SHOWS, INC., 6 E. 39 St., 10016; (212) 679-8230.

MOVIETONEWS, INC. FILM LIBRARY, (Subsidiary of 20th Century Fox), 460 W. 54 St., 10019; (212) 408-8450.

MUSEUM OF MODERN ART FILM LIBRARY, 11 W. 53 St., 10019; (212) 245-8900.

NBC NEWS ARCHIVES, 30 Rockefeller Plaza, 10112; (212) 664-5031.

NEWSREEL ACCESS SYSTEMS, INC., 340 E. 93 St., 10128; (212) 996-3035.

PETRIFIED FILMS INC., 430 W. 14 St., 10014; (212) 242-5461.

PRELINGER ASSOC., INC., 430 W. 14 St., 10014; (212) 255-8866.

THE PORT AUTHORITY OF NY & NJ, 1 World Trade Center, 10048; (212) 466-7646.

SECOND LINE SEARCH, 330 W. 42 St., Room 2901, (212) 594-5544.

STOCK SHOTS TO ORDER, 521 Fifth Ave., 10017; (212) 682-5844.

STREAMLINE FILM ARCHIVES, 109 E. 29 St., 10016; (212) 696-2616.

TELENEWS FILM CORP., 235 E. 45 St., 10019; (212) 682-5600.

TIMESTEPS PRODUCTIONS, (201) 669-1930.

WTN-WORLDWIDE TV NEWS CORP., 31 W. 44 St., 10035; (212) 265-4520

Services for Producers

Advertising, In-Theatre

MOONDIAL MANUFACTURING CORP. (dba) Barnett Film Service, 8969 Sunset Blvd., Hollywood, CA 90069; (213) 272-5928. Gabriel Barnett, pres.; Matilda Barnett, v.p.; Morton Bregman, sec.-treas. (Sponsored theatre clocks especially designed and perfected for advertising use in motion picture theatres.)

MOVIE MEDIA NETWORK, INC., 2600 Douglas Rd., Coral Gables, FL 33134; (305) 448-0008. David I. Weiss, pres. (National program of in-theatre poster advertising; company installs posters of products and services for the general consumer public on the walls of theatre lobbies)

Animals and Trainers

EAST COAST

ACTORPETS, Ruth Krebs; (914) 235-3172; (914) 235-3540.
ALBA'S PARROT FANTASIES, 125 Wilbur Pl., Bohemia, NY 11716; (516) 271-6953.
ALL-TAME ANIMALS INC., 250 W. 57 St., Suite 1429, New York, NY 10107; (212) 245-6740.
ANIMAL ACTORS, INC., Steve and Carol McAuliff; (201) 689-7539.
ANIMALS FOR ADVERTISING, Linda Hanrahan, 310 W. 55 St., New York, NY 10019; (212) 245-2590.
WILLIAM BERLONI THEATRICAL ANIMALS, INC., Suite 42-Q, 484 W. 43 St., New York, NY 10036; (212) 714-1291.
CAPT. HAGGERTY'S THEATRICAL DOGS, 2968/A Jerome Ave., bsmt., Bronx, NY; (212) 220-7771.
CHATEAU ANIMALS, INC., 608 W. 48 St., New York, NY 10036; (212) 246-0520.
CLAREMONT RIDING ACADEMY, 175 W. 89 St., New York, NY 10024; (212) 724-5101.
CLOVE LAKE STABLES INC., 348 Van Pelt Ave., Staten Island 10303; (718) 448-1414.
DAWN ANIMAL AGENCY, INC., 750 Eighth Ave., New York, NY 10036; (212) 575-9396; (813) 422-4080.
HORSES FOR COURSES, 349 Plainfield St., Westbury, L.I. 11590; (516) 333-5831; (212) 533-7557.
VIDBEL PERFORMING ANIMALS, Mitchell Howell Rd., Windham, NY 12496; (518) 734-4137.

WEST COAST

A & R LIVESTOCK, 12682 Kagel Canyon Rd., Lake View Terrace, CA 91342; (818) 899-6553; 897-2873.
ALL ACTING ANIMALS, 3540 Wilshire Blvd., #310, Los Angeles, CA 90010; (213) 387-8214.
ALL GOD'S CREATURES, P.O. Box 4621; Valley Village Sta, N. Hollywood, CA 91607; (818) 784-4177.
ALVIN ANIMAL RENTALS, P.O. Box C B, Bloomington, CA 92316; (714) 823-9437.
THE AMERICAN MONGREL, P.O. Box 2406, Lancaster, CA 93539; (805) 942-7550.
ANIMAL ACTORS OF HOLLYWOOD, 864 W. Carlisle Rd., Thousand Oaks, CA 91360; (805) 495-2122.
THE ANIMAL CONNECTION, 6500 Sepulbeda Blvd., Van Nuys, CA 91411; (818) 997-6007.
ANIMAL HOUSE, 9771 Sunland Blvd., Sunland, CA 91040; (818) 352-4291.
ANIMAL WORLD U.S.A., 19013 Ingomar St., Reseda, CA 91335; (818) 993-4611.
AQUACULTURE U.S.A., 6019 Hazelhurst Pl., North Hollywood, CA 91606; (818) 769-3474.
AQUARIUM STOCK CO., 8070 Beverly Blvd., Los Angeles, CA 90048; (213) 653-8930.
BELLA VISTA STABLE, 10515 McBroom St., Sunland, CA 91040; (818) 353-9896.
BIRDS AND ANIMALS UNLIMITED, 25191 Rivendell Dr., El Toro, CA 92630; (714) 830-7845.
BLAIR BUNCH INC., 7561 Woodman Pl., Van Nuys, CA 91405; (818) 994-1136.

CALIFORNIA ANIMAL OWNERS ASSN., 1014 W. Laurel Dr., Salinas, CA 93907; (418) 424-7441.
CAREY LIVESTOCK, 9932 La Tuna Canyon, Sun Valley, CA 91352; (818) 768-4187.
CASA DE PETS, 13323 Ventura Blvd., Sherman Oaks, CA 91423; (818) 986-2660.
CREATURES FOR FEATURES, 3917 E. Anaheim St., Long Beach, CA 90804; (213) 494-3334; (619) 471-2446.
CRITTERS OF THE CINEMA, 9580 Clybourn Ave., Sun Valley, CA 91352; (818) 896-8888.
MOE DI SESSO'S TRAINED WILDLIFE, 24233 Old Rd., Newhall, CA 91321; (805) 255-7969.
BOB DUNN'S ANIMAL RENTALS, 16001 Yarnell St., Sylmar, CA 91342; (818) 896-0394.
ENTERTAINMENT ENTERPRISES, 1680 Vine St., Suite 519, L.A., CA 90028; (213) 462-6001.
EXOTIC PAWS, 206 15th St., Newport Beach, CA 92663; (714) 673-4152.
GARY GERO, BIRDS & ANIMALS UNLIMITED, 25191 Rivendell Dr., El Toro, CA 92630; (714) 830-7845.
GENTLE JUNGLE INC., 15840 Cedarfort Dr., Saugus, CA 91350-3601; (818) 841-5300.
RICK GLASSEY'S JUNGLE BOOKINGS, 28819 Loretta La., Canyon Country, CA 91350; (805) 252-7971.
DENNIS GRISCO'S ANIMAL RENTAL, P.O. Box 54, Mira Loma, CA 91752; (714) 685-4081.
HOLLYWOOD ANIMAL RENTALS (BOON NARR), P.O. Box 832, Lebec, CA 93243; (805) 248-6195; (805) 259-6081.
GARY JOHNSON'S HAVE TRUNK WILL TRAVEL, 27575 Highway 74, Perris, CA 92370; (714) 351-1768.
KIM'S EXOTIC CRITTERS, 8123 Foothill Blvd., Sunland, CA 91040; (818) 353-2717.
STEVEN KUTCHER—BUGS ARE MY BUSINESS, 1737 N. Sinaloa Ave., Pasadena, CA 91104; (818) 353-6851.
LION'S COUNTRY SAFARI, 8800 Irvine Center Dr., Laguna Hills, CA 92653; (714) 837-1200.
LION, THE TRAINED WILD ANIMALS/LAURA LISA, 3518 Cahuenga Blvd. W. #100, Los Angeles, CA 90068; (213) 462-2301.
LUNDIN FARM, 27506 N. Oak Sprngs Canyon Rd., Canyon Country, CA 91351; (805) 252-6140
MARINE WORLD/AFRICA USA, Marine World Parkway, Vallejo, CA 94589; (707) 644-4000.
MOORPARK COLLEGE, 7075 Campus Rd., Moorpark, CA 93021; (805) 529-2324.
MOTION PICTURES LIVESTOCK & EQUIPMENT RENTALS, 30509 Romero Canyon Rd., Saugus, CA; (805) 257-2714; (923) 462-2301.
MOVIELAND ANIMALS, P.O. Box 422, Norco, CA 91760; (714) 687-8914.
MYERS & WILLIS STABLES, 11035 Osborne St.; 9917 Foothill Blvd., Lake View Terrace, CA 91342; (818) 896-1333.
PAW PRODUCTIONS, 3 Shell Rd., Mill Valley, CA 94941; (415) 383-1529.
THE PECKING ORDER, 3412 W. Victory Blvd., Burbank, CA 91505; (818) 842-1343.
PERFORMING ANIMALS WELFARE SOCIETY, P.O. Box 842, Galt, CA 95632; (916) 441-3041; (209) 745-2606.
POWAY STABLES, P.O. Box 624, Poway, CA 92064; (619) 566-1993; 748-4179.
PULLIS CANINE TRAINING, 2040 Fallon Rd., Petaluma, CA 94952; (707) 778-6252.
PYRAMIDBIRDS/PARROTDISE, 1407 W. Magnolia Blvd., Burbank, CA 91506; (818) 843-5505.
RAINBOW FARMS ANDALUSIAN HORSES, 20700 Northridge Rd., Chatsworth, CA 81311; (818) 998-5170.
THE SHAMBALA PRESERVE, P.O. Box 189, Acton, CA 93510; (805) 268-0380.
LOU SHUMACHER, ANIMAL RENTALS, 14453 Cavette Pl., Baldwin Park, CA 91706; (818) 338-4614.
THE TRAINING ACADEMY INC., 15102 Martha St., Van Nuys, CA; (818) 901-8131.
WEATHERWAX TRAINED DOGS, 16133 Soledad Canyon Rd., Canyon Country, CA 91351; (805) 252-6499.
JOHN WEINHART'S WILD ANIMALS, 9478 Bellegrave Ave., Riverside, CA 92630; (714) 685-0368.
WILDLIFE ASSOCIATES, P.O. Box 982, Pacifica, CA 94044; (415) 355-8808.
WORKING WILDLIFE, Box 65, Acton, CA 93510; (805) 947-4041.
ZOOVET PRODS., 9316 Soledad Canyon Rd., Saugus, CA 91350; (805) 268-0501.

Animation

CALIFORNIA

A I A PRODUCTIONS, INC., 15132 LaMaida St., Sherman Oaks, CA 91403; (818) 501-4406.

ROBERT ABEL & ASSOCIATES, 953 N. Highland Ave., Los Angeles, CA 90038; (213) 462-8100.

ADAMS PRODS., 961 Vernon Ave., Venice, CA 90291; (213) 465-6428; 396-3416.

DAVID ALLEN PRODS., 918 W. Oak St., Burbank, CA 91506; (818) 845-9270.

ANGEL ARTS DESIGN INC., 11729 King St., North Hollywood, CA 91607; (818) 763-8023.

APOGEE PRODUCTIONS, INC., 6842 Valjean Ave., Van Nuys, CA 91406; (818) 989-5757.

ARCCA ANIMATION, 180 N. Rexford, Beverly Hills, CA 90210; (213) 271-5928.

ATLANTIC/KUSHNER-LOCKE, INC., 10880 Wilshire Blvd., Los Angeles, CA 90024; (213) 470-0400.

AVAILABLE LIGHT LTD., 3110 W. Burbank, Burbank, CA 91505-2313; (818) 842-2109.

THE BAER ANIMATION CO., 4729 Lankershim Blvd., North Hollywood, CA 91603; (818) 505-0447; (818) 656-0976.

BASS/YAGER & ASSOCS., 7039 Sunset Blvd., Los Angeles, CA 90028; (213) 466-9701.

DON BLUTH PRODUCTIONS, 12229 Ventura Blvd., Studio City, CA 91604; (818) 506-5440.

BOSUSTOW VIDEO, 2207 Colby Ave., Santa Monica, CA 90064; (213) 478-0821.

BRAVERMAN PRODS. INC., 1861 S. Bundy Dr., Los Angeles, CA 90025; (213) 826-6466.

THE BRUBAKER GROUP, 10560 Dolcedo Way, Los Angeles, CA 90077; (213) 472-4766.

CARTOON A WORLD, 2547 Glen Green, Hollywood, CA 90068; (213) 464-8093.

CELESTIAL MECHANIX INC., 612 Hampton Dr., Venice, CA 90291; (213) 392-8771.

CINESONG CORP., 3942 Murietta Ave., Sherman Oaks, CA 91423; (818) 905-1298.

BOB CLAMPETT PRODS. INC., 729 Seward St., Los Angeles, CA 90038; (213) 466-0264.

COAST PRODS., 1001 N. Poinsetta Pl., Los Angeles, CA 90046-6795; (213) 876-2021.

DIC ENTERPRISES, INC., 5445 Balboa Blvd., Encino, CA 91306; (818) 995-3800.

DOUD FILM INC., 8444 Wilshire Blvd. #700, Beverly Hills, CA 90211; (213) 651-1346.

DREAM QUEST INC., 5887 Blackwelder St., Culver City, CA 90232; (213) 558-4051.

DREAMLIGHT IMAGES INC., 932 N. La Brea Ave., Suite C, Hollywood, CA 90038; (213) 850-1996.

DUCK SOUP PRODUCTIONS, 1026 Montana Ave., Santa Monica, CA 90403; (213) 451-0771.

ENERGY PRODUCTIONS, 2690 Beachwood Dr., Los Angeles, CA 90068; (213) 462-3310.

ENTERTAINMENT EFFECTS GROUP, 13335 Maxella Ave., Marina Del Rey, CA 90292; (213) 823-0433.

FANTASY II FILM EFFECTS, 504 S. Varney, Burbank CA 91502; (818) 843-1413.

FILMFAIR, 10900 Ventura Blvd., Studio City, CA 91604; (818) 766-9441.

FINE ARTS PRODUCTIONS, INC., 3960 Laurel Canyon, Studio City, CA 91604; (818) 985-1556.

FLINT PRODUCTIONS, 7758 Sunset Blvd., West Hollywood, CA 90046; (213) 851-1060.

FORMAT PRODUCTIONS INC., 4253 Reyes Dr., Tarzana, CA 91356; (818) 987-2390.

HANNA BARBERA, 3400 W. Cahuenga Blvd., Hollywood, CA 90028; (213) 851-5000.

INTERACTIVE PRODUCTION ASSOCIATES, 3310 Airport Ave., Santa Monica, CA 90405; (213) 390-9466.

JEAN-GUY JACQUE & COMPANY, 225 N. Rose, Suite 102, Toluca Lake, CA 91505-3902; (818) 841-0965.

KURTZ & FRIENDS, 2312 W. Olive Ave., Burbank, CA 91506; (818) 841-8188.

THE L.A. EFFECTS GROUP, INC., 14411 Vanowen St., Suite 217, Van Nuys, CA 91405; (818) 901-9677.

WALTER LANTZ, 4444 Lakeside Dr., Suite 310, Burbank, CA 91505; (818) 569-3625.

WILLIAM LITTLEJOHN PRODS., INC., 23425 Malibu Colony Dr., Malibu, CA 90265; (213) 456-8620

MARKS COMMUNICATIONS, 5550 Wilshire Blvd., Suite 306, Los Angeles, CA 90036; (213) 937-3464.

PLAYHOUSE PICTURES, 1401 N. La Brea Ave., Hollywood, CA 90028; (213) 851-2112.

QUARTET FILMS, INC., 12345 Ventura Blvd., Studio City, CA 91604; (818) 509-0100.

RUBY-SPEARS PRODUCTIONS, 3330 Cahuenga Blvd., West Los Angeles, 90068; (213) 874-5100.

SABAN PRODUCTIONS, 11724 Ventura Blvd., Suite A, Studio City, CA 91604; (818) 985-3805.

SINGLE FRAME FILMS, 437½ N. Genessee Ave., Los Angeles, CA 90036; (213) 655-2664.

SIR REEL PICTURES, 8036 Shady Glade Ave., North Hollywood, CA 91605; (818) 768-9778.

SOUND CONCEPTS INC., 3485 Meier St., Los Angeles, CA 90066; (213) 390-7406.

RICK ZETTNER & ASSOCIATES, INC., 211 N. Victory Blvd., Burbank, CA 91502; (818) 848-7673.

ORLANDO

WALT DISNEY/MGM STUDIOS, P.O. Box 10200, Lake Buena Vista, FL 32830; (407) 560-5353.

NEW YORK

APA STUDIOS INC., 230 W. 10 St., New York, NY 10014; (212) 929-9436; 675-4894.

ABACUS PRODUCTIONS, 124 E. 24 St., New York, NY 10010; (212) 532-6677.

ANI LIVE FILM SERVICE INC., 222 E. 46 St., New York, NY 10017; (212) 983-1918.

ANIMATED ARTS, 1466 Broadway, New York, NY 10036; (212) 354-4750; 13 Northern Blvd., Albany, NY 12210; (518) 465-6448.

ANIMATED PRODUCTIONS, INC., 1600 Broadway, New York, NY 10019; (212) 265-2942.

ANIMOTION, 501 W. Fayette St., Syracuse, NY 13204; (315) 471-3533.

ARTBEAR PIGMATION, 64 White Ave., South Nyack, NY 10960; (212) 869-3911; (914) 353-0192.

BASKT, EDWARD, 160 W. 96 St., New York, NY 10025; (212) 666-2579.

BEBELL LABS, 630 Ninth Ave., New York, NY 10019; (212) 315-2660.

BECKERMAN, HOWARD, ANIMATION, 45 W. 45 St., New York, NY 10036; (212) 869-0595.

BIGMAN PICTURES, 133 W. 19 St., New York, NY 10011; (212) 242-1411.

BLECHMAN, R.O., 2 W. 47 St., New York, NY 10036; (212) 869-1630.

BROADCAST ARTS, INC., 632 Broadway, 2nd floor, New York, NY 10012; (212) 254-5400.

ELINOR BUNIN PRODUCTIONS, INC., 30 E. 60 St., New York, NY 10022; (212) 688-0759.

BUZZCO ASSOCIATES, INC., 110 W. 40 St., New York, NY 10010; (212) 840-0411.

CAESAR VIDEO GRAPHICS, INC., 137 E. 25 St., New York, NY 10010; (212) 684-7673.

CAGED BEAGLE PRODUCTIONS, INC., 24 Elizabeth St., Port Chester, NY 10573; (914) 967-5379.

CEL-ART PRODUCTIONS, INC., 20 E. 49 St., New York, NY 10017; (212) 751-7515.

CHARLEX, 2. W. 45 St., New York, NY 10036; (212) 719-4600.

CHEAP ANIMATION, 27 Old Mill Rd., West Nyack, NY 10994; (914) 358-2964.

CHELSEA ANIMATION CO., 36 E. 23 St., New York, NY 10010; (212) 473-1646.

CLARK, IAN 229 E. 96 St., New York, NY 10028; (212) 289-0998.

COREY DESIGN STUDIO, 42 E. 23 St., New York, NY 10010; (212) 692-9260.

DARINO FILMS, 222 Park Ave. S., New York, NY 10003; (212) 228-4024.

DA SILVA INC., 311 E. 85 St., New York, NY 10028; (212) 535-5760.

DOROS ANIMATION STUDIO, INC., 156 Fifth Ave., New York, NY 10010; (212) 627-7220.

EDITEL, 222 E. 44 St., New York, NY 10017; (212) 867-4600.

F-STOP STUDIO, (Gary Becker Animation/Motion Graphics), Suite 901, 114 E. 32 St., New York, NY 10016; (212) 686-2292.

THE FANTASTIC ANIMATION MACHINE, INC., 12 E. 46 St., New York, NY 10017; (212) 697-2525.

FEIGENBAUM PRODUCTIONS, INC., 25 W. 43 St., New York, NY 10036; (212) 840-3744.

FILIGREE FILMS, INC., 155 Ave. of the Americas, 10th floor, New York, NY 10013; (212) 627-1770.

FILM PLANNING ASSOCIATES, INC., 44 W. 24 St., New York, NY 10010; (212) 989-0611.

FOCH, BILL, GRAPHICS, 25 W. 45 St., #203, New York, NY 10036; (212) 921-9414.

J. FREEMAN ASSOCIATES, 15 W. 38 St., New York, NY 10018; (212) 307-6936.
FRIEDMAN, HAROLD, CONSORTIUM, 420 Lexington Ave., New York, NY 10017; (212) 697-0858.
GATI, JOHN, FILM EFFECTS, INC., 154 W. 57 St., Suite 832, New York, NY 10019; (212) 582-9060.
GIFFORD ANIMATION, 45 W. 45 St., New York, NY 10036; (212) 719-2530.
R/GREENBERG ASSOC. INC., 350 W. 39 St., New York, NY 10018; (212) 239-6767.
GROSSMAN BROS., 19 Crosby St., New York, NY 10013; (212) 925-1965.
HARVEY FAMOUS CARTOONS, 888 Seventh Ave., New York, NY 10019; (212) 582-2244.
HUBLEY STUDIO, 200 East End Ave., New York, NY 10028; (212) 410-2767.
ICE TEA PRODUCTIONS, 307 E. 37 St., New York, NY 10016; (212) 557-8185.
THE INK TANK, 2 W. 47 St., New York, NY 10036; (212) 869-1630.
KCMP PRODUCTIONS, INC. 50 W. 40 St., New York, NY 10018; (212) 944-7766.
KIMMELMAN ANIMATION, 50 W. 40 St., New York, NY 10018; (212) 944-7766.
KURTZ & FRIENDS Block Film Group, 1 Union Sq. W., Suite 211, New York, NY 10003; (212) 989-3535.
K. LANDMAN INC., 156 Fifth Ave., Suite 325, New York, NY 10010; (212) 924-4254.
LEO ANIMATION CAMERA SERVICE, 25 W. 43 St., New York, NY 10036; (212) 997-1840.
LIBERTY STUDIOS, INC., 238 E. 26 St., New York, NY 10010, (212) 532-1865.
LIEBMAN, JERRY, PRODUCTIONS, 76 Laight St., New York, NY 10013; (212) 431-3452.
MTI/COMPUGRAPH DESIGNS, 885 Second Ave., New York, NY 10017; (212) 355-0510.
MAGNO SOUND & VIDEO, 729 Seventh Ave., New York, NY 10019; (212) 302-2505.
RB/MAVERICKS MOTION GRAPHICS, 35 W. 45 St., New York, NY 10036; (212) 382-2424.
METROPOLIS GRAPHICS, 28 E. 4 St., New York, NY 10003; (212) 677-0630.
MIMONDO PRODUCTIONS LTD., 15 W. 26 St., New York, NY 10010; (212) 686-9620.
MOTIONPICKER STUDIOS, INC., (Clay Animation), 416 Ocean Ave., Brooklyn, NY 11226; (718) 856- 2763.
MUSICVISION, INC., 185 E. 85 St., New York, NY 10028; (212) 860-4420.
NEW YORK ANIMATION, 200 W. 79 St., New York, NY 10024; (212) 362-6992.
NOYES & LAYBOURNE ENTERPRISES, INC., 77 Hudson St., New York, NY 10013; (212) 406-7377.
OVATION FILMS INC., 15 W. 26 St., New York, NY 10010; (212) 686-4540.
PAN PRODUCTIONS, 223 Water St., Brooklyn, NY, 11201; (718) 237-1945.
PERPETUAL ANIMATION, INC., 841 Broadway, New York, NY 10013; (212) 353-9655; 353-9656.
PLANET PICTURES, 66 E. 7 St., New York, NY 10003; (212) 477-1032.
POLESTAR FILM & ASSOC., 15 W. 26 St., New York, NY 10010; (212) 213-0806.
PRISM FILM & TAPE, 15 W. 38 St., New York, NY 10018; (212) 944-0420.
RANKIN/BASS PRODUCTIONS (div. of Lorimar Telepictures), 1 Dag Hammerskjold Pl., New York, NY 10016; (212) 759-7721.
REMBRANDT FILMS, 59 E. 54 St., New York, NY 10022; (212) 758-1024.
SHADOW LIGHT PRODUCTIONS, INC., 12 W. 27 St., New York, NY 10001; (212) 689-7511.
SPORN, MICHAEL, ANIMATION, 34 W. 38 St., New York, NY 10018; (212) 730-1314.
STREAMLINE FILM MANUFACTURING, 109 E. 29 St., New York, NY 10016; (212) 696-2616.
TELMATED MP, P.O. Box 176, Prince Station, New York, NY 10012; (212) 475-8050.
TELEZIGN, 460 W. 42 St., New York, NY 10036; (212) 279-2000.
TRILOGY DESIGN AT JSL, INC., 25 W. 45 St., New York, NY 10036; (212) 382-3592.
VIDEART, INC., 39 W. 38 St., New York, NY 10018; (212) 840-2163.
VIDEO WORKS, 24 W. 40 St., New York, NY 10018; (212) 869-2500.
WALLACH, PETER, PRODUCTIONS, 419 Broome St,. New York, NY (212) 966-1970.
WOO ART INTERNATIONAL, 133 W. 19 St., New York, NY 10011; (212) 989-7870.
ZANDER, MARK, PRODUCTIONS, 118 E. 25 St., New York, NY 10010; (212) 477-3900.

Camera Sales, Rental, Repairs

NEW YORK

ARRIFLEX CO. OF AMERICA, 500 Rte. 303, Blauvelt, NY 10913; (914) 353-1400.
BELDEN COMMUNICATIONS INC., 534 W. 25 St., New York, NY 10001; (212) 691-1910.
BROADCAST EQUIPMENT SUPPLY CORP, Box 133, Rego Park, Queens, NY 11374; (718) 843-6839.
CTL ELECTRONICS, INC., 116 W. Broadway, New York, NY 10013; (212) 233-0754.
THE CAMERA GROUP OF NEW YORK, INC., 25-20 30th Rd., Suite G, Astoria, NY 11102; (212) 254-3600.
CAMERA MART, INC., 456 W. 55 St., New York, NY 10019; (212) 757-6977.
CAMERA SERVICE CENTER 625 W. 54 St., New York, NY 10019; (212) 757-0906.
CECO INTERNATIONAL CORP., 440 W. 15 St., New York, NY 10011; (212) 206-8280.
CHAMPOUX/CORSO, 501 E. 87 St., #5B New York, NY 10128; (212) 472-0309.
CINO 60, 630 Ninth Ave., New York, NY 10019; (212) 586-8782.
FERCO-FILM EQUIPMENT RENTAL CO., 707 Eleventh Ave., New York, NY 10019; (212) 245-4800.
GENERAL CAMERA CORP., 540 W. 36 St., New York, NY 10018; (212) 594-8700.
HIRSCH PHOTO, 699 Third Ave., New York, NY 10017; (212) 557-1150.
KINGSWAY FILM EQUIPMENT LTD., Pier 62, Northriver, New York, NY 10011; (212) 929-7345.
MOVIE MOBILE INC., 30-15 Vernon Blvd., Astoria, NY 11102; (718) 545-7200.
MOVIECAM CORP. OF AMERICA, 625 W. 54 St., New York, NY 10019; (212) 757-2345.
OLDEN CAMERA & LENS CO., INC., 1265 Broadway; (212) 725-1234.
PROCAMERAS & LIGHTING RENTALS, INC., 511 W. 33 St., New York, NY 10001; (212) 695-1517.
RANK PRECISION INDUSTRIES, 260 N. Route 303, West Nyack, NY 10994; (914) 353-1914.
ROESSEL CINE PHOTO TECH INC., 48-20 70th St., Woodside, NY 11377; (718) 424-1600.
ROSS-GAFFNEY, 21 W. 46 St., New York, NY 10036; (212) 719-2744.
SWISS PROFESSIONAL MOVIE EQUIPMENT LTD., 38 W. 32 St., New York, NY 10001; (212) 695-3861.
TECHNOLOGICAL CINEVIDEO SERVICES, INC., 630 Ninth Ave., New York, NY 10019; (212) 247-6517.
TELETECHNIQUES, (Matthews Studio Equipment Dealer) 1 W. 19 St., New York, NY 10011; (212) 206-1475; 633-1868.
WILLOUGHBY CAMERA STORES, 110 W. 32 St., New York, NY 10001; (212) 564-1600.

HOLLYWOOD

AKKAD INTERNATIONAL PRODS. INC., 9229 W. Sunset Blvd., Los Angeles, CA 90069; (213) 657-7670.
AMERICAN VIDEOGRAM INC., 12020 W. Pico Blvd., Los Angeles, CA 90064; (213) 477-1535; 477-1536.
APOGEE PRODUCTIONS, INC., 6842 Valjean Ave., Van Nuys, CA 91406; (818) 989-5757.
ARMISTEAD CAMERA RENTALS, INC., 1638 N. Cherokee, Hollywood, CA 90028; (213) 461-0903.
BACH AURICON, INC., 6950 Romaine St., Hollywood 90038; (213) 462-0931.
BELL & HOWELL, 3333 Wilshire Blvd., Los Angeles, CA; (213) 383-6645.
BERC/BROADCAST RENTAL COMPANY, 4545 Chermak St., Burbank, CA 91505-1063; (818) 841-3000; (213) 464-7655.
BIRNS & SAWYER, 1026 N. Highland Ave., Hollywood 90038; (213) 466-8211.
CENTURY PRECISION OPTICS, 10713 Burbank Blvd., North Hollywood, CA 91601; (818) 766-3715.
CHAPMAN/LEONARD STUDIO EQUIPMENT, 12950 Raymer St., North Hollywood, CA 91605; (818) 764-6726; (213) 877-5309.
CINELEASE INC., 140 S. Victory Blvd., Burbank, CA 91502; (818) 996-9345; 841-8262.
CINEMA ENGINEERING COMPANY INC., 7243 Atoll Ave., North Hollywood, CA 91605; (818) 765-5340.
CINEMA PRODUCTS CORPORATION, 3211 S. La Cienega Blvd., Los Angeles, CA 90016; (213) 478-0711; 836-7991.
CONTINENTAL CAMERA RENTALS, 7240 Valjean Ave., Van Nuys, CA 91406; (818) 989-5222.
GENERAL CAMERA WEST, 6779 Hawthorn Ave., Hollywood, CA 90028; (213) 464-3800.

GORDON ENTERPRISES, 1430 N. Cahuenga Blvd., North Hollywood 90078; (213) 466-3561; (818) 985-5500.
HILL PRODUCTION SERVICE INC., 1139 N. Highland Ave., Hollywood, CA 90038; (213) 463-1182.
HOLLYWOOD FILM CO., 3294 E. 26th St., Hollywood, 90023; (213) 263-9661; 462-3284.
KENWORTHY SNORKEL CAMERA SYSTEMS INC., P.O. Box 49851, Los Angeles 90049; (213) 476-4100.
LEE PANAVISION, 3800 W. Alameda Ave., Suite 1120, Burbank, CA 91505; (818) 972-4956; FAX: (818) 972-3624.
LEONETTI CINE RENTALS, 5609 Sunset Blvd., Los Angeles, CA 90028; (213) 469-2987.
MITCHELL CAMERA CORP., P.O. Box 279, 11630 Tuxford St., Sun Valley, CA 91352; (818) 768-6400.
MOLE-RICHARDSON CO., 937 N. Sycamore Ave., Hollywood, 90038; (213) 851-0111.
MORGAN CAMERA SHOP, 6262 Sunset Blvd., Hollywood, CA 90028; (213) 465-3101.
MOVIECAM SUPER RENTAL, 2037 Granville Ave., Los Angeles, CA 90025; (213) 278-4956; 278-4958.
OTTO NEMENZ INT'L INC., 870 N. Vine St., Hollywood, CA 90038; (213) 469-2774.
PANAVISION INC., 18618 Oxnard St., Tarzana, CA 91356; (818) 881-1702.
PARAMOUNT PICTURES, CORP., (Joel Kirschner, dept. head), 5555 Melrose Ave., Los Angeles, CA 90038; (213) 467-7189.
PASADENA CAMERA RENTAL, 37 E. Walnut St., Pasadena, CA 91103; (818) 796-3300.
RANK PRECISION INDUSTRIES, 13340 Saticoy St., Unit -F, North Hollywood, CA 91605; (818) 765-7265.
RENTACAM, 15016 Ventura Blvd., Suite 1, Sherman Oaks, CA 91403; (818) 501-7368.
UNITED TELEPRODUCTION SERVICES, 15055 Oxnard St., Van Nuys, CA 91411; (818) 997-0100.

MIAMI

IMAGE DEVICES, 1825 NE 149 St., Miami, FL 33181; (305) 945-1111; FAX (305) 945-1117.

SAN FRANCISCO

GASSER, ADOLPH, RENTAL SERVICES, 750 Bryant St., San Francisco, CA 94107; (415) 543-3888.

Checking Theatre Attendance

CERTIFIED REPORTS, INC., Kinderhook, NY 12106; (518) 758-6403. Theatre checking open and blind nationwide. Jack J. Spitzer, bd. chm.
DI-AN RESEARCH, INC. Kinderhook, NY 12106; (518) 758-1492. Theatre checking; industry research. Joe Sugar, pres.
DALE SYSTEM INC., 1101 Stewart Ave., Garden City, NY 11530; (516) 794-2800. Harvey Yaffe, pres.

Colorization by Computer

AMERICAN FILM TECHNOLOGIES, 12100 Wilshire Blvd., Brentwood, CA 90049; (213) 826-4766.
COLOR SYSTEMS TECHNOLOGY, INC., 4553 Glencoe Ave., Marina Del Rey, CA 90292; (213) 822-6567.

Commercial Jingles

CALIFORNIA

ASSOCIATED PRODUCTION MUSIC, 6255 Sunset Blvd., Suite 724, Hollywood, CA 90028; (213) 461-3211.
AUSPEX RECORDS, 12188 Laurel Terrace Dr., Studio City, CA 91604; (213) 877-1078; (818) 763-1955.
JOHN BAHLER ASSOCIATES, 1606 N. Highland Ave., Hollywood, CA 90028; (213) 464-1106.
BERTUS PRODUCTIONS, 2273 Berdon St., Woodland Hills, CA 91367; (818) 883-1920.
BLUE DOLPHIN STUDIO, 650 N. Bronson Ave., Hollywood, CA 90004; (213) 467-7660.
BULLETS—TOTAL MUSIC CO., 4520 Callada Place, Tarzana, CA 91356; (818)708-7359.

CALIFORNIA STAR PRODUCTIONS, 8843 Shirley Ave., Northridge, CA 91324; (818) 993-4584.
CANDLEWICK PRODUCTIONS, 1161 N. Highland Ave., Hollywood, CA 90038; (213) 462-7979.
CREATIVE SERVICES GROUP, 17456 Emelita St., Encino, CA 91316; (818) 343-7005.
DANA PRODUCTIONS, 6249 Babcock Ave., North Hollywood, CA 91606; (213) 877-9246.
WILLIAM ERICSON AGENCY, 1024 Mission St., South Pasadena, CA 91030; (213) 461-4969; (818) 799-2404.
FIRELIGHT PUBLISHING, 4706 New York Ave., La Crescenta, CA 91214; (818) 249-2416.
FULLER SOUND AV RECORDING, 1948 Riverside Dr., Los Angeles, CA 90039; (213) 660-4914.
GRAND STAFF MUSIC PRODUCTIONS, 5740 Tujunga Ave., N. Hollywood, CA 91601; (818) 760-2205.
GRIZZEL PRODUCTIONS, INC., 6033 W. Century Blvd., Suite 400; Los Angeles, CA 90045; (213) 412-8410; (818) 761-7773.
HARK'S SOUND STUDIO, 1041 N. Orange Dr., Hollywood, CA 90038; (213) 463-3288.
CRAIG HARRIS MUSIC, P.O. Box 110, North Hollywood, CA 91603; (818) 508-8000.
HOOK, LINE & SINGERS, 10700 Ventura Blvd., Suite E., North Hollywood, CA 91604; (818) 761-7773.
KAFKA MUSIC CO., P.O. Box 241724, Los Angeles, CA 90024; (213) 556-3723.
KAM/LAGER & ASSOC., 8621 Wilshire Blvd., Suite 105; Beverly Hills, CA 90211; (213) 275-0677.
L.A./NY MUSIC CO., 9034 Sunset Blvd., Suite 101, Los Angeles, CA 90069; (213) 273-1667.
L.A. TRAX INC., 8033 N. Sunset Blvd., Suite 1010, Los Angeles, CA 90046; (213) 852-1980.
LEE MAGID INC, P.O. Box 532, Malibu, CA 90265; (213) 463- 5998.
EDDY MANSON PRODUCTIONS, INC., 7245 Hillside Ave., Suite 216, Los Angeles, CA 90046; (213) 874-9318.
McKOWN & COMPANY, P.O. Box 25134, Los Angeles, CA 90025; (213) 479-1941.
MEDIA MASTERS PRODUCTIONS, 1800 S. Robertson Blvd., Suite 306, Beverly Hills, CA 90035; (213) 451-8823.
911 MUSIC, (213) 850-6911; 850-M911.
RICK NOWELS PRODUCTIONS, 7469 Melrose Ave., Suite 33, Hollywood, CA 90046; (213) 655-7990.
PIECE OF CAKE, INC., 4425 Clybourn Ave., North Hollywood, CA 91602; (818) 763-2087.
RITZ & ASSOCIATES ADVERTISING, 517 N. Robertson Blvd., Los Angeles, CA 90048; (213) 858-8456.
RUSK SOUND STUDIO, 1556 N. La Brea Ave., Hollywood, CA 90028; (213) 462-6477.
SHADOW STEVENS, 9100 Sunset Blvd., Suite 215, Los Angeles, CA 90069; (213) 274-1244.
SUNWEST RECORDING STUDIOS, 5533 Sunset Blvd., Los Angeles, CA 90028; (213) 463-5631.
TAV SOUND INC., 6200 W. Third St., Los Angeles, CA 90036; (213) 937-2460.
TARTAGLIA MUSIC PRODUCTIONS, 3815 W. Olive Ave., Suite 102, Burbank, CA 91505; (818) 841-3585.
TRIANON RECORDING STUDIOS, 1435 South St., Long Beach, CA 90805; (213) 422-2095.
WESTLAKE AUDIO, INC., 7265 Santa Monica Blvd., Los Angeles, CA 90046; (213) 851-9800; 655-0303.
WIRTH-HOWARD PRODUCTIONS, 5706 Ostin St., Woodland Hills, CA 91367; (818) 888-6198.
Y.L.S. PRODUCTIONS, P.O. Box 34, Los Alamitos, CA 90720; (213) 430-2890.

NEW YORK

MAMORSKY, ZIMMERMANN, HAMM, & FORREST, INC., 52 W. 45 St., New York, NY 10036; (212) 575-5180.
MUSIC MAKERS, INC., 57 W. 57 St., New York, NY 10019; (212) 644-5757.
SHELTON LEIGH PALMER & CO., 19 W. 36 St., New York, NY 10018; (212) 714-1710.

Completion Guarantees and Bonding

A.I.G. ENTERTAINMENT RISKS, 3699 Wilshire Blvd., Los Angeles, CA 90010; (213) 480-3570.
ALEXANDER & ALEXANDER, 3550 Wilshire Blvd., Los Angeles, CA 90010; (213) 385-5211.

AMERICAN NATIONAL GENERAL AGENCIES, INC., 3801 Barham Blvd., Suite 320, Los Angeles, CA 90068-1007; (213) 850-5880.
CINE GUARANTORS INC. (div. Taft Entertainment Co.), 3330 Cahuenga Blvd., Los Angeles, CA 90068; (213) 969-2800.
THE COMPLETION BOND COMPANY, INC., 2121 Ave. of the Stars, Suite 830, Century City, CA 90067-5001; (213) 553-8300.
DISC INSURANCE SERVICES, 3601 W. Olive Ave., Burbank, CA 91505; (818) 955-6000.
ENTERTAINMENT COMPLETIONS, INC., 4217 Coldwater Canyon Ave., Studio City, CA 91604; (818) 960-8172.
ENTERTAINMENT FINANCIAL SERVICES, P.O. Box 5120, Sherman Oaks, CA 91413; (818) 905-9518.
FILM FINANCES INC., 9000 Sunset Blvd., Suite 808, Los Angeles, CA 90069; (213) 275-7323.
FIREMAN'S FUND INSURANCE CO., Entertainment Industry Div., 9601 Wilshire Blvd., Beverly Hills, CA 90210; (213) 387-5566.
HOLLINGSWORTH INSURANCE, 1930 Wilshire Blvd., Los Angeles, CA 90057; (213) 473-2522.
PERCENTERPRISES COMPLETION SERVICES INC., 1801 Ave. of the Stars, #1106, Los Angeles, CA 90067; (213) 551-0371.
PERFORMANCE GUARANTEES INC., 1554 S. Sepulveda Blvd., #202, Los Angeles, CA 90025; (213) 478-3355.
ALBERT G. RUBEN & CO., INC., 2121 Ave. of the Stars, Suite 700, Los Angeles, CA 90067; (213) 551-1101.
WORLDWIDE COMPLETION SERVICES, INC., 9200 Sunset Blvd., #401, Los Angeles, CA 90069, (213) 276-4084; New York office: 888 Seventh Ave., 10106, (212) 489-7666. Services include payroll, cash flow projections, budget analysis, accounting, etc.

Consultants

CALIFORNIA

BLUE MOUNTAIN PRODUCTIONS INC., 1800 N. Highland Ave., #411, Hollywood, CA 90068; (213) 465-6515.
CASCADE FILMS LTD., 674 Hermosa Beach, CA 90254; (213) 318-3921.
THE CORPORATE SEAL, 1310 N. Cherokee Ave., Los Angeles, CA 90028; (213) 466-1237.
CAROLE LIEBERMAN, 465 N. Roxbury Dr., #810, Beverly Hills, CA 90210; (213) 456-2458.
M 2 RESEARCH, 1020 N. La Brea Ave., Los Angeles, CA 90038; (213) 464-7414.
MIRAMAR ENTERPRISES, 13416 Magnolia Blvd., #1, Sherman Oaks, CA 91423; (818) 784-4177.
MOTION PICTURE MARINE, 616 Venice Blvd., Marina Del Rey, CA 90291; (213) 822-1100.
2nd UNIT INC., 616 Venice Blvd., Venice, CA 90291; (213) 822-8648.

NEW YORK

AUDIO SERVICES CORP., 326 W. 48 St., 4th floor, New York, NY 10036; (212) 977-5150.
BOOZ, ALLEN & HAMILTON INC., 101 Park Ave., New York, NY 10178; (212) 697-1900.
BROADCAST BUSINESS CONSULTANTS, LTD., 41 E. 42 St., New York, NY 10017; (212) 687-3525.
CINEMAKERS INC., 1974 Broadway, New York, NY 10036; (212) 595-7327.
CONSULTANTS FOR TALENT PAYMENT INC., 22 W. 27 St., New York, NY 10001; (212) 696-1100.
DALE SYSTEM INC., 200 Garden City Plaza, Garden City, NY 11530; (516) 794-2800; 250 W. 57 St., New York, NY 10019; (212) 586-1320. Harvey Yaffe, pres.
DELTA CONSULTANTS INC., 333 W. 52 St., #410, New York, NY 10019; (212) 245-2570.
F.H. EZZES, 25 Central Park W., New York, NY 10023; (212) 757-3539.
FILM COUNSELORS, INC., 630 Ninth Ave., New York, NY 10019; (212) 315-3950.
FILM PLANNING ASSOCIATES, INC., 36 E. 20 St., New York, NY 10003; (212) 260-7140.
GRAPHIC MEDIA COMMUNICATIONS, 12 W. 27 St., 12th floor, New York, NY 10001; (212) 696-0880.
KTV CONSULTANTS INC., 226 E. 54 St., New York, NY 10022; (212) 223-0520.
KOLMOR VISIONS INT'L LTD., 286 Fifth Ave., New York, NY 10001; (212) 947-7517.
LAWRENCE, ALLAN, CO. 279 E. 44 St., New York, NY 10017; (212) 697-4015.
MANDELL ASSOCS. INC., 575 Madison Ave., New York, NY 10022; (212) 605-0174.

MEDIA RESOURCES ASSOCS., 420 E. 64 St., #W2H, New York, NY 10021; (212) 935-9040.
PRODUCTION MANAGEMENT ASSOCS., 333 W. 42 St., #2901, New York, NY 10036; (212) 594-6766.
REEVES COMMUNICATIONS CORP., 708 Third Ave., New York, NY 10017; (212) 573-8888; 573-8600.
ROSS-GAFFNEY, 21 W. 46 St., New York, NY 10036; (212) 719-2744.
SECOND LINE SEARCH, 330 W. 42 St., #2901, New York, NY 10036; (212) 594-5544.
SOUND ENTERPRISES, 305 E. 40 St., #18G, New York, NY 10016; (212) 986-2097.

Costumes & Uniforms

NEW YORK

ALLAN UNIFORM RENTAL SERVICE INC., 112 E. 23 St., New York, NY 10010; (212) 529-4655.
ANIMAL OUTFITS FOR PEOPLE CO., 252 W. 46 St., New York, NY 10036; (212) 840-6219.
CHENKO STUDIO, 167 W. 46 St., New York, NY 10036; (212) 944-0215.
COSTUME ARMOUR INC., Shore Rd., Cornwall-on-Hudson, NY 12520; (914) 534-9120.
THE COSTUME COLLECTION, 601 W. 26 St., New York, NY 10001; (212) 989-5855.
THE COSTUME SHOP INC., 253 W. 35 St., New York, NY 10001; (212) 947-2105.
CREATIVE COSTUME CO., 330 W. 38 St., New York, NY 10018; (212) 564-5552.
DAVID'S OUTFITTERS, INC., 36 W. 20 St., New York, NY 10011; (212) 691-7388.
EAVES-BROOKS COSTUME CO., INC., 21-07 41st Ave., Long Island City, NY 11101; (718) 729-1010.
HOUSE OF COSTUMES LTD., 166 Jericho Turnpike, Mineola, NY 11501; (516) 294-0170.
IN COSTUME, 37 W. 20 St., New York, NY 10011; (212) 255-5502.
IZQUIERDO STUDIOS, 118 W. 22 St., New York, NY 10011; (212) 807-9757.
LAZAR, CATHY, INC., 155 E. 23 St., New York, NY 10010; (212) 473-0363.
LILLIAN COSTUME CO. OF L.I. INC. 226 Jericho Turnpike, Mineola, NY 11501; (516) 746-6060.
ODDS RENTAL, 233 W. 42 St., #506, New York, NY 10036; (212) 575-5927.
RUBIE'S COSTUME CO., INC., 120-08 Jamaica Ave., Richmond Hill, Queens, NY 11418; (718) 846-1008.
UNIVERSAL COSTUME CO., INC., 535 Eighth Ave., New York, NY 10018; (212) 239-3222.

WEST COAST

ADELE'S OF HOLLYWOOD, 5034 Hollywood Blvd., Los Angeles, 90027; (213) 663-2231.
AMERICAN COSTUME CORP., 12980 Raymer St., North Hollywood, CA 91605; (818) 764-2239.
BERMANS COSTUME CO., 2019 Stradella Rd., Los Angeles, CA 90077; (213) 472-1844.
THE BURBANK STUDIOS, 4000 Warner Blvd., Burbank, CA 91522; (818) 954-6000.
CALIFORNIA COSTUME/NORCOSTO, 5867 Lankershim Blvd., N. Hollywood, CA 91601; (818) 760-2911.
CENTER THEATRE GROUP COSTUME SHOP, 3301 E. 14th St., Los Angeles, CA 90023; (213) 267-1230.
THE COSTUME PLACE, 7211 Santa Monica Blvd., Los Angeles, CA 90046; (213) 876-7979.
COSTUME RENTALS CO., 7007 Lankershim Blvd., North Hollywood, CA 91605; (818) 765-8877.
ELIZABETH COURTNEY COSTUMES, 8636 Melrose Ave., Los Angeles, CA; (213) 657-4360.
HOLLYWOOD TOYS & COSTUMES, 6562 Hollywood Blvd., Hollywood, CA 90028; (213) 465-3119.
INTERNATIONAL COSTUME, 1269 Sartori Ave., Torrance, CA 90501; (213) 320-6392.
FANTASY COSTUMES, 4649 San Fernando Rd., Glendale, CA 91204; (213) 245-7367.
FORMAL TOUCH ANTIQUE TUXEDO SERVICE, 842 N. Fairfax Ave., West Hollywood, CA 90046; (213) 658-5553.
IC COSTUME RENTALS, 6121 Santa Monica Blvd., Los Angeles 90038; (213) 462-9003.
TUXEDO CENTER, 7360 Sunset Blvd., Los Angeles, 90046; (213) 874-4200.
URSULA'S COSTUMES INC., 9067 Venice Blvd., Los Angeles, CA 90034; (213) 559-8210.

VALLEY STUDIO, 150 W. Cypress Ave., Suite G, Burbank, CA 91502; (818) 843-1861.

WESTERN COSTUME CO., 5335 Melrose Ave., Hollywood, CA 90038; (213) 469-1451.

Cutting Rooms

LOS ANGELES

ASTROFILM SERVICE, 932 N. La Brea Ave., Los Angeles, CA 90038; (213) 851-1673.

CINEMAPHILE AMALGAMATED PICTURES, P.O. Box 8054, Universal City, CA 91608.

COAST SPECIAL EFFECTS, 4907 N. Lankershim Blvd., N. Hollywood, CA 91601; (818) 762-1182.

CONSOLIDATED FILM INDUSTRIES, 959 Seward St., Hollywood, CA 90038; (213) 462-3161.

CREST NATIONAL FILM & VIDEOTAPE LABS, 1141 N. Seward St., Hollywood, CA 90038; (213) 466-0624; 462-6696.

DELTA PRODUCTIONS, 3333 Glendale, Los Angeles, CA 90039; (213) 663-8754.

THE EDITING COMPANY, 8300 Beverly Blvd., Los Angeles, CA 90048; (213) 653-3570.

F&B/CECO EDITING CENTER, 7051 Santa Monica, Los Angeles, CA 90038; (213) 464-9361.

THE FILM PLACE, 1311 N. Highland Ave., Los Angeles, CA 90028; (213) 466-8361.

HORIZONTAL EDITING STUDIOS, 2625 W. Olive Ave., Burbank, CA 91505; (818) 841-6750.

INDEPENDENT PRODUCERS STUDIO INC., 1604 Vista Del Mar Ave., Hollywood, CA 90028; (213) 461-6960; 461-6966.

MOVIE TECH INC., 832 N. Seward St., Hollywood, CA 90038; (213) 467-8491; 467-5423.

PRODUCTIONS WEST, 6311 Romaine, Suite 7319-25, Los Angeles, CA 90038; (213) 464-0169; 462-4827.

UNIVERSAL CITY STUDIOS INC., 100 Universal City Plaza, Universal City, CA 91608; (818) 777-3000.

YAMAHA INTERNATIONAL CORP., P.O. Box 6600, Buena Park, CA 90622; (714) 522-9011.

NEW YORK

ANIMATED PRODS., INC., 1600 Broadway, New York, NY 10019; (212) 265-2942.

CAMERA MART, THE, 456 W. 55 St., New York, NY 10019; (212) 757-6977.

JOHN CARTER ASSOCS., INC., 300 W. 55 St., #10-V, New York, NY 10019; (212) 541-7006.

CINERGY COMMUNICATIONS CORP., 321 W. 44 St., 10036; (212) 582-2900.

CINEMA ARTS ASSOCS., INC., 333 W. 52 St., New York, NY 10019; (212) 246-2860.

CINETUDE FILM PRODS., 295 W. 4 St., New York, NY 10014; (212) 924-0400.

CUTTING EDGE, 630 Ninth Ave., 14th floor, New York, NY 10036; (212) 541-9664.

DARINO FILMS, 222 Park Ave. S, #2A, New York, NY 10003; (212) 228-4024.

EARTHRISE PRODUCTIONS, 1974 Broadway, #200, New York, NY 10023; (212) 724-3250.

EASY EDIT, 630 Ninth Ave., New York, NY 10036; (212) 541-9664.

THE EDITING MACHINE, INC., 630 Ninth Ave., New York, NY 10036; (212) 757-5420.

FILM/VIDEO ARTS INC., 817 Broadway, 2nd floor, New York, NY 10003-4797; (212) 673-9361.

KOPEL FILMS INC., 630 Ninth Ave., #910, New York, NY 10036; (212) 757-4742.

MARATHON INTERNATIONAL PRODS., INC., 211 E. 51 St., New York, NY 10022; (212) 688-1130.

MAYSLES FILM INC., 250 W. 54 St., New York, NY 10019; (212) 582-6050.

THE MULTIVIDEO GROUP LTD., 50 E. 42 St., #1107, New York, NY 10017; (212) 986-1577; 972-1015.

NATIONAL BROADCASTING CO., 30 Rockefeller Plaza, #412, New York, NY 10112; (212) 664-4754.

PHANTASMAGORIA PRODS., 630 Ninth Ave., #801, New York, NY 10036; (212) 586-4890.

REFLECTIONS XXII M.P. CO., 263 W. 54 St., New York, NY 10019; (212) 247-5370.

ROBERT RICHTER PRODS., INC. 330 W. 42 St., New York, NY 10036; (212) 947-1395.

ROSS-GAFFNEY, INC., 21 W. 46 St., New York, NY 10036; (212) 719-2744.

SOUND ONE CORP., 1619 Broadway, 8th floor, New York, NY 10019; (212) 765-4757.

TODD-AO STUDIOS EAST, 259 W. 54 St., New York, NY 10019; (212) 265-6225.

TRANS/AUDIO, INC., 259 W. 54 St., New York, NY 10019; (212) 265-6225.

UPTOWN EDIT, 21 W. 86 St., New York, NY 10024; (212) 580-2075.

VALKHN FILMS INC., 1600 Broadway, Suite 404, New York, NY 10019; (212) 586-1603.

Editing Equipment

LOS ANGELES

AMPEX CORP., 340 Parkside Dr., San Fernando, CA 91340; (818) 365-8627.

BEXEL CORP., 801 S. Main St., Burbank, CA 91506; (818) 841-5051.

BIRNS & SAWYER, INC., 1026 N. Highland Ave., Hollywood, CA 90038; (213) 466-8211.

CALIFORNIA COMMS. INC., 6900 Santa Monica Blvd., Los Angeles, CA 90038; (213) 466-8511.

CHENOWETH FILMS, 1860 E. N. Hills Dr., La Habra, CA 90631; (213) 691-1652.

CHRISTY'S, 135 N. Victory, Burbank, CA 91502; (818) 845-1755; (213) 849-1148.

CINEMA PRODUCTS CORP., 3211 S. La Cienega Blvd., Los Angeles, CA 90016-3112; (213) 836-7991.

EDIQUIP, 6820 Romaine St., Hollywood, CA 90038; (213) 467-3107.

ALAN GORDON ENTERPRISES, INC., 1430 Cahuenga Blvd., Hollywood, CA 90028; (213) 466-3561.

THE GRASS VALLEY GROUP INC., 21243 Ventura Blvd., #206, Woodland Hills, CA 91364; (818) 999-2303.

HOLLYWOOD FILM CO., 3294 E. 26th St., Vernon, CA 90023; (213) 263-9661.

HOLLYWOOD NATIONAL STUDIOS, 6605 Eleanor Ave., Los Angeles, CA 90038; (213) 467-6272.

J & R FILM CO., INC., 6820 Romaine St., Hollywood, CA 90038; (213) 467-3107.

JACOBSON, GARY, 1248 S. Fairfax, Malibu, CA 90265; (213) 937-6588.

KEM EDITING SYSTEMS INC., 7237 Santa Monica Blvd., Los Angeles, CA (213) 850-0200.

MAGNASYNC/MOVIELA CORP. P.O. Box 707, 5539 Riverton Ave., North Hollywood, CA 91601,; (818) 763-8441.

MARKET STREET SOUND, 73 Market St., Venice, CA 90291; (213) 396-5937.

MAIER-HANCOCK INDUSTRIES INC., 6820 Romaine St., Los Angeles, CA 90038; (213) 467-3107.

PLASTIC REEL CORP. OF AMERICA, 8140 Webb Ave., North Hollywood, CA 91605; (818) 504-0400.

RBC ENTERPRISES, 1860 E. North Hills Dr., La Habra, CA 90631; (213) 691-1652.

STEENBECK INC., 9045 Vasser Ave., Chatsworth, CA 91311; (818) 998-4033.

VIDEO SUPPORT SERVICES, 3473½ Cahuenga Blvd., W. Los Angeles, CA 90068; (213) 469-9000.

ORLANDO

WALT DISNEY/MGM STUDIOS, P.O. Box 10200, Lake Buena Vista, FL 32830; (407) 560-5353.

NEW YORK

AVCOM CINE EQUIPMENT INC., 653 Eleventh Ave., New York, NY 10036; (212) 541-9229.

BROADCAST EQUIPMENT SUPPLY CORP., Box 133, Rego Park, Queens, NY 11374; (718) 843-6839.

THE CAMERA MART, INC., 456 W. 55 St., New York, NY 10019; (212) 757-6977.

CAMERA SERVICE CENTER INC., 625 W. 54 St., New York, NY 10019; (212) 757-0906.

CINECRAFT INC. 866 Ave. of the Americas, New York, NY 10001, (212) 686-2411.

CINERGY COMMUNICATIONS, CORP., 321 W. 44 St., New York, NY 10036; (212) 582-2900.

COMPREHENSIVE SERVICE AV INC., Box 881, New York, NY 10108; (212) 586-6161.

CUTTING EDGE, 630 Ninth Ave., New York, NY 10036; (212) 541-9664.

EASY EDIT, 630 Ninth Ave., New York, NY 10036; (212) 541-9664.

THE EDITING MACHINE, 630 Ninth Ave. #1000 New York, NY 10036; (212) 757-5420.

J & R FILM CO., INC., 636 Eleventh Ave., New York, NY 10036; (212) 247-0972.
KEM EDITING SYSTEMS, 315 W. 57 St., New York, NY 10019; (212) 582-7338.
KINGSWAY FILM EQUIPMENT LTD., Pier 62, NorthRiver, NY 10011; (212) 929-7345.
LAUMIC CO., INC., 306 E. 39 St., 10016; (212) 889-3300.
MM EDITING SYSTEMS, 118 E. 25 St., 7th floor, New York, NY 10010; (212) 460-8810.
MPCS VIDEO INDUSTRIES INC., 514 W. 57 St., New York, NY 10019; (212) 586-3690; (800) 223-0622.
MAYSLES FILM, INC., 250 W. 54 St., New York, NY 10019; (212) 582-6050.
MONTAGE GROUP LTD., 1 W. 85 St., New York, NY 10024; (212) 362-0892.
MOTION PICTURES ENTERPRISES, INC. 430 W. 45 St., New York, NY 10036; (212) 245-0969.
NEUMADE, P.O. Box 5001, Norwalk, CT 06856; (203) 866-7600.
PHANTASMAGORIA PRODUCTIONS, 630 Ninth Ave., New York, NY 10036; (212) 586-4890.
PLASTIC REEL CORP. OF AMERICA, Brisbin Ave., Lyndhurst, NJ 07071; (201) 933-5100; (212) 541-6464.
PREVIEW EQUIPMENT CO., 432 W. 45 St., New York, NY 10036; (212) 245-0969.
ROSS-GAFFNEY INC., 21 W. 46 St., 9th floor, New York, NY 10036; (212) 719-2744.
SPERA CORP., 511 W. 33 St., New York, NY 10001-1302; (212) 629-0009.
STUDIO FILM & TAPE INC., 630 Ninth Ave., New York, NY 10036; (212) 977-9330.

Editing Services

LOS ANGELES

ACE & EDIE FILM & VIDEO TAPE POST PRODUCTION, 722 N. Seward St., Los Angeles, CA 90038; (213) 462-2185.
ADVENTURE FILM & TAPE, 1027 N. Cole Ave., Hollywood, CA 90038; (213) 460-4557.
ARRIFLEX CORP., 600 N. Victory Blvd., Burbank, CA 91502; (818) 841-7070.
THE BURBANK STUDIOS, 4000 Warner Blvd., Burbank, CA 91522; (818) 954-6000.
CFI (CONSOLIDATED FILM INDUSTRIES), 959 Seward St., Hollywood, CA 90038; (213) 462-3161; 960-7444.
CHRISTY'S EDITORIAL FILM SUPPLY, INC., 135 N. Victory Blvd., Burbank, CA 91502; (818) 845-1755; (213) 849-1148.
THE CINEASTE GROUP, 813 N. Highland Ave., Hollywood, CA 90038; (213) 464-8158.
COMPACT VIDEO SERVICES, INC., 2813 W. Alameda Ave., Burbank, CA 91105; (818) 840-7000.
CRAWFORD EDITORIAL, 2440 El Contento Dr., Hollywood, CA 90068; (213) 463-7939; (213) 462-2818.
CROSS CUTS, 1330 N. Vine St., Hollywood, CA 90028; (213) 854-3308.
ECHO FILM SERVICES, INC., 4119 Burbank Blvd., Burbank, CA 91505; (818) 841-4114.
THE EDITING COMPANY, 8300 Beverly Blvd., Los Angeles, CA 90048; (213) 653-3570.
ELECTRONIC ARTS & TECHNOLOGY, 3655 Motor Ave., Los Angeles, CA 90034; (213) 836-2556.
FILM CORE, 849 N. Seward St., Hollywood, 90038; (213) 464-7303.
FILM PLACE, THE, 1311 N. Highland Ave., Los Angeles 90028; (213) 464-0116.
FREUD & KLEPPEL INC., 6290 Sunset Blvd., #603, Los Angeles, CA 90028; (213) 469-1444.
HOLLYWOOD ASSOCIATES, INC., 2800 W. Olive Ave., Burbank, CA 91505; (818) 841-4136.
IMAGE TRANSFORM LAB., 4142 Lankershim Blvd., No. Hollywood, CA 91602; (818) 985-7566; (800) 423-2652.
INDEPENDENT PRODUCERS STUDIO INC., 1604 Vista Del Mar Ave., Hollywood, CA 90028; (213) 461-6960; 461-6966.
KEM EDITING SYSTEMS, 7237 Santa Monica Blvd., Los Angeles 90066; (213) 850-0200.
LION'S GATE STUDIOS, 1861 S. Bundy Dr., Los Angeles, CA 90025; (213) 820-7751.
MATHERS, JIM, FILM COMPANY, P.O. Box 1973, Studio City, CA 91604; (818) 762-2214.
MOFFIT, WILLIAM ASSOCS., 747 N. Lake Ave., #B, Pasadena, CA 91104; (818) 791-2559.
PARAMOUNT STUDIO GROUP, 5555 Melrose Ave., Hollywood 90038; (213) 468-5000.

POST PLUS INC., 6650 Santa Monica Blvd., 2nd floor, Hollywood, CA 90038; (213) 463-7108.
PRO VIDEO/CINETAPE, 801 N. La Brea Ave., Los Angeles, CA 90038; (213) 934-8836.
RED CAR, 1040 N. Las Palmas Ave., Los Angeles, CA 90038; (213) 466-4467.
REEL THING OF CALIFORNIA INC., 1253 N. Vine St., Suite 14, Hollywood, CA 90038; (213) 466-8588.
RENCHER'S EDITORIAL SERVICE, 738 Cahuenga Blvd., Hollywood, CA 90038; (213) 463-9836.
SCREEN IMAGES, INC., 1041 N. Orange Dr., Hollywood 90038; (213) 462-4383.
UNIVERSAL FACILITIES RENTAL DIVISION, 100 Universal City Plaza, Universal City 91608; (818) 777-3000.
WILDWOOD FILM SERVICE, 6855 Santa Monica Blvd., Suite 400, Los Angeles, CA 90038; (213) 462-6388.
WOLLIN PRODUCTION SERVICES, INC., 666 N. Robertson Blvd., Los Angeles, CA 90069; (213) 659-0175.

NEW YORK

A & R, INC., 214 E. 49 St., New York, NY 10017; (212) 371-3221.
ALSCHULER, JANE & CO., 205 E. 42 St., New York, NY 10017; (212) 697-7185.
ANI-LIVE FILM SERVICE, INC., 222 E. 46 St., New York, NY 10017; (212) 983-1918.
ANIMATED PRODS., INC., 1600 Broadway, 10019; (212) 265-2942.
ANOTHER DIRECTION, 231 E. 51 St., 10022; (212) 753-8250.
BENDER EDITORIAL SERVICE, INC., 27 E. 39 St., New York, NY 10016; (212) 867- 1515.
BERT'S PLACE, 141 E. 44 St., 10017; (212) 682-5891.
B. CANARICK'S CO., LTD., 50 E. 42 St., New York, NY 10017; (212) 972-1015.
CHARLES, MICHAEL, EDITORIAL, 6 E. 45 St., New York, NY 10017; (212) 953-2490.
CHUNG GROUP, INC., 11 E. 47 St., 5th floor, New York, NY 10017; (212) 832-0530.
CINE METRIC, INC., 290 Madison Ave., New York, NY 10017; (212) 532-4140.
CINE TAPE, INC., 241 E. 51 St., New York, NY 10022; (212) 355-0070.
COLEMAN, KEN, EDITING, 310 E. 44 St., New York, NY 10022; (212) 986-0170.
COUNTDOWN EDITORIAL SERVICES, INC., 5 E. 47 St., New York, NY 10017; (212) 838-2383.
CRESCENT CUTTERS, INC., 304 E. 45 St., New York, NY 10017; (212) 687-2802.
CREW CUTS FILM & TAPE, INC., 9 E. 47 St., New York, NY 10017; (212) 371-4545.
A CUT ABOVE, EDITORIAL INC., 17 E. 45 St., New York, NY 10017; (212) 661-4949.
THE CUTTING EDGE/EDITORIAL, 420 Lexington Ave., New York, NY 10017; (212) 599-4233.
DJM FILMS, INC., 4 E. 46 St., New York, NY 10017; (212) 687-0111.
DEE, DAVID, 62 W. 45 St., New York, NY 10036; (212) 764-4700.
DELL, JEFF, FILM SERVICE, 241 E. 51 St., New York, NY 10022; (212) 371-1915.
EDITING CONCEPTS, 214 E. 50 St., New York, NY 10022; (212) 980-3340.
THE EDITING HOUSE, INC., 304 E. 45 St., New York, NY 10017; (212) 286-0666.
THE EDITORS, 220 E. 48 St., New York, NY 10017; (212) 371-0862.
EDITORS CORNER, 211 E. 51 St., New York, NY 10022; (212) 688-4334.
EDITOR'S GAS, 16 E. 48 St., New York, NY 10017; (212) 832-6690.
EDITORS HIDEAWAY, INC., 219 E. 44 St., New York, NY 10022; (212) 661-3850.
FILM BILLDERS, 10 E. 40 St., New York, NY 10016; (212) 683-4004.
FILM-RITE, INC., 1185 Ave. of the Americas, New York, NY 10036; (212) 575-6801.
FILMPOWER, 304 E. 45 St., New York, NY 10017; (212) 286-0666.
FINAMORE, D.P., 619 W. 54 St., New York, NY 10019; (212) 582-5265.
FIRST EDITION/COMPOSITE FILMS, 5 E. 47 St., New York, NY 10017; (212) 838-3044.
FREDERIC FISCHER FILMS, 28 Verandah Pl., Brooklyn, NY 11201; (718) 852-2643.
GOLD, JAY, INC., 342 Madison Ave., #424, New York, NY 10173; (212) 681-7171.
GRENADIER PRODS., INC., 141 E. 44 St., New York, NY 10017; (212) 687-2638.
HARVEY'S PLACE, 919 Third Ave., 10022; (212) 688-5510.
HORN/EISENBERG FILM & TAPE EDITING, 16 W. 46 St., New York, NY 10036; (212) 391-8166.
HOROWITZ, ROBERT, FILMS, 216 E. 49 St., New York, NY 10017; (212) 751-1441.
HUDSON, SCOTT, EDITORIAL, 245 E. 50 St., New York, NY 10022; (212) 758-4155.

354

JPC VISUALS, 11 E. 47 St., New York, NY 10017; (212) 223-0555.
ROBERT JUBIN LTD., 11 E. 47 St., New York, NY 10017; (212) 319-4747.
JUPITER EDITORIAL SERVICE, 201 E. 16 St., New York, NY 10003, (212) 460-5600.
KOPEL FILMS, INC., 630 Ninth Ave., New York, NY 10036; (212) 757-4742.
LFR EDITORIAL, INC., 20 E. 46 St., New York, NY 10017; (212) 682-5950.
LM COMMUNICATIONS, CORP., 60 Hamilton Terr., New York, NY 10031; (212) 283-2509.
LANDA, SAUL, INC., 35 W. 87 St., New York, NY 10024; (212) 877-5553; 764-4700.
MAGNO SOUND & VIDEO, 729 Seventh Ave., 10019; (212) 302-2505.
MESSINA EDITORIAL, INC., 18 E. 41 St., New York, NY 10017; (212) 481-3456.
MS EDITORIAL, INC. 200 W. 57 St., New York, NY 10019; (212) 333-7590.
MORTY'S FILM SERVICES, LTD., 10 E. 40 St., New York, NY 10016; (212) 696-5040.
OASIS FILM & TAPE EDITORIAL SERVICES, INC., 341 E. 44 St., New York, NY 10017; (212) 983-3131.
P.A.T. FILM SERVICES, 630 Ninth Ave., New York, NY 10036; (212) 247-0900.
PDR PRODUCTIONS, INC., 747 Third Ave., New York, NY 10017; (212) 755-9019.
PALESTRINI FILM EDITING, INC., 477 Madison Ave., New York, NY 10022; (212) 752-EDIT.
PELCO EDITORIAL INC., 757 Third Ave., New York, NY 10017; (212) 319-EDIT.
PHOTOSONIC EDITING, INC., 420 Lexington Ave., 10017; (212) 599-4233.
PINEYRO, GLORIA, FILM SERVICES CORP., 19 W. 21 St., New York, NY 10010; (212) 627-0707.
POWER POST PRODUCTION, 25 W. 43 St., New York, NY 10036; (212) 840-3860.
REFLECTIONS XXII M.P. CO., 263 W. 54 St., New York, NY 10019; (212) 247-5370.
RICH ENTERPRISES CORP., 15 W. 26 St., New York, NY 10010; (212) 685-0040.
ROSEBUD PRODUCTIONS, INC., 141 E. 44 St., New York, NY 10017; (212) 993-3133.
ROSS-GAFFNEY, INC., 21 W. 46 St., New York, NY 10036; (212) 719-2744.
SALAMANDRA IMAGES, INC., 6 E. 39 St., New York, NY 10016; (212) 779-0707.
SANDPIPER EDITORIAL SERVICE, 50 W. 40 St., New York, NY 10018; (212) 921-1570.
SPECTRUM ASSOCS. INC., 536 W. 29 St., New York, NY 10001, (212) 563-1680.
SPLICE IS NICE, 141 E. 44 St., New York, NY 10017; (212) 599-1711.
STONE-CUTTERS, 422 Madison Ave., New York, NY 10017; (212) 421-9404.
SYLIANOU, MICHEL, PRODUCTIONS, NC., 301 Madison Ave., New York, NY 10017; (212) 687-5708.
SYNCRO-FILM SERVICES, INC., 72 W. 45 St., New York, NY 10036; (212) 719-2966.
TAKE 5 EDITORIAL SERVICES, INC., 681 Lexington Ave., New York, NY 10022; (212) 759-7404.
THE TAPE HOUSE EDITORIAL, 216 E. 45 St., New York, NY 10017; (212) 557-4949.
TAPESTRY PRODUCTIONS, LTD., 924 Broadway, 2nd floor, New York, NY 10010; (212) 677-6007.
THE TRAILER SHOP, INC., 21 W. 46 St., New York, NY 10036; (212) 944-0318.
TRAIMAN, HENRY, ASSOCIATES, 160 Madison Ave., New York, NY 10016; (212) 889-3400.
TRIM BIN EDITORIAL SERVICES INC., 9 E. 38 St., New York, NY 10016; (212) 696-0050.
UPPERCUT EDITORIAL INC., 25 W. 43 St. New York, NY 10016; (212) 704-9760.
VALKHN FILMS INC., 1600 Broadway, Suite 404, New York, NY 10019; (212) 586-1603.

Film Carriers

ALBANY

CLARK SERVICE, INC., 24 N. Third St., 12204; (518) 434-1289. John Pemberton, mgr.
WESCO FILM SERVICE, INC., 24 N. Third St., 12204; (518) 434-1289. John Pemberton.

ATLANTA

BENTON FILM FORWARDING CO., INC., 168 Baker St., N.W., 30313; (404) 577-2821. Walken Calloway.
THEATRES SERVICE CO., 830 Willoughby Way, N.E., 30313; (404) 422-8369. W. B. Langston.

BOSTON

NFS OPERATING CORP., 20 Freeport Way, Dorchester, MA 02122; (617) 288-1600. Jimmie Choukas.

BUFFALO

WESCO FILM SERVICE, INC., 108 Gruner Rd., 14225; (716) 897-0467. Robert Neffke.

CHARLOTTE

CAROLINA FILM SERVICE, INC., 522 Penman St., P.O. Box 30845, 28230; (704) 333-2115. Ernest J. Poole.

CHICAGO

ALLIN EXPRESS SERVICE, P.O. Box 14, Skokie, IL 60076; (312) 935-6886. Bruce Brown.
CLARK FILM SERVICE, 222 N. Laflin St., 60607; (312) 829-3700. William Saley.
EMERY AIRFREIGHT, Chicago O'Hare Airport, 60666; (312) 686-7300. George Brown, mgr.
LAVIN BROS. FILM DELIVERY SERVICE, 6328 N. Richmond Ave.; (312) 274-6450. William Lavin and Lewis Lavin, owners.

CINCINNATI

CLARK FILM SERVICE, 421 Bauer St., 45214; (513) 621-4240. Harry Jansen.

CLEVELAND

CLEVELAND FILM SERVICE, INC., 1625 E. 45 St., 44103; (216) 431-9491. John Remec.

DALLAS

CENTRAL SHIPPING & INSPECTION, 2500 S. Harwood, 75215; (214) 421-5411. Wallace Jack, mgr.

DENVER

DENVER SHIPPING AND INSPECTION, 5355 Harrison St., 80216; (303) 296-3793. Alan Castle, mgr.

DES MOINES

IOWA FILM DEPOT, 3123 Delaware Ave., 50313; (515) 265-1469. Robert Boots, mgr.
KING, H. W. DELIVERY SERVICE, 1320 Grand Ave., 50316; (515) 243-5269. Floyd L. King, mgr.

DETROIT

NFS OPERATING CORPORATION, 6111 Concord Ave., 48211; (313) 923-2150. Terry McCauley.

INDIANAPOLIS

CLARK FILM SERVICE, 429 N. Senate Ave., 46204; (317) 638-3531. George Davenport.

JACKSONVILLE, FL

JACKSONVILLE FILM SERVICE, INC., 2208 W. 21 St., 32209; (904) 355-5447. Bert D. Benton.

KANSAS CITY, MO

HIGHWAY FILM SERVICE, 120 West 17th Ave. 64108; (816) 471-0884. Pat Rafter.

LOS ANGELES

AIR SEA FORWARDERS, 9009 La Cienega Blvd., Inglewood, CA 90045; (213) 776-1611.
GATEWAY FORWARDERS INTERNATIONAL, 3911 E. Floral Dr., Los Angeles, CA 90063; (213) 261-4833.
GILBOY, INC., 8401 Slauson Ave., Pico Rivera, CA 90660; (213) 949-9397. Mrs. Pat Hanna.
NOVO INTERNATIONAL CORP., 8635 Aviation Blvd., Inglewood, CA 90301; (213) 776-1178.

MEMPHIS

FILM TRANSIT, INC., 291 Hernando St., 38118; (901) 365-7550. Guilbert Brandon, president.
MEMPHIS FILM SERVICE, INC., 3931 Homewood Rd., 38118; (901) 794-6601. A. S. Crews.

MILWAUKEE

MILWAUKEE FILM CENTER, INC., 333 N. 25th St., 53233; (414) 344-0300. Oliver Trampe, mgr.

MINNEAPOLIS-ST. PAUL

HYMAN FREIGHTWAYS, INC., 2690 Wycliffe Ave. N., St. Paul; 645-0381. Eugene Pikovsky, pres.
INDEPENDENT FILM SERVICE, INC., 245 Second Ave. N., Minneapolis 55401; (612) 332-2203. Jim Perrin.
TWIN CITY FREIGHT, 2280 Ellis, St. Paul, 55414; (612) 636-6270. W. E. Elshotz, Sr., pres.

NEW HAVEN

NEW HAVEN FILM SERVICE, 90 Woodmont Rd., 06460, Milford CT 06460; (203) 878-1465. William Rosen.

NEW ORLEANS

FILM INSPECTION SERVICE, INC., 2411 Edenborn Ave., Metairie, LA 70001; (504) 833-5552. S.C. Brandon.

NEW YORK CITY

BONDED FILM DISTRIBUTORS, 550 Main St., Fort Lee, NJ 07024; (212) 557-6733. Mike Berg.
NFS OPERATING CORP., 902 E. Hazlewood Ave., Rahway, NJ 07065; 38 W. 39 St., New York, NY (212) 944-1788. Dan Fuchs.
RAPID FILM DISTRIBUTORS, INC., 37-02 27th St., Long Island City, NY 11101; (212) 786-4600.
STATE FILM DELIVERY, 560 Main, Fort Lee, NJ 07024; (201) 947-5200.

OKLAHOMA CITY

MISTLETOE EXPRESS SERVICE, INC., 111 N. Harrison 73125; (405) 235-5566. Jack LaMonte, mgr.
OKLAHOMA CITY SHIPPING & INSPECTION, 809 S. West 7th St., 73109; (405) 235-2553. Charles Baird.

OMAHA

OMAHA FILM DEPOT, 1441 N. 11th St., 68102; (402) 342-6576. Charles Janousek.

PHILADELPHIA

INTERNATIONAL FILM SERVICE, INC., 130 Ferry Ave., Camden, NJ 08104; (215) 232-3500. David Adleman.

PITTSBURGH

PITTSBURGH FILM SERVICE, 16 Nichol Ave., McKees Rocks, 15136; (412) 771-2665. John Callahan, mgr.

PORTLAND, OR

PORTLAND NATIONAL FILM SERVICE, 3567 N.W. Yeon 97210; (503) 224-6205. Cathy Slade.

ST. LOUIS, MO

KAHAN FILM DISTRIBUTORS, 3974 Page Blvd., 63113; (314) 371-6572. Meyer Kahan, mgr.

SALT LAKE CITY, UT

NFS OPERATING CORP., 190 N. 640 West, North Salt Lake, 84054; (801) 292-7626. Rulon Hammer.

SAN FRANCISCO

NFS OPERATING CORP., 701 Bradford Way, 94587; (415) 471-9400. Jack Thompson.

SEATTLE

SEATTLE NATIONAL FILM SERVICE, 900 Maynard Ave., S., 98134; (206) 682-6685. Norman Jones.

WASHINGTON, DC

HIGHWAY DISTRIBUTION SERVICE, 15113 Old Marlboro Pike; Upper Marlboro, MD 20772; (301) 952-1320. Brad Buchanan.

Financing Companies & Banking Services

J.E. ANDARY PRODUCTIONS & FINANCING, 7080 Hollywood Blvd. #114, Los Angeles, CA 90028; (213) 466-3379.
BANK OF AMERICA ENTERTAINMENT INDUSTRIES DIVISION, 555 S. Flower St., Los Angeles, CA 90071; (213) 228-4096.
BANK OF CALIFORNIA ENTERTAINMENT DIVISION, 9401 Wilshire Blvd., Beverly Hills, CA 90212; (213) 273-7200.
BANKERS TRUST, 280 Park Ave., 15th floor, New York, NY 10017; (212) 850-3220.
CHARTER FINANCIAL INC., One Rockefeller Plaza, New York, NY 10020; (212) 399-7777.
CHASE MANHATTAN BANK, N.A., Media & Communications Component, 1 Chase Manhattan Plaza, 5th floor, New York, NY 10081; (212) 552-2222.
CHEMICAL BANK ENTERTAINMENT INDUSTRIES GROUP, 277 Park Ave., New York, NY 10172; (212) 310-5624; 333 S. Grand Ave., Suite 2600, Los Angeles, CA 90071; (213) 253-5041.
CINEMA GROUP, 8758 Venice Blvd., Los Angeles, CA 90212; (213) 204-0102.
CITICORP, USA, INC., 725 S. Figueroa St., Los Angeles, CA 90017; (213) 239-1400.
CITY NATIONAL BANK ENTERTAINMENT DIVISION, 400 N. Roxbury Dr., Suite 400, Beverly Hills, CA 90210; (213) 550-5696.
CONSTANT FINANCIAL SERVICES INC., 8749 Holloway Dr., Los Angeles, CA 90069; (213) 650-5227.
THE CROCKER BANK, ENTERTAINMENT INDUSTRIES GROUP, 10100 Santa Monica Blvd., Suite 420-A, Los Angeles, CA 90067; (213) 550-2764.
ENTERTAINMENT FINANCIAL SERVICES, P.O. Box 5120, Sherman Oaks, CA 91413; (818) 905-9518.
FILM FINANCES, INC., 9000 Sunset Blvd., Suite 808, Los Angeles, CA 90069; (213) 275-7323; FAX: (213) 275-1706; TELEX: 183-205.
FIRST CHARTER BANK ENTERTAINMENT DIVISION, 9300 Wilshire Blvd., Beverly Hills, CA 90212; (213) 275-2225.
FIRST INTERSTATE BANK OF CALIFORNIA, ENTERTAINMENT DIVISION, 9601 Wilshire Blvd., Beverly Hills, CA 90210; (213) 858- 5585.
FIRST LOS ANGELES BANK ENTERTAINMENT DIVISION, 9595 Wilshire Blvd., Beverly Hills, CA 90212; (213) 557-1211.
FIRST NATIONAL BANK OF MINNEAPOLIS, 444 S. Flower St., Suite 1730, Los Angeles, CA 90017; (213) 623-8267.
FLEET CREDIT CORPORATION, 3990 Westerly Place, Suite 100, Newport Beach, CA 92660; (714) 955-2574.
HERITAGE ENTERTAINMENT, INC., 11500 W. Olympic Blvd., Suite 300, Los Angeles, CA 90064; (213) 477-8100.
IMPERIAL BANKING, ENTERTAINMENT BANKING, 9777 Wilshire Blvd., Beverly Hills, CA 90212; (213) 858-1430.
THE LEWIS HORWITZ ORGANIZATION, 1840 Century Park East, Los Angeles, CA 90067; (213) 275-7171.
MERCANTILE NATIONAL BANK, 1840 Century Park East, Los Angeles, CA 90067; (213) 277-2265.
METRO BANK ENTERTAINMENT DIVISION, 10900 Wilshire Blvd., Los Angeles, CA 90024; (213) 824-5700.
MOTION PICTURES INVESTMENT CO., 430 S. Burnside Ave., Los Angeles, CA 90036; (213) 931-9241.
PHOENIX FINANCIAL GROUP, 630 Third Ave., New York, NY 10017; (212) 687-2121.
L.F. ROTHSCHILD & CO., INC., 55 Water St., New York, NY 10041; (212) 412-1116; 3250 Wilshire Blvd., Suite 1100, Los Angeles, CA 90010; (213) 382-1450.

SECURITY PACIFIC NATIONAL BANK, 333 S. Hope St., H14-60, Los Angeles, CA 90071; (213) 345-5353.
THIRD EYE PRODUCTION CO., 100 S. Doheny Dr., Los Angeles, CA 90048; (213) 858-4939.
TOKAI BANK OF CALIFORNIA, 200 E. Colorado Blvd., Pasadena, CA 91105; (818) 570-6391.
TOUCHE ROSS, 10537 Santa Monica Blvd., Los Angeles, CA 90025; (213) 475-1100.
UNION BANK, 9460 Wilshire Blvd., Beverly Hills, CA 90213; (213) 555-6627.
WALKER CORPORATE FINANCIAL CONSULTING, P.O. Box 93-543, Sunset Station, Hollywood, CA 90093.
WELLS FARGO BANK ENTERTAINMENT LOAN CENTER, 9600 Santa Monica Blvd., Beverly Hills, CA 90210; (213) 550-2262.
WESTERN SECURITY BANK, ENTERTAINMENT DIVISION, 4100 W. Alameda Ave., Toluca Lake, CA 91505; (818) 843-0707.

Lighting Equipment

CALIFORNIA

ACEY-DECY EQUIPMENT CO., 5420 Vineland Ave., N. Hollywood, CA 91601; (818) 766-9445.
AMERICAN NEONICS, INC., 5542 Satsuma Ave., North Hollywood, CA 91601; (818) 982-0316; (213) 875-1815.
AMETRON RENTALS, 1200 N. Vine St., Hollywood, CA 90038; (213) 466-4321.
AUTOMATED STUDIO LIGHTING, 545 Rodier St., Glendale, CA 91201; (818) 500-1646.
BARDWELL & MC ALISTER INC., 2621 Empire Ave., Burbank, CA 91504; (213) 849-5533; (818) 843-6821.
BERC (BROADCAST EQUIPMENT RENTAL COMPANY), 4545 Chermak St., Burbank, CA 91505; (818) 841-3000; (213) 464-7655.
BERLIN LIGHTING & GENERATORS, 12752 Tiara St., N. Hollywood, CA 91607; (818) 341-5105.
BIRNS & SAWYER INC., 1026 N. Highland Ave., Hollywood, CA 90038; (213) 466-8211.
CALIFORNIA VIDEO CENTER, 15303 Ventura Blvd., Sherman Oaks, CA 91403; (818) 789-5000.
CASTEX RENTALS, INC., 6863 Willoughby Ave., Los Angeles, CA 90038; (213) 462-1468.
CINE VIDEO, 948 N. Cahuenga Blvd., Hollywood, CA 90038; (213) 464-6200.
CINELEASE INC., 140 S. Victory Blvd., Burbank, CA 91502; (818) 996-9345; 841-8282.
CINEVANS LOCATION EQUIPMENT, P.O. Box 2390, Toluca Lake Station, North Hollywood, CA 91602; (818) 846-5386.
CINEWORKS—CINERENTS, 5724 Santa Monica Blvd., Los Angeles, CA 90038; (213) 464-0296.
COOL LIGHT COMPANY INC., 5723 Auckland Ave., North Hollywood, CA 91601; (818) 761-6116.
CUSTOM NEON, 2210 S. La Brea Ave., Los Angeles, CA 90016; (213) 937-NEON.
EXPENDABLE SUPPLY STORE, 7830 N. San Fernando Rd., Sun Valley, CA 91352; (818) 767-5065; (213) 875-2409; 1316 N. Western Ave., Hollywood, CA 90027; (213) 465-3191.
FAX COMPANY, 1430 N. Cahuenga Blvd., Hollywood, CA 90028; (213) 466-3561; (818) 985-5500.
IMERO FIORENTINO ASSOCIATES, 7060 Hollywood Blvd., Suite 1000, Los Angeles, CA 90028; (213) 467-4020.
G-FORCE INTERNATIONAL ENTERTAINMENT CORP., 279 S. Beverly Dr., Suite 1038, Beverly Hills, CA 90212; (213) 271-0700.
GMT STUDIOS, 5751 Buckingham Pkway, Unit C, Culver City, CA 90230; (213) 649-3733.
ALAN GORDON ENTERPRISES, INC., 1430 N. Cahuenga Blvd, Hollywood, CA 90028; (213) 466-3561; (818) 985-5500.
HARRAH'S THEATRE SERVICE & SUPPLY, 624B S. San Fernando Blvd., Burbank, CA 91502; (818) 842-5111.
HOLLYWOOD CENTER STUDIOS INC., 1040 N. Las Palmas Ave., Los Angeles, CA 90038; (213) 469-5000.
HOLLYWOOD RENTAL COMPANY, INC., 7848 N. San Fernando Rd., Sun Valley, CA 91352; (818) 768-8018; (213) 849-1326.
INTER VIDEO/TRITRONICS, INC., 733 N. Victory Blvd., Burbank, CA 91502; (818) 843-3633; 569-4000.
J L SERVICE, 11347 Victory Blvd., North Hollywood, CA 91601; (818) 508-7780.
JLW STUDIO RENTALS, 8033 Sunset Blvd., Suite 5010, Los Angeles, CA 90046; (818) 763-4965.
KEYLITE PSI, 333 S. Front St., Burbank, CA 91502; (818) 841-5483.
L.A. MARQUEE INC., 12023 Ventura Blvd., Studio City, CA 91604; (818) 505-6572.
LASER MEDIA, INC., 2046 Armacost Ave., Los Angeles, CA 90025; (213) 820-3750.

LEE AMERICA WEST INC., 3620 Valhalla Dr., Burbank, CA 91505; (818) 848-1111.
LEE COLORTRAN, INC., 1015 Chestnut St., Burbank, CA 91506; (818) 843-1200.
LEE PANAVISION INTL., 3800 W. Alameda Ave., Burbank, CA 91505; (818) 972-3600; 972-3624.
LEONETTI CINE RENTALS, 5609 Sunset Blvd., Los Angeles, CA 90028; (213) 469-2987.
LTM CORP. OF AMERICA, 1160 N. Las Palmas Ave., Los Angeles, CA 90038; (213) 460-6166.
MOLE-RICHARDSON CO., 937 N. Sycamore Ave., Hollywood, CA 90038; (213) 851-0111.
NIGHTS OF NEON, 7337 Varna Ave., North Hollywood, CA 91605; (818) 982-3592.
NORCOSTCO, INC., 5867 Lankersheim Blvd., North Hollywood, CA 91601; (213) 461-6555; (818) 760-2911.
ONE PASS FILM & VIDEO, One China Basin Bldg., San Francisco, CA 94107; (415) 777-5777.
THE PALADIN GROUP, INC., 7356 Santa Monica, Los Angeles, CA 90046; (213) 851-8222.
PALINKO'S STUDIO, 9901 Edmore Pl., Sun Valley, CA 91352; (818) 767-5925; 768-2013.
RALEIGH STUDIOS, 650 N. Bronson Ave., Los Angeles, CA 90004; (213) 466-3111.
ROSCO LABORATORIES INC., 1135 N. Highland Ave., Hollywood, CA 90038; (213) 462-2233.
SELLULOID LIGHTING, GRIP & ELECTRIC, 3620 Overland Ave., Los Angeles, CA 90034; (213) 202-8990.
SHANEON, 9909 Canoga Ave., Chatsworth, CA 91311; (818) 709-NEON.
SIGNS AND WONDERS NEON, 12440 Moorpark St., Suite 303, Studio City, CA 91604; (818) 766-1981.
S.I.R. LIGHTING INC., 6048 Sunset Blvd., Hollywood, CA 90028; (213) 466-3417; 466-1314.
STAGE FIFTEEN, 1015 N. Cahuenga Blvd., Stage 15, Hollywood, CA 90038; (213) 466-9015.
STRAND CENTURY LIGHTING, 18111 S. Santa Fe Ave., Rancho Dominguez, CA 90221; (213) 637-7500.
STUDIO SPECTRUM INC., 1056 N. Lake St., Burbank, CA 91502; (818) 843-1610.
SUPERSTAGE, 5724 Santa Monica Blvd., Hollywood, CA 90038; (213) 464-0296.
TM MOTION PICTURE EQUIPMENT RENTALS, 7365 Greenbush Ave., North Hollywood, CA 91605; (818) 764-7479.
TRIANGLE SCENERY/DRAPERY/LIGHTING CO., 1215 Bates Ave., Los Angeles, CA 90029; (213) 662-8129.
THEATRE VISION INC., 5426 Fair Ave., North Hollywood, CA 91601; (818) 769-0928.
ULTRAVISION INC., 7022 Sunset Blvd., Hollywood, CA 90028; (213) 871-2727.
UNITED TELEPRODUCTION SERVICES, 15055 Oxnard St., Van Nuys, CA 91411; (818) 997-0100.
UNIVERSAL FACILITIES RENTAL DIVISION, 100 Universal City Plaza, Universal City, CA 91608; (818) 777-3000.
UT PHOTO SERVICE, 3088 N. Clybourn Ave., Burbank, CA 91505; (213) 245-6631.

EAST COAST

BARBIZON ELECTRIC, 426 W. 55 St., New York, NY 10019; (212) 586-1620.
BERKEY-COLORTRAN, INC., (A division of Berkey Photo, Inc.), 842 Broadway, New York; (212) 475-8700.
BIG APPLE CINE SERVICE, 49-05 108th St., Corona, NY 11368; (212) 699-0497.
BOKEN, INC., 513 W. 54 St., New York, NY 10019; (212) 581-5507.
BOSTON GAFFERS BLAKE FILMS, 160 S. Hampton St., Rear. Boston, MA 02118; (617) 445-4700.
THE CAMERA MART, 456 W. 55 St., New York, NY 10019; (212) 757-6977.
CAMERA SERVICE CENTER, 625 W. 54 St., New York, NY 10019 (213) 757-0906.
CECO, 440 W. 15 St., New York, NY 10011; (212) 206-8280.
CESTARE, THOMAS, INC., 188 Herricks Rd., Mineola, NY, 11501; (516) 642-5550.
CHELSEA FILM & VIDEO, INC., 1 W. 19 St., New York, NY 10011; (212) 243-8923.
ERIK LIGHTING INC., 4077 Park Ave., New York, NY 10457; (212) 901-3100; (800) 858-4450.
FEATURE SYSTEMS, INC., 512 W. 36 St., New York, NY 10018; (212) 736-0447.
FILMTRUCKS, INC., Pier 40 North River, New York, NY 10014; (212) 243-1500.
FIORENTINO, IMERO, ASSOCIATES, 44 W. 63 St., New York, NY 10023; (212) 246-0600.
GOBLIN MARKET FILM SERVICE, 52 St. Marks Pl., Staten Island, NY 10301; (718) 447-7157.

HOTLIGHTS, 133 W. 19 St., New York, NY 10011; (212) 645-5295.
LTM CORP. OF AMERICA, 437 W. 16 St., New York, NY 10011; (212) 243-9288.
LEE LIGHTING AMERICA, LTD., 534 W. 25 St., New York, NY 10001; (212) 691-1910.
LEGS/MANHATTAN, Pier 62, North River, New York, NY 10011; (212) 807-6644.
LIBERTY LIGHTING LIMITED, 236 W. 27 St., #4A, New York, NY 10001; (212) 627-9455.
LIGHTING & PRODUCTION EQUIPMENT, INC., 1676 DeForrest Circle, Atlanta, GA 30318; (404) 352-0464. W. Bruce Harlan, pres.
LOWEL-LIGHT MANUFACTURING, 475 Tenth Ave., New York, NY 10018; (212) 947-0950.
MOVIE LITES LTD., 460 W. 24 St., New York, NY 10011: (212) 989-2318.
MOVIE MOBILE, INC., 30-15 Vernon Blvd., Astoria, NY 11102; (718) 548-7200.
PARIS FILMS PRODS., 47-02 31st Pl., Long Island City, NY 11101; (718) 740-2020.
PROCAMERA & LIGHTING RENTALS, INC., 511 W. 33 St., New York, NY 10001; (212) 695-1517.
PRODUCTION ARTS LIGHTING, INC., 636 Eleventh Ave., New York, NY 10036; (212) 489-0312.
R.D. SPARKS LTD., 16 Jane St., New York, NY 10014; (212) 633-1969.
TELETECHNIQUES SALES AND RENTALS, 1 W. 19 St., New York, NY 10011; (212) 206-1475; 633-1868.
TEMMER LIGHTING, 1 W. 19 St., New York, NY 10011; (212) 206-1475; 633-1868.
TIMES SQUARE THEATRICAL & STUDIO SUPPLY CORP., 318 W. 47 St., New York, NY 10036; (212) 245-4155.

Market Research

LOS ANGELES

THE RICHARD ADLAI CORP., 15760 Ventura Blvd., Suite 1107, North Hollywood, CA 91602; (213) 851-6532; (818) 784-6567. Telex: 756943.
AMERICAN MARKETING ASSOCIATION, 5301 Laurel Canyon Blvd., Suite 250, North Hollywood, CA 91607; (818) 762-4669.
ARBITRON CO., 5670 Wilshire Blvd., Suite 2560, Los Angeles, CA 90036; (213) 937-6420.
BLACK & HART ASSOCIATES, 9016 Wilshire Blvd., Suite 282, Beverly Hills, CA 90211-9960; (800) AIR-MAIL.
CASSIDY-WATSON ASSOCIATES (CWA), 1614 N. Argyle Ave., Hollywood, CA 90028; (213) 462-1739.
CRA INC., DR. IRVING S. WHITE, 908 Tiverton Ave., Los Angeles, CA 90024; (213) 824-1811.
ENTERTAINMENT DATA, INC., 331 N. Maple Dr., Beverly Hills, CA 90210; (213) 271-2105.
ALLAN FREEMAN MARKETING & RESEARCH ASSOCIATES, 9696 Moorgate Rd., Beverly Hills, CA 90210; (213) 276-2140.
ROBIN GERBER & ASSOCIATES, INC., 15910 Ventura Blvd., Suite 706, Encino, CA 91436; (818) 501-8881; (213) 274-6014.
GLOBAL MEDIA ASSOCIATES/USA, 22837 Ventura Blvd., Suite 302, Woodland Hills, CA 91367; (818) 888-1033; Telex: 9102504157.
MAX GOLDBERG & ASSOCIATES, INC., 4289 Bakman Ave., Studio City, CA 91602; (818) 980-5879.
HILTON COMMERCIAL GROUP, INC., 15760 Ventura Blvd., Suite 1107, Encino, CA 91436-3095; (818) 784-6567; Telex: 756943.
HISPANIC ENTERTAINMENT SPECIALIST, 6381 Hollywood Blvd., Suite 410, Hollywood, CA 90028; (213) 466-9060.
IDC SERVICES INC., 2600 W. Olive Ave., Burbank, CA 91505; (818) 569-5100.
JEFFREY IMMEDIATO & ASSOCIATES, P.O. Box 5611, Long Beach, CA 90805; (213) 422-9295.
SIGMUND LOWELL, 11930 Montana Ave., Los Angeles, CA 90049; (213) 207-5947.
MANPEAN RESEARCH & CONSULTING, INC., 9624 Wendover Dr., Beverly Hills, CA 90210; (213) 278-8613.
McCANN-ERICKSON INC., 5420 Wilshire Blvd., Los Angeles, CA 90048; (213) 655-9420.
MICHAELS, HARMON & ASSOCIATES, 7335 Topanga Canyon Blvd., Suite 111, Canoga Park, CA 91303; (818) 702-8011.
MORRIS VIDEO, INC., 2730 Monterey St., Suite 105, Torrance, CA 90503; (213) 533-4800.
CHARLES A. MOSES., 3219 W. Alameda Ave., Burbank, CA 91505; (818) 848-0513.
MUSIC SEARCH, P.O. Box 69954, Los Angeles, CA 90069; (213) 275-4790.
A.C. NIELSEN COMPANY, 6255 Sunset Blvd., Suite 1006, Los Angeles, CA 90028; (213) 466-4391.
PENLAND PRODUCTIONS, INC., 303 N. Glenoaks Blvd., Suite 780, Burbank, CA 91502; (818) 840-9461.

QWEST AUDIENCE RESEARCH & DEVELOPMENT, 574 Lillian Way, Los Angeles, CA 90004; (213) 465-2696.
RADIO TV REPORTS, 7033 Sunset Blvd., Suite 200, Los Angeles, CA 90028; (213) 466-6124.
RESEARCH EXPERIENCE/CINEMA SURVEY, 6777 Hollywood Blvd., Suite 206, Los Angeles, CA 90028; (213) 469-9880.
RESEARCH FRONTIERS CORPORATION, 3524 Caribeth Dr., Encino, CA 91436-4101; (818) 783-1620.
RITZ & ASSOCIATES ADVERTISING, 517 N. Robertson Blvd., Los Angeles, CA 90048; (213) 858-8456.
SHULMAN RESEARCH, 672 S. Lafayette Park Place, Los Angeles, CA 90057; (213) 383-1281.
JANET SNOW & ASSOCIATES, 327 Reeves Dr., Beverly Hills, CA 90212; (213) 552-0082.
VACANTI/McMAHON COMMUNICATIONS, 2700 Cahuenga Blvd., Los Angeles, CA 90068; (213) 850-1990.
VIDEO MARKETING NEWSLETTER, 1680 Vine St., Suite 820, Hollywood, CA 90028; (213) 462-6350.
VIDEO MONITORING SERVICES OF AMERICA, 2301 W. Third St., Los Angeles, CA 90057; (213) 380-5011.
WESTERN INTERNATIONAL RESEARCH, 8544 Sunset Blvd., Los Angeles, CA 90069; (213) 659-5711.
WORLD CLASS SPORTS, 9171 Wilshire Blvd., Suite 404, Beverly Hills, CA 90210; (213) 278-2010.

NEW YORK

MARKET RESEARCH CORP. OF AMERICA, 4 Landmark Sq., Stamford, CT; (203) 324-9600; (212) 582-0065; 624 S. Michigan Ave., Chicago, IL 60605, (312) 939-1500.
CERTIFIED MARKETING SERVICES, INC. (CMS), Route 9, Kinderhook, NY 12106; (518) 758-6405. (National field coverage for in-theatre research/audience reaction cards and tabulation. Trailer monitoring and tracking programs.) William P. Smith, pres.; Bridget Flynn, research dir.; Donna Card, mgr.
NIELSEN, A. C., CO., Nielsen Plaza, Northbrook, IL 60062, (312) 498-6300; 1290 Ave. of the Americas, New York, NY 10019, (212) 956-2500; 6255 Sunset Blvd., Los Angeles, CA 90028; (213) 466-4391.
OPINION RESEARCH CORP., Research Park, Princeton, NJ 08540; (212) 489-1955; (609) 924-5900.
POLITZ, ALFRED, MEDIA STUDIES, 300 Park Ave. South, New York, NY 10010; (212) 982-7600.
THE PULSE OF BROADCASTING, 150 E. 58 St., New York, NY 10022; (212) 980-4618.
ROPER ORGANIZATION, THE, 205 E. 42 St., New York, NY 10017; (212) 599-0700.
SINDLINGER & CO., INC., 405 Osborne St., Wallingford, PA 19086; (215) 565-0247.
STARCH INRA HOOPER, INC., East Boston Post Rd., Mamaroneck, NY 10543; (914) 698-0800.
VIDEODEX, INC., 445 W. 45 St., New York, NY 10017; (212) 687-8837; 342 Madison Ave., New York, NY 10002; (212) 408-3379.

Merchandisers

DISNEY, WALT, PRODUCTIONS, (Character Merchandising Division), 500 Madison Ave., New York, NY 10022; (212) 593-8900.
HARVEY FAMOUS CARTOONS, 888 Seventh Ave., New York, NY 10019; (212) 582-2244.
LICENSING COMPANY OF AMERICA, 75 Rockefeller Plaza, New York, NY 10019; (212) 484-8807; 4000 Warner Blvd., Burbank, CA 91522; (818) 954-6640.
LUCASFILM LICENSING, P.O. Box 2009, San Rafael, CA 94912; (415) 662-1800.

Music, Music Libraries and Music Cutting

AQUARIUS MUSIC PRODS., 12 E. 46 St., New York, NY 10017; (212) 581-0123.
ARIES SOUND INTERNATIONAL, 245 E. 63 St., New York, NY 10021; (212) 838-4940.
EMIL ASCHER, INC., 145 E. 49th St., New York, NY 10017; (212) 750-9339.
ASSOCIATED PRODUCTION MUSIC, 888 Seventh Ave., New York, NY 10106; (212) 977-5680; 6255 Sunset Blvd., Hollywood, CA 90028; (213) 461-3211.
AUDIO DIRECTORS, INC., 325 W. 19 St., New York, NY 10011; (212) 924-5850.

CHAPELL MUSIC LIBRARY, 810 Seventh Ave., New York, NY 10019; (212) 399-7373.

CORELLI-JACOBS FILM MUSIC INC., 25 W. 45 St., New York, NY 10036; (212) 382-0220.

DE WOLFE MUSIC LIBRARY, 25 W. 45 St., New York, NY 10036; (212) 382-0220.

ELIAS ASSOCIATES 6 W. 20 St., New York, NY 10011; (212) 807-6151.

FILM SCORES BY JERRY MARKOE, 11 Fort George Hill 13c, New York, NY 10040; (212) 942-0004. Jerry Markoe, composer-conductor.

HASTINGS SOUND EDITORIAL INC., (914) 478-0227.

KARP, MICHAEL, MUSIC, INC., 260 W. 39 St., New York, NY 10018; (212) 840-3285.

NORMAN KASOW-MUSIC/SFX, INC., 460 W. 42 St., New York, NY 10036; (212) 279-2000.

LAVSKY MUSIC, 16 E. 42 St., New York, NY 10017; (212) 697-9800.

MSP MUSIC, INC., 476 Broadway, New York, NY 10013; (212) 226-1030.

MUSIC HOUSE INC., 16 E. 42 St., New York, NY 10017; (212) 697-9800.

PICTURE SCORES, INC., 42 W. 38 St., New York, NY 10018; (212) 869-5885.

PISCES MUSIC LTD., 12 E. 46 St., New York, NY 10017; (212) 682-1860.

ROSS-GAFFNEY, INC., 21 W. 46 St., New York, NY, 10036; (212) 719-2744.

SLP & CO., 19 W. 36 St., New York, NY 10018; (212) 714- 1710.

SCORE PRODUCTIONS, INC., 249 E. 49 St., New York, NY 10017; (212) 751-2510.

SOUND PATROL, LTD., 6 E. 39 St., New York, NY 10016; (212) 213-6666.

SOUND SHOP, 321 W. 44 St., New York, NY 10036; (212) 757-5700.

VALENTINO, THOMAS J., INC, 151 W. 46 St., New York, NY 10036; (212) 869-5210.

Properties and Scenery

LOS ANGELES

ANTIQUARIAN TRADERS WAREHOUSE, 4851 S. Alameda St., Los Angeles, CA 90058; (213) 627-2144.

ANTIQUE & CLASSIC CAR RENTALS, 611 W. Vernon Ave., Los Angeles, CA 90037; (213) 232-7211.

BEVERLY HILLS FOUNTAIN CENTER, 7856 Santa Monica Blvd., Los Angeles, CA 90046; (213) 651-5252.

BREUNERS FURNITURE RENTAL, 14255 Ventura Blvd., Sherman Oaks, CA 91423; 3281 Wilshire Blvd., Los Angeles, CA 90010; (818) 382-8262.

BRICK PRICE'S MOVIE MINIATURES (WONDERWORKS), 7231 Remmet Ave., #F, Canoga Park, CA 91303-1532; (818) 992-8811.

CAMERA READY CARS, 1577 Placentia, Newport Beach, CA 92663; (714) 645-4700.

CARTHAY SET SERVICES, 5176 Santa Monica Blvd., Los Angeles, CA 90029; (213) 469-7475.

CINEMAFLOAT, 1624 W. Ocean Front, Newport Beach, CA 92663; (714) 675-8888.

CONTINENTAL SCENERY, 1022 N. La Brea Ave., Los Angeles, CA 90038; (213) 464-4139.

EXPENDABLE SUPPLY STORE, 1316 N. Western Ave., Hollywood, CA 90027; (213) 465-3191; 7830 N. San Fernando Rd., Sun Valley, CA 91352; (818) 767-5065; (213) 875-2409.

FLORA SET, INC., 1021 N. McCadden Pl., Los Angeles, CA. (213) 465-9480. Specializes in artificial foliage.

GROSH, R. L. (Scenic Studios), 4114 Sunset Blvd.; Los Angeles CA, 90029; (213) 662-1134.

HB VENDING MACHINES, 10623 Magnolia Blvd., North Hollywood, CA 91601; (818) 766-3400; 877-5841.

HAND PROP ROOM, INC., 5700 Venice Blvd., Los Angeles, CA 90019; (213) 931-1534; 938-2982.

HISTORY FOR HIRE, 11401 Chandler Blvd., North Hollywood, CA 91601; (818) 762-9937.

HOLLYWOOD CENTRAL PROPS, 525 W. Elk Ave., Glendale, CA 91204; (818) 240-4504.

HOLLYWOOD PICTURE VEHICLES, 7046 Darby Ave., Reseda, CA 91301; (818) 506-7562.

HOUSE OF PROPS, 1117 Gower St., Hollywood, CA 90038; (213) 463-3166.

INDEPENDENT STUDIO SERVICES, 11907 Wicks St., Sun Valley, CA 91352; (818) 764-0840; 768-5711.

KREISS COLLECTION, 8619 Melrose Ave., Los Angeles, CA 90069-5010; (213) 656-1606.

MGM/UA COMMUNICATIONS, 10000 Washington Blvd., Culver City, CA 90230; (213) 280-6000.

MINIATURE ESTATES, 1451 S. Robertson Blvd., Los Angeles, CA 90035; (213) 552-2200.

MODERN PROPS, 4063 Redwood Ave., Los Angeles, CA 90066; (213) 306-1400.

NIGHTS OF NEON, 7337 Varna Ave., N. Hollywood, CA 91605; (818) 982-3592.

OMEGA CINEMA PROPS., 5857 Santa Monica, Blvd., Los Angeles, 90038; (213) 466-8201.

PROP CITY/LAIRD INT'L STUDIOS, 9336 W. Washington Blvd., Culver City, CA 90230; (213) 466-3350.

PROP MASTERS, INC., 420 S. First St., Burbank, CA 91502; (818) 846-3915.

PROP SERVICES WEST INC., 915 N. Citrus Ave., Los Angeles, CA 90038; (213) 461-3371.

ROSCHU, 6514 Santa Monica Blvd., Los Angeles 90038; (213) 469-2749.

SCENERY WEST, 1126 N. Citrus Ave., Hollywood, CA 90038; (213) 467-7495.

SCENIC ARTS, 5005 Exposition Blvd., Los Angeles, CA 90016; (213) 731-1151.

SCENIC EXPRESS, 12435 Foothill Blvd., Sylmar, CA 91342; (818) 897-4322.

SILVESTRI STUDIOS, 1733 Cordova, Los Angeles, CA 90007; (213) 735-1481.

SPECIAL EFFECTS UNLIMITED, 752 N. Cahuenga Blvd., Los Angeles, CA 90038; (213) 466-3361.

STUDIO PICTURE VEHICLES, 10901 Sherman Way, Sun Valley, CA 91352; (818) 765-1201; 781-4223.

TRIANGLE SCENERY/DRAPERY/LIGHTING CO., 1215 Bates Ave., Los Angeles, CA 90029; (213) 662-8129.

NEW YORK

ATI MEDICAL STUDIO RENTALS, 532 Fifth Ave., Pelham, NY 10803; (914) 738-5777.

ADVERTISING IN MOVIES INC., Kaufman Astoria Studios, 34-12 36th St., Astoria, Queens, NY 11106; (718) 729-9288.

ALTMAN'S LUGGAGE, 135 Orchard St., New York, NY 10002; (212) 254-7275.

ANTIQUE & CLASSIC AUTOS, (Leonard Shiller), 811 Union St., Brooklyn, NY 11215; (718) 788-3400.

ARTS & CRAFTERS INC., 175 Johnson St., Brooklyn, NY 11201; (718) 875-8151.

BROOKLYN MODEL WORKS, 60 Washington Ave., Brooklyn, NY 11205; (718) 834-1944.

CENTRE FIREARMS CO, INC., 10 W. 37 St., New York, NY 10018; (212) 244-4040.

CINEMA GALLERIES, 517 W. 35 St., New York, NY 10001; (212) 627-1222.

CINEMA WORLD PRODUCTS, INC., 2621 Palisade Ave., Riverdale, NY 10463; (212) 548-1928.

DARROW'S FUN ANTIQUES, 309 E. 61 St., New York, NY 10021; (212) 838-0730.

DIMMLER STUDIO, (718) 387-9788.

EAST COAST FILM CARS, 749-53 Hicks St., Brooklyn, NY 11231; (718) 624-6050.

ECLECTIC/ENCORE PROPERTIES INC., 620 W. 26 St., 4th floor, New York, NY 10001; (212) 645-8880.

GALI KITCHEN RENTAL EQUIPMENT, INC., 404 E. 88 St., New York, NY 10028; (212) 289-5405.

GREAT AMERICAN SALVAGE CO., 34 Cooper Sq., New York, NY 10003; (212) 505-0070.

GEORGE J. KEMPLER CO., INC., 160 Fifth Ave., New York, NY 10010; (212) 989-1180.

KUTTNER ANTIQUES INC., 56 W. 22 St., New York, NY 10010; (212) 242-7969.

MARONE, RICHARD, POLICE MOTORCYCLES & EQUIPMENT, Bellmore, Long Island, NY 11710; (516) 783-7181.

MERCURY NEON SIGN SHOP, 86 Hester St., New York, NY 10002; (212) 219-0542.

OMNI PROPS, 179 Grand St., Brooklyn, NY 11211; (718) 387-3744.

PICTURE CARS, EAST, 156 Sixth Ave., Brooklyn, NY 11215; (718) 852-2300.

THE PROP HOUSE, INC., 653 Eleventh Ave., New York, NY 10036; (212) 713-0760.

PROPS FOR TODAY, 15 W. 20 St., New York, NY 10011; (212) 206-0330.

RENT-A-THING, Box 337, Rt. 6, Baldwin Pl., New York, NY 10505; (914) 628-9298.

SCHOEPFER STUDIO, 120 W. 31 St., New York, NY 10001; (212) 736-6934.

SHOWROOM OUTLET, 625/35 W. 55 St., New York, NY 10019; (212) 581-0570.

STARBUCK STUDIO, 162 W. 21 St., New York, NY 10011; (212) 807-7299.

VISUAL SERVICES, 40 W. 72 St., New York, NY 10023; (212) 580-9551.

WEAPONS SPECIALISTS, 61 Lexington Ave., New York, NY 10010; (212) 683-9349.

Rental Studios and Production Facilities

ATLANTA

LIGHTING & PRODUCTION EQUIPMENT, INC., 1676 DeFoor Circle; 30316; (404) 352-0464.

BOSTON

FILMARTS STUDIO & PRODUCTION CENTER, 1380 Soldiers Field Rd., Boston, MA 01235; (617) 783-3535; FAX: (617) 782-8860.

LOS ANGELES

BURBANK STUDIOS, 4000 Warner Blvd., Burbank, CA 91522; (213) 954-6000.

CARTHAY STUDIOS, INC., 5903-07 W. Pico Blvd., Los Angeles 90035; (213) 938-2101.

CBS/FOX STUDIOS, 4024 N. Radford Ave., Studio City, CA 91604; (818) 760-5000.

CHAPLIN STAGE, 1416 N. La Brea Ave., Hollywood, CA 90028; (213) 469-2411; 856-2682.

CINEWORKS-SUPERSTAGE, 5724 Santa Monica Blvd., Los Angeles, CA 90038; (213) 464-0296.

COLUMBIA PICTURES INDUSTRIES, 4000 Warner Blvd., Columbia Plaza S., Burbank, 91505; (213) 954-6000.

CULVER CITY STUDIOS, INC., 9336 W. Washington, Culver City, CA 90230; (213) 836-5537.

FALCON STUDIOS, 5526 Hollywood Blvd., Los Angeles, CA 90028; (213) 469-9701.

GLENDALE STUDIOS, 1239 S. Glendale Ave., Glendale, CA 91205; (818) 502-5300.

GOLDWYN, SAMUEL STUDIOS, 1041 N. Formosa Ave., Los Angeles, CA 90046; (213) 850-2999.

HAWK'S SOUND STUDIOS, 1041 N. Orange Dr., Hollywood, CA 90036; (213) 463-3288.

HOLLYWOOD CENTER STUDIOS, INC., 1040 N. Las Palmas Ave., Los Angeles, CA 90038; (213) 469-5000.

HOLLYWOOD GENERAL STUDIOS, 1040 N. Las Palmas Ave., Los Angeles, CA 90038; (213) 469-9011; 463-7191.

LEE PANAVISION INTERNATIONAL, 3800 W. Alameda Ave., Suite 1120, Burbank, CA 90038; (818) 972-3600; 972-3624.

MGM/UA COMMUNICATIONS, 10000 W. Washington Blvd., Culver City, CA 90230; (213) 836-3000; 558-5000.

MELROSE STAGE, 4361 Melrose Ave., Los Angeles, CA 90020; (213) 660-8466.

MOLE-RICHARDSON CO., 937 N. Sycamore Ave., Los Angeles 90038; (213) 654-3060.

PARAMOUNT PICTURES CORP., 5555 Melrose Ave., Los Angeles, CA 90038; (213) 468-5000.

PRODUCERS STUDIO, INC., 650 N. Bronson Ave., Los Angeles, CA 90004; (213) 466-8111.

RALEIGH STUDIOS, 650 N. Bronson Ave., Los Angeles, CA 90004; (213) 466-3111.

REN-MAR STUDIOS, 846 N. Cahuenga Blvd., Los Angeles, CA 90038; (213) 463-0808.

S.A. GLOBAL STUDIOS, 201 N. Occidental Blvd., Los Angeles, CA 90026; (213) 384-3331.

S.I.R. MUSIC FILM STUDIOS, INC., 6048 Sunset Blvd., Hollywood, CA 90028; (213) 466-3417; 466-1314.

STAGE 15, 1015 N. Cahuenga Blvd., Hollywood, CA 90038; (213) 466-9015.

U.P.A. STUDIOS, INC., 1875 Century Park E. #2140, Los Angeles, CA, 90067; (213) 556-3800.

UNIVERSAL CITY STUDIOS, 100 Universal City Plaza, Universal City, 91608; (818) 777-3000.

THE VALENCIA STUDIOS, 28343 Ave. Crocker, Valencia, CA 91355; (800) 257-1202.

MIAMI

GREAT SOUTHERN STUDIOS, 15221 N.E. 21 Ave., N. Miami Beach, FL 33162; (305) 944-2464.

LIMELIGHT, 7335 N.W. 41st St., Miami, FL 33666; (305) 593-6969.

LUKE MOBERLY STUDIOS AND PRODUCTIONS, 4810 S.W. 54, Ft. Lauderdale, FL; (305) 581-7508.

NEW YORK

ATELIER FOURTH ST. STAGES, 295 W. 4 St., New York, NY 10014; (212) 243-3550.

BOKEN SOUND STUDIO, 513 W. 54 St., New York, NY 10019; (212) 581-5507; 111 LeRoy St., New York, NY 10014; (212) 924-0438; 511 W. 55 St., New York, NY 10019; (212) 247-0170.

BREITROSE-SELTZER STAGES, INC., 383 W. 12 St., New York, NY 10014; (212) 807-0664.

BROADWAY STUDIOS, 25-09 Broadway, Astoria, New York, NY 11106; (718) 274-9121.

CAMERA MART STAGES, 460 W. 54 St., New York, NY 10019; (212) 757-6977.

CESTARE STUDIOS, INC., 188 Henricks Rd., Mineola, NY 11501; (516) 742-5550.

CINE STUDIO, 241 W. 54 St., New York, NY 10019; (212) 581-1916.

COM/TECH, 770 Lexington Ave., New York, NY 10021; (212) 826-2935.

DE FILIPPO STUDIO, 215 E. 37 St., New York, NY 10016; (212) 986-5444.

FARKAS FILMS, INC., 385 Third Ave., New York, NY 10016; (212) 679-8211.

HBO STUDIO PRODS., 120 E. 23 St., 10010; (212) 512-7800.

HORVATH & ASSOCIATES STUDIOS LTD., 95 Charles St., New York, NY 10014; (212) 741-0300.

INTERNATIONAL PRODUCTION, CENTER, 514 W. 57 St., New York, NY 10019; (212) 582-6530.

KAUFMAN ASTORIA MOTION PICTURE AND TELEVISION PRODUCTION CENTER, 34-12 36th St., Astoria, NY 11106; (212) 392-5600.

LRP VIDEO, 3 Dag Hammarskjold Plaza, New York, NY 10017; (212) 759-0822.

LITTLE HOUSE, ASTORIA, 11-44 31st Ave., Astoria, NY 11106; (718) 726-3231.

MAGNO SOUND & VIDEO, 729 Seventh Ave., 10019; (212) 302-2505.

MATRIX VIDEO, 727 Eleventh Ave., New York, NY 10019; (212) 254-8500.

MODERN TELECOMMUNICATIONS/MTI, 885 Second Ave., New York, NY 10017; (212) 355-0510.

MOTHERS SOUND STAGE, 210 E. 5 St., New York, NY 10003; (212) 260-2050.

NATIONAL VIDEO CENTER/RECORDING STUDIOS, INC., 460 W. 42 St., New York, NY 10036; (212) 279-2000.

THE 95TH STREET STUDIO, INC., 206 E. 95 St., New York, NY 10028; (212) 831-1946.

OVERLAND STAGE COMPANY, 511 W. 54 St., New York, NY 10019; (212) 581-4469.

PHOENIX STAGES, 537 W. 59 St., New York, NY 10019; (212) 581-7670.

PRIMALUX VIDEO & FILM, 30 W. 26 St., New York, NY 10010; (212) 206-1402.

PRODUCTION CENTER, 221 W. 26 St., New York, NY 10001; (212) 675-2211.

REEVES COMMUNICATIONS, 708 Third Ave., New York, NY 10017; (212) 573-8600.

RIVERVIEW STUDIOS, 30-15 Vernon Blvd., Astoria, NY 11102; (718) 573-8600.

SMA VIDEO INC., 84 Wooster St., New York, NY 10012; (212) 226-7474.

SHINBONE ALLEY STAGE, 680 Broadway, New York, NY 10012; (212) 420-8463.

SILVERCUP STUDIOS, 42-25 21st St., Long Island City, NY 11101; (718) 784-3390.

STUDIO 39, 144 E. 39 St., New York, NY 10016; (212) 685-1770.

SYNAPSE TELECOMMUNICATIONS INC., 304 E. 45 St., New York, NY 10017; (212) 370-9191.

TELETECHNIQUES, INC., 1 W. 19 St., New York, NY 10011; (212) 206-1475; 633-1868.

3-G STAGE CORP., 236 W. 61 St., New York, NY 10023; (212) 247-3130.

TITRA SOUND CORPORATION, 1600 Broadway, NY 10019; (212) 757-7129.

UNITED FILM ENTERPRISES, INC., 37 W. 57 St., New York, NY 10019; (212) 758-0870.

UNITEL VIDEO INC., 515 W. 57 St., New York, NY 10019; (212) 265-3600.

VCA TELETRONICS, CENTER STAGE, 503 W. 33 St., New York, NY 10001; (212) 736-7677; 736-7717.

VERITAS STUDIOS, 527 W. 45 St., New York, NY 10036; (212) 581-2050.

VIDEO PLANNING PLUS!, 325 W. 56 St., New York, NY 10019; (212) 582-5066.

WALLACH, PETER, PRODS., 419 Broome St., New York, NY 10013; (212) 966-1970.

ORLANDO

WALT DISNEY/MGM STUDIOS, P.O. Box 10200, Lake Buena Vista, FL 32830-0200; (407) 560-5353.

TEMPE, AZ

WONDER BROTHERS, 2244 S. Industrial Park Ave., Tempe, AZ 85282; (602) 921-0139.

Screening Rooms

ATLANTA

CINEVISION CORP., 1771 Tully Circle, N.E., Atlanta 30329; (404) 321-6333.
20th-CENTURY FOX EXCHANGE, 2200 Century Parkway, 30345; (404) 321-1178.

BOSTON

BOSTON LIGHT & SOUND, 124 Brighton Ave., #134; Boston, MA 02134; (617) 787-3131.
E.M. LOEW THEATRES, 164 Tremont St., Boston, 02111; (617) 482-9200.
UNIVERSAL FILM EXCHANGE, 44 Winchester St., 02116; (617) 426-8760.

CHICAGO

CHICAGO INTERNATIONAL FILM FESTIVAL, 235 Eugenie, Chicago 60614; (312) 644-3400.
ESSANESS THEATRES CORPORATION, 54 West Randolph, Chicago 60601; (312) 332-7465.

KANSAS CITY

COMMONWEALTH THEATRES, 215 W. 18th St., 64108; (816) 474-3050.
DICKINSON OPERATING CO., 5913 Woodson Rd., Mission, KS 66202; (913) 432-2334.

LOS ANGELES

ACADEMY AWARD THEATRE, 8949 Wilshire Blvd., Beverly Hills, 90211; (213) 278-8990.
AIDIKOFF, CHAS., SCREENING ROOM, 9255 W. Sunset Blvd., 90069; (213) 274-0866.
AMERICAN FILM INSTITUTE, 2021 N. Western Ave., Los Angeles, CA 90027; (213) 856-7600.
BEVERLY HILLS SCREENING ROOM, 8949 Sunset Blvd., Beverly Hills, CA 90069; (213) 275-3088.
BURBANK STUDIOS, 4000 Warner Blvd., Burbank, CA 91522; (818) 954-6000.
CENTRE FILMS INC., 1103 N. El Centro Ave., Hollywood 90038; (213) 466-5123.
CONSOLIDATED FILM INDUSTRIES, 959 Seward St., Los Angeles 90038; (213) 462-3161.
DAUGHERTY AUDIO/VIDEO DESIGN, 2172 Ridgemont, Los Angeles, CA 90046; (213) 650-5665; 718-5531.
DE LUXE GENERAL, 1546 N. Argyle Ave., Los Angeles 90028; (213) 462-6171.
DIRECTORS GUILD OF AMERICA, 7950 W. Sunset Blvd., Los Angeles 90046; (213) 656-1220.
HARRAH'S THEATRE SERVICE & SUPPLY, 624B S. San Fernando Blvd., Burbank, CA 91502; (818) 842-5111.
HOLLY-VINE SCREENING ROOM, 6253 Hollywood Blvd., Los Angeles, CA 90028; (213) 462-3498.
HOLLYWOOD SCREENING ROOM, 1800 N. Highland Ave., Suite 509, Hollywood 90028; (213) 466-1888.
JDH WORLD, 12156 Olympic Blvd., Los Angeles 90064; (213) 820-8802.
MARTIN NOSSECK PROJECTION THEATRE, 9118½ Sunset Blvd., Hollywood, 90069; (213) 275-3037.
PREVIEW HOUSE, 7655 Sunset Blvd., Los Angeles 90046; (213) 876-6600.
RALEIGH STUDIOS, 650 N. Bronson Ave., Los Angeles, CA 90004; (213) 466-3111.
SAMUEL GOLDWYN THEATRE, 8949 Wilshire Blvd., Beverly Hills, CA 90211; (213) 278-8990.
JOE SHORE'S SCREENING ROOM, 9118½ W. Sunset Blvd., Los Angeles 90069; (213) 274-4888.

MILWAUKEE

MARCUS THEATRES, 212 W. Wisconsin Ave., 53203; (414) 272-6020.

RKO-STANLEY WARNER THEATRES, INC., 5341 W. Fond du Lac Avenue (Capitol Court Theater); (414) 871-2213.

NEW YORK

(All major producers-distributors have screening rooms at their home offices in New York for their own use. Most also have screening room facilities at their New York exchanges).
CINE-METRIC THEATRE CORP., 290 Madison Ave., New York, NY 10017; (212) 532-4140.
MAGNO PREVIEW THEATRE, 1600 Broadway, New York, NY 10019; (212) 302- 2505.
MAGNO SOUND SCREENING ROOM, 729 Seventh Ave., New York, NY 10019; (212) 302-2505.
MOVIELAB THEATRE SERVICE, INC., 619 W. 54 St., New York, NY 10019; (212) 586-0360.
NAVESYNC SOUND, 513 W. 54 St., New York, NY 10019; (212) 246-0100.
PRECISION FILM LABS' SCREENING THEATRE, 630 Ninth Ave., New York, NY, 10036; (212) 489-8800.
PREVIEW THEATRE, 1600 Broadway, New York, NY 10019; (212) 246-0865.
ROSS-GAFFNEY INC., 21 W. 46 St., New York, NY 10036; (212) 582-3744.
TECHNICOLOR, 321 W. 44 St., New York, NY 10036; (212) 582-7310.

SAN FRANCISCO

THE EXPLORATORIUM, McBEAN THEATER, 3601 Lyon St., San Francisco, CA 94123; (415) 561-0348.
MOTION PICTURE SERVICE CO., 125 Hyde St., San Francisco, CA 94107; (415) 673-9162.
PACIFIC FILM ARCHIVE, 2625 Durant Ave., Berkeley, CA 94720; (415) 642-1412.

WASHINGTON

CAPITAL FILM LABORATORIES, INC., 470 "E" St., S.W., 20002; (202) 347-1717.

ORLANDO

WALT DISNEY/MGM STUDIOS, P.O. Box 10200, Lake Buena Vista, FL 32830; (407) 560-5353.

Slides-Telops

BEBELL LABS, 420 E. 55th St., New York, NY 10022; (212) 486-6577.

Sound and Recording Services

DETROIT

MOTION PICTURE SOUND INC., (MPS), 3026 E. Grand Blvd., Detroit, MI 48202; (313) 873-4655.

HOLLYWOOD

ALTEC, 1515 S. Manchester Ave., Anaheim; (714) 630-8130.
ARTISAN SOUND RECORDERS, 1600 N. Wilcox Ave., Hollywood 90028; (213) 461-2751.
AUDIO EFFECTS COMPANY, 1600 N. Western Ave., Hollywood 90027; (213) 469-3692. (Complete recording services).
B & B SOUND STUDIOS, 3610 W. Magnolia Blvd., Burbank, CA 91505; (818) 848-4496.
BARNUM RECORDING STUDIO, 1944 N. Cahuenga Blvd., Hollywood, CA 90028; (213) 462-0723.
BURBANK STUDIOS, THE, 4000 Warner Blvd., Burbank, CA 91522; (818) 954-6000.
CALIFORNIA RECORDING STUDIOS, 5203 Sunset Blvd., Los Angeles, CA 90027; (213) 666-1244.
CINESOUND, 915 N. Highland Ave., Hollywood, CA 90038; (213) 464-1155.
COLUMBIA PICTURES TELEVISION, 300 S. Colgens Square, Burbank, 91522; (213) 954-6000.
COMPACT VIDEO SERVICES, 2813 Alameda Ave., Burbank, CA 91505; (818) 840-7000; (800) 423-2277; FAX: (818) 846-5197.

CONSOLIDATED FILM INDUSTRIES, 959 N. Seward St., Los Angeles 90038; (213) 462-3161.
DOLBY LABORATORIES, INC., 1610 N. Las Palmas Ave., Los Angeles, CA 90028; (213) 464-4596.
GLEN GLENN SOUND CO., 900 N. Seward St., Hollywood, CA 90038; (213) 469-7221.
MGM/UA COMMUNICATIONS, 10000 W. Washington Blvd., Culver City, CA 90230; (213) 836-3000.
NEWJACK SOUND RECORDERS, 1956 N. Cahuenga Blvd., Los Angeles, CA 90068; (213) 466-6141.
PARAMOUNT RECORDING STUDIOS, 6245 Santa Monica Blvd., Hollywood, CA 90038; (213) 461-3717.
PRODUCERS 1 & 2 RECORDING STUDIOS, 6035 Hollywood Blvd., Los Angeles, CA 90028; (213) 466-7766.
QUALITY SOUND, 5625 Melrose Ave., Los Angeles, CA 90038; (213) 467-7154.
RYDER SOUND SERVICES, INC., 1611 Vine St., Hollywood, CA; (213) 469-3511.
SCOTTSOUND, INC., 6110 Santa Monica Blvd., Los Angeles, CA 90038; (213) 462-6981.
SOUND CASTLE RECORDING STUDIO, 2840 Rowena Ave., Los Angeles, CA 90039; (213) 665-5201.
SOUND SERVICES, INC., (SSI), 7155 Santa Monica Blvd., Los Angeles, CA 90046; (213) 874-9344.
SOUNDS UNLIMITED, P.O. Box 69C, West Hollywood, CA 90069; (213) 659-9578.
TTG RECORDING STUDIOS, 1441 N. McCadden Pl., Los Angeles, CA 90028; (213) 464-7391.
TODD-AO GLEN-GLEN STUDIOS, 1021 N. Seward St., Hollywood, CA 90038; (213) 463-1136.
UNIVERSAL CITY STUDIOS, 100 Universal City Plaza, Universal City, CA 91608; (213) 985-4321.
WARNER HOLLYWOOD STUDIOS, 1041 N. Formosa, Los Angeles, CA 90046; (213) 850-2500.

NEW YORK

A & J RECORDING STUDIOS, INC., 225 W. 57 St., New York, NY 10019; (212) 247-4860.
AR-VEE SOUND SERVICES, 630 Ninth Ave., #400, New York, NY 10036; (212) 459-9588.
AQUARIUS TRANSFER, 12 E. 46 St., New York, NY 10017; (212) 581-0123.
THE AUDIO DEPARTMENT, 119 W. 57 St., New York, NY 10019; (212) 586-3503.
AURA RECORDING, INC., 136 W. 52 St., New York, NY 10019; (212) 582-8105.
BEE VEE SOUND INC., 211 E. 43 St., #603, New York, NY 10017; (212) 949-9170.
BLANK TAPES, INC., RECORDING STUDIOS, 37 W. 20 St., New York, NY 10011; (212) 255-5313.
CP SOUND, 200 Madison Ave., New York, NY 10016; (212) 532- 5528.
CINEQUIP, INC., 241 E. 51 St., New York, NY 10022; (212) 308-5100.
CORELLI-JACOBS RECORDING, 25 W. 45 St., New York, NY 10036; (212) 382-0220.
CREATIVE AUDIO RECORDING SERVICES, 19 W. 36 St., New York, NY 10018; (212) 714-0976.
CUE RECORDINGS, INC., 1156 Ave. of the Americas, New York, NY 10036; (212) 921-9221.
DB SOUND STUDIOS, INC., 25 W. 45 St., New York, NY 10036; (212) 764-6000.
DOLBY LABORATORIES INC., 10 Downing St., #5J, New York, NY 10014; (212) 645-1522.
DOWNTOWN TRANSFER, 167 Perry St., New York, NY 10014; (212) 255-8698.
EAST SIDE FILM & VIDEO CENTER, 216 E. 45 St., New York, NY 10017; (212) 867-0730.
ELECTRO-NOVA PRODUCTIONS, 342 Madison Ave., New York, NY 10017; (212) 687-5838.
EMPIRE SOUND, 18 W. 45 St., New York, NY 10036; (212) 302-2505.
HIT FACTORY, THE, INC., 237 W. 54 St., 10019; (212) 664-1000.
IBERO-AMERICAN PRODUCTIONS, 630 Ninth Ave., New York, NY 10036; (212) 245-7826.
MAGNO SOUND & VIDEO, 729 Seventh Ave., 10019; (212) 302-2505.
THE MIX PLACE, 663 Fifth Ave., New York, NY 10022; (212) 759-8311.
NATIONAL VIDEO CENTER RECORDING STUDIOS, 460 W. 42 St., New York, NY 10036; (212) 279-2000.
NAVESYNC SOUND, 513 W. 54 St., New York, NY 10019; (212) 246-0100.
NEP PRODUCTIONS, INC., 56 W. 45 St., New York, NY 10036; (212) 382-1100.
NEW BREED STUDIOS, 251 W. 30 St., New York, NY 10001; (212) 714-9379.
PHOTO MAG. SOUND STUDIOS, 222 E. 44 St., New York, NY 10017; (212) 687-9030.

PRINCZKO PRODUCTIONS, 9 E. 38 St., New York, NY 10016; (212) 683-1300.
RKO SOUND STUDIOS, 1440 Broadway, New York, NY 10018; (212) 564-8000.
REGENT SOUND STUDIOS, 1619 Broadway, New York, NY 10019; (212) 245-2630.
ROSS-GAFFNEY, INC., 21 W. 46 St., New York, NY 10018; (212) 582-3745.
SCHWARTZ, HOWARD M., RECORDING, INC., 420 Lexington Ave., New York, NY 10017; (212) 687-4180.
SOUND ONE CORP., 1619 Broadway, New York, NY 10019; (212) 765-4757.
SOUND PATROL, LTD., 6 E. 39 St., New York, NY 10016; (212) 213-6666.
SOUND SHOP, THE, 321 W. 44 St., New York, NY 10036; (212) 757-5700.
TITRA SOUND CORP., 1600 Broadway, New York, NY 10019; (212) 757-7129.
TODD-AO STUDIOS EAST, 259 W. 54 St., New York, NY 10019; (212) 265-6225.
TRACK TRANSFERS, INC., 45 W. 45 St., New York, NY 10036; (212) 921-7878.
TRANSFERMATION STUDIOS, INC., 17 E. 45 St., New York, NY 10017; (212) 687-6500.
UNITED RECORDING, 681 Fifth Ave., New York, NY 10036; (212) 751-4660.
THOMAS J. VALENTINO, 151 W. 46 St., #803, 10036; (212) 869-5210.
VOICES, 16 E. 48 St., New York, NY 10017; (212) 935-9820.
WAREHOUSE RECORDING, 320 W. 46 St., New York, NY 10036; (212) 265-6060.

ORLANDO

WALT DISNEY/MGM STUDIOS, P.O. Box 10200, Lake Buena Vista, FL 32830; (407) 560-5353.

SAN FRANCISCO

DOLBY LABORATORIES, INC.Head Office & U.S. Sales, 100 Potrero Ave., 94103; (415) 558-0200; Telex: 34409.
LUCASFILM LTD. (Sprocket Systs., Inc., P.O. Box 2009, San Rafael, CA 94912; (415) 662-1800.
MUSIC ANNEX INC., 69 Green St., San Francisco, CA 94111; (415) 421-6622.
RECORDING ETC., 633 Cowper, Palo Alto, CA 94301; (415) 327-9344.
RUSSIAN HILL RECORDING, 1520 Pacific Ave., San Francisco, CA 94109; (415) 474-4520.
THE SAUL ZAENTZ FILM CENTER, 2600 Tenth St., Berkeley, CA 94710; (415) 549-2500.

TALLAHASSEE

PEGASUS SOUND STUDIOS, P.O. Box 38190, 32315; (904) 574-3350.

WASHINGTON, DC

BYRON MOTION PICTURES INC., 65 K St., N.E., 20002; (202) 429-2056.
CAPITAL FILM LABORATORIES, INC., 470 E. St., S.W., 20024; (202) 347-1717.

Special Effects
NEW YORK

APA, 230 W. 10 St., New York, NY 10014; (212) 929-9436.
ACTION PRODUCTIONS, INC., 14 E. 39 St., New York, NY 10016; (212) 684-4250.
ACTORS MAKE UP STUDIO, 165 W. 47 St., New York, NY 10036; (212) 719-3772.
ALFIE & ASSOCIATES, 222 E. 44 St., New York, NY 10017; (212) 983-2686.
AMERICAN FILM ANIMATION, 151 W. 28 St., New York, NY 10001; (212) 563-5720.
ANIMATED PRODUCTIONS, INC., 1600 Broadway, New York NY 10019; (212) 265-2942.
BROADCAST ARTS, INC., 632 Broadway, New York, NY 10012; (212) 254-5400.
BROOKLYN MODEL WORKS, 60 Washington Ave., Brooklyn, NY 11205; (718) 834-1944.
CHARLEX, 2 W. 45 St., New York, NY 10036; (212) 719-4600.

CIMMELLI INC., 120 N. Pascack Rd., Spring Valley, NY 10977; (914) 356-2232.

CLELAND STUDIO, INC., 122 Spring St., New York, NY 10012; (212) 431-9185.

D'ANDREA PRODUCTIONS INC., 20 E. 49 St., New York, NY 10017; (212) 593-0077.

DOM DE FILIPPO STUDIO, INC., 215 E. 37 St., New York, NY 10016; (212) 986-5444; 867-4220.

DENARO, SAL, AND PUPPETS, 174 DeGraw St., Brooklyn, NY 11231; (718) 875-1711.

DOROS ANIMATION STUDIO, INC., 156 Fifth Ave., Suite 1119, New York, NY 10010; (212) 627-7220.

EDITEL/NEW YORK, 222 E. 44 St., New York, NY 10017; (212) 867-4600.

EFEX SPECIALISTS, 35-39 37th St., Long Island City, NY 11101; (718) 937-2417.

EFX UNLIMITED, 321 W. 44 St., New York, NY 10036; (212) 541-9220.

EUE/SCREEN GEM PRINTS, 222 E. 44 St., New York, NY 10017; (212) 867-4030.

THE FANTASTIC ANIMATION MACHINE, INC., 12 E. 46 St., New York, NY 10017; (212) 697-2525.

FILM OPTICALS, INC., 144 E. 44 St., New York, NY 10017; (212) 697-4744.

FRIEDMAN, HAROLD CONSORTIUM, 420 Lexington Ave., New York, NY 10017; (212) 697-0858.

GATI, JOHN, FILM EFFECTS, INC., 154 W. 57 St., Suite 832, New York, NY 10019; (212) 582-9060.

GLOBUS BROTHERS STAGES, 44 W. 24 St., New York, NY 10010; (212) 243-1000.

R/GREENBERG ASSOCIATES, 350 W. 39 St., New York, NY 10018; (212) 239-6767.

HOLOGRAPHIC LASERLAND, 240 E. 26 St., New York, NY 10010; (212) 686-9397.

I.F. STUDIOS, INC., 15 W. 38 St., New York, NY 10018; (212) 819-1880.

JPC VISUALS, 11 E. 47 St., New York, NY 10017; (212) 223-0555.

KUNZ, PETER, CO., INC., SPECIAL EFFECTS. RDl Box 223, High Falls, NY 12440; (914) 687-0400.

LIBERTY STUDIOS, INC. 238 E. 26 St., New York, NY 10010; (212) 532-1865.

MS25, 516 W. 25 St., New York, NY 10001; (212) 989-2100.

MALLIE, DALE, & COMPANY, INC., 35-30 38th St., Astoria, NY 11101; (718) 706-1233.

MANTELL, PAUL, SPECIAL CREATIONS, 181 Hudson St., New York, NY 10013; (212) 645-8565.

MERCURY NEON, 86 Hester St., New York, NY 10002; (212) 219-0542.

MILLER, MICHAEL, MODEL MAKING, (718) 875-0381.

OPTICAL HOUSE, INC., 25 W. 45 St., New York, NY 10036; (212) 869-5840.

PROP EFFECTS & RIGGING, 780 Carroll St., Brooklyn, NY 11215; (718) 531-0357.

PUPPET PROJECTS, 97 Eagle St., Brooklyn, NY 11222; (718) 383-6110.

DEED ROSSITER SPECIAL EFFECTS, (914) 359-8884.

SMA VIDEO, INC., 84 Wooster St., New York, NY 10012; (212) 226-7414.

SPECIAL MAKE-UP EFFECTS STUDIO, 68 Colonial Ave., Dobbs Ferry, NY 10522; (914) 693-2752.

THEATER EFFECTS, INC., 152 W. 25 St., New York, NY 10001; (212) 242-6754.

TRILOGY DESIGN AT JSL, INC., 25 W. 45th St., New York, NY 10036; (212) 382-3592.

WALLACH, PETER, PRODS., 419 Broome St., New York, NY 10013; (212) 966-1970.

WEISS, PETER, DESIGNS, 32 Union Sq. E., New York, NY 10003; (212) 477-2659.

WIZARDWORKS, 39-40 21st St., Long Island City, NY 11101; (718) 786-8383.

ZELLER INTERNATIONAL, (212) 627-7676; (607) 363-7792.

HOLLYWOOD

ANDERSON, HOWARD A., CO., TV Center, 1016 N. Cole Ave., Hollywood, CA 90038; (213) 463-2336; 3767 Overland, #109. Culver City, CA 90034; (213) 559-4369.

APOGEE, INC., 6842 Valjean Ave., Van Nuys, CA 90066; (818) 989-5757.

CINEMA SERVICE, INC., 6518½ Santa Monica Blvd.; (213) 463-3178.

COAST SPECIAL EFFECTS, 4907 N. Lankershim Blvd., North Hollywood, 91601; (818) 762-1182.

CONSOLIDATED FILM INDUSTRIES, 959 N. Seward St., Los Angeles, CA 90038; (213) 462-3161.

ENERGY PRODUCTIONS, 2690 Beachwood Dr., Hollywood, CA 90068; (213) 462-3310.

FANTASY II FILM EFFECTS, 504 S. Varney St., Burbank, CA 91502; (818) 843-1413.

FILM FAIR, 10900 Ventura Blvd., Studio City, CA 91604; (213) 877-3191.

THE L.A. EFFECTS GROUP, INC., 14411 Vanowen St., Suite 217, Van Nuys, CA 91405; (818) 901-9677.

LASER MEDIA, 2046 Armacost, Los Angeles, CA 90025; (213) 820-3750.

MASTER FILM EFFECTS, 1034 N. Seward St., Los Angeles, CA 90038; (213) 466-4381.

MODERN FILM EFFECTS, 6860 Lexington Ave., Los Angeles, CA 90038; (213) 460-4111.

PACIFIC TITLE & ART STUDIO, 6350 Santa Monica Blvd., Los Angeles 90038; (213) 464-0121.

SCENIC EXPRESS, 12435 Foothill Blvd., Sylmar, CA 91342; (818) 897-4322.

SPECIAL EFFECTS UNLIMITED, 752 N. Cahuenga Blvd., Los Angeles, CA 90038; (213) 466-3361.

SAN RAFAEL

LUCASFILM, INDUSTRIAL LIGHT & MAGIC, P.O. Box 2009, San Rafael, CA 94912; (415) 258-2000.

ORLANDO

WALT DISNEY/MGM STUDIOS, P.O. Box 10200, Lake Buena Vista, FL 32830; (407) 560-5353.

Stop Watches

DUCOMMUN, M., CO., 48 Main St., Warwick, NY 10990; (914) 986-5757.

MARCEL WATCH CORP., 1115 Broadway, New York, NY 10010; (212) 620-8181.

RACINE, JULES & CO., 85 Executive Rd., Elmsford, NY 10523; (914) 277-8450.

Subtitles

CALIFORNIA

AND/OR, P.O. Box 445, Burbank, CA 91503; (818) 577-4142.

CAPTIONS, INC., 2479 Lanterman Terr., Los Angeles, CA 90039; (213) 665-4860.

CINETYP, INC., 843 Seward St., Hollywood, CA 90038; (213) 463-8569.

FOREIGN LANGUAGE GRAPHICS, 4099 N. Mission Rd., Los Angeles, CA 90032; (213) 221-4992.

GLOBAL LANGUAGE SERVICES, 2027 Las Lunas, Pasadena, CA 91107; (818) 792-0862.

GOOSI, 13273 Ventura Blvd., #212, Studio City, CA 91604; (818) 906-9946.

HEADLEY INTERNATIONAL PICTURES, 738 N. Cahuenga Blvd., #F, Los Angeles, CA 90038; (213) 969-9650.

HOMER AND ASSOCIATES, INC., Sunset Gower Studios, 1420 N. Beachwood Dr., Hollywood, CA 90028; (213) 462-4710.

INTEX AUDIOVISUALS, 9021 Melrose Ave., Suite 205, Los Angeles, CA 90069; (213) 271-1319.

LINGUATHEQUE OF L.A., P.O. Box 44281, Van Nuys, CA 91412; (818) 894-2882.

PACIFIC TITLE & ART STUDIO, 6350 Santa Monica Blvd., Los Angeles, CA 90038; (213) 464-5451.

ROLAND FRENCH TRANSLATION SERVICES, 10711 Wellworth Ave., Los Angeles, CA 90024; (213) 475-4547.

TITLES, P.O. Box 1151, Hollywood, CA 90028; (818) 784- 2210.

NEW YORK

THE CAPTION CENTER, 231 E. 55 St., New York, NY 10022; (212) 223-4930.

DEVLIN PRODUCTIONS, INC., 231 E. 55 St., New York, NY 10022; (212) 391-1313.

EISENMAN, HELEN, 630 Ninth Ave., Suite 909, New York, NY 10036; (212) 757-5969; 749-3655.

FRIEDMAN, SONYA, 853 Broadway, Suite 1501, New York, NY 10011; (212) 505-1990.

FIMA NOVECK PRODUCTIONS, 231 W. 44 St., 4th floor, New York, NY 10036; (212) 315-4220.

RENNERT BILINGUAL TRANSLATIONS, 2 W. 45 St., 5th floor, New York, NY 10036; (212) 819-1776.

Trailers

ATLANTA

CINEMA CONCEPTS THEATRE SERVICE, INC., P.O. Box 720576, Atlanta, GA 30328; (404) 956-7460.

CHICAGO

FILMACK CORP., 1327 S. Wabash Ave., Chicago, IL 60605; (312) 427-3395. Joseph R. Mack, pres.

KANSAS CITY, MO

NATIONAL SCREEN SERVICE GROUP, INC., 1800 Baltimore Ave., Kansas City, MO 64108; (816) 842-5893. David J. Farkes.
UNIVERSAL IMAGES, LTD., P.O. Box 9313, Kansas City, MO 64133; (816) 358-6166. (Produces advertising commercials, for showing on theatre screens, and special trailers, e.g., "No Smoking," "Intermission," etc.)

LOS ANGELES

ANDERSON, HOWARD A., CO., 1016 N. Cole Ave., Los Angeles, CA 90038; (213) 463-2336.
BOSUSTOW VIDEO, 2207 Colby Ave., West Los Angeles, CA 90064; (213) 478-0821.

COMING ATTRACTIONS, 861 Seward, Los Angeles, CA 90038; (213) 465-4129.
THE CREATIVE PARTNERSHIP, INC., 7525 Fountain Ave., Hollywood, CA 90046; (213) 850-5551.
CRUSE & CO., 7000 Romaine St., Hollywood, CA 90038; (213) 851-8814.
PABLO FERRO & ASSOCIATES, 1756 N. Sierra Bonita Ave., Hollywood, CA 90046; (213) 850-6193.
HOMER & ASSOCIATES, INC., 1420 N. Beachwood Dr., Hollywood, CA 90028; (213) 469-7307.
LAJON PRODUCTIONS, INC., 2907 W. Olive Ave., Burbank, CA 91505; (213) 841-1440.
NATIONAL SCREEN SERVICE GROUP INC., 2001 S. La Cienega Blvd., Los Angeles, CA 90034; (213) 836-1505. Mitchell Wilen.

NEW YORK CITY

EAST END PRODUCTIONS, 513 W. 54 St., New York, NY 10019; (212) 489-1865.
R/GREENBERG ASSOCIATES INC., 350 W. 39 St., New York, NY 10018; (212) 239-6767.
NATIONAL SCREEN SERVICE, GROUP INC., 1600 Broadway, New York, NY 10019; (212) 246-5700.

PHILADELPHIA

NATIONAL SCREEN SERVICE GROUP, INC., 130 Ferry Ave., Camden, NJ 08104. Patricia Chamberlain.

Talent and Literary Agencies

HOLLYWOOD

(Telephone area code is 213, unless otherwise indicated.)

ABRAMS-RUBALOFF & ASSOC., INC., 8075 West 3rd, 90048; 935-1700
ACTORS ARTISTS AGENCY, 435 S. La Cienega Blvd., Suite 201, 90048; 205-0720.
AGENCY FOR PERFORMING ARTS, 9000 Sunset Blvd., #315, 90069; 273-0744
AIMEE ENTERTAINMENT ASSOCIATES, 13743 Victory Blvd., Van Nuys, CA 91401; (818) 994-9354
ALL TALENT AGENCY, 2437 E. Washington Blvd., Pasadena, 91104; (818) 797-2422.
ALVARADO, CARLOS, AGENCY, 8820 Sunset Blvd., 90069; 652-0272
AMARAL/MURPHY AGENCY, 10000 Riverside Dr., Toluca Lake, 91602; (818) 980-1013
BLANCHARD, NINA, 7060 Hollywood Blvd., 90028; 462-7274
BLOOM, MICHAEL J., 9200 Sunset Blvd., Suite 1210, 90069; 275-6800
CALDER AGENCY, 4150 Riverside Dr., Burbank, 91505; (818) 845-7434
CAREY-PHELPS-COLVIN, 121 N. Robertson, 90211; 659-6671
CENTURY ARTISTS, LTD., 9744 Wilshire Blvd., Beverly Hills, 90212; 273-4366
THE CHASIN AGENCY, 190 N. Canon Dr., Beverly Hills, CA 90212; 278-7505.
COMMERCIALS UNLTD., INC., 7461 Beverly Blvd., 90036; 937-2220
CONTEMPORARY-KORMAN, 132 Lasky Dr., Beverly Hills 90212; 278-8250
COUGLIN AGENCY, KERWIN, 436 E. Palm Ave., #312, Burbank, 91501; (818) 848-7929
CREATIVE ARTISTS AGENCY, 1888 Century Park E. #1400, 90067; 277-4545.
CUMBER, LIL, ATTRACTIONS AGENCY, 6515 Sunset Blvd., 90028; 469-1919
CUNNINGHAM & ASSOC. 261 S. Robertson, Beverly Hills, 90211; 855-1700
DIAMOND ARTISTS AGENCY, LTD., 9200 Sunset Blvd., 90069; 278-8146
ENTERTAINMENT ENTERPRISES, 1680 Vine St., 90028; 462-6001
FELBER, WM., 2126 Cahuenga Blvd., 90068; 466-7629
FILM ARTISTS ASSOCIATES, 470 S. San Vicente Blvd., 90048; 661-6347.
FRINGS, KURT, AGENCY, 328 S. Beverly Dr., Beverly Hills, 90210; 277-1103.
GERSH AGENCY, THE, 222 N. Canon Dr., Beverly Hills, 90210; 274-6611
GOLD, HARRY & ASSOCIATES, 12725 Ventura Blvd., #E, Studio City, 91604; (818) 769-5003.
GORDEAN AGENCY, INC., 809 N. Foothill Rd., Beverly Hills, 90210; 273-4195
GREEN AGENCY, IVAN, 9911 W. Pico Blvd., #1490, 90035, 277-1541
GROSSMAN & ASSOCIATES, 211 S. Beverly Dr., 90212; 550-8127
HAMILBURG, MITCHELL, 292 S. La Cienega, Beverly Hills, 90211; 657-1501
HECHT, BEVERLY, 8949 Sunset Blvd., 90069; 278-3544
HUNT, GEORGE B., 8350 Santa Monica Blvd., 90069; 654-6600
INT'L CREATIVE MANAGEMENT, 8899 Beverly Blvd., 90048; 550-4000
KELMAN/ARLETTA AGENCY, 7813 Sunset Blvd., 90046; 851-8822
KING AGENCY, HOWARD, 118 S. Beverly Dr., Beverly Hills, 90069; 858-8048
KOHNER-LEVY, 9169 Sunset Blvd., 90069; 550-1060
LAZAR, IRVING PAUL, 211 S. Beverly Dr., Beverly Hills, 90212; 275-6153
LEONETTI TALENT AGENCY, 6526 Sunset Blvd., 90028; 463-5610
LYONS, GRACE, MANAGEMENT, 8350 Melrose Ave., Suite 202, 90069; 655-5100.
MAJOR TALENT AGENCY, 1900 Ave. of the Stars, #2375, 90067; 277-4998
McCARTT ORECK BARRETT, 10390 Santa Monica Blvd., #310, 90025; 553-2600
McHUGH AGENCY, JAMES, 8150 Beverly Blvd., 90048; 651-2770
McMILLIAN, HAZEL, 126 N. Doheny Dr., 90211; Beverly Hills, 276-9823
MEDIA ARTISTS GROUP, 6255 Sunset Blvd., 90028; 463-5610.
MESSENGER, FRED, 8235 Sunset Blvd. 90046; 656-2633

MISHKIN AGENCY, 9255 Sunset Blvd., 90069; 274-5261
MORRIS, WILLIAM, 151 El Camino Dr., Beverly Hills, 90212; 274-7451
PEARSON, BEN, 606 Wilshire Blvd. Santa Monica, 90401; 451-8414
PREFERRED ARTISTS, 16633 Ventura Blvd., Suite 1421, Encino, 91436; (818) 990-0305.
PRESCOTT, GUY, 8920 Wonderland Ave., 90046; 656-1963
RAPER ENTERPRISES AGENCY, P.O. Box 22100, Azusa, 91702; (602) 525-9091
ROBINSON-WEINTRAUB, GROSS & ASSOCIATES, 8428 Melrose Place, 90069; 653-5802
RUSH, ART, 10221 Riverside Dr., North Hollywood, 91602; 985-3033
SACKHEIM AGENCY, 9301 Wilshire Blvd., Beverly Hills, 90210; 858-0606
SCHWARTZ & ASSOC., DON, 8721 Sunset Blvd., 90069; 657-8910
SHAW, GLENN, 3330 Barham Blvd., 90068; 851-6262
SHERRELL AGENCY LEW, 7060 Hollywood Blvd., 90028; 461-9955
SMITH-FREEDMAN & ASSOCIATES, 123 N. San Vicente Blvd., Beverly Hills, 90211; 852-4777.
SWANSON, H.N., 8523 Sunset Blvd., 90069; 652-5385.
TANNEN & ASSOC. HERB, 6640 Sunset Blvd., 90028; 466-6191
TRIAD ARTISTS, 10100 Santa Monica Blvd., 16th floor, 90067; 556-2727.
TWENTIETH CENTURY ARTISTS, 3800 Barham Blvd., #303, 90068; 850-5516.
WRIGHT ASSOC., ANN, 13400 Riverside Dr. #104, Sherman Oaks 91423; (818) 655-5040.

NEW YORK

(Area telephone code is 212.)

ABRAMS ARTISTS & ASSOCIATES, LTD., 420 Madison Ave., 10017; 935-8980.
AGENCY FOR PERFORMING ARTS, 888 Seventh Ave., 10106; 582-1500.
ALEXANDER INC., WILLARD, 660 Madison Ave., 10021; 751-7070
AMERICAN-INT'L TALENT 303 W. 42 St., 10036; 245-8888
ANDERSON, BEVERLY, 1472 Broadway, Ste. 806, 10036; 944-7773
ASSOCIATED ARTISTS MANAGEMENT, 311 W. 43rd St., #6806, 10036; 974-0044.
ASSOCIATED BOOKING CORP., 1995 Broadway, 10023; 874-2400
ASTOR, RICHARD, 1697 Broadway, 10019; 581-1970
CASE, BERTHA, % Albert Avedon, 300 W. 53 St., 10019; 247-2982.
COLEMAN-ROSENBERG AGCY., 210 E. 58 St., 10022; 838-0734
COOPER ASSOC., BILL, 224 W. 49 St., #411, 10019; 307-1100
DEACY, JANE, 181 Revolutionary Rd., Scarborough, 10510; (212) 752-4865
DIAMOND ARTISTS, LTD., 119 W. 57 St., 10019; 247-3025
GAGE GROUP, THE, 1650 Broadway, #406,, 10019; 541-5250
HARTIG, MICHAEL, 114 E. 28 St., #203,, 10016; 684-0010
HENDERSON/HOGAN AGENCY, 405 W. 44 St., 10036; 765-5190
HUNT, DIANA, 44 W. 44 St., 10036; 391-4971
INT'L CREATIVE MANAGEMENT, 40 W. 57 St., 10019; 556-5600
JACOBSON/WILDER, INC., 419 Park Ave. S., 10016; 686-6100.
JAN J. AGENCY, 328 E. 61 St., 10021; 759-9775
JORDAN, JOE TALENT AGCY., 156 Fifth Ave., #711,, 10010; 463-8455
KENNEDY ARTISTS REP., 237 W. 11 St., 10014; 675-3944
KROLL LUCY, 390 West End Ave., 10024; 877-0556
LARNER, LIONEL LTD., 130 W. 57 St., 10019; 246-3105
LEIGH ENTERPRISES, LTD., SANFORD, 440 E. 62 St., 10021; 752-4450
LEWIS ASSOC., LESTER, 110 W. 40 St., 10018; 921-8370
McDERMOTT, MARGE, 216 E. 39 St., 10016; 889-1583
MARTINELLI MANAGEMENT, 888 Eighth Ave., 10019; 586-0963
MORRIS AGENCY, WM., 1350 Ave. of the Americas, 10019; 586-5100
OPPENHEIM-CHRISTIE ASSOC., 13 E. 37 St., 10016; 213-4330
OSCARD/FIFI AGENCY, 19 W. 44 St., 10036; 764-1100
OSTERTAG, BARNA 501 Fifth Ave., 10017; 697-6339
PITT AGENCY, JOEL, 144 W. 57 St., 10019; 765-6373
PREMIER TALENT ASSOC., 3 E. 54 St., 10022; 758-4900
RUBENSTEIN, BERNARD, 215 Park Ave. S., 10016; 460-9800
RYAN, CHARLES VERNON, 200 W. 57 St., 10019; 245-2225
SCHULLER AGENCY, WM., 276 Fifth Ave.,, 10001; 532-6005.
SILVER, MONTY, 200 W. 57 St., 10019; 765-4040
TALENT REPS., INC., 20 E. 53 St., 10022; 752-1835
THOMAS, MICHAEL, 18 E. 53 St., 10022; 983-2360

365

TRIAD ARTISTS, 888 Seventh Ave., Suite 1602, 10106; 489-8100.
WATERS AGENCY, BOB, 1501 Broadway, #705, 10036; 302-8787
WOLTERS, HANNS, 10 W. 37 St., 10018; 714-0100
WRIGHT REPS., ANN, 136 E. 57 St., 10022; 832-0110

Advertising & Publicity Representatives

HOLLYWOOD-LOS ANGELES-BEVERLY HILLS

(Area code is 213 unless otherwise indicated.)

ABRAMS, BOB, AND ASSOCIATES, 2030 Prosser Ave., Los Angeles 90025; 475-7739.
BBDO/CATALINA ISLAND, P.O. Box 397, Avalon 90704; 510-2624; 833-4030.
BARLOR ASSOCIATES, 428 N. Palm Dr., BH 90210; 278-1998.
BRAVERMAN-MIRISCH, INC., 1517 Schuyler Rd., Beverly Hills, CA 90210; 274-5204.
BROCATO & KELMAN, INC., 8425 W. 3rd St., Los Angeles 90048; 653-9595.
DICK BROOKS UNLIMITED, 9465 Wilshire Blvd., Beverly Hills, CA 90212; 273-8477.
CLEIN & FELDMAN INC., 8584 Melrose Ave., W. Hollywood 90069; 659-4141.
DANCER-FITZGERALD-SAMPLE INC., 3501 Sepulveda, Torrace 90505; 214-6000.
D'ARCY, MASIUS, BENTON & BOWLES, 6500 Wilshire Blvd., Los Angeles 90048; 658-4500.
DENNIS DAVIDSON & ASSOCS. INC., 211 S. Beverly Dr., #200, BH 90212; 275-8505.
DELLA FEMINA TRAVISANO & PARTNERS, 5900 Wilshire Blvd., #1900, Los Angeles 90036; 937-8540.
DENTSU INC., 4751 Wilshire Blvd., #203, Los Angeles 90010, 939-3452.
DORN, LARRY, ASSOCS. INC., 5550 Wilshire Blvd., Suite 303, Los Angeles 90036; 935-6266.
DOUGHERTY & ASSOCS. PUBLIC RELS., 139 S. Beverly Dr., Suite 311, Beverly Hills, 90212; 273-8177.
EDELMAN, DANIEL, INC., 1925 Century Park East, Los Angeles 90067; 553-1560.
GELFOND, GORDON AND ASSOCIATES, 11500 Olympic Blvd., Suite 377, Los Angeles, CA 90064; 478-3600.
GUTTMAN & PAM LTD., 8500 Wilshire Blvd., Suite 801, Beverly Hills, 90211; 659-6888.
HANSON & SCHWAM, 9200 Sunset Blvd., Los Angeles 90069; 278-1255.
LEE & ASSOCIATES, 145 S. Fairfax Ave., Los Angeles 90036; 938-3300.
LEVINE, MICHAEL, PUB. REL. CO., 8730 Sunset Blvd., Los Angeles, CA 90069; (213) 659-6400.
LEWIS & ASSOCIATES, 3600 Wilshire Blvd., Los Angeles 90010; 739-1000.
LIBERMAN, FRANK, AND ASSOCIATES, 9021 Melrose Ave., Los Angeles 90069; 278-1993.
MAHONEY/WASSERMAN & ASSOCIATES, 117 N. Robertson Blvd., Los Angeles 90048; (213) 550-3922.
McKENZIE, KING & GORDON, 1680 N. Vine St., Hollywood 90028; (213) 466-3421.
MILLER, RENEE PUBLIC RELATIONS, P.O. Box 35237, Los Angeles, CA 90035; 273-5173.

PMK INC., 8436 W. Third St., Suite 650, Los Angeles, 90048; 658-5800.
PUBLICITY WEST, 2155 N. Ridgemont Dr., Los Angeles, 90046; 654-3816; (818) 954-1951.
ROGERS & COWAN, 10000 Santa Monica Blvd., Los Angeles, 90067; 201-8800.
SAATCHI & SAATCHI/DFS, 3501 Sepulveda Blvd., Torrence, 90505; 214-6000.
THOMPSON, J. WALTER CO., 10100 Santa Monica Blvd., Los Angeles, 90067; 553-8383.

NEW YORK

(Area code is 212 unless otherwise indicated)

AYER, INC., N.W., 260 Madison Ave., 10016; 683-4900.
BATES & CO., INC., TED, 1515 Broadway, 10036; 869-3131.
BATTEN, BARTON, DURSTINE & OSBORNE, INC., 1285 Ave. of the Americas, 10019; 415-5000.
BENTON & BOWLES, INC., 909 Third Ave., 10022; 758-6200.
BILLINGS, M/S, PUBLICITY LTD, 250 W. 57 St., #2420, 10019; 581-4493.
BYOIR, CARL & ASSOCIATES, INC., 380 Madison Ave., 10017; 986-6100.
COMMUNICATIONS PLUS INC., 360 Park Ave. So., 10010; 686-9570.
DDB/NEEDHAM, 437 Madison Ave., 10022; 758-7600.
DANCER, FITZGERALD, SAMPLE, 405 Lexington Ave., 10017; 661-0800.
DAVIS, AL, PUBLICITY, 6 E. 39 St., 10016; 725-0850.
DELLA FEMINA, TRAVISANO & PARTNERS, 625 Madison Ave., 10022; 421-7180.
DIENER, HAUSER & BATES, 1515 Broadway, 10036; 840-3300.
DOYLE, DANE, BERNBACH, 437 Madison Ave., 10022; 415-2000.
EISEN, MAX, 234 W. 44 St., 10036; 391-1072.
FURST, RENEE, 303 E. 57 St., 10022; 758-8535.
GIFFORD/WALLACE, INC., 1211 Park Ave., 10028; 427-7600.
GOODMAN, FRANK, 1776 Broadway, 10019; 246-4180.
GREY ADVERTISING AGENCY, 777 Third Ave., 10017; 546-2000.
GREY ENTERTAINMENT MEDIA, 875 Third Ave. 10022; 303-2400.
LYNN, BRUCE, PUBLICITY, 345 Park Ave. So., 10010; 213-0444.
McCANN-ERICKSON, INC., 485 Lexington Ave., 10017; 697-6000.
OGILVY & MATHER, 2 E. 48 St., 10017; 907-3400.
PMK (PICKWICK, MASLANSKY, KOENIGBERG) 1 Lincoln Plaza, 10023; 580-1700.
POST, MYRNA ASSOCIATES, 145 E. 49 St., 10022; 935-7122.
ROFFMAN, RICHARD H., ASSOCIATES, 697 West End Ave., 10025; 749-3647.
ROGERS & COWAN, INC., 122 E. 42 St., 10016; 490-8200.
RUDER, FINN & ROTMAN, INC., 110 E. 59 St. 10022; 593-6400.
SCHLAIFER & CO., INC., CHARLES, 150 E. 69 St., 10155; 879-4310.
SAATCHI, SAATCHI, DFS & COMPTON, 625 Madison Ave., 10022; 661-0800.
SEIFERT-WHITE ASSOCIATES, 18 E. 53 St., 10022; 838-0888.
SOLTERS, ROSKIN, AND FREIDMAN, INC., 45 W. 34 St., 10001; 947-0515.
THOMPSON, J. WALTER, 466 Lexington Ave., 10017; 210-7000.
WAX, MORTON D. PUBLIC RELATIONS, 1560 Broadway, 10019; 302-5360.
WELLS, RICH, GREENE, 9 W. 57 St., 10019; 303-5000.
WOLHANDER, JOE, ASSOCIATES, INC., 11 W. 30 St., 10001; 947-6015.
YOUNG & RUBICAM INTERNATIONAL, 285 Madison Ave., 10017; 210-3000.

Equipment and Supplies

* MANUFACTURERS &
  SERVICES

* STUDIO EQUIPMENT

* REFRESHMENT
  PRODUCTS, EQUIPMENT

* MANUFACTURERS &
  SERVICES
  (By Product Classification)

* THEATRE SUPPLY DEALERS

Manufacturers & Services

A-Wagner Zip Change, Inc.

(formerly Wagner Sign Service)
3100 Hirsch Street, Melrose Park, IL 60160; (312) 681-4100, (800) 323-0744; FAX: (312) 681-4165.
Branch Office: 720 N. 16th Ave., Suite 8, Yakima, WA, 98902. (509) 457-5147.

Changeable marquee letters. Three styles. Wagner "slotted" dimensional red or black in 4″, 6″, 8″, 10″ and 17″. Zip-Change® flat red, black, blue or green halftone or solid stroke in 4″, 6″, 8″, 10″, 12″, 15″, 17″ and 24″ and Zip-Lite® reverse black/clear or bronze/clear in 2½″, 4″, 6″, 8″, 10″ and 12″. Wagner marquee background with stainless steel frames and unbreakable Lumasite, Enduronamel Panel assembly non-lighted metal marquees and clear plastic or aluminum tracks. Letter storage cabinets, mechanical hands and movie Rating Units. Catalog, samples on request.

Advance Seating & Repair, Inc.

2204 E. 57th St., Los Angeles, CA 90001; (213) 583-2727.

Larry Kleinman, president.
Reconditions and installs chairs in motion picture theatres.

Altec Lansing Corp.

10500 W. Reno, Oklahoma City, OK 73128.

Manufacturers of amplifiers, loudspeakers, electronic devices, microphones and transformers "Voice of the theatre" speaker systems.

American Desk Manufacturing Co.

P.O. Box 6107, Temple, TX; (817) 773-1776.

James Brown, chairman of bd.; Paul Kerr, pres.; Charles Sole, Ben Yoshinaga, sr. v.p.s.
Manufacturers of theatre seating.

American Playground Device Co.

Main Offices: 1801-1831 S. Jackson, P.O. Drawer 2599, Anderson, IN 46011; (317) 642-0288.
Branch Office: Nahma Blvd., Nahma, MI 49864; (317) 642-0288.

Manufacturers of playground equipment, park benches, picnic tables, charcoal grills, flood lights and swimming pool equipment for drive-in theatres, and bicycle racks for theatres. Complete line of American approved extra-heavy-duty Park, Picnic, Playground, Swimming Pool, Beach and Dressing Room Equipment.

American Seating Company

901 Broadway, N.W., Grand Rapids, MI 49504; (616) 456-0600.
(District offices in principal cities)

Manufacturers of auditorium and theatre chairs and portable stacking chairs.

American Theatre Products, Inc.

6650 Lexington Avenue, Hollywood, CA 90038; (213) 462-7750.

Leonard Pincus, president; Edward Burke, national sales manager.
Importer and distributor of movie theatre projection equipment.

ASC Technical Services Corp.

(formerly Altec Service Corporation)
Executive offices: P.O. Box 706, Piano, TX 75074; (214) 422-2160.

J. B. Waddell, pres.; R. V. Gandolfi, v.p.

Nationwide sound service and full booth maintenance.
National Director of Field Operations: Lamar Michael, 5857 N. Winthrop, Indianapolis, IN; (317) 257-1807.

Atlantic Audio Visual Corp.

630 Ninth Ave., New York, NY 10036.

Projection system for mini or maxi theatres. Exclusive U.S. Distributors of Zeiss Ikon Projection Equipment.

Automatic Devices Co.

2121 S. 12th St., Allentown, PA 18103; Tel: (215) 797-6000.

Abram Samuels, chairman of bd.
Manufacturers of stage, television, drapery and cubicle hardware.

Ballantyne of Omaha, Inc.

(See Strong International)

Barcto Co.

924 N. Formosa, Hollywood, CA 90046; (213) 851-5411.

Suppliers of film inspection and cleaning equipment and solvent.

Bauer Division, AIC Photo, Inc.

168 Glen Cove Rd., Carle Place, NY 11514; (516) 742-7300.

Super 8 movie cameras and projectors, 16 mm projectors.

Bevelite-Adler

14824 S. Main St., Gardena, CA 90248; Tel.: (800) 421-1256, (213) 321-5641.

Changeable Marquee letters: "Snap Lok" - "Pronto Glo" - "Regency" - 3″ (only in Pronto Style) - 4″ - 6″ - 8″ - 10″ - 12″ - 15″ (only in Pronto Style) - 17″ - 24″. Red, Black, Blue, Green, White for Snap Lok. Pronto, Regency. Brite Glo is Black/Clear or Black/Yellow. Background support available in complete Stainless steel frames or stainless steel, plastic or aluminum track for self mounting. Pronto change arms and storage cabinets for Pronto and Brite Glo.

Brandt, Inc.

705 12th St., Watertown, WI 53094; Tel.: (414) 261-1780.

Manufacturers of coin sorting and counting machines, automatic coin wrappers, currency and document counters.

Bulletin & Directory Board Mfg. Co.

2317 W. Pico Blvd., Los Angeles, CA 90006; (213) 382-1111.

Manufacturer of changeable letter boards, magnetic & write-on boards, cork & chalk boards, glass cases/indoor & outdoor free-standing & wall mounted.

Butler Fixture and Mfg. Co.

3939 William Street, Denver, CO 80205; (303) 296-3939.

John Karpan, president.
Manufacturer of concession stands and boxoffices.

Butterful, Inc.

P.O. Box 558, Dover, DE 19901; (302) 674-1400.

Courtland A. Bell, Jr., president & C.E.O.; Donald Jacobs, product manager; Patsy Shiller, Customer Service.
Butterful Inc. is a wholly owned division of National Cup Company. Manufacturers of cups for popcorn and soda.

Canrad-Hanovia, Inc.

(See Strong International)

Cardinal Systems Corporation

2426 Linden Lane, Silver Spring, MD 20910; (301) 589-3700.

Neal Rockman, president; Scott Reidinger, sr. vice president; Steven Auerbach, general manager.
Sales, service, and installation of complete sound and projection systems and all booth and film handling equipment.

CEMCORP (Consolidated Engineering & Manufacturing Corp.)

1515 Melrose Lane, P.O. Box 105, Forest Hill, MD 21050; (301) 838-0036 and (301) 879-3022.

Manufacturers and designers of ticket issuing equipment: "Automaticket" line, including Ticketaker control boxes, drive-in equipment, ticket control systems and complete box office control system.

Century Projector Corporation

1690 Oak, Lakewood, NJ; (201) 367-4434.

Manufacturers and distributors of motion picture equipment.

Century Projector Corporation

1300 Optical Drive, Azusa, CA 91702; (818) 969-3344.

Manufacturers of motion picture projection and sound equipment.

Cerwin-Vega

555 E. Easy Street, Simi Valley, CA 93065; (818) 896-0777.

Manufacturer of electrical equipment and speakers.

Christie Electric Corp.

20665 Manhattan Place, Torrance, CA 90501; (213) 320-0808.

Tom Christie, pres.; Fred Benjamin, sr. v.p.; Lynn Shubert, v.p.; Jack Kline, natl. sls. mgr.
Manufacturers of Xenolite consoles (lamphouse, rectifier power supply and projector based housed in one unit), dual sound system, and automatic system.

Cinecare International

P.O. Box 1983, Santa Monica, CA 90406; (213) 453-5444 or (800) 421-6534.

James Stanfield, Bill Wenzel.
Manufacturer of film perforation repair machines and repair tapes. Sells worldwide through dealers.

Cinema Film Systems, Inc.

950 E. Renwick Rd., Glendora, CA 91740; (213) 963-6049 and (213) 335-1402. Telex: 67-4668.

Ron E. Offerman, pres.; Richard E. Niccum, sr. v.p.
Manufacture a complete line of projection booth equipment, including platters (3-stack, 5-stack and 35/70), lamphouses, consoles, sound, automation, dimmers, reel arms and projectors. Act as National Sales Representatives for D.O. Industries (KOWA), North American Philips Lighting and Ultra Sound low voltage aisle lighting.

Cinematograph International, Inc.

341 W. 44 St., New York, NY 10036; Tel.: (212) 246-6285.

Distributors of automated theatre equipment and supplies; Cinemeccanica Victoria 70/35mm projectors in U.S.; complete Drive-In theatre equipment; projection-sound equipment and supplies; speaker systems; projection arclamps-rectifiers-generators; Xenon light systems; stage lighting, spotlighting, stage draperies; auditorium seats, carpets; display frames, marquee letters, box office equipment; equipment for Studios, Schools, Auditoriums.

Cinemeccanica U.S., Inc.

5475-115th Ave., N., Clearwater, FL 34620; (813) 573-3011.

Victor Nicelli, pres.; Thomas H. Brenner, gen. mgr.
Distributor of Cinemeccanica projection and sound equipment.

Cinetronix Inc.

11303 Hessler Road, Cleveland, OH 44106; (216) 791-2515.

Robert Sheppard, president.
Custom automation and sound systems.

Ciro Equipment

6820 Romaine Street, Hollywood, CA 90038; (213) 467-1296; (213) 467-3107.

Ron Powell, vice president sales; Jim Frank, vice president marketing.
Manufacturers of splicers and tapes for 70mm, 35mm and 16mm film.

Country Roads, Inc.

1122 So. Bridge St., Belding, MI 48809; (616) 794-3350.

Frank Southwell, chairman of the board; George E. Meeter, Wendy Southwell, sr. vice presidents.
Restoration of theatre, auditorium and stadium seating. Inventories Parts for most major kinds of theatre seating incl. arms, cupholder arms, seat and back covers and foam.

Di/An Controls, Inc.

944 Dorchester Avenue, Boston, MA 02125; (617) 288-7700.

Robert Kodis, president.
Manufacturer of high speed printers and computerized ticketing systems for movie theatres.

Dolby Laboratories Inc.

100 Potrero Ave., San Francisco, CA 94103-4813; (415) 558-0200. Telex: 34409.

Manufacturer of a full line of equipment for motion picture sound.

Econo-Pleat—Phil Sperling

(A division of Eastwest Carpet Mills)
2664 S. La Cienega Blvd., Los Angeles, CA 90034; (213) 871-1690.

Manufacturers of acoustical fabric wall coverings.

EPRAD, Inc.

2573 Tracey Rd., Northwood, OH 43619; (800) 782-0170; (419) 666-3266. FAX: (419) 666-6534.

Manufacturers/suppliers of a complete range of motion picture theatre booth equipment & accessories, including Starscope/Starlet/Galaxy series SVA sound processors and power amps, Universal Xenon lamp houses and consoles, Sword and DBL-MUT large reel film handling devices, and Co-Operator automation sysems.

Forest Bay Construction Corp.

2 Lawson Ave., East Rockaway, NY 11518; Tel: (516) 599-0070.

Experts in theatre design.

Glatz-Jacobsen Theatre Design Consultants, Inc.

1420 Vance St., Suite 100, Lakewood, CO 80215; (303) 238-6415.

Architects for complete motion picture theatre design, remodeling, interior redecorating since 1965.

Goldberg Brothers, Inc.

P.O. Box 38819, Denver, CO 80217; (303) 321-1099.

Manufacturers of motion picture film accessories, including reels, cans, cases, splicing equipment, auomatic rewinds, film rack & cabinets, video tape reels, box office & lobby accessories.

Globe Ticket Company

680 Blair Mill Road, Horsham, PA 19044; (215) 657-4230.

Bob Weikers, divisional sales; Clyde Almy, manager.
Designer and producer of effective systems of admission and revenue control, from a single roll ticket to a computerized ticketing system.

Griggs International Inc.

805 E. 4th St., Belton, TX 76513; (817) 939-3761.

Manufacturers of conventional and Push-Back theatre chairs, lobby and office furniture.

Gulistan Carpet, Division of J. P. Stevens & Co., Inc.

1185 Ave. of the Americas, New York, NY 10036; (212) 575-2282.

Manufacturers of Gulistan carpets.

Heywood-Wakefield Company

National Sales Office, Public Seating Division: 3010 Tenth St., Menominee, MI 49858.

Manufacturers of theatre seating and lounge furniture.

Hurley Screen Corp.

A subsidiary of CEMCORP. 1610 Robin Circle, P.O. Box 217, Forest Hill, MD 21050; (301) 836-9333 and 879-6757.

Manufacturers of custom-made motion picture screens and frames, including Superglo, pearlescent; Silverglo, aluminized; MW-16, matte white; glassmatte, beaded and rear projection surfaces. Frames in wood, steel, aluminum, and rope and pulley style.

Hussey Manufacturing Co., Inc.

One Dyer St., North Berwick, ME 03906; (207) 676-2271; 4012 Richmond NW, Grand Rapids, MI 49504; (616) 453-5435.

Manufacturers of theatre seating.

The Imperial Electric Company

64 Ira Ave., Akron, OH 44309; (216) 253-9126.

Indiana Cash Drawer Company

P.O. Box 236, Shelbyville, IN 46176; (317) 398-6643.

Manufacturers of cash drawers.

International Cinema Equipment Company

6750 N.E. 4th Court, Miami, FL 33138; (305) 756-0699. Telex: 522071 INT CINEMA MIA

Sells, services and distributes all type of 16/35 mm and 70mm projection and sound equipment, representing all major manufacturers of this type of equipment. (Is parent company of Westar Sales and Services Mfg. in the United Kingdom. See listing in British-based Equipment/Services)

Irwin Seating Company

3251 Fruitridge Rd., P.O. Box 2429, Grand Rapids, MI 49501; (616) 784-2621; FAX (616) 784-5819.

Manufacturers of theatre seating.

Kalart Victor Corporation

Hultenius St., Plainville, CT 06062; (203) 747-1663.

Manufacturers of audio-visual equipment and educational television systems including: 16mm sound and silent motion picture projectors: Tele-Beam large screen TV projectors; 16mm TV projectors; Kalart Victor overhead and opaque projectors; 16mm TV uniplex film chain; Craig film editing and viewing equipment for super 8mm and 16mm film.

K-Hill® Signal Company, Inc.

326 W. Third St., Uhrichsville, OH 44683; Tel.: (614) 922-0421.

Manufacturers of drive-in traffic counters. "One way" for box office and flashing light for "exit" sneak-in protection.

Kelmar Systems, Inc.

284 Broadway, Huntington Station, NY 11746; (516) 692-6131.

Andrew J. Marglin, president. Margaret Pearsall, sr. vice president.
Design and manufacture sound systems/automation/film inspection-rewind/film cleaners/reel arms and film guidance systems.

Kinotone, Inc.

257 Tenth Avenue, Paterson, NJ 07524; Tel.: (201) 279-9700.

Distributors of projection and sound equipment.

Kneisley Electric Company

2501-9 Lagrange Street, P.O. Box 4692, Toledo, OH 43620; Tel.: (419) 241-1219.

Manufacturers of Xenon lamphouses, pedestals, and power supplies for 35mm and 70mm motion picture projectors, Xenon conversion kits for carbon arc lamphouses and carbon arc follow spotlights.

Kollmorgen Corporation

347 King St., Northampton, MA 01060; Tel.: (413) 586-2330.

Manufacturers of special optics, and optical instruments.

Koneta Matting Division

700 Lunar Drive, Wapakoneta, OH 45895; Tel.: (419) 738-2155.

Manufacturers of rubber and vinyl entrance mats and matting, nylon top-vinyl back wipe off mats.

LPB Inc.

28 Bacton Hill Road, Frazer, PA 19355; (215) 644-1123.

Richard H. Crompton, president.
Manufacturers of Radio Cine-drive-in theatre AM broadcast equipment.

LaVezzi Precision, Inc.

900 North Larch Avenue, Elmhurst, IL 60126; Tel.: (312) 832-8990.

Manufacturers of parts for projector mechanisms and soundheads, including complete intermittent movement assemblies. Also special high precision machine parts for all types of motion picture equipment.

370

Liberty Brand Co. Inc.

1650 Locust Ave., Bohemia, NY 11716; (516) 589-4500.

Alan Bronson, chairman of the board & president.
Manufacturers of syrup, popcorn, candy and distributors of popcorn and soda equipment.

Lightworks

3345 West Hunting Park Ave., Philadelphia, PA 19132; (215) 223-9200; FAX (215) 227-7332.

Peter Altman, president.
Lighting manufacturer specializing in low voltage, linear-type lighting fixtures and systems.

Lucasfilm, Ltd.

THX Sound System Program
P.O. Box 2009, San Rafael, CA 94912; (415) 662-1977; FAX (415) 662-2186.

Geoff Smith, director operation; Clyde McKinney, technical director.
Motion picture sound system design.

M.J.M. Industries, Inc.

136 Claywell Drive, San Antonio, TX 78209; (512) 828-4687.

E. L. Roberson, chairman of the board & president; Mark Roberson, vice president.
Manufacturer of Dura-rain used for platter systems. Supplier of motion picture theatre equipment.

Manko Seating Company

50 W. 36 St., New York, NY 10018; Tel.: (212) 695-7470.

Specialists in manufacturing seat covers, backs, etc. Large inventory nylons, vinyls, mohair fabrics.

The Marble Company, Inc.

P.O. Box 160080, 421 Hart Lane, Nashville, TN 37216; (615) 227-7772.

National distributor of Marble "Double Eagle" carbons, X-Cel© Xenon bulbs lens, reflectors, Exciter lamps, splicers, tape and other projection room suppliers.

Marks Polarized Corp.

25 B Jeffryn Blvd., West Deer Park, NY 11729; (516) 242-1300.

Ronald Miller, president; Lou Presti, sales manager.
Manufacturer and supplier of 3D viewers and leasors of projection units for projecting 3D, lease patented 3D camera to the industry; 3D installation; 24 hr. hotline.

Massey Seating Company, Inc.

100 Taylor Street, Nashville, TN 37208; (615) 242-2561.

Manufacturers of theatre seating, polyurethane foam cushions, tailored upholstery units and general seating supplies. Products distributed by leading theatre equipment dealers.

Miracle Equipment Co.

Box 275, Grinnell, IA 50112; Tel.: (515) 236-7536.

Manufacturers of drive-in playground equipment, outdoor fiberglass picnic tables and benches. Also coin-operated carousels, stadium seating, water slides, and liter-liminaters (trash receptacles).

NRD Inc.

2937 Alt Blvd. North Grand Island, NY 14072; (716) 773-7634.

Lawrence Keating, J. David McGraw, vice presidents.
Manufacturer of nuclear self-luminous exit signs.

National Electrical Carbon Corporation

25111 Country Club Blvd., North Olmsted, OH 44070-5330; (216) 779-0201.

Sales Office: P.O. Box 94760, Cleveland, OH 44101; (800) 543-6322.

In Canada: National Electrical Carbon Canda, 6300 Northern Dr., Mississauga, Ont L4V 1H7; (416) 678-6660.

Manufacturers of carbons for brushes, carbon, graphite and metal-graphite for electric motors, generators and converters.

National Ticket Company

1650 Broadway, New York, NY 10019; (212) 757-1426.

Ticket printers to theatres; roll-machine-reserved.

Neumade Products Corporation

200 Connecticut Ave., P.O. Box 5001, Norwalk, CT 06856; (203) 866-7600. FAX: 20126 74903. PLANT: 2485 Walden Ave., Buffalo, NY 14225; Tel.: (716) 684-0051.

Manufacturers of motion picture, audio visual, and television equipment and accessories, 8mm, 70mm, 35mm, and 16mm fields.

Nick Mulone & Son

Pittsburgh St., Cheswick, PA 15024; Tel.: (412) 274-6646 or 274-5994.

Manufacturers of wide screen frames, all types.

Norcon Electronics, Inc.

1260 Ralph Ave., Brooklyn, NY 11236; (718) 451-1112.

Manufacturer of "Talk-Thru," a communicating device between patron and box office attendant.

Novelty Scenic Studios

40 Sea Cliff Ave., Glen Cove, NY 11542; Tel.: (718) 895-8668, (516) 671-5940.

Stage curtains and drapes, wall coverings, tracks and stage equipment.

Optical Radiation Corporation

1300 Optical Drive, Azusa, CA 91702; Tel.: (213) 969-3344.

Manufacturer of ORCON lamphouses, OPTIMAX consoles, Xenon bulbs, automation sound systems, and platters. Also exclusive North American distributor of ISCO projection lenses.

Osram Corporation

110 Bracken Rd., Montgomery, NY 12549; (914) 457-4040. FAX: (914) 457-4004; TTX: 3112-23600154.

OSRAM Theatre Xenon lamps.

Panavision, Inc.

18618 Oxnard St., Tarzana, CA 91356; (818) 609-7011.

Manufacturers and lessors of motion picture processes—Ultra Panavision 70, Super Panavision 70, Panavision 70 and Panavision 35.

Perey Turnstiles

535 Fifth Ave., New York, NY 10017; (212) 599-0077.

Manufacturers of theatre turnstiles. Application engineering available.

Poblocki and Sons

620 South First St., Milwaukee, WI 53204; Tel.: (414) 273-3333.

Manufacturers of marquees and canopies, signs, poster cases, etc.

Potts Inc.

201 E. Sangamon, Box 867, Grand Toole, IL 61868; (217) 893-0443.

Robert L. Potts, president.
Manufacturer of platter systems.

Prestoseal Corp.

545 Meacham Ave., Elmont, NY 11003; Tel.: (516) 488-1155.

Manufacturers of motion picture and microfilm splicers.

Projected Sound, Inc.

469 Avon Ave., P.O. Box 112, Plainfield, IN 46168; Tel.: (317) 839-4111.

Manufacturers and suppliers of In-Car Speakers, Junction Boxes, cone units and component parts.

Proctor Companies Inc.

2335 S. Inca, Denver, CO 80223; (303) 934-5455.

Designers and manufacturers of concession stands, popcorn warmers, and concession canopies. Manufacturers of candy cases, box offices, doorman stub boxes, trash receptacles and lobby benches. Distributors of ice makers, popcorn poppers, post mix drink systems, hot dog machines, time clocks, water filters, shelving, sinks, safes, nacho equipment, acoustical sound panels, ticket window enclosures, sneeze guards, crowd control supplies, and lid, napkin, straw & cup dispensers.

RCA

30 Rockefeller Plaza, New York, NY 10020; Tel.: (212) 689-7200.

RCA Service Company, Cherry Hill Offices, Camden, NJ 08101; Tel.: (609) 963-8000.

Theatre Service Field Offices

JERSEY CITY, 43 Edward J. Hart Road, Liberty Industrial Park; W. P. Browski, mgr.
CLEVELAND, OH, 20338 Progress Drive, Strongsville, OH; M. J. Duffield, mgr.
ATLANTA, 4508 Bibb Blvd., Tucker, GA; L. N. Howard, mgr.
SKOKIE, IL, 7620 Gross Pointe Rd.; R. H. Bunting, mgr.
HOLLYWOOD, 1501 Beach St., Montebello, CA; M. B. Solomon Jr., mgr.

Radio Systems, Inc.

5113 West Chester Pike, Edgemont, PA 19028; (215) 356-4700.

Daniel Braverman, president.
Manufacturer of AM radio sound equipment used in drive-in theatres.

Reed Speaker Mfg. Co., Inc.

7530 W. 16th Ave., Lakewood, CA 80215; (303) 238-6534 or (303) 233-1150.

Sam Reed, president.
Drive-in speakers and accessories.

Research Technology International

4700 Chase Avenue, Lincolnwood, IL 60646; (312) 677-3000.

Ray L. Short, Jr., president; Thomas W. Boyle, v.p. media products. Manufacturer of film and video tape inspection, cleaning, editing equipment. Major supplier of film, video and audio-visual supplies, equipment, storage systems and film library furnishings of all kinds.

Schneider Corp. of America

400 Crossways Drive, Woodbury, NY 11797; (516) 496-8500.

Manufacturers of the CINELUX-ULTRA motion picture projection lenses and CINELUX-ULTRA wide angle lenses with focal lengths from 26mm to 150 mm Cinelux Anamorphic 2× for Cinema-Scope.

Selby Industries, Inc.

P.O. Box 277, Richfield, OH 44286; Tel.: (216) 659-6631.

Manufacturers and erectors of drive-in screen towers and prefabricated box offices; drive-in design consultants; speaker posts; canopies, and fencing.

Simplex Projector Co.

(Division of National Screen Service Corp.)
1600 Broadway, New York, NY 10019; (212) 245-6900.

Richard J. Green, vice pres. & gen. mgr.
Product: Simplex projection equipment.

Smart Theatre Systems

3856 Green Industrial Way, Atlanta, GA 30341; (404) 452-1820; FAX (404) 455-4066.

Norman Schneider, president.
Manufacturer of sound systems for motion picture theatres.

Soundfold, Inc.

Box 2125, Dayton, OH 45429; (513) 228-3773 and (513) 293-2671.

Manufacturers of Soundfold, the original patented pleated acoustical wallcovering system. Soundfold also carries a wide variety of fabrics and colors; pleated trim; decorative wall carpet; fiberglass insulation; and Ultra 2000 high tech acoustical wall panels with an N.R.C. rating of .80.

Standard Theatre Supply Co.

125 Higgins Street, Greensboro, NC 27406; (919) 272-6165.

Jim Bellows, president.
Screen frames, drapery, automation and sound systems.

Stewart Filmscreen Corp.

1161 W. Sepulveda Blvd., Torrance, CA 90502; Tel.: (213) 326-1422.

Manufacturers of complete line of Stewart seamless, professional projection screens for front and rear projected backgrounds of all sizes. Also makers of blue screens for travelling matte process.

Strand Lighting, Inc.

20 Bushes Lane, Elmwood Park, NJ 07407; Tel.: (201) 791-7000.

18111 S. Santa Fe Ave., Rancho Dominguez, CA; (213) 637-7500.

Manufacturers of studio, stage and auditorium lighting fixtures and all types of dimmer control equipment.

Strand Lighting (Rank Strand Limited)

P.O. Box 51, Great West Road, Brentford, Middlesex, England TW8 9HR. Tel: 01-568 9222. Telex: 27976. Cables: Rankaudio Brentford.

Strong International

1712 Jackson St., Omaha, NE 68102; (402) 342-4444.
Marketing Division for:

Canrad-Hanovia, Inc., 100 Chestnut St., Newark, NJ 07105; (201) 589-4300.

Ballantyne of Omaha, Inc., 1712 Jackson St., Omaha, NE 68102; (402) 342-4444.

Strong Electric, 1712 Jackson St., Omaha, NE 68102; (402) 342-4444.

Manufacturers of Canrad projection bulbs, Simplex & Ballantyne projectors, soundheads, automation, sound systems, pedestals, Strong lamphouses and consoles with associate power supplies, Tufcold and silver reflectors and Strong follow spotlights.

Systems & Products Engineering Company

709 North 6th St., Kansas City, KS 66101; (913) 321-3978. FAX: (913) 32174 39.

Manufacturers of 35 & 70mm Platter Systems, Analog Light Dimmers, Automation, 35 & 35-70mm Split Film Cue Detectors, Reel Arms, Emergency Paging Systems and Drive-In Theatre Products.

Technikote Corporation

63 Seabring Street, Brooklyn, NY 11231; Tel.: (718) 624-6429/6430.

Manufacturers of seamless projection screens—Anti-static XR-171 Pearlescent Dust-resistant screen, Jetwhite screen, Lenticolar screens, Hilux metallic screen, Matte white screen; drive-in screen paints, wood & metal screen frames; rope and pulley screens.

Theatrical Electronics

Box 706, Matthews, NC 28105.

Reel brackets, rewinds plastic reels, sankor lens, rebuilt used equipment and platters. Everything for the booth.

Weldon, Williams & Lick

P.O. Box 168, Fort Smith, AR 72902; (501) 783-4113; FAX (501) 783-7050.

S. W. Jackson, Jr., chairman of the board; James D. Walcott, Jr., president.

Specialists on numbered printing manufacturing admission tickets of all kinds.

Williams Screen Company

1674 Summit Lake Blvd., Akron, OH 44314; Tel.: (216) 745-0521.

Manufacturers of projection screens.

Edw. H. Wolk, Inc.

1241 S. Wabash Ave., Chicago, IL 60605; Tel.: (312) WE 9-2720-21-22(-)45.

Manufacturers of replacement parts for all American made projectors, arc lamps and sound reproducers, 26½" Reel Arms for regular and automated projection. Deluxe & "Moto-Matic" Hand Rewinders. "Solfonic" Solar Cells & Power Pacs. Distributor of Naren Spot Lights, Ex-Cell Sand/Water Urns, G.E. & Westinghouse Projection and Exciter Lamps, Cetron Photo-Electric Cells, Bausch & Lomb Glass Silvered Reflectors & "Wolk" Rectifier Bulbs; Sav-A-Reel kits.

Studio Equipment

Ampex Corporation

U.S. SALES OFFICES:
California: 401 Broadway, Redwood City, CA 94063; (415) 367-2296 and 340 Parkside Dr., San Fernando, CA 91340; (818) 365-8627.
Colorado: 10604 W. 48th Ave., Wheat Ridge, CO 80033-2293; (303) 423-1300.
Georgia: 1872 Montreal Road, Tucker, GA 30084; (404) 491-7112.
Illinois: 719 W. Algonquin Rd., Arlington Heights, IL 60005; (312) 593-6000.
Maryland: 10215 Fernwood Road, Bethesda, MD 20817; (301) 530-8800.
New Jersey: 5 Pearl Court, Allendale Industrial Park, Allendale, NJ 07401; (201) 825-9600; (212) 947-8633 from NY.
Texas: 3353 Earhart Drive, Carrollton, TX 75006; (214) 960-1162.
Washington: 6627 S. 191st Pl., Suite F-101, Kent, WA 98032; (206) 251-8682.

Audio/Video recording equipment for industry/studios/radio & TV stations.

Amusement Supply Co.

208 W. Montcalm, Detroit 48201; (313) 961-3440.
R. Ruben, owner.

Automatic Devices Co.

2121 South 12th St., Allentown, PA 18103; (215) 797-6000.

Manufacturers of stage and drapery hardware.

BHP, Inc.

1800 Winnemac Ave., Chicago, IL 60640; (312) 989-2140.

Professional motion picture film printers, film/video tape editing systems, and related accessories for motion picture film and video laboratories.

Bach Auricon, Inc.

6950 Romaine St., Hollywood, CA 90038; (213) 462-0931.

Manufacturers of "Filmagnetic" sound-on-film recording equipment and "Auricon" motion picture cameras.

The Camera Mart, Inc.

456 W. 55 St., New York, NY 10019; (212) 757-6977. FAX: (212) 582-2498.

Sale & rental of motion picture and TV equipment, both film & videotape.

CECO, Inc.

440 W. 15 St., New York, NY 10001; (212) 206-8280.

Rental, sale and service of photographic equipment for motion picture and TV studios. Manufacturer of professional tripods, tripod heads, editing viewers, camera motors, editing tables and other professional motion picture production equipment. Distributor for Hajnal Snorkel lens systems. Camera towers to 75 ft. (mobile); lighting towers to 125 ft. (mobile).

Digital Entertainment Corporation

Quad Eight/Westrex

(Member of Mitsubishi Pro Audio Group)
International Headquarters: 225 Parkside Dr., San Fernando, CA 91340; (818) 898-2341.
Offices of Digital Entertainment: 555 W. 57 St., New York, NY 10019; (212) 713-1600; 2200 Hillsboro Road, Nashville, TN 37212; (615) 298-6613.

Products include digital tape recorders; audio mixing consoles; magnetic film recorders; reproducers; photographic film sound recorders.

Fiberbilt Cases, Inc.

601 W. 26 St., New York, NY 10001; (800) 847-4176 and (212) 675-5820.

Manufacturers of cases and trunks for all types of motion picture equipment; also film cases.

Jack A. Frost

234 Piquette Ave., Detroit, MI 48202; (313) 873-8030.

Studio and motion picture lighting equipment. HMI lights—temporary power—transformers.

Grosh Scenic Studios

4114-4122 Sunset Blvd., Hollywood, CA 90029; (213) 662-1134.

Design, manufacture and installation of theatrical stage draperies; custom and standard theatrical hardware.

JBL Professional

8500 Balboa Blvd., Northridge, CA 91329; (818) 893-8411.

Ron Means, pres.; Ken Lopez, v.p., sls.; Mark Gander, v.p., mktg. Professional audio equipment manufacturer, including loudspeakers, signal processing, mixing consoles and multi-track tape recorders (brand names: JBL, UREI, Soundcraft).

Kinotone, Inc.

257 Tenth Avenue, Paterson, NJ 07524; (201) 279-9700.

Distributors of projection and sound equipment.

Kintek, Inc.

224 Calvary St., P.O. Box 9143, Waltham, MA 02254-9143; (617) 894-6111.

David E. Blackmer, chm. of bd.; Zaki Abdun Nabi, pres.; Daniel M. Taylor, v.p., mktg./sls.; Roberta Allis, sls. mgr.
Designer and manufacturer of innovative audio products for motion picture sound recording and reproduction, including film sound processors, power amplifiers, monitors and exciter supplies, surround speakers, a self powered subwoofer, and turn-key stereo sound systems.

Kliegl Bros. Universal Electric Stage Lighting Company, Inc.

32-32 48th Ave., Long Island City, NY 11101; (212) 786-7474.

Manufacturers of Klieglights and lighting control equipment for TV studios, stage, auditorium and architectural lighting specialties.

374

Magnasync-Moviola Corp.

5539 Riverton Ave., North Hollywood, CA 91601; (213) 763-8441. Telex: 67-3199 MAGNA/MOVIS LAS.

Manufacturers and marketers of Videola film-to-video transfer and broadcast equipment. Microprocessor controlled multi-channel voice logging recorders.

OXBERRY Div. of Richmark Camera Service Inc.

180 Broad St., Carlstadt, NJ 07072; (201) 935-3000.

Manufacturers of Animation Stands, Optical Printers, Media Pro Equipment, Registration devices, etc.

RCA

30 Rockefeller Plaza, New York, NY 10020; (212) 598-5900.

Commercial Communications Systems Division, Broadcast Systems, Front and Cooper St., Camden, NJ 08102; (609) 963-8000.

Commerical Communications Systems Division, Photophone Systems, 2700 West Olive Ave., Burbank, CA 91505; (213) 849-6741.

Complete theatre service.

Ringold Theatre Equipment Co.

6504 28th St., S.E. Grand Rapids, MI 49506; (616) 957-2684; nights: (616) 949-0124. (800) 992-2589 (MI); (800) 624-9638 (OH & IN).

Paul Voudouris, pres.; William Thorne, v.p.; Carlton Colthorp, dir., mktg.

Roctronics Lighting, Lasergraphics and Special Effects, Inc.

100-MPA Roctronics Park, Pembroke, MA 02359; (617) 826-8888.

Designers, manufacturers and sellers of entertainment lighting electronics (dimmers and color synthesizers) and special effects (foggers, bubblers, stroboscopes, laser beam scanners, large screen video, animated displays).

Charles Ross, Inc.

333 W. 52 St., New York, NY 10019; (212) 246- 5470.

Rental, sale and service of motion picture and TV lighting, grip equipment and generators. Distributors of Mole-Richardson Co. products in the state of New York.

Soundcraft

JBL Professional, 8500 Balboa Blvd., Northridge, CA 91329; (818) 893-8411. FAX: (818) 893-3639.

Ron Means, pres.; Mark Gander, v.p., mktg.; Ken Lopez, v.p., sls,; Hugh Miller, v.p., finance.

Manufactures audio mixing consoles for all applications, including recording, theatre, concert sound reinforcement, and broadcasting; exclusive distributor for Soundcraft consoles in the U.S. and Mexico.

6000 console, TS-12 console, 200 B/VE video editor, SAC 200 broadcasting console, 200B console, twister automation, TS-12 automation.

Special Effects Unlimited

3325 Cahuenga Blvd., Hollywood, CA 90068; (213) 874-9183.

Gas and electric wind machines, also special effects weaponry.

Tru-Roll Corporation

622 Sonora Ave., Glendale, CA 91201; (213) 243-9567, 245-5741.

Designers and manufacturers of custom and standard theatrical hardware. Curved and straight drapery tracks, contour drapery rigging, motion picture screen frames, top and side screen masking rigging motors and controls, motorized revolving stages, motorized bandwagons, orchestra enclosures, sliding panels, disappearing motion picture screens.

UREI

8500 Balboa Blvd., Northridge, CA 91329; (818) 893-8411; FAX: (818) 893-3639.

Ron Means, pres.; Mark Gander, v.p., mktg.; Ken Lopez, v.p., sls.; Hugh Miller, v.p., finance.

Manufacturers of high quality sound and signal processing equipment for studio, broadcast, live and other applications.

XETRON, Division of Neumade Products Corp.

10 Saddle Rd., Cedar Knolls, NJ 07927; (201) 267-8200.

Lorraine Carbons—Carbon electrodes for all motion picture applications—Xetron Products—Professional 16, 35, 70mm projection equipment and accessories manufactured by Prevost S.P.A. Xetron Xenon lamphouses, consoles, bulbs, film transports, electronic dimming systems, 16MM and 35MM projection lenses. HM1, H1D, HQ1,—Ballast and starters manufactured by IREM. 16MM and 35MM Prevost flat bed editing tables.

Refreshment Products and Equipment

Adams and Brooks, Inc.

1915 S. Hoover St., Los Angeles, CA 90007; (213) 749-3226.

John Brooks, presi.; Wayne K. Zardnik, v.p.; Harry Payne, sls. opns. mgr.

Candy manufacturer.

Alco Dispensing Systems

455 Kehoe Blvd., Carol Stream, IL 60188; (312) 462-8100.

Morgan P. Morgan, pres. & gen. mgr.

Manufacturer of post-mix soft drink equipment.

Alto Shaam Inc.

P.O. Box 450, Menomonee Falls, WI 53051; (800) 558-8744; (414) 251-3800.

Jerry Maahs, pres.

Manufacturer of food warming equipment and hot dog/popcorn merchandisers.

American Can Co.

Kesslerville Rd., Easton, PA 18042; (215) 258-5371; American Lane, Greenwich, CT 06830; (203) 552-2000; One International Blvd., Rexdale, Ont., Canada M9W1A1; (416) 675-3490.

Ralph Palsiano, purchasing agent.

Manufacturers of paper products.

American Popcorn Company

P.O. Box 178, 4332 Grant, Sioux City, IA 51102; (712) 239-1232.

Wrede H. Smith, chm. of bd.; James Fowler, sr. v.p.; Carlton P. Smith, v.p.; Ronald R. Rohlena, sls. rep.

Processor and packager of Jolly Time popcorn.

American Wyott Corporation

1938 Wyott Dr., P.O. Box 1188, Cheyenne, WY 82003; (307) 634-5801.

William Schneider, pres.; James Wilson, Richard Rothwell, v.p.; Kevin Maurer, Jeff Cabana, mktg. mgrs.

Manufacturer of food service equipment.

Armour Food Co.

1514 E. Katella Avenue, Anaheim, CA 92805; (714) 634-2913.

T. C. Smith, dist. sls. mgr; W.B. DeSmith, zone mgr.

Hot dogs and meat suppliers.

B & H Company

1828 8th Street NW, Albuquerque, NM 87102; (505) 247-4501.

George Buffet, owner.

Suppliers of raw popcorn and sno-kone machines.

Bagcraft Corporation of America

10 Minue St., Carteret, NJ 07008; (201) 969-1234.

Manufacturers of popcorn packaging; foil and wax sandwich wraps and bags; french fry, hero, pizza slice packaging; over 150 stock food service packages.

Banner Candy Mfg. Corp.

700 Liberty Ave., Brooklyn, NY 11208; (718) 647-4747.

Peter Stone, pres.; Andrew Grunther, v.p.

Manufacturer of Jordan Almonds, Chocolate Almonds and Fruit & Nut mixes for theatre concessions.

Paul F. Beich Co.

Bloomington, IL 61701; (309) 828-1311.

Manufacturers of 10¢ Bike Whiz. Complete line of other 10¢ bars and 15¢ milk chocolate caramel-filled shells.

Blevins Popcorn Co.

Popcorn Village, Memphis, TN 38117; 813 Ridge Lake Blvd., P.O. Box 171233; (901) 761-2062.

Processing Plants in Ridgway, IL and North Bend, NB Concession supply branches in Atlanta, GA 30325: P.O. Box 20176 Sta. N., 2023 Hills Ave., N.W.; Cincinnati, OH 45246: 11699 Chesterdale Rd.; Dallas, TX 75042: P.O. Box 25264, 2729 Market St.; Houston, TX 77018: P.O. Box 10243, 202 W. 38th St.; Jacksonville, FL 32205: P.O. Box 2752, 5599 Commonwealth Ave.; Louisville, KY 40214: 6224 Strawberry Lane; Memphis, TN 38116: P.O. Box 16834, 3070 Fleetbrook Dr.; Miami, FL 33166: 7760 N.W. 62nd St.; Nashville, TN 37228: P.O. Box 90766, 744 Freeland Station Rd.; New Orleans, LA 70181: P.O. Box 10585, 1017 Jefferson Hwy.; Omaha, NE 68102: P.O. Box 1282, 1009 Capitol Ave.; Tampa, FL 33605: P.O. Box 5461, 1212 N. 39th St.; West Terre Haute, IN 47885: Highway 40 West.

Warehouses in Little Rock, AR, Knoxville, TN & North Loup, NE

Processors of raw popcorn and distributors of all high profit concession supplies and equipment.

Bon-Bon Co. of America

1620 North Spring Street, Los Angeles, CA 90012; (213) 221-4131 or (213) 226-1714.

Ed Gassman, pres.; Frank Becker III, gen. mgr.

Manufacturer of Bon-Bon ice creams.

Canada Dry Corp. (Food Service Division)

2600 Century Pkwy., Atlanta, GA 30345; (404) 982-8870.

Manufacturers of beverage syrups: Sunkist Orange Soda, Ginger Ale, Cola, Tahitian Treat, Root Beer and others.

Carnation Co.

5045 Wilshire Blvd., Los Angeles, CA 90036; (213) 932-6722.

Dana Quiellen, dir., mktg.

Manufacturer of food products.

Castleberry's Food Co.

Box 1010, Augusta, GA 30903; (404) 733-7765.

Fast foods, sauces, packed foods.

Coca-Cola USA

P.O. Drawer 1734, Atlanta, GA 30301; (404) 676- 2121.
Manufacturers of soft drink syrups, Coca-Cola, Tab, Sprite, Fanta flavors, Fresca.

Consolidated Popcorn Inc.

P.O. Box 309, Schaller, IA 51053; (712) 275-4242.
Wayne Blewitt, pres.
Manufacturer of popcorn.

Continental Bondware

17C, Golf Road, Tower Three, Rolling Meadows, IL 60008; (312) 228-0888; 1201 N. Watson, Suite 206, Arlington, TX 76006; (817) 649-5278; 1420 East Edinger, Suite 103, Santa Ana, CA 92705; (714) 547-9285; 5624 Executive Center Dr., Charlotte, NC 28212; (704) 568-7412.
P. O'C. White Jr., vice pres. and gen. mgr.; J. A. Lucas, gen. sales and marketing mgr.; Gary Carter, Southwest regional mgr.; E. Stewart Hein, Western regional mgr.; James K. Caughman, Eastern regional mgr.
Paper hot and cold cups, paper plates, popcorn and food tubs.

C. Cretors and Co.

3243 North Carolina Avenue, Chicago, IL 60618; (312) 588-1690.
C. J. Cretors, chm. of bd.; C. D. Cretors, pres.; Henry Cretors, sr. v.p.; Ned McKnight, sr. v.p.; Van D. Neathery, v.p.; Mark Hamilton, Eastern regional sls. mgr.; Joanne Lee, Western regional sls.
Complete line manufacturer of popcorn and cotton candy equipment.

Delmonte Franchise Beverages, USA

A division of General Cinema Corp.
2600 Century Parkway, Atlanta, GA 30345; (404) 321-1776.
Suppliers of Sunkist Orange Soda Fountain syrup, bottles, cans.

Dixie/Marathon

800 Connecticut Ave., Norwalk, CT 06856; (203) 854-2000.
Charles Beck, merchandise mgr.
Manufacturer of paper products and dispensing systems.

Dr Pepper/Seven Up Companies, Inc.

5523 E. Mockingbird Lane, P.O. Box 665086, Dallas, TX 75265; (214) 824-0331.
Manufacturers of Dr Pepper and Diet Dr Pepper concentrates and fountain syrups, Seven-Up and Diet Seven-Up concentrates and fountain syrups, Welch's concentrates and fountain syrups, IBC Root Beer concentrates and finished product, IBC Cream Soda concentrates and finished product.

Durkee Food Service

925 Euclid Avenue, Cleveland, OH 44115; (216) 344-8000.
Dick Winger, v.p., sales.
Manufacturers of popcorn toppings and seasonings.

Goetze's Candy Co., Inc.

3900 E. Monument St., Baltimore, MD 21205; (301) 342-2010.
Candy designed exclusively for theatres; 3½ oz. 12 pack.

Gold Medal Products Company

2001 Dalton Avenue, Cincinnati, OH 45214-2089; (513) 381-1313.
David B. Evans, chm. of bd. & pres.; J. C. Evans, Edmond Tschan, sr. v.p.; Dan Kroeger, natl. sls. mgr.; Nelson Drummond, mktg. mgr.
Manufacturer of concession equipment and fun food equipment and all related supplies. Product line includes popcorn machines, cotton candy machines, sno-Kone machines, fried pastry snack machines, nachos, caramel corn, hot dog machines and complete snack bars.

Good Time Foods, Inc.

48839 Kato Road, Fremont, CA 94539; (415) 490-3434.
Steve Lazar, pres.
Wholesale distribution of fast food snack bar equipment and supplies to theatres, concessions, schools and fast food restaurants throughout Northern California.

Greer Enterprises, Inc.

281 N. Grant Ave., Columbus, OH 43215; (614) 221-3245. Factory and Sales: 31 Chicago St., Quincy, MI 49082; (517) 639-9825.
Manufacturers of combination frankfurter barbecue unit and bun warmer, Glenray manufacturers of Moist Heat Portable Steam Table (steamette).

Henry Heide, Inc.

P.O. Box 271, New Brunswick, NJ 08903; (201) 846-2400.
Manufacturers of candy—Jujyfruits, Jujubes, Chocolate Flavor Babies, Candy Corn, Red Hot Dollars, Gummi Bears, and drops.

Hershey Foods Corp., Hershey Concession Program

19 East Chocolate Avenue, Hershey, PA 17033; (717) 534-7500.
Manufacturers of chocolate and cocoa.

M. J. Holloway & Company

308 West Ontario, Chicago, IL 60610; (312) 642- 2700.
Manufacturers of candy—Milk Duds, Slo-Poke and Black Crow Suckers, Hi-noon bars, Zooper Dooper bars.

Hollywood Brands, Inc.

A subsidiary of Consolidated Foods Corp.
836 South Chestnut Street, Centralia, IL 62801; (618) 532-4767.
Manufacturers of Pay Day, Butternut, Milk Shake, and Zero.

James River Corp.

605 Kuebler Road, Easton, PA 18042; (215) 250-1400.
Manufacturers of paper products: plates, cups, bowls, towels, tissues, etc.

Jet Spray Corp.

P.O. Box 8250, 825 University Ave., Norwood, MA 02062; (617) 769-7500.
Manufacturers of visual display, electrically refrigerated carbonated and non-carbonated beverage dispensers, hot chocolate dispensers, freeze-dried coffee dispensers, coin operated coffee and chocolate dispensers, instant mashed potato dispensers, hot and cold tea dispenser.

Manley, Inc.

1920 Wyandotte, Kansas City, MO (Mail: P.O. Box 419006, Kansas City, MO 64141); (816) 421-6155.

Manufacturers of popcorn machines and theatre concession stands. Sale of popcorn.

M & M/Mars

High St., Hackettstown, NJ 07840; (201) 852-1000.

Manufacturers of Mars Bar, 3 Musketeers Bar, Milky Way Bar, Snickers Bar, Starburst Fruit Chews, Twix Caramel Cookie Bars, Twix Peanut Butter Cookie Bars, Holidays Plain Chocolates, Holidays Peanut Chocolates, Skittles Bite Size Candies, Munch Bar, M & M's Plain Chocolate Candies, M & M's Peanut Chocolate Candies, Kudos Granola Snack (Peanut Butter), Kudos Granola Snack (Nutty Fudge), Kudos Granola Snack (Chocolate Chip), Combos Bite Size Food.

Nabisco Confections, Inc.

810 Main Street, Cambridge, MA 02139; (617) 491-2500.

Henry Bornhofft, Jr., pres.; Edward Bjornson, exec. v.p.; William Jones, v.p., sales.
Manufacturer of confectionary products.

Nestlé Foods Corporation

100 Manhattanville Rd., Purchase, NY 10577; (914) 251-3000.

Manufacturers of movie snacks: Raisinets, Goobers, Sno Caps, CRUNCH, Alpine White with Almonds, Superior Milk Chocolate, Superior Milk Chocolate with Almonds, $100 Grand, Oh Henry!, Chunky, Laffy Taffy and Bit-O-Honey.

Odell's

7275 Potamac Drive, Boise, ID 83704; (800) 635-0436; FAX (208) 376-9938.

Art Anderson, pres.; Michael Blout, natl. sales mgr.
Manufacturer of popcorn toppings.

Ogden Food Service

One Bills Dr., Orchard Park, NY 14127; (716) 649-6780.

Ogden Foods, Inc.

3660 S. Lawrence St., Philadelphia, PA 19148.

Operators of theatre food concessions—both indoor houses and drive-ins.

Parker Popcorn Company, Inc.

101 E. Poplar St., Murray, KY 42071; (502) 753-5451.

Herman K. Ellis, pres.
Popcorn growers, processors and shippers.

Pepsi-Cola Company

Rt 35, Somers, NY 10589; (914) 767-7814; 4000 Westerly Pl., Suite 200, Newport Beach, CA 92660; (714) 851-9783; #202 2680 Bishop Dr., POB 5100, San Ramon, CA 94583; (415) 830-0700; (714) 851-9783.

Wayne D. Calloway, chm. of bd.; Roger Enrico, pres.
Manufacturers of Pepsi-Cola syrup and bottlers of Pepsi-Cola, Diet-Pepsi, Teem.

Peter Paul, Inc.

(A Division of Hershey Chocolate)
New Haven Rd, Naugatuck, CT 06770; (203) 729-0221.

Manufacturers of candy; Mounds, Almond Joy, York Peppermint Patties, Cadbury chocolate.

Poppers Supply Co., Inc.

1211 N. 2nd St., Philadelphia, PA 19122; (215) 426-1616.

Dave Freedman, pres.; Steve Johnston, gen. mgr.
Concession equipment and supplies.

Proctor Companies Inc.

2335 S. Inca, Denver, CO 80223; Tele: (303) 934-5455.

Designers and manufacturers of concession stands, popcorn warmers, and concession canopies. Manufacturers of candy cases, box offices, doorman stub boxes, trash receptacles and lobby benches. Distributors of ice makers, popcorn poppers, post-mix drink systems, hot dog machines, time clocks, water filters, shelving, sinks, safes, Nachos equipment, acoustical sound panels, ticket window enclosures, sneeze guards, crowd control supplies, and lid, napkin, straw & cup dispensers.

Quinn Popcorn Co., Inc.

Route 1, Lake View, IA 51450; (712) 657-8561.

Kenneth E. Quinn, pres.
Growing, processing, packaging and merchandising of popcorn.

H. B. Reese Candy Company, Inc., Subsidiary of Hershey Chocolate Co.

Hershey, PA 17033; (717) 534-4100.

Manufacturers of Peanut Butter Cups.

Ross-Temp

2421 15th St. S.W./P.O. Box 1527, Mason City, IA 50401; (515) 424-6150.

James Tjaden, v.p., sales.
Manufacturer of commercial ice and beverage and energy systems.

Roundup Food Equipment

1045 W. National, Addison, IL 60101; (312) 543-8650; FAX (312) 543-0359.

August J. Antunes, chm. of bd.; James Antunes, pres.; Thomas Krisch, sales mgr.; Tom Miles, service mgr.
Hot dog grills, heated display cases, toasters, steam warming equipment.

Rowe International, Inc.

75 Troy Hills Rd., Whippany, NJ 07981; (201) 887-0400.

Manufacturers of automatic venders, music systems and bill and coin changers.

Royal Crown Cola Co.

Gould Center East Tower, Suite 500, 2550 Golf Rd., Rolling Meadows, IL 60008; (312) 981-4000.
Branch: 1000 Tenth Ave., P.O. Box 1440, Columbus, GA 31994; (404) 571-6451.

Manufacturers of soft drinks.

Sani Serv

2020 Production Drive, Indianapolis, IN 46241; (317) 247-0460.

G. E. Aguirre, pres.; Jack Farley, gen. mgr.
Manufacturer of food service equipment.

Scotsman Ice Systems

505 Front St., Albert Lea, MN 56007; (507) 373-3961.

Manufacturers of Scotsman ice cube and flake machines, combination ice machines and drink dispensers.

Server Products, Inc.

P.O. Box 249, Menomonee Falls, WI 53051; (414) 251-7100.

Alfred W. Wickesberg, chm. of bd., pres.; Norman Bochlke, v.p.
Manufacturer and originator of melted butter dispensers for buttering popcorn. Also manufacturers of popcorn warmers, Nachos equipment, mustard & ketchup pumps and food warmers.

The Seven-Up Company

121 S. Meramec, St. Louis, MO 63105; (314) 889-7777; (800) 325-7777.

7-UP and Diet 7-UP are available in bottles, cans, pre-mix, and post-mix from the local 7-UP bottling company. The 7-UP bottler is a source for pre-mix and post-mix dispensing equipment and bottle and can vendors.

Simonin's C. F. Sons, Inc.

Tioga & Belgrade Sts., Philadelphia, PA 19134; (215) 426-2300.

Manufacturers of popcorn oils and colored and flavored seasonings.

Smithfield Ham & Products Company

Smithfield, VA 23430; (804) 357-2121.

James River and Smitty Pig brands beef barbeque, pork barbeque, hot dog chili and Smithfield hams.

Sno-Ball Food Service & Concession Supply Inc.

5740 Jarvis, Jefferson, LA; (504) 733-6182.

Avery Stirratt, pres.; Rocky Solar, mgr.
Concessionaires with a complete line of paper, plastic and styrofoam disposables, concession food products and equipment.

Solo Cup Company

1700 Old Deerfield Rd., Highland Park, IL 60035; (312) 831-4800.

Supplier of plastic & paper goods for the concession industry.

Stein Industries, Inc.

22 Sprague Ave., Amityville, NY 11701; (516) 789-2222.

Manufacturers and designers of concession stands, popcorn warmers, display frames, doormen's boxes, and box offices.

Weaver Popcorn Co.

P.O. Box 395, Van Buren, IN 46991; (317) 934-2101.

W. I. Weaver, pres.; Michael E. Weaver, sr. v.p.; Richard P. Lintner, v.p.
Popcorn processors.

379

Manufacturers and Services
By Product Classification

Acoustical Sound Panels
Proctor Companies Inc.

Admission Tickets
Weldon, Williams & Lick

Animation Equipment
Oxberry Berkey Technical

Attraction Advertising Equipment
A-Wagner Zip Change
Bevilite-Adler

Beverages and Beverage Dispensers
Alco Dispensing Systems
Canada Dry Corp.
Coca-Cola USA
Dr Pepper Co.
Jet Spray Corp.
Manley, Inc.
Pepsi-Cola Co.
Ross-Temp
Royal Crown Cola Corp.
Seven-Up Company
Sunkist Soft Drinks
Vendo Co.

Camera Equipment
Bell & Howell Company
Camera Mart, Inc.
CECO, Inc.
Mauer, J. A., Inc.
Mitchell Camera Corp.
Oxberry Berkey Technical

Candy and Candy Machines
Adams and Brooks, Inc.
Banner Candy Mfg. Corp.
Beich, Paul F., Co.
Heide, Henry, Inc.
Hershey Chocolate Corp.
Holloway, M. J. Co.
Hollywood Brands, Inc.
M&M/Mars
Nabisco Confections, Inc.
Nestle Foods Corp.
Quaker City Chocolate & Confectionery Co., Inc.
H. B. Reese Candy
Vendo Co.

Carbons, Carbon Savers & Carbon Coolers
The Marble Co., Inc.
Union Carbide Corp.
Xetron

Coin Changing Machines
National Rejectors, Inc.

Concession Stands
Butler Fixture & Mfg. Co.
Proctor Companies, Inc.
Roundup Food Equipment
Stein Industries, Inc.

Cups & Trays
American Can Company
Continental Bondware
Continental Can Co.
Dixie/Marathon
Lily-Tulip Cup Corp.
Sno-Ball Food Service & Concession Supply Inc.
Solo Cup Company

Curtains and Curtain Controls and Acoustical Drapes
Automatic Devices Co.
Econo-Pleat
Novelty Scenic Studios
Soundfold, Inc.
Standard Theatre Supply

Drive-In Admissions Control
Eprad
K-Hill Signal Corp.

Drive-In Screens and Towers
Ballantyne of Omaha
Selby Industries, Inc.
Technikote

Equipment Cases
Fiberbilt, Division of Ikelheimer-Ernst, Inc.

Exit Signs
NRD Inc.

Film
Research Technology International

Film Editing
A.V.E. Corporation

Film Inspection & Cleaning Equipment
Bartco Co.

Film Perforation Repair Machines
Cincecare International

Film Splicers
Ciro Equipment
Prestoseal Mfg. Corp.

Floor Coverings
Gulistan Carpet

Koneta Matting
Smith, Alexander, Inc.

Food and Food Concessions Suppliers
Armour Food Co.
Bon-Bon Co. of America
Carnation Co.
Castleberry's Food Co.
Poppers Supply Co. Inc.
Roundup Food Equipment
Rowe Mfg. Co.
Sani Serv
Server Products Inc.
Smithfield Ham & Products Co.
Sno-Ball Food Service & Concession Supply
    Inc.
Stein Industries, Inc.
Tri-State Refreshments, Inc.
Vendo Co.

Food Equipment
Alto Shaam Inc.
American Wyott Corporation
Gold Metal Products Company
Good Time Foods Inc.
Greer Enterprises, Inc.

In-Car Speakers and Heaters
Ballantyne of Omaha
Eprad, Inc.
LPB Inc.
The Marble Co., Inc.
Projected Sound, Inc.
Reed Speaker Mfg. Co., Inc.

Interior Decoration
Novelty Scenic Studios

Lenses, Projection
Atlantic Audio Visual Corp.
Cinema Film Systems, Inc.
Kollmorgen Corp.
The Marble Co., Inc.
Panavision, Inc.
Schneider Corp. of America

Lighting Equipment, Studio
Kliegl Bros. Universal Electric Stage Lighting
    Co., Inc.
Charles Ross, Inc.

Lighting Systems
Lightworks

Playground Equipment
American Playground Device Co.
Herschell, Allan, Co., Inc.
Miracle Space Equipment Co.

Platter Systems
M.J.M. Industries, Inc.
Potts Inc.

Popcorn Machines and Supplies
American Popcorn Company
B & H Company

Blevins Popcorn Co.
Butterful, Inc.
Consolidated Popcorn
C. Cretors & Co.
Durkee Food Service
Gold Metal Products Co.
Liberty Brand Co. Inc.
Manley, Inc.
Odell's
Parker Popcorn Co., Inc.
Proctor Companies Inc.
Quinn Popcorn Co., Inc.
Rex Packaging
Server Products, Inc.
Simonin's C. F. Sons, Inc.
Stein Industries, Inc.
Weaver Popcorn Co.

Projection Light Equipment
Ballantyne of Omaha
Canrad-Hanovia, Inc.
Cinema Film Systems, Inc.
Imperial Electric Co.
The Marble Co., Inc.
Kneisley Electric Co.
Optical Radiation Corp.
Osram Sales Corporation
RCA
Rank Organisation
Strong Electric Co.
Xetron

Projection Room Accessories
Neumade Products Corp.
Theatre Equipment Co.

Projectors and Parts
A.V.E. Corporation
American Theatre Products, Inc.
Ballantyne of Omaha
Century Projector Corp.
Cinema Film Systems, Inc.
Kinotone, Inc.
La Vezzi Machine Works
National Theatre Supply
RCA
Simplex Equipment Corp.
Edward H. Wolk

Recording Equipment
Ampex Corporation
Bach Auricon, Inc.
Magnasync Corp.
Maurer, J. A., Inc.
RCA
Reeves Equipment Corp.
S.O.S. Photo-Cine-Optics, Inc.
Westrex-Litton Industries, Inc.

Screen Frames
Standard Theatre Supply Co.
Stewart Filmscreen Corp.

Screens and Screen Paint
Hurley Screen Co.
Stewart Filmscreen Corp.
Technikote Corp.
Williams Screen Co.

Seating for Auditoriums
Advance Seating & Repair, Inc.
American Desk Co.
American Seating Co.
Country Roads, Inc.
Griggs Int'l. Inc.
Heywood-Wakefield Co.
Irwin Seating Co.
Mannk Fabrics Co., Inc.
Massey Seating Co.

Sound Equipment
Altec-Lansing
Ballantyne of Omaha
Cardinal Systems Corporation
Century Projector Corp.
Cerwin-Vega
Cinema Film Systems, Inc.
Cinematograph International, Inc.
Cinetronix Inc.
Kelmar Systems, Inc.
Kinotone, Inc.
Kintek, Inc.
Lucasfilm Ltd/The Sound System Program
RCA
Radio Systems, Inc.
Simplex Equipment Corp.
Smart Theatre Systems
Soundcraft
Urei
Westrex-Litton Industries, Inc.

Spotlights
Kneisley Electric Co.
Strong Electric Co.

Stage Lighting
Century Strand, Inc.
Kliegl Bros.

Studio Lighting
Century Strand, Inc.
Frost Inc., Jack A.
Charles Ross, Inc.

Theatre Design
Forest Bay Construction

3-D Viewers & Projectors
Marks Polarized Corp.

Ticket Machines and Boxes
DI/AN Controls Inc.
Eprad
Globe Ticket Company

Videotape
Research Technology International

Theatre Supply Dealers

ALABAMA
Birmingham
QUEEN CONCESSION SUPPLY CO., 2409 First Ave., North 35203; (205) 251-8665.

ARIZONA
Phoenix
ARIZONA THEATRE EQUIPMENT, 1410 E. Washington, 85026; (602) 437-0215.

CALIFORNIA
Culver City
BUDD THEATRE SUPPLY, INC., 8537 West Washington Blvd., 90230; (213) 870-9301.

Inglewood
CARTER EQUIPMENT CO., LTD., 15430 Condon Ave., Lawndale, CA 90260; (213) 772-1177.

Los Angeles
AUTOMATIC DEVICES CO., 553 Oak Knoll Ave., Pasadena 91109; (213) 681-4338.
BARRETT-ROBINSON CO., 9165 Las Tunas Dr., Temple City 91780; (213) 285-1229.
FILBERT, JOHN P., 1100 Flower, Glendale; (213) 247-6550.
GROSH, SCENIC STUDIOS, 4114 Sunset Blvd.; (213) 662-1134.
HARRAH'S THEATRE SERVICE & SUPPLY, INC., 624 So. San Fernandino Blvd., Burbank, CA 91502; (818) 842-5111.
NATIONAL THEATRE SUPPLY, 2001 S. La Cienega Blvd. 90034; (213) 838-1821.
OLESEN CO., 1535 Ivar Ave., L.A.; (213) 461-4631.
PEMBREX THEATRE SUPPLY, 1100 Flower, Glendale 91209; (213) 247-6550.
THEATRE UPHOLSTERING CO., 1358 W. 24th, L.A.; (213) 733-3200.

San Francisco
PACIFIC THEATRE EQUIPMENT CO., 142 Leavenworth St., 94101; (415) 771-2950.

COLORADO
Denver
MID-CONTINENT THEATRE SUPPLY, 6743 East 50th Ave., Commerce City, CO 80022; (303) 289-5727. Dick Lutz, mgr.
PROCTOR COMPANIES, INC., 2335 S. Inca, Denver, CO 80223; (303) 934-5455.
WESTERN SERVICE & SUPPLY, 4081 South Eliot St., Englewood, CO 80110; (303) 762-8100. R. K. Tankersley, mgr.

DISTRICT OF COLUMBIA
Washington
BEN LUST, 623 Sligo Ave., Silver Spring, MD 20910; (301) 589-6606. Irwin Lust, pres.
R&S THEATRE SUPPLY CO., 4701 42nd St., N.W.; (202) 244-1500.
WILMO CORP., 3322 M St., N.W., 20013; (202) 337-6680.

FLORIDA
Jacksonville
JACKSONVILLE FILM SERVICE, INC., 2208 West 21st, 32209; (904) 355-5447.
Miami
JOE HORNSTEIN, INC., 759 W. Flagler St., 33152; (305) 545-5842.

GEORGIA
Albany
DIXIE THEATRE SERVICE & SUPPLY, 1010 N. Slappey Dr., 31701.
Atlanta
AMERICAN THEATRE SUPPLY, P.O. Box 54553, 30303; (404) 875-3167.
CAPITAL CITY SUPPLY, 2124 Jackson Parkway, N.W., 30304; (404) 792-9424.
NATIONAL THEATRE SUPPLY, 1325 Logan Circle, N.W., 30318; (404) 351-1419.

Savannah
RHODES SOUND & PROJECTION SERVICE, 218 E. 56th St., 31401.

ILLINOIS
Chicago
NATIONAL THEATRE SUPPLY (National Screen Service), 1322 S. Wabash Ave., 60605; (312) 427-8211.

IOWA
Des Moines
MTS NORTHWEST SOUND, INC., 1005 High St., 50309; (515) 243-6520.

KENTUCKY
Louisville
FALLS CITY THEATRE EQUIPMENT, 427 S. Third St., 40201.
HADDEN THEATRE SUPPLY, 909 Emerson Ave., P.O. Box 4151, 40201.

LOUISIANA
New Orleans
NATIONAL CINEMA SUPPLY CORP., 5624 Jefferson Hwy., Harahan, LA 70123.
SOUTHERN THEATRE SUPPLY, INC., 3822 Airline Highway, Metairie; (504) 831-1001.

MASSACHUSETTS
Boston
MAJOR THEATRE EQUIPMENT CORP., 28 Piedmont St., 02116; (617) 542-0445 or 542-6797.

MICHIGAN
Detroit
ALTEC SERVICE CO., 401 Commerce Bldg., 48403; (313) 963-3180.
AMUSEMENT SUPPLY CO., 208 W. Montcalm, 48233; (313) 961-3440.
NORTHWEST STUDIOS, INC., 36419 Groesbeck Highway, Mt. Clemens, MI 48043; (313) 792-1380.

Garden City
RINGOLD THEATRE EQUIPMENT CO., 30948 Ford Road; (313) 522-4650.

Grand Rapids
RINGOLD THEATRE EQUIPMENT CO., 6504-28 St., S.E., 49506; (616) 957-2684.

MINNESOTA
Minneapolis
MTS NORTHWEST SOUND, INC., 51 Glenwood Ave., 55403; (612) 332-1166.

MISSOURI
Kansas City
MID CONTINENT THEATRE SUPPLY, 1800 Wyandotte, 64108; (816) 221-0480.
NATIONAL THEATRE SUPPLY, 1800 Baltimore, 64108; (816) 221-9858.

St. Louis
RINGOLD CINEMA EQUIPMENT CORP., 4547 Green Park Rd., 63123; (314) 487-3283.

NEBRASKA
Omaha
SLIPPER THEATRE SUPPLY, INC., 1502 Davenport St., 68102; (402) 341-5715.

NEVADA
Las Vegas
PEMBREX THEATRE SUPPLY CO., 3519 Algonquin Dr., 89109; (702) 735-5542.

NEW JERSEY
Camden
NATIONAL THEATRE SUPPLY CO., 130 Ferry Ave., 08104; (609) 962-9200.

NEW YORK
Albany
ALBANY THEATRE SUPPLY, 443 N. Pearl St.; (518) 465-8894. Jack McGrath.
Buffalo
THEATRE EQUIPMENT & SERVICE CO., 688 Main St., 14202; (716) 854-1736.
Kingston
SUMMIT ENTERPRISES, Gov. Clinton Hotel; (914) 338-5095.
Tarrytown
MOTION PICTURE ENTERPRISES, P.O. Box 276, 10591; (212) 245-0969. Herbert R. Pilzer, pres.
New York City
CAPITOL MOTION PICTURE SUPPLY, CORP., 630 Ninth Ave.; (212) 757-4510.
JOE HORNSTEIN, INC., 341 W. 44 St., 10036; (212) 246-6285.
STAR CINEMA SUPPLY, 217 W. 21 St., 10011; (212) 675-3515.

NORTH CAROLINA
Charlotte
AMERICAN THEATRE SUPPLY CO., 529 S. Tryon St., 28202; (704) 333-5076.
CHARLOTTE THEATRE SUPPLY CO., 704 Morris St., 28233; (704) 333-9651.
WIL-KIN, INC., 800 S. Graham St., 28202; (704) 333-6101.
Greensboro
STANDARD THEATRE SUPPLY CO., 125 Higgins St., 20660; (919) 272-6165.

OHIO
Cleveland
OHIO THEATRE SUPPLY CO., 7976 Broadview Rd., 44101; (216) 526-2783.

OKLAHOMA
Oklahoma City
OKLAHOMA THEATRE SUPPLY, 628 W. Sheridan Ave., 73125; (405) 236-8691.

PENNSYLVANIA
Philadelphia
BLUMBERG BROS., 1305 Vine St., 19104; (215) 925-7240.
Pittsburgh
NATIONAL THEATRE SUPPLY, 107 6th St. (Fulton Bldg.), 15233; (412) 471-4630.
THEATRE EQUIPMENT & SERVICE CO., 100 Lighthill St., 15233; (412) 322-4600 or (412) 322-0320.

TENNESSEE
Memphis
TRI-STATE THEATRE SUPPLY, 151 Vance Ave., 38101; (901) 525-8249.
Nashville
CAPITAL CITY SUPPLY CO., INC., 6028 Neighborly Ave., 37209; (615) 256-0347.
MID-SOUTH THEATRE SERVICE, 439 Brewer Drive, 37209; (615) 832-5660.

TEXAS
Dallas
MODERN SALES & SERVICE, 2200 Young St., 75247; (214) 747-3191.
TEXAS INTERNATIONAL THEATRE SUPPLY, 7138 Envoy Court, 75247; (214) 634-7150.
Houston
SOUTHWESTERN THEATRE EQUIPMENT, 500-C North Shepherd Dr., 77007; (713) 861-3344.
San Antonio
INDEPENDENT THEATRE SUPPLY, 2750 E. Houston, 78205.
TEXAS THEATRE SUPPLY, 915 S. Alamo St., 78205; (214) 222-1002.

UTAH
Salt Lake City
CLACO EQUIPMENT & SERVICE, 1212 South State St., 84111; (801) 355-1250.
UNIVERSAL THEATRE SUPPLY, 264 East First South St.; (801) 328-1641.

VIRGINIA
Alexandria
STANDARD THEATRE SUPPLY CO., 82 South Early St., 22304; (703) 370-4500.
Roanoke
PERDUE MOTION PICTURES EQUIPMENT, INC., 2315 Williamson Rd., N.E., 24012; (703) 366-0295.
Norfolk
STANDARD THEATRE SUPPLY, 1540 Norview Ave., 23513; (804) 855-8029.

WASHINGTON
Seattle
BROCKLIND'S INC., 901 Olive Way, 98109; (206) MU 2-5898.
BURNS, S. F. & CO., INC., 2319 2nd Ave.; (206) 624-2515.
FACTORY DIRECT DRAPERIES INC., 8300 Aurora N; (206) LA 5-7932.
FAIRBANKS HARLAN CO., 1405 Elliott W; (206) 284-7420.
NATIONAL THEATRE SUPPLY CO., 2413 2nd Ave., 98121; (206) 624-7710.

WEST VIRGINIA
Charleston
MOORE THEATRE EQUIPMENT, 213 Delaware Ave. P.O. Box 782, 25301; (304) 344-4413.

WISCONSIN
Milwaukee
HARRY MELCHER ENTERPRISES, 3607 W. Fond Du Lac Ave., 53220; (414) 442-5020.

Federal Government Film & Media Services

EXECUTIVE DEPARTMENTS

DEPARTMENT OF AGRICULTURE

Video and Teleconference Division, 1614 South Bldg., USDA, Washington, DC 20250; (202) 447-2592; Larry Quinn, chief of division.
Produces video, film, and teleconference presentations for use and distribution both inside and outside of the department.
(For information on obtaining USDA productions, see *National Archives and Records Administration*, below.)

DEPARTMENT OF COMMERCE

Audiovisual Section, Office of Public Affairs, 14th St., Rm. 5521, Washington, DC 20230; (202) 377-3263; Bob Amdur, section chief.
Productions of department (by individual bureaus) videos and films are contracted out; distribution is free of charge and handled by an outside company. Contact this number for more information.
International Trade Administration, Office of Service Industries, Entertainment Division, 14th St. and Constitution Ave., Washington, DC 20230; (202) 377-4781; John Siegmund, International Trade Specialist.
Studies and reports statistics of the industry at home and abroad; the material gathered is published in department reports along with comparative information from other industries. Also concerned with promoting the industry abroad and overcoming trade barriers.
National Telecommunications and Information Administration, Main Commerce Bldg., Washington, DC 20230; (202) 377-1840; Alfred Sikes, Asst. Secretary for Communications and Information.
Develops telecommunications policy for executive branch; conducts technical research on various aspects of telecommunications; makes and administers grants to noncommercial public telecommunications services for construction of facilities.

DEPARTMENT OF DEFENSE

Broadcast-Pictorial Branch, The Pentagon Bldg., Rm. 2E765, Washington, DC 20301-1400; (202) 695-0168; Lt. Col. Steve Titunik, branch chief.
Provides public affairs assistance to non-government electornic and print news media, documentary producers, industrial firms, ad and marketing agencies, publishers, independent producers, educational institutions, and other commercial enterprises with visual informative materials.
Federal Audiovisual Contract Management Office, 601 N. Fairfax St., Alexandria, VA 22314-2007; (202) 274-4876; Florence Harley, Audiovisual management specialist.
This office maintains lists of qualified film and video producers; contracts throughout the federal government will only be awarded to producers who appear on these lists. For information on criteria and selection, contact Ms. Harley at the above address.
Military Departments
Department of the Air Force, Public Affairs, Public Communications Branch, The Pentagon Bldg., Rm. 4A120, Washington, DC 20330-1000; (202) 697-2769; Maj. P. J. Crowley, chief of branch.

Department of the Army, Media Relations Division, Army Public Affairs, The Pentagon Bldg., Rm. 2E641, Washington, DC 20310-1500; (202) 697-2564; Col. Bill Smullen, chief of division.

Department of the Navy, Chief of Information, The Pentagon Bldg., Rm. 2E341, Washington, DC 20350-1200; (202) 697-5342; Cdr. Mark Baker, Asst. Chief of Information.

U.S Marine Corps Headquarters, Attention P.A.M., Washington, DC 20380-0001; (202) 694-1492; Brig. Gen. H. W. Jenkins Jr., Director of Public Affairs.
(The above public affairs offices all have regional branches; contact the Washington addresses for more information.)
Special Assistant for Audiovisual, The Pentagon Bldg., Rm. 2E789, Washington, DC 20301-1400; (202) 695-2936; Donald Baruch, head of division; Capt. Susan Hankey, assistant.
Acts on all requests for Department of Defense assistance from any segment of the film and television industries concerned with dramatic productions and documentaries not dealing with news.

DEPARTMENT OF EDUCATION

Office of Public Affairs, Audiovisual Division, 400 Maryland Ave. SW, Rm. 2089, FOB #6, Washington, DC 20202; (202) 732-4559; Greg Grafson, Audiovisual officer.
Monitors all film video, and audio materials generated by department contracts with, or grants to, companies or non-profit organizations. Distribution of these materials is through the National Audiovisual Center (see *National Archives and Records Administration*, below) or by special arrangements with producers.
Office of Special Education and Rehabilitation Services, 400 Maryland Ave. SW, Switzer Bldg., Rm. 4629, Washington, DC, 20202; (202) 732-1172; Ernest Harrston, acting branch chief, captioning.

This division purchases already produced films and captions them for use by the hearing impaired; contact Mr. Harrston for a catalogue of titles.

DEPARTMENT OF ENERGY

Office of Public Affairs, 1000 Independence Ave. SW, CP24, Washington, DC 20585; (202) 586-6250; Chett Gray, Public Information Specialist.
This department contracts film and video productions to a private company.

DEPARTMENT OF HEALTH AND HUMAN SERVICES

Office of Public Affairs, 200 Independence Ave. SW, Washington, DC, 20201; (202) 245-1897; Jim Miller, Director of Communications.
Produces, distributes, and contracts out video and radio productions. Each of the five branches of HHS has its own public affairs and audivisual office, listed below.
Family Support Administration, 370 L'Enfant Promenade SW, 6th floor, Washington, DC 20447; (202) 252-4518; Nancy Keever, Administrator of Public Affairs.
FSA contracts to produce videos outside of the department.
Health Care Financing Administration, 200 Independence Ave. SW, Rm. 435H, Washington, DC 20201; (202) 245-7257; Dennis Siebert, Director of Public Affairs.
Produces, distributes, and contracts out films and tapes.
Office of Human Development Services, 200 Independence Ave. SW, Rm. 356G, Washington, DC 20201; (202) 472-7257; Sharon Messinger, Director of Public Affairs.
This division contracts to produce films and tapes outside of the department.
Social Security Administration, Office of Government Affairs, 4200 West High Rise, 641 Security Blvd., Baltimore, MD 21235; (301) 965-1720; Mary Ann Hatchitt, Associate Commissioner.
Produces and distributes films and tapes.
U.S. Public Health Service (including *Alcohol, Drug Abuse, and Mental Health Administration, Centers for Disease Control, Food and Drug Administration, Health Resources and Services Administration, Indian Health Service, National Institutes of Health*) Office of Public Affairs, 200 Independence Ave. SW, Rm. 717H, Washington, DC 20201; (202) 245-6867; James Brown, Director of Public Affairs.
Produces, distributes, and contracts out films and tapes.

DEPARTMENT OF HOUSING AND URBAN DEVELOPMENT

Office of Public Affairs, HUD Bldg., 451 7th St. SW, Rm. 10132, Washington, DC 20410; (202) 755-5685; Jane Gallagher, Director of Public Affairs.
This department occasionally contracts outside of the government for video productions.

DEPARTMENT OF THE INTERIOR

Bureau of Mines,
Audiovisual Library, Cochransmill Road, P.O. Box 18070, Pittsburgh, PA 15236; (412) 892-6845; Evelyn Donnelly, librarian (for distribution and purchase of films and tapes).
Office of Public Information, Audiovisual Program, 2401 E St. NW, Washington, DC 20241; (202) 634-1335; William Gage, Director of Audiovisual Program (for information about the department's programs).
The bureau maintains a library of 16mm films and 3/4 inch videos depicting mining, metallurgical operations, and related manufacturing processes. One branch of the program, Mineral Resource Series, is composed of broad-based documentaries directed toward a general audience; the films are produced by independent producers and industrial concerns (they do not carry trademarks, trade names, or other direct advertising). The second branch, Technology Transfer Film Program, is produced by bureau research divisions and is directed toward industry and specialized educational programs. All films and tapes are loaned free of charge (except for return postage) to educational institutions, industries, training workers, engineering and scientific societies, and civic and business associations. Information and catalogues may be obtained from both of the above addresses.

DEPARTMENT OF JUSTICE

Audiovisual Services, 10th St. and Pennsylvania Ave., Rm. 1313, Washington, DC 20530; (202) 633-4694; Mathew White, supervisor.
Records department ceremonies and functions; no distribution.

DEPARTMENT OF LABOR

Audiovisual and Photographic Services Branch, Audiovisual Division, 200 Constitution Ave. NW, N6311, Washington, DC 20210; (202) 523-7820; Stan Hankin, chief of branch.

Produces 16mm, 35mm, and video productions and documents department ceremonies; contracts work outside the department as well.

DEPARTMENT OF STATE

International Communications and Information Policy, Department of State, Rm. 6313, Washington, DC 20520; (202) 647-5727; Diana Lady Dougan, U.S. Coordinator and Director.
Develops, implements, and oversees international communication policy for the department; acts as a liaison for other federal agencies and the private sector in international communications issues.
Office of International Trade, Department of State, Rm. 3831, Washington, DC 20520; (202) 647-2325; Donald McConville, Director.
Concerned with commercial aspects of film industry, trade treaties, restrictions, quotas, copyrights, etc; call for information on specific questions.
Special Projects Staff, Office of Public Communications, Bureau of Public Affairs, Department of State, Rm. 4827A, Washington, DC 20520; (202) 647-8926; James Murray, Director of Staff.
Produces video documentaries on foreign policy topics; available for free educational and public distribution through the Washington office and a number of regional centers. Contact the above address for more information and a catalogue.

DEPARTMENT OF TRANSPORTATION

Office of Public Affairs, 400 7th St. SW, Rm. 10413, Washington, DC 20590; (202) 366-5580; Bill Mosley, Public Affairs officer.
Departmental productions contracted out, although individual agencies do produce films and tapes. Three of the ten agencies are listed below.
Federal Highway Administration, Audiovisual and Visual Aids, 400 7th St. SW, Rm. 4429, HMS24, Washington, DC 20590; (202) 366-9125; Norma Lesser, section chief.
Produces and distributes videos and films to transportation professionals; loans are free of charge.
National Highway and Traffic Safety Administration, Public Affairs, Audiovisual Section, 400 7th St. SW, Rm. 5232, Washington, DC 20590; (202) 366-9550; Tina Foley, Public Affairs Specialist.
Produces and distributes videos and films; also, contracts work outside of the department.
United States Coast Guard, Public Affairs, Audiovisual Branch, Commandante, G-TPA-1, 2100 2nd St. SW, Washington, DC 20593; (202) 267-0923; Wayne Paul, branch chief.
Oversees film and video production and distribution (collection also handled by the National Audiovisual Center, see below), and coordinates the work of the regional film liaison offices.
U.S. Coast Guard Hollywood Liaison, Public Affairs Liaison, Federal Bld., Suite 10125, 1100 Wilshire Blvd., Los Angeles, CA 90024-3612; (213) 209-7817; Cdr. John McElwaine, Hollywood Liaison.

DEPARTMENT OF TREASURY

Office of Public Affairs, 1500 Pennsylvania Ave. NW, Rm. 3414, Washington, DC 20220; (202) 566-8773; Charlie Powers, chief.
Productions are made by individual bureaus within the department (such as the Internal Revenue Service). Contact this address and phone number for more information.

EXECUTIVE AGENCIES

ENVIRONMENTAL PROTECTION AGENCY

Audiovisual Division, Office of Public Affairs, 401 M St. SW, A-107, Washington, DC 20460; (202) 382-2044; Michael Scott, Director.
Produces and distributes videos and films on the environment, pollution, conservation, and related subjects; contracts some productions outside of the agency. Catalog is available on request and loans are mostly free of charge (videos are dubbed on to blank tapes mailed to the division).

FEDERAL COMMUNICATIONS COMMISSION

1919 M St. NW, Washington, DC 20554; (202) 632-6600; Dennis Patrick, Chairman.
Regulates interstate and foreign communications by television, radio, satellite, cable, wire, and microwave. Reviews applications for construction permits and licenses for such services. Selected divisions listed below; for further information, contact *Office of Public Affairs;* (202) 632-5050; John Kamp, chief.
Cable Television; (202) 632-7480; Stephen Ross, chief.
Processes applications and notifications for licensing of cable television relay service stations; registers cable television systems; develops, administer, and enforces regulation of cable TV and CARS.
Engineering and Technology; (202) 632-7060; Thomas Stanley, chief engineer;
Advises FCC on all technical matters and assists in development of telecommunications policy. Reviews develpments in telecommunication technology. Technical library open to the public.
Mass Media Bureau; (202) 632-6460; Alex Felker, chief.
Licenses, regulates, and develops audio and video services in traditional broadcasting, cable, and emerging systems including high definition television; processes applications for licensing of commercial and non-commercial television and radio broadcast equipment

and facilities; handles renewals and changes of ownership; investigates public complaints.

FEDERAL TRADE COMMISSION

6th St. and Pennsylvania Ave. NW, Washington, DC 20580; (202) 326-2180.
Administers statutes designed to promote fair competetion; institutes proceedings to prevent unfair or deceptive practices, combinations in restraint of trade, false advertising, and illegal price discrimination. Supervises associations of exporters under the Export Trade Act. (For specific bureaus or further information, contact the *Public Affairs Office* at the above address and phone number.)

LIBRARY OF CONGRESS

Audiovisual Section of the *Special Materials Cataloging Division, Processing Services Department,* Madison Bldg., Rm. 547, Washington, DC 20540; (202) 287-6758; Richard Thaxter, chief of section.
Supervises the cataloging of approximately 3,000 motion pictures, videos, and sets of slides and transparencies a year, largely on the basis of information supplied by producers and media libraries.
Copyright Office, Madison Bldg., Rm. 403, Washington, DC 20540; (202) 287-8350; Ralph Oman, Register of Copyrights.
Registers films and videos for copyrights.
Copyright Cataloging Division, Rm. 513; (202) 287-8040; Peter Young, chief of division.
Supervises the preparation of the semi-annual *Catalog of Copyright Entries: Motion Pictures and Film Strips* which is distributed by the Superintendent of Documents, Government Printing Office, Washington, DC 20402. This publication contains descriptive data for all theatrical and non-theatrical films and videos registered for copyright during each six-month period.
Motion Picture, Broadcast and Recorded Sound Division of the *Research Services Department,* Madison Bldg., Rm. 338, Washington, DC 20540; (202) 287-5840; Robert Saudek, chief of division.
Supervises the library's collection of more than 331,000 films and videos. The collection is an archive of copyright deposits plus some gift materials. It contains 35mm, 16mm, and 3/4 inch features and television programs, and some documentary, educational, scientific, religious, and industrial proudctions. The collection is chiefly American, but includes German, Italian, and Japanese films. The division has an entensive film and video preservation program and houses historically important films from the early days of the industry.

NATIONAL ARCHIVES AND RECORDS ADMINISTRATION

Motion Picture Sound and Video Branch, Washington, DC 20408; (202) 786-0041; William Murphy, chief of branch.
Houses one of the world's largest audiovisual archives, including more than 120,000 films and 13,000 videos; collection includes documentaries, newreels, combat films, and raw historical footage (government productions as well as gift collections from film corporations and television networks).
National Audiovisual Center, Customer Services Section, 8700 Edgeworth Dr., Capitol Heights, MD 20743; (301) 763-1896; Kevin Hood, director.
Holds relatively current collection of over 8,500 U.S. audiovisual productions for sale and rental (available in all formats). Distributes the collections of many government departments and agencies, in addition to those specifically noted above.
Presidential Libraries Central Office, Washington, DC 20408; (202) 523-3212; John Fawcett, Director.
The eight presidential libraries, located throughout the country, can be reached from this office. Each library has extensive audiovisual materials relevant to that administration; the collection begins with President Coolidge.

NATIONAL ENDOWMENT FOR THE ARTS

Media Arts Program: Film/Radio/Television, 1100 Pennsylvania Ave. NW 20506; (202) 682-5452; Brian O'Doherty, director.
Provides grants to individuals and non-profit organizations for film, video, and radio productions; supports arts programming for public television and radio.

NATIONAL ENDOWMENT FOR THE HUMANITIES

Humanities Projects in Media, 1100 Pennsylvania Ave. NW, 20506; (202) 786-0278; James Dougherty, director.
Provides grants for non-profit media projects aimed at advancing the use and understanding of the humanities.

SECURITIES AND EXCHANGE COMMISSION

Division of Corporation Finance, 450 5th St. NW, Washington, DC 20549.
Reviews financial statements and disclosures.
Radio, Television, and Telegraph, Rm. 3113; (202) 272-2683; H. Christopher Owings, Asst., Director.
Motion Pictures, Rm. 3134; (202) 272-3275; Ann Wallace, Asst. Director.
(For further information concerning registration of security offerings and supervision of trading, contact *Public Affairs,* (202) 272-2650.)

SMITHSONIAN INSTITUTION

Film Archives, Information Management Division, National Air and Space Museum, Washington, DC 20560; (202) 357-4721; Mark Taylor, Film Archivist.

Houses about 10,000 films and videos from Smithsonian, government, other museums, and industry collections.

Smithsonian World, 955 L'Enfant Plaza, Washington, DC 20560; (202) 488-4500; Adrian Malone, Executive Producer.

One hour program broadcast on public television stations.

Telecommunications Office, National Museum of American History, Rm. BB40, Washington, DC 20560; (202) 357-1935; Paul Johnson, Director.

Produces films and videos which are distributed for a fee through a private company. Contact this office for more information.

(Other museums and galleries have small archive collection; contact the *Office of Public Affairs* for more information, (202) 357-2627.

U.S. INFORMATION AGENCY

Television and Film Service, 601 D St. NW, Rm. 5000, Washington, DC 20547; (202) 376-1127; Alvin Snyder, Director.

USIA produces and acquires about 200 film and television documentaries annually for information and cultural programs in 117 countries. In addition, close to 350 targeted, and 150 worldwide new clips are made for use on foreign television. These are seen abroad in commercial theatres, in television, in schools and community centers, and by clubs, universities, and other audiences. Television and Film Service also cerifies the exemption of import duties if a film is educational.

U.S. INTERNATIONAL TRADE COMMISSION

Office of the Secretary, 500 E Street, Rm. 112, Washington, DC 20436; (202) 252-1000; Kenneth Mason, Secretary.

Conducts countervailing duty, anti-dumping, and patent and trademark infringement investigations; the commission is a fact-finding body which addresses business complaints, holds hearings, and makes recommendations to the Department of Commerce.

Distributors of 16mm Feature Films

Following is a listing of distributors having substantial selections of 16mm films for lease or rental. Additionally, some of the companies may have prints available for outright purchase. Inquiries for catalogs listing complete product should be made to the addresses given below.

BENCHMARK FILMS
145 Scarborough Road, Briarcliff Manor, NY 10510; (914) 762-3838.

BLACKHAWK CATALOG
12636 Beatrice St., Los Angeles, CA 90066; (213) 306-4040.

BUDGET FILMS
4590 Santa Monica Blvd., Los Angeles, CA 90029; (213) 660-0187.

CAROUSEL FILMS
241 E. 34 St., room 304, New York, NY 10016; (212) 683-1160.

CINECOM PICTURES
1250 Broadway, New York, NY 10001; (212) 239-8360.

CINEMA GUILD
1697 Broadway, New York, NY 10019; (212) 246-5522.

CIRCLE RELEASING
1101 23rd St. NY, Washington, DC 20037; (202) 331-3838.

CLEM WILLIAMS
2240 Noblestown Rd., Pittsburgh, PA 15205; (412) 921-5810.

COLUMBIA CLASSICS
Columbia Pictures, The Burbank Studios, Burbank, CA 91505; (818) 954-4485.

CORINTH FILMS
34 Gansevoort St., New York, NY 10014; (212) 463-0305.

DIRECT CINEMA
P.O. Box 69589, Los Angeles, CA 90069; (213) 652-8000.

DISNEY PRODUCTIONS
500 S. Buena Vista St., Burbank, CA 91521; (818) 840-1000.

EM GEE FILM LIBRARY
6924 Canby Ave., Suite 103, Reseda, CA 91335; (818) 981-5506.

EUROPEAN CLASSICS
4818 Yuma St. NW, Washington, DC 20016; (202) 363-8800.

FILM-MAKERS COOPERATIVE
175 Lexington Ave., New York, NY 10016; (212) 889-3820.

FILMS INCORPORATED
5547 N. Ravenswood Ave., Chicago, IL 60640; (312) 878-2600.

FIRST RUN/ICARUS
200 Park Ave. South, Suite 1319, New York, NY 10003; (212) 674-3375.

HURLOCK CINE-WORLD, INC.
Box 34619, Juneau, AK 99803; (907) 789-3395.

IFEX FILMS/INTERNATIONAL FILM EXCHANGE LTD.
201 W. 52 St., New York, NY 10019; (212) 582-4318.

THE IMAGES FILM ARCHIVE, INC.
300 Phillips Park Rd., Mamaroneck, NY 10543; (914) 381-2993.

INTERAMA
301 W. 53 St., Suite 19E, New York, NY 10019; (212) 977-4836.

IVY FILM
165 W. 46 St., New York, NY 10036; (212) 382-0111.

KINO INTERNATIONAL
333 W. 39 St., Suite 503, New York, NY 10018; (212) 629-6880.

KIT PARKER
1245 10th St., Monterey, CA 93940; (408) 649-5573.

MANBECK PICTURES CORP.
3621 Wakonda Dr., Des Moines, IA 50321; (515) 285-8345.

MODERN SOUND
1402 Howard St., Omaha, NE 68102; (402) 341-8476.

MUSEUM OF MODERN ART FILM LIBRARY
11 W. 53 St., New York, NY 10019; (212) 708-9433.

NEW LINE CINEMA
575 Eighth Ave., New York, NY 10018; (212) 239-8880.

NEW YORKER FILMS
16 W. 61 St., New York, NY 10023; (212) 247-6110.

PRESTIGE FILM CORPORATION
18 E. 48 St., Suite 1601, New York, NY 10017; (212) 888-2662.

PYRAMID FILMS
P.O. Box 1048, Santa Monica, CA 90406; (213) 828-7577.

REPUBLIC PICTURES CORPORATION
12636 Beatrice St., Los Angeles, CA 90066; (213) 306-4040.

SAMUEL GOLDWYN COMPANY
10203 Santa Monica Blvd., Los Angeles, CA 90067; (213) 552-2255.

SWANK MOTION PICTURES
201 S. Jefferson Ave., St. Louis, MO 63166; (314) 534-6300.

THIRD WORLD NEWSREEL
335 W. 38 St., New York, NY 10018; (212) 947-9277 (feature documentaries and short fiction).

TRANS-WORLD FILMS
332 S. Michigan Ave., Chicago, IL 60604; (312) 922-1530.

Home Video

Statistics & History

Freedom of choice—the control of one's own viewing habits—has been the major impact of home video on the leisure-time industry in America. Owners of videocassette recorders can view what they want when they want and are no longer subject to the programming schedules of the television networks and cable stations. The VCR owner is able to watch yesterday's motion pictures today (by renting or owning vintage Hollywood films, foreign features and television product, as well as films released theatrically as recently as six months ago) and today's television programming tomorrow—along with how-to tapes, music videos and home movies.

Time shifting, the ability of the viewer to tape a show for later viewing (as well as eliminating commercials—by editing them out or fast forwarding past them), is the most common usage of VCRs. One can watch one program while taping another, or tape with the tv set off and nobody home. One can select entertainment or instruction from the more than 50,000 prerecorded tapes now available from the more than 30,000 video specialty stores, supermarkets, hardware stores and libraries. There are more than 40 brands of VCRs with 150 models now available, offering electronic tuner-timers and such special effects as freeze-frame and forward-reverse picture scan as basic features and such extra options as wireless remote control, variable slow and fast motion and full stereo sound. Home video has had a revolutionary effect on the entertainment habits of the nation.

Video History

1923: Though the patent for a video-camera-like device was filed in Germany one hundred years ago, the first practical product was devised by Vladimir Zworykin, a Russian/American immigrant in 1923.

1938: A primitive video disk was on sale at Selfridges of London.

Post World War II: With the development in the early 1930s of an electronic television signal and the audio tape recorder, and their coming into broadcast use in the mid-1940s, it was not long before experiments (by Ampex and RCA in the US, and BBC and Decca in Great Britain) in recording television shows and playing them back were made in earnest. Freeing directors to edit or re-shoot, and attempting to loosen the stranglehold live television broadcasting imposed on the medium, the first recorders were longitudinal machines that looked like audio recorders and used large reels of tape at high speeds.

Early 1955: BBC went on the air with its VERA (Vision Electronic Recording Apparatus) with a head gap of 20 microns and a tape speed of 200 inches per second. A reel about 5 feet in diameter was needed for taping a half-hour program.

April 1956: An American company, Ampex, produced the first working video recorders for broadcast use, using four (quad) recording heads on a rotating drum, and two-inch wide magnetic tape which was reusable. They were first used over the air at CBS's Hollywood studios in November, 1956. (A more portable system using narrower tape and a helical scan system had been patented in Germany in 1953, but the prototypes were far too expensive and difficult to use; a tape could be used only once, and each time it was used the machine had to be cleaned of tape particles.)

1967: A Japanese company, Sony, introduced the first transportable video system which used reel-to-reel tape and recorded in black and white only.

1970: Home video arrived when the first video cassette systems were produced, in the Philips Video Cassette Recorder or VCR. (Philips had also developed and licensed the compact audio cassette.) Sony introduced its ¾-inch U-Matic format intended for professional use in the film and television industries.

1972: Philips launched its N1500, the first video recorder with a tuner-timer, making domestic video recording a reality.

The simple video game, the first interactive use of the television, was introduced into viewing households, altering perception of the TV screen from one of passive reception of broadcast programs to participation.

Late 1975: Sony introduced the Betamax system, utilizing narrower 1½-inch tape (the narrower tape size resulted in lowered costs of recording and recorders). An optional timer was included to enable a viewer to tape even when he was not at home and offered the capability of recording one program while watching another. The cost was approximately $2,200 for a recorder with TV set. Blank tape cost $20.

1976: Cartrivision, V-Cord, and VHS (Video Home System) introduced systems incompatible with Betamax machines. The first two fell by the wayside while VHS (backed by Matsushita Electronics Corporation) emerged as the challenger to Sony's Betamax by making it possible to record up to 2 hours of broadcast material for the first time. Magnavox came out with a videodisc machine, strictly a playback system which used a disc similar in size and substance to a record album that is "read" by a laser beam. RCA manufactured a rival, incompatible videodisc system.

1977: The video software market was born when a small midwestern company called Magnetic Video Corporation licensed 50 feature-length films from 20th Century-Fox and released them for sale on Beta and VHS formats at retail prices of $49.95 to $79.95.

1983: Paramount Pictures paved the way for burgeoning cassette sales when it lowered the price of some of its strongest titles to $39.95 from $79.95. Other prerecorded cassette distributors soon followed suit.

Jan. 1984: United States Supreme Court, after lengthy consideration of a suit brought by MCA Inc. and Walt Disney Productions against Sony, ruled that home taping of broadcast programming is not a violation of copyright laws, in effect legitimizing what viewers were already doing.

1984: The FCC approved the start of Multi-Channel TV Sound Broadcasting, adding stereo sound to the home video experience.

May 1987: Super-VHS or S-VHS (with an expanded band width of up to 5.5 megahertz thus increasing the sharpness of picture image, and 400 lines of horizontal resolution as opposed to conventional VCR's 240) made its debut at the Consumer Electronics Show in Chicago, with anticipated production scheduled for fall of 1987. Another innovation was the introduction of 5-inch CD Video singles at a $7–8 list price, that can hold up to 20 minutes of recorded music videos.

Trends: 1988

- In 1986 the media coined a new term, "couch potato," to describe those who enjoy staying at home and watching TV or a VCR as their pastime of choice. This trend is borne out in the fact that in 1987, while theatrical exhibition grossed $4.2 billion, the home video market (including the sale and rental of videocassettes) generated $7.46 billion.

- A continuing trend from 1987 into 1988 was the commercial sponsorship of videocassettes, with ads for Diet Pepsi prefacing the top-selling Top Gun videotape as the groundbreaker.

- To counter the stagnant growth rate of video recorder sales, novel technology introduced to peek consumer interest included P.I.P. (Picture-in-Picture), a system what when hooked up to a television and videocassette receiver allows the viewer to watch two channels on one screen simultaneously.

- Toshiba displayed a three-dimensional video camera that requires viewers to wear special glasses attached to an electronic adapter. OVC marketed its "3-D Hawaiian Swimsuit Spectacular," reputedly the first 3-D video.

- Go-Video, manufacturer of the prototype VCR-2, a two-deck videocassette player with the ability to duplicate tapes, encountered further legal difficulties that prevented its marketing the machine.

- Bar coding (like that used in supermarkets for inventory control) was introduced to eliminate the pushing of buttons and reduce the chance of errors in VCR programming. A hand-held wireless LED (light emitting diode) code scanner reads and transmits the time, date, and channel information directly to the VCR.

- Three feature films ("Julia and Julia," "Crack in the Mirror" and "Do It Up") as well as a made-for-television movie ("Innocent Victims") were shot using HDV, high definition video, then converted to 35mm using a tape-to-film transfer process which converts the tape's thirty pictures per second to twenty-four frames per second on film. Though unwieldy (HDV must be hooked up to a video tape recorder by means of cables) and with a lower ASA rating than film, this new technology is a step in breaking down the traditional barriers between film and video.

- Though many "A" videos were priced at $89.95, up from $79.95, they dropped in price to an average $29.95 after their first exposure on cable TV (usually in six months).

- While the glut of "B" films made by smaller independent companies to fill the voracious needs of the expanding video industry bottomed out (proving that limited theatrical release of middle level small films did not translate into video sales and rentals) other films bypassed theatrical distribution altogether, resulting in an increase of direct-to-video-features.

Facts and Statistics

- While the Japanese and Koreans dominate the hardware market of the video industry, American producers, distributors, and marketers and retailers fill the programming needs of the ever expanding industry.

- Estimates regarding the number of United States TV households that currently own a VCR vary from 52% (E.I.A.) to 53.3% (Nielsen Station Index) (with New York VCR penetration estimated at 62%; L.A. 64% and Chicago 62%). Media analyst Paul Kagan anticipates that by the early 1990s, 70% of U.S. homes will have a VCR. Moreover an estimated 1 out of every 5 VCR households also owns a second VCR.

- Electronic Industries Association (E.I.A.) figures show that 13.306 million VCRs were sold in to dealers 1987, while 13.174 million were sold in 1986. The E.I.A. calculates that an estimated 110 million prerecorded videocassettes were sold to dealers in 1987.

- Estimated sales of prerecorded videocassettes increased in dollar sales to $2.77 billion and unit sales to 110 million in 1987 and were expected to rise again in 1988 to 135 million units worth $2.97 billion; blank videocassette sales rose to an estimated 280 million units sent to dealers.

- While table model and portable VCR sales declined, camcorder sales (increasing 25% annually since their introduction) were expected to rise to 2 million units in 1988 while sales of color video cameras fell to 113,000 units in 1986 and are expected to continued falling in 1988. (E.I.A.)

- A.C. Nielsen's annual VCR Tracking Report dated May, 1987 showed that prime-time TV shows accounted for 42% of VCR recording time. Daytime programs earned a 23% share.

- Nielsen's report also revealed that 46% of off-TV recording was done while sets were off, and 72% of all recordings was of programs broadcast by network affiliates. 21% of VCR recording occurred on Sunday evening while playback was strongest on Saturday evening (20%) the survey showed.

- While film companies are enjoying healthy growth from selling videocassettes, they are prohibited by law from garnering any of the rental revenues. The First Sale Doctrine states that once the cassette is sold to the retailer, the merchant can rent the cassette as many times as he can without giving back any royalties to the producers.

- A 1987 membership survey by the Video Software Dealers Association revealed that in 1986 a videocassette of "A" theatrical quality rented 80 times on the average while copies of "B" pictures were rented 42 times and "C" pictures 31 times.

- Price per prerecorded tape sold on the average for $17.41 in 1987 as compared to $29 in 1986 and $37.23 in 1985. Rental price average dropped to $2.12 in 1987 from $2.40 in 1986 at video stores and to $1.91 at other rental outlets (video stores account for 67% of rental transactions).

- Cambridge Associates' president Dick Kelly at the Intl. Tape/Disc Assn. estimated that total video revenues for programmers (about 80% of which go to Hollywood majors) would reach $3.7 billion in 1988 and $4.4 billion in 1990, up from the $2.95 billion figure of 1987.

- Six billion hours of prerecorded video was watched per year as compared to 221 billion hours of broadcast TV watched per year (Fairfield Group).

- An AGB research study from April, 1988 indicated that children under 18 spend an average of 50% more viewing time than adults watching prerecorded and home-recorded video tapes in VCR households. Those under 18 watch 3.4 hours per week while adults average 2.3 hours/week.

- An American Video Association survey of member video stores showed that in 1987 stores rented an average of 1,258 tapes per week (up 4% from 1986); sold 21.7 new tapes per month (up 1%) and sold 22.4 used tapes per month (up 87%). The average number of titles was up 44% to 2,563 per store, but the number of new titles purchased per month was down by 21% to 31.5. Average number of copies per "A" title was 5.2 and 1.4 per "B" title. 75% of the stores surveyed no longer carried any Beta tapes (compared to 68% in 1986).

- VCRs are used an average of 7 hours/week per household with 2.4 hours devoted to recording programs and 4.7 hours used playing prerecorded and home-recorded tapes. Some 49% of the 7 hours per week of VCR usage are spent playing rented or purchased tapes, 17% playing home recorded material. Twenty-three percent is spent recording when the television set is off or tuned to another channel while 10% is spent recording the same program the viewer is watching. The AGB Television Research study (released March, 1988) showed VCRs are more prevalent in pay-cable households (64%) than basic cable and non-cable homes (48% each). Of families with children under 18, 65% have VCRs while 48% of households without children do.

The same study found 40% of all home recordings are made in primetime, 31% in daytime. Sunday night has more recording (26%) than any other night, while Saturday is the preferred night for playback (23%).

- A Fairfield Group survey found that in 1987, 54% of the country's VCRs were at least three years old, 22% of them two years old, and 24% under a year old. Machines tended to be used less as the novelty wore off and they got older. Also rentals of videotapes fell off as the machines aged.

Retail Data

At its seventh annual convention, held August, 1988, the Video Software Dealers Association reported that video software dollar volume derived from sales (as opposed to rentals) increased 4.3% in 1987 over 1986. Rentals still accounted for 81.1% of total dollar volume but that was down from 85.4% in 1986. The VSDA commissioned survey revealed that the average prerecorded video software sales transaction was $24.51 per tape, with 1.1 the average number of titles sold (compared to 2.3 titles rented in 1987 at $2.45 per tape rental). The survey estimated that the average number of titles per store was 2832, with the average store owner operating 6.8 stores. The average number of fulltime employees was 2.6 and parttime 3.9. More than 66% of video store owners responded that business was up in 1987.

Another VDSA study showed that as the day progressed video store traffic increased, with the average time spent in the store 4–8 minutes in the morning, 5–12 minutes during the afternoon, and 12–15 minutes in the evening. There are twice as many browsers in the new release section as in the comedy section, but 2–3 times as many in the comedy section as in horror. The percentage of "walkaways" in the video stores is particularly high, often with 30% of the potential customers leaving without a sale or rental.

TOP-SELLING VIDEO TITLES OF 1987

Title		Price	Unit Sales (Thousands)	Wholesale Dollars (Millions)
Top Gun	Paramount	$26.95	3,000	50.1
Lady and the Tramp	Walt Disney	$29.95	2,700	50.8
Crocodile Dundee	Paramount	$29.95	1,900	35.1
Star Trek IV	Paramount	$29.95	1,500	28.3
An American Tail	MCA	$29.95	700	13.0
Karate Kid Part II	RCA/Columbia	$79.95	300	14.8
Lethal Weapon	Warner	$89.95	300	17.1
The Golden Child	Paramount	$79.95	275	13.8
The Color Purple	Warner	$89.95	265	15.0
Aliens	CBS/Fox	$89.95	250	13.9
The Secret of My Success	MCA	$89.95	240	13.4
Peggy Sue Got Married	CBS/Fox	$89.98	235	13.3
Ferris Bueller's Day Off	Paramount	$79.95	230	11.4
Heartbreak Ridge	Warner	$89.95	225	12.7
The Color of Money	Touchstone	$89.95	220	12.4
Outrageous Fortune	Touchstone	$89.95	220	12.4
Stand by Me	RCA/Columbia	$89.95	210	11.7
Nightmare on Elm Street III	Media	$89.95	200	11.2
Ruthless People	Touchstone	$89.95	200	11.2
Blind Date	RCA/Columbia	$89.95	190	10.7
Hoosiers	HBO	$89.95	190	10.7
The Three Amigos	HBO	$89.95	190	10.7
The Fly	CBS/Fox	$89.95	180	10.0
Nothing in Common	HBO	$89.95	180	10.0
Tin Men	Touchstone	$89.95	180	10.0
Hannah and Her Sisters	HBO	$89.95	175	9.9
Little Shop of Horrors	Warner	$89.95	175	9.9
Over the Top	Warner	$89.95	175	9.9
Black Widow	CBS/Fox	$89.98	170	9.5
Children of a Lesser God	Paramount	$79.95	170	8.6
Jumpin' Jack Flash	CBS/Fox	$89.95	170	9.5
Legal Eagles	MCA	$89.95	170	9.5
Mannequin	Media	$89.95	170	9.5
The Mosquito Coast	Warner	$89.95	170	9.5
Police Academy 4	Warner	$89.95	170	9.5
Project X	CBS/Fox	$89.95	170	9.5
Burglar	Warner	$89.95	165	9.2
The Morning After	Lorimar	$79.95	165	8.2
Running Scared	MGM/UA	$79.95	165	8.2
Short Circuit	CBS/Fox	$79.95	160	7.9
Soul Man	New World	$79.95	160	7.9
Angel Heart	IVE	$89.95	150	8.5
Firewalker	Media	$79.95	150	7.4
No Mercy	RCA/Columbia	$89.95	150	8.5
Raising Arizona	CBS/Fox	$89.95	150	8.5
Some Kind of Wonderful	Paramount	$79.95	150	7.4
Superman IV	Warner	$89.95	150	8.5
Tough Guys	Touchstone	$79.95	150	7.4
The Bedroom Window	Vestron	$79.95	140	6.9
Club Paradise	Warner	$79.95	140	6.9
Critical Condition	Paramount	$79.95	140	6.9
Harry and the Hendersons	MCA	$89.95	140	7.9
Ishtar	RCA/Columbia	$89.95	140	7.9
Labyrinth	Embassy	$79.95	140	6.9
Wanted Dead or Alive	New World	$79.95	140	6.9
Light of Day	Vestron	$79.95	135	6.8
About Last Night	RCA/Columbia	$79.95	130	6.4
Crimes of the Heart	Lorimar	$89.95	125	7.3
Manhunter	Lorimar	$79.95	125	6.2
Shanghai Surprise	Vestron	$79.95	125	6.2

SOURCE: TWICE
(This Week in Consumer Electronics)

DEMOGRAPHICS OF CURRENT VIDEO TAPE RENTERS
As of November 1987

No. of People in the Household

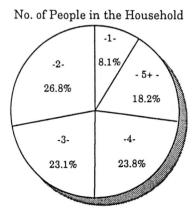

Age of the Head of the Household

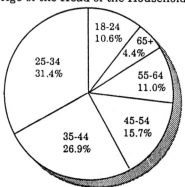

Ages of Children

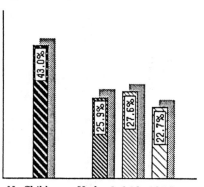

Employment Status

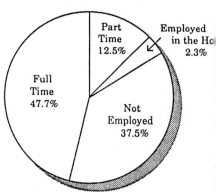

Education Level

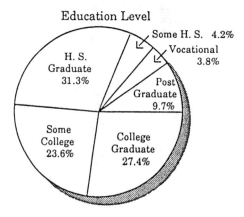

Household Income

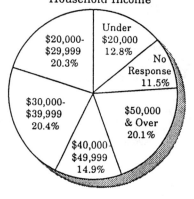

SOURCE: American Video Association

DEMOGRAPHIC CHARACTERISTICS
(As of November 1987)
Classified by VCR Owners and Non-Owners

No. of People in the Household		Owners	Non-Owners
	One	45.3%	54.7%
	Two	49.8%	50.2%
	Three	70.3%	29.7%
	Four	80.7%	19.3%
	Five or more	75.9%	24.1%

Household Income		Owners	Non-Owners
	Under $20,000	34.4%	65.6%
	$20,000 - $29,999	62.6%	37.4%
	$30,000 - $39,999	79.2%	20.8%
	$40,000 - $49,999	82.2%	17.8%
	$50,000 & Over	82.9%	17.1%

Ages of Children		Owners	Non-Owners
	No Children	50.9%	49.1%
	Under 6	75.8%	24.2%
	6 - 12	75.7%	24.3%
	13 - 17	80.2%	19.8%

Employment Status		Owners	Non-Owners
	Full-Time	73.1%	26.9%
	Part-Time	68.2%	31.8%
	Not Employed	51.8%	48.2%
	Emp. in the Home	53.8%	46.2%

Age of the Head of the Household		Owners	Non-Owners
	18 - 24	70.1%	29.9%
	25 - 34	77.0%	23.0%
	35 - 44	71.0%	29.0%
	45 - 54	71.6%	28.4%
	55 - 64	47.0%	53.0%
	65 & Over	22.5%	77.5%

Education Level		Owners	Non-Owners
	Some H.S. or less	33.3%	66.7%
	H.S. Graduate	56.5%	43.5%
	Some College	69.2%	30.8%
	College Graduate	74.6%	25.4%
	Post Graduate	76.5%	23.5%
	Vocational School	80.8%	19.2%

Marital Status		Owners	Non-Owners
	Single	64.3%	35.7%
	Married	67.4%	32.6%
	Wid/Div/Sep	42.8%	57.2%

Racial Background		Owners	Non-Owners
	White	62.2%	37.8%
	Black	60.6%	39.4%
	Hispanic	69.7%	30.3%
	Oriental	75.0%	25.0%
	Other	90.1%	18.9%

Own or Rent		Owners	Non-Owners
	Own	63.1%	36.9%
	Rent	60.8%	39.2%

SOURCE: American Video Association

TOTAL FACTORY SALES OF
VIDEOCASSETTE RECORDERS

1988

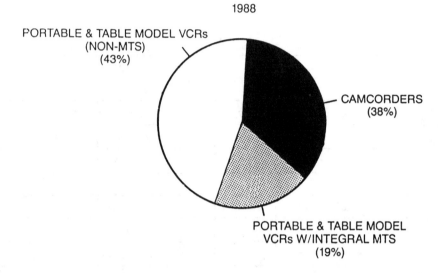

PORTABLE & TABLE MODEL VCRs
(NON-MTS)
(43%)

CAMCORDERS
(38%)

PORTABLE & TABLE MODEL
VCRs W/INTEGRAL MTS
(19%)

1989

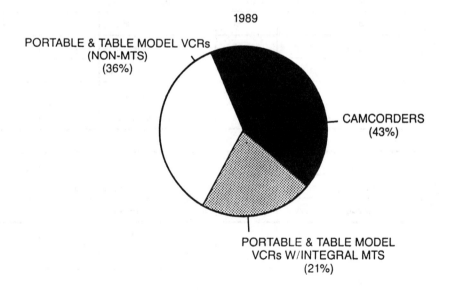

PORTABLE & TABLE MODEL VCRs
(NON-MTS)
(36%)

CAMCORDERS
(43%)

PORTABLE & TABLE MODEL
VCRs W/INTEGRAL MTS
(21%)

FROM TABLES 10, 11, 12, 13, 14
(on following page)

SOURCE: Electronic Industries Association

VIDEOCASSETTE RECORDERS

	Total Sales to Dealers in Units (Thousands)	Total Factory Sales in Dollars (Millions)	Average Value (Dollars per Unit)

TABLE 10

TABLE MODEL VIDEOCASSETTE RECORDERS

1985	10,750	3,771	351
1986	11,810	3,893	330
1987	11,602	3,399	293
1988 (est.)	10,500	3,045	290
1989 (est.)	10,300	2,885	280

TABLE 11

PORTABLE VIDEOCASSETTE RECORDERS
(Excluding Camcorders)

1985	586	402	686
1986	195	85	436
1987	100	43	430
1988 (est.)	*	*	*
1989 (est.)	*	*	*

*Included with table-model VCRs (table 10)

TABLE 12

CAMCORDERS

1985	517	565	1,093
1986	1,169	1,280	1,095
1987	1,604	1,651	1,029
1988 (est.)	2,000	1,900	950
1989 (est.)	2,400	2,200	915

TABLE 13

TOTAL VIDEOCASSETTE RECORDERS
(Sum of Tables 10, 11 and 12)

1985	11,853	4,738	400
1986	13,174	5,258	399
1987	13,306	5,093	383
1988 (est.)	12,500	4,945	395
1989 (est.)	12,700	5,085	400

TABLE 14

VIDEOCASSETTE RECORDERS WITH MTS
(BUILT-IN STEREO CAPABILITY)
(Included above)

1986 (est.)	1,200	590	490
1987 (est.)	2,000	900	450
1988 (est.)	2,500	925	370
1989 (est.)	3,000	1,080	360

SOURCE: Electronic Industries Association

OTHER VIDEO PRODUCTS

	Total Sales to Dealers in Units (Thousands)	Total Factory Sales in Dollars (Millions)	Average Value (Dollars per Unit)
TABLE 15			
VIDEODISC PLAYERS*			
1985 (est.)	75	23	300
1986 (est.)	85	26	300
1987 (est.)	100	30	300
1988 (est.)	120	42	350
1989 (est.)	180	63	350

*Non-commercial.

	Total Sales to Dealers in Units (Thousands)	Total Factory Sales in Dollars (Millions)	Average Value (Dollars per Unit)
TABLE 16			
VIDEOCASSETTE PLAYERS			
1985 (est.)	125	22	175
1986 (est.)	150	26	175
1987 (est.)	160	26	165
1988 (est.)	170	26	155
1989 (est.)	190	29	150

	Total Sales to Dealers in Units (Thousands)	Total Factory Sales in Dollars (Millions)	Average Value (Dollars per Unit)
TABLE 17			
HOME SATELLITE SYSTEMS			
1985 (est.)	600	900	1,500
1986 (est.)	375	750	2,000
1987 (est.)	250	625	2,500
1988 (est.)	275	635	2,300
1989 (est.)	300	675	2,250

SOURCE: Electronic Industries Association

RELATED PRODUCTS
Software

	Total Sales to Dealers in Units (Thousands)	Total Factory Sales in Dollars (Millions)	Average Value (Dollars per Unit)

TABLE 38

BLANK AUDIO CASSETTES—Sales to Consumer Distribution

1985	245,682	263	N/A
1986	296,681	292	N/A
1987 (est.)	335,000	315	N/A
1988 (est.)	370,000	360	N/A
1989 (est.)	400,000	390	N/A

TABLE 39

BLANK VIDEOCASSETTES—Sales to Consumer Distribution

1985	233,021	1,055	N/A
1986	296,253	1,235	N/A
1987 (est.)	280,000	1,045	N/A
1988 (est.)	290,000	1,100	N/A
1989 (est.)	310,000	1,200	N/A

TABLE 40

PRE-RECORDED VIDEOCASSETTES*

1985 (est.)	53,000	1,800	34
1986 (est.)	75,000	2,100	28
1987 (est.)	110,000	2,770	25
1988 (est.)	135,000	2,970	22
1989 (est.)	145,000	3,190	22

*Not included in Total Factory Sales of Consumer Electronics

TABLE 41

HOME COMPUTER SOFTWARE

1985 (est.)	N/A	750	N/A
1986 (est.)	N/A	1,000	N/A
1987 (est.)	N/A	1,600	N/A
1988 (est.)	N/A	2,000	N/A
1989 (est.)	N/A	2,400	N/A

Home Computer Software—Software programs (on disk) compatible with computers priced less than $3,000 and sold to consumers for use in the home.

N/A—Not Applicable

SOURCE: Electronic Industries Association

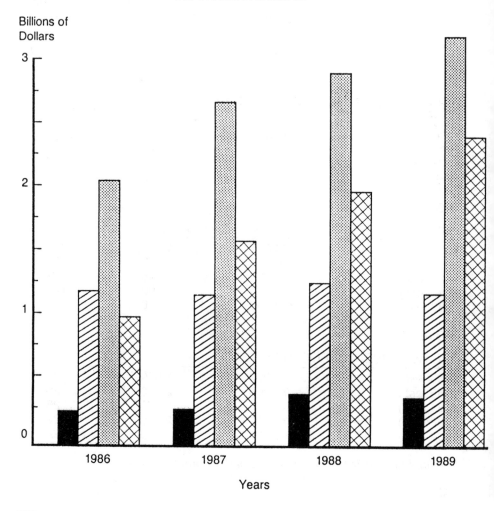

TOTAL FACTORY SALES OF
SOFTWARE PRODUCTS

Billions of
Dollars

Years

 BLANK AUDIOCASSETTES

 BLANK VIDEOCASSETTES

 PRE-RECORDED
VIDEOCASSETTES

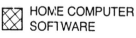 HOME COMPUTER
SOFTWARE

FROM TABLES 38, 39, 40, 41

SOURCE: Electronic Industries Association

10 LEADING COUNTRIES IN TERMS OF VCR HOMES[1]

Rank	Country	Cumulative 1986 Homes	Est. Cum. 1987 Homes	Estimated 1987 Gain	% Growth	Est. 1987 Penetration of TV Homes
1	United States	34.4 million	44.8 million	10.4 million	30%	51%
2	Japan	22.0 million	25.4 million	3.4 million	15%	71%
3	United Kingdom	10.0 million	11.4 million	1.4 million	14%	60%
4	West Germany	8.3 million	9.9 million	1.6 million	19%	44%
5	France	4.4 million	6.2 million	1.8 million	41%	31%
6	Canada	4.3 million	4.8 million	500,000	25%	48%
7	Australia	2.9 million	3.5 million	600,000	21%	57%
8	Spain	2.2 million	3.1 million	950,000	43%	31%
9	Netherlands	1.7 million	2.0 million	375,000	22%	44%
10	Korea	1.6 million	1.9 million	250,000	16%	22%

[1]Estimate of actual VCR homes is based on cumulative sales of VCRs, after allowances for obsolescence and multi-set homes.

SOURCE: Electronic Industries Association

Home Video Companies

* **PRODUCTION COMPANIES**

* **WHOLESALE DISTRIBUTORS**

Home Video Companies

ABC Distribution Company

(A division of Capital Cities ABC Video Enterprises, Inc.)

825 Seventh Ave., New York, NY 10019; (212) 887-1725. Organized 1986. (1979 under parent co.). (Licenses theatrical and television rights to movie exhibitors and television stations internationally. Licenses television and theatrical product to home video and cable distributors worldwide. Produces, co-produces and develops programming for domestic and international distribution.)

PRESIDENT
John T. Healy
SENIOR VICE PRESIDENT
Archie Purvis
DIRECTOR, CASSETTE/CABLE MARKETING
Marvinia Hunter
DIRECTOR, INT'L TV SALES
Bill Vitale
DIRECTOR, INT'L SALES
Armando Nunez, Jr.
DIRECTOR, THEATRICAL SALES
June Shelley
BRANCH
2040 Ave. of the Stars, Century City, CA 90067; (213) 557-6600.
AFFILIATION
A division of Capital Cities/ABC Video Enterprises.

ABC Video Enterprises

2040 Ave. of the Stars, Los Angeles, CA 90067; (213) 557-6600. Subsidiary of American Broadcasting Co., Inc.

PRESIDENT
Herb Granath
PRESIDENT, ABC DISTRIBUTION CO.
John T. Healy
SENIOR VICE PRESIDENT, ABC DISTRIBUTION CO.
Archie Purvis
DIRECTOR, WORLDWIDE CABLE/CASSETTE SALES
Marvinia Hunter

A.C. Video Distribution, Inc.

P.O. Box 8522, New York, NY 10150; (212) 223-0100, ext. 46. Associated with VPI/AC Video Inc., 381 Park Ave. South, Suite #1601, New York, NY 10016.

PRESIDENT
Anna Canepa

A.E.C. Corporation

1977 Spruce Hills Dr., Bettendorf, IA 52722; (319) 359-6666. Organized 1988. (Manufacturer and distributor of prerecorded video programming.)

PRESIDENT
Stephen D. Durbin
VICE PRESIDENT
Carolyn Hamilton
SECRETARY
Thomas Williams
TREASURER
Brad Tregloan

A & M Video

1416 N. La Brea Ave., Hollywood, CA 90028; (213) 469-2411.

V.P., BUSINESS DEVELOPMENT
Milton E. Olin, Jr.

DIRECTOR VIDEO SALES AND MARKETING
Steve Macon
ADMINISTRATIVE MANAGER
Barbara LeBlanc

A M Productions Home Video

46 S. De Lacey Ave., Suite 15, Pasadena, CA 91105; (818) 449-0683.

ANE Home Video

106 West, 2950 South, Salt Lake City, UT 84115; (801) 486-3155.

ANS International Video, Ltd.

396 Fifth Ave., New York, NY 10018; (212) 736-1007. Organized 1980. (Video/film production/post house.)

PRESIDENT
Apo Oguz
GENERAL MANAGER
Marilyn Cohen
PRODUCTION COORDINATOR
Meri Chermak
SALES
Edna Ozcan

ARC Video, Inc.

88 Lexington Ave., Suite 3-K, New York, NY 10016; (212) 725-5530. Organized 1976. (Produces performing arts TV programming—education/informational/performance-oriented.)

CO-DIRECTOR/TECHNICAL DIRECTOR
Jeff Bush
CO-DIRECTOR/ARTISTIC DIRECTOR
Celia Ipiotis

AV Designs

1233 Hermosa Ave., Suite 208, Hermosa Beach, CA 90254; (213) 379-5818. Organized 1984. (Producers of video, film and multi-image media for marketing, promotion, training and education.)

PRESIDENT
Genie Davis
VICE PRESIDENT
Don Davis
PRODUCTION COORDINATOR
Joy Gaston

AVG Inc./SQN Corp.

27 Dryden Lane, Providence, RI 02904; (401) 521-3143. Organized 1971. (Audio/video producing, manufacturing, marketing of quality children's, instructional, music, self-help audio, videocassettes, compact discs.)

CHAIRMAN & CHIEF EXECUTIVE OFFICER
Samuel S. Attenberg
PRESIDENT & C.O.O.
Joan Grow
BOARD OF DIRECTORS
Samuel S. Attenberg, Joan Grow, Richard Carbeau
AFFILIATIONS
VSDA, ABA, NACS

AVS, Inc.

4660 Maryland Ave., Room #13, St. Louis, MO 63108; (314) 361-7072. (Consultants and producers of video and audio.)
PRESIDENT
Susan Meryl Greenberg

AW Industries

8415 Ardmore Rd., Landover, MD 20785; (301) 322-1000.

Academy Entertainment, Inc.

1 Pine Haven Shore Rd., Shelburne, VT 05482; (800) 972-0001.
PRESIDENT
Robert Baruc

Acorn Sports, Inc.

5816 Shakespeare Rd., Suite D, Columbia, SC 29204; (803) 735-0733. Organized 1981. (Golf videos.)
PRESIDENT
D. Swing Meyer

Active Home Video

9300 West Pico Blvd., Los Angeles, CA 90035; (213) 274-8233; (800) 824-6109. Organized 1984. (Video production and distribution.)
PRESIDENT
Ron Levanson
VICE PRESIDENT, SALES
Rod Hurley
CREATIVE SERVICES DIRECTOR
Juanita Weber
SALES
Lisa Jamner
Alice de Buhr

Admit One Video Presentations

185 Frederick St., Toronto, Canada M5A 4L4; (416) 863-6836. ("B" movies, schlock horror, classics.)
PRESIDENT
Len Curtis
OPERATIONS
Joe Mancuso

Adventures in Cassettes

1401-B West River Rd., North, Minneapolis, MN 55411; (800) 328-0108. (Division of Metacom, Inc.)
MAIL ORDER MANAGER
Diane A. Goddard

Alameda County Office of Education

313 W. Winton Ave., Hayward, CA 94544-1198; (415) 887-0152 (ext 210).

All Seasons Entertainment

18121 Napa St., Northridge, CA 91325; (818) 886-8680; (800) 423-5599. Organized 1984. (Acquisition and distribution of feature films and programming to home video market.)
PRESIDENT
Fred Hirsch
VICE PRESIDENT
Kirk Benefiel
AFFILIATIONS
VSDA, IVPA

Lewis Allen/Peter Newman Productions

1500 Broadway, Suite 2805, New York, NY 10036; (212) 221-2400. Organized 1983. (Film and television production.)
PARTNERS
Lewis Allen
Peter Newman
HEAD OF PRODUCTION
Walker Stuart
ADMINISTRATIVE ASSOCIATE
Deborah Stillwell
AFFILIATIONS
Guadalupe Productions, 2700 Bee Cave Rd., Austin, TX 78746

Alpine Film & Video Exchange

1024 N. 250 East, P.O. Box 1254, Orem, UT 84057; (801) 226-8209. (Science and educational videos.)
PRESIDENT
Lorie Fowlker

AmbreCorp, Incorporated

805 S. Main St., Suite 5, Lombard, IL 60148; (312) 629-7070. Organized 1985. (Distributes or obtains video distribution rights to works produced by independent video producers.)
PRESIDENT
John F. Moran, Ph.D.
VICE PRESIDENT
Edward Guy

American Home Video Library

1500 Broadway, Suite 1807, New York, NY 10036; (212) 869-2616.

American Humanist Association

Television Dept., P.O. Box 146, Amherst, NY 14226-0146; (716) 839-5085.

American Medical Association

535 N. Dearborn, Chicago, IL 60610; (312) 645-4420. (Original programming, production and distribution capabilities for broadcast, cable and satellite on healthcare and medical issues.)

American Red Cross

Production Center, 5816 Seminary Rd., Falls Church, VA 22041; (703) 379-8160. (Health, science and safety videos.)

American Sports Network, Inc.

P.O. Box 6100, Rosemead, CA 91770; (818) 572-4727. Organized 1976. (Sports production/video, television and cable.)
PRESIDENT
Louis Zwick

American Video Tape

1116 Edgewater Ave., Ridgefield, NJ 07657; (201) 941-4404.

American Video Works

Box 333, Evanston, IL 60204; (312) 328-0400. Organized 1979. (Home video.)

Amrit Productions Inc.

206 W. 99 St., Room 5D, New York, NY 10025; (212) 877-3623. Organized 1982. (Produces and distributes film, video and how to tapes.)
PRODUCER/DIRECTOR/PRESIDENT
    Tirlok Malik
DIRECTOR/VICE PRESIDENT
    Chander Malik
BRANCHES
    Amrit Productions Inc., H-58 Shiva Jee Park, New Delhi 11006, India

Amstar Productions

2020 Ave. of the Stars, Suite 240, Century City, CA 90067; (213) 556-1325.
PRESIDENT
    R. J. Barich

Anovid Inc.

Box 180, Nesconset, NY 11767; (516) 724-4119. Organized 1980. (Film and video production company.)
PRESIDENT
    E. Divona

Anti-Defamation League of B'Nai B'rith

823 United Nations Plaza, Audio-Visual Dept., New York, NY 10017; (212) 490-2525.
MARKETING DIRECTOR
    Jay West
DIRECTOR OF TV & FILM
    Steve Brody

Morris Anton Associates

301 W. 22 St., New York, NY 10011; (212) 989-2098.
PRESIDENT
    Morris Anton

Anubis Productions International

P.O. Box 50859, Tucson AZ 85703; (602) 293-8088. Organized 1988. (Film and video production and distribution of documentaries, commercials and overseas assignments, specializing in dance, fine arts, cultural, and trade).
PRESIDENT
    Gerald Harwood
VICE PRESIDENT
    Sarajean Allen Harwood
AFFILIATIONS
    Bastet Productions, Video Safaris International, Llamavision Productions.

Apex Productions, Inc.

1778 Palisades Dr., Pacific Palisades, CA 90272; (213) 459-8278. Organized 1985. (Produces feature films and video programs.)
PRESIDENT
    Jim Silverman

Appalshop, Inc.

306 Madison St., Whitesburg, KY 41858; (606) 633-0108. Organized 1969. (Documents and presents history, culture and social issues of rural America.)

Arizona Peddler

790 S. Main, Cottonwood, AZ 86326; (602) 634-5565.
PRESIDENT
    Jack Poland

Arnold & Associates Production, Inc.

2159 Powell St., San Francisco, CA 94133; (415) 989-3490. Organized 1978. (Corporate image and marketing film and video production; TV commercials.)
PRESIDENT
    John Arnold
VICE PRESIDENTS
    Jim Morris
    Jadine Wa

Artec Distributing, Inc.

One Pine Haven Shore Rd., Shelburne, VT 05482; (802) 985-9411. (Provides software and support services to video retailers and rack jobbing services to mass merchandisers, supermarkets and other outlets.)
CHIEF EXECUTIVE OFFICER
    Martin Gold
CHIEF FINANCE OFFICER
    Howard Goldberg
VICE PRESIDENT, OPERATIONS
    Matt Brown
VICE PRESIDENT, SALES
    Ken Miller
CONTROLLER
    Fred Ames
DIRECTOR OF SERVICE
    David Borgendale
VICE PRESIDENT, MANAGEMENT INFORMATION SERVICES
    Greg Casto
BRANCHES
    Canton, MA; Middletown, CT; Pittsburgh, PA; Long Island, NY
AFFILIATIONS
    VSDA, NAVD

Artists' Video Productions

32 Narrow Rocks Rd., Westport, CT 06880; (203) 226-0397. Organized 1986. (Produces and distributes videocassettes for artists.)
PARTNERS
    William Schael
    Joanna Foster

Artmusic, Inc.

522 W. 47th St., #3F, New York, NY 10036; (212) 265-8995. Organized 1980. (Presents and produces TV series/PBS video exhibitions and large scale music events.)
PRESIDENT
    Wendy Chambers
SECRETARY
    Tim Jensen
VICE PRESIDENT
    Barbara Mayfield
BOARD OF DIRECTORS
    Kelly Knauer, Andy Feigenbaum

artsAmerica, Inc.

12 Havemeyer Pl., Greenwich, CT 06830; (203) 869-4693. Organized 1984. (Producer and distributor of videotapes and films about the visual arts. Publisher of artsAmerica Film Art, Film & Video Source Book.)
PRESIDENT
    Bronwyn Dunne
DIRECTOR
    Dorothy Tucker
BOARD OF ADVISORS
    Philip Eliasoph, Phd., Mary Delahoyd, John Sharnik, Robert Sturgeon, Marilyn Boren

Asia Society

725 Park Ave., New York, NY 10021; (212) 288-6400.

Atlantic Film

102 Harbor Rd., Kittery Point, ME 03905; (207) 439-3739. (Outdoor and educational videos.)

Atlantic Video Co. Inc.

725 S. Central Expressway, #C-3, Richardson, TX 75080; (214) 699-1014. Organized 1983. (Manufactures and distributes foreign films.)
PRESIDENT
  Mohammed A. Molubhoy
VICE PRESIDENTS
  Perwez M. Molubhoy
  Salim M. Molubhoy
BOARD OF DIRECTORS
  Mohammed A. Molubhoy, Perwez M. Molubhoy, Salim M. Molubhoy

Atlantis Productions, Inc.

1252 La Granada Dr., Thousand Oaks, CA 91362; (805) 495-2790. Organized 1952. (Production and distribution of motion pictures in film and video.)
PRESIDENT
  Dr. J. Michael Hagopian
VICE PRESIDENT
  Becci Meadors

Aura Productions

7911 Willoughby Ave., Los Angeles, CA 90046; (213) 656-9373.
PRESIDENT
  Richard Bock

Aurora Educational Media, Inc.

74-10 35 Ave., Suite 607W, Jackson Heights, NY 11372; (718) 898-5327. Organized 1985. (Develops, produces and distributes dramatic and documentary film and video.)
PRESIDENT
  Robert Spencer

Avant Communications, Partnership

370 Lexington Ave., Suite 1509; New York, NY 10016; (212) 759-3051.
C/O
  Stan Ferbear

Avetka Productions Inc.

164 Madison Ave., 4th floor, New York, NY 10016; (212) 686-4550. Organized 1982. (Video production and computer animation.)
PRESIDENT
  Maria Avgerakis
VICE PRESIDENT & CREATIVE DIRECTOR
  George Avgerakis

BFA Educational Media

468 Park Ave. S., New York, NY 10016; (212) 684-5910, (800) 221-1274. (Subsidiary of Phoenix Films Inc.)
PRESIDENT
  H. Gelles
MARKETING AND SALES
  Robert Dunlap

B.T. Supply, Inc., t/a Blank Tape Supply

1323-I Shepard Dr., P.O. Box 237, Sterling, VA 22170; (703) 450-6776; (800) 722-3300. Organized 1979. (Wholesale audio, video and computer products.)
PRESIDENT
  Bob Vanjani
VICE PRESIDENT
  Gayle Vanjani

Bandera Enterprises Inc.

Box 1107, Studio City, CA 91604; (818) 985-5050.
PRESIDENT
  Don Flagg

Barnholtz Organization

10966 Le Conte Ave., Suite D., Westwood, CA 90024; (213) 208-6444.
PRESIDENT
  Barry Barnholtz

Barr Films

12801 Schabarum Ave., Irwindale, CA 91706; (818) 338-7878. Organized 1957. (Produces informational, educational, motivational film and video for all markets.)
CEO & CFO
  Allen Dohra
PRESIDENT
  Donald Barr
EXECUTIVE VICE PRESIDENT
  B.L. Earle
VICE PRESIDENT, PRODUCT DEVELOPMENT
  George Holland
NATIONAL SALES MANAGER
  Bob Gergen
BOARD OF DIRECTORS
  Donald Barr (chairman), B.L. Earle, Allen Dohara

Basic Skills Video

P.O. Box 1555, Conaway, SC 29526; (803) 248-7160. Organized 1985. (Production, distribution, duplication of special interest, how-to videos.)
OFFICERS
  Dennis J. Allen
  Frankie B. Allen

Bay Port Productions

4901 Morena Blvd., Suite #127, San Diego, CA 92117; (619) 581-6550. (Produces TV commercials, marketing and public relations videos.)
PRESIDENT & EXECUTIVE PRODUCER
  Bill Polick
PRODUCTION MANAGER
  Horace Barge III
ASSOCIATE PRODUCER
  Amy Blum

Beacon Films, Inc.

(An Altschul Group Company.)
930 Pitner Ave., Evanston, IL 60202; (312) 328-6700. Organized 1978. (Distributor of curriculum-based and special interest AV programming to libraries, schools, and other educational organizations.)
PRESIDENT
  Joseph Farragher
CHAIRMAN OF BOARD
  Joel Altschul

408

Bee Gee Records & Tapes, Inc.

10 Northway Lane, N. Latham, NY 12110; (518) 785-1122. Subsidiary of Bee Gee Distributing Corp.

Norman Beerger Productions

3217-A29, Arville St., Las Vegas, NV 89102-7612; (702) 876-2328. Organized 1984. (Produces and distributes wilderness home video programs.)
OWNER
Norman Beerger

Bellevue Home Entertainment

(A division of Astral Bellevue Pathé Inc.)
7215 Trans Canada Highway, Montreal, Quebec H4T 1A2; Canada; (514) 333-7555.
PRESIDENT
Sidney Greenberg
VICE PRESIDENT, FINANCE
Isar Klaiman
VICE PRESIDENT, OPERATIONS
Gordon Halliday
VICE PRESIDENT, SALES AND MARKETING
Paul Bronfman

Bellevue Home Entertainment

98 Orfus Rd., North York, Toronto, Ontario M6A 1C8, Canada; (416) 785-5580.

Bennett Marine Video

730 Washington St., Marina del Rey, CA 90292; (213) 821-3329. Organized 1982. (Supplier and distributor of marine-oriented video, worldwide.)
PRESIDENT/OWNER
Michael S. Bennett
OPERATIONS MANAGER
Roderic P. Kavanagh

Bennu Productions, Inc.

165 Madison, Ave., New York, NY 10016; (212) 213-8511. Organized 1985. (Film and video production and distribution.)
PRESIDENT
Wayne J. Keeley
SENIOR VICE PRESIDENT
Kevin F. Cavaliere
VICE PRESIDENTS
Joanne Birkmann
Paul D. Sansone
BOARD OF DIRECTORS
Wayne J. Keeley, Kevin F. Cavaliere, Paul D. Sansone, Joanne Birkmann
AFFILIATIONS
NSSEA, AIVF, AFTRA, SIG

Best Film & Video

98 Cutter Hill Rd., Great Neck, NY 11021; (800) 527-2189; 20501 Ventura Blvd., Suite 375, Woodland Hills, CA 91364; (818) 999-2244.
PRESIDENT
Roy Winnick

The Blackhawk Catalog

12636 Beatrice Street, Los Angeles, CA 90066; (213) 306-4040.
VICE PRESIDENT
Philip J. Kromnick
OPERATIONS COORDINATOR
Kimberly Baker

Michael Blackwood Productions, Inc.

251 W. 57 St., Suite 415, New York, NY 10019; (212) 247-4710. (Produces and distributes documentaries on 20th-Century painters, sculptors, architects, choreographers and composers.)
PRESIDENT
Michael Blackwood

Les Blank's Flower Films and Video

10341 San Pablo Ave., El Cerrito, CA 94530; (415) 525-0942. Organized 1967. (Seeks out and documents America's vanishing minority cultures, their music and traditions. Also produces music videos and independent films on such subjects as gap-toothed women, garlic and Werner Herzog.)
PRODUCER/DIRECTOR/CAMERA
Les Blank
DISTRIBUTION MANAGER
Susan Kell
FOLKLORIST/2nd CAMERA
Christine Simon
EDITOR
Maureen Gosling

Book-of-the-Month Club, Inc.

485 Lexington Ave., New York, NY 10017; (212) 867-4300.
DIRECTOR OF VIDEO DIVISION
George Spitzer

Bookshelf Video

301-B West Dyer Rd., Santa Ana, CA 92707; (714) 556-7918.
PRESIDENT
Charles F. Burbage

Bosustow Video

3030 Pennsylvania Ave., Santa Monica, CA 90404; (213) 453-7973. FAX: (213) 828-4053. Organized 1983. (Producers of award winning home videos, corporate videos, electronic press kits, point of sale videos, employee video newsletters, public relations videos, video white papers, training videos, and commercials. Distributors of television educational and home video product.)
PRESIDENT
Tee Bosustow
AFFILIATIONS
AMPTAS, ATVAS, IDA

Box Office Hits Inc.

10660 Westheimer, Houston, TX 77042; (713) 850-8500. Organized 1969. Wholesale distributor of used movies. Retail stores trading as National Video Superstores.)
PRESIDENT
Barry Lotz
VICE PRESIDENT, SALES
Linda Milligan
VICE PRESIDENT, RETAIL OPERATIONS
D. Craig Butler
AFFILIATIONS
Smash Hits Video Inc., Hollywood Hits Inc.

Breger Video, Inc.

915 Broadway, Room 1601, New York, NY 10010; (212) 254-3900. Organized 1983. (Produces cooking videos and PBS series "Madeleine Cooks.")

PRESIDENT
  Sue Breger
PRODUCER/DIRECTOR
  Charles Pinsky
ASSOCIATE
  Barbara Prisco

Brighton Video

(Division of Cortech Communications, Inc.
250 W. 57 St., Suite 916, New York, NY 10019; (212)
315-2502; (800) 542-5554. (Home-video program sup-
plier.)
PRESIDENT
  Gene Feldman
EXECUTIVE VICE PRESIDENT
  Suzette Winter
VICE PRESIDENT
  Stephen Janson
DIRECTOR OF SALES AND MARKETING
  Elaine Reed
OPERATIONS MANAGER
  Hillary Zemlock

Broadcast Quality Inc.

7800 S.W. 57th Ave., Suite 219, South Miami, FL 33142;
(305) 665-5416.
VICE PRESIDENT
  Diana Udel
PRODUCTION MANAGER
  Steve Bradley
VICE PRESIDENT, ACQUISITIONS
  Stephen Kabak

Broadman

127 Ninth Ave. N., Nashville, TN 37234; (615) 251-3697.
(800) 251-3225, (800) 342-0021. (Tennessee).

Brooklyn College

Dept. of Television and Radio, 018 Whitehead Hall,
Bedford Ave. H., Brooklyn, NY 11210; (718) 780-5555.
CHAIRMAN
  Robert C. Williams

Budget Video Inc.

(d/b/a Hollywood Home Theatre)
1540 N. Highland Ave., Suite 110, Hollywood CA 90028;
(213) 466-0121, (213) 466-0127. Organized 1979. (Dealer,
distributor, retailer of video cassettes and laser discs.)
PRESIDENT
  Larry S. Fine
VICE PRESIDENT
  Stephen Stumbris

Bullfrog Films, Inc.

Oley, PA 19547; (215) 779-8226. Organized 1973.
(Distributes programs for personal self-reliance—how-
to's on gardening, home improvements, energy-saving,
etc.—and environmental responsibility.)
PRESIDENT
  John Hoskyns-Abrahall
SECRETARY & TREASURER
  Winifred Scherrer
CUSTOMER SERVICE MANAGER
  Jeanne Badman
BOARD OF DIRECTORS
  John Hoskyns-Abrahall, Winifred Scherrer

Butterfly Video Productions

Box 184, High St., Antrim, NH 03440; (603) 588-2105.
Organized 1986. (Produces and distributes how-to
videos.)
PRODUCER
  Sherry Smythe-Green

CBS/Fox Video

1211 Ave. of the Americas, New York, NY 10036; (212)
819-3200. (Subsidiary of CBS, Inc./20th-Century Fox)
PRESIDENT & CEO
  George Krieger
SENIOR VICE PRESIDENT, PROGRAMMING
  Steven Poe
VICE PRESIDENT, PROGRAMMING
  Jed Daly
PRESIDENT, NORTH AMERICA
  Bob DeLellis
VICE PRESIDENT, INTL. MARKETING
  Chris Windle
VICE PRESIDENT, PROGRAM ACQUISITION
  Francesca Barra

CBS Video Club/CBS Video Library

1400 N. Fruitridge Ave., Terre Haute, IN 47811, and 51
W. 52nd St., New York, NY 10019; (212) 975- 4875. (A unit
of Columbia House, a division of CBS Records Inc.)
VICE PRESIDENT, MARKETING
  Brian Wood

CBS Worldwide Enterprises

51 W. 52 St., New York, NY 10019; (212) 975-4515.
(Subsidiary of CBS Broadcast Group, CBS Inc.)

CC Studios/Children's Circle

389 Newtown Turnpike, Weston, CT 06883; (203)
222-0002. Organized 1963. (Produces and markets home
audio/video cassettes to consumers; adaptations of chil-
dren's books.)
PRESIDENT & TREASURER
  Morton Schindel
VICE PRESIDENT
  Paul J. Schindel
SECRETARY
  Elisabeth Rommel
TREASURER
  Paula J. Gaus
BOARD OF DIRECTORS
  Morton Schindel, Paul Schindel, Elisabeth Rommel
AFFILIATIONS
  Weston Woods; Georgetown Studios

CVI/Cirace Video International

115 Clermont Ave., Alexandria, VA 22304; (703) 461-
9600; (800) 222-3992. Organized 1980. (Television pro-
duction company.)
PRESIDENT
  Robert H. Cirace
VICE PRESIDENT
  Verdine O. Palmer
SECRETARY & TREASURER
  Debra D. Palmer
BOARD OF DIRECTORS
  Robert H. Cirace, Verdine O. Palmer, Wendie L. Wachtel, Barry B.
  Wright, Cherry Wyman
AFFILIATIONS
  Majority stockholder in Uplink Corp., Satellite Service Company

Cable Films & Video

#7171 County Club Station, Kansas City, MO 64113; (913) 362-2804. Organized 1976. (300 classic films in all formats—PAL, SECAM, NTSC—for worldwide distribution; cable, TV and home video.)

PRESIDENT
Herb Miller
GENERAL MANAGER
Todd Randall
AFFILIATIONS
NCTA, NATPE, National Academy of TV Arts & Sciences, Mid-America Cable TV Association

Calypso Video, Inc.

2000 Bay Area Blvd., Suite 123, Houston, TX 77058-2001; (713) 480-3168.

PRESIDENT
C. Opfermann

Camp Motion Pictures/Camp Video

2412 So. Thurman Ave., Los Angeles, CA 90293; (213) 935-8650. Organized 1986. (Manufacturers, producers, distributors of horror/sci-fi home videos and theatricals.)

CEO
Sal Richichi
PRESIDENT
James Golff
NATIONAL SALES MANAGER
Eileen Ward

Steve Campus Productions, Inc.

24 Depot Square, Tuckahoe, NY 10707; (914) 961-1900. Organized 1936. (Full service video production company—commercial, industrial, educational—satellite tele-conferencing; A/V design/production.)

PRESIDENT
Steve Campus
EXECUTIVE VICE PRESIDENT
Jonathan B. Pace
SENIOR VICE PRESIDENT
Andrea Sherman, Ph.D.

Camrac Studios

1775 Kuenzli St., Reno, NV 89502; (702) 323-0965. Organized 1979. (Independent studio/location production company that specializes in all film and video formats. Productions include regional commercials, corporate presentations, and home entertainment.)

PRESIDENT
Shirley Mitchell
DIRECTOR/PRODUCER
Jim Mitchell
EDITOR
Larry Neroda
ACCOUNT REPRESENTATIVE & RESEARCH
Mitch Larson
AFFILIATIONS
Postmasters (subsidiary), Showmasters (subsidiary), Mitchell Productions (subsidiary).

Candlelight Studios

P.O. Box 627, Little River, CA 95456; (707) 937-5424. Organized 1981. (Provides fine art instruction for all ages on videotape.)

PRESIDENT
E. John Robinson

Cape Cod Writers' Conference

309 Green Dunes Dr., Box 111, West Hyannisport, MA 02672; (617) 775-4811. Organized 1963. (Promotes writing through video, audio, conferences, writer-in-the-schools, TV shows, books and the world.)

EXECUTIVE DIRECTOR
Marion Vuilleumier
PROGRAM DIRECTOR
Tom O'Connell
PRESIDENT
Katherine Fitzgerald
VICE PRESIDENT
Elinor Titus
SECRETARY & CLERK
Marian Logan
TREASURER
Olive St. Germaine
REGISTRAR
Jeannette Wilson
AFFILIATION
Cape Arts Workshops, Box 12, Cummaquid, MA 02637

Capezio Ballet Makers

33 W. 60 St., 8th floor, New York, NY 10023; (212) 247-7660.

Capital Communications

3807 Dickerson Rd., Nashville, TN 37207; (615) 868-2040. Organized 1965. (Provides programming for commercial, cable television, along with educational markets. Also provides home video programming.)

CHIEF EXECUTIVE OFFICER
Robert Springer
PRESIDENT
James Springer
SECRETARY—TREASURER
Nancy Springer
BOARD OF DIRECTORS
Robert Springer, James Springer, Nancy Springer
BRANCHES
Nashville, TN; Beverly Hills, CA

Capitol Records-EMI

1750 North Vine St., Tower-6, Hollywood, CA 90028. Organized 1940s. (Record label).

NATIONAL VIDEO PROMOTION MANAGER
Lee A. Fehr

Capt. Nemo's Video

P.O. Box 15, Hat Creek, CA 96040: (916) 335-7467. (Video software leasing and video distribution.)

Care Video Productions

1650 Crossings Parkway, Westlake, OH 44145; (216) 835-5872. Organized 1982. (Producer and distributor of medical education video.)

PRESIDENT
Priscilla L. (Pat) Lehman
VICE PRESIDENT
Darlene M. Hall
AFFILIATION
Distributor: Programming for 25 hospitals.

Cassette Express

3123 Sylvania Ave., Toledo, OH 43613; (419) 472-7727. Subsidiary of Video Connection.

PRESIDENT
John Day

Catalina Video Distributing

6611 Santa Monica Blvd., Los Angeles, CA 90038; (213) 485-9105, (800) 421-3269.

411

Catholic Television Network/Bay Area Dioceses

324 Middlefield Rd., Menlo Park, CA 94025; (415) 326-7850.

CONTACT
Shirley Connolly

Celebrity Home Entertainment

6320 Canoga Ave., Penthouse Suite, Woodland Hills, CA 91365; (818) 715-1980. Organized 1987. (Video manufacturer, distributor, producer.)

CHAIRMAN
Noel C. Bloom
SENIOR VICE PRESIDENT, SALES/MARKETING
Pete Pidutti
VICE PRESIDENT, ACQUISITIONS
Krickett Wertz
VICE PRESIDENT, PRODUCTION
Don Spielvogel
VICE PRESIDENT, BUSINESS/LEGAL AFFAIRS
Robert Norton

Central Sun Video Co.

P.O. Box 3135, Reston, VA 22091; (703) 444-2990. Organized 1985. (Produces, acquires and distributes video folk and bluegrass, acoustic music.)

PRESIDENT & CEO
C.W. Weinberger, Jr.

Centre Films Inc.

1103 N. El Centro Ave., Hollywood, CA 90038; (213) 466-5123. Organized 1971. (Videotape production, stage and equipment rental.)

DIRECTOR/PRESIDENT
Winter D. Horton Jr.
SECRETARY/TREASURER
Carol Horton
PRODUCTION MANAGER
Steven Finkelstein

Century Distributing West, Inc.

16153 Cohasset St., Van Nuys, CA 91406; (818) 786-2846, (800) 423-2304.

Champions on Film and Video

745 State Circle, Box 1941, Ann Arbor, MI 48106; (313) 761-5176.

PRESIDENT
Donald N. Canham

Doris Chase Productions

222 W. 23 St., Suite #722, New York, NY 10011; (212) 243-3700. Organized 1972. (Produces for television, film and video art.)

AFFILIATIONS
Museum of Modern Art, Coe Films, Women Make Movies, Video Data Bank, Coronet Films, Jane Balfour Films Ltd.

Children's Video Library

P.O. Box 4000, 60 Long Ridge Rd., Stamford, CT 06902; (203) 967-9200.

DIRECTOR, SPECIAL MARKETS
Dan Markim

Christ for the Nations Inc.

P.O. Box 24910, Dallas TX 75224; (214) 376-1711.

DIRECTOR
Gene Steiner

Christian Media

P.O. Box 748, Ogden, UT 84402; (801) 399-4006.

PRESIDENT
Joe Burdett

Christophers

12 E. 48 St., New York, NY 10017; (212) 759-4050.

DIRECTOR
Rev. John Catoir

Chronicle Videocassettes

2855 Mitchell Dr., Suite 225, Walnut Creek, CA 94598-1627; P.O. Box 4610, Walnut Creek, CA 94596; (415) 778-8117.

Churchill Films, Inc.

662 N. Robertson Blvd., Los Angeles, CA 90069; (213) 657-5110. Organized 1961. (Educational producers and distributors—documentary, theatrical, television.)

PRESIDENT
George McQuilkin
VICE PRESIDENTS
Robert B. Churchill
Robert L. Glore
BOARD OF DIRECTORS
George McQuilkin, Robert B. Churchill, Robert L. Glore

Cinema Concepts, Inc.

2461 Berlin Turnpike, Newington, CT 06111; (203) 667-1251. Organized 1971. (Non-theatrical distribution of entertainment motion pictures in 16mm, Beta, VHS, U-Matic, 8mm to schools, libraries and home market. Mail-order plus three retail stores.)

PRESIDENT
Joel G. Jacobson
BRANCHES
210 Main St., Old Saybrook, CT 06475; (203) 388-1481
Rt. 72 Plaza, 859 Mill St., East Berlin, CT 06023; (203) 828-1815
AFFILIATIONS
Video Software Dealers Association (Joel Jacobson is a board director of CT chapter)

The Cinema Guild

1697 Broadway, Suite 802, New York, NY 10019; (212) 246-5522. Organized 1975. (Film and video distribution.)

PRESIDENT
Philip S. Hobel
VICE PRESIDENTS
Gary Crowdus
Mary-Ann Hobel
DISTRIBUTION MANAGER
Steven Ringel
TELEVISION AND NON THEATRICAL SALES
Amanda Hass

Cinemagreats

15825 Rob Roy Dr., Oak Forest, IL 60452; (312) 687-7881.

Cinetel Productions

9701 Madison Ave., Knoxville, TN 37932; (615) 690-9950. Organized 1973. (Video production and post production. Programming, commercials, home video, training.)
CHIEF EXECUTIVE OFFICER
 Ross K. Bagwell, Sr.
PRESIDENT
 Ross K. Bagwell, Jr.
VICE PRESIDENT, DIRECTOR OF OPERATIONS
 Patrick Leigh-Bell
VICE PRESIDENT, PRODUCTION COORDINATOR
 Shirley Romine
VICE PRESIDENT, DIRECTOR OF ENGINEERING
 Jerry Nantz
BOARD OF DIRECTORS
 Ross K. Bagwell, Sr.; Ross K. Bagwell, Jr.; Sue B. Bagwell; Dee Haslam
AFFILIATION
 A division of Bagwell Communications, Inc.

Circle Video Productions

2901 W. 16th St., Indianapolis, IN 46222; (317) 638-1066.

City Lights Home Video

8981 Sunset Blvd., #310, W. Hollywood, CA 90069; (213) 859-9702. Organized 1986.
PRESIDENT
 Ronald L. Gilchrist
VICE PRESIDENT, INERNATIONAL SALES
 Talaat Captan
VICE PRESIDENT, NATIONAL SALES
 Robert Komisar
BOARD OF DIRECTORS
 Ronald L Gilchrist, Richard Pepin, Joseph Merhi

City One Stop

2551 S. Alameda St., Los Angeles, CA 90058; (213) 234-3336. Subsidiary of Show Industries.
PRESIDENT
 Lou Fogelman

Classic Family Entertainment

6649 Odessa Ave., Van Nuys, CA 91406; (818) 780-7100.
PRESIDENT
 Sidney Niekerk

Coast Telecourses

11460 Warner Ave., Fountain Valley, CA 92708-2597; (714) 241-6109. (Educational videos.)

Coast Video Distributing Inc.

500 N. Ventu Park Rd., P.O Box 2520, Newbury Park, CA 91320; (805) 499-5827; CA: (800) 362-6278; out of state: (800) 322-6278.
NATIONAL SALES MANAGER
 Pat Sierchio

Color Leasing, Inc.

330 Route 46, Fairfield, NJ 07006; (201) 575-1118, (212) 662-2655. Organized 1966.
PRESIDENT
 Jack Berberian

Columbia Video Bible Series

P.O. Box 3122, Columbia, SC 29230; (803) 754-4100, ext. 131. (Provides quality Biblical teaching on video.)
DIRECTOR, COLUMBIA VIDEO BIBLE SERIES
 Rick H. Byers

Comet Video

2320 Cotner Ave., Los Angeles, CA 90064; (213) 477-8055.
PRESIDENT & C.O.O.
 Robin Montgomery

Comex Systems

The Mill Cottage, Mendham, NJ 07945; (201) 234-1616.
VICE PRESIDENT
 Loe Brovalowski

Commtron Corp.

1501 50 St., Suite 300, West Des Moines, IA 50265; (515) 224-1784. Subsidiary of Bergen Brunswig Corp.
VICE PRESIDENT, SALES
 John Farr

Communicorp, Inc.

220 S. Westmore Ave., Lombard, IL 60148; (312) 629-7070; FAX: 629-7106. Organized 1983. (Video production of corporate, sports, healthcare and consumer videos.)
PRESIDENT
 John F. Moran, Ph.D.
VICE PRESIDENT
 Timothy Bukowski
PRODUCTION MANAGER
 Andy Lock

Compuvid

815 N. Royal St., Alexandria, VA 22314; (703) 683-3234. (Computer and educational videos.)

Concepts Unlimited

600 S. Main St., Oshkosh, WI 54901; (414) 426-0863.
PRESIDENT
 M. J. Beckman

Concord Video

(Admission of American Educational Computer, Inc.)
7506 N. Broadway Ext., Suite 505, Oklahoma City, OK 73116; (405) 840-6031. Organized 1984. (Manufacturer and distributor of children's educational videos and various other video categories.)
CEO
 David Catlin
PRESIDENT
 Clive Fox
BRANCHES
 801 S. Main St., Burbank, CA 91506
AFFILIATIONS
 Division of American Educational Computer, Inc., Affiliate of United Coupon Corp.

Concord Video

801 So. Main St., Burbank, CA 91506.

Concordia Publishing House

3558 S. Jefferson, St. Louis, MO 63118-3968; (314) 664-7000.
PRESIDENT & CEO
John W. Gerber

Congress Video Group, Inc.

1776 Broadway, Suite 1010, New York, NY 10019; (212) 581-4880. Organized 1985. (Publisher and distributor of videos on the sell-through home video market.)
PRESIDENT & CEO
Lawrence Kieves
FINANCIAL CONTROLLING OFFICER
Thomas Schmitz
BOARD OF DIRECTORS
Howard Curd, Ronald Leeds, Jonathan Furer, Kirk C. Kirkorian, Tom E. Constance, Myron M. Blumenthal, Dr. Donald Shapiro
AFFILIATIONS
Congress Video Group, Inc., P.O. Box 12209, 4520 Beech St., Cincinnati, OH 45212; (513) 351-5577.

Corinth Films & Video

34 Gansevoort St., New York, NY 10014; (212) 463-0305. Organized 1977. (Film and video distribution.)
PRESIDENT
John M. Poole
EXECUTIVE VICE PRESIDENT
Peter J. Meyer
TECHNICAL DIRECTOR
Richard Evangelista
COMPTROLLER
Marjory Sassine

Cornell University Audio Visual Center

8 Research Park, Ithaca, NY 14850; (607) 255-2091. Organized 1929. (Provides educational programs to Co-operative Extension agents, consumers, schools and other orgs.)
AFFILIATIONS
Consortium of University Film Centers, Educational Film Library Association

Coronet MTI Film & Video & Coronet Feature Video

108 Wilmot Rd., Deerfield, IL 60015; (312) 940-1260; (800) 621-2131.
PRESIDENT
Joe Elliot

Courier Productions

P.O. Box 291285, Hollywood, CA 90027; (818) 707-6355.
PRESIDENT
Linda D. Roberts

Covenant Video

3200 W. Foster Ave., Chicago, IL 60625; (312) 478-4676; (800) 621-1290. (Religious videos.)
MANAGER
Carol A. Nordstrom

Creative Programming, Inc.

30 E. 60 St., New York, NY 10022; (212) 688-9100. Organized 1982. (Television and home video production.)
EXECUTIVE PRODUCER
Peter Wild

DIRECTOR
Nancy Fisher

Creative Tax Planning Association

225 Broadway, Suite 1100, New York, NY 10007; (212) 227-4000.
OWNER
Howard Einbinder

Creative Visions Video

721 S. San Pedro St., Los Angeles, CA 90014; (213) 623-9254, (800) 421-8528. (Subsidiary of Image Laboratories, Inc.)
PRESIDENT
Robert Hoffman

Crocus Entertainment, Inc.

Twelve Oaks Center, 15500 Wayzata Blvd., #762, Wayzata, MN 55391; (612) 473-9002. Organized 1986. (Manufacturer-supplier/wholesale distributor).
PRESIDENT, CEO
Henry T. Morrison, Jr.
VICE PRESIDENT & TREASURER
Cecil H. Bell
VICE PRESIDENT & SECRETARY
P.R. Peterson
BOARD OF DIRECTORS
Henry T. Morrison, Jr., Cecil H. Bell, P.R. Peterson
BRANCHES
Minneapolis
AFFILIATIONS
VSDA, RARM

Crown Video

225 Park Ave. S., New York, NY 10003; (212) 254-1600.

Crystallus Films, Inc.

11 Fayette St., Cambridge, MA 02139; (617) 492-6739. Organized 1979. (Produces and distributes films and television works of artistic and educational interest.)
PRESIDENT
Elliot Hoffman

A.S. Csaky Motion Picture and Video Productions

420 Legato Terrace, Silver Spring, MD 20901; (301) 681-3333 and 681-3390. Organized 1968. (Develops, produces and distributes motion picture and video productions and screenplays nationally and internationally.)
CHAIRMAN OF THE BOARD & PRESIDENT
A.S. Csaky
VICE PRESIDENT, PRODUCTION
Ramzi D. Seikaly
VICE PRESIDENT, SCREENPLAY DEVELOPMENT
Bud Fleischer
VICE PRESIDENT, TRAVEL MANAGEMENT
Albert Cambata
VICE PRESIDENT, PUBLIC RELATIONS
Cecilia Korda-Bros
VICE PRESIDENT, SALES & MARKETING
Catherine White
GRAPHICS DIRECTOR
John Franey
BRANCHES
Washington, DC, New York, NY

Cunningham Dance Foundation, Inc.

463 West St., New York, NY 10014; (212) 255-3130. (Cultural and arts videos.)

Custom Films/Video, Inc.

11 Cob Dr., Westport, CT 06880; (203) 226-0300. Organized 1962. (Produces film and video.)
PRESIDENT
Lester S. Becker

Cycle Vision Tours, Inc.

1020 Green Valley Rd. NW, Albuquerque, NM 87107; (505) 345-5217; (800) 624-4952. Organized 1983. (Production, marketing and distribution of the Videocycle series. Scenic video tapes for exercise bicycles.)
PRESIDENT
George L. Dixon, Jr., M.D.
VICE PRESIDENT
Margery M. Dixon
EXECUTIVE VICE PRESIDENT
Mark S. Lange
OPERATIONS
Martha D. Lange
BOARD OF DIRECTORS
George L. Dixon, Jr., M.D.; Margery M. Dixon; Mark S. Lange; Martha D. Lange
AFFILIATIONS
Video Software Dealers Assoc., National Bicycle Dealers Assoc., National Sporting Goods Assoc.

Czar Productions, Inc.

809 New Britain Ave., Hartford, CT 06106; (203) 953-0809.
PRESIDENT
Gene Czarnecki

H. W. Daily, Inc.

3409 Brinkman, Houston, TX 17018; (713) 861-9251, (800) 347-5137
PRESIDENT
Don Daily
SECRETARY/TREASURER
H. W. "Bud" Daily
MARKETING & SALES
David Bennett

Damon & Grace Corporation

Mind Fitness Company
9000 Sunset Blvd., Suite #601, Los Angeles, CA 90069; (213) 274-0211. Organized 1972. (Videos to better the quality of life for individuals through behavior modification.)
PRESIDENT
Grace A. Reinbold
VICE PRESIDENT
Jay Michaels

Dawn's Video

519 W. Foothill, Suite C, Rialto, CA 92376; (714) 874-1414. Organized 1980. (Video specialty store.)
OWNER
Gregory C. George
BRANCHES
2085 E. Highland Ave., San Bernardino, CA 92404; (714) 864-3113
9725 Sierra, Fontana, CA 92335; (714) 350-8833
267 E. 40th, San Bernardino, CA 92404; (714) 883-5737
1330 Massachusetts Ave., Riverside, CA 92507; (714) 784-1414

Daya, Inc.

6 Lookout La., Westport, CT 06880; (203) 226-1964. (Needlecraft, educational videos.)

De Luz Video

P.O. Box 1431, Fallbrook, CA 92028; (619) 433-7220. Organized 1978. (Produces railroad home video tapes, VHS only.)
OWNER & PRESIDENT
Frank C. Boulter
PRODUCER & CAMERAMAN
Edward F. Boulter

Development Communications Incorporated

815 N. Royal St., Alexandria, VA 22314; (703) 638-3100. Organized 1978. (Training tapes.)
PRESIDENT
Welby A. Smith, Jr.
VICE PRESIDENT
Lawrence M. Franks
SECRETARY-TREASURER
Elizabeth P. Smith
BOARD OF DIRECTORS
Welby A. Smith, Jr., Lawrence M. Franks, Betsy P. Smith
AFFILIATIONS
ITVA, Dept. of Defense QVPL, ADPA, ASTD, Washington Film Council

Dial Productions

3220 Colony View, Malibu, CA 90265; (213) 456-6980.
PRESIDENT
Charlotte Dial

Digital Touch Ltd.

303 W. 42 St., Suite 4034, New York, NY 10036; (212) 246-3811, ext. 683. Organized 1985. (Multi-media development and production.)
PRESIDENT
Jeffrey Selig
VICE PRESIDENT
Bruce E. Colfin
COUNSEL
Jeffrey E. Jacobson
BOARD OF DIRECTORS
Jeffrey Selig, Bruce E. Colfin, J.E. Jacobson
BRANCH
Boston
AFFILIATION
AES

Direct Cinema Limited, Inc.

P.O. Box 69799, Los Angeles, CA 90069; 291 S. La Cienega Blvd., PH, Beverly Hills, CA 90211; (213) 652-8000. Organized 1974. (Specialized distributor of short videos and films, documentaries, independent features, animation.)
PRESIDENT
Mitchell W. Block
VICE PRESIDENTS
Joan Von Herrmann
Betsy A. McLane
COMPTROLLER
Sharon Levine

Discount Video Tapes, Inc.

P.O. Box 7122, Burbank, CA 91510; (818) 843-3366. Organized 1979. (Specializing in rare and unusual prerecorded videos. Retail and wholesale.)
PRESIDENT
Woody Wise

Disney Educational Productions

2600 W. Olive Ave., Tenth Floor, Burbank, CA 91505; Creative Dev.: (818) 972-3415. Marketing: (818) 972-3410. FAX: (818) 845-4570.

DIRECTOR OF MARKETING
  James N. Gentry
DIRECTOR OF CREATIVE DEVELOPMENT
  Sallie Zemlin-Kisor

Dixie Entertainment Productions Inc.

215 Long Beach Blvd., Box 2, Long Beach, CA 90802; (213) 491-0332. (Formerly See Hear Industries).
PRESIDENT
  Raymond Jacobs

Dobovan Productions, Inc.

1313 Kalakaua Ave., Honolulu, HI 96826.
PRESIDENT
  John B. Dobovan

Documentary Educational Resources, Inc.

101 Morse St., Watertown, MA 02172; (617) 926-0491. Organized 1971. (Produces and distributes 16mm films, videotapes and supplementary written materials to educational audiences.)
PRESIDENT
  John K. Marshall
EXECUTIVE VICE PRESIDENT/SECRETARY AND TREASURER
  Sue Marshall Cabezas
BOARD OF DIRECTORS
  Peter B. Dow (chair), Timothy Asch, Sue Marshall Cabezas, Napoleon A. Chagnon, John K. Marshall, Judith Nierenberg, Stephen M. Thomas, Mary Anne Wolff

Doko Communications

509 Madison Ave., Suite 1400, New York, NY 10022; (212) 686-6160. Organized 1985. (Video production and distribution.)
PRESIDENT
  Reuven Dorot
BRANCHES
  Tel Aviv, Israel

Double Vision Video Productions

401 S St., Sacramento, CA 95814; (916) 448-8220. (Instructional videos.)

Dudkowski-Lynch Associates, Inc.

150 Shoreline Highway, Bldg. E, Mill Valley, CA 94941; (415) 332-5825. Organized 1974. (Video production and post-production.)
PRESIDENT
  Ed Dudkowski
VICE PRESIDENT
  Marijane Lynch

Eagle Productions Ltd.

7860 Mission Center Court, Suite 106, San Diego, CA 92108; (619) 297-8870.

East Texas Distributing

7171 Grand Blvd., Houston, TX 77504; (713) 748-2520, (800) 231-6648; 2732 W. McDowell, Phoenix, AZ 85009; (602) 233-3741, (800) 231-3218.
PRESIDENT
  Ron Eisenberg
MARKETING & SALES
  Jan Moore (Houston)
  Janet Wheeler (Phoenix)

Eastin Phelan Corp.

P.O. Box 4528, Davenport, IA 52808; (319) 323-9735.
PRESIDENT
  Robert Evans

Echo Film Productions

Box 4692, Aspen, CO 81612; (303) 925-5605. Organized 1968. (Sports films, environmental documentaries, adventure films, new age health and arts.)
OFFICERS
  Wilk Wilkinson
  Tulasi Wilkinson
  Jama Wilkinson
AFFILIATIONS
  AFI, 659

Educational Activities Video

(Division of Educational Activities, Inc.)
1937 Grand Ave., Baldwin, NY 11501; (516) 867-7878. Organized 1983. (Produces and distributes educational videotapes.)
PRESIDENT
  Alfred S. Harris
VICE PRESIDENT
  Richard E. Harris

Educational Cable Consortium Inc.

24 Beechwood Rd., Summit, NJ 07901; (201) 277-2870. (Family-oriented educational videos.)
EXECUTIVE DIRECTOR
  Lyle Fisher

Educational Development Corporation

10302 E. 55th Place, Tulsa, OK 74146; (918) 622-4522.
PRESIDENT
  Randall W. White
VICE PRESIDENT, SCHOOL DIV.
  C. Jan Tucker

Educational Dimensions Group

792 Pacific St., Stamford, CT 06904; (203) 327-4612.
PRESIDENT
  Richard A. Byrnes

Educational Video, Inc.

27601 Schoolcraft Rd., Suite C, Livonia, MI 48150; (313) 427-5980. Organized 1983. (Production and marketing of original pre-recorded videocassettes and custom productions.)
PRESIDENT
  Robert Tollini
VICE PRESIDENTS
  Pamela Bonk
  Petra Pepellashi

Electronic University

P.O. Box 938, Pt. Reyes Station, CA 94956; (415) 663-9102. (Subsidiary of Electronic Educational Programs.)
PRESIDENT
  Mark Watts

Emory Medical Television Network

1440 Clifton Rd., N.E., Atlanta, GA 30322; (404) 688-8736. (A subsidiary of Emory University School of Medicine.)
MARKETING & SALES
Julie M. Slavik

Encyclopedia Britannica Educational Corp.

310 S. Michigan Ave., Chicago, IL 60604; (800) 558-6968; (312) 321-6800.

Enter-Tel, Inc.

24400 Chagrin Blvd., Suite 301, Beachwood, OH 44122; (216) 831-6110.
CHAIRMAN
S. Michael Loveman

Entertainment Productions, Inc.

2210 Wilshire Blvd., Suite 744, Santa Monica, CA 90403; (213) 456-3143. Organized 1971. (Motion picture and television productions produced for worldwide markets, including home video, cable, theatrical, etc.)
PRESIDENT
Edward Coe

Environmental Video, Inc.

1116 8th St., Suite A, P.O. Box 577, Manhattan Beach, CA 90266; (213) 546-4581. Organized 1981. (Manufactures and produces pre-recorded videocassettes for the home video market.)
PRESIDENT
James R. Spencer

Episcopal Radio-TV Foundation, Inc.

3379 Peachtree Rd., N.E., Suite 230, Atlanta, GA 30326; (404) 233-5419

Equestrian Video Library

8841 Exposition Blvd., Culver City, CA 90232; (213) 202-1555. Subsidiary of Mercedes Maharis.
PRESIDENT
Mercedes Maharis
NATIONAL SALES DIRECTOR
Jim Renier

Equinox Entertainment Corp.

P.O. Box 5195, Norman, OK 73070-9594; (405) 360-6595.
PRESIDENT
Jerry Colclazier

Ergo Media

P.O. Box 2037, Teaneck, NJ 07666; (201) 692-0404. Organized 1987. (Video publisher, manufacturer of pre-recorded videos of Jewish nature.)
PRESIDENT
Eric A. Goldman
SECRETARY-TREASURER
Susan Goldman
VICE PRESIDENT, MARKETING
Dan Rappoport
ASSOCIATE
Jane Zylberman

Esquire Publishing Corp.

2 Park Ave., New York, NY 10016; (212) 561-8226.

Euro-American Home Video

4818 Yuma St., N.W., Washington, D.C. 20016; (202) 363-8800. (Home video distributor.)
PRESIDENT
Ronald K. Goldman
V.P., MARKETING & SALES
Ted Goldberg

Evergreen Video Society

213 W. 35 St., New York, NY 10001; (212) 714-9860. Organized 1985. (Mail order videotape distribution.)
PRESIDENT
Steve Feltes
VICE PRESIDENT
Karen Chaikin
TREASURER
Roz Chaikin

Everything Video

P.O. Box 313, New Brunswick, NJ 08903; (201) 753-5826. Organized 1982. (Production of railroad videos and distribution of rare historical railroad video tapes.)
PRESIDENT
Norman Skolnick
VICE PRESIDENT
Murray Skolnick

Eye Contact, Inc.

1435 Center St., Oakland, CA 94607; (415) 836-1180. Organized 1982. (Provides multilingual production services in film and video.)
PRESIDENT
Carla Itzkowich
VICE PRESIDENT
Norma Armon

FFH Video

(Subsidiary of Films for the Humanities & Sciences.)
743 Alexander Rd., Princeton, NJ 08540; (609) 452-1128.
PRESIDENT
Harold Mantell

FJC-Intellimedia, Inc.

8332 Zenith Dr., Baldwinsville, NY 13027; (315) 622-1683.
PRESIDENT
Joseph Crisafulli
MARKETING AND SALES
D. LoSurdo

Facets Multimedia, Inc.

1517 W. Fullerton Ave., Chicago, IL 60614; (312) 281-9075. Organized 1975. (Film exhibition—arts films—and video distribution.)
PRESIDENT
David Edelberg, M.D.
VICE PRESIDENT
Constance Qonleg
CO-DIRECTORS
Milos Stehlik
Nicole E. Dreiske

Fairview Audiovisuals

17909 Groveland Ave., Cleveland, OH 44111; (216) 476-7054. Organized 1974. (Produces and distributes

health-related videotapes for personnel and/or patients of healthcare facilities and agencies.)
EXECUTIVE DIRECTOR
  Phyllis Blenkhorn
ADMINISTRATIVE ASSISTANT
  Lillian Zahara
BOARD OF DIRECTORS
  John Mc Fadden (president), Jack Hunger (vice president), Dudley E. Lavely, Jr. (secretary/treasurer)

Family Home Entertainment

500 N. Ventu Park Rd., Newbury Park, CA 91320; (805) 499-5827; (800) 423-7455. (Children's video.)
SENIOR VICE PRESIDENT & GENERAL MANAGER
  Ralph King

Fanlight Productions

47 Halifax St., Boston, MA 02130; (617) 524-0980. Organized 1982. (Non-theatrical distributor of film and video programs dealing with health, mental health and family life issues.)
PRESIDENT (OWNER)
  Ben Achtenberg
DISTRIBUTION MANAGER
  Brenda Shanley
AFFILIATIONS
  Plainsong Productions (film/video/AV production co. Also owned by Ben Achtenberg)

Ferde Grofe Films

3100 Airport Ave., Santa Monica, CA 90405; (213) 397-7524; (800) 854-0561, ext. 925. (Science and educational films.)

Festival Films

2841 Irving Ave. S., Minneapolis, MN 55408; (612) 870-4744. (Wholesale distributors).
PRESIDENT
  Ronald A. Hall

Film Ideas, Inc.

3575 Commercial Ave., Northbrook, IL 60062; (312) 480-5760. Organized 1979. (Educational film and video distribution.)
PRESIDENT
  Mike Collins
SECRETARY
  Alice Collins

Films for the Humanities & Sciences

Box 2053, Princeton, NJ 08543; (609) 452-1128. Organized 1971. (Video distribution and production.)
PRESIDENT
  Harold Mantell
VICE PRESIDENT, SALES AND MARKETING
  Jeff Morris

Financial Video Resources

1365 N. Broadway, Walnut Creek, CA 94596; (415) 674-3574. Organized 1985. (Produces and distributes educational videotapes on financial subjects.)
CEO
  William P. Koch
CFO
  Timothy Salisbury
GENERAL MANAGER
  Susan Pace

First Movie Exchange of Colorado

3011 W. 74th Ave., Westminster, CO 80030; (303) 427-7788. Subsidiary of Wickman Ltd.
PRESIDENT
  Dianne Lynn Wickman

First Run/Icarus Films, Inc.

200 Park Avenue South, #1319, New York, NY 10003; (212) 674-3375.

First Run Features

153 Waverly Place, NY 10014; (212) 243-0600. Organized 1980. (Distributes film and video to theatrical, non-theatrical, cable, home video and foreign markets.)
PRESIDENT
  Seymour Wishman
VICE PRESIDENT
  Nancy Gerstman

First Video Exchange

17503 S. Figueroa, Gardena, CA 90248; (213) 516-6422, (800) 247-2351. Organized 1981. (National movie exchange, stock rotation specialist for video movie dealers.)
PRESIDENT
  Jeff Leyton

Focus International, Inc.

14 Oregon Dr., Huntington Station, NY 11746; (516) 549-5320. Organized 1976. (Producers and distributors of film and video for sex education, research and therapy.)
PRESIDENT
  Mark Schoen, Ph.D.

Forum Home Video

(Division of Management Company Entertainment Group, Inc.)
11355 W. Olympic Blvd., Suite 500, Los Angeles, CA 90064; (213) 208-8899; TELEX: 188198; FAX: (213) 479-7429.; 575 Fifth Ave., Suite 24C, New York, NY 10017; (212) 983-5799; FAX: (212) 867-1565.
PRESIDENT & CEO
  Michael Olivieri
VICE PRESIDENT, ADVERTISING AND PUBLICITY
  Cathy Mantegna

Four Point Entertainment, Inc.

3575 Cahuenga Blvd. W., Suite 600, Los Angeles, CA 90068; (213) 850-1600. Organized 1984. (Television production, videocassette production.)
PRESIDENT
  Ron Ziskin
CHAIRMAN
  Shukri Ghalayini

Fox Hills Video

2730 Wilshire Blvd., Suite 500, Santa Monica, CA 90403; (213) 829-7441. Organized 1986. (Distributes and produces programming for sell-through and rental markets.)
PRESIDENT
  Jack Bernstein
VICE PRESIDENT, SALES
  Michael Meyer

418

VICE PRESIDENT, MARKETING
  Mark Gilule
VICE PRESIDENT, PUBLIC RELATIONS
  Jim Gullo

Fox/Lorber Associates, Inc.

432 Park Ave. S., New York, NY 10016; (212) 686-6777. (Home video sales agent and producer.)
PRESIDENT
  Richard Lorber

Freewheelin' Films Ltd.

P.O. Box 599, Aspen, CO 81611; (303) 925-2640. (Sports and educational videos.)
DIRECTOR
  Rodney Jacobs

Fries Home Video

(Division of Fries Entertainment)
6922 Hollywood Blvd., Los Angeles, CA 90028; (213) 466-2266; (800) 248-1113.

G.G. Communications, Inc.

111 French Ave., Braintree, MA 02184; (617) 843-4860, (800) 525-3503.
PRESIDENT
  Nicholas Russo

GME Piano Video

4150 Chestnut Ave., Long Beach, CA 90807; (213) 427-8586. Organized 1982. (Worldwide distribution of the piano video course Beginning Piano—An Adult Approach—15 cassettes, 3 books).
PRESIDENT AND TREASURER
  Dr. Allen Giles
VICE PRESIDENT
  Anne Diener Giles
BOARD OF DIRECTORS
  Dr. Allen Giles, Anne Diener Giles

GN Communications, Ltd.

2600 W. Peterson Ave., Chicago, IL 60659; (312) 465-0085. Organized 1984. (Sells and produces special interest programming to the television and home market.)
PRESIDENT
  Steven Polydoris

Galaxy Group

3790 Dunn Dr., Suite C., Los Angeles, CA 90034; (213) 204-3392.

Gateway Films Inc.

Box A, Lansdale, PA 19446; (215) 584-1893. Organized 1972. (Motion picture production and distribution.)
PRESIDENT
  A. Kenneth Curtis

Gaylord Production Company

9255 Sunset Blvd., Suite 800, Los Angeles, CA 90069; (213) 274-7769. Organized 1982. (Producer of programming for all television markets including network, first and 2nd syndication, cable and home video.)
PRESIDENT
  Alan Courtney

EXECUTIVE VICE PRESIDENT
  Peter Alex
SENIOR VICE PRESIDENT, BUSINESS AFFAIRS
  Mort Smithline
VICE PRESIDENT, DEVELOPMENT
  Jim Mahoney
VICE PRESIDENT, CREATIVE
  Steve Syatt
AFFILIATIONS
  Parent Company: Oklahoma Publishing. Affiliations: Gaylord Broadcasting (5 station group); The Nashville Network; Opryland/Opryland Hotel/Grand Ol' Opry, (3 radio stations) Texas Rangers

Genesis Project, Inc.

630 Fifth Ave., Suite 1510, New York, NY 10020; (212) 399-1020, (800) 336-4545. (Religious videos.)
PRESIDENT
  Michael Manuel

Glenn Video Vistas

6924 Canby Ave., Suite 103, Reseda, CA 91335; (818) 981-5506. Organized 1980. (Sale of videotapes.)
OWNER/MANAGER
  Murray Glass
AFFILIATION
  Glenn Photo Supply

Global Video Distributors, Inc.

7213 N.W. 79th Terrace, Medley, FL 33166; (305) 887-1986. Organized 1980. (Distribution of video-cassettes.)
PRESIDENT
  Angel Tomorgo
TREASURER
  Xiomara Tomorgo

Global Village

454 Broome St., New York, NY 10013; (212) 966-7526.

Golden Bay Video

20 Sunnyside Ave., Suite A 183, Mill Valley, CA 94941; (415) 381-2566. Organized 1982. (Video production.)
PRESIDENT
  Vinton W. Medbury, Jr.

Golden Productions

249 Sunset Dr., Encinitas, CA 92024; (619) 942-2614. Organized 1983. (Education and training programs for mental health professionals.)
PRESIDENT
  Dr. Kenneth M. Golden

Gorgon Video

15825 Rob Roy Dr., Oak Forest, IL 60452; (312) 687-7881. (Horror videos.)
PRESIDENT
  Jaffa Ali

Gospel Films, Inc.

P.O. Box 455, Muskegon, MI 49443; (616) 773-3361.
PRESIDENT
  Rev. Billy Zeoli

Gospel Video

3790 Dunn Dr., Suite C, Los Angeles, CA 90034; (213) 204-3392.

Granada TV International

1221 Ave. of the Americas, Suite 3468, New York, NY 10020; (212) 869-8480.
DIRECTOR OF GTVI, NY
  Leica Maw
SENIOR SALES EXECUTIVE
  Merry Mullings
SALES ASSISTANT
  Sally Millwood
BOARD OF DIRECTORS
Vivien Wallace (Chief Executive), David Plowright (managing director)
BRANCHES
6 Golden Square, London W1, England; 01-734-8080.
  18 Rue Volney, Paris 75002, France; 4261 7910 (Sales manager: Sara de St. Hubert)

Grand Award Video Inc.

2170 W. Broadway, Room 526, Anaheim, CA 92801; (714) 995-0707. Organized 1983. (Manufacturer of video pre-recorded software and TV's wide screen.)
PRESIDENT
  Jeffrey M. Scheirer
VICE PRESIDENT
  Harry F. Scheirer
BOARD OF DIRECTORS
  Jeffrey Scheirer, Harry F. Scheirer

Grass Roots Network, Inc.

300 Pacific Ave., Suite F, Aspen, CO 81611; (303) 925-8000.
EXECUTIVE DIRECTOR
  David B. Harding

Gravity Sports Films, Inc.

100 Broadway, Jersey City, NJ 07306; (800) 346-4884; (201) 860-9633 in NJ. Organized 1982. (Video distribution of action-sports titles.)
PRESIDENT
  Charles Mathieu
VICE PRESIDENT
  Chris Hawkesworth
SECRETARY
  Bruce Stafford
BOARD OF DIRECTORS
  Charles Mathieu, Chris Hawkesworth, Bruce Stafford

Great Mountain Productions

233 Broadway, Suite 3715, New York, NY 10279; (212) 227-5820. (Educational and children's videos.)

Green Mountain Post Films

37 Ferry Rd., P.O. Box 229, Turners Falls, MA 01376; (413) 863-4754; 863-8248.
PRESIDENT
  Daniel Keller

Grunko Films, Inc.

856 Coffeen Ave., Sheridan WY 82801; (307) 672-2487. Organized 1984. (Video production and distribution of wildlife, hunting, fishing, travel and children's videos.)
PRESIDENT
  G. Wm. Grunkenmeyer
VICE PRESIDENT
  Frank F. Johnson

HBO/Cannon Video

1370 Ave. of the Americas, New York, NY 10019; (212) 977-8990, (800) 648-7650. (Subsidiary of The Cannon Group.)

PRESIDENT
  Curt Viebranz
SENIOR VICE PRESIDENT, MARKETING
  Eric Kessler
SENIOR VICE PRESIDENT, PROGRAMMING
  Henry McGee
VICE PRESIDENT, MARKETING
  Tracy Dolgin

HCP Research

20655 Sunrise Dr., Cupertino, CA 95104; (408) 727-1864.
PRESIDENT
  H.C. Pellow
VICE PRESIDENT
  M.R. Faix

HPG Home Video

400 South Houston, Suite 230, Dallas, TX 75202; (214) 741-5544. Organized 1985. (Produces and markets special interest videos.)
PRESIDENT
  Mickey Holden
DIRECTOR OF MARKETING
  Karlene Lewis
AFFILIATIONS
  VSDA, SIVA

Hands on Productions

633 Post St., Room 500, San Francisco, CA 94109; (415) 771-2055. Organized 1987. (Produces gay/lesbian interest videos.)
PRESIDENT
  David Stuart

Harmony Vision

116 N. Robertson Blvd., Suite 701, Los Angeles, CA 90048; (213) 652-8844. (Music and concert videos.)
PRESIDENT
  Jerry Percell

Hartly Film Foundation, Inc.

Cat Rock Rd., Cos Cob, CT 06807; (203) 869-1818. Organized 1970. (Produces educational films.)
PRESIDENT
  Elda Hartley
VICE PRESIDENT
  James Porter
OFFICE MANAGER
  David R. Sotnik

Health Media of America, Inc.

11300 Sorrento Valley Rd., #250, San Diego, CA 92121; (619) 453-3887.
PRESIDENT
  Robert H. Garrison, Jr.

Hearst Marine Books

105 Madison Ave., New York, NY 10016; (212) 889-3050. (Division of William Morrow, Inc.)

Henwood Cinema Video

Box 376, Jamison, PA 18929; (215) 639-8806. Organized 1976. (Television programming of motion pictures and videocassette programming of feature films.)
PRESIDENT
  Alan Henwood, Jr.

SALES MANAGER
  Mary Henwood
OFFICE MANAGER
  Ron Hagen
ASSISTANT SALES MANAGER
  Ann Miller

Hewlett-Packard

1819 Page Mill Rd., Palo Alto, CA 94304; (415) 857-2381. (How-to and educational videos.)

Hi-Tops Video

(See Media Home Entertainment).

Alfred Higgins Productions Inc.

9100 Sunset Blvd., Los Angeles, CA 90069; (213) 272-6500.
PRESIDENT
  Alfred Higgins

High Gate Pictures

16 W. 61 St., New York, NY 10023; (212) 397-9330.
PRESIDENT
  William F. Deneen

Hollywood Home Theatre

1540 N. Highland Ave., #110, Hollywood, CA 90028; (213) 466-0121, (213) 466-0127.
PRESIDENT
  Larry S. Fine

Hollywood International Film Corporation of America

1044 S. Hill St., Los Angeles, CA 90015; (213) 749-2067. Organized 1969. (Film production and distribution.)
PRESIDENT
  Efrain Tobalina
VICE PRESIDENT
  Maria-Pia Tobalina

Home Entertainment Distributors

9549 Pen Ave. S., Minneapolis, MN 55431; (612) 887-9500, (800) 328-2960, (800) 352-2802 (MN). (Division of Lieberman Enterprises.)
PRESIDENT
  Robert Okinow
MARKETING
  Jeff Abrams
BRANCHES
  1631 Deramus Rd., Kansas City, MO 64120
  2781 Peterson Place, Norcross, GA 30071
  3014 N. Wygant St., Portland, OR 97217

Home and Industrial Distributors

300-1 Rte. 17S., Lodi, NJ 07644; (202) 777-4700, (800) 213-1586.
PRESIDENT
  Alfred Goldberger

Home Vision

5547 N. Ravenswood, Chicago, IL 60640; (312) 878-2600, ext. 325. Organized 1985. (Source for fine and performing arts videos.)
EXECUTIVE SENIOR V.P., PUBLIC MEDIA, INC.
  Gale Livengood

EXECUTIVE DIRECTOR OF HOME VISION
  Christine Lundberg
NATIONAL SALES MANAGER
  John Hillsman
CHAIRMAN OF PUBLIC MEDIA INC.
  Charles Benton

Hot Licks Productions, Inc.

P.O. Box 337, Pound Ridge, NY 10576; (914) 763-8013. FAX: (914) 763-9453. Organized 1979. (Produces video and audio music instruction.)
PRESIDENT
  Arlen Roth
VICE PRESIDENT
  Deborah Roth
BOARD OF DIRECTORS
  Arlen Roth, Deborah Roth
AFFILIATIONS
  Labtek in U.K., Music Sales in Australia and New Zealand, Rumark Video in Canada.

Houghton Mifflin Company

One Beacon St. (executive offices); 2 Park St. (trade and reference divisions), Boston, MA 02108; (617) 725-5000. (Bird-watching and "Watching Birds with Roger Tony Peterson" video.)

Hyde Park Media

1314 Howard St., Suite 2, Chicago, IL 60626; (312) 274-3337.
PRESIDENT
  A. E. De Bartolo

IFEX Films/International Film Exchange Ltd.

201 W. 52 St., New York, NY 10019; (212) 582-4318. Cable: IFEXREP-New York; Telex: 420748; Fax: (212) 956-2257; 9200 Sunset Blvd. PH 9, Los Angeles, CA 90069; (213) 278-6490; FAX: (213) 278-7939; TELEX: 4972966. Organized 1959. (Domestic and international distribution of feature films, documentaries, shorts and video programs.)
PRESIDENT
  Gerald J. Rappoport
SENIOR VICE PRESIDENT
  Richard Grisar
EXECUTIVE VICE PRESIDENT
  Christopher Wood
DIRECTOR, THEATRICAL SALES & MARKETING
  Robert Newman
VICE PRESIDENT, INTERNATIONAL SALES
  Joy Pereths

IRS Video

8335 Sunset Blvd., Suite 300, Los Angeles, CA 90069; (213) 650-8010. (Music videos.)

I.T.A. Publications

P.O. Box 281, Grand Blanc, MI 48439; (313) 655-6434. Organized 1974. (Produces, sells and distributes educational videos, training aids and publications.)
PRESIDENT
  James S. Benko
EXECUTIVE SECRETARY
  Siew-Hiang Benko
SALES MANAGER
  Maureen Juno
EXECUTIVE DIRECTOR
  Anne-Marie Curell

BOARD OF DIRECTORS
James S. Benko, Siew-Hiang Benko, Maureen Juno, Anne-Marie Curell, Nelson Curell, Michael Gould, Bruce A. Benko, Margaret Naessens
AFFILIATIONS
National Association of Deans

ITV Productions Ltd.

3941 Madison Ave., Culver City, CA 90232; (213) 559-7670. Organized 1986. (Video-film production.)
PRESIDENT
David Shapiro
SECRETARY/TREASURER
Cid Hunter

IVCC

2035-39 S. 7th St., Philadelphia, PA 19148; (215) 271-1500; (800) 523-7676. Organized 1982. (Produces and distributes educational material on video tape.)
PRESIDENT
Stan Nicotera

Image Entertainment

6311 Romaine St., Hollywood, CA 90038; (213) 468-8867. (Licensor and distributor of laser videodiscs.)
SENIOR VICE PRESIDENT
Lee Kasper

Image Makers of Pittsford

6 Wood Gate, Pittsford, NY 14534; (716) 385-4567. Organized 1976. (Produces videotapes for industry, educational programs.)
PRESIDENT
Richard H. Roberts

Image Organization, Inc.

9000 Sunset Blvd., Suite 915, Los Angeles, CA 90069; (213) 278-8751. Organized 1987. (International distribution of motion pictures, home video and television.)
CHAIRMAN-CEO
Pierre David
SENIOR VICE PRESIDENT, OPERATIONS
Lawrence Goebel
VICE PRESIDENT, INTERNATIONAL SALES
Mark A. Horowitz
DIRECTOR OF ACQUISITIONS
James Botko
DIRECTOR OF MARKETING
W. Lee Matis
BOARD OF DIRECTORS
Pierre David, Rene Malo, Michael Hirsh, Dimitri Villard, Robby Wald
BRANCHES
Los Angeles (head office), Paris, Montreal, Toronto
AFFILIATIONS
New Star Entertainment, Malofilm Group, Nelvana Entertainment, Pierre David Enterprises.

Images Video & Film Archive, Inc.

300 Phillips Park Rd., Mamaroneck, MY 10543; (914) 381-2994.
PRESIDENT
Robert A. Harris

Imperial Entertainment, Corp.

6430 Sunset Blvd., Suite 1500, Hollywood, CA 90028; (213) 463-4003. Organized 1987. (Film production, finance, distribution worldwide and video distribution, U.S.A.)

PRESIDENT
Sunil R. Shah
SENIOR VICE PRESIDENT
Sundip R. Shah
VICE PRESIDENT OF SALES AND MARKETING (U.S.)
Brian Clendenen
VICE PRESIDENT OF OPERATIONS
Juan Collas
VICE PRESIDENT OF FINANCE
Stan Falkenstein

Imperial Entertainment, Inc.

6430 Sunset Blvd., Suite 1500, Los Angeles, CA 90028; (213) 463-4003. Organized 1987. (Motion picture production and distribution, video manufacturing, foreign sales distributor.)
PRESIDENT
Sunil R. Shah
SENIOR VICE PRESIDENT
Sundip R. Shah
VICE PRESIDENT
Juan Collas
VICE PRESIDENT, SALES AND MARKETING
Brian Clendenen
VICE PRESIDENT, FOREIGN SALES
Chris Davis
BOARD OF DIRECTORS
Sunil R. Shah, Sundip R. Shah, Juan Collas
BRANCHES
Los Angeles: 6430 Sunset Blvd., Los Angeles, CA 90028
London: Bldg. No., GEC Estate, East Lane, Wembley, Middx. HA9 7FF, England

Imperial Video Corp.

P.O. Box 475, Bethpage, NY 11714; (516) 935-5050, (800) 645-5060.
PRESIDENT
B. Rubinowitz

Important Records

187-07 Henderson Ave., Hollis, NY 11423; (718) 740-5700.
VICE PRESIDENT, MARKETING & SALES
Howard Gabriel

Increase Video

6914 Canby Ave., Suite 110, Reseda, CA 91335-4313; (818) 342-2880. FAX: (818) 342-4029.
PRESIDENT
Howard Silvers
DIRECTOR OF MARKETING
Len Chapman

Indiana University Audio-Visual Center

Field Services Division, Bloomington, IN 47405-5901; (812) 855-8087. Organized 1940. (Audiovisual media marketing and distribution.)
EXECUTIVE DIRECTOR (AVC)
Thomas M. Schwen
DIVISION DIRECTOR
Chris Wagner
AFFILIATION
American Film & Video Assocation

Ingram Video, Inc.

347 Reedwood Dr., Nashville, TN 37217; (615) 361-5000, (800) 759-5000. (Subsidiary of Ingram Industries, Inc.)
PRESIDENT
John Taylor

VICE PRESIDENT MARKETING AND OPERATIONS
Ray Capp
VICE PRESIDENT, SALES
Ed Jackson

Innerquest Communications Corp.

6383 Rose La., Carpinteria, CA 93013; (805) 684-9977.
PRODUCER
Don L. Higley

Instant Replay Video Magazine

2951 S. Bayshore Dr., Miami, FL 33133; (305) 448-7088. Organized 1976. (Videotape magazine format about the video industry and TV Broadcasting. Sold on subscription basis. Available in ¾" and ½" Beta and VHS and 8 mm.)
PUBLISHER
Charles Azar

Instructional Video Cassette Corp.

2035 S. 7th St., Philadelphia, PA 19148; (215) 271-1500. (Produces and distributes special interest videocassette, PRO CHESS and PRO Blackjack).
PRESIDENT
Stan Nicotera

Intermedia Arts Minnesota

(formerly UC Video)
425 Ontario St., SE, Minneapolis, MN 55414; (612) 627-4444. (Non-profit media arts center producing, distributing and presenting social issue and contemporary interdisciplinary art and video.)
EXECUTIVE DIRECTOR
Tom Borrup

Inter-Global Communications

(div. Radio's Reliable Resources)
630 Park La., 2nd floor, Philadelphia, PA 19144-3713; (215) 849-3997. Organized 1962. (International film/tape program buying service for television stations and small dealers of home video.)
GENERAL MANAGER
F. O. Pease
OFFICE MANAGER
A. E. Pease
FOREIGN MANAGER
A. P. Taylor
BUYER
B. P. Weber
SALES MANAGER
J. K. Sperling
AFFILIATIONS
Inter-Global News div.

International Audio-Visual, Inc.

100 Northill Dr. #23, Brisbane, CA 94005; (415) 467-1032; 467-4663. (Chinese videos.)
PRESIDENT
S. S. Ling

International Film Foundation, Inc.

155 W. 72nd St., Suite 306, New York, NY 10023; (212) 580-1111. Organized 1945. (Produces and distributes educational films and videos.)
EXECUTIVE DIRECTOR
Dr. Sam Bryan
BOARD OF DIRECTORS
Richard Ford (president)

International Historic Films, Inc.

3533 South Archer Ave., Chicago, IL 60609; (312) 927-2900. Orders: P.O. Box 29035, Chicago, IL 60629. Organized 1976. (Distribution and production of military and political features and documentaries. Also distribution of Eastern European films. Provides stock footage to producers. Sales of films on videocassette through store and direct mail internationally. Videocassettes available on NTSC, PAL and SECAM videostandards.)
PRESIDENT
Peter Bernotas
MARKETING MANAGER
Frank Weinberg
AFFILIATION
Lithuanian Historical Society

International Home Video

431 N. Figueroa, Wilmington, CA 90744; (213) 513-1149. Organized 1983. (Manufactures and distributes prerecorded videocassettes.)
CHAIRMAN
Irving Katzef
PRESIDENT
Russell Greene
SECRETARY & TREASURER
Wayne Jones
BOARD OF DIRECTORS
Russell Greene, Irving Katzef
BRANCH
Video Latino, Country Video USA

International Marketing Services Inc.

2170 W. Broadway, Bldg. 522, Anaheim, CA 92804; (714) 891-6015.
VICE PRESIDENT
Jeff Scheirer

International Sailing Products

P.O. Box 355, Oyster Bay, NY 11771; (516) 922-5182, (800) 645-7676.
PRESIDENT
Steve Benjamin
VICE PRESIDENT
Paul Dickey

International Sunday School Lesson, Inc. (Bible Lessons International)

P.O. Box 1289, Marshall, TX 75671. Organized 1976. (Exegetical verse-by-verse Bible teaching using historical-grammatical hermeneutics.)
FOUNDER & HOST
Dr. Bob Utley

International Video Entertainment

500 N. Ventu Park Rd., Newbury Park, CA 91320; (805) 499-5827. Organized 1986. (Home video manufacturer and distributor.)
CHAIRMAN OF THE BOARD & CEO
Jose E. Menendez
CHIEF FINANCIAL OFFICER
Roger Smith
VICE PRESIDENT, ADMINISTRATION
David Campbell
PRESIDENT OF VIDEO TECHNOLOGY SERVICES
Dave Mishra
SENIOR VICE PRESIDENT & GENERAL MANAGER
David Mount
SENIOR VICE PRESIDENT, SALES AND MARKETING
Ralph King

SENIOR VICE PRESIDENT, PROGRAMMING
Ronna Wallace
AFFILIATIONS
Parent Co. of Video Technology Services, manufacturing division

Ivy Video

165 W. 46 St., New York, NY 10036; (212) 382-0111. (Subsidiary of Ivy Entertainment, Inc.)
PRESIDENT
Sidney Tager
VICE PRESIDENT
Joshua Tager

J2 Communications, Inc.

10850 Wilshire Blvd., Suite 1000, Los Angeles, CA 90024; (213) 474-5252. Organized 1987. (Produces and distributes quality, original home videos in the sell-thru market.)
PRESIDENT & CEO
James P. Jimirro
VICE PRESIDENT & CFO
James Toll
VICE PRESIDENT OF SALES
Duncan Murray
VICE PRESIDENT, MARKETING
James Levin
VICE PRESIDENT, CORPORATE COMMUNICATIONS
David Bowers
VICE PRESIDENT, PROGRAM DEVELOPMENT
Ellen Pittleman
VICE PRESIDENT, BUSINESS AFFAIRS
Scott Roth

JEF Films Inc.

Film House, 143 Hickory Hill Circle, Osterville, MA 02655; (617) 428-7198. Organized 1973. (Production and distribution of films, TV shows [network and syndication] and video programs throughout the world.)
CHIEF EXECUTIVE OFFICER
Jeffrey H. Aikman
VICE PRESIDENT
Elsie Aikman
SALES MANAGER
Jo-Anne Polak
PROMOTION MANAGER
Janie Barber
BOARD OF DIRECTORS
Jeffrey H. Aikman, Elsie Aikman, Donald Aikman, Janie Barber, Jo-Anne Polak
BRANCHES
Film Classic Exchange, Los Angeles, CA
JEF Films Inc.—England, Canada, Australia, France, Spain, Portugal, Greece, Switzerland, Austria, Italy, Monaco, New Zealand, Norway, Denmark, Germany, Sweden, Hong Kong, Fiji, Ireland, Belgium, Luxembourg, Algeria, Morocco, Tunisia
AFFILIATIONS
Owner of Film Classic Exchange (founded 1916), VIP Video, XTC Video, WHAM! Video, JEF Video Line, JEF Films International, PHD Video, The Stock Exchange (stock footage).

JMJ Productions

P.O. Box 4449, Hollywood, FL 33083; (305) 652-3952. (Railroad related documentaries.)
PRESIDENT
Morry Farcus

Jem Records

3619 Kennedy Rd., South Plainfield, NJ 07080; (201) 753-6100. (Distributes and manufactures records, tapes, compact discs, music video.)
PRESIDENT
Marty Scott

VICE PRESIDENT
Ed Grossi
TREASURER
Jeff Tenenbaum
BRANCHES
Grand Prairie TX; Reseda, CA

J & R Film Co. Inc.

6820 Romaine, Hollywood, CA 90038; (213) 467-3107. Organized 1963. (Film and video post production.)
PRESIDENT
Joe Paskal
EXECUTIVE VICE PRESIDENT
Jim Reichow
VICE PRESIDENT, SALES
Ron Powell
BRANCHES
New York, Chicago, Columbus

Journal Films, Inc.

930 Pitner Ave., Evanston, IL 60202; (312) 328-6700; (800) 323-5448.. Organized 1955. (Distributor of educational videos and films for the school and library markets.)
PRESIDENT
Joe Farragher
CHAIRMAN
Joel Altschul
EXECUTIVE VICE PRESIDENT
Esther Altschul
VICE PRESIDENT
Bruce Colling
NATIONAL SALES MANAGER
John Kelly
AFFILIATION
An Altschul Group Company

Joyce Media, Inc.

32003 Crown Valley Rd., Acton, CA 93510; (805) 269-1169. Organized 1971. (Produces and publishes videos.)
PRESIDENT
John Joyce
SECRETARY
M. Gayle Joyce
COMPTROLLER
Lois Knight

K-Video Productions

157 Wiltshire Rd., Claymont, DE 19703; (302) 798-2229. Organized 1980. (Educational tapes, corporate and private videos.)
PRESIDENT
John Kay
VICE PRESIDENT
Stan Kay
SECRETARY & TREASURER
Charmaine Imburgia
AFFILIATIONS
DBE, GWVCB, Delaware State Chamber of Commerce

Kalmbach Publishing Co.

1027 N. 7th St., Milwaukee, WI 53233; (414) 272-2060.
PRESIDENT
Walter J. Mundschau
MARKETING & SALES
Susan Poole

Kartes Productions Inc.

10 E. 106th St., Indianapolis, IN 46280; (317) 844-7403, (800) 582-2000

Keep the Faith Inc.

810 Belmont Ave., North Haledon, NJ 07508; (201) 423-5395, (800) 221-1564. (Catholic, family videos.)

Allan Keith Productions, Inc.

630 Ninth Ave., Suite 714, New York, NY 10036; (212) 246-0239. Organized 1961. (Produces and distributes educational subjects—film and video—speech, make up, sex equity, auto body repair, hairstyling videos, etc.)
PRESIDENT
Allan Keith
VICE PRESIDENT
Michael Keith
SECRETARY
Laurie Schilling

Kennen Publishing Company

150 Shoreline Highway, Bldg. E., Mill Valley, CA 94941; (415) 332-5828. (How-to computer videos.)
PRESIDENT
Ed Dudkowski

Key Video

1211 Ave. of the Americas, New York, NY 10036; (212) 819-3200, (619) 459-0500. (Subsidiary of CBS/Fox Video.)
PRESIDENT
Herb Fischer
DIRECTOR OF PROD. MANAGEMENT
Joseph Annechino

King of Video, Inc.

3529 S. Valley View Blvd., Las Vegas, NV 89103; (800) 634-6143, (702) 362-2520. Organized 1979. Public: 1981. (Manufacture and wholesale distribution of pre-recorded videocassette tapes.)
PRESIDENT & CHIEF EXECUTIVE OFFICER
Steven Vincent
VICE PRESIDENT, SECRETARY & TREASURER
Nancy E. Kelly
VICE PRESIDENT
Marvin L. Tragerman
VICE PRESIDENT OF SALES
John J. Lago
BOARD OF DIRECTORS
Steve Vincent, Marvin L. Tragerman, Daniel Rubenstein

Walter J. Klein Company, Ltd.

6311 Carmel Rd., Box 2087, Charlotte, NC 28247-2087; (704) 542-1403. Organized 1948. (Production and distribution of sponsored films and tapes.)
PRESIDENT
Walter J. Klein
VICE PRESIDENTS
Richard A. Klein
Terry Losazdo
David Jordan
SECRETARY
Elizabeth G. Klein
TREASURER
Betsy J. Klein
BOARD OF DIRECTORS
Walter J. Klein, Richard A Klein, Elizabeth G. Klein, Betsy J. Klein, Terry Losazdo, David Jordan
BRANCH
Seven Devils, NC

Kultur International Films

121 Highway 36, West Long Branch, NJ 07764; (201) 229-2343. Organized 1980. (Home video company dedicated solely to the performing arts with emphasis on ballet, opera, classical music, dance and performing artist profiles.)
PRESIDENT
Dennis M. Hedlund
VICE PRESIDENT
Pearl Lee
BUSINESS ADMINISTRATOR
Lynne Zecca
SALES MANAGER
Johanna Kelly
MANAGING DIRECTOR
Ron Davis
MARKETING DIRECTOR
Peter Frisch

Lawren Productions, Inc.

930 Pitner Ave., Evanston, IL 60202; (312) 328-6700. Organized 1961. (Distributes special education, child development, and attitude challenging AV programming to schools, colleges, hospitals and clinics.)
PRESIDENT
Joseph Farragher
CHAIRMAN OF BOARD
Joel Altschul
AFFILIATION
An Altschul Group Company

Learn Incorporated

113 Gaither Dr., Mt. Laurel, NJ 08054; (609) 234-6100. Organized 1968. (Publishes and markets "How to" video programs and audio programs with print materials.)
PRESIDENT
Bruce E. Corley
VICE PRESIDENT, FINANCE
Andrew S. Myers

Learning Corporation of America

6007 Sepulveda Blvd., Van Nuys, CA 91411; (818) 988-8300.

Legalvision, Inc.

%Jacobson & Colfin, 150 Fifth Ave., Room 1103, New York, NY 10011, (212) 691-5630. Organized 1982. (Produces educational and instructional videotapes for attorneys and businesses.) Distributed by Totaltape Publishers.

Leisure Enterprises Ltd.

309 Rue Bourbon, New Orleans, LA 70130; (504) 561-0531; 561-8323. Organized 1961. (Television productions, broadcast and home video.)
PRESIDENT
John Shoup
VICE PRESIDENT
John Beyer
SECRETARY
Cybil Curtis
TREASURER
Nick Kokoron
BRANCHES
3509 18th St., Metairie, LA 70002
AFFILIATIONS
Great Chef Television Productions, Leisure Video Productions

Leisure Time Products/3M

(See 3M)

Life Video Gospel Association

1435 Central Ave., College Place, WA 99324; (509) 522-0784. Organized 1979. (Produces and distributes religious videotapes.)
PRESIDENT
  Donald M Vories
TREASURER
  Walter Anderson
SECRETARY
  Jeanne Vories
BOARD OF DIRECTORS
  Donald M. Vories, Walter Anderson, Jeanne Vories, Fred E.J. Harder, Vernon Shafer, Paul Turpel, D.K. Smith

Ligonier Ministries, Inc.

270 S. North Lake Blvd., Suite 1270, Altamonte Springs, FL 32701; (800) 435-4343; (407) 834-1633; video hotline: (407) 767-8831. (Adult Scripture/theological training materials).
DIRECTOR OF PUBLIC MINISTRY
  Steven S. Fogerty

Listening Library

One Park Ave., Old Greenwich, CT 06870; (203) 637-3616.
PRESIDENT
  Timothy Ditlow

The Little Red Filmhouse

P.O. Box 691083, Los Angeles, CA 90069; (213) 653-0407. Organized 1975. (Produces and distributes film and video programming.)
PRESIDENT
  Larry Klingman
VICE PRESIDENT
  Anette Klingman

Llamavision Productions

P.O. Box 50859, Tucson, AZ 85703; (602) 293-8088. Organized 1984. (Video production from script to finished product. Producers of award-winning dance and international travel videos.)
PRESIDENT
  Gerald D. Harwood, Ph.D.
VICE PRESIDENT
  Sarajean A. Harwood
AFFILIATIONS
  Anubis Productions, Bastet Productions and Video Safaris International

Lorimar Home Video

17942 Cowan Ave., Irvine, CA 92714; (714) 474-0355.
CHAIRMAN/CEO
  Jerry Gottlieb
SENIOR VICE-PRESIDENT, FINANCE
  Michael A. Piraino
SENIOR VICE-PRESIDENT
  Neal S. Baseman

MAS Productions

18434 Bermuda St., Northridge, CA 91326; (818) 360-0371.

MCA Distributing Corp.

70 Universal City Plaza, 3rd Floor, Universal City, CA 91608; (818) 777-4000. (Distributor of prerecorded video cassettes and records.) A division of MCA/Universal.

EXECUTIVE VICE PRESIDENT, DISTRIBUTION
  John Burns
VICE PRESIDENT, VIDEO DISTRIBUTION
  Bill Hickman
DIRECTOR OF NATIONAL VIDEO ACCOUNTS
  Janis Durr
DIRECTOR OF SALES ADMINISTRATION
  June Morishita
BRANCHES
REGIONAL VIDEO DIRECTOR (NORTHEAST)
  Chet Furmanek
REGIONAL VIDEO DIRECTOR (SOUTHEAST)
  Kip Puiia
REGIONAL VIDEO DIRECTOR (SOUTH)
  Ron Gibson
REGIONAL VIDEO DIRECTOR (MIDWEST)
  Dan Grant
REGIONAL VIDEO DIRECTOR (WEST)
  Barbara Berger

MGM/UA Home Video, Inc.

Filmland, 10000 W. Washington Blvd., Culver City, CA 90232-2728; (213) 280-6000; (800) 468-7600.

OFFICERS
PRESIDENT
  Bernard "Bud" O'Shea
SENIOR VICE PRESIDENT—FINANCE
  Thomas P. Carson
SENIOR VICE PRESIDENT AND GENERAL COUNSEL—ENTERTAINMENT
  Karla Davidson
SENIOR VICE PRESIDENT—MARKETING AND SALES
  Herbert M. Fischer
SENIOR VICE PRESIDENT—CORPORATE GENERAL COUNSEL & SECRETARY
  William A. Jones
SENIOR VICE PRESIDENT—INTERNATIONAL
  Patrick John Leone
SENIOR VICE PRESIDENT, ACQUISITION, PROGRAMMING AND DEVELOPMENT
  John Ruscin
VICE PRESIDENT—SALES
  David Bishop
VICE PRESIDENT & CONTROLLER
  Kathleen A. Coughlan
VICE PRESIDENT & TREASURER
  Walter C. Hoffer
VICE PRESIDENT—TAXES
  Daniel Taylor
VICE PRESIDENT—MARKETING
  Ralph Tribbey

MMI Video Incorporated

57 W. Grand Ave., #401, Chicago, IL 60610; (312) 644-2775. Organized 1983. (Produces and markets behavioral modification, self-help, and heatlh related video-cassettes.)
PRESIDENT
  Mitchell Morris

MPI Home Video

15825 Rob Roy Dr., Oak Forest, IL 60452; (312) 687-7881. (Production and distribution of programming for home video.)
PRESIDENT
  Waleed B. Ali
VICE PRESIDENT
  Malik B. Ali
MARKETING DIRECTORS
  Jaffer Ali
  Nasser Zegar
MARKETING DIRECTOR, WEST COAST
  Peter Blachely
BOARD OF DIRECTORS
  Waleed B. Ali, Malik B. Ali, Jeanean Othman

M.S. Distributing Co.

1050 Arthur Ave., Elk Grove, IL 60007; (312) 364-2888.
PRESIDENT
Tony Dalesandro
MARKETING & SALES
Rick Chrzan

M.S.V. Distributors

40 S. Carolina St., Baltimore, MD 21231; (301) 675-1400, (800) 992-7799, (800) 492-1443. (Subsidiary of Musical Sales.)
PRESIDENT
Michael J. Bereson
MARKETING & SALES
J. Anthony Ray

Macmillan Video

866 Third Ave., New York, NY 10022; (212) 702-3241, 702-2000. (Children's and educational videos.)
EXECUTIVE PRODUCER
James P. MacGuire

Magic Window

2901 W. Alameda Ave., Burbank, CA 91505; (818) 954-4950; 3500 W. Olive Ave., Burbank, CA 91505; (818) 953-7900. (A division of RCA/Columbia Home Video.) (Children's videos.)

Magna Systems, Inc.

W. Countyline 95, Barrington, IL 60010; (312) 382-6477. Organized 1978. (Produces and markets video learning programs.)
PRESIDENT
Wilbur S. Edwards
TREASURER
Jane H. Edwards
SECRETARY
Wilbur S. Edwards
BOARD OF DIRECTORS
Wilbur S. Edwards, Jane H. Edwards, Ashton S. Edwards, William J. Edwards II

Magnum Entertainment

9301 Wilshire Blvd., Room 602, Beverly Hills, CA 90210; (213) 278-9981. Organized 1984. (Manufactures pre-recorded videocassettes for home use.)
PRESIDENT
Walter Gernert
EXECUTIVE VICE PRESIDENT
Danny Kopels
VICE PRESIDENT, SALES
Jim Brown
AFFILIATIONS
VSDA, NAVD, NAD

Mercedes Maharis Productions

8841 Exposition Blvd., Culver City, CA 90232; (213) 202-1555. (Horse-related educational and how-to videos.)
PRESIDENT
Mercedes Maharis

Major League Baseball Productions

(See The Phoenix Communications Group, Inc.)

Major Video Concepts

8399 Zionsville Rd., Indianapolis, IN 46268; (317) 875-8000, (800) 428-1400, (800) 732-1452 (IN) (Subsidiary of ADI/Mayflower Corp.)
VICE PRESIDENT & GENERAL MANAGER
Paul Guhl

Maljack Productions, Inc.

15825 Rob Roy Dr., Oak Forest, IL 60452; (800) 323-0442. (Educational and documentary videos.)

The Market Place

4112 Marsh Ave., Rockford, IL 61111, (815) 877-1514. Organized 1985. (Videocassette distribution of inspirational programs to the home and church markets. Children's programs, music concert videos, financial planning seminar and a how-to fishing program.)
PRESIDENT
Max Anderson

Market W Productions, Inc.

3605 Earnscliff Place, Ste. 56, San Diego, CA 92111; (619) 576-1014. Organized 1984. (Home video, video production, scripting, marketing, distribution.)
PRESIDENT
Lois Winsen

Mass Media Video Ministries

2116 N. Charles St., Baltimore, MD 21218; (301) 727-3270. Organized 1964. (A nationwide agency providing the educational and religious communities and other service organizations quality video programs.)
PRESIDENT
Clifford J. York
VICE PRESIDENT & TREASURER
Janice P. York
BOARD OF DIRECTORS
Clifford J. York, Janice P. York

Master Arts Video

15635 Saticoy St., Unit H, Van Nuys, CA 91406-3235; (818) 909-0233. Subsidiary of Multiple Development Corp. (Martial arts feature films.)
PRESIDENT
Joseph A. Pershes

MasterVision

969 Park Ave., Suite 8F, New York, NY 10028; (212) 879-0448. Organized 1980. (Special interest cultural and educational videocassettes and discs in the arts, humanities, science, sports and how-to's.)
PRESIDENT
Richard Stadin

Mattingly Productions, Ltd.

10100 Main St., Fairfax, VA 22031; (703) 385-6625. Organized 1971. (Video production and training services.)
PRESIDENT
E. Grayson Mattingly
EXECUTIVE VICE PRESIDENT
Suzanne Fisher Mattingly
VICE PRESIDENT-EDITORIAL
Allan C. Fisher, Jr.
SECRETARY & TREASURER
William E. Mattingly

Cameron McKay Productions, Inc.

1011 N. Cole Ave., Hollywood, CA 90038; (213) 463-6073.
PRESIDENT
Cameron McKay

Medallion Productions

4909 Wyandotte, Kansas City, MO 64112; (816) 753-3358.
PRESIDENT
Rebecca B. Newman

Media Bus, Inc.

P.O. Box 718, Woodstock, NY 12498; (914) 679-7739.
PRESIDENT
Bart Friedman

Media Concepts, Inc.

559 49th St. S., St. Petersburg, FL 33707; (813) 321-2122. Organized 1974. (Video production and specialty house.)
PRESIDENT
Charles W.R. (Bob) Skidmore
VICE PRESIDENT
John P. Gallagher
GENERAL MANAGER
R. Edward Schmidt
MARKETING & SALES
Richard E. Smith
John Gallagher
BRANCHES
Fort Myers, FL; Naples, FL

Media Home Entertainment, Inc.

5730 Buckingham Parkway, Culver City, CA 90230; (213) 216-7900, (800) 421-4509. Organized 1978. (Subsidiary of Heron Communications). (One of the largest independent home video companies—providing sports, fitness, and children's programming, as well as theatrically released films.) Hi-Tops Video is one of its brands.
PRESIDENT
Pete Pirner
SENIOR VICE PRESIDENT, MARKETING
Janice Whiffen
SENIOR VICE PRESIDENT
Jack Bernstein

Mediacast T.V.

2350 E. Devon, Suite 250, Des Plaines, IL 60018; (312) 298-1300.
PRESIDENT
Tom Edinger

Meeting House Productions

Mennonite Church and Schuylkill Rds., Spring City, PA 19475; (215) 948-4800. (Family entertainment. Producers of American Video Magazine and original music tapes.)

Mercury Films

211 Arizona Ave., Santa Monica, CA 90401; (213) 451-5510. Organized 1986. (Pre-recorded videotape distribution.)

PRESIDENT
S. Leigh Savidge
VICE PRESIDENT
Arnie Lakeyn

Metacom Audio Publishing Group

1401-B West River Rd. N., Minneapolis, MN 55427; (612) 588-2781. Organized 1970. (Manufactures and distributes—through direct mail—audio and video cassettes of subliminal self help and public domain movies, PD Films and special interest, old-time radio shows, kiddie product, languages.)
PRESIDENT
Dennis Levin
CHIEF EXECUTIVE OFFICER
Phillip T. Levin
VICE PRESIDENT OF FINANCE/CONTROLLER
David Benson

Metro Video

92 Railroad Ave., Hasbrouck Hts., NJ 07604; (201) 288-0400; Toll-free number (800) 87-METRO. Fax: 201/288-5503; Telex: 13943. (Largest independently owned distributor of pre-recorded video cassettes in the country.)
PRESIDENT
Arthur Morowitz
SENIOR VICE PRESIDENT
Henry Schwartzstein
DIRECTOR OF SALES
Bob Shavelson
SUPERVISOR, ADVERTISING/PROMOTIONS
Francine LaMarr
SUPERVISOR, CREATIVE SERVICES
Donna LoScrudato
PRODUCT MERCHANDISERS
Don Goldberg, Robert Mayo, Carl Van Kell, Chris Khrin
BRANCHES
Los Angeles: 5441 W. 104 St., 90045; (213) 417-8447; (800) 727-3876.
San Diego: 7853 El Cajon Blvd., La Mesa, CA 92041; (619) 463-5545; (800) 621-2190.
Pompano Beach, FL: 1985 N.W. 18th St., Pompano Beach, FL 33309, (305) 960-0006; (800) 888-3876.
Minneapolis, MN: 2724 Summer St., 55413; (612) 331-1590; (800) 248-4412 (Minn.only); (800) 328-0280 (out-of-state).
Phoenix, AZ: 1425 W. 12 Place, Ste. 103, Tempe, AZ 85281; (602) 966-5795; (800) 523-4912.
Puerto Rico: Calle B Lote 67, URB Industrial Mario Julia, Puerto Nuevo, PR 00922; (809) 793-3233.

Metro Video Productions

36 Virginia Ave., Edgewater, MD 21037; (307) 261-7660. Organized 1981. (Video production and post production facility.)
PRESIDENT
Thomas Kreazburg
VICE PRESIDENT
Troy J. Jones
TREASURER
Dan Wolf

Metropolitan Museum of Art

Fifth Ave. and 82 St., New York, NY 10028; (212) 879-5500. (Art-related videos.)

Mike Milkovich Enterprises

4505 W. 78th St., Prairie Village, KS 66208; (913) 341-1421.

Mill City Entertainment

Twelve Oaks Center, 15500 Wayzata Blvd., #762, Wayzata, MN 55391; (612) 473-7940. Organized 1985. (Program supplier, home video corporation.)

428

PRESIDENT, CEO
  Henry T. Morrison, Jr.
VICE PRESIDENTS
  Ford Watson Bell
  Cecil H. Bell
SECRETARY
  Robert O. Mathson
BOARD OF DIRECTORS
  Henry T. Morrison, Jr., Ford Watson Bell, Cecil H. Bell
BRANCH
  Minneapolis

Million Dollar Video Corp.

5900 Wilshire Blvd., #500, Los Angeles, Ca 90036; (213) 931-1616. Organized 1985. (Produces Spanish language home videocassettes and TV programs, and distributes Mexican motion picture films in U.S.)
PRESIDENT
  Miguel Kahan
VICE PRESIDENT, DEV. AND FINANCE
  Alberto Abdo
VICE PRESIDENT, VIDEO AND FILM
  Juan Almazan
VICE PRESIDENT, TELEVISION
  Gabriel Manjarrez
VICE PRESIDENT, TELEVISION PRODUCTION
  Luis De Llano
CONTROLLER
  Fred Rigaud
BOARD OF DIRECTORS
  Miguel Kahan (chairman), Bruce C. Corin, Irving Fuller, Esq., Allen Gilbert, Esq.
AFFILIATIONS
  Metropolitan Theatres Corp, Los Angeles, and Productora Metropolitana S.A. de C.V., Mexico City

Mindware Video Programming

P.O. Box 641, Kalaheo, HI 96741; (808) 332-9242. Organized 1976. (Produces stress reduction videos.)
PRESIDENT
  Terry Kamen
AFFILIATION
  Nebulae Productions

Mogul Communications, Inc.

1311 N. Mansfield Ave., Hollywood, CA 90028; (213) 650-2122.
PRESIDENT
  Joseph D. Dolan
VICE PRESIDENT
  Phyllis Dolan
MANAGER
  Judy V. Dundee (Slater)
BOARD OF DIRECTORS
  Joseph D. Dolan, Phyllis Dolan
BRANCHES
  Mogul Comm. Ltd., 35-37 Wardour St., London W1, England

Arthur Mokin Productions, Inc.

P.O. Box 1866, Santa Rosa, CA 95402; (707) 542-4868.
PRESIDENT
  William Mokin

Monterey Home Video

P.O. Box 2648, Malibu, CA 90265; (213) 457-5595.
PRINCIPAL
  Scott Mansfield
SENIOR VICE PRESIDENT & CHIEF FINANCIAL OFFICER
  Jere Rae-Mansfield

Morcraft Films Inc.

Box 65157, Los Angeles, CA 90065; 837 N. Cahuenga Blvd., Hollywood, CA 90038; (213) 464-2009. Organized 1976. (Restoring, re-releasing and printing old public domain films, cartoons and newsreels.)
PRESIDENT
  Dermott W. Morgan

Morris Video

2730 Monterey, Suite #105, Monterey Business Park, Torrance, CA 90503; (213) 533-4800. Organized 1984. (Produces and distributes quality information and entertainment video.)
PRESIDENT
  Dawn Morris
VICE PRESIDENT
  George Morris, Ph.D.
DIRECTOR OF PUBLIC RELATIONS
  Wendy Fulton
NATIONAL SALES MANAGER
  Kandra Inga
NATIONAL SALES REP. MANAGER
  Micki Smallman
BOARD OF DIRECTORS
  Dawn Morris, George Morris, Ph.D., George Bott, David Van Horn.
BRANCH
  663 The Village, Redondo Beach, CA 90277; (213) 374-4984.

Mossman Williams Productions

Box 7135, Kansas City, MO 64113; (816) 363-4352; (816) 921-3845.
PRESIDENT
  Wade Williams

Motor Cycle Video/Power Sport Video

P.O. Drawer 30337, Las Vegas, NV 89030-1537; UPS: Suite 200, 1973 N. Nellis Blvd., Las Vegas, NV 89115; 24-hr. order#: (800) 628-2828, extension 916.
PRESIDENT
  James W. Elbon, Jr.

Movie Buff Video

250 W. 95 St., New York, NY 10025; (212) 666-0331. (Subsidiary of Manhattan Movietime.)
MARKETING AND SALES
  Bruce Goldstein

Movie Merchants, Inc.

3254 Youngfield St., Wheat Ridge, CO 80033; (303) 234-9282.
PRESIDENT
  Shelley Gooch

Multi-Video Inc.

P.O. Box 35444, Charlotte, NC 28235; (704) 536-6928. ("Video Tape Repair" VHS Tape and repair supplies). (Educational and music videos.)

MultiVision of Denver

720 S. Colorado Blvd., Denver, CO 80222; (303) 691-2700.
PRESIDENT
  William Peterson

Muppet Home Video

117 E. 69 St., New York, NY 10021; (212) 794-2400.
EXECUTIVE PRODUCER
  Harriet Yassky

Museum of Modern Art of Latin America

1889 F St., N.W., Washington, DC 20006; (202) 789-6021.
MARKETING & SALES
Angel Hurtado

Music Media

5730 Buckingham Parkway, Culver City, CA 90230; (213) 216-7900, (800) 421-4509. Subsidiary of Media Home Entertainment.
VICE PRESIDENT, SALES
Alan Ostroff
VICE PRESIDENT, MARKETING
Jack Bernstein

NFL Films

330 Fellowship Rd., Mt. Laurel, NJ 08054; (609) 778-1600. Organized 1961. (Produces programming for the National Football League.) A subsidiary of the NFL.
PRESIDENT
Ed Sabol
EXECUTIVE VICE PRESIDENT
Steve Sabol
DIRECTOR OF VIDEO SALES
David Grassman

NSI Video

P.O. Box 895, Hermosa Beach, CA 90254; (213) 374-7476. Subsidiary of Native Son International. (Manufacturer and distributor of skateboard and other action sports videos.)
VICE PRESIDENT, DISTRIBUTION
Gerard Ravel

Naidoff Associates

65 Richard Rd., Ivyland, PA 18974; (215) 674-5410.
PRESIDENT
Bert Naidoff
MARKETING & SALES
Michael Smeyene

National Film Board of Canada

1251 Ave. of the Americas, 16th floor, New York, NY 10020; (212) 586-5131. (Film agency of Canada. Produces and distributes motion pictures.)

National Geographic Television

1145 17th St., N.W., Washington, D.C. 20036; (202) 857-7680. Organized 1965.
VICE PRESIDENT, DIRECTOR OF TELEVISION AND EDUCATIONAL FILMS
Dennis B. Kane
BOARD OF TRUSTEES
Gilbert M. Grosvenor (President and Chairman)
BRANCH
New York EXPLORER Office: 1251 Ave. of the Americas, New York, NY 10020.

National Golf Foundation

1150 South U.S. Highway One, Jupiter, FL 33477; (407) 744-6006. (Sports videos.)

National Hockey League

(See The Phoenix Communications Group, Inc.)

National Peregrine, Inc.

106 W. 2950 South, Salt Lake City, UT 84115; (801) 486-3155; FAX: (801) 466-2407. Organized 1965. (Film production and distribution to the world market.)
PRESIDENT
Hal Brown
CHIEF EXECUTIVE OFFICER
Neil Rosenstein
VICE PRESIDENT AND CHIEF FINANCIAL OFFICER
Larry Whitlock
BOARD OF DIRECTORS
Neil Rosenstein, Hal Brown, Aaron Grunfeld
BRANCHES
9229 Sunset Blvd., 9th Fl., Los Angeles, CA 90069; (213) 859-8250; FAX: 274-6731.

Natural Reflections Video

P.O. Box 476, Coloma, CA 95667; (916) 621-1771. Organized 1980. (Broadcast productions—industrial, prime-time specials, home video productions—specializes in white water productions.)
PRESIDENT
Michael Dennis

Nebulae Productions

400 E. 85 St., New York, NY 10021; (212) 697-9800. Organized 1978. (Produces and distributes nature, relaxation and self-help video programs.)
PRESIDENT
Terry Kamen
VICE PRESIDENT
Roy Kamen

Sara Needham Gallery

Mink Hollow Road, Lake Hill, NY 12448; (914) 679-2807. Organized 1970. (Presents to the general public, knowledge of artist, writer, philosopher, Sara Needham, founder of Disabled Friends of Ulster County.)
CHIEF EXECUTIVE OFFICER
Sara Needham
BOARD OF DIRECTORS
Sara Needham, Henry Needham
BRANCHES
Woodstock, NY; Charleston, SC

Nelson Entertainment (North American Home Video)

(Subsidiary of Nelson Holdings International Ltd.)
335 North Maple Drive, Beverly Hills, CA 90210-3899; (213) 285-6150; FAX: (213) 285-6190.
CHAIRMAN OF THE BOARD AND CHIEF EXEC. OFFICER
F. Richard Northcott
PRESIDENT AND CHIEF OPERATING OFFICER
Barry P. Spikings
ACTING CHIEF FINANCIAL OFFICER
Ronald B. Cushey
SENIOR EXEC. VICE PRESIDENT AND CO-SECRETARY
Walter W.J. Olesiuk
SECRETARY
Nigel Sinclair
SENIOR VICE PRESIDENT, NELSON ENTERTAINMENT GROUP
Peter D. Graves
PRESIDENT AND CHIEF OPERATING OFFICER, NELSON ENTERTAINMENT AND EXEC. VICE PRESIDENT, NELSON HOLDINGS
Richard B. Childs
PRESIDENT AND CHIEF OPERATING OFFICER, NELSON ENTERTAINMENT INTL., AND EXEC. VICE PRESIDENT NELSON HOLDINGS
Ian R. Jessel
PRESIDENT OF PRODUCTION, NELSON FILMS AND SENIOR EXEC. VICE PRESIDENT NELSON GROUP
Richard M. Finkelstein

New Age Video Inc.

1500 Broadway, New York, NY 10036; (212) 869-2616. (Educational, sports, music and dance videos.)

New & Unique Videos

2336 Sumac Dr., San Diego, CA 92105; (619) 282-6126. Organized 1981. (Produces and distributes educational and entertainment videos for diverse audiences.)
PRESIDENT AND PRODUCER
Mark Schulze
VICE PRESIDENT AND CO-PRODUCER
Patricia Mooney
CREATIVE DIRECTOR
Glen Merritt
ASSOCIATE PRODUCER/DIRECTOR
Steve Gruber
BRANCHES
San Diego
AFFILIATIONS
Crystal Pyramid Productions, Art of Love Videos

New Breed Music

P.O. Box 661, Pomona, CA 91768; (714) 623-1999.
PRESIDENT
Jesse Mac Lynum, Jr.

New Liberty Films

P.O. Box 25662, Shawnee Mission, KS 66225; (913) 451-2359. (Christian and issue-oriented videos.)

New Orleans Video Access Center

2010 Magazine St., New Orleans, LA 70130; (504) 524-8626. (Cultural/arts and educational videos.)
DIRECTOR
Karen Kern

New Star Video

260 S. Beverly Dr., Suite 200, Beverly Hills, CA 90212; (213) 205-0666. Organized 1987. (Pre-recorded video-cassettes.)
VICE PRESIDENT, SALES AND MARKETING
Cheryl Lynne Gersch
SALES AND MARKETING MANAGER
Lynn Baldwin
DIRECTOR OF MARKETING AND ACQUISITIONS
Ann Greer
ADVERTISING/MERCHANDISING MANAGER
Maggie Leatherman
NATIONAL ACCTS. MANAGER
Jeffrey Fink
EASTERN REGIONAL SALES MANAGER
Mike Pascuzzi
SOUTHERN REGIONAL SALES MANAGER
Toni Denny
WESTERN REGIONAL SALES MANAGER
Bryce Anderson

New Video Center, Inc.

276 Third Ave., New York, NY 10003; (212) 473-6000.
VICE PRESIDENT, ACQUISITIONS
Mike Tollack

New World Video

1440 S. Sepulveda, Los Angeles, CA 90025; (213) 444-8100. Organized 1984. (Video distribution.)

PRESIDENT
Paul Culberg
SENIOR VICE PRESIDENT, SALES AND MARKETING
David Pierce
EXECUTIVE DIRECTOR, CREATIVE SERVICES
Kim Yost
DIRECTOR, CREATIVE SERVICES
Susan Fields
DIRECTOR OF PROMOTION/MARKETING
Steve Okin
VICE PRESIDENT, CONTROLLER
Burton Messer

New York Times Productions

130 Fifth Ave., New York, NY 10011; (212) 645-3000. Organized 1978. (Produces programming for home video, network and syndication domestically and internationally.) A division of The New York Times Syndication Sales Corporation, an affiliate of The New York Times Company.
CHAIRMAN
Arthur Ochs Sulzberger
VICE CHAIRMAN
Sydney Gruson
PRESIDENT
Sam Summerlin
EXECUTIVE PRODUCER
Ted Harbert

Nightingale-Conant Corp.

7300 N. Lehigh Ave., Niles, IL 60648; (312) 467-0300. (Self-help and psychology videos.)
CUSTOMER CONTACT
Don Reaser

Norstar Instructional Video Corp.

1580 Old Bayshore Highway, San Jose, CA 95112; (408) 436-2882. Organized 1984. (Instructional "How To" distribution company.)
PRESIDENT
Stephen K. Troy
PARTNER
Ray Oltman
BOARD OF DIRECTORS
Stephen K. Troy, Ray Oltman

Northeast Productions, Inc.

1450 Penobscot Bldg., Detroit, MI 48226; (313) 963-2257.
PRESIDENT
W. Beauford

Nostalgia Merchant

5730 Buckingham Parkway, Culver City, CA 90230; (213) 216-7900, (800) 421-4509. (Subsidiary of Media Home Entertainment.)
VICE PRESIDENT, SALES
Alan K. Ostroff

Nostalgia Merchant

6233 W. Sunset Blvd., Suite 1019, Hollywood, CA 90028; (800) 421-4495.

Nova Video Art

10583 Felton Way, Cupertino, CA 95014; (408) 725-0708. Organized 1983. (Produces instructional dance videotapes—e.g., "Learn Classical Ballet and Enjoy It.")
OWNER/PRODUCER
Lilia Peloquin

MARKETING DIRECTOR
Mike Peloquin
GRAPHIC DESIGNER/NARRATOR
Katalin Maritza Balogh
AFFILIATIONS
Video Productions: Vertex Video Associates
Music: Silver Label Recording Co.

Ocean Video Inc.

#601, 4605 Lankershim Blvd., North Hollywood, CA 91602; (818) 506-3216. (Martial arts videos.)
VICE PRESIDENT
Aaron Yeung

On-Site Video

101 W. Main St., Bremen, OH 43107; (614) 569-4601. Organized 1982. (Video distribution.)
OWNER
Allen P. Brand

One Up Productions

1129A Folson St., San Francisco, CA 94103; (415) 558-8688. Organized 1982. (Produces, markets and distributes videotapes for the home video market.)
PRESIDENT
Hamilton V. Bryan II
DIRECTOR OF MARKETING
David Wren
BRANCHES
Super Source Video (distributor of Super VHS prerecorded videotapes exclusively.)

O'Neil and Jeffries Film Productions

3855 Lankershim Blvd., North Hollywood, CA 91604; (818) 760-6666. (Subsidiary of Jeffries Film Int'l.)
PRESIDENT
Hugh Jeffries

Optical Data Corp.

P.O. Box 97, 66 Hanover Rd., Florham Park, NJ 07932; (201) 377-0302; (800) 524-2481.

Optical Programming Associates

%Ira Roth, 11812 San Vicente Blvd., Suite 200, Los Angeles, CA 90049; (213) 207-4355. Organized 1980. (Produces interactive Laser discs.)
BUSINESS MANAGER
Ira Roth

Original Face Video

6116 Merced Ave., #165, Oakland, CA 94611; (415) 339-3126.
PRESIDENTS
Johanna Luther
Joseph Tiefer

Orion Home Video

540 Madison Ave., New York, NY 10022; (212) 888-4500. Organized 1987. (Manufacturer of pre-recorded videocassettes.)
PRESIDENT & CHIEF OPERATING OFFICER
Leonard White
SENIOR VICE PRESIDENT, SALES
Eugene Silverman
SENIOR VICE PRESIDENT, ADMINISTRATION OPERATIONS
Gerald Sobczak

VICE PRESIDENT, PUBLIC AFFAIRS
Paul Wagner
VICE PRESIDENT, MARKETING
Susan Blodgett
VICE PRESIDENT, MERCHANDISING & BUSINESS DEVELOPMENT
Joseph Annechino
BRANCHES
Livonia, MI; Toronto, Canada
AFFILIATION
Division of Orion Pictures Corp.

Ozman Inc.

496-A Hudson St., #K-17, New York, NY 10014; (212) 620-3832. Organized 1984. (Producer/distributor of educational and children's programs.)
PRESIDENT
Merav Ozeri
VICE PRESIDENT
Eytan Kaufman
BRANCH
Washington, D.C.
AFFILIATION
O-Tone Productions, Inc. (Music Productions)

Pacific Arts Video

50 N. LaCienega Blvd., Suite 210, Beverly Hills, CA 90211-2205; (213) 657-2233.
PRESIDENT
George Steele III

Pacific International Enterprises, Inc.

1133 S. Riverside, Suite #1, P.O. Box 1727, Medford, OR 97501; (503) 779-0990.
PRESIDENT/PRODUCER
Arthur R. Dubs
VICE PRESIDENT INTERNATIONAL SALES
Arn S. Withol
SECRETARY/TREASURER
Barbara J. Brown
MEDIA/PUBLICITY DIRECTOR
Paul W. Blumer
PROJECT DEVELOPMENT/ACQUISITIONS
George R. Elsom, Jr.
NATIONAL BOOKING MANAGER
Howard H. Lackey
OFFICE MANAGER
Andy Gough

Pacific Trade Group

94-527 Puahi St., Waipahu, HI 96782; (808) 671-6735. Organized 1977. (Publisher and distributor of books and video tapes.)
PRESIDENT & MANAGER
Richard E. Pultz
SALES
Bill Emerson
SECRETARY
Jane W. Pultz
CONTROLLER
Bill Creps
BOARD OF DIRECTORS
Richard E. Pultz, David A. Jasper, Jane W. Pultz, Faith Higshiguchi

Palmer Video Corporation

1767 Morris Ave., Union, NJ 07083; (201) 686-3030. Organized 1981. (Franchisor—video stores.)
PRESIDENT
Peter Balner
VICE PRESIDENT
Peter Margaritondo
VICE PRESIDENT, FINANCE
Joseph Berger

Panic Distributing Co.

2999 Silver Dr., Columbus, OH 43224; (614) 267-1211.

Paperback Video, Inc.

1060 E. 800 S., Orem, UT 84058; (801) 226-0155. Organized 1986. (Video production.)
PRESIDENT
Linda H. Thomson

Paragon Video Productions

3529 S. Valley View Blvd., Las Vegas, NV 89103; (702) 362-2520, (800) 634-6143. Subsidiary of King of Video.
PRESIDENT
Steve Vincent
VICE PRESIDENT/SECRETARY/TREASURER
Nancy E. Kelly
VICE PRESIDENT-SALES
John J. Lago

Paramount Home Video

5555 Melrose Ave., Los Angeles, CA 90038; (213) 468-5000.
PRESIDENT
Robert Klingensmith
EXECUTIVE VICE PRESIDENT, VIDEO DIVISION
Timothy Cloutt
VICE PRESIDENT, ADVERTISING
Hollace Brown
SR. VICE PRESIDENT, GENERAL MANAGER
Eric Doctorow
SENIOR VICE PRESIDENT, BUSINESS AFFAIRS &
INTERNATIONAL
James Gianopulos

Parent's Magazine

685 Third Ave., New York, NY 10017; (212) 878-8700. (How-to videos.) Subsidiary of Gruner & Jahr, U.S.A., Inc.

Pat Film & Video Services Inc.

630 Ninth Ave., 5th floor, New York, NY 10036; (212) 247-0900. Organized 1964. (Production and distribution of television shows and commercials. Film to tape transfers, ½" VHS-BETA and ¾" duplication. 2" and 1" duplication.)
PRESIDENT
Ervin Rosenfeld
VICE PRESIDENT/SALES
Andrew Cuomo
GENERAL MANAGER
Peter Economos
SECRETARY/TREASURER
Charles Haydon
VIDEO MANAGER
Leonard Laxer

Peak Performance Inc.

P.O. Box 2829, Duxbury, MA 02332; (617) 837-3398. (Sports and how-to videos.)
PRESIDENT
John Gillis

Perennial Education, Inc.

930 Pitner Ave., Evanston, IL 60202; (312) 328-6700. Organized 1966. (Distributor of sex education, family planning, reproductive health and social issues, AV programming to schools, planned parenthoods, health depts, libraries, hospitals, etc.)
PRESIDENT
Joseph Farragher
CHAIRMAN OF BOARD
Joel Altschul
AFFILIATIONS
An Altschul Group Company

Phipps and Company Productions

11375 E. 61st St., Suite 102, Broken Arrow, OK 74012. (Educational and sports videos.)
PRESIDENT
Terry L. Phipps

The Phoenix Communications Group, Inc.

1212 Ave. of the Americas, New York, NY 10036; (212) 921-8100. (Operates Major League Baseball productions under license from Major League Baseball. Licensed by National Hockey League as official production company.)
CHAIRMAN
Joseph L. Podesta
PRESIDENT
James E. Holland
SENIOR VICE PRESIDENT, EXECUTIVE PRODUCER
Geoff Belinfante
SENIOR VICE PRESIDENT, SALES AND SYNDICATION
Terry Kassel

Phoenix Films Inc.

468 Park Ave. S., New York, NY 10016; (212) 684-5910.
PRESIDENT
H. Gelles
MARKETING AND SALES
Robert Dunlap

Picture Start, Inc.

204 W. John St., Champaign, IL 61820; (217) 352-7353.
PRESIDENT
Ron Epple
MARKETING & SALES
Jeff Hellyer

Playhouse Video

1211 Ave. of the Americas, New York, NY 10036; (212) 819-3238. (Division of CBS/Fox Video.)

Plainsong Productions

47 Halifax St., Boston, MA 02130; (617) 524-0980. Organized 1980. (Full production and production services in film and video, both documentary and dramatic. Health care issues specialization.)
PRESIDENT & OWNER
Ben Achtenberg
AFFILIATION
Fanlight Productions (distribution co. also owned by Ben Achtenberg)

Plus A Video Ltd.

158 Godwin Ave., Midland Park, NJ 07482; (201) 447-1501, (800) 524-0195.
PRESIDENT
Lee Friedman

Pola Productions, Inc.

18662 MacArthur Blvd., Room 200, Irvine, CA 92715; (714) 752-5700. Organized 1984. (Video production/distribution.)
PRESIDENT
  James Polakof
EXECUTIVE DIRECTOR
  Gloria J. Polakof
ASSOCIATE PRODUCER
  Tina Maxwell

Polo Trade Corp.

688 Main St., New York, NY 10044; (212) 759-7779.
MARKETING & SALES
  Bill O'Leary

Polygram Music Video U.S.

810 Seventh Ave., New York, NY 10019; (212) 333-8559. Polygram Records, Inc.
SENIOR VICE PRESIDENT, MUSIC VIDEO
  Len R. Epand

Potentials Unlimited, Inc.

4025 Broadmoor, S.E., Grand Rapids, MI 49508; (616) 940-2723. Organized 1979.
PRESIDENT
  Gregg A. Banfill
VICE PRESIDENT
  Stephanie L. Konicov
NATIONAL SALES MANAGER
  Timothy J. Kelley
DISTRIBUTOR SALES MANAGER
  Cheryl L. Moore
INTERNATIONAL SALES MANAGER
  Michael L. Lankes
BOARD OF DIRECTORS
  Barrie Konicov (chairman of the board)

Price Stern Sloan, Inc.

360 N. La Cienega, Los Angeles, CA 90048; (213) 657-6100.
DIRECTOR, VIDEO DIVISION
  Claudia Sloan

Prince Leopard Film Productions, Inc.

307 E. 93 St., Suite 3E, New York, NY 10128; (212) 505-5508. Organized 1984. (Special interest home video tapes, programming and production.)
PRESIDENT
  Sylvia Grodin
VICE PRESIDENT
  Lenny Grodin
PRODUCTION COORDINATOR
  Arietta Venizelos

Prism Entertainment Corporation

1888 Century Park E., Suite 1000, Los Angeles, CA 90067; (213) 277-3270. Organized 1983. (Home video and pre-recorded music, television syndication, film production.)
CHAIRMAN—DIRECTOR
  Paul Levinson
PRESIDENT—DIRECTOR
  Barry Collier
SENIOR VICE PRESIDENT
  Earl Rosenstein

Producers International Corporation

3921 N. Meridian St., Indianapolis, IN 46208; (317) 924-5163. Organized 1968. (Business communications producer. Carries "Jerry Yeagley's Fundamentals of Soccer" for the home video market.)
DIRECTOR OF MARKETING
  Lori A. Feeney

Professional Research, Inc.

930 Pitner Ave., Evanston, IL 60202; (312) 328-6700. Organized 1965. (Produces and distributes health care and patient education AV programming to hospitals, clinics, HMO's, health depts., government agencies and private physicians.)
PRESIDENT
  Joseph Farragher
CHAIRMAN OF BOARD
  Joel Altschul
SALES MANAGER
  Margaret Dugan
AFFILIATION
  An Altschul Group Company

Progress Research, Inc

355 Grand Ave., Oakland, CA 94610; (415) 832-0305. (How-to, sports.)
PRESIDENT
  Richard E. Johnson

Public Access Producers Association

2652 N. Winchell, Portland, OR 97217; (503) 289-2309.
DIRECTOR
  R. S. Kolemaine

Public Production Group

733 15th St. N.W., Washington, DC 20005; (202) 347-7788. (Educational and public interest videos.)
PRESIDENT
  Sam Love

PyraVid International

61 Camino Alto, #108, Mill Valley, CA 94941; (415) 381-2567.
PRESIDENT
  L. Lee Buschel

Quadrus Media Ministry Inc.

128 Kishwaukee St., Rockford, IL 61104; (815) 987-3970. (Children's, music and dramatic videos.)
PRESIDENT
  Joe Musser

Quality Video Service

P.O. Box 2622, Redmond, WA 98052; (206) 788-6840.
PRESIDENT
  James P. Kehoe

Questar/Travel Network

680 N. Lake Shore, Chicago, IL 60611; (312) 266-9400. Organized 1986. (Produces and distributes high-quality non-theatrical videos.)
PRESIDENT
  Albert J. Nader

Questar Video Productions

3529 S. Valley View Blvd., Las Vegas, NY 89103; (702) 362-2520; (800) 634-6143. (Subsidiary of King of Video.)

434

PRESIDENT
  Steve Vincent
VICE PRESIDENT/SECRETARY-TREASURER
  Nancy E. Kelly
VICE PRESIDENT—SALES
  John J. Lago

RCA/Columbia Pictures Home Video

3500 West Olive Ave., Burbank, CA 91505; (818) 953-7900.
PRESIDENT
  Robert Blattner
EXECUTIVE VICE PRESIDENT
  Gary Khammar
VICE PRESIDENT, SALES & MARKETING
  Richard Pinson

RICON Enterprises

5863 Village Forest Court, Houston, TX 77092; (713) 683-0105. Organized 1983. (Production and distribution of videos about the space shuttle program and other NASA projects.)
OWNER
  Richard C. Colton

RKM Video Publishing Co.

2001 Wilshire Blvd., #400, Santa Monica, CA 90403-4622; (213) 274-8072. (How-to and diet videos.)
PRESIDENT
  Alan Riseman

RKO Pictures Home Video

(Subsidiary of RKO Pictures)
1900 Ave. of the Stars, Suite #1562, Los Angeles, CA 90067; (213) 277-3133. Organized 1983. (Ancillary distribution—home video and cable.)
VICE PRESIDENT
  Ellen S. Wander
DIRECTOR, SALES & MARKETING, ANCILLARY DISTRIBUTION
  Robert D. Lazarus
SALES & MARKETING SUPERVISOR
  Maggie Leatherman
BOARD OF DIRECTORS
  C. Robert Manby (Chairman), Mark Seiler (President)

RMI Media Productions, Inc.

2807 W. 47 St., Shawnee Mission, KS 62205; (913) 262-3974. (Instructional videos.)
PRESIDENT
  David L. Little

Radio Vision International

7060 Hollywood Blvd., #525, Hollywood, CA 90028; (213) 469-5750. Organized 1982. (Distributor of music-based programming.)
PRESIDENT/CEO
  Kevin Wall
CHIEF FINANCIAL OFFICER
  Karl T. Wall
SENIOR VICE PRESIDENT, SALES
  David Wyler
BUSINESS AFFAIRS
  Jeff Flower
INTERNATIONAL SALES
  Melek Demir
ACQUISITIONS
  Kevin Lenahan
BOARD OF DIRECTORS
  Ed Simons, Harvey Goldsmith, Kevin Wall, Karl T. Wall, Seth Willenson

BRANCHES
  Radio Vision Int'l (UK), Avon House, 360 Oxford St., 4th Floor, London, W1N 9HA England; Tel: (01) 493-0439.
  Radio Vision Int'l (Japan), 17-7 Akasaka 4-Chome, Minato-ku, Tokyo, 107 Japan; Tel: (03) 582-0211.

Radio Vision Video

7060 Hollywood Blvd., Suite 516, Hollywood, CA 90028; (213) 462-3690. Organized 1988. (Markets and distributes HIP vid clips and concerts.)
CHIEF EXECUTIVE OFFICER
  Karl Wall
SENIOR V.P., SALES AND MARKETING
  Kevin Johnston
BOARD OF DIRECTORS
  Kevin Wall (chairman)
BRANCH
  Avon House, 360 Oxford St., 4th floor, London W1N 9HA England
AFFILIATION
  Radio Vision International

Random House, Inc.

201 E. 50 St., New York, NY 10022; (212) 751-2600. Organized 1955. (Publishing company.)
EXECUTIVE VICE PRESIDENT, HOME VIDEO
  Gerald Harrison
CREATIVE DIRECTOR, HOME VIDEO
  Sharon Lerner
MARKETING DIRECTOR
  Robert Singer
VICE PRESIDENT, SALES
  Edward Martin

Ravenswood Productions

25410 Dodge Ave., Suite J, Harbor City, CA 90710; (213) 549-5422.
PRESIDENT
  James Sudalnik

Reader's Digest

Pleasantville, NY 10570; (914) 769-7000.

Reel Images

Box 137, Monroe, CT 06468; (800) 243-9289.

Reeves Corporate Services

708 Third Ave., 8th floor, New York, NY 10017; (212) 573-8570. Subsidiary of Communications Corp. (Film, video, meetings, multi-image presentations.)
PRESIDENT
  Kevin P. Ward

Regency Home Video

9911 W. Pico Blvd., PH-M, Los Angeles, CA 90035; (213) 552-2431. Organized 1986. (Produces, markets and distributes prerecorded videocassettes.)
CHAIRMAN
  Alan Silverbach
PRESIDENT
  Herb Lazarus
GENERAL MANAGER
  Terry Bochanty
BRANCHES
  New York office—Toby Rogers
  London office—George Blaug
AFFILIATIONS
  Division of Silverbach-Lazarus Group, majority owned by London Weekend Television (LWT)

Rego Irish Records and Tapes, Inc.—Rego Video

64 New Hyde Park Rd., Garden City, NY 11530; (516) 328-7800. Organized 1974. (Manufactures and distributes Irish recordings. Also manufactures and imports Irish videos.)
PRESIDENT
Patrick J. Noonan
VICE PRESIDENT
Margaret E. Noonan
MANAGER
Vincent Mitchell
AFFILIATION
Paddy Noonan Entertainments, Inc.

Rehabfilm

1123 Broadway, New York, NY 10010; (212) 741-5160. (Subsidiary of Rehabilitation Int'l., U.S.A.)
DIRECTOR OF MEDIA
John F. Moses

Republic Pictures Home Video

12636 Beatrice St., Los Angeles, CA 90066; (213) 306-4040. Organized 1952. (Film and video distribution.)
SENIOR VICE PRESIDENT
Vallery Kountze
VICE PRESIDENT
Phil Kromnick
VICE PRESIDENT, FINANCE
David Kirchheimer
VICE PRESIDENT, MARKETING
Glenn Ross
DIRECTOR OF SALES
Gary Jones
BOARD OF DIRECTORS
Russell Goldsmith (Chairman of the Board); Paul J. O'Brien (Secretary), Robert Magness, George Hatch, Bram Goldsmith, Tom Werner

Research Press

2612 N. Mattis, Box 3177, Champaign, IL 61821; (217) 352-3273. (Psychology and educational videos.)
PRESIDENT
Ann Wendel

Rhapsody Films Inc.

P.O. Box 179, New York, NY 10014; (212) 243-0152. Organized 1982. (Distributes jazz and blues films for all markets television, home video and non-theatrical.)
PRESIDENT
Bruce Ricker

Rhino Video

2225 Colorado Bl., Santa Monica, CA 90404, (213) 450-6323; (Horror feature films.)
PRESIDENT
Randi Freeman
MANAGING DIRECTOR
Arny Schor

Ed Rich Productions Inc.

1950 S. Ocean Dr., Hallandale, FL 33009; (305) 454-8068.
PRESIDENT
Ed Rich

Bob Richards/Chatham Films

P.O. Box 41158, Minneapolis, MN 55441-0158; (612) 339-8123. Organized 1980. (Distributes Bob Richards' films and videocassettes.)
PRESIDENT
S.H. Stenulson

Richman Brothers

6935 Airport Highway Lane, Pennsauken, NJ 08109; (609) 665-8085.
PRESIDENT
Jerry Richman
MARKETING & SALES
Charlene Engelbrecht

Riverside Distributing Co.

1208 W. Isabel St., Burbank, CA 91506; (818) 954-0880. Organized 1975. (Distributes video home movies and video accessories.)
PRESIDENT
Bernie Kirtin
VICE PRESIDENT
Saul Gerber
NATIONAL SALES MANAGER
Cliff Sawyer
WEST, REGIONAL MANAGER
Arnold Himmelstein
SECRETARY-TREASURER
Herb Bashkin
BOARD OF DIRECTORS
Saul Gerber, Cliff Sawyer, Bernie Kirtin, Herb Bashkin
BRANCHES
320 W. Madison St., Chicago IL 60606
AFFILIATIONS
Majestic Duplicating Service

Rizzoli Video

597 Fifth Ave., New York, NY 10017; (212) 223-0100. Organized 1985.
DIRECTOR
John Brancati

Robb Mavins Productions, Inc.

1210-240 Stradrook, Winnipeg, Manitoba R3B 0W5, Canada; (204) 477-6165. (Home video producer.)

Rocky Mountain Motion Pictures

P.O. Box 2850, Park City, UT 84060; (801) 649-1030. (Sports videos.)
PRESIDENT
Dean Lyras

Rodale Press Inc.

33 E. Minor St., Emmaus, PA 18049; (215) 967-5171.

Henry Rosenberg & Assoc.

550 Sylvan Ave., Englewood Cliffs, NJ 07632; (201) 569-6560.
PRESIDENT
Henry Rosenberg

SBI Video

4901 Forbes Blvd., Lanham, MD 20706; (202) 459-8000, (800) 638-0243. (Subsidiary of Schwartz Bros. Inc.)
GENERAL MANAGER/VIDEO DIVISION
Patrick Lawrence

SALES MANAGER
Jake Lamb
BRANCHES
1165 Marlkress Rd., Cherry Hill, NJ 08003; (609) 424-2211.
Richie Salvador, branch mgr.
1231 E. 26th St., Cleveland, OH 44114 (216) 696-2701. Harvey
Korman, branch mgr.
1129 Bloomfield Ave., W. Caldwell, NJ 07006; (201) 882-2955.
Andy Miele, sales mgr.

S.I. Video

4111 W. Alameda, #508, Burbank, CA 91505; (818)
845-5599. Organized 1986. (Full service marketing and
distribution for special interest videos.)
PRESIDENT
Patricia M. Leonard
VICE PRESIDENT, BUSINESS DEVELOPMENT
Anne V. Lieberman

STG Distributing, Inc.

4974 E. Clinton Ave., Suite 112, Fresno, CA 93727;
(209) 454-0800. Organized 1984. (Video distribution and
rack jobber.)
PRESIDENT
Jerry Welch
EXECUTIVE VICE PRESIDENT & SECRETARY
James Daily
TREASURER
Fred Atchity, Jr.
CHIEF FINANCIAL OFFICER
Frank Ryason
BOARD OF DIRECTORS
Bernard Horton, Fred Atchity, Jr., Howard Freedland, John Eng-
vall

San Francisco Rush Video

1554 Grove Street, San Francisco, CA 94117; (415)
921-8273. Organized 1983. (Video post-production, home
video producers.)
OWNER-PRESIDENT
William Anthony Longen
VICE PRESIDENT
Stanton Schaffer

Saturn Productions, Inc.

1697 Broadway, New York, NY 10019; (212) 489-2460.
Organized 1984. (Pre-recorded videocassettes.) Parent
company is Telefilm Inc.
PRESIDENT
Tom Ward

Schwartz Brothers, Inc.

4901 Forbes Blvd., Lanham, MD 20706; (301) 459-
8000. Organized 1946. (Wholesale distributor of video-
cassettes, compact discs, records, blank tapes, pre-re-
corded tapes, and accessories.)
PRESIDENT
James Schwartz
CHAIRMAN OF THE BOARD & EXECUTIVE VICE PRESIDENT
Stuart Schwartz
VICE PRESIDENT, FINANCE
Melvin C. Davis
VICE PRESIDENT, SALES
Jerome Jacobs
BOARD OF DIRECTORS
Milton Lyons, Joseph R. Cassidy, Howard Kolodny
BRANCHES
1165 Marlkress Rd., Cherry Hill, NJ 08003; (609) 424-2211
(Richard Salvador, branch manager)
1129 Bloomfield Ave., W. Caldwell, NJ 07006; (201) 882-2955
(Andy Miele, sales manager)
1231 E. 26th St., Cleveland, OH 44114; (216) 696-2701 (Harvey
Korman, branch manager)

AFFILIATIONS
National Association of Record Merchandisers
National Association of Video Distributors
Video Software Dealers Association
Country Music Association

Sea-TV

1619 Chapel St., New Haven, CT 06511; (203)
624-0470. Organized 1983. (Marketing and production of
nautical video cassettes.)
PRESIDENT
Charles P. Croft
BOARD OF DIRECTORS
Herb Hild

See Hear Industries

P.O. Box 4529, Carson, CA 90749-4529; (213) 516-
0315. Division of RJA Inc.
PRESIDENT
Raymond L. Jacobs

Select-A-Tape

8756 Holloway Dr., Los Angeles, CA 90069; (213)
657-2706, (800) 421-4465. (Distributes midnight videos
[horror films] and adult films.)
PRESIDENT
Alan Roberts

Self Improvement Video, Inc.

Suite 283, 77 Ives St., Providence, RI 02906; (401)
351-3770. Organized 1983. (Produces and markets home
video programming.)
PRESIDENT
John R. Koenig
VICE PRESIDENT
Maria P. Koenig
BOARD OF DIRECTORS
John R. Koenig, Maria P. Koenig
AFFILIATION
Engaged in joint ventures with Corporate Image Productions,
Inc.

Self Reliance Foundation

207 Montoya St., Santa Fe, NM 87501; (505) 984-0080.
PRESIDENT
Jeff Kline

Serendipity Communications

4141-B Directors Row, Houston, TX 77092; (713) 680-
1300.
PRESIDENT
Fred R. Brison
DIRECTOR OF MARKETING
Jim Scott

Sherwood Video Production Co.

676 N. St. Clair St., Suite 1880, Chicago, IL 60611; (312)
275-9191. (Educational videos.)
PRESIDENT
Barry Torman

Shokus Video

P.O. Box 8434, Van Nuys, CA 91409; (818) 704-0400.
Organized 1979. (Preservation of vintage TV films and
kinescopes in the public domain.)

PRESIDENT
Stuart Shostak
AFFILIATIONS
AFTRA (since 1982), VSDA 1981–85

Sight and Sound Distributors

2055 Walton Rd., St. Louis, MO 63114; (314) 426-2388; (800) 325-9232.
DIRECTOR
Dan Thompson
BRANCHES
1144 Booth St., Kansas City, KS 66103; (913) 371-8152
2201 Brookwood Dr., Little AK 72202; (501) 664-1630

Single Concept Films

2 Terrain Dr., Rochester, NY 14618; (716) 442-9740. (Educational and medical videos.)
PRODUCER
Jack Ruda

Snoopy's Home Video Library

2730 Wilshire Blvd. #500, Santa Monica, CA 90403; (213) 453-7929; (800) 421-4509. (Children's videos.) Subsidiary of Media Home Entertainment.

Society of Manufacturing Engineers

1 SME Dr., P.O. Box 930, Dearborn, MI 48121-0930; (313) 271-1500; (800) 535-8005; in MI (800) 533-9303.
PRESIDENT
Nathan Chiantello
MANAGER VIDEO COMMUNICATIONS
Timothy Savage

Sonoma Video Productions

553 Mendocino Ave., Santa Rosa, CA 95401; (707) 579-3902. (Producer of instructional and travel video programs.)
GENERAL MANAGER
Ron Schilling

Sony Video Communications

(Division of Sony Corp. of America)
Sony Dr., Park Ridge, NJ 07656; (201) 930-1000.
CORPORATE PRESIDENT
Kenji Tamiya
PRESIDENT
Philip J. Stack
VICE PRESIDENT, SALES
Robert Mueller
NATIONAL SERVICE MANAGER
Philip Hart

Sony Video Software Company, Inc.

1700 Broadway, New York, NY 10019; (212) 757-4990.
PRESIDENT
John O'Donnell
VICE PRESIDENT, SALES
Michael Holzman
DIRECTOR OF BUSINESS AFFAIRS
Jeffrey Ringler

Sound Video Unlimited

7000 N. Austin Ave., Niles, IL 60648; (312) 647-0800.

Source Video Distributing Co., Inc.

1100 Hillsboro Rd., Franklin, TN 37064; (615) 790-5300; (800) 342-5014 (TN).
PRESIDENT
Lee Cowen
MARKETING & SALES
Fred W. Phister

Special Interest Video

1717 Darby Rd., Sebastopol, CA 95472; (707) 829-0127. Organized 1980. (Distribution of instructional and special interest video tapes.)
PRESIDENT
Michael Heumann
MARKETING VICE PRESIDENT
Faison Jordan
SECRETARY & TREASURER
Marcia Ludwig
AFFILIATION
VSDA

Spectrum Video

18121 Napa St., Northridge, CA 91325; (818) 886-8680, (800) 423-5599. (Acquisition and production of alternative non-theatrical, how-to programming for distribution to home video market place.)
PRESIDENT
Fred Hirsch
VICE PRESIDENT
Dwight Krizman
AFFILIATION
VSDA

Sperry Corporation Information Group

P.O. Box 2191, Princeton, NJ 08540; (201) 329-3899; (800) 222-0966. (Science and how-to videos.)

Spinnaker Software Corp.

1 Kendall Square, Cambridge, MA 02139; (617) 494-1200.
VICE PRESIDENT
Priscilla Seuss

Sports Films & Talents, Inc.

12755 State Highway 55, Minneapolis, MN 55441; (612) 540-5972. (Sports videos.)

Sports World Cinema

P.O. Box 17022, Salt Lake City, UT 84117; (801) 266-9300.
PRESIDENT
Gary B. Ewing

Sportsmen on Film

5038 N. Parkway Calabasas, #100, Calabasas, CA 91302. Organized 1984. (Produces video for hunters, shooters and outdoorsmen.)
PRESIDENT
Ken Wilson
VICE PRESIDENT
Greg Summitt
SECRETARY
Sandy Oliveira
BOARD OF DIRECTORS
Lorraine Wilson, (chairman)

Spotlight Video

12636 Beatrice St., Los Angeles, CA 90066; (213) 306-4040. (Subsidiary of Public Pictures Home Video Co.)
SENIOR VICE PRESIDENT
    Nick Draklich

Star Classics Inc.

4301 Glenwood Rd., Brooklyn, NY 11210; (718) 434-1100. Organized 1985. (Produces and distributes video cassettes for the home entertainment market.)
PRESIDENT, C.E.O. & TREASURER
    Martin Chopp
VICE PRESIDENT
    Gerald Schwebel
SECRETARY
    Manny Chopp
BOARD OF DIRECTORS
    Martin Chopp (chairman); Gerald Schwebel, Manny Chopp

Star Video Entertainment, Inc.

550 Grand St., Jersey City, NJ 07302-4112; (201) 333-4600.
PRESIDENT
    Bernard Herman

Star Video Productions

10701 Wilshire Blvd., Room 2001, Los Angeles, CA 90024; (213) 470-6522. Organized 1980. (Production and distribution of How-to home videos.)
PRESIDENT
    Alfredo Ringel
EXECUTIVE VICE PRESIDENT
    Deborah Taper Ringel

Martha Stuart Communications, Inc.

Box 246, 2 Anthony St., Hillsdale, NY 12529; (518) 325-3900. (Educational and general interest videos.)
PRESIDENT
    Martha Stuart
MARKETING & SALES
    Victoria Simons

Summit Media Co.

27811 Hopkins Ave., Unit 1, Valencia, CA 91355; (805) 295-0675. Organized 1987. (Video production and distribution.)
PRESIDENT
    William C. Hutten
VICE PRESIDENT
    Tony Love

Sun Video

15 Donnybrook Dr., Demarest, NJ 07627; (201) 784-0662. Organized 1979. (Home videocassette production and distribution.)
CO-PRESIDENTS
    Henry J. Stern
    Serafim Karalexis
BOARD OF DIRECTORS
    Henry J. Stern, Serafim Karalexis

Sunshine Communications

P.O. Box 1711, Tempe, AZ 85281; (602) 968-3217. Organized 1981. (Produces feature films, videocassettes and TV shows.)

PRESIDENT
    David Belskis
VICE PRESIDENT
    Geri Caswell
SECRETARY
    Michelle Caswell
MARKETING
    Robert Levy
AFFILIATION
    Member: American Film Institute

Supreme Video Works

15 E. 61 St., New York, NY 10021; (212) 753-1050. (Video production for corporate, documentary, fashion, music, performance videos.)
PRODUCER/DIRECTOR/DIRECTOR, PHOTOGRAPHY
    Tony Arzt

Surf Video Network, Inc.

825 Onstott Rd., Lompoc, CA 93436; (805) 733-1200. Organized 1980. (Produces and distributes surfing, skateboarding, windsurfing, BMX, snowboarding, skiing videos.)
PRESIDENT
    Chris Darling
VICE PRESIDENT
    David Natal

SyberVision Systems, Inc.

7133 Koll Center Parkway, Pleasanton, CA 94566; (415) 846-2244. Organized 1977. (Produces self-achievement and sports video and audio tapes.)
PRESIDENT
    Michael Doepke
CO-FOUNDERS
    Steven DeVore
    Nasser Hamedani
VICE PRESIDENT, FINANCE
    John Heinke
VICE PRESIDENT, OPERATIONS
    Regan Jones
VICE PRESIDENT, PRODUCT DEVELOPMENT
    Howard Jamison
AFFILIATIONS
    Professional Ski Instructors of America, Direct Marketing Association, National Sporting Goods Association, International Tape/Disc Association, Video Software Dealers Association.

Syndistar, Inc.

648 Hickory Ave., New Orleans, LA 70123; (504) 737-4486. Organized 1979. (Produces and distributes information films and video.)
PRESIDENT
    Greg Fox
VICE PRESIDENT, SALES & MARKETING
    Lynn Bourgeois
VICE PRESIDENT, OPERATIONS
    Norman Landry
VICE PRESIDENT, PRODUCTION
    Billie Rodrigue
AFFILIATIONS
    ICIA, VSDA

TV Collector

P.O. Box 188, Needham, MA 02192; (508) 238-1179. (Old television programs and nostalgia; Memorabilia catalogs, published separately.)
PRESIDENTS
    Stephen W. Albert
    Diane L. Albert

439

TV Sports Scene, Inc.

(TVSS, Inc.)
5804 Ayrshire Blvd., Minneapolis, MN 55436; (612) 925-9661. Organized 1970. (TV program distribution, national and international.)
PRESIDENT & CHAIRMAN OF THE BOARD
　Donald L. Herrick
VICE PRESIDENT
　Robert C. Bruce
SECRETARY & TREASURER
　Barbara Conley
BOARD OF DIRECTORS
　Donald L. Herrick, Robert C. Bruce, Barbara Conley
AFFILIATIONS
　Owner of U.S. Television Communications, Inc. (USTC)
　Owner—Division Northwest Advertising & Marketing
　Owner—Division MED TV
　Owner—Division Consumer Products Division TV Sports Scene, Inc.

Tamarelle's French Film House

110 Cohasset Stage Rd., Chico, CA 95926; (916) 895-3429.
PRESIDENT
　Claire Tamarelle

Teaching Films, Inc.

930 Pitner Ave., Evanston, IL 60202; (312) 328-6700; (800) 323-9084. (Distributor of educational films and videos for the professional medical and allied health markets.)
PRESIDENT
　Joe Farragher
CHAIRMAN
　Joel Altschul
EXECUTIVE VICE PRESIDENT
　Esther Altschul
VICE PRESIDENT
　Bruce Colling
MARKETING MANAGER
　Beth Kon

Telecine Spanish Video

2151 Belmont Ave., New York, NY 10457; (212) 798-7028.
PRESIDENT
　Peter Velez
MARKETING AND SALES
　Ed Freeberg

Telefilm Co. Inc./Saturn Productions Inc.

1780 Broadway, Room 1100, New York, NY 10019; (212) 489-2460. Organized 1981. (Theatrical, television, cable Saturn Productions pre-recorded videocassettes.)
PRESIDENT
　Tom Ward

Telequest Inc.

14 Washington Road, Princeton Jct., NJ 08550; (609) 799-2105. Organized 1977. (Film and video production for broadcast and industry.)
PRESIDENT
　Richard Blofson
VICE PRESIDENT
　Sam Russell
SECRETARY/TREASURER
　Scott Nielsen

Telstar Inc.

Bob Miller, 1400 Energy Park Drive, Suite 24, St. Paul, MN 55108; (612) 644-4726. Organized 1968. (Produces and markets video training and instructional materials to industry, home and education.)
PRESIDENT
　J.K. Wasley
VICE PRESIDENT
　Bob Miller
BOARD OF DIRECTORS
　J.K. Wasley, Bob Miller

Theta Mark Home Video, Inc.

1721 W. Plano Parkway, Plano, TX 75075; (214) 578-7651. Organized 1986. (Alternative video distributor/rack jobber)
PRESIDENT
　Patrick J. Roper

Third Coast Productions

6125 Airport Freeway, Fort Worth, TX 76117; (817) 831-0916; 831-0559. Organized 1976. (Film and video tape producer.)
GENERAL MANAGER
　Perry W. Tong

Thomson Productions, Inc.

1060 E. 800 S., Orem, UT 84058; (801) 226-0155. Organized 1984. (Video distribution.)
PRESIDENT
　Linda H. Thomson

3M Company/Leisure Time Products

3M Center, Building 223-3S-03, St. Paul, MN 55144; (612) 733-2665. (Sportsman's video collection.)
PROJECT MANAGER
　Howard West
SALES SUPERVISOR
　Tom Diehl
SENIOR MARKETING COORDINATOR
　Carol Bystrzycki

Thriller Video

500 N. Ventu Park Rd., Newbury Park, CA 91320; (805) 499-5827; (800) 423-7455. (Subsidiary of International Video Entertainment.)
SENIOR VICE PRESIDENT & GENERAL MANAGER
　Ralph King
DIRECTOR OF SALES
　Jeanie Mason

Today Home Entertainment

6464 Sunset Blvd., Suite 1100, Hollywood, CA 90028; (213) 461-0467; (800) 521-0107.
CHAIRMAN
　Emanuel L. Wolfe
PRESIDENT
　Adriana Shaw
DIRECTOR, SALES & MARKETING, VIDEO DIVISION
　Michael Craft
DIRECTOR OF DEVELOPMENT
　Dhani Lipsus

Touchstone Home Video

500 S. Buena Vista St., Burbank, CA 91521; (818) 840-6056. Subsidiary of Walt Disney.
DIRECTOR, NATIONAL SALES
　Dick Longwell

Tournament Video Tapes

1615 W. Burbank Blvd., Burbank, CA 91506; (213) 843-0373. Division of Richard J. Soltys Productions. (Sports business videos.)
PRESIDENT
Richard J. Soltys

Tower Productions, Inc.

175 Fifth Ave., Suite 1101, New York, NY 10010; (212) 941-0702. Organized 1983. (Produces programming for broadcast, cable, corporate and home video.)
PRESIDENT
Donald A. Roosa

Trans World Entertainment (USA)

6464 Sunset Blvd., Suite 1100, Hollywood, CA 91601; (213) 461-0467. Organized 1983. (Production of feature films, sales of all media worldwide, domestic video distribution.)
CO-CHAIRMEN
Moshe Diamant
Eduard Sarlui
PRESIDENT
Yoram Pelman
AFFILIATION
TWE Group, Inc.

Tri-Coast Video, Inc.

134 Westgate Parkway, Dothan, AL 36303; (205) 677-1111.
PRESIDENT
C. A. Malugen

Troma, Inc.

733 Ninth Ave., 2nd floor, New York, NY 10019; (212) 757-4555. Organized 1974. (Produces and distributes high-concept, low budget films.)
PRESIDENT
Lloyd Kaufman
VICE PRESIDENT
Michael Herz
DIRECTOR OF THEATRICAL DISTRIBUTION
Carl Morano
DIRECTOR OF ANCILLARY SALES
Jeffrey W. Sass
DIRECTOR OF INTERNATIONAL SALES
Alexandra Platt
DIRECTOR OF BUSINESS AFFAIRS
David Greenspan
DIRECTOR OF MARKETING
Arthur P. Ajzenman
ANCILLARY SALES
Ron Goldberg

Trophy Video

2814 Hickory St., Yorktown Heights, NY 10598; (914) 245-1728. Organized 1985. (Hunting, fishing and adventure videos.)
OFFICERS
Don Todd
Virginia Todd

Two Star Films Inc.

Box 495, St. James, NY 11780; (516) 584-7283.

U.S.A. Homevideo

7920 Alabama Ave., Canoga Park, CA 91304-4991; (818) 888-3040, (800) 423-7455. (Subsidiary of International Video Entertainment.)

SENIOR VICE PRESIDENT & GENERAL MANAGER
Len Levy
NATIONAL SALES MANAGER
David Solomon

Understanding Personal Computers

P.O. Box 5849, Stanford, CA 94305; (415) 494-3737. (How-to videos.)
PRESIDENT
Colin Mick

Unicorn Video Inc.

20822 Dearborn St., Chatsworth, CA 91311; (818) 407-1333. Organized 1981. (Manufactures pre-recorded cassettes.)
PRESIDENT
Joanne Goldstein
VICE PRESIDENT
Edward Goldstein
SECRETARY & TREASURER
Anita Goldstein

United Artists

(see MGM/UA Entertainment Group)

United Entertainment, Inc.

4111 S. Darlington St., Suite 600, Tulsa, OK 74135; (918) 622-6460. Organized 1983. (Distributes pre-recorded video.)
CHAIRMAN OF THE BOARD
Bill Blair
PRESIDENT
Robert Blair
BRANCH
3575 Cahuenga Blvd. W., Culver City, CA 90068

United Home Video

4111 S. Darlington, Suite 600, Tulsa, OK 74135; (918) 622-6460; (800) 331-4077. (How-to, general entertainment, religious, and science-fiction videos.)
PRESIDENT
Robert A. Blair

Universal

(see MCA Home Video)

Universal Home Video

919 N. Broad St., Philadelphia, PA 19123; (215) 232-1100. (Subsidiary of Universal Record Distributing Corp.)
PRESIDENT
Harold B. Lipsius
MARKETING & SALES
Tony Putnick
Lou Reeve

Upswing Artists Management, Ltd.

%Jacobson and Colfin, 150 Fifth Ave., Room 1103, New York, NY 10011; (213) 691-5630. Organized 1979. (Produces music video.)
PRESIDENT
Martin Steckler
VICE PRESIDENT
Bruce Colfin
BOARD OF DIRECTORS
Martin Steckler, Bruce E. Colfin
AFFILIATION
Performance Video

VC II Home Video

13402 Wyandotte Ave., North Hollywood, CA 91605; (800) 221-4274. Organized 1978. (Acquires program licensing for video distribution. Produces, manufactures and distributes [worldwide] theatrical, cable and video.)
CHIEF OPERATING OFFICER
  Rudy Sutton
MARKETING DIRECTOR
  Dave Stevens
ACQUISTIONS
  Mike Fredrychs

V.I.E.W. Video Inc. (Video International Entertainment World)

34 E. 23 St., New York, NY 10010; (212) 674-5550. (Production, packaging, syndication, distribution, home video for programs in art, dance, jazz, opera, classical music, children's interactive, modern lifestyle.)
PRESIDENT
  Bob Karcy
VICE PRESIDENT
  Jack Arel
OPERATIONS
  Maria Buerkli
SALES
  Gerard Speno
BRANCH
  28/30 Rue Mederic, 75017 Paris, France; (14) 267-1516

VIP Video

143 Hickory Hill Circle, Osterville, MA 02655; (617) 428-7198. Subsidiary of JEF Films.
PRESIDENT
  Jeffrey H. Aikman
MARKETING & SALES
  Elsie Aikman

VTR Distributors, Inc.

105 Broadway Ave., Carnegie, PA 15106; (412) 279-9100, (800) 245-1172.
PRESIDENT
  Paul Pasquarelli
CHAIRMAN
  Zack Pilossoph

Van Dam Productions

15 Van Dam St., New York, NY 10013; (212) 807-1877. Subsidiary of Teleculture, Inc.
PRESIDENT
  Jordan Bock

Vanguard Video

4111 S. Darlington, Suite 600, Tulsa, OK 74135; (918) 622-6460; (800) 331-4077. Subsidiary of United Entertainment.
PRESIDENT
  Bill Blair

Vencompass, Inc.

824 Peach St., 3rd floor, Erie, PA 16501; (814) 453-7704. Organized 1983. (Produces educational corporate videos.)
PRESIDENT/CHAIRMAN OF THE BOARD
  Pamela J. Venable
SECRETARY
  Atty. John Leemhuis
TREASURER
  John Petersen
BOARD OF DIRECTORS
  Thomas L. Venable

Vestron Video

1010 Washington Blvd., P.O. Box 10382, Stamford, CT 06901; (203) 978-5400; 2029 Century Park East, Suite 200, Los Angeles, CA 90067; (213) 551-1723.
PRESIDENT & CHAIRMAN, VESTRON, INC.
  Austin O. Furst
PRESIDENT, VESTRON VIDEO
  Jon Peisinger
EXECUTIVE VICE PRESIDENT, VESTRON, INC.
  Strauss Zelnick
SENIOR VICE PRESIDENT, MARKETING, SALES AND DISTRIBUTION
  Al Reuben
SENIOR VICE PRESIDENT, INTERNATIONAL
  Rob Straight
VICE PRESIDENT, SALES
  Michael Karaffa
VICE PRESIDENT, ACQUISITION
  Anne Heekin-Canedy
DIRECTOR OF SPECIAL MARKETS
  Dan Markim
DIRECTOR, NON-THEATRICAL PROGRAMMING
  Jeffrey Peisch
NATIONAL MARKETING MANAGER
  William Perrault
VICE PRESIDENT/GENERAL MANAGER-VESTRON VIDEO ESPAÑOL
  Edwin Friendly

VidAmerica

(Subsidiary of Video Corp. of America)
231 E. 55 St., New York, NY 10022; (212) 355-1600.

Vid-Dimension, Inc.

4221 W. Sierra Madre, #109, Fresno, CA 93722; (209) 276-6000. Organized 1985. (Manufactures and distributes prerecorded educational, religious and entertainment videos in Spanish—subtitled, dubbed.)
PRESIDENT
  Abe G. Osuna
SECRETARY
  Leo Lobato Kelly
BOARD OF DIRECTORS
  Abe G. Osuna, Leo Lobato Kelly

Video Action

237 Ogden Ave., Jersey City, NJ 07307; (201) 792-3833. (Health videos.)
OWNER
  Bob Brennan

Video Action

708 W. First St., Los Angeles, CA 90012; (213) 687-8262. Organized 1981. (Video production and distribution.)
OWNER (PARTNER)
  Leslie T. Hamasaki
OWNER (PARTNER)
  Ruth Watanabe
OPERATIONS MANAGER
  Gregg S. Yokoyama

Video Aided Instruction, Inc.

182 Village Rd., East Hills, NY 11577; (516) 621-6176. Organized 1983. (Produces instructional, educational videocassettes.)
PRESIDENT
  Peter Lanzer
VICE PRESIDENT
  Mona Lanzer
BOARD OF DIRECTORS
  Peter Lanzer, Mona Lanzer

Video Album Ltd.

P.O. Box 24683, 4936 Maple Rd., Edina, MN 55424; (612) 925-9804; FAX: (612) 929-9581. Organized 1975. (Produces educational videos including How to Play the Piano videos.)
OFFICERS
  Yakov Gelfand
  Thelma Hunter
BOARD OF DIRECTORS
  Ruth K. Noack, Charlene Witherell, Maren Mahowald M.D.

Video Artists International, Inc.

2112 Broadway, Room 401, (P.O. Box 153, Ansonia Sta., 10023) New York, NY 10023; (212) 799-7798. Organized 1983. (Manufactures home videocassettes.) Distributed exclusively in the U.S. and Canada by RCA/Ariola International.
PRESIDENT
  Ernest J. Gilbert
VICE PRESIDENT, ACQUISITIONS
  Glenn A. Smith
VICE PRESIDENT, NATIONAL SALES & MARKETING
  Duncan Hutchinson
DIRECTOR CONSUMER MARKETING
  Marc E. Jacoby
PRODUCT MANAGER
  Natasha J. Hinkson

Video Cassette Marketing Corp.

137 Eucalyptus, El Segundo, CA 90245; (213) 322-1140.
PRESIDENT
  James Spencer

Video City Productions

4266 Broadway, Oakland, CA 94611; (415) 428-0202. Organized 1983. (Manufactures and distributes pre-recorded VHS and Beta film product.)
MARKETING DIRECTOR
  Bob Brown
OTHER COMPANY OWNED LABELS:
  Combat Video, Art House Video, Chop 'Em Ups Video, World Aviation Video, Black Action Video.

Video Connection

3123 Sylvania Ave., Toledo, OH 43613; (419) 472-7727.
PRESIDENT
  John Day

Video Dimensions

530 W. 23 St., New York, NY 10011; (212) 929-6135.

Video Dynamics

Box 9550, Jackson, MS 39206; (601) 957-2722, (800) 647-2284. (Children's, educational, religious, and special interest.)
PRESIDENT
  Pat Robinson
MARKETING & SALES
  Steve Robinson

Video Gems

P.O. Box 38188, Los Angeles, CA 90038; (213) 398-3332. Organized 1979. (Manufacturer and distributor of pre-recorded videocassettes.)
PRESIDENT
  Mary L. Greiner

Video International Publishers, Inc.

118 6th St. S., Great Falls, MT 59405; (406) 727-7133. Organized 1980. (Production and distribution of corporate communication, educational and how-to video programming.)
PRESIDENT
  James M. Colla
VICE PRESIDENT
  Penny L. Adkins
SECRETARY/TREASURER
  Penny L. Adkins

Video Knowledge Inc.

29 Bramble Lane, Melville, NY 11747; (516) 367-4250.
PRESIDENT
  Sally Dubrowsky
VICE PRESIDENT
  Ed Dubrowsky
BOARD OF DIRECTOR
  Geoffrey S. Dubrowsky

Video Latino

409 N. Figueroa, Wilmington, CA 90744; (213) 549-4490. (Spanish language general interest videos.)
PRESIDENT
  Russell C. Greene

Video Library of Arts

716 S. Main, Broken Arrow, OK 74012; (918) 251-0466. Division of Ken Meyer Productions.
PRESIDENT
  Ken Meyer

Video Marketing and Distributing Inc.

4301 Hwy. 7, St. Louis Park, MN 55416; (612) 920-8400.
PRESIDENT
  Mark Saliterman

The Video Naturals Company

2590 Glen Green, Suite #6, Los Angeles, CA 90068; (213) 469-0019. Organized 1982. (Produces and distributes "mood videos" such as "Video Fireplace" and "Ocean Waves" for the home video market.)
PRESIDENT/OWNER
  Steve Siporin
AFFILIATIONS
  Distributors: Videotakes (1-800-526-7002)

Video One Video Inc.

1600 124 Ave. N.E. Suite E., Bellevue, WA 98005; (206) 454-5992.
VICE PRESIDENT, SALES
  Jim Koch

Video Paradise, Inc.

115 W. Main St., Westboro, MA 01581; (617) 366-8890.
PRESIDENT
  Donald Rogers

Video Presentations, Inc.

2326 Sixth Ave., Suite 230, Seattle, WA 98121; (206) 728-9241. Organized 1979. (Video off-line editing, production and duplication services in prof. BETACAM, ¾" U-matic and S-VHS.)

PRESIDENT
 H. V. Wright
VICE PRESIDENT
 Nancy L. Wright

Video Products

2428 Glendale Lane, Sacramento, CA 95825; (916) 971-9111 or 971-1809.
PRESIDENT
 Tim Shannahan
BRANCHES
 2350 E. Artesia, Long Beach, CA 90805
 4551 Brickell Privado, Ontario, CA 91761

Video Properties, Inc.

33 E. 68 St., New York, NY 10021; (212) 570-1200.
PRESIDENT
 John A. Friede

Video RX

7115 N. Austin, Niles, IL 60648; (312) 647-8400. (Video distributor.)
OWNERS
 Marvin Steinberg
 Burt Steinberg
OPERATIONS MANAGER
 Marc Barnett

Video Reel, Inc.

28231 N. Ave. Crocker, Suite 120, Valencia, CA 91355; (805) 257-1035. Organized 1983. (Produces and duplicates how-to sports videos.)
PRESIDENT
 Robert Mann
VICE PRESIDENT
 Robert Mann
TREASURER
 Robert Mann
SECRETARY
 Robert Mann
BOARD OF DIRECTORS
 Robert S. Mann, Bonnie L. Krolop
AFFILIATIONS
 Recording Association of America, International Tape and Disc Assn.

Video Releasing Co. of Hawaii

1313 Kalakaua Ave., Honolulu, HI 96826; (808) 946-1000. Organized 1975. (Wholesale distribution of video-cassette programs.)
DIRECTOR OF SALES
 Judy Bottalico

Video Research

18 Ellery St., Cambridge, MA 02138; (617) 576-0864. Organized 1983. (Home video product development.)
PRESIDENT
 David Burke
EXECUTIVE VICE PRESIDENT
 Fred Surr
VICE PRESIDENT, FINANCE
 Jane Lytle-Manns
VICE PRESIDENT, MARKETING
 Bitsy McKay
BOARD OF DIRECTORS
 David Burke, Fred Surr, Lila Hexner, Barry Unger, Judy Obermayer

Video Resources New York Inc.

220 W. 71 St., #91, New York, NY 10023; (213) 724-7055. Organized 1980. (Video and film production;

stock footage, film restoration, film and TV library of history books, home video distributor of nostalgia films and early TV shows. Large collection of commercials from the 1940s through early 1970s. Also ½" and ¾" editing and dubbing.)
PRESIDENT, DIRECTOR, EDITOR, HISTORIAN, EXEC. PRODUCER
 Ira H. Gallen
CO-PRODUCER, WRITER
 John A. Gallagher
VIDEO TECHNICAL ADVISOR
 Vic Tannenberg
CAMERA (D.P.)
 Bill Coleman, Marc Hirschfeld

Video-Sig

1030 East Duane Ave., Suite C, Sunnyvale, CA 94086; (408) 730-9291. Organized 1987. (Video publishers of primarily independent productions.)
FOUNDER
 Richard Petersen
PROJECT COORDINATOR AND DIRECTOR OF SALES
 Julie Hutton
ACQUISITIONS COORDINATOR
 Anne Olson
EDITOR/PUBLICIST
 Dan Steele
PRODUCER AND VIDEOGRAPHER
 Bruce Kent
ADMINISTRATIVE ASST.
 Susan Powers

Video Sports Productions

1704 Sweeney, Las Vegas, NV 89104; (702) 384-7514. (Golf and other sports videos.)
PRESIDENT
 C. A. Montana

Video Tech

19346 Third N.W., Seattle, WA 98177; (206) 546-5401.
PRESIDENT
 Eugene Ekblad

Video Ticket

11811 W. Olympic Blvd., Los Angeles, CA 90064; (213) 478-8499.
PRESIDENT
 Peter Bieler

Video Travel, Inc.

153 W. Fourth St., Williamsport, PA 17701; (717) 326-6525. (Sports, how-to and travel videos.)
PRESIDENT
 Larry Seaman

Video Trend, Inc.

12900 Richfield Court, Livonia, MI 48150; (313) 591-0200. Organized 1979. (Distributor of pre-recorded video.)
PRESIDENT
 Glenn A. Greene
VICE PRESIDENTS
 Robert Tollini (Detroit)
 Robert Fortunel (Detroit)
 John Gallagher (Tampa)
 Jim Weiss (Seattle)
BRANCHES
 Detroit, Chicago, Tampa, Seattle, Salt Lake City, Sacramento, San Francisco

Video Update Inc.

1636 Gervais, St. Paul, MN 55109; (612) 770-3779.
PRESIDENT
John Bedard
MARKETING & SALES
Bruce Carlson

Video Visa Inc.

11845 W. Olympic Blvd., Suite 900, Los Angeles, CA 90064; (213) 478-6868. Subsidiary of UNIVISA.

Video Yesteryear

Box C, Sandy Hook, CT 06482. Organized 1978.
PRESIDENT
Jon Sonneborn

Videoactive Company (a Delaware Corp.)

29169 W. Heathercliff, #216, Malibu, CA 90265; (213) 457-1144. Organized 1982. (Producer and distributor of film and video tape programs: How-to, entertainment, advertising and promotional, and public relations. Also motion picture, full feature scripts and budget prep service.)
PRESIDENT
Bill Myers
VICE PRESIDENT, TECHNICAL
Bill Darst
VICE PRESIDENT, OPERATIONS
Linda Shockley
VICE PRESIDENT, TAPE DUPLICATION
Rock Walton
VICE PRESIDENT, PRODUCTION
Josh Golden
BOARD OF DIRECTORS
Bill Myers (chairman)
BRANCHES
Florida, London, Switzerland

Videobrary

3518 Cahuenga Blvd. W., Suite 301, Hollywood, CA 90068; (213) 851-5811.
PRESIDENT
Tom Corradine
MARKETING & SALES
Paul Lisy

Videocassette Marketing Corporation

137 Eucalyptus Dr., El Segundo, CA 90245; (213) 322-1140, (800) 332-1140. Organized 1984. (Distributes children's, how-to, non-theatrical, environmental and subliminal pre-recorded videocassettes to video stores and consumers.)
GENERAL MANAGER
Cindy E. Greisdorf

Videocom

502 Sprague St., Dedham, MA 02026; (617) 329-4080; FAX: (617) 329-8534; TELEX: 4430135 VIDEOCOM. Organized 1967. (Commercial and industrial production, satellite uplink and distribution, multi-format duplication, videoconferencing, post production.)
PRESIDENT
Dan Swartz
GENERAL MANAGER
Frank Cavallo
VICE PRESIDENT/DUPLICATION MANAGER
Harvey Hecker

EXECUTIVE PRODUCER/DIRECTOR
Andy Abrams
OPERATIONS MANAGER/SATELLITE
Bob Hanson
CONTROLLER
Paul Colao
CHIEF EDITOR
Chris Gambon
CHIEF ENGINEER
Johnny Parker
TRAFFIC
Ken Fischer

Videocraft Classics

1790 Broadway, New York, NY 10019; (212) 246-9849. (Produces and distributes educational videos.)
PRESIDENT
Lee Kraft
VICE PRESIDENT
Marc Weinstein

Videodisc Publishing Inc.

381 Park Ave. S., #1601, New York, NY 10016; (212) 685-5522.
PRESIDENT
Gene Fairly

Videofashion

1 W. 37 St., 5th floor, New York, NY 10018; (212) 869-4666. Telex: 225707. Vidmo UR. FAX: 869-8208. Organized 1976. (World's first "videomagazine." Internationally focused, magazine-format, fashion and lifestyle programs, available for worldwide distribution on videocassette, cable and broadcast. 40 ½-hour programs are produced each year in 4 program lines: Videofashion Monthly (12/year); Videofashion News (12/year) Videofashion Men (4/year); Videofashion Specials (21 available).
CHAIRMAN & PRESIDENT
Nicholas H. Charney
INTERNATIONAL MARKETING
Marlene B. McGinnis
MANAGING EDITOR
Anne V. Adami

Videograph

2833 25th St., San Francisco, CA 94110; (415) 282-6001. (English and Spanish health and educational videos.)
PRESIDENT
Jim Locker

Videolearning Systems, Inc.

354 W. Lancaster Ave., Haverford, PA 19041; (215) 896-6600.
PRESIDENT
Homer H. Hewitt, III

Videoplan, Inc.

1448 W. Rosecrans Ave., Gardena, CA 90249; (213) 532-9024.
PRESIDENT
Peter Jacobs

Videosmith Inc.

2006 Chancellor St., Philadelphia, PA 19103; (215) 665-3690. Organized 1974. (Video/film production and post production, computer animation.)

PRESIDENT
Steve Smith
VICE PRESIDENT
Steve O'Driscoll
TREASURER/SECRETARY
Martha Smith
BRANCHES
3 Independence Way, Princeton, NJ 08540

Videotakes, Inc.

187 Route 71, Manasquin, NJ 08736; (201) 528-5000; (800) 526-7002. Organized 1982. (Marketing of non-feature film videocassettes.)
PRESIDENT
Joe Kennedy, 509 Fisk Ave., Brielle, NJ 08730
SECRETARY
Jenny Peters, 26 W. 83 St., New York, NY 10024

Vidmark, Inc.

2901 Ocean Park Blvd., Suite 213, Santa Monica, CA 90405-2906; (213) 399-8877, (800) 424-7070, (CA); (800) 351-7070.
PRESIDENT
Mark Amin
SENIOR VICE PRESIDENT
Barry Barnholtz
VICE PRESIDENT, MARKETING AND SALES
Sam Pirnazar

Virgin Vision, Inc.

2980 Beverly Glen Circle, Suite 302, Los Angeles, CA; (213) 474-4225.
PRESIDENT
Steven Bickel
VICE PRESIDENT, FINANCE AND ADMINISTRATION
Bern Galvin
VICE PRESIDENT, MARKETING AND PROGRAMS
David R. Bixler

Vision Media

625 Broadway, #902, New York, NY 10012; (212) 529-6880. Organized 1984. (Consulting, production and development services, specializing in original programming for home video.)
PRESIDENT/EXECUTIVE PRODUCER
Paul Tandlies

Vision Productions, Ltd.

311 E. 6th St., #2, Moscow, ID 83843; (208) 883-0105. Organized 1979. (Video production and marketing.)
PRESIDENT
John A. L. Francis
VICE PRESIDENT
E. A. Francis

Vista Home Video

1350 Ave. of the Americas, New York, NY 10019; (212) 582-0500; (800) 443-0519.
PRESIDENT
Nick Santrizos

Vistar International Productions

3790 Dunn Dr., Suite C, Los Angeles, CA 90043; (213) 204-3392.

WEA, Corp. (Warner/Elektra/Atlantic Corp.)

111 N. Hollywood Way, Burbank, CA 91505; (818) 843-6311. (Subsidiary of Warner Communications, Inc.)

PRESIDENT
Henry Droz
MARKETING & SALES
George Rossi

WRI Education

World Research Incorporated, Campus Studies Institute, 968 Emerald St., Suite 6700, P.O. Box 9359, San Diego, CA 92109; (619) 456-5278.
PRESIDENT
Daniel T. Loeffler

Walt Disney Home Video

500 S. Buena Vista St., Burbank, CA 91521; (818) 840-1859.
VICE PRESIDENT, RETAIL PROD.
Ben Tenn
MARKETING
Richard Fried

Walt Disney Educational Media Co.

500 S. Buena Vista St., Burbank, CA 91521; (818) 840-1000. (Division of Walt Disney Productions.)
MARKETING COORDINATOR
Linda Capuano

Ken Walz Productions Inc.

219 E. 60 St., 4th floor, New York, NY 10022; (212) 826-6010. Organized 1972. (Produces television programs, music videos, home videos, commercials, corporate films and motion pictures.)
PRESIDENT
Ken Walz

Warner Home Video Inc.

4000 Warner Blvd., Burbank, CA 91522; (818) 954-6000. Organized 1979. (Brings the motion picture and entertainment-media productions of Warner Bros. Inc. to the prerecorded home video marketplace.) A subsidiary of Warner Bros. Inc., a Warner Communications company.
PRESIDENT
Warren N. Lieberfarb
SENIOR VICE PRESIDENT/GENERAL MANAGER, INTERNATIONAL
Edward J. Byrnes
SENIOR VICE PRESIDENT, NORTH AMERICA
James F. Cardwell
VICE PRESIDENT/MARKETING & DEVELOPMENT
Barbara O'Sullivan
VICE PRESIDENT/SALES
John Quinn
DIRECTOR OF ACQUISITIONS & DEVELOPMENT
Elyse Eisenberg
SALES & PROMOTION MANAGER
Michael Finnegan
DIRECTOR OF PRODUCTION
Lewis Ostrover

Wax Works/Video Works National Distributor

325 E. 3rd St., Owensboro, KY 42301;, (800) 626-1918. Organized 1979. (Video distributor of all national major lines. Also audio distributor.)
PRESIDENT
Terry Woodward
SALES MANAGER
Kirk Kirkpatrick
CREDIT MANAGER
Bill Burton

446

BUYER
    Noel Clayton
BRANCH
    4011 Winchester Rd., Memphis, TN 38118; (800) 331-0993, (901) 366-4088

Weiss Global Enterprises

2055 Saviers Rd., Suite 12, Oxnard, CA 93033-3693; (805) 486-4495. Cable: Weisspict. Organized 1974. (Distributes television and motion picture programming.)
PRESIDENT
    Adrian Weiss
SECRETARY & TREASURER
    Steven A. Weiss
VICE PRESIDENTS
    Ethel L. Weiss
    Laurie Weiss
OPERATIONS MANAGER
    Beverly S. Verman
INFORMATION SERVICES
    Alex Gordon
REPRESENTATIVES
    Exclusive Rep.-15 Western States: Donal Joannes & Assocs., Inc., Donal Joannes; 11340 W. Olympic Blvd., Suite 375, Los Angeles, CA 90064; (213) 478-2561.
    Midwest: E. Melvin Pinsel, 505 N. Lake Shore Drive, Chicago, IL 60611, (312) 645-1144
    Southeast/Southwest: Hank Profenius, 3207 W. Friendly Ave., Greensboro, NC 27408; (919) 292-1434
    Account Executive-"Make Room For Daddy": Gray-Schwartz Enterprises, Inc., Marv Gray, P.O. Box 9239, Calabasas, CA 91302; (818) 702-9888
    Home Video: Carlton Entertainment Corp., Richard S. Ellman, 5521 Grosvenor Blvd., Marina Del Rey, CA 90066; (213) 558-4668
    Foreign: Turner International, Howard Karshan, 25 Old Burlington St., London W1X 1LB, (01) 434-4341

West Glen Communications

1430 Broadway, New York, NY 10018; (212) 921-2800.
EXECUTIVE VICE PRESIDENT
    Vincent Capuzzi
V.P. TELEVISION DISTRIBUTION
    Annette Minkalis
V.P. THEATRICAL DISTRIBUTION
    Sy Perry

West Star Productions

699 E. South Temple, #300, Orem, UT 84057; (801) 532-3909. Organized 1985. (Produces and distributes film and video productions.)
PRESIDENT
    R. Conrad Teichert
CHAIRMAN OF THE BOARD
    Jack Dunlop
BOARD OF DIRECTORS
    R. Conrad Teichart
AFFILIATIONS
    Kappa Tau Alpha, AFI, SMPTE

Westcom Productions Inc.

1925 Bailey Hill Rd., Eugene, OR 97405; (503) 683-2236. Organized 1984. (Complete video production, post production, duplication and marketing services.)
PRESIDENT
    Bruce O'Neil
VICE PRESIDENT, OPERATION
    John Wray
VICE PRESIDENT, MARKETING
    Mark Lange
BUSINESS DEVELOPMENT
    Jack Loe

Western Film & Video, Inc.

30941 W. Agoura Rd., Building 302/304, Westlake Village, CA 91361; (818) 889-7350. FAX: (818) 707-3937.

Organized 1974. (Motion picture laboratory and complete video-tape facility. Productions, duplication, editing, film to tape transfers and standards conversions.)
PRESIDENT & CHIEF EXECUTIVE OFFICER
    Gary R. Guenot
LAB MANAGER
    Glenn White
SECRETARY & TREASURER
    Jim Guenot
BRANCH
    Video Magic (mail-order software)
AFFILIATION
    Part of the Westlake Media Center

Western Publishing Company, Inc.

1220 Mound Ave., Racine, WI 53404; (414) 633-2431. Subsidiary of Western Publishing Group, Inc. (How-to, children's, educational.)
PRESIDENT
    Joseph Marino
VICE PRESIDENT, SALES
    James O'Donnell
NATIONAL SALES MANAGER-VIDEO DISTRIBUTION
    Robert Komisar

Westlamb Associates

2781 Las Ramblas, Suite 200, Mission Viejo, CA 92691; (714) 643-9031.
PRESIDENT
    James Polakof

Weston Woods Studios, Inc.

389 Newtown Turnpike, Weston, CT 06883; (203) 226-3355. Organized 1956. (Producers and distributors of film and video adaptations of children's picture books.)
PRESIDENT
    Morton Schindel
VICE PRESIDENT
    Paul J. Schindel
DIRECTOR OF MARKETING
    Jerri Shales
SECRETARY
    Elisabeth Rommel
TREASURER
    Paula J. Gaus
MARKETING COMMUNICATIONS
    Lynn F. Joffe
BOARD OF DIRECTORS
    Morton Schindel, Paula J. Gaus, Elisabeth Rommel, Cathy S. Knowles, and Paul Schindel

White Janssen, Inc.

604 Davis St., Evanston, IL 60201; (312) 328-2221. Organized 1983. (Home video development company.)
OWNERS
    Stefaan Janssen
    Matthew White
AFFILIATIONS
    Member: VSDA; Center for New Television; AIFV

Wild Wing Productions

7240 Valjean Ave., Van Nuys, CA 91406; (818) 994-4955. Organized 1984. (Creates and produces documentary films and original home video programming in how-to, general entertainment, children's, and educational categories. Acquires special interest programming for home video distribution and TV syndication.)
PRESIDENT & CHIEF EXECUTIVE OFFICER
    Drew Michaels
VICE PRESIDENT, MARKETING & PROMOTION
    Andrew Rapaport
VICE PRESIDENT, ADMINISTRATIVE OPERATIONS
    Kathryn Grossman

Wilderness Video

P.O. Box 2175, Redondo Beach, CA 90278; (213) 973-7544. Organized 1982. (Produces wilderness videos of national parks—Glacier, Yosemite, Yellowstone, Grand Canyon, Bryce/Zion, Big Sur.)
OWNER
R. W. Glusic

Wade Williams Productions

5500 Ward Parkway, Kansas City, MO 64113; (816) 523-2699. Organized 1980. (Production and distribution of science fiction motion pictures and home videos.)
PRESIDENT
Wade Williams
VICE PRESIDENT
Brian Mossman
SECRETARY
Ben Mossman

Win Records and Video, Inc.

76-05 51st Avenue, Elmhurst, NY 11373; (800) 221-1220, (800) 851-2525 (NY state). Organized 1955. (Wholesale distribution of home entertainment products: video software [full line]; records: tapes; CD's; and specially selected accessories.)
PRESIDENT
Sam Weiss
VICE PRESIDENT
George Weiss

Windward Video

P.O. Box 613, Paia, Maui, HI 96779; (808) 579-9313. (Film and video production—educational, corporate, and documentary.)
PRESIDENT
Jerry Rochford

Wishing Well Distributing Co.

P.O. Box 529, Graton, CA 95444; (707) 823-9355. Organized 1978. (Markets and sells over 2000 videos—educational, documentary, entertainment.)
PRESIDENT
Debra Giusti
GENERAL MANAGER
Denise Cordos
SALES MANAGER
Sue Lancaster

Wizard Video Inc.

1551 N. La Brea Ave., Los Angeles, CA 90028; (213) 850-6563.

Wombat Productions

(Division of CorTech Communications, Inc.)
250 W. 57 St., Suite 916, New York, NY 10019; (212) 315-2502. Organized 1970. (Produces television specials and entertainment documentaries.)
PRESIDENT
Gene Feldman

EXECUTIVE VICE PRESIDENT
Suzette Winter
VICE PRESIDENT, MARKETING
Stephen Janson

Women Make Movies, Inc.

225 Lafayette St., Room 212, New York, NY 10012; (212) 925-0606. Organized 1972. (Facilitates the production, exhibition and distribution of media by and about women.)
PRESIDENT
Linda Gibson
VICE PRESIDENT
Elizabeth Merena
TREASURER
Joanne Sandler
SECRETARY
Wendy Lidell
BOARD OF DIRECTORS
Janet Benn, Linda Gibson, Karen Jaehne, Wendy Lidell, Bienvenida Matias, Berenice Reynaud, Tani Takagi, Joanne Sandler, Linda Young, Ariel Doughtery
AFFILIATIONS
Association of Independent Video and Filmmakers
The Women's Funding Coalition

Wonderland Video

3529 S. Valley View Blvd., Las Vegas, NV 89103; (702) 362-2520; (800) 634-6143. (Children's videos.) Subsidiary of King of Video.
PRESIDENT
Steve Vincent
VICE PRESIDENT/SECRETARY-TREASURER
Nancy E. Kelly
VICE PRESIDENT—SALES
John J. Lago

Woodenboat Publications, Inc.

Naskeag Rd., Brooklin, ME 04616; (207) 359-4651. (Wooden boat construction and repair; sailors' knots and splices.)
PRESIDENT
Jonathan Wilson

World Video Pictures

12401 Wilshire Blvd., Suite 102, Los Angeles, CA 90025; (213) 820-6100. (Formerly Program Hunters.)
PRESIDENT
George Atkinson

World Vision Home Video, Inc.

660 Madison Ave., 3rd floor, New York, NY 10021; (212) 832-3838. Organized 1980. (Domestic home video distribution, marketing and sales.)
VICE PRESIDENT & GENERAL MANAGER
Tom Devlin
EASTERN DIVISION MANAGER
Carl Sansarica
MIDWEST DIVISION MANAGER
Brian O'Sullivan
WESTERN DIVISION MANAGER
Kathy Rost
SOUTHERN DIVISION MANAGER
Bruce Knox
MANAGER, SALES ADMINISTRATION
Shari Nowak
BRANCHES
Midwest, 625 N. Michigan Ave., Suite 410, Chicago, IL 60611
Southern, 14 Perimeter Center E., Suite 1406, Atlanta, GA 30346
Western, 9465 Wilshire Blvd., Suite 628, Beverly Hills, CA 90212
AFFILIATION
Worldvision Enterprises

448

Worldwide Tape Distributors

223 Keats Dr., Sicklerville, NJ 08081; (609) 228-0205.
PRESIDENT
Ted Klempner

Xenon Home Video

712 Wilshire Blvd., #25, Santa Monica, CA 90401; (213) 451-5510. Organized 1986. (Manufacturer of Black action and general video programming.)
PRESIDENT
S. Leigh Savidge
VICE PRESIDENT
Arnie Lakeyn
AFFILIATION
VSDA

Xerox Information Resources Group

P.O. Box 1600; Stamford, CT 06904-1288; (203) 625-5634. (Subsidiary of Xerox Corp.)
PRESIDENT
William J. Senter

ZBS Industries

701 Beta Dr., Cleveland, OH 44143; (800) 321-8774. Organized 1979. (Distributes pre-recorded video.)
PRESIDENT
Larry Beyer
VICE PRESIDENT
Earl Stein
SECRETARY/TREASURER
Jay Schultz
BOARD OF DIRECTORS
Larry Beyer, Earl Stein, Jay Schultz

Major Video Retailers

Aardvark Video

811 W. 11th St., Coffeyville, KS 67337; (316) 251-6165.
OWNER
Tim Kilpatrick

Academy Video

18122 Brookhurst St., #B, Fountain Valley, CA 92708;
(714) 964-1691. (Video independent.)
OWNER
Don Rubin

Acorn Sports, Inc.

5816 Shakespeare Rd., Suite D, Columbia, SC 29204;
(803) 735-0733. (Golf videos.)
PRESIDENT
D. Swing Meyer

Alice In Videoland Ltd.

738 Ulster Ave., P.O. Box 2000-H, Kingston, NY 12401;
(914) 338-5288. Organized 1983. (Video sales/rentals—
televisions, stereo. Related products' sales.)
PRESIDENT
Paula DeCesare
BRANCHES
Kingston, NY (2 locations); Saugerties, NY; Phoenicia, NY;
Great Barrington, MA

All American Video-Los Osos

950 Los Osos Valley Rd., Los Osos, CA 93402; (805)
528-2820. (Franchise.)
PRESIDENT
Keith Lilley

All-In-One-Video

2806 N. Highway 441-27, Fruitland, FL 32731; (904)
326-3633. (Video chain.)
PRESIDENT
Sharen Gonzalez

Alternative Video

604 Davis St., Evanston, IL 60201; (312) 328-2221.
Organized 1983. (Direct marketing of special interest
home video programs.)
OWNER
Division of White Janssen, Inc.
AFFILIATIONS
Member: VSDA; Center for New Television; AIFV

American Box Office Video Inc.

40 E. Main St., Hopkinton, MA 01748; (617) 435-5174,
(617) 435-4270. Organized 1984. (4 video stores, video
rack jobbers.)
PRESIDENT
Rachel Dworkin
BUYER
Steve Dworkin
CLERK
Mellissa Dworkin
BRANCHES
Milford, MA; Westboro, MA; Clinton, MA; Hudson, MA.
AFFILIATES
Somerville, Fitchburg, Framingham

American Video Tape

1116 Edgewater Ave., Ridgefield, NJ 07657; (201) 941-
4404, (800) 645-7186. (Subsidiary of American Tape.)
Video, independent.

VICE PRESIDENT, MARKETING & SALES
Marc Gottlieb

Arizona Peddler

790 S. Main, Cottonwood, AZ 86326; (602) 634-5565.
Independent video chain (3).
PRESIDENT
Jack Poland

At the Movies

1312 Round Rock Ave., Round Rock, TX 78664; (512)
255-6021. Independent video.

Audio Visuals of Tampa, Inc.

4333 W. Kennedy Blvd., Box 10099, Tampa, FL 33609;
(813) 876-8718. Independent audio/visual.
PRESIDENT
Murray Segal

Barnes & Noble Inc.

122 Fifth Ave., New York, NY 10003; (212) 206-8800.
Bookstore—independent chain.
DIRECTOR OF MARKETING
Barry Denenberg
SOFTWARE BUYER
Susan Barkan

Bee Gee Records & Tapes, Inc.

10 Northway Lane N., Latham, NY 12110; (518) 785-
1122. Video chain (11).
PURCHASING
Mike Raikowski

Norman Beerger Productions

3127-A29, Arville St., Las Vegas, NV 89102-7612; (702)
876-2328. Organized 1984. (Produces and distributes wilderness home video programs.)
OWNER
Norman Beerger

Beverly Hills Videocentre, Inc.

145 S. Beverly Drive, Beverly Hills, CA 90212; (213)
550-1092. Organized 1980. (Sale and rental of pre-re-
corded videocassettes.)
PRESIDENT
Emil Reisman
SECRETARY
Jane Hamilton
BOARD OF DIRECTORS
Emil Reisman
BRANCH
West Hollywood, CA 90046

The Blackhawk Catalog

12626 Beatrice St., Los Angeles, CA 90066; (213)
306-4040.
VICE PRESIDENT
Philip J Kromnick
OPERATIONS COORDINATOR
Kimberly Baker

Les Blank's Flower Films and Video

10341 San Pablo Ave., El Cerrrio, CA 94530; (415)
525-0942. Organized 1967. (Seeks out and documents

America's vanishing minority cultures, their music and traditions.)
PRODUCER/DIRECTOR/CAMERA
Les Blank
DISTRIBUTION MANAGER
Susan Kell
FOLKLORIST/2nd CAMERA
Christine Simon
EDITOR
Maureen Gosling

Blockbuster Entertainment Corporation

901 E. Las Olas Blvd., Ft. Lauderdale, FL 33301; (305) 524-8200. Organized 1985. (Retail rental of prerecorded video cassettes.)
CHAIRMAN, C.E.O.
H. Wayne Huizenga
PRESIDENT, C.O.O.
Luigi Salvaneschi
SENIOR VICE PRESIDENT/CHIEF FINANCIAL OFFICER
Steven R. Berrard
VICE PRESIDENT/CHIEF MARKETING OFFICER
Thomas A. Gruber
SENIOR VICE PRESIDENT
Robert E. Castleberry
SENIOR VICE PRESIDENT
James F. Ellis
SENIOR VICE PRESIDENT
Barry L. Rosenblatt
VICE PRESIDENT
Charles H. Martin
VICE PRESIDENT
Douglas M. Kinney
VICE PRESIDENT
Robert A. Guerin
CORPORATE CONTROLLER
Joseph J. Burke
BOARD OF DIRECTORS
H. Wayne Huizenga (chairman), John J. Melk (vice chairman), Donald F. Flynn, A. Clinton Allen III, John W. Croghan
SUBSIDIARIES
Movies to Go, Video Library

Bradford Video

394 S. Main St., Bradford, MA 01830; (617) 372-3160. Independent video.
OWNER
David Court

Bridgeport Video

742 W. 31st St., Chicago, IL 60616; (312) 326-1467. Independent video.

Britannica Video/Encyclopaedia Britannica

425 N. Michigan Ave., Chicago, IL 60611; (312) 321-6841. Direct mail.

Broadway Video

168 S. Lake St., Forest Lake, MN 55025; (612) 464-8231. Organized 1982. (Videotape sales and rental.)
MANAGER/OWNER
Thomas M. Houle
OWNER
Stuart J. Houle
BRANCHES
Broadway Video, Rack Jobbing, Video Store of Spring Lake Park

Brookshire Brothers Inc.

P.O. Box 1688, Lufkin, TX 75901; (409) 634-8155. Video chain (50).

PRESIDENT
W. Eugene Brookshire
SOFTWARE & HARDWARE BUYER
M.L. Colmer

Budget Video Inc.

(D/B/A Hollywood Home Theatre)
1540 N. Highland Ave., Suite 110, Hollywood, CA 90028; (213) 446-0121, (213) 466-0127. Organized 1979. (Dealer, distributor, retailer of video cassettes and laser discs.)
PRESIDENT
Larry S. Fine
VICE PRESIDENT
Stephen Stumbris

Calypso Video, Inc.

1706 Secor Rd., Toledo, OH 43607; (419) 536-5394. Independent video.
PRESIDENT
C. Opfermann

Canadian Tire Corp. Ltd.

P.O. Box 770, Station K, Toronto, Ont., Canada M4P 2V8; (416) 480-3000. Mass merchant. Chain (400 stores).
SOFTWARE BUYER
Patti Mills-Roy

Capt. Nemo's Video

P.O. Box 15, Hat Creek, CA 96040; (916) 335-7467. (Video software leasing and video distribution.)
PARTNERS
Steve Barkett, Fred Jorgensen, John Morgan, Trisha Drake, Christopher Barkett

Captain Video

1326 Broad St., Central Falls, RI 02863; (401) 724-1297. Video, independent.
PRESIDENT
Fred Kilsey
VICE PRESIDENT & TREASURER
Mark Feinstein

Carousel Music & Video

121 Winter Haven Mall, Winter Haven, FL 33880; (813) 294-8346; 293-0372. (Complete audio and video store.)
OWNERS
Gary E. Stewart
Ron Edmonds

Christopher's Video West, Inc.

8 S. 101st St., Rt. 59, Naperville, IL 60540; (312) 369-8993. Video independent.
PRESIDENT
P. A. Christopher
SECRETARY & TREASURER
S. L. Christopher

Cinema Concepts, Inc.

2461 Berlin Turnpike, Newington, CT 06111; (203) 667-1251. Organized 1971. (Non-theatrical distribution of entertainment motion pictures in 16mm, Beta, VHS, U-Matic, 8mm to school, libraries and home market. Mail-order plus three retail stores.)
PRESIDENT
Joel G. Jacobson

BRANCHES
Porter Plaza, Main St., Old Saybrook, CT 06475; (203) 388-1481
Rt. 72 Plaza, 859 Mill St., East Berlin, CT 06023; (203) 828-1815
AFFILIATION
Video Software Dealers Association (Joel Jacobson is a board director of CT chapter)

City Lights Video, Inc.

82 Front St. S., Issaquah, Washington, 98027; (206) 392-6700. Organized 1983. (Sales and rental of video software.)
PRESIDENT
Alan Ligda
AFFILIATIONS
VSDA (National and Washington State)

The Copps Corp.

2828 Wayne St., Stevens Point, WI 54481; (715) 344-5900. (Food and non-food distribution.)
CHAIRMAN
Michael Copps
PRESIDENT
Tim Copps
EXEC. VICE PRESIDENT, WHOLESALE DISTRIBUTION
Fred Copps
VICE PRESIDENT, MERCHANDISING
Don Copps
VICE PRESIDENT, PUBLIC AFFAIRS
Tom Copps
EXEC. VICE PRESIDENT, RETAIL OPERATIONS
Darrell Scherwinski
VICE PRESIDENT, FINANCE
Tom Sievwright

B. Dalton Bookseller

7505 Metro Blvd., Minneapolis, MN 55435; (612) 893-7000. (Subsidiary of Dayton Hudson.) Bookstore, chain.
SOFTWARE BUYER
Lesli Casciaro

Dawn's Video

519 W. Foothill, Suite C, Rialto, CA 92376; (714) 874-1414. Organized 1980. (Video specialty store.)
OWNER
Gregory C. George
BRANCHES
2085 E. Highland Ave., San Bernardino, CA 92404; (714) 864-3113
9725 Sierra, Fontana, CA 92335; (714) 350-8833
267 E. 40th, San Bernardino, CA 92404; (714) 883-5737
1330 Massachusetts Ave., Riverside, CA 92507; (714) 784-1414

Discount Video Tapes, Inc.

P.O. Box 7122, Suite B, Burbank, CA 91510; (818) 843-3366. Organized 1979. (Specializing in rare and unusual pre-recorded videos. Retail and wholesale.)
PRESIDENT
Woody Wise

Dodd Camera & Video

27179 Chagrin Blvd., Woodmere, OH 44122; (216) 292-2825. (Subsidiary of The Dodd Co.) Electronics, video chain (10 stores).
PRESIDENT
Richard L. Greiner, Sr.
MANAGER & SOFTWARE BUYER
Don Carter

VICE PRESIDENT & HARDWARE BUYER
Rick Greiner
GENERAL MANAGER
Don Carter

Doubleday Book and Record Clubs, Inc.

245 Park Ave., New York, NY 10167; (212) 984-7309. Mail order.
VICE PRESIDENT
Bernard Schwartz

Downtown Video

3110 W. Peterson, Chicago, IL 60659; (312) 338-1600. (Subsidiary of Downtown Records Inc.) Video chain (6 stores).
PRESIDENT
Howard Rosen
DIRECTOR & SOFTWARE BUYER
Ronald W. Kehr
HARDWARE BUYER
Ron Fischell

Erol's Inc.

6621 Electronic Dr., Springfield, VA 22151; (703) 451-8812. (Video chain with 165 locations.)

Everybody's Records Tapes & Video

5279 N. Lombard, Portland, OR 97203; (503) 286-9841. Organized 1971. (Home entertainment software.)
PRESIDENT
Tom Keenan
AFFILIATION
VSDA, NARM

Family Video

740 Mt. View Dr., Rapid City, SD 57702; (605) 348-7572. Video independent.
PRESIDENTS & BUYERS
Richard Ireland
Christine Ireland

The Federated Group

2161 Hutton, Carrollton, TX 75006; (214) 243-5700. (65 stores).
AUDIO/VIDEO BUYER
Armand Phillipi

Flower Films & Video

(see Les Blank's Flower Films & Video.)

French & Spanish Book Corp.

115 Fifth Ave., New York, NY 10003; (212) 673-7400. Bookstore, independent.
PRESIDENT
Emanuel Molho

G&A Stores, Inc. /d/b/a Curtis Mathes

2500 S. Center, Marshalltown, Iowa 50158; (515) 752-5541. Organized 1984. (Sells TVs, VCRs, video cameras, and movie rental.)
PRESIDENT & TREASURER
Glenn Stalzer
VICE PRESIDENT & SECRETARY
Ann Stalzer

Great American Movie Emporium

5702 W. Maplewood Dr., Littleton, CO 80127; (303) 972-8200. (Subsidiary of Charvin Enterprises, Inc.) Video, franchise.

PRESIDENT
Charles E. De Shazer
VICE PRESIDENT, SOFTWARE & HARDWARE BUYER
Garvin De Shazer

Greenleaf Video, Inc.

3230 Nebraska Ave., Santa Monica, CA 90404; (213) 829-7675. Organized 1984. (Sells informational videos to schools, libraries and consumers.)

PRESIDENT
Barbara K. Greenleaf
SECRETARY
Jon W. Greenleaf

Grolier Book Clubs

Sherman Turnpike, Danbury, CT 06816. (Subsidiary of Times Mirror Co.) Book club.

EDITORIAL DIRECTOR
Grace Mishkin

Hearst Marine Books

105 Madison Ave., New York, NY 10016; (212) 889-3050. (Division of William Morrow, Inc.) Catalog sales.

Home Film Festival

305 Linden St., Scranton, PA 18503; (717) 342-2185; (800) 258-3456. (Rents and sells hard-to-find videos, both foreign and domestic.)

PRESIDENT
Dan Jury
SOFTWARE BUYER
Linda Goodrich

Home Movies, Inc.

1016 Juan Tabo N.E., Albuquerque, NM 87112; (505) 292-8578. Organized 1983. (Video sales and rentals.)

CHIEF EXECUTIVE OFFICER & PRESIDENT
Troy D. Richards
VICE PRESIDENT
Kent Richards
BRANCHES
Home Movies II, 1115 San Mateo S.E., Albuquerque, NM 87108
Home Movies LTD., 7120 Wyoming Blvd., Albuquerque, NM 87109
Home Movies, Downtown, 505½ Fifth St., downtown Albuquerque, NM.

Home Theater Video

1504-A Wyoming N.E., Albuquerque, NM 87112; (505) 293-5784. Video independent.

PROPRIETOR
William R. Leonards

Home Video Network, Inc.

Route 93, Conyngham, PA 18219; (717) 788-5211. Video, drugstores, independent.

PRESIDENT
Walter Haentjens, Jr.
HARDWARE & SOFTWARE BUYERS
Joseph Bayzick
Rick Haentjens

IFEX Films/International Film Exchange Ltd.

201 W. 52 St., New York, NY 10019; (212) 582-4318. Cable: IFEXREP-New York. Telex: 420748; FAX: (212) 956-2257. Also 9200 Sunset Blvd., PH 9, Los Angeles, CA 90069; (213) 278-7939. FAX: (213) 278-7939; TELEX: 4972966. Organized 1959. (Domestic and international distribution of feature films, documentaries, shorts & video programs.)

PRESIDENT
Gerald J. Rappoport
SENIOR VICE PRESIDENT
Richard Grisar
EXECUTIVE VICE PRESIDENT
Christopher Wood
DIRECTOR, THEATRICAL SALES & MARKETING
Robert Newman
VICE PRESIDENT, INTERNATIONAL SALES
Joy Pereths

Image Factory

29 W. Main, Bozeman, MT 59715; (406) 587-8918. Organized 1981. (Video transfers and production, also movie rentals.)

OWNER
Steve Flagg

International Sailing Products

P.O. Box 355, Oyster Bay, NY 11771; (516) 922-5182, (800) 645-7676. Catalog, franchise (3 stores).

PRESIDENT
Steve Benjamin
VICE PRESIDENT
Paul Dickey

International Video

9576 Quivira Rd., Lenexa, KS 66215; (913) 492-2311. Organized 1983. (Retail video software.)

OWNER
Michael Rupani

JBC Video Vesting d/b/a Video Show

546 N. State College Blvd., Fullerton, CA 92631; (714) 871-0711. Organized 1981. (Sale and rental of video cassettes.)

OWNERS
Christine and Rudolph Neely

Kaleidoscope Home Video

700 E. Maple, Centerville, Iowa 52544; (515) 437-1674. Organized 1984. (Home video rental and sales.)

OWNERS
Russell K. Davis
Donna S. Davis
BRANCH
Video "Show" Room, Ottumwa, IA; (515) 682-8231

King's Video Center

1325 W. Warner, Santa Ana, CA 92704; (714) 662-2898. Organized 1982. (Retail video hardware and software, sales and rental.)

Leading Edge Video

2325 Harrison Avenue, Butte; MT 59701

BUYER
Robert C. Wilson

Listening Library

One Park Ave., Old Greenwich, CT 06870; (203) 637-3616.
PRESIDENT
Timothy Ditlow

Long Drug Stores

141 N. Civic Dr., Walnut Creek, CA 94596; (415) 937-1170. Drugstores, chain (192 stores).
MERCHANDISE MANAGER
Terry Sandin

MAS Productions

18434 Bermuda St., Northridge, CA 91326; (818) 360-0371. Mail order.
CUSTOMER CONTACT
Richard Stark

MSI Video

5020 Sunnyside Ave., Suite 112, Beltsville, MD 20705; (301) 474-2220. Organized 1981. (National mail order sales of videocassettes.)
PRESIDENT
Lee Masser

Manzi Video Sales, Inc.

261 Halstead Ave., Harrison, NY 10528; (914) 835-5005. (d/b/a The Video Connection #130.) Video franchise.
PRESIDENT & BUYER
Michael S. Manzi

Meredith Corp. Better Homes & Gardens Book Club

750 Third Ave., New York, NY 10017; (212) 551-7040. Mail order.
CUSTOMER CONTACT
Jane Hamada

Montgomery Video Inc.

18268 Village Mart Dr., Olney, MD 20832; (301) 774-2014. Video chain (5 stores.)
PRESIDENT & BUYER
Lou Kaufman

Morris Video

2730 Monterey, Suite #105, Monterey Business Park, Torrance, CA 90503; (213) 533-4800. Organized 1984. (Produces and distributes quality information and entertainment video. Mail order.)
PRESIDENT
Dawn Morris
VICE PRESIDENT
George Morris, Ph.D.
DIRECTOR OF PUBLIC RELATIONS
Wendy Fulton
NATIONAL SALES MANAGER
Kandra Inga
NATIONAL SALES REP. MANAGER
Micki Smallman
BOARD OF DIRECTORS
Dawn Morris, George Morris, Ph.D., George Bott, David Van Horn.
BRANCH
663 The Village, Redondo Beach, CA 90277; (213) 374-4984.

The Movie Exchange

Box 61, Anderson, PA 19407; (215) 265-0150. Organized 1983. (Video sale and rental, 200 locations.)
PRESIDENT
Shellie Tibbitz
CHAIRMAN OF BOARD
Lamont R. Tibbitz
DIRECTOR, STORE OPERATIONS
Glenn Gasser
DIRECTOR, FIELD OPERATIONS
Brian K. Ward
DIRECTOR, COMPUTER OPERATIONS
Mike Balik
DIRECTOR, OFFICE OPERATIONS
Karen Pastino
BOARD OF DIRECTORS
Peter Morse, Peter Dale, Shellie Tibbitz, Lamont Tibbitz
AFFILIATIONS
VSDA

The Movie Merchants

3254 Youngfield St., Wheat Ridge, CO 80033; (303) 234-9282. Organized 1980. (Video retailer.)
PRESIDENT & TREASURER
Shelley Gooch
VICE PRESIDENT & SECRETARY
Patrick Gooch
BOARD OF DIRECTORS
William Rahmig, Ramon Morton
BRANCH
7562 S. University, Littleton, CO 80122
AFFILIATIONS
VSDA, Wheat Ridge Chamber of Commerce

Movies Tonite

935 E. Broad St., Columbus, OH 43205; (614) 253-0193. Video independent.
PRESIDENT
John Sandefur
VICE PRESIDENT, SOFTWARE BUYER
Debra Harrington
VICE PRESIDENT, HARDWARE BUYER
Jane Sandefur

Movies Unlimited

7421 Manchester, St. Louis, MO 63143; (314) 781-4111. (Subsidiary of Video Information Corp.) Video chain (4 stores).
PRESIDENT
Kevin R. Toal

Movies Unlimited

6736 Castor Ave., Philadelphia, PA 19149; (215) 722-8298. Retail stores, mail order.
GENERAL MANAGER
Mr. Weiss

Music Plus

2551 S. Alameda St., Los Angeles, CA 90058; (213) 234-3336. (Subsidiary of Show Industries d/b/a Music Plus.) Audio and video chain (60 stores).
PRESIDENT
Lou Fogelman
SOFTWARE BUYER
Mitch Perliss

Musical Sales Company

40 S. Caroline St., Baltimore, MD 21231; (301) 675-1400. (One-stop record, tape, CD, video [pre-recorded], and related accessories.)

PRESIDENT
Milton I. Bereson
VICE PRESIDENT
Molly E. Bereson

Nantucket Video Inc.

30 Main St., Nantucket, MA 02554; (617) 228-6870.
Video independent.
PRESIDENT & BUYER
Gene Mahon

National Video, Inc.

7325 NE 55th Ave., Portland, OR 97218; (503) 284-
2965. Organized 1980. (Franchisor of retail video spe-
cialty stores.)
PRESIDENT
Ron Berger
EXECUTIVE VICE PRESIDENT
Troy Cooper
VICE PRESIDENT, FINANCE
F. Kim Cox
BOARD OF DIRECTORS
Ron Berger, William LeVine, Jack Silverman, L. Barton Alex-
ander, Lon Werner, Ken Koger, Peter Dal Bianco

New Breed Music

P.O. Box 661, Pomona, CA 91768; (714) 623-1999.
Independent video.
PRESIDENT
Jesse Mac Lynum, Jr.

Nightingale-Conant Corp.

7300 N. Lehigh Ave., Niles, IL 60648; (312) 647-0300.
Catalog sales.
CUSTOMER CONTACT
Don Reaser

Opening Night Video

9007 Willowbrook Mall, Wayne, NJ 07470; (201) 890-
0066. Video chain (3 stores).
PRESIDENT
Harold Rosenbaum
VICE PRESIDENT & SOFTWARE BUYER
Joyce Mendelowitz

Osco Drug Inc.

1818 Swift Dr., Oak Brook, IL 60521; (312) 572-5000.
Drug, chain (650 stores).
ELECTRONICS BUYER
James H. Seifert

Palmer Video Corporation

1767 Morris Ave., Union, NJ 07083; (201) 686-3030.
Organized 1981. (Franchisor, owner, operator video
stores.)
PRESIDENT
Peter Balner
VICE PRESIDENT
Peter Margaritondo
VICE PRESIDENT, FINANCE
Joseph Berger

Paradise Video, Inc.

1063 Lower Main St., Suite C-109, Wailuku, Maui, HI
96793; (808) 244-9790. Organized 1981.
PRESIDENT
Calvin H. Inouye

VICE PRESIDENT
Jeffrey K. Yamanishi
SECRETARY & TREASURER
Alfred Cantorna
BRANCHES
250 Alamaha St., Kahului, Maui, HI 96732
7 Aewa Pl., Pukalani, Maui, HI 96768
2995 South Kihei Rd., Kihei, Maui, HI 96753
AFFILIATION
VSDA

Pathmark

301 Blaire Rd., Woodbridge, NJ 07095; (201) 499-3000.
Supermarket chain. Rental only.
CUSTOMER CONTACT
Gordon Keil

Public Access Producers Association

2652 N. Winchell, Portland, OR 97217; (503) 289-2309.
Video, direct mail, independent.
DIRECTOR & SOFTWARE BUYER
R. S. Kolemaine

Publishers Central Bureau

225 Park Ave. S., New York, NY 10003; (212) 254-1600.
Catalog, mail order. Independent video.
DIRECTOR OF VIDEO
Judy Harper

Pueblo Home Video, Inc.

1302 N. Elizabeth, Pueblo, CO 81003; (303) 546-3555.
Video, independent.
PRESIDENT & BUYER
Warren E. Lombard
VICE PRESIDENT & BUYER
Carol Lombard

Quality Life Publishing, Inc.

P.O. Box 800, Boulder, CO 80306; (303) 440-9109. (Direct mail catalog distributor of instructional and documentary videos to the home VCR owner.)
PRESIDENT
Robin Sutherland

Rare Bird Video, Inc.

482 Broome St., New York, NY 10013; (212) 334-8150.
Video chain (3 stores).
PRESIDENT
Jack Morris
SOFTWARE & HARDWARE BUYERS
Jack Morris
Wayne Quackenbush

Record & Video Warehouse

3110 W. Peterson, Chicago, IL 60659; (312) 338-1600.
(Subsidiary of Record & Video Warehouse Inc.) Video,
chain (6 stores).
PRESIDENT
Howard Rosen
SOFTWARE BUYER & DIRECTOR
Ronald W. Kehr
HARDWARE BUYER
Ron Fischell

Red Fox Video

110 W. Main St., Lyrens, PA 17048; (717) 453-7165.

456

Rehabfilm

1123 Broadway, New York, NY 10010; (212) 741-5160. Non-profit, private organization. (Subsidairy of Rehabilitation Int'l, U.S.A.)
DIRECTOR OF MEDIA
John F. Moses

Rite Aid Corp.

Trindle Rd. and Railroad Ave., Shiremanstown, PA 17091; (717) 761-2633. Drug chain (1053 stores).
DIRECTOR
Jerry Cardinale
VIDEO BUYER
Sue Schuck

Rizzoli Video

597 Fifth Ave., New York, NY 10017; (212) 223-0100. Organized 1985. Bookstore chain.
DIRECTOR
John Brancati

Schnuck Markets, Inc.

12921 Enterprise Way, Bridgeton, MO 63044; (314) 344-9600. Food markets, chain.
PRESIDENT
Craig D. Schnuck
BUYER
Cynthia Parentin

Sears and Roebuck, Co.

Sears Tower, Dept. 40-15, Chicago, IL 60684; (312) 875-8306. Department store, chain (810 stores).
MARKETING MANAGER
Mike Mangan

Shows To Go Video Centers of America, Inc.

4974 E. Clinton Way #112, Fresno, CA 93727-1520; (209) 299-4306. Video chain (92 stores).
PRESIDENT
Bernard Horton
EXECUTIVE VICE PRESIDENT, SOFTWARE & HARDWARE BUYER
Mike Sherlock

Sound Warehouse

10911 Petal St., Dallas, TX 75238; (214) 343-4700. Video chain (100 stores).
SOFTWARE BUYER
Robert Kallish

Stansbury Stereo and Video Center

6330 Frankford Ave., Baltimore, MD 21206; (301) 488-9600. Electronics, independent video.
PRESIDENT
Jim Disney
VICE PRESIDENT & SOFTWARE BUYER
Dale Bennett
HARDWARE BUYERS
Jim Disney and Dale Bennett

Stars To Go, Inc.

4751 Wilshire Blvd., Suite #140, Los Angeles, CA 90010; (213) 930-9300. Organized 1984. (Rents feature films on prerecorded videocassettes through its Stars To Go Video Centers located in convenience stores.)
CHAIRMAN OF THE BOARD
Fred J. Atchity, Jr.
PRESIDENT & CEO
Jerry R. Welch
VICE PRESIDENT, FINANCE, CFO
Richard D. Vermeer
VICE PRESIDENT, CORP. CONTROLLER
A. Duncan Longworth
VICE PRESIDENT, CUSTOMER SALES & SERVICE
Ronald W. Dunagan
VICE PRESIDENT, MOVIE MANAGEMENT
Peer Ghent
BOARD OF DIRECTORS
Fred J. Atchity, Jr. (chairman), Jerry R. Welch (director)

Studio Associates Video Division

4072 Webber St., Sarasota, FL 34232; (813) 371-5798. (Subsidiary of Studio Associates, Inc.) Photographic darkroom, and independent video retailer.
SOFTWARE & HARDWARE BUYER
Charles Cyphers

Sunset Software

2265 Westwood Blvd., #140, Los Angeles, CA 90064; (213) 474-2446 (not for orders). (Producer and direct mail marketer of R-rated video tapes.)
PRESIDENT & SOFTWARE BUYER
Will Swan

TV Collector

P.O. Box 188, Needham, MA 02192; (508) 238-1179. Organized 1976. (TV nostalgia magazine/tape trading marketplace.)
PUBLISHER
Stephen W. Albert
EDITOR
Diane L. Albert

Tele-Video Enterprises, Inc.

813 W. Main St., Suite 22, Battle Ground, WA 98604; (206) 687-7239 (d/b/a Video City USA) Independent.
PRESIDENT & BUYER
Curt Siebold

Toys "R" Us

395 W. Passaic St., Rochelle Park, NJ 07662; (201) 845-5033. Chain (199 stores). Children's programs.

Transworld Video Inc.

18100 W. Dixie Highway, North Miami Beach, FL 33160; (305) 944-0298. (Subsidiary of Video Connection of America.) National procurement office for Video Connection franchise stores.
NATIONAL SALES MANAGER
Peter Barry

United Video, Inc.

500 Church St. N., Concord, NC 28025; (704) 788-2012. Organized 1981.
PRESIDENT & SECRETARY
Margaret R. Flower
VICE PRESIDENT & TREASURER
Kenneth G. Flower

Universal Video

2935 Pat Booker Rd. #138; Universal City, TX 78148-2748; (512) 659-7131. Independent.

PRESIDENT
Alice Haskell
BRANCH
9179 FM 471 West, #119, San Antonio, TX 78250; (512) 647-1096.

University of Southern California

Davidson Conference Center, University Park, Los Angeles, CA 90089-0871; (213) 743-5219. Independent.
EXECUTIVE DIRECTOR
Philip J. Rapa

Video 1

8611 W. 95th St., Hickory Hills, IL 60457; (312) 598-1000. 8065 W. 95th St., Hickory Hills, IL 60457; (312) 598-0001; 8082 W. IIIth St., Palos Hills, IL 60465; (312) 974-1000. Independent (3 stores).
PRESIDENT
Carole Bartolini
SOFTWARE & HARDWARE BUYER
Dave Able

Video Action

708 W. First St., Los Angeles, CA 90012; (213) 687-8262. Organized 1981. (Video production and distribution.)
OWNER (PARTNER)
Leslie T. Hamasaki
OWNER (PARTNER)
Ruth Watanabe
OPERATIONS MANAGER
Gregg S. Yokoyama

Video Age, Inc.

4820 Excelsior Blvd., Suite 112, Minneapolis, MN 55416; (612) 927-7484. Mail order, telephone sales.
PRESIDENT
William J. Hudlow

Video Biz

113 S. Third St., Richmond, VA 23219; (804) 788-1902. Video chain (7 stores). (Subsidiary of Video Products, Inc.)
PRESIDENT & HARDWARE BUYER
Scott Moffett
SOFTWARE BUYERS
Scott Moffett
Sharon Krohn

Video Biz—North Shore, Inc.

50 Maplewood Ave., Gloucester, MA 01930; (617) 283-3721. Video, franchise.
PRESIDENT & BUYER
Sarah S. Wall

Video Boulevard, Inc.

241 Haverford Ave., Narberth, PA 19072; (215) 664-4136. Organized 1981. (Video rentals and sales.)
PRESIDENT
Steven J. Freid

Video Center Stores

802 S. Solano, Las Cruces, NM 88001; (505) 523-8907. (Subsidiary of Pata Corp.) Video, chain (6 stores).
PRESIDENT & SOFTWARE BUYER
Pat Kilpatrick

Video Centre

P.O. Box 1982, Winter Park, FL 32790; (305) 628-3070. Video, independent.
CHIEF EXECUTIVE OFFICER
Philip Lashinsky

Video Channel Inc.

20103 Saticoy St., Room 2, Canoga Park, CA 91306; (818) 993-8273. Organized 1984. (Video tape sales and rentals.)
PRESIDENT & BUYER
Jeff S. Dickel

The Video Circuit

11507 S.W. Pacific Hwy., Portland, OR 97223; (503) 246-8852. Video chain (3 stores). (Subsidiary of Video Futures, Inc.)
PRESIDENT & BUYER
Leo A. Jerman

Video City Productions

4266 Broadway, Oakland, CA 94611; (415) 428-0202. Organized 1983. (Manufactures and distributes pre-recorded VHS and Beta film product.) Video, chain (9 stores).
MARKETING DIRECTOR
Bob Brown
OTHER COMPANY OWNED LABELS:
Combat Video, Art House Video, Chop 'Em Ups Video, World Aviation Video, Black Action Video

Video Connection

3123 Sylvania Ave., Toledo, OH 43613; (419) 472-7727. Video specialty, chain (76 locations).
PRESIDENT
John Day

Video Connection of America, Inc.

18100 W. Dixie Highway, North Miami Beach, FL 33160; (305) 944-0298. National headquarters for 200 franchised video stores.
PRESIDENT
Bert Tenzer
DIRECTOR OF FRANCHISE SALES
John Barry

Video Corner

553 49th St. S., St. Petersburg, FL 33707; (813) 321-2122. Video, chain (3 stores).
PRESIDENT & HARDWARE BUYER
Bob Skidmore
VICE PRESIDENT & SOFTWARE BUYER
John P. Gallagher
GENERAL MANAGER & HARDWARE BUYER
Richard E. Smith

Video Cove

4747 E. Elliot Rd., Suite 27, Phoenix, AZ 85044; (602) 893-9609. Video, independent.
PRESIDENT & BUYER
Bob Mulvihill

Video Crossroads

5448 Beach Blvd., Buena Park, CA 90621; (714) 521-3870. Video, franchise.

PRESIDENT
  Ralph Zink
SOFTWARE & HARDWARE BUYER
  Corinne Zink

The Video Exchange, Inc.

198 Union Blvd., Room 100, Lakewood, CO 80228; (303) 988-8540, (800) 423-9357. Organized 1981. (Sale of video rental store franchises.) Chain (85 stores).

PRESIDENT
  Allen Kenfield
VICE PRESIDENTS
  David Kenfield
  James Perry
BOARD OF DIRECTORS
  Allen Kenfield, David Kenfield, James Perry, Martin Kenfield
AFFILIATION
  Venture capital backed by Allied Capital Corp., Wash., DC

Video Experience

401 I St., Suite B., Arcata, CA 95521; (707) 826-1105. Video, independent.

PRESIDENT & BUYER
  Doug Simas

Video Flicks

141 Caldwell Blvd., Nampa, ID 83651; (208) 465-5773. Video, independent.

PRESIDENT & BUYER
  Dale R. Durbin

Video Galore

4456 Lake St., Lake Charles, LA 70605; (318) 474-9791. Video, franchise.

OWNER & SOFTWARE BUYER
  Michael K. O'Carroll

Video General/American Video Tape Library

5809 S. Broadway, Suite B, Littleton, CO 80121; (303) 798-3389. Organized 1978. (Tape rental and selling by mail and retail.)

MANAGERS
  Mardell Peterson
  Sandra Cornish
BOARD OF DIRECTORS
  Mardell Peterson, Sandra Cornish
AFFILIATION
  United Independent Video Dealers Association

Video Joe

1203 Eastridge Dr., Slidell, LA 70458; (504) 646-2482. Video, independent.

OWNER & BUYER
  Joe B. Howard
BUYER
  Rusty Howard

Video King

7360 N. Lincoln Ave., Lincolnwood, IL 60646; (312) 675-2910. Video, chain (14 stores).

MERCHANDISE MANAGER
  Vance Frederico

The Video Library

4184 Woodruff Ave., Lakewood, CA 90713; (213) 420-8383. Organized 1982. (Rentals and sales of video tapes and VCRs.)

PRESIDENT
  Steve Cantril
SECRETARY & TREASURER
  Debbie Cantril
BOARD OF DIRECTORS
  Richard Burdick, Kathleen Burdick

Video Marts

7827 S. Redwood Rd., West Jordan, UT 84088; (801) 565-0064. Video chain (12 stores)

PRESIDENT
  Clyde Roper

Video One

5055 Town North Dr., Shreveport, LA 71107; (318) 221-5837. Organized 1981. (Video software.)

OWNERS
  Mary L. West
  Samuel E. West
PURCHASING AGENT
  Samuel L. West

Video Palace

4537 Duke St., Alexandria, VA 22304; (703) 823-5466. Video, independent.

PRESIDENT & BUYER
  Rick Brooks
VICE PRESIDENT & BUYER
  Doc Brooks

Video Paradise Inc.

115 W. Main St., Westboro, MA 01581; (617) 366-8890.

PRESIDENT
  Donald Rogers

Video Playback

137 Route 516, Old Bridge, NJ 08857; (201) 254-5874. Video, independent chain (5 stores).

PRESIDENT & HARDWARE BUYER
  Myron S. Kozak
SOFTWARE BUYER
  Mary T. Kozak

Video Plus, Inc.

Box 8350, Albuquerque, NM 87198; (505) 298-7705. Video, chain (3 stores).

PRESIDENT
  Patrick Riley
SOFTWARE & HARDWARE BUYER
  Lynne Landers

Video Product, Inc. T/A Video Biz

4736 N. Southside Plaza, Richmond, VA 23224; P.O. Box 24285; (804) 233-9703. Organized 1980. (Retail video.)

PRESIDENT & TREASURER
  Scott Moffett
VICE PRESIDENT
  Tabetha Moffett
SECRETARY
  Deborah J. Moffett
BOARD OF DIRECTORS
  Scott Moffett, Deborah Moffett, Tabetha Moffett, Robert Moffett

BRANCHES
Richmond, VA—4 locations; Colonial Heights, VA; Roanoke, VA; Salem VA—1 location
AFFILIATIONS
Video Biz, Inc., VSDA

Video Replay

1668 Merriman Rd., Akron, OH 44313; (216) 836-9773. Video, chain (3 stores).
PRESIDENT & HARDWARE BUYER
J. Dwight Taylor
SOFTWARE BUYER
Jane Friedhoff

Video Revolution

20948 Mission Blvd., Hayward, CA 94541; (415) 481-2880. Video, independent.
OWNER & BUYER
Ole Nordhavn
BRANCH
1339 Washington Ave., San Leandro, CA 94577; (415) 483-9620.

Video Shack, Inc.

1608 Broadway, New York, NY 10019; (212) 581-6260. Video, independent (14 stores).

Video Shoppe

Suite 12, 1325 Kass Circle, Spring Hill, FL 34606; (904) 683-8839. Video, independent (2 stores).
MANAGER & BUYER
Bob Hall

Video Show

(See JBC Video Vesting)

Video Specialties Company

153 Town and Country, Houston, TX 77024; (713) 465-0702. Organized 1972. (Sale and rental of video-cassettes.)
PRESIDENT
John F. Dinwoodie
VICE PRESIDENT
Ann C. Dinwoodie
BUYER
David C. Dinwoodie

Video Station

513 McDowell, St., Asheville, NC 28803; (704) 258-1145. Video, electronics, independent.
PRESIDENT
Mariano Raigo
SECRETARY/TREASURER & BUYER
Robin Raigo

Video Station

3689 Sheridan Dr., Amherst, NY 14226; (716) 835-2577. Video chain (500 stores). (Subsidiary of Rob-Mer Corp.)
PRESIDENT & HARDWARE BUYER
R. A. Lozinak
SOFTWARE BUYER & MANAGER
M. Lozinak

Video Station

240 E. 1300 South, Orem, UT 84058; (801) 226-6626. Organized 1981. (Video rental, duplication, and production.)

OWNER
Mark Greer
MANAGER
Eve Greer
BRANCHES
346 W. 100 South, Orem, UT 84058; 1476 N. Freedom Blvd., Provo, UT 84058.

The Video Station

494A Main St., Woburn, MA 01801; (617) 933-1445. Organized 1980. (Consumer electronics, video retailing.)
PRESIDENT
Joseph V. Elia
VICE PRESIDENT
Jeanne M. Elia
BOARD OF DIRECTORS
Joseph V. Elia, Jeanne M. Elia, Vincent I. Melendy

Video Station, Inc.

374 Springfield Ave., Summit, NJ 07901; (201) 273-0024. Organized 1980. (Sales and rental of videocassettes, recorders, TVs, record-a-calls, radios, CDs; video production studio, ½" and ¾" video editing studio.)
PRESIDENT
Roger Cooper
VICE PRESIDENT
Sandi Cooper
BOARD OF DIRECTORS
Roger Cooper, Sandi Cooper

Video Stop

810 W. 21st St., Clovis, NM 88101; (505) 763-4553. (Subsidiary of Let Us Entertain You.) Video, chain (5 stores).
PRESIDENT
B. Lyons
MANAGER & BUYER
V. Starkey

Video Take #1

432 Paxon Ave., Trenton, NJ 08690-1915; (609) 587-2882. Video, independent.
PARTNERS
James Carlucci, Jr., Janet D. Carlucci

Video Today Inc.

63 E. 8th, Holland, MI 49423; (616) 392-2877. Organized 1981. (Video sales, rental and mail order.) Chain (4 stores).
PRESIDENT
Al Wagenaar
BRANCHES
977 Butternut, Holland, MI; (616) 399-2092
9505 School St., Jenison, MI; (616) 457-3150
755 Michigan, Holland, MI; (616) 392-6210
AFFILIATIONS
VSDA, SBA of Michigan

Video USA

13 W. Broadway, Derry, NH 03038; (603) 432-3236. Video.
PRESIDENT & HARDWARE BUYER
Donald Phelps
VICE PRESIDENT & SOFTWARE BUYER
Hollie Dustin

Video Vantage Inc.

1005 S. Gaylord St., Denver, CO 80209; (303) 777-0710. Organized 1983. (Supplies the Washington Park neighborhoods with their video needs.)

PRESIDENT
Hugh M. Boyd
VICE PRESIDENT
William Boyd
SECRETARY & TREASURER
Karen P. Taylor
AFFILIATIONS
Denver Chamber of Commerce, Video Software Dealers Association

Video Ventures, Inc.

262 W. Cottage Ave., Sandy, UT 84070-1431; (801) 255-0505. Video, 65 branches in drug and food chains.
PRESIDENT
Jerry Burke

Video Village

P.O. Box 38 (449 E. I-30), Rockwall, TX 75087; (214) 722-2222. Organized 1981. (VCR and television sales, movie rentals.)
MANAGER
Lisa Allen
BRANCH
Rowlett, TX

Video Village/The Video House

P.O. Box 2595, Canyon Country, CA 91351; (805) 252-3048. Video, chain (4 stores).
PRESIDENT & HARDWARE BUYER
David M. Smith
OPERATION MANAGER & SOFTWARE BUYER
Maureen Brown

Video Worx

3011 W. 74th Ave., Westminster, CO 80030; (303) 427-1237. Video, independent.
PRESIDENT & BUYER
Don Wickman

Video Yesteryear

Box C, Sandy Hook, CT 06482. Organized 1978. Independent, mail order.
PRESIDENT & MARKETING & SALES
Jon Sonneborn

Video's To Go

9348½ Corbin Ave., Northridge, CA 91324; (818) 701-1115. Video, independent.
PRESIDENT & BUYER
Michael A. Meehan

Video-Forum

96 Broad St., Guilford, CT 06437; (203) 453-9794. (Subsidiary of Jeffrey Norton Publishers, Inc.) Catalog sales.

Videobrary, Incorporated

3518 Cahuenga W., Suite 301, Hollywood, CA 90068; (213) 851-5811. Organized 1979. (Video store set-up. Buying service.)
PRESIDENT
Paul Lisay
GENERAL MANAGER
Richard Rothstein

Videon, Inc.

6443 Fairview, Boise, ID 83704; (208) 375-8899. Video, chain (3 stores).
PRESIDENT
Brent Estep
MARKETING DIRECTOR & SOFTWARE BUYER
Jeff Troup
HARDWARE BUYER
Russ Riley

Visions

P.O. Box 341, 110 Midland Ave., Rye, NY 10580; (914) 937-8601, (212) 824-7711. Mail order.
GENERAL MANAGER
Grace Babtist

Waldenbooks

201 High Ridge Rd., Stamford, CT 06904; (203) 356-7500. (Subsidiary of K Mart Corp.) Bookstore, chain (900 stores).
PRESIDENT
Harry Hoffman
MANAGER, MARKETING DEVELOPMENT & BUYER
George Hodgkins

Ric Webb's Video City

2610 W. Nob Hill Blvd., Yakima, WA 98902; (509) 452-4200. Video, independent.
PRESIDENT, MANAGER & BUYER
Ric Webb

Wegmans Food Markets Inc.

1500 Brooks Ave., P.O. Box 844, Rochester, NY 14692; (716) 328-2550. Food stores, chain (37 stores).
ASSISTANT DIRECTOR, GENERAL MERCHANDISING
Kevin Kamholtz

Wilson's Video

213 E. Dakota, Pierre, SD 57501; (605) 224-0530. Video, independent.
PRESIDENT
Roger R. Wilson

Equipment Manufacturers

* **VIDEO MONITORS**

* **VIDEOCASSETTE RECORDERS**

* **VIDEOTAPE**

Video Monitors

Advanced Technology Division

(Subsidiary of ATD, Inc.)
6431 Independence Ave, Woodland Hills, CA 91367;
(818) 999-1393.
CORP. PRESIDENT
Kenneth K. Kaylor
DIRECTOR OF MARKETING
W. David Patton
NATIONAL SERVICE MANAGER
Charlie Shade

Amtron Corp.

2260 De La Cruz Blvd., Santa Clara, CA 95050; (408)
748-8500.
VICE PRESIDENT, RESEARCH/DEVELOPMENT
W. G. Widera
VICE PRESIDENT, SALES
L. Hamner

Asaca/Shibasoku Corp. of America

12509 Beatrice St., Los Angeles, CA 90066; (213)
827-7144, (800) 423-6347, Fax (213) 306-1382.
CORPORATE PRESIDENT
T. Shigezaki
VICE PRESIDENT & GENERAL MANAGER
Alan Davis
OPERATIONS MANAGER
Sumio Ohya

Ball Electronic Systems Division

(Subsidiary of Ball Corp.)
P.O. Box 589, 9300 W. 108 Circle, Broomfield, CO
80020-0589; (303) 457-5260.
CORPORATE PRESIDENT
Richard Ringeon
PRESIDENT
H. Robert Gill
VICE PRESIDENT, MARKETING
H. Jurgen Mammitzch
NATIONAL SALES MANAGER
Richard Scarle

Burle Industries, Inc.

(Formerly RCA Corporation, New Products Division)
Security Products Division, 1000 New Holland Ave.,
Lancaster, PA 17601-5688; (717) 295-6000.
EXECUTIVE V.P., SECURITY PRODUCTS DIV.
C. L. Rintz
VICE PRESIDENT, MARKETING, SECURITY PRODUCTS DIV.
G. S. Brody

Cetec Gauss

(Division of Cetec Corp.)
9130 Glenoaks Blvd., Sun Valley, CA 91352; (213)
875-1900. FAX: (818) 767-4479. Telex 194989.
CORPORATE PRESIDENT
Robert A. Nelson
PRESIDENT
James R. Williams

Cohu, Inc.

5755 Kearny Villa Rd., PO Box 85623, San Diego, CA
92138-5623; (619) 277-6700. Organized 1957. CCTV sys-
tem equipment—manufacturer and distributor.
PRESIDENT & CHIEF EXECUTIVE OFFICER
James W. Barnes
VICE PRESIDENT
A. Mack Rodgers
VICE PRESIDENT, FINANCE
Charles A. Schwan
BOARD OF DIRECTORS
William S. Ivans, William N. Jenkins, Jack M. Keeney, Charles L.
Blake, James W. Barnes, Gene E. Leary, Raymond C. Sebold, Frank
W. Davis, John E. Goode, Jr.
AFFILIATIONS
Cohu, Inc., Electronics, Division; Delta Design Inc.; BMS, Inc.;
FRL, Inc.

Cohu, Inc. Electronics Division

5755 Kearny Villa Rd., P.O. Box 85623, San Diego, CA
92138-5623; (619) 277-6700.
PRESIDENT & GENERAL MANAGER
James R. Brown
MARKETING MANAGER
John R. Foster
ENGINEERING MANAGER
William W. Steger
MANUFACTURING MANAGER
Gerald C. Samuel

Display Products Group, Conrac Corporation, A Mark IV Industries Company

1724 S. Mountain Ave., Duarte, CA 91010; (818) 303-
0095. Organized 1947. (Manufacturer and marketer of
precision video display monitors for the broadcast, computer graphics, medical imaging, and process control industries.)

Display Products Group

PRESIDENT
Vincent Hewitt
OPERATIONS MANAGER
Michael Taranto
MANAGER OF ENGINEERING
Monte Voigt
Q.A. MANAGER
Rey Roque
CONTOLLER
Michael Whitten
DIRECTOR OF PERSONNEL
Lou Tirapelle
DIRECTOR OF SALES—COMPUTER PRODUCTS
John Keenan
DIRECTOR OF SALES—BROADCAST
William A. Ems
DIRECTOR OF MARKETING AND SALES
Gene D. Ornstead
PRODUCT MARKETING MGR., COMPUTER PRODUCTS
Art Garcia
BOARD OF DIRECTORS (Mark IV Industries.)
Sal H. Alfiero, Clement R. Arrison, Joseph G. Donohoo, Gerald
S. Lippes, Esq; Herbert Roth, Jr.

Electrohome Limited

809 Wellington St., N., Kitchener, Ont., Canada
N2G 4J6; (519) 744-7111.
CHAIRMAN, PRESIDENT & CHIEF EXECUTIVE OFFICER
J. A. Pollock
CHIEF FINANCIAL OFFICER
J. G. Gingerich
VICE PRESIDENT, MOTORS
H. H. LaPier

VICE PRESIDENT, ELECTROHOME LIMITED, & PRESIDENT, C A P COMMUNICATIONS LIMITED
  W. D. McGregor
SECRETARY/TREASURER
  R. A. Bolden
VICE PRESIDENT, ELECTRONICS
  W. M. Nobbs
DIRECTOR HUMAN RESOURCES
  J. R. Boehmer

GBC CCTV Corp.

315 Hudson St., New York, NY 10013; (212) 989-4433, (800) 221-2240; (800) GBC-CCTV.
CORPORATE PRESIDENT
  Stephen Lefkowitz

Hitachi Denshi America

(Division of Hitachi Denshi)
175 Crossways Park W., Woodbury, NY 11797; (516) 921-7200.
CORPORATION PRESIDENT
  J. Tosaka
GENERAL MANAGER
  S. Hotta
VICE PRESIDENT, SALES
  Bernard V. Munzelle

Ikegami Electronics (U.S.A.), Inc.

37 Brook Ave., Maywood, NJ 07607; (201) 368-9171. Organized 1964. (Manufactures and markets professional TV cameras and monitors.)
PRESIDENT
  N. Nishi
SENIOR VICE PRESIDENT
  S. La Conte
VICE PRESIDENT (DISPLAY MONITOR DIVISION)
  Y. Sato
DIRECTOR, SALES & MARKETING
  H. Winch
COMMUNICATIONS MANAGER
  R. Estony
BRANCHES
  Northeast: 37 Brook Avenue, Maywood, NJ 07607; (201) 368-9171. John Chow, regional sales manager.
  Southeast: 6201 Johns Rd., Suite #5, Tampa, FL 33614; (813) 884-2046. John Webb, regional sales manager.
  Midwest: 747 Church Rd., Units C4 & C5, Elmhurst, IL 60126; (312) 834-9774. Bob Johnston, regional sales manager.
  West Coast: 23105 Kashiwa Ct., Torrance, CA 90505; (213) 534-0050. Bill Warnke, regional salesman.
  Southwest: Three Dallas Communications Complex, 6311 N. O'Connor Rd., Suite 100, Lock Box 100, Irving, TX 75039-3510; (214) 869-2363. Michael Mackin, sales mgr.
  Hawaii: Ward Industrial Center, 1020 Auahi St., Bldg. 7, Bay 3A, Honolulu, HI 96814; (808) 946-5955. Kuniko Yamashiro, office administrator.
  Networks and Canada: 37 Brook Ave., Maywood, NJ 07607; (201) 368-9171. Gordon Tubbs, regional sales manager.

Image Amplification Inc.

P.O. Box 699, 30 Chapin Rd., Pine Brook, NJ 07058; (201) 882-0584. Telex: 130236.
V.P. MARKETING & SALES
  A. C. Ginsburg

JVC/Professional Products Co.

(Division of US JVC Corp.)
41 Slater Dr., Elmwood Park, NJ 07407; (201) 794-3900.
PRESIDENT
  Shinzo Nakao
VICE PRESIDENT
  Daniel D. Roberts

Javelin Electronics, Inc.

19831 Magellan Dr., Torrance, CA 90502; (213) 327-7440, (800) 421-2716. Telex 19-444860 JAVELIN TRNC.
PRESIDENT
  Donald T. Heckel
SALES OPERATIONS MANAGER
  Michael M. Burton
NATIONAL SALES MANAGER
  Russ Mayworm

Lectrotech, Inc.

5810 N. Western Ave., Chicago, IL 60659; (312) 769-6262.
PRESIDENT
  William Grossman
VICE PRESIDENT
  Barry Grossman

Lenco, Inc.

Electronics Division, 300 N. Maryland St., Jackson, MO 63755; (314) 243-3147. TWX 910-760-1382. FAX: (314) 243-7122.
PRESIDENT
  Jerry Ford
GENERAL MANAGER
  Paul Gerlach
DIRECTOR, MARKETING
  Don Ford
NATIONAL SALES MANAGER
  Von Haney
NATIONAL SERVICE MANAGER
  Dave Aufdenberg

Matsushita Electric of Canada Ltd.

5770 Ambler Dr., Mississauga, Ont., L4W 2T3 Canada; (416) 624-5010.
CORPORATE PRESIDENT
  A. Higashi
MANAGER, AUDIO VIDEO SYSTEMS GROUP
  A. M. Evans
MANAGER, INDUSTRIAL VIDEO SYSTEMS DEPARTMENT
  J. McDonald
MANAGER, CLOSED CIRCUIT TELEVISION DEPT.
  E. Cameron
MANAGER, PROFESSIONAL AUDIO-VIDEO DEPT.
  A. M. Evans
NATIONAL PARTS MANAGER
  S. Wan
NATIONAL SERVICE MANAGER
  A. Gillespie

Mitsubishi Electronics of America, Inc.

(Division of Mitsubishi Electric.)
991 Knox St., Torrance, CA 90502; (213) 515-3993.
PRESIDENT
  Takeshi Sakurai
NATIONAL SALES MANAGER
  Don Arrons

NEC Home Electronics (USA) Inc.

(Video Products Division.)
1225 Michael Dr., Wood Dale, IL 60191-1094; (312) 860-9500.
PRESIDENT
  Yuzi Ohashi
SENIOR VICE PRESIDENTS
  Akira Sugiyama
  Stanley Gray
VICE PRESIDENT, SALES
  C. K. McCusker
DIRECTOR MARKETING
  Bob Hana

DIRECTOR, MERCHANDISING & PRODUCT PLANNING
  Brian Williams
SALES, VICE PRESIDENT
  K. McCusker
SENIOR VICE PRESIDENT, OEM
  A. Sugiyama
SENIOR VICE PRESIDENT, MANUFACTURING
  N. Maeda

Panasonic Broadcast Systems Company

(Subsidiary of Matsushita Electric Corp. of America.)
  One Panasonic Way, Secaucus, NJ 07094; (201) 348-7000.
PRESIDENT
  Stan Basara

Pioneer Video Inc.

  200 W. Grand Ave., Montvale, NJ 07645, (201) 573-1122.
PRESIDENT
  Ken Kai
DIRECTOR, SPECIAL MARKETS
  Brew Merrill

Quantel-Link Systems Group

  Pear Tree Lane, Newbury, Berkshire, Eng., RG 13 2LT; Tel.: 0635-521303; FAX: 0635-49207; TELEX: 846091 Q LINK G
CHIEF EXECUTIVE
  Stephen Christie
GENERAL MANAGER
  Malcolm Brock

Quasar Company

(Division of Matsushita Electric Corp. of America)
  1325 Pratt Blvd., Elk Grove Village, IL 60007; (312) 228-6366. Organized 1974. (Marketer of broad line of consumer electronics products.)
PRESIDENT
  Jack Pluckhan
EXECUTIVE VICE PRESIDENT
  Keith Nishikawa

RCA, New Products Division

  (See Burle Industries, Inc.)

Sharp Electronics Corporation

  P.O. Box 650, Sharp Plaza, Mahwah, NJ 07430; (201) 529-8200. Organized 1962 (in USA), 1912 (worldwide). (Manufacturer of quality electronics products for home, office, industrial and broadcast use.)
CHAIRMAN OF THE BOARD & DIRECTOR
  Mr. T. Mitsuda
PRESIDENT & DIRECTOR
  Mr. S. Hirooka
EXECUTIVE VICE PRESIDENT & DIRECTOR, CONSUMER
  Mr. C. Daigneault

EXECUTIVE VICE PRESIDENT & DIRECTOR, ADMINISTRATION
  Mr. K. Okuda
EXECUTIVE VICE PRESIDENT & DIRECTOR, INDUSTRIAL
  Mr. T. Tajima
SENIOR EXECUTIVE VICE PRESIDENT
  Mr. S. Okamato
BOARD OF DIRECTORS
  Mr. T. Mitsuda, Mr. S. Hirooka, Mr. S. Okamoto, Mr. C. Daigneault, Mr. K. Okuda
BRANCHES
  Atlanta, GA; Chicago, IL; Los Angeles, CA
AFFILIATION
  Wholly owned subsidiary of Sharp Corporation, Osaka, Japan.

Sony Video Communications

(Division of Sony Corp. of America.)
  Sony Dr., Park Ridge, NJ 07656; (201) 930-1000.
CORPORATE PRESIDENT
  Kenji Tamiya
PRESIDENT
  Philip J. Stack
VICE PRESIDENT, SALES
  Robert Mueller
NATIONAL SERVICE MANAGER
  Philip Hart

Tektronix, Inc.

  P.O. Box 500, Beaverton, OR 97077; (503) 627-7111. TWX 910-467-8708.
CORPORATE PRESIDENT
  Dave Friedley
GENERAL MANAGER
  Dan Castles
MARKETING MANAGER
  Steve Kerman
SALES MANAGER
  Austin Basso

Toshiba America, Inc.

  Corporate Headquarters: 375 Park Ave., Suite 1705, New York, NY 10152; (212) 308-2040; FAX: (212) 836-1179.
CHAIRMAN OF THE BOARD
  Noburo Ishizaka

Toshiba America, Inc.

CONSUMER PRODUCTS BUSINESS SECTOR
  82 Totowa Rd., Wayne, NJ 07470; (201) 628-8000. FAX: (201) 628-1875.
PRESIDENT
  Kenichico Hiyama
VICE PRESIDENT, NATIONAL SERVICE
  John Newman

Videotek, Inc.

  243 Shoemaker Rd., Pottstown, PA 14964; (215) 327-2292. TWX 710-653-0125.
CORPORATION PRESIDENT
  Philip G. Steyaert
VICE PRESIDENT, NATIONAL SALES MANAGER
  Peter H. Choi
NATIONAL SERVICE MANAGER
  Rick Hollowbush

Videocassette Recorders

Ampex Corp. Audio-Video Systems Division

401 Broadway, Redwood City, CA 94063; (415) 367-2011, TELEX 348464.
CORPORATE PRESIDENT
Max O. Mitchell
VICE PRESIDENT & GENERAL MANAGER, MARKETING SALES & SERVICE
Bob Wilson
MARKETING DIRECTOR
Bland McCartha
DIRECTOR, WORLDWIDE SALES & SERVICE
Pat Burns

Curtis Mathes

P.O. Box 2096, Athens, TX 75751; (800) 527-7646; (214) 675-2292.

Hitachi Denshi America

(Division of Hitachi Denshi)
175 Crossways Park W., Woodbury, NY 11797, (516) 921-7200.
CORPORATION PRESIDENT
J. Tosaka
GENERAL MANAGER
S. Hotta
VICE PRESIDENT, SALES
Bernard V. Munzelle

Ikegami Electronics (U.S.A.), Inc.

37 Brook Ave., Maywood, NJ 07607; (201) 368-9171. Organized 1964. (Manufactures and markets professional TV cameras and monitors.)
PRESIDENT
N. Nishi
SENIOR VICE PRESIDENT
S. La Conte
VICE PRESIDENT (DISPLAY MONITOR DIVISION)
Y. Sato
DIRECTOR, SALES & MARKETING
H. Winch
COMMUNICATIONS MANAGER
R. Estony
BRANCHES
Northeast: 37 Brook Ave., Maywood, NJ 07607; (201) 368-9171. John Chow, regional sales manager.
Southeast: 6201 Johns Road, Suite #5, Tampa, FL 33614; (813) 844-2046. John Webb, regional sales manager.
Midwest: 747 Church Rd., Units C4 & C5, Elmhurst, IL 60126; (312) 834-9774. Bob Johnston, regional sales manager.
West Coast: 23105 Kashiwa Court, Torrance, CA 90505; (213) 534-0050. Bill Warnke, regional sales manager.
Southwest: Three Dallas Communications Complex, 6311 North O'Connor Rd., Suite 100, Lock Box 100, Irving, TX 75039-3510; (214) 869-2363. Michael Mackin, sales manager.
Hawaii: Ward Industrial Center, 1020 Auahi St., Bldg. 7 Bay 3A, Honolulu, HI 96814; (808) 946-5955. Kuniko Yamashiro, office administrator.
Networks and Canada: 37 Brook Ave., Maywood, NJ 07607; (201) 368-9171. Gordon Tubbs, regional sales manager.

Instant Replay

2951 S. Bayshore Dr., Miami, FL 33133; (305) 448-7088. Organized 1976. (Manufactures specialized VCRs: RGB output, multistandard, built in caption decoder. VHS Hi Fi Multistd.)

PRESIDENT
Charles Azar
VICE PRESIDENT
Petra Azar

JVC Professional Products Company

(Division of U.S. JVC Corp.)
41 Slater Dr., Elmwood Park, NJ 07407; (201) 794-3900.
PRESIDENT
Shinzo Nakao
VICE PRESIDENT
Daniel D. Roberts

NEC Home Electronics (USA) Inc.

Video Products Division
1255 Michael Dr., Wood Dale, IL 60191-1094; (312) 860-9500.
PRESIDENT
Yuzi Ohashi
SENIOR VICE PRESIDENTS
Akira Sugiyama
Stan Gray
DIRECTOR, MARKETING
Robert Hana
DIRECTORS
Bob Hana
Brian Williams
SALES VICE PRESIDENT
C. K. McCusker
SENIOR VICE PRESIDENT, OEM
A. Sugiyama
SENIOR VICE PRESIDENT, MANUFACTURING
N. Maeda

Panasonic (Consumer Video Div.)

(Subsidiary of Matsushita Electric Corp. of America)
One Panasonic Way, Secaucus, NJ 07094; (201) 348-7000.
CORPORATE PRESIDENT
A. Imura
PRESIDENT
Stan Basara

Quasar Co.

(Division of Matsushita Electric Corp. of America)
1325 Pratt Blvd., Elk Grove Village, IL 60007; (312) 451-1200. Organized 1974. (Marketer of broad line of consumer electronics products.)
PRESIDENT
Jack Pluckhan
EXECUTIVE VICE PRESIDENT
Keith Nishikawa

Sanyo Electric Inc.

1200 W. Artesia Blvd., Compton, CA 90220; (213) 537-5830
CORPORATE PRESIDENT
T. Takyama
EXECUTIVE VICE PRESIDENT, SALES & MARKETING
Jeff Berkowitz
NATIONAL SERVICE MANAGER
Jose Balbin

Sony Video Communications

(Division of Sony Corp. of America.)
Sony Dr., Park Ridge, NJ 07656; (201) 930-1000.
CORPORATE PRESIDENT
Kenji Tamiya
PRESIDENT
Philip J. Stack
VICE PRESIDENT, SALES
Robert Mueller
NATIONAL SERVICE MANAGER
Philip Hart

Toshiba America, Inc.

Consumer Products Business Sector
82 Totowa Rd., Wayne, NJ 07470; (201) 628-8000. FAX:
(201) 628-1875.
PRESIDENT
Ken Hiyama
VICE PRESIDENT NATIONAL SERVICE
John Newman

Zenith Electronics Corporation

1000 Milwaukee Ave., Glenview, IL 60025; (312)
391-7000. (Color television, video cassette recorders,
camcorders, accessories, cable television decoders, teletext products, personal computers, high-resolution monitors, peripherals, high technology components and sub-
systems.)
CHAIRMAN & PRESIDENT
Jerry K. Pearlman
VICE PRESIDENT, GENERAL COUNSEL
John Borst, Jr.

VICE PRESIDENT, HUMAN RESOURCES & PUBLIC AFFAIRS
Michael J. Kaplan
CORPORATE CONTROLLER
Kell B. Benson
TREASURER
David S. Levin
SECRETARY
Dennis J. Waldeck
DIRECTOR, CORPORATE PUBLIC RELATIONS AND
COMMUNICATIONS
John I. Taylor
CONSUMER PRODUCTS GROUP
PRESIDENT, CONSUMER PRODS. GP.
Robert B. Hansen
PRES., ZENITH SALES CO.
Gerald M. McCarthy
VICE PRESIDENT, MARKETING
Bruce A. Huber
VICE PRESIDENT, MANUFACTURING
H. Vincent Kamler
VICE PRESIDENT, PURCHASING
Peter C. Skerlos
VICE PRESIDENT, PURCHASING
James A. Stark
PRESIDENT, ZENITH CABLE PRODUCTS
James L. Faust
COMPUTER GROUP
PRESIDENT COMPUTER GROUP
Carl A. Michelotti
PRESIDENT, ZENITH DATA SYSTEMS
John P. Frank
PRESIDENT, HEATH COMPANY
William E. Johnson
COMPONENTS GROUP
PRESIDENT, COMPONENTS GROUP
Otto M. Genutis
VICE PRESIDENT, VIDEO DISPLAY OPERATIONS
Michael S. Tamkin
CRT GROUP
PRESIDENT
Melvin L. Moore

Videotape

Agfa-Gevaert, Inc.

(Magnetic Tape Division)
100 Challenger Rd., Ridgefield Park, NJ 07660; (201) 440-2500.
CORPORATE PRESIDENT
 Robert A. M. Coppenrath
VICE PRESIDENT & GENERAL MANAGER
 Maria A. Curry
NATIONAL SALES MANAGER
 Andrew Da Puzzo
NATIONAL MARKETING MANAGER, AUDIO PRODUCTS
 Joe Tibensky
NATIONAL MARKETING MANAGER, VIDEO PRODUCTS
 Chris Emery
NATIONAL TECHNICAL MANAGER
 John Matarazzo
MARKETING COMMUNICATIONS MANAGER
 Teri Sosa

Ampex Corporation, Magnetic Tape Division

401 Broadway, M.S. 22-02, Redwood City, CA 94063; (415) 367-3809; Telex 345363.
CORPORATE PRESIDENT
 Max Mitchell
VICE PRESIDENT, DIVISION MANAGER
 Thomas J. Wheeler
DIRECTOR OF SALES AND CUSTOMER SERVICE
 Richard Antonio

Fuji Photo Film USA, Inc., Magnetic Products Division

555 Taxter Rd., Elmsford, NY 10523; (914) 789-8100. TELEX ITT 423298.
CORPORATE PRESIDENT
 Bernie Yasunaga
GENERAL MANAGER
 Stan Bauer

JVC Professional Products Company

(Division of U.S. JVC Corp.)
41 Slater Dr., Elmwood Park, NJ 07407; (201) 794-3900.
PRESIDENT
 Shinzo Nakao
VICE PRESIDENT
 Daniel D. Roberts

Magnetic Media Video Corp.

500 Eastern Parkway, Farmingdale, NY 11735; (516) 293-1010, Telex 14-3223.
VICE PRESIDENT, GENERAL MANAGER
 John Cristiano
VICE PRESIDENT, SALES MANAGER
 Paul Mastroianni

Matsushita Electric of Canada Ltd.

5770 Ambler Dr., Mississauga, Ont., L4W 2T3 Canada; (416) 624-5010.
CORPORATE PRESIDENT
 A. Higashi
MANAGER, INDUSTRIAL VIDEO DEPT.
 M. Ueda
MANAGER, AUDIO-VIDEO SYSTEMS GROUP
 A. M. Evans
MANAGER, INDUSTRIAL VIDEO SYSTEMS DEPT.
 J. McDonald
MANAGER, CLOSED CIRCUIT TELEVISION DEPT.
 E. Cameron
MANAGER, PROFESSIONAL AUDIO VIDEO DEPT.
 A. M. Evans
NATIONAL PARTS MANAGER
 S. Wan
NATIONAL SERVICE MANAGER
 A. Gillespie

Maxell Corp. of America

(Subsidiary of Hitachi)
60 Oxford Dr., Moonachie, NJ 07074; (201) 440-8020. Telex 134538.
CORPORATE PRESIDENT
 H. Matsumoto
VICE PRESIDENT, GENERAL MANAGER
 Ted Ozawa
NATIONAL SALES MANAGER, PROFESSIONAL/INDUSTRIAL PRODUCTS
 James J. Ringwood

Maxima Magnetics, Inc.

300 Bonair Ave., Hatboro, PA 19040; (215) 443-0700, (800) 3 MAXIMA. Organized 1982. (Sells blank video and audio tape to professional users.)
PRESIDENT
 William R. Goss
EXECUTIVE VICE PRESIDENT
 Susan R. Goss
VICE PRESIDENT, SALES AND MARKETING
 Carol M. Moore
BOARD OF DIRECTORS
 W.R. Goss, president; S.R. Goss, secretary/treasurer.

Panasonic Industrial Co.

(Subsidiary of Matsushita Electric Corp. of America)
One Panasonic Way, Secaucus, NJ 07094; (201) 348-7000.
CORPORATE PRESIDENT
 A. Imura

Sony Video Communications

(Division of Sony Corp. of America)
Sony Drive, Park Ridge, NJ 07656; (201) 930-1000.
CORPORATE PRESIDENT
 Kenji Tamiya
PRESIDENT
 Philip J. Stack
VICE PRESIDENT, SALES
 Robert Mueller
NATIONAL SERVICE MANAGER
 Philip Hart

Sunkyong International, Inc.

30 Congress Dr., Moonachie, NJ 07074; (201) 440-5006, Telex WU 642177.
VICE PRESIDENT, MARKETING
 George T. Saddler

TDK Electronics Corp.

12 Harbor Park Dr., Port Washington, NY 11050; (516) 625-0100, Telex 144535.

CORPORATION PRESIDENT
Takashi Tsujii
VICE PRESIDENT, SALES & MARKETING
Koyo Yokoi

Thor Electronics Corp.

321 Pennsylvania Ave., Linden, NJ 07036; (201) 486-3300. Telex 138968 THORLIND

CORPORATE PRESIDENT
Angelo Crudele
GENERAL MANAGER
Roy Gettis
MARKETING & SALES
D. Delane

NATIONAL PARTS MANAGER
Frank Destefano

3M/Magnetic Media Division

223-5S-01, 3M Center, St. Paul, MN 55125; (612) 733-1387. (Manufactures and sells blank audio and video cassettes, floppy disks, systems care products and accessories.)

DIVISION VICE PRESIDENT
D. Drew Davis
MARKETING DIRECTOR
Robert F. Burnett
MARKETING OPERATIONS MANAGER
George F. Burr

469

Consumer and Trade Publications

Quigley Publishing Company

Publishers of Motion Picture Almanac (Annual), Television and Video Almanac (Annual). 159 W. 53 St., New York, NY 10019; (212) 247-3100. Cable: Quigpubco, New York.

PRESIDENT & PUBLISHER
Martin Quigley, Jr.
EDITOR
Jane Klain
VICE PRESIDENT & EXECUTIVE DIRECTOR
Robert McDonald

LONDON BUREAU

William Pay, Manager and London Editor; 15 Samuel Road, Langdon Hills, Basildon, Essex, England; 0268-417-055.

CANADIAN BUREAU

Patricia Thompson, Editor; 1430 Yonge St., Suite 214, Toronto, Ontario M4T 1Y6 Canada; (416) 922-5772.

FOREIGN CORRESPONDENTS

CHILE: Alan Hootnick, Camino Mirasol 1955, Las Condes, Santiago, Chile.
EGYPT: Ahmed Sami, 4 El Ommara St., Apt. 13, Abbassia, Cairo.
FRANCE: Vernice Klier-Moskowitz, 80 Ave. Charles de Gaulle, Neuilly Sur Seine 92200 France.
GREECE: Rena Velissariou, 8432, Kolokotroni Str., Agia Paraskevi, Attikis, Athens. (804).
HOLLAND: Paul Silvius, 467 West Halfront, 1183 JD Amstelveen, Netherlands.
INDIA: B. R. Garga, 55 Anita, Mt. Pleasant Rd., Bombay 4 00006, India
JAPAN: A. C. Pinder, Whaley-Eaton, Service, Central P.O. Box 190, Tokyo, Japan.
PAKISTAN: A. R. Slote, P.O. Box 7426, Karachi 1-3.
SRI LANKA: Chandra Perera, 437 Pethiygoda, Kelanuja, Sri Lanka, Ceylon.
SWITZERLAND: Gabriella Broggi, Via E. Maraini 20 B, 6900 Massagnas, Switzerland

Motion Picture Almanac

(Annually) 159 W. 53 St., New York, NY 10019; (212) 247-3100; Cable: Quigpubco, New York.

EDITOR
Jane Klain
BRITISH EDITOR
William Pay
CANADIAN EDITOR
Patricia Thompson

Television & Video Almanac

(Annually) 159 W. 53 St., New York, NY 10019; (212) 247-3100; Cable: Quigpubco, New York.

EDITOR
Jane Klain
BRITISH EDITOR
William Pay
CANADIAN EDITOR
Patricia Thompson

artsAmerica, Inc. Fine Art Film & Video Source Book

12 Havemeyer Pl., Greenwich, CT 06830; (203) 869-4693. Organized 1984. (Publisher of artsAmerica Fine Art Film & Video Source Book)

PRESIDENT
Browyn Dunne

DIRECTOR
Dorothy Tucker
BOARD OF ADVISORS
Philip Eliasoph, Ph.D., Mary Delahoyd, John Sharnik, Robert Sturgeon, Marilyn Baron.

Back Stage

(See Television Press Section)

Back Stage Television, Film, Tape & Production Directory

(See Television Press Section)

Billboard

(See Television Press Section)

Classic Images

Box 809, Muscatine, IA 52671; (319) 263-2331.

Coming Attractions

(Published monthly by Star Video Entertainment LP and distributed to 2000 video stores.)

550 Grand St., Jersey City, NJ 07302; (201) 333-4600.
PUBLISHER
Carla Edwards

Daily Variety

(See Television Press Section)

Electronic Media

(Weekly publication covering the broadcast TV industry including radio, cable and video.) Crain Communications Inc., 740 N. Rush St., Chicago, IL 60611, (312) 649-5293.

Entertainment Business Media

1700 E. Dyer Rd., Suite 250, Santa Ana, CA 92715; (714) 250-8060. Organized 1979. (Publishes entertainment business and video magazines). Department of HBJ Publications, division of Harcourt Brace, Jovanovich, Inc.

PUBLISHER
David Rowe
PUBLISHER
Tom Adams

Hollywood Reporter, The

(See Television Press Section)

Home Video Publisher

(Weekly, analyzing home video publishing opportunities for special interest programming and feature film.) Knowledge Industry Publications, Inc., 701 Westchester Ave., White Plains, NY 10604; (914) 328-9157.

EXECUTIVE EDITOR
Leslie Grey

Home Viewer

11 N. Second St., Philadelphia, PA 19106; (215) 629-1588.

In Motion Film & Video Production Magazine

(Film and video production trade magazine published 12 times a year.) 421 Fourth St., Annapolis, MD 21403; (301) 269-0605.
EDITOR & PUBLISHER
Steve Lehuray

Independent Film & Video Makers Guide

(Guidebook for the independent film and video maker.) Michael Wiese Film Productions, P.O. Box 406, Westport, CT 06881; (203) 226-6979. Also publishes: Film & Video Budgets and Home Video: Producing for the Home Market (video distributing and marketing book); Fade In: The Screenwriting Process; Hollywood Gift Catalog (comedy book); Goin' Hollywood; The Movie-Making Game (game board).

Instant Replay Video Magazine

2951 S. Bayshore Dr., Miami, FL 33133; (305) 448-7088. Organized 1976. (Videotape magazine format about the video industry and TV Broadcasting. Sold on subscription basis. Available in 3/4" and 1/2" Beta and VHS and 8 mm.)
PUBLISHER
Charles Azar

Millimeter

(Published monthly. Motion picture and TV production industry magazine.) 826 Broadway, New York, NY 10003; (212) 477-4700.

Optic Music's Film & Video Production

(A monthly international film and video production magazine.) Organized 1983. 800 S. Robertson Blvd., Suite 7, Los Angeles, CA 90035; (213) 652-2067.
PUBLISHER/PRESIDENT
David Swartz
SECRETARY/ASSOCIATE PUBLISHER/MANAGING EDITOR
Paula Swartz
VICE PRESIDENT/DIRECTOR OF ADVERTISING
Steven Rich

Photo Business

(Photographic trade publication.) Organized 1956. Published by Billboard Publications, Inc., 1515 Broadway, New York, NY 10036; (212) 536-5193.
EDITOR & ASSOCIATE PUBLISHER
Willard Clark
ASSOCIATE PUBLISHER, MARKETING & SALES
Doris Burke
MANAGING EDITOR
Richard Brandes
PRODUCTION MANAGER
Phyllis Hall

The Producer's Masterguide

(See Television Press Section)

Rockamerica Magazine

(Monthly magazine dealing with the music industry.) 27 E. 21 St., New York, NY 10010; (212) 475-5791.

Show Business

1501 Broadway, Suite 2900, New York, NY 10036. Organized 1941. (Trade paper.)
OWNER
Leo Shull

Tape Business

(Monthly news publication). Published by Knowledge Industry Publications, Inc., 701 Westchester Ave., White Plains, NY 10604; (914) 328-9157.
EXECUTIVE EDITOR
Leslie Grey

Television Digest

(See Television Press Section)

TWICE (This Week in Consumer Electronics)

902 Broadway, New York, NY 10010; (212) 447-2200. Organized 1986. (Weekly news magazine.)
PUBLISHER
Marsha Grand
PRESIDENT
Richard Ekstract
EDITORIAL DIRECTOR
Robert Gerson

Variety

(See Television Press Section)

Video

(Monthly consumer magazine covering hardware, video technology and its impact on lifestyles, and programming.) Published by Reese Communications, 460 W. 34 St., 20th floor, New York, NY 10001; (212) 947-6500. Organized 1978.
PRESIDENT & MANAGING DIRECTOR
Jay Rosenfield
PUBLISHER
Debra Halpert
EDITOR
Judith H. Sawyer

Video Business

(Published 4 times per year by parent company International Thomson Retail Press. A business-to-business magazine for video dealers.) 345 Park Ave. S., 6th floor, New York, NY 10010; (212) 686-7744. Organized 1981.
PUBLISHER
Bill O'Brien
EDITOR
John Gaffney
PRESIDENT & CHIEF EXECUTIVE OFFICER
Robert B. Doll
VICE PRESIDENT/CORP. EDITORIAL DIRECTOR
Art Levis
EASTERN ADVERTISING
Stacey Kelley
WESTERN ADVERTISING
Mitchell Wallis
Robert O'Connor

Video Insider

(Weekly news magazine for the video industry.) 223 Conestoga Rd., Wayne, PA 19087; (215) 688-7030.

Video Marketing Newsletter

(24 issues a year. News service for marketers of consumer video programs and hardware.) 1680 Vine St., Suite 820, Hollywood, CA 90028; (213) 462-6350.

The Video Register and Teleconferencing Resources Directory

(Annual. Directory listing organizations using video—manufacturers, dealers, program distributors, consultants/producers, production facilities.) Published by Knowledge Industry Publications, Inc., 701 Westchester Ave., White Plains, NY 10604; (914) 328-9157.

Video Review Magazine

(Monthly. Home video consumer magazine.) Published by Viare Publishing, 902 Broadway, New York, NY 10010; (212) 477-2200.

The Video Source Book

(A listing of more than 50,000 programs available on video tape from more than 1200 sources.) The National Video Clearinghouse, Inc., 100 Lafayette Dr., Syosset, NY 11791; (516) 364-3686.

Video Store Magazine

(Monthly. Provides information to video retailers nationally on new releases, trends in the industry, industry statistics and promotional ideas.) 1700 E. Dyer Rd., #250, Santa Ana, CA 92705; (714) 250-8060. Organized 1979.
PRESIDENT OF PUBLICATIONS
Richard Moeller
GROUP PUBLISHER
Eileen Paulin
PUBLISHER
David Allen Shaw
EDITOR
Frank Moldstad
NATIONAL ADVERTISING SALES MANAGER
Colette Kreins
BRANCH
545 Fifth Ave., New York, NY 10017; (212) 503-2949.

Video Systems Magazine

9221 Quivira Rd., Overland Park, KS 66215; (913) 888-4664. Organized 1975. (How-to magazine for video professionals, serving the corporate/industrial video marketplace.)
SENIOR MANAGING EDITOR
Tom Cook
EDITOR
Ned Soseman
EDITORIAL DIRECTOR
Jerry Whitaker

PUBLISHER
Duane Hefner
GROUP VICE PRESIDENT
Cameron Bishop
TECHNICAL EDITOR
Rick Lehtinen
AD PRODUCTION MANAGER
Pat Eisenman
AFFILIATIONS
Member: American Business Press; Business Publications Audit of Circulation; Acoustical Society of America; International Television Assn; Professional Film and Video Equipment Association.

Video Tape and Disc Guide to Home Entertainment

(Updated reference guide containing titles and descriptive information about 10,000 available videocassettes and discs for the consumer market.) Published by National Video Clearinghouse, Inc., 100 Lafayette Dr., Syosset, NY 11791; (516) 364-3686.

Video Trade News

(Monthly—for manufacturers and dealers who sell professional video equipment.) Published by C.S. Tepfer Publishing Co. Inc., 56 Branchville Rd., Ridgefield, CT 06877; (203) 438-7224.

Video Vision Magazine

9241 S.W. 12th St., Miami, FL 33174; (305) 262-1505. Organized 1984. (Nationally circulated bilingual video magazine for the Hispanic market.)
PRESIDENT
Lomberto Perez
VICE PRESIDENT
Cary M. Perez

Video Week

(Weekly. Newsletter covering the business of program sales and distribution for videocassettes, disc, pay TV and news media.) Published by Warren Publishing, Inc. 2115 Ward Court N.W., Washington, D.C. 20037; (202) 872-9200.

Videography Magazine

(Monthly. Professional video production trade magazine.) Organized 1976. 50 W. 23 St., New York, NY 10010; (212) 645-1000.
PUBLISHER
John Rice
EDITOR
Brian McKernan
BRANCHES
Media Horizons, 360 N. Michigan Ave., Chicago, IL 60601.
Media Horizons, 5455 Wilshire Blvd., Los Angeles, CA 90036.

Trade Associations

American Video Association

557 E. Juanita Ave., Suite #3, Mesa, AR 85204; (602) 892-8553. Organized 1980. (National retailer owned and operated co-op. Provides buying, merchandising, and informational services to independent video dealers. Sponsors annual convention. Publishes weekly newsletter and price references.)

CHAIRMAN
Danny Shull
PRESIDENT
John Power
SECRETARY/TREASURER
Jerry Ulibarri
BOARD MEMBERS
Danny Shull, John Power, Frank Curreri, Nate Sherer, Tom Daugherty, Roger Barielle, William Patterson, Ken Hosteter, Bill Mitchell

Association of Independent Video and Filmmakers

625 Broadway, 9th floor, New York, NY 10012; (212) 473-3400. (Provides advocacy and professional services for the independent media community.)

EXECUTIVE DIRECTOR
Lawrence Sapadin
MEMBERSHIP/PROGRAMMING DIRECTOR
Ethan Young
FESTIVAL BUREAU DIRECTOR
Kathryn Bowser
BUSINESS MANAGER
Morton Marks
BOARD OF DIRECTORS
Rachel Field (chair), Robert Richter (president), Loni Ding (vice president), Wendy Lidell (secretary), Richard Lorber (treasurer), Robert Aaronson, Adrianne Benton, Christine Choy, Regge Life, Deanna Morse, Barton Weiss

Association of Visual Communicators, Inc.

900 Palm Ave., Suite Room B, S. Pasadena, CA 91030, (818) 441-2274. (Promotes and encourages excellence in the informational audio-visual industry.)

EXECUTIVE DIRECTOR
Chris Carlisle
NATIONAL PRESIDENT
Patricia Rye
DATE OF ORGANIZATION
1957

International Tape/Disc Association

505 Eighth Ave., New York, NY 10018; (212) 643-0620.

CHAIRMAN OF THE BOARD
J. Philip Stack
PRESIDENT
Alfred Markim
SENIOR VICE PRESIDENT
Maria A. Curry
VICE PRESIDENTS
R. Patrick Leonard, Jr.
Nicholas Santrizos
EUROPEAN VICE PRESIDENT
Andrew Bourne
TREASURER
Larry Finley
EXECUTIVE VICE PRESIDENT
Henry Brief
BOARD OF DIRECTORS
Officers are the following: Frank Day, Jurgen Blank, Howard Schwartz, James Fiedler, R. Stanton Bauer, Michael Upton, Daniel Roberts, James MacKay, Donald Winquist, James Ringwood, Peter Pirner, Bud O'Shea, Drew Davis, Reg Childs, Steve Yuhas, Roel Buis, Larry Bennett, Tony Gelardi, Keizo Ito, Daniel Grynberg
DATE OF ORGANIZATION
1970

International Communications Industries Association (ICIA)

3150 Spring St., Fairfax, VA 22031; (703) 273-7200. (A trade association of the communications technologies industry dedicated to expanding and improving communications methods through the effective use of all types of media. As communications technologies become increasingly advanced and more widely used, ICIA members strive to help the world use these technologies more efficiently and cost-effectively.)

CHAIRMAN OF THE BOARD
Jerome Raymond
PRESIDENT
Thomas Roberts
PRESIDENT-ELECT
Edward Goodman
VICE PRESIDENT
Robert Mueller
SECRETARY-TREASURER
John Moore, Jr.
EXECUTIVE VICE PRESIDENT
Harry R. McGee
DATE OF ORGANIZATION
1939

International Teleproduction Society, Inc.

990 Ave. of the Americas, Suite 21E, New York, NY 10018; (212) 629-3266. (Not-for-profit international trade association. Promotes and furthers excellence in the use of video as a medium of communication; provides a source of information and education regarding video production and a forum for exchange of ideas. Establishes one unified voice which addresses common goals.)

EXECUTIVE DIRECTOR
Janet Luhrs
BOARD OF DIRECTORS
Tom Angell (president); Sam Holtz, executive vice president; Ron Herman, vice president; Dick Millais, vice president; Lou Di Giusto, secretary; Robert Henderson, treasurer; Walter Hamilton, Steve Carlisle, Jim Harmon, Scott Kane, Stan Kronquest, Dan McGuire, board members.
CHAPTERS
New York, Mid-Atlantic, Michigan, Chicago, Southern California, Northern California, Toronto

International Television Association

6311 N. O'Connor Rd., LB51, Irving, TX 75039; (214) 869-1112. (Furthers the development of the professional video communicator; has 90 chapters in USA and 10 affiliates in foreign countries.)

PRESIDENT 1988–89
Len Magsamen
PRESIDENT ELECT 1988–89
Joe Maiella
VICE PRESIDENT 1988–89
Beverly Hare
EXECUTIVE DIRECTOR
Fred Wehrli
CHAIRMAN OF THE BOARD 1988–89
Michael Schwarz
DATE OF ORGANIZATION
1973

National Association of Video Distributors

1255 23rd St. NW, Suite 850, Washington DC 20037; (202) 452-8100. Organized 1983. (Promotes and enhances the video distribution industry.)

DIRECTOR, MEMBER SERVICES
Mark T. Engle

National Federation of Local Cable Programmers

P.O. Box 27290, Washington, DC 20038-7290; (202) 829-7189.
EXECUTIVE DIRECTOR
vacant

New York Women in Film

(see Television Organizations)

Video Software Dealers Association

3 Eves Drive, Suite 307, Marlton, NJ 08053; (609) 596-8500.
PRESIDENT 1988–89
Lou Berg

EXECUTIVE VICE PRESIDENT
Mickey Granberg
VICE PRESIDENT
Gary Messenger
TREASURER
David Ballstad
SECRETARY
Brad Burnside

Videotape Production Association, Inc.

565 Fifth Ave., New York, NY 10017; (212) 986-1414.
CHAIRMAN OF BOARD
Morton Dubin
PRESIDENT, NEW YORK CHAPTER
Joe DiBuono
EXECUTIVE DIRECTOR
Janet Luhrs

Video Services

* **ANIMATION**

* **AUDIO MIXING & SWEETENING**

* **CLEANING & EVALUATION OF TAPES**

* **DUPLICATION**

* **EDITING & POST PRODUCTION**

* **EQUIPMENT—SALES & RENTAL**

* **EQUIPMENT REPAIR**

* **MOBILE UNITS**

* **PRODUCTION STUDIOS & STAGES**

* **SCREENING ROOMS**

* **TRANSFERS—FILM TO TAPE**

* **TRANSFERS—TAPE TO FILM**

Videotape Animation

LOS ANGELES

ACTION VIDEO, 6616 Lexington Ave., Los Angeles, CA 90038; (213) 461-3611; FAX: 460-4023.

AMERICAN VIDEO FACTORY, 4150 Glencoe Ave., Marina Del Rey, CA 90292; (213) 823-8622, (800) 367-8433.

AUDIO-VIDEO CRAFT, INC., 6753 Santa Monica Blvd., Los Angeles, CA 90038; (213) 655-3511.

BERC, BROADCAST EQUIPMENT RENTAL COMPANY, 4545 Chermak St., Burbank, CA 91505; (818) 841-3000, (213) 464-7655.

BOSUSTOW VIDEO, 2207 Colby Ave., W. Los Angeles, CA 90064-1504; (213) 478-0821.

CALIFORNIA COMMUNICATIONS, INC., 6900 Santa Monica Blvd., Los Angeles, CA 90038; (213) 466-8511.

CALIFORNIA VIDEO CENTER, 15303 Ventura Blvd., Sherman Oaks, CA 91403; (818) 789-5000.

COTTON CANDY/EYE ON VIDEO, 224 N. Juanita Ave., Los Angeles, CA 90004; (213) 382-4048.

DEVONSHIRE AUDIO/VIDEO STUDIOS, 10729 Magnolia Blvd., N. Hollywood, CA 91601; (818) 985-1945.

GORDON, ALAN, ENTERPRISES, INC., 1430 Cahuenga Blvd., Hollywood, CA 90028; (213) 466-3561; (818) 985-5500.

HAMM, GENE, & ASSOCIATES, 6547 DeLongpre Ave., Los Angeles, CA 90028; (213) 465-2289.

HORIZONTAL EDITING STUDIOS, 2625 W. Olive Ave., Burbank, CA 91505; (818) 841-6750.

IMAGE WEST, 11846 Ventura Blvd., Studio City, CA 91604; (818) 506-5577.

INTER VIDEO, 733 N. Victory Blvd., Burbank, CA 91502; (818) 843-3633; (818) 569-4000.

JP VIDEO SERVICE BETA CAM PRODUCTIONS, 9538 W. Pico Blvd., Los Angeles, CA 90035; (213) 859-9903; 271-1209.

MILLER, FRITZ, ANIMATION/GRAPHICS, 10806 Ventura Blvd., Suite 11, Studio City, CA 91604; (818) 985-6074.

MISKIN, LEE, ANIMATION, 1463 Tamarind Ave., Hollywood, CA 90028; (213) 461-5977.

MULTI-MEDIA WORKS, 7227 Beverly Blvd., Los Angeles, CA 90036; (213) 939-1185.

NEWMAN/FRANKS, 2956 Nicada Dr., Los Angeles, CA 90077; (213) 470-0140; 470-0145.

PACIFIC TITLE & ART STUDIO, 6350 Santa Monica, Hollywood, CA 90038; (213) 464-0121.

PACIFIC VIDEO, 809 N. Cahuenga Blvd., Los Angeles, CA 90038; (213) 462-6266.

PAINT BOX PLUS, 6464 Sunset Blvd., Suite 1000, Hollywood, CA 90028; (213) 856-8530.

THE POST GROUP, 6335 Homewood Ave., Los Angeles, CA 90028; (213) 462-2300.

SABAN PRODUCTIONS, INC., 11724 Ventura Blvd., Studio City, CA 91604; (818) 985-3805.

SCHULMAN VIDEO CENTER, 861 Seward St., Hollywood, CA 90038; (213) 465-8110.

SUNBREAK PRODUCTIONS, 256 S. La Cienega Blvd., Beverly Hills, CA 90211; (213) 659-2324.

TELEMEDIA PRODUCTIONS, 18321 Ventura Blvd., Suite 660, Tarzana, CA 91356.

VARITEL VIDEO, 3575 Cahuenga Blvd. W., Los Angeles, CA 90068; (213) 850-1165.

VID-U PRODUCTIONS, 612 N. Sepulveda Blvd., Los Angeles, CA 90049; (213) 472-7023.

VIDEO IMAGE, 4121 Redwood Ave., Suite 215, Los Angeles, CA 90066; (213) 822-8872.

NEW YORK

ANIMATED VIDEO, 1600 Broadway, New York, NY 10019; (212) 265-2942.

CHARLEX, 2 W. 45 St., New York, NY 10036; (212) 719-4600.

COMP ART PLUS, 12 W. 27 St., New York, NY 10001; (212) 689-8670.

COM/TECH, 770 Lexington Ave., New York, NY 10021; (212) 826-2935.

DEVLIN PRODUCTIONS INC., 1501 Broadway, New York, NY 10036; (212) 391-1313.

DIGIMATION, INC., 10 E. 40th St., New York, NY 10016; (212) 213-6098.

DOLPHIN PRODUCTIONS, 140 E. 80 St., New York, NY 10021; (212) 628-5930.

EDITEL, 222 E. 44 St., New York, NY 10017; (212) 867-4600.

THE FANTASTIC ANIMATION MACHINE, INC., 12 E. 46 St., New York, NY 10017; (212) 697-2525.

MTI TV CITY, 1443 Park Ave., New York, NY 10029; (212) 722-1818.

MAGNO SOUND & VIDEO, 729 Seventh Ave., New York, NY 10019; (212) 302-2505.

MODERN TELECOMMUNICATIONS INC., 1443 Park Ave., New York, NY 10029; (212) 722-1818.

NAPOLEON VIDEOGRAPHICS, 460 W. 42nd ST., New York, NY 10036; (212) 279-2000.

NORTHEAST VIDEO, INC., 420 Lexington Ave., New York, NY 10017; (212) 661-8830.

RVI/RUTT VIDEO, 137 E. 25 St., New York, NY 10010; (212) 685-4000.

STARGATE PRODUCTIONS, INC., 231 W. 55th St., New York, NY 10022; (212) 333-3636.

SYNAPSE TELECOMMUNICATIONS, INC., 304 E. 45th St., New York, NY 10017; (212) 370-9191.

TELETECHNIQUES, INC., 1 W. 19th St., New York, NY 10011; (212) 206-1475; 633-1868.

TODAY VIDEO, 45 W. 45th St., New York, NY 10036; (212) 391-1020.

TRILOGY DESIGN AT JSL, INC., 25 W. 45th St., New York, NY 10036; (212) 382-3592.

UNITEL VISUAL DYNAMICS, 515 W. 57 St., New York, NY 10019; (212) 265-3600.

VIDEO WORKS, 24 W. 40 St., New York, NY 10018; (212) 869-2500.

VISUAL CREATIONS, INC., 305 E. 46 St., New York, NY 10017; (212) 935-0145.

WINDSOR TOTAL VIDEO, 8 W. 38th St., New York, NY 10018; (212) 944-9090.

SAN FRANCISCO

ONE PASS FILM & VIDEO, One China Basin Bldg., San Francisco, CA 94107; (415) 777-5777.

Video Audio Mixing & Sweetening

LOS ANGELES

ALTAVIDEO, 3501 Cahuenga Blvd. W., Los Angeles, CA 90068; (213) 876-8008.

AMERICAN VIDEO FACTORY, 4150 Glencoe Ave., Marina Del Rey, CA 90292; (213) 823-8622; (800) 367-8433.

AUDIO ACHIEVEMENTS RECORDING STUDIO, 1327 Cabrillo Ave., Torrance, CA 90501; (213) 533-9531.

AUDIO ARTS PUBLISHING CO., 5617 Melrose Ave., Los Angeles, CA 90038; (213) 461-3507.

AUDIO POST, 3755 Cahuenga Blvd. W., Suite C, Studio City, CA 91604; (818) 761-5220.

AUDIO RENTS INC., 7237 Santa Monica Blvd., Hollywood, CA 90046; (213) 874-1000.

AUDIO-VIDEO CRAFT INC., 6753 Santa Monica Blvd., Los Angeles, CA 90038; (213) 655-3511.

AUDIO VISUAL HEADQUARTERS CORP., 361 N. Oak St., Inglewood, CA 90302; (213) 419-4040.

BLUE DOLPHIN STUDIO, 650 N. Bronson Ave., Hollywood, CA 90004; (213) 467-7660.

BURBANK STUDIOS, 4000 Warner Blvd., Burbank, CA 91522; (818) 954-6000.

BUZZY'S RECORDING SERVICES, 6900 Melrose Ave., Los Angeles, CA 90038; (213) 931-1867.

CFI, 959 Seward St., Hollywood, CA 90038; (213) 462-3161.

CALIFORNIA COMMUNICATIONS INC., 6900 Santa Monica Blvd., Los Angeles, CA 90038; (213) 466-8511.

CALIFORNIA RECORDING & VIDEO, 5203 Sunset Blvd., Los Angeles, CA 90027; (213) 666-1244.

CANDLEWICK PRODUCTIONS, 1161 N. Highland Blvd., Hollywood, CA 90038; (213) 462-7979.

CARMEN PRODUCTIONS, INC., 15456 Cabrito Rd., Van Nuys, CA 91406; (213) 873-7370; (818) 787-6436.

COMPACT SOUND SERVICES, 2813 W. Alameda Ave., Burbank, CA 91505; (818) 840-7000.

COMPACT VIDEO SERVICES, INC., 2813 W. Alameda Ave., Burbank, CA 91505; (818) 840-7000.

CONSOLIDATED FILM INDUSTRIES, 959 Seward St., Los Angeles, CA 90038; (213) 462-3161.

CREST NATIONAL FILM & VIDEOTAPE LABS, 1141 N. Seward St., Los Angeles, CA 90038; (213) 466-0624; 462-6696.

CRYSTAL SOUND RECORDING, 1014 N. Vine St., Los Angeles, CA 90038; (213) 466-6452.

DSR PRODUCTION, 607 N. 64th St., Los Angeles, CA 90042; (213) 258-6741.

DEVONSHIRE SOUND STUDIOS, 10729 Magnolia Blvd., North Hollywood, CA 91601; (818) 985-1945.

DIGITAL SOUND RECORDING, 607 N. Ave. 64, Los Angeles, CA 90042; (213) 258-6741.

EYE ON VIDEO, 224 N. Juanita Ave., Los Angeles, CA 90004; (213) 382-4048.

FIDELITY RECORDING STUDIO, 4412 Whitsett Ave., Studio City, CA 91604; (818) 508-3263.

FOX TAPE, 5746 Sunset Blvd., Los Angeles, CA 90028; (213) 856-1000.

GRACE & WILD STUDIOS, 3501 Cahuenga Blvd. West, Los Angeles, CA 90068; (213) 876-8008.

GROUP IV RECORDING, 1541 N. Wilcox Ave., Los Angeles, CA 90028; (213) 466-6444.

GROUP W CABLE VIDEO PRODUCTION CENTER, 2939 Nebraska Ave., Santa Monica, CA 90404; (213) 829-2676; 829-5111.

HARMONY GOLD USA, INC., 8831 Sunset Blvd., Suite 300, Los Angeles, CA 90069; (213) 652-8720.

HARRIS, CRAIG (sound composer), P.O. Box 110, N. Hollywood, CA 91603; (818) 508-8000.

HIT CITY, 6146 W. Pico Blvd., Los Angeles, CA 90035; (213) 852-0186.

HOLLYWOOD NATIONAL STUDIOS, 6605 Eleanor Ave., Los Angeles, CA 90038; (213) 467-6272.

HOLLYWOOD SOUND SYSTEMS, 7237 Santa Monica Blvd., West Hollywood, CA 90046; (213) 466-2416.

HOMER & ASSOCIATES, INC., Sunset Gower Studios, 1420 Beachwood Dr., Hollywood, CA 90028; (213) 462-4710.

HORIZONTAL EDITING STUDIOS, 2625 W. Olive Ave., Burbank, CA 91505; (818) 841-6750.

INSTITUTE OF AUDIO/VIDEO ENGINEERING, 1831 Hyperion Ave., Hollywood, CA 90027; (213) 666-3003.

INTERLOK STUDIOS, 1522 Crossroads of the World, Hollywood, CA 90028; (213) 469-3986.

INTERMIX, INC., 2505 S. Robertson Blvd., Los Angeles, CA 90034; (213) 870-2121.

INTERSOUND, INC., 8746 Sunset Blvd., Los Angeles, CA 90069; (213) 652-3741.

INTEX AUDIOVISUALS, 9021 Melrose Ave., Suite 205, Los Angeles, CA 90069; (213) 275-9571; FAX: (213) 271-1319.

KEY WEST, 5701 Buckingham Parkway, Suite C, Culver City, CA 90230; (213) 645-3348.

LAJON PRODUCTIONS INC. 2907 W. Olive Ave., Burbank, CA 91505; (818) 841-1440.

LION SHARE RECORDING STUDIOS, 8255 Beverly Blvd., Los Angeles, CA 90048; (213) 658-5990.

M.F.I. VIDEO CENTER, 1905 Grace Ave., Hollywood, CA 90068; (213) 851-0373.

MASTER DIGITAL INC., 1749 14th St., Santa Monica, CA 90404; (213) 452-1511.

MEDIA MASTERS PRODUCTIONS, 1800 S. Robertson Blvd., Suite 306, Beverly Hills, CA 90035, (213) 451-8823.

MERIDIAN, P.O. Box 1941, Hollywood, CA 90028; (213) 874-4367.

METAVISION, 347 S. Ogden Dr., Suite 220, Los Angeles, CA 90036; (213) 936-8281.

MODERN VIDEOFILM, 7165 Sunset Blvd., Hollywood, CA 90046; (213) 851-8070; FAX: (213) 851-0704.

MUSIC LAB INC., 1831 Hyperion Ave., Hollywood, CA 90027; (213) 666-3003.

NEWMAN/FRANKS, 2956 Nicada Dr., Los Angeles, CA 90077; (213) 470-0140; 470-0145.

ONE PASS FILM & VIDEO, One China Basin Building, San Francisco, CA 94107; (415) 777-5777.

PACIFIC VIDEO, 809 N. Cahuenga Blvd., Los Angeles, CA 90038; (213) 462-6266.

PARAMOUNT RECORDING STUDIOS, 6245 Santa Monica Blvd., Hollywood, CA 90038; (212) 461-3717.

POSITIVE MEDIA, 5422 A. Fair Ave., North Hollywood, CA 91601; (818) 461-0092.

THE POST GROUP, 6335 Homewood Ave., Los Angeles, CA 90028; (213) 462-2300.

POWERHOUSE AUDIO/VIDEO, 19347 Londelius St., Northridge, CA 91324; (818) 993-4778.

PRO VIDEO/CINETAPE, 801 N. La Brea Ave., Los Angeles, CA 90038; (213) 934-8836.

PRECISION FOLEY & ADR., 6353 Homewood Ave., Hollywood, CA 90028; (213) 462-8235.

PREMORE INC., 5130 Klump Ave., North Hollywood, CA 91601; (818) 506-7714.

ROCK SOLID PRODUCTIONS, 801 S. Main St., Burbank, CA 91506; (818) 841-8220.

ROLAND, GLENN, FILMS, 10711 Wellworth Ave., Los Angeles, CA 90024; (213) 475-0937.

RUBBER DUBBERS, INC., 626 Justin Ave., Glendale, CA 91201; (818) 241-5600.

RUSK SOUND STUDIO, 1556 N. La Brea Ave., Hollywood, CA 90028; (213) 462-6477.

RYDER SOUND SERVICES, INC., 1611 N. Vine St., Los Angeles, CA 90038; (213) 469-3511.

SAR PRODUCTIONS, 22801 Ventura Blvd., Suite 211, Woodland Hills, CA 91364; (818) 884-5646.

SALTY DOG RECORDING STUDIO, 14511 Delano St., Van Nuys, CA 91411; (818) 994-9973.

SCHULMAN VIDEO CENTER, 861 Seward St., Hollywood, CA 90038; (213) 465-8110.

SCOTTSOUND INC., 6110 Santa Monica Blvd., Los Angeles, CA 90038; (213) 462-6981.

SIERRA VIDEO, 11320 Chandler, N. Hollywood, CA 91601; (818) 985-1531; 579-7045.

SKYLAND SOUND, INC., 8611 Lookout Mountain Ave., Los Angeles, CA 90046; (213) 650-1440.

SOUND CHAMBER, 27 S. El Molino Ave., Pasadena, CA 91101; (818) 449-8133.

SOUND IMAGE STUDIOS INC., 6556 Willkinson Ave., North Hollywood, CA 91606; (818) 762-8881.

SOUND MASTER, 10747 Magnolia Blvd., North Hollywood, CA 91601; (213) 650-8000.

SOUND SERVICES INC. (S.S.I.), 7155 Santa Monica Blvd., Los Angeles, CA 90046; (213) 874-9344; (818) 986-3255.

SPALLA, RICK VIDEO PRODUCTIONS, 1622 N. Gower St., Hollywood, CA 90028; (213) 469-7307.

SPLIT REEL RECORDING, 870 N. Vine St., Suite B, Hollywood, CA 90038; (213) 466-3817.

STEVENS, KRIS ENTERPRISES INC., 14241 Ventura Blvd., Suite 204, Sherman Oaks, CA 91423; (818) 981-8255.

SUNSET POST INC., 1813 Victory Blvd., Glendale, CA 91201; (818) 956-7912.

SUNSET SOUND FACTORY, 6357 Selma Ave., Hollywood, CA 90028; (213) 467-2500.

SUNWEST STUDIOS, 5533 Sunset Blvd., Hollywood, CA 90028; (213) 463-5631.

SYNC, INC., 931 N. Gardner St., W. Hollywood, CA 90046; (213) 851-6624.

TAJ SOUNDWORKS, 8207 W. Third St., Los Angeles, CA 90048; (213) 655-2775.

TAV SOUND INC., 6200 W. 3rd St., Los Angeles, CA 90038; (213) 937-2460.

TODD-AO GLEN GLENN SOUND, 900 N. Seward St., Hollywood, CA 90038; (213) 469-7221.

TRACK RECORD, 5249 Melrose Ave., Hollywood, Ca 90038; (213) 467-9432.

UNITED VIDEO INDUSTRIES INC., 5533 Sunset Blvd., Hollywood, CA 90028; (213) 465-1000.

VIDCOM ENTERTAINMENT, INC., P.O. Box 2926, Hollywood, CA 90078; (213) 301-8433.

VIDEO ADVENTURES, 1015 Cahuenga Blvd., Hollywood, CA 90038; (213) 461-3288.

VIDEO CIRCUIT STUDIOS, 11440 Chandler Blvd., Studio 1400, N. Hollywood, CA 91601; (818) 506-5493.

THE VIDEO TAPE CO., 10545 Burbank Blvd., North Hollywood, CA 91601; (818) 985-1666.

VIDEO TECHNOLOGY & SERVICES, 500 N. Ventu Park Rd., Newbury Park, CA 91320; (818) 888-3040; (805) 499-5827.

VIDE-U PRODUCTIONS, 612 N. Sepulveda Blvd., Los Angeles, CA 90049; (213) 472-7023.

VILLAGE POST, 1616 Butler Ave., W. Los Angeles, CA 90025; (213) 478-8227.

THE VILLAGE RECORDING STUDIOS, 1616 Butler Ave., West Los Angeles, CA 90025; (213) 478-8227.

VISUAL EYES PRODUCTIONS, 2401 Main St., Santa Monica, CA 90405; (213) 392-8300.

VITELLO & ASSOCIATES, 1612 W. Olive, Suite 203, Burbank, CA 91506; (818) 848-5919.

VOICE OVER L.A. INC., 1717 N. Highland Ave., Suite 620, Hollywood, CA 90028; (213) 463-8652.

WAVES SOUND RECORDERS, 1956 N. Cahuenga Blvd., Hollywood, CA 90068; (213) 466-6141.

WESTLAKE STUDIOS, 7265 Santa Monica Blvd., Los Angeles, CA 90046; (213) 851-9800; 655-0303.

WESTLAKE STUDIOS A & B, 8447 Beverly Blvd., Los Angeles, CA 90048; (213) 654-2155.

WILLIAM SOUND SERVICE, 1343 N. Highland Ave., Los Angeles, CA 90028; (213) 461-5321.

NEW YORK

CINE-MIX, 72 W. 45 St., New York, NY 10036; (212) 869-0100.

EDITEL, NEW YORK, 222 E. 44 St., New York, NY 10017; (212) 867-4600.

MAGNO SOUND & VIDEO, 729 Seventh Ave., New York, 10019; (212) 302-2505.

MODERN TELECOMMUNICATIONS, 1 Dag Hammarskjold Plaza, New York, NY 10017; (212) 355-0510.

NEP PRODUCTIONS, 56 W. 45 St., New York, NY 10036; (212) 382-1100.

NATIONAL RECORDING STUDIOS, 460 W. 42 St., New York, NY 10036; (212) 279-2000.

NEW BREED STUDIOS, 251 W. 30 St., New York, NY 10001; (212) 714-9379.

SECRET SOUND STUDIO INC., 147 W. 24 St., New York, NY 10011; (212) 691-7674.

SOUND SHOP, 321 W. 44 St., New York, NY 10036; (212) 757-7500.

SYNC SOUND INC., 450 W. 56 St., New York, NY 10019; (212) 246-5580.

VCA/TELETRONICS, 231 E. 55 St., New York, NY 10022; (212) 355-1600.

WINDSOR TOTAL VIDEO, 8 W. 38 St., New York, NY 10036; (212) 944-9090.

Videotape Cleaning & Evaluation

LOS ANGELES

CALIFORNIA VIDEO CENTER, 15303 Ventura Blvd., Sherman Oaks, CA 91403; (818) 789-5000.

CREATIVE VIDEO SERVICES, 500 Ventu Park Rd., Newbury Park, CA 91320; (818) 888-3040.

THE EDITING COMPANY, 8308 Beverly Blvd., Los Angeles, CA 90048; (213) 653-3570.

FILM ARTISTS ASSOCIATES, 470 S. San Vicente Blvd., Suite 104, Los Angeles, CA 90048; (213) 651-1700.

FILM PROCESSING CORP., 3602 S. Crenshaw Blvd., Los Angeles, CA 90016; (213) 737-8273.

GRACE & WILD STUDIOS HOLLYWOOD, 3501 Cahuenga Blvd. West, Los Angeles, CA 90068; (213) 876-8008.

IMAGE TRANSFORM INC., 4142 Lankershim Blvd., North Hollywood, CA 91602; (818) 985-7566.

INTER VIDEO, 733 N. Victory Blvd., Burbank, CA 91502; (818) 843-3633; 843-2288.

MAJESTIC DUPLICATING & VIDEO SERVICE, 1208 W. Isabel St., Burbank, CA 91506; (213) 849-1535; (818) 843-1806.

MODERN VIDEOFILM, 7165 Sunset Blvd., Hollywood, CA 90046; (213) 851-8070.

SOUND MASTER, 10747 Magnolia Blvd., North Hollywood, CA 91601; (213) 650-8000.

STUDIO FILM & TAPE INC. 6674 Santa Monica Blvd., Los Angeles, CA 90038; (213) 466-8101; (800) 824-3130.

THE VIDEO TAPE CO., 10545 Burbank Blvd., North Hollywood, CA 91601; (818) 985-1666.

NEW YORK

MTI TV CITY, 1443 Park Ave., New York, NY 10029; (212) 722-1818.

P.A.T. FILM SERVICES, 630 Ninth Ave., New York, NY 10036; (212) 247-0900.

ROSENBERG, WARREN, VIDEO SERVICE INC., 308 E. 79 St., Suite 17A, New York, NY 10021; (212) 744-1111.

T.F.I., TAPE-FILM INDUSTRIES, 619 W. 54 St., New York, NY 10019; (212) 708-0500. Branch offices: 941 N. Highland Ave., Los Angeles, CA 90038; (213) 461-3361; 640 N. La Salle St., Chicago, IL 60610; (312) 957-6700.

VCA/TELETRONICS, 231 E. 55 St., New York, NY 10022; (212) 355-1600.

VIDEO RESOURCES NEW YORK INC., 220 W. 71st, New York, NY 10023; (212) 724-7055.

Videotape Duplication Service

LOS ANGELES

A.M.E. INC., 1133 N. Hollywood Way, Burbank, CA 91505; (818) 841-7440.

AT&T RECORDING, 501 N. Larchmont Blvd., Los Angeles, CA 90004; (213) 466-7756.

ABBEY TAPE DUPLICATORS INC., 9525 Vassar Ave., Chatsworth, CA 91311; (818) 882-5210.

ABERDEEN VIDEO, 3349 Cahuenga Blvd. W., Suite 1A, Los Angeles, CA 90068; (213) 874-3050.

ADVANCED VIDEO TECHNOLOGIES, INC., 9562 Topanga Canyon Blvd., Chatsworth, CA 91311; (213) 463-4220; (818) 718-1270.

ALPHA STUDIOS VIDEO INC., 4720 W. Magnolia Blvd., Burbank, CA 91505; (818) 760-2825.

ALTAVIDEO, 3501 Cahuenga Blvd. W., Los Angeles, CA 90068; (213) 876-8008.

AMERICAN VIDEO FACTORY, 4150 Glencoe Ave., Marina Del Rey, CA 90292; (213) 823-8622; (800) 367-8433.

AMERICAN VIDEOGRAM, INC., 12020 W. Pico Blvd., Los Angeles, CA 90064; (213) 477-1535; 477-1536.

AMETRON RENTALS, 1200 N. Vine St., Hollywood, CA 90038; (213) 466-4321.

AMPAC VIDEO, 3637 Cahuenga Blvd. W., Hollywood, CA 90068; (213) 851-7200.

ANDERSON, HOWARD A. & COMPANY, 1016 N. Cole Ave., Los Angeles, CA 90038; (213) 463-2336.

APOLLO PRODUCTION FACILITY, 1503 Cahuenga Blvd., Hollywood, CA 90028, (213) 464-7871.

AUDIO ARTS PUBLISHING CO., 5617 Melrose Ave., Los Angeles, CA 90038; (213) 461-3507.

AUDIO GRAPHIC FILMS AND VIDEO, 6509 De Longpre Ave., Hollywood, CA 90028, (213) 462-6596; (213) 467-1234.

AUDIO PLUS VIDEO INTERNATIONAL INC., 1438 N. Gower St., Hollywood, CA 90028; (213) 856-0152.

AUDIO-VIDEO CRAFT INC., 6753 Santa Monica Blvd., Los Angeles, CA 90038; (213) 655-3511.

AUDIO VISUAL HEADQUARTERS CORP., 361 N. Oak St., Inglewood, CA 90302; (213) 419-4040.

BOSUSTOW VIDEO, 2207 Colby Ave., W. Los Angeles, CA 90064; (213) 478-0821.

BURBANK PRODUCTION PLAZA, 801 S. Main St., Burbank, CA 91506; (818) 846-7677.

CAL VISTA INTERNATIONAL LTD., 6649 Odessa Ave., Van Nuys, CA 91406; (818) 780-9000.

CALIFORNIA COMMUNICATIONS INC., 6900 Santa Monica Blvd., Los Angeles, CA 90038; (213) 466-8511.

CALIFORNIA VIDEO CENTER, 15303 Ventura Blvd., Sherman Oaks, CA 91403; (818) 789-5000.

CENTURY SOUTHWEST PRODUCTIONS, 2939 Nebraska Ave., Santa Monica, CA 90404; (213) 859-5111; 829-7624.

CINEMA GROUP ENTERTAINMENT, 1875 Century Park East, Los Angeles, CA 90067; (213) 785-3100; (800) 821-3427.

CLOCKWORK WINDOW DUBS., 1316 Third St. Mall, Suite 102, Santa Monica, CA 90401; (213) 395-4484.

COAST FILM LAB CO., 837 N. Cahuenga Blvd., Los Angeles, CA 90038; (213) 464-7293.

COMPACT VIDEO SERVICES INC., 2813 W. Alameda Ave., Burbank, CA 91505; (818) 840-7000; 843-3232.

COMPOSITE IMAGE SYSTEMS, 815 N. Cahuenga Blvd., Hollywood, CA 90038; (213) 461-5734.

COMTEL, 2201 N. Hollywood Way, Burbank, CA 91505; (213) 849-6701; (818) 846-0770; 3152 E. La Palma, Suite D, Anaheim, CA 92806; (714) 630-4470; 5046 Ruffner St., San Diego, CA 92111; (619) 292-1090.

CONSOLIDATED FILM INDUSTRIES, 959 Seward St., Los Angeles, CA 90038; (213) 462-3161.

THE CREATIVE PARTNERSHIP, INC., 7525 Fountain Ave., Hollywood, CA 90046; (213) 850-5551.

CREATIVE SOUND PRODUCTIONS, 6290 Sunset Blvd., Suite 1026, Hollywood, CA 90028; (213) 871-1010.

CREST NATIONAL FILM & VIDEOTAPE LABS, 1141 N. Seward St., Los Angeles, CA 90038; (213) 462-6692.

CUSTOM DUPLICATION INC., 3404 Century Blvd., Inglewood, CA 90303; (213) 776-4810.

DELUXE LABORATORIES, INC., 1377 N. Serrano Ave., Hollywood, CA 90027; (213) 462-6171; (800) 233-5893.

DEVONSHIRE SOUND STUDIOS, 10729 Magnolia Blvd., North Hollywood, CA 91601; (818) 985-1945.

DUBS, INC., 6360 DeLongpre Ave., Hollywood, CA 90028; (213) 461-6171.

DUPLITAPE, 15016 Ventura Blvd., Suite 1, Sherman Oaks, CA 91403; (818) 501-7370.

EDITEL LOS ANGELES, 729 N. Highland Ave., Hollywood, CA 90038; (213) 931-1821.

THE EDITING COMPANY, 8308 Beverly Blvd., Los Angeles, CA 90048; (213) 653-3570.

EMC PRODUCTIONS, 6855 Santa Monica Blvd., Suite 308, Hollywood, CA 90038; (213) 463-3282.

ENVIRONMENTAL VIDEO INC., P.O. Box 577, Manhattan Beach, CA 90266; (213) 546-4581.

FILM TECHNOLOGY CO., 6900 Santa Monica Blvd., Hollywood, CA 90038; (213) 464-3456.

FILMCORE PRINT AND TAPE, 901 N. Seward St., Los Angeles, CA 90038; (213) 464-7303; 464-8600.

FOTO-KEM INDUSTRIES INC., 2800 W. Olive Ave., Burbank, CA 91505; (818) 846-3101.

FOTO-TRONICS SYSTEMS INC., 2800 W. Olive Ave., Burbank, CA 91505; (818) 846-9350.

FOX TAPE, 5746 Sunset Blvd., Los Angeles, CA 90028; (213) 856-1000.

G & B VIDEO LAB, 255 E. Colorado Blvd., Pasadena, CA 91101; (818) 440-1909

GLEN-WARREN PRODUCTION, LTD., 9911 W. Pico Blvd., Los Angeles, CA 90035; (213) 553-9233.

GLOBAL VISION CORPORATION, 3255 Cahuenga Blvd., Hollywood, CA 90068; (213) 851-1190.

GOLDEN WEST VIDEOTAPE, 5800 Sunset Blvd., Los Angeles, CA 90028; (213) 460-8989.

GRACE & WILD STUDIOS HOLLYWOOD, 3501 Cahuenga Blvd. W., Los Angeles, CA 90068; (213) 876-8008.

H.C.V., 3034 Glendale Blvd., Los Angeles, CA 90039; (213) 662-1112.

HOLLYWOOD NEWSREEL SYNDICATE INC., 1622 N. Gower St., Los Angeles, CA 90028; (213) 469-7307.

HORIZONTAL EDITING STUDIOS, 2625 W. Olive Ave., Burbank, CA 91505; (818) 841-6750.

IMAGE TRANSFORM INC., 4142 Lankershim Blvd., North Hollywood, CA 91602; (818) 985-7566; (800) 423-2652.

IMAGE TRANSFORM LABORATORY, 3611 N. San Fernando Rd., Burbank, CA 91505; (818) 841-3812.

IMAGE WEST, 11846 Ventura Blvd., Studio City, CA 91604; (818) 506-5577.

IMMEDIATO, JEFFREY, & ASSOCIATES, P.O. Box 5611, Long Beach, CA 90805; (213) 422-9295.

INSTANT REPLAY COMMUNICATIONS CO., 11122 W. Washington Blvd., Culver City, CA 90232; (213) 870-1231; 5520 Westlawn Ave., Los Angeles, CA; (213) 870-9435.

INTER VIDEO, 733 N. Victory Blvd., Burbank, CA 91502; (818) 843-3633.

INTERNATIONAL VIDEO CONVERSIONS, 815 N. Cahuenga Blvd., Hollywood, CA 90038; (213) 463-7884.

INTERNATIONAL VIDEO ENTERTAINMENT, INC., 7920 Alabama Ave., Canoga Park, CA 91304; (805) 499-5827.

INTERSOUND, 8746 Sunset Blvd., Los Angeles, CA 90069; (213) 652-3741.

J.P. VIDEO SERVICES, 9538 W. Pico Blvd., Los Angeles, CA 90035; (213) 271-1209, 859-9903.

KWHY-TV, CHANNEL 22, 5545 Sunset Blvd., Los Angeles, CA 90028; (213) 466-5441.

KAPPA VIDEO, 801 S. Main St., Burbank, CA 91506; (818) 843-3400.

LP PRODUCTIONS, 223 Strand St., Suite K, Santa Monica, CA 90405; (213) 399-1101; (714) 857-1310.

LEVIN, KARL M., 20959 Elkwood St., Los Angeles, CA 91304; (818) 882-7262.

LION SHARE RECORDING STUDIOS, 8255 Beverly Blvd., Los Angeles, CA 90048; (213) 658-5990.

LIONEL TELEVISION PRODUCTIONS, 417 Colorado Ave., Santa Monica, CA 90401; (213) 394-9697.

MFI VIDEO CENTER, 1905 Grace Ave., Hollywood, CA 90068; (213) 851-0373.

MGS SERVICES, 10507 Burbank Blvd., North Hollywood, CA 91601; (818) 508-5488.

MACROVISION, 10201 Torre Ave., Suite 330, Cupertino, CA 95014; (408) 252-9600.

MAJESTIC DUPLICATION & VIDEO SERVICE, 1208 W. Isabel St., Burbank, CA 91506; (213) 849-1535; (818) 843-1806.

MASTER DIGITAL INC., 1749 14th St., Santa Monica, CA 90404; (213) 452-1511.

McINTIRE-HOFFMAN, INC., 11969 Ventura Blvd., Studio City, CA 91604; (818) 762-2077.

McKAY, CAMERON PRODUCTIONS, 6311 Romaine,, Los Angeles, CA 90038; (213) 463-6073.

MEDIA HOME ENTERTAINMENT INC., 5730 Buckingham Pkway, Culver City, CA 90230; (213) 216-7900.

MIDTOWN VIDEO, 8439 W. Third St., Suite 67, Los Angeles, CA 90048; (213) 651-2420.

MODERN VIDEOFILM, 7165 Sunset Blvd., Hollywood, CA 90046; (213) 851-8070.

MORRIS VIDEO INC., 2730 Monterey St., Suite 105, Torrance, CA 90503; (213) 533-4800.

MUSIC LAB INC., 1831 Hyperion Ave., Hollywood, CA 90027; (213) 666-3003.

NEWMAN/FRANKS, 2956 Nicarda Dr., Los Angeles, CA 90077; (213) 470-0140; 470-0145.

ORION ENTERPRISES, INC., 1015 N. Cahuenga Blvd., Los Angeles, CA 90038; (213) 461-3844.

PACIFIC VIDEO LAB. INC., 5224 Santa Monica Blvd., Los Angeles, CA 90029; (213) 661-1144.

PAL VIDEO, 19061 Tina Pl., Tarzana, CA 91356; (818) 344-1603.

POSITIVE MEDIA, 5422 A Fair Ave., North Hollywood, CA 91601; (818) 761-5192.

THE POST GROUP, 6335 Homewood Ave., Los Angeles, CA 90028; (213) 462-2300.

POST PLUS INCORPORATED, 6650 Santa Monica Blvd., Hollywood, CA 90038; (213) 463-7108.

PROFESSIONAL ARTISTS GROUP, 845 N. Highland Ave., Hollywood, CA 90038; (213) 871-2222.

PROJECT ONE, 6669 Sunset Blvd., Hollywood, CA 90028; (213) 464-2285.

R. PRODUCTIONS & VIDEO EVENTS, 1741 N. Ivar, Suite 210, Hollywood, CA 90028; (213) 464-2285.

RED CAR EDITING, 1040 N. Las Palmas Ave., Los Angeles, CA 90038; (213) 466-4467.

REEL TIME DUPLICATORS, INC., 801 S. Main St., Burbank, CA 91506; (818) 849-1823.

RENCHER'S JOY EDITORIAL SERVICE, 738 Cahuenga Blvd., Hollywood, CA 90038; (213) 463-9836.

ROLLING VIDEO, 18730 Oxnard, Tarzana, CA 91356; (818) 993-6912.

RUSK SOUND STUDIO, 1556 N. La Brea Ave., Hollywood, CA 90028; (213) 462-6477.

SCHULMAN VIDEO CENTER, 861 Seward St., Hollywood, CA 90038; (213) 465-8110.

SELL PICTURES INC., 9701 Wilshire Blvd., Beverly Hills, CA 90212; (213) 874-5402.

SIERRA VIDEO DIVERSIFIED VIDEO INDUSTRIES, INC., 11320 Chandler, N. Hollywood, CA 91601; (818) 985-1531.

SKYLIGHT PRODUCTIONS INC., 6815 Willoughby, Suite 201, Los Angeles, CA 90038; (213) 464-4500.

SOUND MASTER, 10747 Magnolia Blvd., North Hollywood, CA 91601; (213) 650-8000.

SOUND SERVICES, INC. (S.S.I.), 7155 Santa Monica Blvd., Los Angeles, CA 90046; (213) 874-9344.

SOUTHLAND VIDEO, 3255 Cahuenga Blvd., Hollywood, CA 90068; (213) 851-1190.

SPALLA, RICK VIDEO PRODUCTIONS, 1622 N. Gower, Los Angeles, CA 90028; (213) 469-7307.

STAGE FRIGHT PRODUCTIONS, 8817 Amboy Ave., Sun Valley, CA 91352; (818) 768-3333.

STEVENS, KRIS ENTERPRISES INC., 14241 Ventura Blvd., Suite 204, Sherman Oaks, CA 91423; (818) 981-8255.

SUNSET POST INC., 1813 Victory Blvd., Glendale, CA 91201; (818) 956-7912.

SUNSHINE COMMUNICATIONS, 565 N. Gower St., Hollywood, CA 90004; (213) 464-2223.

SUPERCINE INC., 2214 W. Olive Ave., Burbank, CA 91506; (818) 843-8260.

TAPE-FILM INDUSTRIES (TFI), 941 N. Highland Ave., Hollywood, CA 90038; (213) 461-3361.

TELE VIDICS, 2223 E. 223rd St., Long Beach, CA 90810; (213) 830-5296.

TELEPRINT OF LOS ANGELES, 3779 Cahuenga Blvd., West, Studio City, CA 91604; (818) 760-3191.

TRANS-AMERICAN VIDEO INC., 1541 N. Vine St., Los Angeles, CA 90028; (213) 466-2141.

TRANSWORLD VIDEO LAB INC., 1811 W. Magnolia Blvd., Burbank, CA 91506; (818) 843-2416.

TRITONICS INC., 733 N. Victory Blvd., Burbank, CA 91502; (818) 569-0400.

TYLIE JONES & ASSOC. INC., 10718 Riverside Dr., North Hollywood, CA 91602; (818) 980-7300.

UCL VIDEO, 823 N. Seward St., Los Angeles, CA 90038; (213) 469-7291.

UDELL, BILL PRODUCTIONS, 6006 Vantage Ave., North Hollywood, CA 91606; (818) 985-6606.

UNITED COLOR LAB, INC., 823 N. Seward St., Hollywood, CA 90038; (213) 461-9921.

UNITEL VIDEO, 5555 Melrose Ave., Studio G, Los Angeles, CA 90038; (213) 468-4606.

VCI DUPLICATION, 915 Hollywood Way, Burbank, CA 91505; (818) 650-8550.

V.M.G. INC, 16042 Ventura Blvd., Suite 206, Encino, CA 91426; (818) 905-5311.

VIDEO ADVENTURES INC., 1015 Cahuenga Blvd., Hollywood, CA 90038; (213) 461-3288.

VIDEO CIRCUIT STUDIOS, 11440 Chandler Blvd., Studio 1400, N. Hollywood, CA 91601; (818) 506-5493.

VIDEO CRAFTSMEN INC., 6311 Romaine St., Los Angeles, CA 90038; (213) 464-4351.

VIDEO-IT INC., 1016 N. Sycamore Ave., Hollywood, CA 90038; (213) 876-4055; (213) VID-EOIT.

THE VIDEO TAPE CO., 10545 Burbank Blvd., North Hollywood, CA 91601; (818) 985-1666.

VIDEO TAPE TRANSFER LABS, 450 S. Central Ave., Glendale, CA 91204; (818) 956-1669.

VIDEO TRANSITIONS, 910 N. Citrus Ave., Hollywood, CA 90038; (213) 465-3333.

VIDEO VISION, 9100 Sunset Blvd., Suite 350, Los Angeles, CA 90069; (213) 278-4875.

VIDEO WEST, 805 Larrabee St., W. Hollywood, CA 90069; (213) 659-5762

VIDE-U PRODUCTIONS, 612 N. Sepulveda Blvd., Los Angeles, CA 90049; (213) 472-7023.

WEISBARTH, JACOB & ASSOC. INC., 9903 Santa Monica Blvd., Suite 256, Beverly Hills, CA 90212; (213) 277-9616.

WESTERN FILM INDUSTRIES, 30941 W. Agoura Rd., Suite 302, Westlake Village, CA 91360; (818) 889-7350.

WILDER BROTHERS VIDEO, 10327 Santa Monica Blvd., Los Angeles, CA 90025; (213) 557-3500.

WOLD COMMUNICATIONS, 10880 Wilshire Blvd., Suite 2204, Los Angeles, CA 90024; (212) 474-3500.

NEW YORK

A N S INTERNATIONAL VIDEO LTD., 396 Fifth Ave., New York, NY 10018; (212) 736-1007.

ACE AUDIO VISUAL CO., 118 E. 28 St., Fifth Floor, New York, NY 10016; (212) 685-3344; 33-49 55th St., Woodside, NY; (718) 458-3800.

ALL STAR FILM TO VIDEO, 156 Fifth Ave., New York, NY 10011; (212) 645-8529.

AMERICAN INC., 122 E. 42 St., New York, NY 10017; (212) 758-8300.

AMERICAN VIDEO—CHANNELS INC., 321 W. 44 St., New York, NY 10036; (212) 765-6324.

ANIMATED VIDEO, INC., 1600 Broadway, New York, NY 10019; (212) 265-2942.

AQUARIUS TRANSFER, 12 E. 46 St., New York, NY 10017; (212) 581-0123.

BOGAZICI VIDEO LTD., 460 Seventh Ave., New York, NY 10001; (212) 563-9022; 594-1707.

BROWN, TONY PRODUCTIONS, 1501 Broadway, New York, NY 10036; (212) 575-0876.

C & C VISUAL, 12 W. 27 St., New York, NY 10001; (212) 684-3830.

CALAMAR PRODUCTIONS, 38 Greene St., New York, NY 10013; (212) 334-4952.

CINE MAGNETICS FILM & VIDEO LABORATORIES, 50 W. 40 St., New York, NY 10018; (212) 542-0700.

DEVLIN PRODUCTIONS INC., 1501 Broadway, New York, NY 10036; (212) 391-1313.

DOLPHIN PRODUCTIONS, 140 E. 80 St., New York, NY 10021; (212) 628-5930.

EDITEL, NEW YORK, 222 E. 44 St., New York, NY 10017; (212) 867-4600.

EDITING CONCEPTS PRINTS, INC., 216 E. 45 St., New York, NY 10017; (212) 697-9630.

EXPRESS VIDEO INC., 244 W. 49 St., New York, NY 10019; (212) 246-2311.

FAMA II PRODUCTIONS, 2750 Richmond Terrace, Staten Island, NY 10303; (718) 273-1780.

FOTO-VIDEO TRANSFER CENTER, 1 Times Square, New York, NY 10036; (212) 302-1866.

GML VIDEO INC., 137 Varick St., New York, NY 10013; (212) 645-3700.

GLOBE VIDEO SERVICES, INC., 286 Fifth Ave., New York, NY 10001; (212) 695-6868.

HK VIDEO REPRODUCTIONS INC., 2 W. 32 St., New York, NY 10001; (212) 967-7528.

HALLENDAL ENTERPRIZES, 15 W. 28 St., New York, NY 10010; (212) 481-1568.

INTERNATIONAL PRODUCTION CENTER, 514 W. 57 St., New York, NY 10019; (212) 582-6530.

INTERNATIONAL VIDEO SERVICES, 1501 Broadway, New York, NY 10036; (212) 730-1411.

JSL VIDEO SERVICES, INC., 25 W. 45 St., New York, NY 10036; (212) JSL-5082.
JVL ELECTRONICS CO., 500 E. 82 St., New York, NY 10028; (212) 535-4970.
MPCS COMMUNICATIONS, 514 W. 57 St., New York, NY 10019; (212) 586-3690.
MAGNO SOUND & VIDEO, 729 Seventh Ave., New York, NY 10019; (212) 302-2505.
MEDIATECH EAST, 515 W. 57 St., New York, NY 10019; (212) 463-8300; 765-8720.
MODERN TELECOMMUNICATIONS INC., 1443 Park Ave., New York, NY 10029; (212) 722-1818.
MOVIE LAB VIDEO, INC., 619 W. 54 St., New York, NY 10019; (212) 586-0360; 956-3900.
NATIONAL RECORDING STUDIOS, INC., 460 W. 42 St., New York, NY 10036; (212) 279-2000.
NATIONAL VIDEO INDUSTRIES, INC., 15 W. 17 St., New York, NY 10011; (212) 691-1300.
OCCASIONAL VIDEO, 534 E. 84 St., New York, NY 10028; (212) 737-3058.
P.A.T. FILM SERVICES, 630 Ninth Ave., New York, NY 10036; (212) 247-0900.
PDR PRODUCTIONS, INC., 747 Third Ave., New York, NY 10017; (212) 755-9019.
PELCO PRINTS, INC., 757 Third Ave., New York, NY 10017; (212) 319-3348.
PICSONIC PRODUCTIONS CORP., 25 W. 45 St., New York, NY 10036; (212) 575-1910.
RAFIK, 814 Broadway, New York, NY 10001; (212) 475-7884.
REEVES TELETAPE, 708 Third Ave., New York, NY 10012; (212) 573-8600.
REILLY VIDEO COMMUNICATIONS, 508 W. 26th St., New York, NY 10001; (212) 463-0058.
ROSENBERG, WARREN, VIDEO SERVICES, INC., 308 E. 79 St., New York, NY 10021; (212) 744-1111.
ROSS-LEVINE, 594 Broadway, New York, NY 10003; (212) 925-2020.
SYNESTHETICS INC., 58 Walker St., New York, NY 10013; (212) 431-4112.
TFI, TAPE-FILM INDUSTRIES, 619 W. 54 St., New York, NY 10019; (212) 708-0500.
TABCO FILM & VIDEO SERVICES, 850 Seventh Ave., New York, NY 10019; (212) 315-3880.
TELETECHNIQUES, 1 W. 19 St., New York, NY 10011; (212) 206-1475; 633-1868.
IIIDB VIDEO SPECIALISTS, INC., 121 E. 24 St., New York, NY 10010; (212) 677-6856.
TODAY VIDEO, INC., 45 W. 45 St., New York, NY 10036; (212) 391-1020.
TYLIE JONES/EAST, 248 E. 48 St., New York, NY 10017; (212) 753-9015.
UNI VISION, 481 Eighth Ave., New York, NY 10001; (212) 563-1320.
UNITEL VIDEO, 515 W. 57 St., New York, NY 10019; (212) 265-3600.
VCA TELETRONICS, 231 E. 55 St., New York, NY 10022; (212) 355-1600.
VIDEO CASSETTE TRANSFERS, 1501 Broadway, New York, NY 10036; (212) 575-8433.
VIDEO CENTRAL INC., 225 W. 36 St., New York, NY 10018; (212) 947-6960.
VIDEO DUB, INC., 423 W. 55 St., New York, NY 10019; (212) 757-3300.

VIDEO PLANNING INC., 250 W. 57 St., New York, NY 10019; (212) 582-5066.
VIDEO PORTFOLIOS, 142 W. 24 St., New York, NY 10011; (212) 989-3858.
VIDEO RESOURCES NEW YORK, INC., 220 W. 71 St., New York, NY 10023; (212) 724-7055.
VIDEO 3000, 1400 Broadway, Penthouse Loft, New York, NY 10018; (212) 302-1313.
VIDEOROOM, 1487 Third Ave., New York, NY 10028; (212) 879-5333.
VIDEOWORKS, 24 W. 40 St., New York, NY 10018; (212) 869-2500.
VIDLO VIDEO, 40 E. 21 St., New York, NY 10010; (212) 475-4140.
WINDSOR TOTAL VIDEO, 8 W. 38 St., New York, NY 10018; (212) 944-9090.
WINKLER VIDEO DUPLICATION, 248 E. 48 St., New York, NY 10017-1598; (212) 980-6110; 5801 Westside Ave., No. Bergen, NJ 07047; (201) 861-6500.

CALIFORNIA

CARROL FILM & VIDEO, INC., 3535 Ross Ave., Bldg. II, Suite 205, San Jose, Ca 91524; (408) 978-2784.
TELEVISION ASSOCIATES, INC., 2410 Charleston Rd., Mountain View, CA; (415) 967-6040.

ILLINOIS

AV CENTER, 5153 N. Lincoln Ave., Chicago, IL 60659; (312) 275-7098.
TELEMATRON PRODUCTIONS, INC., 3210 W. West Lake Ave., Glenview, IL 60025; (312) 729-5215.

MICHIGAN

PREMIERE VIDEO, INC., 35687 Industrial Rd., Livonia, MI 48150; (313) 464-4650; (800) 248-6646.

PENNSYLVANIA

MEDIA CONCEPTS, 331 N. Broad St., Philadelphia, PA 19107; (215) 923-2545.

WASHINGTON

VIDEO PRESENTATIONS, 2326 Sixth Ave., Room 230, Seattle, WA 98121; (206) 728-9241.

CANADA

BELLEVUE PATHE QUEBEC VIDEO DUPLICATION CENTER, 5588 Cote de Liesse, Montreal, Que., H4P 1A9; (514) 737-2777.
MANTA VIDEO LABS, 311 Adelaide St. E., Toronto, Ont., M5A IN2; (416) 863-9316.
PATHÉ VIDEO INC., 720 King St. W., Toronto, Ont., M5V 2T3;, (416) 364-6720.

Videotape Editing & Post Production Facilities and Services

WEST COAST

—A—

A.M.E. Inc., 1133 N. Hollywood Way, Burbank, CA 91505; (818) 841-7440.

ABERDEEN VIDEO, 3349 Cahuenga Blvd. West, Suite 1A, Los Angeles, CA 90068; (213) 874-3050.

ACE AND EDIE 2, 722 N. Seward St., Hollywood, CA 90038; (213) 462-2185.

ACTION VIDEO, 6616 Lexington Ave., Los Angeles, CA 90038; (213) 461-3611; FAX: (213) 460-4033.

ADVENTIST MEDIA PRODUCTIONS, 1100 Rancho Conejo Blvd., Newbury Park, CA 91320; (805) 373-7771; 373-7777.

ADVENTURES IN FILM & TAPE, 1027 N. Cole Ave., Hollywood, CA 90038; (213) 460-4557.

ALDAN CO. INC., 355 S. Mansfield Ave., Los Angeles, CA 90036; (213) 936-1032.

ALL SEASONS ENTERTAINMENT, 18121 Napa St., Northridge, CA 91325; (818) 886-8680; (800) 423-5599.

ALPHA CINE LABORATORY, INC., 5724 W. Third St., Suite 311, Los Angeles, CA 90036; (213) 934-7793.

ALPHA STUDIOS VIDEO INC., 4720 W. Magnolia Blvd., Burbank, CA 91505; (818) 760-2825.

ALTAVIDEO, 3501 Cahuenga Blvd. W., Los Angeles, CA 90068; (213) 876-8008.

AME, INC., 1133 N. Hollywood Way, Burbank, CA 91505; (818) 841-7440; FAX: (818) 842-8409.

AMERICAN VIDEO FACTORY, 4150 Glencoe Ave., Marina Del Rey, CA 90292; (213) 823-8622; (800) 367-8433.

AMERICAN VIDEOGRAM INC., 12020 W. Pico Blvd., Los Angeles, CA 90064-1504; (213) 477-1535.

AMPAC VIDEO, 3637 Cahuenga Blvd. W., Hollywood, CA 90068; (213) 851-7200.

ANDERSON, HOWARD A., COMPANY, 1016 N. Cole Ave., Los Angeles, CA 90038; (213) 463-2336.

AQUARIUS THEATRE, 6230 Sunset Blvd., Hollywood, CA 90028; (213) 460-6700.

APOLLO VIDEO FACILITY, 1503 Cahuenga Blvd., Hollywood, CA 90028; (213) 464-7871; 465-6154.

AUDIO ARTS PUBLISHING CO., 5617 Melrose Ave., Los Angeles, CA 90038; (213) 461-3507.

AUDIO GRAPHIC FILMS AND VIDEO, 6509 De Longpre Ave., Hollywood, CA 90028; (213) 462-6596; (213) 467-1234.

AUDIO-VIDEO CRAFT INC., 6753 Santa Monica Blvd., Los Angeles, CA 90038; (213) 655-3511.

—B—

BERC, 4545 Chermak St., Burbank, CA 91505; (818) 841-3000; (213) 464-7655.

BELOW THE LINE LEASING, 1351 Third St., Suite 201, Santa Monica, CA 90401; (213) 458-1723.

BLUE RIDGE EDITORIAL, 1019 N. Cole Ave., Hollywood, CA 90038; (213) 461-2846

BOSUSTOW VIDEO, 2207 Colby Ave., West Los Angeles, CA 90064; (213) 478-0821.

BOULEVARD VIDEO PRODUCTIONS, 15016 Ventura Blvd., Suite 1, Sherman Oaks, CA 91403; (818) 501-7369.

BOWEN VIDEO FACILITIES, 7826 Clybourn Ave., Sun Valley, CA 91352; (818) 504-0070.

BURBANK PRODUCTION PLAZA, 801 S. Main St., Burbank, CA 91508; (818) 846-7677.

—C—

CCR VIDEO CORPORATION, 6410 Santa Monica Blvd., Los Angeles, CA 90038; (213) 464-7151.

CALIFORNIA COMMUNICATIONS INC., 6900 Santa Monica Blvd., Los Angeles, CA 90038; (213) 466-8511.

CALIFORNIA VIDEO CENTER, 15303 Ventura Blvd., Sherman Oaks, CA 91403; (818) 789-5000.

CENTURY SOUTHWEST PRODUCTIONS, 2939 Nebraska Ave., Santa Monica, CA 90404; (213) 829-5111; 829-7624.

CHOICE TELEVISION, 800 S. Date Ave., Alhambra, CA 91803; (818) 576-2906; 289-7719.

CHOOKOLINGO ELECTRONICS, 5328 Alfonso Dr., Agoura, CA 91301; (818) 991-7865.

CINETYP INC., 843 Seward St., Hollywood, CA 90038; (213) 463-8569.

CLARASOL PRODUCTION CO., 1028 La Brea Ave., Hollywood, CA 90038; (213) 462-7212; 464-0180.

CLOCKWORK WINDOW DUBS, 1316 3rd St. Mall, Suite 102, Santa Monica, CA 90401; (213) 395-4484.

COMPACT VIDEO SERVICES INC., 2813 W. Alameda Ave., Burbank, CA 91505; (818) 840-7000; 843-3232.

COMPLETE POST INC., 6087 Sunset Blvd., Hollywood, CA 90028; (213) 467-1244.

THE COMPLEX, 2323 Corinth St., Los Angeles, CA 90064; (213) 477-1938.

COMPOSITE IMAGE SYSTEMS, 815 N. Cahuenga Blvd., Hollywood, CA 90038; (213) 461-5734.

CONSOLIDATED FILM INDUSTRIES, 959 Seward St., Los Angeles, CA 90038; (213) 462-3161.

CORNERSTONE PRODUCTIONS, 6430 Sunset Blvd., Suite 1013, Hollywood, CA 90028; (213) 871-2255.

CRAVEN PRODUCTIONS, 727 N. Victory Blvd., Burbank, CA 91502; (818) 843-6009.

THE CREATIVE PARTNERSHIP, 7526 Fountain Ave., Hollywood, CA 90046; (213) 850-5551.

CREATIVE VIDEO SERVICES, 500 Ventu Park Rd., Newbury Park, CA 91320; (818) 888-3040.

CREST NATIONAL FILM & VIDEOTAPE LABS, 1141 N. Seward St., Hollywood, CA 90038; (213) 466-0624; 462-6696.

CROSS CUTS, 1330 N. Vine St., Hollywood, CA 90028; (213) 854-3308.

—D—

DSR PRODUCTIONS, 607 N. 64th Ave., Los Angeles, CA 90042; (213) 258-6741.

DELTA PRODUCTIONS, 3333 Glendale Blvd., Suite 3, Los Angeles, CA 90039; (213) 663-8754.

DEVONSHIRE SOUND STUDIOS, 10729 Magnolia Blvd., North Hollywood, CA 91601; (818) 985-1945.

DIGITAL POST, 629 N. La Brea Ave., Los Angeles, CA 90036; (213) 936-7181.

DIGITAL SOUND RECORDING, 607 N. Ave. 64, Los Angeles, CA 90042; (213) 258-6741.

—E—

ECHO FILM SERVICES INC., 4119 Burbank Blvd., Burbank, CA 91505; (818) 841-4114.

EDIT POINT, P.O. Box 1243; S. Pasadena, CA 91030; (818) 799-5611.

EDITEL-LOS ANGELES, 729 N. Highland Ave., Hollywood, CA 90038; (213) 931-1821.

THE EDITING COMPANY, 8300 Beverly Blvd., Los Angeles, CA 90048; (213) 653-3570.

ELECTRONIC ARTS & TECHNOLOGY, 3655 Motor Ave., Los Angeles, CA 90034; (213) 836-2556.

ELFMAN, RICHARD, PRODUCTIONS, 723 Ocean Front Walk, Venice, CA 90291; (213) 399-9118.

ENCORE VIDEO INC., 6344 Fountain Ave., Hollywood, CA 90028; (213) 466-7663.

EYE ON STUDIO, 224 N. Juanita Ave., Los Angeles, CA 90004; (213) 465-7777.

EYE SQUARE VIDEO INC., 1749 14th St., Santa Monica, CA 90404; (213) 452-9076.

—F—

FBC PRODUCTION SERVICES, 12401 W. Olympic Blvd., Los Angeles, CA 90064; (213) 826-5264.

FALCON COMMUNICATIONS, 800 S. Date Ave., Alhambra, CA 91803; (818) 576-2906.

FIDELITY RECORDING STUDIO, 4412 Whitsett Ave., Studio City, CA 91604; (818) 508-3263.

FILM CORE PRINT & TAPE, 849 N. Seward St., Los Angeles, CA 90038; (213) 464-7303.

THE FILM PLACE, 1311 N. Highland Ave., Los Angeles, CA 90028; (213) 464-0116.

FILMLAND CORPORATE CENTER, 10000 Washington Blvd., Culver City, CA 90232; (213) 558-0071.

FILMSERVICE LABORATORIES, INC., 6327 Santa Monica Blvd., Los Angeles, CA 90038; (213) 464-5141.

FORSHER, JAMES, COLLECTION OF ARCHIVAL FOOTAGE & STILLS, 6363 Sunset Blvd., Suite 714, Hollywood, CA 90028; (213) 461-0177

FRAME BY FRAME, 729 Seward St., Suite 115, Los Angeles, CA 90038; (213) 469-8264; 463-0145.

FREUND & KLEPPEL INC., 6290 Sunset Blvd., Suite 603, Los Angeles, CA 90028; (213) 469-1444.

—G—

GLEN-WARREN PRODUCTIONS, LTD., 9911 W. Pico Blvd., Penthouse M, Los Angeles, CA 90035; (213) 553-9233.

GLOBAL ENTERTAINMENT NETWORK, INC., 1832 N. Gower St., Hollywood, CA 90028; (213) 461-2534.

GRACE & WILD STUDIOS HOLLYWOOD, 3501 Cahuenga Blvd. West., Los Angeles, CA 90068; (213) 876-8008.

GROUP W CABLE VIDEO PRODUCTION CENTER, 2939 Nebraska Ave., Santa Monica, CA 90404; (213) 829-2676.

GROUP W PRODUCTIONS, One Lakeside Pl., 3801 Barham Blvd., Los Angeles, CA 90068; (213) 850-3800.

—H—

H.C.V., 3034 Glendale Blvd., Los Angeles, CA 90039; (213) 662-1112.

HEALTH TELEVISION CORP., PRODUCTION GROUP INC., 6605 Eleanor Ave., Hollywood, CA 90038; (213) 463-1713.

HIDEAWAY PRODUCTIONS, 16820 Solana Lane, Canyon Country, CA 91351; (805) 252-4508.

HOLLYWOOD NATIONAL STUDIOS, 6605 Eleanor Ave., Santa Fe Springs, CA 90038; (213) 467-6272.

HOLLYWOOD NEWSREEL SYNDICATE INC., 1622 N. Gower St., Los Angeles, CA 90028; (213) 469-7307.

HOLLYWOOD PACIFIC STUDIOS, 6290 Sunset Blvd., Hollywood, CA 90028; (213) 463-8118.

HOLLYWOOD VAULTS, 742 N. Seward St., Los Angeles, CA 90038; (213) 461-6464.

HOMER & ASSOCIATES, INC., Sunset Gower Studios, 1420 N. Beachwood Dr., Hollywood, CA 90028; (213) 462-4710.

HORIZONTAL EDITING STUDIOS, 2625 W. Olive Ave., Burbank, CA 91505; (818) 841-6750.

—I—

IMAGE PRODUCTIONS, 1812 W. Victory Blvd., Burbank, CA 91506; (818) 846-2047.

IMAGE TRANSFORM INC., 4142 Lankershim Blvd., North Hollywood, CA 91602; (818) 985-7566; (800) 423-2652.

IMMEDIATO, JEFFREY & ASSOCIATES, P.O. Box 5611, Long Beach, CA 90805; (213) 422-9295.

INDEPENDENT PRODUCERS STUDIO, INC., 1604 Vista Del Mar Ave., Hollywood, CA 90028; (213) 461-6966.

INNOVATION UNLIMITED, 4444 Via Marina, Penthouse-81, Marina Del Rey, CA 90291; (213) 823-4251.

INSTANT REPLAY COMMUNICATIONS CO., 11122 W. Washington Blvd., Culver City, CA 90232; (213) 870-9435.

INSTITUTE OF AUDIO/VIDEO ENGINEERING, 1831 Hyperion Ave., Hollywood, CA 90027; (213) 666-2380.

INTER VIDEO, 733 N. Victory Blvd., Burbank, CA 91502; (818) 843-3633; 569-4000; FAX: (818) 843-6884.

INTERMIX INC., 2505 S. Robertson Blvd., Los Angeles, CA 90034; (213) 870-2121.

—J—

JKR PRODUCTIONS/JIM RUXIN, 12140 W. Olympic Blvd., Suite 21, Los Angeles, CA 90064; (213) 826-3666.

J.P. VIDEO SERVICES, 9538 W. Pico Blvd., Los Angeles, CA 90035; (213) 271-1209; 859-9903.

JAMAR/ACLA PRODUCTIONS, 11969 Ventura Blvd., Studio City, CA 91604; (818) 762-2077.

TYLIE JONES/WEST, 10718 Riverside Dr., N. Hollywood, CA 91602; (818) 980-7300.

—K—

KCET, 4401 Sunset Blvd., Los Angeles, CA 90027, (213) 666-6500.

KTEH VIDEOSERVICES, 100 Skyport Dr., San Jose, CA 95115; (408) 947-6654.

KWHY-TV, CHANNEL 22, 5545 Sunset Blvd., Los Angeles, CA 90028; (213) 466-5441.

KAPPA VIDEO, 801 S. Main St., Burbank, CA 91506; (818) 843-3400.

KEY WEST EDITING, 5701 Buckingham Parkway, #C, Culver City, CA 90230; (213) 645-3348.

KLASKY/CSUPO, 729 Seward St., Suite 101, Hollywood, CA 90038; (213) 463-0145.

KRAMER, JERRY & ASSOCIATES, 8640 W. Third St., Suite 11, Los Angeles, CA 90048; (213) 278-2947.

KUTT, DANIEL, 921 10th St., Santa Monica, CA 90403; (213) 394-6008.

—L—

LP PRODUCTIONS, 223 Strand St., Suite K, Santa Monica, CA 90405; (213) 399-1101.

LAJON PRODUCTIONS INC., 2907 W. Olive Ave., Burbank, CA 91505; (818) 841-1440.

LASER EDIT INC., 540 N. Hollywood Way, Burbank, CA 91505; (818) 842-0777.

LE DUC VIDEO PRODUCTIONS, 2002 21st St., Suite A, Santa Monica, CA 90404; (213) 450-8275; 450-2840.

LEVIN, KARL M., 20959 Elkwood St., Canoga Park, CA 91304; (818) 882-7262.

LIONEL TELEVISION PRODUCTIONS, 3329 Brookside Dr., Malibu, CA 90265; (213) 456-5809.

LUCASFILM LTD., P.O. Box 2009, San Raphael, CA 94912; (415) 662-1800.

—M—

M.A.T.E. VIDEOTAPE, 1653 18th St., Suite 3, Santa Monica, CA 90404; (213) 828-8807.

M.F.I. VIDEO CENTER, 1905 Grace Ave., Hollywood, CA 90068; (213) 851-0373.

MACPHERSON'S FILM CONTINUITY SERVICE, 13371 Gladstone Ave., Sylmar, CA 91342; (818) 367-4769.

MACROVISION, 10201 Torre Ave., Suite 330, Cupertino, CA 95014, (408) 252-9600.

MASTER DIGITAL INC., 1749 14th St., Santa Monica, CA 90404; (213) 452-1511.

MEDIA MASTERS PRODUCTIONS, 1800 S. Robertson Blvd., Suite 306, Beverly Hills, CA 90035; (213) 451-8823.

MEGA PRODUCTIONS INC., 1714 N. Wilton Pl., Hollywood, CA 90028; (213) 462-6342.

MERIDIAN, P.O. Box 1941, Hollywood, CA 90028; (213) 874-4367.

METAVISION, 347 S. Ogden Dr., Suite 200, Los Angeles, CA 90036; (213) 936-8281.

METROTAPE, (division of Metromedia), 5746 Sunset Blvd., Los Angeles, CA 90028; (213) 856-1356.

MIDTOWN VIDEO, 8489 W. Third St., Suite 67, Los Angeles, CA 90048; (213) 651-2420.

MOBILEFAX, 710 N. Seward St., Hollywood, CA 90038, (213) 467-4000.

MODERN TALKING PICTURE SERVICE INC., 6735 San Fernando Rd., Glendale, CA 91201; (818) 240-0519; (813) 541-7571.

MODERN VIDEOFILM, 7165 Sunset Blvd., Hollywood, CA 90046; (213) 851-8070.

MUSIC LAB INC., 1831 Hyperion Ave., Hollywood, CA 90027; (213) 666-3003.

—N—

NATARNO'S, JAN, VIDEOTAPE EDITING, 6132 DeLongpre Ave., Hollywood, CA 90028; (213) 462-5511.

NATIONAL TELEVISION NEWS INC., 213A, 23480 Park Sorrento, Calabasas Park, CA 91302; (818) 883-6121.

NEWMAN/FRANKS, 2956 Nicada Dr., Los Angeles, CA 90077; (213) 470-0140; 470-0145.

—O—

ONE PASS FILM & VIDEO, One China Basin Building, San Francisco, CA 94107; (415) 777-5777.

ORION ENTERPRISES, 1015 N. Cahuenga Blvd., Los Angeles, CA 90038; (213) 461-3844.

—P—

PRC OF AMERICA (PLASTIC REEL CORPORATION), 8140 Webb Ave., N. Hollywood, CA 91605; (818) 504-0400.

PACIFIC VIDEO, 809 N. Cahuenga Blvd., Los Angeles, CA 90038; (213) 462-6266.

PAINT BOX PLUS, 6464 Sunset Blvd., Suite 1000, Hollywood, CA 90028; (213) 856-8530.

POLYCOM DIGITAL POST, 2911 W. Olive, Burbank, CA 91504; (818) 845-1917.

POSITIVE MEDIA, 5422A Fair Ave., North Hollywood, CA 91601; (213) 461-0092.

THE POST GROUP, 6335 Homewood, Los Angeles, CA 90028; (213) 462-2300.

POST PLUS INC., 6650 Santa Monica Blvd., 2nd Floor, Hollywood, CA 90038; (213) 463-7108.

POST-PRODUCTION SYSTEMS, 2433 28th St., Suite H, Santa Monica, CA 90405; (213) 450-5094.

POST TIME EDITORIAL INC., 1777 N. Vine St., Suite 303, Los Angeles, CA 90028; (213) 462-6968.

POST 2, 115 N. Pacific Ave., Suite B, Glendale, CA 91202; (818) 242-7642.

PRECISION FOLEY & ADR, 6353 Homewood Ave., Hollywood, CA 90028; (213) 462-8235.

PREMORE INC., 5130 Klump Ave., North Hollywood, CA 91601; (818) 506-7714.

PRO VIDEO & CINETAPE, 801 N. La Brea Ave., Los Angeles, CA 90038; (213) 934-8836.

PRODUCERS ASSOCIATES, 7243 Santa Monica Blvd., W. Hollywood, CA 90046; (213) 851-4123.

PROFESSIONAL ARTISTS GROUP, 845 N. Highland Ave., Hollywood, CA 90038; (213) 871-2222.

R. PRODUCTIONS & VIDEO EVENTS, 1741 N. Ivar, Suite 210, Hollywood, CA 90028; (213) 465-4197.

RED CAR EDITING, 1040 N. Las Palmas, Los Angeles, CA 90038; (213) 466-4467.

REEL MAGIC, 11684 Ventura Blvd., Suite 325, Studio City, CA 91604; (818) 762-5670.

RENCHER'S EDITORIAL SERVICE, 738 Cahuenga Blvd., Hollywood, CA 90038; (213) 463-9836.

ROCK SOLID PRODUCTIONS, 801 S. Main St., Burbank, CA 91506; (818) 841-8220.

ROLAND, GLENN FILMS, 10711 Wellworth Ave., Los Angeles, CA 90024; (213) 475-0937.

RUBBER DUBBERS, INC., 626 Justin Ave., Glendale Ave., CA 91201; (818) 241-5600.

RUSSIAN HILL RECORDING, 1520 Pacific Ave., San Francisco, CA 94109; (415) 474-4520.

RUXIN, JIM, 12140 Olympic Blvd., Los Angeles, CA 90064; (213) 826-3666.

SAR PRODUCTIONS, 22801 Ventura Blvd., Suite 211, Woodland Hills, CA 91364; (818) 884-5646.

SCHULMAN VIDEO CENTER, 861 Seward St., Hollywood, CA 90038; (213) 465-8110.

SCOTTSOUND INC., 6110 Santa Monica Blvd., Los Angeles, CA 90038; (213) 462-6981.

SHORELINE PROFESSIONAL VIDEO SYSTEMS, 1622 N. Highland Ave., Hollywood, CA 90028; (213) 461-9800.

SIERRA VIDEO, 11320 Chandler, N. Hollywood, CA 91601; (818) 985-1531; 579-7045.

SKYLIGHT PRODUCTION INC., 6815 W. Willoughby, Suite 201, Los Angeles, CA 90038; (213) 464-4500.

SKYLINE PRODUCTIONS, 6309 Eleanor Ave., Hollywood, CA 90038; (213) 856-0033.

SOUND IMAGE STUDIOS, INC., 6556 Wilkinson Ave., N. Hollywood, CA 91606; (818) 762-8881.

SOUND MASTER, 10747 Magnolia Blvd., North Hollywood, CA 91601; (213) 650-8000.

SOUTH, LEONARD, PRODUCTIONS, 4500 Forman Ave., Suite 1, Toluca Lake, CA 91602; (818) 760-8383.

SPALLA, RICK VIDEO PRODUCTIONS, 1622 N. Gower, Los Angeles, CA 90028; (213) 469-7307.

SPECTRA IMAGE INC., 540 N. Hollywood Way, Burbank, CA 91505; (818) 842-1111.

SPRINGBOARD STUDIOS, 12229 Montague St., Los Angeles, CA 91331; (818) 896-4321.

SQUARE WHEEL PRODUCTIONS/THE CONSULTANCY, P.O. Box 675, Van Nuys, CA 91408-0675; (818) 508-0332.

STAGE FRIGHT PRODUCTIONS, 8817 Amboy Ave., Sun Valley, CA 91352; (818) 768-3333.

STARFAX, 654 Hawthorne St., Glendale, CA 91204; (818) 244-3600.

STARLIGHT EDITING SERVICES, 5250 Strohm, North Hollywood, CA 91601; (818) 769-3874.

SUNSET POST INC., 1813 Victory Blvd., Glendale, CA 91201; (818) 956-7912.

SUNSHINE COMMUNICATIONS, 565 N. Gower St., Hollywood, CA 90004; (213) 464-2223.

SUNWEST STUDIOS, 5533 Sunset Blvd., Hollywood, CA 90028; (213) 463-5631.

SUPERIOR VIDEO SERVICES, 13423 Saticoy St., North Hollywood, CA 91605; (818) 786-7060.

SYNC INC., 931 N. Gardner St., West Hollywood, CA 90046; (213) 851-6624.

TAJ SOUNDWORKS, 8207 W. 3rd St., Los Angeles, CA 90048; (213) 655-2775.

TAURO PRODUCTIONS, 5019 York Blvd., Highland Park, CA 90042; (213) 258-2379.

TELEMEDIA PRODUCTIONS, 18321 Ventura Blvd., Suite 660, Tarzana, CA 91356; (818) 708-2005.

TELE VIDICS, 2223 E. 223rd St., Long Beach, CA 90810, (213) 830-5296.

TELEPRINT OF LOS ANGELES, 3779 Cahuenga West, Studio City, CA 91604; (818) 760-3191.

TODD-AO GLEN GLENN STUDIOS, 900 N. Seward St., Hollywood, CA 90038; (213) 469-7221.

TOP VIDEO SERVICES INC., 10153 Riverside Dr., Suite 1B, Toluca Lake, CA 91602; (818) 763-1295.

TRANS-AMERICAN VIDEO INC., 1541 N. Vine St., Los Angeles, CA 90028; (213) 466-2141.

TRITRONICS INC., 733 N. Victory Bl., Burbank, CA 91502; (818) 569-4000.

TYLIE JONES & ASSOC. INC., 10718 Riverside Dr., North Hollywood, CA 91602; (818) 980-7300.

UCL VIDEO, 823 N. Seward St., Los Angeles, CA 90038; (213) 469-7291.

UDELL, BILL, PRODUCTIONS, 6006 Vantage Ave., North Hollywood, CA 91606; (818) 985-6866.

UNITEL VIDEO, 5555 Melrose Ave., Studio G, Los Angeles, CA 90038; (213) 468-4606.

USA PRODUCTIONS, RCA Building, 6363 Sunset Blvd., Suite 810, Hollywood, CA 90028; (213) 467-5256.

VRA TELEPLAY PICTURES, P.O. Box 8471, Universal Plaza Station, North Hollywood, CA 91608; (213) 462-1099.

VTR SERVICE COMPANY, 3169 Barbara Ct., Suite D, Hollywood, CA 90068; (213) 851-9700.

VALLEY VIDEO, 4209 W. Burbank Blvd., Burbank, CA 91505; (818) 841-2387.

VANTAGE POINT PRODUCTIONS, 228 Santa Monica Blvd., Suite 6, Santa Monica, CA 90401; (213) 394-5534; 394-3836.

VARITEL VIDEO, 3575 Cahuenga Blvd. West, Los Angeles, CA 90068; (213) 850-1165.

VECTOR PRODUCTIONS INC., P.O. Box 7000-645, Redondo Beach, CA 90277; (213) 757-0520, (213) 316-6031.

VENTURA COUNTY CABLEVISION, 30901 Agoura Rd., Westlake Village, CA 91361; (818) 889-0282.

VIA VISION PRODUCTIONS, 5919 Franklin Ave., Los Angeles, CA 90028; (213) 851-9607.

VIDCOM PRODUCTION FACILITY, 2426 Townsgate Rd., Suite K, Westlake Village, CA 91361; (818) 991-1974.

VIDEO ADVENTURES INC., 1015 Cahuenga Blvd., Hollywood, CA 90038; (213) 461-3288.

VIDEOASIS, 317 S. Verdugo Rd., Glendale, CA 91205; (818) 507-1037.

VIDEO CIRCUIT STUDIOS, 11440 Chandler Blvd., Studio 1400, N. Hollywood, CA 91601; (818) 506-5493.

VIDEO CRAFTSMEN INC., 6311 Romaine St., Los Angeles, CA 90038; (213) 464-4351.

VIDEO EVENTS INC., 6410 Santa Monica Blvd., Los Angeles, CA 90038; (213) 465-4197.

VIDEO HOUSE, 201 N. Hollywood Way, Suite 202, Burbank, CA 91505; (818) 954-9559.

VIDEO SUPPORT SERVICES INC., 3473½ Cahuenga Blvd. W., Los Angeles, CA 90068; (213) 469-9000.

THE VIDEO TAPE CO., 10545 Burbank Blvd., North Hollywood, CA 91601; (818) 985-1666.

VIDEO TECHNOLOGY & SERVICES, 500 N. Ventu Park Rd., Newbury Park, CA 91320; (818) 888-3040.

VIDEO TRANSITIONS INC., 910 N. Citrus Ave., Hollywood, CA 90038; (213) 465-3333.

VIDEOWERKS, 1316 Third St., Suite 102, Santa Monica, CA 90401; (213) 393-8754.

VIDEO WEST, 805 Larrabbee St., W. Hollywood, CA 90069; (213) 659-5762.

VIDEO-IT INC., 1016 Sycamore Ave., Hollywood, CA 90038; (213) 876-4055; (818) VID-EOIT; (213) 876-4055.

VIDE-U PRODUCTIONS, 612 N. Sepulveda Blvd., Los Angeles, CA 90049; (213) 472-7023.

VISUAL EYES PRODUCTIONS, 2401 Main St., Santa Monica, CA 90405; (213) 392-8300.

VITELLO & ASSOCIATES, 1612 W. Olive, Suite 203, Santa Monica, CA 91506; (818) 848-5919.

WEISBARTH, JACOB & ASSOC. INC., 9903 Santa Monica Blvd., Suite 256, Beverly Hills, CA 90212; (213) 277-9616.

WESTERN FILM INDUSTRIES, 30941 W. Agoura Rd., Suite 302, Westlake Village, CA 91361; (818) 889-7350.

WILDER BROTHERS VIDEO, 10327 Santa Monica Blvd., Los Angeles, CA 90025; (213) 557-3500.

WILDWOOD FILM SERVICE, 6855 Santa Monica Blvd., Suite 400, Los Angeles, CA 90038; (213) 462-6388.

WINTERS, GLENN, PRODUCTIONS, INC., P.O. Box 920, Montrose, CA 91020; (818) 790-4201.

WOLLIN PRODUCTION SERVICES INC., 666 N. Robertson Blvd., Los Angeles, CA 90069; (213) 659-0175.

NEW YORK

A.D.M. VIDEO PRODUCTIONS, 40 Seaview Blvd., Pt. Washington, NY 11050; (516) 484-6900.

A N S INTERNATIONAL VIDEO LTD., 396 Fifth Ave., New York, NY 10018; (212) 736-1007.

ALBA/EDITORIAL, 330 W. 42 St., New York, NY 10036; (212) 967-7345.

ALL CHANNELS VIDEO, INC., 630 Ninth Ave., New York, NY 10036; (212) 247-3428.

ALL-MOBILE VIDEO, 630 Ninth Ave., New York, NY 10036; (212) 757-8919.

AMERICAN TV VIDEO, 248 E. 48 St., New York, NY 10017; (212) 688-6222.

AQUARIUS TRANSFER, 12 E. 46 St., New York, NY 10017; (212) 581-0123.

ARANESS COMMUNICATIONS, 244 W. 49 St., Suite 400, New York, NY 10019; (212) 582-6246.

ARTEL VIDEO, INC., 1600 Broadway, New York, NY 10019; (212) 315-5665.

BNS VIDEO SERVICES, INC. (division of Broadcast News Service, Inc.), GPO 2360, Pier 62, W. 23 St., New York, NY 10011; (213) 466-0234, (212) 223-0909.

BETELGEUSE PRODUCTIONS, 44 E. 32 St., New York, NY 10016; (212) 213-1333.

BROADWAY VIDEO, 1619 Broadway, New York, NY 10019, (212) 265-7600.

BURTON, PHILIP, PRODUCTIONS, 1776 Broadway, Room 1810, New York, NY 10019; (212) 333-7710.

C & C VISUAL, 12 W. 27 St., New York, NY 10001; (212) 684-3830.

CAESAR VIDEO GRAPHICS, INC., 137 E. 25 St., New York, NY 10010; (212) 684-7673.

CAROB VIDEO, 250 W. 57 St., New York, NY 10107; (212) 957-9525.

CENTERLIGHT TELEVISION, 245 W. 19 St., New York, NY 10011; (212) 919-4745.

CHROMAVISION, 119 W. 22 St., New York, NY 10011; (212) 463-8997.

CINERGY COMMUNICATIONS CORP., 321 W. 44 St., New York, NY 10036; (212) 582-2900.

CINETAPE, INC., 241 E. 51 St., New York, NY 10022; (212) 355-0070.

CINE-VID POST PRODUCTION, INC., 25 W. 45 St., New York, NY 10036; (212) 704-4000.

COMMUNICATIONS PLUS VIDEO, 360 Park Ave. S., New York, NY 10010; (212) 686-9570.

COM/TECH, INC., 770 Lexington Ave., New York, NY 10021; (212) 826-2935.

THE CUTTING EDGE/EDITORIAL, 420 Lexington Ave., New York, NY 10017; (212) 599-4233.

DC VIDEO, 270 Lafayette St., New York, NY 10012; (212) 431-1646.

DJM FILMS INC., 4 E. 46 St., New York, NY 10017; (212) 687-0111.

DEVLIN PRODUCTIONS, INC., 1501 Broadway, New York, NY 10036; (212) 391-1313; FAX: (212) 391-2744.

EDITEL NEW YORK, 222 E. 44 St., New York, NY 10017; (212) 867-4600.

EDITING CONCEPTS, 214 E. 50 St., New York, NY 10022; (212) 980-3340.

EDITORS GAS VIDEO, INC., 16 E. 48 St., New York, NY 10017; (212) 832-6690.

ELECTRIC FILM, 87 Lafayette St., New York, NY 10013; (212) 925-3429.

EMPIRE VIDEO, 216 E. 45 St., New York, NY 10017; (212) 687-2060.

EVEN TIME LTD., 62 W. 45 St., New York, NY 10036; (212) 764-4700.

FAMA II PRODUCTIONS INC., 2750 Richmond Terrace, Staten Island, NY 10303; (718) 273-1780.

FRAMERUNNER, INC., 1995 Broadway, Suite 1100, New York, NY 10023; (212) 874-1730.

GROUND CONTROL VIDEO, 49 W. 27 St., Suite 903, New York, NY 10001; (212) 683-5455.

HORN/EISENBERG FILM & TAPE EDITING, 16 W. 46 St., New York, NY 10036; (212) 391-8166.

IMAGE MIX, INC., 305 E. 46 St., New York, NY 10017; (212) 752-3010.

INTERNATIONAL PRODUCTION CENTER, 514 W. 57 St., New York, NY 10019; (212) 582-6530.

INTERNATIONAL VIDEO SERVICES, 1501 Broadway, New York, NY 10036; (212) 730-1411.

JPC VIDEO INC., 11 E. 47 St., 4th floor, New York, NY 10017; (212) 223-0555.

JSL VIDEO SERVICES, INC., 25 W. 45th St., New York, NY 10036; (212) JSL-5082.

KTV CONSULTANTS, 226 E. 54 St., New York, NY 10022; (212) 223-0520.

KALEIDOSCOPE PRODUCTIONS, 601 W. 50 St., New York, NY 10019; (212) 489-7150.

KOPEL FILMS, 630 Ninth Ave., New York, NY 10036; (212) 757-4742.

L & D FILM/VIDEO, 630 Ninth Ave., New York, NY 10036; (212) 315-0410.

LM COMMUNICATIONS CORP., 60 Hamilton Terr., New York, NY 10031; (212) 283-2509.

LRP VIDEO, 3 Dag Hammarskjold Plaza, New York, NY 10017; (212) 759-0822.

MAGNO SOUND & VIDEO, 729 Seventh Ave., New York, NY 10019; (212) 302-2505.

MANHATTAN TRANSFER/EDIT, 545 Fifth Ave., New York, NY 10017; (212) 687-4000.

MANHATTAN VIDEO PRODUCTIONS, 12 W. 27 St., New York, NY 10001; (212) 683-6565.

MARKLE, WILLIAM, ASSOCIATES, 630 Ninth Ave., Suite 1409, New York, NY 10036; (212) 246-8642.

MATRIX VIDEO, 727 Eleventh Ave., New York, NY 10019; (212) 265-8500.

MODERN TELECOMMUNICATIONS, 1 Dag Hammarskjold Plaza, New York, NY 10017; (212) 355-0510.

MOVIELAB VIDEO, INC., 619 W. 54 St., New York, NY 10019; (212) 956-3900.

MULTI-VIDEO GROUP LTD., 50 E. 42 St., New York, NY 10017; (212) 986-1577.

MYRVIK, RON, PRODUCTIONS, 34 E. 29 St., New York, NY 10016; (212) 685-0726.

NEP PRODUCTIONS, INC., 56 W. 45 St., New York, NY 10036; (212) 382-1100.

NATIONAL VIDEO CENTER, 460 W. 42 St., New York, NY 10036; (212) 279-2000.

NATIONAL VIDEO INDUSTRIES, 15 W. 17 St., New York, NY 10011; (212) 691-1300.

NEXUS PRODUCTIONS, INC., 10 E. 40 St., New York, NY 10016; (212) 679-2180.

NORTHEAST VIDEO, INC., 420 Lexington Ave., New York, NY 10017; (212) 661-8830.

OCCASIONAL VIDEO, 534 E. 84 St., New York, NY 10028, (212) 737-3058.

OTTERSON TV, INC., 251 W. 30 St., 14 W, New York, NY 10001; (212) 695-7417.

P.A.T. FILM SERVICES, 630 Ninth Ave., New York, NY 10036; (212) 247-0900.

PHANTASMAGORIA PRODUCTIONS, INC., 630 Ninth Ave., New York, NY 10036; (212) 586-4890.

PICSONIC PRODUCTIONS, 25 W. 45 St., New York, NY 10036; (212) 575-1910; 575-1911.

PICTURE PERFECT PRODUCTIONS, 630 Ninth Ave., New York, NY 10036; (212) 333-5220.

POST EXPRESSIONS, 5 E. 47 St., New York, NY 10017; (212) 838-5130.

PRIMA LUX VIDEO, 30 W. 26 St., New York, NY 10010, (212) 206-1402.

PRINCZKO PRODUCTIONS, 9 E. 38 St., New York, NY 10016; (212) 683-1300.

R.G. VIDEO, 21 W. 46 St., New York, NY 10036; (212) 997-1464.

RVI/RUTT VIDEO INC., 137 E. 25 St., New York, NY 10010; (212) 685-4000.

REBO ASSOCIATES, 530 W. 25 St., New York, NY 10001; (212) 989-9466.

REEVES TELETAPE, 708 Third Ave., New York, NY 10017; (212) 573-8600.

ROSENBERG, WARREN, VIDEO SERVICES, 308 E. 79 St., New York, NY 10021; (212) 744-1111.

ROSS-GAFFNEY, 21 W. 46 St., New York, NY 10036; (212) 719-2744.

SAGA PRODUCTIONS, INC., 16 W. 19 St., New York, NY 10011; (212) 645-9600.

SALAMANDRA IMAGES, INC., 6 E. 39 St., New York, NY 10016; (212) 779-0707.

SHADOW LIGHT PRODUCTIONS, INC., 12 W. 27 St., New York, NY 10001; (212) 689-7511.

SPLICE IS NICE, 141 E. 44 St., New York, NY 10017; (212) 599-1711.

SYNAPSE TELECOMMUNICATIONS, INC., 304 E. 45 St., New York, NY 10017; (212) 370-9191.

TFI, TAPE-FILM INDUSTRIES, 619 W. 54 St., New York, NY 10019; (212) 708-0500.

TV-R/MASTER COLOR TRANSFER, INC., 333 W. 52 St., New York, NY 10019; (212) 541-4030.

TVC VIDEO, 225 E. 43 St., New York, NY 10017; (212) 599-1616.

TAKE THREE EDITORIAL INC., 141 E. 44 St., New York, NY 10017; (212) 687-3344.

THE TAPE HOUSE EDITORIAL CO., 216 E. 45 St., New York, NY 10017; (212) 557-4949.

TAPESTRY PRODUCTIONS, LTD., 924 Broadway, New York, NY 10010; (212) 677-6007.

TEATOWN VIDEO INC., 165 W. 46 St., New York, NY 10036; (212) 302-0722.

TELETECHNIQUES, INC., 1 W. 19 St., New York, NY 10011; (212) 206-1475; 633-1868.

TELSTAR EDITING, INC., 29 W. 38 St., New York, NY 10018; (212) 730-1000.

TODAY VIDEO, INC., 45 W. 45 St., New York, NY 10036; (212) 391-1020.

TRAIMAN, HENRY, ASSOCIATES, 160 Madison Ave., New York, NY 10016; (212) 889-3400.

TRANSCOM MEDIA, 902 Broadway, New York, NY 10010; (212) 529-1000.

TULCHIN STUDIOS, 240 E. 45 St., New York, NY 10017, (212) 986-8270.

UNITEL, 515 W. 57 St., New York, NY 10019; (212) 265-3600.

488

VCA TELETRONICS, 231 E. 55 St., New York, NY 10022, (212) 355-1600.

VALKAN FILMS, INC., 1600 Broadway, Suite 404, New York, NY 10019; (212) 586-1603.

VIDEO CASSETTE TRANSFERS, 1501 Broadway, New York, NY 10036; (212) 575-8433.

VIDEO CENTRAL, INC., 225 W. 36 St., New York, NY 10018; (212) 947-6960.

VIDEO MEDIA PRODUCTIONS, 1493-33 88 St., Howard Beach, NY; (718) 845-3709.

VIDEO PLANNING INC., 250 W. 57 St., New York, NY 10019; (212) 582-5066.

VIDEO PORTFOLIOS, 142 W. 24 St., New York, NY 10011, (212) 989-3858.

VIDEO RESOURCES NEW YORK, INC., 220 W. 71st St., New York, NY 10023; (212) 724-7055.

VIDEO TEAM, INC., 522 W. 36 St., New York, NY 10018; (212) 629-8010.

VIDEO 3000, 1400 Broadway, Penthouse Loft, New York, NY 10018; (212) 302-1313.

VIDEOGENIX OF NY, INC., 503-11 Broadway, New York, NY 10012; (212) 925-0445.

VIDEOWORKS, INC., 24 W. 40 St., New York, NY 10018; (212) 869-2500.

VIDLO VIDEO, 40 E. 21 St., New York, NY 10010; (212) 475-4140.

WINDSOR TOTAL VIDEO, 8 W. 38th St., New York, NY 10018; (212) 944-9090.

CONNECTICUT

E.C.A. STUDIO, Wilton, CT 06897; (203) 762-3380; (212) 333-5656.

ENCORE TELEPRODUCTIONS CORP., 600 Main St., Monroe, CT 06468; (203) 268-7487.

IMAGE PRODUCTIONS INC., 50 Water St., South Norwalk, CT 06854; (203) 853-3486.

PENNSYLVANIA

VIDEOSMITH, INC., 2006 Chancellor St., Philadelphia, PA 19103; (215) 864-0658.

CENTER CITY VIDEO, INC., 1503 Walnut St., Philadelphia, PA 19018; (215) 568-4134.

WASHINGTON, DC

CAPITOL VIDEO COMMUNICATIONS, INC., 2121 Wisconsin Ave., N.W., Washington, DC 20007; (202) 965-7800.

CIRACE VIDEO/INTERNATIONAL, P.O. Box 3510, Arlington, VA 22203; (703) 486-1555.

VOX-CAM ASSOCIATES, 813 Silver Springs Ave., Silver Spring, MD 29010; (301) 589-5377.

CANADA

MANTA VIDEO LABS, 311 Adelaide St. E., Toronto, Ont., M5A 1N2; (416) 863-9316.

PATHÉ SOUND & POST PRODUCTION CENTRE, 121 St. Patrick St., Toronto, Ont.; (416) 598-2521.

Video Equipment, Sales and Rental

WEST COAST

AMERICAN VIDEO FACTORY, 4150 Glencoe Ave., Marina Del Rey, CA 90292; (213) 823-8622; (800) 367-8433.
AMERICAN VIDEOGRAM INC., 12020 W. Pico Blvd., Los Angeles, CA 90064-1504; (213) 477-1535.
AMETRON RENTALS, 1200 N. Vine St., Los Angeles, CA 90038; (213) 466-4321.
AMPEX CORPORATION, 340 Parkside Dr., San Fernando, CA 91340-3098; (818) 365-8627.
AQUASTAR SYSTEMS, 3960 Laurel Canyon Blvd., #406, Studio City, CA 91604; (818) 880-5639; (800) 227-5606.
AUDIO GRAPHIC FILMS AND VIDEO, 6509 De Longpre Ave., Hollywood, CA 90028; (213) 462-6596, (213) 467-1234.
AUDIO SERVICES CORPORATION, 10639 Riverside Dr., N. Hollywood, CA 91602; (818) 980-9891; (800) 228-4429.
AUDIO-VIDEO CRAFT INC., 6753 Santa Monica Blvd., Los Angeles, CA 90038; (213) 655-3511.
AUDIO VISUAL HEADQUARTERS CORP., 361 N. Oak St., Inglewood, CA 90302; (213) 419-4040.
BERC (BROADCAST EQUIPMENT RENTAL COMPANY), 4545 Chermak St., Burbank, CA 91505; (818) 841-3000, (213) 464-7655.
BACKGROUND ENGINEERS INC., 1213 Flower St., Glendale, CA 91201; (818) 500-0454.
BETACAM SPECIALISTS, 3917 Riverside Dr., Suite 9137, Burbank, CA 91505; (818) 845-6480.
BEXEL CORPORATION, 801 S. Main St., Burbank, CA 91506; (818) 841-5051.
BOSUSTOW VIDEO, 2207 Colby Ave., W. Los Angeles, CA 90064-1504; (213) 478-0821.
BOWEN VIDEO FACILITIES & STAGE, 7826 Clybourn Ave., Sun Valley, CA 91352; (818) 504-0070.
BROADCAST REMOTE, 415 S. Flower, Burbank, CA 91502; (818) 841-0919.
BUDGET VIDEO, 1534 N. Highland Ave., Los Angeles, CA 90028; (213) 466-2431, (213) 464-7655.
CCR VIDEO CORPORATION, 6410 Santa Monica Blvd., Los Angeles, CA 90038; (213) 464-7151.
CALIFORNIA COMMUNICATIONS INC., 6900 Santa Monica Blvd., Los Angeles, CA 90038; (213) 466-8511.
CALIFORNIA VIDEO CENTER, 15303 Ventura Blvd., 11th Fl., Sherman Oaks, CA 91403; (818) 789-5000.
CINEMA PRODUCTS CORPORATION, 3211 S. La Cienega Blvd., Los Angeles, CA 90016-3112; (213) 836-7991.
CINE VIDEO, 948 N. Cahuenga Blvd., Hollywood, CA 90038; (213) 464-6200.
COLOR-VUE VIDEO ASST. INC., 1800 S. Victory Blvd., Building A, Burbank, CA 91201; (818) 244-7774.
COMTEL, 2201 N. Hollywood Way, Burbank, CA 91505; (213) 849-6701; (818) 846-0770; 5046 Ruffner St., San Diego, CA 92111; (619) 292-1090; 3152 E. La Palma, Suite D, Anaheim, CA 92806; (714) 630-4470.
COMPREHENSIVE SERVICE CORPORATION, P.O. Box 38339; Los Angeles, CA 90038; (213) 462-0969.
CONTINENTAL CAMERA SYSTEMS, 7240 Valjean Ave., Van Nuys, CA 91406; (818) 989-5222.
THE CREATIVE PARTNERSHIP, 7525 Fountain Ave., Hollywood, CA 90046; (213) 850-5551.
DAVIS, WALT ENTERPRISES, INC., 931 N. Cole Ave., Hollywood, CA 90038; (213) 461-0700.
GORDON, ALAN ENTERPRISES INC., 5362 Cahuenga Blvd., Beverly Hills, CA; (818) 985-5500.
GREENE, COWE & CO., 3083 N. Lima St., Burbank, CA 91504; (818) 841-7821.
H.C.V., 3034 Glendale Blvd., Los Angeles, CA 90039; (213) 662-1112.
HARRISON, STAN, 39039 Willowvale Rd., Palmdale, CA 93551; (818) 569-4528.
HOFFMAN VIDEO SYSTEMS, 870 N. Vine St., Hollywood, CA 90038; (213) 465-6900.
HORIZONTAL EDITING STUDIOS, 2625 W. Olive Ave., Burbank, CA 91505; (818) 841-6750.
ILLUMINATION, 20548 Pacific Coast Highway, Malibu, CA 90265; (213) 456-3423.
INSTANT REPLAY EQUIPMENT CO., 1122 W. Washington Blvd., Culver City, CA 90232; (213) 837-5507.
INTER VIDEO, 733 N. Victory Blvd., Burbank, CA 91502; (818) 843-3633; 569-4000.
KAPPA VIDEO, 801 S. Main St., Burbank, CA 91506; (818) 843-3400.
L.A. VIDEO, 273 S. Western Ave., Los Angeles, CA 90004; (213) 487-0524.

MAGNASYNC MOVIOLA, 5539 Riverton Ave., North Hollywood, CA 91601; (818) 763-8441.
MAJESTIC DUPLICATING & VIDEO SERVICE, 1208 W. Isabel St., Burbank, CA 91506; (213) 849-1535; (818) 843-1806.
MEGA PRODUCTIONS INC., 1714 N. Wilton Pl., Hollywood, CA 90028; (213) 462-6342.
MILES & COMPANY, 1418 Dodson Ave., San Pedro, CA 90732; (213) 548-0462.
ONE PASS FILM & VIDEO, One China Basin Building, San Francisco, CA 94107; (415) 777-5777.
P.D.S. VIDEO PRODUCTIONS, 1102 W. Chestnut St., Burbank, CA 91506; (818) 841-4711.
PRC OF AMERICA (PLASTIC REEL CORPORATION), 8140 Webb Ave., North Hollywood, CA 91605 (818) 504-0400.
PAL VIDEO, 19061 Tina Place, Tarzana, CA 91356; (818) 344-1603.
POSITIVE MEDIA, 5422A Fair Ave., North Hollywood, CA 91601; (818) 461-0092.
POST-PRODUCTION SYSTEMS, 2433 28th St., Suite H, Santa Monica, CA 90405; (213) 450-5094.
PREMIUM BROADCAST VIDEO RENTAL, 2141 Ventura Blvd., Suite 177, Woodland Hills, CA 91367; (818) 704-8884.
RANK PRECISION IND. INC., 13340 Saticoy, Unit F, North Hollywood, CA 91605; (818) 765-7265.
RENTACAM, 15016 Ventura Blvd., Suite 1, Sherman Oaks, CA 91403; (818) 501-7368.
ROCK SOLID PRODUCTIONS, 801 S. Main St., Burbank, CA 91506; (818) 841-8220.
SAWYER CAMERA VIDEO SERVICE, 1208 W. Isabel St., Burbank, CA 91506; (818) 843-1781; (213) 849-1535.
SCHULMAN VIDEO CENTER, 861 Seward St., Hollywood, CA 90038; (213) 465-8110.
SHORELINE PROFESSIONAL VIDEO SYSTEMS, 1622 N. Highland Ave., Hollywood, CA 90028; (213) 461-9800.
SIERRA VIDEO DIVERSIFIED VIDEO INDUSTRIES, INC., 4216 N. Maxson Rd., El Monte, CA 91732; (818) 579-7023; 579-7045.
SPRINGBOARD STUDIOS, 12229 Montague St., Los Angeles, CA 91331; (818) 896-4321.
STARFAX, 654 Hawthorne St., Glendale, CA 91204; (818) 244-3600.
STARLIGHT EDITING SERVICES, 5250 Strohm Ave., N. Hollywood, CA 91601; (818) 769-3874.
STATE OF THE ART AUDIO VISUAL EQUIPMENT, 23520 Telo Ave., Suite 10, Torrance, CA 90505; (213) 530-8711.
STEENBECK INC., 9554 Vassar Ave., Chatsworth, CA 91311; (818) 998-4033.
STUDIO & REMOTE VIDEO, 10650 Magnolia Blvd., North Hollywood, CA 91601; (818) 508-6010.
STUDIO SPECTRUM INC., 1056 N. Lake St., Burbank, CA 91502; (818) 843-1610.
TELEMEDIA PRODUCTIONS, 18321 Ventura Blvd., Suite 660, Tarzana, CA 91356; (818) 708-2005.
TIME LOGIC SYSTEMS, 5555 Melrose Ave., Studio G, Hollywood, CA 90038; (213) 468-4608.
UNITED TELEPRODUCTION SERVICES, 15055 Oxnard St., Van Nuys, CA 91411; (818) 997-0100.
U.T. PHOTO SERVICE INC., 3088 N. Clybourn Ave., Burbank, CA 91505; (213) 245-6631.
VTR SERVICE AND SALES, 3169 Barbara Ct., Suite D, Hollywood, CA 90068; (213) 851-9700.
VECTOR ENGINEERING, P.O. Box 7000-645, Redondo Beach, CA 90277; (213) 757-0520; (213) 316-6031.
VIDEO ADVENTURES INC., 1015 Cahuenga Blvd., Hollywood, CA 90038; (213) 461-3288.
VIDEO EQUIPMENT RENTALS, 450 S. Central Ave., Glendale, CA 91204; (818) 956-0212.
VIDEO IMAGE, 4121 Redwood Ave., Suite 215, Los Angeles, CA 90066; (213) 822-8872.
VIDEO-IT INC., 1016 N. Sycamore Ave., Hollywood, CA 90038; (213) 876-4055; (213) VID-EOIT.
VIDEO POOL, 1832 N. Gower St., Hollywood, CA 90028; (213) 461-7665; (818) 798-4336.
VIDEO SUPPORT SERVICES INC., 3473½ Cahuenga Blvd. W., Los Angeles, CA 90068; (213) 469-9000.
VIDEOTAPE PRODUCTS INC., 320 N. Madison Ave., Los Angeles, CA 90004; (213) 664-1144; (800) 422-2444.
VISUAL EYES PRODUCTIONS, 2401 Main St., Santa Monica, CA 90405; (213) 392-8300.
WESTERN FILM INDUSTRIES, 30941 W. Agoura Rd., Suite 302, Westlake Village, CA 91360; (818) 889-7350.
WEXLER VIDEO INC., Burbank Prod. Plaza, 801 S. Main St., Burbank, CA 91506; (818) 846-9381.
Z & A SERVICE, 9707 W. Washington Blvd., Culver City, CA 90232; (213) 836-3194.

490

NEW YORK

ANS LABS, 396 Fifth Ave., New York, NY 10018; (212) 736-1007.
ARC VIDEO EQUIPMENT, 511 W. 33 St., New York, NY 10001; (212) 629-0009.
A/T SCHARFF, 599 Eleventh Ave., New York, NY 10036; (212) 582-4400.
ALL-MOBILE VIDEO, INC., 630 Ninth Ave., New York, NY 10036; (212) 757-8919.
AMERICAN VIDEO INC., 717 Lexington Ave., New York, NY 10022; (212) 888-0888.
AUDIO SERVICES CORPORATION, 326 W. 48 St., New York, NY 10036; (212) 977-5151.
AUDIO VIDEO SALON INC., 1553 Second Ave., New York, NY 10028; (212) 249-4104.
BNS VIDEO SERVICES, INC., Pier 62, W. 23 St., New York, NY 10011; (212) 466-0234; 223-0900.
BARGAIN SPOT, 64 Third Ave., New York, NY 10003; (212) 674-1188.
BIG APPLE VIDEO, 367 First Ave., New York, NY 10010; (212) 420-0370.
BOGAZICI VIDEO LTD., 460 Seventh Ave., New York, NY 10001; (212) 563-9022.
BROADCAST VIDEO RENTALS, LTD., 333 W. 52 St., New York, NY 10019; (212) 541-5390.
BROTHERS CAMERAS, INC., 466 Lexington Ave., 10017; (212) 986-3323.
BRYCE AUDIO VIDEO CO., 115 W. 40 St., New York, NY 10018; (212) 575-8600.
CTL ELECTRONICS INC., 116 W. Broadway, New York, NY 10013; (212) 233-0754.
THE CAMERA GROUP OF NEW YORK, INC., 25-50 30th Rd., Suite 4G, Astoria, NY 11102; (212) 254-3600.
THE CAMERA MART, 456 W. 55 St., New York, NY 10019; (212) 757-6977.
CAMERA SERVICE CENTER, INC., 625 W. 54 St., New York, NY 10019; (212) 757-0906.
CITICAM VIDEO SERVICES, 630 Ninth Ave., Suite 910, New York, NY 10036; (212) 315-4855.
COLUMBUS TV & VIDEO CENTER, 529 Columbus Ave., New York, NY 10024; (212) 496-2626.
COMPREHENSIVE SERVICE A-V INC., Box 881, New York, NY 10108; (212) 586-6161.
COSMOPHONIC SOUND INC., 1614 Second Ave., New York, NY 10028; (212) 734-0459.
FERCO VIDEO, 707 Eleventh Ave., New York, NY 10019; (212) 245-4800.
FIRST RUN VIDEO INC., 1390 Third Ave., New York, NY 10021; (212) 772-3838; 1147½ Second Ave., New York, NY 10021; (212) 935-1212.
FORTY-SEVENTH ST. PHOTO INC., 38 E. 19 St., New York, NY 10003; (212) 260-4410; 116 Nassau St., New York, NY 10038; (212) 608-6934; 67 W. 47 St., New York, NY 10036; (212) 398-1410; 115 W. 45 St., New York, NY 10036; (212) 398-1410.
FOX TELEVISION OF AMERICA, INC., 333 W. 52 St., Suite 702, New York, NY 10019; (212) 246-4300.
G & R VIDEO, 522 W. 36 St., New York, NY 10018; (212) 564-7260.
GRAND CENTRAL RADIO, 155 E. 45 St., New York, NY 10017; (212) 682-3869.
HARVEY ELECTRONICS, 2 W. 45 St., New York, NY 10036; (212) 575-5000.
INTERCONTINENTAL TELEVIDEO INC., 29 W. 38 St., New York, NY 10018; (212) 719-0202.
INTERNATIONAL ELECTRONICS CO., 211 Eighth Ave., New York, NY 10011; (212) 243-2362.
J & R MUSIC WORLD, 23 Park Row, New York, NY 10038; (212) 732-8600.
JEMS SOUND LTD., 785 Lexington Ave., New York, NY 10021; (212) 838-4716.
K V L AUDIO VISUALS INC., 529 W. 46 St., New York, NY 10036; (212) 977-4488.
L & D FILM/VIDEO, 630 Ninth Ave., New York, NY 10036; (212) 315-0410.
LAST STOP VIDEO INC., 4979 Broadway, New York, NY 10034; (212) 304-9311.
LAUMIC CO., 306 E. 39 St., New York, NY 10016; (212) 889-3300.
LEONARD RADIO, 55 W. 44 St., New York, NY 10036; (212) 840-2025.
LONGWOOD VIDEO, 32 W. 22 St., New York, NY 10010; (212) 741-3733.
MPCS VIDEO INDUSTRIES, 514 W. 57 St., New York, NY 10019; (212) 586-3690.
MAR VIDEO INC., 10 W. 30 St., New York, NY 10001; (212) 683-7966.
MARTIN AUDIO-VIDEO CORP., 423 W. 55 St., New York, NY 10019; (212) 541-5900.
MAYA VIDEO PRODS. INC., 172 Madison Ave., New York, NY 10001; (212) 532-6206.

METRO ELECTRONICS CORP., 81 West Broadway, New York, NY 10007; (212) 406-2760.
MIDTOWN AUDIO & VIDEO CENTER, INC., 158 W. 29 St., New York, NY 10010; (212) 629-8633.
MILLER L. MATTHEW, ASSOCIATES, LTD., 48 W. 21 St., New York, NY 10010; (212) 741-8011.
MODERN TELECOMMUNICATIONS, INC., 1 Dag Hammarskjold Plaza, New York, NY 10017; (212) 355-0510.
MOVIE MOBILE INC., 3015 Vernon Blvd., Long Island City, NY 11102; (718) 545-7200.
NATIONAL TELE-RENT INC., 150-09 12th Rd., Whitestone, NY 11357; (212) 829-1600.
NATIONAL VIDEO INDUSTRIES, 15 W. 17 St., New York, NY 10011; (212) 691-1300.
NEW YORK VIDEO, 717 Lexington Ave., New York, NY 10022; (212) 755-4640.
NORTHEAST ELECTRONIC & VIDEO STORES, 420 Lexington Ave., New York, NY 10017; (212) 661-8830.
OLDEN CAMERA VIDEO & COMPUTER STORE, 1265 Broadway, New York, NY 10001; (212) 725-1234.
OMNI VIDEO SERVICES, INC., 511 W. 33 St., New York, NY 10001; (212) 629-4303.
REEVES COMMUNICATIONS, 708 Third Ave., New York, NY 10017; (212) 573-8888; 573-8600.
RELIANCE AUDIO-VISUAL CORP., 623 W. 51 St., New York, NY 10019; (212) 586-5000.
RODNEY'S VIDEO WAREHOUSE, 128 Mamaroneck Ave., White Plains, NY; (914) 946-9696.
S RENTAL CO., 13 E. 31 St., New York, NY 10010; (212) 685-3344; 33-49 55th St., Woodside, NY; (718) 458-3800.
SAVEMART INC., 88 Chambers St., New York, NY 10007; (212) 267-8130; 7 E. 14 St., New York, NY 10003; (212) 243-8456; 599 W. 181 St., New York, NY 10033; (212) 928-2000.
SELECT AUDIO VISUAL INC., 902 Broadway, New York, NY 10010; (212) 598-9800.
SONOCRAFT CORP., 360 W. 31st St., New York, NY 10001; (212) 760-9300.
SOUND & VISION INC., 83 Leonard St., New York, NY 10012; (212) 219-3007.
SOUNDVIEW AV CO., 347 W. 39 St., New York, NY 10018; (212) 594-0183.
SPATARO, CHARLIE, A. V. WORKSHOP, 333 W. 52nd St., New York, NY 10019; (212) 397-5020.
STREET VISIONS REMOTE INC., 34 Gansevoort St., New York, NY 10014; (212) 242-4324.
TECHNISPHERE, 29 E. 19 St., New York, NY 10003; (212) 777-5100.
TELE-CASSETTE SERVICES, INC. 3315 Sycamore La., Yorktown Heights, NY 10598; (914) 245-5005.
TELESTAR VIDEO, 206 E. 29 St., New York, NY 10016; (212) 689-1040.
TELETECHNIQUES, INC., 1 W. 19 St., New York, NY 10011; (212) 206-1475; 663-1868.
TEMMER LIGHTING, 1 W. 19 St., New York, NY 10011; (212) 206-1475; 633-1868.
TOWN VIDEO SALES, 21 Ann St., New York, NY 10038; (212) 267-9760.
VICOM COMMUNICATIONS, 248 W. 33 St., New York, NY 10001; (212) 685-5232.
VIDEO CENTRAL, 225 W. 36 St., New York, NY 10018; (212) 947-6960.
VIDEO OVERSEAS INC., 249 W. 23 St., New York, NY 10011; (212) 645-0797.
VIDEO POWER USA INC., 511 W. 54 St., New York, NY 10019; (212) 315-0810.
VIDEO RENTALS INC., 100 Stonehurst Ct., Northvale, NJ 07647; (201) 768-3181; (800) 255-2874.
VIDEO STOP INC., 367 Third Ave., New York, NY (212) 685-6199.
VIDEO 35, 254 W. 98th St., New York, NY 10025; (212) 864-1408.
VISUAL WORD SYSTEMS INC., 17 E. 45 St., New York, NY 10017; (212) 661-3366.
WEST VILLAGE VIDEO, 680 Washington St., New York, NY 10014; (212) 691-7430.
WILLOUGHBYS, 110 W. 32 St., New York, NY 10001; (212) 564-1600.
WINDSOR TOTAL VIDEO, 8 W. 38 St., New York, NY 10018; (212) 944-9090.
THE WIZ, 12 W. 45 St., New York, NY 10036; (212) 302-2000; 2577 Broadway, New York, NY 10025; (212) 662-9000; 17 Union Sq. W., New York, NY 10003; (212) 741-9500; 1922 Third Ave., New York, NY 10029; (212) 369-0600; 404 Ave. of the Americas, New York, NY 10011; (212) 677-2100; 230 W. 125 St., New York, NY 10027; (212) 866-4200.
YK VIDEO, 432 Park Ave. S., New York, NY 10037; (212) 686-8515.
ZAZY INTERNATIONAL, 49 W. 24 St., New York, NY 10011; (212) 807-8060.

Video Equipment Repair

LOS ANGELES

AMERICAN VIDEO FACTORY, 4150 Glencoe Ave., Marina Del Rey, CA 90292; (213) 823-8622.
AMETRON RENTALS, 1200 N. Vine St., Los Angeles, CA 90038; (213) 466-4321; 464-1144.
AMPAC VIDEO, 3637 Cahuenga Blvd. W., Hollywood, CA 90068; (213) 851-7200.
AMPEX CORP., 340 Parkside Dr., San Fernando, CA 91340; (818) 365-8627.
ATLAS VIDEO, 8113 State S Gt., Los Angeles, CA; (213) 569-1393.
AUDIO ARTS PUBLISHING CO., 5617 Melrose Ave., Los Angeles, CA 90038; (213) 461-3507.
AUDIO GRAPHICS FILMS & VIDEO, 6509 De Longpre Ave., Hollywood, CA 90028; (213) 462-6596; 467-1234.
AUDIO VISUAL HEADQUARTERS CORP., 361 N. Oak St., Inglewood, CA 90302; (213) 419-4040.
BERC (BROADCAST EQUIPMENT RENTAL CO.), 4545 Chermak St., Burbank, CA 91505; (818) 841-3000; (213) 464-7655.
BACKGROUND ENGINEERS INC., 1213 Flower St., Glendale, CA 91201; (818) 500-0454.
BEVERLY HILLS VIDEOCENTER, 187 S. Beverly Dr., Beverly Hills, CA 90212; (213) 550-1092.
BROADCAST REMOTE FAX, 415 S. Flower St., Burbank, CA 91502; (818) 841-0919.
BUDGET VIDEO, 1534 N. Highland Ave., Los Angeles, CA 90028; (213) 466-2431.
BURBANK PRODUCTION PLAZA, 801 S. Main St., Burbank, CA 91506; (818) 846-7677.
CCR VIDEO CORP., 6410 Santa Monica Blvd., Los Angeles, CA 90038; (213) 464-7151.
CINE VIDEO, 948 N. Cahuenga Blvd., Hollywood, CA 90038; (213) 464-6200.
CINEMA PRODUCTS CORPORATION, 3211 S. La Cienega Blvd., Los Angeles, CA 90016-3112; (213) 836-7991; 478-0711.
COMPREHENSIVE SERVICE CORP., P.O. Box 38339, Los Angeles, CA 90038; (213) 462-0969.
CONTINENTAL CAMERA RENTALS, 7240 Valjean Ave., Van Nuys, CA 91406; (818) 989-5222.
CREATIVE PARTNERSHIP, 7526 Fountain Ave., Hollywood, CA 90046; (213) 850-5551.
DAVIS, WALT ENTERPRISES, INC., 931 N. Cole, Hollywood, CA 90038; (213) 876-6400.
EDIT POINT, 316 Pasadena Ave., S. Pasadena, CA 91030; (818) 799-5611.
ELECTRONIC SERVICE CENTER, 1141 Westminister, Suite 4, Alhambra, CA 91803; (818) 282-8684; 282-8719.
ELFMAN, RICHARD, PRODUCTIONS, 723 Ocean Front Walk, Venice, CA 90291; (213) 399-9118.
EYE ON STUDIO, 224 N. Juanita Ave., Los Angeles, CA 90004; (213) 465-7777.
EYE SQUARE VIDEO INC., 1749 14th St., Santa Monica, CA 90404; (213) 452-9076.
GORDON, ALAN ENTERPRISES INC., 5362 Cahuenga Blvd., Hollywood, CA; (818) 985-5500; (213) 466-3561.
H.C.V., 3034 Glendale Blvd., Los Angeles, CA 90039; (213) 662-1112.
HOFFMAN VIDEO SYSTEMS, 1945 S. Figueroa St., Los Angeles, CA 90007; (213) 749-3311.
HUCHINGSON MARTIN, 3169 Barbara Court, Suite A, Los Angeles, CA 90068; (213) 876-4001.
IMMEDIATO, JEFFREY & ASSOCIATES, P.O. Box 5611, Long Beach, CA 90805; (213) 422-9295.
INSTANT REPLAY COMMUNICATIONS CO., 11122 W. Washington Blvd., Culver City, CA 90232; (213) 870-9435.
INTERVIDEO/TRITRONICS, INC., 733 N. Victory Blvd., Burbank, CA 91502; (818) 569-4400; 843-3633.
KAPPA VIDEO, 801 S. Main St., Burbank, CA 91506; (818) 843-3400.
KEM FILM/VIDEO SYSTEMS, 662 N. Van Ness Ave., Suite 303, Los Angeles, CA 90004; (213) 467-1547.
L.A. VIDEO, 273 S. Western, Los Angeles, CA 90004; (213) 487-0524.
LIONEL TELEVISION PRODUCTIONS, 3329 Brookside Dr., Malibu, CA 90265; (213) 456-5809.
MAGNASYNC MOVIOLA, 5539 Riverton Ave., N. Hollywood, CA 91601; (818) 763-8441.
MILES & COMPANY, 1418 Dodson Ave., San Pedro, CA 90732; (213) 548-0462.
ONE PASS MOBILE SERVICES, 729 N. Highland Ave., Hollywood, CA 90038; (213) 937-4095.
PDS VIDEO PRODUCTIONS, 1102 W. Chestnut St., Burbank, CA 91506; (818) 841-4711.

PRC OF AMERICA (PLASTIC REEL CORP.), 8140 Webb Ave., N. Hollywood, CA 91605; (818) 504-0400.
PAL VIDEO, 19061 Tina Pl., Tarzana, CA 91356; (818) 344-1603.
POSITIVE MEDIA, 5422A Fair Ave., North Hollywood, CA 91601; (818) 461-0092.
RANK CINETEL INC., 13340 Saticoy, Unit F, N. Hollywood, CA 91605; (818) 765-7265.
ROCK SOLID PRODUCTIONS, 801 S. Main St., Burbank, CA 91506; (818) 841-8220.
SAWYER CAMERA & VIDEO SERVICE, 1208 W. Isabel St., Burbank, CA 91506; (818) 843-1781.
SCHULMAN VIDEO CENTER, 861 Seward St., Hollywood, CA 90038; (213) 465-8110.
SHORELINE LTD., 1622 N. Highland Ave., Hollywood, CA 90028; (213) 461-9800.
SIERRA VIDEO DIVERSIFIED VIDEO INDUSTRIES, INC., 4216 N. Maxson Rd., El Monte, CA 91732; (818) 579-7023; 579-7045.
SPECTRA IMAGE INC., 540 N. Hollywood Way, Burbank, CA 91505; (818) 842-1111.
STARFAX, 654 Hawthorne St., Glendale, CA 91204; (818) 244-3600.
STARLIGHT EDITING SERVICES, 5250 Strohm, North Hollywood, CA 91601; (818) 769-3874.
STATE OF THE ART AUDIO-VISUAL EQUIPMENT, 23520 Telo Ave., Suite 10, Torrance, CA; (213) 530-8711.
STEENBECK INC., 9554 Vassar Ave., Chatsworth, CA 91311; (818) 998-4033.
STUDIO SPECTRUM INC., 1056 N. Lake St., Burbank, CA 91502; (818) 843-1610.
TOP VIDEO SERVICES INC., 10153 Riverside Dr., Suite 1B, Toluca Lake, CA 91602; (818) 763-1295.
U.T. PHOTO SERVICE INC., 3088 N. Clybourn Ave., Burbank, CA 91505; (213) 245-6631.
VCR DOCTOR, 12471 Washington Blvd., Los Angeles, CA 90066; (213) 301-3322.
VTR SERVICE AND SALES, 3169 Barbara Ct., Suite D, Hollywood, CA 90068; (213) 851-9700.
VECTOR ENGINEERING, P.O. Box 7000-645, Redondo Beach, CA 90277; (213) 757-0520; 316-6031.
VIDEO ADVENTURES, INC., 1015 Cahuenga Blvd. Hollywood, CA 90038; (213) 461-3288.
VIDEO CIRCUIT STUDIOS, 11440 Chandler Blvd., Studio 1400, N. Hollywood, CA 91601; (818) 506-5493.
VIDEO SUPPORT SERVICES, 3473½ Cahuenga Blvd. West, Los Angeles, CA 90068; (213) 469-9000.
VIDEO-IT INC., 1016 N. Sycamore, Hollywood, CA 90038; (213) 876-4055; (818) VIDEOIT
VIDEOTAPE PRODUCTS INC., 320 N. Madison Ave., Los Angeles, CA 90004; (213) 664-1144; (800) 422-2444.
WESTERN FILM INDUSTRIES, 30941 W. Agoura Rd., Suite 302, Westlake Village, CA 91360; (818) 889-7350.
WEXLER VIDEO INC., Burbank Production Plaza, 801 S. Main St., Burbank, CA 91506; (818) 846-9381.
Z & A SERVICE, 9707 W. Washington Blvd., Culver City, CA 90232; (213) 836-3194.

NEW YORK

AABCO CO., 1588 York Ave., New York, NY 10028; (212) 535-9578.
AJ'S VIDEO INC., 205 East Broadway, New York, NY 10002; (212) 477-4880.
ADVISORY TV & RADIO LABS, 175 Seventh Ave., New York, NY 10011; (212) 243-0786.
ALL CITY ELECTRONICS SERVICE INC., 1 E. 36 St., New York, NY 10016; (212) 689-7180.
ALL-WAYS SALES & SERVICE INC., 325 Third Ave., 10010; (212) 685-6285.
AMERICAN VIDEO SERVICE DEPT., 516 Amsterdam Ave., New York, NY 10024; (212) 724-4870.
APEX VIDEO TV REPAIR, 1235 First Ave., New York, NY 10021; (212) 517-4300.
AUDIO VIDEO SALON INC., 1553 Second Ave., New York, NY 10028; (212) 249-4104.
AUDIOVISIONS, 1319 Second Ave., New York, NY 10021; (212) 988-5756.
AUTHORIZED FACTORY SERVICE CO., 902 Broadway, New York, NY 10010; (212) 598-4822.

492

BERRY CAMERA REPAIR, 152 Fourth Ave., New York, NY 10003; (212) 677-8407.

BOGAZICI VIDEO LTD., 460 Seventh Ave., New York, NY 10001; (212) 563-9022; 594-1707.

BRYCE AUDIO/VIDEO CENTER, 115 W. 40 St., New York, NY 10018; (212) 575-8600; (800) 223-1346.

CTL ELECTRONICS, 150 Duane St., New York, NY 10013; (212) 233-0754.

CINE MAGNETICS VIDEO, 50 W. 40 St., New York, NY 10018; (212) 542-0700.

COLUMBUS TV & VIDEO CENTER, 529 Columbus Ave., New York, NY 10024; (212) 496-2626.

COSMOPHONIC SOUND, INC. 1614 Second Ave., New York, NY 10028; (212) 734-0459.

E C ELECTRONICS, 254 W. 51 St., New York, NY 10019; (212) 586-6156.

EMPIRE STATE TELEPHONE SYSTEMS INC., 218 E. 82nd St., New York, NY 10028; (212) 737-3556.

FAMAVISION, FAMA II PRODUCTIONS, 2750 Richmond Terr., Staten Island, NY 10303; (718) 273-1780.

GENERAL VIDEO, 250 W. 57 St., New York, NY 10019; (212) 956-4150.

GERMAN HI-FI SERVICE, 1574 Third Ave., New York, NY 10128; (212) 369-3366.

HARVEY ELECTRONICS, 2 W. 45 St., New York, NY 10036; (212) 575-5000.

INTERNATIONAL ELECTRONICS CO., 211 Eighth Ave., New York, NY 10011; (212) 243-2362.

JAPANESE AMERICAN TRANSITOR SERVICE, 86 West Broadway, New York, NY 10007; (212) 964-8286.

LUNAR VIDEO LTD., 138 E. 26 St., New York, NY 10010; (212) 686-4802.

MARTIN AUDIO-VIDEO CORP., 423 W. 55 St., New York, NY 10019; (212) 541-5900.

MERCURY VIDEO SERVICE, 301 W. 56 St., New York, NY 10019; (212) 246-6711.

MIRACLE VIDEO, 693 Ninth Ave., New York, NY 10036; (212) 246-0831.

MOTTO TV SALES & SERVICE, 428 Second Ave., New York, NY 10010; (212) 532-2839.

NATIONAL TELE-RENT INC., 150-09 12th Rd., Whitestone, NY 11357; (212) 829-1600.

PYRAMID ELECTRONICS INC., 353 E. 76 St., New York, NY 10021; (212) 628-6500.

RELIANCE AUDIO-VISUAL CORP., 623 W. 51 St., New York, NY 10019; (212) 586-5000.

RIDGE RADIO & TELEVISION SERVICE CO., 51 University Place, New York, NY 10003; (212) 673-6400.

SELECT AUDIO VISUAL INC., 902 Broadway, New York, NY 10010; (212) 598-9800.

SUPERIOR ELECTRONIC CO., 122 Madison Ave., New York, NY 10016; (212) 962-6274.

TECHNETRON ELECTRONICS INC., 43 E. 29 St., New York, NY 10016; (212) 725-8778; 725-8779.

TECHNISPHERE CORP., 29 E. 19 St., New York, NY 10003; (212) 777-5100.

TELETECHNIQUES, 1 W. 19 St., New York, NY 10011; (212) 633-1868.

TELEVIDEO ELECTRONIC CORP., 233 W. 77 St., New York, NY 10024; (212) 874-7722.

TRIBORO TELEVISION SERVICE, 1626 First Ave., New York, NY 10028; (212) 249-0327.

UNISON ELECTRONIC CORP., 98-102 E. 12 St., New York, NY 10003; (212) 673-2032.

UNIVERSITY HI-FI & TAPE, 15 Third Ave., New York, NY 10003; (212) 477-5240.

VI-AUD, SALES & SERVICE, 300 W. 43 St., New York, NY 10036; (212) 245-7966.

VIDCOM COMMUNICATIONS, 248 E. 33 St., New York, NY 10016; (212) 867-7335.

VIDEO CENTRAL, 225 W. 36 St., New York, NY 10018; (212) 947-6960.

VIDEO DIAGNOSTICS, 17 E. 45 St., New York, NY 10017; (212) 557-6690.

VIDEO INSTALLATIONS PLUS INC., 360 S. Broadway, Yonkers, NY; (914) 968-3636.

VIDEO SERVICE CENTER, 225 W. 36 St., New York, NY 10018; (212) 947-6960.

VIDEO WORLD, 138 W. Houston, New York, NY 10012; (212) 673-2435.

WAVE ELECTRONICS, 910 West End Ave., New York, NY 10025; (212) 222-0909.

WILLOUGHBY'S, 110 W. 32 St., New York, NY 10001; (212) 564-1600.

Video Mobile Units

LOS ANGELES

ABC TELEVISION CENTER, 4151 Prospect Ave., Los Angeles, CA 90027; (213) 557-7777.

ALL SEASONS ENTERTAINMENT, 18121 Napa St., Northridge, CA 91325; (818) 886-8680; (800) 423-5599.

AMERICAN VIDEO FACTORY, 4150 Glencoe Ave., Marina Del Rey, CA 90292; (213) 823-8622; (800) 367-8433.

AMERICAN VIDEOGRAM INC., 12020 W. Pico Blvd., Los Angeles, CA 90064; (213) 477-1535, 477-1536.

AQUASTAR SYSTEMS, 3960 Laurel Canyon Blvd., #406, Studio City, CA 91604; (818) 880-5639; (800) 227-5600.

BERC (BROADCAST EQUIPMENT RENTAL COMPANY), 4545 Chermak St., Burbank, CA 91505; (818) 841-3000; (213) 464-7655.

BETACAM SPECIALISTS, 3719 Riverside Dr., Suite 9137, Burbank, CA 91505; (818) 845-6480.

BEXEL CORPORATION, 801 S. Main St., Burbank, CA 91506; (818) 841-5051.

BOWEN VIDEO FACILITIES, 7826 Clybourn Ave., Sun Valley, CA 91352; (818) 504-0070.

BROADCAST REMOTE, 415 S. Flower, Burbank, CA 91502; (818) 841-0919.

CCR VIDEO CORPORATION, 6410 Santa Monica Blvd., Los Angeles, CA 90038; (213) 464-7151.

COLOR-VUE VIDEO ASSIST INC., 1800 S. Victory Blvd., Bldg. A, Burbank, CA 91201; (818) 244-7774.

EDIT POINT, 316 Pasadena Ave., Suite 6, S. Pasadena, CA 91030; (818) 799-5611.

EYE ON VIDEO, 224 N. Juanita Ave., Los Angeles, CA 90004; (213) 382-4048.

EYE SQUARE VIDEO INC., 1749 14th St., Santa Monica, CA 90404; (213) 452-9076.

HOLLYWOOD NATIONAL STUDIOS, 6605 Eleanor Ave., Los Angeles, CA 90038; (213) 467-6272.

HOLLYWOOD NEWSREEL SYNDICATE, INC., 1622 N. Gower St., Los Angeles, CA 90028; (213) 469-7307.

HUTCHINGSON MARTIN, 3169 Barbara Court, Suite A, Los Angeles, CA 90068; (213) 876-4001.

IMMEDIATO, JEFFREY, & ASSOCIATES, P.O. Box 5611, Long Beach, CA 90805; (213) 422-9295.

INTER VIDEO/TRITRONICS, INC., 733 N. Victory Bl., Burbank, CA 91502; (818) 569-4000; 843-3633.

JP VIDEO SERVICES, (BETA CAM PRODUCTIONS), 9538 W. Pico Blvd., Los Angeles, CA 90035; (213) 271-1209; 859-9903.

KCOP, 915 N. La Brea Ave., Los Angeles, CA 90038; (213) 851-1000.

KNBC, 3000 W. Alameda St., Burbank, CA 91523; (818) 840-4444.

KTEH VIDEOSERVICES, 100 Skyport Dr., San Jose, CA 95115; (408) 947-6654; 947-6655.

LEVIN, KARL M., 20959 Elkwood St., Canoga Park, CA 91304; (818) 882-7262.

M.F.I. VIDEO CENTER, 1905 Grace Ave., Hollywood, CA 90068; (213) 851-0373.

MEDIA MASTERS PRODUCTIONS, 1800 S. Robertson Blvd., Suite 306, Los Angeles, CA 90035; (213) 451-8823.

MILES & CO., 1418 Dodson Ave., San Pedro, CA 90732; (213) 548-0462.

MOBILE IMAGE, 2944 W. Mountain Pine Dr., La Crescenta, CA 91214; (213) 873-5203, (818) 248-6905.

ONE PASS MOBILE SERVICES, 729 N. Highland Ave., Hollywood, CA 90038; (213) 937-4095.

P.D.S. VIDEO PRODUCTIONS, 1102 W. Chestnut St., Burbank, CA 91506; (818) 841-4711.

POSITIVE MEDIA, 5422A Fair Ave., North Hollywood, CA 91601; (818) 461-0092.

ROLAND, GLENN, FILMS, 10711 Wellworth Ave., Los Angeles, CA 90024; (213) 475-0937.

SCHULMAN VIDEO CENTER, 861 Seward St., Hollywood, CA 90038; (213) 465-8110.

SIERRA VIDEO, 11320 Chandler, N. Hollywood, CA 91601; (818) 985-1531; 579-7045.

SKYLINE PRODUCTIONS, 6309 Eleanor Ave., Hollywood, CA 90038; (213) 856-0033.

SOUND MASTER, 10747 Magnolia Blvd., North Hollywood, CA 91601; (213) 650-8000.

SPALLA, RICK VIDEO PRODUCTIONS, 1622 N. Gower St., Los Angeles, CA 90028; (213) 469-7307.

STARFAX, 654 Hawthorne St., Glendale, CA 91204; (818) 244-3600.

SUNRISE CANYON VIDEO, P.O. Box 10968, Burbank, CA 91510; (818) 845-7473.

TBA PRODUCTION GROUP, 1925 Park East, Suite 260; Los Angeles, CA 90067; (213) 551-0898.

TELE VIDICS, 2223 E. 223 St., Long Beach, CA 90810; (213) 830-5296.

TOP VIDEO SERVICES, INC., 10153 Riverside Dr., Suite 1B, Toluca Lake, CA 91602; (818) 763-1295.

UNITEL VIDEO, 5555 Melrose Ave. Studio G, Los Angeles, CA 90038; (213) 468-4606.

VTE TELEVISION, 8610 Sunset Blvd., Hollywood, CA 90069; (213) 659-4801.

VALLEY PRODUCTION CENTER, 6633 Van Nuys Blvd., Van Nuys, CA 91405; (818) 988-6601.

VENTURA COUNTY CABLEVISION, 30901 Agoura Rd., Westlake Village, CA 91361; (818) 889-0282.

VIDCOM, 2426 Townsgate Rd., Suite K, Westlake Village, CA 91361; (818) 991-1974.

VIDEO ADVENTURES INC., 1015 Cahuenga Blvd., Hollywood, CA 90038; (213) 461-3288.

VIDEO CIRCUIT STUDIOS, 11440 Chandler Blvd., Studio 1400, N. Hollywood, CA 91601; (818) 506-5493.

VIDEO WEST, 805 Larrabee St., West Hollywood, CA 90069; (213) 659-5762.

VIDE-U PRODUCTIONS, 612 N. Sepulveda Blvd., Los Angeles, CA 90049; (213) 472-7023.

NEW YORK

A.D.M. VIDEO PRODUCTIONS, 40 Seaview Blvd., Port Washington, NY 11050; (516) 484-6900.

ALL MOBILE VIDEO, 630 Ninth Ave., New York, NY 10036, (212) 757-8919.

BNS VIDEO SERVICES (Division of Broadcast News Service, Inc.), GPO 2360, New York, NY 10116; Pier 62, W. 23 St., New York, NY 10011; (212) 466-0234.

CECO INTERNATIONAL CORP., 440 W. 15 St., New York, NY 10011; (212) 206-8280.

DEVLIN PRODUCTIONS, INC., 1501 Broadway, New York, NY 10036; (212) 391-1313.

FAMA II PRODUCTIONS, 2750 Richmond Terrace, Staten Island, NY 10303; (718) 273-1780.

FEATURE SYSTEMS, 512 W. 36 St., New York, NY 10018; (212) 736-0477.

FLYING TIGER COMMUNICATIONS, INC., 155 W. 18 St., New York, NY 10011; (212) 929-1156.

LEE PRODUCTIONS, INC., 12 W. 27 St., New York, NY 10001; (212) 213-4110.

MTI TELEVISION CITY, 1443 Park Ave., New York, NY 10029; (212) 722-1818.

MALICK PRODUCTION SERVICES/MTI, 885 Second Ave., New York, NY 10017; (212) 355-0510.

MANHATTAN BRIDGE STUDIO, 156 Tillery St., Brooklyn Heights, NY; (718) 330-0555.

MODERN TELECOMMUNICATIONS, 1 Dag Hammarskjold Plaza, New York, NY 10017; (212) 355-0510.

NEP PRODUCTIONS, INC., 56 W. 45 St., New York, NY 10036; (212) 382-1104.

OMNI VIDEO SERVICES, LTD., 511 W. 33 St., New York, NY 10019; (212) 629-4303.

UNITEL VIDEO, 515 W. 57 St., New York, NY 10019; (212) 265-3600.

VIDEO PLANNING INC., 250 W. 57 St., New York, NY 10019; (212) 582-5066.

WINDSOR TOTAL VIDEO, 8 W. 38 St., New York, NY 10018; (212) 944-9090.

Video Production Facilities

LOS ANGELES

ABC TELEVISION CENTER, 4151 Prospect Ave., Los Angeles, CA 90027; (213) 557-7777.

ABERDEEN VIDEO, 3349 Cahuenga Blvd., Los Angeles, CA 90068; (213) 874-3050.

ALPA STUDIOS, 4720 W. Magnolia Blvd., Burbank, CA 91505; (818) 760-2825.

AMERICAN VIDEO FACTORY, 4150 Glencoe Ave., Marina Del Rey, CA 90292; (213) 823-8622; 367-8433.

AMERICAN VIDEOGRAM INC., 12020 W. Pico Blvd., Los Angeles, CA 90064; (213) 477-1535; 477-1536.

ANDERSON, HOWARD A., & CO., 1016 N. Cole Ave., Los Angeles, CA 90038; (213) 463-2336.

APOLLO PRODUCTION FACILITY, 1503 Cahuenga Blvd., Hollywood, CA 90028; (213) 464-7871.

ATLANTIC/KUSHNER-LOCKE, 10880 Wilshire Blvd., Suite 2404, Westwood, CA 90024; (213) 470-0400.

AUDIO ARTS PUBLISHING CO., 5617 Melrose Ave., Los Angeles, CA 90038; (213) 461-3507.

AUDIO-VIDEO CRAFT INC., 6753 Santa Monica Blvd., Los Angeles, CA 90038; (213) 655-3511.

BERC (BROADCAST EQUIPMENT RENTAL COMPANY), 4545 Chermak St., Burbank, CA 91505; (818) 841-3000; (213) 464-7655.

BAKER-NISBET INC., 451 N. La Cienega Blvd., Suite 12, Los Angeles, CA 90048; (213) 657-5687.

BETACAM SPECIALISTS, 3917 Riverside Dr., Suite 9137, Burbank, CA 91505; (818) 845-6480.

BOSUSTOW VIDEO, 2207 Colby Ave., West Los Angeles, CA 90064; (213) 478-0821.

BOWEN VIDEO FACILITIES, 7826 Clybourn Ave., Sun Valley, CA 91352; (818) 504-0070.

BURBANK PRODUCTION PLAZA, 801 S. Main St., Burbank, CA 91506 (818) 846-7677; 841-5051.

CALIFORNIA VIDEO CENTER, 15303 Ventura Blvd., Sherman Oaks, CA 91403; (818) 789-5000.

CENTRE FILMS INC., 1103 N. El Centro Ave., Los Angeles, CA 90038; (213) 466-5123.

CENTURY SOUTHWEST PRODUCTIONS, 2939 Nebraska Ave., Santa Monica, CA 90404; (213) 829-5111; 829-7624.

CHELSEA VIDEO STUDIOS, 6534 Sunset Blvd., Hollywood, CA 90028; (213) 464-5360.

CHOICE TELEVISION, 800 S. Date Ave., Alhambra, CA 91803; (818) 576-2906; 289-7719.

CINETYP, INC., 843 Seward St., Hollywood, CA 90038; (213) 463-8569.

CLARASOL PRODUCTION CO., 1028 N. La Brea Ave., Hollywood, CA 90038; (212) 462-7212; 464-0180.

COMPACT VIDEO SERVICES INC., 2813 W. Alameda Ave., Burbank, CA 91505; (818) 840-7000; 840-7243.

COMPLETE POST INC., 6087 Sunset Blvd., Hollywood, CA 90028; (213) 467-1244.

CONSOLIDATED FILM INDUSTRIES, 959 Seward St., Los Angeles, CA 90038; (213) 462-3161.

DEVONSHIRE SOUND STUDIOS, 10729 Magnolia Blvd., N. Hollywood, CA 91601; (818) 985-1945.

DUBS, INC., 6360 DeLongpre Ave., Hollywood, CA 90028; (213) 461-3726.

EYE ON VIDEO, 224 N. Juanita Ave., Los Angeles, CA 90004; (213) 382-4048.

EYE SQUARE VIDEO INC., 1749 14th St., Santa Monica, CA 90404; (213) 452-9076.

FIESTA SOUND & VIDEO, 1655 S. Compton Ave., Los Angeles, CA 90021; (213) 748-2057.

FOX TAPE, 5746 Sunset Blvd., Los Angeles, CA 90028; (213) 856-1000.

GLENDALE STUDIOS, 1239 S. Glendale Ave., Glendale, CA 91205; (818) 502-5300.

GLOBAL ENTERTAINMENT NETWORK, INC., 1832 N. Gower St., Hollywood, CA; (213) 461-2534.

GOLDEN WEST VIDEOTAPE, 5800 Sunset Blvd., Los Angeles, CA 90028; (213) 460-8989.

GREENE, CROW & CO., 3083 N. Lima St., Los Angeles, CA 91504; (818) 841-7821.

GROUP W PRODUCTIONS, 3801 Barham Blvd., Los Angeles, CA 90068; (213) 850-3800.

HOLLYWOOD NATIONAL STUDIOS, 6605 Eleanor Ave., Los Angeles, CA 90038; (213) 467-6272.

HOLLYWOOD NEWSREEL SYNDICATE, INC., 1622 N. Gower St., Los Angeles, CA 90028; (213) 469-7307.

HOLLYWOOD PACIFIC STUDIOS, 62900 Sunset Blvd., Hollywood, CA 90028; (213) 463-8118.

IMAGE TRANSFORM INC., 4142 Lankershim Blvd., North Hollywood, CA 91602 (818) 985-7566.

IMAGE WEST, 11846 Ventura Blvd., Studio City, CA 91604; (818) 506-5577.

IMMEDIATO, JEFFREY & ASSOCIATES, P.O. Box 5611, Long Beach, CA 90805; (213) 422-9295.

INTER VIDEO TRITRONICS INC., 733 N. Victory Blvd., Burbank, CA 91502; (818) 569-4000, (800) 232-2141.

INTERMIX INC., 2505 S. Robertson Blvd., Los Angeles, CA 90034; (213) 870-2121.

J.P. VIDEO SERVICES, 9538 W. Pico Blvd., Los Angeles, CA 90035; (213) 271-1209; 859-9903.

KCET, 4401 Sunset Blvd., Los Angeles, CA 90027; (213) 666-6500.

KCOP TELEVISION INC., 915 N. La Brea Ave., Los Angeles, CA 90038; (213) 851-1000.

KWHY-TV, CHANNEL 22, 5545 Sunset Blvd., Los Angeles, CA 90028; (213) 466-5441.

KEY WEST, 5701 Buckingham Pkwy, Suite C, Culver City, CA 90230; (213) 645-3348.

LMI PRODUCTIONS, %Lee Magid, Inc., P.O. Box 532, Malibu, CA 90265; (213) 463-7210.

LA BREA STUDIOS, 1028 N. La Brea Ave., Hollywood, CA 90038; (213) 462-7210.

LEVIN, KARL M., 20959 Elkwood St., Los Angeles, CA 91304; (818) 882-7262.

LIGHT-HOUSE PRODUCTIONS, 427 Linnie Canal, Venice, CA 90291; (213) 827-1537.

LIONEL TELEVISION PRODUCTIONS, 3329 Brookside Dr., Malibu, CA 90265; (213) 456-5809.

LOS ANGELES NEWS NETWORK, 1730 Camino Palmero, Suite 206, Los Angeles, CA 90046; (213) 850-5411.

MARSH INTERNATIONAL FILMS, 629 N. La Brea Ave., Los Angeles, CA 90036; (213) 936-7181.

MAXIMILLIAN TELEVISION & VIDEO, 411 W. 7th St., Los Angeles, CA 90014; (213) 624-8688.

McINTIRE-HOFFMAN, INC., 11969 Ventura Blvd., Studio City, CA 91604; (818) 762-2077.

MEDIA MASTERS PRODUCTIONS, 1800 S. Robertson Blvd., Suite 306, Beverly Hills, CA 90035; (213) 451-8823.

MILES & COMPANY, 1418 Dodson Ave., San Pedro, CA 90732; (213) 548-0462.

MORRIS VIDEO INC., 2730 Monterey St., Torrance, CA 90503; (213) 533-4800.

NEWMAN/FRANKS, 2956 Nicada Dr., Los Angeles, CA 90077; (213) 470-0140; 470-0145.

ONE PASS FILM & VIDEO, One China Basin Bldg., San Francisco, CA 94107; (415) 777-5777.

P.D.S. VIDEO PRODUCTIONS, 1102 W. Chestnut St., Burbank, CA 91506; (818) 841-4711.

PARALLAX PRODUCTIONS, P.O. Box 2413, Beverly Hills, CA 90213; (213) 459-2719.

POSITIVE MEDIA, 5422A Fair Ave., North Hollywood, CA 91601; (818) 761-5192.

THE POST PLACE, 12401 W. Olympic Blvd., Los Angeles, CA 90064; (213) 820-2900.

PREMORE INC., 5130 Klump Ave., N. Hollywood, CA 91601; (818) 506-7714.

THE PRODUCTION GROUP, 1330 N. Vine St., Hollywood, CA 90028; (213) 469-8111.

PROFESSIONAL ARTISTS GROUP, 845 N. Highland Ave., Hollywood, CA 90038; (213) 871-2222.

PROFESSIONAL MEDIA SERVICE, 18301 Pammey Lane, Huntington Beach, CA 92648; (714) 964-0542.

REN-MAR STUDIOS, 846 N. Cahuenga Blvd., Los Angeles, CA 90038; (213) 463-0808.

S.A. GLOBAL STUDIOS, 201 N. Occidental Blvd., Los Angeles, CA 90026; (213) 384-3331.

SCHULMAN VIDEO CENTER, 861 Seward St., Hollywood, CA 90036; (213) 465-8110.

SOUND MASTER AUDIO/VIDEO, 10747 Magnolia Blvd., N. Hollywood, CA 91601; (213) 650-8000.

SOUTHLAND VIDEO, 3255 Cahuenga Blvd., Los Angeles, CA 90068; (213) 851-1190.

SPALLA, RICK PRODUCTIONS, 1622 N. Gower St., Los Angeles, CA 90028; (213) 469-7307.

SPRINGBOARD STUDIOS, 12229 Montague St., Los Angeles, CA 91331; (818) 896-4321.

STUDIO & REMOTE VIDEO, 10650 Magnolia Blvd., North Holly-wood, CA 91601; (818) 508-6010.
SUNRISE CANYON VIDEO, P.O. Box 10968, Burbank, CA 91510; (818) 845-7473.
SUPERCOLOSSAL PICTURES CORP., 3413 Cahuenga Blvd. W., Los Angeles, CA 90068; (213) 222-5550.
TBA PRODUCTION GROUP, 1925 Century Park East, Suite 260, Los Angeles, CA 90067; (213) 551-0898.
TAPE-FILM INDUSTRIES (TFI), 941 N. Highland Ave., Hollywood, CA 90038; (213) 461-3361.
TELEVISION MATRIX, 1438 N. Gower St., Hollywood, CA 90028; (213) 465-9616.
TOP VIDEO SERVICES, INC., 10153 Riverside Dr., Suite 1B, Toluca Lake, CA 91602; (818) 763-1295.
TRANS-AMERICAN VIDEO INC., 1541 N. Vine St., Los Angeles, CA 90028; (213) 466-2141.
TRANSWORLD FILM CORP., 1520 S. Beverly Glen Blvd., Suite 304, Los Angeles, CA 90024; (213) 277-4250.
UNITEL VIDEO, 5555 Melrose Ave., Studio G, Los Angeles, CA 90038; (213) 468-4606.
THE VALENCIA STUDIOS, 28343 Avenue Crocker, Valencia, CA 91355; (800) 782-4348; (805) 257-1202.
VALLEY PRODUCTION CENTER, 6633 Van Nuys Blvd., Van Nuys, CA 91405; (818) 988-6601.
VARITEL VIDEO, 3375 Cahuenga Blvd. W., Los Angeles, CA 90068; (213) 850-1165.
VIA VISION PRODUCTIONS, 5919 Franklin Ave., Los Angeles, CA 90028; (213) 460-4864.
VIDCOM ENTERTAINMENT, INC., P.O. Box 2926, Hollywood, CA 90078; (213) 301-8433.
VIDE-U PRODUCTIONS, 612 N. Sepulveda Blvd., Los Angeles, CA 90049; (213) 472-7023.
VIDEO ADVENTURES INC., 1015 Cahuenga Blvd., Hollywood, CA 90038; (213) 461-3288.
VIDEO CIRCUIT STUDIOS, 11440 Chandler Blvd., Studio 1400, N. Hollywood, CA 91601; (818) 506-5493.
VIDEO HOUSE, 201 N. Hollywood Way, Suite 202, Burbank, CA 91505; (818) 954-9559.
VIDEO IMAGE, 4121 Redwood Ave., Suite 215, Los Angeles, CA 90066, (213) 822-8872.
VIDEO TECHNICS, 1052B N. 5th St., San Jose, CA; (408) 275-1066; 1833 Evergreen St., San Mateo, CA 94402; (415) 343-8040.
VIDEO WEST, 805 Larrabee St., West Hollywood, CA 90069; (213) 659-5762.
VIDEO-IT INC., 1016 N. Sycamore Ave., Hollywood, CA 90038; (818) 876-4055; (818) VID-EOIT.
VIDEO-PAC SYSTEMS LTD., 800 N. Seward St., Hollywood, CA 90038; (213) 469-7244.
WEXLER VIDEO INC., Burbank Production Plaza, 801 S. Main St., Burbank, CA 91506; (818) 846-9381.
WILDER BROTHERS VIDEO, 10327 Santa Monica Blvd., Los An-geles, CA 90025; (213) 557-3500.
WINTERS PRODUCTIONS, Box 920, Montrose, CA 91020; (818) 790-4201.

NEW YORK

ADM VIDEO PRODUCTIONS INC., 40 Seaview Blvd., Port Washing-ton, NY 11050; (516) 484-6900.
ANS INTERNATIONAL VIDEO LTD., 396 Fifth Ave., New York, NY 10018; (212) 736-1007.
BROADWAY STUDIOS, 25-09 Broadway, Astoria, NY 11106; (718) 274-9121.
BROADWAY VIDEO, 1619 Broadway, New York, NY 10019; (212) 265-7600; 713-0540.
CALAMAR PRODUCTIONS, 38 Greene St., New York, NY 10012; (212) 334-4952.
CAMERA MART STAGES, INC., 460 W. 54 St., New York, NY 10019; (212) 757-6977.
CHARLEX, INC., 2 W. 45 St., New York, NY 10036; (212) 719-4600.
CHROMAVISION, 119 W. 22 St., New York, NY 10011; (212) 463-8997.
CINE-VID POST PRODUCTION, INC., 25 W. 45 St., New York, NY 10036; (212) 704-4000.
CREATIVE WAYS/VISUAL CREATIONS, INC., 305 E. 46 St., New York, NY 10017; (212) 935-0145.
DEVLIN PRODUCTIONS, INC., 1501 Broadway, New York, NY 10036; (212) 391-1313; FAX: (212) 391-2744.
EMPIRE STAGES OF NY, 50-20 St., Long Island City, NY 11101; (718) 392-4747.
E.U.E. SCREEN GEMS, 222 E. 44 St., New York, NY 10017; (212) 867-4030.
FAMA II PRODUCTIONS, 2750 Richmond Terrace, Staten Island, NY 10303; (718) 273-1780.
GLEN-WARREN PRODUCTIONS LTD., 551 Fifth Ave., #414, New York, NY 10017; (212) 883-0090.

HBO STUDIO PRODUCTIONS, 120A E. 23 St., New York, NY 10010; (212) 512-7800.
INTERNATIONAL PRODUCTION CENTER, 514 W. 57 St., New York, NY 10019; (212) 582-6530.
JPC VIDEO INC., 11 E. 47 St., #400, New York, NY 10017; (212) 223-0555; 755-4028.
KAUFMAN-ASTORIA STUDIOS, 34-12 36th St., Astoria, NY 11106; (718) 392-5600.
LRP VIDEO, 3 Dag Hammarskjold Plaza, New York, NY 10017; (212) 759-0822.
KOLMOR VISIONS INT'L LTD., 286 Fifth Ave., New York, NY 10001; (212) 947-7517.
MPCS VIDEO INDUSTRIES, 514 W. 57 St., New York, NY 10019; (212) 586-3690.
MTI TV CITY, 1443 Park Ave., New York, NY 10029; (212) 722-1818.
MAGNO SOUND & VIDEO, 729 Seventh Ave., New York, NY 10019; (212) 302-2505.
MANHATTAN BRIDGE STUDIOS & VIDEO, 156 Tillary St., Brook-lyn Heights, NY 11201; (718) 330-0555.
MANHATTAN VIDEO PRODUCTIONS, INC., 12 W. 27 St., New York, NY 10001; (718) 330-0555.
MATRIX VIDEO, 727 Eleventh Ave., New York, NY 10019; (212) 265-8500.
MICROVIDEO LEARNING SYSTEMS, 119 W. 22 St., New York, NY 10011; (212) 255-3108.
MODERN TELECOMMUNICATIONS INC., 1 Dag Hammarskjold Plaza, New York, NY 10017; (212) 355-0510; 885 Second Ave., New York, NY 10017; (212) 355-0510.
MOTHERS SOUND STAGES, 210 E. 5 St., New York, NY 10003; (212) 529-5097; 260-2050.
NBC TELESALES, 30 Rockefeller Plaza, New York, NY 10112; (212) 664-4754.
NATIONAL VIDEO CENTER/RECORDING STUDIOS, INC., 460 W. 42 St., New York, NY 10036; (212) 279-2000.
NATIONAL VIDEO INDUSTRIES, INC., 15 W. 17 St., New York, NY 10011; (212) 691-1300.
NORTHEAST VIDEO, 420 Lexington Ave., New York, NY 10017; (212) 661-8830.
NORTHSTAR VIDEO LTD., 423 E. 90 St., New York, NY 10028; (212) 996-9666.
PRIMA LUX VIDEO, 30 W. 26 St., New York, NY 10010; (212) 206-1402.
PROFESSIONAL COMMUNICATION SERVICES, 1776 Broadway, New York, NY 10019; (212) 247-7965.
REBO ASSOCIATES, 530 W. 25 St., New York, NY 10001; (212) 989-9466.
REEVES TELETAPE, 708 Third Ave., New York, NY 10019; 841 Ninth Ave., New York, NY 10019; (213) 573-8600; 53 St. and Broadway, New York, NY; 573-8600.
SILVER CUP STUDIOS, 42-25 21st St., Long Island City, NY 11101; (718) 784-3390.
SPALLA, RICK VIDEO PRODUCTIONS, 301 W. 45 St., New York, NY 10036; (212) 765-4646.
TELETECHNIQUES, 1 W. 19 St., New York, NY 10011; (212) 206-1475; 580-9511.
TELESTAR VIDEO, 206 E. 29 St., New York, NY 10016; (212) 689-1040.
TODAY VIDEO, 45 W. 45 St., New York, NY 10036; (212) 391-1020.
TULCHIN STUDIOS, 240 E. 45 St., New York, NY 10017; (212) 986-8270.
UNITEL VIDEO, 515 W. 57 St., New York, NY 10019; (212) 265-3600.
VCA/TELETRONICS INTERNATIONAL, 231 E. 55 St., New York, NY 10022; (212) 355-1600; 503 W. 33 St., New York, NY 10001; (212) 736-7717.
VIDEO PLANNING PLUS!, 250 W. 57 St., New York, NY 10019; (212) 582-5066.
VIDEO PORTFOLIOS, 142 W. 24 St., New York, NY 10011; (212) 989-3858.
VIDEOWORKS, 24 W. 40 St., New York, NY 10018; (212) 869-2500.
VIDLO VIDEO, 40 E. 21 St., New York, NY 10010; (212) 475-4140.
WNET, 356 W. 58 St., New York, NY 10019; (212) 560-2068.
WINDSOR TOTAL VIDEO, 8 W. 38 St., New York, NY 10017; (212) 944-9090.

NEW JERSEY

CENTENNIAL STUDIO, 140 Centennial Ave., Pisctaway, NJ 08854; (201) 457-8880.
COLOR LEASING STUDIO, 330 Rt. 46, Fairfield, NJ 07006; (201) 575-1118; (212) 662-2655.
PRESS BROADCASTING, Press Plaza, Asbury Park, NJ 07712; (201) 774-7700.
VIDEOCENTER OF NJ INC., 228 Park Ave. E., Rutherford, NJ 07073; (201) 509-0900.

Video Screening Rooms

LOS ANGELES

ALTAVIDEO, 3501 Cahuenga Blvd. W., Los Angeles, CA 90068; (213) 876-8008.

AMERICAN VIDEO FACTORY, 4150 Glencoe Ave., Marina Del Rey, CA 90292; (213) 823-8622; (800) 367-8433.

AMPAC VIDEO, 3637 Cahuenga Blvd., Hollywood, CA 90068; (213) 851-7200.

AUDIO ARTS PUBLISHING CO., 5617 Melrose Ave., Los Angeles, CA 90038; (213) 461-3507.

AUDIO-VIDEO CRAFT INC., 6753 Santa Monica Blvd., Los Angeles, CA 90038; (213) 655-3511.

AUDIO VISUAL HEADQUARTERS CORP., 361 N. Oak St., Inglewood, CA 90302; (213) 419-4040.

BERC (BROADCAST EQUIPMENT RENTAL CO.), 4545 Chermak St., Burbank, CA 91505; (818) 841-3000, (213) 464-7655.

BOSUSTOW VIDEO, 2207 Colby Ave., West Los Angeles, CA 90064; (213) 478-0821.

CHELSEA VIDEO STUDIOS, 6534 Sunset Blvd., Hollywood, CA 90028; (213) 464-5360.

CHOICE TELEVISION, 800 S. Date Ave., Alhambra, CA 91803; (818) 576-2906; 289-7719.

THE CREATIVE PARTNERSHIP, 7526 Fountain Ave., Hollywood, CA 90046; (213) 850-5551.

DAUGHERTY AUDIO/VISUAL DESIGN, 2172 Ridgemont, Los Angeles, CA 90046; (213) 650-5665; 718-5531.

DIGITAL SOUND RECORDING, 607 N. Ave. 64, Los Angeles, CA 90042; (213) 258-6741.

THE EDITING COMPANY, 8300 Beverly Blvd., Los Angeles, CA 90048; (213) 653-3570.

ENGEL, RAY, PRODUCTIONS, 1730 Camino Palmero, Suite 206, Los Angeles, CA 90046; (213) 850-5411.

FOTO-KEM INDUSTRIES, 2800 W. Olive St., Burbank, CA 91505; (818) 846-3101.

GLOBAL VISION CORPORATION, 3255 Cahuenga Blvd., Hollywood, CA 90068; (213) 851-1190.

GRACE & WILD STUDIOS, HOLLYWOOD, 3501 Cahuenga Blvd. W., Los Angeles, CA 90068; (213) 876-8008.

HARRAH'S THEATRE SERVICE & SUPPLY, 624B S. San Fernando Blvd., Burbank, CA 91502; (818) 842-5111.

HORIZONTAL EDITING STUDIOS, 2625 W. Olive Ave., Burbank, CA 91505; (818) 841-6750.

IMAGE TRANSFORM, 4142 Lankershim Blvd., North Hollywood, CA 91602; (818) 985-7566.

IMAGE WEST, 11846 Ventura Blvd., Studio City, CA 91604; (818) 506-5577.

IMMEDIATO, JEFFREY, & ASSOCIATES, P.O. Box 5611, Long Beach, CA 90805; (213) 422-9295.

INDEPENDENT PRODUCERS STUDIO INC., 1604 Vista Del Mar Ave., Hollywood, CA 90028; (213) 461-4966.

INSTANT REPLAY COMMUNICATIONS CO., 11122 W. Washington Blvd., Hollywood, CA 90232; (213) 870-9435.

INTER VIDEO/TRITRONICS, 733 N. Victory Blvd., Burbank, CA 91502; (818) 569-4000.

INTERMIX INC., 2505 S. Robertson, Los Angeles, CA 90034; (213) 870-2121.

J.P. VIDEO SERVICES, 9538 W. Pico Blvd., Los Angeles, CA 90035 (213) 271-1209; 859-9903.

KWHY-TV, CHANNEL 22, 5545 Sunset Blvd., Los Angeles, CA 90028; (213) 466-5441.

LEVIN, KARL M., 20959 Elkwood St., Canoga Park, CA 91304; (818) 882-7262.

MARKET STREET SCREENING ROOM, 73 Market St., Venice, CA 90291; (213) 396-5937.

MEDIA MASTERS PRODUCTIONS, 1800 S. Robertson Blvd., Suite 306, Beverly Hills, CA 90035; (213) 451-8823.

NEWMAN/FRANKS, 2956 Nicada Dr., Los Angeles, CA 90077. (213) 470-0140; 470-0145.

PACIFIC VIDEO, 809 N. Cahuenga Blvd., Los Angeles, CA 90038; (213) 462-6266.

POSITIVE MEDIA, 5422A Fair Ave., North Hollywood, CA 91601; (213) 461-0092.

THE POST GROUP, 6335 Homewood Ave., Los Angeles, CA 90028; (213) 462-2300.

POST PLUS INCORPORATED, 6650 Santa Monica Blvd., 2nd floor, Hollywood, CA 90038; (213) 463-7108.

RUBBER DUBBERS, INC., 626 Justin Ave., Glendale, CA 91201; (818) 241-5600.

S.A. GLOBAL STUDIOS, 201 N. Occidental Blvd., Los Angeles, CA 90026; (213) 384-3331.

SOUND MASTER, 10747 Magnolia Blvd., North Hollywood, CA 91601; (213) 650-8000.

SOUTHLAND VIDEO, 3255 Cahuenga Blvd., Hollywood, CA 90068; (213) 851-1190.

STARLIGHT EDITING SERVICES, 5250 Strohm, North Hollywood, CA 91601; (818) 769-3874.

UCL VIDEO, 823 N. Seward St., Hollywood, CA 90038; (213) 469-7291.

UNITEL VIDEO, 5555 Melrose Ave., Studio G, Los Angeles, CA 90038; (213) 468-4606.

VALLEY VIDEO, 4209 W. Burbank Blvd., Burbank, CA 91505; (818) 841-2387.

VARITEL VIDEO, 3575 Cahuenga Blvd. W., Los Angeles, CA 90068; (213) 850-1165.

VIDEO ADVENTURES INC., 1015 Cahuenga Blvd., Hollywood, CA 90038; (213) 461-3288.

VIDEO CIRCUIT STUDIOS, 11440 Chandler Blvd., Studio 1400, N. Hollywood, CA; 91601; (818) 506-5493.

VIDEO CRAFTSMEN INC., 6311 Romaine St., Los Angeles, CA 90038; (213) 464-4351.

THE VIDEO HOUSE, 201 N. Hollywood Way, Suite 202, Burbank, CA 91505; (818) 954-9559.

VIDEO-IT INC., 1016 N. Sycamore Ave., Hollywood, CA 90038; (213) 876-4055; (213) VID-EOIT.

THE VIDEO TAPE CO., 10545 Burbank Blvd., North Hollywood, CA 91601; (818) 985-1666.

VIDE-U PRODUCTIONS, 612 N. Sepulveda Blvd., Los Angeles, CA 90049; (213) 472-7023.

WILDER BROTHERS VIDEO, 10327 Santa Monica Blvd., Los Angeles, CA 90025; (213) 557-3500.

NEW YORK

ALL MOBILE VIDEO INC., 630 Ninth Ave., New York, NY 10036; (212) 757-8919.

DEVLIN PRODUCTIONS INC., 1501 Broadway, New York, NY 10036; (212) 391-1313.

DU ART VIDEO, 245 W. 55 St., New York, NY 10019; (212) 757-3681.

LRP VIDEO, 3 Dag Hammarskjold Plaza, New York, NY 10017; (212) 759-0822.

MPCS VIDEO INDUSTRIES, 514 W. 57 St., New York, NY 10019; (212) 586-3690.

MAGNO SOUND & VIDEO, 729 Seventh Ave., New York, NY 10019; (212) 302-2505.

MODERN TELECOMMUNICATIONS INC., 885 Second Ave., New York, NY 10017; (212) 355-0510.

MOVIELAB THEATRE SERVICE, 619 W. 54 St., New York, NY 10019; (212) 586-0360.

NATIONAL VIDEO INDUSTRIES INC., 15 W. 17 St., New York, NY 10011; (212) 691-1300.

P.A.T. FILM SERVICES, 630 Ninth Ave., New York, NY 10036; (212) 247-0900.

TELETECHNIQUES, INC., 1 West 19 St., New York, NY 10011; (212) 206-1475; 580-9551.

VCA/TELETRONICS, 231 E. 55 St., New York, NY 10022; (212) 355-1600.

VIDEO CENTRAL, 225 W. 36 St., New York, NY 10018; (212) 847-6960.

WINDSOR TOTAL VIDEO, 8 W. 38 St., New York, NY 10018; (212) 944-9090.

Videotape Transfer, Film to Tape

LOS ANGELES

A.M.E. INC., 1133 N. Hollywood Way, Burbank, CA 91505; (818) 841-7740.

ACTION VIDEO, 6616 Lexington Ave., Los Angeles, CA 90038; (213) 461-3611.

ALPHA CINE LABORATORY, 5724 W. Third St., Suite 311, Los Angeles, CA 90036; (213) 934-7793.

ALTAVIDEO, 3501 Cahuenga Blvd. W., Los Angeles, CA 90068; (213) 876-8008.

AMERICAN VIDEO FACTORY, 4150 Glencoe Ave., Marina Del Rey, CA 90292; (213) 823-8622; (800) 367-8433.

AMPAC VIDEO, 3637 Cahuenga Blvd. W., Hollywood, CA 90068; (213) 851-7200.

ANDERSON, HOWARD A., CO., 1016 N. Cole Ave., Los Angeles, CA 90038; (213) 463-2336.

APOLLO VIDEO FACILITY, 1503 Cahuenga Blvd., Hollywood, CA 90028; (213) 464-7871; 465-6154.

ASHFIELD FILM LAB, 747 N. Seward St., Hollywood, CA 90038; (213) 462-3231.

AUDIO ARTS PUBLISHING, CO., 5617 Melrose Ave., Los Angeles, CA 90038; (213) 461-3507.

AUDIO GRAPHICS FILMS AND VIDEO, 6509 De Longpre Ave., Hollywood, CA 90028; (213) 462-6596, (213) 467-1234.

AUDIO-VIDEO CRAFT INC., 6753 Santa Monica Blvd., Los Angeles, CA 90038; (213) 655-3511.

BABYLON POST, 6671 Sunset Blvd., Suite 1583, Hollywood, CA 90028; (213) 460-4088.

BEVERLY HILLS HOME VIDEOCENTRE, 187 S. Beverly Dr., Beverly Hills, CA 90212; (213) 550-1092.

BONDED SERVICES, 5260 Vineland Ave., North Hollywood, CA 91601; (818) 761-4058.

BOULEVARD VIDEO PRODUCTIONS, 15016 Ventura Blvd., Suite 1, Sherman Oaks, CA 91403; (818) 501-7369.

BUDGET VIDEO, 1534 N. Highland Ave., Los Angeles, CA 90028; (213) 466-2431.

CFI, 959 Seward St., Hollywood, CA 90038; (213) 462-3161; 960-7444.

CAL VISTA INTERNATIONAL INC., 6649 Odessa Ave., Van Nuys, CA 91406; (818) 780-9000.

CALIFORNIA COMMUNICATIONS INC., 6900 Santa Monica Blvd., Los Angeles, CA 90038; (213) 466-8511.

CHELSEA VIDEO STUDIOS, 6534 Sunset Blvd., Hollywood, CA 90028; (213) 464-5360.

COMPACT VIDEO SERVICES INC., 2813 W. Alameda Ave., Burbank, CA 91505; (818) 840-7000.

COMPLETE POST INC., 6087 Sunset Blvd., Hollywood, CA 90028; (213) 467-1244

COMPOSITE IMAGE SYSTEMS, 815 N. Cahuenga Blvd., Hollywood, CA 90038; (213) 461-5734.

CONRAD FILM DUPLICATING CO., 6750 Santa Monica Blvd., Hollywood, CA 90038; (213) 463-5614.

CONSOLIDATED FILM INDUSTRIES, 959 Seward St., Los Angeles, CA 90038; (213) 462-3161.

CREST NATIONAL FILM & VIDEOTAPE LABS, 1141 N. Seward St., Los Angeles, CA 90038; (213) 466-0624; 462-2696.

DELUXE LABORATORIES, INC., 1377 N. Serrano Ave., Hollywood, CA 90027; (213) 462-6171.

DEVONSHIRE AUDIO/VIDEO STUDIOS, 10729 Magnolia Blvd., N. Hollywood, CA 91601; (818) 985-1540.

EDITEL-LOS ANGELES, 729 N. Highland Ave., Hollywood, CA 90038; (213) 913-1821.

THE EDITING COMPANY, 8300 Beverly Blvd., Los Angeles, CA 90048; (213) 653-3570.

ENCORE VIDEO INC., 6344 Fountain Ave., Hollywood, CA 90028; (213) 466-7663.

EYE ON VIDEO, 224 N. Juanita Ave., Los Angeles, CA 90004; (213) 382-4048.

FILM & THEATRE SOCIETY, 1730 Camino, #206, Los Angeles, CA 90004; (213) 850-5411.

FILM TECHNOLOGY CO. INC., 6900 Santa Monica Blvd., Los Angeles, CA 90038; (213) 464-3456.

FOTO-KEM INDUSTRIES INC., 2800 W. Olive Ave., Burbank, CA 91505; (818) 846-3101.

G & B PROFESSIONAL PHOTOGRAPHY, 255 E. Colorado Blvd., Pasadena, CA 91101; (818) 440-1909.

GLEN-WARREN PRODUCTIONS, LTD., 9911 W. Pico Blvd., Los Angeles, CA 90035; (213) 553-9233.

GLOBE TELEVISION, 1954 Cotner Ave., Los Angeles, CA 90025; (213) 479-8081.

GRACE & WILD STUDIOS HOLLYWOOD, 3501 Cahuenga Blvd. W., Los Angeles, CA 90068; (213) 876-8008.

H.C.V., 3034 Glendale Blvd., Los Angeles, CA 90039; (213) 662-1112.

HOLLYWOOD NEWSREEL SYNDICATE INC., 1622 N. Gower St., Los Angeles, CA 90028; (213) 469-7307.

IMAGE TRANSFORM INC., 4142 Lankershim Blvd., North Hollywood, CA 91602; (818) 985-7566.

IMAGE TRANSFORM LABORATORY, 3611 N. San Fernando Rd., Burbank, CA 90028; (818) 841-3812.

INDEPENDENT PRODUCERS STUDIO INC., 1604 Vista Del Mar Ave., Hollywood, CA 90028; (213) 461-6966.

INTER VIDEO/TRITRONICS INC., 733 N. Victory Blvd., Burbank, CA 91502; (818) 843-2288, (800) 232-2141.

INTERSOUND, INC., 8746 Sunset Blvd., Los Angeles, CA 90069; (213) 652-3741.

IPS/INDEPENDENT PRODUCERS STUDIO INC., 1604 Vista Del Mar Ave., Hollywood, CA 90028; (213) 461-6966.

INTERNATIONAL VIDEO CONVERSIONS, 815 N. Cahuenga Blvd., Hollywood, CA 90038; (213) 463-7884.

JP VIDEO SERVICE, 9538 W. Pico Blvd., Los Angeles, CA 90035; (213) 859-9903; (213) 271-1209.

KWHY-TV, CHANNEL 22, 5545 Sunset Blvd., Los Angeles, CA 90028; (213) 466-5441.

LP PRODUCTION, 223 Strand St., Suite K, Santa Monica, CA 90405; (213) 399-1101; (714) 857-1310.

LAJON PRODUCTIONS, INC., 2907 W. Olive Ave., Burbank, CA 91505; (818) 841-1440.

M.F.I. VIDEO CENTER, 1905 Grace Ave., Hollywood, CA 90068; (213) 851-0373.

MAJESTIC DUPLICATING & VIDEO SERVICE, 1208 W. Isabel St., Burbank, CA 91506; (213) 849-1535; (818) 843-1806.

MAXIMILLIAN TELEVISION & VIDEO, 411 W. Seventh St., Los Angeles, CA 90014; (213) 624-8688.

McINTIRE-HOFFMAN INC., 11969 Ventura Blvd., Studio City, CA 91604; (818) 762-2077.

MEDIA MASTERS PRODUCTIONS, 1800 S. Robertson Blvd., Suite 306; Beverly Hills, CA 90035; (213) 451-8823.

MODERN TALKING PICTURE SERVICE INC., 6735 San Fernando Rd., Glendale, CA 91201; (818) 240-0519; (813) 541-7571.

MODERN VIDEOFILM, 7165 Sunset Blvd., Hollywood, CA 90046; (213) 851-8070.

MUSIC LAB INC., 1831 Hyperion Ave., Hollywood, CA 90027; (213) 666-3003.

ONE PASS FILM & VIDEO, One China Basin Building, San Francisco, CA 94107; (415) 777-5777.

PACIFIC TITLE & ART STUDIO, 6350 Santa Monica Blvd., Hollywood, CA 90038; (213) 464-0121.

PACIFIC VIDEO, 809 N. Cahuenga Blvd., Los Angeles, CA 90038; (213) 462-6266.

PAL VIDEO, 19061 Tina Pl., Tarzana, CA 91356; (818) 344-1603.

THE POST GROUP, 6335 Homewood, Los Angeles, CA 90028; (213) 462-2300.

PRO VIDEO/CINETAPE, 801 N. La Brea Ave., Los Angeles, CA 90038; (213) 934-8836.

R. PRODUCTIONS & VIDEO EVENTS, 1741 N. Ivar, Suite 210, Hollywood, CA 90028; (213) 465-4197.

RALEIGH STUDIOS, 650 N. Bronson Ave., Los Angeles, CA 90004; (213) 466-3111.

RENCHER'S EDITORIAL SERVICE, 738 Cahuenga Blvd., Hollywood, CA 90038; (213) 463-9836.

RUBBER DUBBERS INC., 626 Justin Ave., Glendale, CA 91201; (818) 241-5600.

RUSK SOUND STUDIO, 1556 N. La Brea Ave., Hollywood, CA 90028; (213) 462-6477.

RUSSIAN HILL RECORDING, 1520 Pacific Ave., San Francisco, CA 94109; (415) 474-4520.

RUXTON LTD., 611 N. Orchard Dr., Burbank, CA 91506; (818) 845-3724.

SIERRA VIDEO, 11320 Chandler, N. Hollywood, CA 91601; (818) 985-1531.

SKYLINE PRODUCTIONS, 6309 Eleanor Ave., Hollywood, CA 90038; (213) 856-0033.

SOUND SERVICES INC. (S.S.I.), 7155 Santa Monica Blvd., Los Angeles, CA 90046; (213) 874-9344; 986-3255.

SOUND WEST, INC., 12166 Olympic Blvd., Los Angeles, CA 90064; (213) 826-6560.

SPALLA, RICK, VIDEO PRODUCTIONS, 1622 N. Gower St., Los Angeles, CA 90028; (213) 469-7307.

498

SPRINGBOARD STUDIOS, 12229 Montague St., Los Angeles, CA 91331; (818) 896-4321.

STARFAX, 654 Hawthorne St., Glendale, CA 91204; (818) 244-3600.

STUDIO TELEVISION SERVICE, 7550 W. Sunset Blvd., Los Angeles, CA 90046; (213) 460-4400.

SUPERCINE INC., 2214 W. Olive Ave., Burbank, CA 91506; (818) 843-8260.

TAV/COMMAND, INC., 1541 N. Vine St., Los Angeles, CA 90028; (213) 466-2141.

TAV SOUND INC., 6200 W. Third St., Los Angeles, CA 90038; (213) 937-2460.

TELEPRINT OF LOS ANGELES, 3779 Cahuenga Blvd. W., Studio City, CA 91604; (818) 760-3191.

TODD-AO GLENN STUDIOS, 900 N. Seward St., Hollywood, CA 90038; (213) 469-7221.

TRANS-AMERICAN VIDEO INC., 1541 N. Vine St., Los Angeles, CA 90028; (213) 466-2141.

TRANSWORLD VIDEO LAB INC., 1811 W. Magnolia Blvd., Burbank, CA 91506; (818) 841-2416.

U C L VIDEO, 823 N. Seward St., Los Angeles, CA 90038; (213) 469-7291.

U P A PRODUCTIONS OF AMERICA, 1875 Century Park E., Suite 2140, Los Angeles, CA 90067; (213) 556-3800.

UNITED COLOR LAB, INC., 823 N. Seward St., Hollywood, CA 90038; (213) 461-9921.

UNITEL VIDEO, 5555 Melrose Ave., Studio G, Los Angeles, CA 90038; (213) 468-4606.

V C I SERVICES, 1631 Gardena, Glendale, CA 91204; (818) 500-9090; (213) 650-8550.

VALLEY VIDEO, 4209 W. Burbank Blvd., Burbank, CA 91505; (818) 841-2387.

VIDEO ADVENTURES INC., 1015 Cahuenga Blvd., Hollywood, CA 90038; (213) 461-3288.

VIDEO CIRCUIT STUDIOS, 11440 Chandler Blvd., Studio 1400, N. Hollywood, CA 91601; (818) 506-5493.

VIDEO CRAFTSMEN INC., 6311 Romaine St., Los Angeles, CA 90038; (213) 464-4351.

VIDEO EVENTS INC., 1741 N. Ivar, Suite 210, Hollywood, CA 90028; (213) 465-4197.

VIDEO IMAGE, 4121 Redwood Ave., Suite 215, Los Angeles, CA 90066; (213) 822-8872.

THE VIDEOTAPE CO., 10545 Burbank Blvd., North Hollywood, CA 91601; (818) 985-1666.

VIDEO TECHNOLOGY & SERVICES, 500 N. Ventu Park Rd., Newbury Park, CA 91320; (818) 888-3040; (805) 499-5827.

VIDEO VIEW, 1617 N. El Centro Ave., Hollywood, CA 90038; (213) 463-4179.

VIDE-U PRODUCTIONS, 612 N. Sepulveda Blvd., Los Angeles, CA 90049; (213) 472-7023.

WESTERN FILM INDUSTRIES, 30941 W. Agoura Rd., Suite 302, Westlake Village, CA 91360; (818) 889-7350.

WILDER BROTHERS VIDEO, 10327 Santa Monica Blvd., Los Angeles, CA 90025; (213) 557-3500.

WILLIAM SOUND SERVICE, 1343 N. Highland Ave., Los Angeles, CA 90028; (213) 461-5321.

WORLD COMMUNICATIONS, 10880 Wilshire Blvd., Suite 2204, Los Angeles, CA 90024; (213) 474-3500.

YALE LABS, 1509 N. Gordon, Los Angeles, CA 90028, (213) 464-6181.

NEW YORK

A & D FILM/VIDEO, INC., 630 Ninth Ave., New York, NY 10036; (212) 315-0410.

ANS INTERNATIONAL VIDEO LTD., 396 Fifth Ave., New York, NY 10018; (212) 736-1007.

ACE AUDIO VIDEO CO., 118 E. 28 St., New York, NY 10016; (212) 685-3344.

ALL CHANELS VIDEO, INC. 630 Ninth Ave., New York, NY 10036; (212) 247-3428.

ALL MOBILE VIDEO, 630 Ninth Ave., New York, NY 10036; (212) 757-8919.

ALL STAR, 156 Fifth Ave., New York, NY 10011; (212) 645-8529.

AMERICAN TV VIDEO, 248 E. 48 St., New York, NY 10017; (212) 688-6222.

AMERICAN VIDEO CHANNELS, INC., 321 W. 44 St., New York, NY 10036; (212) 765-6324.

BOGAZICI VIDEO LTD., 460 Seventh Ave., New York, NY 10001; (212) 563-9022.

CINE MAGNETICS FILM & VIDEO LABORATORIES, 650 Halstand Ave., Mamaroneck, NY; 50 W. 40 St., New York, NY 10018; (212) 542-0700.

DEVLIN PRODUCTIONS, 1501 Broadway, New York, NY 10036; (212) 391-1313.

DOLPHIN PRODUCTIONS, 140 E. 80 St., New York, NY 10021; (212) 628-5930.

DU ART FILM LABS, 245 W. 55 St., New York, NY 10019; (212) 757-4580.

EUE/SCREEN GEMS, 222 E. 44 St., New York, NY 10017; (212) 867-4030.

EDITEL—NEW YORK, 222 E. 44 St., New York, NY 10017; (212) 867-4600.

86TH ST. PHOTO, 1525 Third Ave., New York, NY 10028; (212) 737-2265.

FAMA II PRODUCTIONS, 2750 Richmond Terrace, Staten Island, NY 10303; (718) 273-1780.

FOTO-VIDEO TRANSFER CENTER, 1 Times Square, New York, NY 10036; (212) 302-1866.

HBO STUDIO PRODUCTIONS, 120A E. 23 St., New York, NY 10010; (212) 512-7800.

IMAGE MIX, INC., 305 E. 46 St., New York, NY 10017; (212) 752-3010.

INTERNATIONAL VIDEO MARKET, 926 Second Ave., New York, NY 10022; (212) 826-1996.

INTERNATIONAL VIDEO SERVICES, 1501 Broadway, New York, NY 10036; (212) 730-1411.

JSL VIDEO SERVICES, INC., 25 W. 45 St., New York, NY 10036; (212) JSL-5082.

LRP VIDEO, 3 Dag Hammerskjold Plaza, New York, NY 10017; (212) 759-0822.

LANDMARK VIDEO INC., 350 Fifth Ave., New York, NY 10001; (212) 947-8637.

LANDYVISION, 400 E. 83 St., Suite 4A, New York, NY 10028; (212) 734-1402.

LASER VIDEO INC., 384 Bleecker St., New York, NY 10014; (212) 947-8637.

MPCS VIDEO INDUSTRIES, 514 W. 57 St., New York, NY 10019; (212) 586-3690.

MAGNO SOUND & VIDEO, 729 Seventh Ave., New York, NY 10019; (212) 302-2505.

MANHATTAN TRANSFER/EDIT, 545 Fifth Ave., New York, NY 10017; (212) 687-4000.

MODERN TELECOMMUNICATIONS INC., 1443 Park Ave., New York, NY 10029; (212) 722-1818; 1 Dag Hammarskjold Plaza, New York, NY 10017; (212) 355-0510.

MOVIELAB VIDEO INC., 619 W. 54 St., New York, NY 10019; (212) 956-3900.

MULTI-VIDEO GROUP LTD., 50 E. 42 St., New York, NY 10017; (212) 986-1577.

NATIONAL VIDEO CENTER/RECORDING STUDIOS, INC., 460 W. 42 St., New York, NY 10036; (212) 279-2000.

PICSONIC PRODUCTIONS CORP., 25 W. 45 St., New York, NY 10036; (212) 575-1910.

R.G. VIDEO, 21 E. 46 St., New York, NY 10036; (212) 719-2744.

REEVES TELETAPE, 708 Third Ave., New York, NY 10017; (212) 573-8888; 1697 Broadway, New York, NY 10019; (212) 307-4880.

REGENT SOUND STUDIOS INC., 1619 Broadway, New York, NY 10019; (212) 245-2630.

ROSENBERG, WARREN, VIDEO SERVICES, 308 E. 79 St., New York, NY 10021; (212) 744-1111.

S/T VIDEOCASSETTE DUPLICATION CORP., 500 Willowtree Rd., Leonia, NJ; (212) 239-4653.

SOUND ONE CORP., 1619 Broadway, New York, NY 10019; (212) 765-4757.

SPALLA, RICK, PRODUCTIONS, 301 W. 45 St., New York, NY 10036; (212) 765-4646.

SPECTRUM LIGHT PRODUCTIONS, 208 E. 21 St., New York, NY 10010; (212) 477-0346.

SYNAPSE TELECOMMUNICATIONS, INC., 304 E. 45 St., New York, NY 10017; (212) 370-9191.

TVC VIDEO, 225 E. 43 St., New York, NY 10017; (212) 599-1616.

TFI (TAPE FILM INDUSTRIES), 619 W. 54 St., New York, NY 10019; (212) 708-0500.

THE TAPE HOUSE EDITORIAL, 216 E. 45 St., New York, NY 10017; (212) 557-4949.

TV-R/MASTER COLOR TRANSFER, INC., 333 W. 52 St., New York, NY 10019; (212) 541-4030.

UNITEL VIDEO, 515 W. 57 St., New York, NY 10019; (212) 265-3600.

VCA/TELETRONICS, 231 E. 55 St., New York, NY 10022; (212) 355-1600.

VIDEO CASSETTE TRANSFERS, 1501 Broadway, Suite 406, New York, NY 10036; (212) 575-8433.

VIDEO CENTRAL, 225 W. 36 St., New York, NY 10018; (212) 947-6960.

VIDEO CONNECTION, 2244 Broadway, New York, NY 10024; (212) 724-2727.

VIDEO DUB, INC., 423 W. 55 St., New York, NY 10019; (212) 757-3300.

VIDEO FEX, 321 W. 44 St., New York, NY 10036; (212) 541-9200.

VIDEO MEDIA PRODUCTIONS, 149-33 88th St., Howard Beach, NY; (718) 845-3709.

VIDEO PLANNING INC., 250 W. 57 St., New York, NY 10019; (212) 582-5066.

VIDEO RESOURCES NEW YORK, INC., 220 W. 71 St., New York, NY 10023; (212) 724-7055.

VIDEO STOP, 367 Third Ave., New York, NY 10016; (212) 685-6199.

VIDEOROOM, 1487 Third Ave., New York NY 10028; (212) 879-5333.

VIDEOWORKS, 24 W. 40 St., New York, NY 10018; (212) 869-2500.

WINDSOR TOTAL VIDEO, 8 W. 38 St., New York, NY 10018; (212) 944-9090.

CANADA

BELLEVUE PATHÉ QUEBEC VIDEO DUPLICATION CENTER, 5588 Cote de Liesse, Montreal, Que., H4P 1A9; (514) 737-2777.

MANTA VIDEO LABS, 311 Adelaide St. E, Toronto, Ont., M5A IN2; (412) 863-9316.

PATHÉ SOUND & POST PRODUCTION CENTRE, 1212 St. Patrick St., Toronto, Ont.; (416) 598-2521.

Videotape Transfer, Tape to Film

LOS ANGELES

AMERICAN VIDEO FACTORY, 4150 Glencoe Ave., Marina Del Rey, CA 90292; (213) 823-8622.

APOLLO VIDEO FACILITY, 1503 Cahuenga Blvd., Hollywood, CA 90028; (213) 464-7871; 465-6154.

AUDIO GRAPHIC FILMS AND VIDEO, 6509 De Longpre Ave., Hollywood, CA 90028; (213) 462-6596, (213) 467-1234.

BEVERLY HILLS HOME VIDEOCENTRE, 145 S. Beverly Dr., Beverly Hills, CA 90212; (213) 550-1092; 8205 Santa Monica Blvd., W. Hollywood, CA 90046; (213) 656-4477.

COMPACT VIDEO SERVICES INC., 2813 W. Alameda Ave., Burbank, CA 91505; (818) 840-7000.

CONSOLIDATED FILM INDUSTRIES, 959 Seward St., Los Angeles, CA 90038; (213) 462-3161.

CREATIVE VIDEO SERVICES, 500 Ventu Park Rd., Newbury Park, CA 91320; (818) 888-3040.

CREST NATIONAL FILM & VIDEOTAPE LABS, 1141 N. Seward St., Los Angeles, CA 90038; (213) 462-0624; 462-6696.

DEVONSHIRE SOUND STUDIOS, 10729 Magnolia Blvd., N. Hollywood, CA 91601; (818) 985-1945.

THE EDITING COMPANY, 8300 Beverly Blvd., Los Angeles, CA 90048; (213) 653-3570.

ENCORE VIDEO, INC., 6344 Fountain Ave., Hollywood, CA 90028; (213) 466-7663.

IMAGE TRANSFORM INC., 4142 Lankershim Blvd., North Hollywood, CA 91602; (818) 985-7566.

IMAGE TRANSFORM LABORATORY, 3611 N. San Fernando Rd., Burbank, CA 91505; (818) 841-3812.

INTER VIDEO/TRITONICS INC., 733 N. Victory Blvd., Burbank, CA 91502; (818) 843-3633; 569-4000.

INTERNATIONAL VIDEO CONVERSIONS, 815 N. Cahuenga Blvd., Hollywood, CA 90038; (213) 463-7884.

KWHY-TV, CHANNEL 22, 5545 Sunset Blvd., Los Angeles, CA 90028; (213) 466-5441.

MEDIA MASTERS PRODUCTIONS, 1800 S. Robertson Blvd., Suite 306, Beverly Hills, CA 90035; (213) 451-8823.

MODERN TALKING PICTURE SERVICE, INC., 6735 San Fernando Rd., Glendale, CA 91201; (818) 240-0519; (813) 541-7571.

MODERN VIDEOFILM, 7165 Sunset Blvd., Hollywood, CA 90046; (213) 851-8070.

ONE PASS FILM & VIDEO, One China Basin Bldg., San Francisco, CA 94107; (415) 777-5777.

RVS—TAPE TO FILM TRANSFER SERVICES, 2408 W. Olive Ave., Burbank, CA 91506; (818) 954-8621.

RENCHER'S EDITORIAL SERVICE, 738 Cahuenga Blvd., Hollywood, CA 90038; (213) 463-9836.

RINGER VIDEO SERVICES, 2408 W. Olive Ave., Burbank, CA 91506; (818) 954-8621.

ROUZER STUDIO, 451 N. Mansfield, Los Angeles, CA 90036-2621; (213) 935-6124.

SOUND SERVICES INC., 7155 Santa Monica Blvd., Los Angeles, CA 90038; (213) 874-9344.

SPALLA, RICK, PRODUCTIONS, 1622 N. Gower St., Los Angeles, CA 90028; (213) 469-7307.

TAV SOUND INC., 6200 W. Third St., Los Angeles, CA 90038; (213) 937-2460.

TAPE-FILM INDUSTRIES, 941 N. Highland Ave., Hollywood, CA 90038; (213) 461-3361.

TELEPRINT OF LOS ANGELES, 3779 Cahuenga Blvd. W., Studio City, CA 91604; (818) 760-3191.

TODD-AO GLEN GLENN STUDIOS, 900 N. Seward St., Hollywood, CA 90038; (213) 469-7221.

VECTOR PRODUCTIONS INC., P.O. Box 7000-645, Redondo Beach, CA 90277; (213) 757-0520, (213) 316-6031.

VIDEO CIRCUIT STUDIOS, 8103 Orion Ave., Van Nuys, CA 91406; (818) 785-6220.

VIDEO VIEW, 1617 N. El Centro Ave., Hollywood, CA 90028; (213) 463-4179.

WEISBARTH, JACOB & ASSOCIATES, INC., 9903 Santa Monica Blvd., Suite 256, Beverly Hills, CA 90212; (213) 277-9616.

WESTERN FILM INDUSTRIES, 30941 W. Agoura Rd., Suite 302, Westlake Village, CA 91360; (818) 889-7350.

NEW YORK

A & D FILM/VIDEO, 630 Ninth Ave., New York, NY 15036; (212) 315-0410.

AVPS CORP., 31 W. 60 St., New York, NY 10023; (212) 765-5060.

CINELAB CORP., 1600 Broadway #1008, New York, NY 10019; (212) 315-0600.

DEVLIN PRODUCTIONS, INC., 1501 Broadway, New York, NY 10036; (212) 391-1313; (212) 582-5572.

DU ART FILM LABS INC., 245 W. 55 St., New York, NY 10019; (212) 757-4580.

EUE/SCREEN GEMS, 222 E. 44 St., New York, NY 10017; (212) 867-4030.

MPCS VIDEO INDUSTRIES, INC., 514 W. 57 St., New York, NY 10019; (212) 586-3690; (800) 223-0622.

MAGNO SOUND & VIDEO, 729 Seventh Ave., New York, NY 10010; (212) 302-2505.

MAYFAIR RECORDING STUDIO INC., 701 Seventh Ave., New York, NY 10036; (212) 719-2810.

MODERN TELECOMMUNICATIONS INC., 885 Second Ave., New York, NY 10017; (212) 355-0510.

NATIONAL FILM CENTER, 232 E. 46 St., New York, NY 10017; (212) 279-2000.

PICSONIC PRODUCTIONS CORP., 25 W. 45 St., #703; New York, NY 10036; (212) 575-1910.

POSITIVE TRANSFER LTD., 545 Fifth Ave., New York, NY 10017; (212) 888-2722.

SPALLA, RICK VIDEO PRODUCTIONS, 301 W. 45 St., New York, NY 10036; (212) 765-4646.

TFI, 619 W. 54 St., New York, NY 10019; (212) 708-0500.

TV-R INC., 333 W. 52 St., New York, NY 10019; (212) 541-4030.

VIDEO PRODUCTION INC., 333 W. 52 St., New York, NY 10019; (212) 581-7312.

VIDEO TRANSCRIPTS INC., 509 Madison Ave., New York, NY 10022; (21) 752-3131.

WARREN ROSENBERG VIDEO SERVICES, 308 E. 79 St., New York, NY 10021; (212) 744-1111.

WINDSOR TOTAL VIDEO, 565 Fifth Ave., New York, NY 10017; (212) 725-8080.

The Home Video World Market

The Home Video World Market

ARGENTINA

Number of VCRs: 300,000–350,000
Format Share: About 78% VHS, 22% Beta
TV System: PAL N
TV Distributors: AVH, Gati-Video, LK-TEL, Video Espagna, Legal Video, Transeuropa Video Entertainment, Transmundo Homevideo and some 20 smaller ones
Number of Retail Video Outlets or Video Clubs: About 800
Sell-In Price to Retailer: $60–$80
Average Rental: Two cassettes for one day, three over weekend
Best Seller: About 3,000 units
Piracy: 35%
Hardware: $1,800–$2,000 for a VCR
Product: Almost entirely feature films; some miniseries. Small percentage of adult films
Videodisks: Negligible
Subtitles: Argentines prefer electronically subtitled films to dubbed versions. Subtitling is done locally.
Price Argentines pay for average cassette rental: $2.00–$4.00.

The extraordinary expansion in Argentina's home video industry in 1986 experienced a shakeout in 1987 as the market became saturated with product and the numerous videoclubs shuttered. Of the more than 100 videocassette traders operating in 1986, only 30 distributors remained by the end of 1987. Estimates of the number of VCRs in the country vary widely from 300,000 to 800,000 because of the large number smuggled into the country.

During 1987 almost 70 legal actions were taken throughout Argentina against video piracy resulting in an estimate that while pirated copies accounted for 40–45% of all tapes previously, the figure is currently down to about 35%.

Videoclubs have set up an association to represent their interests, the Argentine Federation of Video Clubs (FAVIC).

High governmental taxes have also slowed the industry's previous rapid growth. A 100% levy on foreign goods including videocassette recorders, plus an import tax has actually raised the price of a VCR to about $2,000, therefore resulting in maintaining the number of VCRs in the country at about a constant 300,000 to 325,000.

AUSTRALIA

Estimates indicate that approximately 58% of the households with television sets also have video cassette recorders (90% VHS; 10% Beta).

The following figures showing the number of VCRs sold here each year since 1979 reveal the rapid penetration of the market:

1979	26,000
1980	72,000
1981	150,000
1982	350,000
1983	500,000
1984	685,000
1985	600,000

The average time spent viewing VCRs is 1 hour 52 minutes per week, and is divided equally between pre-recorded and recorded off-air material. VCRs cost between A$399 to more than A$1000, and cassette rentals average A$3 per night. There are currently approximately 2800 active retail outlets.

VCR imports dropped from a 1984 high of AUS $295.25 million to AUS $153.94 in 1987.

Major video distributors total nine, while there are some 20 smaller outfits. Nearly all the majors have links to other Australian media groups as well as to leading world-wide film distributors.

For example, the major VCR wholesalers include CBS-Fox, Warner Video, and RCA/Columbia/Hoyts (latter is a leading theatre circuit) as well as CIC Video (film distributor with links to Paramount), Syme Video (media conglomerate with ties to Disney), and PBV (TV station owners with ties to MGM and United Artists). Other distributors are Thorn-EMI Video, Video Classics and Roadshow.

A Joint Federal Parliamentary Select Committee on video material (which also includes film material) was established in 1985 and is expected to make a report affecting the label and rating of videos for violence and sexual violence and to address the issue of establishing uniform national standards on video classification and availability.

AUSTRIA

VCR Penetration: 43% of Austria's 1,800,000 households.
Number of Retail Stores: 900 (rentals account for 90% of market)
Industry Income: 300,000,000 schillings ($28,700,000)
Product: Adventure films top the rental list
Format: VHS recorders predominate

A recent bill in parliament called for the federal government to start a study of violence and pornography in video software, a major concern in Austria. Currently federal laws differ from state laws, and state laws vary state to state. Youths may enter video stores but must show identity cards, meeting the local age limits.

The Austrian government imposed a levy of 3 schillings per tape hour in 1982 to offset losses from home taping and has collected 50,000,000 schillings ($5,000,000 to date) paid by the dealers. 51% of the blank tape tax goes into a special fund for cultural and social purposes (old age pension, health insurance, aid to film schools and producers).

BRAZIL

Population (1988): 144,000,000
Inflation (February 1988): 18% month
Exchange rate (Feb. 23, 1988): $1=94,80 cruzados
TV sets: 40,000,000
Viewers reached: 130,000,000
VCRs: 2.5–3 million
Sealed titles: 3,200; **Sealed tapes:** 6,000,000
Total revenues in 1987: $60,000,000 (official), $20–25,000,000 (pirated)
Retail Outlets: 5–6,000
Average whole price per copy: $40
Average rental per day: $0.90
Principal markets: São Paulo, Rio Grande do Sul, Rio de Janeiro

Home video distribution was the fastest growing segment of Brazil's entertainment industry in 1987, despite the inhibiting factors of government regulation and piracy. Resolution 136 of Concine, Brazil's film and Video regulatory agency imposed a 25% quota for Brazilian product in number of titles and tapes in every distributor's catalog and mandated that all mastering and duplicating work be performed in local labs. It defined legal tapes as only those carrying a seal issued by Embrafilme after proof of copyright ownership and local lab work. Nearly 500 dealers have joined Abevc, one of several retailer organizations to remove illegal product from their shelves.

Although technically there are 120 home video distributors registered by Concine, only half of them are operational and only 30–35% operate at significant levels.

In the past two years there has been a 400% rise in the number of VCRs (up to 2.5–3 million) in Brazil. Sony, Mitsubishi, Philco, Sanyo, Sharp, CCE and Gradiente all assemble 12 different types of VCRs here and the retail price has dropped from $1,200 in 1986 to an average of $850 in 1987. Preference, however, is for smuggled Panasonic and JVC models available for $550.

90% of the market is in VHS format and Brazilian system is the unique PAL-M (PAL 525 lines) however, conversion from NTSC can be easily done for $50. All tapes are manufactured in NTSC system.

Approximately 3,200 titles (6 million tapes) are available and rental is dominant. Wholesale price (for stores) is $40 and 24-hour rental average $1. Rental stores (almost 5,000) have overtaken videoclubs (in which tapes were exchanged among members). Due to high taxes (the 17% ICM or municipal tax, the 15% IPI or federal tax, and a 10% import tax for blank tape) 50% of the wholesale price for a tape goes for taxes, resulting in piracy. However, because of strict regulation, piracy has declined from an 80% level to 40%. An organization of pirates called "Pool" has circumvented the new law by printing new films over sealed tapes containing legitmate films already having the seal of control on their boxes.

Organizations

Concine: (Film/hv regulatory agency); Head: Roberto Farias, Rua da Imprensa, 16, Rio de Janeiro.

UBV: (Copyright owners assn.); Head: Roberto Mendes, Rua Mexico, 31, Rio de Janeiro.

ABEVC: (Retailers assn.); Head: Irapuã Valverde, Avenida Reboucas, 1206 cj 4, São Paulo.

CANADA

VCRs were in 45% of all households in Canada as of May 1987, compared to 35% in 1986 (as reported by Statistics Canada, a federal government agency). As of November 1987, A.C. Nielsen Co. of Canada reported that 51% of all households with TV also had a VCR, a 4% climb since March, 1987. As of January 1988, Canada's population was 24,823,000.

It is estimated VCR sales (in units) will decrease from 950,000 in 1987 to 930,000 in 1988. The rental-sales ratio is 80–20. 90% of all English-language cassettes (VHS & Beta) are manufactured in Toronto and 10% in Montréal; 95% of the English market in Canada is serviced by two companies, Video I and Bellevue Video. Canadian sales of cassette are estimated at about 10% of the U.S. market.

Other data recently compiled by A.C. Nielsen of Canada:
About 72% of VCRs are VHS format.

Films are the most frequently recorded programs.
More than 50% of the usage occurs while the TV set is off, and the same percentage eliminates commercials while recording.
More than 20% of households watch more TV since purchase of a VCR.
Nearly 75% of households sampled cited recording of programs that would otherwise be missed as the chief reason for use.

CHILE

By the end of 1987 the number of VCRs in Chile is estimated at 150,000, and a substantial number of VCPs (videocassette players) were imported and sold at a lower price in Beta format.
Video industry gained legal status in 1986 and as of January 1, 1987 law No. 18,443 established penalties for piracy protecting legitimate videocassette distributors which at that time numbered only three; Video Chile, CCN Video and Videoman. Piracy is currently estimated to be 45%. By the end of 1987 import duties on VCRs were slashed by 40% encouraging sales.

EGYPT

Number of production companies for recording and distributing tapes: 1988—217.
Number of fully registered video clubs selling and renting video tapes: 1988—19800. In addition, more than 2000 small shops and magazines also sell and rent video tapes to viewers.
Number of VCR owners: Near 7 million up from 5 million in 1987 (still growing).
The Censorship Dept., which is headed by Mrs. Naiema Hamdy, and connected to the Ministry of Culture, is in charge of viewing, rating and granting the approval on general release to all and any local and/or foreign production on tapes.
Now in Egypt there is available a wireless video sender manufactured in Japan that can transmit from any VCR set to any number of TV sets within a range of 300 meters.
General: There's no doubt that video is spreading rapidly in Egypt and is beginning to have a serious effect on theatrical film business. The Indian public enjoys watching films in its own homes at inexpensive prices with all members of the family on hand and the ability to invite friends and neighbors if they wish. Going to a movie theatre is annoying to them for many reasons, including crowded streets, the cost of transportation, and the lack of parking areas.

—AHMED SAMI

FRANCE

After years of being stymied by heavy taxes, piracy and restrictive windowing, France's video companies are scrambling back on their feet. Producers are hopeful that the VAT on recorders will be slashed from 18.6% to 7% in the coming year. A total of 4.9 million recorders (mostly VHS) sold by 1987. 27.5 million non-recorded cassettes sold in 1987. 3 million pre-recorded cassettes sold in 1987. 85% of the market is in rentals, with a total of some 4,000 video clubs.
Trends: The European Economic Community's executive branch has levied a provisional tax on Korean and Japanese imports which undercut European prices, skimming off 30% of the market in 1987. Aside from the anti-dumping measures, Europe hardly presents a common front in regard to recorder prices which are 40% higher in France than in the United Kingdom.

—VERNICE KLIER-MOSKOWITZ

GREAT BRITAIN

With an annual income to distributors exceeding £200 million and a weekly audience of over 25 million, the home video business in the UK remains a thriving one. Films on cassettes have helped the industry achieve a £500 million turnover, probably the biggest market in Europe. Some 11 million people have video recorders in their home (55% of TV households), and it is probably the second most popular home leisure pastime after television itself. Another encouraging statistic is that 31% of these households rent videotapes as frequently as once a week. Viewers bought 2,155,000 VCRs in 1987—an 11% increase over 1986, while sales to the trade (2,200,000) increased only 2%. The average price for VCRs were estimated to be £350 ($650) in 1987, a drop from £440 in 1984. There are some 7–8000 outlets in the UK and the average charge for a cassette rental has increased to £1.31 a night. Leading distributors include Warner Home Video, CIC, RCA/Columbia, CBS/FOX, Entertainment in Video, Virgin, Vestron Home Video (UK), MGM/UA, Guild and New World. As with the theatrical market, the majority of the product screened at home hails from America.
Commenting on the state of the industry, Steward Till, chairman of the British Video Association (BVA), stressed that the "long term health of the video market depends on the ability to persuade the majority of VCR owners to rent pre-recorded cassettes more often." Answering attacks on

the video trade by politicians and the media, to counter its early reputation for showing violent and sleazy product, the BVA moved towards self-regulating of trade advertising and cassette jacket designs, with the result that it received an assurance from the government that the proposed Broadcasting Standards Council will not change the status or integrity of the British Board of Film Classification to which the industry conforms.
The Rank Organisation, with a view to the world market, acquired the American company BHCP Video, now called Rank Video Services America, and currently operates the leading video duplication business in the world. Prior to the takeover Rank was already Europe's leader in this field.
As has been stated previously, like cinemas and 'free' television, the video business is dependent on quality entertainment. Given that, there is no reason why home viewing should not continue to expand despite the development of cable, Pay-TV and Satellite broadcasting.

—WILLIAM PAY

GREECE

Home video invaded Greek homes, cafes, and other places in 1983. More and more videocassettes are produced every year to supply the numerous video clubs operating in the country.
Number of Videocassettes: It is estimated that more than 3000 titles are produced legally locally at the rate of 500 every year. They are rented at the rate of drs. 70 per day.
Price of a Videocassette: The price to wholesalers of a videocassette by it producer is about drs. 6,000–8,000. Each copy is rented by video clubs for drs. 250–300 per day, but the competition is so keen that some minor dealers are renting them for drs. 50, especially those from pirated sources.
Videocassette Piracy: There is an extensive traffic of illegal video cassette operators who import masters illegally and/or duplicate imported titles or local ones and sell their inferior copies cheaper to regional places. Even good pictures which have not as yet been released theatrically in Athens are out in the market as videocassettes. As there is not a law against this piracy, an organization was established by several producers to protect their interests. It is called Protection Society of Videocassette Producers (EPPVE), which acts according to a decision of the Supreme Court by which the illegal reproduction of a videocassette is considered a forgery and the culprits are sentenced to imprisonment and/or heavy fines.
Hardware and Software Dealers: There are many dealers selling hardware and software equipment in Athens, operating or acting as agents of Akai, Asa, Blaupunkt, Grundig, Hitachi, Lowe, Panasonic, Magnasonic, Philips, Siemens, Telefunken, Salora, etc.
Producers, Wholesalers, Agents: There are more than one hundred videocassette producers in Greece, but it is expected that only the important ones will survive after the video boom subsides. Some of the most important ones are: Home Video Hellas S.A., 275, Messoguion Str., Athens 162 31; Audiovisual Enterprises, 7 Sochou Str., Athens 115 25; Key Video, 16-18 Skalidi Str., Athens 115-25; Nea Kinissi Video, 13 Gravias Str., Athens 106 78; Video Elit, 41-43 Kifissias Str. 151 23; Spentzos Films Video, 49 Themistocleous Str., Athens 106 85; Liberty Video, 292 Messoguion Str., Athens, 155 62; Mediterranean Trading Company (MTC), 5 Aristotelous Str., Callithea Athens 175 71; EMGEE Home Video, 70 Homerou Str., Nea Smyrni Athens 171 21; VideoSonic I Evrydamantos Str. Athens 117 43; CBS Enterprises, 311 Messoguion Str., Athens 152 31; Georguiadis Electroniki, 20 Lagoumutzi Str., Athens 176 71. Festival Home Video, 3 George Str. Athens 106 77; Hellas World Video, 442 Acharnon Str., Athens 111 43; International Video Business, 29 Mavromateon Str., Athens 104 34; Kino Video, Messoguion 230 Athens 151 61; Pap Video, 47 Didotou Str. Athens 106 80; AudioVideo Magnetics, Vassileos Constantinou & Kifissias Str., Athens 152 33; Home Video Center, 96 Academias Str., Athens 106 77; Libero Video, 10-12 Gravias Str., Athens 106; Master Home Video, 96 Academias Str., Athens 106 77, etc.

—RENA VELISSARIOU

HOLLAND

Population: 14,700,000
Number of VCRs: 2,000,000. This means that some 35% of Dutch families own VCRs.
Number of Distributors: some 40 of which only 23 are active. The most important are Esselte-CIC (Paramount, Universal), Warner Home Video (WB and UA), RCA-Columbia, CBS-Fox, RCV (Orion), CNR (MGM) Cannon (Cannon and Touchstone).
Number of Rental Shops: around 1000.
Rental Price: from Dfl. 3.50 to Dfl. 10. per day. Estimated number of rentals per year: 39,000,000.
Video Sales: A growing market (1987: some Dfl. 11,000,000) at this moment mainly dealing in B-pictures, soft pornography and documentaries.
Sales Prices: Some Dfl. 40–80. for soft pornography and B-pix. For documentaries between Dfl. 27.50 and Dfl 40. Blank tapes sell for around Dfl 10.(3 hours)
Total Video Turnover: Dfl. 211,000,000. generated by some 3,000 titles.
Window: 6 months from first theatrical release.
Video Systems: 73% VHS, 15% V2000, 12% Betamax. The purchase price of a VHS recorder starts at some Dfl. 800.

Philips, Blaupunkt and Gründig (West Germany), Sharp, Japanese video recorders (Sony, Akai, Hitachi), practically all VHS systems, are sold here.

Trade Associations: Producers & Importers: Nederlandse Vereniging van Producenten en Importeurs van Beeld en Geluidsdragers (NVPI), Albertus Perkstraat 36, 1217 NT Hilversum. Rental Shops: Nederlandse Vereniging van Detail Ondernemingen (NVDO) Twijnstraat 46, 3511 ZL Utrecht.

Piracy: Still important, but slowly going down. Now estimated at some Dfl. 55,000,000 per year. Last year some 26.000 illegal video tapes were seized. The government has still not prepared new legislation which would enable more severe punishment for copyright-infringement. VIDEO VEILIG (Video Safe) is the venture which is constantly alert on copyright-infringement. Members are the NVPI (Video distributors), Stemra-Buma (Mechanical Copyright Organization), NBB (Filmdistributors, Exhibitors and Producers Organization), NOS (Television Organization) and the MPAA.

Top 10 of 1987: 1) Back To The Future; 2) Police Academy III; 3) Commando; 4) Indiana Jones and the Temple of Doom; 5) Iron Eagle; 6) Jewel of the Nile; 7) Cobra; 8) Deathwish III; 9) Weird Science; 10) The Hitcner.

General: Video is obviously hurting the cinema trade. For a family of 4 it is obviously much cheaper to rent a film for Dfl. 10 than to go to a cinema which would cost Dfl. 45.

Purchase of a recorder is relatively high by those with a good income, mostly by those living in the west of the Netherlands (the most prosperous provinces), those who look often to TV, and by members of the most important TV organizations: A.V.R.O, T.R.O.S. and V.O.O. 70% of the owners of a recorder rent a print of pictures for instance with video companies. There are many stores in many cities and villages. TV programs are often copied (recorded) by 86% of the owners of a recorder.
—PAUL SILVIUS

INDIA

With the expansion of TV networks throughout the country an increasing number of VCRs have made their appearance in Indian homes. A rough estimate puts the total number of VCRs in the country around 2,500,000. There are well over 75,000 video libraries renting out cassettes. Besides, there are about 100,000 video parlours in the country. The number is still growing as video is making its appearance in the small towns and villages. In the absence of legitimate cassettes, they have been screening only pirated prints, thus depriving the national exchequer and the film industry of millions of rupees. In addition, there are over 5,000 video coaches and 30,000 hotel rooms having closed circuit TV. Many metropolitan cities have now started having closed circuit TV in buildings and housing societies and the numbers are growing. Clubs, schools, hospitals and other institutions also have regular screenings of films on video.

Widespread video piracy has undoubtedly affected the film industry's export earnings. For example: UK, which had nearly a hundred cinema halls showing Indian films, now practically has none. Similar is the case in Canada and U.S.A. In India, however, the situation is different. The number of feature films produced in 1987 though less than the previous year is still fairly high. But box office receipts have registered a decline. In Bombay alone there are nearly 5,000 video parlours—as against 150 cinema houses—which screen Hindi films openly, thus depriving the film industry of a sizeable revenue.

Through the film industry's concerted efforts the government has now passed a law against video piracy. Any person who exhibits or permits the exhibition of a video film in any place without proper certification is liable for imprisonment for a period of three years and a fine which may extend to Rs. 100,000. Taking advantage of the stringent laws the producers are now selling the video rights of their films; thus a new source of revenue has been opened to them.

Most Hindi and regional films, old and new are available fairly cheaply on video cassettes. The entire work—18 films of the late Raj Kapoor—is now available in a package deal for Rs.2,500/- (about 180 US Dollars).

The proliferation of video libraries and the vast improvements in video exhibition technology through anti-glare enlarged screens, has opened up exciting possibilities for cheap entertainment through video. A defense organization in Bombay organizes free video shows for defense personnel and their families, which are open to civilians for a dime.
—B. D. GARGA

ITALY

Gross Revenue: for video distributors belonging to Univideo (an association of 21 major video producers and distributors which controls 70% of the video cassette market): $77,000,000 on 1,669,000 videocassettes sold (up from $61,000,000 in 1986); with an additional gross revenue for non-member legitimate (non-porno, non-pirate) distributors of $20,000,000. Revenue for porno and pirate tapes is estimated to be $100,000,000 resulting in a total of $200,000,000 for the software business.

VCR Price: lowest cost of owning a VCR continued to drop from $900 in 1986 to $600 in 1987. Prices are elevated by a 12% custom duty, an 18% value added tax and a 16% luxury tax. High taxes also hurt the sales of videocassettes which often cost $75 or more at the retail level.

VCR Penetration: 13.8% (up from 10% in 1986) with an anticipated 3 million VCRs in Italian households by the end of 1989 and 4 million in

1990 (with a penetration rate of 20%) but still one of the lowest in Europe partly due to the fact that Italy has the largest free television transmission of any country—national networks and over 600 local stations. Only 50% of VCR owners rent videocassettes. Most use their machines only for home taping.

Video titles: approximately 5,000 non-porno.

Retail outlets: an estimated 2,000 which rent or sell (a special license is needed to sell). Retailers must report each title they buy from a distributor to the local police. Sell through is put at 15–20% of the total.

Sales of blank tape: 8,000,000 units, mostly used for taping from TV or making pirated copies of video cassettes.

Piracy: It is estimated that piracy has fallen from 50% or more in 1986 to 35% in 1987. Video pirates face prison terms ranging from 3 months to 3 years and $5,000 in fines. Polar-proof stamps (with Polaroid tamperproof images of the SIAE logo) placed on legitimate tapes makes it easier to catch violators.

In January, 1988, members of Italy's motion pciture association joined the home video industry and the MPAA to form the Federation Against Audiovisual Piracy to cooperate with SIAE, the Italian copyright association in investigating and prosecuting copyright infringements by pirates.

Top Videocassettes in Italy—1987 (Sold by distributors to dealers.) 1) Pinnochio; 2) Platoon; 3) The Name of the Rose; 4) Top Gun; 5) Rocky IV; 6) Over the Top; 7) Cobra; 8) Out of Africa; 9) Crocodile Dundee; 10) Back to the Future.

JAPAN

The Latin word video, to see, has been adopted for use in our modern world as a term which covers a rather large field in the electronics sector including videocassette recorders (VCRs) or video tape recorders (VTRs), and the compact disks (CDs) using laser beam technology. The Japanese, who are the most skillful people in the world in adapting ideas and improving on them, are the world leaders in video manufacturing. At present they make 90% of the world VCRs or VTRs produced, have close to 90% of the most lucrative American market, and perhaps 99% of the Japanese market, which includes 38.5 million households.

At present, American production of videocassette recorders is negligible, as is production of CD systems, thus leaving 90 percent of sales to Japanese makers and the remainder mostly to South Korean or European makers. The report that Tandy Corp. (USA) had developed a new type of erasable CD system caught the Japanese by surprise and they were very skeptical that it could be done by the American company at the low price of $500 as claimed. Last year Japanese VTR production was down 12.2 percent (27.5 million units) to $20.159 billion of which $8 billion worth was exported (down 30.9 percent) while imports increased 288.6 percent to $90 million due mostly to cheap imports from South Korea. VTR production reached its peak in 1986 at 33,879,000 units, 27,689,000 of which were exported, decreasing to 30,544,000 of which 22,801,000 were exported.

Video has an important relationship with television as well as with the movie industry in the past decade in two ways: from legal sales of cassettes or solid discs of movies, and the adverse factor, illegal pirating of copyrighted material or sale to the public, which hurts both producers and exhibitors and is rampant in many countries.

Consumer use in Japan is considerable as one can see from these figures: the 53 video software-related industries in the past year reported total revenues of yen 205,017,000,000 (about $1.55 billion at the exchange rate of yen 132 to $1 as written), a 25.2 percent gain over the previous year comprising compact disk production of yen 96,867 million, cassettes yen 68,695 million, and other software production yen 9,612 million. Copyright income was yen 488 million according to Japan Video Association which admits this does not include producers who are not associated members. Cassette rentals given by them were yen 19,044 million. Taken on an item basis disk sales were 15,739,947, up 5 percent; cassette sales 7,625,177, up 80 percent; and cassette rentals 1,901,186, up 20 percent. Of course, these figures do not include exports.

Foreign feature films are most popular with sales of yen 32,096 million (up 47.2 percent) and overshadow Japanese movies (Yen 12,180 million, up 17.9 percent), followed by Japanese music and soft porn movies on tapes or disks. Videocassette rental indicated a slight preference for foreign films with yen 7,656 million (up 40.2 percent) compared to yen 7,225 (up 37.9 percent) for domestic feature films.

Part of sales of compact disks are due to the opening up in 1985 of a number of one-man-operated video theatres usually with seats for around 100 customers willing to pay from $4 to $10. These may have contributed to the admissions figure for regular movie- goers dropping from over 160 million to about 144 million but the fault is really that of VTRs or CDs shown in 53 percent of Japanese Homes.

Although film attendance in Japan has dropped, there have been diatribes by cinema importers, distributors, producers and exhibitors complaining of lost revenues due to black market or legal cassettes or compact discs. The Motion Picture Assoc. of America has set up teams to patrol video rental stores to warn them to refrain from sales of pirated tapes or discs of American films. Since there are over 8,000 regulated shops and an estimated 4,000–7,000 not regulated and selling pirated tapes, this is quite a task. What action has been taken by the authorities was limited to piracies of domestic Japanese software. At present 50% of tapes sold are pirated, resulting in losses of up to $1 billion to copyright holders. The Ministry of Education has submitted an amendment to the present copyright law which imposes a penalty on "display of pirated cassettes," including heavier fines and prison sentences (usually suspended).

While Japan has flooded the world with video exports, the public's use has been nowhere near the enthusiasm engendered in America, and to a lesser extent, Europe. The answer to this lies in the Japanese character and customs. It is true that increasing numbers of Japanese have been resorting to setting a timer to tape TV shows they are liable to miss and want to view later, and there are smaller numbers who tape the shows to send to family members working outside Japan and wish to keep up with what goes on in their homeland.

Going to the movies in Japan is either a habit or compulsion for youngsters, a "ceremony" for others and a chance to get out of the home. In general, the average Japanese would hesitate to pay out a goodly sum to purchase a cassette or solid disc for showing at home for his family, though admittedly the male members of the household might invest in soft pornography. A Japanese home is not meant for entertaining outsiders so there is no question of inviting neighbors or friends to a viewing. Entertaining is done outside the home and in no way consists of running a VTR for outsiders.

Of course, one cannot say with certainty that in the future these customs may not change and there may be a revolution in the use of VTRs or CDs such as took place in America or Europe. Thus, if there is blame to be handed out regarding competition with movies it still goes to TV.

What then will be done by the cinema industry, especially the exhibitors, if there is an explosive spread of video theatres in the future? Will they fight them or come to some sort of compromise, or even join them? Thus far there appears to be no opposition to them but that could change if box office profits fall and they begin to hurt the movie theatres or any other branch of the industry. Since they normally use imported features, producers and importers from abroad seem not worried.

Japan is foremost in the world in production and export of video tape recorders (VTRs) which now have a diffusion rate in households in the world's major market countries reaching 30% (compared to 40% in Japan's urban areas and 31% nationwide), a phenomenon which took only 20 years since introduction of black-and-white in 1964 by Sony and development of a color model in 1966, followed by introduction of its Betamax in 1975 for home use.

Here again is the example of how the Japanese lifted the technological know how and research of foreign companies such as RCA and Zenith in America, and Philips of Holland, estimated at costing as much as a billion dollars, and developed them to the advantage of Japanese business in the case of the CDs. The history of VTRs shows the same trends.

What Philips and the Japanese companies are working on now includes an erasable disc, a further improvement—which may control the future. Both Matsushita and Hitachi have begun production of VTRs in America and expect to increase production 5 times within 3 years. The appreciated yen means lower production costs in the USA and defuses American criticisms of the Japanese trade surplus as well as the American charges of dumping. Sony is making VTRs in France. CDs for use in automobiles have now reached over 114,000 units and the trend is accelerating, and is expected to reach 300,000 this year.

In the past year video software industries rose from 38 to 50 with billings rising to yen 130 billion.

When any discussion of CDs is made, it is necessary to mention the battle between Sony's Betamax system and the rival VHS systems which are incompatible in that the cassettes are not interchangeable on the other equipment. That battle has resulted in defeat by Sony with only an estimated 12% of the market with 88% for VHS (Video Home System) developed by Victor of Japan.

Sony replied to this by introducing the 8mm single-unit video system, whose recording time is 120 minutes, which VTR makers are already copying. It was also Sony who, when the large American companies decided against putting CDs in production because of the huge capital outlay despite the fact that they had paid for research, went into CD production, along with, on a much smaller scale, Philips of Holland.

In 1970 Sony discovered that Philips of Holland, as well as RCA and Zenith, both American, had spent hundreds of millions of dollars on research and development of a laser diode disc to record, and spent four years unsuccessfully trying to develop a system. In 1978 Philips, after the American companies had written off videodiscs as risky because of the expense, came to them with their technological data in order to prevent a second Betamax-VHS video tape problem by producing two incompatible competing systems.

This move was regarded by some as foolish since Sony then picked the ball up and carried it from there, in 1982 producing their first CD system with picture for $800. Other firms followed and now Japan has gone on to dominate not only the American market but also a lion's share of the world market to such an extent that the average person thinks it was Sony and not Philips who invented it. Sony still dominates the US market for CDs with Matsushita Electronics second. Philips has a good piece of the European market, and a very small bit of the Japanese market with Zenith dropping out before production, while RCA only produces some esoteric disk systems for the US government. A third American company MCA sold its factories to Pioneer Electronics of Japan. Apparently few American companies are interested in trying to buck the Japanese.

A random sampling by the Video Software Promotion Council indicated 27.9% of Japanese households used VTRs daily, 32% once in 2–3 days, and 25.4% once a week. Over 50% of units used were rental cassettes or discs, with 64.1% of foreign origin.

The Economic Planning Agency say 53 percent of Japan's 38.5 million households now have VTRs or CDs and diffusion in the Tokyo and Osaka regions is at a 40% rate and in rural districts 31%, terming it "the video revolution in Japan."

Toho-Towa established Towa Video to deal exclusively in cassette sales, contracting for Cannon's Over the Top series, joining Nikkatsu Video

Films, Shochiku CBS/Fox Video, Toei Video, Herald Enterprises, Shochiku-Fuji, et al.

—A. C. PINDER

New Zealand

Population: 3,500,000
VCR penetration: 50% (up from 30% in 1986)
Number of video titles: 7,800 (up from 6,200 in 1986)
Wholesale value of market: NZ$31–32,000,000 (up from NZ$ 27,000,000 previous year)
Retail dealers: 400
Retail value of market: NZ$120–150,000,000
Rental cost: Overnight rental NZ$4–5

New Zealand home video has experienced continued growth in 1987. Contributing factors are the limited viewing choice offered by the monopolistic 2-channel TV broadcasting and the isolation of the rural population.

Responding to pressure from public interest groups and the video industry itself, a new Video Recordings Act has set up two rating authorities (the industry-based Labelling Body and the government-appointed Video Recording Authority) to determine video censorship and penalties for breaching the new regulations. All tapes now released must be labeled with a colored rating sticker indicating content. A green label indicates G for general viewing; yellow is PG, PG-13 and PG-16 and red stickers indicate R, videotapes restricted to those 18 and over. The penalty for making, copying, selling, renting or exhibiting indecent videos is up to 3 months in jail for a fine of up to NZ$3,000 for individuals and NZ$10,000 for companies.

PAKISTAN

The sub-Divisional Magistrate, Karachi East and many parts of Pakistan have prohibited the exhibition of films on videocassette recorders in hotels, restaurants, and other public places and public shows (by charging any amount) in shops, houses or any other places in their jurisdictions. The decision was taken as unauthorized public shows of uncensored foreign and Pakistani films on VCRs were causing adverse effects on the minds of the general public, especially the young and children, and was diverting them into immoral activity which was creating annoyance to the people of those areas and disturbing public tranquility.

It was also in response to demands from people connected with the film industry and trade, as the unrestricted exhibition of illegally imported films was depriving them of their clientele. They have welcomed the step and demanded the imposition of such a ban throughout the country in the absence of any law against the business of video films. However the government has not yet accepted any such proposal to ban the video business to protect the national film industry.

Video has reached almost all well-to-do houses in the country. The young generation and cinemas are the most affected by video because there is no censorship of video films which are smuggled in from abroad in large quantities. Indian films have the biggest viewership, as their language, customs, costumes, songs, etc. are very similar to those of Pakistani films and the official import of Indian films has been banned for the last 30 years. Of movie fans, hardly 1 per cent goes to cinemas, the remaining 99 per cent watching video films, including Pakistani features. There are about 50,000 videocassette shops in the country. Each of these shops has an average of 10 VCRs or VCPs for renting out to viewers who pay between Rs.30 and Rs.50 for 24 hours. Every shop has about 500 copies of Indian and foreign films. Almost the same number of VCRs (500,000) are privately owned. The number of video copies in the country is about 2 million, if not more. About half a million prints are added each year. The leaders of the domestic film industry trade have demanded the destruction of all of these copies, following the directive of President Zia-ul-Haq to burn all smuggled goods, except for currency notes and gold, in mid-1988.

There are license fees of Rs.200 and Rs.400 for the domestic and commercial use, respectively, of a VCR/VCP. The custom duty on the import of a VCR/VCP is Rs.3,000 per piece. The government's decision to extend legal cover to the VCR and its manufacture and assembly in the country followed the permission for the assembly of 80,000 VCRs a year against the official estimates for 40,000 to 60,000 sets. The Industrial Investment Schedule for the sixth Five Year Plan has earmarked an investment of Rs.24 million for the establishment of new plants to manufacture and assemble VCRs. However, for one or the other reason, not a single VCR set (manufactured/assembled in Pakistan) has come on the market so far, in spite of strong protests by the manufacturers.

For the last seven years, the illegal exhibition of the latest uncensored foreign films, mainly Indian, on VCRs remained the biggest opposition to Pakistan cinema for a number of reasons, including the high cost of cinema tickets (Rs.12/- and Rs.10/- for a balcony seat) strict censorship, poor maintenance of cinema houses, transportation problems, disturbances, etc., whereas video copies of the lastest Indian and foreign films are freely available for Rs.5 for 24 hours.

In affluent localities like Clifton, Defence Society, Bahadurabad, PSCH Society (in Karachi), Gulberg, Iqbal Town, Muslim Town (in Lahore), a home delivery scheme has been introduced. In response to a telephone call, the video dealer sends the requested tape to the door-step of subscribers. In thickly populated poor areas of cities like Karachi, Hyderabad, Lahore, Peshawar, Quetta, Sukkur, etc., leads are supplied to houses for a monthly subscription of Rs.50 or so for one picture a day and two on holidays. Elderly people prefer to enjoy Indian films produced in the 1950s and 1960s and censored pictures made in Pakistan as they can be seen with family members. Films produced in India in the 1970s and 1980s are self-censored with a remote controller by the head of the family, as they have lots of vulgar and sexy scenes.

Video prints of Pakistani feature films are also made available the next day of their release, without the permission of their makers. In the absence of law, producers are helpless to take legal action against piracy. The National Film Development Corporation exports video prints of Pakistani pictures throughout the world, particularly to those countries where large populations from Pakistan and India live. We earn about Rs.3 million in foreign exchange a year through the export of these films. We also export popular TV plays in video to a number of countries, including India (unofficially).

A Pakistani firm in Rawalpindi claims to have built a 30-foot dish antenna "giant radio telescope" to scan and receive signals from different satellites. The radiotelescope is said to have gain of 50 decibels at 4 gigahertz frequency and be able to track all kinds of satellites viewable on the Pakistan horizon.

—A. R. SLOTE

SPAIN

With a population of 38 million, there are 2.7–3.0 million VCRs in Spanish households; 21% of homes now have a VCR. About 70% of those are VHS format while the remaining 30% includes Beta and the Philips 2000 systems.

There are 3,000 retail video outlets and the average rental is approximately $3 for one or two nights. VCRs cost between $800 and $1200. Legal sales and rentals are estimated at $100 million a year. The current price for an "A" film ranges from $70–$80 per tape to video clubs who rent it to customers for $3 per night. Cassettes are also sold in department stores and through video clubs and the average price is $26.

All the major American distributors are in the Spanish market and American studios dominate about 80% of the market. Virtually all home video films are released in Spanish-dubbed versions and feature films dominate the market with a small percentage for pornography and music videos.

A major impediment to video growth is piracy and the local Anti-Piracy Federation, back by the MPEA spent $700,000 to combat piracy in Spain. Another problem is "community video" where apartment houses are wired and a master VCR shows 4–5 rented videos daily throughout the building. The legal status of community video has yet to be defined.

SRI LANKA

Sri Lanka has hit the world headlines as one of the centers in the East for pirating Western TV videos. The government of Sri Lanka on several occasions threatened to legislate laws to curb pirating of video tapes but so far nothing has happened or effective measures taken. The latest ploy is the pirating of video tapes of Western films in Sri Lanka and smuggling to the Middle East. There are more than 800,000 Sri Lankan workers in the Middle East employed in various projects, who smuggle them from Sri Lanka when they return after their holiday vacation.

At present there are more than 1500 video lending libraries in the city of Colombo and in the immediate suburbs; now it is booming business to have a video lending library or a video parlour. There are about 4,000 video libraries on the island and about 750 video parlours or mini video cinemas, compared to 370 permanent 35mm film exhibition theatres in the country. Many video cinemas show mainstream films, while some video parlours are engaged in the lucrative business of showing sex videos: blue films. The Film Corporation of Sri Lanka, which is state-owned under the President J.R. Jayawardhena, has not been able to take any steps to curb the video cinemas. The State Film Corporation's income has fallen very badly due to the video cinemas competing with cinema theatres. Films that are banned or not imported to the country come in video cassette form, are duplicated and publicly exhibited in video cinemas.

Weak laws and widespread corruption allow these to proliferate. The Police turn deaf and blind to raid these cinemas as the law is weak. Local tele-drams are also pirated by home video makers and smuggled to the Sri Lankan communities abroad especially in the Middle East. Last year, the Presidential Committee's recommendation to curb the video cinema menace and save the National Film Industry has not been implemented to date. The intelligentsia lobby to stop them, but without any success.

There are more than 400 video rental outlets in the city of Colombo alone. An ad hoc survey into the home video business shows that there are more than 2,500 video outlets in the country's main cities. There are about ten bona fide importers of video films on the island and most of them have their main centers of business in the city of Colombo from where they rent and distribute. The average rental system calls for an initial deposit of Rs.500 (U.S. $18.00) to Rs.1,000 ($36.00) and a daily charge of Rs.25 to Rs.50 ($1.00 to $2.00) Many of the small video rental centers which deal in pirated copies of Western (European and American), Eastern (Hong Kong, Japanese, Singaporean and Taiwan) and Indian films, rent the tapes for almost 50% below the rental charged by legitimate shops.

—CHANDRA S. PERERA

SWITZERLAND

In Switzerland in 1987, there were some 750 videoshops which mostly work on a rental basis, while the outright sale of videocassettes is mainly done by the major distributors and by mail order. As Switzerland is trilingual, the turnover of videocassettes is divided: 60% German, 26% French and 6% Italian; only 6% are spoken in English. By genre, 58% of the hired or sold movies on cassettes are action dramas or thrillers (2–3% horror), 28% are family programs and 14% erotic films. Among the evergreens is the whole Disney family catalogue. Still selling and renting at a steady clip are film musicals.

According to estimated statistics of the Swiss Videogram Association, by the end of 1988 nearly 700,000 VCRs are in Swiss homes, this corresponds to a VCR penetration of 22% of the Swiss German part of the country, 36% in French part and 19% of the Italian speaking part of Switzerland. The gross turnover of the official importers is estimated to amount to 40,000,000 SFr, while 5,000,000 SFr. is grossed by "pirates" operating on the gray market, concentrating mainly on porno films.

So far piracy has been sued on basis of the copyright law only, which has been proved to be inefficient. Now, a revision of this law is under way. The revised copyright law will introduce the application of penal law in case of great abuses: disregard of copyrights will be severely punished, in extreme cases with up to three years in jail. Now, the top fine is 5,000 SFr.

New laws would also provide a legal basis for prohibiting violent tv-movies (the so called "Brutalos") and a revised one would put limits on the spread of pornography. All these new propositions have yet to undergo discussion in the Federal Parliament.

Almost 100% of the recorders sold are the Japanese type Video Home System (VHS). The European device, Video 2000, a co-production of Philips and Grundig, has completely vanished, as well as Sony's Beta-System.

Governmental subsidy: January 1, 1986, the Federal Department of Culture, Federal Bureau of Cultural Promotion decided to extend subsidies on video productions, too, i.e. this authority grants contributions not only for national film productions but also for VHS- and U-matic video films which have artistic qualities.

Government Departments: Bundesamt fuer Kulturpflege, Sektion Film, Thunstrasse 20, 3000 BERNE 6.

Associations: Schweizerischer Video-Verband, Schwarztorstrasse 7, P.O. Box 2485, 3001 BERNE.

—GABRIELLA BROGGI

USSR

While there are no published official statistics on the USSR's video industry, it is estimated there are approximately 500,000 videocassette records in the country, all in VHS format. The Soviet Union exports about 300 video features to 80 countries but restricts the import of videos to about 10–12 per year. Video trade organizations include: VNITIK (All-Union Institute Theory and History of Cinema); NIKFI (Research Institute for Film Equipment & Technology); VGIK (All-Union Institute of Cinematography) and LIKI (Leningrad Institute of Film Engineers).

VENEZUELA

Number of VCRs: Estimated to be 850,000 of which 65% are still in Beta format and 35% in VHS.

Retail outlets: about 780 throughout the country.

Price of tapes: legal price ranges from 500–700 bolivares ($16–$23).

Income: estimated billings from legal video operations $10,000,000.

Video cassettes: 120 titles are released each month, usually with 750 cassettes per title.

Piracy: Venezuela has one of the lowest piracy rates in Latin America, reportedly between 15–25%.

Leading distributors include: Blancic Video; Videos de Venezuela; Videovision; Videorama; Rodven. Rodven and Videorama also own retail shops.

WEST GERMANY

Rentals and sales volume: Market worth 420,000,000 marks ($250,000,000).

VCR Sales: A record 2,150,000 sold in 1987, (up from the previous record of 1,750,000 in 1986); 97% of the country's VCRs utilize VHS format. Betamax and Video 2000 share the remaining 3%.

Household VCR Penetration: 34% of 26,000,000 households (up from 29% in 1986; 38% predicted by the end of 1988).

Blank Cassette Sales: 70,000,000 in 1987 (up from 63,000,000 in 1986).

Prerecorded Videocassettes: A record 4,200,000 cassettes were shipped to the trade in 1987 (up from 3,300,000 in 1986).

Video Premieres: Out of the 1,175 films released on videocassette in 1987, features without previous theatrical release soared to 808 last year from 316 in 1986.

Piracy: Despite better detection and stricter legislation with stiffer penalties, loss to the trade is still an estimated 300,000,000 marks ($175,000,000) annually.

Retail Outlets: Somewhere between 5–7,000 vidshops, 4,000 dealers, with rentals over 90% of volume. Sell-through handled by mail order houses, department stores and supermarkets.

While VCR sales climbed once again in West Germany in 1987, video rentals fell of sharply with deliveries to dealers down 30–50%. While VCR users increased to 14,900,000 in 1987 (up nearly 2 million) the number of video renters dropped from 6,500,000 to 6,400,000. According to the Assn. of Video Distributors (BVV) video rentals grossed 1.2 billion marks ($2 billion) in 1987, down from 1.615 billion in 1986. The Bundesverband Video, however reported a 1987 retailer gross of $706 million for the 7,800 German video shops and a $309 million gross of video distributors, but other sources find these figures overly optimistic.

While price-breakers and the import of new low-priced VCRs from South Korea selling from as little as 600 marks (a little over $400) to 2,000 marks ($1,250), stimulated the sale of VCRs, only 40% of VCR owners rented in 1987. One factor was the strong competition from West Germany's two national public television networks and cable services which often air popular films before their release to video stores.

The major video distributors in West Germany are: CBS/Fox; C.I.C. Video; Constantin Video; Euro Video; RCA/Columbia Pictures Video; Taurus Video; VCL/Virgin Communications; Vestron Video; Video Medien Pool; Warner Home Video.

Principal Video Distributors in the World Market

Principal Video Distributors in the World Market

ARGENTINA

ARGENTINA VIDEO HOME SA (AVH), Viamonte 2146, Piso 7, (1356) Buenos Aires. Tel: 48-8275/9800. Tlx: 21821.
BUENOS AIRES VIDEO PRODUCCIONES, Independencia 3090, (1225) Buenos Aires. Tel: 93-5630.
LATIN FILMS VIDEO HOME, Lavalle 2773, (1051) Buenos Aires. Tel: 49-4659. Tlx: 24247 ARCO AR.
LEDAFILMS VIDEO HOME, Av Belgrano 406, Piso 1, (1092) Buenos Aires. Tel: 30-0260/0556. Tlx: 23163 LEDAF AR.
LEGAL VIDEO, Tucuman 2235, (1051) Buenos Aires. Tel: 48-3465/5305. Tlx: 17238 SCAL AR.
LK-TEL VIDEO ENTRETENIMIENTO SA, Lavalle 652, (1047) Buenos Aires. Tel: 394-7428.
MAGNUM GOLDEN VIDEO, Callao 420, Piso 11, (1022) Buenos Aires. Tel: 49-5549, 46-8100. Tlx: 22751 SUDAM AR.
PARIS FILMS VIDEO HOME, Lavalle 1763, (1048) Buenos Aires. Tel: 40-0902.
TAURO VIDEO SA, Ayacucho 490, Piso 2, (1026) Buenos Aires. Tel: 40-5784/49-7803. Tlx: 24835/24836 SEDEM AR.
TELECINEMA VIDEO HOME, Sanchez de Bustamante 1952, (1425) Buenos Aires. Tel: 826-1062/1067. Tlx: 22778 TELEC AR.
TRANSEUROPA VIDEO ENTERTAINMENT, Ayacucho 586, (1026) Buenos Aires. Tel: 46-0558/2137. Tlx: 17387 TRAFI AR.
TRANSMUNDO HOME VIDEO SA, Lavalle 1977/79, (1051) Buenos Aires. Tel: 40-4338/3862. Tlx: 18468 ELECT AR.
VANGUARDIA VIDEO, Lavalle 2032, (1051) Buenos Aires. Tel: 49-5712.
VEA VIDEO EDITORES ASOCIADOS, Corrientes 2422, Piso 3, (1046) Buenos Aires. Tel: 48-9714/2658. Tlx: 21171 ARLUR AR.
VIDECO SA, Ave de Mayo 981, Piso 5, (1084) Buenos Aires. Tel: 38-2572/0871. Tlx: 18506 MILIA AR.
VIDEOCLAUEN, Lavalle 1924, (1051) Buenos Aires. Tel: 40-4399/45-8448.
VIDEO ESPAÑA SA, Callao 429, Piso 11, (1022) Buenos Aires. Tel: 49-5549, 46-8100.
VIDEO LASER PRODUCCIONES, Lavalle 1994, (1051) Buenos Aires. Tel: 49-0607.
VIDEOMAN INTERNACIONAL, Tucuman 2235, (1051) Buenos Aires. Tel: 48-3465/5305. Tlx: 17238 SCAL AR.
VIDEO STAR, Ayacucho 467, Piso 2, (1026) Buenos Aires. Tel: 49-1872.
VIDEO VESTAL SRL, Ave Cordoba 785, Piso 8, (1054) Buenos Aires. Tel: 392-7506. Tlx: 24590 AFAIN AR.
VIDEO WORLD SRL, Florida 833, Piso 3, (1005) Buenos Aires. Tel: 312-5877/5870. Tlx: 17046 MMM AR.

AUSTRALIA
New South Wales

CANNON SCREEN ENTERTAINMENT, 301 Castlereagh St, Sydney, NSW 2000. Tel: (02) 271 711. Tlx: EMI 24812.
CBS-FOX VIDEO (SOUTH PACIFIC), 100 Miller St, North Sydney, NSW 2060. Tel: (02) 92 0225. Tlx: 70959.
CIC-TAFT VIDEO, 176 South Creek Rd, Dee Why, NSW 2099. Tel: (02) 981 0577. Tlx: 121546. Fax: (02) 981 5983.
COMMUNICATIONS AND ENTERTAINMENT LTD, 185 Elizabeth St, Sydney, NSW 2000. Tel: (02) 268 9000. Tlx: 72900.
DELTA HOME VIDEO PTY LTD, 1/47-51 Parraweena Rd, Caringran 2229. Tel: (02) 525 9144. Tlx: AA23744.
PACIFIC TELECASTERS PTY LTD, Suite 1403 Office Tower, Bondi Junction Plaza, Bondi Junction, NSW 2022. Tel: (02) 387 4622. Tlx: AA24178.
PALACE HOME VIDEO, 168 Day St, Sydney, NSW 2000. Tel: (02) 267 2533. Tlx: 177413.
RCA-COLUMBIA-HOYTS VIDEO PTY LTD, 8th flr, Strathfield Plaza, The Boulevarde, Strathfield, NSW 2135. Tel: (02) 764 3888. Tlx: VIDEOS AA74388.
ROADSHOW HOME VIDEO, 49 Market St, Sydney, NSW 2000. Tel: (02) 267 3522. Tlx: AA24161. Fax: (02) 264 2913.
SEVEN KEYS VIDEO, 68 Alfred St, Milsons Point, NSW 2061. Tel: (02) 922 4188. Tlx: AA25641.
SHOWCASE VIDEO, Unit 89, 106 Canterbury Rd, Bankstown, NSW 2200. Tel: (02) 708 4133.
SUNDOWNER FILM & VIDEO, 275 Alfred St, Nth Sydney 2060. Tel: (02) 923 1877. Tlx: AA27935.
VESTRON VIDEO INTERNATIONAL, Clemenger Building, 5th flr, 120 Pacific Hwy, St Leonards, 2065 NSW. Tel: (02) 436 4988. Tlx: AA 72047.
VIDEO CLASSICS, 286 Pacific Hwy, Crows Nest, 2065 Sydney. Tel: (02) 438 4856. Tlx: AA25043 EFFO.
WARNER HOME VIDEO, 1st flr, 15-19 Parraweena St, Cremorne, NSW 2090. Tel: (02) 908 3088. Tlx: AA74409 WEAWHV.

Victoria

CANNON SCREEN ENTERTAINMENT, 117-125 York St, South Melbourne, VIC 3205. Tel: (03) 690 3022.
CBS-FOX VIDEO (SOUTH PACIFIC), Suite 8, St Kilda Rd, St Kilda VIC 3182. Tel: (03) 534 0937. Tlx: 33540.
CIC-TAFT VIDEO, 1st flr, 484 St Kilda Rd, Melbourne, VIC 3004. Tel: (03) 269 4731.
NILSON PREMIERE, 200 Berkeley St, Carlton, VIC 3053. Tel: (03) 347 8111. Tlx: 31185.
PALACE HOME VIDEO, 1051A High St, Armadale, VIC 3143. Tel: (03) 20 6911/20 8694.
RCA-COLUMBIA PICTURES-HOYTS HOME VIDEO, 1st flr, 418 St Kilda Rd, Melbourne, VIC 3004. Tel: (03) 267 6566. Tlx: 31437.
ROADSHOW HOME VIDEO, 206 Bourke St, Melbourne, or PO Box 1498N, VIC 3000. Tel: (03) 667 6555. Tlx: AA32502.
ROADSHOW INTERNATIONAL PTY, 500 Collins St, Melbourne 3000. Tel: (03) 613 811. Tlx: 32502.
SYME HOME VIDEO, The Age Bldg 250 Spencer St, Melbourne, 3000 VIC. Tel: (03) 677 911. Tlx: 151483
WARNER HOME VIDEO, 520 King St, Melbourne, VIC 3000. Tel: (03) 329 7922. Tlx: 38689.

Queensland

CANNON SCREEN ENTERTAINMENT, 7 Marie St, Milton, QLD 4064. Tel: (07) 369 7388.
CBS-FOX (SOUTH PACIFIC), Suite 2, 10 Benson St, Toowong, QLD 4066. Tel: (07) 229 8588.
CIC-TAFT VIDEO, 6 Zamia St, Sunnybank, QLD 4109. Tel: (07) 345 7255.
COMMUNICATIONS AND ENTERTAINMENT LTD, 22 Mayneview St, Milton, QLD 4064. Tel: (07) 369 9177.
PALACE HOME VIDEO, 418 Adelaide St, Brisbane, QLD 4000. Tel: (07) 831 0033.
RCA-COLUMBIA PICTURES-HOYTS VIDEO PTY LTD, 301 Coronation Dr, Milton, QLD 4064. Tel: (07) 369 1877.
WARNER HOME VIDEO, 476 Milton Rd, Auchenflower, QLD 4066. Tel: (07) 371 9100.

Western Australia

CANNON SCREEN ENTERTAINMENT, 292 Rokeby Rd, Subiaco, WWA 6006. Tel: (09) 382 4411.
CBS-FOX VIDEO (SOUTH PACIFIC), 77 Hay St, Subiaco, WA 6006. Tel: (09) 382 4411.
CIC-TAFT VIDEO, 15 Oxford Cl., Leederville, WA 6007. tel: (09) 382 3655.
COMMUNICATIONS AND ENTERTAINMENT LTD, 292 Rokeby Rd, Subiaco, WA 6008. Tel: (09) 382 2533.
RCA-COLUMBIA PICTURES-HOYTS VIDEO PTY LTD, 22 Thorogood St, Victoria Pk, WA 6100. Tel: (09) 361 8666.
ROADSHOW HOME VIDEO, 36 Milligan St, Peth, WA 6000. Tel: (09) 481 0479.
WARNER HOME VIDEO, 185 Stirling St, Perth, WA 6000. Tel: (09) 328 999.

AUSTRIA

THORN EMI SCREEN ENTERTAINMENT, Endgasse 13, A-1188 Wien. Tel: 0222-478951. Tlx: 3222526
VIDEO TEAM COMPUTER HERBST, A 5090 Lofev No 2, Salzburg. Tel: 0662-38100. Tlx: 916520072.
VIDEO VERTIEL, Webgasse 43, A-1060 Wien. Tel: 0222-5979795. Tlx: 13-3274.

BELGIUM

ALL VIDEO, Groenstraat 29, 3588 Hechtel, Eksel. Tel: (011) 73 59 89
BILL INTERNATIONAL, St Katelijnestraat 45, 2800 Mechelen. Tel: (015) 20 40 80
BLEUMERS, Boomgaardstraat 66, 2600 Berchem. Tel: (03) 230 94 53
CANNON DISTRIBUTORS/THORN EMI ENTERTAINMENT SA, Ave Eugene Plasky 157, 1040 Brussels. Tel: (02) 735 81 64. Tlx: 20814
CBS SA, Pl Stéphanie 20, 1050 Brussels. Tel: (02) 513 84 45. Tlx: 22642
CNR VIDEO BELGIUM, De Limburg Stirumlaan 132, 1810 Wemmel. Tel: (02) 460 07 07. Tlx: 62455
DELTA VIDEO BELGIE, Staatsbaan 69, 2360 Oud-Turnhout. Tel: (014) 67 01 82.
ELECTRIC VIDEO, Frans Halsvest 24, 2800 Mechelen. Tel: (015) 21 10 95.
ESSELTE CIC VIDEO NV, Ave. du Péage 95, 1940 Woluwé-Saint-Etienne. Tel: (02) 720 97 20. Tlx: 20311
EVC EDITIONS CENTRE VIDEO, Rue Gendebien 4, 6070 Chatelineau. Tel: (071) 38 37 15
RCA/COLUMBIA PICTURES VIDEO BV, Rue Souveraine 38, 1050 Brussels. Tel: (02) 513 86 83. Tlx: 26124

SDA, Kasteelstraat 48, 2540 Hove. Tel: (03) 455 50 74.
SPRL BPV, Rue du Collège 5, 6000 Charleroi. Tel: (071) 32 27 33. Tlx: 51840
SPVB BELGA FILMS VIDEO, Rue Royale 241, 1030 Brussels. Tel: (02) 218 72 80.
VDS DIFFUSION, Ruzenhoflaan 10, 1860 Meise. Tel: (02) 269 31 69
VESTRON VIDEO BELGIUM NV, Kalenbergstraat 31, 1710 Dilbeek
VIDEO PLAY, Quai de Flandres 7, 6000 Charleroi. Tel: (071) 33 08 36.
VRP SPRL, Rue de la Régence 6, 6000 Charleroi. Tel: (071) 31 34 42. Tlx: 51725
WARNER HOME VIDEO SA, Blvd Lambermont 79, 1030 Brussels. Tel: (02) 242 57 57. Tlx: 61218

BRAZIL

CIC VIDEO, Ave Rio Branco 245/906, Rio de Janeiro. Tel: 220-6211. Tlx: 35522.
CINEMATOGRAFICA F J NETTO LTDA, Ave São João 1588, 2a Sobreloja, Sao Paulo. Tel: 220-5622. Tlx: (011) 32472.
DIF PRODUTORA E DISTRIBUTORA LTDA., Rua Paraiso, 694, Sao Paulo-SP 04103. Tel.: 055011 2899655; Tlx: (011) 21083 EEPR BR
GLOBO VIDEO, Praia de Botatogo 440, Rio de Janeiro. Tel: 266-1698. Tlx: 35558.
JOTA HOME VIDEO, Ave Marechal Camara 160/1422, Rio de Janeiro. Tel: 262-6659. Tlx: 30904.
JZ TV & CINEMA, Av Brig Faria Lima 1857/10°, São Paulo. Tel: 212-6533. Tlx: 22888 XPSP BR.
LOOK VIDEO PROD E DISTRIBUIDORS LTDA, Ave Juruce 783, CEP 04080 São Paulo. Tel: 533-7666. Tlx: 1122289.
MACVIDEO, Rua Uruguai 287, Rio de Janeiro. Tel: 571-0042. Tlx: 34746.
MANCHETE VIDEO, Rua do Russell 804, Rio de Janeiro. Tel: 285-0033.
NETWORK DISTRIBUIDORA DE FILMES SA, Rua da Lapa 120, 3rd flr, 20021 Rio de Janeiro. Tel: 232-1550. Tlx: 2123018.
PHOENIX HOME VIDEO, Rua Stella 515, Villa Marlana, São Paula. Tel: 572-1863
POLE VIDEOCOMUNICACOES LTDA, Ruados Andradas 241, Sala 4, 01208 São Paulo. Tel: 220-5022. Tlx: 1137806.
SMI, Rua Emilio Berla 105, Copacabana, Rio de Janeiro. Tel: 236-0352.
TOP TAPE VIDEO, Rua Alice 97, Laranjeiras, Rio de Janeiro. Tel: 205-5552. Tlx: 23923.
TRANS VIDEO LTD, Rua Tabapua 594, São Paulo CEP04533. Tel: 881-6764. Tlx: 24062 AUTU BR.
VIACOM VIDEO AUDIO COMMUNICATIONS LTD, Alameda Jau 1742, 11 Andar, Caixa Postal 51521 São Paulo. Tel: 853-4633. Tlx: 1121773
VIDEOLAB LTD, R Tabapuan, 594, 3rd flr, São Paulo Sp CEP 04533. Tel: 853-1255. Tlx: 24062 AUTU BR.
VIRGIN VIDEO, Rua do Acre 47/1101, Rio de Janeiro. Tel:233-3484. Tlx: 34807.

BULGARIA

VIDEO BULGARE, 7 ru Levsky, 1000 Sofia. Tlx: 22652 KOMKUL.

CANADA

Direct Distributors
BELLEVUE HOME ENTERTAINMENT INC. (A division of Astral Bellevue Pathe Inc.), 7215 Trans Canada Hwy., Monreal, Que. H4T 1A2 (514) 333-7555. Branches: 98 Orfus Rd., North York, Ont. M6A 1C8 (416) 785-5580. 1420 Kootenay St., Vancouver, B.C. (604) 324-4343. 15043A-118th Ave., Edmonton, Alta. T5V 1H9. 6143 - 4th St. S.E., Unit 9, Calgary, Alta. T2H 2H9 (403) 258-2113, Westview Pl., 1421 St. James St., Winnipeg, Man. R3H 0Y9 (204) 786-3488. 100 Ilsley Ave., Unit T, Dartmouth, N.S. B3B 1L3 (902) 465-4448. 104 - 2301 Ave. "C" N., Saskatoon, Sask. S7L 5Z5 (306) 244-7292.
PROLUSION GROUP, 225 Montee de Liesse, Ville Saint-Laurent, Que. H4T 1P5 (514) 737-4774, Telex: 05-824579 (Prolusion Montreal)
VIDEO ONE CANADA LTD., Head Office, 1001 Bldg. B, 93 Skyway Ave., Etobicoke, Ont. M9W 6C7 (416) 674-0192, Fax: (416) 674-7825. Branches: Video One Canada Ltd., 105 - 2250 Boundary Rd., Burnaby, B.C. V5M 3Z3 (604) 437-4473; (800) 242-0648. Video One Canada Ltd., B-18 - 6020 2nd St. S.E., Calgary, Alta. T2H 2L8 (403) 258-3880; (800) 352-8245. Video One Canada Ltd., 11616 - 149th St., Edmonton, Alta. T5M 3R3 (403) 451-9060; (800) 661-9605. Video One Canada Ltd., 515 - 45th St. W., Saskatoon, Sask. S7L 5Z9 (306) 933- 4930. Video One Canada Ltd., Unit 12, 1832 King Edward, Winnipeg, Man. R2R 0N1 (204) 694-6007. Video One Canada Ltd. (Ont.) Ltd., 1110 Dearness Dr., Unit 12, London, Ont. N6E 1N9 (519) 685-1502; (800) 265-6054. Video One Canada (Ont.) Ltd., 1 Mobile Dr., Toronto, Ont. M4A 1H5 (416) 751-9600; (800) 387-4535. Video One Canada (Ont.) Ltd. 5360 Canotek Rd., Gloucester, Ont. K1J 8Y6 (613) 744-5102. Crawford/Video One Canada Ltd., 20 Hallet Cr., Unit 102, St. John's, Nfld. A1B 4C5 (709) 739-5924. Video Globe 1, 341 Isabey, Ville St. Laurent, Qué. H4T 1Y2 (514) 738-6665; (800) 361-7151

Wholesalers
BELLEVUE HOME ENTERTAINMENT INC. (A division of Astral Bellevue Pathé Inc.), 7215 Trans Canada Hwy., Montréal, Qué. H4T

1A2 (514) 333-7555/1-800-361-3320. Showrooms/branch offices in Vancouver, Edmonton, Calgary, Winnipeg, Saskatoon, Toronto, Montréal, Dartmouth
R.O.W. ENTERTAINMENT, 255 Shields Ct., Markham, Ont. L3R 8V2 (416) 475-3550
THE SHANNOCK CORP.,4222 Manor St., Burnaby, B.C. V5G 1B2 (604) 433-3331, Fax: (604) 433-4815. 610-C 70th Ave. S.E., Calgary, Alta. T2H 2J6 (403) 253-2113, Fax: (403) 255-3359 #23-156 Duncan Mill Rd., Don Mills, Ont. M3B 3N2 (416) 445-3906

Distribution
ASTRAL VIDEO, (A Division of Astral Bellevue Pathé Inc.), 720 King St. W., Ste. 600, Toronto, Ont. M5V 2T3 (416) 364-3894
MALOFILM GROUP, 1207 rue St.-André, 4e étage, Montréal, Qué. H2L 3S8 (514) 844-4555, Fax: (514) 844-1471, Telex: 055- 61301
NORSTAR ENTERTAINMENT INC., 86 Bloor St. W., 5th fl., Toronto, Ont. M5M 1M5 (416) 961-6278, Telex: 06219870 SIMCOM TOR, Fax: (416) 961-5608. 1176 Georgia St. W. Ste. 310 Vancouver, B.C. V6E 4B9 (604) 681-9298
NORTH AMERICAN RELEASING INC., 808 Nelson St., Ste. 2204, Vancouver, B.C. V6Z 2H2 (604) 681-2165, Telex: 04-352823 Ambleside VCR
VIDEOVILLE SHOWTIME INC., 4610 Côte Vertu, Ville St. Laurent, Qué. H4S 1C7 (514) 336-0038; (800) 361-5508, Telex: 0524692 ATT: VIDEOVILLE
WHITE KNIGHT VIDEO INC., 1861 Welch St., Ste. 107, N. Vancouver, B.C. V7P 1B7 (604) 986-9311; (800) 663-4474

DENMARK

ABCOLLECTION A/S, Revetlowsgade 30, DK-1651, Copenhagen V. Tel: (01) 310093
ABCOLLECTION VIDEOFILM, Reventlowsgade 30, DK-1651, Copenhagen V. Tel: (01) 313144. Tlx: 16449 ABCOLDK.
CINNAMON FILM, Pantheonsgade 29, 5000 Odense C. Tel: (9) 121716. Tlx: 16600 Cinnamon Film.
ESSELTE VIDEO A/S, Koebmagergade 19, 1150 Copenhagen K. Tel: (1) 154710. Tlx: 21136.
SAGA VIDEO OG/KORT FILM A/S, Fimaktiesel Skabct, Groennegade 27, 1107 Copenhagen 12. Tel: (01) 125758, (01) 142266. FILMCOM A/S, Allegade 23, DK-2000, Copenhagen F. Tel: (01) 881811. Tlx: 27272 FILMCO DK.
IRISH LYDBAND A/S, Handvaerkerbyen 7, 2670 Greve Strand. Tel: (02) 902700.
METRONOME VIDEO/WARNER HOME VIDEO, 16 Sondermarksvej DK-2500, Copenhagen/Valby. Tel: (1) 468822. Tlx: 19497 Unique DK.
NORDISK FILMS VIDEO A/S, Axeltorv F, 1609 Uobenhavnv. Tlx: 15286 Filmxo DK.
POLYGRAM VIDEO, Emdrupvei 115A, 2400 Copenhagen NV. Tel: (01) 692522. Tlx: 19202.
VIDEO INTERNATIONAL, L, 16 Gasvaerksvej, DK-1656, Copenhagen V. Tel: (01) 229999. Tlx: 22922 Video DK.

FINLAND

ARBITRAGE LTD, Sf-65280 Vasa 28. Tel: 61213622. Tlx: 74129 ARBIT SF.
BEST SELLER FILM AND VIDEO, Itaportti 4C, 02210 Espoo 21. Tel: 8036266.
FILM & VIDEO OY, Sammalkalliontie 5, 02210 Espoo. Tel: 8036266. Tlx: 125871 SKT SF.
OY MANDAG AB, Sarkiniementi 5, 00210 Helsinki. Tel: 673351. Tlx: 122144.
OXFORD VIDEO FINLAND OY, Uudenmaankaty 7 A6, SF 00120, Helsinki. Tel: 603683, 603853.
SKT GROUP INC, Itaportti 4C, 02210 Espoo 21. Tel: 8036266.
STARVIDEO OY, Karnaistenkatu 43, 08100 Lohja 10. Tel: 1223676.
VIDEO EXPRESS OY, SF-65630 Karpero. Tel: 291720. Tlx: 74299.
VIDEOFORM FINLAND OY, Laiturik 10, 08100 Lohja 10. Tel: 1222189. Tlx: 1458 VIDEO SF.
VIDEOGRAMM OY, Laiturik 10, 08100 Lohja 10. Tel: 1222012. Tlx: 1458 VIDEO SF.

FRANCE

ADES VIDEO, 54 rue Saint-Lazare, 75009 Paris. Tel: 48 74 85 30. Tlx: 280422.
ALPHA VIDEO, 126 rue La Boétie, 75008 Paris. Tel: 45 63 44 11/45 63 55 53. Tlx: 641486.
CARRERE VIDEO, 27 rue de Surène, 75008 Paris. Tel: 42 68 13 00. Tlx: 641591.
CIC 3M FRANCE VIDEO, blvd de l'Oise, 95006 Cergy Pontoise Cedex, 15 rue de la Faisander, 75116 Paris. Tel: 704 62 65. Tlx: 615082.
CINETHEQUE, 130 rue de Courcelles, 75017 Paris. Tel: 42 67 37 42. Tlx: 240918.
CONCORDE, 276 rue des Pyrénées, 75020 Paris. Tel: 47 97 33 74. Tlx: 212052.
DELTA VIDEO DIFFUSION, 116 ave Champs-Elysées, 75008 Paris. Tel: 45 63 17 27. Tlx: 641605.
DOUNIA VIDEO, 116 blvd de Belleville, 75020 Paris. Tel: 47 97 47 92. Tlx: 212650.

511

FILMS 44 VIDEO, 1 rue de Bourbon Le Château, 75006 Paris. Tel: 43 25 89 14. Tlx: 270700.
FOUAD ANTOUN PRODUCTIONS, 167 Ave Victor Hugo, 75016 Paris. Tel: 45 53 97 17. Tlx: 614067.
GCR (GAUMONT COLUMBIA FILMS RCA VIDEO), 9 ave Matignon, 75008 Paris. Tel: 42 99 19 25. Tlx: 650703.
MK2 VIDEO, 55 rue Treversière, 75012 Paris. Tel: 43 07 92 74. Tlx: 214720 F.
POLYGRAM SA, 53 ave Franklin D Roosevelt, 75008 Paris. Tel: 225 70 40. Tlx: 642589.
REGIE CASSETTES VIDEO, 104 Champs Elysées, 75008 Paris. Tel: 46 05 76 80. Tlx: 643335.
RENE CHATEAU VIDEO, 72 rue Lauriston, 75116 Paris. Tel: 47 27 99 68. Tlx: 649932 F.
SCHERZO VIDEO PRODUCTION, 50 ave Champs-Elysées, 75008 Paris. Tel: 43 59 48 10. Tlx: 640411.
STE NOUVELLE DE CINEMATOGRAPHIE, 5 rue Lincoln, 75008 Paris. Tel: 43 59 74 50. Tlx: 660586.
SUPER PRODUCTION VIDEO, 19 rue de Berri, 75008 Paris. Tel: 45 62 65 54. Tlx: 643067.
SWAN VIDEO DIFFUSION, 4 fg St-Antoine, 75011 Paris. Tel: 43 43 76 90/48 83 80 41
UGC VIDEO, 24 ave Charles de Gaulle, F-92522 Neuilly-sur-Seine. Tel: 46 37 11 11. Tlx: 614487.
VIDEO MARC DORCEL, 6 rue Bargue, 75015 Paris. Tel: 45 67 93 20. Tlx: 201838.
VIDEO MARKETING (IFM), 18 rue d'Armenonville, 92200 Neuilly-sur-Seine. Tel: 47 45 47 16. Tlx: 615262.
VIDEO 72, 45 rue de Ponthieu, 75008 Paris. Tel: 43 59 44 57. Tlx: 660312.
VIDEO PRESTIGE, 78 ave des Champs-Elysées, 75008 Paris. Tel: 43 59 59 90.
VIP VIDEO CLUB INTERNATIONAL, 41 rue du Colisée. 75008 Paris. Tel: 45 62 55 09. Tlx: 290441.
WALT DISNEY DISTRIBUTION, 44 Champs-Elysées, 75008 Paris. Tel: 43 59 17 80. Tlx: 640062.
WARNER FILIPACCHI VIDEO/WARNER HOME VIDEO, 25 ave Marceau, 75116 Paris. Tel: 47 23 00 46. Tlx: 620367 F.

GREECE

AUDIOVISUAL ENTERPRISES (MGM, UA, Warner, Disney), 7 Sohou St, Athens 11525. Tel: 6710263. Tlx: 223282.
APOLLO TELEVISION INTERNATIONAL ENTERPRISES LTD, 46 Leoforos Vas Konstantinou, Athens 11635. Tel: 7224243. Tlx: 221880.
CBS/FOX VIDEO, 311 Mesogion St, Chalandri, Athens 15231. Tel: 6725284.
EMGEE HOME VIDEO (BBC Video, Thames Video), 70 Omirou St, Nea Smyrni, Athens. Tel: 9353930.
HELLAS TELEVISION INTERNATIONAL, 96 Akadimias. St, Athens 10677. Tel: 3620533. Tlx: 215083.
HOME VIDEO HELLAS LTD, 15 Adrianiou St, Athens 11525. Tel: 6473170. Tlx: 225537.
J T TELEVISION INTERNATIONAL, 129 Queen Sofia Ave, Athens 11521. Tel: 6461735. Tlx: 210582.
JOY VIDEO—VIDEO ELLT (ABC Video, Lorimar-Telepictures), 41-43 Kifislas Ave, 15123 Paradisos Amarousiou, Athens. Tel: 6833970-5. Tlx: 216686.
MEDUSA VIDEO, SYMBOL VIDEO, FLY VIDEO, 198 Kifisias Ave, Neo Psyhiko, Athens 11525. Tel: 6726346/6716560/6473627. Tlx: 224312.
MTC VIDEO (Cannon), 8 Aristotelous St, Athens 17671. Tel: 9234032.
NEA KINISI VIDEO, 9-13 Gravias St, 10878 Athens. Tel: 3628454/6. 91-81 Akadimias St, 10677 Athens. Tel: 3621162.
PLUS VIDEO, 57 Vas Sofias Ave, Athens 11521. Tel: 7225058. Tlx: 225767.
SYMBOL VIDEO SA, 198 Kifisias Ave, N Psyhiko, 15451 Athens. Tel: 6716560/6473627. Tlx: 224312 FLY.
TELEVISION ENTERPRISES SA, 28 Kapodistriou St, Athens 10682. Tel: 3626423. Tlx: 218712.
VIDEO CITY INTERNATIONAL (WMF, UGC, ORC), 23-25 Themistocleous St, Athens. Tel: 3608255. Tlx: 223722.
VIDEOSONIC, 1 Evridamantos and Lagoumitzi St, Athens 11745. Tel: 9225350. Tlx: 223858.

HOLLAND

BESTVIDEO, Stadhouderslaan 165, 2983 CT Ridderkerk. Tel: 01804-17469.
BOUDISQUE, De Ruytferkade 41-43, 1012 AA Amsterdam. Tel: 020-260311. Tlx: 12589.
BRABANT VIDEO BV, Jorisstraat 26, 4834 VD Breda. Tel: 076-611254. Tlx: 74014.
CANNON VIDEO BENELUX, De Lairessestraat 111-115, 1075 HH Amsterdam. Tel: 020-711818. Tlx: 71073.
CBS/FOX VIDEO, Herenweg 115, 2105 MG Heemstede. Tel: 023-233233, 233211. Tlx: 41051-41388.
CNR VIDEO, Gouwzeestraat 1-3, 1382 KD Weesp. Tel: 02940-17661, 18416.
BV COR KOPPIES VIDEO, Oranje Nassaulaan 53, Amsterdam. Tel: 020-767841. Tlx: 18287.

DELTA PRODUCTIONS S'HERTOGENBOSCH BV, Nieuwe Markt 2, Schinnen. Tel: 04493-4646. Tlx: 30366 DELTA NL.
EMPIRE VIDEO, Raadhuisplein 50, 2981 ES Ridderkerk. Tel: 01804-25971. Tlx: 620041.
ESSELTE CIC VIDEO BV, Ampereweg 13, Woerden. Tel: 03480-22254. Tlx: 40332.
ARPA VIDEO, Belijersweg 18, 1093 KR Amsterdam. Tel: 020-932333, 937476.
UMBRELLA VIDEO BV, Magnesiumweg 15, 3812 PW Amersfoort. Tel: 033-15235. Tlx: 79239.
VIDEOCASION BV, Hallenweg 10, 5683 CT Best. Tel: 04998-99600.
VIDEO CLUB SPECTRUM, Ligusterstraat 20, 6504 AA Nijmegen. Tel: 080-770508.
VIDEO EXCLUSIEF, Florijnhof 25, 5551 VM Valkenswaard. Tel: 04092-43866. Tlx: 10436.
VIDEO ENTERTAINMENT SERVICES BV, Catharijnesingel 55, 3511 GD Utrecht. Tel: 030-316844. Tlx: 70276.
VIDEO FOR PLEASURE, Virulystraat 6, 9716 JV Groningen. Tel: 050-717788. Tlx: 77185.
VIDEO NETWORK BV, Nieuw Loosdrechtsedijk 239, Nieuw Loosdrecht. Tel: 02158-4194. Tlx: 43110.
VIDEO SCREEN, Edisonbaan 18, Nieuwegein. Tel: 03402-70933. Tlx: 47847 FILEX.
VIDEO STAR, Mangesiumweg 15, Amersfoort. Tel: 033-634127. Tlx: 79239.
VPR BV, Thomas Van Aquinostraat, 43 Tilburg, Tel: 013-637563. Tlx: 41550.
VSR NEDERLAND, De Lairessestraat 16b, Amsterdam. Tel: 020-629214. Tlx: 11802 INTER NL.
VUH VIDEO HOLLAND BV, Venloweg 34, Almere. Tel: 03240-30390. Tlx: 73520 VUHOL.
WARNER HOME VIDEO (NETHERLANDS) BV, Franse Akker 8, Breda. Tel: 076-480911. Tlx: 74460 WEABR NL.
WINDMILL, Luikerweg 14A, Valkenswaard. Tel: 04902-44119.
ELKAZ VIDEO, Illegaliteitslaan 166, Groningen. Tel: 02240-17070.
VIDEO FILM MARKT, Koninginneweg 9, 1211 AN Hilversum. Tel: 035-16457. Tlx: 73324.
EP VIDEO, De Roeden 9, Bolsward. Tel: 05157-4933.
VAN GILS VIDEO BV, Eekboerplein 4, 7575 BA Oldenzaal. Tel: 05410-19148. Tlx: 72000.
GOLD MEDAL VIDEO BV, Nieuwe Uilenburgerstraat 3, 1064 NR Amsterdam. Tel: 020-265551. Tlx: 15340.
HAFBO BV, Nieuwe Baanstraat 7, Baarn. Tel: 02154-13213.
HDN, Filmamentlaan 2, 5632 AB Eindhoven. Tel: 040-421480.
KING MOVIE PRODUCTIONS BV, Koninginneweg 93, 1211 AN Hilversum. Tel: 035-16457. Tlx: 73324.
MANHATANN INTERNATIONAL VIDEO, Cardanuslaan 34, 6865 HK Doorwerth. Tel: 085-333383. Tlx: 75019 VIMAR
MOVIES SELECT VIDEO BV, Haarlemmerdijk 163, 1013 KH Amsterdam. Tel: 020-238630. Tlx: 11223 MOVIE NL.
PALMA VIDEO, Industrieweg 3M, 5262 GL Vught. Tel: 073-566899.
RCA/COLUMBIA PICTURES VIDEO BV, Vreelandseweg 42b, Hilversum. Tel: 035-13246. Tlx: 73534.
RCV 2001 NEDERLAND BV, Energieweg 45a, 2382 NC Zoeterwoude. Tel: 071-899373. Tlx: 39495.
SPRINGBOARD VIDEO, Havikstraat 55a, 3514 TM Utrecht. Tel: 030-719174/732733. Tlx: 76242 S VID.
TELEVIZIER VIDEO, 's-Graveland seweg 52, 1217 ET Hilversum. Tel: 035-717253. Tlx: 73142

HONG KONG

CEL, Rms 113-115 11th flr, New Henry Ho, 10 Tea Ho St Central
COMMUNICATIONS AND ENTERTAINMENT INTL, 8th flr, Printing Ho, 6 Duddell St Central.
KAM PRODUCTIONS STUDIOS LTD, 12th flr, Park Tower, 15 Austin Rd, Kowloon.
WORLD VIDEO LTD, 1st flr, D&E, Imperial Bldg, 54-56 Canton Rd, Kowloon. Tel: 3 7214143. Tlx: 34372.

INDIA

AMIT ELECTRONICS, 3 Velders St, Mount Rd, Madras 600 002. Tel: 849879/848130.
ARF VIDEO, Natraj Studio, 194 Andheri Kurla Rd, Bombay 400 069. Tel: 6360845/6141189
BOMBINO VIDEO PVT LTD, 7/8 Udyog Nagar, 7 Shilay Industrial Estate, Goregoan (W), SV Rd, Bombay 400 062. Tel: 2046233/2048625/694554/692151
ESQUIRE VIDEO, unit 1A & 1B, Gr fl, Rehmat Manzil 75 Veer, Nariman Rd, Churchgate, Bombay 400 020. Tel: 230811/234226.
HIBA VIDEO, Vijaya Villas, 3rd floor, Warden Rd, Bombay 400 026. Tel: 8224807
INFOCOM, 230 B Acharya, J C Bose Rd, Calcutta 700 020. Tel: 435107. Tlx: 021-7381 RONG IN
MULTI VIDEO PVT LTD, 341 Lajpatrai Market, New Delhi. Tel: 230079.
NAMDHARI ELECTRICALS, 1668 Bhagirath Palace, Chandni Chowk, Old Delhi 110 006
NFDC (NATIONAL FILM DEVELOPMENT CORPORATION), D block, 5th flr, Shivsagar Estate, Dr Annie Besant Rd, Worli Bombay 400 018. Tel: 4929096/4922393. Tlx: 011-73489 NFDC IN.

SAGAR VIDEO INTERNATIONAL (PREM SAGAR), Nataraj Studio, 194 Andheri Kurla Rd, Bombay 400 069. Tel: 6360845/6141189
SUN VIDEO (LIMELITE), 31 Kailash Darshan, Kennedy Bridge, Bombay 400 007. Tel: 356966/385597/388170. Tlx: 1175476 GOLD INDT
VIDEO KING (INDIA) PVT LTD, 1009 Dalamal Tower, Nariman Point, Bombay 400 021. Tel: 231187/226139. Tlx: 011-3668 HHGE-IN
IMAGE VIDEO PVT LTD, Atlanta, 17th flr, Nariman Point, Bombay 400 021. Tel: 223747/223777
KAZEM BUNARIS, 7 Shaly Industrial Estate, 8 Udyog Nagar, S V Rd, Goregaon, Bombay 400 062. Tel: 694554/692151
MAGNEM VIDEO, 68 Hill Rd, Natraj Shopping Centre, Bandra, Bombay 400 050. Tel: 6427274/6429377
M G VIDEO ELECTRIC (P) LTD, M G House, Plot no 22, Santacruz Electronic Export Processing Zone, Andheri (E), Bombay 400 096. Tel: 6301851/6327246
NAVINA INVESTMENT CO, 3/33 Tardeo AC Mkt, Tardeo, Bombay 400 034
OSCAR TRADING CO PVT LTD, 309 Arun Chambers, Tardeo Rd, Bombay 400 034. Tel: 4947602/4941735
ORSON VIDEO (P) LTD, Unit 46 and 47, Santacruz Electronic Export Processing Zone, Andheri (E), Bombay 400 096. Tel: 6329808/6321526/6323128
RADHKA VIDEO, 58/64 Hari Chambers, S B Rd, Fort, Bombay 400 001. Tel: 2862339/2863319
SPECTRA VIDEO PVT LTD, 78 SDF III, Santacruz Electronic Export Processing Zone, Andheri (E), Bombay 400 096. Tel: 6300528/6301472
SURYA BHARTI, Trisandhya A, 97 Dada Saheb Phalke Rd, Dadar, Bombay 400 014. Tel: 447261/447938
TELEVIDEO ELECTRONIC, Trisandhya A, Dada Saheb Phalke Rd, Dadar, Bombay 400 014. Tel: 447261/448036
TEISCO VIDEO VISION, 9/10/11 Amar Industrial Estate, Andheri Kurla Rd, Sakinaka, Bombay 400 072. Tel: 8220889/8121833. Fax: 5123602/5123315/5123022
VGP VIDEO VISION OF INDIA, Unit 51, 2nd SDF bldg, Santacruz Electronic Export, Andheri (E), Bombay 400 096
VIDEO MASTER, 39/40 Ratnajyot Industrial Estate, Irla Lane, Vile Parle (E), Bombay 400 056. Tel: 6360061/6362136

ITALY

RCA-COLUMBIA, 7 Via S Alessandro, 00137 Rome
DOMOVIDEO, 77 Via A Do Casperi, 38100 Trento
WALT DISNEY HOME VIDEO, 18 Via Agnello, 20121 Milan
MULTIVISION, 9 Via Dante, 20123 Milan
DB VIDEO, Via C Poma, 20129 Milan
CREAZIONI HOME VIDEO, 18 Via Agnello, 20121 Milan
GENERAL VIDEO, 28 Via Panziera, 50047 Prato (Florence)
RICORDI, 2 Via Berchet, 20121 Milan
AVO FILM, 20 Via C Ravizza, 20149 Milan
PLAYTIME, 4 Via E Fermi, 20090 Noverasco di opera (Milano)

JAPAN

CHANNEL COMMUNICATIONS, INC, 1101 Silver Plaza Azabu, 1-2-16 Mita, Minato-Ku, Tokyo 108. Tel: (03) 798-3304. Tlx: 2423783 CHCOMMJ.
COMSTOCK LTD, Sofia Roppongi 310, 7-8-5 Roppongi Minato-ku, Tokyo 106. Tel: (03) 403-0140. Tlx: 2423210. EVRGRN.
DISC CENTER CO LTD, PO Box 874, Osaka 530-91. Tel: (06) 323-6350. Tlx: 64488 Discarea J.
FUJI TELEVISION NETWORK INC, 7 Kawada-cho, Ichigaya, Shinjukuku, Tokyo 162. Tel: 353-1111. Tlx: 22560.
MODERN PROGRAMS INC, 501 Akasaka New Plaza, Minato-ku, Tokyo 107. Tel: (03) 585-4604, 585-2800. Tlx: J23415 Modpro.
NIHON VICTOR CO LTD, 4-1 Nihonbashi-honcho, Chuo-ku, Tokyo 103. Tel: 241-7811
NIKKATSU VIDEO FILMS, 2-16-2 Higashi-Azabu, Minato-ku, Tokyo 106. Tel: 505-2411
NIPPON COLUMBIA CO LTD, 4-14-14 Akasaka, Minato-ku, Tokyo 107. Tel: 584-8111
NIPPON TELEVISION NETWORK CORP, 14 Niban-cho, Chiyoda-ku, Tokyo 102. Tel: 265-2111. Tlx: J24566.
PACK-IN VIDEO CO LTD, 1-7-1 Shinbashi, Minato-ku, Tokyo 105
PONY INC, 4-3-31 Kudan-kita, Chiyoda-ku, Tokyo 102. Tel: (03) 265-4164. Tlx: 0232408.
TDK CORE CO LTD, 1-9-6 Hatchobori, Chuo-ku, Tokyo 104. Tel: 555-1131
TELECAS JAPAN CO LTD, 214 Azabu Heights, 1-5-10 Roppongi, Minatoku, Tokyo. Tel: (03) 583-2900. Tlx: J23693.
TOEI VIDEO CO LTD, 15-10, 3-chome, Ginza, Chuo-ku, Tokyo 104. Tel: (03) 545-4511. Tlx: 2524541.
TOKUMO COMMUNICATIONS CO LTD, No 1 Hibiya Bldg, 1-18-21 Shinbashi, Minato-ku, Tokyo 105. Tel: 591-9161.
TOKYO BROADCASTING SYSTEM INC, 5-3-6 Akasaka, Tokyo 107. Tel: (03) 584-3111. Tlx: J24883.
TOKYO CHANNEL 12 LTD, 4-4-7 Shibakoen, Minato-ku, Tokyo.
TOSHIBA-EMI LTD, 2-2-17 Akasaka, Minato-ku, Tokyo 107. Tel: 587-9111.
VIDEO FILMS INC, Komeido Bldg, 3-9 Yoesuya, Shinjuku-ku, Tokyo. Tel: (03) 357-6574/5. Tlx: 2324084. Videofj.

VAP CO LTD, NTV Yonbancho Annex, 4th fl, 5-6 Yonbancho, Chiyoda-ku, Tokyo 102. Tel: 234-5711
VICTOR MUSICA INDUSTRIES INC, 4-26-18 Jungumae, Shibuya-ku, Tokyo 150. Tel: 405-5151. Tlx: 2424293 VICREC J
WORLD FILM & TELEVISION CORP, Ginza-8-10 Bldg, 6th flr, 8-10-8 Ginza, Chuo-ku, Tokyo. Tel: (03) 571-8047/9. Tlx: J25640 WORLDTYO.

NEW ZEALAND

CANNON SCREEN ENTERTAINMENT (NZ LTD), Private Bag, Newmarket, Auckland. Tel: 09 398 416. Tlx: NZ21341.
KERRIDGE ODEON AMALGAMATED VIDEO SERVICES, PO Box 422, Auckland. Tel: 09 32 206.
CIC TAFT VIDEO (NZ LTD), PO Box 3097, Auckland. Tel: 09 444 1824. Tlx: NZ60849.
WARNER HOME VIDEO, PO Box 2195, Auckland. Tel: 09 792 964. Tlx: NZ2839.
VIDEOCORP INTERNATIONAL, PO Box 39476, Auckland West. Tel: 09 389 899. Tlx: NZVideoNZ60191.
RCA COLUMBIA PICTURES, HOYTS VIDEO, PO Box 68490, Newton, Auckland. Tel: 09 790 661. Tlx: NZ2208.
CBS FOX VIDEO, PO Box 37720 Parnell, Auckland. Tel: 09 31 513. Tlx: NZ21490.
SHOWCASE VIDEO, PO Box 78115 Grey Lynn, Auckland. Tel: 09 762 750.
VIDEO WHOLESALERS, 25a East St, Newton, Auckland. Tel: 09 395 496.
CEL COMMUNICATIONS AND ENTERTAINMENT, 16 Liverpool St, Auckland. Tel: 09 389 706

NORWAY

ARONSEN VIDEO DIVISION, Drammensveien 130A, N-0277 Oslo 2. Tel: 02-555320. Tlx: 76181.
AS HJEMMET AVD/SELECT VIDEO, Kr Augustsgt 14, 0164 Oslo 1. Tel: 02-429470. Tlx: 76677.
AS INTERVIDEO, PO Box 32, Ljabruvn 32, 1113 Oslo 11. Tel: 02-297200.
AS VIDA, Mollergaten 20, PO Box 8383, Hammersborg 0129, Oslo. Tel: 02-200707. Tlx: 71896.
BIG PARTNER FILM AS, Betmannsgt 4, PO Box 1010, 7001 Trondheim. Tel: 07-514455. Tlx: 55473.
CCV AS, PO Box 36 Alnabru, 0614 Oslo. Tel: 02-647770. Tlx: 76465.
CD INTERNATIONAL AS, Konstaddalin 26, 5061 Kokstad PO Box 641, 5001 Bergen. Tel: 05-228211. Tlx: 40119 CDINT N.
HVC VIDEO VISION AS HEIDI FILM, Strandgt 116, 5500 Haugesund. Tel: 47-42985.
INTER PRESS AS, Mollergt 20, 0129 Oslo 1. Tel: 02-426890. Tlx: 78451.
JBJ VIDEO DISTRIBUTION, Klostergaten 19, N-1500 Moss. Tel: 032-54843.
NON STOP VIDEO AS, PO Box 52, Lilleaker, 0216 Oslo 2. Tel: 47-2505220. Tlx: 76553.
NORSK VIDEOGRAMFORENING, Teatergt 5, 0180 Oslo. Tel: 2-60407.
POLYGRAM VIDEO, Marcus Thranes Gt 2, PO Box 4352 Torshov, 0473 Oslo 4. Tel: 02-372905. Tlx: 78521 N.
SCANDINAVIAN TELEVISION & VIDEO AS, Fladeby Gaard, Flatebyveien 6, PO Box 64, 1790 Tistedal. Tel: 31-91500.
SCREEN ENTERTAINMENT AS, Teatkgt 5, 01180 Oslo 1. Tel: 02-426890. Tlx: 78451.
T & O FILM AS, Teatergarten 3, 0180 Oslo 1. Tel: 470-211704.
VCL VIDEO AS, Eviebakken 19, 1346 Gjetturn. Tel: 02-392006.

PORTUGAL

ECOVIDEO, Av Da Liberdade 563, PO Box 62, 3701 S Joao Da Madiera. Lisbon.
EDIVIDEO, Rua Manuel Ferreira, De Andrade 6-B, 1500 Lisbon.
VISTA-VIDEO-PRODUCOES VIDEO-SARL, Rua Antonio Pedro, 68-1 D1, Lisbon.

SINGAPORE

AMARJIT PICTURES, 1 North Bridge Rd., 09-06 High St. Centre, Singapore 0617. Tel: 3371054. Tlx: 24275.
BURNEO FILM ORGANISATION SDN BHD, 3rd flr, Pawagam BFO Dalit, Jalan Bukit Merah (Bukit Merah Town Centre), Singapore 0315. Tel: 2739066. Tlx: 51020.
CATHAY ORGANISATION PTE LTD, 11 Dhoby Ghaut, 05-00 Cathay Bldg., Singapore 0922. Tel: 3378181. Tlx: 21124.
CEL VIDEO (S) PTE LTD, 14-07, 190 Middle Rd., Singapore 0718. Tel: 3361800.
SHAW & SHAW PTE LTD, 13th & 14th flrs, Shaw Centre, 1 Scotts Rd., Singapore 0922. Tel: 2532077. Tlx: 23957.
VIDEOVAN ENTERPRISES (S) PTE LTD, 04-10 Beach Centre, Beach Rd., Singapore 0718. Tel: 3398870.
VISIONEX PRODUCTION PTE LTD, 08-19/20, 101 A Upper Cross St., Singapore 0106. Tel: 5343288.

SPAIN

J J BARROSO PRODUCCIONES VIDEOGRAFICAS, %Conil 11, Pozuelo De Alarcon, Madrid.

CB FILMS, Diagonal 407, Principal, 08008 Barcelona. Tel: (903) 2179354.

CIA IBEROAMERICANS DE TV SA, Calle Velazquez 18 70, Madrid 2.

CIC—RCA/COLUMBIA PICTURES VIDEO SRC, Edificio AGF, Albacate 5, 28027 Madrid. Tel: (901) 4054362.

CYDIS VIDEO, Doce de Octubre 28, 28009 Madrid. Tel: (01) 2749008.

DISPREVSA, Francesco Carbonell 35-37, Barcelona 34. Tel: (903) 2050913.

FARANDULA/DUMBY HOME VIDEO, San Bernadino 17, Leganitos 9 y 11, Madrid. Tel: (901) 4791261.

FILMAYER VIDEO SA, Matires De Alcala 4, 28015 Madrid. Tel: (901) 2489205.

HISPAVIDEO SA, Nunez De Balboa 121-5 C, Madrid 6. Tel: (901) 2612546.

GRUPO AGUILA SA, Aguila 124, 28006 Madrid. Tel: (901) 4318862.

IVE DISTRIBUTORS SA, Ave Hospital Militar 52, 08023 Barcelona. Tel: (93) 2179354.

IVEX FILMS, Mariano Cubi 4, Entrasuelo, 08006 Barcelona. Tel: (93) 2185409.

IVS INTERNACIONAL VIDEO SYSTEMS, Olite 37, PO Box 1290, Pamplona. Tel: 242630.

J F VIDEO, Gran Via 70-60 III, Madrid 13. Tel: (901) 2415586.

KALENDER VIDEO SA, Pintor Juan Gris 5, 28020 Madrid. Tel: (901) 4554477.

LAUREN FILMS, Video Hogar, Balmes 87, pral., 08008 Barcelona. Tel: (93) 50910 LAFL E; FAX: (93) 323 5400; Tlx: (93) 323 6155.

LAX VIDEO SA, Jarama 19, 28002 Madrid. Tel: (901) 4582162.

METROMEDIA VIDEO, Doce de Octubre 28, 28009 Madrid. Tel: (901) 2749005. Tlx: 43455 SELI E1.

MGM/UA HOME VIDEO, Doce de Octubre, 28009 Madrid

OMNIVIDEO SA, Berlin 95-97 Ent A. Barcelona 29. Tel: (903) 2397807.

POLYGRAM IBERICA SA, Avenida America Esq, Hernadez De Tejeda, 28027 Madrid. Tel: (901) 2674200.

ROLLER SA VIDEO PRODUCCIONES, Nazalmanzano 17 "Las Calabazas," Ciudad Puerta Hierro, Madrid 35.

TELE JACTOR ESPANA SA, Travesia San Juan Bosco 7, 31007 Pamploma. Tel: (948) 272811.

UNIVERSAL VIDEO SA, Avenida de Los Toraros SA, 28028 Madrid. Tel: (901) 2563901

VIDEO DISCO, Avenida de Los Toreros 10, 28028 Madrid. Tel: (901) 2562002.

VIDEO DISTRIBUCION INTERNATIONAL, Calle Valencia 553, Barcelona 26. Tel: (03) 243 2600.

VIDEO FAMILIAR, Mandarina 7, Madrid 28027. Tel: (01) 4085613. Tlx: 45233.

VIDEO FRAME INTERNACIONAL SA, Duque de Sevilla n°2, 28002 Madrid. Tel: (901) 4114177. Tlx: 47846.

VIDEOMAN INTERNACIONAL SA, Doce de Octubre 28, 28009 Madrid. Tel: (01) 2749065. Tlx: 45829 DIFI.

VIDEO SERVICE SA, Canos del Peral 2, 28013 Madrid 13. Tel: (901) 2470086. Tlx: 43175 LOTU E

VIDEO SEVEN, San Bernardo 17, 28015 Madrid. Tel: (901) 2474499, 4791261.

WALSH VIDEO, Hilarion Eslava 60, 28015 Madrid.

WARNER HOME VIDEO, Alfonso Rodriguez Santamaria 18, 28002 Madrid. Tel: (901) 2509905.

WEEKEND VIDEO, Ventura Rodriguez 7, 28008 Madrid. Tel: (901) 2420733/0856.

SWEDEN

AUDIOVISION INVESTMENT AB, Sodra Kungsvagen 293, 181 63 Lidingo. Tel: 08-7662600.

CENTRUM RADIO VIDEOFILMER, Ranhammarsvagen 28, S-161 85 Bromma. Tel: 468-987590. Tlx: 12669.

CROWN VIDEO INTERNATIONAL, PO Box 8093, S-252 08 Helsingborg. Tel: 42-133599. Tlx: 12442. CIA.

DIRECT VIDEO, PO Box 53228, 400 16 Gothenburg. Tel: 031-112244. Tlx: 2330 CONTR S.

EH INTERNATIONAL SWEDEN AB, Box 1106, 171 22 Solna. Tel: 08-824582. Tlx: 40227 NORWAY.

ESSELTE VIDEO AB, PO Box 9006, Hornsgaten 166, S-102 71 Stockholm. Tel: 08-7772500. Tlx: 17924. Fax: 08-845980.

FREKVENSIA GETE AB, Stockholm SV 37, 194 54 Upplands Vaesby. Tel: 0760-92190. Tlx: 12205 FREKV GT.

IVIDEOGROSSISTEN AB, Sveavagen 17, 111 57 Stockholm. Tel: 08-112255. Tlx: 19409.

NORDISK BETAL TV, Grev Turegatan, 18, 114 46 Stockholm. Tel: 08-626322. Tlx: 13326.

PRISMA FILM AND VIDEO, Birger Svenssons Vag 40, S-432 00 Varberg. Tel: 340-89065. Tlx: 27538 VIKING.

SCANDINAVIAN FILM & VIDEO, PO Box 1332, S-111 83 Stockholm. Tel: 08-232910.

SCAND-VIDEO AB, PO Box 66055, 500 06 Boras. Tel: 033-127520. Tlx: 36111.

SELECT VIDEO, S-212 05 Malmö. Tel: 040-934560. Tlx: 32449.

TRANS WORLD VIDEO AB, PO Box 230, S-201 22 Malmo.

VIDEO EXPRESS AB, PO Box 30066, 104 25 Stockholm. Tel: 08-132540. Tlx: 15488.

VIDEOGROSSISTEN AB, Sveavagen 17, S-111 57, Stockholm. Tel: 46-31112255. Tlx: 2330 MAXS S.

VIDEO TAPE CENTER, Hagaparkagatan 19, 723 36 Vaesteraas.

VIKING VIDEO/PRISMA FILM & VIDEO, Drottninggatan 47, 432 00 Varberg. Tel: 340-85650. Tlx: 20120Y FOTEX S.

VTC SCANDINAVIA, Ulvsundavagen 174, S-161 85 Bromma. Tel: 46-87339100. Tlx: 15321.

SWITZERLAND

UPC FILM AG, Postfach 436, Basle.

TPC—THE PRODUCERS CORP, Hauserstrasse 14, 8030 Zurich.

TAIWAN

HWA AN MOTION PICTURE & INVEST INC, Room 402 Northwest Bldg, 58 Kun-ming St., PO Box 22158, Taipei, Taiwan.

UNITED KINGDOM

A & M SOUND PICTURES, 136-140 New Kings Rd., London SW6 4LZ. Tel: 01-736 3311. Tlx: 916342 ALMOSS G.

AMARAY INTERNATIONAL, Oak House, Oak End Way, Gerrards Cross, Bucks.

ANGLO AMERICAN FILM DISTRIBUTORS/VIDEO MEDIA LTD, 70 Wardour St., London W1. Tlx: 291565 AA FILM.

APEX VIDEO, 3 Standard Rd, Park Royal Ind. Est., London NW10 6EX. Tel: 01-965 5354. Tlx: 914382

ARIEL FILMS & VIDEO DISTRIBUTORS, 3 High St., Christchurch, Dorset DH23 1AB. Tel: 0202 479868. Tlx: 41594.

ATLANTIS VIDEO PRODUCTIONS LTD, Atlantis House, 60 Wapping High St., London E1 9LX. Tel: 01-481 3333. Tlx: 893970 ATLANT G.

AVATAR COMMUNICATIONS, Imperial Studios, Imperial Rd., London SW6 2AG. Tlx: 8950127.

BBC VIDEO, Woodlands, 80 Wood Lane, London W12 0TT. Tel: 01-743 5588. Tlx: 928937 BBCENT

BORDEAUX FILMS INTERNATIONAL LTD, 3rd flr, 92 Wardour St., London W1. Tel: 01-434 3459. Tlx: 21879/25267 BOROFILMS LONDON W1.

BRENT WALKER VIDEO, Knightsbridge House, 197 Knightsbridge, London SW7 1RB. Tel: 01-225 1941. Tlx: 23639.

CANNON VIDEO, 30631 Golden Sq., London W1A 4DX. Tel: 01-437 9234.

CAREYVISION, Unit 4, Whitworth Rd. Ind. Est., Pin Green, Stevenage SG1 4QS. Tel: 0438 350660. Tlx: 825422 POURRI G.

CBS/FOX VIDEO, Perrivale Ind. Est., Greenford, Middx. UB6 7RU. Tel: 01-997 2552. Tlx: 268763.

CHANNEL 5 DISTRIBUTION LTD, 1 Rockley Rd., London W14 0DL. Tel: 01-743 3473. Tlx: 298816.

CHRYSALIS, 12 Strafford Pl., London W1N 9AF. Tel: 01-408 2355. Tlx: 21753.

CIC VIDEO, 4th flr, Glenthorne House, 5-17 Hammersmith Gr., London W6 0ND. Tel: 01-846 9433. Tlx: 268763.

CINEPLEX, Unit 4, The Whitworth Road Industrial Estate, Whitworth Road, Stevenage SG1 4QS. Tel: 0438 350660.

CITY VISION PIC, Unit 1 McKay Trad. Est., Kensal Rd., London W10 5BX. Tel: 01-960 8211. Tlx: 291877 VISION G.

DERANN FILM SERVICES LTD, 99 High St., Dudley, W. Midlands. Tel: 0384 233191. Tlx: 335893 DERANN.

ELECTRIC VIDEO, 41 Paddington St., London W1M 3RN. Tel: 01-935 7288. Tlx: 24583.

EMBASSY HOME ENTERTAINMENT, Sloane Sq. House, Holbein Pl., Sloane Sq., London SW1 8NS. Tel: 01-730 3455. Tlx: 895 0483.

ENTERTAINMENT AND VIDEO DISTRIBUTORS LTD, 27 Soho Sq., London W1. Tel: 01-439 1979. Tlx: 262428 ENTVIF.

FILMCENTRE OVERSEAS CORP, 113-117 Wardour St., London W1. Tel: 01-439 7491.

FILMTOWN VIDEO, 36 Soho Sq., London W1V 5DG. Tel: 01-434 9729. Tlx: 297648.

FUTURE VISION LTD, Unit 10, Brunswick Ind. Pk., Waterfall Rd., New Southgate N11 1JL. Tel: 01-368 1276.

GMH ENTERTAINMENTS, 22 Manasty Road, Orton, Southgate, Peterborough.

GO VIDEO LTD, PO Box 4BT, 35-37 Wardour St., London W1A 4BT. Tel: 01-734 7195/6. Tlx: 922488.

GRANADA VIDEO, 36 Golden Sq., London W1R 4AH. Tel: 01-734 8080. Tlx: 27937.

GTO FILMS & VIDEO INTERNATIONAL, 27A Queens' Ter., St John's Wood, London NW8. Tel: 01-580 7576. Tlx: 267811 MUSIC IQ.

GUILD HOME VIDEO, Crown House, 2 Church St., Walton-on-Thames, Surrey KT12 2QS. Tel: 0932 228899. Tlx: 269651.

HENDRING LTD., Garden Suite, 21 Tower St., London, WC2H 9NS. Tel: 01-379 5526.

HERON HOME ENTERTAINMENT, Unit 4, Brunswick Ind. Pk., Brunswick Pk. Rd., New Southgate, London N11 1JL. Tel: 01-368 1226. Tlx: 897654.

IMPACT, 44 Gt Marlborough St., London W1V 1DB. Tel: 01-734 6813. Tlx: 264660 OVIDEO G.

INTERMOVIE, Agra House, 964 North Circular Rd., London NW2 7JR. Tel: 01-450 5477/78/79. Tlx: 928706.
ISLAND VISUAL ARTS, 334-336 King St., London W6 0RA. Tel: 01-846 9566. Tlx: 934541.
KINGS FEATURES ENTERTAINMENTS INC, 18 Hanover Sq., London W1R 9HG. Tel: 01-491 3382. Tlx: 266570 KINGSN G.
LONGMAN VIDEO, Longman House, Burnt Mill, Harlow, Essex CM20 2JE. Tel: 0279 26721.
MEDUSA COMMUNICATIONS, 109 Regal House, 51 Bancroft, Hitchin, Herts SG5 1LL. Tel: 0462 53612. Tlx: 826552.
MGM/UA HOME VIDEO, Hammer House, 113-117 Wardour St., London W1V 3TD. Tel: 01-439 9932. Tlx: 28527.
MISSING IN ACTION, Handle House, 1 Derby St., London W1Y 7HD. Tel: 10-493 9637. Tlx: 892756 HANDLE G.
NELSON ENTERTAINMENT, 8 Queen St., London W1X 7PM.
NEW REALM ENTERTAINMENTS LTD, Townsend House, 22-25 Dean St., London W1V 5AL. Tel: 01-437 9143/786 5818. Tlx: 892604 NRDLON G NUREALMPIC.
NEW WORLD VIDEO, 27 Soho Sq., London W1V 5FL. Tel: 01-434 0497. Tlx: 27950 ref: 2794. Fax: 01-836 4871.
NICKELODEON PICTURES LTD, 74 Queensway, 2nd flr, London W2. Tlx: 265905 HALEPI G.
ODYSSEY VIDEO, 44 Gt Marlborough St., London W1V 1DB. Tel: 01-439 2244. Tlx: 264660 OVIDEO.
PALACE VIDEO, 16-17 Wardour Mews, London W1V 3DG. Tel: 01-734 7060. Tlx: 263900 PALACE G.
PALAN ENTERTAINMENT CORPORATION, 1 Euston Centre, London NW1 3JG. Tel: 01-388 5034. Tlx: 268710 PALAN G.
PENDULUM COMMUNICATIONS LTD., 18 Great Marlborough Street, London, W1V 1AF. Tel: 01 - 437 0885.
PICTURE MUSIC INTERNATIONAL, 20 Manchester Sq., London W1A 1ES. Tel: 01-486 4488. Tlx: 22643. Fax: 01-935 3852.
PICKWICK VIDEO LTD., The Hyde Industrial Estate, The Hyde, London, NW9 6JU.
POLYGRAM VIDEO, 1 Rockley Rd., London W14 0DL. Tel: 01-743 3474. Tlx: 298816. Fax: 01-743 2074.
(PVG) PALACE VIRGIN & GOLD DISTRIBUTION, 69 Flempton Rd., London E10 7NL. Tel: 01-539 5566. Tlx: 894793 S GOLD.
QUADRANT VIDEO, 37a High St., Carshalton, Surrey SM3 3BB. Tel: 01-669 1114. Tlx: 269556.
RCA/COLUMBIA PICTURES VIDEO (UK), Metropolis House, 22 Percy St., London W1P 9FF. Tel: 01-636 8373. Tlx: 23876.
SELECT VIDEO, PO Box 111, Gt Ducie St., Manchester M60 3BL. Tel: 061-834 4842. Tlx: 668609.
S GOLD AND SONS (RECORDS LTD), 69 Flempton Rd., Leyton, London E10 7 NL. Tel: 01-539 3600. Tlx: 894793.
SONY VIDEO SOFTWARE EUROPE, 41-42 Berners St., London W1P 3AA. Tel: 01-631 4000. Tlx: 268054.
SPAN PICTURES LTD., 1-2 John Princes Street, London, W.1. Tel: 01 - 491 4997.
STABLECANE, Unit 10, Brunswick Ind. Pk., Waterfall Rd., New Southgate London N11 1JL. Tel: 01-368 1276. Tlx: 269023 PREST G.
THAMES VIDEO, 149 Tottenham Court Rd., London W1P 9LL. Tel: 01-387 9494. Tlx: 25286.
TREDEGAR WHOLESALE VIDEO CENTRE, The House, 21 Greycaine Road, North Watford, WD2 4QT. Tel: 0923 226936.
VESTRON VIDEO (UK), 69 New Oxford St., London WC1 1DG.
VIDEO BOX OFFICE LTD., 22 Manasty Road, Orton Southgate, Peterborough PE2 0UP. Tel: 0733 233464.
VIDEO COLLECTION UNIT, 10 Brunswick Ind. Pk., Waterfall Rd., New Southgate N11 1JL. Tel: 01-368 1276.
VIDEO GEMS (A.M.T. Ltd), 3 Standard Rd., Park Royal Ind. Est., London NW10 6EX. Tel: 01-961 5646. Tlx: 914382 MSDLON G.
VIDEO INSTANT, 9 Sentinel House, Sentinel Sq., Brent St., Hendon, London N1 2EN. Tel: 01-202 9879.
VIDEO PROGRAMME DISTRIBUTORS LTD, Bldg 1, GEC Est, East Lane, Wembley, Middx. HA9 7FF. Tel: 01-904 0921. Tlx: 295369 VIDPRO G.
VIRGIN VISION VIDEO, 328 Kensal Rd., London W10 5XJ. Tel: 01-968 8888. Tlx: 892890.
WARNER HOME VIDEO, 135 Wardour St., London, W1V 4AP.
WIERNERWORLD LTD, 90 Old Church Lane, Stanmore, Middx. HA7 2RR. Tel: 01-954 8777. Tlx: 923753 MONREF or 946240 CWEASY.
WEEKEND VIDEO, Seymour Mews House, Seymour Mews, Wigmore St., London W1H 9PE. Tel: 01-935 9000. Tlx: 228726 FVFILM G.

WEST GERMANY

ALEXANDRA-VERLAG GMBH, Dachauerstr 37, 8000 Munich 2. Tel: 089-297194. Tlx: 529096.
ALL-VIDEO VERTRIEBS GMBH, Industriestr 49, 4044 Kaarst 1. Tel: 02101-604042. Tlx: 8518065.
ALL VIDEO PROGRAMM VERTRIEBSGESELLSCHAFT GMBH, Lazarettstr 19, 4300 Essen 1. Tel: 0201-202866/69. Tlx: 8579531.
ARCADE VIDEO (DEUTSCHLAND) GMBH, Buckower, Chaussee 60-68, 1000 Berlin 48. Tel: 030-7215042.
ARIOLA-EURODISC GMBH, Carl Bertelsmann-Str 161, Postfach 3306, 4830 Gütersloh 1. Tel: 05241-805151. Tlx: 933787
ATLAS FILM & AV GMBH & CO KG, Verleih und Vertrieb, Ludgeristr 14-16, 4300 308280. Tlx: 8551126.
AV-FILM GMBH, Max-Planck-Str 38, 8056 Neufahrn. Tel: 08165-5536.
BEATE UHSE-VIDEO, Gutenbergstr 12, Postfach 2955, 2390 Flensburg. Tel: 0461-809206, 809271, 809275. Tlx: 17461307.

BENRA FILMVERLEIH KG/VIDEO, Raschigstr 100, 6700 Ludwigshafen/Rh. Tel: 0621-552088/89.
REINHARD BERG FILMPRODUKTION, Körnerstr 5, 6200 Wiesbaden. Tel: 06121-305919.
BRUCKMANN VERLAG MUNCHEN, Nymphenburger Str 86, Postfach 27, 8000 Munich 20. Tel: 089-1257308. Tlx: 523739.
CALIG VERLAG GMBH, Schuhstr 4, Postfach 1047, 3200 Hildesheim. Tel: 05121-169225.
CANNON SCREEN ENTERTAINMENT, Frankfurter Ring 115, 8000 Munich 40. Tel: 089-315063. Tlx: 5213397.
CBS/FOX VIDEO (GERMANY) GMBH, Am Forsthaus, Gravenbruch 7, 6078 Neu-Isenburg 2. Tel: 06102-5552. Tlx: 4185555.
CD-FILM, Lützowstr 20, 4100 Duisburg 1. Tel: 0203-355164, 356623.
CHRONOS FILMVERLEIH GMBH, Schopenhauerstr 50, 1000 Berlin 38. Tel: 030-8033051/52. Tlx: 181511.
CIC VIDEO GMBH, Frankfurter Str 74, 6236 Eschborn/Ts. Tel: 06196-46054/8. Tlx: 418193.
CONSTANTIN VIDEO GMBH, Kaiserstr 39, 8000 Munich 40. Tel: 089-38609/0.
DATAKONTEXT VERLAG GMBH, Postfach 400253, 5000 Köln 40. Tel: 0221-486503, 02234-78913.
EKSTASE-VIDEO, Postfach 2171, 4322 Sprockhövel 2.
ELECTRONIC CENTER GMBH, ECG TV-Studio, Adalbertstr 44-48, 6900 Frankfurt/Main 90. Tel: 069-770611. Tlx: 412980.
EMBASSY VIDEO GMBH, Maria-Theresia-Str 32, 8000 Munich 80. Tel: 089-985491/95. Tlx: 521478.
EMI ELECTROLA GMBH, Maarweg 149, 5000 Köln 30. Tel: 0221-4902/0. Tlx: 8881290.
ERL VERLAG VIDEO, Berliner Ring 62, Postfach 1444, 6330 Wetzlar. Tel: 06441-5050.
ERNST KLETT VERLAG, Rotebühlstr 77, Postfach 809, 7000 Stuttgart 1. Tel: 0711-6672/0. Tlx: 722225.
EUROVIDEO BILDPROGRAMM GMBH, Oskar-Messter-Str 15, 8045 Ismaning. Tel: 089-96123/7. Tlx: 5215946.
FWU, Institut für Film und Bild in Wissenschaft und Unterricht gemeinnützige GmbH, Postfach 260, 8022 Grünwald. Tel: 089-64971.
GBM VERLAG BILDUNG UND MEDIEN GMBH, Schwedenstr 10, 8137 Berg 2/Starnberger See. Tel: 08151-51156.
VERKAUF EXCLUSIVE ÜBER ALL VIDEO PROGRAMM VERTRIEBSGESELLSCHAFT, Lazarettstr 19, 4300 Essen 1. Tel: 0201-202866/69.
GLOBAL FILM & VIDEO GMBH, Nederlingerstr 21, 8000 Munich 19. Tel: 089-151063. Tlx: 5215019.
GLORIA VIDEO GMBH, Gutenbergstr 23-25, 6800 Mannheim 1. Tel: 0621-371055. Tlx: 462906.
IVH INTERNATIONAL HOME VIDEO VERTRIEBS GMBH, Lazarettstr 19, 4300 Essen 1. Tel: 0201-233551. Tlx: 8579685.
IMV-VERTRIEBS INTERNAT MEDIEN, Oskar-Messter-Str 15, 8045 Ismaning. Tel: 089-96123/7. Tlx: 5215946.
INSTITUT FÜR VIDEO INFORMATIONS SYSTEME VIS GMBH, Lakronstr 59, 4000 Düsseldorf 12. Tel: 0211-283031.
INTER-PATHÉ GMBH & CO KG, Bolongarostr 141, 6230 Frankfurt/Main 80. Tel: 069-304043/315680. Tlx: 411981.
ITALVIDEO GIACINTO SOLL IMPORT-EXPORT, Video und Tonträger, Schwalbenweg 3, 7258 Heimsheim. Tel. 07033-31411, 31461. Tlx: 783374.
JAHRESZEITEN TV UND VIDEO PRODUKTION GMBH, Prossmoorweg 5, 2000 Hamburg 60. Tel: 040-27717/0. Tlx: 213214.
JAPAN HOME VIDEO TATSUNOKO FILM PRODUCTION GMBH, Heinrich-Berbalk-Str 56, 6000 Frankfurt/Main 56. Tel: 069-5083540. Tlx: 4189533.
KLASING & CO GMBH, Delius Klasing Verlag, Siekerwass 21, 4800 Bielefeld 1. Tel: 0521-559/0. Tlx: 932934.
KV KOMPLETT-VIDEO, Flemingstr 15, 8000 Munich 81. Tel: 089-928020. Tlx: 5216059.
LANGENSCHEIDT KG, Neusser Str 3, 8000 Munich 40. Tel: 089-36096/0. Tlx: 5215379.
MARKT & TECHNIK VERLAG AKTIENGESELLSCHAFT, Hans-Pinsel-Str 2, 8013 Haar. Tel: 089-4613/0. Tlx: 522052.
MARKETING FILM BOCHUM GMBH, Viktoriastr 23-25, 4630 Bochum T. Tel: 0234-60745. Tlx: 825786.
MEDIENVILM VIDEO MAGAZIN GMBH, Alt Seulberg 73, Postfach 1360 6382 Friedrichsdorf/Ts. Tel: 06172-72055/56. Tlx: 410884.
MERKUR FILM AGENCY GMBH, Krünerstr 65, 8000 Munich 70. Tel: 089-7693424. Tlx: 5216092.
MIKE HUNTER VIDEO GMBH, Hohe Pforte 4-6, 5000 Köln 1. Tel: 0221-210041/43. Tlx: 888900.
NB FILM & VIDEO ENTERTAINMENT GMBH & CO KG, Postfach 2120, 4150 Krefeld 1. Tel: 02151-801122. Tlx: 8531121.
NEUE ATLAS MEDIEN PRODUKTIONSUND VERTRIEBS GMBH & CO KG, Ludgeristr 14-16, 4100 Duisburg 1. Tel: 0203-3080. Tlx: 855126.
OTTO MAIER VERLAG GMBH, Postfach 1860, 7980 Ravensburg. Tel: 0751-861. Tlx: 732921.
PÄDAGOGISCHER VERLAG SCHWANN-BAGEL GMBH, Am Wehrhahn 100, Postfach 7640, 4000 Düsseldorf 1. Tel: 0211-360301. Tlx: 8581345.
PIONEER-MELCHERS GMBH, Hansaallee 191, Postfach 110942, 4000 Düsseldorf 1. Tel: 0211-5953/0. Tlx: 8587326.
POLYBAND GESELLSCHAFT F BILD-U TONTRÄGER GMBH & CO BETRIEBS KG, Am Moosfeld 37, 8000 Munich 82. Tel: 089-420030. Tlx: 522636.
POLYGRAM MUSIK VERTRIEB, Glockengiesserwall 3, 2000 Hamburg 1. Tel: 040-308701. Tlx: 2163924.

RDS RAINBOW DISTRIBUTION SERVICES GMBH, Peterweilstr 4-8, 6000 Frankfurt am Main 60. Tel: 069-430175. Tlx: 413037.

RIBU FILM PRODUKTION GMBH & CO KG, Güntherstr 39, 2000 Hamburg 76. Tel: 040-257151. Tlx: 2173812.

SELECT VIDEO GMBH, Raiffeisenstr 13, 7024 Filderstadt 4. Tel: 0711-77-716. Tlx: 7255154.

SPRINGER-VERLAG GMBH & CO KG, Heidelberger Platz 3, 1000 Berlin 33. Tel: 030-8207/1. Tlx: 183319.

STARLIGHT-FILM PRODUKTIONS-UND VERTRIEBS GMBH, Steinring 45, 4630 Bochum 1. Tel: 0234-37601/4. Tlx: 825351.

TAURUS-FILM VIDEO GMBH, Betastr 1, 8043 Unterföhring. Tel: 089-9590/0. Tlx: 523222/30.

TELEWISEEN GMBH, Plannmüllerweg 17a, 6100 Darmstadt. Tel: 06151-76299.

SUNRISE VIDEO GMBH, Lorsbacher Str 1, 6238 Hoafheim/Ts. Tel: 06192-28901.

TOPAZ CLASSIC MEDIENPROGRAMM GESELLSCHAFT, Pfisterstr 5, 8000 Munich 2. Tel: 089-222122, 2283630. Tlx: 5218565.

UFA-VIDEO GMBH, Steinhauser Str 1-3, Postfach 800149, 8000 Munich 80. Tel: 089-4136347. Tlx: 523487.

USI RHENANIA-FACHVERLAG GMBH, Possmoorweg 1, 2000 Hamburg 60. Tel: 040-27172234. Tlx: 213214.

UVG, UNTERHALTUNGS-UND VIDEO VERKAUFS GMBH, Alt Seulberg 73, Postfach 1360, 6382 Friedrichsdorf/Ts. Tel: 06172-72055/56. Tlx: 410884.

VCL, COMMUNICATIONS GMBH, Martin-Kollar-Str 1, 8000 Munich 82. Tel: 089-42008/0. Tlx: 5212360 vcld.

VERLAG DAS FREIE BUCH GMBH, Buch und Zeitlungsverlag, Tulbeckstr 4, 8000 Munich 2. Tel: 089-5024834.

VERLAG E S MITTIER & SOHN GMBH, Steintorwall 17, Postfach 2352, 4900 Herford. Tel: 05221-50001. Tlx: 934801.

VERTRIEBSGESELLSCHAFT RCA/COLUMBIA PICTURES VIDEO GMBH & CO KG, Osterstr 116, 2000 Hamburg 20. Tel: 040-4902/1. Tlx: 2164193. Fax: 4902304.

VESTRON VIDEO INTERNATIONAL, Southern Star Promotion GmbH, Am Moosfeld 85, 8000 Munich 82. Tel: 089-429057. Tlx: 5218088 SSP D.

VFL VIDEO-FILM LEASING GMBH, Obertorstr 38, 6490 Schlüchtern 1. Tel: 06661-3001/3. Tlx: 49566.

VGS VERLAGSGESELLSCHAFT, Breite Str 118/120, Postfach 180269, 5000 Köln 1. Tel: 0221-219641.

VIA VIDEO GESELLSCHAFT FÜR VIDEO-WERBUNG UND VERTRIEB GMBH, Eidigweg 23, Postfach 1173, 2077 Trittau. Tel: 04154-81880. Tlx: 2189453.

VIDEAL VERTRIEB VON AUDIOVISUELLEN PRODUKTEN GMBH, Alsterkampt 17, 2000 Hamburg 13. Tel: 040-4101027. Tlx: 2164167.

VMP VIDEO MEDIEN POOL PRODUKTIONS-UND VERTRIEBS GMBH, Frankfurter Ring 115, 8000 Munich 40. Tel: 089-3509020.

VMV VESTISCHER MEDIEN VERLAG, Scheideweg 120, 4390 Gladbeck. Tel: 02043-64774.

VPS VIDEO PROGRAMM SERVICE GMBH, Saarstr 7, 8000 Munich 40. Tel: 089-386010. Tlx: 5212767.

VTB VIDEO + TONBILD GMBH, Audiovisuelle Medien im Kollektiv, Spohrstr 26, 6000 Frankfurt/Main 1. Tel: 069-5974016.

VTD VIDEO TONTRÄGER DR DRESSLER GMBH, Gollierstr 5, 8000. Munich 2. Tel: 089-5026344. Tlx: 5214499.

WARA FILM UND TON GMBH & CO KG, Wittekindstr 15, 5000 Köln 41. Tel: 0221-445007.

WARNER HOME VIDEO GMBH, Eine Warner Communications Gesellschaft, Arndtstr 16, 2000 Hamburg 76. Tel: 040-22805/0. Tlx: 214881.

YUGOSLAVIA

FILMOTEKA 16, Savska 9, 41000 Zagreb. Tel: 041-444 425.

Companies

* **NETWORKS**

* **SET MANUFACTURERS**

* **MAJOR PRODUCERS**

Companies

Capital Cities/ABC, Inc.

1330 Ave. of the Americas, New York, NY 10019; (212) 887-7777; 41 Prospect Ave., Los Angeles, CA 90027; (213) 557-7777.

CHM. OF BOARD & CHIEF EXECUTIVE OFFICER
Thomas S. Murphy
PRESIDENT & CHIEF OPERATING OFFICER
Daniel B. Burke
EXECUTIVE VICE PRESIDENT
Joseph P. Dougherty
EXECUTIVE VICE PRESIDENT; CHAIRMAN & CHIEF
EXECUTIVE OFFICER, FAIRCHILD PUBLICATIONS
John B. Fairchild
EXECUTIVE VICE PRESIDENT;
PRESIDENT, ABC TELEVISION NETWORK GROUP
John B. Sias
SENIOR VICE PRESIDENT; CHIEF FINANCIAL OFFICER
Ronald J. Doerfler
SENIOR VICE PRESIDENT; PRESIDENT, BROADCAST GROUP
Michael P. Mallardi
SENIOR VICE-PRESIDENT; PRESIDENT, PUBLISHING GROUP
Phillip J. Meek
SENIOR VICE PRESIDENT & GENERAL COUNSEL
Stephen A. Weiswasser
VICE PRESIDENT, CORPORATE COMMUNICATIONS
Patricia J. Matson
VICE PRESIDENT, POLICY & STANDARDS
Alfred R. Schneider
VICE PRESIDENT & CONTROLLER
Allan J. Edelson
VICE PRESIDENT
Joseph M. Fitzgerald
VICE PRESIDENT
John E. Frisoli
VICE PRESIDENT
James M. Goldberg
VICE PRESIDENT
Robert T. Goldman
VICE PRESIDENT
Ann Maynard Gray
VICE PRESIDENT
Andrew E. Jackson
VICE PRESIDENT & ASSISTANT CONTROLLER
David S. Loewith
VICE PRESIDENT
Jeffrey Ruthizer
VICE PRESIDENT & TREASURER
David J. Vondrak
SECRETARY
Gerald Dickler
ASSISTANT SECRETARY
Philip R. Farnsworth
ASSISTANT TREASURER
Allen S. Bomes
BOARD OF DIRECTORS
Thomas S. Murphy (chmn. of the bd., CEO); Daniel B. Burke (pres., COO); Robert P. Bauman (chmn. of the bd., CEO, Beecham Group p.l.c.); Warren E. Buffett (chmn. of the bd., CEO, Berkshire Hathaway Inc.); Frank T. Cary (former chmn. of the bd., IBM); Gerald Dickler (secty.; senior counsel, Hall, Dickler, Lawler, Kent & Friedman, Attorneys at Law); Joseph P. Dougherty (exec. v.p.); John B. Fairchild (exec. v.p., chmn., CEO, Fairchild Publications); Leonard H. Goldenson (chmn., executive committee; retired chmn. of the bd., American Broadcasting Companies, Inc.); Leon Hess (chmn. of the bd., CEO, Amerada Hess Corp.); George P. Jenkins (consultant to W.R. Grace & Co.; retired chmn. of the bd., Metropolitan Life Insurance Company); Thomas M. Macioce (partner, Shea & Gold, Attorneys at Law; former chmn. of the bd., CEO, Allied Stores Corporation); John H. Muller Jr. (chmn., pres., CEO, General Housewares Corp.); Frederick S. Pierce (former pres., COO, American Broadcasting Companies Inc.); John B. Poole (retired chmn. of the bd., Poole Broadcasting Company); John B. Sias (exec. v.p.; pres., ABC Television Network Group); William I. Spencer (retired pres., chief admin. officer, Citicorp and Citibank, N.A.); M. Cabell Woodward, Jr (vice chmn., CFO, ITT Corp.).

FINANCIAL (ALL CAPITAL CITIES/ABC, INC.)

SENIOR VICE PRESIDENT AND CHIEF FINANCIAL OFFICER
Ronald J. Doerfler
SENIOR VICE PRESIDENT FINANCE
Ann Maynard Gray
VICE-PRESIDENT OF MANAGEMENT INFORMATION SYSTEMS
Edward D. Williams
TREASURER
David S. Vondrak
COMPTROLLER
Allan J. Edelson
ASSISTANT COMPTROLLERS
David S. Loewith, Allen Bomes
VICE PRESIDENT, CORPORATE INTERNAL AUDIT
Joseph H. Lock
VICE PRESIDENT, TAXES
Arnold Agree

ADMINISTRATION

VICE-PRESIDENT, ADMINISTRATION,
CAPITAL CITIES/ABC, INC.
Robert T. Goldman
DIRECTOR, CORPORATE SERVICES
Robert M. Sammon
VICE PRESIDENT OF REAL ESTATE AND CONSTRUCTION,
ABC
Richard E. Hockman
VICE PRESIDENT, ADMINISTRATION, WEST COAST, ABC
Roger K. Lund
VICE PRESIDENT, HUMAN RESOURCES,
CAPITAL CITIES/ABC, INC.
John E. Frisoli
VICE PRESIDENT, PERSONNEL, CAPITAL CITIES/ABC, INC.
Anita Hecht
VICE PRESIDENT, LABOR RELATIONS,
CAPITAL CITIES/ABC, INC.
Jeffrey Ruthizer

OFFICE OF COMMUNICATION

PRESIDENT, OFFICE OF COMMUNICATION
James E. Duffy
VICE PRESIDENT, OFFICE OF COMMUNICATION
John E. (Jack) Harr

PUBLIC RELATIONS

VICE PRESIDENT, PUBLIC RELATIONS,
ABC BROADCAST GROUP
Richard J. Connelly
VICE PRESIDENT, PLANNING AND VISUAL COMMUNICATION
Rick Giacalone
VICE PRESIDENT, PROGRAM INFORMATION
Tom Mackin
VICE PRESIDENT, PUBLIC RELATIONS, WEST COAST
Bob Wright
DIRECTOR, NEWS PUBLIC RELATIONS, ABC
Carol Olwert
DIRECTOR, NEWS INFORMATION, WASHINGTON
Joyce Kravitz
DIRECTOR, BUSINESS INFORMATION
Jeffrey R. Tolvin
DIRECTOR, VISUAL COMMUNICATION, EAST COAST
Peter Murray
DIRECTOR, VISUAL COMMUNICATION, WEST COAST
Hal Garb
DIRECTOR, COMMUNITY RELATIONS
Jane Paley
MANAGER, NEWSPAPER, PUBLICITY
Vic Ghidalia
MANAGER, ENTERTAINMENT PUBLICITY
David Horowitz
MANAGER, MAGAZINE PUBLICITY
Anne Marie Riccitelli
MANAGER, BROADCAST PUBLICITY
Regina DiMartino
MANAGER, NEWS PUBLIC RELATIONS
Elise Adde

518

MANAGER, COMMUNITY RELATIONS
Janice Gretemeyer Adams
DIRECTOR, PROGRAM PUBLICITY
Rosalind Jarrett
MANAGER, BUSINESS INFORMATION, WEST COAST
Jim Brochu
DIRECTOR, BROADCAST PUBLICITY
Jerry Hellard

LEGAL

SENIOR VICE PRESIDENT AND GENERAL COUNSEL,
CAPITAL CITIES/ABC, INC.
Stephen A. Weiswasser
VICE PRESIDENT, GENERAL ATTORNEY AND DIRECTOR
OF BUSINESS AFFAIRS, ABC NEWS
Samuel Antar

CORPORATE COMMUNICATIONS

VICE PRESIDENT, CORPORATE COMMUNICATIONS, ABC, INC.
Patricia J. Matson
VICE PRESIDENT, CORPORATE PROJECTS
Julie Hoover
DIRECTOR, VIDEO ENTERPRISES AND CORPORATE
COMMUNICATIONS
Roann Rubin

EXECUTIVE AND RESEARCH

VICE PRESIDENT, MARKETING AND RESEARCH SERVICES
Marvin Mord
VICE PRESIDENT, AUDIENCE AND AFFILIATE RESEARCH
Paul Sonkin
VICE PRESIDENT, PRIMARY AND SOCIAL RESEARCH
Henry Schafer
VICE PRESIDENT, MARKET PLANNING AND TECHNOLOGY
RESEARCH
Richard Montesano

BROADCAST GROUP

PRESIDENT
Michael P. Mallardi
PRESIDENT, BROADCAST OPERATIONS AND ENGINEERING
Julius Barnathan
PRESIDENT, ABC VIDEO ENTERPRISES
Herbert A. Granath
PRESIDENT, TELEVISION STATIONS, EAST
Lawrence J. Pollock
PRESIDENT, TELEVISION STATIONS, WEST
Kenneth M. Johnson
PRESIDENT, NATIONAL TELEVISION SALES
John B. Watkins
PRESIDENT, RADIO
James B. Arcara
PRESIDENT, RADIO STATIONS
Don B. Bouloukos
PRESIDENT, RADIO NETWORKS
Aaron M. Daniels

ABC TELEVISION NETWORK GROUP

PRESIDENT
John B. Sias
PRESIDENT, ABC ENTERTAINMENT
Brandon Stoddard
GROUP PRESIDENT, ABC NEWS AND SPORTS, AND
PRESIDENT, ABC NEWS
Roone Arledge
PRESIDENT, ABC SPORTS
Dennis Swanson
PRESIDENT, ABC TELEVISION NETWORK
Mark Mandala
PRESIDENT, ABC COMMUNICATIONS
James E. Duffy
EXECUTIVE VICE PRESIDENT
Robert Iger
SENIOR VICE PRESIDENT, SALES
H. Weller Keever
SENIOR VICE PRESIDENT, AFFILIATE RELATIONS
George M. Newi
SENIOR VICE PRESIDENT, FINANCE
Ann M. Gray
VICE PRESIDENT, OPERATIONS
Mark Roth
VICE PRESIDENT, PUBLIC RELATIONS
Richard J. Connelly

VICE PRESIDENT, PUBLIC RELATIONS, WEST COAST
Bob Wright
DIRECTOR, PROGRAM PUBLICITY
Rosalind Jarrett
DIRECTOR, BROADCAST PUBLICITY
Jerry Hellard
DIRECTOR, PHOTOGRAPHY, ADVERTISING AND PUBLICITY
Tony Rezza
VICE PRESIDENT, BROADCAST STANDARDS AND PRACTICES,
WEST COAST
Brett A. White
VICE PRESIDENT, SALES, WEST COAST
William Harmond

AFFILIATE RELATIONS

SENIOR VICE PRESIDENT IN CHARGE OF AFFILIATE
RELATIONS
George H. Newi
VICE PRESIDENT AND DIRECTOR OF AFFILIATE OPERATIONS
William (Buzz) Mathesius
VICE PRESIDENT & DIRECTOR OF STATION RELATIONS
Bryce Rathbone
DIRECTOR PLANNING AND FINANCIAL ANALYSIS
Arnold Marfoglia

NETWORK SALES

EXECUTIVE VICE PRESIDENT IN CHARGE OF SALES
H. Weller (Jake) Keever
SENIOR VICE PRESIDENT AND NATIONAL SALES MANAGER
John Tiedemann, Jr.
VICE PRESIDENT, MARKETING
Madeline Nagel
VICE PRESIDENT, DAYTIME SALES
Alfred A. Smith
VICE PRESIDENT, SPORTS SALES
J. Larre Barrett
VICE PRESIDENT AND DIRECTOR, SPORTS SALES
James Wasilko
VICE PRESIDENT, NEWS AND EARLY MORNING SALES
Lawrence Fried
VICE PRESIDENT, SALES ADMINISTRATION
Charles C. Allen
VICE PRESIDENT, SPECIAL PROGRAM SALES
Robert Cagliero
VICE PRESIDENT, REVENUE, PLANNING & SALES
ADMINISTRATION
Robert T. Wallen
VICE PRESIDENT, TELEVISION NETWORK SALES, DETROIT
Richard C. Wozniak
VICE PRESIDENT, TELEVISION NETWORK SALES,
WESTERN DIVISION
William A. Harmond
VICE PRESIDENT, TELEVISION NETWORK SALES,
CENTRAL DIVISION
Edward J. Wollock
VICE PRESIDENT, NEWS SALES,
CENTRAL DIVISION, CHICAGO
William C. Gillogly
VICE PRESIDENT, REGIONAL SALES
Ed Ryan
VICE PRESIDENT AND DIRECTOR OF EASTERN SALES
Marvin Goldsmith
VICE PRESIDENT AND DIRECTOR, DAYTIME SALES
Fred Cohen
DIRECTOR, SALES SERVICE, NIGHTTIME
Harold Geary
VICE PRESIDENT, PRIME TIME SALE PROPOSALS
Elaine Chin
VICE PRESIDENT, EASTERN SALES MANAGER
George Cain
DIRECTOR, SALES SERVICE
Tom Mahoney
DIRECTOR, SPORTS MERCHANDISING AND PROMOTION
Al Cohen
DIRECTOR, SALES PROPOSALS AND DEVELOPMENT,
CENTRAL DIVISION
John Saddler
VICE PRESIDENT, SALES MANAGER, CENTRAL DIVISION
Michael R. Rubin

ADVERTISING & PROMOTION

VICE PRESIDENT AFFILIATE MARKETING SERVICES
Paul W. (Pete) Barrett

VICE PRESIDENT, SALES DEVELOPMENT AND CREATIVE
SERVICES
  Chuck Gabelmann
DIRECTOR, ADVERTISING
  Russell Roney
DIRECTOR, STATION ADVERTISING SERVICES
  Alan Morris
DIRECTOR, GRAPHIC DESIGN, SALES DEVELOPMENT
& CREATIVE SERVICES
  Bill Dueuell
DIRECTOR, SALES DEVELOPMENT
  Allen Hirschman

ABC SPORTS, INC.

PRESIDENT, SPORTS
  Dennis Swanson
SENIOR VICE PRESIDENT OF SPORTS PLANNING
& ADMINISTRATION
  Stephen J. Solomon
SENIOR VICE PRESIDENT, PRODUCTION COORDINATION
  Dennis Lewin
VICE PRESIDENT OF ADMINISTRATION AND FINANCIAL
CONTROLS
  Bob Apter
VICE PRESIDENT, OLYMPICS OPERATIONS
  Marvin Bader

CAPITAL CITIES/ABC NATIONAL TELEVISION
SPOT SALES, INC.

PRESIDENT
  John B. Watkins
VICE PRESIDENT
  Philip J. Sweenie
GENERAL SALES MANAGER, EASTERN SALES
  Joseph Cohen
GENERAL SALES MANAGER, NEW YORK
  Ed Pearson
SALES MANAGER, EAST
  Mike Colleran
SALES MANAGER, MIDWEST
  Scott Thomas
SALES MANAGER, SAN FRANCISCO
  Franklin Lowe
SALES MANAGER, WEST
  Mary Webb Ellis
SALES MANAGER, DALLAS
  Mike Irvine
SALES MANAGER, ATLANTA
  Deborah Shay
SALES MANAGER, LOS ANGELES
  Michael Jack
DIRECTOR, RESEARCH SYSTEMS & SALES PLANNING
  Christine McCaughey
SALES MANAGER, BOSTON
  Ted Ryan
SALES MANAGER, CHARLOTTE
  Geralyn Stynes
SALES MANAGER, PHILADELPHIA
  Steve Cobble
SALES MANAGER, ST. LOUIS
  Jerry Lyles

CAPITAL CITIES/ABC-OWNED
TELEVISION STATIONS

PRESIDENT—EAST
  Lawrence J. Pollock
PRESIDENT—WEST
  Kenneth M. Johnson
SENIOR VICE PRESIDENT, BROADCAST GROUP
  Jim Allegro
PRESIDENT AND GENERAL MANAGER, WABC-TV, NEW YORK
  Walter C. Liss
PRESIDENT AND GENERAL MANAGER, WLS-TV, CHICAGO
  Joseph Ahern
PRESIDENT AND GENERAL MANAGER, WTVD,
DURHAM-RALEIGH
  G. Alan Nesbitt
PRESIDENT AND GENERAL MANAGER, KFSN-TV, FRESNO
  Marc Edwards
PRESIDENT AND GENERAL MANAGER, KTRK-TV, HOUSTON
  Paul Bures
PRESIDENT AND GENERAL MANAGER, KABC-TV,
LOS ANGELES
  John Severino

PRESIDENT AND GENERAL MANAGER, WPVI,
PHILADELPHIA
  Rick Spinner
PRESIDENT AND GENERAL MANAGER, KGO-TV,
SAN FRANCISCO
  Len Spagnoletti

ABC VIDEO ENTERPRISES

PRESIDENT, ABC VIDEO ENTERPRISES
  Herbert Granath
VICE PRESIDENT
  John Healy
VICE PRESIDENT AND GENERAL MANAGER
  Archie Purvis
VICE PRESIDENT, INTERNATIONAL DEVELOPMENT
  Phil Boyer
VICE PRESIDENT
  Bruce Maggin
VICE PRESIDENT, FINANCIAL CONTROLS & PLANNING
  Jerry Sullivan
VICE PRESIDENT, GENERAL ATTORNEY & DIRECTOR
OF BUSINESS AFFAIRS
  Larry M. Loeb
DIRECTOR OF FINANCIAL PLANNING
  Robert Wong
DIRECTOR, TELEVISION AND SALES,
ABC PICTURES INTERNATIONAL, INC.
  William Vitale

ABC ENTERTAINMENT

PRESIDENT
  Brandon Stoddard

WEST COAST:

VICE PRESIDENT, CURRENT SERIES PROGRAMS
  John Barber
VICE PRESIDENT, COMEDY & VARIETY SERIES
DEVELOPMENT
  Stuart Bloomberg
VICE PRESIDENT, CREATIVE SERVICES, ON-AIR PROMOTION
  Stuart Brower
VICE PRESIDENT, FILM PRODUCTION, ABC CIRCLE FILMS
  Ted Butcher
VICE PRESIDENT, SPECIAL PROGRAMS
  John Hamlin
VICE PRESIDENT, PRIME TIME MOTION PICTURES
  Ted Harbert
VICE PRESIDENT, TAPE PRODUCTION
  Edgar Hirst
VICE PRESIDENT, DRAMATIC SERIES DEVELOPMENT
  Chad S. Hoffman
VICE PRESIDENT, PRODUCTION
  Herbert Jellinek
VICE PRESIDENT, PROGRAM PLANNING & SCHEDULING
  George Keramidas
VICE PRESIDENT, ADMINISTRATION
& ASST. TO THE PRESIDENT
  Deirdre A. Paulino
VICE PRESIDENT, CASTING
  Donna L. Rosenstein
VICE PRESIDENT, MOTION PICTURES FOR TELEVISION &
MINISERIES
  Allen Sabinson
VICE PRESIDENT, CHILDREN'S PROGRAM SERIES
  Jennie Trias
VICE PRESIDENT, POST PRODUCTION, ABC Circle Films
  Rob Wieland
VICE PRESIDENT, MARKETING
  Mark Zakarin
DIRECTOR, CURRENT SERIES PROGRAMS
  Dennis Burgess
  Stephanie Tuttle
DIRECTOR, COMEDY SERIES DEVELOPMENT
  Cynthia Bell
DIRECTOR, SPECIAL PROJECTS
  Donald Colhour
DIRECTOR, DAYTIME PROGRAMS, WEST COAST
  Geanne Finney
DIRECTOR, COMEDY SERIES DEVELOPMENT
  Kim Fleary
DIRECTOR, ARTIST RELATIONS
  Dottie Gagliano
DIRECTOR, ADVERTISING
  Jill Green
DIRECTOR, BUSINESS ADMINISTRATION
  Karle Koerbling

DIRECTOR, CURRENT SERIES PROGRAMS
  Susan Leeper
  Lowell Mate
DIRECTOR, DRAMATIC SERIES DEVELOPMENT
  Gary Levine
DIRECTOR, PROGRAM ADMINISTRATION
  Hank Miller
DIRECTOR, VARIETY/LATE-NIGHT PROGRAMS
  Launa Newman-Minson
DIRECTOR, SPECIAL PROGRAMS
  Henry Cohen
EXEC. PRODUCER, MOTION PICTURES FOR TELEVISION
  Judd Parkin
EXEC. PRODUCER, MOTION PICTURES FOR TELEVISION
  Wendy Riche
DIRECTOR, CASTING
  Nick Wilkinson
  Robin Stoltz Nassif
EXEC. PRODUCER, ABC NOVELS FOR TELEVISION
& LIMITED SERIES
  Nina Rosenthal
DIRECTOR, CHILDREN'S PROGRAMS
  Ame Simon
DIRECTOR, DRAMATIC SERIES DEVELOPMENT
  Susan Sands
EXEC. PRODUCER, MOTION PICTURES FOR TELEVISION
  Scott Spiegel

BUSINESS AFFAIRS—WEST COAST

SENIOR VICE PRESIDENT, BUSINESS AFFAIRS & CONTRACTS
  Ronald V. Sunderland
VICE PRESIDENT, BUSINESS AFFAIRS
  Barry Gordon
VICE PRESIDENT, BUSINESS AFFAIRS & CONTRACTS
  Alan Kaplan
VICE PRESIDENT, BUSINESS AFFAIRS ADMINISTRATION
  Ronald Pratz
DIRECTOR, BUSINESS AFFAIRS
  Pat Thompson

EAST COAST:
VICE PRESIDENT, EARLY MORNING PROGRAMMING
  Philip A. Beuth
VICE PRESIDENT, DAYTIME PROGRAMS, EAST COAST
  Mary Alice Dwyer-Dobbin
VICE PRESIDENT, MOTION PICTURE POST PRODUCTION
  Andre De Szekely
VICE PRESIDENT, DAYTIME PROGRAMS
  JoAnn Emmerich
VICE PRESIDENT, PROGRAM ADMINISTRATION
  Stephen K. Nenno
VICE PRESIDENT, TAPE PRODUCTION, EAST COAST
  Rod Rodomista
VICE PRESIDENT, LATE NIGHT & CHILDREN'S TELEVISION
  Squire D. Rushnell
VICE PRESIDENT, FINANCE
  P. Thomas Van Schaick
DIRECTOR, EARLY MORNING PROGRAMMING
  Amy Dorn Kopelan
DIRECTOR, DAYTIME WRITER & SERIAL DEVELOPMENT
  Eleanor Timberman
DIRECTOR, DAYTIME CASTING
  Mari Lyn Henry
DIRECTOR, BUSINESS ADMINISTRATION
  Phillip Burnett
DIRECTOR, PLANNING & SCHEDULING, ON-AIR PROMOTION,
EAST COAST
  Frank Cuciti
DIRECTOR, PROGRAM SERVICES
  Judy Ahlborg
DIRECTOR, DAYTIME MERCHANDISING
  Jenny Davis
DIRECTOR, PROGRAM ADMINISTRATION, EAST COAST
  Maureen Domal
DIRECTOR, PRIMETIME CASTING, EAST COAST
  Alexa Fogel
DIRECTOR, CHILDREN'S SPECIALS
  Eda Hallman
DIRECTOR, TAPE PRODUCTION
  William Herlihy
DIRECTOR, DIRECT RESPONSE MARKETING
  Amy Kopelan
DIRECTOR, NON-SERIAL PROGRAMMING AND SERIAL
SUPPORT, DAYTIME PROGRAMS
  Maxine Levinson

DIRECTOR, CURRENT DAYTIME SERIALS, EAST COAST
  Gail Starkey

BUSINESS AFFAIRS: EAST COAST

VICE PRESIDENT, BUSINESS AFFAIRS AND CONTRACTS
  Donal L. Flynn
VICE PRESIDENT, BUSINESS AFFAIRS
  Anthony Farinacci
VICE PRESIDENT, CONTRACTS
  David Sherman
DIRECTOR, MUSIC & MUSIC PUBLISHING
  Ronald Schubert
DIRECTOR, COMPLIANCE/BUSINESS AFFAIRS, EAST
  Peter Rosenberg

ABC NEWS

GROUP PRESIDENT, ABC NEWS & SPORTS
  Roone Arledge
EXECUTIVE VICE PRESIDENT & ASSISTANT
TO THE PRESIDENT
  David Burke
SR. VICE PRESIDENT
  Richard Wald
V.P. & EXECUTIVE PRODUCER, POLITICAL BROADCASTS
  Jeff Gralnick
VICE PRESIDENT OF ABC NEWS FOR PROGRAM
DEVELOPMENT, EXECUTIVE PRODUCER, "20/20"
  Av Westin
VICE PRESIDENT & WASHINGTON BUREAU CHIEF
  George Watson
VICE PRESIDENT AND EXECUTIVE PRODUCER OF ABC'S
"WORLD NEWS TONIGHT"
  William Lord
VICE PRESIDENT, NEWS PRACTICES
  Robert Siegenthaler
VICE PRESIDENT, EXECUTIVE PRODUCER, DOCUMENTARIES
  Pamela Hill
EXECUTIVE PRODUCER, "NIGHTLINE"
  Richard Kaplan

BROADCAST OPERATIONS AND ENGINEERING

PRESIDENT
  Julius Barnathan
VICE PRESIDENT AND GENERAL MANAGER,
BROADCAST OPERATIONS, EAST COAST
  Herbert Kraft
V.P., BROADCAST ENGINEERING
  Max Berry
DIRECTOR, TELEVISION NETWORK OPERATIONS, NEW YORK
  Richard W. Stubbe
VICE PRESIDENT AND GENERAL MANAGER, BROADCAST
OPERATIONS & ENGINEERING, WEST COAST
  Jack Neitlich
VICE PRESIDENT AND DIRECTOR, TV OPERATIONS,
WASHINGTON
  James Truelove
VICE PRESIDENT & DIRECTOR, INTERNATIONAL TECHNICAL
PRODUCTION AND BROADCAST OPERATIONS, PARIS
  Jacques Lesgards
DIRECTOR NETWORKING SERVICES, NEW YORK
  John Gilmore
DIRECTOR OF PRODUCTION SERVICES, NEW YORK
  J. Deet Jonker
DIRECTOR OF TELECOMMUNICATIONS, NEW YORK
  Brent Stranathan
DIRECTOR OF TV OPERATIONS, LOS ANGELES
  Randy Hooper
DIRECTOR OF PRODUCTION SERVICES, LOS ANGELES
  James Kussman
DIRECTOR, EQUIPMENT PLANNING
  Michael Fisher
DIRECTOR, AUDIO/VIDEO SYSTEMS, NEW YORK
  Ben Greenberg
DIRECTOR, ALLOCATIONS AND R.F. SYSTEMS
  Tony Uyttendaele

BROADCAST STANDARDS & PRACTICES

VICE PRESIDENT, WEST COAST
  Brett White

CBS Inc.

51 W. 52 St., New York, NY 10019; (212) 975-4321; 7800 Beverly Blvd., Los Angeles, CA 90036; (213) 852-2345.

BOARD OF DIRECTORS
William Paley, Roswell L. Gilpatric, Franklin A. Thomas, Henry B. Schact, Marietta Tree, Newton N. Minow, Harold Brown, James R. Houghton, James D. Wolfensohn, Michel Bergerac, Walter Cronkite, Laurence A. Tisch, Edson W. Spencer.
CHAIRMAN
William Paley
PRESIDENT & CHIEF EXECUTIVE OFFICER
Laurence A. Tisch
SENIOR VICE PRESIDENT, CORPORATE AFFAIRS
Jay Kriegel
SENIOR VICE PRESIDENT
Edward Grebow
CHAIRMAN, CBS/BROADCAST GROUP
Gene F. Jankowski

CBS ENTERTAINMENT (HOLLYWOOD)

PRESIDENT, CBS ENTERTAINMENT
Kim LeMasters
EXECUTIVE VICE PRESIDENT, PRIMETIME PROGRAMS
Barbara Corday
VICE PRESIDENT, BUSINESS AFFAIRS, WEST COAST
Layne Britton
VICE PRESIDENT, DAYTIME, CHILDREN'S & LATE-NIGHT PROGRAMS
Michael S. Brockman
VICE PRESIDENT, TALENT AND CASTING
Lisa Freisberger
VICE PRESIDENT, TALENT AND GUILD NEGOTIATIONS
Leola Gorius
VICE PRESIDENT, BUSINESS AFFAIRS, MUSIC OPERATIONS
Harry Heitzer
VICE PRESIDENT, BUSINESS AFFAIRS
William B. Klein
VICE PRESIDENT, BUSINESS AFFAIRS, CONTRACT NEGOTIATIONS
Sid Lyons
VICE PRESIDENT, BUSINESS AFFAIRS, ADMINISTRATION
James F. McGowan
VICE PRESIDENT, MOTION PICTURES FOR TV, MINISERIES
Pat Faulstich
VICE PRESIDENT, CBS ENTERTAINMENT PRODUCTIONS
Norman Powell
VICE PRESIDENT, CHILDREN'S PROGRAMS AND DAYTIME SPECIALS
Judy Price
VICE PRESIDENT, VARIETY AND INFORMATIONAL SPECIALS
Fred Rappoport
VICE PRESIDENT, PLANNING AND SCHEDULING
Peter F. Tortorici
DIRECTOR, MINISERIES
Kit Anderson
PROGRAM EXECUTIVE
Joe Bowen
DIRECTOR, MOTION PICTURES FOR TV
Robert Drummel
DIRECTOR, CASTING
Christopher Gorman
VICE PRESIDENT, CURRENT PROGRAMS
Maddy Horne
DIRECTOR, DAYTIME PROGRAMS
Barbara Hunter
DIRECTOR, PROGRAM PLANNING AND SCHEDULING
Carol Lem
DIRECTOR, DRAMATIC PROGRAM DEVELOPMENT
Jonathan Levin
DIRECTOR, MOTION PICTURES FOR TV
Adoley Odunton
DIRECTOR, CASTING
Holly Powell
DIRECTOR, CASTING
Renee Rousselot
DIRECTOR, MINISERIES
Dighton Spooner
DIRECTOR, MOTION PICTURES FOR TV
Larry Strichman
DIRECTOR, ENTERTAINMENT & INFORMATIONAL SPECIALS
Suzan Sosna

CBS ENTERTAINMENT (NEW YORK)

DIRECTOR, PRESS INFORMATION
Enid Moore
VICE PRESIDENT, DAYTIME PROGRAMS, NEW YORK
Laurence A. Caso
DIRECTOR, DAYTIME
Judy Jensen
DIRECTOR CHILDREN'S PROGRAMS, NEW YORK
Carolyn Ceslik
DIRECTOR, DAYTIME CASTING, NEW YORK
Laura Marino

CBS/BROADCAST GROUP (NEW YORK)

PRESIDENT, CBS BROADCAST GROUP
Howard Stringer
SENIOR VICE PRESIDENT, COMMUNICATIONS
George F. Schweitzer
SENIOR VICE PRESIDENT, PLANNING & RESEARCH
David F. Poltrack
VICE PRESIDENT, COMMUNICATIONS
Alice Henderson
PRESIDENT, CBS RADIO
Nancy C. Widmann
PRESIDENT, CBS SPORTS
Neal H. Pilson

CBS/BROADCAST GROUP (HOLLYWOOD)

VICE PRESIDENT, PROGRAM PRACTICES
Carol A. Altieri
VICE PRESIDENT, OPERATIONS, TELEVISION CITY
Charles Cappleman
VICE PRESIDENT, ON-AIR PROMOTIONS, ENTERTAINMENT
Jerold Goldberg
VICE PRESIDENT, MEDIA RELATIONS, WEST COAST
Ann Morfogen
VICE PRESIDENT, ADVERTISING & PROMOTION
Michael Mischler

CBS MARKETING DIVISION

PRESIDENT, CBS MARKETING DIVISION
Thomas F. Leahy
VICE PRESIDENT, ADMINISTRATION
Mary Lou Jennerjahn
VICE PRESIDENT, SALES
Jerome Dominus

CBS AFFILIATE RELATIONS DIVISION

PRESIDENT, CBS AFFILIATE RELATIONS DIVISION
Anthony C. Malara
VICE PRESIDENT & DIRECTOR, AFFILIATE RELATIONS
Scott Michels

CBS NEWS DIVISION

PRESIDENT
David Burke
VICE PRESIDENT, NEWS COVERAGE & OPERATIONS
David Buksbaum
VICE PRESIDENT, NEWS BROADCASTS
Mark Harrington
VICE PRESIDENT & DIRECTOR SPECIAL EVENTS
Joan Richman
DIRECTOR NEWS COVERAGE
Theodore Savalgio

CBS TELEVISION STATIONS DIVISION

PRESIDENT, CBS TELEVISION STATIONS
Eric Ober
VICE PRESIDENT, NEWS ADMINISTRATION & STATION SERVICES
Allen Y. Shaklan
VICE PRESIDENT, SALES; GENERAL MANAGER, NATIONAL SALES & MARKETING
Eglon Simons
VICE PRESIDENT, FINANCE
Carl Wenhold

Children's Television Workshop

1 Lincoln Plaza, New York, NY; (212) 595-3456. (Educational Broadcasting.)
CHAIRMAN—CEO
Joan Ganz Cooney

PRESIDENT—COO
  David V. B. Britt
SENIOR VICE PRESIDENT, CORPORATE AFFAIRS
  Emily Swenson
VICE PRESIDENT, GENERAL COUNSEL AND SECRETARY
  David C. Condliffe
VICE PRESIDENT AND EXECUTIVE PRODUCER
  David D. Connell
VICE PRESIDENT, FINANCE
  Kenneth J. Gruber
VICE PRESIDENT, COMMUNITY EDUCATION SERVICES
  Evelyn P. Davis
VICE PRESIDENT, PUBLIC AFFAIRS
  Fran Kaufman
VICE PRESIDENT, PRODUCTION
  Alfred Hyslop
VICE PRESIDENT AND PUBLISHER, MAGAZINE GROUP
  Nina B. Link
VICE PRESIDENT AND TREASURER
  Wayne W. Luteran
VICE PRESIDENT, INTERACTIVE TECHNOLOGY & SCHOOL
SERVICES
  Robert L. Madell
VICE PRESIDENT, RESEARCH
  Keith W. Mielke
PRESIDENT, CTW PRODUCTS AND INTERNATIONAL
TELEVISION
  William F. Whaley

Columbia Pictures Television

(A unit of Columbia Pictures Entertainment, Inc.)
3300 Riverside Dr., Burbank, CA 91505; (818)
954-6000; 1438 North Gower St., Los Angeles, CA 90028;
(213) 460-7200.
CHAIRMAN AND CHIEF EXECUTIVE OFFICER
  Gary Lieberthal
PRESIDENT
  Scott Siegler
PRESIDENT, SYNDICATION
  Barry Thurston
EXECUTIVE VICE PRESIDENT, DRAMA
  Steven H. Berman
EXECUTIVE VICE PRESIDENT, EMBASSY
  Frances C. McConnell
EXECUTIVE VICE PRESIDENT, BUSINESS AFFAIRS
  Valerie Cavanaugh
EXECUTIVE VICE PRESIDENT, COMEDY
  Frances C. McConnell
SENIOR VICE PRESIDENT, BUSINESS AFFAIRS
  Jan E. Abrams
SENIOR VICE PRESIDENT, SYNDICATION, WESTERN &
SOUTHEASTERN REGIONS
  Meade Camp
SENIOR VICE PRESIDENT, CURRENT PROGRAMS, COMEDY
  Deborah Curtan
SENIOR VICE PRESIDENT, MARKETING
  Michael Zucker
VICE PRESIDENT, SYNDICATION OPERATIONS
  Francine Beougher
VICE PRESIDENT, CURRENT PROGRAMS, COMEDY
  Eduardo G. Cervantes
VICE PRESIDENT, TALENT & CASTING
  Dennis Cornell
VICE PRESIDENT, CORPORATE COMMUNICATIONS/PUBLICITY
  Don DeMesquita
VICE PRESIDENT, BUSINESS AFFAIRS
  Richard Frankie
VICE PRESIDENT, POST-PRODUCTION
  Christine J. Friedgen
VICE PRESIDENT, COMEDY DEVELOPMENT
  Marla Ginsburg
VICE PRESIDENT, BUSINESS AFFAIRS
  Harvey Harrison
VICE PRESIDENT, STUDIO OPERATIONS
  David Holman
VICE PRESIDENT
  Andrew J. Kaplan
VICE PRESIDENT, TAPE PRODUCTION
  Edward Lammi
VICE PRESIDENT, SYNDICATION, EASTERN REGION
  Gary Lico
VICE PRESIDENT, RESEARCH
  David Mumford

VICE PRESIDENT, SYNDICATION, MIDWEST REGION
  John Rohrs
VICE PRESIDENT, MOTION PICTURE SALES AND
ACQUISITIONS
  Leslie Z. Tobin
VICE PRESIDENT, DRAMA DEVELOPMENT
  Jimmy Veres
VICE PRESIDENT, SYNDICATION, EASTERN REGION
  Herbert O. Weiss

Columbia Pictures International Television

(A unit of Columbia Pictures Entertainment, Inc.)
711 Fifth Ave., New York, NY 10022; (212) 751-4400.
PRESIDENT
  Nicholas Bingham
SENIOR VICE PRESIDENT, INTERNATIONAL TELEVISION
SALES
  Michael Grindon
VICE PRESIDENT AND GENERAL MANAGER,
LATIN/SOUTH AMERICA
  Helios Alvarez
VICE PRESIDENT, JAPAN/KOREA
  Toru Ohnuki
VICE PRESIDENT, AUSTRALIA/FAR EAST
  Tony McMullen

Walt Disney Pictures and Television

500 S. Buena Vista St., Burbank, CA 91521; (818)
840-1000. (Programming producer.)
CHAIRMAN OF THE BOARD
  Jeffrey Katzenberg
PRESIDENT
  Richard Frank

TELEVISION DIVISION

SENIOR VICE PRESIDENT—PRODUCTION/DISNEY SUNDAY
MOVIE
  Gary Barton
VICE PRESIDENT—NETWORK TELEVISION DEVELOPMENT
  Grant Rosenberg
SENIOR VICE PRESIDENT—DOMESTIC TELEVISION
DISTRIBUTION
  Robert Jacquemin
EXECUTIVE VICE PRESIDENT—MOTION PICTURE &
TELEVISION PRODUCTION
  Marty Katz
SENIOR VICE PRESIDENT—BUSINESS & LEGAL AFFAIRS
  Bill Kerstetter
SENIOR VICE PRESIDENT—VIDEO
  John Reagan
VICE PRESIDENT—EASTERN OPERATIONS
  Peter Afee
VICE PRESIDENT—TELEVISION PRODUCTION
  Mitch Ackerman
VICE PRESIDENT—PROGRAMMING AND PRODUCTION
  Jamie Bennett
VICE PRESIDENT—INTERNATIONAL VIDEO & PAY TV
  Richard B. Cohen
VICE PRESIDENT—MARKETING
  Ann Daly
VICE PRESIDENT—SALES/DOMESTIC TV
  Richard Goldman
VICE PRESIDENT—POST PRODUCTION, MOTION PICTURES &
TV
  Don Hall
VICE PRESIDENT—BUSINESS AFFAIRS
  Jere R. Hausfater
VICE PRESIDENT—PROGRAMMING & PRODUCTION
  Mary Kellogg-Joslyn
VICE PRESIDENT—TELEVISION ANIMATION
  Michael Webster
VICE PRESIDENT—WORLDWIDE MARKETING
  Carol Black
VICE PRESIDENT—PRODUCTION/DISNEY SUNDAY MOVIE
  Donald Deline
VICE PRESIDENT—CENTRAL REGION/DOMESTIC
TELEVISION
  Larry Frankenbach
VICE PRESIDENT—DOMESTIC HOME VIDEO SALES
  Richard Longwell

VICE PRESIDENT—LEGAL AFFAIRS
David Mayer
VICE PRESIDENT—POST PRODUCTION
David McCann
VICE PRESIDENT—VIDEO PRODUCTION
Pam McKissick
VICE PRESIDENT—TV RESEARCH, SYNDICATION
& NETWORK
Michael Mellon
VICE PRESIDENT—MUSIC
Christopher Montan
VICE PRESIDENT—WESTERN REGION
David Morris
VICE PRESIDENT—SOUTHERN REGION/DOMESTIC TV
Peter Newgard
VICE PRESIDENT—PRODUCTION ESTIMATING & AUDITING
Sandra Rabins
VICE PRESIDENT—CASTING
Gretchen Rennell
VICE PRESIDENT—PAY TV & ACQUISITIONS
Hal Richardson
VICE PRESIDENT—ADMINISTRATION
Anne Waldeck

Eastman Kodak Company

343 State St., Rochester, NY 14650; (716) 724-4000;
1901 W. 22nd St., Oakbrook, IL 60521; (312) 654-5300;
6706 Santa Monica Blvd., Hollywood, CA 90038; (213)
464-6131; 1133 Ave. of the Americas, New York, NY 10036;
(212) 930-8000; 6300 Cedar Springs Rd., Dallas, TX
75235; (214) 351-3221 (Motion Picture and Audiovisual
Products Division offices.)
CHAIRMAN OF THE BOARD & CHIEF EXECUTIVE OFFICER
Colby H. Chandler
PRESIDENT & EXECUTIVE OFFICER
Kay R. Whitmore
VICE CHAIRMAN & EXECUTIVE OFFICER
J. Phillip Samper
GROUP VICE PRESIDENT & GENERAL MANAGER,
PHOTOGRAPHIC PRODUCTS GROUP
Wilbur J. Prezzano
VICE PRESIDENT & GENERAL MANAGER, MOTION PICTURE
& AUDIOVISUAL PRODUCTS DIVISION
Joerg D. Agin
GENERAL MANAGER, MARKETING, AND VICE PRESIDENT,
MOTION PICTURE & AUDIOVISUAL PRODUCTS DIVISION
Leonard F. Coleman

Fox Inc.

P.O. Box 900, Beverly Hills, CA 90213; (213) 277-2211.
Fox Inc. is the parent company of Fox Broadcasting Co.,
Fox Television Stations Inc., Twentieth Century Fox Film
Corporation.
CHAIRMAN AND CHIEF EXECUTIVE OFFICER
Barry Diller
PRESIDENT
Jonathan Dolgen
EXECUTIVE VICE PRESIDENT
Chase Carey
SENIOR VICE PRESIDENT, EMPLOYEE RELATIONS
Dean Ferris
SENIOR VICE PRESIDENT, ADMINISTRATION
Donn Fletcher
SENIOR VICE PRESIDENT, GENERAL COUNSEL
David Handleman
SENIOR VICE PRESIDENT, FINANCE
J. Mark Hattendorf
SENIOR VICE PRESIDENT, BANKING
John Meehan
SENIOR VICE PRESIDENT, BROADCAST OPERATIONS &
ENGINEERING
Andrew Setos
VICE PRESIDENT, CORPORATE COMMUNICATIONS
Michael Binkow
VICE PRESIDENT AND ASSISTANT TO THE CHAIRMAN
Beth Colloty
VICE PRESIDENT, LABOR RELATIONS
Pamela DiGiovanni
VICE PRESIDENT, LEGAL AFFAIRS
Daphne Gronich

VICE PRESIDENT, ASSISTANT GENERAL COUNSEL
Mary Anne Harrison
VICE PRESIDENT, COMPENSATION/BENEFITS
George Litterini

Fox Broadcasting Company

P.O. Box 900, Beverly Hills, CA 90213; (213) 277-2211;
New York office: 40 W. 57 St., New York, NY 10019; (212)
977-5500. Chicago office: 625 N. Michigan Ave., Suite
401, Chicago, IL 60611; (312) 440-0012.
CHAIRMAN AND CHIEF EXECUTIVE OFFICER, FOX, INC.
Barry Diller
PRESIDENT AND CHIEF OPERATING OFFICER
Jamie Kellner
PRESIDENT, FBC ENTERTAINMENT
Garth Ancier
EXECUTIVE VICE PRESIDENT, ENTERTAINMENT
Kevin Wendle
SENIOR VICE PRESIDENT, FINANCE AND ADMINISTRATION
Tom Allen
SENIOR VICE PRESIDENT, PROGRAMMING
Robert Kenneally
SENIOR VICE PRESIDENT, PUBLICITY AND CORPORATE
CREATIVE SERVICES
Brad Turell
VICE PRESIDENT, ON-AIR PROMOTION AND CREATIVE
MARKETING
Bobb Bibb
VICE PRESIDENT, RESEARCH
Andy Fessel
VICE PRESIDENT, ON-AIR PROMOTION & SPECIAL PROJECTS
Lewis Goldstein
VICE PRESIDENT, DEVELOPMENT
Charles Hirschhorn
VICE PRESIDENT, BUSINESS AFFAIRS
Ira Kurgan
VICE PRESIDENT, AFFILIATE RELATIONS—WESTERN REGION
David Ferrara
VICE PRESIDENT, WESTERN SALES
Deborah Myers
VICE PRESIDENT, PROGRAMMING & PRIMETIME
SCHEDULING
Alan Sternfeld
VICE PRESIDENT, LEGAL AFFAIRS
Eric Yeldell
NEW YORK OFFICE
SENIOR VICE PRESIDENT, ADVERTISING SALES
Patricia Mastandrea
VICE PRESIDENT, EASTERN SALES
David Cassaro
VICE PRESIDENT, AFFILIATE RELATIONS, EASTERN
REGION
Gregory Gush
CHICAGO OFFICE
VICE PRESIDENT, AFFILIATE RELATIONS, CENTRAL REGION
Bob Mariano
VICE PRESIDENT, CENTRAL SALES
Larry Widrig

Fox Television Stations Inc.

5746 Sunset Blvd., Los Angeles, CA 90028; (213) 856-
1000.
CHAIRMAN AND CHIEF EXECUTIVE OFFICER, FOX INC.
Barry Diller
PRESIDENT AND CHIEF OPERATING OFFICER
Robert M. Kreek
VICE PRESIDENT, DEVELOPMENT
Stephen Chao
VICE PRESIDENT, LEGAL AFFAIRS
Gerald Friedman
VICE PRESIDENT, CORPORATE AND LEGAL AFFAIRS
Tom Herwitz
VICE PRESIDENT, GENERAL MANAGER—FOX TAPE
Steve McPeek
VICE PRESIDENT, LEGAL AFFAIRS
Muriel Reiss
VICE PRESIDENT, LABOR RELATIONS
Hugo Rossiter
VICE PRESIDENT, PROGRAMMING
David Simon

VICE PRESIDENT AND CHIEF FINANCIAL OFFICER
  Mitchell Stern
VICE PRESIDENT, FIRST RUN PROGRAMMING
  Jake Tauber

FOX TELEVISION STATION GROUP

WNYW/New York—Channel 5, Carolyn Wall gen. mgr.; KTTV/Los Angeles—Channel 11, Robert Morse gen. mgr.; WFLD/Chicago—Channel 32, Cary Jones gen. mgr.; WFXT/Boston—Channel 25, Joseph Robinowitz gen. mgr.; KDAF/Dallas—Channel 33, Gayle Brammer gen. mgr.; WTTG/Washington—Channel 5, Betty Endicott gen. mgr.; KRIV/Houston—Channel 26, Jerry Marcus gen. mgr.

GTG Entertainment

(A partnership formed between the Gannett Co. and Grant A. Tinker.)
9336 W. Washington Blvd., Culver City, CA (213) 202-3260. Organized 1986. (Develops and produces television programs, both entertainment and reality-based.)
PRESIDENT
  Grant A. Tinker
EXECUTIVE VICE PRESIDENT
  Stuart P. Erwin, Jr.
SENIOR VICE PRESIDENT
  Jay Sandrich
SENIOR VICE PRESIDENT
  M.S. Rukeyser, Jr.
VICE PRESIDENT, BUSINESS AFFAIRS
  Richard Katz
VICE PRESIDENT, PRODUCTION
  Jack Clements
BRANCHES
  GTG East/New York; GTG Marketing/New York

The Great American Broadcasting Co.

(Subsidiary is Taft Entertainment)
3330 Cahuenga Blvd., Los Angeles, CA 90068; (213) 969-2800 (Producer).
CHAIRMAN & CHIEF EXECUTIVE OFFICER
  Charles S. Mechen
PRESIDENT
  Sy Fischer
EXECUTIVE VICE PRESIDENT
  Karl Honeystein
SENIOR VICE PRESIDENT, CREATIVE
  Joel Cohen

DIVISIONS INCLUDE:

Cine Guarantors, 3330 Cahuenga Blvd., Los Angeles, CA 90068; (213) 969-2800.
Hanna-Barbera Productions, Inc., 3400 Cahuenga Blvd., Hollywood, CA 90068; (213) 851-5000.
Ruby-Spears Enterprises, 3330 Cahuenga Blvd., Los Angeles, CA 90068; (213) 874-5100.
The Sy Fischer Company, Inc., 3330 Cahuenga Blvd., Los Angeles, CA 90068; (213) 969-2800.
Taft Entertainment Motion Pictures/Keith Barish Prods., 1800 Century Park East, Los Angeles, CA 90067; (213) 551-1911.
Taft Entertainment Television Production, 14144 Ventura Blvd., Sherman Oaks, CA 91422; (818) 905-6644.
Taft Merchandising Group, 415 Madison Ave., New York, NY 10017; (212) 751-1057.
Titus Productions, 211 E. 51 St., New York, NY 10022; (212) 752-6460.

Merv Griffin Enterprises

(A unit of Columbia Pictures Entertainment, Inc.)
1541 N. Vine St., Hollywood, CA 90028; (213) 461-4701.
CHAIRMAN
  Merv Griffin
PRESIDENT
  Robert J. Murphy
VICE PRESIDENT OF MOTION PICTURES AND FILMS FOR TELEVISION
  Peter Barsocchini
VICE PRESIDENT OF GAMES SHOWS AND VARIETY
  Ray Sneath

International Creative Management, Inc.

40 W. 57 St., New York, NY 10019; (212) 556-5600. 8899 Beverly Blvd., Los Angeles, CA 90048; (213) 550-4000. (Representatives of performing and creative talent in the entertainment industry.) A subsidiary of Josephson International Inc.
PRESIDENT
  Jeff Berg

Lorimar-Telepictures Corp.

10202 W. Washington Blvd., Culver City, CA 90232; (213) 202-2000.
CHAIRMAN AND CHIEF EXECUTIVE OFFICER
  Merv Adelson
OFFICE OF THE PRESIDENT
  Dick Robertson, David E. Salzman, Michael Jay Solomon

Lorimar Television

PRESIDENT
  David Salzman
EXECUTIVE PRESIDENT, CREATIVE AFFAIRS
  Leslie Moonves
EXECUTIVE VICE PRESIDENT, BUSINESS & FINANCIAL AFFAIRS
  David Stanley
SENIOR VICE PRESIDENT, NETWORK CURRENT PROGRAMS
  Ken Horton
SENIOR VICE PRESIDENT, NETWORK PRODUCTION
  Robert Rosenbaum
SENIOR VICE PRESIDENT, PUBLICITY & NETWORK PROMOTION & ADVERTISING
  Barry Stagg
SENIOR VICE PRESIDENT, BUSINESS AFFAIRS
  Julie Waxman

Network Television Group

SENIOR VICE PRESIDENT, BUSINESS AFFAIRS
  Irv Sepkowitz
VICE PRESIDENT, CREATIVE AFFAIRS
  Joanne Brough
VICE PRESIDENT, PUBLICITY & ADVERTISING
  Robert Crutchfield
VICE PRESIDENT, SERIES DEVELOPMENT
  David Goldsmith
VICE PRESIDENT, BUSINESS AFFAIRS
  Wilton Haff
VICE PRESIDENT, DAYTIME & CHILDREN'S PROGRAMMING
  Lucy Johnson
VICE PRESIDENT, MOVIES & MINISERIES
  Leslie Moonves
VICE PRESIDENT, NEW YORK STORY DEPARTMENT
  Susan Pollock
VICE PRESIDENT, PRODUCTION
  Robert Rosenbaum

First-Run Television Group

SENIOR VICE PRESIDENT, FIRST-RUN COMEDY DEVELOPMENT
  Bob Jacobs
VICE PRESIDENT, PROGRAMMING
  Jay Feldman
VICE PRESIDENT, PRODUCTION
  Scott Stone

Domestic Distribution Group

PRESIDENT, OFF-NETWORK SYNDICATION
  Pat Kenney
PRESIDENT, FIRST-RUN SYNDICATION
  Jim McGillen
EXECUTIVE VICE PRESIDENT, PERENNIAL SYNDICATION
  Scott Carlin
EXECUTIVE VICE PRESIDENT, MEDIA SALES
  Karl Kuechenmeister
SENIOR VICE PRESIDENT, FIRST-RUN COMEDY MARKETING
  Bob Jacobs
SENIOR VICE PRESIDENT, FIRST-RUN MIDWESTERN SALES
  Mark Robbins
VICE PRESIDENT, PERENNIAL EASTERN SALES
  Rob Barnett

VICE PRESIDENT, OFF-NETWORK NORTHEASTERN SALES
  Tom Byrnes
VICE PRESIDENT, PAY CABLE & FEATURE FILM
SYNDICATION
  Dalton Danon
VICE PRESIDENT, MEDIA SALES
  James Engleman
VICE PRESIDENT, DISTRIBUTION SERVICES
  Roslyn Fisch
VICE PRESIDENT, OFF-NETWORK SOUTHWESTERN SALES
  Bruce Genter
VICE PRESIDENT, NETWORK, OFF-NETWORK & THEATRICAL
RESEARCH
  Garry Hart
VICE PRESIDENT, FIRST-RUN MIDWESTERN SALES
  Jeff Hufford
VICE PRESIDENT, FIRST-RUN EASTERN SALES
  Jeannie Kadow
VICE PRESIDENT, MEDIA SALES
  Peter Kranzler
VICE PRESIDENT, OFF-NETWORK SOUTHEASTERN SALES
  Maury Lanken
VICE PRESIDENT, CREATIVE SERVICES
  Jim Moloshok
VICE PRESIDENT, FIRST-RUN, PERENNIAL & SPORTS
RESEARCH
  Bruce Rosenblum
VICE PRESIDENT, SPORTS MEDIA SALES
  Marc Solomon
VICE PRESIDENT, FIRST-RUN WESTERN SALES
  Tom Straszewski
VICE PRESIDENT
  Peter Temple
VICE PRESIDENT, FIRST RUN EASTERN SALES
  Alicia Windroth

International Distribution Group

SENIOR VICE PRESIDENT, INTERNATIONAL SALES
  Stuart Graber, Jeff Schlesinger
VICE PRESIDENT, INTERNATIONAL DISTRIBUTION SERVICES
  Bonnie Adamson
VICE PRESIDENT, INTERNATIONAL DISTRIBUTION
ADMINISTRATION
  Rosemary Mazzo

MCA Television

(Distributor. A subsidiary of MCA, Inc. as is Universal Television, the production arm. See listing.) 445 Park Ave., New York, NY 10022; (212) 759-7500. 100 Universal Plaza, Universal City, CA 91608; (818) 777-1000.

CHAIRMAN, MCA TELEVISION GROUP
  Al Rush
PRESIDENT, MCA TV
  Don Menchel
PRESIDENT, MCA-TV ENTERPRISES
  Shelly Schwab
SENIOR VICE PRESIDENT, DIRECTOR OF SALES
  Jim Kraus
SENIOR VICE PRESIDENT, MARKETING
  Marc Grayson
SENIOR VICE PRESIDENT, CREATIVE SERVICES
  Mort Slakoff
VICE PRESIDENT, MANAGER OF RESEARCH
  Bert Herbert
VICE PRESIDENT, MIDWEST AREA
  Paul Hoffman
SALES EXECUTIVE, MIDWEST AREA
  Steve Saltman
DIVISION MANAGER, SOUTHEAST AREA
  Jeff McElheney
VICE PRESIDENT, SOUTHWEST AREA
  Tom Maples
VICE PRESIDENT, WESTERN AREA
  Richard Nailling
DIVISION MANAGER, NORTHEAST AREA
  Robert Raleigh
SENIOR VICE PRESIDENT, ADVERTISER SALES
  David Brenner
SENIOR VICE PRESIDENT, SALES DEV. & SPECIAL PROJECTS
  Bobbi Fisher
SALES EXECUTIVE
  Stephanie Beatty

DIRECTOR, ADVERTISER SALES/EAST
  Karen Volkman
EASTERN REGION MANAGER
  Steve Rosenberg
VICE PRESIDENT, RESEARCH & SALES DEVELOPMENT
  Don Micallef
VICE PRESIDENT, PROGRAM DEVELOPMENT
  Ken Arber
DIRECTOR, PROGRAM ANALYSIS & DEVELOPMENT
  Tom Russo
VICE PRESIDENT, CREATIVE SERVICES
  Kate Kelleher
DIRECTOR OF PROMOTION & PUBLICITY
  Gerri Pare
DIRECTOR OF SALES SERVICES
  Steve Teamkin
ASSISTANT DIRECTOR OF OPERATIONS
  Kathy Fenus
WESTERN REGION MANAGER
  Bill Trotter
SOUTHEAST REGION MANAGER
  Charlotte Sweet
SALES EXECUTIVE, WESTERN AREA
  Gary Wendt
VICE PRESIDENT, LEGAL & BUSINESS AFFAIRS
  Sara Rutenberg
VICE PRESIDENT, TV DISTRIBUTION
  Fran Toll
SENIOR VICE PRESIDENT, MCA TV ENTERPRISES
  Lin Oliver
VICE PRESIDENT, SYNDICATION SERVICES
  David Darley
VICE PRESIDENT, SYNDICATION SERVICES
  Bill Vrbanic
DIRECTOR, ADVERTISER SALES/MIDWEST
  Dan Zifkin
MIDWEST REGION MANAGER
  Chris Rovtar
VICE PRESIDENT, INT'L. LEGAL AND BUSINESS AFFAIRS
  Ernie Goodman
VICE PRESIDENT, ADVERTISING, PROMOTION & PUBLICITY
  Bob Crutchfield
DIRECTOR OF PUBLICITY
  Debbie Darr
SOUTHWEST REGION MANAGER
  Steve Hackett
BRANCH OFFICES:
  Atlanta, Chicago, Dallas, New York, Universal City, Toronto, Canada; London, England; Paris, France; Amsterdam, Netherlands; Tokyo, Japan; Sydney, Australia; São Paulo, Brazil; Beirut, Lebanon.

MGM/UA Communications Co.

450 Roxbury Dr., Beverly Hills, CA 90210; (213) 281-4000. Consists of the following companies: United Artists Pictures, Inc., Metro-Goldwyn-Mayer Pictures, Inc., MGM/UA Television Productions, Inc., MGM-UA Distribution Co., MGM/UA Telecommunications, MGM/UA Home Video, Inc., MGM/UA Licensing & Merchandising.

BOARD OF DIRECTORS
  Fred Benninger, Terry Christensen, Willie D. Davis, Ann Getty, Edward A. Horrigan, Jr., Kirk Kerkorian, Arthur G. Linkletter, Frank Rothman, Sidney Sapsowitz, Walter M. Sharp, Stephen D. Silbert, Kenneth L. Trefftzs
EXECUTIVE COMMITTEE
  Fred Benninger, Terry Christensen, Kirk Kerkorian, Frank Rothman, Sidney H. Sapsowitz, Walter H. Sharp, Stephen D. Silbert
CHAIRMAN OF THE BOARD, PRESIDENT & CHIEF
EXECUTIVE OFFICER
  Jeffrey C. Barbakow
EXECUTIVE VICE PRESIDENT
  Kenin M. Spivak
SENIOR VICE PRESIDENT
  Trevor Fetter
SENIOR EXECUTIVE VICE PRESIDENT
  Sidney H. Sapsowitz
SENIOR VICE PRESIDENT—FINANCE AND CHIEF FINANCIAL
OFFICER
  Thomas P. Carson
SENIOR VICE PRESIDENT AND GENERAL COUNSEL—
ENTERTAINMENT
  Karla Davidson

SENIOR VICE PRESIDENT, CORPORATE GENERAL COUNSEL
AND SECRETARY
  William Allen Jones
SENIOR VICE PRESIDENT—LABOR RELATIONS
  Benjamin B. Kahane
SENIOR VICE PRESIDENT—CORPORATE DEVELOPMENT
  Mary M. McCarthy
VICE PRESIDENT AND CONTROLLER
  Kathleen A. Coughlan
VICE PRESIDENT—HUMAN RESOURCES
  Sherry Harris
VICE PRESIDENT AND TREASURER
  Walter C. Hoffer
VICE PRESIDENT—MANAGEMENT INFORMATION SERVICES
  John Sanders
VICE PRESIDENT—CORPORATE LEGAL AFFAIRS
  Sally Suchil
VICE PRESIDENT—TAXES
  Daniel Taylor

MGM/UA TELEVISION PRODUCTIONS, INC.

BOARD OF DIRECTORS
  Fred Benninger, David Gerber, Frank Rothman, Sidney H. Sapsowitz, Walter M. Sharp, Stephen D. Silbert
EXECUTIVE COMMITTEE
  David Gerber, Sidney H. Sapsowitz, Stephen D. Silbert
PRESIDENT
  David Gerber
EXECUTIVE VICE PRESIDENT
  Lynn Loring
SENIOR VICE PRESIDENT—FINANCE
  Thomas P. Carson
SENIOR VICE PRESIDENT AND GENERAL COUNSEL—
ENTERTAINMENT
  Karla Davidson
SENIOR VICE PRESIDENT, CORPORATE GENERAL COUNSEL
AND SECRETARY
  William A. Jones
SENIOR VICE PRESIDENT—LABOR RELATIONS
  Benjamin B. Kahane
SENIOR VICE PRESIDENT—BUSINESS AFFAIRS
AND ADMINISTRATION
  Mark Pedowitz
SENIOR VICE PRESIDENT—TELEVISION PRODUCTION
  Christopher Seitz
SENIOR VICE PRESIDENT—MOVIES AND MINI-SERIES
  Diane Sokolow
VICE PRESIDENT—VIDEOTAPE OPERATIONS
  Dee Baker
VICE PRESIDENT—BUSINESS AFFAIRS
  Susan E. Brooks
VICE PRESIDENT—LABOR RELATIONS
  Ronald M. Bruno
VICE PRESIDENT AND CONTROLLER
  Kathleen Coughlan
VICE PRESIDENT—DEVELOPMENT
  Ellen Endo-Dizon
VICE PRESIDENT—ADMINISTRATION
  Leslie H. Frends
VICE PRESIDENT AND TREASURER
  Walter C. Hoffer
VICE PRESIDENT—CURRENT PROGRAMMING
  Ron Levinson
VICE PRESIDENT—FINANCIAL ADMINISTRATION
  Thomas Malanga
VICE PRESIDENT—SYNDICATION AND SPECIAL PROJECTS
  Mark Massari
VICE PRESIDENT—DEVELOPMENT
  Judy Palnick
VICE PRESIDENT—POST PRODUCTION
  Bruce Pobjoy
VICE PRESIDENT—ADVERTISING, PUBLICITY AND
PROMOTION
  Kim Reed
VICE PRESIDENT—BUSINESS AFFAIRS
  Lorna Shepherd
VICE PRESIDENT—CASTING
  Mary Jo Slater
VICE PRESIDENT—TAXES
  Daniel Taylor

MGM/UA TELECOMMUNICATIONS, INC.

CHAIRMAN AND CHIEF EXECUTIVE OFFICER
  Sidney H. Sapsowitz

PRESIDENT AND CHIEF OPERATING OFFICER
  Norman Horowitz
SENIOR EXECUTIVE VICE PRESIDENT
  Randolph Blotky
EXECUTIVE VICE PRESIDENT—DOMESTIC TELEVISION
DISTRIBUTION
  Richard Cignarelli
EXECUTIVE VICE PRESIDENT—INTERNATIONAL
TELEVISION DISTRIBUTION & WORLDWIDE PAY TELEVISION
  Anthony J. Lynn
SENIOR VICE PRESIDENT—FINANCE
  Thomas P. Carson
SENIOR VICE PRESIDENT AND GENERAL COUNSEL—
ENTERTAINMENT
  Karla Davidson
SENIOR VICE PRESIDENT—FINANCE & ADMINISTRATION
  Jeffrey D. Ivers
SENIOR VICE PRESIDENT, CORPORATE GENERAL COUNSEL
AND SECRETARY
  William A. Jones
VICE PRESIDENT—PAY TELEVISION
  Joseph Abrams
VICE PRESIDENT—EASTERN DIVISION
  Charles Atkins
VICE PRESIDENT—GENERAL SALES MANAGER—DOMESTIC
SYNDICATION
  Robert Corona
VICE PRESIDENT AND CONTROLLER
  Kathleen Coughlan
VICE PRESIDENT—INTERNATIONAL TELEVISION
DISTRIBUTION
  Marion Edwards
PRESIDENT—BUSINESS AFFAIRS
  Myron Dubow
VICE PRESIDENT AND TREASURER
  Walter C. Hoffer
VICE PRESIDENT—MIDWESTERN DIVISION
  Robert Horen
VICE PRESIDENT—BUSINESS AFFAIRS
  William E. Josey
VICE PRESIDENT—WESTERN DIVISION
  Peter Preis
VICE PRESIDENT—DIVISION MANAGER—
SOUTHWEST TERRITORY
  Victoria Quoss
VICE PRESIDENT—MARKETING
  Jack Smith
VICE PRESIDENT—SOUTHEASTERN DIVISION
  Philip Smith
VICE PRESIDENT—TAXES
  Daniel Taylor
VICE PRESIDENT—SALES—EUROPE
(Foreign TV syndication division)
  James R. Wills

MTM Enterprises, Inc.

4024 Radford Avenue, Studio City, CA; (213) 760-5000.
(TV program production)
CHAIRMAN OF THE BOARD
  Mary Tyler Moore
PRESIDENT
  Arthur Price
SENIOR EXECUTIVE VICE PRESIDENT
  Mel D. Blumenthal
EXECUTIVE VICE PRESIDENT
  Tom Palmierei
PRESIDENT, TELEVISION
  Peter Grad
DATE OF ORGANIZATION
  1970

Magno Sound & Video

729 Seventh Ave., New York, NY 10019; (212) 302-
2505. (Full production services)
PRESIDENT
  Ralph Friedman
VICE PRESIDENT
  Robert Friedman
VICE PRESIDENT
  David Friedman

National Broadcasting Co., Inc.

30 Rockefeller Plaza, New York, NY 10112; (212) 664-4444. Registered Telegraphic Address: NAT-BROCAST, NY; West Coast: 3000 W. Alameda Blvd., Burbank, CA 91523; (818) 840-4444.

CHAIRMAN OF THE BOARD, NBC, INC.
John F. Welch, Jr.
PRESIDENT AND CHIEF EXECUTIVE OFFICER
Robert C. Wright
VICE CHAIRMAN
Irwin Segelstein
PRESIDENT, NBC ENTERPRISES
Jerome Wexler
GROUP EXECUTIVE VICE PRESIDENT
Raymond Timothy
GROUP EXECUTIVE VICE PRESIDENT
Robert Butler
PRESIDENT, NBC ENTERTAINMENT
Brandon Tartikoff
PRESIDENT, NBC TELEVISION NETWORK
Pierson Mapes
EXECUTIVE VICE PRESIDENT OPERATIONS AND TECHNICAL SERVICES
Michael Sherlock
GROUP EXECUTIVE VICE PRESIDENT
Robert Walsh
PRESIDENT, NBC RADIO
Randall Bongarten
PRESIDENT, NBC TELEVISION STATIONS
Albert Jerome
PRESIDENT, NBC NEWS
Lawrence Grossman
PRESIDENT, NBC SPORTS
Arthur Watson
EXECUTIVE VICE PRESIDENT & GENERAL COUNSEL
Corydon Dunham
EXECUTIVE VICE PRESIDENT PERSONNEL AND LABOR RELATIONS
Eugene McGuire
EXECUTIVE VICE PRESIDENT CORPORATE COMMUNICATIONS
M. S. Rukeyser
SENIOR VICE PRESIDENT BUSINESS AFFAIRS AND EXECUTIVE VICE PRESIDENT, NBC PRODUCTIONS
John Agoglia
VICE PRESIDENT CORPORATE PLANNING
Ellen Agress
VICE PRESIDENT RESEARCH
William Rubens

EXECUTIVE DIVISION

PRESIDENT AND CEO
Robert C. Wright
EXECUTIVE VICE PRESIDENT
Alfred F. Barber
GROUP EXECUTIVE VICE PRESIDENT
Raymond Timothy
GROUP EXECUTIVE VICE PRESIDENT
Robert Walsh

Corporate Planning

VICE PRESIDENT
Ellen Agress
VICE PRESIDENT, BUSINESS PLANNING
Barbara Watson

NBC Enterprises

PRESIDENT
Jerome Wexler
VICE PRESIDENT, FINANCE & ADMINISTRATION
John Daly
VICE PRESIDENT, INTERNATIONAL SALES
Miguel Perez-Colon
VICE PRESIDENT, BUSINESS AFFAIRS
Susan Beckett

NBC Entertainment

PRESIDENT
Brandon Tartikoff
EXECUTIVE VICE PRESIDENT, PRIMETIME PROGRAMS
Warren Littlefield
VICE PRESIDENT, PROGRAM PRODUCTION
Perry Massey, Jr.
VICE PRESIDENT, MOTION PICTURES FOR TV
Anthony Masucci

VICE PRESIDENT, MINI-SERIES AND NOVELS FOR TV
Susan Baerwald
SENIOR VICE PRESIDENT, EAST COAST, PROGRAM AND PROGRAM PLANNING
Lee Currlin
SENIOR VICE PRESIDENT, SERIES PROGRAMS
Perry Simon
VICE PRESIDENT, PROGRAMS, EAST COAST
David Wedeck
VICE PRESIDENT, COMEDY DEVELOPMENT
David Neuman
VICE PRESIDENT, CASTING
Lori Openden
VICE PRESIDENT, ON-AIR PROMOTION
John Luma
VICE PRESIDENT, CHILDREN'S AND FAMILY PROGRAMS
Phyllis Vinson
VICE PRESIDENT, SPECIALS AND VARIETY PROGRAMS
Richard Ludwin
VICE PRESIDENT, DAYTIME PROGRAMS
Brian Frons
VICE PRESIDENT, GAME PROGRAMS
Joel Stein
VICE PRESIDENT, FINANCE & ADMINISTRATION CONTROL, WEST COAST
Joseph Cicero
VICE PRESIDENT, DRAMA DEVELOPMENT
Dan Filie
VICE PRESIDENT, CURRENT COMEDY PROGRAMS
Vicki Horwitz
VICE PRESIDENT DAYTIME DRAMA
Susan Lee
VICE PRESIDENT, CURRENT DRAMA PROGRAMS
Brian Pike
VICE PRESIDENT, CREATIVE AFFAIRS, NBC PRODUCTIONS
Ivan Fecan
VICE PRESIDENT, FILM PRODUCTION
Charles Goldstein
VICE PRESIDENT, DRAMA DEVELOPMENT
Michele Brustin
VICE PRESIDENT, ENTERTAINMENT PRODUCTION
Timothy Quealy
VICE PRESIDENT, FAMILY PROGRAMS
Winifred White
VICE PRESIDENT, PROGRAM & MEDIA PLANNING
Paul Wang
VICE PRESIDENT, TALENT AND CASTING
Joel Thurm

NBC Network

GROUP EXECUTIVE VICE PRESIDENT
Raymond Timothy
PRESIDENT, NBC-TV NETWORK
Pierson Mapes
EXECUTIVE VICE PRESIDENT, NBC-TV NETWORK
Robert Blackmore
VICE PRESIDENT, FINANCE AND ADMINISTRATION
David Bivins
VICE PRESIDENT, NETWORK POLICY AND PLANNING
George Hiltzik
VICE PRESIDENT, PART PROGRAM SALES
Ron Dobson
SENIOR VICE PRESIDENT, NATIONAL SALES
Larry Hoffmer
VICE PRESIDENT, SALES DEVELOPMENT AND MARKETING
Diane Seamans
VICE PRESIDENT, EASTERN SALES
Richard Plastine
VICE PRESIDENT, SALES DEVELOPMENT
Robert Conrad
VICE PRESIDENT AND GENERAL SALES MANAGER, EAST
Jon Nesvig
VICE PRESIDENT, MARKETING
Robert Niles
VICE PRESIDENT, SPORTS SALES AND MARKETING
James Burnette
VICE PRESIDENT, OLYMPIC SALES AND MARKETING
Bert Zeldin
VICE PRESIDENT, SALES ADMINISTRATION
Joseph Iaricci
VICE PRESIDENT, WEST COAST AND SPECIAL PROGRAMS SALES
Carl Meyer
VICE PRESIDENT, PLANNING AND PRICING
William Caulfield
VICE PRESIDENT, SPORTS SALES
Arthur Miller

VICE PRESIDENT, CENTRAL AND NATIONAL FIELD SALES
Richard Schade
VICE PRESIDENT, DETROIT SALES
John Spain Jr.
VICE PRESIDENT, AFFILIATE RELATIONS AND OPERATIONS
William Kelley
VICE PRESIDENT, AFFILIATE SERVICES
James Ritter
VICE PRESIDENT, AFFILIATE OPERATIONS RELATIONS
John Damiano
VICE PRESIDENT, AFFILIATE RELATIONS, OPERATIONS WITH
AFFILIATE MARKETING
William Fouch
VICE PRESIDENT, AFFILIATE ADVERTISING AND PROMOTION
SERVICES
Martha Stanville
VICE PRESIDENT, SPECIAL PROMOTION PROJECTS
Charles Stepner

Legal

EXECUTIVE VICE PRESIDENT AND GENERAL COUNSEL
Corydon Dunham
VICE PRESIDENT, WASHINGTON, D.C.
Robert Hynes
VICE PRESIDENT, GOVERNMENT RELATIONS
Sallie Forman
VICE PRESIDENT, GOVERNMENT RELATIONS
Terence Mahony
VICE PRESIDENT, WASHINGTON OPERATIONS
Tom Sawyer
VICE PRESIDENT, LAW, NEW YORK
Steve Stander
VICE PRESIDENT, LAW, WEST COAST
Don Zachary
VICE PRESIDENT, LAW, WASHINGTON
Howard Monder
VICE PRESIDENT, LAW BROADCAST ADMINISTRATION
Alan Gerson
VICE PRESIDENT, PROGRAM INFORMATION RESOURCES
Bettye Hoffman
VICE PRESIDENT, BROADCAST STANDARDS, WEST COAST
Maurice Goodman
VICE PRESIDENT, BROADCAST STANDARDS, EAST COAST
Richard Gitter
VICE PRESIDENT, COMPLIANCE & PRACTICES, WEST COAST
Meryl Marshall

News Division

PRESIDENT, NBC NEWS
Michael Gartner
VICE PRESIDENT AND ASSISTANT TO THE PRESIDENT
Timothy J. Russert
VICE PRESIDENT, AFFILIATE NEWS SERVICES
Jo Moring
VICE PRESIDENT, FINANCE AND ADMIN.
Natalie Parks Hunter
VICE PRESIDENT, NEWS EUROPE
Edward Planer (London)
VICE PRESIDENT, NEWS, WASHINGTON
Robert McFarland
VICE PRESIDENT, EDITORIAL PRODUCTION SERVICES
Thomas Wolzien

Operations & Technical Services

EXECUTIVE VICE PRESIDENT
Michael Sherlock
VICE PRESIDENT, ENGINEERING
Steve Bonica
VICE PRESIDENT, OPERATIONS AND TECHNICAL SERVICES,
WEST COAST
Crawford McGill
VICE PRESIDENT, MATERIALS AND SERVICES, WEST COAST
Fred Kigerl
VICE PRESIDENT, BROADCAST OPERATIONS AND
TECHNICAL SERVICES
John Frishette
VICE PRESIDENT, PROGRAM PRODUCTION OPERATIONS
Maurice Corwin
VICE PRESIDENT, OPERATIONS SYSTEMS SOFTWARE
Eric Koopmann
VICE PRESIDENT, SYSTEMS DEVELOPMENT
Rachele Lowenbraun
VICE PRESIDENT, OPERATIONS AND TECHNICAL
MAINTENANCE
Crawford McGill
VICE PRESIDENT, PRODUCTION AND SERVICES
Leonard Lucas

VICE PRESIDENT, PRODUCTION OPERATIONS
Steven Seidenfrau
VICE PRESIDENT, MANAGEMENT INFORMATION SERVICES
Maurice Greenfield
VICE PRESIDENT, MANAGEMENT INFORMATION SERVICES,
WEST COAST
Gerald Reeves
VICE PRESIDENT, FINANCE AND ADMINISTRATION, WEST
COAST
John O'Neill, Jr.
VICE PRESIDENT, MATERIALS AND SERVICES
Anthony Pedalino
VICE PRESIDENT, BROADCAST OPERATIONS
Dave Baylor

Personnel & Labor Relations

EXECUTIVE VICE PRESIDENT, EMPLOYEE RELATIONS, NBC
Edward L. Scanlon
VICE PRESIDENT, EMPLOYEE RELATIONS, WEST COAST
Wayne Rickert
VICE PRESIDENT, LABOR RELATIONS, WEST COAST
Bernard Gehan

Corporate Communications

VICE PRESIDENT CORPORATE AND MEDIA RELATIONS
Elizabeth Hudson
VICE PRESIDENT CORPORATE INFORMATION, WEST COAST
Jay Rodriguez
VICE PRESIDENT, MEDIA OLYMPICS
Alan Baker
VICE PRESIDENT, TALENT RELATIONS & MEDIA SERVICES,
WEST COAST
Kathleen Tucci
VICE PRESIDENT, MEDIA RELATIONS, EAST COAST
Curtis Block
VICE PRESIDENT, MEDIA RELATIONS, WEST COAST
Michael O'Hara
VICE PRESIDENT, CORPORATE AFFAIRS
Robert Cornet
VICE PRESIDENT, ADVERTISING AND PROMOTION
John Miller
VICE PRESIDENT, ADVERTISING AND PROMOTION, EAST
COAST
Tim Miller
VICE PRESIDENT, PRINT ADVERTISING
Jenness Brewer
VICE PRESIDENT, ON-AIR PROMOTION
John Luma
VICE PRESIDENT, AFFILIATE ADVERTISING AND PROMOTION
SERVICES
Martha Stanville
VICE PRESIDENT, SPECIAL PROMOTION PROJECTS
Charles Stepner

Research

VICE PRESIDENT
William Rubens
VICE PRESIDENT PROGRAM RESEARCH
Edward Frank

Sports

PRESIDENT
Arthur A. Watson
EXECUTIVE VICE PRESIDENT
Kenneth Schanzer
EXECUTIVE VICE PRESIDENT, OLYMPICS
Mike Estridge
VICE PRESIDENT PROGRAM PLANNING AND DEVELOPMENT
Sean McManus
VICE PRESIDENT SPORTS NEGOTIATIONS
Bertram Zeldin
VICE PRESIDENT, SPORTS NEGOTIATIONS
Jeff Cokin
VICE PRESIDENT OPERATIONS
Kenneth Aagaard
VICE PRESIDENT FINANCE AND ADMINISTRATION
E. James Greiner
VICE PRESIDENT SPORTS PROJECTS PLANNING AND
BUSINESS DEVELOPMENT
Jarobin Gilbert, Jr.

Television Business Affairs

EXECUTIVE VICE PRESIDENT, NBC-TV BUSINESS AFFAIRS
John Agoglia
VICE PRESIDENT, PROGRAM ACQUISITIONS
Joseph Bures

VICE PRESIDENT, BUSINESS AFFAIRS, PRIMETIME
PROGRAMS
  Gary Newman
VICE PRESIDENT, BUSINESS AFFAIRS
  Leigh Brecheen
VICE PRESIDENT, PROGRAM AND TALENT CONTRACTS
  Jay Goldberg
VICE PRESIDENT, STRATEGIC PLANNING
  Barbara Watson

Television Stations

GROUP EXECUTIVE VICE PRESIDENT
  Robert Walsh
PRESIDENT, NBC TELEVISION STATIONS
  Albert Jerome
VICE PRESIDENT, PROGRAMS
  Weston Harris
VICE PRESIDENT FINANCE AND ADMINISTRATION
  Robert Finnerty
VICE PRESIDENT TV OPERATIONS AND ENGINEERING
  Duffy Sasser II
VICE PRESIDENT, TV STATIONS OPERATIONS AND
ENGINEERING
  Mark Mousky
VICE PRESIDENT, NEWS, TV STATIONS
  Paul Beavers
VICE PRESIDENT, PROGRAMS
  Wes Harris
VICE PRESIDENT, ADVERTISING AND PROMOTION
  Ann Berk
VICE PRESIDENT, SALES
  Bud Hirsch
VICE PRESIDENT, SPOT SALES
  James Zafiros
VICE PRESIDENT AND GENERAL MANAGER, WMAQ-TV
  Robert Morse
VICE PRESIDENT AND GENERAL MANAGER, KNBC-TV
  John Rohrbeck
VICE PRESIDENT AND GENERAL MANAGER, WKYC-TV
  John Llewellyn
VICE PRESIDENT AND GENERAL MANAGER, WNBC-TV
  Carl Carey
VICE PRESIDENT AND GENERAL MANAGER, WRC-TV
  Allan Horlick
PRESIDENT AND GENERAL MANAGER, WTVJ
  Richard Lobo
PRESIDENT AND GENERAL MANAGER, KCNC
  Roger Ogden

NBC Productions

PRESIDENT, NBC PRODS.
  Brandon Tartikoff
EXECUTIVE VICE PRESIDENT, NBC PRODS.
  John Agoglia
SENIOR VICE PRESIDENT, NBC PRODS.
  Don Loughery
VICE PRESIDENT, PRODUCTION OPERATIONS
  Gary Considine
VICE PRESIDENT, PRODUCTION, NBC PRODS.
  William Phillips
VICE PRESIDENT, MEDIA PLANNING, NBC PRODS.
  Gene Walsh
VICE PRESIDENT, CREATIVE AFFAIRS, NBC PRODS.
  Leslie Lurie
VICE PRESIDENT, FINANCE, NBC PRODS.
  Gerard Petry

New World Television

1440 S. Sepulveda Blvd., Los Angeles, 90025; (213)
444-8100. (Producer and distributor)

NEW WORLD TELEVISION GROUP

PRESIDENT AND CHIEF EXECUTIVE OFFICER
  Edward B. Gradinger
EXECUTIVE VICE PRESIDENT & GENERAL COUNSEL
  Peter R. Bierstedt
EXECUTIVE VICE PRESIDENT AND CHIEF FINANCIAL
OFFICER
  Robert A. Stein
VICE PRESIDENT, MARKETING
  Gloria LaMont

NEW WORLD TELEVISION PRODUCTIONS

PRESIDENT
  Jon Feltheimer
EXECUTIVE VICE PRESIDENT
  George Reeves
SENIOR VICE PRESIDENT, CREATIVE AFFAIRS
  Freyda Rothstein
SENIOR VICE PRESIDENT, PRODUCTION
  Lorin B. Salob
VICE PRESIDENT OF PROGRAMS
  Lea Stalmaster
VICE PRESIDENT, MOVIES & MINI SERIES
  Todd Baker
VICE PRESIDENT, DRAMATIC DEVELOPMENT
  Michael Levine
VICE PRESIDENT, CREATIVE AFFAIRS
  Marla Ginsberg
VICE PRESIDENT, TAPE PROGRAMS
  Mary-Ellis Bunim
DIRECTOR, DRAMATIC DEVELOPMENT
  Eric Tannenbaum
EXECUTIVE PRODUCTION MANAGER
  Tony Bishop
MANAGER OF COMEDY DEVELOPMENT
  Debbie Ingram
DEPARTMENT COORDINATOR
  J. B. Lyon
DIRECTOR OF PRODUCTION & BUDGETS
  Al d'Ossche

*NEW WORLD TELEVISION GROUP BUSINESS
& LEGAL AFFAIRS/FINANCE*

EXECUTIVE VICE PRESIDENT, NEW WORLD TELEVISION
GROUP
  George Reeves
SENIOR VICE PRESIDENT FINANCE
  Peter Knepper
VICE PRESIDENT, BUSINESS AFFAIRS
  Neil Shenker
VICE PRESIDENT, BUSINESS AFFAIRS
  Honi Almond
VICE PRESIDENT, LEGAL AFFAIRS
  Karen Magid
VICE PRESIDENT, BUSINESS AFFAIRS
  Sandra Stern
VICE PRESIDENT, BUSINESS AFFAIRS
  Jacquelyn Gail Snyder
DIRECTOR OF PRODUCTION BUDGETS & BUSINESS AFFAIRS
ADMINISTRATION
  Doug Beatty
DIRECTOR, LEGAL AFFAIRS
  Estelle Radin
ASSOCIATE DIRECTOR OF LEGAL AFFAIRS
  Ray Gross
MANAGER, ADMINISTRATION OF LEGAL AFFAIRS
  Karen Ragni

NEW WORLD TELEVISION DISTRIBUTION

SENIOR VICE PRESIDENT/GENERAL SALES MANAGER
  Tony Brown
SENIOR VICE PRESIDENT, INTERNATIONAL DISTRIBUTION
  James McNamara
V.P./NATIONAL SALES MANAGER
  Joe Middelburg
V.P./WESTERN SALES MANAGER
  Jim Weathers
V.P./MIDWESTERN SALES MANAGER
  Monte Lounsbury
V.P./SOUTHEAST SALES MANAGER
  Tony Fasola
EASTERN SALES REPRESENTATIVE
  Frank L. Browne
WESTERN SALES REPRESENTATIVE
  Sandy Lang
DIRECTOR SALES & SERVICE
  Dorothy Hamilton-Corona
MANAGER OF INTERNATIONAL SALES & PROMOTIONS
  Thea Diserio

LEARNING CORPORATION OF AMERICA

CHIEF EXECUTIVE OFFICER
  Robert C. Peters
PRESIDENT
  B. Donald Greene

HIGHGATE PICTURES, INC.

PRESIDENT, LCA/HIGHGATE
Steven Maier
SENIOR VICE PRESIDENT CREATIVE AFFAIRS
Helen Verno
DIRECTOR OF SERIES DEVELOPMENT
Susan Aronson
DIRECTOR OF MOVIES/MINI SERIES
Abby Wolf

NEW WORLD TELEVISION
MARKETING/PUBLICITY/PROMOTION

VICE PRESIDENT, PUBLICITY
Justin Pierce
DIRECTOR OF MARKETING
Gloria Lamont
MANAGER, NATIONAL PROMOTIONS
Mark Shulte

Orion Home Entertainment Corporation

711 Fifth Ave., New York, NY 10022; (212) 758-5100.
CHAIRMAN OF THE BOARD, CHIEF EXECUTIVE OFFICER
Lawrence B. Hilford
EXECUTIVE VICE PRESIDENT
William Bernstein
SENIOR VICE PRESIDENT, GENERAL COUNSEL AND
SECRETARY
Leonard B. Pack
SENIOR VICE PRESIDENT FOR BUSINESS AFFAIRS
Robert A. Mirisch
SENIOR VICE PRESIDENT, CFO & TREASURER
Edwin L. Schwartz
VICE PRESIDENT FOR BUSINESS AFFAIRS
Kimberle A. Aronzon
VICE PRESIDENT, CHIEF ACCOUNTING OFFICER
Lawrence Bernstein
ASSISTANT SECRETARY
John W. Hester
ASSISTANT TREASURER
Richards T. Matthews

ORION TELEVISION, INC.

1888 Century Park E., Los Angeles, CA 90067; (213) 282-0550
CHAIRMAN OF THE BOARD
Eric Pleskow
PRESIDENT
Richard M. Rosenbloom
EXECUTIVE VICE PRESIDENT
William Bernstein
SENIOR VICE PRESIDENT
Gary A. Randall
SENIOR VICE PRESIDENT, BUSINESS AFFAIRS
Robert Mirisch
VICE PRESIDENT, BUSINESS AFFAIRS
Douglass Bergmann
VICE PRESIDENT, DEVELOPMENT
Jeff Wachtel
VICE PRESIDENT
Robert A. Mirisch
VICE PRESIDENT & TREASURER
Edwin L. Schwartz
VICE PRESIDENT, CURRENT PROGRAMS
Ann E. Stich
SECRETARY
Leonard B. Pack
ASSISTANT TREASURER
Richards T. Matthews

ORION TV PRODUCTIONS, INC.

1888 Century Park East, Los Angeles, CA 90067; (213) 282-0550.
CHAIRMAN OF THE BOARD
Eric Pleskow
PRESIDENT
Richard M. Rosenbloom
EXECUTIVE VICE PRESIDENT
William Bernstein
SENIOR VICE PRESIDENT, BUSINESS AFFAIRS
Robert Mirisch
VICE PRESIDENT, POST PRODUCTION
Mick McAfee

VICE PRESIDENT, BUSINESS AFFAIRS
Robert A. Mirisch
VICE PRESIDENT & TREASURER
Edwin L. Schwartz
VICE PRESIDENT, PRODUCTION
Stan Neufeld
VICE PRESIDENT & CONTROLLER
Steven C. Smith
SECRETARY
Leonard B. Pack
ASSISTANT TREASURER
Richards T. Matthews

ORION TELEVISION SYNDICATION

(A Division of Orion Pictures Corporation) 1888 Century Park East, Los Angeles, CA 90067; (213) 282-0550.
CHAIRMAN
Lawrence B. Hilford
PRESIDENT
J. Scott Towle
SENIOR VICE PRESIDENT—SALES AND MARKETING
Larry Hutchings
SENIOR VICE PRESIDENT, BUSINESS AFFAIRS
Robert A. Mirisch
VICE PRESIDENT—SOUTHERN DIVISION
James Ricks, Jr.
VICE PRESIDENT—WESTERN DIVISION
Stephen Mulderrig
VICE PRESIDENT—CENTRAL DIVISION
Donald Frehe
VICE PRESIDENT—EASTERN DIVISION
Thomas Cerio
VICE PRESIDENT OF ADVERTISING, PUBLICITY &
PROMOTION
Robert Oswaks
VICE PRESIDENT, OPERATIONS
Kathy Haynsworth

Paramount Television Group

(A Division of Paramount Pictures Corporation) 5555 Melrose, Hollywood, CA 90038; (213) 468-5000. 1 Gulf & Western Plaza, New York, NY 10023; (212) 333-7600.

TELEVISION GROUP

PRESIDENT
Melvin Harris
SENIOR VICE PRESIDENT, BUSINESS DEVELOPMENT
Alan Cole-Ford
VICE PRESIDENT, CONTROLLER
Mark Lebowitz
VICE PRESIDENT, RESEARCH
Thomas Mazza
VICE PRESIDENT, PLANNING
Jack Waterman

DOMESTIC TELEVISION DIVISION

PRESIDENT, DOMESTIC TV & VIDEO PROGRAMMING
Lucille Salhany
EXECUTIVE VICE PRESIDENT, SALES & MARKETING
Steven Goldman
SENIOR VICE PRESIDENT, ADVERTISING & PROMOTION
Meryl Cohen
SENIOR VICE PRESIDENT, PROGRAMMING
Frank Kelly
SENIOR VICE PRESIDENT, GENERAL SALES MANAGER
R. Gregory Meidel
SENIOR VICE PRESIDENT, BUSINESS AFFAIRS/FINANCE
Robert Sheehan
SENIOR VICE PRESIDENT, BUSINESS AFFAIRS
Vance Scott Van Petten
VICE PRESIDENT, PROGRAMMING
Alan Baker
VICE PRESIDENT, LEGAL AFFAIRS
Thomas Fortuin
VICE PRESIDENT, ADMINISTRATION, SALES—CONTRACTS
Howard Green
VICE PRESIDENT, CENTRAL REGIONAL MANAGER
Dick Montgomery
VICE PRESIDENT, OPERATIONS
Philip Murphy
VICE PRESIDENT, CREATIVE AFFAIRS
Steven Nalevansky

VICE PRESIDENT, SOUTHERN REGIONAL MANAGER
  Al Rothstein
VICE PRESIDENT, PRODUCTION
  Jack Wartlieb
VICE PRESIDENT, EASTERN REGION
  R. Edward Wilson

NETWORK TELEVISION DIVISION

PRESIDENT
  John Pike
EXECUTIVE SENIOR VICE PRESIDENT, BUSINESS AFFAIRS
  Cecelia Andrews
SENIOR VICE PRESIDENT, LEGAL AFFAIRS
  Howard Barton
SENIOR VICE PRESIDENT, CREATIVE AFFAIRS
  Jeffrey Hayes
SENIOR VICE PRESIDENT, DEVELOPMENT
  Paul J. Heller
SENIOR VICE PRESIDENT, PROGRAMS
  John Symes
VICE PRESIDENT, FINANCE
  Gerald Goldman
VICE PRESIDENT, SERIES DEVELOPMENT
  Paul Heller
VICE PRESIDENT, BUSINESS AFFAIRS
  Ronald Jacobson
VICE PRESIDENT, TALENT & CASTING
  Helen Mossler
VICE PRESIDENT, PRODUCTION
  Michael Schoenbrun
VICE PRESIDENT, COMEDY DEVELOPMENT
  Constance Kaplan
EXECUTIVE DIRECTOR OF PRODUCTION
  Tim Iacofano

INTERNATIONAL TELEVISION DIVISION (Bermuda)

PRESIDENT
  Bruce Gordon
VICE PRESIDENT, OPERATIONS
  Joseph Lucas
VICE PRESIDENT, EUROPEAN SALES
  Peter Cary
VICE PRESIDENT, FAR EAST SALES
  George Mooratoff
VICE PRESIDENT, TV SALES, CANADA
  Malcolm Orme
VICE PRESIDENT, LATIN AMERICA SALES
  Ramon Perez

INTERNATIONAL SALES OFFICES

ENGLAND: Paramount TV Ltd., 23 Berkeley House, Hay Hill, London, W1X 8JB, England.
VICE PRESIDENT, EUROPEAN SALES
  Peter Cary
AUSTRALIA: Paramount Pictures Pty., Ltd., Suite 3209, Australia Square, Box 4272 GPO, Sydney, 2001, N.S.W. Australia.
VICE PRESIDENT, FAR EAST SALES
  George Mooratoff
CANADA: Paramount Pictures Corp. Ltd., 146 Bloor Street W., Toronto, Ontario M5S 1M4, Canada.
VICE PRESIDENT, TV SALES, CANADA
  Malcolm Orme
LOS ANGELES:
VICE PRESIDENT, LATIN AMERICA
  Ramon Perez

Public Broadcasting Service

Headquarters: 1320 Braddock Place, Alexandria, VA 22314; (703) 739-5000; New York Office: 609 Fifth Ave., New York, NY 10017; (212) 753-7373; Los Angeles office: 4401 Sunset Blvd., Suite 335, Los Angeles, CA 90027; (213) 667-9289. (A private non-profit corporation providing national programming, distribution, and related services for public TV stations.)

CHAIRMAN
  Alfred R. Stern
PRESIDENT AND CHIEF EXECUTIVE OFFICER
  Bruce L. Christensen
VICE PRESIDENT AND CHIEF OPERATIONS OFFICER
  Neil B. Mahrer
SENIOR VICE PRESIDENT, PROGRAM SUPPORT GROUP
  M. Peter Downey

SENIOR VICE PRESIDENT, GENERAL COUNSEL & CORPORATE SECRETARY
  Paula A. Jameson
SENIOR VICE PRESIDENT, BROADCAST OPERATIONS & ENGINEERING
  Richard R. Green
SENIOR VICE PRESIDENT, POLICY AND PLANNING
  Michael E. Hobbs
SENIOR VICE PRESIDENT, EDUCATION SERVICES
  William T. Reed
SENIOR VICE PRESIDENT, NATIONAL PROGRAMMING & PROMOTION SERVICES
  Suzanne S. Weil
SENIOR VICE PRESIDENT, TREASURER & CHIEF FINANCIAL OFFICER
  Amy S. Fleishman
SENIOR VICE PRESIDENT, ADMINISTRATION & COMPUTER SERVICES
  Eric L. Sass
SENIOR VICE PRESIDENT, DEVELOPMENT
  Michael B. Soper
VICE PRESIDENT, NATIONAL PROGRAMMING & PROMOTION SERVICES
  Daniel C. Agan
VICE PRESIDENT, ADULT LEARNING AND ELEMENTARY/SECONDARY SERVICES
  Dee F. S. Brock
VICE PRESIDENT, NEWS & PUBLIC AFFAIRS PROGRAMMING
  Barry O. Chase
VICE PRESIDENT, PROGRAM ADMINISTRATION & INFORMATION
  Lance W. Ozier

RCA Consumer Electronics Division

Box 1976, Indianapolis, IN 46206; (317) 267-5000. (Set manufacturer.)

GROUP VICE PRESIDENT
  Jack K. Sauter
DIVISION VICE PRESIDENT OPERATIONS
  D. Joseph Donahue
DIVISION VICE PRESIDENT MARKETING
  S. S. Stepnes
DIVISION VICE PRESIDENT PUBLIC AFFAIRS
  F. V. McCann

Rank Cintel Inc.

(Marketing of telecine equipment) PO Box 710, 704 Executive Blvd., Valley Cottage, NY 10989-009, USA; (914) 268-8911; FAX: (914) 268-5939.

EXECUTIVE VICE PRESIDENT
  Colin Brown

Rank Precision Industries

RANK CINTEL LTD.

(Manufacturer of telecine equipment for broadcast and film/tape transfer) Watton Road, Ware, Hertfordshire SC12 OAE. Tel. (Ware) 3939; Telex: 81415; FAX: 0920 60803.

GENERAL MANAGER
  Jack R. Brittain

RANK TAYLOR HOBSON LTD.

(Manufacturer of precision measurement equipment, professional cine lenses and suppliers of industrial thermal imaging equipment) P.O. Box 36, 1 New Star Road, Thurmaston Lane, Leicester LE3 7JQ. Tel: (Leicester) 763771; Telex: 3422338.

MANAGING DIRECTOR
  Christopher Waldron

RANK PRECISION INDUSTRIES Gmbh (West German Office)

(Marketing of telecine equipment and motion picture camera lenses) Postfach 4827, Kreuzberger Ring 6 6200 Wiesbaden, West Germany; Tel: 06121 702495; Telex: 04186175; FAX: 06121 702495.
GESCHAFTSFUHRER
H-U Rathgeber

RANK PRECISION INDUSTRIES S.p.A. (Italian Office)

(Marketing of telecine equipment and motion picture camera lenses) Via Vassallo 31, 20125 Milan, Italy; Tel: 392 688 9451; Telex: 330362; FAX: 392 607 0180.
DIRECTOR AND GENERAL MANAGER
A. Resasco

RANK PRECISION INDUSTRIES, INC. (U.S. Office)

(Marketing of motion picture camera lenses) 411 East Jarvis Ave., Des Plaines, IL 60018; Tel: (312) 699-0581; Telex: 23 726441; FAX: (312) 699-0581.
PRESIDENT
John Campbell

RANK PRECISION INDUSTRIES MARKETING Ges.m.b.H. (Austrian Office)

(Marketing of telecine equipment) Amalienstrasse 68, A-1130 Wien-Austria; Tel: 43 222 825571; FAX: 43 222 82557116.
GESCHAFTSFUHRER
Eric Pelz

RANK TAYLOR HOBSON K.K. (Japanese Office)

(Marketing of professional cine lenses) Kokudokan Buildings, 9-13, 4-chome, Chuo-Ku, Ginza, Tokyo 336, Japan; Tel: 813 545 1451; Telex: 7227684; FAX: 813 545 6522.
PRESIDENT
K. Fujimoto

International Division

STRAND LIGHTING, INC.

(Marketing of lighting and lighting control equipment) 18111 Santa Fe Ave., Rancho Dominquez, CA 90221; (213) 637-7500; FAX: (213) 632-5519; Telex: 200473.
PRESIDENT
W.J. Griffiths (Temporary)

RANK STRAND LTD. (U.K. Office)

(Manufacturer of lighting and lighting control equipment) Grant Way, Off Syon Lane, Isleworth, Middx: TW7 5QD. Tel: 01 560 3171; Telex: 27976; FAX: 01 568 2103.
MANAGING DIRECTOR
Oliver Hartreee

STRAND LIGHTING PTY. LTD. (Australian Office)

(Marketing of lighting and lighting control equipment) 264-270 Normanby Road, South Melbourne, Victoria 3205, Australia; Tel: 0106 3 646 4522; FAX: 0106 13 646 5020; Telex: 34732.
GENERAL MANAGER
I. Haddon

STRAND LIGHTING CANADA LIMITED (Canadian Office)

(Marketing of lighting and lighting control equipment) 6490 Viscount Road, Mississauga, Ont. L4V 1H3, Canada; (416) 677-7130; Telex: 06968646; FAX: 0101 416 677 6859.
PRESIDENT
Mrs. D. Appleton

STRAND LIGHTING FRANCE S.A. (French Office)

(Marketing of lighting and lighting control equipment) 26 Villa des Fleurs, 92400 Courbevoie, France; Tel: 010 331 478 86666; FAX: 010 331 433 37175; Telex: 214593.
GENERAL MANAGER
B. Bouchet

STRAND LIGHTING ASIA LIMITED (Hong Kong Office)

(Marketing of lighting and lighting control equipment) 802 Houston Centre, 63 Mody Road, Tsimshatsui East, Kowloon, Hong Kong; Tel: 010 852 3 685161; Telex: 449553; FAX: 010 852 3 694890.
MANAGING DIRECTOR
P. O'Donnel

STRAND LIGHTING S.p.A. (Italian Office)

(Marketing of lighting and lighting control equipment) 00137 Roma, 80 Via Cermenati, Italy; Tel: 010 396 6120241; FAX: 010 396 8171845.
MANAGING DIRECTOR
A. Rossi

STRAND LIGHTING GmbH (West German Office)

(Marketing of lighting and lighting control equipment) P.O. Box 4449, 3300 Braunschweig, West Germany; Tel: 010 49 5331 7951; Telex: 95641; FAX: 010 49 5331 78883.
GENERAL MANAGER
H.J. Fritz

Republic Pictures Corporation

12636 Beatrice St., P.O. Box 66930, Los Angeles, CA 90066-0930; (213) 306-4040; Telex/Twx: 910-343-7417.
CHAIRMAN OF THE BOARD
Russell Goldsmith
PRESIDENT
Charles W. Larsen
VICE PRESIDENT
Stephen P. Beeks
VICE PRESIDENT—ACQUISITIONS
Sidney Levine
VICE PRESIDENT—FINANCE & CONTROLLER
David Kirchheimer
VICE PRESIDENT, INTERNATIONAL SALES
Joe Levinsohn
VICE PRESIDENT—MARKETING
Vallery Kountze
CANADA: Kaleidoscope Entertainment, Inc./Randy Zalken, pres., 101 Duncan Mill Road, Suite 102, Don Mills, Ontario, M3B 1Z3.
UNITED KINGDOM & SELECTED PORTIONS OF WESTERN EUROPE: TV Programmes International, Ltd./Bernard Shaw, sales repr., 21 Cherry Garden Lane, Folkestone, Kent, England. Telephone: 303-76897; Telex: 966560 SHAW TV.
GREECE AND BALKANS: 46 King Constantine Ave./Panos Spyropoulos, sales repr., Athens, 516 Greece. Telephone: 7224-243/7234-896; Telex: 221880 APOL GR.
TURKEY: Umut Sanat Urunleri/Seher Karabol, sales repr., Istiklal Caddesi Lale Han No. 87/6, Beyoglu, Istanbul, Turkey. Telephone: 149-77-35/143-44-39, Telex: 23359 BOTX TR.
AUSTRIA: Post Box 192, Postamt 1140, Vienna, Austria, Mounir J. Chammas, sales rep.

Sony Corp. of America

One Sony Dr., Park Ridge, NJ 07656; (201) 930-1000.
(Set manufacturer)
PRESIDENT, SONY CORP. OF AMERICA
Neil Vander Dussen
PRESIDENT, SONY COMMUNICATIONS PRODUCTS CO.
Richard Wheeler
PRESIDENT, SONY MAGNETIC PRODUCTS COMPANY
John Hollands
PRESIDENT, SONY CONSUMER AUDIO PRODUCTS CO.
Thomas Harvey
PRESIDENT, SONY CONSUMER VIDEO PRODUCTS CO.
Shinichi Takagi
PRESIDENT, SONY CONSUMER DISPLAY PRODUCTS CO.
Michael Heil
PRESIDENT, SONY CONSUMER SALES CO.
John Briesch
PRESIDENT, SONY INFORMATION SYSTEMS CO.
Henry Klerx

Twentieth Century Fox Television Division

P.O. Box 900, Beverly Hills, CA 90213; (213) 277-2211. A
division of Twentieth Century Fox Film Corp.

TELEVISION DIVISION
PRESIDENT, TWENTIETH CENTURY FOX TELEVISION
DIVISION
Jonathan Dolgen

TELEVISION PRODUCTION
PRESIDENT, TELEVISION PRODUCTION
Harris L. Katleman
EXECUTIVE VICE PRESIDENT, TV BUSINESS AFFAIRS
David Freedman
SENIOR VICE PRESIDENT, PRODUCTION AND FINANCE
Charles Goldstein
EXECUTIVE VICE PRESIDENT, CREATIVE AFFAIRS
Dayna A. Kalins
SENIOR VICE PRESIDENT, BUSINESS AFFAIRS
Larry Jones
VICE PRESIDENT, TELEVISION POST—PRODUCTION
James A. (Skip) Lusk
VICE PRESIDENT, CURRENT PROGRAMMING
Stephen Gelber
VICE PRESIDENT, PRODUCTION MANAGEMENT
Bob Gros
VICE PRESIDENT, BUSINESS AFFAIRS
David Robinson
VICE PRESIDENT, TAPE PRODUCTION
Joel Hornstock
VICE PRESIDENT, LEGAL AFFAIRS
Walter Swanson

DOMESTIC SYNDICATION
PRESIDENT, DOMESTIC SYNDICATION
Michael J. Lambert
SENIOR VICE PRESIDENT, ADMINISTRATION AND
OPERATIONS, TELEVISION OPERATIONS
Leonard J. Grossi
SENIOR VICE PRESIDENT, SALES, DEVELOPMENT AND
FEATURE FILM PLANNING
Joseph Greene
SENIOR VICE PRESIDENT, SALES, EASTERN DIVISION
Daniel Greenblatt
SENIOR VICE PRESIDENT, SALES, WESTERN DIVISION
Anthony Bauer
VICE PRESIDENT, BUSINESS AFFAIRS
Benson H. Begun
VICE PRESIDENT, LEGAL AFFAIRS
David Grant
VICE PRESIDENT, CREATIVE SERVICES
Frank Bierman
VICE PRESIDENT, CREATIVE SERVICES
Cynthia Lieberman
VICE PRESIDENT, RESEARCH
Steve Leblang
VICE PRESIDENT, ADMINISTRATIVE AND STRATEGIC
PLANNING
Alan Winters
VICE PRESIDENT, WESTERN DIVISION
John J. Campagnolo

SALES EXECUTIVE WESTERN DIVISION
Timothy Mudd
VICE PRESIDENT, MIDWEST SALES
Matthew F. Jacobson
VICE PRESIDENT, SOUTHEASTERN DIVISION
Michael Newsom
VICE PRESIDENT, SOUTHWESTERN DIVISION
Vic Zimmerman
DIRECTOR, DOMESTIC SALES AND CLEARANCES
Barbara Van Buskirk
DIRECTOR, PLANNING & ADMINISTRATION
Diana Ritchie
MANAGER, STATION RELATIONS
Wendy Ehrlich
MANAGER, CREATIVE SERVICES
Tanya Neimark

INTERNATIONAL SYNDICATION
EXECUTIVE VICE PRESIDENT, INTERNATIONAL
SYNDICATION
William Saunders
VICE PRESIDENT, AUSTRALIA AND FAR EAST TERRITORIES
Peter Broome
VICE PRESIDENT, LATIN AMERICA
Elie Wahba
VICE PRESIDENT, TELEVISION SALES—EUROPE
Malcolm Vaughan
SALES MANAGER, MEXICO
Gustavo Montaudon
SALES MANAGER, LONDON
Steve Cornish
SALES MANAGER, FRANCE
Gilles Meunier

VIDEO AND PAY TELEVISION
SENIOR VICE PRESIDENT, VIDEO AND PAY TELEVISION
Jim Griffiths
VICE PRESIDENT, PAY TV SALES
George Krieger
VICE PRESIDENT, WORLDWIDE NON-THEATRICAL SALES
Sam Weinstein

BRANCH OFFICES
- NEW YORK: 40 W. 57 St., New York, NY 10019; (212) 977-5500;
  Joseph Greene, sr. v.p., domestic syndication; Ted Baker, North-
  eastern division sls. mgr. Harry Mulford, v.p, natl. sls.
- CHICAGO: 35 E. Wacker Dr., Suite 1234, Chicago, Illinois 60601;
  (312) 372-1589; Dennis Juravic, central division v.p.
- DALLAS: 11551 Forest Central Dr., Suite 300, Dallas, Texas 75243;
  (214) 343-9252; Al Shore, southwestern division v.p.
- ATLANTA: 2200 Century Parkway, Suite 560, Atlanta, Georgia
  30345; (404) 634-0011; Michael Newson, southeastern division v.p.
- LOS ANGELES: Box 900, Beverly Hills, California 90213; (213)
  203-2841; Tony Bauer, western division v.p.

FOREIGN SALES OFFICES:
Twentieth Century-Fox France, Inc., 114 Rue la Boetie, 75008, Paris,
France. Gilles Meunier, sales mgr.
Twentieth Century-Fox Film Company, Ltd., 31-32 Soho Square, Lon-
don, W1V 6AP, England. Malcolm Vaughn, vice president, United King-
dom, Europe Middle/Near East and Africa. Stephen Cornish, sls. mgr.
Twentieth Century-Fox Film Corp. (Australia), P.O. Box Q301, Queen
Victoria Building, Sydney 2000, Australia. Peter Broome, vice president,
Australia Far East. Paul Herbert, sls. mgr.
Twentieth Century-Fox Far East, Inc., Fukide Building, 1-13
Toranomon 4, Chome Minato-Ku, Tokyo 105, Japan. Goro Uzaki tv sls.
rep.
Fox Interamericana, S.A., Apartado 6-1023, Mexico, D.F. 06600
Gustavo Montaudon, sls. mgr.
Fox Film do Brazil, S.A.–TV Division, Rua Dr. Costa Jr. 230 C.E.P.,
05002 São Paulo, Brazil. Elie Wahba, v.p., Latin America.

Universal Television

(A division of Universal City Studios Inc, a subsidiary of
MCA Inc.)
Universal City Studios, Universal City, CA 91608; (213)
985-4321. (Producer of TV programs)
PRESIDENT, UNIVERSAL TELEVISION
Kerry McCluggage
EXECUTIVE VICE PRESIDENT, ADMINISTRATION
Ed Masket
EXECUTIVE VICE PRESIDENT IN CHARGE OF PRODUCTION
Earl Bellamy

EXECUTIVE VICE PRESIDENT, CREATIVE AFFAIRS
  Richard Lindheim
VICE PRESIDENT, CURRENT PROGRAMMING
  Garrett Hart
VICE PRESIDENT, DRAMATIC DEVELOPMENT
  Charmaine Balian
VICE PRESIDENT, PUBLICITY, PROMOTION AND
ADVERTISING
  Robert Crutchfield
VICE PRESIDENT, TELEVISION CASTING
  Joan Sittenfield
VICE PRESIDENT, TELEVISION CASTING/SERIES
  Mark Malis
VICE PRESIDENT, COMEDY DEVELOPMENT
  Brad Johnson
VICE PRESIDENT, COMEDY PROGRAMS
  Barbara Romen
VICE PRESIDENT, BUSINESS AFFAIRS
  Robert Kelley
VICE PRESIDENT, BUSINESS AFFAIRS
  Paul Miller
VICE PRESIDENT, BUSINESS AFFAIRS
  Arnold Shane
VICE PRESIDENT, TALENT DEVELOPMENT & ACQUISITIONS
  Pete Terranova
VICE PRESIDENT, MOVIES FOR TELEVISION
  Tom Thayer
VICE PRESIDENT, TELEVISION PRODUCTION MANAGEMENT
  Ralph Sariego

Univision Holdings, Inc.

330 Madison Ave., 26th floor, New York, NY 10017; (212) 983-8500. (Producers of Spanish-language programming for television; has 450 satellite interconnected TV affiliates and 6 non-connected TV affiliates.)

PRESIDENT & CHIEF EXECUTIVE OFFICER
  William Grimes
MANAGER, CORPORATE OFFICE
  William D. Stiles
SENIOR VICE PRESIDENT, DIRECTOR OF SALES &
MARKETING
  Browning Holcombe, Jr.
SENIOR VICE PRESIDENT, BUSINESS DEVELOPMENT
  Blaine Decker
VICE PRESIDENT, PROGRAM DIRECTOR
  Rosita Peru
VICE PRESIDENT, NEWS DIRECTOR
  Guillermo Martinez

Warner Bros. Television

4000 Warner Blvd., Burbank CA 91522; (818) 954-6000. 75 Rockefeller Plaza, New York, NY 10019; (212) 484-8000.

TELEVISION PROGRAMMING

PRESIDENT
  Harvey Shephard
EXECUTIVE VICE PRESIDENT
  Barry M. Meyer
VICE PRESIDENT, SPECIAL PROJECTS
  Karen Cooper Minnides
SENIOR VICE PRESIDENT, BUSINESS AFFAIRS
  Art Stolnitz
SENIOR VICE PRESIDENT, CREATIVE AFFAIRS
  Larry Lyttle
VICE PRESIDENT, SENIOR ADVERTISING, PUBLICITY &
PROMOTION EXECUTIVE
  Doug Duitsman
SENIOR VICE PRESIDENT, PRODUCTION
  Gary Credle
VICE PRESIDENT, MOVIES FOR TELEVISION AND MINI-
SERIES
  Norman Stephens
VICE PRESIDENT, CURRENT PROGRAMMING
  David Sacks
VICE PRESIDENT, MOVIES & MINISERIES
  Gregg Maday
  Jane Rosenthal
VICE PRESIDENT, COMEDY DEVELOPMENT
  Scott Kaufer

VICE PRESIDENT, MOVIES & MINI-SERIES DEVELOPMENT
  Elly Sidel
VICE PRESIDENT, TALENT
  Phyllis Huffman
VICE PRESIDENTS, BUSINESS AFFAIRS
  Beverly Nix, Joe Reilly, Art Horan
VICE PRESIDENT, LEGAL AFFAIRS
  Milt Segal
VICE PRESIDENT, FILM & TAPE PRODUCTION
  Steve Papazian
VICE PRESIDENT, POST PRODUCTION
  Karen Pingitore
VICE PRESIDENT, PRODUCTION & OPERATIONS
  Tom Treloggen
VICE PRESIDENT, STORY & VOCATIONAL ADMINISTRATION
  Gus Blackmon
DIRECTOR, PUBLICITY, PROMOTION & ADVERTISING
  Claire Lee
DIRECTOR, FINANCIAL ADMINISTRATION
  Rosalee Jeffries
DIRECTOR, TV ESTIMATING
  Mike McKnight
DIRECTOR, TALENT
  Kathleen Letterie
DIRECTOR, DRAMA DEVELOPMENT
  Susan Horowitz
DIRECTOR, COMEDY DEVELOPMENT
  David Himelfarb
DIRECTOR, CURRENT PROGRAMMING
  Shelley Raskov

NETWORK FEATURES, PAY TV & ANIMATION
(WARNER BROS. CARTOONS, INC.)

75 Rockefeller Plaza, New York, NY 10019; (212) 484-8000.

PRESIDENT & PRESIDENT, WARNER BROS. ANIMATION
  Edward Bleier
VICE PRESIDENT, PAY TV SALES & ADMINISTRATION
  Stanley Solson
VICE PRESIDENT, MARKETING
  Eric Frankel
DIRECTOR, FINANCIAL AFFAIRS
  J. T. Shadoan
DIRECTOR, CLIENT SERVICES, PAY TV & NETWORK
  Margaret Jelcich

DOMESTIC DISTRIBUTION

PRESIDENT WORLDWIDE DISTRIBUTION
  Charles D. McGregor
EXECUTIVE VICE PRESIDENT, WORLDWIDE OPERATIONS
  Mauro A. Sardi
VICE PRESIDENT, DOMESTIC SALES MANAGER
  William S. Hart
VICE PRESIDENT, WESTERN SALES
  Ed Donaldson
VICE PRESIDENT, SOUTHERN SALES
  Bill Seiler
VICE PRESIDENT, MIDWESTERN SALES
  John Louis
EASTERN SALES DIRECTOR
  Gary Cozen
NORTH CENTRAL SALES DIRECTOR
  John Laing
VICE PRESIDENT RESEARCH
  Paul Simon
VICE PRESIDENT, ADVERTISING, PROMOTION AND
PUBLICITY
  Ken Fournier
VICE PRESIDENT, FINANCIAL ADMINISTRATION
  John Chickering
DIRECTOR PRODUCT COORDINATION
  Dee Eulberg
VICE PRESIDENT, DOMESTIC SALES CONTRACTS
  Dan McRae
DIRECTOR PUBLICITY & PROMOTION
  Sharon Kneller
DOMESTIC SALES ADMINISTRATION
  Eleanor Liebs

WARNER BROS. ANIMATION, INC.

4000 Warner Blvd., Burbank, CA 91522; (818) 954-3713.

VICE PRESIDENT, GENERAL MANAGER
  Steven Greene

VICE PRESIDENT, PRODUCTION
Kathleen Helppie

BOOKING & SERVICES DEPARTMENT

New York: 630 Ninth Avenue, New York, NY 10036; (212) 484-8000.
TECHNICAL SERVICE DIRECTOR
Erwin Markisch
MANAGER, BOOKING SERVICES
Joe Kivlehan
MANAGER, PROGRAM INFORMATION
Louis B. Marino
ASSISTANT TECHNICAL SERVICE MANAGER
Bruce Hoffman

BRANCH OFFICES:

Covington: Lowe Davis Rd., P.O. Box 999, Covington, LA 70434; (504) 892-2703.
VICE PRESIDENT, SOUTHEASTERN SALES DIRECTOR
Bill Seiler

Los Angeles: 143 Patricia Way, P.O. Box 2749, Grass Valley, CA 95945; (916) 272-5343.

Ft. Mitchell: 3058 Brookwood Circle, Ft. Mitchell, KY 41017; (606) 341-2585.
VICE PRESIDENT, MIDWESTERN SALES
John H. Louis

Chicago: 4000 Warner Blvd., Burbank, CA 91522; (818) 954-6097.
NORTH CENTRAL SALES DIRECTOR
John Laing

Pennsylvania: 50 Belmont Ave., Apt. 316, Bala Cynwyd, PA 19004; (215) 664-7307.
EASTERN SALES DIRECTOR
Gary Cozen

FOREIGN DISTRIBUTION

Warner Bros. TV Distribution, 4000 Warner Blvd., Burbank, CA 91522.
EXECUTIVE VICE PRESIDENT, WORLDWIDE OPERATIONS
Mauro A. Sardi
VICE PRESIDENT, INTERNATIONAL SALES AND ADMINISTRATION
John Whitesell
INTERNATIONAL SALES
John Laing
VICE PRESIDENT PRODUCT COORDINATION
Dee Eulberg
VICE PRESIDENT, FINANCIAL ADMINISTRATION
John Chickering
VICE PRESIDENT, RESEARCH
Paul Simon
VICE PRESIDENT, ADVERTISING, PROMOTION AND PUBLICITY
Ken Fournier
DIRECTOR, INTERNATIONAL CONTRACTS
Jaime Ruiz
INTERNATIONAL ADMINISTRATION
Carolyn Hewitt
DIRECTOR PUBLICITY & PROMOTION
Sharon Kneller
INTERNATIONAL RECORDS & DATA
Charlene Pollock
BOOKING & SERVICES DEPT. serviced through New York office at 630 Ninth Ave., New York, NY 10036. For staff see personnel under domestic distribution at that address.

FOREIGN SALES OFFICES

EUROPE, MIDDLE EAST & AFRICA: 135/141 Wardour St., London W1V 4AP, England.
VICE PRESIDENT SALES & ADMINISTRATION
Bryan Hambleton
ASSISTANT DIRECTOR SALES & ADMINISTRATION
Gary Phillips
SALES REPRESENTATIVE
Kevin Williams

FRENCH SPEAKING TERRITORIES: 20 Rue Troyon, 75017 Paris, France.
VICE PRESIDENT, TELEVISION
Michel Lecourt

AUSTRALIA, NEW ZEALAND & SOUTHEAST ASIA: 154 Castlereagh St.—5th floor, Alfred Moss House, Sydney, N.S.W., 2000 Australia, Box 2661, G.P.O. Sydney, N.S.W., 2001 Australia.
SALES DIRECTOR
Matt Brown

JAPAN: P.O. Box 762, Tokyo Central, Japan.
TELEVISION SALES
Ken Sugizaki

LATIN AMERICA: Acapulco 37, Mexico 7 D.F., Mexico.
VICE PRESIDENT SALES
Jorge Sanchez

BRAZIL: Warner Bros. (South) Inc., Rua Senador Dantas, 19-10 Andar, Rio de Janeiro, Brazil.
BRAZIL TELEVISION SUPERVISOR
Louremerg do Nascimento

ARGENTINA: Tucuman 1938, Buenos Aires, Argentina.
TELEVISION MANAGER
Luis D'Alterio

CANADA: Warner Bros. Distributing, (Canada) Ltd., 70 Carlton St., Toronto, Ontario, Canada, M5B 1L7; (416) 922-5145.

William Morris Agency, Inc.

1350 Ave. of the Americas, New York, NY 10019; (212) 586-5100. Beverly Hills Office: 151 El Camino, Beverly Hills, CA 90212; (213) 274-7451. Nashville Office: 2325 Crestmoor Rd., Nashville, TN 37215; (615) 385-0310. Overseas offices: London, Rome,* Sydney* & Munich.* (Representatives for artists and all creative talent in the entertainment and literary worlds.) *Corresponding offices.

OFFICE OF THE CHAIRMEN
Norman Brokaw (Beverly Hills), Lou Weiss (New York)
PRESIDENT
Lee Stevens (New York)
EXECUTIVE VICE PRESIDENTS
Roger Davis, Tony Fantozzi, Walt Zifkin
VICE PRESIDENT, TREASURER
Larry Lewis (New York)

MOTION PICTURE DEPARTMENT

Beverly Hills—Department Head, Sue Mengers
John Burnham, Jim Crabbe, Ames Cushing, Dodie Gold, David Goldman, Elaine Goldsmith, J. J. Harris, Jean-Pierre Henreaux, Leonard Hirshan, Andy Howard, Toni Howard, Joan Hyler, Alan Iezman, Ron Mardigian, Fred Milstein, Mike Peretzian, John Ptak, Judy Scott-Fox, Mike Simpson, Bobbi Thompson, Peter Turner, Irene Webb, Fred Westheimer, Cary Woods, Carol Yumkas, Scott Zimmerman, Mike Zimring
New York—Department Head, Boaty Boatwright
Anne Carey, Peter Franklin, Myrna Jacoby, George Lane, Owen Laster, Phyllis Levy, Biff Liff, Dan Mizell, Gilbert Parker, Johnnie Planco, Ed Robbins, Katy Rothacker, Risa Shapiro, Esther Sherman, Steven Starr.

TELEVISION DEPARTMENT

Worldwide Head, Jerry Katzman
Beverly Hills—Department Head, Robert Crestani
Jeff Alpern, Larry Auerbach, Arthur Axelman, Bruce Brown, Aaron Cohen, Lee Cohen, Greg DeFatta, Ruth Engelhardt, Steve Glick, Sam Haskell, Dick Howard, Adam Isaacs, Mark Itkin, Sol Leon, Greg Lipstone, Deborah Miller, Larry Noveck, Bonnie Owens, Gary Rado, Elizabeth Ramsland, Leonard Rosenberg, Hal Ross, Mark Schwartz, Kathy Smith, Mark Teitlebaum, Steve Weiss, Jeff Witjas.
New York—Department Head, Leo Bookman.
Lucy Aceto, Sean Crowley, Art Fuhrer, Jim Griffin, Stephen Lane, Michael Naso, David Segal, Ron Yatter.
DIRECTOR OF PUBLICITY
Florence Gaines

Zenith Electronics Corporation

1000 Milwaukee Ave., Glenview, IL 60025; (312) 391-8181.

(Consumer home entertainment products; electronic do-it-yourself kits, instruments, home study education materials; microcomputer systems, video display terminals, components, and cable and subscription TV and videotex products.)

PRESIDENT AND CHIEF EXECUTIVE OFFICER
Revone W. Kluckman
SENIOR VICE PRESIDENT AND GROUP EXECUTIVE, CONSUMER PRODUCTS
Robert B. Hansen
GENERAL MANAGER CATV/STV OPERATIONS
James Faust

Producers-Distributors

* **PROGRAMS**

* **COMMERCIALS**

* **FEATURE FILMS**

* **SHORTS**

Producers and Distributors

ABC Distribution Co.
(A division of Capital Cities/ABC Video Enterprises)
825 Seventh Ave., New York, NY 10019; (212) 887-1725. Telex: 234337. Fax: (212) 887-1708; 2040 Avenue of the Stars, Century City, CA 90067; (213) 557-6600; Fax: (213) 557-7925; Telex: 673127. John T. Healy, president, ABC Distribution Company; Archie Purvis, senior vice president; Paul Coss, vice president, acquisitions & development; Marvinia Hunter, director, worldwide cable/cassette marketing; Bill Vitale, director, international TV sales; Armando Nunex, Jr., director, international TV sales.

- Series: Moonlighting, Secrets & Mysteries.
- Mini-Series: Baby M, Amerika, Ike, Out on A Limb.
- Made-For-TV Movies: Lady-Killers, Acceptable Risks, Amazons, Best Kept Secrets, A Bunny's Tale, Embassy, The Hearst and Davies Affair, Infidelity, Jacqueline Bouvier Kennedy, The Jericho Mile; Long Time Gone, Love Lives On, The Midnight Hour, My Mother's Secret Life, Triplecross, Who Will Love My Children? (95 titles available).
- Features: Cabaret, The Day After, The Flamingo Kid, Impulse, National Lampoon's Class Reunion, Prizzi's Honor, Silkwood, SpaceCamp, Young Doctors in Love, etc.
- Sports.
- News Specials.
- Documentaries.
- Children's Programming (72 titles).
- Academy Awards Special—International version.

ABR Entertainment Company
32123 Lindero Canyon Rd., Suite 2067, Westlake Village, CA 91361; (818) 706-7727. (Producer and distributor) Alexander B. Rosen, chm. & CEO; Ed Hawkins, exec. v.p.; Celinda Glickman, v.p., operations.

A.L.S. Production Services
6381 Virginia Hills Dr., Salt Lake City, UT 84121; Alvin Simmons, pres. (Motion picture & television producer's services, equipment rentals, sales, lease and servicing. All facets of production equipment & services.)

APA Studios, Inc.
230 W. 10 St., New York, NY 10014; (212) 929-9436. Organized 1963. (Special effects motion picture firm working in commercials, features, industrials; stop-motion, 3-D Animation hi-speed, time-lapse, locals and graphics, total production). Lee Howard, pres.; David Rogers, art director; Robert Self, production mgr.

Academy Film Productions, Inc.
3918 W. Estes Ave., Lincolnwood, IL 60645; (312) 674-2122. Bernard Howard, pres. (Produce live and filmed or video-taped shows and commercials, slides, animation, slide films and industrial films).

Act III Entertainment of Tennessee, Inc.
631 Mainstream Drive, Nashville, TN 37228; (615) 244-1717. Steve A. Womack, exec. vice president and gen. manager. (Producer.)

Alden Films
7820-20th Ave., Brooklyn NY 11214; (718) 331-1045. Paul Weinberg, pres. (Film and video distributors for Jewish Chautauqua Society, Hadassah, Natl. Council of Jewish Women, Eternal Light Film Library, Jewish Natl. Fund, Women's American ORT, Pioneer Women/Namaat, United Jewish Appeal, American Red Magen David, American Society for Technion.)

All American Television
304 E. 45 St., New York, NY 10017; (212) 818-1200. (Distributor) George Back, pres.; Joseph E. Kovacs, exec. v.p.; Joan Marcus, v.p. synd.; Conrad Roth, sr. v.p.; John Reisenbach, senior v.p., national advertising sales; Carl W. Menk, Jr., v.p., station sales and marketing; Todd C. Jackson, v.p., international sales.

Allend'or Productions, Inc.
15036 Valley Vista Blvd., P.O Box 5550, Sherman Oaks, CA 91413; (213) 872-1332. Algernon G. Walker, pres.; Irene J. Brooks, v.p.; Marcia J. Walker, secy., treas.; (Motion-picture and TV production.)

Almi Television Productions
1900 Broadway, New York, NY 10023; (212) 769-6400. Martin Schildkraut, exec. v.p.; Debbie Von Ahrens, sr. acct. exec.; Mary Voll, sr. acct. exec.

- Theatrical feature packages: Almi Film Festival (10); Children's Cinema Classics (65); Kung-Fu (13); She's A Lady (19); Hot Rocks (8); Thriller (18); Almi Passport (33); Great Comedy Volume I (32); Great Comedy—Volume II (15); ½ hour animated special: Kitten's Christmas.

American Adventure Productions, Inc.
314 C Mediterranean Ave., Aspen, CO 81611; (303) 920-3777. John Wilcox, pres.; Josiah Wilcox, secty. (Producers of adventure and wildlife documentaries)

Amrit Productions, Inc.
206 W. 99 St., Suite 5-D, New York, NY 10025; (212) 222-1170. Tirlok Malik, pres.; Chander Malik, v.p. (Producer and arranger of production and co-production of films for TV and video; arranges casting for Indian actors; also distributes video films.)

Animated Productions, Inc.
1600 Broadway, New York, NY 10019; Columbus 5-2942. Al Stahl, pres.; Richard Stahl, v.p.; Shirlee Debrier, production dir.; Peter Puzzo, exec. dir. (Producers of programs, television commercials, cartoons and shorts, industrial films, specialists in animation, stop motion, and fotomation.) Fully-animated with punched tape—animation stand, precision Super 8 blow-up optical bench, Super 8 with opticals.)

Arlington Film Studios
120–37 101st Ave. No., Seminole, FL 34642. Organized 1962. (Produce all types sound and silent motion picture films.) Producer: Frank Ruzz.

Arztco Pictures, Inc.
15 E. 61 Street, New York, NY 10021; (212) 753-1050. Organized 1967. (Production of motion pictures, commercials, industrials, and video.) Tony Arzt, pres., prod./dir.

Associated Press Broadcast Services
1825 K Street, N.W., Suite 615, Washington, D.C. 2007; (202) 955-7243. Jim Williams, deputy director. (TV Direct, the first nonexclusive video news service available to all TV news operations, including Washington Direct, BeatChecks, and AP Videographs; APTV Wire, the AP's high-speed selectable wire for TV stations.)

Associated Television Int'l.
650 N. Bronson St., Suite 300, Hollywood, CA 90004; (213) 871-1340. Organized 1976. Trevor Batkin, pres.; Paul Sharratt, v.p.; John Collins, v.p. marketing. (TV and motion picture production and distribution.)

Associated Television International
P.O. Box 4180, Hollywood, CA 90078; (213) 871-1340. Organized 1979. John Campbell Collins, v.p. marketing; Mark Melville, v.p. development; David McKenzie, C.O.O.; Diane Newman, office manager. (Television syndication and distribution.)

Atlantic Television, Inc.
Operational Headquarters, sales and distribution office: 8255 Sunset Blvd., Los Angeles, CA 90046; (213) 650-2500. Jonathan M. Dana, pres., m.p. & TV; Patricia Furnare, v.p., worldwide operations.

539

Atlantis Films Limited

Cinevillage, 65 Heward Ave., Toronto, Ontario, Canada M4M 2T5; (416) 462-0246. Organized 1982. Michael MacMillan, pres; Janice Platt, Seaton McLean, v.p.s; Peter Sussman, exec. prod. (Television and film production.)

Atlantis Television International Inc.

65 Heward Ave., Toronto, Ontario, Canada M4M 2T5; (416) 462-0016. Organized 1983. Ted Riley, pres.; Jacqueline Scott, manager of sales; Anna Mastromattei, distribution assistant. Affiliated with Atlantis Films Limited. (Markets, sells and distributes films to Canadian and international television and home video marketplace.)

Audio Productions

(A division of Reeves Teletape, Inc.) 227 E. 45 St., New York, NY 10017. (212) 573-8656. Peter J. Mooney, pres.; (Producers of Educational-Documentary and Industrial Films).

Aurora General Entertainment Corp.

5950 West Oakland Park Blvd., Fort Lauderdale, FL 33313 (305); 733-3500.

- War Chronicles, Judy Garland specials, The Littlest Angel, Raggedy Ann and Andy, feature film packages, James Michener Specials, Upstairs at Xenon, The Amazing World of Kreskin.

B

BBC Enterprises Limited

Head Office: Woodlands, 80 Wood Lane, London W12 0TT. Tel.: (01) 546-0202. James Arnold-Baker, Chief Executive, BBC Australia, Hugh Sheppard, Westfield Towers, 100 William St., Sydney; Tel: Sydney 35866411. USA Television Sales: Lionheart Television International Inc., 1762 Westwood Blvd., Los Angeles, CA 90024; (213) 470-3939. Canada, Educational & Training Sales, Hilary Read, 214 King St. W., Toronto; (416) 585-2583. (BBC Enterprises distributes all types of BBC TV programming, licenses BBC titles for merchandising including the BBC microcomputer, produces BBC Video, BBC Records and BBC Books and provides facilities for other broadcasters.)

BBC/Lionheart Television

630 Fifth Avenue, #2220, New York, NY 10111; (212) 541-7342 (Distributor.) John Reynolds, head of BBC U.S., Maq Jawed, sr. exec. v.p.; Ray Krafft, sr. exec. v.p.; Richard Golden, sr. v.p.; Brian Sloman, dir., publicity & promo.

Bob Banner Associates, Inc.

132 S. Rodeo Dr., Suite 402, Beverly Hills, CA 90212; (213) 274-0442. Bob Banner, pres.; J. William Hayes, first v.p.; Stephen Pouliot, v.p. (Production of television programs, motion pictures and theatrical productions.)

Barbre Productions, Inc.

Div. of Combined Communications Corporation, P.O. Box 5667, 1089 Bannock St., Denver, CO 80217, (303) 266-3601. Alvin G. Flanagan, pres.; Jon D. Ackelson, producer/director. (Producer, distributor of filmed shows, producer of film commercials and business films.)

- Prairie World of the Kit Fox (1); Valley of the Standing Rocks (1); Harry Jackson—A Man and His Art; The Troopers Are Coming; Rocky Mountain Conquest.

Robert Baron & Associates

63-33 98th Pl., Forest Hills, NY 11374; (212) 302-1515. Robert Baron, pres., prod.; John Whited, director; West Coast studio facilities, Helen Miles, mgr. & Prod.; Jules Brenner & Gayne Rascher, cameramen; Angie Ross, supervising editor. (Producers of TV commercials, industrials, sales promotion film & multi-media presentations; complete video tape facilities.)

Barry & Enright Productions

1888 Century Park East, Suite 1100, Los Angeles, CA, 90067; (213) 556-1000. Organized 1975. Dan Enright, pres.; Don Enright, v.p., development; Les Alexander, v.p., development; Louis "Deke" Heyward, v.p., development; Robert Doben, v.p., development,

games shows; Chris Sohl, v.p. administration; Jeff Weiss, v.p., business affairs. (Produces network and syndicated programs, games, quizzes, sitcoms, movies-of-the-week, features.)

Ben Barry & Associates, Inc.

10246 Briarwood Dr., Los Angeles, CA 90077; (213) 274-1523. Ben Barry, pres.

- Feature films, including The Family, Honey Comb, Sabra, Action Man, Assassination, I Killed Rasputin, Peking Blonde, Singapore, Singapore, Johnny Banco, Black Sun, Restless Breed, Magnificent Matador, Sword of Monte Cristo, One Russian Summer, etc.

- Feature films, under House of Horrors heading, including The She Beast, Death Dream, Fangs of the Living Dead, The Night Evelyn Came Out of the Grave, Murder Clinic, Children Shouldn't Play with Dead Things, Blood Spattered Bride, Don't Look in the Basement, Nightmare Hotel, Kiss of the Tarantula, Invisible Terror, Zombies. Science fiction features: Star Pilot, Invaders from Mars, Fantastic Invasion from Planet Earth, No Survivors Please, Electronic Monster, Fabulous World of Jules Verne. New: A Swingin' Summer, Invaders From Mars, Restless Breed, Magnificent Matador, Blood on the Arrow. Samuel Fuller classics: Shock Corridor, Naked Kiss.

The Beagle Group

110 E. 59th St., 37th floor, New York, NY 10022; (212) 750-1000. Michael Bennahum, pres. & CEO; Helen Verno, vice president, creative; Dan Farrell, vice president, business affairs; Sharon Hall, dir. of development; Joanna Gleason, vice president. (Television and film production company.)

Beck, Alexander, Films, Inc.

1560 Broadway, Suite 1101, New York, NY 10036; (212) 575-9494. Alexander Beck, president. (Distributes feature films, shorts and Westerns.)

The Behrens Company, Inc.

51 S.W. 9th St., Miami, FL 33130; (305) 371-6077. Robert A. Behrens, pres.; Elizabeth H. Behrens, secty.

Bergman-Harris Productions, Inc.

850 Seventh Ave., Suite 404, New York, NY 10019; (212) 757-7921. Organized 1980. David Bergman, pres.; Paul Harris v.p. (Television production.)

Best Film & Video Corporation

98 Cutter Mill Rd., Great Neck, NY 11021; (516) 487-4515. Roy Winnick, pres.; Ben Tenn, exec. v.p.; Harvey Urman, sls. mgr. (Cable, video, cassette and disc distribution and production).

Binder Entertainment, Inc.

1040 N. Las Palmas, Bldg. #16, Hollywood, CA 90038; (213) 871-8102. Organized 1988. Steve Binder, pres. (Television and film production. Formerly BRB Entertainment, Inc.)

Milton Blackstone/Associates

P.O. Box 1892, La Jolla, CA 92038; (619) 459-8255. Milton H. Blackstone, exec. prod. (Talent, promotion and special events direction, true-life commercials, pr. films.)

- Comedians' Golf Classic; Comedy Hall of Fame (special); Wonderful World of Water (special); Beach Ball; (Pro) Am Team Golf Championship; Mother Goose Parade (special); Jr. World Golf Championship (special); Defending Champion (series); Let There Be Balls (special); Golf Derby; Show Biz Salutes (series and specials); Sports City (in preparation) '76 Andy Williams Open (90 min.); Feature Film: Cockeyed Charley; New Series in Development; Hobo; Pilot; Something to Celebrate; Days of Pleasure—Nights of Despair.

Blair Entertainment

(A division of John Blair Communications, Inc.) 1290 Ave. of the Americas, New York, NY 10104; (212) 603-5990. Alan Bennett, pres.; Mitch Sallitt, v.p./gen. sales manager; Ken Dubow, Northeast reg. mgr.; Christine Lafroscia, Jr. A/E; Chris Lacey, A/E; Paul Franklin, Midwest reg. mgr.; Bill Featherstone, Southern reg. mgr.

- First Run: Divorce Court (52 week first-run series); Fan Club.
- Series: Death Valley Days (130 half-hours in color); The Cisco Kid (156 half-hours in color).

- Feature Films: Revenge Movie Package (12 features).
- Sports: Road to the Super Bowl '88 (1-hour special); NFL Update '87 (1-hour special); Super Stars of the Super Bowl (1-hour special); NFL's Strange But True Football Stories (1-hour special); NFL All Time, All Pro Teams (1-hour special); Road to the Super Bowl Vignettes; Baseball's All-Star Comedy Classics '88; Baseball's World Series Comedy Classics '88.
- Children's: Beachcombers (130 half-hours in color); Lollipop Dragon (2 half-hour specials).

Borden Productions

Great Meadows Rd., Concord, MA 01742 (617) 369-5030. Dick Borden, pres.; William Sweney, Gordon M. Beck, v.p.

Braverman Productions, Inc.

1861 S. Bundy Dr., Los Angeles, CA 90025; (213) 826-6466. Charles Braverman, pres.; Greg Griffin, development. (Producers of feature films, TV specials, documentaries, commercials, titles and special montages, specialists in kinestasis animation.)

Bray Studios, Inc.

19 Ketchum St., Westport, CT 06880; (203) 226-3777. Paul Bray, Jr., pres. (Producers and distributors of films, film strips, slides and multi-media presentations on wide variety of subject matter; services for producers include animation art and photography as well as location crews and equipment.)

Brookfield Productions, Inc.

11600 Washington Pl., Suite #201, Los Angeles, CA 90066; (213) 390-9767. Organized 1978. Norman G. Brooks, pres.; Fern Field, dir. of development. (Television film production.)

Barry Brown Brillig Prod., Inc.

770 Amalfi Dr., Pacific Palisades, CA 90272; (213) 459-4455. Organized 1959; Barry Brown, pres. (Feature motion pictures, industrial films & TV commercials.)

Buena Vista TV

(A subsidiary of Walt Disney Productions) 350 S. Buena Vista St., Burbank, CA 91521; (818) 840-5414. Robert Jacquemin, sr. v.p.; Peter Affe, v.p., eastern div. mgr.; Jamie Bennett, v.p., production/ programming; Larry Frankenbach, v.p., midwest div. mgr.; Rich Goldman, v.p., gen. sls. mgr., Mary Kellogg, v.p., production; Michael Mellon, v.p., research, David Morris, v.p., western div. mgr.; Peter Newgard, v.p., southern div. mgr.

Buena Vista International, Inc.

(A subsidiary of Walt Disney Productions) 350 S. Buena Vista St., Burbank, CA 91521; (818) 840-5414. John Elia, dir. distribution; Etienne de Villiers, pres. Buena Vista International TV.

C

CCW Productions, Inc.

8915 Yolanda Ave., Northridge, CA 91324; (818) 993-7816; Branches: CCW Productions, Inc., Valley Bank Plaza, 300 South Fourth St., Suite 1501, Las Vegas, NE 89101. Organized 1983. Robert M. Cawley, pres./CEO; Philip L. Cuppett, v.p./CFO; Rena L. Winters, v.p., production; Bob Corrigan, prod. coordinator. (Production of feature films, TV movies and television specials.)

Camelot Entertainment Sales

1700 Broadway, New York, NY 10019; (212) 315-4000. Steve Hirsch, pres.; Marsha Diamond, v.p., research.
- Wheel of Fortune; Jeopardy!; The Oprah Winfrey Show; Oprah Specials.

Steve Campus Productions, Inc.

24 Depot Square, Tuckahoe, NY 10707; (914) 961-1900. Steve Campus, pres. (Producer of educational, industrial, medical, documentary films, and multi-media productions.)

Stephen J. Cannell Prods.

7083 Hollywood Blvd., Hollywood, CA 90028; (213) 465-5800.

- The A-Team (NBC); Hardcastle & McCormick (ABC); Hunter (NBC); Riptide (NBC); The Lost Precinct (NBC), Stingray (NBC); J.J. Starbuck (NBC); Wiseguy (CBS); 21 Jump Street (FBC); Sonny Spoon (NBC).

George Carlson & Associates

2512 Second Ave., #306, Seattle, WA 98121; (206) 441-1466. George Carlson, producer. (Program producers.)
- The Traveler/Northwest Traveler series.

Carthay Sound Stage

5907 W. Pico Blvd., Los Angeles, CA (213); 938-2101. (Complete film videotape services & rental center.) Contact: Helen Miles.

Casablanca Productions

8544 Sunset Blvd., Los Angeles, CA 90069; (213) 659-2067. Organized 1974. Dennis Holt, chm./chief exec. officer; David Nelson, pres./director; Gary Geweniger, v.p./exec. producer; Holly Vega, sales rep.; Penny Johnson, post-production sprv.; Chrissa Vayos, office coordinator. (Television commercial production.)

Castle Hill Television

1414 Ave. of the Americas, New York, NY 10019; (212) 888-0800. (Distributor)
- Regal Gold (20 theatrical features); Sterling Collection (12 theatrical features; Made in Hollywood USA (27 classic films); Fright Night (16 horror features); Muscles, Monsters & Myths (7 classics); The Best of Steve Allen (2 one-hr. specials).

CEL Communications, Inc.

515 Madison Ave., New York, NY 10022; (212) 421-4030. Merton Y. Koplin, chm. (A&E); Charles D. Grinker, vice chm., creative director; Martin L. Waldman, CEO, pres. (Creators of The Video Encyclopedia of the Twentieth Century, a visual encyclopedia of America in the 20th Century on videotape and laserdisc)
- Series: Creativity with Bill Moyers (A&E); A Walk Thru the 20th Century with Bill Moyers (A&E); Dining in France, 13 half-hours hosted by Pierre Salinger (PBS); The Magic Years in Sports (ESPN).

Centerpoint Productions, Inc.

320 E. 46 St., New York, NY 10017 (212) 355-3160. Bill Ellis, chief exec. officer.

Charisma Artists Corporation

9348 Civic Center Dr., Suite 101, Beverly Hills, CA 90210; (213) 281-5915. Organized 1985. Nick Edenetti, exec. producer; Larry West, production mgr.; Kathryn Lemon, secretary/treas., Aric Edenetti, casting coordinator; Fernando Alverado, associate prod.; Francois Favre, corp. attorney. (Television and motion picture production.)

Cinar Films Inc.

1207 St. Andre, Montreal, Quebec, H2W 1T1, Canada; (514) 843-7070. Organized 1976. Micheline Charest, pres.; Ronald A. Weinberg, William Litwack, dir. Branches in Montreal, Toronto. (Film/TV production, distribution).

Cinecraft, Inc.

2515 Franklin Blvd., Cleveland, OH 44113; (216) 781-2300. Neil McCormick, pres.; Maria Keckan, CEO; (Production facility and services for video and film, for broadcast and corporate.)

Cinema Shares International Television, Ltd.

450 Park Ave., New York, NY 10022; (212) 421-3161. Beverly J. Partridge, pres. (TV distribution.)

Cinetudes Film Productions, Ltd.

295 W. 4 St., New York, NY 10014; (212) 924-0400. Christine Jurzykowski, pres.; Gale Goldberg, exec. prod.; Anita Cinnamon, mktg. dir.; Alex Gartner, dir. of devel., prod. & acquisition. (Production of TV programs, motion pictures and theatrical productions)

Cineworld Corporation

2670 N.E. 24 St., Pompano Beach, FL 33064; (305) 781-2627. John F. Rickert, pres.; Ildiko M. Rickert, secty./treas. (Distribution, production, international co-production, financing and packaging.)

City Film Productions, City Film Center, Inc.

64-12 65th Place, Middle Village, Queens, NY 11379-1624; (718) 456-5050; John R. Gregory, exec. prod. (Producers of 8 mm/16 mm/35 mm motion pictures, for the fields of business, industry, advertising, sales, science, religion, education, health, entertainment and TV. Creative, consultation and production facilities.)

Dick Clark Productions, Inc.

3003 W. Olive Ave., Burbank, CA 91505; (213) 841-3003. Dick Clark chm. & CEO; Francis La Maina pres., COO; Ken Ferguson, CFO; Martin Weisberg, secty.; Neil Sterns, senior v.p., creative affairs; Ellen Glick, v.p., creative affairs; Karen Clark, v.p.-admin.; Michael Tenzer, v.p. bus. affairs; Richard Levine, v.p., pgm. & sls.; Bryan Thompson, cont.; Barry Ademlan, v.p., TV dept.; Richard Al Clark, producer; Lisa Demberg, v.p., creative affairs; Larry Klein, producer; Al Schwartz, v.p. prods.; Bruce Sterten, v.p. game show develp.; Gene Weed, v.p., TV.

Claster Television Productions

9630 Deereco Rd., Timonium, MD 21093; (301) 561-5500. (Distributor) John Claster, pres.; Sally C. Bell, exec. v.p.; Janice Corter, sr. v.p. sls.; Terri Akman, prog. dir.; John Russell and Peggy Powell, acct. execs.

Coast Special Effects

4907 N. Lankershim Blvd, North Hollywood, CA 91601; (818) 762-1182. Nancy Evelyn, v.p.; Ron Seawright, sr. prod.; Joe Rayner & Peter Kleinow, spec. effects directors. (Special effects for TV commercials and feature films.)

Columbia Pictures Television

(A unit of Columbia Pictures Entertainment, Inc.) Columbia Plaza North, 3300 Riverside Dr., Burbank, CA 91505; (818) 954-6000. (For officers see listing in Companies section). Syndication personnel: Gary Lieberthal, chairman and CEO; Barry Thurston, president, syndication; Michael Zucker, senior v.p., marketing; Meade Camp, senior v.p., southeastern and western regions; Terry Mackin, account exec., western region; Jeff Gallop, account exec., western region; Leslie Tobin, vice pres., motion picture sales & acquisitions; David Mumford, vice pres., research; Francine Beougher, vice pres., distribution operations; William L. Clark, dir., special marketing; Leslie Glenn, dir., research; Alan Daniels, dir., advertising and promotion; Elise Keen, mgr., synd. contracts; Bill Coveny, mgr., publicity. **Branch Offices:** *NEW YORK:* Columbia Pictures Television, 711 Fifth Ave., New York, NY 10022; (212) 702-2920; Gary Lico, v.p., eastern region; Herb Weiss, v.p., eastern region. *CHICAGO:* Columbia Pictures Television, 645 N. Michigan Avenue, Suite 834, Chicago, IL 60611; (312) 915-0230; John Rohrs, Jr., v.p., midwestern region. *ATLANTA:* Columbia Pictures Television, One Atlantic Center, 1201 W. Peachtree Street, #4820, Atlanta, GA 30309; (404) 892-2725; Susan Grant, account exec., southeastern region; Joe Kissack, account exec., southeastern region.

- SYNDICATION FEATURE FILM PACKAGES: Columbia Classics (34 titles); Columbia Gems I (242 titles); Columbia Gems II (32 titles); Columbia Night at the Movies (ad hoc quarterly barter network); Embassy II (20 titles); Embassy III (20 titles); Entertainer of the Year (15 titles); Prime 4 (3 titles); TV 20 (20 titles); TVM One (19 titles); Volume I (28 titles); Volume IV (15 titles); Volume V (26 titles); Volume VI (21 titles).

- SYNDICATION OFF-NETWORK COMEDY SERIES: Archie Bunker's Place (97 ½-hour episodes); Barney Miller (170 ½-hour episodes); Benson (158 ½-hour episodes); Carson's Comedy Classics (130 ½-hour episodes); Carter Country (44 ½-hour episodes); Diff'rent Strokes (189 ½-hour episodes); The Facts of Life (209 ½-hour episodes); Fish (35 ½-hour episodes); Good Times (133 ½-hour episodes); The Jeffersons (253 ½-hour episodes); Maude (141 ½-hour episodes); One Day at a Time (209 ½-hour episodes); Punky Brewster (88 ½-hour episodes); Snaford & Son (136 ½-hour episodes); Silver Spoons (116 ½-hour episodes); Soap (93 ½-hour episodes); Square Pegs (20 ½-hour episodes); That's My Mama (39 ½-hour episodes); The Three Stooges (190 ½-hour episodes); Who's the Boss? (120 ½-hour episodes).

- SYNDICATION OFF-NETWORK DRAMA SERIES: Charlie's Angels (115 one-hour episodes); Fantasy Island (200 ½-hour episodes, 152 one-hour episodes); Hart to Hart (112 one-hour episodes); Police Story (105 ½-hour episodes); Police Woman (91 one-hour episodes); S.W.A.T. (37 one-hour episodes); Starsky and Hutch (92 one-hour episodes); T.J. Hooker (90 one-hour episodes).

Communication Arts Corporation

P.O. Box 144, Hollywood, CA 90078; (213) 274-8600. Organized 1972. Gilbert A. "Gil" Cabot, exec. v.p., program and talent development; Kaye Merrill, casting v.p.; Thomas G. Barfield, v.p., prod.; Terry DeLyle, opns. mgr.; Nancy K. Austin, prod. coordinator.

- Divisions: Gil Cabot Associates, Inc.; StoryBrokers, Inc.; JenStar Productions, Inc.; Sundi Records, Inc.; TOBAC Music Pubberies, Inc.; Tic Toc Bunny Productions, Inc; Sweet Breeze Productions, Inc.

Communication Commission of National Council of the Churches of Christ in the USA.

475 Riverside Dr., New York, NY 10115; (212) 870-2575. William F. Fore, assistant general secretary for communication; D. Williams McClurken, executive director for broadcasting and film; David W. Pomeroy, director, media resources.

- Davey and Goliath (60 films for children); Davey and Goliath specials: Christmas, Lost and Found, Happy Easter, Hallowe'en Who-Dun-It, New Year Promise, To the Rescue, School Who Needs It!, others (including information about network religious TV programs).

Condor Pictures, Inc.

1536 Viewsite Terrace, Hollywood, CA 90069; (213) 652-7447. Milton Simon, gen. mgr. (TV pilot films. Films made to order.)

Contempo Communications Inc.

1841 Broadway, Suite 1111, New York, NY 10023; (212) 247-4444. Joan F. Marshall, pres. (Theatrical, business, documentary, award-winning live shows, mixed-media, motion pictures, video sales mtgs.)

Coproducers Corporation

2670 N.E. 24 St., Pompano Beach, FL 33064; (305) 781-2627. John F. Rickert, pres.; Ildiko M. Rickert, secty./treas. (Distribution, production, international co-production, financing and packaging.)

Coral International Television Corporation

Suite 404, 6850 Coral Way, Miami FL 33155; (305) 661-8922. Sy Shapiro, exec. v.p. & CEO; Manolo Vidal, dir. Latin American sls.

Corniche Productions, Ltd.

101 East Victoria, Santa Barbara, CA 93101; (805) 564-8790. Organized 1982. Robert C. Acosta, managing partner; Venita Vancaspel, partner; Ann Trimbach Acosta, exec. prod.; Elizabeth Scott, co. mgr. (Creates, develops, produces and markets TV product.)

Corradine, Tom J., & Associates

3518 W. Cahuenga Blvd., Suite 301, Hollywood, CA., 90068; (213) 851-5811. Branch office in New York. Tom Corradine, pres.; Mark Deemer, v.p.; Bob Morgan, head booker; Edward Reagan, v.p., marketing; Paul Lisy, v.p., video cassette dir. (Distribute filmed series, feature films. Western representative for Weiss Global Enterprises and Bloom Film Group. National reps for TV National Releasing Corp., Lippert Pictures, Inc., and Film Video Releasing Corp.)

- 700 feature films, 192 Westerns, 500 cartoons, 6 series.

William G. Cox Film Enterprises

9726 Edward Dr., Sun City, AZ 85351. William G. Cox, owner-producer. (Produce commercials, news clips informational & public relations films.)

Thomas Craven Film Corporation

5 W. 19 St., New York, NY 10011; (212) 463-7190. Michael Craven, pres.; Ernest Barbieri, v.p.; Frynne Hamden, secty. (Producers of films and videotapes. Producers of educational, informational, training, fund-raising, documentary, public relations and television films and tapes for corporate, non-profit and governmental clients. Producers of commercials and public service announcements. Producers of international films and tapes, with extensive overseas production experience. Brochure and additional info available on request.)

- Representative Credits: Recruiting films for Peace Corps; training and promotion films for Volkswagen, Porsche, Peugeot and Audi; training and informational tapes and films for several United

Nations agencies; television specials on David Lean; Dylan Thomas and Samuel Taylor Coleridge; numerous films and tapes for U.S. military and governmental agencies.

Creative Programming, Inc.
30 E. 60 St., Room 1103, New York, NY 10022; (212) 688-9100. Organized 1982. Peter Wild, exec. prod.; Nancy Fisher, prod. (Television and home video production.)

Bing Crosby Productions, Inc.
610 South Ardmore, Los Angeles, CA 90005; (213) 487-7150. James C. Kennedy, pres.; Stanley G. Mouse, v.p.; John G. Boyette, v.p. & treas. (Motion pictures, television (film & tape) syndication.)

Crossover Programming Company
1861 S. Bundy Dr., Los Angeles, CA 90025; (213) 826-6466. Charles Braverman, pres.; Greg Griffin, development. (Producers of pay television series, specials, variety shows. Specialists in kinestasis animation.)

Crystal Pictures, Inc.
1560 Broadway, New York, NY 10036; (212) 840-6181. Joshua Tager, president; S. Tager, dir. of sls. (Distribute features, Westerns, packages & reissue TV series.) Telex: 620852
● 60 features; 200 short subjects; comedies (Charlie Chaplin & other old time comedies) (112); TV series (one hr. and ½ hrs.) (410).

D

DIC Animation City, Inc.
3601 W. Olive, Burbank, CA 91505; (818) 955-5400. Organized 1982. Andy Heyard, pres.; Jeff Wernick, v.p.; Mel Woods, chief fin. off.; Gregory B. Payne, secty. (Television production company.)
● The Real Ghostbusters, ALF, Dennis the Menace, Beverly Hills Teens, The New Archie's

Depicto Films Corp.
504-A Aspen Lane, Wyckoff, NY 07481. J. R. von Maur, president. (Producers of filmed commercials and industrial motion pictures. Sales meeting and conventions, road shows.)

Devillier Donegan Enterprises
1608 New Hampshire Ave. NW, Washington, D.C. 20006; (202) 232-8200. Organized 1981. Ron Devillier, pres.; Brian Donegan, exec. v.p.; Frank Liebert, dir., domestic sales; Linda Ekizian, dir., international sales; Joan Lanigan, dir., acquisitions; John Estaban, business mgr. (Movie and television distributor to broadcast and cable domestically and worldwide. Exclusive distributor in North America for NHK Tokyo, Film Australia, Channel Four and Lionheart and Monty Python, London.)

Digital Vision Entertainment
7080 Hollywood Blvd., Suite 901, Los Angeles, CA 90028; (213) 462-3790. Organized 1981. Geoffrey de Valois, president. (Motion picture and television production and distribution.)

Walt Disney Productions
500 S. Buena Vista, Burbank, CA., 91521; (818) 840-1000; 500 Park Ave., New York, NY, 10022; (212) 593-8900. (For officers and personnel see listing under Companies.)

Dixie Entertainment Productions, Inc.
215 Long Beach Blvd., 2nd floor, Long Beach, CA 90802; (213) 491-0332. Irene Jacobs, pres.; S. Giovannoli, chm.; Gil Benzeevi, senior v.p., marketing; Rudy Gerren, v.p. (Full service television production house, 1″, ¾″, ½″; also producer and distributor of video and motion pictures.)

Dubie-Do Productions, Inc.
New York City (212) 765-4240 or 1 Laurie Dr., Englewood Cliffs, NJ 07632; (201) 568-4214. Richard S. Dubelman, pres. (TV and theatrical productions.)

Dunn Cal. Studios, Inc.
P.O. Box 388670, Chicago IL 60638; (312) 644-7600. Deborah Rezzardi, pres. (Producers of motion pictures, multi-screen presenta-

tions, TV commercials, slidefilms for sales, training, promotion, indoctrination.)

E

Eagle/Horowitz Productions, Ltd., Inc.
2230 Hillsboro Ave., Los Angeles, CA 90034; (213) 837-1773. Organized 1984. David J. Eagle, pres.; David Horowitz, v.p.; Nancy Weingrow Eagle, secty.; Suzanne Horowitz, treas. (Television and motion picture production.)

Ralph Edwards Productions
1717 N. Highland Ave., Hollywood, CA 90028. Ralph Edwards, owner. (Creator, packager, producer television shows.)
● The People's Court-syndication.
● This is Your Life-syndication.
● Truth or Consequences—syndication

Ralph Edwards/Stu Billett Productions
1717 N. Highland Ave., Hollywood, CA 90028. (Creator, packager, producer television shows.)
● Superior Court—syndication.

Empire Television
1551 N. LaBrea Ave., Los Angeles, CA 90028; (213) 850-6110. Telex: 4790597 EMPIREINC.
● Theatrical features: Ghoulies; The Dungeonmaster; Walking the Edge; Trancers; The Alchemist; Zone Troopers; Ghost Warrior; Re-Animator; Troll; Mutant Hunt.
● Heroes, Pirates, and Warriors: 14-picture adventure package.

Entertainment Productions, Inc.
2210 Wilshire Blvd., Room 744, Santa Monica, CA 90403; (213) 456-3143. Organized 1971. Edward Coe, pres. (Motion picture and television productions for worldwide markets, including home video, cable, theatrical, etc.)

F

Family Films
P.O. Box 14328, St. Louis, MO 63178. Iris Austin, mgr.

Doris Faye Productions
325 W. 45 St., New York, NY 10036; (212) 246-0430. Organized 1959; Doris Faye, pres. (TV and film packagers; specialists in "educating through comedy" programs; on/off camera talent, script writing, video home-viewing.)

Don Fedderson Productions
16255 Ventura Blvd., Suite 1117, Encino, CA 91436; (818) 986-3118. Don Fedderson, chairman of the board.
● My Three Sons (network); Family Affair (network).

The Film Company
111 Barrow St., New York, NY 10014; (212) 620-5654. Peter Bergmann, Anthony Lidelicato, Ronald Saland. (Motion picture production.)

Film/Jamel Productions, Inc.
195 S. Beverly Dr., Suite 412, Beverly Hills, CA 90212; (213) 273-7773. Gil Cates, pres. (Producers theatre, films, TV.)

Filmack Studios
1327 S. Wabash Ave., Chicago, IL 60605; (312) 427-3395. Joseph R. Mack, pres.; Robert Mack, v.p. (Motion picture film producer for theatres, TV and industry, as well as filmstrips and slides for education.)

Filmation
(A division of Group W. Productions, a Westinghouse Broadcasting Co. subsidiary) 6464 Canoga Ave., Woodland Hills, CA 91367; (818)

712-4900. (Production of children's programming for TV and theatrical release; animation.) Lou Scheimer, pres.; Arthur Nadel, v.p., creative affairs; Joe Mazzuca, v.p., prod.; Alice Donenfeld, v.p., sls.; John Grusd, v.p., art direction, Majid Saee, v.p., MIS systems.

Films Five, Inc.

42 Overlook Rd., Great Neck, NY 11020; (516) 487-5865. Walter Bergman, head of studio oper. (Producers of industrials, documentaries, commercials, live film, videotape & animation. Editorial department & massprint distribution on premises.)

Films of the Nations

7820 20th Ave., Brooklyn, NY 11214; (718) 331-1045. Jerome Schapiro, mgr. (Distributors of TV, industrial and educational free sponsored films.) Color and b/w.

Fima Noveck Productions

321 W. 44 St., New York, NY 10036. (212) 315-4220. Fima Noveck, pres. (Production and post-production; commercials; features; MTV.)

Format Productions

4253 Reyes Dr., Tarzana, CA 91356; (818) 987-2390. Herbert Klynn, pres.; Marvin L. Klynn, exec. v.p. Selma Klynn, v.p.; Ruth Page, secty./treas. (Animation films for TV commercials, TV programming, theatrical shorts, feature and industrial films.)

Four Star International, Inc.

2831 W. Alameda Ave., Burbank, CA 91505-4455; (818) 842-9016. Lance Thompson, v.p.; Robert Neece, v.p., domestic distribution.
- Series: Big Valley; Wanted Dead or Alive; Achievers (13½ hrs.).
- Movies: Star Two (15 new films); Star One (15 new films); No Restrictions (13 new films); Cisco Kid Features (13 features); Dick Tracy (8 features); 200 feature films.

44 Blue Productions

1755 E. Bayshore Dr. #7, Redwood City, CA 94063; (415) 364-4445. Organized 1984. Rasha Drachkovitch, Stephanie Noonan-Drachkovitch, co-owners. (Produces television programming.)

Fox/Lorber Associates, Inc.

432 Park Ave. S., Suite 705, New York, NY 10016; (212) 686-6777. Richard Lorber, pres; David M. Fox, C.E.O.
- Specials: The Elvis Collection (Elvis '56, Aloha From Hawaii, '68 Comeback Special, One Night With You); Great Performers (Mel Brooks, Rich Little, Bette Midler, Pee-wee Herman, Gladys Knight); King . . . Montgomery to Memphis; Legacy of a Dream; Country.
- Series—First Run: The Dr. Fad Show
- Series—Off Network: Romance Theatre, Extra! Extra!
- Features: Fox/Lorber's Greatest Hits (3 music driven suspense dramas); Classic All-Stars (Mr. Ace, Dark Waters, The Mask of Dijion); Bad Girls (feature films starring Joan Collins, Raquel Welch, Susannah York, Deborah Harry); Romance Theatre (17 feature films introduced & hosted by Louis Jourdan); Young Duke (15 westerns with John Wayne); Trailblazers I & II Westerns from the 1940s
- Sports: U.S. Pro Ski Tour

Sandy Frank Entertainment, Inc.

115 E. 57 St., Suite 1410, New York, NY 10022; (212) 759-9199. Sandy Frank, pres.

Woody Fraser Productions, Inc.

3500 W. Olive Ave., Suite 500, Burbank, CA 91505; (818) 953-7600. Woody Fraser, pres. (Television production.)

Fremantle International, Inc.— Talbot Television, Ltd.

660 Madison Ave., New York, NY 10021; (212) 421-4530. (Distributor) Paul Talbot, pres.; Julie Zulueta-Corbo, dir.; homevideo and Latin American sls.; Josh Braun, v.p., global operations; Ellen Windemuth, v.p. bus. affairs & intl. coproductions; Russell Becker, dir., Far Eastern sls.; Richard Becker, asst. dir., Far Eastern sls.; Tony Gruner, chief exec. officer, Talbot TV Ltd. (U.K.); Peter Baker,

European sls. chief; Dorothy Skeoch, operations, Talbot Television Ltd. (U.K.); Skip Braun, v.p., Fremantle of Canada; Randy Zalken, v.p., Fremantle of Canada; Marshall Kesten, dir. of finance, Fremantle of Canada.

Fries Distribution Company

(A subsidiary of Fries Entertainment, Inc.), 6922 Hollywood Blvd., Los Angeles, CA 90028; (213) 466-2266. Telex: 3781675; FDC Fax: (213) 466-9407. Regional offices: New York (212) 593-2220; Chicago (312) 751-3483. (Production and distribution of features and series for TV, cable & home video.)
- TV movie packages: Fries Frame I—27 made-for-TV movies including Adam, Bill, The Burning Bed, The Jayne Mansfield Story and the two-part Dempsey; Fries Frame 2—20 made-for-TV movies including Do You Remember Love, Toughlove, Bitter Harvest, Rosie: The Rosemary Clooney Story and the two-part Martian Chronicles; Fries Frame 3—25 made-for-TV movies including An Early Frost, the two-part Fatal Vision, Poison Ivy and the Wilma Rudolph Story; Fries Frame 4—23 made-for-TV movies including the two-part Inside the Third Reich, Blood Vows: The Story of a Mafia Wife, The Jericho Mile and Mafia Princess; Fries Dynamite—11 films including 4 world premiere theatricals: Viper, The Siege of Firebase Gloria, Deadly Intent and Edge of Darkness; Fries Family Theatre: The Mark Twain Collection—6 films based on Twain classics including The Adventures of Huckleberry Finn.

G

GGP (Golden Gaters Productions)

400 Tamal Plaza, Corte Madera, CA 94925; (415) 924-7500. David L. Peterson, pres.; Robert C. Horowitz, v.p.-gen. mgr.; Henry S. Schneidman, v.p., gen. sls. mgr.; Alphonse H. Carignan, controller. (TV sales, syndication and production; post-production; sports marketing).

GN Communications, Ltd.

2600 W. Peterson, Chicago, IL 60659; (312) 465-0085. Organized 1984. Steven N. Polydoris, president. (Distributes quality TV programs from television.)

Galaxie Productions, Inc.

P.O. Box 1933, Washington, DC 20013; (202) 775-1113. Edward Jasen, president; Dr. Edward von Rothkirch, exec. v.p. & exec. prod.; S. McCormick, secty.-treas.; Paul Malec, chief engineer (Produce & distribute films for non-theatrical motion pictures & television: commercials, travelogues, documentaries, language dubbing on film, complete sound stage for audio recording, custom recording on tape or disk. Fully equipped audio visual, motion picture, & VTR remote truck for sound motion picture, VTR, & still photography. Branch offices: %A. L. Weintraub, 5th floor, 2250 S.W. 3rd Ave., Miami, FL 33129 & C.P.O. Box 1711, Tokyo 100-91 Japan; %V. J. Pandhi, Suite 6G, 102—45 62nd Rd., Rego Park, NY 11375.

Gaylord Production Company

9255 Sunset Blvd., Suite 800, Los Angeles, CA 90069; (213) 274-7769. Alan Courtney, president; Peter Alex, executive vice president; Mort Smithline, senior vice president, business affairs; Jim Mahoney, vice president, development; Steve Sytt, vice president, creative services. (Producer of programming for all television markets, including network, first and second syndication, cable and home video.)

Gaynes Productions Ltd.

6918 Oporto Dr., Hollywood, CA 90068; (213) 874-6909. Organized 1985. Lloyd H. Gaynes, pres.; Kirsten Tellerz, v.p.; Joyce Taylor, writer. (Television productions.)

Gilson International

9200 Sunset Blvd., Los Angeles, CA 90069.
- Series: Hill Street Blues, Remington Steele, St. Elsewhere, Newhart, White Shadow, WKRP in Cincinnati, Last Resort, MTM Variety Hour, Paris, Duck Factory, Betty White Show, Doc, Three for the Road, Tony Randall Show, We've Got Each Other, Phyllis, Mary, Popcorn Kid, Beverly Hills Buntz, Eisenhower & Lutz, Tattingers, Mary Tyler Moore project.
- Films: Boy Who Drank Too Much, Fighting Back, First You Cry, In Defense of Kids, Nowhere to Run, Something for Joey, Thornwell, Vampire, Critical List (4-hr. mini-series), Carly's Web, Independence, Riviera, Fresno (6-hr. mini-series).
- Sports: For the Honor of Their Country (13-part Olympic series), Time Capsule: The 1936 Berlin Olympic Games (special).

Glen Glenn Sound Co.
(Todd-Ao Corp.)
900 N. Seward St., Hollywood, CA 90038; (213) 469-7221. Robert Knudson, pres.; Ron Ward, opns. (Complete film and video-tape sound recording services for feature motion pictures and television programs).

Glenar Studios
211 S. Rose, Burbank, CA, 91505; (213) 848-0408. Sid Glenar, owner. (Produces films, commercials & animation.)

Global American Television, Inc.
Shearer Rd., Colrain, MA 01340; (413) 625-9893. Organized 1982. Pamela M. Roberts, and Edward Wierzbowski, officers. (Produces socially relevant and cultural programming.)

Melvin L. Gold Enterprises
301 E. 48 St., New York, NY 10017; (212) 688-0897. Mel Gold, pres. (Consultant, producer and packager of live and film TV programs, industrial films, commercials, features.)

Samuel Goldwyn Television
10203 Santa Monica Blvd., Los Angeles, CA 90067; (213) 552-2255; FAX: (213) 284-8493. Dick Askin, pres., television distribution. Branches: 200 W. 57 St., Suite 808, New York, NY 10010; (212) 315-3030. 1112 Chickasaw Dr., Brentwood, TN 37027; (615) 373-5972. One Magnificent Mile, 980 N. Michigan Ave., Chicago, IL 60611-4597; (312) 664-4013.

Mark Goodson Productions
375 Park Ave., New York, NY 10152; (212) 751-0600. 6430 Sunset Blvd., Hollywood, CA 90028; (213) 464-4300. Mark Goodson, owner; Giraud Chester, exec. v.p., Alan R. Sandler, v.p., finance; Gil Fates, exec. prod.; Howard Felsher, Chester Feldman, Jonathan Goodson, Mimi O'Brien, producers; Paul Alter, Marc Breslow, directors.
- The Rebel (film); The Richard Boone Show, Branded (film); Beat the Clock; To Tell The Truth; What's My Line; Password; The Price Is Right; Match Game PM; Tattletales; I've Got A Secret (all tape); Family Feud; Card Sharks; Match Game; Mind Readers; Password Plus; Child's Play; Body Language; Trivia Trap; Super Password, Classic Concentrations, Blockbusters, New Family Feud.

Goulding-Elliott-Greybar Productions, Inc.
420 Lexington Ave., New York, NY 10017; (212) 532-9014. Organized 1955. Ray Goulding pres./secty.; Bob Elliott, v.p./treas. (Production of radio and TV commercials and radio & TV programs.)

Granada Television International
400 Madison Ave., Suite 1511, New York, NY 10017; (212) 869-8480.
- First Among Equals; Game, Set and Match; Lost Empires; Floodtide; Death of the Heart; Man and Music; 7 Up, 28 Up; The Jewel in the Crown; The Return of Sherlock Holmes.

Sherry Grant Enterprises
17915 Ventura Blvd., Suite 208, Encino, CA 91316; (818) 705-2535.

Gray-Schwartz Enterprises, Inc.
Teleflix Division, P.O. Box 9239, Calabasas, CA 91302; (818) 702-9888. Marv Gray, pres.

Greatest Fights of the Century, Inc.
9 E. 40 St., New York, NY 10016; William D. Cayton, pres. (Produce and distribute fight films.)
- Big Fights of the Decades Series (formerly titled Greatest Fights of the Century) 500 quarter-hour programs from 1900 to 1988, featuring all the world champions, each in his greatest, and most memorable fight, including George Foreman, Joe Frazier, Muhammad Ali, Floyd Patterson, Rocky Marciano, Joe Louis, Jack Dempsey, Sugar Ray Robinson, Rocky Graziano, Archie Moore, Larry Holmes, Marvin Hagler, Boom Boom Mancini, 31 Mike Tyson fights (28 by KO), etc.

The Earl Greenburg Organization
8730 Sunset Blvd., Suite 290, Los Angeles, CA 90069; (213) 657-2225. Organized 1988. Earl Greenburg, pres.; Stephan Mat-

suo, senior v.p.; Marcia Lewis, v.p., development. (Produces television and motion pictures.)

Greystone Communications, Inc.
1239 S. Glendale Ave., Glendale, CA 91205; (818) 502-5562. Organized 1986. Craig A. Haffner, pres.; Steven Lewis, Donna E. Lusitana, exec. v.p.s (Television production company for network, first run, cable, home video.)

Merv Griffin Enterprises
1541 N. Vine St., Hollywood, CA 90028; (213) 460-2231. Merv Griffin, chm. and CEO; Robert J. Murphy, pres. and COO; Peter Barsocchini, v.p., motion pictures and films for television, Ray Sneath, v.p., game shows and variety. (Production company.)

Group W Productions
(Westinghouse Broadcasting Company)
3801 Barham Blvd., Los Angeles, CA 90068; (213) 850-3800. Derk Zimmerman, pres. & CEO; George E. Resing Jr., sr. v.p.; Kevin Tannehill, v.p., sls. & mktg.; Owen S. Simon v.p., creative services. Gerard Farrell, v.p., sls. research; Sam Cue, v.p., controller; Dan Cosgrove, v.p., media sls.; Tony Dwyer, v.p., domestic sls.; Cornell Chulay, v.p., business affairs; Meryl Marshall, v.p., pgm. devel.
- Hour Magazine (5 shows weekly, 60 mins.), LifeQuest (6 one-hour specials per year), BraveStarr (65 half-hours), Ghostbusters (65 half-hours), He-Man and the Masters of the Universe (130 half-hours), She-Ra: Princess of Power (93 half-hours), Bill Cosby's Fat Albert and the Cosby Kids (90 half-hours), Teenage Mutant Ninja Turtles (13 half-hours), Life's Most Embarrassing Moments (weekly half-hour).

Reg Grundy Productions, Inc.
9911 W. Pico Blvd., Suite 720, Los Angeles, CA 90035; (213) 557-3555. N.Y. rep.: McManus & Co., 425 E. 63 St., Apt E-5F, New York, NY 10021. Organized 1979. Reg Grundy, O.B.E., pres. and chm.; Robert Crystal, v.p.; Sue McIntosh, secty. and treas. (Produces TV programs for network and syndication. All day parts.)

Gutman, Leo A., Inc.
230 Park Ave., New York, NY; (212) 682-5652.
- Hennessey—96 half-hours (b & w), starring Jackie Cooper and a host of guest stars.

Guymark Studios, Inc.
3019 Dixwell Ave., Hamden, CT 06518. Anthony Guarino, Jr., pres.; Guy Guarino, v.p., chg. of photo; Mark Guarino, v.p., chg. of audio & video. (Producers facilities and technical services for sound film video animation, product photography. 1200 sq. ft. sound stage w/ cyclorama complete ¼□ & 16 mm sound studios, all format still photography studio, 16 mm animation studio, slide to film transfer, film to video transfer, ¾" video editing, Time Code, digital video effects, character & graphics generator.)

H

H-R Productions, Inc.
159 W. 53 St., New York, NY 10019; (212) 541-8015. Herbert Rosen, president. (Producer of films, package shows.)

Handel Film Corporation
8730 Sunset Blvd., W. Hollywood, CA 90069; (213) 657-8990. Leo A. Handel, pres.; Peter Mertens, producer. (Produces filmed series.)
- Magic of the Atom (10); The Age of the Atom (color special); Sweden-Vikings Today Style (color special); (color special); Police Dog; 1-hr TV special (1972); Art in America (series 1983–10); Thailand 1983; Philippines 1984; Computer Series 1983–; Measuring Things (series 3) 1985; Singapore 1986; Puerto Rico, 1988; Fiber Optics, 1988.

Hanna-Barbera Productions, Inc.
(A Division of The Taft Entertainment Company) 3400 Cahuenga Blvd., Hollywood, CA 90068; (213) 851-5000. Joseph Barbera, pres.; William Hanna, sr. v.p.; Martyn S. Weinberg, exec. v.p. & chief operating officer; Richard Sigler, v.p. bus. affairs; Jean

MacCurdy, v.p., children's programs; John Michaeli, v.p. communications; Ross Sutherland, v.p. dir., personnel & labor relations; Iwao Takamoto, v.p. creative design; Maurice Morton, v.p. & gen. mgr; Joseph Taritero, v.p., creative affairs; Sam Edwing, v.p., development; Paul DeKorte, v.p. music; Jayne Barbera, v.p., animation production.

- Animated Series: The 13 Ghosts of Scooby-Doo (ABC); The Super Powers Team Galactic Guardians (ABC); The Snorks (NBC); The Jetsons (SYN); Challenge of the Gobots (SYN); Paw Paws (SYN); Funtastic Treasure Hunt (SYN); Galtar and the Golden Lance (SYN); The Greatest Adventure: Stories from the Bible (SYN).
- Animated Specials: Star Fairies (SYN); Pound Puppies (SYN).

Larry Harmon Pictures Corp.
650 N. Bronson Ave., Hollywood, CA 90004 (213) 463-2331. Larry Harmon, pres.

Harmony Gold U.S.A.
8831 Sunset Blvd., Los Angeles, CA 90069; (213) 652-8720. (Producer-distributor)

- Animated cartoon series: Captain Harlock (65 half-hr. episodes); Robotech (85 half-hr. episodes).
- Shaka Zulu (10 hour mini-series).
- Raggedy Ann & Andy (3 holiday specials).
- Family Animation Showcase (20 animated features).
- 2-Part Classics (six 2-part, 4-hour series).
- Harmony Golden I (mini-package of 5 first-run features).
- Animals of Africa (52 half-hrs.).
- The King of the Olympics (4-hr. mini-series).
- The Man Who Lived at the Ritz (4-hr. mini-series).
- Animation Adventure Theatre (3 animated features).
- Travelin' Gourmet (13 half hours).
- Around the World in 80 Days (6 hour mini-series).
- The Secret Identity of Jack the Ripper (live special event).

Harris-Tuchman Productions, Inc.
4293 Sarah St., Burbank, CA 91505; (818) 841-4100. Ralph G. Tuchman, pres. & gen. mgr.; Fran Harris, v.p. & creative dir. (Producers of sales, training and industrial films.)

Harriscope Corporation
10889 Wilshire Blvd., Suite 1240, Los Angeles, CA 90024. Burt I. Harris, pres.; Harvey Simpson, finance dir. (Distribution of filmed programs and radio & TV broadcasting and CATV.)

- Jalopy Races From Hollywood (26); Main Event Wrestling (65); All Girl Wrestling (26); So This Is Hollywood (24).

Hartley Film Foundation Inc.
59 Cat Rock Rd., Cos Cob, CT 06807; (203) 869-1818. Elda Hartley, pres. (Producer of films and video tapes on philosophy, psychology, religion, and health.)

Helios Productions
4140 Warner Blvd., Suite 314, Burbank, CA 91505; (818) 845-6888. Organized 1983. Joseph Maurer, Bradley Wigor, partners. (Produces quality television entertainment.)

Henley, Arthur, Productions
234 Fifth Ave., New York, NY 10001; (718) 263-0136. Arthur Henley, president. (Production, writing consultation, live and film.)

- Make Up Your Mind.

ITC Entertainment Group
12711 Ventura Blvd., Studio City, CA 91604; (213) 760-2110.

Domestic Distribution: James C. Stern, exec. v.p. & gen. sls. mgr.; Charles Keys, v.p., western div. sls. mgr.; John Herrin, v.p. southern div. sls. mgr.; Reid Davis, v.p., midwestern sls. mgr.; Don Toye, v.p., eastern sls. mgr.

International Distribution: James P. Marrinan, exec. v.p. & gen. mgr. intl.; Armando Nuñez, exec. v.p., foreign sales; Doralea Rosenberg, gen. mgr., ITC of Canada; Josh Elbaum, v.p. intl. sls.

Creative & Production Services: Margo Raport, dir. of worldwide advertising, promotion & publicity.

- Series: The Muppet Show (120 half-hours, color); Thunderbirds 2086 (24 half-hours, color); The Saint (114 hrs., 43 color); Return

of The Saint (22, color); Edward The King (13 one-hours, color); When Havoc Struck (12 half-hours, color); The Protectors (52 half-hours); My Partner the Ghost (26 hours); Department S (28 hours); The Persuaders (22 hours); The Adventurer (26 half-hours); The Baron (26 hours); Man in a Suitcase (28 hours); The Prisoner (17 hours); Secret Agent (45 hours); Fury (114 half-hours); Space: 1999 (40 hours, color).

- Features: Entertainment Volume Eight (18 features in color, including "The Big Easy," "Billionaire Boys Club," "Young Doctors in Love"); Entertainment Volume Seven (16 features in color, including "High Road to China," "Lassiter," The Boys in Company C"); Entertainment Volume Six (16 features in color, including "Amos," "Not My Kid," & "Malice in Wonderland"); Entertainment Volume Five (16 features in color, including "All of Me," "Halloween," & "Sophie's Choice"); Entertainment Volume Four (16 features in color, including "On Golden Pond," "The Great Muppet Caper," & "The Elephant Man"); Entertainment Volume Three (16 features in color including "The Muppet Movie," All Quiet on the Western Front," & "The Jazz Singer"); Entertainment Volume Two (16 features in color, including "The Boys from Brazil," "Capricorn One," & "Movie, Movie"); Entertainment Volume One (14 features in color, including "The Return of the Pink Panther," "The Eagle Has Landed," and "Great Expectations"); The Thrillers (43 made-for-television movies, color). SST: Super Space Theatre (13 science fiction films); Hammer House of Horror Double Feature (6 double features or 12 one-hr. features); Cinema 12 (12 features).
- Specials: Superlative Seven (musical-variety hour specials, color, starring Julie Andrews, Steve Lawrence, Eydie Gorme, Ethel Merman, etc.); The Very Special Seven (musical-variety hour specials, color, starring Julie Andrews, Peggy Lee, Dick Van Dyke, etc.)

Image Organization, Inc.
9000 Sunset Blvd., Suite 915, Los Angeles, CA 90069; (213) 278-8751. Pierre David, chairman and CEO; Lawrence Goebel, senior vice president; Mark A. Horowitz, vice president, international sales; James Botko, director of acquisitions; W. Lee Matis, director of marketing. (International distribution of motion pictures, home video and television.)

Independent-International Pictures Corp.
Executive Plaza, 223 Route 18, East Brunswick, NY 08816; (201) 249-8982. Samuel M. Sherman, pres.; Dan Q. Kennis, chmn.; Al Adamson, exec. v.p. (Television distributor and packager-producer of feature film packages, TV specials, TV series.)

- Feature packages: Scream Showcase: Beyond the Living, Demons of the Dead, Doctor Dracula, Exorcism at Midnight, In Search of Dracula, Man with the Synthetic Brain, Midnight, Ship of Zombies, Terror of Frankenstein, Vampire Men of the Lost Planet, Hand of Power, Night Fiend, Horror of the Werewolf, Voice from the Grave; Action Group: The Gun Riders, Mission to Death, The Fakers, Queen of Sheba, The Barbarians, Submarine Attack, Fighting Rats of Tobruk, Money; Drive In Theatre: The Murder Gang, Intrigue in the Orient, Blazing Stewardesses, The Naughty Stewardesses, Trapped in the Desert, The Smiling Maniacs, Syndicate Sadists.

Independent Network, Inc.
11150 Olympic Blvd., Suite 1100, West Los Angeles, CA 90064; (213) 479-6755; TELEX: 662612 INITEL FV LSA; FAX: (213) 479-1582. Irv Holender, pres.; Irving D. Ross, Dir. of U.S. sls. (Distribution & syndication; producers of films.)

- 26 hours of G.L.O.W. (Gorgeous Ladies of Wrestling).
- 16 features—Movie Madness #1.
- 14 features—Ninja/Kung Fu Theatre.

Interlingual Television, K.K.
Mori Bldg. No. 7, No. 2 Nishikubo Tomoecho, Shiba, Minato-Ku Tokyo, Japan. Tel.: 434-2506; Cable Interlingual Tokyo; Telex: J22862, Interlin, Tokyo. Largest independent distributor of Television films in the Far East, with affiliate offices in Australia, USA, Europe. Sub-licenses in Japan and other countries over 4,000 half-hours of telecasting film of U.S., European and Australian origin.

- Adventures of Long John Silver; Space Angel Cartoons; Four Seasons of Japan; Speed and Action; Big Challenge; Golf Around the World; Wings to Adventure; Let's Travel; World's Great Adventures; Filopat and Pitafil; Popeye the Sailor; Funny Company; Joe & The Bees; New Avengers; Spunky & Tadpole; The Living Ocean; In the Kingdom of the Dolphin; Wild World of the East; The Lighthouse; Alburria—A Trip to Remember; Here Comes the Grump; Texas Jack and His Pals; Famous Fairytales; Wonderful World of Brother Buzz; Feature films (color, 27 titles); George; Color Classics—The Best of the Past.

International Film Bureau Inc.

332 S. Michigan Ave., Chicago, IL 60604; (312) 427-4545. Wesley Greene, pres. (Distributes live action, animated shorts, documentaries. Curriculum and general audience films for television.)

International Film Exchange, Ltd.
(A Today Home Entertainment Company)

201 W. 52 St., New York, NY 10019; (212) 582-4318; Cable: IFEX-REP—New York; Telex: 420748. FAX: (212) 956-2257; 9200 Sunset Blvd., Los Angeles, CA 90069; (213) 278-6490; Telex: 4972966; FAX: (213) 278-7939. Gerald J. Rappoport, Emanuel L. Wolf, Richard Grisar, Christopher Wood, Beulah Rappoport, Joy Pereths, exec. officers. (International distributors and producers of theatrical, non-theatrical, educational and television films.)

J

JEF Films Inc.

Film House, 143 Hickory Hill Circle, Osterville, MA 03265; (617) 428-7198. Organized 1973. Branches: Los Angeles, CA (Film Classic Exchange); Australia, New Zealand, England, France, Spain, Portugal, Greece, Canada, Fiji, Switzerland, Austria, West Germany, Italy, Monaco, Ireland, Denmark, Finland, Sweden, Norway, Belgium, Luxembourg, Algeria, Morocco, Tunisia. Owns: Film Classic Exchange, XTC Video, WHAM! Video!, VIP Video, JEF Video line, JEF Films International, PHD Video, The Stock Exchange (stock footage). Jeffrey H. Aikman, CEO; Elsie Aikman, v.p.; Jo-Anne Polak, sls. mgr.; Janie Barber, promotions mgr; (Produces and distributes in the following media: television (network and syndication), motion pictures, home video, pay per view, non-theatrical. Also stock footage library of 30,000 films.)

K

KLW International Inc.

Route 9, P.O. Box 806, Marmora, NJ 08223; (609) 391-0872. Organized 1985. Kevin L. Weakland, chairman/pres.; George Weakland, vice pres.; Shannon Weakland, secretary; Helyn Weakland, treasurer. (Entertainment production, financing, and consulting.)

Stacy Keach Productions

5216 Laurel Canyon Blvd., North Hollywood, CA 91607; (213) 877-0472. Stacy Keach, Sr., pres.; Mary Keach, v.p.; James Keach, secty. (Producer of films, commercials, public information films.)

● Properties: Living Proof; Back in Action; Approved Exercises for Senior Citizens; Approved Exercises for the Heart Patient.

M. A. Kempner, Inc.

4699 N. Federal Highway, #102, Pompano Beach, FL 33064; (305) 946-7660; FAX: (305) 946-7013. Marvin A. Kempner, pres.

Killiam Shows, Inc.

6 E. 39 St., New York, NY 10016; (212) 679-8230. Paul Killiam, pres.; John Rogers, v.p. (Produces and distributes programs about silent films.)

King Features Entertainment Inc.

235 E. 45 St., New York, NY 10017; (212) 682-5600. Telex: 7105812391. J. F. D'Angelo, chm.; Bruce L. Paisner, pres.; William E. Miller, exec. v.p.; Leonard Soglio, v.p. domestic sls. mgr.; Samuel Gang, intl. sls. mgr.

King International Corporation

124 Lasky Dr., Beverly Hills, CA 90212; (213) 274-0333. Frank King, pres.; Herman King, v.p. (Produces TV series.)

● Maya

King World Productions, Inc.

1700 Broadway, New York, NY 10019; (212) 315-4000. 150 El Camino Dr., Suite 305, Beverly Hills, CA 90212; (213) 858-1833. 980 N. Michigan Ave., Suite 1400, Chicago, IL 60611; (312) 337-6765. Roger M. King, bd. chm.; Steve Palley, COO; Michael G. King, pres.; Sid Cohen, sr. v.p., sls.; Jeffrey Epstein, chief financial

officer, Jonathan Birkhann, v.p. legal & business affairs; Kevin Stein, v.p. dev., West Coast; Allyson Kossow, v.p., public relations.

● Properties: ½ hr. strips: Wheel of Fortune, Jeopardy!, Headline Chasers. Movie Packages: Classic Detectives (34); Epics (5); Spotlight 10 (10); Popcorn Theatre (15). Off-net: Topper, Guns of Will Sonnett, Branded. Specials: Drug Wars (1 hr.), Wards of the Street (1 hr.).

Walter J. Klein Company, Ltd.

6311 Carmel Rd., Box 2087, Charlotte, NC 28211-2087; (704) 542-1403. Walter J. Klein, pres.; Richard A. Klein, v.p. sales; David Jordan, controller; Betsy Klein, print sales dir.; Roxanne Mason, distribution dir.; Terry Losardo, production dir.; David Sherwin, editorial dir.; Charles Shedd, Jonathan Quade, Salvatore Messina, directors; Brady Brandwood, editor; Elizabeth Norkum, Barbara Cade, distribution assts.; Denise Joseph, Sandra Newton, Betty Stephens, Mary Babcock, John Edwards, administration. (Production and free distribution of sponsored films for industry, TV, government, associations for 40 years. complete film facilities on 2-acre lot.)

L

LBS Communications, Inc.

875 Third Ave., New York, NY 10022; (212) 418-3000; 9220 Sunset Blvd., Suite 101-A, Los Angeles, CA 90069; (213) 859-1055; 625 N. Michigan Ave., Suite 1200, Chicago, IL 60611 (312) 943-1717. Henry Siegel, pres. & chairman, LBS Communications; Paul Siegel, pres., LBS Entertainment; Phil Howort, pres., Global Tele Com; Mike Welden, pres., TV Horizons; Jon Nottingham, exec. v.p., sales & marketing; Joseph Tirinato, exec. v.p., programming & dev.

● Programming: Family Feud

● LBS Live Event Specials: UFO Cover-Up . . . Live! (2 hour event), A Chance to End the Nightmare

● Children: Police Academy; The Animated Series (65 half hour episodes); The Adventures of Teddy Ruxpin (65); Care Bears & Friends at the Movies (6 movies); Mask (75); Inspector Gadget (86)

● Features/Packages: LBS Spectrum II (Bonanza: The Next Generation, Vietnam War Story, Miracle of the Heart); Hope Diamonds (11 Bob Hope feature films)

● Specials: Scared Straight! Ten Years Later (2 hours); The Treasures of the Titanic; Smithsonian Treasures; Test Series

● Series/Off-Network: Gidget (80 episodes); Hardcastle & McCormick (67); Family (85)

The Landsburg Co., Inc.

11811 W. Olympic Blvd., Los Angeles, CA 90064; (213) 478-7878. Alan Landsburg, chm. of bd.; Howard Lipstone, pres; Kay Hoffman, exec. v.p.; Joan Barnett, v.p., movies & mini-series; Jane Lipstone, v.p., pub.; Victor Paddock, v.p., business affairs; Thomas Igner, controller. (Producer for TV and theatrical films and TV film and tape series.)

Don Lane Pictures, Inc.

35 W. 45 St., New York, NY 10036; (212) 840-6355. Donald J. Lane, pres.; Sheva Scheingarten, producer/director; Thomas Lalicki, v.p., producer; Carol Laufer, prod. mgr. (Produces industrial motion pictures, slide films and video cassettes; news films.)

Herbert S. Laufman & Company

8140 Rideway, Skokie, IL 60076; (312) 675-4578. Herbert S. Laufman,. pres. (Producers and distributors of live & film programs.)

● It's Baby Time (52).

Robert Lawrence Enterprises

305 Madison Ave., Suite 411, New York, NY 10165; (212) 996-2836. Robert L. Lawrence.

Herbert Leonard Enterprises, Inc.

5300 Fulton Ave., Van Nuys, CA 91401; (818) 783-0457. Herbert B. Leonard, pres.; Walter Bernstein, v.p.; James P. Tierney, Esq., secty. (Producers of filmed series and feature films.)

● Herbert B. Leonard produced Rin Tin Tin (164); Naked City (138); Route 66 (116); Popi (U.A.); produced and directed Going Home (MGM); Ladies Man (series); Breaking Away (pilot).

Levinson Entertainment Ventures International, Inc.

650 North Bronson Ave., Suite 250, Los Angeles, CA 90004; (213) 460-4545. Organized 1982. Robert S. Levinson, pres.; Sandra S. Levinson, vice pres.; Jed Leland, Jr., director of dev.; Deborah Scott, prod. associate. (Video, television, and film development and production. Affiliated with Program Partners Corp., NY; Edge Records, L.A. and Together Productions, LA on co-prods.)

Liberty Studios, Inc.

238 E. 26 Street, New York, NY 10010; (212) 532-1865. Organized 1961. Anthony Lover, pres., producer-director; David Bruce, George Apostol, directors. (Complete live action and special effects production, including motion control graphics, blue screen. Owns and operates fully equipped sound stages, editing/optical facilities, camera lighting, grip and sound equipment, equipment transfer trucks for sound stage as well as location shooting. Video production includes off-line room and on-line Beta.)

Jack Lieb Productions, Inc.

100 West #4 Erie St., Chicago, IL 60610. Warren H. Lieb, pres.; Charles Kite, editor; Toba J. Cohen, prod.-dir. (Audio-visual producers.)

Lionheart Television International

1762 Westwood Blvd., Los Angeles, CA 90024; (213) 470-3939. (Distributor) Frank R. Miller, pres. & CEO; Tay Voye, exec. v.p.; David Friedman, sr. v.p. com. sls.; Ray Krafft, v.p. pub. TV sls.

Lorimar Television

10202 Washington Blvd., Culver City, CA 90230; (213) 280-8000.

- Network series: Dallas; Falcon Crest; Knots Landing; Perfect Strangers; The Hogan Family, Full House, Midnight Caller, Paradise.
- First-run syndication: Mama's Family; It's a Living; ThunderCats; Love Connection; The People's Court; SilverHawks; Superior Court; She's the Sheriff; Freddy's Nightmares, Fun House, Family Medical Center, Gumby, N.I.W.S. (New Information Weekly Service).
- Mini-series: Jack the Ripper

Lott Video Productions

The Lott Bldg., P.O. Box 1107, Santa Monica, CA; (213) 397-4217. D. N. Lott, owner. (Producers of film commercials.)

M

MCA Television

445 Park Ave., New York, NY 10022; (212) 759-7500. West Coast: 100 Universal Plaza, Universal City, CA 91608; (818) 777-1000. (For officers see listing under Companies)

- Latest product: Out Of This World (24); Bustin' Loose (26); Bionic Six (65); Charles in Charge (52 half-hr. episodes); Kate & Allie (122 half-hrs.); Knight Rider (90 hrs. or 91 half-hrs.); Universal Pictures Prestige 13 (features, including Hitchcock's Rope and The Trouble with Harry); Universal Pictures Exploitable 13 (films including Repo Man, Terror in the Aisles, Streets of Fire, etc.); The A Team (98 hrs.); Harper Valley (29 half-hrs.); Operation Petticoat (32 half-hrs.); Universal's Marvelous Ten (movies, including Captain America, Munster's Revenge, etc.); Amen (half-hours); The Munsters Today (24 half hours); My Secret Identity (24 half hours); Morton Downey Jr. Show (hour strip); Airwolf (80 hours).
- Series: One-hour: Simon & Simon (156); Black Sheep Squadron (35); Magnum (129); The Columbo/McCloud/McMillan Mystery Movies (162); Quincy (148); Buck Rogers (37 1-hr. or 25 1-hrs. & 6 two-hrs.); Kojak (118); The Rockford Files (125); BJ/Lobo Show (86 half-hrs. or 86 hrs.); The Incredible Hulk (85); Emergency! (136); Half-hours: Gimme a Break (137); That's Incredible (165); House Calls (57); Leave It to Beaver (234); The Munsters (70); 90-min.: Banacek (16); Baretta (82); Alias Smith & Jones (43); The Six Million Dollar Man (108); The Bionic Woman (58); Switch (70); Five Star Mystery (87); The Bold Ones (98); Ironside (198); It Takes a Thief (65); The Name of the Game (76 half-hrs.); Rod Serling's Night Gallery (97 half-hrs.); Run for Your Life (85); Rich Man, Poor Man Book 1 (12 hrs. in 1-hr., 2-hrs. or 90-min.); Best Sellers II (33); The Deputy (76 half-hrs.); Mickey Spillane's Mike Hammer (78 half-hrs.); Thriller (67); Men from Shiloh (23 ninety-min. movies); Wagon Train (32 ninety-min. episodes); Dead End Kids Movies (7 movies).
- Features: Universal Pictures Debut Network (33 features); Debut Network II (35); Film Fest I (22); Universal Prestige 13 & Exploit-

able 13 (26); Universal's Marvelous Ten (10); Universal's Most Wanted List (23); The Hit List (36); Universal Network Movies 85 (52 two-hr., 33 1½ hrs.); Battlestar Galactica (12 two-hr. movies or 24 one-hrs.); Champagne Movies 34 (34); Ninety Minute Movies (49); Universal Grand 50 (48); Universal Star Spangled 33 (48); Universal World Premieres (35 two-hr movies); Comedy Festival I (26); Comedy Festival II (26); Universal 40 (39); Universal 49 (49); Universal 52 (52); Universal 50 (45); Paramount Pre '48 (496); Paramount 100 Select (100); Universal 53 (52); Universal 123 (116); Universal 260 Select List (260 features, 90 color); Universal Color One Hundred (99); Universal 36 Black and White Elite (36); 77 Horror Greats (77); Western Roundup (26); Reserve (259); Diabolic Dozen (12).

MCA Television International

100 Universal City Plaza, Universal City, CA 91608; (818) 777-1000. Colin P. Davis, pres. Foreign Offices: Brazil: Rua Said Aiach, 305, São Paulo, Brazil; 884-0166. Wanderley Fucciolo, v.p. Australia: Universal House, Poplst & Pelican St., Sydney, NSW, Australia 2000; 267-0944. Pat Cleary, v.p. Japan: Maison Kirakawa Bldg., 2-5-2 Hirakawa-cho, Chiyoda-ku; 265-5726. Keinosuke Kuragaki, v.p. Canada: 2450 Victoria Park Ave., Willowdale, Toronto, Ontario M2J 4A2, Canada; (416) 491-3000. Peter Hughes, v.p., Ron Suter, sales exec.; Beirut, Lebanon: 1324 Mme. Curie St., Sammakieh Bldg., Beirut; 369-175. Kamal Sayegh, v.p. France: 8 Rue La Boetie, Paris 75008, France; 265-9780. Hendrik van Daalen, v.p. England: 139 Piccadilly, London W.1, England. 629-7211; Roger Cordjohn, v.p., U.K.

- New for 1988–89 Season: Coach (13 ½-hr); Coming of Age (15 ½-hr); Almost Grown (1 2-hr, 12 1-hr); Men (13 1-hr.); The Mystery Wheel (18 2-hr); The Munsters Today (24 ½-hr); My Secret Identity (24 ½-hr).
- Renewals: The Equalizer IV (22 1-hr); Murder, She Wrote (22 1-hr); Miami Vice V (1 2-hr, 20 1-hr); Amen III (22 ½-hr); Simon & Simon VIII (13 1-hr.); Alfred Hitchcock Presents (41 ½-hr); Charles in Charge IV (26 ½-hr); Out of this World II (24 ½-hr).

M.C.E.G., Inc./Manson International

11355 W. Olympic Blvd., Suite 500, Los Angeles, CA 90064; (213) 208-8899; Telex: 188198 TRT, 691242 WUI; FAX: (213) 479-7429. Andrew Milner, senior v.p., international sales; Maura Hoy, director of international sales; Andrea Miller, director of international sales.

- Distributors of 300 plus feature films, documentaries and entertainment specials to the international theatrical, video, cable TV and broadcast TV markets.

MGM/UA Television Distribution

1350 Ave. of the Americas, New York, NY 10019; (212) 708-0300. (For officers and personnel see listing under Companies.)

MGS Services

A subsidiary of Viacom International Inc., 619 W. 54 St., New York, NY 10019; (212) 765-4500. Chicago, IL: 201 E. Erie St., 60611; (312) 337-3761; Los Angeles, CA: 10507 Burbank Blvd., N. Hollywood, CA 91601; (818) 508-5488.

MPO Videotronics, Inc.

2580 Turquoise Circle, Newbury Park, CA 91320; (805) 499-8513; FAX: (805) 499-8206; Mark Barker, West. Reg. Mgr. New York: 619 W. 54 St., New York, NY 10019; (212) 708-0550; FAX: (212) 977-9458; Jeff Greenberg, East Reg. Mgr. Chicago: 5999 New Wilke Rd., Suite 204, Rolling Meadows, IL 60008; (312) 806-6780; FAX: (312) 806-6873; Bill Bailey, M.W. Reg. Mgr. Atlanta: (404) 875-0015; FAX: (404) 642-0138; Skip Bulkley, S.E. Reg. Mgr. Canada: 85 Curlew Drive, Don Mills, ONT M3A 2P8; (416) 445-2538; FAX: (416) 445-4051.

MRC Films & Video

71 W. 23 St., New York, NY 10010; (212) 989-1754. Lawrence Mollot, exec. producer. (Producer of industrial, documentary, television films and TV commercials.)

Madison Square Garden Network

2 Pennsylvania Plaza, New York, NY 10121; (212) 563-8000. Robert Gutkowski, exec. v.p., MSG Communications Group; Martin Brooks, v.p., programming & network operations; Lee Berke, v.p., marketing; Doug Moss, v.p., advertising sales; Paul Schneider, dir., public relations; Pete Silverman, v.p., exec. producer.

- Live Events: New York Knickerbockers basketball; New York Rangers hockey; College football and basketball, pro wrestling, pro boxing, track and field, tennis.

Manley Productions, Inc.

111 W. 57 St., New York, NY 10019; (212) 541-7733. Walter H. Manley, gen. mgr.; Pat Hart, sls. mgr. Telex: 421832; FAX: (212) 957-9006; Cable: WALTMANLY. (Producers and distributors.)

Marathon International Productions, Inc.

211 E. 51 St., New York, NY 10022; (212) 688-1130. Konstantin Kalser, pres. and exec. producer. (Produce & distribute motion pictures and public information films.)

Medallion TV Enterprises, Inc.

8831 Sunset Blvd., West Hollywood, CA 90069; (213) 652-8100. Telex: 910-490-1139. FAX: (213) 659-8512. John A. Ettlinger, production. (Producers and distributors of film programs for TV, commercials, packages of live programs, local and network.)

● Celebrity Billiards (30); Wrestling Stars of the 60s; High Road To Danger (39); Kingdom of the Sea (41); Wonders of the World (117); Star Route (26); Creeping Terror Package—Volumes I, II, III & IV, 20/20 Feature Package; Las Vegas Fight of the Week (26); The New Roller Derby (26 hrs.); Wrestling Spectacular (26 hrs.); Man Who Skied Down Mt. Everest (90 min. special); Dinah East (95 min. special); Something Else (39 half hrs.); Scrooge 'n' Jud; The Making of. . . (39 half-hrs.); Action I-Action II (60 min. specials).

Milner-Fenwick, Inc.

2125 Greenspring Dr., Timonium, MD 21093; (301) 252-1700. David Milner, pres.; Richard Milner, v.p.; Michael Quitt, sales mgr., v.p. (Producers of medical, educational, training and documentary films and video-tapes—16mm, Super 8mm, ¾″ and ½″ video. Full motion picture services including sound recording, animation, live photography and editing.)

Mode-Art Pictures

3075 W. Liberty Ave., Pittsburgh, PA 15216; (412) 343-8700. Robert L. Stone, gen. mgr.; James M. Seng, mgr. (Producers of documentary and industrial sales and safety films and television commercials. Also owns and operates a 930-seat theatre for motion pictures, live stage, teleconferences, meetings & seminars.)

Mode 2 Productions

P.O. Box 8050, Pittsburgh, PA 15216; (412) 343-8700. Robert L. Stone, pres.; James M. Seng, v.p. (Producers of documentary and industrial sales and safety films and television commercials.)

Modern Sound Pictures, Inc.

1402 Howard St., Omaha, Nebraska, 68102; (402) 341-8476. Keith T. Smith, pres. (Distributor of over 200 feature films and 300 shorts.)

Modern Talking Picture Service, Inc.

General Offices: 5000 Park St., North, St. Petersburg, FL 33709; (813) 541-7571. (Distributor of free-loan sponsored films and videocassettes, and collateral materials.)

Divisions

Modern TV: Distributor of free-loan 16mm-sound and color motion pictures and videocassettes. TV NewsBridge produces and distributes VNRs to TV stations and cable systems. PR-NewsBridge produces and distributes PSA to TV stations and cable systems. TV spot newsclips and public service announcements for television stations.

Modern Video Programs: Distributor of programs and series for Cable Television Stations.

Modern Satellite Services: Distributor of programs and services.

Affiliations

Modern Telecommunications, Inc.

One Dag Hammarskjold Plaza, New York, NY 10017; (212) 355-0510. Robert Weisgerger, pres. (A post-production company specializing in videotape services.)

Moffitt-Lee Productions

1438 N. Gower St., Suite 250, Hollywood, CA 90028; (213) 557-4052. Organized 1978. John Moffitt, exec. prod.-dir.; Pat Tourk Lee, exec. prod.; Amy Kimelman, coord. prod.; Matt Neuman, prod.; Not Necessarily the News; Vic Kaplan, prod. consultant; Nancy Kurshner, assoc. producer. (Television production.)

Motion Picture Service Co., Inc.

125 Hyde St., San Francisco, CA 94102; (415) 673-9162. Lino Kwong, operations mgr. (Theatre advertising, special trailers, animated film strips, optical sound services, color film lab, computer graphics.)

Movietonews, Inc. (20th Century-Fox Film Corp.)

460 W. 54 St., New York, NY 10019; (212) 977-5500. (Stock film library, international newsreels.)

N

NBC International, Ltd.

30 Rockefeller Plaza, New York, NY 10112; (212) 664-4444. Robert C. Blackmore, exec. vice pres., NBC-TV; Mike Perez, v.p., intl. sls.; Eric J. Stanley, dir., intl. sls.

● Movies, mini-series, children's shows, comedy and drama series, sporting events, information programs, news programs, etc.

NBC News Video Archives

30 Rockefeller Plaza, New York, NY 10112; (212) 664-3797.

● Complete archives of NBC News.

New Century Telecommunications

545 Madison Ave., New York, NY 10022; (212) 371-9750. (Producer and distributor) Robert B. Morin, pres.; David Skillman, v.p., sls.; Jack E. Dube, v.p. intl.; Gene Lavelle, v.p., opns.; Steven Orr, v.p. sls.

New World Television

1440 S. Sepulveda Blvd., Los Angeles, CA 90025; (213) 444-8100. (For officers and personnel see listing under companies.)

Nostalgia Productions

1555 S. Cardiff, Los Angeles, CA 90035; (213) 277-5865. Carla Howard, pres.; Scott Ben-Yashar, dir. opns. (Producer of custom family documentaries—histories.)

O

Odyssey Filmakers

1001 N. Poinsettia Place, Hollywood, CA 90046; (213) 876-2021; 111 Barrow Street, New York, NY 10021; (212) 620-5654. Peter Bergmann, president; Sherri Seckel, George Ellison, executive prods.; Bob Abel, Ron Phillips, Bob Reagan, Ray Rivas, Henry Winkler, directors; Frank Coppolla, David Russell, Alison Rumery, sales reps. (Producers of TV commercials.)

Odyssey Productions, Inc.

24 E. 51 St., New York, NY 10022; (212) 421-9595.

● Lowell Thomas Television series, High Adventure (color-11); World of Lowell Thomas (half-hour-41).

Lillian Okun Productions

307 E. 44 St., New York, NY 10017; (212) 661-3958, ext. 311N. (Live shows—children and teen-age, women's.)

Orbis Communications, Inc.

432 Park Avenue South, New York, NY 10016; (212) 685-6699; Robert L. Turner, pres.; John C. Ranck, exec. vice pres., international and domestic program sales; Brian T. Byrne, exec. vice pres., advertising sales; Ethan J. Podell exec. vice pres., business affairs; Hilary Hendler, senior vice pres., station sales; Frank Buquicchio, senior vice pres., finance. BRANCH OFFICES: 8800 Sunset Blvd., Suite 501, Los Angeles, CA 90067; (213) 289-7100. Neil Russell, senior vice pres., program acquisitions & dev.; Dana Ardi, vice pres.; 35 East Wacker Dr., Suite 1356, Chicago, IL 60601; (617) 346-6333. (Distributes films of Carolco Pictures, and Pacific International Enterprises. Also handles distribution of: Orbis Premiere Movies, Platinum 139 Films, and Orbis Color Classics.)

Orion Pictures Television, Inc.

711 Fifth Ave., New York, NY 10022; 1888 Century Park E., Los Angeles, CA 90067. (For officers see listing under Companies)

- Films: Orion III Film Package, including Back to School.
- Series: Cagney & Lacey.
- First Run: Hollywood Squares, High Rollers.

Outdoor News Network

3176 Pullman, Suite 105, Costa Mesa, CA 92626; (714) 556-0330. Organized 1983. Sean Foxen, pres.; Bill Rico, vice pres.; Sandy Rice, secty./treas. (Television show.)

Jim Owens Companies

1525 McGavock St., Nashville, TN 37203; (615) 256-7700. James W. Owens, pres.; Judy McCracken, secretary. (Program producers of music entertainment and information programs for television syndication and cable network release.)

Earl Owensby Studios

P.O. Box 184, Shelby, NC 28150; (704) 482-0611. Earl Owensby, pres.; Linda Comer, secty.

P

P.A.T. Film Services Inc.

630 Ninth Ave., New York, NY 10036; (212) 247-0900. Ervin Rosenfeld, pres.; Charles Haydon, v.p. secretary; Andrew Cuomo, v.p.; Len Laxter, mgr.; Michael Rosenfeld, video mgr. (Produces and distributes TV shows and commercials; ¾" VHS & Beta cassettes for distribution. Standards conversion and videotape editing.)

Pacific International Enterprises, Inc.

1133 S. Riverside, Ste. #1, P.O. Box 1727, Medford, OR 97501; (503) 779-0990. Arthur R. Dubs, pres.-prod.; Arn S. Wihtol, v.p. sales/acquisitions; Barbara J. Brown, secty.-treas.; Paul W. Blumer, media-pub. dir.; Andy Gough, controller/office mgr.

- Features: Vanishing Wilderness, Wonder of It All, Challenge To Be Free, American Wilderness, The Adventures of the Wilderness Family, Wilderness Family Part 2, Mountain Family Robinson, Across the Great Divide, Cold River, Great Adventure, Young and Free, The Fourth Wish, Sacred Ground, Windwalker, Mystery Mansion, The Dream Chasers.

Pakula Productions, Inc.

330 W. 58 St., Suite 5H, New York, NY 10019; (212) 664-0640. (Motion picture and TV production) Alan J. Pakula, pres.; Hannah C. Pakula, v.p.; Eric Weissmann, secty.

Palladium Entertainment, Inc.

444 Madison Ave., 26th floor, New York, NY 10022; (212) 355-7070. Gary Dartnall, Nathaniel T. Kwit, Sr. (Producers & distributor of film series). Subsidiaries include Lassie Television, Inc. and Lone Ranger Television, Inc.

- Lassie; Lone Ranger; Lone Ranger Cartoon, Sgt. Preston; Skippy the Bush Kangaroo; Magic of Lassie; Lassie the New Beginning.
- America at the Movies; An American Christmas Carol; Antonio and the Mayor; Aunt Mary; Bushido Blade; Chu Chu and the Philly Flash; City in Fear; Coffee, Tea or Me; Crime Club; Crisis in Mid-Air; Cutter's Trail; Daddy, I Don't Like It Like This; Deadly Harvest; Death of Innocence; Dr. Max; Escape; Face of Fear; Family Rico; The Four Feathers; Goodbye Raggedy Ann; Graduation Day; Horror at 37,000 Feet; Hunter; I Want to Keep My Baby; Legend of Walks Far Woman; Migrants; Mongo's Back in Town; Mother and Daughter; My Bodyguard; Nightmare; On the Right Track; Orphan Train; Relentless; Revenge of the Stepford Wives; The Seduction of Miss Leona; Something Evil; Thaddeus Rose and Eddie; That Lucky Touch; Travis Logan, D.A.; Visions of Death; When She Was Bad; Zorro the Gay Blade.
- Additional movie titles: Agatha, Beyond Reason, Blade in Hong Kong, Cease Fire, The Coca Cola Kid, Consenting Adult, The Empty Beach, An Enemy of the People, Escape From El Diablo, The Grey Fox, Heartaches, Hercules in New York, The Gold & Glory (aka The Coolangatta Gold), Invisible Stranger, Oliver Twist, The Pilot, Straight Time, Stranger's Kiss, Tell Me That You Love Me, Too Scared to Scream, Torchlight, Touched.

Paramount Television

5555 Melrose St., Hollywood, CA 90038: (213) 468-5000. For officers and personnel see listing under Companies.

- Features & Specials: Portfolios I-XII; The Jesse Owens Story; Star Trek Memories; Paramount First-Run Network II: Concerts starring Sinatra, Cher, Diana Ross, etc.
- Operation Prime-Time (OPT) Projects: Solid Gold '79 (2 hrs.); The Girl, The Gold Watch & Everything (2 hrs.); The Top of the Hill (4 hrs.); The Way They Were (2 hrs.); Golda (4 hrs.); Smiley's People (6 hrs.); Solid Gold (48 hrs.); The Girl, The Gold Watch & Dynamite (2 hrs.)
- Series: Entertainment Tonight (first-run, live, 52 wks.); Taxi (66 half-hrs.); Solid Gold (48 hrs.); Laverne & Shirley (134 half-hrs.); Happy Days Again (189 half-hrs.); Make Me Laugh (195 half-hrs.); The Odd Couple (114 half-hrs.); The Brady Bunch (117 half-hrs.); Star Trek (79 hrs.); Love, American Style (224 half-hrs.); Star Trek Animated (22 half-hrs.); The Brady Kids (22 half-hrs.); Mission: Impossible (171 hrs.); The Untouchables (114 hrs.); The Lucy Show (156 half-hrs.); The Best of the West (13 half-hrs.); Bosom Buddies (19 half-hrs.); The Brady Brides (10 half-hrs.); Fonz & The Happy Days Gang (13 half-hrs.); Foul Play (10 hrs.); The Greatest American Hero (8 hrs.); Mean Jeans (13 half-hrs.); Nero Wolfe (14 hrs.); Happy Days (189 half-hrs.); Here's Boomer (24 half-hrs.); Mork & Mindy (73 half-hrs.); Number 96 (6 hrs.); Taxi (66 half-hrs.)
- Mini-Series: (hours in parentheses): A Town Like Alice (60); Backstairs at the White House (90); Evita Peron (4); Flesh and Blood (4); Golda (4); The Last Outlaw (8); The Moneychangers (6); Shogun (12); Smiley's People (6); The Timeless Land (8); Tinker, Tailor, Soldier, Spy (6); The Top of the Hill (4); Washington: Behind Closed Doors (12); Winds of War (16).
- Movies of the Week (hrs. in parentheses): An Act of Love (2); The Greatest American Hero (2); Midnight Offerings (2); Tenspeed and Brown Shoe (2); A Time for Love (2); Act of Violence (2); The Alternative (1½); Assault on the Wayne (1½); Big Bob Johnson (2); Call to Danger (1½); Barbary Coast (2); The Caper (1½); Case for the Defense (1½); Chopper Squad (1½); Cindy (2); Clone Master (2); The Cops and Robin (2); The Deadly Game (2); Death in the Family (1½); The Defection of Simas Kudirka (2); Delancey Street (1½); and others.

Tom Parker Motion Pictures

18653 Ventura Blvd., Tarzana, CA 91536; (818) 342-9115. Telex: 858964; FAX: (818) 347-6208. Tom Parker, dir. of prod. & sls. (Licensing agent and distributor for intl. theatrical, home video and TV.)

Pathe Pictures, Inc.

161 W. 54 St., New York, NY 10019; (212) 247-4767. Joseph P. Smith, pres.; Samuel A. Costello, v.p., secty. & treas.; James J. Harrington, v.p. & gen. counsel.; Joseph A. Volatile, dir. opns. (Producer of documentaries, educational films and children's programs.)

- Milestones of the Century (365); Men of Destiny (130); Pathe Educational Shorts (103); Showtime at the Apollo (13); Musical Parade of Stars (1100); Captain David Grief (39); Showtime (39); When the Music's Over (hr. musical variety special).

John Pearson International

2980 Beverly Glen Circle, Suite 302, Los Angeles, CA 90077; (213) 933-5879. Arnie Frank, pres. (Distribution of TV series, features, specials, etc.)

- Features: Horror Film Package (15); Adventure Film Package (10); Comedy Film Package (2); Mystery Film Package (5); Frankenstein's Great Aunt Tillie; Guyana; Treasure of the Amazon; Sketches of a Stranger; Every Girl Should Have One.
- Sports Programs: (all half-hour and in color) Andy at Indy (13 episodes); Chase the Wind, King Richard the Racer, Iron Men Steel Machines, Rodeo Cowboy, Twilight Cheat, Wings of the Wind. Hour programs in color: Roller Super Stars (26 eps.); World Championship Kick-Boxing (26 eps.); Salute to Baseball, The Winning Blow.
- Family Programs: (all half-hour and in color) Trick and Treat (130 episodes).
- Children's Programs: The Fabulous Storybook Lady (13 half-hours); Domingo (30 half-hour episodes).
- Music Specials: Lucille Ball Specials (7); Something Special (22 eps.—60 mins.); Soul to Soul (60 min.); Rock and Roll Revival (67 min.); Televisa Musical Specials (4—60 min.); Superstars— Las Vegas! including The Ben Vereen Special (86 min.); The John Davidson Special (70 min.); The Strange Case of Alice Cooper (72 min.); 11th World Popular Song Fest (60 min.); A Night in Las Vegas (60 min.); Today's Jazz (3—30 min.).
- Documentary Specials: Karate, Kung-Fu (60 min.); Sharks (60 min.); Giants of the Deep (60 min.), Other Roads, Other Ways (30

min.); Shanghai Shadows (60 min.); Energy—The Alternatives (30 min.); Ghosts and Gold (30 min.); Great American Hobo (30 min.); Great American Lumberjack (60 min.); Living with Grace (30 min.); The Wilson Crisis (30 min.); Voyage to Understanding (60 min.).

● Special Interest Programs: Baja Giants (30 min.); Ghosts & Gold (30 min.); Lucy in Disguise (60 min.). Country Rhapsody (7 films—various):

Pohlman Film Productions, Inc.

527 N. 27th St., Milwaukee, WI 53208; (414) 342-6363. (Produces industrial motion pictures, multi-media slide shows; slide product.)

Premier Film, Video & Recording Corp.

3033 Locust St., St. Louis, MO 63103; (314) 531-3555. Wilson Dalzell, pres. (Producers of motion pictures, TV spots, strip films & carts, recording and record pressings and video productions, film to video transfer, etc.)

Prijatel Productions, Inc.

1612 Prosser Ave., Dayton, OH 45409; (513) 298-8134. (Producer and distributor) Donald F. Prijatel, pres.; Julie Smith Prijatal, v.p., adv. & pub. rel.

Prime T.V. Films, Inc.

509 Madison Ave., New York, NY 10022; (212) 421-2170. Elsa Jane Campbell, pres.; Eduardo La Madrid, treas.

● Features: March of the Wooden Soldiers, When Comedy Was King, Golden Age of Comedy, Lady Take a Chance, D'Jango (color, western), Day the Sky Exploded, Incredible Petrified World, Teenage Zombies, Ape Man, Corpse Vanishes, Limping Man, White Fire, Memory of Love, Orient Express, Stars Look Down, Spotlight Scandals, Nine East Side Kids: East Side Kids, Boys of the City, That Gang of Mine, Flying Wild, Bowery Blitzkrieg, Mr. Wise Guy, Let's Get Tough, Smark Alecks, Neath Brooklyn Bridge.

● Series: Charlie Chaplin Comedy Theatre (26 half-hrs.); The Goldbergs; Courageous Cat (130 episodes, color, 5½ mins.).

Program Syndication Services, Inc.

375 Hudson St., New York, NY 10014-3620; (212) 463-3900.

ProServ Television, Inc.

10935 Estate Lane, #100, Dallas, TX 75238; (214) 343-1400. Bob Briner, pres.; Dennis Spencer, sr. v.p.; Herb Swan, v.p. of intl. sls. (Producers of live events, made-for-TV specials, weekly series, industrials, and home videocassettes.)

Q

Qintex Entertainment, Inc.

345 N. Maple Dr., Suite 210, Beverly Hills, CA 90210; (213) 281-2600. Branches: 720 Fifth Ave., New York, NY 10012. Organized 1971. David Evans, pres., COO; Jonathan D. Lloyd, exec. v.p., CFO; Mort Marcus, exec. v.p., sls. and mktg. (Television syndication/film distribution company, first run sales and production.)

Quality Program Sales, Inc.

824 Rome Dr., Los Angeles, CA 90065; (213) 222-8803. Kyle C. Thomas, pres. (Distributes films for TV.)

Quanta, Ltd.

1100 17th St., N.W., Washington, D.C. 20036; (202) 775-0334. W.G. Williams, U.S. representative. (British television and video production company specializing in interpreting and science and technology to general audiences.)

R

Radio and Television Packagers, Inc.

9 E. 40 St., New York, NY 10016; (212) 532-1711. William Cayton, pres. (Producer and distributor of filmed series.)

● Jungle: (59 ¼-hr. programs); Cartoon Classics—The Amazing Gift, Beauty and the Beast, The Brave Duckling, The Ice Witch, The Enchanted Princess, The Fisherman and the Fish, Tale of the Northern Lights, Gunnar the Sailor, The Valiant Knight, The Magic Antelope, The Tiny Oxen, Omar and the Ogres, The Strange Circus, Wanda and the Wicked Princess, The Wild Swans, The Woodcutter's Wish, The Frog Princess, The Fire Bird, The Space Explorers, New Adventures of the Space Explorers, Mr. E. from Tau Ceti, The Undersea Explorers, Journey to the Beginning of Time (also available in episode form); Treasure Island Revisited; The Adventures of Mutt & Jeff and Bugoff; When Funnies Were Funny (42 full-color cartoons from the geniuses of early animation); Animations (32 language arts subjects).

Carl Ragsdale Associates, Ltd.

4725 Stillbrooke, Houston, TX 77035; (713) 729-6530. Carl V. Ragsdale, pres. (Producer of documentaries and industrial motion pictures, television commercials, and theater short subjects.)

● Branches: Suite 200, 2120 "L" St. NW, Wash., DC 20037; (202) 347-7095, Arthur Neuman, exec. prod. in charge; 12522 Argyle Dr., Los Alamitos, CA 90720; (213) 598-4201, Frank Coghlan, exec. prod. in charge.

Harry Rasky Productions, Inc.

(Production of feature films and TV specials.) CBC, P.O. Box 500, Terminal A, Toronto, Canada; (416) 975-6867. (World-wide co-productions.)

Raymond International

11 Soho St., Suite 104, Toronto, Ont., Canada M5T 1Z6; (416) 340-0130; FAX: (416) 340-0130. Bruce Raymond, pres.; Donovan B. Raymond, gen. mgr.; Antony B. Armstrong, mgr. prod. services. (Producers and distributors)

Redlin Productions, Inc.

19116 Lanark, Reseda, CA; (213) 885-8462. William A. Redlin, pres.; Emil F. Redlin, secty., treas. (Producer live and film programs, features.)

Republic Pictures Corporation

12636 Beatrice St., Los Angeles, CA 90066-0930; (213) 306-4040. Telex/Twx: 910-343-7417. (For officers see listing under Companies.)

● First Run: On Trial (35 strips).

● Off Network series: Beauty & the Beast (44 hours, available 9/91); Bonanza (310 hours), Get Smart (138 half hours); High Chaparral (98 hours).

● Film Packages: Classic Television Series (48 different series); Color-Imaged Specials (8 by 8/90); The John Wayne Collection (16 features); Hollywood Stars (16 features); Hollywood 1-2-3 (89 features); Action-Packed Package (28 features); Animated Features (5 features); Christmas Features (4 features); Home of the Cowboys (22 features); Classic Comedy (13 features); Serial Movies (26-100 minute features); Cartoons (15).

Ring-Ting-A-Ling Productions

161 W. 54 St., Suite 403, New York, NY 10019; (212) 245-8298. Robert Weiner, pres. (Producer of films and TV programs; casting director and talent coordinator.)

Riviera Productions

31628 Saddletree Dr., Westlake Village, CA 91361; (818) 889-5778. F. W. Zens, exec. producer; Leif Rise, assoc. producer. (Produces filmed series, commercials, features.)

● Punch and Trudy (6); Teletunes (15); Aqua-Lung Adventures (13).

Richard H. Roffman Associates

697 West End Ave., New York, NY 10025; (212) 749-3647. Richard H. Roffman, pres.; Malvina Cohn, John Bowman, Don Lester, Leo Blau, v.p.s. (Producers and distributors of shows also do Public Relations and publicity and promotion for shows—also do casting for shows, etc.; also use guests and feature information on numerous cable TV and UHF-TV and AM-FM radio shows in N.Y. area.)

Jack Rourke Productions

Box 1705 Burbank, CA 91507. Jack Rourke, pres.; William Hagens, v.p.; Jim Rourke, v.p., productions; sales; Hank Edwards, v.p., promotion.

Ruby-Spears Enterprises, Inc.

(A division of The Taft Entertainment Co.) 3255 Cahuenga Blvd., Hollywood, CA 90068; (213) 874-5100. Joseph Ruby, bd. chm.; Kenneth Spears, pres.

- Series: Punky Brewster (NBC); Lazer Tag (NBC); The Chipmunks (NBC); The Puppy's Great Adventures (CBS); The Centurions (syn.); Rambo (syn.); Chuck Norris Karate Kommandos (syn.)

S

SFM Entertainment

1180 Ave. of the Americas, New York, NY 10036; (212) 790-4800.

- SFM Holiday Network (package of family feature films.) March of Time series, Zoobilee Zoo; The Hugga Bunch, The Indomitable Teddy Roosevelt, Crusade in the Pacific, The Care Bears Crusade in Europe.

Saban International Services

11724 Ventura Blvd., Studio City, CA 91604; (818) 985-3805. Stan Golden, president. (Producer & distributor.)

Saban Productions/Haim Saban/dba

11724 Ventura Blvd., Studio City, CA 91604; (818) 985-3805. Organized 1980. Haim Saban, owner. Branches in Paris and Tel-Aviv. (Producers of music, cartoons, game shows programming.)

Schaefer/Karpf/Eckstein Productions

3500 W. Olive Ave., Suite 730, Toluca Lake, CA 91505; (818) 953-7770.

George Schlatter Productions

8321 Beverly Blvd., Los Angeles, CA 90048; (213) 655-1400. Organized 1964. George H. Schlatter, pres.; Jolene B. Schlatter, v.p.; Nathan Golden, secty./treas. (Produces television shows and motion pictures.)

Scotti/Vinnedge Television

1037 North Cole Ave., Los Angeles, CA 90038; (213) 466-1006. Tony Scotti and Syd Vinnedge, exec. producers.

Arnold Shapiro Productions

5800 Sunset Blvd., Los Angeles, CA 90028; (213) 460-5202. Organized 1981. Arnold Shapiro, pres. (Produces documentaries and reality programs.)

The Silverbach-Lazarus Group

9911 W. Pico Blvd., Penthouse M, Los Angeles, CA 90035; (213) 552-2660. (Distributor) Alan Silverbach, chm.; Herb Lazarus, pres.; Toby Rodgers, sr. v.p.

The Fred Silverman Company

12400 Wilshire Blvd., Los Angeles, CA 90025; (213) 826-6050. Organized 1981. Fred Silverman, pres.; Gigi Levangie, dir., creative affairs. (Produces television and motion picture entertainment.)

- Matlock (series); Jake and the Fatman (CBS series); Perry Mason movies (NBC); In the Heat of the Night (NBC); Father Dowling Mysteries (NBC).

Slesinger, Stephen, Inc.

1111 N. Westshore Blvd., Tampa, FL 33607; (813) 879-6968 or (813) 837-8773. Shirley A. Lasswell, pres. (Produces films.)

Rick Spalla Video Productions

Subsidiaries: Hollywood Newsreel Syndicate, Inc., and Rick Spalla Production, Inc.

1622 North Gower St., Hollywood, CA 90028 (213); 469-7307; 301 W. 45 St., New York, NY 10036; (212) 765-4646. Organized 1957. Rick Spalla, pres.; Anthony J. Spalla, v.p.; Jeff Spalla, prod. suprv.; Mike Spalla, music dir.; Maralee Spalla, p.r. (Film and video tape production-producer and packager of TV programs, commercials and industrial films.)

- Syndicated TV shows: Portrait of a Star; Hollywood Backstage; High Road to Danger; Hollywood Guest Shot; Hobby Nobbing . . . with the Stars; Century of Fashion; The Open Road, Hollywood's Fantastic Artists' and Models' Ball; Hollywood Star Newsreel, Holiday on Wheels, Portrait: The New Breed; Century of Fashion . . . in Motion Pictures; The Great Getaway; Live two-hr. special: California State network hook-up. Miss California International Beauty Pageant (2 hours) (Annual Competition in April.); The Wild . . . Wild . . . World of Spirit; Kay Crawford's Pep Arts Training Series (14 hrs.).

Aaron Spelling Productions, Inc.

1401 N. Formosa, Hollywood, CA 90046; (213) 850-2413. Organized 1965. Aaron Spelling, chm.of the bd., chief exec. officer; Jules Haimovitz, president & chief operating officer; Douglas S. Cramer, vice chm. of bd.; E. Duke Vincent, pres. of the exec. comm.; Ronald Lightstone, exec. v.p.; John T. Brady, sr. v.p., chief financial officer; Norman Henry, v.p., prod.; Alan Greisman, v.p., motion pictures, Renate Kamer, v.p. & secty.; Arthur Frankel, v.p., business and legal affairs; Ilene Chaiken, v.p., television dev.; Joseph Dervin, v.p., post prod.; Marcia Basichis, vice pres., current programming; Tony Shepherd, v.p., talent; Miki Dahlgren, sr. dir. business affairs; Pam Bottaro, dir. of dev., motion pictures; Board of directors: Aaron Spelling, Jules Haimovitz, Douglas S. Cramer, E. Duke Vincent, Arthur H. Bilger, J. William Hayes . (Development and production of all forms of TV programming, as well as the production of feature films.)

- Series: The Colbys, Dynasty, Hotel.

Bob Stewart Productions

1717 N. Highland Ave., Suite #807, Hollywood, CA 90028; (213) 461-3721. Organized 1964. Robert Steward, pres. (Television production company.)

Sunbow Productions, Inc.

130 Fifth Ave., New York, NY 10011; (212) 337-6100. Organized 1978. (Television production.) Thomas L. Griffin, chairman; Joe Bacal, pres.; Fred Cohen, exec. v.p.-dev.; Jay Bacal, senior v.p.-creative dir.; Eve Silverman, senior v.p.-dev.; Carole Weitzman, v.p./prod. & business affairs; v.p.-dev.; Anne Newman, v.p.-dev.; C. J. Kettler, senior v.p. Sunbow Intl.

Survival Anglia Ltd.

420 Lexington Ave., New York, NY 10017; (212) 867-6979 . John F. Ball, pres.; James T. de Kay, senior v.p.; Victor Simpkins, v.p., business affairs & corporate communications.

- Properties: Tales of the Unexpected (66 half-hrs., bizarre, mystery-suspense anthology with international stars); Tales of the Unexpected, Series Three (22 half-hrs.); World of Survival (21 half-hr. wildlife episodes hosted by John Forsythe); For a Better World (6 one-hr. wildlife/natural history adventures from around the world); Lions of Etosha (one-hr. special on lions filmed by cinematographer Des Bartlett); Warriors of the Gods (one-hr. special on Asian elephants by Dieter Plage).

Syndicast Services, Inc.

360 Madison Ave., New York, NY 10017; (212) 557-0055. (Distributor) Leonard V. Koch, pres.; Gerry Lepkanich, v.p. sls.; Terry Paolillo, v.p., opns.; William Madden, dir. sta. sls.

T

TFI (Tape Film Industries)

619 W. 54 St., New York, NY 10019; (212) 708-0500; 941 N. Highland Avenue, Los Angeles, CA 90038; (213) 461-3361; 640 N. LaSalle St., Chicago, IL; (312) 951-6700. Charles A. Ahto, pres. (Duplication and distribution of TV commercials, film and video tape, complete storage facilities in N.J. & Delaware, post-production services; fulfillment services.)

TMS Entertainment, Inc.

3575 Cahuenga Blvd W., Suite 370, Los Angeles, CA 90068; (213) 850-5550. Organized 1983 in U.S., 1964 in Tokyo. Eiji Katayama, exec. v.p., CEO; Sander Schwartz, sr. v.p. Branches: Tokyo Movie Shinsa (TMS). (Creates and produces fully-animated TV shows and feature films.)

TV Art International Inc.

300 Central Park West, Suite 2G, New York, NY 10024; (212) 580-2152. Organized 1987. Jorge De Gregorio, pres.; Graciela Abelin, vice president; Freda Luang, exec. secretary; Midalys DeLualle, secretary. Jorge De Gregorio, Graciela Abelin, Charles Luetke, board of directors. (Distribution of programs in U.S.A. and Latin America—branch: TV Art Argentina.)

D. L. Taffner/Limited

31 W. 56 St., New York, NY 10019; (212) 245-4680. Donald L. Taffner, pres.; John P. Fitzgerald, chief exec. officer; Rick Levy, pres., sales and marketing/syndication; Joe Ceslik, v.p., gen. sales mgr/syndication; Dennis E. Doty, sr. v.p.; David Dreilinger, v.p., business & legal affairs, Dennis Ellis, v.p., chief financial officer; Leon Memoli, v.p., development; Martha Strauss, v.p., intl. sales; Christina Thomas, v.p., sales and development. (Distributor).

- Comedy: Benny Hill (85 half hrs.); Thames Comedy Originals (156 half hrs.); After Benny (40 half hrs.); Robins Nest (48 half hrs.); Man About the House (39 half hrs.); George & Mildred (38 half hrs.); Keep it in the Family (31 half hrs.).
- Feature Films: Best of Benny (90 mins.).
- Mini-Series: Blood & Honor (5 hrs.).
- Series/First Run: Too Close for Comfort (104 weeks); Check It Out (52 weeks); Ted Knight Show (52 weeks).
- Documentaries: Hollywood (13 hrs.); World at War (36 hrs.); Destination America (9 hrs.).
- Series/Off Network: Three's Company (222 half hrs.); Too Close for Comfort (107 half hrs.); The Ropers (26 half hrs.); Three's A Crowd (22 half hrs.).
- Specials: Benny Hill Specials I (5 hrs.).
- Animation: Danger Mouse (50 half hrs.).

Telecine Film Studios, Inc.

R2 Box 7A1, Winterset, IA 50273. Byron L. Friend, pres. (Producers of motion pictures, TV series, TV commercials, videotape.)

- Zoo Parade; Magic Ranch.

Telemated Motion Pictures

137 S.W. 54th St., Cape Coral, FL 33914. Saul Taffet, producer-director. (Producer of documentaries, commercials, industrial, corporate image, public relations, training, sales promotion, and educational films.)

Telemount Pictures, Inc.

P.O. Box 1106, Santa Monica, CA 90406. Henry B. Donovan, pres. and producer. (Producers of Cowboy G-Men film series.)

- 39 Westerns; 13 shorts.

Television Program Enterprises

875 Third Ave., New York, NY 10022; (212) 759-8787. (Producer and distributor) Philbin S. Flanagan, v.p. & gen. mgr.; Mary Jane Hastings, dir. opns.

Teleworld, Inc.

245 W. 55 St., New York, NY 10019; (212) 489-9310. Robert Seldelman, pres. West Coast: 11340 W. Olympic Blvd., Los Angeles, CA 90064; (213) 478-2561. Donal Joannes.

Foreign Offices: United Kingdom: Dandelion, 49 St. Peter's St., London N1 8JP, England; 354-2472. Noel Cronin, sls. rep. Mid East: Transworld Television Corp., 81 Piccadilly, London, W1V 9HB, England; 499-7419. Issam Hamaoul, sls. rep. Spain: Apartdao 33009, Madrid-23, Spain; 637-5560. Antoniette Brughera Miranda, sls. rep. Australia: Telepix Pty. Ltd., 155 Alexander St., Crows Nest NSW, 2065 Australia; 439-7377. Robert Lapthorne, sls. rep.

- Mini-Series: Chiefs (6 hrs.); Kennedy (U.S. only; 7 hrs.); Mistral's Daughter (U.S. only; 8 hrs.); Civilization & The Jews (intl. only; 9 hrs.)
- Features/Packages: Spiderman (U.S. only—7 live-action features); Teleworld's Top 50 (chiller & action features).
- Series/First Run: Powerhouse (16 half-hrs.).
- Series: Star Maidens (U.S. only—13 half-hrs.); Castaway (U.S. only—13 half-hrs.).
- Specials: Dinosaur (intl. only; 1 hr.).

Michael R. Terr Productions

2473 Crestview Dr., Hollywood, CA 90046; (213) 654-7506. John Rienhardt, director; Michael Terr, producer. (Film programs and commercials.)

- Wildcat Rider (26); Dancing Age (13); Native Son; Gods of Bali; Black Man in the White World; Lolita Go Go; Here Comes the Sexy; Aliki; Two Kids That Stole a Moon; Songs of Siberia (Musical); The Enemies; Jazz at Its Level Best (13 one-half hour color musical); Jazz on Stage (13) one-half hour color-musical; A Tribute to Louis Armstrong and Mahalia Jackson (2½ hr. show); Manchurian Massacre (1976); Opium War Atom Boy (90 min.); (1976); Animation; The Open Heart; Mauricette; Cry in the Wind; Our Soviet Sister. New Films: Aba—The Black Superman, Walk the Walk, Deadwood 76, Eegah, Spies-a-Go-Go, The Face of Terror, Fallguy, The Choppers, A Fourth for Marriage.

Bob Thomas Productions

60 E. 42 St., New York, NY 10165; (212) 221-3602. Robert G. Thomas, pres. (Motion picture and TV producer; program syndication & satellite services to reach 270 independent television stations.)

Titus Productions, Inc.

211 E. 51st St., New York, NY 10022; (212) 752-6460. Herbert Brodkin, pres.; Robert Buzz Berger, v.p. (Producers of motion pictures, television series and specials.)

Herb Tobias and Associates, Inc.

1901 Ave. of the Stars, Suite 840, Century City, Los Angeles, CA 90067; 277-6211. (Talent Agency.)

Tower Productions

11541 Landale St., No. Hollywood, CA 91602. H. G. and Barbara J. Rhinelander, owners. (Live programs.)

- Space Patrol (live, plus 300 half-hr. and 200 15-min. kinescopes).

Transvue TV International Co.

A Division of Transvue Pictures Corp., 5131 Colbath Ave., Sherman Oaks, CA 91423; (818) 990-5600. Herbert B. Schlosberg, pres.; K. Galloway, secty.

Tribune Entertainment Company

(A subsidiary of Tribune Broadcasting Co., Inc.) 435 N. Michigan Ave., Suite 1800, Chicago, IL 60611; (312) 222-4484. Sheldon Cooper, pres.; Donald Hacker, exec. v.p.; David Sifford, exec. v.p., marketing & sales; Peter Marino, v.p., programming; George Paris, v.p., programming (West Coast); Melvyn Smith, v.p., programming; Joseph Antelo, v.p., exec. prod., At the Movies; Carol Forace, v.p., dir. of research & sales; Jack Devlin, dir. creative svcs.; Allan I. Grafman, dir. business affairs; Dale Laackman, dir. of operations (Producer-distributor) National media sales and station clearances by Teletrib, 875 Third Ave., New York, NY 10022; (212) 450-9190.

- Series: Geraldo (1 hour, weekly); At the Movies (½ hour weekly movie review); U.S. Farm Report (weekly); Soul Train (weekly); Monsters (½ hour, first run)
- Specials: On Trial: Lee Harvey Oswald (2 hrs. with host Geraldo Rivera); The Geraldo Rivera Specials (2 hrs.); Soul Train Music Awards (2 hrs.); Nadia (2 hrs.); Living the Dream: A Tribute of Dr. Martin Luther King Jr. and Black History Notes (in association with Tribune Central City Productions); Hollywood Christmas Parade; The Tournament of Rose Parade.
- Sports: Chicago Cubs Baseball television network.

Turn of the Century Fights, Inc.

9 E. 40 St., New York, 10016; (212) 532-1711. William D. Cayton, pres. (Produce and distribute fight films.)

- Knock-Out (now total of 600 subjects, from 1897 through 1988).
- The Legendary Champions (90-min. feature)

Turner Program Services

1050 Techwood Dr., N.W., Atlanta, GA 30318; (404) 827-2085. Henry A. Gillespie, chm.; Russ Barry, pres.; Bob Schuessler, v.p.-CNN-special projects; Sid Pike, v.p., intl.; Howard Karshan, v.p., Europe; John Walden, v.p., mktg.; Bob Rierson, dir. programming; Ken Christensen, dir. adv. promo.

Twentieth Century Fox Film Corporation, Television Distribution Division

P.O. Box 900, Beverly Hills, CA 90213; (213) 277-2211. (For officers and personel see listing in Companies.)

- Series: Circus (52); That's Hollywood (74).

- Series/First Run: A Current Affair (daily live half-hour magazine show); Animal Express (130); 9 to 5 (52 first-run episodes, plus 33 existing half-hours); Small Wonder (96 first-run); Miller's Court (65); Expedition Danger (26); Audubon Wildlife Theater (78)
- Series/Off-Network: Batman (120); Daniel Boone (120); Fall Guy (112); The Ghost and Mrs. Muir (50); Jackie Gleason Show (100); Julia (86); Lancer (51); Land of the Giants (51); Lost in Space (83 hours, 29 b & w); M*A*S*H (255); Nanny and the Professor (54); Room 222 (113); Trapper John (151); Voyage to the Bottom of the Sea (78 color, 32 b & w); 12 O'Clock High (17 color, 61 b & w); Dynasty (204); Vegas (68); The Ann Sothern Show (190); Movin' On (44); The Untamed World (106); Mr. Belvedere (95 available Fall '89).
- Specials: Charles Dickens' Classics (8); Hollywood: The Gift of Laughter (6); The Making of M*A*S*H (1); Time of Man (1); The President's Command Performance (2); Inside Russia (1); Future Shock (1); Assassins Among Us (1); The Cancer Confrontation (1); Divorce, Kids in the Middle (1); Sex, Teenage Style (1); The Undersea World of Jacques Cousteau (36); Jane Goodall and the World of Animal Behavior (4).
- First Run Syndication: 9 to 5; Dream Girl USA; 100,000 Pyramid; Small Wonder; Dance Fever.
- Features: Big 36 (36, 5 color); Century 5, 6, 7, 8, 9, 10, 11, 12 (total of 212 color and 8 b & w); Century 13 (26), Century 14 (21, includes Predator, Cocoon, Aliens); Charlie Chan (20 b & w); Fox IV, V, VI (total, 102 color, 103 b & w); Fox Hollywood Theatre '88 (advertiser supported, includes Miracle on 34th Street, Boy in Blue, Careful, He Might Hear You, Paris, Texas, Countdown to Looking Glass), Fox Premiere Movies (8, barter), Fox Mystery Theatre (13 90-min. specials); Laurel and Hardy (6); Planet of the Apes (5); Premiere One (20); Premiere 2 (22); Premiere 3 (22); Time Tunnel (5); Mark II (16, 90-min. features); Premium Plus (28); Mark III (25, 2–2½-hour features); MPC-20 (20); Carry On (11).
- News/News Stories: Fox Movietone News (520 original newsreels).
- Domestic Late-Night Network: The New Avengers (26 hours).
- Domestic Miniseries: Sara Dane (8 hours); Wild Times (4 hours); Roughnecks (4 hours); The Far Pavilions (6 hours); Empire, Inc. (6 hours); Jamaica Inn (4 hours); Mussolini and I (4 hours); Flying Doctors (6 hours); Spearfield's Daughter (6 hours)
- Domestic Cartoons: Groovie Goolies & Friends (104 half-hours); Crusader Rabbit (13 color hours, 260 4-minute color episodes, 195 4-minute b & w episodes); Doctor Doolittle (17 half-hours); Fantastic Voyage (17 half-hours); The Hardy Boys (17 half-hours); Journey to the Center of the Earth (17 half-hours); Return to the Planet of the Apes (13 half-hours).

Twyman Films, Inc.

4409 Forest Park Plaza, Dayton, OH 45405; (513) 276-5941. John F. Heck, pres. (Distributor of feature films from Warner Bros., Disney, Fox, Learning Corp., Columbia, Rank & the Rohauer Collection.)

- A Paris; Josef von Sternberg's Anatahan; Louis Malle's Calcutta; Jean Luc Godard's Le Gai Savoir; The Fables of Jean de la Fontaine (33) (in French or English); Frederic Rossif's A Wall In Jerusalem; Tristana, Nosferatu, Merveilleuse Visit, Miracle of Intervale Avenue Heureux Anniversaire, Codine, The Mad Adventures of "Rabbi" Jacob La Caza, Kwaidan, Das Tagebuch Einer Verlorenen (Diary of a Lost Girl), Un Chien Andalou.

U

UPA Productions of America

1875 Century Park E., Suite 2140, Los Angeles, CA 90067; (213) 556-3800. Henry G. Saperstein, pres.; (Distributes Mr. Magoo, Dick Tracy, Gerald McBoing-Boing color cartoons, family specials, and features, Godzilla, Rodan, sci-fi features etc. Produces animated commercials, theatrical films, industrial & TV programs.)

United Press International

1400 I St., NW, Washington, DC 20005; (202) 898-8000. Dr. Earl Brian, chm.; Paul Steinle, pres.; Al Rossiter, Jr., exec. editor. (Distributes news, audio and information services.) Entertainment queries should be directed to UPI Features, (202) 898-8051.

Universal Television

A Division of Universal City Studios, Inc. Universal City, CA 91608, (213) 985-4321. (For officers see listing under companies.)

- 1987–88 season: A Year in the Life; Family Man; Magnum, P.I.; Miami Vice; Murder, She Wrote; Private Eye; Simon & Simon; The Equalizer; The Law and Harry McGraw.

V

Valiant International Pictures

4774 Melrose Ave., Hollywood, CA 90029; (213) 665-5257. Harry Novak, pres.; Ivan Levitan, v.p.; Carmen Novak, secty./treas. (Distributor.)

Van Praag Productions, Inc.

135 E. 55 St., New York, NY 10022; (212) 838-2111. William Van Praag, exec. dir., Eugene Van Praag, Anita Palumbo, Ray Van Praag, staff directors.

Veritas Productions, Inc.

1 Laurie Dr., Englewood Cliffs, NJ 07632; (201) 568-4214 or New York City (212) 765-4240. Richard S. Dubelman, pres.; Joan D. Morley, asst. to pres. (TV and motion picture production)

Versatile Television Production, Inc.

324 Broadway, Cape Girardeau, MO 335-8816. TWX Cape Girardeau 968; Robert O. Hirsch, press.; Jerry Hollis, mgr. (Producers of animated, live action film and video tape commercials and industrial.)

Vestron Television

1010 Washington Blvd., Box 10382, Stamford, CT 06901; (203) 978-5400. Julian Levin, v.p., Vestron TV; David Armstrong, v.p., domestic sales; Bruce Casino, mgr, East Coast sales; Tim Lavender, account exec.; Su Corbin, mgr., operations & admin. West Coast office: 2029 Century Park East, Los Angeles, CA 90067; (213) 551-1723. Central office: 1128 White Lake Court, Fort Worth, TX 76103; (817) 654-2401; Timothy Lavender, acct. exec.

- Over 40 theatrical motion pictures, including Empire of Terror; Lovely & Deadly; Heroes, Pirates and Warriors; The Beach Boys: An American Band, etc.

Viacom International Inc.

1211 Ave. of the Americas, New York, NY 10036; (212) 575-5175.

Corporate personnel: Summer Redstone, chm.; Frank J. Biondi, pres. & CEO; Viacom Entertainment Group; Gus Lucas, exec. v.p., Viacom Entertainment Group; Neil Baum, sr. v.p., corp. dev. & administration, Raymond A. Boyce, sr. v.p., corporate relations; George Castell, v.p., corporate dev. & administration; Kenneth Meyer, v.p., Human Resources; Gordon E. Belt, v.p. & CFO, treas.; Dennis Ellis, v.p., controller; John Brady, sr. v.p., finance/Viacom Entertainment Group; David Fluhrer, dir., corporate communications.

Viacom Enterprises Personnel: Arthur Kananack, pres., domestic syndication; Dennis Gillespie, sr. v.p., mktg; Michael H. Gerber, sr. v.p.; Paul Kalvin, v.p., natl mktg. mgr.; Toby Martin, v.p., programs; Charles Tolep, v.p. & gen. mgr., licensing & merchandising; Eric Veale, v.p., sls. opns; Elissa Lebeck, v.p., res. & mktg. svcs.; Tony Guido, v.p., bus. affairs; Katherine Hogan, v.p., counsel entertainment; Kenneth Werner, dir., bus. affairs; Gerald Pinks, dir., domestic sls. svc.; Lisa Merians, dir, creative svcs.; Betsy Vorce, dir, public rels.; George Faber, dir, communications (L.A. office); Kim Schlotman, dir., mkt. strategy; Richard Dorfman, dir, advertiser sls.; Sean Deneny, mgr., Mid-Atlantic domestic sls.; Joe DiSalvo, sls. mgr., Northeastern div.

Viacom Productions: Tom Tannenbaum, pres., Viacom Productions.

Viacom World Wide: Willard Block, pres., Viacom World Wide Ltd.; Neil McHugh, v.p., new business & admin.; Raul Lefcovich, v.p., international; James Marrinan, v.p., international marketing, Viacom Latino Americana; Noreen Brittenham, assoc. dir., sls. admin., Viacom Latino Americana

Regional Offices: New York: 1211 Ave. of the Americas, New York, NY 10036; (212) 575-5175. Joseph DiSalvo, mgr., Northeast div.; Sean Deneny, mgr.; Mid-Atlantic domestic sls.; Los Angeles: 10900 Wilshire Blvd., Los Angeles, CA 90024; (213) 208-2700. Brooks Carroll, v.p., sls., Western div.; Al Miller, acct. exec., Western div.; Atlanta: 400 Perimeter Center Terrace, Suite 982, Atlanta, GA 30346; (404) 395-7795; Frank Flanagan, v.p., Southeastern div.; Mary Crescas, acct. exec., Southeastern div.; Irving: 433 E. Las Colinas Blvd., Suite 1160, Irving, TX 75039; (214) 556-2255; David Campbell, mgr., Southwestern div.; Gloria Martin, acct. exec., Southwestern div.; Chicago: 10 S. Riverside Plaza, Suite 316; Chicago, IL 60606; (312) 648-5858; Dennis Emerson, v.p., Midwest; Dennis Boyle, mgr., Central Western div.

International Offices: London: Viacom International Limited, 40 Conduit St., London, W1R 9FB, England; (441) 434-4483; Cable: VIACOM London; Telex: 851-919122. Martha Burke-Hennessy, man. dir., Viacom S.A. & Viacom International Ltd. New York:

Viacom Latino Americana, 1211 Ave. of the Americas, New York, NY 10028; (212) 575-5175; Telex: 620-235 VIA. James Marrinan, v.p., gen. mgr., Viacom Latino Americana; Sydney: Viacom International Pty. Ltd., 16th floor, St. Martins Tower, 31 Market St., Sydney, N.S.W. 2000, Australia; (612) 29-4391; Cable: TELECAST, Sydney; Telex: 790-20698; Peter Press, v.p., man. dir.; Lloyd Fryer. All mail to: P.O. Box 0342, Queen Victoria Bldg., Sydney, N.S.W. 2000, Australia. São Paulo: Viacom Video Audio Communicacoes Ltda., Alameda Jau', 1742, Il Andar, Caixa Postal 51521, 01499 São Paulo, Brazil; (55-11) 853-4633; Cable: NEWSHOWS, São Paulo; Telex: 391-01131773. Contact: Ivan Aragon, gen. mgr. Tokyo: Viacom Japan, Inc., 4F, Mitsuwa Bldg., 7-2 Ginza 6-Chome, Chuo-Ku, Tokyo 104, Japan; (81-3) 573-0551; Cable: VIACOMINTL, Tokyo; Telex: 781-24204. Jiro Sugiyama, pres., Viacom Japan, Inc. Toronto: Viacom Enterprises Canada Ltd., 45 Charles St., East, Toronto 5, Ont., Canada M4Y 1S2; Phone: (416) 925-3161; Cable: VIACOMCAN, Toronto; Telex: 369-06219596. Alastair Banks, v.p., gen. mgr. Zug: Viacom S.A., Chamerstrasse 18, 6300 Zug, Switzerland; Phone: 41-42-21-8122; Cable: VIACOM, Zug; Telex: 845-868-750. Contact: Manfred Metzger.

- Series, first-run: What a Country! (26 half-hr. originals); MTV top 20 Video Countdown (52 hour originals); The New Honeymooners (68 discovered half-hrs.); Newly-Released Perry Mason (26 hr. episodes not seen since original airdates); Bizarre (130 half-hrs.)
- Ad Hoc Network (offered jointly with Tribune Entertainment): TV Net (one per month: first-run primetime features never before seen on broadcast television).
- Animated Series: Terrytoons (689 cartoon units); Harlem Globetrotters (22 half-hrs.); The Alvin Show (26 half-hrs.)
- Series, Off-Network: All in the Family (207 half-hrs.); Andy Griffith (249 half-hrs.); The Best of the Beverly Hillbillies (168 half-hrs.); The Bob Newhart Show (142 half-hrs.); Cannon (124 half-hrs.); Circus (24 half-hrs. & 1 1-hr. special); Clint Eastwood in Rawhide (217 half-hrs.); December Bride (154 half-hrs.); Dick Van Dyke (158 half-hrs.); Family Affair (138 half-hrs.); Family Feud (260 half-hrs.); Gomer Pyle (226 hrs.); Gunsmoke (226 hrs.); Have Gun Will Travel (156 half-hrs.); Hawaii Five-O (200 hrs.); Hogan's Heroes (168 half-hrs.); The Honeymooners (107 half-hrs.; 68 newly-recovered, 39 that have been in syndication); I Love Lucy (179 half-hrs.); I Spy (6 hrs.); The Life and Times of Grizzly Adams (35 hrs., 2 90-min. specials); Marshall Dillon (233 half-hrs.); The Mary Tyler Moore Show (168 half-hrs.); Millionaire (188 half-hrs.); My Three Sons (160 half-hrs.) Our Miss Brooks (127 half-hrs.); Perry Mason (271 hrs; 26 newly-recovered, 50 seen twice since their original airdates, 195 that have been in syndication); Petticoat Junction (148 half-hrs.); The Rookies (90 hrs.); Trackdown (71 half-hrs.); The Twilight Zone (168 half-hrs. & hrs.); The Wild, Wild West (104 hrs.); You Are There (65 half-hrs.)
- Packages/Features: Viacom I, II, III,IV, V, VI, VII, VIII, IX, V, XI; Viacom Movie Greats; The Legend Group; The Exploitables; The Explodables; Gasp; Thematics; Young and Reckless.

Vidistrib, Inc.

4209 Troost Ave., Studio City, CA 91604; Tel.: (818) 762-3535. John P. Ballinger, pres.; Rita Cross, v.p.-treas. (TV show sales & distribution syndication, barter, consultation).

Viking Films, Inc.

1600 Broadway, New York, NY 10019; (212) 255-8858. Israel M. Berman, pres., exec. producer. (Produce educational, children's subjects, sciences, cartoons & puppets.)

W

WW Entertainment

(A division of World Northal Corporation) 205 E. 42 St., New York, NY 10017; (212) 661-3350; Telex: 4973939; FAX: (212) 808-5469. Tony Elmaleh, v.p., prod.; James R. Mayer, v.p.; Zita Siegel, dir. sls. adm.; Bernice Farnan, administrator/sales & research.

- Feature Films—Martial Arts Feature Films: Black I (13 titles); Black Belt II (26 titles); Black Belt III (13 titles); Black Belt IV (29 titles); Black Belt V (13 titles); Action Flicks (7 titles); WW Entertainment I (16 titles).
- Series—The Best of Groucho (130 half-hrs.); Skyways (130 hrs.)
- Co-productions-BBC: 24 feature films.

Roger Wade Productions, Inc.

15 W. 44 St., New York, NY 10036; (212) 575-9111. Roger W. Wade, pres. (Producers of motion pictures and videotape for industry, sound slide films, multi-media, slides.)

Warner Bros. Television

4000 Warner Blvd., Burbank, CA 91522; (818) 954-6000. (For officers and personnel, see listing under Companies.)

Series and specials available for domestic sales (all color unless otherwise indicated)

- Miniseries: Hollywood Wives (6 hrs.); "V" (10 hrs.); Bare Essence (4 hrs. or 4½ hrs.); The Thorn Birds (10 hrs.); Pearl (6 hrs.); Scruples (6 hrs.); Roots (12 hrs.); Roots: The Next Generation (14 hrs.)
- Series/Off Network: Head of the Class (half-hrs.); Growing Pains (half-hrs.); Night Court (half-hrs.); Scarecrow and Mrs. King (88 hours); Matt Houston (68 hours); Private Benjamin (39 half-hrs.); The Dukes of Hazzard (147 hrs.); Alice (202 half-hrs.); Welcome Back, Kotter (95 half-hrs.); Chico and the Man (88 half-hrs.); F-Troop (65 half-hrs., 31 color); Superman (104 half-hrs., 52 color); Batman/Superman/Aquaman (69 animated half-hrs.) Harry-O (44 hrs.); Wonder Woman (61 hrs); Kung Fu (62 hrs.); The Waltons (221 hrs.); The FBI (234 hrs.); Tarzan (57 hrs.); Maverick (124 hrs.)
- Specials: The Phenomenon of Roots (1 hr.); David L. Wolper Specials of the Seventies (30 one-hr. specials)
- Features/Packages: Volume 27 (18 features); TV4 (13 features); Volume 26 (24 features); TV3 (13 features); Volume 25 (24 features); TV2 (13 feature titles); Volume 24 (18 features); 13 Classic Thrillers II (13 features); TVI (13 features); Volume 23 (20 features); Volume 22 (38 features); Volume 21 (26 features); The FBI Story (4 features); Volume 20 (30 features); Volume 19 (29 features, 28 in color); Volume 18 (28 features, 25 in color); Volume 17 (23 features, 21 in color); Volume 16 (18 features, 16 in color); Volume 14-15 (13 features, 12 in color); Volume 13 (25 features, 17 in color); Volume 2-A (22 features, 13 in color); Volume 1-A (24 features, 17 in color); 13 Classic Thrillers (13 features); Tarzan Features (32 features, 9 in color); The Bowery Boys (48 features); Starlite 6 (26 features, 12 in color); Starlite 5 (28 features, 18 in color); Starlite 4 (30 features, 16 in color); Starlite 3 (30 features, 19 in color); Special Features (17 features).
- Cartoons: Bugs Bunny & Friends (100 cartoons); Porky Pig & Friends (156 cartoons)

INTERNATIONAL

- Cartoons: Bugs Bunny & Friends (100 cartoons); Bugs Bunny cartoons (234 cartoons); Looney Toons (190 cartoons, 78 color, 112 black-and-white)
- Features/Packages: International 33 (36); International 21 (51); International 21 (34); International 30 (66); International 29 (44); International 28 (7); International 27 (5); International 26 (11); International 25 (32); International 24 (80); International 23 (99); International 22 (135); International 21 (56); International 20 (3); International 19 (28); International 18 (26); International 17 (28); International 16 (92); International 15 (33); International 14 (36); International 13 (35); International 12 (36); International 11 (36); International 9 (1); International 5 (48); International 4 (127)
- Miniseries: Napoleon and Josephine: A Love Story (6 hrs.); Nutcracker: Money, Madness and Murder (6 hrs.); Dream West (7 hrs.); Crossings (6 hrs.); Dress Gray (4 hrs.); North and South—I (12 hrs.); North and South—II (12 hrs.); Hollywood Wives (6 hrs.); The Thorn Birds (10); "V" (10); Roots (12); Roots: The Next Generation (14); The Mystic Warrior (5); Bare Essence (4); Scruples (6); Pearl (6); The Phenomenon of Roots (1); The Awakening Land (7); Born to the Wind (4); Hanging by a Thread (4); Haywire (4); Moviola (6); Night the Bridge Fell Down (4); Pirate (4); Salem's Lot (4)
- One-Hour Series: O'Hara (6); Scarecrow and Mrs. King (88); Hotel; The Colbys (49); Spenser: For Hire; Shell Game (6); Shadow Chasers (12); Hollywood Beat (14); "V" (19); Matt Houston (68); The Dukes of Hazzard (147); Harry O (44); Kung Fu (62); Tarzan (57); I Had Three Wives (6); MacGruder & Loud (13); Eye to Eye (6); Double Dare (6); Finder of Lost Loves (23); Glitter (13); The Yellow Rose (22); The Mississippi (23); Bare Essence (11); The Alaskans (36); Banyon (15); Bourbon Street Beat (39); Bret Maverick (16); Bronco (63); California Fever (10); Casablanca (5); Cheyenne (107); Code R (13); The Dakotas (19); Delphi Bureau (8); Dial M for Murder (13); Drama (42); Enos (17); The F.B.I. (238); Fitzpatricks (13); Freebie and the Bean (9); Gallant Men (25); Hawaiian Eye (134); High Performance (4); Life on Earth (13); Maverick (124); The New Land (13); Nichols (24); Notorious Woman (7); Rafferty (13); Roaring 20's (45); Search (23); 77 Sunset Strip (205); The Streets of San Francisco (119); Sugarfoot (69); Superfriends (93); Challenge of Superfriends (16); Surfside Six (74); Time Express (4); The Tribal Eye (7); The Waltons (219); Wizards and Warriors (8); Wonder Woman (13); New Adventures of Wonder Woman (46); The Yeagers (4); Young Maverick (6)
- Half-Hour Series: Night Court; Growing Pains; Life with Lucy (13); My Sister, Sam; Head of the Class; Welcome Back, Kotter (95); Love, Sidney (44); Porky Pig Show (26); Private Benjamin (39); Roadrunner Show (26); Superman (104); Tarzan, Lord of the Jungle (34); Alice (202); Rubik, the Amazing Cube (13); Off the Rack (7); A.E.S Hudson Street (5); Another Day (13); Aquaman (18); At Ease (14); Batman (17); New Adventures of Batman (16); B.C. Archaelogy of Bible Lands (12); Bugs Bunny Show (78); Chicago Teddy Bears (13); Chico and the Man (88); Colt .45 (67);

The Cowboys (12); Dorothy (4); The Dukes—Animated (20); Fat Albert and the Cosby Kids (60); Flo (29); F Troop (65); Goodnight, Beantown (8); Jimmy Stewart Show (24); Lassie's Rescue Rangers (17); Lawman (156); Little People, The Brian Keith Show (46); Marine Boy (78); Me and Maxx (10); Merrie Melodies Show (24); Mr. Roberts (30); New Adventures of Superman (34); No Time for Sergeants (34); Park Place (5); Shazam! (28); TV Funnies (16)

Weiss Global Enterprises

2055 S. Saviers Rd., Suite 12, Oxnard, CA 93033-3693; (805) 486-4495. Cable: WEISSPICT. Adrian Weiss, pres.; Steven A. Weiss, secty./treas.; Ethel L. Weiss, v.p.; Laurie Weiss, v.p.; Beverly S. Verman, opns. mgr.; Alex Gordon, information services.

- Features: Galaxy "15": fifteen features including Ginger in the Morning, Molly and Promises! Promises!; Golden Showmanship "9": nine features including Cattle Queen of Montana, Slightly Scarlett; Westerns: 60 action features starring Johnny Mack Brown, Harry Carey, Fred Kohler, Jr., Rex Lease, Buddy Roosevelt and Bob Steele; Vintage Flicks: 24 features from the '30's and '40's; One-Hour Documentaries: The Brave Rifles (51 mins.), Our Time in Hell (51 mins.); Those Crazy Americans (54 mins.); Impact "120": 120 films produced by Robert L. Lippert, including Baron of Arizona, I Shot Jesse James, King Dinosaur, etc.
- Serials: Custer's Last Stand (15 episodes); The Black Coin (15 episodes); The Clutching Hand (15 episodes).
- Series, First-Run: The Stan Kann Show (52 half-hrs.); Kids Say the Darndest Things (600 episodes, 5 min. each).
- Series, Off-Network: Make Room For Daddy (161 half-hr. programs); Canine Comments (13 quarter-hr. short subject); I Married Joan (98 half-hr. sit-coms); The Bill Dana Show (42 half-hrs.); Craig Kennedy, Crimonologist (26 half-hr. mysteries); Good Morning World (26 half-hr. sit-coms); Thrill of Your Life (13 half-hrs.); My Little Margie (126 half-hrs.); Rocky Jones, Space Ranger (39 half-hrs.); Waterfront (78 half-hrs.); The Adventures of Jim Bowie (76 half-hours).
- Comedy Shorts: The Chuckle Heads (150 five-min. slapstick comedy shorts).
- Cartoons: Alice by Walt Disney (10 ten-min. cartoons); Krazy Kid Kartunes (4 six-min. cartoons); Nursery Rhymes (6 1½-min. cartoons).

Worldvision Enterprises, Inc.

660 Madison Ave., New York, NY 10021; (212) 832-3838. John D. Ryan, pres. & chief exec. officer; Bert Cohen, exec. v.p. & C.O.O; Lawrence Gottlieb, exec. v.p., finance & admin.; Burt Rosenburgh, exec. v.p. & g.m., Evergreen Programs, Inc.; Steve Blank, senior v.p., finance; Randy Hanson, senior v.p., domestic sales; Gary G. Montanus, senior v.p., marketing; Tom Devlin, v.p. & g.m., Worldvision Home Video, Inc.; Bill Baffi, v.p., eastern division mgr.; Jerry Kaufer, v.p., creative services; Rita Scarfone, v.p., advertising & promotion; Dan Willis, v.p., international sales admin.; Mitch Black, v.p., operations; Andrea Furman, v.p., office management & personnel; Philip Marella, v.p., legal & business affairs; Adam Lloyd, account exec., eastern div.; Karen Davidson, account exec., advertiser sales; Robert J. Day, mgr., eastern div., Worldvision Home Video, Inc.; Gerald Bizenspan, dir., research & sales dev.; Andy Samet, dir. of promotion; Noreen McGrath, dir., marketing & strategic planning; Phil Martzolf, dir., domestic sales admin.; Doreen Muldoon, dir., advertiser sales admin.

DOMESTIC DIVISION

CENTRAL: 625 N. Michigan Avenue, Chicago, IL 60611; (312) 642-2650. Brian O'Sullivan, acct. exec., Central Division; Jim Kauss, acct. exec., Cent. Div., Evergreen Programs; Ken Williams, Central Div. mgr., Worldvision Home Video, Inc.

SOUTHERN: 400 Perimeter Center Terrace, Atlanta, GA 30346; (404) 394-7444. Jim Thomson, v.p., Southern Division mgr.; Reggie Jester, acct. exec., Southern Division; Karl Middelburg, acct. exec., Southern Division; Bruce Knox, Southern Div. mgr., Worldvision Home Video, Inc.

WESTERN: 9465 Wilshire Blvd., Beverly Hills, CA 90212; (213) 273-7667. Paul Danylik, v.p., Western Division mgr.; Martin Weisman, acct. exec., Western Division, Lawrence A. Forsdick, v.p., Special Projects.

- Hour Series: Barnaby Jones (177); Ben Casey (153); Breaking Point (30); Combat (152); Don Lane Show (130); Fugitive (120); The Invaders (43); Little House on the Prairie (216.5); Love Boat I (140); Love Boat II (115); Mod Squad (124 1-hr.); Man from Atlantis (13 1-hr;, 3 2-hr., 1 1½-hr.); Return to Eden (22); Streets of San Francisco (119).
- Half-Hour Series: Adventures of Champion (26); Annie Oakley (80); Buffalo Bill, Jr. (40); Come Along (13); Dark Shadows (780); Dickens & Fenster (32); Doris Day Show (128); Douglas Fairbanks Presents (115); F.D.R (25 ½-hr., 1 1-hr.); High Road (31); It Pays to Be Ignorant (39); Love Boat II (115 ½ or 1 hour); Mickey Rooney (17); Next Step Beyond (24); N.Y.P.D. (49); On the Mat (52); One Step Beyond (94); People's Choice (104); Range Rider

(76); The Rebel (76); Starring the Actors (13); Starting From Scratch (24); Take My Word for It (130); That Girl (136); Throb (48); Wendy and Me (34); Wonders of the Wild (26); Trivial Pursuit (195).

- Mini-Series: Return to Eden (6 hours); Holocaust (10 hours); Against the Wind (13 hours).
- Features: Prime VIII (20 color features); Prime VII (25 color features); Prime VI (19); Prime V (26); Prime IV (26); Prime III (16); Prime II (16); Prime I (10); Hanna Barbera Superstars (10).
- Animated & Children's Programming: Fun World of Hanna-Barbera (84 half-hrs.); H-B's World of Super Adventure (129 half-hrs.); Banana Splits (125 half-hrs.); Saturday at the Movies (6 specials); Top Cat (30 half-hrs.); Wait Till Your Father Gets Home (48); Josie & The Pussycats (16); Josie & the Pussycats in Outer Space (16); Harvey/Casper, (244 cartoons) The Jackson Five (23 half-hrs.); The Jerry Lewis Show (17 half-hrs.); King Kong (26 half-hrs.); Lancelot Link-Secret Chimp (17 half-hrs.); Milton the Monster (26 half-hrs.); Professor Kitzel (104 cartoons); The Reluctant Dragon & Mr. Toad (17 half-hrs.); Smokey the Bear (51 half-hrs.); George of the Jungle (17 half-hrs.); The Funtastic World of Hanna-Barbera (2 hour); The Jetsons (75 half-hours); Rambo (65 half-hrs.); Centurions (65 half-hrs.); Chuck Norris Karate Kommandos (5 half-hours; mini-series); Snorks (65 half-hour); The Yogi Bear Show (65 half-hour); Hanna Barbera's Superstars 10 (10 2 hours movies); Discover (103 half-hour); Yogi Bear's First Christmas (2 hour movie).
- Specials: Jack Nicklaus at the Home of Golf (3 hrs.); The Fabulous Sixties (10 one-hrs.); The Bay City Rollers (1 hr.); Echo 1 (17 1 hour); Herbie Mann/Roland Kirk (half-hr.); Is It Christ? (1 hr.); The Last Nazi (1 hour); Raphael (1 hr.); Roberta Flack/Donny Hathaway (half-hr.); The World of Miss World (1 hr.); The New Fangled Wandering Minstrel Show (1 hr.); The Musical Ambassadors, Kenny Rogers & The First Edition in New Zealand (1 hr.); Ron Luciano's Lighter Side of Sports (half-hr.); A Christmas Carol (animated half-hr.); An Evening with Irish Television (1 hr.); Russian Festival of Music and Dance; The Bobby Vinton Show (1 hr.); A Shark's Paradise (2 hours); Amahl & the Night Visitors (1 hr.); Children of the Gael (1 hr.); Irish Rovers Special (1 hr.); The Night the Animals Talked (half-hour); Sunshine Specials (eight 1-hr.); A Little Bit of Irish: Bing Crosby (1 hr.).

Worldvision International:

AUSTRALIA: Worldvision Enterprises of Australia Pty. Ltd., 5–13 Northcliff St., Milsons Point 2061, Sydney; Tel.: 922-4722. Brian Rhys-Jones, mgr. dir., Australia & Far East.

BRAZIL: Worldvision Filmes do Brasil Ltd., Rua Macedo Sobrinho 50, Botafogo, CEP 22271, Rio de Janeiro; Tel.: 286-8992. Raymund Lopes Rodgigues, mgr. dir., Brazil.

CANADA: Worldvision Enterprises of Canada, 1200 Bay St., Suite #203, Toronto M5R 2A5, Canada; Tel.: (416) 967-1200. Bruce Swanson, v.p. and gen. mgr.

ENGLAND: Worldvision Enterprises, U.K. Ltd., 54 Pont St., London, S.W. 1, England, Tel.: 584-5357. William Peck, mng. dir., England.

FRANCE: Worldvision Enterprises S.A.R.L., 28, rue Bayard 75008, Paris, France; Tel.: 4273-3995. Mary Jane Fourniel, mng. dir., France & French-speaking countries.

GERMANY: Worldvision GmbH, Postfach 906, 8 München 33, Germany; Tel.: 26-4091. Mex Hartmann, mng. dir.

ITALY: Worldvision Enterprises, Inc., Adalia Anstalt, Via Del Corso, 22/Int. 10, 00186, Rome, Italy; Tel.: 67-87-056. Martin Michael Kiwe, v.p., European operations.

JAPAN: Worldvision Enterprises, Inc., Tsukiji Hamarikyu Bldg., 7th floor, 5-3-3, Tsukiji, Chou-ku, Tokyo 104, Japan; Tel.: 545-3977. Mie Horasawa, sls. rep., Japan and Korea.

- New Releases: Theatrical Films: Ironweed, The Running Man, Light of Day, Monster Squad; Internal Affairs (4 hour mini-series); Stone for Ibarra (2 hour movie); Stranger on My Land (2 hours); Starting From Scratch (24 half-hours); Streets of San Francisco (119 hours); A.F.I. Life Achievement Award (90 mins); Home Fires (4 hr. mini-series); Hanna-Barbera's Superstars (10 animated films, 2hrs.); General Hospital (serial, hours); One Life to Live (serial, hours); All My Children (serial, hours); Hands of a Stranger (4-hr. mini-series); Highway to Heaven (1 hr. series); Dallas (1 hr. series); Angel in Green (2-hr. movie); Kids Like These (2-hr. movie); Little Troll Prince (1 hr. animated Christmas special); A Mouse, A Mystery and Me (half-hour special).
- Series and Specials (U.S. Networks, 1987–88): The Last Frontier (4-hour mini-series); The Stepford Children (2 hours); The Day They Came to Arrest the Book (1 hour special); Stone Fox (2 hours); Shark's Paradise (2 hours); When the Bough Breaks (2 hours); Night of Courage (2 hours); Stranger In My Bed (2 hours); The High Price of Passion (2 hours); Sable (1 hour series); Throb (48 half-hours); You Again? (26 half-hours); The Love Boat (hour); On Wings of Eagles (4 hour mini-series); Doubletake (4 hour mini-series); Key to Rebecca (4 hour mini-series); Sam's Son (2 hours); A Deadly Business (2 hours); My Two Loves (2 hours); Welcome Home Bobby (2 hours); Smurfs (224 animated half-

hours (available only in U.K., Ireland, Canada); The Jetsons (75 animated half-hours); Wildfire (13 animated half-hours); Berenstain Bears (26 animated half-hours); The Flintstones 25th Anniversary (1 hour animated special); The 13 Ghosts of Scooby Doo (13 animated half- hours); Mr. T (30 animated half-hours); The Flintstone Kids (34 animated half-hours); Alvin & the Chipmunks (54 animated half- hours); Yogi's Treasure Hunt (27 animated half-hours); Sky Commanders (13 animated half-hours); Snorks (36 animated half-hours (available only in U.K., Ireland and Canada); Roboforce (half-hour animated special).

• Special Presentation Programming: Three Little House on the Prairie Special Presentations—Look Back to Yesterday (2 hrs.), Bless All the Dear Children (2 hrs.), The Last Farewell (2 hrs.); An Act of Love: The Patricia Neal Story (2 hrs.); Worldvision Dramatic Specials (10 one-hr. specials); Holocaust (9½ hrs.); Against the Wind (13 hrs.); The Ordeal of Patty Hearst (3 hrs.); The Trial of Lee Harvey Oswald (4 hrs.); The Last Nazi (90 min.); Russian Festival of Music and Dance (1 hr.); Reincarnation (2 hrs.); Little Mo (3 hrs.); Freedom Road (4 hrs.); Candid Camera Special (5 one-hrs.); Remember Me (2 hrs.).

• Feature Films: More than 200 titles—Prestige Package; 21 features in color including: "Night Watch," "A Touch of Class," "Hedda," "Baker's Hawk," "Black Market Baby," "Breakthrough," "Book of Numbers," "Fingers," "Cry For Me Billy," "Sweet Hostage," "Nasty Habits," and "Thieves"; Paragon Features; over 80 features in color. Stars include Robert Preston, Patty Duke Astin, Valerie Perrine, Dom DeLuise, Patricia Elliott, Gary Coleman, Mickey Rooney, George C. Scott, Henry Fonda, James Whitmore, Dennis Weaver, David Janssen, James Woods, Lee Majors, James Earl Jones, Ed Asner, Suzanne Pleshette, William Devane; Prime I, II, III, IV and V; 84 made-for-TV movies, all in color. Among the stars: Alan Ladd, Fred Astaire, Ernest Borgnine, Walter Brennan, LeVar Burton, Sammy Davis Jr., Helen Hayes, Susan Hayward, Hal Holbrook, Janet Leigh, Ray Milland, Agnes Moorehead, Ryan O'Neal, Jack Palance, Lee Remick, Burt Reynolds, Jill St. John, Gloria Swanson, Barbara Stanwyck, Shelley Winters; Selznick Classics; 22 films including "Intermezzo," "Duel in the Sun," "Notorious," "Spellbound," "Rebecca," "The Spiral Staircase," "Portrait of Jenny," "The Farmer's Daughter," "The Garden of Allah," "Bill of Divorcement," "Made For Each Other," and "The Wild Heart"; ABC Pictures; including "Cabaret," "They Shoot Horses Don't They?," "Charly," "Take the Money and Run," "Straw Dogs," "For Love of Ivy," "Song of Norway," "The Killing of Sister George," and "Krakatoa, East of Java" (all in color).

• Children's Programming: Hanna-Barbera/Ruby-Spears; representing thousands of half-hours of animated programming; Casper the Friendly Ghost; Milton the Monster; Jerry Lewis Show; Jackson 5; Lancelot Link.

• Holiday Specials: Little Troll Prince; A Mouse, A Mystery and Me; 'Tis the Season to Be Smurfy; The Cabbage Patch Kids' First Christmas; Smurfily Ever After (U.K. & Ireland & Canada only); I Love the Chipmunks Valentine Special; Alvin & The Chipmunks Reunion (Easter); A Flintstone Christmas; Yogi's First Christmas; Casper's First Christmas; Christmas Comes to Pacland; Smurfs Christmas Special (U.K., Ireland, Canada only); My Smurfy Valentine (U.K., Ireland & Canada only); Smurfs Springtime

Special/Easter (U.K., Ireland & Canada only); The Gathering; The Gathering II; Casper Halloween Special; The Pumpkin Who Couldn't Smile; The Thanksgiving Visitor; The Thanksgiving That Almost Wasn't; The Great Santa Claus Caper; A Christmas Story; A Christmas Memory; A Christmas Carol; The Night the Animals Talked; Amahl and the Night Visitors; A Little Bit of Irish; Russian Festival of Music and Dance.

• Series: Little House on the Prairie (216 1 hr.); Eight is Enough (112 one-hr. comedy-drama); Kaz (22 one hr.); Project UFO (26 fact-based action-adventure, one-hr.); The Andros Targets (13 one hr.); Spencer's Pilots (11 one-hr.); Man From Atlantis (20 hours); Married: The First Year (4 one-hr. drama); Pruitts of Southampton (starring Phyllis Diller, 130 half-hr. comedy); The Doris Day Show (128 half hrs.); Hunter (13 one hr.); Mod Squad (124 hr.); The Invaders (43 hrs.); The Fugitive (120 hrs., 30 in color); The Next Step Beyond (John Newland, 24 half hr.); Thunder (12 half hrs.); Garrison's Gorillas (World War II drama, 26 hrs.); Cowboy in Africa (26 hrs., color) Ben Casey (153 one-hr., b/w); That Girl (136 half-hour); Lucie Arnaz Show (6 half-hr.); Return to Eden (22 one hrs.).

Worldwide Television News

1995 Broadway, New York, NY 10023; (212) 362-4440. Kenneth Coyte, pres.; William H. Dudar, bureau chief; Michael Harbert, rgl. exec. for corporate video sls; Scott Michaeloff, rgl. exec. for TV facilities sls. (Produces and distributes intl. news coverage; produces weekly news cassettes including 2 programs—Roving Report & Earthwatch; video news releases, corporate promotional videos, crewing & production services.)

FILM LIBRARY: 1995 Broadway, New York, NY 10036; (212) 362-4440. Vincent O'Reilly, library mgr.

Wright, Carter, Enterprises

6533 Hollywood Blvd., Hollywood, CA 90028; (213) 469-0944. Carter Wright, pres.; June Wright, talent coordinator. (Live and film shows, commercials).

Ziv International

1875 Century Park E., Suite 1610, Los Angeles, CA 90067; (213) 277-9064. Telex: 698619.

• Series: Angel (50), Animator's Film Library (60), Candy Candy (65), Captain Future (52), Captain Harlock (42), Captain Nemo (15), Fables of the Green Forest (52), Gumby (34), King Arthur, (44), Robot Festival, (130), Space Angel (52), Spunky & Tadpole (15), Villa Alegre (260), Man from Buttonwillow (52), Children of the World (13).

• Specials: Tom Jones Live in Vegas, Tony Bennett/Nancy Wilson, Crystal Gayle, Bal Du Moulin Rouge, Peter Cottontail, Silent Knight, Les Miserables.

• Feature length films: 300.

• Merchandising and licensing.

Programs

* NETWORK PRIMETIME SHOWS

* SYNDICATED

* MOVIES AND MINI-SERIES MADE FOR TELEVISION

1988–89 Prime Time Shows

Series titles are listed alphabetically by network, along with time slots, suppliers, production staff heads (executive producer: EP; executive supervising producer: ESP; supervising producer: SP; senior producer: Sr. P; producer: P; co-producer: CP; director: D), cast regulars and semi-regulars.

ABC-TV

Series Title	Day	Hr.	Mins.	Supplier	Production Principals	Cast Regulars & Semi-Regulars
ABC Sunday Night Movie	Sun	9:00	120	Various		
China Beach	Wed	10:00	60	Sacret Inc.-Warner Bros. TV	EP: John Sacret Young SP: Patricia Green P: John Wells CP: Chris Nelson, Geno Escarrega	Dana Delany, Nan Woods, Michael Boatman, Marg Helgenberger, Robert Picardo, Tim Ryan, Concetta Tomei, Brian Winner, Megan Gallagher, Nancy Giles, Jeff Kober
Dynasty	Thu	9:00	60	Aaron Spelling Progs.-Richard & Esther Shapiro Prods.	EP: Aaron Spelling, Douglas S. Cramer, Richard & Esther Shapiro SP: David Paulsen P: Dennis Hammer	John Forsythe, Linda Evans, John James, Gordon Thomson, Michael Nader, Heather Locklear, Emma Samms, Joan Collins, Stephanie Beacham, Ray Abruzzo, Stella Hall, Liza Morrow
Full House	Fri	8:30	30	Jeff Franklin Prods.-Miller-Boyett Prods.-Lorimar TV	EP: Jeff Franklin, Thomas L. Miller, Robert L. Boyett SP: Rob Dames & Bob Fraser P: Don Van Atta, Lenny Ripps, Marc Warren, Dennis Rinsler	John Stamos, Bob Saget, David Coulier, Lori Loughlin, Candace Cameron, Jodie Sweetin, Mary Kate Olsen, Ashley Fuller Olsen
Growing Pains	Wed	8:00	30	Warner Bros. TV	EP: Mike Sullivan, Steve Marshall, Dan Guntzelman P: Henry Johnson, David Kendall	Alan Thicke, Joanna Kerns, Kirk Cameron, Tracey Gold, Jeremy Miller
Head of the Class	Wed	8:30	30	Eustis/Elias Prods.-Warner Bros. TV	EP: Michael Elias & Rich Eustis P: Alan Rosen	Howard Hesseman, William G. Schilling, Jeannette Arnette, Leslie Bega, Dan Frischman, Robin Givens, Khrystyne Haje, Jory Husain, Tony O'Dell, Brian Robbins, Kimberly Russell, Dan Schneider, Tannis Vallely
Hooperman	Wed	9:30	30	Adam Prods.-20th Fox TV	EP: Rick Kellard, Robert M. Myman, Michael Wagner SP: R. W. Goodwin CP: Phil Kellard & Tom Moore	John Ritter, Barbara Bosson, Felton Perry, Sydney Walsh, Alix Elias, Clarence Felder, Joseph Gian, Debrah Farentino, Britches (dog)
Incredible Sunday	Sun	7:00	60	Woody Fraser Prods.-Reeves Entertainment Group	EP:-D: Woody Fraser SP: Bill Paolantonio, Earl Durham P: Alex Gregory	John Davidson, Christina Ferrare
Just The Ten Of Us	Fri	9:30	30	GSM Prods.-Warner Bros. TV	EP: Dan Guntzelman, Steve Marshall, Mike Sullivan P: Henry Johnson	Bill Kirchenbauer, Deborah Harmon, Heather Langenkamp, Brooke Theiss, Jamie Luner, Jo Ann Willette, Matt Shakman, Heidi Zeigler
Knightwatch	Thu	8:00	60	MGM/UA TV-Astor III Prods.	EP: Kevin Sullivan	Benjamin Bratt, Joshua Cadman, Don Franklin, Ava Haddad, Calvin Levels, Paris Vaughan, Tom Bower
MacGyver	Mon	8:00	60	Henry Winkler/John Rich Prods.-Paramount Network TV	EP: Henry Winkler, John Rich, Steve Downing	Richard Dean Anderson, Dana Elcar
Mission: Impossible	Sun	8:00	60	Paramount Network TV	SP: Michael Fisher CP: Walter Brough	Peter Graves, Tony Hamilton, Phil Morris, Thaao Penghlis, Terry Markwell
Mr. Belvedere	Fri	9:00	30	Lazy B/Fox Prods.-20th Fox TV	EP: Frank Dungan & Jeff Stein SP: Liz Sage P: Patricia Rickey, Ric Weiss & Jeff Ferro CP: Geri Maddern	Christopher Hewett, Ilene Graff, Rob Stone, Tracy Wells, Brice Beckham, Bob Uecker
Monday Night Football	Mon	9:00	120+	ABC Sports	EP: Geoffrey Mason P: Ken Wolfe D: Craig Janoff	Al Michaels, Frank Gifford, Dan Dierdorf
Moonlighting	Tue	9:00	60	Picturemaker Prods.-ABC Circle Films	EP: Jay Daniel SP: Artie Mandelberg P: Charles H. Eglee CP: Chris Welch, Barbara Hall	Cybill Shepherd, Bruce Willis, Allyce Beasley, Curtis Armstrong

559

Series Title	Day	Hr.	Mins.	Supplier	Production Principals	Cast Regulars & Semi-Regulars
Murphy's Law	Sat	8:00	60	Zev Braun Pictures-New World TV	EP: Zev Braun, Michael Gleason, Leonard Stern P: Lee Zlotoff, Lynn Rainer	George Segal, Maggie Han, Josh Mostel
Perfect Strangers	Fri	8:00	30	Miller-Boyett-Prods.-Lorimar TV	EP: Thomas L. Miller, Robert L. Boyett, William Bickley & Michael Warren P: Paula Roth	Bronson Pinchot, Mark Linn-Baker, Melanie Wilson, Rebeca Arthur, Belita Moreno, Jo Marie Payton-France, Sam Anderson
Police Story	Sat	9:00	120	Columbia Pictures TV	CP: Jim O'Keefe	
Roseanne	Tue	8:30	30	Carsey-Werner Co.-Wind Dancer Prods.	EP: Matt Williams, Marcy Carsey, Tom Werner P: Gayle S. Maffeo, Laurie Gelman, Danny Jacobson	Roseanne Barr, John Goodman, Laurie Metcalf, Sal Barone, Sara Gilbert, Lecy Goranson, George Clooney, Natalie West
thirtysomething	Tue	10:00	60	Bedford Falls Co.-MGM/UA TV	EP: Marshall Herskovitz, Edward Zwick SP: Scott Winant P: Richard Kramer CP: Ellen Pressman	Timothy Busfield, Polly Draper, Mel Harris, Peter Horton, Melanie Mayron, Ken Olin, Patricia Wettig
20/20	Fri	10:00	60	ABC News	EP: Victor Neufeld Sr. P: Jeff Diamond D: Michael Buddy	Hugh Downs, Barbara Walters, Bob Brown, Tom Jarriel, Stone Phillips, Lynn Sherr, John Stossel
Who's the Boss?	Tue	8:00	30	Columbia Pictures TV-Hunter/Cohan Prods.	EP: Martin Cohan, Blake Hunter SP: Karen Wengrod, Ken Cinnamon P: John Anderson, Danny Kallis	Tony Danza, Judith Light, Alyssa Milano, Danny Pintauro, Katherine Helmond
Wonder Years, The	Wed	9:00	30	Black/Marlens Co.-New World TV	EP: Neal Marlens, Carol Black, Bob Brush P: Jeff Silver	Fred Savage, Dan Lauria, Alley Mills, Jason Hervey, Olivia d'Abo, Josh Saviano

CBS-TV

Series Title	Day	Hr.	Mins.	Supplier	Production Principals	Cast Regulars & Semi-Regulars
Almost Grown	Mon	10:00	60	Universal TV	EP: William Sackheim, David Chase SP: Stephen Cragg, Andrew Schneider P: Frank South CP: Mark Horowitz	Timothy Daly, Eve Gordon, Rita Taggart, Michael Alldredge, Anita Gillette, Richard Schaal, Albert Macklin, Ocean Hellman
Annie McGuire	Wed	8:30	30	MTM Enterprises	EP: Elliot Shoenman, Paul Wolff SP: Tom Cherones	Mary Tyler Moore, Denis Arndt, Eileen Heckart, John Randolph, Adiren Brody, Cynthia Marie King, Bradley Warden
Beauty & the Beast	Fri	8:00	60	Witt/Thomas Prods.-Republic Pictures	EP: Paul Junger Witt, Tony Thomas, Ron Koslow SP: Stephen Kurzfeld P: Kenneth R. Koch, George R. R. Martin CP: Alex Gansa, Howard Gordon	Linda Hamilton, Ron Perlman, Roy Dotrice, Jay Acovone
CBS Sunday Movies	Sun	9:00	120	Various		
CBS Tuesday Movies	Tue	9:00	120	Various		
Coming Of Age	Mon	8:30	30	Bungalow Prods. 78-Universal TV	EP: Barry Kemp, Emily Marshall P: Alan Eisenstock & Larry Mintz	Paul Dooley, Phyllis Newman, Alan Young, Glynis Johns, Kevin Pollak, Ruta Lee
Dallas	Fri	9:00	60	Lorimar TV	EP: Leonard Katzman, Larry Hagman SP: Arthur Bernard Lewis P: Mitchell Wayne Katzman, Cliff Fenneman	Barbara Bel Geddes, Patrick Duffy, Linda Gray, Larry Hagman, Steve Kanaly, Howard Keel, Ken Kercheval, Charlene Tilton, Sheree J. Wilson, Andrew Stevens, George Kennedy
Designing Women	Mon	9:30	30	Bloodworth/Thomason Mozark Prods.-Columbia Pictures TV	EP: Harry Thomason, Linda Bloodworth-Thomason SP: Pamela Norris P: Douglas Jackson, Tommy Thompson CP: David Trainer	Delta Burke, Dixie Carter, Annie Potts, Jean Smart, Meshach Taylor, Hal Holbrook, Alice Ghostley
Dirty Dancing	Sat	8:00	30	Vestron TV-Steve Tisch Co.	EP: Steve Tisch, Mitchell Camold, Steven Reuther SP: Barra Grant P: Mireille Soria, Chris Morgan CP: Cyrus Yavneh	Patrick Cassidy, Melora Hardin, Paul Feig, Constance Marie, John Wesley, Mandy Ingber, Charles Stratton, McLean Stevenson
Equalizer, The	Wed	9:00	60	Universal TV	EP: James McAdams, Coleman Luck SP: Stuart Cohen, Robert Eisele CP: Gail Morgan Hickman, Marc Laub	Edward Woodward, Keith Szarabajka, Robert Lansing, Chad Redding, William Zabka, Maureen Anderman
Falcon Crest	Fri	10:00	60	Amanda/MF Prods.-Lorimar TV	EP: Michael Filerman, Joanne Brough, Camille Marchetta P: Phil Parslow CP: Stephen Black, Henry Stern, Rena Down	Jane Wyman, David Selby, Ana-Alicia, Lorenzo Lamas, Margaret Ladd, Chao-Li Chi, Susan Sullivan, Mariska Hargitay, Kristian Alfonso, Rod Taylor, Cesar Romero

Series Title	Day	Hr.	Mins.	Supplier	Production Principals	Cast Regulars & Semi-Regulars
48 Hours	Thu	8:00	60	CBS News	EP: Andrew Heyward Sr. P. Catherine Lasiewicz, Steve Glauber, Al Briganti	Dan Rather, Bernard Goldberg
High Risk	Tue	8:00	60	The Landsburg Co.	EP: Alan Landsburg P: Kay Hoffman	Wayne Rogers, David Frost
Knots Landing	Thu	10:00	60	Roundelay/MF Prods.- Lorimar TV	EP: David Jacobs, Michael Filerman, Lawrence Kasha P: Mary-Catherine Harold, Lynn Lathan, Bernard Lechowich	William Devane, Kevin Dobson, Michele Lee, Donna Mills, Ted Shackelford, Joan Van Ark, Teri Austin, Lynne Moody, Pe- ter Reckell, Larry Riley, Pat Petersen, Tonya Crowe, Nicolette Sheridan, Robert De- siderio
Murder, She Wrote	Sun	8:00	60	Universal TV	EP: Peter S. Fischer SP: Robert F. O'Neill P: Robert Van Scoyk, Robert Swanson	Angela Lansbury, Tom Bosley, William Windom, Michael Horton
Murphy Brown	Mon	9:00	30	Shukovsky/English Prods.-Warner Bros. TV	EP: Diane English, Joel Shu- kovsky SP: Korby Siamis P: Tom Seeley, Norm Gun- zenhauser, Russ Woody	Candice Bergen, Pat Corley, Faith Ford, Charles Kimbrough, Ro- bert Pastorelli, Joe Regalbuto, Grant Shaud
Newhart	Mon	8:00	30	MTM Prods.	EP: Mark Egan, Mark Solomon SP: Bob Bendetson, Shelley Zellman P: Stephen C. Grossman	Bob Newhart, Mary Frann, Peter Scolari, Julia Duffy, Tom Poston, William Sanderson, Tony Papenfuss, John Voldstad
Paradise	Thu	9:00	60	Roundelay Prods.- Lorimar TV	EP: David Jacobs SP: James L. Conway P: James H. Brown	Lee Horsley, Jenny Beck, Mat- thew Newmark, Brian Lando, Michael Patrick Carter, Dehl Berti, Sigrid Thornton, Nicolas Surovy
Raising Miranda	Sat	8:30	30	GTG Entertainment	EP: Deborah Aal P: Jane Anderson, Martha Will- iamson CP: Andrew J. Selig, Bob Rosenfarb	James Naughton, Royana Black, Miriam Flynn, Steve Vinovich, Michael Manasseri, Bryan Cranston
Simon & Simon	Sat	9:00	60	Universal TV	EP: John G. Stephens SP: Richard C. Okie P: Mark A. Burley CP: Rick Mittleman, Sam Shaw, Sally Hope	Jameson Parker, Gerald McRaney, Mary Carver, Joan McMurtrey
60 Minutes	Sun	7:00	60	CBS News	EP: Don Hewitt Sr. P: Philip Scheffler D: Arthur Bloom	Mike Wallace, Morley Safer, Harry Reasoner, Ed Bradley, Diane Sawyer, Andy Rooney
TV 101	Tue	8:00	60	GTG Entertainment	EP: Karl Schaefer, Scott Brazil P: Michael Cassutt	Sam Robards, Andrew Cassese, Stacey Dash, Alex Desert, Stewart Goddard, Matthew LeBlanc, Teri Polo, Mary B. Ward, Andrew White, Leon Russom, Brynn Thayer
Van Dyke Show, The	Wed	8:00	30	GTG Entertainment	EP: Sam Bobrick, Ron Clark SP: George Tricker & Neil Rosen P: Jim Geoghan CP: Walter Barnett	Dick Van Dyke, Barry Van Dyke, Karin Lizer, Billy O'Sullivan, Whitman Mayo, Maura Tierney, Paul Scherrer
West 57th	Sat	10:00	60	CBS News	EP: Andrew Lack Sr. P: Tom Yellin SP: Maurice Murad	John Ferrugia, Meredith Vieira, Steve Kroft, Karen Burnes, Se- lina Scott, Stephen Schiff
Wiseguy	Wed	10:00	60	Stephen J. Cannell Prods.	EP: Stephen J. Cannell, Les Sheldon SP: David Burke, Jo Swerling Jr., Stephen Kronish P: Alex Beaton, Alfonse Rug- giero Jr.	Ken Wahl, Jonathan Banks, Jim Byrnes

NBC-TV

Series Title	Day	Hr.	Mins.	Supplier	Production Principals	Cast Regulars & Semi-Regulars
A Different World	Thu	8:30	30	Carsey-Werner Co.- Bill Cosby	EP: Marcy Carsey, Tom Werner, Margie Peters, Thad Mum- ford P: Joanne Curley, Debbie Allen CP: Susan Fales D: Debbie Allen	Dawnn Lewis, Jasmine Guy, Ka- deem Hardison, Mary Alice, Glynn Turman, Cree Summer, Charnele Brown, Darryl Bell, Sinbad
ALF	Mon	8:00	30	Alien Prods.	EP: Bernie Brillstein, Tom Patchett SP: Lisa A. Bannick P: Paul Fusco CP: Steve Hollander	Max Wright, Anne Schedeen, Andrea Elson, Benji Gregory, ALF, Liz Sheridan, John LaMotta
Amen	Sat	8:30	30	Carson Prod. Group	EP: Ed Weinberger, Arthur Ju- lian SP: Marsha Posner Williams P: Terry Hart & Marshall Karp CP: Reuben Cannon & Ken Johnston D: Bill Foster	Sherman Hemsley, Clifton Davis, Anne Maria Horsford, Barbara Montgomery, Roz Ryan, Jester Hairston

Series Title	Day	Hr.	Mins.	Supplier	Production Principals	Cast Regulars & Semi-Regulars
Baby Boom	Wed	9:30	30	Pipeline Prods.-Finnegan-Pinchuk Co.-MGM/UA TV	EP: Charles Shyer, Nancy Meyers P: Bruce Block	Kate Jackson, Daniel Bardol, Joy Behar, Susie Essman, Robyn Peterson, Sam Wanamaker, Michelle & Kristina Kennedy
Cheers	Thu	9:00	30	Charles/Burrows/Charles Prods.-Paramount Network TV	EP: Glenn & Les Charles, James Burrows SP: Cheri Eichen & Bill Steinkellner P: David Angell, Peter Casey, David Lee CP: Tim Berry, Phoef Sutton	Ted Danson, Kirstie Alley, Rhea Perlman, John Ratzenberger, Woody Harrelson, Kelsey Grammer, George Wendt, Bebe Neuwirth
Cosby Show, The	Thu	8:00	30	Carsey-Werner Co.-Bill Cosby	EP: Marcy Carsey, Tom Werner, John Markus SP: Carmen Finestra, Gary Kott P: Terri Guarnieri CP: Matt Robinson, Janet Leahy	Bill Cosby, Phylicia Rashad, Lisa Bonet, Malcolm-Jamal Warner, Tempestt Bledsoe, Keshia Knight Pulliam, Sabrina LeBeauf, Geoffrey Owens
Day By Day	Sun	8:30	30	UBU Prods.-Paramount Network TV	EP: Andy Borowitz SP: Janis Hirsch P: June Galas	Doug Sheehan, Linda Kelsey, Julia Louis-Dreyfus, Christopher Daniel Barnes, Courtney Thorne-Smith, Thora
Dear John	Thu	9:30	30	Ed. Weinberger Prods.-Paramount Network TV	EP: Ed. Weinberger, Peter Noah SP: Robert Stevens P: Mark Grossman, David Hackel, Bob Ellison	Judd Hirsch, Jere Burns, Jane Carr, Isabelle Hofmann, Harry Groener
Empty Nest	Sat	9:30	30	Witt-Thomas-Harris Prods.-Touchstone Films & TV	EP: Paul Junger Witt, Tony Thomas, Susan Harris, Rod Parker, Hal Cooper SP: Arnie Kogan, David Tyrone King CP: Gil Junger, Susan Beavers	Richard Mulligan, Kristy McNichol, Dinah Manoff, David Leisure, Park Overall
Family Ties	Sun	8:00	30	UBU Prods.-Paramount Network TV	EP: Gary David Goldberg, Alan Uger SP: Bruce Ferber P: Linda Nieber, Bruce Ferber CP: Russell Marcus	Meredith Baxter Birney, Michael Gross, Michael J. Fox, Justine Bateman, Tina Yothers, Brian Bonsall, Courteney Cox, Marc Price
Golden Girls, The	Sat	9:00	30	Witt-Thomas-Harris Prods.-Touchstone Films & TV	EP: Paul Junger Witt, Tony Thomas, Susan Harris, Terry Grossman, Kathy Speer, Mort Nathan & Barry Fanaro SP: Eric Cohen CP: Robert Bruce & Marty Weiss D: Terry Hughes	Beatrice Arthur, Betty White, Rue McClanahan, Estelle Getty
Hogan Family, The	Mon	8:30	30	Miller-Boyett Prods.-Lorimar TV	EP: Thomas L. Miller, Robert L. Boyett SP: Chip & Doug Keyes, Judy Pioli P: Rich Correll, Bob Keyes, Deborah Oppenheimer CP: Harriet Ames-Regan	Sandy Duncan, Jason Bateman, Danny Ponce, Jeremy Licht, Edie McClurg, Josh Taylor, Tom Hodges, Steve Witting
Hunter	Sat	10:00	60	Stephen J. Cannell Prods.	EP: George Geiger SP: Jo Swerling Jr., Tom Chehak P: Paul Waigner, John Kousakis	Fred Dryer, Stepfanie Kramer, Charles Hallahan, Garrett Morris
In The Heat Of The Night	Tue	9:00	60	MGM/UA TV-Fred Silverman Co.-Juanita Bartlett Prods.	EP: Fred Silverman, David Moessinger SP: Jeri Taylor P: Edward Ledding CP: Lee Maddux	Carroll O'Connor, Howard Rollins, Anne-Marie Johnson, Alan Autry, David Hart, Hugh O'Connor, Lois Nettleton, Geoffrey Thorne
L.A. Law	Thu	10:00	60	20th-Fox TV	EP: Steven Bochco, Rick Wallace SP: David E. Kelley P: Scott Goldstein, Michele Gallery CP: William M. Finkelstein, Judith Parker	Harry Hamlin, Jill Eikenberry, Corbin Bernsen, Susan Dey, Alan Rachins, Michael Tucker, Jimmy Smits, Michele Greene, Susan Ruttan, Richard Dysart, Blair Underwood, Larry Drake
Magical World Of Disney, The	Sun	7:00	60	Walt Disney TV	EP: William Blinn	Michael D. Eisner
Davy Crockett					EP: William Blinn SP: Mark Ovitz P: Frank Fischer	Tim Dunigan, Gary Grubbs
Absent-Minded Professor, The Action-adventure element					EP: William Dial, Richard Chapman, William Blinn	Harry Anderson, Cory Danziger
Matlock	Tue	8:00	60	Fred Silverman Co.-Strathmore Prods.-Viacom	EP: Fred Silverman, Dean Hargrove SP: Joel Steiger P: Richard Collins CP: Jeff Peters	Andy Griffith, Nancy Stafford, Kene Holliday, Julie Sommars, Don Knotts
Miami Vice	Fri	10:00	60	Michael Mann Co.-Universal TV	EP: Michael Mann, Robert Ward, Richard Brams SP: Scott Shepard CP: Don Gold, Michael Attanasio	Don Johnson, Philip Michael Thomas, Saundra Santiago, Michael Talbott, Olivia Brown, Edward James Olmos
Midnight Caller	Tue	10:00	60	Lorimar TV	EP: Robert Singer, Robert Butler P: Richard DiLello, John F. Perry CP: David Israel & Steve Zito	Gary Cole, Wendy Kilbourne, Arthur Taxier, Dennis Dun
NBC Monday Night at the Movies	Mon	9:00	120	Various		
NBC Sunday Night at the Movies	Sun	9:00	120	Various		

Series Title	Day	Hr.	Mins.	Supplier	Production Principals	Cast Regulars & Semi-Regulars
Night Court	Wed	9:00	30	Starry Nights Prods.-Warner Bros. TV	EP: Reinhold Weege SP: Jeff Melman P: Gary Murphy, Larry Strawther, Nancy Steen, Neil Thompson CP: Tim Steele	Harry Anderson, Markie Post, John Larroquette, Charles Robinson, Richard Moll, Marsha Warfield
Something Is Out There ..	Fri	9:00	60	Columbia Pictures TV	EP: Frank Lupo, John Ashley	Joe Cortese, Maryam d'Abo, Gregory Sierra
Sonny Spoon	Fri	8:00	60	NBC Prods.-Stephen J. Cannell Prods.	EP: Stephen J. Cannell SP: Jo Swerling Jr., Stuart Segall P: Randall Wallace, Robert Bielak	Mario Van Peebles, Terry Donahoe, Bob Wieland, Melvin Van Peebles, Mark Thomas Miller, Nestor Serrano
Tattingers	Wed	10:00	60	Paltrow Group, NY-LA-MTM Prods.	EP: Bruce Paltrow, Tom Fontana, Mark Tinker P: Robert DeLaurentis, Channing Gibson, John Tinker	Stephen Collins, Blythe Danner, Mary Beth Hurt, Jerry Stiller, Roderick Cook, Zach Grenier, Patrice Colihan, Chay Lentin, Rob Morrow, Sue Francis Pai
227	Sat	8:00	30	Columbia Pictures TV	EP: Ron Bloomberg, Bill Boulware P: Roxie Wenk-Evans CP: Al Gordon D: Gerren Keith	Marla Gibbs, Hal Williams, Alaina Reed, Jackee, Helen Martin, Regina King, Curtis Baldwin, Kia Goodwin, Countess Vaughn
Unsolved Mysteries	Wed	8:00	60	Cosgrove-Meurer Prods.	EP: Terry Dunn Meurer, John Cosgrove SP: Chris Pye, Edward R. Horwitz	Robert Stack

Syndicated Shows, 1988–89

Half-Hour Off-Network Shows

Title	No. of Episodes (Original/Repeat)	Distributor
9 to 5	85	20th Century Fox
Alice	202	Warner Bros.
All in the Family	207	Viacom
Andy Griffith	249	Viacom
Angie	37	Paramount
Archie's Place	97	Embassy
Barney Miller	170	Columbia
Batman	120	20th Century Fox
Benson	120	Columbia
Best of Groucho	130	WW Ent
Beverly Hillbillies	274	Viacom
Bewitched	252	DFS
BJ/Lobo	86	MCA
Bob Newhart Show	142	Viacom
Bob Newhart (current)	134	MTM
Bosom Buddies	37	Paramount
Brady Bunch	117	Paramount
Branded	48	King World
Car 54, Where Are You?	60	Republic Pictures
Carol Burnett Show	150	C.B. Distribution
Carson Comedy	130	Columbia
Cheers	112	Paramount
Cosby	125 (est.)	Viacom
Dick Van Dyke	158	Viacom
Diff'rent Strokes	144	Embassy
Facts of Life	153	Embassy
Fame, Fortune & Romance	115	Teletrib
Family Affair	138	Viacom
Family Ties	98	Paramount
Fantasy Island	200	Columbia
Flying Nun	82	Columbia
Get Smart	138	Republic
Gilligan's Island	98	Turner Ent.
Gimme a Break	85	MCA
Gomer Pyle	150	Viacom
Good Times	133	Embassy
Guns of Will Sonnett	50	King World
Happy Days	255	Paramount
Harper Valley P.T.A.	29/23	MCA
Here's Lucy	144	Lorimar Telepictures
Hitchcock Presents	265	MCA
Hogan's Heroes	168	Viacom
Honeymooners	107	Viacom
I Dream of Jeannie	139	DFS
I Love Lucy	179	Viacom
I Married Joan	98	Weiss-Global
Jeffersons	207	Embassy
Kate & Allie	96	MCA
Knight Rider	90	MCA
Laugh-In	130	Lorimar/Telepictures
Laverne & Shirley	178	Paramount
Leave It to Beaver	234	MCA
Love Boat II	115	Worldvision
M*A*S*H	255	20th Century Fox
Maude	142	Embassy

564

Title	No. of Episodes (Original/Repeat)	Distributor
Mayberry RFD	78	Lorimar/Telepictures
Mork & Mindy	95	Paramount
My Favorite Martian	107	Lorimar/Telepictures
My Little Margie	126	Weiss-Global
Night Court	101	Warner Bros.
Night Gallery	97	MCA
One Day at a Time	187	Embassy
Operation Petticoat	32/20	MCA
Partridge Family	96	DFS
Punky Brewster	44	Columbia
Private Benjamin	39	Warner Bros.
Real McCoys	130	Columbia
Real People	195	Lorimar/Telepictures
Rifleman	168	Colbert
Sanford & Son	136	Embassy
Saturday Night Live	102	Orion
Show of Shows (Best of)	65	Ziv
Silver Spoons	116	Columbia/Embassy
Soap	92	Columbia
Square Pegs	20	Embassy
Tales of the Texas Rangers	52	Screen Gems
Taxi	93	Paramount
That Girl	136	Worldvision
That's Incredible	165	MCA
That's My Mama	39	Columbia
The Ropers	26	Taffner
Three's a Crowd	22	Taffner
Three's Company	174	Taffner
Too Close for Comfort	122	Taffner
Topper	78	King World
Twilight Zone	136	Viacom
We Love Lucy	26	Viacom
Webster	98	Paramount
What's Happening	65	Columbia
WKRP in Cincinnati	90	Victory
Wyatt Earp	130	Screen Gems

Hour Off-Network Shows

Title	No. of Episodes	Distributor
12 O'Clock High	78	20th Century Fox
A-Team	128	MCA
Avengers	83	Orion
Barnaby Jones	177	Worldvision
BJ/Lobo	86	MCA
Black Sheep Squadron	33	MCA
Blue Knight	23	Lorimar/Telepictures
Bonanza	268	Republic
Buck Rogers	37	MCA
Cannon	124	Viacom
Charlie's Angels	115	Columbia
CHiPS	138	MGM/UA
Dallas	161	Lorimar/Telepictures
Dukes of Hazzard	143	Warner Bros.
Dynasty	178	20th Century Fox
Eight Is Enough	112	Lorimar/Telepictures
Falcon Crest	157	Lorimar/Telepictures
Fall Guy	111	20th Century Fox
Fantasy Island	130	Columbia
Flamingo Road	37	Lorimar Telepictures

Title	No. of Episodes (Original/Repeat)	Distributor
Fridays	52	All American
Gunsmoke	402	Viacom
Hart to Hart	112	Columbia
Hawaii 5-0	200	Viacom
Here Come the Brides	52	Columbia
Hill St. Blues	146	Victory
Hitchcock Hour	93	MCA
Incredible Hulk	85	MCA
Ironhorse	47	Columbia
Knight Rider	90	MCA
Knots Landing	128	Lorimar/Telepictures
Kojak	118	MCA
Little House on the Prairie	216	Worldvision
Lost in Space	83	20th Century Fox
Lou Grant	114	Victory
Love Boat I	140	Worldvision
Love Boat II	115	Worldvision
Magnum	129	MCA
Mannix	130	Paramount
Matt Houston	68	Warner Bros.
Mission Impossible	171	Paramount
Mystery Movies	124	MCA
Naked City	99	Screen Gems
Perry Mason	271	Viacom
Police Story	84	Columbia
Police Woman	91	Columbia
Quincy	148	MCA
Rawhide	144	Viacom
Rockford Files	125	MCA
Saturday Night Live	102	Orion
Scarecrow & Mrs. King	88	Warner Bros.
Simon and Simon	125	MCA
St. Elsewhere	116	MTM
Star Trek (NBC epsiodes)	79	Paramount
Streets of San Francisco	119	Worldvision
T.J. Hooker	90	Columbia
That's Incredible	107	MCA
The Man from U.N.C.L.E.	132	Turner Ent.
The Prisoner	17	ITC
Thriller	67	MCA
Tom Jones	24	ABR Entertainment
Trapper John	132	20th Century Fox
Twilight Zone	18	Viacom
Vegas	68	20th Century Fox
Voyage to the Bottom of the Sea	110	20th Century Fox
Waltons	221	Warner Bros.
We Love Lucy	13	Viacom
Wonder Woman	61	Warner Bros.
Wonderful World of Disney	185 (est.)	Buena Vista

Children's: Animated Half Hours

Title	No. of Episodes (Original/Repeat)	Distributor
Alvin & the Chipmunks	65	Lorimar/Telepictures
Bionic 6	48	MCA
Bravestarr	65	Group W
Bullwinkle	98	DFS
C.O.P.S.	65	Claster
Care Bears	65	SFM
Children's Animated Classics	28	ABR Entertainment

Title	No. of Episodes (Original/Repeat)	Distributor
Comic Strip	65	Lorimar/Telepictures
Danger Mouse	50	Taffner
Danger Mouse	50	Taffner
Dennis the Menace	65	DFS
Denver the Last Dinosaur	13	World Events
Devlin	16	DFS
Duck Tales	65	Buena Vista
Dudley Do Right	38	DFS
Fat Albert	65	Group W
Felix the Cat	65	Screen Gems
Flintstones	166/94	DFS
Fantastic World/Hanna-Barbera	17	Worldvision
G.I. Joe	100	Claster
Ghost Busters	65	Group W
Gumby	130	Ziv Intl.
Gumby	65	Lorimar/Telepictures
He-Man/Masters of the Universe	65	Group W
Heathcliff	86	Lexington
Heathcliff	86	Lexington
Inch High Private Eye	13	DFS
JEM	75	Claster
Jetsons	75	Worldvision
King Leonardo	39	DFS
Marvel Universe (13 episodes each of 5 series)	65	New World
Mighty Mouse & Friends	130	Viacom
My Little Pony and Friends	65	Claster
Popeye	65	Access Media
Rambo	65	Worldvision
Real Ghostbusters	65	Columbia
Rocky & Friends	78	DFS
Roman Holiday	13	DFS
Scooby Doo	110/110/40	DFS
She-Ra	93	Group W
Silverhawks	65	Lorimar/Telepictures
Smurfs	130	Tele-Trib
Snorks	65	Worldvision
Space Kidettes	20	DFS
Super Sunday	14	Claster
Superfriends	110/110/40	Lexington
Teddy Ruxpin	65	Lexington
Teddy Ruxpin	65	Lexington
Teenage Mutant Ninja Turtles	13	Group W
Tennessee Tuxedo	140	DFS
Thunderbirds	24	ITC
Thundercats	65	Lorimar/Telepictures
Thundercats II	65	Lorimar/Telepictures
Thundersub	27	Lionheart
Transformers	65	Claster
Uncle Waldo	52	DFS
Valley of the Dinosaurs	16	DFS
Visionaries	13	Claster
Wheelie & the Chopper Bunch	13	DFS
Yogi Bear	65	Worldvision
Young Samson	20	DFS

Children's: Live Action

Title	No. of Episodes	Distributor
Cisco Kid	156	Blair Ent.
Double Dare	130	Viacom

Title	No. of Episodes (Original/Repeat)	Distributor
Dr. Fad	26	Fox/Lorber
Finders Keepers	130	Viacom
Fun House	170/90	Lorimar/Telepictures
Kideo TV	49	Lexington
Kids Songs	26	Orbis
Littlest Hobo	96	Lorimar/Telepictures
Muppets	120	ITC
Superboy	13	Viacom
Superman	104	Warner Bros.
Young Universe	26	Behrens

1987–88 Motion Pictures Made for Television

Listed herewith are new films especially made for television and shown for the first time during the 1987–88 season. Key for credits: P is Producer; Exec. P: Executive Producer; Sprv. P: Supervising Producer; D: Director; W: Writer. Running time indicated includes commercials. Mini-series (made for television movies shown in three parts or more) are in the list at the end of this section.

ADDICTED TO HIS LOVE
Green/Epstein Prod.; Columbia Pictures Entertainment. Exec. P: Jim Green, Allen Epstein. Sprv. P: Allen Esptein. P: Danielle Alexandra. D: Arthur Allan Seidelman. W: Roni Simon, Richard Alfieri. Shown on ABC March 28, 1988. (2 hrs.)
Cast: Barry Bostwick, Polly Bergen, Colleen Camp, Erin Gray, Linda Purl, Dee Wallace Stone, Hector Elizondo, Peggy Lipton, Rosemary Forsyth, Nicholas Walker.

AFTER THE PROMISE
CBS Entertainment Prod. P: Tamara Asseyev. D: David Greene. W: Robert W. Lenski. Shown on CBS Oct. 11, 1987. (2 hrs.).
Cast: Mark Harmon, Diana Scarwid, Rosemary Dunsmore, Donnelly Rhodes.

ALONE IN THE NEON JUNGLE
Robert Halmi, Inc. Exec. P: Bill Brademan, Ed Self. P: Robert Halmi. Sprv. P: Ira Halberstadt. D: Georg Stanford Brown. W: Mark Rogers, Stephen Downing. Shown on CBS Jan. 17, 1988. (2 hrs.)
Cast: Suzanne Pleshette, Danny Aiello, Jon Tenney, Joe Morton, Raymond Serra, Jon Polito, Priscilla Lopez, Charlotte D'Amboise, W.T. Martin, Jude Cicolella, Patty Owen, Brad Greenquist, Alex Coleman, Georg Stanford Brown, Frank Converse.

ANGEL IN GREEN
Aligre Prods. Inc.; Taft Hardie Group Ltd. P: Harry A. Sherman. D: Marvin J. Chomsky. W: Michael Patrick Goodman. Shown on CBS Sept. 22, 1987. (2 hrs.)
Cast: Bruce Boxleitner, Susan Dey, Milo O'Shea, Pete Smith, Dan Lauria, Bobby Hosea, Michael Novack, Jose Santana.

THE ANN JILLIAN STORY
9J Inc., ITC. Exec. P: Andrea Baynes. P: Peter Thompson. Exec. in charge of prod: Dennis A. Brown. D: Corey Allen. W: Audrey Davis Levin. Shown on NBC Jan. 4, 1988. (2 hrs.)
Cast: Ann Jillian, Tony Lo Bianco, Viveca Lindfors, George Touliatos, Tim Wibber, Kate Lynch, Peter Millard, Pam Hyatt, Elizabeth Lennie, Tod Waite.

APRIL MORNING
The Samuel Goldwyn Company; Robert Halmi, Inc. Exec. P: Robert Halmi, Samuel Goldwyn Jr. Sprv. P: David J. Patterson. P: Robert Halmi Jr., Delbert Mann. D: Delbert Mann. W: James Lee Barrett. Shown on CBS April 24, 1988. (2 hrs.)
Cast: Tommy Lee Jones, Robert Urich, Chad Lowe, Susan Blakely, Meredith Salenger, Rip Torn.

ASSAULT & MATRIMONY
Michael Filerman Prods., NBC Prods. Exec. P: Michael Filerman. Sprv. P: Joel Dean. P: Karen Moore. D: Jim Frawley. W: John Binder. Shown on NBC Sept. 28, 1987. (2 hrs.)
Cast: Jill Eikenberry, Michael Tucker, John Hillerman, Michelle Phillips, Raf Mauro, Joe Cortese, Doreen Ramus, Duncan MacGregor, Antony Holland, Endi Saunders, Ken Camroux.

THE ATTIC: THE HIDING OF ANNE FRANK
Telecom Entertainment Inc., Yorkshire Television. Exec. P: Michael Lepiner, Kenneth Kaufman. Co-exec: David Cunliffe, William Hanley. P: Marjorie Kalins, Timothy J. Fee, Nick Gillott. Sprv. P-D: John Erman. W: William Hanley, based on the book "Anne Frank Remembered" by Miep Gies with Alison Leslie Gold. Shown on CBS April 17, 1988. (2 hrs.)
Cast: Mary Steenburgen, Paul Scofield, Huub Stapel, Eleanor Bron, Frances Cuka, Miriam Karlin, Ronald Pickup, Gary Raymond, Victor Spinetti, Tom Wilkinson, Lisa Jacobs, Isabelle Amyes, Ian Sears, Georgia Slowe, Jeffrey Robert, Edda Barends.

BABY M
ABC Circle Films. Exec. P: Ilene Amy Berg. P: Gordon Freeman. D-W: James Steven Sadwith. Shown on ABC May 22 & 23, 1988. (4 hrs.)
Cast: JoBeth Williams, John Shea, Bruce Weitz, Robin Strasser, Anne Jackson, Bruce McGill, Dakin Matthews, Jenny Lewis, Dana Wheeler-Nicholson, Annabella Price, Dabney Coleman, Lonny Chapman, Nancy Addison, Tricia O'Neil, Ben Slack, Brian Peter Green, Lesley Woods, Allan Wasserman, Matt Roe.

BAJA OKLAHOMA
HBO Pictures. P: Marykay Powell. Exec. P: Hunt Lowry. D: Bobby Roth. W: Bobby Roth, Dan Jenkins, based on Jenkins' novel. Shown on HBO Feb. 20, 1988. (102 mins.)
Cast: Lesley Ann Warren, Peter Coyote, Swoosie Kurtz, Anthony Zerbe, William Forsythe, Billy Vera, Willie Nelson, Emmylou Harris, Alice Krige, Bruce Abbott, Jordan Charney, Julia Roberts, Bob Wills Jr.

BAY COVEN
A Guber-Peters Entertainment Co. prod; Phoenix Entertainment Group. Exec. P: Jon Peters, Peter Guber, Roger Birnbaum. P: Michael Rhodes. Sprv. P: Stanley M. Brooks. D: Carl Schenkel. W: R. Timothy Kring. Shown on NBC Oct. 25, 1987. (2 hrs.)
Cast: Tim Matheson, Pamela Sue Martin, Barbara Billingsley, Jeff Conaway, Woody Harrelson, Susan Ruttan, James Sikking.

BERYL MARKHAM: A SHADOW ON THE SUN
Tamara Assayev Prods. and New World TV. Exec. P: Tamara Assayev. P: Tamara Assayev, Stefanie Powers. D: Tony Richardson. W: Allan Scott, based on Vanity Fair article "The Beryl Markham Mystery" and interviews conducted by James Fox. Shown on CBS May 15 & 17, 1988. (4 hrs.)
Cast: Stefanie Powers, Claire Bloom, Peter Bowles, Brian Cox, Niamh Cussack, Trevor Eve, Frederic Lehne, James Fox, Rupert Frazer, Joseph Mydell, Sverre Anker Ousdal, Nicola Pagett, John Rubinstein, Jack Thompson, Frederick Treves, Timothy West, Serena McGuinnes, Duncan Lindsay, Richard Olivier.

BILLIONAIRE BOYS CLUB
A Donald March/Gross-Weston Prod.; ITC Prods. Exec. P: Donald March. P: Marcy Gross, Ann Weston. Sprv. P: Marvin Chomsky. W: Gy Waldron, suggested by stories by Sue Horton and Greg Critser. Shown on NBC Nov 8 & 9, 1987. (4 hrs.)
Cast: Judd Nelson, Fredric Lehne, Raphael Sbarge, John Stockwell, Ron Silver, Brian McNamara, Barry Tubb, John Dye, Robert Krantz, Stan Shaw, Jill Schoelen, James Sloyan.

BLUEGRASS
The Landsburg Company. Exec. P: Alan Landsburg, Joan Barnett. P: Arthur Fellows, Terry Keegan. D: Simon Wincer. W: Matt Crowley. Shown on CBS Feb. 28 & 29, 1988. (4 hrs.)

Cast: Cheryl Ladd, Brian Kerwin, Anthony Andrews, Shawnee Smith, Diane Ladd, Kieran Mulroney, Mickey Rooney, Wayne Rogers, Arthur Rosenberg, Judith-Marie Bergan, Jerry Hardin.

BLUFFING IT
Ohlmeyer Communications. Exec. P: Don Ohlmeyer. P: Linda Jonsson, Christopher Sands. Co-P: Karen Danaher. D-W: James Sadwith. Shown on ABC Sept. 13, 1987. (2 hrs.)
Cast: Dennis Weaver, Janet Carroll, Michelle Little, Robert Sean Leonard, Cleavant Derricks, Vickie Wauchope, Wanda Cannon.

BODY OF EVIDENCE
CBS Entertainment Prods. P-D: Roy Campanella II. Sprv. P: Henry Colman. W: Cynthia Whitcomb. Shown on CBS Jan. 24, 1988. (2 hrs.)
Cast: Margot Kidder, Barry Bostwick, Caroline Kava, Jennifer Barbour, David Hayward, Tony Lo Bianco.

BONANZA: THE NEXT GENERATION
Gaylord Prod. Co.; LBS Communications; Bonanza Ventures, Inc. Exec. P: Tom Sarnoff, Bill Claxton. Sprv. P: Stacy Williams. P: David Dortort. D: Bill Claxton. W: Paul Savage. Shown in syndication (N.Y.) March 8, 1988. (2 hrs.)
Cast: John Ireland, Robert Fuller, John Amos, Barbara Anderson, Michael Landon Jr., Brian A. Smith, Jack Lilley, Rex Lynn, Robert Hoy, Jerry Gatlin, Richard Bergman, Peter Mark Richman, Gary Reed, Jeff Myer, Robert Jauregui.

THE BOURNE IDENTITY
Alan Shayne Prods. Inc; Warner Bros. Television. Exec. P: Alan Shayne. P: Frederick Muller. Co-P: Martin Rabbett. D: Roger Young. W: Carol Sobieski, based on the novel by Robert Ludlum. Shown on ABC May 8 & 9, 1988. (4 hrs.)
Cast: Richard Chamberlain, Jaclyn Smith, Anthony Quayle, Donald Moffat, Yorgo Voyagis, Peter Vaughan, Denholm Elliott, Kate Howard, Bruce Boa, Shane Rimmer, James Laurenson, William Roberts, Jacqueline Pearce, James Faulkner, Philip Madoc, Terry Richards.

BRING ME THE HEAD OF DOBIE GILLIS
20th Century Fox Television. Exec. P-D: Stanley Z. Cherry. P: Dwayne Hickman, Steve Clements, Marc Summers. W: Deborah Zoe Dawson, Victoria Johns, Stanley Z. Cherry. Shown on CBS Feb. 21, 1988. (2 hrs.)
Cast: Dwayne Hickman, Bob Denver, Connie Stevens, Sheila James, Steve Franken, William Schallert, Mike Jolly, Lisa Wilcox, Tricia Leigh Fisher, Scott Grimes, Nicholas Worth.

BROKEN ANGEL
Stan Margulies Co.; MGM/UA. Exec. P: Stan Margulies. P: Robin S. Clark. D: Richard T. Heffron. W: Cynthia Cherbak. Shown on ABC March 14, 1988. (2 hrs.)
Cast: William Shatner, Susan Blakely, Roxann Biggs, Jason Horst, Millie Perkins, Nicole Mercurio, Carmen Zapata, Brock Peters, Erika Eleniak, Collin Davis.

C.A.T. SQUAD: PYTHON WOLF
NBC Prods. Exec. P-D: William Friedkin. P: David Salvern. W: Robert Ward. Shown on NBC May 23, 1988. (2 hrs.)
Cast: Joe Cortese, Jack Youngblood, Steve James, Deborah Van Valkenburgh, Miguel Ferrer, Alan Scarfe, Brian Delate, Michael Fletcher, William Mooney, Alan Coates.

THE CAINE MUTINY COURT-MARTIAL
The Maltese Companies; Wouk/Ware Prods. and Sandcastle 5 Prods. Exec. P: Ray Volpe, Joseph Wouk. Co-exec. P: Edd Griles. P: Robert Altman, John Flaxman. Sprv. P: Scott Bushnell. D: Robert Altman. W: Herman Wouk. Shown on CBS May 8, 1988. (2 hrs.)
Cast: Eric Bogosian, Jeff Daniels, Brad Davis, Peter Gallagher, Michael Murphy, Kevin J. O'Connor, Daniel Jenkins, Danny Darst, Ken Michaels.

CASE CLOSED
Houston Motion Picture Entertainment Inc.; CBS Entertainment. P: Andres Gottlieb. Co-P: Byron Allen. D: Dick Lowry. W: Byron Allen, Steve Crider. Shown on CBS April 19, 1988. (2 hrs.)
Cast: Charles Durning, Byron Allen, Marc Alaimo, James Green, Eddie Jones, Christopher Neame, Charles Weldon, Erica Gimpel.

THE CHILD SAVER
Michael Filerman Prod.; NBC Prods. Exec. P: Michael Filerman. P: Karen Moore. Co-P: Grace Gilroy. D: Stan Lathan. W: Charles Rosin. Shown on NBC Jan. 18, 1988. (2 hrs.)
Cast: Alfre Woodard, Michael Warren, Mario Van Peebles, Constance McCashin, Martin Balsam, Deon Richmond, Marina Durrell, Matthew Kaye, Fernando Lopez, Margo Martindale.

CHRISTMAS COMES TO WILLOW CREEK
Blue Andre Prod; ITC Prods. Inc. P: Blue Andre. Co-P: Jeffrey Fischgrund. D: Richard Lang. W: Michael Norell. Shown on CBS Dec. 20, 1987. (2 hrs.)
Cast: John Schneider, Tom Wopat, Kim Delaney, Zachary Ansley, Joy Coghill, Antony Holland, Hoyt Axton.

THE CHRISTMAS VISITOR
Entertainment Media, The Disney Channel and Wonderworks. P: Peter Beilby, Robert Le Tet. D: George Miller. W: Jeff Peck. Shown on the Disney Channel, Dec. 5, 1987. (101 mins.)
Cast: Dee Wallace Stone, John Waters, Charles Tingwell, Bill Kerr, Nadine Garner, Grant Piro, Andrew Ferguson, Francis Bell, Christopher Stevenson, Kim Gyngell, David Ravenswood.

CLINTON AND NADINE
HBO Pictures; ITC Entertainment Group. P: Donald March. D: Jerry Schatzberg. W: Robert Foster. Shown on HBO May 28, 1988. (2 hrs.)
Cast: Andy Garcia, Ellen Barkin, Morgan Freeman, Michael Lombard, John C. McGinley, Brad Sullivan, Alan North, Bill Raymond.

CODENAME: KYRIL
An Incito Production; HTV. Exec. P: Stein Monn-Iverson, Patrick Dromgoole. P: Beryl Vertue. D: Paul Sarony. D: Ian Sharp. W: John Hopkins. Shown on Showtime April 17 & 18, 1988. (4 hrs.)
Cast: Edward Woodward, Ian Charleson, Denholm Elliott, Joss Ackland, Richard E. Grant, John McEnery, Peter Vaughan, James Laurenson, Espen Skjonberg, Catherine Neilson, Sven-Bertil Taube, Hugh Fraser, Charles Simon, Terence Harvey, Alec Linstead.

CONSPIRACY OF LOVE
New World Pictures. Exec. P: Nelle Nugent. D: Noel Black. W: Barry Morrow. Shown on CBS Oct. 18, 1987. (2 hrs.)
Cast: Robert Young, Drew Barrymore, Glynnis O'Connor, Elizabeth Wilson, Mitchell Laurance, John Fujioka, Alan Fawcett.

CRASH COURSE
Fries Entertainment Inc. Exec. P: Charles Fries. P: Irv Wilson. D: Oz Scott. W: William A.A. Schwartz. Shown on NBC Jan. 17, 1988. (2 hrs.)
Cast: Jackee, Brian Bloom, Harvey Korman, Alyssa Milano, Charlie Robinson, Rob Stone, Tina Yothers, Dick Butkus, Olivia D'Abo, Edie McClurg, Ray Walston, Bradd Wong.

DANGER DOWN UNDER
Hoyts Prods. Ltd.; Weintraub Entertainment Group Inc. Exec. P: Reuben Leder, Lee Majors. P: Jane Scott. D: Russ Mayberry. W: Reuben Leder. Shown on NBC March 14, 1988. (2 hrs.)
Cast: Lee Majors, Rebecca Gilling, Martin Vaughan, William Wallace, Bruce Hughes, Morgan Lewis, Paul Chubb, Natalie McCurry, Moya O'Sullivan, Warwick Moss, Emily Stocker.

DANGEROUS AFFECTION
A Freyda Rothstein Production and Litke-Grossbart Prod.; New World Television. Exec. P: Freyda Rothstein, Jack Grossbart. P: Renee Valente. D: Larry Elikann. W: Annabel Davis-Goff, Susan Rice. Shown on NBC Nov. 1, 1987. (2 hrs.)
Cast: Judith Light, Jimmy Smits, Audra Lindley, Michael Parks, Billy Sullivan, Rhea Perlman, Joseph Hacker, John Aylward, John Lisbon Wood, Spice Williams.

DEEP DARK SECRETS
Fries Entertainment; Gross-Weston Prods. Exec. P: Charles Fries. P: Marcy Gross, Ann Weston. D: Robert Lewis. W: Nancy Sackett. Shown on NBC Oct. 26, 1987. (2 hrs.)
Cast: James Brolin, Melody Anderson, Pamela Bellwood, Morgan Stevens, Joe Spano, Mona Abiad, Drew Borland, Beverley Elliott, Jill Diane Filion, Merrilyn Gann, Michele Goodger, Don Granberry, Lee Jeffrey, Campbell Lane, Marcle Maillard, Walter Marsh, Roman Podhora, Ric Reid, Dana Still.

DENNIS THE MENACE: THE LIVE-ACTION MOVIE
DIC Enterprises Prod.; Coca-Cola Telecommunications Inc. P: Philip D. Fehrle. Exec. P: Andy Heyward. D: Doug Rogers. W: Ernest Chambers, Jack Mendelsohn, based on characters created by Hank Ketcham. Shown in syndication (N.Y.) Sept. 26, 1987. (2 hrs.)
Cast: Victor DiMattia, William Windom, Jim Jansen, Patricia Estrin, Patsy Garrett, Zachary Bostrom, Jarrett Lennon, Molly Morgan, Kirstan Price, Barton Tinapp.

DESPERADO: AVALANCHE AT DEVIL'S RIDGE
Walter Mirisch Prods., Charles E. Sellier Jr. and Universal TV. Exec. P: Andrew Mirisch. P: Charles E. Sellier Jr. D: Richard Compton. W: Larry Cohen. Shown on NBC May 24, 1988. (2 hrs.)
Cast: Alex McArthur, Hoyt Axton, Alice Adair, Dwier Brown, Lise Cutter, Rod Stieger, Lee Paul, Arch Archamboult, John Barks, Jack Caffrey, Tom Connor, Ben Connors, Blake Conway, Steve Cormier, Dan Mart, Clifton Doran.

DESPERATE
Warner Bros. TV. P: Alex Beaton. Exec. P: Michael Braverman. D: Peter Markel. W: Michael Braverman. Shown on NBC Sept. 19, 1987. (2 hrs.)
Cast: John Savage, Meg Foster, Chris Burke, Liane Langland, Andrew Robinson, J.A. Preston, George Dickerson, Castulo Guerra, Frances Foster, Byrne Piven.

THE DIRTY DOZEN: THE FATAL MISSION
MGM/UA TV. P: Mel Swope. D: Lee H. Katzin. W: Mark Rodgers. Shown on NBC Feb. 14, 1988. (2 hrs.)
Cast: Telly Savalas, Ernest Borgnine, Hunt Block, Matthew Burton, Jeff Conaway, Alex Cord, Erik Estrada, Ernie Hudson, James Carroll Jordan, Ray Mancini, John Matuszak, Natalia Nogulich, Heather Thomas, Anthony Valentine, Richard Yniguez.

DOWNPAYMENT ON MURDER
Adam Prod.; 20th Century-Fox Television. Exec. P: Robert M. Myman. P: Carole Bloom. Sprv. P: R.W. Goodwin. D: Waris Hussein. W: Barry Schneider, Bill Driskill. Shown on NBC Dec. 6, 1987. (2 hrs.)
Cast: Connie Sellecca, Ben Gazzara, G.W. Bailey, Jonathan Banks, John Karlen, Sheila Larken, David Morse, Miguel Ferrer, Jenny Beck, Brandon Bluhm, Conrad Bachmann, John Durbin, Kimberly Pistone.

DREAMS LOST, DREAMS FOUND
Atlantic Video Ventures Prod.; Yorkshire Television. P: Pat Sandys. Exec. P: John Goldstone, Jonathan Dana. D: Willi Patterson. W: William Corlett, based on the novel by Pamela Wallace. Shown on Showtime Sept. 13, 1987 (102 mins.)
Cast: Kathleen Quinlan, David Robb, Betsy Brantley, Colette O'Neill, Charles Gray, Louise Breslin, Tom Watson, Anne Kristen, Fiona Mollison, Tom Mannion, Kay Gallie.

DROP-OUT MOTHER
Fries Entertainment Inc.; Comco Prod. Inc. Prod. Exec. P: Charles Fries, Julie Corman. P: Ann Shanks. Co-P-W: Bob Shanks. D: Charles S. Dubin. Shown on CBS Jan. 1, 1988. (2 hrs.)
Cast: Valerie Harper, Wayne Rogers, Carol Kane, Danny Gerard, Jane Eastwood, Alyson Court, Kim Hunter, Bruce Gray, Tim Henry, Meg Howarth, Diane Stapley, Marilyn Smith, Allen Stewart-Coates.

EARTH*STAR VOYAGER
Marstar Prods. Inc.; Walt Disney Television. Exec. P: Martin Starger. Co-P: Dennis E. Doty. P: Howard Alston. D: James Goldstone. W: Ed Spielman. Shown on ABC Jan. 17 & 24, 1988. (4 hrs.)
Cast: Duncan Regehr, Brian McNamara, Julia Montgomery, Jason Michas, Tom Breznahan, Margaret Langrick, Sean O'Byrne, Peter Donat, Henry Kingi, Ric Reid, Frank C. Turner, Dinah Gaston.

ECHOES IN THE DARKNESS
A Litke-Grossbart Prod.; New World Television. Exec. P: Jack Grossbart. P-D: Glenn Jordan. Assoc. P: Paul Rubell. W: Joseph Wambaugh. Shown on CBS Nov. 1 & 2, 1987. (5 hrs.)
Cast: Peter Coyote, Stockard Channing, Robert Loggia, Peter Boyle, Cindy Pickett, Gary Cole, Zeljko Ivanek, Alex Hyde-White, Treat Williams, Brenda Bazinet, Philip Bosco, Eugene A. Clark, Richard Comar, Diane D'Aquila, Scott Denton, Tony De Santis, Jayne Eastwood, David Ferry, Pat Hamilton, Vincent Irizarry, Susannah Hoffman, Alan Jordan, Isabelle Mejias.

EIGHT IS ENOUGH: A FAMILY REUNION
An Echo Cove Prod; Lorimar Telepictures. Exec. P: William Blinn. P: Frank Fischer. D-Sprv. P: Harry Harris. W: Gwen Bagni-Dubov. Shown on NBC Oct. 18, 1987. (2 hrs.)
Cast: Dick Van Patten, Mary Frann, Adam Rich, Willie Aames, Grant Goodeve, Dianne Kay, Connie Needham, Lani O'Grady, Susan Richardson, Laurie Walters.

ELVIS AND ME
New World Television. Exec. P: Priscilla Beaulieu Presley, Bernard Schwartz, Joel Stephens. P: Robert Lovenheim. Assoc. P: Vicki Niemi-Gordon, Eric Sears. D: Larry Peerce. W: Joyce Eliason. Shown on ABC Feb. 7 & 8, 1988. (4 hrs.)
Cast: Dale Midkiff, Susan Walters, Billy Greenbush, Linda Miller, Jon Cypher.

EMMA, QUEEN OF THE SOUTH SEAS
Fries Entertainment; Andros Prods. Pty, Ltd. P: Ann Chapman, Ross Matthews. Exec. P: Rob Chapman, Anthony I. Ginnane. D: John Banas. W: Ann Chapman, Rob Chapman, Petru Popescu, based on the novel "Queen Emma of the South Seas" by Geoffrey Dutton. Shown in OPT syndication (N.Y.) June 13 & 14, 1988. (4 hrs.)
Cast: Barbara Carrera, Steve Bisley, Hal Holbrook, E.G. Marshall, Thaao Penghlis, Barry Quin, Ron Haddrick, Rebecca Rigg, Henk Johannes, Anna-Maria Monticelli, Nathaniel Lees.

EVIL IN CLEAR RIVER
Steve Tisch Company and Lionel Chetwynd Prods. in association with Phoenix Television Prods. Inc. Exec. P: Steve Tisch, Lionel Chetwynd. P: Barbara Black. D: Karen Arthur. W: William Schmidt. Shown on ABC Jan. 11, 1988. (2 hrs.)
Cast: Lindsay Wagner, Randy Quaid, Thomas Wilson Brown, Michael Flynn, Stephanie Dees, Carolyn Croft, Gloria Carlin, George Sullivan.

EYE ON THE SPARROW
Sarabande Production in association with Republic Pictures Corp. Exec. P: David Manson. P-W: Barbara Turner. Co-P: Cyrus Yavneh. D: John Korty. Shown on NBC Dec. 7, 1987. (2 hrs.)
Cast: Mare Winningham, Keith Carradine, Sandy McPeak, Kaaren Lee, Conchata Ferrell, Bianca Rose, Joy Carlin, Anne Lawder, Winifred Mann.

FAMILY SINS
London Films. Exec. P: Jerry London. P: Mel Bishop. D: Jerrold Freedman. W: George Rubino. Shown on CBS Oct. 15, 1987. (2 hrs.)
Cast: James Farentino, Jill Eikenberry, Andrew Bednarski, Mimi Kuzyk, Brent Spinner, Michael Durrell, Tom Bower, Richard Venture, Michelle Casey, Ben Dickson, Michael Halton, Kate Hawley, Yuri Lane, Shane Miner, Thomas Wilson Brown.

FATAL CONFESSION: A FATHER DOWLING MYSTERY
Fred Silverman Co., Strathmore Prods. and Viacom. Exec. P: Fred Silverman, Dean Hargrove. P: Peter Katz. Sprv. P: Joel Steiger. D: Christopher Hibler. W: Donald E. Westlake, based on characters from Ralph McInerny's Father Dowling books. Shown on NBC Nov. 30, 1987. (2 hrs.)
Cast: Tom Bosley, Tracy Nelson, Robert Prescott, Mary Wickes, Susan Blakely, Leslie Nielsen, Peter Scolari, Sada Thompson, Kevin Crowley, Holly Fulger, Ted Liss, Mike Nussbaum, Stella Stevens, Guy Fricano, Joe Greco, Sarah Long.

THE FATHER CLEMENTS STORY
Zev Braun Prod.; Interscope Communications Inc. Exec. P: Zev Braun, Ted Field. P: Phil Parslow. Co-P: Chet Walker. D: Ed Sherin. W: Arthur Heinemann, Ted Tally. Shown on NBC Dec. 13, 1987. (2 hrs.)
Cast: Louis Gossett Jr., Malcolm-Jamal Warner, Carroll O'Connor, Larry Fishburn, Glenn Plummber, Ron McClarty, Rosetta Lenoire, Irv Kupcinet, Pat Bowie, Rob Brueler.

A FATHER'S HOMECOMING
NBC Productions. P: R.W. Goodwin. Exec. P-W: Gloria Katz, Willard Huyck. D: Rick Wallace. Shown on NBC June 19, 1988. (2 hrs.)
Cast: Michael McKean, Jonathan Ward, Nana Visitor, Marcianne Warman, Bryon Thames, Brandon Douglas, Peter Michael Goetz, Jadrien Steele, Billy Morrisette.

A FATHER'S REVENGE
Shadowplay/Rosco Prod.; Phoenix Entertainment Group, Inc. Exec. P: Gerald W. Abrams. Co-P: Hans Brockman, Mel Frohman. P: Hans Proppe. D: John Herzfeld. W: Mel Frohman. Shown on ABC Jan. 24, 1988. (2 hrs.)

Cast: Brian Dennehy, Ron Silver, Anthony Valentine, Christoph M. Ohrt, Claudia Matschulla, Alexander Radszun, Angus McInnes, Helen Patton, Joanna Cassidy.

14 GOING ON 30
Walt Disney Television. Exec. P: James Orr, Jim Cruickshank. P: Susan B. Landau. D: Paul Schneider. W: Richard Jeffries. Shown on ABC March 6 & 13, 1988. (2 hrs.)

Cast: Steve Eckholdt, Daphne Ashbrook, Adam Carl, Gabey Olds, Irene Tedrow, Patrick Duffy, Harry Morgan, Loretta Swit, Alan Thicke, Dick Van Patten, Rick Rossovich, Kit McDonough, Richard McGonagle, John Ingle, Sal Viscuso, John (Bunky) Butler.

FOXFIRE
Marian Rees Associates, Inc. Exec. P: Marian Rees. P: Dorothea Petrie. D: Jud Taylor. W: Susan Cooper. Shown on CBS Dec. 13, 1987. (2 hrs.)

Cast: Jessica Tandy, Hume Cronyn, John Denver, Gary Grubbs, Harriet Hall.

FREEDOM FIGHTER
A Bill McCutchen Prod., HTV Limited and Columbia Pictures Television. Exec. P: Bill McCutchen. Co-exec. P: Tony Danza. P: Frederic Golchan, William Hill. Sprv. Exec. P: Patrick Dromgoole. D: Desmond Davis. W: Gerald DiPego, suggested by the book "The Berlin Wall" by Pierre Galante. Shown on NBC Jan. 11, 1988. (2 hrs.)

Cast: Tony Danza, Neil Dickson, Geraldine James, David McCallum, David Robb, Colette Stephenson, Sid Caesar.

GOD BLESS THIS CHILD
The Indie Prod. Co.; Phoenix Entertainment Group. Exec. P: Bruce J. Sallan. P: Andras Hamori. Co-P-W: Dennis Nemec. D: Larry Elikann. Shown on ABC March 21, 1988. (2 hrs.)

Cast: Mare Winningham, Grace Johnston, L. Scott Caldwell, Obba Babatunde, Dorian Harewood.

GORE VIDAL'S LINCOLN
Chris/Rose Prods. Inc.; Finnegan-Pinchuk Co. Exec. P: Sheldon Pinchuk, Bill Finnegan, Pat Finnegan. P: Bob Christiansen, Rick Rosenberg. D: Lamont Johnson. W: Ernest Kinoy, based on Gore Vidal's novel. M: Ernest Gold. Shown on NBC March 27 & 28, 1988. (4 hrs.)

Cast: Sam Waterston, Mary Tyler Moore, Richard Mulligan, Deborah Adair, Tom Brennan, Gregory Cooke, Steven Culp, Ruby Dee, Jerome Dempsey, Jeffrey DeMunn, Jon DeVries, George Ede, Robin Gammell, James Gammon, Thomas Gibson, Tim Guinee, David Leary, Cleavon Little, John McMartin, John Houseman.

THE GUNFIGHTERS
Gross-Jacobson Entertainment; Alliance Entertainment. Exec. P: Sonny Gross, Larry Jacobson, Sprv. P: Stephen J. Roth. P: Jeff King. Co-P: Clay Borris. W: Jim Byrnes. Shown in syndication (N.Y.) Oct. 27, 1987. (2 hrs.)

Cast: Art Hindle, Reiner Shoene, George Kennedy, Tony Addabbo, Michael Kane, Lori Hallier, Francis Damberger, Howard Kruschke, Beverly Hendry, Eric Kramer, Mike Evans, Brian Fustukiah, Dale Wilson, Moira Wally, Wendall Smith.

GUNSMOKE: RETURN TO DODGE
CBS Entertainment Prod. P: John Mantley. Sprv. P: Stan Hough. D: Vincent McEveety. W: Jim Byrnes. Shown on CBS Sept. 26, 1987. (2 hrs.)

Cast: James Arness, Amanda Blake, Buck Taylor, Fran Ryan, Earl Holliman, Ken Olandt, Steve Forrest.

HAUNTED BY HER PAST
A Norton Wright Prod. ITC Prods. Inc. Exec. P: Norton Wright. P: Terry Morse. D: Michael Pressman. W: Barry Schneider. Shown on NBC Oct. 5, 1987. (2 hrs.)

Cast: Susan Lucci, Marcia Strassman, Robin Thomas, Finola Hughes, Douglas Seale, John James.

A HAZARD OF HEARTS
The Grade Company; Gainsborough Pictures. P: Albert Fennell, John Hough. D: John Hough. W: Terence Feely. Shown on CBS Dec. 27, 1987. (2 hrs.)

Cast: Diana Rigg, Edward Fox, Helena Bonham Carter, Fiona Fullerton, Neil Dickson, Marcus Gilbert, Christopher Plummer, Stewart Granger, Anna Massey, Eileen Atkins, Gareth Hunt.

HEMINGWAY
A co-prod. of Daniel Wilson Prod. and Alcor Film GmbH. Exec. P: Daniel Wilson, Bobo Scriba. P: Gerhard Von Halem, Linda Marmelstein, Ully Pickardt. Sprv. P: Goetz Weidner. D-W: Bernhard Sinkel. Shown in syndication on April 25 & 27, 1988. (6 hrs.)

Cast: Stacy Keach, Josephine Chaplin, Marisa Berenson, Lisa Banes, Pamela Reed, Priscilla Pointer, Stuart Whitman, Myron Natwick, Rebecca Potok, Geoffrey Carey, Zoey Wilson, Jerry di Giacomo, Consuelo de Haviland, Fiona Fullerton, Red Robbins, James Villers, Jesse Doran, Dudly Sutton, Peter Hallwachs, Rozel Zech, Ana Torrent.

THE HIGHWAYMAN
Glen Larson Prod.; 20th Century-Fox TV. P: Harker Wade. Co-P: J.C. Larson. Exec. P: Glen A. Larson. Sprv. P: Mark Clafferty. D: Doug Heyes. W: Glen A. Larson, Doug Heyes. Shown on NBC Sept. 20, 1987. (2 hrs.)

Cast: Sam Jones, Claudia Christian, Stanford Egi, Jimmy Smits, Wings Hauser, Jennifer Runyon, Lyle Alzado, Rowdy Roddy Piper, Theresa Saldana, G. Gordon Liddy.

A HOBO'S CHRISTMAS
A Joe Byrne/Falrose Prod.; Phoenix Entertainment Group. Exec. P: Joe Byrne. P: Paul Freeman. D: Will Mackenzie. W: Jeb Rosebrook. Shown on CBS Dec. 6, 1987. (2 hrs.)

Cast: Barnard Hughes, Gerald McRaney, Wendy Crewson, William Hickey, Lee Weaver, Jamie Mills, Harley Cross, Helen Stenborg, Michael Ruud.

HOOVER VS. THE KENNEDYS: THE SECOND CIVIL WAR
A Sunrise Films Limited Prod.; Selznick/Glickman Productions. Exec. P: Daniel Selznick, Joel Glickman, Michael O'Herlihy. P: Paul Saltzman. D: Barbara Kelly. W: Lionel E. Siegel. Shown in OPT syndication (N.Y.) Nov. 17 & 24, 1987. (4 hrs.)

Cast: Jack Warden, Nicholas Campbell, Robert Pine, Barry Morse, Richard Anderson, Leland Gantt, Heather Thomas, Marc Strange, Tom Butler, Errol Slue, Elliott McIvor, Paul Taylor, Paul Soles, Michael Hogan, August Schellenberg, Djanet Sears.

HOSTAGE
CBS Entertainment Prods. P: Diana Kerew. D: Peter Levin. W: Stephen J. Foreman. Shown on CBS Feb. 14, 1988. (2 hrs.)

Cast: Carol Burnett, Carrie Hamilton, Leon Russom, Annette Bening, Priscilla Caroline Smith, Doris Belack.

HOT PAINT
Catalina Production Group Ltd. Exec. P: Franklin R. Levy, Gregory Harrison. P: Mike Rauch, Matthew Ruston. Co-P-W: Eliot Wald, Andrew Kurtzman. D: Sheldon Larry. Shown on CBS March 20, 1988. (2 hrs.)

Cast: Gregory Harrison, John Larroquette, Cyrielle Claire, John Glover, Jonathan Cecil, Maury Chaykin, Julie Bovasso, Don Francks, Graeme Campbell, Elias Zarou, Sam Moses.

I SAW WHAT YOU DID
Universal TV. Exec. P: Jon Epstein, Wendy Riche. P: Barry Greenfield. D: Fred Walton. W: Cynthia Cidre, based on Ursula Curtiss' novel "Out of the Dark." Shown on CBS May 20, 1988. (2 hrs.)

Cast: Shawnee Smith, Tammy Lauren, Candace Cameron, David Carradine, Robert Carradine, Rosanna Huffman, Jo Anderson, Bob Brundin, Patrick O'Bryan, Dana Gladstone, Alan Fudge, Susan Kellerman, Michael Ross, Robert Winley.

IF IT'S TUESDAY, IT STILL MUST BE BELGIUM
John J. McMahon Prods.; MGM/UA TV. P: Mel Swope. Exec. P: John J. McMahon, Alan Eisenstock, Larry Mintz. D: Bob Sweeney; W: Alan Eisenstock, Larry Mintz. Shown on NBC Sept. 21, 1987. (2 hrs.)

Cast: Claude Akins, Lou Liberatore, Courteney Cox, Faith Ford, Stephen Furst, Peter Graves, Kene Holliday, Anna Maria Horsford, Lou Ja-

cobi, Bradley Kane, David Leisure, Kiel Martin, Richard Moll, Tracy Nelson, David Oliver, Doris Roberts, Bruce Weitz.

THE IMPOSSIBLE SPY
BBC-TV Prods.; Quartet Intl.; IMGC. Exec. P: Harvey Chertok. P: Graham Massey, David Goldstein, Sarah Frank. D: Jim Goddard. W: Marty Ross, Douglas Livingston. Shown on HBO Nov. 28, 1987. (1½ hrs.)
Cast: John Shea, Eli Wallach, Sasson Gabay, Michal Bat-Adams, Rami Danon, Haim Girafi, Jack Cohen, Anat Barzilay, Yossi Kenan, Judith Mlilo, Victor Kammar.

THE INCREDIBLE HULK RETURNS
B & B Prods.; New World TV. Exec. P: Nicholas Corea, Bill Bixby. Sprv. P: Daniel McPhee. D-W: Nicholas Corea. Shown on NBC May 22, 1988. (2 hrs.)
Cast: Bill Bixby, Lou Ferrigno, Jack Colvin, Lee Purcell, Charles Napier, John Gabriel, Jay Baker, Tim Thomerson, Eric Kramer, Steve Levitt, William Riley, Tom Finnegan.

INHERIT THE WIND
Vincent Pictures; David Greene/Robert Papazian Prod. Exec. P: Peter Douglas. P: Robert A. Papazian. D: David Greene. W: John Gay. Shown on NBC March 20, 1988. (2 hrs.)
Cast: Kirk Douglas, Jason Robards, Darren McGavin, John Harkins, Megan Follows, Kyle Secor, Michael Ensign, Don Hood, Jean Simmons.

INTIMATE CONTACT
Zenith Prods. & Central TV. Exec. P: Ted Childs. P: Chris Burt. D: Waris Hussein. W: Alma Cullen. Shown on HBO Showcase Sept. 5 & 6, 1987. (3 hrs.)
Cast: Claire Bloom, Daniel Massey, David Phelan, Abigail Cruttenden, Mark Kingston, Sylvia Sims, Sally Jane Jackson, Maggie Steed, Paul Jesson, John Murtagh, David Webb, Neil Pearson, John Joyce, Mack Penfold, Sebastian Breaks, James Wooley, Derek Benfield.

INTO THE HOMELAND
HBO Pictures; Capistrano Pictures. Exec. P-W: Anna Hamilton Phelan. P: Kevin McCormick. D: Lesli Linka Glatter. Shown on HBO Dec. 26, 1987. (2 hrs.)
Cast: Powers Boothe, C. Thomas Howell, Paul LeMat, Cindy Pickett, David Caruso, Shelby Leverington, Arye Gross, Emily Longstreth.

JUSTIN CASE
Blake Edwards Co. and Walt Disney TV. Exec. P-D-W: Blake Edwards. P: Tony Adams. Shown on ABC May 15, 1988. (1½ hrs.)
Cast: George Carlin, Molly Hagan, Gordon Jump, Timothy Stack, Kevin McClarnon, Douglas Sills, Paul Sand, Valerie Wildman, Todd Susman, Rob McCary, Philippe Denham, Richard McGonagle, Jay Thomas, Kenneth Tigar, Kay Perry, John Lavachielli, Dotty Colorso.

KENNY ROGERS AS "THE GAMBLER" III— THE LEGEND CONTINUES
Wild Horses Production. Exec. P: Ken Kragen, Lelan Rogers, Dick Lowry. P: Patrick Markey. Co-P: Peter Burrell. D: Dick Lowry. W: Jeb Rosebrook, Roderick Taylor. Shown on CBS Nov. 22 & 24, 1987. (4 hrs.)
Cast: Kenny Rogers, Bruce Boxleitner, Linda Gray, Melanie Chartoff, Matt Clark, George Kennedy, Marvin J. McIntyre, Dean Stockwell, Jeffrey Jones, Charles Durning, Richard Chaves, Tony Plana, George American Horse, James Greene, Marco Rodriguez.

KIDS LIKE THESE
Taft Entertainment/Nexus Prods. Exec. P: Georg Stanford Brown. P: Ed Gold. Sprv. P: Bert Gold. W: Emily Perl Kingsley, Allan Sloane. Shown on CBS Nov. 8, 1987. (2 hrs.)
Cast: Tyne Daly, Richard Crenna, Martin Balsam, Joey McFarland, Joshua O'Neill, Ted Polito, David Kaufman, Amy Van Nostrand, Zachary M. Allen, Brian Personette, Dr. Margaret Giannini.

THE KING OF LOVE
Sarabande Productions; MGM/UA Television. Exec. P: David Manson. P: Cyrus Yavneh. D: Anthony Wilkinson. W: Donald Freed. Shown on ABC Nov. 19, 1987. (2 hrs.)
Cast: Nick Mancuso, Rip Torn, Sela Ward, Michael Lerner, Alan Rosenberg, Katy Boyer, Robin Gammell.

LAGUNA HEAT
A Jay West Prod. of an HBO Pictures Presentation. Exec. P: Jay Weston. P: Bill Badalato. D: Simon Langton. W: Pete Hamill, D.M. Eyre, David Burton Morris. Shown on HBO Nov. 15, 1987. (2 hrs.)
Cast: Harry Hamlin, Jason Robards, Rip Torn, Catherine Hicks, Anne Francis, James Gammon, Dehl Berti, Jeff Kober, Rutayn Alda, Clyde Kusatsu, Gary Pagett, Fred Ponzlov, Peter Janson, Peter Brocco, Ryan McWhorter.

LAURA LANSING SLEPT HERE
A Schaefer/Karpf/Eckstein Prod.; Gaylord Prod. Co. Exec. P: Merrill H. Karpf. P-D: George Schaefer. Co-P-W: James Prideaux. Shown on NBC March 7, 1988. (2 hrs.)
Cast: Katharine Hepburn, Karen Austin, Brenda Forbes, Joel Higgins, Lee Richardson, Nicolas Surovy.

LENA: MY 100 CHILDREN
Robert Greenwald Prods.; Alliance Entertainment Group. Exec. P: Robert Greenwald. Assoc. P: Gregory Prange. Co-P: Tova Laiter, Steve McGlothen. Sprv. P: Philip K. Kleinbart. D: Edwin Sherin. W: Jonathan Rintels, Yabo Yablonsky. Shown on NBC Nov. 23, 1987. (2 hrs.)
Cast: Linda Lavin, Torquil Campbell, Lenore Harris, Cynthia Wilder, George Touliatos, Suzannah Hoffman, John Evans, Sam Malkin, Victoria Wauchope, Megal Fahlenbock.

LITTLE GIRL LOST
Marian Rees Associates Production. Exec. P: Marian Rees. P: Robert Huddleston. Co-P: Angela Shelly, C. Scott Alsop, David Graham. D: Sharron Miller. W: Ann Beckett. Shown on ABC April 25, 1988. (2 hrs.)
Cast: Tess Harper, Frederic Forrest, Patricia Kalember, Lawrence Pressman, Christopher McDonald, Sandy Martin, Joel Colodner, William Edward Phipps.

THE LITTLE MATCH GIRL
NBC Prods. Inc. Exec. P: Michael Manheim. P: Robert Hargrove. Sprv. P: Andre R. Guttfreund. D: Michael Lindsay-Hogg. W: Maryedith Burrell. Shown on NBC Dec. 21, 1987. (2 hrs.)
Cast: Keisha Knight Pulliam, William Daniels, John Rhys-Davies, Jim Metzler, William Youmans, Hallie Foote, Maryedith Burrell, Rue McClanahan,

THE LONG JOURNEY HOME
Andrea Baynes Prods. and Grail Prods.; Lorimar Television. Exec. P: Andrea Baynes. Co-exec. P: David Birney, Meredith Baxter Birney. P: Ervin Zavada. D: Rod Holcomb. W: Karen Clark. Shown on CBS Nov. 29, 1987. (2 hrs.)
Cast: Meredith Baxter Birney, David Birney, Ray Baker, James Sutorius, Daphne Maxwell, Kevin McCarthy, Mike Preston.

LONGARM
Universal TV. Exec. P-W: David Chisholm. Sprv. P: Ken Topolsky. P: Charles E. Sellier Jr. D: Virgil W. Vogel. Shown on ABC March 6, 1988. (1½ hrs.)
Cast: John T. Terlesky, Whitney Kershaw, Deborah Dawn Slaboda, Daphne Ashbrook, Lee de Broux, John Dennis Johnston, John Quade, Malachi Throne, Shannon Tweed, Noble Willingham.

MAN AGAINST THE MOB
Frank von Zerneck Films. Exec. P: Frank von Zerneck, Robert M. Sertner. Co-P: John Rester. Assoc. P: Susan Weber-Gold. P: Phillips Wylly Sr. D: Steven Hilliard Stern. W: David J. Kinghorn. Shown on NBC Jan. 10, 1988. (2 hrs.)
Cast: George Peppard, Kathryn Harrold, Stella Stevens, Max Gail, Barry Corbin, Fredric Lehne, Mark Lonow, Paul Tuerpe, Paul Sylvan, Michael Gregory.

THE MAN WHO BROKE 1000 CHAINS
HBO Pictures and Journey Entertainment. Exec. P: Michael Campus. P: Yoram Ben-Ami. D: Daniel Mann. W: Michael Campus, David Wyles, based on the book by Vincent Godfrey Burns. Shown on HBO Oct. 31, 1987. (113 mins.)
Cast: Val Kilmer, Charles Durning, Kyra Sedgwick, James Keach, Clancy Brown, Elisha Cook, William Sanderson, Sonia Braga, Taj Mahal, Paul Benjamin, Bill Bollender.

MANDELA
HBO Pictures. Exec. P: Herbert Brodkin. P: Robert Berger. D: Phillip Saville. W: Ron Harwood. Shown on HBO Sept. 20, 1988. (135 mins.)
Cast: Danny Glover, Alfre Woodard, John Indi, John Matshikiza, Nathan Danbusa Mdledle.

MARIO PUZO'S THE FORTUNATE PILGRIM
Carlo & Alex Ponti Prods., RETEITALIA, S.P.A. Exec. P: Carlo Ponti. P: Alex Ponti. D: Stuart Cooper. W: John McGreevey, based on the novel by Mario Puzo. Shown on NBC April 3 & 4, 1988. (5 hrs.)
Cast: Sophia Loren, Edward James Olmos, Hal Holbrook, John Turturro, Anna Strasberg, Yorgo Voyagis, Mirjana Karanovic, Annabella Sciorra, Ron Marquette.

MAYFLOWER MADAM
Robert Halmi, Inc. P: Robert Halmi. Sprv. P: Ira Halberstadt. D: Lou Antonio. W: Elizabeth Gill, Charles Israel. Shown on CBS Nov. 15, 1987. (2 hrs.)
Cast: Candice Bergen, Chris Sarandon, Caitlin Clarke, Jim Antonio, Debra Rogers, Leslie Hardy, Victoria Loving, Robert Silver, Chita Rivera.

MISTRESS
A Jaffe/Lansing Prod; Republic Pictures. P: Stephanie Austin. Exec. P: Sherry Lansing, Richard Fischoff. Sprv. P: David Permut, Joyce Eliason. D: Michael Tuchner. W: Joyce Eliason. Shown on CBS Oct. 4, 1987. (2 hrs.)
Cast: Victoria Principal, Kerri Keane, Joanna Kerns, Alan Rachins, Guy Boyd, Darrell Larson, Grace Zabriskie, Spiros Focas, William Bumiller, Don Murray.

MOVING TARGET
Lewis B. Chesler Prods., Bateman Company Prods.; The Finnegan/Pinchuk Co., MGM/UA Television Prods. Inc. Exec. P: Lewis B. Chesler, Kent Bateman. P: Bill Finnegan, Christopher Morgan. Co-P: Andy Tennant, Ed Hunsaker. D: Chris Thomson. W: Andy Tennant. Shown on NBC Feb. 8, 1988. (2 hrs.)
Cast: Jason Bateman, John Glover, Jack Wagner, Chynna Phillips, Donna Mitchell, Claude Brooks, Bernie Coulson, Richard Dysart, Tom Skerritt.

THE MURDER OF MARY PHAGAN
George Stevens Jr. Prod. in association with Century Tower Prods. P: George Stevens Jr. D: Billy Hale. W: Jeffrey Lane, George Stevens Jr. based on the story by Larry McMurtry. Shown on NBC Jan. 24 & 26, 1988. (5 hrs.)
Cast: Jack Lemmon, Richard Jordan, Robert Prosky, Peter Gallagher, Kathryn Walker, Rebecca Augusta Miller, Paul Dooley, Charles Dutton, Kevin Spacey, Cynthia Nixon, Kenneth Welsh.

MY FATHER, MY SON
Fred Weintraub Prod.; John J. McMahon Prod.; MGM-UA Television. P: Fred Weintraub. Exec. P: John J. McMahon. D: Jeff Bleckner. W: Jacqueline Feather, David Seidler, based on the book by Adm. Elmo Russell Zumwalt Jr. and Elmo R. Zumwalt III. Shown on CBS May 22, 1988. (2 hrs.)
Cast: Keith Carradine, Karl Malden, Margaret Klenck, Michael Horton, Dirk Blocker, Mack Dryden, Tim Choate, Jenny Lewis, Billy Sullivan, Grace Zabriskie.

NECESSITY
20th Century Fox Film Corp. Exec. P: Dan Enright. P: Les Alexander, Dan Enright. Co-P: Ed Fields. Sprv. P: Richard Briggs. D: Michael Miller. W: Michael Ahnemann, based on the novel by Brian Garfield. Shown on CBS May 3, 1988. (2 hrs.)
Cast: Loni Anderson, James Naughton, John Heard, Harris Laskawy, Sherman Howard, Dendrie Allyn Taylor, Diana Bellamy.

NIGHTINGALES
Aaron Spelling Prods. Exec. P: Aaron Spelling, Douglas S. Cramer. P: Rita Lakin, Frank Farino. D: Mimi Leder. W: Howard Lakin. Shown on NBC June 27, 1988. (2 hrs.)
Cast: Mimi Kuzyk, Susan Waters, Britta Phillips, Chelsea Field, Kristy Swanson, Neith Hunter, Galyn Gorg, Larry Poindexter, Reed Rudy, Fran Bennett, John Bennett Perry.

NIGHTMARE AT BITTER CREEK
Swanton Films; Guber-Peters Entertainment Co.; Phoenix Entertainment Group. Exec. P: Jon Peters, Peter Guber. P: Scott Swanton.

Sprv. P: Ron Roth. D: Tim Burstall. W: Scott Swanton, Greg McCarty. Shown on CBS May 24, 1988. (2 hrs.)
Cast: Lindsay Wagner, Tom Skerritt, Constance McCashin, Joanna Cassidy, Janne Mortil, Ray Guth, Dwight McFee, J.C. Roberts, Walter Marsh.

NITTI: THE ENFORCER
Leonard Hill Films. Exec. P: Leonard Hill, Robert O'Connor. Sprv. P: Ron Gilbert. Co-P: Daniel Cahn, Joel Fields. P-W: Lee David Zlotoff. D: Michael Switzer. Shown on ABC April 17, 1988. (2 hrs.)
Cast: Anthony LaPaglia, Vincent Guastaferro, Trini Alvarado, Michael Moriarty, Michael Russo, Louis Guss, Clayton Landey, Bruce Kirby, Renata Vanni, Michael Collins, Mike Starr, Wayne Grace, Peter Iacangelo.

NORMAN ROCKWELL'S BREAKING HOME TIES
A John Wilder Nightwatch Prod.; Telecom Entertainment Inc. Exec. P: Michael Lepiner, Kenneth Kaufman, John Wilder. P: Graham Cottle. D-W: John Wilder. Shown on ABC Nov. 26, 1987. (2 hrs.)
Cast: Jason Robards, Eva Marie Saint, Doug McKeon, Erin Gray, Claire Trevor.

NOT QUITE HUMAN
Sharmhill Prods; Walt Disney TV. Exec. P-D: Steven H. Stern, P: Noel Resnick. W: Alan Ormsby. Shown on ABC Dec. 20 & 27, 1987. (2 hrs.) (Premiered on Disney Channel June 19, 1987).
Cast: Alan Thicke, Robyn Lively, Robert Harper, Joseph Bologna, Jay Underwood, Brian Cole, Brandon Douglas, Lili Haydn, Sasha Mitchell, Greg Monaghan, Lonny Price, Carey Scott, Kristy Swanson.

ONASSIS: THE RICHEST MAN IN THE WORLD
The Konigsberg/Sanitsky Co.; K & S Partnership. Exec. P: Frank Konigsberg, Larry Sanitsky. P: Alfred R. Kelman. Assoc. P: Ron Binkowski, Jane Bieber. D: Waris Hussein. W: Jacqueline Feather, David Seidler. Shown on ABC May 1 & 2, 1988. (4 hrs.)
Cast: Raul Julia, Jane Seymour, Anthony Quinn, Francesca Annis, Elias Koteas, Beatie Edney, Anthony Zerbe, John Kapelos, Robert Krantz, Lorenzo Quinn, Richard Chaves.

ONCE UPON A TEXAS TRAIN
Robert Papazian Production; Brigade Prods. and Rastar. Exec. P: Doreen Bergesen, Robert A. Papazian. P-D-W: Burt Kennedy. Shown on CBS Jan. 3, 1988. (2 hrs.)
Cast: Willie Nelson, Richard Widmark, Shaun Cassidy, Chuck Connors, Ken Curtis, Royal Dano, Jack Elam, Gene Evans, Kevin McCarthy, Dub Taylor, Stuart Whitman, Angie Dickinson.

PERFECT PEOPLE
Robert Greenwald Prods. Exec. P: Robert Greenwald. P: Heidi M. Frey. Sprv. P: Philip K. Kleinhart. D: Bruce Seth Green. W: Gregory Goodell. Shown on ABC Feb. 29, 1988. (2 hrs.)
Cast: Lauren Hutton, Perry King, Priscilla Barnes, Cheryl Pollak, David Leisure, Robert Estes, June Lockhart, Karen Valentine, Jennifer Rhodes, Roger Nolan, Twink Caplan, Vincent Howard, Ronnie Schell.

PERRY MASON: THE CASE OF THE AVENGING ACE
The Fred Silverman Co.; Strathmore Prods.; Viacom. Exec. P: Dean Hargrove, Fred Silverman. Exec. Spvr. P: Philip Saltzman. Sprv. P: Joel Steiger. D: Peter Katz. D: Christian I. Nyby II. W: Lee David Zlotoff. Shown on NBC Feb. 28, 1988. (2 hrs.)
Cast: Raymond Burr, Barbara Hale, William Katt, David Ogden Stiers, Erin Gray, Larry Wilcox, Charles Siebert, James Sutorius, Arthur Taxier, James McEachin, Don Galloway, Richard Sanders, Patty Duke.

PERRY MASON: THE CASE OF THE LADY IN THE LAKE
The Fred Silverman Co.; Strathmore Prods. Viacom Prod. Exec. P: Fred Silverman, Dean Hargrove. Exec. Sprv. P: Philip Saltzman. Sprv. P: Joel Steiger. Assoc. P: David Solomon. P: Peter Katz. D: Ron Satlof. W: Shel Williams. Shown on NBC May, 15, 1988. (2 hrs.)
Cast: Raymond Burr, Barbara Hale, William Katt, David Ogden Stiers, David Hasselhoff, John Beck, Audra Lindley, Lianna Langland, Doran Clark, John Ireland, George DeLoy, Darrell Larson.

THE PERRY MASON: THE CASE OF THE MURDERED MADAM

The Fred Silverman Co.; Strathmore Prods.; Viacom. Prod. Exec. P: Fred Silverman, Dean Hargrove. Sprv. P: Philip Saltzman, Joel Stieger. P: Peter Katz. D: Ron Satlof. W: Patricia Green. Shown on NBC Oct. 4, 1987. (2 hrs.)

Cast: Raymond Burr, Barbara Hale, William Katt, Daphne Ashbrook, Vincent Baggetta, Jason Bernard, Anthony Geary, Bill Macy, James Noble, John Rhys-Davies, Ann Jillian, David Ogden Stiers, Kim Ulrich, Jamie Horton, Richard Portnow, Mike Moroff, Wendeline Harstone, John Nance, Michael Osborn.

PERRY MASON: THE CASE OF THE SCANDALOUS SCOUNDREL

The Fred Silverman Co.; Strathmore Prods.; Viacom Prod. P: Peter Katz. Sprv. P: Joel Steiger. Exec. P: Dean Hargrove, Fred Silverman. D: Christian I. Nyby II. W: Anthony Spinner, based on characters created by Erle Stanley Gardner. Shown on NBC Nov. 15, 1987. (2 hrs.)

Cast: Raymond Burr, Barbara Hale, William Katt, David Ogden Stiers, Robert Guillaume, Morgan Brittany, Eugene Butler, Rene Enriquez, George Grizzard, Wings Hauser, Yaphet Kotto, Susan Wilder, James McEachlin.

POOR LITTLE RICH GIRL: THE BARBARA HUTTON STORY

ITC Entertainment. Exec. P: Lester Persky. P: Nick Gillott. D: Charles Jarrott. W: Dennis Turner, based on the book by C. David Heymann. Shown on NBC Nov. 16 & 17, 1987. (5 hrs.)

Cast: Farrah Fawcett, David Ackroyd, Stephane Audran, Amadeus August, Nicholas Clay, Bruce Davison, Carmen Du Sautoy, Anne Francis, Sacha Hehn, Burl Ives, Kevin McCarthy, Tony Peck, Janes Read, Zoe Wanamaker.

PROMISED A MIRACLE

Roni Weisberg Prods.; Dick Clark Prods.; Republic Pictures. Exec. P: Preston Fischer, Dick Clark, Fran LaMaina. P: Roni Weisberg. Co-P: Dan Paulson, Lisa Demberg. D: Stephen Gyllenhaal. W: David Hill, based on "We Let Our Son Die" by Larry Parker as told to Don Tanner. Shown on CBS May 19, 1988. (2 hrs.)

Cast: Rosanna Arquette, Judge Reinhold, Tom Bower, Vonni Ribisi, Robin Pearson Rose, John Vickery, Gary Bayer, Shawn Elliott, Maria O'Brien, Jennifer Puscas, America Martin, Michael Cavanaugh, Wyatt Knight, Amy Michelson, Terry Wills, Kathy Kinney, Tuesday Knight.

THE PROUD MEN

Cowboy Prods., Inc.; Agamemnon Films Prod.; Von Zerneck-Samuels Prods. Exec. P: Stu Samuels, Frank Von Zerneck. P: Robert M. Sertner. Co-P: Fraser C. Heston. D: William A. Graham. W: Jeff Andrus. Shown on ABC Oct. 1, 1987. (2 hrs.)

Cast: Charlton Heston, Peter Strauss, Nan Martin, Alan Autry, Belinda Balsaki, Maria Mayenzet, Red West, Billy Ray Sharkey, Buck Taylor, Gregory Kupiec, Dale Swann, Steve Whittaker.

RED RIVER

Catalina Prod. Group Ltd. MGM/UA Television. Exec. P: Franklin R. Levy, Gregory Harrison P: Michael Rauch, Matthew Rushton. D: Richard Michaels. W: Richard Fielder. Shown on CBS April 10, 1988. (2 hrs.)

Cast: James Arness, Bruce Boxleitner, Gregory Harrison, Ray Walston, Laura Johnson, Zachary Ansley, L.Q. Jones, Jerry Potter, Burton Gilliam, Stan Saw, Ty Hardin, Robert Horton, John Lupton, Guy Madison, Travis Swords, Temple Williams.

THE RED SPIDER

CBS Entertainment Prods. P: Paul King, Timothy King. Co-P: Derek Kavanagh. D: Jerry Jameson. W: Paul King. Shown on CBS April 21, 1988. (2 hrs.)

Cast: James Farentino, Amy Steel, Philip Casnoff, Soon-Teck Oh, Stephen Joyce, Earl Hindman, Kario Salem, Blu Mankuma, Jennifer O'Neill.

THE RETURN OF BEN CASEY

Cooper Canadian Films. Exec. P: Robert Cooper. P: Julian Marks. D: Joseph L. Scanlan. W: Barry Oringer, based on characters created by James E. Moser. Shown in syndication (N.Y.) Feb. 13, 1988. (2 hrs.)

Cast: Vince Edwards, Al Waxman, Gwynyth Walsh, Lynda Mason Green, Jason Blicker, Harry Landers, August Schellenberg.

THE RETURN OF DESPERADO

Walter Mirisch Prods; Charles E. Sellier Jr.; Universal TV. Exec. P: Andrew Mirisch. P: Charles E. Sellier Jr. D: E.W. Swackhammer. W: John Mankiewicz, Daniel Pyne, Charles Grant Craig. Shown on NBC Feb. 15, 1988. (2 hrs.)

Cast: Alex McArthur, Robert Foxworth, Marcy Walker, Victor Love, Vanessa Bell, Shelby Leverington, Charles Boswell, Billy Dee Williams, Vivan Bonnell, Hal Havins, J. Jay Saunders, John Barks, Greg Brinkley, Rahda Delamarter, Rusty Dillen, Jerry Gardner.

THE RETURN OF THE SHAGGY DOG

Walt Disney Television. Exec. P: Michael S. McLean. P: Harvey Marks. D: Stuart Gillard. W: Diane Wilk, Paul Haggis. Shown on ABC Nov. 1 & 8, 1987. (2 hrs.)

Cast: Gary Kroeger, Todd Waring, Michelle Little, Cindy Morgan, Jane Carr, Gavin Reed, K Callan, James MacKrell, Jack Ammon, Paul Batten, Lorena Gale, Gary Hetherington, Antony Holland, Don MacKay, Betty Phillips, Leroy Schultz.

RIGHT TO DIE

A Don Ohlmeyer Production. Exec. P: Don Ohlmeyer. P: Karen Danaher Dorr. D: Paul Wendkos. W: Phil Penningroth. Shown on NBC Oct. 12, 1987. (2 hrs.)

Cast: Raquel Welch, Michael Gross, Bonnie Bartlett, Peter Michael Goetz, Joanna Miles, Ed O'Neill, Diane Salinger, Mark Shera, Castulo Guerra, Jacklyn Bernstein, David Wohl.

ROCK 'N' ROLL MOM

Walt Disney Television. P: Stan Rogow. D: Michael Schultz. W: Gen Le Roy. Shown on ABC Feb. 7, 1988. (2 hrs.)

Cast: Dyan Cannon, Michael Brandon, Telma Hopkins, Nancy Lenehan, Josh Blake, Amy Lynne, Frank Drescher, Alex Rocco, Joe Pantoliano, Heather Locklear.

ROMAN HOLIDAY

Jerry Ludwig Enterprizes Inc; Paramount. Exec. P-W: Jerry Ludwig. P: Mel Efros. D: Noel Nosseck. Shown on NBC Dec. 28, 1987. (2 hrs.)

Cast: Tom Conti, Catherine Oxenberg, Ed Begley Jr., Paul Daneman, Eileen Atkins, Patrick Allen, Francis Matthews, Shane Rimmer, Christopher Muncke, Tessa Hood, Andrew Bicknell, David Rolfe.

SADIE AND SON

Norton Wright Prod./Kenny Rogers Org.; ITC. Exec. P: Norton Wright. P: Richard L. O'Connor. D: John Llewellyn Moxey. W: Carl Kleinschmitt. Shown on CBS Oct. 21, 1987. (2 hrs.)

Cast: Debbie Reynolds, Brian McNamara, Sam Wanamaker, Cynthia Dale, David Ferry, Robert Morelli.

SAVE THE DOG!

Elsboy Prods.; Walt Disney Television. P: Lynn Bigelow, Jim Kouf. Sprv. P: George W. Perkins. Exec. P: Paul Aaron. Co-exec. P: Erwin Stoff. D: Paul Aaron. W: John McNamara, based on a screenplay by Harris Orkin. Shown on The Disney Channel March 19, 1988. (95 mins.)

Cast: Cindy Williams, Tony Randall, Katherine Helmond, Tom Poston, Charlotte Rae, Billie Bird, Al Lewis.

SCANDAL IN A SMALL TOWN

Carliner/Rappaport Prod. P: Michele Rappaport, Mark Carliner. D: Anthony Page. W: Robert Avrech. Shown on NBC April 10, 1988. (2 hrs.)

Cast: Raquel Welch, Christa Denton, Frances Lee McCain, Peter Van Norden, Robin Gammell, Ronny Cox.

THE SECRET GARDEN

Rosemont Prods. Ltd. Exec. P: Norman Rosemont. P: Steve Lanning. D: Alan Grint. W: Blanche Hanalis, based on the book by Frances Hodgson Burnett. Shown on CBS Nov. 30, 1987. (2 hrs.)

Cast: Gennie James, Barret Oliver, Jadrien Steele, Michael Hordern, Billie Whitelaw, Derek Jacobi, Lacy Gutteridge, Colin Firth, Julian Glover.

SHAKEDOWN ON THE SUNSET STRIP

CBS Entertainment Prod. P: Harold Gast, Walter Grauman. D: Walter Grauman. W: Harold Gast. Shown on CBS April 22, 1988. (2 hrs.)

Cast: Perry King, Season Hubley, Joan Van Ark, Vincent Baggetta, Alan Blumenfeld, David Graf, Robert Hirschfeld, Michael McGuire, Joan McMurtrey, Charles Siebert.

SHARING RICHARD

Houston Motion Picture Entertainment, Inc. in cooperation with CBS Entertainment. Sprv. P: Ian Sanders. P: Roni Weisberg. D: Peter Bonerz. W: Ann Donahue and Marion Zola. Shown on CBS April 26, 1988. (2 hrs.)

Cast: Ed Marinaro, Eileen Davidson, Nancy Frangione, Hillary Bailey Smith, Janet Carroll, Lisa Jane Persky, Roger Bowen, Kelly Minter, Murphy Dunne.

SHATTERED INNOCENCE

Green/Epstein Prods.; Lorimar Television. Exec. P: Jim Green, Allen Epstein. P: Milton Sperling. D: Sandor Stern. W: Thanet Richard, Sandor Stern. Shown on CBS March 9, 1988. (2 hrs.)

Cast: Jonna Lee, Melinda Dillon, John Pleshette, Kris Kamm, Ben Frank, Dennis Howard, Stephen Schnetzer, Richard Cox, Nadine van der Velde.

SIDE BY SIDE

Avnet/Kerner Prod. Exec. P: Jon Avnet, Jordan Kerner. P: Rosemary Edelman. D: Jack Bender. W: Rosemary Edelman, Sheldon Keller. Story: Rosemary Edelman, Anthony Velona. Shown on CBS March 6, 1988. (2 hrs.)

Cast: Milton Berle, Sid Caesar, Danny Thomas, Morey Amsterdam, Marjorie Lord, Georgann Johnson, Richard Kline, Edith Fields, Michael Lembeck, Laura Owens, Jennifer Bassey, Jeff Lampert, Maidie Norman, Ben Slack.

SOMETHING IS OUT THERE

Columbia Pictures Television. Exec. P: Frank Lupo, John Ashley. D: Richard Colla. W: Frank Lupo. Shown on NBC May 8 & 9, 1988. (4 hrs.)

Cast: Joe Cortese, Maryam d'Abo, Robert Webber, George Dzundza, Kim Delaney, Gregory Sierra, John Putch, John O'Hurley, Joseph Cali.

SPLASH, TOO

Mark H. Ovitz Prod. and Walt Disney Television. P: Mark H. Orvitz. D: Greg Antonacci. W: Bruce Franklin Singer, based on characters created by Bruce Jay Friedman. Shown on ABC May 1 & 8, 1988. (2 hrs.)

Cast: Todd Waring, Amy Yasbeck, Donovan Scott, Rita Taggart, Noble Willingham, Dody Goodman, Mark Blankfield, Barney Martin, Doris Belack, Timothy Williams, Jana Marie Hupp, Joey Travolta, Kirk Fyson, Roger Hewlett, Russell J. McConnell.

STONES FOR IBARRA

Titus Prods. Inc. Exec. P: Herbert Brodkin, Robert Berger. P: Bruce S. Pustin. D: Jack Gold. W: Ernest Kinoy, based on the novel by Harriet Doerr. Shown on CBS Jan. 29, 1988. (2 hrs.)

Cast: Glenn Close, Keith Carradine, Alfonso Arau, Jorge Cervera, Jr., Ron Joseph, Lupe Ontiveros, Diane Rodriguez, Trinidad Silva, Ray Oriel, Joaquin Martinez, Marco Rodriguez.

STRANGE VOICES

The Landsburg Company; Forrest Hills Prod. Inc. in association with Dacks-Geller Prods. Exec. P: Alan Landsburg, Joan Barnett. Co-exec. P: Greg H. Sims, Nancy McKeon. P: Roberta Dacks, Nancy Geller. D: Arthur Allan Seidelman. W: Donna Dottley Powers, Wayne Powers. Shown on NBC Oct. 19, 1987. (2 hrs.)

Cast: Valerie Harper, Nancy McKeon, Stephen Macht, Tricia Leigh Fisher, Millie Perkins, Robert Krantz, Jack Blessing, Gerald Hiken, Marta Kristen, Fay Hauser, Gary Bisig.

STRANGER ON MY LAND

Edgar J. Scherick Associates Prods.; Taft Entertainment Television. Exec. P: Edgar J. Scherick, Gary Hoffman. P: Michael Barnathan. D: Larry Elikann. W: Edward Hume, I.C. Rapaport. Shown on ABC Jan. 17, 1988. (2 hrs.)

Cast: Tommy Lee Jones, Dee Wallace Stone, Terry O'Quinn, Pat Hingle, Barry Corbin, Richard Anderson, Ned Romero, Natalie Gregory, Stephen Joyce, Lyman Ward, Ben Johnson.

STUDENT EXCHANGE

Walt Disney Television. P: Charlie Milhaupt. D: Mollie Miller. W: William Davies, William Osborne. Shown on ABC Nov. 29 & Dec. 6, 1987. (2 hrs.)

Cast: Viveka Davis, Todd Field, Mitchell Anderson, Heather Graham, Maura Tierney, Gavin MacLeod, Lisa Hartman, O.J. Simpson, Rob Estes, Lee Garlington, David Selburg.

SUSPICION

HTV Ltd. Exec. P: Patrick Dromgoole. P: Barry Levinson. Co-P: Patric Lynch, Sebastian Robinson. D: Andrew Grieve. W: Jonathan Lynn, Barry Levinson. Shown on PBS April 20, 1988. (1½ hrs.)

Cast: Anthony Andrews, Jane Curtin, Betsy Blair, Ellis Dale, Eric Dodson, Tricia George, Michael Hordern, Jonathan Lynn, Brian Culton, Vivian Pickles, Donald Pickering.

THE TAKING OF FLIGHT 847: THE ULI DERICKSON STORY

Columbia Pictures Television. Exec. P: Jim Calio, David Hume Kennerly. P: Jay Benson. D: Paul Wendkos. W: Norman Morrill. Shown on NBC May 2, 1988. (2 hrs.)

Cast: Lindsay Wagner, Eli Danker, Sandy McPeak, Ray Wise, Leslie Easterbrook, Laurie Walters, Joseph Nasser, Barry Jenner, Valorie F. Armstrong, James McMullan, Steven Eckholdt, Phillip Levien.

TERRORIST ON TRIAL: THE UNITED STATES VS. SALIM AJAMI

George Englund Prod.; Robert Papazian Prod. Exec. P: George Englund. Co-exec. P-W: Richard Levinson, William Link. P: Robert Papazian. D: Jeff Bleckner. Shown on CBS Jan. 10, 1988. (3 hrs.)

Cast: Sam Waterston, Ron Leibman, Robert Davi, Joe Morton, Jo Henderson, Stephen Lee, Frances Conroy, James Greene.

THE THREE KINGS

An Aaron Spelling Prod. Exec. P: Aaron Spelling, Douglas S. Cramer, Esther Shapiro. P-W: Stirling Silliphant, Mel Damski. Sprv. P: E. Duke Vincent. D: Mel Damski. Shown on ABC Dec. 17, 1987. (2 hrs.)

Cast: Jack Warden, Lou Diamond Phillips, Stan Shaw, Jane Kaczmarek, Vic Tayback, Charles Nelson Reilly.

TO HEAL A NATION

Lionel Chetwynd Prods., Orion TV; Von Zerneck-Samuels Prods. Exec. P: Frank von Zerneck, Stu Samuels, Lionel Chetwynd. P: Robert M. Sertner. Co-P: Gordon L. Freedman, Ian Sander. D: Michael Pressman. W: Lionel Chetwynd, based on the book by Jan C. Scruggs, Joel L. Swedlow. Shown on NBC May 29, 1988. (2 hrs.)

Cast: Eric Roberts, Glynnis O'Connor, Marhsall Colt, Scott Paulin, Lee Purcell, Brock Peters, Gloria Carlin, Jordan Charney, Tamlyn Tomita, Laurence Luckinbill, Linden Chiles, James F. Kelly, Eloy Casados, Tom Everett.

TOO YOUNG THE HERO

Rick-Dawn Prods.; Pierre Cossette Prods.; Landsburg Company. Exec. P: Pierre Cossette, Alan Landsburg, Joan Barnett. P-D: Buzz Kulik. W: David J. Kinghorn, based on a manuscript by Calvin Graham, Gray Thomas. Shown on CBS March 27, 1988. (2 hrs.)

Cast: Ricky Schroder, Jon DeVries, Debra Mooney, Mary Louise, Rick Warner, Thomas Mills Wood, Christopher Curry, John Linton, Markus Flanagan.

THE TOWN BULLY

Dick Clark Prods., Inc. Exec. P: Dick Clark. Co-exec. P: Dan Paulsen. Co-P: Lisa Demberg, Jonathan Rintels. P: Ian Sander. D: Noel Black. W: Jonathan Rintels. Shown on ABC April 24, 1988. (2 hrs.)

Cast: Bruce Boxleitner, Pat Hingle, Isabella Hofmann, Jerry Hardin, Timothy Scott, Jordan Charney, John Jackson, Sandy Ward, Katy Boyer, Macon McCalman, David Graf, Royce D. Applegate, Ellen Geer, Christine Elise.

THE TRACKER

HBO Pictures. Lance Hool Prods. Exec. P: Alan Trustman. P: Lance Hool. D: John Guillermin. W: Kevin Jarre. Shown on HBO March 16, 1988 (2 hrs.)

Cast: Kris Kristofferson, Mark Moses, Scott Wilson, David Huddleston, John Quade, Geoffrey Black, Jennifer Snyder, Karen Kopins, Don Swayze, Brynn Thayer, Ernie Lively.

WEEKEND WAR

Pompian/Atamian Prods.; Columbia Pictures TV. Exec. P: Paul Pompian, Gil Atamian. P: Paul Pompian. Co-P: Gregory Widen. D: Steven H. Stern. W: Dennis Hackin, Steven Hackin, Gregory Widen. Shown on ABC Feb. 1, 1988. (2 hrs.)

Cast: Stephen Collins, Daniel Stern, Evan Mirand, Michael Beach, Scott Paulin, James B. Tolkan, Victor Mohica, Kidany Lugo Santiago, Charles Haid, Christine Healy.

WHAT PRICE VICTORY
David L. Wolper Prod.; Warner Bros. Television. Exec. P: David L. Wolper, Bernard Sofronski. P: Mark M. Wolper. D: Kevin Connor. W: D.M. Eyre Jr. Shown on ABC Jan. 18, 1988. (2 hrs.)
Cast: Mac Davis, George Kennedy, Robert Culp, Susan Hess, Warren Berlinger, Guy Boyd, Eriq La Salle, Brian Wimmer.

A WHISPER KILLS
Sandy Hook Prods., Steve Tisch Co. and Phoenix Entertainment Corp. P: Hans Proppe. Co-P: Jody Brockway Paonessa. D: Christian I. Nyby II. W: John Robert Bensink. Shown on ABC May 16, 1988. (2 hrs.)
Cast: Loni Anderson, Joe Penny, June Lockhart, James Sutorius, Jeremy Slate, Martin Ponch, Bob Parnell.

WHO GETS THE FRIENDS?
CBS Entertainment. Prod. Sprv. P: Andrew Gottlieb. P-D: Lila Garrett. W: Lila Garrett, Sandy Krinski. Shown on CBS May 10, 1988. (2 hrs.)

Cast: Jill Clayburgh, James Farentino, Lucie Arnaz, Leigh Taylor Young, Robin Thomas, Laura Waterbury, James Sloyan, Greg Mullavey.

WINDMILLS OF THE GODS
Dove, Inc.; ITC Entertainment Group. Exec. P: Sidney Sheldon. P: Michael Viner. Co-P: Deborah Raffin. D: Lee Phillips. W: John Gay, based on the novel by Sidney Sheldon. Shown on CBS Feb. 7 & 9, 1988. (4 hrs.)
Cast: Jaclyn Smith, Robert Wagner, Franco Nero, Christopher Cazenove, David Ackroyd, Jean Pierre Aumont, Nicholas Ball, Ruby Dee, Jeffery DeMunn, Stephanie Faracy, Ian McKellen, Ari Meyers, Michael Moriarty, Lisa Pelikan, John Pleshette, John Standing, Susan Tyrrell, John van Dreelen, J.T. Walsh.

THE WOMAN HE LOVED
Larry A. Thompson Prods; New World Television. Exec. P: Larry A. Thompson. P: William Hill. D: Charles Jarrott. W: William Luce. Shown on CBS April 3, 1988. (2 hrs.)
Cast: Jane Seymour, Anthony Andrews, Olivia de Havilland, Lucy Gutteridge, Tom Wilkinson, Julie Harris, Robert Hardy, Phyllis Calvert.

1987–88 Mini-Series

Mini-series are movies made for television shown in three parts or more.

JAMES CLAVELL'S NOBLE HOUSE

Noble House Prods. Ltd.; DeLaurentiis Entertainment Group. Exec. P: James Clavell. P-W: Eric Bercovici. D: Gary Nelson. Based on the novel by James Clavell. Shown on NBC Feb. 21–24, 1988. (8 hrs.)

Cast: Pierce Brosnan, Deborah Raffin, Ben Masters, John Rhys-Davies, Julia Nickson, Khigh Dhiegh, Gordon Jackson, Bert Kwouk, Nancy Kwan, John Houseman, Denholm Elliott.

NAPOLEON AND JOSEPHINE: A LOVE STORY

David L. Wolper Production in association with Warner Bros. Television. Exec. P.: David L. Wolper, Bernard Sofronski. P. Alfred R. Kelman. Co-P/Prod. Supervisor: Suzanne Wiesenfeld. D. Richard Heffrom. W: James Lee. Shown on ABC Nov. 10, 11, 12, 1987. (6 hrs.)

Cast: Armand Assante, Jacqueline Bisset, Anthony Perkins, Stephanie Beacham, Anthony Higgins, Nickolas Grace, Jane Lapotaire, Patrick Cassidy, William Lucking, Jean-Pierre Steward, Leigh Taylor-Young, Jon Vickery, Ione Skye.

Television Stations

* **CHANNEL ALLOCATIONS**

* **PERSONNEL**

Television Stations

[A listing of television stations in the United States. All stations are authorized by and operate under the approval of the Federal Communications Commission, Washington, DC]

ALABAMA
Anniston

WJSU-TV (Channel 40) CBS
P.O. Box 40, Anniston, AL 36202 (205) 237-8651.
Bob Ford, gen. mgr.; Jim Kidd, prog. dir.; Bill Hagler, gen. sales mgr.; John Murrell, chief eng.
Operation: 1969.

Birmingham

WBMG (Channel 42) CBS
Birmingham Television Company, Box 6146, Birmingham, AL 35209 (205) 252-9821.
Roy H. Park, pres.; Hoyle S. Broome, v.p. & gen. mgr.; Gary Andrick, natl. sls. mgr.; Sara M. Coleman, lcl. sls. mgr.; Frank Morock, news dir.; Susan Ellenberg, traf. mgr.; Fred Vinson, chief eng.
Operation: 1965. TV homes in area: 541,000.

WBRC-TV (Channel 6) ABC
Taft Broadcasting Company, P.O. Box 6, Birmingham, AL 35201 (205) 322-6666.
Nick Bolton, gen. mgr.; Bob Fanning, gen. sales mgr.; Jerry Thorn, chief eng.; Telerep Agency, nat'l rep.
Operation: 1949; TV sets in area: 695,500.

WCAJ (Channel 68)
Shelley Bdcstg. Co., 800 Lakeshore Dr., Sanford U., Birmingham, AL 35229 (205) 871-6801.
Sid Burgess, gen. mgr.; Harry Lawson, chief eng.
Operation: 1986.

WTTO (Channel 21)
HR Bdcstg. Corp. of Birmingham, 2021 Golden Crest Dr., Birmingham, AL 35029 (205) 251-2100.
Gary Gardner, gen. mgr.; Robert Cleary, gen. sls. mgr.; Marilyn Greene, prog. dir.; Michel Wilk, promo. mgr.; Ross Howard, lcl. sls. mgr.
Operation: 1982.

WVTM-TV (Channel 13) NBC
WVTM-TV, Inc., P.O. Box 10502, Birmingham, AL 35202 (205) 933-2720.
John J. McCrory, pres.; Jack Harrison, v.p. & gen. mgr.; Frank Landers, gen. sls. mgr.; Everett Holle, film buyer & prog. dir.; Robin Cooper, prom. mgr. rep: HRP
Operation: 1949; TV sets in area: 593,000.

Dothan

WDHN (Channel 18) ABC
Morris Network, Inc., P.O. Box 6237, Dothan, AL 36302 (205) 793-1818.
H. Dean Hinson, pres.; Aubrey Wood, gen. mgr.; Charles Scott, prom. dir.; Linda Prescott, gen. sls. mgr.; Lisa Hill, prog. dir.; Dan Billings, chief eng.

WTVY (Channel 4) CBS
WTVY, Inc., P.O. Box 1089, Dothan, AL 36302; (205) 792-3195.
Charles Woods, owner-mgr.; Reginald Mitchell, prgm. dir.; Jerry Vann, news dir.; Joe Earl Holloway, prodn. mgr.; John Gause, sales mgr.; Carl Blackmon, nat'l sls. mgr.; Doug Dansby, chief eng.; regional rep., nat'l rep.: Seltel, Inc.
Operation: 1955; TV sets in area: 587,300.

Florence

WOWL-TV (Channel 15)
Television Muscle Shoals, Inc., 840 Cypress Mill Road, P.O. Box 2220, Florence, AL 35630 (205) 767-1515.
Dick Biddle, chm. of bd. & CEO; Jack Worley, pres.; Lincoln Williams, operations mgr.; Larry Rohling, chief eng.; Sara Biddle, community relations dir.; Alicia Smith, news desk mgr.
Operation: 1957; TV homes in area: approx. 234,000.

WTRT (Channel 26)
Bridgeland Television, Inc., 4600 Jackson Hwy., Sheffield, AL 35660. (205) 381-2600.
Les W. White, pres.; Barry Ross, v.p.

Gadsden

WNAL-TV (Channel 44)
WNAL-TV, Inc., 2729 11th Ave. South, Birmingham, AL 35205 (205) 547-4444.
Anthony J. Fant, pres. & gen. mgr.; Joe Al Holland, gen. sls. mgr.; Robert D. Hill, Jr., prog. dir. & film buyer; Kyla B. Fant, prom. mgr.; Mike Hathcock, chief eng.; natl. rep.: ITS.
Operation: April, 1986.

Huntsville

WAAY-TV (Channel 31)
Rocket City Television, Inc., 1000 Monte Sano Blvd., S.E.; Huntsville, AL 35801 (205) 533-3131.
M.D. Smith IV, pres.; Dan Whitsett, vp. & sls. mgr.; Robert A. Gay, chief eng.
Operation: 1959.

WAFF-TV (Channel 48) NBC
American Valley Corp., Huntsville, AL 35801 (205) 533-4848.
Lee Brantley, v.p. & gen. mgr.; David Stagnitto, opns. mgr.; Lamar Reid, gen. sls. mgr.; Rod Hughes, chief eng.; Pat Brown, news dir.
Operation: 1954.

WHNT-TV (Channel 19) CBS
The Times Alabama Broadcasting, Inc., 200 Holmes Ave., P.O. Box 19, Huntsville, AL 35804 (205) 533-1919.
Bob Browning, pres. & gen. mgr.; Bill Ambrose, v.p. & sls. mgr.; Dick Wright, v.p. & opns. mgr.; Dan Roden, chief eng.; Frank Verdel, news dir.
Operation: 1963.

WZDX (Channel 54)

Community Svc. Broadcasting, Suite 600, Osborne Office Center, Chattanooga, TN 37411 (615) 894-4980.

Media Central, Inc., gen. mgr.; Kevin Mirck, gen. sls. mgr.

Operation: April, 1985.

Mobile

WALA-TV (Channel 10) NBC

Knight-Ridder Bdcst., Inc., 210 Government St., Mobile, AL 36602, P.O. Box 1548 (205) 433-3754. TWX 810 741-2642. FAX-FFB.

Joe Cook, pres. & gen. mgr.; Becky Farrell, gen. sls. mgr.; John Reese, chief eng.; Dave Cochran, news dir.; Darrel Taylor, promo. mgr.; nat'l rep.: HRP

Operation: 1953; TV sets in area: 425,900.

WKRG-TV (Channel 5) CBS

WKRG-TV, Inc., 555 Broadcast Drive, Mobile, AL 36606 (205) 479-5555.

Toulmin Greer, bd. chm.; D.H. Long Jr., pres. & film buyer; Thomas W. Diamond, sr. v.p. & sta. mgr.; James C. Hall, opns. mgr.; Curtis B. Willard, chief eng.; nat'l rep.: Katz Agency.

Operation: 1955; TV sets in area: 422,400.

WPMI (Channel 15) FOX

WPMI TV Co., Inc., 764 St. Michael St., Mobile, AL 36602 (205) 433-1500.

William G. Evans, pres., gen. mgr.; Ray Chumley, dir. sls.; Debby Hunt, prog. dir.; Harold Johnson, chief eng.; nat'l rep.: Seltel.

Operation: 1982.

Montgomery

WAKA-TV (Channel 8) CBS

Alabama Telecasters, Inc., 3020 East Blvd., Montgomery, AL 36117 (205) 279-8787.

Jack Long, gen. mgr.; Mark Smith, pgm. dir. & opns. mgr.; Johnny Wright, chief eng.; Bill Byrd, sta. mgr.

Operation: 1960.

WCOV-TV (Channel 20) FOX

WCOV, Inc., P.O. Box 2505, Montgomery, AL 36105 (205) 288-7020.

David Woods, pres. & gen. mgr.; Phil Witt, chief eng.; nat'l rep.: Seltel.

Operation: 1953; TV sets in area, 172,300.

WKAB-TV (Channel 32) ABC

Montgomery Alabama Channel 32, P.O. Box 3236, Montgomery, AL 36192 (205) 272-5331.

Joseph D. Tydings, pres.; John Rogers, gen. mgr. & gen. sls. mgr.; Leesa Hood, natl., regl. sls. mgr.; David Murphy, opns. mgr.; Jerry Garvin, chief eng. nat'l rep., Petry TV.

Operation: March 24, 1962; TV households: 156,000.

WMCF-TV (Channel 45)

Word of God Fellowship, Inc., 135 Bell Rd., Montgomery, AL 36117 (205) 821-2204.

John Stalls, pres.

WSFA-TV (Channel 12) NBC

Cosmos Broadcasting Corp., 10 E. Delano, P.O. Box 2566, Montgomery, AL 36105 (205) 281-2900.

James Sefert, pres.; Mel Stebbins, v.p. & gen. mgr.; Bill Byrd, gen. sls. mgr.; Carl M. Stephens, prog. mgr.; Leslie

Morris, prom. dir.; Charles Halsten, chief eng.; nat'l rep: Blair.

Operation: 1954; TV sets in area: 367,300.

Tuscaloosa

WCFT-TV (Channel 33) CBS

WCFT-TV, Inc., Box 5239, Tuscaloosa, AL, 35401 (205) 553-1333.

S.A. Rosenbaum, pres.; Jim Caruthers, v.p. & gen. mgr.; Don Rankin, lcl. sls. mgr.; Ed Clark, news dir.; nat'l rep.: Adam Young Inc.

Operation: Oct. 29, 1965; TV households: 79,900.

WDBB (Channel 17)

Channel 17 Associates, Ltd., 651 Beacon Pkwy., West, Birmingham, AL 35209; (205) 942-1717.

David R. Dubose, pres. & gen. mgr.; Mark Gray, promo. mgr.; John Batson, chief eng.

Operation: October, 1984.

ALASKA
Anchorage

KIMO (Channel 13) ABC

Alaska 13 Corp. dba Alaska TV Network, 2700 E. Tudor Rd., Anchorage, AK 99507; (907) 561-1313.

Duane L. Triplett, pres. & CEO; Thomas Tierney, sta. mgr.; Larry Hogue, dir. mktg. & sls.; Lance Hopkins, chief eng.; nat'l rep., Katz.

Operation: 1967.

KTBY (Channel 4) FOX

Totem Broadcasting Corp., 510 L St., Anchorage, AK 99501. Robert C. Ely, sec.; Huntly Gordon, treas.

Operation: 1983.

KTUU-TV (Channel 2) NBC

P.O. Box 102880, Anchorage, AK 99501; (907) 257-0200.

Jessica Longston, pres.; Al Bramstedt, Jr., gen. mgr.; Nancy Johson, dir. mktg. & natl. sls. mgr.; Andrew McLeod, lcl. sls. mgr.; Nancy Johnson, dir. mktg.; Leeland Verschuesen, chief eng.; nat'l rep.: Blair.

Operation: 1953; TV sets in area: 116,820.

KTVA (Channel 11) CBS

Northern Television, Inc., Box 10-2200, Anchorage, AK 99510; 272-3456.

A. G. Hiebert, chm.; Ron Moore, pres., Anchorage Div.; Bruce Sloan, operations mgr.; nat'l rep., Art Moore, Inc., Adam Young, Inc.

Operation: 1953; TV sets in area: 70,000.

Fairbanks

KATN-TV (Channel 2) ABC, NBC

Fairbanks TV, Inc., Box 74730, Fairbanks, AK 99707.

Duane L. Triplett, pres.; David L. Geesin, v.p., sta. mgr.; J.B. Krause, gen. sls. mgr.; Ralph Gillette, chief eng.; nat'l rep: Katz.

Operation: 1955; TV sets in area: 23,000.

KTVF (Channel 11) CBS

Northern Television, Inc., Box 950, Fairbanks, AK 99707 (907) 452-5121.

A. G. Hiebert, chm.; Henry Hove, pres.; nat'l rep., Art Moore, Inc.

Operation: 1955; TV sets in area: 27,000.

Juneau

KJUD (Channel 8) ABC, CBS, NBC
1107 West Eighth St., Suite 2, Juneau, AK 99801 (907) 586-3145.
Duane Triplett, pres.; John Kaknos, sta. mgr.; Charles Payne, chief eng.; Terence O'Malley, news dir.; nat'l rep.: Katz, Tacher.
Operation: 1956.

Sitka

KTNL (Channel 13) CBS
520 Lake St., Sitka, AK 99835. (907) 747-6626.
Dr. Dan Etulain, pres. & gen. mgr.; Ivan Benson, prog. dir.; Garth Kanen, chief eng.
Operation: 1966.

ARIZONA
Flagstaff

KNAZ-TV (Channel 2) NBC
Grand Canyon TV Co., Box 1843, Flagstaff, AZ 86002 (602) 526-2232.
Don Purnell, gen. mgr.; Ed Bouchard, chief engr.
Operation: 1970.

Nogales-Tucson

KMSB (Channel 11) FOX
Mountain States Broadcasting, 2445 N. Tucson Blvd., Tucson, AZ 85716; (602) 795-0311.
Randy Cantrell, v.p. & gen. mgr.; Harry West, prog. dir. & film buyer; Larry Lominac, prom. mgr.; Rich Heatley, chief eng.; nat'l rep.: Seltel.
Operation: February, 1967; TV households: 275,000.

Phoenix

KNXV-TV (Channel 15)
Scripps Howard Bdcstg. Co., 4625 S. 33 Pl., Phoenix, AZ 85040 (602) 243-4151.
Stuart Powell, gen. mgr.; Mike Norten, gen. sls. mgr.; Matt Cooperstein, prog. & promo. dir.; Don Thomas, opns. & eng. mgr.; nat'l rep.: Katz.
Operation: 1979.

KPAZ (Channel 21)
Trinity Broadcasting of Arizona, Inc., 3351 E. McDowell Rd., Phoenix, AZ 85008 (602) 273-1477.
Paul F. Crouch, pres.
Operation: December, 1969; TV households: 310,000.

KPHO-TV (Channel 5)
Broadcasting Division, Meredith Corporation, 4016 N. Black Canyon, Phoenix, AZ 85017 (602) 264-1000.
Richard Q. DeAngelis, v.p. & gen. mgr.; Don Pauly, gen. sls. mgr.; Chuck Alvey, sta. mgr.; Chris Sehring, nat'l sls. mgr.; Greg Brannan, pgm. & promo. mgr.
Operation: 1949; Total TV Homes: in survey area, 1,707,300; metro area, 745,500.

KTSP-TV (Channel 10) CBS
KTSP-Great American Television: Radio Co., Inc., 511 W. Adams St., Phoenix, AZ 85003; (602) 257-1234.
Bill Stough, v.p. & gen. mgr.; Eric Land, gen. sls. mgr.; Donna Johannes, adv. & promo. mgr.; Dave Howell, news dir.; Gary Rockey, prog. mgr.; Al Hillstrom, chief eng.; Sherree Lucas, bus. mgr.; nat'l rep.: HRP.

Operation: 1953; TV households in total survey area: 1,475,800.

KTVK (Channel 3) ABC
Arizona Television Company, 3435 North 16th St., P.O. Box 5068, Phoenix, AZ.
Delbert F. Lewis, pres. & gen. mgr.; Bill Lawrence, chief eng.; James G. Tuton, bus. mgr.; nat'l rep.: Edward Petry Co., Inc.
Operation: 1955; TV homes in area: 480,000.

KTVW (Channel 33)
Seven Hills TV Co., 3019 E. Southern Ave., Phoenix, AZ 85040. (602) 243-3333.
Jose C. Cancela, gen. mgr.; Barry Levisohn, ops. mgr.; Lawrence Beckman, chief eng.
Operation: 1979.

KUTP (Channel 45)
United Television, Inc., 4630 S. 33 St., Phoenix, AZ 85040 (602) 268-4500.
Jerry Braet, v.p. & gen. mgr.; Mike Durand, gen. sls. mgr.; Tom Foy, chief eng.; nat'l rep.: Petry.
Operation: December, 1985.

Phoenix-Mesa

KPNX-TV (Channel 12) NBC
KPNX Broadcasting Co., 1101 N. Central Ave., P.O. Box 711, Phoenix, AZ 85001; (602) 257-1212.
C. E. Cooney, pres., gen. mgr.; Bob Allingham, v.p., prog. dir.; Leon Anglin, v.p., eng.; nat'l rep., Blair Television.
Operation: 1954; TV sets in area: 795,300.

Prescott

KUSK (Channel 7)
3211 Tower Rd., Prescott, AZ 86301; (602) 778-6770.
William H. Sauro, pres.; Rich Howe, gen. mgr. & sls. mgr.; Patricia Gray, opns. mgr.; Thayne Higgins, chief eng.
Operation: 1982.

Tucson

KGUN-TV (Channel 9)
May Broadcasting Co., P.O. Box 5707, Tucson, AZ 85703 (602) 792-9933.
Jack Parris, v.p. & gen. mgr.; Bruce Franzen, prog. mgr.; Bob Tobey, gen. sls. mgr.; John Sawyer, chief acct. Phil Aaland, chief eng.; nat'l rep.: Katz Continental.
Operation: 1956; TV sets in area: 238,970.

KOLD-TV (Channel 13) CBS
Knight-Ridder Bdcstg. Inc., Tucson, AZ 85705; (602) 624-2511.
Jay Watson, pres. & gen. mgr.; Wanda Myers, gen. sls. mgr.; Tom Foos, prog. dir. & film buyer; Phil Dunton, chief eng.; Gerald Jensen, news dir.; nat'l rep., MMT.
Operation: 1953; TV sets in area, 190,000.

KPOL (Channel 40)
2475 Jack Rabbit Ave., Tucson, AZ 85745; (602) 884-9001.
Julius Polan, pres.; David M. Reaban, v.p., gen. mgr. & film buyer; Frank C. Idaspe, gen. & gen. sls. mgr.; David J. Polan, sta. mgr.; nat. rep.: Avery-Knodel.
Operation: December, 1984.

KVOA-TV (Channel 4) NBC
Channel 4-TV, Inc., P.O. Box 5188, 209 W. Elm, Tucson, AZ 85703 (602) 792-2270.
Jon F. Ruby, pres. & gen. mgr.; Jim Joslyn, exec. v.p.; Dave Kerrigan, v.p.-prod.; Brink Chipman, news dir.; Dave Hatfield, v.p.-prog.; Ralph Turk, v.p.-eng.; Renee Bear, controller, nat'l. rep., Petry.
Operation: 1953; TV sets in area: 274,500.

Yuma

KYEL-TV (Channel 13) NBC
Beam Broadcasters, Ltd., Box 592, Yuma, AZ 85364; (602) 782-5113.
Peter Rosella, v.p. & gen. mgr.; Boyce Holt, gen. sls. mgr.; Dick Sampson, chief eng.; nat'l rep.: Katz.
Operation: December 1963; TV households, 755,900.

KYMA (Channel 11) ABC
Yuma Bdcstg. Co., 1385 S. Pacific Ave., Yuma, AZ 85365 (602) 342-2205.
Clyde E. Pettit Jr., pres.; Ralph Toddre, gen. mgr.; natl. rep.: Blair.

ARKANSAS
El Dorado

KTVE (Channel 10) NBC
KTVE, Inc., 2909 Kilpatrick Blvd., Monroe, LA 71201; (318) 323-1300.
Terry McKenna, pres.; George Singleton, v.p. & gen. mgr.; David Brown, gen. sls. mgr.; Mike Caruso, chief eng.; Jerry Mayer, news dir.; Tommy Walker, opns.
Operation: 1955.

Fayetteville-Springdale

KHOG (Channel 29) ABC
Sigma Broadcasting (An Arkansas partnership), P.O. Box 4150, Fort Smith, AR 72914 (501) 783-4105.
Robert Hernreich, partner; Cynthia Hernreich, partner; Darrel Cunningham, gen. mgr.; Cliff Walker, sta. mgr.; Ron Evans, local sls. mgr.; Marvin Macedo, chief eng.
Operation: December, 1977; TV households: 41,300.

Ft. Smith

KFSM-TV (Channel 5) NBC, ABC
Times Southwest Bdcstg. Co., 318 N. 13th St., Ft. Smith, AR 72901 (501) 783-3131.
Robert H. Eoff, pres. & gen. mgr.; Gene Graham, gen. sls. mgr.; James Anhalt, chief eng.
Operation: 1956.

KHBS (Channel 40) ABC
Sigma Broadcasting (An Arkansas partnership), 2415 N. Albert Pike, Ft. Smith, AR 72914 (501) 783-4105.
Robert E. Henreich, partner; Cynthia Hernreich, partner; Darrel Cunningham, gen. mgr.; Jarrel Wyatt, gen. sls. mgr.; Tim Bass, prog. dir.; Don Vest, chief eng.
Operation: 1971.

KPOM-TV (Channel 24)
Box 4610, 4624 Kelley Highway, Ft. Smith, AR 72914 (501) 785-2400.
Ken Taishoff, v.p.-gen. mgr.; Bill Oltman, news dir.; Ken Hansen, chief eng.; nat'l rep.: Telerep.
Operation: 1978.

Jonesboro

KAIT-TV (Channel 8) ABC
Cosmos Bdcstg. Co., P.O. Box 790, Jonesboro, AR 72403 (501) 932-4288.
Harold Culver, v.p. & gen. mgr.; Mike Rickwald, gen. sls. mgr.; Al Banks, lcl. sls. mgr.; nat'l rep., MMT.
Operation: July, 1963; TV households: 157,600.

Little Rock

KARK-TV (Channel 4) NBC
United Bdcstg. Corp., 201 W. Third, Little Rock, AR 72203 (501) 376-2481; TWX 910-722-7417.
M. L. Waddington, gen. mgr.; Clyde Anderson, gen. sls. mgr.; Tom Bonner, exec. v.p. & prog. dir.; Susan Newkirk, prom. mgr.; Dean Howard, v.p. eng.; nat'l rep., Katz.
Operation: 1954; TV sets in area: 546,310.

KLRT (Channel 16)
11711 West Markham, Little Rock, AR 72211 (501) 375-1616.
Stephen G. Scollard, v.p. & gen. mgr.; Joe Swaty, prog. & promo. dir.; Lanny Kiest sls. mgr.; Miguel Copello, opns. mgr.; Bill Van Duynhoven, chief eng.; Roger Hines, bus. mgr.
Operation: June, 1983.

KTHV (Channel 11) CBS
Arkansas Television Co., 8th & Izard Sts., P.O. Box 269, Little Rock, AR 72203 (501) 376-1111.
Robert L. Brown, pres. & gen. mgr., KTHV, Channel 11; C. S. Berry, chm. of bd., ARK Television Co.; Marcus George, pres. & treas., ARK Television Co.; Lonnie Gibbons, nat'l sales mgr.; Bob Hicks, prog. mgr.; nat'l rep: Seltel.
Operation: 1955; TV sets in area: 647,500.

Little Rock-Pine Bluff

KATV (Channel 7) ABC
Albritton Communications, Inc., 401 Main, Box 77, Little Rock, AR 72203 (501) 372-7777.
Dale Nicholson, pres. & gen. mgr.; Joe Delgrosso, gen. sls. mgr.; Richard Farrester, prog. dir.; James Roddey, prom. mgr.; Jim Pitcock, news dir.; nat'l rep.: Petry.
Operation: 1953; TV sets in area; 647,500.

Pine Bluff

KJTM-TV (Channel 38) FOX
TVX Bdcstg. Group, Inc., 7123 I-30, Suite 54, Little Rock, AR 72209 (501) 561-3838.
Tim McDonald, pres.; Ed Groves, v.p. & gen. mgr.; Chris Bailey, gen. sls. mgr.; Carol Humphries-Smith, prog. dir.; Michael Price, prom. mgr.; Richard Duncan, chief eng.; natl. rep.: Telerep.

CALIFORNIA
Anaheim

KDOC-TV (Channel 56)
1730 Clementine St., Anaheim, CA 92802 (714) 999-5000.
Pat Boone, pres.; Calvin Brack, v.p. & gen. mgr.; Calvin Brack, dir. bus. affairs; Hoshang Moaddeli, prod. mgr.; Roger Knipp, chief eng.
Operation: 1982.

Arcata

KREQ (Channel 23) FOX
The Mad River Bdcstg. Co., Inc., 1485 L St., Arcata, CA 95521-5742 (707) 826-2323.

Lawrence Rogow, pres. & gen. mgr.; Charles Lohr, gen. sls. mgr. & prog. dir.; John Doyle, prod. mgr.; Lynn Mackay, prom. mgr.; Steve Keeva, news dir.; Don Wilson, dir. eng.; natl. rep.: Adam Young.
Operation: August, 1987.

Bakersfield

KBAK-TV (Channel 29) ABC
Burnham Broadcasting Co., Box 2929, Bakersfield, CA 93303 (805) 327-7955.
Wayne W. Lansche, pres. & gen. mgr.; Bob Banks, chief eng'.; nat'l rep.: Katz.
Operation: 1953; TV sets in area: 560,100.

KERO-TV (Channel 23) CBS
McGraw-Hill Bdctg. Co., Inc., 321 21 Street, Bakersfield, CA 93303 (805) 327-1441. P.O. Box 2367.
Ronald E. Mires, v.p. & gen. mgr.; Norman Hall, dir. of eng.; Walt Brown, news dir.
Operation: 1953; TV sets in area: 280,000.

KGET-TV (Channel 17) NBC
Ackerley Communications, Inc., P.O. Box 1700, Bakersfield, CA 93301 (805) 327-7511.
Raymond A. Watson, v.p. & gen. mgr.; Tom Randour, gen. sls. mgr.; Shirley Sanford, prog. dir.; Doug Caldwell, news dir.; Tom Ballew, chief eng.
Operation: 1959; TV sets in area: 147,000.

Chico

KCPM (Channel 24) NBC
Chico Broadcasting Co., Box 4406, Chico, CA 95927.
Melvin Querio, pres. & gen. mgr.; Ron Gittelson, gen. sls. mgr.; Donna O'Connor, prom. mgr.; Dan McGrath, prod. mgr.; Jack Koonce, chief eng.
Operation: September, 1985.

KHSL-TV (Channel 12) CBS
Golden Empire Broadcasting Co., Box 489, Chico, CA 95927 (916) 342-0141.
C. H. Kinsley, Jr., exec. v.p.; Dino Corbin, gen. mgr.; Bill Meyer, gen. sls. mgr.; Steve Sorenson, prod. mgr.; Russell B. Pope, dir. of eng.; Donna Schiague, chief eng. nat'l rep.: Seltel.
Operation: 1953; TV sets in area: 101,460.

Concord

KFCB (Channel 42)
First Century Bcstg., Inc. 5101 Port Chicago Hwy., Concord, CA 94520 (415) 676-8969.
Ronn Haus, pres.; Debra Fraser, prog. dir.-sls.; Steve Harris, promos, mgr.; Gary Johnson, prod. mgr.; Linda Demars, traf. mgr.
Operation: June, 1983.

Cotati

KRCB-TV (Channel 22)
Rural California Broadcasting Corp., Box 2638, Rohnert Park, Cotati, CA 94928; (707) 585-8522.
Leroy Lounibos, pres.; Nancy Dobbs-Dixon, gen. mgr.; Steve McConnell, sta. mgr.; Dawn Smith, prog. mgr.; Leslie Swanson, devel. dir.

El Centro

KECY-TV (Channel 9) CBS
Pacific Media Corporation, 646 Main Street, El Centro, CA 92243; (619) 353-9990.
Robert Zimmer, gen. sls. mgr.; Deborah Weekes, prog. dir.; Kristine Karter, news dir.; nat'l rep.: Seltel.
Operation: Dec. 1968; TV Households: 60,300.

Eureka

KIEM (Channel 3) NBC
Precht Communications, Inc., 5650 S. Broadway, Eureka, CA (707) 443-3123.
Robert Precht, pres.; Peter McNair, gen. mgr.; Donald King, operations mgr.; Peggy Worden, nat'l sls. mgr.; H. Hank Ingham, lcl. sls. mgr.; nat'l rep.: Katz.
Operation: 1953.

KVIQ (Channel 6)
Miller Bdcstg. Co., 1800 Broadway, Eureka, CA 95501 (707) 443-3061.
Ronald W. Miller, pres.; Pattison J. Christensen, v.p.; Mike Fiest, chief eng.
Operation: 1958.

Fresno

KAIL (Channel 53)
Trans-America Broadcasting Corp., P.O. Box 5188, Fresno, CA 93755 (209) 299-9753.
Albert J. Williams, pres.; C.B. Reis, gen. mgr.; Kathleen Jones, prog. dir. & film buyer; Vincent Brown, chief eng.
Operation: 1961.

KFSN-TV (Channel 30) ABC
Capital Cities/ABC Inc., 1777 G. St., Fresno, CA 93706. (209) 442-1170.
Mark Edwards, v.p. & gen. mgr.; Dudley Few, gen. sls. mgr.; Mark Arminio, lcl. sls. mgr.; Dave Converse, chief eng.; Fernando Grando, prog. dir.
Operation: 1956.

KJEO (Channel 47) CBS
Retlaw Broadcasting Co., Box 5455, Fresno, CA (209) 222-2411.
Joseph C. Drilling, pres.; Donald C. Drilling, v.p. & gen. mgr.; Mark Libby, gen. sls. mgr.; Kathleen Williams, natl. sls. mgr.; Kenneth Holden, chief eng.; Patricia Houlihan, prog. mgr.; Andrew Mastoras, v.p.-finance; Patrice Coulter, traffic mgr.; nat'l. rep.: Petry.
Operation: 1953; Sets in area: 577,300.

KMPH (Channel 26)
Pappas Telecasting, Inc., 5111 McKinley Ave., Visalia, CA 93727 (209) 733-2600.
Harry J. Pappas, pres. & gen. mgr.; Edward G. Aiken, v.p./TV; Michael Granados, sta. mgr.; Joseph Shaffer, v.p./prog.; Lise Markham, natl. sls. mgr.; Joel Cheatwood; news dir.; Dale Kelly, chief eng.
Operation: October, 1971.

KSEE (Channel 24) NBC
San Joaquin Communications Corp., 5035 East McKinley Ave., Fresno, CA 93727; (209) 454-2424.
Todd Holmes, v.p. & gen. mgr.; Bill Spellman, gen. sls. mgr.; Ken Preston, dir. eng.; Lee Jason, prog. dir.; Doug Stewart, promo. mgr.; Ken Coy, news dir.
Operation: 1953; TV sets in area: 405,100.

Hanford-Fresno

KFTV (Channel 21)
Spanish International Communications Corp., 8515 E. Lacey Blvd., Hanford, CA 93230 (209) 584-3362.

August Ruiz, gen. mgr.; Ray Carrasco, gen. sls. mgr.; Mac McKenzie, chief eng.

Operation: 1962.

Los Angeles

KABC-TV (Channel 7) ABC
Capital Cities ABC Inc., Hollywood, CA 90027 (213) 557-7777.

John C. Severino, pres. & gen. mgr.; John Riedl, gen. sls. mgr.; Robert Burris, creative svcs. dir.; Don Corsini, prog. dir.; Bruce Gordon, fin. dir.; Robert Billeci, dir. eng.; nat'l rep.: ABC Television Spot Sales, Inc.

Operation: 1949.

KCBS (Channel 2) CBS
CBS, Inc. 6121 Sunset Blvd., Los Angeles, CA 90028

Robert Hyland, v.p. & gen. mgr.; Steve Gigliotti, sls. dir.; Jay Strong, dir. prog.; Edward Spray, bdcst. dir.; Erik Sorenson, news dir.; Robert Davis, dir. tech. opns.; Elizabeth Vendely, dir. comms.; Andi Sporkin, dir. press inf.

Operation: 1950; TV sets in area: 10,300,000.

KCOP (Channel 13)
KCOP Television Inc., a Chris Craft Industries, station, 915 N. La Brea Ave., Hollywood, CA 90038 (213) 851-1000.

Bill Frank, pres. & gen. mgr.; Rick Feldman, gen. sls. mgr.; Peter Mathes, nat'l sls. mgr.; Suzann Thomason & Jill Thomason, lcl. sls. mgrs.; Win Korabell, dir. of eng.; Jane Clark, bus. mgr.; Peter Schlesinger, dir. of prgm. opns.; Carol Myers Martz, prgm. mgr.; Gary Davis, dir. of creative svcs.

Operation: 1948; TV sets in area: 4,132,100.

KHJ-TV (Channel 9)
KHJ-TV (Division of RKO General, Inc.), 5515 Melrose Avenue, Hollywood, CA 90038 (213) 467-5459.

Chuck Velona, gen. mgr., KHJ-TV; Hank Oster, gen. sls. mgr.; Walt Baker, program dir.; Dick Paradise, promo. dir.; Buck Evans, chief eng.; Richard Tripaldi, controller, KHJ Division; nat'l rep., Blair.

Operation: 1948; TV sets in area: 3,511,000.

KMEX-TV (Channel 34)
Spanish International Bcstg. Co., 5420 Melrose Ave., Los Angeles, CA 90038 (213) 466-8131.

Daniel Villanueva, gen. mgr.; Robert Porter, v.p., eng.; Louis Sweeney, v.p., nat'l sls.; Charles Barry, sls. mgr.; rep., Spanish International Network Sales Inc.

Operation: September, 1962; TV households: 1,500,000.

KNBC (Channel 4) NBC
National Broadcasting Co., Inc., 3000 W. Alameda Ave., Burbank, CA 91523 (818) 840-4444.

John Rohrbeck, v.p. & gen. mgr.; Jim Sterling, gen. sls. mgr.; Carole Cartwright, prog. dir.; Regina Miyamoto, mgr. press & pub.; Tom Capra, news dir.; Harry Burbidge, chief eng.; Rep: NBC Spot Sales.

Operation: Jan. 1949.

KTLA (Channel 5)
KTLA, Inc., 5800 Sunset Blvd., Hollywood, CA 90028 (213) 460-550.

Steve Bell, sr. v.p. & gen. mgr.; Michael Eigner, v.p. & sta. mgr.; Tom Arnost, gen. sls. mgr.; Jeff Wald, news dir.; Ira Goldstone, eng. dir.

Operation: 1947; TV sets in area: 4,138,000.

KTTV (Channel 11) FOX
5746 Sunset Blvd., Los Angeles, CA 90028 (213) 856-1000.

Bob Morse, v.p. & gen. mgr.; Martin Bergman, v.p. & gen. sls. mgr., Don Tillman, v.p. and prog. dir.; Hanna Gryncwajc, nat'l sls. mgr.; Bill Klusman, commercial operations dir.; Elizabeth Saunders, tv. promo.; Ray Green, exec. prod.; Lee Pardee, v.p. eng.; Walter R. Kalb, v.p. finance & admin.; Steve Blue, news dir. Rep: Petry..

Operation: Jan. 1949.

KWHY-TV (Channel 22)
Harriscope of Los Angeles,Inc., 5545 Sunset Blvd., Los Angeles, CA 90028 (213) 466-5441.

Burt I. Harris, pres.; Burt I. Harris, Jr., v.p. & gen. mgr.; Mike Wagner, acct. exec.; John H. Nelson, acct. exec.; Eugene A. Harris, David J. Zulli, chief eng.

Operation: 1963.

Modesto

KCSO (Channel 19) Spanish language
Sainte Limited., P.O. Box 3689, Modesto, CA 95352 (209) 578-1900.

Chester Smith, Naomi L. Smith, gen. partners.

Monterey

KMST-TV (Channel 46)
Retlaw Broadcasting Co., P.O. Box 1938, Monterey, CA 93940 (408) 649-0460.

Joseph Drilling, pres.; Ben Tucker, gen. mgr.; Dick Drilling, sta. mgr.; Tom Tucker, sls. mgr.; Kathy Nash, public affairs dir.; Mark Walker, prod. mgr.; Ken Warren, chief eng.; Bob Stock, pro. dir.; Michelle McCullouch, traffic mgr.

Operations: February, 1969. TV households: 184,800.

Oxnard

KADY (Channel 63)
KADY-TV, Entertainment Partnership, L.P., 663 Maulhardt, Oxnard, CA 93030; (213) 278-4274.

John Huddy, pres.; Peter Leone, gen. mgr.; Ed Branca, gen. sls. mgr.; Roger Terneuzen, dir. opns.; Erica Huddy, prog. mgr.

Operation: August, 1985.

Palm Springs

KESQ-TV (Channel 42, Cable 3) ABC
P.O. Box 4200, Palm Springs, CA 92263. Owned by EFG Broadcast Corp., Dallas, TX; (619) 328-8881.

Scott Vaughan, gen. mgr.; Bill Evans, lcl. sls. mgr.; Kirk Gregory, natl. sls. mgr.; nat'l rep.: Katz.

Operation: October 1968; TV households: 63,700.

KMIR-TV (Channel 36) NBC
Desert Empire TV Corp., P.O. Box 1506, Palm Springs, CA 92263 (619) 568-3636.

John Conte, pres. & gen. mgr.; Jan Pearce, chief exec.; Tina Stein, news dir.; rep.: Seltel.

Operation: Oct. 1968; TV households: 65,400.

Redding

KRCR TV (Channel 7) ABC
California-Oregon Broadcasting, Inc., 755 Auditorium Dr., Redding (Shasta Co.), CA 96001 (916) 243-7777.
Richard W. Green, v.p. & gen. mgr.; Doreeta Domke, operations mgr.; nat'l rep., Blair.

Sacramento

KCRA-TV (Channel 3) NBC
Kelly Broadcasting Co., 310 10th St., Sacramento, CA 95814 (916) 444-7300.
Robert E. Kelly, partner; Jon S. Kelly, partner; Nina N. Kelly, partner; Don Saraceno, gen. mgr.; nat'l rep.; Blair Television, Inc.
Operation: 1955; TV sets in area: 558,900.

KRBK-TV (Channel 31)
500 Media Pl., Sacramento, CA 95815 (916) 929-0300
Barry Baker, sr. v.p., dir. bdcst. div.; Elliott Troshinsky, v.p. & gen. mgr.
Ted Koplar, pres.
Operation: 1974.

KTXL (Channel 40)
Camellia City Telecasters, Inc., P.O. Box 40, Sacramento, CA 95801 (916) 454-4422.
Business Men's Assurance Co. of America, Kansas City, MO; Michael A. Fisher, v.p. & gen. mgr.; Rod Bacon, gen. sls. mgr.; Cal Bollwinkel, prog.-oper. mgr.; Audrey Farington, promo. mgr.; Bob Cook, news dir.
Operation: 1968.

KXTV (Channel 10) CBS
Belo Broadcasting Corp., 400 Broadway, Sacramento, CA 95818 (916) 441-2345.
Ward Huey, pres.; Allan Howard, v.p. & gen. mgr.; Robert Mahlman, gen. sls. mgr.; Kurt Eichsteadt, prog. mgr.; Sheila Gumtow, mktg./promo. mgr.; nat'l rep.: Tele-Rep.
Operation: 1955; TV sets in area: 931,800.

Salinas

KCBA (Channel 35)
Cypress Broadcasting Inc., Box 3560, Salinas, CA 93912; (408) 422-3500.
Barbara Etrick, v.p. & gen. mgr.; Karl Kauffman, chief, eng.; Bill Kline, prog. mgr.
Operation: November, 1981

KSBW-TV (Channel 8) NBC
Gillett of California, Inc., P.O. Box 81651, 238 John St. Salinas, CA 93912 (408) 758-8888. (Affiliated with KSBY-TV, San Luis Obispo, CA)
Jeffrey H. Lee, pres. & gen. mgr.; Cynthia Lindsay, gen. sls. mgr.; Teresa Burgess, prog. mgr.; Mike Kronley, news dir.; Willis Wells, chief eng.
Operation: 1953; TV homes in area: 212,700.

San Bernardino

KAGL (Channel 30)
Marantha Broadcasting Co., Box 10070, Anaheim, CA 92802 (714) 535-5456.
Robert Billman, pres.; Timothy Waisanem, gen. mgr.; Vera Waisanem, gen. sls. mgr.; Will Welty, prog. dir.
Operation: March, 1986.

KSCI (Channel 18)
KSCI, Inc., 1954 Cotner Ave., West Los Angeles, CA 90025; (213) 479-8081.
Ray Beindorf, pres.; Rosemary Fincher, sta. mgr., gen. sls. mgr. & prog. dir.
Operation: June, 1977.

San Diego

KCST-TV (Channel 39) NBC
KCST-TV, Inc., 8330 Engineer Rd., San Diego, CA 92111 (619) 279-3939.
Neil E. Derrough, pres. & gen. mgr.; Jay Belbey, controller; Joseph M. Collins, gen. sls. mgr.; Tom Wimberly, dir. of tech. svcs.; Ron Miller, news dir.; Ric Schwartz, prod. mgr.; Penny Martin, prog. mgr.
Operation: 1965.

KFMB-TV (Channel 8) CBS
Midwest Television, Inc., 7677 Engineer Road, San Diego, CA 92111 (714) 292-5362.
August C. Meyer, Jr., pres.; Robert L. Myers, vice-pres. & gen. mgr.; Bill Moylan, v.p., operations; John Weigand, chief eng.; nat'l rep.. Petry.
Operation: 1949, TV sets in area: 1,015,800.

KGTV (Channel 10) ABC
McGraw-Hill Broadcasting Co., P.O. Box 85347, San Diego, CA 92138 (619) 237-1010.
Edward J. Quinn, v.p. & gen. mgr.; William Christensen, dir. of eng.; Howard Oleff, local sls. mgr.; Mark Wilcox, natl. sls. mgr.; Darrell Brown, gen. sls. mgr.; Helen Hutchings, dir., business affairs; Don Lundy, prog. dir.
Operation: 1953.

KTTY (Channel 69)
San Diego Family TV, Inc., 1696 Frontage Rd., Chula Vista, CA 92016; (619) 575-6969.
James M. Harmon, pres. & gen. mgr.; Joseph Alvarez, sr. v.p.; Andy Feldman, lcl. sls. mgr.; Gayle Garrett, natl. sls. mgr.; Richard Thiriot, prog. consult.; Judy Albrecht, promo. mgr.
Operation: October, 1984.

KUSI-TV (Channel 51)
7377 Convoy Ct., San Diego, CA 92111 (619) 571-5151.
William Rust, pres.; Michael McKinnin, gen. mgr.; William E. Moore, sta. mgr.; Bruce Stein, gen. sls. mgr.; nat'l rep.: Katz.
Operation: 1982.

XETV (Channel 6) FOX
Bay City Television, Inc., 8253 Ronson Road, Television Heights, San Diego, CA 92111 (619) 279-6666.
Martin M. Colby, v.p. & gen. mgr.; Robert C. Taylor, treas./bus. mgr.; Joan O'Laughlin, sta. mgr. and gen. sls. mgr.; Valerie Hoffman, prog. mgr., Bob Anderson, prod. mgr.; Philip Paluso, promo. mgr.; Felipe Fernandez, chief eng.; Julian Kaufman, consultant; nat'l rep.: Telerep.
Operation: 1953; TV sets in area: 582,450.

XEWT-TV (Channel 12) Spanish language
Televisora de Calimex, S.A., P.O. Box 12, Tijuana, Baja California, Mexico (706) 685-9201 and 685-9202.
Jose Marquez, gen. mgr.; Carlos H. Luna, prog. prom. mgr.; Roberto Espinoza, business mgr.

San Francisco

KBHK-TV (Channel 44)
UTV of San Francisco Inc., 420 Taylor St., San Francisco, CA 94102 (415) 885-3750.

Robert Qudeen, v.p. & gen. mgr.; Heather Farnsworth, gen. sls. mgr.; Richard Jones, lcl. sls. mgr.; Larry Young, nat'l sls. mgr.; Suzanne Guyette, news & p.a. mgr.; Ed Hippe, eng. mgr.; Jo Russell, prod. mgr.

Operation: January, 1968. TV households: 3,953,400.

KDTV (Channel 14) Spanish language
Univision Station Group, Inc., 2200 Palou Ave., San Francisco, CA 94124. An affiliate of Univision, Inc.

August Ruiz, gen. mgr.; Jorge Belon, prod. & programming dir.; Sharon Michelucci, bus. mgr.; Kenneth Schreiner, chief eng.

Operation: 1975.

KGO-TV (Channel 7) ABC
Capital Cities ABC, Inc., 900 Front St., San Francisco, CA 94111 (415) 954-7777.

Leonard Spagnoletti, gen. mgr.; Bob Young, gen. sls. mgr.; John Moczulski, prog. svcs. mgr.; Harry Fuller, news dir.; Rosemary Roach, rsch. dir.; Ed Johnson, chief eng. rep.: ABC-TV

Operation: 1949; TV homes in area: 2,143,900.

KOFY (Channel 20)
Pacific FM Inc., 2500 Marin St., San Francisco, CA 94124. (415) 821-2020.

James J. Gabbert, pres.; Michael P. Lincoln, gen. mgr.; Richard Blue, v.p.; Hal Capron, dir. sls.

Operation: 1980; TV households, 1,200,000.

KPIX (Channel 5) CBS
Group W (Westinghouse Broadcasting Co.), 855 Battery St., San Francisco, CA 94111 (415) 362-5550.

Carolyn Wean, v.p. & gen. mgr.; Kenneth Williams, gen. sls. mgr.; Marty Edelman, lcl. sls. mgr.; Ann Miller, prog. dir.; Bruno Cohen, news dir.

Operation: 1948; TV households in area: 1,894,000.

KRON-TV (Channel 4) NBC
Chronicle Broadcasting Co., subsidiary of The Chronicle Publishing Company, 1001 Van Ness Avenue, San Francisco, CA (415) 441-4444.

F.A. Martin III, pres. and chief exec. officer of Chronicle Bdcst. Co.; Amy McCombs, pres. & gen. mgr.; G.E. "Tom" Pickell, v.p. of finance and admin.; Rich Cerussi gen. sls. mgr.; David Wilson, prog. mgr.; Herb Dudnick, news dir.; Bruce Lindgren, dir., creative services; nat'l rep.: Petry Television.

Operation: 1949; TV households in area: 2,143,990.

KTSF-TV (Channel 26)
Lincoln Broadcasting Co., 100 Valley Dr., Brisbane, CA 94005; (415) 468-2626.

Lillian L. Howell, owner; Brian Holton, gen. mgr.; Michael Sherman, sta. mgr.

KTVU (Channel 2)
KTVU, Inc. No. 2 Jack London Square, Oakland, CA 94623 (415) 834-1212.

Kevin O'Brien, v.p. & gen. mgr.; William McGowan, gen. sls. mgr.; Thomas Jermain, nat'l sales mgr.; Jeff Block, lcl. sls. mgr.; Caroline Chang, prog. dir.; Marlene Belles, contr.; Micki Byrnes, mktg. dir.; Ray Jacobs, dir. of operations; Fred Zehnder, news dir.; Sterling Davis, chief eng.

Operation: 1958.

KWBB (Channel 38)
45 Franklin St., San Francisco, CA 94102 (415) 558-8268.

Huntly Gordon, pres. & gen. mgr. & gen. sls. mgr., news dir.; John T. Anderson, prog. dir. & film buyer; Joe Shackleford, chief eng.; nat'l rep.: Adam Young.

Operation: 1986.

Sanger

KMSG-TV (Channel 59)
Sanger Telecasters, Inc., 706 W. Herndon Ave., Fresno, CA 93650 (209) 435-5900.

Diane D. Cocola, pres.; James K. Zahn, gen. mgr.; Gary M. Cocola, gen. sls. mgr.; Jeff Wiedenhoeff, prog. dir.; Steve Weber, chief eng.

Operation: July, 1985.

San Jose

KICU-TV (Channel 36)
Ralph C. Wilson Industries, Inc., 1585 Schallenberger Rd., San Jose, CA 95131. (408) 298-3636. Studio: same address and phone.

William Hirshey, pres.; John Davidson, v.p. & gen. mgr.; Brent Scheiner, nat'l sls. mgr., Jim Kraenzel, chief eng.

Operation: 1967.

KNTV (Channel 11)
Landmark Communications, 645 Park Avenue, San Jose, CA 95110; (408) 286-1111.

Richard A. Fraim, v.p. & gen. mgr.; Stewart B. Park, prog. dir.; Martin Edelman, gen. sls. mgr.; Tom Moo, news dir.; Lou Bell, engr. mgr.; Barbara Smith, contr.; nat'l rep., Katz.

Operation: 1955.

KSTS (Channel 48)
Telemundo of Northern California, Inc., 2349 Bering Dr., San Jose, CA 95131 (408) 435-8848.

Paul Niedermeyer, gen. mgr.; Kenneth Elkin, cont.; Jose Cruz, gen. sls. mgr.; David Hudson, chief eng.

Operation: 1981.

San Luis Obispo

KSBY-TV (Channel 6)
KSBY, Inc., 467 Hill St., San Luis Obispo, CA 93401 (805) 541-6666.

D. R. Oswald, pres. & gen. mgr.; James Brodsky, dir. tech. opns.; Vivi Zigler, sta. mgr.; Ken Reid, chief eng.

Operation: 1953.

Santa Ana

KTBN-TV (Channel 40)
Trinity Broadcasting Network, P.O. Box A, Santa Ana, CA 92711 (714) 832-2950.

Paul F. Crouch, pres.; Cindy Tatum, prog. dir.; Ben Miller, v.p., eng.; Rich Bemillez, sls.

Operation: 1967.

Santa Barbara

KEYT (Channel 3) ABC
Smith Broadcasting of California, P.O. drawer X, Santa Barbara, CA 93102.

Sandra G. Benton, v.p. & gen. mgr.; Steve Lakey, promo. mgr.; Renee Foley, prog. supvr.; King Harris, news dir.; Charles Good, chief eng.; nat'l rep.: Seltel.

Operation: 1953; TV sets in area: 393,300.

Santa Maria

KCOY-TV (Channel 12) CBS
Stauffer Communications, Inc., 1503 N. McClelland, Santa Maria, CA 93454 (805) 922-0505.

Charles Stauffer, gen. mgr.; Tom Murphy, prod. mgr.; Bill Pierce, news dir.; Dennis Bornhoft, chief eng. Rep.: Katz.

Operation: 1964; TV households: 193,000.

Santa Rosa

KFTY (Channel 50)
Sonoma Broadcasting, Inc., Box 1150, Santa Rosa, CA 95402 (707) 526-5050.

James D. Johnson, exec. v.p. & gen. mgr.; Paul Sacks, sls. mgr.; Joe Perez, v.p., engineering; Chuck Snyder, news dir.

Operation: 1981.

Stockton/Sacramento

KOVR—TV (Channel 13)
Outlet Broadcasting, 225 E. Miner Ave., Stockton, CA 95202 (209) 466-6981. Sacramento Studio and Main Business Office: 1216 Arden Way, Sacramento, CA 95815 (916) 927-1313.

Edwin Pfeiffer, pres. & gen. mgr.; Chris Pike, sls. mgr.; Robert Hess, chief eng.; Henry Urick, prog. mgr.; nat'l rep: Katz Agency.

Operation: 1954; TV sets in area (Sacramento/Stockton Mkt.) 932,000.

KSCH-TV (Channel 58)
Pegasus Bdcstg. of Stockton-Sacramento California, Inc., Box 269058, Sacramento, CA 95826-9058; 3033 Gold Canal Dr., Sacrafenton, CA 95826-9058.

Gary Anderson, pres. & gen. mgr.; Cece Hayes, gen. sls. mgr.; Donna Reith, prog. dir.; Julie Wood, prom. mgr.; Bob Olson, chief eng.

Operation: April, 1986.

COLORADO
Colorado Springs/Pueblo

KKTV (Channel 11) CBS
KKTV Inc., P.O. Box 2110, 80901; 3100 N. Nevada Ave., Colorado Springs, CO (719) 634-2844.

Barry Ackerley, pres.; James Lucas, v.p./gen. mgr.; nat'l rep.: Katz, West.

Operation: 1952; TV households in area: 367,300; Total households in survey area: 375,200.

KOAA-TV (Channel 5) NBC
Sangre de Cristo Communications, Inc., 2200 7th Avenue, Pueblo, CO 81003 (303) 544-5782.

John O. Gilbert, pres. & gen. mgr.; Kenneth Renfrow, chief eng.; Jack Sinclair, prog. dir.; Flo Isringhausen, nat'l sls. mgr.; Dave Rose, news dir.; Dori Walls, lcl. sls. mgr.

Operation: 1953; TV sets in area: 296,700.

KRDO-TV (Channel 13) ABC
Pikes Peak Broadcasting Co., P.O. Box 1457, Colorado Springs, CO 80901 (719) 632-1515.

Harry W. Hoth, Jr., pres.; Neil O. Klocksiem, gen. mgr.; Charles H. Upton, chief eng.

Operation: 1953; TV sets in area: 199,500.

KXRM-TV (Channel 21)
KXRM, Inc., 5050 Edison Ave., Colorado Springs, CO 80915.

Larry W. Douglas, pres., gen. mgr., prog. dir. & film buyer; Chip Lusko, gen. sls. mgr.; Larry Frost, promo. mgr.; Joe Duckett, chief eng.

Operation: December, 1984.

Denver

KCNC (Channel 4) NBC
General Electric Property Management Company of Colorado, Inc., 1044 Lincoln Street, P.O. Box 5012 T.A., Denver, CO 80217 (303) 861-4444.

Roger L. Ogden, pres./gen. mgr.; J.H. MacDermott, v.p./sta. mgr.; David Layne, mgr. engineering; Rick Wardell, gen. sls. mgr.; Marv Rockford, v.p./news dir.; Lon Lee, v.p./prm. mgr.; Tom Edwards, production mgr.; Mike Jackson, promotion mgr.

KDVR (Channel 31)
Centennial Bcstg. Corpl., 501 Wazee St., Denver, CO 80204; (303) 595-3131.

Terence J. Brown, v.p. & sta. mgr.; Peter McCampbell, gen. sls. mgr.; Chris Bryan, promo. mgr.; Steve Coulan, dir. eng.; Stephanie A. Campbell, dir. prog.; P. Bradley Short, cont. & secty.; nat'l rep.: MMT.

Operation: August, 1983.

KMGH-TV (Channel 7) CBS
McGraw-Hill Co., Inc., 123 Speer Blvd., Denver, CO 80203 (303) 832-7777.

Edward T. Reilly, pres.; Bob White, v.p. & gen. mgr.; Jim Birschbach, gen. sls. mgr.; Mary Carole McDonnell, dir. of prog.; Robert A. Chernet, dir. of adv. & promo.; Shirley Thompson, traffic mgr.; Roger Bell, news dir.; Larry Pozzi, dir. of eng.

Operation: 1953.

KUSA (Channel 9) ABC
Gamnett Broadcasting., 1089 Bannock St., Denver, CO 80204 (303) 893-9000.

Ken Tonning, pres. & gen. mgr.; Colleen Broton, v.p. & controller; Butch Montoya, news dir.; Darla Ellis, prog. dir.

Operation: 1952; TV sets in area: 1,008,000.

KWGN (Channel 2)
WGN of Colorado, Inc., 6160 S. Wabash Way, Englewood, CO (303) 740-2222.

John Suder, v.p. & gen. mgr.; Tom Shannon, prog. mgr.; Charles Biondo, creative svcs. dir.; Tom Burton, sr. producer/director; Tarey Thornburg, film dir.; Kent Gratteau, chief eng.; Royce Nation, v.p., treas. & CFO.

Operation: 1952; TV sets in area: 1,004,850.

Durango

KREZ-TV (Channel 6) NBC, CBS
(Satellite of KREX-TV, Grand Junction, CO)
Withers Broadcasting Co. of Colorado, Box 789, Grand Junction, CO 81502 (303) 242-5000.

Thomas McGill, gen. mgr.

Operation: Nov., 1963.

Grand Junction

KJCT-TV (Channel 8)
ABC, P.O. Box 3788, Grand Junction, CO 81502

Harry W. Hoth, pres.; Jan Hammer, sta. mgr.; Roger Hightower, chief eng.

Operation: 1979; TV households: 66,100.

KREX-TV (Channel 5) CBS, NBC
Withers Bdcst. of Colorado, 345 Hillcrest Manor, Grand Junction, CO (303) 242-5000.
Thomas McGill, gen. mgr. nat'l rep.: Katz.
Operation: 1954; TV sets in area: 61,000 (ARB).

Montrose

KREY-TV (Channel 10) NBC, CBS
(Satellite of KREX-TV, Grand Junction, CO)
Withers Broadcasting Co. of Colorado, Box 789, Grand Junction, CO 81502 (303) 249-9601.
Tom McGill, gen. mgr.; nat'l rep.: Katz.
Operation: 1956.

Steamboat Springs

KSBS-TV (Channel 24)
Wodlinger Bdcstg. Co., 6439 Wenoga Rd., Mission Hills, KS 66207.
Constance J. Wodlinger, pres.; Mark L. Wodlinger, gen. sls. mgr.
Operation: January, 1988.

Sterling

KTVS (Channel 3) CBS
Stauffer Communications, Inc., 224 N. 3rd St., Sterling, CO 80751 (303) 522-5743.
John Stauffer, pres.; Gene L. Huston, sta. mgr.; Barbara Parenti, prog. dir.; nat'l rep.: Katz.
Operation: Dec. 1963.

CONNECTICUT
Bridgeport

WBCT (Channel 43)
101 Ansonia Rd., Woodbridge, CT 06525.
L. Vlock, pres.
Operation: October, 1987

Hartford

WFSB-TV (Channel 3)
Post-Newsweek Stations, Connecticut, Inc., 3 Constitution Plaza, Hartford, CT 06115 (203) 728-3333.
Barry Barth, v.p. & gen. mgr.; Dick Ahles, v.p. news; Lois Koteen, v.p. CRTV svcs.
Operation: 1957; TV sets in area: 1,327,800.

WTIC (Channel 61)
Arch Communications, Inc., One Corporate Center, Hartford, CT 06103; (203) 527-6161.
Arnold L. Chase, pres.; Edward T. Karlick, gen. mgr.; Robert Gluck, v.p. & gen. sls. mgr.; Jim Perry, chief eng.; nat'l rep.: Katz.
Operation: September, 1984.

New Britain

WVIT (Channel 30) NBC
1422 New Britain Ave., West Hartford, CT 06110 (203) (203) 521-3030.
Al Bova, v.p./gen. mgr.; Art DePasqua, gen. sls. mgr.
Operation: 1953; TV sets in area: 820,000.

New Haven-Hartford

WTNH-TV (Channel 8) ABC
Cook Intlet Communications, Corp., Box 1859, New Haven, CT 06508 (203) 784-8888.
Lewis Freifeld, pres. & gen. mgr.; Fran Tivald, gen. sls. mgr.; Larry Manne, prog. dir.; Don Cohen, promo. mgr.; Mike Sechrist, news dir.; Bob Russo, chief eng.; nat'l rep.: Blair TV, Inc.
Operation: 1948; TV sets in area: 1,949,200.

New London

WTWS (Channel 26)
R&R Media Corp., 216 Broad St., New London, CT 06320; (203) 444-2626.
Richard R. Rangoon, pres.; Jim Kontoleon, gen. mgr., prog. dir., film buyer; Jay McSorley, gen. sls. mgr.; Steven Ellis, chief eng.
Operation: March, 1985.

Waterbury

WTXX (Channel 20) IND
Channel 20 Enterprises, 414 Meadow St., Waterbury, CT 06702 (203) 575-2020.
Michael Finkelstein, gen. partner; Geoffrey Rose, v.p. & gen. mgr.; Nancy McCormick, prog. dir.; Charles Allen, chief eng.; nat'l rep.: MMT, Inc.
Operation: 1953; TV sets in area: 813,000.

DELAWARE
Wilmington

WTGI-TV (Channel 61)
Delaware Broadcasters Ltd., One Christina Plaza, 303 A St., Wilmington, DE 19801 (302) 654-6161.
Daniel G. Slape, pres. & gen. mgr.; Jack Kline, gen. sls. mgr.; Everett Pettiecord, prom. mgr.; Don Borowitcz, chief eng.
Operation: July, 1986.

DISTRICT OF COLUMBIA
Washington

WDCA-TV (Channel 20)
Channel 20 Inc., 5202 River Rd., Washington, DC 20016.
Timothy M. Lynch, v.p. & gen. mgr.; Gregg Pittman, gen. sls. mgr.; Glen Dyer, prog. mgr.; Russ Elkin, dir. of eng.; rep.: Seltel.
Operation: April, 1966; TV households: 1,724,500.

WFTY (Channel 50)
Hill Broadcasting, Inc., 12276 Wilkins Ave., Rockland, MD 20852 (202) 230-1550.
Nolanda Hill, pres. & gen. mgr.; Lisa Brannock, exec. v.p. & sta. mgr.; Ken White, v.p., chief fin. off.; Mike Jones, gen. sls. mgr.; Don Hazen traffic opns.; Donn Fraser, bus. mgr.; Pat Myers, traffic mgr.; Robert Thurber, chief eng.
Operation: 1981.

WJLA-TV (Channel 7) ABC
Allbritton Communications Co. 4461 Connecticut Avenue, N.W. Washington, DC 20008.
Thomas B. Cookerly, pres. & gen. mgr.; James E. Griffin, Jr., v.p., dir. bdcst. opns.; Thursa C. Thomas, dir. public affairs; John Tollefson, v.p., eng.; John C. Long, v.p., dir. sls.; nat'l rep.: Petry Co.

WRC-TV (Channel 4) NBC
National Broadcasting Co., 4001 Nebraska Ave., N.W., Washington, DC 20016 (202) 885-4000.
Allan Horlick, v.p. & gen. mgr.; Larry Spero, dir. sls.; Kathy McCampbell, dir. prog.; Bret Marcus, news dir.; Tom Mann, dir. eng.
Operation: June, 1947; TV households: 4,637,400.

WTTG (Channel 5) FOX
Fox TV Stations, Inc., 5151 Wisconsin Ave., N.W. Washington DC 20016 (202) 244-5151.
Betty Endicott, v.p. & gen. mgr.; Michael Wortsman, v.p. & gen. sls. mgr.; Gary Quinn, chief eng.; William Cunningham, v.p. & bus. mgr.; Lindy Spero, v.p. & creative srvcs. dir.; nat'l rep.: Telerep.
Operation: 1947; TV sets in area: 2,647,100.

WUSA-TV (Channel 9) CBS
A division of the Evening News Association, Inc., 4001 Brandywine St., NW, Washington, DC 20016 (202) 364-3900.
Ronald Townsend, v.p. & gen. mgr.; Lawrence P. Herbster, dir. bus. aff.; Henry K. Yaggi, gen. sls. mgr.; Henry E. Price, prog. dir.; Harry Owen, chief eng.; rep: MMT Sales.
Operation: 1949; TV households in ADI area: 1,390,300.

FLORIDA
Cape Coral

WFTX (Channel 36) FOX
Wabash Valley Bdcstg., Inc., 621 Pine Island Rd., Cape Coral, FL 33991 (813) 574-3636.
Chris Duffy, pres.; Chris Andrews, gen. mgr. & film buyer; Bruce Stano, sls. mgr.; Merrilly Huff, prog. dir.; Joe Lenders, prom. mgr.; Jeffry Blevins, chief eng.; natl. rep.: ITS.
Operation: October, 1985.

Clearwater

WCLF (Channel 22)
Christian Television Corp., Inc., 6922 142nd Ave., N., Largo, FL 33541 (813) 535-5622.
Robert D'Andrea, gen. mgr.; Carl Berger, chief eng.
Operation: 1979.

Cocoa

WTGL-TV (Channel 52)
Box 1852, 26 Forrest Ave., Cocoa, FL 32922 (305) 631-2730.
Robert D'Andrea, pres.; Ken Mieksell, gen. mgr.; Phil Grace, v.p.; Jim Goodling, treas.; Gene Polino, secty.; Ken Mikesell, opns. dir.; Clay Mullins, prog. dir.; Bill Bryan, chief eng.
Operation: 1982.

Daytona Beach-Orlando

WESH-TV (Channel 2) NBC
WESH-TV Broadcasting, Inc., P.O. Box 1551, Daytona Beach, FL 32015; (904) 252-2222; P.O. Box 547697, Orlando, FL 32854 (407) 645-2222.
Noaln Quam, pres. & gen. mgr.; Kenneth Smith, sta. mgr.; Frank C. Biancuzzo, mktg. & adv. dir.; Robert Fowler, v.p. & dir. sls.; nat'l rep.: Petry.
Operation: 1956; TV households: 2,100,000.

Fort Lauderdale

WSCV (Channel 51)
Telemundo Group, Inc., 4035 N. 29th Ave., Hollywood, FL 33022 (305) 947-0051.
Julio Rumbaut, pres.
Operation: 1980.

Fort Myers

WBBH-TV (Channel 20) NBC
Waterman Broadcasting Corp. of Texas, 3719 Central Ave., Fort Myers, FL 33901 (813) 939-2020.
Howard L. Hoffman, v.p. & gen. mgr.; Bob Cleveland, chief eng.; Rosie Rose, compt.; Doug Kight, sales & mgr.; Jim Bradley, news admin.
Operation: December, 1968; TV households: 173,900.

WINK-TV (Channel 11) CBS
Fort Myers Broadcasting Co., 2824 Palm Beach Blvd., Fort Myers, FL 33902 (813) 334-1331.
Edward J. McBride, pres.; Robert F. Doty, v.p. & gen. mgr.; Jr.; Mike Dixon, gen. sls. mgr.; Clarence Mosley, dir. eng.; Jim Bennett, news dir.; Fred Greene, public affairs dir.; nat'l rep.: Blair Television.
Operation: 1954.

Fort Pierce

WTVX (Channel 34) CBS
WTVW, Inc., Box 3434, Ft. Pierce, FL 34954 (407) 464-3434.
Frank K. Spain, pres.; Lynwood N. Wright, gen. mgr.; Eric Reed, prog. dir.; Valerie Hinton, promo. dir.; Max Berryhill, chief, eng.; nat'l rep.: Seltel.
Operation: April 5, 1966; TV households: 69,400.

Fort Walton Beach

WPAN (Channel 53)
Ft. Walton Beach Broadcasting, 11 Tupelo Ave., S.E., Ft. Walton Beach, FL 32548; (904) 244-5353.
Elbert R. Davis, pres. & gen. mgr.; Hank Taylor, sta. mgr., prog. dir. & film buyer; Jim Riggs, gen. sls. mgr.; Patty Vogt, promo. mgr.; Jerry O'Laughlin, news dir.; Richard Gilbert, chief eng.; nat'l rep.: Adam Young.
Operation: February, 1984.

Gainesville

WCJB (Channel 20) ABC
Gainesville Television, Inc., P.O. Box WCJB, Gainesville, FL 32602 (904) 377-2020.
Carolyn Catlin, v.p. & gen. mgr.; Robert Salat, gen. sls. mgr.; Karen Woolfstead, prog. dir.; Michael A. Sherrill, chief eng.
Operation: 1971.

Jacksonville

WAWS-TV (Channel 30)
Malrite of Jacksonville, Inc., 8675 Hogan Rd., Jacksonville, FL 33216 (904) 642-3030.
Lynn Fairbanks, sta. gen. mgr.; Dan Gasby, gen. sls. mgr.; Joe Gersh, nat'l sls. mgr.; Richard M. Sullivan, dir. of prog. & operations.; nat'l rep.: I.N.T.V.
Operation: 1981.

WJKS-TV (Channel 17) NBC
9117 Hogan Rd., Box 17000, Jacksonville, FL 32216 (904) 641-1700.

L. W. White, v.p. & gen. mgr.; David Ayotte, eng. mgr.; John C. Boles, promo. mgr.; Michael Crew, news dir.; Joyce Lueders, bus. mgr.; Roy Tym, gen. sls. mgr.; Russ Myerson, prgm. mgr.
Operation: Feb. 1966.

WJXT (Channel 4) CBS
WJXT, operated by the Post-Newsweek Stations, Florida Inc., P.O. Box 5270, 1851 Southampton Road, Jacksonville, FL 32207 (904) 399-4000.
Gus Bailey, Jr., v.p. & gen. mgr.; Ann Pace, prog. dir.; Christy Birong, dir. community affairs; Don Carmichael, v.p. & gen. sls. mgr.; Mel Martin, v.p./news dir.; Ken Kaminski, bdcst. opns. mgr.; Cindy Hass, op. mgr.; Jim Biggers, eng. mgr.; nat'l rep.: Petry.
Operation: 1949; TV sets in area: 546,000.

WNFT (Channel 47)
North Florida 47, Inc., 2117 University Blvd., So., Jacksonville, FL 32216 (904) 725-4700.
Ray Davis, v.p. & gen. mgr.; Bill Schrader, prom. mgr.; Rob Fields, sls. mgr.; Dave Murphy, opns. mgr.; Karen Gorman, prog. dir.; Marci Hunter, news dir.; Charles McHan, chief eng.
Operation: 1980.

WTLV (Channel 12) ABC
Television 12 of Jacksonville, Inc., Television P.O. Box TV-12, Jacksonville, FL 32231 (904) 354-1212.
Linda Rios Brook, pres. & gen. mgr.; Ken Bauder, gen. sls. mgr.; Marc McKinney, nat'l sls. mgr.; Dave Richardson, news dir.; Clyde Smith, chief eng.
Operation: 1957.

Lakeland

WTMV (Channel 32)
4332 S. Florida Ave., Lakeland, FL 33803 (813) 376-4224
Dan L. Johnson, gen. mgr.; Betty Jo Johnson, sta. mgr.; Robert Hughes, promo. mgr.; Taylor Bracey, news dir.; Bill Brister, chief eng.
Operation: Arpil, 1986.

Leesburg

WIYE (SuperChannel 55)
Sharp Communications, Inc., 4520 Parkbreeze Ct., Orlando, FL 32808 (407) 297-0155.
Claud Bowers, pres. & gen. mgr.; Randy Rivers, prog. dir.; Carol Gentry & Ann Borderick, office mgrs.; Gary Hawkins, chief eng.; Jo Arrington, traf. dir.; Clairece Kibler, sls. mgr.
Operation: 1982.

Melbourne

WAYK (Channel 56)
TV 56 Ltd., 6525 Babcock St., S.E., Palm Bay, FL 32909 (305) 725-0056.
William Varecha, pres. & film buyer; Fred Procise, gen. sls. mgr.; Michelle Phillips, asst. prog. dir.; Wilma Schrader, prom. mgr.; Donna Skattum, news dir.; Steve Schrader, chief eng.; natl. rep.: Mutual TeleSales.
Operation: June, 1986.

WMOD (Channel 43)
Seewall Operating Co., 4450 Enterprise Ct., Melbourne, FL 32935(305) 254-4343.
E. Donald Lass, pres.; Carlo Anneke, gen. mgr.; Frederick

Painton, gen. sls. mgr.; Paul Williamson, prog. dir., Carmen Colluci, chief eng.; nat'l rep.: Adam Young.
Operation: 1982.

Miami

WBFS (Channel 33)
Ch. 33, Inc., 16550 N.W. 52 Ave., Miami, FL 33014; (305) 621-3333.
Milt Grant, pres.; Jerry Carr, gen. mgr.; Michael Turner, gen. sls. mgr.
Operation: December, 1984.

WCIX-TV (Channel 6)
TVX Bdcstg. Group, Inc., 8900 NW 18th Terrace, Miami, FL; (305) 593-0606.
Jack Sander, pres.; Skipp Moss, v.p. & gen. mgr.; Bernie Wimmers, dir. eng.; nat'l rep.: Seltel.
Operation: Sept. 1967; TV households: 1,213,200.

WDZL (Channel 39)
39 Bcstg. Ltd., 2055 Lee St., Hollywood, FL 33020 (305) 925-3939.
Odyssey Partners, owner; Harvey Cohen, exec. v.p. & gen. mgr.; Cyrus Russell, gen. sls. mgr.; Henry Hirsch, promo. mgr.; Robert Castillo, chief eng.; nat'l. rep.: Katz.
Operation: October, 1982.

WHFT-TV (Channel 45)
Trinity Bdcstg. of Florida, 3324 Pembroke Rd., Pembroke, FL 33021; (305) 962-1700.
Paul F. Crouch, pres.; Charles L. Quinn, sta. mgr.; David Hall, chief eng.
Operation: 1975.

WLTV (Channel 23)
Spanish International Communications Corp., 695 N.W. 199th St., Miami, FL 33169 (305) 856-2323 (sales) (305) 652-4000 (operations).
Joaquin Blaya, v.p. & gen. mgr.; Harold M. Parks, nat'l sls. mgr.; Vivian Quevedo, sta. mgr.; Tony Segredo, sls. mgr.
Operation: 1954.

WPLG (Channel 10) ABC
Post-Newsweek Stations of FL Inc., 3900 Biscayne Blvd., Miami, FL 33137 (305) 576-1010.
G. William Ryan, pres. & gen. mgr.; Don Hain, chief eng.
Operation: November 1961; TV households: 1,925,000.

WSVN (Channel 7) NBC
Sunbeam Television Corp., 1401 79th Street Causeway, Miami, FL 33141 (305) 751-6692.
Edmund N. Ansin, pres.; Robert W. Leider, v.p. & gen. mgr.; John Fenwick, sls. mgr.; Mark Mayo, contr.; Merlin Haynie, chief eng.; Dan Johnson, ops. mgr.; Charmaine Meyer, creative services mgr.; nat'l rep.: Harrington, Righter & Parsons, Inc. Southern: Clem & Lowrance.
Operation: 1956; TV Households: 1,156,700.

WTVJ (Channel 4) CBS
WBC Bdcstg. Co., 316 N. Miami Ave., Miami, FL 33128 (305) 377-8241.
Alan Perris, gen. mgr.; Alan Thiel, bus. mgr.; Al Buch, news dir.; Dick Wexo, gen. sls. mgr.; Barry Allentuck, na'l. sls. mgr.; Judy Girrard, dir. pgrm.; Eddie Reno, dir. adv./promo.; nat'l rep.: MMT Sales, Inc.
Operation: 1949; TV homes in area: 1,390,500.

Naples

WEVU (Channel 26) ABC
Caloosa TV Corp., 28950 Old 41 Rd., SE, Bonita Springs, FL 33923 (813) 332-0076.
Ray Karpowicz, pres. & gen. mgr.; Larry Landaker, sta. mgr. & gen. sls. mgr.; John Buckey, creative svcs. dir.; David McKelvey, v.p. eng.; Ann Merkley, controller; Sue Peters, prog. dir.; nat'l rep.: Seltel.
Operation: 1974.

Ocala

WOGX (Channel 51)
Wabash Valley Bdcstg. Corp., Box 3985, Ocala, FL 32678 (904) 351-5551.
Mel Grossman, v.p. & gen. mgr.; Randy Keiser, pgm. dir.
Operation: January, 1983.

Orlando

WCPX-TV (Channel 6) CBS
First Media Corp., P.O. Box 606000, Orlando, FL 32860 (305) 291-6000.
Glenn Potter, pres.; Michael Schweitzer, v.p.-gen. mgr.; Jim Posey, gen. sls. mgr.; Everett Hughes, prog. mgr.; Robert Diehl, chief eng.; nat'l rep.: Katz.
Operation: 1954; TV homes in area: 1,087,500.

WFTV (Channel 9) ABC
WFTV, Inc., 639 W. Central, Orlando, FL 32802 (305) 841-9000.
Clifton L. Conley, v.p. & gen. mgr.; Lou Sopowitz, gen. sls. mgr.; Paul Warnock, chief eng.; Bill Templeton, contr.

WOFL-TV (Channel 35)
Meredith Corp., 35 Skyline Dr., Lake Mary, FL 32746.
Norris Reichel, v.p. & gen. mgr.; Martin Ross, gen. sls. mgr.; Tom Calato, natl. sls. mgr.; Sharon DeLuca, lcl. sls. mgr.; Jim Miotke, sls.-rsrch. dev. dir.; Mark Simonsen, reg. sls. mgr.; Kate McSweeny, prog. mgr.; nat'l rep.: MMT Sales.
Operation: 1979.

Palm Beach

WPTV (Channel 5) NBC
Scripps-Howard Bcastg. Co., P.O. Box 510, Palm Beach, FL 33480. Studio: 622 N. Flagler Drive, West Palm Beach, FL (305) 655-5455.
William J. Brooks, gen. mgr.; Jim Knight, asst. gen. mgr. & gen.sls.mgr.; Arvo O. Katajisto, ops. dir.; Ed Roos, chief eng.; nat'l rep.: Blair.
Operation: Aug. 1954. TV households: 1,152,800.

Panama City

WJHG-TV (Channel 7) NBC
WJHG-TV, P.O. Box 2349, Panama City, FL 32401 (904) 234-2125.
James H. Gray, Jr., pres.; Ray H. Holloway, v.p. & gen. mgr.; Roger Jones, sales mgr.; Jack Crusan, prod. mgr.; Jerry Smithnick, sta. mgr.; Scott Clark, chief eng.; nat'l rep.: Katz.
Operation: 1953; TV households: 293,700.

WMBB (Channel 13) ABC
Buford Television, Inc., Box 1340, Panama City, FL 32401 (904) 769-2313.
Bob Buford, pres.; David Jernigan, exec. v.p. & gen. mgr.; Patti Clements, prog. dir.; Steve Cook, creative svcs. mgr.;

Wendell Nelson, chief eng.; Kiat Thosakul, bus. mgr.; Judi Barnes, lcl. sls. mgr.; Tom Najjar, regl. sls. mgr.; Jerry Fisher, news dir.
Operation: October, 1973; TV households: 255,200.

Pensacola

WEAR-TV (Channel 3) ABC
Heritage Media Corp., Box 12278, Pensacola, FL 32581 (904) 455-7311.
David N. Walthall, pres.; Jack J. Robinette, pres., TV div.; M. J. Groothand, gen. mgr. & film buyer; Bob Shields, gen. sls. mgr.; Joe Smith, op. mgr.; Harry Babb, chief eng.; A. P. Neumann, news. dir.; Kathy Musial, promo. dir.
Operation: 1954; TV households: 483,400.

WJTC (Channel 44)
Carnex, TV, Inc., 700 S. Palafox St., Pensacola, FL 32501; (904) 438-4444.
Tom Eaton, pres.
Operation: November, 1984.

St. Petersburg

WTOG (Channel 44) FOX
Hubbard Broadcasting Inc., 365-105th Terrace, N.E. St. Petersburg, FL 33716 (813) 576-4444.
Stanley S. Hubbard, pres.; Edward G. Aiken, gen. mgr.; Alan B. Frank, gen. sls. mgr.; John Kays, chief eng.
Operation: 1968.

WTSP-TV (Channel 10) ABC
WTSP-TV, St. Petersburg/Tampa, FL, P.O. Box 10,000, St. Petersburg, FL 33733.
Lawrence M. Clamage, gen. mgr.; Paul Siracuse, gen. sls. mgr.; Larry Cazavan, prgm. mgr.; Ken Middleton, news dir.; Peter Ford, chief eng.; Bob Mack, promo. mgr.

Sarasota

WWSB (Channel 40) ABC
Southern Bdcst. Corp. of Sarasota, 5725 Lawton Dr., Sarasota, FL 34233 (813) 922-0777.
Douglas C. Backer, pres. & gen. mgr.; J. Manuel Calvo, v.p. & sta. mgr.; Jack Lyons, v.p., dir. sls.; Linda Des Marais, v.p., prog. & news.
Operation: 1971.

Tallahassee

WTWC (Channel 40) NBC
Holt-Robinson TV, Inc., 8440 Deerlake Rd., Tallahassee, FL 32312 (904) 893-4140.
Stan Lightsey, pres.; Don Neil, gen. mgr.; John Burns, gen. sls. mgr.; Tina Johnson, prog. coor.; Mike Brown, chief eng.; nat'l rep.: Young.
Operation: April, 1983.

WTXL-TV (Channel 27) ABC
Tallahassee 27 Ltd. Partnership, P.O. Box 13899, Tallahassee, FL 32317; (904) 898-3127.
Joseph D. Tydings, pres.; Mack Keoun, gen. mgr.; Chris Aldridge, gen. sls. mgr. & dir. opns.
Operation: September, 1976.

Tampa

WFTS (Channel 28)
Tampa Bay TV, Inc., 4501 E. Columbus Dr., Tampa, FL 33605; (813) 623-2828.

Jim Major, gen. mgr.; Larry Jopek, gen. sls. mgr.; Joseph Logsdon, prog. dir.; Laura Barton, promo. mgr.; Lee Melvin, chief eng.; Marsha Hames, nat'l sls. mgr.; nat'l rep.: Blair.

Operation: November, 1981.

WTVT (Channel 13) CBS

WTVT Holdings, Inc., 3213 West Kennedy Blvd., Box 31113, Tampa, FL 33631; Transmitter, Route 1, Box 767, Riverview, FL 33569 (813) 876-1313.

Clarence V. McKee, pres. & CEO; Harry M. Apel, v.p. & gen. mgr.; John Westerberg, gen. sls. mgr.; Carol Mountain, prod. mgr.; Dick A'Hearn, oper. mgr.; Jim West, news dir.; Lowell Otto, chief eng.; nat'l rep.: Tele Rep.

Operation: 1955; TV sets in area: 1,131,400.

WXFL (Channel 8) NBC

905 East Jackson St., P.O. Box 1410, Tampa, FL 33601 (813) 228-8888.

Robert T. Sutton, pres. & CEO; Jim Saunders, v.p. & gen. mgr.; Ed Whatley, prod. mgr.; Marshall Hites, dir. adv. & promo.; Paul Catoe, gen. sls. mgr.; Andrew Capone, nat'l sls. mgr.; Doug Duperrault, prog. dir.; Ardell Hill, dir. eng. & opns. mgr.

Operation: 1955; TV sets in area: 1,199,760.

W. Palm Beach

WFLX (Channel 29)

4119 West Blue Heron Blvd., West Palm Beach, FL 33404 (305) 845-2929.

Murray J. Green, v.p. & gen. mgr.; John C. Chaffee, pres., TV div.; nat'l rep.: Petry.

Operation: 1982.

WPEC-TV (Channel 12) ABC

Fairfield Drive, P. O. Box 24612, West Palm Beach, FL 33416 (305) 844-1212.

Alex W. Dreyfoos, Jr., pres.; Robert C. Wiegand, exec. v.p. & gen. mgr.; Allen Sternberg, prog. dir.

Operation: 1955.

GEORGIA
Albany

WALB-TV (Channel 10) NBC)

Gray Communications Systems, Inc., P.O. Box 3130, Albany, GA 31708 (912) 883-0154.

James H. Gray, Jr., pres.; Connie Greene, secty.; Phillip R. Greene, v.p. & gen. mgr.; Barbara Jones, treas.; William N. Williams, chief eng.; nat'l rep.: Katz.

Operation: 1954.

WTSG (Channel 31) FOX

Newsouth Bdcstg. Inc., P.O. Box 4050, Albany, GA 31708 (912) 453-3100.

Timothy Brumlik, pres.; Manny Cantu, gen. mgr.; David Antoniak, prog. & promo. mgr.; Tony Gainous, chief eng.

Operation: 1982.

Atlanta

WAGA-TV (Channel 5) CBS

Gillett Communications of Atlantica, Inc., Box 4207, Atlanta, GA 30302 (404) 875-5551.

Jack Sander, pres. & gen. mgr.; John Dolive, dir. bdcst. opns.; nat'l rep.: Gillett TV sales.

Operation: 1949.

WATL (Channel 36)

WATL-TV, One Monroe Place, Atlanta, GA 30324 (404) 881-3600.

David Henderson, pres.; John Serrao, v.p. & gen. mgr.; Gene McHugh, gen. sls. mgr.; Don Hess, prog. dir.; Doug Furce, prod. mgr.; David Jones, chief eng.; nat'l rep.: Katz.

Operation: 1954.

WGNX-TV (Channel 46)

Tribune Broadcasting Co., 1810 Briarcliff Rd., P.O. Box 98097, Atlanta, GA 30359 (404) 325-4646.

Herman Ramsey, v.p. & gen. mgr.; Len Graziano, gen. sls. mgr.; Lorrie Shilling, prog. mgr.

Operation: 1971.

WSB-TV (Channel 2) NBC

Cox Broadcasting Corporation, 1601 W. Peachtree Street, N.E., Atlanta, GA 30309 (404) 897-7000.

Clifford M. Kirtland, Jr., pres., Cox; Stanley G. Mouse, exec. v.p., Cox; William A. Schwartz, pres. bdstg. div., Cox; Don Elliot Heald, v.p. & gen. mgr., WSB-TV; Dale Smith, station mgr., WSB-TV; Ed Godfrey, news dir., WSB-TV; A. R. Van Cantfort, prgm. mgr., WSB-TV; John Carpenter, gen. sls. mgr., WSB-TV; William Powers, dir. of engineering, WSB-TV.

Operation: 1948.

WTBS (Channel 17)

Superstation, Inc., 1050 Techwood Dr., N.W., Atlanta, GA 30318 (404) 892-1717.

R. E. Turner, chm.; Gerald Hagan, pres.; Jack Petrik, exec. v.p. pgrmng.; Robert Levi, v.p. & gen. mgr.; William Merriam, exec. v.p. prod. & oper.; Jack Verner, chief eng.

Operation: 1967.

WVEU (Channel 69)

Broadcasting Corp. of Georgia, 2700 N.E. Expressway, Bldg. A, Phoenix Business Park, Atlanta, GA 30345 (404) 325-6929.

David J. Harris, pres.; Vance L. Eckersley, v.p. & gen. mgr.; Mann Reed, gen. sls. mgr. & sta. mgr.; Gary Kelly, chief eng.; Marti Chitwood, p.a. mgr.; Peter L. Mandell, promo. mgr.; Sheldon Moss, lcl. sls. mgr.; David Hickman, natl. sls. mgr.; Mary F. McKee, prog. mgr.

Operation: 1981.

WXIA-TV (Channel 11) ABC

Pacific & Southern Broadcasting Co., Inc., 1611 W. Peachtree St., N.E., Atlanta, GA 30309.

Harvey Mars, pres.; Jack Lease, prog. mgr.; Howard Kaufman, gen. sls. mgr.; Wayne Freedman, nat'l sls. mgr.; Bill Spell, lcl. sls. mgr.; Steve Smith, news dir.; Mike Howey, dir. eng.; Sheryl Gripper, community affairs; John Heinen, dir. creative svcs.

Operation: Sept., 1951; TV households: 1,568,400.

Augusta

WAGT-TV (Channel 26) NBC

P.O. Box 1526, Augusta, GA 30903 (404) 722-0026.

Nick Evans, Jr., gen. mgr.; Lee Sheridan, sta. mgr.; James Halpin, gen. sls. mgr.; Al Van Dinteren, chief eng.

Operation: Dec. 24, 1968; TV households: 183,700.

WJBF (Channel 6) ABC

Pegasus Bdcst. of Augusta, Georgia, Inc., Box 1404, Augusta, GA 30903 (803) 722-6664.

Terry R. Sams, pres. & gen. mgr.; John R. Bennett, v.p.-opns. & sta. mgr.; Ray Erb, v.p.-sls. & gen. sls. mgr.; Marty

Bosshart, nat'l sls. mgr.; Mary Miller, bus. mgr.; Art Cabot, v.p.-prog. & promo.; Gerald Levy, v.p.-community relations; William Doker, chief eng.; Jimmy Thomas, prod. mgr.; Peter Michenfelder, news dir.
Operation: 1953; TV sets in area: 608,000.

WRDW-TV (Channel 12)
Television Station Partners, Drawer 1212, Augusta, GA 30903.
Ralph E. Becker, pres.; Stan Marinoff, v.p. & gen. mgr.; Louis S. Wall, gen. sls. mgr.; Lee Davis, chief eng.; Steve Johnston, program mgr.
Operation: Feb. 1954; TV households: 678,600.

Columbus
WLTZ (Channel 38) NBC
Columbus TV, Inc., Box 12289, Columbus, GA 31995; (404) 561-3838.
J. Curtis Lewis, Jr., pres.; Bob Walton, v.p. & gen. mgr.; Tom Breazeale, gen. sls. mgr.; R.C. Bartlett, prog. dir.; Sandra Stouder, promo mgr.; Borden Black, news dir.; Bob Hoor, chief eng.; nat'l rep.: Adam Young.
Operation: October, 1970.

WRBL-TV (Channel 3) CBS
Columbus Broadcasting Co., Inc., 1350 13th Ave., Columbus, GA 31994 (404) 322-3333.
Mark Prather, v.p. & gen. mgr.; R. W. Mack, dir. opns.; Mike Loew, gen. sls. mgr.; John Simmons, chief eng.
Operation: 1953; TV sets in area: 767,600.

WTVM (Channel 9) ABC
Pegasus Bdcstg., Inc., Box 1848, Columbus, GA 31902 (404) 324-4671.
Wayne Daugherty, pres. & gen. mgr.; W. Carroll Ward, prog. dir.; Richard Heath, sls. mgr.; Dick Byrd, news dir.; David Williams, chief eng.; nat'l rep.: Blair Television.
Operation: 1953; TV sets in area: 719,900.

WXTX (Channel 54)
Columbus Family TV, Inc., 6524 Buena Vista Rd., Box 12188, Columbus, GA 31907; (404) 561-5400.
Ed Groves, gen. mgr.; Reid Walls, gen. sls. mgr.; Denise Murray, prog. dir.; Joy Scarbrough, promo. mgr.; Cliff Curley, film buyer, April Henry, film dir.; Karen Krieger, news dir.; Rick Liverett, chief eng.
Operation: June, 1983.

Macon
WGXA (Channel 24) ABC
Russell Rowe Communications, Box 340, Macon, GA 31297 (912) 745-2424.
Ken Gerdes, v.p. & gen. mgr.; Frank Shurling, gen. sls. mgr.; Jim Baker, opns. mgr.; Kelly Causey, promo. mgr.; Ron Wildman, news dir.; Richard Blanton, chief eng.; nat'l rep.: Blair.
Operation: 1982.

WMAZ-TV (Channel 13) CBS
Multimedia Broadcasting Company, Box 5008, Macon, GA 31213 (912) 746-1313.
Don McGouirk, v.p. & gen. mgr.; Gostin Freeney, gen. sls. mgr.; Sydney Thum, prog. dir,; Lacy Worrell, dir. of eng.; nat'l rep.: Katz Agency, Inc.

WMGT Channel 41) NBC
Morris Network, Inc., Box 4328, Macon, GA (912) 745-4141.

Dean Hinson, pres.; Charles Morris, chmn.; Aubrey Wood, gen. sls. mgr.; Lisa Hill, prom. mgr.; John Gimlin, news dir.; Joe Sears, chief eng.; nat'l rep.: Seltel.
Operation: 1968.

Savannah
WJCL (Channel 22) ABC
Lewis Bcstg. Corp., 10001 Abercorn St., Extension, Savannah, GA 31406 (912) 925-0022.
J. Fred Pierce, exec. v.p. & gen. mgr.; Christopher A. Barbieri, v.p., sls. & prgm.; Mary Poythress, opns. dir.
Operation: 1970.

WSAV (Channel 3) NBC
WSAV-TV, P.O. Box 2429, 1430 East Victory Drive., Savannah, GA 31402 (912) 651-0300. Station is owned by News-Press & Gazette Co., St. Joseph, MO; David R. Bradley, Jr., pres.
David R. De Armond, gen. mgr.; Robert B. Beall, gen. sls. mgr.; Keith Young, news dir.; Cecil K. Daniel, Jr., prod. mgr.; Byron Strong, chief eng.; nat'l rep.: Petry.
Operation: 1956; TV sets in area: 206,500.

WTOC-TV (Channel 11) CBS
American Savannah Broadcasting Co., 516 Abercorn St., Savannah, GA 31401 (912) 234-1111.
Jess Mooney, v.p. & gen. mgr.; Bud Bradbury, prom. dir.; LaVaughn Thompson, chief eng.; nat'l rep.: Katz Agency Inc.
Operations: 1954; TV sets in area: 394,800.

Thomasville, GA-Tallahassee, FL
WCTV (Channel 6) CBS
John H. Phipps, P.O. Box 3048, Tallahassee, FL 32315 (904) 893-6666.
John E. Phipps, chm.; Dennis O. Boyle, pres.; Frank Watson, v.p. & gen. mgr.; Jerry L. Williams, prm. mgr.; Melvin Blank, opns. mgr.; nat'l rep.: Blair TV.
Operation: 1955; TV sets in area: 416,500.

Toccoa
WNEG-TV (Channel 32)
Stephens County Broadcasting Co., 100 Blvd., Box 907, Toccoa, GA 30577; (404) 886-0032.
Roy E. Gaines, pres. & gen. mgr.; David Austin, gen. slsl. mgr.; Connie Gaines, prog. dir. & film buyer; Tony Garrison, promo. mgr.; Cindy Wood, prod. mgr.
Operation: September, 1984.

Valdosta
WVGA (Channel 44) ABC
Morris Network, Inc., Box 1588, Valdosta, GA 31601 (912) 242-4444.
Dean Hinson, pres.; Aubrey Wood, gen. mgr.; Marvin L. Keene, gen. sls.-sta. mgr.; Bianca Short, prog. dir.
Operation: 1980.

HAWAIIAN ISLANDS
Hilo, Hawaii

KGMD-TV (Channel 9) CBS
(Satellite of KGMB-TV, Honolulu)
Lee Enterprises, Inc., 58 Manaolana Pl., Hilo, HI 96720 (808) 935-6221

Lee Carlson, gen. mgr.; Morris Nimi, asst. chief eng.
Operation: 1955.

KHBC-TV (Channel 2)
Hilo Bdcstg. Corp., 400 Hualani St., Hilo, HI 96720 (808) 969-2000.
Marvin S. Chupack, pres.; Bill Evans, pres.; Abe Lagadon, studio mgr.; Gerri Shimada, prog. dir.; Nick Hutchings, sls. mgr.; Richard Schaller, film buyer; Tina Louise Esteban, news dir.; Charles Epperson, chief eng.
Operation: August, 1983.

KHVO (Channel 13) ABC
(Satellite of KHVH-TV, Honolulu)
Shamrock Bdcstg. Co., Nani Loa Surf Hotel, Hilo, HI 96720 (808) 935-8289.
Operation: May, 1960; TV sets in area.

Honolulu, Oahu
KGMB TV (Channel 9) CBS
Lee Enterprises, Incorporated 1534 Kapiolani Blvd., Honolulu, HI 96814 P.O. Box 581, Honolulu, HI 96809 (808) 944-5200.
Lee Carlson, gen.. mgr.; Sharon Kanaley, nat'l & gen. sls. mgr.; Phil Arnone, prog. dir., James Manke, news dir.; nat'l rep.: Katz Agency.
Operation: 1952. TV households (State): 261,170.

KHAI (Channel 20)
Media Central, Inc., 735 Sheridan St., Honolulu, HI 96814 (808) 943-1169.
Dan T. Kawakami, gen. mgr.; Gregg Mueller, gen. sls. mgr.; Sam F. Sugano, prog. dir.; Mark Miyashiro, chf. oper.
Operation: December, 1983.

KHNL-TV (Channel 13)
King Bdcstg. Co., 150-B Puuhale Road, Honolulu, HI 96819
Richard J. Blangiardi, gen. mgr.; Shirley Feliciano, bus. mgr.
Operation: July, 1962; TV homes: 320,000.

KHON-TV (channel 2) Honolulu
KAII-TV WAILUKU SATELLITE
KHAW-TV HILO SATELLITE
KHON-TV, Inc. 615 Piikoi St., Honolulu HI 96814.
William S. Snyder, pres. & gen. mgr.; nat'l rep.: Blair TV
Operation: 1952; TV sets in area: 323,720.

KITV (Channel 4) ABC
Tak Communications, Inc., 1290 Ala Moana Blvd., Honolulu, HI 96814; 545-4444.
Tom Hartman, pres. & gen. mgr.; Bob McCall, acting gen. mgr.; Bob Kato, chief eng.; Muneo Hamada, bus. mgr.; Paul Udell, news dir.; Mike Ainsworth, prod. mgr.; Tracy Keliihoomalu, prog. dir.
Operation: 1954.

Wailuku, Maui
KAII-TV (Channel 7) NBC
(Satellite of KHON-TV, Honolulu) KHON-TV, Inc., 1170 Auahi St., Honolulu, HI 96814.
Personnel: same as KHON-TV, Honolulu.
Operation: Nov. 1958.

KGMV-TV (Channel 3) CBS
(Satellite of KGMB-TV; Honolulu, Heftel Broadcasting-Maui, Inc., P.O. Box 1574, Kahului, HI 96732.

Cecil Heftel, pres., treas. & gen. mgr.; Earl McDaniel, gen. mgr.; Thomas Yoshida, chief eng. & sta. mgr.
Operation: 1955.

KMAU (Channel 12) ABC
(Semi-satellite of separately-owned, KITV, Honolulu)
Maui Publishing Co., Ltd., Box 550, Wailuku, HI 96814.
Operation: Dec., 1955.

IDAHO
Boise
KBCI-TV (Channel 2) CBS
Eugene Television, Inc., 1007 Jefferson St., Boise, ID 83707 (208) 336-5222.
Donald E. Tykeson, pres.; Timothy J. Bever, gen. mgr. & film buyer; Mark Jollie, gen. sls. mgr.; Gary Rogers, chief eng.; rep.: Katz Television, Art Moore & Associates, Inc. (Pacific Northwest).
Operation: 1953; TV sets in area: 212,000.

KTVB-TV (Channel 7) NBC, ABC
KTVB, Inc. 5407 Fairview Ave., P.O. Box 7 Boise, ID 83707 (208) 375-7277.
Ancil Payne, pres.; Robert E. Krueger, v.p. & gen. mgr.; Phil Wenstrand, news dir.; nat'l rep.: Avery-Knodel, Inc.

Idaho Falls
KIDK-TV (Channel 3) CBS
Retlaw Bdcstg. Co., P.O. Box 2008, Idaho Falls, ID 83403; (208) 522-5100.
Gerry Cornwell, sta. & gen. sls. mgr. & natl. sls. mgr.; Barbara Henricksen, nat'l sls. mgr.; Kim Southwick, opns. dir.; Gary Smith, chief eng.; nat'l rep.: Katz.
Operation: 1953; TV sets in area: 107,900.

KIFI-TV (Channel 8)
The Post Company, P.O. Box 2148, Idaho Falls, ID 83401 (208) 523-1171.
Jerry M. Brady, v.p. & gen. mgr.; Herman G. Haefele, sta. mgr.; Don Larsen, chief eng.; nat'l rep.: Seltel.
Operation: 1961.

Lewiston
KIVI (Channel 6) ABC
Sawtooth Communications, Inc., 1866 East Chisholm Dr., Nampa, ID 83651 (208) 336-0500.
Larry J. Chase, pres./gen.mgr.; Ken Ritchie, sls. mgr.; Susu Mahood, local sls. mgr.; Dan Smede, news dir.; Andy Suk, chief eng.; nat'l rep.: Seltel; regional rep.: Tacher.
Operation: 1974.

KLEW-TV (Channel 3) CBS
Retlaw Bdcstg. Co., 2626 17th St., Lewiston, ID 83501; (208) 746-2636.
Steven Crow, mgr.; Marlin Jackson, chief eng.; Gene Haagenson, news dir.; nat'l rep.: Seltel
Operation: 1955.

Nampa
KTRV (Channel 12)
679 Sixth St., Nampa, ID 83651 (208) 466-1200.
Rex L. McArthur, v.p./gen. mgr.; Diane Frisch, prog. dir.;

Francis Wilson, chief eng.; Jim Barto, bus. mgr.; nat'l rep.: Petry.
Operation: 1981.

Pocatello-Blackfoot
KPVI (Channel 6) ABC
Ambassador Media Corp., P.O. Box 667, Pocatello, ID 83204 (208) 233-6667.
Sen. William Armstrong, pres.; Brian Hogan, v.p. & gen. mgr.; Mike Tracy, gen. sls. mgr.; Tony Divesti, chief eng.; Greg Licht, news dir.; nat'l rep.: Blair.
Operation: 1974; TV households: 102,000.

Twin Falls
KMVT (Channel 11) CBS, ABC
KMVT Broadcasting, Inc., 1100 Blue Lakes Blvd., N., Twin Falls, ID 83301 (208) 733-1100.
Jim Underwood, pres.; Lee Wagner, gen. mgr.; George Brown, ops. mgr.; George Brown, prog. dir.; Dennis Lowe, chief eng.; nat'l rep.: Katz.
Operation: 1955; TV sets in area: 45,830.

ILLINOIS
Aurora
WPWR-TV (Channel 50)
Channel 50 TV Corp., 2151 N. Elston Ave., Chicago, IL 60614 (312) 276-5050.
Fred Eychaner, pres.; Al DeVaney, v.p. & gen. mgr.; Brent Stephenson, v.p. & sta. mgr.; Elizabeth Hertel, pub. svc. mgr.; Neal Sabin, prog. mgr.
Operation: April, 1982.

Bloomington
WYZZ (Channel 43)
Bloomington Comco, Inc., 2714 East Lincoln St., Bloomington, IL 61701 (309) 662-4373.
G.J. Robinson, pres.; Richard S. Plotkin, gen. mgr.; Larry Halcomb, sls. mgr.; Mary Anne Renne, prog. dir.; John Wamsley, chief eng.
Operation: 1982.

Champaign
WCIA (Channel 3) CBS
Midwest Television, Inc., 509 S. Neil St., Champaign, IL 61820 (217) 356-8333.
A. C. Meyer, Jr., pres.; Guy Main, exec. v.p.; Jack B. Everette, exec. v.p. & treas.; Gerald P. Johnson, sls. mgr.; Leonard Davis, nat'l sales mgr.; Ed Mathais, prod. mgr.; Sheila Hickman, prog. dir. & film buyer; nat'l rep.: Petry.
Operation: 1953; TV sets in area: 329,000.

WICD-TV (Channel 15) NBC
Plains Television Partnership, 250 Country Fair Dr., Champaign, IL 61821 (217) 351-8500.
Elmer Balaban, partner; Joe Norris, stn. mgr; Ginger Rush, nat'l sls. mgr. Ed Mason, local sales mgr.; David Boyer, chief eng.; Larry Waters, ops. mgr.; nat'l rep., Katz Television Continental.
Operation: 1959.

Chicago
WBBM-TV (Channel 2) CBS
CBS, Inc., 630 N. McClurg Court, Chicago, IL 60611 (312) 944-6000.

Rod Perth, sta. mgr.; Johnathan Rodgers, v.p. & gen. mgr.; Sam Stallworth, sls. dir.; Karen Miller, bcstg. dir.; Joan Zucker, dir. press reltns.
Operation: 1946; TV sets in area: 2,679,260.

WCFC (Channel 38)
Christian Communications of Chicagoland, Inc., 1 N. Wacker Dr., Chicago, IL 60606. (312) 977-3838.
Jerry K. Rose, pres.; Kevin L. San Hamel, gen. sls. mgr.; Phillip Mowbray, dir. opns.; David Oseland, prog. dir.; Alan Bolds, prom. mgr.; Jim Tillery, chief eng.
Operation: 1976.

WCIU-TV (Channel 26)
Weigel Bdg. Co., Board of Trade, Chicago, IL 60604.
Howard Shapiro, pres. & gen. mgr.; Peter Zomaya, asst. gen. mgr. & sls. mgr.; Merri Houser, film dir.; Bernie Hoelting, chief eng.; Ben Larson, Eng. news dir.; Don Aguirre, Span. news. dir.; Norman Shapiro, dir. bus. & lgl. affairs.
Operation: 1964.

WFLD-TV (Channel 32) Fox
Fox TV Stations, Inc., 205 N. Michigan Ave., Chicago, IL 60601.
Cary Jones, v.p. & gen. mgr.; Rich Engberg, v.p. & gen. sls. mgr.; Dwain Schoonover, eng. mgr.; nat'l rep: Petry.
Operation: Jan., 1966; TV households: 3,138,000.

WGN-TV (Channel 9)
WGN, Continental Broadcasting Company, 2501 W. Bradley Pl., Chicago, IL 60618 (312) 528-2311.
Dennis Fitzsimons, v.p./gen. mgr.; Peter Walker, lcl. sls. mgr.; Pam Pearson, dir. creative svcs.; Paul Davis, news dir.; Charlotte O'Brien, dir. of community svcs; Marc Schacher, dir. prog.

WLS-TV (Channel 7) ABC
Capital Cities/ABC, Inc., 190 N. State St., Chicago, IL 60601 (312) 750-7777.
Mark Mandala, pres.; Joe Ahern, gen. mgr.; Mark Grant, gen. sls. mgr.; Tim Bennett, prog. dir.; James Hattendorf, news dir.; nat'l rep.: ABC TV Spot Sales.
Operation: Oct., 1943; TV homes: 2,995,000.

WMAQ-TV (Channel 5) NBC
National Bdcstg. Co., Merchandise Mart, Chicago, IL 60654 (312) 861-5555.
Richard Lobo, v.p. & gen. mgr.; Ken Hall, dir. sls.; Lisa Churchville, sls. mgr.; Jim Powell, dir. bdcst. opns. & eng.; Dave Mayber, sls. mgr.; David Finney, prog. dir.; Jim Powell, chief eng. nat'l rep.: NBC Spot Sales.
Operation: 1949; TV sets in area: 3,530,230

WSNS-TV (Channel 44)
Video 44, a Joint Venture, 430 W. Grant Pl., Chicago, IL 60614 (312) 929-1200.
Burt I. Harris, pres., Harriscope (L.A.); Alan Silverman, pres., Essaness Theatre Corp.; Jose F. Lamas, gen. mgr.; Charles Breeding, chief eng.; John Dickinson, ops. mgr.
Operation: April, 1970.

Decatur
WAND (Channel 17) ABC
(Serving Decatur, Springfield & Champaign)
WAND-Television, Inc. (subsidiary of Lin Broadcasting Corp., Inc.), 904 Southside Drive, Decatur, IL 62525 (217) 424-2500.

D. Adams, pres. & gen. mgr.; T. J. Vaughan, v.p. sta. mgr.; Larry Katt, v.p. sls.; Nat'l Rep.: Blair.
Operation: 1953; TV sets in area: 569,506.

WFHL (Channel 23)
Decatur Foursquare Broadcasting, 2510 Parkway Ct., Decatur, IL 62526; (217) 428-2323.
Gregory L. Barnes, pres.; Mark Siegal, sta. mgr. & prog. dir.; Rita Gray, sls. mgr.; Paul Osborne, news dir.; Steve Wallace, chief eng.
Operation: May, 1984.

Harrisburg

WSIL-TV (Channel 3) ABC Primary
21 W. Poplar St., Harrisburg. IL; 62946.
Steve Wheeler, pres.
Operation: 1953.

Joliet/Chicago

WGBO-TV (Channel 66)
Grant Bcstg. Co., 875 N. Michigan Ave., Suite 3141, Chicago, IL 60611 (312) 751-6666.
Steve Freidheim, gen. mgr.; George Leh, prog. dir.; Chuck Jennings, chief eng.
Operation: 1981.

Marion

WTCT-TV (Channel 27)
Tri-State Christian TV, Rt. 37, Marion, IL 62959 (618) 997-9333.
Garth Coonce, pres. & gen. mgr.; Steve McKeown, prod. mgr.; Christina M. Coonce, prog. dir.; nat'l rep.: Spot Time Ltd.
Operation: 1981.

Moline

WQAD-TV (Channel 8)
3003 Park 16 St., Moline, IL 61625 (309) 764-8888.
H. Oliver Gillespie, pres. & gen. mgr.; Peggy Vyncke, v.p. & contr.; Gene Smith, gen. sls. mgr.; Lloyd Bolkcom, dir. of pgm. & comm. affairs; Joh Riches, news dir.; Rick Serre, chief eng.
Operation: 1963.

Mount Vernon

WCEE (Channel 13)
Sudbrink Broadcasting Corp. of Ill., Box 1300, Mount Vernon, IL 62864 (618) 822-6900.
Vic Rumore, pres.; Ric Gorman, v.p. & gen. mgr., Steve Epstein, chief eng.
Operation: 1983.

Peoria

WEEK-TV (Channel 25) NBC
Eagle Broadcasting Corporation, 2907 Springfield Rd., E. Peoria, IL 61611 (309) 698-2525.
Patrick Devlin, v.p. & gen. mgr.; Dennis Upam, opns. & promo. mgr.; Ken Tofanelli, chief eng.; Phil Supple, news dir. nat'l rep.: Katz Agency.
Operation: 1953; TV sets in area: 475,000.

WHOI-TV (Channel 19) ABC
Forward of Illinois, Inc. 500 N. Stewart St., Creve Coeur, IL 61611 (309) 698-1919.

Charles E. Sherman, pres. & gen. mgr.; William Thorson, sr. v.p. & gen. sls. mgr.; nat'l rep.: Blair.
Operation: Oct. 1953; TV households; 475,300.

WMBD (Channel 31) CBS
Midwest Television, Inc., 3131 N. University, Peoria, IL 61611 (309) 688-3131.
August C. Meyer, Jr., pres.; Guy F. Main, exec. v.p.: Gene Robinson, v.p. and gen. mgr.; Gene C. Robinson, stat. mgr.; Lloyd Peterson, op. mgr.; Paul Baumgartner, chief eng.; nat'l rep.; Petry
Operation: 1958; TV sets in area: 338,300.

Quincy

WGEM-TV (Channel 10) NBC
Quincy Broadcasting Co., 513 Hampshire, P.O. Box 80, Quincy, IL 62306 (217) 228-6600.
T. A. Oakley, pres.; Ralph M. Oakley, v.p. & gen. mgr.; Fred Colgan, op. mgr.; Ben Stewart, v.p.-sls.; Jim Martens, chief eng.; nat'l rep.: Blair.
Operation: 1953; TV sets in area: 372,400.

Rockford

WIFR-TV (Channel 23) CBS
WIFR Television, Inc., 2523 N. Meridian Rd., Rockford, IL 61103.
Dennis Blake West, pres.; Arles Hendershott, news dir.; Jim Brady, opns. mgr.; Doug Warkenthien, prod. mgr.; Roy Bilsbarrow, cont.; Barbara Schobinger, prog. supvr.
Operation: 1965.

WQRF-TV (Channel 39)
Family Group Ltd. IV, 401 S. Main St., Rockford, IL 61101 (815) 987-3950.
Robb Gray, Jr., gen. mgr.; Kemp Nichol, gen. sls. mgr.; Jan Bacino, promo. mgr.; Dean Turman, chief eng.
Operation: 1978.

WREX-TV (Channel 13) ABC
WREX-TV, West Auburn at Winnebago Rds., Rockford, IL 61105 (910) 642-0770.
Member of The Gilmore Broadcasting Corp.
James S. Gilmore, owner; John McWeeny, gen. mgr.; Jim Smith, dir. of nat'l sls.; Warren A. Anderson, local sls. mgr.; Gene Hines, film mgr.; nat'l rep.: Seltel.
Operation: September, 1953; TV households: 401,600.

WTVO (Channel 17) NBC
Winnebago Television Corp., N. Meridian Rd. & State, Rockford, IL 61105 (910) 963-5413.
Harry Balaban, pres.; Hal Froelich, mgr.; Richard McDaniel, prgm. dir.; Tom Anderson, sales mgr.; Al Petzke, chief eng.; Frank Sanders, film dir.; nat'l rep.: Adam Yound, Inc.
Operation: 1953; TV sets in area: 580,300.

Rock Island

WHBF-TV (Channel 4) CBS
Rock Island Broadcasting Co., Telco Bldg., 231 18 St., Rock Island, IL 61201 (309) 786-5441.
Anne Potter DeLong, pres.; Edward E. DeLong III, exec. v.p.; Charles F. Harrison, v.p. & gen. mgr.; Dewey I.. Nelsen, asst. gen. mgr. & v.p. sls.; Wesley C. Hoots, chief eng. ; nat'l rep.: Petry Television, Inc.
Operation: 1950; TV sets in area: 486,000.

Springfield

WICS (Channel 20) NBC

2680 East Cook St., Springfield, IL 62703 (217) 753-5620.
John DiMatteo, pres.; Mike Bock, v.p., dir. bdcst. opns.;
John V. Connors, v.p. & gen. mgr.; Don Squires, gen. sls. mgr.;
Virginia Rush, nat'l sls. mgr.; Jerrold Merritt, chief eng.; Gary
Spears, prog. mgr.; Demetrios Hadjis, creative svcs. dir.; H.K.
Springer, comtr.; nat'l rep.: Katz Agency.
Operation: 1953: TV sets in area: 805,000.

WRSP (Channel 55)

Springfield Independent TV Co., 3440 Clearlake Ave.,
Springfield, IL 62702; (217) 523-8855.
Tom Mochel, gen. mgr.; Michael T. Burns, gen. sls. mgr.;
Ken Myers, chief eng.; nat'l rep.: Indep. TV Sls.
Operation: June, 1979.

INDIANA
Bloomington-Indianapolis

WTTV (Channel 4) Independent

TEL-AM Corp., 3490 Bluff Road, Indianapolis, IN 46217
(217) 787-2211.
Elmer C. Snow, pres. & gen. mgr.; Mike Davis, prgm. mgr.;
Clyde Dutton, gen. sls. mgr.; Bernie Souers, lcl. sls. mgr.; Tom
Weber, dir. eng.
Operation: 1949; TV sets in area; 2,500,000.

Elkhart-South Bend

WSJV (Channel 28) ABC

WSJV, Inc. (owner)—Subsidiary of Quincy Newspapers
(Illinois) Inc., Box 1646, Elkhart, IN 46515 (219) 293-8616;
South Bend (219) 674-5106.
Thomas A. Oakley, pres.; Don E. Fuller, v.p. & gen. mgr.;
Jon Hart, gen. sls. mgr.; natl rep., Blair.
Operation: 1954; TV sets in ADI: 281,300.

Evansville

WEHT-TV (Channel 25) CBS

Gilmore Broadcasting Corp., P.O. Box 25, Evansville, IN
47701 (812) 424-9215.
James S. Gilmore, Jr., pres.; Ernest D. Madden, gen. mgr.;
Mike Riley, gen. sls. mgr.; Jenny Gager, div. contrl.; Mike
Peckenpaugh, chief eng.; nat'l rep.: Katz.
Operation: 1953; TV sets in area: 290,600.

WEVV (Channel 44) Fox Affiliate

Ralph C. Wilson Industries, Inc., 629 Walnut St., Evans-
ville, IN 47708; (812) 424-9201.
Michael Brooks, gen. mgr.; John Sandwell, gen. sls. mgr.;
Alice Lovell, prog. dir.; Don Hollingsworth, chief eng.; nat'l
rep.: MMT Sales.
Operation: November, 1983.

WFIE (Channel 14) NBC

WFIE, Inc., 1115 Mt. Auburn Rd., Evansville, IN 47712
(812) 426-1414.
Conrad L. Cagle, pres. & gen. mgr.; Ralph S. Jackson, exec.
v.p.; Bob West, dir. ops; Bill Hollander, news dir.
Operation: 1953; TV sets in area: 214,000.

WTVW (Channel 7)

Woods Communications Group, Inc., 477 Carpenter St., P.
O. Box 7, Evansville, IN 47701; (812) 422-1121.
Ken Schreiber, gen. mgr.; nat'l rep.: Seltel.
Operation: 1956; TV sets in area: 247,480.

Fort Wayne

WANE-TV (Channel 15) CBS

Indiana Broadcasting Corp., 2915 W. State Blvd., Fort
Wayne, IN 46808 (219) 424-1515.
Robert A. Fishman, pres. & gen. mgr.; Meredith Smith, fin.
mgr.; Mark Meger, prog. dir.; Herb Lyons, chief eng.; nat'l rep.:
Petry.
Operation: 1954; TV sets in area: 253,000.

WFFT-TV (Channel 55)

Great Trails Bdcstg. Corp., 3707 Hillegas Rd., Ft. Wayne, IN
46808 (219) 424-5555.
Alexander Williams, pres.; Clark Davis, exec. v.p.; Jeff
Evans, v.p. & gen. mgr.; Jim Glendening, nat'l sls. mgr.
Operation: December, 1977.

WKJG-TV (Channel 33) NBC

Thirty-Three, Inc., 2633 W. State Blvd., Ft. Wayne, IN
46808 (219) 422-7474.
Joseph R. Cloutier, pres. & treas.; Hilliard Gates, v.p. & gen.
mgr.; William Kline, gen. sls. mgr.; Ed Schmidt, chief eng.;
nat'l rep., Blair Television.
Operation: 1953; TV sets in area: 280,000.

WPTA (Channel 21) ABC

WPTA-TV, Inc, 3401 Butler Road, Ft. Wayne, IN 46808
(219) 483-0584.
Edwin C. Metcalfe, v.p./gen. mgr.; Marvin Gottlieb, gen. sls
mgr.; Barbara Wigham, sta. mgr. & dir. of prgm. & promo.;
Bill MacDonald, sls. mgr.; Wayne Ludkey, news dir.; Ray
Krueger, chief eng.; nat'l rep.: Blair Television.
Operation: 1956.

Gary

WPWR-TV (Channel 50)

Channel 50 TV Corp., 2151 N. Elston Ave., Chicago, IL
60614 (219) 276-5050.
Fred Eychaner, pres. & gen. mgr.; Mike Dunlop, v.p. & gen.
sls. mgr.; Brent Stephenson, v.p. & sta. mgr.; Neal Sabin, prog.
dir.; Bob Minor, chief eng.; natl. rep.: MMT.
Operation: September, 1967.

Indianapolis

WHMB-TV (Channel 40)

LeSea Bldg., Co., Box 12, South Bend, IN (317) 773-5050.
Lester Sumrall, pres.; Doug Garlinger, chief eng.; Wanda
Linville, traffic mgr.
Operation: 1971.

WISH-TV (Channel 8) CBS

Indiana Broadcasting Corp., 1950 N. Meridian St., Indianapolis, IN 46202 (317) 923-8888.
Peter K. Orne, pres. & gen. mgr.; Scott Blumenthal, gen. sls.
mgr.; Terry VanBibber, chief eng.; nat'l rep.: Petry.
Operation: 1954; TV sets in area: 1,950,000.

WRTV (Channel 6) ABC

McGraw-Hill Broadcasting Company, Inc., 1330 North Meridian St., Indianapolis, IN 46206 (317) 635-9788.
John Proffitt, v.p. & gen. mgr.; Sharon Chalfin, gen. sls.
mgr.; Ken Ladage, prog. dir.; Robert Flanders, v.p./dir. bus.
systems develop. & eng.; Sharon Malmstone, promo. dir.;
Martin Siddall, bus. mgr.; MMT Sales, Inc.
Operations: 1949.

WTHR (Channel 13) NBC
Video Indiana, Inc., 1000 N. Meridian St., Indianapolis, IN 46204 (317) 639-2311.

Michael J. Corken, gen. mgr.; Linda Kirby, publ. affairs dir.; Robert Shire, gen. sls. mgr.; Tom Rose, prog. dir.; William Hineman, chief eng.; Bob Campbell, news dir.; Mark Dillon, bus. mgr.; nat'l rep.: John Blair & Co.

Operation: 1957; Ownership change: 1975. TV sets in area: 1,284,200.

WXIN (Channel 59)
Outlet Communications, Inc., 1440 N. Meridian St., Indianapolis, IN 46202; (317) 632-5900.

Joseph A. Young, v.p. & gen. mgr.; Raymond Hunt, gen. sls. mgr.; Michael McKinnon, chief eng.

Operation: February, 1984.

Lafayette

WLFI-TV (Channel 18)
WLFI-TV, Inc., 2605 Yeager Rd., West Lafayette, IN 47906; (Studio); P.O. Box 7018, Lafayette, IN 47906 (mailing). (317) 463-3516.

Robert A. Ford, gen. mgr.; Thomas C. Combs, sls. mgr.; Ken Gardner, chief eng.; Nina Hart, prog. mgr.

Operation: May, 1953; TV households: 319,900.

Richmond

WKOI (Channel 43)
Trinity Broadcasting of Indiana, 1702 S. Ninth St., Richmond, IN 47374 (317) 935-2390.

Paul Crouch, pres.; Mary L. Laird, supvr.; Joe Hoyer, prod./dir.; Carl Dole, chief eng.

Operation: 1982.

South Bend

WHME-TV (Channel 46)
Lester Sumrall Evangelistic Assn. Inc., Box 12, South Bend, IN 46624 (219) 291-8200.

Lester Sumrall, pres.; Steve Sumrall, group v.p.; Peter Sumrall, v.p. & gen. mgr.

Operations: July, 1974.

WNDU-TV (Channel 16) NBC
Michiana Telecasting Corp., Juniper Road, Box 1616, South Bend, IN 46634.

Bazil O'Hagan, pres. & gen. mgr.; Gregory Giczi, opns. mgr.; nat'l rep.; Adam Young, Inc.

Operation: 1955; TV homes in area: 270,000.

WSBT-TV (Channel 22) CBS
WSBT, Inc., 300 W. Jefferson Blvd., South Bend, IN 46601 (219) 233-3141.

E. Berry Smith, pres. & gen. mgr.; Jerry Bleck, nat. sales mgr.; N. J. Gassensmith, program dir. & film dir.; Robert Bell, chief eng.; nat'l rep.; Katz Agency.

Operation: 1952; Sets in area: 327,200.

Terre Haute

WBAK-TV (Channel 38) ABC
WBAK Television Co., P.O. Box 719, Terre Haute, IN 47808 (812) 238-1515.

Cy N. Bahakel, pres.; Hal Edwards, gen. mgr.; David Pierce, chief eng.; Barry Sinnock, prod. mgr.; nat'l rep.: Seltel.

Operation: 1973.

WTHI-TV (Channel 10) CBS
Wabash Valley Broadcasting Corp., 918 Ohio St., Terre Haute, IN 47808 (812) 232-9481.

David L. Bailey, v.p. & gen. mgr.; Phil Johnson, gen. sls. mgr.; Rod Garvin, dir. opns., prog.; nat'l rep. Katz Agency.

Operation: 1954; TV sets in area: 876,000.

WTWO (Channel 2) NBC
Illiana Telecasting Corp., P.O. Box 299, Terre Haute, IN 47808.

Mark Allen, exec. v.p. & gen. mgr.; Jerry Tiller, gen. sls. mgr.; Phylis Martindale, opns. mgr.; nat'l rep.: Blair.

Operations: Sept., 1965.

IOWA
Ames

WOI-TV (Channel 5) ABC
Iowa State Univ. Bdcstg. Corp., Ames, IA 50011 (515) 294-5555.

Bob Helmers, pres. & gen. mgr.; Ed Powers, chief eng.; Vicky Cordes, film dir.; nat'l rep.: Katz.

Operation: 1950; TV sets in area: 552,600.

Cedar Rapids

KCRG-TV (Channel 9) ABC
Cedar Rapids Television Co., 2nd Ave. at 5th St. S.E., Cedar Rapids, IA 52401 (319) 398-8422.

Joseph F. Hladky, Jr., pres.; Ed Lasko, v.p. & gen. mgr.; Ron Stack, gen. sls. mgr.; Edna A. Herbst, v.p. & promotion dir.; Walt Alliss, chief eng. & ops. dir.; Paul Dicker, prog. dir.; James Laymon, bus. mgr.; nat'l rep.: H-R.

Operation: 1953; TV homes in area: 493,300.

KGAN-TV (Channel 2) CBS
KGAN-TV, Broadcast Park, Box 3131, Cedar Rapids, IA 52406 (319) 395-9060.

Richard Herbst, v.p. & gen. mgr.; Dick Aune, gen. sls. mgr.; John Ganahl, opns. mgr.; Bob Burns, chief eng.; nat'l rep.: The Katz Agency, Inc.

Operation: 1953; TV sets in area: 373,800.

Davenport

KLBJ-TV (Channel 18)
937 East 53 St., Suite D, Davenport, IA 52807 (319) 386-1818.

Gary Brandt, pres. & gen. mgr.; Bridget Bowen, gen. sls. mgr.; Dan Olson, nat'l sls. mgr.; Kathleen DeBoeuf, controller; Don Bargmann, chief eng.; Sue Passe, prod. mgr.; Randy Belk, prog. mgr.; Joy Boruff, promo. mgr.; Penny Foy, traffic mgr.; nat'l rep.: Seltel.

Operation: July, 1985.

KWOL-TV (Channel 6) NBC
KWOL Broadcasting Co., 805 Brady St., Davenport, IA 52808 (319) 324-1661.

Joseph Lentz, sta. mgr.; John Sloan, sls. mgr.; John Hegamen, chief eng.; Kenneth H. MacQueen, v.p.,; William Ryan, pres.; Joseph Lentz, sta. mgr.

Operation: 1949; TV sets in area: 670,200.

Des Moines

KCCI-TV (Channel 8) CBS
H & C Communications, Inc., P.O. Box 10305, Des Moines, IA 50306 (515) 247-8800.

Paul Fredericksen, pres. & gen. mgr.; Guy Koenigsberger, v.p., programs; Ron Briggs, gen. sls. mgr.; Paul Rhoades, v.p./news; John Pascuzzi, v.p., opns.; Robert Day, dir. prog.; Pam Kulik, dir. promo. & comm. affairs.
Operation: 1955; TV sets in area: 529,200.

KDSM-TV (Channel 17)
Duchossois Communications of Iowa, 4023 Fleur Dr., Des Moines, IA 50321 (515) 287-1717.
Rolland Johnson, pres.; Tommy Thompson, v.p. & gen. mgr.; Ted Stephens, gen. sls. mgr.; Jerry Johnson, prom. mgr.; Marty Morfeld, chief eng.
Operation: March, 1983.

WHO-TV (Channel 13) NBC
Palmer Communications, Inc., 1801 Grand Ave., Des Moines, IA 50308 (515) 242-3500.
William J. Ryan, pres.; Tom Heston, gen. sls. mgr.; nat'l rep.: Blair.
Operation: 1954; households: 379,500.

Dubuque

KDUB-TV (Channel 40) ABC
Dubuque TV, One Dubuque Plaza, Dubuque, IA 52001; (319) 556-4040.
Thomas Bond, gen. ptnr.; Marshal Porter, gen. sls. mgr.; Dave Basinger, opns. mgr.; Gary Haverland, chief eng.
Operation: June, 1970.

Kirksville, MO-Ottumwa, IA

KTVO (Channel 3) ABC
P.O. Box 949, Highway 63 N, Kirksville, MO 63501; (816) 627-3333.
Jerry Heilman, gen. mgr.; Dan Havens, sls. mgr.; Keith Reynolds, chief eng.; Ed Spell, dir. pub. info.; nat'l rep.: MMT.
Operation: 1955: TV sets in area: 146,600.

Mason City

KIMT-TV (CHANNEL 3) CBS
Spartan Radiocasting, Inc., Second & Pennsylvania, Mason City, IA 50401; 423-2540.
John Shine, gen. mgr.; Vern Schofield, gen. sls. mgr.; Dale Byre, chief eng.; nat'l rep.: Katz Agency.
Operations: 1954; TV sets in area: 449,000.

Sioux City

KCAU-TV (Channel 9) ABC-TV
Citadel Communications, Ltd., 7th & Douglas Sts., Sioux City, IA 51101 (712) 277-2345.
Ray Cole, v.p. & gen. mgr.; Don Hale, natl. sls. mgr.; Gary Seaberg, lcl. sls. mgr.; J. D. Walls, bdcst. opns. mgr. & prog. dir.; Joe Corcoran, news dir.; Mark LeValley, tech. opns. dir.; natl. rep.; Katz.
Operation: 1953; TV homes in area: 169,500.

KMEG-TV (Channel 14) CBS
KMEG Television, Inc., Box 657, 7th & Floyd Blvd., Sioux City, IA 51105 (712) 277-3554.
Bruce McGorrill, pres.; Bruce Lewis, gen. mgr.; Carl Keller, gen. sls. mgr.; Lyle Johnson, chief eng.; Greg Funk, bus. mgr.
Operation: Sept., 1967; TV homes: 167,700.

KTIV (Channel 4) NBC
KTIV Television Co., 3135 Floyd Blvd., Sioux City, IA 51105; (712) 239-4100.

Jim Waterbury, pres.; Mike Smith, v.p. & gen. mgr.; Mary Bracken, v.p./programming; Dale Russell, v.p., eng.; Jack Baker, v.p. sls.; nat'l rep.: John Blair Co.
Operation: 1954; TV sets in area: 372,200.

Waterloo

KWWL-TV (Channel 7) NBC
American Black Hawk Broadcasting Co., E. 4th & Franklin, Waterloo, IA 50703 (319) 291-1200.
James Waterbury, pres. & gen. mgr.; nat'l rep., Blair.
Operation: 1953; TV sets in area: 412,700.

KANSAS
Colby

KLBY (Channel 4) ABC
999 S. Range, Colby, KS 67701; (913) 462-8644.
Bob Surber, gen. mgr.; Wayne Roberts, sta. mgr.; Josie Taylor, news dir.; Tom Cook, farm dir., R. K. Wellman, chief eng.
Operation: July, 1984.

Ensign

KTVC (Channel 6) CBS
Southwest Kansas Television Co., Box 157, Dodge City, KS 67801.
Sid Warner, pres.; W. H. Bailey, gen. mgr.;
Operation: 1957.

Garden City

KSNG-TV (Channel 11) NBC
(Satellite of KSNW-TV, Wichita, KS
Part of Kansas State Network)
Kansas State Network, Inc., South Highway 83, Garden City, KS 67846 (316) 276-2311. Rep.: Katz.
Stan Orth, sta. mgr.
Operation: Nov. 1958.

KUPK-TV (Channel 13) ABC
Satellite of KAKE-TV, Wichita, KS)
KAKE-TV, Box 10, Wichita, KS 67201.
Ron Collins, pres. & gen. mgr.; Bob Surber, sta. mgr.; Larry Hatteberg, news dir.; Paul Hinderliter, chief eng.; Roxie Tucker, prog. dir.
Operation: Oct., 1964.

Goodland

KLOE-TV (Channel 10) ABC, CBS
Kays, Inc., Broadcast Plaza Box 569, Goodland, KS 67735 (913) 899-2321.
Kay Melia, gen. mgr.; nat'l rep.: Blair.
Operation: 1958.

Great Bend

KSNC (Channel 2) NBC
(Satellite of KSNW-TV, Wichita, KA)
Kansas State Network, Inc., P.O. Box 689, Great Bend, KS 67530 (316) 793-7868. Bill Ranker, gen. mgr.; Gary Gore, sls. mgr.; Tim McQuade, news. dir.; Jim Bowers, chief eng.
Operation: November, 1954.

Hays

KAYS-TV (Channel 7) CBS, ABC
(Satellite KLOE-TV Goodland, KS)

KAYS Inc., Box 817, Hays, KS, 67601.
Bernard Brown, sta. mgr.; Dannia Massier, chief engineer; Ken Fitch, prod. mgr.
Operation: Sept., 1958; TV households: 97,000.

Pittsburg

KOAM-TV (Channel 7) CBS
KOAM, Limited Partnership, Owned by TA Associates, Boston, MA. P.O. Box 659, Pittsburg, KS 66762 (316) 231-0400.
Donald J. Hicks, gen. mgr.; natl. rep.: Seltel.
Operation: 1953.

Salina

KAAS-TV (Channel 18)
Channel 24 Ltd., 316 N. West Street, Wichita KS 67203 (316) 942-2424. Operates as S-1 satellite station of KSAS-TV, Wichita.
Alan Rudy, pres.; Harlan Reams, v.p., gen. mgr.; John Friend, gen. sls. mgr.; Lee Reams, promos.-opns. mgr.; Mac Mac Shane, chief eng.; natl rep.: Seltel.
Operation: April 3, 1988.

Topeka

KTKA-TV (Channel 49) ABC
Mid-America Bcstg. of Topeka, 101 S.E. Monroe, Topeka, KS 66603 (913) 234-4949.
Joseph Brechner, pres.; Dennis Czechanski, gen. mgr.; Sandi Wilber, gen. sls. mgr.; Kevin Goodman, prom. mgr.; Bob Totten, news dir.; Gary Krohe, chief eng.; nat'l rep.: Seltel.
Operation: June, 1983.

KSNT (Channel 27) NBC
Topeka Television, Inc., P.O. Box 2700, Topeka, KS 66601 (913) 582-4000.
Richard L. Pexton, gen. mgr.; Herbert L. Brown, gen. sls. mgr.; Douglas M. Retherford, news dir.
Operation: 1967; TV households: 814,900.

WIBW-TV (Channel 13) CBS
Stauffer Communications, Inc., Box 119, Topeka, KS 66601 (913) 272-3456.
John H. Stauffer, pres.; Jerry Holley, v.p., brdgt.; George Logan, gen. mgr.; Vince Frye, gen. sls. mgr.; Kent Cornish, opns. mgr./prog. dir.; nat'l rep.: Blair.
Operation: November, 1953; TV households: 514,800.

Wichita

KAKE-TV (Channel 10) ABC
KAKE-TV, 1500 North West St., Box 10, Wichita, KS (316) 943-4221.
Ron Collins, pres. & gen. mgr.; Dale Morrell, chief eng.; Jerry Watson, v.p. and gen. sales mgr.; Larry Hatteberg, exec. news dir.; Don Golledge, prod. mgr.; Darrell Ewalt, prog. dir.; Mark Chanbesh, promo. dir.; Tom McBroom, compt.; nat'l rep.: Petry.
Operation: 1954.

KSAS-TV (Channel 24)
Channel 24 Ltd., 316 N. West St., Wichita, KA 67203 (316) 942-2424.
Alan Rudy, pres.; Harlan Reams, v.p., gen. mgr. & prom. mgr.; John Friend, gen. sls. mgr.; Lee Reams, promos.-opns. mgr.; Mac MacShane, chief eng.; nat'l rep.: Seltel.
Operation: August, 1985.

KSNW-TV (Channel 3) NBC
(Satellites—KSNC-TV, Great Bend, KS, Ch. 2; KSNG-TV, Garden City, KS, Ch. 11; KSNK-TV, McCook, NB, Ch. 8)
Kansas State Network, Inc., P.O. Box 333; 833 North Main St., Wichita, KS 67201 (316) 265-3333.
Al Buch, gen. mgr.; Gary Sotir, natl. sls. mgr.; Jonna Buch, creative svcs. dir.; Marc Luedtke, opns. mgr.; Paul Fanning, prod. mgr.; natl. rep.; Katz.
Operation: 1955; TV sets in area: 417,000.

Wichita-Hutchinson

KWCH (Channel 12) CBS
Kansas Broadcasting System, 2815 E. 37th St., North, P.O. Box 12, Wichita, KS 67201 (316) 838-1212; 1800 N. Plum St., Hutchinson, KS (316) 665-5503.
Ronald J. Bergamo, v.p. & gen. mgr.; Steve Merren, gen. sls. mgr.; John Mileham, v.p./admin.; Jay Zacharias, chief eng.; Terry Cole, news dir.; Robert Wine, contr.
Operation: 1953; TV sets in area: 427,400.

KENTUCKY

Ashland

WTSF (Channel 61)
Tri-State Family Bcstg., Inc., 3100 Bath Ave., Ashland, KY 41101 (606) 329-2700.
Claude H. Messinger, gen. mgr. & chief exec. off.; Anne Bledsoe, prog. dir.; Virgil Adkins, chief eng.
Operation: April, 1983.

Beattyville

WLJC-TV (Channel 65)
North Route 11, Beattyville, KY 41311 (606) 464-3600.
Forest Drake, pres.; Jonathan Drake, gen. mgr. & chief eng.; Debra Green, sls. mgr.; Rachel Drake, prog. dir.; Bonnie West, office mgr.; John Stone, news dir.
Operation: 1982

Bowling Green

WBKO (Channel 13) ABC
Bluegrass Television, Inc., 2727 Russellville Rd., P.O. Box 13000, Bowling Green, KY 42101.
Clyde Payne, v.p. & gen. mgr.; Dennis Bradford, natl. sls. mgr.; Gene Prather, opns. mgr.; Dave Chumley, chief eng.; Steve Crabtree, news dir.; nat'l rep.: Katz.
Operation: June, 1962; TV households: 265,600.

Campbellsville

WGRB (Channel 34)
Green River Bcstg., Inc., Box 400, Campbellsville, KY 42718 (502) 465-2223.
Mike Harding, gen. mgr.; Gloria Davis, gen. sls. mgr.; Joe DeSpain, asst. mgr.; Anita Begley, bus. mgr.; Larry Nelson, chief eng.; nat'l rep.: Spot Time Ltd.
Operation: April, 1983.

Danville

WDKY-TV (Channel 56) FOX
WDKY License Co., 434 Interstate Ave., Lexington, KY 40505 (606) 299-3856.
David Godbout, v.p., gen. mgr., prog. dir. & film buyer; John Maybin, gen. sls. mgr.; John Keel, prom. mgr.; Scott Wills, chief eng.; natl. rep.: MMT.
Operation: February, 1986.

Hazard

WYMT-TV (Channel 57) CBS
Kentucky Central TV, Inc., P.O. Box 929, Hazard, KY 41701 (606) 436-4444, 436-2522.

Ralph W. Gabbard, exec. v.p.; Wayne M. Martin, sta. mgr.; E. Scott Mason, prom. mgr.; Jim Combs, chief eng.

Operations: Oct., 1969.

Lexington

WKYT-TV (Channel 27) CBS
Kentucky Central Television Inc., Box 5037, Lexington, KY 40505; Offices: Rt. 4, Winchester Rd.; (606) 299-0411.

Ralph Gabbard, v.p. & gen. mgr.; Al Taylor, v.p., op.; Jere Pigue, v.p. sls.; Hall Schumacher, dir. of eng'.

Operation: June 1967; TV households: 409,800.

WLEX (Channel 18) NBC
WLEX-TV, Inc., P.O. Box 1457, Russell Cave Road, Lexington, KY 40591 (606) 255-4404.

Harry C. Barfield, pres. & gen. mgr.; John G. Atchison, secty.; Joe Oliver, v.p. & nat'l sls. dir.; Hays McMakin, local sales; L. Neuzel, chief prog.; Al Scheer, v.p. & chief eng.; nat'l rep.: Blair.

Operation: 1955; TV households in area: 585,000.

WTVQ-TV (Channel 36) ABC
Shamrock Broadcasting Co., P.O. Box 5590 Lexington, KY 40555 (606) 233-3600.

William L. Service, v.p. & gen. mgr.; Dave White, news dir.; Jerry Fox, prog. mgr.; Jerry W. Fox, sta. mgr.; Jack Lackey, chief eng.; Rep.: Katz TV.

Operation: 1968; TV households: 212,100.

Louisville

WAVE-TV (Channel 3) NBC basic
Cosmos Broadcasting Corp., P.O. Box 32970, Louisville, KY 40232; 725 S. Floyd Street, Louisville, KY 40203 (502) 585-2201.

Guy Hempel, v.p. & gen. mgr.; Steve Langford, gen. sls. mgr.; Nick Ulmer, nat'l sls. mgr.; Roger Roebuck, prgm. dir.; Bill Eschback, chief eng.; Ed Godfrey, news dir.; Mark Young, prom. dir.; nat'l rep.: MMT.

Operation: 1948; TV sets in area: 950,400.

WDRB-TV (Channel 41)
Independence Television Co., Independence Square, Louisville, KY 40203 (502) 584-6441.

Elmer F. Jaspan, pres. & gen. mgr.; Robert Hurtman, gen. sls. mgr.; Glen Cook, chief eng.

Operation: 1971.

WHAS-TV (Channel 11) CBS
Journal Bdcstg. of Kentucky, Inc., P.O. Box 1100, Louisville, KY 40201; 582- 7840.

Jake C. Clifford, v.p., bdcstg.; N. Neil Kuvin, pres. & gen. mgr., Richard Sweeney, prog. dir.; Bill Bratton, dir. eng.; nat'l rep., Harrington, Righter and Parsons, Inc.

Operation: 1950; TV sets in area: 912,000.

WLKY-TV (Channel 32) ABC
Pulitzer Broadcasting Co., 1918 Mellwood Ave., P.O. Box 6205, Louisville, KY 40206 (502) 893-3671.

Lyn P. Stoyer, v.p. & gen. mgr.; Jim Oetken, gen. sls. mgr.; Jack Shafer, prog. dir.; Andy Barton, news dir.; Paul Kelley, v.p. & chief eng.; Lora Bradshaw, community affairs dir.

Operation: September, 1961; households: 610,900.

Madisonville

WLCN (Channel 19)
Life Anew Ministries, Inc., Box 1087, 721 Princeton Pike, Madisonville, KY 42431; (502) 821-5433.

John Stalls, pres.; John Price, v.p.

Operation: September, 1983.

Paducah

WPSD-TV (Channel 6) NBC
Paducah Newspapers, Inc., P.O. Box 1197, 100 Television Lane, Paducah, KY 42001 (502) 442-8214.

Fred Paxton, pres. & mgring dir.; John Williams, gen. mgr.; nat'l rep., Blair.

Operation: 1957; TV sets in area: 325,000.

LOUISIANA
Alexandria

KALB-TV (Channel 5) NBC
Lanford Telecasting Co., Inc., 605-11 Washington St., Alexandria, LA 71301 (318) 445-2456.

Robert E. Miller, v.p. & gen. mgr.; Lesly Golmon, asst. gen. mgr. & gen. sls. mgr.; Berton Chaudoir, nat'l & regl. sls. mgr.; Dowell Bushnell, sls. mgr.; Tom Webb, news dir.; Jimmy Fox, mgr. creative svcs.; nat'l rep.: The Katz Agency.

Operation: 1954; TV sets in area; 507,900.

KLAX-TV (Channel 31)
Cypress Comm. Corp., 1811 England Dr., Alexandria, LA 71301 (318) 473-2231.

James C. Richards, pres. & gen. mgr.; John Boyle, opns. mgr.; Charles Tarver, chief eng.

Operation: 1982.

Baton Rouge

WAFB-TV (Channel 9) CBS
Guaranty Broadcasting Corp., 844 Government St., Baton Rouge, LA 70821.

Ronald E. Winders, v.p. & gen. mgr.; David Ward, asst. gen. mgr.; Ed Lamy, prog. dir.; Wayne Bettoney, gen. sls. mgr.; Margie Larson, dir., community relations; Carlton Cremeens, news dir.; Steve Schneider, sports dir.; Bill Comeaux, chief eng.; Ronnie Melancon, prod. mgr.

Operation: 1953; TV sets in area: 460,000.

WBRZ (Channel 2) ABC
Louisiana Television Broadcasting Corp., P.O. Box 2906, Baton Rouge, LA 70821; (504) 387-2222.

Douglas L. Manship, pres.; Charles Manship, treas.; Richard Manship, secty. & gen. mgr.; Pat Cheramie, asst. gen. mgr. & dir. sls.; Denise Akers, mktg. dir.; Barbara Bree Shab, prog. mgr. & dir. comm. affairs; William R. Yordy, chief eng.; Raymond Drago, prod. mgr.; Kim Kirkendoll, bus. mgr.; Gus Luckett, finance mgr.; Fred Reno, sls. mgr.; James Daboual III, nat'l regnl., sls. mgr.; John Spain, news dir.; Jamie Politz, personnel dir.; nat'l rep.: Blair Television.

Operation: 1955; TV HH TSA: 775,900; TV HH 258,600.

WVLA (Channel 33) NBC
WVLA Television, Inc., P.O. Box 14685, Baton Rouge, LA 70808 (504) 766-3233.

Cyril E. Vetter, pres. & sta. mgr.; Bill Hathorn, gen. sls. mgr.

Operation: 1971.

Lafayette

KADN (Channel 15)
KADN Broadcasting, Inc., 1506 Eraste Landry Rd., Lafayette, LA 70506 (318) 237-1500.

Charles Chatelain, gen. mgr.; Eddie Blanchard, prog. dir.; Clark White, gen. sls. mgr.; Dave Pierce, sls. mgr.; Keith Towndsin, chief eng.; nat'l rep.: ITS.

Operation: 1980.

KATC (Channel 3) ABC
Adams TV of Lafayette, Box 3347, Lafayette, LA 70502 (318) 235-3333.

J. Michael Early, pres. & gen. mgr.; James Reardon, sls. dir.; rep.: Katz.

Operation: 1962; TV households: 357,600.

KLFY-TV (Channel 10) CBS
Texoma Broadcasters, Co., Box 90665, Lafayette, LA 70509 (318) 981-4823.

M. N. Bostick, pres.; Thomas G. Pears, gen. mgr.; Terry Dover, op. mgr.; Dave Hebert, chief eng.; Dan Coleman, prod. spvsr.; nat'l rep.: Seltel.

Operation: 1955; TV sets in area: 321,000.

Lake Charles

KPLC-TV (Channel 7) NBC
Cosmos Bcstg. Corp., 320 Division St., P.O. Box 1488, Lake Charles, LA 70602 (318) 439-9071.

Jim Serra, gen. sls. mgr.; Ron Blansett, chief eng.; Ron Loewen, v.p.-gen. mgr.; James Smith, news dir.; Jim Brandenburg, opns. dir.; Paula Dupuis, mktg. mgr.; Robin Daugereau, prog. co-ord.; Peter Hemphill, creative svcs. dir.

Operation: 1954; TV sets in area: 76,500.

KVHP (Channel 29)
KVHP-TV, Partners, 129 W. Prien Lake Rd., Lake Charles, LA 70601; (318) 474-1316.

Gary D. Hardesty, pres.-gen. mgr.; Paul Jimmy Martin, sta. mgr.; Charles Anderson, prod. mgr.; Cathy High, bus. mgr.; Bill Leger, news dir.; natl. rep.: ITS.

Operation: December, 1982.

Monroe

KARD (Channel 14) ABC
Woods Communications Group, Inc., 701 Parkwood Dr., West Monroe, LA 71291 (318) 323-1972.

Charles Woods, pres.; Gwen Kidd, gen. mgr.; Rodney Evans, chief eng.

Operation: August, 1967; TV households: 182,600.

KNOE-TV (Channel 8) CBS
Noe Enterprises Inc., 1400 Oliver Rd., P.O. Box 4067, Monroe, LA 71211 (318) 322-8155.

James A. Noe, Jr., pres. & gen. mgr.; Allen Jones, nat'l sls. mgr.; Jack McCall, prog. dir.; Raymond Boyd, dir. of eng.; Lloyd Voorhees, mgr. regional/local sls. mgr.; Ansel Smith, ops. mgr.; rep.: Blair.

Operation: 1953; TV sets in area: 800,000.

KTVE (Channel 10) NBC
(A Gray Communications System Station)
KTVE, Inc., 400 West Main, El Dorado, AR 71730 (318) 323-1300; 2909 Kilpatrick Blvd., Monroe, LA.

George Singleton, v.p. & gen. mgr.; Mike Caruso, chief eng.; David Brown, reg. sls. mgr.; Fran Rogers, nat'l sls. mgr.;

Helen Johnson, prog. dir.; rep.: Katz.

Operation: 1955; TV sets in area: 298,200.

New Orleans

WDSU-TV (Channel 6) NBC
Cosmos Broadcasting Corp., 520 Royal St., New Orleans, LA 70130 (504) 527-0666.

Jim Keelor, v.p. & gen. mgr.; Evan Wiggins, opns. mgr.; Tano Compagno, prod. dir.; Anne Coleman, sta.-pgm. dir.; Mike Kibbey, gen. sls. mgr.; Mary McCarthy, news dir.; Linda Nix, adv.-mktg. dir.; Steve Mohammed, bus. mgr.; Bill Laughlin, chief eng.; nat'l rep.: HRP.

WGNO-TV (Channel 26) IND
Tribune Broadcasting Co., 2800 World Trade Center, 2 Canal St., New Orleans, LA 70130; (504) 581-2600.

James Dowdle, pres.; Robert Gremillion, sta. mgr.; Randy Davis, chief eng.; sales rep.: Telerep.

Operation: 1967; TV households: 657,600.

WNOL-TV (Channel 38)
TVX of New Orleans, 1661 Canal St., New Orleans, LA 70112; (504) 525-3838.

John Trinder, pres.; Madelyn Mix Bonnot, v.p. & gen. mgr.; Cheryl Faust, gen. sls. mgr.; nat'l rep.: Seltel

Operation: March, 1984.

WVUE-TV (Channel 8) ABC
Burnham Bdcstg. Co., 1025 S. Jefferson Davis Pkwy., New Orleans, LA 70125 (504) 486-6161; TWX 810-951-6090.

Phil Nye, pres. & gen. mgr.; Ron Jones, gen. sls. mgr.; Greg Buisson, mktg. dir.; Kevin Brennan, news dir.; nat'l rep.: Petry.

Operation: 1959; TV sets in area: 2,000,000.

WWL-TV (Channel 4) CBS
Loyola University, 6363 St. Charles Ave., New Orleans, LA 70118.

J. Michael Early, v.p. & gen. mgr.-prog. dir.; Jerrold Whaley, gen. sls. mgr.; Everett Bonner, natl. sls. mgr.; Ms. Jimmie Phillips, lcl. sls. mgr.; Joe Duke, news dir.; Phil Johnson, asst. gen. mgr.; nat'l rep.: Katz TV.

Operation: September, 1957; TV households: 684,000.

Shreveport

KMSS-TV (Channel 33)
SWMM/Shreveport Corp., Box 30033, Shreveport, LA 71130 (318) 631-5677.

Arthur A. Lanham, gen. mgr.-v.p.; Susan K. Newman, gen. sls. mgr.; Douglas Ginn, prog. dir.; Don Adams, chief eng.; Phyliss Phillips, bus. mgr.; Holland McDaniel, prom. dir.

Operation: October, 1985.

KSLA-TV (Channel 12) CBS basic
Viacom Bdcst., Inc., P.O. Box 4812, Shreveport, LA 71134 (318) 222-1212.

Dan Bates, v.p. & gen. mgr.; David Loveland, sls. mgr.; Art Shiver, promo. dir.; Roger Herring, chief eng.; nat'l rep.: Telerep.

Operation: 1954; TV sets in area: 743,000.

KTAL-TV (Channel 6) NBC
KTAL-TV, Inc., 3150 No. Market St., Shreveport, LA 71104 (318) 425-2422. Texas: 3227 Summerhill Rd., Texarkana; (214) 793-1133.

W. E. Hussman, pres.; H. Lee Bryant, v.p. for bdcst'.; Doug Yoder, nat'l sls. mgr.; Kenny Gardner, sta. mgr.; Jean Byrd,

prog. dir.; George Tracy, dir. of eng.
Operation: 1953; TV sets in area: 490,900.

KTBS-TV (Channel 3) ABC
KTBS, Inc., 312 E. Kings Highway, Shreveport, LA 868-3644.
E. Newton Wray, pres. & gen. mgr.; George D. Wray, Jr., vice-pres.; Charles W. Wray, secy-treas.; Edwin Wray, sta. mgr. & promo. mgr.; Marvin L. Perry, Jr., film dir.; Dave Hendricks, chief eng.; nat'l rep.: Katz Agency.
Operation: 1955; TV sets in area: 732,300.

MAINE
Bangor
WABI-TV (Channel 5) CBS
Community Broadcasting Service, 36 Hildreth St., Bangor, ME 04401 (207) 947-8321.
George J. Gonyar, v.p. & gen. mgr.; Dale Carter, chief eng.; nat'l rep.: Blair.
Operation: 1953; TV sets in area: 140,000.

WLBZ-TV (Channel 2) NBC
WLBZ Television, Inc., Box 934, Mt. Hope Ave., Bangor, ME 04401 (207) 942-4822.
Fred Thompson, pres.; Bruce McGorrill, exec. v.p.; Margo Cobb, v.p./gen. mgr.; J. Hopkins, chief eng.; nat'l rep.: Katz Agency.
Operation: 1954; TV sets in area: 125,000.

WVII-TV (Channel 7) ABC
Bangor Communications, Inc., 371 Target Industrial Circle, Bangor, ME 04401 (207) 945-6457.
Barbara J. Cyr, exec. v.p. & gen. mgr.; Michele Slater, lcl./Canadian sls. mgr.; Gary Kasparek prod. mgr.; Ron Wolfe, news dir.; Judy Vardamis, prog. dir.; nat'l sls. mgr.; rep.: Seltel.
Operation: 1965, TV households: 220,000.

Poland Spring
WMTW-TV (Channel 8)
Mt. Washington TV, a division of Harron Communications Corp., Inc., Auburn, ME 04210; (207) 782-1800. Sales dept., Portland; (207) 775-1800.
Paul Harron, pres.; Al Ritter, v.p. & gen. mgr.; Bernie Aiello, sta. mgr.; John Ricker, chief eng.; nat'l rep.: Petry.
Operation: 1954.

Portland
WCSH-TV (Channel 6) NBC
Maine Radio and TV Co., 579 Congress St., Portland, ME 04101; (207) 772-0181.
Bruce McGorill, exec. v.p.; Lew Colby, gen. mgr.; nat'l rep.: Katz Agency.
Operation: 1953; TV sets in area: 210,000.

WGME-TV (Channel 13) CBS
Guy Gannett Broadcasting Services, Northport Plaza, Portland, ME 04104 (207) 797-9330.
Jean Gannett Hawley, pres.; Robert L. Gilbertson, exec. v.p.; David King, v.p. & gen. mgr.; Fred Desjardins, chief eng.; Jerry Senger, treas. nat'l rep., Blair TV assoc.
Operation: 1954; TV sets in area: 288,000.

WPXT (Channel 51) FOX
Portland Bdcstg., Inc., 2320 Congress St., Portland, ME 04102.

Josh McGraw, v.p. & gen. mgr.; Tony Palminteri, gen. sls. mgr.; Jennifer Dennison, prog. dir.; Doreen Morgan, prom. mgr.; Mark Beck, chief eng.; natl. rep.: Seltel.
Operation: September, 1986.

Presque Isle
WAGM-TV (Channel 8)
NEPSK, Inc., P.O. Box 1149, Presque Isle, ME 04769 (207) 764-4461.
Thom Shelburne III, pres.; Norm Johnson, v.p. & gen. mgr.
Operation: 1956.

MARYLAND
Baltimore
WBAL-TV (Channel 11) CBS
The Hearst Corp., 3800 Hooper Ave., Baltimore, MD 21211 (301) 467-3000.
John C. Conomikes, v.p. & gen. mgr., Hearst Broadcasting Stations; Malcolm D. Potter, v.p. & gen. mgr., WBAL-TV; Lynn McIntyre, prog. dir.; Jack Gilmore, v.p. sls.; Kristin Long, nat'l sls. mgr.; David Elmore, lcl. sls. mgr.; nat'l rep.: Blair.
Operation: March, 1948; TV households: 2,613,200.

WBFF (Channel 45)
Chesapeake TV Inc., 3500 Parkdale Ave., Baltimore, MD 21211 (301) 462-4500.
Julian S. Smith, bd. chm.; Robert Simmons, pres.; Bruce Lumpkin, gen. mgr. & gen. sls. mgr.; Kim Laxton, nat'l sls. mgr.; Robert Smith, prog. mgr.; Mike Schroeder, promo. mgr.; Dwight Weems, prod. mgr.; Sharon Christopher Wylie, public affairs mgr.; Dennis Winters, chief eng.
Operation: 1971.

WHSW-TV (Channel 24)
Silver King Bdcstg. of MD, Inc., 4820 Seton Dr., Baltimore, MD 21215 (301) 358-2400.
Ken Becker, v.p. & sta. mgr., Barbara Brown, sls. mgr.; Brad Foltyn, prog. dir.; Sue Gallion, traffic mgr.; Jim Vest, chief eng.
Operation: December, 1985.

WJZ-TV (Channel 13) ABC
Westinghouse Broadcasting Co., Inc., 3725 Malden Ave., Baltimore, MD 21211 (301) 466-0013.
Daniel L. Ritchie, pres. & chief exec. off., Westinghouse Broadcasting Co.; Paul Yates, v.p. & gen. mgr.; H. Brian O'Neill, creative svcs. mgr.; Stan Rudick, prgm. mgr.; Steven Engles, gen. sls. mgr.; Glenn Lahman, chief eng.; Richard Reingold, news dir.; Harold Murphy, bus. mgr.
Operation: 1948; TV sets in area: 2,653,500.

WMAR-TV (Channel 2) NBC
WMAR, Inc., 6400 York Road, Baltimore, MD 21212 (301) 377-2222.
Arnold J. Kleiner, pres. & gen. mgr.; Joseph Bruno, v.p. eng.; Charlotte M. English, v.p. prog.; John Butte, v.p. news; Howard Zeiden, v.p. sls.
Operation: 1947; TV sets in area: 2,390,600.

WNUV-TV (Channel 54)
New Vision, Assoc. Ltd. Partnership, 3001 Druid Park Dr., Baltimore, MD 21215 (301) 462-5400.
Samuel S. Kravetz, pres. & gen. mgr.; Mark Salditch, prog. dir. & film buyer; Paul Garnet, chief eng.
Operation: July, 1982.

Hagerstown

WHAG-TV
Williams Communications, Inc., 13 East Washington Street, Hagerstown, MD 21740 (301) 797-4400.
Alexander Williams, pres.; Hugh J. Breslin III, gen. mgr. & gen. sls. mgr.; Chuck Noland, prog. dir.; rep.: Katz.
Operation: 1970.

Salisbury

WBOC-TV (Channel 16) CBS
WBOC-TV, Inc., 17291 N. Salisbury Blvd., Salisbury, MD 21801; (301) 749-1111.
Thomas Draper, pres.; William Kenton, gen. mgr.; Carol Hess, prog. dir.; Robert Getz, gen. sls. mgr.; Sally Cannon, news dir.; Vincent Donovan, chief eng.; rep.: Katz
Operation: 1954; TV sets in area: 139,150.

WMDT (Channel 47) ABC, NBC
Delmarva Broadcast Svc. Genl. Partnership, P.O. Box 4009, Salisbury, MD 21801; (301) 742-4747.
Frank Pilgrim, gen. mgr.; Rich Dipilla, reg. & nat'l sls. mgr.; Susan Kelly, lcl. sls. mgr.; Clay Spurrier, chief eng.; Ray Carter, news dir.; nat'l rep.: Seltel.
Operation: 1980.

MASSACHUSETTS
Adams-Pittsfield

WCDC (Channel 19) ABC
(Satellite of WTEN, Albany, NY)
Knight-Ridder Broadcasting, Inc. 341 Northern Blvd., Albany, NY 12204 (518) 436-4822.
Dow C. Smith, gen. mgr.; John Hirsch, gen. sls. mgr.; Robert Peterson, prog. dir.; James Holland, news dir.

Boston

WBZ TV (Channel 40) NBC
Westinghouse Broadcasting Co., Inc., 1170 Soldiers Field Road, Boston, MA 02134 (617) 787-7000.
John J. Spinola, v.p. & gen. mgr.; Tony Vinciquerra, gen. sls. mgr.; Stan Hopkins, news dir.; George St. Andre, dir. eng.; Barry Schulman, prog. mgr.; Shelley Hobson, creative services dir.; Nance Guilmartin, information services mgr.; Bob Houghton, cont.; Bob Hayes, sls. svc. dir.; Bill Ferrick, commercial ops. mgr.
Operation: 1948; TV sets in area: 2,700,000.

WCVB-TV (Channel 5) ABC
The Hearst Corp., 5 TV Place, Needham, MA 02192.
S. James Coppersmith, v.p. & gen. mgr.; Deborah Sinay, v.p., gen. sls. mgr.; Paul La Camera, v.p. & sta. mgr.; Philip Balboni, v.p. news; Burt Peretsky, pub. rel. mgr.; Edward Aaronson, dir. promos.; Donna Latson-Gittens, v.p. comm. prog.
Operation: 1972.

WFXT-TV (Channel 25) Fox
Fox TV Stations, Inc., 100 Second Ave., Needham Heights, MA 02194 (617) 449-4200.
Joe R. Robinowitz, gen. mgr.; David D. Leahy, gen. sls. mgr.; Arthur Carr, natl. sls. mgr.; Peter Hennessey lcl. sls. mgr.; Richard D. Beach, prog. dir.; Gayton Masters, promo. mgr.; Dennis Correia, chief eng.
Operation: 1977.

WNEV-TV (Channel 7) CBS
New England TV Corp., 7 Bulfinch Pl., Government Center, Boston, MA 02114 (617) 725-0777.
Seymour Yanoff, pres.; Vic Lai, v.p.-admin. fin.; Mike Wach, v.p. sls.; Bruce Marson, v.p. prog.; Jennifer Gillespie, dir. p.r.; Jim Thistle, v.p. news; Jackie Comeau, v.p. rsch; Richard Weisberg, v.p.-mktg. & creative svcs.; Karl Renwanz, v.p.-eng.; nat'l rep.: Telerep.
Operation: June, 1948; homes in area: 2,034,200.

WQTV (Channel 68)
Monitor TV, Inc., 1660 Soldiers Field Rd., Boston, MA 02135 (617) 787-6868.
Allan Ginsberg, acting gen. mgr.; William Spitzer, sta. mgr.; Christine Howe, bus. mgr.; Michael Roessler, sls. mgr.; James Dunford, promo. mgr.; David Folsom, chief eng.; nat'l rep.: ITS
Operation: January, 1979.

WSBK-TV (Channel 38) NBC, ABC, CBS
New Boston TV, Inc., 83 Leo Birmingham Pkwy, Brighton, MA 02135 (617) 783-3838.
Joseph C. Dimino, gen. mgr.; Daniel J. Berkery, sta. mgr.; B. J. Anderson, promo. mgr.; William B. Knight, compt.; John Anderson, dir. of sls. develop.; Stuart Tauber, nat'l sls. mgr.; Ron Pulera, local sls. mgr.; Dick Beach, op. mgr. promo. mgr.; Doug Henderson, chief eng.
Operation: 1964.

Boston-Cambridge

WLVI-TV (Channel 56)
Gannett Massachusetts Broadcasting, Ind., 75 Morrissey Bldg., Boston, MA 02125 (617) 265-5656.
Gerald R. Walsh, pres. & gen. mgr.; Victoria Gregorian, prog. mgr.; Thom Neeson, v.p. & gen. sls. mgr.; Denis Dowdle, natl. sls. mgr.; Bob McCaughey, lcl. sls. mgr.; Ron Becker, v.p. news & opns.; Mike Izor, cont.; Gail Satz, prod. mgr.; Natalie McIver, news & pub. affairs mgr.
Operation: 1953.

Marlborough

WHSH (Channel 66)
Silver King. Bcstg. of Mass., 111 Speen St., Framingham, MA 01701 (617) 350-6666.
Merrill Buchhalter, gen. mgr.; David O'Leary, prog. dir.; Charles Fitch, chief eng.
Operation: March, 1983.

Springfield-Holyoke

WGGB-TV (Channel 40) ABC
The WHYN Stations Corp., 1300 Liberty Street, Springfield, MA 01101 (413) 785-1911.
Clifford Lefkovich, gen. mgr.; Dick Wylie, natl sls. mgr.; Rep.: Katz Agency.
Operation: 1953; TV sets in area: 1,213,500.

WWLP (Channel 22) NBC
Adams TV of Springfield, Inc., Box 2210, Springfield, MA 01102-2210 (413) 786-2200.
William M. Pepin, pres., gen. mgr.; Constance O'Brien, bus. mgr.; E. Holland Low, v.p., nat'l sls.; Daniel T. Sullivan, Jr., v.p., lcl. sls. mgr.; Max Marek, chief eng.; nat'l rep.: Blair.
Operation: 1953; TV sets in area: 714,900.

Vineyard Haven

WCVX-TV (Channel 58)
29 Bassett Lane, Hyannis, MA 02601 (617) 775-4242.
Daniel Carney, gen. mgr.; Fred Lungo, pgm. dir.; Ben Emery, gen. sls. mgr.; Greg Bush, news dir.; Don Moore, chief eng.
Operation: July, 1985.

Worcester

WHLL-TV (Channel 27)
Central Mass. TV, Inc., 27 Parker Rd., Shewsbury, MA 01545.
Robert Thurber, gen. mgr.; Mike Jones, gen. sls. mgr.; Jim Barnett, prod. mgr.; Cathy Martin, traffic mgr.; Mike Krasner, news dir.; Moses Primo, chief eng.
Operation: 1970; TV households: 2,037,700.

MICHIGAN
Alpena-Oscoda

WBKB-TV (Channel 11) CBS
Thunder Bay Broadcasting Co., 1390 Bagley St., Alpena, MI 49707 (517) 356-3434.
Stephen A. Marks, pres. & gen. mgr.; Daniel H. Springer, news dir.; Michael Campbell, prod. mgr.; Mark Nowak, chief eng.; Jodie Bryant, prog. dir.
Operation: 1975.

Ann Arbor

WIHT (Channel 31)
Satellite Television Systems, Inc., 3975 Varsity Dr., Ann Arbor, MI 48104; (313) 973-7900.
Christopher Webb, gen. mgr. & gen. sls. mgr.; Robert Thompson, chief eng.
Operation: 1981.

Battle Creek-Kalamazoo

WUHQ-TV (Channel 41) ABC
Channel 41, Inc., 5200 West Dickman Road, Battle Creek, MI 49016 (616) 968-9341.
John W. Lawrence, pres.; William J. Lawrence, Jr., bd. chmn.; Jerry Colvin, exec. v.p. & gen. mgr.; Phil Hartman, prog. & prom. mgr.; Michael J. Laemers, chief eng. & ops. mgr.; Denny Monroe, controller; Brett Bowers, film dir.
Operation: 1971; Receivers in area: 938,000.

Bay City-Saginaw

WNEM-TV (Channel 5) NBC
WNEM-Television; Broadcasting div./Meredith Corp.; Offices and studios, 107 N. Franklin, Saginaw, MI (517) 755-8191. Sales office & studio: G-3426 Miller Road, Flint, MI (313) 732-2050.
Paul Virciglio, v.p. & gen. mgr.; Bill Avery, prog. dir.; Paula Morrissey, gen. sls. mgr.; Greg Surma, chief eng.; Barbara Handley-Miller, news dir.; nat'l rep.: MMT Sales, Inc.
Operation: 1954; TV households in area: 433,300.

Cadillac

WWTV (Channel 9) CBS
Wilson Communications, Inc. P.O. Box 627; Cadillac, MI 49601 (616) 775-3478.
Ralph C. Wilson, Jr., chmn.; William R. Hirshey, pres.; J.A. Skip Simms, v.p. & gen. mgr.; nat'l rep.: Blair.
Operation: Jan. 1, 1954; TV sets in area: 1,234,200.

Cheboygan

WPBN-TV & WTOM-TV NBC
WPBN-TV & WTOM-TV, Inc., Box 546, Traverse City, MI 49684 (616) 947-7770.
Frank L. Beam, pres.; Peter S. Good, v.p. & gen. mgr.; Chuck O'Connor, natl. sls. mgr.; Leon Bush, chief eng.; nat'l rep.: Katz.
Operation: 1959.

Detroit

WDIV-TV (Channel 4) NBC
Post-Newsweek Station, Michigan, Inc. 550 Lafayette Blvd., Detroit, MI 48231 (313) 222-0444.
Alan W. Frank, v.p. & gen. mgr.; Robert Warfield, v.p. news & dir. bdcst. opns.; Ann Wise, exec. asst. & gen. mgr.
Operation: 1947; TV sets in area; U.S. total survey area: 3,324,00, total coverage area (inc. Canada): 3,525,000.

WGPR-TV (Channel 62)
WGPR, Inc., 3140-6 E. Jefferson Ave., Detroit, MI 48207 (313) 259-8862.
George Mathews, pres. & gen. mgr.; James W. Panagos, v.p. & gen. sls. mgr.; Joe Spencer, prog. dir.; Ulysses W. Boykin, v.p. public affairs.
Operation: 1975.

WJBK-TV (Channel 2) CBS
Gillett Communications of Detroit, Inc., Box 2000, Southfield, MI 48037 (313) 557-2000.
George U. Lyons, pres. & gen. mgr.; James Clayton, gen. sls. mgr.; Steve Antoniotti, v.p. bdcst.
Operation: 1948; TV sets in area: 2,034,000.

WKBD-TV (Channel 50) FOX
Cox Communications, P.O. Box 359, Southfield, MI 48037.
George H. Williams, v.p. & gen. mgr.; Duane Kell, gen. sls. mgr.; Ellen Bramson, sls. mgr.; Paul Prange, prog. mgr.; G. R. Fitzgerald, business mgr.; David Jerrell, dir. of eng.; Toby Cunningham, prod. mgr.
Operation: 1965.

WXON-TV (Channel 20)
27777 Franklin Rd., Suite 708, Detroit, MI 48034 (313) 355-2900.
Aben E. Johnson Jr., pres.; Doug Johnson, v.p., gen. mgr. & prog. dir.; A.J. Schweizer, opns., mgr.; Gary King, chief eng.; Melanie Churell, news dir.; nat'l rep.: MMT.
Operation: September, 1968.

WXYZ-TV (Channel 7) ABC
WXYZ, Inc., Broadcast House, 20777 W. Ten Mile Rd., Detroit, MI 48231 (313) 444-1111.
Thomas C. Griesdorn, gen. mgr.; Grace Gilchrist, gen. sls. mgr.; Robert Sliva, natl. sls. mgr.; Joseph Trondle, lcl. sls. mgr.; Mimmi Mathis, creative svcs. dir.; Marla Drutz, dir. rsch. & sls. devel.; Jan Qualtiere, bus. mgr.; Wallace Rodammer chief eng. natl. rep.: Katz.
Operation: 1948; TV sets in area: 1,823,423.

Detroit-Windsor (Canada)

CBET (Channel 9) CBC
Canadian Bdg. Corp., 825 Riverside Drive West, Windsor, Ont. N9A 5K9 (519) 254-2831.
Bruce Taylor, dir. of TV; Fred Stecher, mgr. TV opns.; R. Kryger, mgr., TV tech. svcs.; J. Molnar, communications.
Operation: 1954.

Escanaba

WJMN-TV (Channel 3) ABC
(Satellite of WFRV-TV, Green Bay, WI)
WFRV Inc., P.O. Box 19055, Green Bay, WI 54307.
Rep.: Telerep.
Operation: 1969.

Flint

WJRT-TV (Channel 12) ABC
Knight-Ridder Broadcasting, Inc., 2302 Lapeer Rd., Flint
MI 48503 (313) 233-3130.
P. Thomas Bryson, pres. & gen. mgr.; nat'l rep.; HRP.
Operation: 1958; TV households in area: 1,156,700.

Grand Rapids

WOTV-TV (Channel 8) NBC basic
Lin Central Broadcasting Corp., 120 College Ave., P.O. Box
B, Grand Rapids, MI 49501; (616) 456-8888.
Lilliane Clary, bus. mgr.; Jim Thomas, prom. mgr.; Donald
P. Gallagher, chief eng.; Sue McDonnell, gen. sls. mgr.; nat'l
rep.: Blair.
Operation: 1951; TV sets in area: 532,500.

WXMI-TV (Channel 17)
3117 Plaza Drive, N.E., Grand Rapids, MI 49505; (616)
364-8722.
Harold Shively, , pres. & gen. mgr.; Richard J. Stawicki,
opns. dir.; Pat Mullen, sls. dir.; Mark Krause, prog. mgr.;
Bonnie Hunter, dir. of off.; Pam Swenk, prom. mgr.; Carleen
Gordon, news; Dale Scholten, dir. of eng.; nat'l rep.: Petry.
Operation: March, 1982.

WZZM (Channel 13)
Western Michigan Bdcstg. Corp., P.O. Box Z, 645 Three
Mile Rd., N.W., Grand Rapids, MI 49501.
Jack Mazzie, v.p.-gen. mgr.; Michael Seagly, prog.-opns.
mgr.; Buss Kunst, gen. sls. mgr; Tim Siegel, nat'l sls. mgr.;
Dale Wolters, chief eng.

Kalamazoo

WWMT (Channel 3) CBS
Busse Bcstg., Corp., 590 W. Maple St., Kalamazoo, MI
49008 (616) 388-3333.
Larry Busse, pres. & gen. mgr.; Gil Brettner, sta. mgr.;
Michael Brunette, gen. sls. mgr.; Phil Parsons, promo. mgr.;
James Garrett, chief eng.; nat'l rep.: MMT
Operation: 1950; TV sets in area: 932,000.

Lansing

WLNS-TV (Channel 6) CBS
Young Bdcstg., Inc., 2820 E. Saginaw, Lansing, MI 48912
(517) 372-8282.
Donald J. Kuasick, pres.; Robert E. Sene, gen. sls. mgr.;
Dennis R. Selenka, corp. controller; Carl Onken, chief eng.;
nat'l rep.: Adam Young.
Operation: 1950; TV homes in area: 1,063,100.

WSYM-TV (Channel 47)
600 West St. Joseph St., Lansing, MI 48933 (517) 484-7747.
Pete Bannister, lcl. sls. mgr.; Tom Bennett, nat'l sls. mgr.;
Larry Estlack, chief eng.; rep.: MMT Sales.
Operation: December, 1982.

Lansing-Onondaga

WILX-TV (Channel 10) NBC
Adams TV of Lansing, Inc., P.O. Box 30380, Lansing, MI
48909 (517) 783-2621.
Bill Snider, pres. & gen. mgr.; Steve Hillman, sta. mgr.;
Steve Danowski, gen. mgr.; Sandy Rushton, natl. sls. mgr.;
Pamela Bobzien, bus. mgr.; Nancie Gee, prog. dir.; Dan Tam-
bellini, news dir.; natl rep: Katz.
Operation: 1959.

Marquette

WLUC-TV (Channel 6) CBS, NBC
Federal Bdcstg. Co., P.O. Box 460, Marquette, MI 49855
James Kizer, gen. mgr.; Brad Vansluyters, gen. sls. mgr.;
Jack LaForest, prog. mgr.; Jack Truitt, chief eng.; Kim Parker,
promo. mgr.; Ed Kearney, news dir.; Dale Hemmila, assign.
mgr.; Bruce Saari, film dir.; nat'l rep.: MMT.
Operation: 1956.

Saginaw-Bay City

WEYI-TV (Channel 25) CBS
WEYI, Inc., 2225 W. Willard Rd., Clio, MI 48420 (517)
755-0525.
Michael Florile, v.p. & gen. mgr.; Diane Watkins, promo.
mgr.; Robert Volz, chief eng.
Operation: 1953.

Sault Ste. Marie

WGTQ (Channel 8) ABC
201 East Front St., Traverse City, MI 49684
Michael D. Khouri, v.p. & gen. mgr.
Operation: 1982

WWUP-TV (Channel 10) CBS
Wilson Communications, Inc., Box 627, Cadillac, MI
49601.
Personnel: See WWTV, Cadillac.
Operation: 1962.

Traverse City

WGTU (Channel 29) WGTQ (Channel 8) ABC
Adams Communication Corp., 201 E. Front St., Traverse
City, MI 49684; (616) 922-2900.
Gregg Brissette, v.p. & sta. mgr.; Nancy M. Sundstrom,
prog. dir., Bill Wagman, news dir.
Operation: 1971.

WPBN-TV (Channel 7) NBC
WPBN-TV, Inc., P.O. Box 546, Traverse City, MI 49685-
0546 (616) 947-7770.
Frank Beam, pres.; Peter S. Good, v.p. & gen. mgr.; Leon
Bush, chief eng.
Operation: 1954.

MINNESOTA
Alexandria

KCCO-TV (Channel 7) CBS
Midwest Call Letters, Inc., 720 Hawthorne St., Alexandria,
MN 56308 (612) 763-5166.
Bruce Barnes, pres.; Glenn Flint, v.p. & gen. mgr.; John
Ginther, sls. mgr.; Carl Iverson, chief eng.; rep.: Seltel; Rams-
land (MN)
Operation: 1958.

Austin

KAAL-TV (Channel 6) ABC
MDM, Inc., P.O. Box 577, Austin, MN 55912 (507) 433-8836.
Clark Cipra, pres. & gen. mgr.; Janet Anderson, prog. dir.; Jerald Jones, v.p./eng.; Dennis Fisher, news dir.; Greg Grimley, prod. mgr.

Duluth-Superior (WI)

KBJR-TV (Channel 6) NBC
RJR Communications, Inc., KBJR Building, Duluth MN 55802 (218) 727-8484.
Robert J. Rich, CEO; R. W. Pearson, v.p.; Steven Rich, prog. dir.; John Rich, gen. sls. mgr.; Julie Nippet, pub. aff. dir.; nat'l rep.: Katz Agency.
Operation: 1954; TV sets in area: 336,500.

WDIO-TV (Channel 10) ABC
Channel 10, Inc., 10 Observation Road, Duluth, MN 55811 (218) 727-6864.
Frank P. Befera, pres. & gen. mgr.; George Couture, sta. mgr.; Dave Poirier, prog. mgr.; George W. Woody, chief eng.; Joel Anderson, news dir.; Lucy Reichert, promo. mgr.
Operation: 1966.

KDLH-TV (Channel 3) CBS
Benedek Broadcasting of Minnesota, Inc., 425 West Superior St., Duluth, MN 55802 (218) 727-8911.
John LaForge, gen. mgr.; Steve Hasskamp, chief eng.; Stu Lunsford, dir. sls.; James Cuzzo, prog. dir.; nat'l rep.: MMT.
Operation: 1954; TV sets in area: 326,090.

Hibbing

WIRT (Channel 13) ABC
Channel 10, Inc., 10 Observation Rd., Duluth, MN 55811 (218) 727-6864.
Satellite of WDIO-TV, Duluth.
Operation: 1967.

Mankato

KEYC-TV (Channel 12) CBS
United Communications, Corp., P.O. Box 128, Mankato, MN 56001 (507) 890-8128.
Howard J. Brown, pres.; Hap Halligan, v.p. & gen. mgr.; Eugene W. Schulte, v.p.-secty.-treas.
Operation: October, 1960; TV households: 202,200.

Minneapolis-St. Paul

KARE-TV (Channel 11)
8811 Olson Memorial Hwy., Minneapolis, MN 55427 (612) 546-1111.
Joseph H. Franzgrote, pres. & gen. mgr.; Elliot Bass, gen. sls. mgr.; Lou Morline, lcl. sls. mgr.; Michael Hanrahan, nat'l sls. mgr.; Steven Thaxton, promo. mgr.; Tom Kirby, news dir.; Hillis Aldrich, chief eng.; nat'l rep.: Blair.
Operation: 1965; TV homes in area: 1,766,100.

KITN (Channel 29)
7325 Aspen Lane N., Minneapolis, MN 55428 (612) 424-2929.
Gail L. Brekke, gen. mgr.; Marty Sokoler, gen. sls. mgr.; Gene Steinberg, stn. mgr.; Robert Thaman, prom. mgr.; Don Kirby, chief eng.; nat'l rep.: MMT.
Operation: October, 1982.

KMSP-TV (Channel 9)
United Television, Inc. 6975 York Ave. So., Minneapolis, MN 55435 (612) 926-9999.
Evan Thompson, pres.; Stuart Swartz, sta. mgr.; Roger Werner, gen. sls. mgr.; Joe Carney, op. mgr.; Penny Parrish, news dir.; Darold Arvidson, dir. of eng.; nat'l rep.: Katz.
Operation: 1955; TV sets in area: 1,838,700.

KSTP-TV (Channel 5) ABC
Hubbard Broadcasting, Inc., 3415 University Ave., Minneapolis, MN 55414 (612) 646-5555.
Robert Regalbuto, pres. & gen. mgr.; John Degan, sta. mgr.; Karl Gersheimer, dir. sls.; nat'l rep.: Petry Television, Inc.
Operation: 1948.

KTMA-TV (Channel 23)
KTMA Acquisition Corp., 2505 N.D. Kennedy St., Minneapolis, MN 55403 (612) 623-0200.
Donald O'Connor, pres. & gen. mgr.; Mary O'Neill, prom. mgr.; James Clark, gen. sls. mgr.; Carolyn Greene, lcl. sls. mgr.; nat'l rep.: ITS.
Operation: September, 1982.

WCCO-TV (Channel 4) CBS
90 South 11th St., Minneapolis, MN 55403 (612) 339-4444.
Ron Handberg, v.p. & gen. mgr.; Bob McGann, gen. sls. mgr.; Greg Keck, bus. mgr.; Mike Sullivan, dir. p.a. & comm. reltns.; Reid Johnson, dir. news; Anne Birch, dir. adv. & promo.; nat'l rep.: Katz.
Operation: 1949; TV sets in area 1,199,800.

Rochester

KTTC-TV (Channel 10) NBC
KTTC Television, Inc., 601 First Ave., S.W., Rochester, MN 55901.
Clark L. Wideman, v.p. & gen. mgr.; Russ Hamilton, gen. sls. mgr.; Ronald E. Gruber, op. mgr.; C. H. Sanders, chief eng.; nat'l rep.: Seltel.
Operation: July, 1953; TV households: 363,300.

St. Cloud

KXLI (Channel 41)
L.E.O. Bcstg., Inc., 800 St. Germain, St. Cloud, MN 56301 (612) 252-0110.
Douglas McMonagle, gen. mgr.; Diana Fuhrman, prog. dir.; Larry Enter, chief eng.; nat'l rep.: Adam Young.
Operation: November, 1982.

Walker

KCCW-TV (Channel 12) CBS
Midwest Call Letters, Inc., Box 168, Alexandria, MN 56452. Satellite to KCMT.
Bruce Barnes, pres.; Glenn W. Flint, v.p. & gen. mgr.; Carl Iverson, chief eng.; rep.; Seltel; Ramsland (MN)
Operation: 1964.

MISSISSIPPI
Biloxi-Gulfport-Pascagoula

WLOX-TV (Channel 13) ABC
WLOX Television, Inc., Box 4596, Biloxi, MS 39531 (601) 896-1313.
John Hash, pres.; Leon Long, v.p. & gen. mgr.; Don Moore, v.p. & opns. mgr.; rep.: Blair
Operation; 1962; TV households: 369,100.

Columbus

WCBI-TV (Channel 4) CBS
Columbus Television, Inc., owner, P.O. Box 271, Columbus, MS 39701 (601) 327-4444.

Frank Imes, gen. mgr.; Brett Smith, prod. mgr.; Bill Doss, chief eng.; Vallory Williamson, prog. dir.; nat'l rep.: Seltel.

Operation: 1956; TV sets in area: 237,200.

Greenville

WXVT (Channel 15) CBS
Big River Broadcasting Co., 3015 E. Reed Rd., Greenville, MS 38701. (601) 334-1500.

Marshall Noecker, pres.; Joe Macione, Jr., v.p. & gen. mgr.; Peter Sparks, chief eng.

Operation: 1980.

Greenwood

WABG-TV (Channel 6) ABC
Mississippi Telecasting Co., Inc., P.O. Drawer 720, Greenwood, MS 38931 (601) 453-4001

Cy N. Bahakel, pres.; Ralph Robinson, sta. mgr.; Ada Mitchell, office mgr.; Robert Askew, chief eng.

Operation: 1959; TV households: 336,700.

Gulfport

WXXV-TV (Channel 25)
Four-O of Gulfport, Inc., Hwy. 49, P.O. Box 2500, Gulfport, MS 39505; (601) 832-2525.

David C. Hopper, gen. mgr.; Terry Smith, cheif eng.

Operation: January, 1985.

Jackson

WAPT (Channel 16) ABC
Clay Broadcasting of Mississippi, Inc., Box 10297, Jackson, MS 39209 (601) 922-1607.

Ben Strickland, v.p. & gen. mgr.; Joe Root, station mgr.; Danny Bardin, dir. of eng.

Operation: 1970; TV household: 538,600.

WDBD (Channel 40)
Jackson Television, Ltd., P.O. Box 10888, Jackson, MS 39209.

Don Kent, pres.

Operation: November, 1984.

WJTV (Channel 12) CBS
News Press & Gazette Co., P.O. Box 8887, Jackson, MS 39204 (601) 372-6511.

John MacGregor, pres.; William H. Dilday, Jr., exec. v.p. & gen. mgr.; Jim Stembridge, chief eng.; Phyllis Brooks, prog. dir.; Walter Saddler, news dir.; rep.: Petry.

Operation: 1954; TV sets in area: 434,600.

WLBT (Channel 3) NBC
TV-3, Inc., 715 South Jefferson, Jackson, MS 39205 (601) 948-3333.

Frank E. Melton, gen. mgr. & CEO; Brad Streit, sta. mgr.; Dan Modisett, gen. sls. mgr.; Floyd Kinard, chief eng.; Larry Keeler, prod. mgr.; nat'l rep.: Blair.

Operation: 1953; TV sets in area: 342,000.

Laurel-Hattiesburg

WDAM-TV (Channel 7)
Beam Communications Corp., P.O. Box 1978, Hattiesburg, MS 39401.

Frank L. Beam, pres.; Marvin Reuben, exec. v.p.; Cliff Brown, gen. mgr.; Bobby Smith, chief eng. and oper. mgr.; Diane Schilling, prog. mgr.; nat'l rep.: Katz.

Operation: 1956; TV set in area: 204,500.

Meridian

WLBM-TV (Channel 30) NBC
TV-3, Inc., 4608 Skyland Dr., Meridian, MS 39201 (601) 485-3030.

Frank Melton, CEO & pres.; Glenn Rose, gen. mgr. & sls. mgr.; Bert Case, news dir.; Floyd Kinard, chief eng.; nat'l rep.: Katz.

Operation: October, 1982.

WTOK-TV (Channel 11) ABC
WTOK-TV, Inc., Southern Bldg., Box 2988, Meridian, MS 39402 (601) 693-1441.

Robert Ward, pres. & gen. mgr.; John L. Buffington, sta. mgr.; Bob Ford, gen. sls. mgr.; Cecil Germany, nat'l sls. mgr.; nat'l rep.: Katz.

Operation: 1953; TV sets in area: 151,900.

WTZH (Channel 24) ABC, NBC
Meridian Bdcstg. Partnership, Box 5185, Meridian, MS 39301 (609) 693-2933.

Nory LeBrun, pres. & gen. mgr.; Ray Denton, sta. mgr.

Operation: June, 1968; TV households: 76,300.

Natchez

WNTZ (Channel 48)
MSLA Bdcstg., Inc., Television Plaza, Beltline Hwy., Natchez, MS 39120 (601) 442-4800.

Donald B. Wilburn, gen. & gen. sls. mgr., film buyer; Mark McKay, prog. dir. & prom. mgr.; Gwen Belton, news dir.; Charles Fisher, chief eng.; natl. rep.: Mutual.

Operation: November, 1985.

Tupelo

WTVA (Channel 9) NBC
WTWV, Inc., Beech Springs Rd., Box 350, Tupelo, MS 38801 (601) 842-7620.

Frank K. Spain, pres.; Mark Ledbetter, exec. v.p. & gen. mgr.; Bob Leech, dir. nat'l sls; Charles Ed Bishop, prog. dir.; Wendell Robionson, chief eng.

Operation: 1957; TV sets in area: 433,900.

West Point

WVSB-TV (Channel 27) ABC
Venture Systems, Inc., Box 777, West Point, MS 39773 (601) 494-8327.

David C. Hopper, pres. & gen. mgr.; Kathy Poulin, gen. sls. mgr.; Lynda Mize, prom. mgr.; Chuck Govan, news dir.; Terry Smith, chief eng.; nat'l rep.: Avery-Knodel.

Operation: May, 1983.

MISSOURI
Cape Girardeau

KBSI (Channel 23) FOX
Cape Girardeau Family TV Ltd., 806 Enterprise, Cape Girardeau, MO 63701 (314) 334-1223.

Michael D. De Clue, gen. mgr.; Glenn Rose, gen. sls. mgr.; Mark Culbertson, prog. dir.; Bryan Uptain, prom. mgr.; Doug Goodson, chief eng.; natl. rep.: Seltel.
Operation: September, 1983.

KFVS-TV (Channel 12) CBS
American Hirsch Broadcasting Co., Box 310 Broadway, Cape Girardeau, MO 63701 (314) 335-1212.
Walter H. McCroba, pres.; Joe Goleniowski, v.p. & gen. mgr.; George W. Jeter, sect-treas.; nat'l rep.: Katz Agency.
Operation: 1954.

Columbia
KMIZ-TV (Channel 17) ABC
Stauffer Communications, Inc., 501 Business Loop 70 East, Columbia, MO 65201 (314) 449-0917.
Carlos Fernandez, gen. mgr.; Alan Parker, lcl. sls. mgr.; Jean Viox, nat'l sls. mgr.; Gale Clevenger, news dir.; Ron Rowe, chief eng.; Judy Reich, prog. dir.; Shelia Carpenter, prom. mgr.; nat'l rep.: Blair.
Operation: 1971.

KOMU-TV (Channel 8) NBC
The Curators of the University of Missouri, Highway 63, South, Columbia, MO 65201 (314) 442-1122.
Thomas R. Gray, gen. mgr.; Don Ruggles, sales mgr.; Robert Austin, dir. of prog.; James Moore, chief eng.; John Quarderer, dir. of news; nat'l rep.: Seltel.
Operation: 1953; TV sets in area: 505,200.

Hannibal-Quincy (IL)
KHQA-TV (Channel 7) CBS
Benedek Bcstg. 510 Main St., Quincy, IL 62301 (217) 222-6200.
Richard Belkin, v.p., bcstg. div.; Gary N. Schmedding, gen. mgr.; Tim Thompson, nat'l tv sls. mgr.; Robert Fruehe, nat'l radio sls. sales mgr.; rep.: Katz.
Operation: 1953; TV sets in area: 212,000.

Jefferson City
KRCG-TV (Channel 13) CBS
Box 659, Jefferson City, MO 65102 (314) 896-5144.
Owned by Price Communications, Inc.
Robert Price, pres.; John C. Denshane, v.p.-gen. mgr.; Duane Lammers, sls. mgr.; Cleon Crum, chief eng.; Lee Gordon, prgm. dir.; Roger Wellman, news dir.; nat'l rep.: Katz.

Joplin
KODE-TV (Channel 12) ABC
Gilmore Broadcasting Corp. (licensee), 1928 W. 13th St., Joplin, MO (417) 623-7260.
Douglas A. Padgett, v.p./gen. mgr.; Bill Acker, sta. mgr.; Randy Collard, gen. sls. mgr.; Gayle Kirchner, dir. comm. affairs/promo. mgr.; nat'l rep.: Seltel.
Operation: 1954; TV sets in area: 440,900 TV households per May '81 ARB.

KSNF (Channel 16) NBC
Tri-State Bdcstg. Corp., P.O. Box 1393, Joplin, MO 64801 (417) 781-2345.
Bill Bengtson, v.p. & gen. mgr.; Bill Ward, gen. sls. mgr.; Mel Brooks, chief eng.; Jim Lobbey, prod. prom. opns. mgr.; Steve Russell, news dir.
Operation: September, 1967; TV households: 290,600.

Kansas City
KCTV (Channel 5) CBS
4500 Shawnee Mission Parkway, Fairway, KS 66205 (913) 677-5555.
Philip A. Jones, v.p. & gen. mgr.; Pat North, gen. sls. mgr.; Erv Parthe, prog. dir.; Owen Uridge, promo. dir.; nat'l rep.: MMT Sales.
Operation: 1953.

KMBC-TV (Channel 9) ABC
Division—The Hearst Corp., 1049 Central, Kansas City, MO 64105 (816) 221-9999.
Paul Dinovitz, v.p. & gen. mgr.; Bill Lind, gen. sls. mgr.; Cheryl Craigie Parker, nat'l sls. mgr.; Robert Twibeli, lcl. sls. mgr.; Deb McDermott, prog. dir.; Gerald Golden, resident controller; Michael Sullivan, news dir.; Joe Todaro, creative svs. dir.
Operation: August, 1953; TV households; 2,098,000.

KSHB-TV (Channel 41)
Scripps-Howard Broadcasting, 4720 Oak St., Kansas City, MO 64112 (816) 753-4141.
Bob Wormington, gen. mgr.; Peter D. Brake, asst. gen. mgr. & film buyer; Harold DeGood, chief eng.
Operation: September, 1970; TV households: 1,225,400.

KYFC (Channel 50)
Kansas City Youth for Christ., Inc. 4715 Rainbow Blvd., Shawnee Mission, KS 66205 (913) 262-1700.
Ronnie Metsker, exec. dir.
Operation: 1978.

KZKC-TV (Channel 62)
Media Central, Inc., 2111 Blue Summit Dr., Kansas City, MO 64126 (816) 254-6262.
Bob Harris, gen. mgr.; Jay Rabin, gen. sls. mgr.; Todd Powers, prog. dir.; Karen Underwood, news dir.; Greg Fugate, chief eng.; nat'l rep.: Seltel.
Operation: December, 1983.

WDAF-TV (Channel 4) NBC
Taft Broadcasting Company, Signal Hill, Kansas City, MO 64108 (816) 753-4567.
Dudley Taft, pres.; Earl Beall, v.p. & gen. mgr.; Randy Smith, gen. sales mgr.; Buddy Turner, operations mgr.; James Schmidt, chief eng.; nat'l rep.: Telerep.
Operation: 1949; TV sets in area: 1,510,400.

Poplar Bluff
KPOB-TV (Channel 15) ABC
(Satellite of WSIL-TV, Harrisburg, IL)
Mel Wheeler, Inc., 1710 Westminster, Suite F, Denton, TX 76205; nat'l rep.: MMT.
Operation: 1961.

St. Joseph
KQTV (Channel 2) ABC
Elba Development Corp., 270 Commerce Dr., Rochester, NY 14623. (716) 359-3000.
George Loar, v.p. & gen. mgr.; Denise Dailey, gen. sls. mgr.; Dave Tillery, news dir.
Operation: 1953.

St. Louis

KDNL-TV (Channel 30)
KDNL, Inc., 1215 Cole St., St. Louis, MO 63106 (314) 436-3030.
William L. Viands, Jr., v.p. & gen. mgr.; William J. Tynan, gen. sls. mgr.; Bob West, prog. dir.; Otis Thomas, news dir.; Gene Faulkner, chief eng.; nat'l rep.: MMT.
Operation: 1969.

KMOV-TV (Channel 4) CBS
Viacom Bdcstg., Inc. One Memorial Drive, St. Louis, MO 63102 (314) 621-4444.
Allan Cohen, v.p., gen. mgr.; Peggy Milner, bus. mgr.; Jim Rothschild, opns. dir.; Bob Grissom, gen. sls. mgr.; Al Holzer, news dir.; Wilbur Allmeyer, asst. chief eng.; natl. rep.: Telerep.
Operation: 1959; est. TV sets in area: 1,037,390.

KPLR (Channel 11)
Koplar Communications, Inc., 4935 Lindell Blvd., St. Louis, MO. 63108 (314) 367-7211.
Marie Koplar, bd. chmn.; Edward Koplar, pres.; Barry Baker, sr. v.p. & dir. bdcst. div.; Gregory Filandrinos, dir. sls.; Larry Marcus, v.p. bus. affairs; James Wright, v.p., opns.; Denny Van Valkenburgh, nat'l sls. mgr.; Howard Stevens, prog. mgr.; nat'l rep.: Petry.
Operation: 1959; TV sets in area: 1,067,500.

KSDK (Channel 5) NBC
Multimedia Broadcasting Co. Div. Multimedia Inc., 1000 Market St., St. Louis, MO 63101 (314) 421-5055.
W. L. Bolster, v.p. & gen. mgr.; Wm. J. Katsafanas, gen. sls. mgr.; Edward J. Piette, dir. bdgst. opns.; Richard Brase, dir. creative svcs.; Maryanne Brandmeier, lcl. sls. mgr.; Terry Doll, dir. pub. rels.; Ron Turner, news dir.
Operation: 1947; TV households in area: 1,000,000.

KTVI (Channel 2) ABC
Times Mirror Broadcasting, 5915 Berthold Ave., St. Louis, MO 63110 (314) 647-2222.
John McCrory, pres.; Carson W. Capps, v.p. & gen. mgr.; Marshall W. Galliers, v.p. & sta. mgr.; V. Noble Redmon Jr., chief eng.; nat'l rep.: Harrington, Righter, & Parsons.
Operation: 1953; TV sets in area: 1,498,000.

Springfield

KDEB-TV (Channel 27) ABC
Woods Communications Group, Inc., 3000 Cherry St., Springfield, MO 65802 (417) 862-2727.
Charles Woods, pres.; Deborah Corbett, gen. mgr.; Rick Lipps, film buyer; Mike Scott, gen. sls. mgr.; Nancy Bingaman, prog. dir.; Paul Katona, chief eng.; nat'l rep.: Seltel.
Operation: 1968.

KOLR-TV (Channel 10) CBS
Independent Broadcasting Co., P.O. Box 1716 S.S.S., Springfield, MO 65805 (417) 862-1010.
J.H. Cooper, pres.; Ellis Shook, v.p. & gen. mgr.; John O. Cooper, treas.; Howard Frost, chief eng.; Bill Ferrell, gen. sls. mgr.; Al Riggs, lcl. sls. mgr.; nat'l rep., Katz.
Operation: 1953; TV sets in area: 494,300.

KSPR (Channel 33)
Telepictures Broadcasting KSPR Corp., 3754 S. Glenstone St., Springfield, MO 65804 (417) 887-1333.
Jack Stuart, gen. mgr.; Mike McMellon, opns. mgr.; Malcolm Hukriede, sls. mgr.; Paul Katona, chief eng.
Operation: January, 1983.

KYTV (Channel 3) NBC
KY-3, Inc., P.O. Box 3500, Springfield, MO 65808 (417) 866-2766.
Stanley M. Pederson, v.p. & gen. mgr.; Franklin D. Schurz, Jr., pres., Schurz Comm., Inc.
Operation: 1953; TV sets in area: 459,600.

MONTANA
Billings

KTVQ (Channel 2) CBS
SJL of Monta Ltd. Partnership, 3203 3rd Ave. N., P.O. Box 2557, Billings, MT (406) 252-5611.
Kelly Sugai, gen. mgr., sls. mgr. & film buyer; Lee Lareva, opers. dir.; Duane Grants, prod. mgr.; Ron Jacobson, chief eng.; nat'l rep.: Blair.
Operation: 1953; TV sets in area: 105,350.

KULR-TV (Channel 8) NBC
KULR Corp., P.O. Box 23909, Billings, MT 59104.
E. D. "Bob" Merrill, pres. & gen. mgr.
Operation: 1958; TV households: 100,300.

Butte

KTVM (Channel 6) ABC, NBC
(Satellite of KECI-TV, Missoula, MT)
Eagle Communications Inc., 750 Dewey Blvd., Butte MT 59701.
Bob Precht, chm.; Ann Ragsdale, v.p. & gen. mgr.; Larry Sem, sta. mgr.; Billy Ward, chief eng.

KXLF-TV (Channel 4) CBS
KXLF Communications, Inc., 1003 S. Montana St., Butte, MT 59701 (406) 792-9111.
Ron Cass, pres., gen. mgr., & nat'l sls. mgr.; Marla Wilkin, sls. mgr.; John Mizelle, chief eng.
Operation: 1953; TV households: 65,600.

Glendive

KXGN-TV (Channel 5) CBS, NBC
Glendive Broadcasting Corp., Broadcast Bldg., 210 South Douglas, Glendive, MT 59330 (406) 365-3377.
Lewis W. Moore, pres.; Dan Frenzel, mgr.; Mikel Huseby, chief eng.; Winnifred Norton, office mgr.
Operation: 1957.

Great Falls

KFBB-TV (Channel 5) ABC, NBC, CBS
KFBB Corp., P.O. Box 1139, Great Falls, MT (406) 453-4377.
Stan Whitman, gen. mgr.; Jack Fisher, gen. sls. mgr.; Ted Schroeder, ops./prog. mgr.; Don Ayers, prod./promo. mgr.; Joyce Stele, acct. supvr.; Ron Schlosser, chief eng.; Dick Pompa, news dir.; nat'l rep.: Katz.
Operation: 1954; TV homes in area: 92,700.

KRTV (Channel 3) CBS
KRTV Communications, Inc., P.O. Box 1331, Great Falls, MT 59403.
Peter B. Friden, pres.
Operation: 1958.

KTGF (Channel 16) NBC
Continental Television Network, Inc., 118 Sixth St., So., Great Falls, MT 59405 (406) 761-8816.

James M. Colla, pres. & gen. mgr.; Penny L. Adkins, corp. v.p. & prom. mgr.; Chuck Outland, gen. sls. mgr.; & prog. dir.; M. Thomas Beam, admin. asst.; Cheryl Cordeiro, compt.; natl. rep.: Seltel.
Operation: September, 1986.

Hardin

KOUS-TV (Channel 4) NBC
KOUS-TV, Inc., Drawer D. Hardin, MT (406) 665-3320.
Daniel W. Coon, pres.; Thom Curtis, gen. mgr.; Debbie Stoddard, prog. dir.; Vicki Stern, traffic mgr.; nat'l rep.: Seltel.
Operation: 1980.

Helena

KTVH-TV (Channel 12) NBC
KTVH, Inc., Box 6125, Helena, MT 59604 (406) 443-5050.
Bill Stebbins, lcl. sls. mgr.; Hal Peck, promo. mgr. & film buyer; rep.: Adam Young.
Operation: Jan., 1958; TV households; 91,200.

Kalispell

KCFW-TV (Channel 9) ABC, NBC
(Satellite of KECI-TV: Missoula, MT)
401 First Ave. E., P.O. Box 857, Kalispell, MT 59901.
Anne Ragsdale, v.p.-gen. mgr., Eagle Communications; Steve Fetueit, sta. mgr.; Mark Holston, news dir.; Mike Stocklin, sls. mgr.; Chris Neuhausen, chief eng.
Operation: June, 1968.

Miles City

KYUS-TV (Channel 3) ABC
KYUS-TV, Inc., Box 1074, Miles City, MT 59301 (406) 232-3540.
Daniel Coon, pres.; Dana L. Kehr, v.p. & gen. mgr.; J. R. Middleton, eng.
Operation: Sept., 1969.

Missoula

KECI-TV (Channel 13) ABC, NBC
Eagle Communications, 340 West Main, Missoula, MT (406) 721-2063.
Bob Precht, chmn.; Anne Ragsdale, v.p. & gen. mgr.; Jean Crepeau, prog. dir.; Sharikay Hettick, traffic dir.
TV households in area: 140,000 (ARB).

KPAX-TV (Channel 8) ABC, CBS
KPAX Communications, Inc., Box 4827, Missoula, MT 59801
Bill Sullivan, pres. gen. mgr. & natl. sls. mgr.; Bob Hermas, sls. mgr.; Mark Rapson, chief eng.
Operation: May, 1970.

NEBRASKA
Albion

KCAN-TV (Channel 8)
Amaturo Group, Inc., Rt. 1, Box 31A, Genoa, NE 68640.
Franny E. Brosseau, pres.; Wayne Lansche, gen. sls. mgr.
Operation: December, 1964.

Grand Island

KGIN-TV (Channel 11) CBS
Busse Bdcstg. Inc., Box 1069, Grand Island, NE 68801 (308) 382-6100.

Cal Coleman, gen. sls. mgr.; Laura Parks, news dir.; nat'l rep.: Avery-Knodel.
Operation: Oct., 1961.

Hastings

KHAS-TV (Channel 5) NBC
Nebraska Television Corp., Highway 281, Box 578, Hastings, NE 68901 (402) 463-1321.
John T. Benson, gen. mgr.; Donald R. Seaton, v.p.; James D. Conway, secty.-treas.; Randy Nicholson, film dir.; nat'l rep.: Seltel.
Operation: 1956; TV sets in area: 169,000.

Hayes Center

KWNB-TV (Channel 6) ABC
(Satellite of KHGI-TV, Kearney, NE)
Same personnel as KHGI-TV; nat'l rep.: Katz.
Operation: 1956; TV sets in area; 52,000.

Kearney

KHGI-TV (Channel 13) ABC
Gordon Bcstg., Inc., Box 220, Kearney, NE 68847; (308) 743-2494. (Also operates KWNB-TV, Hayes Center, NE; KSNB-TV, Superior, NE.)
Robert D. Gordon, pres. & gen. mgr.; Larry Landaker, v.p. sls.; Ron Tillery, v.p. opns. & film buyer; Mary Beth Richmond, promo. mgr.; Jerry Fuehrer, chief eng.; nat'l rep.: Katz.
Operation: 1953; TV households in area 615,800.

Lincoln

KOLN-TV/KGIN-TV (Channel 10) CBS
KOLN, Inc., Box 30350, Lincoln, NE 68503 (402) 467-4321.
Frank Jonas, pres. & gen. mgr.; Clyde Helton, gen. sls. mgr.; Lyle Kaufman, opns. mgr. & chief eng.; Robert Flinn, creative svcs. & prog. dir.; John Denney, news dir.; Christine McPike, contr.; natl. rep. MMT.
Operation: 1953; TV sets in area: 371,000.

McCook-Oberlin

KSNK (Channel 8) NBC
(Satellite of KARD-TV, Wichita, KS)
Kansas State Network Inc., P.O. Box 238, Oberlin, KS 67749.
Sherman Simpson, gen. mgr.; Gary Gore, gen. sls. mgr.; Bill Sykes, prog. dir.; rep.: Katz.
Operation: November, 1959.

North Platte

KNOP-TV (Channel 2) NBC
North Platte Television, Inc., Box 749, North Platte, NE 69101. (308) 532-2222.
Ulysses A. Carlini, gen. mgr.; Jodi Ritacca, news dir.; Chris Davies, chf. eng.
Operation: 1958.

Omaha

KETV (Channel 7) ABC
Channel 7, 27th & Douglas Sts., Omaha, NE 68131 (402) 345-7777.
John F. Carpenter, v.p. & gen. mgr.; Howard Shrier, sls. mgr.; Richard S. Spark, bus. mgr.; nat'l rep.: Blair TV.
Operation: 1957; TV sets in area: 578,100.

KMTV (Channel 3) CBS

Lee Enterprises, Inc., 10714 Mockingbird Dr., Omaha, NE 68131 (402) 592-3333.

Howard Kennedy, v.p. & gen. mgr., KMTV; Don Browers, prog. mgr.; Larry Steele, chief eng.; David Kuehn, gen. sls. mgr.; nat'l rep.: Katz.

Operation: 1949; TV sets in area: 415,000.

KPTM (Channel 42)

Pappas Telecasting of the Midlands, 4625 Farnam St., Omaha, NE 68132 (402) 558-4200.

Harry J. Pappas, pres. & gen. mgr.; Gary R. Nielsen, v.p. & sta. mgr.; Neil Schwartz, gen. mtkg. mgr.; Maureen Kelly, traf. mgr.; Susan Christensen, natl. mktg. mgr.; Jim McKernan, retail mktg. mgr.; Bruce Binenfeld, prom. mgr.; Marilyn Rothe, film dir.; Jace Anderson, prod. mgr.; Kevin Drewes, chief eng.; natl. rep.: Telerep.

Operation: April, 1986.

WOWT (Channel 6) CBS

3501 Farnam St., Omaha, NE 68131 (402) 346-6666.

James H. Smith, pres. & gen. mgr.; Don Grubaugh, v.p. & sls. mgr.; John Dixon, prog. dir.; Steve Murphy, news dir.; Judy Horan, dir. promo. & merch.; Bruce Lee, lcl-reg. sls. mgr.; nat'l rep.: Petry.

Operation: 1949; TV sets in area 573,900.

Scottsbluff

KDUH-TV (Channel 4) NBC

Duhamel Bcstg. Enterprises, 1523 1st Ave., Scottsbluff, NE 69341 (308) 632-3071.

William F. Duhamel, pres.; Jerry Dishong, gen. mgr.; Wes Haugan, gen. sls. mgr.; Monte Loos, prog. dir., prom. mgr. & film buyer; Richard Rose, news dir.; Dale Brye, chief eng.; nat'l rep.: Katz.

Operation: March, 1958.

KSTF (Channel 10) CBS

(Satellite of KGWN-TV, Cheyenne, WY.)

Stauffer Comm., Inc., 2923 E. Lincolnway, Cheyenne, WY (307) 634-7755.

Carl J. Occhipinti, gen. mgr.; Timothy H. Daniels, res. mgr.; Tony Schaeffer, chief eng.; nat'l rep.: Katz.

Operation: 1955.

Superior

KSNB-TV (Channel 4) ABC

(Satellite of KHGI-TV, Kearney, NE.)

Same personnel as KHGI-TV.; nat'l rep.: Katz.

Operation: October, 1965.

NEVADA
Henderson-Las Vegas

KVVU-TV (Channel 5)

KVVU Broadcasting Corp., 25 TV5 Drive, Henderson, NV 89014 (702) 435-5555.

William C. McReynolds, pres.; Rusty Durante, gen. mgr.; Bill Utton, gen. sls. mgr.; Jack Smith, dir. of eng.

Operation: Sept., 1967; TV households: 155,000.

Las Vegas

KLAS-TV (Channel 8) CBS

3228 Channel 8 Dr., P.O. Box 15047, Las Vegas, NV 89114 (702) 733-8850.

Wayne Simmons, v.p./gen. mgr.; Carole Henderson, gen. sls. mgr.; Tony Malone, loc. sls. mgr.; Greg Carroll, promo. mgr; John Nelson, chief eng.; nat'l rep.: Katz Television.

Operation: 1953; TV sets in area: 213,000.

KRLR (Channel 21)

Dres Media, Inc., Box 26815, Las Vegas, NV 89126; (702) 382-2121.

Charlene Scott, pres.; Rick Scott, gen. mgr.; Carol Patton, sls. mgr.; Wayne Cartley, prog. dir.; Gigi Koury, promo. mgr.; Steve Scott, chief eng.

Operation: July, 1984.

KTNV-TV (Channel 13) ABC

KTNV-TV, 3355 S. Valley View, Las Vegas, NV 89102 (702) 876-1313.

Jim Behling, v.p. & gen. mgr.; Gary Plumlee, gen. sls. mgr.; Tim Foster, nat'l sls. mgr.; Stormi Lloyd-Drake, prog. dir.; Ron Futrell, sports dir.; Michael Williams, production mgr.; Steve Minium, news dir.; Terry Ostlund, chief eng.; William A. Kellogg, controller; Phyllis Gemma, promotions mgr.

Operation: 1956; TV households: TSA 682,600.

KVBC (Channel 3) NBC

Valley Broadcasting Co., Box 44169, Las Vegas, NV 89116 (702) 649-0500.

Rolla D. Cleaver, gen. mgr.; Buzz Floyd, prog. mgr.; nat'l rep.: Blair TV.

Operation: 1955.

Reno

KAME-TV (Channel 21)

Page Enterprises, P.O. Box 11129, Reno, NV 89510 (702) 786-2121.

Bill Andrews, pres. & gen.mgr.; Mike Andrews, sls. mgr.; B.J. Andrews, sta. mgr.; Maggie Verhoef, prog. dir.; Al Ruch, chief eng.; nat'l rep.: Seltel.

Operation: October, 1981.

KCRL-TV (Channel 4) NBC

Circle L. Inc., 1790 Vassar St., Reno, NV 89510 (702) 322-9145.

Edward Neuhoff, pres.; Jim Elliott, v.p. & gen. mgr.; John Firpo, news dir.; Norvel Seyler, chief eng.; rep.: MMT

Operation: 1962; TV households: 166,600.

KOLO-TV (Channel 8) ABC

Donrey of Nevada, Box 10,000, Reno, NV 89510 (702) 786-8880.

Fred Smith, pres.; James C. Herzig. gen. mgr.; Jack Hartman, gen. sales mgr.; John Csia, prog. mgr.; Earl Ling, promo. dir.; Robert Northam, chief eng.; nat'l rep.: Blair.

Operation: 1953; TV sets in area: 234,000.

KREN-TV (Channel 27)

Sainte Limited, P.O. Box 4159, Modesto, CA 95352-4159 (209) 523-0777.

Chester Smith, gen. partner; Herbert G. Crenshaw, eng.

Operation: November, 1985.

KTVN (Channel 2) CBS

Sarkes Tarzian, Inc., 4925 Energy Way, Reno, NV 89502 (702) 786-2212.

Dennis Slewert, gen. mgr; John Richardson, sta. & gen. sls. mgr.; Al Richards, chief eng.; Matt James, news editor; rep.: Katz.

Operation: 1967; TV households: 161,000.

NEW HAMPSHIRE
Concord

WNHT (Channel 21)
The Flatley Co., Box 2100, Concord, NH 03301 (603) 225-2100.
Thomas J. Flatley, pres.; Ronald Polera, gen. mgr.; Bob Joyce, prog. dir.; R. Gregg Chadwick, chief eng.
Operation: April, 1984.

Derry

WNDS (Channel 50)
CTV of Derry, Inc., TV-50 Place, Derry, NH 03038 (603) 434-8050.
James L. Lannin, gen. mgr.; Kent Ohlman, prod. & promo. mgr.; Brooke Willis, news dir.; Paul Hunter, chief eng.
Operation: September, 1983.

Manchester

WMUR-TV (Channel 9) ABC
WMUR, Inc., 1819 Elm St., Manchester, NH 03104 (603) 623-8061.
J.A. Simms, gen. mgr.; Pete Morrison, news dir.; nat'l rep.; Seltel.
Operation: 1954; TV sets in area: 965,576.

NEW JERSEY
Atlantic City

WWAC-TV (Channel 53)
Channel 53 Corp., 3600 Conshohocken Ave., Philadelphia, PA 19131 (215) 473-9060.
William S. Gross, owner.
Operation: February, 1988.

Vineland

WHSP (Channel 65)
Silver King Bdcstg. of Vineland, Inc., 4449 N. Delsea Dr., Newfield, NJ 08344 (609) 691-6565.
Carmen J. Colucci, gen. mgr.; Brian Eckert, prog. & news dir.; Dan Merlo, chief eng.
Operation: July, 1981.

Wildwood

WMGM-TV (Channel 40) NBC
South Jersey Broadcasting Corp., 15 Shore Rd., Linwood, NJ 08221 (609) 927-4440.
Howard Green, pres.; Jane B. Stark, sta. mgr. & gen. sls. mgr.; Kim Dougherty, prgm. prod. mgr.; Michael Schurman, news dir.
Operation: 1966; TV households: 400,000.

NEW MEXICO
Albuquerque

KGGM-TV (Channel 13) CBS
New Mexico Broadcasting Co., Inc., 1414 Coal Ave., S.W., Albuquerque, NM 87104 (505) 243-2285.
Bruce A. Hebenstreit, pres.; Paul Thorne, v.p. & sls. mgr.; Jack Mahoney, gen. mgr.; Brenda Yager, promo. dir.; Dick Doyle, chief eng.; Bud Holgerson, operations mgr.

KGSW (Channel 14)
Mountain States Broadcasting/Providence Journal Broadcasting, Box 25200, Albuquerque, NM 87125 (505) 842-1414.

Erick B. Steffens, gen. mgr.; Shirley Mix, sls. mgr.; Dudley Bullock, chief eng.; nat'l rep.: Seltel.
Operation: 1981

KNAT (Channel 23)
Trinity Bcstg. of Arizonia, Inc., 1510 Coors Blvd., N.W., Albuquerque, NM 87105 (505) 836-1992.
Bob Brewer, v.p. & gen. mgr.; Dave Cavileer, gen. sls. mgr.; Sandie Zolman, prog. dir.; Bill Frost, chief eng.
Operation: 1975.

KOAT-TV (Channel 7) ABC
KOAT-TV, Inc., Box 25982, Albuquerque, NM 87125 (505) 884-7777.
Max A. Sklower, gen. mgr.; Elvin Smith, nat'l sls. & op. mgr.; James Sharman, chief eng.; Monty Salisbury, news dir.; nat'l rep.: Blair.
Operation: 1953, TV homes in area: 276,000.

KOB-TV (Channel 4) NBC
Hubbard Broadcasting, Inc., 4 Broadcast Plaza, S.W., Albuquerque, NM (505) 243-4411.
Stanley S. Hubbard, pres.; Jerry Danziger, gen. mgr.; Dave Herman, sta. mgr.; Bob Evans, sls. mgr.; Sam Tikkanen, chief eng.; nat'l rep.: Edward Petry Co.
Operation: 1948; TV sets in area: 442,700.

Carlsbad

KVIO-TV (Channel 6) ABC
Marsh Media of El Paso, Box 12077, Texas American Bank Bldg., Amarillo, TX 79101 (806) 372-5555.
Doyle Hadden, gen. mgr.; Robert Lancaster, chief eng.
Operation: 1956; TV sets in area: 15,600.

Clovis

KVIH-TV (Channel 12) ABC
One Broadcast Center, Amarillo, TX 79101 (806) 373-7787
James R. McCormick, pres. & gen. mgr.; John Patrick, gen. sls. mgr.; Mac Douglas, prog. dir. & film buyer; John McKissack, news dir.; Bill Canady, chief eng.; natl. rep.: Katz.
Operation: December, 1957.

Farmington

KOBF (Channel 12) NBC
P.O. Box 1620, Farmington, NM 87499 (505) 326-1141.
Bettie Cleveland, gen. mgr.; Bill Hirshey, prod. mgr.; Dan Bibeau, chief eng.
Operation 1972.

Las Cruces

KASK (Channel 48)
Las Cruces Full Power Television, Inc., 900 First National Tower, Las Cruces, NM 88001 (505) 524-2103.
Logan D. Matthews, pres. & gen. mgr.; Albert F. Gabalis, gen. sls. mgr.; Christopher Jackson, opns. mgr.; Gary Worth, news dir.; Keith Peterson, chief eng.; nat'l rep.: Spot Time.
Operation: October, 1984.

Roswell

KBIM-TV (Channel 10) CBS
Caprock Telecasting, Inc., Box 910, Roswell, NM 88201 (505) 622-2120.
Joseph A. Carriere, pres.; Marc Reischman, sta. mgr.; E.C. Rader, dir. of eng.; Dave Brown, v.p., news; nat'l rep.: Katz.
Operation: 1966; TV homes: 113,300.

KOBR (Channel 8) NBC

Hubbard Bdcstg., Inc., 124 E. Fourth St., Roswell, NM 88201 (505) 625-8888.

Stanley S. Hubbard, pres.; John Amodeo, sta. mgr.; Larry Oldrup, gen. sls. mgr.; Julie Roberts, news dir.; Dave Atkins, chief eng.; natl. rep.: Petry.

Operation: June, 1953.

Santa Fe

KCHF (Channel 11)

Son Broadcasting, Inc., Box 4338, Albuquerque, NM 87106 (505) 983-1111.

Belarmino R. Gonzales, pres. & gen. mgr.; Susan Stein, gen. sls. mgr.; Mary Kay Gonzales, opns. & promo. mgr.; Luther Kent, chief eng.

Operation: November, 1983.

KNMZ-TV (Channel 2)

Coronado Communications, Co., P.O. Box 580, Santa Fe, NM 87504 (505) 473-2002.

Carl F. Floyd, v.p., gen. mgr.; Eva Lopez, prog. dir.; Cassie Travaini, gen. sls. mgr.

Operation: October, 1983.

Silver City

KWNM-TV (Channel 10) ABC

Box 25982 Albuquerque, NM 87125 (505) 884-7777.

Fred J. Steurer, v.p., eng.; natl. rep.: Blair.

NEW YORK

Albany

WNYT (Channel 13) NBC

Viacom Broadcasting Corp., P.O. Box 4035, Albany, NY 12204 (518) 436-4791.

Donald D. Perry, v.p. & gen. mgr.; Richard Klein, chief eng.; James Moore, dir. prod.; Noelle Wall, promo dir.; Stephen Baboulis, news dir.; Tom Raponi, gen. sls. mgr.; Robert Gilbert, natl sls. mgr.; Linda Cummings, traffic mgr.; Thomas Blau, bus. mgr.; Douglas Jones, dir. prog. & pub. aff.

Operation: 1954.

WRGB (Channel 6) CBS

WRGB Bdcstg., Inc., 1400 Balltown Rd., Schenectady, NY 12309; (518) 346-6666.

David Lynch, v.p. & gen. mgr.; Terry Walden, mgr. prog.; Beverly Wittner, mgr. pub. affairs; Gary Whitaker, news. dir.; William Brandt, mgr., prom.

Operation: 1947.

WTEN (Channel 10)

Knight-Ridder Broadcasting Company, Incorporated, 341 Northern Blvd., Albany, NY 12204 (518) 436-4822.

Don C. Smith, pres. & gen. mgr.; John Hirsh, gen. sls. mgr.; Judy Seabridge, opns. mgr.; James Holland, news dir

WUSV (Channel 45)

Union St. Video, Inc., 165 Freemans Bridge Rd., Scotia, NY 12302; (518) 346-4545.

Keith Wheeler, pres.; Willard J. Stone, gen. mgr.; Jonathan Miles, news dir.; James Grich, chief eng.; rep.: ITS.

Operation: 1984.

WXXA-TV (Channel 23)

Albany TV 23, Inc., P.O. Box 6423, Albany, NY 12206 (518) 438-8700.

James Boaz, pres., gen. mgr. & prog. dir.; David Low, gen. sls. mgr. & sta. mgr.; Janet Gray, prom. mgr.; Catherine Castracane, bus. mgr.; Sargent Cathrall, chief eng.; natl rep.: Petry.

Operation: July, 1982.

Binghamton

WBNG-TV (Channel 12) CBS

Gateway Communications, Inc., 50 Front Street, Binghamton, NY 13902 (607) 723-7311.

John S. Mucha, v.p. & gen. mgr.; Mark Prutisto, prog. mgr.; Joseph McNamara, gen. sls. mgr.; Ronald Shoemaker, chief eng.

WICZ-TV (Channel 40)

Stainless, Inc., 70 Henry St., Binghamton, NY 13902 (607) 723-8251.

Jesse Pevear, v.p. & gen. mgr.; G. Ricciardelli, tech. dir.; natl rep.: MMT.

WMGC-TV (Channel 34) ABC

Citadel Communications, Ltd., Box 813, Binghamton, NY 13902.

Philip J. Lombardo, mng. gen. partner, gen. mgr.; Brad Worthen, gen. sls. mgr.; Mary Ann Connerton, lcl. sls. mgr.; M. Susan Boncek, bus. mgr.; Darcy Thorton, news dir.; natl rep.: Katz.

Operation: 1962; TV households: 171,000.

Buffalo

WGRZ-TV (Channel 2) NBC

WGRZ-TV, Inc., 259 Delaware Ave., Buffalo, NY 14202 (716) 856-1414.

Richard Tarr, pres.; Lyn P. Stoyer, sr. v.p. & gen. mgr.; Raymond P. Maselli, v.p. & gen. mgr.; Sue Pearce, v.p. & bus. mgr.; Tom Cochran, lcl. sls. mgr.; Joe Rape, prog. & mktg. mgr.; Pam Curtis, prom. mgr.; Gary Legters, opns. mgr.; Tim Rudell, news dir.; Richard Westlund, chief eng.; Joe Lentini, dir. community reltns.; natl rep.: TeleRep.

Operation: August, 1954.

WIVB-TV (Channel 4) CBS

Buffalo Broadcasting Co., Inc., 2077 Elmwood Ave., Buffalo, NY 14207; (716) 874-4410.

Leslie G. Arries, Jr., pres.; John Hayes, sta. mgr.; Wilson Shepard, gen. sls. mgr.; Ralph Thompsom, dir. of eng. natl rep.: Harrington, Righter & Parsons, Inc.

Operation: 1948; TV households in area: 1,038,700; U.S. & Canada: 2,700,300.

WKBW-TV (Channel 7)

WKBW-TV, Queen City Bdcstg., Inc., 7 Broadcast Plaza, Buffalo, NY 14202.

Steve Kimatian, v.p. & gen. mgr.; Clifford Fisher, gen. sales mgr.; Rom Martzolf, program mgr.; Don Holland, chief engineer; rep.: Blair TV.

Operation: 1958.

WNBY-TV (Channel 49)

Aud Enterprises, Inc., 699 Hertal Ave., Buffalo, NY 14207 (716) 875-4919.

Paul A. Mooney, pres.; Bill Saltzgiver, gen. mgr.; Linda Lynch, gen. sls. mgr.; Joe Cayton, prog. dir.; Rick Mortellaro, prom. mgr.; Mike Anger, chief eng.; natl. rep.; Seltel.

Operation: September, 1987.

WUTV (Channel 29)

Citadel Communications Co., Ltd., 951 Whitehaven Rd., Grand Island, NY 14072 (716) 773-7531

Philip J. Lombardo, pres.; Frank B. Gregg, v.p. & gen. mgr.; Dennis Majewicz, chief eng.; Ken Kaszubowski, mgr. bdcst. opns.; Tony McMahon, gen. sls. mgr.; Lois M. Ringle, prog. dir.

Operation: December, 1970; TV households: 1,213,100.

Carthage-Watertown

WWNY-TV (Channel 7) CBS, NBC

United Communication Corp., 120 Arcade St., Watertown, NY 13601 (315) 788-3800.

Howard J. Brown, pres.; Eugene W. Schulte, v.p.; Kevin Mastellon, gen. mgr.; Ed Dempsey, sls. mgr.; Lois Dempster, prog. dir.; Don Rohr, chief eng.; nat'l rep.: Katz TV.

Operation: 1954; TV sets in area: 156,920.

Elmira

WENY-TV (Channel 36) ABC

WENY, Inc., P.O. Box 208, Elmira, NY 14902 (707) 739-3636.

Howard L. Green, exec. v.p.; Patrick M. Parish, gen. mgr.; Meade Murtland, sta. mgr.; Conrad Schwenzer, dir. of eng.

Operation: Nov., 1969.

WETM-TV (Channel 18) NBC

(Satellite of WSTM-TV, Syracuse, NY)

WETM-TV, Inc., Box 1207, Elmira, NY 14902 (607) 733-5518.

Robert N. Smith, pres.; John Wingate, v.p. & gen. mgr.; Larry Taylor, chief eng.

Operation: 1956; TV sets in area: 83,600.

New York City

WABC-TV (Channel 7) ABC

Capital Cities/ABC, Inc., 7 Lincoln Square, New York, NY 10023 (212) 887-7777.

Walter C. Liss, Jr., pres. & gen. mgr.; Tom Kane, gen. sls. mgr.; Brooke Bailey-Johnson, pgm. dir.; Cliff Love, editorial dir.; Howard Rothstein, bus. mgr.; Kimball Howell, dir. of creative services; James Baker, chief eng.

Operation: 1948; TV sets in area: 6,000,000.

WCBS-TV (Channel 2) CBS

CBS Television Stations, Division of Columbia Broadcasting System, Inc., 524 W. 57 St., New York, NY 10019 (212) 975-4321.

Neil E. Derrough, pres.; Roger Colloff, v.p. & gen. mgr.; Robert Fogarty, sls. dir.; Dolores Danska, dir. bcstg.; Bill Lacey, dir. bcst. admin.; Steve Wasserman, news dir.; Toni Johnson, opns. mgr.

Operation: 1941; TV sets in area: 6,000,000.

WNBC-TV (Channel 4) NBC

WNBC-TV, 30 Rockefeller Plaza, New York, NY 10112 (212) 664-4444.

Carl V. Bud Carey, v.p. & gen. mgr.; Karen Lee Copeland, prog. dir.; Lou Abitabilo, dir. sls.; Linda Lipman, dir. adv. & promo.; Dave Vacheron, mgr. bdcst. standards; Julian Phillips, mgr. community relns.

Operation: 1941; TV sets in area: 6,000,000.

WNYW-TV (Channel 5) FOX

Fox TV Stations, Inc., 205 E. 67 St., New York, NY 10021 (212) 535-1000.

Kevin O'Brien, gen. mgr.; Charles Meehan, v.p. & gen. sls. mgr.; Robert Friedman, prog. dir.; John Parsons Peditto, news dir., William Kelly, v.p. & chief eng.; nat'l rep.: Katz.

Operation: 1944; TV households in area: 6,471,396.

WWOR-TV (Channel 9) Secaucus, NJ

MCA Bdcstg., Inc., 445 Park Ave., New York, NY 10022 (212) 564-8000.

Bob Kuneth, v.p. & gen. mgr.; Thomas Ryan, v.p./gen. sls. mgr.; Farrell Meiser, prog. dir.; Tom Petner, news dir. Cam Pardo, bus. mgr.

WPIX (Channel 11)

WPIX Inc., 11 WPIX Plaza, New York, NY 10017; (212) 949-1100.

Leavitt J. Pope, pres.; David Polinge, sr. v.p. asst. to pres.; Gerald Mulderring, sr. v.p. sls.; Otis Freeman, sr. v.p., eng.; John Corporon, sr. v.p. news; Pat Austin, sr. v.p., finance; Julie Nunnari, v.p. prog.; Paul Bisonette, v.p. creative svcs.; Liz Goldberg, v.p. opns.; Bob Murch, v.p., eng.; Fred Witte, contr.; Jane Perlman, v.p. rsrch.; Claudia Gasparini, v.p., human resources; Martin Appel, v.p. sports & pub. reltns.; Don Carney, v.p. spts. & spec. events; Kathleen Shepherd, v.p. prod. & community affairs; Laurence Linehan, Gerard Puccio, John McGowan, v.p., sls.

Operation: 1948; TV households in area: 6,878,000 (ARB).

New York-Newark (NJ)

WNJU-TV (Channel 47)

47 Industrial Ave., Newark, NJ 07608 (201) 288-5550.

Carlos Barba, pres. & gen. mgr.; Thomas Johansen, v.p. & sls. dir.; Julio Omana, sta. mgr.; George Kraus, v.p., sta. mgr. & chief eng.; Sylvia Pascual, prog. dir.

Operation: May, 1965; TV households: 2,300,000.

WWHT-TV (Channel 68/60)

WWHT, Inc., 390 W. Market St., Newark, NJ 07107.

Herb Lefkowitz, gen. mgr.; Joe Giardina, v.p. of engineering; Lia Afriat, mgr. of programming.

Operation: July, 1977.

New York-Paterson (NJ)

WXTV (Channel 41)

Spanish International Communications Corp., 24 Meadowland Parkway, Secaucus, NJ 07094.

Ivan Egas, gen. mgr.; George Kraus, chief eng.; rep.: Blair TV.

Operation: 1968.

Plattsburgh-Burlington (VT)

WPTZ (Channel 5) NBC

Rollins Telecasting Inc., P.O. Box 647, Atlanta, GA 30301.

W. P. Eaton, Jr., gen. mgr.; Lincoln Dixon, chief eng.; nat'l rep.: Blair Television.

Operation: 1956; TV homes in area: 252,600 (U.S.); 954,880 (Canada).

Poughkeepsie

WTBY (Channel 54)

Trinity Broadcasting of New York, Box 534, Fishkill, NY 12524 (914) 896-4610.

Paul Crouch, pres. & gen. mgr.; Stan Hollin, gen. sls. mgr.; Terry Hickey, prog. dir. & film buyer; Lindy Dressler, promo. mgr.; Dale Osborn, chief eng.

Operation: April, 1981.

Riverhead

WLIG (Channel 55)
WLIG-TV 55, Inc. 300 Crossways Park, Drive, Woodbury, NY 11797 (516) 364-1500.
Michael C. Pascucci, pres.; Marvin R. Chauvin, v.p. & gen. mgr.; Robert Bee, gen. sls. mgr.; Bruce David Klein, prog. dir.
Operation: January, 1985.

Rochester

WHEC-TV (Channel 10) CBS
WHEC, Inc., 191 East Avenue, Rochester, NY 14604 (716) 546-5670.
Arnold Klinsky, v.p. & gen. mgr.; Alan Cartwright, sls. dir.; John Walsh, chief eng.; Al Holzer, news dir.; nat'l rep.: Telerep.
Operation: 1953; TV sets in area, 453,500.

WOKR (Channel 13) ABC
WOKR Partners, 4225 W. Henrietta Rd., Rochester, NY 14623 (716) 334-8700.
Vincent T. DeLuca, pres./gen. mgr.; Donald J. Loy, prog. dir.-creative svcs.; Margaret Camera, controller; Clyde Parker, eng. mgr.; Kent Beckwith, gen. sls. mgr.; Jim Sanders, nat'l sls. mgr.; nat'l rep.: MMT.
Operation: 1962; TV households: 1,191,800.

WROC-TV (Channel 8) NBC
Television Station Partners, 201 Humboldt St., Rochester, NY 14610 (716) 288-8400.
Thomas F. Kenney, v.p. & gen. mgr.; Geoff Proud, nat'l sls. mgr.; Alicia Rodriguez, prog. mgr.; Jeff Ulrich, prom. mgr.; David Nolan, news dir.; John Coon, chief eng.
Operation: 1949; TV sets in area: 479,000.

WUHF (Channel 31) FOX
Mairite TV of New York, Inc., 360 East Ave., Rochester, NY 14604 (716) 232-3700.
Milton Matitz, chm.; Rick Rambaldo, v.p. & gen. mgr.; nat'l rep.: Blair TV.
Operation: 1980.

Smithtown

WHSI-TV (Channel 67)
Silver King Bcstg. of New Jersey, Inc. 390 West Market St., Newark NJ 07107; (516) 360-0771.
Ella Connors, sta. mgr.; Bill Roller, prog. mgr.; John Neuhaus, chief eng.
Operation: November, 1973.

Syracuse

WIXT-TV (Channel 9) ABC
WIXT-TV, Inc., 5904 Bridge St., East Syracuse, NY 13057 (315) 446-4780.
Steve Kronquest, v.p. & gen. mgr.; Angela Roach, nat'l sls. mgr.; John King, chief eng.
Operation: 1962.

WSTM-TV (Channel 3) NBC
WSTM-TV, Inc., 1030 James St., Syracuse, NY 13203 (315) 474-5100.
Ronald W. Philips, pres. & gen. mgr.; William P. McManus, gen. sls. mgr.; Nancy DeMartino, creative svcs. dir.
Operation: 1950; TV sets in area: 525,000.

WSYT (Channel 68) FOX
1000 James St., Syracuse, NY, 93203 (315) 472-6800.
Vincent Arminio, gen. mgr.; Thomas Disinger, sta. mgr.; Rick Herrmann, prom. dir.; Rick Finnie, chief eng.; natl. rep.: Seltel.
Operation: February, 1986.

WTVH-TV (Channel 5) CBS basic
Meredith Corp. 980 James St., Syracuse, NY 13203 (315) 425-5555.
Larry Rhodes, v.p. & gen. mgr.; Robert Stettner, gen. sls. mgr.; Edward F. Merritt, dir. of eng.; nat'l rep.: MMT Sales Inc.
Operation: 1948 as WHEN-TV; TV sets in area: 480,000.

Utica

WKTV (Channel 2) NBC
Harron Communications Corp., P.O. Box 2, Utica, NY 13503 (315) 733-0404.
Shell Storrier, sr. v.p. & gen. mgr.; Paul Harron, Jr., pres.; Daniel German, program. dir. & promo. mgr. & film dir.; Marie Zumpano, traffic mgr.; Merv Ainsworth, chief eng.; nat'l rep.: Katz.
Operation: 1949; TV homes in area: 340,100.

WTUV (Channel 33) FOX
Mohawk Valley Bdcstg., Inc., Greenfield Rd., Rome, NY 13440 (315) 337-3300.
Craig Fox, Joel Friedman, Kevin O'Kane, owners.
Operations: October, 1986.

WUTR (Channel 20) ABC
Roy H. Park Bcstg. of Utica-Rome Inc., P.O. Box 20, Utica, NY 13503 (315) 797-5220.
Roy H. Park, pres.; Paul Kennedy, gen. mgr.; rep.: Blair.
Operation: Feb., 1970.

Watertown

SFYF (Channel 50)
Moreland Broadcast Associates, Box 6250, Watertown, NY 13601.
David J. Altieri, gen. mgr.
Operation: December, 1986.

NORTH CAROLINA
Asheville

WHNS-TV (Channel 21)
Pappas Telecasting of the Carolinas, 521 College Ave., Asheville, NC 28813; (704) 258-2100.
Harry J. Pappas, pres.; Joseph A. Shaffer, v.p.-gen. mgr.; Henry Boyce, prog. mgr.; Tom Post, gen. sls. mgr.; Steve Crook, dir. eng.
Operation: 1964; TV sets in area: 625,000.

WLOS-TV (Channel 13) ABC
WLOS TV, Inc., Box 1300, Asheville, NC 28802 (704) 255-0013. 105 N. Spring St., P.O. Box 2666, Greenville, SC 29602 (803) 271-1313.
Michael J. Fiorile, v.p. & gen. mgr.; Cliff Pine, prog. mgr.; Ken Glover, gen. sls. mgr.; Bill Walsh, bus. mgr.; nat'l rep.: HRP.
Operation: 1954; TV households in area: 1,254,300 TSA.

Belmont

WJZY (Channel 46)
Metro-Crescent Communications, Inc., Box 668400, Charlotte, NC 28266-8400.; 3501 Performance Red., Charlotte, NC 28214 (704) 398-0046.
Loretta Webber, pres.; Mark Conrad, gen. mgr.; Thomas Schenk, natl. sls. mgr.; Dale Synder, prog. dir.; Jan Bailey-Sugg, lcl. sls. mgr.; Kip Cozart, prom. mgr.; Ed Merritt, chief eng.; natl. rep.: Seltel.
Operation: March, 1987.

Burlington

WRDG (Channel 16)
Box 16, Burlington, NC 27215 (919) 376-9868.
Jack Rehburg, pres.; Steve Rehburg, gen. mgr. & prom.-adv. mgr.
Operations: August, 1984.

Charlotte

WBTV (Channel 3) CBS
Jefferson Pilot Broadcasting Co., One Julian Price Place, Charlotte, NC 28208 (704) 374-3500.
Joseph M. Bryan, chm. bd.; Wallace J. Jorgenson, pres.; James G. Babb, Jr., exec. v.p.; Cullie M. Tareton, sr. v.p. & gen. mgr.; William F. Foy, news and info. mgr.; Marion Meginnis, program oprs. mgr.; Joseph B. McCoy III, gen. sls. mgr.; George K. Reynolds, tech. op. mgr.; Paul Cameron, sports dir.; Mrs. Tommi L. Jones, v.p./personnel; Joseph B. Young, v.p./ research & planning; George B. Grills, Jr., dir. of eng.; Larry M. Harding, v.p./public aff.
Operation: 1949; TV sets in area; 1,150,540.

WCCB-TV (Channel 18)
WCCB-TV, Inc., 1 Television Place, Charlotte, NC 28205 (704) 372-1800.
Cy N. Bahakel, pres.; Steven Soldinger, gen. mgr.; William Riordan, gen sls mgr.; Howard Trivette, prog. dir.; Robert Phillips, chief eng.; nat'l rep.: Katz.
Operation: Dec., 1953.

WPCQ-TV (Channel 36)
Channel 36 Partners, Channel 36, Inc., General Partner, P.O. Box 18665, Charlotte, NC 28218 (704) 536-3636.
Jeff B. Davidson, v.p. & gen. mgr.; Tim Bloodworth, prog. dir.; Rick Anderson, chief eng.; Richard Herd, gen. sls. mgr.
Operation: 1967; TV households: 2,165,200.

WSOC-TV (Channel 9) ABC
Carolina Broadcasting Company, P.O. Box 34665, Charlotte, NC 28234 (704) 335-4999.
Grey Stone, v.p., gen. mgr.; Jack Callaghan, sta. mgr.; Merritt Rose, gen. sls. mgr.; Martin Fenton, lcl. sls. mgr.; A. Bruce Chastine, contr.; Alan Batten, dir., adv./promo.; Richard Moore, news dir.; Merle Thomas, chief eng.; nat'l rep.: Telerep.
Operation: 1957; TV sets in area. 2,892,800.

Durham

WTVD (Channel 11) ABC
Capital Cities/ABC, Inc., Box 2009, 411 Liberty St., Durham, NC 27702 (919) 683-1111.
Alan Nesbitt, pres./gen. mgr.; Denis O'Connor, gen. sls. mgr.; Jon L. Miller, prog. mgr.; Chrystle Swain, dir. of community affairs.; Dave Davis, news dir.; William Higgs, bus. mgr.; Edward Wall, chief eng.
Operation: 1954; TV homes in area: 621,000 (ADI).

Durham-Raleigh

WPTF-TV (Channel 28) NBC
Durham Life Broadcasting Service, Inc., 29521, 3012 Highwoods Blvd., Raleigh, NC 27604 (919) 832-8311.
Felton P. Coley, pres.; William M. Dunaway, v.p. & gen. mgr.; Robert Wolfe, prog. dir.; Christy Hinson, promo. mgr.; Kevin Kelly, news dir.; nat'l rep.: Blair.
Operation: November, 1968; TV households, 598,000.

Fayetteville

WFCT (Channel 62)
Fayetteville Cumberland Telecasters, Inc., Drawer 62, Lumber Bridge, Fayetteville, NC 28357 (919) 843-3884.
John Bishop , v.p. & gen. mgr.; Bob Peretic, dir. sls.; Ernie Whitmeyer, prog. opns.; George Johnson, chief eng.; nat'l rep.: Adam Young.
Operation: March, 1985.

WKFT (Channel 40)
SJL of No. Carolina Associates, 230 Donaldson St., Fayetteville, NC 28301 (919) 323-4040.
Richard Armfield, gen. mgr.; Jerry K. Moore, sta. mgr.
Operation: 1981.

Greensboro

WFMY-TV (Channel 2) CBS
WFMY Television Corp., P.O. Box TV2, Greensboro, NC 27420 (919) 379-9639.
Mike Conly, v.p. & gen. mgr.; Jack Foreitand, prog. dir.; nat'l rep.: Blair
Operation: 1949; TV homes in area: 797,800.

WGGT (Channel 48)
Guilford Telecasters, Inc., 330 S. Greene St., Greensboro, NC 27401 (919) 274-4848.
Eugene Bohi, pres. & gen. mgr.; Norm Cissna, gen. sls. mgr.; Kenneth Gonzalez, dir.-prog., opns.; Robert Juelich, promo. dir.; nat'l rep.: Petry.
Operation: May, 1981.

WLXI-TV (Channel 61)
Box TV-61, Greensboro, NC 27420 (919) 855-5610.
Gary S. Smithwick, pres.; Richard C. Snowden, gen. mgr.; Jeff Johnson, prog. dir.
Operation: January, 1983.

Greenville

WNCT-TV (Channel 9) CBS
Roy A. Park Broadcasting, Inc., P.O. Box 898, Greenville, NC 27834 (919) 756-3180.
Roy H. Park, bd. chm.; Mrs. Dorothy D. Park, secretary; K. B. Skinner, dir.; Randall Stair, v.p. & treas.; Wright M. Thomas, pres.; Edward J. Adams, v.p.-gen. mgr.; Luther Griffin, gen. sls. mgr.; Herb Grady, prod. mgr.; Shirley Dale, prog. mgr.; Heber Adams, chief eng.; nat'l rep.: Blair TV.
Operation: 1953; TV sets in area: 476,300.

Hickory

WHKY-TV (Channel 14)
The Long Family Partnership, Box 1059, Hickory, NC 28603 (704) 322-5115.
Thomas E. Long, gen. mgr.; Jeffrey B. Long, sta. mgr.; nat'l sls. mgr.; Jim Carr, sls. mgr.; Frank Jones, news dir.; JuJu

Phillips, sports dir.; Lynne Critcher, traffic mgr.
Operation: 1968; TV households: 125,700.

High Point

WGHP-TV (Channel 8)
P.O. Box TV 8, Greensboro, NC 27420; (919) 841-8888.
David Boylan, v.p./gen. mgr.; Frank Terry, bus. mgr.; Quinn
Koontz, gen. sls. mgr.; Jim Ogle, news dir.
Operation: October, 1963; TV households: 1,618,000.

Lexington

WEJC (Channel 20)
Koinonia Ministries, Inc., Rt. 1, Box 2020, Lexington, NC
27292 (704) 246-2020.
William P. Register, pres. & gen. mgr.; Steve Anderson,
prog. dir.
Operation: October, 1985.

New Bern

WCTI-TV (Channel 12) ABC
Diversified Communications, P.O. Box 2325, New Bern, NC
28561.
Woodie Webb, v.p. & gen. mgr.

Raleigh

WLFL-TV (Channel 22)
TVX of Raleigh-Durham, Inc., 1205 Front St., Raleigh, NC
27609 (919) 821-2200.
Linda Cochran, v.p. & gen. mgr.; Kathy Bennett, natl. sls.
mgr.; Jenny Zoeller, prog. dir.; Don Ingram, chief eng.; rep.:
Seltel.
Operation: December, 1981.

WRAL-TV (Channel 5) CBS
Capitol Broadcasting Co., P.O. Box 12,000, Raleigh, NC
27605 (919) 821-8500.
James F. Goodmon, pres. & chief exec. off.; John M. Bren-
nan, sr. v.p. & treas.; John L. Greene, sr. v.p.; Louise S.
Stephenson, secty.; Paul Quinn, sta. mgr.; Wilbur Brann, chief
eng.; nat'l rep.: Katz Television American.
Operation: 1956; TV sets in area: 950,000.

Washington

WITN-TV (Channel 7) NBC
WITN-TV Inc., U.S. 17 South, Box Office 468, Washington,
NC 27889 (919) 946-3131.
Howard W. Meagle, Jr., v.p./gen. mgr.; David Jernigan, gen.
sls. mgr.; Frank Brady, reg./lcl. sls. mgr.; Paul Oughton, opns.
mgr.; Al Manning, eng.; Glen Denny, promo. mgr.; Fran Williams, bus. mgr.; Greg Albrecht, news dir.; Dick Jones, farm.
dir.; nat'l rep.: Seltel.
Operation: Sept. 1955; TVHH: 724,000.

Wilmington

WECT-TV (Channel 6) NBC, CBS
Atlantic Telecasting Corp., 322 Shipyard Blvd., Wilming-
ton, NC 28401 (919) 791-8070.
Dan D. Cameron, pres.; Wayne Jackson, sta. mgr.; Bill Elks,
Oper. dir.; C. D. Martin, Jr., sls. mgr.; Paul A. Brissette, Jr.,
exec. v.p. & gen. mgr.; Mike Loizides, chief eng.; Ernie
Whitmeyer, prod. dir.; nat'l rep.: Adam Young.
Operation: 1954; TV sets in area: 325,000.

WJKA (Channel 26) CBS
Wilmington Telecasters, Inc., 1926 Oleander Dr., Wilming-
ton, NC 28403 (919) 343-8826.
Kathrine Everett, pres.; Ty Watts, gen. mgr.; Bob Watson,
gen. sls. mgr.; Jan Ammons, asst. gen. sls. mgr.; Aileen
LeBlanc, dir. prog.; promo., public affairs.; Jim Bordeaux,
chief eng.; Gina Klinefeltee, bus mgr.; nat'l rep.: Seltel.
Operation: September, 1984.

WWAY (Channel 3) ABC
Old North Broadcasting Corp., Box 2068, 615 N. Front St.
Wilmington, NC (919) 762-8581.
Robert Price, pres.; Bill Ferrell, sls. mgr.; Mitchell Saieed,
v.p./gen. mgr.; George Allen, sta. mgr.; Elliott Hunter, chief
engineer; rep., Seltel.
Operation: 1964; TV households: 570,450.

Winston-Salem

WNRW-TV (Channel 45)
Act III Bdcst. of Greensboro, 3500 Myer-Lee Dr., Winston-
Salem, NC 27101 (919) 722-4545.
Bert Ellis, pres.; Jim Fletcher, gen. mgr.; Jason Elkin, gen.
sls. mgr.; Peter Wickwire, prog. dir. & film buyer; nat'l rep.:
Telerep.
Operation: September, 1979.

WXII-TV (Channel 12) NBC
700 Coliseum Drive, P.O. Box 11847, Winston-Salem, NC
27116 (919) 721-9944.
Reynard A. Corley, v.p. & gen. mgr.; Allan Simmons, mktg.
dir.; David L. Summers, gen. sls. mgr.; Roger Bergson, news
dir.; Phyllis Sheffield, prog. dir.; Henry Hunt, dir. of engineering; nat'l rep.: Katz Television.
Operation: 1953; households: 1,603,900 (TSA-May '83
ARB).

NORTH DAKOTA
Bismarck

KFYR-TV (Channel 5) NBC
Meyer Broadcasting Co., Broadway at Fourth, Bismarck,
ND 58501 (701) 223-0900.
William Ekberg, pres.; Judith Johnson, v.p.; Tom Barr, gen.
mgr.; Jerry Hegel, gen. sls. mgr.; Jim Sande, prog. & opns.
mgr.; Rich Beierle, dir. eng.; nat'l rep: Blair Television Associ-
ates.
Operation: 1953; TV homes in area: 144,000.

KXMB-TV (Channel 12) CBS
Reiten Television, Inc., 1811 N. 15th, Bismarck, ND 58501
(701) 223-9197.
John VonRueden, gen. mgr. & gen. sls. mgr.; Darrell Dor-
gan, news dir.; George McDonald, prod. mgr.; Rocky Hefty,
chief eng.; nat'l rep.: Seltel.
Operation: 1955; TV sets in area: 55,000.

WBMY (Channel 17) ABC
WDAY, Inc., 4007 State St., Bismarck, ND 58501 (710)
223-1700.
Charles Bohnet, exec. v.p.; Dewey Heggen, gen. mgr.;
Chuck Peterson, gen. sls. mgr.; Susan J. Elder, prog. dir.; Bob
Prowse, prom. mgr.; Becky Jones, news dir.; Jerry Grimstad,
chief eng.; natl. rep.: Katz.
Operation: March, 1985.

Devil's Lake-Grand Forks

WDAZ-TV (Channel 8) ABC
(Satellite of WDAY-TV, Fargo, ND)
WDAY Inc., 301 So. 8th St. N, Fargo, ND 58102 (701)
237-6500.
Robert Keer, gen. mgr.; Bonnie Moore, promo. mgr.; rep.:
Katz; Andy McDermott Ltd. (Canada).
Operation: 1967.

Dickinson

KQCD-TV (Channel 7) NBC
Meyer Broadcasting Co., Radar Base Road, Dickinson, ND
58601 (201) 225-6843.
Penny Borg, mgr.; nat'l rep.: Blair TV
Operation: 1980.

KXMA-TV (Channel 2) CBS
Reiten Television, Inc., Drawer B, Dickinson, ND 58602
(701) 227-1400.
David Reiten, pres. & gen. mgr. & sls. mgr.; Louis Tysver,
chief eng.; nat'l rep.: Seltel.
Operation: 1956; TV sets in area: 52,000.

Fargo

KTHI-TV, (Channel 11) NBC
Spokane Television, Inc., Box 1878, Fargo, ND 58102 (701)
237-5211; Box 127, Grand Forks, ND 58201 (701) 772-3481.
John Hrubesky, v.p. & gen. mgr.; Greg Holder, gen. sls. mgr.;
Dale Bosch, sta. mgr.; Carol Gillett, traffic mgr.; Roger John-
son, chief eng.

KVRR (Channel 15)
Red River Bdcstg. Corp., 4015 9th Ave., SW Fargo, ND
58103 (701) 277-0515.
Jane Boler, gen. mgr.; Greg Baldwin, sls. mgr.; Kent Lien,
prog. dir. & film buyer; Gary Goodrich, bctg. group coor.;
Timothy Anderson, chief eng.
Operation: January, 1983.

WDAY-TV (Channel 6) ABC
WDAY, Inc., 301 So. 8th St., Fargo, ND 58102 (701)
237-6500.
Charles Bohnet, exec. v.p.-gen. mgr.; Robert Prowse, pro-
mo. mgr.; Cole Carley, gen. sls mgr.; nat'l rep: Katz.
Operation: 1953; TV sets in area: 174,700.

Minot

KMCY (Channel 14) ABC
WDAY, Inc., Box 2276, Minot, ND 58702 (701) 838-6614.
Staff: same as WBMY, Bismarck, except Richard Beierle,
chief. eng. Natl. rep.: Katz.
Operation: June, 1985.

KMOT (Channel 10) NBC
Meyer Broadcasting Co., Box 1120, Minot, ND 58701 (701)
852-4101.
W. A. Ekberg, pres.; Wayne L. Sanders, sta. mgr.

KXMC-TV (Channel 13) CBS, ABC
KXMC TV, Inc., 3425 S. Broadway, Box 1686, Minot, ND,
58702 (701) 852-2104.
Chester Reiten, pres. & gen. mgr.; Henry Buechler, mgr.;
Rod Romine, prog. dir.; Duane Aase, chief eng.; nat'l rep.:
Seltel.
Operation: 1953; TV sets in area: 129,000.

Valley City-Fargo

KXJB-TV (Channel 4) CBS
North American Communications Corp., 4302 13th Ave. So.
Fargo, ND 58103 (701) 282-0444.
Bruce Barnes, pres. & gen. mgr.; Paul Wickre, gen. sls. mgr.;
Arvid Sonstelie, chief eng.; nat'l rep., Seltel.
Operation: 1954; TV sets in area: 214,000.

Williston

KUMV-TV (Channel 8)
Box 1287, Williston, ND 58801; Meyer Broadcasting Co.,
602 Main St., Williston, ND 58802
William A. Ekberg, pres.; Cherie Olson Harms, sta. mgr.
Operation: 1957.

KXMD-TV (Channel 11) ABC, CBS
1219 Knoll, P.O. Box 790, Williston, ND 58801
Marilyn Karst, sta. mgr.; Seltel.
Operation: 1969

OHIO
Akron

WAKC-TV (Channel 23) ABC
Group One Bcstg., 853 Copley Rd., Akron, OH 44309 (216)
535-7831.
Roger G. Berk, pres.; Bob Bostian, v.p. & gen. mgr.; Wm. F.
O'Neil, Jr., prog. dir.; Leo Zody, film ed.; Earl Miller, chief
eng.; nat'l rep.: Spot Time.
Operation: 1953; TV sets in area: 340,000.

WBNX-TV (Channel 55)
Winston Bdcstg., Network, Inc., 2690 State Rd., Cuyahoga
Falls, OH 44223 (216) 928-5711.
Lou Spangler, pres. & gen. mgr.; Terry Schultz, gen. sls.
mgr.; Anne Catherine, Keith, sta. mgr. & prog. dir.; Margie
Coger, prom. mgr.; Steven Nelson, chief eng.
Operation: December, 1985.

Canton

WDLI (Channel 17)
David Livingston Missionary Foundation, Inc., 6600 Atlan-
tic Blvd., Louisville, OH 44641 (216) 875-5542.
Denny Hazen, gen. mgr. & prog. dir.; Mike Tonges, opns.
dir. & chief eng.
Operation: January, 1967.

WOAC (Channel 67)
Canton 67, 4867 Fulton Dr., NW, Canton, OH 44718 (216)
492-5267.
Morton Kent, pres.; Mike Larson, gen. mgr.; Phil Sherck,
gen. sls. mgr.; Kevin Hoffman, prog. dir.; Scott Davis, news
dir.; Les Carpenter, chief eng.
Operation: September, 1981.

Cincinnati

WCPO-TV (Channel 9) CBS
Scripps-Howard Broadcasting Co., 500 Central Ave., Cin-
cinnati, OH 45202 (513) 721-9900.
Frank Gardner, gen. mgr.; J.B. Chase, asst. gen. mgr. & gen.
sls. mgr.; Rick Reeves, dir. of ops.; J.B. Chase, gen. sls. mgr.;
Jeff Sales, nat'l sls. mgr.; Jack Calalan, news dir.; Hasker
Nelson, dir. of community affairs; Ruth Ackerman, lcl. sls.

mgr.; Robbin Holliday, bus. mgr.; Leon Brown, chief eng.; nat'l rep.: Blair-TV, Inc.
Operation: 1949; TV sets in area: 1,000,000.

WIII (Channel 64)
5177 Fishwick Dr., Cincinnati, OH 45216; (513) 641-4400.
Stephen Kent, pres.; Greg Currell, gen. sls. mgr.; Doug Miller, chief eng.
Operation: 1980.

WKRC-TV (Channel 12) ABC
Taft Broadcasting Company, 1906 Highland Avenue, Cincinnati, OH 45219 (513) 651-1200.
Charles Mechem, bd. chm.; John Rose, gen. mgr. & v.p.; Ann Bryant, prog. dir.; Craig Millar, gen. sls. mgr.; Carl Moorehead, chief eng.; Bob Weinstein, nat'l sls. mgr.; Chuck DeVendra, lcl. sls. mgr.; Don North, news dir.; John Hill, film dir.
Operation: 1949; TV sets in area: 1,004,100.

WLWT (Channel 5) NBC
140 W. Ninth St., Cincinnati, OH 45202; (513) 352-5000.
Anthony H. Kiernan, v.p. & gen. mgr.; Cliff Abromats, news dir.; Diana Richardson, prog. dir.; Harry Schneider, controller; Florence Parker, dir. community svcs.; Jerry Blankenbeker, chief eng.; Mickey Fisher, traf. mgr.; Thomas Storey, film dir.; natl rep.: Katz Television.
Operation: 1948; households: 2,221,800 (TSA—May '83 ARB).

WXIX-TV (Channel 19) FOX
Malrite Communications Group, Inc., 10490 Taconic Terrace, Cincinnati, OH 45215 (513) 772-1919.
John Chaffee, pres.; Bill Jenkins, v.p. & gen. mgr.; Patrice Mohn, prog. dir.; Gracelyn Brown, prom. mgr.; Suzanne Kay, news dir.; Jim Parker, chief eng.; natl. rep.: Petry.
Operation: November, 1983.

Cleveland

WEWS (Channel 5) ABC
Scripps Howard Broadcasting Co., 3001 Euclid Ave., Cleveland, OH 44115 (216) 431-5555.
Richard J. Janssen, pres. & CEO; James H. Knight, v.p. & gen. mgr.; Jane Sherwin, gen. sls. mgr.; John Tamerlano, natl. sls. mgr.; Gary Stark, prog. dir.; Seth Alspaugh, creative svcs. dir.; John L. Ray, news dir.; rep. Blair-TV, Inc.
Operation: 1947; Total TV households: 1,824,400.

WJW-TV (Channel 8) CBS
Gillett Communications of Ohio, Inc., 5800 S. Marginal Rd., Cleveland OH 44103 (216) 431-8888.
C. David Whitaker, pres.; Spencer Koch, dir. sls.; Mike Renda, nat'l sls. mgr.; Louis Gattozzi, dir. opns.; Robert Green, dir. tech. svcs.; Joann Stern, dir. creative svcs.; Thomas Flavelle, controller; Virgil Dominic, news dir.
Operation: 1949.

WKYC-TV (Channel 3) NBC
National Broadcasting Co., 1403 East Sixth Street, Cleveland, Ohio 44114 (216) 344-3333.
John Llewellyn, v.p. & gen. mgr.; Dan Klintworth, adv. & promo. mgr.; David Boylan, dir. of sls.; Raymond Smith, dir., tech. ops.; Kathleen McNulty, bus. mgr.; Gregory R. Stehlin, prog. dir.; Ron Bilek, news dir.; nat'l rep.: NBC Spot Sales.
Operation: 1948; TV sets in area: 3,663,800.

Columbus

WBNS-TV (Channel 10) CBS
Dispatch Printing Co., 770 Twin Rivers Drive, Columbus, OH 43216 (216) 460-3700.
Gene D'Angelo, pres. & gen. mgr.; Arnold Routson, v.p. sls.; William Orr, v.p., eng'.; John A. Haldi, vice pres., prgm.; Dale Laackman, prod. dir.; Gerald Cary, treas.; Larry Maisel, News dir.; Jay Scafone, dir. adv. & promo.; nat'l rep.:. Blair TV Inc.
Operation: 1949; TV sets in area: 557,400.

WCMH-TV (Channel 4) NBC
Outlet Broadcasting, 3165 Olentangy River Rd., Columbus, OH 43202 (614) 263-5441.
David E. Henderson, pres.; Gary Robinson, v.p. & gen. mgr.; Jeff Cash, gen. sls. mgr.; Bill Lanesey, natl. sls. mgr.; Robert Shaw, prog. dir.; Janna Petry, promo. mgr.; Richard Tuininga, news dir.; Ralph Landon, chief eng.; Paul Ernst, prog. dir.; Lance Carwile, film dir.; natl. rep.: Katz.
Operation: 1949; TV homes in area: 1,494,000.

WTTE (Channel 28)
WTTE Channel 28, Inc., 6130 Sunbury Rd., Box 280, Columbus, OH 43216; (614) 895-2800.
John T. Quigley, gen. mgr.; Steve Marks, gen. sls. mgr.; Oran D. Gough, opns. dir.; Joe Subich, chief eng.; nat'l rep.: Seltel.
Operation: June, 1984.

WSYX (Channel 6) ABC
Anchor Media, 1271 Dublin Road, Columbus, 43216 (614) 481-6666.
Jack Sander, pres.; Charles Wing, v.p. & gen. mgr.; Jim Conshafter, gen. sls. mgr.; Russ Reed, prog. mgr.; Kathy Ward, promo. dir.; Bill Seaman, chief eng.; nat'l rep.: MMT.
Operation: 1949; TV sets in area: 727,000.

Dayton

WDTN (Channel 2) ABC
4595 South Dixie Ave., P.O. Box 741, Dayton, OH 45401.
Philip M. Stolz, exec. v.p. & gen. mgr.; Larry Ryan, gen. sls. mgr.; Kirk Szesney, promo. mgr.; Steve Fisher, sta. mgr.; O. Ted Lester, chief eng.; nat'l rep.: Blair.
Operation: 1949; TV homes in area: 1,029,500.

WHIO-TV (Channel 7) CBS
Miami Valley Broadcasting Corp., 1414 Wilmington Avenue, Dayton, OH 45401 (513) 259-2111.
Stanley G. Mouse, pres.; Neil Pugh, v.p. & gen. mgr.; Don Kemper, sta. mgr.; John Hayes, gen. sls. mgr.; John Hanley, cont.; Robert Wells, dir. of info. svcs.; John Clark, prog. dir.; Sim Kollinger, chief eng.; nat'l rep.: Tele-rep.
Operation: 1949; TV sets in area: 437,160.

WKEF (Channel 22) ABC
Adams TV of Dayton, 1731 Soldiers Home Road, Dayton, OH 45418 (513) 263-2662.
James Graham, pres., gen. mgr. & prog. dir.; Doug Gealy, lcl. sls. mgr.; Mike Thomas, prod. spvr.; Darrell Hunter, chief eng.; Sandy Patton, promo dir.; Johnny Walker, news dir.; rep.: Katz.
Operation: 1964; TV households: 1,399,000.

WRGT-TV (Channel 45)
Dayton Telecasting, Inc., 45 Broadcast Plaza, Dayton, OH 45408; (503) 263-4500.
Dave Miller, gen. mgr.; Ken Beedle, gen. sls. mgr.; Linda Triplett, opns. mgr.; Miles Ptacek, chief eng.; nat'l rep.: MMT.
Operation: September, 1984.

Lima

WLIO-TV (Channel 35) NBC, ABC
Lima Communications Corporation, 1424 Rice Ave., Lima, Ohio 45802 (419) 228-8835.
James C. Dages, pres. & gen. mgr.; James Garling, prog. dir; Fred Vobbe, chief eng.; Bruce A. Opperman, sls. mgr.; nat'l rep.: The Katz Co.
Operation: 1952; TV sets in area: 464,300.

WTLW (Channel 44)
American Christian TV Services, Inc., 1844 Baty Rd., Lima, OH 45807; (419) 339-4444.
Gary Cooper, pres.; Robert Placie, sta. mgr.; Ron Mighell, v.p., dir.; Jeffrey G. Millslagle, prog. dir.; John Owens, prod. dir.; Robert Armistead, devel. dir.; Ray Tanner, chief eng.
Operation: June, 1982.

Lorain-Cleveland

WUAB (Channel 43)
Gaylord Broadcasting Co. of Ohio, 8443 Day Dr., Parma, OH 44129 (216) 845-6043.
James R. Terrell, pres.; Michael E. Schuch, v.p. & gen. mgr.; Rex Rickly, chief eng.; rep.: MMT.

Newark

WSFJ (Channel 51)
Christian Television of Ohio, Inc., 10077 Jacksontown Rd., Thornville, OH 43076 (614) 833-0771.
Jean Rodabaugh, acting pres. & gen. mgr.; Betty J. Stanley, v.p.; Charlotte Reichley, prog. dir.; nat'l rep.: Hugh Wallace.
Operation: 1980.

Sandusky

WGGN-TV (Channel 52)
Christian Faith Bcstg., Box 2397, Sandusky, OH 44870 (419) 684-5311.
Rusty Yost, gen. mgr.; Gene Asberry, chief eng.
Operation: December, 1982.

Shaker Heights

WOIO (Channel 19) FOX
Channel 19, Inc., 2720 Van Aken Blvd., Cleveland, OH 44120; (216) 561-1919.
Hubert Payne, pres.; Dennis Thatcher, gen. mgr.; Dave Smith, gen. sls. mgr.; Val King, natl. sls. mgr.; Jackie Krejcik, lcl. sls. mgr.; Richard Sullivan, prog. dir.; Craig Wright, promo. mgr.; Curtis Garris, chief eng.; natl. rep.: Petry.
Operation: May, 1985.

Springfield

WTJC (Channel 26)
Miami Valley Christian Television Inc., Box 26, Dayton, OH 45401 (513) 323-0026.
Marvin D. Sparks, pres.; John Elliott, chief eng.; Rod Robison, dir. develop.
Operation: 1980

Steubenville

WTOV-TV (Channel 9) ABC, NBC
Television Station Partners, Box 9999, Steubenville, OH 43952.
I. Martin Pompadur, CEO; Ziff Corp.; Ralph E. Becker, COO; Stephen W. Dant, v.p. & gen. mgr.; James McCreary, v.p., cont.; Toni Ventresca, prog. mgr.

Toledo

WNWO-TV (Channel 24) ABC
Toledo Television Investors Ltd. Partnership, 300 S. Byrne Rd., Toledo, OH 43615 (419) 535-0024.
Brett Cornwell, v.p./gen. mgr.; Linda Blackburn, gen. sls. mgr.; Susan Roberts, bus. mgr.; James Bowe, v.p. eng./ops.; rep.: Petry.
Operation: 1966; TV households: 1,775,100.

WTOL (Channel 11) CBS
Cosmos Broadcasting Corp., P.O. Box 715, Toledo, OH 43695 (419) 248-1111.
S. Wheeler Rudd, v.p. & gen. mgr.; John Cottingham, gen. sls. mgr.; Rita Wissman, nat'l sls. mgr.; Paul Ladrow, lcl. sls. mgr.; Rick Gevers, news dir.; Steve Israel, prog. dir.; Wayne Thing, prod. mgr.; Sharon Newson, pub. affairs dir.; Jeff Bell, promo. mgr.; Paul Lentz, chief eng.; Nancy Gruhler, traffic mgr.; nat'l rep.: MMT Sales.
Operation: 1958; TV sets in area: 1,405,800.

WTVG-TV (Channel 13) NBC
SCI Holdings, Inc., 4247 Dorr St., Toledo OH 436074 (419) 255-1313.
H. W. Ray, v.p. & gen. mgr.; George Carlino. nat'l sls. mgr.; Doug Sinn, sls. dir.; nat'l rep.: Storer Television Sales, Inc.
Operation: 1948; TV sets in area: 751,100.

Youngstown

WFMJ-TV (Channel 21) NBC
WFMJ-TV, Inc., 101 W. Boardman St., Youngstown, OH 44503 (216) 744-8611.
Betty H. Brown Jagnow, pres.; John A. Grdic, gen. mgr.; Homean Baxter, film dir.; Larry Oleson, chief eng.; nat'l rep., Blair TV.
Operation: 1953; TV households in area: 280,500.

WKBN-TV (Channel 27) CBS
WKBN Broadcasting Corp., 3930 Sunset Blvd., Youngstown, OH 44501 (216) 782-1144.
W. P. Williamson, Jr., bd. chm.; Ruth L. Cruikshank, secty.; W. P. Williamson, III, pres. & gen. mgr.; David V. Stewart, treas.; W.F. Decker, sta. mgr.; C.R. Wade, sls. mgr.; Norm Berger, prog. dir.; nat'l rep.: Katz Agency.
Operation: 1953; TV sets in area: 514,000.

WYTV (Channel 33)
WYTV, 3800 Shady Run Rd., Youngstown, OH 44502.
Geoffrey Pearce, gen. mgr.

Zanesville

WHIZ-TV (Channel 18) NBC, ABC
Southeastern Ohio Television System, Downard Rd., Zanesville, OH 43701 (614) 453-0361.
Allan Land, group mgr.; Barbara Mitter, prog. dir.; Elmer Hartmeyer, chief eng.; Franklin Young, film oper. mgr.; nat'l rep.: Katz.
Operation: 1953; TV sets in area: 80,000.

OKLAHOMA
Ada

KTEN (Channel 10) ABC, CBS, NBC
Eastern Oklahoma Television Co., Inc., P.O. Box 728, Ada, OK 74820 (405) 332-3111.
Tom Johnson, gen. & gen. mgr.; Bill Green, chief eng.; Dan Hoover, v.p. & prog. dir.; nat'l rep.: Katz.
Operation: 1954; TV sets in area: 178,310.

Ardmore

KXII-TV (Channel 12)
Texoma Broadcasters, Inc., Box 1175, Sherman, TX.
M.N. Bostick, pres.; Richard R. Adams, gen. mgr.; Dennis Lite, chief eng.; Mike Leucke, prod. mgr.; nat'l rep.: Seltel.
Operation: 1956.

Bartlesville

KDOR (Channel 17)
All American TV, Inc., Box 1700, Talala, OK 45069 (918) 275-4219.
Sonny Arguinzoki, pres.; Linda Hernandez, gen. mgr.; Leonard Wallace, chief eng.
Operation: February, 1984.

Lawton

KSWO-TV (Channel 7) ABC
KSWO Television Co., Inc., P.O. Box 708, Lawton, OK 73502 (405) 355-7000.
R. H. Drewry, pres.; Larry Patton, gen. mgr.; Jim Lockerd, chief eng.
Operation: 1953; TV sets in area: 225,000.

Oklahoma City

KAUT (Channel 43)
Rollins Telecasting of Oklahoma, Box 14843, Oklahoma City, OK 73113; (405) 478-4300.
Don Richards, gen. mgr.; Rusty Hoyle, gen. sls. mgr.; Bill Finch, prom. mgr.; Eldon Brown, chief eng.; nat'l rep.: Petry.
Operation: November, 1980.

KGMC (Channel 34)
Oklahoma City Bdcstg. Co., 1501 NE 85th, Oklahoma City, OK 73131 (405) 478-3434.
Ted Baze, gen. mgr.; Ken Belford, gen. sls. mgr.; Greg Miller, v.p & chief eng.; Judy Lisenby, prog. dir.; nat'l rep.: Seltel.
Operation: 1979.

KOCO-TV (Channel 5) ABC
Gannett Broadcast Group, 1300 E. Britton Road, Oklahoma City, OK 73113.
Tom Kirby, pres. & gen. mgr.; Lou Morlino, v.p. & gen. sls. mgr.; Ted Newcomb, v.p. & chief eng.; Lynette Rodriguez, compt.; Mike Palmer, v.p., bdcst. op.
Operation: 1954; TV households: 834,600.

KOKH (Channel 25)
Blair Broadcasting of Oklahoma, Inc., 1228 E. Wilshire Blvd., Oklahoma City, OK 73111 (405) 843-2525.
James Harmeyer, pres. & gen. mgr.
Operation: 1979.

KTBO-TV (Channel 14)
Trinity Bcstg. of Oklahoma, 3705 NW 63rd St., Oklahoma City, OK 73116 (405) 848-1414.
Paul F. Crouch, pres.; Al Brown, gen. mgr.; John Gordon, chief eng.
Operation: March, 1981.

KTVY (Channel 14) NBC
Knight-Ridder Bdcstg. Inc., 500 East Britton Road, Oklahoma City, OK 73114 (405) 478-1212.
Robert F. Finke, pres. & gen. mgr.; Paul Wise, gen. sls. mgr.;

Rick Grossman, mktg. dir.; Fred Heinemann, chief eng.
Operation: 1949; TV sets in area: 613,500.

KWTV (Channel 9) CBS
Griffin Television, Inc. P.O. Box 14159, Oklahoma City, OK 73113 (405) 843-6641.
Duane Harm, pres. & gen. mgr.; Al Sandubrae, sta. mgr.; Russ Elkin, chief eng.; Rick Buchanan, mktg. man.; nat'l rep.: Telerep.
Operation: 1953; TV sets in area: 847,800.

Sayre

KVIJ-TV
(Satellite of KVII-TV, Amarillo, TX)
Marsh Media, Inc., One Broadcast Center, Amarillo, TX 79101 (405) 928-3233.
Rep.: Katz Television.
Operation: 1961.

Tulsa

KGCT-TV (Channel 41)
5807 S. Garnett St., Tulsa, OK 74145 (918) 252-9589.
Leonard Anderson, pres.; William Dan Harley, mgr. & gen. sls. mgr.; Peggy Marsh, office mgr.; C.E. Martin, chief eng.; nat'l rep.: Spot Time.
Operation: May, 1981.

KJRH-TV (Channel 2) NBC
Scripps-Howard Broadcasting Company, P.O. Box 2, Tulsa, OK 74101 (918) 743-2222.
Ben Hevel, gen. mgr.; William J. Donahue, asst. gen. mgr.; Tom Allen, news dir.; Michael J. Vrabec, gen. sls. mgr.; Vic Turner, chief eng.; nat'l rep.; Blair Television.
Operation: 1954; TV sets in area: 460,300.

KOKI-TV (Channel 23)
Tulsa 23, 7422 E. 46 Place, Tulsa, OK 74135 (918) 663-6880.
James U. Lavenstein, pres. & gen. mgr.; Mike Braker, gen. sls. mgr.; Eugene Wilkin, prog. dir. & film buyer; Ben Frizzell, creative svcs. mgr.; Robert G. Hardie, chief eng.; nat'l rep.: Katz.
Operation: November, 1980.

KOTV (Channel 6) CBS
KOTV, Inc., 320 S. Frankfort St., Tulsa, OK 74120 (918) 582-6666.
Ward Huey, pres.; Phil Keller, gen. mgr.; Bob Allen, prog. mgr.; Foster Morgan, news dir.; nat'l rep.: Petry.
Operation: 1949

KTUL-TV (Channel 8) ABC
KTUL-TV, Inc., Box 8, Tulsa, OK 74101 (918) 446-3351.
John G. Garwood, pres. & gen. mgr.; Stephen W. Dant, gen. sls. mgr.; Terry Wilson, prog. dir.; P. Kent Doll, prom. mgr.; Roman Hlohowskyj, chief eng.; nat'l rep.: Telerep.
Operation: 1954; TV homes in area: 481,400.

KWHB (Channel 47)
Television Communications, Inc., Box 470047, Tulsa, OK 74147 (918) 250-9402.
Peter Sumrall, gen. mgr.; Jim Shaffer, gen. sls. mgr.; Steve Morgan, opns. mgr.; Gary Murphy, lcl. sls. mgr.; Darryl Ferguson, chief eng.
Operation: April, 1985.

OREGON

Bend

KTVZ (Channel 21) CBS, NBC
Resort Bdcstg. Co., Box 149, Bend, OR 97709 (503) 389-6511.
John Larkin, gen. mgr.; Duncan Laing, sls. mgr.; Teresa Bollard, ops. mgr.; nat'l rep.: Katz.
Operation: 1977.

Coos Bay

KCBY-TV (Channel 11) CBS
(Satellite of KVAL-TV, Eugene, OR)
Northwest Television, Inc., P.O. Box 1156, Coos Bay, OR 97420 (503) 269-1111.
Bruce Bennett, sta. mgr.; Tim Hershiser, chief eng.

Eugene

KEZI-TV (Channel 9) ABC
KEZI, Inc., P.O. Box 7009, Eugene, OR 97401 (503) 485-5611.
Carolyn S. Chambers, pres.; Bruce Liljegren, gen. mgr.; Dave Larson, asst. sta. mgr.; Beth Cookson, nat'l/reg. sls.; Bruce A. Barrett, gen. sls. mgr.; Joe Smelser, prod. mgr.; Dennis Hunt, chief eng.
Operation: 1960; TV households: 226,200.

KMTR-TV (Channel 16) NBC
KMTR, Inc., Box 7308, Eugene, OR 97401 (503) 746-1600.
Robert W. Davis, pres. & gen. mgr.; Cam Wilson, v.p. & gen. sls. mgr. Julie Strandlien, prog. dir.; Cambra Ward, promo. mgr.; Paul Riess, news dir.; Jerry Madsen, chief eng.; nat'l rep.; Seltel.
Operation: October, 1982.

KVAL-TV (Channel 13) Primary NBC
Northwest Television, Inc., Blanton Heights, P.O. Box 1313, Eugene, OR 97401 (503) 342-4961.
James W. Putney, v.p., gen. mgr.; John Doyle, news dir.; Dave Weinkauf, gen. sls. mgr.; Greg Raschio, lcl. sls. dir.; Paul Greene, prog. dir.; Jim Bowen, chief eng.; nat'l rep.: Katz Television, Inc.
Operation: 1954; TV sets in area: 469,700.

Klamath Falls

KOTI-TV (Channel 2)
California/Oregon Broadcasting Co., P.O. Box 2K, Klamath Falls, OR 97601 (503) 882-2222.
Wm. B. Smullin, pres.; Ed Zander, gen. mgr.; nat'l rep.: Blair; reg. rep.: Art Moore & Associates.
Operation: 1956.

Medford

KDRV (Channel 12)
Sunshine TV, Inc., 1090 Knutson Ave., Medford, OR 97504 (503) 773-1212.
John Hash, pres.; Keith Lollis, gen. mgr; Rick Carrara, chief eng.
Operation: January, 1984.

KOBI-TV (Channel 5) NBC
Oregon Broadcasting Co., P.O. Box 5M, Medford, OR 97501 (503) 779-5555.
William B. Smullin, pres.; Ed Zander, v.p. & gen. mgr.;

Patricia D. Smullin, v.p.; Patricia C. Smullin, treas; Bill Kirk, chief eng.; nat'l rep.: Blair.
Operation: 1953.

KTVL-TV (Channel 10) CBS
Freedom Communications, Inc., Box 10, Medford, OR 97501 (503) 773-7373.
Ed Ivey, v.p. & gen. mgr.; Cliff Williams, gen. sls. mgr.; Marvin Rhodes, prog. dir.; Mel Tynan, chief eng.
Operation: 1961; TV households: 127,800.

Portland

KATU (Channel 2) ABC
Fisher Broadcasting, Inc., 2153 N.E. Sandy Blvd., Portland, OR 97232 (503) 231-4222.
Sherwood V. Hinman, v.p. & gen. mgr.; Robert D. Kalstad, v.p. & sta. mgr.; Leland Petrik, prog. dir.; Robert Moore, chief eng.; Thomas Oberg, gen. sls. mgr.; Jim Rogers, nat'l sls. mgr.; Joella Werlin, pub. affairs mgr.; rep.: Telerep.
Operation: 1962; TV households: 795,100.

KGW-TV (Channel 8)
King Broadcasting Company, 1501 S. W. Jefferson St., Portland, OR 97201 (503) 226-5000.
Irwin P. Starr, v.p. & gen. man.
Operation: 1956.

KOIN-TV (Channel 6) CBS
KOIN-TV, Inc., 222 S.W. Columbia St., Portland, OR 97201 (503) 464-0600.
R. M. Schafbuch, gen. mgr.; Steve Currie, bdcst. opr. mgr.; Brian Holmes, gen. sls. mgr.; Dusty Davidsen, sta. mgr.; Karen Lee Bice, promo. mgr.; Lee Wood, chief eng.; nat'l rep.: Harrington, Righter & Parsons.
Operation: 1953; TV sets in area: 1,148,500.

KPTV (Channel 12)
Oregon Television, Inc., P.O. Box 3401, Portland, OR 97208; 735 S. W. 20th Place, Portland, OR (503) 222-9921.
Marty Brantley, pres. & gen. mgr.; Connie Martin, gen. sls. mgr.; Gregg Shelby, nat'l sls. mgr.; Gordon White, prog. mgr. & film buyer; Barbara Deaton, promo. mgr.; Bob Nelson, chief eng.; rep.: Tele-Rep.
Operation: 1952; TV households: 785,700.

Roseburg

KPIC (Channel 4) CBS Primary
(Affiliate of KVAL-TV, Eugene, OR)
Southwest Oregon Television Broadcasting Corp., studio & office: 655 West Umpqua, Roseburg, OR 97470; (503) 672-4481.
Don Tykeson, pres.; Don Cithero, sta. mgr.; Jim Putney, gen. mgr.; nat'l rep.: Katz.
Operation: 1956.

Salem

KHSP (Channel 22)
Silver King Bdcstg. of Oregon, Inc., 4923 Indian School Rd., N.E., Salem, OR 97305 (503) 390-2202.
Christopher Desmond, pres., gen. & gen. sls. mgr.; Judy Koeney, prog. dir. & film buyer; Bob Ridgeway, chief eng.
Operation: November, 1981.

PENNSYLVANIA

Allentown

WFMZ-TV (Channel 69)
Maranatha Broadcasting Co., Inc., E. Rock Rd., Allentown, PA 18103 (215) 797-4530.
Richard C. Dean, pres. & gen. mgr.; David G. Hinson, prog. dir.; Brad Rinehart, news dir.; Dean Dallmann, sls. mgr.; Kathy Craine, office mgr.; Barry Fisher, chief eng.
Operation: November, 1976.

Altoona

WWPC (Channel 23) FOX
Evergreen Bdcstg. Corp., 211 Townsend, Birmingham, MI 48009 (814) 266-8088.
Robert N. Smith, pres.; Martin Ostrow, gen. & gen. sls. mgr.; Chris Taylor, prog. dir. & film buyer; Bob Andrade, chief eng.
Operation: 1974.

WTAJ-TV (Channel 10) CBS
A Gateway Station; 5000 Sixth Avenue, Altoona, PA 16603 (814) 944-2031.
Donald F. Snyder, v.p. & gen. mgr.; Bob Eger, nat'l sls. mgr.; David Metz, prog. mgr.; Richard Kline, chief eng.
Operation: 1953.

Erie

WICU (Channel 12) NBC
Great Lakes Communications, Inc., 3514 State St. Erie, PA 16508 (814) 454-5201.
Priscilla Lamb Schwier, pres.; Clarence Paolella, gen. mgr. & film buyer; Mike Csop, chief eng.; nat'l rep.: Katz
Operation: 1949; TV sets in area: 274,000.

WJET-TV (Channel 24) ABC
JET Broadcasting Co., Inc., 8455 Peach St., Erie, PA 16509 (814) 864-4902.
Myron Jones, pres.; John Kanzius, exec. v.p./gen. mgr.; John Kanzius, prog. dir.; Steve Drexler, news dir.; nat'l rep.: Blair.
Operation: 1966; TV households: 160,500.

WSEE (Channel 35) CBS
Keystone Bdcstg. Co., 1220 Peach St., Erie, PA 16501 (814) 455-7575.
Jerry Montgomery, v.p. & gen. mgr.; William Podbielski, chief eng.; nat'l rep.: MMT.
Operation: 1954; U.H.F. sets in area 245,400.

Greensburg/Pittsburgh

WPCB-TV
Cornerstone TeleVision, Inc., Wall, PA, Greensburg, PA 15148 (412) 824-3930.
R. Russell Bixler, pres.; Oleen Eagle, gen. mgr.; David Skeba, prog. mgr.; Blake Richert, chief eng.
Operation: April, 1979.

Harrisburg

WHP-TV (Channel 21) CBS-TV
WWHP, Inc., P.O. Box 1507, Harrisburg, PA 17105 (717) 238-2100.
Tom Girocco, pres.; Donald C. Yeiser, v.p. & gen. mgr.; Chris Fickes, news dir.; Tom Miller, nat'l sls. mgr.; Maurice Gannaway, dir. eng.; nat'l rep.: Katz.
Operation: 1953; TV households in ADI: 527,900.

WHTM-TV (Channel 27) ABC
Box 2775, Harrisburg, PA 17105 (717) 236-2727.
Robert Smith, pres.; John Purcell, v.p. & gen. mgr.; Frank Ratermann, gen. sls. mgr.; Paul O'Dell, prog. dir.; Janice Dexter, prom. mgr.; Jon McCall, news dir.; Donald Landis, chief eng.; Joseph Fry, contrl.; nat'l rep.: Harrington, Righter & Parsons.
Operation: June, 1953; TV sets in area: 527,130.

Johnstown

WFAT-TV (Channel 19)
P.O. Box 19, Johnstown, PA 14907-0019 (814) 266-1919.
Leon A. Crosby, owner; Timothy Lee Crosby, gen. mgr.; George S. Plenderleith, sta. mgr.; Michael D. Forosisky, sls. mgr.; William Caramana, chief eng.
Operation: 1953.

WJAC-TV (Channel 6) NBC
WJAC, Inc., Hickory Lane, Johnstown, PA 15905 (814) 255-7600.
James M. Edwards, Sr., pres.; Richard D. Schrott, v.p.; Philip A. Marcinek, prog. dir.; Rob Abele, chief eng.; nat'l rep.: Harrington, Righter & Parsons.
Operation: 1949; TV sets in area, 1,372,860.

Lancaster

WGAL-TV (Channel 8) NBC
WGAL Television, Inc., 1300 Columbia Ave., Lancaster, PA 17604 (717) 393-5851.
David R. Dodds, v.p. & gen. mgr.; Rigby Wilson, gen. sls. mgr.; John Feeser, lcl. sls. mgr.; Mike Tully, lcl. sls. mgr.; Nelson Sears, prog. mgr.; Ed Wickenheiser, news dir.; nat'l rep.: Blair.
Operation: March, 1949; TV households: 1,267,900.

Lancaster/Lebanon

WLYH-TV (Channel 15)
P.O. Box 1283, Television Hill, Lebanon, PA 17042 (717) 273-4551.
Licensee: Gateway Communications, Inc., Suite 612, Executive Building, Cherry Hill, NJ 08034 (609) 667-8100.
Robert W. Eolin, v.p. & gen. mgr.
Operation: May 2, 1957.

Philadelphia

WKYW-TV (Channel 3) NBC
Group W (Westinghouse Broadcasting Co.), Independence Mall East, Philadelphia, PA 19106 (215) 238-4700.
James B. Thompson, vice pres. & gen. mgr.; Bob Jones, prgm. mgr.; Brian O'Neill, creative svcs. dir.; Allen Murphy, gen. sls. mgr.; Glenn Romsos, chief eng.; nat'l rep.: TVAR.
Operation: 1941; TV sets in area: 2,275,000.

WCAU-TV (Channel 10) CBS
WCAU-TV, Inc., City Ave. & Monument Rd., Philadelphia PA 19131 (215) 668-5510.
Steve Cohen, vice-pres. & gen. mgr.; Gordon Hughes, v.p. & sta. mgr.; Jay Newman, news dir.; Dan Sitarski, dir. of opns. & eng.; Dave Harvey, dir. tech. opns.; Dave Kenworthy, dir. creative svcs.; Jim Diaz, dir. sls.; Martin Blair, dir. p.r.; nat'l rep.: CBS Television National Sales.
Operation: 1948; TV sets in area: 2,373,100.

WGBS-TV (Channel 57)
Grant Bdcstg. of Phila., Inc., 420 N. 20th St., Philadelphia, PA 19130 (215) 563-5757.

Robert O'Connor, gen. mgr.; Carol Healey, sta. mgr.; Mark Cooper, promo dir.; Dick Quinto, chief eng.

Operation: October, 1985.

WPHL-TV (Channel 17)
WPHL-TV Inc., 5001 Wynnefield Ave., Philadelphia, PA 19131 (215) 878-1700.

Randall E. Smith, exec. v.p. & gen. mgr.; Steve Mosko, sta. mgr.; Karen Corbin, prog. & mktg. mgr.; Jan Dickler, dir. sls.; Eric Gordon, prod. mgr.; David Smith, chief eng.; Bruce Wetusbach, v.p., finance & treas.

Operation: July, 1960; TV households: 3,407,700.

WPVI (Channel 6) ABC
Capital Cities/ABC, Inc., 4100 City Line Ave., Philadelphia, PA 19131 (215) 878-9700.

Richard Spinner, pres. & gen. mgr.; Art Moore, dir. sta. promo. & adv.; Irwin L. Ross, chief eng.

Operation: 1947; TV sets in area: 4,556,200.

WTAF-TV (Channel 29)
Taft Broadcasting Co., 330 Market St., Philadelphia, PA 19106 (215) 925-2929

Randall E. Smith, gen. mgr.; Elliott Troshinsky, gen. sls. mgr.; Chuck Wing, lcl. sls. mgr.; Gregg Miller, prog. mgr.; Karen Corbin, prom. mgr.; Richard Owens, chief eng.; rep.: Telerep.

Operation: 1965; TV households: 3,037,000.

Pittsburgh

KDKA-TV (Channel 2) CBS
Westinghouse Broadcasting Co., Inc., 1 Gateway Center, Pittsburgh, PA 15222 (412) 392-2200.

Thomas L. Goodgame, v.p. & gen. mgr.; Carolyn Wean, sta. mgr.; Deb Zeyen, prog. mgr.; Joe Berwanger, gen. sls. mgr.; Jack Cvetic, chief eng.; Brad Crum, creative svcs. dir.; Carolyn McClair, info. svcs. dir.

WPGH-TV (Channel 53)
Lorimar Bdcst. Group—A Lorimar-Telepictures Company, 750 Ivory Ave., Pittsburgh, PA 15214 (412) 931-5300.

Michael A. Liff, v.p. & gen. mgr.; Bill Butler, dir. prog. & promo.; Kathy Saunders, gen. sls. mgr.; Mike Wolff, lcl. sls. mgr.; Jack Papson, prod. mgr.; Terry Caywood, promo. mgr. Households (TV): 1,678,900.

WPTT-TV (Channel 22)
Commercial Radio Institute, Inc., 500 Seco Rd., Pittsburgh, PA 15230 (412) 856-9010.

Julian S. Smith, CEO.; Robert Simmons, pres.; Charles L. Hobbs, gen. mgr.; Kenneth Zuckerman, gen. sls. mgr.; Keith King, lcl. & regl. sls. mgr.

Operation: 1978.

WPXI (Channel 11) NBC
WPXI Corp., 11 Television Hill, Pittsburgh, PA 15230 (412) 237-1100.

John A. Howell III, v.p. & gen. mgr.; Bruno M. Graziano, gen. sls. mgr.; Mark W. Barash, prog. dir.; Steve Riley, promo. mgr.; Mike Sechrist, news dir.; Linc-Reed Nickerson, chief eng.

Operation, 1957.

WTAE-TV (Channel 4) ABC
400 Ardmore Blvd., Pittsburgh, PA 15221 (412) 242-4300.

Jim Hefner, v.p. & gen. mgr.; Rick Henry, v.p. sls.; Viki Gedrys-Regan, dir. creative svcs.; Marty Faubell, dir. of eng.; David Crantz, dir. of p.r. & spec. projects; Joe Rovitto, news dir.; nat'l rep.: Katz Agency Inc.

Reading

WTVE (Channel 51)
Reading Broadcasting, Inc., 1729 N. 11th St., Reading, PA 19604 (215) 921-9181.

Jeffrey D. Miller, gen. mgr.; Robert Pritchard, chief eng.; Carol White, sls. mgr.; Mark Hauck, prod. adm.; Daniel Bendetti, prod. mgr.

Operation: 1980.

Red Lion

WGCB-TV (Channel 49)
Red Lion Television Inc., Box 88, Red Lion, PA 17356 (717) 246-1681.

John H. Norris, pres.; Fred W. Wise, v.p.; John E. Stockstill, gen. mgr.; Sally Horne, prog. dir.; nat'l rep.: Spot Time.

Operation: 1979.

Scranton/Wilkes-Barre

WNEP-TV (Channel 16) ABC
The New York Times Co., Wilkes-Barre/Scranton Airport, Avoca, PA 18641 (717) 826-1616.

Elden A. Hale Jr., exec. v.p. & gen. mgr.; Warren A. Reed, gen. sls. mgr.; Bill Christian, exec. prog. prod.; rep.: Katz.

Operation: 1954; TV sets in area: 352,375.

WOLF-TV (Channel 38)
Scranton TV Partners, Ltd., 916 Oak St., Scranton, PA 18508 (717) 347-9653.

Guyon Turner, CEO; Gilbert Hoban, gen. sls. mgr.; Peter Kilcollen, prog. & promo.; Dave Swartz, chief eng.; nat'l rep.: ITS.

Operation: June, 1985.

WYOU-TV (Channel 22) CBS
Diversified Communications, 415 Lackawana Ave., Scranton, PA 18503 (717) 961-2222.

Garry Ritchie, v.p. & gen. mgr.; Harry McClintock, prog. dir.; David Bunnell, gen. sls. mgr.; nat'l rep.: Blair.

Operation: 1953; TV sets in area: 843,200.

Wilkes-Barre

WBRE-TV (Channel 28) NBC
Northeastern Television Investor, Ltd. Partnership, 62 S. Franklin St., Wilkes-Barre, PA 18773; (717) 823-2828.

Terry S. Baltimore, v.p. & gen. mgr.; Tom Rosing, gen. sls. mgr.; Ben Justus, chief eng.; nat'l rep.: Petry.

Operation: 1953; TV sets in area: 939,300.

York

WPMT (Channel 43) IND
Westport-York Ltd. Partnership, 2005 S. Queen St., York, PA 17403.

Jonathan Hayes, pres. & gen. mgr.; Michael Lape, v.p. & gen. mgr.; Jon Piana, gen. sls. mgr.; Cindy Hunt, prog. opns. & prom. mgr.; Jack Schuster, chief eng.; nat'l rep.: Petry.

Operation: December, 1986; TV sets in area: 850,000.

RHODE ISLAND
Providence

WJAR-TV (Channel 10) NBC
Outlet Communications, Inc., 111 Dorrance St., Providence, RI 02903 (401) 751-5700.

Bruce G. Sundlun, chm. and CEO; David E. Henderson, pres. & COO; John Sawhill, v.p. & gen. mgr.; Fred Weiss, chief eng.; Charles Compagnone, nat'l sls. mgr.; Linda Sullivan, nat'l sls. mgr.; nat'l rep.: Katz.

Operation: 1949; TV sets in area: 1,891,000.

WLNE (Channel 6) CBS
430 County St., New Bedford, MA 02741; (617) 992-6666.

John D. Quinlan, gen. mgr.; Paul A. Karpowicz, gen. sls. mgr.; Doreen Dawson-Wade, sls. mgr.; Truman B. Taylor, prog. mgr.; George C. Wolf, news dir.; Philip B. Taylor, chief eng.; Robert B. Rieske, mgr. spec. projects.

Operation: 1963; TV households: 533,700.

WNAC-TV (Channel 64) FOX
Sudbrink Bcstg. of New England, Inc., 33 Pine St., Rehoboth, MA 02769 (617) 252-9711.

Vic Rumore, pres.; Ric Gorman, v.p. & gen. mgr.; Bruce Sohigian, sls mgr.; Keith Fotz, prog. dir.; B. Bates, chief eng.; rep.: Seltel.

Operation: December, 1981.

WPRI-TV (Channel 12) ABC
Knight-Ridder Broadcasting, Inc., 25 Catamore Boulevard, East Providence, RI 02914 (401) 438-7200.

Robert E. Rice, pres. & gen. mgr.; Matthew L. Krein, gen. sls. mgr.; Hayden Williams, nat'l sls. mgr.; Sandi Morvillo, reg. sls. mgr.; Edward Passarelli, bus. mgr.; T. Arthur Bone, v.p. & chief eng.; Cathy Perron, prog. mgr.; Jim Vescera, promo. mgr.; Edwin Hart, news dir.; Joseph Fogarty, admin. asst. to gen. mgr.; nat'l rep.: MMT Sales, Inc.

Operation: 1955; TV Households: 2,737,600 (ARB 5-81).

SOUTH CAROLINA
Anderson

WAXA (Channel 40)
Mark III Bcstg. Co., P.O. Box 40, Anderson, SC 29622.
Mary Kupris, pres.
Operation: October, 1984.

Charleston

WCBD-TV (Channel 2) ABC
Charleston Television, Inc., P.O. Box 879, Charleston, SC 29402.

Joseph W. (Bill) Evans, III, v.p. & gen. mgr.; Joan McMahon, gen. sls. mgr.; Alicia Wertimer, lcl. sls. mgr.; Steve Gleason, prog. mgr.; Brian Bogner, promo. mgr.; Richard Fordham, prod. mgr.; Michael Sullivan, news dir.; Jerry Walthall, chief eng.

Operation: 1954.

WCIV (Channel 4) NBC
First Charleston Corp., Highway 703, Mt. Pleasant, SC 29464 (803) 884-8513.

Stephen G. Brock, pres. & gen. mgr.; Foster Morgan, news mgr.; Ken Adkins, sls. mgr.; Carl Shaw, chief eng.

WCSC-TV (Channel 5) CBS
WCSC, Inc. 485 East Bay St., P.O. Box 186, Charleston, SC 29402 (803) 723-8371.

Harold Crump, CEO of WCSC-TV; Dave Allen Petry CEO, co-owner of WCSC; Mark Pierce, exec. v.p.; gen. mgr.; WCSC-TV; Larry Shrum, v.p. & gen. sls. mgr.; Eddie Bolling, v.p. & nat'l/reg. sls. mgr.; Lovell Waugh, v.p. & lcl. sls. mgr.; Jack Becknell, v.p., dir. of eng.; Charlie Thompson, v.p. & dir. prog.; Miriam McManus, v.p., contr.; Andy Hunt, v.p. & prom. dir.; natl rep: Petry.

Operation: 1953; TV Households: 197,100.

WTAT-TV (Channel 24) FOX
Charleston Community Television Ltd., 4301 Arco Lane, Charleston, SC 29418 (803) 744-2424.

David S. Low, gen. mgr. & film buyer; Bill Littleton, prog. dir.; Lawrence Pink, chief eng.; natl. rep.: ITS.

Operation: September, 1985.

Columbia

WCCT-TV (Channel 57)
Carolina Christian Bcgst. Inc., 1221 Sunset Blvd., W., Columbia, SC 29169 (803) 796-7757.

James H. Thompson, pres.; Paul B. Gorman, gen. mgr. & chief eng.; Ginger S. Bruce, sls. mgr. & pub. rel. dir.; Lisa Cruz, prog. mgr.; Joyce Dickerson, traffic mgr.; Ginger S. Bryce, pub. rel. dir.

Operation: September, 1981.

WIS-TV (Channel 10) NBC
1111 Bull St., P.O. Box 367, Columbia, SC 29202; (803) 799-1010.

Dixon C. Lovvorn, sr. v.p. & gen. mgr.; Scott Parks, news dir.; Diane K. Bagwell, prog./promo./mgr.; C. Joseph Tonsing, gen. sls. mgr.; John Augustine, chief eng.

Operation: 1953; TV sets in area: 853,400.

WLTX-TV (Channel 19) CBS
Capital Communications, Inc., P.O. Drawer M, Columbia, SC 29250 (803) 776-3600.

Richard T. Laughridge v.p. & gen. mgr.; Donald M. Bryant, prog. dir.; Bill Aull, chief eng.; Richard T. Laughridge, nat'l sls. mgr.; nat'l rep.: Katz Television.

Operation: 1953; TV sets in area: 289,800.

WOLO-TV (Channel 25) ABC
Columbia TV Broadcasters Inc., Box 4217, Columbia, SC 29240 (803) 754-7525.

David Aiken, gen. mgr.; Joe Mahan, sls. mgr.; Reggie Hall, news dir.; Rick Sprott, chief eng.; rep.: Katz.

Operation: 1961; TV households in area: 273,000.

Florence

WBTW (Channel 13) CBS
Spartan Radiocasting Co., 3430 N. TV Road, Florence, SC 29501 (803) 662-1565.

Bruce R. Miller, gen. mgr.; Tom Wall, gen. sls. mgr.; Jim Griffin, news dir.; natl. rep.: Katz.

Operation: 1954; TV households: 613,300.

WPDE-TV (Channel 15)
Diversified Communications, Inc., Box F-15, Florence, SC 29501 (803) 665-1515.

Bill Christian, v.p. & gen. mgr.; Lynn Young, nat'l sls. mgr.; Mike Reed, gen. sls. mgr.; Charl Jackson, opns. mgr.; Joyce Jordan, bus. mgr.; Jimmy Gamble, chief eng.; nat'l rep.: Blair.

Operation: 1980.

Greenville

WYFF-TV (Channel 4) NBC

Pulitzer Broadcasting Co., 505 Rutherford St., Greenville, SC 29602.

Douglas A. Smith, sr. vice pres. & gen. mgr.; Bill Wheless, sta. mgr.; John Scott, sls. dir.; Fritzie Mumford, prog. dir.; Bob King, chief eng.; Penny Henderson, bus. mgr.; Andy Scott, promo. mgr.; nat'l rep.: Petry.

Operation: 1953; TV sets in area: 956,230.

Spartanburg

WSPA-TV (Channel 7) CBS

Spartan Radiocasting Co., Box 1717, Spartanburg, SC 29304 (803) 576-7777.

Walter J. Brown, pres.; K. Nick Evans, exec. v.p.; Joe Varholy, gen. mgr.; Boyd Bunting, secty.,-treas.; Jimmy Sanders, prgm./stn. mgr.; Fred Tuck, chief eng.; Tom Ahner, trans. engineer; Bill Shatten, promo. mgr.; Rick McCue, gen. sales mgr.; Jerry Smith, local/reg. sales mgr.; Harvey Cox, news dir.; nat'l rep.: Blair.

Operation: 1956; TV sets in area: 2,300,000.

SOUTH DAKOTA
Aberdeen

KPRY-TV (Channel 4) ABC

SDTV, Inc., North Highway 281, Box 1520, Aberdeen, SD 57401 (605) 225-9200.

Eric Davis, mgr.; Ken Walker, news dir.; Earl Miller, chief eng.

Operation: 1958.

Florence

KDLO-TV (Channel 3) CBS

(Satellite of KELO-TV, Sioux Falls, SD)

Midcontinent Broadcasting Co., % KELO-TV, Phillips Ave. & 13th St., Sioux Falls, SD 57102 (605) 336-1100.

Joe Floyd, pres.; N. L. Benston, v.p.; E. R. Ruben, secty.-treas.; Evans Nord, pres. & gen. mgr. of KELO; Joe H. Floyd. v.p.; nat'l rep.: Seltel.

Operation: 1955; TV sets in area: 375,500.

Lead

KHSD-TV (Channel 11) ABC

Duhamel Broadcasting Enterprises, Box 1760, Rapid City, S.D. 57709.

William F. Duhamel, pres. & gen. mgr.; Monte Loos, opns. dir.; Frank Ethrington, dir. of eng.; rep.: Katz.

Operation: November, 1966.

KIVV-TV (Channel 5) NBC

Heritage Media, Inc., Box 677, Rapid City, SD 57709 (605) 394-7777.

Ray Moser, gen. mgr.; Harvey Sachau, mgr. of eng.; Gerry Fenske, gen. sls. mgr.; Les Hofland, prod. mgr.; Robert Slocum, contr.; Dan Schillinger, news dir.; rep.: Blair.

Operation: July, 1976.

Pierre

KPRY-TV (Channel 4) ABC

(Satellite of KSFY-TV, Sioux Falls)

300 N. Dakato Ave., Sioux Falls, SD 57102 (605) 336-1300.

Personnel: See KSFY-TV, Sioux Falls

Operation: 1976.

Rapid City

KEVN-TV (Channel 7) NBC

Heritage Media, Inc., Box 677, Rapid City, SD 57709 (605) 394-7777.

Ray Moser, gen. mgr.; Harvey Sachau, mgr. of eng.; Gerry Fenske, gen. sls. mgr.; Les Hofland, prod. mgr.; Robert Slocum, contr.; Dan Schillinger, news dir.; rep.: Blair.

Operation: July, 1976.

KOTA-TV (Channel 3) ABC

KDUH Channel 4, KHSD Channel 11, KSGW Channel 12 (satellites).

Duhamel Broadcasting Enterprises, Duhamel Bldg., 6th & St. Joe Streets, P.O. Box 1760, Rapid City, SD 57709 (605) 342-2000.

William F. Duhamel, pres. & gen. mgr.; Monte Loos, opns. mgr.; Frank Ethrington, dir. of engineering; Lindell Peterson, farm dir.; nat'l rep: Katz.

Operation: 1955; TV sets in area: 80,200.

Reliance

KPLO-TV (Channel 6) CBS

(Satellite of KELO-TV, Sioux Falls, SD)

Midcontinent Broadcasting Co., % KELO-TV., Phillips Ave. & 13th St., Sioux Falls, SD 57102 (605) 336-1100.

Joe Floyd, pres.; N. L. Bentson, v.p.; E. R. Ruben, secty.-treas.; Evans A. Nord, pres. & gen. mgr. of KELO; Joe H. Floyd, v.p.; nat'l rep.: Seltel.

Operation: 1957; TV sets in area, 375,500.

Sioux Falls

KDLT-TV (Channel 5) NBC

Dakotaland Broadcasting, Inc. P.O. Box 1200, Mitchell SD 57301; (605) 996-7501.

Hal Greene, gen. mgr.; Jim Brady, chief eng.

Operation: 1983; TV households: 235,000.

KELO-TV (Channel 11) CBS

Midcontinent Broadcasting Co., Phillips at 13th, Sioux Falls, SD 57102 (605) 336-1100.

Joe Floyd, pres.; N. L. Bentson, v.p.; E. R. Ruben, secty.-treas.; Evans A. Nord, pres. & gen. mgr. of KELO; Joe H. Floyd, v.p.; Dale Larson, prog. dir.; Jack Townsend, sls. devel. dir.; Scott Burri, prod. mgr.; Cynthia Nord, promo mgr.; Jerry Lofgren, natl. sls. mgr., nat'l rep.: Seltel.

Operation: 1953; TV sets in area: 375,500.

KSFY-TV (Channel 13)

SDTV, Inc., 300 N. Dakota Ave., Sioux Falls, SD 57102.

Harvey Libow, gen. mgr.; Wayne Gudgel, dir. eng.; Craig Sepllerberg, prom. dir.; Marge Hokenstad, prog. dir.; Kenneth Walker, news dir.; sales rep.: Katz.

Operation: July, 1960; TV households: 309,300.

TENNESSEE
Chattanooga

WDEF-TV (Channel 12) CBS

Roy H. Park, Broadcasting of Tennessee, Inc., Broadcast Center, 3300 Broad St., Chattanooga, TN 37402 (615) 267-3392.

Roy H. Park, pres.; Mark Keown, v.p. & gen. mgr.; D. Michael Hood, gen. sls. mgr.; Doris A. Ellis, prog. dir.; William M. Christman, chief eng.; Charles Wilkie, bus. mgr.; nat'l rep.: Blair Television.

Operation: 1954; TV sets in area: 300,000.

WDSI (Channel 61)

WDSI Limited Partnership, 2401 E. Main St., Chattanooga, TN 37404 (615) 697-0661.

Mike Starr, gen. partner; Clifford Pine, gen. mgr. & prog. dir.; Cal Cass, gen. sls. mgr.; Cheryal Morgan, prog. asst.; Jeff Gregory, chief eng.; nat'l rep.: ITS

Operation: January, 1972.

WRCB-TV (Channel 3) NBC

WRCB-TV, Sarkes Tarzian, Inc. 900 Whitehall Road, Chattanooga, TN 37405 (615) 267-5412.

Tom Tolar, gen. mgr.; Lawson Fox, prog. dir.; Doug Short, sls. mgr.; Patti Duffy, promo. mgr.

Operation: 1956; TV sets in area: 571,800.

WTVC (Channel 9) ABC

WTVC, Inc., Box 1150, Chattanooga, TN 37401 (615) 266-4151.

F. Lewis Robertson, v.p., gen. mgr. & progr. mgr.; Dennis Brown, chief eng.; nat'l rep.: Petry.

Operation: 1958; TV homes in area: 466,100.

Crossville

WINT-TV (Channel 20)

Cumberland Communications Corp., Box 608, Crossville, TN 38555; (615) 484-8424.

John A. Cunningham, gen. mgr. & chief eng.; James P. Young, sls. mgr.; Rita L. Young, prog. mgr.; Helen L. Cunningham, office mgr.; Wilda Golob, news & pub. affairs dir.; Robin Cunningham, film dir.

Operation: October, 1976.

Greeneville

WETO (Channel 39) FOX

East Tennessee's Own, Inc., Box 1074, Greeneville, TN 37744.

Jay D. Austin, pres. & gen. sls. mgr.; Bob Lochte, gen. mgr. & prog. dir.; Bobby Rader, prom. mgr.; Larry Bentley, chief eng.; natl. rep.: Busby.

Operation: November, 1985.

Jackson

WBBJ-TV (Channel 7) ABC

Jackson Telecasters Inc.; Box 2387, Muse Street, Jackson, TN 38301 (901) 424-4515.

Al Marra, gen. mgr.; Harvey Hutchinson, gen. sls. mgr.; Rip Ward, chief eng.; nat'l rep.: Katz.

Operation: 1965; TV homes in area: 426,200.

WJWT (Channel 16)

Goldeon Circle Broadcasting, Inc., 364 N. Royal, Jackson, TN 38301; (901) 424-1600.

Bud Borchert, gen. mgr. & prog. dir.; Bill King, gen. sls. mgr.; Pat McKnight, prom. mgr.

Operation: April, 1985.

Johnson City

WJHL-TV (Channel 11) CBS-ABC

Roy H. Park Broadcasting of the Tri-Cities, Inc., 338 East Main St., Johnson City, TN 37602 (615) 926-2151.

Roy H. Park, pres.; W. H. Lancaster, Jr., v.p. & gen. mgr.; Jack Dempsey, sls. mgr.; Al Gregory, prog. dir.; K. B. Skinner, treas.; Mrs. Dorothy Park, secy.; Carl E. Dickenson, chief eng.; nat'l rep.: Blair-TV.

Operation: 1953; TV sets in area: 1,023,400 (ARB).

Kingsport-Johnson City-Bristol

WKPT-TV (Channel 19) ABC

Holston Valley Broadcasting Corp., 222 Commerce, Kingsport, TN 37660. Mail: Box WKPT, Kingsport, TN 37662.

George DeVault, Jr., pres. & gen. mgr.; Ray Walker, v.p., sta. mgr. & gen. sls. mgr.; Harold T. Dougherty, v.p. eng.; rep.: Seltel.

Operation: 1969; TV homes in ADI: 287,600.

Knoxville

WATE-TV (Channel 6) ABC

Nationwide Communications Inc., 1306 Broadway, N.E. Knoxville, TN 37917 (615) 637-9666.

Clark Pollock, pres.; Jim Mikels, gen. mgr.; Jim Abbott, sta. mgr.; Bob Williams, chief eng.; Steve Slack, gen. sls. mgr.; Ray Sylvester, promo. dir.; nat'l rep.: Blair.

Operation: 1953; TV sets in area: 420,500.

WBIR-TV (Channel 10) CBS

Multimedia Broadcasting Co., 1513 Hutchinson, Knoxville, TN 37901 (615) 637-1010.

James T. Lynagh, pres.; James M. Hart, v.p. & gen. mgr.; Robert E. Horton, chief eng.; nat'l rep.: The Katz Agency.

Operation: 1956; TV sets in area: 384,800.

WTVK (Channel 26) NBC

South Central Broadcasting Corp., Box 1388, Knoxville, TN 37901; Memorial Park Road on Sharps Ridge, Knoxville, TN 37901 (615) 687-2312.

John D. Engelbrecht, pres.; George F. Stoltz, v.p.; Leighman D. Groves, secty.-treas.; Duane V. Eastvold, gen. mgr.; Jerry Whitener, sls. mgr.; Robert Glenn, chief eng.; nat'l rep.: Seltel.

Operations: 1953; TV sets in ara: 302,700.

Memphis

WHBQ-TV (Channel 13) ABC

RKO General Inc. (NY), 485 So. Highland Ave., P.O. Box 11407, Memphis, TN 38111 (901) 320-1313.

Alex Bonner, v.p. & gen. mgr.; Jack Bolton, v.p. & gen. sls. mgr.; Dick Kvale, nat'l sls. mgr.; Jimmie Mitchell, lcl. sls. mgr.; Robert Lewis, prog. dir.; Larry Caughlan, chief eng.; nat'l rep.: Harrington, Righter & Parsons.

Operation: 1953; TV households in area: 554,400.

WMC-TV (Channel 5) NBC

Scripps-Howard Broadcasting Co., 1960 Union Ave., Memphis, TN 38104 (901) 726-0555.

Ronald G. Klayman, Jr., v.p. & gen. mgr.; Edw. F. Greaney, Jr., asst gen. mgr. news & public affairs; Joe W. Cooper, asst. gen. mgr., sls.; Charlotte Moore English, asst. gen. mgr.-prog.; J. Philip Slavick, opns. mgr.; Mason Granger, news. dir.; Michael I. Schwartz, eng. mgr.; Robert B. Mize, creative sbcs. mgr.; Oliva Holmes, prom. mgr.; William S. Fee, nat'l sls. mgr.; nat'l rep.: Blair-TV, Inc.

Operation: 1948; TV sets in area: 944,100.

WMKW-TV (Channel 30)

TVX Broadcast Group, Inc., Box 30030, Memphis, TN 38130 (901) 346-3030.

John Trinder, pres.; Morrie P. Beitch, v.p. & gen. mgr.; DeShon Darnell, gen. sls. mgr.; Randy Whitaker, lcl. sls. mgr.; Denise G. Reber, dir. finance; Jean Anders, dir. promo.; Liz Mullen, dir. prog.; Jim Mattson, dir. eng.

Operation: April, 1983.

WPTY-TV (Channel 24)

WPTY Television, a Ltd. Partnership, 2225 Union Ave., Memphis, TN 38104; (901) 278-2424.

Kent E. Lillie, v.p. & gen. mgr.; Steve Barry, nat'l sls. mgr.; Steve Pickell, chief eng.; nat'l rep.: Petry Television.

Operation: 1978.

WREG-TV (Channel 3) CBS

New York Times Broadcasting Service, Inc., 803 Channel 3 Drive, Memphis, TN 38103 (901) 525-1313.

C. Frank Roberts, pres. & gen. mgr.; Olin Morris, v.p. & dir. mgt., dir. pub. affairs; nat'l rep.: The Katz Agency, Inc.

Operation: 1956; TV sets in area: 515,000.

Nashville

WCAY-TV (Channel 30)

TVX of Nashville, 300 Peabody St., Nashville, TN 37210 (615) 256-3030.

John Trinder, pres. & CEO; Dick Williams, gen. mgr.; Dale Fashee, gen. sls. mgr.; Kristen Bailey, prog. dir.; Damon Fultz, lcl. sls. mgr.; Deborah Little, promo. mgr.; Bruce Elder, chief eng.; nat'l rep.: Seltel.

Operation: February, 1984.

WKRN-TV (Channel 2) ABC

441 Murfreesboro Rd., Nashville, TN 37210 (615) 248-7222.

Art Elliot, gen. mgr.; Gene Parker, chief eng.; Bill Lord, news dir.; nat'l rep.: HRP.

Operation: 1953; TV sets in area: 634,500.

WSMV-TV (Channel 4) NBC

WSMV-TV, Inc., P.O. Box 4, Nashville, TN 37202 (615) 749-2244.

Mike Kettenring, pres. & gen. mgr.; Dan Akens, sta. mgr.; Brenda Jordan, prog. coord.; David Byars, chief eng.; nat'l rep.: MMT Sales.

Operation: 1950; TV homes in area: 1,083,200.

WTVF-TV (Channel 5) CBS

Channel Five Television Co., 474 James Robertson Pkwy., Nashville, TN 37219 (615) 244-5000.

Thomas E. Ervin, pres. & gen. mgr.; Carrie Brooks, v.p., treas.; Chris Clark, v.p., news dir.; Bill Jay Bumpus, v.p. prog.

Operation: 1954; TV sets in area: 813,000.

WZTV (Channel 17)

Reel Broadcasting Co., Inc., Multimedia, Inc., P.O. Box 90764, Nashville, TN 37209 (615) 244-1717.

Bob Jay, gen. sls. mgr.; Michael Sambor, natl. sls. mgr.; Tom Bumbera, prog. dir.; Leesa Crawford, traf. mgr.; Ray McInturff, chief eng.

Operation: March, 1976.

TEXAS

Abilene

KRBC-TV (Channel 9) NBC

Abilene Radio & Television Co., 4510 S. 14th St., Abilene, TX (915) 692-4242; TWX: 910-897-5414.

Dale Ackers, pres. & gen. mgr.; Ken Knox, sta. mgr.; Jerry Shackelford, prog. mgr.; Bob Lloyd, chief eng.; nat'l rep.: Blair Television.

Operation: 1953; TV sets in area: 200,000.

KTAB-TV (Channel 32) CBS

Big Country Television Co., Box 5676, Abilene, TX (915) 695-2777.

Bill Terry, gen. mgr.; Wayne Roy, gen. sls. mgr.; Bryan Mundy, ops. mgr.; Jerry Marshall, lcl. sls. mgr.; Bob Bartlett, news dir.; Leland Ohlhausen, chief eng.; nat'l rep.: Katz Television.

Operation: 1979; sets in area: 138,000.

Abilene-Sweetwater

KTXS-TV (Channel 12) ABC

Abilene-Sweetwater Bdcstg. Co., 4420 N. Clack, Abilene, TX 79603 (915) 677-2281.

Clay Milstead, gen. mgr.; Monte Williams, chief eng.; rep.: Seltel.

Amarillo

KAMR-TV (Channel 4) NBC

Cannan Communications, Inc., P.O. Box 1224, Wichita Falls, TX 76307 (806) 383-3321.

Darrold A. Cannan, Jr., pres.; Ray Poindexter, v.p. & gen. mgr.; Larry Taylor, sls. mgr.; John Schnabel, bus. mgr.; Ken High, chief eng.; Joe Sherrill, op. mgr.; Lynn Walker, news dir.

Operation: 1953

KCIT (Channel 14) FOX

1019 S. Fillmore, Amarillo, TX 79101 (806) 374-1414.

Ralph C. Wilson Jr., pres.; Fred M. Hutching, gen. & gen. sls. mgr.; Scott McIver, prog. dir. & film buyer; Harry L. Strader, prom. mgr.; Dick Stafford, chief eng.; natl. rep.: MMT.

Operation: October, 1982.

KFDA-TV (Channel 10) CBS

Panhandle Telecasting Co., P.O. Box 1400, Amarillo, TX 79189; (806) 383-2226.

R. H. Drewry, pres.; Mike Lee, gen. mgr.; J. P. Goode, bus. mgr.; Walt Howard, news dir.; Tim Winn, chief eng.; Joy Sherrod, sls. mgr.

Operation: 1953; TV sets in area: 222,200.

KVII (Channel 7) ABC

Marsh Media, Inc., One Broadcast Center, Amarillo, TX 79101 (806) 373-1787.

James R. McCormick, pres. & gen. mgr.; John Patrick, gen. sales mgr.

Operation: 1957.

Austin

KBVO (Channel 42)

Drawer 2728, Austin, TX 78768.

Steve Beard, gen. mgr.; Ray McEachern, sta. mgr.; Curt Prince, lcl. sls. mgr.; George Gould, natl. sls. mgr.; Patti Smith, prom. mgr.; Bill Enloe, chief, eng.; nat'l rep.: Katz.

Operation: December, 1983.

KTBC-TV (Channel 7) CBS

The Times Mirror Co., Box 2223, Austin, TX 78767 (512) 476-7777.

Jack E. Harrison, v.p. & gen. mgr.; Charlie King, gen. sls. mgr.

KVUE (Channel 24) ABC

KVUE-TV, Inc. Box 9927, Austin TX 78766 (512) 459-6521.

Joe Jerkins, pres. & gen. mgr.; Al Helton, prog. mgr.; Michael J. Wenglar, chief eng.

Operation: 1971.

KXAN (Channel 36) NBC
Kingstip Communications, Inc., P.O. Box 490, Austin TX 78767 (512) 476-3636.
Jane Wallace, pres. & gen. mgr.; Lyle Banks, gen. sls. mgr.; George Csahanin, chief eng.
Operation: 1965.

Beaumont

KBMT-TV (Channel 12) ABC
Texas Telecasting, Inc., Box 1550, Beaumont, TX 77706 (713) 883-7512.
Michael D. McKinnon, pres.; Max A. Sklower, exec. v.p. & gen. mgr.; Tom Michalk, gen. sls. mgr.; Austin Hodges, chief eng.; nat'l rep.: Blair Television.
Operation: 1961.

KFDM-TV (Channel 6) CBS
Freedom TV Sub, Inc., P.O. Box 7128, 2955 Interstate 10 East, Beaumont, TX 77706 (409) 892-6622.
Larry Beaulieu, v.p. & sta. mgr.; Richard Kihn, chief eng.; nat'l rep., Petry & Co.
Operation: 1955; TV sets in area: 241,000.

Brownsville

KVEO (Channel 23) NBC
394 N. Expressway, Brownsville, TX 78520 (512) 544-2323.
L. William Heyman, Jr., gen. mgr.; Brent Skinner, gen. sls. mgr.; Brad Levy, prog. dir.; Ignacio Cantu, dir. eng.; nat'l rep.: Seltel.
Operation: 1981.

Bryan

KBTX-TV (Channel 3) CBS
Brazos Broadcasting Co., 4141 E. 29th St., P.O. Drawer 3730, Bryan, TX 77805 (409) 846-7777.
M. N. Bostick, pres.; Ulman McMullen, sta. mgr.; nat'l rep.: Seltel.
Operation: May, 1957; TV sets in area: 220,000.

Corpus Christi

KIII (Channel 3) ABC
Texas Television, Inc., 4750 S. Padre Island Dr., Corpus Christi, TX 78404.
Michael D. McKinnon, pres.; Max Sklower, gen. mgr.; Leonard Roper, bus. mgr.; Billy Brotherton, sta. mgr.; rep.: Blair Television.
Operation: 1964; TV households: 318,900.

KORO (Channel 28)
Telecorpus, Inc., 102 N. Mesquite, Corpus Christi, TX 78401 (512) 883-2823.
Servando Caballero, gen. mgr.; Felipe Franco, chf. eng.
Operation: 1977.

KRIS-TV (Channel 6) NBC
Gulf Coast Broadcasting Co., Box 840, Corpus Christi, TX 78403 (512) 883-6511.
T. Frank Smith, pres. & gen. mgr.; Van Johnson, sr. v.p.; sta. mgr.; Charlie Barte, sls. mgr.; Marvin Born, dir. of eng.; nat'l rep.: Petry.
Operation: 1956; TV sets in area: 116,780.

KZTV (Channel 10) CBS
K-Six Television, Inc., 301 Artesian, Corpus Christi, TX; 78401.

Vann M. Kennedy, pres. & gen. mgr.; Eugene Looper, prog. dir.; Jim Bixler, comm. mgr.; Walter Furley, news dir.; Dale Taylor, chief eng.
Operation: 1956.

Dallas-Fort Worth

KDAF-TV (Channel 33) FOX
Fox TV Stations, 8001 Carpenter Freeway, Dallas, TX 75247; (214) 634-8833.
Raymond J. Schonbak, v.p. & gen. mgr.; Katy Ellitt-Atteberry, gen. sls. mgr.; Joe Maggio, chief eng.; nat'l rep.: Katz.
Operation: 1980.

KDFI-TV (Channel 27)
P.O. Box 561427, Dallas, TX 75356-1427; (214) 637-2727.
John McKay, pres.; Thoren Schroeck, v.p., sls.; Ed Murlatt, chief eng.
Operation: January, 1981.

KDFW-TV (Channel 4) CBS
KDFW-TV, Inc., 400 North Griffin St., Dallas, TX 75202 (214) 720-4444.
Bill Baker, v.p. & gen. mgr.; Tom Collier, gen. sls. mgr; Joe Bell, prog. dir.; Warren Farrar, chief eng.; rep.: Harrington, Righter & Parsons.
Operation: 1949; TV sets in area: 1,645,980.

KTXA (Channel 21)
Channel 21, Inc., 1712 E. Randol Mill Rd., Arlington, TX (817) 265-2100. Owned by Taft Bdcst. Co.
William P. Castleman, v.p./gen. mgr.; Dirk Brinkerhoff, gen. sls. mgr.; Kathy Daume, lcl. sls. mgr.; Glen P. Dyer, prod. mgr.; Jerry Stretch, mgr. bus. affairs.
Operation: 1981.

KXAS-TV (Channel 5) NBC
North Texas Broadcasting Corp., 3900 Barnett St., Ft. Worth, TX 76101 (817) 429-1550.
Frank O'Neill, pres. & gen. mgr.; Russ Thornton, dir., admin. & devel.; Patty Parker, gen. sls. mgr.; Bill Shock, eng. dir.
Operation: 1948.

KXTX-TV (Channel 39)
CBN Continental Bcstg., 3900 Harry Hines Blvd., Dallas, TX 75219 (214) 521-3900.
Dick Bove, v.p. & gen. mgr; Phil Mazur, gen. sls. mgr.; Harold Nash, chief eng.; sales rep.: Adam Young, Inc.
Operation: February, 1968; TV households: 2,006,100.

WFAA-TV (Channel 8) ABC
A. H. Belo Corp. (parent organization of The Dallas Morning News and WFAA-TV), Communications Center, Dallas, TX 75202 (214) 748-9631.
David T. Lane, pres. & gen. mgr.; Buff Parham, gen. sls. mgr.; Bob Robinson, opns. mgr.; Marty Haag, v.p. & exec. news dir.; Beaven Els, chief engr.; Michael Grant, exec. dir. prog. & promo; Pat Oswald, controller; nat'l rep.: Telerep.
Operation: 1949; TV sets in area: 1,647,700.

El Paso

KCIK (Channel 14)
Cristo Rey Corp., 3100 N. Stanton St., El Paso, TX 79903 (915) 533-1414.

Robert Munoz, genl mgr.; Jay Duncan, prog. mgr.; Vaquero Cooper, chief eng.; nat'l rep: ITS.
Operation: 1979; sets in area: 283,200.

KDBC-TV (Channel 4) CBS
El Paso Television Co., 2201 Wyoming Ave., El Paso, Texas 79903 (915) 532-6551.
Sam Kobren, gen. mgr.; Richard Morales, bus. mgr.; Charles Maly, prog. dir.; Walter Ward, chief eng.; Ron McDaniel, sls. dir.; nat'l rep.: Seltel.
Operation: 1953; TV sets in area: 222,000.

KINT-TV (Channel 26)
Paso Del Norte Bcstg. Corp., 5426 N. Mesa Dr., El Paso, TX 79912 (916) 581-1126.
Richard A. Najera, bd. chm.; Mary S. Ponce, pres.; Walt Dalton, sta. mgr.-sls. mgr.; Karl W. Moran, contr.; Jose Luis Torres, news dir.; Sylvia Martinez, traf.-prog. dir.; Alfredo Durand, chief eng.
Operation: January, 1984.

KTSM-TV (Channel 9) NBC
Tri-State Broadcasting Co., Inc., 801 N. Oregon St., El Paso, TX 79903 (915) 532-5421.
Karl O. Wyler, pres. & gen. mgr.; Jack Rye, exec. v.p. & progs.; John Phelan, v.p., sls.; W. T. McGill, v.p., eng'.; nat'l rep.: Blair.
Operation: 1953; TV households in area: 306,260.

KVIA-TV (Channel 13)
KVIA-TV Marsh Media—El Paso, Box 12277, El Paso, TX 79912.
Richard E. Pearson, gen. mgr.; Cathy Franco, prog. dir.; Steve Giust, gen. sls. mgr.; Jack Wilkinson, chief eng.; natl rep.: Katz Television.
Operation: 1956; TV sets in area: 168,600.

Fort Worth

KTVT (Channel 11)
Gaylord Broadcasting Co., 5322 Bridge St., Fort Worth, TX 76103 (817) 738-1951; Branch office: 10111 N. Central Expressway, Dallas, TX 75231.
Charles L. Edwards, v.p. & gen. mgr.; Harry J. Delanmey, sta. mgr.; nat'l rep.: Telerep.

Harlingen

KGBT-TV (Channel 4) CBS
Draper Communications, Inc., P.O. Box 2567, Harlingen, TX 78551. (512) 421-4444.
Thomas H. Draper, pres.; Don E. Locke, v.p. & gen. mgr.; John S. Clark, gen. sls. mgr.; Frank Ogden, chief eng.; nat'l rep.: Katz.
Operation: 1953. TV sets in area: 177,500.

Houston

KHOU-TV (Channel 11) CBS
Gulf Television Corp., P.O. Box 11, Houston, TX 77001 (713) 526-1111.
Allen E. Howard, pres. & gen. mgr.; Craig Bland, gen. sls. mgr.; Hal Kemp, prog. mgr.; Andrew Klarer, prod. mgr.; Paula Walker, news dir.; nat'l rep.: Telerep.
Operation: March, 1953; TV households: 1,326,000.

KHTV (Channel 39)
KHTV, Gaylord Bdcstg. Co., 7700 Westpark Drive, P.O. Box 630129, Houston, TX 77263-0129; (713) 781-3939.

Ed Trimble, v.p. & gen. mgr.; John De Roche, gen. sls. mgr.; Bob Clark, prog. dir.; Trish Naber, prom. mgr.; John R. Schilberg, chief eng.; nat'l rep.: MMT.
Operation 1967.

KPRC-TV (Channel 2) NBC
H & C Communications, Inc., 8181 Southwest Freeway, Houston, TX 77074 (713) 771-4631.
William P. Hobby, bd. chmn.; James E. Crowther, pres. bdcst. group; Tom Reiff, pres. & gen. mgr. Ch. 2; Red Koch, v.p., prog.; Art Biggs, v.p. eng.; Paul Paolicelli, v.p. news; Dick Daggett, gen. sls. mgr.; Bruce Bryant, creative svcs. dir.; nat'l rep.: Petry.
Operation: 1949; TV sets in area: 1,409,530.

KRIV-TV (Channel 26) FOX
Fox TV Stations, Inc., P.O. Box 22810, 3935 Westheimer, Houston, TX 77227 (713) 626-2610..
M. Jerry Marcus, v.p. & gen. mgr.; Gayle Brammer, v.p. & gen. sls. mgr.; Roz Brown, prog. dir.; Mary Delaney, prom. mgr.; nat'l rep.: Katz.
Operation: August, 1971; TV households: 1,115,900.

KTRK-TV (Channel 13) ABC
Capital Cities Communications, Inc.; mailing address: P.O. Box 12, Houston, TX 77001; offices and studios: 3310 Bissonnet, Houston, TX (713) 666-0713; TWX: 910-881-1511; Transmitter: Alameda, TX.
Thomas S. Murphy, pres. & chmn.; Paul Bures, v.p. & gen. mgr.; Jim Masucci, oper. dir.; Charles Wolf, creative svcs. mgr.; Gerald Kennedy, prod. supvr.; Margaret Shilstone, prom. supvr.; Jim Topping, news dir.; J. L. Hamilton, chief studio eng.; Art Giddings, chief transmitter eng.; spot sales rep., Capital Cities/ABC.
Operation: 1954; TV homes in area: 1,457,400.

KTXH (Channel 20)
TVX of Houston, Inc., 8950 Kirby Drive, Houston, TX 77054 (713) 661-2020.
Julio Bermudez, v.p. & gen. mgr.; Scott Sanders, gen. sls. mgr.; Patty Duncan, prog. dir.; Lennie Philyaw, promo. dir.; Jim Aldendorf, bus. mgr.; Thomas Daniels, chief eng.; nat'l rep.: Seltel.
Operation: November, 1982.

Irving

KHSX (Channel 49)
Cela, Inc., 1957 E. Irving Blvd., Irving, TX 75060 (214) 721-0104.
Eldred Thomas, pres. & gen. mgr.; Mario Montes, prog. mgr.; Richie Martin, prom. mgr.; Steve Fjordbak, news dir.; Tom Long Jr., chief eng.
Operation: April, 1984.

Jacksonville

KETK-TV (Channel 56) NBC
Texas American Bdcstg. Ltd., 5656 N. Jackson St., Jacksonville, TX 75766 (214) 586-5644.
Phil Hurley, pres. & gen. mgr.; John Gaston, gen. sls. mgr.; Jean Pavelka, prog. dir.; Mike Stanford, opns. mgr.; Bece Cantu, prom. mgr.; John Jenkins, news dir.; Moe Strout, chief eng.; natl. rep.: Blair.
Operation: February, 1987.

Kerrville

KRRT (Channel 35) FOX
TVX of San Antonio, 6218 N.W. Loop 410, San Antonio, TX 78238 (512) 684-0035.
Richard B. Lowe, v.p. & gen. mgr.; Steve Scollard, gen. sls. mgr.; Kem Maher, prog. dir.; Lennie Philyaw, prom. mgr.; Brian Coombs, chief eng.; natl. rep.: Seltel.
Operation: November, 1985.

Laredo

KGNS-TV (Channel 8) NBC
Fabri Development Corp., Box 2829, Laredo, TX 78041 (512) 727-8888.
Michael Clark, gen. mgr.; T. Frank Smith IV, gen. sls. mgr.; Velia Herrera, prog. dir.; rep.: Katz.
Operation: 1956; TV sets in area: 23,000

KLDO (Channel 27) ABC
Panorama Broadcasting Co., 1600 Water St., Riverdrive Mall, Laredo, TX 78040; (512) 727-0027.
Elia Johnston, gen. mgr., film buyer, gen. sls. mgr. & prog. dir.; Cindy Rodriguez, promo. mgr.; Randy Kent, news dir.; Rene Gonzalez, chief eng.; nat'l rep.: Adam Young.
Operation: December, 1984.

KVTV (Channel 13) CBS
Shea & Anna St., Laredo, TX 78040; P.O. Box 2039, Laredo, TX 78044.
Vann M. Kennedy, pres. & gen. mgr.; Jay Dickey, sta. mgr.; Debbie Shoup, news dir.; Ralph Quiroz, chief eng.; sls. rep.: Seltel.
Operation: December, 1973.

Longview

KLMG-TV (Channel 51) CBS
East Texas TV Network, 701 N. Access Rd., Box 5151, Longview, TX 75608.
Clara J. McLaughlin, pres. & CEO; J. Wesley Ferns, v.p. & gen. mgr.; Ron Cooke, gen. sls. mgr.; Cathy Smith, prog. dir.; Mary Hobbs, promo mgr., Steve Walker, news dir.
Operation: September, 1984.

Lubbock

KAMC-TV (Channel 28) ABC
McAlister TV Enterprises Inc., Box 2805, Lubbock, TX 79408 (806) 745-2828.
Bob Nash, pres. & gen. mgr.; Bill Maddox, sls. mgr.; Bill Baker, chief eng.; A. C. Wimberly, prog. dir.
Operation: 1968; TV homes in area: 147,180.

KCBD-TV (Channel 11) NBC
Caprock Telecasting Co., Inc., Box 2190, Lubbock, TX 79408 (806) 744-1414.
Bill de Tournillon, gen. mgr.; Peggy Sullivan, prog. dir.; Sherrell Lambert, dir. of eng.; Craig Wells, sls. mgr.; nat'l rep.: Katz.
Operation: 1953: TV sets in area: 224,00.

KJTV (Channel 34)
Box 3757, Lubbock, TX, 79452 (806) 745-1134.
Ray Moran, pres.; Brad Moran, gen. mgr. & prog. dir.; Randy Roberts, gen. sls. mgr.; Guy Smith, chief eng.; nat'l rep.: Seltel.
Operation: January, 1982.

KLBK-TV (Channel 13) CBS
Charles Woods TV Corp., 7400 University Ave., Lubbock, TX 79423 (806) 745-2345.
Charles Woods, pres.; David Underwood, gen. mgr. & sls. mgr.; Chris Alexander, news dir.; Don King, chief eng.; nat'l rep.: Blair.
Operation: 1952; TV sets in area: 188,000.

Lufkin

KTRE-TV (Channel 9) ABC
Buford Television Inc. of Lufkin, Box 729, Lufkin, TX 75901 (409) 853-5873.
Errol R. Kapellusch, gen. mgr.; Duane Dargis, sls. mgr.; nat'l rep.: Katz.
Operation: 1955.

Midland

KMID-TV (Channel 2) ABC
Telepictures Broadcasting Corp., Inc., KMID-TV, Midland, TX 79711 (915) 563-2222.
John Foster, gen. mgr.; nat'l rep.: Katz.
Operation: 1953; TV sets in area: 166,7000.

Monahans

KTPX-TV (Channel 9) NBC
MSP Television of Midland-Odessa, Box 6699, Midland, TX 79701 (915) 563-4210.
Dan Robbins, gen. mgr.; Richard Howard, news dir.; Grady Woodward, dir. of eng.
Operation: 1958; TV homes in area: 173,800.

Odessa

KOSA-TV (Channel 7) CBS
Adams TV of Texas, Inc., 1211 N. Whitaker, Odessa, TX 79760 (915) 337-8301.
Ben Strickland, v.p., gen. mgr. & gen. sls. mgr.; Vic Ludington, lcl. sls. mgr.; Al Harris, chief eng.; Dan Scott, news. dir.; nat'l rep.: Blair.
Operation: 1956; TV homes in area: 119,500.

KPEJ (Channel 24)
Southwest Multi Media-Odessa-Midland, Box 11009, Odessa, TX 79763 (915) 337-2424.
Dan J. Roberts, gen. mgr.; Michael T. Walenta, opns. mgr.; Stan Kaye, gen. sls. mgr.; Catherine Young, prog. dir.; Rod McGehee, prom. mgr.; nat'l. rep.: ITS.
Operation: June, 1986.

Port Arthur

KJAC-TV (Channel 4) NBC
Southeast Texas Television Corp., P.O. Box 3257, Port Arthur, TX 77643 (409) 985-5557.
Rush Evans, v.p.-gen. mgr.; Gary Powers, comm. mgr.; Charles Ravell, chief eng.; nat'l rep.: Katz.
Operation: 1957; TV sets in area: 167,000.

San Angelo

KACB-TV (Channel 3) NBC
(Satellite of KRBC-TV, Abilene)
Abilene Radio & TV Co., 4510 14th St., P.O. Box 178, Abilene, TX 79604 (915) 692-4242.
Dale Ackers, pres.; Ken Knox, sta. & sls. mgr.; Jerry Shackelford, prog. dir.; Glen Welch, chief eng.; rep.: Blair TV.
Operation: 1962.

KIDY (Channel 6)

Sage Bcstg. Co., 3901 W. Heimer, Suite 190, Houston, TX 77027.

Raymond Schindler, pres.

Operation: July, 1983.

KLST (Channel 8) CBS

Jewell Television, 2800 Armstrong, San Angelo, TX 76903 (915) 655-7383.

Phil Brassie, gen. mgr.; Lou Kordek, news dir.; Darryl Naramore, chief eng.; nat'l rep.: Katz.

Operation: July, 1953; sets in area: 89,800.

San Antonio

KENS-TV (Channel 5) CBS

5400 Fredericksburg Rd., San Antonio, TX 78229; P.O. Box TV5, 78299; (512) 366-5000.

Mike Conly, pres. bdcst./gen. mgr.; Dave Sankovich, v.p., gen. sls. mgr.; Jack Forehand, v.p.-sta. mgr.; Bob Rogers, v.p., news; Susan Korbel, dir. mktg.; Rebecca Dewan, dir., finance; Jerry Nordsiek, chief eng.; nat'l rep.: Katz.

Operation: 1950; TV sets in area: 1,112,600.

KMOL-TV (Channel 4) NBC

United TV, Inc., P.O. Box 2641, San Antonio, TX 78205 (512) 226-4251.

Robert P. Donohue, v.p., gen. mgr.; Kevin Donohue, gen. sls. mgr.; John Seabers, natl. sls. mgr.; Dennis Marshall, creative svcs. dir.; Gene Hansbauer, bus. mgr.; Mort Barrett, mktg. develop. mgr.; Phil Johnson, lcl. sls. mgr.; Jack Carroll, prog. dir.; Ron Harris, news dir.; Harold Friesenhahn, chief eng.; Ray Laube, prod. dir.; rep.: Telerep.

Operation: 1949; TV homes: 531,000.

KSAT-TV (Channel 12) ABC

H&C Communications, Inc., Box 2478, San Antonio, TX 78298 (512) 228-1200.

James Schiavone, pres. & gen. mgr.; Rick Andrycha, prog. mgr.; Jack Dix, gen. sls. mgr.; rep.: Petry.

Operation: 1957; TV homes in area: 945,300.

KWEX-TV (Channel 41)

The Spanish International Communications Corp., 411 E. Durango Blvd., San Antonio, TX 78204; (512) 227-4141.

Jose C. Cancela, gen. mgr.; Heberto Gutierrez, gen. sls. mgr.; Armando Solis, contr.; James R. Meek, dir. eng.

Temple-Waco

KCEN-TV (Channel 6) NBC

Channel 6, Inc., P.O. Box 6103, Temple, TX 76503 (817) 773-6868; Waco office, 4716 W. Waco Drive, Waco, TX 76710 (817) 776-7016; TWX 910-890-4870.

Anyse Sue Mayborn, pres.; Dan Lesmeister, v.p. & gen. mgr.; Ken Smith, chief eng.; nat'l rep.: Blair TV.

Operation: 1953; TV sets in area: 245,600.

Tyler-Longview

KLTV (Channel 7) ABC

Channel 7, Inc., Box 957, Tyler, TX 75710 (214) 597-5588.

Robert P. Buford, Gerald B. & Geoffrey R. Buford, owners; Larry Harris, exec. v.p. & gen. mgr.; Bob Way, chief eng.; Gayle Helms, prog. dir.; nat'l rep.: Katz Agency.

Operation: 1954; TV sets in area: 178,500.

Victoria

KAVU-TV (Channel 25) NBC

Community Bcstg. of Coastal Bend, Inc., Box 4929, Victoria, TX 77903 (512) 576-5288.

Doug McDougal, pres. & gen. mgr.; Bob Hesse, gen. sls. mgr.; Helen Villarreal, prog. dir.; Mike Burch, news dir.; Fred Berrad, tech. eng.; nat'l rep.: Adam Young.

Operation: July, 1982.

KVCT (Channel 19) ABC

Victoria Communications Corporation, P.O. Box 1879, Victoria, TX 77902.

William Murphy, pres.; Betty Grimsinger, gen. mgr. & gen. sls. mgr.; Doris Littles, prog. dir.; Brenda Simpson, news dir.

Operation: 1969.

Waco

KWTX-TV (Channel 10) CBS

KWTX Broadcasting Company, 6700 American Plaza, Waco, TX 76712. Mail: P.O. Box 2636, Waco, TX 76702.

M. N. Bostick, pres. Ray Deaver, v.p., sta. mgr. & sls. mgr.; Robert Levy, sec.-treas.; Lisa Oatman, natl.-regl. sls. mgr.; Ken Musgrave, chief eng.; Ralph Webb, prog. dir.; natl. rep.: Seltel.

Operation: 1955; TV sets in area: 245,600.

KXXV (Channel 25) ABC

Shamrock Bdcstg., Box 2522, Waco, TX 76702 (817) 754-2525.

Robert A. Mann, gen. mgr.; Bob Good, sta. mgr.; Don Shores, gen. sls. mgr.; Jinx Dennix, prog. dir.; Don Marion, news dir.; Lou Strowger, chief eng.; natl. rep.: Katz.

Operation: January, 1985.

Weslaco

KRGV-TV (Channel 5) ABC

Mobile Video Tapes, Inc., 900 E. Expressway Avenue, Weslaco, TX 78596 (512) 968-5555.

Douglas L. Manship, pres.; Ray Alexander, gen. mgr.; Jim Cook, lcl. sls. mgr.; Tom Hagner, gen. sls. mgr.; Julian Adame, prgm. dir.; Rick Diaz, news dir.; nat'l rep.: Blair Television.

Operation: 1954; TV sets in area: 218,000.

Wichita Falls

KAUZ-TV (Channel 6) CBS

Adams TV of Wichita Falls, P.O. Box 2130, Wichita Falls, TX 76307.

Mark Cumming, v.p. & gen. mgr. & natl. sls. mgr.; Linda Hilden, prog. dir.; Leon Hoeffner, chief eng.; Sandy Berthelot, natl. sls. asst.; nat'l rep.: Blair Television.

KFDX-TV (Channel 3) NBC

Price Communications, Box 4000, Wichita Falls, TX 76308 (817) 692-4530.

Bob Price, chmn.; Dick Appleton, sr. v.p., TV; Jack West, gen. mgr.; Mike Muirhead, natl. sls. mgr.; Jack Young, lcl.-rgnl. sls. mgr.; Jim Smith, dir. of eng.; Peggy Edgar, film ed.; nat'l rep.: Katz.

Operation: 1953; TV sets in area: 250,000.

KJTL (Channel 18)

Wichita Falls TV, Ltd., Box 4865, Wichita Falls, TX 76308 (817) 691-1808.

Peter D'Acosta, v.p. & gen. mgr.; Karen Dickins, sls. mgr.; Ken Thomason, chief eng.; nat'l rep.: Seltel.

Operation: May, 1985.

UTAH
Ogden

KOOG-TV (Channel 30)
Ogden Television, Inc., 1309 16th St. 84404 (801) 621-3030.
E. Russell Sorensen, gen. mgr.; Steve Pluim, gen. sls. mgr.;
John Mason, prog. dir., film buyer & prom. mgr.; Lee Latham,
chief eng.; natl. rep.: Mutual TeleSales.
Operation: October, 1985.

Salt Lake City

KSL-TV (Channel 5) CBS
KSL, Inc., Broadcast House, 5 Triad Center, Salt Lake City,
UT 84110-1160 (801) 575-5555.
Jack Adamson, pres.; William R. Murdoch, v.p., gen. mgr.;
Jim Monroe, mktg. dir.; J. Talmage Ball, chief eng.; J. Spencer
Kinard, v.p./news dir.; David Manookin, dir. prog.; nat'l rep.:
Petry
Operation: 1949; TV homes in area: 841,900.

KSTU (Channel 13)
Mountain West Television, 5020 W. Amelia Earhart Dr., Salt
Lake City, UT 84116 (801) 532-1300.
Vickie Street, gen. mgr.; Jo-Ann Wong, prog. dir.; Susan
Adams, nat'l sls. mgr.; Milt Jouflas, lcl. sls. mgr.; nat'l rep.:
Blair.
Operation: 1978.

KTVX (Channel 4) ABC
United TV, Inc., 1760 Fremont Dr., Salt Lake City, UT
84104.
Evan Thompson, pres.; David J. Woodcock, v.p. & gen.
mgr.; Robert Galle, gen. sls. mgr.; Gordon Acker, prog. dir.;
Randy Hoffman, promo. mgr.; Jim McDermaid, tech dir.
Operation: 1948; TV sets in area: 901,000.

KUTV (Channel 2) NBC
KUTV Inc., 2185 S. 3600 West, Salt Lake City, UT 84119
(801) 973-3000.
George C. Hatch, pres.; Al Seethaler, v.p. & gen. mgr.; John
Mason, prog. dir.; Dick Thiriot, film buyer, nat'l rep.: katz.
Operation: 1954; TV set in area: 771,200.

VERMONT
Burlington

WCAX-TV (Channel 3) CBS
Mt. Mansfield Television, Inc., P.O. Box 608, Joy Dr., So.
Burlington, VT 05402 (802) 862-5761.
S. T. Martin, pres. & gen. mgr.; Peter R. Martin, exec. v.p. &
prog. dir.; Ken Jarvis, gen. sls. mgr.; Stuart Hall, v.p. & prod.
mgr.; Charles Liese, chief eng.; Judy Clark, film mgr.; Ken
Greene, dir. prom.-pub. affairs; Dolores Drolette, v.p., cont.
nat'l rep., HRP, NY.
Operation: 1954; TV sets in area: U.S. 1,168,000, Canada
1,328,000.

WVNY-TV (Channel 22) ABC
Citadel Communications Co., Ltd., 100 Market Square,
Burlington, VT 05401 (802) 658-8022.
Philip J. Lombardo, pres./gen. mgr.; William Bradley, gen.
mgr. v.p.; Tom Hansen, dir. bdct. opns.; Brad Worthen, gen. sls.
mgr.; Richard Meyers, chief eng.
Operation: 1982.

Hartford-Hanover

WNNE-TV (Channel 31) NBC
WNNE-TV, Inc., Box 1310, White River Junction, VT 05001
(802) 295-3100.
Karen J. Creighton, pres. & gen. mgr.; Steve Rozov, v.p. &
gen. sls. mgr.; Ginny Doyle, prog. dir.; Joseph Alvin v.p. &
chief eng.
Operation: 1978.

VIRGINIA
Bristol

WCYB-TV (Channel 5) NBC, ABC
Appalachian Broadcasting Corporation, 101 Lee St., Bristol,
VA 24201 (703) 669-4161.
Robert H. Smith, Jr., exec. v.p. & gen. mgr.; Jack Shaver, v.p.
sls. & asst. to gen. mgr.; Echel Edens, chief eng.; Charles
Lineberger, prog. mgr.; Terry Dugas, opns. mgr.; Sandhi Ko-
zsuch, dir. prod./creative svcs.; Steve Hawkins, news dir.; nat'l
rep.: Petry.
Operation: 1956; TV sets in area: 1,125,000.

Charlottesville

WVIR-TV (Channel 29) NBC
Virginia Broadcasting Corp., P.O. Box 769, Charlottesville,
VA 22902 (804) 977-7082.
Lloyd T. Smith, Jr., pres.; Harold B. Wright, Jr., v.p. & gen.
mgr.; Jim Fernald, gen. sls. mgr.
Operation: March, 1973; TV households: 82,000.

Hampton-Norfolk

WVEC-TV (Channel 13) ABC
1930 E. Pembroke Ave., Hampton, VA 23663; 613 Woodis
Ave., Norfolk, VA 23510; (804) 625-1313.
J. William Beindorf, v.p. & gen. mgr.; Rick Keilty, gen. sls.
mgr.; Meyer Davis, opns. & prog. mgr.; Cil Frazier, adv./
promo. mgr.; Dick Cannon, chief eng.; nat'l rep.: Petry.
Operation: 1953; TV sets in area: 502,900.

Harrisonburg

WHSV-TV (Channel 3) ABC
Benedek Bcstg. Corp., P.O. Box TV 3, Highway 33 West,
Harrisonburg, VA 22801 (703) 433-9191.
Michael R. Lennon, gen. mgr.; Bob Bolyard, nat'l sls. mgr.;
Christopher Jones, opns. mgr.
Operation: 1953; TV households: 293,500.

Lynchburg

WSET-TV (Channel 13) ABC
WSET, Inc. 2320 Langhorne Rd., P.O. Box 11588, Lynchburg, VA 24506 (804) 528-1313.
David F. McAtee, pres. & gen. mgr.; Beve Lutz, business
mgr., Jack Tackett, v.p. & sls. mgr.; Douglas Daniel, chief eng.;
nat'l rep.: Katz Agency.
Operation: 1953; TV households in area: 350,630.

Manassas

WTKK (Channel 66)
National Capital Christian Broadcasting, Inc., 9008 Center
St., Manassas, VA 22110 (703) 369-3400.
Lester R. Raker, pres.; Phil DeLorme, chief eng.; Dawn

Morales, traffic mgr.; Tom Fultz, sta. mgr.; Kevin Thomas, sls. mgr.
Operation: 1978.

Norfolk

WTKR-TV (Channel 3) CBS
WTKR-TV, Inc., 720 Boush St., Norfolk, VA 23510 (804) 446-1000.
Bill Peterson, pres. & gen. mgr.; Rufus DeVane, gen. sls. mgr.; Joe Perkins, prog. dir.; Julie McCollum, dir. of community affairs/personnel; Gene Gildow, dir. of eng..
Operation: 1950; TV sets in area: 485,900.

WTVZ (Channel 33)
TVX Broadcast Group of Virginia, Box 148, Norfolk, VA 23501 (804) 622-3333.
Richard Kitelyn, v.p. & gen. mgr.; Elise Tucker, gen. sls. mgr.
Operation: 1979.

Norfolk-Portsmouth-Newport News

WAVY-TV (Channel 10) NBC
WAVY Television, Inc. (Division of LIN Broadcasting Corporation), 801 Wavy St., Portsmouth, VA 23704 (804) 393-1010.
Mike McGrew, pres. & gen. mgr.; Bill Logan, sta. mgr.; Jack Paris, gen. sls. mgr.; Ted Hand, chief eng.; nat'l rep: Blair Television.
Operation: 1957.

Portsmouth

WYAH-TV (Channel 27)
CBN-Continental Broadcasting Network, Box 1338, Portsmouth, VA 23704 (804) 393-2501.
Tim Robertson, pres.; Thomas Smith, v.p. & gen. mgr.; Ken Reichenbach, chief eng.; David Whitener, prog. mgr.; Larry Harris, prod. mgr.; Bob Walker, mgr., p.r.
Operation: 1961; TV homes in area: 535,000.

Richmond

WRLH-TV (Channel 35)
Busse Bdcstg. Corp., 1925 Westmoreland St., Richmond, VA 23230 (804) 358-3535.
Greg Graber, pres. & gen. mgr. Paul Wachsmith, gen. sls. mgr.; Anne Driscoll, prog. asst.; Larry Cole, chief eng.; rep.: MMT.
Operation: February, 1982.

WTVR (Channel 6) CBS
Roy H. Park Broadcasting of Virginia, Inc., 3301 W. Broad St., P.O. Box 11064, Richmond, VA 23201 (804) 254-3600.
Richard Pegram, exec. v.p. & gen. mgr.; Wanda Lewis, v.p. sls.; Ed Herbert, lcl. sls. mgr.; Ken Miller, chief eng.; Charles Fishburne, news dir. Bailey Dwiggins, prog. & opns. mgr.
Operation: 1948; TV sets in area: 665,900.

WVRN-TV (Channel 63)
Sudbrink Bdcstg., 458 Southlake Blvd., Richmond, VA 23236 (804) 794-7777.
Vic Rumore, pres.; John Riggle, gen. mgr.; Dan Peltier, gen. sls. mgr.; Harold J. Pontious, prog. dir. & film buyer; Dale Robinson, prom. mgr.; Bill Price, chief eng.; natl. rep.: Seltel.
Operation: January, 1984.

WWBT (Channel 12) NBC
Jefferson Pilot Broadcasting Company of Virginia, P.O. Box 12, 5710 Midlothian Pike, Richmond, VA 23201 (804) 233-5461.
W. J. Jorgenson, pres.; John H. Hutchinson, Jr., v.p. & gen. mgr.; Ellen Shuler, gen. sales mgr.; Dave Frasier, tech. op. mgr.; John Shreves, prgrm./oper. mgr.; nat'l rep.: Petry.
Operation: 1956; TV sets in area: 498,700.

Richmond-Petersburg

WXEX-TV (Channel 8) ABC
Nationwide Communications, Inc. 21 Buford Rd., Richmond, VA 23235 (804) 320-3201.
H. Joseph Lewin, gen. mgr.; Jack Porray, gen. sls. mgr.; Gene Walsh, prgm. dir.; nat'l rep.: Katz.
Operation: 1955.

Roanoke

WDBJ-TV (Channel 7) CBS
WDBJ Television, Inc. Mailing Address: P.O. Box 7, Roanoke, VA 24022; Street Address: 2001 Colonial Ave., S.W., Roanoke, VA 24015 (703) 344-7000.
C. H. McKeever, pres. & gen. mgr. & promo. dir.; Kay Hall, prog. dir.; George Bassett, dir.–sls. mktg.; Carl Guffey, dir. of opns.; Barbara Nicely, promo. dir.; Al Dyson, chief eng.; nat'l rep.: Harrington, Righter & Parsons, Inc.
Operation: 1955; TV homes in area: 985,100.

WEFC (Channel 38)
612 Bullitt Ave., S.E., Roanoke, VA 24013.
C. Kenneth Wright, pres.; R.B. Stewart, Sr., gen. mgr.; E.T. Griffis, prog. dir.; Andrew Wright, chief eng.
Operation: November, 1984.

WSLS-TV (Channel 10) NBC
Roy H. Park Broadcasting of Roanoke, Inc., Church Ave. & Third Street, Roanoke, VA 24011 (703) 981-9110.
James J. DeSchepper, v.p./gen. mgr.; Pete Watkins, gen. sls. mgr.; Mike Berkey, chief eng.; nat'l rep.: Blair TV.
Operation: 1952; TV sets in area: 680,900.

WVFT (Channel 27)
Family Group Ltd., 2618 Colonial Ave., Roanoke, VA 24015 (703) 345-7227.
Ian N. Wheeler, pres.; Howard D. Trickey, gen. mgr.; Suzanne Montgomery, gen. sls. mgr.; Jerry M. McCook, chief eng.; natl. rep.: ITS.
Operation: November, 1985.

WASHINGTON
Bellingham

KVOS-TV (Channel 12) CBS
KVOS TV, Inc., 1151 Ellis St., Bellingham, WA 98225 (206) 671-1212.
Barry Ackerly, pres.; David Reid, v.p. & gen. mgr.; Robert Lewis, prog. dir.; Margot Wilson, promo. mgr.; rep.: Seltel.
Operation: 1953; TV sets in area: 2,000,000.

Pasco

KEPR-TV (Channel 19) CBS
Retlaw Enterprises, Inc., P.O. Box 702, Yakima, WA 98907 (509) 452-9111.
Gary Nieman, mgr.; Stu Seibel, prog. dir.; Ken Christensen,

news dir.; Don Eckis, chief eng.; nat'l rep.: Seltel; northwest: Art Moore & Associates, Inc.
Operation: 1954; TV sets in area: 334,400.

Richland-Pasco-Kennewick

KNDU (Channel 25) NBC
(Associated with KNDO, Yakima, WA)
Columbia Empire Broadcasting Corp., 1608 S. 24th Ave., Yakima, WA 98901; 3312 Kennewick Ave., Kennewick, WA 99336.
Elliott Kleeman, gen. mgr. & film buyer; Jerry Rogers, sta. mrg. & sls. mgr.; Ron Rutherford, news, dir.; Ed Lyon, chief eng.; nat'l rep.: Katz.
Operation: 1961.

KVEW (Channel 42) ABC
(A Satellite of KAPP, Yakima, WA)
Apple Valley Broadcasting, Inc., 601 N. Edison, Kennewick, WA 99336 (509) 735-8369.
H. Darrell Blue, v.p. & gen. mgr.; J. Marcus Wood, sta. mgr.; Neil Bennett, chief eng.
Operation: 1970.

Seattle

KCPQ (Channel 13)
Kelly TV Co., Box 98828, 4400 Steilacoom Blvd., SW, Tacoma, WA 98499 (206) 582-8613.
Roger Ottenbach, gen. mgr.; Robert E. Kelly, prog. dir./owner; Jay Maxey, gen. sls. mgr.; Dan Jensen, sta. mgr.; Robert Galvin, prom. mgr.; Larry Brandt, chief eng.; nat'l rep.: Telerep.
Operation: 1954.

KING-TV (Channel 5) NBC
King Broadcasting Co., 333 Dexter Ave., Seattle, WA 98109 (206) 485-5555.
Steven C. Clifford, pres.; Eric S. Bremmer, pres.; bdcstng; Steve Welch, v.p., finance; Stan Mak, v.p. radio; Suzanne Sorknes, v.p., gen. cnsl.; Sturges Dorrance, v.p. & gen. mgr., King TV; Patricia Chappell, prog. dir.; Don Varyu, news dir.; Ellen Hansen, p.a. dir.; Barbara Kersey, mktg. & adv. dir.; Robert Gover, gen. sls. mgr.; Tyrone Mortensen, chief eng.; rep.: Blair.
Operation: 1948; TV sets in area: 941,600.

KIRO-TV (Channel 7) CBS
KIRO, Inc., Broadcast House, Third & Broad, Seattle, WA. 98121 (206) 624-7077.
Kenneth L. Hatch, pres.; Al F. Mladenich, sen. v.p.; Glenn C. Wright, v.p. & sta. mgr.; Michael Poth, local sls. mgr.; Charles Morris, eng. dir.; Nick Freeman, prog. dir.; nat'l rep.: Petry Television, Inc.
Operation: February, 1958; TV households: 976,800.

KOMO-TV (Channel 4) ABC
Fisher Broadcasting Inc., 100 Fourth Ave., N., Seattle WA 98109.
John F. Behnke, pres. & CEO, Fischer Bdcstg.; Jay W. Giesa, exec. v.p. for adm., & secty. Fisher; Patrick M. Scott, v.p. & gen. mgr., KOMO; Don Wilkinson, v.p. dir. eng., Fisher; Ed J. Lackner, v.p. corp. affairs, Fisher; nat'l rep.: Katz.
Operation: 1953; TV sets in area: 1,133,700.

KTZZ-TV (22 UHF STEREO)
United States Television Seattle, 945 Dexter Ave., N., Seattle, WA 98109-3515 (206) 282-2202.

Dan Lutgen, sta. mgr.; Shelley Olds, prog. mgr.; Gina Huggerty, bus. mgr.; Karl Paulsen, chief eng.; natl. rep.: ITS.
Operation: June, 1985.

Spokane

KAYU-TV (Channel 28)
KAYU-TV Partners, Ltd., Box 8115, Spokane, WA 99203 (509) 448-2828.
Robert Hamacher, gen. mgr.; Lane Guin, gen. sls. mgr.; Tim Burrows, film buyer; Kelly Bundy, promo. mgr.; Ronald Valley, eng. dir.; nat'l rep.: Petry.
Operation: October, 1982.

KHQ-TV (Channel 6) NBC
KHQ, Inc., 4202 S. Regal, Spokane, WA 99223 (509) 448-6000.
John Reber, pres. & gen. mgr.; Robt. L. Busse, contr.; Michael Gee, v.p., gen. sls. mgr.; Bill Storms, lcl. sls. mgr.; Larry W. Gants, dir. prog. & promo.; Don Carmichael, opns. mgr.; William Isbel, chief eng.; nat'l rep.: Katz Agency.
Operation: 1952; TV sets in area: 528,800 ARB.

KREM-TV (Channel 2) CBS
King Broadcasting Co., S-4103 Regal St., Spokane, WA 99223 (509) 448-2000.
Dennis Williamson, v.p. & gen. mgr.; John Rowland, sls. mgr.; Meg Antonius, prog. dir.; Jeff Orgega, chief eng.; nat'l rep.: Blair.
Operation: 1954; TV sets in area: 393,200.

KXLY-TV (Channel 4) ABC
KXLY-TV (Spokane Television, Inc.) W. 500 Boone Ave., Spokane, WA 99201 (509) 328-9084.
Elizabeth M. Burns, pres.; Stephen R. Herling, v.p. & gen. mgr.; Eileen McKinnon, prog. dir.; Brian Williams, opns. mgr.; Don Pope, chief. eng.; Teddie Gibbon, sls. mgr.; nat'l rep: HRP.
Operation: 1953; TV sets in area: 358,600.

Tacoma

KSTW (Channel 11)
Gaylord Bdg. Co., Box 11411, Tacoma, WA 98411 (206) 572-5789.
Edward L. Gaylord, chm.; Kevin T. Hale, v.p. & gen. mgr.; Donald M. Lacy, asst. gen. mgr.; Tom Shannon, prog. mgr.; Paul Crittenden, chief eng.; rep.: Telerep.
Operation: 1953; TV households: 1,038,500.

KTBW-TV (Channel 20)
Trinity Bcstg. of Washington, 1909 S. 341 St., Tacoma, WA 98003 (206) 927-7720.
Paul F. Crouch, pres.; Jim Fuller, gen. mgr.; Dick F. Engh, acting chief eng.
Operation: March, 1984.

Vancouver/Portland (OR)

KPDX (Channel 49)
Columbia River TV, Inc., Vancouver, WA 98660 (206) 254-4949; 910 N.E. Union, Portland, OR 97232 (503) 239-4949.
Jack F. Matranga, pres.; Richard Williams, gen. sls. mgr.; Dennis Updegraff, prog.-opns. mgr.; Dennis Beauchamp, chief eng.
Operation: October, 1983.

Wenatchee

KCWT (Channel 27)
Bingham Communications Group, 32B North Mission St., Wenatchee WA 98801 (509) 662-5298.
Michaɔl O. Barry, pres. & gen. mgr.; David C. Herald, gen. sls. mgr.; Melanie Dahl, prog. dir.; Robert Wyatt, chief eng.; natl. rep.: Adam Young.
Operation: April, 1984.

Yakima

KAPP (Channel 35) ABC
Apple Valley Bcstg. Co., 1610 South 24th Ave., Yakima, WA 98902 (509) 453-0351.
Elizabeth Burns, pres., Darrell Blue, gen. mgr.; Ron Simmons, prog. dir.; Judy Ernesti, gen. sls. mgr.; Jim Sollers, promo. mgr.; Dave Ettl, news dir.; rep.: Harrington.
Operation: September, 1970; TV households: 148,700.

KIMA-TV (Channel 29) CBS
Retlaw Enterprises, Inc., P.O. Box 702, Yakima, WA 98907 (509) 575-0029. Affiliated stations: KEPR-TV, Pasco, WA; KLEW-TV, Lewiston, ID.
John J. Noel, Jr., pres.; Dale Hazen, gen. mgr.; Stu Seibel, prog. dir.; Mike Rastovich, dir. of eng.; rep.: Seltel; Pacific Northwest: Art Moore & Associates, Inc.
Operation: 1953; TV sets in area 768,900.

KNDO (Channel 23) NBC
(Operates associated station KNDU, Richland-Pasco-Kenewick, WA)
Columbia Empire Broadcasting Corp., 1608 S. 24th Ave., Box 10028, Yakima, WA 98909 (509) 248-2300.
Elliott R. Kleeman, gen. mgr.; natl. rep.: Katz.
Operation: 1959.

WEST VIRGINIA
Bluefield

WVVA (Channel 6) NBC
WVVA Television, Inc., P.O. Box 1930, Bluefield, WV 24731 (304) 325-5487.
Thomas Oakley, pres.; Charles E. Webb, v.p., gen. mgr.; Todd Andrick, opns. mgr.; Daniel Kurtz, promo. mgr.; Kenneth Dick, chief eng.; nat'l rep.: Seltel.
Operation: 1955; TV sets in area: 635,700.

Charleston

WCHS-TV (Channel 8) CBS
Heritage Media, Inc., 1111 Virginia St. E., Charleston, WV (304) 346-5358.
Dennis Adkins, gen. mgr.; Steve Herman, gen. sls. mgr.; Jo Corey, prog. dir.; Michael Hooper, promo. mgr.; Tim Sharp, news dir.; Robert Roush, chief eng.; nat'l rep.: Petry.
Operation: 1954.

WVAH-TV (Channel 11)
W.V. Telecasting, Inc., 11 Broadcast Plaza, Hurricane, WV 25526 (304) 757-0011.
Bert Ellis, pres. & CEO; William Castleman, COO; Gary Dreispul, gen. mgr.; George Panicza, chief eng.
Operation: September, 1982.

Clarksburg

WBOY-TV (Channel 12)
912 West Pike Street, Clarksburg, WV 26301 (304) 623-3311.

B. Imes, pres.; Stan Siegel, v.p. & gen. mgr.; Joe Wright, chief eng.; nat'l rep.: Seltel.
Operation: 1957.

WLYJ (Channel 46)
Christian Communication Center, 775 West Pike St., Clarksburg, West VA 26301 (304) 623-5782.
Joseph Rose, pres.; Jack L. Kincaid, mgr.; Wayne Fast, chief eng.
Operation: February, 1981.

Huntington-Charleston

WOWK-TV (Channel 13) CBS
Television Center, 555 Fifth Ave., Huntingon, WV 25701 (304) 525-7661.
Leo M. MacCourtney, v.p. & gen. mgr.; Paul N. Dicker, prog. dir.; Billie Sue Graybeal, nat'l sls. mgr.; Mike Ferko, gen. sls. mgr.; Andy Footo, regl. sls. mgr.; Brian Peterson, news dir.; Bob Willis, mktg. dir.; Al Grossniklaus, chief eng.; sls. rep.: Blair TV.
Operation: October, 1955; TV households: 877,300.

WSAZ-TV (Channel 3) NBC
Lee Enterprises, Inc., 645 Fifth Avenue, Huntington, WV 25701 (304) 697-4780.
Richard Gottlieb, pres. & COO; Gary Schmedding, gen. mgr.; Don Ray, gen. sls. mgr.; Chris Leister, nat'l sls. mgr.; Robert Harris, Charleston operations mgr.; George M. Curry, prog. dir.; Bill Cummings, news dir.; Bob Dean, mgr. eng.
Operation: 1949; TV sets in area: 684,700.

Oak Hill

WOAY-TV (Channel 4) ABC, Primary
Thomas Broadcasting Co., Box 251, Oak Hill, WV 25901 (304) 469-3361.
Robert R. Thomas III, pres.; Curtis W. Butler, v.p. & gen. mgr.; Don Watkins, prod. mgr.; nat'l rep.: Katz.
Operation: 1954; TV sets in area: 377,820.

Parkersburg

WTAP (Channel 15) NBC
Benedek Broadcasting Inc., 121 W. 7th St., Parkersburg, WV 26102 (304) 485-4588.
Sherman A. Grimm, gen. mgr.; Charles Helmick, prog. dir. & chief eng.; nat'l rep.: MMT.
Operation: 1953; TV households in area: 70,620.

Weston-Clarksburg

WDTV (Channel 5) CBS
Withers Broadcasting Co. of WV P.O. Box 480, Bridgeport, WV 26330 (304) 842-3558.
W. Russell Withers, Jr., Pres.; Dusty Wayman, gen. mgr.; Nick Pelligrin, prog. dir. & traffic dir.; rep.: Avery-Knodel.
Operation: 1960; TV households, 798,200.

Wheeling

WTRF-TV (Channel 7) ABC, CBS
Forward Tele-Production, Inc., 96 16th St., Wheeling, WV 26003 (304) 232-7777.
James G. Squibb, Jr., pres. & gen. mgr.; Jim Davis, lcl. sls. mgr.; Pat Gaughan, promo. mgr.; Sandra Hamm, news dir.; Joe Dumas, chief eng.
Operation: 1953; TV sets in area: 523,000.

WISCONSIN

Appleton

WXGZ-TV (Channel 32)
Appleton Midwestern TV Ltd., 3025 N. Marshall Rd., Appleton, WI 54915 (414) 731-3232.
Roy Smith, gen. mgr.; Jonie Pave, gen. sls. mgr.; John Kremer, prog. dir.; John Rysso, chief eng.
Operation: December, 1983.

Eau Claire

WEAU-TV (Channel 13) NBC
WEAU-TV, 1907 South Hastings Way, Eau Claire, WI 54701.
Alvin K. Leitl, pres. & gen. mgr.; Dick Dionne, opr. mgr.; Ron Wiedemeier, chief eng.; nat'l rep.: MMT.
Operation: 1953; TV households: 421,640.

WQOW-TV (Channel 18) ABC
(A satellite of WXOW-TV, LaCrosse, WI) TAK Communications, Inc., 2881 S. Hastings Way, Eau Claire, WI 54701 (715) 835-1881.
Chuck Roth, gen. mgr.; Dave White, chief eng.; Bob Braun, sls. mgr.; Larry Wentz, news dir.
Operation: 1980.

Green Bay

WBAY-TV (Channel 2) CBS
A division of Nationwide Communications Inc., 115 So. Jefferson St., Green Bay, WI 54301 (414) 432-3331.
Ted Kohl, gen. mgr.; Robert Krieghoff, gen. sls. mgr.; Richard Millhiser, prog. dir.; nat'l rep.: Katz.
Operation: 1953; TV sets in area: 707,700.

WFRV-TV (Channel 5) ABC
WFRV Inc., P.O. Box 19055, Green Bay, WI 54307 (414) 437-5411.
Robert B. Forrow, gen. mgr.; Mitch Lambert, gen. sls. mgr.; Alan Eaton, dir. opns. & prog.; Norm Koelbl, chief eng.; nat'l rep.: TeleRep.
Operation: 1955; TV households in area: 485,040.

WGBA (Channel 26) IND
Family Group Ltd., III, 1391 North Rd., P.O. Box 19099, Green Bay, WI 54307 (414) 4949-2626.
James Tomlin, gen. mgr.; Nancy Martinson, sta. mgr.; Michael Schuster, natl. sls. mgr.; nat'l rep.: Blair.
Operation: 1980.

WLUK-TV (Channel 11) NBC
WLUK-TV, Inc., P.O. Box 19011, Green Bay, WI 54307 (414) 494-8711.
Bill Fyffe, gen. mgr.; Rick Morein, dir. sls.; Sam Hutchison, prog. dir.; Jim Steffey, chief eng.; nat'l rep.: HPR.
Operation: 1954.

LaCrosse

WKBT (Channel 8) CBS
Young Bdcstg. Inc., 141 So. 6th St., La Crosse WI 54601 (608) 782-4678.
David F. Peschau, v.p. & gen. mgr.; Art Fahey, gen. sls. mgr.; Dick Konrad, opns. mgr.; nat'l rep.: Adam Young.
Operation: 1954; TV homes: 379,460 (NSI).

WLAX (Channel 25)
Family Group Partnership, 1305 Interchange Place, La Crosse, WI 54603 (608) 781-0025.

Ian Wheeler, pres.; Howard R. Trickey, gen. mgr.; Del Lonnquist, gen. sls. mgr.; Doug Maszka, prog. dir.; Barbara Smith, film buyer; Scott Neader, prom. mgr.; Roger Lonnquist, chief eng.; natl. rep.: ITS.
Operation: September, 1986

WXOW-TV (Channel 19) ABC
(S-2 Satellite, Eau Claire, WI, Channel 18)
TAK Communications, P.O. Box C-4019, LaCrosse, WI 54602.
Sharad Tak, gen. partner; rep.: Katz.
Operation: March, 1970; TV households: 154,200.

Madison

WISC-TV (Channel 3) CBS
7025 Raymond Road, Madison, WI 53719 (608) 271-4321.
Elizabeth Murphy Burns, pres.; Gary DeHaven, gen. mgr.; Donna Kirner, nat'l sls. mgr.; Chris Cain, chief eng.; nat'l rep.: HRP.
Operation: 1956; TV sets in area: 635,000.

WKOW-TV (Channel 27) ABC
TAK Communications, Inc., 5727 Tokay Blvd., Madison WI 53701 (608) 274-1234.
Thomas Hartman, pres.; Jim Matthews, gen. mgr.; nat'l rep.: Katz Agency.
Operation: 1953; TV households in area: 214,800.

WMSN-TV (Channel 47)
Channel 47 Ltd. Partnership, 7847 Big Sky Dr., Madison, WI 53719 (608) 833-0047.
Phyllis A. Lourien, pres.; Bill Franks, gen. mgr. & film buyer; Jason Elkin, gen. sls. mgr.; John Noonan, prog. dir. & promo. mgr.; Andy Murphy, chief eng.; natl. rep.: ITS.
Operation: June, 1986.

WMTV (Channel 15) NBC
Adams TV of Madison, Inc., 615 Forward Dr., Madison, WI 53711 (608) 274-1515.
Vickie Street, pres. & gen. mgr.; Fred Sole, opns. mgr.
Operation: 1953; TV households in area: 266,500.

Milwaukee

WCGV-TV (Channel 24)
HR Broadcasting Corp. of Milwaukee, Inc., 5445 N. 27th St., Milwaukee, WI 53209 (414) 527-2424.
Robert J. Furlong, gen. mgr. & film buyer; Mitch Nye, gen. sls. mgr.; Betty Hertz, prog. mgr.; Walter White, chief eng.; nat'l rep.: Katz.
Operation: 1980.

WISN-TV (Channel 12) ABC
WISN Division—The Hearst Corp., 759 No. 19 St., Milwaukee, WI 53233 (414) 342-8812.
C. Wayne Godsey, v.p. & gen. mgr.; Rick Henry, gen. sls. mgr.; Jim Killoran, nat'l sls. mgr.; Terry Dolan, lcl. sls. mgr.; Bill Lowery, prod. mgr.; John Stewart, dir. of bdcst. ops.; Tim Morrisey, news dir.; James Wagner, promo. mgr.; Noel Enders, resident cont.
Operation: 1954; TV sets in area: 675,600.

WITI-TV (Channel 6) CBS
SCI Holdings, Inc., 9001 North Green Bay Road, Milwaukee, WI 53217 (414) 355-6666.
Andrew P. Potos, pres. & gen. mgr.; Ray Engelhart, prog. dir.; Donald Roering, chief eng.
Operation: 1956; TV sets in area: 1,380,400.

WTMJ-TV (Channel 4) NBC
WTMJ Inc., 720 East Capitol Drive, Milwaukee, WI 53201 (414) 332-9611.

Steve Smith, pres.; Wayne Barnett, v.p. & gen. mgr.; Norb Ryan, gen. sls. mgr.; Mark Le Grand, lcl. sls. mgr.; Tom Mikkelsen, mgr. of eng.; Gerald McGrath, prgm. mgr.; Ed Hinshaw, ed. dir.; Tom Luljak, news dir.; Glenn Kleiman, mng. editor; Gerry Skowronski, film supvr.; Rod Synnes, comm. rel. dir.

Operation: 1947; TV households in area: 700,000.

WVTV (Channel 18)
Gaylord Broadcasting Co., P.O. Box 1818, Millwaukee, WI 53201 (414) 442-7050.

Harold E. Prohe, v.p. & gen. mgr.; rep.: Petrey.

Operation: 1966; TV homes: 694,400.

Rhinelander (Wausau)
WJFW-TV (Channel 12) NBC
Northland TV Inc., Box 858, Rhinelander, WI 54501 (715) 369-4700.

James Buckner, pres.; Mike Meyer, gen. & natl. sls. mgr.; Bette Henning, lcl. sls. mgr.; Brian Henning, chief eng. rep.: Seltel.

Operation: 1966; TV homes in area: 230,000.

Wausau
WAOW-TV (Channel 9) ABC
(Outlet of The Wisc. TV Network)
Wisconsin TV Network Assn., 1908 Grand Ave., Wausau WI 54401 (715) 842-2251.

Laurin Jorstad, gen. mgr., prog. dir. & film buyer; Ron Montezon, nat'l sls. mgr.; Sharon Reyer, promo. mgr.; Russ Crass, chief eng.; rep.: Katz Television.

Operation: 1965; TV households: 170,310.

WSAW-TV (Channel 7) CBS
Forward Communications Corp., 1114 Grand Ave., Wausau, WI 54401 (715) 845-4211.

Richard D. Dudley, chmn./pres., Forward Comm.; Bart Kellenhauser, pres. WSAW-TV; Gene R. Anderson, sr. v.p., finance; Bill Jones, lcl. sls. mgr.; Jack Crowley, v.p., prog.; Mark Zelich, v.p., news; Joe Kamenick, chief eng.; nat'l rep.: Seltel.
Operation: 1954.

WYOMING
Casper
KFNB-TV (Channel 20) ABC, CBS
First National Bcstg., 7075 Salt Creek Hwy., Casper, WY 82601 (307) 237-2020.

A.J. Stanton, pres.; Pete Sieler, gen. mgr.; Charles Vick, chief eng.; nat'l rep.: Avery Knodel, Bob Hix Co.

Operation: October, 1984.

KGWC-TV (Channel 14) CBS
Stauffer Communications, Inc., Box 170, Casper, WY 82601 (307) 234-1111.

Robert Calvert, gen. mgr.; Jeremy Patey, dir. prog.; Tim Swanson, sls. mgr.; Bob Spain, chief eng.

Operation: 1980.

KTWO-TV (Channel 2) NBC
KTWO Corp., 4200 E. Second Street, Casper, WY 82601 (307) 237-3711.

Jack Rosenthal, pres.; Bob Price, v.p. and gen. mgr.; Steve Broomell, chief eng.; Dave Borino, prog. dir.; nat'l rep.: Katz; regional rep.: Jonn McGuire, Denver.

Operation: 1957; TV homes in area: 109,200.

Cheyenne
KGWN-TV (Channel 5) CBS, ABC
Stauffer Communications, Inc., 2923 East Lincolnway, Cheyenne, WY; 82001 (307) 634-7755.

Gerald Holley, v.p.; Carl Occhipinti, gen. mgr.; Dusty Thein, gen. sls. mgr.; Barbara Parenti, prog. dir.; Tony Schaefer, dir. eng.; rep.: Katz.

Operation: 1954; TV sets in area: 501,900.

KLWY (Channel 1 27)
Heart of Wyoming TV, Inc., 7020 Salt Creek Rte., Box 5, Casper, WY 82601 (307) 237-2020.

Peter C. Sieler, gen. mgr.; nat'l rep.: Adam Young.

Operation: November, 1987.

Lander
KGWL-TV (Channel 5) CBS
Stauffer Communications, Inc., 340 N. Center, Casper, WY 82601 (307) 234-1111.

John H. Stauffer, pres.; Robert L. Calvert, gen. mgr.; Tim Swanson, gen. sls. mgr.; Jeremy Patey, opns. dir.; Craig Kennedy, news dir.; Bob Spain, eng.; nat'l rep.: Blair.

Operation: September, 1982.

Rawlins
KFNR (Channel 11) ABC, CBS
First National Bdcstg. Corp., Box 1, 7075 Salt Creek Rte., Casper, WY 82601 (307) 237-2020.

Peter Sieler, gen. mgr.; George Vavra, promo. mgr.; Charles D. Vick, chief eng.; natl. rep.: Adam Young, Box Hix Co.

Operation: April, 1986.

Riverton
KFNE-TV (Channel 10) ABC, CBS
First National Bdcst. Corp., Box 1, Casper, WY 82601 (307) 237-2020.

Peter G. Sieler, gen. mgr.

Operation: 1980; Households: 17,800.

Rock Springs
KGWR-TV (Channel 13) CBS
Stauffer Communications, Inc., Box 170 Rock Springs, WY 82601 (307) 234-1111.

John H. Stauffer, pres.; Robert L. Clavert, gen. mgr. & film buyer; Tim Swanson, gen. sls. mgr.; Jeremy Patey, prog. dir.; Kim Sherwood, news dir.; Bob Spain, chief eng.; nat'l rep.: Blair.

Operation: 1977.

Sheridan
KSGW-TV (Channel 12) ABC
(A satellite of KOTA-TV, Rapid City, SD) Duhamel Broadcasting Enterprises, Box 1760, Rapid City, SD 57709.

Personnel: See KOTA-TV, Rapid City, SD

Operation: 1977.

Public Broadcasting Service Station Affiliates

Alabama
Birmingham .... WBIQ
Demopolis .... WIIQ
Dozier .... WDIQ
Florence .... WFIQ
Huntsville .... WHIQ
Louisville .... WGIQ
Mobile .... WEIQ
Montgomery .... WAIQ
Mount Cheaha State Park .... WCIQ

Alaska
Anchorage .... KAKM
Bethel .... KYUK-TV
Fairbanks .... KUAC-TV
Juneau .... KTOO-TV

Arizona
Phoenix .... KAET
Tucson .... KUAS-TV
Tucson .... KUAT

Arkansas
Arkadelphia .... KETG
Fayetteville .... KAFT
Jonesboro .... KTEJ
Little Rock .... KETS
Mountain View .... KEMV
Newark .... KLEP

California
Cotati .... KRCB-TV
Eureka .... KEET
Fresno .... KMTF
Huntington Beach .... KOCE-TV
Los Angeles .... KCET
Los Angeles .... KLCS
Redding .... KIXE
Sacramento .... KVIE
San Bernardino .... KVCR-TV
San Diego .... KPBS-TV
San Francisco .... KQED
San Francisco .... KQEC
San Jose .... KTEH
San Mateo .... KCSM-TV

Colorado
Broomfield .... KBDI-TV
Denver .... KRMA-TV
Pueblo .... KTSC

Connecticut
Bridgeport .... WEDW
Hartford .... WEDH
New Haven .... WEDY
Norwich .... WEDN

Delaware
Seaford .... WDPB
Wilmington .... WHYY-TV

District of Columbia
Washington .... WETA-TV
Washington .... WHMM

Florida
Ft. Myers .... WSFP-TV
Gainesville .... WUFT
Jacksonville .... WJCT
Miami .... WPBT
Miami .... WLRN-TV
Orlando .... WMFE-TV
Pensacola .... WSRE
Tallahassee .... WFSU-TV
Tampa .... WUSF-TV
Tampa/St. Petersburg .... WEDU
West Palm Beach .... WXEL-TV

Georgia
Athens .... WGTV

Atlanta .... WPBA
Chatsworth .... WCLP-TV
Cochran .... WDCO-TV
Columbus .... WJSP-TV
Dawson .... WACS-TV
Pelham .... WABW-TV
Savannah .... WVAN-TV
Waycross .... WXGA-TV
Wrens .... WCES-TV

Guam
Agana .... KGTF

Hawaii
Honolulu .... KHET
Wailuku .... KMEB-TV

Idaho
Boise .... KAID
Moscow .... KUID-TV
Pocatello .... KISU-TV

Illinois
Carbondale .... WSIU-TV
Chicago .... WTTW
Chicago .... WYCC
Jacksonville .... WJPT
Macomb .... WIUM-TV
Moline .... WQPT
Olney .... WUSI-TV
Peoria .... WTVP
Quincy .... WQEC
Urbana .... WILL-TV

Indiana
Bloomington .... WTIU
Evansville .... WNIN
Gary .... WYIN
Indianapolis .... WFYI
Muncie .... WIPB
South Bend .... WNIT
Vincennes .... WVUT

Iowa
Council Bluffs .... KBIN
Des Moines .... KDIN-TV
Fort Dodge .... KTIN
Iowa City .... KIIN-TV
Mason City .... KYIN
Red Oak .... KHIN
Sioux City .... KSIN
Waterloo .... KRIN

Kansas
Hays .... KOOD
Hutchinson .... KPTS
Topeka .... KTWU

Kentucky
Ashland .... WKAS
Bowling Green .... WKGB
Covington .... WCVN
Elizabethtown .... WKZT
Hazard .... WKHA
Lexington .... WKLE
Louisville .... WKPC-TV
Louisville .... WKMJ
Madisonville .... WKMA
Morehead .... WKMR
Murray .... WKMU
Owensboro .... WKOH
Owenton .... WKON
Paducah .... WKPD
Pikeville .... WKPI
Somerset .... WKSO

Louisiana
Alexandria .... KLPA-TV
Baton Rouge .... WLPB-TV
Lafayette .... KLPB-TV

Lake Charles	KLTL-TV		New Jersey	
Monroe	KLTM-TV		Camden	WNJS
New Orleans	WLAE-TV		Montclair	WNJM
New Orleans	WYES-TV		New Brunswick	WNJB
Shreveport	KLTS-TV		Trenton	WNJT

Lake Charles ..... KLTL-TV
Monroe ..... KLTM-TV
New Orleans ..... WLAE-TV
New Orleans ..... WYES-TV
Shreveport ..... KLTS-TV

Maine
Augusta ..... WCBB
Biddeford ..... WMEA
Calais ..... WMED-TV
Orono ..... WMEB-TV
Presque Isle ..... WMEM-TV

Maryland
Annapolis ..... WMPT
Baltimore ..... WMPB
Frederick ..... WFPT
Hagerstown ..... WWPB-TV
Oakland ..... WGPT
Salisbury ..... WCPB

Massachusetts
Boston ..... WGBH-TV
Boston ..... WGBX-TV
Springfield ..... WGBY-TV

Michigan
Alpena ..... WCML-TV
Bad Axe ..... WUCX-TV
Cadillac ..... WCMV
Detroit ..... WTVS
East Lansing ..... WKAR-TV
Flint ..... WFUM
Grand Rapids ..... WGVU-TV
Kalamazoo ..... WGVK
Manistee ..... WCMW
Marquette ..... WNMU-TV
Mt. Pleasant ..... WCMU-TV
University Center ..... WUCM-TV

Minnesota
Appleton ..... KWCM-TV
Austin ..... KSMQ-TV
Bemidji ..... KAWE
Duluth-Superior, WI ..... WDSE-TV
Minneapolis-St. Paul ..... KTCA-TV
St. Paul ..... KTCI-TV

Mississippi
Biloxi ..... WMAH
Booneville ..... WMAE
Bude ..... WMAU
Greenwood ..... WMAO
Jackson ..... WMAA
Meridian ..... WMAW
Oxford ..... WMAV
State College ..... WMAB

Missouri
Joplin ..... KOZJ
Kansas City ..... KCPT
St. Louis ..... KETC
Sedalia-Warrensburg ..... KMOS-TV
Springfield ..... KOZK

Montana
Bozeman ..... KUSM

Nebraska
Alliance ..... KTNE-TV
Bassett ..... KMNE-TV
Hastings ..... KHNE-TV
Lexington ..... KLNE-TV
Lincoln ..... KUON-TV
Merriman ..... KRNE-TV
Norfolk ..... KXNE-TV
North Platte ..... KPNE-TV
Omaha ..... KYNE-TV

Nevada
Las Vegas ..... KLVX
Reno ..... KNPB

New Hampshire
Durham ..... WENH
Keene ..... WEKW-TV
Littleton ..... WLED-TV

New Jersey
Camden ..... WNJS
Montclair ..... WNJM
New Brunswick ..... WNJB
Trenton ..... WNJT

New Mexico
Albuquerque ..... KNME-TV
Las Cruces ..... KRWG
Portales ..... KENW

New York
Binghamton ..... WSKG
Buffalo ..... WNED-TV
Buffalo ..... WNEQ-TV
Garden City ..... WLIW
New York ..... WNYC-TV
New York ..... WNYE-TV
New York ..... WNET
Norwood ..... WNPI-TV
Plattsburgh ..... WCFE-TV
Rochester ..... WXXI-TV
Schenectady ..... WMHT
Syracuse ..... WCNY-TV
Watertown ..... WNPE-TV

North Carolina
Asheville ..... WUNF-TV
Chapel Hill ..... WUNC-TV
Charlotte ..... WTVI
Columbia ..... WUND-TV
Concord ..... WUNG-TV
Greenville ..... WUNK-TV
Jacksonville ..... WUNM-TV
Linville ..... WUNE-TV
Wilmington ..... WUNJ-TV
Winston-Salem ..... WUNL-TV

North Dakota
Bismarck ..... KBME
Dickinson ..... KDSE
Fargo-Moorhead, Minn. ..... KFME
Grand Forks ..... KGFE
Minot ..... KSRE
Williston ..... KWSE

Ohio
Akron ..... WEAO
Alliance ..... WNEO
Athens ..... WOUB-TV
Cambridge ..... WOUC-TV
Cincinnati ..... WCET
Cleveland ..... WVIZ-TV
Columbus ..... WOSU-TV
Dayton ..... WPTD
Lima-Bowling Green ..... WBGU-TV
Oxford ..... WPTO
Portsmouth ..... WPBO-TV
Toledo ..... WGTE-TV

Oklahoma
Cheyenne ..... KWET
Claremore ..... KXON-TV
Eufaula ..... KOET
Oklahoma City ..... KETA
Tulsa ..... KOED-TV

Oregon
Bend ..... KOAB-TV
Corvallis ..... KOAC-TV
La Grande ..... KTVR
Medford ..... KSYS
Portland ..... KOAP-TV

Pennsylvania
Bethlehem-Allentown ..... WLVT-TV
Clearfield ..... WPSX-TV
Erie ..... WQLN
Harrisburg ..... WITF-TV
Pittsburgh ..... WQED
Pittsburgh ..... WQEX
Scranton-Wilkes-Barre ..... WVIA-TV

Puerto Rico
Caguas ..... WUJA
Mayaguez ..... WIPM-TV
Ponce ..... WQTO

San Juan .... WIPR-TV

Rhode Island
Providence .... WSBE-TV

Samoa
Pago Pago .... KVZK

South Carolina
Allendale .... WEBA-TV
Beaufort .... WJWJ-TV
Charleston .... WITV
Columbia .... WRLK-TV
Conway .... WHMC
Florence .... WJPM-TV
Greenville .... WNTV
Greenwood .... WNEH
Rock Hill .... WNSC-TV
Spartanburg .... WRET-TV
Sumter .... WRJA-TV

South Dakota
Aberdeen .... KDSD-TV
Brookings .... KESD-TV
Eagle Butte .... KPSD-TV
Lowry .... KQSD-TV
Martin .... KZSD-TV
Pierre .... KTSD-TV
Rapid City .... KBHE-TV
Vermillion .... KUSD-TV

Tennessee
Chattanooga .... WTCI
Cookeville .... WCTE
Lexington .... WLJT-TV
Memphis .... WKNO-TV
Nashville .... WDCN-TV
Sneedville .... WSJK-TV

Texas
Austin-San Antonio .... KLRN-TV
Austin .... KLRU-TV
Beaumont .... KITU
Belton .... KNCT
College Station .... KAMU-TV
Corpus Christi .... KEDT
Dallas .... KERA-TV
El Paso .... KCOS
Harlingen .... KLUJ
Harlingen .... KMBH
Houston .... KUHT
Lubbock .... KTXT

Odessa .... KOCV-TV
San Antonio .... KLRN-TV

Utah
Provo .... KBYU-TV
Salt Lake City .... KUED

Vermont
Burlington .... WETK
Rutland .... WVER
St. Johnsbury .... WVTB
Windsor .... WVTA

Virginia
Fairfax .... WNVC
Goldvein .... WNVT
Marion .... WMSY-TV
Norfolk .... WHRO-TV
Norton .... WSBN-TV
Richmond .... WCVE-TV
Richmond .... WCVW
Roanoke .... WBRA-TV
Staunton .... WVPT

Virgin Islands
Charlotte Amalie .... WTJX-TV

Washington
Centralia .... KCKA
Pullman .... KWSU-TV
Richland .... KTNW
Seattle .... KCTS-TV
Spokane .... KSPS-TV
Tacoma .... KTPS
Yakima .... KYVE-TV

West Virginia
Grandview .... WSWP-TV
Huntington .... WPBY-TV
Morgantown .... WNPB-TV

Wisconsin
Green Bay .... WPNE
La Crosse .... WHLA
Madison .... WHA-TV
Menomonie-Colifax .... WHWC-TV
Milwaukee .... WMVS
Milwaukee .... WMVT
Park Falls .... WLEF-TV
Wausau .... WHRM-TV

Wyoming
Lander .... KCWC-TV

Corporate Histories
of the Networks

Corporate Histories of the Networks

Capital Cities/ABC, Inc.

Like the other major U.S. television networks, ABC had its origins in radio. In the beginning Radio Corporation of America (RCA) owned two radio networks: the Blue and the Red. In 1941 the FCC decreed that the same company could not own two networks, so RCA incorporated the Blue under the name of American Broadcasting System and established it as an independent subsidiary with 116 stations. RCA then sold this network to Edward J. Noble, founder and chairman of the Life Savers Corporation, for $8 million. The name was changed to the American Broadcasting Company in 1944, at which time the network had 197 radio affiliates.

Television arrived for ABC in 1948 when, on April 19, ABC carried its first TV program: "On the Corner," with Henry Morgan, which was sponsored by the Admiral Radio Corp. Later in the year ABC scored two "firsts": the live broadcast of an opera (Verdi's "Otello") from the Metropolitan Opera House in New York and a TV documentary, "The Marshall Plan."

The next big step for ABC came in 1952 with its merger with United Paramount Theatres, the motion picture theatre circuit founded when Paramount Pictures was required under the Sherman Anti-Trust Act to separate its film production unit from its theatres. This merger was engineered by Leonard H. Goldenson, then the president of UPT. The new company was called American Broadcasting-Paramount Theatres, Inc.

During the 1950's ABC began operation at a profit although it had to struggle fiercely to acquire new affiliates. In 1954 ABC made a deal with Walt Disney to acquire a 35 per cent interest in Disneyland and all TV programs produced by Disney. The following year ABC signed an exclusive rights contract with Warner Bros. for TV programming.

The 1960's brought many changes to ABC beginning with the introduction of color programming for the fall season of 1962; this was expanded in 1966 to include full color broadcasting. In 1965 AB-PT's name was changed to American Broadcasting Companies, Inc. and the company's corporate headquarters were moved from West 66th Street in New York to 1330 Avenue of the Americas, where they have remained.

High points in the decade of the '60s also included the introduction of the blockbuster theatrical movie to TV with spectacular rating results when "The Bridge on the River Kwai" was viewed (in 1966) by 60 million Americans.

In 1967 the ABC evening news was expanded from 15 minutes to a half hour, and Joey Bishop inaugurated ABC's late-night programming with his talk show.

An attempt to gain control of ABC by Howard Hughes was circumvented by Goldenson in 1968. Hughes said publicly that he abandoned his efforts to acquire the network because of the strong resistance of Goldenson; however, it was speculated elsewhere that he gave up because as new owner of ABC he would have had to attend a public hearing under the auspices of the FCC. The fanatically reclusive Hughes, it was assumed, would never have agreed to come out of seclusion for such an event.

The decade of the Seventies was an eventful one for ABC, too, not the least because in 1972 it was able to operate at a profit for the first time in ten years. Also in the 1976–77 season ABC moved for the first time into first place in the ratings race. It held the lead for the next two years and then dropped back into second place in 1979–80, a position it held until 1983–84 when it dropped to third position. It was unable to rise above that until 1987–88 when it displaced CBS in second place, primarily because of special sports programming, such as the World Series and the Superbowl.

In 1976 Barbara Walters joined ABC, becoming the first anchorwoman in television history. Her almost $1 million a year salary caused lifted eyebrows among her fellow anchor persons, including Harry Reasoner and Howard K. Smith.

In 1977 the mini-series "Roots" appeared on ABC and became the all-time highest-rated program. This helped immensely in the ratings race, and credit must go in large part to Fred Silverman who two years before had joined the company as president of ABC international. He left in 1978 to go to NBC.

The decade of the Eighties was a turbulent one for the television industry as cable TV and home video began whittling away at their audiences. ABC was no exception. Halfway through the period—in 1985—ABC agreed to be purchased by Capital Cities Communications at a cost of $3.5 billion. 1986 saw formal completion of the takeover and the merged company's name was changed to Capital Cities/ABC, Inc.

With the departure of Goldenson, that year also brought other important changes in management. Daniel B. Burke replaced Frederick J. Pierce as president and chief operating officer. There were also sweeping reductions in personnel in the interests of economy and streamlining. (At least 1,000 employees were fired.)

Budget cuts notwithstanding Capital Cities/AAC chairman Thomas Murphy pledged ABC would not scrimp on programming. Instead the focus was to be on the network's non-programming expenses which accounted for about 30 per cent of the budget. One result was to cut out internally-generated research which was to be contracted for on an ad hoc basis as needed.

Capital Cities/ABC owns eight television stations and is a partner in ESPN, the highly successful cable TV sports channel. It also owns publishing operations which include nine daily newspapers, several weeklies and a variety of trade and consumer magazines.

Columbia Broadcasting System, Inc.

CBS first saw the light of day in 1927 as a radio network with 16 stations—United Independent Broadcasters, Inc.—founded by Arthur Judson, a concert tour manager. In need of money, Judson secured backing from Louis Sterling, president of the Columbia Phonograph Company, and changed the network name to Columbia Phonograph Broadcasting System. Later other investors were invited in, the most prominent of whom was William S. Paley, who, on September 26, 1928, at the age of 27, became president of the firm whose name was changed again. Now it was called the Columbia Broadcasting System.

Paley introduced many innovations to radio broadcasting, most significant of which was the signing of an agreement in 1931 with Paramount Pictures whereby film stars were heard on radio for the first time. This laid the groundwork for the CBS policy in television from the outset to feature shows built around stars (Ed Sullivan, Lucille Ball, Arthur Godfrey, Jack Benny, Burns & Allen, Garry Moore, etc.).

Actually CBS was in TV as early as 1931 when it began regularly scheduled TV programming over experimental station W2XAB in New York City. In 1941 CBS began weekly broadcast of black-and-white TV programming over WCBS-TV in New York. By 1948 it had 30 affiliated stations.

The decade of the 1950's brought many important advances. In 1951 CBS broadcast the first live coast-to-coast TV transmission between New York and San Francisco. In 1952 there came opening of Television City in Hollywood—the industry's first self-contained TV production facility. In 1956 "Playhouse 90" made its debut and set new high standards for drama originated on TV.

But the big event of the decade came along early—in 1951—with the debut of "I Love Lucy." The road to creating that phenomenal success was a rocky one. For one thing CBS did not want Desi Arnaz, and signed him only on the insistence of Lucille Ball. Second, the couple wanted to work before a live audience—a practice also anathema to the CBS powers-that-be. Ball and Arnaz persisted, and their efforts led to what is regarded as the invention of the situation-comedy format.

1951 was also the year that Bill Gordon designed the CBS Eye—destined to become one of the most famous logos in the world.

In the field of soap operas CBS was both leader and winner, virtually monopolizing that market from 1951 to 1956. In 1951 it introduced "Search for Tomorrow," which was to become the longest-running show ever in that genre. This was followed by "Love of Life" (1951) "The Guiding Light" (1952)—both overnight hits. "Guiding Light" was still on the air in 1988, as was the fourth soap CBS introduced, "As the World Turns" (1956).

In the late '50s and through the '60s and '70s CBS reigned as king of prime time ratings as tallied by the Nielsen Company. It had tied with NBC in 1969–70 and 1970–71 and ABC led in three seasons; but the rest of the time CBS was Number One. Thus it was quite a jolt to the company when in 1985–86 it slipped to second place and stayed there through the following season. Then came the worst blow of all: in 1987–88 CBS came in third for the first time in TV history.

CBS maintained its long-running lead with such successes as "Gunsmoke" (1957), "The Defenders" (1961), "The Beverly Hillbillies" (1962), "All in the Family" (1972) and "Dallas" (1978). Also helping was "60 Minutes," the news-oriented show, which in 1988 had remained in the Top Ten prime time shows for 11 consecutive seasons.

CBS began the turbulent Eighties with a new president, Thomas Wyman (replacing John D. Backe). Worst year for the company so far in that decade was surely 1985 when the company was sent reeling under three major assaults.

First, Gen. William C. Westmoreland filed a $120 million law suit, charging he had been libeled during a 1982 "CBS Reports" documentary. The subsequent trial ended 18 weeks after it began in New York Federal Court after the general heard some of his closest advisers during the Vietnam War testify they supported the CBS documentary contention in that he had deliberately underestimated the enemy troop strength on the field. Fearing he would lose, Westmoreland dropped the action before it could go to a jury.

Second, Senator Jesse Helms (Rep., N.C.) and his Fairness in Media committee launched an unfriendly takeover bid to "become Dan Rather's boss." (Rather had replaced Walter Cronkite as chief news anchor in 1981.)

Third, Atlanta broadcast entrepreneur Ted Turner made an unfriendly junk-bond bid for CBS. In a clever move the network bought up 21 per cent of its own stock for $956 million and thwarted the takeover. Turner went after MGM/UA instead.

Meanwhile Laurence A. Tisch, a former theatre chain executive, had become the major stockholder in CBS and in 1986 he instigated some sweeping changes in the interests of cost-cutting and efficiency. Some 700 jobs were eliminated at the CBS Broadcast Group. Tisch also removed Wyman as president, named himself chief executive officer and induced founder William Paley to return to active duty as acting chairman of the board.

In 1988, stung by CBS' worst prime time rating performance ever, Tisch shuffled executive ranks again, naming Howard Stringer, previously president of CBS News, as president of the Broadcasting Group. He replaced Gene F. Jankowski, who was named to the newly created position of chairman of the Broadcast Group. At the same time Tisch reported the CBS second-

quarter income for 1988 rose 40 per cent to a new quarterly record. He attributed this to higher sales achieved despite a slow adverting market and to improvement of operating margin through reduction of costs and making operations more efficient.

It was all, said Tisch, the beginning of "a new era" for CBS.

National Broadcasting Company

Television began for NBC in 1928, when on April 4, it acquired from the Federal Communications Commission a permit to operate an experimental station, W2XBS. Actual transmission from the Empire State Building did not begin, however, until October 30, 1931. Some eight years late the network began broadcasting on a regular basis, beginning with the opening of the New York World's Fair on April 30, 1939.

NBC, like the other networks, was an outgrowth of radio operations. Radio Corp. of America, General Electric and Westinghouse jointly launched a network in 1926 which had 31 stations; 25 in a network called Red and 6 in one called Blue. A year later it was forced to sell the Blue network to ABC (see history of that network), keeping for itself the one known as Red.

In 1930 RCA bought out its partners, GE and Westinghouse, and NBC became its wholly owned subsidiary.

NBC became a TV network on January 12, 1940, when two stations, WNBC-TV, New York, and WRGB-TV, Schenectady, New York, carried the first network programming. In June, 1941, the FCC granted NBC the first commercial TV license and a month later it had four advertisers signed up: Procter & Gamble, Lever Brothers, Sun Oil and Bulova.

After World War II NBC scored two big "firsts." On June 19, 1946, Gillette became the first advertiser to sponsor a TV network show, the Joe Louis-Billy Conn boxing match. That same year Bristol-Myers became the first sponsor of a network TV series, "Geographically Speaking."

NBC can also claim to be the first to introduce coast-to-coast network TV coverage. On September 4, 1951, when the U.S.-Japanese peace treaty was signed in San Francisco, its cameras were on hand.

In 1952 NBC pioneered early morning programming when it introduced "The Today Show."

NBC can also claim the first regularly scheduled network color series: "The Marriage," launched in 1954. That same year it achieved the first west-to-east TV transmission with the television of the Tournament of Roses Parade in color. At the start of the 1965–66 season it could declare it was the "only all-color network."

In 1968 NBC introduced new forms of TV programming with "The Name of the Game," a series that incorporated feature-film elements into a 90-minute show. This then spawned the "NBC Mystery Movie"—a series of programs composed of "Colombo," "Hec Ramsey", "McMillan and Wife," "McCloud," "Amy Prentiss," "McCoy," and "Quincy, M.E.".

In 1972 NBC broke new ground again when it introduced "The Tomorrow Show" shown from 1:00 a.m. to 2:00 a.m. This was a talk program and it demonstrated that in the wee small hours of the morning something more than re-runs and old movies could be shown. In 1974 another late-night show called "Weekend" was begun.

In 1976 NBC's telecast of "Gone with the Wind" drew the largest audience to that date for an entertainment program. In 1978 its "Holocaust" mini-series attracted 107 million viewers and won 21 major awards.

Such programs helped NBC in the ratings, but in 1976–77 it fell to third place, where it stayed until 1983–84. (Ironically 1976 was the year in which NBC celebrated its 50th anniversary in broadcasting with a four-hour, star-filled special.) In 1984–85 it edged up to second place, and the following year it was ranked Number One in prime-time viewing for the first time in the three decades of such tallying by Nielsen. (For the record NBC did tie for first place with CBS in 1969–70 and 1970–71.)

NBC held on solidly to its first place standing for 1986–87 and 1987–88.

Along with the other networks NBC moved into a period of turmoil during the decade of the Eighties, fighting off rising costs and competition from cable TV and home video. In 1986 General Electric Corporation purchased RCA (NBC's parent) for $6.28 billion; GE, it will be remembered, helped launch the radio network in 1926 which led to the development of NBC-TV. This brought personnel changes led by the replacement of Grant A. Tinker as NBC chief executive officer by Robert Wright, although Wright was not given Tinker's chairman title, that being taken by John F. Welch of GE. Instead Wright was

named president as well as chief executive officer. Along with its competition NBC started cutting staff and budgets in 1986.

NBC owns television stations located in Chicago, Cleveland, Los Angeles, New York City and Washington, D.C. GE, the parent company, also owns TV station subsidiaries in Denver and Miami, which are operated under the aegis of NBC.

In 1987 NBC owned eight radio stations in various cities, but it is reconfiguring these operations and plans to sell some of them and also to acquire other stations in different cities.

In 1987 NBC released some interesting figures about costs of television production. It revealed the average prime time half-hour series program for the 1986–87 season cost about $500,000 for two showings; that the average hour program costs $1 million or more; and that a feature film made for TV runs to about $3 million.

Cable Television

* **STATISTICS AND HISTORY**

* **MAJOR CABLE SYSTEM OPERATORS**

* **MAJOR PROGRAM SUPPLIERS**

Cable Television

STATISTICS

HISTORICAL DATES

FIRST OVER-THE-AIR TOLL-TV EXPERIMENTS: 1950, Skiatron system tested over WOR-TV in New York City. 1951, Telemeter system tested over KTLA-TV, Los Angeles; Zenith tested its system over its own experimental station in Chicago.

FEBRUARY 10, 1955: Federal Communications Commission started proceedings to determine whether it should authorize TV stations to transmit programs paid for on a subscription basis. Study involved 92 docket volumes reflecting the views of over 25,000 persons on legal, technical and policy questions.

MAY 23, 1957: FCC concluded it had authority to authorize use of TV broadcast frequencies for subscription operations if it found it were in the public interest to do so. Did not define whether this service should be classified as "broadcasting" or some other.

OCTOBER 17, 1957: FCC adopted its first report on the proceedings and declared it would consider applications to conduct trial pay-TV operations over TV stations provided certain conditions were met.

MARCH 24, 1959: FCC issued third report saying it was ready to consider any pay-TV application by a commercial TV station conforming with requirements, among which were limitation of three-year trial authorizations to markets where there were at least four commercial TV stations (including the pay-TV one), and one trial system allowed per market.

JUNE 22, 1960: Hartford Phonevision Co. (later RKO General Phonevision Co.), a licensee of WHCT (Channel 18), Hartford, CT, applied for authority to conduct a three-year trial subscription-TV operation. Application granted February 23, 1961. Operations began June 29, 1962, and concluded in January, 1969.

JULY 3, 1967: FCC's subscription TV committee submitted a fourth report proposing an over-the-air subscription TV service. Rules were designed to integrate subscription TV into the total TV system so good programming would continue to be available over regular TV stations.

DECEMBER 12, 1968: FCC formally established over-the-air subscription TV as a regular broadcast service.

1975: Home Box Office became the first in the television industry to use a satellite for regular transmission of programming.

1984: The FCC officially deregulated the cable industry, permitting pricing flexibility and enabling operators to raise charges for basic cable services by adding new channels while reducing service charges for premium channels.

1985: The Court of Appeals struck down the "must carry" rules which required cable operators to carry all local broadcast stations.

Statistics for 1987

In 1987 there were 23,000 communities being served by cable television with over 43.2 million subscribers. This represents over 49 percent of U.S. TV households.

Cable systems reached a total of 8,000 with another 500 franchises approved but not yet built. Texas has the most systems with 552 and California has the most subscribers at 4.2 million.

Industry revenues in 1987 were estimated at about $11.4 billion.

The national average monthly subscriber rate for basic services rose to $13 by 1988, compared to $11 the year before and less than $8 in 1981.

Over 1600 systems accept advertising on the local origination channels (excluding automated channels) with rates from $2 to $300 per 30-second spot. Most cable systems derive less than 5 percent of their gross revenues from advertising, but cable revenues from advertising continue to grow and had reached $41 billion in 1987. Projections were that the figure would reach $1.5 billion in 1988.

Cable systems are required by law to offer a minimum 20-channel capacity which is the average; however many systems offer more.

Pay cable (Home Box Office, Showtime, etc.) now operates on about 7200 systems, reaching 32 million subscribers in all 50 states.

Almost 32 percent of all cable systems have ties with broadcast interests; over 20 percent with program producers; and about 18 percent with newspapers. Many systems have multiple cross-ownership ties.

Tele-Communications, based in Denver, is the nation's largest developer and operator of cable systems. It has more than 5 million subscribers. Second largest is American Television, also based in Colorado, which has 3.6 million subscribers.

United Artists Communications, also based in Colorado, has 800,000 subscribers. In 1988 it announced plans to acquire the United Cable TV Corporation of Denver to form United Artists Entertainment which would become the country's third-largest cable TV operation with some 2.4 million subscribers. Since Tele-Communications owns 65.5 percent of United Artists Communications and 23.7 percent of United Cable it will have a majority interest in the new company—some 52 percent.

The Turner Broadcasting System, operators of the Cable News Network and "Superstation" WTBS, planned to begin operation of a new cable entertainment network late in 1988. The company said it has signed up nearly 10 million TV households through local cable systems for its commencement date.

Cable System Operators

American TV & Communications Corp.

160 Inverness Drive West, Englewood, CO 80112; (303) 799-1200. (A subsidiary of Time, Inc.)
CHAIRMAN OF THE BOARD & CHIEF EXECUTIVE OFFICER
Trygve E. Myhren
VICE CHAIRMAN OF THE BOARD & VICE PRESIDENT
N.J. Nicholas, Jr.
EXECUTIVE VICE PRESIDENT & CHIEF OPERATING OFFICER
James H. Doolittle
EXECUTIVE VICE PRESIDENTS
Thomas W. Binning, Gary S. Bryson, John F. Gault, Kevin H. Rorke
SENIOR VICE PRESIDENTS
James P. Cottingham, Henry J. Gerken, John G. Dawson, Edward McCarthy, Richard B. Holcomb, Richard J. Davies, David E. O'Hayre

Cablevision Systems Corporation

One Media Crossways, Woodbury, NY 11797; (516) 364-8450.
CHAIRMAN & CHIEF EXECUTIVE OFFICER
Charles F. Dolan
PRESIDENT & CHIEF OPERATING OFFICER
John Tatta

Cardinal Communications, Inc.

1800 N Meridian St., Indianapolis, IN 46202; (317) 923-6358.
CHAIRMAN & CHIEF EXECUTIVE OFFICER
James F. Ackerman
PRESIDENT & CHIEF OPERATING OFFICER
Myron T. Pattison

Comcast Cable Communications, Inc.

1 Belmont Ave., Bala Cynwyd, PA 19004; (215) 667-4200.
PRESIDENT
Robert B. Clasen

Continental Cablevision, Inc.

The Pilot House, Lewis Wharf, Boston, MA 02110; (617) 742-9500.
CHAIRMAN & CHIEF EXECUTIVE OFFICER
Amos B. Hostetter, Jr.
PRESIDENT & CHIEF OPERATING OFFICER
Timothy P. Neher
SENIOR VICE PRESIDENTS—OPERATIONS
John P. Rakoske, Michael J. Ritter, Charles J. Younger
SENIOR VICE PRESIDENT, MARKETING
Frederick C. Livingston
SENIOR VICE PRESIDENT, PROGRAMMING
Robert A. Stengel
SENIOR VICE PRESIDENT & TREASURER
Nancy Hawthorne
SENIOR VICE PRESIDENT, LEGAL CORPORATE COUNSEL
Robert J. Sachs

Cox Cable Communications, Inc.

1400 Lake Hearn Dr., Atlanta, GA 30319; (404) 843-5000. (A subsidiary of Cox Enterprises.)
PRESIDENT
James O. Robbins

SENIOR VICE PRESIDENT FINANCE
Robert C. O'Leary
SENIOR VICE PRESIDENTS—OPERATIONS
Barry R. Elson, Wayne D. Knighton and G. Lewis Davenport
VICE PRESIDENT MARKETING & PROGRAMMING
Ajit M. Dalvi
VICE PRESIDENT, TECHNICAL OPERATIONS
Alex B. Best
VICE PRESIDENT, CORPORATE AFFAIRS
David C. Andersen

Heritage Communications, Inc.

2195 Ingersoll Ave., Des Moines, IA 50312; (515) 246-1440. (Owned by Tele-Communications Inc.)
CORPORATE OFFICERS
CHAIRMAN
James M. Hoak, Jr.
PRESIDENT
James S. Cownie
EXECUTIVE VICE PRESIDENT/OPERATIONS
Rod Thole
EXECUTIVE VICE PRESIDENT/SECRETARY
Wayne Kern
EXECUTIVE VICE PRESIDENT/FINANCE
David Lundquist
SENIOR VICE PRESIDENT/ENGINEERING
Doug Truckenmiller
VICE PRESIDENT/OPERATIONS
Nile McDonald
VICE PRESIDENT/OPERATIONS
Kevin Rice
VICE PRESIDENT/MARKETING
Dale Parker
VICE PRESIDENT/DEVELOPMENT
David Oman
VICE PRESIDENT/CONTROLLER
Loran Schlitz

NewChannels Corp.

112 Northern Concourse, North Syracuse, NY 13212; (315) 455-5826. (A subsidiary of Newhouse Broadcasting Corp.)
PRESIDENT
Robert Miron
EXECUTIVE VICE PRESIDENT
Leo A. Calistri

Post-Newsweek Cable

2621 East Camelback Rd., Suite 150, Phoenix, AZ 85016; (602) 468-1177. (A subsidiary of The Washington Post Co.)
PRESIDENT
Howard E. Wall

Prime Cable

One American Center, Suite 3000, 600 Congress Ave., Austin, TX 78701; (512) 476-7888.
PRESIDENT
Robert W. Hughes
CHIEF OPERATIONS OFFICER
C. Ronald Dorchester

Rogers Communications, Inc.

Box 249, Toronto M5K 1J5 Ontario, Canada; (416) 864-2338.

CHAIRMAN
John W. Graham
VICE CHAIRMAN & CHIEF EXECUTIVE OFFICER
Edward S. Rogers
PRESIDENT
Colin D. Watson

Sammons Communications, Inc.

Box 15216, Dallas, TX 75201; (214) 742-9828.
PRESIDENT
James Whitson
VICE PRESIDENT/OPERATIONS
Mark S. Weber

Service Electric Cable TV, Inc.

201 West Centre St., Mahanoy City, PA 17948; (717) 773-2585.
PRESIDENT/DIRECTOR
John Walson
SECRETARY/DIRECTOR
Margaret Walson

Spectradyne (Hotels/Motels)

1501 N. Plano Road, Richardson, TX 75081; (214) 234-2721.
PRESIDENT
John M. Lewis
VICE PRESIDENT OF PROGRAMMING
Bill Coleman

Storer Communications, Inc.

Box 61-8000, Miami, FL 33161; (305) 899-1000.
PRESIDENT/CHIEF EXECUTIVE OFFICER
Kenneth L. Bagwell
EXECUTIVE VICE PRESIDENT
William P. Whelan

TCA Cable TV

Box 130489, Tyler, TX 75713; (214) 595-3701.

TeleCable Corp.

Box 2098, 740 Duke St., Norfolk, VA 23510; (804) 624-5000.
CHAIRMAN OF THE BOARD
Frank Batten
PRESIDENT
Richard D. Roberts
VICE PRESIDENTS
Gordon R. Herring, James S. Key, Nicholas E. Worth
VICE PRESIDENT & TREASURER
Alfred F. Ritter, Jr.

Tele-Communications, Inc.

Regency Plaza One, 4643 S. Ulster Street, Ste. 600, Denver, CO 80237; (303) 771-8200. Mailing: P.O. Box 5630 T.A., Denver, CO 80217.
CHAIRMAN
Bob Magness
PRESIDENT & CHIEF EXECUTIVE OFFICER
John C. Malone
SENIOR VICE PRESIDENT & TREASURER
Donne F. Fisher
SENIOR VICE PRESIDENT
John Sie

Texas Community Antennas, Inc.

3027 S.E. Loop 323, Tyler, TX 75701; (214) 595-3701.
PRESIDENT
Robert Rogers
VICE PRESIDENTS
R. Don Cowan, Wayne McKinney

Times Mirror Cable Television, Inc.

2381 Morse Ave., Irvine, CA 92714; (714) 660-0500.
PRESIDENT & CHIEF EXECUTIVE OFFICER
Larry W. Wangberg
EXECUTIVE VICE PRESIDENT/ENGINEERING
Gilbert L. Tash
SENIOR VICE PRESIDENT/CHIEF FINANCIAL OFFICER
James F. Guthrie
SENIOR VICE PRESIDENT/GROUP OPERATIONS
James "Trey" Smith
SENIOR VICE PRESIDENT/GROUP OPERATIONS
Kent D. Franke

United Artists Cablesystems Corp.

60 Craig Rd., Montvale, NJ 07645; (201) 930-9191. (Owned by Tele-Communications & United Artists Communications.)
CHAIRMAN
Stewart Blair
PRESIDENT & CHIEF EXECUTIVE OFFICER
Marvin J. Jones

UACC Midwest, Inc.

1430 Balltown Road, Schenectady, NY 12309; (518) 385-1229.
PRESIDENT
G.W. Oswald
SENIOR VICE PRESIDENT
C. Skelly
ENGINEERING VICE PRESIDENT
P. Pappas

United Cable Television Corp.

Denver Technological Center, 4700 S. Syracuse Pkwy., Denver, CO 80237; (303) 779-5999. (Owned by Tele-Communications, Inc.
CHAIRMAN & CHIEF EXECUTIVE OFFICER
Gene W. Schneider
PRESIDENT & CHIEF OPERATING OFFICER
Fred A. Vierra

Viacom Cable

1211 Ave. of the Americas, New York, NY 10036; (212) 575-5175. P.O. Box 13, Pleasanton, CA 94566; (415) 463-0870. (A division of Viacom International.)
PRESIDENT
John W. Goddard
EXECUTIVE VICE PRESIDENT
Edward Bennett
SENIOR VICE PRESIDENTS
Garrett Girvan, Kurt Jorgensen, Bill Lilly

Vision Cable Communications, Inc.

270 Sylvan Ave., Englewood Cliffs, NJ 07632; (201) 894-5555. (A division of Newhouse Group, Inc.)
EXECUTIVE VICE PRESIDENT & GENERAL MANAGER
Joel Fleming
VICE PRESIDENT
V. Mitchell Roberts

VICE PRESIDENT PROGRAMMING
Pamela T. Hammond
VICE PRESIDENT/ENGINEERING
Richard M. White

Warner Cable Communications, Inc.

400 Metro Place North, Dublin, OH 43017; (614) 792-7000. (A division of Warner Communications, Inc.)

PRESIDENT & CHIEF OPERATING OFFICER
James L. Gray
EXECUTIVE VICE PRESIDENT & CHIEF FINANCIAL OFFICER
Jack L. Messman

Western Communications, Inc.

Suite 225, 2855 Mitchell Dr., Box 4610, Walnut Creek, CA 94596; (415) 935-3055. (Owned by Chronicle Publishing Co.)

Cable and Pay TV Program Suppliers

Pay cable services and pay-per-view services are designated as such. All others are basic cable services.

American Movie Classics

Rainbow Program Enterprises, 150 Crossways Park West, Woodbury, NY 11797; (516) 364-2222. A Pay-TV system.

Arts & Entertainment Network (A&E)

555 Fifth Ave., New York, NY 10017. (212) 661-4500. (A joint venture of Hearst Corp., ABC and NBC)
PRESIDENT & CHIEF EXECUTIVE OFFICER
Nickolas Davatzes

Black Entertainment Television (BET)

1232-31st St., N.W., Washington, D.C. 20007; (202) 337-5260.
PRESIDENT
Robert L. Johnson
VICE PRESIDENT OF ADVERTISING
Janis P. Thomas
VICE PRESIDENT OF NETWORK OPERATIONS
Jeff Lee
VICE PRESIDENT OF FINANCE
Antonia O. Duncan

Bravo

Rainbow Program Enterprises, 150 Crossways Park West, Woodbury, NY 11797; (516) 364-2222. A Pay-TV System.
PRESIDENT & CHIEF OPERATING OFFICER
Joshua Sapan
VICE PRESIDENT—PROGRAMMING
Jonathan D. Sehring

Cable News Network

Turner Broadcasting System, One CNN Center, P.O. Box 105366, Atlanta, GA 30348-5366; (404) 827-1500.
BOARD CHAIRMAN & PRESIDENT OF TBS
R. E. (Ted) Turner
CNN EXECUTIVE VICE PRESIDENT
Burt Reinhardt
CNN SENIOR VICE PRESIDENT
Ed Turner

Cable News Network Headline News

One CNN Center, P.O. Box 105366, Atlanta, GA 30348-5366; (404) 827-1500.
BOARD CHAIRMAN & PRESIDENT
R. E. (Ted) Turner
PRESIDENT
Burt Reinhardt
VICE PRESIDENT—HEADLINE NEWS
Paul R. Amos

Christian Broadcasting Network

CBN Center, Virginia Beach, VA 24363; (804) 424-7777.
FOUNDER AND CHIEF EXECUTIVE OFFICER
M.G. (Pat) Robertson

C-SPAN Cable Satellite Public Affairs Network

Suite 412, 444 N. Capitol, St., N.W., Washington, DC 20001; (202) 737-3220.
CHAIRMAN AND CHIEF EXECUTIVE OFFICER
Brian P. Lamb
EXECUTIVE VICE PRESIDENT
Mike Michaelson
VICE PRESIDENT, BUSINESS AFFAIRS
Robert Kennedy
VICE PRESIDENT, CORPORATE COMMUNICATIONS
Susan Swain
VICE PRESIDENT, NETWORK OPERATIONS
Brian Lockman
VICE PRESIDENT, CORPORATE DEVELOPMENT
Bruce Collins

Cinemax

1271 Ave. of the Americas, New York, NY 10020; (212) 484-1000. A second pay-TV service created by Home Box Office, Inc. and designed to complement the foundation HBO service.
PRESIDENT AND CHIEF OPERATING OFFICER
Michael Fuchs
SENIOR VICE PRESIDENT, CINEMAX
Larry Carlson
SENIOR VICE PRESIDENT, CINEMAX PROGRAMMING
Lee deBoer
SENIOR VICE PRESIDENT, CINEMAX MARKETING & SALES
Dick Beahrs
VICE PRESIDENT, CORPORATE AFFAIRS
David Pritchard

Discovery Channel

8201 Corporate Dr., Landover, MD 20785; (301) 577-1999.
CHAIRMAN & CHIEF EXECUTIVE OFFICER
John S. Hendricks
PRESIDENT & CHIEF OPERATING OFFICER
Ruth L. Otte
SENIOR VICE PRESIDENT, ADVERTISING SALES
Kathy Clinton
SENIOR VICE PRESIDENT, PROGRAM ACQUISITIONS & DEVELOPMENT
Suzanne Hayes
SENIOR VICE PRESIDENT, AFFILIATE SALES
Sandra McGovern

The Disney Channel

3800 West Alameda, Burbank, CA 91505; (818) 564-7500. (A Pay-TV system and a subsidiary of The Walt Disney Company)
PRESIDENT
John F. Cooke

ESPN, Inc.

ESPN Plaza, Bristol, CT 06010, (203) 585-2000; and 355 Lexington Ave., New York, NY 10017, (212) 661-6040. (Entertainment & Sports Programming Network)
PRESIDENT & CHIEF EXECUTIVE OFFICER
J. William Grimes
EXECUTIVE VICE PRESIDENT/PROGRAMMING PRODUCTION
Steven M. Bornstein

SENIOR VICE PRESIDENT/INTERNATIONAL & LEGAL AFFAIRS
Andrew P. Brilliant
VICE PRESIDENT, ADVERTISING SALES
John S. Bonanni

Financial News Network

2525 Ocean Park Blvd., Santa Monica, CA 90405; (213) 450-2412.
CHAIRMAN OF THE BOARD
Earl W. Brian, M.D.
SENIOR VICE PRESIDENT, PROGRAMMING, GENERAL MANAGER
Michael Wheeler
SENIOR VICE PRESIDENT, AFFILIATES & GENERAL MANAGER, SCORE
Arnie Rosenthal
SENIOR VICE PRESIDENT, SALES
A. Scott Hults
SENIOR VICE PRESIDENT TELSHOP, GENERAL MANAGER
Elio Betty, Jr.
VICE PRESIDENT PRODUCTION
Keith Manasco
DIRECTOR AFFILIATE RELATIONS
Christopher Taylor

Home Box Office, Inc.

1100 Ave. of the Americas, New York, NY 10036; (212) 512-1000. (A Pay-TV system and a subsidiary of Time, Inc.)
CHAIRMAN AND CHIEF EXECUTIVE OFFICER
Michael Fuchs
PRESIDENT
E. Thayer Bigelow
SENIOR VICE PRESIDENT, MARKETING
John Billock
EXECUTIVE VICE PRESIDENT, AFFILIATE SALES & OPERATIONS
Peter Frame
SENIOR VICE PRESIDENT, NETWORK OPERATIONS AND CORPORATE DEVELOPMENT
Ed Horowitz
VICE PRESIDENT, CORPORATE AFFAIRS
David Pritchard

Home Premiere Television

800 Third Ave., 16th floor, New York, NY 10022; (212) 486-6600. (A pay-per-view cable network.)
PRESIDENT & CHIEF EXECUTIVE OFFICER
James O. Heyworth
VICE PRESIDENT/FINANCE
William A. Futera
VICE PRESIDENT/AFFILIATE RELATIONS & MARKETING
J. Robert Bedell
VICE PRESIDENT/PROGRAMMING
James L. English

Home Shopping Networks I & II

1529 U.A. 19S, Clearwater, FL 34624; (813) 530-9455. (live, discount shop-at-home TV service).
CHAIRMAN
Roy M. Speer
PRESIDENT
Lowell W. Paxton

The Learning Channel

1525 Wilson Blvd., Rosslyn, VA 22209; (703) 276-0881.
CHAIRMAN & CHIEF EXECUTIVE OFFICER
Harold E. Morse
PRESIDENT
Robert J. Shuman

Lifetime

1211 Ave. of the Americas, New York, NY 10036; (212) 719-8950. (Hearst/ABC-Viacom Entertainment Services)
PRESIDENT & CHIEF EXECUTIVE OFFICER
Thomas F. Burchill
VICE PRESIDENT/PROGRAMS
Charles B. Gingold
VICE PRESIDENT/MARKETING
Laurence E. Rebich

MTV Networks, Inc.

1775 Broadway, New York, NY 10019; (212) 713-6510. (Provides MTV-24 hr. a day music video channel; VH-1/Video Hits One; and Nickelodeon, Nick at Nite children's and young adults' programming service)
PRESIDENT & CHIEF OFFICER
Tom Freston

The Nashville Network

Box 10210, Stamford, CT 06904; (203) 965-6000. (A service of Opryland USA, Inc. and Group W Satellite Communications.) Production Center address: 2806 Opryland Dr., Nashville, TN 37214; (614) 889-6840
PRESIDENT
Don Mitzner
SENIOR VICE PRESIDENT, SALES & MARKETING
Lloyd Werner

The Playboy Channel

Playboy Enterprises, Inc., 8560 Sunset Blvd., Los Angeles, CA 90069; (213) 659-4080. (A Pay-TV system distributed by Playboy Programming Distribution Co.)

PRISM

225 City Line Ave., Bala Cynwyd, PA 19004; (215) 668-2210. (A Pay-TV system)
VICE PRESIDENT AND GENERAL MANAGER
Donald L. Heller
VICE PRESIDENT AND ASSISTANT GENERAL MANAGER
Sam Schroeder

Rainbow Program Enterprises

150 Crossways Park West, Woodbury, NY 11797; (516) 364-2222. (Bravo, American Movie Classics, Sports-Channel New York, Sports Channel New England, Sports-Vision Chicago, PRISM of Philadelphia, SportsChannel Florida, Rainbow Home Video, Rainbow Network Communications, News 12 Long Island)
PRESIDENT
Marc Lustgarten

Request Television

Reiss Media Enterprises, Inc., 140 East 45th St., New York, NY 10017; (212) 984-5900. (A pay-per-view cable network)
CHAIRMAN & CHIEF EXECUTIVE OFFICER
Jeffrey C. Reiss
EXECUTIVE VICE PRESIDENT
Leonard Fertig
SENIOR VICE PRESIDENT & GENERAL COUNSEL
Bruce Karpas
VICE PRESIDENT, SALES, MARKETING & PROGRAMMING
Paul FitzPatrick

SelecTV of California, Inc.

4755 Alla Rd., Marina del Rey, CA 90291; (213) 827-4400. (WHT Pay-TV system)
PRESIDENT
  Thomas C. Hunt
VICE PRESIDENT SALES & MARKETING
  Ronald E. Ruppe

Showtime/The Movie Channel, Inc.

1633 Broadway, New York, NY 10019; (212) 708-1600. (A Pay-TV system)
CHAIRMAN AND CHIEF EXECUTIVE OFFICER
  Winston H. (Tony) Cox
EXECUTIVE VICE PRESIDENT, MARKETING & CREATIVE SERVICES
  Matthew Blank
EXECUTIVE VICE PRESIDENT, PROGRAMMING
  Fred Schneier
EXECUTIVE VICE PRESIDENT, BUSINESS DEVELOPMENT & AFFILIATE MARKETING
  Jack Heim
PRESIDENT, VIACOM NETWORK ENTERPRISES
  Ron Bernard
CHIEF FINANCIAL OFFICER & SENIOR VICE PRESIDENT
  Jerry Cooper
PRESIDENT, VIEWER'S CHOICE
  Scott Kurnit
SENIOR VICE PRESIDENT, GENERAL COUNSEL, VIACOM NETWORKS GROUP
  Greg Ricca
SENIOR VICE PRESIDENT, PROGRAM PLANNING
  Jim Miller
EXECUTIVE VICE PRESIDENT & GENERAL MANAGER, VIAMCOM SATELLITE NETWORKS
  Stephan Wm. Schulte
SENIOR VICE PRESIDENT, ADMINISTRATION
  Dwight Tierney

Silent Network

6363 Sunset Blvd., Ste. 930-B, Hollywood, CA 90028; (213) 464-SIGN. Organized 1980. (Cable TV network for deaf and hearing-impaired audiences utilizing sign language, voice and open captions.)
CHAIRMAN/CEO
  Sheldon I. Altfeld
PRESIDENT
  Herbert W. Larson
SR. PRODUCER/VICE PRESIDENT, OPERATIONS
  Dawn Jeffory-Nelson
VICE PRESIDENT, SALES & MARKETING
  Carol Mau
DIRECTOR, AFFILIATE RELATIONS
  Suzan G. Hendershot
DIRECTOR, SPECIAL PROMOTIONS
  Susan H. Moore
AFFILIATIONS
  National Academy of Cable Programming, National Association for the Deaf, Academy of Television Arts & Sciences

Telstar Channel

555 Madison Ave., 6th floor, New York, NY 10022; (212) 838-3377. (A Pay-TV system).
CHAIRMAN OF THE BOARD
  Gerald A. Bartell
VICE CHAIRMAN & CHIEF EXECUTIVE OFFICER
  Joseph A. Corazzi
VICE PRESIDENT & SECRETARY-TREASURER
  Stan Irwin
EXECUTIVE VICE PRESIDENT
  Carl A. Sambus
SENIOR VICE PRESIDENT, PROGRAMMING & MARKETING
  Dr. Gerry D. Jordan

TEMPO Television Network

(Formerly SPN) 6918 S. Yorktown, Tulsa, OK 74136; (918) 496-3200
PRESIDENT
  R. B. Smith
VICE PRESIDENT/NATIONAL SALES & PROGRAMMING
  Ray Klinge
VICE PRESIDENT/EASTERN DIVISION
  Jim Trecek
VICE PRESIDENT, WESTERN DIVISION
  Seth Kittey

Tower Productions Inc.

175 Fifth Ave., Suite 1101, New York, NY 10010; (212) 941-0702. Organized 1983. (Produces programming for broadcast, cable, corporate and home video.)
PRESIDENT
  Donald A. Roosa

Trinity Broadcasting Network

Box A, Santa Ana, CA 92711; (714) 832-2950.
PRESIDENT
  Paul F. Crouch
DIRECTOR AFFILIATE SERVICES
  Stan Hollon

Univision

Univision Holdings, Inc., 330 Madison Ave., New York, NY 10017; (212) 983-8500.
MANAGER—CORPORATE OFFICE
  William D. Stiles
SENIOR VICE PRESIDENT, DIRECTOR OF SALES & MARKETING
  Browning Holcombe, Jr.
SENIOR VICE PRESIDENT, BUSINESS DEVELOPMENT
  Blaine Decker
VICE PRESIDENT, PROGRAM DIRECTOR
  Rosita Peru
VICE PRESIDENT, NEWS DIRECTOR
  Guillermo Martinez

USA Network

1230 Ave. of the Americas, New York, NY 10020; (212) 408-9100
PRESIDENT & CHIEF EXECUTIVE OFFICER
  Kay Koplowitz
EXECUTIVE VICE PRESIDENT & CHIEF OPERATING OFFICER
  Kent Replogle
VICE PRESIDENT, FINANCE & ADMINISTRATION
  Doug Hamilton
VICE PRESIDENT, RESEARCH
  David Bender
VICE PRESIDENT, MARKETING
  Andrew Besch
SENIOR VICE PRESIDENT, BUSINESS AFFAIRS, OPERATIONS AND GENERAL COUNSEL
  Stephen Brenner
SENIOR VICE PRESIDENT, AFFILIATE RELATIONS
  Gil Faccio
SENIOR VICE PRESIDENT, PROGRAMMING
  David Kenin
SENIOR VICE PRESIDENT, AD SALES
  John Silvestri

WTBS

Turner Broadcasting System, 1050 Techwood Drive, N.W., Atlanta, GA 30318; (404) 827-1717.
CHAIRMAN/PRESIDENT
  R.E. (Ted) Turner

The Weather Channel

2840 Mt. Wilkinson Parkway, Suite 200, Atlanta, GA 30039; (404) 434-6800.

PRESIDENT
Michael J. Eckert

VICE PRESIDENT, SPECIAL PROJECTS
Douglas S. Holladay

VICE PRESIDENT, ADVERTISING SALES
Ed Peters

VICE PRESIDENT/AFFILIATE SALES & SERVICES
Rebecca Ruthuen

Trade Names of Basic Cable & Pay-TV Suppliers

(See company listings)

American Movie Classics (Rainbow)
BET (Black Entertainment Network)
Bravo (Rainbow Programming Services)
CNN (Cable News Network—Turner Broadcasting)
Cinemax (Cinemax—Time, Inc.)
C-SPAN (Cable Satellite Public Affairs Network)
The Disney Channel (Group W/Disney)
ESPN (Entertainment & Sports Programming Network—Getty Oil)
FNN (Financial News Network)
Home Box Office (Home Box Office—Time, Inc.)
Home Premiere Television (ATC, Cox TeleCable, Continental, Newhouse)

Lifetime (Hearst/ABC/Viacom)
MTV (MTV Network)
The Movie Channel (Showtime/The Movie Channel)
Nashville Network (NLT Corp.)
Nickelodeon (MTV Networks)
The Playboy Channel (Playboy Enterprises)
Request Television (Reiss Media Enterprises)
Showtime (Showtime/The Movie Channel)
Telstar (Telestar Channel)
Univision (Spanish International Network)
USA Network (USA Cable Network)
Video Hits One (MTV Networks)
The Weather Channel (The Weather Channel)
WHT (SelecTV of California)
WTBS (Turner)

657

Advertising Agencies

* **STATION REPRESENTATIVES**

Advertising Agencies

A. D. ADAMS ADVERTISING, 9 E. 38 St., New York, NY 10016; (212) 685-9060.
A. D. ADAMS, pres.

ALLIED ADVERTISING AGENCY, INC., 830 Statler Office Bldg., Boston, MA 02116; (617) 482-4100.
HOWARD SHAMBAN, TV dir.; MARC F. SHAMBAN, TV time buyer.

ANDERSON DAVID & SEEDS, INC., Colonial Bldg., Clinton, NY 13323; (212) 853-6141.
JAY C. ANDERSON, pres.; MARK ANDERSON, acct. exec.

ARNOLD & COMPANY, INC., Park Square Bldg., Boston, MA 02116; (617) 357-1900.
GERARD GOLDEN, pres.; ARNOLD Z. ROSOFF, chairman & treasurer; LEN KARSAVOL, creative dir.; DENNIS LEE, copy chief; MARIE KACHINSKI, media dir.; STAVROS COSMOPULOS, exec. v.p., creative services; FRED SIEGEL, media; PHYLLIS MAYNARD, media; ANNE GOTZ, JOAN BENNETT, GINNY MEANEY, media.

N. W. AYER INCORPORATED, 1345 Ave. of the Americas, New York, NY 10105; (212) 974-7400.
MARCELLA ROSEN, sr. v.p. & media dir.; DAVID LEHMKUHL, group media dir., planning; JANE TWYON, group media dir., planning; RICHARD WELSH, group media dir., network & negotiation; DIANE ZGONC, group media dir., planning; SUSAN BELL, mgr. spot buying.

BBDO CHICAGO, INC., 410 N. Michigan Ave., Chicago, IL 60611; (312) DElaware 7-7860.
ROGER MOHR, chmn. of the bd.; ERIC HARKNA, pres.; CHUCK SHELDON, exec. prod.

TED BATES ADVERTISING/NEW YORK, 1515 Broadway, New York, NY 10036; (212) 869-3131.
ROBERT E. JACOBY, Chm.; ROBERT A BRUNS, Pres.; WALTER E. REICHEL, Sr. v.p.-Exec. Dir. Media & Programs Dept.; JOEL M. SEGAL, Sr. V.P.-Dir. TV/Radio Div. Division of TED BATES WORLDWIDE, INC. (same address) with affiliates in Fort Lauderdale, Chicago, Minneapolis, San Francisco, Los Angeles, Canada, Mexico, Argentina, Brazil, Chile, Colombia, Ecuador, Peru, Venezuela, United Kingdom, Norway, Sweden, Denmark, West Germany, Austria, Netherlands, Belgium, France, Spain, Italy, Greece, South Africa, Malaysia, Thailand, Singapore, Hong Kong, Japan, Philippines, Australia, New Zealand.

BEHRENDS, BODLE & PARSONS, INC., 7031 Albert Pick Rd., Ste. 200, Greensboro, NY 27409; (919) 668-7272.

RICHARD D. BEHRENDS, pres.; RICHARD FURMANSKI, v.p. & senior art dir.; ROBERT A. BODLE, JR., v.p. & exec. creative dir.; SYLVIA Y. PASSAVANT, secty.-treas.; JERRY BLACKWELDER, media dir.

HERBERT S. BENJAMIN ASSOCIATES, INC., 2736 Florida St., Baton Rouge, LA 70802; (504) 387-0611.
LEE HERZBERG, JR., chm./pres.; MARGARET S. WEBB, exec. v.p.; PATTI HASSELL, treas.; JACKLYN ROBBINS, secty.; LENORE USHER, v.p., acct. exec.; GUS WALES, v.p./creative dir.; RICHARD J. BARRA, v.p.; mgr. Lafayette branch office; ELISE GANETT, asst. v.p., exec. admin.

WALTER F. BENNETT CO., 20 N. Wacker Dr., Chicago, IL 60606; (312) 372-1131.
FRED DIENERT, pres.; TED DIENERT, exec. v.p.; JAN KLUTS, media dir.-time buyer. Other offices: 1634 Spruce St., Philadelphia, PA 19103; (215) 545-2003; 16479 Dallas Pkwy., Dallas, TX 72348; (214) 380-1122.

BENTON & BOWLES 909 Third Ave., New York, NY 10022; (212) 758-6200.
JOHN S. BOWEN, pres. & chief exec. officer; VICTOR G. BLOEDE, chm. of bd. & chm., Benton & Bowles International; GEORGE SIMKO, sr. v.p & group exec.

RALPH BING ADVERTISING CO., 16109 Selva Dr., San Diego, CA 92128; (714) 487-7444.
RALPH BING, TV dir.

FRANK BLOCK ASSOC., The Chase, 10th floor, St. Louis, MO 63108; (314) 367-9600.
DAVID STOBLE, dir. mktg.

BOTSFORD, KETCHUM, INC., 55 Union St., San Francisco, CA 94111.
DENIS HITCHMOUGH, senior v.p., media; MORTY BARAN, dir. broadcast prod.; PATTY MORAN, v.p. mgr. broadcast business affairs.

BRAVERMAN-MIRISCH INC., 1517 Schuyler Rd., Beverly Hills, CA 90210; (213) 274-5204.
MILLICENT BRAVERMAN, pres.

BURLINGAME/GROSSMAN, INC., 6160 N. Cicero Ave., Chicago, IL 60646; (312) 777-0610.
S. J. BRICHTA, TV dir.

LEO BURNETT COMPANY, INC., Prudential Plaza, Chicago, IL 60601; (312) 565-5959.
JOHN J. KINSELLA, pres. & CEO; NORM L. MUSE, chm. of the board; WAYNE A. (AL) WIGGINS, vice chm., chief administrative officer; THOMAS D. HEATH, vice chm., corporate development; JOHN C. (JACK) KRAFT, exec. v.p., administration & finance.; HALL (CAP) ADAMS, Chm. & CEO, Leo Burnett U.S.A.; RICHARD (RICK) FIZDALE, pres. & chief creative officer, Leo Burnett, U.S.A.; HENRY J. (HANK) FEELEY, chm. & CEO, Leo Burnett International; MICHAEL CONRAD, pres. & chief creative officers, Leo Burnett International.

HAROLD CABOT & CO., INC., One Constitution Plaza, Boston, MA 02129; (617) 242-6200.
WILLIAM H. MONAGHAN, pres.; PETER CROWELL, media dir.; LOUIS STAMOULIS, dir. radio-TV.

CALDWELL VAN RIPER/FORT WAYNE, 701 S. Clinton St., Fort Wayne, IN 46802; (219) 422-7495.
DENISE DOUVILLE, media director.

CAMPBELL-MITHUN, INC., Northstar Center, Minneapolis, MN 55402; (612) 339-7383; and 111 East Wacker Drive, Chicago, IL 60601; (312) 565-3800.
WILLIAM D. DUNLOP, chm.-exec. comm. & CEO (Mpls.); WILLIAM E. STEIN, pres. & COO (Chicago); RAYMOND L. SACHS, vice chm. & vice chm./exec. comm. (Mpls.); EARL HERZOG, v.p., media dir. (Mpls.); ART EDELSTEIN, v.p., media dir. (Chicago); ALAN GERSTEN, v.p., media planning services dir. (Mpls.); LORNA TWEED, v.p., spot buying bdcst. mgr. (Mpls.); GAIL BURCH, assoc. media dir., (Mpls.); JANET BAK, v.p., assoc. media dir. (Chicago); JEANNE O'NEILL, assoc. media dir. (Chicago); TESS ZYCH, assoc. media dir. (Chicago).

THE CRAMER-KRASSELT CO., 733 N. Van Buren St., Milwaukee, WI 53202; (414) 276-3500.
ROBERT L. CHRISTIANSEN, chmn. of bd. & treas.; TED WING, pres; C. ROSS LITTIG, vice chm. of bd.; DONALD E. POM, media dir.-TV/radio; CAROL WALCZAK, buyer/planner; KATHY HARRISON, buyler/planner; CATHY POCHERT, bdcst. svs. mgr.

CRESWELL, MUNSELL, FULTZ & ZIRBEL, INC., 4211 Signal Ridge Road, N.E., Cedar Rapids, IA 54202; (319) 395-6500.
F.BAKER, pres.; J. MEEKS, S. CUSTER, M. WHITE, G. ANDERSON, B. CLINE, W. FRITZ, J. MEEKS, I. WAY, sr. v.p.'s-radio/TV producers; T. F. TAYLOR, v.p. exec. broadcast prod.; M. MURRAY, prod.

CUNNINGHAM & WALSH, CHICAGO INC., 875 Michigan Ave., Chicago, IL 60611; (312) 943-9400.
CHARLES C. HATCHER, sr. v.p. dir. operations & bdcst. prod.; GREGG DEARTH, sr. v.p. dir. creative svcs; JOHN DOHERTY, pres. & CEO.

D'ARCY MASIUS BENTON & BOWLES, INC., 909 Third Ave., New York, NY 10022; (212) 758-6200.
New York: MICHAEL MOORE, sr. v.p., corporate media dir.; RICHARD LEVENSON, sr. v.p., exec. creative dir. Atlanta: REGIS C. NAPOLITANO, sr. v.p., media dir.; B.A. ALBERT, sr. v.p., creative dir. Bloomfield Hills: GEORGE M. ROGERS, JR., sr. v.p. dir. of media services; STEPHEN C. KOPCHA, exec. v.p., creative dir. Chicago: JOSEPH P. ZELLER, sr. v.p. dir. media services; GARY J. HORTON, deputy mng. dir., chief creative officer. Houston: HEIDI ASKEW, v.p., media dir.; KEN THOREN, sr. v.p., creative dir.; Los Angeles: RON LAWRENCE, v.p., media dir.; KEN BERRIS, sr. v.p., creative dir. Minneapolis-St. Paul: GEORGE C. SCOTT, v.p., media and research dir.; DICK BRINER, v.p., creative dir. St. Louis: JAMES PORCARELLI, sr. v.p., dir. of media services; ALBERT LERMAN, chief creative officer/deputy mng. dir. San Francisco:

ROGER BARON, v.p. media dir.; SCOTT YOUNG, v.p., exec. creative dir.

DIENER/HAUSER/BATES CO., INC., 116 N. Robertson Blvd., Suite 210, Los Angeles, CA 90048; (213) 855-1900.
EUGENE B. COFSKY, pres. West Coast div., BILL ISENBERGER, sr. v.p.; HICKEY SHAPIRO, v.p.

W. B. DONER & CO., 25900 Northwestern, Southfield, MI 48075; (313) 354-9700; also 2305 N. Charles St., Baltimore, MD 21218; (301) 338-1600.
W. B. DONER, chm. of exec. comm.; HERBERT D. FRIED, chm. of bd.; MICHAEL SHAPIRA, pres.; SEYMOUR (SKIP) RO- BERTS, exec. v.p.; H.B. LEVINE, secy./treas.; JAMES DALE, vice chairman.

DOREMUS & COMPANY (Subsidiary of BBDO Intl., Inc.), 120 Broadway, New York, NY 10005; (212) 964-0700.
FRANKLIN E. SCHAFFER, chairman; G. BARRY McMEN- NAMIN, president; WILLIAM B. PALMER, creative dir.; LOUIS CROSSIN, media dir.
Branch offices; Boston, Chicago, San Francisco, Washington, Los Angeles, Miami, Minneapolis, Rockford, London.
Corresp. offices: Akron, Denver, Baltimore, Detroit, Cleveland, Pittsburgh, Dallas, Hartford, Houston, Atlanta, Kansas City, St. Louis.

DOYLE DANE BERNBACH INC., 437 Madison Ave., New York, NY 10022; (212) 826-2000.
GEORGE NILES, v.p., media; JOSEPH R. DALY, chm. of the bd.; ROBERT LEVENSON, vice chm., creative; BARRY LOS- GHRANE, pres. & CEO.

EARLE PALMER BROWN & SPIRO, 100 S. Broad St., Philadelphia, PA 19102; (215) 923-5400.
HERB SMITH, exec. v.p., general mgr.

EISNER & ASSOCIATES, INC., 12 W. Madison St., Baltimore, MD 21201; (301) 685-3390.
H. W. EISNER, chm.; STEVE EISNER, pres.; GEORGE NILES, v.p., media.

MIKE FADELL ADVERTISING AGENCY, 6101 York, S. Minneapolis, MN 55410; (612) 922-5606.
MIKE FADELL, SR., TV dir. & timebuyer.

FAHLGREN & SWINK, 655 Metro Place S., Dublin, OH 43017; (614) 766-3500.
CHRIS CLEMENTS, sr. v.p. media & mktg. svcs.; WILLIAM KIGHT, vice chairman, president, Columbus.

FAHLGREN & SWINK, PARKERSBURG, Rosemar Rd. & Seminary Dr., Parkersburg, WV 26101; (304) 424-3591.
WILLIAM FARSON, treasurer; H. SMOOT FAHLGREN, chair- man/chief exec. officer.

FAIRFAX INC., ADVERTISING, 635 Madison Ave., New York, NY 10022; (212) 350-1800.
STANLEY I. FISHEL, dir. of television; ROBERT McQUADE, producer; RICHARD MIRENDA, art director; MIKE COHN, media dir.

FOOTE, CONE & BELDING COMMUNICATIONS, INC., 101 Park Ave., New York, NY 10178; (212) 907-1000; 401 North Michigan Ave., Chicago, IL 60611; (312) 467-9200.
JOHN O'TOOLE, chm. (New York); NORMAN W. BROWN, pres. & CEO (Chicago).
ADVERTISING OFFICES: Chicago, New York, San Francisco, Los Angeles, Greenwich, CT, Philadelphia, Toronto, Montreal, Mexico City, Kingston (Jamaica), San Juan (Puerto Rico), Caracas, Port of Spain (Trinidad), São Paulo (Brazil), Buenos Aires, Stock- holm, Gothenburg (Sweden), Oslo, Copenhagen, Hamburg, Berlin, Amsterdam, Rotterdam, London, Nottingham, Brussels, Paris, Mar- seille, Lisbon, Madrid, Barcelona, Frankfurt-am-Main, Zurich, Vienna, Milan, Rome, Athens, Johannesburg, Durban, Cape Town, Tokyo, Hong Kong, Kuala Lumpur, Singapore, Jakarta, Sydney, Melbourne.

FOSTER & DAVIES, INC., Hanna Bldg., Cleveland, OH 44115; (216) 241-0711.

ALBERT FRANK-GUENTHER LAW, INC., 71 Broadway, New York, NY 10006; (212) 248-5200.
STEPHEN J. WITT, chm.; JOHN F. COWELL III, pres.
Branch office: San Francisco.

GERBER ADVERTISING AGENCY, 209 S.W. Oak Ave., Portland, OR 97204; (503) 221-0100.
BETTY CHIMENTI, media dir.; KAREN ANDRUS-HUGHES, media buyer.

GILLHAM ADVERTISING INC., Fourth Floor, 102 W. 500 So., Salt Lake City, UT 84101; (801) 328-0281.
RONALD W. GRIFFITHS, senior v.p.; WENDY SARIS, media dir.; TERESA WESEMANN, traffic mgr.

GREY ADVERTISING, INC., 777 Third Ave., New York, NY 10017; (212) 546-2000.
EDWARD H. MEYER, pres. & chief exec. officer; ALEC GER- STER, v.p., dir. of media & programming.
Branch offices: Amsterdam-Baarn, Auckland, Brussels, Buenos Aires, Caracas, Chicago, Copenhagen, Detroit, Dusseldorf, Glas- gow, Gothenburg, Hong Kong, Johannesburg, London, Los An- geles, Madrid, Malmoe, Milan, Minneapolis/St. Paul, Montevideo, Montreal, New York, Oslo, Paris, Rio de Janeiro, San Francisco, Santiago, Singapore, Stockholm, Sydney, Tokyo, Toronto, Vienna.

GRISWOLD, INC., Landmark Office Towers, 101 Prospect Ave., Cleve- land, OH 44115; (216) 696-3400.
PATRICK J. MORIN, pres. and CEO; NEAL B. DAVIS, exec. vice pres., dir. of client services; THOMAS PAPADIMOULIS, senior vice pres., co-creative dir.; WALTER WOODWARD, exec. vice pres., co- creative dir.

GRUBB, GRAHAM & WILDER, INC., Century 21 Plaza, Champaign, IL 61820; (217) 344-4334.
ROBERT F. GRUBB, chm.; JOHN A. GRUBB, pres.; PATRICK CHELF, media dir.

HARRIS & LOVE, INC./ADVERTISING, 136 East So. Temple, Salt Lake City, UT 84111; (801) 532-7333.
DONALD G. WARE, pres.

HART-CONWAY CO., INC., 300 Triangle Bldg., Rochester, NY 14604; (716) 232-2930.
PETER B. WHITCOMBE, pres.; WILLIAM WESTERFELD, exec. v.p.

HENDERSON ADVERTISING, INC., 60 Pelham Pointe, Greenville, SC 29615; P.O. Box 2247, Greenville, SC 29602 (Mailing Address); (803) 271-6000.
RALPH W. CALLAHAN JR., chm. & pres.; BILL REYNOLDS, sr. v.p. media dir.

HICKS AND GREIST, INC., 220 E. 42 St., New York, NY 10036; (212) 370-9600.
CHARLES V. SKOOG, JR., chm.; D. EDWARD RICCHIUTO, pres.; S. PARKER, media dir.; DEMETRI KONTUPOULOS, TV prod. dir.

HOLLAND ADVERTISING, 252 Ludlow Ave., Cincinnati, OH 45220; (513) 221-1252
MARK S. HOLLAND, executive v.p.

HOUCK ADVERTISING, 1402 Grandin Rd., Roanoke, VA 24015; (703) 989-6655.
WILLIAM B. HOUCK, chm.; WILLIAM B. HOUCK, JR., pres.; CYNTHIA G. CALDWELL, media buyer.

HUTCHINS/YOUNG & RUBICAM INC., 400 Midtown Tower; Roches- ter, NY 14604; (716) 546-6480.
FRANK M. HUTCHINS, chm.; JAMES N. MOREY, pres. & chief exec. officer; ROBERT H. MAHARRY, v.p., creative dir.; CHARLES E. RELLER, v.p. finance & adm., treasurer; OWEN J. CRUMB, v.p. & gen. mgr., pub. rel. div.; HARVEY J. BOZZI, JR., v.p./director of special projects.

HENRY J. KAUFMAN & ASSOCIATES, INC., 2233 Wisconsin Ave., N.W., Washington, DC 20007; (202) 333-0700.
STUART E. KARU, chm. & CEO; MICHAEL G. CARBERRY, pres. & COO; MARY D. YERRICK, sr. v.p., development; J. ROGER VILSACK, exec. v.p. creative svcs.; MERRICK MUR- DOCK, exec. prod.

KELLY, ZAHRNDT & KELLY INC., 10805 Sunset Office Dr., St. Louis, MO 63127.
ROBERT W. KELLY, dir.; WILLIAM A. WILSON, MARY HOP- PER, CHARLES CROWE, DAVE ERICH, acct. execs.

KERR, WEST & GISH, INC., 104 Kenner Ave., Suite 203, Nashville, TN 37205; (615) 297-9770.
AL KERR, pres.

KETCHUM COMMUNICATIONS, INC., Six PPG Place, Pittsburgh, PA 15222; (412) 456-3500.
Pittsburgh: WILLIAM H. GENGE, chm.; GERALD J. VOROS, pres.; HERBERT D. GORDON, sr. v.p., media services; JUDITH HOFSCHER, v.p., media dir.; RICHARD SLEEMAN, v.p. & broad- cast services mgr.
New York office: Ketchum New York. THOMAS MILLER, pres.; JIM McHUGH, v.p., dir. media network, res. (N.Y.).

KEYES MARTIN GABY LINETT, 841 Mountain Ave., Springfield, NJ; (201) 376-7300.
Specialist: ROBYN GREEN-TAYLOR, media director.

KRUPNICK & ASSOCIATES, INC., 135 N. Meramec, St. Louis, MO 63105; (314) 862-9393.
WILLIAM W. QUADE, TV production.

KUTTNER & KUTTNER, INC., 212 W. Superior St., Chicago, IL 60610; (312) 787-7940.

LEWIS, GILMAN & KYNETT, INC., 1700 Market St., Philadelphia, PA 19103; (215) 568-3775.
ROBERT G. WILDER, CEO, pres. & chm.; CARL E. CASSELMAN, exec. v.p., exec. creative dir.; EDWIN R. BATES, v.p., creative dir.; STEPHEN J. BARCUS, v.p., group supervisor; WESLEY G. HOTCHKISS, v.p.; CHESTER D. HARRINGTON, v.p. & exec. dir. of media services, MICHAEL A. WALSH, v.p., media dir.; FREDERIC C. MOFFATT, media acct. mgr.; GLORIA PEDALINO, media acct. mgr.; RICHARD BONDS, media acct. mgr.; GLORIA F. HARTMAN, media acct. mgr.; GUY S. MOSS, media acct. mgr.; JAMES J. SLOAN, media acct. mgr.

LINTAS: CAMPBELL-EWALD CO., 30400 Van Dyke, Warren, MI; (313) 574- 3400.
RICHARD D. O'CONNOR, chm.; PETER A. DOW, pres.; LOUIS M. SCHULTZ, exec. v.p., media dir.
Branch Offices: Atlanta, Chicago, Los Angeles, New York, San Francisco, Dallas, Washington, Miami, Pittsburgh.

THE W. E. LONG ADVERTISING AGENCY, 300 W. Washington St., Chicago, IL 60606; (312) 726-4606.
PAUL FRANK, gen. mgr. & creative dir.; THOMAS E. RADIKE, dir. mktg.; ANITA RAUH, media supervisor.

LOWE & HALL ADVERTISING, INC., 215 East Stone Ave., P.O. Box 3357, Greenville, SC; (803) 242-5350.
EDWARD E. BROWER, JR., pres.; KENNETH BROWER, exec. v.p.; W. T. HALL, v.p.; VALERIE VURNAKES, v.p.

McCANN-ERICKSON, 485 Lexington Ave., New York, NY 10017; (212) 697-6000.
JOHN M. OTTER, sr. v.p. dir., natl. bdcast.; JOHN MATTIMORE, v.p., network supvsr.; WILLIAM SHERMAN, v.p., network supvsr.; CLARE SIMPSON, v.p., dir., Coca-Cola natl. bdcast.; ANN KOHL, network supvsr.; RICHARD FORESTER, LORI ISOLA, WENDY RICH, buyers.

EDWARD J. McELROY ADV., INC., 3600 Wilshire Blvd., Los Angeles, CA 90005; (213) 381-3045.
E. D. BROTSOS, pres. & acct. sup.; VICKI PANAGIOTIS, media dir.; LISA C. MOLLER, acct. exec./prod. mgr.

McKENZIE, KING & GORDON, 1680 N. Vine St., Suite 710, Hollywood, CA 90028; (213) 466-3421.
MARIE McKENZIE, pres.; DON McKENZIE, creative dir.; MARIE SELTZER, media dir.; KEVIN MCKENZIE, assoc. creative dir.

MELDRUM & FEWSMITH, INC., 1220 Huron Rd., Cleveland 15, OH; (216) 241-2141.
CHRIS PERRY, chmn./CEO & creative dir.; ROBERT IREDELL IV, president; ROBERT P. HUDDILSTON, exec. v.p., CFO; JEFFREY H. BRYDEN, exec. v.p.; BRUCE S. CHILDERS, exec. v.p.; CATHERINE V. VOITLEIN, v.p., broadcast services; CYNTHIA E. HOLUB, broadcast prod.; MICHAEL LERNER, broadcast prod.

NEEDHAM & GROHMANN, INC., 30 Rockefeller Plaza, New York, NY 10112; 245-6200.
HOWARD A. HEINSIUS, president; WILLIAM R. HOGAN, art dir.; PETER R. WELLS, ANTHONY R. WRIGHT, ANTHONY E. F. CORNWELL, v.p.'s.

NEEDHAM, HARPER & STEERS ADVERTISING, INC., 909 Third Ave., New York, NY 10022; (212) 758-7600.
PAUL C. HARPER, JR., chmn. of the bd. & chief exec. officer; JOEL P. BAUMWOLL, pres. NH&S New York; BARRON Z. BIEDERMAN, pres. NH&S/Issues & Images; LOIS KOREY, exec. v.p. & creative dir.; 303 E. Wacker Dr., Chicago, IL 60601 (312) 861-0200. B. BLAIR VEDDER, JR.; chief op. officer; KEITH L. REINHARD, pres. NH&S Chicago; JOEL M. HOCHBERG, sr. v.p. & creative dir.; 10889 Wilshire Blvd., Los Angeles, CA 90024 (213) 208-5000. BRADLEY H. ROBERTS, pres. NH&S West; RICHARD KELLEY, sr. v.p. & creative dir.

NOWAK BARLOW JOHNSON, 117 Highbridge St., Fayetteville, NY 13066; (305) 637-9895.
DONALD G. NOWAK, pres. & CEO; Ed Gabriel, audio-visual dir.

OHLMEYER ADVERTISING, 9 W. 57 St., New York, NY 10019; (212) 418-6900.

DON OHLMEYER, chm.; PHIL HOWERT, pres.; LEE PRATT, v.p., media dir.; DEAN HEITLER, v.p. mgr. supvsr.; PETER CHRISANTHUPOULUS, v.p. bdcst. supvr.

THE PITLUK GROUP, 45 N.E. Loop 410, San Antonio, TX 78216; (512) 366-3100.
LOUIS H. PITLUK, pres.; JACK N. PITLUK, JR., v.p.; HELEN THOMPSON, med. dir.; JOHN HOEMANN, creative dir.

ROCKLIN, IRVING & ASSOCIATES, 65 E. South Wacker Place, Suite 2400, Chicago, IL 60601; (312) 726-2324.
ROBERT ROCKLIN, pres.; MARK ROCKLIN, v.p.; PATTY JO WONG, creative dir.; SUE McKINNEY, writer; KENT GERBER, acct. exec.; ROBERT TOUROUNJIAN, art dir.; JEAN CARMOSINO, comptroller; YVONNE DAUGHERTY, traffic mgr.

RUDER, FINN & ROTMAN, INC., 110 E. 59 St. New York, NY 10022; (212) 593-6400.
DAVID FINN, chmn. of bd.; KATHY BLOOMGARDEN, pres.; AMY BORDE, pres. NY; CHARLOTTE LIPTON, vice chairman, bdcst. communications dept.

RUMRILL-HOYT, INC., 60 Corporate Woods, Rochester, NY 14623; (716) 272-6100.
RICHARD D. THOMPSON, chairman & CEO; NICK ORLOFF, pres./COO; DONNA FARRINGTON, mgr. radio/TV prod.; FRANK KOPEC, v.p., dir. of media services.

LOWE RUNKLE CO., 6801 N. Broadway, Oklahoma City, OK 73114 (405) 848-6800.
OSCAR HEUSER, pres. & CEO; MARK BAUSKE, dir. bdcst. prod.

SAATCHI & SAATCHI COMPTON, INC., 405 Lexington Ave., New York, NY 10174; (212) 661-0800.
O. MILTON GOSSETT, pres. & CEO; C. CAPUANO, v.p. art & TV commercial production; BRUCE COX, sr. v.p./dir. bdcst. programming. Branch offices: Los Angeles, CA; Southfield, MI.

SHOTWELL AND PARTNERS, INCORPORATED, 801 East Blvd., Charlotte, NC 28203; (704) 372-8880
SIMONS MICHELSON ZIEVE INC., 900 Wilshire Dr., Troy, MI 48084-1600; (313) 362-4242.
MORTON ZIEVE, JAMES A. MICHELSON, officers; JON KATZ, TV dept. dir.

SPITZ ADVERTISING INC., 530 Oak St., Syracuse, NY; (315) 479-5581.
WILLIAM SPITZ, president; CHRIS SLATER, radio-TV dir.; NICK BIBKO, acct. exec.; FAN SPITZ, single sls. & prod.

TATHAM-LAIRD & KUDNER, 980 N. Michigan Ave., Chicago, IL 60611; (312) 337-4400.
CHARLOTTE BEERS, chm. & CEO; WILLIAM YOUNGCLAUS, pres. & COO; RALPH RYDHOLM, mgr. partner, chief creative officer; JOHN J. VALVERDE, sr. partner, chief financial officer; PHILLIP GERBER, sr. partner, media opns. dir.; WERNER WOLFF, mgr. broadcast business affairs.

J. WALTER THOMPSON COMPANY, 466 Lexington Ave., New York, NY 10017; (212) 210-7000.
DON JOHNSON, bd. chm. & chief exec. officer; JOSEPH W. O'DONNELL, chm.-elect. DENIS LANIGAN, vice-chm. & chief operating officer; JACK CRONIN, vice-chm.; BURT MANNING, vice chm.—Creative Resources, JACK PETERS, pres.
J. Walter Thompson USA Inc., (subsidiary of J. Walter Thompson Co.) offices: Atlanta, Chicago, Detroit, Los Angeles, New York, San Francisco, Washington, DC.
Service offices: Charlotte, Dallas, Denver, Houston, Indianapolis, Kansas City, Memphis, Miami, New Orleans, Oklahoma City, Omaha, Philadelphia, Phoenix, Rochester, Salt Lake City, St. Louis.
J. Walter Thompson Co. International offices: Buenos Aires, Sydney, Melbourne, Perth, Brisbane, Vienna, Brussels, São Paulo, Rio de Janeiro, Toronto, Montreal, Vancouver, Santiago, Copenhagen, Santo Domingo, Quito, Guayaquil, Helsinki, Lyon, Paris, Frankfurt, Dusseldorf, Hamburg, Athens, Guatemala City, Hong Kong, Milan, Rome, Osaka, Tokyo, Kuala Lumpur, Mexico City, Amsterdam, Wellington, Auckland, Zug, Lima, Manila, Lisbon, San Juan, Singapore, Johannesburg, Cape Town, Madrid, Barcelona, Colombo, Stockholm, Zurich, Asuncion, Bangkok, Istanbul, Izmir, Dubai, London, Manchester, Caracas, Montevideo.

TRACY-LOCKE ADVERTISING INC., Plaza of the Americas, South Tower, P.O. Box 50129, Dallas, TX 75250; (214) 742-3131.
MORRIS HITE, bd. chm.; NORM CAMPBELL, pres.; BOB BELTON, v.p. bdcst prod.; LARRY SPIEGEL, sr. v.p. dir. media & research; WALT ATKINSON, v.p. media serv. dir.; CLAUDE CAYLOR, v.p., media dir.; JUDY MILLER, v.p., media buying director; GINA BURKS, dir. of network; CAROL CASTELLANO, dir. of spot.

VAN BRUNT & CO., ADVERTISING-MARKETING INC., 300 E. 42 St., New York, NY 10017; (212) 949-1300.
EDWIN VAN BRUNT, chm. bd.; ALBERT VAN BRUNT, pres.; WILLIAM BUCKLEY, dir. of broadcast.

VICTOR VAN DER LINDE CO., INC., 381 Broadway, Westwood, NJ 07675; (201) 664-6830.
A. K. KINGSLEY, v.p.

MORTON DENNIS WAX AND ASSOCIATES, 1560 Broadway, New York, NY 10036; (212) 302-5360
MORTON DENNIS WAX, pres.; SANDRA WAX, v.p./gen. mgr.

WILLIS/CASE/HARWOOD, INC., 3411 Office Park Drive, Dayton, OH 45439; (513) 299-7394.
MICHAEL G. HEALY, pres.; RONDA L. McCALL, broadcast producer.

YOUNG & RUBICAM INC., 285 Madison Ave., New York, NY 10017; (212) 953-2000.
EDWARD N. NEY, chm., pres. & chief exec. officer; ALEXANDER KROLL, exec. v.p.; pres. Y&R USA div.; JOSEPH W. OSTROW, exec. v.p., dir. communications svcs.; RICHARD H. LOW, exec. v.p., dir. bdcst, programming & purchasing.
Y&R USA OFFICES: Cedar Rapids & Des Moines, IA; Chicago; Cincinnati, OH; Denver, CO; Detroit, MI; Houston, TX; Kansas City, MO; New York, NY; Los Angeles, San Diego & San Francisco, CA; Rochester, NY; St. Petersburg, FL.
Y&R International Offices: Adelaide, Melbourne & Sydney, Australia; Madrid, Spain; Berne & Zurich, Switzerland; Brussels, Belgium; Buenos Aires, Argentina; Copenhagen, Denmark; Frankfurt & Munich, Germany; Stockholm & Gothenburg, Sweden; Hong Kong; London, England; Mexico City, Mexico; Milan, Italy; Montreal & Toronto, Canada; Oslo, Norway; Paris, France; San Juan, Puerto Rico; Santo Domingo, Dominican Republic; São Paulo, Brazil; Singapore; Tokyo, Japan; Vienna, Austria; Amsterdam, The Netherlands; Santiago, Chile.

Station Representatives

ABC-TV TELEVISION SPOT SALES, INC., 1345 Ave. of the Americas, New York, NY 10019; (212) 887-7777.
JOHN B. WATKINS, pres.; PHILIP J. SWEENIE, v.p.; JOSEPH COHEN, east. sls. mgr.; MICHAEL COLLERAN, est. sls. mgr.; MARY WEBB ELLIS, east. sls. mgr.
Branch Offices: Chicago 60601, Two Illinois Center; (312) 750-7777, SCOTT THOMAS, sls. mgr.; Los Angeles 90067, 2040 Ave. of Stars; (213) 557-6241, MICHAEL JACK; San Francisco 94111, 900 Front St.; (415) 863-0077, FRANKLIN LOWE; Southfield, MI (Detroit) 48075, 3000 Town Center, (313) 355-4490., ED PEARSON; Dallas 75251, 2 Forest Plaza/12201 Merit Dr.; (214) 960-7981, MICHAEL IRVINE; Atlanta 30339, 200 Galleria Parkway, NW; (404) 956-0822, DEBBIE SHAW.

AVERY-KNODEL TELEVISION, 437 Madison Ave., New York, NY 10022; (212) 421-5600.
J. W. KNODEL, chmn.; ROBERT J. KIZER, pres.; F. ROBERT KALTHOFF, exec. v.p.
Branch Offices: Chicago 60601, 2600 Prudential Plaza; (312) 467-6111, F. ROBERT KALTHOFF; Los Angeles 90004, 155 Montgomery St.; (415) 986-8082, JOSEPH FRIEDMAN; Los Angeles 90005, 633 S. Shatto Place; (213) 385-6394; Atlanta 30326, 3340 Peachtree Road, N.E., (404) 233-4474, JAMES GOSSETT; Dallas 75219, 3626 N. Hall St., Suite 608; (214) 528-1741 WALLIS S. IVY; Detroit, 48084, DAVID BRANGAN; St. Louis 63102, 410 Mansion House Center; (314) 241-5051, FRED W. JOHNSON; Minneapolis, St. Paul: toll free exchange, 929-1300, Edna, MN 55435, 6700 France Ave., Suite 155, MAUREEN KVAM; Denver 80206, 280 Columbine Ave.; (303) 321-1086, BOB HIX; Portland 97204, 620 SW 5th Suite 907; (503) 223-5980, RON HILLBURY; Seattle 98109, P.O. Box 19417; (206) 624-9200, JACK DAVIES; Haddonfield 08033, 537 Mt. Vernon Avenue, TOM WOOD.

BLAIR TELEVISION, 1290 Ave. of the Americas, New York, NY 10104; (212) 603-5000.
HARRY B. SMART, chairm/CEO; WALTER A. SCHWARTZ, pres./COO; PATRICK J. DEVLIN, exec. v.p./dir. of sls. operations; JAMES R. KELLY, sr. v.p./dir. of client services; WILLIAM E. BREDA, JR., sr. v.p./dir. of affiliate/IND sls.; FLOYD J. GELINI, sr. v.p./dir. of regional sls.; SANFORD S. ACKERMAN, v.p./dir. of finance/planning/admin.; KENNETH P. DONNELLON, v.p.; STEVEN A. MURPHY, v.p./management systems & services.
Branch offices: Chicago, Atlanta, Boston, Charlotte, Cleveland, Dallas, Detroit, Houston, Jacksonville, Los Angeles, Miami, Minneapolis, Philadelphia, St. Louis, San Francisco, Seattle.

CBS TELEVISION STATIONS NATIONAL SALES, 51 W. 52 St., New York, NY 10019; (212) 975-4321.
RHODERIC H. PERTH, v.p. & gen. mgr.; GARY MONTANUS, dir. eastern sales; Branch offices: Chicago, 630 North McClurg Court, (312) 944-6000, INGER JENSON, dir., midwest sales; Detroit, 26877 Northwest Hwy., (313) 352-2800, CHET COLLINS, mgr.; San Francisco, 1 Embarcadero Center, (415) 433-0500, FRANKLIN WHEELER, mgr.; Los Angeles, Sunset Blvd., (213) 460-3000, ROBERT BERGLUND; Atlanta: 6 Piedmont Center, (404) 261-2227, SAM STOLWORTH, mgr.

GROUP W TELEVISION SALES, 90 Park Ave., New York, NY 10016; (212) 883-6100.
EDWARD GOODMAN, pres.; JOEL SEGALL, senior v.p. & gen. sls. mgr.; GREG SCHAEFER, v.p. NY sales mgr.; BOB KAPLAN, group sales mgr.; KENT ATHERTON, natl sales mgr.; JEFF OSBORNE, v.p., admin. sls. & mktg.; ANTHONY DeTHOMAS, controller; JOSEPH PICCIRILLO, dir. research.
Branch offices: Atlanta, GA 30326, 3330 Peachtree Rd. NE, Suite 345; (404) 885-5336; Boston, MA 02134, 1170 Soldiers Field Rd.; (617) 787-7220, DAVID BIGGS; Chicago, IL 60611, 625 N. Michigan Ave., Suite 400; (312) 454-6910, STEPHANIE LEVINE; Dallas, TX 75251, 12221 Merit Drive, Suite 620; (214) 458-9767, JERRY DANFORD; Detroit (Oak Park), MI 48237, 25900 Greenfield Rd., Suite 243; (313) 968-2160, ROBERT E. NEWSHAM; Los Angeles, CA 90048, 6500 Wilshire Blvd., Suite 1150; (213) 655-3556, ALAN BUCKMAN; Philadelphia, PA 19106, Independence Mall East; (215) 238-4966, THOMAS HOLLINGSHEAD; San Francisco, CA 94111, 825 Battery St.; (415) 765-8793, CHUCK PREWITY; Baltimore, MD 21211; 3725 Malden Ave., (301) 466-0013.

KATZ COMMUNICATIONS, INC., One Dag Hammarskjold Plaza, New York, NY 10017; (212) 572-5500.
JAMES L. GREENWALD, chm., CEO; RICHARD D. MENDELSON, pres., CEO; MICHAEL I. PACKMAN, sr. v.p., chief finan. off.; LUCILLE F. LUONGO, v.p., corp. relations.
KATZ TELEVISION: PETER GOULAZIAN, pres.; PAUL D. ARNZEN, sr. v.p., dir. new business; DICK WEINSTEIN, v.p., planning & devel.; LEN GRAZIANO, v.p., regnl. operations; JOHN VON SOOSTEN, v.p., dir. prog.; BOB EINHORN, v.p., dir. sls. research; GEORGE FELDMAN, v.p., dir. mgt. serv.; MARK SHOTTLAND, v.p., natl. sls. projects; CATHY EGAN, v.p., dir., marketing; LAURA NILON, mgr., TV admin.
KATZ AMERICAN TELEVISION: JAMES E. BELOYIANIS, pres.; MICHAEL HUGGER, v.p., gen. sls. mgr., Red, Stars & Eagles; IBRA MORALES, v.p., gen. sls. mgr., White & Blue; KEITH GREEN, v.p., natl. sls. mgr., White; KENNETH PERREN, v.p., natl. sls. mgr., Blue; JOHN SHANNON, natl. sls. mgr., Red; SWAIN WEINER, v.p., natl. sls. mgr., Eagles; RUSSELL WHITE, v.p., natl. sls. mgr., Stars & New York Office Manager; BOB SCUTARI, N.Y. team mgr., Red; FRANK QUAGLIARIELLO, NY team mgr., Eagles; JOHN ROSSI, NY team mgr., Stars; JONATHAN SMITH, NY team mgr., Eagles; JAY ZEITCHIK, v.p., NY team mgr., Blue; BILL CARROLL, v.p., dir. prog.; BUD BOWLIN, v.p., dir., Direct-Response Advertising Sls.; LISA SCHOENBACK, v.p., dir. sls. research; DONNA MOREAU-CUPP, assoc. dir., natl. sls. devel.
KATZ TELEVISION CONTINENTAL: TOM OLSON, pres.; JACK HIGGINS, v.p., gen. mgr.; ARDIE BIALEK, v.p., natl. sls. mgr., West; JERRY CIFARELLI, natl. sls. mgr., East; JAY FRIESEL, v.p., natl. sls. mgr., Southeast; BOB SWAN, v.p., natl. sls. mgr., East Central; JOHN WALL, v.p., natl. sls. mgr., West Central; MAURY WIND, v.p., natl. sls. mgr., South Central; MARGARET CAPUTO, v.p., mgr., West Central; CHRIS JORDAN, mgr., East; CAREY MOLER, mgr., West; MARK RYAN, v.p., mgr., South Central; MICHAEL SPIESMAN, v.p., mgr. Southeast; MARGARET TJEPKEMA, mgr., East Central; MITCHELL PRAVER, v.p., dir., prog.; BUB BOWLIN, v.p., dir., Direct-Response Advertising Sls.; MICHAEL STEINBERG, v.p., dir., sls. research; WILLIAM REED, dir., marketing.
KATZ INDEPENDENT TELEVISION: MARTY OZER, pres.; MICKY COLEN, v.p., regnl. sls. mgr.; PAT GARVEY, v.p., natl. sls. mgr., Lancers; MICHAEL RAOUNAS, v.p. natl sls. mgr., Sabers; SUSAN ZILLER BRAZELL, v.p., natl. sls. mgr., Swords; KERRY ANDREWS, NY mgr., Lancers; JILL NOVORRO, v.p., NY mgr., Sabers; JOE WHITE, v.p., NY mgr., Swords; STUART ZUCKERMAN, v.p., NY mgr., Swords; ANDI POCH, v.p., dir., sports & specials sls. unit; JOAN RUTMAN, v.p., dir., sls. research; DONNA FEE, dir., marketing.

MMT SALES, INC., 150 E. 52 St., New York, NY 10022; (212) 391-8008.
GARRY SCOLLARD, chm.; NEIL KENNEDY, exec. v.p.; JACK OKEN, pres.; ROGER GOLDHAMER, sr. v.p., dir. natl. sls.; TED VAN ERK, v.p. dir. sls.; ELAINE LINKER, v.p. dir. sls.; JON GLUCK, v.p. dir. prog.; AL CANNARELLA, v.p., dir. rsch.
Branch offices in Atlanta, Boston, Charlotte, Chicago, Cleveland, Dallas, Detroit, Los Angeles, Miami, Minneapolis, Philadelphia, St. Louis, San Francisco, Seattle.

ART MOORE INC., 220 W. Mercer, Seattle, WA 98119; (206) 282-3400.
GREG SMITH, EARLE BAKER, SANDY RUNNION, RICK STAEB, RUTH HALLETT. Branch: Portland, OR 97214, 516 S.E. Morrison; (503) 228-2451, DARRELL RUTTER, BRUCE WORKMAN, TEDDI JONES, LYNN THORSEN.

NBC SPOT TELEVISION SALES, NATIONAL BROADCASTING COMPANY, INC., 30 Rockefeller Plaza, New York, NY 10020 (212) 664-4444.
BUD HIRSCH, v.p.; JIM ZAFIROS, v.p.; J. FRISCHER, J. HARRIS, mgrs. Eastern sls.

NATIONAL TIME SALES, 9 E. 41 St., New York, NY 10016; (212) 661-6550.
H. FRANKLIN, sales mgr.
Branch offices: Chicago, 60645, 3322 W. Peterson Ave.; (312) 478-5544, HOOPER JONES; Atlanta, 30309, 1819 Peachtree Rd. N.E.; (404) 355-7961, BERNARD OCHS; Dallas, 75202, 1407 Main St.; (214) 748-2172, JACK RILEY; San Francisco, 94133, 559 Pacific Ave.; SAM POSNER; Beverly Hills, 90028, 111 N. La Cienega Blvd.; CHUCK DWYER; San Jose, 95129, 4320 Stevens Creek Blvd.; (408) 249-5287, GENE BERNALD.

THE BERNARD I. OCHS CO., 805 Longleaf Dr., N.E., Atlanta, GA 30342 (404) 262-1200.
BARNEY OCHS; PAT CASTLEBERRY, sec.

PETRY TELEVISION, INC., 3 E. 54th St., New York, NY 10022; (212) 688-0200.
PETRY INC.: DAVID S. ALLEN, president; C.W. SCHELLENGER, sr. v.p., finance & administration; HARRY STECKER, exec. vice pres., dir. of client services; JOHN SCOGNAMILLO, vice pres., controller; TOM BELVISO, vice pres., sales administration, regional office; WILLIAM WIEHE, vice pres., The Petry Marketing Group; GEORGE DENNIS, v.p., director of manpower dev.; MARIE IMBESI- CHIECA, v.p., dir. of personnel.

PETRY TELEVISION: WILLIAM FAGAN, pres.; George Blinn, sr. v.p., gen. sls. manager; JERRY LINEHAN, v.p., director of sls.; STEVE EISENBERG, v.p., dir. of sls.; ROBERT MIGGINS, v.p., regional area (West Coast); GREG MOLOZNIK, v.p., regional area mgr. (Midwest); PAT McNEW, v.p., regional area mgr. (North); LAVERNE COLE, v.p., regional area mgr. (South); PATRICK TWYON, director of sports; DAVID HANDLER, director of sports; TEDDY S. REYNOLDS, v.p., Director of Research; JOANNE DIPRISCO, director of sales development, The Petry Marketing Group; NEIL HITZIG, national sales director, The Petry Marketing Group; RICHARD KURLANDER, v.p., director of programming; JOHN DORKIN, director of programming; KEVIN NUGENT, v.p., group sales mgr., FALCONS; BILL SHAW, v.p., group sls. mgr., HAWKS; ROB FRIEDMAN, v.p., group sls. mgr., ROADRUNNERS; RICHARD LARCADE, v.p., group sales mgr., RAVENS; DONALD O'TOOLE, v.p., group sales mgr., THUNDERBIRDS.
PETRY NATIONAL: MICHAEL T. MEMBRADO, pres.; JOHN I. HEISE, senior v.p., gen. sales mgr; PAUL MORRISSEY, v.p. of sales; ROBERT HEBENSTREIT, v.p., dir. of research; JACK FENTRESS, v.p., dir. of programming; JOHN DORKIN, dir. of programming; DEBORAH HACKENBERRY, dir. of sales development, The Petry Marketing Group; JOSEPH LYONS, v.p., group sales mgr, RED; CHUCK HANRAHAN, v.p., group sls. mgr., WHITE; AL WESTERMANN, v.p., sr. group sales mgr., BLUE; BILL HAHN, group sales mgr, GREEN; PATRICK TWYON, dir. of sports; DAVID HANDLER, dir. of sports; NEIL HITZIG, national sales director, The Petry Marketing Group.
BRANCH OFFICES: CHICAGO: 410 Michigan Ave., Suite 1180, 60611; Greg Moloznick, v.p., regional area mgr. (Midwest); James Ottolin, v.p., group sls. mgr., RED; Stewart Strizak, group sls. mgr., BLUE; Kent Francis, dir. of agri-marketing; Bill Carney, v.p., group sls. mgr., CHARGERS; Lynn Evans, group mgr., MUSTANGS; Stu Lutz, v.p., grp. mgr., BRONCOS; LOS ANGELES: 8383 Wilshire Blvd., Suite 626, Beverly Hills, CA 90211; Robert Miggins, v.p., dir. of West Coast Operations; Jim Valice, group sls. mgr., RED; Eleanor Gottleib, group sls., BLUE; Jack Devine, v.p., group mgr., COMETS; Jim Baral, group mgr., METEORS; ATLANTA: 950 E. Paces Ferry Rd., Suite 2940, Atlanta, GA 30326, Val Napolitano, v.p., sales mgr.; Chris Teter, group sls. mgr.; BOSTON, 419 Boylston St., Boston, MA 02116; Diane Gosdanian, v.p., sls. mgr.; Craig McMurray, group mgr.; CHARLOTTE: Two Fairview Plaza, 5950 Fairview Rd., Suite 804, Charlotte, NC 28210; Stockton Holt, mgr.; CLEVELAND: 1111 Superior Ave., Suite 7A, Cleveland, OH 44114, Roger Stepic; DALLAS: 3811 Turtle Creek Blvd., Suite 520, Dallas, TX 75219; Laverne Cole, v.p., regional area mgr. (South); Cliffe Hahne, mgr.; DENVER: 6025 South Quebec, Suite 250, Englewood, CO 80111; Tony Kirk, mgr.; DETROIT, 3221 W. Big Beaver Rd., Suite 102, Troy, MI 48084; Patrick McNew, v.p., regional area mgr., (North); Dave Wygant, group mgr; Carol Charron, group mgr.; HOUSTON: 3000 Post Oak Blvd., Suite 1590, Houston, TX 77056; Chuck Sitta, mgr.; MINNEAPOLIS: 706 Second Ave. S., Minneapolis, MN 55402; Tom Vannelli, mgr.; PHILADELPHIA: Two Penn Center Plaza, Suite 406, Philadelphia, PA 19102; Dave Bell, mgr.; ST. LOUIS, Ten South Broadway, Suite 525, St. Louis, MO 63102; Bruce Farber; SAN FRANCISCO: 909 Montgomery St., Suite 402, San Francisco, CA 94133, Don Brownstein, mgr.; SEATTLE, 2001 6th Ave., 1600 Westin Bldg., Seattle, WA 98121; Marc F. Meahl, mgr.; TAMPA/ST. PETERSBURG: 9800 Fourth St. N., Suite 108, St. Petersburg, FL 33702; Judy Obernier, mgr.

RADIO-TELEVISION REPRESENTATIVES LIMITED, 10 Price St., Toronto, Ont. M4W 1Z4; (416) 962-3221. FAX: (416) 962-1162. ROBERT H. QUINN, pres. & gen. mgr.; MARK BURKO, v.p./tv sls. mgr.
Branch offices: Montreal: 1118 St. Catherine St., W., Room 201, Montreal, Que. H3B 1H5; (514) 866-3446, MARK BURKO, JOHN AONSO; Calgary: 300–5th Ave., SW, Suite 2050, Calgary, Alta. T2P 3C4; Mark Swanson (403) 269-3496, FAX: (403) 265-6523; Vancouver: 999 W. Broadway, Vancouver, B.C. V5Z 1K5; (604) 736-6634, FAX: (604) 736-8059; FRANK JOBES; Winnipeg: 305-326 Broadway Ave., Winnipeg, Man. R3C 0S5; (204) 943-9574, FAX: (204) 943-6016; HENRY BOSCHMAN.

SELTEL, INC., 750 Third Ave., New York, NY 10017; (212) 697-0944. TWX: 710-581-3801/3791/5065/6768/2512.
JACK MULDERRIG, pres. & CEO, RAYMOND J. JOHNS, exec. v.p.; STEVE BOUTIS, SR., v.p., finance; JOSEPH CUSENZA, sr. v.p., affiliate operations; DAVID SCHWARTZ, sr. v.p., independent operations; C. WILLIAM COLDWELL, v.p., natl. sls. mgr., affiliate Red & Blue Teams; JUDY KLEINBERGER, v.p., natl. sls. mgr., affiliate White Team; PHYLLIS TAORMINE, v.p., natl. sls. mgr., Indy-Raiders Team; DAN PARISI, natl. sls. mgr., Indy-Rangers & Rebels Team; JANEEN BJORK, v.p., dir. of programming; DOUGLAS DARFIELD, v.p., research dir.
Chicago: 211 E. Ontario, Suite 700, Chicago, IL 60611; (312) 642-2450. TWX: 910-221-0241, 0242, 5195. MARTY MILLER, sr. v.p., central region mgr.; JIM PARKET, v.p., sls. mgr. affiliate Red Team; RANDY BROWN, sls. mgr. affiliate White Team; TODD ROHDE, sls. mgr. Indy-Raiders Team; DAN POPRAVAK, sls. mgr., Indy-Rangers Team.
Atlanta: 1819 Peachtree Rd., N.E. Atlanta, GA 30309; (404) 355-7701. TWX: 810-751-3101. PAUL BREWER, mgr.
Boston: 545 Boylston St., 7th floor, Boston, MA 02116; (617) 236-8666. TWX: 710-321-0016. PETER DURAN, mgr.

Charlotte: 5821 Park Rd., Suite 112, Charlotte, NC 28209; (704) 554-7124. SUZY PLETTNER, mgr.
Dallas: 3010 LBJ Freeway, Suite 1130, Dallas, TX 75234; (214) 484-4871.. TWX: 910-861-4210. MICHAEL CUSTARDO, mgr.
Denver: 222 Milwaukee St., Suite 210, Denver, CO; (303) 333-4845. Telex: 100-230-450296. CHRIS MATTHEWS, mgr.
Detroit: 26211 Central Park Blvd., Suite 202, Southfield, MI 48076-4107; (313) 354-3611. TWX: 810-224-4502. JESS CHALKER, v.p., mgr.
Houston: 4848 Loop Central Dr., Suite 710, Houston, TX 77081. (713) 660-8881. TWX: 910-881-0063. SABRINA LEONARD, mgr.
Los Angeles: 5757 Wilshire Blvd., Los Angeles, CA 90036; (213) 930-2450. TWX: 910-321-4124. LAVADA HEALTH, v.p., mgr.; DAVE WARE, sls. mgr. Indy-Raiders; ED TINNEY, sls. mgr. Indy-Rangers; JUDY MALCOLM-GRAGG, sls. mgr. affiliate team; RALPH CLAUSSEN, sls. mgr. affiliate White Team.
Miami: 6101 Blue Lagoon Dr., Suite 460, Miami, FL 33126; (305) 266-4066. TWX: 810-848-0197. ENID BLUESTONE, mgr.
Minneapolis: 623 Second Ave. South, Suite 408, Minneapolis, MN 55402; (612) 338-7707. TWX: 910-576-3419. MIKE CLEARY, mgr.
Philadelphia: 1411 Walnut St., Suite 1125, Philadelphia, PA 19103; (215) 563-5400. TWX: 710-670-1017. JOSEPH PEDRI, mgr.
Portland: 1512 S.W. 18th Ave., Portland, OR 97201; (503) 226- 2911. EASY LINK: 629-275-56+. RICHARD GOHLMAN, mgr.
St. Louis: St. Louis Place, 200 N. Broadway, Suite 1125, St. Louis, MO 63102; (314) 241-4193. TWX: 910-761-0400. RICHARD J. QUIGLEY III, v.p., mgr.
San Francisco: 50 Francisco St., San Francisco, CA 94133; (415) 391-8890. TWX: 910-372-7361. EDWARD OUTLAND, mgr.
Seattle: 701 Dexter Ave., North, Suite 216, Seattle, WA 98109; (206) 285-1913. EASY LING: 627-625-31. BOB TACHER, mgr.

SPOT TIME LTD., 1 Times Square, New York, NY 10036; (212) 575-5077. CARMINE PATTI, pres.; TONY PATTI, v.p., sls. mgr.; ANDREW PATTI, v.p
Branches in Chicago, Detroit, Los Angeles, and Oakland, CA.

STAUFFER COMMUNICATIONS, INC., 100% owner of WIBW-TV, Box 119, Topeka, KA 66601; (913) 272-3456.
GEORGE LOGAN, TV gen. mgr.; VINCE FRYE, natl. sales mgr. (and gsm.) Represented nationally by Blair, New York, Chicago, Dallas, Detroit, Atlanta, San Francisco, Los Angeles, Seattle, Charlotte, Cleveland, Memphis, Portland, Boston, Jacksonville, Minneapolis, St. Louis, Philadelphia.

STORER TELEVISION SALES, INC., 800 Third Ave., New York, NY 10022; (212) 935-6000.
FRANCIS BARRON, pres.; PETER E. MURRAY, exec. v.p., sales; PETER STORER, JR., research director.
Branch Offices: Chicago: 410 No. Michigan Ave., (312) 329-1930; CHARLES LIEBER, v.p., Midwest sales; Detroit: Number Two Storer Place, (313) 557-0300; ELAINE CARPENTER, Det. sls. mgr.; Atlanta: Three Piedmont Ctr., (404) 233-9935; RICHARD GOLDSTEIN, Southern sls. mgr.; San Francisco: 150 Lombard Street, (415) 981-8860, SHAWN McGREEVY, v.p., S.F. sls.; Los Angeles, 6420 Wilshire Blvd., (213) 651-0841, JOSEPH MERTENS, v.p., West Coast sls.

TELEREP, INC., 875 Third Ave., New York, NY 10022; (212) 759-8787. ALFRED M. MASINI, pres. & gen. mgr.; STEVEN HERSON, v.p., dir. opns.; LARRY GOLDBERG, v.p., gen. sls. mgr., COUGAR STNS.; THOMAS BELVISO, v.p., gen. sls. mgr., TIGER STNS.; THOMAS TILSON, v.p., gen. sls. mgr. JAGUAR STNS.; SUSAN ZILLER BRAZELL, v.p., sls., LION STNS.
Branches in Atlanta, Chicago, Detroit, Los Angeles, Minneapolis, St. Louis, San Francisco, Philadelphia, Boston, Dallas, Cleveland, Houston, Memphis, Miami, Charlotte, Seattle.

ADAM YOUNG, INC., 3 E. 54 St., New York, NY 10022; (212) 688-5100. ADAM YOUNG, chm. of the bd.; VINCENT J. YOUNG, pres.; ARTHUR W. SCOTT JR., exec. v.p./gen'l sales mgr.; MARIANNE O'LEARY, mgr., research & programming services.
BRANCH OFFICES: ATLANTA: 2 Piedmont Center, Suite 506, Atlanta, GA 30305; (404) 261-8800. TWX: 810-751-0057, CAL CASS, mgr.; BOSTON: contact MARION CHIOFALO, account exec.; (212) 688-5100. CHICAGO: 444 N. Michigan Ave., Suite 920, Chicago, IL 60611; (312) 744-1313. TWX: 910-221-1191. LOIS HAMELIN, mgr.; DALLAS: 1701 N. Market St., Suite 205, Dallas, TX; (214) 748-2660. TWX: 910-861-0089; SUSAN WAGNER, mgr.; DENVER: Box 61498, Denver, CO 80206-8498; (303) 377-6526; BOB HIX, mgr.; DETROIT: 2855 Coolidge, Suite 222, Troy, MI 48084; (313) 649-3999. ESLNK: 62872846, ALLAN BAUR, mgr.; LOS ANGELES: 6100 Wilshire Blvd., Suite 50, Los Angeles, CA 90048; (213) 938-2081. TWX: 910-321- 2897; KEITH THOMPSON, v.p., western sales; MINNEAPOLIS: 630 Baker Bldg., Minneapolis, MN 55402; (612) 339-3397. Easylink: 62615840. JAMES O. RAMSLANI, mgr.; PHILADELPHIA & PITTSBURGH: contact JOE COHEN, account exec.; (212) 688-5100; ST. LOUIS: Box 50269, St. Louis, MO 63105; (314) 991-5249. TWX: 910-761-1145; BRUCE SCHNEIDER, mgr.; SAN FRANCISCO: 425 California St., Suite 1150, San Francisco, CA 94104; (415) 986-5366. TWX: 910-372-6010; CHRIS KELLY, sales mgr.

Organizations

* NATIONAL GROUPS

* REGIONAL UNITS

* GUILDS AND UNIONS

Organizations

Academy of Television Arts and Sciences

3500 W. Olive Ave., Suite 700, Burbank, CA 91505; (818) 953-7575. (Formed in 1948 to advance the arts and sciences of television.) Awards Emmys for nighttime programming and publishes Emmy Magazine, Hank Rieger, editor.

PRESIDENT
  Doug Duitsman
FIRST VICE PRESIDENT
  Leo Chaloukian
SECOND VICE PRESIDENT
  Jan Scott
VICE PRESIDENT, LOS ANGELES
  Jay Strong
SECRETARY
  John Furia, Jr.
TREASURER
  Mel Sawelson
IMMEDIATE PAST PRESIDENT
  Richard H. Frank
EXECUTIVE DIRECTOR
  James Loper
CHIEF FINANCIAL OFFICER
  John Macker
AWARDS DIRECTOR
  John Leverence
BOARD OF GOVERNORS
  Stu Berg, Barbara Brogliatti, Hazel Catmull, Patrick Collins, Fred Chulack, Robert Crutchfield, Marc Danields, William Finnegan, Preston Fischer, Ian Fraser, John Furia, Lee Gabler, Mike Gavin, Dan Gingold, Bill Hargate, Tom Huth, Jerry Immel, Jordan Kerner, Herb Klynn, A. Richard Larson, Linda Lavin, Sydney Litwack, Margaret Loesch, Ellis Marcus, Mina Mittelman, Richard Mulligan, J.H. Rowland Perkins II, Sally Powers, Jeane Renick, Phil Roman, Stu Rosen, Peter Schlesinger, Howard Schwartz, Jan Scott, Gary Shaffer, Susan Simons, Howard Smit, Jerry Smith, Jim Smith, Jay Strong, Bob Sweeney, Russ Tinsley, Ed Vane, Harry Wolf

Actor's Equity Association (AAAA-AFL-CIO-CLC)

(Organized May 16, 1913; Membership, 38,000) 165 W. 46 St., New York, NY 10036, (212) 869-8530.

PRESIDENT
  Colleen Dewhurst
FIRST VICE-PRESIDENT
  Patrick Quinn
SECOND VICE-PRESIDENT
  Mary Lou Westerfeld
THIRD VICE-PRESIDENT
  Arne Gundersen
FOURTH VICE PRESIDENT
  Werner Klemperer
TREASURER
  Conrad Fowkes
RECORDING SECRETARY
  Lynn Archer
EXECUTIVE SECRETARY
  Alan Eisenberg
EXECUTIVE CONSULTANT
  Willard Swire
COUNSEL
  Cohn, Glickstein, Lurie
MIDWEST REGIONAL V.P.
  Madeleine Fallon
WESTERN REGIONAL V.P.
  Joseph Ruskin

Advertising Council, The

825 Third Ave., New York, NY 10022; (212) 758-0400.
CHAIRMAN
  Walter E. Mattson

PRESIDENT
  Ruth A. Wooden
SENIOR VICE PRESIDENT, MEDIA
  Gordon C. Kenney
VICE PRESIDENT, FINANCIAL DEVELOPMENT
  Jane K. Dean
SENIOR VIDE PRESIDENT, CAMPAIGN ADMINISTRATION
  Elenore Hangley
EDITOR, PUBLIC SERVICE ADVERTISING BULLETIN
  Thomas P. Fowler
VICE PRESIDENT OF PUBLIC AFFAIRS
  William F. Rhatican
BRANCH OFFICES
  The Advertising Council, 1717 N. Highland Ave., Los Angeles, CA; The Advertising Council, 1930 Rhode Island Ave., N.W., Washington, DC 20036.

Advertising Research Foundation

3 E. 54 St., New York, NY 10022; (212) 751-5656.
CHAIRMAN
  John C. Webber
VICE CHAIRMAN
  David F. Poltrack
PRESIDENT
  Michael J. Naples
SENIOR VICE PRESIDENT, DIRECTOR OF OPERATIONS
  James H. Moore
SENIOR VICE PRESIDENT, MEDIA RESEARCH
  Lawrence R. Stoddard
SECRETARY
  Tod Johnson
GENERAL COUNSEL
  Gilbert H. Weil

Alliance of Motion Picture and Television Producers

(Membership: Major studios, independent production companies, and film processing laboratories) 14144 Ventura Blvd., 3rd floor, Sherman Oaks, CA 91423; (818) 995-3600.
PRESIDENT
  J. Nicholas Counter III
VICE PRESIDENT-LEGAL AFFAIRS
  Carol A. Lombardini
VICE PRESIDENT-CONTRACT ADMINISTRATION
  Paul A. Westefer
CHIEF FINANCIAL OFFICER
  Kathy Grotticelli

American Advertising Federation

1400 K St., NW, Suite 1000, Washington, DC 20005; (202) 898-0089.
CHAIRMAN OF THE BOARD
  Robert Blackmore
PRESIDENT
  Howard H. Bell

American Association of Advertising Agencies

666 Third Ave., New York, NY 10017; (212) 682-2500.
CHAIRMAN OF THE BOARD
  William V. Weithas, Lintas Worldwide, New York
VICE CHAIRMAN
  Glen W. Fortinberry, Ross Roy Group, Michigan
SECRETARY-TREASURER
  Jack Painter, Benito Advertising, Inc., Tampa
PRESIDENT
  Leonard S. Matthews, A.A.A.A., New York

WASHINGTON REPRESENTATIVE
  John E. O'Toole, Executive Vice President
WESTERN OFFICE REPRESENTATIVE
  Robert P. Stephens, Vice President, Beverly Hills, CA
EXECUTIVE VICE PRESIDENT
  Harry Paster
SENIOR VICE PRESIDENTS
  Tony Gruber, Marilyn Bockman, Donald C. Lewis, Donald
Ambuhl, Gloria Lanza-Bajo, Bernard Ryan, James C. Martucci,
Jr.
VICE PRESIDENT
  Robert J. Finn

American Cinema Editors

(Organized November 28, 1950; Membership: 2500)
4416-1/2 Finley Ave., Los Angeles, CA 90027; (213)
660-4425.

PRESIDENT
  Bob Bring
VICE PRESIDENT
  Eve Newman
SECRETARY
  Bernie Balmuth
TREASURER
  Ernest V. Milano
BOARD OF DIRECTORS
  Scott C. Eyler, Robert L. Kimble, Frederic L. Knudtson, Alan C.
Marks, Chuck Montgomery, Millie Moore, Peter Parasheles

American Federation of Musicians (AFL-CIO)

(Organized October, 1896; Membership: 280,000) Suite
600, Paramount Bldg., 1501 Broadway, New York, NY
10036; (212) 869-1330.

PRESIDENT
  J. Martin Emerson, Suite 600, Paramount Bldg., 1501 Broadway,
New York, NY 10036; (212) 869-1330.
VICE PRESIDENT
  John Glasel, 5020 Stacey Ave., Las Vegas, NV 89108.
CANADA VICE PRESIDENT
  J. Alan Wood, 25 Overlea Blvd., Toronto, Ont., Canada
M4H 1B1.
SECRETARY-TREASURER
  Kelly L. Castleberry II, Suite 600, Paramount Bldg.,1501 Broad-
way, New York, NY 10036.
EXECUTIVE BOARD
  Eugene Frey, John Glasel, Bob D'Arcy, Richard Q. Totusek.
PRESIDENT EMERITUS
  Victor W. Fuentealba

American Federation of Television and Radio Artists (AAAA-AFL-CIO)

(Organized August, 1937; Membership 60,000) 1350
Ave. of the Americas, New York, NY 10019; (212) 265-
7700.

PRESIDENT
  Frank Maxwell
FIRST VICE PRESIDENT
  Ann Loring
SECOND VICE PRESIDENT
  Len Dresslar
VICE PRESIDENTS
  K.T. Stevens, Peter Hackes, Belva Davis, Shelby Scott, Kenneth
Barry, Chris Ward, Lee Lawson
TREASURER
  Kenneth Roberts
RECORDING SECRETARY
  Mike Botula
NATIONAL EXECUTIVE DIRECTOR
  John C. Hall Jr.
DIRECTOR, CENTRAL REGION
  Herbert Neuer
DIRECTOR, WESTERN REGION
  Donald S. Tayer
DIRECTOR, EASTERN REGION
  Dan Mallinger

CONTROLLER
  Dan Friedenreich
NATIONAL REPRESENTATIVES
  Harold Kocin, Walter Grinspan, Louis Santillana, Jr.

American Guild of Musical Artists (AFL-CIO), Branch of Associated Actors and Artistes of America

(Organized 1936; Membership 5,500) 1727 Broadway,
New York, NY 10019-5214; (212) 265-3687.

PRESIDENT
  Nedda Casei
FIRST VICE PRESIDENT
  Eileen Schauler
SECOND VICE PRESIDENT
  Chester Ludgin
THIRD VICE PRESIDENT
  Robert Manno
FOURTH VICE PRESIDENT
  Muriel Costa-Greenspon
FIFTH VICE PRESIDENT
  Betty Baisch
TREASURER
  Lawrence Davidson
RECORDING SECRETARY
  Yolanda Antoine
NATIONAL EXECUTIVE SECRETARY
  Gene Boucher
ASSOCIATE EXECUTIVE SECRETARY
  Alan Olsen
ASSISTANTS TO THE EXECUTIVE SECRETARY
  Thomas Jamerson, Alexander Dube
COUNSEL
  Becker and London
DIRECTOR OF MEMBERSHIP
  Annelise Kamada
FINANCIAL SECRETARY
  Grace Pedro
DIRECTOR OF PUBLIC RELATIONS
  Michael Rubino

CANADA: Graham Spicer, 615 Yonge St., Toronto, Ontario M4Y
2T4, (416) 967-4252; CHICAGO: Barbara J. Hillman, 343 S. Dearborn St., Chicago, IL 60604, (312) 372-8081; LOS ANGELES:
Dennis Moss, 12650 Riverside Dr., Suite 205, North Hollywood, CA
91607, (213) 877-0683; NEW ENGLAND: Robert M. Segal, 11
Beacon St., Boston, MA 02108, (617) 742-0208; NEW ORLEANS:
Rosemary Le Boeuf, 619 N. Hennessy, New Orleans, LA, (504)
486-9410; NORTHWEST: Carolyn Carpp, 5051 148 Ave., NE,
Bellevue, WA 98007, (206) 881-7235; PHILADELPHIA: Mark P.
Muller, Lafayette Bldg., 8th floor, 5th and Chestnut St., Phila-
delphia, PA 19106, (215) 925-8400; SAN FRANCISCO: Harry
Polland/Donald Tayer, 100 Bush St., Suite 1500, San Francisco, CA
94104, (415) 986-4060; TEXAS: Benny Hopper, 3915 Fairlakes Dr.,
Dallas, TX 75149, (214) 279-4720; WASHINGTON/BALTIMORE:
Joshua J. Kaufman, 918 16th St., NW, Suite 503, Washington, DC
20006, (202) 466-3030.

American Guild of Variety Artists (AAAA-AFL-CIO)

(Organized July 14, 1939; Registered Membership:
35,000; Active Membership: 5,000) 184 Fifth Ave., New
York, NY 10010; (212) 675-1003.

HONORARY PRESIDENT
  George Burns
HONORARY FIRST VICE PRESIDENT
  Rod McKuen
HONORARY THIRD VICE PRESIDENT
  Ann Corio
EXECUTIVE PRESIDENT
  Alan Jan Nelson
EXECUTIVE VICE PRESIDENT
  Will Aherne
SECRETARY TREASURER
  Jack London
REGIONAL VICE PRESIDENTS
  Dick Martin, Margie Coate, Ronald Puckett, Stanley Burns, Bob
Freed, Tommy Spencer, Harry Lewis, Thomas Merriweather, Tina
Marie, Steve Stephens, Ted Monson, Bobby Faye, Don George, Etta
Rollins, Ralph Shaw.

American Humane Association

(Organized 1877) Hollywood office: 14144 Ventura Blvd., Sherman Oaks, CA 91423; (818) 501-0123; National Headquarters: 9725 E. Hampden, Denver, CO 80231; (303) 695-0811. (Liaison with the television and motion picture industry as supervisors of animal action in television and motion picture production.)
NATIONAL PRESIDENT
Donald Anthony
VICE PRESIDENT
Hortense Landau
TREASURER
Charles W. Ennis
DIRECTOR—L.A. REGIONAL OFFICE
Betty Denny Smith

American Society of Cinematographers, Inc.

(Organized 1919; Membership: 286) 1782 N. Orange Dr., Hollywood, CA 90028; (213) 876-5080.
PRESIDENT
Harry Wolf
FIRST VICE PRESIDENT
Leonard South
SECOND VICE PRESIDENT
Howard Schwartz
THIRD VICE PRESIDENT
Charles Wheeler
SECRETARY
Joseph Westheimer
TREASURER
Linwood G. Dunn

American Society of Composers, Authors and Publishers (ASCAP)

(Organized February 13, 1914; Membership: 26,000 Music Writers, 1,645 Associate Writer Members, 9,900 Publishers) One Lincoln Plaza, New York, NY 10023, (212) 595-3050; 6430 Sunset Blvd., Hollywood, CA 90028.
PRESIDENT
Morton Gould
VICE PRESIDENTS
Arthur Hamilton, Irwin Z. Robinson
SECRETARY
Marilyn Bergman
TREASURER
Leon J. Brettler
ASSISTANT SECRETARY
John Green
ASSISTANT TREASURER
Sidney Herman
COUNSEL
Bernard Korman
MANAGING DIRECTOR
Gloria Messinger
WESTERN REGIONAL DIRECTOR
Todd Brabec, ASCAP, 6430 Sunset Blvd., Hollywood, CA 90028
SOUTHERN REGIONAL EXECUTIVE DIRECTOR
Connie Bradley, ASCAP, Two Music Square W., Nashville, TN37203

Asian Cinevision, Inc.

32 East Broadway, New York, NY; (212) 925-8685. (A not-for-profit organization dedicated to encouraging the creation and presentation of Asian and Asian American media arts. Current programs include film festival exhibitions; media services (information and referral); archive library; publications; production services; video documentation editing, duplication, transfer screening.)

Associated Actors and Artistes of America (AAAA-AFL-CIO)

(Organized July 18, 1919; Membership: 85,000) 165 W. 46 St., New York, NY 10036; (212) 869-0358.
PRESIDENT
Frederick O'Neal
VICE PRESIDENTS
Ken Orsatti, Sanford I. Wolff, Jack Rechtzeit, Rod McKuen
TREASURER
Willard Swire
EXECUTIVE SECRETARY
John C. Hall, Jr.
AFFILIATES
Actors' Equity Association, American Federation of Television and Radio Artists, American Guild of Musical Artists, American Guild of Variety Artists, Asociacion Puertorrique/tna de Artistas y Tecnicos del Espectaculo, Hebrew Actors Union, Italian Actors Union, Screen Actors Guild, Screen Extras Guild.

Association of Independent Commercial Producers

P.O. Box 2007, San Francisco, CA 94126-2007; (415) 771-6268. Organized 1972. (Seeks to improve the dialogue and working relationship between clients and the commercial production industry.)
PRESIDENT
Ron Lakis (Starrion Productions)
VICE PRESIDENTS
Ron Eveslage (Eveslage Film & Video)
Bill Bayne (Landvoight-Bayne Productions)
Robert Gondell (Group One)
SECRETARY/TREASURER
Roy Diner (Diner & Allied Film & Video Services)
VICE PRESIDENT ASSOC.
Emily Riddel (Aardvark Productions)
BOARD OF DIRECTORS
Ron Lakis, Ron Eveslage, Bill Bayne, Robert Gondell, Roy Diner, Emily Riddel
BRANCHES
National—New York; Chicago, Denver, Miami, Dallas, Seattle, Los Angeles, San Francisco.

Association of Independent Television Stations

1200 18th St., N.W., Suite 502, Washigton, DC 20036; (202) 887-1970; FAX (202) 887-0950.
CHAIRMAN
Charles L. Edwards
VICE CHAIRMAN
John A. Serrao
PRESIDENT
Preston R. Padden
SECRETARY
L. Martin Brantley
TREASURER
Randall E. Smith
VICE PRESIDENT, GOVERNMENT RELATIONS
James B. Hedlund
VICE PRESIDENT, MARKETING
Ronald C. Inman
BOARD OF DIRECTORS
Edward G. Aiken, Steven A. Bell, L. Martin Brantley, John C. Chaffee, Charles L. Edwards, Robert J. Hamacher, Robert Kreek, Preston R. Padden, Harry J. Pappas, Norris D. Reichel, John A. Serrao, Randall E. Smith, John A. Trinder, Ian N. Wheeler

Association of Independent Video and Filmmakers, Inc.

625 Broadway, New York, NY 10012; (212) 473-3400. (Membership: over 5,000 independent professionals, including producers, directors, writers and technicians in film and video; publishes The Independent Magazine.)
EXECUTIVE DIRECTOR
Lawrence Sapadin

Association of National Advertisers, Inc.

155 E. 44 St., New York, NY 10017; (212) 697-5950.
PRESIDENT
  DeWitt F. Helm, Jr.
SENIOR VICE PRESIDENT, WASHINGTON, D.C.
  Daniel L. Jaffe
VICE PRESIDENTS
  Peter Eder, Clark Holt, Monica Madariaga

Association of Talent Agents

(Organized April, 1937; Membership: 150) (Official organization of talent agents in Hollywood.) 9255 Sunset Blvd., Suite 318, Los Angeles, CA 90069; (213) 274-0628.
EXECUTIVE DIRECTOR
  Chester L. Migden
FIRST VICE PRESIDENT
  Roger Davis
VICE PRESIDENTS
  Carter Gibson, Eric Klass, Sid Craig, Sandy Bresler, Sonjia Warren Brandon
SECRETARY-TREASURER
  Nina Blanchard

Authors' Guild, Inc.

(Membership: 6,600) 234 W. 44 St., New York, NY 10036; (212) 398-0838.
PRESIDENT
  Robert K. Massie
VICE PRESIDENT
  Roger Angell
TREASURER
  Carolyn G. Heilburn
EXECUTIVE DIRECTOR
  Helen A. Stephenson

The Authors League of America, Inc.

(Membership: 15,000) Authors League, 234 W. 44. St., New York, NY 10036; (212) 391-9198.
PRESIDENT
  Garson Kanin
VICE PRESIDENT
  Robert Anderson
SECRETARY
  Eve Merriam
TREASURER
  Garson Kanin
ADMINISTRATOR
  Peggy Randall

Banff Television Festival

P.O. Box 1020, Banff, Alberta, Canada, T0L 0C0; (403) 762-3060. TELEX: TV FEST BNF 03-822804; FAX: (403) 762-5357. (Honors excellence in world TV)
EXECUTIVE DIRECTOR
  Carrie Hunter
FESTIVAL DIRECTOR
  Jerry Ezekiel
BUSINESS MANAGER
  Jim Bertram

BMI (Broadcast Music, Inc.)

320 W. 57 St., New York, NY 10019 (212) 586-2000; 230 Half Mile Rd., Red Bank, NJ (201) 758-0700; 8730 Sunset Blvd., Los Angeles, CA 90069 (213) 656-9109; 6767 Forest Lawn Dr., Hollywood, CA 90068 (213) 851-6440; 1111 Bayhill Dr., San Bruno, CA 94066 (415) 583-8355; 727 N. 1st St., St. Louis, MO 63102 (314) 621-3100; 10 Music Square E., Nashville, TN 37203 (615) 259-3625; 8500 S.W. 117th Rd., Suite 116, Miami, FL 33183 (305) 271-8220; 3701 Algonquin Rd., Two Crossroads, Suite 360, Rolling Meadows, IL 60008 (312) 870-8060; Royal Bank Center, suite 710, Hato Rey, PR 00917 (809) 754-6490; 1325 S. Dairy Ashford, Suite 260, Houston, TX 77077, (713) 558-3500; Shovel Shop Square 3A, North Easton, MA 02356 (508) 238-0174; Ponce de Leon Ave., Pan Am Bldg., Suite 905, Hato Rey, Puerto Rico 00917 (809) 754-6490.
BOARD CHAIRMAN
  Joseph Carriere
PRESIDENT
  Frances W. Preston
SENIOR VICE PRESIDENT, SPECIAL COUNSEL TO THE PRESIDENT
  Theodora Zavin
VICE PRESIDENT, NASHVILLE
  Roger Sovine
VICE PRESIDENT, CALIFORNIA
  Ronald M. Anton
VICE PRESIDENT FINANCE & CHIEF FINANCIAL OFFICER
  Jeff White
VICE PRESIDENT, CORPORATE RELATIONS
  Robbin Ahrold
VICE PRESIDENT, INTERNATIONAL
  Ekke Schnabel
VICE PRESIDENT, SYSTEMS & DATA PROCESSING
  Richard Mack
VICE PRESIDENT, LICENSING
  Lawrence P. Sweeney
VICE PRESIDENT, ADMINISTRATION
  Alan H. Smith
VICE PRESIDENT, SECRETARY, AND GENERAL COUNSEL
  Edward W. Chapin
CONTROLLER AND TREASURER
  Thomas Curry

Broadcast Pioneers

320 W. 57 St., New York, NY 10019; (212) 586-2000.
PRESIDENT
  Sol J. Paul
VICE PRESIDENT
  Wallace Dunlap
VICE PRESIDENT
  Jim Greenwald
EXECUTIVE DIRECTOR
  Edward J. DeGray

Cable Television Information Center (CTIC)

1500 N. Beauregard St., Suite 205, Alexandria, VA 22311; (703) 845-1705. Organized 1972. (Provides community governments and consumers with objective information about the cable industry.)
PRESIDENT
  Harold E. Horn
DIRECTOR OF INFORMATION
  Peter Krasilovsky

Catholic Actors Guild of America

(Organized April, 1914; Membership: 550) 165 W. 46th St., Suite 710, New York, NY 10036; (212) 398-1868.
PRESIDENT
  William J. O'Malley
FIRST VICE PRESIDENT
  Frederick O'Neal
SECOND VICE PRESIDENT
  Hildegarde
TREASURER
  Martin Kiffel
EXECUTIVE SECRETARY
  Suzanne Richardson
CHAIRMAN OF EXECUTIVE BOARD
  Lisa Di Julio

Catholic Broadcasting Office

(See Office for Film & Broadcasting)

Catholic Communications Foundation

Ste. 198, Box 9000, Carlsbad, CA 92008; (714) 942-1120. Established by the Catholic Fraternal Benefit Societies to assist the national, regional and local radio and television activities of the Catholic Church in the United States. The Foundation awards communications training scholarships to the Institute for Religious Communications. The CCF's board of directors is composed of Bishops of the Catholic Church, fraternal benefit society executives and representatives from the communications industry.

CHAIRMAN
Most Reverend Anthony G. Bosco, Auxiliary Bishop of Pittsburgh
PRESIDENT
Most Reverend Kenneth Povish, Bishop of Lansing, MI.
EXECUTIVE DIRECTOR
James R. Bastis

Catholic Conference (U.S.), Department of Communication

Suite #1300, 1011 First Ave., New York, NY 10022; (212) 644-1898.
SECRETARY OF COMMUNICATION
Richard H. Hirsch

The Department of Communication of the U.S. Catholic Conference (the public policy agency of the Catholic Bishops of America) addresses the Church's apostolate in and through the print and electronic media. It provides advice and technical assistance on more than 100 radio and 50 network television programs a year.

The Department also publishes a weekly guide to current films and television programs that appear in 100 plus papers of the Catholic Press in the United States. In this activity the Department reviews all current nationally-released 35mm films, and provides information about resources for film utilization and education (16mm films, books, magazines, festivals). The critical reviews are addressed to the moral, as well as the aesthetic, dimensions of motion pictures, and are the result of a consensus based on the reactions of the Department's professional staff and Board of Consultors. All films reviewed are also classified according to the Department's rating system. In addition, this weekly service carries information and evaluative studies on trends and issues pertinent to television, with an emphasis on educational material.

The Department also plays a liaison role for the USCC with the film and broadcasting industries, national media, and religious agencies and organizations. It is a member of OCIC and UNDA, the international Catholic organizations for film and broadcasting, respectively. Consultation and information services are also provided for the Pontifical Commission for Social Communications and the communication offices of national episcopal offices throughout the world.

With staff assistance, the episcopal members of the Communication Committee administer funds raised through the Catholic Communication Campaign, an annual collection. These funds are used to support a variety of media programs, projects, and studies in this country and the Third World.

Clear Channel Broadcasting Service

1776 K St., N.W., Washington, DC 20006; (202) 429-7020.
PRESIDENT
Wayne Vriesman, WGN, Chicago
LEGAL COUNSEL
John L. Bartlett, Wiley Rein & Fielding, Washington, DC.

Communication Commission of National Council of Churches of Christ in the USA

475 Riverside Dr., New York, NY 10027; (212) 870-2567.
CHAIRPERSON
Beverly Chain
ASSISTANT GENERAL SECRETARY FOR COMMUNICATION, NCC
William F. Fore
EXECUTIVE DIRECTOR FOR BROADCASTING AND FILM
D. Williams McClurken
DIRECTOR FOR MEDIA RESOURCES
David W. Pomeroy

Corporation for Public Broadcasting

1111 16th St., N.W. Washington, DC 20036; (202) 955-5100.
PRESIDENT
Donald E. Ledwig
SENIOR VICE PRESIDENT
Vacant
VICE PRESIDENT AND TREASURER
Frederick L. DeMarco
VICE PRESIDENT, CORPORATE COMMUNICATIONS
Rozanne Weissman
GENERAL COUNSEL AND SECRETARY
Paul E. Symczak

Directors Guild of America, Inc. (DGA)

National office: 7950 Sunset Blvd., Hollywood, CA 90046; (213) 656-1220. 110 W. 57 St., New York, NY 10019; (212) 581-0370. Chicago: 520 N. Michigan Ave., Suite 400, Chicago, IL 60611; (312) 644-5050.
PRESIDENT
Franklin Schaffner
NATIONAL VICE PRESIDENT
Larry Auerbach
NATIONAL EXECUTIVE DIRECTOR
Glenn Gumpel
VICE PRESIDENTS
Franklin Schaffner, Jane Schimel, Gene Reynolds, Max Schindler, Arthur Hiller, Yael Woll, Burt Bluestein
SECRETARY/TREASURER
Sheldon Leonard
ASSISTANT SECRETARY/TREASURER
Marilyn Jacobs

The Dramatists Guild, Inc.

(Membership: 903 Active; 6,869 Associate; 520 Subscribing) 234 W. 44 St., New York, NY 10036; (212) 398-9366.
PRESIDENT
Peter Stone
VICE PRESIDENT
Terrence McNally
SECRETARY
Sheldon Harnick
TREASURER
Ruth Goetz
EXECUTIVE DIRECTOR
David E. LeVine
COUNSEL
Cahill Gordon & Reindel

Electronic Industries Association

2001 Eye St., N.W., Washington, DC 20006; (202) 457-4900.
CHAIRMAN OF THE BOARD
John Mitchell, Motorola, Inc.
PRESIDENT
Peter F. McCloskey
TREASURER
C. Travis Marshall, Vice President, Motorola, Inc.
VICE PRESIDENT PUBLIC AFFAIRS
Mark V. Rosenker

Episcopal Actors Guild of America, Inc.

(Organized 1926; 750 members) 1 E. 29 St., New York, NY 10016; (212) 685-2927.

HONORARY PRESIDENTS PRESIDING BISHOP
The Right Rev. Edmond L. Browning
BISHOP OF NEW YORK
The Right Reverend Paul Moore, Jr., S.T.D.
RETIRED BISHOP OF NEW YORK
The Right Reverend Horace W. B. Donegan, D.D.
PRESIDENT EMERITUS
Ray Heatherton
PRESIDENT
Barnard Hughes
VICE PRESIDENTS
Rev. Norman J. Catir, Jr., Warden of the Guild, Joan Fontaine, Rex Harrison, Mike Mearian
RECORDING SECRETARY
Joan Warren
TREASURER
L. Herndon Werth
EXECUTIVE SECRETARY
Lon C. Clark
EXECUTIVE ASSISTANT
Michelle Trudeau

Federal Communications Commission

1919 M St., N.W., Washington, DC 20554, (202) 632-6600.

CHAIRMAN
Dennis R. Patrick
COMMISSIONERS
James H. Quello, Patricia Diez Dennis
CHIEF, OFFICE OF PLANS AND POLICY
John Haring
CHAIRMAN, REVIEW BOARD
Joseph A. Marino
CHIEF JUDGE, OFFICE OF ADMINISTRATIVE LAW JUDGES
Thomas B. Fitzpatrick
GENERAL COUNSEL
Diane Killory
MANAGING DIRECTOR
Edward Minkel
ACTING CHIEF/MASS MEDIA BUREAU
Alex D. Felker
CHIEF, COMMON CARRIER BUREAU
Gerald Brock
CHIEF, FIELD OPERATIONS BUREAU
Richard M. Smith
CHIEF, OFFICE OF LEGISLATIVE AFFAIRS
Sherrie Marshall
CHIEF, OFFICE OF PUBLIC AFFAIRS
John F. Kamp

The Harry Fox Agency

205 E. 42 St., New York, NY 10017; (212) 370-5330. (Music Licensing Bureau)
PRESIDENT
Edward P. Murphy

Girls Friday of Show Business

(See Women in Show Business)

Institute of Electrical and Electronics Engineers, Inc.

345 E. 47 St., New York, NY 10017 (212) 705-7900.
PRESIDENT
Dr. Bruno O. Weinschel
PRESIDENT-ELECT
Henry L. Bachman
EXECUTIVE VICE PRESIDENT
Dr. Emerson W. Pugh
VICE PRESIDENT—EDUCATIONAL ACTIVITIES
Dr. Cyrill J. Tunis
VICE PRESIDENT—PROFESSIONAL ACTIVITIES
Carleton A. Bayless

VICE PRESIDENT—PUBLICATION ACTIVITIES
Charles H. House
VICE PRESIDENT—REGIONAL ACTIVITIES
Dennis Bodson
VICE PRESIDENT—TECHNICAL ACTIVITIES
Merlin G. Smith
SECRETARY/TREASURER
Dr. Michiyuko Uenohara
TREASURER
Edward J. Doyle
GENERAL MANAGER AND EXECUTIVE DIRECTOR
Eric Herz

International Alliance of Theatrical Stage Employes & Moving Picture Machine Operators of the U.S. and Canada (AFL-CIO)

(Organized nationally, July 17, 1893; internationally, October 1, 1902.) 1515 Broadway, New York, NY 10036; (212) 730-1770.

INTERNATIONAL PRESIDENT
Alfred W. Ditolla
INTERNATIONAL PRESIDENTS EMERITUS
Walter F. Diehl
Richard F. Walsh
GENERAL SECRETARY-TREASURER
James J. Riley
FIRST VICE PRESIDENT
Frank A. Hobbs, Niles, IL
SECOND VICE PRESIDENT
John J. Nolan, Paramus, NJ
THIRD VICE PRESIDENT
J. E. Johnson, Karnack, TX
FOURTH VICE PRESIDENT
John J. Ryan, Burtonsville, MD
FIFTH VICE PRESIDENT
Edward C. Powell, San Francisco, CA
SIXTH VICE PRESIDENT
Michael W. Proscia, New York, NY
SEVENTH VICE PRESIDENT
Alan L. Cowley, Hamilton, Ont.
EIGHTH VICE PRESIDENT
Nick Long, Los Angeles, CA
NINTH VICE PRESIDENT
Daniel J. Kerins, Chicago, IL
TENTH VICE PRESIDENT
Donald T. Rohrbach, Hollywood, CA
ELEVENTH VICE PRESIDENT
Thomas C. Short, Cleveland, OH
INTERNATIONAL TRUSTEES
Michael J. Sullivan, Hartford, CT; Nels L. Hansen, Las Vegas, NV; Ada S. Philpot, San Francisco, CA.

The Alliance is comprised of approximately 900 local unions covering the United States, Canada and Hawaii. Following is a list of the New York, Chicago and Hollywood locals:

PRODUCTION

AFFILIATED PROPERTY CRAFTSMEN LOCAL 44 (IATSE-AFL-CIO), HOLLYWOOD

(Organized May 15, 1939) 7429 Sunset Blvd., Hollywood, CA 90046; (213) 876-2320 and 838-7788.

ART DIRECTORS, LOCAL 876 (IATSE) HOLLYWOOD

(Chartered January 7, 1960) 14724 Ventura Blvd., Sherman Oaks, CA 91403; (818) 905-0599.

BROADCASTING STUDIO EMPLOYEES, LOCAL 782 (IATSE), NEW YORK

(Chartered Jan. 5, 1945) 41 Nottingham Rd., Glen Rock, NJ 07452; (201) 445-7372.

FIRST AID EMPLOYEES, LOCAL 767 (IATSE), LOS ANGELES

(Chartered Oct. 30, 1942) 8736 Swinton Ave., Sepulveda, CA 91343; (213) 894-3781.

INTERNATIONAL PHOTOGRAPHERS OF THE MOTION PICTURE INDUSTRIES (Cameramen) IPMPI LOCAL 666, CHICAGO

(Chartered Jan. 1, 1929) Suite 1122, 327 S. La Salle St., Chicago, IL; (312) 341-0966.

IPMPI, LOCAL 659 (IATSE), LOS ANGELES

(Organized 1928) 7715 Sunset Blvd., Hollywood, CA 90046; (213) 876-0160.

IPMPI, LOCAL 644 (IATSE), NEW YORK

(Organized Nov. 15, 1926) 250 W. 57 St., New York, NY 10019; (212) 247-3860.

INTERNATIONAL SOUND TECHNICIANS OF THE MOTION PICTURE BROADCAST AND AMUSEMENT INDUSTRIES, LOCAL 695 (IATSE-AFL), LOS ANGELES

(Organized Sept. 15, 1930) 15840 Ventura Blvd., Encino, CA 91436; (818) 985-9204.

LABORATORY TECHNICIANS, LOCAL 780 (IATSE), CHICAGO

(Chartered Nov. 10, 1944) 327 S. La Salle St., Room 1720, Chicago, IL; (312) 922-7105.

LABORATORY TECHNICIANS, LOCAL 683 (IATSE-AFL-CIO), LOS ANGELES

(Organized Sept. 29, 1919) 6721 Melrose Ave., Hollywood, CA 90038; (212) 935-1123.

LABORATORY TECHNICIANS, LOCAL 702 (IATSE-AFL), NEW YORK

(Organized September, 1937) Room 1405, 165 W. 46 St., New York, NY 10036; (212) 869-5540.

MAKE-UP ARTISTS & HAIR STYLISTS, LOCAL 706 (IATSE), HOLLYWOOD

11519 Chandler Blvd., No. Hollywood, CA 91601; (213) 877-2776.

MAKE-UP ARTISTS AND HAIR STYLISTS, LOCAL 798 (IATSE), NEW YORK

(Chartered Feb. 18, 1949) 1790 Broadway, New York, NY 10019; (212) 757-9120.

MOTION PICTURE COSTUMERS, LOCAL 705 (IATSE-AFL), HOLLYWOOD

(Chartered Nov. 1, 1937) 1427 N. La Brea Ave., Hollywood, CA 90028; (213) 851-0220.

MOTION PICTURE AND VIDEO EDITORS GUILD, LOCAL 776 (IATSE), LOS ANGELES

(Chartered Aug. 2, 1944) Secretary's address: 7715 Sunset Blvd., Hollywood, CA 90046; (213) 876-4770.

MOTION PICTURE FILM & VIDEO TAPE EDITORS, LOCAL 771 (IATSE), NEW YORK

(Chartered Aug. 18, 1943) 353 W. 48 St., New York, NY 10036; (212) 765-1069.

MOTION PICTURE SCRIPT SUPERVISORS AND PRODUCTION OFFICE COORDINATORS LOCAL 161

250 W. 57 St., Room 1202, New York, NY 10019; (212) 245-4562.

MOTION PICTURE SET PAINTERS, LOCAL 729 (IATSE), HOLLYWOOD

(Chartered Aug. 1, 1953) 11365 Ventura Blvd., Studio City, CA 91604; (818) 784-3000.

MOTION PICTURE STUDIO CINETECHNICIANS, LOCAL 789 (IATSE), HOLLYWOOD

(Chartered April 16, 1945) 1635 Vista Del Mar, Hollywood, CA 90028; (213) 462-7288.

MOTION PICTURE SCREEN CARTOONISTS, LOCAL 839 (IATSE), HOLLYWOOD

(Chartered Jan. 18, 1952) 4729 Lankershim Blvd., North Hollywood, CA 91602; (213) 766-7151.

MOTION PICTURE SCREEN CARTOONISTS, LOCAL 841 (IATSE), NEW YORK

(Chartered April 16, 1952) 127 E. 35 St., New York, NY 10016; (212) 684-0760.

MOTION PICTURE STUDIO ELECTRICAL TECHNICIANS, LOCAL 728 (IATSE), AND M.P.M.O. OF U.S. AND CANADA-AFL-CIO

(Chartered May 15, 1939) 14629 Nordhoff St., Panorama City, CA 91406; (213) 851-3300.

MOTION PICTURE CRAFTS SERVICE, LOCAL 727 (IATSE), HOLLYWOOD

(Organized May 15, 1939) 12754 Ventura Blvd., Suite 205, North Hollywood, CA 91604.

MOTION PICTURE STUDIO ART CRAFTSMEN, (Illustrators and Matte Artists) LOCAL 790 (IATSE), HOLLYWOOD

(Chartered April 17, 1945) Suite 210, 7715 Sunset Blvd., Los Angeles, CA 90046; (213) 876-2010.

MOTION PICTURE STUDIO GRIPS, LOCAL 80 (IATSE), HOLLYWOOD

(Organized May 15, 1939) 6926 Melrose Ave., Los Angeles, CA 90038; (213) 931-1419.

MOTION PICTURE STUDIO TEACHERS AND WELFARE WORKERS, LOCAL 884 (IATSE) HOLLYWOOD

(Chartered September 1, 1960) 9617 Haas Ave., Los Angeles, CA 90047; (213) 754-8419.

PUBLICISTS, LOCAL 818 (IATSE), HOLLYWOOD

(Chartered July 11, 1955) 1427 N. La Brea Ave., Hollywood CA 90028.

RADIO AND TELEVISION SOUND EFFECTS, LOCAL 844 (IATSE), NEW YORK

(Chartered July 17, 1952), Box 637, Ansonia Station, New York, NY 10023.

SCENIC & TITLE ARTISTS, LOCAL 816 (IATSE) LOS ANGELES

(Chartered March 31, 1949) 6180 Laurel Canyon Blvd., No. Hollywood, CA 91606; (818) 769-0816.

SCRIPT SUPERVISORS, LOCAL 871 (IATSE), HOLLYWOOD

(Chartered January 1, 1958) 7061 Hayenhurst, Van Nuys, CA 91906; (818) 782-7063.

SET DESIGNERS AND MODEL MAKERS, LOCAL 847 (IATSE), HOLLYWOOD

(Chartered Nov. 14, 1952) Suite 210, 7715 Sunset Blvd., Los Angeles, CA 90046; (213) 876-2010.

STORY ANALYSTS, LOCAL 854 (IATSE), HOLLYWOOD

(Chartered Oct. 18, 1954) 7715 Sunset Blvd., Los Angeles, CA 90046; (213) 876-2010.

MOTION PICTURE STUDIO MECHANICS, LOCAL 476 (IATSE), CHICAGO

(Chartered Feb. 2, 1931) Room 1743; 327 S. La Salle St., Chicago, IL 60604; (312) 922-5215.

STUDIO MECHANICS, LOCAL 52 (IATSE-AFL), NEW YORK

(Organized 1924) 221 W. 57 St., New York, NY 10019; (212) 765-0741.

STUDIO PROJECTIONISTS AND VIDEO PROJECTION TECHNICIANS, LOCAL 165 (IATSE), HOLLYWOOD

(Chartered May 15, 1939) 14724 Ventura Blvd., Sherman Oaks, CA 91403; (213) 462-6385.

TELEVISION BROADCASTING STUDIO EMPLOYEES, LOCAL 794 (IATSE), NEW YORK

(Chartered June 7, 1945) 144 Aster Ave., Hawthorn, New York, NY 10532.

DISTRIBUTION

FILM EXCHANGE EMPLOYEES, BACK ROOM, LOCAL B-45 (IATSE), CHICAGO

(Chartered May 1, 1937) 5455 Sheridan Ave., Chicago, IL 60640.

FILM EXCHANGE EMPLOYEES, BACK ROOM, LOCAL B-61 (IATSE), LOS ANGELES

(Chartered May 1, 1937) 7715 Sunset Blvd., Room 226, Hollywood, CA 90046.

FILM EXCHANGE EMPLOYEES, FRONT OFFICE, LOCAL F-45 (IATSE), CHICAGO

(Chartered Sept. 4, 1942) #G. R. Kuehnl, Apt. 1611, 5455 Sheridan Rd., Chicago, IL 60640.

In addition to the above, there are 34 locals of Back Room Employees and 29 locals of Front Office Employees in the other exchange cities.

MOTION PICTURE HOME OFFICE AND FILM EXCHANGE EMPLOYEES, LOCAL H-63 (IATSE), NEW YORK

(Chartered Mar. 19, 1945) 29 E. 49 St., New York, NY 10017; (212) 759-0686.

EXHIBITION

AMUSEMENT AREA EMPLOYEES, LOCAL B-192 (IATSE) LOS ANGELES

(Chartered Oct. 1, 1965) 7715 Sunset Blvd., Room 226, Los Angeles, CA 90046.

EXHIBITION EMPLOYEES, LOCAL 829 (IATSE), NEW YORK

(Chartered December 11, 1950) 150 E. 58 St., New York, NY 10022; (212) 752-4427.

PROJECTIONISTS LOCAL 110 (IATSE), CHICAGO

(Chartered Feb. 4, 1915) 875 N. Michigan Ave. Suite 4160, Chicago, IL 60611; (312) 787-0220.

PROJECTIONISTS LOCAL 150 (IATSE), LOS ANGELES

(Chartered July 16, 1908) 1800 S. Vermont Ave., Los Angeles, CA 90006; (213) 733-1191.

PROJECTIONISTS LOCAL 306 (IATSE), NEW YORK

(Organized July, 1913) 745 Seventh Ave., New York, NY 10019; (212) 586-5157, and 55 Flatbush Ave., Brooklyn, NY; (212) 852-2700.

STAGE EMPLOYEES, LOCAL 4 (IATSE), BROOKLYN

(Chartered April 8, 1888) 2917 Glenwood Rd., Brooklyn, NY 11210; (212) 252-8777.

STAGE EMPLOYEES, LOCAL 2 (IATSE), CHICAGO

(Chartered July 17, 1893) 222 W. Adams St., Room 1345, Chicago, IL 60606.

STAGE EMPLOYEES, LOCAL 33 (IATSE), LOS ANGELES

(Chartered Mar. 1, 1896) 4605 Lankershim Blvd. Suite 833, N. Hollywood, CA 91602; (213) 985-0633-4.

STAGE EMPLOYEES, LOCAL 1 (IATSE), NEW YORK

(Chartered July 17, 1893) 1775 Broadway, New York, NY 10019; (212) 489-7710.

THEATRE EMPLOYEES, LOCAL B-46 (IATSE), CHICAGO

(Chartered May 1, 1937) 875 N. Michigan Ave. Suite 4160, Chicago, IL 60611; (312) 787-0220.

THEATRE EMPLOYEES, LOCAL B-183 (IATSE), NEW YORK

(Chartered May 6, 1942) 235 W. 46 St., Rm. 320, New York, NY 10036; (212) 245-2331, 2332.

THEATRICAL WARDROBE ATTENDANTS, LOCAL 769 (IATSE), CHICAGO

3314 Lake Shore Dr., Apt. 805, Chicago, IL 60657.

THEATRICAL WARDROBE ATTENDANTS, LOCAL 768 (IATSE), LOS ANGELES

(Chartered Dec. 3, 1942) 5909 Melrose Ave. Suite 17, Los Angeles, CA 90038.

THEATRICAL WARDROBE ATTENDANTS, LOCAL 764 (IATSE), NEW YORK

(Chartered Sept. 4, 1942) 1501 Broadway, Room 1604, New York, NY; (212) 221-1717.

TREASURERS AND TICKET SELLERS & CASHIERS, LOCAL 750 (IATSE), CHICAGO

(Chartered Aug. 1, 1941) 188 W. Randolph St., Room 1920, Chicago, IL 60601.

TREASURERS AND TICKET SELLERS, LOCAL 857 (IATSE), LOS ANGELES

(Chartered June 1, 1955) 6513 Hollywood Blvd., Room 204, Hollywood, CA 90028.

TREASURERS AND TICKET SELLERS, LOCAL 751 (IATSE), NEW YORK

(Chartered Aug. 1, 1941) 257 W. 52 St., New York, NY 10019; (212) 315-0544.

Outside the three cities covered by the above listings, there are over 900 IATSE locals in the exhibition field.

International Brotherhood of Electrical Workers (AFL)

(Organized November 28, 1891; Membership over 1 million) 1125 15th St., N.W., Washington, DC 20005; (202) 833-7000.

INTERNATIONAL PRESIDENT
John J. Barry, 1125 15th St., N.W., Washington, DC 20005
INTERNATIONAL SECRETARY
Jack F. Moore, 1125 15th St., N.W., Washington, DC 20005
INTERNATIONAL TREASURER
Thomas Van Arsdale, Jr., 158-11 Jewel Ave., Flushing, NY 11365
DISTRICT OFFICES
Willowdale, Ontario: 45 Sheppard Ave. East, Suite 401; Ken Woods.
Braintree, MA: Battery March Park, Quincy, MA 02169, John E. Flynn
Hackensack, NJ, 171 Main St., Rm. 104. A. W. Giles
Cincinnati, OH: 7710 Reading Rd., Suite 9, B. G. Williamson
Birmingham, AL: No. 2 Metroplex Dr., Suite 113, D. H. Waters
Lombard, IL; 2200 S. Main St., Ste. 303, James P. Conway.
Oklahoma, OK; 4400 Will Rogers Pkwy. #309, Orville A. Tate, Jr.
Idaho Fall, ID 83402: P.O. Box 1216, Jon Walters
Walnut Creek, CA: 150 N. Wiget Lane, Suite 700, S. R. McCann
Rosemont, IL: 10400 W. Higgins Rd., Suite 400, Edward P. McEntee
Springfield, MO: 300 So. Jefferson, Suite 300, Ray Edwards
Chattanooga, TN: Franklin Bldg., Suite 515, John A. Hightower

IBEW LOCAL 349 (FILM)

(Organized April 24, 1904) 1657 N.W. 17th Ave. Miami, FL 33125; (305) 325-1330.

BUSINESS MANAGER
Art Fernandez

IBEW LOCAL 40 (FILM)

(Organized March 5, 1923) 5643 Vineland Ave., No. Hollywood, CA 91601; (213) 877-1171.

BUSINESS MANAGER
Russell J. Bartley

International Radio and Television Society Inc.

420 Lexington Ave. Suite 531, New York, NY 10170; (212) 867-6650.

PRESIDENT
Betty Hudson
FIRST VICE PRESIDENT
James H. Rosenfeld

VICE PRESIDENTS
Mark H. Cohen, Gerald M. Levin, Neal H. Pilson, Ralph M. Baruch
SECRETARY
Jerome S. Boros
TREASURER
Robert C. Butler
EXECUTIVE DIRECTOR
Stephen B. Labunski

National Academy of Television Arts and Sciences, The

National Office: 111 W. 57 St., New York, NY 10019; (212) 586-8424. (Formed to advance the arts and sciences of television.) (Organized 1957) Awards Emmys for daytime, children's, religious, sports and news documentary programming.

CHAIRMAN OF THE BOARD
Robert Wussler
PRESIDENT
John Cannon
VICE CHAIRMAN
Richard Schneider
VICE PRESIDENT
Irvin Davis
SECRETARY
Sandra Pastoor
TREASURER
Isadore Miller

National Association of Broadcasters

1771 N St., N.W., Washington, DC 20036; (202) 429-5300. (Organized 1922 to foster and promote the development of the arts of aural and visual broadcasting in all its forms; to protect its members in every lawful and proper manner from injustices and unjust exactions; to do all things necessary and proper to encourage and promote customs and practices which will strengthen and maintain the broadcasting industry to the end that it may best serve the public.)

CHAIRMAN
Wallace J. Jorgenson
PRESIDENT
Edward O. Fritts
TELEVISION BOARD OF DIRECTORS
Benjamin McKeel (chm.), Margo Cobb (vice-chm.), Gary R. Chapman, Michael J. Conley, William F. Duhamel, Frank J. Flynn, Jr., Daniel E. Gold, Thomas L. Goodgame, Harold Protter, Patricia C. Smullin, Cullie M. Tarleton, Glenn C. Wright, Leavitt J. Pope, Daniel Villanueva. Networks: Eugene S. Cowen (Capital Cities/ABC), Robert D. Hynes, Jr. (NBC), John F. Strum (CBS).

National Association of Public Television Stations

1818 N. Street, N.W., Suite 410, Washington, D.C. 20036; (202) 887-1700. Organized 1979. (Does research, planning and representation for member public television stations throughout the U.S.)

ACTING PRESIDENT/VICE PRES. & GEN. COUNSEL
Baryn S. Futa
BOARD OF TRUSTEES
Donald J. Carlyon, Henry J. Cauthen, Dr. Margaret Chisholm, Dr. Thomas W. Cole, Jr., J. Michael Collins, W. Wayne Godwin, Charlotte Hill, Dr. Teruo Ihara, Sue T. Keene, R. Bruce MacGregor, Richard O. Moore, F. Lee Morris, Dr. Richard Ottinger, Dr. Glenn Terrell, Anthony Tiano, Dr. Albert C. Van Dusen, Charles W. Vaughan, Arnold D. Wallace, Viviane Warren
AFFILIATIONS
Works closely with Corp. for Public Broadcasting & Public Broadcasting Service (PBS) but is not "affiliated."

NATPE INTERNATIONAL (National Association of Television Program Executives, Inc.)

10100 Santa Monica Blvd., Ste. 300, Los Angeles, CA 90067; (213)282-8801.
PRESIDENT
A. Philip Corvo
CHAIRMAN OF THE BOARD
Joseph Weber, MMT Sales, New York

National Cable Television Association

1724 Massachusetts Ave., N.W., Washington, DC 20036; (202) 775-3550. Organized 1951. (Trade association that lobbies for cable television interest.)
PRESIDENT
James P. Mooney
EXECUTIVE VICE PRESIDENT
Decker Anstrom
VICE PRESIDENT, SCIENCE & TECHNOLOGY
Wendell Bailey
VICE PRESIDENT, PROGRAMMING & MARKETING
Char Beales
VICE PRESIDENT, ADMINISTRATION
Phylis Eagle
VICE PRESIDENT, SPECIAL POLICY PROJECTS
Brenda Fox
VICE PRESIDENT, ASSOCIATION AFFAIRS
Jadz Janucik
DEPUTY VICE PRESIDENT, GOVERNMENT RELATIONS
Katherine Meier
VICE PRESIDENT, INDUSTRY COMMUNICATIONS
Louise Rauscher
VICE PRESIDENT, INDUSTRY AFFAIRS
Barbara York
VICE PRESIDENT, RESEARCH & POLICY ANALYSIS
Cynthia Brumfield
BOARD OF DIRECTORS
John W. Goddard (chairman); Jerry D. Lindauer (secretary); James S. Cownie (immediate past chm.); Daniel Aaron; Edward M. Allen; Kenneth L. Bagwell; Robert Miron (vice chairmen); James O. Robbins (treas.); James P. Mooney (president); Gregory Bryan Blow; David A. Bohmer; William J. Bresnan; Carolyn S. Chambers; Joseph Collins; Winston H. Cox; Jerry D. Craft; Boyce Booley; Frank M. Drendel; John D. Evans; Michael J. Fuchs; Alan Gerry; James L. Gray; J. William Grimes; David W. Hamilton; Amos ("Bud") B. Hostetter, Jr.; Marvin L. Jones; Kay Koplovitz; Philip B. Lind; John C. Malone; John J. Rigas; Richard D. Roberts; Clive Runnells; Gene W. Schneider; William B. Strange, Jr.; John Tatta; Charles C. Townsend, III; June E. Travis; R.E. "Ted" Turner; Larry W. Wangberg; Maggie Wilderotter; John ("Dubby") O. Wynne.
AFFILIATIONS
National Academy of Cable Programmming, National Cable Forum

National Federation of Local Cable Programmers

P.O.Box 27290, Washington, DC 20038-7290; (202) 829-7186.
EXECUTIVE DIRECTOR
Vacant

National Music Publishers' Association, Inc.

205 E. 42 St., New York, NY 10017; (212) 370-5330.
CHAIRMAN
Irwin Z. Robinson
PRESIDENT AND CEO
Edward P. Murphy
VICE PRESIDENTS
William Lowery, Ralph Peer II, Leon J. Brettler
SECRETARY
Samuel Trust
TREASURER
Sidney B. Herman

New York Women in Film

1100 Ave. of the Americas, Suite 1440B, New York, NY 10036; (212) 512-8022. Organized 1977. (Serves as a networking, educational, and informational organization for professional women in film and television.)
PRESIDENT
Pat Fili
VICE PRESIDENT, ADMINISTRATION
Rosalind Lichter
VICE PRESIDENT, OPERATIONS
Maria Nation
SECRETARY
Emily Squires
TREASURER
Laura Fieber
NEWSLETTER EDITOR
Nancy Leff
BOARD OF DIRECTORS
Yanna Kroyt Brandt; Margot Breier; Pat Herold; Willa Hoffner; Jayne Keyes; Linda Kline; Susan Lazarus; Joy Pereths; Diane Sokolow; Francia White; (Board terms are for two years with rotating dates of completion).
CHAPTERS
Los Angeles, San Francisco, Atlanta, Dallas, Boston, Chicago, Washington, D.C., Toronto and worldwide

Permanent Charities Committee of The Entertainment Industries

Samuel Goldwyn-Permanent Charities Building, 463 N. La Cienega Blvd., Los Angeles, CA 90048; (213) 652-4680. (A donor federation within the entertainment industries supporting community wide charities.)
CHAIRMAN OF THE BOARD
Daniel E. Slusser
PRESIDENT & CHIEF EXECUTIVE OFFICER
Paul C. Masterson
FIRST VICE PRESIDENT
Gene Allen
SECOND VICE PRESIDENT
Barbara Corday
SECRETARY
William K. Howard
TREASURER
Robert S. Colbert, CPA
VICE PRESIDENT, OPERATIONS AND DEVELOPMENT
Irwin J. Kaplan

Producer-Writers Guild of America Pension Plan

1015 No. Hollywood Way, Burbank, CA 91505; (818) 846-1015.
CHAIRMAN
David Karp
VICE CHAIRMAN
Jean Butler
SECRETARY
Marshall Wortman
VICE SECRETARY
Robert Key

SESAC, INC.

(One of the world's foremost music licensing organizations. A special projects department handles scoring for motion pictures, slide films, syndicated TV series and agency produced commercials; programming for background music and premium albums.)
The Coliseum Tower, 10 Columbus Circle, New York, NY 10019; (212) 586-3450.
CHAIRMAN & PRESIDENT
A. H. Prager
EXECUTIVE VICE PRESIDENT
Vincent Candilora

Screen Actors Guild (AAAA-AFL-CIO)

(Organized July, 1933; Membership: 70,000) 7065 Hollywood Blvd., Hollywood, CA 90028; (213) 465-4600. Branches— New York, 1515 Broadway, 44th Floor, New York, NY 10036, John T. McGuire; Chicago, 307 N. Michigan Ave., Herbert H. Neuer; Boston, 11 Beacon St., Robert M. Segal; Lathrup Village, MI 48076, 28690 Southfield Rd., Jane Ford, Dallas, TX 75204, 3220 Lemmon Ave., Clinta Dayton; San Francisco, CA 94104, 100 Bush St., Don Tayer; FL. 3266 Ponce de Leon Blvd., Coral Gables, FL, Melvin B. Karl.
PRESIDENT
Barry Gordon
PRESIDENT EMERITUS
Leon Ames
SECOND VICE PRESIDENT
Maureen Donnelly
THIRD VICE PRESIDENT
Joseph Ruskin
FOURTH VICE PRESIDENT
Jordan Derwin
FIFTH VICE PRESIDENT
Reed Farrell
SIXTH VICE PRESIDENT
Dan Caldwell
VICE PRESIDENTS
Bruce McLaughlin, Larry Keith, J. Carlton Adair, Daryl Anderson, Frank Aletter, Dan Ingram
RECORDING SECRETARY
Sumi Haru
TREASURER
Yale Summers

NATIONAL EXECUTIVE STAFF
NATIONAL EXECUTIVE DIRECTOR
Ken Orsatti
ASSOCIATE NATIONAL EXECUTIVE DIRECTOR
John McGuire
PUBLIC RELATIONS DIRECTOR
Mark Locher
COUNSEL
Leo Geffner
CONTROLLER
Gerald Wilson

Society of Motion Picture and Television Engineers

(Organized 1916; Membership: 8,800) 595 W. Hartsdale Ave., White Plains, NY 10607; (914) 761-1100.
PRESIDENT
M. Carlos Kennedy
PAST PRESIDENT
Harold J. Eady
EXECUTIVE VICE PRESIDENT
Maurice L. French
ENGINEERING VICE PRESIDENT
Stanley N. Baron
EDITORIAL VICE PRESIDENT
Howard L. LaZare
FINANCIAL VICE PRESIDENT
Stephen D. Kerman
CONFERENCE VICE PRESIDENT
Blaine Baker
SECTIONS VICE PRESIDENT
Irwin W. Young
SECRETARY/TREASURER
Richard K. Schafer
EXECUTIVE DIRECTOR
Lynette Robinson

The Songwriters Guild of America

276 Fifth Ave., Suite 306, New York, NY 10001; (212) 686-6820; California Office: 6430 Sunset Blvd., Hollywood, CA 90028; (213) 462-1108. Nashville Office: 50 Music Square W., Nashville, TN 37203; (615) 329-1782.

PRESIDENT
George David Weiss
EXECUTIVE DIRECTOR
Lewis M. Bachman

Station Representatives Association, Inc.

230 Park Ave., New York, NY 10017; (212) 687-2484.
PRESIDENT
Steve Herson
VICE PRESIDENT/RADIO
Jerry Cregan
VICE PRESIDENT/TV
Peter Ryan
SECRETARY
Dave Kaufman
TREASURER
Tony Miraglia
MANAGING DIRECTOR
Jerry Feniger
ADMINISTRATIVE ASSISTANT
Audrey Tanzer
DIRECTORS
(Radio board) Eduardo Caballero, George Pine, Stu Olds, Jerry Cregan, Tom Turner, Tony Miraglia, Dave Kaufman. (TV board) Peter Ryan, Pete Goulazian, Steve Herson, Ed Goldman, Art Scott, Tim McAuliffe, Ray Johns.

Television Bureau of Advertising

477 Madison Ave., New York, NY 10022; (212) 486-1111. (Organized 1954.); 3060 Mercer University Dr., Suite 310, Atlanta, GA 30341; (404) 451-2727; 3625 N. Hall, Dallas, TX 75219; (214) 520-2240; 400 No. Michigan Ave., Suite 616, Chicago, IL 60611; (312) 527-3373; 3155 W. Big Beaver Rd., Suite 217, Troy, MI 48084; (313) 649-6688; 5900 Wilshire Blvd., Los Angeles, CA 90036; (213) 653-8890.

PRESIDENT
William G. Moll
CHAIRMAN OF THE BOARD
James G. Babb
VICE PRESIDENT
Peter Ryan
TREASURER
David Allen
CHAIRMAN EX-OFFICIO
E. Blake Byrne
EXECUTIVE VICE PRESIDENT GENERAL MANAGER
Richard Severance
SENIOR VICE PRESIDENT RESEARCH & MARKETING
Harvey Spiegel
SENIOR VICE PRESIDENT, RESOURCE DEVELOPMENT
Beverly Keene
SENIOR VICE PRESIDENT NATIONAL SALES
James A. Joyella
VICE PRESIDENT, CREATIVE DIRECTOR
Margaret Davis
SENIOR VICE PRESIDENT, COMMUNICATIONS
Robert M. Grebe
SENIOR VICE PRESIDENT, EDUCATION AND TRAINING
Barbara Zeiger
SENIOR VICE PRESIDENT, DEVELOPMENT
Diane Healey Linen
SENIOR VICE PRESIDENT, RETAIL MARKETING
Wallace Westphal
VICE PRESIDENT CENTRAL DIVISION
Michael Smythe
VICE PRESIDENT, AUTOMOTIVE MARKETING
Richard O'Donnell
VICE PRESIDENT, PACIFIC
Arthur Trudeau
VICE PRESIDENT, SOUTHWEST
Chuck Hanson
VICE PRESIDENT, SOUTHEAST
Perry Bascom
VICE PRESIDENT, WESTERN SALES
Robert Fairbanks

VICE PRESIDENT, LOCAL SALES MANAGER
John Krubski, Patrick J. Ryan
VICE PRESIDENT, FINANCE
Robert D. Brady

Television Information Office

745 Fifth Ave., New York, NY 10022; (212) 759-6800.
DIRECTOR
Robert Mulholland
EXECUTIVE EDITOR
Steven Miller
MANAGERS, STATION SERVICES
Henry Levinson, Lynne Grasz
MANAGER, RESEARCH SERVICES
James Poteat
LIBRARIAN
Leslie Slocum

Theatre Authority, Inc.

(Organized May 21, 1934) 16 East 42nd St., Suite 202,
New York, NY 10017-6907; (212) 682-4215.
PRESIDENT
Willard Swire
EXECUTIVE SECRETARY
Helen Leahy
TREASURER
Joan Greenspan
COUNSEL
Fred Krones

United Nations—Information Products Division, Department of Public Information

United Nations, New York, NY 10017; (212) 963-6945.
DIRECTOR, INFORMATION PRODUCTS DIVISION
Georges Leclère

Women in Communications, Inc.

3724 Executive Center Dr., Room 165, Austin, TX
78731; (512) 346-9875. Organized 1909. (Promotes advancement of women in communications, protects First
Amendment, encourages professionalism in the field.)
PRESIDENT
Sharon Watson
PRESIDENT ELECT
Karen Carnahan
ACTING SUPERVISOR
Naomi Sparks
BRANCHES
Public Affairs Office, Washington, D.C. Over 200 chapters.

Women in Film

(Non-profit organization formed in 1973 by professional
women in the motion picture and television industries;
purpose is to serve as a support group and act as a
clearing house and resource of information on qualified

professional women in those industries) 6464 Sunset
Blvd., #660, Los Angeles, CA; (213) 463-6040. Branches
in New York, Washington, D.C. and Atlanta, GA
PRESIDENT EMERITUS—FOUNDER
Tichi Wilkerson
CHAIRMAN
Diane Asselin
SECRETARY-TREASURER
Johanna Levine
EXECUTIVE ADMINISTRATOR
Debbie Supnik

Women in Show Business

(A philanthropic organization composed of women in
the entertainment industry dedicated to providing funds
for reconstructive and restorative surgery for children)
P.O. Box 2535, North Hollywood, CA 91602; (818) 762-
4669.
PRESIDENT
Sherry Tischler
EXECUTIVE VICE PRESIDENT/WAYS & MEANS
Linda Desiante
FIRST VICE PRESIDENT/PROGRAM
Jeanne Taylor
EXECUTIVE VICE PRESIDENT
Lynn Helsel
SECOND VICE PRESIDENT/MEMBERSHIP
Anne Parlapiano
RECORDING SECRETARY
Frances Wright
CORRESPONDING SECRETARY
Janet Taylor
TREASURER
Margaret Weiner

Writers Guild of America

NATIONAL CHAIRMAN
Edward Adler

WRITERS GUILD OF AMERICA, EAST, INC.

555 W. 57 Street, New York, NY 10019; (212) 245-6180.
PRESIDENT
Edward Adler
VICE PRESIDENT
Adrian J. Meppen
SECRETARY-TREASURER
Jane C. Bollinger
EXECUTIVE DIRECTOR
Mona Mangan

WRITERS GUILD OF AMERICA, WEST, INC.

8955 Beverly Blvd., Los Angeles, CA 90048; (213)
550-1000.
PRESIDENT
George Kirgo
VICE PRESIDENT
Del Reisman
SECRETARY-TREASURER
Alfred Levitt
EXECUTIVE DIRECTOR
Brian Walton

State Associations of Broadcasters

ALABAMA BROADCASTERS ASSOCIATION
Ben K. McKinnon, exec. dir.
Box 43525, Birmingham 35243; (205) 942-4571.

ALASKA BROADCASTERS ASSOCIATION
Roy Robinson, pres.
Box 102424, Anchorage, 99510; (907) 258-2424.

ARIZONA BROADCASTERS ASSOCIATION
Ken Heady, exec. dir.
Box 654, Scottsdale 85252; (602) 991-1700.

ARKANSAS BROADCASTERS ASSOCIATION
Dale Nicholson, pres.; Pat Willcox, exec. dir.
2024 Arkansas Valley Drive, Suite 201, Little Rock 72212; (501) 227-7564.

CALIFORNIA BROADCASTERS ASSOCIATION
Victor J. Biondi, exec. dir.; Karmi A. Speece, exec. asst.
1127 11th St., Suite 730, Sacramento 95814; (916) 444-2237.

COLORADO BROADCASTERS ASSOCIATION
Cliff Dodge, exec. dir.; Judy Gaughan, admin. asst.
1660 Lincoln #2202, Denver 80264; (303) 894-0911.

CONNECTICUT BROADCASTERS ASSOCIATION
Paul K. Taff, exec. dir.
101 Tall Timbers La., Glastonbury 06033; (203) 633-5031.

FLORIDA ASSOCIATION OF BROADCASTERS, INC.
514 E. College, Tallahassee, 32301; (904) 681-6444.

GEORGIA ASSOCIATION OF BROADCASTERS, INC.
William G. Sanders, exec. dir.; Eve Moffa, exec. dir.
500 Sugar Mill Rd., Atlanta 30350; (404) 993-2200.

HAWAIIAN ASSOCIATION OF BROADCASTERS
Dick Schaller (KIKU-TV, Honolulu), pres.
Station KIKI-TV, 150 B Puhale Rd., Honolulu 96819; (808) 847-1178. %KNUI Radio, Box 35, Kahului 96732; (808) 877-5566.

IDAHO STATE BROADCASTERS ASSOCIATION
Connie Searles, exec. dir.; Gerry Cornwell (KIDK-TV Pocatello), pres.
Box 884, Boise 83701; (208) 345-3072.

ILLINOIS BROADCASTERS ASSOCIATION
Wally Gair, exec. dir.
2126 S. MacArthur Rd., Springfield 62704; (217) 753-2636.

INDIANA BROADCASTERS ASSOCIATION, INC.
Joyce Martello, exec. dir..
310 N. Alabama, Suite A, Indianapolis 46204; (317) 638-1332.

IOWA BROADCASTERS ASSOCIATION
William F. Sanders (KICD, Spencer), pres.; Nolan Quam (KCCI-TV, Des Moines), v.p.; Glenn Olson (KQWC, Webster City), treas.; Jack Shelley, exec. secty.
1230 Marston Ave., Ames 50010; (515) 232-1449.

KANSAS ASSOICATION OF BROADCASTERS
Harriet J. Lange, exec. dir.
818 Merchants Nat'l Bank Bldg., Topeka 66612; (913) 235-1307.

KENTUCKY BROADCASTERS ASSOCIATION
J.T. Whitlock, exec. dir. & treas.
Box 680, Lebanon 40033; (502) 692-3126.

LOUISIANA ASSOCIATION OF BROADCASTERS
Manuel Broussard, pres.; Hugh Hyman, exec. dir.
732 North Blvd., Suite C, Baton Rouge 70802; (504) 383-7486.

MAINE ASSOCIATION OF BROADCASTERS
Helen Dudman, pres.; Norman Johnson, pres.-elect; Norman G. Gallant, exec. dir.
Box PI, 385 Western Ave., Augusta 04330; (207) 623-3870.

MARYLAND-DISTRICT OF COLUMBIA-DELAWARE BROAD-CASTERS ASSOCIATION, INC.
Edward Wetter (WABS, Arlington, VA), pres.; Malcolm D. Potter (WBAL-TV, Baltimore), v.p.; C. Robert Taylor (WDEL/WSTW, Wilmington, Del.), secty.; Robert B. Cochrane, exec. dir.
Route 1-Box 559, St. Michaels, MD 21663; (301) 745-5155.

MASSACHUSETTS BROADCASTERS ASSOCIATION
Robert S. Mehrman, exec. dir.
250 Summer St., 4th Floor, Boston 02210; (617) 439-7636.

MICHIGAN ASSOCIATION OF BROADCASTERS
Charles D. Mefford, pres.; Karole White, exec. dir.
819 N. Washington Ave., Lansing 48906; (517) 484-7444..

MINNESOTA BROADCASTERS ASSOCIATION
Ned Goodwin (KBUN/KBHP, Bemidji) pres.; Ray Foslid, exec. dir.
3517 Raleigh Ave., So., St. Louis Park 55416; (612) 926-8123.

MISSISSIPPI BROADCASTERS ASSOCIATION
Robert Ward, pres.; Jackie Lett, exec. dir.
Box 4561, Jackson 39216; (601) 362-5444.

MISSOURI BROADCASTERS ASSOCIATION
Terry King, pres.; Ted Griffin, exec. v.p.
1800 Southwest Blvd., Jefferson City 65101; (314) 636-6692.

MISSOURI PUBLIC RADIO ASSOCIATION
% Arlen Diamond, pres.
KSMU, 901 S. National, Springfield 65804; (417) 836-5878.

MONTANA BROADCASTERS ASSOCIATION
Robert W. Hoene, exec. dir.; Dean Williams, pres.
Box 503, Helena 59624; (406) 442-3961.

NEBRASKA BROADCASTERS ASSOCIATION
Ed Schafer, pres.; Ken Fearnow (WOW, Omaha) chm., Larry Rice (KBRB, Ainsworth) vice chmn.; Larry Walkin (KRNU, Lincoln), secty.-treas.
7101 Mercy Rd., Suite 419, Omaha 68106; (402) 391-8236.

NEVADA BROADCASTERS ASSOCIATION
David T. Newman, pres.
P.O. Box 1928, Reno 89505.

NEW HAMPSHIRE ASSOCIATION OF BROADCASTERS
B. Allan Sprague, exec. dir.
Box 900, Manchester 03105; (603) 669-5144.

NEW JERSEY BROADCASTERS ASSOCIATION
Arnold Zucker, exec. dir.; Joe Knox Jr., pres.; Michael Levine, v.p.
NJBA, 31 Wine, St., Rutgers University, New Brunswick 08903; (201) 247-3337.

NEW MEXICO BROADCASTERS ASSOCIATION
Art Schreiber (KKOB-AM-FM, Albuerque), pres.; Paul Thorne (KGGM-TV), pres. elect; Dee Schelling, exec. dir.
790-9D Tramway Lane NE, Albuquerque 87122; (505) 299-6908.

NEW YORK STATE BROADCASTERS ASSOCIATION, INC.
Joseph A. Reilly, pres. & exec. dir.; Belinda Bouchard, admin. asst.
90 State St., Suite 530, Albany, 12207; (518) 434-6100.

NORTH CAROLINA ASSOCIATION OF BROADCASTERS
John Greene, pres.; Wade H. Hargrove, exec. dir.
Box 627, Raleigh 27602; (919) 821-7300.

NORTH DAKOTA BROADCASTERS ASSOCIATION
Dewey Heggen, pres.
Box 8116, Grand Forks 58202; (701) 777-2577.

OHIO ASSOCIATION OF BROADCASTERS, INC.
Dale V. Bring, exec. v.p.
100 E. Broad St., Suite 1206, Columbus 43215; (614) 228-4052.

OKLAHOMA ASSOCIATION OF BROADCASTERS
Richard Adams (KXII-TV, Ardmore), pres.; Linda Saunders, exec. dir.
4545 N. Lincoln, Oklahoma City 73105; (405) 528-2475.

OREGON ASSOCIATION OF BROADCASTERS
Sherwood "Skip" Hinman, pres.; Vern Mueller, exec. dir.
Box 20037, Portland 97220; (503) 257-3041.

PENNSYLVANIA ASSOCIATION OF BROADCASTERS
Richard Wyckoff, pres.; Robert Eolin, Jr., (WLYH-TV, Lancaster), chmn; Brian Danzis (WCMB/WMIX-FM, Harrisburg), vice chmn.
114 South St., Harrisburg 17101; (717) 233-3511.

RHODE ISLAND BROADCASTERS ASSOCIATION
John D. Sawhill, pres.; Roger E. Bouchard, exec. dir.
%WNRI Radio, 786 Diamond Hill Rd., Woonsocket 02895; (401) 769-0600.

ROCKY MOUNTAIN BROADCASTERS ASSOCIATION
Bernard J. Bustos, pres.; Henry Fletcher, exec. dir.
Box 220, Pocatello, Idaho 83204; (208) 233-5020.

SOUTH CAROLINA BROADCASTERS ASSOCIATION
William Saunders, pres.; Dr. Richard M. Uray, exec. mgr.
Univ. of South Carolina College of Journalism, Columbia
29208; (803) 777-6783.

SOUTH DAKOTA BROADCASTERS ASSOCIATION
John Goeman, pres.; Joe Copper, exec. dir.
1018 S. Lyndale, Sioux Falls 57105; (605) 334-2682.

TENNESSEE ASSOCIATION OF BROADCASTERS
Thomas R. King, exec. dir.; Dan Newberg, pres.
Box 40185, Nashville 37204; (615) 331-4535.

TEXAS ASSOCIATION OF BROADCASTERS
Ann Arnold, exec. dir.; Stephanie Glass, office mgr.
400 W. 15th St., Suite 305, Austin 78701; (512) 322-9944.

UTAH BROADCASTERS ASSOCIATION
James Burgoyne (KBLQ) pres.; Earl J. Glade Jr., exec. dir.
Box 401, Provo 84603; (801) 226-3094.

VERMONT ASSOCIATION OF BROADCASTERS
Mark Brady, pres.
%WFAD, Middlebury; (802) 388-2490.

VIRGINIA ASSOCIATION OF BROADCASTERS
Peter Easter, exec. dir.
620 Stagecoach Rd., Charlottesville 22901; (804) 977-3716.

VIRGINIA PUBLIC RADIO ASSOCIATION
Jim Miskimen, pres.; Jerry Glass, secty.-treas.
%WMRA Radio, Harrisonburg 22607; (703) 568-6221.

WASHINGTON STATE ASSOCIATION OF BROADCASTERS
Ron Hughes, pres.; Val Linburgh, secty.-treas.; Karmi Speece,
exec. dir.
111 Third Ave., Suite 712, Seattle 98101; (206) 625-0714.

WEST VIRGINIA BROADCASTERS ASSOCIATION
Dale B. Miller (WAJR/WVAQ, Morgantown), pres.; Marilyn
Fletcher, exec. dir.
2120 Weberwood Dr., South Charleston 25303; (304) 344-
3798.

WISCONSIN BROADCASTERS ASSOCIATION
Gary DeHaven (WISC-TV, Madison), chmn. of board; John
Laabs, pres.
44 E. Mifflin St., Suite 205, Madison 53703; (608) 255-2600.

WYOMING ASSOCIATION OF BROADCASTERS
Ray Lansing, exec. secty.-treas.
Box 1873, Cheyenne 82003; (307) 632-7622.

The Press

* **TRADE PUBLICATIONS**

* **NEWSPAPER LISTING**

Trade Publications

Quigley Publishing Company

Publishers of Motion Picture Almanac (Annual), Television and Video Almanac (Annual). 159 W. 53 St., New York, NY 10019; (212) 247-3100; Cable: Quigpubco, New York.

PRESIDENT AND PUBLISHER
 Martin Quigley, Jr.
VICE PRESIDENT & MANAGING DIRECTOR
 Robert McDonald
EDITOR-IN-CHIEF
 Jane Klain

LONDON BUREAU
 William Pay, Manager and London Editor; 15 Samuel Rd., Langdon Hills, Basildon, Essex, England. Tel.: 0268-417-055.

CANADIAN BUREAU
 Patricia Thompson, Editor; 1430 Yonge St., Suite 214, Toronto, Ont. M4T 1Y6 Canada.

FOREIGN CORRESPONDENTS
CHILE: Alan Hootnick, Camino Mirasol, 1955 Las Condes, Santiago, Chile.
EGYPT: Ahmed Sami, 4 El Ommara St., Apt. 13, Abbassia, Cairo.
FRANCE: Vernice Klier-Moskowitz, 80 Ave. Charles de Gaulle, Neuilly Sur Seine 92200 France.
GREECE: Rena Velissariou, 8432, Kolokotroni Str., Agia Paraskevi, Attikis, Athens. (804).
HOLLAND: Paul Silvius, 467 W. Halfront, 1183 JD Amstelveen, Netherlands.
INDIA: B. D. Garga, 55 Anita, Mt. Pleasant Rd., Bombay 400006, India.
JAPAN: A. C. Pinder, Whaley-Eaton Service, Central P.O. Box 190, Tokyo, Japan.
PAKISTAN: A.R. Slote, P.O. Box 7426, Karachi, 1–3.
SWITZERLAND: Gabriella Broggi, Via E. Maraini 20B, 6900 Massagna, Switzerland.

Motion Picture Almanac

(Annually) 159 W. 53 St., New York, NY 10019; (212) 247-3100; Cable: Quigpubco, New York.

EDITOR
 Jane Klain
BRITISH EDITOR
 William Pay
CANADIAN EDITOR
 Patricia Thompson

Television & Video Almanac

(Annually) 159 W. 53 St., New York, NY 10019; (212) 247-3100; Cable: Quigpubco, New York.

EDITOR
 Jane Klain
BRITISH EDITOR
 William Pay
CANADIAN EDITOR
 Patricia Thompson

Advertising Age

(Weekly) 740 Rush St., Chicago, IL 60611; (312) 649-5200; 220 E. 42 St., New York, NY 10017; (212) 210-0100.

CHAIRMAN
 Mrs. G. D. Crain
CHAIRMAN, EXECUTIVE COMMITTEE
 S. R. Bernstein
PUBLISHER
 Louis F. Demarco
PRESIDENT & EDITOR-IN-CHIEF
 Rance Crain

The American Cinematographer

(Monthly on the 1st—Semi-technical) Published by American Society of Cinematographers, Inc., 1782 N. Orange Dr., Hollywood, CA 90028; (213) 876-5080.

EDITOR
 George Turner
ASSISTANT EDITOR
 Jean Turner
ADVERTISING
 Angie Gollmann
CIRCULATION MANAGER
 Patty Armacost

Back Stage

(Weekly dealing with theatrical and nontheatrical films, television shows and commercials, cassettes, radio, and theater, published Friday), 330 W. 42 St., New York, NY 10036; (212) 947-0020; 5150 Wilshire Blvd., Los Angeles, CA 90036; (213) 936-5200; 100 E. Ohio St., Chicago, IL 60611; (312) 943-0051.

ADVERTISING DIRECTOR & PUBLISHER
 Ira Eaker
ASSOCIATE PUBLISHER
 Anthony Vagnoni
EDITOR
 Richard Miller

Back Stage TV, Film & Tape Production Directory

(Annually, March), 330 W. 42 St., New York, NY 10036; (212) 947-0020.

EDITOR
 Theresa Piti

Billboard

(Weekly dealing with records, music, entertainment artists, video hardware and software, etc., published Saturdays), 9107 Wilshire Blvd., Beverly Hills, CA 90210; (213) 273-7040; 1515 Broadway, New York, NY 10036, (212) 764-7300; 49 Music Square W., Nashville, TN 37203; (615) 321-4290; 806 15 St., N.W., Washington, D.C. 20005; (202) 783-3282.

PUBLISHER/EDITOR-IN-CHIEF
 Sam Holdsworth
ASSOCIATE PUBLISHER/DIRECTOR OF RESEARCH
 Marty Feely
MANAGING EDITOR
 Ken Schlager

Broadcasting—The News Magazine of the Fifth Estate

(Weekly on Monday; also publishes Broadcasting Yearbook every March.) Washington Headquarters: 1705 DeSales St., N.W., 20036; (202) 659-2340; New York: 630 Third Ave., 10017; (212) 599-2830; Hollywood: 1680 N. Vine St., 90028; (213) 463-3148.

PRESIDENT AND PUBLISHER
 Lawrence B. Taishoff
VICE PRESIDENT/OPERATIONS
 David N. Whitcombe
VICE PRESIDENT/MANAGING EDITOR
 Donald V. West

Celebrity Bulletin

(A chronicle of the day-to-day activities of celebrities in New York, Hollywood, London, Paris and Rome. Published daily.) 1780 Broadway, New York, NY 10019; (212) 757-7979.
PUBLISHER
Celebrity Service, Inc.

Celebrity Register

(A biographical index, published every two years) 1780 Broadway, Suite 300, New York, NY 10019; (212) 757-7979; 1 (800) FOR CELEBS.
PUBLISHER
Celebrity Service, Inc.
EDITOR
Earl Blackwell

Contact Book

(An entertainment industry directory, published annually) 1780 Broadway, New York, NY 10019; (212) 757-7979.
PUBLISHER
Celebrity Service, Inc.
EDITOR
Donnali Shor

Daily Variety

(Motion picture, television, homevideo, pay-TV, cable, radio, theatre, night clubs, daily) 1400 N. Cahuenga Blvd., Hollywood, CA 90028; (213) 469-1141.
EDITOR
Peter P. Pryor
ASSOCIATE PUBLISHER
Michael Silverman
MANAGING EDITOR
Richard Bozanich
MARKETING DIRECTOR
Pattikay Lee
PRODUCTION MANAGER
Bob Butler

Electronics

(Industry management magazine covering technology and business. Published monthly) VNU Business Publication Inc., Ten Holland Dr., Hasbrook Heights, NJ 07604; (201) 393-6000.
PUBLISHER
Jim Uhl
EDITOR-IN-CHIEF
J. Robert Lineback
EXECUTIVE EDITOR
Jeremy Young

Film News

(Published 4 times in the year by Film News Company. Spring, Summer, Fall, Winter) The international review of AV materials and equipment. Editoral and business office: Box 619, LaSalle, IL 61301.
EDITOR
J. Paul Carvico

Film Quarterly

(Quarterly; published Fall, Winter, Spring and Summer. A critical journal of motion pictures and their related arts; successor to *The Quarterly of Film, Radio and Television* and *The Hollywood Quarterly*.) Editorial, Sales, and Advertising office: University of California Press, Berkeley, CA 94720; (415) 642-6333.
EDITOR
Ernest Callenbach
Published by University of California Press

Hollywood Creative Directory

(Who's what and where in motion picture and television production and development. Published every four months.) 451 Kelton Ave., Los Angeles, CA 90024; (213) 208-1961. Organized 1987.
PUBLISHER/OWNER
David Sterling

Hollywood Report

(Quarterly) 917 S. Tremaine Ave., Hollywood, 90019, CA; (213) 939-2345.
EDITOR
Syd Cassyd

Hollywood Reporter, The

(Film, TV, entertainment daily) 6715 Sunset Blvd., Hollywood, 90028 CA; (213) 464-7411; and 1501 Broadway, New York, NY, 10036; (212) 354-1858.
PUBLISHER & EDITOR-IN-CHIEF
Tichi Wilkerson Kassel
EDITOR
Teri Ritzer
BUREAUS
NEW YORK: 1501 Broadway, New York, NY 10036; (212) 354-1858.
WASHINGTON D.C.: Rm. 1139, National Press Bldg., Washington DC, 20045; (202) 737-2828.
LONDON: 57 Duke St., London W.1.; 01-629/6765, 6766.

I.A.T.S.E. Official Bulletin

(Quarterly) 1515 Broadway, New York, NY 10036; (212) 730-1770.
EDITOR
James J. Riley

International Photographer

(Monthly, on the 5th) 7715 Sunset Blvd., Hollywood, CA 90046; (213) 876-0160.
PUBLISHER
International Photographer
EDITOR
George Toscas

International Motion Picture Almanac

(See Quigley Publications)

International Television and Video Almanac

(See Quigley Publication)

Journal of the Syd Cassyd Archives Academy of Television Arts & Sciences

(Quarterly) 917 S. Tremaine, Hollywood 90019, CA; (213) 939-2345.
EDITOR
Syd Cassyd

The Producer's Master-Guide

(Annual) 611 Broadway, Suite 807, New York, NY 10012; (212) 777-4002. International reference guide for producers in the motion picture, television, commercials, cable and videotape industries in the U.S., Canada, the Caribbean Islands, Bermuda, Ireland, the United Kingdom, New Zealand, and Australia.

PUBLISHER AND TREASURER
Shmuel Bension

QV Publishing, Inc.

250 E. Hartsdale Ave., Suite 36, Hartsdale, NY 10530; (914) 946-0590. Organized 1982. (Provides information about cable/television sports and addressability/pay-per-view, via newsletters, directories and other publications and seminars.)
PRESIDENT
Dantia Quirk

Radio-Electronics

(Monthly dealing with technical aspects of electronics, including TV, radio, computers, and electronic service technicians, high-fidelity enthusiasts and experimenters) 500B Bicounty Blvd., Farmingdale, NY 11735; (516) 293-3000.
PUBLISHER
Larry Steckler
EDITORIAL DIRECTOR
Art Kleiman
MANAGING EDITOR
Brian Fenton

SMPTE Journal

(Technical monthly) 595 West Hartsdale Ave., White Plains, NY 10607; (914) 761-1100.
EDITOR
Jeffrey B. Friedman
ADVERTISING MANAGER
Janice Baio

TV Facts, Figures, Film & TV

A Division of C.C. Publishing (Magazine for syndicated programming and promotion). 19 W. 44 St., Suite 812, New York, NY 10036; (212) 302-2680.
PUBLISHER
Harvey Seslowsky
VICE PRESIDENT & EDITOR-IN-CHIEF
Miss Avra Fliegelman

Television Digest

(Published weekly. Television Digest with Consumer Electronics, TV & Cable Action Update; Annual Television & Cable Factbook, Annual Cable & Station Coverage Atlas, Satellite Week, Video Week, Biweekly Public Broadcasting Report, Monthly Early Warning Report, Communications Daily, Bi-weekly Space Commerce Bulletin, Weekly Common Carrier) 2115 Ward Court, N.W., Washington, DC 20037; (202) 872-9200.
EDITOR & PUBLISHER
Albert Warren
EDITORIAL DIRECTOR
David Lachenbruch
EXECUTIVE EDITOR
Dawson B. Nail
SENIOR EDITOR & ASSOCIATE PUBLISHER
Paul L. Warren

Television Factbook

(Published annually by Warren Publishing, Inc.) 2115 Ward Court, N.W., Washington, DC 20037; (202) 872-9200.
EDITOR & PUBLISHER
Albert Warren
MANAGING EDITOR
Michael C. Taliaferro
EDITORIAL DIRECTOR
Mary Appel

Television Index

40-29 27th St., Long Island City, NY 11101, (718) 937-3990.
EDITOR & PUBLISHER
Jerry Leichter

Television/Radio Age

(Bi-weekly trade magazine) 1270 Ave. of the Americas, New York, NY 10020; (212) 757-8400.
PUBLISHER
Sol J. Paul
EDITOR
Jack Loftus
EXECUTIVE EDITOR
Alfred J. Jaffe
MANAGING EDITOR
Ed Rosenthal
ASSISTANT EDITORS
Bob Sobel, George Swisshelm, Jim Forkan
PRODUCTION DIRECTOR
Marvin Rabach
BRANCH OFFICES
6290 Sunset Blvd., Suite 315, Los Angeles, CA 90028; Keepers Lodge, Hatfield Park, Hatfield Herts, England, AL9 5P5; 716 S. Wayne St., Arlington, VA 22204.

Variety

(A Cahners Publication) (International entertainment business weekly, published Wednesdays) 475 Park Ave. S., New York, NY 10016; (212) 779-1100; 1400 N. Cahuenga Blvd., Hollywood, CA 90028; (213) 469-1141; 1483 Chain Bridge Rd., McLean, VA 22101; (703) 448-0510; 400 North Michigan Ave., Chicago, IL 60611; (312) 337-4984; *Paris:* 33 Champs Elysees, 75008 France; Phone 720-19-56; *Rome:* VARIETY, Via Bissolati, 20, 00187 Italy; 463-290. *London:* 34/35 Newman St., W1P 3PD England, 637-3663; *Madrid:* Calle Lagasca, 104, 28006, Spain; Phone 276-4262; *Sydney, Australia:* 1-7 Albion Place, 2000, N.S.W. Phone: 61-3124; *Toronto:* 74 Albany Ave., Ont.; (416) 531-1600; *Scandinavia:* 8 Skindegrade, Copenhagen, Denmark; Phone: 91-0040; *Munich:* Zittelstrasse, 4 Germany; Phone: 30-89130.
PUBLISHER
Syd Silverman
EDITOR
Roger Watkins
SALES
Martin Feldman

GREAT BRITAIN

Image Technology

(Technical monthly) Journal of the British Kinematograph, Sound and Television Society. 549 Victoria House, Vernon Place, London, WC1B 4DJ. Tel.: 01 242-8400.

Screen International

Published by King Publications Ltd. Weekly, covering news, reviews, comment and pictures of the film and television industries. 6-7 Great Chapel Street, London, W.1. Tel.: 01 43 5741.
PUBLISHER
Peter King
EDITOR
Peter Noble

FRANCE

Le Film Français

(Weekly French motion picture trade magazine) 103
Blvd. St. Michel Paris, France, 75005; U.S. office: 1403
Elevado, Los Angeles, CA 90026 (213) 556-3800.

PUBLISHER
Denis Jacob
EDITOR
Pierre Rival
U.S. EDITOR
Patricia Saperstein

Newspapers in Principal Markets of the U.S.

Arranged alphabetically by states, this list gives the names and addresses of newspapers in cities and market areas of over 100,000 population which maintain regular motion picture and television departments.

Alabama

Birmingham, **The News,** 2200 N. 4th Ave., 35202.
Birmingham, **Post-Herald,** 2200 N. 4th Ave., 35202.
Huntsville, **Times,** 2317 Memorial Pkway., 35807.
Mobile, **Mobile Press Register.,** 304 Government St., 36602.
Montgomery, **Advertiser,** 200 Washington Ave., 36104.

Arizona

Phoenix, **Gazette,** 120 E. Van Buren St., 85004.
Phoenix, **Republic,** 120 E. Van Buren St., 85004.
Tucson, **Arizona Daily Star,** 4850 S. Park Ave., 85726.

Arkansas

Little Rock, **Democrat,** Capitol Ave. & Scott, 72203.
Little Rock, **Arkansas Gazette,** 112 W. Third St., 72203.

California

Fresno, **Bee,** 1626 E St., 93706.
Glendale, **News Press,** 111 N. Isabel, 91209.
Long Beach, **Press-Telegram,** 604 Pine Ave., 90801.
Los Angeles, **Daily News,** P.O. Box 4200, 90042.
Los Angeles, **Herald-Examiner,** 1111 S. Broadway., 90054.
Los Angeles, **Times,** Times Mirror Sq., 90053.
Oakland, **The Tribune,** 401 13th St., 94612.
Pasadena, **Star News,** 525 E. Colorado St., 91109.
Riverside, **Press-Enterprise Co.,** 3512 14th St., 92502.
Sacramento, **Bee,** 2100 Q St., 95813.
Sacramento, **Sacramento Union Inc.,** 301 Capitol Mall, 95812.
San Bernardino, **Sun,** 399 "D" St., 92401.
San Diego, **DBA Union-Tribune,** 351 Camino de la Reina, 92108.
San Francisco, **Chronicle,** 901 Mission St., 94119.
San Francisco, **The Examiner,** 110 5th St., 94119.
San Jose, **Mercury-News,** 750 Ridder Park Dr., 95131.
San Pedro, **News Pilot,** 362 W. 7th St., 90733.
Santa Ana, **Orange County Register,** 625 N. Grand Ave., 92711.
Stockton, **Stockton Daily Record,** 530 E. Market St., 95202.
Torrance, **South Bay Breeze,** 5215 Torrance Blvd., 90503.
West Covina, **Tribune-San Gabriel Valley,** 1210 N. Azusa Canyon Rd., 91790.

Colorado

Denver, **The Post,** 650 15th St., 80202.
Denver, **Rocky Mountain News,** 400 W. Colfax Ave., 80204.

Connecticut

Bridgeport, **Post,** 410 State St., 06602.
Hartford, **Courant,** 285 Broad St., 06101.
New Haven, **Register,** 40 Sargent Dr., 06511.
Waterbury, **American-Republican, Inc.,** 389 Meadow St., 06702.

Delaware

Wilmington, **News-Journal Co.,** 831 Orange St., 19899.

District of Columbia

Washington, **Post,** 1515 "L" St., N.W., 20005.
Washington, **Times,** 3600 New York Ave., N.E., 20002.
Washington, **USA Today,** 1001 16th St. N.W., 20036.

Florida

Fort Lauderdale, **News,** 101 N. New River Drive E., 33301.
Fort Lauderdale, **Sun Sentinel,** 101 N. New River Drive E., 33301.
Jacksonville, **Florida Times-Union,** One Riverside Ave., 32201.
Miami, **Herald,** 1 Herald Plaza, 33101.
Miami, **The News,** 1 Herald Plaza, 33101.
Orlando, **Sentinel,** 633 N. Orange Ave., 32801.
St. Petersburg, **Times,** 1301 34th St. N., 33713.
Sarasota, **Herald Tribune,** 801 S. Tamiami Trail, 34236.
Tampa, **Tribune,** 202 S. Parker, 33606.

Georgia

Atlanta, **Journal-Constitution,** 72 Marietta St. N.W., 30303.
Columbus, **Ledger-Enquirer Newspapers,** 17 W. 12th St., 31902.
Macon, **Telegraph & News,** 120 Broadway, 31201.
Savannah, **Savannah News-Press,** 105-111 W. Bay St., 31402.

Hawaii

Honolulu, **Advertiser,** P.O. Box 3110, 96802.
Honolulu, **Honolulu Star-Bulletin, Inc.,** P.O. Box 3080, 96802.
Honolulu, **Hawaii Hochi,** 917 Kokea St., 96817.

Illinois

Chicago, **The Sun-Times,** 401 N. Wabash, 60611.
Chicago, **Tribune,** 435 N. Michigan Ave., 60611.
Joliet, **Herald News,** 300 Caterpillar Dr., 60436.
Lansing, **Daily Calumet & Pointer,** 18127 William, 60438.
Moline, **Daily Dispatch,** 1720 5th Ave., 61265.
Peoria, **Peoria Journal Star Inc.,** 201 S.W. Jefferson Ave., 61602.
Rock Island, **Argus,** 1724 4th Ave., 61202.
Rockford, **Register-Star,** 99 E. State St., 61105.
Waukegan, **News-Sun,** 100 W. Madison St., 60085.

Indiana

Evansville, **Courier & Press,** 201 N.W. 2nd St., 47701.
Fort Wayne, **Journal-Gazette,** 600 W. Main St., 46802.
Fort Wayne, **News Sentinel,** 600 W. Main St., 46802.
Gary, **Post-Tribune,** 1065 Broadway, 46402.
Hammond, **Times,** 417 Fayette St., 46320.
Indianapolis, **Star & News,** 307 N. Pennsylvania St., 46206.
South Bend, **Tribune,** 225 W. Colfax, 46626.

Iowa

Cedar Rapids, **Gazette,** 500 3rd Ave., S.E., 52401.
Davenport, **Quad City Times,** 124 E. 2nd St., 52808.
Des Moines, **Register & Tribune,** 715 Locust St., 50304.
Sioux City, **Journal,** 515 Pavonia St., 51101.
Waterloo, **Courier,** 501 Commercial St., 50704.

Kansas

Kansas City, **Kansan,** 901 N. 8th St., 66101.
Topeka, **Capital-Journal,** 616 Jefferson, 66607.
Wichita, **The Eagle and Beacon,** 825 E. Douglas St., 67201.

Kentucky

Lexington, **Herald-Leader,** Main & Midland, 40507.
Louisville, **The Courier-Journal & Times,** 525 W. Broadway, 40202.

Louisiana

Baton Rouge, **Advocate,** 525 Lafayette St., 70821.
New Orleans, **The Times-Picayune,** 3800 Howard Ave., 70140.
Shreveport, **Journal-Times,** 222 Lake St., 71102.

Maryland

Baltimore, **Sun,** 501 North, 21230.

685

Massachusetts

Boston, **Christian Science Monitor**, One Norway St., 02115.
Boston, **Globe**, 135 Morrissey Blvd., 02107.
Boston, **Boston-Herald**, 1 Herald Square, 02106.
New Bedford, **Standard-Times**, 555 Pleasant St., 02742.
Springfield, **Republican**, 1860 Main St., 01101.
Worcester, **Worcester Telegram & Gazette**, 20 Franklin St., 01601.

Michigan

Ann Arbor, **News**, 340 E. Huron St., 48106.
Detroit, **Free Press**, 321 W. Lafayette Blvd., 48231.
Detroit, **News**, 615 W. Lafayette Blvd., 48231.
Flint, **The Journal**, 200 E. 1st St., 48502.
Grand Rapids, **The Press**, 155 Michigan N.W., 49503.
Kalamazoo, **Kalamazoo Gazette**, 401 S. Burdick St., 49003.
Lansing, **State Journal**, 120 E. Lenawee St., 48919.
Muskegon, **Chronicle**, 981 Third St., 49443.
Royal Oak, **Tribune**, 4500 Delemere Blvd., 48073.
Saginaw, **News**, 203 S. Washington Ave., 48605.

Minnesota

Duluth, **News-Tribune**, 424 W. 1st., 55801.
Minneapolis, **Star & Tribune**, 425 Portland Ave., 55415.
St. Paul, **Pioneer Press Dispatch**, 345 Cedar St., 55101.

Mississippi

Biloxi-Gulfport, **Sun-Herald**, 1320 De Buys Rd., 39531.
Jackson, **Clarion Ledger-News**, 311 E. Pearl, 39201.

Missouri

Kansas City, **Star Times**, 1729 Grand Ave., 64108.
St. Louis, **The Post-Dispatch**, 900 N. Tucker Blvd., 63101.
Springfield, **Springfield News & Leader**, 651 Boonville, 65801.

Nebraska

Lincoln, **Journal-Star**, 926 "P" Street, 68501.
Omaha, **World-Herald**, 14th & Dodge, Sts., 68102.

Nevada

Las Vegas, **Review-Journal**, 1111 W. Bonanza, 89106.
Las Vegas, **Sun**, 121 S. Highland Ave., 89104.

New Hampshire

Manchester, **Union Leader**, 35 Amherst St., 03105.

New Jersey

Cherry Hill, **Courier-Post**, P.O. Box 5300, 08034.
Elizabeth, **Journal**, 295-299 N. Broad St., 07207.
Hackensack, **The Record**, 150 River St., 07601.
Jersey City, **Journal**, 30 Journal Square, 07306.
Neptune, **Asbury Park Press**, 3601 State Hwy. 66, 07753.
Newark, **Newark Star Ledger**, 1 Star Ledger Plaza, 07101.
Passaic-Clifton, **Herald-News**, 988 Main Ave., 07055.
Paterson, **News**, News Plaza & Straight St., 07509.
Trenton, **Times**, 500 Perry St., 08618.

New Mexico

Albuquerque, **Journal**, 7777 Jefferson N.E., 87109.
Albuquerque, **Tribune**, 7777 Jefferson N.E., 87109.

New York

Buffalo, **The Evening News**, 1 News Plaza, 14203.
Colonie, **Times-Union**, News-Plaza, 12211.
Melville, **Newsday**, 235 Pinelawn Rd., 11747.
New York City:
Brooklyn **Daily, Inc.**, 129 Montague St., Brooklyn, 11201.
The Daily News, 220 E. 42 St., 10017.
The Post, 210 South St., 10002
The Times, 229 W. 43 St.,10036.
The Village Voice, 842 Broadway, 10003.
Wall Street Journal, 200 Liberty St., 10281.
Niagara Falls, **Gazette**, 310 Niagara St., 14302.
Rochester, **Gannett News**, 55 Exchange St., 14614.

Rochester, **Times-Union**, 55 Exchange St., 14614.
Syracuse, **The Post-Standard**, Clinton Square, 13202.
Utica, **Observer-Dispatch**, 221 Oriskany Plaza, 13503.
Yonkers, **The Herald Statesman**, 733 Yonkers Ave., 10704.

North Carolina

Charlotte, **Observer**, 600 S. Tryon St., 28201.
Durham, **Durham Morning Herald**, 115-19 Market St., 27702.
Raleigh, **News & Observer**, 215 S. McDowell St., 27601.
Winston-Salem, **Journal**, 418 N. Marshall, 27102.

North Dakota

Fargo, **Forum**, 101 5th St., 58102.

Ohio

Akron, **The Beacon Journal**, 44 E. Exchange St., 44309.
Canton, **The Repository**, 500 Market Ave., South, 44702.
Cincinnati, **The Enquirer**, 617 Vine St., 45201.
Cincinnati, **Post**, 617 Vine St., 45201.
Cleveland, **The Plain Dealer**, 1801 Superior Ave., 44114.
Columbus, **The Dispatch**, 34 S. Third St., 43216.
Dayton, **News Journal-Herald**, 45 S. Ludlow St., 45402.
Toledo, **The Toledo Blade**, 541 Superior St., 43604.
Youngstown, **The Vindicator**, 107 Vindicator Square, 44501.

Oklahoma

Oklahoma City, **Daily Oklahoman**, 500 N. Broadway, 73125.
Tulsa, **The Tribune**, 315 S. Boulder Ave., 74102.
Tulsa, **The World**, 315 S. Boulder Ave., 74102.

Oregon

Portland, **The Oregonian**, 1320 SW Broadway, 97201.

Pennsylvania

Allentown, **The Morning Call**, 101 N. 6th St., 18105.
Erie, **The Times**, 20 E. 12th St., 16501.
Philadelphia, **The Inquirer**, 400 N. Broad St., 19101.
Philadelphia, **The News**, 400 N. Broad St., 19101.
Pittsburgh, **Post Gazette**, 50 Blvd. of Allies, 15222.
Pittsburgh, **Pittsburgh Press Co.**, 34 Blvd. of Allies, 15222.
Reading, **The Eagle**, 345 Penn St., 19601.
Scranton, **Tribune**, 338 N. Washington Ave., 18501.
Scranton, **The Times**, Penn & Spruce, 18501.

Rhode Island

Providence, **The Journal-Bulletin**, 75 Fountain St., 02902.

South Carolina

Columbia, **The State-Record**, P.O. Box 1333, 29202.

Tennessee

Chattanooga, **The News-Free Press**, 400 E. 11th St., 37401.
Knoxville, **The Journal**, 210 W. Church Ave., 37901.
Knoxville, **The News-Sentinel**, 208 W. Church Ave., 37901.
Memphis, **Commercial Appeal**, 495 Union Ave., 38103.
Nashville, **The Banner**, 1100 Broadway, 37203.
Nashville, **The Tennessean**, 1100 Broadway, 37203.

Texas

Abilene, **Reporter News**, 100 Cypress St., 79604.
Amarillo, **The Globe News**, 900 S. Harrison St., 79105.
Austin, **American-Statesman**, 166 E. Riverside Dr., 78704.
Beaumont, **The Enterprise**, 380 Walnut St., 77704.
Corpus Christi, **The Caller-Times**, 820 N. Broadway, 78401.
Dallas, **The Morning News**, Communications Center, 75222.
Dallas, **The Times Herald**, 1101 Pacific, 75202.
El Paso, **Herald-Post**, 401 Mills Ave., 79901.
El Paso, **Times**, 401 Mills Ave., 79901.
Fort Worth, **The Star-Telegram**, 400 W. 7th St., 76101.
Houston, **The Chronicle**, 801 Texas St., 77002.
Houston, **The Post**, 4747 Southwest Freeway, 77001.
Lubbock, **The Avalanche-Journal**, 710 Avenue "J", 79401.
San Antonio, **The Express News**, Avenue "E" & 3rd St., 78205.
San Antonio, **The Light**, 420 Broadway, 78205.

Waco, **Tribune-Herald,** 900 Franklin, 76703.
Wichita Falls, **The Times,** 1301 Lamar St., 76307.

Utah

Salt Lake City, **Deseret News,** 30 E. 1st St., South, 84110.
Salt Lake City, **The Tribune,** 143 S. Main St., 84101.

Virginia

Alexandria, **Gazette,** 717 N. St. Asaph St., 22313.
Arlington, **Northern Va. Sun,** 1227 N. Ivy St., 22201.
Newport News-Hampton, **The Daily Press,** 7505 Warwick Blvd., 23607.
Norfolk, **Virginian-Pilot,** 150 W. Brambleton Ave., 23501.

Richmond, **Times-Dispatch,** 333 E. Grace St., 23213.
Roanoke, **Times-World,** 201-09. W. Campbell Ave., 24011.

Washington

Seattle, **The Post-Intelligencer,** 101 Elliot Ave. West, 98119.
Seattle, **The Times,** Fairview Ave. N & John, 98111.
Seattle, **Daily Journal of Commerce,** 83 Columbia St., 98104.
Tacoma, **The News-Tribune,** 1950 S. State, 98405.

Wisconsin

Madison, **Capital-Times,** 1901 Fish Hatchery Rd., 53713.
Milwaukee, **The Journal,** 333 W. State St., 53201.
Milwaukee, **Sentinel,** 333 W. State St., 53201.

The Industry in
Great Britain and Ireland

* **INDUSTRY DEVELOPMENTS**

* **BRITISH ACADEMY OF FILM AND TELEVISION ARTS
  AWARDS (1987)**

* **PROGRAM CONTRACTORS**

* **SATELLITE CABLE BROADCASTERS**

* **PRODUCERS, DISTRIBUTORS & SERVICE COMPANIES
  AND PERSONNEL**

* **ORGANIZATIONS**

* **SERVICES**

* **BRITISH BASED EQUIPMENT/SERVICES**

British Year in Review

THE WINDS OF CHANGE dominated the television scene in Britain during 1988. The BBC (British Broadcasting Corporation) which is funded by the government-imposed licence fee on owners of TV sets faces a situation whereby the government might introduce legislation ending this system (estimated at £1,000 million annually), moving towards some form of subscription payment. It would be a revolutionary move with the BBC having to earn its keep. On the other hand, the commercial contractors, due to re-negotiate their contracts in 1992, have the IBA (Independent Broadcasting Authority) considering the possibility of offering their franchises to the highest bidder.

Alongside all this debate, the UK and indeed European industry is about to be hit by the PAY-TV invasion. However, the government has received a warning from an all-party group report expressing the need to preserve the best of British television, including its tradition for making high quality programmes. It recommends the BBC, funded by a licence fee of 'remarkable value' continue virtually unchanged in the medium-term but with all advertising-support television, Cable and Satellite regulated by a new Commercial Television Authority replacing the present IBA. Public service broadcasting would remain at the centre of a re-cast British service, with the interests of viewers rather than advertisers at the forefront. Other recommendations are that a fifth channel based on a network of local stations be established as soon as possible; Channel 4 would remain substantially as it is at present; British Satellite Broadcasting would be given a fair trial, at least until 1992, to establish its film subscription channel and franchises on two remaining DBS channels to be awarded as soon as possible after 1992.

Next year, instead of the current four channels, British viewers will be able to receive some twenty channels. Rupert Murdoch's News International plans an extensive involvement in satellite presentation with his SKY TV broadcasting a service of news, entertainment and free films. The Amstrad electronics company and others will be offering low-priced receivers to receive the new services. But that is very much for the future. At this reporting, there is very much a fluid situation with the cable market still relatively small in the UK and satellite yet to be launched. In the meantime, despite some fall-off in viewers, the industry here remains a very lucrative one.

Although a commercial television contract is no longer 'a licence to print money,' advertising revenue remains buoyant (estimated at £1,500 million in 1988) and has permitted the majority of contractors to earn good profits, thereby enabling them to expand into other areas such as investments in the Super Channel project which provides a satellite-to-cable service outside the IBA's jurisdiction, aimed at cable services in Western Europe.

A significant development has been the need to improve the quality and variety of programming. It is a trend that has led to increased access for independent producers to the schedules of both BBC and ITV, the commercial channel. ITV hopes to commission up to 175–225 hours of new networked material and 200–400 hours of new regionally-shown material, per calendar year. Currently, 15 regionally-based ITV companies each present on average some 107 hours of programming each week and an additional 24 hours of breakfast-time programmes. A few companies have extended their schedules and are now broadcasting through the night. Over 70% of the programmes shown on ITV are made by ITV companies themselves. The five major companies—Central, Granada, LWT, Thames and Yorkshire—take the prime responsibility for the provision of network programming for the rest of ITV.

The BBC's programme budget, reaching £20 million a year by the summer of 1990, would be earmarked for the independent sector, with such production accounting for 600 hours of the BBC's output in 1991–2.

All this, together with the proposed new PAY-TV outlets, certainly augurs well for the British, and other, production industries.

The vast majority of overseas material on the networks here still originates in the USA. ITV's and Channel 4's quota of overseas material is 14 percent of total programme output. This comprises theatrical motion pictures, TV films and series. Estimates of the prices paid by local contractors and the BBC for American shows are around $13,000 for half-hour episodes to between $50,000 and $3 million for a feature film.

The CEA (Cinematograph Exhibitors Association) continues to maintain its three-year holdback for theatrical films released in UK cinemas although it has conceded that there will be an automatic exclusion (in addition to that for short and foreign films) for any cinema film made for an audited production cost not exceeding £1.25 million. It has been a decision that led to a boost for Channel 4's Film on Four (two of its early successes were "My Beautiful Laundrette" and "Wish You Were Here") as more and more companies made both films and television programmes. However, this TV holdback by the exhibitors is again under threat by producers who claim it is now redundant. They maintain that video distributors can negotiate the early video release of a film and Satellite broadcasting makes the holdback outdated.

It is a move that will be strongly opposed by the CEA which states in its annual report that 'the implications to the whole of the film industry of a material reduction in the revenues which at present accrue from cinema exhibition would be extremely serious. At present, the initial audience for a film in the cinema pays a very high proportion of the total revenues accruing to film production. Later, films are acquired for showing on television, which is a secondary market and which plays a far less important role in recouping the original production costs. Apart from other markets, such as video, there are at present two quite separate box-offices for films, one derived from the cinema and one, albeit much smaller derived from television.'

Also, continues the report, 'any further reduction in the cinema-going audience will have serious social implications. Fewer cinemas, particularly in suburban and smaller town situations, would seriously reduce the already very limited number of places of entertainment and leisure available to the cinema audiences who are the least likely members of society to stay at home to watch any form of television.'

Although under threat by the plans for cable and satellite, home video remains a thriving business with the annual income to distributors exceeding £200 million with weekly audiences of over 25 million receiving their entertainment on cassettes. Both BBC Enterprises and the commercial contractors report increasing sales overseas. Two recent significant indications of the international nature of the business were the Rank Organisation's acquisition of the American company BHCP Video, now called Rank Video Services America, giving them the leading video duplication business in the world; and Television South's decision to takeover the American MTM group. So, on the threshold of its PAY-TV revolution, home entertainment via the TV set—whether transmitted by film, tape or laser—remains big business, for television is now a virtually universal feature of people's lives in the UK, with 97% of the population having access to it in their homes.

British Academy of Film and Television Arts (BAFTA) Awards (1987)

Film Production and Performance

The Michael Balcon Award for Outstanding British Contribution to Cinema: The Monty Python Team

The Best Film: Claude Berri, Jean de Florette

The Best Achievement in Direction: Oliver Stone, Platoon

The Best Original Screenplay: David Leland, Wish You Were Here

The Best Adapted Screenplay: Claude Berri/Gerard Brach, Jean de Florette

The Best Actress in a leading role: Anne Bancroft, 84 Charing Cross Road

The Best Actor in a leading role: Sean Connery, The Name of the Rose

The Best Actress in a supporting role: Susan Wooldridge, Hope and Glory

The Best Actor in a supporting role: Daniel Auteuil, Jean de Florette

The Best Score for a Film: Ennio Morricone, The Untouchables

The Best Foreign Language Film: Anna-Lena Wibom/Andrei Tarkovsky, The Sacrifice (Sweden/France)

The Best Short Film: Jonas Grimås, Artisten

Television Production and Performance

The Desmond Davis Award for Outstanding Creative Contribution to Television: Julia Smith

Best Single Drama: Mick Jackson, Lifestory

Best Drama Series/Serial: Andy Park/Tony Smith, Tutti Frutti

Best Factual Series: Paul Hamann, The Duty Men

Best Light Entertainment Programme: Geoff Posner, Victoria Wood on TV Special

Best Comedy Series: John Lloyd/Mandie Fletcher, Blackadder the Third

Best Children's Programme (Entertainment/Drama): Colin Shindler/Carol Wiseman, A Little Princess

Best Children's Programme (Documentary/Educational): Mike Beynon, The Really Wild Show

Best News or Outside Broadcast: Stewart Purvis, Special Edition of Channel 4 News—Coverage of the Zeebrugge Diaster

Best Actress: Emma Thompson, Fortunes of War/Tutti Frutti

Best Actor: David Jason, Porterhouse Blue

Best Light Entertainment Performance: Nigel Hawthorne, Yes, Prime Minister

Best Original Television Music: Christopher Gunning/Rick Lloyd, Porterhouse Blue

The Huw Wheldon Award: Ian Squires/Gillian Lynne, A Simple Man (L.S. Lowry)

The Writer's Award: Jonathan Lynn/Anthony Jay

The Richard Dimbleby Award: Esther Rantzen

The Foreign Television Programme: Gunther Walraff, Lowest of the Low (Ganz Unten)

1987 Television Award for Originality: Network 7

The Flaherty Documentary Award: Phil Agland, Baka—People of the Rainforest

The Best Animated Film: Bridget Appleby, The Reluctant Dragon

Government Units and Program Contractors

HOME OFFICE
Queen Anne's Gate, London, SW1H 9AT. Tel: 01-213-3000.

The Secretary of State for the Home Department is empowered to licence persons or corporate bodies to operate broadcasting stations as laid down in the Wireless Telegraphy Act, 1949. The BBC is incorporated by Royal Charter and operates under this and a License and Agreement granted on the 2nd April 1981. The provisions of the Charter and the License Agreement run to 31st December 1996. The Independent Broadcasting Authority operates under the Broadcasting Act 1981 which extends the life of the Authority until 31st December 1996 and under a licence that runs to the same dates.

BRITISH BROADCASTING CORPORATION
TELEVISION SERVICE
Television Centre, Wood Lane, London W.12. Tel: 01-743 8000.

Chairman of Governors: Marmaduke Hussey
Deputy Director General: John Birt
Managing Director, Television: Paul Fox
Controller BBC-1: Jonathan Powell
Controller BBC-2: Alan Yentob
Head of Presentation Department: (vacancy)
Community Programme Unit Editor: Tony Laryea
Head of Drama Group: Mark Shievas
Head of Light Entertainment Group: James Moir
Head of Sports Group and Events Group: Jonathan Martin
Head of Features and Documentary Group: Will Wyatt
Head of Science and Features: Mick Rhodes
Head of Music and Arts: Leslie Megahey
Head of School Broadcasting: Alan Rogers
Head of Religious Programmes: John Whale
Deputy Director News and Current Affairs: Ron Neil
Managing Editor News and Current Affairs: Ian Hargreaves
Editor News and Current Affairs Television: Tony Hall
Deputy Editor News and Current Affairs Television: Samir Shah
Head of Scenic Operations Television: W. O. Parkinson
Head of Costume Department: Mrs. J. Shardlow
Head of Television Make-up Department: Miss I. Mair
Head of Television Script Units: Miss S. Capon
BBC Enterprises Ltd. Chief Executive: J. Arnold-Baker
Head of Television Publicity: Keith Samuel
Controller Resource Operations, TV: Charles Paton
Assistant Controller, Resource Development Operations, Television: John Jarvie
Head of Engineering, Studio and Network TV: J. Hughes
General Manager International Relations: Malcolm Walker

INDEPENDENT BROADCASTING AUTHORITY
70 Brompton Road, London, SW3 1EY. Tel: 01-584 7011.

The Authority was created by Parliament in 1954 as the Independent Television Authority, to provide a comprehensive television service additional to that of the BBC. Under the terms of the Sound Broadcasting Act, 1972, the Authority was renamed the Independent Broadcasting Authority and its functions were extended to cover the provision of Independent Local Radio.

The Broadcasting Act 1980 provided for the setting up of the Channel Four Television Company as a subsidiary of the IBA; it started broadcasting in England, Scotland and Northern Ireland on November 2, 1982. A separate Welsh Fourth Channel Authority was also established by this Act; broadcasting on November 1, 1982. The Broadcasting Act 1981 has consolidated a number of Acts relating to the IBA.

The Authority selects and appoints the ITV & ILR programme companies; supervises the programmes provided by the contractors—and the Channel Four Television Company—and their scheduling; controls advertising, and builds, owns and operates transmitting stations. Fifteen ITV programme companies provide programmes in 14 regions of the United Kingdom (two companies operate in London). As a part of its review of the ITV system, the Authority, in December 1980, offered a contract to broadcast a new national breakfast-time television service, which started in February 1983, to TV-AM. In addition, changes were made to some ITV companies.

Some 46 Independent Local Radio stations now provide a programme service in areas of the United Kingdom (two companies operating in London).

Both ITV and ILR are financed mainly by the sale of advertising time.

The Members of the Authority are appointed by the Home Secretary and consist of a Chairman and Deputy Chairman and ten other members, of whom three make the interests of Scotland, Wales and Northern Ireland, respectively, their special care.

Chairman: The Rt. Hon. the Lord Thomson of Monifieth
Director General: John Whitney
Deputy Director General: Lady Littler
Director of Television: David Glencross
Director of Radio: Peter Baldwin
Director of Engineering: Dr. John Forrest
Director of Finance: Peter Rogers
Controller of Public Affairs: Colette Bowe
Controller of Advertising: Frank Willis
Deputy Director of Television: Miss Clare Mulholland
Head of Research: Barrie Gunter

INDEPENDENT BROADCASTING AUTHORITY GENERAL
ADVISORY COUNCIL

Drawn from various walks of life, the Council is appointed to give the IBA impartial advice on the general pattern and content of ITV and Channel 4 programmes.
Chairman: Mrs. D. D. Jackson, A.C.I.S.

INDEPENDENT BROADCASTING AUTHORITY ADVERTISING
ADVISORY COMMITTEE

The Committee, under the terms of the Broadcasting Act 1981, must be representative of organizations, authorities and persons concerned with standards of conduct of advertising including, in particular, the advertising of medical or surgical goods or services, and the public as consumers.
Chairman: Prof. A. L. Diamond

INDEPENDENT BROADCASTING AUTHORITY SCOTTISH
COMMITTEE

Chairman: J. R. Purvis

INDEPENDENT BROADCASTING AUTHORITY NORTHERN
IRELAND COMMITTEE

Chairman: Prof. J. F. Fulton

INDEPENDENT BROADCASTING AUTHORITY WELSH
COMMITTEE

Chairman: G. R. Peregrine.

INDEPENDENT TELEVISION NEWS LTD.
ITN House, 48 Wells Street, London, W1P 4DE. Tel: 01-637 2424. Telex 22101.

Chairman: George Russell
Editor and Chief Executive: David Nicholas, CBE

PROGRAM CONTRACTORS
(Appointed by the Independent Broadcasting Authority).

ANGLIA TELEVISION LTD.
Head office: Anglia House, Norwich, NR1 3JG. Tel: 0603 615151. Telex: 97424; FAX: 0603 631032. London Office: Brook House, Park Lane, London, W.1. Tel: 01408 2288. Telex: 25353. FAX: 01-493 2598.

EAST OF ENGLAND CONTRACTOR
Chairman: P.W. Gibbins
Directors: The Lord Buxton, D. S. McCall, D. T. Puttnam, P. C. Garner, P. W. Gibbins, Mrs. J. Nutting, P. G. Sharman, T. P. Wootton, Dr. Mary Archer, Timothy Colman, DCL, JP, M. J. Hughes.
Director of Programmes: P. C. Garner
Group Marketing Director: T. P. Wootton
General Manager: M. J. Hughes
Company Secretary: G. M. Rae

BORDER TELEVISION
The Television Centre, Carlisle, CA1 3NT, Cumbria. Tel: 0228 25101; London Office: 33 Margaret Street, London, W1N 7LA. Tel: 01-637 4363.

NORTHWEST ENGLAND—SOUTH SCOTLAND, NORTH NORTHUMBERLAND, AND ISLE OF MAN
Directors: The Earl of Lonsdale (Chairman), James L. Graham (Managing), T. M. Glover (Sales Director), P. Brownlow (Financial Director), M. Bragg, J. R. Wills, P. Corlay, M. Sutherland, H. J. Brewis, Miss M. E. Burkett, O.B.E., B.A., F.M.A., J.I.M. Smail, O.B.E., M.C., T.D., D.L., J. C. Clucas, Dr. June Paterson-Brown, D. W. Trimble, M.A.

Secretary: P. Brownlow
Chief Engineer: R. Dale
Controller of Programmes: P. Gorley
Assistant Controller of Programmes (Planning): E. Hadwin
Editor: L. Howell

CENTRAL INDEPENDENT TELEVISION PLC
(Transmission Area—The Midlands. Period—All Week)
West Midlands: Central House, Broad Street, Birmingham B1 2JP. Tel: 021 643 9898. *East Midlands:* TV Centre, Lenton Lane, Nottingham NG7 2NA. Tel: 0602 863322. *London:* 35/38 Portman Square, London W1H 9FH. Tel: 01-486 6688.

MIDLANDS CONTRACTOR
Chairman: Sir Gordon Hobday
Managing Director: Robert Phillis
Directors

Andy Allan	*(Director of Programmes)*
Cliff Baty	*(Director of Finance)*
Ellis Birk	
Charles Denton	*(Chief Executive Zenith)*
David Justham	*(Chairman, West)*
John Madocks, C.B.E. DL	*(Chairman, East)*
Howard Perlin	
Robert Maxwell, M.C.	
Dick Emery	*(Director of Sales)*
Alan Pankhurst	*(Director of Personnel & Industrial Relations)*

Jean Parker
Sir Leo Pliatzky, K.C.B.
John Jackson
L. Murray Thomson
Secretary: Colin A. Campbel
HEADS OF DEPARTMENTS
Director of Operations: Peter Gardner
Director of Personnel & Industrial Relations: Alan Pankhurst
Director of Programmes: Andy Allan
Director of Public Affairs: Marshall Stewart
Cable & Satellite Executive: Jeremy Taylor
Controller of Drama: Ted Childs
Controller, Education & Religion: Philip Grosset
Controller of Entertainment & Music: Jon Scoffield
Controller of Features Group: Richard Creasey
Controller of News & Current Affairs: Robert Southgate
Controller of Programme Planning & Presentation: John Terry
Controller of Sport: Billy Wright, C.B.E.
Controller of Young People' Programmes: Lewis Rudd
Controller of Public Affairs: Keith Smith
Studio Controller (West): Dave Davidovitz
Studio Controller (East): Peter Pearson
Chief of Press & Publicity Officer, West: John Palmer
Head of Production Planning: Tony Page
Head of Sport (West): Gary Newbon
Head of Rights Negotiations: Dorothy Viljoen
Chief of Engineering: Gerry Kaye
Chief Press Officer: Alan Deeley
Legal Adviser: Colin A. Campbell

CHANNEL FOUR TELEVISION
60 Charlotte Street, London, W1P 2AX. Tel: 01-631 4444. Telex 892355. FAX: 01-637 4872.

Chairman: Sir Richard Attenborough
Chief Executive: Michael Grade
Managing Director: Justin Dukes
Director of Programmes: Liz Forgan
Director of Finance: David Scott
Director of Acquiring and Sales: Colin Leverthal
Director and General Manager: Frank McGettigan

CHANNEL TELEVISION
The Television Centre: Rouge Bouillon St. Heller, Jersey. Tel: Jersey 73999. Telex 4192265 (TVJYG).

Chairman: Major J. R. Riley.
Directors: Mrs. M. Kay Mouat, J. C. Rowe, D. le Marquand, G. R. Dorey, Mrs. A. Wonfor.
Managing Director: John Henwood.
Director of Programmes: John P. Henwood.
Director of Sales and Marketing: Michael J. Le Cocq
Director of Finance: Euan MacGregor

GRAMPIAN TELEVISION LTD.
Queen's Cross, Aberdeen, AB9 2XJ: Scotland. Tel: 0224 646464; Telex: 73151. Fax: 0224 635127 Albany House, 68 Albany Road, West Ferry, Dundee DD5 1NW Tel: 0382-739363; Advertising: 0382-739149, Telex 76563. 6 Manor Place, Edinburgh EH3 7DD Tel: 031- 226-3926, Telex 728139. 23-25 Huntly Street, Inverness IV3 5PR Tel: 0463-242624; Advertising 0463-242626, Telex 75655. 29 Glass-house Street, London W1R 5RG Tel: 01-439-3141, Telex 267912, Fax 01-439-1498.

NORTH SCOTLAND CONTRACTOR
NON-EXECUTIVE DIRECTORS:
Chairman: Sir Iain Tennant, K.T.
Deputy Chairman: Dr. Calum A. MacLeod, M.A., LL.B., LL.D.

Douglas F. Hardie, C.B.E., J.P., Fiona Lyall, M.B., Ch.B., D.P.H., Alistair Mair, M.B.E., B.Sc., Angus Stewart Macdonald, C.B.E., Sir George Sharp, O.B.E., J.P.
EXECUTIVE DIRECTORS:
Chief Executive: Donald H. Waters, C.A.
Director of Television: Robert Christie
Company Secretary: Graham Good, C.A.
Sales and Marketing Director: Neil R. Welling Dip M, MInst M
EXECUTIVES:
Area Sales Manager: Richard Gow
Head of Documentaries: Ted Brocklebank
Head of News and Current Affairs: Alistair Gracie
Sales Controller: Christopher Kidd MInst M
Publicity & Promotions Executive: Michael J. McLintock, M.A., D.I.P. C.A.M.
Production Executive: John Hughes
Production Services Executive: Eric M. Johnstone
Chief Engineer: Alec Ramsey
Sales Administration Manager: John R. Stacey

GRANADA TELEVISION LTD.
Granada TV Centre, Manchester 3. Tel: 061-832 7211. 36 Golden Square, London W.1. Tel: 01-734-8080. News Centre, Albert Dock, Liverpool L3 4BA; News Centre, White Cross, Lancaster LA1 4XQ; News Centre, Bridgegate House, Chester.

LANCASHIRE CONTRACTOR
Directors: D. E. Plowright (Chairman), A. Bernstein (Deputy Chairman), Prof. J. Ashworth, Lord Evans of Claughton, D. H. Harker, N. Phillips, A. Quinn (Managing Director), S. Towneley, M. Wall, A. Mutch (Secretary).
Granada International: Vivien Wallace (Chief Executive)

HTV LTD.
The Television Centre, Culverhouse Cross, Cardiff CF5 6XJ. Tel: Cardiff 590590. Television Centre, Bristol BS4 3HG. Tel: Bristol 778366. Scottish Life House, Bridge St., Manchester, Tel: 061-834 3765. London Sales Office: 99 Baker Street, London, W1-M 2AJ. Tel: 01-486 4311.

WALES AND WEST OF ENGLAND CONTRACTOR
Chairman: G. E. McWatters
Managing Director: P.S.B.F. Dromgoole
Sales Director: C. D. Romaine
Research Executive: I. Platt
Secretary: G. S. Tovey, FCIS, FCA.

LWT
South Bank Television Centre, London SE1 9LT. Tel: 01-261 3434.

LONDON CONTRACTOR—Friday 5:15 p.m. to Monday 6:00 a.m.
Chairman and Managing Director: Brian Tesler, C.B.E.
Director of Programmes: Greg Dyke
Group Finance Director: Peter McNally
Sales Director: Ron Miller
Secretary: Judith T. Thomas
Director of Personnel and Administration: Roy van Gelder
Director of Production: Peter Cazaly
Director of Corporate Affairs: Barry Cox

RADIO TELEFIS EIREANN
Donnybrook Dublin 4, Ireland: Tel: (01) 693111. London Office: Ireland House, 150 New Bond Street, London, W1Y OHD Tel: 01-493 8921. NATIONAL NETWORK OF THE REPUBLIC OF IRELAND.

Chairman: James P. Culliton
Director-General: Vincent Finn
Asst. Director-General: R. K. Gahan
Asst. Director-General: J. P. Sorohan
Director of Public Affairs: D. Holden
Director of Television Programmes: Bob Collins
Director of Radio Programmes: Michael Carroll
Director of News: Weslay Boyd

SCOTTISH TELEVISION, Plc
Cowcaddens, Glasgow, G2 3PR Scotland. Tel: 041 332 9999. Telex 77388. 7 Adelaide Street, London WC2 N4L Tel: 836 1500. Telex 27622; The Gateway, Edinburgh EH7 4AH, Tel: 031 557 4554; Suite 306, Sunlight House, Quay Street, Manchester M33JY. Tel: 061-834 7621

CENTRAL SCOTLAND CONTRACTOR
DIRECTORS:
Sir Campbell Fraser, LL.D., D.Univ., *Chairman*
William Brown, C.B.E., *Managing Director and Deputy Chairman**
Alan Chilton, *Director of Sales**
Ferdi Coia, *Director of Facilities**
Gus Macdonald, *Director of Programmes**
Alan L. Montgomery, *Finance Director**
Sir Kenneth Alexander, LL.D., D.Univ.
Gavin Boyd, C.B.E.
Rev. Robin D. Buchanan-Smith
Mrs. Dorothy Dunnett
Charles A. Fraser, C.V.O., D.L.
Gavin Laird
  *Members of the Executive Board.

Stevenson *(Controller, UK Regional Sales)*; M. Thornhill *(Controller Personnel and Staff Relations)*; J. Willis *(Contoller of Documentaries and Current Affairs)*; K. R. Bellini *(Head of Programme Purchasing)*; F. W. Cieslik *(Contracts Manager)*; R. J. Coyle *(Company Secretary)*; M. E. Crossley *(Head of Press & Public Relations)*; D. M. Dallas *(Head of Science & Features)*; A. M. Drury *(Head of Casting)*; D. Bould *(Deputy Commercial Director)*; G. Ironside (Head of Local Programmes & Sport); C. Jelley *(Head of Education, Children's Programmes & Religion)*; Miss S. A. Mason *(Head of Publications & Merchandising)*; K. A. Morgan *(Head of Music)*; J. Q. Rogers *(Chief Engineer)*; W. P. Rogers *(Head of Production Operations)*; Mrs. S. E. Ryle *(Head of Publicity)*; P. H. Smale *(Head of Technical Operations)*; J. B. Smith *(Head of Programme Administration)*.

Satellite—Cable Broadcasters

ABERDEEN CABLE SERVICES
303 King Street, Aberdeen, AB2 3AP, Scotland. Tel: 0224 649444

THE ARTS CHANNEL
P.O. Box 7, Ebbw Vale, Gwent NP3 5YP. Tel: 496 306995.

BRIGHTSTAR
Visnews Ltd., Cumberland Avenue, London, NW10 7EH. Tel: 01-965 7733. Telex: 22678. FAX: 01-965 0620.

BRITISH CABLE SERVICES
Southern House, 1-4 Cambridge Terrace, Oxford OX1 1UD. Tel: 0865 250110

BT VISION
Euston Tower, 286 Euston Road, London, NW1 3DG. Tel: 01-728 3798

BRITISH SATELLITE BROADCASTING (BSB)
The Park Lane Suite, 14 Old Park Lane, London, W1Y 3LH. Tel: 01-409 0303. FAX: 01 499 0671.

CABLETEL COMMUNICATIONS
The Fieldway, Bristol Road, Greenford, Middx: UB6 8UN. Tel: 01-575 9000.

CABLEVISION
Central Hall Buildings, High Street, Wellingborough, Northants: NN8 4HT. Tel: 0933 222078

CLYDE CABLE VISION
40 Anderston Quay, Glasgow, G3 8DA, Scotland. Tel: 041 221 7040.

COVENTRY CABLEVISION
Whitley Village, London Road, Coventry CV3 4HE. Tel: 0203 505070.

CNN INTERNATIONAL
25/28 Old Burlington Street, London, W1X 1LB. Tel: 01-434 9323.

THE CHILDREN'S CHANNEL
44-46 Whitfield Street, London, W1P 5RF. Tel: 01-580 6611.

CROYDON CABLE TV
Communications House, Blue Riband Estate, Roman Way, Croydon, Surrey CR2 6RA. Tel: 01 760 0222.

EAST LONDON COMMUNICATIONS
ELT House, 2 Mill Harbour, London, E14 9TE. Tel: 01 538 4510

EUROSPORT
31-36 Foley Street, London, W1P 7LB. Tel: 01-636 4077.

THE LANDSCAPE CHANNEL
South Bank House, Black Prince Road, London, SE1. Tel: 01-587 1011.

THE LIFESTYLE CHANNEL
The Quadrangle, 180 Wardour Street, London, W1V 8AA. Tel: 01 439 1177.

PREMIERE
7 D'Arblay Street, London, W1A 2AD. Tel: 01-434 0611.

SCREENSPORT
The Quadrangle, 180 Wardour Street, London, W1V 4AE. Tel: 01-439 1177.

SKY CHANNEL
31-36 Foley Street, London, W1P 7LB. Tel: 01 636 4077.

SUPER CHANNEL
19-21 Rathbone Place, London, W1P 1DF. Tel: 01 631 5050.

SWINDON CABLE
Newcombe Drive, Hawksworth Estate, Swindon SN2 1TU. Tel: 0793 615601

TELEVISION BROADCASTING COMPANY
New Roman House, 10 East Road, London, N1. Tel: 01 251 1533.

WESTMINSTER CABLE CO.
87-89 Baker Street, London, W1M 1AJ. Tel: 01-935 6699

WINDSOR TELEVISION
The Keep, 21 Victoria Street, Windsor, SL4 1YE. Tel: 0753 856345

TV Program Material—
Producers, Distributors and Service Companies

ABACUS PRODUCTIONS LTD.
731 Shelton Street, London WC2; Tel: 01-240 1277; Cables: ABAFILMS LONDON.

Directors: John Mackey (Chairman), Ron Trainer (Managing), Betty J. Martin.
Producers of TV and cinema commercials on both film and video. Matte process, stop motion, model animation, own studios, 2 stages, cove, 2 cutting rooms, Preview Theatre. Rostrum techniques, front projection screen.

ABC SPORTS INTERNATIONAL INC.
8 Carburton Street, London, W1P 7DT. Tel: 01-636 7366. Telex: 23625 ABC5PT G.

ADVISION LTD.
23 Gosfield Street, London, W1P 7HB. Tel: 01-580 5707. Telex: 28668; FAX: 01-631 1457.

Sound recording facilities: 3 studios, max. capacity 50 musicians. All studios have sound to picture facilities. Digital editing suite. Mobile recording studio for location work.

AEROFILMS
Gate Studios, Station Road, Boreham Wood, Herts: WD6 1EJ; Tel: 01-207 0666. Fax: 01-207 5433.

AIR-TIME PRODUCTIONS LTD.
50-Frith Street, London, W.1. Tel: 01-734 9304.

Director: Johnny Fielder.

ALLIED VISION LTD.
360 Oxford Street, London, W1N 9HA. Tel: 01-409 1984.

ALPHA FILMS LTD.
Unit 1, McKay Trading Estate, Kensal Road, London, W10 5BX. Tel: 01-960 8211. Telex: 291877 Vision G.

JOHN ANDERSON HIRE
Court Lane, Iver, Bucks. Tel: Iver 653737 (production facilities).

ANDERSON BURR PARTNERSHIP LTD.
Bray Studios, Water Oakley, Windsor, Berks. LSL4 5UGTel: 0628 22111. FAX: 0628 784713.

EAMONN ANDREWS STUDIOS LTD.
Television Club, 46/48 Harcourt Street, Dublin, Ireland. Tel: Dublin, 758891.

Directors: Eamonn Andrews, Dermod Cafferky, Lorlan Bourke.
(Tape, disc-recording, filming, Radio & TV programme contractors.)

ANIMALS UNLIMITED
Careys Wood, Smallfield, Surrey: (Animal agency). Tel: 034 284-2400.

(Animal agency.)

ANVIL FILM & RECORDING GROUP LTD.
Denham Studios, North Orbital Rd., Denham, Nr. Uxbridge, Middx. Tel: 0895 833522. Telex: 934704. FAX: 0895 833617.

Directors: R. W. Keen, K. Somerville, C. Eng. MIERE., Peter Gray.
(Documentaries, etc.)

ARMADA PRODUCTIONS
86/88 Wardour Street, London WIV 3LF. Tel: 01-734 6312.

Managing Director: J. D. Dooley.

ATHOS FILM PRODUCTIONS LTD.
65 High Street, Hampton Hill, Middx. TW12 1NH. Tel: 01-783 0533. Telex: 28905 Ref. 325.

Directors: P. G. A. Bucknall, The Viscount Portman, D. B. Bucknall, R. Orr-Ewing.
(Production, video and film, 35/16mm.)

AUSTRALIAN BROADCASTING CORPORATION
54 Portland Place, London, WIN 4DY. Tel: 01-631 4456. Cables: Austcast, London. Telex: 263897 (News) 23494 (Admin.). FAX: 01-323 1125.

Bureau Chief (Europe): J. Highfield.

AUSTRALIAN FILM COMMISSION
2nd Floor, Victory House, 99-101 Regent Street, London W1. Tel: 01-734 9383. Telex: 28711 Ausfilm. G.

AUTOCUE LTD.
Autocue House, 265 Merton Road, London, SW18 5JS. Tel: 01-870 0104. Telex: Autocue Telexir 885039 Autocu G.

Contact: Mick Gould
(Computer & closed circuit prompting facilities for film, TV and conferences; Aston Caption Charactor Generator Hire.)

BBC ENTERPRISES LTD.
Woodlands, 80 Wood Lane, London W12 OTT. Tel: 01-743 5588 & 01-576 0202. Cables: Telecentre London, Telex: 934678 & 265781; Overseas Sales Offices: 80 William Street, Sydney, New South Wales 2011, Australia; Distributors for U.S.A.; Lionheart Television International, 1762 Westwood Boulevard, Los Angeles, CA 90024, U.S.A.; Lionheart Television: 630 Fifth Avenue, Suite 2220, New York, NY 10111, USA.

Director of Programme Sales: Keith Owen.

BOULTON-HAWKER FILMS LTD.
Hadleigh, Ipswich, Suffolk 1P7 5BG. Tel: 0473 82 2235.

Directors: K. P. Boulton, M. J. Boulton, N. H. L. Rea, D.A. Boulton.

BRENT WALKER FILM & THEATRE DIVISION
Knightsbridge House, 197, Knightsbridge, London SW7 1RB. Tel: 01-225 1941. Telex: 23639.

BRITISH DIRECT TELEVISION LTD.
3-4 Woking Business Park, Woking, Surrey GU21 5JY. Tel: 04862 27676.

Directors: Lawrence R. Greetham, Simon D. Currey, Sue M. Greetham.

BRITISH LION SCREEN ENTERTAINMENT
Pinewood Studios, Pinewood Road, Iver, Bucks. 5L0 0NH. Tel: 0753 651700. Telex: 847505.

Chairman and Chief Executive: Peter R. E. Snell.

BRITISH SCREEN
37-39 Oxford Street, London, W1R 1RE. Tel: 01-434 0291. Telex: 888694 BRISCR G. FAX: 01-434 9933.

Executive Officer: Simon Relph.

BRITISH TRANSPORT FILMS LANSDOWNE (VAULTS) LTD.
Imperial Studios, Maxwell Road, Boreham Wood, Hertfordshire, WD6 1WE Tel: 01-207 4664.

BRYON PARKIN ASSOCIATES LTD.
37 Dover Street, London, W1X 3RA. Tel: 01-950 5151.

CAMERA LOCATION SERVICES
16 St. James Close, St. John's Woking, Surrey. Tel: 04862 4645.

(Researchers, suppliers film and photographic locations.)

CANADIAN BROADCASTING CORPORATION
43-51 Great Titchfield Street, London, W1P 8DD Tel: 01-580 0336 Telex: 23771.

CARLTON TELEVISION LTD.
St. John's Wood Studios, St. John's Wood Terrace, London, NW8 6PY. Tel: 01-722 9255. Fax: 01-483 4264.

Managing Director: Barry Johnstone

CASTLE COMMUNICATIONS
Unit 7, Merton Road Industrial Estate, 271 Merton Road, London SW18 5JS Tel: 01-871 2022. Telex: 911515 CASCOM G 01-871 1419, Fax: 01-871 0470

CAVALIER FILMS LTD.
34 Deacon's Hill Road, Elstree, Herts. Tel: 01-953 1403.

Directors: D. T. Rogers, A. V. Kimber.
(Specialized films, documentary, commercials.)

CBS BROADCAST
6 Albemarle Street, London, W.1.

CBS NEWS
100 Brompton Rd., London, S.W.3. Tel: 01-584 3366. Telex: 916 319. Cables: Colnews London.

(News, radio and TV coverage.)

CBS/FOX VIDEO
Perivale Industrial Park, Greenford, Middlesex UB6 7RU. Tel: 01-997 2552. Telex: 8951742. FAX: 01-991 0251

CENTRAL OFFICE OF INFORMATION
Hercules Road, London, SE1 7DU. Tel: 01-261 8495.
Films and Television Division: *Director:* John Hall.
Radio Services: *Head:* Eric Turnbull.

CHATSWORTH TELEVISION
97-99 Dean Street, London, W1V 5RA. Tel: 01-734 4302. Telex: 28604 Ref. 890. FAX: 01-437 3301.

ROGER CHERRILL LTD.
65-66 Dean Street, London W1V 6PL. Tel: 01-437 6411. FAX: 01-437 6411.
(Post sync dialogue, dubbing and effects, film and TV production, post production.)

CHESS VALLEY FILMS LTD.
Film House, Little Chalfont, Bucks: HP7 9PY. Tel: 02-404 2222 and 2020.
Directors: Ronald E. Haddock, F.B.I.P.P., P. M. Trudi Drayton, Heather M. Davies, MBKSTS.
Production 35/16mm film broadcast and non-broadcast TV and allied services.)

CHRYSALIS VISUAL PROGRAMMING
12-13 Stratford Place, London, W1N 9AF. Tel: 01-408 2355. Telex: 21753.

CINE-LINGUAL SOUND STUDIOS LTD.
27-29 Berwick Street, London, W1V 3RF. Tel: 01-437 0136.
Directors: A. Anscombe, P. J. Anscombe, M. Anscombe, D. J. Old.

CINEMA VERITY LTD.
Cannon Elstree Studios, Borehamwood, Herts: WD6 1JG. Tel: 01-953 1600. Telex: 922436 EFILMS G. Cables: EMIFILM Borehamwood. Fax: 01-207 0860.
Producer: Verity Lambert.

CINESOUND EFFECTS LIBRARY LTD.
Imperial Studios, Maxwell Road, Elstree Way, Boreham Wood, Herts WD6 IWE. Tel: 01-953 5837 and 5545, 1587, 4904.
(Sound effects.)

CINE VIDEO LTD.
245 Old Marylebone Road, London NW1 5QT. Tel: 01-402 8385.

CINEVISTA LTD.
Suite 4, 3 Bateman Street, London, W.1. Tel: 01-437 7187.
Directors: John Simmons, Cecilia Simmons.
(Entertainment and sponsored material.)

COLOUR VIDEO SERVICES LTD.
22-5 Portman Close, Baker Street, London, W1H 4BE. Tel: 01-486 2881.
Chairman: Roland Chase.
Managing Director: H. Manley.
(Superscan tape-to-film transfer. 16mm or 35mm, Cassette Duplication, Telecine, Conference Centre, equipment hire.)

COLUMBIA PICTURES TELEVISION
A Division of Columbia Pictures Corporation Ltd. St. Margaret's House, 19/23 Wells Street, London, W1P 3FP. Tel: 01-637 8444. Telex: 263392 COLP1C G. Cables: Columfilm, London.
Vice President, European Production: Tim Vignoles.
Vice President, European Sales: Nicholas Bingham.
(Production and distribution TV film series.)

CRANEZOOM LTD.
28 Saint Mary le Park Court, Albert Bridge Road, London, SW11 4PJ. Tel: 01-223 0034.

CROSSBOW FILMS LTD.
42 Connaught Square, London, W2 2HD. Tel: 01-724 6966. Telex: XBOW 21464.

CROWN TELEVISION PRODUCTIONS PLC.
Crown Television Centre, Church Road, Claygate, Esher, Surrey KT10 0JP. Tel: 0372 69111. Telex: 8811232 GREENS G.

C.T.S. STUDIOS LTD.
The Music Centre, Engineers Way, Wembley, Middlesex. Tel: 01-903 4611. Telex: 923400.
Contact: Peter Harris.

CTVC
Hillside Studios, Merry Hill Road, Bushey, Watford WD2 1DR. Tel: 01-950 4426.
(Production and post production, film and video library hire facilities.)

CUCUMBER STUDIOS LTD.
19/21 Heddon Street, London, W1. Tel: 01-437 0109.

CYGNET LTD.
Bilton Centre, Coronation Road, High Wycombe, Bucks HP12 3TA. Tel: 0494 450541. Telex: 83659 BIGGSC G.
Managing Director: D. N. Plunket.

DANDELION DISTRIBUTION LTD
49 St. Peter's Street, London, N1 8JP. Tel: 01-354 2472. Telex: 27972 TVUIN.

DEE & CO. LTD
46 Potters Lane, Barnet Herts. EN5 5BE. Tel: 01-449 7533. Telex: 946240 CWEASY G Ref: 19028490

DE LANE LEA SOUND CENTRE
75 Dean Street, London, W.1. Tel: 01-439 1721.
(Sound recording, foreign version dubbing, editing facilities.)

DE WOLFE LTD.
80-88 Wardour Street, London, W1V 3LF Tel: 01-439 8481.
Directors: James de Wolfe, Gordon Chambers, Warren de Wolfe. (Library recorded music, original scores, Angel Recording Studios Ltd.)

WALT DISNEY CO. LTD.
31-32 Soho Square, London, W1V 6AP. Tel: 01-734 8111. Telex: 21532. FAX 01-4398741.
Managing Director: Etienne de Villiers.

DRAKE AUDIO VISUAL
89 St. Fagans Road, Fairwater, Cardiff CF5 3AE.
Managing Director: R. G. Drake.
Marketing Director: H. Drake.

DRUMMER FILMS LTD.
14 Haywood Close, Pinner HA5 3LQ.
Managing Director: Martin M. Harris (Producer).

DUCK LANE FILM PRODUCTIONS LTD.
8 Duck Lane, London, W1V1FL Tel: 01-439 3912. Telex: 25554.
Director: R. Andrews.

EDUCATIONAL & TELEVISION FILMS LTD.
247a Upper Street, London, N1-1RU. Tel: 01-226 2298.
General Manager: Stanley Forman.

ELECTRONIC PUBLISHING CO. LTD.
68-70 Wardour Street, London, W1V 3HP. Tel: 01-734 1874. Telex: Peclon 25554.

ELEPHANT VIDEO LTD.
15-17 Old Compton Street, London, W1V 5PJ. Tel: 01-437 9541. Cables: Eaglepix, London, W.1. Telex: 928152 GAL-AFI G.
Directors: Barry Jacobs, A. Jacobs.

ENTERTAINMENT FILM PRODUCTIONS LTD.
27 Soho Square, London, W1V 5FL. Tel: 01-439 1606. FAX: 01-734 2483. Telex: 262428 ENT VIF.
Directors: Michael L. Green, Nigel Green, Trevor H. Green.

ENTERTAINMENT IN VIDEO LTD.
27 Soho Square, London, W1V 5FL. Tel: 01-439 1979. Telex: 262428 ENTVIF. Fax: 734 2483.
Directors: Michael L. Green, Nigel Green, Trevor H. Green.

EPA INTERNATIONAL PROGRAMMERS LTD.
P.O. Box 228, London SW16 1BP. Tel: 01-677 7523.

EUREKA LOCATION MANAGEMENT
16 Broadwick St., London, W1V 1FH. Tel: 01-734 4100, 734 1787, 734 9451. Telex: 265 871, answerback MONREF G, quoting ref. 76:WJJ106. Electronic mail—Telecom gold.
Head of Operations: Ian Lloyd

EUSTON FILMS LTD.
365 Euston Road, London, NW1 3AR. Tel: 01-387 0911
Production Controller: Bill Launder.

EWART TELEVISION
Wandworth Plain, London, SW18 1ET. Tel: 01-874 0131. Telex: 929509. FAX: 01-871 9737.
Managing Director: Keith Ewart.
(Full studio and post production facility.)

EYELINE FILM AND VIDEO LTD.
77 Dean Street, London, W.1. Tel: 01-734 3391. Telex: 265351.

Directors: Harold Orton, Jacki Roblin, George H. Brown, Alfred Shaughnessy, Gordon Grimward.
(Ent. advertising material.)

FALKMAN COMMUNICATIONS LTD.
33 Gresse Street, London, W1P 1PN. Tel: 01-636 1371. FAX: 01-631 1497.

Directors: B. Falk, L. Green, J. Finnis.

FILMSCREEN INT. LTD.
Studio 3, 12 Neals Yard, Covent Garden, London, WC2H 9DP. Tel: 01-379 0733. Telex: 269445 SSINT G. FAX: 01-379 0117.

FLAMINGO FILM PRODUCTIONS
P.O. Box 130, Hove, East Sussex BN3 6QU Tel: 0273 550088. Telex: 877050. FAX: 0273 540969.

Directors: R. Kruger, J. S. Kruger.
(Producers of feature films, musical video films and television programming.)

MARK FORSTATER PRODUCTIONS LTD.
42a, Devonshire Close, Portland Place, London, W.I. Tel: 01-631 0611.

FOWLER-CHAPMAN COMPANY LTD.
28 Saint Mary le Park Court, Albert Bridge Road, London, SW11 4PJ. Tel: 01-223 0034.

FREMANTLE INTERNATIONAL, INC.
Greendon House, 7 c/d Bayham Street, London, NW1 0HE. Tel: 01-380 1189.

President: Paul Talbot.
Chief Executive: Anthony Gruner.
(TV film Distributors.)

FRIDAY PRODUCTIONS LTD.
83 Cadogan Lane, London, S.W.1. Tel: 01-235 1909

JAMES GARRETT & PARTNERS LTD.
25 Bruton Street, London, W1X 7DB. Tel: 499 6452. Telex: 261163. FAX: 409 1797.

Directors: J. L. M. P. Garrett (Chmn.); M. Gilmour (Managing); D. T. Peers (Dep'y. Chmn.); D. T. Cromwell (Prod. Dir.); M. Garrett; F. Bloom.
(Advertising film producers.)

GATEWAY AUDIOVISUAL/VIDEO
470-472 Green Lanes, Palmers Green, London, N. 13 5XF. Tel: 01-882 0177. Telex: 896462.

Director: G. L. Smart, A.R.P.S., M.B.K.S.
(Industrial, advertising, educational and training films.)

GENERAL SCREEN ENTERPRISES LTD.
Film House, 97 Oxford Road, Uxbridge, Middx. Tel: 0895 31931. Telex: 934883. Fax: 0895 35335.

Managing Director: Fred Chandler.
Scriptwriter: Tony Church.
(Main titles, trailers, commercials, opticals, special effects.)

G.H.W. PRODUCTIONS LTD.
52 Queen Anne Street, London, W1M 9LA. Tel: 01-935 1186.

Directors: Peter Rogers, Betty E. Box, O.B.E.; D. G. Truscott.

WILLIAM GILBERT ASSOCIATES LTD
16 Brook Mews North, London, W2 3BW. Tel: 01-258 3620/1/2/3

GLOBAL TELEVISION SERVICES LTD.
159-165, Great Portland Street, London, W1N 6NR. Tel: 01-637 4041. Fax: 01-637 4048

Directors: Ian R. Warren, T. L. Donald, I. L. Donald, V. Glynn. European Purchasing Agent for programmes for Australian Broadcasting Commission and Broadcasting Corporation of New Zealand. World Distributors for Portman Productions.

GLOBO INTERNATIONAL (LONDON) LTD
14-15 Stratford Place, London, W1N 9AF. Tel: 01-409 1712.

BOB GODFREY FILMS LTD
55 Neal Street, London, W.C.2 Tel: 01-240 1793/1889.

(Animation for television and cinema. Commercials. 16/35 mm camera service.)

GOLDCREST FILMS AND TELEVISION LTD.
180 Wardour Street, London, W1V 3AA. Tel: 01-437 8696. Telex: 267458 Goldcr. FAX: 01-437 4448.

GOLDEN COMMUNICATIONS (OVERSEAS) LTD
47 Greek Street, London, W1V 5LQ. Tel: 01-439 1431.

Vice President (International Sales): David A. E. Shepperd

G.P.A. (FILMS) LTD.
22 Romily Street, London, W.1. Tel: 01-734 6994.

Director: Gerry Poulson.

GRADE COMPANY
Embassy House, 3 Audley Square, London, W1Y 5DR. Tel: 01-409 1925. Telex: 297197 EMBCOM.

GRANADA TELEVISION INTERNATIONAL LTD.
36 Golden Square, London, W1R 4AH Tel: 01-734 8080. Telex: 27937; 18 Rue Volney, 75002 Paris, France. Tel: (33 1) 42.61.79.10. Telex: 213008; 1221 Avenue of the Americas, Suite 3468, New York, NY 10020, U.S. Tel: (212) 869 8480. Telex: 62454 UW.

Chief Executive: Vivien Wallace.
(Overseas distributors of TV programmes made by Granada.)

GTO FILMS AND VIDEO INTERNATIONAL LTD.
36 Soho Square, London, W1V 5DG. Tel: 01-734 4334. Telex: 297648 GTO ARL.

ELAINE GREENE LTD.
31, Newington Green, London, N16 9PU. Tel: 01-249 2971.

Directors: Elaine Greene, Ilsa Yardley, Timothy Webb.
(Literary agency.)

GUILD HOME VIDEO LTD.
Crown House, 2 Church Street, Walton-on-Thames, Surrey KT12 2QS. Tel: 01-546 3377. Telex: 269651. Fax: 01 546 4568.

HALLIFORD STUDIOS LTD
Manygate Lane, Shepperton, Middx. TW17 9EG: Tel: 0932 226341. FAX: 0932 246336.

Studio Manager: Allan d'Aguiar.

HAMMER FILM PRODUCTIONS LTD.
Cannon Elstree Studios, Boreham, Herts. Tel: 01-953 1600.

Directors: Roy Skeggs, Timothy L. Kirby, Sir John Terry.

HAMPDEN GURNEY STUDIOS, LTD.
39-41 Hanover Steps, St. Georges Fields, Albion Street, London, W2 2YG. Tel: 01-402 7543 and 01-262 5736.

STEWART HARDY FILMS LTD.
2-4 Wigton Gardens Stanmore, Middx. HA7 I8G. Tel: 01-204 4153.

Director: J. R. Williams.
(Animation, diagram, cartoon films.)

HEMDALE HOLDINGS
21 Albion Street, London, W2 2AS. Tel: 01-724 1010. Telex: 25558.

Directors: J. Daly, A. D. Kerman, D. Gibson.

HENSON INTERNATIONAL TELEVISION
2 Old Brewery Mews, Hampstead High Street, London, NW3 1PZ. Tel: 01-435 7121. Telex: 8955914 (Kermit G)

HERON HOME ENTERTAINMENT
A Heron International Company. Unit 4, Brunswick Industrial Park Road, New Southgate, London N11 1JL. Tel: 01-368 1226. Telex: (London) 897654LTBEST G.

HISTORICA CONSULTANCY
8-9 The Incline, Coalport, Telford, Shrop. TF8 7HR. Tel: 0952 584043

GERARD HOLDSWORTH PRODUCTIONS LTD.
31 Palace Street, London, SW1E 5HW Tel: 01-828 1671.

Directors: Mary V. Holdsworth, P. H. Filmer-Sankey, Don Kelly.
(Documentaries, TV program material.)

I.F.A. (SCOTLAND) LTD.
1 North Claremont Street, Glasgow, C3. Scotland. Tel: 041-332 3620.

INCA FILMS LTD.
76 Brewer Street, London, W1R 4HU. Tel: 01-437 3877.

Directors: Anne Balfour Fraser, Timothy Burrill, Brian Little, Eric Falk, Frances Cockburn.
(Documentary, advertising and entertainment material.)

INDEPENDENT TELEVISION NEWS LTD.
ITN House, 48 Wells Street, London, W1P 4DE Tel: 01-637 2424. Telex: 261779.

Chairman: George Russell.
(Production facilities.)

INTERNATIONAL TELEVISION ENTERPRISES LTD
27 Upper Brook Street, London, WIY IPD. Tel: 01-491 1441.

ISLAND PICTURES
22 St. Peter's Square, London W.6. Tel: 01-741 1511.

ITC ENTERTAINMENT LTD.
45 Seymour Street, London, W1A 1AG. Tel: 01-262 8040. Telex: 261807

698

ITEL
  27 Upper Brook Street, London, W1Y 1PD. Tel: 01-491 1441.
  Telex: 25353. FAX: 01-493 2598.

ITN LTD.
  ITN House, 48 Wells Street, London, W1P 4DE. Tel: 01-637
  2424. Telex 261779.
  (Studio, VTR and Conversion Facilities) Contact: Mike Jessey.

ITV FILM PURCHASE GROUP
  Meridien House, 42 Upper Berkeley Street, London, W1H
  7PL. Tel: 01-258 3570. Telex: 9419024

IVS ENTERPRISES LTD.
  54 Warwick Square, London, SW1V 2AJ. Tel: 01-834 6012;
  Telex: 27151; FAX: 01-630 6270.

BRIAN JACKSON FILMS LTD.
  39-41 Hanover Steps, St. Georges Fields, Albion Street,
  London, W2 2YG. Tel: 01-402 7543 and 01-262 5736. Cables:
  JAKSONFILM London, W1. Telex: 896559 GECOMS-G.

J & M ENTERTAINMENT
  2 Dorset Square, London, NW1 6PU Tel: 01-723 6544. Telex:
  298538 FILMIN G Fax: 01-724 7541 Cables: Filming London
  NW1.

JARAS ENTERTAINMENTS LTD.
  21 Cavendish Place, London, W1M 9DL. Tel: 01-580 5927.

CYRIL JENKINS PRODUCTIONS LTD.
  7 Coniston Court, Carlton Drive, London SW15 2BZ. Tel:
  01-788 2733.
  Directors: Cyril G. Jenkins, J. M. Jenkins.
  Entertainment, documentary and advertising material.)

**KRUGER LEISURE ORGANISATION (FILM, VIDEO & TV
  DISTRIBUTION) LTD.**
  P.O. Box 130, Hove, East Sussex BN3 6QU. Tel: 0273
  550088. Telex: 877050. FAX: 0273 540969.
  Directors: J. S. Kruger, R. Kruger, H. R. Kruger.

KIMPTON WALKER LTD.
  47/49 Acre Lane, London. SW2 5TN. Tel: 01-737 3317. Telex:
  27789. Fax: 01-274 4534
  (Theatre, film and television scenery.)

LEE INTERNATIONAL STUDIOS WEMBLEY
  128 Wembley Park Drive, Wembley, Middx. HA9 81E. Tel:
  01-902 1262. FAX: 01-902 1521. Telex: 893458 LISS G.

LE VIEN FILMS LTD.
  15 Chesterfield Hill, London, W.1. Tel: 01-629 4545 Cables:
  Vienfilms London, W.1.
  Executive Producer: Jack Le Vien.
  (TV films and features.)

LIBRA PRODUCTIONS LTD.
  Marl Cottage, Mark Cross, Crowborough, Sussex. Tel: Ro-
  therfield 2172/2746.
  Directors: Kevin Scott (U.S.A.), Thomas Kyffin.
  (Producers of television programmes.)

LIMEHOUSE PRODUCTIONS LTD
  Limehouse Studios, Canary Wharf, West India Docks, Lon-
  don E14 9SJ. Tel: 01-987 2090. Telex: 296149.
  Group Managing Director: Ian Reed.

LITTLE KING PRODUCTIONS LTD.
  13-14 Bateman Street, London, W.1. Tel: 01-437 9611. FAX:
  01-734 7143.
  Contacts: Dr. Simon C. Nicholas, M.B., B. Chir., Simon Manley-
  Cooper.
  (Medical and industrial films for film & video.)

LONDON FILM PRODUCTIONS LTD
  44a Floral Street, London WC2E 9DA. Tel: 01-379 3366.
  Telex: 896805.

LWTI Ltd.
  Seymour Mews House, Seymour Mews, Wigmore Street,
  London, W1H 9PE. Tel: 01-935 9000. Telex: 22872 TV film G.

LORIMAR DISTRIBUTION LTD.
  16 Berkeley Street, London, W.1. Tel: 01-493 1566.
  Managing Director: Ray Lewis.

LORIMAR-TELEPICTURES INTERNATIONAL LTD.
  49 Berkeley Square, Londno, W1X 5Db. Tel: 01-409 1190.
  Telex: 25153 Lormar G. Fax: 01-629 2064 (2 or 3).
  Managing Director: Stuart B. Graber.

I.R. MAXWELL (FILM DISTRIBUTORS) LTD.
  Headington Hill Hall, Oxford, OX3 0BW. Tel: 0865 64881.
  Telex: 83177.

McCANN INTERNATIONAL PROGRAMME MARKETING LTD.
  88-94 Tottenham Court Road, London, W1P 9HE. Tel:
  01-323 4641. Telex: 297957.

MAJESTIC FILMS INTERNATIONAL
  68A Delancey Street, London, NW1 7RY. Tel: 01-284 0242.
  FAX: 01-384 1019.

MARK I PRODUCTIONS LTD.
  Lee International Studios, 128 Wembley Park Drive, Wembley, Middlesex, HA9 8JE. Tel: 01-902 1262.

MECCA INTERNATIONAL PRODUCTIONS LTD
  14 Oxford Street, London, W1N 0HL. Tel: 01-637 9401.

MEDIA RELEASING DISTRIBUTORS LTD.
  60-66 Wardour Street, London, W.1. Tel: 01-437 2341. Telex:
  943763 CROCOM G(MRD).
  Directors: Trevor H. Green, J. Green.

THE MOVING PICTURE COMPANY
  25 Noel Street, London, W.1. Tel: 01-434 3100. Telex: 27256.
  Fax: 437 3951
  (Production Facilities.)

MUSIC BOX
  19-21 Rathbone Place, London, W1P 1DF. Tel: 01-636 7888.

NBC NEWS WORLDWIDE INC.
  8 Bedford Avenue London, WC1. Tel: 01-637 8655.

NATIONAL FILM AND TELEVISION SCHOOL
  Beaconsfield Studios, Station Road, Beaconsfield, Bucks.
  HP9ILG. Tel: 04946 71234. FAX: 04946 4042.
  Director: Colin Young.

NATIONAL SCREEN
  Studios: 15 Wadsworth Road, Greenford, Middx. UB6 7JN
  Tel: 01-998 2851. Telex: 934522. London Office: Wedge-
  wood Mews, Greek Street London, W1V 5LE. Tel: 01-437
  4851.
  Directors: John Mahony, Norman Darkins, Brian McIlmail

NETWORK TELEVISION LTD.
  47 Poland Street, London WIV 3DF. Tel: 01-734 0496.

NEW CENTRAL FILM SERVICES LTD.
  97-99 Dean Street, London, W.1. Tel.: 01-734 5827-8.
  (Editing equipment hire, cutting rooms, production offices, cutting
  room supplies.)

NEW REALM ENTERTAINMENTS LTD.
  Townsend House, 22/25 Dean Street, London, W.1. Tel: 01
  437 9143.
  Managing Director: Adrienne Fancey.

NIXPARGO ANIMATIONS
  Maidensgrove, Nr. Henley-on-Thames, Oxon. RG9 6EZ Tel:
  049 163-286.
  Producers: Nicholas Spargo, Mary Spargo.

NUMO PRODUCTIONS LTD.
  3 Richmond Mews, London, W.1. Tel.: 01-439 4017.

NVC CABLE LTD.
  32 Eccleston Square, London, SW1V 1PB. Tel: 01-834 2300.
  Telex: 893045 NVCG.

OPTICAL FILM EFFECTS LTD.
  Pinewood Studios, Iver Heath, Bucks. 5L0 0NH. Tel: 0753
  655486. Telex: 847505 G.
  Directors: R. W. Field, R. A. Dimbleby.

OVERSEAS FILM AND TELEVISION CENTRE LTD.
  Overseas House, 19-23 Ironmonger Row, London, EC1.
  Tel.: 01-251 2793.
  Directors: D. S. Bowden, P. Whale, A. Muscat, K. Minchell, C. G.
  E. Gover.
  (Ent. and adv. producers.)

OVERVIEW FILMS LTD.
  113-117 Wardour Street, London, W1V 3TD. Tel: 01-439 7491.
  Telex: 21259 FILM G. FAX: 01-734 4970.

PALLADIUM INTERNATIONAL TELEVISION LTD.
  6 Goodwins Court, St. Martin's Lane, London, WC2N 4LL.
  Tel: 01-836 0576. Telex: 267664. FAX: 01-836 4198.

DAVID PARADINE PRODUCTIONS LTD.
Breakfast Television Centre, Hawley Crescent, London NW1 8EF. Tel: 01-482 2898. Telex: 27613 TALKIN G. Fax: 01-482 0871.

PARAMOUNT TELEVISION
23 Berkeley House, Hay Hill, London, W.1. Tel.: 01-629 1150.
Managing Director: Peter Cary.
(TV film distributors.)

PEARL & DEAN LTD.
27 Sale Place, London, W2 1PT. Tel: 01-262 5000.
Managing Director: R. Elsner

PETROFILMS UK LTD
8 West Street, London W.C.2. Tel: 01-836 2112.

PHOENIX FILMS LTD.
Manor Road, Goring-On-Thames, RG8 9DP. Tel: 04-918 72365.
Directors: B. G. Hanson, M. E. Hanson.
(Live-action, cartoon, stop motion.)

PIZAZZ PICTURESS
30 Berwick Street, London, W.1. Tel: 01-434 3581.
Producer: Pamela Dennis.
Directors: Eric Goldberg, Mario Cavalli.

PLATO FILMS LTD.
247A Upper Street, London, N1 1RU. Tel: 01-226 2298.
Managing Director: Stanley Forman.

POLYGRAM FILMS (UK) Ltd.
(Polygram Music Video)
1, Rockley Road, London, W14 0DL. Tel: 01-743 3474. Telex: 298816.
(Producers, distributors, film and TV material, including music video programming).

POLYGRAM INTERNATIONAL
30 Berkeley Square, London, W1X 5HA. Tel: 01-493 8800. Telex: 263872.

POLYMUSE INTERNATIONAL TELEVISION
22 Cleveland Square, London, W2. Tel: 01-402 9066.

PORTMAN PRODUCTIONS LTD
Tennyson House, 159-165 Great Portland Street, London, W1N 6NR. Tel: 01-637 4041. Telex: 263953 HELPFL G. Fax: 01 637 4041.
Directors: T. L. Donald, I. L. Donald, I. R. Warren, A. R. Warren, Victor Glynn

PRESTWICH HOLDINGS, PLC.
1 Euston Centre, London, NW1 3AJ. Tel: 01-388 5034. FAX: 01-388 5881.

RICHARD PRICE TELEVISION ASSOCIATES LTD
Seymour Mews House, Seymour Mews, London WIH 9PE. Tel: 01-935 9000. Fax: 01-487 3975.

PRIMROSE FILM PRODUCTIONS LTD.
61 Regents Park Road, London, N.W.1. Tel: 01-722 7475 and 01-340 9627.
Directors: Louis Hagen, Anne Hagen.
(Animation, live action, children's programmes.)

PRODUCTIONS ASSOCIATES (UK) LTD
The Stable Cottage, Pinewood Studios, Pinewood Road, Iver Heath, Bucks. SL0 0NH. Tel: 01-486 9921.

PROSPECT STUDIOS LTD.
High Street, Barnes, London, SW13 9LE. Tel: 01-876 6284-5.

QUADRANT TELEVISION
Surrey House, Sutton, Surrey 5M1 4QQ Tel: 01-642 0924.
(Production and post-production facilities.)

QUIGLEY PUBLICATIONS
(Subsidiary of Quigley Publishing Co. Inc. of New York) 15 Samuel Road, Langdon Hills, Basildon, Essex SS16 6EZ. Tel: 0268 417055.
UK Manager: William Pay

RADIO LUXEMBOURG (LONDON) LTD.
38 Hertford Street, London, W1V 8BA. Tel: 01-493 5961.
Director of Sales and Marketing: Brian Mellor.
(Representatives of European television production group Société Internationale de Programmes Pour Telediffusion. British representatives of Radio Tele-Luxembourg.)

RANDOM FILM PRODUCTIONS LTD.
Unit 2, Cornwall Works, Cornwall Avenue, Finchley, London N3 1LD. Tel: 01-349 9155.

Directors: F. G. Woosnam-Mills, M. R. Woosnam-Mills, M. P. Molloy.
(Documentaries and educational.)

RANK ADVERTISING FILMS LTD.
127 Wardour Street, London, W.1. Tel: 01-439 9531. Telex: 262556.
Managing Director: Douglas Thomas.
(Cinema, video, and indoor poster contractors. Producers of industrial cinema and video films, TV cinema and video commercials.)

RANK FILM DISTRIBUTORS LTD.
127 Wardour Street, London, WIV 4AD. Tel: 01-437 9020. Telex: 262556.
Managing Director: F. P. Turner.

RANK VIDEO SERVICES LTD.
Phoenix Park, Great West Road, Brentford, Middlesex, TW8 9PL. Tel: 01-568 4311. Telex: 22345.
Managing Director: Nicholas Watkins.

RAVENSDALE FILM & TELEVISION LTD
34-35 Dean Street, London, W.1. Tel: 01-734 4686.

REDIFFUSION FILMS LTD
P.O. Box 451, Buchanan House, 3 St. James's Square, London SW1Y 4LS. Tel: 01-925 0550. Telex: 919673. Cables: Rediffuse. FAX: (Group 3) 01-839 7135.
Production Executive: Jelte Bonnevie

RKO PRODUCTIONS INTERNATIONAL
33 Dover Street, London, W1X 3RA; Tel: 01-629 4799.

THE ROBERT STIGWOOD GROUP LTD.
118/120 Wardour Street, London, W.1. Tel: 01-437 2512. Telex: 264267.

REX ROBERTS STUDIOS LTD.
22, Glasthule Road, Dun Laoghaire, Co. Dublin, Ireland. Tel: Dublin 808305.
(Adv. material.)

ROYAL SOCIETY FOR THE PROTECTION OF BIRDS (RSPB)
Film and Video Unit, The Lodge Sandy, Beds. SG19 2DL. Tel: 0767 80551. Telex: 82469 RSPB. FAX: 0767 292365.
Head of Unit: Jeffery Boswall.

SAGITTA PRODUCTIONS LTD.
%Pamela Gillis Management, 46 Sheldon Avenue, London, N6 4JR. Tel: 01-340 7868.
Managing Director: John Hawkesworth.
(TV and film series.)

SAMUELSON GROUP PLC
303-315 Cricklewood Broadway, Edgware Road, London, NW2 6PQ. Tel : 01-452 8090. Cables: Samcine London. Telex: 21430.
(Equipment supply)

SATELLITE TELEVISION PLC
31/36 Foley Street, London W1P 7LB. Tel: 01-636 4077. Telex: 268395.

SEVEN SEAS FILMS LTD.
83 Duke Street, Grosvenor Square, London, W.1. Tel: 01-629 0788.
Directors: J. Rayfield, Brian Everett.

SOUTHERN TELEVISION LTD
P.O. Box 15, 2-4 New Road, Southampton SO9 7DF. Tel: 0703 28296/229666. Telex: 296149 LIMHSE G.
Managing Director: Frank Copplestone.

SOVEXPORTFILM
60 Hillway, Highgate, London, N6 6DP. Tel: 01-340 86849.

SURVIVAL ANGLIA LTD.
Brook House, Park Lane, London, W.1. Tel: 01-408 2288.
Executive Director: M. A. Hay

SWIFT FILM PRODUCTIONS
1 Wool Road, Wimbledon, London, S.W.20. Tel: 01-946 2040.
Director: T. Peter Hadingham, M.B.K.S.
(Industrial, advertising and documentary & TV 16mm films, filmstrips, AV programmes.)

SWINDON CABLE LTD.
Newcome Drive, Hawksworth Estate, Swindon, SN2 1TU. Tel: 0793 615601.

700

TALBOT TELEVISION LTD.
Greendon House, 7C/D Bayham Street, London, NW1 0HE.
Tel: 01-380 1189.
President: Paul Talbot.
Chief Executive: Anthony Gruner.
(TV film distributors.)

TELECINE
Video House, 48 Charlotte Street, London, W1P 1LX. Telex: 267283 TELCIN.

TELEVENTURES
5th Floor, 16 Hanover Square, London, W1R 0A. Tel: 01-491 3949.

TELEVISION INTERNATIONAL ENTERPRISES LIMITED
22 South Audley Street, London WIY GES. Tel: 01-499 9252.

TELEVISION REPORTERS INTERNATIONAL LTD.
Cannon Elstree Studios, Borehan Wood, Herts. Tel: 01-953 1600.
Directors: Robert S. Baker, Roger G. Moore, John Goodman.

THAMES TELEVISION INTERNATIONAL
149 Tottenham Court Road, London, W1P 9LL. Tel: 01-387 9494.

TITAN INTERNATIONAL PRODUCTIONS LTD
185A Newmarket Road, Norwich, Norfolk NR4 6AP. Tel: 0603 51139.
Directors: P. Newbrook, E. Newbrook.

TOWN AND COUNTRY PRODUCTIONS LTD
Parry's Lodge, Threapwood, Malpas, Cheshire, SY14 7AW. Tel: 0948 81 309.
Directors: J. C. A. Minoprio, C. P. Minoprio.

TRANSATLANTIC FILMS
100 Blythe Road, London, W14 0HE.

TRANSWORLD INTERNATIONAL (UK) INC.
The Pier House, Strand on the Green, Chiswick, London, W4 3NN. Tel: 01-994 1444. FAX: 01-994 9606. Telex: 8955303 & 267486.

TRIANGLE FILM PRODUCTIONS LTD.
15 Oslo Court, Prince Albert Road, London, N.W.8 Tel: 01-722 5656. Cables: Triphilms London N.W.8. Telex: 885493 WINBNK.

TRIBUNE PRODUCTIONS LTD.
Cannon Elstree Studios, Boreham Wood, Herts. Tel: 01-953 1600.
Directors: Robert S. Baker, A. Baker, M. G. Baker, G. S. Barnett.

TRICKFILM STUDIOS LTD.
13 Charlotte Mews, London W.1. Tel: 01-580 0183.

TRILION VIDEO LTD.
36-44 Brewer Street, London, W.1. Tel: 01-439 4177.
Managing Director: Bill Hope.

TRIUMPH FILMS INC.
10 Blomfield Villas, London, W.2. Tel: 01-286 1711.
Director: Peter Hanmer.
(Producers of advertising film and shorts.)

TURNER INTERNATIONAL
25-58 Old Burlington Street, London, W1X 1LB. Tel: 01-434 4341.

TVI LTD.
142 Wardour Street, London, W1V 3AV. Tel: 01-434 2141. Telex: 268208. Fax: 439 3984.
Managing Director: Debbie Hills.

TWICKENHAM FILM STUDIOS LTD.
Twickenham Studios, The Barons, St. Margarets, Twickenham, Middlesex. Tel: 01-892 4477.
Directors: G. Coen, G. Humphreys, M. Landserger, S. J. Mullens
Secretary: M. Darby

TYBURN PRODUCTION LTD.
Pinewood Studios, Iver Heath, Bucks SL0 0NH. Tel: 0753 651700. Telex: 847505. FAX: 0753 656844.
Directors: P. E. Rogers (chairman) Kevin Francis, Gillian Garrow.
Executive Producer: Kevin Francis
Director of Research & Development: Gillian Garrow
Music Supervisor: Philip Markell
(Producers and distributors of TV and home video programming).

UNICORN PICTURES LTD.
Suite 4, 3 Bateman Street, London, W.1. Tel: 01-437 7187.
Director: John Simmons.

UNITED INTERNATIONAL PICTURES
(A subsidiary of UNITED INTERNATIONAL PICTURES B.V., Postbus 9255, 1006 AG Amsterdam, The Netherlands) UIP House, 45 Beadon Road, Hammersmith, London W6 OEG. Tel: 01-741-9041. Telex: 8956521. Telefax: 01-748-8990 (Distribution)
President & Chief Executive Officer: Michael Williams-Jones
Senior Vice Presidents: Ted McLean (Finance & Administration), Jean Prewitt (General Counsel), Hy Smith (Marketing)
Marketing/Sales Executives: Anne Bennett (VP publicity); Andrew Cripps (Sales Manager—South East Asia); Michael Macclesfield (VP sales—special markets); Michael Murphy (VP sales—Latin America); Howard Rochlin (VP sales); Tony Themistocleous (VP sales—Europe); Gina Wright (VP advertising).
Senior Executive/General Manager—Pay-TV Group: Joan Estes

UNITED VIDEO INTERNATIONAL
54 Warwick Square, London, SW1V 2AJ. Tel: 01-834 6012.

UNIVERSAL PICTURES LTD.
139 Picadilly, London, W1V 9FH. Tel: 01-629 7211.

VESTRON PICTURES (UK) LTD
69 New Oxford Street, London, W.1. Tel: 01-379 0221.
Managing Director: Michael Myers

VIRGIN VISION LTD.
328 Kensal Road, London, W10 5XJ. Tel: 01-968 8888. Telex: 892890 VIRGIN G. Fax: 01-968 8537.
Directors: Robert Devereux, Mike Watts, Stephan Navin, Julian Fortman, Peter Coles.

VISUAL ENTERTAINMENTS LTD
51 South Audley Street, London, W.1. Tel: 01-493 7428.
Directors; Benjamin Fisz, Maude Spector, Sue Carrington-Green.

VIEWSPORT LTD
21 Cavendish Place, London W1M 9DL. Tel: 01-580 5927.
Managing Director: Jarvis Astaire.

VISNEWS LTD.
Cumberland Avenue, London, NW10 7EH. Tel: 01-965 7733. FAX: 01-965 0620.
Managing Director: Julian Kerr.
Company Secretary/Financial Controller: Barry MacDonald.
NEWS DIVISION:
Head of News: Stephen Claypole.
Head of Broadcast Facilities: Howard Barrow.
(International production services supported by Worldwide Communications Network.)

VISUAL PROGRAMME SYSTEMS LTD.
77 Bedford Court Mansions, Bedford Avenue, London, WC1B 3AE.

VOICE OF LONDON LTD.
245 Old Marylebone Road, London, NW1 5RT. Tel: 01-402 8385.
Studio Manager: Miss Pat Smith.
(Studio facilities.)

WARNER BROS. TELEVISION LTD.
Warner House, Pinewood Studios, Iver Heath, Bucks. Tel: Iver 654 545.

WATERLOO PRODUCTIONS
1 Lower James Street, London, W.1. Tel: 01-734 8311.

JOSEF WEINBERGER LTD.
12-14 Mortimer Street, London, W1N 8EL. Tel: 01-580 2827.
(Representing Telemusic Library, France.)

WEINTRAUB SCREEN ENTERTAINMENT
167-169 Wardour Street, London, W1V 3TA. Tel: 01-439 1790. FAX: 01-734 1509. Telex: 269919.
UK Managing Director: Richard Milnes.

RICHARD WILLIAMS ANIMATION LTD.
London Studio: 138 Royal College Street, London, NW1 0TA. Tel: 01-437 4455.
Director: Richard Williams.

WORLD AUDIO VISUAL ENTERTAINMENT PLC
18 Great Marlborough Street, London, W1V 1AF. Tel: 01-439 9596. Telex: 264036 WAVE G.

WORLDMARK PRODUCTIONS LTD.
18 Middle Row, London W10 5AT. Tel: 01-960 3251. Telex: 946240 Cweasy G. (Reply ref. 19017530).
Directors: Tony Maylam, Drummond Challis.

WORLD WIDE INTERNATIONAL TELEVISION
21-25 St. Anne's Court, London, W1V 3AW. Tel: 01-434 1121. Telex: 269 271. FAX: 01-734 0619.

Directors: Lord Willis, R. King, R. Townsend, Brian Redhead, C. Courtenay-Taylor, R. Marshall.

WORLDWIDE TELEVISION NEWS
WTN House, 31–36 Foley Street, London W1P 7LB. Tel: 01-323 3255. Telex: 23915; 1995 Broadway, New York, NY 10023, U.S. Tel: (212) 262-4440. Telex: 237853.

Equipment/facilities/services: Producers of sponsored programmes and video news release worldwide for television and industrial corporate sector. Film and video crews strategically located throughout the world to operate as first or second units to individual producers/directors. Worldwide communications network via regional bureaux in London, New York, Washington DC, Paris, Frankfurt, Rome, Johannesburg, Tel Aviv, Hong Kong, Tokyo and Sydney. Post productions facilities centres in London, New York and Frankfurt, with various format editing, standards conversion, satellite transmission/reception.

WYATT CATTANEO PRODUCTIONS LTD.
Charing Cross Rd., London, W.C.2. Tel; 01-379 6444.

SONNY ZAHL ASSOCIATES LTD.
57 Great Cumberland Place, London, W1H 7LJ. Tel: 01-724 3684 and 723 5699.

ZENITH PRODUCTIONS LTD
8 Great Titchfield Street, London, W1P 7AA. Tel: 01-637 7941. Telex: 23348 ZENITH. FAX: 01-631 1493.

ZOOM PRODUCTION COMPANY
102 Dean Street, London, W1V 5RA. Tel: 01-434 3895. Fax: 01-734 2751.

Trade Publications

Broadcast

Published weekly by International Thomson Business Publishing, 100 Avenue Road, London, NW3 3TP. Tel: 01-935 6611.

EDITOR IN CHIEF AND ASSOCIATE PUBLISHER
Martin Jackson

Image Technology

(Technical monthly) Journal of the British Kinematograph, Sound and Television Society. 549 Victoria House, Vernon Place, London, WC1B 4DJ. Tel.: 01 242-8400.

EDITOR
John Gainsborough
ADVERTISEMENT MANAGER
Andy Pay

Screen International

Published by King Publications Ltd. Weekly, covering news, reviews, comment and pictures of the film and television industries. 6-7 Great Chapel Street, London, W.1. Tel.: 01 43 5741.

PUBLISHER
Peter King
EDITOR-IN-CHIEF
Peter Noble

Televisual

Published monthly by the Centaur Group, St. Giles House, 50 Poland Street, London, W1V 4AX. Tel: 01 439 4222.

EDITOR AND PUBLISHER
Philip Reevell

Home Video Distributors

See listing under Principal Video Distributors in the World Market in the Home Video Section

Services for TV Producers/Distributors

CAMERAS—ACCESSORIES FILM STOCK—TELE-CINE—VIDEO AND EDITING EQUIPMENT

ACMADE INTERNATIONAL
Oakside, (Division of Oakside International Holdings Ltd.), Oxford Road, Uxbridge, Middlesex. Tel: Uxbridge 36313. Telex: 8954606.

ADVANCED VIDEO HIRE LTD
51 The Cut, London, SE1 8LF. Tel: 01-928 1963.

AGFA
27 Great West Road, Brentford, Middlesex. TW8 9AX Tel: 01-560 2131.

AMPEX GREAT BRITAIN LTD.
Acre Road, Reading, Berks. Tel: 0734 875200.

AMSTRAD plc
Brentwood House, 169 Kings Road, Brentwood, Essex: CM14 4EF. Tel: 0277 228888.

AUTOCUE LTD.
265 Merton Road, London. S.W.18 5JS. Tel: 01-870 0104. Telex: Autocue Telexir 885039 Autocu G.

F. W. O. BAUCH LTD.
49 Theobald Street, Boreham Wood, Herts. WD6 4RZ Tel: 01-953 0091. Telex: 27502. FAX: 01-207 5970.

R. R. BEARD LTD.
f10 Trafalgar Avenue, London, SE15 6NR. Tel: 01-703 3136 and 9638.

BELL & HOWELL LTD.
Alperton House, Bridgewater Road, Wembley, Middlesex, HA0 1EG. Tel: 01-902 8812.

STUART BELL & PARTNERS LTD.
40 Frith Street, London, W1V 5TF. Tel: 01-439 2700.

BETTER SOUND LTD.
35 Endell Street, London, WC2. Tel: 01-836 0033.

CFS EQUIPMENT HIRE LTD.
10 Wadsworth Road, Perivale, Greenford, Middx. UB6 7JX. Tel: 01-998 2731. Telex: 24672.

CINESOUND INTERNATIONAL LTD.
Imperial Studios, Maxwell Road, Boreham Wood, Herts. LWD6 1WE. Tel: 01-953 5387.

CINETECHNIC LTD.
169 Oldfield Lane, Greenford, Middlesex. Tel: 01-578 1011; and 35 Briardale Gardens, London, NW3 7PN. Tel: 01-435 2289.

CINEVIDEO LTD.
7 Silver Road, White City Industrial Park, Wood Lane, London W12 7SG. Tel: 01-743 3839. FAX: 01-749 3501. Telex: 915 282 CINEGP G.

DOLBY LABORATORIES INC.
346 Clapham Road, London, SW9 9AP. Tel: 01-720 1111. Telex: 919109. Fax: 01-720 4118.

JOE DUNTON CAMERAS LTD.
Wycombe Road, Wembley, Middlesex, HA0 1QN. Tel: 01-903 7933. Telex: 291843.

EDRIC AUDIO VISUAL LTD.
34-36 Oak End Way, Gerrard's Cross, Bucks. Tel: (02813) 84646/7/8.

ENGLISH ELECTRIC VALVE COMPANY LTD.
Waterhouse Lane, Chelmsford, Essex. Tel: 0245-493493. Telegrams: Enelectico, Chelmsford. Telex: 99103.

FRANSCOPE
Grove House, 551 London Road, Isleworth, Middx. TW7 4DS. Tel: 01-568 0131. Telex: 935054.

FUJI PHOTO FILM (UK) LTD.
Fuji Film House, 125 Finchley Road, London NW3 6JH. Tel: 01-586 5900, (Med. X-Ray Division 01-586 931) Telex: 8812995.

HARKNESS SCREENS LTD.
Gate Studios, Station Road, Boreham Wood, Herts., WD6 1DQ; Tel: 01-953 3611. Cables: Screens, London, Telex: 8955602 PERLUX G. FAX: 01-207 3657.

HAYDEN LABORATORIES LTD.
Hayden House, Chiltem Hill, Chalfront St. Peter, Gerrards Cross, Bucks. SL9 9EW. Tel: 02-813 88447/89221.

HITACHI DENSHI (UK) LTD.
13-14 Garrick Ind. Centre, Irving Way, Hendon, London NW9 6AZ. Tel. 01-202 4311

INTERNATIONAL VIDEO CORPORATION
10 Portman Road, Reading, Berkshire. RG3 1JR. Tel: 0734 585421. Telex: 847579.

ITN LTD.
ITN House, 48 Wells Street, London, W1P 4DE. Tel: 01-637 2424.

KEM ELECTRONIC LTD
24 Vivian Avenue, Hendon Central, London, NW4 3XP. Tel: 01-202 0244. Telex: 28303.

K. G. M. VIDIAIDS LTD.
Clock Tower Road, Isleworth, Midd. Tel: 01-568 0151.

KODAK LTD. Motion Picture AV and Television Division
P.O. Box 66, Kodak House, Station Road, Hemel Hempstead, Herts. HP1 1JU. Tel: Hemel Hempstead (0442) 62331.

LEE COLORTRAN LTD.
Ladbroke Hall, Barlby Road. London, W10 5HH. Tel: 01-968 7000.

LEE ELECTRIC (LIGHTING) LTD.
Ladbroke Hall, 85 Barlby Road, London W10 5HH. Tel: 01-960 2400. Telex: 924743. LEE LEC G; FAX: 01-960 2400.

LEE FILTERS LTD.
Central Way, Walworth Industrial Estate, Andover, Hants. SP10 5AN. Tel: 0264 66245. Telex: 477259.

LIPSNER-SMITH CO. LTD.
Unit 7, Longbridge Way, Cowley Mill Trading Estate, Uxbridge, UB8 2YG. Tel: Uxbridge 52191.

MARCONI COMMUNICATION SYSTEMS LTD.
Marconi House, Chelmsford, Essex, CM1 1PL. Tel: (0245) 353221.

ERNEST F. MOY LTD.
Unit 5, Brunswick Park Ind. Est., New Southgate, London, N11 1JF. Tel: 01-361 1211. Telegraphic Address: Movedor, London, N11.

NEILSON-HORDELL LTD.
Unit 11, Central Trading Estate, Staines, Middlesex, TW18 4UU. Tel: 0784 56456 and 54105.

PHOTOGRAPHIC ELECTRICAL CO. LTD.
71, Dean Street, London, W1V 6 DE. Tel: 01-437 4633/4. Cables: Photoelect London. Telex: 25554.

PYE TELECOMMUNICATIONS LTD.
9 Priestley Way, Eldonwall Estate, Edgware Road, London, NW2 7AF. Tel: 01-452 6411. Head Office: St. Andrews Road, Cambridge. Tel: 0223 61222.

RADAMEC EPO LTD.
Bridge Road, Chertsey, Surrey KT16 8LJ. Tel: 0932 561181. FAX: 0932 568775. Telex: 929945 RADEPOG.

RANK AUDIO VISUAL LTD.
3 Centaurs Business Park, Syon Lane, Isleworth, Middx. TW7 5QD. Tel: 01-568 9222. Telex: 935064. FAX: 01-847 0370.
Managing Director: Ronald Sharp.

RANK CINTEL
Watton Road, Ware, Herts. Tel: Ware 3939. Telex: 81415.
Managing Director: Chris Waldron.

RANK TAYLOR HOBSON LTD.
P.O. Box 36, 2 New Star Road, Leicester LE4 7JQ. Tel: 0533 763-771. Telex: 342338. Cables: Metrology Lestr. FAX: 0533 740167.
Managing Director: Chris Waldron.

PHILIP RIGBY & SONS LTD.
14 Creighton Avenue, Muswell Hill, London, N10 1NU. Tel: 01-883 3703.

RONFORD-BAKER
Braziers, Oxhey Lane, Watford, Herts. WD1 4RJ. Tel: 01-428 5941. FAX: 01-428 4743.

RONFORD LTD.
Lee International Film Studios, Studio Road, Shepperton, Middlesex, TW17 0QD. Tel: 0932-561423.

SAMUELSON GROUP PLC
303-315 Cricklewood Broadway, London, NW2 6PQ. Tel: 01-452 8090. Cables: Samcine London. Telex: 21430.

SHURE ELECTRONICS LTD.
Eccleston Road, Maidstone, Kent, ME15 6AU. Tel: 0622 59881.

STRAND LIGHTING
P.O. Box 51, Great West Road, Brentford, Middlesex, TW8 9HR. Tel: 01-560 3171.

TECHNOVISION CAMERAS LTD.
Unit 4, St. Margaret's Business Centre, Drummond Place, Twickenham, Middlesex. TW1 1JN. Tel: 01-891 5961. Telex: 917408 TECNOV G. FAX: 01 744 1154.

3M UNITED KINGDOM PLC
3M House, P.O. Box 1, Bracknell, Berks: RG12 1JU. Tel: 0344 58571.

VARIAN TUT LTD.
P.O. Box 41, Coldhams Lane, Cambridge, CB1 3JU. Tel: 0223 245115. Telex: 81342. VARTUT G. FAX: 0223 214632.

VIDEO TIME
22/24 Greek Street, London, W1V 5LG. Tel: 01-439 1211. Telex: 27256.

W. VINTEN LTD.
Western Way, Bury St. Edmunds, Suffolk, IP33 3TB. Tel: 0284 75 2121. Telex: 81176 VINTEN G. FAX: 0284 706514.

WESTAR SALES & SERVICES LTD.
Unit 7, Cowley Mill Trading Estate, Longbridge Way, Uxbridge, Middx. UB8 2YG. Tel: 0895 34429. Telex 8954169.

ZONAL LTD.
Holmethorpe Avenue, Redhill, Surrey, RHI 2NX. Tel: 0737 767171. FAX: 0737 767610.

MUSIC LIBRARIES-FACILITIES

ABBEY ROAD STUDIOS
3 Abbey Road, London NW8. Tel: 01-286 1161.

ACME FILM PRODUCTIONS LTD.
174 Wardour Street, London, W1V 3AB. Tel: 01-437 1572/ 1889.

BOOSEY & HAWKES MUSIC PUBLISHERS LIMITED
295 Regent Street, London, W1R 8JH. Tel: 01-580 2060. Telex: 8954613 Boosey G.

BOURNE MUSIC LTD.
34/36 Maddox Street, London, W1R 9PD. Tel: 01-493 6412 and 6583.

C.T.S. STUDIOS LTD.
THE MUSIC CENTRE
Engineers Way, Wembley, Middlesex. Tel: 01-903 4611. Telex: 923400.

DE WOLFE LTD.
80-88 Wardour Street, London, W1V 3LF. Tel: 01-439 8481.

EMI MUSIC LTD.
30 Gloucester Place, London, W1A 1ES.

FILM BOOKING OFFICES, LTD.
(Film Library Ltd.)
174 Wardour Street, London, W1V 3AB. Tel: 01-437 1572.

ITN LTD.
ITN House, 48 Wells Street, London, W1P 4DE. Tel: 01-637 2424.

MOZART EDITION (GREAT BRITAIN) LTD.
5th Floor, Crown House, North Circular Road, London, NW10 7PN.

MUSIC SALES LTD.
8-9 Frith Street, London, W1V 5TZ. Tel: 01-434 0066

PEER INTERNATIONAL LIBRARY LTD.
8 Denmark Street, London, WC2H 8LT. Tel: 01-836 4524.

POLYGRAM MUSIC VIDEO
1 Rockley Road, London, W14 DDL. Tel: 01-743 3474. Telex: 298816.

PORTLAND RECORDING STUDIOS LTD.
35 Portland Place, London, W1N 3AG. Tel: 01-637 2111/4.

SOUTHERN LIBRARY OF RECORDED MUSIC LTD.
8 Denmark Street, London, WC2H 8LT. Tel: 01-836 4524.

STUDIO FILM & VIDEO LABORATORIES LTD.
8-14 Meard Street, London, W1V 6DE. Tel: 01-437-0831.

VISNEWS LIMITED
Cumberland Avenue, London, NW10 7EH. Tel: 01-965 7733. Telex: 22678. Cables Visnews, London. FAX: 01-965 0620.

JOSEF WEINBERGER LTD.
12-14 Mortimer Street, London, W1N 8EL. Tel: 01-580 2827.
(Representing Telemusic Library, France.)

ZOMBA SCREEN MUSIC
11 Greek Street, London, W1V 5LE. Tel: 01-437 4266. Telex: 919884. FAX: 01-451 3900.

FILM LABORATORIES & VIDEO SERVICES

BUCKS MOTION PICTURE LABORATORIES LTD.
714 Banbury Avenue, Slough, Berks. SL1 4LH. Tel: 0753 76611. Telex. 9312100157-TD G. FAX: 0753 691762.

COLOUR FILM SERVICES LTD.
22-25 Portman Close, Baker Street, London, W1A 4BE. Tel: 01-486 2881. Telex. 24672, and 10 Wadsworth Road, Perivale, Greenford, Middx. UB6 7JX. Tel: 01-998 2731. Telex: 24672.

FILMATIC LABORATORIES LTD.
16 Colville Road, London, W11 2BS. Tel: 01-221 6081. Telex: 295046 FILMAT-G.

HALLIFORD STUDIOS
Manygate Lane, Shepperton, Middlesex. Tel: 0932 226341. FAX: 0932 246336.
Studio Manager: Allan d'Aguiar.

KINGLY STUDIOS LTD.
17 Kingley Court, Kingley Street, London, W.1. Tel: Gerrard 6372.

LEE INTERNATIONAL FILM STUDIOS LTD.
128 Wembley Park Drive, Wembley, Middlesex. Tel: 01-902 1262.

METROCOLOR LONDON LTD.
22 Soho Square, London, W.1. Tel: 01-437-7811. Telex: 28463; 91/95 Gillespie Road, Highbury, London, N.5. Tel: 01-226 4422. Telex: 28463.
Managing Director: B. E. Compton.

PORTLAND RECORDING STUDIOS LTD.
35 Portland Place, London, W1N 3AG. Tel: 01-637 2111/4.

RANK FILM LABORATORIES LTD.
Denham, Uxbridge, Middlesex, UB9 5HQ. Tel: Denham (0895) 832323. Telex: 934704. Fax: 0895 833617.
Managing Director: J.W. Downer.
Sales Director: M.A. Levy.

SAMUELSON FILM SERVICE LTD.
303-315 Cricklewood Broadway, London, N.W.2. 6PQ. Tel: 01-452 8090.

STUDIO FILM & VIDEO LABORATORIES LTD.
8-14 Meard Street, London, W1V 6DE. Tel: 01-437 0831.

TECHNICOLOR LTD.
P.O. Box 7, Bath Road, West Drayton, Middlese, UB7 0DB. Tel: 01-759 5432. Fax: 01-897 2666.

TWICKENHAM FILM STUDIOS, LTD.
St. Margarets, Twickenham, Middlesex. TW1 2AW. Tel: 01-892 4477. Telex: 8814497.

UNITED MOTION PICTURES (LONDON) LTD.
3 and 36/38 Fitzroy Square, London, W.1. Tel: 01-580 1171 and 01-388 1234.

WORLD WIDE SOUND
21-25, St. Anne's Court, London, W1V 3AW. Tel: 01-434 1121. Telex: 269271. FAX: 01-734 0619.

RECORDING STUDIOS

ADVISION SOUND STUDIOS
23 Gosfield Street, London, W1P 7HB. Tel: 01-580 5707. Telex: 28668. FAX: 01 631 1457.

AIR STUDIOS
214 Oxford Street, London, W.1. Tel: 01-637 2758.

EAMONN ANDREWS STUDIOS LTD.
The Television Club, 46/48, Harcourt Street, Dublin, Ireland. Tel: Dublin 758891.

ANVIL FILM & RECORDING GROUP LTD.
Denham Studios, North Orbital Road, Denham, Nr. Uxbridge, Middx: UB9 5HH. Tel: 0895 833522. Telex: 934704. FAX: 0895 833617.

AUDIO INTERNATIONAL RECORDING STUDIOS LTD.
18 Rodmarton Street, London, W1H 3FW. Tel: 01-486 6466.

CANNON ELSTREE STUDIOS LTD.
Boreham Wood, Herts. Tel: 01-953 1600. Telegrams: Emifilms, Boreham Wood. Telex: 922436 EFILMS G. Fax 01-207 0860.

CBS RECORDING STUDIOS
CBS Records, 31-37 Whitfield Street, London, W1P 5RE. Tel: 01-636 3434.

CINE-LINGUAL SOUND STUDIOS LTD
27-27 Berwick Street, London, W1V 3RF. Tel: 01-437 0136.

CINESOUND EFFECTS LIBRARY LTD.
Imperial Studios, Maxwell Road, Elstree Way, Boreham Wood, Herts, WD6 IWE. Tel: Elstree 5837 and 5545, 4904, 1587.

C.T.S. STUDIOS LTD.
The Music Centre, Engineer's Way, Wembley, Middlesex. Tel: 01-903 4611. Telex: 923400.

DELTA SOUND SERVICES LTD.
Shepperton Studio Centre, Squires Bridge Road, Shepperton, Middx. TW17 0QD. Tel: Chertsey 62045/46.

ECO LTD.
The Exchange, Mount Stuart Square, Cardiff CF1 6EA, Wales. Tel: 0222-493321. Telex: 497457 (HAVRON).
Contact: John Cross.

MOTIVATION SOUND LTD,
(Voice-over Recording Studios)
35a Broadhurst Gardens, London, NW6 3QT. Tel: 01-624 7785.

NATIONAL SCREEN
15 Wadsworth Road, Greenford, Middlesex. Tel: 01-998-2851; 2. Wedgwood Mews, 12-13 Greek Street, London, W1V 5LE. Tel: 01-437 4851-6. Telex: 934522.

NEW CENTRAL FILM SERVICES LTD.
97-99 Dean Street, London W.1. Tel: 01-734 5827-8.

PORTLAND RECORDING STUDIOS LTD.
35 Portland Place, London, W1N 3AG Tel: 01-637 2111.

RANK FILM LABORATORIES LTD.
Denham, Uxbridge, Middlesex, UB9 5HQ. Tel: Denham (0895) 832323. Telex: 934704. Fax: 0895 833617
Managing Director: J. W. Downer.
Sales Director: M. A. Levy.

STUDIO FILM & VIDEO LABORATORIES LTD.
8-14 Meard Street, London, W1V 6DE. Tel: 01-437 0831.

UNITED MOTION PICTURES (LONDON) LTD.
Boston House, 36/38 Fitzroy Square, London, W.1. Tel: 01-580 1171.

W.F.S. (FILM FACILITIES) LTD.
153 Wardour Street, London, W1V 3TB. Tel: 01-437 5532.

WORLD WIDE SOUND
21-25 St. Anne's Court, London, W1V 3AW. Tel: 01-434 1121. FAX: 01-734 0619.

PRODUCTION SERVICES

AIRtv FACILITIES LTD.
Hawley Crescent, London, NW1 8NP. Tel: 01-485 4121.

AKA FILM SERVICES LTD.
60 Farringdon Road, London EC1R 3BP. Tel: 01-251 3885

BARRY WESTWOOD PRODUCTIONS
231 West Street, Fareham, Hants., PO16 0HZ. Tel: 0329-285941.

CAMERA EFFECTS
8-11 Bateman Street, London W.1. Tel: 01-437 9377.

CHERRILL, ROGER LTD.
65-66 Dean Street, London, W1V 6PL. Tel: 01-437 7972. FAX: 01-437 6411.

CINEBUILD LTD.
1 Wheatsheaf Hall, Wheatsheaf Lane, London S.W.8. Tel: 01-582 8750. Telex: 943763 Crocom G Cinebuild.

CINEVIDEO LTD.
Marylebone Cine Tape Studios, 245 Old Marylebone Road, London, NW1 5QT. Tel: 01-402 8385. Cable: Filmprod London.

CLAPP, NIKKI
18 Cresswell Road, East Twickenham, Middx. TW1 2DZ. Tel: 01-891 0054.
Languages: Greek, Italian & French.

COLOUR FILM SERVICES LTD.
22-25 Portman Close, Baker Street, London, W1A 4BE. Tel: 01-486 2881. Telex: 24672.

COMBINED PRINTS & PRODUCTION SERVICE LTD.
65-66 Dean Street, London, W1V 5HD. Tel: 01-437 7972. FAX: 01-437 6411.

COMPLETE VIDEO
3 Slingsby Place, London, WC2E 9AB. Tel: 01-379 7739.

CROW FILM & TV SERVICES LTD.
12 Wendell Road, London, W12 9RT. Tel: 01-749 6071. Telex: 931458 CROWTVG.

EDINBURGH FILM & TV STUDIOS
Nine Mile Burn, by Penicuik, Midlothian, EH 26 9LT, Scotland. Tel: Penicuik (0968) 72131.

EDIT ART POST PRODUCTION
86 Wardour Street, London, W1V 3LF. Tel: 01-734 8966.

EDIT 142
5th Floor, 142 Wardour Street, London W.1. Tel: 01-439 7934.

FILM PRODUCTION SERVICES
"Shortend," 82 Holywell Road, Studham, Nr. Dunstable, Beds. Tel: 0582 873107.

CHARLES H. FOX LTD.
22 Tavistock Street, Covent Garden, London WC2E 7PY. Tel. 01-240 3111.

GAZELLE FILM PRODUCTIONS LTD.
IPA House, Orange Street, Bristol, BS2 9HG. Tel: 421214/5.

GENERAL SCREEN ENTERPRIZES LTD.
97 Oxford Road, Uxbridge, Middlesex. Tel: 0895-31931. FAX: 0895 35335.

INFOVISION LTD.
Bradley Close, White Lion Street, London, N1 9PN. Tel: 01-837 0012. Telex: 299800 ACTION.

ISLAND FILMS/EDITING
22 St. Peter's Square, London, W6 9NW. Tel: 01-741 1511

KAUFMAN, MIKE (POST PRODUCTIONS) LTD.
80-82 Wardour Street, London, W1V 3LF. Tel: 01-734 8335. Telex: 264864 Answerback MKPPLN G.

LOUIS ELMAN + LEAH INTERNATIONAL PRODUCTIONS LTD.
Denham Studios, Denham, Nr. Uxbridge, Middlesex. Tel 0895 833036 & 853522. Telex: 934704.

MAGPIE FILM PRODUCTIONS LTD.
22 Bodenham Road, Northfield, Birmingham, B31 5DP, West Midlands. Tel: 021-475 6666 & 021-471 1396.

MERCURY PRODUCTION OFFICES
Tel: 01-734 5000 (single offices or suites in Wardour Street, London).

METRO VIDEO
The Old Bacon Factory, 57-59 Great Suffolk Street, London, SE1 0BS. Tel: 01-929 2088.

MILLS, PETER FILM EDITING LTD.
75 Dean Street, London, W1V 5HA. Tel: 01-437 3003 & 01-439 1721.

MOLINARE
34 Fouberts Place, London, W1V 2BH. Tel: 01-439 2244. FAX: 01-734 6813. Telex: 299200 MOLI G.

PMPP FACILITIES
(Formerly Paul Miller Post Production)
69 Dean Street (Entrance Meard Street), London, W1V 5HB. Tel: 01-437 0979.

NORWOOD STUDIOS LTD.
147 Victoria Road, Leeds, LS6 1DU. Tel: 0532-787539.
(For rushes—35mm and 16mm optical and mags.)

N S & H CREATIVE PARTNERSHIP
13 John Street, London, W.C.1. Tel: 01-405 2324.

ONE INCH VIDEO COMPANY
11/13 Neal's Yard, Covent Garden, London, WC2H 9LZ. Tel: 01-831 1900. FAX: 01-836 0914. Telex: 22125 VIDEO G.

PEERLESS CAMERA CO.
15 Neals Yard, London, WC2H 9DP. Tel: 01-836 3367.

PLATYPUS FILMS LTD.
9 Grape Street, London, WC2H 8DR. Tel: 01-240 0351.

POST HOUSE (POST PRODUCTIONS) LTD.
12 D'Arblay Street, London, W1V 3FP. Tel: 01-439 1705/6/7.

PRATER AUDIO VISUAL LTD.
7A College Approach, Greenwich, London, SE10 9HY. Tel: 01-858 8939. FAX: 01-305 1537.

RANK VIDEO SERVICES LTD.
Phoenix Park, Great West Road, Brentford, Middlesex, TW8 9PL. Tel: 01-568 4311. Telex: 22345.
Managing Director: Nicholas Watkins.

SAMUELSON GROUP PLC
303-315 Cricklewood Broadway, London, NW2 6PQ. Tel: 01-452 8090. Telex: 21430 Cables Samcine, London.

SOLUS ENTERPRISES
35 Marshall Street, London, W1V 1LL. Tel: 01-734 0645 and 01-734 3384/5.

TABS
63 Stirling Court, Marshall Street, London W.1. Tel: 01-734 3356/7.
EC: Janet Easton
(Specialities: Technicians answering and booking service.)

TATTOOIST INTERNATIONAL LTD.
9 Lyme Steet, London N.W.1. Tel: 01-267 0242/3.

TELEVISUAL LTD.
58 Kew Road, Richmond, Surrey, TW9 2PQ. Tel: 01-940 1155.

VIDEO EUROPE
31 Ransome's Dock, Parkgate Road, Battersea, London, SW11 4NP. Tel: 01-585 0555.

VIDEO ROOM
155-157 Oxford Street, London, W1R 1TB. Tel: 01-434 0724.

VISNEWS LIMITED
Cumberland Avenue, London, NW10 7EH. Tel: 01-965 7733. Telex: 22678 Cables Visnews, London. FAX: 01-965 0620.
(International production services supported by World-wide Communications Network).

WSTV PRODUCTION LTD.
159-163 Great Portland Street, London, W1N 5FD. Tel: 01-580 5896.
(Video tape and TV production, TV cmml.)

WETFORD FILMS LTD.
Wetford Lodge, 163 Nightingale Lane, London S.W.12. Tel: 01-675 1333.

WOLFF PRODUCTIONS
6a Noel Street, London, W1V 3RB. Tel: 01-439 1838.

WOOD, PATRICK FILM SERVICES
13 South Road, Amersham, Bucks. Tel: 0494 724941.

WORLD WIDE INTERNATIONAL TELEVISION
21-25 St. Anne's Court, London, W1V 3AV. Tel: 01-434 1121. Telex: 269271. FAX: 01-734 0619.

TITLING—SPECIAL EFFECTS

CINE-SOUND EFFECTS LTD.
(Soundefex Ltd., Lansdowne Vaults Ltd.) Imperial Studios, Maxwell Road Boreham Wood, Herts. Tel: 01-953 5837 and 1587, 4904, 5545.

ELECTROCRAFT CONSULTANTS LTD.
Sales Office and Works: Liss Mill, Mill Road, Liss, Hants. Tel: Liss 89 3444.

FILMTEXT LTD.
37 Kew Road, Richmond Surrey, TW9 2NQ. Tel: 01-940 5034.

GENERAL SCREEN ENTERPRISES LTD.
97 Oxford Road, Uxbridge, Middx. Tel: 0895 31931. FAX: 0895 35335.

METROCOLOR LONDON LTD.
91/95 Gillespie Road, Highbury, London, N.5. Tel: 01-226 4422. Telex: 28463. Also, 22 Soho Square, London, W.1. Tel: 01-437 7811. Telex: 28463.

NATIONAL SCREEN
15 Wadsworth Road, Greenford, Middlesex, UB6 7JN. Tel: 01-998 2851; 2 Wedgwood Mews, Greek Street, London, W1V 5LE. Tel: 01-437 4851-6. Telex: 934522.

RANK FILM LABORATORIES LTD.
Denham Uxbridge, Middlesex, UB9 5HQ. Tel: Denham (0895) 832323. Telex 832323. Fax 0895 833617.
Managing Director: J. W. Downer.
Sales Director: M. A. Levy.

STUDIO FILM & VIDEO LABORATORIES LTD.
8-14 Meard Street London, W1V 6DE. Tel: 01-437 0831.

TECHNICOLOR LTD.
(Subsidiary of Technicolor Inc.) P.O. Box No. 7 Bath Road, West Drayton, Middlesex, UB7 0DB5. Tel: 01-759 5432. Telegraphic and Cable Address: Technicolor, West Drayton. Telex: 22344.

UNIVERSAL FILM LABORATORY LTD.
Braintree Road, Ruislip, Middlesex. Tel: 01-841 5101.

STUDIOS

BRAY STUDIOS (Samuelson Group)
Windsor Road, Windsor, Berks. Tel: 0628 22111. Telex: 21430. Cables: Samcine London. FAX: 0628 770381.
(4 stages, total 23,600 sq. ft. All depts. theatre, workshops, bar and catering.)

BUSHEY
(Cygnet Ltd.)
Melbourne Road, Bushey, Herts. Tel: 01-950 1621.
Studio Manager: Philip Lee
2 Stages (66′×33′×15′ high with cycloroma backing; 30′×22′×12′ high with video gallery).

CANNON ELSTREE STUDIOS LTD.
Boreham Wood, Herts. Tel: 01-953 1600. Telex: 922436 EFILMSG. FAX: 01-207 0860.
Managing Director: Andrew Mitchell.
7 sound stages (four 15,000 square feet, two 8,000 square feet, one 5,200 square feet.) 3 silent stages: (one 30,000 sq. ft., one 15,750 sq. ft., one 8,000 sq. ft.)
Theatres: Three viewing, one dubbing, one ADR and looping theatre. RCA sound. Complete Dolby installation in transfers, looping, re-recording and viewing for producing Dolby encoded optical sound tracks.

CARLTON TELEVISION LTD.
St. John's Wood Studios, St. John's Wood Terrace, London, N.W.8. 6PY Tel: 01-722 9255. FAX: 01-483 4264.
Managing Director: Barry Johnstone.

CINEVIDEO LTD.
245 Old Marylebone Road, London, NW1 5QT. Tel: 01-402 8385.

CREATIVE FILM MAKERS LTD.
Pottery Lane House, Pottery Lane, Holland Park, London, W11 4LZ. Tel: 01-229 5131.

C.T.S. STUDIOS LTD.
The Music Centre, Engineers Way, Wembley, Middlesex. Tel: 01-903 4611. Telex: 923400.

CTVC
Hillside Studios, Merry Hill Road, Bushey, Watford WD2 1DR. Tel: 01-950 4426.

GATEWAY AUDIO VISUAL/VIDEO
470-472 Green Lanes, London, NI3 5XF. Tel: 01-882 0177.

HALLIFORD FILM STUDIOS LTD.
Manygate Lane, Shepperton, Middlesex, TW17 9EG. Tel: 0932 226341. FAX: 0932 246336.

Studio Manager: Allan d'Aguiar.
Two stages (60×60×40) totalling 6,000 sq. ft.

ITN LTD.
ITN House, 48 Wells Street, London, WIP 4DE. Tel: 01-637 2424.

Studio VTR and conversion facilities.
Contact: Mike Jessey

LEE INTERNATIONAL STUDIOS SHEPPERTON
Studios Road, Shepperton, Middlesex, TW17 0QD. Tel: 0932 562611. FAX: 0932 568989. Telex: 929416 MOVIES G.

Contact: Cathy Bunce.
14 stages.

LIMEHOUSE STUDIOS
Canary Wharf, West Indian Docks, London, 314 9SJ. Tel: 01-987 2090.

Contact: Ron Payne

MORENO FILM STUDIOS
35 Broadhurst Gardens, London, N.W.6. Tel: Maida Vale 0645.

Directors: George Moreno (Managing), Fred Thompson.

MTM ARDMORE STUDIOS LTD.
Herbert Road, Bray, Co. Wicklow, Ireland. Tel: Dublin 862971. Telex: 91504 PATT E1. Fax: Dublin 861894.

PINEWOOD STUDIOS
Iver Heath, Bucks. SL0 0NH. Tel: 0753 651700; Cables: Pinewood, Iver Heath. Telex: 847505 Pinew G.

Managing Director: Cyril Howard.
A. 165 ft.×110 ft.×35 ft. (with tank 40 ft.×30 ft.×8 ft.)
B. 110 ft.×81 ft.×34 ft.
C. 110 ft.×81 ft.×34 ft.
D. 165 ft.×110 ft.×35 ft. (with tank 40 ft.×30 ft.×8 ft.)
E. 165 ft.×110 ft.×35 ft. (with tank 40 ft.×30 ft.×8 ft.)
F. 100 ft.×75 ft.×35 ft. (with tank 20 ft.× 20 ft.×8 ft.)
G. 55 ft.×49 ft.×23 ft.
H. 90 ft.×37 ft.×28 ft.
J. 110 ft.×80 ft.×29 ft. 3 ins. (dual-purpose, film & TV).
K. 110 ft.×80 ft.×29 ft. 3 ins. (dual-purpose, film & TV).
L. 105 ft.×90 ft.×30 ft. (dual-purpose, film & TV).
M. 105 ft.×90 ft.×30 ft. (dual-purpose, film & TV). South Dock Stage (silent) 174' × 96' × 28'. North Dock Stage (silent) 125' × 54' × 27'. Special effects stage (silent)—89 ft. × 80 ft. × 20 ft. Small Process Stage—75 ft. × 32ft. 6 ins. × 17 ft. Large Process Stage—175 ft. × 28 ft. × 28 ft. 007 Stage—334' × 136' × 40'6". (World's largest silent stage). 5 theatres for viewing, dubbing, and post-sync, effects. Any ratio, 16mm, 35mm, 70mm, viewing available, with sync separate sound. Up to 115 seats. Dubbing in multitrack, stereo, Dolby up to 6 tracks. 50 cutting rooms. Special effects: Matte stage. Vis 35mm. back projection. Fully equipped process projection dept. including front projection and 70m rear and foreground projection. Triple head process system. Models of all kinds including VistaVision Rear Projection and VistaVision Front Projection. Travelling Matte System comprising 70 ft. × 40 ft. Stewart Blue Screen and associated lighting ring. Stills: Stills studio. Dressing rooms. Production and Unit Offices: Many available. Exterior Lot: 72 acres with formal gardens, lake, woods, and concrete service roads. Multi-Purpose Catering Dept. Paddock tank 230 ft. wide narrowing to 110 ft. Backing 240 ft. 2 60 ft. Another tank 75 ft. × 225 ft. Both tanks contain approximately 800,000 gallons. Props available.

PROSPECT STUDIOS LTD.
High Street, Barnes, London, S.W.13. Tel: 876 6284/5.

SHEPPERTON STUDIO CENTRE
Studios Road, Shepperton, Middlesex, TW17 0QD. Tel: 09328 62611. Telex: 929416 Movies G.

Five sound and one silent stages.

TVI LTD
142 Wardour Street, London, W1V 3AV. Tel: 01-434 2141. Telex: 268208. Fax: 439 3984.

Managing Director: Debbie Hills.
Videopost production facilities. VTR copying and standard conversion. Telecine, Studios.

TWICKENHAM
St. Margaret's, Twickenham, Middlesex. Tel: 01-892 4477.

Owned by Twickenham Film Studios, Ltd.
Stage One: 7,192 square feet. Stage Two: 2,000 square feet, Stage Three: 5,700 square feet.
RCA Sound. Re-Recording and dubbing theatres with 36 input 6 track stereo Rock & Roll (High speed 6 times).
Directors: G. Coen, G. Humphreys, M. Landsberger, S. J. Mullens.

W.F.S. (FILM FACILITIES) LTD.
153 Wardour Street, London, W1V 3TB. Tel: 01-437 5532.

WORLD WIDE SOUND
21-25 St. Anne's Court, London, W1V 3AW. Tel: 01-434 1121. FAX: 01-734 0619.

Director of Sound: R. King

NEWS FILM SERVICE

CBS NEWS
100 Brompton Road, London S.W.3. Tel: 01-584 3366.

CCL NEWS & FEATURES
87 Charlotte Street, London, W1P 1LB. Tel: 01-631 5424. Telex: 266685 CCLLDN.

INDEPENDENT TELEVISION NEWS LTD.
ITN House, 48 Wells Street, London, W1P 4DE. Tel: 01-637 2424. Telex: 261779

NBC NEWS WORLDWIDE INC.
8 Bedford Avenue, London W.C.1. Tel: 01-637 8655

VISNEWS LIMITED
Cumberland Avenue, London, N.W.10. 7EH Tel: 01-965 7733. Telex: 22678. Cables: Visnews London, FAX: 01-965 0620.

Managing Director: Julian Kerr
Head of News: Stephen Claypole

WORLDWIDE TELEVISION NEWS
WTN House, 31-36 Foley Street, London, W1P 7LB. Tel: 01-323 3255. Telex: 23915.

COSTUME SUPPLIERS

ANGELS
Morris Angel & Son Ltd.
119 Shaftesbury Avenue, London WC2H 8AE. Tel: 01-836 5678. Telex: 24919 Angels G. FAX: 01-240 9527.

Managing Director: Tim Angel.

BERMAN AND NATHANS LTD.
Head Office: 18 Irving Street, Leicester Square, London, WC2H 7AX. Tel: 01-839 1651.
Main Store: 40 Camden Street, London, NW1 0EN. Tel: 01-387 0999. Telex: Berman G 8952359

TWENTIETH CENTURY COSTUMES
9 Dallington Street, London, EC1V 0BQ. Tel: 01-608 1966. FAX: 01-490 0155. Telex: 94013393 TWEN G.

LEADING ADVERTISING AGENCIES

ABBOTT, MEAD VICKERS/SMS LTD.
32 Aybrook Street, London W1M 3JL. Tel: 01 486 0122.

ALLEN, BRADY AND MARSH LTD.
Lynton House, 7-12 Tavistock Square, London WC1H 9SX. Tel: 01 388 1100.

TED BATES COMMUNICATIONS
Parkwood House, 33-34 Soho Square, London W1A 1BD. Tel: 01 434 3111.

BBDO LTD.
6-10 Cambridge Terrace, Regents Park, London NW1 4JA. Tel: 01 486 1277.

BOASE MASSIMI POLLITT PARTNERSHIP PLC
12 Bishops Bridge Road, London W2 6AA. Tel: 01 258 3979.

LEO BURNETT LTD.
48 St. Martins Lane, London WC2N 4EJ. Tel: 01 836 2424.

COLLETT DICKENSON PEARCE AND PARTNERS LTD.
110 Euston Road, London NW1 2DQ. Tel: 01 388 2424.

D'ARCY MASIUS BENTON AND BOWLES
2 St James' Square, London SW1Y 4SN. Tel: 01 839 3422.

DAVIDSON PEARCE LTD.
67 Brompton Road, London SW3 1EF. Tel: 01 589 4595.

DFS DORLAND LTD.
121-141 Westbourne Terrace, London W2 6JR. Tel: 262 5077.

FOOTE, CONE AND BELDING ADVERTISING LTD.
82 Baker Street, London W1M 2AE. Tel: 01 935 4426.

GEERS GROSS ADVERTISING LTD.
110 St. Martins Lane, London WC2N 4DY. Tel: 01 240 7100.

GOLD GREENLEES TROTT ADVERTISING LTD.
82 Dean Street, London W1V 5AB. Tel: 01 437 0434.

GREY ADVERTISING LTD.
215-217 Great Portland Street, London W1N 5HD. Tel: 01 636 3399.

KHBB-DOWNTON
82 Charing Cross Road, London WC2H 0BA. Tel: 01 379 7350.

LOWE HOWARD-SPINK MARSCHALK
Bowater House, Knightsbridge, London SW1. Tel: 01 584 5033.

McCANN-ERICKSON ADVERTISING LTD.
36 Howland Street, London W1A 1AT. Tel: 01 580 6690.

McCORMICK-PUBLICIS LTD,
24 Nutford Place, London W1H 5YN. Tel: 01 723 3484.

OGILVY AND MATHER LTD.
Brettenham House, Lancaster Place, London WC2E 7EZ. Tel: 01 836 2466.

REEVES ROBERTSHAW NEEDHAM LTD.
5 Princes Gate, London SW7 1QJ. Tel: 01 589 1445.

SAATCHI AND SAATCHI COMPTON LTD.
80 Charlotte St., London W1A 1AQ. Tel: 01 636 5060.

SSC & B: LINTAS WORLDWIDE—LONDON
Lintas House, New Fetter Lane, London EC4P 4EU. Tel: 01 822 8888.

J. WALTER THOMPSON LTD.
40 Berkeley Square, London W1X 6AD. Tel: 01 629 9496.

WIGHT COLLINS RUTHERFORD SCOTT AND PARTNERS LTD (WCRS)
41-44 Great Queen Street, London WC2B 5AR. Tel: 01 242 2800.

YOUNG AND RUBICAM LTD.
Greater London House, Hampstead Road, London NW1 7QP. Tel: 01 387 9366.

FINANCIAL SERVICES

BARCLAYS BANK PLC
The Media Section, Barclays Business Centre, 27 Soho Square, London, W1A 4WA. Tel: 01-439 6951.

BAYLY MARTIN & FAY INTERNATIONAL LTD.
Braintree House, Braintree Road, Ruislip, Middx: HA4 0YA. Tel: 01 841 4461. Telex: 935792 HOWINS G. FAX: 01 842 2124.

BRITISH & COMMONWEALTH MERCHANT BANK PLC
2 St. Mary Axe, London, EC3A 8BP. Tel: 01 623 8788. FAX: 01-626 1086. Telex: 884040 CABANK G.

BRITISH SCREEN LTD.
37-39 Oxford Street, London, W1R 1RE. Tel: 01-434 0291. Telex: 888694 BRISCR G. FAX: 01 434 9933

COMPLETION BOND COMPANY INC.
Pinewood Studios, Iver Heath, Bucks: SL0 0NH. Tel: 0753 652433. Telex: 849003. CPLBND G. FAX: 0753 655697

CONTRACTS INTERNATIONAL LTD.
32 Haymarket, London, SW1Y 4TP. Tel: 01-930 8494. Telex: 295885. FAX: 01-930 5575.

DISTANT HORIZON
4th Floor, 17 Great Cumberland Place, London, W1H 7LA. Tel: 01-724 3440. FAX: 010935 4402. Telex: 917354. PROTAC G.

FILM FINANCES LTD.
1/11 Hay Hill, Berkeley Square, London, W1X 7LF. Tel: 01-629 6557. Telex: 298060 FILFIN G. FAX: 01-491 7530.

FILM TRUSTEES LTD.
2nd Floor, Broadwick House, 8-12 Broadwick Street, London, W1V 1FH. Tel: 01-434 3501. Telex: 23788 FILMTR G. FAX: 01-734 8893.

GENERAL ENTERTAINMENT INVESTMENTS
65-67 Ledbury Road, London, W11 2AD. Tel: 01-221 3512. Telex: 28604. FAX: 0932 868989.

GUINNESS MAHON & CO. LTD.
32 St. Mary at Hill, London, EC3P 3AJ. Tel: 01-623 9333. FAX: 01-283 4811

PARMEAD INSURANCE BROKERS LTD.
Artillery House, 35 Artillery Lane, London, E.1. Tel: 01-467 8656.

PEAT MARWICK McLINTOCK
1 Puddle Dock, Blackfriars, London, EC4V 3PD. Tel: 01-236 8000.

PIERSON, BELDRING & PIERSON
City Tower, Level 15, 40 Basinghill Street, London, EC2V 5DE. Tel: 01-628 5091. Telex: 885119-8812941.

RUBEN SEDGWICK INSURANCE SERVICES
Pinewood Studios, Pinewood Road, Iver, Bucks: SL0 0NH. Tel: 011 44 753 654 555. Telex: 851 848708 SEDFOR G. FAX: 011-44-753 653 152

SARGENT-DISC LTD.
Pinewood Studios, Pinewood Road, Iver, Bucks: Tel: 0753 656631/655388. FAX: 0753 655881.

SPECTRUM ENTERTAINMENT
27 Harley Street, London, W1N 1DA. Tel: 01-351 5410. Telex: 261507. FAX: 01-351 7679.

TOUCHE ROSS
Hill House, 1 Little New Street, London, EC4A 3TR. Tel: 01-353 8011.

WASA FILM FINANCE CORPORATION LTD.
99 Park Lane, London, W1Y 4EQ. Tel: 01-491 2822. Telex: 264833 SAFIN G. FAX: 01-493 3710.

WILLIS WRIGHTSON LONDON LTD.
Wren Court, 15 London Road, Bromley, Kent: BR1 1DE. Tel: 01-466 6711. Telex: 8954048.

PROFESSIONAL & TRADE ASSOCIATIONS

THE ADVERTISING ASSOCIATION
Abford House, 15 Wilton Road, London SW1V 1NJ. Tel: 01-828 2771. FAX: 01-931 0376.

The Advertising Association is the federated organisation representing the shared advertising interests of advertisers, agencies and the media. It is the central spokesman for the UK advertising business, at national and international levels, and as such maintains a continuing programme of research and information retrieval. It is responsible for the collection and dissemination of the UK statistics on advertising expenditure, and runs an annual programme of seminars and courses for people in the communications business.
Director General: Roger Underhill.

THE ADVERTISING STANDARDS AUTHORITY
Brook House, 2-16 Torrington Place, London, WC1E 7HN. Tel: 01-580 5555 (9 lines). Fax: 01-631 3051 (Groups 2 & 3).

ASSOCIATION OF CINEMATOGRAPH, TELEVISION AND ALLIED TECHNICIANS
(Affiliated to Trades Union Congress and Labour Party). 111 Wardour Street, London W.1. Tel: 01-437 8506.

President: Bruce Anderson.
General Secretary: Alan Sapper.
(The Association is the recognized Trade Union for film, television and radio technicians and negotiates salaries and working conditions. It also controls the A.C.T.T. Employment Bureau as an agency exclusively for film and TV technicians.)

ASSOCIATIONS OF INDEPENDENT PRODUCERS
17 Great Pulteney Street, London W1R 3DG. Tel: 01-434 0181. Fax: 01-437 0086.
Director: Steve Pinham.

ASSOCIATION OF PROFESSIONAL RECORDING STUDIOS LTD.
163A High Street, Rickmansworth, Herts, WD3 7AY. Tel: 0923 772907. FAX: 0923 773079.

Secretary General: Philip Vaughan.

ASSOCIATION OF PROFESSIONAL VIDEO DEALERS LTD.
P.O. Box 25, Godalming, Surrey, GU7 1PL. Tel: 04868 23429.

Director and Secretary: Charles Potter, M.B.E.

BRITISH ACADEMY OF FILM AND TELEVISION ARTS
195 Piccadilly, London, W1V 9LG. Tel: 01-734 0022.

President: H. R. H. The Princess Royal
Vice President: Sir Richard Attenborough, C.B.E.
Chairman: Johnny Goodman.
Hon. Treasurer: Richard Price.
Director: Tony Byrne.
The British Academy of Film and Television Arts exists in order to promote, improve and advance original and creative work amongst people engaged in film and television production.

BRITISH ACTORS' EQUITY ASSOCIATION
Incorporating the Variety Artistes Fed.) 8 Harley Street, London, W1N 2AB. Tel: 01-637 9311 and 636 6367. FAX: 01-580 0970.

Honorary Treasurer: Milton Johns.
General Secretary: Peter Plouviez.

BRITISH FILM DESIGNERS GUILD
26-28, Binney Street, London W.1. Tel: 01-499 4336

Executive Consultant: John French

BRITISH FILM INSTITUTE
21-28 Stepton Street, London, W1P 1PL. Tel: 01-255 1444. Telex: 27624 BFILDNG. FAX: 01-436 7950.

Founded 1933. Principal object to encourage the development of the art of the film, to promote its use as a record of contemporary life and manners and to foster public appreciation and study of it from these points of view. The Institute has a similar role in relation to television. The Board of Governors is appointed by the Minister of the Arts, two are selected by a poll of the membership. The National Film Archive and the National Film Theatre are departments of the Institute which publishes Sight and Sound, a quarterly film magazine and the Monthly Film Bulletin, and provides services for education, film availability regions and production.
Chairman: Sir Richard Attenborough, C.B.E.
Director: Anthony Smith.
Deputy Director: Wilf Stevenson.

BRITISH FILM & TELEVISION PRODUCERS ASSOCIATION LTD.
162-170 Wardour Street, London, W1V 4LA. Tel: 01-437 7700. FAX: 01-734 4564.

Chief Executive: Otto Plaschkes
Secretary: Andrew Patrick.

BRITISH KINEMATOGRAPH SOUND AND TELEVISION SOCIETY
547-549 Victoria House, Vernon Place, London, WC1B 4AD. Tel: 01-242 8400.

Secretary: Ray Mobsby
Founded in 1931, the Society was incorporated in 1946 to service the industries of its title, encouraging technical and scientific progress. To further these aims, the Society disseminates to its Members information on technical developments within these industries, arranges technical lectures, international conferences, and demonstrations, and encourages the exchange of ideas. The broad nature of its purpose is made possible by the subscriptions of its Members and by its freedom from political or commercial bias. The *BKSTS Journal; Image Technology*, is published monthly and is sent free to all members.

BRITISH MUSIC INFORMATION CENTRE
10 Stratford Place, London, W1N 9AE. Tel: 01-499 8567.

(Reference library of works by 20th Century British composers.)

THE BRITISH RADIO AND ELECTRONIC EQUIPMENT MANUFACTURERS' ASSOCIATION
Landseer House, 19 Charing Cross Road, London, WC2H 0ES. Tel: 01-930 3206. Telex: 296215 BREMA G.

Director: O. P. Sutton, C.B.E.
Secretary: R. B. S. Purdy, O.B.E.

BRITISH SOCIETY OF CINEMATOGRAPHERS LTD.
%Tree Tops, 11 Croft Road, Chalfont St. Peter, Gerrards Cross, Bucks, SL9 9AE. Tel: 0753 888052.

Secretary and Treasurer: Frances Russell.
(To promote and encourage the pursuit of the highest standards in the craft of motion picture photography.)

BRITISH VIDEOGRAM ASSOCIATION LTD
21-22 Poland Street, London, W1V 3DD. Tel: 01-437 5722. Telex: 295101.

Director General: Norman Abbott.

BROADCASTING AND ENTERTAINMENT TRADES ALLIANCE
181-185 Wardour Street, London, W1V 3AA. Tel: 01-439 7585.

General Secretary: D. A. Hearn.

CABLE TELEVISION ASSOCIATION
50 Frith Street, London, W1V 5TE. Tel: 01-437 0549/0983.

Director: Nicolas Melleash

CENTRAL CASTING LTD.
162-170 Wardour Street, London, W1V 3AT. Tel: 01-437 1881.

Directors: O. Beuselinck, J. Goodman, B. J. Kingham, I. Lewis, O. Plaschkes, , J. A. Walton, B. T. Yeoman.
Managing Director: B. T. Yeoman.
(Licensed annually by the Dept. of Employment.)

CHILDREN'S FILM & TELEVISION FOUNDATION LTD
Cannon Elstree Studios, Borehamwood, Herts., WD6 1JG. Tel: 01-953 1600. Cables: Chififo Borehamwood.

Chief Executive: S. T. Taylor, F.C.I.S.

CINEMA AND TELEVISION BENEVOLENT FUND
Royalty House, 72 Dean Street, London, W1V 6LT. Tel: 01-437 6567.

Executive Director: P. J. C. Ratcliffe, O.B.E.
Secretary: H. V. Hughes, F.C.A.
(The Fund gives relief by financial grants and allowances to needy members or ex-members of the film industry or independent TV, and their widows; maintenance and education of orphans and generally to assist those in distress due to sickness, injury, unemployment or old age. Convalescence is available to assist in recovery after illness or operations at "Glebelands," Wokingham, Berks. Admission to Convalescent Home free upon application to the Secretary.)

COMPOSERS' GUILD OF GREAT BRITAIN
34 Hanway Street, London, W1P 9DE.

General Secretary: Miss Elizabeth Yeoman.
(Objects: To further artistic and professional interests of its members.)

CONFEDERATION OF ENTERTAINMENT UNIONS
60-62 Clapham Road, London, SW9 0JJ.

President: Alan Sapper.
Vice-President: P. Plouviez.
Treasurer: P. Leech.
Secretary: J. Morton.
(Confederation of trades unions engaged in the entertainment industry.)

DIRECTORS GUILD OF GREAT BRITAIN
125 Tottenham Court Road, London, W1P 9HN. Tel: 01-387 7131.

Administrator: Susan Dormer

ELECTRICAL ELECTRONIC TELECOMMUNICATION AND PLUMBING UNION
Hayes Court, West Common Road, Bromley, BR2 7AU. Tel: 01-462 7755. FAX: 01-462 4959.

(Representing electrical electronic lighting operatives engaged in production.)
General Secretary: Eric Hammond.

ELECTRONIC ENGINEERING ASSOCIATION
Leicester House, 8 Leicester Street, London WC2H 7BN. Tel: 01-437 0678; Telex: 263536.

THE ENTERTAINMENT AGENTS' ASSOCIATION LTD.
403 Collingwood House, Dolphin Square, London, SW1V 3NE. Tel: 01-834 0515.

President: Bunny Lewis.
Secretary: Gordon Blackie.
(Founded in 1927 as the Agents' Assoc. and name changed to present one in February, 1966. The Association comprises the principal agencies in all branches of the entertainment industry.)

FEDERATION AGAINST COPYRIGHT THEFT (FACT)
7 Victory Business Centre, Worton Road, Isleworth, Middlesex. TW7 6ER. Tel: 01-568 6646. Telex: 295007.

Director General: P. C. Duffy.

FILM ARTISTES' ASSOCIATION
F.A.A. House, 61 Marloes Road, London W.8. Tel: 01-937 4567.

General Secretary: Michael Reynel.

GENERAL MUNICIPAL BOILERMAKERS & ALLIED TRADES UNION
Thorne House, Ruxley Ridge, Claygate, Esher, Surrey. Tel: 0372 62081. Telex: 27428.

General Secretary: John Edmonds.

GUILD OF BRITISH CAMERA TECHNICIANS
303-315 Cricklewood Broadway, London, NW2 6PQ. Tel: 01-450 3821 and 450 0000.

Chairman. Lou Lavelly.

GUILD OF FILM PRODUCTION ACCOUNTANTS AND FINANCIAL ADMINISTRATORS (GFPA)
Twickenham Film Studios, St. Margaret's, Twickenham, Middx. TW1 2AW. Tel: 01-892 4477. Telex: 884497 TWIKST G. FAX: 01-891 0168.

President: Ron Swinburne
Hon. Secretary: Maurice Landsberger

GUILD OF FILM PRODUCTION EXECUTIVES
Pinewood Studios, Iver Heath, Bucks. Tel: 0753 651700.

President: Stuart Lyons.
(The Guild is an association of many of the more experienced production executives in the UK film industry.)

THE INCORPORATED SOCIETY OF BRITISH ADVERTISERS LTD.
44 Hertford Street, London W1Y 8AE. Tel: 01-499 7502.

(Objects: The protection and advancement of the advertising interests of all member companies.)
Director: K. N. Miles.

INDEPENDENT PROGRAMME PRODUCERS' ASSOCIATION
50-51 Berwick Street, London, W1V 4RD. Tel: 01-439 7034. FAX: 01 494 2700.

INDEPENDENT TELEVISION ASSOCIATION (ITVA)
Knighton House, 56 Mortimer Street, London, W1N 8AN. Tel: 01-636 6866. Telex: 262988. FAX: 01-580 7892.

(The Association exists to represent and promote the interests of the programme companies appointed by the Independent Broadcasting Authority. The members are Anglia Television Ltd., Border Television p.l.c., Central Independent Television, p.l.c., Channel Television, Grampian Television p.l.c., Granada Television Ltd., HTV Ltd., London Weekend Television Ltd., Scottish Television p.l.c., TVS p.l.c., TSW-Television South West Ltd., Thames Television Ltd., Tyne Tees Television Ltd., Ulster Television p.l.c., Yorkshire Television Ltd., TV-a.m. Ltd.)
Director: David Shaw.

INSTITUTE OF PRACTITIONERS IN ADVERTISING
44 Belgrave Square, London, SW1X 8QS. Tel: 01-235 7020. Fax: 01-245 9904.

INTERNATIONAL VISUAL COMMUNICATIONS ASSOCIATION (IVCA)
102 Great Russell Street, London, WC1E 3LN. Tel: 01-580 0962.

(Objects: IVCA is the professional association providing a voice and a network for the promotion and use of screen communications. It is a non-profit making Association and the only British Association whose membership and interests span film, video and multi-image communications. IVCA was formed on January 1st 1988 through the merging of The International Television Association (ITVA UK) and The British Industrial and Scientific Film Association (BISFA), and has over 1500 members.)

MECHANICAL COPYRIGHT PROTECTION SOCIETY LTD.
Elgar House, 41 Streatham High Road, London, SW16 1ER. Tel: 01-769 4400. Cables and Telegrams: Mecolico, London S.W.16. Telex: 946792 MCPSG.

(Objects: The Society has the authority of some ten thousand music copyright owners in the U.K. and Commonwealth, the U.S.A., Germany, Italy and other countries to licence the use of their works for all forms of mechanical reproduction, including sound synchronisation in cinematograph, television and advertising films.)
Managing Director: R. W. Montgomery
Company Secretary and Financial Controller: K. R. D. Lowde.
Commercial Operations Controller: G. J. Churchill.

MOTION PICTURE EXPORT ASSOCIATION OF AMERICA INC.
162-170 Wardour Street, London W1V 3AT. Tel: 01-437 2282.

Senior Vice-President: S. Frederick Gronich.
Deputy Directors: Harlan G. Moen, Georg Eriksson.

MUSICIANS' UNION
60-62, Clapham Road, London, SW9 0JJ Cables: Amuse., London S.W.9. Tel: 01-582 5566.

General Secretary: John Morton.

THE PERFORMING RIGHT SOCIETY LTD.
29-33 Berners Street, London, W1P 4AA. Tel: 01-580 5544. Telex: 892678 PRSLONG. Fax: 6314138.

Chief Executive: M. J. Freeguard, F.C.I.S.
Public Relations Manager: Miss Lesley Brat, B.A.
(Representing the composers and publishers of music.)

THE PERSONAL MANAGERS' ASSOCIATION LTD.
% Secretary: Angela Adler Rvercroft, One Summer Road, East Molesey, Surrey KT8 9LX.

(An association of the principal personal managers who represent stars, feature players, authors, writers, producers, directors and technicians.)
President: Peter Dunlop.

PHONOGRAPHIC PERFORMANCE LTD.
Ganton House, 14/22 Ganton Street, London, W1V 1LB. Tel: 01-437 0311.

(A company founded by the British recording industry to own and exercise the public performance and broadcasting rights in sound recordings in the U.K. and to issue licences for public performances and broadcasting.)
Chairman: J. A. Brooks.
Managing Director: J. V. Love.

THE RADIO, ELECTRICAL AND TELEVISION RETAILERS' ASSOCIATION (RETRA) LTD.
RETRA House, 57-61 Newington Causeway, London, SE1 6BE. Tel: 01-403 1463.

Director: R. T. Edom

THE RADIO INDUSTRY COUNCIL
Landseer House, 19 Charing Cross Road, London, WC2H 0ES. Tel: 01-930 3206. Telex: 296215 BREMAG.

Director: O. P. Sutton, C.B.E.
Secretary: R. B. S. Purdy, O.B.E.

RADIO SOCIETY OF GREAT BRITAIN
Lambda House, Cranborne Road, Potters Bar, Herts., EN6 3JE. Tel: 0707 59015.

Chief Executive/Secretary: David A. Evans.

ROYAL TELEVISION SOCIETY
Tavistock House East, Tavistock Square, London, WC1H 9HR, Tel: 01-387 1970. FAX: 01-387 0358.

SCREEN ADVERTISING WORLD ASSOCIATION LTD.
103A Oxford Street, London, W1R 1TF. Tel: 01-734 7621.

SOCIETY OF AUTHORS
84 Drayton Gardens, London, SW10 9SB. Tel: 01-373 6642.

(An independent trade union representing authors.)

SOCIETY OF AUTHORS BROADCASTING GROUP
84 Drayton Gardens, London, SW10 9SB. Tel: 01-363 6642.

(Representing film, TV and radio writers.)
(A subsidiary group within the Society of Authors.)

SOUND AND COMMUNICATIONS INDUSTRIES FEDERATION
4-B, High Street, Burnham, Slough, SL1 7JH. Tel: 06286 67633.

Chief Executive: Ken Walker.

VARIETY CLUB OF GT. BRITAIN (TENT NO. 36)
32 Welbeck, Street, London, W1M 7PG. Tel: 01-935 4466.

Press Guy: David Jones.

THE WRITERS GUILD OF GREAT BRITAIN
430 Edgware Road, London, W2 1EH Tel: 01-723 8074.

(The Writers Guild of Great Britain is the Trades Union Council-affiliated union which is the recognised representative body for negotiating agreements for writers in film, television, and radio as well as in the field of theatre and of publishing. As well as negotiating industrial agreements, the Guild represents writers wherever their interests need to be represented.)
President: Maureen Duffy.
Hon. Treasurer: Patrick Campbell.
Gen. Sec.: Walter J. Jeffrey.

British-Based Equipment Companies and Services

ABEKAS VIDEO SYSTEMS LTD.

10 Portman Road, Reading, Berks. RG3 1JR. Tel: 0734 585421. Telex: 847579. FAX: 0734 597267.

ACMADE INTERNATIONAL

Oakside Oxford Road, Uxbridge, Middlesex UB9 4DX (0895-36313) Telex: 8954606.

ADVENT COMMUNICATIONS LTD.

Watermeadow House, Watermeadow Chesham, Bucks HP5 1LF. Tel: 0494 774400. Telex: 838870 G.

AEG-TELEFUNKEN (UK) LTD.

217 Bath Road, Slough, Berks. SL1 4AW. Tel: 2-872101.

AGFA
Motion Picture Division

27 Great West Road, Brentford, Middlesex TW8 9AX. Tel: 01-560 2131.

AKG ACOUSTICS LTD.

191 The Vale, London, W3 7QS. Tel: 01-749 2042.

AMEK SYSTEMS AND CONTROLS LIMITED

Islington Mill, James Street, Salford M3 5HW. Tel: 061-834 6747. Telex: 668127.

AMPEX INTERNATIONAL

Acre Road, Reading, Berks. Tel: 0734 85200.

AMSTRAD PLC

Brentwood House, 169 Kings Road, Brentwood, Essex. CM14 4EF. Tel: 0277 228888.

ARRI (G.B.) LTD.

The Movie House, 2/3 Airlinks, Spitfire Way, Heston, Middlesex. Tel: 01-848 8881.

ASTON ELECTRONIC DEVELOPMENTS LIMITED

125 Deepcut Bridge Road, Deepcut, Camberley, Surrey. Tel: 02516 6221.

AUDIX LTD.

Station Road, Wenden, Saffron Walden, Essex.

AUDIO KINETICS

Kinetic House, Theobald St., Boreham Wood, Herts. Tel: 01-953 8118.

AVS BROADCAST

Venture House, Davis Road, Chessington, Surrey KT9 1TT. Tel: 01-391 5678. FAX: 01-391 5409. Telex: 267439 AVS.

AV DISTRIBUTORS (LONDON) LTD.

21-22 St. Albans Place, Upper Street, Islington Green London N1 0NX. Tel: 01-226 1508.

BAL COMPONENTS LTD.

Bermuda Road, Nuneaton, Warwickshire, CV10 7QF. Tel: 0203 341111. Telex: 311563.

BALLANCROFT FILM & TV EQUIPMENT CO., LTD.

292 Worton Road, Isleworth, Middlesex. Tel: 01-560 494.

F.W.O. BAUCH LTD.

49 Theobald Street, Boreham Wood, Herts. WD6 4RZ. Tel: 01-953 0091. Telex: 27502. FAX: 01-207 5970.

BELL & HOWELL LTD.

Alperton House, Bridgewater Road, Wembley, Middlesex HA0 1EG (01-902 8812). FAX: 01-902 1954.

ROBERT BOSCH LTD.

PO Box 166, Rhodes Way, Watford. Tel: 0923 44233.

BOSTON INSULATED WIRE (UK) LTD.

1 Canbury Park Road, Kingston-upon-Thames, Surrey. Tel: 01-546 3384.

BRABURY ELECTRONICS LTD.

Smirham Bridge, Hungerford, Berks. RG17 1OQU. Tel: 04 886 5511.

BOSTON INSULATED WIRE (UK) LTD.

1 Canbury Park Road, Kingston-upon-Thames, Surrey. Tel: 01-5463384.

CANFORD AUDIO

Crowther Road, Washington, Tyne & Wear NE38 0BW. Tel: 091 415 0205. Telex: 538202 CANFRD G. FAX: 091 416 0392.

CARLTON COMMUNICATIONS, PLC.

New Roman House, 10 East Road, London, N1 6AJ. Tel: 01-251 1533. Telex: 28177. FAX: 01-608 2244.

CEL ELECTRONICS LTD.

Chroma House, Shire Hill, Saffron Walden, Essex CB11 3AQ. Tel: 0799 23817. Telex: 817807 CHROMA G. FAX: 0799 28081.

CFS EQUIPMENT LTD.

10 Wadsworth Road, Perivale, Greenford, Middx. UB6 7JX. Tel: 01-998 2731. Telex: 24672.

CINEVIDEO LTD.

7 Silver Road, White City Industrial Park, Wood Lane, London W12 7SG. Tel: 01-743 3839. Telex: 915 282 CINEGP G. FAX: 01-749 3501.

COX ASSOCIATES LTD.

Cox House, Amberley Way, Hounslow, Middlesex TW4 6BH. Tel: 01-570 8283. Telex: 946441 COXAL G.

CROMA RESEARCH LTD.

Croma House, North Way, Walworth Industrial Estate, Andover, Hants SP10 5AZ. Tel: 0264 332132. Telex: 477407.

DOLBY LABORATORIES INC.

346 Clapham Road, London SW9 9AP (01-720 1111). Telex 919109. FAX: 01-720 4118.

PHILLIP DRAKE ELECTRONICS LTD.

37 Broadwater Road, Welwyn Garden City, Herts AL7 3AX. Tel: 0707 333866. Telex: 25415 DRAKE G.

EASTMAN KODAK COMPANY

European Region Office, 245 Hammersmith Road, London, W6 8PL. Tel: 01-748 7979. Telex: 261155. FAX: 01-741 5968.

EDRIC AUDIO VISUAL LTD.

34-36 Oak End Way, Gerrards Cross, Bucks. SL9 8BR. Tel.: 02813 84646 and 86521.

EDS PORTAPROMPT LTD.

Lane End Road Sands, High Wycombe, Bucks HP12 4JQ. Tel: 0494 450414. Telex: 848314 CHACOM G. ATTN EDS. FAX: 0494 37591.

ELECTROSONIC LTD.

815 Woolwich Road, London, SE7 8LT. Tel: 01 855 1101.

ELF AUDIO VISUAL LTD.

836 Yeovil Road, Trading Estate, Slough, Berks. Tel: 75-36123.

ENGLISH ELECTRIC VALVE COMPANY LIMITED

Chelmsford, Essex CM1 2QU. Tel: 0245 493493.

FILM STOCK CENTRE

68-70 Wardour Street, London, W1V 3HP. Tel: 01-734 0038.

FUJI PHOTO FILM (UK) LTD.

125 Finchley Road, Swiss Cottage, London, NW3 6JH. Tel: 01-586 5900.

FUTURE FILM DEVELOPMENTS

114 Wardour Street, London W1A 3DG. Tel: 01-434 3344. Telex: 21624 ALOF FED G.

GEC CABLE SYSTEMS

P.O. Box 53. Copesewood. COVENTRY CV3 1HJ. Tel: 0203 433184. Telex: 31361 GECTEL G.

GEC (LAMPS AND LIGHTING) LTD.

PO Box 17, East Lane, Wembley, Middlesex HA9 7PG. Tel: 01-904 4321.

GML

143-145 Cardiff Road. Reading, Berks. RG1 8JF. Tel: 0734 584948. Telex: 847109 GUNML G.

GORDON AUDIO VISUAL LTD.

28 Market Place, Oxford Circus, London W1N 8PH. Tel: 01-580 9191.

HARKNESS SCREENS LTD.

The Gate Studios, Station Road, Boreham Wood, Herts. WD6 1DQ (01-953 3611). Telex: 8955602 Perlux G. Cables: Screens London. FAX: 01-207-3657. Int. FAX: 44 1 207 3657.

HAYDEN LABORATORIES LTD.

Chiltern Hill, Chalfont St. Peter, Bucks. 9UG. Tel: 0753 888447.

HITACHI DENSHI (UK) LTD.

13-14 Garrick Industrial Centre, Irving Way, Hendon, London, NW9 6A2. Tel: 01-202 4311.

IAN P. KINLOCH AND COMPANY LIMITED

3 Darwin Close, Reading, Berkshire, RG2 0TB. Tel: 0734 311030. Telex: 846787 IPK Co.

INDEPENDENT CAMERA AND EQUIPMENT CO. LTD.

60 Farringdon Road, London EC1R 3BP. Tel: 01-251 3885.

INTERNATIONAL VIDEO CORPORATION (UK) LTD.

10 Portman Road, Reading, Berks, RG3 1JR. Tel: 0734 585421.

JOE DUNTON CAMERAS LTD.

Wycombe Road, Wembley, Middlesex HA0 1QN. Tel: 01-903 7933

IKEGAMI ELECTRONICS

61 High Street, Kingston-upon-Thames, Surrey, KT1 1LO. Tel: 01-546 7772. Telex: 897005 ITCG.

KADEK VISION
P.O. No. 21, Shepperton Studio Centre, Studios Road, Shepperton, Middlesex TW17 0QD. Tel: 093 2866941.

KEM ELECTRONIC LTD.
24 Vivian Avenue, London NW4 3XP. Tel: 01-202 0244.

KODAK LTD.
P.O.Box 66, Kodak House, Station Road, Hemel Hempstead, Herts. HP1 1JU. Tel: 0442-62331.

LEE COLORTRAN
Ladbroke Hall, Barlby Road, London W10 5HH. Tel: 01-968 7000.

LEE ELECTRIC (LIGHTING) LTD.
Ladboke Hall, 85 Barlby Road, London, W10 5HH. Tel: 01-960 2111. FAX: 01-960 2400. Telex: 924743 LEELEC G.

LEE FILTERS LTD.
Walworth Industrial Estate, Andover, Hants. SP10 5AN Tel: 0264-66245.

LIPSNER-SMITH CO. LTD.
Unit 7, Cowley Mill Trading Estate, Longbridge Way, Uxbridge, Middlesex. Tel: 89 52191.

MARCONI COMMUNICATION SYSTEMS LTD.
Marconi House, New Street, Chelmsford, Essex CM1 1PL. Tel: 0245 353221.

NEILSON-HORDELL LTD.
Central Trading Estate, Staines, Middlesex. Tel: 81-56456.

NEVE ELECTRONICS INTERNATIONAL
Cambridge House Melbourn, Nr. Royston, Herts. SG8 6AU. Tel: 0763 60776.

OPTICAL & TEXTILE LTD.
22-26 Victoria Road, New Barnet, Herts. EN4 9PF. Tel: 01-441 2199.

OSRAM (GEC) LTD.
P.O. Box 17, East Lane, Wembley, Middlesex HA9 7PG. Tel: 01-904 4321.

JOHN PAGE LTD.
Wesley House, 75 Wesley Avenue, London, N.W. 10. Tel: 01-961 4181.

P.A.G. FILM LTD., & P.A.G. POWER LTD.
565 Kingston Road, London SW20 85A. Tel: 01-543 3131.

PANDORA'S OTHER BOX LTD.
208A Main Road, Sutton-at-Hone, Dartford, Kent DA4 9HP. Tel: 0322 866 245.

PHOTOGRAPHIC ELECTRICAL CO. LTD.
71 Dean Street, London W1V 6DE. Tel: 01-437 4633.

PHOTOMEC (LONDON) LTD.
(Humphries Group) Valley Road Industrial Estate, St. Albans, AL3 6NU, Herts. Tel: 56 50711.

QUANTEL
31 Turnpike Road, Newbury, Berks: RG13 2NE. Tel: 0635 32222. FAX: 0635 31776.

RADAMEC EPO LTD.
Bridge Road, Chertsey, Surrey, KT16 8LJ. Tel: 0932 561181. FAX: 0932 568775. Telex: 929945 RADEPO G.

RANK AUDIO VISUAL
3 Centaurs Business Park, Syon Lane, Isleworth, Middx. TW7 5QD. Tel: 01-568 9222. Telex: 935064. FAX: 01-847 0370.

RANK CINTEL
Watton Road, Ware, Hertfordshire. Tel: 0920 3939.

RANK FILM LABORATORIES LTD.
North Orbital Road, Denham, Uxbridge, Middlesex UB9 5HQ Tel: 0895 832323 Telex: 934704 FAX: 0895.833617.

RANK TAYLOR HOBSON LTD
P.O. Box 36, 2 New Star Rd., Leicester LE4 7JG. Tel: 0533 763771. Telex: 34411. Cables: Metrology Lestr).

RANK VIDEO SERVICES LTD.
Phoenix Park, Great West Road, Brentford, Middlesex TW8 9PL. Tel: 01-568 4311. Telex 22345

RONFORD-BAKER ENGINEERING CO. LTD.
Braziers, Oxhey Lane, Watford, Herts. WD1 4RJ. Tel: 01-428 5941. FAX: 01-428 4743.

RONFORD LTD.
Lee International Film Studios, Studio Road, Shepperton, Middx. TW17 0QD. Tel: 0932 564111.

RPS BROADCAST FACILITIES
10 Giltway, Giltbrook. Nottingham NG16 2GN. Tel: 0602 384103.

SAMUELSON GROUP PLC
303-315 Cricklewood Broadway, London NW2 6PQ. Tel: 01-452 8090.

SAMUELSON SALES LTD.
303 Cricklewood Broadway, London NW2 6PQ. Tel: 01-450-4557.

SAMUELSON SIGHT & SOUND LTD.

303-315 Cricklewood Broadway, London NW2 6PQ. Tel: 01-452 8090.

SCREEN ELECTRONICS LTD.

19 Anson Road, Martlesham Heath, Nr. Ipswich, Suffolk. Tel: 0473 623748. Telex 988732.

SCREENTECH

23 Wrotham Road, Gravesend, Kent DA11 0PA. Tel: 0474 333111. FAX: 0474 328184. Telex: 966475 VACORP.

SHURE ELECTRONICS LTD.

Eccleston Road, Maidstone, Kent, ME15 6AU. Tel: 0622 59881.

SONY BROADCAST LTD.

Belgrave House, Basing View, Basingstoke, Hants. RG21 2LA. Tel: 0256 55011.

SOUND ASSOCIATES LTD.

56 Ayres Street, London, SW1 1EU. Tel: 01-403 5348.

SPACEWARD MICROSYSTEMS LTD.

The Old School, Haddenham, Cambridge CB6 3XA. Tel: 0353 741 222.

STRAND LIGHTING

P.O. Box 51, Great West Road, Brentford, Middlesex TW8 9HR. Tel: 01-560 3171.

SURVEY & GENERAL INSTRUMENT CO. LTD.

Fircroft Way, Edenbridge, Kent TN8 6HA. Tel: 0732 864111. Telex: 95527 OPTSLS G.

SYLVANIA LIGHTING

Otley Road, Charlestown Shipley, West Yorkshire, BD17 7SN. Tel: 0274 595921.

SYSTEM VIDEO LTD.

Unit A, 120 Oyster Lane, Byfleet, Surrey KT14 7JG. Tel: Byfleet 40408. Telex: 928538. FAX: 09323 54389

TECHNOVISION CAMERAS LTD.

Unit 4 St. Margarets Business Centre, Drummond Place, Twickenham, Middlesex TW1 1JN. Tel: 01-891 5961. Telex: 917408 TECNOV G. FAX: 01-744 1154.

THOMSON-CSF ELECTRONIC TUBES LTD.

Ringway House, Bell Road, Daneshill, Basingstoke.

THORN EMI LAMPS AND COMPONENTS LTD.

Miles Road, Mitcham, Surrey CR4 37X. Tel: 01-640 1221.

3M UNITED KINGDOM PLC

3M House, P.O. Box 1, Bracknell, Berkshire RG12 1JU. Tel: 0344 58571.

VALIANT ELECTRICAL WHOLESALE CO.

20 Lettice Street, Fulham, London SW6. Tel: 01-736 8115.

VARIAN TVT LTD

(Subsidiary of Varian Associates Inc. of California) P.O. Box 41, Coldhams Lane, Cambridge CB1 3JU. Tel: 0223 245115. Telex: 81342 VARTVTG. FAX: 0223 214632.

VG ELECTRONICS LTD

Theaklen Drive, Hastings, East Sussex, TN34 1YQ. Tel: 0424 446888. Telex: 957357 VGELEC. FAX: 0424 435699.

W. VINTEN LTD.

Western Way, Bury St. Edmunds, Suffolk IP33 3TB. Tel: 0284 752121. Telex: 81176 Vinten G. FAX: 0284 706514.

VISTEK ELECTRONICS LTD

Unit C, Wessex Road, Bourne End, Bucks. SL8 5DT. Tel: 06285 31221. Telex: 846077.

WESTAR SALES & SERVICES LTD.

Unit 7, Cowley Mill Trading Estate, Longbridge Way, Uxbridge, Middlesex UB8 2YG. Tel: 0895 34429. Telex: 8954 169.

WINSTED

Units 3/4, Wassage Way, Hampton Lovett Industrial, Estate, Droitwich WR9 10NX. Tel: (0905) 770276. Telex: 334007 WINSTD G.

WOTAN LAMPS LTD

1 Gresham Way, Durnsford Road, London, SW19 8HU. Tel: 01-947 1261.

ZONAL LTD

Holmethorpe Avenue, Redhill, Surrey, RH1 2NX. Tel: 0737 767171. FAX: 0737 767610.

The
World Market

* **MARKET ANALYSES**

* **STATIONS**

* **OUTLOOK**

* **PROGRAM SOURCES**

The World Market

AFGHANISTAN

People's Radio & Television Afghanistan, Post Office Box 544, Kabul; 8 stations, 19,000 sets.

ALBANIA

Radiodiffusion TV Shqiptar, Tirana, government-owned experimental station, broadcasts sixteen hours weekly to some 210,000 sets, many of them located in public places so that segments of the populace not owning sets can view the programs.

ANGOLA

Television Popular de Angola, C.P. 2604, Luanda; 30,000 sets.

ARGENTINA

Television had its debut in this country in 1951 with only one channel (7) in Buenos Aires. Since then it has been joined by Channels 9, 11 and 13 (in 1960–61), all of which are state-owned and operated while channel 9 (under state control since 1974) was licensed back to Alejandro Romay in 1984. There are now 36 channels in the provinces, which have 191 repeating stations.

Of the 36 provincial stations 30 are privately owned. The PAL-N color system has been used since 1980.

Cable outlets now total 150, three of which operate in the northern and western suburbs of Buenos Aires within the metropolitan area.

AUSTRALIA

1986–87 witnessed a major shakeup of Australian commercial television. Partly as a result of the Hawke government's strict cross-ownership rules covering print media and television, the three original network owners, after more than 30 years, sold to relative newcomers to electronic media. The longtime owners, Kerry Packer, Rupert Murdoch and the Fairfax family sold Network Seven (recently renamed Australian Television Network) to Christopher Skase of Qintex/Universal Telecasters, Nine Network to Alan Bond (Bond Media) and Network Ten to Frank Lowy (Westfield Capital Corp/Northern Star Holdings), respectively.

The Australian television industry, which first began broadcasts in 1956 and color transmission in the mid 1970s, consists of a mixture of government and private enterprise with three commercial networks and two government-owned (Australian Broadcasting Corp, or ABC, and Special Broadcasting Service, SBS), each with a distinctive programming identity. ABC's program mix is Australian and British with a majority of its product from the BBC, Thames and Granada with whom it has exclusive agreements. Since it began broadcasting via Ausst satellite in 1986, ABC now has a national saturation of almost 100% of the population including the most remote areas of the Outback. Australia's other cultural public broadcaster, SBS which broadcasts in more than 40 languages, (with an audience of less than 2% in most Australian capital cities) is currently embroiled in a public debate over its funding future. Funded totally by the government for the eight years of its existence, SBS has reached a point where its budgets are stretched and it faces threats of amalgamation with the ABC. SBS is also handicapped in that it has recently been pushed onto the UHF band and cannot be tuned in by a large portion of the audience in the cities where it is transmitted.

Predominantly U.S. and European programming dominates the three commercial networks (each of which has an audience share of 25–30%) and each network has exclusive agreements for programming. Nine Network (the number one network), has agreements with Warner Bros. and Columbia, CBS and ABC networks, MTV, ESPN and WTN. Its new owner Bond Media also operates the country's only private satellite broadcaster, Sky Channel. The Australian Television Network (formerly Seven Network) has established a predominantly Australian image for the network. ATN has a station in each of the five major mainland state capitals with a potential audience reach of almost 70% of the national total. ATN has an ongoing relationship with Paramount, Disney, Lorimar and recently it signed an exclusive agreement with MGM/UA for theatrical and TV product. It also has a long-standing relationship with London Weekend Television, BBC and ITV.

Network Ten recently has attempted to break an unwritten agreement between the three networks over exclusive agreements with American distributors by not waiting until end-of-year for buying agreements.

A recent survey by the Australian Broadcasting Tribunal shows that over the past 10 years, the percentage of households watching TV during the evening dropped from a high of 54.5% in 1979 to the current 51.9%. The fall-offs have been in the daily prime-time area, children's afternoon TV and Friday and Saturday nights. Australian production companies include: Beyond International Group, Revcom (French), McElroy and McElroy, Taft-Hardie's Hanna-Barbera Australia, Crawford Prods., Grundy Organisation, Kennedy-Meller Group.

Viewing Patterns: Total TV households: 4,914,000; families viewing (aggregate): 4,792,000; families viewing (percentage): 98%. Average viewing time per week of all age groups is 18 hours, 26 minutes.

National Top-Ten Programs, 1987–88: (in order) 60 Minutes; Alf; The Cosby Show; Neighbours; News and Weather; Mike Willesee; The Flying Doctors; Family Ties; Sale of the Century; Who's the Boss.

AUSTRIA

Austria's only TV and radio network, the Austrian Broadcasting Corp (ORF), an independent public corporation, operates two TV channels FS1, which broadcasts from 9 a.m. until midnight, and FS 2, which broadcasts from the afternoon to midnight.

Of Austria's 2,760,000 households, 95% have at least one TV set. On an average, ORF TV reaches approximately 72% of the country's 7,500,000 people daily with primetime viewership roughly 55% of the population. Additionally, in each of Austria's nine provinces, ORF has regional studios for local broadcasting of nine hours daily. Approximately 60% of ORF's revenue comes from radio and TV license fees, while 40% comes from radio and TV advertising.

A 35-member board of trustees, the Kuratorium, a 35-member committee of representatives from the radio and TV audience and a commission monitoring ORF compliance with the provisions of the Austrian broadcasting Act, is responsible for supervising ORF.

BAHRAIN

Bahrain TV, P.O. Box 1075, Manama, Bahrain, operates 1 channel and 1 relay for some 176,000 color sets.

BANGLADESH

Pilot station established in 1964 by government. Now includes originating station at Dacca with relay stations at Chittagong, Natore, Khulna, Sylhet, and Rangpur plus two under construction. Address Bangladesh TV, Television Bhaban, Rampura P.O. Box 456, Dacca. 450,000 sets.

BOLIVIA

Television broadcasting began here in 1969. The two networks are government-controlled. Channel 7 is national and the other is via eight university channels (Channel 13 in La Paz). Bolivia has about 450,000 TV sets. There is also a small cable operation, Channel 3. NTSC is the TV system, and there has been color since 1980. As no copyright laws exist in Bolivia, much product is pirated and many producers have stopped supplying product since there are no dollars available.

Empresa Nacional de Televisón Boliviana (Channel 7). Pres., Ricardo Ocampo, Ayacucho, 467, La Paz. Telex 2312 TVBOL.

Dial (Channel 6). Pres., Javier Zuazo Chavez, v.p., Eduardo Quintanilla, Calle Batallón Colorados, Casilla 20574, La Paz, Telex 2531B1CSA.

Illimani de Communicaciones (Channel 9). Pres., Raul Garafulic Gutiérrez. Casilla 6122, La Pax. Telex 3342.

Channel 13 (University Channel). Pres., Eduardo Barrientos. In operation since 1981. Av. 6 de agosto, Ed. Hoy.

Channel 3. Pay-TV channel, headed by Alvaro Valerama and Rolando Chiappe. Avds. Arce, Ed. Ilimani.

BRAZIL

Television was introduced in 1951. Brazil now has some 24,000,000 sets using PAL-M system. The audience is estimated at about 100,000,000, which makes this country the highest selling and fastest growing market in Latin America with TV Globo earning 70% of the revenue.

Brazilian law requires that all owners of radio or TV stations be of Brazilian nationality. A further law stipulates that all foreign films shown on TV be dubbed, and that no station may transmit more than 22 half hours of foreign films for each 72 hours of weekly transmission time. Stations

716

which transmit less than 12 hours per day have a corresponding lower quota. Seven sound studios, four in Rio de Janeiro and three in São Paulo take care of the dubbing of all American and some Italian, Argentine and Mexican films that come into the country.

Professional Association of Radio and TV Station Owners: Sindicato dos Proprietarios de Impresas de Radio Diffusao a Televisao, Avenida Presidente 'Churchill 97 Sala 606, Rio de Janeiro.

BRUNEI

Established 1975 by governmental Radio TV Brunei, Bander Seri Begawan, Brunei. Two channels; 238,000 sets.

BULGARIA

Bulgarian Television, San Stefano Str 29, 1504 Sofia serves 2.6 million sets using 625-line Secam color.

BURMA

Burma Broadcasting Service, Prome Road, Kamayut Post Office, Rangoon. One station. 74,000 sets.

CAMBODIA (Kampuchea)

Radio Kampuchea Television, 28 Ave Preah Mohaksatryany Kossonak, Phnom Penh City, broadcasts daily on Channel 8 with relay to Bokor. Sets are estimated at 43,000.

CANADA

Number of TV Sets: In 1987, 94% of 9,556,000 households had at least one color TV set, a significant increase from a decade ago when the figure was 35% of households in 1977 (as reported by Statistics Canada, a federal government agency).

Number of TV Stations: 118—including 18 Canadian Broadcasting Corp. owned stations and 25 privately-owned affiliates; and 22 CTV Television Network affiliate stations.

TV Corporations: Canadian Broadcasting Corp., 1500 Bronson Ave., P.O. Box 8478, Ottawa, Ont. K1G 3J5 (613) 724-1200; English Networks: 1255 Bay St., P.O. Box 500, Stn. A, Toronto, Ont. M5W 1E6 (416) 975-3311; French Networks: 1400 est boul René Lévesque, P.O. Box 6000, Montréal, Qué. H3C 3A8 (514) 285-3211; CBC Enterprises/Les Enterprises Radio-Canada (English & French Networks), Box 500, Stn. A, Toronto, Ont. M5W 1E6 (514) 975-3500. CTV Television Network Ltd., 42 Charles St. E., Toronto, Ont. M4Y 1T5 (416) 928-6000. Global Communications Limited (Global Television Network), 81 Barber Greene Rd., Don Mills, Ont. M3C 2A2 (416) 446-5311.

Educational TV: Access Network (The Alberta Educational Communications Corporation), 16930-114 Ave., Edmonton, Alta. T5M 3S2 (403) 451-7272. TVOntario (Province of Ontario educational network), 2180 Yonge St., Toronto, Ont. M4T 2T1 (416) 484-2600.

Pay TV: Allarcom Limited, 5325-104th St., Edmonton, Alta. T6H 5B8 (403) 436-1250. The Family Channel, 98 Queen St. E., Ste. 200, Toronto, Ont. M5C 1S6 (416) 867-8866 (National). First Choice Canadian Communications Corp., 98 Queen St. E., Toronto, Ont. M5C 1S6 (416) 364-9115 (covers eastern half of Canada from Ontario to Newfoundland). Superchannel/Alberta, 5324 Calgary Trail, Edmonton, Alta. T6H 4J8 (403) 437-7744 (covers western half of Canada from Manitoba to British Columbia). Television Quatre Saisons (Four Seasons Television Network Inc.), 405 Ogilvy, Montréal, Qué. H3N 1M4 (514) 271-3535 (French-language service in Québec). YTV Canada Incorporated, 525 Lakeshore Blvd. W., Toronto, Ont. H5V 2V8 (416) 340-1221 (Children/teens/families) (National).

Specialty Service: MuchMusic Network, 299 Queen St. W., Toronto, Ont. M5V 2Z5 (416) 591-5757 (National—basic cable). Vision TV: Canada's Faith Network, 315 Queen St. E., Toronto, Ont. M5A 1S7 (416) 366-9211 (Multi-faith) (National satellite to cable).

Cable TV: In 1987, 67%—or 6,424,000 households out of 9,556,000—subscribed to cable TV services, a growth from 46% in 1977, a decade ago. Of these households, 3,652,000 have cable converters (as reported by Statistics Canada, a federal Government agency). There are approx. 1,000 cable companies and, in early 1988, the Canadian Cable Television Association (CCTA) had 655 members, representing about 90% of all cable television subscribers in the country. The number of cable subscribers served by CCTA is around 6,000,000. In 1986 the net profit before taxes of Canadian cable companies amounted to $140,000,000 (Canadian funds).

Industry Organizations: The Federation of Canadian Guilds and Unions in Films and Television, 65 Heward Ave., Ste. 106, Toronto, Ont. M4M 2T5 (416) 462-1022. Canadian Cable Television Association, 85 Albert St., Ste. 400, Ottawa, Ont. K1P 6A4 (613) 232-2631.

—PATRICIA THOMPSON

CHILE

The spectacular surge in the television industry in Chile since 1973 reflects the profound transformation of Chilean society itself.

The Census of 1970 revealed that only 19% of Chilean households possessed a TV set. However by 1982 the Census showed that 78% of households had at least one TV set. By the end of 1987, more than 2 million households had TV sets, which represents 81% coverage. It is estimated that within a few years more than 95% of households will have TV.

The impulse for this boom in television has been what the economists have called "Chile's Quiet Revolution" since 1973 when the Marxist government was ruled illegal and unconstitutional by the Congress and the Supreme Court and the economy was returned to private hands. The freedom to invest and to create produced immediate dividends.

In 1973, almost 2 million people in Santiago lived in subhuman conditions in shacks which had no electricity and no running water. By 1987 however, every home had electricity and running water. Consequently, the younger generation is far better educated and much healthier than their parents. Therefore the youth market for television advertisers is now the most important. The average 10 year-old child has already spent 7,300 hrs. of his life watching TV, and the average 15 year-old has watched 10,000 hrs.

The Structure of Chilean Television: As of July 19, 1988, there are three networks in Chile: Television Nacional de Chile (state-owned); Universidad Catolica de Chile Television and Universidad de Chile Television. There is also a channel in Valparaiso operated by the Universidad Catolica de Valparaiso. The three networks (TVN, U. Cat. & U. de Ch.) each have regional channel-outlets, and therefore all regions of the country (including the Antarctic Zone and Easter Island) are served by at least one network.

A new Law of Television in preparation will end the monopoly of VHF television and permit an unlimited number of channels and networks. The new Law of Television will also allow an unlimited number of UHF channels (only to be restricted by technical factors).

Under existing law (and as contemplated in the new law) there is no limit on the number of hours of transmissions per day. In 1970, the networks transmitted only an average of 6.5 hrs. per day. In 1987, the networks transmit 15–17 hrs. per day. The networks began transmitting regularly in color in April 1978.

Television Programming: According to a survey by the Consejo Nacional de Television (the body which regulates Chilean television, similar to the FCC), foreign-produced programming accounts for 58% of transmission-hrs. per day, with 42% produced in Chile.

Foreign programs include "Miami Vice," "The A-Team," "L.A. Law," "The Cosby Show," "Golden Girls," "Alf," "Moonlighting," "Dynasty," "Dallas," "Falcon Crest," etc., as well as specials such as Miss Universe, Miss World and the Oscars ceremony, and at least one mini-series per week. All foreign programming is dubbed into Spanish.

The Chilean-produced programming consists of news, sports, cultural-educational, children's and "teleseries" (a prime-time "soap" of about 75 mins per day). TVN and U. Cat. each produce one teleseries per year of about 130 episodes. Existing law also requires about 4 hrs. per week in prime-time of "cultural" programs.

The survey by the Consejo Nacional de Television shows the following breakdown of a typical day's programming by category: General Entertainment: 50.24%; Journalistic: 22.98; Cultural-Educational: 14.06; Children's: 12.72; Total: 100.00%

TVN has a second channel which exclusively broadcasts cultural programming.

Trends in Television Advertising: Existing law calculates the maximum number of commercial-minutes per day on the following basis: six minutes of commercials for every hour of transmission, but if time is not sold in a particular time-slot it can be added on to any other hour during the day. The new law under discussion contemplates total abolition of commercial-time regulations.

According to an exhaustive study by Megatec S.A., the total investment in television advertising time in 1987 was about US$150 million. In comparison to advertising in newspapers and magazines, television advertising represented 58.6% of the total invested in these media.

The breakdown by network is as follows: U. Cat.: 53.8%; TVN: 41.3; U. de Ch.: 4.2; U. Cat. de V.: 0.7; Total: 100.00%.

The ranking of the 10 most-advertised types of products on television is as follows: 1) Magazines, 2) Dept. stores, 3) Drinks, 4) Toys, 5) Cinemas, 6) Clothing, 7) Banks, 8) Toothpastes, 9) Newspapers, 10) Yogurt.

In terms of advertising in all media, the largest advertiser in 1987 was Lever Chile, followed by Nestle Chile.

Cable TV: Cable TV service began in late 1987 in Santiago. By early 1988, there were 4,200 homes with cable, and is growing by leaps and bounds. There are four cable channels in operation in Santiago at present. Their programming includes news, entertainment and sports reports, movies, specials, etc.

Sources: Consejo Nacional de Television, Rodrigo Altamirano, jefe dep. control, Moneda 1020, 4th floor, Santiago, Tel.: 82306; Megatec S.A., Harry Thomas, ger. gral., Paulette Ivovic, acct. mgr., Hernando de Aguirre 1111, Providencia, Santiago, Tel.: 225 7016; Film & Television Commission of Chile, Alan Hootnick, Camino Mirasol 1955, Las Condes, Santiago, Tel.: 243 1366, Telex: 341687 ALMAC CK.

—ALAN HOOTNICK

CHINA (People's Republic)

Peking TV, opened in 1969, consists of three networks, one purely local and the other two broadcasting by micro-wave to the rest of the country. Color broadcasts began in 1973. Shanghai, China's largest city, has two channels on the air for about 9 hours daily with some 50% of the programs listed as entertainment, 20% movies, news or documentaries, and 20% sports or children's programs, in addition to educational and foreign language-instruction programs. Chinese officials blame the Cultural Revolution for the slow growth of TV and say that after the Gang of Four was ousted in the following decade TV stations were opened in all 29 of China's provinces and private set ownership rose to 81 million tuned to 70 stations and 130 relays. With some 7 million sets being added annually, China is producing 800 TV dramas a year. Twenty percent of all households now have TV sets and by 1990 this number will be doubled.

The biggest impact on Chinese audiences was the Walt Disney Company release of a 2-year cycle of films to be shown weekly under an agreement to shares revenues from commercials.

In the past 5 years China has sold 10,000 hours of TV programs to 150 countries. Last year Shanghai TV alone imported 200 programs from 24 countries and exported 400 hours of programming.

CCTV began use of International Telecommunications Satellite Organization facilities to reach parts of China where reception is poor to nonexistent but only until they set up their own satellite service for which they are setting up 50 ground stations. Some 62% of the country is covered already as far as reception is concerned.

Some 93.3% of city homes have TV sets but the figure is only 11.5% for rural homes, due to poor reception. CTV broadcasts 30hours weekly, programming news, instruction, cartoons, variety and drama. Audience estimated at 800 million.

China now manufactures some 8.2 million sets annually and it is estimated that the number of sets will soon reach 80 million, including sets open to the public audience. Total number of nation-wide stations (including micro-wave relay stations) is over 40. Black-and-white sets sell for the equivalent of $370 and color sets for about $1,335 and there is a waiting list for the former. Domestic and imported films are broadcast from time to time, including American feature films occasionally.

Central Broadcasting Administration, Hsin Men, Peking, now offers nation-wide TV commercials at rates ranging from about $625 for a 15-second spot to a full minute for $1,800.

CHINA (Taiwan)

Television began in 1962 by the Educational Television Station which later became the private China Television Service in 1971. There are now three networks: Taiwan Television Enterprise (1962), China Television Company (1969) and China Television Service. All three act as private corporations deriving revenues from commercials. These three stations have 24 transmitters with total broadcasts of about 265 hours weekly for some 5.9 million set owners (1.25 sets per family) who pay about $1.50 annually for a license. About 80% of the programs are domestic, with most of the imports from the U.S.A. Over half of the sets are color. Taiwan has two communication satellite stations. A new rule states that commercials must not exceed 15% total broadcast time. Movie theatre owners complain that the three imported feature films shown weekly on television hurt their box office.

All three networks broadcast in color, TTV and CTV 6 hours 25 minutes weekdays and 12 hours weekends and holidays while CTS broadcasts 10.15 hours weekdays, 15 hours on Saturday and 17 hours Sunday or holidays. News takes an average of 21%, public service over 10%, culture and education 20%, entertainment 48%. TTV has 10 transmitters, CTV 6, and CTS 8, plus an equal number of relay stations. Sets number 5,900,000. Of the 20.4 billion yuan spent for advertising 29.07% went to television.

New rules call for no commercials during programs of less than 30 minutes and all commercials to secure government approval. In the future, 80% of all programs must originate in Taiwan with entertainment programs taking up no more than 55% of standard broadcast time and 45% or more devoted to educational, cultural or news types.

With relay stations it is estimated that 100% of the island's population of 18 million receives TV reception. About 12% of programs are imports, mostly from America, and these are broadcast in the original English with Chinese captions, which has served to develop knowledge of the English language among the populace.

TV showings of full-length Chinese-language, feature films imported from Hong Kong were stopped following retaliatory action by local cinema interests but the government may step in later and permit such showings, except on Sundays and holidays when the theatres reap their largest harvest. Inquiries should be addressed: Ministry of Communications, Taipei, Taiwan, Republic of China, or to: China Radio/TV Assoc. 6-144 Hsin Shen (South) Rd., Section 1, Taipei, Taiwan, Republic of China.

CONGO

Radio-TV de Congo, B.P. 2241, Brazzaville. One station; 8,000 sets.

EGYPT

Television broadcasting in Egypt was launched in the early sixties, beaming programs in the European Technical Transmission with an image of 825 Scansions known as Middle East SECAM.

The two main channels now cover large areas of the Middle East including Saudi Arabia, thus boosting advertising rates continuously.

Both channels transmit over 200 hours weekly covering all spheres and are hooked to international satellite for new up-dates and major world events. The capital, Cairo has one more local channel broadcasting over 28 hours weekly. Similar local channels are expected to start operating in 1988–1989 to cover all major cities in Egypt.

The TV receivers in use are well over 20 million, watched by double that number of viewers in a country where television is the major, and sometimes the sole, source of entertainment and information.

Television in Egypt is attached to the Ministry of Information headed by Safwat El Sherif. Mrs. Samia Sadek is the president of Egyptian TV.

—AHMED SAMI

ETHIOPIA

Ethiopia Television, Post Office Box 5544, Addis Ababa. Two stations; 48,000 sets.

FINLAND

Finland has a three-channel television system that differs considerably from the other countries. There is at present in Finland one radio and television operation licence which has been granted to the Finnish Broadcasting Company, Oy Yleisradio Ab. The existence of MTV, Oy Mainow-TV-Reklam Ab, which is a private commercial TV company, is acknowledged in the same license.

Launched in Sept., 1986 semi-public Kolmoskanava (TV-3 Finland) owned by pubcaster YLE, commercial MTV and Nokia Industries, reaches 800,000 Finnish households (50%). Its programming balances foreign and domestic fare, news, documentaries, and feature films, series and soap operas. It now airs 7 hours a day—more on weekends.

The basis for official relations between the companies were laid down in more detail in the basic agreement concluded in 1976. Television broadcasting in Finland is under parliamentary control. The Administrative Council of the Finnish Broadcasting Company appointed by Parliament is the highest organ exercising program policy. It has two functions. The Administrative Council exercises program policy control over both companies. In addition, as its name implies, it is the highest administrative organ in the Finnish Broadcasting Company.

MTV has its own corresponding administrative council.

As a bilingual country Finland also has programs in Swedish on all tv-channels.

Some 19 hours per week—out of the total of 75—are sold by Oy Yleisradio Ab to MTV. At the end of 1981 a one-year price agreement was signed, according to which MTV's levy to the Finnish Broadcasting Company is at least 191.2 million marks in 1982. MTV produces nearly 43% of its programs.

Helsinki TV, owned by Sanoma Publishing is a cable operator with a combination service of free and pay TV reaching 103,000 of Finland's cable households. In 1987 Sanoma set up Eurocable which owns Norway's Janco Cable, 31% of Ireland's Cork Communications and 10% of London's Westminster Cable.

Numbers of color sets is today about 0.9 million (57% of all sets).

The Finnish Broadcasting Company: Head Office, Kesäkatu 2, 00260 Helsinki 26 (Telephone 441141) Broadcasting Center, Yleisradiokeskus, Pasila 00240 Helsinki 24 (Telephone 41811) TV 2 Television Center, Tohloppi, 33270 Tampere 27 (Telephone 445455), MTV, Oy Mainos-TV-Reklam AB, Pasilankatu 44, 00240 Helsinki 24 (Telephone 15001).

FRANCE

TV Households: 19,400,000
Networks: 4 private-held, 2 pubcasters.
Cable Penetration: less than 1%.
Regulatory Body: CNCL (National Commission of Communication and Liberties). Could be replaced or modified per outcome of May 8 presidential election.
Privately-held Networks: *TF-1* (Francis Bouygues, Robert Maxwell, others—50%, traded stock—50%). 99% penetration. Audience share: 39–45%.
La Cinq 19-21 rue Jean Goujon 75008 Paris; tel. 42 89 60 00; Jerome Seydoux, president: Robert Hersant, vice pres.: Silvio Berlusconi. 68% penetration. Share: 12–14%.
Metropole-6 (Compagnie Luxembourgeoise de Telediffusion, Lyonnaise de Eaux, others) 16 Cours Albert 1er, 75008 Paris; Tel. 42 56 66 66 and 45 63 17 17; president: Jean Drucker. 50% penetration. Share: 4%.
Canal Plus (pay-tv and unscrambled broadcast). (Havas, Compagnie Generale des Eaux, others). 2,200,000 subscribers, over-air penetration: 40%. Audience share: 4%.

La Sept 35 quai Andre Citroen, 75015 Paris tel. 40 59 77; president: Georges Duby.

Public Broadcasters: *Antenne-2:* 60% revenues from ads, rest user tax. 99% penetration. Shares: 25–29%.

FR-3: 15% ad revenues. 90%+ penetration. Share: 9–12%. (Shares based on Mediametrie, Monday–Sunday, highest and lowest scores since Jan.)

Networks: France's audiovisual landscape changed with the privitization of TF-1, controlled by Francis Bouygues and Robert Maxwell, and the addition of a fifth (La Cinq) and sixth channel (M-6). The end of the government monopoly in TV was begun in 1982 by Socialist President Francois Mitterand, and continued by the majority government of Prime Minister Jacques Chirac. The last five years have seen France go from three to six national networks—two public, three private and one pay TV—and from strict state control to a comparatively wide diversity.

TF-1 still dominates the field, scoring ratings of 46% despite the success of the fourth channel (Canal-Plus, a pay-TV movie channel). Antenne 2, and the regional FR-3 are still state-operated, funded by the annual TV tax, and commercials. A new cultural channel, La Sept, is slated for satellite broadcast on TDF 1; meanwhile, it is programming on FR-3. La Sept also has a vocation in funding TV and theatrical films. The originality of this station is that it will program European creations, cinemas, festivals, and spotlight events and auteurs.

—VERNICE KLIER MOSKOWITZ

GHANA

Ghana Broadcasting Corporation, Broadcast House, Post Office Broad Box 1633, Accra. Five stations, 147,000 sets.

GREECE

TV is nationwide and one of the most popular entertainments of the Greek public, harming all other kinds of recreation, especially movies.

There are two Channels in Athens operated by the Helliniki Radiophonia Tileorassi ERT merged into one unit now. Its Television Stations ET 1 and ET 2 as well as the Radio Broadcasting ERA (Helliniki Radiophonia) are all under the above mentioned unit, the ERT.

ERT is controlled by the State and responsibility of all its services is invested to its General Director, presently Mr. Antonis Koveos. It operates as an enterprise of Public Benefit open to all trends of the media.

Both TV channels operate in color. ET 1 has one relay station in Thessaloniki telecasting news from Northern Greece and another one in Patras covering the news from Southern Greece. Both Channels ET 1 and ET 2 have many relay towers all over the country. Discussions are underway for the establishment of a 3rd Channel in Thessaloniki.

Privatization of Radio Broadcasting—Radio broadcasting is no more a state monopoly. As of 1987, the year of "Free Radio," it is permitted to municipalities and other individuals to establish and operate radio stations.

The first private Radio Station, which started operating in 1987, is "Radio-Athens" FM 9,84 by the Municipality of Athens. During 1988 more private Radio Stations started the: "Top FM Stereo," "Antenna F.M. Stereo," Channel I of Pireaus, "Channel 10," "Radio FM Stereo," Radio Thessaliniki, Radio Chalkididki, Bolygyros, Free Radio of Zante. There are 30 other applications for private Radio Stations by several municipalities which will start operating shortly.

Supervision of Mass Media: A special service of the Mass Communication media was established recently and its Secretary is responsible for the supervision of all Mass Communication Media.

TV Programs: Both Channels ET 1 and ET 2 put on the air eight to ten hours of programs on weekdays and 10–12 on Sundays and Holidays, which are mostly video-taped. About 60% of this program is covered by news, educational subjects, discussion panels, local movies and serials and the rest by foreign films and movies.

ERT is a full member of E.B.U. and transmits all important international events through satellite.

It is estimated that more than one million B/W sets were sold in this country and the number of color ones is equally high.

The ET 1 offices are located at 16 Miurouzi Str. Athens, and the main offices and Studio are located at 436 Messoguion Str. Agades Paraskevi, Athens. The ET 2 Channel's headquarters are located at 136 Messoguion and Katehaki Str. Athens.

TV Commercials: A great number of spots are sold daily by both channels to several advertising agencies. The price per minute varies according to the popularity of the program.

Agencies: There are several agencies acting on behalf of various foreign TV companies: Hellas Television International, 96 Academias Str. Athens. representing MGM, Screen Gems, Warner Bros., Sacis, RAI, Paramount, Rank, Titanus, Egyptian TV, Aussi TV, Spanish TV, Brazilian TV, World Vision, Rumulus, World Fair Communications and Thames TV; Apollon International Enterprises 46 King Constantinou Avenue, Athens representing Anthony Morris, Children TV Workshop, Embassy Telecommunications, Four Star Enterprise, Hanson International, John Pearson International, Lassis Television, London Films, Marvin Goofman Associates, Metromedia Productions, NBC International, Orion, P.S.O., Samuel Goldwyn, TriStar, Toho, Mexican TV, Strenghold Television etc. Yannis Triantafyllis, 9 Klisovis Str. Athens agent of ITC TV etc. Dennis Petropoulos agent of N,T,A, II Lycavitou Str. Athens, Constantinos Tri-

coupis II, Halkokondyli Str. Athens. Georguiades Electroniki s.a., 20 Lagoumitzi Callithea, Athens.

Local TV production: Both Channels ET 1 and ET 2 produce several films and series for local use and exportation to foreign TV stations. ET 1 is in addition subsidizing some Greek pictures which are shot as serials also. According to the provisions of the new law, an affiliated company of ERT 1 will be established to undertake local TV production.

Independent TV producers: Hellas TV Productions, 96 Academias Str., Athens, Manager Andreas Lappas. Dennis Petropoulos, II Licavitou Str. Athens. Panos Spyropoulos, 46 King Constantinou Avenue, Athens. Andromeda Dyas Epe, 47 Lemnou Str. Athens. Kinimatografiki Epe 4 Tim. Filimond Str. Athens. Basil Maros, 26 Democritou Str. Athens, N. Samaras 14 Strat. Syndesmou Str. Athens. TVEM, 52 Skoufa Str. Athens. Aris Triantafyllis 5–7 Kapodistriou Str. Athens, Astyr Film, Finos Film 53 Hiou Str. Athens, Georgiades Electroniki, 20 Lagoumitzi Str., Athens.

TV studios: Television Enterprises S.A. Head office 28, Kapodistriou Str. Athens. Manager Christos Elmatzoglou. ATA Studios head office Omerou 8 Str. Athens., Fin Films Spata Attikas, Sklavis Studio 59 Zoodochou Peyes Athens. Roussopoulos Bros. Studio. Cinemagic Studio, etc.

Cable TV: A new law will be drafted to cover cable TV and until then cable TV is out of the question legally in Greece. However the Mayor of Pireaus expressed his intention to establish a cable TV service in Pireaus. Greek authorities are considering this possibility.

Satellite: ERT, is open to all trends of mass media and will start transmitting foreign programs through 6–7, and later more European Satellite stations until a new law covering cable and satellite TV is drafted. Only the TV receivers in Athens, Pireaus, Thessaloniki, Ioannina, Patras, Corfu, Herakleon, Komotini, Florina and Rhodes will receive the foreign satellite programs. Negotiations are under way with the foreign satellite stations SKY, PREMIERE, CHILDREN, CHANNEL, CNN, LIFE STYLE, MUSIC BOX, SUPER ART of Great Britain, TV 3, La CINQ, MC of France, SAT i and SAT 3 of West Germany, FILMNET of Holland, RAI UNO of Italy and HORIZON SAT of the Soviet Union.

The above experimental stage of satellite transmission will not require costly antennas. However, many such antennas are already installed on top of several buildings in Athens, Thessaloniki and other key cities.

—RENA VELISSARIOU

GUAM (U.S. Possession)

Guam Television operates one station with two channels for 17 hours daily, servicing an estimated 15,000 sets in the hands of Americans and natives. Owner is Pacific Broadcasting Corp., Agana. Some color is broadcast. The Department of Education, Agana, operates Channel 12, some 14 hours daily.

GUINEA

Radio-Diffusion Guinienne, B.P. 391, Conraky. 11,500 sets.

HOLLAND

The number of TV sets as of December 31, 1987 was some 4,703,000 which, with a population of 14,700,000, means that the market is practically saturated and that 98% of the Dutch families have a set. This obviously means strong competition for motion picture business. Young people, however, still like to go to the cinemas on weekends rather than stay at home to watch TV with their parents.

Holland is very widely cabled, and cable systems reach some 76% of the population. This means in many instances a good reception of the 2 Dutch channels, 3 German, 2 Belgian, 2 English, 1-2 French stations, plus the commercial stations, Sky Channel and Super Channel.

On top of this, the Pay TV station Filmnet is operational and has some 80,000 subscribers in Holland. Filmnet is operated by Esselte Pay TV, division of the Swedish Esselte Group. Their programs are transmitted via the ECS-one Satellite and a subscription costs from Dfl. 22.75 to Dfl. 34.50 (for 24 hours a day) per month, depending on the number of features chosen (plus Dfl. 10. per month for the decoder). The address is: Esselte PayTV, PO Box 132, 3440 AC Woerden.

The NOS (Nederlandse Omroep Stichting) in Hilversum is the central TV and Radio Organization and there are 8 main subdivision stations: a Roman Catholic one: KRO, 2 political (left) ones: VARA and VPRO, 2 Protestant: NCRV and EO and 3 neutrals: AVRO, TROS and VERONICA. These three have the largest number of subscribers.

The 8 major companies are completely independent in their activities and buy a lot of product on the international market. There are also some minor TV organizations like TELEAC, which broadcast educational programs such as mathematical, languages and computer courses.

The yearly contribution for TV and Radio combined is Dfl. 158.

Commercial stations are not allowed in Holland. There are commercials shown on both channels by STER, but programs are never interrupted by these commercials. Sky and Super Channels are only allowed on Dutch cable without Dutch subtitled programs and publicity specifically aimed at Dutch audiences is prohibited.

Radio and TV fall under the Ministry of Welfare, Social Health and Culture (WVC) which is particularly severe on the subject of "hidden" advertising.

As an average, feature films are shown 2–3 nights per week and also regularly in the afternoons. There is a window of 40 months, but it is possible to obtain exceptions to this rule. The decision lies with the Dutch Cinema Organization (NBB). Many American and English films are shown as well as TV series. Popular in 1987 were: St. Elsewhere, Miami Vice, The Cosby Show, Golden Girls, Family Ties. A popular German series is Derek. 2 Dutch series were: Zeg 'ns AAA (Say A) and Medisch Centrum West (Medical Centre West).

The quality of Dutch programs is good, and there are some excellent talkshows.

Prices of colour TV sets start at Dfl. 500. Price is obviously dependant on size of screens, remote control and Teletext.

Philips is the most important manufacturer in Holland. Import of Japan and German sets is also significant.

—PAUL SILVIUS

HONG KONG

Established 1957 by Rediffusion (HK) as closed circuit, converted to conventional TV in 1974. Asia Television (ATV) Central P.O Box 1414, Kowloon, Hong Kong. Additional outlets: Television Broadcast (HK-TVB), 77 Broadcast Drive, P.O. Box 70100, Kowloon, Hong Kong; and, Radio TV Hong Kong, Kowloon Central P.O. Box 200, Hong Kong (governmental unit acting as producer for above). Sets number 1,402,000.

HUNGARY

Magyar Televizio, 1810 Budapest serves 3.4 million sets nationwide using 625-line Secam color, currently with two nationwide programs plus local station specials.

INDIA

At present, there are 14 full fledged TV stations which have independent production facilities. These are located at Delhi, Bombay, Calcutta, Madras, Jullundhur, Srinagar, Lucknow, Cuttack, Hyderabad, UDK Delhi, Bangalore, Ahmedabad, Trivandrum and Gauhati. To augment program production, 10 more centers have been planned.

Apart from these, there are seven relay stations which were set up for the SITE (Satellite Instructional Television Experiment) program which ran for one year, from August 1975. They are in Jaipur, Hyderabad, Gulbarga, Muzaffarpur, Sambalpur, Raipur and Pij, situated near Ahmedabad. At present, programs for Hyderabad and Gulbarga in Telugu and Kannada are recorded at Hyderabad. Cuttack records programs in Oriya and feeds Sambalpur. Jaipur, Muzaffarpur and Raipur are supplied with pre-recorded tapes in Hindi by Delhi. At Pij recording is done at the SAC (Space Application Centre) studios and telecast for one hour daily. Altogether, these terrestrial stations cover 40% of the viewers formerly covered by the SITE program.

The launching of the Indian National Satellite System (INSAT-IB) in 1984 has completely changed the electronic media scene, opening up new possibilities in mass communication. With the addition of 36 low power and very low power transmitters in 1987, Doordarshan now puts out its programs over 220 transmitters.

The launching of INSAT-IC this year will not only augment these facilities but also take the load off the orbiting INSAT-IB. It will also make it possible to cover about 97 percent of the area and 70 percent of the population.

There are an well over 10,000,000 TV sets in the country, with an estimated audience of nearly 80 million, in comparison to 30 million viewers that go to the cinema daily. About half the TV sets are concentrated in metro towns but with LPTs now beaming out to cover over half the country's population, the growth rate of TV sets is expected to go up to 30 million by 1990. While Doordarshan has been quick in stepping up hardware, software development in terms of programmes has not received the attention it deserves. It is still very largely dependent on the mainstream cinema.

Doordarshan has started a weekly telecast of national and international film classics for its late night viewers. In addition it also purchases unreleased "art" films which may otherwise remain in the cans. This has given a fillip to low budget "art" filmmakers.

—B.D. GARGA

INDONESIA

The government-owned RRI-TV, on the air since 1962 as the first developing nation to have complete TV coverage, in 1988 gave permission for one station, Rajawari Citra Televisi Indonesia, Jakarta, to carry commercials which had been banned since 1981. Since 1985 they have banned American or other imported TV shows on the grounds that the public preferred domestic fare, though the last showing of American TV fare indicated an average audience of 24 million viewers.

At present stations are operated on 2 channels in Jakarta, Bandung, Jogakarta, Semarang and Tjiribon, with some 203 relays. Broadcasting

hours average above 40 hours weekly with some programs in color to sets estimated to number over 2 million. Programs are 50% entertainment, 25% educational, 25% public service, live 60% of the time, and 40% video-taped. With the departure of imported shows, the government will increase educational shows based on national culture. Indonesia is building 50 relays under its fourth 5-year plan since its 203 relays now reach only 27% of its population of 114 million. Inquiries to TV Republic Indonesia (TVRI), Yayasan Televisi, Senayan Jakarta. 10 stations; 4,950,000 sets.

IRAN

Islamic Republic of Iran Broadcasting, Post Office Box 98-200, Teheran. Sixteen stations, 2.2 million sets.

IRAQ

Iraq Broadcasting & Television, Broadcasting House, Salihiya, Baghdad. Six stations, 725,000 sets.

IRELAND

Telefis Eireann is the official name of the television service in Ireland. Television, like sound broadcasting, is run as an independent State Statuary body and responsibility for both services is vested in Radio Eireann, the Broadcasting Authority. This Authority, appointed by the Government, consists of nine members serving on a part-time basis under a chairman selected by the Government. The present chairman is T. Andrews.

The Minister for Posts and Telegraphs, who is responsible for the autonomously operated Authority, reserves to himself the duties of fixing and collecting license fees from domestic viewers, licenses transmitting stations, and has a veto on the appointment and conditions of the Authority's top executive. The Director-General, Kevin McCourt, is employed full-time.

The Television service began in 1962. It has five main high power transmitters and thirteen satellite "transposers," serving areas outside the range of the main transmitters. Its national coverage is estimated at 98 per cent of the population. The national technical standard is a 625 line one, but programs are also broadcast on a 405 line in the Eastern and Northwestern parts of the country.

The Authority, which has the responsibility of providing programs of suitable cultural and national content, transmits 44 hours per week, with occasional additional programs. In addition, educational programs for schools, two and a half hours per week, are broadcast for 33 weeks of the year on behalf of the Department of Education.

Of the 44 hours of weekly programs, 22 are of home origin. The balance are imported mainly from Great Britain and America.

There are about 350,000 receiving sets in operation, of which about 200,000 are able to receive programs from Great Britain's BBC-TV and Independent TV stations as well as Radio Telefis Eireann.

ISRAEL

Israel television broadcasts daily in Arabic and Hebrew. Arabic programs start at 6:00 p.m. and continue to 8:00 p.m. Programs include documentaries, round-ups, news, films, variety shows, discussions, games, etc. These programs include, as well, weekly interviews with individuals of the Arab Israeli population who can convey regards to their relatives in neighboring countries, such as Egypt, Syria, Lebanon, Jordan, through this medium.

At 8:00 the Hebrew programs begin, offering the same variety of broadcast as the Arabic programs. Hebrew broadcasts continue up to 11:30 or midnight. The majority of Hebrew programs are subtitled in Arabic; and foreign language broadcasts, including films, are subtitled in both Hebrew and Arabic. Similarly, most of the Arabic programs have Hebrew subtitles.

Besides the above mentioned programs, television broadcasts every morning (except Saturday) educational programs beginning at 8:00 and continuing to 4:00. This is followed by children's programs which continue to 6:30 and include films, puzzles, games, cartoons, etc.

ITALY

From its inception the Italian television industry was dominated by a public network agency, RAI, but toward the end of the 1970's its dominance was finally challenged by private broadcasting. Prime networks are Canale-5, Italia-1 and Rete 4. The first two are part of the Silvio Berlusconi conglomerate while the third is owned by the Mondadori publishing group.

Overseeing RAI is a parliamentary commission which elects 10 of its 16 directors. The others are elected by IRI (Institute for Reconstruction of

Industry) which owns 99.55% of RAI, the rest being held by a publishing association. RAI gets its operating authority from the Ministry of Post and Telecommunications; its finances are reviewed by the Ministry of Finance. RAI is funded by license fees and advertising. (Ads are limited to 5% of airtime.)

RAI operates three TV networks: RAI-1, its main and most successful outlet; RAI-2, an alternate network; and RAI-3, whose viewers are few although it is the only one which does not carry advertising.

RAI has transmitters all over Italy and uses 21 regional offices. It has five production centers and provides the majority of its own programming, including that for a worldwide news service it operates.

Private TV companies are not subject to the same rule as RAI. For instance they carry up to 14–18% advertising in airtime.

Trends: TV in Italy has made tremendous advances in acquiring programming the last several years. It is reported public and private broadcasters have invested close to $500,000,000 in foreign films and TV programs to attract TV viewers.

1988 saw the birth of three syndicated networks that plan to debut in 1989. Competing for the 10% audience share unclaimed by the RAI and Silvio Berlusconi's networks are Italia Network, Cierreti Network (formed by the Cierreti Group Advertising Association) and Five Star which will get programming from SACIS.

IVORY COAST

TV Ivorienne, Television House, Latrille, BP 8883, Abidjan. Operates 11 stations. Sets estimated at 450,000.

JAPAN

Non-commercial TV broadcasting began in Tokyo Feb. 1, 1953, by the quasi-governmental Nippon Hoso Kyokai (NHK) followed seven months later by the first commercial TV broadcast of Nippon Television Network (NTV). Broadcast time for NHK, which began with only 866 set-owners paying a fee of Yen 200 monthly, was 4 hours a day compared to 6 hours by NTV, which was affiliated with the Yomiuri newspapers. By 1960 NHK possessed 60 stations and there were 47 commercial stations broadcasting, while the number of sets had increased to about 7 million, topping the 10 million mark two years later.

Although commercial networks as they are established in the U.S. are legally forbidden, there came about a nationwide grouping of commercial stations with the Tokyo stations acting as pivotal points and providing tieups and programs. Thus in 1959, 16 commercial stations formed Japan News Network which soon spread to other programming areas, with JOKR in Tokyo, followed by three other such groupings centering on NTV, Nippon Educational Television (renamed Asahi National Broadcasting in 1977), and the Fuji TV key stations in Tokyo. It was then apparent that several newspapers with national sales systems, through capital tieups, were virtually in control of the national commercial networks.

Educational broadcasts were begun by NHK in 1959, followed three weeks later by Nippon Educational Television, which later dropped the "educational" pretense and became a regular broadcaster, as TV Tokyo (JOTX) did later, when it was found impossible to operate a private educational TV station in Japan for financial reasons.

The Tokyo Metropolitan area, which comprises almost 30% of Japan's population of 122.4 million, is served by Channel 1 NHK general network station, Channel 3 NHK educational network station, Channels 4, 6, 8 and 10 operated by NTV, TBS, Fuji, TV Asahi commercial network stations, respectively, and semi-independent TV Tokyo (JOTX) on channel 12 and TVK (UHF) 42 in Yokohama.

NHK's general programming lists 16 regional stations throughout the nation, 54 local stations and numerous relay stations in the VHF range to bring general programming to 3,493 outlets (2,851 UHF outlets). NHK educational facilities comprise 9 regional stations, 39 local stations, 2,207 relay stations for a total of 3,417 outlets of which 2,778 are UHF, including use of mini-satellite relays. It must be emphasized that in most cases (but not all) the general and educational services make use of the same facilities.

There are 42 companies operating both radio and TV stations and 63 operating only TV stations. In the VHF sector some 48 companies operate 486 stations; in UHF 55 companies operate 5,841 stations, plus 9 SHF stations.

These four "networks" operate in the 8 key areas of Japan—Tokyo, Osaka, Nagoya, Fukuoka, Sapporo, Hiroshima, Sendai, and Hokkaido—which are 4 commercial-station areas (plus NHK). Other stations located in less populous areas use a cross network arrangement by which programs from plural key stations are received. There is Asahi National Broadcasting with 18 stations, Fuji Telecasting with 27, Tokyo Broadcasting System with 25, and Nippon Television with 29 stations. In addition several independent stations have ties and non-commercial NHK covers 30 million of Japan's 37 million households.

While NHK collects monthly fees from 32,133,475 registered sets, the Home Ministry estimates the total number is 62,495,000 (including households with more than one), of which 9,423,000 are black and white and 53,072,000 are color. Some 98.5% of registered households possess one or more color sets for which they are assessed a flat $7.73 a month versus $4.60 for black-and-white sets. Thus, it is no surprise that NHK is by far the wealthiest broadcasting corporation in the world with 16,000 employees, which it has promised to reduce to 15,000, and a 23-story headquarters in Tokyo.

With 29.8% of the national advertising budget, TV is the leading advertising medium with designated prime time from 7:00 to 11:00 p.m. and ad spot buying rates determined on the gross rating point though, with a seller's market, card rates are often disregarded. Top rate for a 60-second network shop is $48,000 and a 54-minute program for a month about $1.4 million; generally contracts are for 6 months but recently 3-month contracts became available, there being waiting lists for sponsors. Sporting events, especially baseball, in non-prime time bring top prices due to good results. Though rules call for not more than 18% of broadcast time be devoted to commercials, this rule is only loosely followed. In addition some stations persist in intensifying audio volume for favored commercials.

Although an agreement was once reached to restrict broadcasting hours to 16.5 a day to conserve energy, commercial stations are broadcasting past the midnight deadline practically 24 hours a day and even NHK now broadcasts past the deadline. While TV is undoubtedly the most influential medium for both young and old, various polls disagree when attempts are made to determine the average daily time a Japanese watches the tube. NHK says the average Japanese spends 2 hours 53 minutes daily (another poll says 3 hours 18 minutes) viewing TV. Nielsen gives the Tokyo viewing time as 8 hours 12 minutes daily, taking into consideration the viewing by each household member. Favorite shows have veered from soap operas to various kinds of emceed shows, especially quiz shows. Men prefer sports shows, including baseball, sumo wrestling, golf, and, recently, American-style football, though old-type samurai dramas are still popular with both sexes. The younger audience spends much time watching cartoons before graduating to teen-age singing shows, contests or quizzes. These imports, especially those from the U.S. tend to be grade B films or films made in America especially for TV. These are almost always dubbed into Japanese but a few are available in the original language on a different wavelength for the benefit of TV sets equipped with multiplex receivers.

Cable TV is still in its infancy, serving only hotels, high class apartment houses and some people with poor TV reception. The Motion Picture Producers Association contracted with CATV operators obligating them to pay $143 per showing of feature films, later to increase as CATV expands. Satellite dish reception began in 1987 when NHK, after previous satellite failure, finally opened a 24-hour service. Twelve CATV operators charge $540 for installation and monthly fees of $25. Thus far NHK's satellite subscribers number 645,000 with 65 percent representing joint reception in apartment buildings. Antenna and tuner for individuals runs $800 for individuals and joint reception $8,000. Japan Satellite Broadcasting, a private firm, says it will offer DBS service in 1990 when it puts its own satellite in orbit.

As for national advertising expenditures, Japanese TV took 29.8% of the total compared to 25.1% by newspapers. The TV share came to some $88.9 billion, up over last year. Food and beverage advertisers comprised 27% of the total followed by autos, 15.4%, cosmetics, 10.3%, pharmaceuticals, 8.5%, service-entertainment, 7.4%, and department stores, 7%.

A survey indicated imported feature films shown on TV cost more than domestic movies but are shown more often so tend to dominate the medium, so it must be assumed their frequency on TV reflects a response to demand, even taking into consideration the reluctance of Japanese movie studios to contribute to the prosperity of what they consider a dangerous competitor to their own industry.

As with the old TV programs purchased from abroad, Japanese buyers insist on rock bottom prices, the result being a formidable collection of full length feature films which, due to their age and caliber, are mostly trash. With few exceptions, they can only be characterized as mixed second- and third-rate. Despite that films are repeated year after year. Once dubbed into Japanese, some Japanese say, it does not make much difference if the film is good or not. Sellers abroad are advised when contracting to provide a special clause on re-runs without compensation.

Last year a total of 449 Japanese feature films were shown on TV 460 times compared with 1,017 imports from abroad which were shown 1,067 times. Fewer imports are shown on prime time since most are used to fill the late night and early morning hours, being cheaper than ordinary programming. Of imports, NHK showed only 34 compared with 142 for NTV, 165 for TBS, 124 for Fuji, 101 for Asahi TV and 501 for the local station TV Tokyo.

"Sesame Street" returned to NHK after an absence of 7 years. NHK features very few late movies, specializing in a few movie classics and rare imported family dramas. The commercial stations now rarely feature imported TV shows on prime time, screening a few during daylight hours, and more during late night or very early morning hours when this comparatively cheap filler can be sued. "Alfred Hitchcock Presents" is used by Tokyo TV in prime time, while another network does the same for the "Colombo" series. Picked at random, sitcoms from abroad include: "A-Team," "Surfside 6," "Combat," "Hunter," "Star Trek," "Family Ties," "60 Minutes," "CBS Evening News," "That's Hollywood," "Mike Hammer," and "Twilight Zone." Since these are in both Japanese and English (via multiplex attachment) it would seem that their foreign audience was well served, but alas, 90 percent are shown from midnight on, with only 6% audience viewing.

NKH general stations average 19 hours daily, 37.3% devoted to news and commentaries, 21% to entertainment, 27% to culture, and 14% to education. Commercial stations average 23 hours with entertainment 40.6%, cultural 23.9%, news 16.4%, education 12.1%, sports 5.6% and announcements .6%. Of this broadcasting average, over 23 hours consisted of sponsored programs and 3 hr. of sustaining programs. Although broadcasters claimed that advertising commercials (including a daily average of 241 spot announcements) took only 6% of total broadcasting time of each station on the average, anyone with a stop watch knows that this is not true. Over 60% of Japanese polled indicated an opinion that there were far too many commercials, while 50% objected to the ads shown in conjunction with kiddies' programs and thought such programs should carry no ads.

NHK claims the average viewer watches TV on an average of 173 minutes daily, of which 49 minutes are devoted to NHK programs and with 124 minutes devoted to commercial stations, a slight decrease from the year before but these figures are ridiculed by commercial broadcasters.

Sponsors of a 30-minute prime time show pay about $10,000 on a Tokyo station with other spots going for $4,500 per sponsor.

Production cost for a one-hour program is only $90,000, about one-fifth of the cost in the U.S. Payments for authoring a 30-minute script is $500 at NHK and as low as $200 at commercial stations. However, writers with a national reputation get much more.

A study of 107 commercial TV stations reveals that although the UHF outlets located in the periphery of the large cities are doing only moderately well as regards operating profits, the older-established VHF stations, particularly those affiliated with networks and in Tokyo or Osaka, enjoyed a good year.

Japan exports very few TV programs of its own but it is the world's largest exporter of TV sets and in addition sells TV equipment, complete broadcasting studios and nationwide setups abroad.

While a critic would rate Japanese TV in general as somewhat below the not very high American standard, and take umbrage at the great percentage of time taken by commercials on all stations except those of NHK, the average Japanese is satisfied with it. Lately, the government tried steps to prevent further intensification by stations of audio volume for commercials and limited them to 18% of total program time.

Only 15% of viewers said they were satisfied fully with Japanese TV, says an NHK poll.

Quiz games have the highest average ratings followed by prime time cinema feature films. Then comes sports, samurai or home dramas, action dramas, kiddie and cartoon shows, musical, news, imported TV shows, and finally educational broadcasts.

The baseball craze is such that even high school championship games rate prime time coverage and get a huge audience.

There are no national cable TV systems but cable TV stations feed to 4.3 million households where TV reception is poor or non-existent. In the cities, cable TV is piped to hotels (usually in English) and to some high-class apartment houses, and to a few private subscribers. In the suburbs some multi-storied housing complexes have their own cable TV. Very few dishes used for satellite reception now exist though the first private satellite broadcasting company promises it will be in full operation by 1990. Since 1985 NHK and private telecasters have had contracts to use Intelsat and a European satellite on a 24-hour basis but ordinarily they take only a few extra bits daily for inclusion on news broadcasts since they are not too interested in outside world news unless it affects Japan. In fact, this is also true as regards imported TV shows; they prefer their own, and imports are shown only on non-prime time and the late night hours.

Addresses of the commercial networks can be found in the World TV Broadcasters list in this volume and additional information can be obtained from National Association of Commercial Broadcasters in Japan, Bungei Shunjusha Building, 3 Kioi-cho, Chiyoda-ku, Tokyo, All Japan TV Production Companies Assoc., Akasaka White House, 4-1-6 Akasaka, Minato-ku, Tokyo 107, or from Advertising Association of Broadcasters in Japan, 8-10 Nishi Ginza, Tokyo. For non-commercial TV information one should address Nippon Hoso Kyokai (NHK), 2-2-1 Jinnan, Shibuya-ku, Tokyo 150.

—A. C. PINDER

JORDAN

Jordan Television Corporation, Post office Box 1041, Amman. 360,000 sets; 12 stations.

KENYA

Voice of Kenya TV, Broadcasting House, P.O. Box 30456, Nairobi. One channel, 275,000 sets.

LIBERIA

Liberia Broadcasting Corporation, Post Office Box 594, Monrovia. One station, 52,000 sets.

MADAGASCAR

Television Madagascar, P.O. Box 442, Tanarive, Madagascar, operates a single station and three relays. 97,000 sets.

MALAYSIA

TV Malaysia was established in 1963 and serves some 1,846,000 sets on an average of 6 hours daily, half of broadcasts are in color. Originating station is at Kuala Lumpur, serving three networks on the main peninsula. One network extends to Sabah, where there is also a secondary station at Kota Kinabalu, which operates a small network of its own, extending to Sarawak. Inquiries to TV Malaysia (RIM), Broadcasting Dept., Kuala Lumpur 50614.

Malaysia opened its first commercial TV channel in December, 1985.

MEXICO

Television began in 1950. It is estimated there are now 6,500,000 sets using the NTSC system. In Mexico City there are six over-the-air channels, of which four are run by the privately-held Televisia under government concession on the other two by the government. There are five cable channels in Mexico City, all under control of Televisia. In addition there are 29 independent stations around the country.

Televisa (Channels 2, 4, 5, and 8): Chapultepec, 28, Mexico 06724, D.F. Prez, Miguel Alemán; vp, Alejandro Burillo; other top execs, Guillermo Cañedo, etc. Telex 017-73154.

Instituto Mexicana de Television (Imevisión): Government stations, Channel 7, 13, 22. Periférico sur 4121, Mexico 4141. Pres. is Pablo Marentes; other execs are José Ramón Fernandez, Salvador Núñez Sánchez. Telex 017-73878 TVGO.

Televisión de la República Mexicana: Government provincial educational network. Guanajuato 125, Col. Roma, Mexico 6.

Government Organizations

Dirección de Radio-Television-Cine: Headed by Jesus Hernández Torres. Churubusco Studios. Mexico. Dir., Alejandro Ordorica Saavedra.

RTC Televisión: Jose Eduardo Lopez Latorre, director. Colima, 161 Mexico.

Organización de la Televisión Iberoamericana (OTI): TV federation for most Latin American networks; headquartered in Mexico. Varsovia, 44 Mexico City 6. Secretary, Amaury Daumas; Aide, Dario de la Peña; Telex 017-71140.

MICRONESIA

Micronesia Broadcasting Corp., Taga Hotel, Saipan, Mariana Islands, comprises two stations broadcasting 16 hours daily on a commercial basis.

MONGOLIA

This Communist bloc nation established Radio-TV Mongolia in 1970 and now consists of two stations with satellite connection with Soviet Russia. Located in Ulan Bator, broadcasting to 64,000 sets.

NEW CALEDONIA

Societé Nationale de Radio-TV, P.O. Box G3 Cedex, Noumea, broadcasts on 4 channels in color to an estimated 50,000 sets.

NEW ZEALAND

The state-owned and operated Broadcasting Corp. of N.Z. television service operates two national networks in color—the TV1 network which originates programs from the Avalon television complex in Lower Hutt (near Wellington), and the TV2 network which originates programs from the Auckland studios. TV1 transmits some 88 hours of programs a week, and TV2 about 71 hours. Five days are commercial. Sundays are non-commercial on each network. Fridays are non-commercial on TV1, and Saturdays non-commercial on TV2.

A new privately-owned network TV3 is scheduled to begin operation March, 1989.

Locally made programs are estimated at about 3,000 hours annually, which includes drama, news and current affairs, light entertainment, religion, service programs and sports. The balance of program output is purchased from overseas, mainly from Britain (40–45%), the U.S. (48%) and Australia (10%). Use of satellite links permits same-day presentation of world news items and live telecasts, particularly of sports. There are 1 million sets.

NIGERIA

Western Nigeria TV Service, Television House, Bompai Road, Kano. Ten stations, 4,486,500 sets.

NORTH KOREA

Experimental telecasting, using Russian equipment since 1960s, followed by establishment of a national network of 20 stations with regional stations and relays. Korean Central Broadcasting Committee, Television Section, Pyongyang, Democratic Peoples Republic of (North) Korea. Sets: 1,050,000.

OMAN

Oman Color TV, Ministry of Information & Culture, P.O. Box 600, Muscat, Oman. Three stations and 1 relay for 151,000 sets.

PAKISTAN

Television came to Pakistan in 1964, when its first black-and-white station opened on November 26 at Lahore. Since then it has emerged as an important audiovisual medium and a significant national institution. In the beginning, hardly 9.32% of the population of Pakistan (including the East, which is now Bangladesh) could view its programs. Now PTV is a public limited company registered under the Companies Ordinance 1984, with authorized capital of Rs.690,781 million. All shares of the corporation are held by the government of Pakistan.

Progress: From its modest beginning, PTV quickly became one of the leading TV organizations of Southeast Asia. Today in its 25th year, PTV has a national network covering the five main program producing and transmitting centers at Karachi, Lahore, Islamabad, Quetta, and Peshawar. They are linked with 27 high-powered rebroadcasting centers (boosters) to form the PTV hook-up known as the National Network.

About 82.20% of the population of Pakistan (103 million) views PTV color programs in all four provinces and parts of Azad Kashmir. Millions more are expected to be brought under the viewing range with the establishment of additional proposed rebroadcasting centers over the next two years. The area under the umbrella of PTV signals has steadily risen from 8,029 sq. km in 1964 to 280,588 sq. km in 1987.

There are at present approximately 1,485,785 licensed TV sets, with the number of unlicensed sets believed to be about 30% or 445,000 more. The average viewership per TV set is estimated to be 8 persons. PTV has increased its programming up to 66.40 hours per week during the last fiscal year excluding special morning transmissions, "Aaj," which started in early 1988 with 75 minutes, has increased to 120 minutes in September. Transmission via satellite, which commenced as early as 1972 is now a regular feature and covers important international events, including sports, Haj, visits abroad of the head of state, U.N. special meetings, reports from war fronts, etc., which are broadcast in cooperation with various news agencies.

PTV's income from all sources, which reached a new height of Rs.690 million during 1985–86 and even higher in 1986–87, is likely to go down during the current financial year. Because of the Islamic Shariat Ordinance, 1988, dozens of ads were declared unsuitable, causing great loss to the PTV. A number of other restrictions, including women's appearance in ads only where they are very much necessary, the curtailing of musical programs and the discontinuation of Pakistani feature films, a strict check on foreign films and requiring fully dressed women in plays and other TV programs, etc., may further reduce the business of PTV. The main sources of income for PTV are commercials and license fees of Rs.200 per year for domestic sets and Rs.400 per year for commercial sets.

Color Era: Color television came to Paksitan in 1976. Since then PTV productions have been entered in international competitions and festivals and have won a number of awards. There are approximately 600,000 color sets in Pakistan.

PTV has also instituted the PTV Annual Awards to acknowledge and honor excellence in the various professions concerned with television. PTV Awards were first given in 1980. One additional award was introduced in 1988, by organizing a competition, Jashn-e-Tamseel, between the five centers, based on viewers' opinions. PTV has also given awards to advertising agencies since 1971 to improve the standard of TV commercials.

PTV exports a good number of its programs to other countries, particularly those where Pakistani and Indian nationals live in large quantity. Lahore, which produces programs in Arabic, exports programs on child care, economics, population, education, Iqbaliyat, general science, electrical wiring, food and nutrition, Pakistani studies, poultry farming, vegetable growing, etc. In addition to private viewing, these programs are shown in about 500 community centers all over Pakistan.

Training Institute: A Central Training Institute was set up at Islamabad to train program producers and engineering personnel. This institution has been elevated to a full-fledged PTV academy, training in all fields—news, engineering, management, finance, current affairs, program production, etc. Another institute is likely to begin operation in Quetta this year.

PTV presents its viewers with a number of imported programs, including canned feature films every week. The greatest coverage was given to sports and festivals, with 21.46 hours per week; whereas poetry was given shortest duration, 0.14 hours a week during the last year. Religious programs received 4.53 hours of air time; news, 8.34 hours; current affairs, 5.28 hours, children, 1.48 hours, women, 0.19 hours; features, 3.28 hours; dramas, 4.58 hours, commercials, 2.44 hours; and announcements, 5.28 hours.

Pakistan manufactured over 248,000 TV sets in 1987. Apart from this, a considerable number of sets are brought into the country each year as personal baggage and through barter. Customs duty on a set is 80% of its value. However, there is no duty on locally manufactured TV sets. At present, PTV extends technical cooperation to a number of countries, including Uganda, United Arab Emirates and other neighboring countries.

The Federal TV Complex was opened in March 1987 at Islamabad. Built at a cost of Rs.230 million, it includes PTV headquarters, with the most modern studios and machinery, and an audience participation hall, the PTV Academy and the National News Bureau.

Six new booster-rebroadcasting centers are scheduled to be installed within the next two years. A sum of Rs.182 million has been allocated for starting a second RV Channel, developing a transmitter and broadcasting house at Faisalabad and Loralai during 1988–89. Besides ongoing projects of mass media agencies, Rs.64 million will go to the second channel of PTV for education and extension of TV coverage to Azad Kashmir.

PTV has added new technqiues Electronics News Gathering (ENG). It was adopted for action news and location coverage. Lately, teleprompters, frame synchronizers and character generators with Arabic and English fonts have been added to the Islamabad center for news and subtitling of programs in Arabic.

Till June 1988, there were a total of about 5,200 full-time employees with PTV. In addition, there are hundreds of writers, artistes and other talents who are usually engaged on contract fees. They are paid wages according to their work on the programs. The highest and lowest remunerations paid to a performer are Rs.36 and Rs.6 per minute.

The government of Pakistan has approved a project for Rs.100 million for a ground receiving station to receive satellite pictures directly. Accepting the space age concept of viewing TV programs directly from satellite, official clearance has been given for a plan to manufacture special sets for that purpose. A Pakistani firm claims to have built a dish-antenna, 30-foot diameter giant radio telescope to scan and receive signals from different satellites. This radiotelescope is said to have a gain of 50 decibels at 4 gigahertz frequency with the ability to track all kinds of satellites viewable on the Pakistan horizon. Weighing more than two tons and built of steel and aluminum, it can be rotated to the full 360 degrees of horizon and zero to 90 degrees.

—A. R. SLOTE

PHILIPPINES

Broadcasts began in 1953 by DZAQ-TV then owned by Alto Broadcasting. At present 40 stations are on the air for commercial broadcasting and one government station; most are located in Manila. The number of sets is estimated at over 4,000,000. ABS-CBN was replaced by KBS. Others are Associated Broadcasting. Inter-Island Broadcasting, Metropolitan Broadcasting, Philippines Broadcasting. Radio Mindanao Network, Republic Broadcasting and Southern Broadcasting. More provincial outlets are planned.

Commercial ad revenues have averaged 30.8% gains over the past 10 years and now 46% of all advertising money spent is for TV compared to 29% for newspaper ads.

POLAND

Some 9 million TV receivers are registered in Poland tuned in to one of two channels which broadcast in color on the SECAM system. Householders pay a license fee of 2,400 zlotys a year, which is the main source of revenue for the networks.

Poland has seven regional studios and 30% of the schedule is broadcast locally with the balance going out nationally. Most popular shows are news and current affairs, followed by features, documentaries, TV theatre, and music. (Theatrical feature films can be transmitted one year after original release.)

Foreign programs make up some 19% of the scheduling; they are acquired either through cash or barter deals. Advertising is permitted and foreign companies can buy time. There is no official censorship, but each station is responsible for what goes over the airwaves, both in programs and advertising.

As of yet there are no cable or pay-TV systems in Poland.

PUERTO RICO

Television started in 1954, and there are about 750,000 sets using the NTSC system in Puerto Rico. Most public places, such as restaurants and clubs, have television sets for their patrons; the medium is available in local hotels upon request.

Even though most Puerto Ricans know English, and the number of persons who will acquire a working knowledge of English will increase considerably through intensification of English instruction in public schools and the migration of Puerto Rican families to the United States, and workers who come back from the States with more knowledge of English, television programming is in English and Spanish. WKAQ-Telemundo owned Reliance, on channel 4, has 30% of its programming in English of which 10% have Spanish sub-tutles. There are 10 private stations in all.

Kinescope versions of top North American television shows are shown on both stations.

Cable television is on the rise here. The largest operator is Cable TV of Puerto Rico. It is owned by Harris Cable of Los Angeles, which bought the San Juan franchise in 1976, starting with some 8,000 customers. Total subscribers now on the island are about 150,000.

Cable programming is also being expanded. At first the cable company offered only HBO and Virgin Islands stations. Receiving stations were built to bring in programs by satellite and by 1980 programs were being funneled from the states. Puerto Ricans now have a choice of 21 cable channels.

Cable TV charges its subscribers $11 a month for a basic package of 12 channels. HBO and Galavision cost $9.95 each additionally. Cable currently reaches greater San Juan, Bayamon, Carolina, Trujillo Alto and Guaynabo, which have an estimated 300,000 homes.

QATAR

Qatar TV Service (governmental), Ministry of Information, P.O. Box 1836 Doha, Qatar. Color since 1973. One station and relay; 122,000 sets.

SAMOA (AMERICAN)

Three TV stations serve some 42,000 sets on the American part of this Pacific island as well as a number of sets on the part administered by New Zealand. The station is also used daily for educational instructions to local schools. Address: Television of Samoa, Pago Pago. There are six channels.

SAUDI ARABIA

Established 1957, now 56 stations and 2 networks. General Directorate of TV, Ministry of Information, P.O. Box 570, Riyadh, Saudi Arabia; ARAMCO-TV, Box 96, Dhahran, Saudi Arabia. 4 million sets.

SIERRA LEONE

Sierra Leone TV Service, New England, Private Mail Bag, Freetown. One station, 32,000 sets.

SINGAPORE

TV Singapore went on the air in 1963 and now serves an estimated 750,000 sets on four channels in four languages. One channel broadcasts 66 hours weekly the others 40 hours; of this total about 146 hours weekly are in color. Inquiries to Radio-TV Singapore, P.O. Box 1902, Singapore 11. For the fourth consecutive year Singapore Broadcasting Corp. profits dropped-from U.S. $4.36 million to $720,000 most recently.

SOUTH AFRICA

South African Broadcasting Corp., P.O. Box 8606, Johannesburg 2000, started broadcasts in 1976 and now has over 80 stations with four services broadcasting 7 languages over 3 channels to over 3 million sets. From 1978 advertising was accepted.

Associated South West African Broadcasting, P.O. Box 321, Windhoek, Namibia, South West Africa, an autonomous statutory body, broadcasts 6 hours daily from Windhoek.

SOUTH KOREA

Commercial TV broadcasting began in 1956, but the station burned three years later and it was not until 1961 when the government established the Korea Broadcasting Service (KBS-TV) network. The commercial network of Tongyang Broadcasting Co. (TBC) began in 1964 and was followed by the commercial Munwha Broadcasting Co. (MBC) in 1969. The American Forces Korea Network (AFKN-TV) was also established to serve American troops, and now comprises 6 stations.

KBS, which is entirely government-owned and collects a montly fee from each household with a TV set, is somewhat unique since its takes commerical advertising, unlike most governmental networks. Political opponents of the regime are rarely mentioned on broadcasts; this one-sided coverage had led to a boycott by some of the public who refuse to pay fees. KBS also holds a controlling 65% interest in the only other commercial broadcaster, Munhwa Broadcasting. Under the present regime, other stations were compelled by the government to merge with KBS, except for the Christian Broadcasting System which has been restricted since 1980 to broadcasting only religious programs. The government uses KBS profits from advertising revenues for education scholarships and expenses of newsmen traveling abroad.

KBS-TV has its key station in Seoul and 21 local stations, with other local stations, making a total of 33 TV stations, including those operated by MBC and the former TBC. Color broadcasting started in 1980. Almost 10 million sets are in operation, covering almost every household. If armed forces of USA are counted, the total stations number 33.

Korean broadcasts are limited to 6.5 hours of evening time and 4 hours mornings on weekdays, 11 hours on Saturday and 17 on Sunday. Monthly fees of about $1.00 are collected and advertisements are accepted.

On Saturdays and Sundays between 8 and 9 p.m. it is estimated that 60% or more of the population gathers before their sets to view commercial stations' soap operas, far beyond the average 30% viewing for most shows.

In 1981 the Republic of Korea "consolidated" all news media and took over the private stations, so daily listings read: KBS-1 TV (7 cities), KBS-2 TV (2), KBS-3 TV-UHF (6), MBC-TV (6). Korean Broadcasting Advertisement Corporation handles all TV and radio advertising.

SPAIN

The first time Televisión Española—(now Radio-Televisión Española, RTVE)—transmitted on a regular basis was October 29, 1956, on a scan system of 625 lines at 25 frames per second. That program lasted three hours with a range of 70 kilometres, broadcasting for about 400 sets. The First Channel (VHF) was followed by a Second Channel (UHF) in 1967, complementary at first, but then somewhat competitive and with a clearer trend towards "culture." Channel 1 now covers all of Spain, including the Balearic and Canary Islands. Channel 2 reaches 80% of national territory. According to the Director of Television, Channel 2 has a ceiling of 85% of territory, since the investment costs double when the 70% level of coverage is reached. A PAL System in color, RTVE reaches approx. 14,500,000 homes on the mainland and Canary Islands.

RTVE is now an autonomous agency under the Ministry of Culture, Paseo de la Castellana 109, Madrid 16. All programs are controlled by a Censorship Board. Drama, films and episodes of series are classified according to ratings: "general" (no sign on the screen), "older than 14" (a small lozenge), "older than 18" (two small lozenges).

The production of programs is entirely financed by advertising and tie-in merchandising, since the government withdrew its annual subsidy. Both channels carry ad spots. Due to nocturnal habits of Spaniards, the costliest time comes around 10:30 p.m. The ad spots appear on the screen at regular half-hour or one hour intervals, till 7 p.m. Later the spots rhythm accelerates, mainly during feature films in spite of audience and film directors' protests.

Regional TV networks also exist in the Basque provinces, Cataluña and Galicia. The Basque's Euskal Telebista (ETB) has two channels (one in Castilian, with Basque subtitles; one in Basque) headquartered in Durango and San Sebastian. In Cataluña with a 6 million population, Televisio de Catalunya (TV 3) is the most successful of the regional networks. Broadcasting from the outskirts of Barcelona, its programs are in the Catalan language without subtitles. TBG (Television de Galicia) is the newest network, and regional channels are anticipated in Valencia in 1989 and Andalucia by 1990.

In May, 1987, Spanish legislators passed a law approving three private TV channels in Spain and in April, 1988 the Spanish Parliament approved a further law regulating private TV. Modified from the original bill, now allowing ownership by Spanish media companies of up to 25% as compared to an earlier 15%, the law was received with great political opposition. Although the new Transport, Tourism and Communications minister set fall of 1989 as a target date for private TV operation, a National Technical Plan, defining the specific technical requirements the new networks would have to comply with, has yet to first be approved.

Staff and Studios: Director General RTVE (officially called "Ente," Italian style) is Pilar Miro. Director of TVE is Jesus Martin.

RTVE built in Madrid a 210 meter high tower ("Torrespaña") for news and live broadcasts. This "Towerspain" is now one of the landmarks of the capital.

TVE has ten news broadcasting stations in provinces. The Canary Islands set up their own programming. National Headquarters are at Prado del Rey, Madrid 24, with general offices and nine studios with total area of 3,000 square meters. Additional studios are in Barcelona.

Televisió de Catalunya (TV-3): started broadcasting 1984. Offices and studios in San Juan Despi, outside Barcelona. Director: Enric Canals.

Euskal Telebista (ETB): Basque regional TV, began broadcasting, 1983. Offices in Durango and San Sebastian. Director general: Josie Ortuondo.

Television de Galicia (TVG): Started 1985. Broadcasts from Santiago de Compostela. Director general: Abilio Bernaldo de Quiros.

Programming Schedule and Contents: Channel 1 broadcasts 76 h 45' weekly, with accent on week-ends. Same happens with Channel 2, which broadcasts 46 h 45' weekly. Total of weekly broadcasting time: 123 h 30'. Special programs such as prize boxing bouts, sports championships, bullfights, royal and political messages, etc., move or remove normal programming.

Many broadcasting hours consist in theater movies (about seven features weekly) and filmed foreign production, including American series as "Flamingo Road," "Winds of War," "Masada," "The Martian Chronicles," etc. TVE broadcasts too many debate and panel shows, too many heavy music meetings, but lacks comedy fare. From 1982 the Ente has invested in prestige Spanish features, which first are being shown in theaters and then will be adapted to television as miniseries. Many of them have won awards at international film festivals.

Price range for half hour of screening time is $1,500–$2,000. One-hour series generally brings twice the half-hour price. Price range for feature films is $7,800–$17,000, dubbed into Spanish at Madrid studios. Only "Film Society" screenings (Channel 2) accept foreign prints with Spanish subtitles.

SRI LANKA

Indian Television System, "Door Dharshan" which is state-owned, had requested Sri Lanka government, through Indian government, permission to establish a television relay transmission station in the city of Jaffna in the north of Sri Lanka, where the Indian government maintains about 100,000 Indian military troops (occupied forces) under the 1987 Indo-Sri Lanka Peace Accord.

According to the official request, by establishing a TV relay Transmission Centre in Jaffna with a 1,000 kilowatt transmitter, the Indian Doordharshan (TV) will be able to telecast all Indian programs to Pidurutalagala, where the Sri Lankan TV Rupavahini has its main Television Transmitter Antenna. This proposal is now being studied by officials of the Ministry of State and Rupavahini Corporation. If this proposal is accepted, the entire island will be able to see all programs telecast in India. The cost of establishing the relay transmission centre and maintenance will be borne by the Government of India. It is interesting to note that India opposed Sri Lanka giving facilities to the establishment of a Voice Of America transmission center on Sri Lankan soil. This was one of the demands made by Indian Prime Minister and the Indian Government before signing the Indo Sri Lanka Peace Accord.

"Marcos' Dangerous Life" was shot in Colombo, produced by Australian filmmaker Terry Sands and directed by Robert Marcovitz, re-enacting the last days of the reign of Ferdinand Marcos, as seen through the eyes of a journalist, played by Gary Busey. The Australian company was on location for nearly three weeks, mainly in Colombo.

The Raditelevisao Portuguese (The National Television of Portugal) produced a film on Sri Lanka—one of a series of films the Portuguese TV Network hopes to produce. John Bush and Murray Boland were in Sri Lanka recently to film the British adventure program "Survival."

Productions Audiovisuelles in Paris has decided to invest US $1,700,000 producing a TV series titled "Pedro De Gascogne," an historical series re-creating the adventures of a French nobleman at the Court of Sri Lanka in the 18th Century. (The total production is estimated to cost $2,000,000 approximately.)

Tele-dramas are becoming very popular and many commercial firms have come forward to fiance and sponsor tele-dramas in the Sinhala language so that they could advertise and promote their products. At least two tele-dramas are being shown weekly, each running into twenty to twenty-five episodes. The most popular English TV series is "Knight Rider" which has caught on very well. Generally, almost all British and American TV series are popular among all communities irrespective of whether they know the English language or not.

ITN (Independent Television Network) recently opened its new transmitting centre which provides its range to 75 miles from the city of Colombo. Rupavahini Corporation and I.T.N.—Independent Television Network Ltd. is under the Ministry of State and Information. Minister Dr. Ananda Tissa de Alwis, Secretary Minister of State—B.I. Gunatunga, Secretary of Information: Dr. Anura Gunasekera, Additional Sec. G.P.S.U. de Silva. Address of the Ministry: Transworks House, Colombo 1. Tel: 31747-48-49.

Rupavahini Corporation: Chairman: Kumar Abeyasinghe S.L.A.S., Director General Dr. Anura Gunasekera, Address: Torrigton Square, Colombo 7. Tel: Chairman: 580131; Office General: 580123, 580136.

Independent Television Network Ltd., Competent Authority: M.D.T.L. Guruge Address. I.T.N. Studios, Wickremasinghepura, Kotte, Sri Lanka.

Sri Lanka Broadcasting Corporation: Torrigton Square, Colombo 7. Chairman: Mr. Livy Wijemanne Tel: 596439 Office: 597491, 597500

Liaisoning and Promotion of Production of Television Films, Programmes and sales of TV films, for Sri Lanka and Maldive Republic. Chandra S. Perera TV Producer, Director, Cinematographer, and Journalist representing N.B.C. TV News, National Broadcasting Co. of New York, W.T.N.-Worldwide Television News of London, GAMMA PRESS PARIS. Address. 437 Pethiyagoda, Kelaniya, Sri Lanka. Tel: 521885, Cables: Telecinex.

TV Producers: Wicks Studio, Maradana, Colombo-10, Telecine Ltd., Hyde Park Corner, Colombo 2.

—CHANDRA S. PERERA

SWITZERLAND

As of July 30, 1988, the Federal Post Office registered nearly 2,300,000 households in which at least one TV set (mostly color) is operating. As most of the households keep more than one set, the estimated number of TV-sets in operation is about 5 million. The number of transmitters and boosters has increased from 1,318 (1987) to 1,330.

Commercial TV was introduced on a limited basis on February 1, 1965. From November 1, 1985, 23 minutes weekly, only on workdays, were allowed; the cost per minute as of January 1, 1987, was 20,600 Swiss francs. On October 1, 1987, the cost of annual licenses was fixed at 184,80 Swiss francs for private sets. As of December, 1987, 95% of all Swiss households had color TV sets.

Swiss TV viewers have recently shown a certain tiredness, diminishing the daily TV-sessions: Swiss Italians dedicated an average 2 hours and 13 minutes a day to TV-watching; French language watchers 2 hours 4 minutes a day and Swiss Germans 1 hour 32 minutes a day.

National channels (in German, French and Italian language) are tuned in only 46 minutes a day by Swiss Germans, who prefer foreign channels for the remaining 54 minutes; French-language watchers tune in a national channel for an average 48 minutes a day and select foreign channels for 73 minutes; Swiss Italians watch national channels for 42 minutes a day (mainly the news) and switch to foreign channels for some 85 minutes of the daily TV-session. Cable TV is expanding steadily and is now the second highest in Europe: as of January 1988, there were nearly 2,000,000 subscribers; 68% of them are Swiss Germans, 64% French lingo watchers, 54% Swiss Italians.

Local TV Stations: So far, in Switzerland 7 local TV stations are active; they need a special governmental authorization which allows them to finance themselves partially by commercials. Their reach is limited to a radius of about a dozen miles and the daily time dedicated to TV commercials is restricted.

—GABRIELLA BROGGI

TAHITI

Office of Radiodiff-Television Française, Papeete, operates four channels 34 hours weekly to serve the estimated 24,000 sets of this French possession. It is owned by the government and buys canned programs in Paris.

THAILAND

Thai Television Company (government-owned) opened its first station in 1955 and there are four stations (two using color) and 8 relays on a commercial basis. Stations are also operated under names of Bangkok Broadcasting & TV, Bangkok Entertainment Co. and Mass Communication Organization of Thailand, all located in Bangkok. Sets are estimated at 4 million, some color.

In 1980 a ban on broadcasts from 6:30 to 8:00 p.m., as a power-saving measure, allegedly improved "family relationships," so at present broadcasts are limited to 8 hours on weekdays, and 16 hours on weekends and holidays.

TURKEY

Turkish Radio Television Corp., P.O. Box 98, Kizilay-Ankara serves 5.8 million TV sets via 37 stations.

UNITED ARAB EMIRATES

Established 1969 by Thompson TV International and Abu Dhabi TV Service. In 1971 United Arab Emirates TV Service, P.O. Box 637 Abu Dhabi established separate facilities which now consist of three stations and three relays. Dubai Radio and Color TV, P.O. Box 1695, Kubai, now broadcasts on two channels from 1 station and 1 relay in Arabic, French and English. 147,000 sets.

U.S.S.R.

Soviet Television, TV Center, 12 Korolyov Street, Moscow, originating all TV programs direct and via satellite. Sets number 272,500,000.

VIETNAM

Since 1968 the Government Information Department of the Democratic Republic of Vietnam has operated one non-commercial station in Hanoi. Number of sets is about 2 million.

A second station was added in Saigon (now known as Ho Chi-Minh City) when South Vietnam was "liberated" and the divided country became one.

Hanoi has initiated use of a Russian satellite and 7 hours of color telecasts on weekdays and all day Saturday and Sunday, compared with the previous 4 hours a day in black and white.

WEST GERMANY

TV Households: Out of approximately 25,800,000 German households, 23,364,322 households have television sets with 47,456,000 viewers. Of these, about 16,000,000 have at least one color set. Some 23,000,000 households have at least one radio. Total TV set sales per year: about $2.2 billion.

TV Networks: West Germany has two state-owned networks, ARD and 2DF. Recently two privately owned networks were established: SAT I and RTL Plus. ARD is the national hookup of nine regional stations; and ZDF or second channel, a single nationally-beamed station based in Mainz near Frankfurt. ARD's nine stations each contribute to one joint national broadcasting operation, five regional channels and several radio channels. ARD has a budget of about $1,640-billion; ZDF, $556,000,000. Commercials are aired on both stations in sharply limited timeslots. Stations are supported largely by $6.50 monthly license fees paid by TV set owners.

Cable penetration in Germany was as of 1987 30% with 2.7 million homes hooked up to cable and 2.3 able to receive satellite. There are 5 national, ad-supported-only private satellite to cable services: Eureka, RTL Plus, SAT I (latter two also receive terrestrially), Tele 5, and Unser Kleines Theater—all in German. Sky Channel and Super Channel satellite to cable services broadcast programming in English while TV 5 broadcasts in French.

The Federal Office of Post and Communications in Bonn is responsible for the technical side of the TV medium, while the nation's 11 states, which under the consitution are allowed to formulate their own media policy, have supervisory TV and cable boards.

YEMEN (Arab Republic)

San'a Television, Ministry of Information, San'a, established in 1977, currently broadcasts on 3 channels to some 120,000 sets.

YEMEN (People's Republic)

Established in 1964, People's Democratic Republic of Yemen, P.O. Box 1264, Aden, broadcasts on 3 channels to an estimated 55,000 sets.

ZIMBABWE

Established in 1960 as Rhodesia TV, and now named Zimbabwe Broadcasting Corp., P.O. Box H.G. 200, Highlands, Harare, its 6 stations serve some 560,000 sets.

World TV Broadcasters

Europe

ALBANIA
RADIOTELEIZIONI SHQIPTAR
Rrga Ismail Qemali, Tirana.

AUSTRIA
OSTERREICHISCHER RUNDFUNK
GmbH ORF
Argentinierstrasse 30a, 1041 Vienna Postfach 700.

BELGIUM
RADIODIFFUSION-TELEVISION BELGE
(FRENCH)
Boulevard A. Reyers, 1040, Bruxelles.

BELGISCHE RADIO EN TELEVISIE
(B.R.T.) (FLEMISH)
Omreopcentrum A. Reyerslaan, 1040, Brussel.

BULGARIA
BULGARIAN TELEVISION
San Stefano Str. 29, Sofia 1504.

CYPRUS
CYPRUS BROADCASTING
CORPORATION
P.O. Box 4824, Nicosia.

CZECHOSLOVAKIA
CESKOSLOVENSKA TELEVIZIE
M. Gorkeho 30, Prague 1.

DENMARK
RADIO DENMARK
Television Service, Radio Denmark, Radiohuset, Rosenornsalle, Alle 22, Copenhagen.

FINLAND
FINNISH BROADCASTING CO.
Kesakatu 2, Helsinki 26.

FRANCE
TELEDIFFUSION DE FRANCE
116, avenue du President Kennedy. F-75790 Paris Cedex 16.

GERMANY

GERMAN FEDERAL REPUBLIC
DEUTSCHE RUNDFUNK-UND
FERNSEHANSTALTEN
BAYERISCHER RUNDFUNK
Rundfunkplatz 1, 8 Munich 2.

HESSISCHER RUNDFUNK
Frankfurt (Main), Bertramstr. 8.

NORDEUTSCHER RUNDFUNK
Hamburg, 13, Rothenbaumchaussee 132/134.

RADIO BREMEN
Heinrich-Hertz-Str. 13, Bremen, 33.

SAARLANDISCHER RUNDFUNK
66 Saarbrucken, Funkhaus Halberg, Postfach 1050.

SENDER FREIES BERLIN
Berlin 19, Masurenallee 8-14.

SUEDDEUTSCHER RUNDFUNK
7000 Stuttgart 1, Neckarstr. 145.

SUEDWESTFUNK
757 Baden-Baden, Hans-Bredow-Strass.

WESTDEUTSCHER RUNDFUNK
Appellhofplatz 1, 5 Cologne 1. Postfach 101950.

ZWEITES DEUTSCHES FERNSEHEN
Essenheimer Landstrasse, 65 Mainz-Lerchenberg, Postfach 4040.

GIBRALTAR
GIBRALTAR BROADCASTING, LTD.
Television House, Wellington Front.

GIBRALTAR TELEVISION
28 John Mackintosh Square, Gibraltar.

GREECE
GREEK RADIO TELEVISION
ERT 1 Channel, Messoguion Str. 436 Athens. ERT 2 Channel Messoguion and Katehaki Str. Athens.

HOLLAND
NEDERLANDSE OMROEP STICHTING
(N.O.S.)
P.O. Box 10, Hilversum.

HUNGARY
MAGYAR RADIO ES TELEVIZIO
Television Direction, V. Szabadsagter, 17, Budapest.

IRELAND
RADIO EIREANN TELEFIS
Donnybrook, Dublin 4.

ITALY
RADIO-TELEVISIONE ITALIANA
Viale Mazzini 14, 00195, Rome.

LUXEMBOURG
TELE LUXEMBOURG
Villa Louvigny.

MALTA
THE MALTA TELEVISION SERVICE LTD.
Television House, P.O. Box 384, Gwardamanga.

MONACO
TELE MONTE CARLO
16, Blvd. Princesse Charlotte, Monte Carlo.

POLAND
POLSKIE RADIO I TELEWIZJA
Woronicza St., Warsaw.

PORTUGAL
**RTP-RADIOTELEVISAO PORTUGUESA
S.A.R.L.**
Rua de S. Domingos (a Lapa) 26, Lisboa.

ROMANIA
**RADIODIFUZIUNEA TELEVIZUNEA
ROMANA**
Calea Dorobantilor, 191, Bucarest O. Romania.

SPAIN
TELEVISION ESPAÑOLA
de Prado del Rey, Madrid.

SWEDEN
SVERIGES RADIO
AB S-105 10 Stockholm.

SWITZERLAND
SWISS BROADCASTING CORPORATION
Giacommettistrasse 3, CH-3000 Berne 15.

U.S.S.R.
SOVJET TELEVISION
Akademika Koroljova 12, Moscow.

YUGOSLAVIA
TELEVISION YOUGOSLAVE
Boriso Kidrica 70/1 Belgrade.

Africa

ALGERIA
**RADIODIFFUSION-TELEVISION
ALGERIENNE**
21 Blvd. des Martyrs, Algiers.

BOURKINA FASSO (Upper Volta)
TELEVISION NATIONALE DE BOURKINA
Post Office Box 7029, Ouagadougou.

BENIN
**OFFICE DE RADIODIFFUSION ET DE
TELEVISION DU BENIN**
BP 366, Cotonou.

CAMEROUN
**UNITE TC, RADIO DIFFUSION DU
CAMEROUN**
Ministry of Information, Yaonde.

CENTRAL AFRICAN REPUBLIC
TELEVISION CENTRAFRICAINE
Ministry of Information, B.P. 940, Bangui.

DJIBOUTI
RADIO TELEVISION DE DJIBOUTI
B.P. 97, Ave. St. Laurent du Var, Djibouti.

EGYPT
**U.A.R. BROADCASTING CORPORATION
OF CAIRO**
Television Bldg., Cornish Road, P.O. Box 1186, Cairo.

GABON
RADIO TELEVISION GABONAISE
B.P. 10150, Libreville.

GHANA
GHANA BROADCASTING CORPORATION
P.O. Box 1633, Accra.

KENYA
KENYA BROADCASTING SERVICE
P.O. Box 30456, Nairobi.

LIBYA
LIBYA JAMAHIRIAYH BROADCASTING TV
P.O. Box 33, Tripoli.

MOROCCO
**RADIODIFFUSION TELEVISION
MAROCAINE**
1, Zankat al Brihi, Rabat.

NIGERIA
**BROADCASTING COMPANY OF
NORTHERN NIGERIA, LTD.**
Television House, P.O. Box 250, Kaduna.

NIGERIAN BROADCASTING CORP.
P.M.B. 12005, Victoria Island, Lagos, Nigeria.

**WESTERN NIGERIA RADIOVISION
SERVICE**
Television House, P.O. Box 1460, Ibadan.

SIERRA LEONE
SIERRA LEONA TV BROADCASTING
New England, Private Mail Bag, Freetown.

SUDAN
SUDAN TELEVISION
Box 1094, Omduran, Sudan (107,000 sets).

TANZANIA
TV ZANZIBAR
TV Zanzibar, P.O. Box 314, Zanzibar (7,500 sets).

TUNISIA
RADIODIFFUSION TV TUNISIA
71 Ave. de la Liberté, Tunis.

ZAIRE
ZAIRE TELEVISION
Box 3171, Kinshasa, Zaire (71,000 sets).

ZAMBIA
ZAMBIA TELEVISION
P.O. Box 50015, Lusaka, Zambia (70,000 sets).

Asia

NATIONALIST CHINA
**TAIWAN TELEVISION ENTERPRISES
LTD.**
No. 10, Pa Te Road, Sec 3, Taipei.

CHINESE TELEVISION SERVICE
N. 100, Kuang Fu South Road, Taipei.

GUAM
GUAM TELEVISION
Pacific Broadcasting, Box 368, Agana, Guam.

HONG KONG
TELEVISION BROADCASTS, LTD.
77 Broadcast Drive, Hong Kong.
REDIFFUSION (Hong Kong Ltd.)
81 Broadcast Drive, Kowloon, Hong Kong.

INDIA
ALL INDIA TELEVISION
Television Centre, All India Radio, Akashwani Bhawan, 5th Floor, Parliament Street, New Delhi, 110001.

INDONESIA
JAJASAN TELEVISI RI (RRI-TV)
Senajan, Jakarta

IRAN
IRAN REPUBLIC BROADCASTING
P.O. Box 19395, Tehran 17-74.

IRAQ
TV-STATION OF THE REP. OF IRAQ
Ministry of Guidance, Broadcasting House, Salhiya, Baghdad.

JAPAN
NIPPON HOSO KYOKAI (NHK)
2-2-1 Jinnan, Shibuya-ku, Tokyo 150.
ASAHI BROADCASTING CO. LTD. (ABC) JOBX-TV
Osaka.
KANSAI TELEVISION CORP. (KTV) JONR-TV
Osaka.
MAINICHI BROADCASTING SYSTEM (MBS) JOQR-TV
Osaka.
FUJI TELECASTING CO.
7 Kawada-cho, Ichigaya, Shinjuku, Tokyo.
ASAHI NATIONAL BROADCASTING CO. (TV ASAHI or ANB) formerly Nippon Educational Television (NET)
6-4-10 Roppongi, Tokyo.
NIPPON TELEVISION NETWORK (NTV)
14 Niban-cho, Chiyoda-ku, Tokyo.
TOKYO BROADCASTING SYSTEM (TBS)
5-3-6, Akasaka, Minato-ku, Tokyo.
NATIONAL ASSOCIATION OF COMMERCIAL BROADCASTERS
Bungei Shunju Bldg., 3 Kioi-cho, Chiyoda-Ku, Tokyo.
MCA JAPAN LTD.
Maison Hirakawa, 2-5-2 Hirakawa-cho, Chiyoda-ku, Tokyo.
JAPAN (Audience Research) A.C. NIELSEN CO.
1-1-71 Naka-Meguro, Meguro-ku, Tokyo 153.
VIDEO RESEARCH CORP.
2-16-7 Ginza, Chuo-ku, Tokyo 104.
TOKYO CHANNEL 12 TV (JOTX)
4-4 Shiba Koen, Tokyo.

CABLE TELEVISION JCTV
%ANB, 6-4/10 Roppongi, Minato-ku, Tokyo.
TVK (UHF) CHANNEL 42
Yokohama, 231.
TELEVI OSAKA (JOBH)
2-2 Kyobashi, Higashi-ku, Osaka 530.
YOMIURI TELEV (JOIX)
1-8-11 Higashi-Tenma, Osaka 530.
HOKKAIDO BUNKA HOSO (JOBM)
14-1-5 Nishi Kita-Ichijo, Sapporo 060.
HOKKAIDO BROADCASTING (JOHR)
5-2 Nishi Kita Ichijo, Chuo-ku, Sapporo 060.
HOKKAIDO TELEVI HOSO (JOHH)
4-13-10-17 Hiragishi, Toyohira-ku Sapporo.
SAPPORO TELEVI (JOKX)
8-1-1 Nishi Kita-Ichijo, Sapporo 060.
OKINAWA TELEVI (JOOF)
1-2-20 Kumoji, Naha 900.
RYUKU HOSO (JORR)
2-3-1 Kumoji, Naha 900.
RKB MAINICHI HOSO (JOFR)
4-1-10 Watanabe-dori Fukuoka 810.
FUKUOKA HOSO (JOFH)
1-1-1 Watanabe-dori, Fukuoka 810.
KAGOSHIMA HOSO (JOTI)
4-31 Yamano-kuchi-machi, Kagoshima.

SOUTH KOREA
KOREA BROADCASTING SYSTEM
33-3 ga, Namsan-Rong, Chung-Ku, Seoul.

KUWAIT
KUWAIT-TV
P.O. Box 621, Kuwait.

LEBANON
COMPAGNIE LIBANAISE DE TELEVISION
P.O. Box 4848, Beirut.

MALAYSIA
TELEVISION MALAYSIA
Dept. of Broadcasting, P.O. Box 1047, Kuala Lumpur.

PHILIPPINES
INTERCONTINENTAL BROADCASTING CORPORATION
P. Guevarra Ave., San Juan, Rizal.
KANLAON BROADCASTING SYSTEM, INC.
Broadcast Plaza, Bohol Ave., Quezon City.
REPUBLIC BROADCASTING SYSTEM
E de los Santos Avenue, Diliman, Quezon City.

SAUDI ARABIA
SAUDI ARABIAN TELEVISION
P.O. Box 570, Riyadh.

THAILAND
THAI TELEVISION CO. LTD.
Bangkhunprom, Bangkok.
THAI ARMY TELEVISION STATION
Pahol Youthin Road, Bangkok.

BANGKOK ENTERTAINMENT
2357 New Petchburi, Bangkok.

Pacific

AMERICAN SAMOA
TELEVISION OF SAMOA
Department of Education, Pago Pago, 96799.

AUSTRALIA
AUSTRALIAN BROADCASTING
COMMISSION
Government owned.
145 Elizabeth St., P.O. Box 487 G.P.O., Sydney, N.S.W. 2001.

AMALGAMATED TELEVISION SERVICES
Pty. Ltd. Television Station A.T.N., Channel 7
Television Centre, Epping, 2121, Sydney, N.S.W.

TELEVISION CORPORATION LIMITED
Television Station TCN, Channel 9
Artarmon Road, Willoughby, 2068, Sydney, N.S.W.

UNITED TELECASTERS LIMITED
(Channel A-10)
Epping & Pittwater Rds., North Ryde 2113, N.S.W.

HERALD-SUN TV
Pty. Ltd. Television Station HSV Channel 7
Cnr. Dorcas and Wells St., South Melbourne, Victoria.

GENERAL TELEVISION COR.
Pty. Ltd. Television Station GTV, Channel 9
22-46 Bendigo Street, Richmond, Melbourne, Victoria.

AUSTRAMA TELEVISION (Channel 0)
ATC C/Ansett Transport Industries Ltd.
489 Swanston Street, Melbourne, Victoria.

CANBERRA TELEVISION LTD.
Television Station CTC, Channel 7
Canberra Television Centre, Black Mountain, ACT, P.O. Box 633,
Canberra.

BRISBANE TV LIMITED
Sir Samuel Griffiths Drive, Mt. Coot-tha, Brisbane, Queensland.

QUEENSLAND TELEVISION LIMITED
Sir Samuel Griffiths Drive, Mt. Coot-tha, Brisbane, Queensland.

TELEVISION BROADCASTER LTD.
Television Station ADS, Channel 7
125 Strangeways Terrace, North Adelaide, South Australia.

SOUTHERN TELEVISION CORP. LTD.
Television Station NWS, Channel 9
202-208 Tynte Street, North Adelaide, South Australia.

TVW LIMITED
Television Station TVW, Channel 7
Osborne Park Road, Tuart Hill, Perth, W.A.

TASMANIAN TELEVISION LIMITED
TVT, Channel A-6
G.P.O. Box 1209M, Hobart, Tas.

MARIANAS ISLANDS
GUAM TELEVISION
P.O. Box 368, Agana.

NEW CALEDONIA
RADIODIFFUSION TV, NOUMEA
Box 327, Noumea.

NEW ZEALAND
NEW ZEALAND BROADCASTING
COUNCIL
P.O. Box 30, 355, Lower Hutt, New Zealand.

TAHITI
TELEVISION FRANCE L
Box 125, Papeete.

Central America

COSTA RICA
TELEVISORA DE COSTA RICA LTDA.
Apt. 3376, San Jose.

CUBA
CMQ-TV
Radiocentre, Habana.

CMBF-TV
Mazon y San Miguel, Habana.

DOMINICAN REPUBLIC
RAHINTEL TELEVISION
P.O. Box 1220, zone 7.

GUATEMALA
RADIO-TELEVISION GUATEMALA, S.A.
Apt. 1367, Guatemala.

HAITI
TELE-HAITI
P.O. Box 1126, Port-au-Prince.

HONDURAS
RADIO Y TELEVISION HONDURENA,
S.A.
Tegucigalpa.

JAMAICA
JAMAICAN BROADCASTING CORP.
5-9 South Ocean Avenue., P.O. Box 100, Kingston.

MEXICO
TELEVISION DE LA FRONTERA, S.A.
Vincente Guerrero num. 704 Ciudad Juarez, Chih.

RADIO PANAMERICANA, S.A.
Av. Chapultepec num. 18 Mexico, D.F.

TELEVISION DEL NORTE, S.A.
Aparatado Postal num. 1833 Monterrey, N.L.

TELEVIMEX, S.A.
Av. Chapultepec num. 18 Mexico D.F.

RADIO TELEVISION S.A.
Calle Quinta num. 210 Desps. 14–16 Edificio Barbachano
Tijuana, B.C.

CADENA TELEVISION DEL NORTE, S.A.
Monterrey, N.L. (Dom. Av. Chapultepec num. 18 Mexico, D.F.)

RAFAEL TIJERINA CARRANZA
Aldama num. 2611 Nuevo Laredo, Tams.

TELEVISION TAPATIA, S.A. de C.V.
Circunvalacion num. 265 Guadalajara, Jal.

TELEVISORA DE LA LAGUNA, S.A.
Torreon, Coah. (Dom. Av. Chapultepec mun. 18, Mexico, D.F.)

TELEVISION PASO DE CORTES, S.A.
Av. Chapultepec num. 18 Mexico, D.F.

SERGIO R. MOLINAR FERNANDEZ
Apartado Postal num. 271 Ciudad Juarez, Chih.

TELEVISORA DE CHIHUAHUA, S.A.
Chihuahua, Chih. (Dom. Av. Chapultepec num. 18 Mexico, D.F.)

TELEVISORA DE HERMOSILLO, S.A.
Hermosillo, Son. (Dom. Av. Chapultepec num. 18 Mexico, D.F.)

TELEVISORA DE GUADALAJARA, S.A.
Guadalajara, Jal. (Dom. Av. Chapultepec num. 18 Mexico, D.F.)

TELEVISORA DE CALIMEX, S.A.
Tijuana, B.C. (Dom. Av. Chapultepec num. 18 Mexico. D.F.)

TELEVISORA DE OCCIDENTE, S.A.
Guadalajara, Jal. (Dom. Av. Chapultepec num. 18, Mexico, D.F.)

TELEVISORA DEL NORTE, S.A.
Monterrey, N.L. (Dom. Av. Chapultepec num. 18 Mexico, D.F.)

TELEVISORA DE YUCATAN, S.A.
Merida, Yrc. (Dom. Av. Chapultepec num. 18 Mexico, D.F.)

TELEVISION DE GUANAJUATO, S.A.
Cerro del Zamorano, Qro. (Dom. Av. Chapultepec mun. 18 Mexico, D.F.)

TV DE CULIACAN, S.A.
Culiacan, Sin. (Dom. Av. Chapultepec num. 18 Mexico, D.F.)

TELEVISORA DE MEXICALI, S.A.
Apartado Postal num. 1356 Mexicali, B.C. (Dom. Av. Chapultepec num. 18 Mexico, D.F.)

TELEVISION DE COLIMA, S.A. de C.V.
Anillo Cirunvalacion num. 1080 Nte. Colima, Col.

FELIPE ARRIOLA GANDARA
Av. Alvaro Obregon num. 138 Nogales, Son.

CARLOS FERRAEZ MATOS
Calle Bolivar entre Diaz Miron y Boulevard Miguel Aleman Veracruz, Ver.

TELEVISION GONZALES CAMERENA, S.A.
Av. Chapultepec num. 18 Mexico, D.F.

TELEVISORA DEL GOLFO, S.A.
Ciudan Madero, Tams. (Dom. Av. Chapultepec num. 18 Mexico, D.F.)

TELEVISION DE MEXICO, S.A.
Av. Chapultepec num. 18 Mexico, D.F.

ANTONIO SUAREZ REYES
Av. Punta Banda y Eugenia, Frallion-Amiento Chapultepec Ensenada, B.C.

NETHERLANDS ANTILLES
TELECURAÇAO
P.O. Box 415, Curaçao.

NICARAGUA
TELEVISION DE NICARAGUA, S.A.
Apdo 1505, Managua.

PANAMA
CIRCUITO RPC-TELEVISION
Direccion de Correos y Telecomunicaciones, Ministerio de Gobierno y Justicia, Panama.

TELEVISORA NACIONAL S.A. PANAMA
Ric. Chiari, Panama.

PUERTO RICO
WKAQ-TV
Telemundo Inc., Box W.

WIPM-TV
Dept. of Education
Hato Rey, San Juan.

WAPA-TV
WAPA-TV Broadcasting Corp.
P.O. Box 2050, San Juan.

WORA-TV
Quality Telecasting Corp.
Box 43, Mayaguez.

WIPR-TV
Dept. of Education
Hato Rey, San Juan.

WRIK-TV
Ponce TV Corp.
Darlington Bldg.

WSUR-TV
American Colonial Broadcasting Corp.
Box 4189, San Juan.

WKBM-TV
American Colonial Broadcasting Corp.
Box 4189, San Juan.

WOLE-TV
Western Broadcasting Corp.
Box 415, Aguadilla.

TRINIDAD
TRINIDAD AND TOBAGO TELEVISION CO. LTD.
Television House
12a Maraval Road, Port-of-Spain.

VIRGIN ISLANDS
ISLAND TELERADIOSERVICE, INC.
P.O. Box 1947, St. Thomas.

South America

ARGENTINA
PRIMERA TELEVISION ARGENTINA
Av. Alem 735, Buenos Aires.

COMPANIA ARGENTINA DE TELEVISION, S.A.
Castex 3345, Buenos Aires.

PRODUCCIONES ARGENTINA DE TV
Lima 1261, Buenos Aires.

TELEONCE
Calle Pavon 2444, Buenos Aires.

RIO DE LA PLATA
San Juan, 1160, Buenos Aires.

DIFUSORA MARPLATENSE
Av. Luro 2907, Mar del Plata.

SOCIEDAD DIFUSORA MENDOZA
Garibaldi 7, Mendoza.

TELECOLOR, S.A.
Av. Gral Paz 266, Cordoba.

BRAZIL
TELEVISAO—TUPI
Av. Joao Luiz Alves, 13-Urca, Rio de Janeiro.

TELEVISAO—RIO
Av. Atlantica 4264, Rio de Janeiro.

EMISSORA DE TELEVISAO CONTINENTAL
Rue das Laranjeiras 291, Rio de Janeiro.

TELEVISAO MAYRINK VEIGA
Rio de Janeiro.

RADIO GLOBO DO RIO DE JANEIRO
Rua Irineau Marinho 35, Rio de Janeiro.

CHILE
TV CHILE
Bellavista 0990, Casilla Postal 16.104, Correo 9, Santiago.

COLOMBIA
R. TELEVISORA NACIONAL
Direccion General de la Radiotelevisora National de Colombia
Apartado Nacional 1824, Bogota.

ECUADOR
LA VOZ DE LOS ANDES—TELEVISION
Cas: 691, Quito.

PRIMERA TELEVISION ECUATORIANA
S.A.
Illingworth 114 y Pichincha, Guayaquil.

PERU
MINISTRY OF EDUCATION
Ministerio de Educacion Publica
Direccion de Cultera, Lima.

TELEVISORA AMERICA
Montero Rosas, Lima.

TELEVISORA PANAMERICANA
Ave. Arequipa 1110, Lima.

TELEVISORA VICTORIA
Av. Tacna 543, Lima.

TELEVISORA EXCELSIOR
Ave. Manco Capac, Lima.

TELEVISORA EL SOL
Jose Galvez 1040, Lima.

TELEVISORA SUR PERUANA
P.O. Box 514, Arequipa.

URUGUAY
TV MONTE CARLO
18 DE Julio 1855, Montevideo.

SAETA-TV
Lorenzo Carnelli 1234, Montevideo.

VENEZUELA
TELEVISORA NACIONAL
Apt. 3979, Caracas.

CORPORACION VENEZOLANA DE
TELEVISION
Apartado 6674, Caracas.

R. CARACAS TV
Apartado 2057, Caracas.